WITHDRAWN
KT-547-957

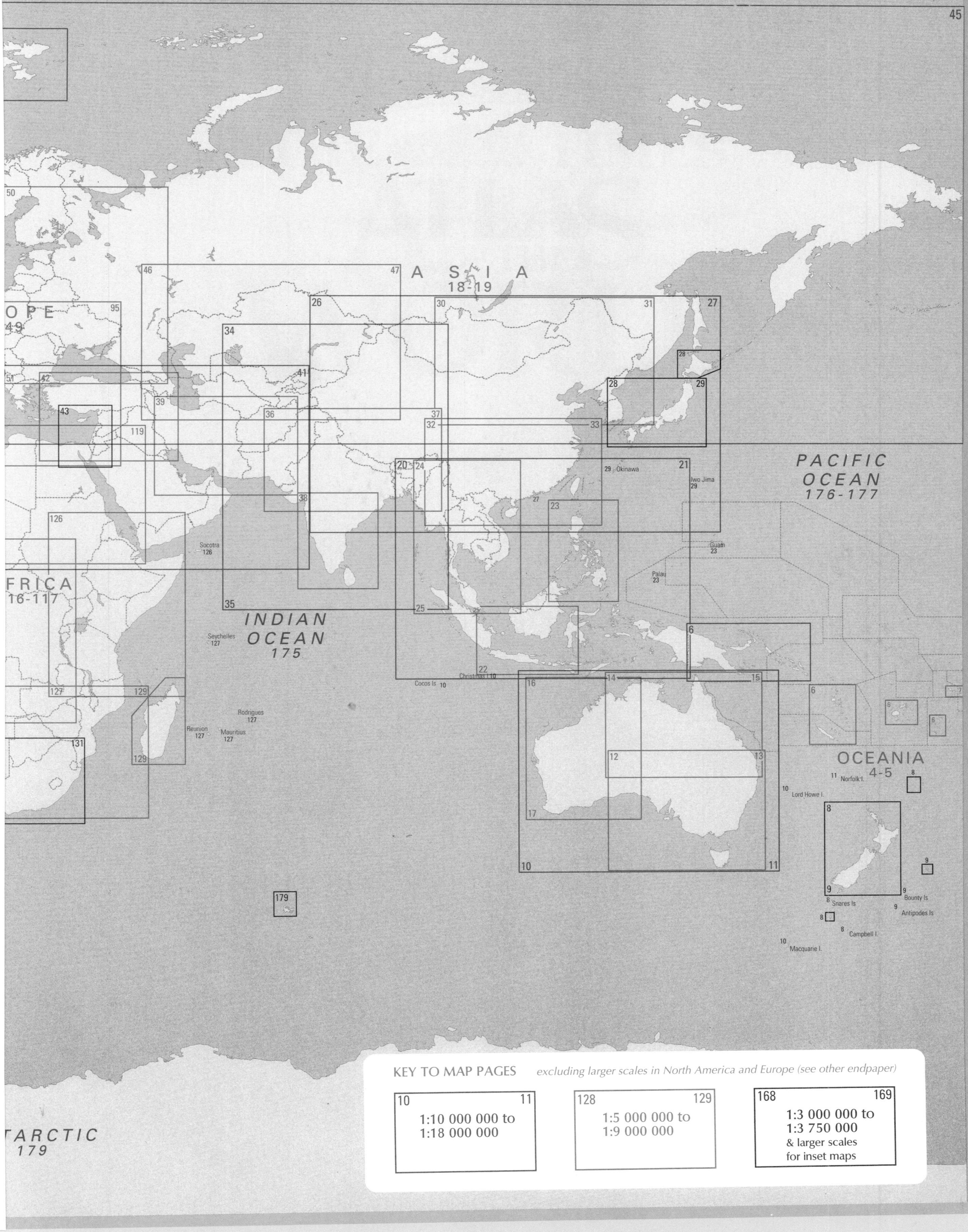
TIC OCEAN
178
ASIA
18-19
OPE
49
FRICA
16-117
INDIAN
OCEAN
175
PACIFIC
OCEAN
176-177
OCEANIA
4-5
TARCTIC
179
Socotra 126
Seychelles 127
Rodrigues 127
Reunion 127
Mauritius 127
Cocos Is 10
Christmas I. 10
Okinawa 29
Iwo Jima 29
Guam 23
Palau 23
Norfolk I. 11
Lord Howe I. 10
Snares Is 8
Bounty Is 9
Antipodes Is 9
Campbell I. 8
Macquarie I. 10

KEY TO MAP PAGES

excluding larger scales in North America and Europe (see other endpaper)

10 — 11: 1:10 000 000 to 1:18 000 000	128 — 129: 1:5 000 000 to 1:9 000 000	168 — 169: 1:3 000 000 to 1:3 750 000 & larger scales for inset maps

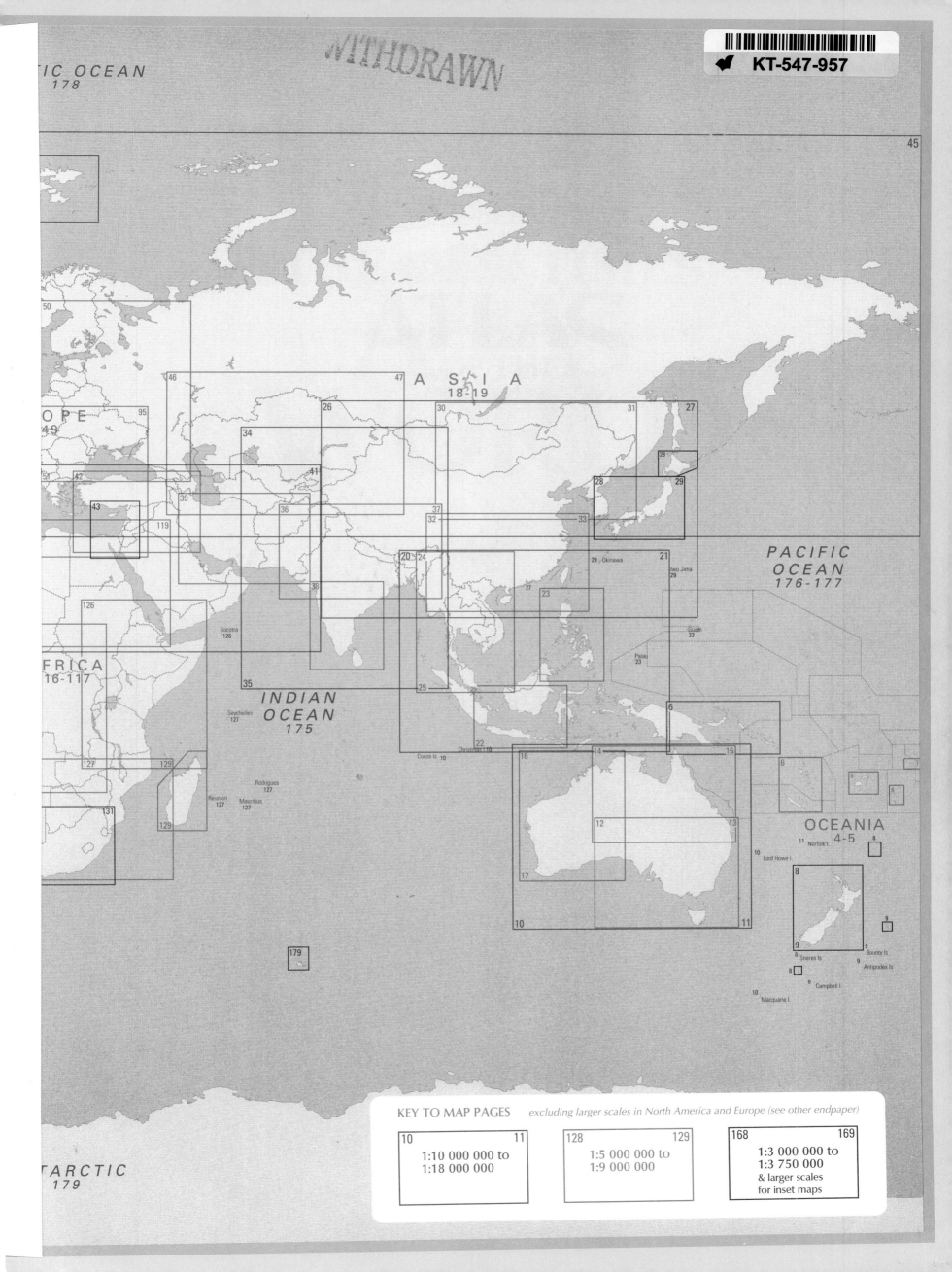

THE TIMES ATLAS OF THE WORLD

CONCISE EDITION

TIMES BOOKS
London

REF 912 TIM
95184

Times Books, London
77-85 Fulham Palace Road
London W6 8JB

First Edition 1972
Second Edition 1975
Third Edition 1978
Fourth Edition 1980
Fifth Edition 1986
Sixth Edition 1992

Seventh Edition 1995
Reprinted with changes 1996
Reprinted 1996, 1997
Revised 1997
Reprinted 1998

Copyright © Times Books Group Ltd 1997

Maps © Bartholomew Ltd 1997

Geographical Consultants

Mr H A G Lewis OBE
Geographical Consultant to The Times and Chairman of The Permanent Committee on Geographical Names

Mr B L D Winkleman

All rights reserved. No part of this publication may be reproduced, stored in a retrieval system, or transmitted, in any form or by any means, electronic, mechanical, photocopying, recording or otherwise without the prior written permission of the publisher and copyright owners.

The contents of this edition of The Times Atlas of the World Concise Edition are believed correct at the time of printing. Nevertheless the publisher can accept no responsibility for errors or omissions, changes in the detail given or for any expense or loss thereby caused.

Printed in the UK by The Bath Press

Physical Earth Maps pages 34-47:
Duncan Mackay

Picture credits pages 50-51:
Science Photo Library

ISBN 0 7230 0960 0

MH10126 Imp 002

The maps in this product are also available for purchase in digital format, from Bartholomew Data Sales.
Tel: +44 (0) 181 307 4065.
Fax: +44 (0) 181 307 4813

The publishers would like to thank all National Survey Departments, Road, Rail and National Park authorities, Statistical Offices and national Place-Name Committees throughout the World for their valuable assistance, and in particular the following:

Antarctic Place-Names Committee, London

Australian Surveying & Land Information Group, Belconnen, Australia

Automobile Association of South Africa, Johannesburg, Republic of South Africa

Mr John C. Bartholomew, Edinburgh

British Antarctic Survey, Cambridge

British Geological Survey, Keyworth, Nottinghamshire

The British Petroleum Company Ltd., London

Bureau of Coast and Geodetic Survey, Manila, Republic of the Philippines

Chief Directorate: Surveys and Land Information, Mowbray, Republic of South Africa

Commission de toponymie du Québec, Québec, Canada

Defense Mapping Agency, Aerospace Center, St Louis, Missouri, USA

Department of Survey and Land Information, Wellington, New Zealand

Department of National Development, Director of National Mapping, Canberra, Australia

Federal Survey Division, Lagos, Nigeria

Food and Agriculture Organisation of the United Nations, Rome, Italy

Foreign and Commonwealth Office, London

French Railways, London

Mr P J M Geelan, London

General Directorate of Highways, Ankara, Turkey

General Bathymetric Chart of the Oceans (GEBCO), International Hydrographic Organisation, Monaco

HM Stationery Office, London

Hydrographic Office, Ministry of Defence, Taunton

Institut Géographique National, Brussels, Belgium

Institut Géographique National, Paris, France

Instituto Brasileiro de Geografia e Estatistica, Rio de Janeiro, Brazil

Instituto Geografico e Cadastral, Lisbon, Portugal

Instituto Geografico Nacional, Lima, Peru

Instituto Geografico Nacional, Madrid, Spain

International Atomic Energy Agency, Vienna, Austria

International Boundaries Research Unit, Durham

International Road Federation, Geneva, Switzerland

International Union for the Conservation of Nature, Gland, Switzerland and Cambridge, UK

Kort- og Matrikelstyrelsen, Copenhagen, Denmark

Lands and Surveys Department, Kampala, Uganda

The Meteorological Office, Bracknell, Berkshire

National Geographic Society, Washington, DC, USA

National Library of Scotland, Edinburgh

Permanent Committee on Geographical Names, London

Royal Geographical Society, London

Royal Scottish Geographical Society, Glasgow

Scott Polar Research Institute, Cambridge

Scottish Development Department, Edinburgh

Statens Kartverket, Hønefoss, Norway

Survey of Israel, Tel Aviv, Israel

Survey Department, Singapore

Survey of India, Dehra Dun, India

Survey of Kenya, Nairobi, Kenya

Surveyor General, Harare, Zimbabwe

Surveyor General, Ministry of Lands and Natural Resources, Lusaka, Zambia

Surveys and Mapping Branch, Department of Energy, Mines and Resources, Ottawa, Canada

Surveys and Mapping Division, Dar-es-Salaam, Tanzania

The United States Board on Geographic Names, Washington, DC, USA

The United States Department of State, Washington, DC, USA

The United States Geological Survey, Earth Science Information Center, Reston, Virginia, USA

United Nations, specialised agencies, New York, USA

Marcel Vârlan, University 'Al. I. Cuza', Iaşi, Romania

THE TIMES ATLAS OF THE WORLD

IN ITS VARIOUS editions the Times Atlas of the World has been established for many years, as amongst the most authoritative in the world. The Atlas was described, in 1944, by Lord Shackleton, then President of the Royal Geographical Society, as 'the finest reference atlas ever produced'.

In 1972 the first Concise Edition of the Times Atlas of the World was published in the form of an abridged version of the Comprehensive Edition. Since then there have been six editions of the Concise, each extensively up-dated, but each containing essentially the same selection of maps, and the map scales and areas covered remained the same. This new seventh Edition, however, is a completely new atlas.

The methods employed by cartographers to create maps and atlases have evolved gradually over the centuries. Some of the changes have been small and others have been significant leaps, but none have compared with the revolution brought about by computer cartography.

Extensive databases, covering the world at a variety of scales, and computer cartography have allowed the creation of this new edition of the Concise with substantial changes in the selection of the areas mapped, the map scales and the design of the maps. The content of this seventh Edition reflects the world at the end of the 20th century.

In contrast to these radical changes in map production technology, the extensive editorial research, the accuracy and depth of detail, the effort to ensure the maps are as up-to-date as possible remain the same. The Introduction to the Atlas, located at the beginning of the reference map section, explains the sequence of the maps, the scales and projections used, the editorial policies on name forms and on international boundaries.

CONTENTS

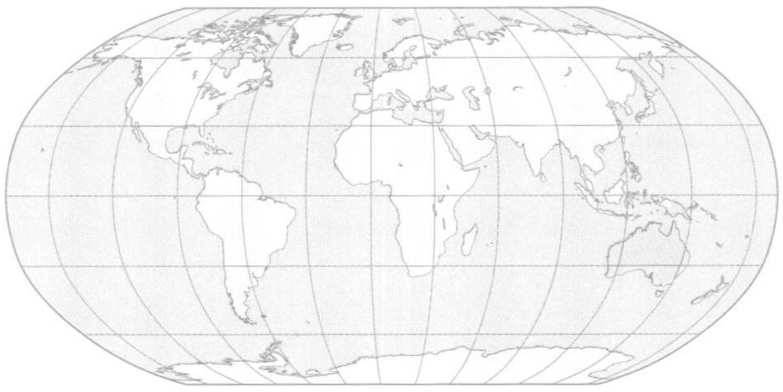

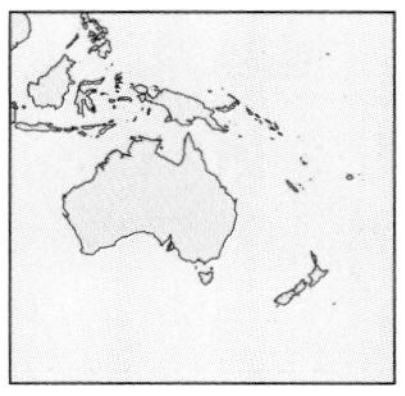

COUNTRYFINDER

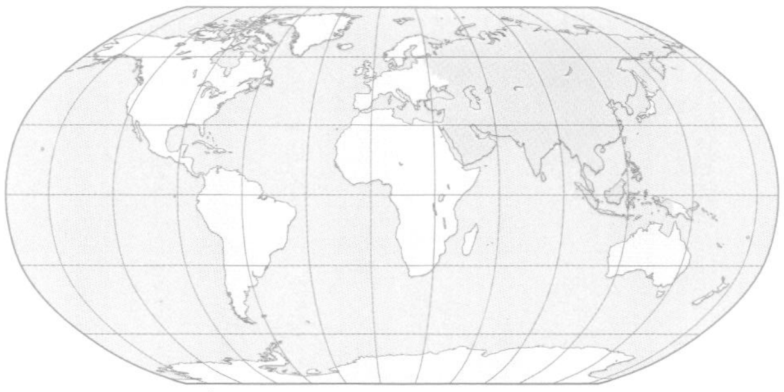

ASIA

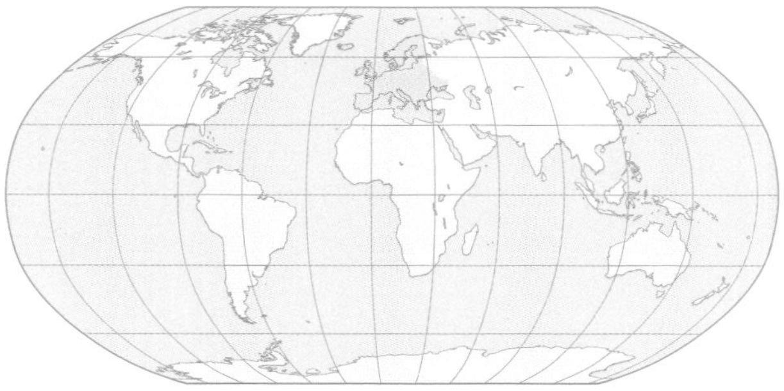

EUROPE

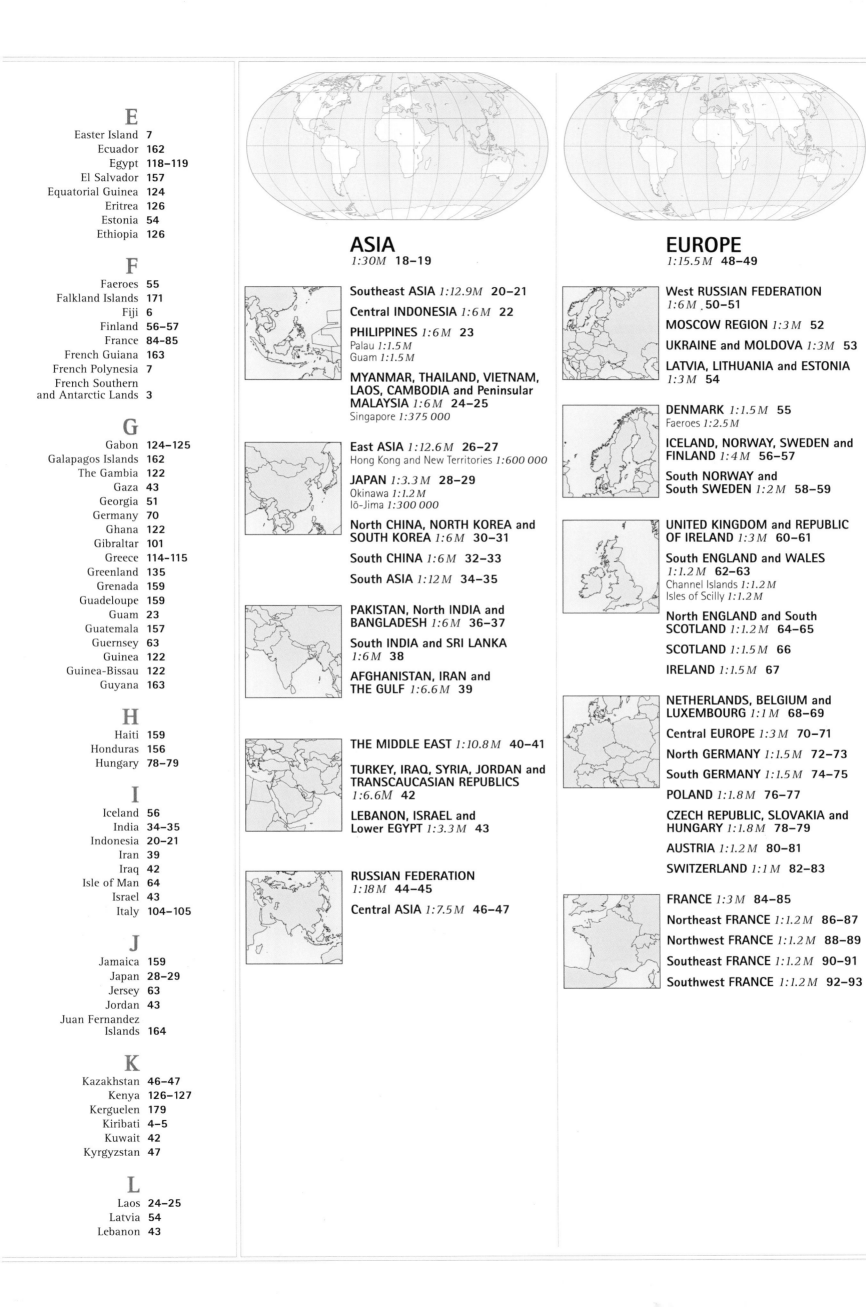

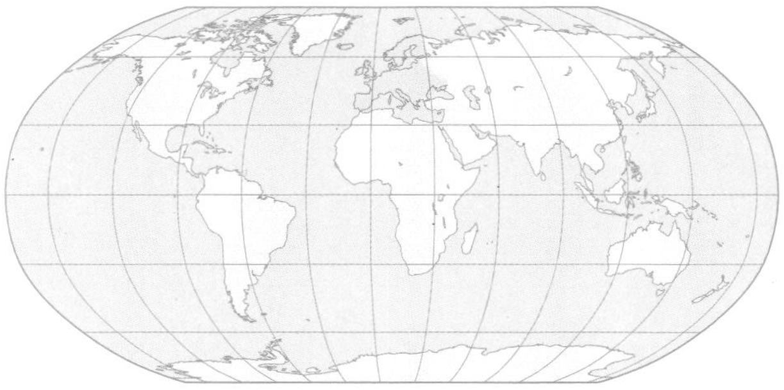

EUROPE continued

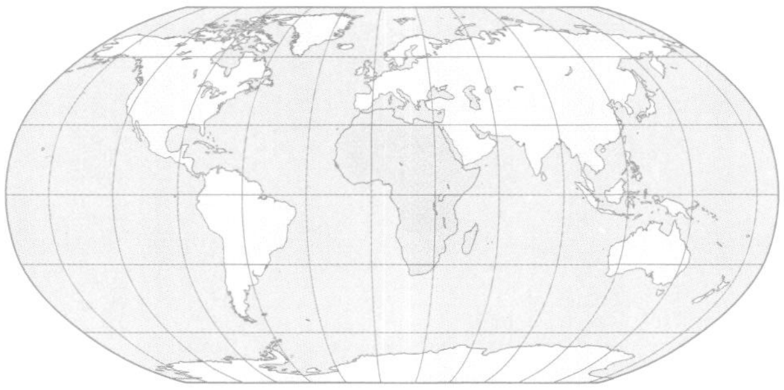

AFRICA

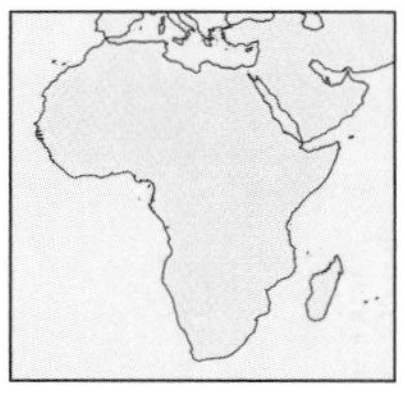

S

T

U

V

W

Y

Z

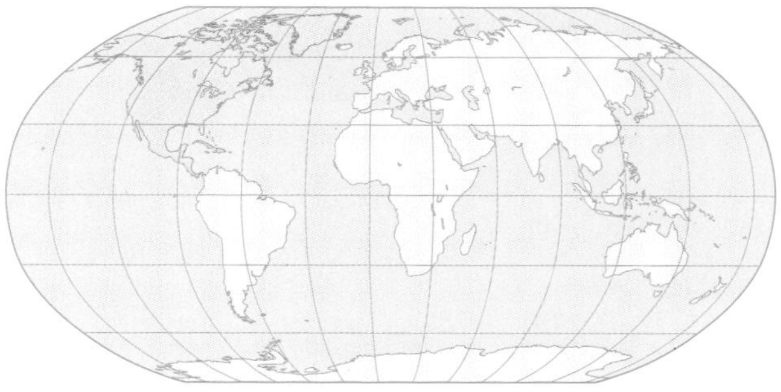

NORTH AMERICA

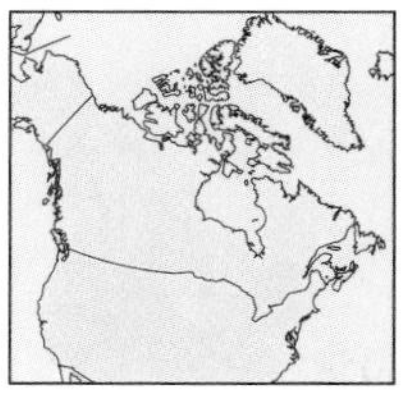

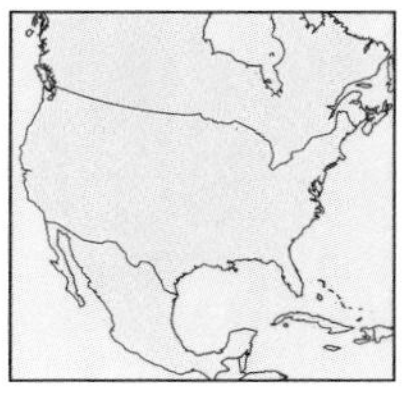

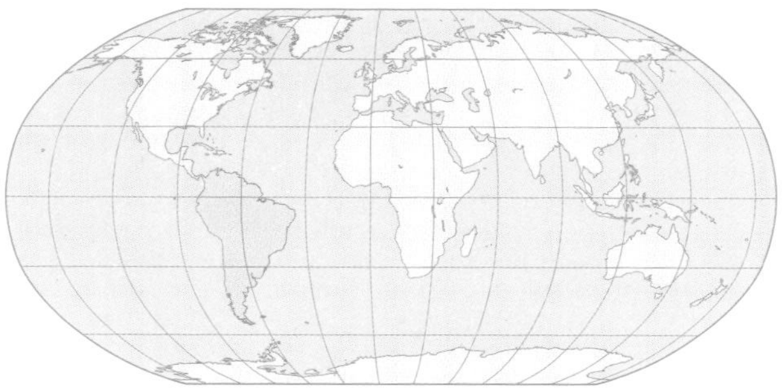

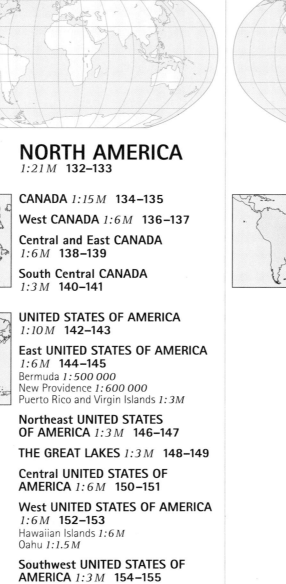

SOUTH AMERICA

IN THIS GUIDE to States and Territories all independent states and all major territories appear. The states and territories are arranged in alphabetical order using the same English-language conventional name form as is used on the maps. The name of the capital city is also given in its English-language form, while on the maps it is given in its local form with the English-language form in brackets.

The statistics used for the area and population, and as the basis for languages and religions, are from the latest available sources. The information for the internal divisions in federal states may be for a less recent date than that for the entire country, but are the latest available.

The order of the different languages and religions reflects their relative importance within the country; generally all languages and religions with over one or two per cent speakers or adherents are mentioned.

For independent states membership of the following international organizations is shown by the abbreviations below. Territories are not shown as having separate membership of these international organizations.

ASEAN	Association of Southeast Asian Nations
CARICOM	Caribbean Community
CIS	Commonwealth of Independent States
COMM.	Commonwealth
EU	European Union
NAFTA	North American Free Trade Area
OAU	Organization of African Unity
OECD	Organization for Economic Cooperation and Development
OPEC	Organization of Petroleum Exporting Countries
SADC	Southern African Development Community
UN	United Nations

AFGHANISTAN

Status : REPUBLIC
Area : 652,225 sq km (251,825 sq mls)
Population : 20,141,000
Capital : KABUL
Language : DARI, PUSHTU, UZBEK, TURKMEN
Religion : SUNNI MUSLIM, SHI'A MUSLIM
Currency : AFGHANI
Organizations : UN

MAP PAGE: 39

A LANDLOCKED COUNTRY in central Asia, Afghanistan borders Pakistan, Iran, Turkmenistan, Uzbekistan, Tajikistan and China. Its central highlands are bounded by the Hindu Kush to the north and desert to the south and west. Most farming is on the plains round Kabul, the most populated area, and in the far northeast. The climate is dry, with extreme temperatures. Civil war has disrupted the rural-based economy. Exports included dried fruit, nuts, carpets, wool, hides and cotton.

ALBANIA

Status : REPUBLIC
Area : 28,748 sq km (11,100 sq mls)
Population : 3,645,000
Capital : TIRANA
Language : ALBANIAN (GHEG, TOSK DIALECTS), GREEK
Religion : SUNNI MUSLIM, GREEK ORTHODOX, R.CATHOLIC
Currency : LEK
Organizations : UN

MAP PAGE: 112-113

ALBANIA LIES IN the western Balkans of south Europe, on the Adriatic Sea. It is mountainous, with coastal plains which support half the population. The economy is based mainly on agriculture and mining, chiefly chromite. The fall of communism brought reform and foreign aid for the ailing economy.

ALGERIA

Status : REPUBLIC
Area : 2,381,741 sq km (919,595 sq mls)
Population : 28,548,000
Capital : ALGIERS
Language : ARABIC, FRENCH, BERBER
Religion : SUNNI MUSLIM, R.CATHOLIC
Currency : DINAR
Organizations : OAU, OPEC, UN

MAP PAGE: 120-121

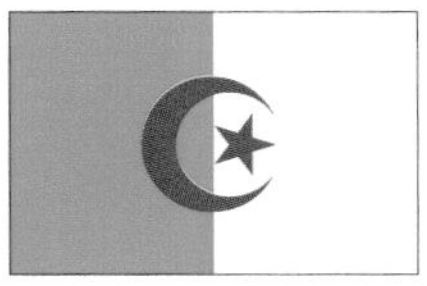

ALGERIA IS ON the Mediterranean coast of North Africa. The second largest country in Africa, it extends southwards from the coast into the Sahara Desert. Over 85 per cent of the land area is a dry sandstone plateau, cut by valleys and rocky mountains, including the Hoggar Massif in the southeast. Though hot, arid and largely uninhabited, the region contains oil and gas reserves. To the north lie the Atlas Mountains, enclosing the grassland of the Chott Plateau. The mountains separate the arid south from the narrow coastal plain which has a Mediterranean climate and is well suited to agriculture. Most people live on the plain and on the fertile northern slopes of the Atlas. Hydrocarbons have been the mainstay of the economy. Though reserves are dwindling, oil, natural gas and related products still account for over 90 per cent of export earnings. Other industries produce building materials, food products, iron, steel and vehicles. Agriculture employs a quarter of the workforce, producing mainly food crops. Political unrest including Islamic militancy in the early 1990s weakened the economy.

AMERICAN SAMOA

Status : US TERRITORY
Area : 197 sq km (76 sq mls)
Population : 56,000
Capital : PAGO PAGO
Language : SAMOAN, ENGLISH
Religion : PROTESTANT, R.CATHOLIC
Currency : US DOLLAR

MAP PAGE: 7

LYING IN THE South Pacific Ocean, American Samoa consists of five islands and two coral atolls. The main island is Tutuila.

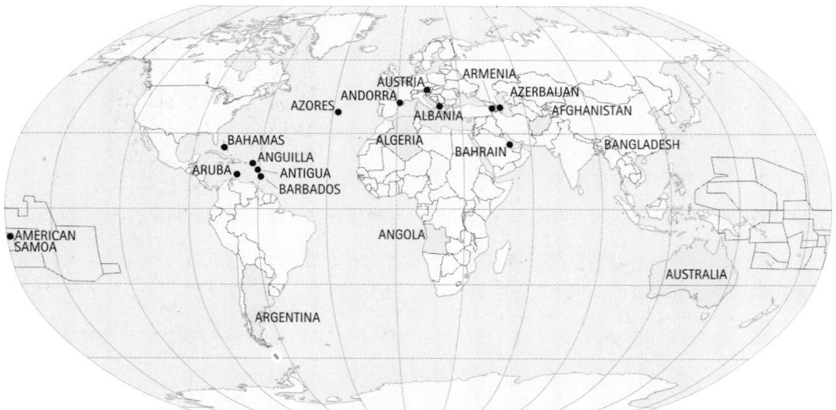

ANDORRA

Status : PRINCIPALITY
Area : 465 sq km (180 sq mls)
Population : 68,000
Capital : ANDORRA LA VELLA
Language : CATALAN, SPANISH, FRENCH
Religion : R.CATHOLIC
Currency : FRENCH FRANC, SPANISH PESETA
Organizations : UN

MAP PAGE: 102

A LANDLOCKED STATE in southwest Europe, Andorra nestles in the Pyrenees between France and Spain. It consists of deep valleys and gorges, surrounded by mountains. Winter lasts six months, with heavy snowfalls; spring and summer are warm. One-third of the population lives in the capital. Tourism (about 12 million visitors a year), trade and banking are the main activities. Livestock, tobacco and timber are also important. Exports include clothing, mineral water, cattle, electrical equipment, and paper and paper products.

ANGOLA

Status : REPUBLIC
Area : 1,246,700 sq km (481,354 sq mls)
Population : 11,072,000
Capital : LUANDA
Language : PORTUGUESE, MANY LOCAL LANGUAGES
Religion : R.CATHOLIC, PROTESTANT, TRAD.BELIEFS
Currency : KWANZA
Organizations : OAU, SADC, UN

MAP PAGE: 125

ANGOLA LIES ON the Atlantic coast of southern central Africa. Its northern province, Cabinda, is separated from the rest of the country by part of Congo (Zaire). Much of Angola is high plateau, with a fertile coastal plain where most people live. The climate is equatorial in the north but desert in the south. Over half the workforce are farmers, growing cassava, maize, bananas, coffee, cotton and sisal. Angola is rich in minerals. Oil and diamonds account for 90 per cent of exports. Civil war has slowed economic development.

ANGUILLA

Status : UK TERRITORY
Area : 155 sq km (60 sq mls)
Population : 8,000
Capital : THE VALLEY
Language : ENGLISH
Religion : PROTESTANT, R.CATHOLIC
Currency : E. CARIB. DOLLAR

MAP PAGE: 159

ANGUILLA LIES AT the northern end of the Leeward Islands in the Caribbean Sea. Tourism and fishing are the basis of the economy.

ANTIGUA AND BARBUDA

Status : MONARCHY
Area : 442 sq km (171 sq mls)
Population : 66,000
Capital : ST JOHN'S
Language : ENGLISH, CREOLE
Religion : PROTESTANT, R.CATHOLIC
Currency : E. CARIB. DOLLAR
Organizations : CARICOM, COMM., UN

MAP PAGE: 159

THE STATE COMPRISES Antigua, Barbuda and Redonda, three of the Leeward Islands in the eastern Caribbean. Antigua, the largest and most populous, is mainly hilly scrubland, with many beaches and a warm, dry climate. The economy relies heavily on tourism.

ARGENTINA

Status : REPUBLIC
Area : 2,766,889 sq km (1,068,302 sq mls)
Population : 34,768,000
Capital : BUENOS AIRES
Language : SPANISH, ITALIAN, AMERINDIAN LANGUAGES
Religion : R.CATHOLIC, PROTESTANT, JEWISH
Currency : PESO
Organizations : UN

MAP PAGE: 170-171

ARGENTINA OCCUPIES ALMOST the whole of the southern part of South America, from Bolivia to Cape Horn and from the Andes to the Atlantic Ocean. The second largest South American state has four geographical regions: the subtropical forests and swampland of the Chaco in the north; the temperate fertile plains or Pampas in the centre, which support most of the farming and the bulk of the population; the wooded foothills and valleys of the Andes in the west; and the cold, semi-arid plateaux of Patagonia, south of the Colorado river. Farming was the making of Argentina and still plays an important part in terms of export earnings. Beef, mutton and wool are the main produce but grains, sugarcane, soybeans, oilseeds and cotton are also important. Industry now makes the biggest contribution to the economy. Oil and gas are being produced and some mineral resources, chiefly iron ore, are being exploited. Manufacturing has expanded to include not only food processing but also textiles, motor vehicles, steel products, iron and steel, industrial chemicals and machinery.

ARMENIA

Status : REPUBLIC
Area : 29,800 sq km (11,506 sq mls)
Population : 3,599,000
Capital : YEREVAN
Language : ARMENIAN, AZERI, RUSSIAN
Religion : ARMENIAN ORTHODOX, R.CATHOLIC, SHI'A MUSLIM
Currency : DRAM
Organizations : CIS, UN

MAP PAGE: 42

A LANDLOCKED STATE in southwest Asia, Armenia is in southwest Transcaucasia and borders Georgia, Azerbaijan, Iran and Turkey. It is mountainous, with a central plateau-basin, and dry, with warm summers and cold winters. One-third of the population lives in Yerevan. War over Nagorno-Karabakh, the majority-Armenian enclave in Azerbaijan, has crippled the economy. Manufacturing and mining were the main activities. Agriculture was also important, producing mostly grapes (for brandy), vegetables, wheat and tobacco.

ARUBA

Status : NETHERLANDS TERRITORY
Area : 193 sq km (75 sq mls)
Population : 70,000
Capital : ORANJESTAD
Language : DUTCH, PAPIAMENTO, ENGLISH
Religion : R.CATHOLIC, PROTESTANT
Currency : FLORIN

MAP PAGE: 158

THE MOST SOUTHWESTERLY of the islands in the Lesser Antilles, Aruba lies just off the coast of Venezuela. Tourism and offshore finance are the most important activities.

AUSTRALIA

Status : FEDERATION
Area : 7,682,300 sq km (2,966,153 sq mls)
Population : 18,054,000
Capital : CANBERRA
Language : ENGLISH, ITALIAN, GREEK, ABORIGINAL LANGUAGES
Religion : PROTESTANT, R.CATHOLIC, ORTHODOX, ABORIGINAL
Currency : DOLLAR
Organizations : COMM., OECD, UN

MAP PAGE: 10-11

AUSTRALIA, THE WORLD'S sixth largest country, occupies the smallest, flattest and driest continent. The western half of the continent is mostly arid plateaux, ridges and vast deserts. The central-eastern area comprises lowlands of river systems draining into Lake Eyre, while to the east is the Great Dividing Range, a belt of ridges and plateaux running from Queensland to Tasmania. Climatically more than two-thirds of the country is arid or semi-arid. The north is tropical monsoon: the south is subtropical in the west, temperate in the east. A majority of Australia's highly urbanized population lives in cities along on the east, southeast and southwest coasts. Australia is richly endowed with natural resources. It has vast mineral deposits and various sources of energy. Over 50 per cent of the land is suitable for livestock rearing, though only 6 per cent can be used for crop growing. Forests cover 18 per cent of the land and fishing grounds off the coasts are teeming with marine life. Agriculture was the main sector of the economy, but its contribution to national income has fallen in recent years, as other sectors have grown. Sheep-rearing is still the main activity and Australia is the world's leading wool producer. It is also a major beef exporter and wheat grower. Wool, wheat, meat (beef and mutton), sugar and dairy products account for a third of export earnings. Minerals have overtaken agricultural produce as an export earner. As well as being among the world's leading producers of iron ore, bauxite, nickel and uranium, Australia also exploits lead, gold, silver, zinc and copper ores, tungsten and gems. Its is a major producer of coal; petroleum and natural gas are also being exploited. Manufacturing and processing has shifted from being based on agricultural produce (chiefly food processing and textiles) to being based on mineral production. The main products are: iron and steel, construction materials, petrochemicals, motor vehicles, electrical goods. Along with manufacturing, trade and services are the key growth sectors of the economy. Tourism is a major foreign exchange earner, with 1.5 million visitors a year.

AUSTRALIAN CAPITAL TERRITORY

Status: FEDERAL TERRITORY
Area: 2,400 sq km (927 sq mls)
Population: 299,000
Capital: CANBERRA

NEW SOUTH WALES

Status: STATE
Area: 801,600 sq km (309,499 sq mls)
Population: 6,009,000
Capital: SYDNEY

NORTHERN TERRITORY

Status: TERRITORY
Area: 1,346,200 sq km (519,771 sq mls)
Population: 168,000
Capital: DARWIN

QUEENSLAND

Status: STATE
Area: 1,727,200 sq km (666,876 sq mls)
Population: 3,113,000
Capital: BRISBANE

SOUTH AUSTRALIA

Status: STATE
Area: 984,000 sq km (379,925 sq mls)
Population: 1,462,000
Capital: ADELAIDE

TASMANIA

Status: STATE
Area: 67,800 sq km (26,178 sq mls)
Population: 472,000
Capital: HOBART

VICTORIA

Status: STATE
Area: 227,600 sq km (87,877 sq mls)
Population: 4,462,000
Capital: MELBOURNE

WESTERN AUSTRALIA

Status: STATE
Area: 2,525,000 sq km (974,908 sq mls)
Population: 1,678,000
Capital: PERTH

AUSTRIA

Status : REPUBLIC
Area : 83,855 sq km (32,377 sq mls)
Population : 8,053,000
Capital : VIENNA
Language : GERMAN, SERBO-CROAT, TURKISH
Religion : R.CATHOLIC, PROTESTANT
Currency : SCHILLING
Organizations : EU, OECD, UN

MAP PAGE: 80-81

A LANDLOCKED STATE in central Europe, Austria borders the Czech Republic, Italy, Slovenia, Hungary, Germany, Switzerland and Liechtenstein. Two-thirds of the country, from the Swiss border to eastern Austria, lies within the Alps, with the low mountains of the Bohemian Massif to the north. The only lowlands are in the east. The Vienna Basin and Danube river valley in the northeast contain almost all the agricultural land and most of the population. Austria also has a large forested area, minerals, chiefly iron ore, and fast-flowing rivers for hydroelectric power. The climate varies according to altitude, but in general summers are warm and winters cold with heavy snowfalls. Industry is the mainstay of the economy. Manufactures include machinery, iron and steel, electrical goods, chemicals, food products, vehicles, and paper products. Agricultural output covers 90 per cent of food needs. Crops include cereals, fruit (chiefly grapes) and vegetables as well as silage, sugar beet and rapeseed. Dairy and timber products are exported. With 15 million visitors a year, tourism is a major industry.

AZERBAIJAN

Status : REPUBLIC
Area : 86,600 sq km (33,436 sq mls)
Population : 7,499,000
Capital : BAKU
Language : AZERI, ARMENIAN, RUSSIAN, LEZGIAN
Religion : SHI'A MUSLIM, SUNNI MUSLIM, RUSSIAN AND ARMENIAN
Currency : MANAT
Organizations : CIS, UN

MAP PAGE: 42

AZERBAIJAN IS IN east Transcaucasia, southwest Asia, on the Caspian Sea. Its region of Nakhichevan is separated from the rest of the country by part of Armenia. It has mountains in the northeast and west, valleys in the centre and a coastal plain. The climate is continental. It is rich in energy and mineral resources. Oil production onshore and offshore is the main industry and the basis of heavy industries. Agriculture is still important, with cotton and tobacco the main cash crops. War with Armenia has reduced output.

AZORES

Status : PORTUGUESE TERRITORY
Area : 2,247 sq km (868 sq mls)
Population : 237,800
Capital : PONTA DELGADA
Language : PORTUGUESE
Religion : R.CATHOLIC, PROTESTANT
Currency : PORT. ESCUDO

MAP PAGE: 100

A GROUP OF islands in the Atlantic Ocean around 1500 kilometres (1000 miles) west of Portugal.

THE BAHAMAS

Status : MONARCHY
Area : 13,939 sq km (5,382 sq mls)
Population : 278,000
Capital : NASSAU
Language : ENGLISH, CREOLE, FRENCH CREOLE
Religion : PROTESTANT, R.CATHOLIC
Currency : DOLLAR
Organizations : CARICOM, COMM., UN

MAP PAGE: 145

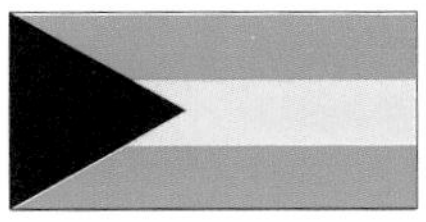

THE BAHAMAS IS an archipelago of about 700 islands and 2,400 cays in the northern Caribbean between the Florida coast of the USA and Haiti. Twenty-two islands are inhabited, and two thirds of the population live on the main island of New Providence. The climate is warm for much of the year, with heavy rainfall in the summer. Tourism is the islands' main industry. Banking, insurance and ship registration are also major foreign exchange earners. Exports include oil transhipments, chemicals, pharmaceuticals, crayfish and rum.

BAHRAIN

Status : MONARCHY
Area : 691 sq km (267 sq mls)
Population : 586,000
Capital : MANAMA
Language : ARABIC, ENGLISH
Religion : SHI'A MUSLIM, SUNNI MUSLIM, CHRISTIAN
Currency : DINAR
Organizations : UN

MAP PAGE: 39

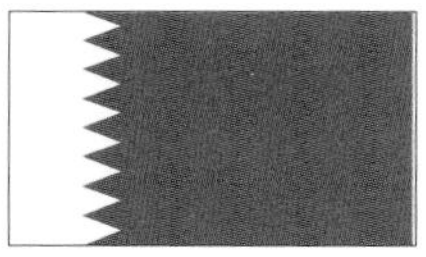

BAHRAIN'S 33 ARID islands lie in a bay in The Gulf, southwest Asia, off the coasts of Saudi Arabia and Qatar. Bahrain Island, the largest, has irrigated areas in the north where most people live. Oil is the main sector of the economy. Banking is also strong.

BANGLADESH

Status : REPUBLIC
Area : 143,998 sq km (55,598 sq mls)
Population : 120,433,000
Capital : DHAKA
Language : BENGALI, BIHARI, HINDI, ENGLISH, LOCAL LANGUAGES
Religion : SUNNI MUSLIM, HINDU, BUDDHIST, CHRISTIAN
Currency : TAKA
Organizations : COMM., UN

MAP PAGE: 37

THE SOUTH ASIAN state of Bangladesh is in the northeast of the Indian subcontinent, on the Bay of Bengal. It consists almost entirely of the low-lying alluvial plains and deltas of the Ganges and Brahmaputra rivers. The southwest is swampy, with mangrove forests in the delta area. The north, northeast and southeast have low forested hills. With a cultivable area of 70 per cent and few other natural resources, Bangladesh has a strong agricultural base, engaging two-thirds of the workforce. Food crops include rice, wheat, fruit and pulses; cash crops include jute, sugar cane, oilseeds, spices and tea. The main industries produce fertilizers, iron and steel, paper and glass as well as agricultural, marine and timber products. Exports include garments, raw and manufactured jute, fish and prawns, leather and tea. Bangladesh faces problems of overpopulation, low world commodity prices and the vagaries of climate. Floods and cyclones during the summer monsoon season often destroy crops. As a result, the country relies on foreign aid and remittances from its workers abroad.

BARBADOS

Status : MONARCHY
Area : 430 sq km (166 sq mls)
Population : 264,000
Capital : BRIDGETOWN
Language : ENGLISH, CREOLE (BAJAN)
Religion : PROTESTANT, R.CATHOLIC
Currency : DOLLAR
Organizations : UN, COMM., CARICOM

MAP PAGE: 159

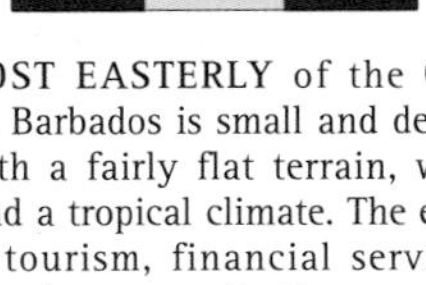

THE MOST EASTERLY of the Caribbean islands, Barbados is small and densely populated, with a fairly flat terrain, white-sand beaches and a tropical climate. The economy is based on tourism, financial services, light industries and sugar production.

© Bartholomew

BELARUS

Status: REPUBLIC
Area: 207,600 sq km (80,155 sq mls)
Population: 10,141,000
Capital: MINSK
Language: BELORUSSIAN, RUSSIAN, UKRAINIAN
Religion: BELORUSSIAN ORTHODOX, R.CATHOLIC
Currency: ROUBLE
Organizations: CIS, UN

MAP PAGE: 50-51

BELARUS IS A landlocked state in east Europe, bounded by Lithuania, Latvia, Russia, Ukraine and Poland. Belarus consists of low hills and forested plains, with many lakes, rivers and, in the south, extensive marshes. It has a continental climate. Agriculture contributes a third of national income, with beef cattle and grains as the major products. Manufacturing produces a range of items, from machinery and crude steel to computers and watches. Output has fallen since the ending of cheap Soviet energy supplies and raw materials.

BELGIUM

Status: MONARCHY
Area: 30,520 sq km (11,784 sq mls)
Population: 10,113,000
Capital: BRUSSELS
Language: DUTCH (FLEMISH), FRENCH, GERMAN (ALL OFFICIAL), ITALIAN
Religion: R.CATHOLIC, PROTESTANT
Currency: FRANC
Organizations: EU, OECD, UN

MAP PAGE: 69

BELGIUM LIES ON the North Sea coast of west Europe. Beyond low sand dunes and a narrow belt of reclaimed land are fertile plains which extend to the Sambre-Meuse river valley from where the land rises to the forested Ardennes plateau in the southeast. Belgium has mild winters and cool summers. It is densely populated and has a highly urbanized population. The economy is based on trade, industry and services. With few mineral resources, Belgium imports raw materials for processing and manufacture, and exports semi-finished and finished goods. Metal working, machine building, food processing and brewing, chemical production, iron and steel, and textiles are the major industries. External trade is equivalent to over 70 per cent of national income. Exports include cars, machinery, chemicals, foodstuffs and animals, iron and steel, diamonds, textiles and petroleum products. The agricultural sector is small, but provides for most food needs and a tenth of exports. A large services sector reflects Belgium's position as the home base for over 800 international institutions.

BELIZE

Status: MONARCHY
Area: 22,965 sq km (8,867 sq mls)
Population: 217,000
Capital: BELMOPAN
Language: ENGLISH, CREOLE, SPANISH, MAYAN
Religion: R.CATHOLIC, PROTESTANT, HINDU
Currency: DOLLAR
Organizations: CARICOM, COMM., UN

MAP PAGE: 157

BELIZE IS ON the Caribbean coast of central America and includes cays and a large barrier reef offshore. Belize's coastal areas are flat and swampy; the north and west are hilly, and the southwest contains the Maya mountain range. Jungle covers about half of the country. The climate is tropical, but tempered by sea breezes. A third of the population lives in the capital. The economy is based primarily on agriculture, forestry and fishing. Exports include sugar, clothing, citrus concentrates, bananas and lobsters.

BENIN

Status: REPUBLIC
Area: 112,620 sq km (43,483 sq mls)
Population: 5,561,000
Capital: PORTO-NOVO
Language: FRENCH, FON, YORUBA, ADJA, LOCAL LANGUAGES
Religion: TRAD.BELIEFS, R.CATHOLIC, SUNNI MUSLIM
Currency: CFA FRANC
Organizations: OAU, UN

MAP PAGE: 123

BENIN IS IN west Africa, on the Gulf of Guinea. The Atakora range lies in the northwest; the Niger plains in the northeast. To the south are plateaux, then a fertile plain and finally an area of lagoons and sandy coast. The climate is tropical in the north, but equatorial in the south. The economy is based mainly on agriculture and transit trade. Agricultural products, chiefly cotton, coffee, cocoa beans and oil palms, account for two thirds of export earnings. Oil, produced offshore, is also a major export.

BERMUDA

Status: UK TERRITORY
Area: 54 sq km (21 sq mls)
Population: 63,000
Capital: HAMILTON
Language: ENGLISH
Religion: PROTESTANT, R.CATHOLIC
Currency: DOLLAR

MAP PAGE: 145

IN THE ATLANTIC Ocean to the east of the USA, Bermuda is a group of small islands. The climate is warm and humid. The economy is based on tourism, insurance and shipping.

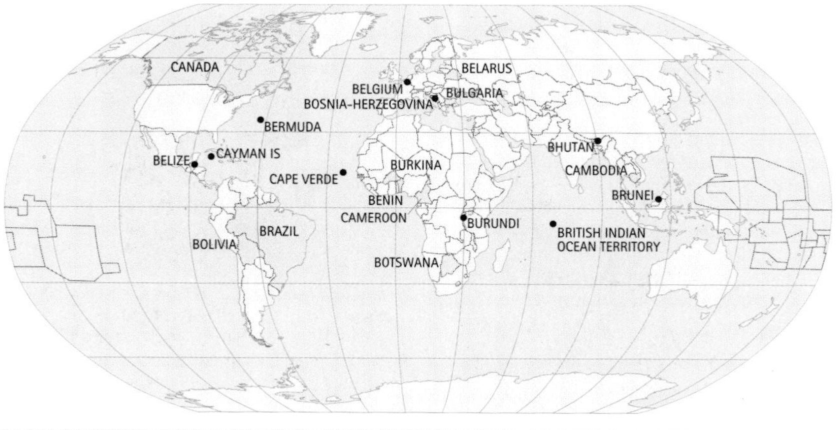

BHUTAN

Status: MONARCHY
Area: 46,620 sq km (18,000 sq mls)
Population: 1,638,000
Capital: THIMPHU
Language: DZONGKHA, NEPALI, ASSAMESE, ENGLISH
Religion: BUDDHIST, HINDU
Currency: NGULTRUM, INDIAN RUPEE
Organizations: UN

MAP PAGE: 37

BHUTAN NESTLES IN the eastern Himalayas of south Asia, between China and India. It is mountainous in the north, with fertile valleys in the centre, where most people live, and forested lowlands in the south. The climate ranges between permanently cold in the far north and subtropical in the south. Most of the working population is involved in livestock raising and subsistence farming, though fruit and cardamon are exported. Electricity, minerals, timber and cement are the main exports. Bhutan relies heavily on aid.

BOLIVIA

Status: REPUBLIC
Area: 1,098,581 sq km (424,164 sq mls)
Population: 7,414,000
Capital: LA PAZ/SUCRE
Language: SPANISH, QUECHUA, AYMARA
Religion: R.CATHOLIC, PROTESTANT, BAHA'I
Currency: BOLIVIANO
Organizations: UN

MAP PAGE: 164-165

A LANDLOCKED STATE in central South America, Bolivia borders Brazil, Paraguay, Argentina, Chile and Peru. Most Bolivians live in the high plateau within the Andes ranges. The lowlands range between dense Amazon forest in the northeast and semi-arid grasslands in the southeast. Bolivia is rich in minerals, and sales (chiefly zinc, tin, silver and gold) generate half of export income. Natural gas and timber are also exported. Subsistence farming predominates, though sugar, soya beans and, unofficially, coca are exported.

BOSNIA-HERZEGOVINA

Status: REPUBLIC
Area: 51,130 sq km (19,741 sq mls)
Population: 4,484,000
Capital: SARAJEVO
Language: SERBO-CROAT
Religion: SUNNI MUSLIM, SERBIAN ORTHODOX, R.CATHOLIC, PROTESTANT
Currency: DINAR
Organizations: UN

MAP PAGE: 104

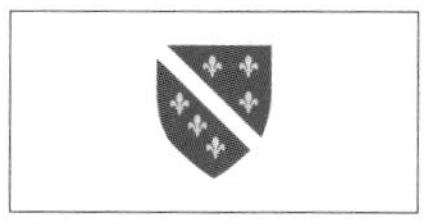

BOSNIA-HERZEGOVINA LIES IN the western Balkans of south Europe, on the Adriatic Sea. It is mountainous, with ridges crossing the country northwest-southeast. The main lowlands are around the Sava valley in the north. Summers are warm, but winters can be very cold. Civil war has ruined the economy, which was based on agriculture, sheep rearing and forestry. All production has ceased, the currency is worthless and only the black economy operates. Much of the population relies on UN relief.

BOTSWANA

Status: REPUBLIC
Area: 581,370 sq km (224,468 sq mls)
Population: 1,456,000
Capital: GABORONE
Language: ENGLISH (OFFICIAL), SETSWANA, SHONA, LOCAL LANGUAGES
Religion: TRAD.BELIEFS, PROTESTANT, R.CATHOLIC
Currency: PULA
Organizations : COMM., OAU, SADC, UN

MAP PAGE: 128-129

BOTSWANA, A LANDLOCKED state in south Africa, borders South Africa, Namibia, Zambia and Zimbabwe. Over half of the country lies within the upland Kalahari desert, with swamps to the north and salt-pans to the northeast. Most people live near the eastern border. The climate is subtropical, but drought-prone. The economy was founded upon cattle rearing, and beef is an important export, but now it is based on mining and industry. Diamonds account for 80 per cent of export earnings. Copper-nickel matte is also exported.

BRAZIL

Status: REPUBLIC
Area: 8,511,965 sq km (3,286,488 sq mls)
Population: 155,822,000
Capital: BRASÍLIA
Language: PORTUGUESE, GERMAN, JAPANESE, ITALIAN, AMERINDIAN LANGUAGES
Religion: R.CATHOLIC, SPIRITIST, PROTESTANT
Currency: REAL
Organizations: UN

MAP PAGE: 162-167

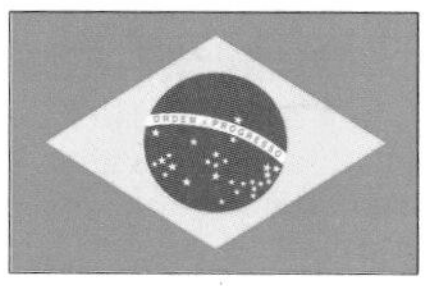

BRAZIL, IN EASTERN South America, covers almost half of the continent - making it the world's fifth largest country - and borders ten countries and the Atlantic Ocean. The northwest contains the vast Amazon Basin, backed by the Guiana Highlands. The centre west is largely a vast plateau of savannah and rock escarpments. The northeast is mostly semi-arid plateaux, while the east and south contain the rugged mountains and fertile valleys of the Brazilian Highlands and narrow, fertile coastal plains. The Amazon basin is hot, humid and wet; the rest of Brazil is cooler and drier, with seasonal variations. The northeast is drought-prone. Most Brazilians live in urban areas along the coast and on the central plateau, chiefly São Paulo, Rio de Janeiro and Salvador. Brazil is well endowed with minerals and energy resources. Over 50 per cent of the land is forested and 7 per cent is cultivated. Agriculture employs a quarter of the workforce. Brazil is the world's largest producer of coffee and a leading producer of sugar, cocoa, soya beans and beef. Timber production and fish catches are also important. Brazil is a major producer of iron, bauxite and manganese ores, zinc, copper, tin, gold and diamonds as well as oil and coal. Manufacturing contributes a quarter of national income. Industrial products include food, machinery, iron and steel, textiles, cars, pharmaceuticals, chemicals, refined oil, metal products and paper products. The main exports are machinery, metallic ores, cars, metal products, coffee beans, soya products, electrical and electronic

goods, and orange juice. Despite its natural wealth and one of the largest economies in the world, Brazil has a large external debt and growing poverty gap.

BRITISH INDIAN OCEAN TERRITORY

Status: UK TERRITORY
Area: 60 sq km (23 sq mls)
Population: 3,100

MAP PAGE: 18

THE TERRITORY CONSISTS of the Chagos Archipelago in the middle of the Indian Ocean. The islands are uninhabited apart from the joint British-US military base on Diego Garcia.

BRUNEI

Status: MONARCHY
Area: 5,765 sq km (2,226 sq mls)
Population: 285,000
Capital: BANDAR SERI BEGAWAN
Language: MALAY, ENGLISH, CHINESE
Religion: SUNNI MUSLIM, BUDDHIST, CHRISTIAN
Currency: DOLLAR (RINGGIT)
Organizations: ASEAN, COMM., UN

MAP PAGE: 20

THE SOUTHEAST ASIAN state of Brunei lies on the northwest coast of the island of Borneo, on the South China Sea. Its two enclaves are surrounded inland by Malaysia. The western part is hilly with a narrow coastal plain which supports some crops and most of the population. The eastern part is mountainous and more forested. Tropical rainforest covers over two thirds of Brunei. The economy is dominated by the oil and gas industries.

BULGARIA

Status: REPUBLIC
Area: 110,994 sq km (42,855 sq mls)
Population: 8,402,000
Capital: SOFIA
Language: BULGARIAN, TURKISH, ROMANY, MACEDONIAN
Religion: BULGARIAN ORTHODOX, SUNNI MUSLIM
Currency: LEV
Organizations: UN

MAP PAGE: 112

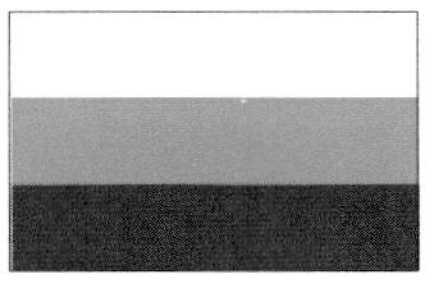

BULGARIA, IN SOUTH Europe, borders Romania, Yugoslavia, Macedonia, Greece, Turkey and the Black Sea. The Balkan Mountains separate the Danube plains in the north from the Rhodope massif and the lowlands in the south. The climate is subject to regional variation. The economy is based on agriculture and manufacturing, chiefly machinery, consumer goods, chemicals and metals. Disruption of Soviet-dominated trade has reduced output.

BURKINA

Status: REPUBLIC
Area: 274,200 sq km (105,869 sq mls)
Population: 10,200,000
Capital: OUAGADOUGOU
Language: FRENCH, MORE (MOSSI), FULANI, LOCAL LANGUAGES
Religion: TRAD.BELIEFS, SUNNI MUSLIM, R.CATHOLIC
Currency: CFA FRANC
Organizations: OAU, UN

MAP PAGE: 122-123

BURKINA, A LANDLOCKED country in west Africa, borders Mali, Niger, Benin, Togo, Ghana and Côte d'Ivoire. The north of Burkina lies in the Sahara and is arid. The south is mainly semi-arid savannah. Rainfall is erratic and droughts are common. Settlements centre on the country's rivers. Livestock rearing and farming are the main activities. Cotton, livestock, groundnuts and some minerals are exported. Burkina relies heavily on aid.

BURUNDI

Status: REPUBLIC
Area: 27,835 sq km (10,747 sq mls)
Population: 5,982,000
Capital: BUJUMBURA
Language: KIRUNDI (HUTU, TUTSI), FRENCH
Religion: R.CATHOLIC, TRAD.BELIEFS, PROTESTANT, SUNNI MUSLIM
Currency: FRANC
Organizations: OAU, UN

MAP PAGE: 127

THE DENSELY POPULATED east African state of Burundi borders Rwanda, Congo (Zaire), Tanzania and Lake Tanganyika. It is hilly with high plateaux and a tropical climate. Burundi depends upon subsistence farming, coffee exports and foreign aid.

CAMBODIA

Status: MONARCHY
Area: 181,000 sq km (69,884 sq mls)
Population: 9,836,000
Capital: PHNOM PENH
Language: KHMER, VIETNAMESE
Religion: BUDDHIST, R.CATHOLIC, SUNNI MUSLIM
Currency: RIEL
Organizations: UN

MAP PAGE: 25

CAMBODIA LIES IN southeast Asia, on the Gulf of Thailand. It consists of the Mekong river basin, with the Tonle Sap (Great Lake) at its centre. To the north, northeast and east are plateaux and to the southwest are mountains. The climate is tropical monsoon, with forests covering half the land. Most people live on the plains and are engaged in farming (chiefly rice growing), fishing and forestry. Devastated by civil war, Cambodia is dependent on aid.

CAMEROON

Status: REPUBLIC
Area: 475,442 sq km (183,569 sq mls)
Population: 13,277,000
Capital: YAOUNDÉ
Language: FRENCH, ENGLISH, FANG, BAMILEKE, MANY LOCAL LANGUAGES
Religion: TRAD.BELIEFS, R.CATHOLIC, SUNNI MUSLIM, PROTESTANT
Currency: CFA FRANC
Organizations: OAU, UN, COMM.

MAP PAGE: 124

CAMEROON IS IN west Africa, on the Gulf of Guinea. The coastal plains, southern and central plateaux are covered with tropical forest. The northern lowlands are semi-arid savannah, and the western highlands, around Mount Cameroon, support a range of crops. A majority of Cameroonians are farmers. Cocoa, coffee and cotton are the main cash crops, though crude oil, sawn wood and logs account for over half of export earnings.

CANADA

Status: FEDERATION
Area: 9,970,610 sq km (3,849,674 sq mls)
Population: 29,606,000
Capital: OTTAWA
Language: ENGLISH, FRENCH, AMERINDIAN LANGUAGES, INUKTITUT (ESKIMO)
Religion: R.CATHOLIC, PROTESTANT, GREEK ORTHODOX, JEWISH
Currency: DOLLAR
Organizations: COMM., NAFTA, OECD, UN

MAP PAGE: 134-135

THE WORLD'S SECOND largest country, Canada covers the northern two-fifths of North America and has coastlines on the Atlantic, Arctic and Pacific Oceans. On the west coast, the Cordilleran region contains coastal mountains, interior plateaux and the Rocky Mountains. To the east lie the fertile prairies. Further east, covering about half the total land area, is the Canadian, or Laurentian, Shield, fairly flat U-shaped lowlands around the Hudson Bay extending to Labrador. The Shield is bordered to the south by the fertile Great Lakes-St Lawrence lowlands. In the far north climatic conditions are polar. In general, however, Canada has a continental climate. Winters are long and cold with heavy snowfalls, while summers are hot with light to moderate rainfall. Most Canadians live in the south, chiefly in the southeast, in the urban areas of the Great Lakes-St Lawrence basin, principally Toronto and Montreal. Canada is well endowed with minerals, energy resources, forests and rich coastal waters. Only 5 per cent of land is classified as arable, but that is still a large area. Canada is among the world's leading exporter of wheat. Other major agricultural exports are apples, beef cattle, potatoes, oilseeds and feed grain. Canada is also a leading exporter of wood from its vast coniferous forests, and fish and seafood from its rich Atlantic and Pacific fishing grounds. It is a top producer of iron ore, uranium, nickel, copper, zinc and other minerals, as well as crude oil and natural gas. Its abundant raw materials are the basis of for manufacturing industries. The principal ones are car manufacture, food processing, chemical production, lumber, woodpulp and paper making, oil refining, iron and steel, and metal refining, Canada is an important trading nation. External trade is equivalent to about 30 per cent of national income. Exports include cars, crude materials, minerals fuels (chiefly oil and gas), food (chiefly wheat), newsprint, lumber, wood pulp, industrial machinery and aluminium. Canada has an important banking and insurance sector.

ALBERTA

Status: PROVINCE
Area: 661,190 sq km (255,287 sq mls)
Population: 2,672,000
Capital: EDMONTON

BRITISH COLUMBIA

Status: PROVINCE
Area: 947,800 sq km (365,948 sq mls)
Population: 3,570,000
Capital: VICTORIA

MANITOBA

Status: PROVINCE
Area: 649,950 sq km (250,947 sq mls)
Population: 1,117,000
Capital: WINNIPEG

NEW BRUNSWICK

Status: PROVINCE
Area: 73,440 sq km (28,355 sq mls)
Population: 751,000
Capital: FREDERICTON

NEWFOUNDLAND

Status: PROVINCE
Area: 405,720 sq km (156,649 sq mls)
Population: 581,000
Capital: ST JOHN'S

NORTHWEST TERRITORIES

Status: TERRITORY
Area: 3,426,320 sq km (1,322,910 sq mls)
Population: 63,000
Capital: YELLOWKNIFE

NOVA SCOTIA

Status: PROVINCE
Area: 55,490 sq km (21,425 sq mls)
Population: 925,000
Capital: HALIFAX

ONTARIO

Status: PROVINCE
Area: 1,068,580 sq km (412,581 sq mls)
Population: 10,795,000
Capital: TORONTO

PRINCE EDWARD ISLAND

Status: PROVINCE
Area: 5,660 sq km (2,158 sq mls)
Population: 132,000
Capital: CHARLOTTETOWN

QUEBEC

Status: PROVINCE
Area: 1,540,680 sq km (594,860 sq mls)
Population: 7,226,000
Capital: QUÉBEC

SASKATCHEWAN

Status: PROVINCE
Area: 652,330 sq km (251,866 sq mls)
Population: 1,002,000
Capital: REGINA

YUKON TERRITORY

Status: TERRITORY
Area: 483,450 sq km (186,661 sq mls)
Population: 33,000
Capital: WHITEHORSE

CAPE VERDE

Status: REPUBLIC
Area: 4,033 sq km (1,557 sq mls)
Population: 392,000
Capital: PRAIA
Language: PORTUGUESE, PORTUGUESE CREOLE
Religion: R.CATHOLIC, PROTESTANT, TRAD.BELIEFS
Currency: ESCUDO
Organizations: OAU, UN

MAP PAGE: 122

CAPE VERDE COMPRISES ten semi-arid volcanic islands and five islets off the coast of west Africa. The economy is based on fishing and subsistence farming, but relies on workers' remittances and foreign aid.

CAYMAN ISLANDS

Status: UK TERRITORY
Area: 259 sq km (100 sq mls)
Population: 31,000
Capital: GEORGE TOWN
Language: ENGLISH
Religion: PROTESTANT, R.CATHOLIC
Currency: DOLLAR

MAP PAGE: 158

IN THE CARIBBEAN, northwest of Jamaica, there are three main islands: Grand Cayman, Little Cayman and Cayman Brac. They form one of the world's major offshore financial centres, though tourism is also important.

© Bartholomew

CENTRAL AFRICAN REPUBLIC

Status: REPUBLIC
Area: 622,436 sq km (240,324 sq mls)
Population: 3,315,000
Capital: BANGUI
Language: FRENCH, SANGO, BANDA, BAYA, LOCAL LANGUAGES
Religion: PROTESTANT, R.CATHOLIC, TRAD. BELIEFS, SUNNI MUSLIM
Currency: CFA FRANC
Organizations: OAU, UN

MAP PAGE: 124

THE LANDLOCKED CENTRAL African Republic borders Chad, Sudan, Congo (Zaire), Congo and Cameroon. Most of the country is savannah plateaux, drained by the Ubangi and Chari river systems, with mountains to the north and west. The climate is hot with high rainfall. Most of the population live in the south and west, and a majority of the workforce is involved in subsistence farming. Some cotton, coffee, tobacco and timber are exported. However, diamonds and some gold account for more than half of export earnings.

CHAD

Status: REPUBLIC
Area: 1,284,000 sq km (495,755 sq mls)
Population: 6,361,000
Capital: NDJAMENA
Language: ARABIC, FRENCH, MANY LOCAL LANGUAGES
Religion: SUNNI MUSLIM, TRAD.BELIEFS, R.CATHOLIC
Currency: CFA FRANC
Organizations: OAU, UN

MAP PAGE: 118

CHAD IS A landlocked state of central Africa, bordered by Libya, Sudan, Central African Republic, Niger, Nigeria and Cameroon. It consists of plateaux, the Tibesti massif in the north and Lake Chad basin in the west. Climatic conditions range between desert in the north and tropical forest in the southwest. Most people live in the south and near Lake Chad. Farming and cattle herding are the main activities, cattle and raw cotton the chief exports. Impoverished by civil war and drought, Chad relies upon foreign aid.

CHILE

Status: REPUBLIC
Area: 756,945 sq km (292,258 sq mls)
Population: 14,210,000
Capital: SANTIAGO
Language: SPANISH, AMERINDIAN LANGUAGES
Religion: R.CATHOLIC, PROTESTANT
Currency: PESO
Organizations: UN

MAP PAGE: 170 -171

CHILE HUGS THE Pacific coast of the southern half of South America. Between the High Andes in the east and the lower coastal ranges is a central valley, with a mild climate, where most Chileans live. To the north is arid desert, to the south is cold, wet forested grassland. Chile is a leading exporter of copper, and is rich in other minerals and nitrates. Agriculture, forestry and fishing are important activities. Timber products, chemicals products and other manufactures account for a third of exports.

CHINA

Status: REPUBLIC
Area: 9,560,900 sq km (3,691,484 sq mls)
Population: 1,221,462,000
Capital: BEIJING
Language: CHINESE (MANDARIN OFFICIAL), MANY REGIONAL LANGUAGES
Religion: CONFUCIAN, TAOIST, BUDDHIST, SUNNI MUSLIM, R.CATHOLIC
Currency: YUAN
Organizations: UN

MAP PAGE: 26-27

CHINA, THE WORLD'S third largest country, occupies almost the whole of east Asia, borders fourteen states and has coastlines on the Yellow, East China and South China seas. It has an amazing variety of landscapes. The southwest contains the high Tibetan plateau, flanked by the Himalayas and Kunlun mountains. The northwest is mountainous with arid basins and extends from the Tien Shan and Altai ranges and vast Taklimakan desert in the west to the Mongolian plateau and Gobi desert in the centre-east. Eastern China is predominantly lowland and is divided broadly into the basins of the Huang He (Yellow River) in the north, Chang Jiang (Yangtze) in the centre and Xi Jiang (Pearl River) in the southeast. The main exceptions are the Manchurian uplands, loess plateau, Qin Ling range, southeast mountains and the Yunnan plateau in the far south. Climatic conditions and vegetation are as diverse as the topography. Northern China has an extreme continental climate, much of the country experiences temperate conditions, while the southwest enjoys a moist, warm subtropical climate. More than 70 per cent of China's huge population live in rural areas, chiefly in the northern part of the eastern lowlands and along the coast. Agriculture and livestock rearing involves two thirds of the working population. China is the world's largest producer of rice, wheat, soya beans and sugar and is self-sufficient in cereals, fish and livestock. Cotton, soya bean and oilseeds are the major cash crops. China is rich in coal, oil, natural gas and many minerals, chiefly iron ore, wolfram (tungsten ore), tin and phosphates. Industrial and agricultural production were given a boost by the economic reforms of the 1980s which introduced a degree of private enterprise. Industry also benefited from the setting up of joint ventures and the inflow of foreign investment. The major industries produce iron and steel, machinery, textiles, processed foods, chemicals and building materials. China's chief exports are textiles and clothing, petroleum and products, machinery and transport equipment, agricultural products, metal products, iron and steel.

ANHUI (ANHWEI)

Status: PROVINCE
Area: 139,000 sq km (53,668 sq miles)
Population: 58,340,000
Capital: HEFEI

BEIJING (PEKING)

Status: MUNICIPALITY
Area: 16,800 sq km (6,487 sq miles)
Population: 11,020,000
Capital: BEIJING

FUJIAN (FUKIEN)

Status: PROVINCE
Area: 121,400 sq km (46,873 sq miles)
Population: 31,160,000
Capital: FUZHOU

GANSU (KANSU)

Status: PROVINCE
Area: 453,700 sq km (175,175 sq miles)
Population: 23,140,000
Capital: LANZHOU

GUANGDONG (KWANGTUNG)

Status: PROVINCE
Area: 178,000 sq km (68,726 sq miles)
Population: 65,250,000
Capital: GUANGZHOU

GUANGXI ZHUANG (KWANGSI CHUANG)

Status: AUTONOMOUS REGION
Area: 236,000 sq km (91,120 sq miles)
Population: 43,800,000
Capital: NANNING

GUIZHOU (KWEICHOW)

Status: PROVINCE
Area: 176,000 sq km (67,954 sq miles)
Population: 33,610,000
Capital: GUIYANG

HAINAN

Status: PROVINCE
Area: 34,000 sq km (13,127 sq miles)
Population: 6,860,000
Capital: HAIKOU

HEBEI (HOPEI)

Status: PROVINCE
Area: 187,700 sq km (72,471 sq miles)
Population: 62,750,000
Capital: SHIJIAZHUANG

HEILONGJIANG (HEILUNGKIANG)

Status: PROVINCE
Area: 454,600 sq km (175,522 sq miles)
Population: 36,080,000
Capital: HARBIN

HENAN (HONAN)

Status: PROVINCE
Area: 167,000 sq km (64,479 sq miles)
Population: 88,620,000
Capital: ZHENGZHOU

HONG KONG

Status: SPECIAL ADMINISTRATIVE REGION
Area: 1,075 sq km (415 sq mls)
Population: 6,190,000
Capital: HONG KONG
Language: CHINESE (CANTONESE, MANDARIN), ENGLISH
Religion: BUDDHIST, TAOIST, PROTESTANT
Currency: DOLLAR

HUBEI (HUPEI)

Status: PROVINCE
Area: 185,900 sq km (71,776 sq miles)
Population: 55,800,000
Capital: WUHAN

HUNAN

Status: PROVINCE
Area: 210,000 sq km (81,081 sq miles)
Population: 62,670,000
Capital: CHANGSHA

JIANGSU (KIANGSU)

Status: PROVINCE
Area: 102,600 sq km (39,614 sq miles)
Population: 69,110,000
Capital: NANJING

JIANGXI (KIANGSI)

Status: PROVINCE
Area: 166,900 sq km (64,440 sq miles)
Population: 39,130,000
Capital: NANCHANG

JILIN (KIRIN)

Status: PROVINCE
Area: 187,000 sq km (72,201 sq miles)
Population: 25,320,000
Capital: CHANGCHUN

LIAONING

Status: PROVINCE
Area: 147,400 sq km (56,911 sq miles)
Population: 40,160,000
Capital: SHENYANG

NEI MONGOL (INNER MONGOLIA)

Status: AUTONOMOUS REGION
Area: 1,183,000 sq km (456,759 sq miles)
Population: 22,070,000
Capital: HOHHOT

NINGXIA HUI (NINGHSIA HUI)

Status: AUTONOMOUS REGION
Area: 66,400 sq km (25,637 sq miles)
Population: 4,870,000
Capital: YINCHUAN

QINGHAI (TSINGHAI)

Status: PROVINCE
Area: 721,000 sq km (278,380 sq miles)
Population: 4,610,000
Capital: XINING

SHAANXI (SHENSI)

Status: PROVINCE
Area: 205,600 sq km (79,383 sq miles)
Population: 34,050,000
Capital: XI'AN

SHANDONG (SHANTUNG)

Status: PROVINCE
Area: 153,300 sq km (59,189 sq miles)
Population: 86,100,000
Capital: JINAN

SHANGHAI

Status: MUNICIPALITY
Area: 6,300 sq km (2,432 sq miles)
Population: 13,450,000
Capital: SHANGHAI

SHANXI (SHANSI)

Status: PROVINCE
Area: 156,300 sq km (60,348 sq miles)
Population: 29,790,000
Capital: TAIYUAN

SICHUAN (SZECHWAN)

Status: PROVINCE
Area: 569,000 sq km (219,692 sq miles)
Population: 109,980,000
Capital: CHENGDU

TIANJIN (TIENTSIN)

Status: MUNICIPALITY
Area: 11,300 sq km (4,363 sq miles)
Population: 9,200,000
Capital: TIANJIN

XIZANG (TIBET)

Status: AUTONOMOUS REGION
Area: 1,228,400 sq km (474,288 sq miles)
Population: 2,280,000
Capital: LHASA

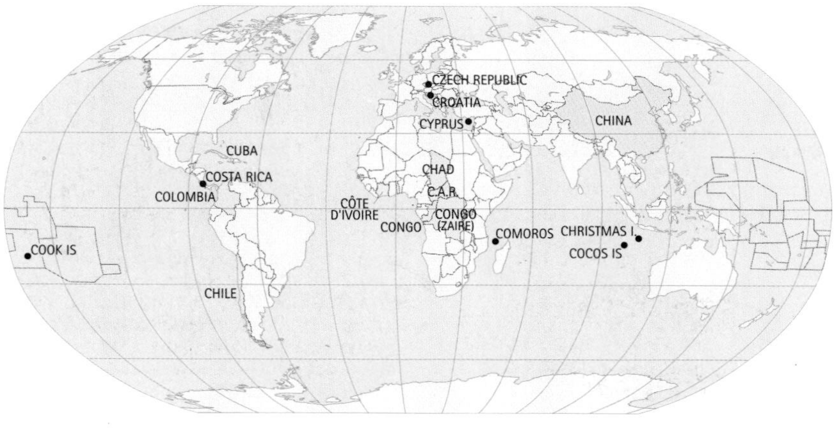

XINJIANG UYGUR (SINKIANG UIGHUR)
Status: AUTONOMOUS REGION
Area: 1,600,000 sq km (617,763 sq miles)
Population: 15,810,000
Capital: ÜRÜMQI

YUNNAN
Status: PROVINCE
Area: 394,000 sq km (152,124 sq miles)
Population: 38,320,000
Capital: KUNMING

ZHEJIANG (CHEKIANG)
Status: PROVINCE
Area: 101,800 sq km (39,305 sq miles)
Population: 42,360,000
Capital: HANGZHOU

CHRISTMAS ISLAND
Status: AUSTRALIAN TERRITORY
Area: 135 sq km (52 sq mls)
Population: 2,000
Capital: THE SETTLEMENT
Language: ENGLISH
Religion: BUDDHIST, SUNNI MUSLIM, PROTESTANT, R.CATHOLIC
Currency: AUSTR. DOLLAR

MAP PAGE: 10

COCOS ISLANDS
Status: AUSTRALIAN TERRITORY
Area: 14 sq km (5 sq mls)
Population: 1,000
Capital: HOME ISLAND
Language: ENGLISH
Religion: SUNNI MUSLIM, CHRISTIAN
Currency: AUSTR. DOLLAR

MAP PAGE: 10

THE COCOS ISLANDS are two separate coral atolls in the east of the Indian Ocean between Sri Lanka and Australia. Most of the population live on West Island and Home Island.

COLOMBIA
Status: REPUBLIC
Area: 1,141,748 sq km (440,831 sq mls)
Population: 35,099,000
Capital: BOGOTÁ
Language: SPANISH, AMERINDIAN LANGUAGES
Religion: R.CATHOLIC, PROTESTANT
Currency: PESO
Organizations: UN

MAP PAGE: 162

A STATE IN northwest South America, Colombia has coastlines on the Pacific Ocean and the Caribbean Sea. Behind coastal plains lie three ranges of the Andes, separated by high valleys and plateaux where most Colombians live. To the southeast are the prairies and then the jungle of the Amazon. Colombia has a tropical climate, though temperatures vary with altitude. Only 5 per cent of land can be cultivated, but a range of crops are grown. Coffee (Colombia is the world's second largest producer), sugar, bananas, cotton and flowers are exported. Petroleum and its products are the main export. Coal, nickel, gold, silver, platinum and emeralds (Colombia is the world's largest producer) are mined. Industry involves mainly processing minerals and agricultural produce. In spite of government efforts to stop the drugs trade, coca growing and cocaine smuggling are rife.

COMOROS
Status: REPUBLIC
Area: 1,862 sq km (719 sq mls)
Population: 653,000
Capital: MORONI
Language: COMORIAN, FRENCH, ARABIC
Religion: SUNNI MUSLIM, R.CATHOLIC
Currency: FRANC
Organizations: OAU, UN

MAP PAGE: 126-127

THE STATE COMPRISES three volcanic islands Grande Comore, Anjouan and Mohéil and some coral atolls in the Indian Ocean, off the east African coast. The tropical islands are mountainous, with poor soil. Subsistence farming predominates, but vanilla, cloves and ylang-ylang (an essential oil) are exported.

CONGO
Status: REPUBLIC
Area: 342,000 sq km (132,047 sq mls)
Population: 2,590,000
Capital: BRAZZAVILLE
Language: FRENCH (OFFICIAL), KONGO, MONOKUTUBA, LOCAL LANGUAGES
Religion: R.CATHOLIC, PROTESTANT, TRAD. BELIEFS, SUNNI MUSLIM
Currency: CFA FRANC
Organizations: OAU, UN

MAP PAGE: 124-125

CONGO, IN CENTRAL Africa, is for the most part forest or savannah-covered plateaux drained by the Ubangi-Congo river systems. Sand dunes and lagoons line the short Atlantic coast. The climate is hot and tropical. Most Congolese live in the southern third of the country. Oil is the main source of export revenue. Diamonds, lead, zinc and gold are also mined. Hardwoods are the second biggest export earner. Half of the workforce are farmers, growing food crops and cash crops including sugar, coffee, cocoa and oil palms.

CONGO (ZAIRE)
Status: REPUBLIC
Area: 2,345,410 sq km (905,568 sq mls)
Population: 43,901,000
Capital: KINSHASA
Language: FRENCH, LINGALA, SWAHILI, KONGO, MANY LOCAL LANGUAGES
Religion: R.CATHOLIC, PROTESTANT, SUNNI MUSLIM, TRAD. BELIEFS
Currency: ZAÏRE
Organizations: OAU, UN

MAP PAGE: 124-125

THE CENTRAL AFRICAN state of Congo consists of the basin of the Congo river flanked by plateaux, with high mountain ranges to the north and east and a short Atlantic coastline to the west. The climate is tropical with rainforest close to the Equator and savannah to the north and south. Congo has fertile land that grows a range of food crops and cash crops, chiefly coffee. It has vast mineral resources, copper and diamonds being the most important. However economic mismanagement and political turmoil have ruined the economy.

COOK ISLANDS
Status: NEW ZEALAND TERRITORY
Area: 293 sq km (113 sq mls)
Population: 19,000
Capital: AVARUA
Language: ENGLISH, MAORI
Religion: PROTESTANT, R.CATHOLIC
Currency: DOLLAR

MAP PAGE: 4-5

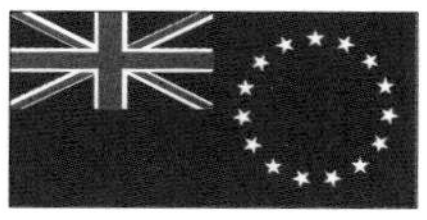

COSTA RICA
Status: REPUBLIC
Area: 51,100 sq km (19,730 sq mls)
Population: 3,333,000
Capital: SAN JOSÉ
Language: SPANISH
Religion: R.CATHOLIC, PROTESTANT
Currency: COLÓN
Organizations: UN

MAP PAGE: 156

COSTA RICA HAS coastlines on the Caribbean Sea and Pacific Ocean. From the tropical coastal plains the land rises to mountains and a temperate central plateau where most people live. Farming is the main activity and exports include bananas, coffee, sugar, flowers and beef. There is some mining and a strong manufacturing sector, producing a range of goods from clothing (the main export) and electrical components to food products and cement.

CÔTE D'IVOIRE
Status: REPUBLIC
Area: 322,463 sq km (124,504 sq mls)
Population: 14,230,000
Capital: YAMOUSSOUKRO
Language: FRENCH (OFFICIAL), AKAN, KRU, GUR, LOCAL LANGUAGES
Religion: TRAD.BELIEFS, SUNNI MUSLIM, R.CATHOLIC
Currency: CFA FRANC
Organizations: OAU, UN

MAP PAGE: 122

CÔTE D'IVOIRE (IVORY Coast) is in west Africa, on the Gulf of Guinea. In the north are plateaux and savannah, in the south are low undulating plains and rainforest, with sand-bars and lagoons on the coast. Temperatures are warm, and rainfall is heavier in the south. Most of the workforce is engaged in farming. Côte d'Ivoire is a major producer of cocoa and coffee, and agricultural products (including cotton and timber) are the main export. Gold and diamonds are mined and some oil is produced offshore.

CROATIA
Status: REPUBLIC
Area: 56,538 sq km (21,829 sq mls)
Population: 4,495,000
Capital: ZAGREB
Language: SERBO-CROAT
Religion: R.CATHOLIC, ORTHODOX, SUNNI MUSLIM
Currency: KUNA
Organizations: UN

MAP PAGE: 104-105

THE SOUTH EUROPEAN state of Croatia has a long coastline on the Adriatic Sea and many offshore islands. Coastal areas have a Mediterranean climate, inland is colder and wetter. Croatia was strong agriculturally and industrially, but secessionist and ethnic conflict, the loss of markets and the loss of tourist revenue have caused economic difficulties.

CUBA
Status: REPUBLIC
Area: 110,860 sq km (42,803 sq mls)
Population: 11,041,000
Capital: HAVANA
Language: SPANISH
Religion: R.CATHOLIC, PROTESTANT
Currency: PESO
Organizations: UN

MAP PAGE: 158

CUBA COMPRISES THE island of Cuba, the largest island in the Caribbean, and many islets and cays. A fifth of Cubans live in and around Havana. Sugar, with molasses and rum, account for two thirds of export earnings. Severe recession followed the disruption of traditional trade with east Europe and the ending of Russian subsidies.

CYPRUS
Status: REPUBLIC
Area: 9,251 sq km (3,572 sq mls)
Population: 742,000
Capital: NICOSIA
Language: GREEK, TURKISH, ENGLISH
Religion: GREEK (CYPRIOT) ORTHODOX, SUNNI MUSLIM
Currency: POUND
Organizations: COMM., UN

MAP PAGE: 43

THE MEDITERRANEAN ISLAND of Cyprus has hot summers and mild winters. The economy of the Greek south is based mainly on specialist agriculture and tourism, though shipping and offshore banking are also major sources of income. The Turkish north depends upon agriculture, tourism and aid from Turkey.

CZECH REPUBLIC
Status: REPUBLIC
Area: 78,864 sq km (30,450 sq mls)
Population: 10,331,000
Capital: PRAGUE
Language: CZECH, MORAVIAN, SLOVAK
Religion: R.CATHOLIC, PROTESTANT
Currency: KORUNA
Organizations: UN, OECD

MAP PAGE: 78

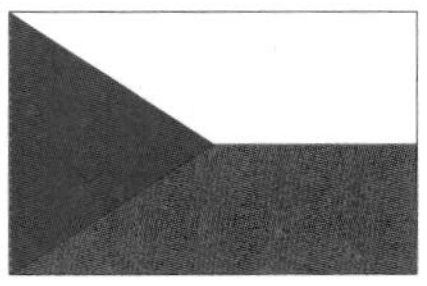

THE LANDLOCKED CZECH Republic in central Europe consists of rolling countryside, wooded hills and fertile valleys. The climate is temperate, but summers are warm and winters fairly cold. The country has substantial reserves of coal and lignite, timber and some minerals, chiefly iron ore, graphite, garnets and silver. It is highly industrialized and major manufactures include industrial machinery, consumer goods, cars, iron and steel, chemicals and glass. Since separation from Slovakia in January 1993, trade between the two countries has declined, exacerbating the difficulties the economy was already experiencing from the introduction of a free-market economy. There is, however, a growing tourist industry.

© Bartholomew

DENMARK

Status: MONARCHY
Area: 43,075 sq km (16,631 sq mls)
Population: 5,228,000
Capital: COPENHAGEN
Language: DANISH
Religion: PROTESTANT, R.CATHOLIC
Currency: KRONE
Organizations: EU, OECD, UN

MAP PAGE: 55

THE KINGDOM OF Denmark in north Europe occupies the Jutland Peninsula and nearly 500 islands in and between the North and Baltic seas. The country is low-lying, with a mixture of fertile and sandy soils, and long, indented coastlines. The climate is cool and temperate, with rainfall throughout the year. A fifth of the population lives in Greater Copenhagen on the largest of the islands, Zealand. Denmark's main natural resource is its agricultural potential; two thirds of the total area is fertile farmland or pasture. Agriculture, forestry and fishing are all important sectors of the economy. The chief agricultural products are cheese and other dairy products, beef and bacon, much of which is exported. Some oil and natural gas is produced from fields in the North Sea. Manufacturing, largely based on imported raw materials, now accounts for over half of exports. The main industries are iron and metal working, food processing and brewing, chemicals and engineering. Exports include machinery, food, chemicals, furniture, fuels and energy, and transport equipment.

DJIBOUTI

Status: REPUBLIC
Area: 23,200 sq km (8,958 sq mls)
Population: 577,000
Capital: DJIBOUTI
Language: SOMALI, FRENCH, ARABIC, ISSA, AFAR
Religion: SUNNI MUSLIM, R.CATHOLIC
Currency: FRANC
Organizations: OAU, UN

MAP PAGE: 119

DJIBOUTI LIES IN northeast Africa, on the Gulf of Aden. It consists mostly of low-lying desert, with some areas below sea level and a mountainous area to the north. Temperatures are high and rainfall is low. Most people live in the coastal strip. There is some camel, sheep and goat herding, and cattle, hides and skins are the main exports. With few natural resources, the economy is based on services and trade. The deep-water port and the railway line to Addis Ababa account for about two thirds of national income.

DOMINICA

Status: REPUBLIC
Area: 750 sq km (290 sq mls)
Population: 71,000
Capital: ROSEAU
Language: ENGLISH, FRENCH CREOLE
Religion: R.CATHOLIC, PROTESTANT
Currency: E. CARIB. DOLLAR, POUND STERLING, FRENCH FRANC
Organizations: CARICOM, COMM., UN

MAP PAGE: 159

DOMINICA IS THE most northerly of the Windward Islands in the eastern Caribbean. It is mountainous and forested, with a coastline of steep cliffs, and features geysers and hot springs. The climate is tropical and rainfall abundant. A quarter of Dominicans live in the capital. The economy is based on agriculture, with bananas (the major export), coconuts and citrus fruits the most important crops. There is some forestry, fishing and mining. Manufactured exports include soap, coconut oil, rum and bottled water. Tourism is growing.

DOMINICAN REPUBLIC

Status: REPUBLIC
Area: 48,442 sq km (18,704 sq mls)
Population: 7,915,000
Capital: SANTO DOMINGO
Language: SPANISH, FRENCH CREOLE
Religion: R.CATHOLIC, PROTESTANT
Currency: PESO
Organizations: UN

MAP PAGE: 159

THE STATE OCCUPIES the eastern two thirds of the Caribbean island of Hispaniola. It has a series of mountain ranges, including the highest peaks in the region, fertile valleys and a large coastal plain in the east. The climate is hot tropical, with heavy rainfall. A third of the population lives in the capital. Sugar, coffee and cocoa are the main cash crops. Bauxite, nickel (the main export), gold and silver are mined, and there is some light industry. Tourism is the main foreign exchange earner.

ECUADOR

Status: REPUBLIC
Area: 272,045 sq km (105,037 sq mls)
Population: 11,460,000
Capital: QUITO
Language: SPANISH, QUECHUA, AMERINDIAN LANGUAGES
Religion: R.CATHOLIC, PROTESTANT
Currency: SUCRE
Organizations: UN

MAP PAGE: 162

ECUADOR IS IN northwest South America, on the Pacific coast. It consists of a broad coastal plain, the high ranges of the Andes and the forested upper Amazon basin to the east. The climate is tropical, moderated by altitude. Most people live on the coast or in the mountain valleys. Ecuador is one of the continent's leading oil producers. Mineral reserves include gold, silver, zinc and copper. Most of the workforce depends on agriculture. Ecuador is the world's leading producer of bananas. Shrimps, coffee and cocoa are also exported.

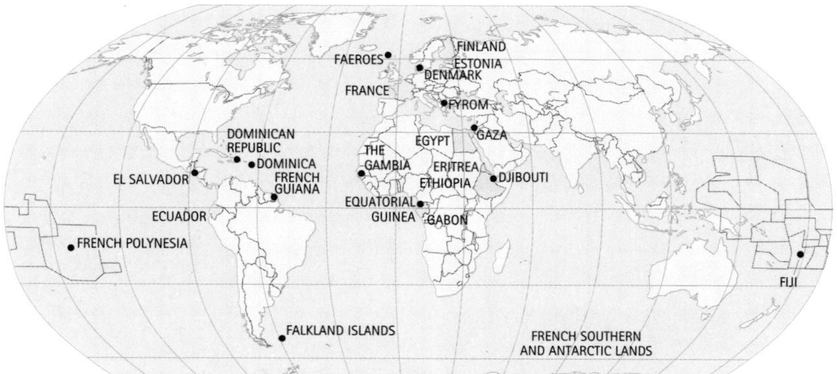

EGYPT

Status: REPUBLIC
Area: 1,000,250 sq km (386,199 sq mls)
Population: 59,226,000
Capital: CAIRO
Language: ARABIC, FRENCH
Religion: SUNNI MUSLIM, COPTIC CHRISTIAN
Currency: POUND
Organizations: OAU, UN

MAP PAGE: 118-119

EGYPT, ON THE eastern Mediterranean coast of North Africa, is low-lying, with areas below sea level in the west, and in the Qattara depression, and mountain ranges along the Red Sea coast and in the Sinai peninsula. It is a land of desert and semi-desert, except for the Nile valley, where 99 per cent of Egyptians live, about half of them in towns. The summers are hot, the winters mild and rainfall is negligible. Less than 4 per cent of land (chiefly around the Nile floodplain and delta) is cultivated, but farming employs half the workforce and contributes a sixth of exports. Cotton is the main cash crop. Rice, fruit and vegetables are exported, but Egypt imports over half its food needs. It has major reserves of oil and natural gas, phosphates, iron ore, manganese and nitrates. Oil and its products account for half of export earnings. Manufactures include cement, fertilizers, textiles, electrical goods, cars and processed foods. Workers' remittances, Suez canal tolls and tourist receipts are major sources of income, though attacks on tourists by Islamic militants has reduced the latter.

EL SALVADOR

Status: REPUBLIC
Area: 21,041 sq km (8,124 sq mls)
Population: 5,768,000
Capital: SAN SALVADOR
Language: SPANISH
Religion: R.CATHOLIC, PROTESTANT
Currency: COLÓN
Organizations: UN

MAP PAGE: 157

A DENSELY POPULATED state on the Pacific coast of central America, El Salvador has a coastal plain and volcanic mountain ranges that enclose a plateau where most people live. The coast is hot, with heavy summer rainfall, the highlands are cooler. Coffee (the chief export), sugar and cotton are main cash crops. Shrimps are also exported. Manufactures include processed foods, cosmetics, pharmaceuticals, textiles and clothing.

EQUATORIAL GUINEA

Status: REPUBLIC
Area: 28,051 sq km (10,831 sq mls)
Population: 400,000
Capital: MALABO
Language: SPANISH, FANG
Religion: R.CATHOLIC, TRAD.BELIEFS
Currency: CFA FRANC
Organizations: OAU, UN

MAP PAGE: 124

THE STATE CONSISTS of Rio Muni, an enclave on the Atlantic coast of central Africa, and the islands of Bioco, Annobón and Corisco group. Most people live on the coastal plain and upland plateau of the mainland; the capital is on the fertile volcanic island of Bioco. The climate is hot, humid and wet. Cocoa and timber are the main exports, but the economy depends heavily upon foreign aid.

ERITREA

Status: REPUBLIC
Area: 117,400 sq km (45,328 sq mls)
Population: 3,531,000
Capital: ASMARA
Language: TIGRINYA, ARABIC, TIGRE, ENGLISH
Religion: SUNNI MUSLIM, COPTIC CHRISTIAN
Currency: ETHIOPIAN BIRR
Organizations: OAU, UN

MAP PAGE: 126

ERITREA, ON THE Red Sea coast of northeast Africa, consists of high plateau in the north and a coastal plain that widens to the south. The coast is hot, inland is cooler. Rainfall is unreliable. The agricultural-based economy has suffered from 30 years of war and occasional poor rains. Coffee and cotton were the main cash crops, though food crops were important to reduce food aid.

ESTONIA

Status: REPUBLIC
Area: 45,200 sq km (17,452 sq mls)
Population: 1,530,000
Capital: TALLINN
Language: ESTONIAN, RUSSIAN
Religion: PROTESTANT, RUSSIAN ORTHODOX
Currency: KROON
Organizations: UN

MAP PAGE: 54

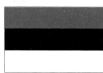

ESTONIA IS IN north Europe, on the Gulf of Finland and Baltic Sea. The land, one third of which is forested, is generally low-lying, with many lakes. The climate is temperate. About one third of Estonians live in Tallinn. Forests and oil-shale deposits are the main natural resources. Agriculture is limited to livestock and dairy farming. Industries include timber, furniture production, shipbuilding, leather, fur and food processing.

ETHIOPIA

Status: REPUBLIC
Area: 1,133,880 sq km (437,794 sq mls)
Population: 56,677,000
Capital: ADDIS ABABA
Language: AMHARIC, OROMO, LOCAL LANGUAGES
Religion: ETHIOPIAN ORTHODOX, SUNNI MUSLIM, TRAD.BELIEFS
Currency: BIRR
Organizations: OAU, UN

MAP PAGE: 126

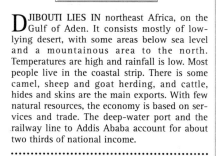

ETHIOPIA, IN NORTHEAST Africa, borders Eritrea, Djibouti, Somalia, Kenya and Sudan. The western half is a mountainous region traversed by the Great Rift Valley. To the east is mostly arid plateaux. The highlands are warm with summer rainfall, though droughts occur; the east is hot and dry. Most people live in the centre-north. Secessionist

wars have hampered economic development. Subsistence farming is the main activity, though droughts have led to famine. Coffee is the main export and there is some light industry.

FAEROES

Status: DANISH TERRITORY
Area: 1,399 sq km (540 sq mls)
Population: 47,000
Capital: TÓRSHAVN
Language: DANISH, FAEROESE
Religion: PROTESTANT
Currency: DANISH KRONE

MAP PAGE: 55

A SELF GOVERNING territory, the Faeroes lie in the north Atlantic Ocean between the UK and Iceland. The islands benefit from the Gulf Stream which has a moderating effect on the climate. The economy is based on deep-sea fishing and sheep farming.

FALKLAND ISLANDS

Status: UK TERRITORY
Area: 12,170 sq km (4,699 sq mls)
Population: 2,000
Capital: STANLEY
Language: ENGLISH
Religion: PROTESTANT, R.CATHOLIC
Currency: POUND

MAP PAGE: 171

LYING IN THE southwest Atlantic Ocean, northeast of Cape Horn, the Falklands consists of two main islands, West Falkland and East Falkland, where most of the population live, and many smaller islands. The economy is based on sheep farming and the sale of fishing licences, though oil has been discovered offshore.

FIJI

Status: REPUBLIC
Area: 18,330 sq km (7,077 sq mls)
Population: 784,000
Capital: SUVA
Language: ENGLISH, FIJIAN, HINDI
Religion: PROTESTANT, HINDU, R.CATHOLIC, SUNNI MUSLIM
Currency: DOLLAR
Organizations: UN

MAP PAGE: 6

FIJI COMPRISES TWO main islands, of volcanic origin and mountainous, and over 300 smaller islands in the South Pacific Ocean. The climate is tropical and the economy is based on agriculture (chiefly sugar, the main export), fishing, forestry, gold mining and tourism.

FINLAND

Status: REPUBLIC
Area: 338,145 sq km (130,559 sq mls)
Population: 5,108,000
Capital: HELSINKI
Language: FINNISH, SWEDISH
Religion: PROTESTANT, FINNISH (GREEK) ORTHODOX
Currency: MARKKA
Organizations: EU, OECD, UN

MAP PAGE: 56-57

FINLAND IS IN north Europe, on the Gulf of Bothnia and the Gulf of Finland. It is low-lying apart from mountainous areas in the northwest. Forests cover 70 per cent of the land area, lakes and tundra over 20 per cent. Only 8 per cent is cultivated. Summers are short and warm, and winters are long and severe, particularly in the north. Most people live in the southern third of the country, along the coast or near the many lakes. Timber is the main resource and products of the forest-based industries account for a third of exports. Finland has a large fishing industry and its agricultural sector produces enough cereals and dairy products to cover domestic needs. It has some mineral deposits, chiefly zinc, copper, nickel, gold and silver. Finland is a highly industrialised country, though it must import most of the raw materials. Apart from the timber and related industries, it has important metal working, shipbuilding and engineering industries. Other industries produce chemicals, pharmaceuticals, plastics, rubber, textiles, electronic equipment, glass and ceramics.

F.Y.R.O.M. (MACEDONIA)

Status: REPUBLIC
Area: 25,713 sq km (9,928 sq mls)
Population: 2,163,000
Capital: SKOPJE
Language: MACEDONIAN, ALBANIAN, SERBO-CROAT, TURKISH, ROMANY
Religion: MACEDONIAN ORTHODOX, SUNNI MUSLIM, R.CATHOLIC
Currency: DENAR
Organizations: UN

MAP PAGE: 112-113

FYROM, FORMERLY THE Yugoslav republic of Macedonia, is a landlocked state of south Europe, bordered by Yugoslavia, Bulgaria, Greece and Albania. Lying within the south Balkans, it is a rugged country, traversed north-south by the Vardar valley. It has fine, hot summers, but very cold winters. The economy is based on industry, mining and, to a lesser degree, agriculture. But conflict with Greece and UN sanctions against Yugoslavia have reduced trade, caused economic difficulties and discouraged investment.

FRANCE

Status: REPUBLIC
Area: 543,965 sq km (210,026 sq mls)
Population: 58,143,000
Capital: PARIS
Language: FRENCH, FRENCH DIALECTS, ARABIC, GERMAN (ALSATIAN), BRETON
Religion: R.CATHOLIC, PROTESTANT, SUNNI MUSLIM
Currency: FRANC
Organizations: EU, OECD, UN

MAP PAGE: 84-85

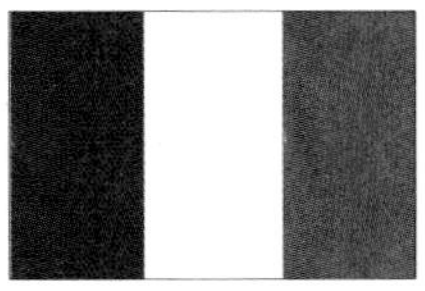

FRANCE LIES IN southwest Europe, with coastlines on the North Sea, Atlantic Ocean and Mediterranean Sea; it includes the Mediterranean island of Corsica. Northern and western regions consist mostly of flat or rolling countryside, and include the major lowlands of the Paris basin, the Loire valley and the Aquitaine basin, drained by the Seine, Loire and Garonne river systems respectively. The centre-south is dominated by the Massif Central. Eastwards, beyond the fourth major lowland area of the Rhône-Saône valley, are the Alps and the Jura mountains. In the southwest, the Pyrenees form a natural border with Spain. The climate of northern parts is temperate and wet, but in the centre and east it is continental, with warmer summers and milder winters. Along the south coast a Mediterranean climate prevails, with hot, dry summers and mild winters with some rainfall. Some 75 per cent of the population live in towns, but Greater Paris is the only major conurbation, with a sixth of the French population. Rich soil, a large cultivable area and contrasts in temperature and relief have given France a strong and varied agricultural base. It is a major producer of both fresh and processed food and the world's second largest exporter of agricultural products, after the USA. Major exports include cereals (chiefly wheat), dairy products, wines and sugar. France has relatively few mineral resources, though iron ore, potash salts, zinc and uranium are mined. It has coal reserves, some oil and natural gas, but it relies mainly for its energy needs on nuclear and hydroelectric power and imported fuels. France is the world's fourth largest industrial power after the USA, Japan and Germany. Heavy industries include iron, steel and aluminium production and oil refining. Other major industries are food processing, motor vehicles, aerospace, chemicals and pharmaceuticals, telecommunications, computers and armaments as well as luxury goods, fashion and perfumes. The main exports are machinery, agricultural products, cars and other transport equipment. France has a strong services sector and tourism is a major source of revenue and employment.

FRENCH GUIANA

Status: FRENCH TERRITORY
Area: 90,000 sq km (34,749 sq mls)
Population: 147,000
Capital: CAYENNE
Language: FRENCH, FRENCH CREOLE
Religion: R.CATHOLIC, PROTESTANT
Currency: FRENCH FRANC

MAP PAGE: 163

FRENCH GUIANA, ON the northeast coast of South America, is densely forested and is mountainous in the south. The climate is tropical with high rainfall. Most people live in the coastal strip and most workers are involved in subsistence farming, though sugar is exported. Livestock rearing and fishing are also important. Timber and mineral resources are largely unexploited and industry is limited. French Guiana depends upon French aid.

FRENCH POLYNESIA

Status: FRENCH TERRITORY
Area: 3,265 sq km (1,261 sq mls)
Population: 220,000
Capital: PAPEETE
Language: FRENCH, POLYNESIAN LANGUAGES
Religion: PROTESTANT, R.CATHOLIC, MORMON
Currency: PACIFIC FRANC

MAP PAGE: 7

EXTENDING OVER A vast area of the southeast Pacific Ocean, French Polynesia comprises more than 130 islands and coral atolls. The main island groups are the Marquesas, the Tuamotu Archipelago and the Society Islands. The capital, Papeete, is on Tahiti in the Society Islands. The climate is subtropical and the economy is based on tourism.

FRENCH SOUTHERN AND ANTARCTIC LANDS

Status: FRENCH TERRITORY
Area: 7,781 sq km (3,004 sq mls)

MAP PAGE: 3

THIS TERRITORY INCLUDES Crozet Island, Kerguelen, Amsterdam Island and St Paul Island. All are uninhabited apart from scientific research staff. In accordance with the Antarctic Treaty, French territorial claims in Antarctica have been suspended.

GABON

Status: REPUBLIC
Area: 267,667 sq km (103,347 sq mls)
Population: 1,320,000
Capital: LIBREVILLE
Language: FRENCH, FANG, LOCAL LANGUAGES
Religion: R.CATHOLIC, PROTESTANT, TRAD.BELIEFS
Currency: CFA FRANC
Organizations: OAU, UN

MAP PAGE: 124-125

GABON, ON THE Atlantic coast of central Africa consists of low plateaux, with a coastal plain lined by lagoons and mangrove swamps. The climate is tropical and rainforests cover 75 per cent of the land. Half of the population lives in towns, chiefly Libreville and Port Gentil. The economy is heavily dependent on mineral resources, mainly oil but also manganese and uranium. Timber, chiefly okoumé, is exported. Agriculture is mainly at subsistence level, but oil palms, bananas, sugarcane and rubber are grown.

THE GAMBIA

Status: REPUBLIC
Area: 11,295 sq km (4,361 sq mls)
Population: 1,118,000
Capital: BANJUL
Language: ENGLISH (OFFICIAL), MALINKE, FULANI, WOLOF
Religion: SUNNI MUSLIM, PROTESTANT
Currency: DALASI
Organizations: COMM., OAU, UN

MAP PAGE: 122

THE GAMBIA, ON the coast of west Africa, occupies a strip of land along the lower Gambia River. Sandy beaches are backed by mangrove swamps, beyond which is savannah. The climate is tropical, with rainfall in the summer. Over 70 per cent of Gambians are farmers, growing chiefly groundnuts (the main export) but also seed cotton, oil palms and food crops. Livestock rearing and fishing are important, while manufacturing is limited. Re-exports, mainly from Senegal, and tourism are major sources of income.

GAZA

Status: AUTONOMOUS REGION
Area: 363 sq km (140 sq mls)
Population: 756,000
Capital: GAZA
Language: ARABIC
Religion: SUNNI MUSLIM, SHI'A MUSLIM
Currency: ISRAELI SHEKEL

MAP PAGE: 43

GAZA IS A narrow strip of land on the southeast corner of the Mediterranean Sea, between Egypt and Israel. The territory has limited autonomy from Israel. The economy is based on agriculture and remittances from work in Israel.

© Bartholomew

GEORGIA

Status: REPUBLIC
Area: 69,700 sq km (26,911 sq mls)
Population: 5,457,000
Capital: TBILISI
Language: GEORGIAN, RUSSIAN, ARMENIAN, AZERI, OSSETIAN, ABKHAZ
Religion: GEORGIAN ORTHODOX, RUSSIAN ORTHODOX, SHI'A MUSLIM
Currency: LARI
Organizations: CIS, UN

MAP PAGE: 51

GEORGIA IS IN northwest Transcaucasia, southwest Asia, on the Black Sea. Mountain ranges in the north and south flank the Kura and Rioni valleys. The climate is generally mild, but subtropical along the coast. Agriculture is important, with tea, grapes, citrus fruits and tobacco the major crops. Mineral resources include manganese, coal and oil, and the main industries are iron and steel, oil refining and machine building. However, economic activity has been seriously affected by separatist wars and political unrest.

GERMANY

Status: REPUBLIC
Area: 357,868 sq km (138,174 sq mls)
Population: 81,642,000
Capital: BERLIN
Language: GERMAN, TURKISH
Religion: PROTESTANT, R.CATHOLIC, SUNNI MUSLIM
Currency: MARK
Organizations: EU, OECD, UN

MAP PAGE: 70

THE WEST EUROPEAN state of Germany borders nine countries and has coastlines on the North and Baltic seas. It includes the southern part of the Jutland peninsula and Frisian islands. Behind the indented coastline and covering about one third of the country is the north German plain, a region of fertile farmland and sandy heaths drained by the country's major rivers. The central highlands are a belt of forested hills and plateaux which stretches from the Eifel region in the west to the Erzgebirge (Ore mountains) along the border with the Czech Republic. Farther south the land rises to the Swabian and Jura mountains, with the high rugged and forested Black Forest in the southwest and the Bavarian plateau and Alps to the southeast. The climate is temperate, with continental conditions in eastern areas where winters are colder. Rainfall is evenly spread throughout the year. Divided in 1945 after defeat in the second world war, Germany was reunified in 1990, barely a year after the collapse of communism in eastern Europe. It had been thought that west Germany, the world's third largest industrial economy and second largest exporter, would easily absorb east Germany, less than half the size and with a quarter of the population. But the initial cost of unification was high. The overhaul of east German industry led to 30 per cent unemployment there, while the high level of investment and the rising social security bill led to tax increases in the west. In addition unification coincided with recession in the west German economy and rising unemployment, which created social tensions. However, by 1994 there were signs that the economy was pulling out of the recession. Germany lacks minerals and other industrial raw materials, with the exception of lignite and potash. It has a small agricultural base, though a few products (chiefly wines and beers) enjoy an international reputation. It is predominantly an industrial economy, dominated by the mechanical and engineering, iron and steel, chemical, pharmaceutical, motor, textile and high-tech industries. It also has a large service sector, with tourism, banking and finance being important.

BADEN-WÜRTTEMBERG

Status: STATE
Area: 35,751 sq km (13,804 sq miles)
Population: 10,344,009
Capital: STUTTGART

BAYERN (BAVARIA)

Status: STATE
Area: 70,554 sq km (27,241 sq miles)
Population: 12,014,674
Capital: MÜNCHEN

BERLIN

Status: STATE
Area: 889 sq km (343 sq miles)
Population: 3,467,322
Capital: BERLIN

BRANDENBURG

Status: STATE
Area: 29,056 sq km (11,219 sq miles)
Population: 2,545,511
Capital: POTSDAM

BREMEN

Status: STATE
Area: 404 sq km (156 sq miles)
Population: 678,731
Capital: BREMEN

HAMBURG

Status: STATE
Area: 755 sq km (292 sq miles)
Population: 1,708,528
Capital: HAMBURG

HESSEN (HESSE)

Status: STATE
Area: 21,114 sq km (8,152 sq miles)
Population: 6,016,251
Capital: WIESBADEN

MECKLENBURG-VORPOMMERN (MECKLENBURG-WEST POMERANIA)

Status: STATE
Area: 23,559 sq kn (9,096 sq miles)
Population: 1,829,587
Capital: SCHWERIN

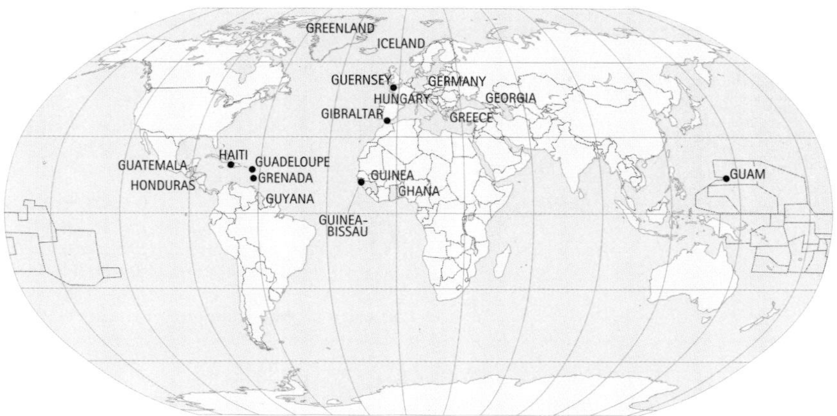

NIEDERSACHSEN (LOWER SAXONY)

Status: STATE
Area: 47,351 sq km (18,282 sq miles)
Population: 7,795,149
Capital: HANNOVER

NORDRHEIN-WESTFALEN (NORTH RHINE-WESTPHALIA)

Status: STATE
Area: 34,070 sq km (13,155 sq miles)
Population: 17,908,473
Capital: DÜSSELDORF

RHEINLAND-PFALZ (RHINELAND-PALATINATE)

Status: STATE
Area: 19,849 sq km (7,664 sq miles)
Population: 3,983,282
Capital: MAINZ

SAARLAND

Status: STATE
Area: 2,570 sq km (992 sq miles)
Population: 1,083,119
Capital: SAARBRÜCKEN

SACHSEN (SAXONY)

Status: STATE
Area: 18,341 sq km (7,081 sq miles)
Population: 4,557,210
Capital: DRESDEN

SACHSEN-ANHALT (SAXONY-ANHALT)

Status: STATE
Area: 20,607 sq km (7,956 sq miles)
Population: 2,731,463
Capital: MAGDEBURG

SCHLESWIG-HOLSTEIN

Status: STATE
Area: 15,731 sq km (6,074 sq miles)
Population: 2,730,595
Capital: KIEL

THÜRINGEN (THURINGIA)

Status: STATE
Area: 16,251 sq km (6,275 sq miles)
Population: 2,496,685
Capital: ERFURT

GHANA

Status: REPUBLIC
Area: 238,537 sq km (92,100 sq mls)
Population: 17,453,000
Capital: ACCRA
Language: ENGLISH (OFFICIAL), HAUSA, AKAN, LOCAL LANGUAGES
Religion: PROTESTANT, R.CATHOLIC, SUNNI MUSLIM, TRAD. BELIEFS
Currency: CEDI
Organizations: COMM., OAU, UN

MAP PAGE: 122

A WEST AFRICAN STATE on the Gulf of Guinea, Ghana is a land of plains and low plateaux covered with savannah and, in the west, rainforest. In the east is the Volta basin. The climate is tropical, with high rainfall in the south, where most people live. Ghana is a major producer of cocoa. Timber is also an important commodity. Bauxite, gold, diamonds and manganese ore are mined, and there are a number of industries around Tema.

GIBRALTAR

Status: UK TERRITORY
Area: 6.5 sq km (2.5 sq mls)
Population: 28,000
Capital: GIBRALTAR
Language: ENGLISH, SPANISH
Religion: R.CATHOLIC, PROTESTANT, SUNNI MUSLIM
Currency: POUND

MAP PAGE: 101

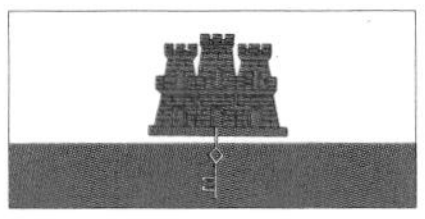

GIBRALTAR LIES ON the south coast of Spain at the western entrance to the Mediterranean Sea. The economy depends on tourism, offshore banking and entrepôt trade.

GREECE

Status: REPUBLIC
Area: 131,957 sq km (50,949 sq mls)
Population: 10,458 ,000
Capital: ATHENS
Language: GREEK, MACEDONIAN
Religion: GREEK ORTHODOX, SUNNI MUSLIM
Currency: DRACHMA
Organizations: EU, OECD, UN

MAP PAGE: 114-115

GREECE OCCUPIES THE southern part of the Balkan Peninsula of south Europe and many islands in the Ionian, Aegean and Mediterranean Seas. The islands make up over one fifth of its area. Mountains and hills cover much of the country. The most important lowlands are the plains of Thessaly in the centre-east and Salonica in the northeast. Summers are hot and dry. Winters are mild and wet, colder in the north with heavy snowfalls in the mountains. One third of Greeks live in the Athens area. Agriculture involves one quarter of the workforce and exports include citrus fruits, raisins, wine, olives and olive oil. A variety of ores and minerals are mined and a wide range of manufactures are produced including food and tobacco products, textiles, clothing, chemical products and metal products. Tourism is an important industry and there is a large services sector. Tourism, shipping and remittances from Greeks abroad are major foreign exchange earners. The war in former Yugoslavia and UN embargo on trade to Serbia have lost Greece an important market and regular trade route.

GREENLAND

Status: DANISH TERRITORY
Area: 2,175,600 sq km (840,004 sq mls)
Population: 58,000
Capital: NUUK
Language: GREENLANDIC, DANISH
Religion: PROTESTANT
Currency: DANISH KRONE

MAP PAGE: 135

SITUATED TO THE northeast of North America between the Atlantic and Arctic Oceans, Greenland is the largest island in the world. It has a polar climate and over 80 per cent of the land area is permanent ice-cap. The economy is based on fishing and fish processing.

GRENADA

Status: MONARCHY
Area: 378 sq km (146 sq mls)
Population: 92,000
Capital: ST GEORGE'S
Language: ENGLISH, CREOLE
Religion: R.CATHOLIC, PROTESTANT
Currency: E. CARIB. DOLLAR
Organizations: CARICOM, COMM., UN

MAP PAGE: 159

THE CARIBBEAN STATE comprises Grenada, the most southerly of the Windward Islands, and the southern Grenadines. Grenada has wooded hills, beaches in the southwest, a warm climate and good rainfall. Agriculture is the main activity, with bananas, nutmeg and cocoa the main exports. Tourism and manufacturing are important. Grenada relies on grant aid.

GUADELOUPE

Status: FRENCH TERRITORY
Area: 1,780 sq km (687 sq mls)
Population: 428,000
Capital: BASSE TERRE
Language: FRENCH, FRENCH CREOLE
Religion: R.CATHOLIC, HINDU
Currency: FRENCH FRANC

MAP PAGE: 159

GUADELOUPE, IN THE Caribbean's Leeward group, consists of two main islands, Basse-Terre and Grande Terre, connected by a bridge, and a few outer islands. The climate is tropical, but moderated by trade winds. Bananas, sugar and rum, tourism and French aid are the main sources of foreign exchange.

GUAM

Status: US TERRITORY
Area: 541 sq km (209 sq mls)
Population: 149,000
Capital: AGANA
Language: CHAMORRO, ENGLISH, TAGALOG
Religion: R.CATHOLIC
Currency: US DOLLAR

MAP PAGE: 23

LYING AT THE south end of the North Mariana Islands in the Western Pacific Ocean, Guam has a humid tropical climate. The island has a large US military base and the economy relies on that and tourism which is beginning to develop.

GUATEMALA

Status: REPUBLIC
Area: 108,890 sq km (42,043 sq mls)
Population: 10,621,000
Capital: GUATEMALA CITY
Language: SPANISH, MAYAN LANGUAGES
Religion: R.CATHOLIC, PROTESTANT
Currency: QUETZAL
Organizations: UN

MAP PAGE: 157

THE MOST POPULOUS country in Central America after Mexico, Guatemala has a long Pacific and a short Caribbean coastline. Northern areas are lowland tropical forests. To the south lie mountain ranges with some active volcanoes, then the Pacific coastal plain. The climate is hot tropical in the lowlands, cooler in the highlands, where most people live. Farming is the main activity, coffee, sugar and bananas are the main exports. There is some mining and manufacturing (chiefly clothing and textiles). Tourism is important. Guerrilla activity is rife in certain areas.

GUERNSEY

Status: UK TERRITORY
Area: 78 sq km (30 sq mls)
Population: 64,000
Capital: ST PETER PORT
Language: ENGLISH, FRENCH
Religion: PROTESTANT, R.CATHOLIC
Currency: POUND

MAP PAGE: 63

ONE OF THE Channel Islands lying off the west coast of the Cherbourg peninsula in northern France.

GUINEA

Status: REPUBLIC
Area: 245,857 sq km (94,926 sq mls)
Population: 6,700,000
Capital: CONAKRY
Language: FRENCH, FULANI, MALINKE, LOCAL LANGUAGES
Religion: SUNNI MUSLIM, TRAD.BELIEFS, R.CATHOLIC
Currency: FRANC
Organizations: OAU, UN

MAP PAGE: 122

GUINEA IS IN west Africa, on the Atlantic Ocean. The coastal plains are lined with mangrove swamps. Inland are the Fouta Djallon mountains and plateaux. To the east are savannah plains drained by the upper Niger river system, while to the southeast are mountains. The climate is tropical, with high coastal rainfall. Agriculture is the main activity, with coffee, bananas and pineapples the chief cash crops. Bauxite, alumina, iron ore, gold and diamonds are the main exports, but Guinea relies upon foreign aid.

GUINEA-BISSAU

Status: REPUBLIC
Area: 36,125 sq km (13,948 sq mls)
Population: 1,073,000
Capital: BISSAU
Language: PORTUGUESE, PORTUGUESE CREOLE, LOCAL LANGUAGES
Religion: TRAD.BELIEFS, SUNNI MUSLIM, R.CATHOLIC
Currency: CFA FRANC
Organizations: OAU, UN

MAP PAGE: 122

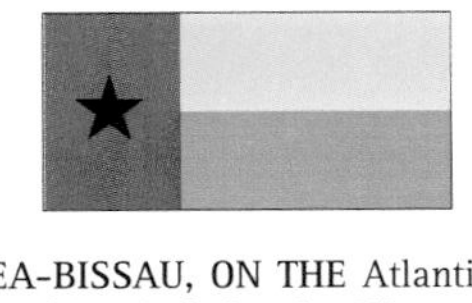

GUINEA-BISSAU, ON THE Atlantic coast of west Africa, includes the Bijagos Archipelago. The mainland coast is swampy and contains many estuaries. Inland are forested plains and to the east are savannah plateaux. The climate is tropical. The economy is based mainly on subsistence farming. There is some fishing, but little industry. Forestry and mineral resources are largely unexploited. The main exports are cashews, groundnuts, oil palms and their products. Donors largely suspended support in 1991 because of payment arrears.

GUYANA

Status: REPUBLIC
Area: 214,969 sq km (83,000 sq mls)
Population: 835,000
Capital: GEORGETOWN
Language: ENGLISH, CREOLE, HINDI, AMERINDIAN LANGUAGES
Religion: PROTESTANT, HINDU, R.CATHOLIC, SUNNI MUSLIM
Currency: DOLLAR
Organizations: CARICOM, COMM., UN

MAP PAGE: 163

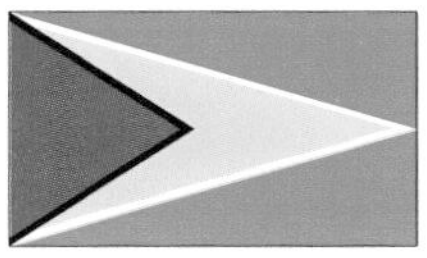

GUYANA, ON THE northeast coast of South America, consists of the densely forested highlands in the west, and the savannah uplands of the southwest. A lowland coastal belt supports crops and most of the population. The generally hot, humid and wet conditions are modified along the coast by sea breezes. The economy is based on agriculture, mining, forestry and fishing. Sugar, bauxite, gold and rice are the main exports. Other exports are shrimps and timber.

HAITI

Status: REPUBLIC
Area: 27,750 sq km (10,714 sq mls)
Population: 7,180,000
Capital: PORT-AU-PRINCE
Language: FRENCH, FRENCH CREOLE
Religion: R.CATHOLIC, PROTESTANT, VOODOO
Currency: GOURDE
Organizations: UN

MAP PAGE: 159

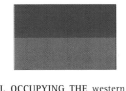

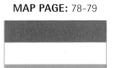

HAITI, OCCUPYING THE western third of the Caribbean island of Hispaniola, is a mountainous state, with small coastal plains and a central valley. The climate is tropical, hottest in coastal areas. Haiti has few natural resources, is overpopulated and relies on exports of local manufactures and coffee, and remittances from workers abroad. Political unrest and UN sanctions from 1991 to 1994 hit the economy badly.

HONDURAS

Status: REPUBLIC
Area: 112,088 sq km (43,277 sq mls)
Population: 5,953,000
Capital: TEGUCIGALPA
Language: SPANISH, AMERINDIAN LANGUAGES
Religion: R.CATHOLIC, PROTESTANT
Currency: LEMPIRA
Organizations: UN

MAP PAGE: 156

HONDURAS, IN CENTRAL America, is a mountainous and forested country with lowland areas along its long Caribbean and short Pacific coasts. Coastal areas are hot and humid with heavy summer rainfall, inland is cooler and drier. Most people live in the central valleys. Coffee and bananas are the main exports, along with shrimps, lead, zinc and timber. Industry involves mainly agricultural processing. Honduras depends on foreign aid.

HUNGARY

Status: REPUBLIC
Area: 93,030 sq km (35,919 sq mls)
Population: 10,225,000
Capital: BUDAPEST
Language: HUNGARIAN, ROMANY, GERMAN, SLOVAK
Religion: R.CATHOLIC, PROTESTANT
Currency: FORINT
Organizations: UN, OECD

MAP PAGE: 78-79

A LANDLOCKED COUNTRY in central Europe, Hungary borders Austria, Slovakia, Ukraine, Romania, Yugoslavia, Croatia and Slovenia. The Danube river flows north-south through central Hungary. To the east lies a great plain, flanked by highlands in the north. To the west low mountains and Lake Balaton separate a small plain and southern uplands. The climate is continental, with warm summers and cold winters. Rainfall is fairly evenly distributed thoughout the year. Half the population lives in urban areas, and one fifth lives in Budapest. Hungary has a predominantly industrial economy. The main industries produce metals, machinery, transport equipment (chiefly buses), textiles, chemicals and food products. Some minerals and energy reources are exploited, chiefly bauxite, coal and natural gas. Farming remains important, though output has fallen. Fruit, vegetables, cigarettes and wine are the main agricultural exports. Tourism is an important foreign exchange earner. Progress towards creating a market economy has been proved slow.

ICELAND

Status: REPUBLIC
Area: 102,820 sq km (39,699 sq mls)
Population: 269,000
Capital: REYKJAVIK
Language: ICELANDIC
Religion: PROTESTANT, R.CATHOLIC
Currency: KRÓNA
Organizations: OECD, UN

MAP PAGE: 56

THE NORTHWEST EUROPEAN island of Iceland lies in the Atlantic Ocean, near the Arctic Circle. It consists mainly of a plateau of basalt lava flows. Some of its 200 volcanoes are active, and there are geysers and hot springs, but one tenth of the country is covered by ice caps. Only coastal lowlands can be cultivated and settled, and over half the population lives in the Reykjavik area. The climate is fairly mild, moderated by the North Atlantic Drift and southwesterly winds. The mainstay of the economy is fishing and fish processing, which account for 80 per cent of exports. Agriculture involves mainly sheep and dairy farming. Iceland is self-sufficient in meat and dairy products, and exports wool and sheepskins. Diatomite is the only mineral resource but hydro-electric and geothermal energy resources are considerable. The main industries produce aluminium, ferro-silicon, electrical equipment, books, fertilizers, textiles and clothing. Tourism is growing in importance.

© Bartholomew

INDIA

Status: REPUBLIC
Area: 3,287,263 sq km (1,269,219 sq mls)
Population: 935,744,000
Capital: NEW DELHI
Language: HINDI, ENGLISH (OFFICIAL), MANY REGIONAL LANGUAGES
Religion: HINDU, SUNNI MUSLIM, SIKH, CHRISTIAN, BUDDHIST, JAIN
Currency: RUPEE
Organizations: COMM., UN

MAP PAGE: 34-35

MOST OF THE South Asian state of India occupies a peninsula that juts out into the Indian Ocean between the Arabian Sea and Bay of Bengal. The heart of the peninsula is the Deccan plateau, bordered on either side by ranges of hills, the Western Ghats and the lower Eastern Ghats, which fall away to narrow coastal plains. To the north is a broad plain, drained by the Indus, Ganges and Brahmaputra rivers and their tributaries. The plain is intensively farmed and is the most populous region. In the west is the Thar Desert. The Himalayas form India's northern border, together with parts of the Karakoram and Hindu Kush ranges in the northwest. The climate shows marked seasonal variation: the hot season from March to June; the monsoon season from June to October; and the cold season from November to February. Rainfall ranges between heavy in the northeast Assam region and negligible in the Thar Desert, while temperatures range from very cold in the Himayalas to tropical heat over much of the south. India is among the ten largest economies in the world. It has achieved a high degree of self-sufficiency and its involvement in world trade is relatively small, though growing. Agriculture, forestry and fishing account for one third of national output and two thirds of employment. Much of the farming is on a subsistence basis and involves mainly rice and wheat growing. India is a major world producer of tea, sugar, jute, cotton and tobacco. Livestock is raised mainly for dairy products and hides. India has substantial reserves of coal, oil and natural gas and many minerals including iron, manganese and copper ores, bauxite, diamonds and gold. The manufacturing sector is large and diverse. The main manufactures are chemicals and chemical products, textiles, iron and steel, food products, electrical goods and transport equipment. The main exports are diamonds, clothing, chemicals and chemical products, textiles, leather and leather goods, iron ore, fish products, electronic goods and tea. However, with a huge population - the second largest in the world - India receives foreign aid to support its balance of payments.

INDONESIA

Status: REPUBLIC
Area: 1,919,445 sq km (741,102 sq mls)
Population: 194,564,000
Capital: JAKARTA
Language: INDONESIAN (OFFICIAL), MANY LOCAL LANGUAGES
Religion: SUNNI MUSLIM, PROTESTANT, R.CATHOLIC, HINDU, BUDDHIST
Currency: RUPIAH
Organizations: ASEAN, OPEC, UN

MAP PAGE: 20-21

INDONESIA, THE LARGEST and most populous country in southeast Asia, consists of 13,677 islands extending along the Equator between the Pacific and Indian oceans. Sumatra, Java, Sulawesi, Kalimantan (two thirds of Borneo) and Irian Jaya (western New Guinea) make up 90 per cent of the land area. Most of Indonesia is mountainous and covered with rainforest or mangrove swamps, and there are over 300 volcanoes, some still active. Two thirds of the population live in the lowland areas of Java and Madura. In general the climate is tropical monsoon. Indonesia is rich in energy resources, minerals, forests and fertile soil. It is among the world's top producers of rice, palm oil, tea, coffee, rubber and tobacco. It is the world's leading exporter of natural gas and a major exporter of oil and timber. In recent years manufacturing output has risen. A range of goods are produced including textiles, clothing, cement, fertilizer and vehicles. Tourism has also increased. However, given its huge population, Indonesia remains a relatively poor country.

IRAN

Status: REPUBLIC
Area: 1,648,000 sq km (636,296 sq mls)
Population: 67,283,000
Capital: TEHRAN
Language: FARSI (PERSIAN), AZERI, KURDISH, REGIONAL LANGUAGES
Religion: SHI'A MUSLIM, SUNNI MUSLIM, BAHA'I, CHRISTIAN, ZOROASTRIAN
Currency: RIAL
Organizations: OPEC, UN

MAP PAGE: 39

IRAN IS IN southwest Asia, on The Gulf, the Gulf of Oman and Caspian Sea. Eastern Iran is high plateaux country, with large salt pans and a vast sand desert. In the west the Zagros Mountains form a series of ridges, while to the north lie the Elburz Mountains. Most farming and settlement is on the narrow plain along the Caspian Sea and the foothills of the north and west. The climate is one of extremes, with hot summers and very cold winters. Most of the light rainfall is in the winter months. Agriculture involves one quarter of the workforce. Wheat is the main crop but fruit (chiefly dates) and pistachio nuts are grown for export. Fishing in the Caspian Sea is important and caviar is exported. Petroleum (the main export) and natural gas are Iran's leading natural resources. There are also reserves of coal, iron ore, copper ore and other minerals. Manufactures include carpets, clothing, food products, construction materials, chemicals, vehicles, leather goods and metal products. The 1979 revolution and 1980-88 war with Iraq slowed economic development.

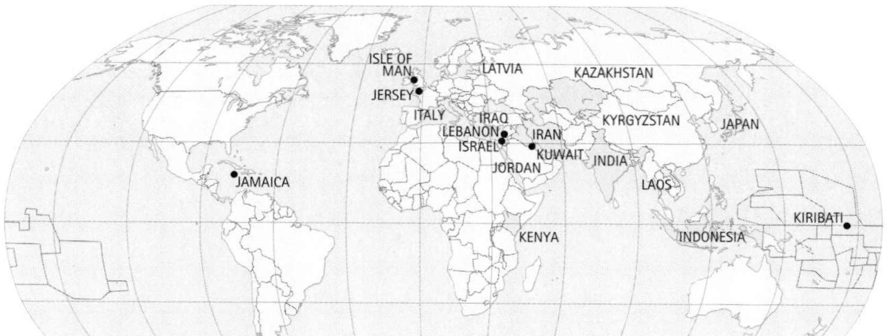

IRAQ

Status: REPUBLIC
Area: 438,317 sq km (169,235 sq mls)
Population: 20,449,000
Capital: BAGHDAD
Language: ARABIC, KURDISH, TURKMEN
Religion: SHI'A MUSLIM, SUNNI MUSLIM, R.CATHOLIC
Currency: DINAR
Organizations: OPEC, UN

MAP PAGE: 42

IRAQ, WHICH LIES on the northwest shores of The Gulf in southwest Asia, has at its heart the lowland valley of the Tigris and Euphrates rivers. In the southeast where the two rivers join are marshes and the Shatt al Arab waterway. Northern Iraq is hilly, rising to the Zagros Mountains, while western Iraq is desert. Summers are hot and dry, while winters are mild with light though unreliable rainfall. The Tigris-Euphrates valley contains most of the arable land and population, including one in five who live in Baghdad. One third of the workforce is involved in agriculture, with dates, cotton, wool, hides and skins exported in normal times. However, the 1980-88 war with Iran, defeat in the 1991 Gulf war and international sanctions have ruined the economy and caused considerable hardship. Petroleum and natural gas sales, which had accounted for 98 per cent of export earnings, were severely restricted. Much of the infrastructure was damaged and industrial output - which had included petroleum products, cement, steel, textiles, bitumen and pharmaceuticals - was reduced.

ISLE OF MAN

Status: UK TERRITORY
Area: 572 sq km (221 sq mls)
Population: 72 ,000
Capital: DOUGLAS
Language: ENGLISH
Religion: PROTESTANT, R.CATHOLIC
Currency: POUND

MAP PAGE: 64

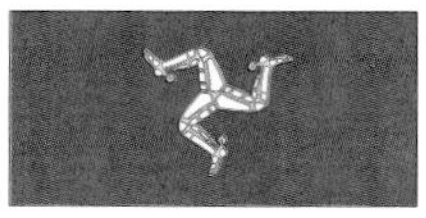

ISRAEL

Status: REPUBLIC
Area: 20,770 sq km (8,019 sq mls)
Population: 5,545,000
Capital: JERUSALEM
Language: HEBREW, ARABIC, YIDDISH, ENGLISH, RUSSIAN
Religion: JEWISH, SUNNI MUSLIM, CHRISTIAN, DRUZE
Currency: SHEKEL
Organizations: UN

MAP PAGE: 43

ISRAEL LIES ON the Mediterranean coast of southwest Asia. Beyond the coastal plain of Sharon are the hills and valleys of Judea and Samaria with the Galilee highlands to the north. In the east is the rift valley, which extends from Lake Tiberias to the Gulf of Aqaba and contains the Jordan river and Dead Sea. In the south is the Negev, a triangular semi-desert plateau. Most people live on the coastal plain or in northern and central areas. Much of Israel has warm summers and mild winters, during which most rain falls. Southern Israel is hot and dry. Agricultural production was boosted by the inclusion of the West Bank of the Jordan in 1967. Citrus fruit, vegetables and flowers are exported. Mineral resources are few but potash, bromine and some oil and gas are produced. Manufacturing makes the largest contribution to the economy. Israel produces finished diamonds, textiles, clothing and food products as well as chemical and metal products, military and transport equipment, electrical and electronic goods. Tourism and foreign aid are important to the economy.

ITALY

Status: REPUBLIC
Area: 301,245 sq km (116,311 sq mls)
Population: 57,187,000
Capital: ROME
Language: ITALIAN, ITALIAN DIALECTS
Religion: R.CATHOLIC
Currency: LIRA
Organizations: EU, OECD, UN

MAP PAGE: 104-105

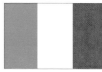

MOST OF THE south European state of Italy occupies a peninsula that juts out into the Mediterranean Sea. It includes the main islands of Sicily and Sardinia and about 70 smaller islands in the surrounding seas. Italy is mountainous and dominated by two high ranges: the Alps, which form its northern border; and the Apennines, which run almost the full length of the peninsula. Many of Italy's mountains are of volcanic origin and its two active volcanoes are Vesuvius near Naples and Etna on Sicily. The main lowland area is the Po river valley in the northeast, which is the main agricultural and industrial area and is the most populous region. Italy has a Mediterranean climate with warm, dry summers and mild winters. Sicily and Sardinia are warmer and drier than the mainland. Northern Italy experiences colder, wetter winters, with heavy snow in the Alps. Italy's natural resources are limited. Only about 20 per cent of the land is suitable for cultivation. Some oil, natural gas and coal are produced, but most fuels and minerals used by industry must be imported. Italy has a fairly diversified economy. Agriculture flourishes, with cereals, wine, fruit (including olives) and vegetables the main crops. Italy is the world's largest wine producer. Cheese is also an important product. However, Italy is a net food importer. The north is the centre of Italian industry, especially around Turin, Milan and Genoa, while the south is largely agricultural with production based on smaller, less mechanized farms. Thus average income in the north is much higher than that in the south. Another feature of the Italian economy is the size of the state sector, which is much larger than that of other European Union countries. Italy's leading manufactures include industrial and office equipment, domestic appliances, cars, textiles, clothing, leather goods, chemicals and metal products and its famous brand names include Olivetti, Fiat and Benetton. Italy has a strong service sector. With over 25 million visitors a year, tourism is a major employer and accounts for 5 per cent of national income. Finance and banking are also important.

JAMAICA

Status: MONARCHY
Area: 10,991 sq km (4,244 sq mls)
Population: 2,530,000
Capital: KINGSTON
Language: ENGLISH, CREOLE
Religion: PROTESTANT, R.CATHOLIC, RASTAFARIAN
Currency: DOLLAR
Organizations: CARICOM, COMM., UN

MAP PAGE: 159

JAMAICA, THE THIRD largest Caribbean island, has beaches and densely populated coastal plains traversed by hills and plateaux rising to the forested Blue Mountains in the east. The climate is tropical, cooler and wetter on high ground. The economy is based on tourism, agriculture, mining and light manufacturing. Bauxite, alumina, sugar and bananas are the main exports. Jamaica depends on foreign aid.

JAPAN

Status: MONARCHY
Area: 377,727 sq km (145,841 sq mls)
Population: 125,197,000
Capital: TOKYO
Language: JAPANESE
Religion: SHINTOIST, BUDDHIST, CHRISTIAN
Currency: YEN
Organizations: OECD, UN

MAP PAGE: 28-29

JAPAN, WHICH LIES in the Pacific Ocean off the coast of east Asia, consists of four main islands - Hokkaido, Honshu, Shikoku and Kyushu - which extend northeast-southwest over 1,600 km (995 miles). It includes more than 3,000 smaller volcanic islands in the surrounding Sea of Japan, East China Sea and Pacific Ocean. The central island of Honshu occupies 60 per cent of the total land area and contains 80 per cent of the population, mostly in the east-central Kanto plain which includes Tokyo, Kawasaki and Yokohama. Behind the long and deeply indented coastline, nearly three quarters of Japan is mountainous and heavily forested. The most rugged range crosses Honshu and includes the country's highest point, Mount Fuji, which reaches a height of 3,776 m (12,388 ft). Japan has over 60 active volcanoes, and is subject to frequent major earthquakes, monsoons, typhoons and tidal waves. The climate is generally temperate maritime, with warm summers and mild winters, except in western Hokkaido and northwest Honshu, where the winters are very cold with heavy snow. Rain falls mainly in June and July, and typhoons sometimes occur in September. Japan has few natural resources. It has a limited land area of which only 14 per cent is suitable for cultivation, and production of its few industrial raw materials (chiefly coal, oil, natural gas and copper) is insufficient for its industry. Most raw materials must be imported, including about 90 per cent of energy requirements. Yet, in a fairly short space of time, Japan has become the world's second largest industrial economy. Its economic success is based on manufacturing, which employs one third of the workforce and accounts for one third of national output. Japan has a range of heavy and light industries centred mainly round the major ports of Yokohama, Osaka and Tokyo. It is the world's largest manufacturer of cars, motorcycles and merchant ships, and a major producer of steel, textiles, chemicals and cement. It is a leading producer of many consumer durables, such as washing machines, and electronic equipment, chiefly office equipment and computers. Recent years have seen the spread of Japanese business overseas, with many industrial plants sited in the European Union and the USA. Japan has a strong service sector, banking and finance are particularly important and Tokyo is one of the world's major stock exchanges. Owing to intensive agricultural production, Japan is 70 per cent self-sufficient in food. The main food crops are rice, barley, fruit, wheat and soya beans. Livestock raising (chiefly cattle, pigs and chickens) and fishing are also important. Japan has one of the largest fishing fleets in the world. In spite of its forestry resources, Japan has to import timber as well as food.

JERSEY

Status: UK TERRITORY
Area: 116 sq km (45 sq mls)
Population: 87,000
Capital: ST HELIER
Language: ENGLISH, FRENCH
Religion: PROTESTANT, R.CATHOLIC
Currency: POUND

MAP PAGE: 63

ONE OF THE Channel Islands lying off the west coast of the Cherbourg peninsula in northern France.

JORDAN

Status: MONARCHY
Area: 89,206 sq km (34,443 sq mls)
Population: 5,439,000
Capital: AMMAN
Language: ARABIC
Religion: SUNNI MUSLIM, CHRISTIAN, SHI'A MUSLIM
Currency: DINAR
Organizations: UN

MAP PAGE: 43

JORDAN, IN SOUTHWEST Asia, has a short coastline on the Gulf of Aqaba. Much of Jordan is rocky desert plateaux. In the west, behind a belt of hills, the land falls below sea level to the Dead Sea and Jordan river. Much of Jordan is hot and dry, the west is cooler and wetter and most people live in the northwest. Phosphates, potash, fertilizers, pharmaceuticals, fruit and vegetables are the main exports. Jordan relies upon tourism, workers' remittances and foreign aid, all of which were affected by the 1991 Gulf crisis.

KAZAKHSTAN

Status: REPUBLIC
Area: 2,717,300 sq km (1,049,155 sq mls)
Population: 16,590,000
Capital: ALMATY
Language: KAZAKH, RUSSIAN, GERMAN, UKRAINIAN, UZBEK, TATAR
Religion: SUNNI MUSLIM, RUSSIAN ORTHODOX, PROTESTANT
Currency: TANGA
Organizations: CIS, UN

MAP PAGE: 46-47

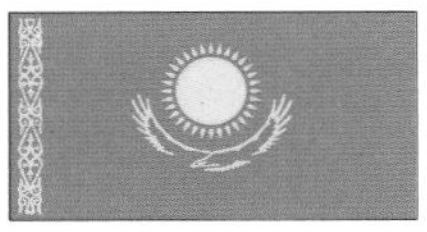

STRETCHING ACROSS CENTRAL Asia, Kazakhstan covers a vast area of steppe land and semi-desert. The land is flat in the west rising to mountains in the southeast. The climate is continental and mainly dry. Agriculture and livestock rearing are the main activities, with cotton and tobacco the main cash crops. Kazakhstan is very rich in minerals, such as oil, natural gas, coal, iron ore, chromium, gold, lead and zinc. Mining, metallurgy, machine building and food processing are major industries.

KENYA

Status: REPUBLIC
Area: 582,646 sq km (224,961 sq mls)
Population: 30,522,000
Capital: NAIROBI
Language: SWAHILI (OFFICIAL), ENGLISH, MANY LOCAL LANGUAGES
Religion: R.CATHOLIC, PROTESTANT, TRAD.BELIEFS
Currency: SHILLING
Organizations: COMM., OAU, UN

MAP PAGE: 126-127

KENYA IS IN east Africa, on the Indian Ocean. Beyond the coastal plains the land rises to plateaux interrupted by volcanic mountains. The Rift Valley runs northwest of Nairobi to Lake Turkana. Most people live in central Kenya. Conditions are tropical on the coast, semi-desert in the north and savannah in the south. Agricultural products, chiefly tea and coffee, provide half export earnings. Light industry is important. Tourism is the main foreign exchange earner; oil refining and re-exports for landlocked neighbours are others.

KIRIBATI

Status: REPUBLIC
Area: 717 sq km (277 sq mls)
Population: 79,000
Capital: BAIRIKI
Language: I-KIRIBATI (GILBERTESE), ENGLISH
Religion: R.CATHOLIC, PROTESTANT, BAHA'I, MORMON
Currency: AUSTR. DOLLAR
Organizations: COMM.

MAP PAGE: 4-5

KIRIBATI COMPRISES 32 coral islands in the Gilbert, Phoenix and Line groups and the volcanic island of Banaba, which straddle the Equator in the Pacific Ocean. Most people live on the Gilbert islands, and the capital, Bairiki, is on Tarawa, one of the Gilbert Islands. The climate is hot, wetter in the north. Kiribati depends on subsistence farming and fishing. Copra and fish exports and licences for foreign fishing fleets are the main foreign exchange earners.

KUWAIT

Status: MONARCHY
Area: 17,818 sq km (6,880 sq mls)
Population: 1,691,000
Capital: KUWAIT CITY
Language: ARABIC
Religion: SUNNI MUSLIM, SHI'A MUSLIM, OTHER MUSLIM, CHRISTIAN, HINDU
Currency: DINAR
Organizations: OPEC, UN

MAP PAGE: 42

KUWAIT LIES ON the northwest shores of The Gulf in southwest Asia. It is mainly low-lying desert, with irrigated areas along the Bay of Kuwait where most people live. Summers are hot and dry, winters are cool with some rainfall. The oil industry, which accounts for 80 per cent of exports, has largely recovered from the damage caused by Iraq in 1991. Income is also derived from extensive overseas investments.

KYRGYZSTAN

Status: REPUBLIC
Area: 198,500 sq km (76,641 sq mls)
Population: 4,668,000
Capital: BISHKEK
Language: KIRGHIZ, RUSSIAN, UZBEK
Religion: SUNNI MUSLIM, RUSSIAN ORTHODOX
Currency: SOM
Organizations: CIS, UN

MAP PAGE: 47

A LANDLOCKED CENTRAL Asian state, Kyrgyzstan is rugged and mountainous, lying in the western Tien Shan range. Most people live in the valleys of the north and west. Summers are hot and winters cold. Agriculture (chiefly livestock farming) is the main activity. Coal, gold, antimony and mercury are produced. Manufactures include machinery, metals and food products. Disruption of Russian-dominated trade has caused economic problems.

LAOS

Status: REPUBLIC
Area: 236,800 sq km (91,429 sq mls)
Population: 4,882,000
Capital: VIENTIANE
Language: LAO, LOCAL LANGUAGES
Religion: BUDDHIST, TRAD.BELIEFS, R.CATHOLIC, SUNNI MUSLIM
Currency: KIP
Organizations: UN

MAP PAGE: 24-25

A LANDLOCKED COUNTRY in southeast Asia, Laos borders Vietnam, Cambodia, Thailand, Myanmar and China. Forested mountains and plateaux predominate. The climate is tropical monsoon. Most people live in the Mekong valley and the low plateau in the south, and grow food crops, chiefly rice. Electricity, timber, coffee and tin are exported. Foreign aid and investment and the opium trade are important.

LATVIA

Status: REPUBLIC
Area: 63,700 sq km (24,595 sq mls)
Population: 2,515,000
Capital: RIGA
Language: LATVIAN, RUSSIAN
Religion: PROTESTANT, R.CATHOLIC, RUSSIAN ORTHODOX
Currency: LAT
Organizations: UN

MAP PAGE: 54

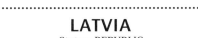

LATVIA IS IN north Europe, on the Baltic Sea and Gulf of Riga. The land is flat near the coast but hilly with woods and lakes inland. Latvia has a modified continental climate. One third of the people live in Riga. Crop and livestock farming are important. Industry is varied but specialist products include telephones, diesel trains, buses and paper. Latvia has few natural resources. Economic priorities are creating a market economy and reducing economic dependence on Russia.

LEBANON

Status: REPUBLIC
Area: 10,452 sq km (4,036 sq mls)
Population: 3,009,000
Capital: BEIRUT
Language: ARABIC, FRENCH, ARMENIAN
Religion: SHI'A, SUNNI AND OTHER MUSLIM, PROTESTANT, R.CATHOLIC
Currency: POUND
Organizations: UN

MAP PAGE: 43

LEBANON LIES ON the Mediterranean coast of southwest Asia. Beyond the coastal strip, where most people live, are two parallel mountain ranges, separated by the Bekaa Valley. In general the climate is Mediterranean. Civil war crippled the traditional sectors of banking, commerce and tourism, but some fruit production and light industry survived. Reconstruction is under way.

© Bartholomew

LESOTHO

Status: MONARCHY
Area: 30,355 sq km (11,720 sq mls)
Population: 2,050,000
Capital: MASERU
Language: SESOTHO, ENGLISH, ZULU
Religion: R.CATHOLIC, PROTESTANT, TRAD.BELIEFS
Currency: LOTI
Organizations: COMM., OAU, SADC, UN

MAP PAGE: 131

LESOTHO IS A landlocked state surrounded by the Republic of South Africa. It is a mountainous country lying within the Drakensberg range. Most people live in the western lowlands and southern Orange and Caledon river valleys. In general Lesotho has hot moist summers and cool, dry winters, with lower temperatures in the mountains. Subsistence farming and herding are the main activities. Exports include livestock, vegetables, wool and mohair. The economy depends heavily on South Africa for transport links and employment.

LIBERIA

Status: REPUBLIC
Area: 111,369 sq km (43,000 sq mls)
Population: 2,760,000
Capital: MONROVIA
Language: ENGLISH, CREOLE, MANY LOCAL LANGUAGES
Religion: TRAD. BELIEFS, SUNNI MUSLIM, PROTESTANT, R.CATHOLIC
Currency: DOLLAR
Organizations: OAU, UN

MAP PAGE: 122

LIBERIA IS ON the Atlantic coast of west Africa. Beyond the coastal belt of sandy beaches and mangrove swamps the land rises to a forested plateau, with highlands along the Guinea border. A quarter of the population lives along the coast. The climate is hot with heavy rainfall. The 1989-93 civil war ruined the economy. Before the war exports included iron ore, diamonds and gold along with rubber, timber and coffee. Ship registration was a major foreign exchange earner. Liberia now relies on foreign aid.

LIBYA

Status: REPUBLIC
Area: 1,759,540 sq km (679,362 sq mls)
Population: 5,407,000
Capital: TRIPOLI
Language: ARABIC, BERBER
Religion: SUNNI MUSLIM, R.CATHOLIC
Currency: DINAR
Organizations: OAU, OPEC, UN

MAP PAGE: 118

LIBYA LIES ON the Mediterranean coast of north Africa. The desert plains and hills of the Sahara dominate the landscape and the climate is hot and dry. Most people live in cities near the coast, where the climate is cooler with moderate rainfall. Farming and herding, chiefly in the northwest, are important but the main industry is oil, which accounts for about 95 per cent of export earnings. There is some heavy industry. In 1993 the UN imposed economic sanctions because of alleged sponsorship of terrorism.

LIECHTENSTEIN

Status: MONARCHY
Area: 160 sq km (62 sq mls)
Population: 31,000
Capital: VADUZ
Language: GERMAN
Religion: R.CATHOLIC, PROTESTANT
Currency: SWISS FRANC
Organizations: UN

MAP PAGE: 83

A LANDLOCKED STATE between Switzerland and Austria in central Europe, Liechtenstein occupies the floodplains of the upper Rhine valley and part of the Austrian Alps. It has a temperate climate with cool winters. Dairy farming is important, but manufacturing is dominant. Major products include precision instruments, dentistry equipment, pharmaceuticals, ceramics and textiles. There is also some metal working. Finance, chiefly banking, is very important. Tourism and postal stamps provide additional revenue.

LITHUANIA

Status: REPUBLIC
Area: 65,200 sq km (25,174 sq mls)
Population: 3,715,000
Capital: VILNIUS
Language: LITHUANIAN, RUSSIAN, POLISH
Religion: R.CATHOLIC, PROTESTANT, RUSSIAN ORTHODOX
Currency: LITAS
Organizations: UN

MAP PAGE: 54

LITHUANIA IS IN north Europe, on the eastern shores of the Baltic Sea. It is mainly lowland with many lakes, small rivers and marshes. The climate is generally temperate. About 15 per cent of people live in Vilnius. Agriculture, fishing and forestry are important, but manufacturing dominates the economy. The main products are processed foods, light industrial goods, machinery and metalworking equipment. Progress towards a market economy is slow. The economy remains heavily dependent on Russia.

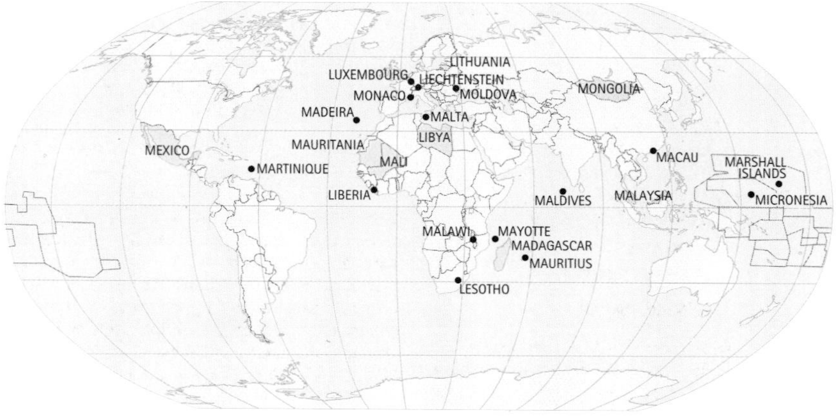

LUXEMBOURG

Status: MONARCHY
Area: 2,586 sq km (998 sq mls)
Population: 410,000
Capital: LUXEMBOURG
Language: LETZEBURGISH, GERMAN, FRENCH, PORTUGUESE
Religion: R.CATHOLIC, PROTESTANT
Currency: FRANC
Organizations: EU, OECD, UN

MAP PAGE: 69

LUXEMBOURG, A LANDLOCKED country in west Europe, borders Belgium, France and Germany. The hills and forests of the Ardennes dominate the north, with rolling pasture to the south, where the main towns, farms and industries are found. Summers are warm and winters mild, though colder in the north. The iron and steel industry is still important, but light industries (including textiles, chemicals and food products) are growing. Luxembourg is a major banking centre and the home base of key European Union institutions.

MACAU

Status: PORTUGUESE TERRITORY
Area: 17 sq km (7 sq mls)
Population: 418,000
Capital: MACAU
Language: CANTONESE, PORTUGUESE
Religion: BUDDHIST, R.CATHOLIC, PROTESTANT
Currency: PATACA

MAP PAGE: 33

AN ENCLAVE ON the south coast of China, Macau consists of an area of the mainland and the two islands of Taipa and Coloane. The territory is scheduled to revert to China in 1999.

MADAGASCAR

Status: REPUBLIC
Area: 587,041 sq km (226,658 sq mls)
Population: 14,763,000
Capital: ANTANANARIVO
Language: MALAGASY, FRENCH
Religion: TRAD.BELIEFS, R.CATHOLIC, PROTESTANT, SUNNI MUSLIM
Currency: FRANC
Organizations: OAU, UN

MAP PAGE: 129

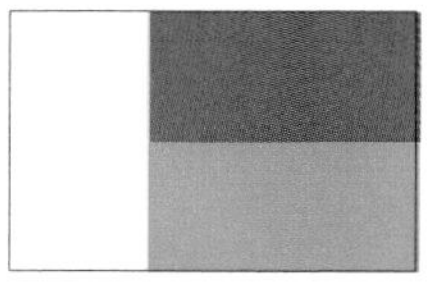

MADAGASCAR AND ADJACENT islets lie off the east coast of south Africa. The world's fourth largest island is in the main a high plateau with a coastal strip to the east and scrubby plain to the west. The climate is tropical with heavy rainfall in the north and east. Most people live on the plateau. Exports include coffee, vanilla, cloves, sugar and shrimps. The main industries are agricultural processing, textile manufacturing, oil refining and mining (chiefly chromite). Tourism and foreign aid are important.

MADEIRA

Status: PORTUGUESE TERRITORY
Area: 794 sq km (307 sq mls)
Population: 253,000
Capital: FUNCHAL
Language: PORTUGUESE
Religion: R.CATHOLIC, PROTESTANT
Currency: PORT. ESCUDO

MAP PAGE: 96

AN ISLAND GROUP in the Atlantic Ocean to the southwest of Portugal. Tourism is important to the economy.

MALAWI

Status: REPUBLIC
Area: 118,484 sq km (45,747 sq mls)
Population: 9,788,000
Capital: LILONGWE
Language: CHICHEWA, ENGLISH, LOMWE
Religion: PROTESTANT, R.CATHOLIC, TRAD. BELIEFS, SUNNI MUSLIM
Currency: KWACHA
Organizations: COMM., OAU, SADC, UN

MAP PAGE: 127

LANDLOCKED MALAWI IN central Africa is a narrow hilly country at the southern end of the East African Rift Valley. One fifth of the country is covered by Lake Malawi, which lies above sea level. Most people live in the southern regions. The climate is mainly subtropical with varying rainfall. The economy is predominantly agricultural. Tobacco, tea and sugar are the main exports. Manufacturing involves mainly chemicals, textiles and agricultural products. Malawi relies heavily on foreign aid.

MALAYSIA

Status: FEDERATION
Area: 332,665 sq km (128,442 sq mls)
Population: 20,140,000
Capital: KUALA LUMPUR
Language: MALAY, ENGLISH, CHINESE, TAMIL, LOCAL LANGUAGES
Religion: SUNNI MUSLIM, BUDDHIST, HINDU, CHRISTIAN, TRAD. BELIEFS
Currency: DOLLAR (RINGGIT)
Organizations: ASEAN, COMM., UN

MAP PAGE: 20-21

THE FEDERATION OF Malaysia, in southeast Asia, comprises two regions, separated by the South China Sea. Peninsular Malaysia occupies the southern Malay peninsula, which has a chain of mountains dividing the eastern coastal strip from the wider plains to the west. To the east, the states of Sabah and Sarawak in the north of the island of Borneo are mainly rainforest-covered hills and mountains with mangrove swamps along the coast. Both regions have a tropical climate with heavy rainfall. About 80 per cent of the population lives in Peninsular Malaysia, mainly on the coasts. The country is rich in natural resources. It is the world's largest producer of tin, palm oil, pepper and tropical hardwoods, and a major producer of natural rubber, coconut and cocoa. It also has vast reserves of minerals and fuels. However high economic growth in recent years has come from manufacturing which now provides most exports and involves mainly processing industries, electronics assembly and engineering (chiefly car production). With over 7 million visitors a year, tourism is also a major industry.

PENINSULAR MALAYSIA

Status: DIVISION
Area: 131,585 sq km (50,805 sq mls)
Population: 14,942,697
Capital: KUALA LUMPUR

SABAH

Status: STATE
Area: 76,115 sq km (29,388 sq mls)
Population: 1,583,726
Capital: KOTA KINABALU

SARAWAK
Status: STATE
Area: 124,965 sq km (48,249 sq mls)
Population: 1,708,737
Capital: KUCHING

MALDIVES
Status: REPUBLIC
Area: 298 sq km (115 sq mls)
Population: 254,000
Capital: MALE
Language: DIVEHI (MALDIVIAN)
Religion: SUNNI MUSLIM
Currency: RUFIYAA
Organizations: COMM., UN

MAP PAGE: 35

THE MALDIVE ARCHIPELAGO comprises 1,190 coral atolls (202 of which are inhabited), in the Indian Ocean, southwest of India. The climate is hot, humid and monsoonal. The islands depend mainly on fishing and fish processing, light manufacturing (chiefly clothing) and tourism.

MALI
Status: REPUBLIC
Area: 1,240,140 sq km (478,821 sq mls)
Population: 10,795,000
Capital: BAMAKO
Language: FRENCH, BAMBARA, MANY LOCAL LANGUAGES
Religion: SUNNI MUSLIM, TRAD.BELIEFS, R.CATHOLIC
Currency: CFA FRANC
Organizations: OAU, UN

MAP PAGE: 122

A LANDLOCKED STATE in west Africa, Mali is low-lying, rising to mountains in the northeast. Northern regions lie within the Sahara desert. To the south, around the Niger river, are marshes and savannah grassland. Rainfall is unreliable. Most people live along the Niger and Senegal rivers. Exports include cotton and groundnuts. Some gold is produced. Mali relies heavily on foreign aid.

MALTA
Status: REPUBLIC
Area: 316 sq km (122 sq mls)
Population: 371,000
Capital: VALLETTA
Language: MALTESE, ENGLISH
Religion: R.CATHOLIC
Currency: LIRA
Organizations: COMM., UN

MAP PAGE: 111

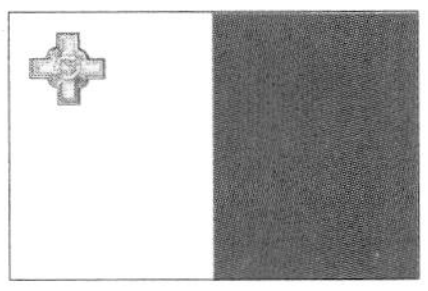

THE ISLANDS OF Malta and Gozo lie in the Mediterranean Sea, off the coast of south Italy. Malta, the main island, has low hills and an indented coastline. Two thirds of the population lives in the Valletta area. The islands have hot, dry summers and mild winters. The main industries are tourism, ship building and repair, and export manufacturing (chiefly clothing). Vegetables, flowers, wine and tobacco are also exported.

MARSHALL ISLANDS
Status: REPUBLIC
Area: 181 sq km (70 sq mls)
Population: 56,000
Capital: DALAP-ULIGA-DARRIT
Language: MARSHALLESE, ENGLISH
Religion: PROTESTANT, R.CATHOLIC
Currency: US DOLLAR
Organizations: UN

MAP PAGE: 4

THE MARSHALL ISLANDS consist of over 1,000 atolls, islands and islets, within two chains, in the North Pacific Ocean. The main atolls are Majuro (home to half the population), Kwajalein, Jaluit, Enewetak and Bikini. The climate is tropical with heavy autumn rainfall. The islands depend on farming, fishing, tourism, financial services, and US aid and rent for a missile base.

MARTINIQUE
Status: FRENCH TERRITORY
Area: 1,079 sq km (417 sq mls)
Population: 379,000
Capital: FORT-DE-FRANCE
Language: FRENCH, FRENCH CREOLE
Religion: R.CATHOLIC, PROTESTANT, HINDU, TRAD.BELIEFS
Currency: FRENCH FRANC

MAP PAGE: 159

MARTINIQUE, ONE OF the Caribbean's Windward Islands, has volcanic peaks in the north, a populous central plain, and hills and beaches in the south. The tropical island depends on fruit growing (chiefly bananas), oil refining, rum distilling, tourism and French aid.

MAURITANIA
Status: REPUBLIC
Area: 1,030,700 sq km (397,955 sq mls)
Population: 2,284,000
Capital: NOUAKCHOTT
Language: ARABIC, FRENCH, LOCAL LANGUAGES
Religion: SUNNI MUSLIM
Currency: OUGUIYA
Organizations: OAU, UN

MAP PAGE: 122

MAURITANIA IS ON the Atlantic coast of northwest Africa and lies almost entirely within the Sahara desert. Oases and a fertile strip along the Senegal river to the south are the only areas suitable for cultivation. The climate is generally hot and dry. A quarter of Mauritanians live in Nouakchott. Livestock rearing and subsistence farming are important. The economy is heavily dependent on iron ore mining and fishing, which together account for 90 per cent of export earnings, and foreign aid.

MAURITIUS
Status: REPUBLIC
Area: 2,040 sq km (788 sq mls)
Population: 1,122,000
Capital: PORT LOUIS
Language: ENGLISH, FRENCH CREOLE, HINDI, INDIAN LANGUAGES
Religion: HINDU, R.CATHOLIC, SUNNI MUSLIM, PROTESTANT
Currency: RUPEE
Organizations: COMM., OAU, UN, SADC

MAP PAGE: 127

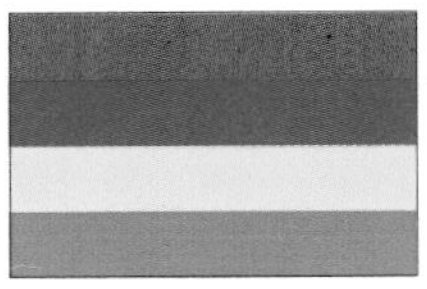

THE STATE COMPRISES Mauritius, Rodrigues and some 20 small islands in the Indian Ocean, east of Madagascar. The main island of Mauritius is volcanic in origin and has a coral coast rising to a central plateau. Most people live on the west side of the island. The climate is warm and humid. Mauritius depends mainly on sugar production, light manufacturing (chiefly clothing) and tourism.

MAYOTTE
Status: FRENCH TERRITORY
Area: 373 sq km (144 sq mls)
Population: 110,000
Capital: DZAOUDZI
Language: MAHORIAN (SWAHILI), FRENCH
Religion: SUNNI MUSLIM, R.CATHOLIC
Currency: FRENCH FRANC

MAP PAGE: 127

LYING IN THE Indian Ocean off the east coast of Central Africa, Mayotte is part of the Comoros Archipelago, but remains a French Territory.

MEXICO
Status: REPUBLIC
Area: 1,972,545 sq km (761,604 sq mls)
Population: 90,487,000
Capital: MEXICO CITY
Language: SPANISH, MANY AMERINDIAN LANGUAGES
Religion: R.CATHOLIC, PROTESTANT
Currency: PESO
Organizations: NAFTA, OECD, UN

MAP PAGE: 156-157

THE LARGEST COUNTRY in central America, Mexico extends southwards from the USA to Guatemala and Belize, and from the Pacific Ocean to the Gulf of Mexico. The greater part of the country is high plateaux flanked by the western and eastern Sierra Madre mountain ranges. The principal lowland is the Yucatán peninsula in the southeast. The climate varies with latitude and altitude: hot and humid in the lowlands, warm in the plateaux and cool with cold winters in the mountains. The north is arid, while the far south has heavy rainfall. Mexico City is one of the world's largest conurbations and the centre of trade and industry. Agriculture involves a quarter of the workforce and exports include coffee, fruit and vegetables. Shrimps are also exported and timber production is important for allied industries. Mexico is rich in minerals, including copper, zinc, lead and sulphur, and is the world's leading producer of silver. It is one of the world's largest producers of oil, from vast oil and gas resources in the Gulf of Mexico. The oil and petrochemical industries are still the mainstay, but a variety of manufactures are now produced including iron and steel, motor vehicles, textiles and electronic goods. Tourism is growing in importance.

FEDERATED STATES OF MICRONESIA
Status: REPUBLIC
Area: 701 sq km (271 sq mls)
Population: 105,000
Capital: PALIKIR
Language: ENGLISH, TRUKESE, POHNPEIAN, LOCAL LANGUAGES
Religion: PROTESTANT, R.CATHOLIC
Currency: US DOLLAR
Organizations: UN

MAP PAGE: 4

MICRONESIA COMPRISES 607 atolls and islands in the Carolines group in the North Pacific Ocean. A third of the population lives on Pohnpei. The climate is tropical with heavy rainfall. Fishing and subsistence farming are the main activities. Copra and fish are the main exports. Income also derives from tourism and the licensing of foreign fishing fleets. The islands depend on US aid.

MOLDOVA
Status: REPUBLIC
Area: 33,700 sq km (13,012 sq mls)
Population: 4,432,000
Capital: CHIȘINĂU
Language: ROMANIAN, RUSSIAN, UKRAINIAN, GAGAUZ
Religion: MOLDOVAN ORTHODOX, RUSSIAN ORTHODOX
Currency: LEU
Organizations: CIS, UN

MAP PAGE: 51

MOLDOVA IS IN east Europe, sandwiched between Romania and Ukraine. It consists of hilly steppe land, drained by the Prut and Dnestr rivers; the latter provides access to the Black Sea through Ukrainian territory. Moldova has long hot summers and mild winters. The economy is mainly agricultural, with tobacco, wine and fruit the chief products. Food processing and textiles are the main industries. Ethnic tension, which erupted into civil war in 1992, has slowed economic reform.

MONACO
Status: MONARCHY
Area: 2 sq km (0.8 sq ml)
Population: 32,000
Capital: MONACO
Language: FRENCH, MONEGASQUE, ITALIAN
Religion: R.CATHOLIC
Currency: FRENCH FRANC
Organizations: UN

MAP PAGE: 91

THE PRINCIPALITY, IN south Europe, occupies a rocky peninsula and a strip of land on France's Mediterranean coast. It depends on service industries (chiefly tourism, banking and finance) and light industry.

MONGOLIA
Status: REPUBLIC
Area: 1,565,000 sq km (604,250 sq mls)
Population: 2,410,000
Capital: ULAN BATOR
Language: KHALKA (MONGOLIAN), KAZAKH, LOCAL LANGUAGES
Religion: BUDDHIST, SUNNI MUSLIM, TRAD.BELIEFS
Currency: TUGRIK
Organizations: UN

MAP PAGE: 26-27

MONGOLIA IS A landlocked country in east Asia between Russia and China. Much of it is high steppe land, with mountains and lakes in the west and north. In the south is the Gobi desert. Mongolia has long, cold winters and short, mild summers. A quarter of the population lives in the capital. Mongolia is rich in minerals and fuels. Copper accounts for half export earnings. Livestock breeding and agricultural processing are important. The demise of the Soviet Union caused economic problems and Mongolia depends on foreign aid.

© Bartholomew

MONTSERRAT

Status: UK TERRITORY
Area: 100 sq km (39 sq mls)
Population: 11,000
Capital: PLYMOUTH
Language: ENGLISH
Religion: PROTESTANT, R.CATHOLIC
Currency: E. CARIB. DOLLAR
Organizations: CARICOM

MAP PAGE: 159

MOROCCO

Status: MONARCHY
Area: 446,550 sq km (172,414 sq mls)
Population: 27,111,000
Capital: RABAT
Language: ARABIC, BERBER, FRENCH, SPANISH
Religion: SUNNI MUSLIM, R.CATHOLIC
Currency: DIRHAM
Organizations: UN

MAP PAGE: 120

LYING IN THE northwest corner of Africa, Morocco has both Atlantic and Mediterranean coasts. The Atlas ranges separate the arid south and disputed Western Sahara from the fertile regions of the west and north, which have a milder climate. Most Moroccans live on the Atlantic coastal plain. The economy is based mainly on agriculture, phosphate mining and tourism. Manufacturing (chiefly textiles and clothing) and fishing are important.

MOZAMBIQUE

Status: REPUBLIC
Area: 799,380 sq km (308,642 sq mls)
Population: 17,423,000
Capital: MAPUTO
Language: PORTUGUESE, MAKUA, TSONGA, MANY LOCAL LANGUAGES
Religion: TRAD.BELIEFS, R.CATHOLIC, SUNNI MUSLIM
Currency: METICAL
Organizations: OAU, SADC, UN, COMM.

MAP PAGE: 129

MOZAMBIQUE LIES ON the east coast of southern Africa. The land is mainly a savannah plateau drained by the Zambezi and other rivers, with highlands to the north. Most people live on the coast or in the river valleys. In general the climate is tropical with winter rainfall, but droughts occur. Reconstruction began in 1992 after 16 years of civil war. The economy is based on agriculture and trade. Exports include shrimps, cashews, cotton and sugar, but Mozambique relies heavily on aid.

MYANMAR

Status: REPUBLIC
Area: 676,577 sq km (261,228 sq mls)
Population: 46,527,000
Capital: RANGOON
Language: BURMESE, SHAN, KAREN, LOCAL LANGUAGES
Religion: BUDDHIST, SUNNI MUSLIM, PROTESTANT, R.CATHOLIC
Currency: KYAT
Organizations: UN

MAP PAGE: 24-25

MYANMAR IS IN southeast Asia, on the Bay of Bengal and Andaman Sea. Most people live in the valley and delta of the Irrawaddy river, which is flanked on three sides by mountains and high plateaux. The climate is hot and monsoonal, and rainforest covers much of the land. Most people depend on agriculture. Exports include teak and rice. Myanmar is rich in oil and gemstones. Political unrest has affected economic development.

NAMIBIA

Status: REPUBLIC
Area: 824,292 sq km (318,261 sq mls)
Population: 1,540,000
Capital: WINDHOEK
Language: ENGLISH, AFRIKAANS, GERMAN, OVAMBO
Religion: PROTESTANT, R.CATHOLIC
Currency: DOLLAR
Organizations: COMM., OAU, SADC, UN

MAP PAGE: 128

NAMIBIA LIES ON the Atlantic coast of southern Africa. Mountain ranges separate the coastal Namib Desert from the interior plateau, bordered to the south and east by the Kalahari desert. Namibia is hot and dry, but some summer rain falls in the north which supports crops, herds and most of the population. The economy is based mainly on agriculture and diamond and uranium mining. Fishing is increasingly important.

NAURU

Status: REPUBLIC
Area: 21 sq km (8 sq mls)
Population: 11,000
Capital: YAREN
Language: NAURUAN, GILBERTESE, ENGLISH
Religion: PROTESTANT, R.CATHOLIC
Currency: AUSTR. DOLLAR
Organizations: COMM.

MAP PAGE: 4

NAURU IS A coral island in the South Pacific Ocean, with a fertile coastal strip, a barren central plateau and a tropical climate. The economy is based on phosphate mining, but reserves are near exhaustion.

NEPAL

Status: MONARCHY
Area: 147,181 sq km (56,827 sq mls)
Population: 21,918,000
Capital: KATHMANDU
Language: NEPALI, MAITHILI, BHOJPURI, ENGLISH, MANY LOCAL LANGUAGES
Religion: HINDU, BUDDHIST, SUNNI MUSLIM
Currency: RUPEE
Organizations: UN

MAP PAGE: 37

THE SOUTH ASIAN country of Nepal lies in the southern Himalayas between India and China. High mountains (including Everest) dominate northern Nepal. Most people live in the temperate central valleys and subtropical southern plains. The economy is based largely on agriculture and forestry. Manufacturing (chiefly textiles) and tourism are important. Nepal relies upon foreign aid.

NETHERLANDS

Status: MONARCHY
Area: 41,526 sq km (16,033 sq mls)
Population: 15,451,000
Capital: AMSTERDAM
Language: DUTCH, FRISIAN, TURKISH
Religion: R.CATHOLIC, PROTESTANT, SUNNI MUSLIM
Currency: GUILDER
Organizations: EU, OECD, UN

MAP PAGE: 68-69

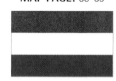

THE NETHERLANDS LIES on the North Sea coast of west Europe. Apart from hills in the far southeast, the land is flat and low-lying, much of it below sea level. The coastal region contains the delta of five rivers and polders (reclaimed land), protected by sand dunes, dikes and canals. The climate is temperate, with cool summers and mild winters. Rainfall is spread evenly throughout the year. The Netherlands is a densely populated country, with the majority of people living in the western Amsterdam-Rotterdam-The Hague area. Horticulture and dairy farming are important activities, with exports of eggs, butter and cheese. The Netherlands is Europe's leading producer and exporter of natural gas from reserves in the North Sea, but otherwise lacks raw materials. The economy is based mainly on international trade and manufacturing industry. Industrial sites are centred mainly around the port of Rotterdam. The chief industries produce food products, chemicals, machinery, electric and electronic goods and transport equipment. Financial services and tourism are important.

NETHERLANDS ANTILLES

Status: NETHERLANDS TERRITORY
Area: 800 sq km (309 sq mls)
Population: 205,000
Capital: WILLEMSTAD
Language: DUTCH, PAPIAMENTO
Religion: R.CATHOLIC, PROTESTANT
Currency: GUILDER

MAP PAGE: 159

THE TERRITORY COMPRISES two separate island groups: Curacao and Bonaire off the northern coast of South America, and Saba, Sint Eustatius and the southern part of Sint Maarten in the northern Lesser Antilles.

NEW CALEDONIA

Status: FRENCH TERRITORY
Area: 19,058 sq km (7,358 sq mls)
Population: 186,000
Capital: NOUMÉA
Language: FRENCH, LOCAL LANGUAGES
Religion: R.CATHOLIC, PROTESTANT, SUNNI MUSLIM
Currency: PACIFIC FRANC

MAP PAGE: 6

AN ISLAND GROUP, lying in the southwest Pacific, with a sub-tropical climate. The economy is based on nickel mining, tourism and agriculture.

NEW ZEALAND

Status: MONARCHY
Area: 270,534 sq km (104,454 sq mls)
Population: 3,542,000
Capital: WELLINGTON
Language: ENGLISH, MAORI
Religion: PROTESTANT, R.CATHOLIC
Currency: DOLLAR
Organizations: COMM., OECD, UN

MAP PAGE: 8-9

NEW ZEALAND, IN Australasia, comprises two main islands separated by the narrow Cook Strait, and a number of smaller islands. North Island, where three quarters of the population lives, has mountain ranges, broad fertile valleys and a volcanic central plateau with hot springs and two active volcanoes. South Island is also mountainous, the Southern Alps running its entire length. The only major lowland area is the Canterbury Plains in the east. The climate is generally temperate, though South Island has cooler winters with upland snow. Rainfall is distributed throughout the year. Farming is the mainstay of the economy. New Zealand is one of the world's leading producers of meat (beef, lamb and mutton), wool and dairy products. Specialist foods, such as kiwi fruit, and fish are also important. Coal, oil and natural gas are produced, but hydroelectric and geothermal power provide much of the country's energy needs. Other industries produce timber, wood pulp, iron, aluminium, machinery and chemicals. Tourism is the largest foreign exchange earner.

NICARAGUA

Status: REPUBLIC
Area: 130,000 sq km (50,193 sq mls)
Population: 4,539,000
Capital: MANAGUA
Language: SPANISH, AMERINDIAN LANGUAGES
Religion: R.CATHOLIC, PROTESTANT
Currency: CÓRDOBA
Organizations: UN

MAP PAGE: 157

NICARAGUA LIES AT the heart of Central America, with both Pacific and Caribbean coasts. Mountain ranges separate the east, which is largely jungle, from the more developed western regions, which include Lake Nicaragua and some active volcanoes. The highest land is in the north. The climate is tropical. The economy is largely agricultural.

Traditional exports include cotton, coffee, bananas and gold. The aid-dependent economy has suffered from civil war (1978-89) and US sanctions.

NIGER

Status: REPUBLIC
Area: 1,267,000 sq km (489,191 sq mls)
Population: 9,151,000
Capital: NIAMEY
Language: FRENCH (OFFICIAL), HAUSA, FULANI, LOCAL LANGUAGES
Religion: SUNNI MUSLIM, TRAD.BELIEFS
Currency: CFA FRANC
Organizations: OAU, UN

MAP PAGE: 123

A LANDLOCKED STATE of west Africa, Niger lies mostly within the Sahara desert, but with savannah land in the south and Niger valley. The Air massif dominates central regions. Much of the country is hot and dry. The south has some summer rainfall, though droughts occur. The economy depends on subsistence farming and herding, uranium exports and foreign aid.

NIGERIA

Status: REPUBLIC
Area: 923,768 sq km (356,669 sq mls)
Population: 111,721,000
Capital: ABUJA
Language: ENGLISH, CREOLE, HAUSA, YORUBA, IBO, FULANI
Religion: SUNNI MUSLIM, PROTESTANT, R.CATHOLIC, TRAD. BELIEFS
Currency: NAIRA
Organizations: COMM., OAU, OPEC, UN

MAP PAGE: 123

NIGERIA IS IN west Africa, on the Gulf of Guinea, and is the most populous country in the African continent. The Niger delta dominates coastal areas, fringed with sandy beaches, mangrove swamps and lagoons. Inland is a belt of rainforest that gives way to woodland or savannah on high plateaux. The far north is the semi-desert edge of the Sahara. The climate is tropical with heavy summer rainfall in the south but low rainfall in the north. Most people live in the coastal lowlands or in western Nigeria. About half the workforce is involved in agriculture, mainly growing subsistence crops, and Nigeria is virtually self-sufficient in food. Cocoa and rubber are the only significant export crops. The economy is heavily dependent on vast oil resources in the Niger delta and shallow offshore waters, which account for about 90 per cent of export earnings. Nigeria also has natural gas reserves and some mineral deposits, but these are as yet largely undeveloped. Industry involves mainly oil refining, chemicals (chiefly fertilizer), agricultural processing, textiles, steel manufacture and vehicle assembly. Economic mismanagement in the oil boom of the 1970s and political instability have left Nigeria with a heavy debt, poverty and rising unemployment.

NIUE

Status: NEW ZEALAND TERRITORY
Area: 258 sq km (100 sq mls)
Population: 2,000
Capital: ALOFI
Language: ENGLISH, POLYNESIAN (NIUEAN)
Religion: PROTESTANT, R.CATHOLIC
Currency: NZ DOLLAR

MAP PAGE: 5

NORFOLK ISLAND

Status: AUSTRALIAN TERRITORY
Area: 35 sq km (14 sq mls)
Population: 2,000
Capital: KINGSTON
Language: ENGLISH
Religion: PROTESTANT, R.CATHOLIC
Currency: AUSTR. DOLLAR

MAP PAGE: 11

NORTH KOREA

Status: REPUBLIC
Area: 120,538 sq km (46,540 sq mls)
Population: 23,917,000
Capital: PYONGYANG
Language: KOREAN
Religion: TRAD.BELIEFS, CHONDOIST, BUDDHIST, CONFUCIAN, TAOIST
Currency: WON
Organizations: UN

MAP PAGE: 31

OCCUPYING THE NORTHERN half of the Korean peninsula in east Asia, North Korea is a rugged and mountainous country. The principal lowlands and the main agricultural areas are the Pyongyang and Chaeryong plains in the southwest. More than half the population lives in urban areas, mainly on the coastal plains, which are wider along the Yellow Sea to the west than the Sea of Japan to the east. North Korea has a continental climate, with cold, dry winters and hot, wet summers. About half the workforce is involved in agriculture, mainly growing food crops on cooperative farms. A variety of minerals and ores, chiefly iron ore, are mined and are the basis of the country's heavy industry. Exports include minerals (chiefly lead, magnesite and zinc) and metal products (chiefly iron and steel). North Korea depends heavily on aid, but has suffered since support from Russia and China was ended in in 1991 and 1993 respectively. Agricultural, mining and maufacturing output have fallen. Living standards are much lower than in South Korea from which it was separated in 1945.

NORTHERN MARIANA ISLANDS

Status: US TERRITORY
Area: 477 sq km (184 sq mls)
Population: 47,000
Capital: SAIPAN
Language: ENGLISH, CHAMORRO, TAGALOG, LOCAL LANGUAGES
Religion: R.CATHOLIC, PROTESTANT
Currency: US DOLLAR

MAP PAGE: 21

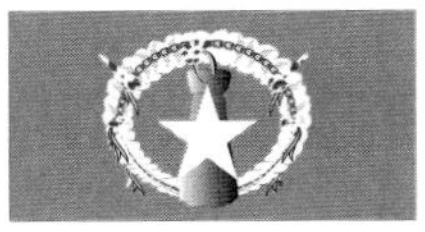

A CHAIN OF islands in the Western Pacific Ocean, tourism is increasingly important to the economy.

NORWAY

Status: MONARCHY
Area: 323,878 sq km (125,050 sq mls)
Population: 4,360,000
Capital: OSLO
Language: NORWEGIAN
Religion: PROTESTANT, R.CATHOLIC
Currency: KRONE
Organizations: OECD, UN

MAP PAGE: 56-57

A COUNTRY OF NORTH Europe, Norway stretches along the north and west coasts of Scandinavia, from the Arctic Ocean to the North Sea. Its extensive coastline is indented

with fjords and fringed with many islands. Inland, the terrain is mountainous, with coniferous forests and lakes in the south. The only major lowland areas are along the southern North Sea and Skagerrak coasts, where most people live. The climate on the west coast is modified by the North Atlantic Drift. Inland, summers are warmer but winters are colder. Norway has vast petroleum and natural gas resources in the North Sea. It is west Europe's leading producer of oil and gas, which account for over 40 per cent of export earnings. Related industries include engineering (such as oil and gas platforms) and petrochemicals. More traditional industries process local raw materials: fish, timber and minerals. Agriculture is limited, but fishing and fish farming are important. Norway is the world's leading exporter of salmon. Merchant shipping and tourism are major sources of foreign exchange.

OMAN

Status: MONARCHY
Area: 309,500 sq km (119,499 sq mls)
Population: 2,163,000
Capital: MUSCAT
Language: ARABIC, BALUCHI, FARSI, SWAHILI, INDIAN LANGUAGES
Religion: IBADHI MUSLIM, SUNNI MUSLIM
Currency: RIAL
Organizations: UN

MAP PAGE: 41

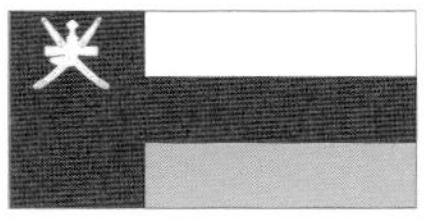

THE SULTANATE OF southwest Asia occupies the southeast coast of Arabia and an enclave north of the United Arab Emirates. Oman is a desert land, with mountains in the north and south. The climate is hot and mainly dry. Most people live on the coastal strip on the Gulf of Oman. The majority depends on farming and fishing, but the oil and gas industries dominate the economy. Copper is mined.

PAKISTAN

Status: REPUBLIC
Area: 803,940 sq km (310,403 sq mls)
Population: 129,808,000
Capital: ISLAMABAD
Language: URDU (OFFICIAL), PUNJABI, SINDHI, PUSHTU, ENGLISH
Religion: SUNNI MUSLIM, SHI'A MUSLIM, CHRISTIAN, HINDU
Currency: RUPEE
Organizations: COMM., UN

MAP PAGE: 39

PAKISTAN IS IN the northwest part of the Indian subcontinent in south Asia, on the Arabian Sea. Eastern and southern Pakistan are dominated by the great basin drained by the Indus river system. It is the main agricultural area and contains most of the population. To the north the land rises to the mountains of the Karakoram and part of the Hindu Kush and Himalayas. The west is semi-desert plateaux and mountain ranges. The climate ranges between dry desert and polar ice cap. However, temperatures are generally warm and rainfall is monsoonal. Agriculture is the main sector of the economy, employing about half the workforce and accounting for over two thirds of export earnings. Cultivation is based on extensive irrigation schemes. Pakistan is one of the world's leading producers of cotton and an important exporter of rice. However, much of the country's food needs must be imported. Pakistan produces natural gas and has a variery of mineral deposits including coal and gold, but they are little developed. The main industries are textiles and food processing, with fabrics and ready-made clothing the leading exports. Pakistan also produces leather goods, fertilizers, chemicals, paper and precision instruments. The country depends heavily upon foreign aid and remittances from Pakistanis working abroad.

PALAU

Status: REPUBLIC
Area: 497 sq km (192 sq mls)
Population: 17,000
Capital: KOROR
Language: PALAUAN, ENGLISH
Religion: R.CATHOLIC, PROTESTANT, TRAD.BELIEFS
Currency: US DOLLAR
Organizations: UN

MAP PAGE: 23

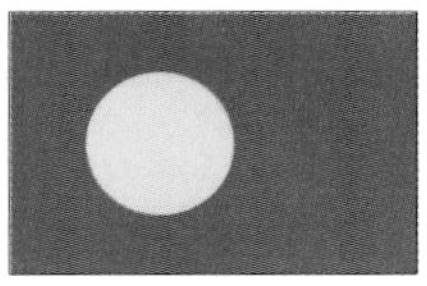

PALAU COMPRISES OVER 300 islands in the western Carolines group of the North Pacific Ocean. Two thirds of the people live on Koror. The climate is tropical. Palau depends on farming, fishing, tourism and US aid.

PANAMA

Status: REPUBLIC
Area: 77,082 sq km (29,762 sq mls)
Population: 2,631,000
Capital: PANAMA CITY
Language: SPANISH, ENGLISH CREOLE, AMERINDIAN LANGUAGES
Religion: R.CATHOLIC, PROTESTANT, SUNNI MUSLIM, BAHA'I
Currency: BALBOA
Organizations: UN

MAP PAGE: 157

PANAMA IS THE most southerly state in Central America and has Pacific and Caribbean coasts. It is hilly, with mountains in the west and jungle near the Colombian border. The climate is tropical. Most people live on the drier Pacific side. The economy is based mainly on services related to the canal, shipping, banking and tourism. Exports include bananas, shrimps, sugar and petroleum products.

PAPUA NEW GUINEA

Status: MONARCHY
Area: 462,840 sq km (178,704 sq mls)
Population: 4,074,000
Capital: PORT MORESBY
Language: ENGLISH, TOK PISIN (PIDGIN), LOCAL LANGUAGES
Religion: PROTESTANT, R.CATHOLIC, TRAD.BELIEFS
Currency: KINA
Organizations: COMM., UN

MAP PAGE: 6

PAPUA NEW GUINEA, in Australasia, occupies the eastern half of New Guinea and includes many island groups. Papua New Guinea has a forested and mountainous interior, bordered by swampy plains, and a tropical monsoon climate. Most of the workforce are farmers. Timber, copra, coffee and cocoa are important, but exports are dominated by minerals, chiefly copper and gold. The country depends on foreign aid.

© Bartholomew

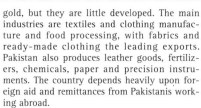

PARAGUAY

Status: REPUBLIC
Area: 406,752 sq km (157,048 sq mls)
Population: 4,828,000
Capital: ASUNCIÓN
Language: SPANISH, GUARANÍ
Religion: R.CATHOLIC, PROTESTANT
Currency: GUARANÍ
Organizations: UN

MAP PAGE: 165

PARAGUAY IS A landlocked country in central South America, bordering Bolivia, Brazil and Argentina. The river Paraguay separates a sparsely populated western zone of marsh and flat alluvial plains from a more developed, hilly and forested region to the east. The climate is subtropical. The mainstay of the economy is agriculture and agricultural processing. Exports include cotton, soya bean and edible oil products, timber and meat. The largest hydro-electric dam in the world is at Itaipú on the river Paraná.

PERU

Status: REPUBLIC
Area: 1,285,216 sq km (496,225 sq mls)
Population: 23,560,000
Capital: LIMA
Language: SPANISH, QUECHUA, AYMARA
Religion: R.CATHOLIC, PROTESTANT
Currency: SOL
Organizations: UN

MAP PAGE: 162, 164

PERU LIES ON the Pacific coast of South America. Most people live on the coastal strip and the slopes of the high Andes. East of the Andes is high plateau country and the Amazon rainforest. The coast is temperate with low rainfall, while the east is hot, humid and wet. Agriculture involves one third of the workforce. Sugar, cotton, coffee and, illegally, coca are the main cash crops. Fishmeal and timber are also important, but copper, zinc, lead, gold, silver, petroleum and its products are the main exports.

PHILIPPINES

Status: REPUBLIC
Area: 300,000 sq km (115,831 sq mls)
Population: 70,267,000
Capital: MANILA
Language: ENGLISH, FILIPINO (TAGALOG), CEBUANO
Religion: R.CATHOLIC, AGLIPAYAN, SUNNI MUSLIM, PROTESTANT
Currency: PESO
Organizations: ASEAN, UN

MAP PAGE: 23

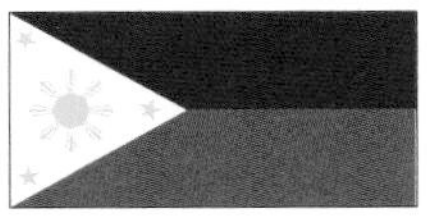

THE PHILIPPINES, IN southeast Asia, consists of 7,100 islands and atolls lying between the South China Sea and the Pacific Ocean. The islands of Luzon and Mindanao occupy two thirds of the land area. They and nine other fairly large islands are mountainous and forested. There are ten active volcanoes and earthquakes are common. Most people live in the intermontane plains on the larger islands or on the coastal strips. The climate is hot and humid with heavy monsoonal rainfall. Coconuts, sugar, pineapples and bananas are the main agricultural exports. Fish and timber are also important. The Philippines produces copper, gold, silver, chromium and nickel as well as oil, though geothermal power is also used. The main industries process raw materials and produce electrical and electronic equipment and components, footwear and clothing, textiles and furniture. Tourism is being encouraged. Foreign aid and remittances from workers abroad are important to the economy, which faces problems of high population growth rate and high unemployment.

PITCAIRN ISLANDS

Status: UK TERRITORY
Area: 45 sq km (17 sq mls)
Population: 71
Capital: ADAMSTOWN
Language: ENGLISH
Religion: PROTESTANT
Currency: DOLLAR

MAP PAGE: 7

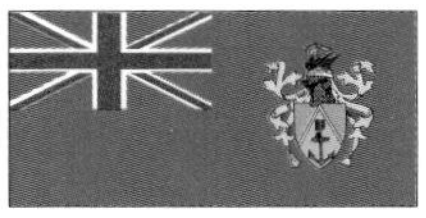

AN ISLAND GROUP in the southeast Pacific Ocean consisting of Pitcairn Island and three uninhabited islands. It was originally settled by mutineers from HMS Bounty.

POLAND

Status: REPUBLIC
Area: 312,683 sq km (120,728 sq mls)
Population: 38,588,000
Capital: WARSAW
Language: POLISH, GERMAN
Religion: R.CATHOLIC, POLISH ORTHODOX
Currency: ZŁOTY
Organizations: UN, OECD

MAP PAGE: 76-77

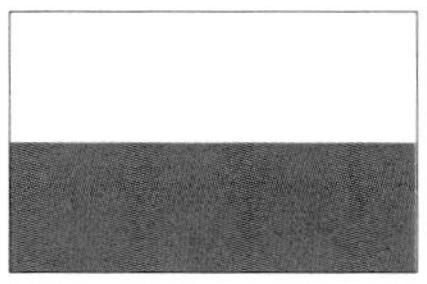

POLAND LIES ON the Baltic coast of central Europe. The Oder and Vistula deltas dominate the coast, fringed with sand dunes. Inland much of Poland is low-lying (part of the North European plain), with woods and lakes. In the south the land rises to the Sudeten and western Carpathian mountains which form the borders with the Czech Republic and Slovakia respectively. The climate is continental, with warm summers and cold winters. Conditions are milder in the west and on the coast. A third of the workforce is involved in agriculture, forestry and fishing. Agricultural exports include livestock products and sugar. The economy is heavily industrialized, with mining and manufacturing accounting for 40 per cent of national income. Poland is one of the world's major producers of coal. It also produces copper, zinc, lead, nickel, sulphur and natural gas. The main industries are ship building, car manufacture, metal and chemical production. The transition to a market economy has resulted in 15 per cent unemployment and economic hardship.

PORTUGAL

Status: REPUBLIC
Area: 88,940 sq km (34,340 sq mls)
Population: 10,797,000
Capital: LISBON
Language: PORTUGUESE
Religion: R.CATHOLIC, PROTESTANT
Currency: ESCUDO
Organizations: EU, OECD, UN

MAP PAGE: 96

PORTUGAL LIES IN the western part of the Iberian peninsula in southwest Europe, has an Atlantic coastline and is flanked by Spain to the north and east. North of the river Tagus are mostly highlands with forests of pine and cork. South of the river is undulating lowland. The climate in the north is cool and moist, influenced by the Atlantic Ocean. The south is warmer, with dry, mild winters. Most Portuguese live near the coast, with one third of the total population in Lisbon and Oporto. Agriculture, fishing and forestry involve 12 per cent of the workfork. Wines, tomatoes, citrus fruit, cork (Portugal is the world's largest producer) and sardines are important exports. Mining and manufacturing are the main sectors of the economy. Portugal produces pyrite, kaolin, zinc, tungsten and other minerals. Export manufactures include textiles, clothing and footwear, electrical machinery and transport equipment, cork and wood products, and chemicals. Service industries, chiefly tourism and banking, are important to the economy as are remittances from workers abroad.

PUERTO RICO

Status: US TERRITORY
Area: 9,104 sq km (3,515 sq mls)
Population: 3,674,000
Capital: SAN JUAN
Language: SPANISH, ENGLISH
Religion: R.CATHOLIC, PROTESTANT
Currency: US DOLLAR

MAP PAGE: 159

THE CARIBBEAN ISLAND of Puerto Rico has a forested, hilly interior, coastal plains and a tropical climate. Half the population lives in the San Juan area. The economy is based on export manufacturing (chiefly chemicals and electronics), tourism and agriculture.

QATAR

Status: MONARCHY
Area: 11,437 sq km (4,416 sq mls)
Population: 551,000
Capital: DOHA
Language: ARABIC, INDIAN LANGUAGES
Religion: SUNNI MUSLIM, CHRISTIAN, HINDU
Currency: RIYAL
Organizations: OPEC, UN

MAP PAGE: 39

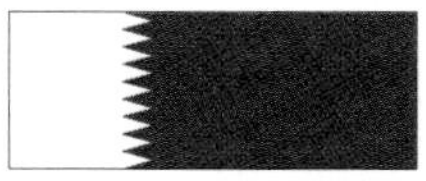

THE EMIRATE OCCUPIES a peninsula that extends northwards from east-central Arabia into The Gulf in southwest Asia. The peninsula is flat and barren with sand dunes and salt pans. The climate is hot and mainly dry. Most people live in the Doha area. The economy is heavily dependent on petroleum, natural gas and the oil-refining industry. Income also comes from overseas investment.

REPUBLIC OF IRELAND

Status: REPUBLIC
Area: 70,282 sq km (27,136 sq mls)
Population: 3,582,000
Capital: DUBLIN
Language: ENGLISH, IRISH
Religion: R.CATHOLIC, PROTESTANT
Currency: PUNT
Organizations: EU, OECD, UN

MAP PAGE: 67

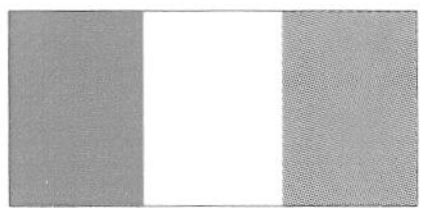

A STATE IN northwest Europe, the Irish republic occupies some 80 per cent of the island of Ireland in the Atlantic Ocean. It is a lowland country of wide valleys, lakes and peat bogs, with isolated mountain ranges around the coast. The west coast is rugged and indented with many bays. The climate is mild due to the North Atlantic Drift and rainfall is plentiful, though highest in the west. Nearly 60 per cent of people live in urban areas, Dublin and Cork being the main cities. Agriculture, the traditional mainstay, involves mainly the production of livestock, meat and dairy products, which account for about 20 percent of exports. Manufactured goods form the bulk of exports. The main industries are electronics, pharmaceuticals and engineering as well as food processing, brewing and textiles. Natural resources include petroleum, natural gas, peat, lead and zinc. Services industries are expanding, with tourism a major foreign exchange earner. The economy could benefit from peace in Northern Ireland, which is part of the United Kingdom.

RÉUNION

Status: FRENCH TERRITORY
Area: 2,551 sq km (985 sq mls)
Population: 653,000
Capital: ST-DENIS
Language: FRENCH, FRENCH CREOLE
Religion: R.CATHOLIC
Currency: FRENCH FRANC

MAP PAGE: 127

THE INDIAN OCEAN island of Réunion is mountainous, with coastal lowlands and a warm climate. It depends heavily on sugar, tourism and French aid. Some uninhabited islets to the east are administered from Réunion.

ROMANIA

Status: REPUBLIC
Area: 237,500 sq km (91,699 sq mls)
Population: 22,680,000
Capital: BUCHAREST
Language: ROMANIAN, HUNGARIAN
Religion: ROMANIAN ORTHODOX, R.CATHOLIC, PROTESTANT
Currency: LEU
Organizations: UN

MAP PAGE: 112

ROMANIA LIES ON the Black Sea coast of east Europe. Mountains separate the Transylvanian plateau from the populous plains of the east and south and the Danube delta. The climate is continental. Romania is rich in fuels and metallic ores. Mining and manufacturing (chiefly metallurgy and machine building) predominate but agriculture

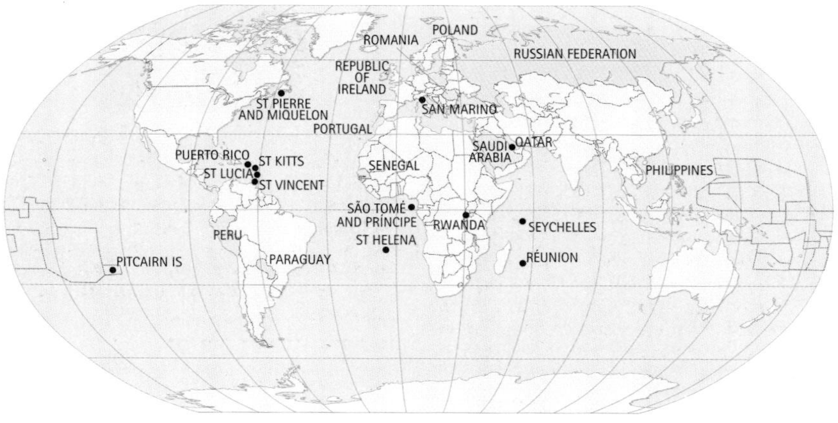

is important. Pre-1989 mismanagement and economic reforms of the 1990s have caused hardship.

RUSSIAN FEDERATION

Status: REPUBLIC
Area: 17,075,400 sq km (6,592,849 sq mls)
Population: 148,141,000
Capital: MOSCOW
Language: RUSSIAN, TATAR, UKRAINIAN, LOCAL LANGUAGES
Religion: RUSSIAN ORTHODOX, SUNNI MUSLIM, OTHER CHRISTIAN, JEWISH
Currency: ROUBLE
Organizations: CIS, UN

MAP PAGE: 44-45

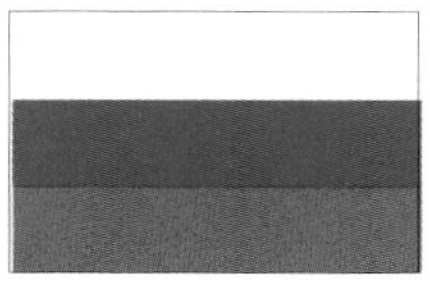

RUSSIA OCCUPIES MUCH of east Europe and all of north Asia, and is the world's largest state, nearly twice the size of the USA. It borders thirteen countries to the west and south and has long coastlines on the Arctic and Pacific oceans to the north and east. European Russia, which lies west of the Ural mountains, is part of the North European plain. To the south the land rises to uplands and the Caucasus Mountains on the border with Georgia and Azerbaijan. East of the Urals lies the flat Siberian plain. Much of central Siberia is plateaux. In the south is Lake Baikal, the world's deepest lake, and the Altai and Sayan ranges on the border with Azerbaijan and Mongolia. Eastern Siberia is rugged and mountainous with active volcanoes, notably in the Kamchatka peninsula. Russia's major rivers are the Volga in the west and the Ob, Yenisey, Lena and Amur in Siberia. The climate and vegetation range between Arctic tundra in the north and semi-arid steppe towards the Black and Caspian Sea coasts in the south. In general, the climate is continental with extreme temperatures. The majority of the population (the sixth largest in the world), industry and agriculture are concentrated in European Russia, but there has been increased migration to Siberia to exploit its vast natural resources. The economy is heavily dependent on exploitation of its raw materials and heavy industry. Russia has a wealth of mineral resources, though they are often difficult to exploit because of the climate. It is one of the world's leading producers of petroleum, natural gas and coal as well as iron and manganese ores, platinum, potash, asbestos and many precious and rare metals. Mining provides important exports and is the basis of heavy industry. Russia is a major producer of steel and machinery such as tractors, motor vehicles and generators, as well as chemicals and textiles. Other light industries are less important to the economy. Forests cover about 40 per cent of the land area and supply an important timber, paper and pulp industry. About 8 per cent of land is suitable for cultivation. However farming is generally inefficient and much of food needs, especially grains, must be imported. Fishing is important and Russia operates a large fleet throughout the world. Economic reforms begun in the late 1980s to liberalize the economy met with mixed success, largely because of political unrest. The transition to a free market economy, which was speeded up in the 1990s has been painful, with rising unemployment.

RWANDA

Status: REPUBLIC
Area: 26,338 sq km (10,169 sq mls)
Population: 7,952,000
Capital: KIGALI
Language: KINYARWANDA, FRENCH, ENGLISH
Religion: R.CATHOLIC, TRAD.BELIEFS, PROTESTANT, SUNNI MUSLIM
Currency: FRANC
Organizations: OAU, UN

MAP PAGE: 127

A DENSELY POPULATED and landlocked state in east Africa, Rwanda consists mainly of mountains and plateaux to the east of the Rift Valley. The climate is warm with a summer dry season. Rwanda depends upon subsistence farming, coffee and tea exports, light industry and foreign aid, but the 1990-93 civil war and ethnic conflict have devastated the country.

ST HELENA

Status: UK TERRITORY
Area: 411 sq km (159 sq mls)
Population: 7,000
Capital: JAMESTOWN
Language: ENGLISH
Religion: PROTESTANT, R.CATHOLIC
Currency: POUND STERLING

MAP PAGE: 128

ST HELENA AND its dependencies, Ascension and Tristan da Cunha are isolated island groups lying in the south Atlantic Ocean. Ascension is over 1000 kilometres (620 miles) northwest of St Helena and Tristan da Cunha over 2000 kilometres (1240 miles) to the south.

ST KITTS-NEVIS

Status: MONARCHY
Area: 261 sq km (101 sq mls)
Population: 42,000
Capital: BASSETERRE
Language: ENGLISH, CREOLE
Religion: PROTESTANT, R.CATHOLIC
Currency: E. CARIB. DOLLAR
Organizations: CARICOM, COMM., UN

MAP PAGE: 159

ST KITTS-NEVIS are in the Leeward group in the Caribbean Sea. Both volcanic islands are mountainous and forested with sandy beaches and a warm, wet climate. Some 75 per cent of the population lives on St Kitts. Agriculture is the main activity, with sugar, molasses and sea island cotton the main products. Tourism and manufacturing (chiefly garments and electronic components) are important.

ST LUCIA

Status: MONARCHY
Area: 616 sq km (238 sq mls)
Population: 145,000
Capital: CASTRIES
Language: ENGLISH, FRENCH CREOLE
Religion: R.CATHOLIC, PROTESTANT
Currency: E. CARIB. DOLLAR
Organizations: CARICOM, COMM., UN

MAP PAGE: 159

ST LUCIA, PART OF the Windward group in the Caribbean Sea, is a volcanic island with forested mountains, hot springs, sandy beaches and a wet tropical climate. Agriculture is the main activity, with bananas accounting for over half export earnings. Tourism, agricultural processing and manufacturing (chiefly garments, cardboard boxes and electronic components) are increasingly important.

ST PIERRE AND MIQUELON

Status: FRENCH TERRITORY
Area: 242 sq km (93 sq mls)
Population: 6,000
Capital: ST-PIERRE
Language: FRENCH
Religion: R.CATHOLIC
Currency: FRENCH FRANC

MAP PAGE: 139

A GROUP OF islands off the south coast of Newfoundland in eastern Canada.

ST VINCENT AND THE GRENADINES

Status: MONARCHY
Area: 389 sq km (150 sq mls)
Population: 111,000
Capital: KINGSTOWN
Language: ENGLISH, CREOLE
Religion: PROTESTANT, R.CATHOLIC
Currency: E. CARIB. DOLLAR
Organizations: CARICOM, COMM., UN

MAP PAGE: 159

ST VINCENT, WHOSE TERRITORY includes 32 islets and cays in the Grenadines, is in the Windward Islands group in the Caribbean Sea. St Vincent is forested and mountainous, with an active volcano, Mount Soufrière. The climate is tropical and wet. The economy is based mainly on agriculture and tourism. Bananas account for about half export earnings. Arrowroot is also important.

SAN MARINO

Status: REPUBLIC
Area: 61 sq km (24 sq mls)
Population: 25,000
Capital: SAN MARINO
Language: ITALIAN
Religion: R.CATHOLIC
Currency: ITALIAN LIRA
Organizations: UN

MAP PAGE: 107

LANDLOCKED SAN MARINO lies on the slopes of Mt Titano in northeast Italy. It has a mild climate. A third of the people live in the capital. There is some agriculture and light industry, but most income comes from tourism and postage stamp sales.

SÃO TOMÉ AND PRÍNCIPE

Status: REPUBLIC
Area: 964 sq km (372 sq mls)
Population: 127,000
Capital: SÃO TOMÉ
Language: PORTUGUESE, PORTUGUESE CREOLE
Religion: R.CATHOLIC, PROTESTANT
Currency: DOBRA
Organizations: OAU, UN

MAP PAGE: 125

THE TWO MAIN islands and adjacent islets lie off the coast of west Africa in the Gulf of Guinea. São Tomé is the larger island and supports over 90 per cent of the population. Both São Tomé and Príncipe are mountainous and tree-covered, and have a hot and humid climate. The economy is heavily dependent on cocoa, which accounts for over 90 per cent of export earnings.

SAUDI ARABIA

Status: MONARCHY
Area: 2,200,000 sq km (849,425 sq mls)
Population: 17,880,000
Capital: RIYADH
Language: ARABIC
Religion: SUNNI MUSLIM, SHI'A MUSLIM
Currency: RIYAL
Organizations: OPEC, UN

MAP PAGE: 40-41

SAUDI ARABIA OCCUPIES most of the Arabian peninsula in southwest Asia. The terrain is desert or semi-desert plateaux, which rise to mountains running parallel to the Red Sea in the west and slope down to plains in the southeast and along The Gulf in the east. Most people live in urban areas, one third in the cities of Riyadh, Jiddah and Mecca. Summers are hot, winters are warm and rainfall is low. Saudi Arabia has the world's largest reserves of oil and gas, located in the northeast, both onshore and in The Gulf. Crude oil and refined products account for over 90 per cent of export earnings. Other industries and irrigated agrculture are being encouraged, but most food and raw materials are imported. Saudi Arabia has important banking and commercial interests. Each year 2 million pilgrims visit Islam's holiest cities, Mecca and Medina, in the west.

SENEGAL

Status: REPUBLIC
Area: 196,720 sq km (75,954 sq mls)
Population: 8,347,000
Capital: DAKAR
Language: FRENCH (OFFICIAL), WOLOF, FULANI, LOCAL LANGUAGES
Religion: SUNNI MUSLIM, R.CATHOLIC, TRAD.BELIEFS
Currency: CFA FRANC
Organizations: OAU, UN

MAP PAGE: 122

SENEGAL LIES ON the Atlantic coast of west Africa. The north is arid semi-desert, while the south is mainly fertile savannah bushland. The climate is tropical with summer rains, though droughts occur. One fifth of the population lives in Dakar. Groundnuts, phosphates and fish are the main resources. There is some oil refining and Dakar is a major port. Senegal relies heavily on aid.

SEYCHELLES

Status: REPUBLIC
Area: 455 sq km (176 sq mls)
Population: 75,000
Capital: VICTORIA
Language: SEYCHELLOIS (SESELWA, FRENCH CREOLE), ENGLISH
Religion: R.CATHOLIC, PROTESTANT
Currency: RUPEE
Organizations: COMM., OAU, UN

MAP PAGE: 127

THE SEYCHELLES COMPRISES an archipelago of 115 granitic and coral islands in the western Indian Ocean. The main island, Mahé, contains about 90 per cent of the population. The climate is hot and humid with heavy rainfall. The economy is based mainly on tourism, transit trade, and light manufacturing, with fishing and agriculture (chiefly copra, cinnamon and tea) also important.

© Bartholomew

SIERRA LEONE

Status: REPUBLIC
Area: 71,740 sq km (27,699 sq mls)
Population: 4,509,000
Capital: FREETOWN
Language: ENGLISH, CREOLE, MENDE, TEMNE, LOCAL LANGUAGES
Religion: TRAD. BELIEFS, SUNNI MUSLIM, PROTESTANT, R.CATHOLIC
Currency: LEONE
Organizations: COMM., OAU, UN

MAP PAGE: 122

SIERRA LEONE LIES on the Atlantic coast of west Africa. Its coast is heavily indented and lined with mangrove swamps. Inland is a forested area rising to savannah plateaux, with the mountains to the northeast. The climate is tropical and rainfall is heavy. Most of the workforce is involved in subsistence farming. Cocoa and coffee are the main cash crops, but rutile (titanium ore), bauxite and diamonds are the main exports. Civil war and economic decline have caused serious difficulties.

SINGAPORE

Status: REPUBLIC
Area: 639 sq km (247 sq mls)
Population: 2,987,000
Capital: SINGAPORE
Language: CHINESE, ENGLISH, MALAY, TAMIL
Religion: BUDDHIST, TAOIST, SUNNI MUSLIM, CHRISTIAN, HINDU
Currency: DOLLAR
Organizations: ASEAN, COMM., UN

MAP PAGE: 25

THE STATE COMPRISES the main island of Singapore and 57 other islands, lying off the southern tip of the Malay Peninsula in southeast Asia. A causeway links Singapore to the mainland across the Johor Strait. Singapore is generally low-lying and includes land reclaimed from swamps. It is hot and humid, with heavy rainfall throughout the year. There are fish farms and vegetable gardens in the north and east of the island, but most food needs must be imported. Singapore also lacks mineral and energy resources. Manufacturing industries and services are the main sectors of the economy. Their rapid development has fuelled the nation's impressive economic growth over the last three decades to become the richest of Asia's four 'little dragons'. The main industries include electronics, oil refining, chemicals, pharmaceuticals, ship building and repair, iron and steel, food processing and textiles. Singapore is a major financial centre. Its port is one of the world's largest and busiest and acts as an entrepot for neighbouring states. Tourism is also important.

SLOVAKIA

Status: REPUBLIC
Area: 49,035 sq km (18,933 sq mls)
Population: 5,364,000
Capital: BRATISLAVA
Language: SLOVAK, HUNGARIAN, CZECH
Religion: R.CATHOLIC, PROTESTANT, ORTHODOX
Currency: KORUNA
Organizations: UN

MAP PAGE: 79

A LANDLOCKED COUNTRY in central Europe, Slovakia borders the Czech Republic, Poland, Ukraine, Hungary and Austria. Slovakia is mountainous along the border with Poland in the north, but low-lying along the plains of the Danube in the southwest. The climate is continental. Slovakia is the smaller, less populous and less developed part of former Czechoslovakia. With few natural resources, uncompetitive heavy industry and loss of federal subsidies, the economy has suffered economic difficulties.

SLOVENIA

Status: REPUBLIC
Area: 20,251 sq km (7,819 sq mls)
Population: 1,984,000
Capital: LJUBLJANA
Language: SLOVENE, SERBO-CROAT
Religion: R.CATHOLIC, PROTESTANT
Currency: TÓLAR
Organizations: UN

MAP PAGE: 104

SLOVENIA LIES IN the northwest Balkans of south Europe and has a short coastline on the Adriatic Sea. It is mountainous and hilly, with lowlands on the coast and in the Sava and Drava river valleys. The climate is generally continental, but Mediterranean nearer the coast. Dairy farming, mercury mining, light manufacturing and tourism are the main activities. Conflict in the other former Yugoslav states, which has affected tourism and international trade, has caused serious economic problems.

SOLOMON ISLANDS

Status: MONARCHY
Area: 28,370 sq km (10,954 sq mls)
Population: 378,000
Capital: HONIARA
Language: ENGLISH, SOLOMON ISLANDS PIDGIN, MANY LOCAL LANGUAGES
Religion: PROTESTANT, R.CATHOLIC
Currency: DOLLAR
Organizations: COMM., UN

MAP PAGE: 6

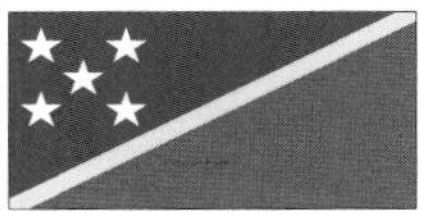

THE STATE CONSISTS of the southern Solomon, Santa Cruz and Shortland islands in Australasia. The six main islands are volcanic, mountainous and forested, though Guadalcanal, the most populous, has a large area of flat land. The climate is generally hot and humid. Subsistence farming and fishing predominate. Exports include fish, timber, copra and palm oil. The islands depend on foreign aid.

SOMALIA

Status: REPUBLIC
Area: 637,657 sq km (246,201 sq mls)
Population: 9,250,000
Capital: MOGADISHU
Language: SOMALI, ARABIC (OFFICIAL)
Religion: SUNNI MUSLIM
Currency: SHILLING
Organizations: OAU, UN

MAP PAGE: 126-127

SOMALIA IS IN the Horn of northeast Africa, on the Gulf of Aden and Indian Ocean. It consists of a dry scrubby plateau, rising to highlands in the north. The climate is hot and dry, but coastal areas and the Jubba and Shebele river valleys support crops and the bulk of the population. Subsistence farming and herding are the main activities. Exports include livestock and bananas. Drought and war have ruined the economy.

SOUTH AFRICA

Status: REPUBLIC
Area: 1,219,080 sq km (470,689 sq mls)
Population: 41,244,000
Capital: PRETORIA/CAPE TOWN
Language: AFRIKAANS, ENGLISH, NINE LOCAL LANGUAGES (ALL OFFICIAL)
Religion: PROTESTANT, R.CATHOLIC, SUNNI MUSLIM, HINDU
Currency: RAND
Organizations: COMM., OAU, SADC, UN

MAP PAGE: 130-131

SOUTH AFRICA OCCUPIES most of the southern part of Africa. It borders five states, surrounds Lesotho and has a long coastline on the Atlantic and Indian oceans. Much of the land is a vast plateau, covered with grassland or bush and drained by the Orange and Limpopo river systems. A fertile coastal plain rises to mountain ridges in the south and east, including Table Mountain near Cape Town and the Drakensberg range in the east. Gauteng is the most populous province, with Johannesburg and Pretoria its main cities. South Africa has warm summers and mild winters. Most of the country has rainfall in summer, but the coast around Cape Town has winter rains. South Africa is the largest and most developed economy in Africa, though wealth is unevenly distributed. Agriculture provides one third of exports, including fruit, wine, wool and maize. South Africa is rich in minerals. It is the world's leading producer of gold, which accounts for one third of export earnings. Coal, diamonds, platinum, uranium, chromite and other minerals are also mined. The main industries process minerals and agricultural produce, and manufacture chemical products, motor vehicles, electrical equipment and textiles. Financial services are also important.

SOUTH KOREA

Status: REPUBLIC
Area: 99,274 sq km (38,330 sq mls)
Population: 44,851,000
Capital: SEOUL
Language: KOREAN
Religion: BUDDHIST, PROTESTANT, R.CATHOLIC, CONFUCIAN, TRADITIONAL
Currency: WON
Organizations: UN, OECD

MAP PAGE: 31

THE STATE CONSISTS of the southern half of the Korean Peninsula in east Asia and many islands lying off the western and southern coasts in the Yellow Sea. The terrain is mountainous, though less rugged than that of North Korea. Population density is high and most people live on the western coastal plains and in the Han basin in the northwest and Naktong basin in the southeast. South Korea has a continental climate, with hot, wet summers and dry, cold winters. Arable land is limited by the mountainous terrain, but because of intensive farming South Korea is nearly self-sufficient in food. Sericulture is important as is fishing, which contributes to exports. South Korea has few mineral resources, except for coal and tungsten. It is one of Asia's four 'little dragons' (Hong Kong, Singapore and Taiwan being the others), which have achieved high economic growth based mainly on export manufacturing. In South Korea industry is dominated by a few giant conglomerates, such as Hyundai and Samsung. The main manufactures are cars, electronic and electrical goods, ships, steel, chemicals, and toys as well as textiles, clothing, footwear and food products. Banking and other financial services are increasingly important.

SPAIN

Status: MONARCHY
Area: 504,782 sq km (194,897 sq mls)
Population: 39,210,000
Capital: MADRID
Language: SPANISH, CATALAN, GALICIAN, BASQUE
Religion: R.CATHOLIC
Currency: PESETA
Organizations: EU, OECD, UN

MAP PAGE: 96-97

SPAIN OCCUPIES THE greater part of the Iberian peninsula in southwest Europe, with coastlines on the Atlantic Ocean (Bay of Biscay and Gulf of Cadiz) and Mediterranean Sea. It includes the Balearic and Canary island groups in the Mediterranean and Atlantic, and two enclaves in north Africa. Much of the mainland is a high plateau, the Meseta, drained by the Duero, Tagus and Guadiana rivers. The plateau is interrupted by a low mountain range and bounded to the east and north also by mountains, including the Pyrenees which form the border with France and Andorra. The main lowland areas are the Ebro basin in the northeast, the eastern coastal plains and the Guadalquivir basin in the southwest. Three quarters of the population lives in urban areas, chiefly Madrid and Barcelona, which alone contain one quarter of the population. The plateau experiences hot summers and cold winters. Conditions are cooler and wetter to the north, though warmer and drier to the south. Agriculture involves about 10 per cent of the workforce and fruit, vegetables and wine are exported. Fishing is an important industry and Spain has a large fishing fleet. Mineral resources include iron, lead, copper and mercury. Some oil is produced, but Spain has to import most energy needs. The economy is based mainly on manufacturing and services. Manufacturing industries account for one third of national income and are based mainly around Madrid and Barcelona. The principal products are machinery and transport equip-

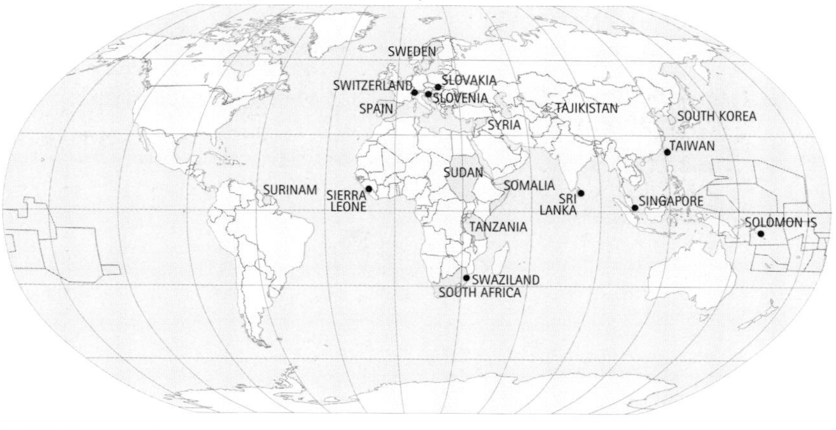

ment. Spain is a leading manufacturer of motor vehicles (SEAT). Other manufactures are agricultural products, chemicals, steel and other metals, paper products, wood and cork products, clothing and footwear, and textiles. With some 50 million visitors a year, tourism is a major industry, accounting for 10 per cent of national income and employing about the same percentage of the workforce. Banking and commerce are also important.

SRI LANKA

Status: REPUBLIC
Area: 65,610 sq km (25,332 sq mls)
Population: 18,354,000
Capital: COLOMBO
Language: SINHALESE, TAMIL, ENGLISH
Religion: BUDDHIST, HINDU, SUNNI MUSLIM, R.CATHOLIC
Currency: RUPEE
Organizations: COMM., UN

MAP PAGE: 38

SRI LANKA LIES in the Indian Ocean off the southeast coast of India in south Asia. It has rolling coastal plains with mountains in the centre-south. The climate is hot and monsoonal and most people live on the west coast. Manufactures (chiefly textiles and clothing), tea, rubber, copra and gems are exported. The economy relies on aid and workers' remittances. Tourism has been damaged by separatist activities.

SUDAN

Status: REPUBLIC
Area: 2,505,813 sq km (967,500 sq mls)
Population: 28,098,000
Capital: KHARTOUM
Language: ARABIC, DINKA, NUBIAN, BEJA, NUER, LOCAL LANGUAGES
Religion: SUNNI MUSLIM, TRAD. BELIEFS, R.CATHOLIC, PROTESTANT
Currency: DINAR
Organizations: OAU, UN

MAP PAGE: 118-119

AFRICA'S LARGEST COUNTRY, Sudan is in northeast Africa, on the Red Sea. It lies within the Upper Nile basin, much of which is arid plain but with swamps to the south. Mountains lie to the northeast and south. The climate is hot and arid with light summer rainfall, though droughts occur. Most people live along the Nile and are farmers and herders. Cotton, gum arabic, livestock and other agricultural products are exported. In southern Sudan civil war has ruined the economy.

SURINAM

Status: REPUBLIC
Area: 163,820 sq km (63,251 sq mls)
Population: 423,000
Capital: PARAMARIBO
Language: DUTCH, SURINAMESE (SRANAN TONGO), ENGLISH, HINDI, JAVANESE
Religion: HINDU, R.CATHOLIC, PROTESTANT, SUNNI MUSLIM
Currency: GUILDER
Organizations: CARICOM, UN

MAP PAGE: 163

SURINAM, ON THE Atlantic coast of northern South America, consists of a swampy coastal plain (where most people live), central plateaux and the Guiana Highlands. The climate is tropical and rainforest covers much of the land. Bauxite mining is the main industry. Alumina and aluminium are the chief exports, with shrimps, rice, bananas and timber. Surinam depends on Dutch aid.

SWAZILAND

Status: MONARCHY
Area: 17,364 sq km (6,704 sq mls)
Population: 908,000
Capital: MBABANE
Language: SWAZI (SISWATI), ENGLISH
Religion: PROTESTANT, R.CATHOLIC, TRAD.BELIEFS
Currency: EMALANGENI
Organizations: COMM., OAU, SADC, UN

MAP PAGE: 131

LANDLOCKED SWAZILAND IN southern Africa lies between Mozambique and South Africa. Savannah plateaux descend from mountains in the west towards hill country in the east. The climate is subtropical, temperate in the mountains. Subsistence farming predominates. Asbestos, coal and diamonds are mined. Exports include sugar, fruit and wood pulp. Tourism and workers' remittances are important.

SWEDEN

Status: MONARCHY
Area: 449,964 sq km (173,732 sq mls)
Population: 8,831,000
Capital: STOCKHOLM
Language: SWEDISH
Religion: PROTESTANT, R.CATHOLIC
Currency: KRONA
Organizations: EU, OECD, UN

MAP PAGE: 56-57

SWEDEN, THE LARGEST and most populous of the Scandinavian countries, occupies the eastern part of the peninsula in north Europe and borders the North and Baltic Seas and Gulf of Bothnia. Forested mountains cover the northern half of the country, part of which lies within the Arctic Circle. Southwards is a lowland lake region, where most of the population lives. Farther south is an upland region, and then a fertile plain at the tip of the peninsula. Sweden has warm summers and cold winters, though the latter are longer and more severe in the north and milder in the far south. Sweden's natural resources include coniferous forests, mineral deposits and water resources. There is little agriculture, though some dairy products, meat, cereals and vegetables are produced in the south. The forests supply timber for export and for the important pulp, paper and furniture industries. Sweden is one of the world's leading producers of iron ore. Copper, zinc, lead, uranium and other metallic ores are also mined. Mineral industries, chiefly iron and steel, are the basis for the production of a range of products, but chiefly machinery and transport equipment of which cars and trucks (Volvo and Saab) are the most important export. Sweden also manufactures chemicals, electrical goods (Electrolux) and telecommunications equipment (Ericsson). Like their Scandinavian neighbours, Swedes enjoy a high standard of living.

SWITZERLAND

Status: FEDERATION
Area: 41,293 sq km (15,943 sq mls)
Population: 7,040,000
Capital: BERN
Language: GERMAN, FRENCH, ITALIAN, ROMANSCH
Religion: R.CATHOLIC, PROTESTANT
Currency: FRANC
Organizations: OECD

MAP PAGE: 82-83

SWITZERLAND IS A landlocked country of southwest Europe that is surrounded by France, Germany, Austria, Liechtenstein and Italy. It is also Europe's most mountainous country. The southern half of the nation lies within the Alps, while the northwest is dominated by the Jura mountains. The rest of the land is a high plateau, which contains the bulk of the population and economic activity. The climate varies greatly, depending on altitude and relief, but in general summers are mild and winters are cold with heavy snowfalls. Switzerland has one of the highest standards of living in the world. Yet it has few mineral resources and, owing to its mountainous terrain, agriculture is based mainly on dairy and stock farming. Most food and industrial raw materials have to be imported. Manufacturing makes the largest contribution to the economy and though varied is specialist in certain products. Engineering is the most important industry, producing precision instruments such as scientific and optical instruments, watches and clocks, and heavy machinery such as turbines and generators. Other industries produce chemicals, pharmaceuticals, metal products, textiles, clothing and food products (cheese and chocolate). Banking and other financial services are very important and Zurich is one of the world's leading banking cities. Tourism and international organisations based in Switzerland are also major foreign currency earners.

SYRIA

Status: REPUBLIC
Area: 185,180 sq km (71,498 sq mls)
Population: 14,186,000
Capital: DAMASCUS
Language: ARABIC, KURDISH, ARMENIAN
Religion: SUNNI MUSLIM, OTHER MUSLIM, CHRISTIAN
Currency: POUND
Organizations: UN

MAP PAGE: 42

SYRIA IS IN southwest Asia, on the Mediterranean Sea. Behind the coastal plain lies a range of hills and then a plateau cut by the Euphrates river. Mountains flank the borders with Lebanon and Israel, east of which is desert. The climate is Mediterranean in coastal regions, hotter and drier inland. Most Syrians live on the coast or in the river valleys. Cotton, cereals and fruit are important, but the main exports are petroleum and its products, textiles and chemicals. Syria receives support from Gulf states.

TAIWAN

Status: REPUBLIC
Area: 36,179 sq km (13,969 sq mls)
Population: 21,211,000
Capital: TAIPEI
Language: CHINESE (MANDARIN OFFICIAL, FUKIEN, HAKKA), LOCAL LANGUAGES
Religion: BUDDHIST, TAOIST, CONFUCIAN, CHRISTIAN
Currency: DOLLAR

MAP PAGE: 33

THE EAST ASIAN state consists of the island of Taiwan, separated from mainland China by the Taiwan Strait, and several much smaller islands. Much of Taiwan itself is mountainous and forested. Densely populated coastal plains in the west contain the bulk of the population and most economic activity. Taiwan has a tropical monsoon climate, with warm, wet summers and mild winters. Agriculture is highly productive. Taiwan is virtually self-sufficient in food and exports some products. Coal, oil and natural gas are produced and a few minerals are mined but none of them are of great significance to the economy. Taiwan depends heavily on imports of raw materials and exports of manufactured goods. The latter is equivalent to 50 per cent of national income. The country's main manufactures are electrical and electronic goods, including television sets, watches, personal computers and calculators. Other products include clothing, footwear (chiefly track shoes), textiles and toys. In contrast to mainland China, Taiwan has enjoyed considerable prosperity.

TAJIKISTAN

Status: REPUBLIC
Area: 143,100 sq km (55,251 sq mls)
Population: 5,836,000
Capital: DUSHANBE
Language: TAJIK, UZBEK, RUSSIAN
Religion: SUNNI MUSLIM
Currency: ROUBLE
Organizations: CIS, UN

MAP PAGE: 47

LANDLOCKED TAJIKISTAN IN central Asia is a mountainous country, occupying the western Tien Shan and part of the Pamir ranges. In less mountainous western areas summers are warm though winters are cold. Most activity is in the Fergana basin. Agriculture is the main sector of the economy, chiefly cotton growing and cattle breeding. Mineral and fuel deposits include lead, zinc, uranium and oil. Textiles and clothing are the main manufactures. Civil war has damaged the economy, which depends heavily on Russian support.

TANZANIA

Status: REPUBLIC
Area: 945,087 sq km (364,900 sq mls)
Population: 30,337,000
Capital: DODOMA
Language: SWAHILI, ENGLISH, NYAMWEZI, MANY LOCAL LANGUAGES
Religion: R.CATHOLIC, SUNNI MUSLIM, TRAD. BELIEFS, PROTESTANT
Currency: SHILLING
Organizations: COMM., OAU, SADC, UN

MAP PAGE: 127

TANZANIA LIES ON the coast of east Africa and includes Zanzibar in the Indian Ocean. Most of the mainland is a savannah plateau lying east of the great Rift Valley. In the north are Mount Kilimanjaro and the Serangeti National Park. The climate is tropical and most people live on the narrow coastal plain or in the north. The economy is mainly agricultural. Coffee, cotton and sisal are the main exports, with cloves from Zanzibar. Agricultural processing and diamond mining are the main industries, though tourism is growing. Tanzania depends heavily on aid.

© Bartholomew

THAILAND

Status: MONARCHY
Area: 513,115 sq km (198,115 sq mls)
Population: 59,401,000
Capital: BANGKOK
Language: THAI, LAO, CHINESE, MALAY, MON-KHMER LANGUAGES
Religion: BUDDHIST, SUNNI MUSLIM
Currency: BAHT
Organizations: ASEAN, UN

MAP PAGE: 24-25

A COUNTRY IN southeast Asia, Thailand borders Myanmar, Laos, Cambodia and Malaysia and has coastlines on the Gulf of Thailand and Andaman Sea. Central Thailand is dominated by the Chao Phraya river basin, which contains Bangkok, the only major urban centre, and most economic activity. To the east is a dry plateau drained by tributaries of the Mekong river, while to the north, west and south, extending halfway down the Malay peninsula, are forested hills and mountains. Many small islands line the coast. The climate is hot, humid and monsoonal. About half the workforce is involved in agriculture. Thailand is the world's leading exporter of rice and rubber, and a major exporter of maize and tapioca. Fish and fish processing are important. Thailand produces natural gas, some oil and lignite, metallic ores (chiefly tin and tungsten) and gemstones. Manufacturing is the largest contributor to national income, with electronics, textiles, clothing and footwear, and food processing the main industries. With over 5 million visitors a year, tourism is the major source of foreign exchange.

TOGO

Status: REPUBLIC
Area: 56,785 sq km (21,925 sq mls)
Population: 4,138,000
Capital: LOMÉ
Language: FRENCH, EWE, KABRE, MANY LOCAL LANGUAGES
Religion: TRAD. BELIEFS, R.CATHOLIC, SUNNI MUSLIM, PROTESTANT
Currency: CFA FRANC
Organizations: OAU, UN

MAP PAGE: 123

TOGO IS A long narrow country in west Africa with a short coastline on the Gulf of Guinea. The interior consists of plateaux rising to mountainous areas. The climate is tropical, drier inland. Agriculture is the mainstay of the economy. Cotton, coffee and cocoa are exported, but phosphates are the main exports. Oil refining and food processing are the main industries. Lomé is an entrepot trade centre.

TOKELAU

Status: NEW ZEALAND TERRITORY
Area: 10 sq km (4 sq mls)
Population: 2,000
Language: ENGLISH, TOKELAUAN
Religion: PROTESTANT, R.CATHOLIC
Currency: NZ DOLLAR

MAP PAGE: 5

TONGA

Status: MONARCHY
Area: 748 sq km (289 sq mls)
Population: 98,000
Capital: NUKU'ALOFA
Language: TONGAN, ENGLISH
Religion: PROTESTANT, R.CATHOLIC, MORMON
Currency: PA'ANGA
Organizations: COMM.

MAP PAGE: 6

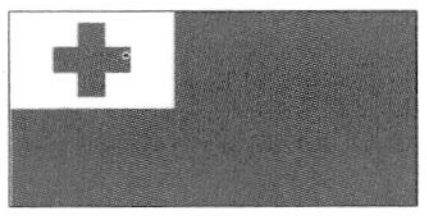

TONGA COMPRISES SOME 170 islands in the South Pacific Ocean, northeast of New Zealand. The three main groups are Tongatapu (where 60 per cent of Tongans live), Ha'apai and Vava'u. The climate is warm with good rainfall and the economy relies heavily on agriculture. Exports include coconut products, root crops, bananas and vanilla. Fishing, tourism and light industry are increasingly important.

TRINIDAD AND TOBAGO

Status: REPUBLIC
Area: 5,130 sq km (1,981 sq mls)
Population: 1,306,000
Capital: PORT OF SPAIN
Language: ENGLISH, CREOLE, HINDI
Religion: R.CATHOLIC, HINDU, PROTESTANT, SUNNI MUSLIM
Currency: DOLLAR
Organizations: CARICOM, COMM., UN

MAP PAGE: 159

TRINIDAD, THE MOST southerly Caribbean island, lies off the Venezuelan coast. It is hilly in the north, with a populous central plain. Tobago, to the northeast, is smaller, more mountainous and less developed. The climate is tropical. Oil and petrochemicals dominate the economy. Asphalt is also important. Sugar, fruit, cocoa and coffee are produced. Tourism is important on Tobago.

TUNISIA

Status: REPUBLIC
Area: 164,150 sq km (63,379 sq mls)
Population: 8,896,000
Capital: TUNIS
Language: ARABIC, FRENCH
Religion: SUNNI MUSLIM
Currency: DINAR
Organizations: OAU, UN

MAP PAGE: 121

TUNISIA IS ON the Mediterranean coast of north Africa. The north is mountanous with valleys and coastal plains, where most people live. Beyond a central area of salt pans are Saharan plains. The north has a Mediterranean climate, the south is hot and arid. Oil and phosphates are the main resources. Olive oil, citrus fruit and textiles are also exported. Tourism is important.

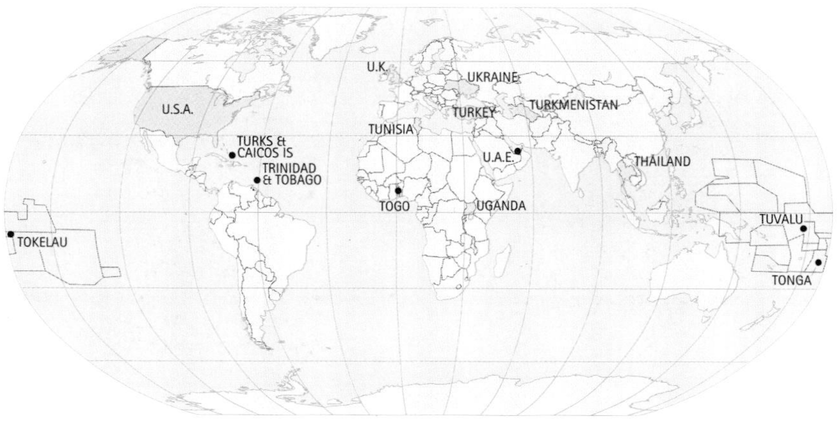

TURKEY

Status: REPUBLIC
Area: 779,452 sq km (300,948 sq mls)
Population: 61,644,000
Capital: ANKARA
Language: TURKISH, KURDISH
Religion: SUNNI MUSLIM, SHI'A MUSLIM
Currency: LIRA
Organizations: OECD, UN

MAP PAGE: 42

TURKEY OCCUPIES THE Asia Minor peninsula of southwest Asia and has coastlines on the Black, Mediterranean and Aegean seas. It includes eastern Thrace, which is in south Europe and separated from the rest of the country by the Bosporus, Sea of Marmara and Dardanelles. The Asian mainland consists of the semi-arid Anatolian plateau, flanked to the north, south and east by mountains. Over 40 per cent of Turks live in central Anatolia and the Marmara and Aegean coastal plains. The coast has a Mediterranean climate, but inland conditions are more extreme with hot, dry summers and cold, snowy winters. Agriculture involves about half the workforce and exports include cotton, tobacco, fruit, nuts and livestock. Turkey is one of the world's major producers of chrome. Coal and lignite, petroleum, iron ore and boron are also exploited. Apart from food products, the main manufactures are textiles (the chief export), iron and steel, vehicles and chemicals. With over 7 million visitors a year, tourism is a major industry. Remittances by workers aboard are also important.

TURKMENISTAN

Status: REPUBLIC
Area: 488,100 sq km (188,456 sq mls)
Population: 4,099,000
Capital: ASHKHABAD
Language: TURKMEN, RUSSIAN
Religion: SUNNI MUSLIM
Currency: MANAT
Organizations: CIS, UN

MAP PAGE: 46

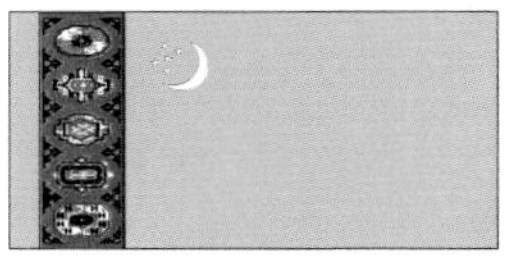

TURKMENISTAN, IN CENTRAL Asia, lies mainly within the desert plains of the Kara Kum. Most people live on the fringes: the foothills of the Kopet Dag in the south, Amudarya valley in the north and Caspian Sea plains in the west. The climate is dry with extreme temperatures. The economy is based mainly on irrigated agriculture, chiefly cotton growing. Turkmenistan is rich in oil, natural gas (the main export) and minerals.

TURKS AND CAICOS ISLANDS

Status: UK TERRITORY
Area: 430 sq km (166 sq mls)
Population: 14,000
Capital: GRAND TURK
Language: ENGLISH
Religion: PROTESTANT
Currency: US DOLLAR

MAP PAGE: 159

THE STATE CONSISTS of 40 or so low-lying islands and cays in the northern Caribbean. Only eight islands are inhabited, two fifths of people living on Grand Turk and Salt Cay. The climate is tropical. The islands depend on fishing, tourism and offshore banking.

TUVALU

Status: MONARCHY
Area: 25 sq km (10 sq mls)
Population: 10,000
Capital: FONGAFALE
Language: TUVALUAN, ENGLISH (OFFICIAL)
Religion: PROTESTANT
Currency: DOLLAR
Organizations: COMM.

MAP PAGE: 4

TUVALU COMPRISES NINE coral atolls in the South Pacific Ocean. One third of the population lives on Funafuti and most people depend on subsistence farming and fishing. The islands export copra, stamps and clothing, but rely heavily on UK aid.

UGANDA

Status: REPUBLIC
Area: 241,038 sq km (93,065 sq mls)
Population: 19,848,000
Capital: KAMPALA
Language: ENGLISH, SWAHILI (OFFICIAL), LUGANDA, MANY LOCAL LANGUAGES
Religion: R.CATHOLIC, PROTESTANT, SUNNI MUSLIM, TRAD. BELIEFS
Currency: SHILLING
Organizations: COMM., OAU, UN

MAP PAGE: 126-127

A LANDLOCKED COUNTRY in east Africa, Uganda consists of a savannah plateau with mountains and lakes. It includes part of Lake Victoria from which the Nile flows northwards to Sudan. The climate is warm and wet. Most people live in the southern half of the country. Agriculture dominates the economy. Coffee is the main export, with some cotton and tea. Uganda relies heavily on aid.

UKRAINE

Status: REPUBLIC
Area: 603,700 sq km (233,090 sq mls)
Population: 51,639,000
Capital: KIEV
Language: UKRAINIAN, RUSSIAN, REGIONAL LANGUAGES
Religion: UKRAINIAN ORTHODOX, R.CATHOLIC
Currency: HRYVNIA
Organizations: CIS, UN

MAP PAGE: 53

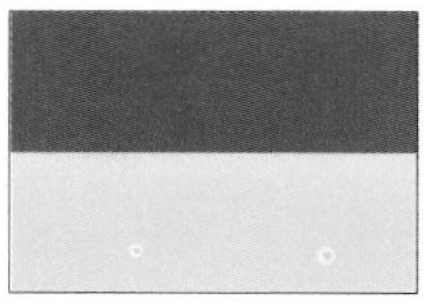

UKRAINE LIES ON the Black Sea coast of east Europe. Much of the land is steppe, generally flat and treeless, but with rich black soil and drained by the river Dnieper. Along the border with Belarus are forested, marshy plains. The only uplands are the Carpathian mountains in the west and smaller ranges on the Crimean peninsula. Summers are warm and

winters are cold, with milder conditions in the Crimea. About a quarter of the population lives in the mainly industrial provinces of Donetsk, Kiev and Dnepropetrovsk. The Ukraine is rich in natural resources: fertile soil, substantial mineral deposits and forests. Agriculture, livestock raising and viticulture are important, but mining and manufacturing predominate, contributing over 40 per cent of national income. Coal mining, iron and steel production, engineering and chemicals are the main industries. Output has fallen and few state enterprises have been privatized since Ukraine became independent in 1991.

UNITED ARAB EMIRATES (UAE)

Status: FEDERATION
Area: 77,700 sq km (30,000 sq mls)
Population: 2,314,000
Capital: ABU DHABI
Language: ARABIC (OFFICIAL), ENGLISH, HINDI, URDU, FARSI
Religion: SUNNI MUSLIM, SHI'A MUSLIM, CHRISTIAN
Currency: DIRHAM
Organizations: OPEC, UN

MAP PAGE: 39

THE UAE IS in east-central Arabia, southwest Asia. Six emirates lie on The Gulf while the seventh, Fujairah, fronts the Gulf of Oman. Most of the land is flat desert with sand dunes and salt pans. The only hilly area is in the northeast. Three emirates - Abu Dhabi, Dubai and Sharjah - contain 85 per cent of the population. Summers are hot and winters are mild with occasional rainfall in coastal areas. Fruit and vegetables are grown in oases and irrigated areas. The state's wealth is based on hydrocarbons, mainly within Abu Dhabi, but with smaller supplies in Dubai, Sharjah and Ras al Khaimah. Dubai is a thriving entrepot trade centre.

ABU DHABI
Status: EMIRATE
Area: 64,750 sq km (25,000 sq miles)
Population: 800,000

AJMAN
Status: EMIRATE
Area: 260 sq km (100 sq miles)
Population: 76,000

DUBAI
Status: EMIRATE
Area: 3,900 sq km (1,506 sq miles)
Population: 500,000

FUJAIRAH
Status: EMIRATE
Area: 1,170 sq km (452 sq miles)
Population: 63,000

RAS AL KHAIMAH
Status: EMIRATE
Area: 1,690 sq km (653 sq miles)
Population: 130,000

SHARJAH
Status: EMIRATE
Area: 2,600 sq km (1,004 sq miles)
Population: 314,000

UMM AL QAIWAIN
Status: EMIRATE
Area: 780 sq km (301 sq miles)
Population: 27,000

UNITED KINGDOM (UK)

Status: MONARCHY
Area: 244,082 sq km (94,241 sq mls)
Population: 58,258,000
Capital: LONDON
Language: ENGLISH, SOUTH INDIAN LANGUAGES, CHINESE, WELSH, GAELIC
Religion: PROTESTANT, R.CATHOLIC, MUSLIM, SIKH, HINDU, JEWISH
Currency: POUND
Organizations: COMM., EU, OECD, UN

MAP PAGE: 60-61

A COUNTRY OF northwest Europe, the United Kingdom occupies the island of Great Britain, part of Ireland and many small adjacent islands in the Atlantic Ocean. Great Britain comprises the countries of England, Scotland and Wales. England covers over half the land area and supports over four-fifths of the population, chiefly in the southeast region. The landscape is flat or rolling with some uplands, notably the Cheviot Hills on the Scottish border, the Pennines in the centre-north and the Cumbrian mountains in the northwest. Scotland consists of southern uplands, central lowlands, highlands (which include the UK's highest peak) and islands. Wales is a land of mountains and river valleys. Northern Ireland contains uplands, plains and the UK's largest lake, Lough Neagh. The climate is mild, wet and variable. The UK has few mineral deposits, but has important energy resources. Over 40 per cent of land is suitable for grazing, over 25 per cent is cultivated, and 10 per cent is forested. Agriculture involves mainly sheep and cattle raising and dairy farming, with crop and fruit growing in the east and southeast. Productivity is high, but about one third of food needs must be imported. Both forestry and fishing are also important. The UK produces petroleum and natural gas from reserves in the North Sea and is self-sufficient in energy in net terms. It also has reserves of coal, though the coal industry has contracted in recent years. Manufacturing accounts for over 20 per cent of national income and relies heavily on imported raw materials. Major manufactures are food and drinks, motor vehicles and parts, aerospace equipment, machinery, electronic and electrical equipment, and chemicals and chemical products. However, the economy is dominated by service industries, including banking, insurance, finance, business services, retail and catering. London is one of the world's major banking, financial and insurance capitals. Tourism is a major industry, with over 18 million visitors a year. International trade is also important, equivalent to a third of national income and the UK has a large merchant fleet.

ENGLAND
Status: CONSTITUENT COUNTRY
Area: 130,423 sq km (50,357 sq miles)
Population: 48,532,700
Capital: LONDON

NORTHERN IRELAND
Status: CONSTITUENT REGION
Area: 14,121 sq km (5,452 sq miles)
Population: 1,631,800
Capital: BELFAST

SCOTLAND
Status: CONSTITUENT COUNTRY
Area: 78,772 sq km (30,414 sq miles)
Population: 5,120,200
Capital: EDINBURGH

WALES
Status: PRINCIPALITY
Area: 20,766 sq km (8,018 sq miles)
Population: 2,906,500
Capital: CARDIFF

UNITED STATES OF AMERICA (USA)

Status: REPUBLIC
Area: 9,809,386 sq km (3,787,425 sq mls)
Population: 263,034,000
Capital: WASHINGTON
Language: ENGLISH, SPANISH, AMERINDIAN LANGUAGES
Religion: PROTESTANT, R.CATHOLIC, SUNNI MUSLIM, JEWISH, MORMON
Currency: DOLLAR
Organizations: NAFTA, OECD, UN

MAP PAGE: 142-143

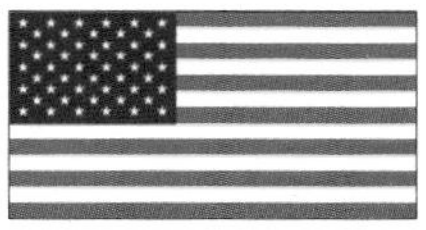

THE USA COMPRISES 48 contiguous states in North America, bounded by Canada and Mexico, and the states of Alaska, to the northwest of Canada, and Hawaii, in the Pacific Ocean. The populous eastern states consist of the Atlantic coastal plain (which includes the Florida peninsula and the Gulf of Mexico coast) and the Appalachian mountains. The central states form a vast interior plain drained by the Mississippi-Missouri river system. To the west lie the Rocky Mountains, separated from the Pacific coastal ranges by the intermontane plateaux. The coastal ranges, which are prone to earthquakes, extend northwards into Alaska. Hawaii is a group of some 20 volcanic islands. Climatic conditions range between arctic in Alaska to desert in the intermontane plateaux. Most of the USA is temperate, though the interior has continental conditions. The USA has abundant natural resources. It has major reserves minerals and energy resources. About 20 per cent of the land can be used for crops, over 25 per cent is suitable for livestock rearing and over 30 per cent is forested. The USA has the largest economy in the world, which is based mainly on manufacturing and services. Though agriculture accounts for only about 2 per cent national income, productivity is high and the USA is a net exporter of food, chiefly grains and fruit. Major industrial crops include cotton, tobacco and sugarbeet. Livestock rearing, forestry and fishing are also important. Mining is well developed. The USA produces iron ore, bauxite, copper, lead, zinc, phosphate and many other minerals. It is a major producer of coal, petroleum and natural gas, though being the world's biggest energy user it must import significant quanities of petroleum and its products. Manufacturing is well diversified. The main products are: iron, steel and aluminium metals and products, machinery, transport equipment (chiefly motor vehicles and aircraft), electrical and electronic goods, food products, chemicals, textiles and clothing. Tourism is a major foreign currency earner. Other important service industries are banking and finance, and Wall Street in New York is a major stock exchange.

ALABAMA
Status: STATE
Area: 135,775 sq km (52,423 sq miles)
Population: 4,273,084
Capital: MONTGOMERY

ALASKA
Status: STATE
Area: 1,700,130 sq km (656,424 sq miles)
Population: 607,007
Capital: JUNEAU

ARIZONA
Status: STATE
Area: 295,274 sq km (114,006 sq miles)
Population: 4,428,068
Capital: PHOENIX

ARKANSAS
Status: STATE
Area: 137,741 sq km (53,182 sq miles)
Population: 2,509,793
Capital: LITTLE ROCK

CALIFORNIA
Status: STATE
Area: 423,999 sq km (163,707 sq miles)
Population: 31,878,234
Capital: SACRAMENTO

COLORADO
Status: STATE
Area: 269,618 sq km (104,100 sq miles)
Population: 3,822,676
Capital: DENVER

CONNECTICUT
Status: STATE
Area: 14,359 sq km (5,544 sq miles)
Population: 3,274,238
Capital: HARTFORD

DISTRICT OF COLUMBIA
Status: FEDERAL DISTRICT
Area: 176 sq km (68 sq miles)
Population: 543,213
Capital: WASHINGTON

DELAWARE
Status: STATE
Area: 6,446 sq km (2,489 sq miles)
Population: 724,842
Capital: DOVER

FLORIDA
Status: STATE
Area: 170,312 sq km (65,758 sq miles)
Population: 14,399,985
Capital: TALLAHASSEE

GEORGIA
Status: STATE
Area: 153,951 sq km (59,441 sq miles)
Population: 7,353,225
Capital: ATLANTA

HAWAII
Status: STATE
Area: 28,314 sq km (10,932 sq miles)
Population: 1,183,723
Capital: HONOLULU

IDAHO
Status: STATE
Area: 216,456 sq km (83,574 sq miles)
Population: 1,189,251
Capital: BOISE

ILLINOIS
Status: STATE
Area: 150,007 sq km (57,918 sq miles)
Population: 11,846,544
Capital: SPRINGFIELD

INDIANA
Status: STATE
Area: 94,327 sq km (36,420 sq miles)
Population: 5,840,528
Capital: INDIANAPOLIS

IOWA
Status: STATE
Area: 145,754 sq km (56,276 sq miles)
Population: 2,851,792
Capital: DES MOINES

KANSAS
Status: STATE
Area: 213,109 sq km (82,282 sq miles)
Population: 2,572,150
Capital: TOPEKA

KENTUCKY
Status: STATE
Area: 104,664 sq km (40,411 sq miles)
Population: 3,883,723
Capital: FRANKFORT

LOUISIANA
Status: STATE
Area: 134,273 sq km (51,843 sq miles)
Population: 4,350,579
Capital: BATON ROUGE

THE LIBRARY
GUILDFORD COLLEGE
of Further and Higher Education

© Bartholomew

USA
continued

MAINE
Status: STATE
Area: 91,652 sq km (35,387 sq miles)
Population: 1,243,316
Capital: AUGUSTA

MARYLAND
Status: STATE
Area: 32,134 sq km (12,407 sq miles)
Population: 5,071,604
Capital: ANNAPOLIS

MASSACHUSETTS
Status: STATE
Area: 27,337 sq km (10,555 sq miles)
Population: 6,092,352
Capital: BOSTON

MICHIGAN
Status: STATE
Area: 250,737 sq km (96,810 sq miles)
Population: 9,594,350
Capital: LANSING

MINNESOTA
Status: STATE
Area: 225,181 sq km (86,943 sq miles)
Population: 4,657,758
Capital: ST PAUL

MISSISSIPPI
Status: STATE
Area: 125,443 sq km (48,434 sq miles)
Population: 2,716,115
Capital: JACKSON

MISSOURI
Status: STATE
Area: 180,545 sq km (69,709 sq miles)
Population: 5,358,692
Capital: JEFFERSON CITY

MONTANA
Status: STATE
Area: 380,847 sq km (147,046 sq miles)
Population: 879,372
Capital: HELENA

NEBRASKA
Status: STATE
Area: 200,356 sq km (77,358 sq miles)
Population: 1,652,093
Capital: LINCOLN

NEVADA
Status: STATE
Area: 286,367 sq km (110,567 sq miles)
Population: 1,603,163
Capital: CARSON CITY

NEW HAMPSHIRE
Status: STATE
Area: 24,219 sq km (9,351 sq miles)
Population: 1,162,481
Capital: CONCORD

NEW JERSEY
Status: STATE
Area: 22,590 sq km (8,722 sq miles)
Population: 7,987,933
Capital: TRENTON

NEW MEXICO
Status: STATE
Area: 314,937 sq km (121,598 sq miles)
Population: 1,713,407
Capital: SANTA FE

NEW YORK
Status: STATE
Area: 141,090 sq km (54,475 sq miles)
Population: 18,184,774
Capital: ALBANY

NORTH CAROLINA
Status: STATE
Area: 139,396 sq km (53,821 sq miles)
Population: 7,322,870
Capital: RALEIGH

NORTH DAKOTA
Status: STATE
Area: 183,123 sq km (70,704 sq miles)
Population: 643,539
Capital: BISMARCK

OHIO
Status: STATE
Area: 116,104 sq km (44,828 sq miles)
Population: 11,172,782
Capital: COLUMBUS

OKLAHOMA
Status: STATE
Area: 181,048 sq km (69,903 sq miles)
Population: 3,300,902
Capital: OKLAHOMA CITY

OREGON
Status: STATE
Area: 254,819 sq km (98,386 sq miles)
Population: 3,203,735
Capital: SALEM

PENNSYLVANIA
Status: STATE
Area: 119,290 sq km (46,058 sq miles)
Population: 12,056,112
Capital: HARRISBURG

RHODE ISLAND
Status: STATE
Area: 4,002 sq km (1,545 sq miles)
Population: 990,225
Capital: PROVIDENCE

SOUTH CAROLINA
Status: STATE
Area: 82,898 sq km (32,007 sq miles)
Population: 3,698,746
Capital: COLUMBIA

SOUTH DAKOTA
Status: STATE
Area: 199,742 sq km (77,121 sq miles)
Population: 732,405
Capital: PIERRE

TENNESSEE
Status: STATE
Area: 109,158 sq km (42,146 sq miles)
Population: 5,319,654
Capital: NASHVILLE

TEXAS
Status: STATE
Area: 695,673 sq km (268,601 sq miles)
Population: 19,128,261
Capital: AUSTIN

UTAH
Status: STATE
Area: 219,900 sq km (84,904 sq miles)
Population: 2,000,494
Capital: SALT LAKE CITY

VERMONT
Status: STATE
Area: 24,903 sq km (9,615 sq miles)
Population: 588,654
Capital: MONTPELIER

VIRGINIA
Status: STATE
Area: 110,771 sq km (42,769 sq miles)
Population: 6,675,451
Capital: RICHMOND

WASHINGTON
Status: STATE
Area: 184,674 sq km (71,303 sq miles)
Population: 5,532,939
Capital: OLYMPIA

WEST VIRGINIA
Status: STATE
Area: 62,758 sq km (24,231 sq miles)
Population: 1,825,754
Capital: CHARLESTON

WISCONSIN
Status: STATE
Area: 169,652 sq km (65,503 sq miles)
Population: 5,159,795
Capital: MADISON

WYOMING
Status: STATE
Area: 253,347 sq km (97,818 sq miles)
Population: 481,400
Capital: CHEYENNE

URUGUAY
Status: REPUBLIC
Area: 176,215 sq km (68,037 sq mls)
Population: 3,186,000
Capital: MONTEVIDEO
Language: SPANISH
Religion: R.CATHOLIC, PROTESTANT, JEWISH
Currency: PESO
Organizations: UN

MAP PAGE: 173

URUGUAY, ON THE Atlantic coast of central South America, is a low-lying land of prairies. The coast and the River Plate estuary in the south are fringed with lagoons and sand dunes. Almost half the population lives in Montevideo. Uruguay has warm summers and mild winters. The economy was founded on cattle and sheep ranching, and meat, wool and hides are major exports. The main industries produce food products, textiles, petroleum products, chemicals and transport equipment. Offshore banking and tourism are important.

UZBEKISTAN
Status: REPUBLIC
Area: 447,400 sq km (172,742 sq mls)
Population: 22,843,000
Capital: TASHKENT
Language: UZBEK, RUSSIAN, TAJIK, KAZAKH
Religion: SUNNI MUSLIM, RUSSIAN ORTHODOX
Currency: SOM
Organizations: CIS, UN

MAP PAGE: 46-47

A REPUBLIC OF central Asia, Uzbekistan borders the Aral Sea and five countries. It consists mainly of the flat desert of the Kyzyl Kum, which rises eastwards towards the mountains of the western Pamirs. Most settlement is in the Fergana basin. The climate is dry and arid. The economy is based mainly on irrigated agriculture, chiefly cotton production. Industry specializes in fertilizers and machinery for cotton harvesting and textile manufacture. Uzbekistan is rich in minerals and has the largest gold mine in the world.

VANUATU
Status: REPUBLIC
Area: 12,190 sq km (4,707 sq mls)
Population: 169,000
Capital: PORT VILA
Language: ENGLISH, BISLAMA (ENGLISH CREOLE), FRENCH (ALL OFFICIAL)
Religion: PROTESTANT, R.CATHOLIC, TRAD.BELIEFS
Currency: VATU
Organizations: COMM., UN

MAP PAGE: 6

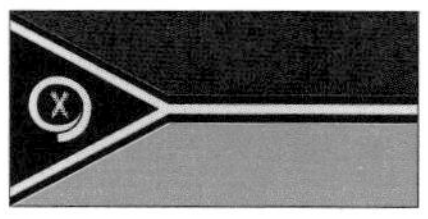

VANUATU OCCUPIES AN archipelago of some 80 islands in Oceania. Many of the islands are mountainous, of volcanic origin and densely forested. The climate is tropical with heavy rainfall. Half the population lives on the main islands of Efate, Santo and Tafea, and the majority of people live by farming. Copra, beef, seashells, cocoa and timber are the main exports. Tourism is growing and foreign aid is important.

VATICAN CITY
Status: ECCLESIASTICAL STATE
Area: 0.4 sq km (0.2 sq ml)
Population: 1,000
Language: ITALIAN
Religion: R.CATHOLIC
Currency: ITALIAN LIRA

MAP PAGE: 109

THE WORLD'S SMALLEST sovereign state, the Vatican City occupies a hill to the west of the river Tiber in the Italian capital, Rome. It is the headquarters of the Roman Catholic church and income comes from investments, voluntary contributions and tourism.

VENEZUELA
Status: REPUBLIC
Area: 912,050 sq km (352,144 sq mls)
Population: 21,644,000
Capital: CARACAS
Language: SPANISH, AMERINDIAN LANGUAGES
Religion: R.CATHOLIC, PROTESTANT
Currency: BOLÍVAR
Organizations: OPEC, UN

MAP PAGE: 162-163

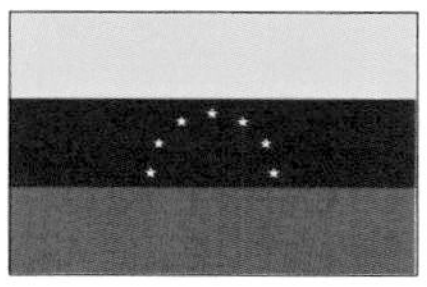

VENEZUELA IS IN northern South America, on the Caribbean Sea. Its coast is much indented, with the oil-rich area of Lake Maracaibo at the western end and the swampy Orinoco delta in the east. Mountain ranges run parallel to the coast then turn southwestwards to form the northern extension of the Andes chain. Central Venezuela is lowland grasslands drained by the Orinoco river system, while to the south are the Guiana Highlands which contain the Angel Falls, the world's highest waterfall. About 85 per cent of the population lives in towns, mostly in the coastal mountain areas. The climate is tropical, with summer rainfall. Temperatures are lower in the mountains. Venezuela is an important oil producer, and sales account for about 75 per cent of export earnings. Bauxite, iron ore and gold are also mined and manufactures include aluminium, iron and steel, textiles, timber and wood products, and petrochemicals. Farming is important, particularly cattle ranching and dairy farming. Coffee, cotton, maize, rice and sugarcane are major crops.

VIETNAM

Status: REPUBLIC
Area: 329,565 sq km (127,246 sq mls)
Population: 74,545,000
Capital: HANOI
Language: VIETNAMESE, THAI, KHMER, CHINESE, MANY LOCAL LANGUAGES
Religion: BUDDHIST, TAOIST, R.CATHOLIC, CAO DAI, HOA HAO
Currency: DONG
Organizations: UN, ASEAN

MAP PAGE: 24-25

VIETNAM EXTENDS ALONG the east coast of the Indochina peninsula in southeast Asia, with the South China Sea to the east and south. The Red River (Song-koi) delta lowlands in the north are separated from the huge Mekong delta in the south by narrow coastal plains backed by the generally rough mountainous and forested terrain of the Annam highlands. Most people live in the river deltas. The climate is tropical, with summer monsoon rains. Over three quarters of the workforce is involved in agriculture, forestry and fishing. Rice growing is the main activity, and Vietnam is the world's third largest rice exporter, after the USA and Thailand. Coffee, tea and rubber are the main cash crops. The north is fairly rich in minerals including some oil, coal, iron ore, manganese, apatite and gold. The food processing and textile industries are important, but the steel, oil and gas and car industries are growing rapidly. The 1992 economic reform programme, inflow of foreign investment and the 1994 lifting of the US trade embargo are boosting an economy which suffered from decades of war and strife.

VIRGIN ISLANDS (UK)

Status: UK TERRITORY
Area: 153 sq km (59 sq mls)
Population: 19,000
Capital: ROAD TOWN
Language: ENGLISH
Religion: PROTESTANT, R.CATHOLIC
Currency: US DOLLAR

MAP PAGE: 159

THE CARIBBEAN TERRITORY comprises four main islands and some 36 islets at the eastern end of the Virgin Islands group. Apart from the flat coral atoll of Anegada, the islands are volcanic in origin and hilly. The climate is subtropical and tourism is the main industry.

VIRGIN ISLANDS (USA)

Status: US TERRITORY
Area: 352 sq km (136 sq mls)
Population: 105,000
Capital: CHARLOTTE AMALIE
Language: ENGLISH, SPANISH
Religion: PROTESTANT, R.CATHOLIC
Currency: US DOLLAR

MAP PAGE: 159

THE TERRITORY CONSISTS of three main islands and some 50 islets in the Caribbean's western Virgin Islands. The islands are mostly hilly and of volcanic origin and the climate is subtropical. The economy is based on tourism, with some manufacturing on St Croix.

WALLIS AND FUTUNA

Status: FRENCH TERRITORY
Area: 274 sq km (106 sq mls)
Population: 14,000
Capital: MATA-UTU
Language: FRENCH, POLYNESIAN (WALLISIAN, FUTUNIAN)
Religion: R.CATHOLIC
Currency: PACIFIC FRANC

MAP PAGE: 4-5

THE SOUTH PACIFIC territory comprises the volcanic islands of the Wallis archipelago and Hoorn Islands. The climate is tropical. The islands depend upon subsistence farming, the sale of licences to foreign fishing fleets, workers' remittances and French aid.

WEST BANK

Status: TERRITORY
Area: 5,860 sq km (2,263 sq mls)
Population: 1,219,000
Language: ARABIC, HEBREW
Religion: SUNNI MUSLIM, JEWISH, SHI'A MUSLIM, CHRISTIAN

MAP PAGE: 43

THE TERRITORY CONSISTS of the west bank of the river Jordan and parts of Judea and Samaria in southwest Asia. The land was annexed by Israel in 1967, but the Jericho area was granted self-government under an agreement between Israel and the PLO in 1993.

WESTERN SAHARA

Status: TERRITORY
Area: 266,000 sq km (102,703 sq mls)
Population: 283,000
Capital: LAÂYOUNE
Language: ARABIC
Religion: SUNNI MUSLIM
Currency: MOROCCAN DIRHAM

MAP PAGE: 120

SITUATED ON THE northwest coast of Africa, the territory of Western Sahara is controlled by Morocco.

WESTERN SAMOA

Status: MONARCHY
Area: 2,831 sq km (1,093 sq mls)
Population: 171,000
Capital: APIA
Language: SAMOAN, ENGLISH
Religion: PROTESTANT, R.CATHOLIC, MORMON
Currency: TALA
Organizations: COMM., UN

MAP PAGE: 7

WESTERN SAMOA CONSISTS of two main mountainous and forested islands and seven small islands in the South Pacific Ocean. Seventy per cent of people live on Upolu. The climate is tropical. The economy is based on agriculture, with some fishing and light manufacturing. Traditional exports are coconut products, timber, taro, cocoa and fruit, but cyclones in recent years devastated the coconut palms. Tourism is increasing, but the islands depend upon workers' remittances and foreign aid.

YEMEN

Status: REPUBLIC
Area: 527,968 sq km (203,850 sq mls)
Population: 14,501,000
Capital: SANA
Language: ARABIC
Religion: SUNNI MUSLIM, SHI'A MUSLIM
Currency: DINAR, RIAL
Organizations: UN

MAP PAGE: 40-41

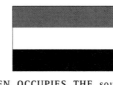

YEMEN OCCUPIES THE southwestern Arabian Peninsula, on the Red Sea and Gulf of Aden. Beyond the Red Sea coastal plain the land rises to a mountain range then descends to desert plateaux. Much of Yemen is hot and arid, but rainfall in the west supports crops and most settlement. Farming and fishing are the main activities, with cotton the main cash crop. Oil production is increasingly important. Remittances from workers abroad are the main foreign exchange earner.

YUGOSLAVIA

Status: REPUBLIC
Area: 102,173 sq km (39,449 sq mls)
Population: 10,544,000
Capital: BELGRADE
Language: SERBO-CROAT, ALBANIAN, HUNGARIAN
Religion: SERBIAN ORTHODOX, MONTENEGRIN ORTHODOX, SUNNI MUSLIM
Currency: DINAR
Organizations: UN

MAP PAGE: 112

THE SOUTH EUROPEAN state comprises only two of the former Yugoslav republics: the large and populous but landlocked Serbia and the much smaller Montenegro on the Adriatic Sea. The landscape is for the most part rugged, mountainous and forested. Northern Serbia (including the formerly autonomous province of Vojvodina) is low-lying, drained by the Danube river system. The climate is Mediterranean on the coast, continental inland. War and economic sanctions have ruined Serbia's economy and damaged that of Montenegro.

ZAIRE

see CONGO *page 15*

MAP PAGE: 124-125

ZAMBIA

Status: REPUBLIC
Area: 752,614 sq km (290,586 sq mls)
Population: 9,373,000
Capital: LUSAKA
Language: ENGLISH, BEMBA, NYANJA, TONGA, MANY LOCAL LANGUAGES
Religion: PROTESTANT, R.CATHOLIC, TRAD. BELIEFS, SUNNI MUSLIM
Currency: KWACHA
Organizations: COMM., OAU, SADC, UN

MAP PAGE: 124-125

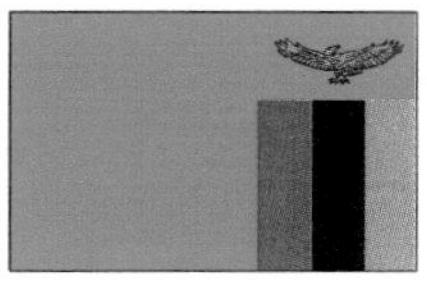

A LANDLOCKED STATE in central Africa, Zambia borders seven countries. It is dominated by high savannah plateaux and flanked by the Zambezi river in the south. Most people live in the central Copperbelt. The climate is tropical with a rainy season from November to May. Agriculture, which involves 70 per cent of the workforce, is mainly at subsistence level. Copper is still the mainstay of the economy, though reserves are declining. Lead, zinc, cobalt and tobacco are also exported. Manufacturing and tourism are important.

ZIMBABWE

Status: REPUBLIC
Area: 390,759 sq km (150,873 sq mls)
Population: 11,526,000
Capital: HARARE
Language: ENGLISH (OFFICIAL), SHONA, NDEBELE
Religion: PROTESTANT, R.CATHOLIC, TRAD.BELIEFS
Currency: DOLLAR
Organizations: COMM., OAU, SADC, UN

MAP PAGE: 128-129

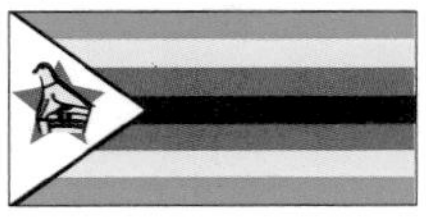

ZIMBABWE, A LANDLOCKED state in southern central Africa, consists of high plateaux flanked by the Zambezi river valley and Lake Kariba in the north and the Limpopo in the south. Climatic conditions are temperate because of altitude. Most people live in central Zimbabwe. Tobacco, cotton, sugar, tea, coffee and beef are produced for export as are a variety of minerals including gold, nickel, asbestos and copper. Manufacturing provides a wide range of goods. Tourism is a major foreign exchange earner.

© Bartholomew

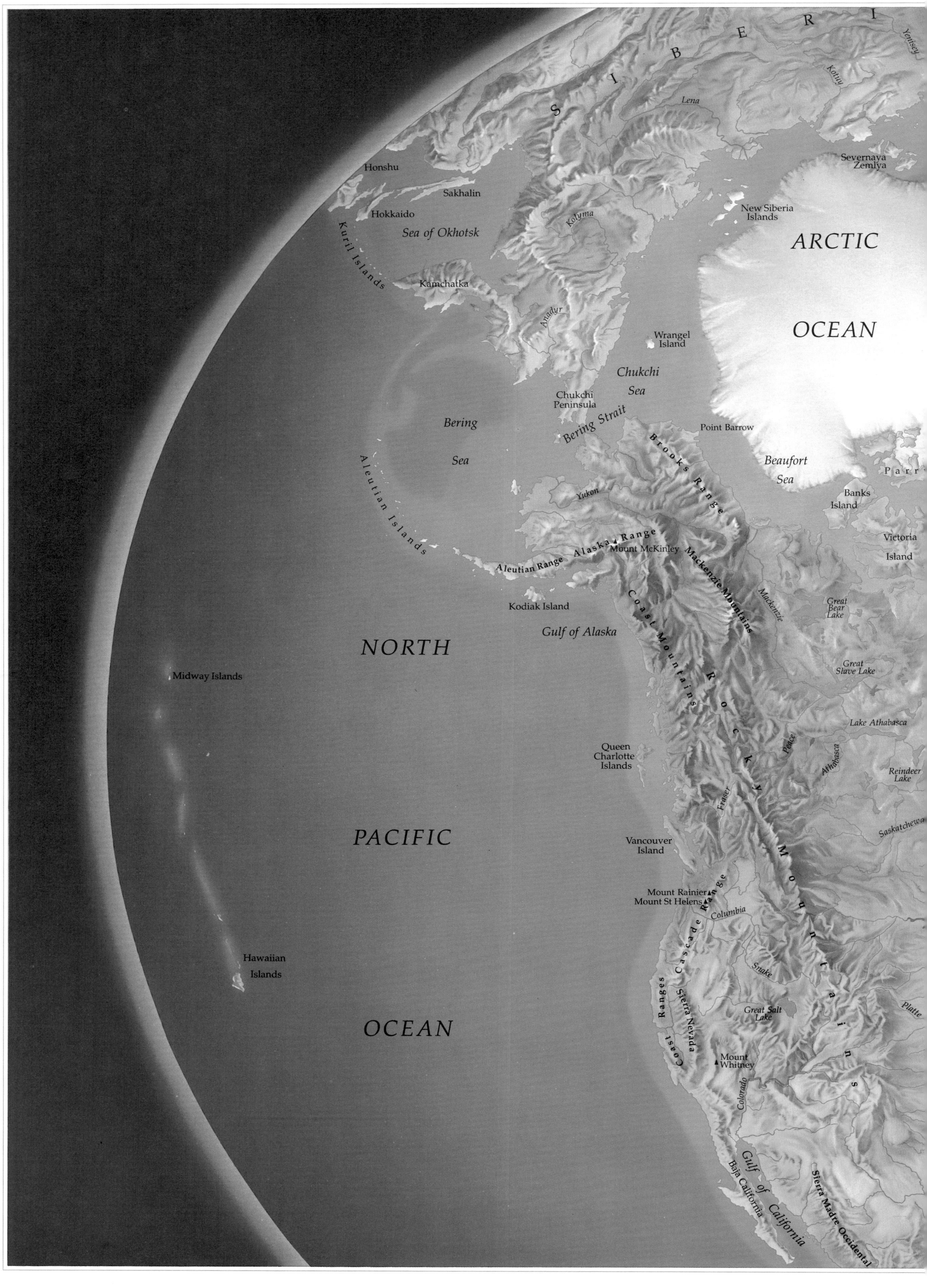
S I B E R I
Yenisey
Kotuy
Lena
Honshu
Sakhalin
Hokkaido
Sea of Okhotsk
Kuril Islands
Kamchatka
Kolyma
Anadyr
Severnaya Zemlya
New Siberia Islands
ARCTIC
OCEAN
Wrangel Island
Chukchi Sea
Chukchi Peninsula
Bering Strait
Bering Sea
Point Barrow
Beaufort Sea
Parr
Banks Island
Victoria Island
Aleutian Islands
Brooks Range
Yukon
Alaska Range
Mount McKinley
Aleutian Range
Mackenzie Mountains
Mackenzie
Great Bear Lake
Kodiak Island
Gulf of Alaska
Coast Mountains
NORTH
PACIFIC
OCEAN
Midway Islands
Great Slave Lake
Rocky Mountains
Lake Athabasca
Peace
Athabasca
Queen Charlotte Islands
Reindeer Lake
Fraser
Saskatchewan
Vancouver Island
Mount Rainier
Mount St Helens
Cascade Range
Columbia
Snake
Hawaiian Islands
Coast Ranges
Sierra Nevada
Great Salt Lake
Platte
Mount Whitney
Colorado
Gulf of California
Baja California
Sierra Madre Occidental

A
Ob
Novaya Zemlya
Black Sea
North Cape
SCANDINAVIA
Limit of permanent pack ice
Svalbard
Norwegian Sea
NORTH POLE
North Sea
Mediterranean Sea
Jan Mayen
Denmark Strait
BRITISH ISLES
Iceland
Bay of Biscay
Greenland
Ellesmere Island
Queen Elizabeth Islands
NORTH AFRICA
Islands
Baffin Bay
Davis Strait
Cape Farewell
Madeira
Baffin Island
NORTH
Canary Islands
Foxe Basin
Azores
Southampton Island
Hudson Strait
Cape Chidley
Labrador Sea
Hudson Bay
Labrador
Churchill
Churchill
Southern Indian Lake
La Grande Rivière
Laurentian Highlands
Newfoundland
Cape Race
James Bay
Rupert
ATLANTIC
Lake Winnipeg
Nova Scotia
Lake Manitoba
Lake of the Woods
St Lawrence
Lake Superior
Cape Cod
Lake Huron
Lake Ontario
Missouri
Mississippi
Lake Michigan
Lake Erie
Mountains
Great Plains
Ohio
OCEAN
Appalachian
Tennessee
Cape Hatteras
Ozark Plateau
Arkansas
Mississippi
Savannah
Red River
Florida
Bahamas
West Indies
Rio Grande
Gulf of Mexico

© Bartholomew

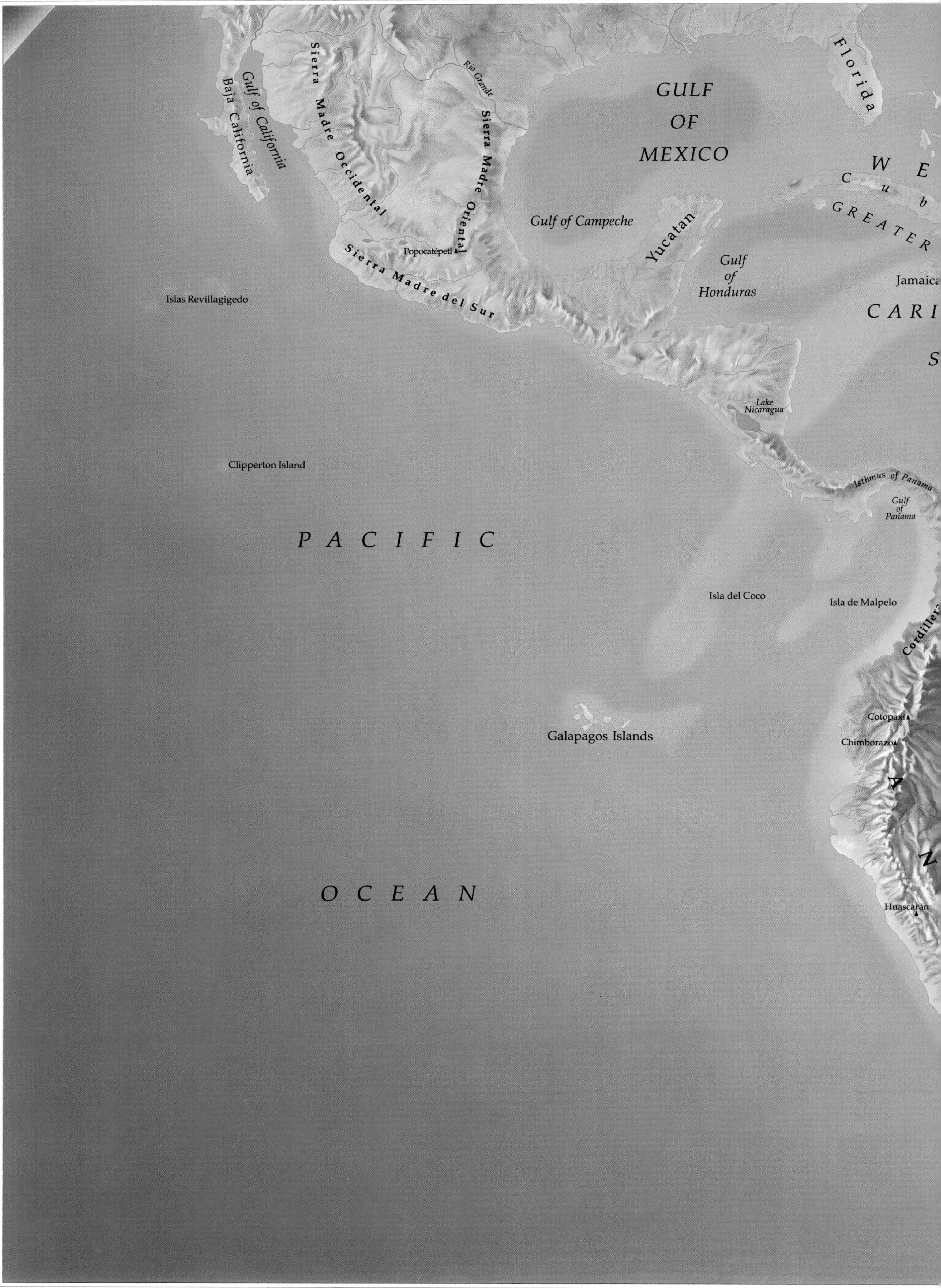
Gulf of California
Baja California
Sierra Madre Occidental
Rio Grande
Sierra Madre Oriental
GULF OF MEXICO
Florida
W E
Cuba
GREATER
Gulf of Campeche
Yucatan
Popocatépetl
Sierra Madre del Sur
Gulf of Honduras
Jamaica
CARI
S
Islas Revillagigedo
Lake Nicaragua
Clipperton Island
Isthmus of Panama
Gulf of Panama
PACIFIC
Isla del Coco
Isla de Malpelo
Cordillera
Galapagos Islands
Cotopaxi
Chimborazo
OCEAN
Huascarán

NORTH
ATLANTIC
OCEAN
BAHAMAS
ST INDIES
Hispaniola
ANTILLES
Puerto Rico
BBEAN
EA
LESSER ANTILLES
Trinidad
Gulf of Darien
Lake Maracaibo
LLANOS
Orinoco
Occidental
Cauca
Magdalena
Cordillera Oriental
Roraima
Guiana Highlands
Branco
Mouths of the Amazon
Negro
Japurá
Putumayo
Amazon
Marañon
Juruá
Purus
Madeira
Tapajós
Xingu
Tocantins
Parnaíba
Ucayali
Araguaia
São Francisco
Madre de Dios
MATO GROSSO
Brazilian Highlands
Lake Titicaca
Ancohuma
Lake Poopó
Salar de Uyuni
Atacama Desert
GRAN CHACO
Pilcomayo
Paraguay
Paraná
© Bartholomew

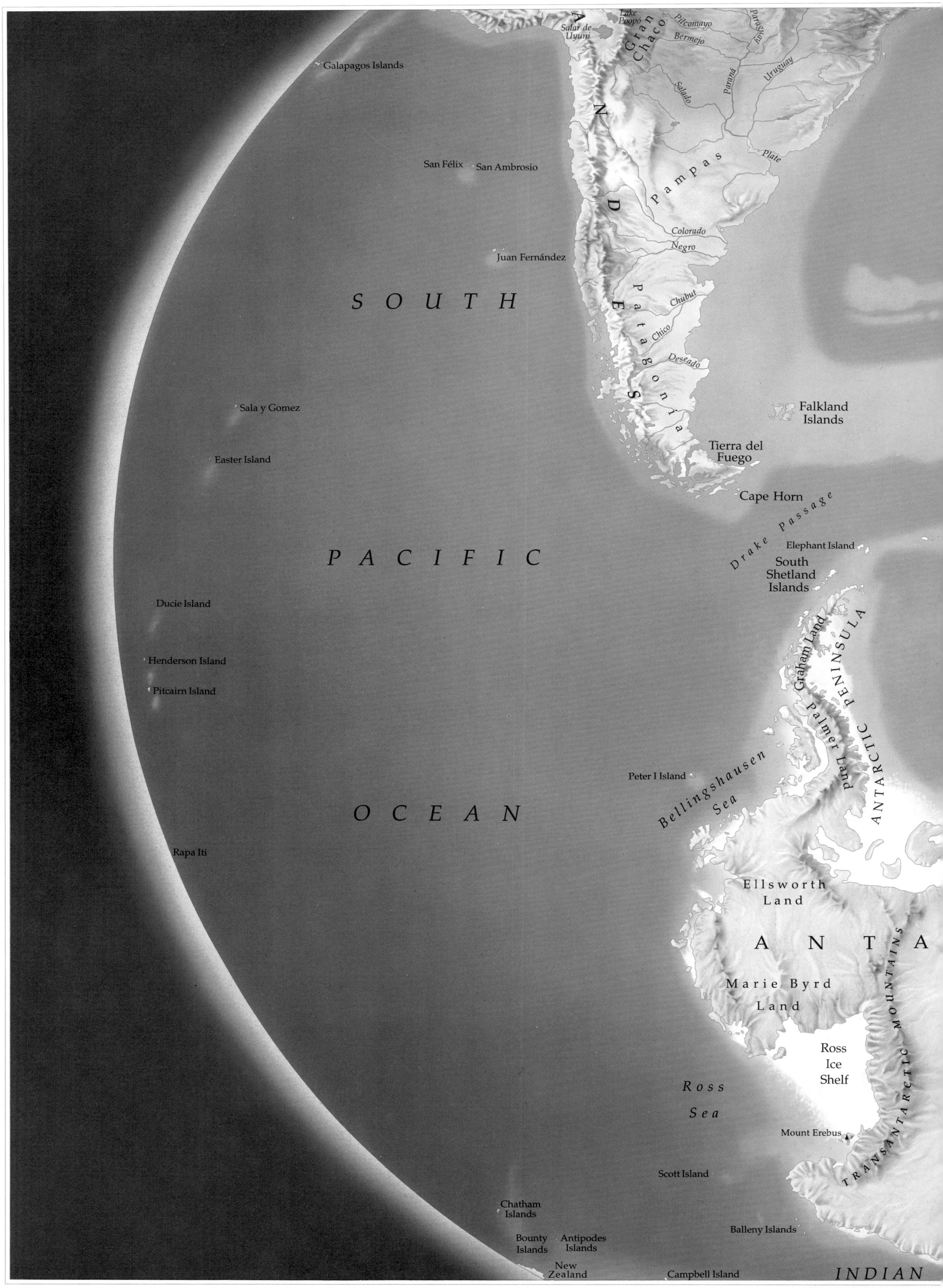
Lake Poopó
Salar de Uyuni
Gran Chaco
Pilcomayo
Bermejo
Paraguay
Salado
Paraná
Uruguay
Galapagos Islands
Plate
Pampas
San Félix
San Ambrosio
A N D E S
Colorado
Negro
Juan Fernández
Patagonia
Chubut
Chico
Deseado
S O U T H
Falkland Islands
Sala y Gomez
Tierra del Fuego
Easter Island
Cape Horn
Drake Passage
Elephant Island
P A C I F I C
South Shetland Islands
Ducie Island
Graham Land
PENINSULA
Henderson Island
Pitcairn Island
Palmer Land
ANTARCTIC
Peter I Island
Bellingshausen Sea
O C E A N
Rapa Iti
Ellsworth Land
A N T A
Marie Byrd Land
TRANSANTARCTIC MOUNTAINS
Ross Ice Shelf
Ross Sea
Mount Erebus
Scott Island
Chatham Islands
Bounty Islands
Antipodes Islands
Balleny Islands
New Zealand
Campbell Island
INDIAN

St Helena
Tristan da Cunha
S O U T H
Gough Island
Cunene
Orange
Kalahari Desert
South Georgia
South Sandwich Islands
South Orkney Islands
Cape of Good Hope
A T L A N T I C
Bouvet Island
Madagascar
Weddell Sea
Limit of permanent pack ice
Queen Maud Land
O C E A N
Prince Edward Islands
Îles Crozet
R C T I C A
SOUTH POLE
Enderby Land
Îles Kerguelen
Macdonald Islands
Heard Island
St Paul
Amsterdam Island
Wilkes Land
OCEAN

© Bartholomew

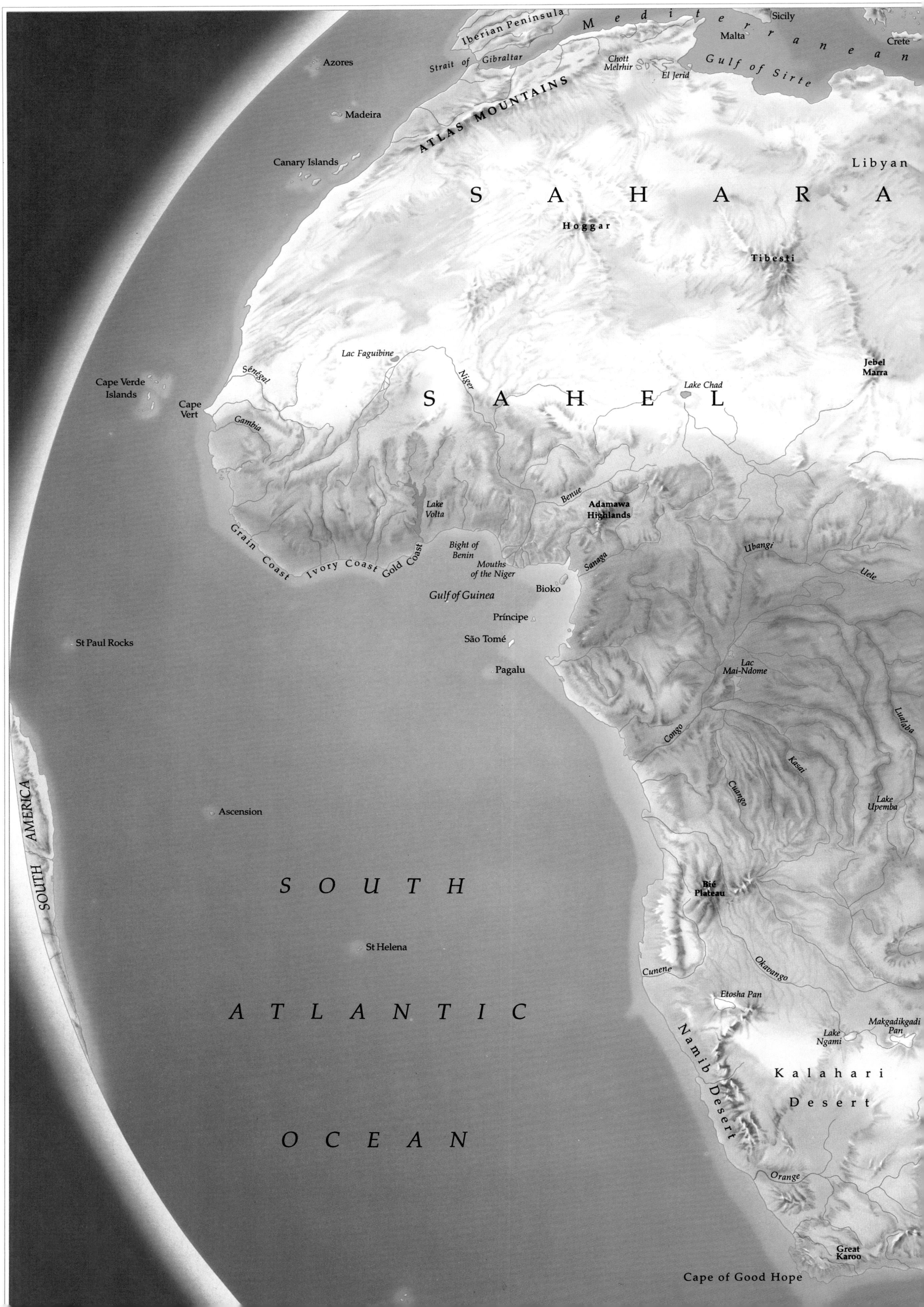
Iberian Peninsula
Mediterranean
Sicily
Malta
Crete
Strait of Gibraltar
Chott Melrhir
El Jerid
Gulf of Sirte
Azores
Madeira
ATLAS MOUNTAINS
Canary Islands
Libyan
SAHARA
Hoggar
Tibesti
Jebel Marra
Lac Faguibine
Sénégal
Niger
Cape Verde Islands
Cape Vert
Gambia
SAHEL
Lake Chad
Benue
Adamawa Highlands
Lake Volta
Grain Coast
Ivory Coast
Gold Coast
Bight of Benin
Mouths of the Niger
Sanaga
Ubangi
Uele
Gulf of Guinea
Bioko
Príncipe
São Tomé
Pagalu
St Paul Rocks
Lac Mai-Ndome
Lualaba
Congo
Kasai
Cuango
Lake Upemba
SOUTH AMERICA
Ascension
SOUTH
ATLANTIC
OCEAN
Bié Plateau
St Helena
Cunene
Okavango
Etosha Pan
Lake Ngami
Makgadikgadi Pan
Namib Desert
Kalahari Desert
Orange
Great Karoo
Cape of Good Hope

Cyprus
Sea
Euphrates
Tigris
Zagros Mountains
Daryācheh-ye-Namak
Amudar'ya
Pamirs
Tarim
Hindu Kush
Karakoram
Plateau of Iran
Plateau of Tibet
HIMALAYA
Helmand
Dead Sea
Gulf of Suez
Gulf of Aqaba
Qattâra
Desert
Nile
The Great Oasis
Lake Nasser
ARABIAN
PENINSULA
RED SEA
Persian Gulf
Gulf of Oman
Brahmaputra
Indus
Thar Desert
Ganges (Ganga)
Nubian Desert
ARABIAN SEA
Deccan
Godavari
Krishna
Blue Nile
White Nile
Bab el Mandeb
Gulf of Aden
Socotra
Lake Tana
Ethiopian Plateau
Danakil Desert
Ogaden
Laccadive Islands
Shabeelle
Maldive Islands
Sri Lanka
Lake Turkana
Lake Kyoga
Lake Albert
Mt Stanley
Mount Kenya
Tana
Juba
Lake Edward
Lake Victoria
Lake Kivu
Rift Valley
INDIAN
Lake Natron
Kilimanjaro
Lake Eyasi
Pemba
Zanzibar
Seychelles
Amirante Islands
Chagos Archipelago
Lake Tanganyika
Lake Rukwa
Mafia Island
Coëtivy Island
Aldabra Islands
Providence Islands
Lake Mweru
Lake Bangweulu
Lake Nyasa
Agalega Islands
Comoro Islands
Mozambique Channel
OCEAN
Lake Chilwa
Zambezi
Lake Kariba
Madagascar
Tromelin
Rodrigues
Mauritius
Réunion
Limpopo
Vaal
Drakensberg

© Bartholomew

NORTH POLE
ARCTIC
Ellesmere Island
Hudson Bay
Baffin Island
Davis Strait
Greenland
Greenland Sea
Svalba
LABRADOR
Jan Mayen
North Ca
Denmark Strait
Norwegian Sea
Iceland
Cape Farewell
Faeroe Islands
NORTH
SCANDINAV
Vänern
Vättern
British Isles
Grampians
North Sea
Irish Sea
Balti
ATLANTIC
Severn
Thames
Elbe
Oder
Vistula
NORT
English Channel
Rhine
Neisse
Seine
Loire
Danube
Bay of Biscay
Hun
Massif Central
Mt Blanc
ALPS
OCEAN
Garonne
Rhône
Po
Azores
Cantabrian Mts
Pyrenees
Adriatic Sea
Dinaric Alps
Apennines
Ebro
Corsica
Tagus
Balearic Islands
Sardinia
Guadalquivir
MEDITERRA
Strait of Gibraltar
Sicily
Madeira
Malta
ATLAS MOUNTAINS
Chott Melrhir
El Jerid
Gulf of Sirte
Canary Islands

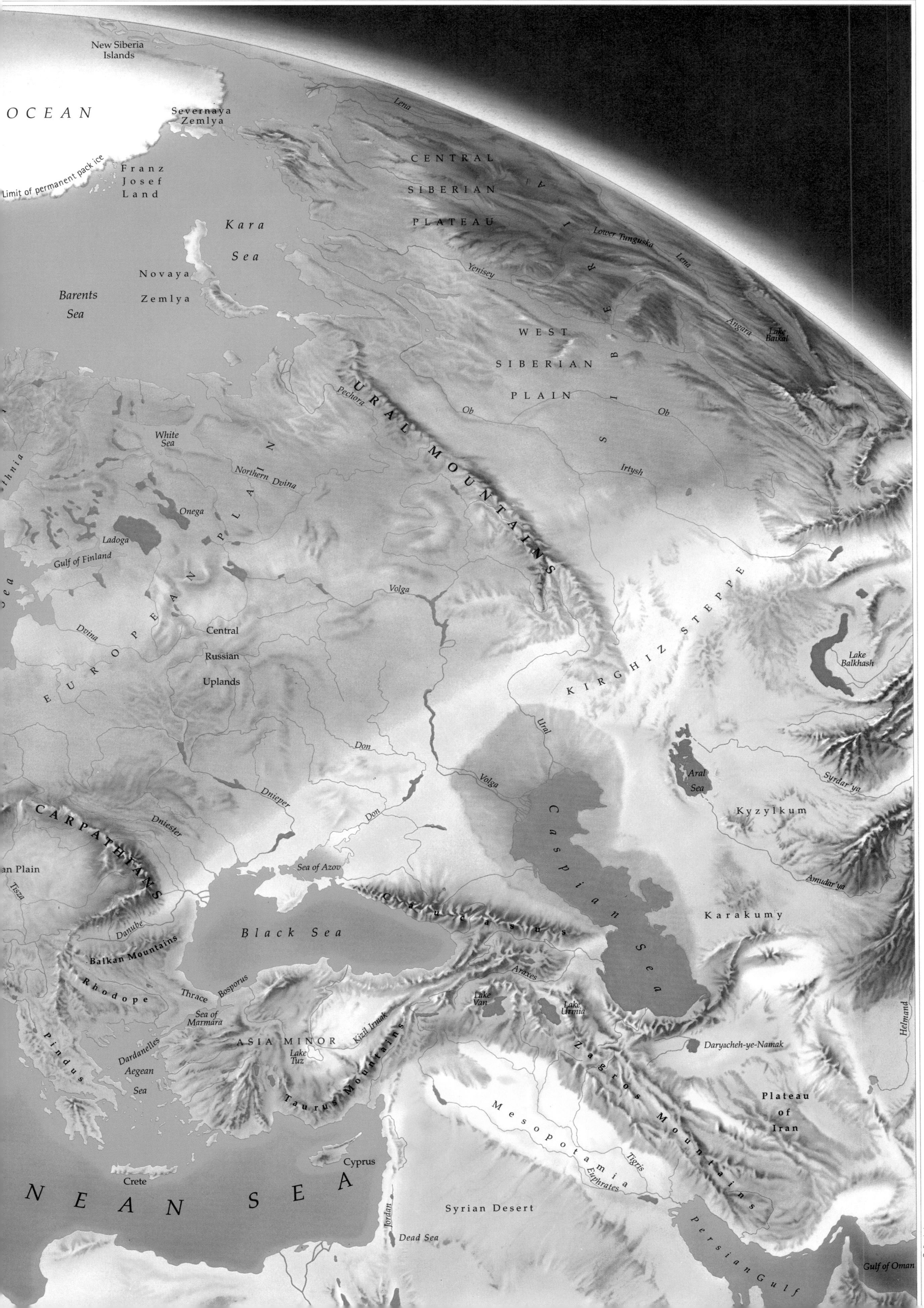
New Siberia Islands
OCEAN
Severnaya Zemlya
Limit of permanent pack ice
Franz Josef Land
CENTRAL SIBERIAN PLATEAU
SIBERIA
Lena
Lower Tunguska
Yenisey
Angara
Lake Baikal
Kara Sea
Novaya Zemlya
Barents Sea
WEST SIBERIAN PLAIN
Ob
Pechora
URAL MOUNTAINS
White Sea
Northern Dvina
Irtysh
Onega
Ladoga
Gulf of Finland
EUROPEAN PLAIN
Volga
KIRGHIZ STEPPE
Lake Balkhash
Dvina
Central Russian Uplands
Ural
Aral Sea
Syrdar'ya
Don
Dnieper
Dniester
CARPATHIANS
Caspian Sea
Kyzylkum
Sea of Azov
Amudar'ya
Tisza
Caucasus
Karakumy
Danube
Black Sea
Balkan Mountains
Rhodope
Thrace
Bosporus
Araxes
Lake Van
Lake Urmia
Sea of Marmara
Kizil Irmak
ASIA MINOR
Zagros Mountains
Daryacheh-ye-Namak
Helmand
Pindus
Dardanelles
Lake Tuz
Aegean Sea
Taurus Mountains
Plateau of Iran
Mesopotamia
Tigris
Euphrates
Cyprus
Crete
NEAN SEA
Jordan
Syrian Desert
Dead Sea
Persian Gulf
Gulf of Oman
© Bartholomew

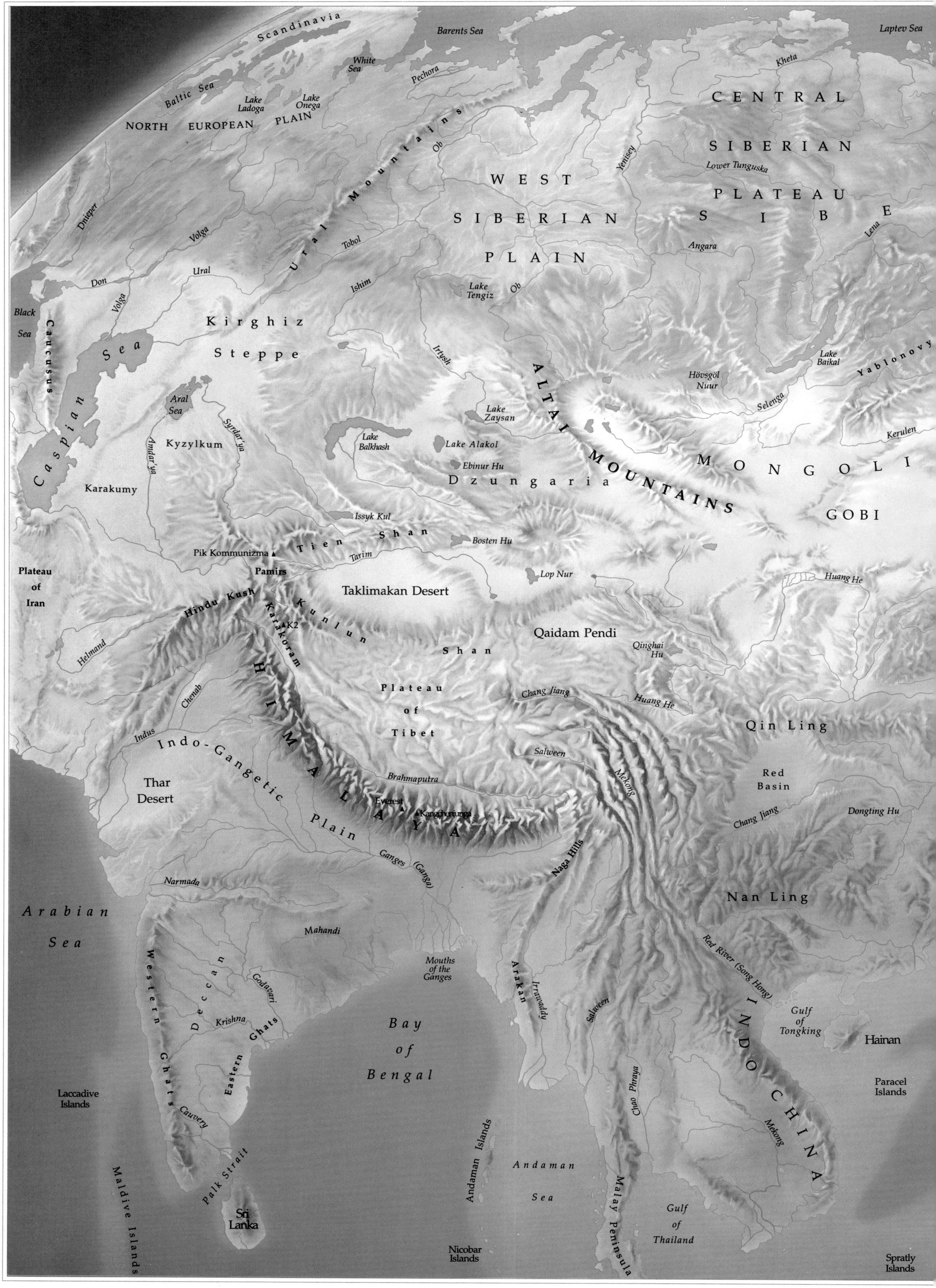
Scandinavia
Barents Sea
Laptev Sea
White Sea
Pechora
Kheta
Baltic Sea
Lake Ladoga
Lake Onega
CENTRAL
NORTH EUROPEAN PLAIN
Ural Mountains
Ob
SIBERIAN
Yenisey
Lower Tunguska
WEST
PLATEAU
SIBERIAN
S I B E
Dnieper
Volga
Tobol
Angara
Lena
PLAIN
Ural
Don
Ishim
Lake Tengiz
Ob
Black Sea
Volga
Kirghiz
Caucasus
Sea
Steppe
Irtysh
ALTAI MOUNTAINS
Lake Baikal
Yablonovy
Hövsgöl Nuur
Caspian
Aral Sea
Lake Zaysan
Selenga
Syrdar'ya
Amdar'ya
Kyzylkum
Lake Balkhash
Lake Alakol
Kerulen
Ebinur Hu
MONGOLI
Karakumy
Dzungaria
Issyk Kul
GOBI
Tien Shan
Bosten Hu
Pik Kommunizma
Tarim
Plateau of Iran
Pamirs
Lop Nur
Huang He
Taklimakan Desert
Hindu Kush
Kunlun
Karakoram
K2
Qaidam Pendi
Helmand
Shan
Qinghai Hu
HIMALAYA
Plateau of Tibet
Chenab
Chang Jiang
Huang He
Qin Ling
Indus
Indo-Gangetic Plain
Salween
Thar Desert
Brahmaputra
Red Basin
Mekong
Everest
Kangchenjunga
Dongting Hu
Chang Jiang
Ganges (Ganga)
Naga Hills
Narmada
Nan Ling
Arabian Sea
Mahandi
Red River (Song Hong)
Mouths of the Ganges
Western Ghats
Deccan
Godavari
Arakan
Irrawaddy
Salween
Gulf of Tongking
Krishna
Ghats
Bay of Bengal
Hainan
Eastern
INDOCHINA
Laccadive Islands
Paracel Islands
Cauvery
Chao Phraya
Mekong
Andaman Islands
Andaman Sea
Palk Strait
Maldive Islands
Sri Lanka
Malay Peninsula
Gulf of Thailand
Nicobar Islands
Spratly Islands

New Siberia Islands
Bering Strait
Alaska
Anadyr
Nunivak Island
Yana
Indigirka
Kolyma
Bering Sea
Aleutian Islands
Lena
R I A
Kamchatka
Dzhugdzhur Range
Sea of Okhotsk
Range
Kuril Islands
Sakhalin
Tatar Strait
Greater Khingan Range
Hulun Nur
Amur
Lake Khanka
Hokkaido
Manchuria
NORTH PACIFIC OCEAN
Midway Island
Sea of Japan
Changbai Shan
Honshu
Korea
Bo Hai
Huang He
Korea Strait
Yellow Sea
Great Plain of China
Shikoku
Kyushu
Chang Jiang
East China Sea
Bonin Islands
Poyang Hu
Ryukyu Islands
Volcano Islands
Taiwan Strait
Taiwan
Marianas
Marshall Islands
PHILIPPINES
South China Sea
Guam
Kiribati
Luzon
Caroline Islands
Mindoro
Samar
Panay
Palawan
Negros
Sulu Sea
Mindanao

© Bartholomew

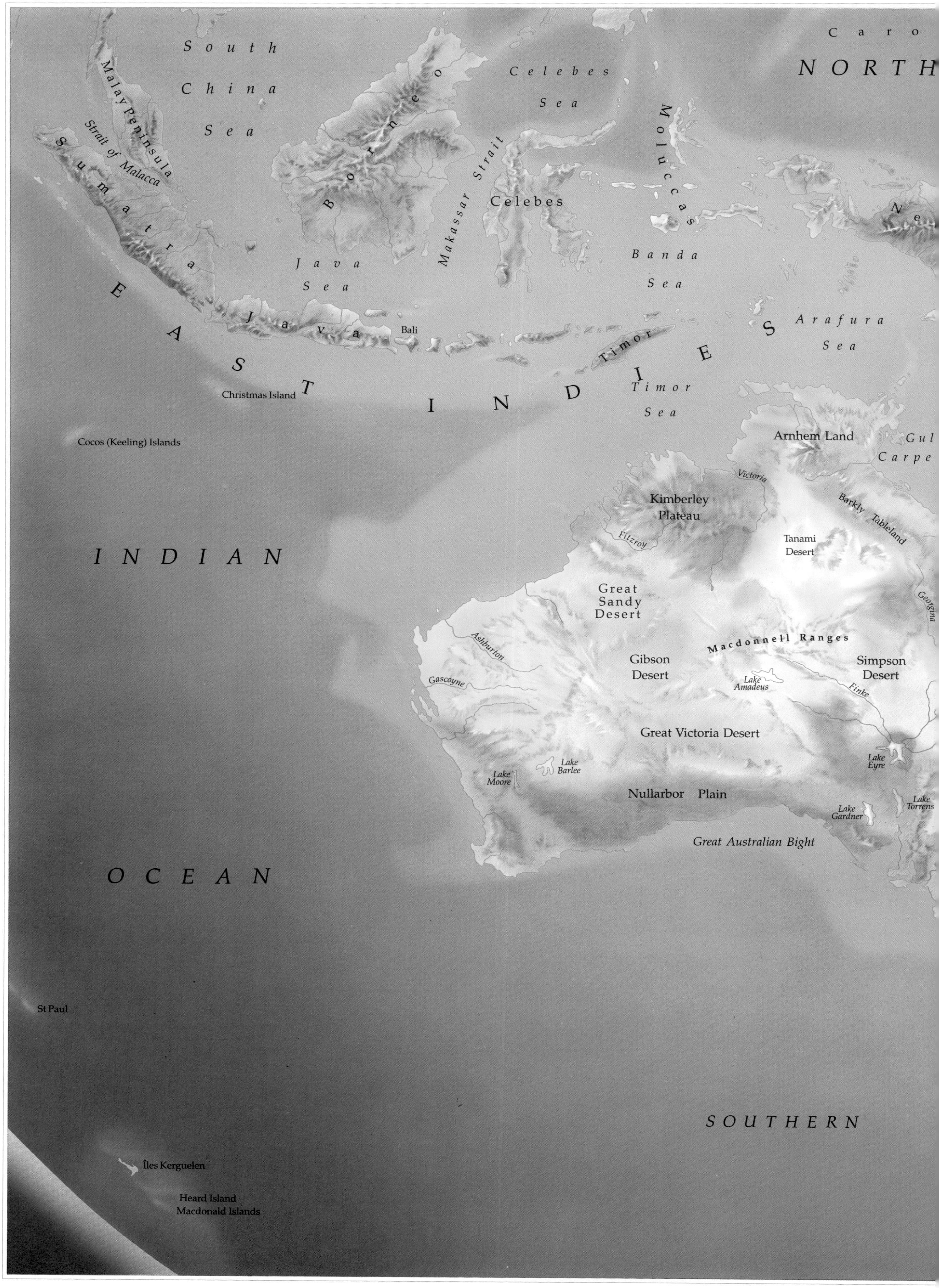
South China Sea
Malay Peninsula
Strait of Malacca
Sumatra
Borneo
Celebes Sea
Makassar Strait
Celebes
Moluccas
Java Sea
Banda Sea
Java
Bali
Timor
Arafura Sea
Timor Sea
EAST INDIES
Christmas Island
Cocos (Keeling) Islands
NORTH
Arnhem Land
Victoria
Kimberley Plateau
Fitzroy
Barkly Tableland
Tanami Desert
Georgina
Great Sandy Desert
Ashburton
Gascoyne
Gibson Desert
Macdonnell Ranges
Lake Amadeus
Simpson Desert
Finke
Great Victoria Desert
Lake Barlee
Lake Moore
Lake Eyre
Nullarbor Plain
Lake Torrens
Lake Gardner
Great Australian Bight
INDIAN OCEAN
St Paul
SOUTHERN
Îles Kerguelen
Heard Island
Macdonald Islands

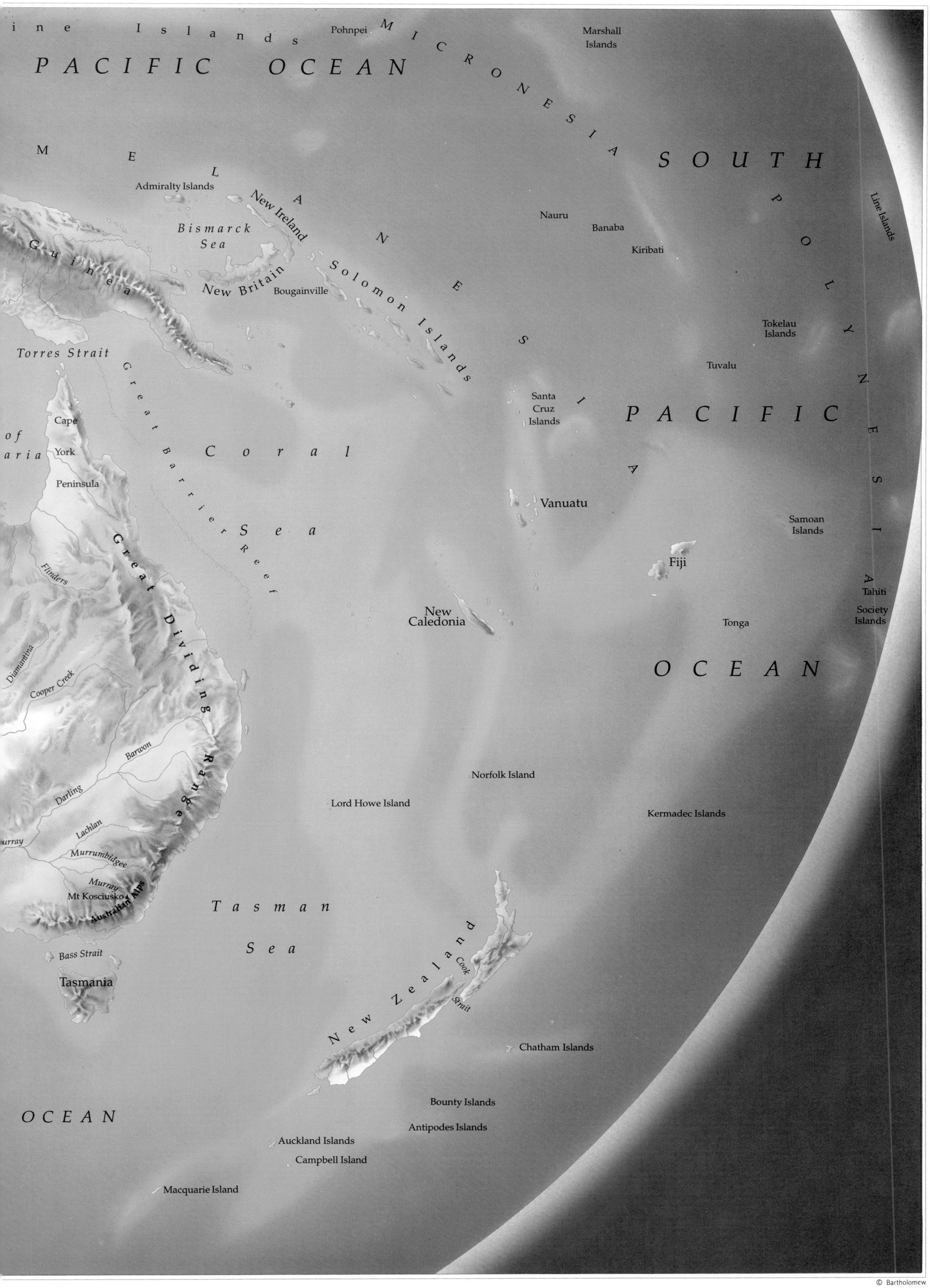

© Bartholomew

Continents and Oceans

Land area = 1,000,000 sq km / *386,000 sq mls*

Water area = 1,000,000 sq km / *386,000 sq mls*

Islands and Inland Waters

Land area = 10,000 sq km / *3,860 sq mls*

Inland water surface area = 1,000 sq km / *386 sq mls*

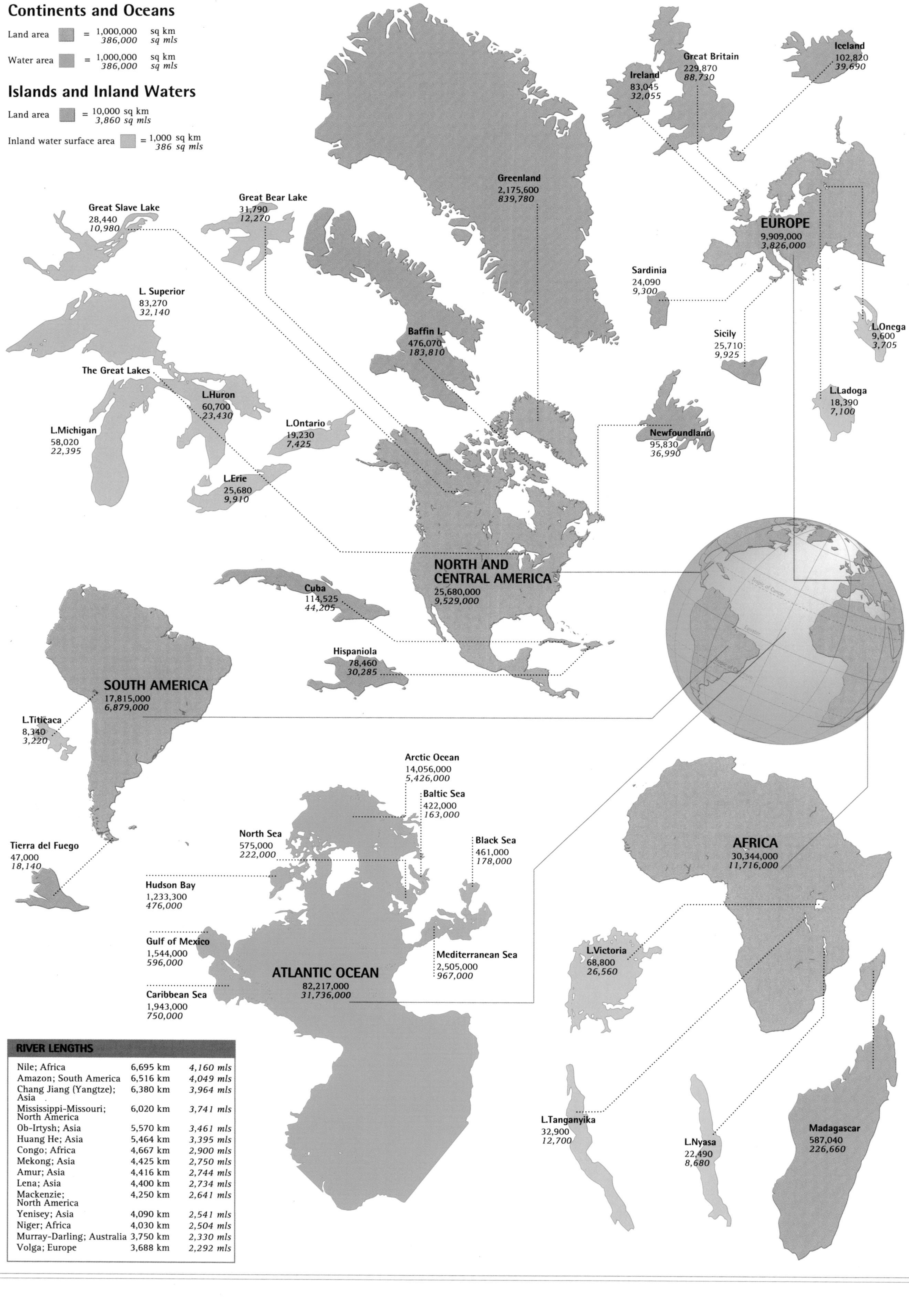
Greenland
2,175,600
839,780
Great Britain
229,870
88,730
Ireland
83,045
32,055
Iceland
102,820
39,690
Great Slave Lake
28,440
10,980
Great Bear Lake
31,790
12,270
L. Superior
83,270
32,140
The Great Lakes
L.Huron
60,700
23,430
L.Michigan
58,020
22,395
L.Ontario
19,230
7,425
L.Erie
25,680
9,910
Baffin I.
476,070
183,810
EUROPE
9,909,000
3,826,000
Sardinia
24,090
9,300
Sicily
25,710
9,925
L.Onega
9,600
3,705
L.Ladoga
18,390
7,100
Newfoundland
95,830
36,990
NORTH AND CENTRAL AMERICA
25,680,000
9,529,000
Cuba
114,525
44,205
Hispaniola
78,460
30,285
SOUTH AMERICA
17,815,000
6,879,000
L.Titicaca
8,340
3,220
Tierra del Fuego
47,000
18,140
Arctic Ocean
14,056,000
5,426,000
Baltic Sea
422,000
163,000
North Sea
575,000
222,000
Black Sea
461,000
178,000
Hudson Bay
1,233,300
476,000
Gulf of Mexico
1,544,000
596,000
Mediterranean Sea
2,505,000
967,000
Caribbean Sea
1,943,000
750,000
ATLANTIC OCEAN
82,217,000
31,736,000
AFRICA
30,344,000
11,716,000
L.Victoria
68,800
26,560
L.Tanganyika
32,900
12,700
L.Nyasa
22,490
8,680
Madagascar
587,040
226,660

RIVER LENGTHS

Nile; Africa	6,695 km	*4,160 mls*
Amazon; South America	6,516 km	*4,049 mls*
Chang Jiang (Yangtze); Asia	6,380 km	*3,964 mls*
Mississippi-Missouri; North America	6,020 km	*3,741 mls*
Ob-Irtysh; Asia	5,570 km	*3,461 mls*
Huang He; Asia	5,464 km	*3,395 mls*
Congo; Africa	4,667 km	*2,900 mls*
Mekong; Asia	4,425 km	*2,750 mls*
Amur; Asia	4,416 km	*2,744 mls*
Lena; Asia	4,400 km	*2,734 mls*
Mackenzie; North America	4,250 km	*2,641 mls*
Yenisey; Asia	4,090 km	*2,541 mls*
Niger; Africa	4,030 km	*2,504 mls*
Murray-Darling; Australia	3,750 km	*2,330 mls*
Volga; Europe	3,688 km	*2,292 mls*

MOUNTAIN HEIGHTS (Selected)		
Everest; Nepal/China	8,848 m	*29,028 ft*
K2; Jammu & Kashmir/China	8,611 m	*28,251 ft*
Kanchenjunga; Nepal/India	8,586 m	*28,169 ft*
Dhaulagiri; Nepal	8,167 m	*26,794 ft*
Annapurna; Nepal	8,091 m	*26,545 ft*
Aconcagua; Argentina	6,960 m	*22,834 ft*
Ojos del Salado; Argentina/Chile	6,908 m	*22,664 ft*
Mt McKinley; Alaska, USA	6,194 m	*20,321 ft*
Mt Logan; Canada	6,050 m	*19,849 ft*
Kilimanjaro; Tanzania	5,895 m	*19,340 ft*
Elbrus; Russian Federation	5,642 m	*18,510 ft*
Kirinyaga; Kenya	5,199 m	*17,057 ft*
Puncak Jaya; Indonesia	5,029 m	*16,499 ft*
Vinson Massif; Antarctica	4,897 m	*16,066 ft*
Mt Blanc; France/Italy	4,808 m	*15,774 ft*

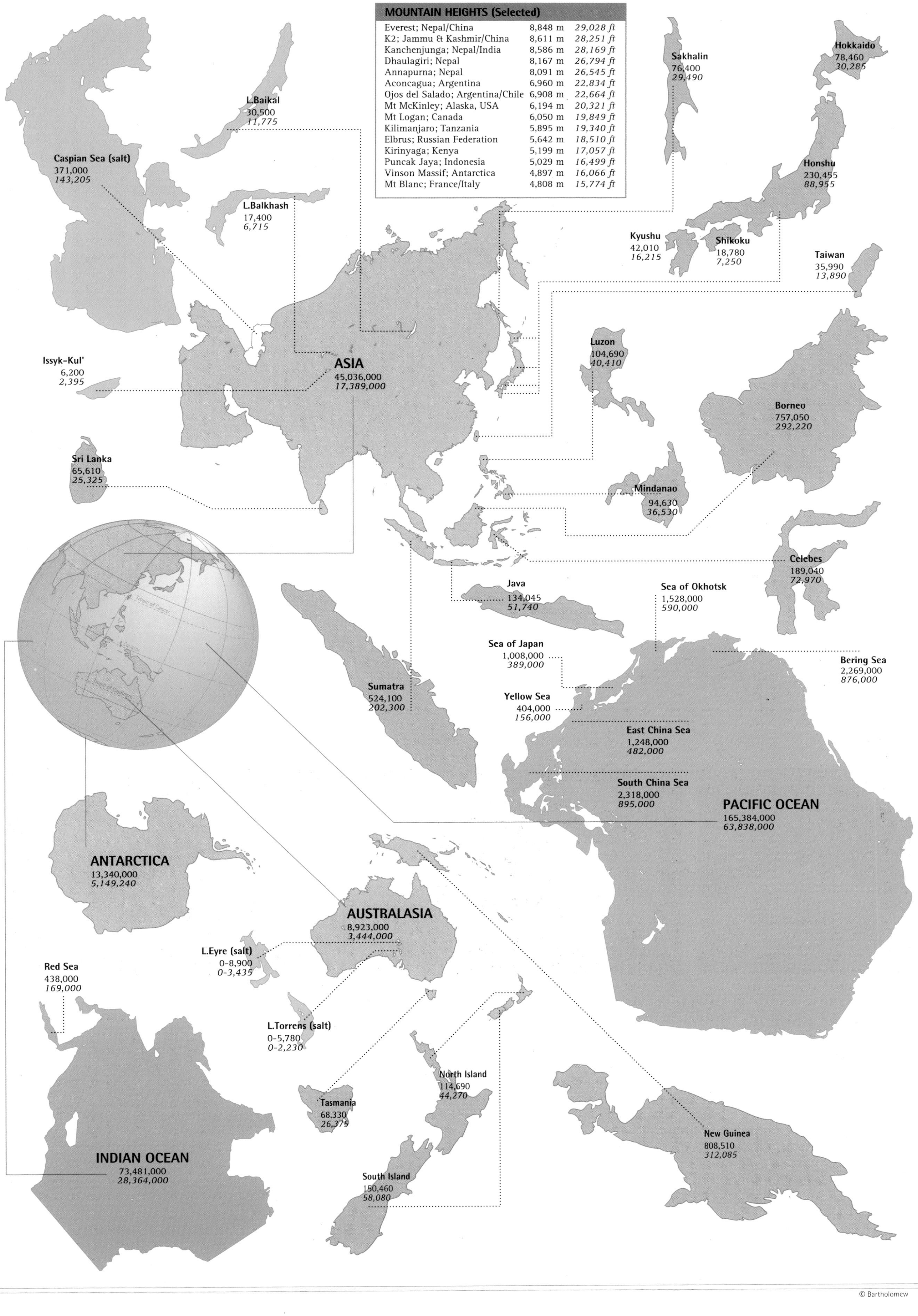
Caspian Sea (salt)
371,000
143,205
L.Baikal
30,500
11,775
L.Balkhash
17,400
6,715
Issyk-Kul'
6,200
2,395
ASIA
45,036,000
17,389,000
Sri Lanka
65,610
25,325
Sakhalin
76,400
29,490
Hokkaido
78,460
30,285
Honshu
230,455
88,955
Kyushu
42,010
16,215
Shikoku
18,780
7,250
Taiwan
35,990
13,890
Luzon
104,690
40,410
Borneo
757,050
292,220
Mindanao
94,630
36,530
Celebes
189,040
72,970
Java
134,045
51,740
Sea of Okhotsk
1,528,000
590,000
Sea of Japan
1,008,000
389,000
Bering Sea
2,269,000
876,000
Sumatra
524,100
202,300
Yellow Sea
404,000
156,000
East China Sea
1,248,000
482,000
South China Sea
2,318,000
895,000
PACIFIC OCEAN
165,384,000
63,838,000
ANTARCTICA
13,340,000
5,149,240
AUSTRALASIA
8,923,000
3,444,000
L.Eyre (salt)
0-8,900
0-3,435
Red Sea
438,000
169,000
L.Torrens (salt)
0-5,780
0-2,230
North Island
114,690
44,270
Tasmania
68,330
26,375
New Guinea
808,510
312,085
INDIAN OCEAN
73,481,000
28,364,000
South Island
150,460
58,080

© Bartholomew

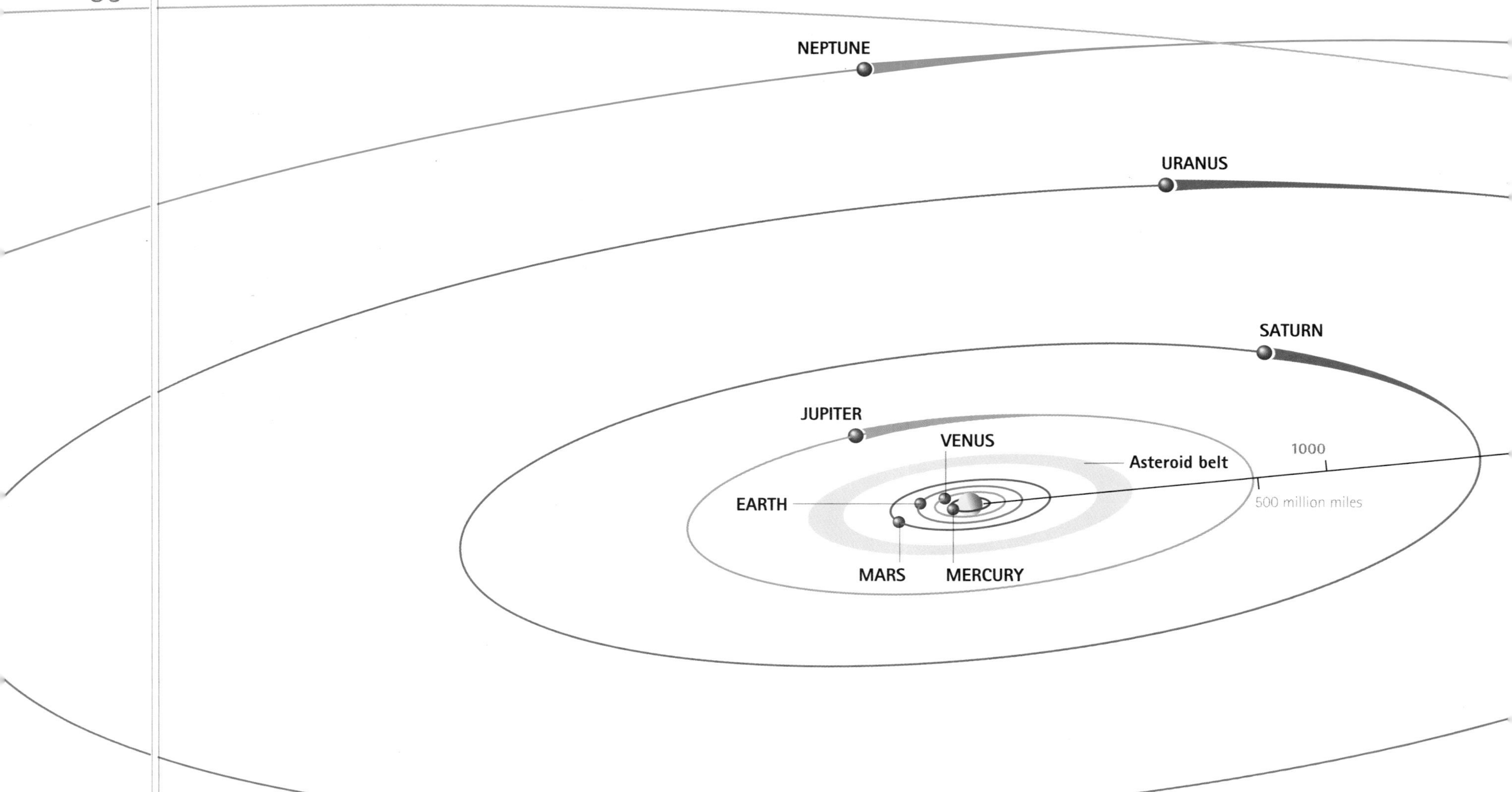

CURRENT THEORY SUGGESTS that the solar system condensed from a primitive solar nebula of gas and dust during an interval of a few tens of millions of years about 4600 million years ago. Gravity caused this nebula to contract, drawing most of its mass into the proto-sun at the centre. Turbulence gave the original cloud a tendency to rotate, and as it contracted, conservation of angular momentum caused the proto-sun to spin faster and faster, forcing the remainder of the cloud into a disc shape. The centre of the cloud heated up as it compressed, and so became hot enough for the Sun to begin to shine, through nuclear energy released at its core. Meanwhile the surrounding disc cooled, allowing material to condense into solid form. Particles stuck together as they collided and progressively larger bodies were built up. These swept up most of the debris to form the planets, which orbit the Sun close to the plane of the now vanished disc. The first materials to condense were the least volatile refractory compounds such as oxides of iron, nickel and aluminium. Decreasing temperature allowed rocky silicate material to appear followed by more volatile compounds such as water and methane. Thus composition of the planets progressed from less refractory cores to more volatile outer layers.

The planets nearest to the Sun are dense with metallic cores mantled by rocky silicate materials; planets farther from the Sun accreted and retained large volumes of volatiles and are thus much more massive. They may have cores of rock and ice, surrounded by solid or liquid hydrogen enveloped in thick gassy atmospheres. These gas giants are accompanied by captured rocky and icy satellites which are mostly too small to have accreted and held atmospheres.

The subsequent evolution of the solar system was dominated by chemical segregation within the planets and surface bombardment by smaller bodies. This bombardment was over by 3 to 4 million years ago, although minor impacts still occur. Traces of these events remain on the surfaces of planets which have insufficient internal heat to drive resurfacing processes.

MERCURY is the nearest planet to the Sun, spinning three times for every two orbits around the Sun. It has an exceptionally large metallic core which may be responsible for Mercury's weak magnetic field. Mercury is an airless world subject to vast extremes of temperature, from -180°C at night to 430°C near the middle of its long day. Photographs taken from the Mariner 10 spacecraft probe during the mid-1970s, revealed the surface to be dominated by heavily cratered areas dating from the early meteorite bombardment of the inner solar system. As the bombardment was tailing off Mercury's radius contracted by between one and two kilometres, forming compressional features (lobate scarps) which may have been caused by a change in the core from liquid to solid. The image above is a mosaic made from photographs taken as Mariner 10 approached the planet.

VENUS has a dense atmosphere of 96 per cent carbon dioxide mixed with nitrogen, oxygen, suphur dioxide and water vapour which hides the surface under permanent cloud and maintains a mean surface temperature of about 480°C. The planet's slow rotation means that weather systems are driven mostly by solar heat, rather than by spin. As a result, beyond 10 kilometres above the surface, westerly winds at speeds up to 100 metres per second cause a bulk rotation of the atmosphere in about four days. Imaging radar has been used to map most of the planet from orbiting spacecraft. The most recent survey by the Magellan probe began in the 1990s. Mountains, valleys, impact craters and other features have been mapped and three dimensional simulations generated by computer from the Magellan data. The false-colour image above, made at ultraviolet wavelengths, shows the upper cloud layers.

MARS has a thin atmosphere of about 95 per cent carbon dioxide mixed with other minor constituents. Day and night surface temperatures vary between about -120°C and -20°C. A variety of landscapes has been identified, including ancient heavily cratered terrains and plains. The large dark area on the right of the image above is Syrtis Major Planitia, this dark material is thought to have originated in eruptions from ancient shield volcanoes. There are several large volcanoes; the best preserved of these, Olympus Mons, rises 26 kilometres above the surface and is 550 kilometres across at its base. Mars shows evidence of erosional processes. Dust storms frequently obscure the surface. The large channels, such as the 5000 kilometre long Valles Marineris, may have been cut by flowing water. Water is abundant in the polar caps and may be widespread held in as perma-frost below the surface.

JUPITER has at least 16 satellites and a debris ring system. The outer atmosphere is all that can be directly observed. It is mostly hydrogen with lesser amounts of helium, ammonia, methane, water vapour and more exotic compounds. Jupiter's rapid rotation causes it to be flattened towards the poles. This rotation, and heat flow convection from the interior, cause complex weather patterns. Where cloud systems interact vast storms can occur. Some last only a few days, but the most persistent of these is the Great Red Spot which can be seen at the lower left centre in the image above. The internal structure of Jupiter can be deduced. At about 1000 kilometres below the cloud tops hydrogen and helium may liquify to form a 10,000 kilometre layer. Convection currents in this region generate the planet's intense magnetic field. The denser core, about 4 per cent of the planet's mass, is mostly of rock and ice, with a little iron near the centre.

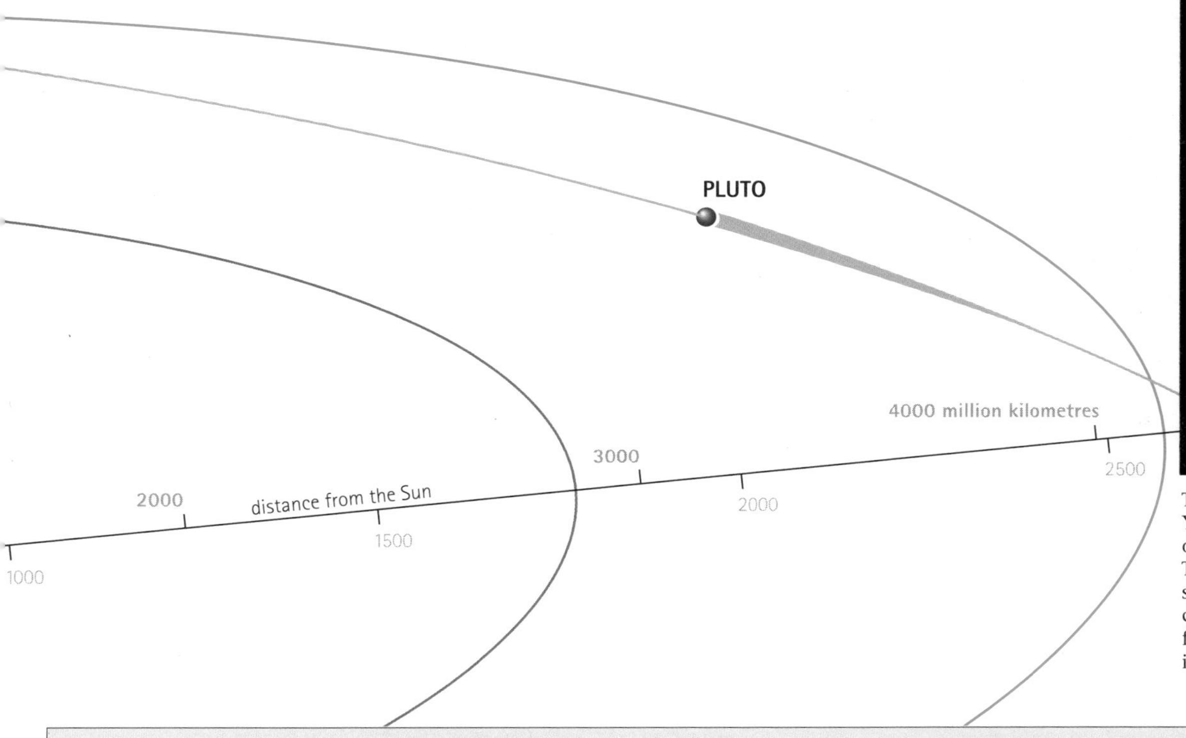

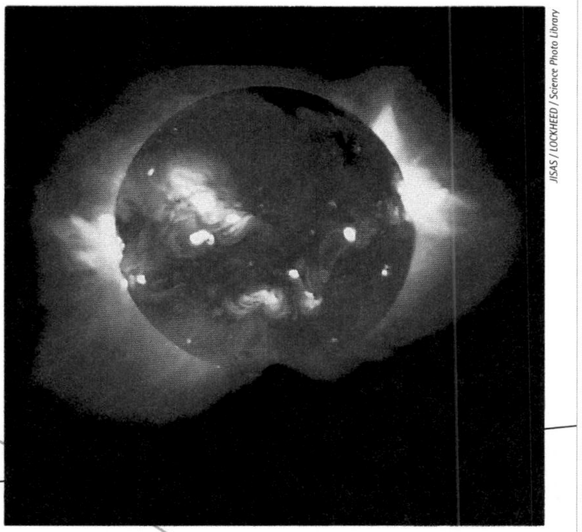

The Sun is seen above, in an x-ray image taken by the YOHKOH satellite in 1992. The image shows the activity of the outer layer of the solar atmosphere, the corona. The brightest areas are solar active regions where sunspots would be seen in visible light; the dark areas are coronal holes where gas density is extremely low and from which the solar wind, a stream of charged particles, is ejected into space.

	SUN	MERCURY	VENUS	EARTH	(MOON)	MARS	JUPITER	SATURN	URANUS	NEPTUNE	PLUTO
Mass (Earth=1)	333 400	0.055	0.815	1 (5.97 10^{24}kg)	0.012	0.107	317.8	95.2	14.5	17.2	0.003
Volume (Earth=1)	1 306 000	0.06	0.88	1	0.020	0.150	1 323	752	64	54	0.007
Density (water=1)	1.41	5.43	5.24	5.52	3.34	3.94	1.33	0.70	1.30	1.64	2.0
Equatorial diameter (km)	1 392 000	4 878	12 104	12 756	3 476	6 794	142 800	120 000	52 000	48 400	2 302
Polar flattening	0	0	0	0.003	0	0.005	0.065	0.108	0.060	0.021	0
'Surface' gravity (Earth=1)	27.9	0.37	0.88	1	0.16	0.38	2.69	1.19	0.93	1.22	0.05
Number of satellites greater than 100km in diameter	–	0	0	1	–	0	7	13	7	6	1
Total number of satellites	–	0	0	1	–	2	16	17	15	8	1
Period of rotation (in Earth days)	25.38	58.65	-243 (retrograde)	23hr 56m 4 secs	27.32	1.03	0.414	0.426	-0.74 (retrograde)	0.67	-6.39 (retrograde)
Length of year (in Earth days and years)	–	88 days	224.7 days	365.26 days	–	687 days	11.86 years	29.46 years	84.01 years	164.8 years	247.7 years
Distance from Sun (max) Mkm	–	69.7	109	152.1	–	249.1	815.7	1 507	3 004	4 537	7 375
Distance from Sun (min) Mkm	–	45.9	107.4	147.1	–	206.7	740.9	1 347	2 735	4 456	4 425
Distance from Sun (mean) Mkm	–	57.9	108.9	149.6	–	227.9	778.3	1 427	2 870	4 497	5 900
Mean orbital velocity km/sec	–	47.9	35.0	29.8	–	24.1	13.1	9.6	6.8	5.4	4.7
Inclination of equator to orbit plane	7.25°	0.0°	177.3°	23.45°	6.68°	25.19°	3.12°	26.73°	97.86°	29.56°	122°
Inclination of orbit to ecliptic	–	7.01°	3.39°	0°	5.15°	1.85°	1.30°	2.48°	0.77°	1.77°	17.13°

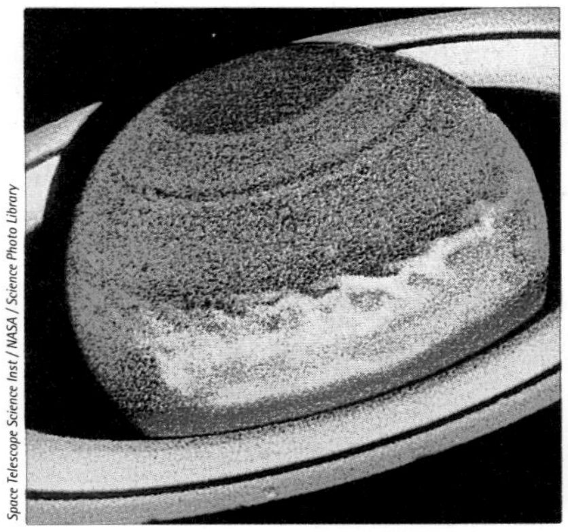

SATURN is the least dense of the planets. It has a stormy atmosphere situated above a 30,000 km layer of liquid molecular hydrogen and helium distorted by the planet's rotation. Below is a thin shell of liquid metallic hydrogen wrapped around a rock and ice core containing 25 per cent of Saturn's mass. The rings of Saturn are thought to be mostly made of icy debris, from 10 metres down to a few microns in size, derived from the break-up of one of its satellites. The rings are less than one kilometre thick but extend from above the cloud layer out to about 170,000 kilometres from the centre. The rings are divided by gaps swept clear by complex gravitational interaction. The Hubble Telescope image above shows an unusual, long-lived storm which first appeared in 1990. The storm is the elongated reddish-white region along the planet's equator.

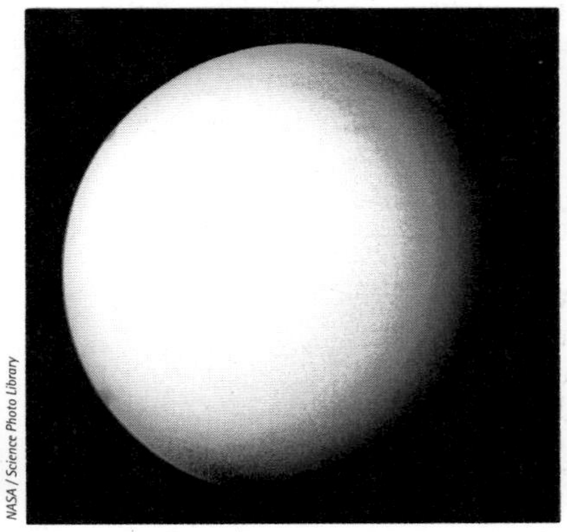

URANUS was little known until Voyager 2 flew past it in January 1986. It has a cloud cover even more featureless than either Jupiter or Saturn, and consists mostly of hydrogen. Unique among the planets, its axis is tilted almost into the plane of its orbit, with the south pole presently facing towards the Sun. Voyager 2 discovered ten more satellites and povided detailed images of the planet's eleven rings of icy debris. The above composite false-coloured image was taken from Voyager 2, 2.7 million kilometres from the planet. The pink areas centred on the poles are due to the presence of hazes high in the atmosphere. The blue areas at mid-latitudes are the most haze-free.

NEPTUNE provided a number of surprises when Voyager 2 flew past in August 1989, travelling within 5000 kilometres of the planet's north pole. It was discovered the planet rotates in 16 hours 3 minutes, one hour faster than was believed to be the rate. Six new satellites were discovered, all irregular in shape, and with impact craters little changed since soon after their formation. Neptune has four rings. The magnetic axis is inclined 50° to the axis of rotation and displaced 10,000 kilometres from the centre. Neptune's atmosphere, a mixture of hydrogen, helium and methane, exhibits great turbulence. The above, virtually true-colour, image, shows two prominent cloud features of this highly active atmosphere. To the left is the Great Dark Spot, a giant storm, which circuits the planet every 18.3 hours. A second, smaller dark spot (lower right) circuits the planet every 16.1 hours.

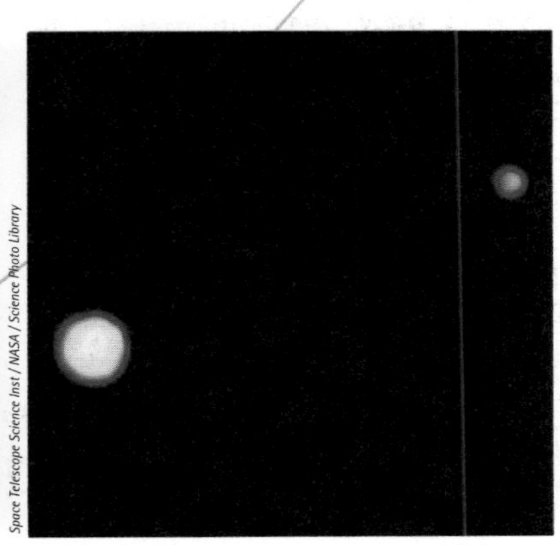

PLUTO, usually the most distant planet, is temporarily within the orbit of Neptune. The atmosphere is thought to be composed mostly of methane. The above image of Pluto (left) and its satellite, Charon, was taken by the Hubble Space Telescope in February 1994. Astronomers were able to see the two bodies clearly for the first time and to measure directly and accurately their diameters. When the image was taken Pluto was 4.4 billion kilometres from the Earth and 19,640 kilometres from Charon.

© Bartholomew

NORTHERN SKY

Star Magnitude

Each unit of magnitude indicates a difference of brightness of 2.512 times. The brightest star is Sirius (mag. −1.45).

0
1
2
3
4
5

Link Line

Variable star

Open star cluster

Globular star cluster

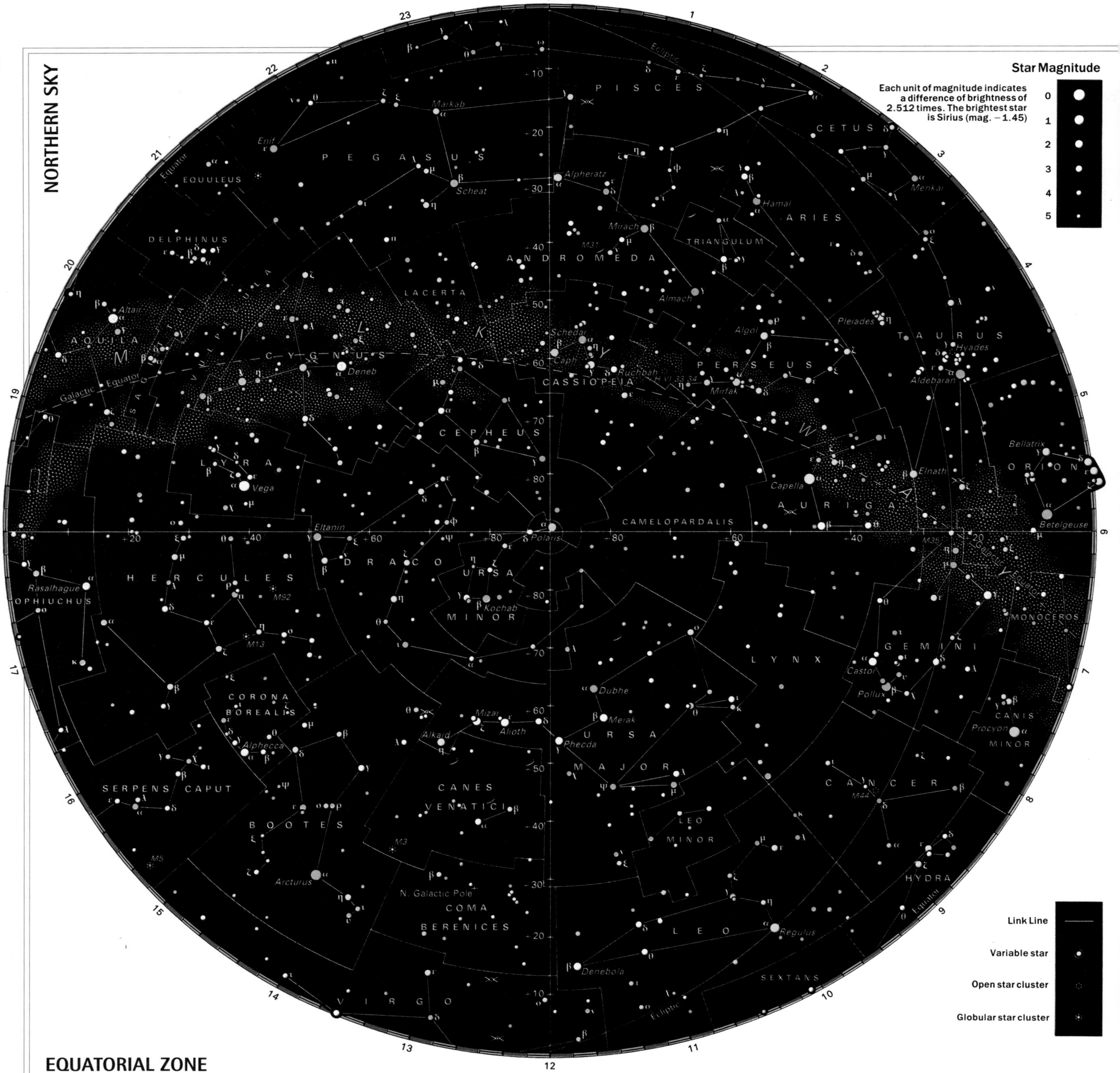

EQUATORIAL ZONE

Declination

+30°
+15°
0°
−15°
−30°

1 h 0 h 23 h 22 h 21 h 20 h 19 h Right 18 h Ascension 17 h 16 h 15 h 14 h 13 h

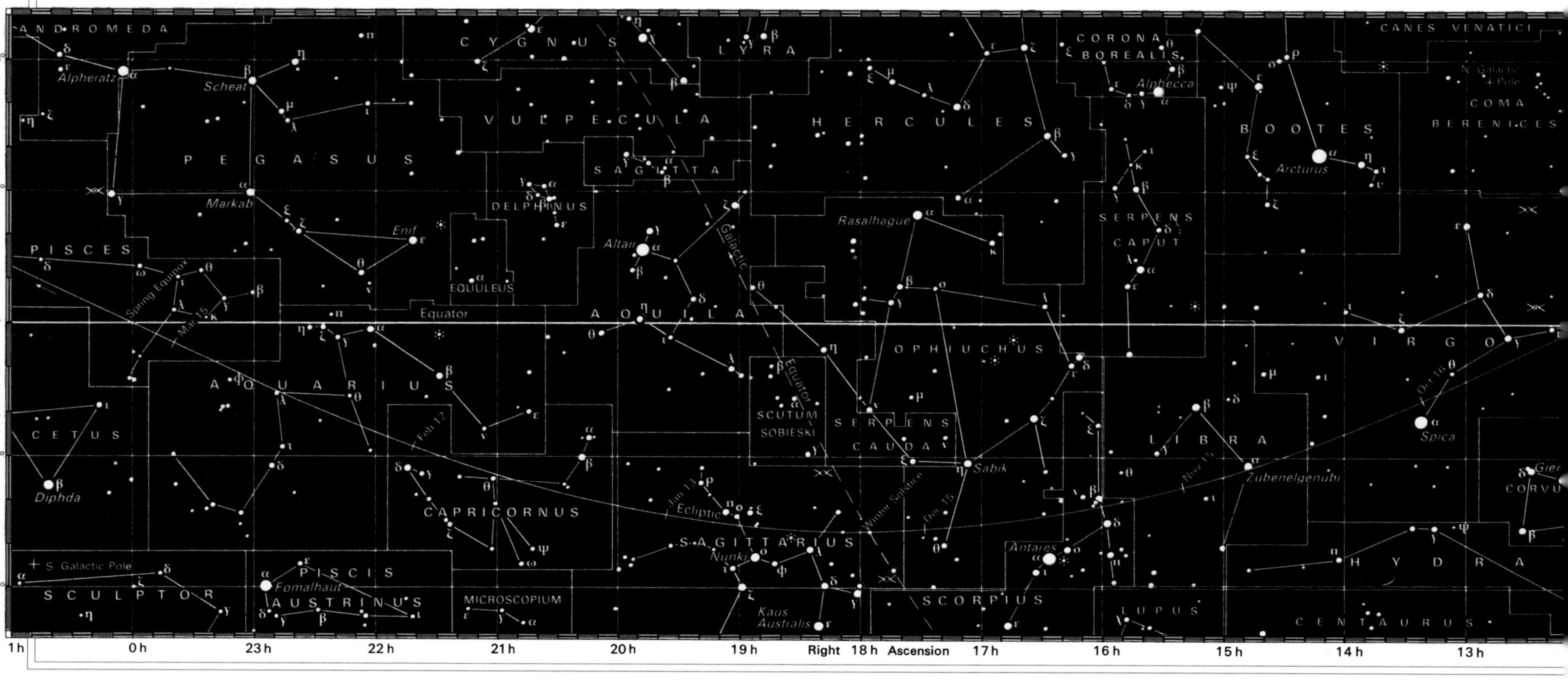

SOUTHERN SKY

Star Colours and Spectral Types

	* Temp in 000°C
O-B	50.0–25.0
A	11.0
F	7.5
G	6.0
K	5.0
M	3.5

The surface temperature of a star is indicated both by its colour and its spectrum

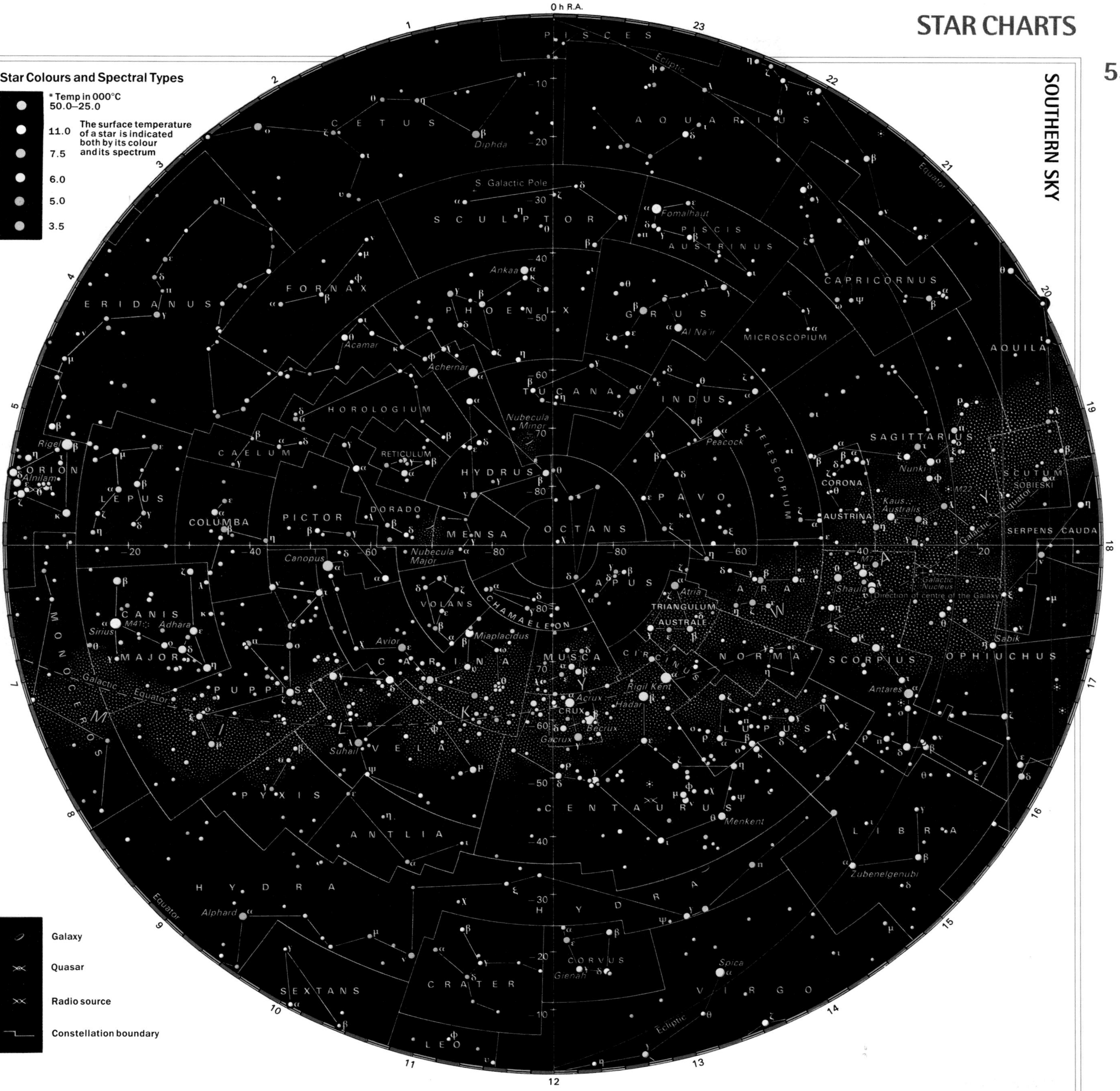

Key

Galaxy

Quasar

Radio source

Constellation boundary

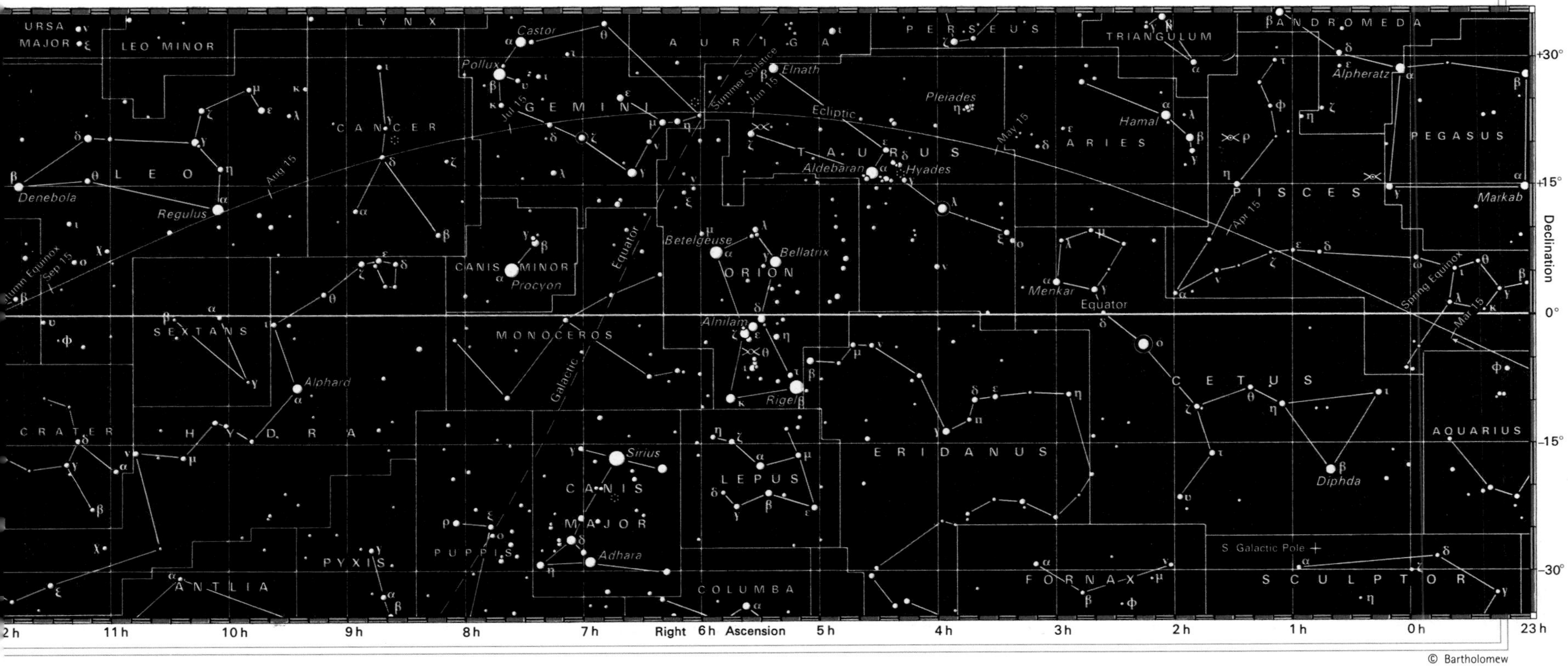

© Bartholomew

Equatorial Scale 1:66 000 000

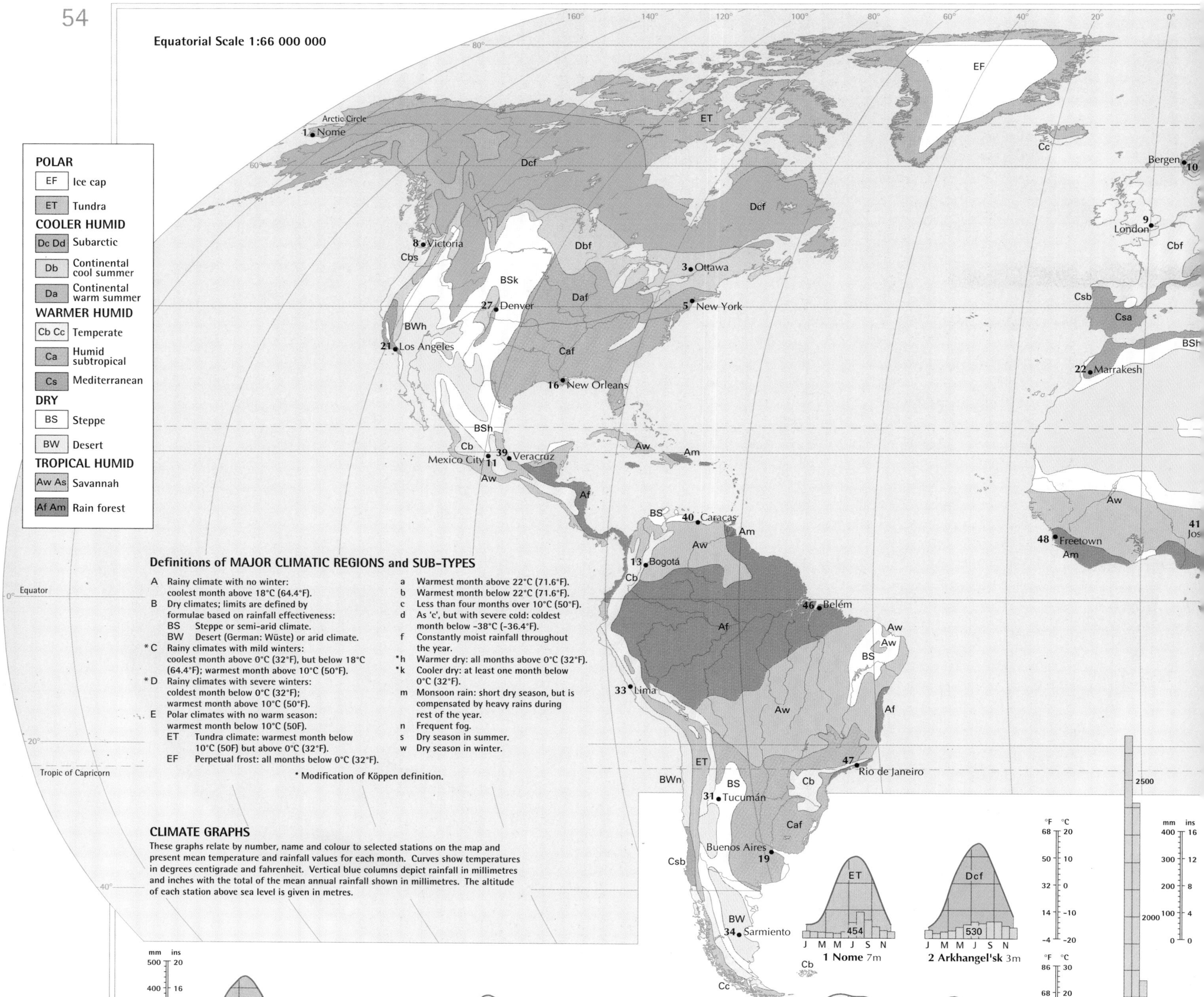
POLAR
EF Ice cap
ET Tundra
COOLER HUMID
Dc Dd Subarctic
Db Continental cool summer
Da Continental warm summer
WARMER HUMID
Cb Cc Temperate
Ca Humid subtropical
Cs Mediterranean
DRY
BS Steppe
BW Desert
TROPICAL HUMID
Aw As Savannah
Af Am Rain forest
Arctic Circle
1 Nome
Dcf
ET
EF
Cc
Bergen 10
9 London
Cbf
8 Victoria
Cbs
Dbf
3 Ottawa
5 New York
BSk
27 Denver
Daf
BWh
21 Los Angeles
Caf
16 New Orleans
Csb
Csa
BSh
22 Marrakesh
BSh
Cb
Mexico City 11
39 Veracruz
Aw
Am
Af
BS
40 Caracas
Am
Aw
48 Freetown
Am
41 Jos
13 Bogotá
Cb
46 Belém
Af
Aw
BS
33 Lima
Aw
Af
47 Rio de Janeiro
ET
BWn
BS
31 Tucumán
Cb
Caf
Csb
Buenos Aires 19
BW
34 Sarmiento
Cb
Cc
Equator
Tropic of Capricorn
80°
60°
40°
20°
0°
160°
140°
120°
100°

Definitions of MAJOR CLIMATIC REGIONS and SUB-TYPES

A Rainy climate with no winter: coolest month above 18°C (64.4°F).
B Dry climates; limits are defined by formulae based on rainfall effectiveness:
BS Steppe or semi-arid climate.
BW Desert (German: Wüste) or arid climate.
*C Rainy climates with mild winters: coolest month above 0°C (32°F), but below 18°C (64.4°F); warmest month above 10°C (50°F).
*D Rainy climates with severe winters: coldest month below 0°C (32°F); warmest month above 10°C (50°F).
E Polar climates with no warm season: warmest month below 10°C (50F).
ET Tundra climate: warmest month below 10°C (50F) but above 0°C (32°F).
EF Perpetual frost: all months below 0°C (32°F).

a Warmest month above 22°C (71.6°F).
b Warmest month below 22°C (71.6°F).
c Less than four months over 10°C (50°F).
d As 'c', but with severe cold: coldest month below −38°C (−36.4°F).
f Constantly moist rainfall throughout the year.
*h Warmer dry: all months above 0°C (32°F).
*k Cooler dry: at least one month below 0°C (32°F).
m Monsoon rain: short dry season, but is compensated by heavy rains during rest of the year.
n Frequent fog.
s Dry season in summer.
w Dry season in winter.

* Modification of Köppen definition.

CLIMATE GRAPHS

These graphs relate by number, name and colour to selected stations on the map and present mean temperature and rainfall values for each month. Curves show temperatures in degrees centigrade and fahrenheit. Vertical blue columns depict rainfall in millimetres and inches with the total of the mean annual rainfall shown in millimetres. The altitude of each station above sea level is given in metres.

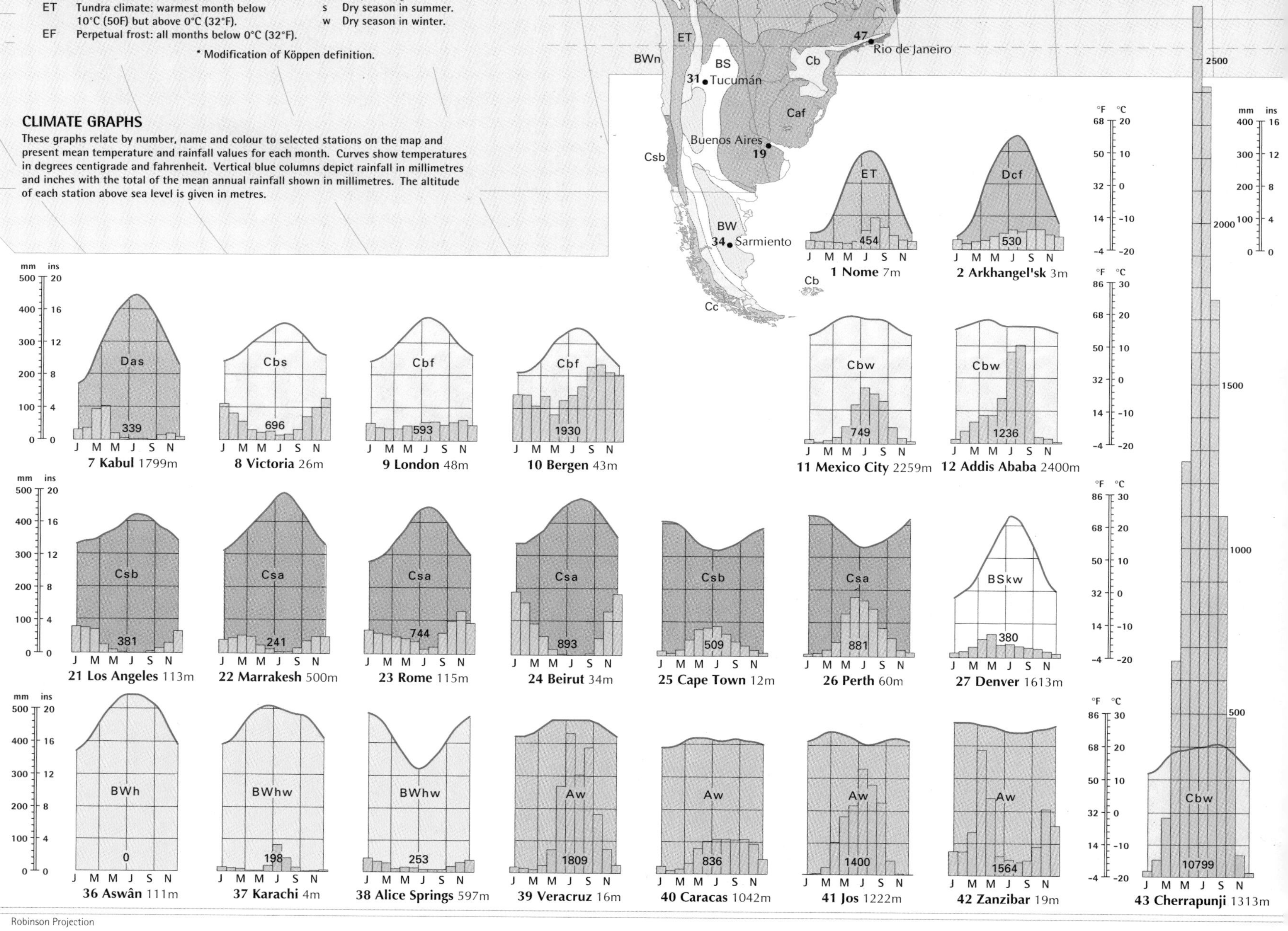
1 Nome 7m
ET 454
2 Arkhangel'sk 3m
Dcf 530
7 Kabul 1799m
Das 339
8 Victoria 26m
Cbs 696
9 London 48m
Cbf 593
10 Bergen 43m
Cbf 1930
11 Mexico City 2259m
Cbw 749
12 Addis Ababa 2400m
Cbw 1236
21 Los Angeles 113m
Csb 381
22 Marrakesh 500m
Csa 241
23 Rome 115m
Csa 744
24 Beirut 34m
Csa 893
25 Cape Town 12m
Csb 509
26 Perth 60m
Csa 881
27 Denver 1613m
BSkw 380
36 Aswân 111m
BWh 0
37 Karachi 4m
BWhw 198
38 Alice Springs 597m
BWhw 253
39 Veracruz 16m
Aw 1809
40 Caracas 1042m
Aw 836
41 Jos 1222m
Aw 1400
42 Zanzibar 19m
Aw 1564
43 Cherrapunji 1313m
Cbw 10799
J M M J S N
mm ins
°F °C

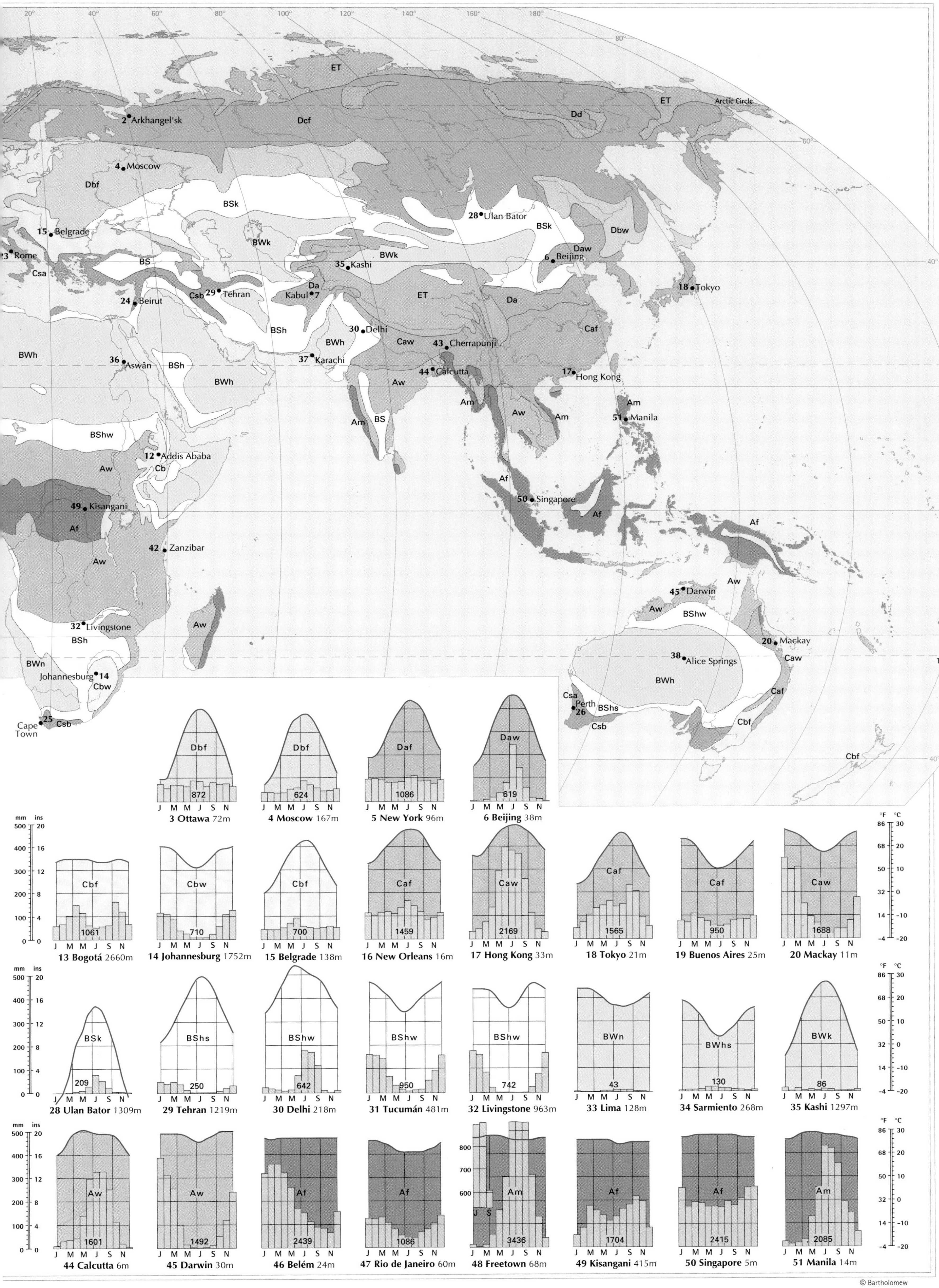

© Bartholomew

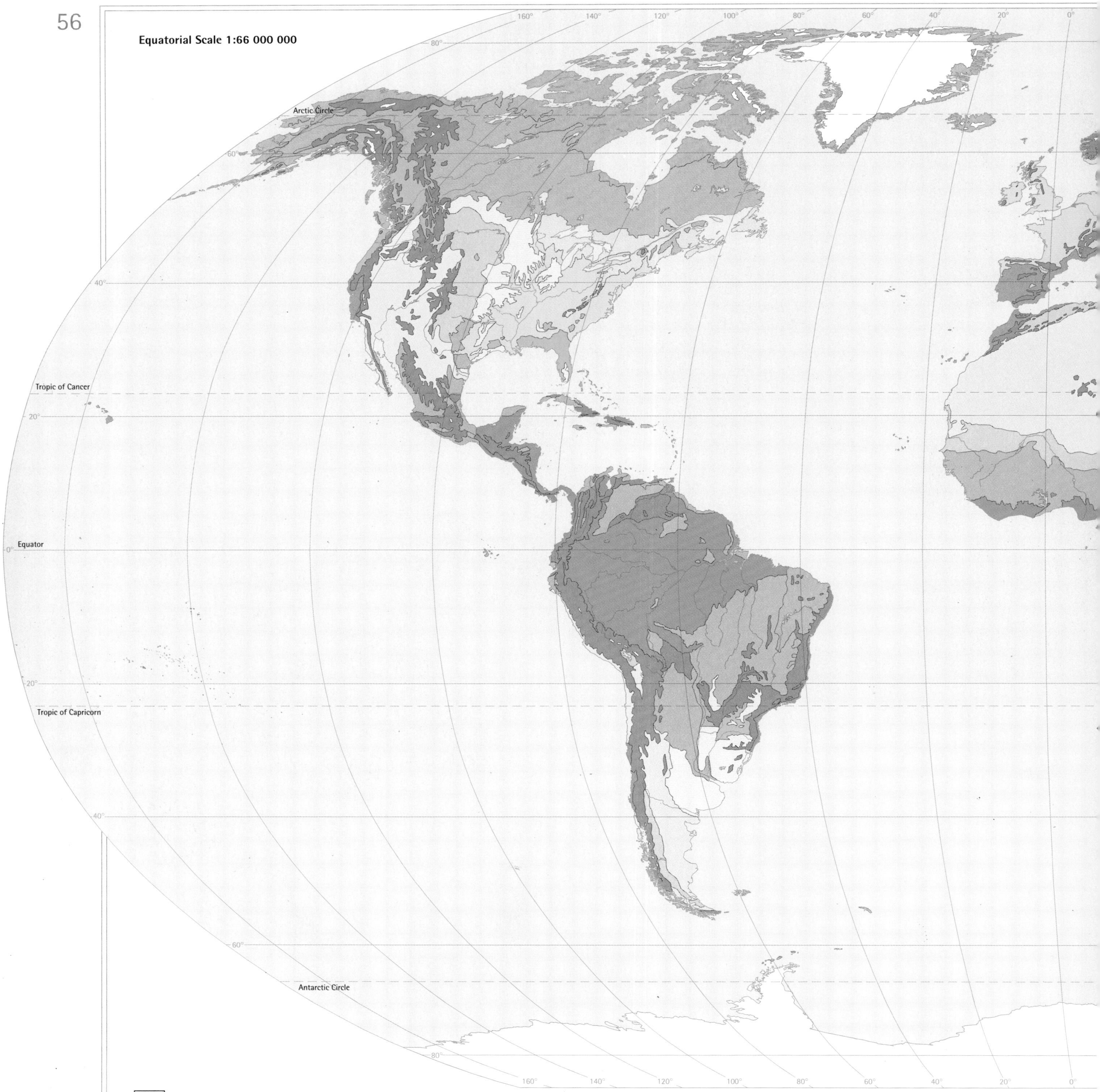

Ice cap and ice shelf

Mountain vegetation
Stunted vegetation growth found on mountains of mid- and high altitudes and at very high altitudes in tropical latitudes. Absence of trees apart from low growing forms of birch and willow. Mosses and lichens are abundant.

Tundra
Region of restricted plant growth confined mostly between latitudes north of 60° N and south of the polar ice cap. Vegetation is characterised by mosses, lichens, rushes, grasses and flowering herbs.

Boreal forest (Taiga)
Continuous zone in northern hemisphere found between latitudes 50° N and 70° N. Characteristic form of vegetation is the coniferous tree with the dominant species being pine, larch, spruce and fir.

Conifer forest
Different formations of coniferous forest to that of the boreal forest, found in western North America, southeastern USA and southern Brazil. Pine, spruce and larch are dominant.

Mixed forest, mid-latitudes
Transition zone in north-central Europe, east-central North America and eastern Asia with a mixture of areas of broadleaf trees and areas of conifer trees in almost equal numbers.

Broadleaf forest
Deciduous forest found mainly in the mid-latitudes of the northern hemisphere. Before 1500 a wide variety of species existed eg. oak, ash, beech, elm, maple, hickory, alder, and birch, but due to exploitation little original forest remains.

Mediterranean scrub
Areas of shrub dominated vegetation located in the Mediterranean basin and similar bio-climatic regions in coastal parts of California, Chile, South Africa and southern Australia. A variety of aromatic herbaceous plants grow beneath low shrub thickets, pines, oaks or gorse.

Prairie
Areas of grassland where long grasses are dominant, found in central North America, the Veld of eastern South Africa and the Pampas of Argentina. Sward grasses and bunch grasses grow up to 1 metre high.

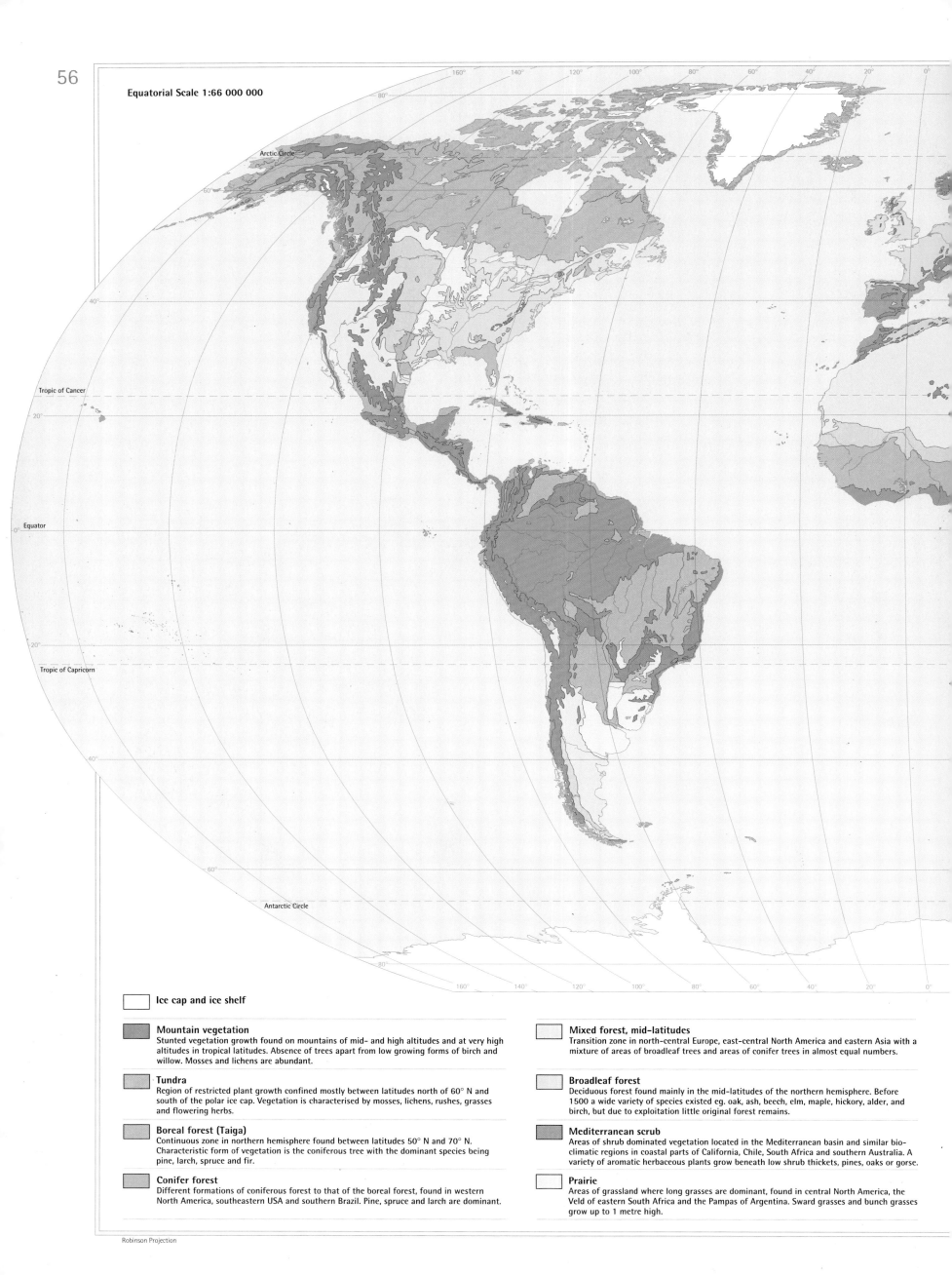

Robinson Projection

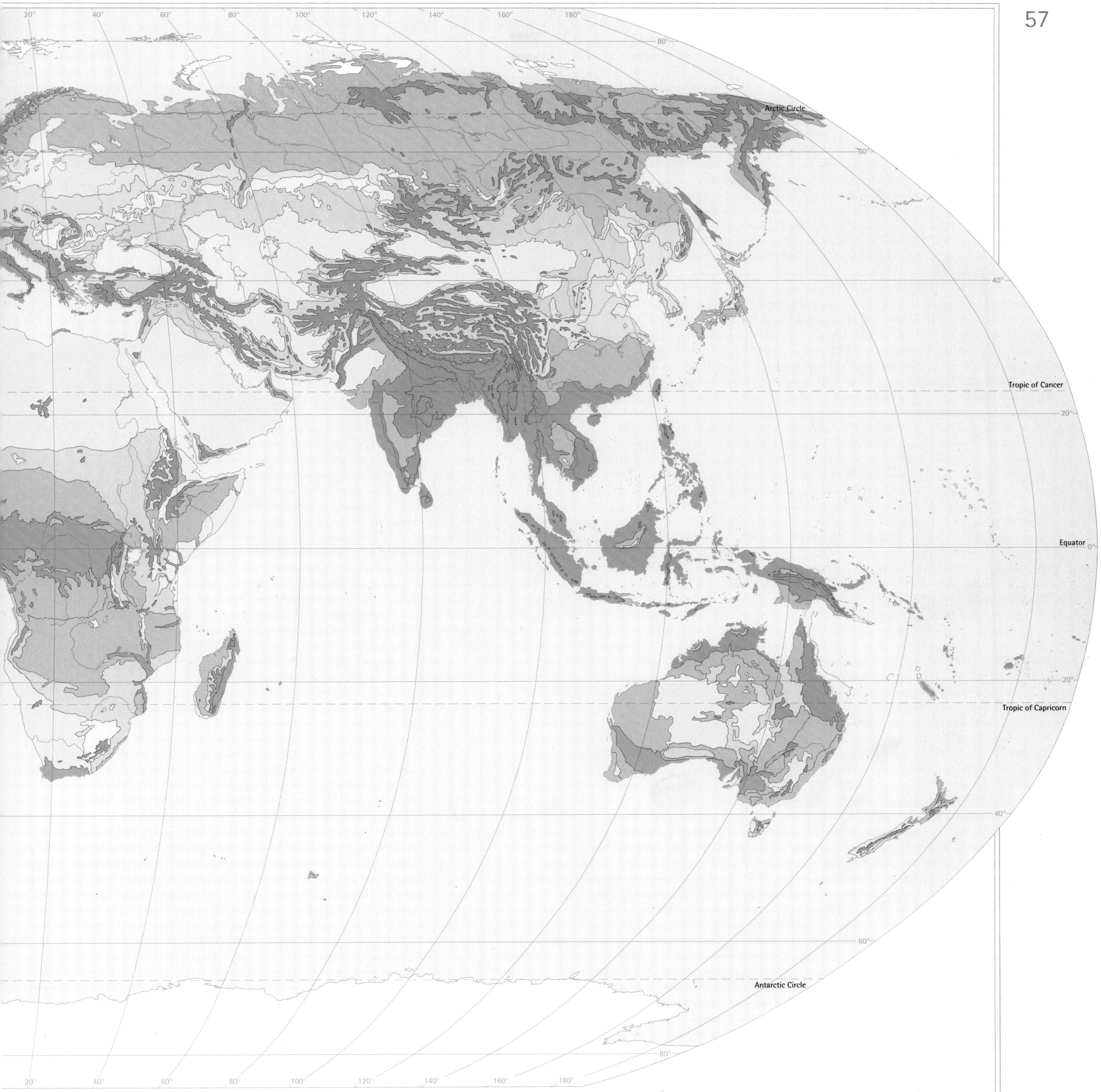

Steppe
Areas of grassland where short grasses are dominant, traditionally the wild grasslands of Euroasia but also found extensively in central North America, central and southern Africa and Australia. Drought resistant grasses grow with colourful flowering herbs.

Savannah
Grassland found in the tropics to the north and south of the tropical rain forests of South America and Africa and around the desert fringes of Australia. Grasses are interspersed with scattered thorn bushes or deciduous trees such as acacia in Africa and eucalypts in Australia.

Tropical rain forest (Selva)
Dense forest located in tropical areas of high rainfall and continuous high temperature, particularly Central America, northern South America, west-central Africa and southeast Asia. Up to three tree layers grow above a variable shrub layer.

Monsoon forest
Deciduous forest mostly occuring in eastern India, parts of Southeast Asia and northern and northeastern Australia, growing in association with the monsoon climate.

Dry tropical forest
Semi-deciduous forest growing in semi-desert areas of South America and the Indian sub-continent where rainfall is usually less than 250mm per annum. Thorny scrub and low to medium sized trees with thick bark and deep roots characterise the vegetation.

Sub-tropical forest
Hardleaf evergreen forests growing between the latitudes of 15° to 40° north and south of the equator in China, Japan, Australia, New Zealand and South Africa.

Dry tropical scrub and thorn forest
Low-growing widely spaced shrubs, bushes and succulents are characteristic of this vegetation growing in extensive areas of Central and South America, Africa, the Indian sub-continent and Australia.

Desert vegetation
Limited vegetation growth in the harsh, dry conditions of desert areas. Xerophytic shrubs, grasses and cacti adapt themselves by relying on the chance occurence of rain, storing water when it is available in short bursts and limiting water loss.

© Bartholomew

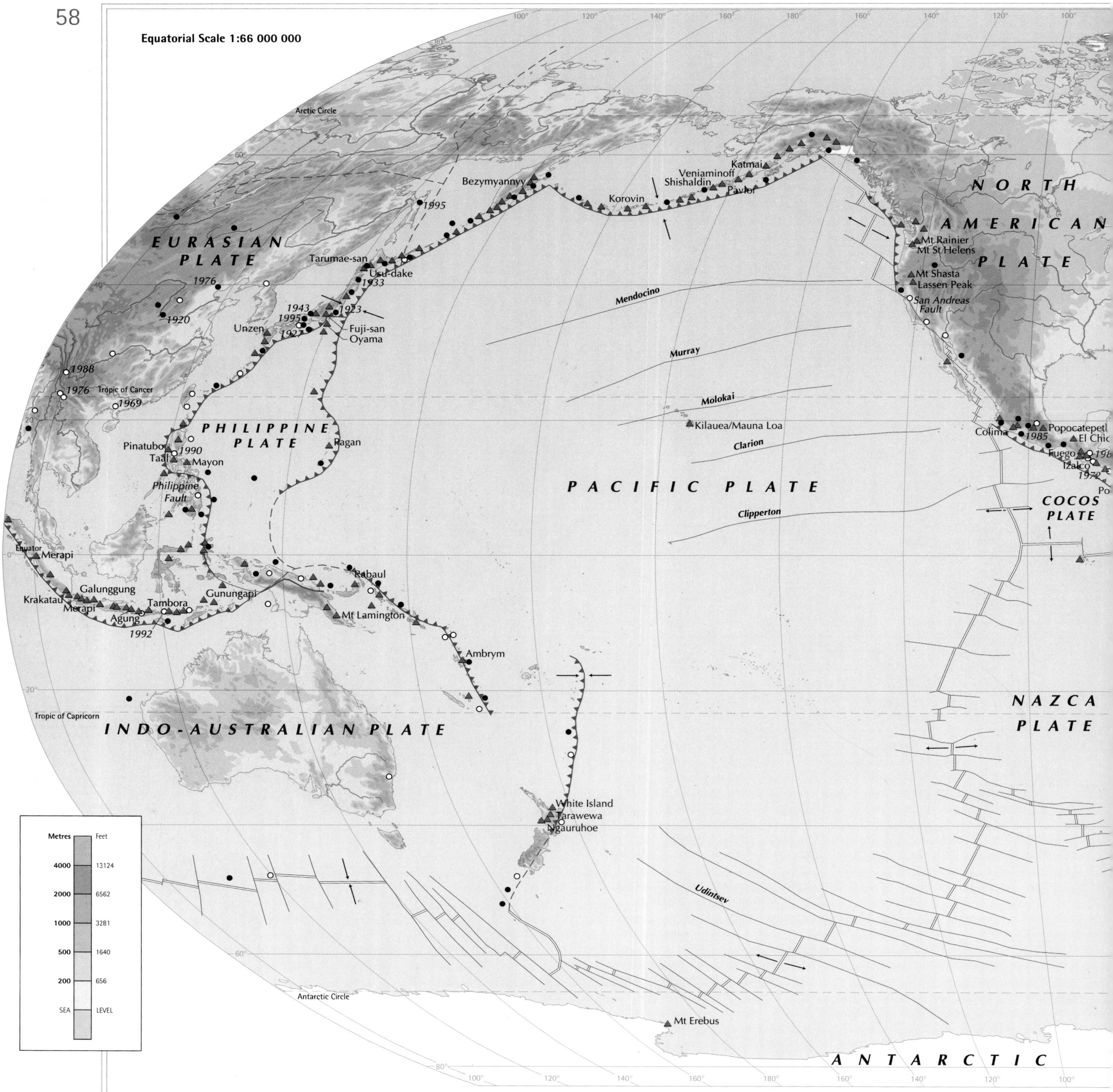

MAJOR EARTHQUAKES SINCE 1980

YEAR	LOCATION	*FORCE	DEATHS
1980	El Asnam, Algeria	7.7	4000
1980	Southern Italy	6.9	3000
1981	Kerman, Iran	7.3	2500
1982	El Salvador	7.4	16
1982	Dhamar, Yemen	6.0	3000
1983	Eastern Turkey	7.1	1500
1985	Santiago, Chile	7.8	177
1985	Xinjiang Uygur, China	7.4	63
1985	Michoacán, Mexico	8.1	20 000
1986	El Salvador	7.5	1000
1987	Ecuador	7.0	2000
1988	Yunnan, China	7.6	1000
1988	Armenia	6.9	25 000
1988	Nepal / India	6.9	1000
1989	San Francisco Bay, USA	7.1	67

YEAR	LOCATION	*FORCE	DEATHS
1990	Northwestern Iran	7.7	50 000
1990	Luzon, Philippines	7.7	1600
1991	Costa Rica / Panama	7.4	82
1991	Georgia	7.1	114
1991	Uttar Pradesh, India	6.1	1600
1992	Kyrgyzstan	7.5	50
1992	Flores, Indonesia	7.5	2500
1992	Erzincan, Turkey	6.8	500
1992	Cairo, Egypt	5.9	550
1993	Northern Japan	7.8	185
1993	Maharashtra, India	6.4	9700
1994	Northern Bolivia	8.3	10
1994	Kuril Islands, Japan	8.3	10
1995	Kobe, Japan	7.2	5200
1995	Sakhalin, Russian Fed	7.6	2500

* Richter scale

MAJOR VOLCANIC ERUPTIONS SINCE 1980

YEAR	LOCATION
1980	Mt St Helens, USA
1981	Hekla, Iceland
1982	El Chichón, Mexico
1983	Kilauea, Hawaii
1983	Oyama, Japan
1985	Nevado del Ruiz, Colombia
1986	Lake Nyos, Cameroon
1988	Gunungapi, Indonesia
1991	Pinatubo, Philippines
1991	Unzen-dake, Japan
1993	Mayon, Philippines
1993	Galeras, Colombia
1994	El Llaima, Chile
1994	Rabaul, PNG
1996	Ruapehu, New Zealand

Robinson Projection

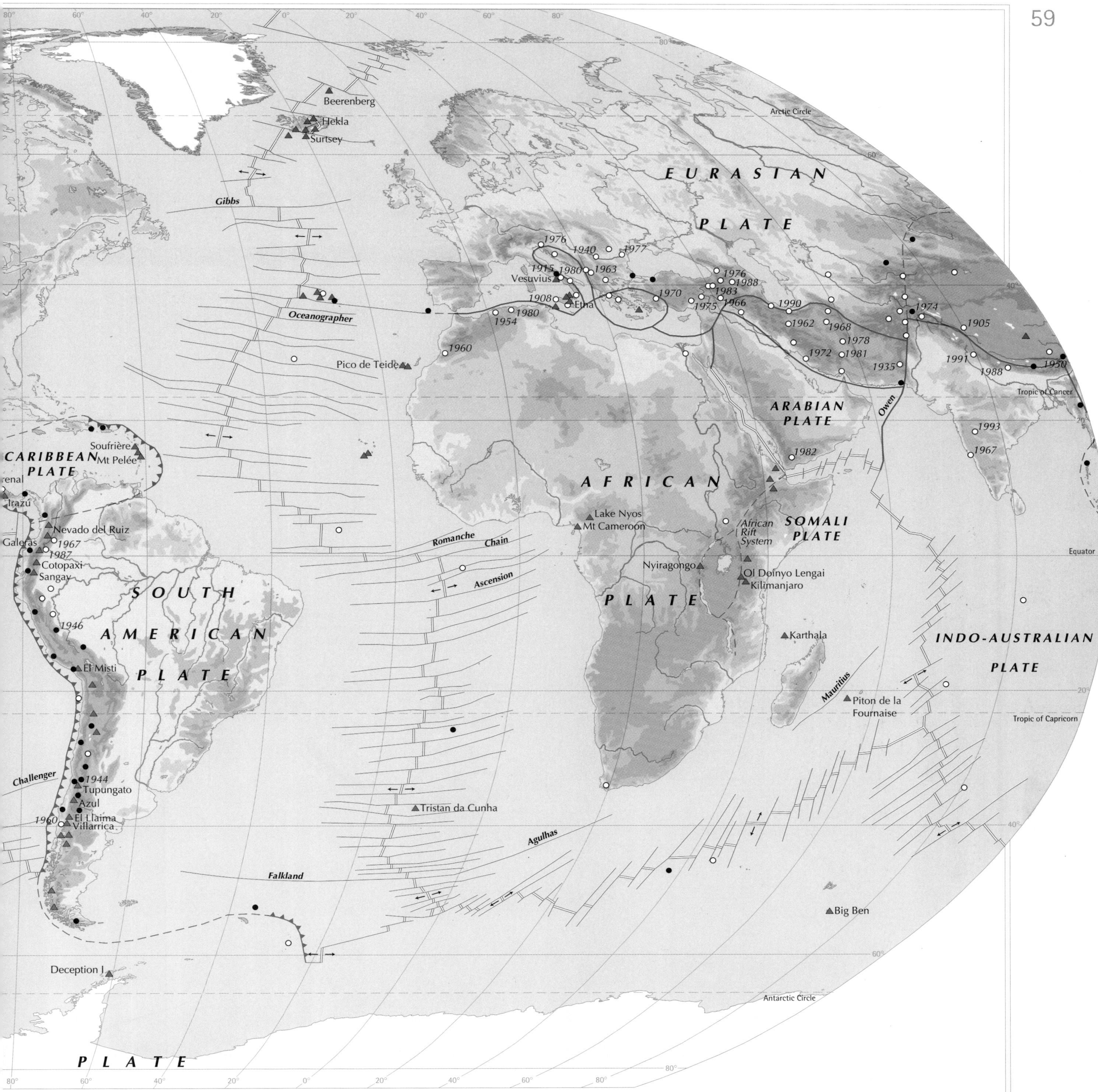

Subduction zone
Where a thick continental plate collides with a thin oceanic plate the latter descends beneath the former in a process known as subduction. Where two oceanic plates collide one plate may subduct under the other . Deep ocean trenches are formed where a convergence has taken place.

Collision zone
Where two continental plates converge the result is that the edge of one plate wedges under the other and throws up rocks from the continental crust which buckle and produce chains of fold mountains.

Spreading ridge
Where two oceanic plates drift apart the edges of the plates lift to form a ridge. Magma rises through the rift in the crust and cools quickly to form new crust. In this way mid-ocean ridges are created on the ocean floor.

Fracture zone
Where two plates move past each other horizontally they leave faults or fractures as a result. Friction between the plates results in a build up of strain. The stress is released either in small movements or sporadic large jolts.

Boundary uncertain

Earthquakes

- ● High magnitude earthquake (over 7.8 Richter scale)
- ○ Lesser magnitude earthquake
- *1954* Date of catastrophic earthquake (over 1000 deaths)

Most earthquakes occur near plate boundaries where there are sudden movements in the earth's crust. The most powerful earthquakes occur along fault lines and at collision zones.

Volcanoes

- ▲ Active volcano

Most volcanoes occur at subduction zones or spreading ridges where magma from inside the earth rises to the surface through a rift in the earth's crust and solidifies on the earth's surface.

Permanent ice

© Bartholomew

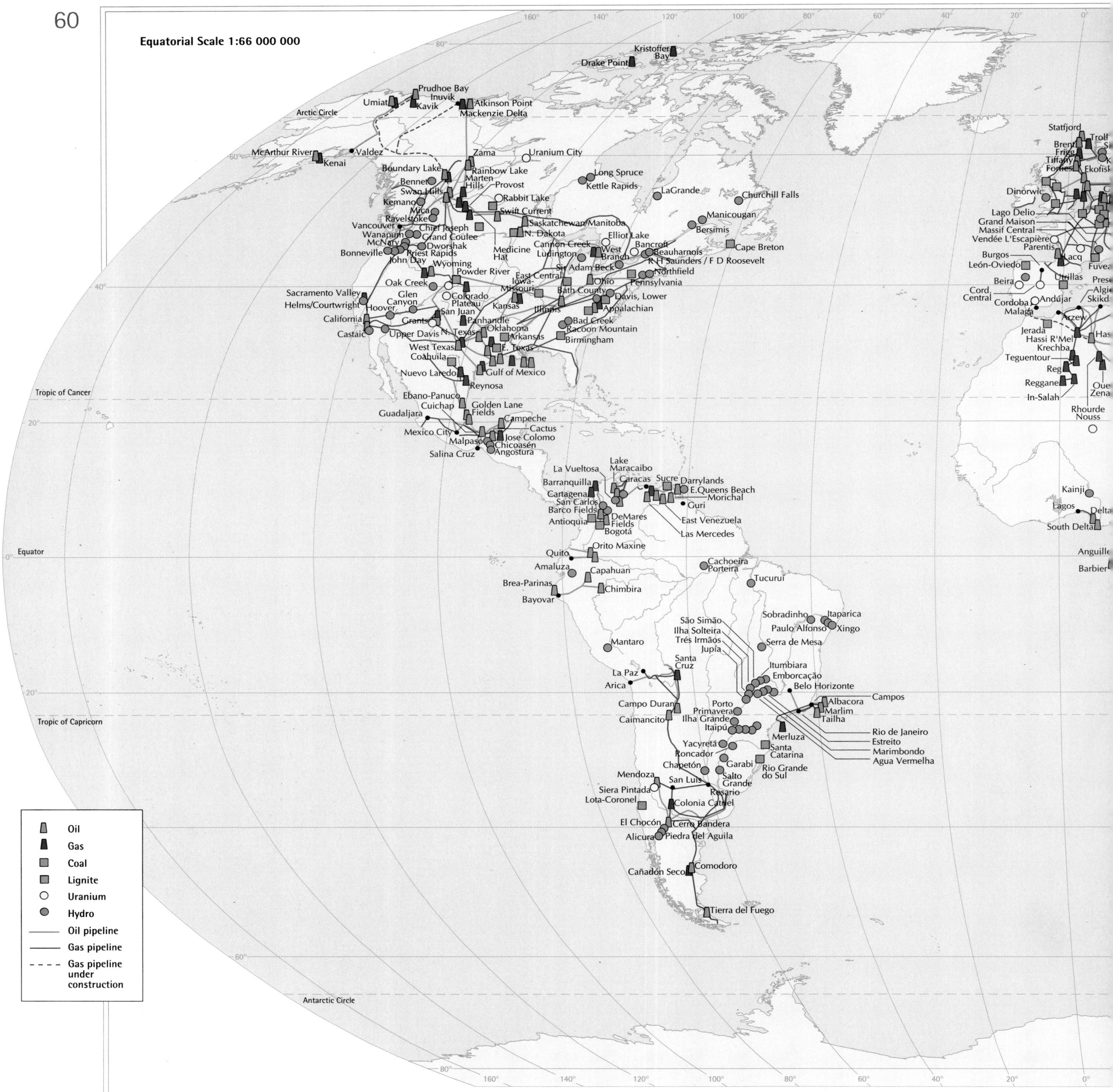
Equatorial Scale 1:66 000 000
Arctic Circle
Tropic of Cancer
Equator
Tropic of Capricorn
Antarctic Circle
Kristoffer Bay
Drake Point
Prudhoe Bay
Inuvik
Umiat
Kavik
Atkinson Point
Mackenzie Delta
McArthur River
Valdez
Kenai
Zama
Uranium City
Boundary Lake
Rainbow Lake
Marten Hills
Provost
Bennett
Swan Hills
Kemano
Rabbit Lake
Swift Current
Mica
Revelstoke
Chief Joseph
Saskatchewan/Manitoba
Vancouver
Wanapum
McNary
Grand Coulee
Dworshak
N. Dakota
Bonneville
Priest Rapids
John Day
Wyoming
Medicine Hat
Cannon Creek
Ludington
West Branch
Elliot Lake
Bancroft
Beauharnois
R H Saunders / F D Roosevelt
Northfield
Long Spruce
Kettle Rapids
LaGrande
Churchill Falls
Manicougan
Bersimis
Cape Breton
Powder River
Oak Creek
East Central
Iowa-Missouri
Sir Adam Beck
Ohio
Pennsylvania
Sacramento Valley
Helms/Courtwright
Glen Canyon
Colorado Plateau
Kansas
Bath County
Davis, Lower
Appalachian
Hoover
San Juan
Illinois
California
Grants
Panhandle
Bad Creek
Racoon Mountain
Castaic
Upper Davis
N. Texas
Oklahoma
Arkansas
Birmingham
West Texas
Coahuila
E. Texas
Nuevo Laredo
Gulf of Mexico
Reynosa
Ebano-Panuco
Cuichap
Golden Lane Fields
Guadaljara
Campeche
Mexico City
Cactus
Malpaso
Jose Colomo
Chicoasén
Angostura
Salina Cruz
La Vueltosa
Lake Maracaibo
Barranquilla
Caracas
Sucre
Darrylands
Cartagena
E.Queens Beach
Morichal
San Carlos
Barco Fields
Guri
DeMares Fields
Antioquia
Bogotá
East Venezuela
Las Mercedes
Orito Maxine
Quito
Amaluza
Capahuan
Cachoeira Porteira
Brea-Parinas
Chimbira
Tucuruí
Bayovar
Sobradinho
Itaparica
Paulo Alfonso
Xingo
São Simão
Ilha Solteira
Três Irmãos
Jupiá
Serra de Mesa
Mantaro
Santa Cruz
Itumbiara
Emborcação
La Paz
Belo Horizonte
Arica
Campos
Albacora
Marlim
Tailha
Campo Duran
Porto Primavera
Caimancito
Ilha Grande
Itaipú
Rio de Janeiro
Merluza
Estreito
Marimbondo
Agua Vermelha
Yacyretá
Santa Catarina
Roncador
Chapetón
Garabi
Rio Grande do Sul
Mendoza
Salto Grande
San Luis
Siera Pintada
Rosario
Lota-Coronel
Colonia Catriel
El Chocón
Cerro Bandera
Alicura
Piedra del Aguila
Cañadón Seco
Comodoro
Tierra del Fuego
Statfjord
Troll
Brent
Frigg
Tiffany
Forties
Ekofisk
Dinorwic
Lago Delio
Grand Maison
Massif Central
Vendée L'Escapière
Parentis
Lacq
Fuvea
Burgos
León-Oviedo
Beira
Utrillas
Cord Central
Cordoba
Andújar
Malaga
Arzew
Jerada
Hassi R'Mel
Krechba
Teguentour
Reg
Reggane
In-Salah
Rhourde Nouss
Kainji
Lagos
South Delta
Oil
Gas
Coal
Lignite
Uranium
Hydro
Oil pipeline
Gas pipeline
Gas pipeline under construction

Robinson Projection

PRIMARY ENERGY CONSUMPTION

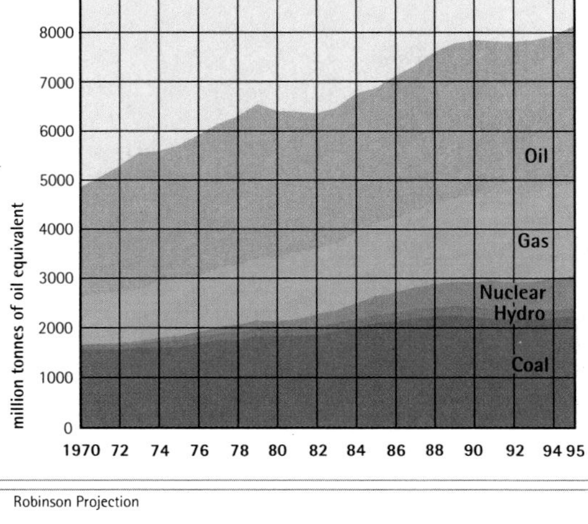
million tonnes of oil equivalent
9000
8000
7000
6000
5000
4000
3000
2000
1000
0
Oil
Gas
Nuclear
Hydro
Coal
1970 72 74 76 78 80 82 84 86 88 90 92 94 95

OIL CONSUMPTION

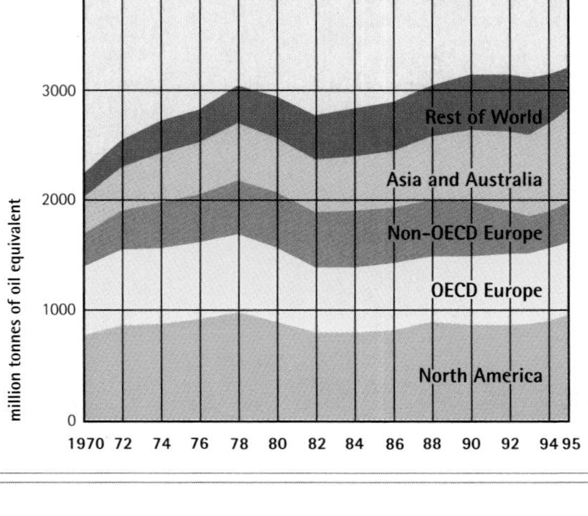
million tonnes of oil equivalent
4000
3000
2000
1000
0
Rest of World
Asia and Australia
Non-OECD Europe
OECD Europe
North America
1970 72 74 76 78 80 82 84 86 88 90 92 94 95

NUCLEAR ENERGY CONSUMPTION

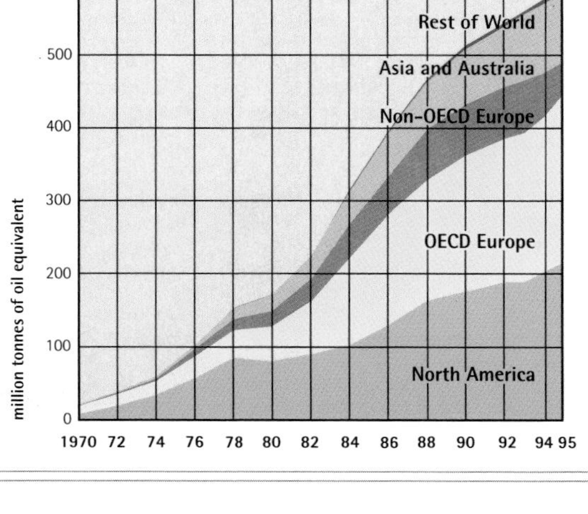
million tonnes of oil equivalent
600
500
400
300
200
100
0
Rest of World
Asia and Australia
Non-OECD Europe
OECD Europe
North America
1970 72 74 76 78 80 82 84 86 88 90 92 94 95

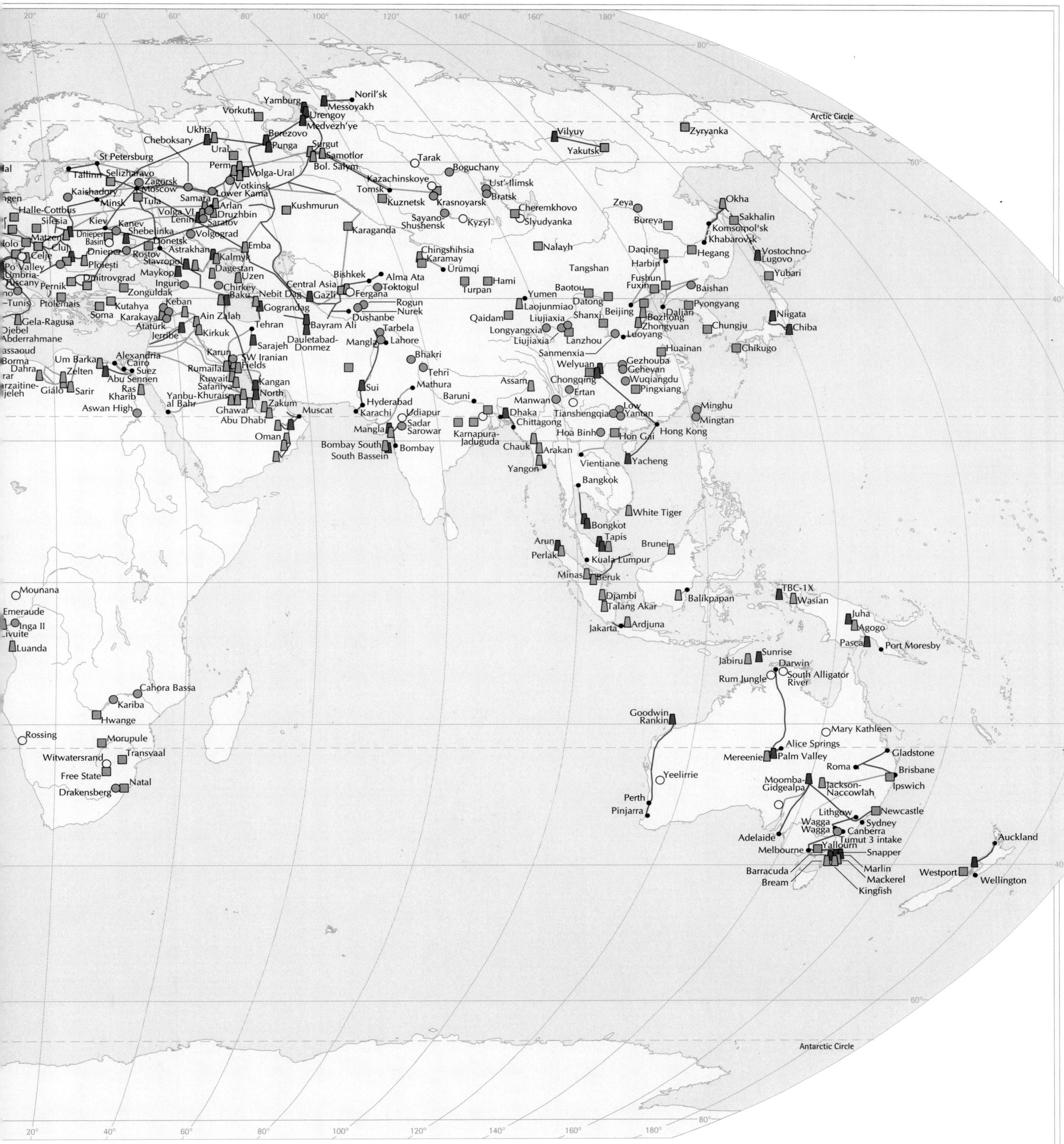

OIL RESERVES 1995
(thousand million tonnes)
Total - 138.3

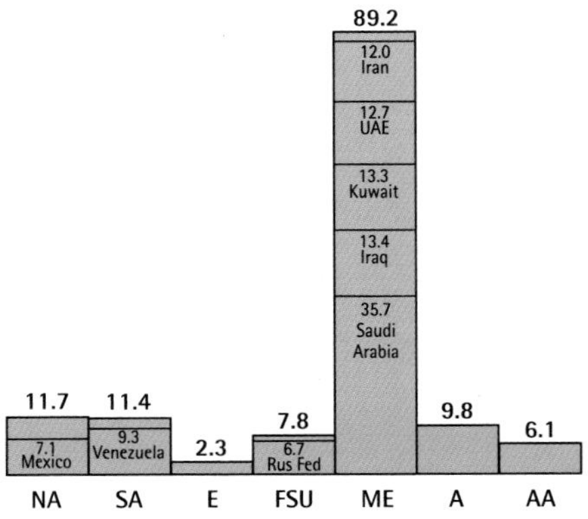

NATURAL GAS RESERVES 1995
(trillion cubic metres)
Total - 139.7

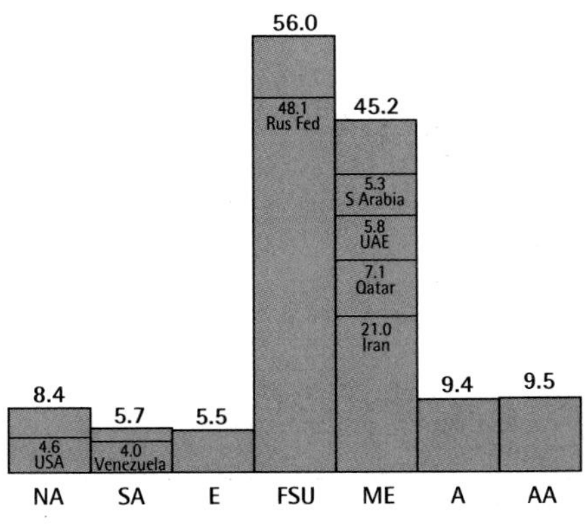

COAL RESERVES 1995
(thousand million tonnes)
Total - 1039

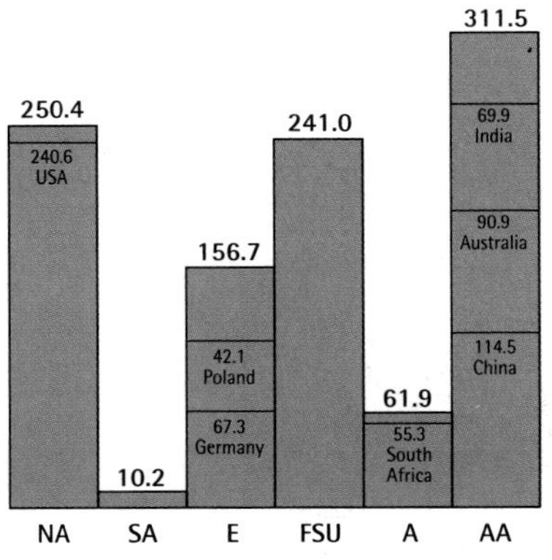

NA North America
SA South and Central America
E Europe
FSU Former Soviet Union
ME Middle East
A Africa
AA Asia and Australasia

© Bartholomew

Equatorial Scale 1:66 000 000

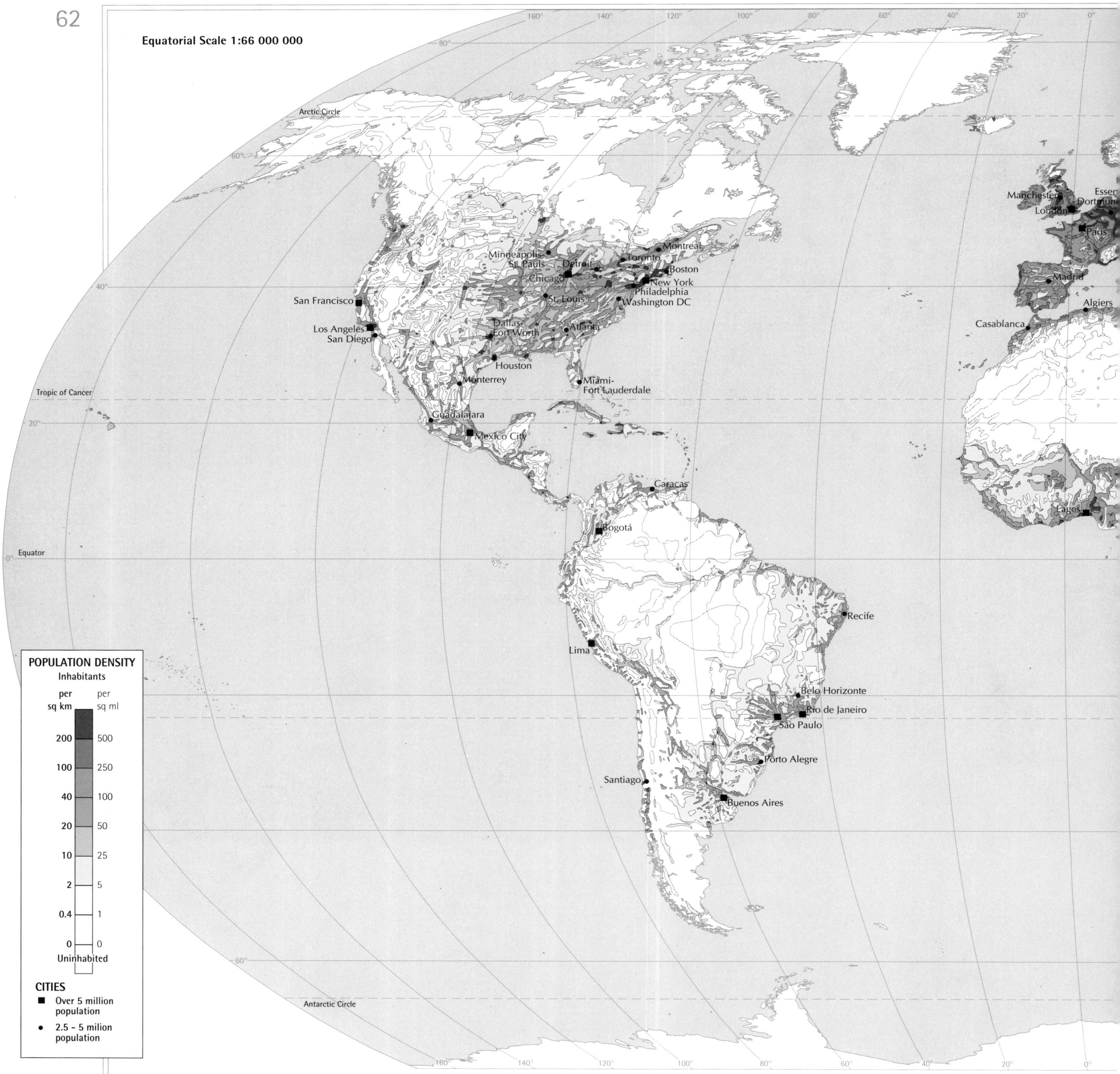

HIGHEST POPULATIONS 1995

	COUNTRY	POPULATION
1	China	1 221 462 000
2	India	935 744 000
3	USA	263 034 000
4	Indonesia	194 564 000
5	Brazil	155 822 000
6	Russian Federation	148 141 000
7	Pakistan	129 808 000
8	Japan	125 197 000
9	Bangladesh	120 433 000
10	Nigeria	111 721 000
11	Mexico	90 487 000
12	Germany	81 642 000
13	Vietnam	74 545 000
14	Philippines	70 267 000
15	Iran	67 283 000

HIGHEST DENSITIES 1995
(persons per sq km)

	COUNTRY	DENSITY
1	Macau	24 588
2	Monaco	16 410
3	Singapore	4 674
4	Gaza	2 083
5	Malta	1 174
6	Bermuda	1 167
7	Maldives	852
8	Bahrain	848
9	Bangladesh	836
10	Barbados	614
11	Taiwan	586
12	Mauritius	550
13	Nauru	524
14	South Korea	452
15	San Marino	410

URBAN / RURAL POPULATIONS 1994
(by continent)

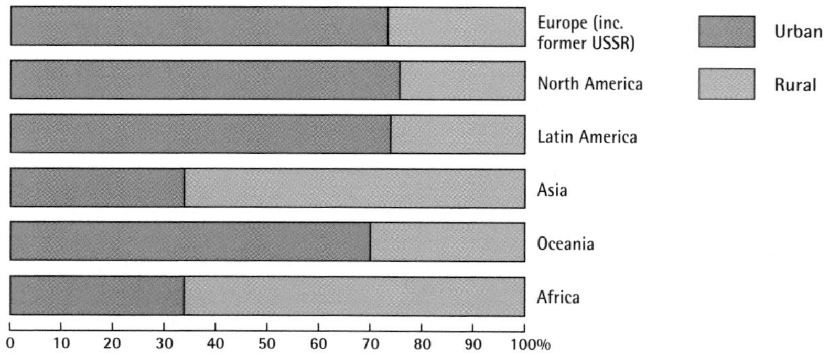

Robinson Projection

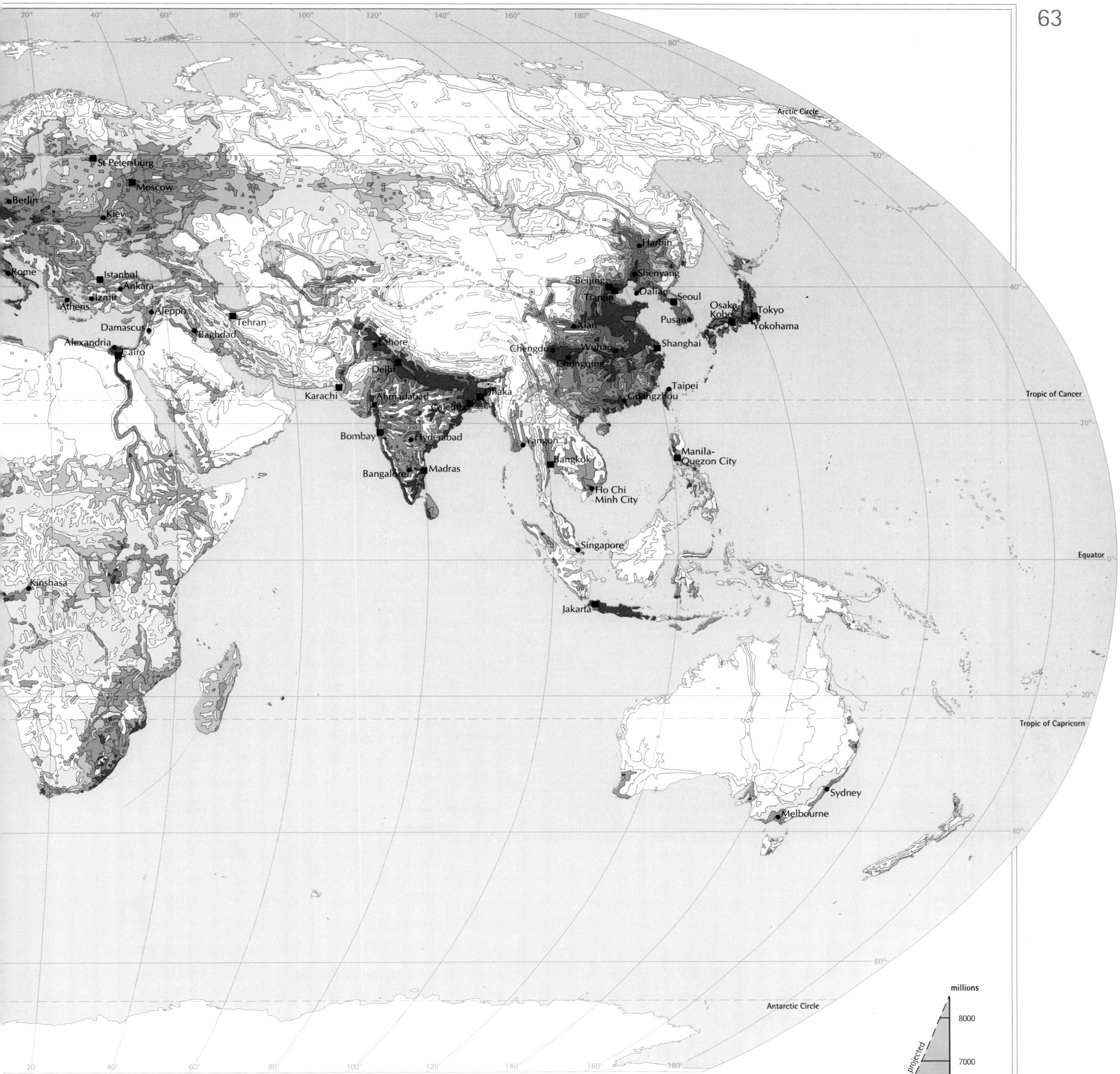

FASTEST GROWING POPULATIONS

(average % per annum 1990-1995)

	COUNTRY	GROWTH
1	Afghanistan	5.83
2	Andorra	5.50
3	Yemen	4.97
4	Jordan	4.89
5	Gaza	4.80
6	French Guiana	4.53
7	Oman	4.23
8	Turks and Caicos Is	3.85
9	The Gambia	3.83
10	Israel	3.78
11	Nicaragua	3.74
12	Angola	3.72
13	Comoros	3.68
14	Macau	3.62
15	Kenya	3.59

POPULATION GROWTH

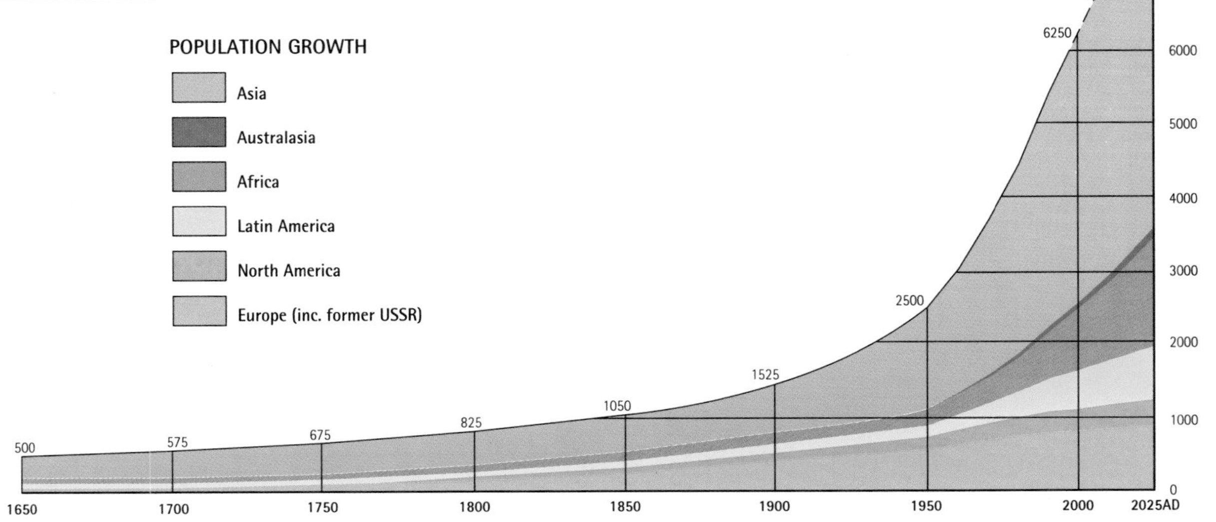

© Bartholomew

METROPOLITAN AREAS

A metropolitan area is a continuous built-up area which may include a number of cities and towns. The population given for the selected metropolitan areas below is from the latest available sources.

POPULATIONS OVER 10 MILLION

Population	Metropolitan area and country
20,200,000	**MEXICO CITY** MEXICO
16,972,000	**NEW YORK** USA
15,199,423	**SÃO PAULO** BRAZIL
13,341,896	**SHANGHAI** CHINA
12,571,720	**BOMBAY** INDIA
12,200,000	**BUENOS AIRES** ARGENTINA
11,642,000	**CAIRO** EGYPT
11,609,735	**TOKYO** JAPAN
11,420,000	**LOS ANGELES** USA
10,916,272	**CALCUTTA** INDIA
10,819,407	**BEIJING** CHINA
10,627,000	**SEOUL** SOUTH KOREA

Population	Metropolitan areas by country
	AFGHANISTAN
2,000,000	KABUL
	ALGERIA
3,033,000	ALGIERS
	ANGOLA
1,717,000	LUANDA
	ARGENTINA
12,200,000	BUENOS AIRES
1,179,067	CORDOBA
1,078,374	ROSARIO
	ARMENIA
1,200,000	YEREVAN
	AUSTRALIA
1,065,000	ADELAIDE
1,386,000	BRISBANE
3,178,000	MELBOURNE
1,215,000	PERTH
3,700,000	SYDNEY
	AUSTRIA
1,565,800	VIENNA
	AZERBAIJAN
1,779,500	BAKU
	BANGLADESH
2,040,663	CHITTAGONG
6,105,160	DHAKA
	BELARUS
1,633,600	MINSK
	BOLIVIA
1,234,000	LA PAZ
	BRAZIL
1,334,460	BELEM
3,461,905	BELO HORIZONTE
1,596,274	BRASILIA
1,975,624	CURITIBA
2,294,524	FORTALEZA
3,015,960	PORTO ALEGRE
2,859,469	RECIFE
9,600,528	RIO DE JANEIRO
2,472,131	SALVADOR
15,199,423	SÃO PAULO
	BULGARIA
1,221,000	SOFIA
	CANADA
3,127,000	MONTREAL
3,893,000	TORONTO
1,603,000	VANCOUVER
	CHILE
4,628,320	SANTIAGO
	CHINA
1,370,000	ANSHAN
1,257,000	BAOTOU
10,819,407	BEIJING
2,214,000	CHANGCHUN
1,362,000	CHANGSHA
3,004,000	CHENGDU
3,151,000	CHONGQING
2,543,000	DALIAN
1,420,000	FUSHUN
1,361,000	FUZHOU
3,671,000	GUANGZHOU
1,587,000	GUIYANG
1,412,000	HANGZHOU
2,966,000	HARBIN
5,574,000	HONG KONG
1,170,000	HUAINAN
1,327,000	JILIN
2,415,000	JINAN
1,718,000	KUNMING
1,566,000	LANZHOU
1,227,000	LUOYANG
1,415,000	NANCHANG
2,265,000	NANJING
2,040,000	QINGDAO
1,460,000	QIQIHAR
13,341,896	SHANGHAI
4,763,000	SHENYANG
1,352,000	SHIJIAZHUANG
2,199,000	TAIYUAN
1,590,000	TANGSHAN
9,371,000	TIANJIN
3,921,000	WUHAN
2,859,000	XIAN
1,759,000	ZHENGZHOU
2,430,000	ZIBO
	COLOMBIA
1,033,951	BARRANQUILLA
5,025,989	BOGOTA
1,655,699	CALI
1,594,967	MEDELLIN
	CONGO (ZAIRE)
3,505,000	KINSHASA
	CÔTE D'IVOIRE
2,168,000	ABIDJAN
	CUBA
2,099,000	HAVANA
	CZECH REPUBLIC
1,214,174	PRAGUE
	DENMARK
1,342,679	COPENHAGEN
	DOMINICAN REPUBLIC
2,055,000	SANTO DOMINGO
	ECUADOR
1,508,444	GUAYAQUIL
1,100,847	QUITO
	EGYPT
3,380,000	ALEXANDRIA
11,642,000	CAIRO
2,096,000	EL GIZA
	EL SALVADOR
1,522,126	SAN SALVADOR
	ETHIOPIA
1,891,000	ADDIS ABABA
	FRANCE
1,230,936	MARSEILLES
9,318,821	PARIS
	GEORGIA
1,400,000	TBILISI
	GERMANY
3,447,916	BERLIN
2,720,400	ESSEN-DORTMUND
1,669,000	HAMBURG
1,236,500	MUNICH
	GREECE
3,097,000	ATHENS
	GUATEMALA
1,132,730	GUATEMALA CITY
	HAITI
1,402,000	PORT-AU-PRINCE
	HUNGARY
1,992,343	BUDAPEST
	INDIA
3,297,655	AHMADABAD
4,086,548	BANGALORE
12,571,720	BOMBAY
10,916,272	CALCUTTA
8,375,188	DELHI
4,280,261	HYDERABAD
1,514,425	JAIPUR
2,111,284	KANPUR
1,642,134	LUCKNOW
5,361,468	MADRAS
1,661,409	NAGPUR
2,485,014	PUNE
	INDONESIA
2,056,915	BANDUNG
9,253,000	JAKARTA
1,730,052	MEDAN
1,249,230	SEMARANG
2,473,272	SURABAYA
	IRAN
1,484,000	ISFAHAN
1,882,000	MASHHAD
6,773,000	TEHRAN
	IRAQ
4,044,000	BAGHDAD
	ISRAEL
1,135,800	TEL AVIV
	ITALY
1,358,627	MILAN
1,071,744	NAPLES
2,723,327	ROME
	JAPAN
1,214,122	FUKUOKA
1,071,898	HIROSHIMA
1,167,604	KAWASAKI
1,015,431	KITAKYUSHU
1,394,964	KYOTO
2,095,393	NAGOYA
8,520,000	OSAKA-KOBE
1,704,135	SAPPORO
11,609,735	TOKYO
3,250,548	YOKOHAMA
	JORDAN
1,272,000	AMMAN
	KAZAKHSTAN
1,151,300	ALMA-ATA
	KENYA
1,503,000	NAIROBI
	LEBANON
1,500,000	BEIRUT
	LIBYA
1,500,000	TRIPOLI
	MALAYSIA
1,711,000	KUALA LUMPUR
	MEXICO
2,846,720	GUADALAJARA
20,200,000	MEXICO CITY
2,521,697	MONTERREY
1,267,000	PUEBLA DE ZARAGOZA
	MOROCCO
3,210,000	CASABLANCA
1,472,000	RABAT
	MOZAMBIQUE
1,098,000	MAPUTO
	MYANMAR
3,295,000	RANGOON
	NETHERLANDS
1,091,338	AMSTERDAM
1,069,356	ROTTERDAM
	NIGERIA
5,689,000	LAGOS
	NORTH KOREA
2,230,000	PYONGYANG
	PAKISTAN
1,507,000	FAISALABAD
7,702,000	KARACHI
4,092,000	LAHORE
1,099,000	RAWALPINDI
	PERU
6,483,901	LIMA
	PHILIPPINES
7,832,000	MANILA - QUEZON CITY
	POLAND
1,655,700	WARSAW
	PORTUGAL
1,742,000	LISBON
1,314,794	OPORTO
	PUERTO RICO
1,390,000	SAN JUAN
	REP OF SOUTH AFRICA
2,350,157	CAPE TOWN
1,137,378	DURBAN
1,916,063	JOHANNESBURG
	ROMANIA
2,350,984	BUCHAREST
	RUSSIAN FEDERATION
1,143,000	CHELYABINSK
1,104,000	KAZAN
8,957,000	MOSCOW
1,441,000	NIZHNIY NOVGOROD
1,442,000	NOVOSIBIRSK
1,269,000	OMSK
1,099,000	PERM
1,027,000	ROSTOV-ON-DON
1,239,000	SAMARA
5,004,000	ST PETERSBURG
1,097,000	UFA
1,006,000	VOLGOGRAD
1,371,000	YEKATERINBURG
	SAUDI ARABIA
1,800,000	JEDDAH
1,500,000	RIYADH
	SENEGAL
1,492,000	DAKAR
	SINGAPORE
2,874,000	SINGAPORE
	SOUTH KOREA
1,818,293	INCHON
3,797,566	PUSAN
10,627,000	SEOUL
2,228,834	TAEGU
	SPAIN
1,625,542	BARCELONA
2,909,792	MADRID
	SUDAN
1,947,000	KHARTOUM
	SWEDEN
1,669,840	STOCKHOLM
	SYRIA
2,768,000	ALEPPO
2,913,000	DAMASCUS
	TAIWAN
1,400,000	KAOHSIUNG
2,720,000	TAIPEI
	TANZANIA
1,657,000	DAR-ES-SALAAM
	THAILAND
5,876,000	BANGKOK
	TUNISIA
1,636,000	TUNIS
	TURKEY
3,022,236	ANKARA
6,407,215	ISTANBUL
2,665,105	IZMIR
	UK
2,329,600	BIRMINGHAM
1,784,000	LEEDS
1,440,900	LIVERPOOL
9,227,687	LONDON
2,578,900	MANCHESTER
	UKRAINE
1,187,000	DNEPROPETROVSK
1,117,000	DONETSK
1,618,000	KHARKOV
2,616,000	KIEV
1,106,000	ODESSA
	URUGUAY
1,383,660	MONTEVIDEO
	USA
3,051,000	ATLANTA
2,414,000	BALTIMORE
4,497,000	BOSTON
1,193,000	BUFFALO
7,498,000	CHICAGO
1,539,000	CINCINNATI
2,213,000	CLEVELAND
1,370,000	COLUMBUS
4,135,000	DALLAS - FORT WORTH
1,668,000	DENVER
4,285,000	DETROIT
3,437,000	HOUSTON
1,406,000	INDIANAPOLIS
1,602,000	KANSAS CITY
11,420,000	LOS ANGELES
3,264,000	MIAMI - FORT LAUDERDALE
1,446,000	MILWAUKEE
2,583,000	MINNEAPOLIS -ST PAUL
1,295,000	NEW ORLEANS
16,972,000	NEW YORK
4,941,000	PHILADELPHIA
2,287,000	PHOENIX
2,404,000	PITTSBURG
1,570,000	PORTLAND
1,073,000	ROCHESTER
1,388,000	SACRAMENTO
1,348,000	SAN ANTONIO
2,549,000	SAN DIEGO
5,240,000	SAN FRANCISCO
2,078,000	SEATTLE
2,507,000	ST LOUIS
2,101,000	TAMPA-ST PETERSBURG
4,293,000	WASHINGTON DC
	UZBEKISTAN
2,094,000	TASHKENT
	VENEZUELA
4,092,000	CARACAS
1,400,643	MARACAIBO
1,274,354	VALENCIA
	VIETNAM
1,447,523	HAIPHONG
1,056,146	HANOI
3,924,435	HO CHI MINH
	YUGOSLAVIA
1,168,454	BELGRADE
	ZIMBABWE
1,000,000	HARARE

© Bartholomew

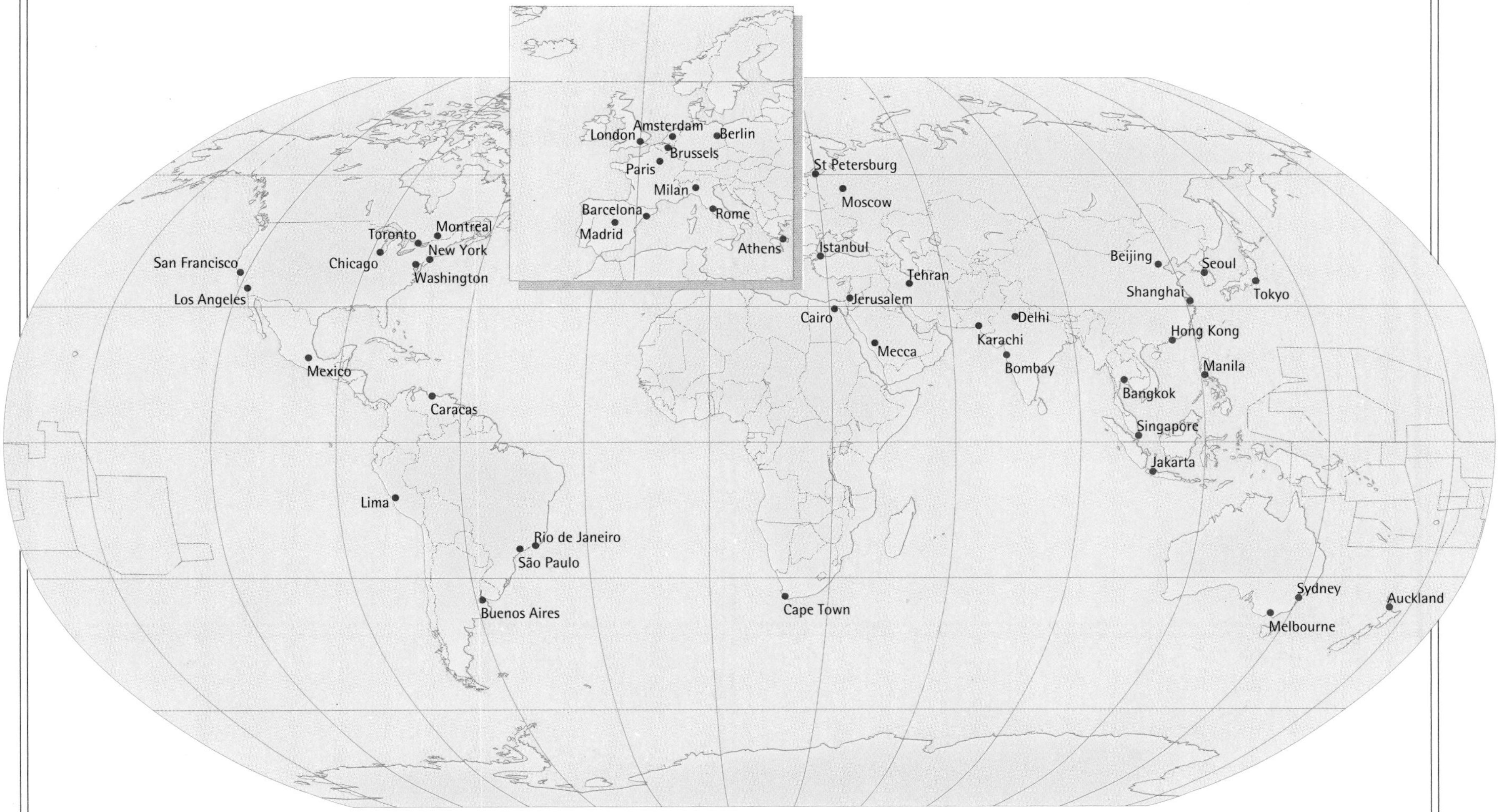

Contents

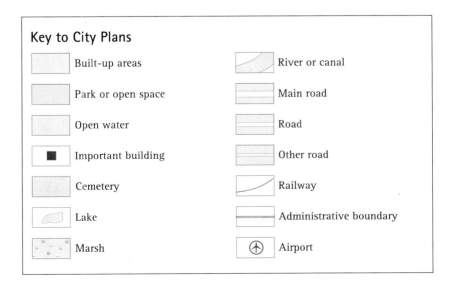

Key to City Plans

- Built-up areas
- Park or open space
- Open water
- Important building
- Cemetery
- Lake
- Marsh
- River or canal
- Main road
- Road
- Other road
- Railway
- Administrative boundary
- Airport

© Bartholomew

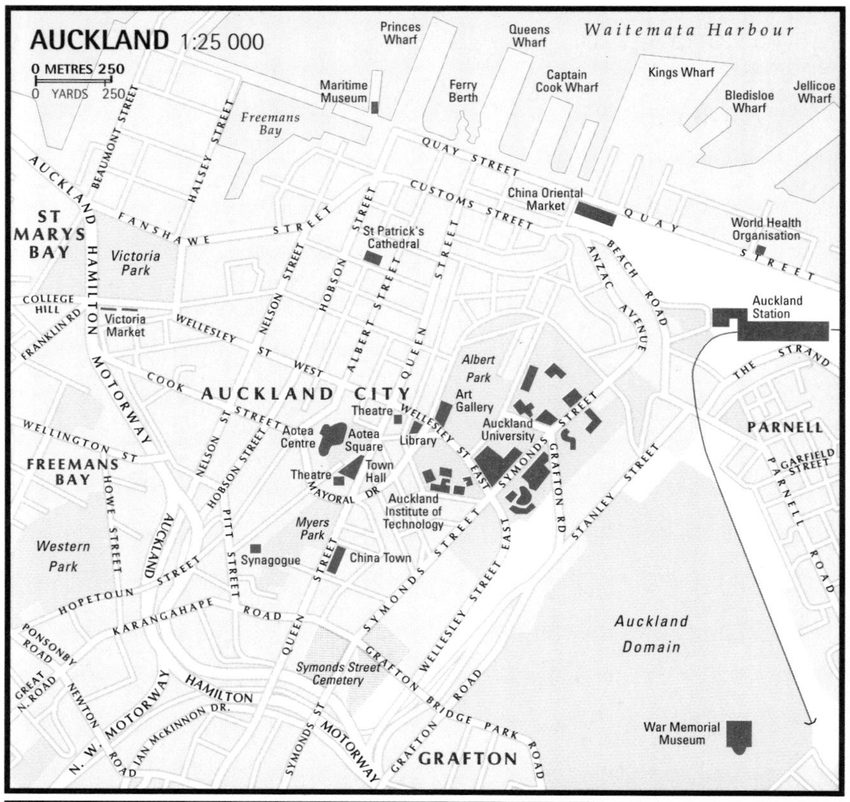

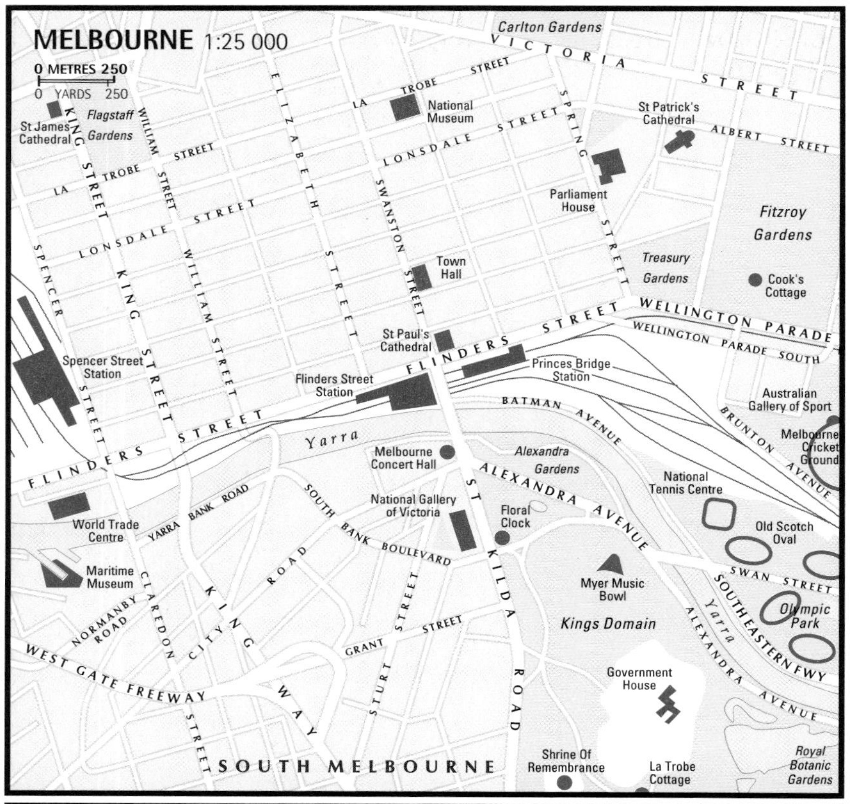

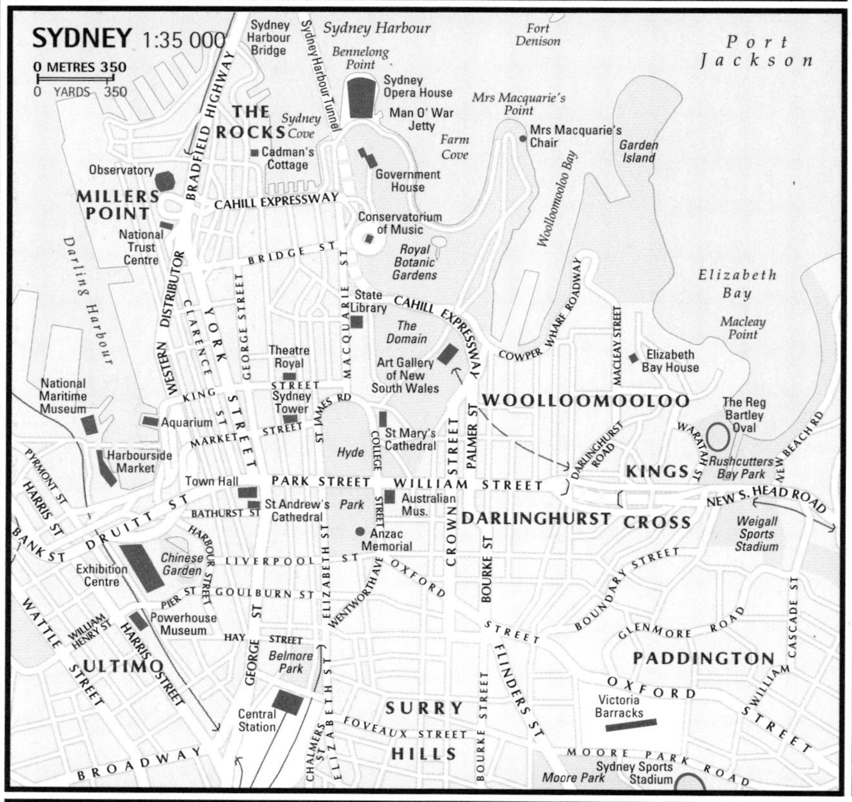

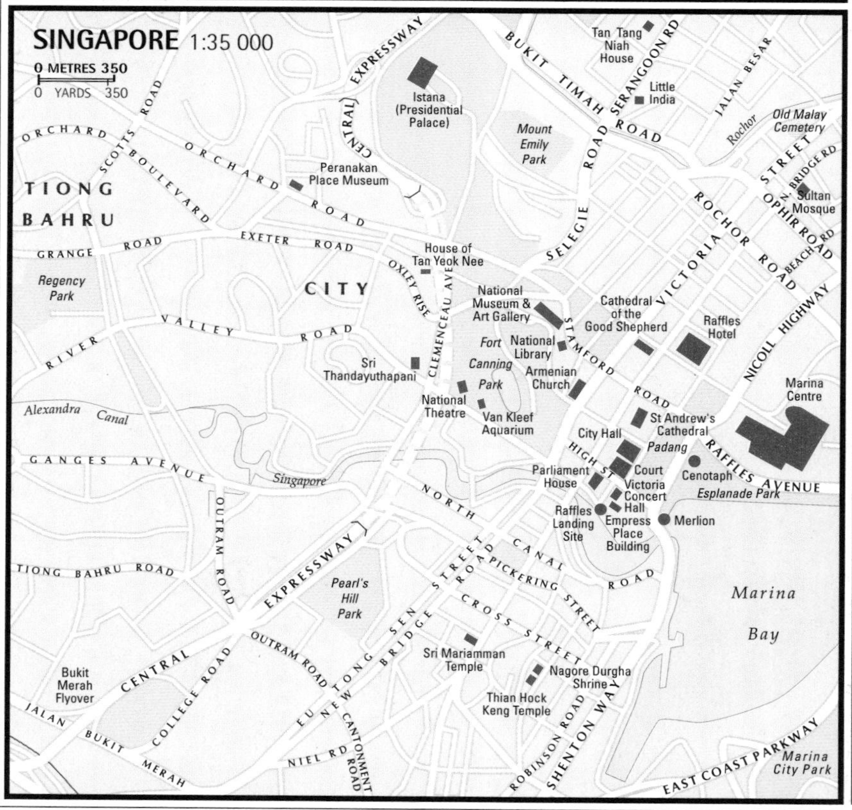

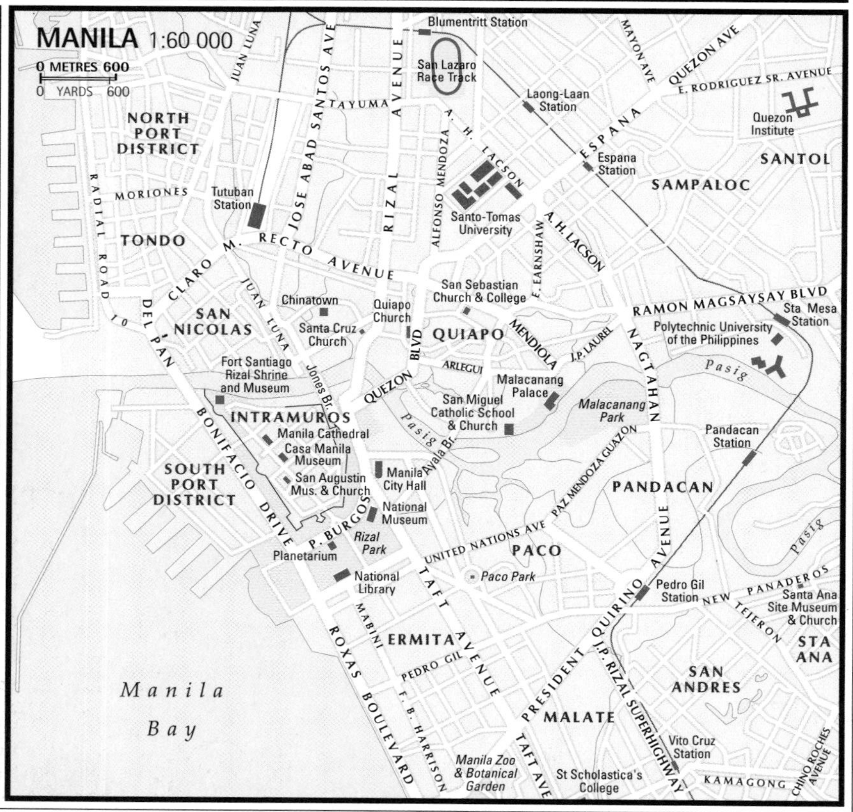

© Bartholomew

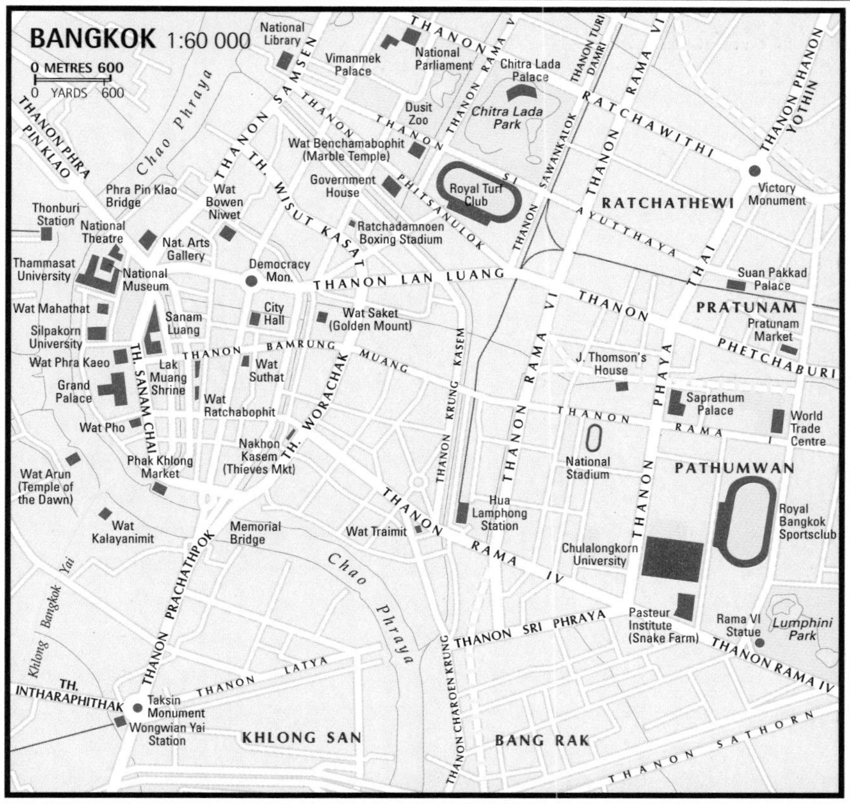

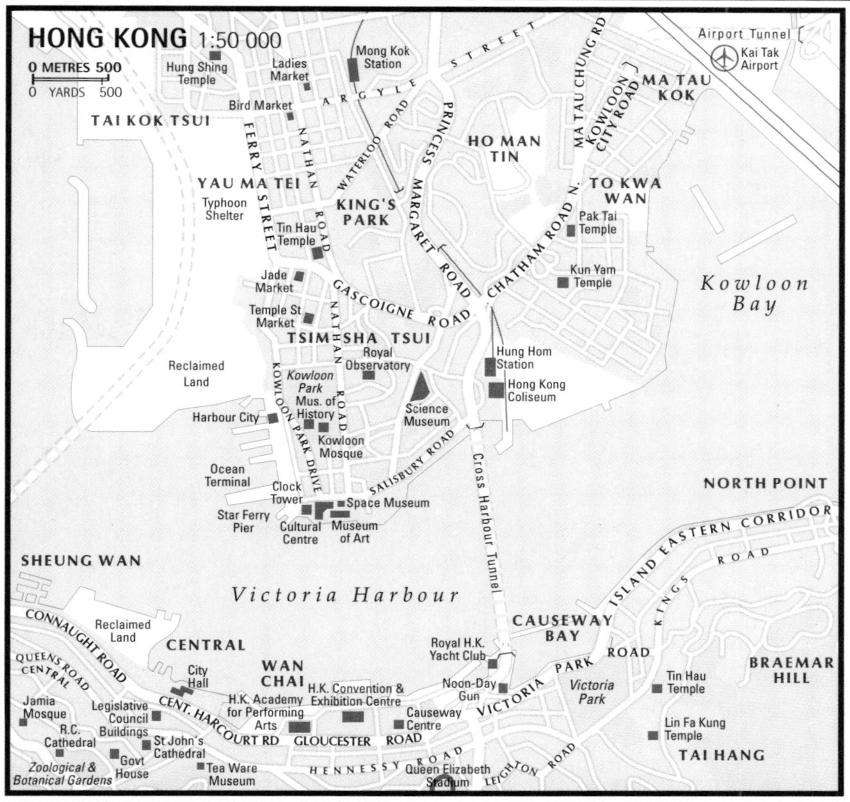

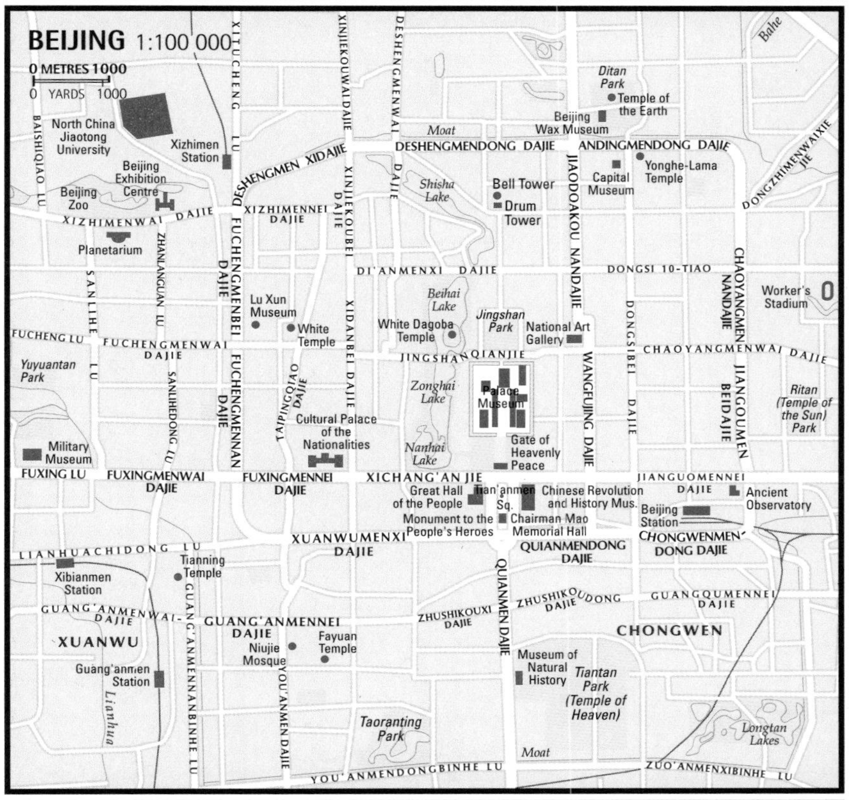

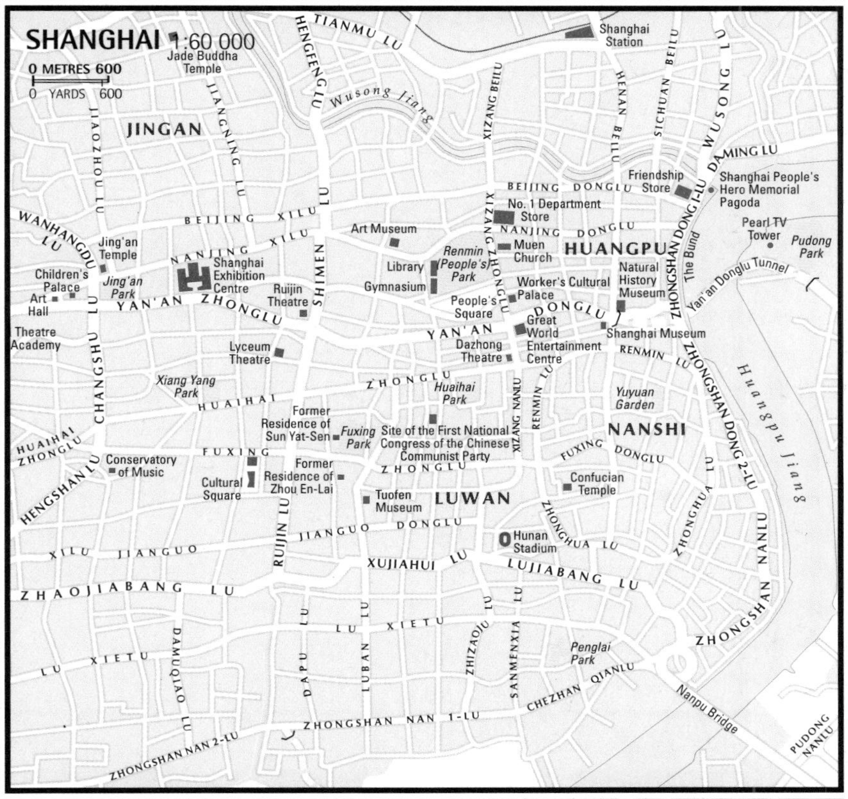

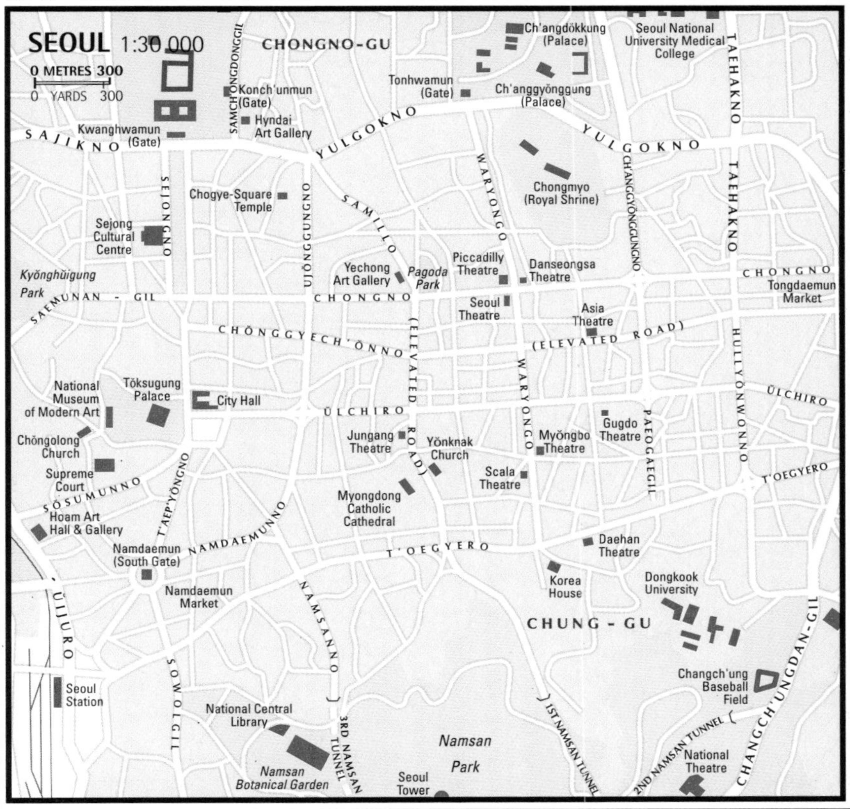

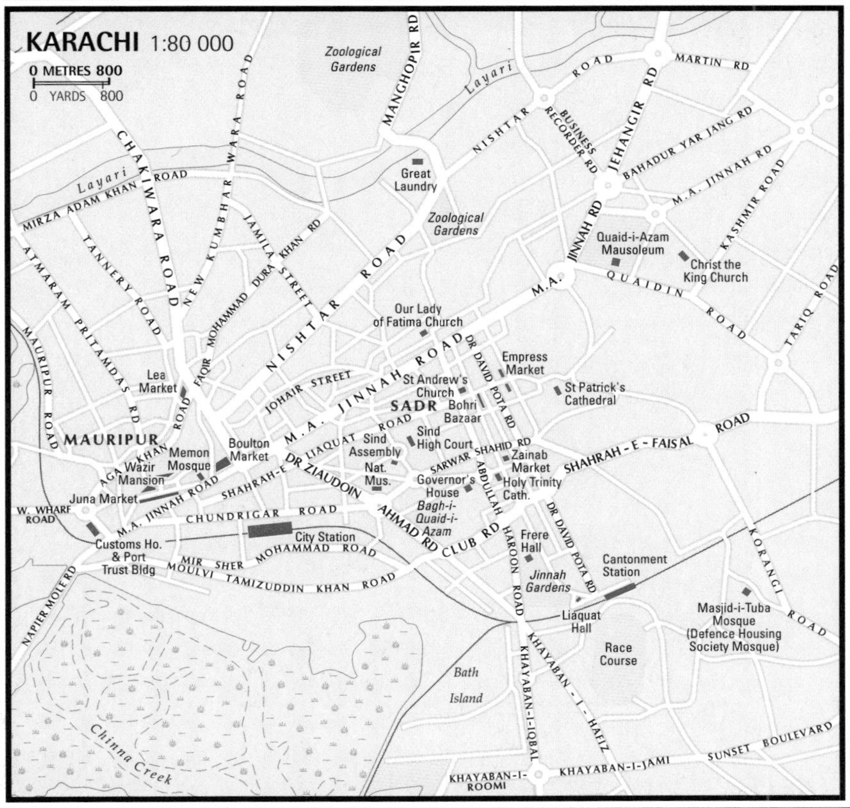

© Bartholomew

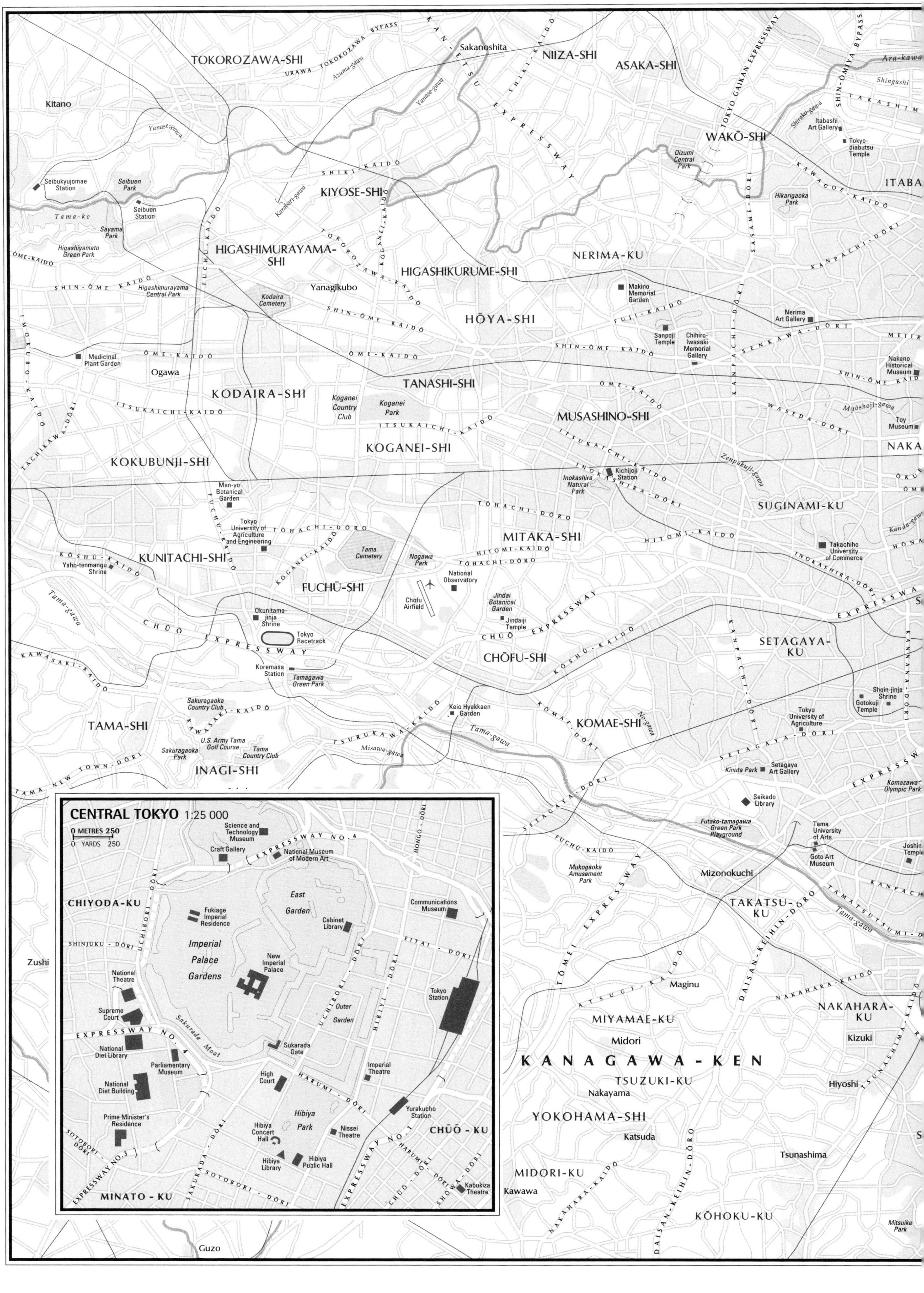
TOKOROZAWA-SHI
NIIZA-SHI
ASAKA-SHI
WAKŌ-SHI
Sakanoshita
Kitano
Ara-kawa
Shingashi
Itabashi Art Gallery
Tokyo-diabutsu Temple
Oizumi Central Park
Hikarigaoka Park
ITABA
Seibukyujomae Station
Seibuen Park
Seibuen Station
Tama-ko
Sayama Park
Higashiyamato Green Park
KIYOSE-SHI
HIGASHIMURAYAMA-SHI
HIGASHIKURUME-SHI
NERIMA-KU
Higashimurayama Central Park
Kodaira Cemetery
Yanagikubo
Makino Memorial Garden
HŌYA-SHI
Nerima Art Gallery
Sanpoji Temple
Chihiro-Iwasaki Memorial Gallery
Nakano Historical Museum
Medicinal Plant Garden
Ogawa
TANASHI-SHI
KODAIRA-SHI
Koganei Country Club
Koganei Park
MUSASHINO-SHI
Toy Museum
KOKUBUNJI-SHI
KOGANEI-SHI
NAKA
Kichijoji Station
Inokashira Natural Park
SUGINAMI-KU
Man-yo Botanical Garden
Tokyo University of Agriculture and Engineering
Tama Cemetery
MITAKA-SHI
Takachiho University of Commerce
KUNITACHI-SHI
Yaho-tenmangu Shrine
Nogawa Park
National Observatory
FUCHŪ-SHI
Chofu Airfield
Jindai Botanical Garden
Jindaiji Temple
Okunitama-jinja Shrine
Tokyo Racetrack
SETAGAYA-KU
CHŌFU-SHI
Koremasa Station
Tamagawa Green Park
Shoin-jinja Shrine
Gotokuji Temple
Sakuragaoka Country Club
Keio Hyakkaen Garden
KOMAE-SHI
Tokyo University of Agriculture
TAMA-SHI
U.S. Army Tama Golf Course
Tama Country Club
Sakuragaoka Park
INAGI-SHI
Kinuta Park
Setagaya Art Gallery
Komazawa Olympic Park
Seikado Library
Futako-tamagawa Green Park Playground
Tama University of Arts
Goto Art Museum
Joshin Temple
Mukogaoka Amusement Park
Mizonokuchi
TAKATSU-KU
Zushi
Maginu
NAKAHARA-KU
MIYAMAE-KU
Kizuki
Midori
KANAGAWA-KEN
TSUZUKI-KU
Hiyoshi
Nakayama
YOKOHAMA-SHI
Katsuda
Tsunashima
MIDORI-KU
Kawawa
KŌHOKU-KU
Mitsuike Park
Guzo
CENTRAL TOKYO 1:25 000
0 METRES 250
0 YARDS 250
Science and Technology Museum
Craft Gallery
National Museum of Modern Art
CHIYODA-KU
East Garden
Communications Museum
Fukiage Imperial Residence
Cabinet Library
Imperial Palace Gardens
New Imperial Palace
National Theatre
Tokyo Station
Supreme Court
Outer Garden
Sakurada Moat
National Diet Library
Sukarada Gate
Parliamentary Museum
Imperial Theatre
National Diet Building
High Court
Yurakucho Station
Prime Minister's Residence
Hibiya Park
Nissei Theatre
CHŪŌ - KU
Hibiya Concert Hall
Hibiya Library
Hibiya Public Hall
MINATO - KU
Kabukiza Theatre

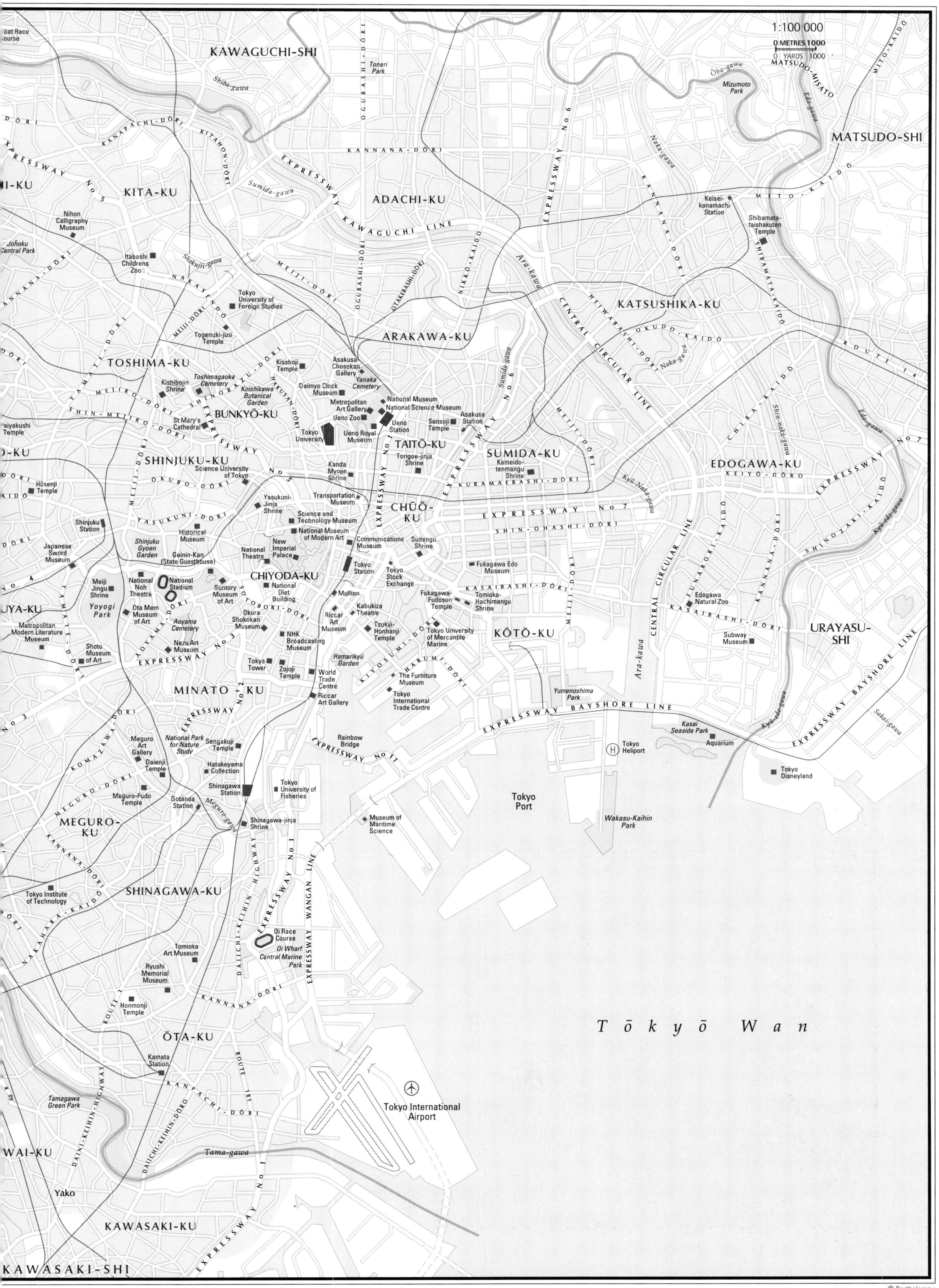

© Bartholomew

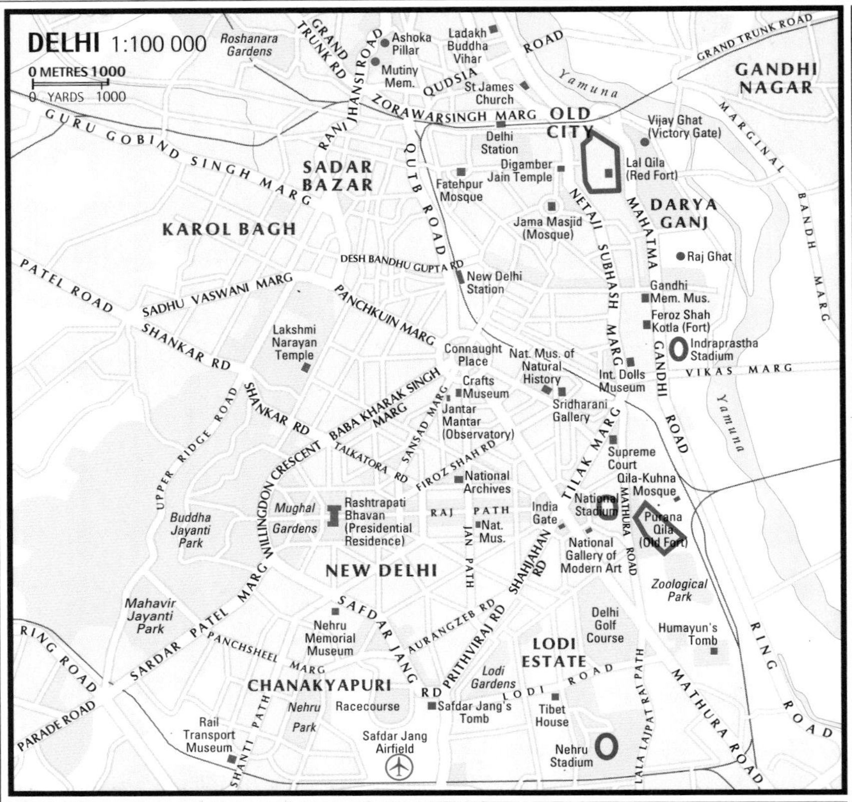

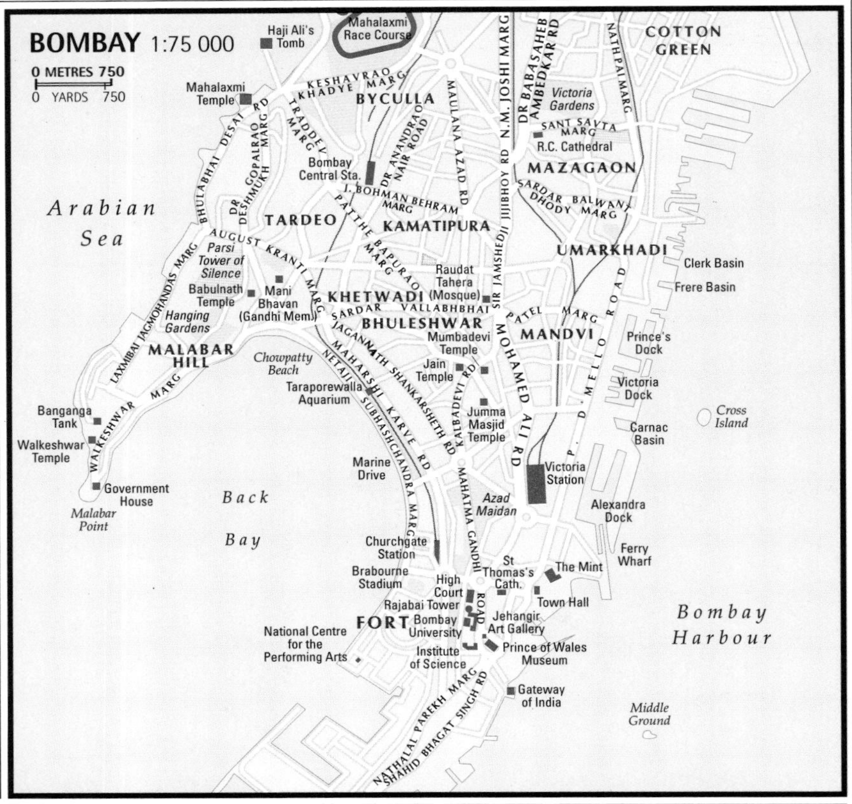

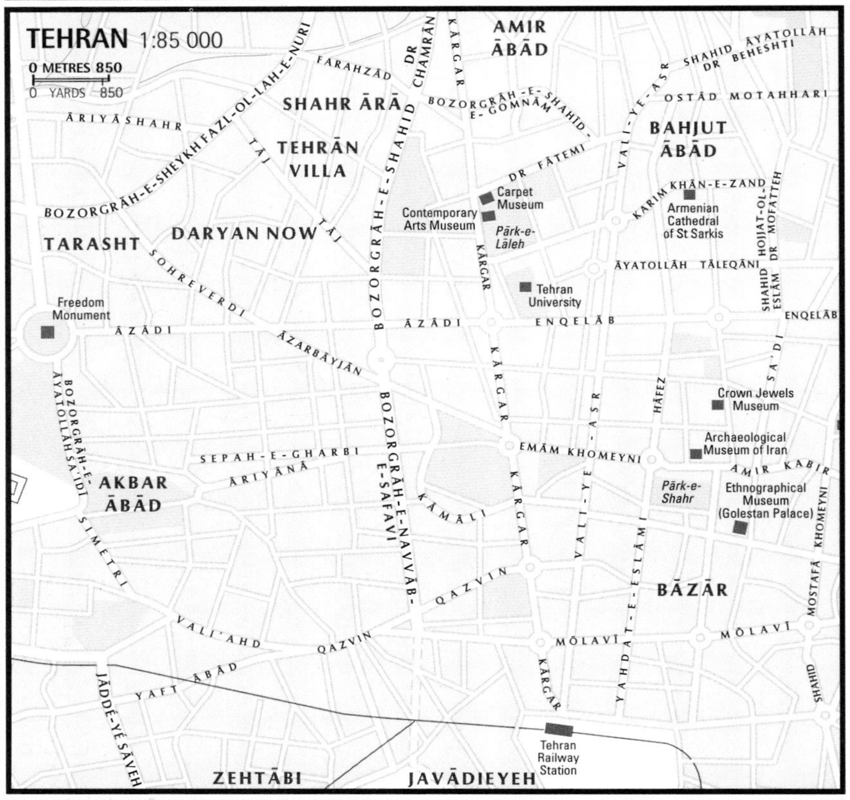

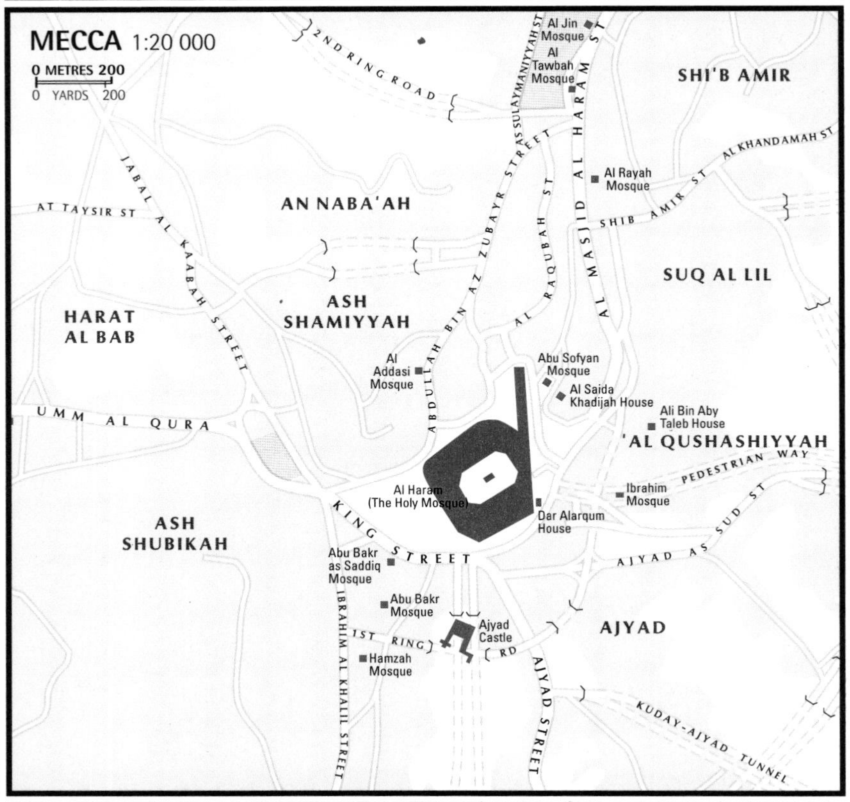

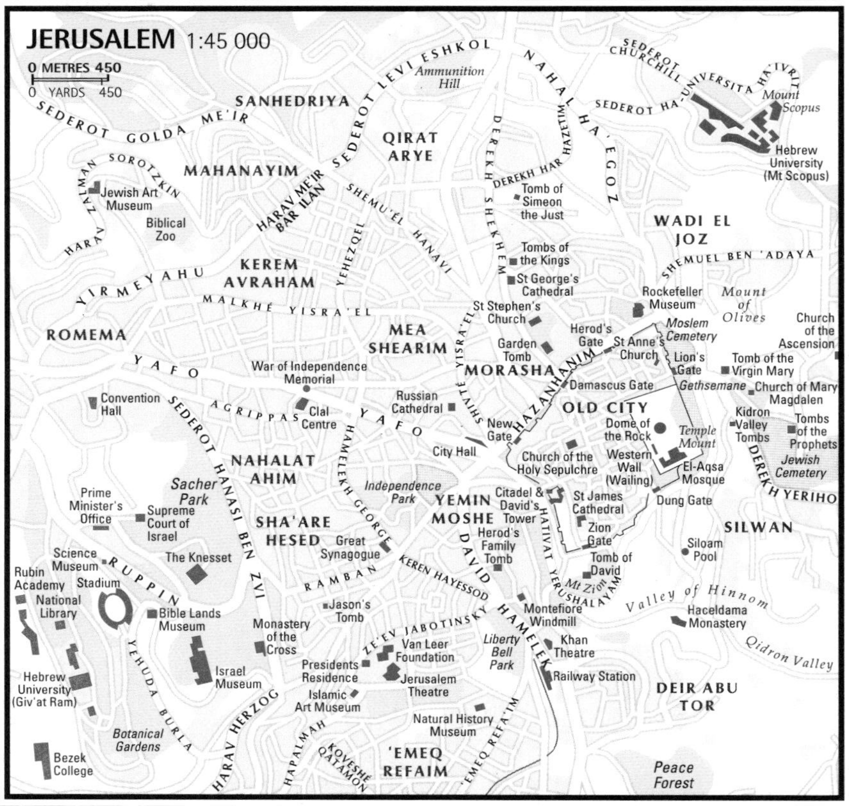

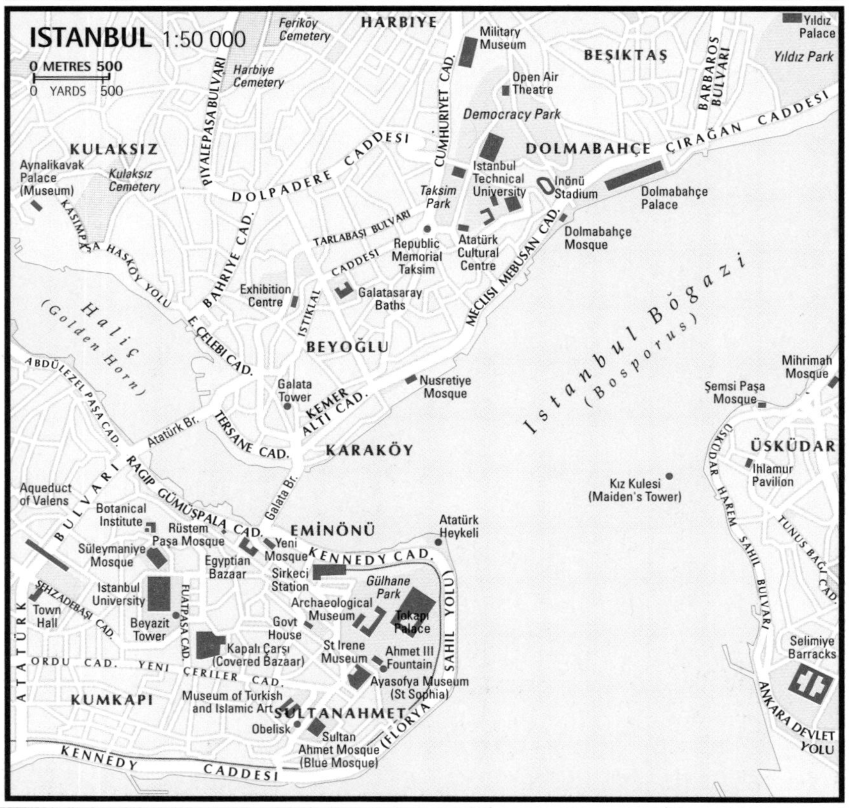

© Bartholomew

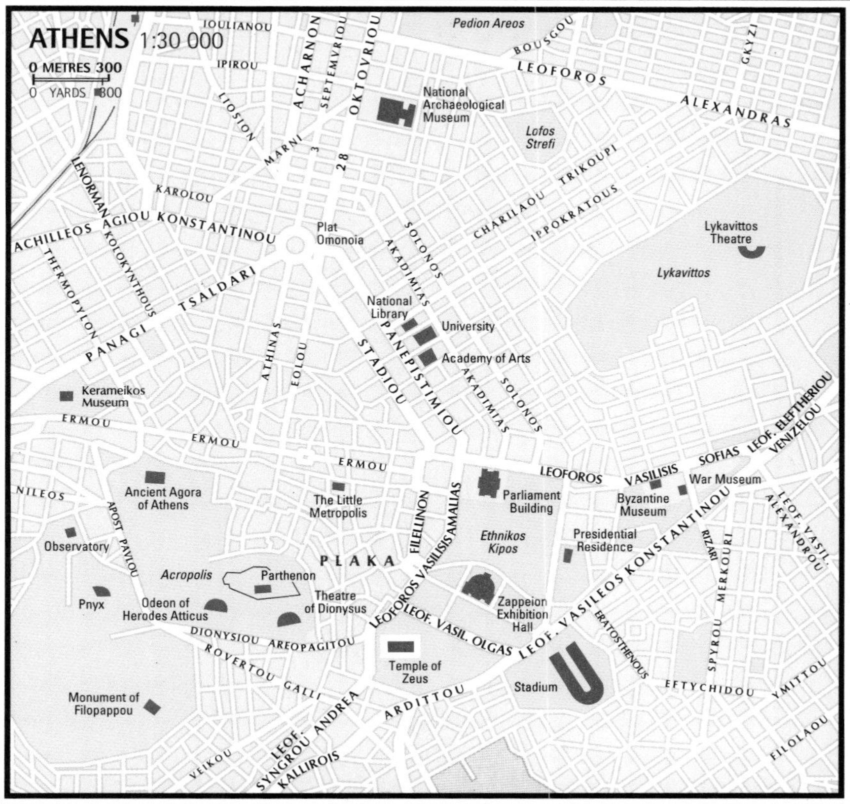

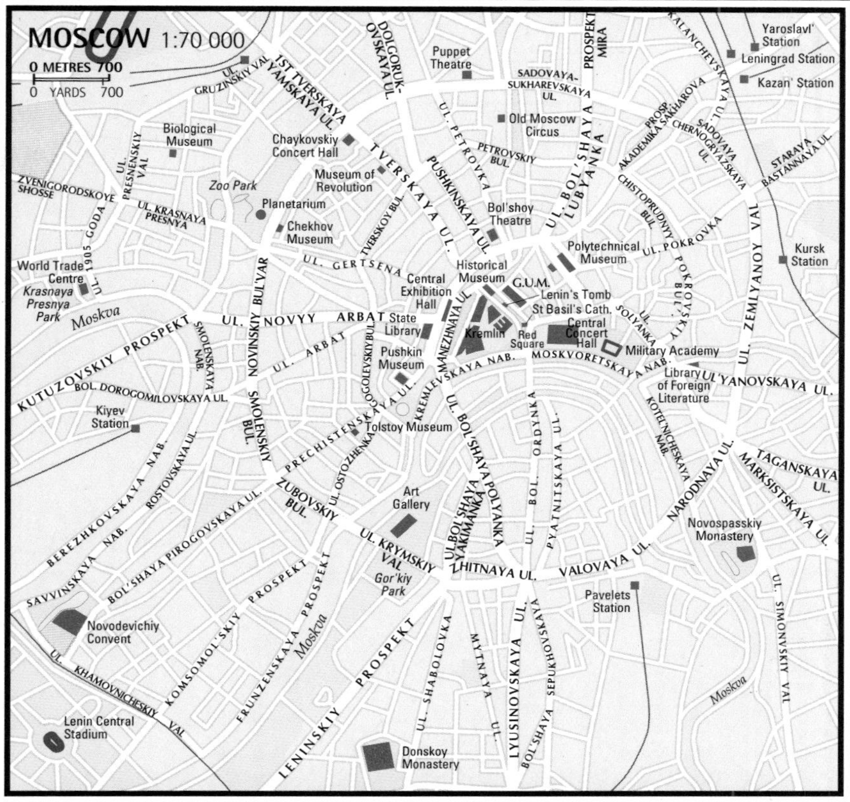

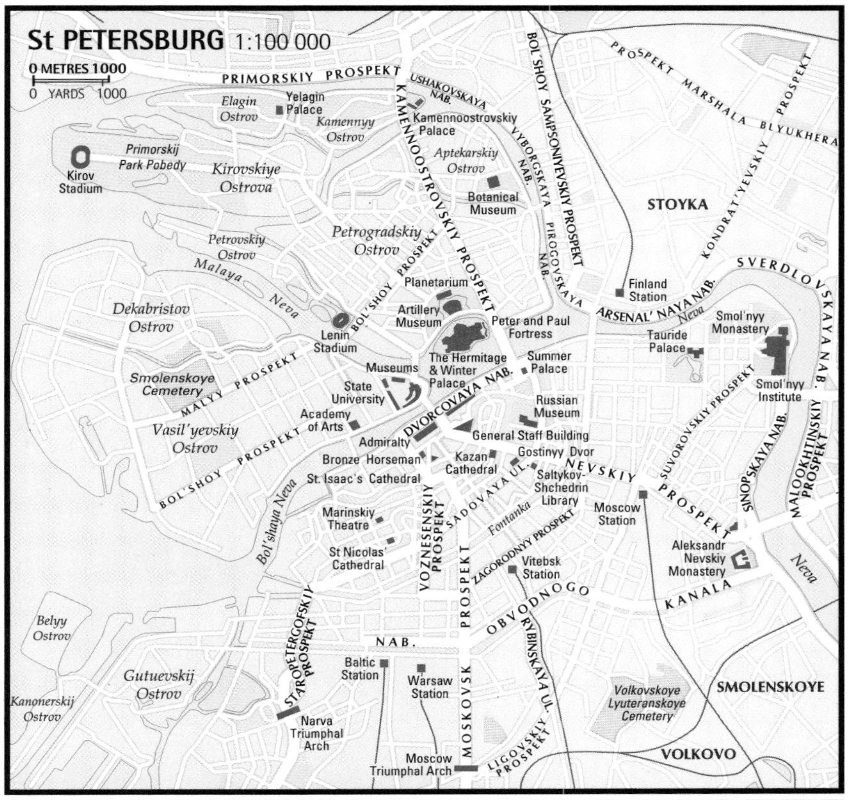

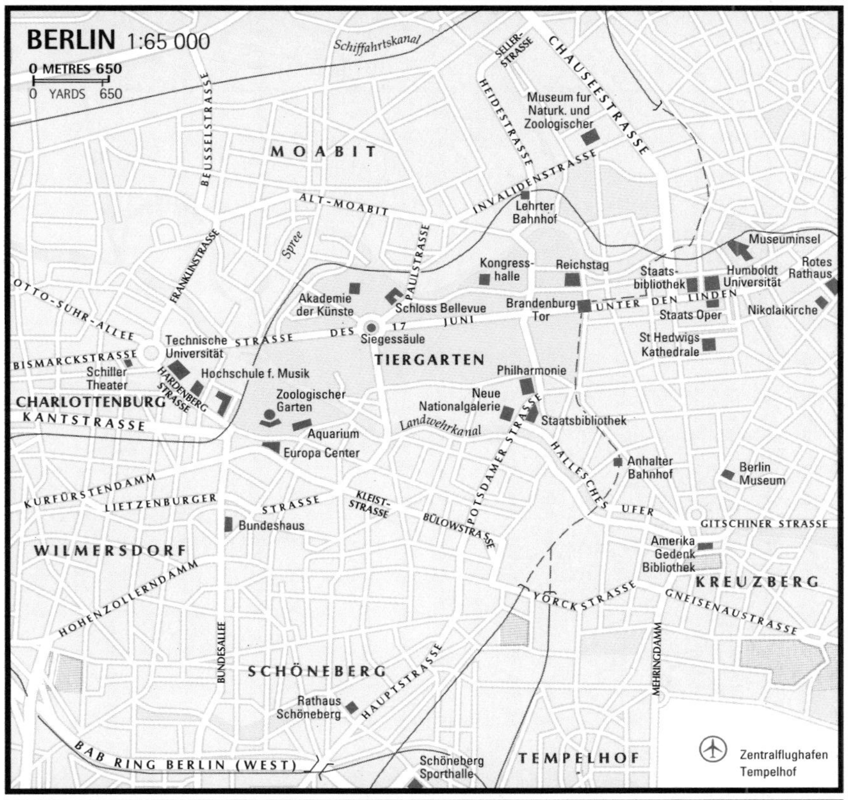

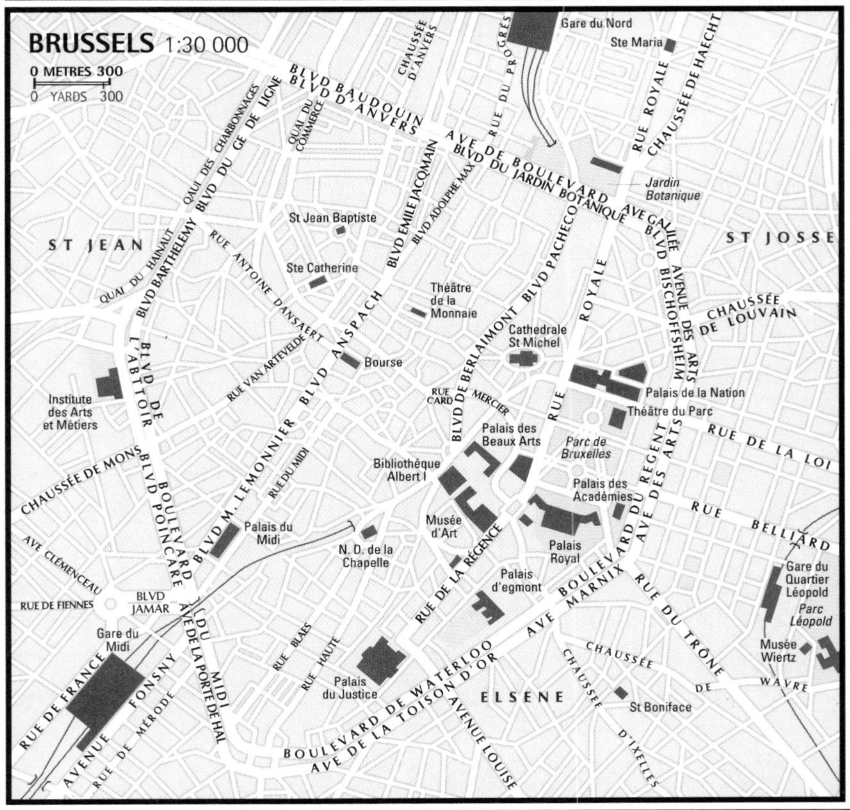

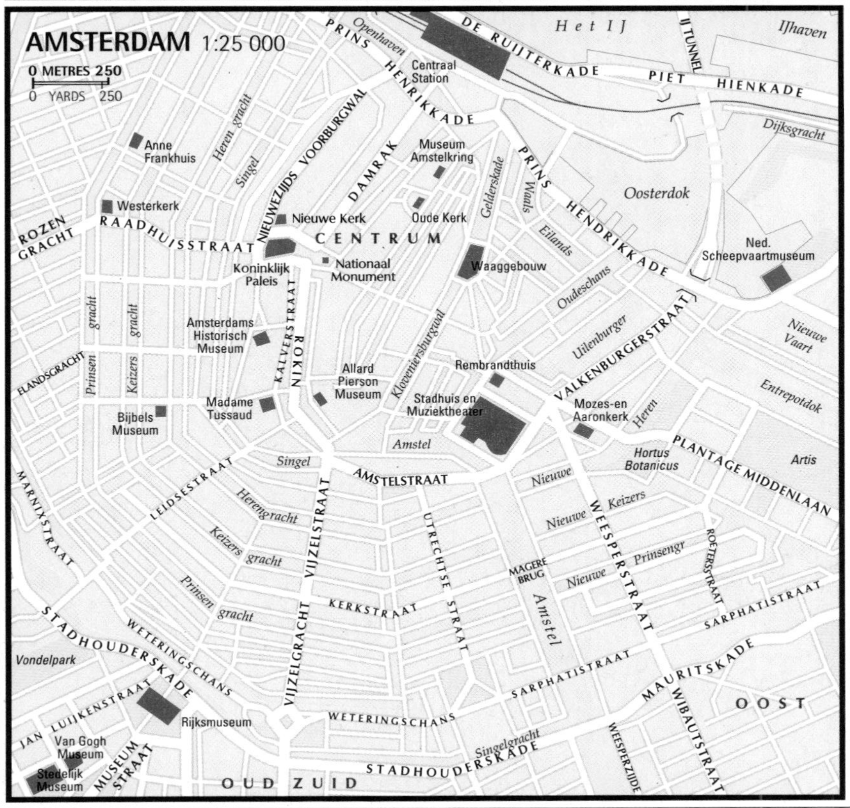

© Bartholomew

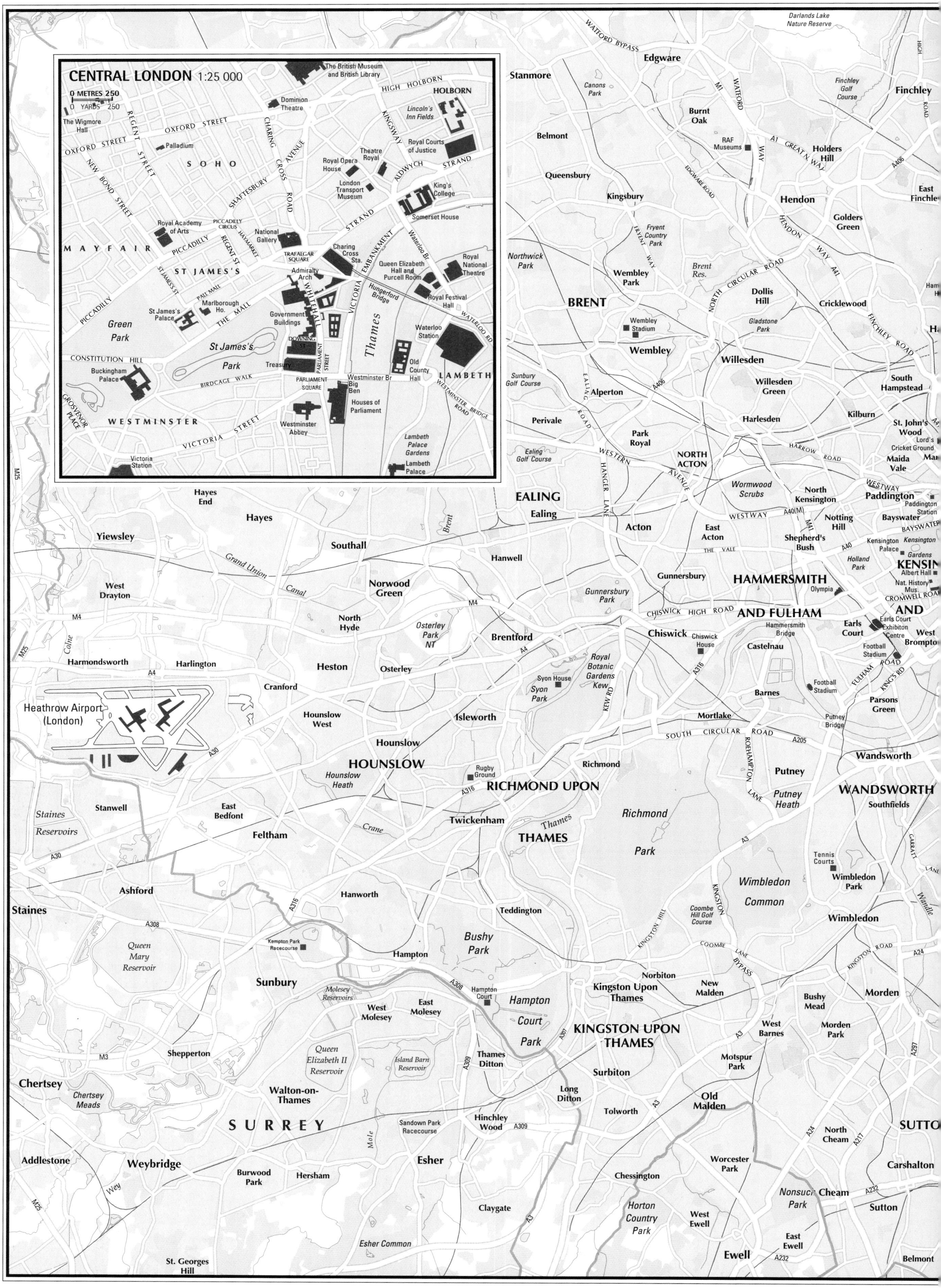
CENTRAL LONDON 1:25 000
0 METRES 250
0 YARDS 250
The British Museum and British Library
HIGH HOLBORN
HOLBORN
Dominion Theatre
Lincoln's Inn Fields
Royal Courts of Justice
The Wigmore Hall
OXFORD STREET
Palladium
S O H O
REGENT STREET
CHARING CROSS ROAD
AVENUE
KINGSWAY
Theatre Royal
Royal Opera House
ALDWYCH
STRAND
London Transport Museum
King's College
NEW BOND STREET
SHAFTESBURY
Somerset House
Royal Academy of Arts
PICCADILLY CIRCUS
National Gallery
M A Y F A I R
PICCADILLY
REGENT ST
HAYMARKET
TRAFALGAR SQUARE
Charing Cross Sta.
EMBANKMENT
Waterloo Br
Royal National Theatre
ST JAMES'S
ST JAMES'S ST
Admiralty Arch
Queen Elizabeth Hall and Purcell Room
PALL MALL
VICTORIA
Hungerford Bridge
Royal Festival Hall
Marlborough Ho.
WHITEHALL
St James's Palace
THE MALL
Government Buildings
Thames
Waterloo Station
WATERLOO RD
Green Park
DOWNING ST
St James's Park
PARLIAMENT STREET
CONSTITUTION HILL
Treasury
Old County Hall
Buckingham Palace
BIRDCAGE WALK
PARLIAMENT SQUARE
Westminster Br
Big Ben
LAMBETH
Houses of Parliament
WESTMINSTER BRIDGE ROAD
GROSVENOR PLACE
WESTMINSTER
Westminster Abbey
VICTORIA STREET
Lambeth Palace Gardens
Victoria Station
Lambeth Palace
Darlands Lake Nature Reserve
WATFORD BYPASS
Edgware
Stanmore
Canons Park
M1
WATFORD WAY
Burnt Oak
Finchley Golf Course
Finchley
HIGH ROAD
Belmont
RAF Museums
A1 GREAT N WAY
Holders Hill
A406
Queensbury
EDGWARE ROAD
Kingsbury
Hendon
East Finchley
Golders Green
HENDON WAY
Fryent Country Park
FRYENT WAY
Northwick Park
Brent Res.
NORTH CIRCULAR ROAD
A41
Wembley Park
Dollis Hill
Cricklewood
BRENT
Gladstone Park
FINCHLEY ROAD
Wembley Stadium
Wembley
Willesden
Sunbury Golf Course
Willesden Green
South Hampstead
Alperton
EALING ROAD
A406
Kilburn
Perivale
Harlesden
St. John's Wood
Lord's Cricket Ground
Park Royal
HARROW ROAD
Maida Vale
Ealing Golf Course
WESTERN AVENUE
NORTH ACTON
HANGER LANE
Wormwood Scrubs
North Kensington
WESTWAY
Paddington
Paddington Station
EALING
Ealing
WESTWAY
A40(M)
Notting Hill
Bayswater
BAYSWATER
Hayes End
Hayes
Brent
Acton
East Acton
M41
Shepherd's Bush
Kensington Palace
Kensington Gardens
Yiewsley
Southall
THE VALE
A40
Holland Park
Albert Hall
Grand Union Canal
Hanwell
Gunnersbury
HAMMERSMITH
Nat. History Mus.
West Drayton
Norwood Green
Gunnersbury Park
Olympia
CROMWELL ROAD
M4
CHISWICK HIGH ROAD
AND FULHAM
AND
M4
North Hyde
Osterley Park NT
Hammersmith Bridge
Earls Court
Earls Court Exhibition Centre
West Brompton
Chiswick
Chiswick House
Colne
Brentford
A4
Castelnau
M25
Harmondsworth
Harlington
Heston
Osterley
Royal Botanic Gardens Kew
Football Stadium
FULHAM ROAD
A4
Syon House
Syon Park
A316
Football Stadium
KING'S RD
Cranford
KEW RD
Barnes
Parsons Green
Heathrow Airport (London)
Hounslow West
Isleworth
Mortlake
Putney Bridge
SOUTH CIRCULAR ROAD
A205
A30
Hounslow
ROEHAMPTON LANE
Wandsworth
HOUNSLOW
Rugby Ground
Richmond
Putney
Hounslow Heath
A316
RICHMOND UPON
WANDSWORTH
Putney Heath
Southfields
Staines Reservoirs
Stanwell
East Bedfont
Richmond Park
Crane
Twickenham
Thames
Feltham
THAMES
A3
GARRATT LANE
A30
Tennis Courts
Wimbledon Park
Ashford
Hanworth
Wimbledon Common
KINGSTON HILL
Wandle
Staines
A316
Teddington
Coombe Hill Golf Course
Wimbledon
A308
Queen Mary Reservoir
Kempton Park Racecourse
Bushy Park
KINGSTON HILL
COOMBE LANE
BYPASS
KINGSTON ROAD
A24
Hampton
Norbiton
Sunbury
Molesey Reservoirs
A308
Hampton Court
Hampton Court Park
Kingston Upon Thames
New Malden
Bushy Mead
Morden
West Molesey
East Molesey
A307
KINGSTON UPON THAMES
West Barnes
Morden Park
A3
M3
Shepperton
Queen Elizabeth II Reservoir
Island Barn Reservoir
A309
Thames Ditton
Surbiton
Motspur Park
A297
Chertsey
Chertsey Meads
Walton-on-Thames
Long Ditton
Old Malden
Tolworth
A3
S U R R E Y
Sandown Park Racecourse
Hinchley Wood
A309
Mole
North Cheam
A217
A24
SUTTO
Addlestone
Weybridge
Burwood Park
Hersham
Esher
Chessington
Worcester Park
Carshalton
Wey
Nonsuch Park
Cheam
A232
M25
Claygate
Horton Country Park
West Ewell
Sutton
A3
Esher Common
East Ewell
Ewell
A232
St. Georges Hill
Belmont

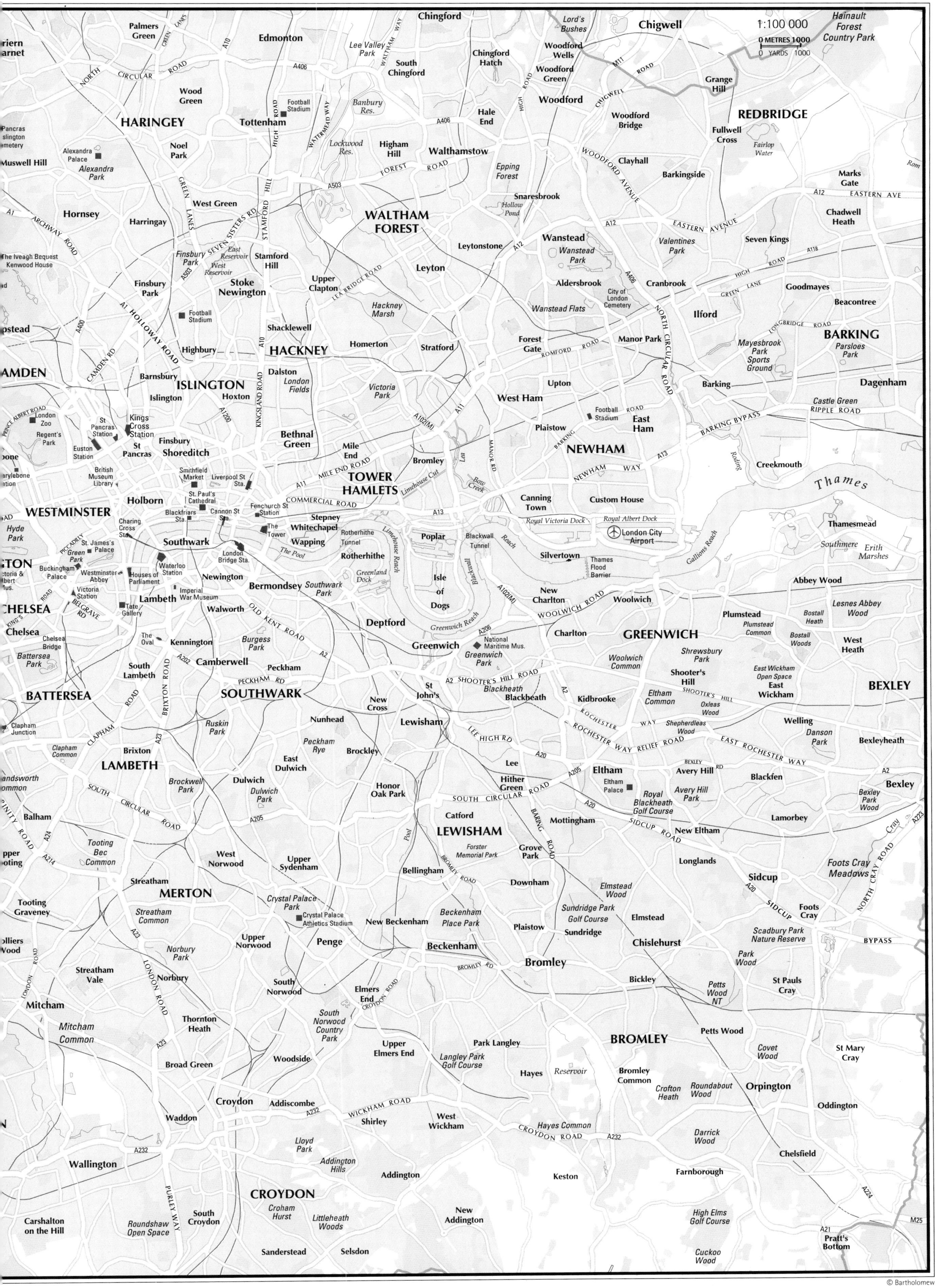

© Bartholomew

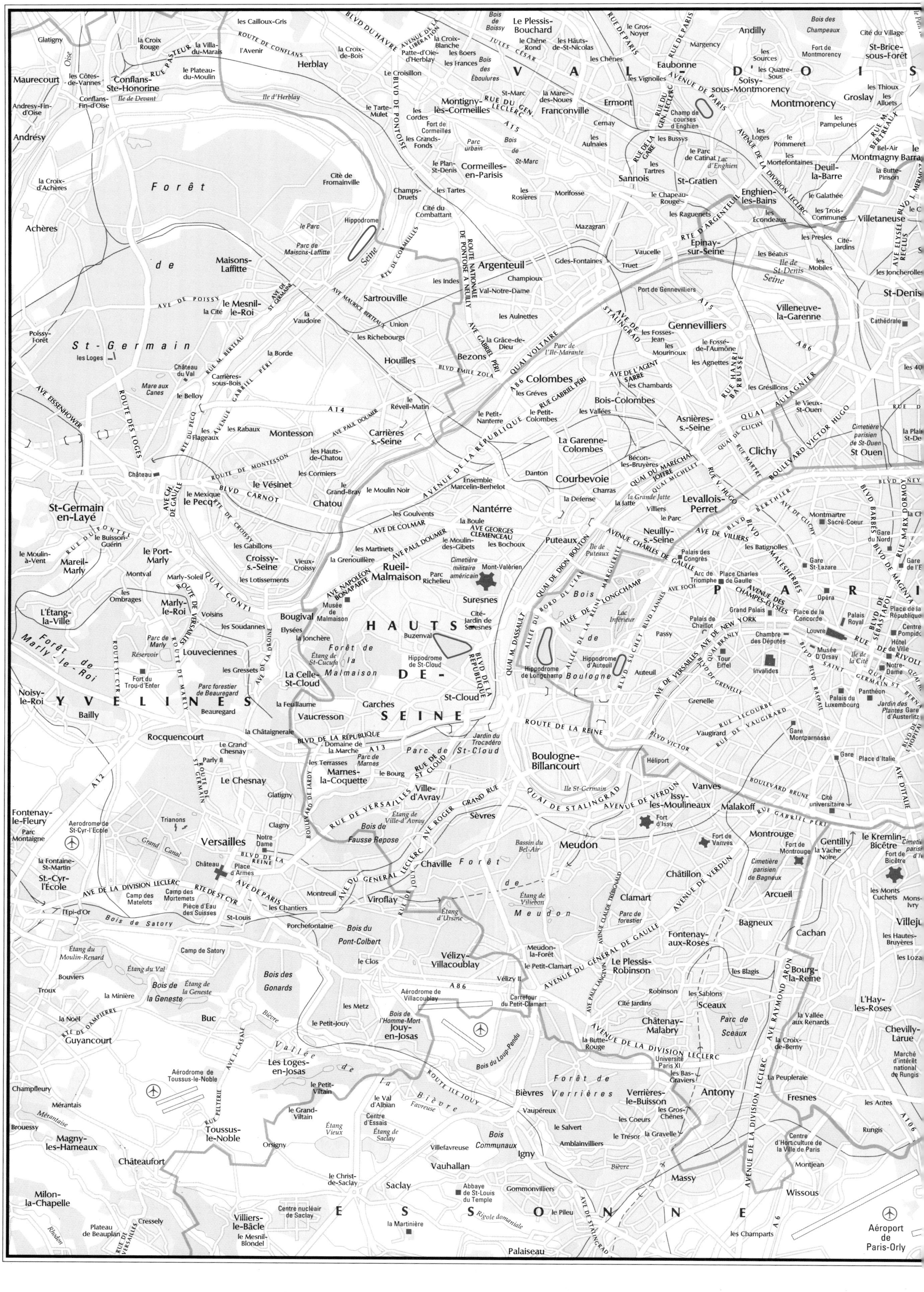
V A L - D' O I S E
Y V E L I N E S
HAUTS-DE-SEINE
E S S O N N E
P A R I S
Forêt de St-Germain
Forêt de Marly-le-Roi
Seine
Glatigny
Maurecourt
Andresy-Fin-d'Oise
Andrésy
Conflans-Ste-Honorine
Conflans-Fin-d'Oise
la Croix Rouge
la Villa-du-Marais
les Côtes-de-Vannes
le Plateau-du-Moulin
Ile de Devant
Ile d'Herblay
les Cailloux-Gris
l'Avenir
la Croix-de-Bois
Herblay
BLVD DU HAVRE
AVENUE DE LA LIBÉRATION
la Croix-Blanche
Patte-d'Oie-d'Herblay
les Boers
les Frances
Bois des Éboulures
Bois de Boissy
Le Plessis-Bouchard
le Chêne Rond
les Hauts-de-St-Nicolas
JULES CÉSAR
les Chênes
RUE DE PARIS
les Gros-Noyer
Eaubonne
Margency
Andilly
Bois des Champeaux
Cité du Village
Fort de Montmorency
St-Brice-sous-Forêt
les Sources
les Quatre-Sous
Soisy-sous-Montmorency
les Vignolles
Montmorency
Groslay
les Thioux
les Alluets
les Pampelunes
Le Croisillon
BLVD DE PONTOISE
le Tarte-Mulet
les Cordes
Montigny-lès-Cormeilles
Fort de Cormeilles
les Grands-Fonds
St-Marc
la Mare-des-Noues
Franconville
Ermont
Cernay
les Aulnaies
Champ de courses d'Enghien
les Bussys
le Parc de Catinat
Lac d'Enghien
les Loges
le Pommeret
les Mortefontaines
Deuil-la-Barre
Montmagny
Bel-Air
la Butte-Pinson
Parc urbain
Bois de St-Marc
le Plan-St-Denis
Cormeilles-en-Parisis
les Rosières
Morifosse
Sannois
les Tartres
St-Gratien
le Chapeau-Rouge
les Raguenets
Enghien-les-Bains
les Écondeaux
le Galathée
les Trois-Communes
Villetaneuse
la Croix-d'Achères
Achères
Cité de Fromainville
Champs-Druets
les Tartes
Cité du Combattant
Hippodrome
le Parc
Parc de Maisons-Laffitte
Maisons-Laffitte
Mazagran
Epinay-sur-Seine
les Presles
Cité-Jardins
les Béatus
Ile de St-Denis
les Mobiles
Argenteuil
Gdes-Fontaines
Vaucelle
Truet
Champioux
les Indes
Val-Notre-Dame
Port de Gennevilliers
St-Denis
les Joncherolles
AVE DE POISSY
le Mesnil-le-Roi
la Cité
Sartrouville
AVE MAURICE BERTEAUX
la Vaudoire
Union
les Richebourgs
les Aulnettes
Gennevilliers
Villeneuve-la-Garenne
Cathédrale
Poissy-Forêt
les Loges
la Borde
Houilles
la Grâce-de-Dieu
Bezons
Parc de l'Ile-Marante
les Fosses-Jean
les Mourinoux
le Fossé-de-l'Aumône
les Agnettes
Château du Val
Carrières-sous-Bois
Mare aux Canes
le Belloy
AVE EISSENHOWER
ROUTE DES LOGES
BLVD EMILE ZOLA
QUAI VOLTAIRE
Colombes
les Grèves
les Chambards
les Grésillons
le Réveil-Matin
A14
les Rabaux
les Flageaux
Montesson
Carrières-s.-Seine
le Petit-Nanterre
le Petit-Colombes
Bois-Colombes
les Vallées
Asnières-s.-Seine
le Vieux-St-Ouen
Cimetière parisien de St-Ouen
St Ouen
QUAI AULAGNIER
QUAI DE CLICHY
La Garenne-Colombes
Clichy
BOULEVARD VICTOR HUGO
Château
les Hauts-de-Chatou
les Cormiers
Bécon-les-Bruyères
Danton
Courbevoie
Charras
la Défense
la Grande Jatte
la Jatte
Levallois-Perret
Le Vésinet
le Grand-Bray
le Moulin Noir
Chatou
Ensemble Marcelin-Berthelot
AVENUE DE LA RÉPUBLIQUE
St-Germain en-Laye
le Mexique
le Pecq
BLVD CARNOT
les Goulvents
AVE DE COLMAR
Nantérre
la Boule
AVE GEORGES CLEMENCEAU
les Bochoux
Puteaux
Ile de Puteaux
Villiers
le Parc
Neuilly-s.-Seine
AVENUE CHARLES DE GAULLE
Palais des Congrès
Arc de Triomphe
Place Charles de Gaulle
les Batignolles
Montmartre
Sacré-Coeur
Gare du Nord
Gare St-Lazare
le Buisson-Guérin
le Moulin-à-Vent
Mareil-Marly
le Port-Marly
les Gabillons
Croissy-s.-Seine
Vieux-Croissy
la Grenouillère
AVE PAUL DOUMER
le Moulin-des-Gibets
Cimetière militaire américain
Mont-Valérien
Rueil-Malmaison
Parc Richelieu
Montval
Marly-Soleil
QUAI CONTI
les Lotissements
AVE NAPOLÉON BONAPARTE
Suresnes
Bois de Boulogne
Lac Inférieur
ALLÉE DE LA REINE MARGUERITE
LONGCHAMP
AVE FOCH
AVENUE DES CHAMPS-ÉLYSÉES
Opéra
Grand Palais
Palais Royal
Place de la Concorde
Place de la République
les Ombrages
Marly-le-Roi
Voisins
L'Étang-la-Ville
Bougival
Musée de Malmaison
les Soudannes
Élysées
la Jonchère
Cité-Jardin de Suresnes
Buzenval
Palais de Chaillot
Passy
Chambre des Députés
Louvre
Hôtel de Ville
Centre Pompidou
Parc de Marly
Réservoir
Louveciennes
Forêt de la Malmaison
Étang de St-Cucufa
Hippodrome de St-Cloud
BLVD DE LA RÉPUBLIQUE
QUAI M. DASSAULT
Hippodrome de Longchamp
Hippodrome d'Auteuil
Auteuil
Musée d'Orsay
Tour Eiffel
Invalides
Ile de la Cité
Notre-Dame
Fort du Trou-d'Enfer
Parc forestier de Beauregard
les Gressets
La Celle-St-Cloud
Boulogne
Panthéon
Palais du Luxembourg
Jardin des Plantes
Gare d'Austerlitz
Noisy-le-Roi
Bailly
Beauregard
la Feuillaume
Vaucresson
Garches
St-Cloud
Grenelle
Rocquencourt
la Châtaigneraie
BLVD DE LA RÉPUBLIQUE
Jardin du Trocadéro
ROUTE DE LA REINE
Vaugirard
Gare Montparnasse
le Grand Chesnay
Domaine de la Marche
A13
Parc de St-Cloud
Boulogne-Billancourt
Héliport
Gare
Place d'Italie
Parly II
les Terrasses
Parc de Marnes
le Bourg
Marnes-la-Coquette
Le Chesnay
Ville-d'Avray
Ile St-Germain
Vanves
Issy-les-Moulineaux
Malakoff
Cité universitaire
A12
Glatigny
Fontenay-le-Fleury
Parc Montaigne
Aerodrome de St-Cyr-l'Ecole
Trianons
Clagny
Bois de Fausse Repose
Étang de Ville-d'Avray
Sèvres
QUAI DE STALINGRAD
Fort d'Issy
Grand Canal
Versailles
Notre Dame
BLVD DE LA REINE
Bassin du Bel-Air
Meudon
Fort de Vanves
Montrouge
Fort de Montrouge
Gentilly
la Vache Noire
le Kremlin-Bicêtre
Fort de Bicêtre
la Fontaine-St-Martin
St.-Cyr-l'École
Château
Place d'Armes
AVE DE PARIS
Chaville
Forêt de Meudon
Châtillon
Cimetière parisien de Bagneux
AVE DE LA DIVISION LECLERC
RTE DE ST CYR
Camp des Matelots
Camp des Mortemets
Pièce d'Eau des Suisses
Montreuil
les Chantiers
Viroflay
Étang de Villebon
Clamart
Arcueil
les Monts Cuchets
l'Epi-d'Or
Bois de Satory
St-Louis
Porchefontaine
Étang d'Ursine
Parc de forestier
Bagneux
Villejuif
Étang du Moulin-Renard
Camp de Satory
Bois du Pont-Colbert
Fontenay-aux-Roses
Cachan
les Hautes-Bruyères
Étang du Val
Bouviers
Bois des Gonards
le Clos
Vélizy-Villacoublay
Meudon-la-Forêt
le Petit-Clamart
Le Plessis-Robinson
les Blagis
Bourg-la-Reine
Troux
la Minière
Bois de la Geneste
Étang de la Geneste
Vélizy II
A86
Aérodrome de Villacoublay
Carrefour du Petit-Clamart
Robinson
les Sablons
Sceaux
L'Hay-les-Roses
la Noël
Buc
Bièvre
les Metz
Bois de l'Homme-Mort
Jouy-en-Josas
le Petit-Jouy
Cité Jardins
Châtenay-Malabry
Parc de Sceaux
la Vallée aux Renards
Chevilly-Larue
RTE DE DAMPIERRE
Guyancourt
Vallée de la Bièvre
Les Loges-en-Josas
Bois du Loup-Pendu
la Butte-Rouge
Université Paris XI
la Croix-de-Berny
Marché d'intérêt national de Rungis
Aérodrome de Toussus-le-Noble
AVE J. CASALE
ROUTE ILE JOUY
Forêt de Verrières
les Bas-Graviers
la Peupleraie
Champfleury
Mérantais
le Petit-Viltain
le Val d'Albian
Favreuse
Bièvres
Vaupéreux
Verrières-le-Buisson
Antony
Fresnes
les Antes
le Grand-Viltain
Centre d'Essais
Étang Vieux
Étang de Saclay
les Gros-Chênes
les Coeurs
le Salvert
Rungis
Brouessy
Magny-les-Hameaux
Toussus-le-Noble
RUE PELTERIE
Orsigny
Villefavreuse
Bois Communaux
Amblainvilliers
le Trésor
la Gravelle
Centre d'Horticulture de la Ville de Paris
Montjean
Châteaufort
Vauhallan
Igny
le Christ-de-Saclay
Saclay
Abbaye de St-Louis du Temple
Gommonvilliers
Massy
Wissous
Milon-la-Chapelle
Plateau de Beauplan
Cressely
Centre nucléaire de Saclay
la Martinière
Rigole domaniale
le Pileu
AVE DE STALINGRAD
Villiers-le-Bâcle
le Mesnil-Blondel
Rhodon
les Champarts
Palaiseau
A6
A106
Aéroport de Paris-Orly

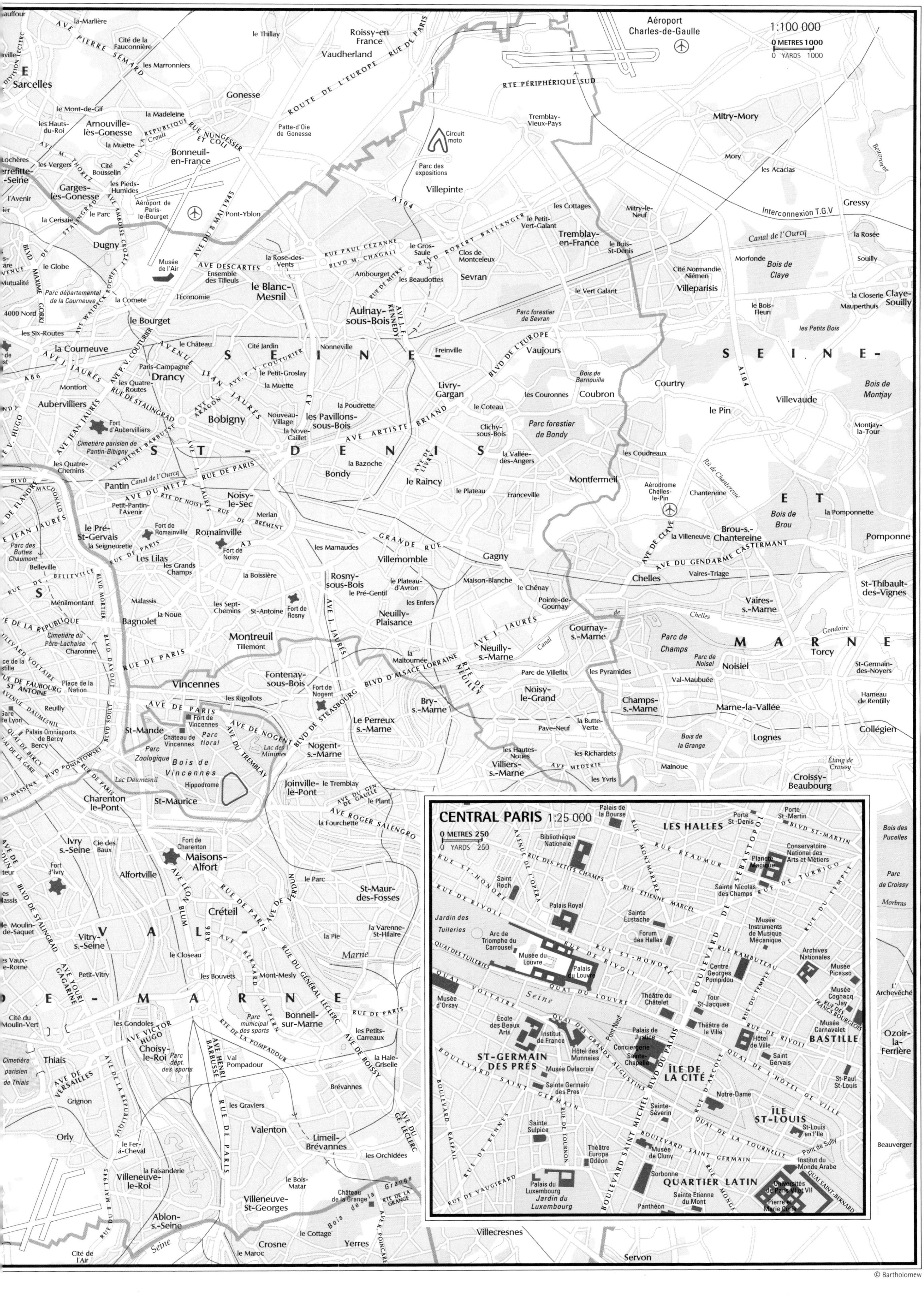

© Bartholomew

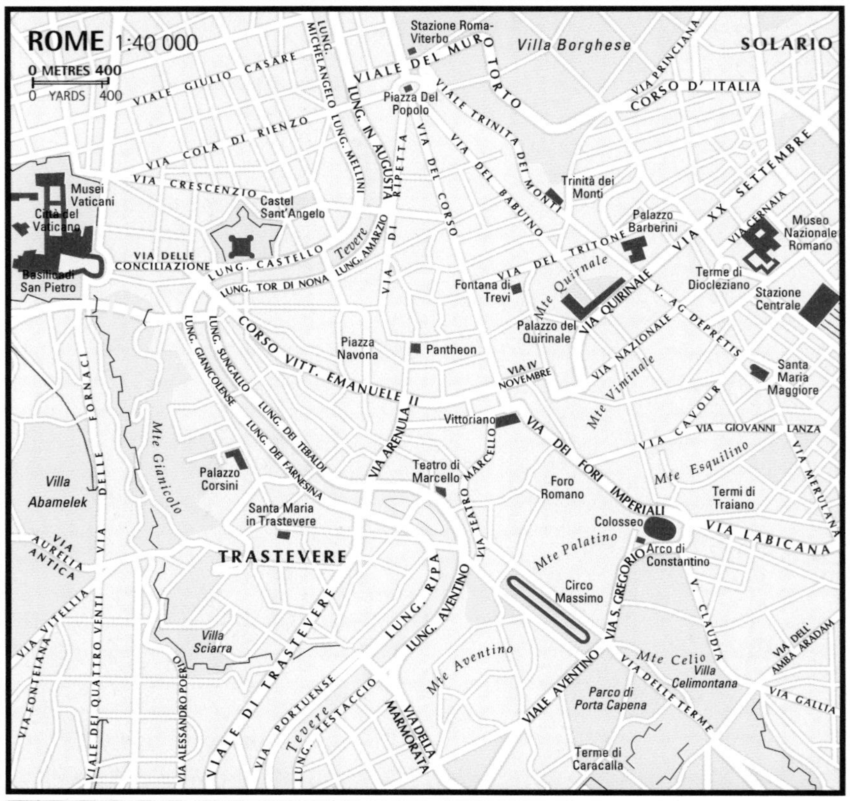

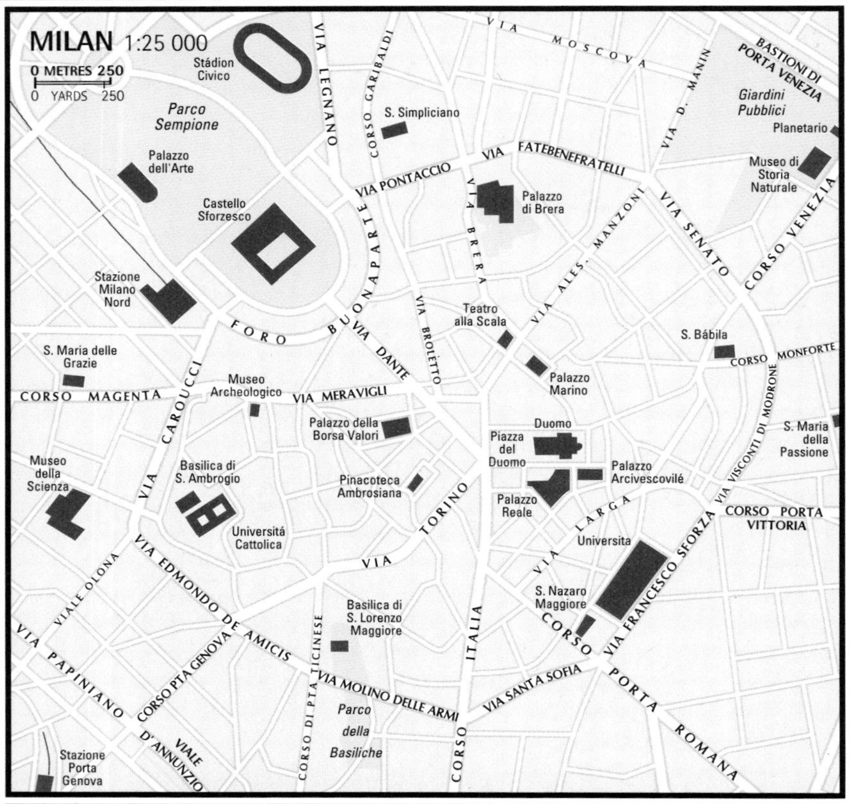

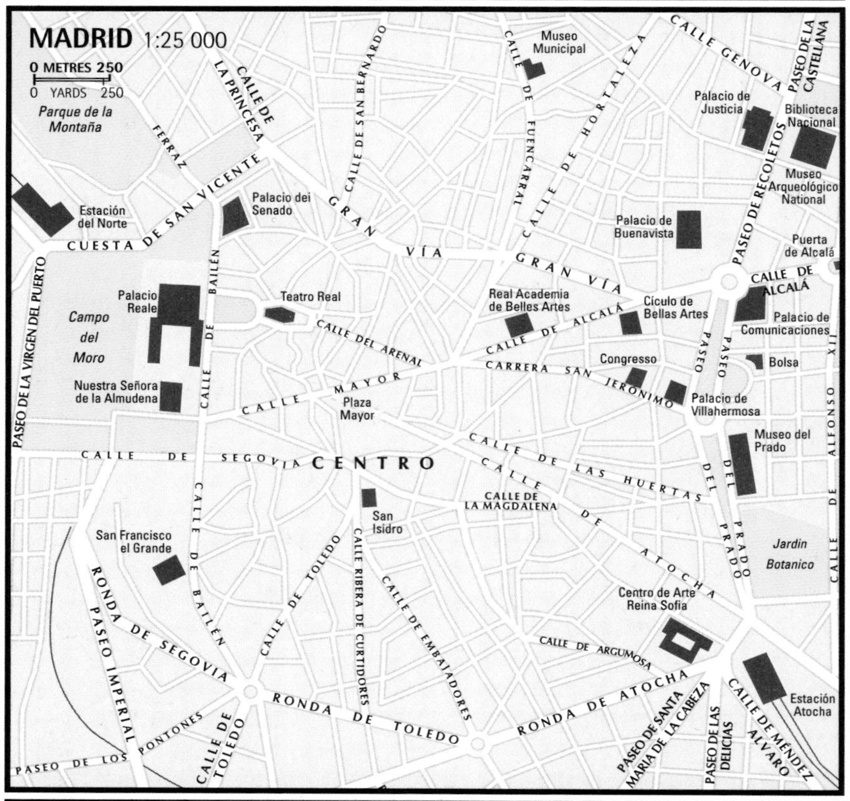

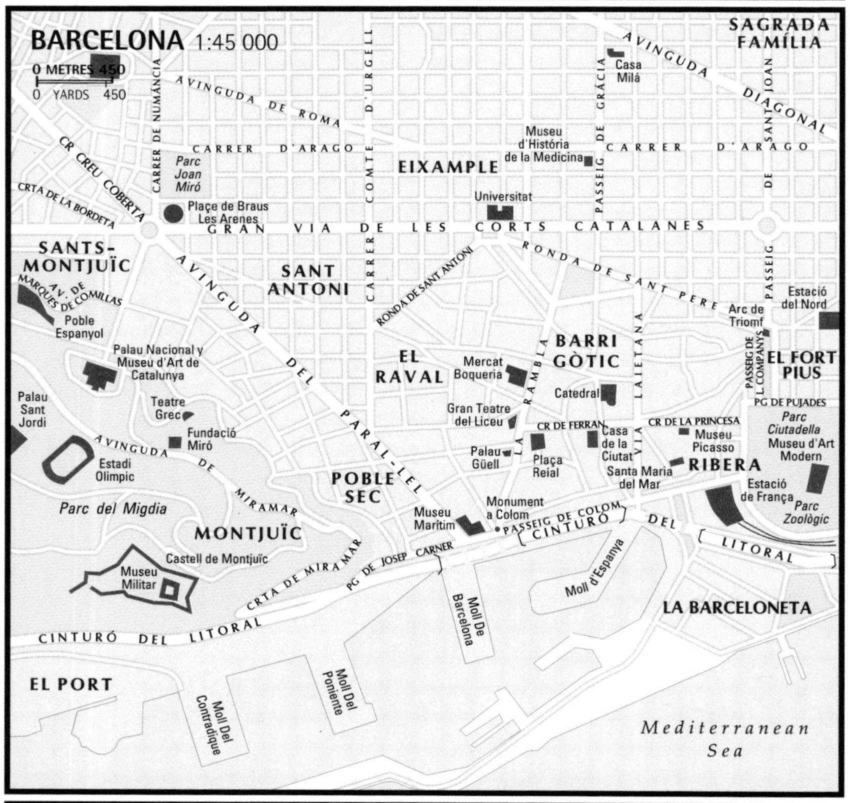

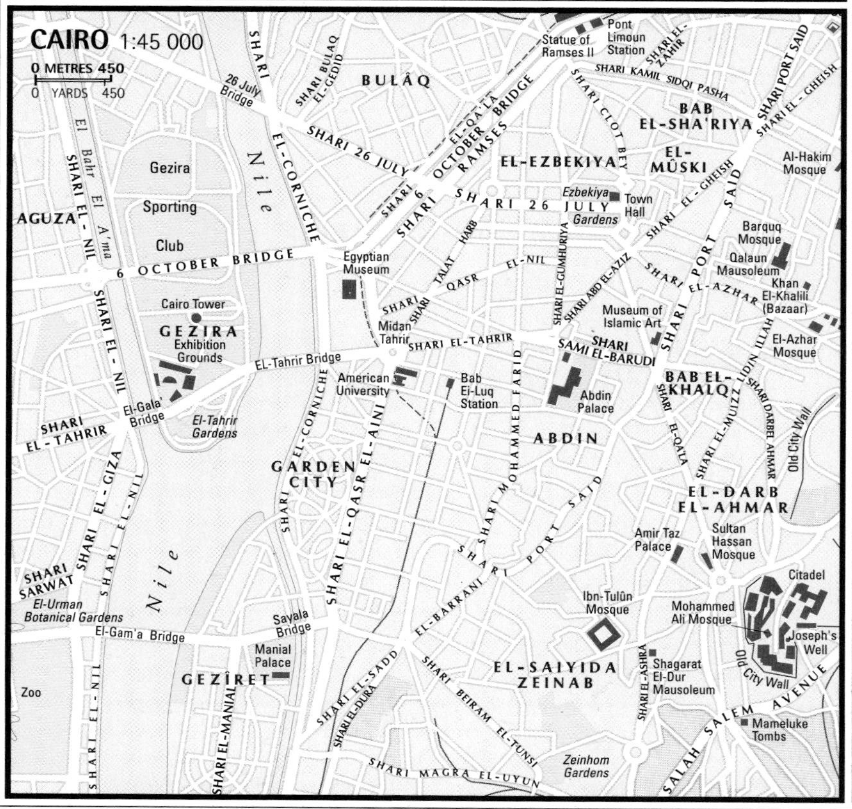

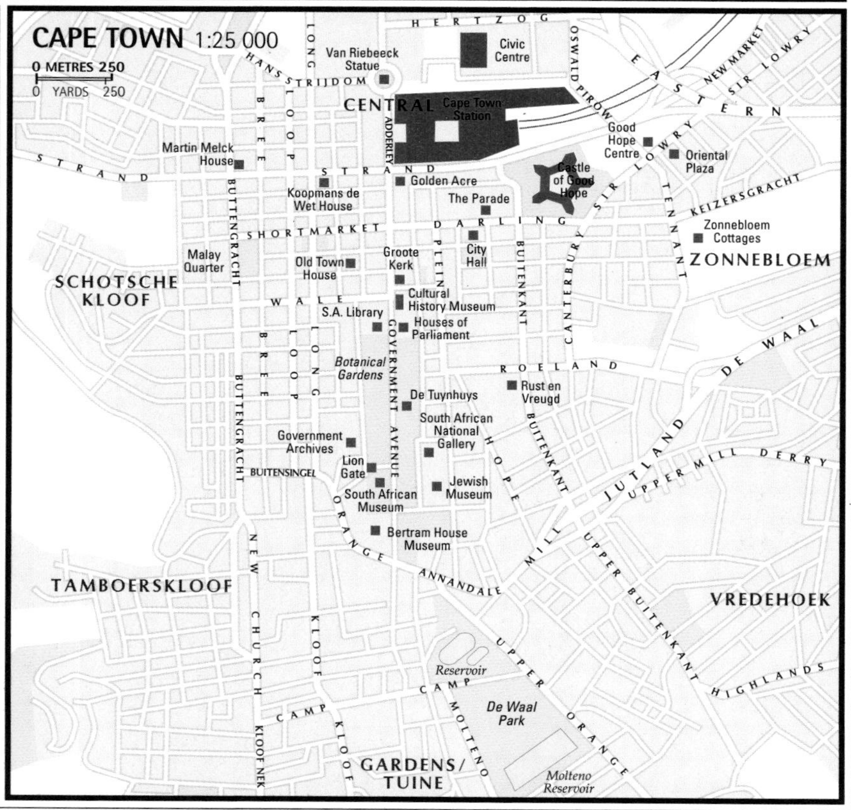

© Bartholomew

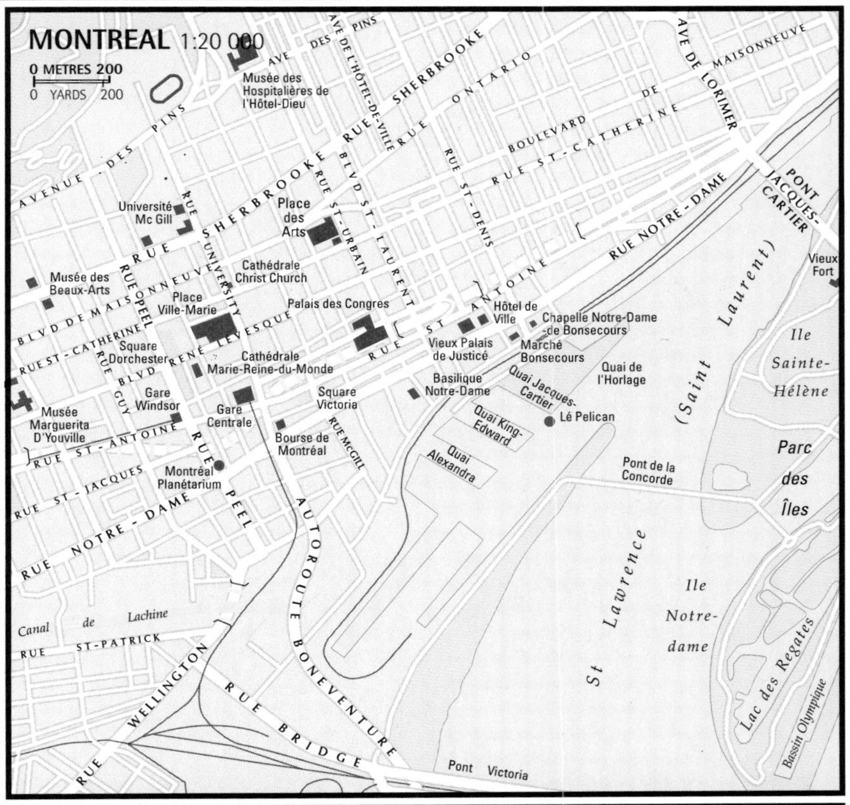

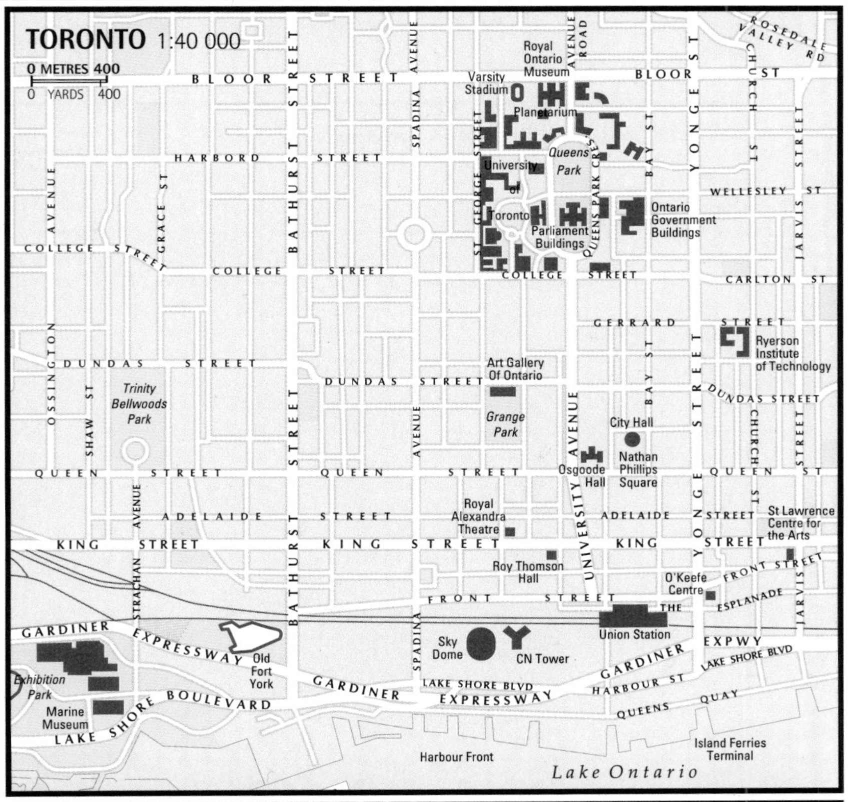

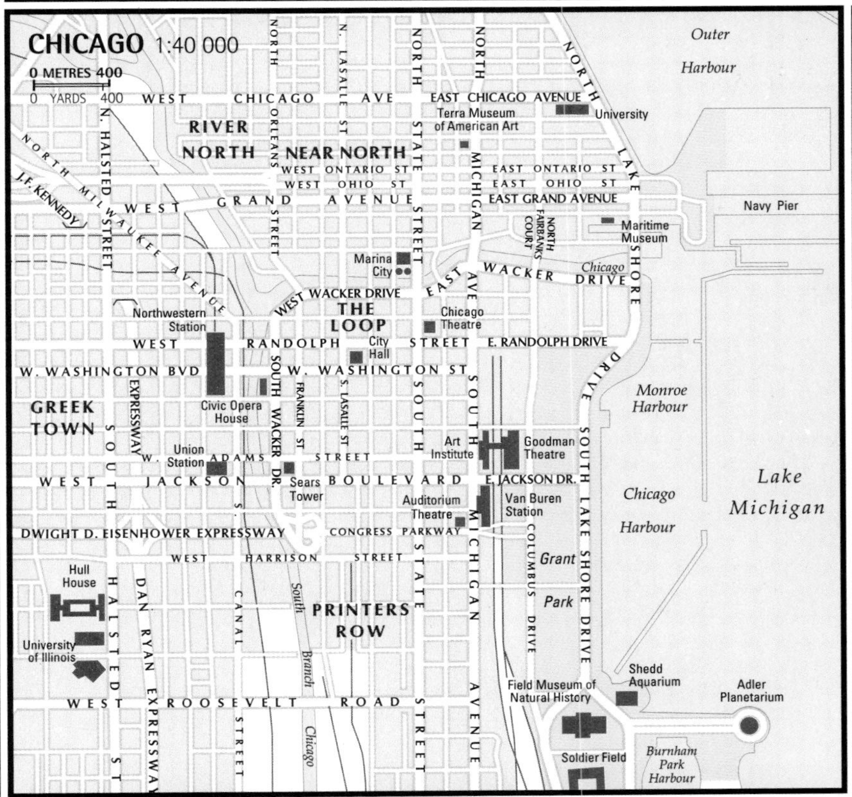

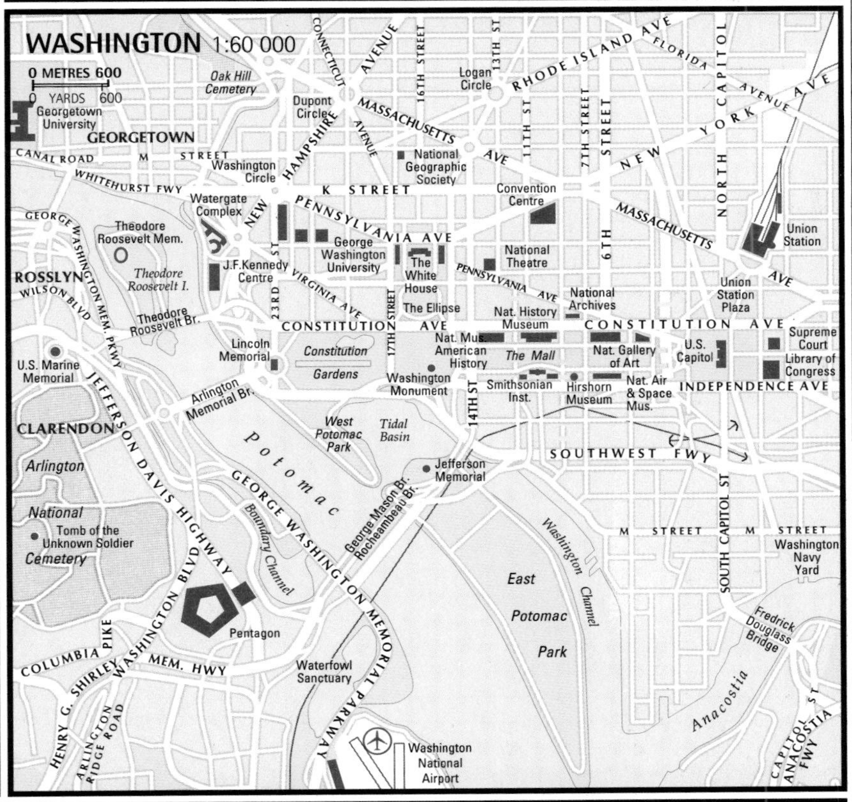

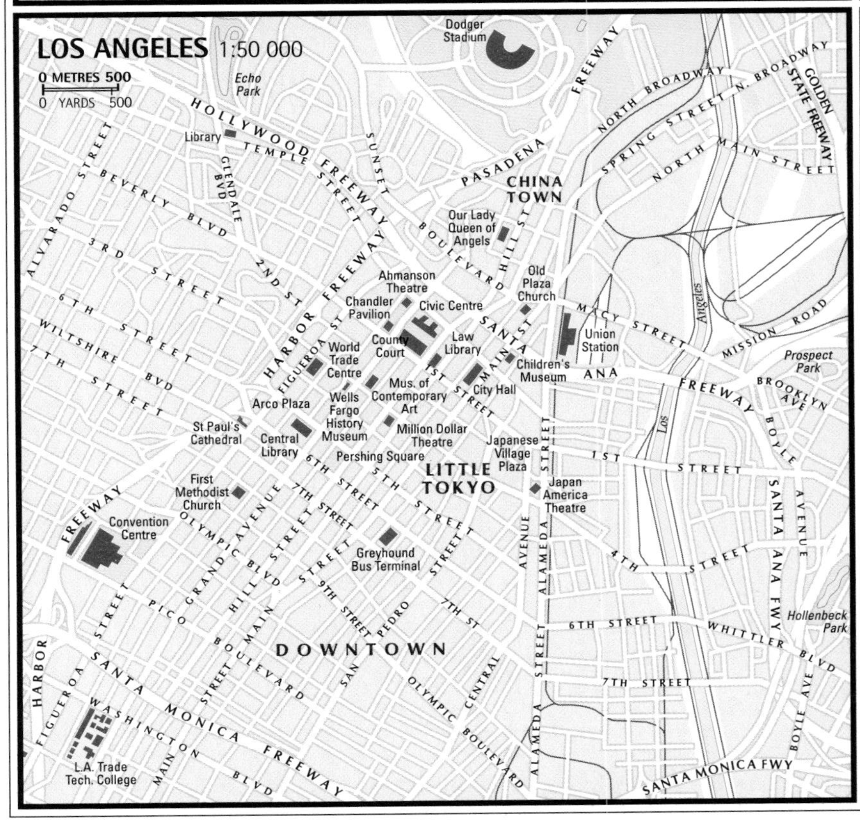

© Bartholomew

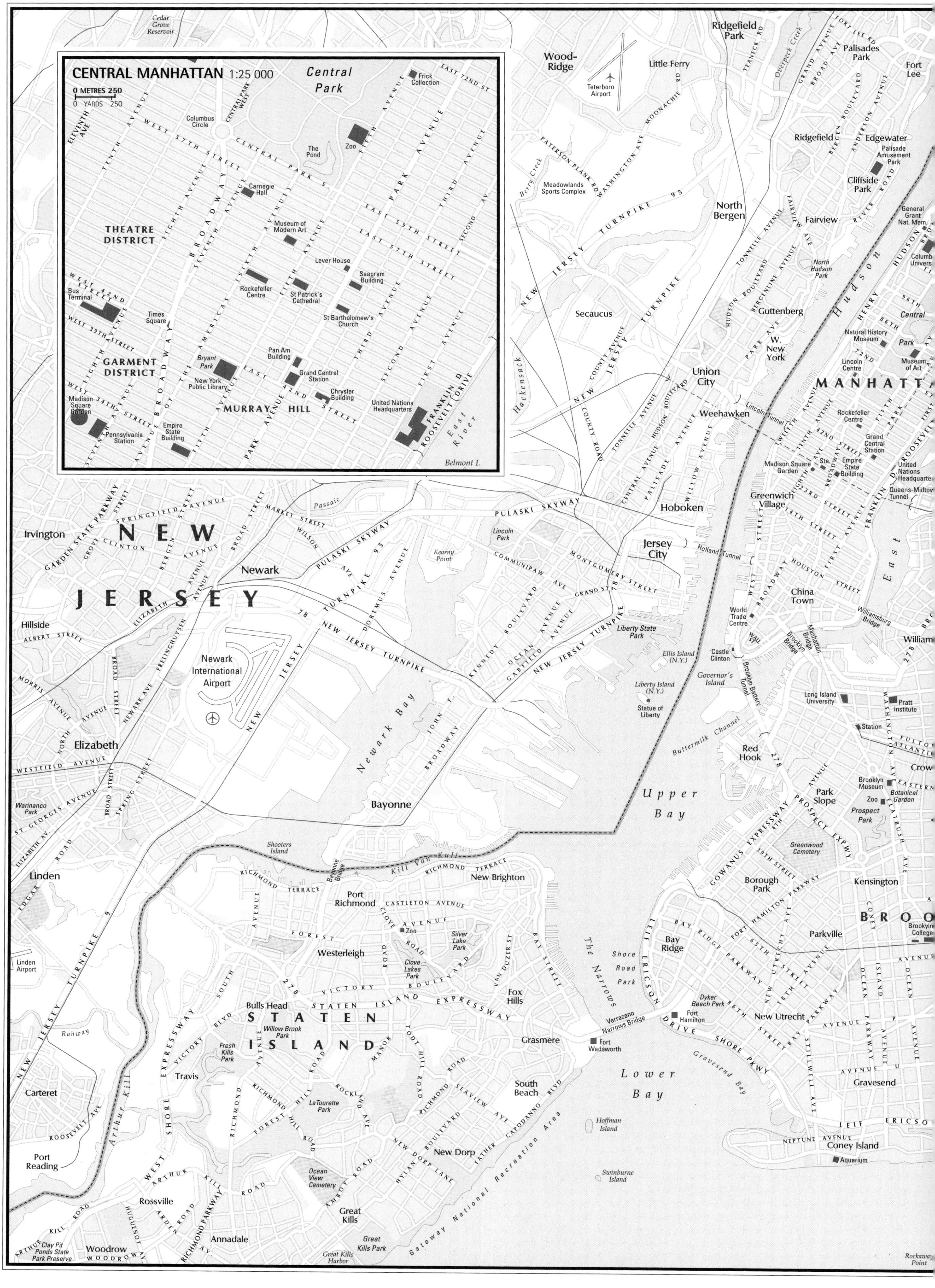
CENTRAL MANHATTAN 1:25 000
0 METRES 250
0 YARDS 250
Central Park
Frick Collection
Columbus Circle
Zoo
The Pond
Carnegie Hall
Museum of Modern Art
Lever House
Seagram Building
THEATRE DISTRICT
Bus Terminal
Times Square
Rockefeller Centre
St Patrick's Cathedral
St Bartholomew's Church
Pan Am Building
Grand Central Station
Chrysler Building
GARMENT DISTRICT
Bryant Park
New York Public Library
MURRAY HILL
United Nations Headquarters
Madison Square Garden
Pennsylvania Station
Empire State Building
East River
Belmont I.
ELEVENTH AVE
TENTH AVENUE
WEST 57TH STREET
CENTRAL PARK WEST
CENTRAL PARK S.
EIGHTH AVENUE
BROADWAY
SEVENTH AVENUE
FIFTH AVENUE
PARK AVENUE
THIRD AVENUE
SECOND AV.
EAST 72ND ST
EAST 59TH STREET
EAST 57TH STREET
WEST 42ND STREET
WEST 39TH STREET
WEST 34TH STREET
EAST 42ND STREET
FIRST AVENUE
FRANKLIN D. ROOSEVELT DRIVE
Cedar Grove Reservoir
Wood-Ridge
Teterboro Airport
Little Ferry
Ridgefield Park
Palisades Park
Fort Lee
Ridgefield
Edgewater
Palisade Amusement Park
Cliffside Park
Fairview
General Grant Nat. Mem.
Meadowlands Sports Complex
North Bergen
North Hudson Park
Secaucus
Guttenberg
W. New York
Union City
Weehawken
Lincoln Tunnel
Hoboken
Jersey City
Holland Tunnel
Hackensack
Passaic
PULASKI SKYWAY
Lincoln Park
Kearny Point
NEW JERSEY
Irvington
Newark
Hillside
Newark International Airport
Elizabeth
Warinanco Park
Linden
Linden Airport
Newark Bay
Bayonne
Liberty State Park
Ellis Island (N.Y.)
Liberty Island (N.Y.)
Statue of Liberty
Governor's Island
Castle Clinton
Brooklyn Battery Tunnel
Buttermilk Channel
Red Hook
Upper Bay
Shooters Island
Kill Van Kull
Bayonne Bridge
New Brighton
Port Richmond
Westerleigh
Zoo
Silver Lake Park
Clove Lakes Park
Bulls Head
STATEN ISLAND
Willow Brook Park
Fresh Kills Park
Travis
Carteret
Rahway
Arthur Kill
Port Reading
Rossville
Woodrow
Clay Pit Ponds State Park Preserve
Annadale
Great Kills
Great Kills Park
Great Kills Harbor
LaTourette Park
Ocean View Cemetery
New Dorp
South Beach
Grasmere
Fox Hills
Fort Wadsworth
Verrazano Narrows Bridge
The Narrows
Shore Road Park
Lower Bay
Hoffman Island
Swinburne Island
Gateway National Recreation Area
Gravesend Bay
Fort Hamilton
Dyker Beach Park
Bay Ridge
New Utrecht
Gravesend
Coney Island
Aquarium
Rockaway Point
Borough Park
Kensington
Parkville
Greenwood Cemetery
Park Slope
Prospect Park
Brooklyn Museum
Botanical Garden
Long Island University
Pratt Institute
Station
Brooklyn College
BROO
Hudson
MANHATTAN
Central Park
Natural History Museum
Museum of Art
Lincoln Centre
Rockefeller Centre
Grand Central Station
Madison Square Garden
Empire State Building
United Nations Headquarters
Queens-Midtown Tunnel
Greenwich Village
China Town
World Trade Centre
Manhattan Bridge
Brooklyn Bridge
Williamsburg Bridge
East
Columbia Univers
NEW JERSEY TURNPIKE
GARDEN STATE PARKWAY
GOWANUS EXPRESSWAY
PROSPECT EXPWY
STATEN ISLAND EXPRESSWAY
SHORE PKWY
LEIF ERICSON DRIVE
RICHMOND PARKWAY
HYLAN BOULEVARD
FATHER CAPODANNO BLVD
VICTORY BLVD
RICHMOND TERRACE
FOREST AVENUE
CASTLETON AVENUE
COMMUNIPAW AVE
MONTGOMERY STREET
KENNEDY BOULEVARD
JOHN F. KENNEDY BOULEVARD
BROADWAY
SPRINGFIELD AVENUE
CLINTON AVENUE
MARKET STREET
FRELINGHUYSEN AVENUE
ELIZABETH AVENUE
WESTFIELD AVENUE
ST GEORGES AVENUE
EDGAR ROAD
ROOSEVELT AVE
FLATBUSH AVE
OCEAN PARKWAY
STILLWELL AVE
NEPTUNE AVENUE
HAMILTON PARKWAY
FORT HAMILTON PARKWAY
HENRY HUDSON PARKWAY
HOUSTON STREET
WILLIAMSBURG
PALISADE AVENUE
BERGENLINE AVENUE
TONNELLE AVENUE
HUDSON BOULEVARD
COUNTY AVENUE
PATERSON PLANK RD
WASHINGTON AVE
MOONACHIE RD
GRAND AVENUE
BERGEN BOULEVARD
ANDERSON AVENUE
RIVER ROAD
FORT LEE RD
Overpeck Creek
Berry Creek

1:100 000
0 METRES 1000
0 YARDS 1000
BRONX
QUEENS
Fordham
Botanical Garden
Baychester
Hunters Island
Pelham Bay Park
Isaac Rice Memorial Stadium
Hart Island
Sands Point
Sands Point Park
Mott Point
Hempstead Harbor
Tremont
Belmont
Bronx Zoo
West Farms
Crotona Park
George Washington Bridge
Manorhaven
Port Washington North
Eastchester Bay
City Island
Kings Point
Manhasset Bay
Hempstead Harbor Park
Port Washington
Yankee Stadium
Melrose
City College
Harlem
Soundview
Sound view Park
Throgs Neck
Ferry Point Park
Mott Haven
Hunts Point
Kings Point
Kings Point Park
Marine Academy
Throgs Neck
Maritime College
Flower Hill
Plandome
Manhasset
Brother Islands
Hunts Point
Clason Point
Bronx Whitestone Bridge
Throgs Neck Bridge
Saddle Rock
Great Neck
Downing Memorial Stadium
New York City Museum
East
Rikers Island
College Point
Whitestone
Fort Totten
Wards Island
Hell Gate
Little Neck Bay
Harbor Hills
Thomaston
Flushing Airport
Astoria
La Guardia Airport
Flushing Bay
Douglaston
Long Island City
Broadway
Bayside
Little Neck
Lake Success
Shea Stadium
Flushing
Jackson Heights
Sunnyside
Woodside
Elmhurst
Hall of Science
Glen Oaks
North New Hyde Park
Flushing Meadows Corona Park
Kissena Park
Oakland Gardens
Alley Park
New Calvary Cemetery
Corona
Meadow Lake
Queens College
Fresh Meadows
Cunningham Park
Garden City Park
Cedar Grove Cemetery
New Hyde Park
Newton Creek
Laurel Hill
Willow Lake
St John's University
Bellaire
Queens Village
Belmont Park Race Track
Floral Park
Forest Hills
Kew Gardens
Station
Glendale
Jamaica
Hillside
Franklin Square
Richmond Hill
Elmont
Mt Carmel Cemetery
Forest Park
Cambria Heights
Bushwick
Beth David Cemetery
Cypress Hills Nat. Cemetery
St Albans
Cemetery of the Evergreens
Highland Park
Wood Haven
Bedford-Stuyvesant
North Valley Stream
Montefiore Cemetery
Springfield Gardens
Ozone Park
Children's Museum
East New York
Aqueduct Race Track
Valley Stream
Malverne
Valley Stream State Park
Brownsville
Howard Beach
Laurelton
Rosedale
New Lots
Flatbush
Brookville Park
Spring Creek Park
Grassy Bay
John F. Kennedy International Airport
South Valley Stream
Lynbrook
North Woodmere Park
Jamaica Bay
Canarsie
Woodmere
Hewlett
Canarsie Beach Park
Head of Bay
Cedarhurst
Flatlands
Gateway National Recreation Area
Woodsburgh
Hewlett Bay
Bay Park
Green Sedge
Bergen Beach Park
Inwood
Lawrence
Mill Basin
Marine Park
Rockaway Park
Far Rockaway
Floyd Bennett Field
The Raunt
Island Park
Broad Channel
Sheepshead Bay
Edgemere
Lawrence Marsh
Channel
Rockaway Park
East Rockaway Inlet
Silver Point Beach Park
Reynolds
Long Beach
Sheepshead Bay
Atlantic Beach
Long Beach
Rockaway Inlet
Rockaway Beach
Jacob Riis Park
Fort Tilden
Breezy Point
© Bartholomew

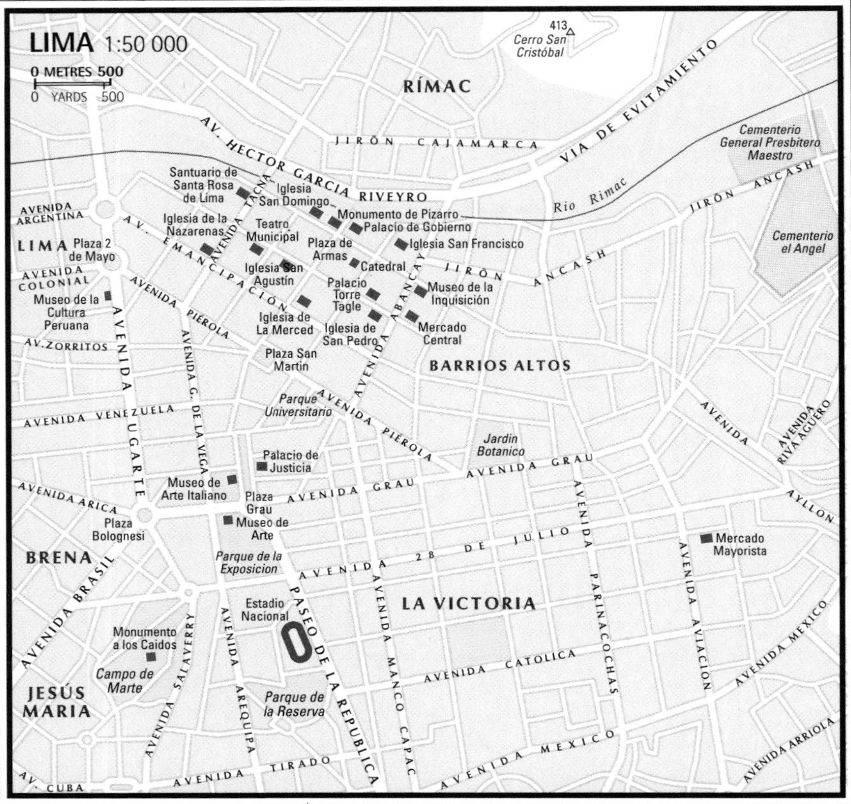

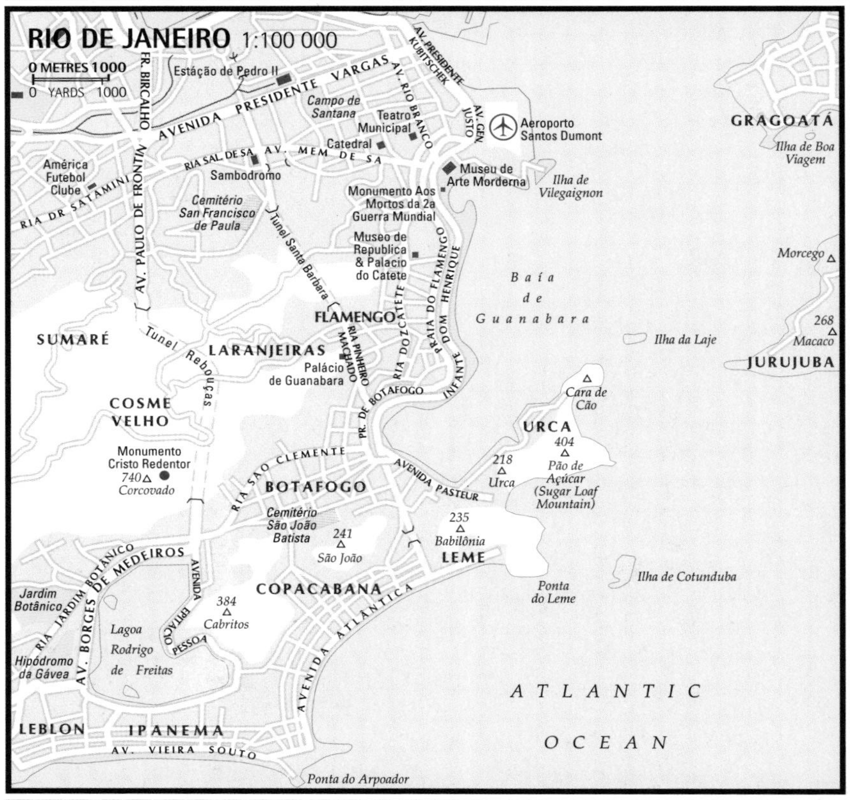

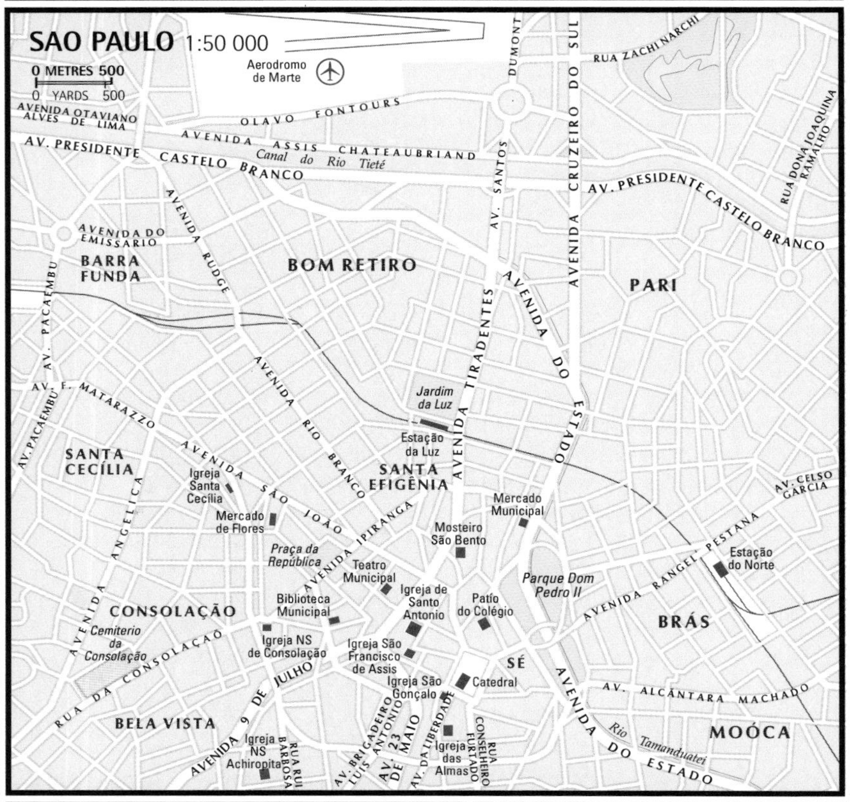

© Bartholomew

THE FIRST CONCISE Edition of the Times Atlas of the World used mapping developed for the larger Comprehensive Edition. This mapping had been compiled using traditional cartographic techniques which placed restrictions on what was possible when planning the Concise Edition pages. While some new mapping was specifically developed, compromises had to be made on many of the derived pages.

This new Seventh Edition of the Concise has been completely redeveloped from Bartholomew digital databases. In planning the map pages, these databases allow the freedom to select the optimum scale and coverage for each region or continent which best suits the format and extent of the new atlas. In order to portray the correct geographical relationships within each map, the use of continuation insets have been avoided wherever possible. Map areas have been selected with historic, cultural, political and economic links in mind as well as their physical geography.

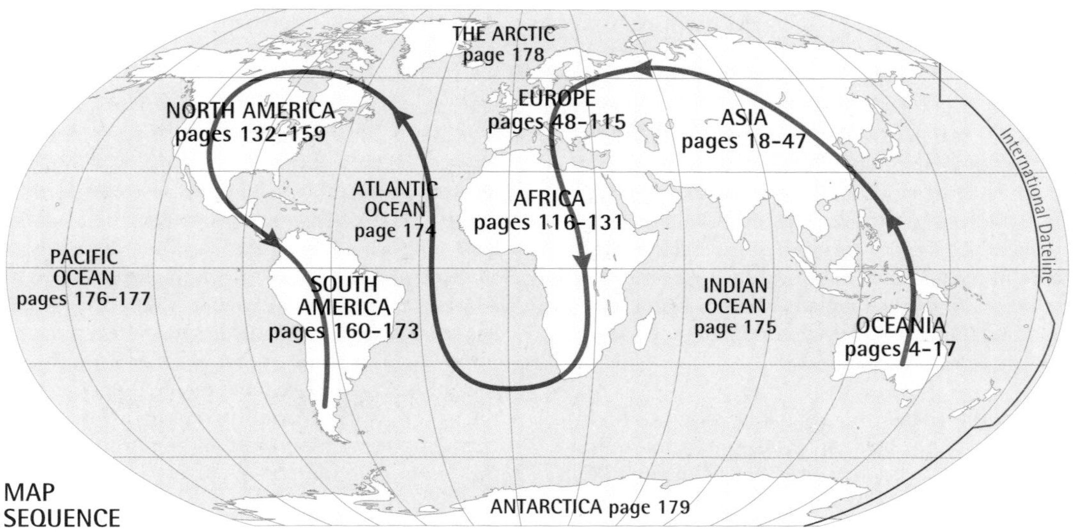

MAP SEQUENCE

In the tradition of the Times Atlas of the World the sequence of coverage starts at the International Date Line in the Pacific Ocean and broadly works westwards, moving from Oceania through Asia, Europe, Africa, North America and finally to South America. Each continent section is prefaced by a politically coloured map highlighting the states and territories within that particular continent. This is followed by reference maps of sub-continent regions, and within each of these in turn, more detailed reference mapping of the relevant individual countries.

While Europe and North America are still well represented in this new edition there is more balanced coverage with much more extensive mapping of Africa, Asia and South America. The new atlas also reflects the changed world scene in the post Cold War era, with new mapping of the re-unified Germany and the now independent Baltic States, for example. A completely new suite of maps covering the World's Oceans concludes the main reference map section.

SCALE

In order to compare like with like throughout the world it would obviously be necessary to maintain a common set of map scales throughout the atlas. However, the desirability of mapping the more densely populated areas of the world at larger scales and practical considerations, such as the need to fit a homogeneous physical region within a uniform rectangular page format, mean that a set of scale bands, as have been used in this atlas, provide the best practical solution. Scales for continental maps range between 1:15.5 million and 1:30 million, depending on the size of the continental land mass being covered. Scales for regional maps are typically in the range 1:7.5 million to 1:12.6 million, though smaller scales are used for remoter parts of Asia and North America. Detailed local mapping for most of the world is at scales between 1:3 million and 1:6.6 million, though for the most densely populated area of Europe this increases to a maximum scale of 1:1 million. Island insets are covered at a variety of scales.

PROJECTIONS

The creation of the new computer generated maps in this atlas presented the opportunity to review the map projections used and to create projections specifically designed for the area and scale of each map, or suite of maps. As the only way to show the earth with absolute accuracy is on a globe, all map projections are compromises. Some projections seek to maintain correct area relationships (equal area projections) or correct angles and shapes (conformal projections), others attempt to achieve a balance between these properties. The choice of projections used in this atlas has been made on an individual continent and regional basis.

For world maps in the atlas, the Robinson projection is used. This projection combines elements of conformality with that of equal area, and shows, over the earth as a whole, relatively true shapes and resonably equal areas. For the continental maps, different projections were selected according to the latitude and longitude and the overall shape of each continent. The projection used for Asia, the Two-Point Equidistant was chosen for its conformal qualities, while for North and South America the Bi-Polar Oblique projection, originally specifically designed for these continents, has been used. For Oceania, Europe and Africa, Lambert Azimuthal Equal Area, Chamberlin Trimetric and Stereographic projections respectively are used.

As with the continental maps, the selection of projections for the series on regional maps within each continent has been made on an individual basis for that region. Oblique Mercator projections have been selected for the regional maps of southeast Asia along the equator, while in higher latitudes in Europe, Conic Equidistant projections have been used extensively. In North America Lambert Conformal Conic projections have been used for regional mapping, while Lambert Azimuthal Equal Area projections have been employed in both South America and Australia. The projection used is indicated at the bottom left of each map.

MAP PRESENTATION

The map pages include a map title, location map showing the position of the region within the continent or, for larger scale maps, the position within the region. A scale bar and a key to the relief colouring are also included on each map. The measurements on the scale bar and the relief key are given in both metric and imperial measures. The symbols used on the maps are fully explained on page 84 of this introductory section. The reference system used in the index is based on the latitude and longitude grid, and the number and letter for each grid square is shown along the sides, top and bottom of each map, within the map frame. The red numbers located within the arrows show the page number for the adjoining map.

One of the criteria used to classify projections is their geometric characteristics. The diagrams on the right show projections based on an open cylinder, a cone and a plane, the groups are known as cylindrical, conic and azimuthal projections respectively.

Diagram A in each group illustrates the patterns of deformation or distortion when the cylinder, cone or plane is at a tangent to the globe, and diagram B illustrates these patterns when the cylinder, cone or plane intersects the globe. The lines or points of intersection may or may not be lines of latitude.

The patterns of deformation are parallel to the lines of intersection on cylindrical and conic projections, and concentric with the point or plane of intersection on azimuthal projections.

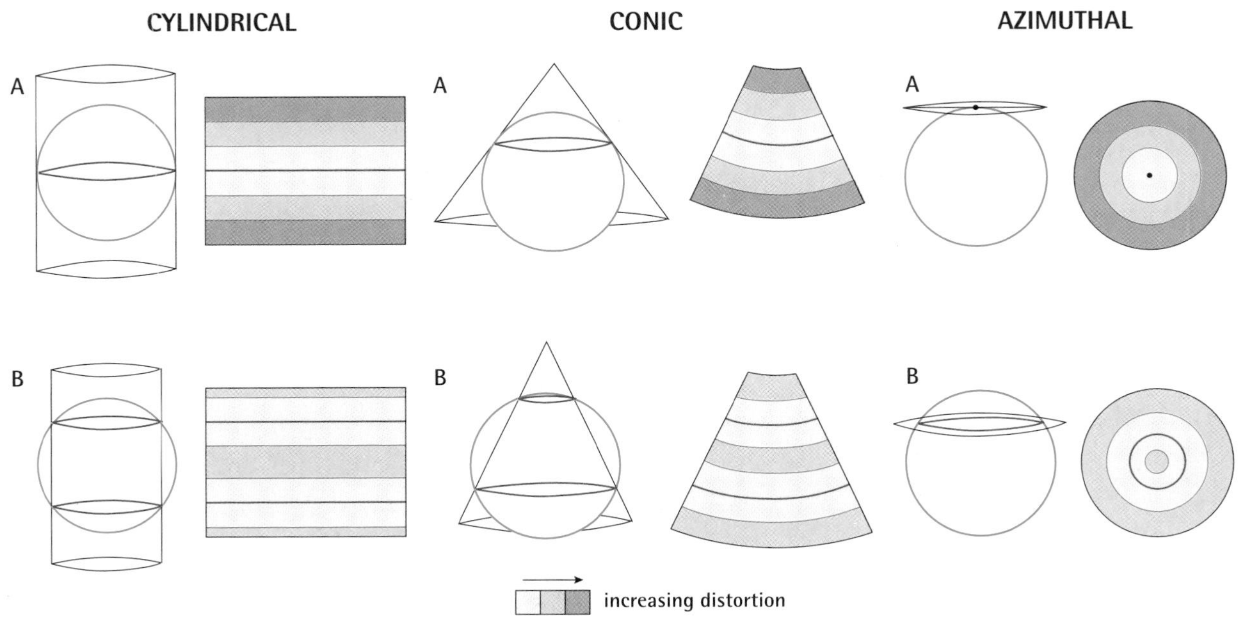

© Bartholomew

THE SPELLING OF place names on maps has always been a matter of great complexity, because of the variety of the world's languages and of the systems used to write them down. There is no single standard way of spelling names or of converting them from one alphabet, or symbol set, to another. Instead, conventional ways of spelling have evolved in each of the world's major languages, and the results often differ significantly from the name as it is spelt in the original. Familiar examples in English include Munich (München in German), Florence (Firenze in Italian) and Moscow (Moskva from Russian).

Continuing changes in official languages, and in writing systems, have to be taken into account by cartographers when creating maps and databases. Other factors also stand in the way of achieving a single standard. In many countries different languages are in use in different regions, or side-by-side in the same region. Sometimes the problem is dealt with in the country concerned by the use of a 'lingua franca' such as English to provide a mutually intelligible standard. In many cases the most-spoken language takes precedence, but there is still the potential for widely varying name forms even within a single country. A worldwide trend towards national, regional and ethnic self-determination is operating at the same time as an inevitable pressure towards more international standardization. There are other complications for the cartographer. For instance, more than one form is often in use for international feature names, such as extensive mountain ranges or long rivers which are shared by two or more countries.

Place names are, to an extent, a mirror for the changes that continue to transform the political globe. As could naturally be expected, changes of territorial control have an effect on name form usage. Yet even in countries where name forms have long been largely standardized, there are still some continuing issues for the cartographer to address: in the UK for example, the relative prominence (and spelling) of Gaelic and Welsh name forms versus anglicized names. Name spelling issues are, in fact, likely to emerge in any part of the world. A close watch is kept on areas where changes might be expected, although sometimes they crop up in unexpected places.

Reflecting trends across the world, systematic alterations have been made in this edition of the atlas compared with previous editions, involving all name forms for the ex-Soviet republics of Belarus, the Ukraine, Moldova, Armenia, Georgia, Azerbaijan, Tajikistan and Kyrgyzstan. A new romanization system is now used for Greece and Cyprus, and name forms in Cambodia, Laos and Vietnam have also been systematically altered.

These changes result, for example, in Kyyiv for Kiyev; Athina for Athínai; Phnum Penh for Phnom Penh; and Ha Nôi for Hanoi. New mapping of Spain takes full account of the official prominence now given to Catalan, Galician and main Basque names, which results in name forms such as Eivissa for Ibiza; A Coruña for La Coruña; and San Sebastián amended to Donostia - San Sebastián.

The local name forms used in this atlas are those which are officially recognised by the government of the country concerned, usually as represented by its official mapping agency. This is a basic principle laid down by the United Kingdom government's Permanent Committee on Geographical Names (PCGN). PCGN and the US Board on Geographic Names (BGN) for the most part use shared romanization principles for non-Roman alphabets and syllabaries. For example, Russian-language names are spelt using the standard BGN/PCGN system, which gives names such as Lipetsk and Yoshkar-Ola as opposed to a system used in eastern Europe which gives Lipeck and Joškar-Ola. However, for Arabic-speaking countries in particular, US policy is to use a single standard system for romanizing names, where PCGN prefers to follow local versions as one would find in the country itself or in its official mapping; an example from Tunisia is Sfax (local usage) as opposed to Şafāqis (strict romanization). In this atlas PCGN usage is followed.

Cartographers are sometimes criticised for giving undue prominence to local name forms instead of using plain English. It is, in fact, impossible to provide English names for the majority of mappable features, and translating names into English is fraught with linguistic hazards. Consequently a

ABBREVIATIONS AND GLOSSARY

A. Alp Alpen Alpi *alp*
Alt *upper*
Abbe Abbaye *abbey*
A.C.T. Australian Capital Territory
Afghan. Afghanistan
Afr. Africa African
Ag. Agia Agioi Agion Agios *saint*
Aig. Aiguille *peak*
Akr. Akra Akrotirion *cape, point*
Anch. Anchorage
Appno Appennino *mountains*
Aqued. Aqueduct
Ar. Arroyo *watercourse*
Arch. Archipel Archipelago
Archipiélago *archipelago*
Arg. Argentina Argentinian
Arr. Arrecife *reef*
Aust. Australia Australian
Azer. Azerbaijan

B. Baai Bahía Baía Baie Baja Bay Bucht Bukhta Bukt *bay*
Bad *spa*
Ban *village*
Bayou *inlet*
Bir *well*
Bc Banc *(sand) bank*
Bca Boca *mouth*
Bel. Belgium Belgian
Bg Berg *mountain*
Bge Barrage
Bge. Barragem *reservoir*
Bgt Bight Bugt *bay*
Bi Bani Beni *tribe (sons of)*
Bj Burj *hills*
Bk Bank
Bn Basin
Bol. Bol'shoy Bol'shoye Bol'shaya Bol'shiye *big*
Bos. Bosanski *town*
Br. Bredning *bay*
Brücke *bridge*
British Britain
Burun Burnu *point, cape*
Bt Bukit *mountain*
Bü. Büyük *big*

C. Cabo Cap *cape, headland*
Cape
Col *high pass*
Ç. Çay *river*
Cabo Cabeço *summit*
Cach. Cachoeira Cachoeiro *waterfall*
Can. Canal Canale *canal, channel*
Cañon Canyon *canyon*
Cat. Cataract
Catena *mountains*
Cd Ciudad *town, city*
Ch. Chaung *stream*
Chott *salt lake, marsh*
Chan. Channel
Che Chaîne *mountain chain*
Cma Cima *summit*
Cno Corno *peak*
Co Cerro *hill, peak*
Cor. Coronel *colonel*
Cord. Cordillera *mountain chain*
Cr. Creek
Cuch. Cuchilla *chain of mountains*
Czo Cozzo *mountain*

D. Da *big, river*
Dag Dagh Dagı *mountain*
Dagları *mountains*
Danau *lake*
Darreh *valley*
Daryacheh *lake*
Diavlos *hill*
-d. -dake *peak*
D.C. District of Columbia
Den. Denmark
Dj. Djebel *mountain*
Dr Doctor
Dz. Dzong *castle, fort*

E. East Eastern
Eil. Eiland *island*
Eilanden *islands*
Emb. Embalse *reservoir*
Equat. Equatorial
Escarp. Escarpment
Est. Estuary Estrecho *strait*
Étg Étang *lake, lagoon*

F. Firth
F.D. Federal District
Fed. Federation
Fj. Fjell *mountain*
Fjord Fjörður *fjord*
Fk Fork
Fl. Fleuve *river*
Fr. France French
Fte Fonte *well*

G. Gebel *mountain*
Göl Gölü Gol *lake*
G. Golfe Golfo Gulf *gulf, bay*
Gora *mountain*
Guba *bay*
Gunung *mountain*
-g. -gawa *river*
Gd Grand *big*
Gde Grande *big*
Geb. Gebergte *mountain range*
Gebirge *mountains*
Gen. General
Gez. Gezira *island*
Ger. Germany
Ghub. Ghubbat *bay*
Gl. Glacier
Gob. Gobernador *governor*
Grp Group
Gr. Graben *trench, ditch*
Gross Grosse Grande *big*
Gt Great Groot Groote *big*
Gy Góry Gory *mountains*

H. Hawr *lake*
Hill
Hoch *high*
Hora *mountain*
Hory *mountains*
Halv. Halvøy *peninsula*
Harb. Harbour
Hd Head
Hg. Hegység *mountains*
Hgts Heights
Hist. Historic
Hond. Honduras
Ht Haut *high*
Hte Haute *high*

I. Île Ilha Insel Isla Island Isle *island, isle*
Isola Isole *island*
im. imeni *in the name of*
In. Inder Indre Inner Inre *inner*
Inlet *inlet*
Ind. India Indian
Indon. Indonesia
Inf. Inferior Inférieure *lower*
Is Islas Îles Ilhas Islands Isles *islands, isles*
Isr. Israel
Isth. Isthmus

J. Jabal Jebel *mountain*
Jibal *mountains*
Jrvi Jaure Jezero Jezioro *lake*
Jökull *glacier*
Jap. Japan Japanese

K. Kaap Kap Kapp *cape*
Kaikyo *strait*
Kato *lower*
Kiang *river or stream*
Ko *island, lake, inlet*
Koh Kuh Kuhha *island*
Kolpos *gulf*
Kopf *hill*
Kuala *estuary*
Kyst *coast*
Kan. Kanal Kanaal *canal*
Kazakh. Kazakhstan
Kep. Kepulauan *archipelago, islands*
Kg Kampong *village*
Kompong *landing place*
Kong *king*
Kh. Khawr *inlet*
Khirbet *ruins*
Khr Khrebet *mountain range*
Kl. Klein Kleine *small*
Kör. Körfez Körfezi *bay, gulf*
K. Küçük *small*
Kyrgyz. Kyrgyzstan

L. Lac Lago Lake Liman Limni Liqen Loch Lough *lake, loch*
Lam *stream*
Lag. Lagoon Laguna Lagôa *lagoon*
Ldg Landing
Liech. Liechtenstein
Lit. Little
Lith. Lithuania
Lux. Luxembourg

M. Mae *river*
Me *great, chief, mother*
Meer *lake, sea*
Muang *kingdom, province, town*
Muong *town*
Mys *cape*
Mal. Malyy Malaya Maloye *small*
Mex. Mexico Mexican
Mf Massif *mountains, upland*
Mgna Montagna *mountain*
Mgne Montagne *mountain*
Mgnes Montagnes *mountains*
Mon. Monasterio Monastery *monastery*
Monument
Moz. Mozambique

local name form map is more internally consistent than a partly-anglicized one; it reflects more closely name forms found in the country itself, and it has the added advantage of being more accessible to readers whose first language is not English. Local name form mapping such as is found in this atlas is the nearest that the cartographer can achieve to an international standard.

However, prominent English-language conventional names and historic names are not neglected; along with significant superseded names, they are included in brackets on the map where space permits and are cross-referenced in the index, while the Guide to States and Territories on pages 10 to 32 and small-scale continental maps use only these familiar forms. Continents, oceans, seas and underwater features in international waters appear in English throughout the atlas, as do other international features where such a name exists in common use. Country names are also shown in English but include recent policy changes promulgated by some national governments and adopted by the United Nations - Myanmar (replacing Burma), Belarus (replacing Belorussia and a variety of other versions as well as the traditional White Russia), Kyrgyzstan (for Kirghizia or Kirgizia), Moldova (Moldavia), and Côte d'Ivoire (Ivory Coast). Many of these alternate name forms are also cross-referenced in the index. In the case of these country names, and with certain cities such as Beijing (replacing Peking), the gradual incorporation of local forms in to the English language can be seen at work. This atlas reflects that process but does not attempt to lead it.

NAME CHANGES

Unequivocal renamings are far more common, particularly affecting towns and cities. The dissolution of the Soviet Union in particular has given rise to a series of reversions away from communist-inspired names. Russian-language spellings are now occasionally being amended for other reasons: eg Ashkhabad is now Ashgabat, which is closer to the Turkmen form. Some name changes have attracted international interest - most notably, perhaps, the reversion of Leningrad to Sankt-Peterburg in the Russian form, and St. Petersburg in the English form; but this atlas also represents the latest state of knowledge as regards less famous names, based on a continuously updated collection of reference sources and on contacts with geographical consultants and authorities around the world.

BOUNDARIES

The status of nations and their boundaries, and the names associated with these, are shown in this atlas as they are in reality at the time of going to press, as far as can be ascertained. The atlas naturally includes the recent change of the status of nations and their boundaries which have included the reunification of Germany, and the partition of the Soviet Union, Yugoslavia and Czechoslovakia. Although many former dependent territories are now independent, new nations such as Eritrea and Palau have also emerged as separate entities quite apart from the above-mentioned schisms.

Where international boundaries are the subject of dispute it may be that no protrayal of them will meet with the approval of the countries involved, but it is not seen as the function of this atlas to try to adjudicate between the rights and wrongs of political issues. Although reference mapping is not a suitable medium for indicating the claims of many separatist and irredentist movements that are active in the world, every reasonable attempt is made to show where a territorial dispute exists, and where there is an important difference between 'de facto' (existing on the ground) and 'de jure' (according to law) boundaries. The territories occupied by Israel are clearly indicated as such rather than simply being incorporated into Israel itself, but at the same time no political entity of 'Palestine' is mentioned. In Kashmir, the long-standing dispute between India and Pakistan is represented by giving prominence to the de facto situation, while suitable boundary symbols also indicate that this is not a settled issue. The atlas aims to take a strictly neutral viewpoint of all such cases, based on advice from expert consultants.

In this atlas changes to the internal administrative divisions of countries are also regarded as being of prime importance, and some attract international interest, such as the changes in the provincial structure in the Republic of South Africa.

Mt	Mont Mount *mountain*
Mt.	Mountain
Mte	Monte *mountain*
Mtes	Montes *mountains*
Mti	Monti Munti *mountains*
Mtii	Muntii *mountains*
Mtn	Mountain
Mth	Mouth
Mths	Mouths
Mts	Monts Mountains
N.	Nam *south(ern), river*
	Neu Ny *new*
	Nevado *peak*
	Nudo *mountain*
	Noord Nord Nörre Nørre North *north*
	Nos *spit, point*
Nac.	Nacional *national*
Nat.	National
N.E.	Northeast
Neth.	Netherlands
Nic.	Nicaragua
Nizh.	Nizhneye Nizhniy Nizhnyaya *lower*
Nizm.	Nizmennost' *lowland*
N.O.	Noord Oost Nord Ost *northeast*
Nor.	Norway Norwegian
Nov.	Novyy Novaya Noviye Novoye *new*
Nr	Nether
N.W.	Northwest
N.Z.	New Zealand
Nva	Nueva *new*
O.	Oost Ost *east*
	Ostrov *island*
Ø.	Østre *east*
Ob.	Ober *upper, higher*
Oc.	Ocean
Ode	Oude *old*
Ogl.	Oglat *well*
Or.	Ori *mountains*
	Oros *mountain*
Orm.	Ormos *bay*
O-va	Ostrova *islands*
Ot	Olet *mountain*
Öv.	Över Övre *upper*
Oz.	Ozero *lake*
	Ozera *lakes*
P.	Pass
	Pic Pico Piz *peak, summit*
	Pulau *island*
	Pou *mountain*
P.P.	Pulau-pulau *islands*
Pak.	Pakistan
Para.	Paraguay
Pass.	Passage
Peg.	Pegunungan *mountain range*
Pen.	Peninsula Penisola *peninsula*
Per.	Pereval *pass*
Phn.	Phnom *hill, mountain*
Pgio	Poggio *hill*
Pl.	Planina Planinski *mountain(s)*
Pla	Playa *beach*
Plat.	Plateau
Plosk.	Ploskogor'ye *plateau*
Pno	Pantano *reservoir, swamp*
Pol.	Poland Polish
Por.	Porog *rapids*
Port.	Portugal Portuguese
P-ov	Poluostrov *peninsula*
Pr.	Proliv *strait*
	Przyladek *cape*
Pres.	Presidente *president*
Presq.	Presqu'île *peninsula*
Prom.	Promontory
Prov.	Province Provincial
Psa	Presa *dam*
Pso	Passo *dam*
Pt	Point
	Pont *bridge*
	Petit *small*
Pta	Ponta Punta *cape, point*
	Puerta *narrow pass*
Pte	Pointe *cape, point*
	Ponte Puente *bridge*
Pto	Porto Puerto *harbour, port*
Pzo	Pizzo *mountain peak, mountain*
Q.	Qala *castle, fort*
R.	Reshteh *mountain range*
	River Rud *river*
Ra.	Range
Rca	Rocca *rock, fortress*
Reg.	Region
Rep.	Republic
Res.	Reserve
	Reservoir
Resp.	Respublika *republic*
Rf	Reef
Rge	Ridge
Riba	Ribeira *coast, bottom of the river valley*
Rom.	Romania Romanian
Rte	Route
Rus. Fed.	Russian Federation
S.	Salar Salina *salt pan*
	San São *saint*
	See *lake*
	Seto *strait, channel*
	Sjö *lake*
	Sör South Süd Sud Syd *south*
	sur *on*
Sa	Serra Sierra *mountain range*
Sab.	Sabkhat *salt flat*
Sc.	Scoglio *rock, reef*
Sd	Sound Sund *sound*
S.E.	Southeast
Seb.	Sebjet Sebkhat Sebkra *salt flat*
Serr.	Serranía *mountain range*
Sev.	Severnaya Severnyy *north(ern)*
Sh.	Sha'ib *watercourse*
	Shat *river (-mouth)*
	Shima *island*
	Shankou *pass*
Si	Sidi *lord, master*
Sk.	Shuikou *reservoir*
Skt	Sankt *saint*
Smt	Seamount
Snra	Senhora *Mrs, lady*
Snro	Senhoro *Mr, gentleman*
Sp.	Spain Spanish
	Spitze *peak*
Sr	Sönder Sønder *southern*
Sr.	Sredniy Srednyaya *middle*
St	Saint Sint
	Staryy *old*
St.	Stor Store *big*
	Stung *river*
Sta	Santa *saint*
Ste	Sainte *saint*
	Store *big*
Sto	Santo *saint*
Str.	Strait Stretta *strait*
Sv.	Sväty Sveti *holy, saint*
Switz.	Switzerland
S.W.	Southwest
T.	Tal *valley*
	Tall Tell *hill*
	Tepe Tepesi *hill, peak*
Tajik.	Tajikistan
Terr.	Territory
Tg	Tanjung Tanjong *cape, point*
Tk	Teluk *bay*
Tmt	Tablemount
Tr.	Trench Trough
Tre	Torre *tower, fortress*
Tte	Teniente *lieutenant*
Turkmen.	Turkmenistan
U.A.E.	United Arab Emirates
Ug	Ujung *point, cape*
U.K.	United Kingdom
U.S.A.	United States of America
Unt.	Unter *lower*
Upr	Upper
Uzbek.	Uzbekistan
V.	Val Valle Valley *valley*
	Väster Vest Vester *west(ern)*
	Vatn *lake*
	Ville *town*
	Vorder *near*
Va	Vila *small town*
Vol.	Volcán Volcan Volcano *volcano*
Vdkhr.	Vodokhranilishche *reservoir*
Vdskh.	Vodoskhovshche Vodaskhovishcha *reservoir*
Vel.	Velikiy Velikaya Velikiye *big*
Ven.	Venezuela Venezuelan
Verkh.	Verkhniy Verkhneye Verkhne *upper* Verkhnyaya *upper*
Vost.	Vostochnyy *eastern*
Vozv.	Vozvyshennost' *hills, upland*
W.	Wadi *watercourse*
	Wald *forest*
	Wan *bay*
	Water *water*
	Well
	West
Wr	Wester
-y	-yama *mountain*
Yt.	Ytre Ytter Ytri *outer*
Yugo.	Yugoslavia
Yuzh.	Yuzhnaya Yuzhno Yuzhnyy *southern*
Zal.	Zaliv *bay*
Zap.	Zapadnyy Zapadnaya Zapadno Zapadnoye *western*
Zem.	Zemlya *land*

© Bartholomew

SYMBOLS

RELIEF

Contour intervals used in layer colouring at scales greater than 1:4 million

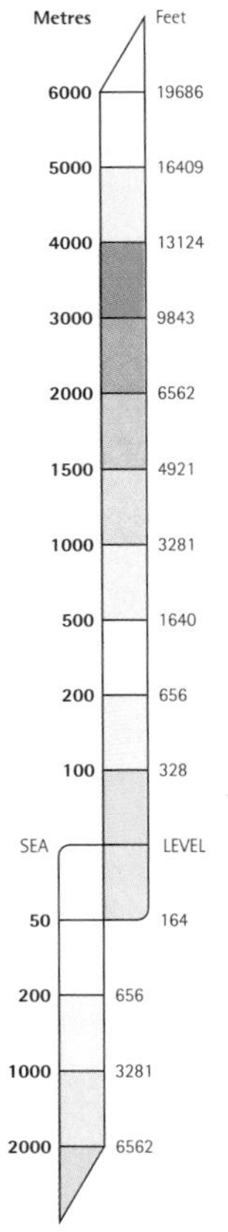

Metres	Feet
6000	19686
5000	16409
4000	13124
3000	9843
2000	6562
1500	4921
1000	3281
500	1640
200	656
100	328
SEA	LEVEL
50	164
200	656
1000	3281
2000	6562

At scales of 1:3 million, additional bathymetric contour lines are shown at 1000 and 3000 metres below sea level.

Contour intervals used in layer colouring at scales of 1:4 million and smaller

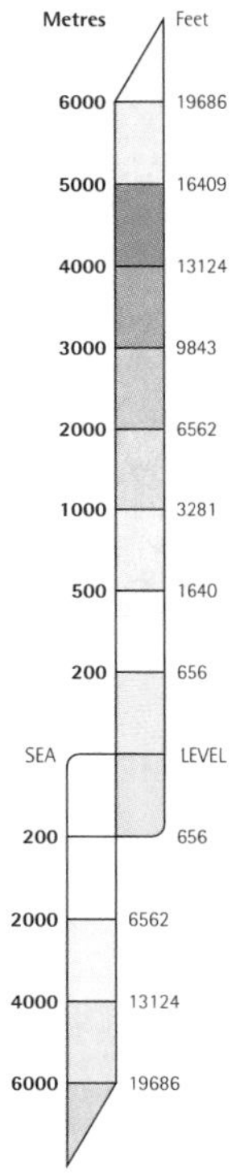

Metres	Feet
6000	19686
5000	16409
4000	13124
3000	9843
2000	6562
1000	3281
500	1640
200	656
SEA	LEVEL
200	656
2000	6562
4000	13124
6000	19686

213 △   Summit
height in metres

PHYSICAL FEATURES

Freshwater lake

Seasonal freshwater lake

Saltwater lake *or* Lagoon

Seasonal saltwater lake

Dry salt lake *or* Salt pan

Marsh

River

Waterfall

Dam *or* Barrage

Seasonal river *or* Wadi

Canal

Flood dyke

Reef

Volcano

Lava field

Sandy desert

Rocky desert

Oasis

Escarpment

Mountain pass

Ice cap *or* Glacier

COMMUNICATIONS

Motorway

Motorway tunnel

Motorways are classified separately at scales greater than 1:4 million, at smaller scales motorways are classified with main roads.

Main road

Main road *under construction*

Main road tunnel

Other road

Other road *under construction*

Other road tunnel

Track

Car ferry

Main railway

Main railway *under construction*

Main railway tunnel

Other railway

Other railway *under construction*

Other railway tunnel

Train ferry

⊕ Main airport

✦ Other airport

BOUNDARIES

International

International *through water*

International *disputed*

Ceasefire line

Main administrative

Main administrative *through water*

Other administrative

Other administrative *through water*

Main administrative *at scales of 1:4 million and smaller*

Other administrative boundaries are not shown at scales of 1:4 million and smaller

National park

Reserve

OTHER FEATURES

Ancient wall

Historic *or* Tourist site

SETTLEMENTS

POPULATION	NATIONAL CAPITAL	ADMINISTRATIVE CAPITAL	CITY OR TOWN
Over 5 million	▣ **Beijing**	◉ **Tianjin**	◉ **New York**
1 to 5 million	▣ **Sŏul**	◉ **Lagos**	◉ **Barranquilla**
500000 to 1 million	▣ **Bangui**	◉ **Douala**	◉ **Memphis**
100000 to 500000	▢ **Wellington**	○ **Mansa**	○ **Mara**
50000 to 100000	▢ Port of Spain	○ Lubango	○ Arecibo
10000 to 50000	▫ Malabo	○ Chinhoyi	○ El Tigre
Less than 10000	▫ Roseau	○ Áti	○ Soledad

Urban area

STYLES OF LETTERING

Country name	**EGYPT**	**BARBADOS**
Main administrative name	**PORTO**	Main administrative names *at scales of 1:4 million and smaller* AGADEZ
Other administrative name	M A N C H E	Area name ARTOIS
Physical feature	ISLAND LAKE	MOUNTAIN RIVER
	Gran Canaria *LAKE ERIE*	*SOUTHERN ALPS* Niger

© Bartholomew

ATLAS OF THE WORLD

© Bartholomew

ARCTIC OCEAN
Parry Islands
Ellesmere Island
Melville I.
Devon I.
Dundas
Greenland
(Den.)
Banks I.
Beaufort Sea
Victoria Island
Baffin Bay
Baffin Island
Davis Str.
Barrow
Point Hope
Inuvik
Coppermine
Bering Strait
U.S.A.
Nome
Yukon
Fairbanks
Mackenzie
Great Bear L.
Great Slave L.
Anchorage
Whitehorse
Seward
Juneau
Hay River
Hudson Bay
Churchill
Ivujivik
Godthåb
Frederikshåb
Scoresbysund
Tasiilaq
Denmark Str.
Jan Mayen (Nor.)
Arctic Circle
ICELAND
Reykjavik
Faeroes (Den.)
NORWAY
Bergen
CANADA
Prince Rupert
Aleutian Is
Fraser
Edmonton
Saskatoon
Regina
Winnipeg
Schefferville
Fort Rupert
Sept-Îles
Goose Bay
Newfoundland
St John's
Vancouver
Victoria
Calgary
Seattle
Portland
L. Superior
Duluth
Quebec
Montreal
Ottawa
St John
Halifax
Minneapolis
Lake Michigan
Toronto
Buffalo
Boston
Detroit
UNITED STATES OF AMERICA
Salt Lake City
Omaha
Chicago
Indian.
Pittsb.
New York
Philadelphia
Washington
Sacramento
San Francisco
Colorado
Denver
Kansas City
St Louis
Cincinnati
Norfolk
Los Angeles
Oklahoma City
Memphis
Phoenix
Mississippi
Atlanta
Birmingham
San Diego
El Paso
Ft Worth
Dallas
Houston
New Orleans
Jacksonville
Rio Grande
San Antonio
Tampa
Miami
Gulf of Mexico
Nassau
THE BAHAMAS
Guadalupe I. (Mex.)
Torreón
Monterrey
Tampico
MEXICO
Havana
CUBA
DOMINICAN REP.
HAITI
San Juan
Puerto Rico (U.S.A.)
ANTIGUA
Santo Domingo
Kingston
JAMAICA
Guadalajara
Revillagigedo Is. (Mex)
Mexico City
Veracruz
Puebla
Belmopan
BELIZE
HONDURAS
Caribbean Sea
DOMINICA
Acapulco
GUAT.
Guatemala City
Tegucigalpa
EL SALVADOR
NICARAGUA
ST LUCIA
ST VINCENT
GRENADA
BARBADOS
TRINIDAD & TOBAGO
Port of Spain
Managua
Barranquilla
Caracas
COSTA RICA
San José
PANAMA
Panama City
VENEZUELA
Orinoco
Georgetown
Paramaribo
GUYANA
SUR.
Fr. Guiana
Medellín
Bucaramanga
Bogotá
Cali
COLOMBIA
Clipperton I. (Fr.)
Quito
ECUADOR
Guayaquil
Galapagos Is (Ecuador)
Macapá
Belém
São Luís
Manaus
Amazon
Fortaleza
Fernando de Noronha (Braz.)
Pôrto Velho
Recife
PERU
BRAZIL
São Francisco
Callao
Lima
Cusco
Salvador
Arequipa
La Paz
BOLIVIA
Brasília
Belo Horizonte
Sucre
Iquique
PARAGUAY
Rio de Janeiro
São Paulo
Trindade (Braz.)
Martin Vaz Is (Braz.)
Antofagasta
Asunción
Curitiba
Tucumán
Paraná
Pôrto Alegre
Coquimbo
Córdoba
Valparaíso
Santiago
Rosario
URUGUAY
Montevideo
Buenos Aires
ARGENTINA
CHILE
Concepción
Bahia Blanca
Puerto Montt
San Félix (Chile)
I. Sala y Gómez (Chile)
Easter I. (Chile)
Juan Fernandez Is (Chile)
Falkland Islands (U.K.)
Stanley
Punta Arenas
Ushuaia
Cape Horn
Drake Passage
Shag Rocks (U.K.)
South Georgia (U.K.)
Scotia Sea
South Sandwich Is (U.K.)
South Shetland Is (U.K.)
South Orkney Is (U.K.)
Antarctic Peninsula
Bouvet I. (Nor.)
Thurston I.
Bellingshausen Sea
Alexander I.
Amundsen Sea
Marie Byrd Land
Ellsworth Land
Weddell Sea
Queen Maud Land
NORTH PACIFIC OCEAN
Hawaiian Is
Honolulu
Hawaii
Hilo
U.S.A.
Equator
Marquesas Is (Fr.)
Samoa (U.S.A.)
Tuamotu Islands (Fr.)
Cook Islands (N.Z.)
Society Islands (Fr.)
Tahiti
French Polynesia
Rarotonga
Pitcairn Is. (U.K.)
SOUTH PACIFIC OCEAN
NORTH ATLANTIC OCEAN
Bermuda (U.K.)
Azores (Port.)
Madeira (Port.)
Canary Is (Sp.)
SOUTH ATLANTIC OCEAN
St Helena (U.K.)
Tristan da Cunha (U.K.)
Gough I. (U.K.)
UNITED KINGDOM
Glasgow
Edinburgh
North Sea
DK
REP. OF IRELAND
Dublin
Birm.
London
NETH.
Amst.
BEL.
Brussels
L.
Paris
Berne
Bay of Biscay
Bordeaux
FRANCE
SW.
Bilbao
Marseille
A.
Oporto
PORT.
Madrid
Barcelona
Lisbon
SPAIN
Valencia
Tangier
Gibraltar (U.K.)
Algiers
Tunis
Casablanca
Rabat
TUNISIA
MOROCCO
Marrakesh
ALGERIA
Laâyoune
Western Sahara
Tamanrasset
MAURITANIA
Nouakchott
Arlit
CAPE VERDE
SENEGAL
Dakar
Gao
MALI
NIGER
THE GAMBIA
GUINEA-BISSAU
Bissau
Bamako
Mopti
Niamey
BURKINA
Niger
Ouagadougou
GUINEA
Conakry
Freetown
SIERRA LEONE
CÔTE D'IVOIRE
Yamoussoukro
GHANA
TOGO
BENIN
Abuja
NIGERIA
Lagos
Monrovia
LIBERIA
Abidjan
Accra
Lomé
Libreville
S.T.
Port Gentil
GABON
90° 165° 150° 135° 120° 105° 90° 75° 60° 45° 30° 15° 0°
75° 60° 45° 30° 15° 0° 15° 30° 45° 60° 75°

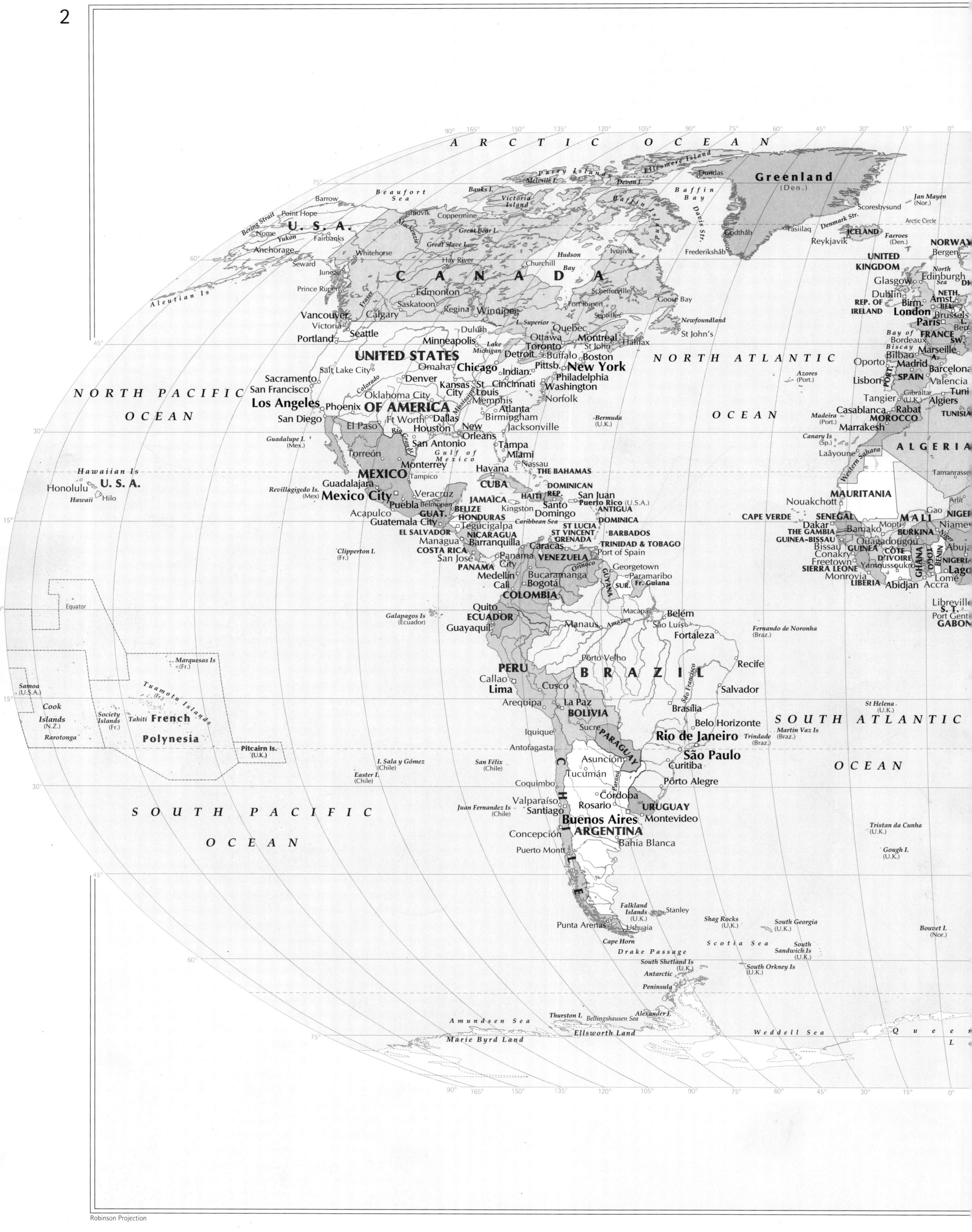

Robinson Projection

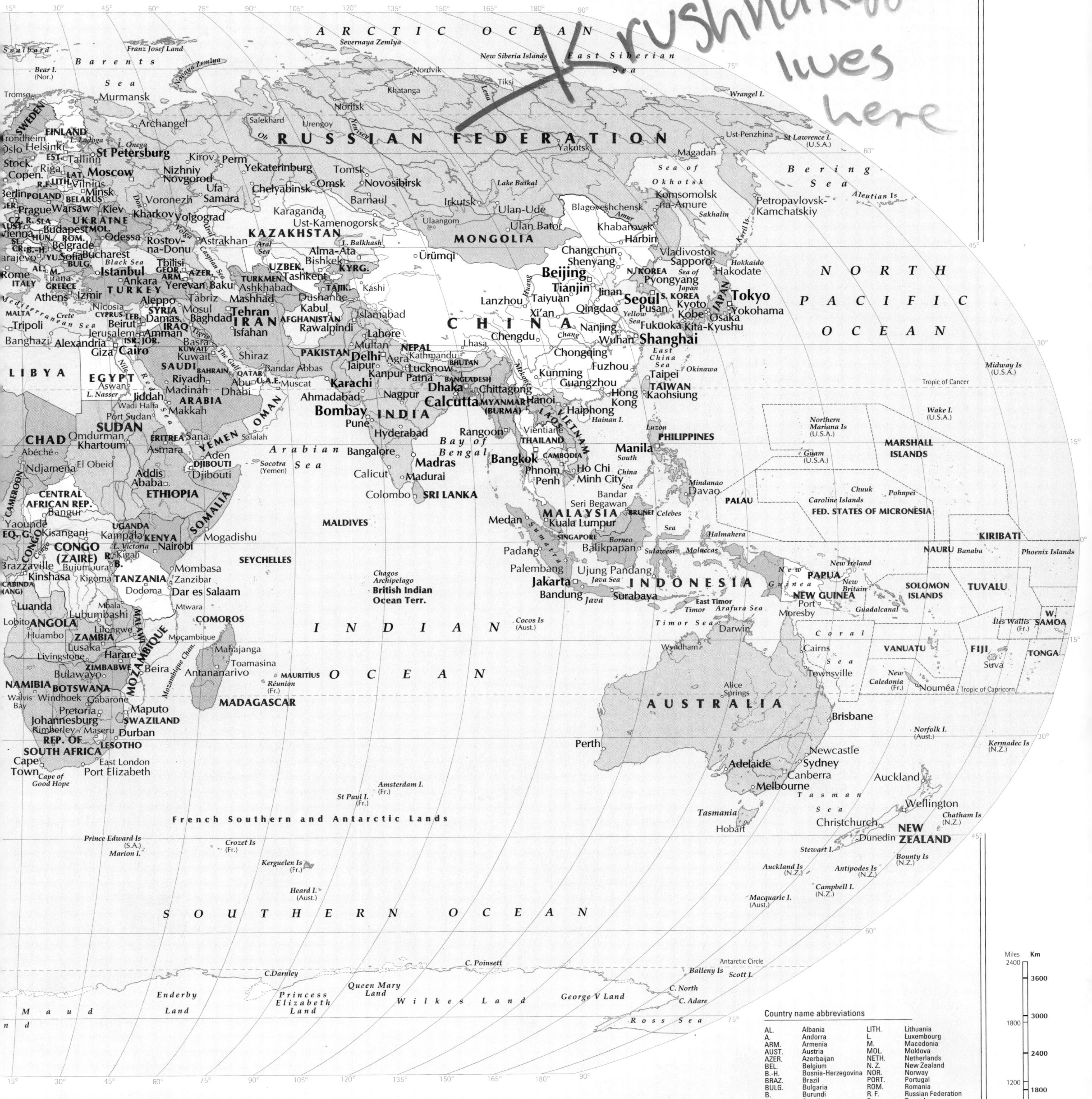
Krushnakoff lives here
ARCTIC OCEAN
Severnaya Zemlya
Franz Josef Land
Svalbard
Barents Sea
Bear I. (Nor.)
Novaya Zemlya
New Siberia Islands
East Siberian Sea
Wrangel I.
Nordvik
Tiksi
Khatanga
Murmansk
Tromsø
Norilsk
Archangel
Salekhard
Urengoy
RUSSIAN FEDERATION
Yakutsk
Ust-Penzhina
St Lawrence I. (U.S.A.)
Magadan
Sea of Okhotsk
Bering Sea
Aleutian Is
Petropavlovsk-Kamchatskiy
Komsomolsk-na-Amure
Sakhalin
Kuril Is.
FINLAND
SWEDEN
Trondheim
Oslo
Helsinki
Ladoga
L. Onega
St Petersburg
Stock.
EST.
Tallinn
Riga
LAT.
Copen.
LITH.
Vilnius
Moscow
Kirov
Perm
Nizhniy Novgorod
Yekaterinburg
Tomsk
Chelyabinsk
Omsk
Novosibirsk
Ufa
Samara
Berlin
POLAND
BELARUS
Minsk
Warsaw
Prague
Kiev
UKRAINE
Voronezh
Kharkov
Volgograd
Barnaul
Irkutsk
Lake Baikal
Ulan-Ude
Ulan Bator
Blagoveshchensk
Amur
Khabarovsk
Harbin
Karaganda
Ust-Kamenogorsk
Ulaangom
MONGOLIA
KAZAKHSTAN
Odessa
Rostov-na-Donu
Astrakhan
Aral Sea
L. Balkhash
Budapest
MOL.
ROM.
Belgrade
Bucharest
Sofia
BULG.
YU.
Rome
ITALY
AL.
Tirana
GREECE
Athens
Black Sea
Istanbul
Ankara
TURKEY
Izmir
Tbilisi
GEOR.
ARM.
AZER.
Yerevan
Baku
Caspian Sea
UZBEK.
Tashkent
TURKMEN.
Ashkhabad
Alma-Ata
Bishkek
KYRG.
TAJIK.
Dushanbe
Ürümqi
Kashi
Tabriz
Mashhad
Tehran
IRAN
Mosul
Baghdad
IRAQ
SYRIA
Nicosia
CYPRUS
LEB.
Beirut
Damas.
Jerusalem
Amman
ISR.
JOR.
Isfahan
Kabul
AFGHANISTAN
Islamabad
Rawalpindi
Lahore
Mediterranean Sea
Crete
MALTA
Tripoli
Banghazi
Alexandria
Cairo
Giza
LIBYA
EGYPT
Aswan
L. Nasser
Basra
KUWAIT
Kuwait
Shiraz
The Gulf
BAHRAIN
QATAR
U.A.E.
Bandar Abbas
Muscat
Abu Dhabi
Riyadh
SAUDI ARABIA
Madinah
Makkah
Jiddah
Port Sudan
Red Sea
Nile
OMAN
Wadi Halfa
SUDAN
Omdurman
Khartoum
ERITREA
Asmara
Sana
YEMEN
Aden
Salalah
DJIBOUTI
Djibouti
Socotra (Yemen)
Addis Ababa
ETHIOPIA
SOMALIA
Mogadishu
CHAD
Abéché
Ndjamena
El Obeid
CENTRAL AFRICAN REP.
Bangui
CAMEROON
Yaoundé
EQ. G.
UGANDA
Kampala
KENYA
Nairobi
L. Victoria
R.
B.
Kigali
Kisangani
CONGO
CONGO (ZAIRE)
Brazzaville
Bujumbura
Kinshasa
Kigoma
TANZANIA
Mombasa
Zanzibar
Dodoma
Dar es Salaam
CABINDA (ANG)
Luanda
Lobito
ANGOLA
Huambo
Lubumbashi
Mbala
Mtwara
MALAWI
Lilongwe
ZAMBIA
Lusaka
COMOROS
Moçambique
MOZAMBIQUE
Mahajanga
Harare
Livingstone
ZIMBABWE
Beira
Mozambique Chan.
Toamasina
Antananarivo
MADAGASCAR
Bulawayo
NAMIBIA
BOTSWANA
Walvis Bay
Windhoek
Gaborone
Pretoria
Maputo
Johannesburg
SWAZILAND
Kimberley
Maseru
Durban
REP. OF SOUTH AFRICA
LESOTHO
Cape Town
Cape of Good Hope
East London
Port Elizabeth
PAKISTAN
Karachi
Delhi
Multan
Jaipur
Agra
NEPAL
Kathmandu
Lucknow
BHUTAN
Kanpur
Patna
Lhasa
BANGLADESH
Dhaka
Chittagong
Ahmadabad
Nagpur
Calcutta
INDIA
Bombay
Pune
Hyderabad
Arabian Sea
Bay of Bengal
Bangalore
Madras
Calicut
Madurai
Colombo
SRI LANKA
MALDIVES
SEYCHELLES
Chagos Archipelago
British Indian Ocean Terr.
MAURITIUS
Réunion (Fr.)
INDIAN OCEAN
CHINA
Chengdu
Chongqing
Kunming
Mekong
Lanzhou
Xi'an
Taiyuan
Huang
Beijing
Tianjin
Jinan
Qingdao
Shenyang
Changchun
Nanjing
Chang
Wuhan
Shanghai
Fuzhou
Guangzhou
Hong Kong
Hainan I.
MYANMAR (BURMA)
Rangoon
Hanoi
LAOS
Haiphong
VIETNAM
Vientiane
THAILAND
Bangkok
CAMBODIA
Phnom Penh
Ho Chi Minh City
South China Sea
N. KOREA
Pyongyang
Sea of Japan
S. KOREA
Seoul
Pusan
Yellow Sea
Fukuoka
Kita-Kyushu
Kyoto
Kobe
Osaka
JAPAN
Tokyo
Yokohama
Sapporo
Hokkaido
Hakodate
Vladivostok
East China Sea
Okinawa
Taipei
TAIWAN
Kaohsiung
Luzon
PHILIPPINES
Manila
Mindanao
Davao
NORTH PACIFIC OCEAN
Midway Is (U.S.A.)
Tropic of Cancer
Wake I. (U.S.A.)
Northern Mariana Is (U.S.A.)
Guam (U.S.A.)
MARSHALL ISLANDS
PALAU
Chuuk
Pohnpei
Caroline Islands
FED. STATES OF MICRONESIA
KIRIBATI
NAURU
Banaba
Phoenix Islands
Bandar Seri Begawan
BRUNEI
MALAYSIA
Kuala Lumpur
SINGAPORE
Medan
Sumatra
Padang
Palembang
Borneo
Balikpapan
Celebes Sea
Halmahera
Sulawesi
Moluccas
Ujung Pandang
INDONESIA
Jakarta
Java Sea
Bandung
Java
Surabaya
New Guinea
New Ireland
PAPUA NEW GUINEA
New Britain
Port Moresby
SOLOMON ISLANDS
Guadalcanal
TUVALU
East Timor
Timor
Arafura Sea
Timor Sea
Darwin
Coral Sea
Cairns
Townsville
W. SAMOA
Îles Wallis (Fr.)
VANUATU
FIJI
Suva
TONGA
New Caledonia (Fr.)
Nouméa
Tropic of Capricorn
Cocos Is (Aust.)
Wyndham
Alice Springs
AUSTRALIA
Brisbane
Perth
Norfolk I. (Aust.)
Kermadec Is (N.Z.)
Newcastle
Sydney
Canberra
Adelaide
Melbourne
Auckland
Tasman Sea
Tasmania
Hobart
Wellington
Chatham Is (N.Z.)
Christchurch
NEW ZEALAND
Dunedin
Stewart I.
Bounty Is (N.Z.)
Auckland Is (N.Z.)
Antipodes Is (N.Z.)
Campbell I. (N.Z.)
Macquarie I. (Aust.)
Amsterdam I. (Fr.)
St Paul I. (Fr.)
French Southern and Antarctic Lands
Prince Edward Is (S.A.)
Marion I.
Crozet Is (Fr.)
Kerguelen Is (Fr.)
Heard I. (Aust.)
SOUTHERN OCEAN
C. Poinsett
C.Darnley
Antarctic Circle
Balleny Is
Scott I.
Queen Mary Land
Enderby Land
Princess Elizabeth Land
Wilkes Land
George V Land
C. North
C. Adare
Ross Sea
Maud Land
15° 30° 45° 60° 75° 90° 105° 120° 135° 150° 165° 180° 90°
75° 60° 45° 30° 15° 0° 15° 30° 45° 60° 75°
Miles Km
2400 3600 3000 1800 2400 1200 1800 1200 600 600
1:66M
© Bartholomew

Country name abbreviations

AL.	Albania	LITH.	Lithuania
A.	Andorra	L.	Luxembourg
ARM.	Armenia	M.	Macedonia
AUST.	Austria	MOL.	Moldova
AZER.	Azerbaijan	NETH.	Netherlands
BEL.	Belgium	N. Z.	New Zealand
B.-H.	Bosnia-Herzegovina	NOR.	Norway
BRAZ.	Brazil	PORT.	Portugal
BULG.	Bulgaria	ROM.	Romania
B.	Burundi	R. F.	Russian Federation
CR.	Croatia	R.	Rwanda
CZ. R.	Czech Republic	S. T.	São Tome & Principe
DK	Denmark	SL.	Slovenia
EQ. G.	Equatorial Guinea	SLA	Slovakia
EST.	Estonia	S. A.	Republic of South Africa
FR.	France	SP.	Spain
GEOR.	Georgia	SUR.	Surinam
GER.	Germany	SW.	Switzerland
GUAT.	Guatemala	TAJIK.	Tajikistan
HUN.	Hungary	TURKMEN.	Turkmenistan
ISR.	Israel	U.A.E.	United Arab Emirates
JOR.	Jordan	U. K.	United Kingdom
KYRG.	Kyrgyzstan	U. S. A.	United States of America
LAT.	Latvia	UZBEK.	Uzbekistan
LEB.	Lebanon	YU.	Yugoslavia

THE LIBRARY
GUILDFORD COLLEGE
of Further and Higher Education

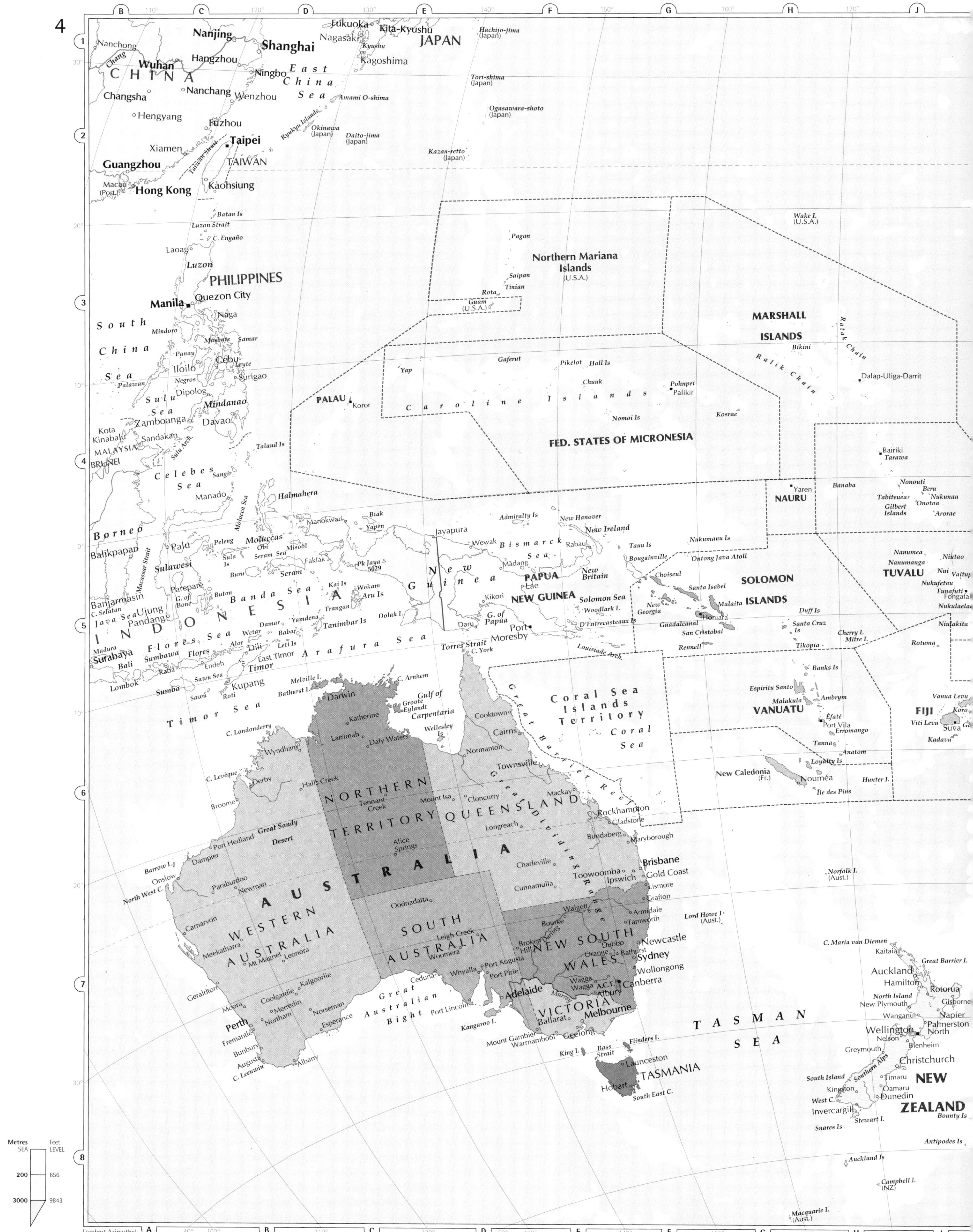
Nanchong
Nanjing
Shanghai
Fukuoka
Kita-Kyushu
Nagasaki
Kyushu
JAPAN
Hachijo-jima (Japan)
Chang
Wuhan
Hangzhou
CHINA
Ningbo
East China Sea
Kagoshima
Tori-shima (Japan)
Changsha
Nanchang
Wenzhou
Amami O-shima
Hengyang
Ogasawara-shoto (Japan)
Fuzhou
Ryukyu Islands
Okinawa (Japan)
Daito-jima (Japan)
Xiamen
Taipei
Taiwan Strait
TAIWAN
Kazan-retto (Japan)
Guangzhou
Macau (Port.)
Hong Kong
Kaohsiung
Batan Is
Luzon Strait
C. Engaño
Wake I. (U.S.A.)
Pagan
Laoag
Luzon
Northern Mariana Islands (U.S.A.)
PHILIPPINES
Saipan
Tinian
Rota
Manila
Quezon City
Guam (U.S.A.)
Naga
South China Sea
Mindoro
Masbate
Samar
MARSHALL ISLANDS
Ratak Chain
Bikini
Panay
Iloilo
Cebu
Leyte
Gaferut
Pikelot
Hall Is
Ralik Chain
Palawan
Negros
Surigao
Yap
Chuuk
Pohnpei
Palikir
Dalap-Uliga-Darrit
Sulu Sea
Dipolog
Mindanao
PALAU
Koror
Caroline Islands
Zamboanga
Davao
Nomoi Is
Kosrae
Kota Kinabalu
Sandakan
MALAYSIA
BRUNEI
Sulu Arch.
Talaud Is
FED. STATES OF MICRONESIA
Bairiki
Tarawa
Celebes Sea
Sangir
Manado
Molucca Sea
Halmahera
Yaren
NAURU
Banaba
Nonouti
Beru
Tabiteuea
Nukunau
Onotoa
Gilbert Islands
Arorae
Borneo
Manokwari
Biak
Yapen
Admiralty Is
New Hanover
New Ireland
Jayapura
Balikpapan
Palu
Peleng
Moluccas
Obi
Misoöl
Wewak
Bismarck Sea
Rabaul
Tauu Is
Nukumanu Is
Sula Is
Seram Sea
Fakfak
Pk Jaya 5029
New Guinea
Madang
Bougainville
Ontong Java Atoll
Nanumea
Niutao
Nanumanga
Nui
Vaitupu
TUVALU
Sulawesi
Macassar Strait
Buru
Seram
PAPUA
Lae
New Britain
Choiseul
SOLOMON ISLANDS
Nukufetau
Funafuti
Fongafale
Nukulaelae
Banjarmasin
Parepare
G. of Bone
Buton
Banda Sea
Kai Is
Wokam
Aru Is
Kikori
NEW GUINEA
Solomon Sea
Santa Isabel
Malaita
C. Selatan
Java Sea
Ujung Pandang
INDONESIA
Trangan
Dolak I.
G. of Papua
Woodlark I.
New Georgia
Honiara
Duff Is
Niulakita
Damar
Yamdena
Tanimbar Is
Daru
Port Moresby
D'Entrecasteaux Is
Guadalcanal
San Cristobal
Santa Cruz Is
Cherry I.
Mitre I.
Madura
Surabaya
Bali
Flores Sea
Wetar
Babar
Alor
Dili
Leti Is
East Timor
Timor
Sumbawa
Flores
Lombok
Raba
Endeh
Arafura Sea
Torres Strait
C. York
Louisiade Arch.
Rennell
Tikopia
Rotuma
Sawu Sea
Sumba
Sawu
Roti
Kupang
Melville I.
Bathurst I.
C. Arnhem
Banks Is
Timor Sea
Darwin
Groote Eylandt
Gulf of Carpentaria
Great Barrier Reef
Coral Sea Islands Territory
Coral Sea
Espiritu Santo
Malakula
Ambrym
VANUATU
Vanua Levu
Koro
Katherine
Wellesley Is
Cooktown
Éfaté
Port Vila
Erromango
FIJI
Viti Levu
Suva
Kadavu
C. Londonderry
Larrimah
Daly Waters
Cairns
Tanna
Anatom
Wyndham
Normanton
Loyalty Is
C. Levêque
Derby
Halls Creek
NORTHERN TERRITORY
Tennant Creek
Townsville
New Caledonia (Fr.)
Nouméa
Île des Pins
Hunter I.
Broome
Mount Isa
Cloncurry
Mackay
QUEENSLAND
Great Dividing Range
Rockhampton
Gladstone
Great Sandy Desert
Port Hedland
Longreach
Bundaberg
Maryborough
Dampier
Alice Springs
AUSTRALIA
Barrow I.
Onslow
North West C.
Paraburdoo
Newman
Charleville
Brisbane
Gold Coast
Toowoomba
Ipswich
Lismore
Norfolk I. (Aust.)
Cunnamulla
Grafton
Oodnadatta
Carnarvon
WESTERN AUSTRALIA
SOUTH AUSTRALIA
Walgett
Armidale
Tamworth
Lord Howe I. (Aust.)
Bourke
Leigh Creek
Newcastle
Meekatharra
Mt Magnet
Leonora
Broken Hill
NEW SOUTH WALES
Dubbo
Orange
Bathurst
Sydney
Woomera
Wollongong
C. Maria van Diemen
Kaitaia
Great Barrier I.
Whyalla
Port Augusta
Port Pirie
Wagga Wagga
A.C.T.
Canberra
Albury
Auckland
Hamilton
Rotorua
Geraldton
Kalgoorlie
Coolgardie
Ceduna
Great Australian Bight
Adelaide
Murray
VICTORIA
North Island
New Plymouth
Gisborne
Moora
Merredin
Northam
Norseman
Esperance
Port Lincoln
Kangaroo I.
Ballarat
Melbourne
Geelong
Wanganui
Napier
Perth
TASMAN SEA
Wellington
Palmerston North
Fremantle
Bunbury
Mount Gambier
Warrnambool
Flinders I.
Nelson
Blenheim
Augusta
C. Leeuwin
Albany
King I.
Bass Strait
Launceston
Greymouth
Christchurch
TASMANIA
Southern Alps
NEW ZEALAND
Hobart
South East C.
South Island
Timaru
Oamaru
Kingston
West C.
Dunedin
Invercargill
Stewart I.
Bounty Is
Snares Is
Antipodes Is
Auckland Is
Campbell I. (NZ)
Macquarie I. (Aust.)
Metres SEA
Feet LEVEL
200
656
3000
9843
Lambert Azimuthal Equal Area Projection

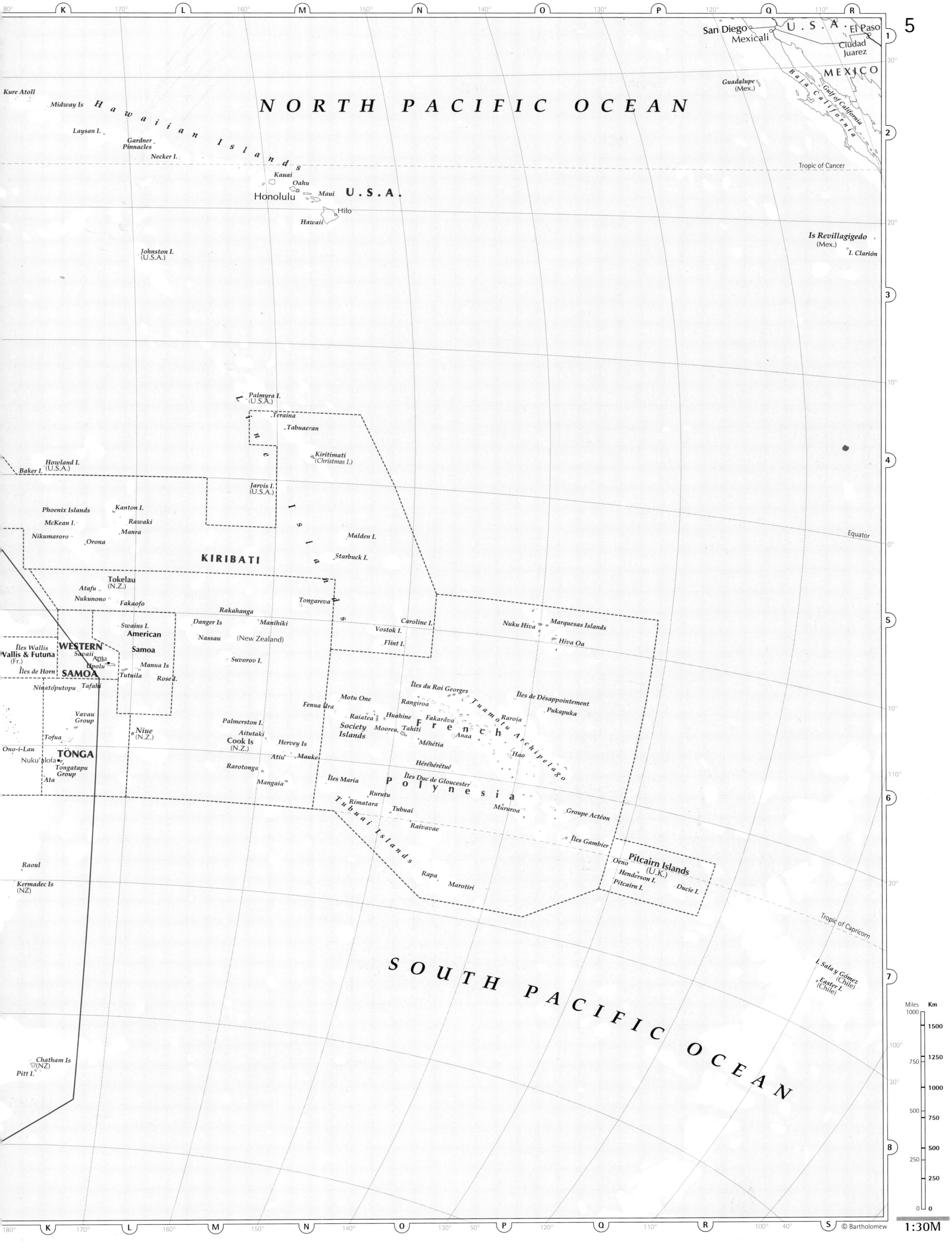
NORTH PACIFIC OCEAN
SOUTH PACIFIC OCEAN
Hawaiian Islands
Kure Atoll
Midway Is
Laysan I.
Gardner Pinnacles
Necker I.
Kauai
Oahu
Honolulu
Maui
U.S.A.
Hilo
Hawaii
Johnston I. (U.S.A.)
San Diego
Mexicali
U.S.A.
El Paso
Ciudad Juarez
MEXICO
Guadalupe (Mex.)
Baja California
Gulf of California
Tropic of Cancer
Is Revillagigedo (Mex.)
I. Clarión
Palmyra I. (U.S.A.)
Line Islands
Teraina
Tabuaeran
Kiritimati (Christmas I.)
Howland I. (U.S.A.)
Baker I.
Jarvis I. (U.S.A.)
Phoenix Islands
Kanton I.
McKean I.
Rawaki
Manra
Nikumaroro
Orona
Malden I.
Starbuck I.
KIRIBATI
Equator
Tokelau (N.Z.)
Atafu
Nukunono
Fakaofo
Tongareva
Rakahanga
Danger Is
Manihiki
Nassau
(New Zealand)
Caroline I.
Vostok I.
Flint I.
Suvorov I.
Swains I.
American Samoa
Manua Is
Tutuila
Rose I.
Îles Wallis
Wallis & Futuna (Fr.)
Îles de Horn
WESTERN SAMOA
Savaii
Apia
Upolu
Niuatoputapu
Tafahi
Vavau Group
Tofua
Ono-i-Lau
TONGA
Nuku'alofa
Tongatapu Group
Ata
Niue (N.Z.)
Palmerston I.
Aitutaki
Cook Is (N.Z.)
Hervey Is
Atiu
Mauke
Rarotonga
Mangaia
Nuku Hiva
Marquesas Islands
Hiva Oa
Îles du Roi Georges
Îles de Désappointement
Pukapuka
Motu One
Rangiroa
Fenua Ura
Raiatea
Huahine
Society Islands
Moorea
Tahiti
Fakarava
Anaa
Raroia
Tuamotu Archipelago
Méhétia
Hao
Héréhérétué
French Polynesia
Îles Duc de Gloucester
Îles Maria
Rurutu
Rimatara
Tubuai
Tubuai Islands
Mururoa
Groupe Actéon
Raivavae
Îles Gambier
Rapa
Marotiri
Pitcairn Islands (U.K.)
Oeno
Henderson I.
Pitcairn I.
Ducie I.
Tropic of Capricorn
I. Sala y Gómez (Chile)
Easter I. (Chile)
Raoul
Kermadec Is (NZ)
Chatham Is (NZ)
Pitt I.
Miles
Km
© Bartholomew
1:30M

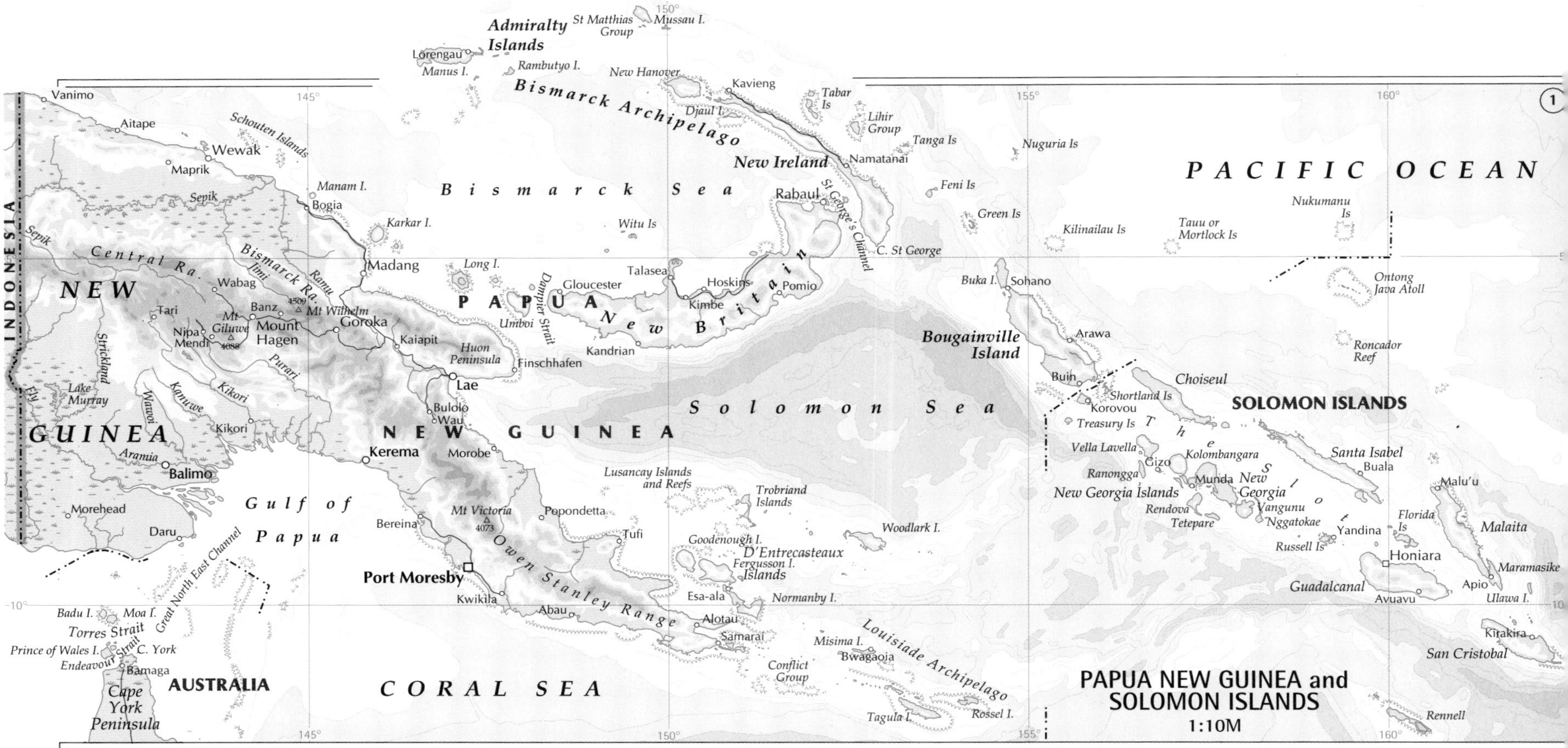
PAPUA NEW GUINEA and
SOLOMON ISLANDS
1:10M
1
PACIFIC OCEAN
Admiralty Islands
St Matthias Group
Mussau I.
Lorengau
Manus I.
Rambutyo I.
New Hanover
Kavieng
Bismarck Archipelago
Djaul I.
Tabar Is
Lihir Group
New Ireland
Namatanai
Tanga Is
Nuguria Is
Bismarck Sea
Rabaul
St George's Channel
C. St George
Feni Is
Green Is
Kilinailau Is
Tauu or Mortlock Is
Nukumanu Is
Ontong Java Atoll
Vanimo
Aitape
Schouten Islands
Wewak
Maprik
Sepik
Manam I.
Bogia
Karkar I.
Witu Is
INDONESIA
Central Ra.
NEW
Bismarck Ra.
Ramu
Madang
Long I.
Talasea
Hoskins
Kimbe
New Britain
Pomio
Buka I.
Sohano
Wabag
Tari
Banz
Mt Giluwe
Mt Wilhelm
Mount Hagen
Goroka
Nipa
Mendi
PAPUA
Gloucester
Umboi
Dampier Strait
Kaiapit
Huon Peninsula
Finschhafen
Kandrian
Bougainville Island
Arawa
Roncador Reef
Strickland
Lake Murray
Purari
Lae
Kikori
Fly
Buin
Choiseul
Shortland Is
Korovou
Treasury Is
SOLOMON ISLANDS
Bulolo
Wau
GUINEA
Kikori
NEW GUINEA
Kerema
Morobe
Solomon Sea
The Slot
Vella Lavella
Kolombangara
Santa Isabel
Buala
Aramia
Balimo
Ranongga
Gizo
Munda
New Georgia
New Georgia Islands
Lusancay Islands and Reefs
Trobriand Islands
Rendova
Tetepare
Vangunu
Nggatokae
Malu'u
Morehead
Gulf of Papua
Mt Victoria
Popondetta
Florida Is
Malaita
Daru
Bereina
Tufi
Woodlark I.
Yandina
Russell Is
Honiara
Goodenough I.
D'Entrecasteaux Islands
Fergusson I.
Guadalcanal
Avuavu
Apio
Maramasike
Great North East Channel
Port Moresby
Owen Stanley Range
Kwikila
Abau
Esa-ala
Normanby I.
Ulawa I.
Badu I.
Moa I.
Torres Strait
Alotau
Samarai
Misima I.
Bwagaoja
Louisiade Archipelago
Kirakira
Prince of Wales I.
C. York
Endeavour Strait
San Cristobal
Bamaga
AUSTRALIA
Cape York Peninsula
CORAL SEA
Conflict Group
Tagula I.
Rossel I.
Rennell

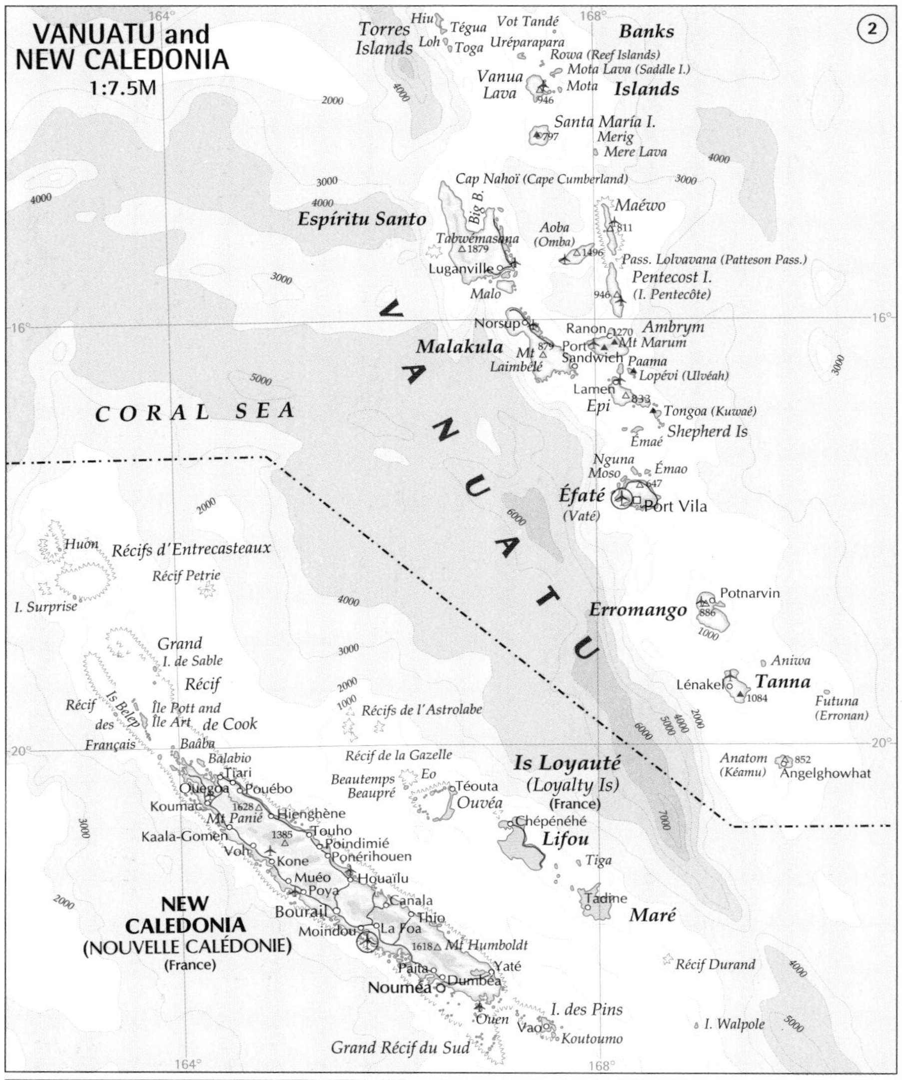
VANUATU and
NEW CALEDONIA
1:7.5M
2
Torres Islands
Hiu
Tégua
Loh
Toga
Vot Tandé
Uréparapara
Banks Islands
Rowa (Reef Islands)
Mota Lava (Saddle I.)
Vanua Lava
Mota
Santa Maria I.
Merig
Mere Lava
Cap Nahoï (Cape Cumberland)
Espíritu Santo
Big B.
Maéwo
Tabwémasana
Aoba (Omba)
Luganville
Pass. Lolvavana (Patteson Pass.)
Pentecost I. (I. Pentecôte)
Malo
Norsup
Ranon
Ambrym
Malakula
Port Sandwich
Mt Marum
Mt Laimbélé
Paama
Lopévi (Ulvéah)
VANUATU
Lamen
Epi
Tongoa (Kuwaé)
Shepherd Is
CORAL SEA
Émaé
Nguna
Moso
Émao
Éfaté (Vaté)
Port Vila
Huon
Récifs d'Entrecasteaux
Récif Petrie
I. Surprise
Potnarvin
Erromango
Grand I. de Sable
Récif
Aniwa
Tanna
Lénakel
Futuna (Erronan)
Récif des Français
Île Pott and Île Art
de Cook
Récifs de l'Astrolabe
Baaba
Balabio
Tiari
Récif de la Gazelle
Ouégoa
Pouébo
Beautemps Beaupré
Eo
Is Loyauté (Loyalty Is) (France)
Anatom (Kéamu)
Angelghowhat
Koumac
Mt Panié
Hienghène
Téouta
Ouvéa
Chépénéhé
Lifou
Kaala-Gomen
Touho
Poindimié
Ponérihouen
Voh
Kone
Houaïlu
Muéo
Poya
Tiga
NEW CALEDONIA (NOUVELLE CALÉDONIE) (France)
Bourail
Canala
Thio
Tadine
Maré
Moindou
La Foa
Mt Humboldt
Païta
Yaté
Récif Durand
Nouméa
Dumbéa
Ouen
Vao
I. des Pins
Koutoumo
I. Walpole
Grand Récif du Sud

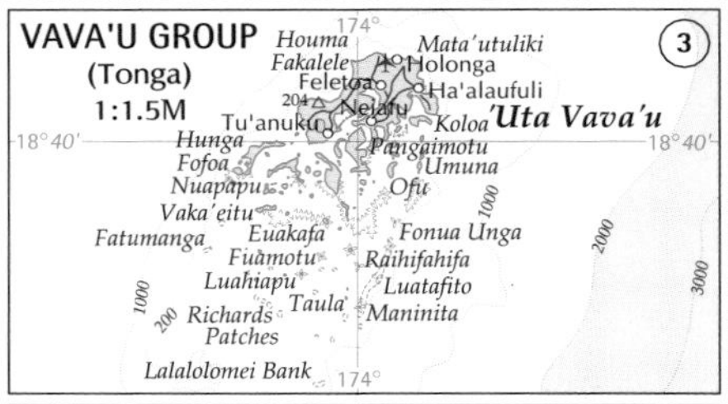
VAVA'U GROUP
(Tonga)
1:1.5M
3
Houma
Fakalele
Mata'utuliki
Holonga
Feletoa
Neiafu
Ha'alaufuli
Tu'anuku
Koloa
Uta Vava'u
Hunga
Fofoa
Pangaimotu
Umuna
Nuapapu
Vaka'eitu
Ofu
Fatumanga
Euakafa
Fonua Unga
Fuamotu
Luahapu
Taula
Maninita
Richards Patches
Lalalolomei Bank

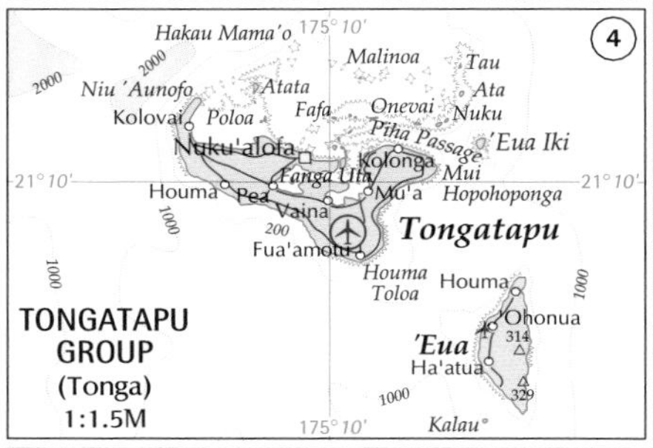
4
Hakau Mama'o
Malinoa
Tau
Niu 'Aunofo
Atata
Ata
Kolovai
Poloa
Fafa
Onevai
Nuku
Nuku'alofa
Kolonga
Piha Passage
'Eua Iki
Houma
Pea
Fanga Uta
Mui
Vaini
Mu'a
Hopohoponga
Fua'amotu
Tongatapu
TONGATAPU GROUP
(Tonga)
1:1.5M
Houma
Toloa
Houma
Ohonua
'Eua
Ha'atua
Kalau

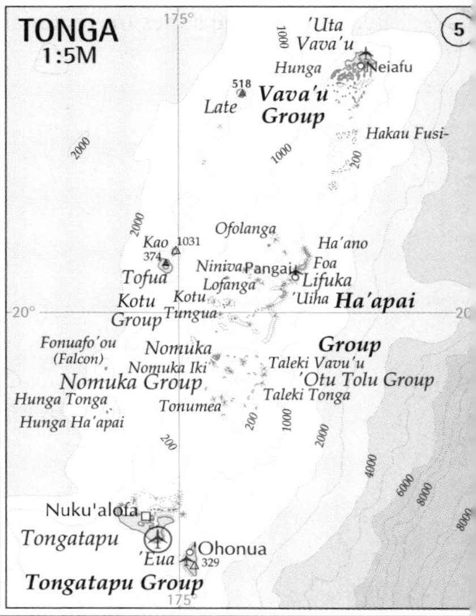
TONGA
1:5M
5
'Uta Vava'u
Neiafu
Hunga
Vava'u Group
Late
Hakau Fusi-
Ofolanga
Ha'ano
Kao
Ninivi
Pangai
Foa
Tofua
Lofanga
Lifuka
Kotu Group
Kotu
'Uiha
Ha'apai
Tungua
Group
Fonuafo'ou (Falcon)
Nomuka
Nomuka Iki
Taleki Vavu'u
Nomuka Group
'Otu Tolu Group
Hunga Tonga
Taleki Tonga
Hunga Ha'apai
Tonumea
Nuku'alofa
Tongatapu
Ohonua
'Eua
Tongatapu Group

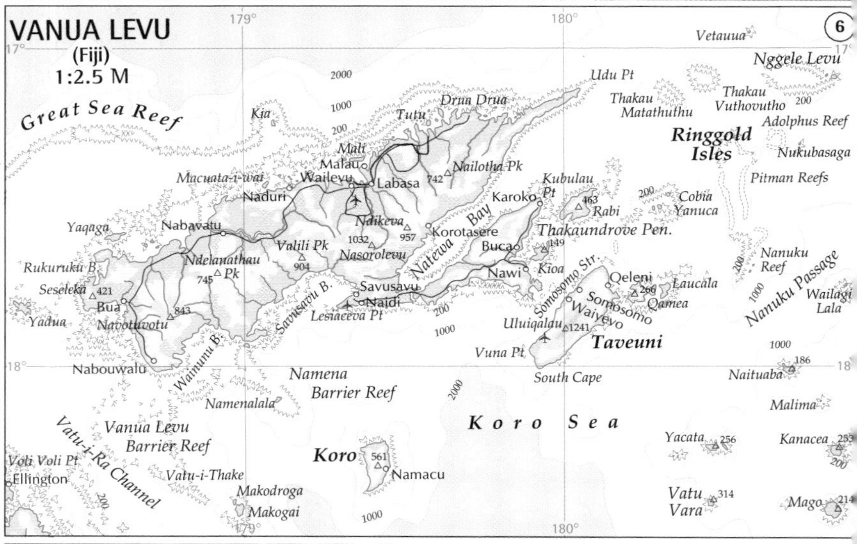
VANUA LEVU
(Fiji)
1:2.5 M
6
Vetauua
Nggele Levu
Udu Pt
Thakau Vuthovutho
Thakau Matathuthu
Adolphus Reef
Great Sea Reef
Kia
Drua Drua
Tutu
Ringgold Isles
Nukubasaga
Mali
Malau
Pitman Reefs
Macuata-i-wai
Waileva
Labasa
Nailotha Pk
Kubulau Pt
Naduri
Karoko
Cobia
Yanuca
Yaqaga
Nabavatu
Nakeva
Korotasere
Thakaundrove Pen.
Rabi
Natewa Bay
Bucalevu
Nanuku Reef
Ndelanathau Pk
Valili Pk
Nasorolevu
Nawi
Kioa
Qeleni
Laucala
Rukuruku B.
Nanuku Passage
Seseleka
Savusavu
Naidi
Somosomo Str.
Somosomo
Qamea
Wailagi Lala
Bua
Savusavu B.
Lesiaceva Pt
Waiyevo
Yadua
Navatuvotu
Uluiqalau
Taveuni
Vuna Pt
Nabouwalu
Wainunu B.
Naituaba
Namena Barrier Reef
South Cape
Malima
Namenalala
Koro Sea
Vatu-i-Ra Channel
Vanua Levu Barrier Reef
Yacata
Kanacea
Voli Voli Pt
Ellington
Koro
Namacu
Vatu-i-Thake
Makodroga
Makogai
Vatu Vara
Mago

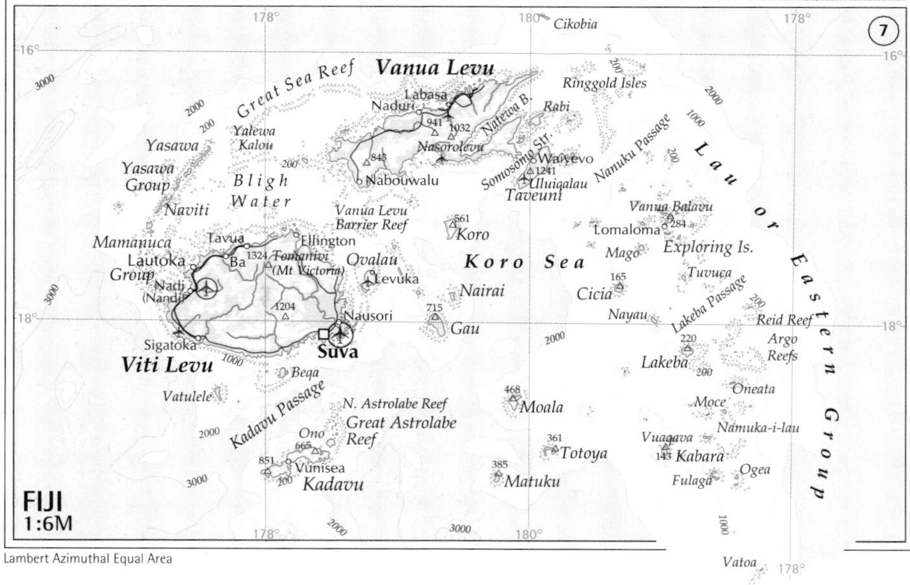
7
Cikobia
Vanua Levu
Great Sea Reef
Labasa
Ringgold Isles
Naduri
Natewa B.
Rabi
Yalewa Kalou
Nasorolevu
Somosomo Str.
Waiyevo
Nanuku Passage
Yasawa
Uluigalau
Taveuni
Yasawa Group
Nabouwalu
Bligh Water
Lau or Eastern Group
Vanua Balavu
Naviti
Vanua Levu Barrier Reef
Koro
Lomaloma
Mamanuca
Tavua
Lautoka
Ba
Tomanivi (Mt Victoria)
Ovalau
Koro Sea
Mago
Exploring Is.
Group
Nadi
Levuka
Tuvuca
Nandi
Nairai
Cicia
Nausori
Gau
Nayau
Lakeba Passage
Reid Reef
Sigatoka
Suva
Viti Levu
Argo Reefs
Lakeba
Vatulele
Beqa
N. Astrolabe Reef
Great Astrolabe Reef
Kadavu Passage
Moala
Oneata
Moce
Namuka-i-lau
Ono
Vunisea
Kadavu
Totoya
Vuagava
Kabara
Matuku
Fulaga
Ogea
Vatoa
FIJI
1:6M

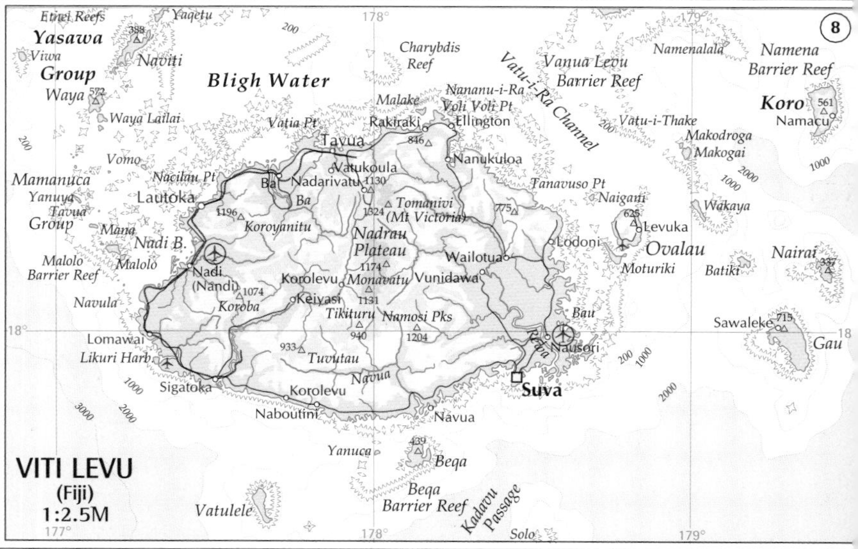
8
Yaqetu
Eitiwi Reefs
Yasawa Group
Viwa
Naviti
Waya
Waya Lailai
Charybdis Reef
Bligh Water
Vatu-i-Ra Channel
Vanua Levu Barrier Reef
Namenalala
Namena Barrier Reef
Koro
Namacu
Malake
Nananu-i-Ra
Voli Voli Pt
Ellington
Rakiraki
Vatia Pt
Vatu-i-Thake
Makodroga
Makogai
Tavua
Vomo
Vatukoula
Nanukuloa
Mamanuca
Nacilau Pt
Ba
Nadarivatu
Tanavuso Pt
Naigani
Yanuya
Lautoka
Tomanivi (Mt Victoria)
Wakaya
Tavua
Group
Mana
Koroyanitu
Nadrau Plateau
Levuka
Ovalau
Lodoni
Malolo
Nadi B.
Malolo Barrier Reef
Moturiki
Nairai
Batiki
Wailotua
Navula
Nadi (Nandi)
Korolevu
Monavatu
Vunidawa
Koroba
Keiyasi
Tikituru
Namosi Pks
Bau
Lomawai
Sawaleke
Likuri Harb.
Tuvutau
Navua
Nausori
Gau
Sigatoka
Korolevu
Rewa
Suva
Naboutini
Navua
Yanuca
Beqa
Beqa Barrier Reef
Kadavu Passage
Vatulele
Solo
VITI LEVU
(Fiji)
1:2.5M

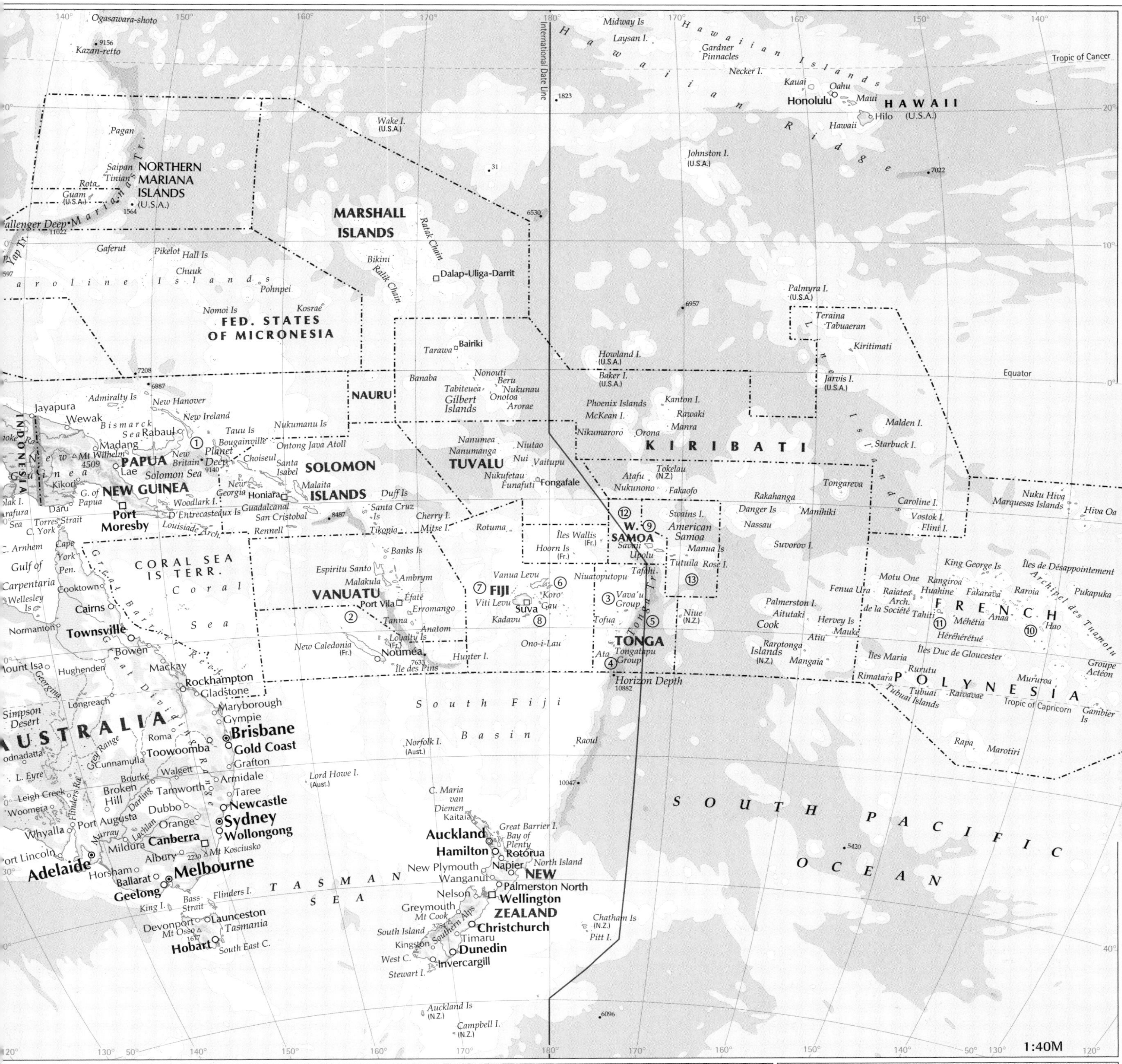

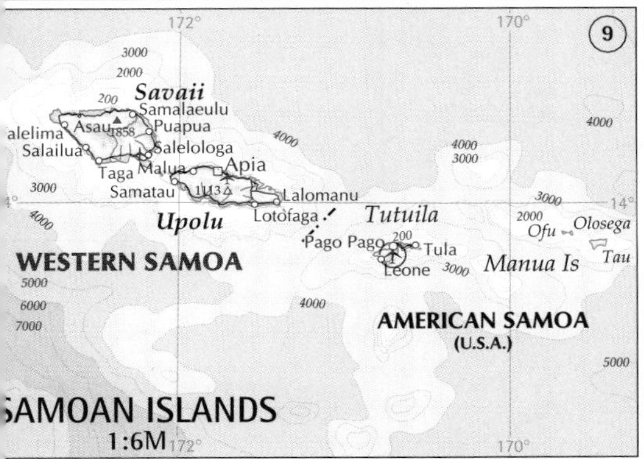

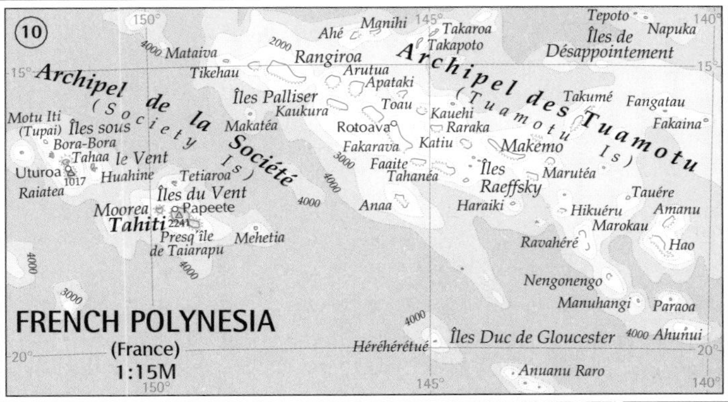

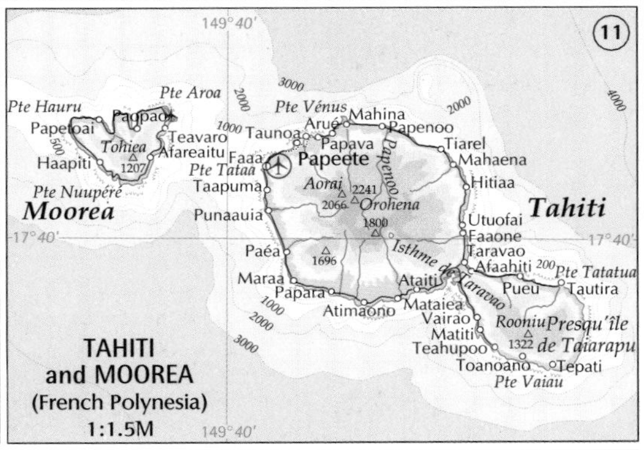

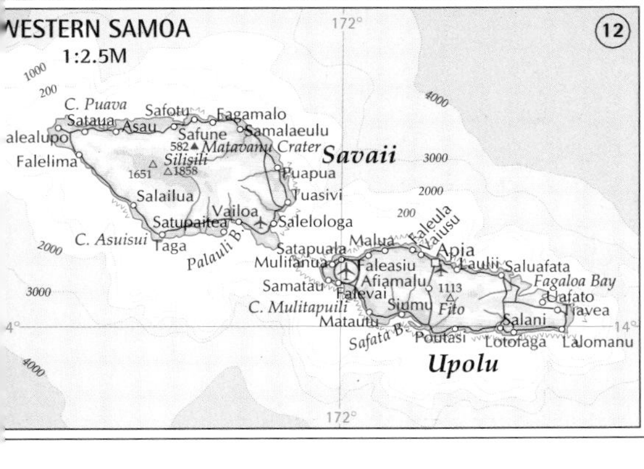

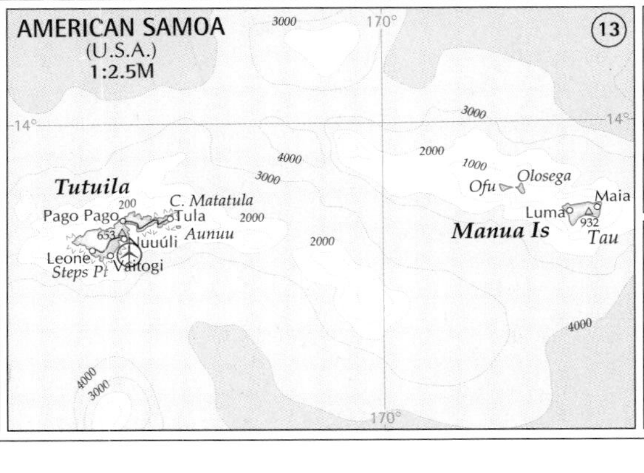

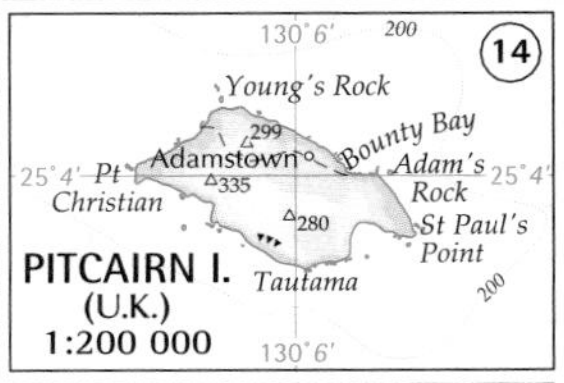

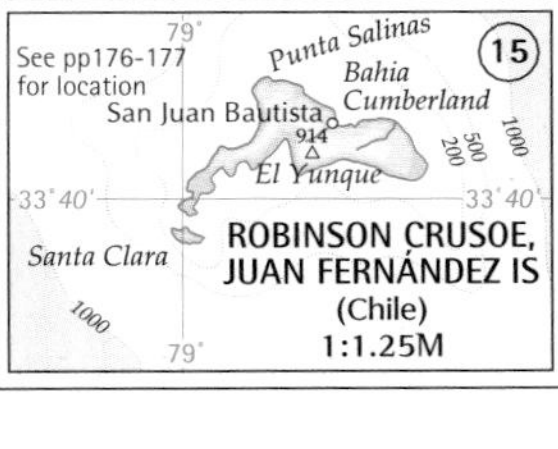

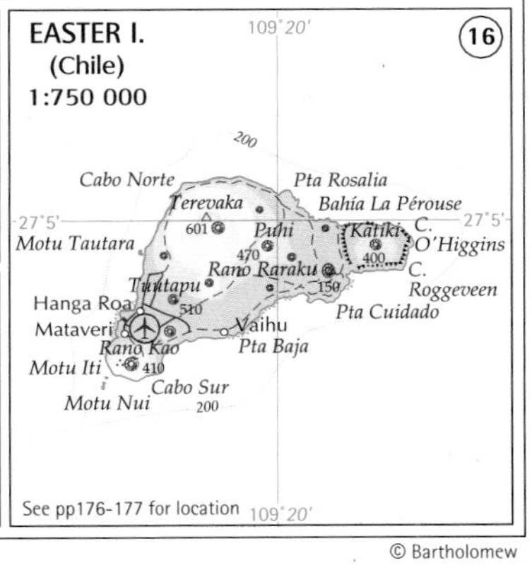

© Bartholomew

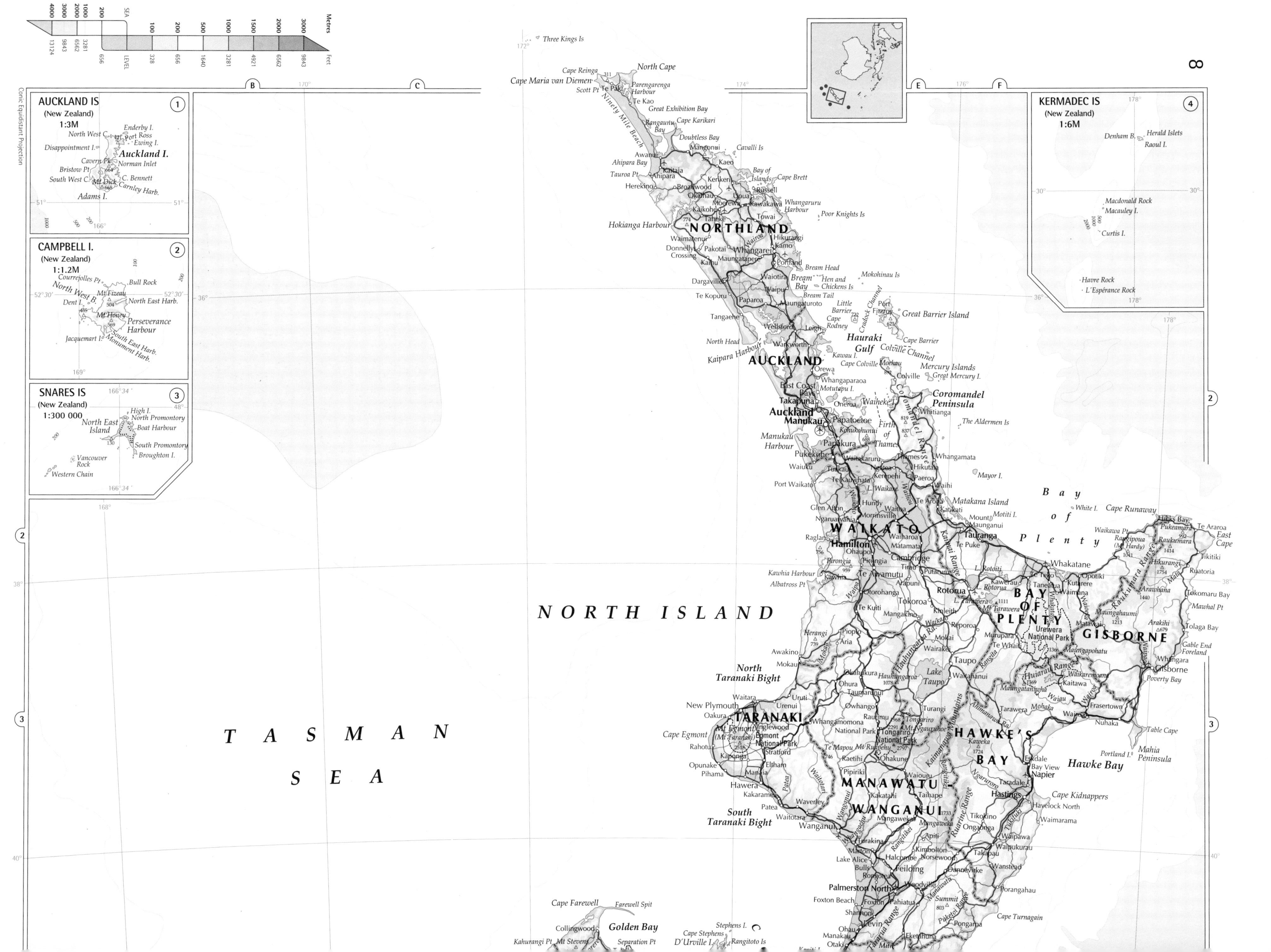
Metres
Feet
3000
9843
2000
6562
1500
4921
1000
3281
500
1640
200
656
100
328
SEA
LEVEL
200
656
1000
3281
2000
6562
3000
9843
4000
13124
Conic Equidistant Projection
AUCKLAND IS
(New Zealand)
1:3M
Auckland I.
Enderby I.
Port Ross
Ewing I.
North West C.
Disappointment I.
Norman Inlet
Cavern Pk
Bristow Pt
C. Bennett
South West C.
Mt Dick
Carnley Harb.
Adams I.
CAMPBELL I.
(New Zealand)
1:1.2M
Courrejolles Pt
Bull Rock
North West B.
Mt Fizeau
North East Harb.
Dent I.
Mt Honey
Perseverance Harbour
Jacquemart I.
South East Harb.
Monument Harb.
SNARES IS
(New Zealand)
1:300 000
High I.
North Promontory
North East Island
Boat Harbour
South Promontory
Broughton I.
Vancouver Rock
Western Chain
KERMADEC IS
(New Zealand)
1:6M
Denham B.
Herald Islets
Raoul I.
Macdonald Rock
Macauley I.
Curtis I.
Havre Rock
L'Espérance Rock
Three Kings Is
Cape Reinga
North Cape
Cape Maria van Diemen
Scott Pt
Te Paki
Parengarenga Harbour
Te Kao
Ninety Mile Beach
Great Exhibition Bay
Rangaunu Bay
Cape Karikari
Doubtless Bay
Mangonui
Cavalli Is
Awanui
Ahipara Bay
Kaitaia
Ahipara
Kaeo
Tauroa Pt
Kerikeri
Bay of Islands
Cape Brett
Herekino
Broadwood
Russell
Okaihau
Opua
Whangaruru Harbour
Moerewa
Kawakawa
Kaikohe
Towai
Poor Knights Is
Hokianga Harbour
NORTHLAND
Waimatenui
Hikurangi
Kamo
Donnellys Crossing
Pakotai
Whangarei
Maungatapere
Kaihu
Portland
Bream Head
Dargaville
Waiotira
Bream Bay
Hen and Chickens Is
Mokohinau Is
Waipu
Bream Tail
Te Kopuru
Paparoa
Maungaturoto
Little Barrier I.
Port Fitzroy
Great Barrier Island
Cradock Channel
Tangaehe
Cape Rodney
Wellsford
Leigh
North Head
Warkworth
Hauraki Gulf
Cape Barrier
Colville Channel
Kaipara Harbour
AUCKLAND
Kawau I.
Cape Colville
Moehau
Mercury Islands
Great Mercury I.
Orewa
Colville
Whangaparaoa
Motutapu I.
East Coast Bays
Coromandel Peninsula
Takapuna
Oneroa
Waiheke I.
Whitianga
Auckland
Manukau
Papatoetoe
Firth of Thames
Coromandel Range
The Aldermen Is
Kohukohunui
Manukau Harbour
Papakura
Pukekohe
Thames
Whangamata
Waiuku
Tuakau
Te Kauwhata
Kerepehi
Hikutaia
Paeroa
Mayor I.
Port Waikato
L. Waikare
Waihi
Huntly
Waitoa
Te Aroha
Matakana Island
Katikati
Glen Afton
Morrinsville
Ngaruawahia
Mount Maunganui
Motiti I.
White I.
Cape Runaway
Bay of Plenty
WAIKATO
Kaimai Range
Tauranga
Te Puke
Raglan
Hamilton
Waiharoa
Matamata
Ohaupo
Pirongia
Cambridge
Tirau
Putaruru
Te Awamutu
Arapuni
Kawhia Harbour
Kawhia
Albatross Pt
Otorohanga
Rotorua
L. Rotoiti
L. Rotorua
Kawerau
Whakatane
Tokoroa
Te Kuiti
Kinleith
Mangakino
Reporoa
Mt Tarawera
BAY OF PLENTY
Te Teko
Taneatua
Waimana
Opotiki
Kutarere
Hicks Bay
Pukeamaru
Te Araroa
East Cape
Waikawa Pt
Raukumara Range
Tikitiki
Ruatoria
Hikurangi
Arawhana
Tokomaru Bay
Mawhai Pt
Matawai
Maungahaumi
Arakihi
Tolaga Bay
GISBORNE
Gable End Foreland
Whangara
Gisborne
Poverty Bay
NORTH ISLAND
Herangi
Piopio
Aria
Mokai
Wairakei
Awakino
Mokau
Taupo
Lake Taupo
Wakahanui
Murupara
Te Whaiti
Urewera National Park
Maungapohatu
North Taranaki Bight
Ohura
Taumarunui
Huiarau Range
Waikaremoana
Kaitawa
Waitara
New Plymouth
Urenui
Uruti
Owhango
Turangi
Tarawera
Mohaka
Wairoa
Frasertown
Nuhaka
Oakura
TARANAKI
Whangamomona
Raurimu
Tongariro
Kaimanawa Mountains
Table Cape
Cape Egmont
Mt Egmont (Mt Taranaki)
Inglewood
Egmont National Park
National Park
Tongariro National Park
Mt Ruapehu
HAWKE'S BAY
Kaweka
Portland I.
Mahia Peninsula
Rahotu
Kaponga
Stratford
Te Mapou
Raetihi
Ohakune
Eskdale
Bay View
Napier
Hawke Bay
Opunake
Pihama
Eltham
Manaia
Pipiriki
Waiouru
MANAWATU-WANGANUI
Hawera
Kakaramea
Patea
Waverley
Kakatahi
Taihape
Taradale
Hastings
Cape Kidnappers
Havelock North
Waimarama
South Taranaki Bight
Waitotara
Wanganui
Mangaweka
Tikokino
Ongaonga
Waipawa
Waipukurau
Turakina
Apiti
Marton
Kimbolton
Norsewood
Takapau
Lake Alice
Halcombe
Bulls
Feilding
Dannevirke
Wanstead
Rongotea
Palmerston North
Woodville
Porangahau
Foxton Beach
Foxton
Pahiatua
Summit
Shannon
Cape Turnagain
Levin
Pongaroa
Ohau
Manakau
Otaki
Tararua Range
Eketahuna
Cape Farewell
Farewell Spit
Collingwood
Golden Bay
Kahurangi Pt
Mt Stevens
Separation Pt
Stephens I.
Cape Stephens
D'Urville I.
Rangitoto Is
TASMAN SEA

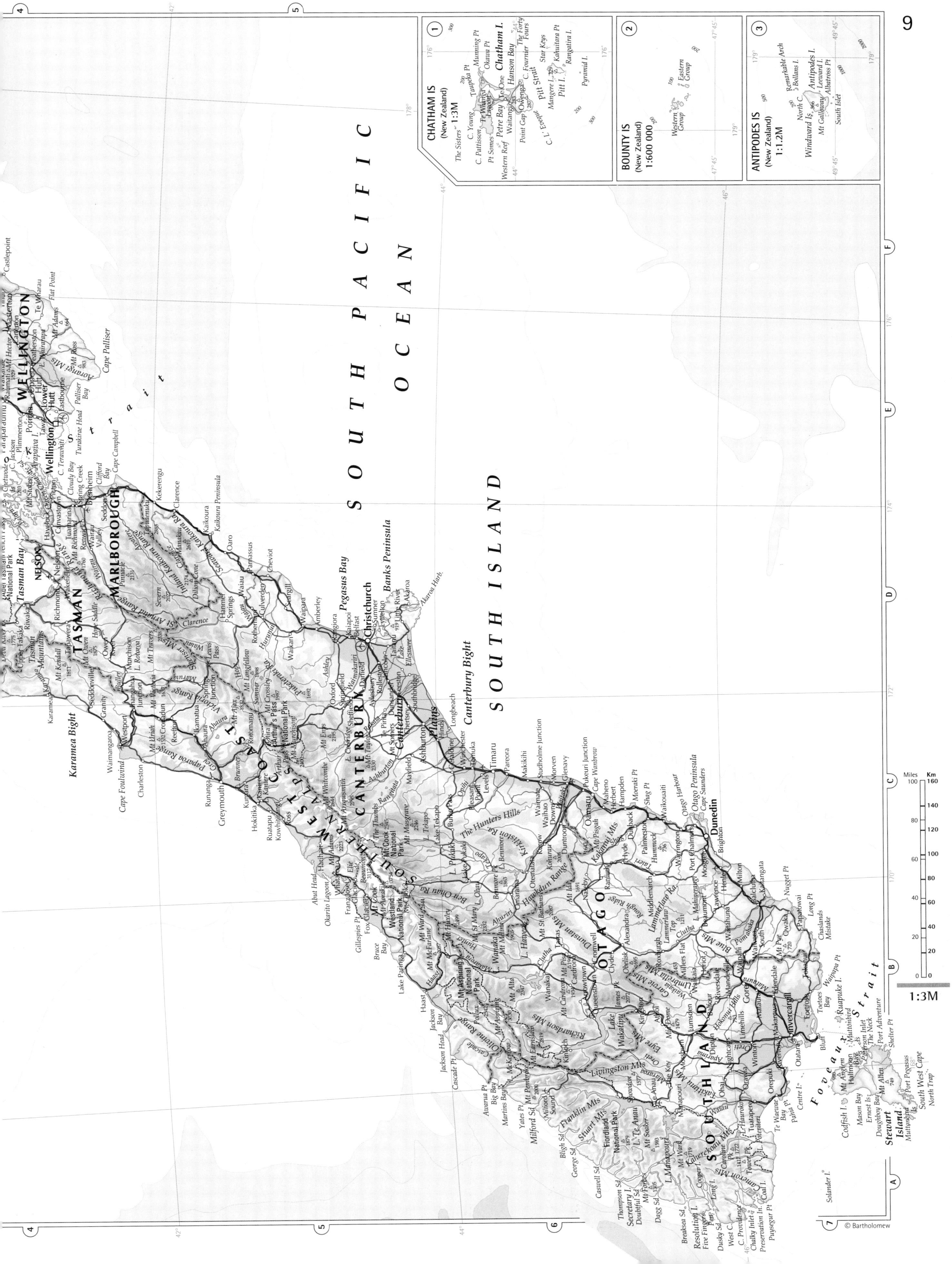
SOUTH PACIFIC
OCEAN
SOUTH ISLAND
CHATHAM IS
(New Zealand)
1:3M
BOUNTY IS
(New Zealand)
1:600 000
ANTIPODES IS
(New Zealand)
1:1.2M
WELLINGTON
TASMAN
NELSON
MARLBOROUGH
CANTERBURY
WEST COAST
OTAGO
SOUTHLAND
Christchurch
Dunedin
Invercargill
Wellington
Blenheim
Nelson
Greymouth
Timaru
Oamaru
Queenstown
Banks Peninsula
Pegasus Bay
Canterbury Bight
Karamea Bight
Tasman Bay
Foveaux Strait
Stewart Island
Southern Alps
Fiordland National Park
Mt Cook
Lake Wakatipu
Miles
Km
1:3M
© Bartholomew

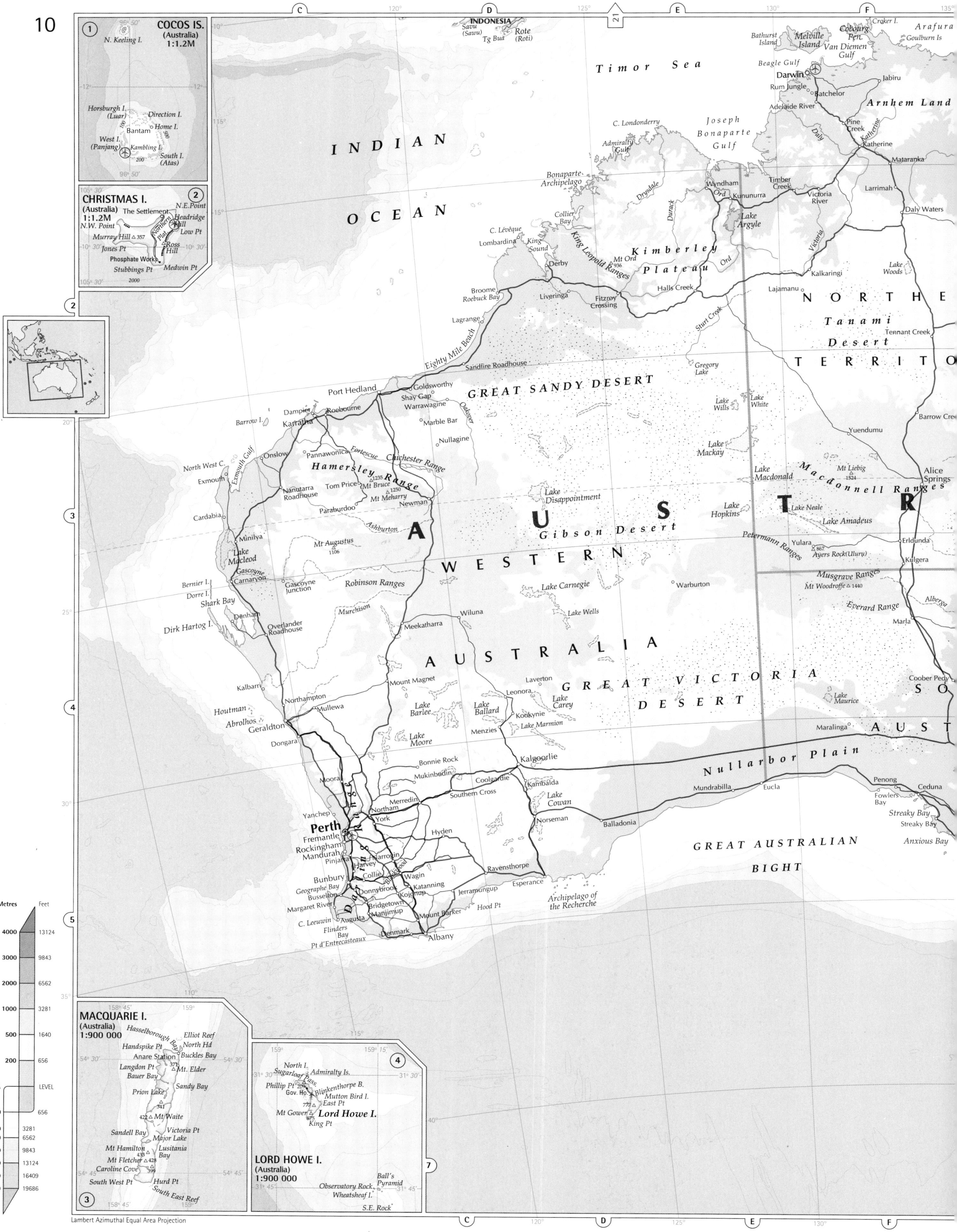
COCOS IS.
(Australia)
1:1.2M
N. Keeling I.
Horsburgh I. (Luar)
Direction I.
Home I.
Bantam
West I. (Panjang)
Kambling I.
South I. (Atas)
CHRISTMAS I.
(Australia)
1:1.2M
The Settlement
N.E.Point
N.W. Point
Headridge Hill
Low Pt
Murray Hill 357
Jones Pt
Ross Hill
Phosphate Works
Stubbings Pt
Medwin Pt
INDONESIA
Savu (Sawu)
Rote (Roti)
Tg Bua
Timor Sea
INDIAN OCEAN
Arafura
Bathurst Island
Melville Island
Cobourg Pen.
Croker I.
Goulburn Is
Van Diemen Gulf
Beagle Gulf
Darwin
Jabiru
Rum Jungle
Batchelor
Adelaide River
Arnhem Land
Pine Creek
Katherine
Daly
Mataranka
C. Londonderry
Joseph Bonaparte Gulf
Admiralty Gulf
Bonaparte Archipelago
Drysdale
Wyndham
Ord
Kununurra
Timber Creek
Victoria River
Larrimah
Daly Waters
Collier Bay
Durack
Lake Argyle
C. Lévêque
Lombardina
King Sound
King Leopold Ranges
Mt Ord 936
Kimberley Plateau
Derby
Kalkaringi
Lake Woods
Broome
Roebuck Bay
Liveringa
Fitzroy Crossing
Halls Creek
Lajamanu
NORTHERN TERRITORY
Tanami Desert
Tennant Creek
Lagrange
Sturt Creek
Eighty Mile Beach
Sandfire Roadhouse
Gregory Lake
Port Hedland
Goldsworthy
Shay Gap
Warrawagine
GREAT SANDY DESERT
Lake Wills
Lake White
Dampier
Roebourne
Karratha
Barrow I.
Marble Bar
Oakover
Nullagine
Barrow Creek
Yuendumu
North West C.
Exmouth
Exmouth Gulf
Onslow
Pannawonica
Fortescue
Chichester Range
Hamersley Range
1235
Mt Bruce
1250
Mt Meharry
Lake Mackay
Lake Macdonald
Macdonnell Ranges
Mt Liebig 1524
Alice Springs
Nanutarra Roadhouse
Tom Price
Paraburdoo
Newman
Lake Disappointment
Cardabia
Ashburton
AUSTRALIA
Gibson Desert
Lake Hopkins
Lake Neale
Lake Amadeus
Minilya
Mt Augustus 1106
WESTERN AUSTRALIA
Petermann Ranges
Yulara
867
Ayers Rock (Uluru)
Erldunda
Kulgera
Lake Macleod
Gascoyne
Carnarvon
Gascoyne Junction
Robinson Ranges
Bernier I.
Dorre I.
Shark Bay
Lake Carnegie
Warburton
Musgrave Ranges
Mt Woodroffe 1440
Everard Range
Alberga
Denham
Dirk Hartog I.
Overlander Roadhouse
Murchison
Wiluna
Meekatharra
Lake Wells
Marla
GREAT VICTORIA DESERT
Laverton
Leonora
Lake Carey
Coober Pedy
Lake Maurice
Kalbarri
Mount Magnet
Northampton
Mullewa
Lake Barlee
Lake Ballard
Kookynie
Lake Marmion
Houtman Abrolhos
Geraldton
Dongara
Lake Moore
Menzies
Maralinga
SOUTH AUSTRALIA
Bonnie Rock
Kalgoorlie
Nullarbor Plain
Mukinbudin
Coolgardie
Kambalda
Moora
Darling Range
Southern Cross
Lake Cowan
Mundrabilla
Eucla
Penong
Ceduna
Fowlers Bay
Streaky Bay
Yanchep
Northam
Merredin
York
Perth
Fremantle
Rockingham
Mandurah
Pinjarra
Norseman
Balladonia
Hyden
Harvey
Narrogin
Collie
Bunbury
Geographe Bay
Busselton
Margaret River
Donnybrook
Blackwood
Wagin
Katanning
Kojonup
Bridgetown
Manjimup
Ravensthorpe
Jerramungup
Esperance
Archipelago of the Recherche
Hood Pt
GREAT AUSTRALIAN BIGHT
Anxious Bay
C. Leeuwin
Augusta
Flinders Bay
Pt d'Entrecasteaux
Denmark
Mount Barker
Albany
Metres
Feet
4000
13124
3000
9843
2000
6562
1000
3281
500
1640
200
656
SEA
LEVEL
200
656
1000
3281
2000
6562
3000
9843
4000
13124
5000
16409
6000
19686
MACQUARIE I.
(Australia)
1:900 000
Hasselborough Bay
Elliot Reef
North Hd
Handspike Pt
Anare Station
Buckles Bay
Langdon Pt
Mt. Elder
Bauer Bay
Sandy Bay
Prion Lake
Mt Waite
Sandell Bay
Victoria Pt
Major Lake
Mt Hamilton
Lusitania Bay
Mt Fletcher
Caroline Cove
South West Pt
Hurd Pt
South East Reef
LORD HOWE I.
(Australia)
1:900 000
North I.
Sugarloaf Pass
Admiralty Is.
Phillip Pt
Gov. Ho.
Blinkenthorpe B.
Mutton Bird I.
East Pt
Mt Gower
Lord Howe I.
King Pt
Ball's Pyramid
Observatory Rock
Wheatsheaf I.
S.E. Rock
Lambert Azimuthal Equal Area Projection

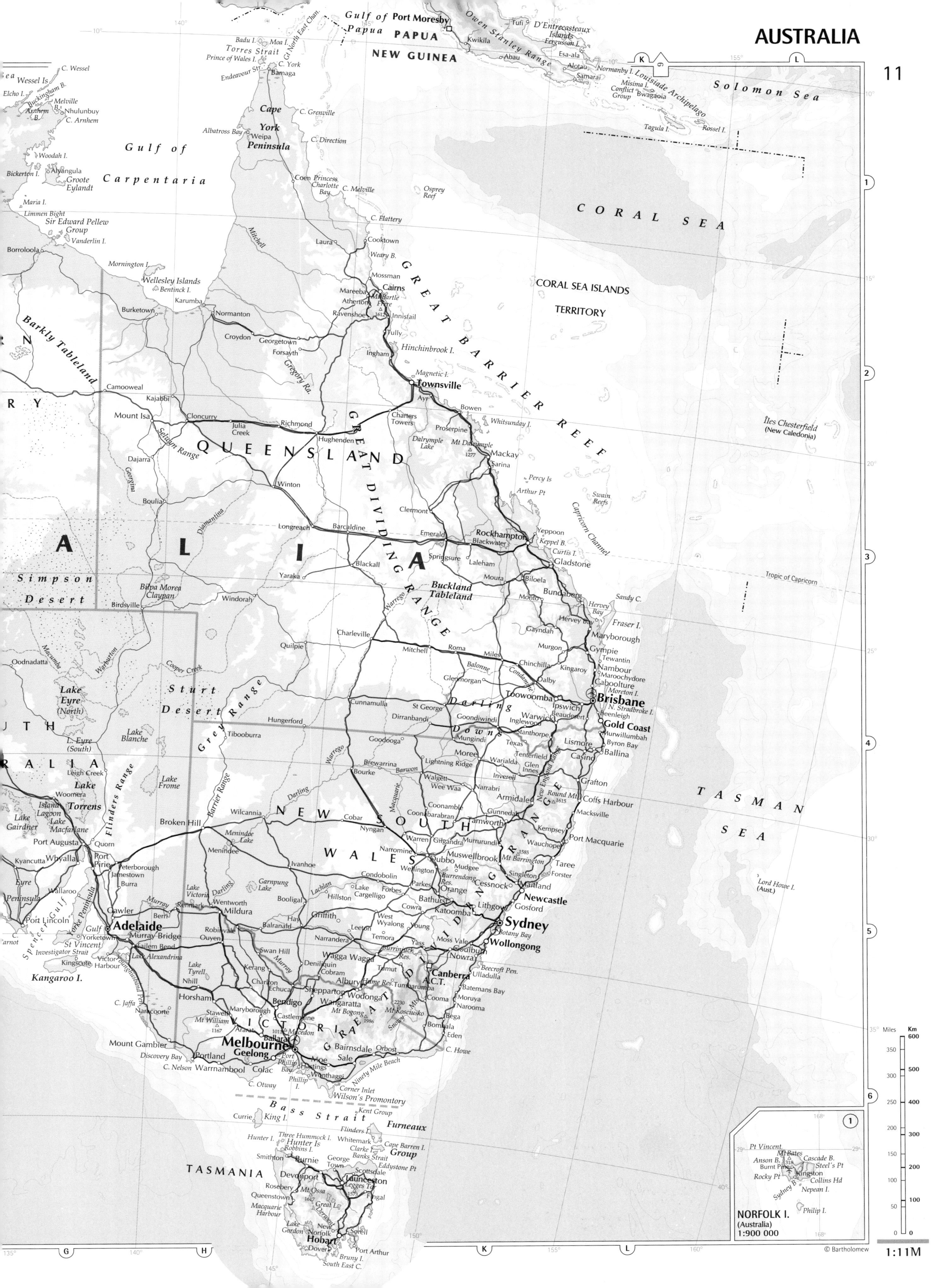
Gulf of Papua
Port Moresby
PAPUA
NEW GUINEA
Owen Stanley Range
D'Entrecasteaux Islands
Louisiade Archipelago
Solomon Sea
Torres Strait
C. York
Cape York Peninsula
Gulf of Carpentaria
Groote Eylandt
CORAL SEA
CORAL SEA ISLANDS TERRITORY
GREAT BARRIER REEF
Îles Chesterfield (New Caledonia)
Cairns
Townsville
Mount Isa
Cloncurry
QUEENSLAND
GREAT DIVIDING RANGE
Mackay
Rockhampton
Gladstone
Tropic of Capricorn
Bundaberg
Fraser I.
Simpson Desert
Lake Eyre (North)
Sturt Desert
Charleville
Toowoomba
Brisbane
Gold Coast
Darling Downs
Lord Howe I. (Aust.)
TASMAN SEA
NEW SOUTH WALES
Broken Hill
Dubbo
Newcastle
Sydney
Wollongong
Canberra
A.C.T.
Port Augusta
Adelaide
Kangaroo I.
Mildura
VICTORIA
Bendigo
Ballarat
Melbourne
Geelong
Mt Kosciusko
Bass Strait
King I.
Furneaux Group
TASMANIA
Launceston
Hobart
NORFOLK I. (Australia) 1:900 000
Miles
Km
© Bartholomew
1:11M

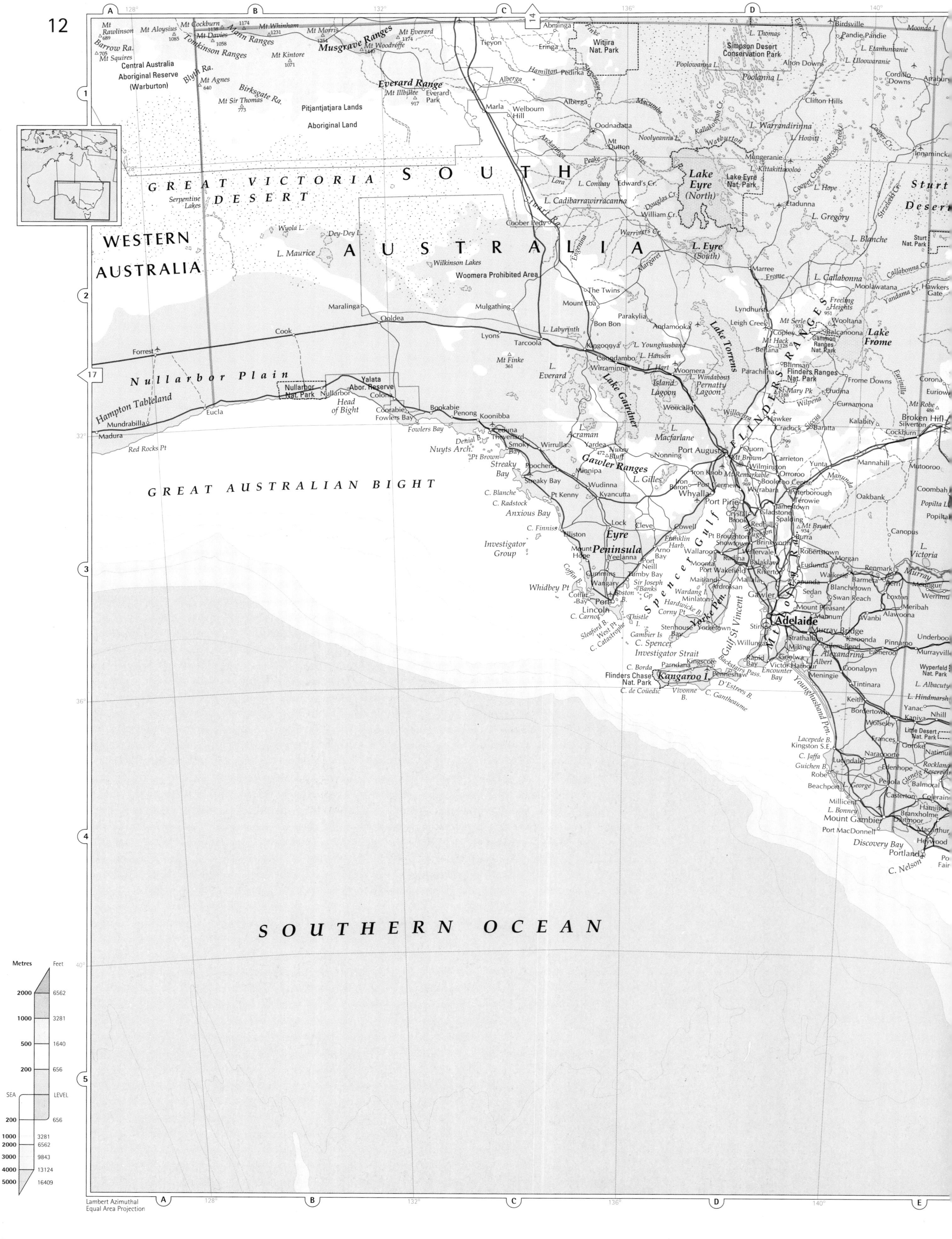
SOUTH AUSTRALIA
WESTERN AUSTRALIA
GREAT VICTORIA DESERT
Nullarbor Plain
Hampton Tableland
GREAT AUSTRALIAN BIGHT
SOUTHERN OCEAN
Central Australia Aboriginal Reserve (Warburton)
Pitjantjatjara Lands Aboriginal Land
Musgrave Ranges
Everard Range
Mann Ranges
Tomkinson Ranges
Birksgate Ra.
Blyth Ra.
Barrow Ra.
Mt Rawlinson
Mt Aloysius
Mt Cockburn
Mt Davies
Mt Whinham
Mt Morris
Mt Everard
Mt Woodroffe
Mt Kintore
Mt Squires
Mt Agnes
Mt Sir Thomas
Mt Illbillee
Everard Park
Witjira Nat. Park
Simpson Desert Conservation Park
Lake Eyre (North)
Lake Eyre Nat. Park
L. Eyre (South)
Sturt Stony Desert
Sturt Nat. Park
Woomera Prohibited Area
Wilkinson Lakes
L. Maurice
Serpentine Lakes
Wyola L.
Dey-Dey L.
Maralinga
Ooldea
Cook
Forrest
Nullarbor Nat. Park
Yalata Abor. Reserve
Nullarbor
Head of Bight
Eucla
Mundrabilla
Madura
Red Rocks Pt
Coorabie
Fowlers Bay
Colona
Bookabie
Penong
Koonibba
Ceduna
Thevenard
Denial B.
Nuyts Arch.
Pt Brown
Smoky Bay
Streaky Bay
Poochera
Wirrulla
Minnipa
Gawler Ranges
Wudinna
Kyancutta
Pt Kenny
C. Blanche
C. Radstock
Anxious Bay
C. Finniss
Elliston
Investigator Group
Eyre Peninsula
Lock
Cleve
Cowell
Franklin Harb.
Arno Bay
Port Neill
Tumby Bay
Sir Joseph Banks Gp
Mount Hope
Yeelanna
Cummins
Wangary
Whidbey Pt
Coffin B.
Coffin Bay
Port Lincoln
Boston B.
C. Carnot
Sleaford B.
West Pt
C. Catastrophe
Thistle I.
Gambier Is
C. Spencer
Investigator Strait
Spencer Gulf
Yorke Pen.
Gulf St Vincent
Whyalla
Iron Knob
Iron Baron
Port Germein
Port Pirie
Port Augusta
Port Broughton
Wallaroo
Kadina
Moonta
Port Wakefield
Maitland
Ardrossan
Minlaton
Wardang I.
Hardwicke B.
Corny Pt
Stenhouse Bay
Yorketown
Adelaide
Gawler
Mallala
Balaklava
Clare
Snowtown
Mount Pleasant
Murray Bridge
Strathalbyn
Tailem Bend
Milang
Goolwa
Victor Harbour
Encounter Bay
Backstairs Pass.
Kangaroo I.
Kingscote
Parndana
Penneshaw
Flinders Chase Nat. Park
C. Borda
C. de Couëdic
Vivonne B.
D'Estrees B.
C. Gantheaume
L. Alexandrina
L. Albert
Meningie
Coonalpyn
Tintinara
Keith
Bordertown
Wolseley
Frances
Naracoorte
Lucindale
Penola
Kingston S.E.
Lacepede B.
C. Jaffa
Guichen B.
Robe
Beachport
Millicent
Mount Gambier
Port MacDonnell
Discovery Bay
Portland
C. Nelson
Younghusband Pen.
FLINDERS RANGES
Flinders Ranges Nat. Park
Lake Torrens
Lake Frome
L. Callabonna
Lake Gairdner
L. Everard
L. Acraman
L. Gilles
L. Macfarlane
L. Labyrinth
L. Younghusband
L. Hanson
L. Hart
Island Lagoon
Pernatty Lagoon
L. Windabout
Tarcoola
Kingoonya
Coondambo
Wirraminna
Woomera
Woocalla
Andamooka
Parakylia
Mulgathing
Mount Eba
The Twins
Bon Bon
Lyons
Mt Finke
Coober Pedy
Marla
Welbourn Hill
Oodnadatta
Mt Dutton
Alberga
Abminga
Eringa
Tieyon
Marree
Leigh Creek
Lyndhurst
Copley
Beltana
Parachilna
Hawker
Quorn
Wilmington
Carrieton
Orroroo
Peterborough
Jamestown
Gladstone
Burra
Mt Bryan
Morgan
Renmark
Waikerie
Barmera
Loxton
Blanchetown
Swan Reach
Mannum
Pinnaroo
Broken Hill
Innamincka
Birdsville
Moolawatana
Frome Downs
Yunta
Mannahill
Oakbank
Canopus
L. Victoria
Mt Serle
Freeling Heights
Gammon Ranges Nat. Park
Balcanoona
Wooltana
Blinman
Wilpena
Arkaroola
Stuart Ra.
Cooper Cr.
Strzelecki Cr.
Warburton
Macumba
Neales
L. Blanche
L. Gregory
L. Hope
L. Cadibarrawirracanna
L. Conway
William Cr.
Etadunna
Mungeranie
Clifton Hills
Alton Downs
Poolowanna L.
L. Thomas
Lambert Azimuthal Equal Area Projection
Metres
Feet
2000 6562
1000 3281
500 1640
200 656
SEA LEVEL
200 656
1000 3281
2000 6562
3000 9843
4000 13124
5000 16409

QUEENSLAND
NEW SOUTH WALES
VICTORIA
TASMANIA
GREAT DIVIDING RANGE
Grey Range
Darling Downs
Riverina
Gippsland
TASMAN SEA
Bass Strait
Furneaux Group
Hunter Is
Banks Strait
JERVIS BAY TERR.
Brisbane
Gold Coast
Toowoomba
Ipswich
Sydney
Newcastle
Wollongong
Canberra
Melbourne
Geelong
Ballarat
Bendigo
Hobart
Launceston
Devonport
Burnie
Dubbo
Tamworth
Armidale
Orange
Bathurst
Wagga Wagga
Albury
Wodonga
Mildura
Griffith
Goulburn
Port Macquarie
Coffs Harbour
Grafton
Lismore
Maryborough
Gympie
Nambour
Bundaberg
Fraser I.
Moreton I.
N. Stradbroke I.
King I.
Flinders I.
Cape Barren I.
Bruny I.
Maria I.
Wilson's Promontory
Port Phillip Bay
Botany B.
Port Stephens
Jervis Bay
C. Howe
C. Otway
C. Byron
South West C.
South East C.
Charleville
Cunnamulla
Bourke
Cobar
Broken Hill
Wilcannia
Menindee
Hay
Deniliquin
Shepparton
Wangaratta
Sale
Traralgon
Warrnambool
Horsham
Moree
Narrabri
Goondiwindi
St George
Roma
Miles
Dalby
Warwick
Kingaroy
Stanthorpe
Glen Innes
Inverell
Tenterfield
Muswellbrook
Singleton
Maitland
Cessnock
Gosford
Katoomba
Lithgow
Queanbeyan
Cooma
Bega
Nowra
Batemans Bay
Eden
Queenstown
Strahan
Ninety Mile Beach
Miles Km
200 320
280
160 240
120 200
160
80 120
40 80
40
0 0

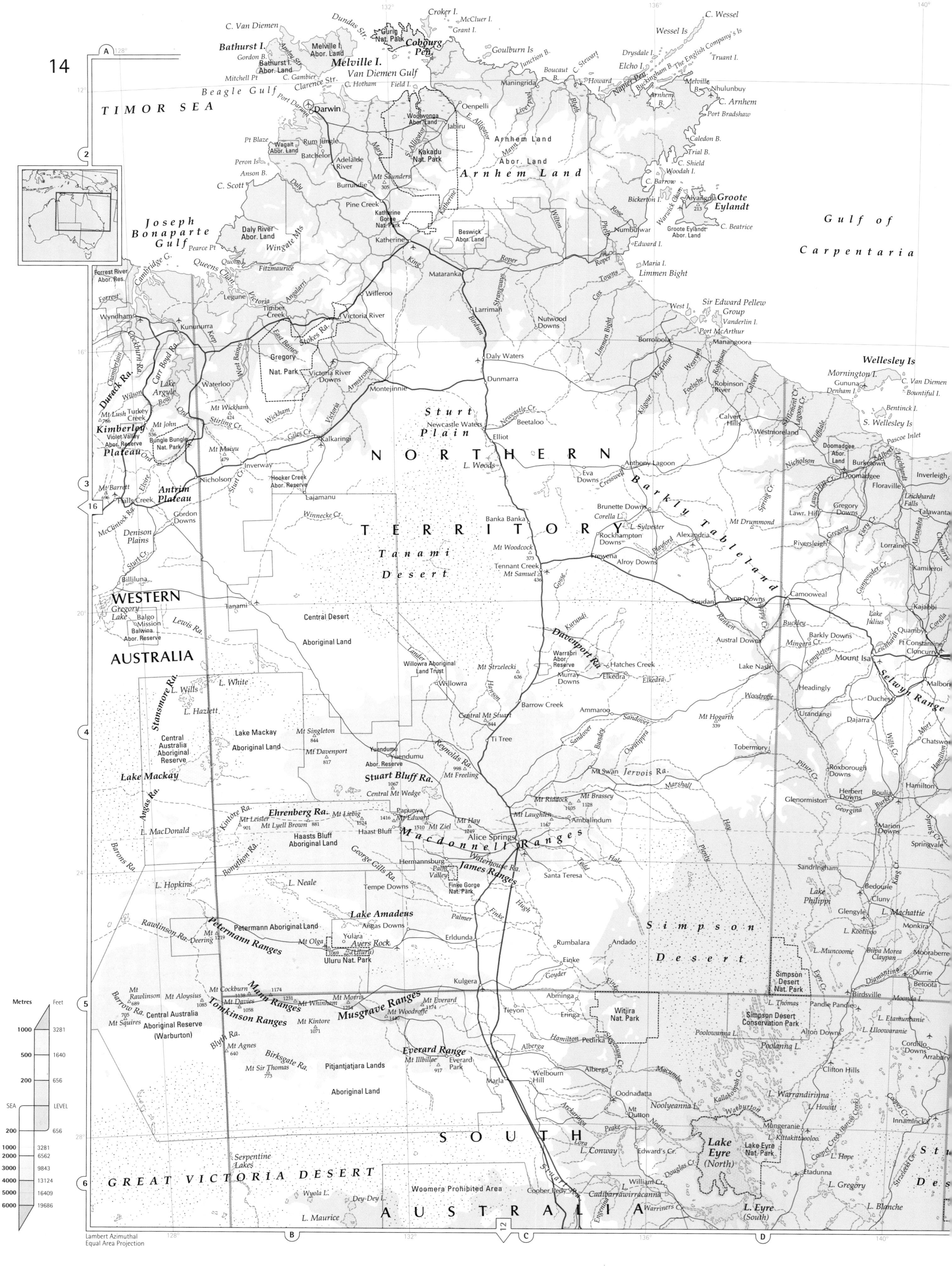
TIMOR SEA
Beagle Gulf
Bathurst I.
Melville I.
Van Diemen Gulf
Cobourg Pen.
Darwin
Arnhem Land
Kakadu Nat. Park
Joseph Bonaparte Gulf
Gulf of Carpentaria
Groote Eylandt
Katherine
Mataranka
Daly Waters
Dunmarra
Sir Edward Pellew Group
Wellesley Is
Mornington I.
Borroloola
Wyndham
Kununurra
Lake Argyle
Kimberley Plateau
Durack Ra.
Gregory Nat. Park
Victoria River Downs
Sturt Plain
Newcastle Waters
Elliott
NORTHERN TERRITORY
Tanami Desert
Barkly Tableland
Tennant Creek
Camooweal
Mount Isa
Cloncurry
Selwyn Range
Halls Creek
Antrim Plateau
WESTERN AUSTRALIA
Gregory Lake
Central Desert Aboriginal Land
Davenport Ra.
Barrow Creek
Central Australia Aboriginal Reserve
Lake Mackay
Lake Mackay Aboriginal Land
Stuart Bluff Ra.
Ehrenberg Ra.
Macdonnell Ranges
Alice Springs
Haasts Bluff Aboriginal Land
James Ranges
Hermannsburg
Finke Gorge Nat. Park
Lake Amadeus
Petermann Aboriginal Land
Petermann Ranges
Avers Rock (Uluru)
Uluru Nat. Park
Simpson Desert
Simpson Desert Nat. Park
Simpson Desert Conservation Park
Witjira Nat. Park
Birdsville
Mann Ranges
Tomkinson Ranges
Musgrave Ranges
Everard Range
Central Australia Aboriginal Reserve (Warburton)
Pitjantjatjara Lands Aboriginal Land
Marla
Oodnadatta
Lake Eyre (North)
Lake Eyre Nat. Park
L. Eyre (South)
SOUTH AUSTRALIA
GREAT VICTORIA DESERT
Woomera Prohibited Area
Coober Pedy
Metres
Feet
1000
3281
500
1640
200
656
SEA
LEVEL
200
656
1000
3281
2000
6562
3000
9843
4000
13124
5000
16409
6000
19686
Lambert Azimuthal Equal Area Projection

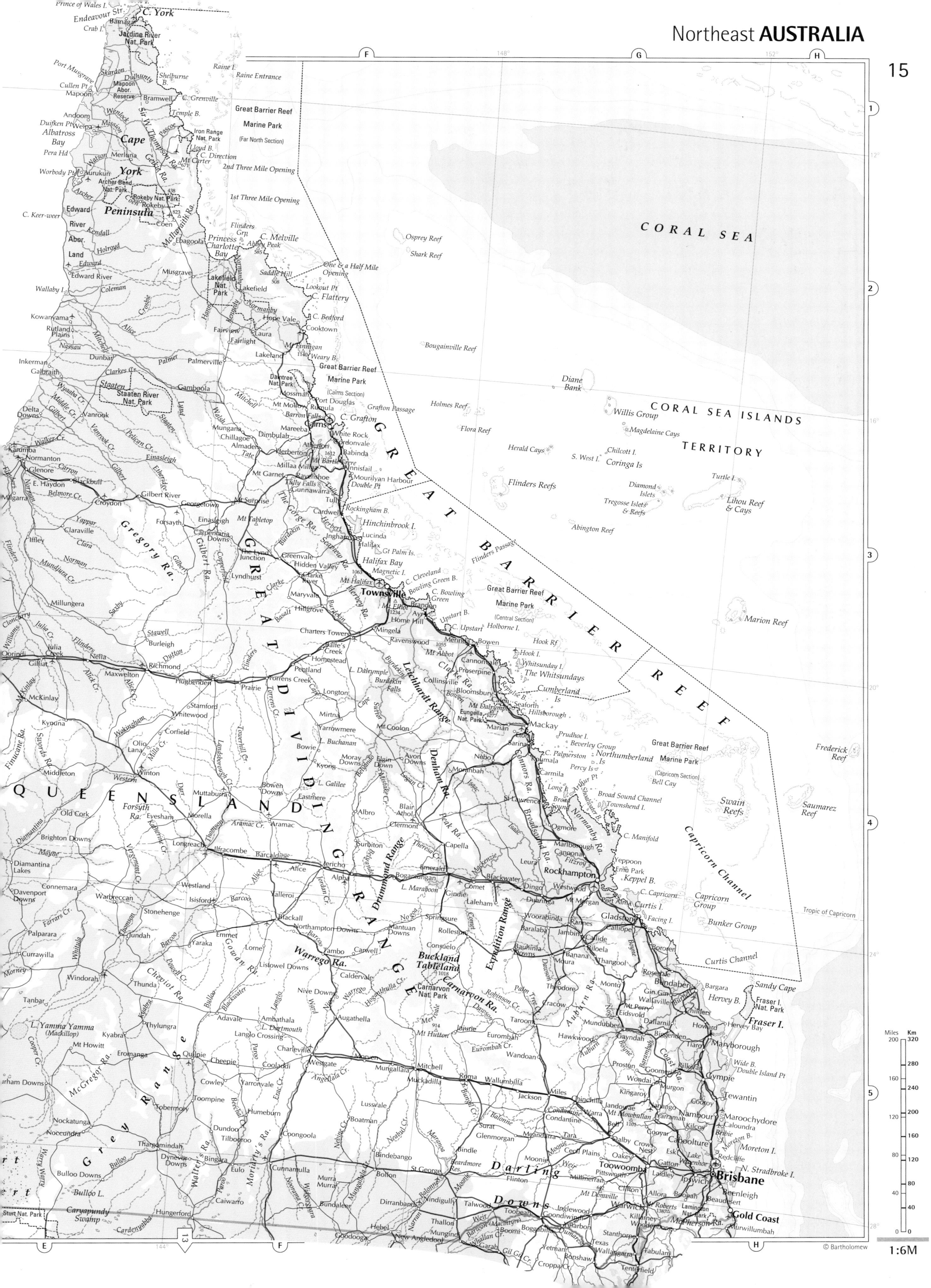
CORAL SEA
CORAL SEA ISLANDS TERRITORY
GREAT BARRIER REEF
QUEENSLAND
GREAT DIVIDING RANGE
Cape York Peninsula
Great Barrier Reef Marine Park (Far North Section)
Great Barrier Reef Marine Park (Cairns Section)
Great Barrier Reef Marine Park (Central Section)
Great Barrier Reef Marine Park (Capricorn Section)
C. York
Cooktown
Cairns
Port Douglas
Townsville
Charters Towers
Bowen
Mackay
Rockhampton
Gladstone
Bundaberg
Maryborough
Gympie
Nambour
Brisbane
Gold Coast
Toowoomba
Warwick
Dalby
Roma
Charleville
Longreach
Barcaldine
Emerald
Hughenden
Richmond
Julia Creek
Karumba
Normanton
Croydon
Georgetown
Winton
Cunnamulla
St George
Goondiwindi
Darling Downs
Fraser I.
Moreton I.
N. Stradbroke I.
Hinchinbrook I.
The Whitsundays
Willis Group
Coringa Is
Flinders Reefs
Lihou Reef & Cays
Marion Reef
Frederick Reef
Saumarez Reef
Swain Reefs
Capricorn Channel
Capricorn Group
Bunker Group
Curtis Channel
Tropic of Capricorn
Osprey Reef
Bougainville Reef
Holmes Reef
Gregory Ra.
Leichhardt Range
Drummond Range
Expedition Range
Warrego Ra.
Grey Range
Buckland Tableland
Carnarvon Nat. Park
© Bartholomew
1:6M
Miles Km

Metres | Feet

Metres	Feet
3000	9843
2000	6562
1000	3281
500	1640
200	656
SEA	LEVEL
200	656
1000	3281
2000	6562
3000	9843
4000	13124
5000	16409

Lambert Azimuthal
Equal Area Projection

WESTERN AUSTRALIA
SOUTH AUSTRALIA
GREAT VICTORIA DESERT
Gibson Desert
Nullarbor Plain
GREAT AUSTRALIAN BIGHT
Archipelago of the Recherche
Darling Range
Perth
Fremantle
Kalgoorlie
Boulder
Coolgardie
Geraldton
Carnarvon
Albany
Esperance
Bunbury
Shark Bay
Houtman Abrolhos
Eucla
Norseman
Warburton
Wiluna
Leonora
Laverton
Meekatharra
Newman
Hamersley Ra. Nat. Park
Robinson Ranges
Kenneth Ra.
Barlee Ra.
Stirling Ra.
Nullarbor Nat. Park
Hampton Tableland
Petermann Ranges
Musgrave Ranges
Mann Ranges
Tomkinson Ranges
Lake Amadeus
Uluru Nat. Park
Ayers Rock (Uluru)
Mt Olga
Maralinga
Ooldea
Cook
Forrest
Rawlinna
Miles
Km
1:6M
© Bartholomew

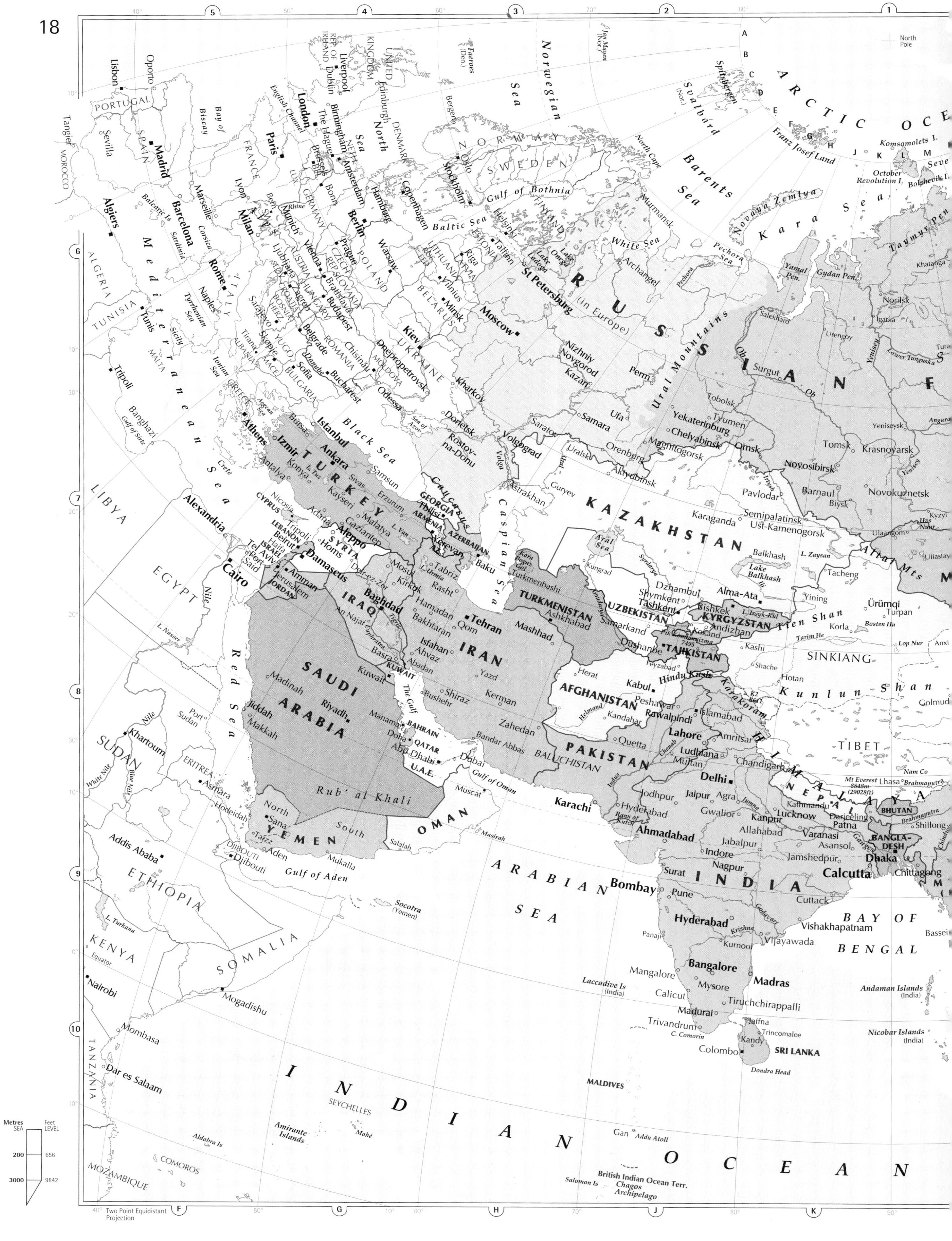
ARCTIC OCEAN
North Pole
Norwegian Sea
Jan Mayen (Nor.)
Faeroes (Den.)
Svalbard (Nor.)
Spitsbergen
Franz Josef Land
Komsomolets I.
October Revolution I.
Bolshevik I.
Barents Sea
Kara Sea
Novaya Zemlya
North Cape
Murmansk
White Sea
Archangel
Pechora Sea
Pechora
Yamal Pen.
Gydan Pen.
Taymyr Pen.
Khatanga
Norilsk
Igarka
Urengoy
Salekhard
Yenisey
Lower Tunguska
Tura
Ob
Surgut
Tobolsk
Tyumen
Yekaterinburg
Chelyabinsk
Magnitogorsk
Omsk
Novosibirsk
Tomsk
Krasnoyarsk
Yeniseysk
Angara
Barnaul
Biysk
Novokuznetsk
Kyzyl
Ulaangom
Uliastay
Altai Mts
RUSSIAN FEDERATION
RUSSIA (in Europe)
Ural Mountains
St Petersburg
Moscow
Nizhniy Novgorod
Kazan
Perm
Ufa
Samara
Saratov
Volgograd
Orenburg
Aktyubinsk
Uralsk
Ural
Volga
Astrakhan
Guryev
Rostov-na-Donu
Donetsk
Kharkov
Dnepropetrovsk
Kiev
UKRAINE
Odessa
Sea of Azov
Black Sea
Lake Ladoga
Lake Onega
Helsinki
FINLAND
Tallinn
ESTONIA
Riga
LATVIA
LITHUANIA
Vilnius
BELARUS
Minsk
Gulf of Bothnia
Baltic Sea
SWEDEN
Stockholm
NORWAY
Oslo
Bergen
DENMARK
Copenhagen
North Sea
UNITED KINGDOM
Edinburgh
Liverpool
Birmingham
London
English Channel
REP. OF IRELAND
Dublin
NETH.
The Hague
Amsterdam
BELG.
Brussels
LUX.
Bonn
GERMANY
Hamburg
Berlin
POLAND
Warsaw
CZECH REP.
Prague
SLOVAKIA
Bratislava
AUSTRIA
Vienna
HUNGARY
Budapest
Munich
Rhine
Bern
SWITZ.
Alps
Milan
Lyon
FRANCE
Paris
Bay of Biscay
Marseille
Corsica
Sardinia
Balearic Is
SPAIN
Madrid
Barcelona
PORTUGAL
Lisbon
Oporto
Sevilla
Tangier
MOROCCO
Algiers
ALGERIA
TUNISIA
Tunis
Tripoli
LIBYA
Banghazi
Gulf of Sirte
Mediterranean Sea
ITALY
Rome
Naples
Tyrrhenian Sea
Sicily
MALTA
Ionian Sea
SLOVENIA
Ljubljana
CROATIA
Zagreb
BOSNIA-HERZ.
Sarajevo
YUGO.
Belgrade
ALBANIA
Tirana
MACE.
Skopje
BULGARIA
Sofia
ROMANIA
Bucharest
Danube
MOLDOVA
Chisinau
GREECE
Athens
Aegean Sea
Crete
Istanbul
Bursa
Izmir
Ankara
TURKEY
Samsun
Sivas
Erzurum
Konya
L. Tuz
Antalya
Kayseri
Malatya
Adana
Gaziantep
L. Van
Caucasus
GEORGIA
Tbilisi
ARMENIA
Yerevan
AZERBAIJAN
Baku
Caspian Sea
CYPRUS
Nicosia
LEBANON
Beirut
Tripoli
SYRIA
Aleppo
Homs
Damascus
ISRAEL
Haifa
Tel Aviv
Port Said
Jerusalem
Amman
JORDAN
Alexandria
Cairo
EGYPT
Nile
L. Nasser
Red Sea
Deir-ez-Zor
Mosul
Kirkuk
IRAQ
Baghdad
Tigris
Euphrates
An Najaf
Basra
KUWAIT
Kuwait
L. Urmia
Tabriz
Rasht
Hamadan
Qom
Tehran
Bakhtaran
Isfahan
Ahvaz
Abadan
IRAN
Yazd
Shiraz
Bushehr
Kerman
Zahedan
Bandar Abbas
Mashhad
SAUDI ARABIA
Madinah
Riyadh
Jiddah
Makkah
Manama
BAHRAIN
Doha
QATAR
Abu Dhabi
U.A.E.
Dubai
The Gulf
Gulf of Oman
Muscat
OMAN
Masirah
Salalah
Rub' al Khali
North YEMEN South
Sana
Hodeidah
Taizz
Aden
Mukalla
Gulf of Aden
Socotra (Yemen)
DJIBOUTI
Djibouti
ERITREA
Asmara
SUDAN
Port Sudan
Khartoum
Nile
White Nile
Blue Nile
ETHIOPIA
Addis Ababa
L. Turkana
KENYA
Equator
Nairobi
SOMALIA
Mogadishu
Mombasa
TANZANIA
Dar es Salaam
SEYCHELLES
Mahé
Amirante Islands
Aldabra Is
COMOROS
MOZAMBIQUE
INDIAN OCEAN
ARABIAN SEA
KAZAKHSTAN
Aral Sea
Kara Bogaz Gol
Turkmenbashi
Kungrad
Syrdarya
Amudarya
TURKMENISTAN
Ashkhabad
UZBEKISTAN
Tashkent
Samarkand
Shymkent
Dzhambul
Alma-Ata
Bishkek
KYRGYZSTAN
L. Issyk-Kul
Andizhan
Kokand
Pik Kommunizma 7495
Dushanbe
TAJIKISTAN
Fayzabad
Karaganda
Semipalatinsk
Ust-Kamenogorsk
Pavlodar
Irtysh
Balkhash
Lake Balkhash
Ili
L. Zaysan
Tacheng
Yining
Ürümqi
Turpan
Bosten Hu
Korla
Tien Shan
Tarim He
Kashi
Lop Nur
Anxi
SINKIANG
Shache
Hotan
Kunlun Shan
Golmud
TIBET
Lhasa
Nam Co
Brahmaputra
Herat
AFGHANISTAN
Kabul
Helmand
Kandahar
Hindu Kush
Karakoram
K2 8611
Peshawar
Rawalpindi
Islamabad
Quetta
PAKISTAN
BALUCHISTAN
Lahore
Amritsar
Chenab
Ludhiana
Multan
Chandigarh
Indus
Karachi
HIMALAYA
Mt Everest 8848m (29028ft)
NEPAL
Kathmandu
BHUTAN
Darjeeling
Delhi
Jaipur
Agra
Jumna
Jodhpur
Hyderabad
Rann of Kutch
Gwalior
Kanpur
Lucknow
Allahabad
Patna
Varanasi
Ganges
Shillong
BANGLADESH
Dhaka
Chittagong
Asansol
Ahmadabad
Jabalpur
Indore
Jamshedpur
Calcutta
Nagpur
Surat
INDIA
Bombay
Pune
Cuttack
Godavari
Hyderabad
Krishna
Vishakhapatnam
Panaji
Kurnool
Vijayawada
BAY OF BENGAL
Bassein
Bangalore
Mangalore
Mysore
Madras
Calicut
Tiruchchirappalli
Madurai
Trivandrum
C. Comorin
Jaffna
Trincomalee
Kandy
Colombo
SRI LANKA
Dondra Head
Laccadive Is (India)
Andaman Islands (India)
Nicobar Islands (India)
MALDIVES
Gan
Addu Atoll
British Indian Ocean Terr.
Chagos Archipelago
Salomon Is
Metres SEA Feet LEVEL
200 656
3000 9842
Two Point Equidistant Projection

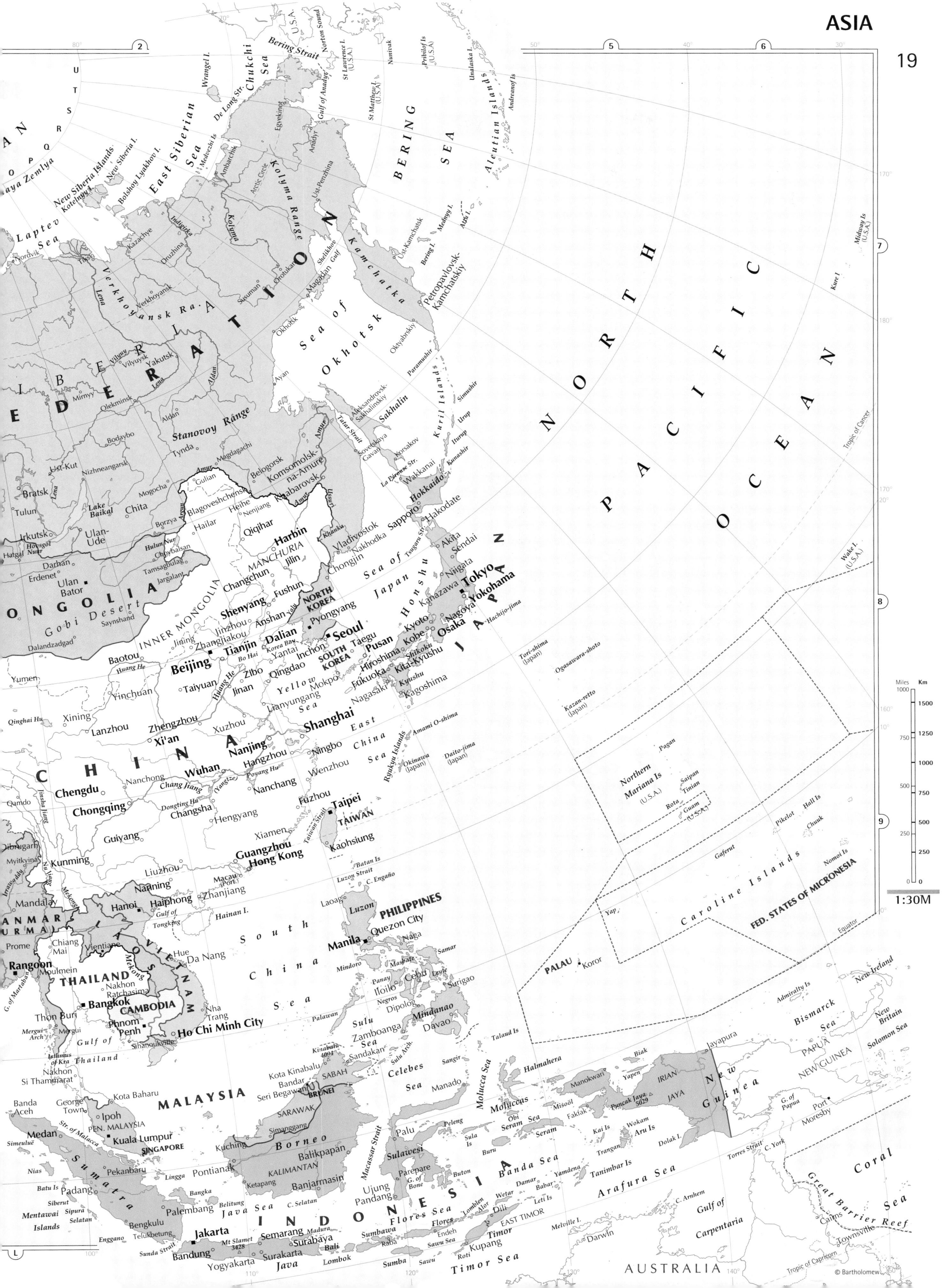
Bering Strait
Chukchi Sea
Wrangel I.
De Long Str.
East Siberian Sea
New Siberia Islands
New Siberia I.
Kotelnyy I.
Bolshoy Lyakhov I.
Laptev Sea
Nordvik
Tiksi
Lena
Verkhoyansk Ra.
Verkhoyansk
Kazachye
Indigirka
Druzhina
Kolyma
Kolyma Range
Ambarchik
Arctic Circle
Medvezhi Is
Egvekinot
Gulf of Anadyr
Anadyr
Ust-Penzhina
St Lawrence I. (U.S.A.)
St Matthew I. (U.S.A.)
Nunivak
Pribilof Is (U.S.A.)
Unalaska I.
Aleutian Islands
Andreanof Is
Norton Sound
U.S.A.
BERING SEA
Shelikhov Gulf
Magadan
Orotukan
Susuman
Kamchatka
Ust-Kamchatsk
Bering I.
Mednyy I.
Attu I.
Petropavlovsk-Kamchatskiy
Sea of Okhotsk
Okhotsk
Oktyabrskiy
Paramushir
Kuril Islands
Simushir
Urup
Iturup
Kunashir
Avan
Aleksandrovsk-Sakhalinskiy
Sakhalin
Tatar Strait
Sovetskaya Gavan
Korsakov
La Pérouse Str.
Wakkanai
NORTH PACIFIC OCEAN
Midway Is (U.S.A.)
Kure I.
Tropic of Cancer
FEDERATION
SIBERIA
Vilyuy
Vilyuysk
Yakutsk
Aldan
Lena
Mirnyy
Olekminsk
Stanovoy Range
Bodaybo
Tynda
Magdagachi
Amur
Belogorsk
Komsomolsk-na-Amure
Khabarovsk
Ussuri
Ust-Kut
Nizhneangarsk
Bratsk
Tulun
Lake Baikal
Chita
Mogocha
Irkutsk
Ulan-Ude
Borzya
Hövsgöl Nuur
Hatgal
Darhan
Erdenet
Ulan Bator
Hulun Nur
Choybalsan
Tamsagbulag
Jargalant
MONGOLIA
Gobi Desert
Saynshand
Dalandzadgad
Gulian
Blagoveshchensk
Heihe
Nenjiang
Hailar
Qiqihar
Harbin
MANCHURIA
Jilin
Khanka
Vladivostok
Nakhodka
Sapporo
Hokkaido
Hakodate
Tsugaru Str.
Akita
Sendai
Niigata
Chongjin
Sea of Japan
Honshu
Kanazawa
Tokyo
Yokohama
Nagoya
Kyoto
Osaka
Kobe
Shikoku
Kyushu
Kita-Kyushu
Fukuoka
Hiroshima
Nagasaki
Kagoshima
Hachijo-jima
JAPAN
Tori-shima (Japan)
Ogasawara-shoto
Kazan-retto (Japan)
Wake I. (U.S.A.)
Changchun
Fushun
Shenyang
NORTH KOREA
Pyongyang
Anshan
Yalu
Dalian
Korea Bay
Seoul
Taegu
Pusan
SOUTH KOREA
Inchon
Yantai
INNER MONGOLIA
Jining
Jinzhou
Zhangjiakou
Tianjin
Bo Hai
Beijing
Baotou
Huang He
Zibo
Jinan
Qingdao
Taiyuan
Yellow Sea
Mokpo
Lianyungang
Yumen
Yinchuan
Qinghai Hu
Xining
Lanzhou
Zhengzhou
Xuzhou
Xi'an
Shanghai
East China Sea
Nanjing
Hangzhou
Ningbo
Wenzhou
Amami O-shima
Ryukyu Islands
Okinawa (Japan)
Daito-jima (Japan)
CHINA
Wuhan
Poyang Hu
Chengdu
Nanchong
Chang Jiang
Yangtze
Nanchang
Chongqing
Dongting Hu
Changsha
Hengyang
Fuzhou
Taipei
TAIWAN
Taiwan Strait
Xiamen
Kaohsiung
Qamdo
Jinsha Jiang
Guiyang
Kunming
Guangzhou
Hong Kong
Macau
Zhanjiang
Liuzhou
Nanning
Dibrugarh
Myitkyina
Irrawaddy
Nu Jiang
Mekong
Mandalay
Hanoi
Haiphong
Gulf of Tongking
Hainan I.
Batan Is
Luzon Strait
C. Engaño
Laoag
Luzon
PHILIPPINES
Quezon City
Manila
Naga
Samar
Mindoro
Masbate
Panay
Leyte
Cebu
Iloilo
Negros
Surigao
Dipolog
Mindanao
Davao
Palawan
Sulu Sea
Zamboanga
South China Sea
MYANMAR (BURMA)
Prome
Rangoon
Moulmein
G. of Martaban
Chiang Mai
Vientiane
LAOS
VIETNAM
Hue
Da Nang
THAILAND
Nakhon Ratchasima
Bangkok
CAMBODIA
Thon Buri
Phnom Penh
Nha Trang
Ho Chi Minh City
Mergui
Mergui Arch.
Gulf of Thailand
Sihanoukville
Isthmus of Kra
Nakhon Si Thammarat
Northern Mariana Is (U.S.A.)
Pagan
Saipan
Tinian
Rota
Guam (U.S.A.)
Hall Is
Pikelot
Chuuk
Gaferut
Caroline Islands
Nomoi Is
FED. STATES OF MICRONESIA
Yap
PALAU
Koror
Equator
New Ireland
Admiralty Is
Bismarck Sea
New Britain
Solomon Sea
PAPUA NEW GUINEA
Talaud Is
Kinabalu 4094
Sandakan
Sulu Arch.
Kota Kinabalu
SABAH
Bandar Seri Begawan
BRUNEI
Celebes Sea
Sangir
Manado
Molucca Sea
Halmahera
Biak
Manokwari
Yapen
Jayapura
IRIAN JAYA
New Guinea
Puncak Jaya 5029
Misoöl
Moluccas
Obi
Seram
Seram Sea
Fakfak
G. of Papua
Port Moresby
Kai Is
Wokam
Aru Is
Dolak I.
Banda Sea
Yamdena
Tanimbar Is
Trangan
Arafura Sea
Torres Strait
C. York
Coral Sea
Great Barrier Reef
Kota Baharu
MALAYSIA
Banda Aceh
George Town
Ipoh
PEN. MALAYSIA
Kuala Lumpur
SINGAPORE
Str. of Malacca
Medan
Simeulue
Sumatra
Nias
Pekanbaru
Batu Is
Padang
Siberut
Mentawai Islands
Sipura
Selatan
Enggano
Bengkulu
Telukbetung
Sunda Strait
Palembang
Bangka
Belitung
Lingga
Pontianak
Kuching
SARAWAK
Simanggang
Borneo
Balikpapan
KALIMANTAN
Ketapang
Banjarmasin
Java Sea
C. Selatan
Jakarta
Bandung
Mt Slamet 3428
Semarang
Madura
Surabaya
Surakarta
Yogyakarta
Java
Bali
Lombok
INDONESIA
Macassar Strait
Palu
Peleng
Sula Is
Buru
Sulawesi
Parepare
Buton
G. of Bone
Ujung Pandang
Flores Sea
Flores
Sumbawa
Raba
Sumba
Sawu Sea
Sawu
Endeh
Lomblen
Alor
Wetar
Dili
EAST TIMOR
Timor
Kupang
Roti
Timor Sea
Damar
Babar
Leti Is
Melville I.
Darwin
C. Arnhem
Gulf of Carpentaria
Cairns
Townsville
Tropic of Capricorn
AUSTRALIA
Miles
Km
1:30M
© Bartholomew

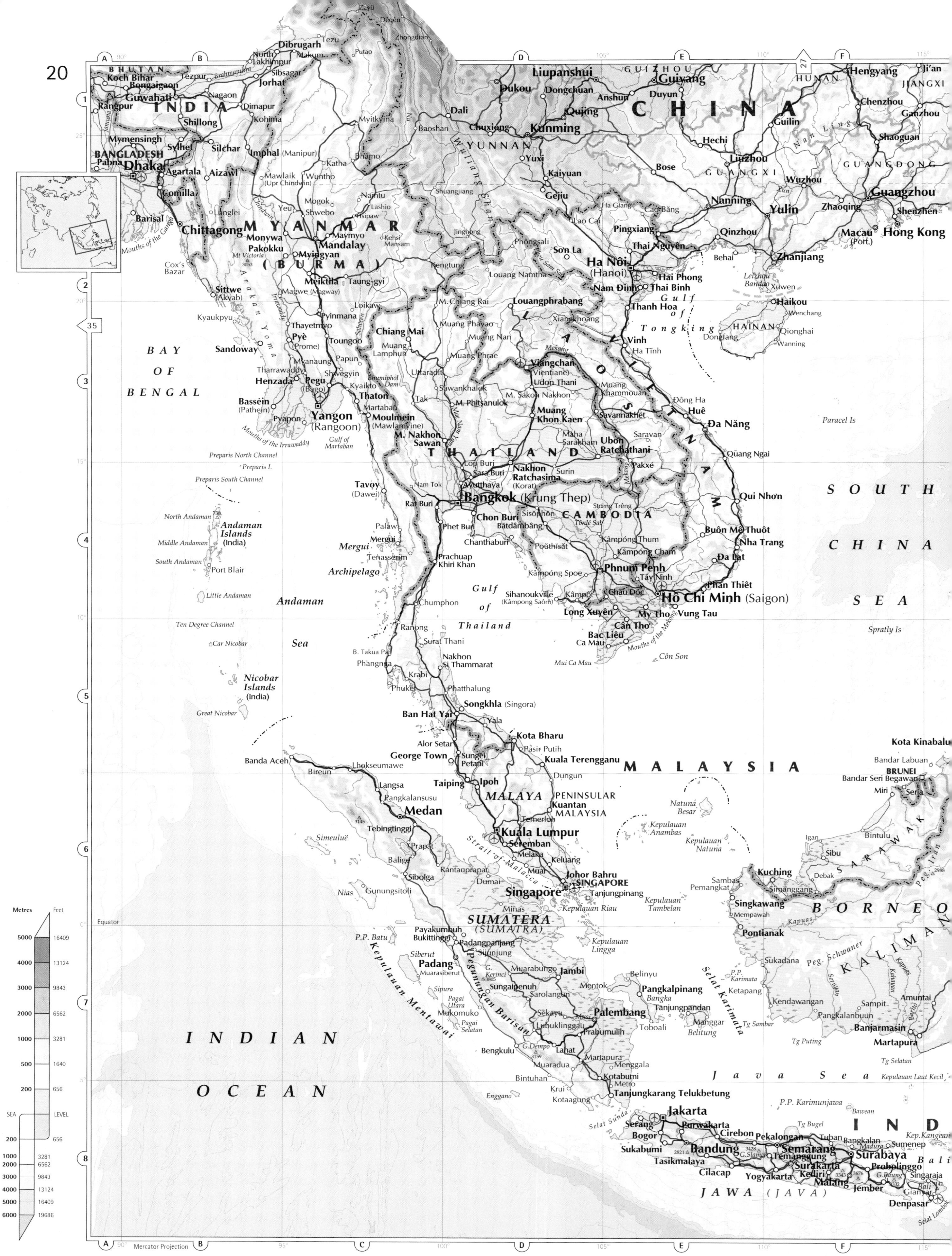
BHUTAN
INDIA
CHINA
BANGLADESH
MYANMAR (BURMA)
THAILAND
LAOS
VIETNAM
CAMBODIA
MALAYSIA
BRUNEI
SINGAPORE
SUMATERA (SUMATRA)
BORNEO
KALIMANTAN
SARAWAK
JAWA (JAVA)
YUNNAN
GUIZHOU
HUNAN
JIANGXI
GUANGXI
GUANGDONG
HAINAN
MALAYA
PENINSULAR MALAYSIA
BAY OF BENGAL
Andaman Sea
Gulf of Thailand
Gulf of Tongking
SOUTH CHINA SEA
INDIAN OCEAN
Java Sea
Strait of Malacca
Selat Karimata
Selat Sunda
Gulf of Martaban
Mouths of the Irrawaddy
Mouths of the Ganges
Mouths of the Mekong
Andaman Islands (India)
Nicobar Islands (India)
North Andaman
Middle Andaman
South Andaman
Little Andaman
Port Blair
Ten Degree Channel
Car Nicobar
Great Nicobar
Preparis North Channel
Preparis I.
Preparis South Channel
Mergui Archipelago
Paracel Is
Spratly Is
Kepulauan Mentawai
Pegunungan Barisan
Kepulauan Riau
Kepulauan Lingga
Kepulauan Anambas
Kepulauan Natuna
Natuna Besar
Kepulauan Tambelan
Equator
Dhaka
Chittagong
Yangon (Rangoon)
Mandalay
Bangkok (Krung Thep)
Viangchan (Vientiane)
Ha Nôi (Hanoi)
Hô Chi Minh (Saigon)
Phnum Penh
Kuala Lumpur
Singapore
Jakarta
Kunming
Guangzhou
Hong Kong
Macau (Port.)
Nanning
Guiyang
Medan
Palembang
Surabaya
Bandung
Semarang
Da Năng
Huê
Hai Phong
Chiang Mai
Moulmein (Mawlamyine)
Kota Bharu
George Town
Ipoh
Johor Bahru
Kuching
Pontianak
Banjarmasin
Padang
Jambi
Bengkulu
Tanjungkarang Telukbetung
Denpasar
Kota Kinabalu
Bandar Seri Begawan
Mercator Projection
Metres
Feet
SEA LEVEL
5000 16409
4000 13124
3000 9843
2000 6562
1000 3281
500 1640
200 656
6000 19686

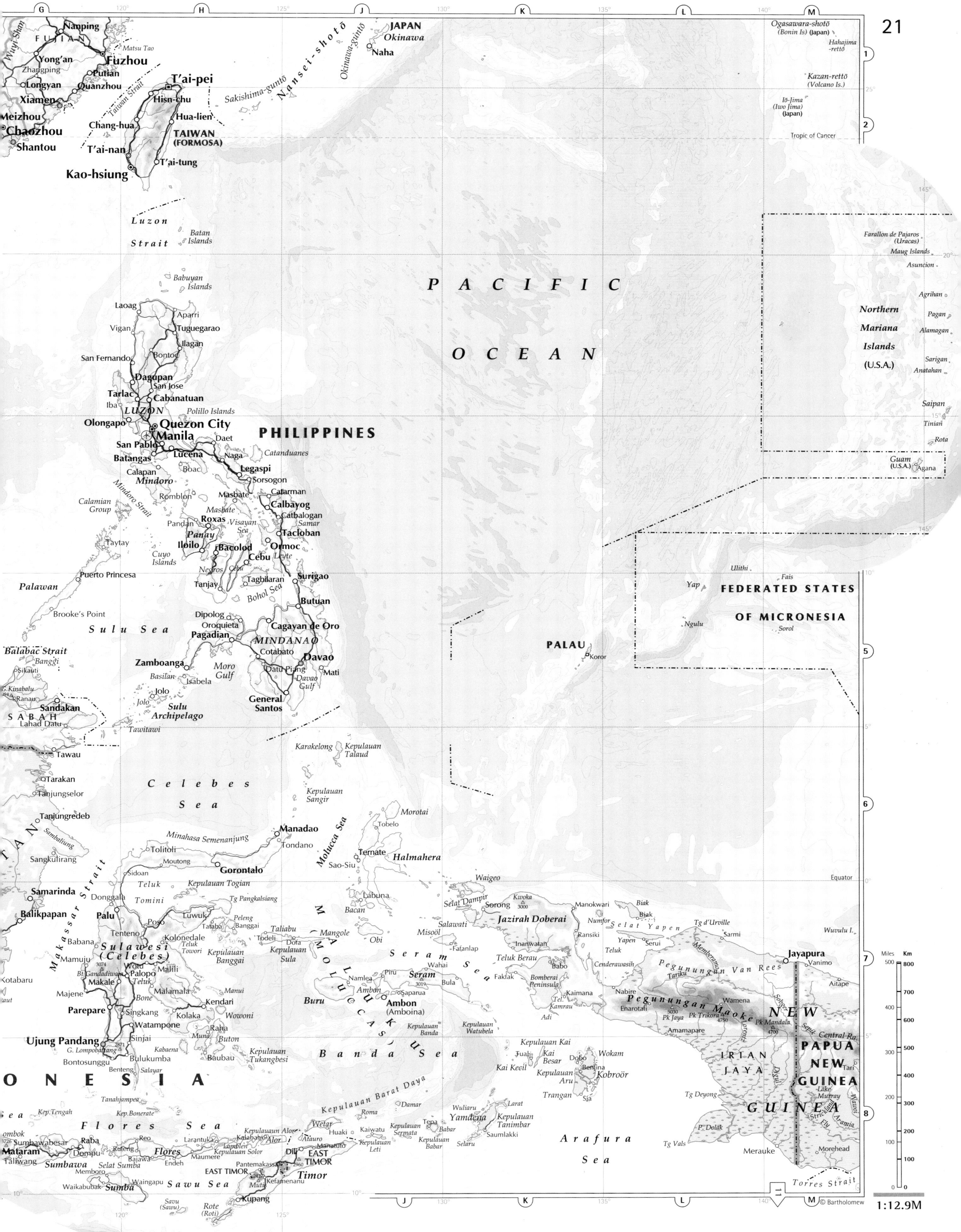
PACIFIC OCEAN
PHILIPPINES
JAPAN
Okinawa
Naha
Nansei-shotō
Okinawa-guntō
Sakishima-guntō
Ogasawara-shotō (Bonin Is) (Japan)
Hahajima -rettō
Kazan-rettō (Volcano Is.)
Iō-Jima (Iwo Jima) (Japan)
Tropic of Cancer
FUJIAN
Wuyi Shan
Nanping
Matsu Tao
Yong'an
Fuzhou
Zhangping
Putian
Quanzhou
Longyan
Xiamen
Meizhou
Chaozhou
Shantou
Taiwan Strait
T'ai-pei
Hsin-chu
Hua-lien
Chang-hua
TAIWAN (FORMOSA)
T'ai-nan
T'ai-tung
Kao-hsiung
Luzon Strait
Batan Islands
Babuyan Islands
Laoag
Aparri
Vigan
Tuguegarao
Ilagan
San Fernando
Bontoc
Dagupan
San Jose
Tarlac
Cabanatuan
Iba
LUZON
Polillo Islands
Olongapo
Quezon City
Manila
Daet
San Pablo
Lucena
Naga
Catanduanes
Batangas
Legaspi
Calapan
Boac
Mindoro
Sorsogon
Mindoro Strait
Romblon
Masbate
Catarman
Calamian Group
Calbayog
Catbalogan
Samar
Pandan
Roxas
Visayan Sea
Tacloban
Panay
Taytay
Iloilo
Bacolod
Ormoc
Cuyo Islands
Cebu
Leyte
Negros
Palawan
Puerto Princesa
Tanjay
Tagbilaran
Surigao
Bohol Sea
Butuan
Brooke's Point
Sulu Sea
Dipolog
Oroquieta
Cagayan de Oro
Pagadian
MINDANAO
Balabac Strait
Banggi
Cotabato
Zamboanga
Moro Gulf
Davao
Sikuati
Datu Piang
Mati
Basilan
Isabela
Davao Gulf
G.Kinabalu 4101
Ranau
Jolo
General Santos
Sandakan
SABAH
Sulu Archipelago
Lahad Datu
Tawitawi
Tawau
Tarakan
Tanjungselor
Celebes Sea
Karakelong
Kepulauan Talaud
Kepulauan Sangir
Tanjungredeb
Sambaliung
Morotai
Tobelo
Molucca Sea
Manadao
Tondano
Minahasa Semenanjung
Tolitoli
Moutong
Gorontalo
Ternate
Halmahera
Sangkulirang
Sao-Siu
Sidoan
Teluk Tomini
Kepulauan Togian
Samarinda
Donggala
Makassar Strait
Tg Pangkalsiang
Balikpapan
Palu
Poso
Luwuk
Peleng
Banggai
Tataba
Tenteno
Kolonedale
Teluk Towori
Sulawesi (Celebes)
Babana
Mamuju
Kepulauan Banggai
Bi Gandadiwata 3074
Wotu
Palopo
Teluk
Malili
Kotabaru
Makale
Majene
Bone
Malamala
Manui
Parepare
Kendari
Singkang
Kolaka
Wowoni
Watampone
Raha
Muna
Buton
Ujung Pandang
Sinjai
G. Lompobatang 2871
Kabaena
Bulukumba
Bontosunggu
Baubau
Benteng
Salayar
INDONESIA
Tanahjampea
Kep.Tengah
Kep.Bonerate
Flores Sea
Lombok
Sumbawabesar
Raba
Reo
Larantuka
Kalabahi
Alor
Kepulauaun Alor
Alauro
Wetar
Huaki
Mataram
Dompu
Ruteng
Flores
Maumere
Lomblen
Kepulauan Solor
Dili
EAST TIMOR
Manatuto
Taliwang
Sumbawa
Selat Sumba
Bajawa
Ende
Memboro
EAST TIMOR
Pantemakassar
2960
Timor
Waikabubak
Sumba
Waingapu
Sawu Sea
Mutis
Kefamenanu
Kupang
Savu (Sawu)
Rote (Roti)
Waigeo
Labuna
Selat Dampir
Sorong
Kwoka 3000
Manokwari
Biak
Bacan
Salawati
Jazirah Doberai
Numfor
Selat Yapen
Tg d'Urville
Sarmi
Taliabu
Mangole
Misoöl
Ransiki
Yapen
Serui
Todeli
Dofa
Obi
Kepulauan Sula
Fafanlap
Inanwatan
Teluk
Wuvulu I.
Seram Sea
Teluk Berau
Wahai
Babo
Cenderawasih
Jayapura
Vanimo
Piru
Seram
Fakfak
Bomberai Peninsula
Pegunungan Van Rees
Tariku
Mamberamo
Namlea
3019
Bula
Kaimana
Nabire
Aitape
Ambon
Saparua
Tel Kamrau
Enarotali
Wamena
Sobger
Buru
Ambon (Amboina)
Pegunungan Maoke
Pk Jaya 5030
Pk Trikora 4750
Pk Mandala 4700
NEW
Sepik
Central Ra.
Adi
MALUKU (MOLUCCAS)
Kepulauan Banda
Kepulauan Watubela
Amamapare
Lorentz
Kepulauan Kai
Fuai
Kai Besar
Wokam
PAPUA
Banda Sea
Dobo
Benjina
Kai Keeil
Kepulauan Aru
Kobroör
IRIAN JAYA
NEW
Tari
Digul
GUINEA
Lake Murray
Trangan
Sia
Tg Deyong
Wahgi
Kepulauan Barat Daya
Damar
Larat
Wuliaru
GUINEA
Strickland
Aramia
Roma
Yamdena
Kepulauan Tanimbar
Fly
Tepa
Babar
Saumlakki
P. Dolak
Kaiwatu
Kepulauan Sermata
Kepulauan Leti
Kepulauan Babar
Selaru
Arafura Sea
Tg Vals
Merauke
Morehead
Torres Strait
PALAU
Koror
Ulithi
Fais
Yap
FEDERATED STATES OF MICRONESIA
Ngulu
Sorol
Farallon de Pajaros (Uracas)
Maug Islands
Asuncion
Agrihan
Pagan
Northern Mariana Islands (U.S.A.)
Alamagan
Sarigan
Anatahan
Saipan
Tinian
Rota
Guam (U.S.A.)
Agana
Equator
Miles
Km
© Bartholomew

1:12.9M

INDONESIA
MALAYSIA
BORNEO
KALIMANTAN
KALIMANTAN BARAT
KALIMANTAN TENGAH
KALIMANTAN TIMUR
KALIMANTAN SELATAN
SARAWAK
SULAWESI (CELEBES)
SULAWESI TENGAH
SULAWESI SELATAN
SUMATERA (SUMATRA)
SUMATERA SELATAN
JAWA (JAVA)
JAWA BARAT
JAWA TENGAH
JAWA TIMUR
YOGYAKARTA
BALI
NUSA TENGGARA BARAT
NUSA TENGGARA TIMUR
LAMPUNG
BENGKULU
JAMBI
RIAU
JOHOR
SINGAPORE
JAVA SEA
FLORES SEA
BALI SEA
INDIAN OCEAN
MACASSAR STRAIT
Selat Karimata
Selat Sunda
Selat Bangka
Selat Gaspar
Selat Makassar
Teluk Tomini
Teluk Bone
Laut
Bangka
Belitung
Madura
Bali
Lombok
Sumbawa
Sumba
Flores
Jakarta
Bandung
Semarang
Surabaya
Surakarta
Yogyakarta
Malang
Cirebon
Bogor
Tegal
Pekalongan
Kediri
Madiun
Jember
Banyuwangi
Denpasar
Mataram
Palembang
Jambi
Pangkalpinang
Tanjungkarang Telukbetung
Serang
Pontianak
Singkawang
Kuching
Banjarmasin
Balikpapan
Samarinda
Palangkaraya
Ujung Pandang
Parepare
Palu
Watampone
Sumbawa Besar
Bima
Raba
Singapore
Johor Bahru
Kepulauan Riau
Kepulauan Lingga
Kepulauan Tambelan
Kepulauan Laut Kecil
Peg. Muller
Peg. Schwaner
Kapuas
Mahakam
Barito
Mercator Projection
© Bartholomew
Miles
Km
1:6M
Metres
Feet
SEA
LEVEL
3000
2000
1000
500
200
9843
6562
3281
1640
656
4000
5000
6000
13124
16409
19686
25

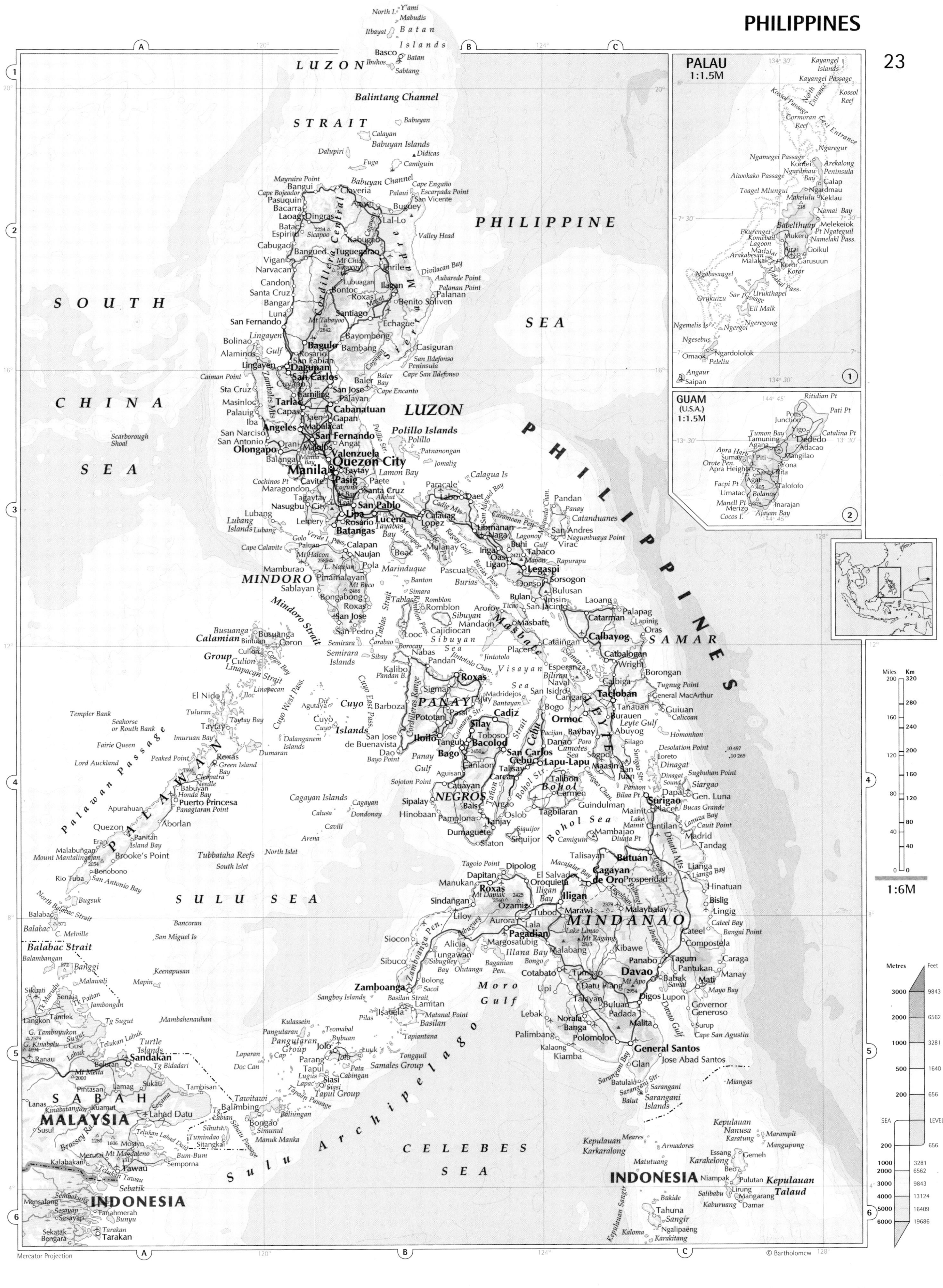

LUZON STRAIT
Balintang Channel
Batan Islands
Babuyan Islands
Babuyan Channel
PHILIPPINE SEA
SOUTH CHINA SEA
LUZON
Polillo Islands
Manila
Quezon City
Baguio
Dagupan
San Fernando
Olongapo
Angeles
Tarlac
Cabanatuan
Batangas
Lucena
Legaspi
Naga
Sorsogon
MINDORO
Mindoro Strait
Calamian Group
PALAWAN
Puerto Princesa
Palawan Passage
Cuyo Islands
Sibuyan Sea
Visayan Sea
SAMAR
LEYTE
PANAY
NEGROS
CEBU
BOHOL
Iloilo
Bacolod
Cebu
Tacloban
Roxas
Catbalogan
Calbayog
Ormoc
Dumaguete
Bohol Sea
Surigao
Butuan
Cagayan de Oro
Iligan
MINDANAO
Davao
Zamboanga
Pagadian
Cotabato
General Santos
Moro Gulf
Davao Gulf
SULU SEA
Sulu Archipelago
CELEBES SEA
Tubbataha Reefs
SABAH
MALAYSIA
Sandakan
Tawau
INDONESIA
Balabac Strait
PALAU 1:1.5M
Babelthuap
Koror
GUAM (U.S.A.) 1:1.5M
Agana
Miles
Km
1:6M
Metres
Feet
SEA LEVEL
Mercator Projection
© Bartholomew

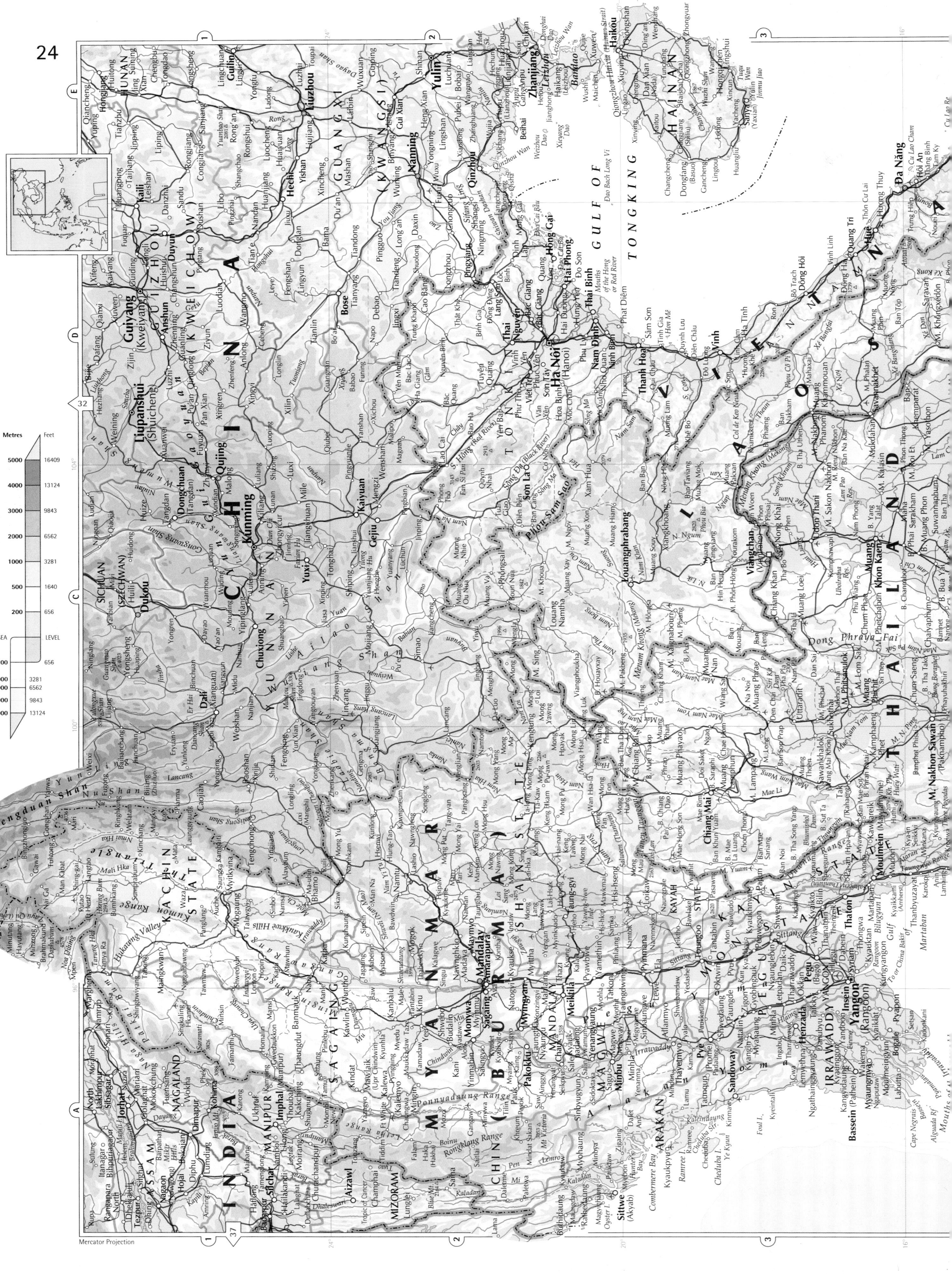

Metres
Feet
5000
16409
4000
13124
3000
9843
2000
6562
1000
3281
500
1640
200
656
SEA
LEVEL
INDIA
CHINA
MYANMAR (BURMA)
LAOS
THAILAND
VIETNAM
GUIZHOU (KWEICHOW)
GUANGXI (KWANGSI)
YUNNAN
SICHUAN (SZECHWAN)
HUNAN
HAINAN
KACHIN STATE
SHAN STATE
SAGAING
MANDALAY
MAGWE
ARAKAN
CHIN
PEGU
IRRAWADDY
KAYAH STATE
MANIPUR
NAGALAND
MIZORAM
ASSAM
TONKIN
GULF OF TONGKING
Kunming
Guiyang (Kweiyang)
Nanning
Ha Nôi (Hanoi)
Hai Phong
Mandalay
Yangon (Rangoon)
Chiang Mai
Vientiane (Viangchan)
Louangphrabang
Liuzhou
Guilin
Zhanjiang
Haikou
Da Nang
Hue
Moulmein (Mawlamyine)
Pegu
Bassein (Pathein)
Sittwe (Akyab)
Imphal
Dali
Hengduan Shan
Mercator Projection

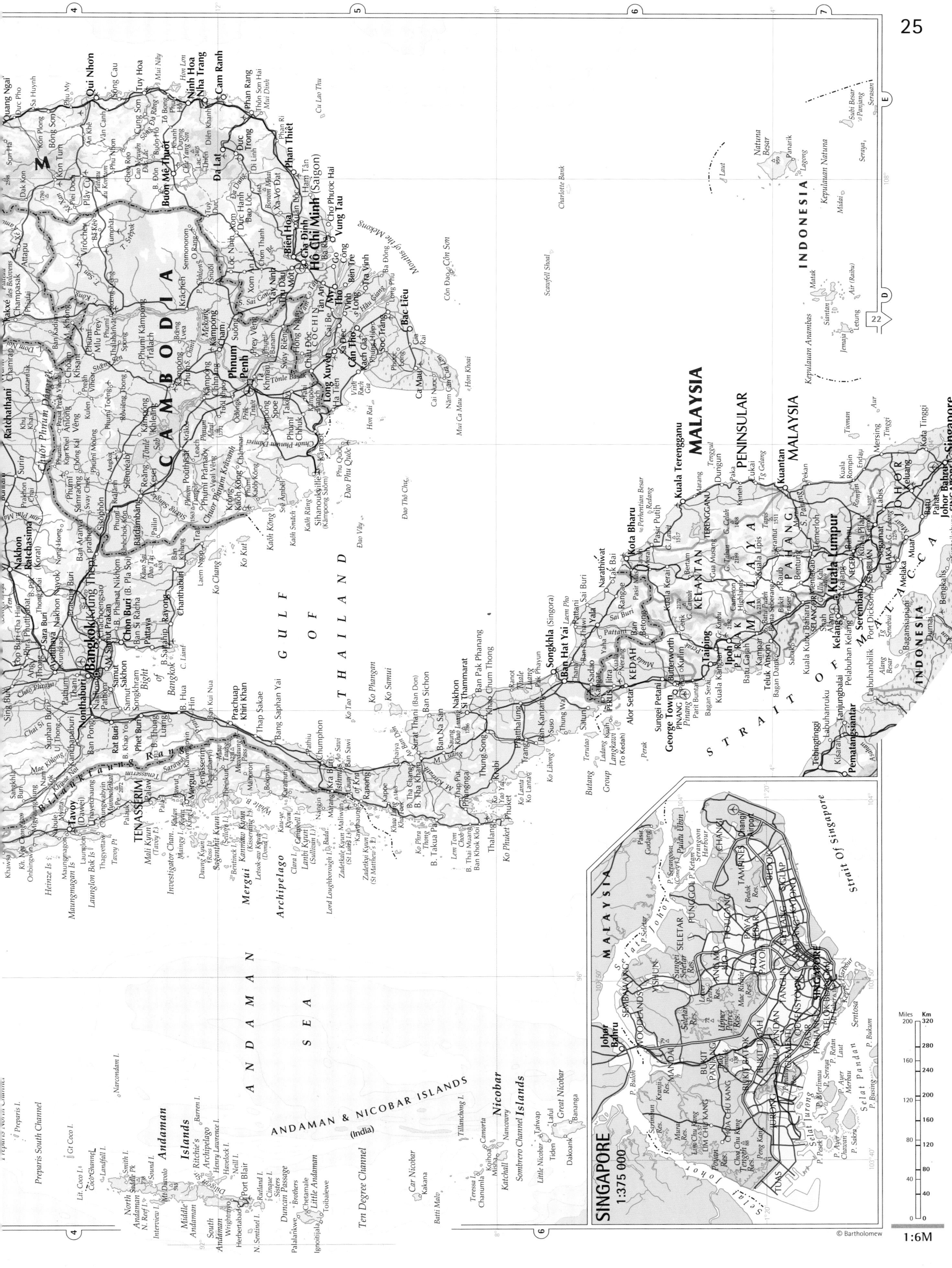

© Bartholomew

RUSSIAN FEDERATION
KAZAKHSTAN
MONGOLIA
KYRGYZSTAN
TAJIKISTAN
CHINA
INDIA
NEPAL
BHUTAN
BANGLADESH
MYANMAR (BURMA)
THAILAND
LAOS
JAMMU AND KASHMIR
AKSAI CHIN
XINJIANG UYGUR ZIZHIQU (SINKIANG UIGHUR AUT. REGION)
XIZANG ZIZHIQU (TIBET AUT. REGION)
QINGHAI
GANSU
SICHUAN
YUNNAN
GUIZHOU
NINGXIA
HIMACHAL PRADESH
UTTAR PRADESH
MADHYA PRADESH
BIHAR
WEST BENGAL
ORISSA
SIKKIM
ARUNACHAL PRADESH
ASSAM
MEGHALAYA
NAGALAND
MANIPUR
MIZORAM
TRIPURA
Melkosopochnik
Ozero Balkhash
TIEN SHAN
Terskey Ala-Too
Tarim Pendi (Tarim Basin)
CHINESE TURKESTAN
Taklimakan Shamo (Taklimakan Desert)
Junggar Pendi (Dzungarian Basin)
ALTAI MTS
Hangayn Nuruu
Gobi Altay Nuruu
KUNLUN SHAN
Altun Shan (Astin Tagh)
Qaidam Pendi
Qilian Shan
Hoh Xil Shan
Xizang Gaoyuan (Plateau of Tibet)
Gangdisê Shan (Kailas Range)
Nyainqêntanglha Shan
HIMALAYA
KARAKORAM
Bayan Har Shan
Hengduan Shan
Daxue Shan
Qionglai Shan
Mt Everest (Qomolangma Feng)
Kaimur Range
Eastern Ghats
Arakan Yoma
BAY OF BENGAL
Mouths of the Ganga
Zapadnyy Sayan
Vostochnyy Sayan
Khrebet Tannu Ola
Badain Jaran Shamo
Tengger Shamo
Almaty
Bishkek
Ürümqi (Urumchi)
Lhasa
Kathmandu
Thimphu (Tashi Chho)
Delhi
Dhaka
Calcutta
Ha Nôi
Lanzhou
Xining
Chengdu
Chongqing
Kunming
Guiyang
Mandalay
Chittagong
Lucknow
Kanpur
Patna
Varanasi
Allahabad
Agra
Chandigarh
Karaganda
Semipalatinsk
Ust'-Kamenogorsk
Barnaul
Irkutsk
Ulan-Ude
Ulaanbaatar
Kashi (Kashgar)
Aksu
Hotan
Yining (Gulja)
Shihezi
Hami
Golmud
Vishakhapatnam
Cuttack
Bhubaneshwar
Jamshedpur
Ranchi
Raipur
Guwahati
Dibrugarh
Imphal
Sittwe
Henzada
Pegu
Chiang Mai
Louangphrabang
Viangchan
Albers Equal Area Conic Projection
Metres
Feet
6000 19686
5000 16409
4000 13124
3000 9843
2000 6562
1000 3281
500 1640
200 656
SEA LEVEL
200 656
1000 3281
2000 6562
3000 9843
4000 13124
5000 16409
6000 19686

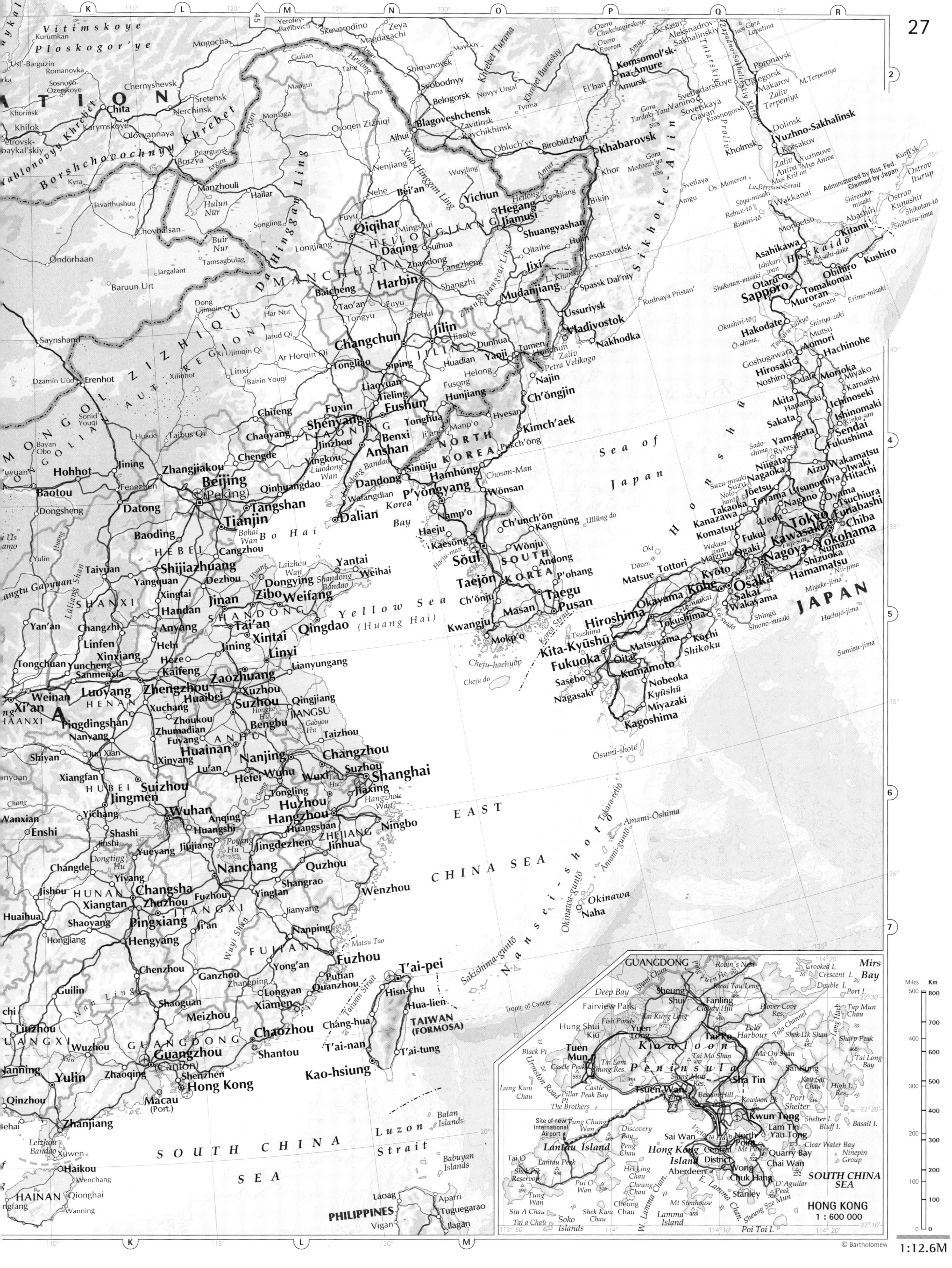
Vitimskoye Ploskogor'ye
Chita
Chernyshevsk
Sretensk
Nerchinsk
Borshchovochnyy Khrebet
Yablonovyy Khrebet
Skovorodino
Zeya
Mogocha
Blagoveshchensk
Svobodnyy
Belogorsk
Komsomol'sk-na-Amure
Amursk
Khabarovsk
Birobidzhan
Yuzhno-Sakhalinsk
Poronaysk
Kholmsk
Korsakov
Sikhote-Alin'
Manzhouli
Hailar
Hulun Nur
Choybalsan
Öndörhaan
Baruun Urt
Da Hinggan Ling
Xiao Hinggan Ling
HEILONGJIANG
MANCHURIA
Qiqihar
Daqing
Harbin
Yichun
Hegang
Jiamusi
Shuangyashan
Jixi
Mudanjiang
Ussuriysk
Vladivostok
Nakhodka
Changchun
Jilin
JILIN
Tongliao
Siping
NEI MONGOL ZIZHIQU (INNER MONGOLIA AUT. REGION)
Erenhot
Saynshand
Hohhot
Baotou
Datong
Zhangjiakou
Beijing (Peking)
Tianjin
Tangshan
Qinhuangdao
Chengde
Chifeng
Shenyang
Fushun
Anshan
Benxi
Jinzhou
LIAONING
Dandong
Dalian
Liaodong Bandao
Bo Hai
Bohai Wan
HEBEI
Baoding
Shijiazhuang
Taiyuan
SHANXI
SHANDONG
Jinan
Zibo
Weifang
Qingdao
Yantai
Weihai
Yellow Sea (Huang Hai)
Korea Bay
NORTH KOREA
P'yŏngyang
Namp'o
Sinŭiju
Hamhŭng
Ch'ŏngjin
Kimch'aek
Wŏnsan
SOUTH KOREA
Sŏul
Inch'ŏn
Taejŏn
Taegu
Pusan
Kwangju
Mokp'o
Masan
P'ohang
Ulsan
Cheju do
Korea Strait
Sea of Japan
Honshū
Hokkaidō
Sapporo
Asahikawa
Hakodate
Aomori
Hachinohe
Sendai
Akita
Niigata
Tōkyō
Yokohama
Kawasaki
Chiba
Nagoya
Kyōto
Ōsaka
Kōbe
Hiroshima
Okayama
Shikoku
Kyūshū
Kita-Kyūshū
Fukuoka
Kumamoto
Kagoshima
Nagasaki
JAPAN
Nansei-shotō
Okinawa
Naha
EAST CHINA SEA
Tropic of Cancer
HENAN
Zhengzhou
Luoyang
Kaifeng
Xi'an
JIANGSU
Xuzhou
Nanjing
Changzhou
Suzhou
Wuxi
Shanghai
ANHUI
Hefei
Huainan
Bengbu
HUBEI
Wuhan
Jingmen
Yichang
Shashi
ZHEJIANG
Hangzhou
Ningbo
Wenzhou
JIANGXI
Nanchang
Jingdezhen
HUNAN
Changsha
Zhuzhou
Xiangtan
Hengyang
FUJIAN
Fuzhou
Xiamen
Quanzhou
T'ai-pei
Hsin-chu
T'ai-chung
T'ai-nan
Kao-hsiung
TAIWAN (FORMOSA)
Taiwan Strait
GUANGDONG
Guangzhou (Canton)
Shenzhen
Hong Kong
Macau (Port.)
Shantou
Chaozhou
Guilin
Liuzhou
Yulin
Zhanjiang
Haikou
HAINAN
SOUTH CHINA SEA
Luzon Strait
Batan Islands
Babuyan Islands
PHILIPPINES
Laoag
Aparri
Tuguegarao
Vigan
Ilagan
HONG KONG 1 : 600 000
Kowloon Peninsula
Lantau Island
Hong Kong Island
Tsuen Wan
Sha Tin
Tai Po
Tuen Mun
Yuen Long
Kwun Tong
Victoria
Aberdeen
Stanley
Mirs Bay
Deep Bay
Lamma Island
Site of new International Airport
Miles
Km
1:12.6M
© Bartholomew

HOKKAIDO
continuation at the same scale
SEA OF OKHOTSK
SEA OF JAPAN
(NIPPON HAI)
HOKKAIDŌ
HOKKAIDO
AOMORI
Wakkanai
Sōya-misaki
Noshappu-misaki
Rebun-tō
Rishiri-zan
Rishiri-tō
Teshio
Hamatonbetsu
Esashi
Enbetsu
Shosanbetsu
Yagishiri-tō
Teuri-tō
Tomamae
Nayoro
Shibetsu
Monbetsu
Yūbetsu
Saroma-ko
Abashiri
Abashiri-wan
Shiretoko-misaki
Shiretoko-hantō
Nemuro-kaikyō
Rausu
M. Dokuchayeva
Rudnaya
Ostrov
Kunashir
Yuzhno-Kuril'sk
Golovnino
ADMINISTERED BY RUSSIAN FEDERATION. CLAIMED BY JAPAN.
Taraku-shima
Shibotsu-jima
Suishō-tō
Nosapu-misaki
Nemuro
Nemuro-wan
Notsuke-saki
Shari-dake
Rumoi
Mashike
Asahikawa
Furano
Kitami
Bihoro
Taisetsu-zan
Asahi-dake
Akan National Park
Kushiro-Shitsugen National Park
Kushiro
Ishikari-wan
Otaru
Sapporo
Ebetsu
Iwamizawa
Yūbari
Obihiro
Chitose
Tomakomai
Shakotan-misaki
Shakotan-hantō
Niseko
Tōya-ko
Shikotsu-Tōya National Park
Date
Muroran
Noboribetsu
Uchiura-wan (Volcano Bay)
Shiraoi
Hidaka-sanmyaku
Urakawa
Erimo-misaki
Hiroo
Okushiri-tō
Esashi
Hakodate
Esan-misaki
Matsumae
Tsugaru-kaikyō
Ōma-zaki
Shiriya-zaki
Shimokita-hantō
Mutsu
Mutsu-wan
Aomori
Hirosaki
Hachinohe
Towada
Misawa
Tok-tō (Take-shima) (Liancourt Rocks)
SOUTH KOREA
Kwangju
Masan
Chinju
Pusan
Ulsan
Kimhae
Miryang
Sunch'ŏn
Yŏsu
KOREA STRAIT
Tsushima
Izuhara
Kamitsushima
Oki-shotō
Dōgo
Dōzen
Shimane-hantō
Matsue
Izumo
Tottori
Hamada
SHIMANE
HIROSHIMA
Hiroshima
Kure
Fukuyama
OKAYAMA
Okayama
Kurashiki
Himeji
Yamaguchi
Shimonoseki
Kita-Kyūshū
Fukuoka
Kurume
Saga
Sasebo
Nagasaki
Kumamoto
Beppu
Ōita
Yatsushiro
Miyazaki
Nobeoka
Kagoshima
Sendai
Miyakonojō
KYŪSHŪ
SHIKOKU
Matsuyama
Imabari
Takamatsu
Tokushima
Kōchi
Muroto-zaki
Ashizuri-misaki
Cheju do (Quelpart I.)
Gotō-rettō
Koshikijima-rettō
EAST CHINA SEA
Danjo-guntō
Uji-guntō
Sata-misaki
Metres
Feet
SEA
LEVEL
Conic Equidistant Projection

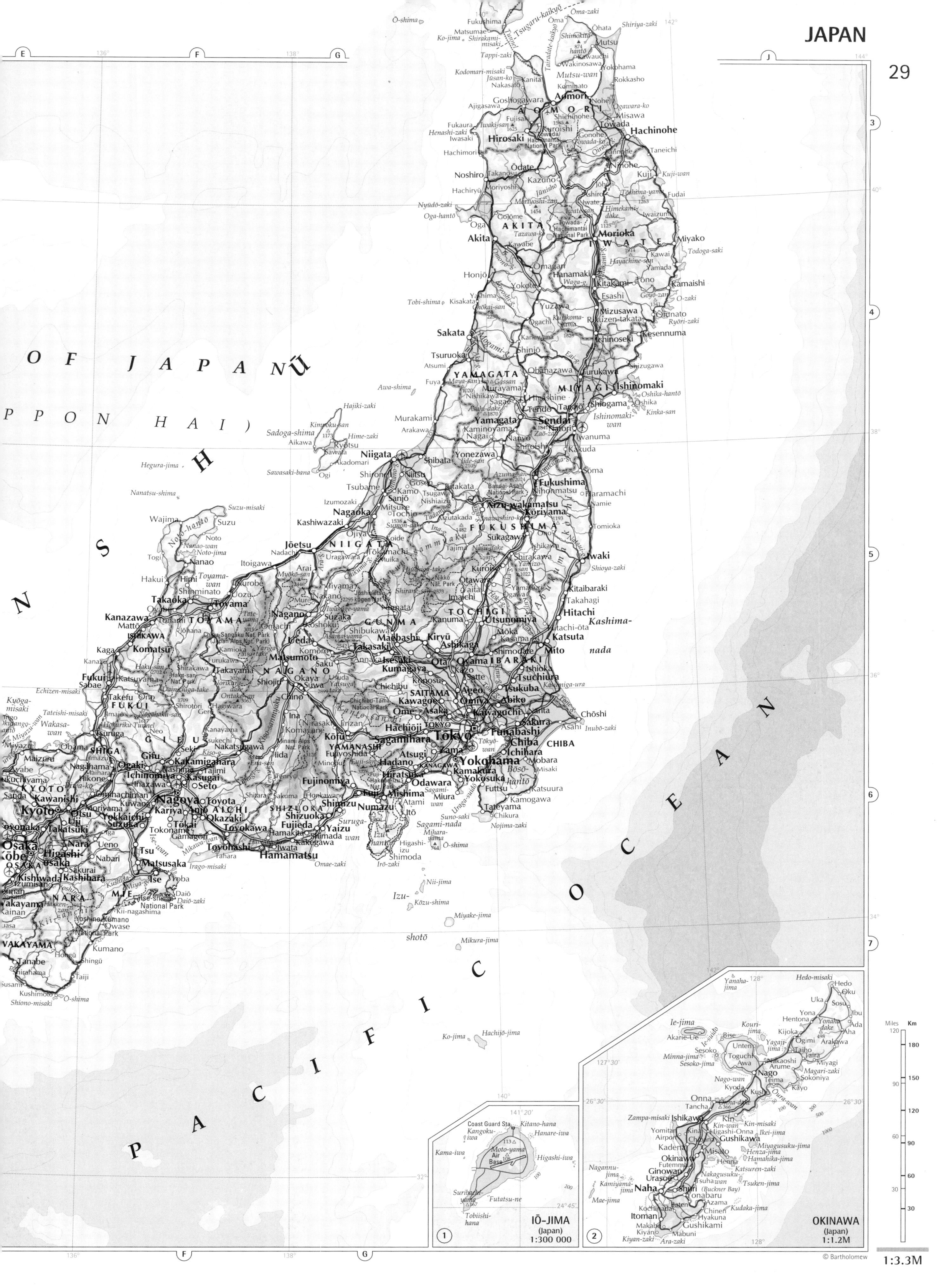
OF JAPAN
PPON HAI
H O N S H Ū
PACIFIC OCEAN
Tsugaru-kaikyō
Mutsu-wan
AOMORI
Aomori
Hirosaki
Hachinohe
Towada
Misawa
Noshiro
Ōdate
AKITA
Akita
Oga
Morioka
IWATE
Miyako
Kamaishi
Hanamaki
Kitakami
Mizusawa
Ōfunato
Kesennuma
Ishinomaki
MIYAGI
Sendai
Shiogama
Sakata
Tsuruoka
YAMAGATA
Yamagata
Yonezawa
Niigata
NIIGATA
Nagaoka
Kashiwazaki
Jōetsu
Sadoga-shima
Fukushima
FUKUSHIMA
Kōriyama
Aizu-wakamatsu
Iwaki
Hitachi
Mito
IBARAKI
Tsuchiura
Tsukuba
Kashima-nada
Utsunomiya
TOCHIGI
Maebashi
Takasaki
GUNMA
Kiryū
Ashikaga
Nagano
NAGANO
Matsumoto
Ueda
Toyama
TOYAMA
Takaoka
Kanazawa
ISHIKAWA
Komatsu
Noto-hantō
Wajima
Fukui
FUKUI
Gifu
GIFU
Takayama
Nagoya
AICHI
Toyota
Okazaki
Toyohashi
Hamamatsu
Shizuoka
SHIZUOKA
Numazu
Kōfu
YAMANASHI
Tōkyō
TOKYO
Hachiōji
Sagamihara
Yokohama
KANAGAWA
Kawasaki
Chiba
CHIBA
Funabashi
Chōshi
Kyoto
KYOTO
Ōtsu
SHIGA
Ōsaka
OSAKA
Kōbe
Nara
NARA
Tsu
MIE
Ise
Wakayama
WAKAYAMA
Shima
Izu-shotō
Ō-shima
Miyake-jima
Hachijō-jima
Kii-nagashima
Shiono-misaki
IŌ-JIMA
(Japan)
1:300 000
Moto-yama
Suribachi-yama
OKINAWA
(Japan)
1:1.2M
Naha
Okinawa
Ginowan
Urasoe
Nago
Ishikawa
Gushikawa
Itoman
Ie-jima
Hedo-misaki
Miles
Km
1:3.3M
© Bartholomew

RUSSIAN FEDERATION
MONGOLIA
CHINA
TYVA (TUVA)
BURYATIYA
HÖVSGÖL
DZAVHAN
ARHANGAY
BULGAN
SELENGE
TÖV
HENTIY
GOVĬALTAY
BAYAN-HONGOR
ÖVÖR-HANGAY
DUNDGOVĬ
DORNGOVĬ
SÜHBAATAR
ÖMNÖGOVĬ
GOBI
GANSU (KANSU)
QINGHAI (TSINGHAI)
NINGXIA (NINGSIA)
SHAANXI (SHENSI)
SHANXI
QILIAN SHAN
Badain Jaran Shamo
Mu Us Shamo
Tengger Shamo
Huang (Yellow River)
Ozero Baykal (Lake Baykal)
Qinghai Hu
Irkutsk
Ulan-Ude
Chita
Ulaanbaatar (Ulan Bator)
Darhan
Erdenet
Erenhot
Hohhot (Huhehot)
Baotou
Datong
Wuhai
Shizuishan (Dawukou)
Yinchuan
Jinchang
Xining
Lanzhou (Lanchow)
Linxia
Yan'an
Taiyuan
Shijiazhuang
Linfen
Changzhi
Handan
Anyang
Xinxiang
Albers Equal Area Conic Projection
Metres
Feet
6000
19686
5000
16409
4000
13124
3000
9843
2000
6562
1000
3281
500
1640
200
656
SEA
LEVEL

CHITA
KHABAROVSK
YEVREYSKAYA AVTONOMNAYA OBLAST'
DORNOD
HEILONGJIANG
MANCHURIA
JILIN
LIAONING
NEI MONGOL ZIZHIQU
(INNER MONGOLIAN AUT. REGION)
HEBEI
TIANJIN
BEIJING
SHANDONG
(SHANTUNG)
NORTH KOREA
SOUTH KOREA
Sea of Japan
(Nippon Hai)
YELLOW SEA
(HUANG HAI)
BO HAI
(GULF OF CHIHLI)
Bohai Haixia
Liaodong Wan
Korea Bay
(So-chaoson-man)
Korea Strait
Chita
Blagoveshchensk
Khabarovsk
Vladivostok
Ussuriysk
Svobodnyy
Belogorsk
Birobidzhan
Manzhouli
Hailar
(Hulun)
Qiqihar
(Tsitsihar)
Harbin
Daqing
Yichun
Hegang
Jiamusi
Shuangyashan
Jixi
Mudanjiang
Changchun
Jilin
Siping
Tonghua
Shenyang
(Mukden)
Fushun
Anshan
Benxi
Dandong
Dalian
(Dairen) (Lüda)
Chifeng
Xilinhot
Tongliao
Jinzhou
Yingkou
Qinhuangdao
Beijing
(Peking)
Tianjin
(Tientsin)
Tangshan
Zhangjiakou (Kalgan)
Baoding
Cangzhou
Jinan (Tsinan)
Zibo
Weifang
Yantai
(Chefoo)
Weihai
Qingdao (Tsingtao)
P'yŏngyang
Hamhŭng
Ch'ŏngjin
Kaesŏng
Sŏul (Seoul)
Inch'ŏn
Taejŏn
Taegu
Kwangju
Pusan
Ulsan
1:6M
© Bartholomew

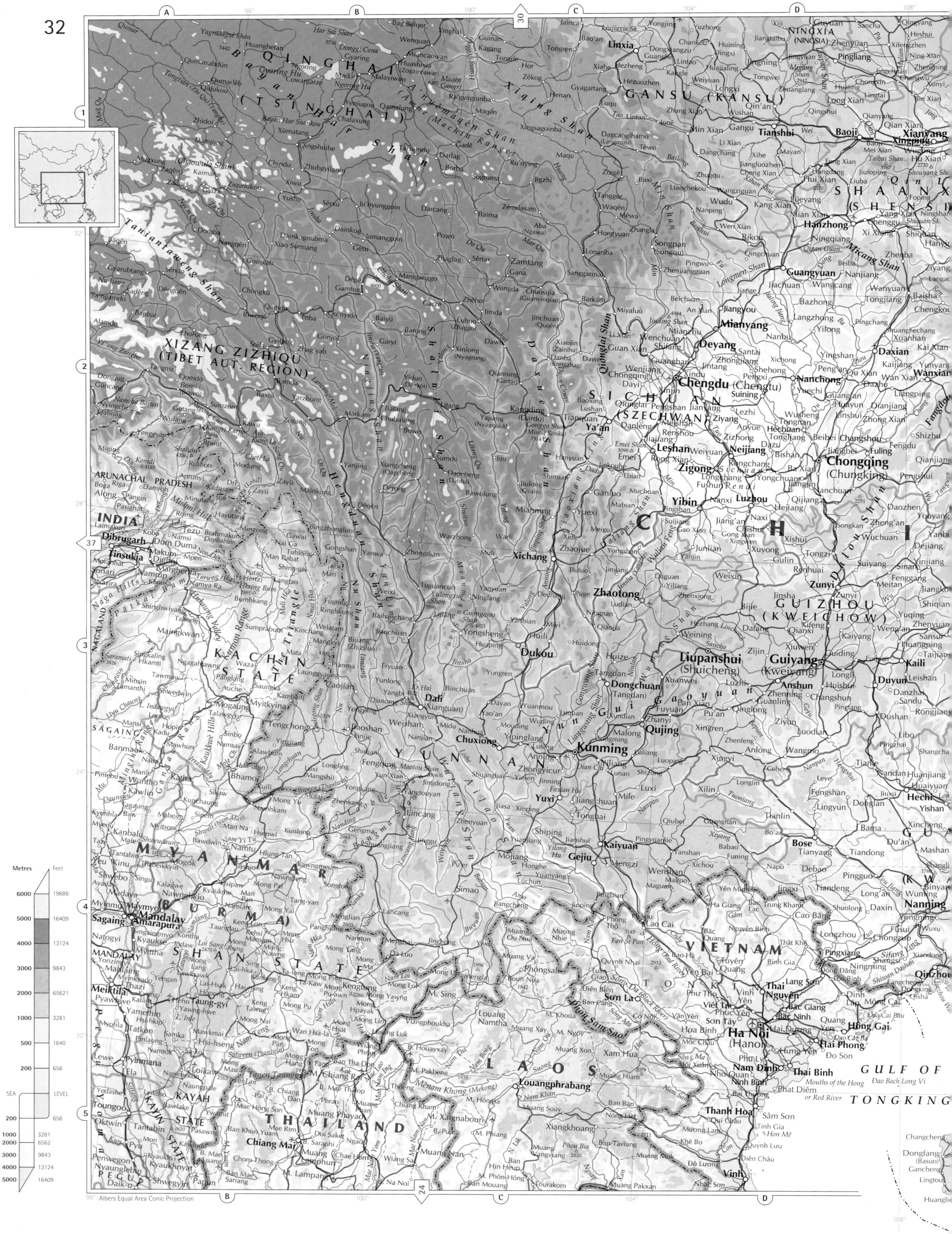
QINGHAI (TSINGHAI)
GANSU (KANSU)
NINGXIA (NINGSIA)
SHAANXI (SHENSI)
SICHUAN (SZECHWAN)
XIZANG ZIZHIQU (TIBET AUT. REGION)
YUNNAN
GUIZHOU (KWEICHOW)
CHINA
INDIA
ARUNACHAL PRADESH
NAGALAND
KACHIN STATE
SAGAING
MANDALAY
MYANMAR (BURMA)
SHAN STATE
KAYAH STATE
KAYIN STATE
PEGU
THAILAND
LAOS
VIETNAM
TONKIN
GULF OF TONGKING
Bayan Har Shan
Anyêmaqên Shan
Xiqing Shan
Tanggula Shan
Taniantaweng Shan
Shaluli Shan
Daxue Shan
Qionglai Shan
Min Shan
Hengduan Shan
Nu Shan
Gaoligong Shan
Wuliang Shan
Ailao Shan
Yun Gui Gaoyuan
Dalou Shan
Linxia
Lanzhou
Tianshui
Baoji
Xianyang
Hanzhong
Guangyuan
Mianyang
Deyang
Chengdu (Chengtu)
Ya'an
Leshan
Zigong
Neijiang
Yibin
Luzhou
Chongqing (Chungking)
Nanchong
Daxian
Xichang
Zhaotong
Dukou
Liupanshui (Shuicheng)
Guiyang (Kweiyang)
Zunyi
Anshun
Kaili
Duyun
Qujing
Kunming
Dali (Xiaguan)
Chuxiong
Yuxi
Gejiu
Kaiyuan
Hechi
Bose
Nanning
Qinzhou
Dibrugarh
Tinsukia
Myitkyina
Bhamo
Mandalay
Amarapura
Sagaing
Meiktila
Taunggyi
Toungoo
Chiang Mai
Chiang Rai
Louangphrabang
Xiangkhoang
Ha Nôi (Hanoi)
Hai Phong
Nam Đinh
Thanh Hoa
Vinh
Lao Cai
Sơn La
Điên Biên
Hong Gai
Albers Equal Area Conic Projection
Metres
Feet
6000
5000
4000
3000
2000
1000
500
200
SEA LEVEL
19686
16409
13124
9843
65621
3281
1640
656

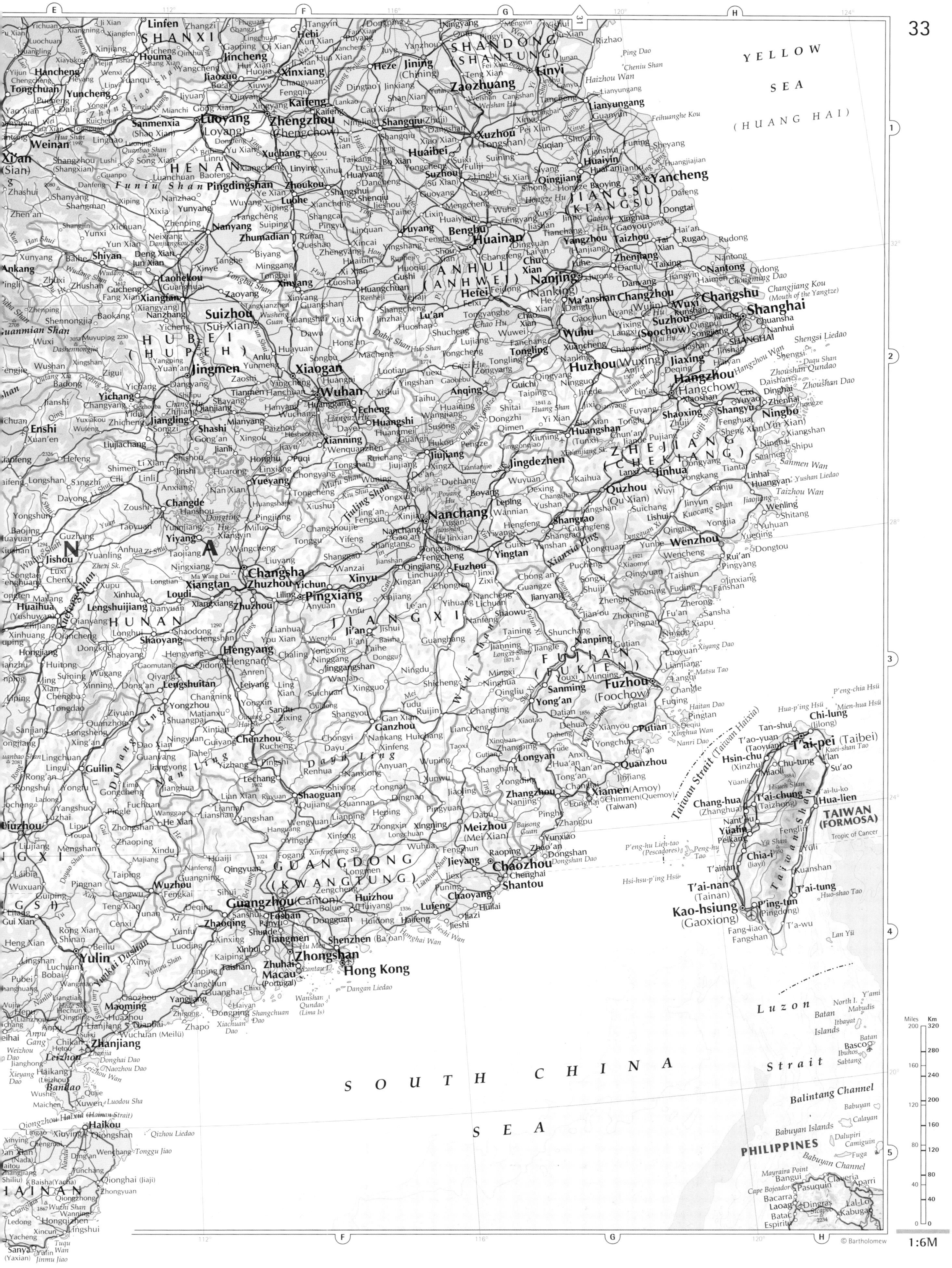
YELLOW SEA (HUANG HAI)
SOUTH CHINA SEA
Luzon Strait
Balintang Channel
Babuyan Channel
Taiwan Strait (Taiwan Haixia)
SHANXI
SHANDONG (SHANTUNG)
HENAN
JIANGSU (KIANGSU)
ANHUI (ANHWEI)
HUBEI (HUPEH)
HUNAN
JIANGXI
ZHEJIANG (CHEKIANG)
FUJIAN (FUKIEN)
GUANGDONG (KWANGTUNG)
HAINAN
TAIWAN (FORMOSA)
PHILIPPINES
Shanghai
Nanjing (Nanking)
Hangzhou (Hangchow)
Wuhan
Changsha
Nanchang
Fuzhou (Foochow)
Guangzhou (Canton)
Hong Kong
Macau (Portugal)
Zhengzhou (Chengchow)
Hefei
Xi'an (Sian)
Luoyang (Loyang)
Kaifeng
Xuzhou (Tongshan)
Suzhou (Soochow)
Ningbo
Wenzhou
Xiamen (Amoy)
Shantou
Chaozhou
Zhanjiang
Haikou
T'ai-pei (Taibei)
Kao-hsiung (Gaoxiong)
T'ai-chung (Taizhong)
T'ai-nan (Tainan)
Tropic of Cancer
Miles
Km
1:6M
© Bartholomew

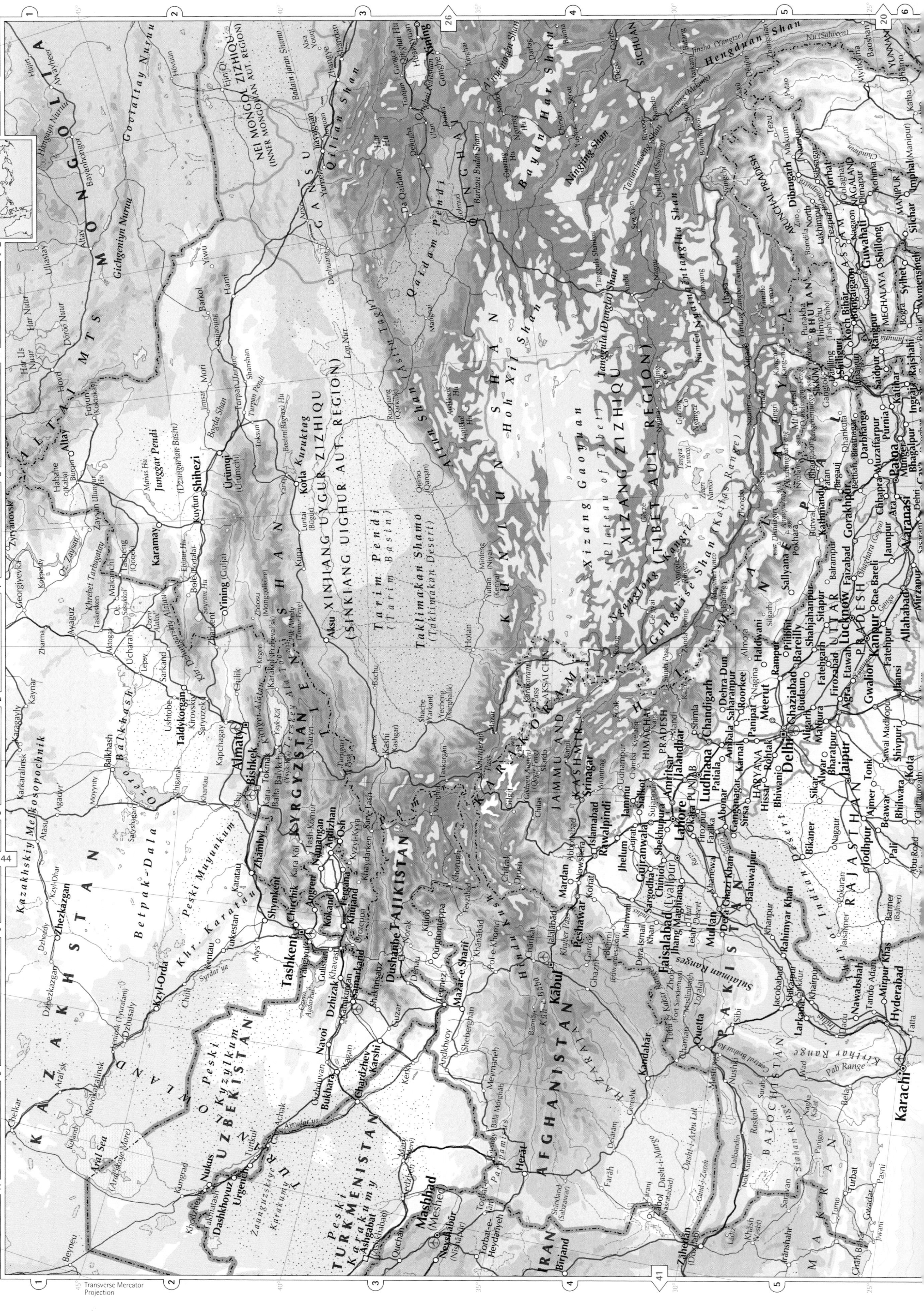
KAZAKHSTAN
UZBEKISTAN
TURKMENISTAN
KYRGYZSTAN
TAJIKISTAN
AFGHANISTAN
PAKISTAN
IRAN
MONGOLIA
NEI MONGOL ZIZHIQU
(INNER MONGOLIAN AUT. REGION)
XINJIANG UYGUR ZIZHIQU
(SINKIANG UIGHUR AUT. REGION)
XIZANG ZIZHIQU
(TIBET AUT. REGION)
QINGHAI
GANSU
SICHUAN
YUNNAN
JAMMU AND KASHMIR
HIMACHAL PRADESH
PUNJAB
HARYANA
UTTAR PRADESH
RAJASTHAN
NEPAL
BHUTAN
ASSAM
MEGHALAYA
NAGALAND
MANIPUR
ARUNACHAL PRADESH
BALOCHISTAN
HAZARAJAT
ALTAI MTS
TIEN SHAN
KUNLUN SHAN
KARAKORAM
HIMALAYA
Hindu Kush
Takla Makan Shamo
(Taklimakan Desert)
Tarim Pendi
(Tarim Basin)
Qaidam Pendi
Junggar Pendi
Xizang Gaoyuan
(Plateau of Tibet)
Betpak-Dala
Peski Kyzylkum
Peski Karakumy
Aral Sea
Ozero Balkhash
Thar or Indian Desert
Sulaiman Ranges
Kirthar Range
Almaty
Bishkek
Tashkent
Dushanbe
Kabul
Islamabad
Delhi
Karachi
Ürümqi
Lhasa
Xining
Samarkand
Herat
Kandahar
Quetta
Lahore
Mashhad
Kathmandu
Thimphu
Transverse Mercator
Projection

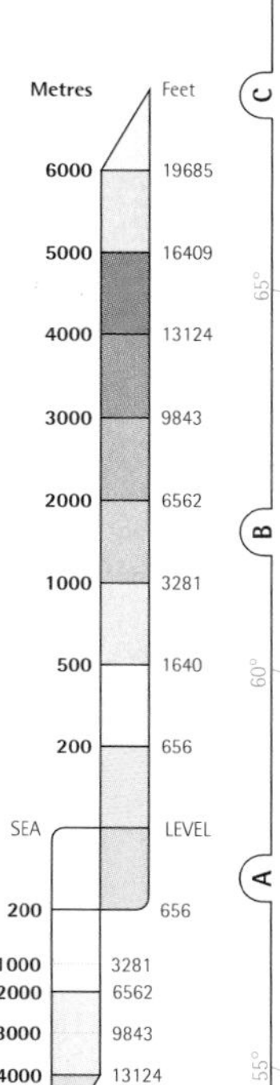
Metres
Feet
6000
19685
5000
16409
4000
13124
3000
9843
2000
6562
1000
3281
500
1640
200
656
SEA
LEVEL
200
656
1000
3281
2000
6562
3000
9843
4000
13124
5000
16409

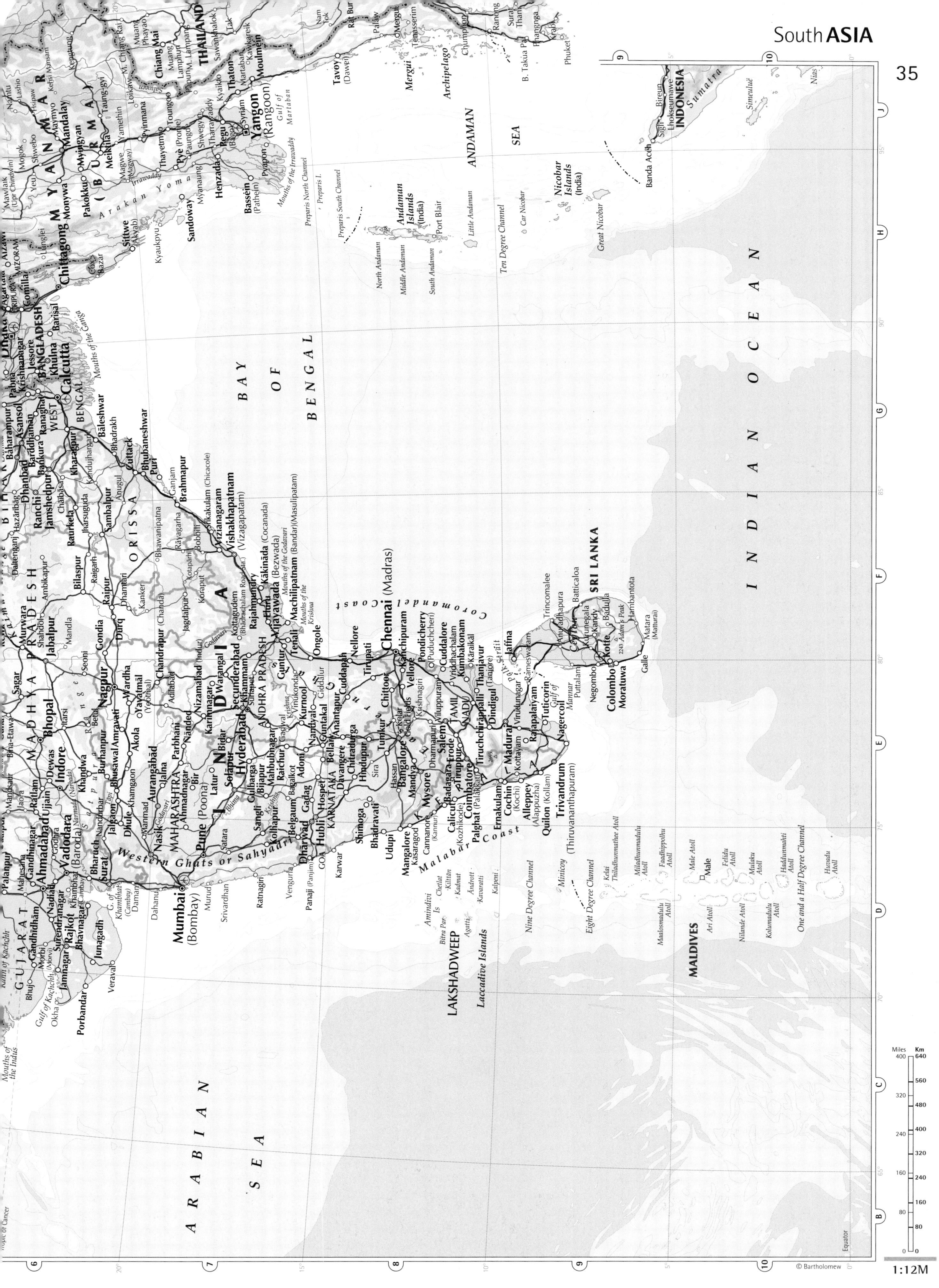

© Bartholomew

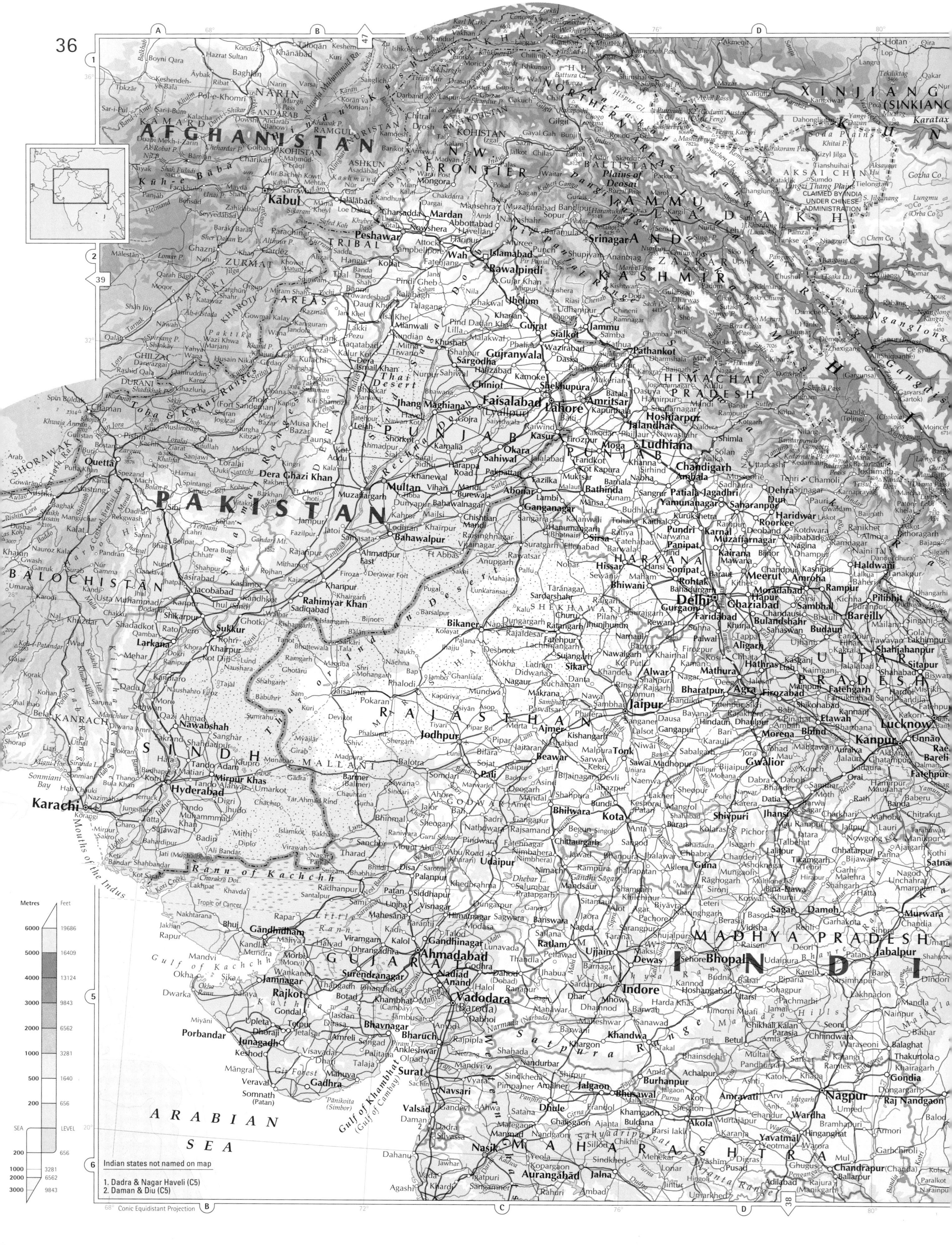

AFGHANISTAN
PAKISTAN
INDIA
XINJIANG (SINKIANG)
NORTHERN AREAS
JAMMU AND KASHMIR
LADAKH
NORTH-WEST FRONTIER
TRIBAL AREAS
PUNJAB
BALOCHISTAN
SINDH
HIMACHAL PRADESH
HARYANA
UTTAR PRADESH
RAJASTHAN
GUJARAT
MADHYA PRADESH
MAHARASHTRA
ARABIAN SEA
CLAIMED BY INDIA UNDER CHINESE ADMINISTRATION
Kābul
Islamabad
Rawalpindi
Peshawar
Lahore
Faisalabad (Lyallpur)
Multan
Quetta
Karachi
Hyderabad
Srinagar
Delhi
Jaipur
Ahmadabad
Bhopal
Indore
Lucknow
Kanpur
Nagpur
Thar or Indian Desert
Rann of Kachchh
Gulf of Kachchh
Gulf of Khambhat (Gulf of Cambay)
Mouths of the Indus
Metres
Feet
6000
19686
5000
16409
4000
13124
3000
9843
2000
6562
1000
3281
500
1640
200
656
SEA
LEVEL
200
656
1000
3281
2000
6562
3000
9843
Indian states not named on map
1. Dadra & Nagar Haveli (C5)
2. Daman & Diu (C5)
Conic Equidistant Projection

CHINA
XIZANG GAOYUAN
(PLATEAU OF TIBET)
XIZANG ZIZHIQU
(TIBET AUT. REGION)
UYGUR ZIZHIQU
(UIGHUR AUT. REGION)
QINGHAI
(TSINGHAI)
KUN LUN SHAN
Hoh Xil Shan
Tanggula (Dangla) Shan
Nyainqentanglha Shan
Taniantaweng Shan
HIMALAYA
NEPAL
Kathmandu
BHUTAN
Thimphu
SIKKIM
Gangtok
Lhasa
Xigazê
ARUNACHAL PRADESH
ASSAM
NAGALAND
MEGHALAYA
MANIPUR
MIZORAM
TRIPURA
BANGLADESH
Dhaka
Chittagong
Rajshahi
Khulna
Sylhet
BIHAR
Patna
WEST BENGAL
Calcutta
ORISSA
Cuttack
Bhubaneshwar
Puri
Ranchi
Jamshedpur
Varanasi
Allahabad
Gorakhpur
Guwahati
Shillong
Imphal
Dibrugarh
Jorhat
MYANMAR
(BURMA)
SAGAING
CHIN
ARAKAN
Sittwe
(Akyab)
Mouths of the Ganga
BAY OF BENGAL
Miles
Km
1:6M
© Bartholomew

South INDIA and SRI LANKA

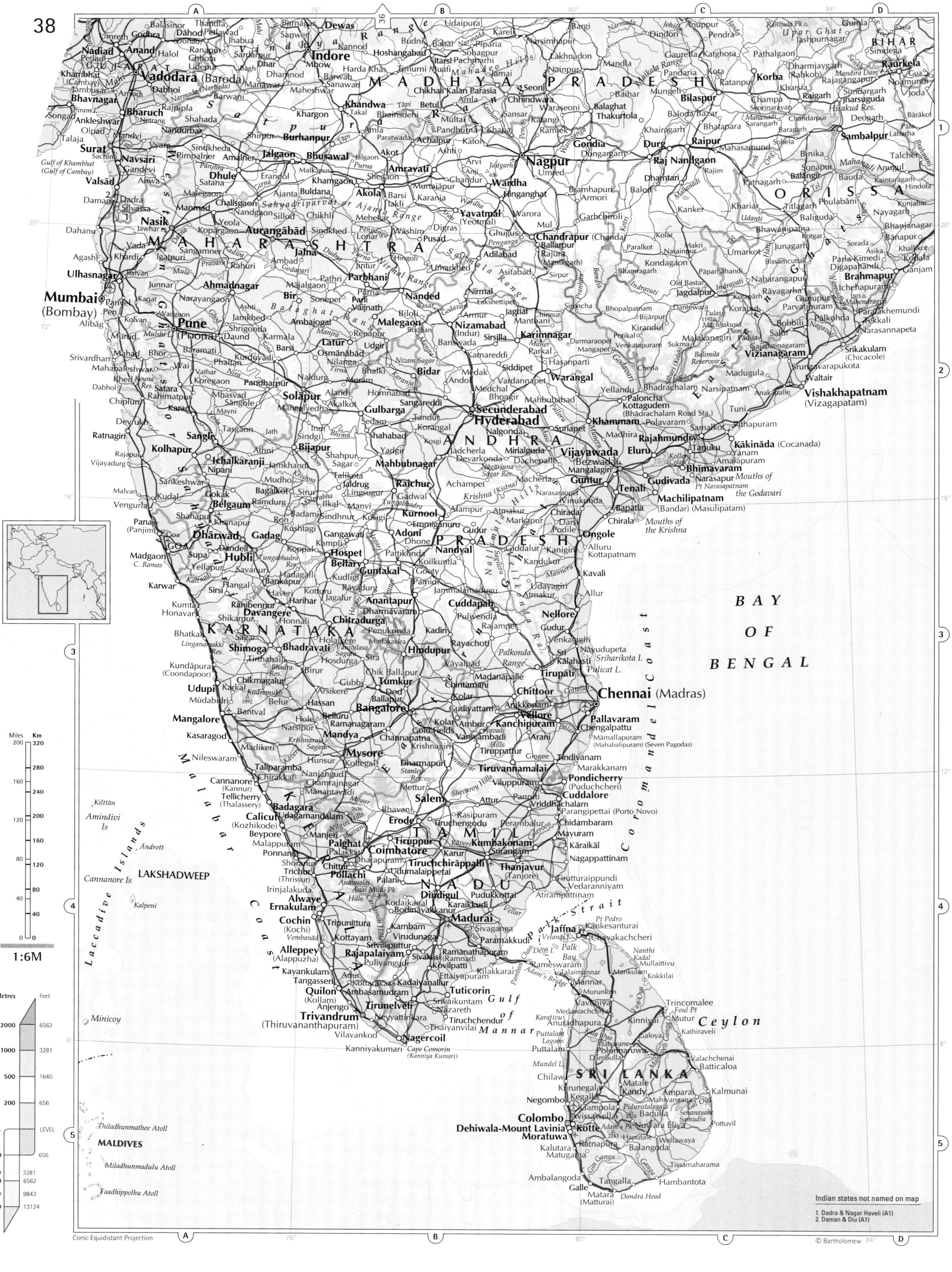

MADHYA PRADESH
MAHARASHTRA
ANDHRA PRADESH
KARNATAKA
TAMIL NADU
KERALA
ORISSA
BIHAR
GUJARAT
BAY OF BENGAL
LAKSHADWEEP
MALDIVES
Laccadive Islands
Malabar Coast
Coromandel Coast
Palk Strait
Gulf of Mannar
Ceylon
Gulf of Khambhat (Gulf of Cambay)
Mouths of the Krishna
Mouths of the Godavari
Eastern Ghats
Western Ghats
Satpura Range
Vindhya Range
Mumbai (Bombay)
Pune (Poona)
Vadodara (Baroda)
Indore
Nagpur
Hyderabad
Secunderabad
Bangalore
Chennai (Madras)
Mysore
Madurai
Coimbatore
Vishakhapatnam (Vizagapatam)
Vijayawada
Colombo
Jaffna
Kandy
Trivandrum (Thiruvananthapuram)
Cochin (Kochi)
Calicut (Kozhikode)
Mangalore
Pondicherry (Puducherry)
Cape Comorin (Kanniya Kumari)
Thiladhunmathee Atoll
Miladhunmadulu Atoll
Faadhippolhu Atoll
Minicoy
Miles
Km
1:6M
Metres
Feet
SEA LEVEL
Conic Equidistant Projection
© Bartholomew
Indian states not named on map
1. Dadra & Nagar Haveli (A1)
2. Daman & Diu (A1)

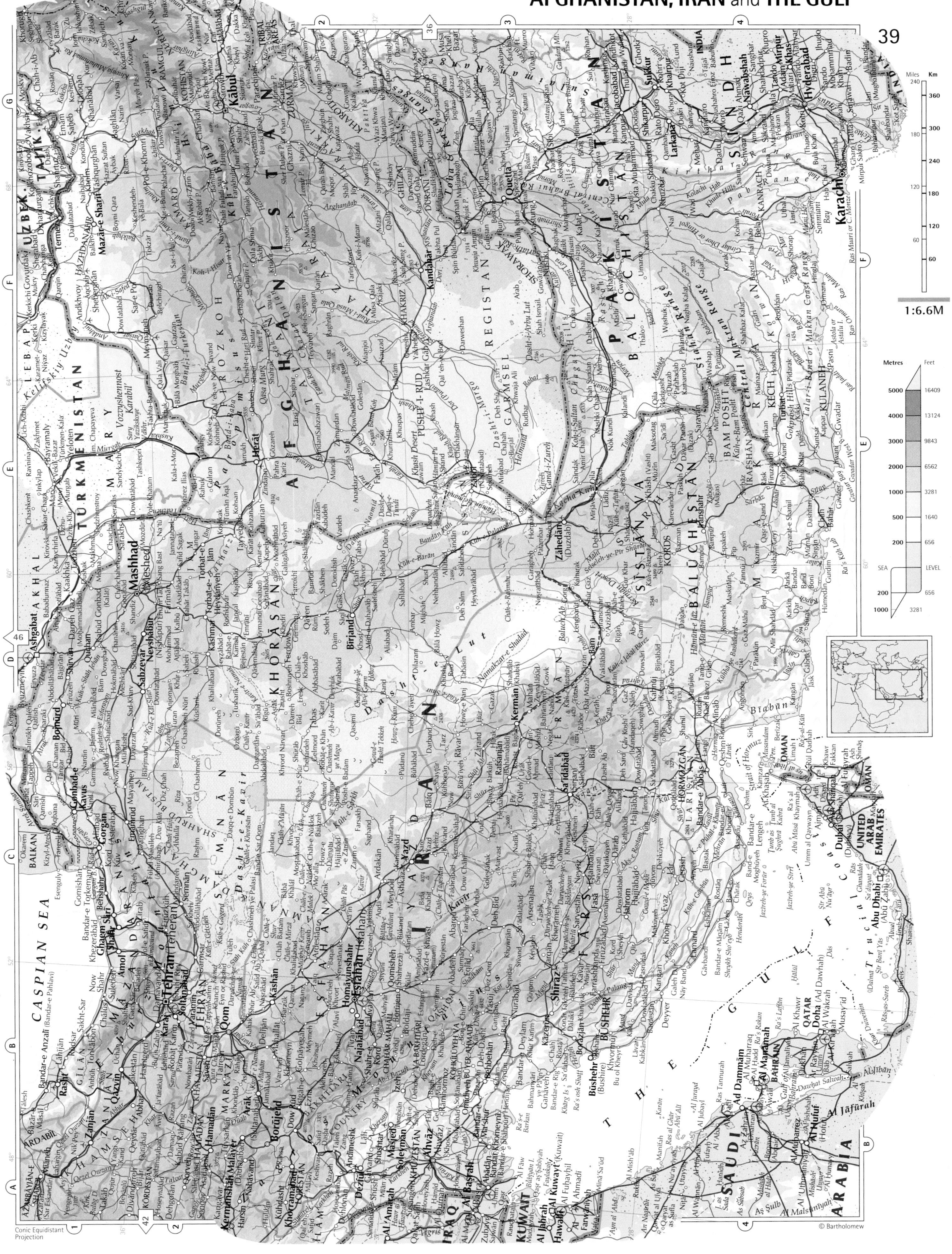
Miles
Km
1:6.6M
Metres
Feet
5000
16409
4000
13124
3000
9843
2000
6562
1000
3281
500
1640
200
656
SEA
LEVEL
200
656
1000
3281
AFGHANISTAN
IRAN
PAKISTAN
TURKMENISTAN
UZBEK.
TAJIK.
IRAQ
KUWAIT
SAUDI ARABIA
QATAR
BAHRAIN
UNITED ARAB EMIRATES
OMAN
INDIA
CASPIAN SEA
THE GULF
Kābul
Tehrān
Mashhad
Karachi
Hyderabad
Quetta
Kandahār
Herāt
Mazār-e Sharīf
Ashgabat
Eşfahān
Shīrāz
Kermān
Zāhedān
Yazd
Tabas
Birjand
Doha
Dubai
Abu Dhabi
Al Kuwayt (Kuwait)
Al Başrah
Ahvāz
Bandar-e 'Abbās
Conic Equidistant Projection
© Bartholomew

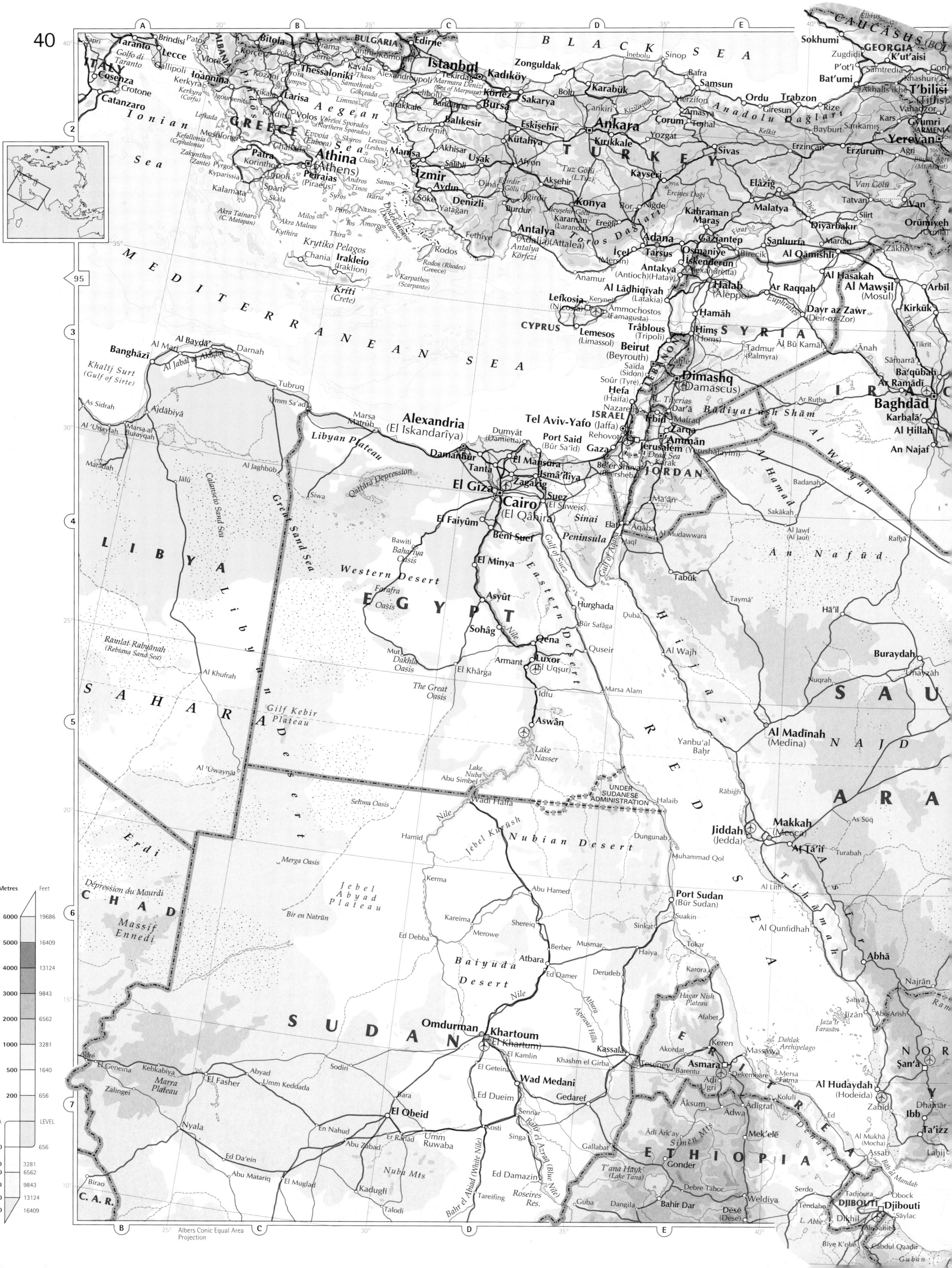
BLACK SEA
MEDITERRANEAN SEA
Ionian Sea
Aegean Sea
RED SEA
TURKEY
GREECE
ALBANIA
ITALY
BULGARIA
GEORGIA
ARMENIA
CYPRUS
SYRIA
LEBANON
ISRAEL
JORDAN
IRAQ
EGYPT
LIBYA
SUDAN
CHAD
C. A. R.
ERITREA
ETHIOPIA
DJIBOUTI
SAUDI ARABIA
YEMEN
SAHARA
Libyan Desert
Western Desert
Eastern Desert
Nubian Desert
Great Sand Sea
Libyan Plateau
Qattara Depression
Sinai Peninsula
Gulf of Suez
Gulf of Aqaba
Nile
Lake Nasser
Lake Nuba
UNDER SUDANESE ADMINISTRATION
Istanbul
Ankara
Izmir
Bursa
Konya
Adana
Antalya
Kayseri
Athina (Athens)
Thessaloniki
Irakleio (Iraklion)
Kríti (Crete)
Lefkosia (Nicosia)
Beirut (Beyrouth)
Dimashq (Damascus)
Halab (Aleppo)
Tel Aviv-Yafo (Jaffa)
Jerusalem (Yerushalayim)
Amman
Gaza
Alexandria (El Iskandarîya)
Cairo (El Qâhira)
El Giza
Port Said (Bûr Sa'îd)
Suez (El Suweis)
Aswân
Luxor (El Uqsur)
Asyût
Baghdad
Al Mawsil (Mosul)
Al Madinah (Medina)
Makkah (Mecca)
Jiddah (Jedda)
Port Sudan (Bûr Sudan)
Khartoum (El Khartum)
Omdurman
Wad Medani
El Obeid
Asmara
Djibouti
Şan'a
Al Hudaydah (Hodeida)
Banghāzī
Tubruq
Yerevan
T'bilisi (Tiflis)
Metres
Feet
6000 19686
5000 16409
4000 13124
3000 9843
2000 6562
1000 3281
500 1640
200 656
SEA LEVEL
200 656
1000 3281
2000 6562
3000 9843
4000 13124
5000 16409
Albers Conic Equal Area Projection
95

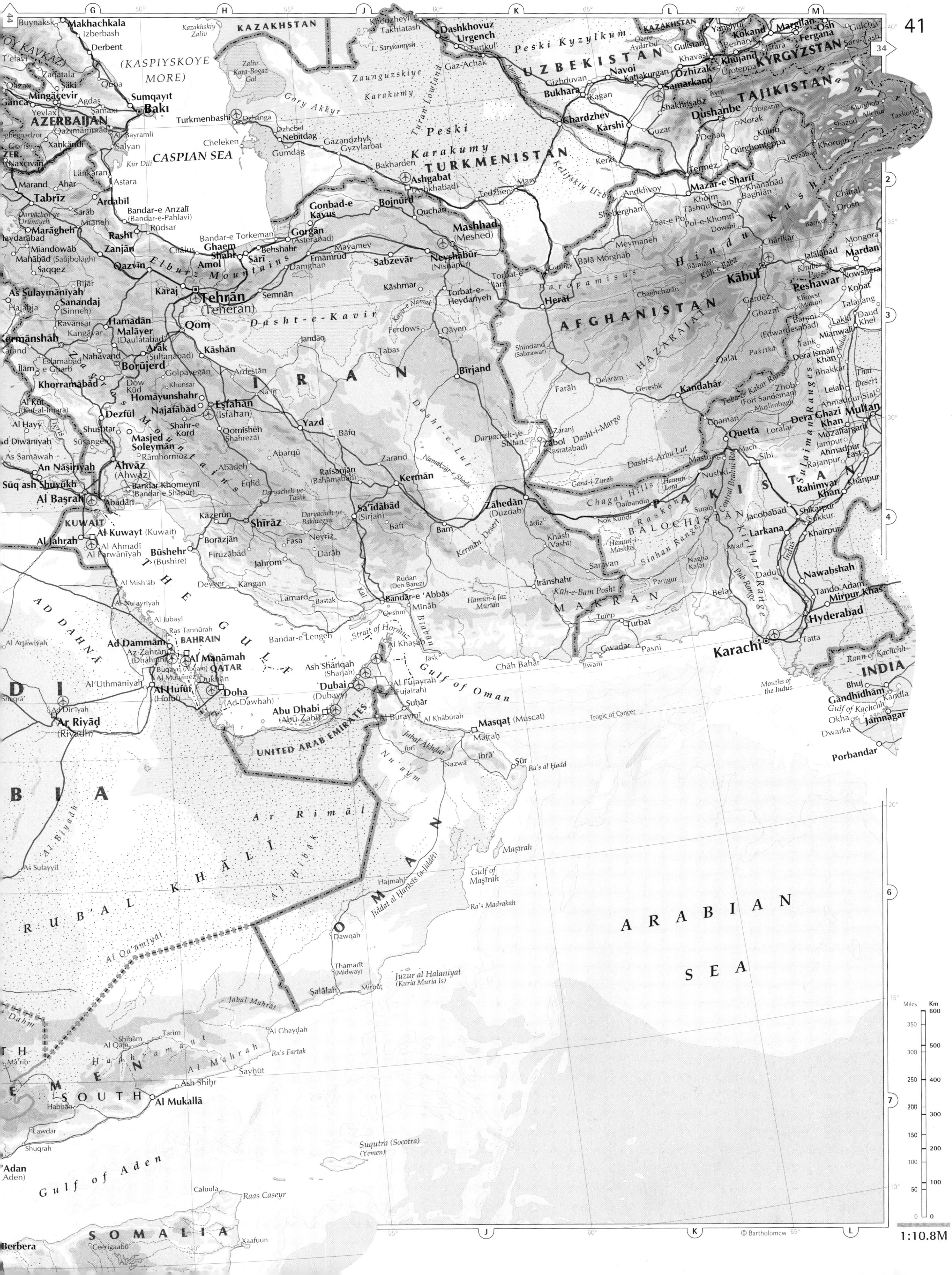
KAZAKHSTAN
UZBEKISTAN
KYRGYZSTAN
TAJIKISTAN
TURKMENISTAN
AZERBAIJAN
AFGHANISTAN
IRAN
PAKISTAN
INDIA
KUWAIT
BAHRAIN
QATAR
UNITED ARAB EMIRATES
OMAN
SOUTH
SOMALIA
CASPIAN SEA
(KASPIYSKOYE MORE)
THE GULF
Gulf of Oman
Strait of Hormuz
ARABIAN SEA
Gulf of Aden
Gulf of Maşīrah
Tropic of Cancer
Mouths of the Indus
Rann of Kachchh
Gulf of Kachchh
Peski Kyzylkum
Zaunguzskiye Karakumy
Peski Karakumy
Turan Lowland
Dasht-e-Kavir
Dasht-e-Lut
Elburz Mountains
Zagros Mountains
Paropamisus
Hindu Kush
Hazarajat
Dasht-i-Margo
Dasht-i-Arbu Lut
Chagai Hills
Balochistan
Makran
Kirthar Range
Sulaiman Ranges
Toba & Kakar Range
Siahan Range
Central Brahui Range
Kermān Desert
Rub' al Khālī
Ar Rimāl
Ad Dahnā
Al Biyadh
Jiddat al Ḩarāsīs
Jabal Akhdar
Jabal Mahrat
Hadhramaut
Al Mahrah
Baku
Tehrān (Teheran)
Qom
Eşfahān (Isfahān)
Shīrāz
Mashhad (Meshed)
Tabrīz
Ashgabat (Ashkhabad)
Dushanbe
Samarkand
Bukhara
Kābul
Kandahār
Herāt
Quetta
Peshawar
Multan
Hyderabad
Karachi
Mazar-e Sharīf
Kermān
Yazd
Zāhedān (Duzdab)
Bandar-e 'Abbās
Al Başrah
Al Kuwayt (Kuwait)
Al Manāmah
Doha (Ad Dawhah)
Abu Dhabi (Abū Zabī)
Dubai (Dubayy)
Masqaţ (Muscat)
Ar Riyāḑ (Riyadh)
Al Hufūf (Hofuf)
Ad Dammām
Şalālah
Al Mukallā
Adan (Aden)
Berbera
Suqutra (Socotra) (Yemen)
Jazur al Halaniyat (Kuria Muria Is)
Maşīrah
Ra's al Ḩadd
Ra's Madrakah
Ra's Fartak
Raas Caseyr
© Bartholomew
Miles
Km
1:10.8M

TURKEY, IRAQ, SYRIA, JORDAN and TRANSCAUCASIAN REPUBLICS

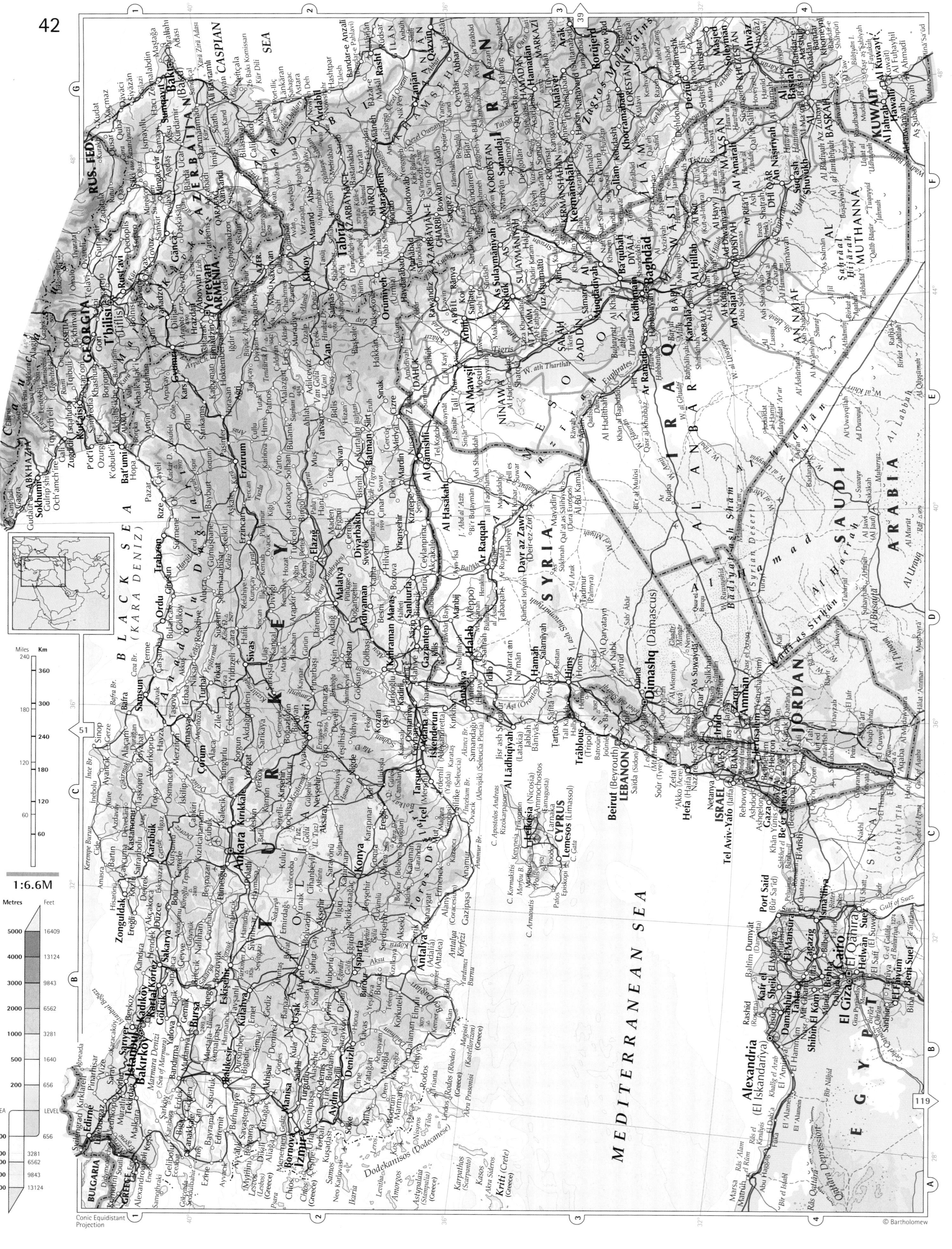

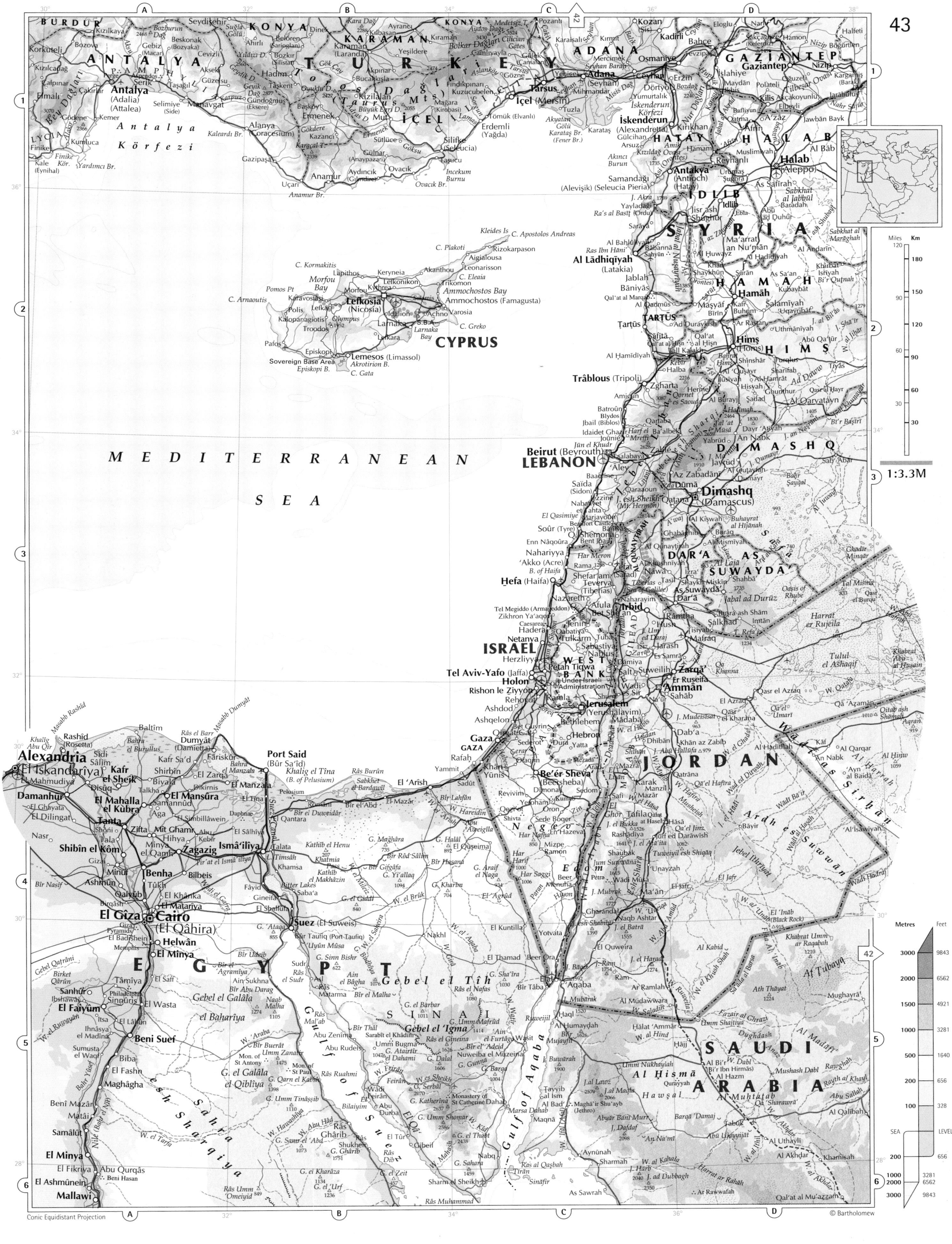

Conic Equidistant Projection

© Bartholomew

RUSSIAN FEDERATION

Chukchi Sea
Bering Strait
U.S.A.
Vostochno-Sibirskaye More
(East Siberian Sea)
Novosibirskiye Ostrova
(New Siberia Islands)
More Laptevykh
(Laptev Sea)
Severnaya Zemlya
Poluostrov Taymyr
BERING SEA
Khrebet Cherskogo
Verkhoyanskiy Khrebet
Khrebet Kolymskiy
Koryakskiy Khrebet
Sredinnyy Khrebet
Kamchatka
Petropavlovsk-Kamchatskiy
Magadan
OKHOTSKOYE MORE
(SEA OF OKHOTSK)
SREDNE-SIBIRSKOYE PLOSKOGOR'YE
FEDERATION
Yakutsk
Stanovoy Khrebet
Stanovoye Nagor'ye
O. Sakhalin
Yuzhno-Sakhalinsk
Kuril'skiye Ostrova
(Kuril Is)
Khabarovsk
Komsomol'sk-na-Amure
Blagoveshchensk
Vladivostok
Sikhote-Alin
Ust'-Ilimsk
Bratsk
Krasnoyarsk
Achinsk
Kansk
Irkutsk
Ulan-Ude
Chita
Ozero Baykal
(Lake Baikal)
Abakan
Kyzyl
MONGOLIA
Ulaanbaatar
GOBI
MANCHURIA
Qiqihar
Harbin
Jilin
Changchun
Shenyang
Fushun
Anshan
Dalian
NORTH KOREA
P'yongyang
SOUTH KOREA
Soul (Seoul)
Taegu
Kwangju
Sea of Japan
Sapporo
Hokkaido
Honshu
JAPAN
Sendai
Tokyo
Yokohama
Nagoya
Osaka
Kobe
Hiroshima
Fukuoka
Kagoshima
Beijing
Tianjin
Shijiazhuang
Hohhot
Baotou
Datong
Zhangjiakou
Jinan
Qingdao
Yellow Sea
(Huang Hai)
Bo Hai
Zhengzhou
Luoyang
Xi'an
Lanzhou
Xining
Yinchuan
Taiyuan
Nanjing
Shanghai
EAST CHINA SEA
CHINA
Qilian Shan
Miles
Km
© Bartholomew
1:18M

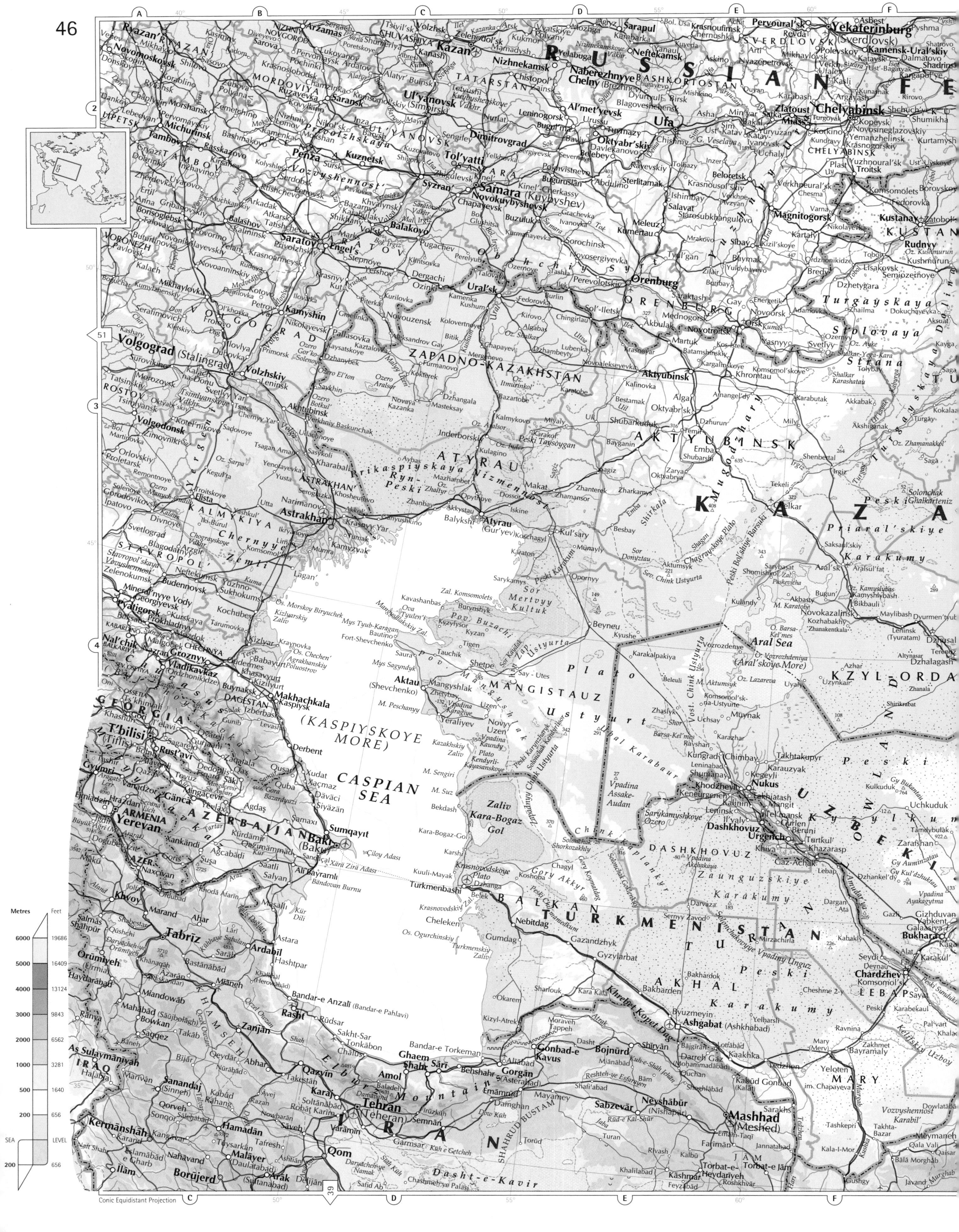
RUSSIAN FE
KAZA
CASPIAN SEA
(KASPIYSKOYE MORE)
Aral Sea
(Aral'skoye More)
TURKMENISTAN
UZBEKI
IRAN
GEORGIA
ARMENIA
AZERBAIJAN
IRAQ
Volgograd (Stalingrad)
Astrakhan'
Atyrau (Gur'yev)
Aktau (Shevchenko)
Makhachkala
Baku (Baku)
Sumqayıt
Tbilisi (Tiflis)
Yerevan
Tabrīz
Tehran (Teheran)
Mashhad (Meshed)
Ashgabat (Ashkhabad)
Turkmenbashi
Nukus
Urgench
Dashkhovuz
Bukhara
Chardzhev
Aktyubinsk
Orenburg
Ural'sk
Saratov
Samara (Kuybyshev)
Tol'yatti
Ul'yanovsk (Simbirsk)
Kazan'
Penza
Ufa
Chelyabinsk
Yekaterinburg (Sverdlovsk)
Magnitogorsk
Kustanay
Zaliv Kara-Bogaz Gol
Plato Ustyurt
Prikaspiyskaya Nizmennost'
Mugodzhary
Karakumy
Elburz Mountains
Dasht-e-Kavir
Metres
Feet
6000
5000
4000
3000
2000
1000
500
200
SEA
LEVEL
200
19686
16409
13124
9843
6562
3281
1640
656
656
Conic Equidistant Projection

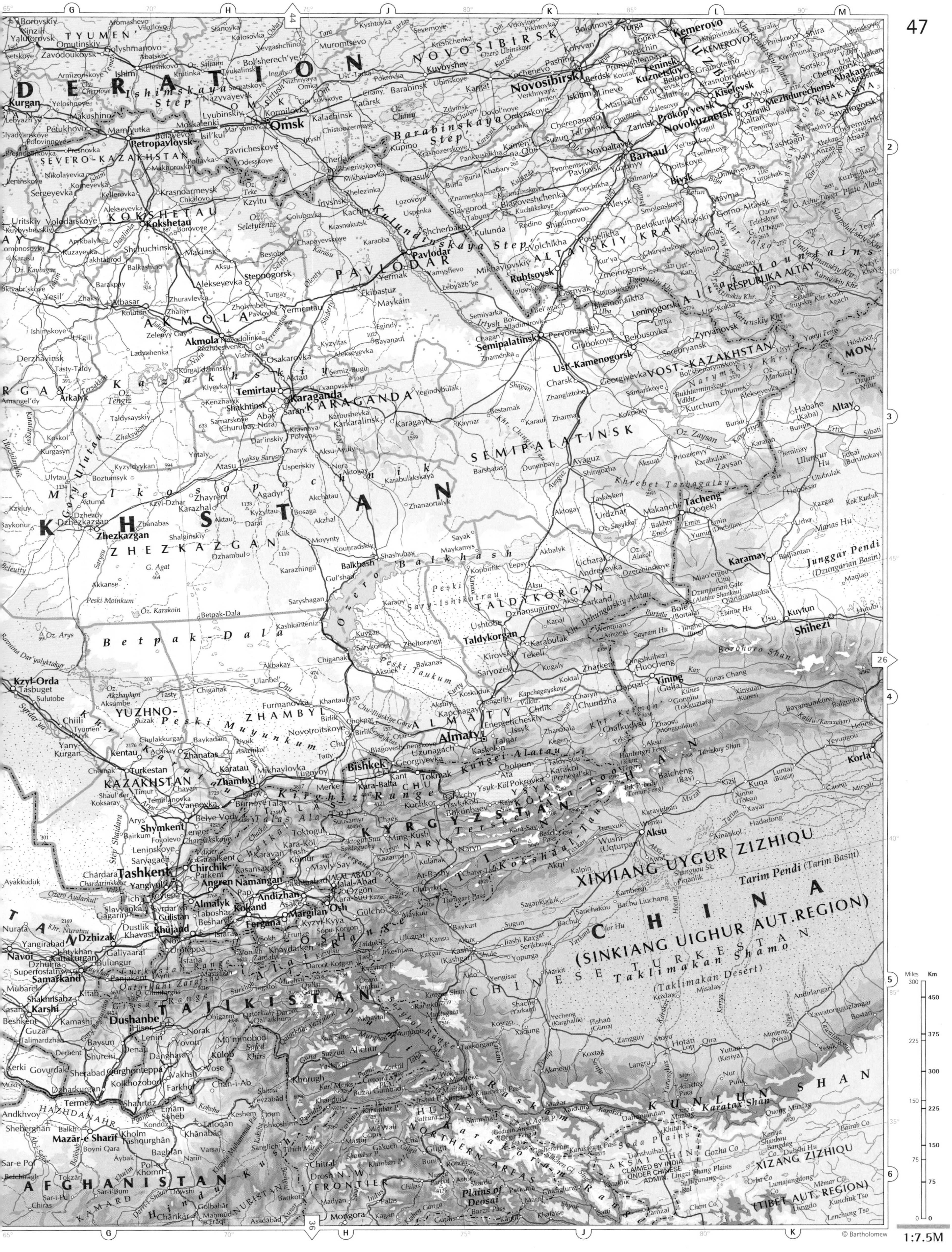
KAZAKHSTAN
KYRGYZSTAN
TAJIKISTAN
AFGHANISTAN
CHINA
(SINKIANG UIGHUR AUT. REGION)
XINJIANG UYGUR ZIZHIQU
XIZANG ZIZHIQU
(TIBET AUT. REGION)
CHINESE TURKESTAN
Taklimakan Shamo
(Taklimakan Desert)
Tarim Pendi (Tarim Basin)
Junggar Pendi
(Dzungarian Basin)
KUNLUN SHAN
TIEN SHAN
Karakoram Range
Hindu Kush
Altai Mountains
Kazakhskiy Melkosopochnik
Betpak-Dala
Ozero Balkhash
Ishimskaya Step
Barabinskaya Step
Kulundinskaya Step'
NOVOSIBIRSK
ALTAYSKIY KRAY
RESPUBLIKA ALTAY
KHAKASIYA
KEMEROVO
KUZBASS
PAVLODAR
AKMOLA
KOKSHETAU
SEVERO-KAZAKHSTAN
KARAGANDA
SEMIPALATINSK
VOST.-KAZAKHSTAN
TALDYKORGAN
ALMATY
ZHAMBYL
ZHEZKAZGAN
YUZHNO-KAZAKHSTAN
NARYN
OSH
TYUMEN'
MON.
Omsk
Novosibirsk
Barnaul
Kemerovo
Novokuznetsk
Biysk
Rubtsovsk
Semipalatinsk
Ust'-Kamenogorsk
Pavlodar
Akmola
Karaganda
Temirtau
Petropavlovsk
Kokshetau
Kurgan
Zhezkazgan
Kzyl-Orda
Balkhash
Taldykorgan
Almaty
Bishkek
Zhambyl
Shymkent
Tashkent
Namangan
Andizhan
Kokand
Fergana
Osh
Khujand
Samarkand
Dushanbe
Karshi
Termez
Mazār-e Sharīf
Kashi (Kashgar)
Aksu
Yining (Gulja)
Karamay
Shihezi
Tacheng (Qoqek)
Altay
Korla
Hotan
Yecheng (Kargilik)
Shache (Yarkant)
KASHMIR
NORTHERN AREAS
N.W. FRONTIER
AKSAI CHIN
CLAIMED BY INDIA UNDER CHINESE ADMIN.
Plains of Deosai
Miles
Km
© Bartholomew

1:7.5M

Greenland
(Den.)
King Christian X Land
King Christian IX Land
King Frederick VI Coast
Frederikshåb
C. Farewell
Labrador Sea
Shannon I.
Traill I.
Scoresbysund
Greenland Sea
Spitsbergen
Longyearbyen
Svalbard
(Nor.)
Bear I.
(Nor.)
Denmark Strait
Jan Mayen
(Nor.)
Ísafjörður
Húnaflói
Siglufjörður
Keflavík
Reykjavík
ICELAND
Vatnajökull
Höfn
Tromsø
Vesterålen
Lofoten
Narvik
Kiruna
NORWEGIAN SEA
Mo i Rana
Faeroes
(Den.)
Tórshavn
Trondheim
Kristiansund
Östersund
Härnösand
Shetland
Orkney
Outer Hebrides
Bergen
Voss
Lillehammer
NORWAY
SWEDEN
Falun
Uppsala
Oslo
Drammen
Stavanger
Karlstad
Stockholm
Örebro
Egersund
Arendal
Larvik
Kristiansand
Skagerrak
Vänern
Vättern
Norrköping
Jönköping
Borås
Göteborg
Skagen
Kattegat
Ålborg
Århus
DENMARK
Copenhagen
Helsingborg
Malmö
Kalmar
Öland
Gotland
Esbjerg
Odense
Bornholm
Baltic
UNITED KINGDOM
SCOTLAND
Inverness
Aberdeen
Dundee
Edinburgh
Glasgow
Londonderry
N. IRELAND
Belfast
Sligo
REP. OF IRELAND
Isle of Man
Irish Sea
Manchester
Newcastle
NORTH SEA
Tralee
Limerick
Dublin
York
Leeds
Liverpool
Cork
WALES
ENGLAND
Birmingham
Swansea
Cardiff
Norwich
London
Bristol
Plymouth
Southampton
Dover
Isles of Scilly
English Channel
Channel Is.
Cherbourg
NETHERLANDS
Groningen
Amsterdam
The Hague
Rotterdam
Hamburg
Bremen
Lübeck
Rostock
Hannover
Berlin
Gdańsk
Szczecin
Bydgoszcz
Toruń
POLAND
Poznań
Płock
Kalisz
Łódź
Legnica
Wrocław
Elbe
Essen
Düsseldorf
GERMANY
Calais
Lille
Brussels
BELGIUM
Bonn
Cologne
Leipzig
Dresden
Koblenz
Rhine
Frankfurt
LUXEMBOURG
Luxembourg
Amiens
Rouen
Caen
Brest
Reims
Seine
Paris
Prague
CZECH REP.
Katowice
Ostrava
Plzeň
České Budějovice
Brno
Mannheim
Saarbrücken
Nürnberg
Stuttgart
Rennes
Le Mans
Angers
Orléans
Loire
Nancy
Strasbourg
St-Nazaire
Nantes
Tours
FRANCE
Mulhouse
Dijon
Freiburg
Zürich
Munich
Danube
Vienna
Bratislava
Salzburg
Innsbruck
AUSTRIA
LIECHTENSTEIN
Bern
SWITZERLAND
Lausanne
Genève
Mt Blanc 4808
Bay of Biscay
La Rochelle
Limoges
Clermont-Ferrand
Lyon
St-Étienne
Grenoble
Budapest
HUNGARY
Balaton
Kecskemét
Szeged
Graz
Maribor
Ljubljana
SLOV.
Zagreb
CROATIA
A Coruña
C. Finisterre
Gijón
Oviedo
Santander
Bilbao
Vigo
Ourense
León
Burgos
Bordeaux
Donostia-San Sebastián
Pyrenees
Toulouse
Nîmes
Montpellier
Rhône
Nice
MONACO
Marseille
Toulon
Milan
Turin
Brescia
Trieste
Venice
Genoa
Parma
La Spezia
Bologna
Rijeka
Pula
Zadar
Split
BOSNIA-HERZ.
Sarajevo
Dubrovnik
Podgorica
Oporto
Braga
Douro
Coimbra
PORTUGAL
Valladolid
Salamanca
Logroño
Pamplona
Andorra
ANDORRA
Perpignan
Zaragoza
Ebro
Lleida
SPAIN
Madrid
Tajo
Toledo
Barcelona
Tarragona
Castelló de la Plana
Lisbon
Setúbal
Badajoz
Ciudad Real
Valencia
Balearic Islands
Menorca
Mallorca
Palma
Ibiza
Pisa
Florence
SAN MARINO
Ancona
Livorno
Perugia
Corsica
Ajaccio
Civitavecchia
VATICAN CITY
Rome
ITALY
Apennines
Adriatic Sea
Foggia
Bari
Tirana
ALBANIA
Naples
Salerno
Taranto
Sardinia
Cagliari
Cosenza
Corfu
C. St Vincent
Huelva
Sevilla
Córdoba
Granada
Málaga
Cádiz
Algeciras
Gibraltar (U.K.)
Str. of Gibraltar
Ceuta (Sp.)
Tangier
Tétouan
Alicante
Murcia
Cartagena
Almería
Melilla (Sp.)
Oran
Algiers
Annaba
Sétif
Sidi Bel Abbès
MEDITERRANEAN
Tunis
Sicilian Channel
Palermo
Messina
Reggio di Calabria
Ionian Sea
Sicily
Mount Etna 3323
Catania
Siracusa
Sousse
MALTA
Valletta
Madeira
(Port.)
Funchal
Casablanca
Rabat
Meknès
Fez
Marrakesh
MOROCCO
Béchar
ALGERIA
TUNISIA
Gabès
Tripoli
Benghazi
Gulf of Sirte
LIBYA
ATLANTIC OCEAN
São Jorge
Pico
Terceira
Azores
(Port.)
São Miguel
Santa Maria
Canary Islands
(Spain)
La Palma
Tenerife
Santa Cruz
Gran Canaria
Las Palmas
Lanzarote
Fuerteventura
Metres
Feet
SEA
LEVEL
200
656
3000
9843
Chamberlin Trimetric Projection

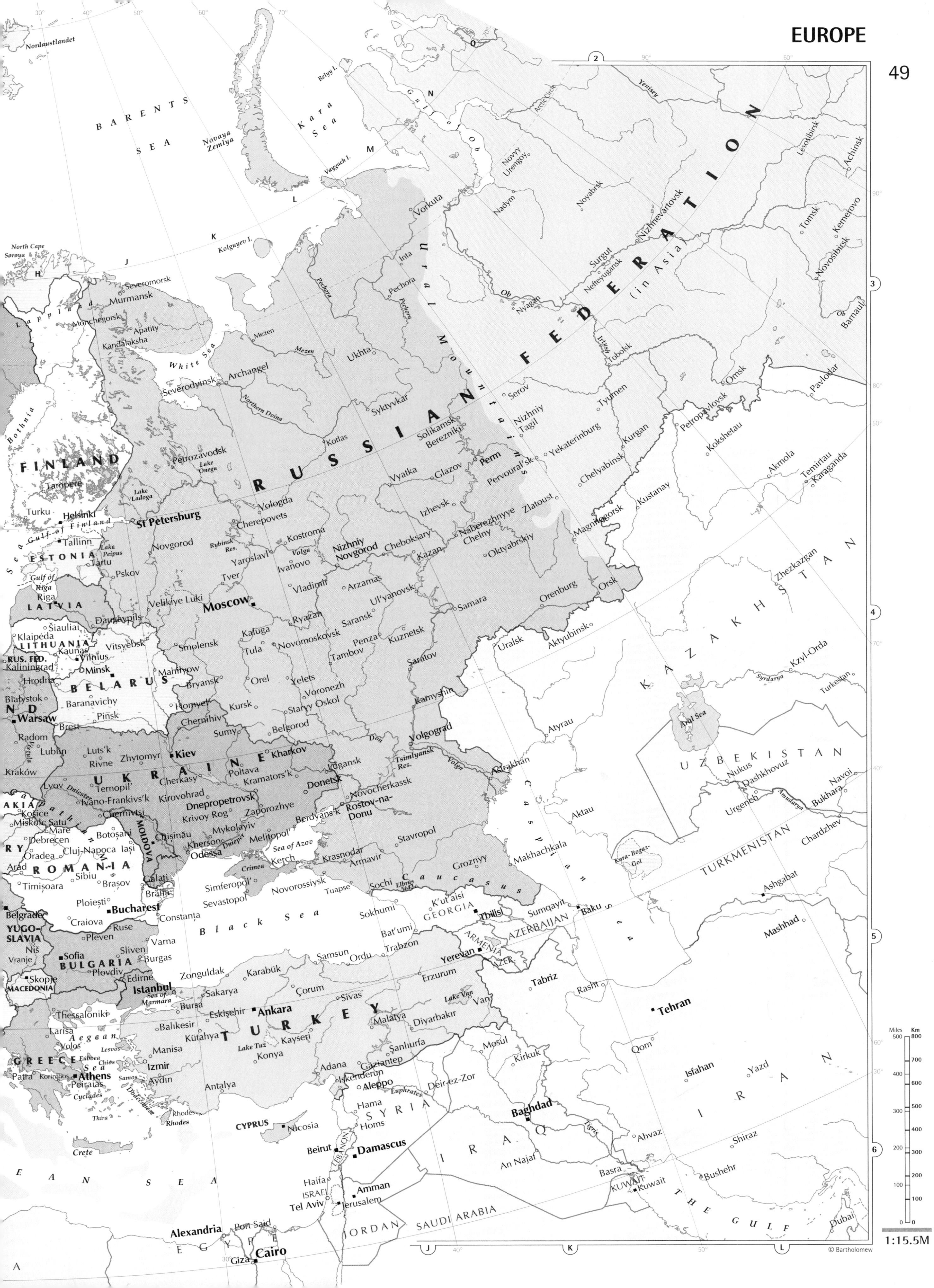
Nordaustlandet
BARENTS SEA
Novaya Zemlya
Kara Sea
Belyy I.
Gulf of Ob
Vaygach I.
Kolguyev I.
North Cape
Sørøya
RUSSIAN FEDERATION
(in Asia)
Ural Mountains
Yenisey
Arctic Circle
Novyy Urengoy
Noyabrsk
Nadym
Vorkuta
Inta
Pechora
Ukhta
Mezen
White Sea
Archangel
Severodvinsk
Severomorsk
Murmansk
Monchegorsk
Apatity
Kandalaksha
Lapland
Bothnia
FINLAND
Tampere
Turku
Helsinki
Gulf of Finland
Tallinn
ESTONIA
Tartu
Lake Peipus
Gulf of Riga
Riga
LATVIA
Daugavpils
Šiauliai
Klaipėda
LITHUANIA
Kaunas
Vilnius
RUS. FED.
Kaliningrad
Hrodna
Minsk
BELARUS
Vitsyebsk
Mahilyow
Homyel'
Baranavichy
Pinsk
Brest
Białystok
Warsaw
Radom
Lublin
Vistula
Kraków
Petrozavodsk
Lake Onega
Lake Ladoga
St Petersburg
Novgorod
Pskov
Velikiye Luki
Smolensk
Moscow
Tver
Yaroslavl
Rybinsk Res.
Vologda
Cherepovets
Kotlas
Syktyvkar
Northern Dvina
Kostroma
Ivanovo
Vladimir
Nizhniy Novgorod
Volga
Cheboksary
Kazan
Arzamas
Vyatka
Glazov
Izhevsk
Perm
Solikamsk
Berezniki
Serov
Nizhniy Tagil
Pervoural'sk
Yekaterinburg
Chelyabinsk
Kurgan
Zlatoust
Magnitogorsk
Naberezhnyye Chelny
Oktyabrskiy
Samara
Orenburg
Orsk
Ul'yanovsk
Saransk
Penza
Kuznetsk
Ryazan
Kaluga
Tula
Novomoskovsk
Tambov
Orel
Yelets
Bryansk
Kursk
Voronezh
Staryy Oskol
Belgorod
Saratov
Kamyshin
Volgograd
Tsimlyansk Res.
Don
Astrakhan
Rostov-na-Donu
Novocherkassk
Krasnodar
Armavir
Stavropol
Groznyy
Makhachkala
Caucasus
Elbrus 5642
Sochi
Novorossiysk
Tuapse
Sea of Azov
Kerch
Crimea
Simferopol'
Sevastopol
Black Sea
Chernihiv
Sumy
Kiev
Kharkov
UKRAINE
Luts'k
Rivne
Zhytomyr
Poltava
Kramators'k
Donetsk
Luhansk
Cherkasy
Kirovohrad
Dnepropetrovsk
Zaporozhye
Krivoy Rog
Mykolayiv
Kherson
Odessa
Melitopol'
Berdyans'k
Dniester
Dnieper
Lvov
Ternopil'
Ivano-Frankivs'k
Chernivtsi
Chişinău
MOLDOVA
Košice
Miskolc
Satu Mare
Debrecen
Oradea
Cluj-Napoca
Iaşi
Botoşani
Arad
ROMANIA
Sibiu
Braşov
Timişoara
Galati
Braila
Ploieşti
Bucharest
Constanţa
Craiova
Belgrade
YUGOSLAVIA
Niš
Vranje
Pleven
Ruse
Varna
Sofia
BULGARIA
Sliven
Burgas
Plovdiv
Skopje
MACEDONIA
Edirne
Istanbul
Sea of Marmara
Thessaloniki
Larisa
Aegean Sea
Volos
Lesvos
Euboea
Chios
GREECE
Patra
Korinthos
Athens
Peiraias
Samos
Cyclades
Dodecanese
Thira
Rhodes
Crete
Bursa
Balıkesir
Manisa
Izmir
Aydın
Kütahya
Eskişehir
Sakarya
Zonguldak
Karabük
Çorum
Ankara
TURKEY
Lake Tuz
Konya
Kayseri
Sivas
Samsun
Ordu
Trabzon
Erzurum
Malatya
Diyarbakır
Lake Van
Van
Sanlıurfa
Gaziantep
Adana
Iskenderun
Antalya
CYPRUS
Nicosia
Aleppo
Hama
Homs
SYRIA
Euphrates
Deir-ez-Zor
Beirut
LEBANON
Damascus
Haifa
ISRAEL
Tel Aviv
Jerusalem
Amman
JORDAN
SAUDI ARABIA
Port Said
Alexandria
EGYPT
Cairo
Giza
Sokhumi
Bat'umi
K'ut'aisi
GEORGIA
Tbilisi
ARMENIA
Yerevan
AZERBAIJAN
AZER.
Sumqayit
Baku
Caspian Sea
Tabriz
Rasht
Tehran
Qom
Isfahan
Yazd
IRAN
Mosul
Kirkuk
Baghdad
IRAQ
Tigris
An Najaf
Basra
KUWAIT
Kuwait
Ahvaz
Shiraz
Bushehr
THE GULF
Dubai
Mashhad
Ashgabat
TURKMENISTAN
Kara-Bogaz-Gol
Aktau
Chardzhev
Bukhara
Navoi
Amudarya
Urgench
Nukus
Dashkhovuz
UZBEKISTAN
Aral Sea
Syrdarya
Kzyl-Orda
Turkestan
KAZAKHSTAN
Atyrau
Uralsk
Aktyubinsk
Zhezkazgan
Kustanay
Kokshetau
Petropavlovsk
Akmola
Temirtau
Karaganda
Pavlodar
Omsk
Tyumen
Tobolsk
Irtysh
Ob
Nyagan
Surgut
Nefteyugansk
Nizhnevartovsk
Tomsk
Kemerovo
Novosibirsk
Barnaul
Lesosibirsk
Achinsk
Miles
Km
1:15.5M
© Bartholomew

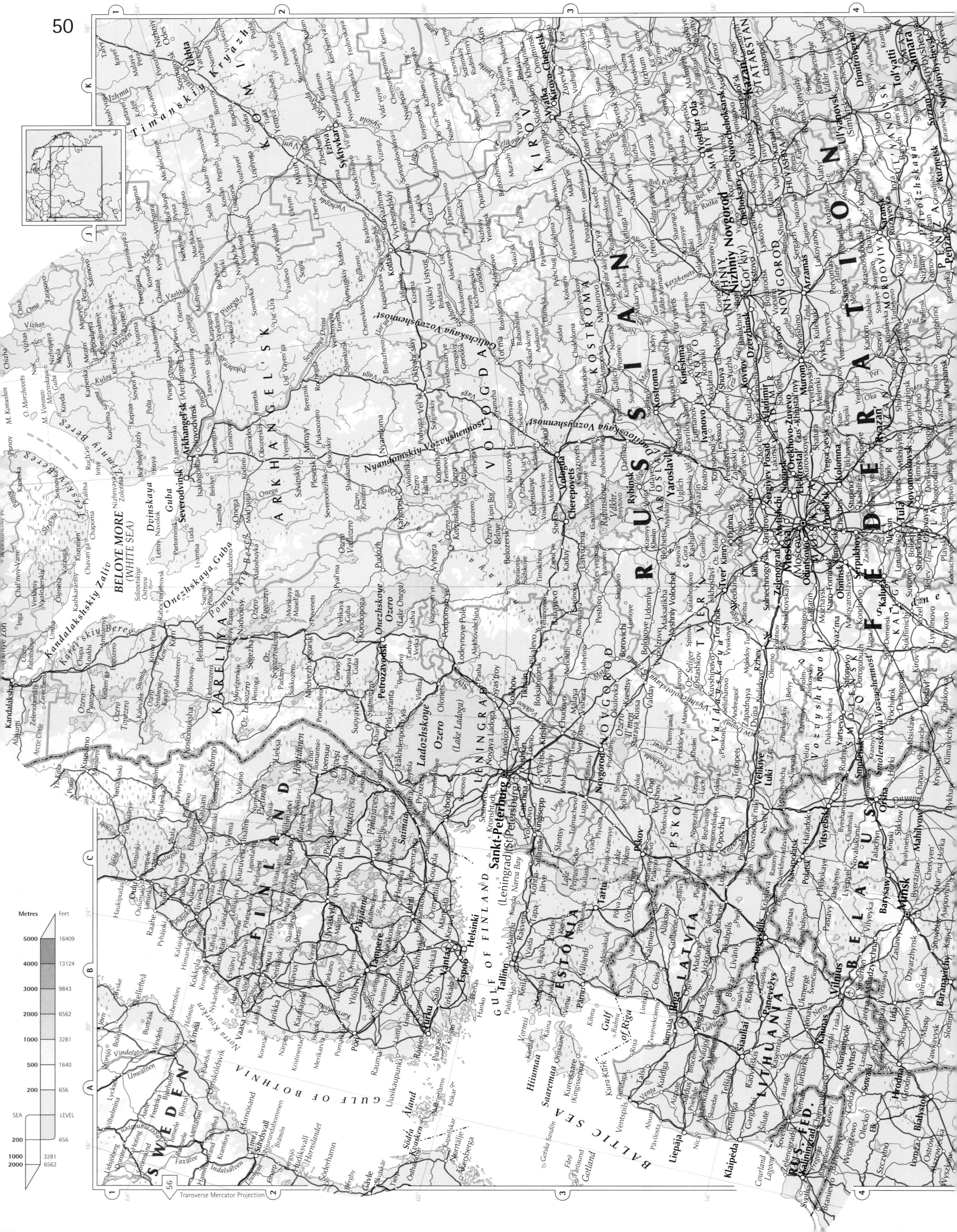
RUSSIAN FEDERATION
FINLAND
SWEDEN
ESTONIA
LATVIA
LITHUANIA
BELARUS
RUS. FED.
KARELIYA
ARKHANGEL'SK
VOLOGDA
KOSTROMA
YAROSLAVL'
TVER'
PSKOV
NOVGOROD
LENINGRAD
SMOLENSK
KALUGA
MOSKVA
VLADIMIR
IVANOVO
NIZHNIY NOVGOROD
KIROV
KOMI
TATARSTAN
CHUVASHIYA
MARIY EL
MORDOVIYA
PENZA
RYAZAN'
TULA
ULYANOVSK
BELOYE MORE (WHITE SEA)
Dvinskaya Guba
Onezhskaya Guba
Kandalakshskiy Zaliv
GULF OF BOTHNIA
GULF OF FINLAND
Gulf of Riga
BALTIC SEA
Ladozhskoye Ozero (Lake Ladoga)
Onezhskoye Ozero (Lake Onega)
Timanskiy Kryazh
Sankt-Peterburg (Leningrad) (St Petersburg)
Moskva (Moscow)
Helsinki
Tallinn
Riga
Vilnius
Minsk
Arkhangel'sk
Petrozavodsk
Vologda
Yaroslavl'
Nizhniy Novgorod (Gor'kiy)
Kazan'
Syktyvkar
Ukhta
Novgorod
Pskov
Smolensk
Kaliningrad
Metres
Feet
5000
16409
4000
13124
3000
9843
2000
6562
1000
3281
500
1640
200
656
SEA
LEVEL
200
656
1000
3281
2000
6562
Transverse Mercator Projection
56

CASPIAN SEA
(KASPIYSKOYE MORE)
BLACK SEA
(CHERNOYE MORE)
(KARA DENIZ)
Sea of Azov
KAZAKHSTAN
UKRAINE
ROMANIA
MOLDOVA
BULGARIA
TURKEY
GEORGIA
ARMENIA
AZERBAIJAN
POLAND
GREECE
1:6M
Miles
Km
© Bartholomew

MOSCOW REGION

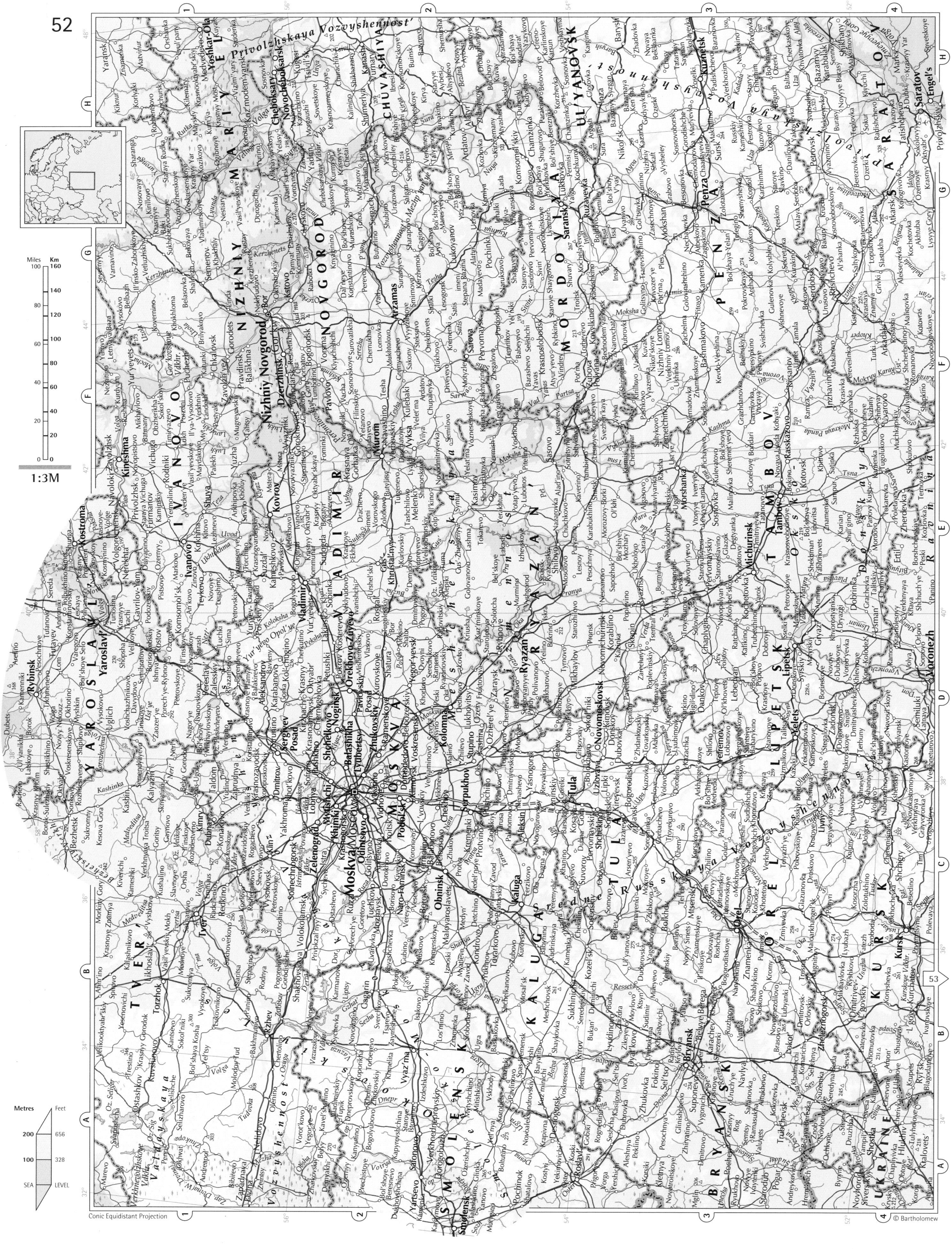

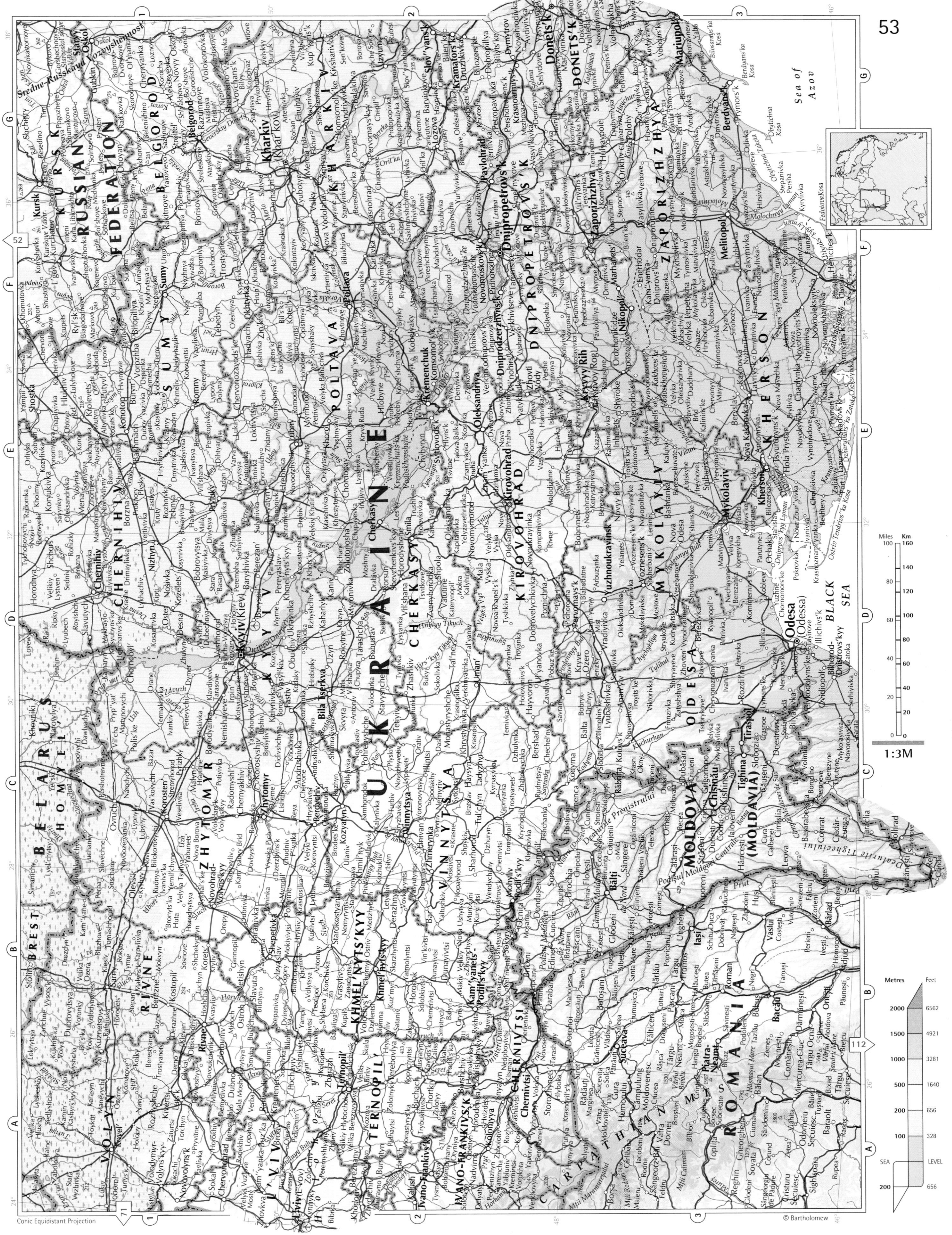

UKRAINE
MOLDOVA
RUSSIAN FEDERATION
BELARUS
ROMANIA
BLACK SEA
Sea of Azov
Kyyiv (Kiev)
Chişinău (Kishinev)
Odesa (Odessa)
Kharkiv (Khar'kov)
Dnipropetrovs'k
Donets'k
Zaporizhzhya
L'viv (L'vov)
Miles
Km
1:3M
Metres
Feet
SEA LEVEL
Conic Equidistant Projection
© Bartholomew

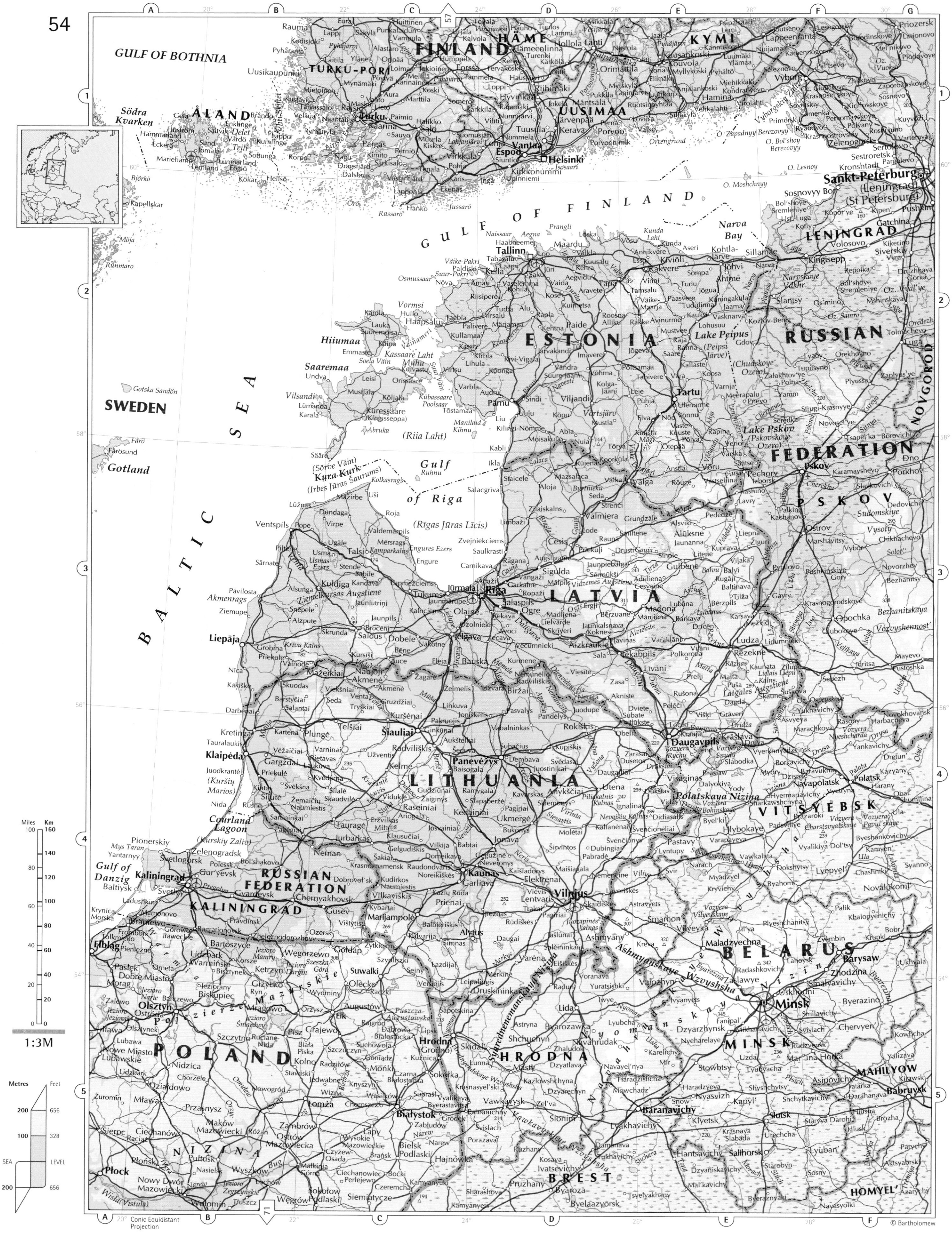

LATVIA, LITHUANIA and ESTONIA
54
GULF OF BOTHNIA
FINLAND
HÄME
KYMI
TURKU-PORI
UUSIMAA
ÅLAND
Södra Kvarken
Helsinki
Sankt-Peterburg (Leningrad) (St Petersburg)
LENINGRAD
GULF OF FINLAND
Narva Bay
Tallinn
ESTONIA
Hiiumaa
Saaremaa
Lake Peipus (Peipsi Järve) (Chudskoye Ozero)
Tartu
Pärnu
Lake Pskov (Pskovskoye Ozero)
Pskov
RUSSIAN FEDERATION
NOVGOROD
PSKOV
SWEDEN
Gotland
BALTIC SEA
Gulf of Riga (Rīgas Jūras Līcis)
Ventspils
Rīga
LATVIA
Liepāja
Jelgava
Daugavpils
LITHUANIA
Klaipėda
Šiauliai
Panevėžys
Kaunas
Vilnius
Courland Lagoon
Kaliningrad
RUSSIAN FEDERATION
KALININGRAD
Gulf of Danzig
VITSYEBSK
Polatsk
BELARUS
Minsk
MINSK
HRODNA
Hrodna (Grodno)
BREST
Baranavichy
MAHILYOW
Babruysk
HOMYEL'
POLAND
Olsztyn
Elbląg
Białystok
Łomża
Płock
1:3M
Miles
Km
Metres
Feet
SEA LEVEL
Conic Equidistant Projection
© Bartholomew

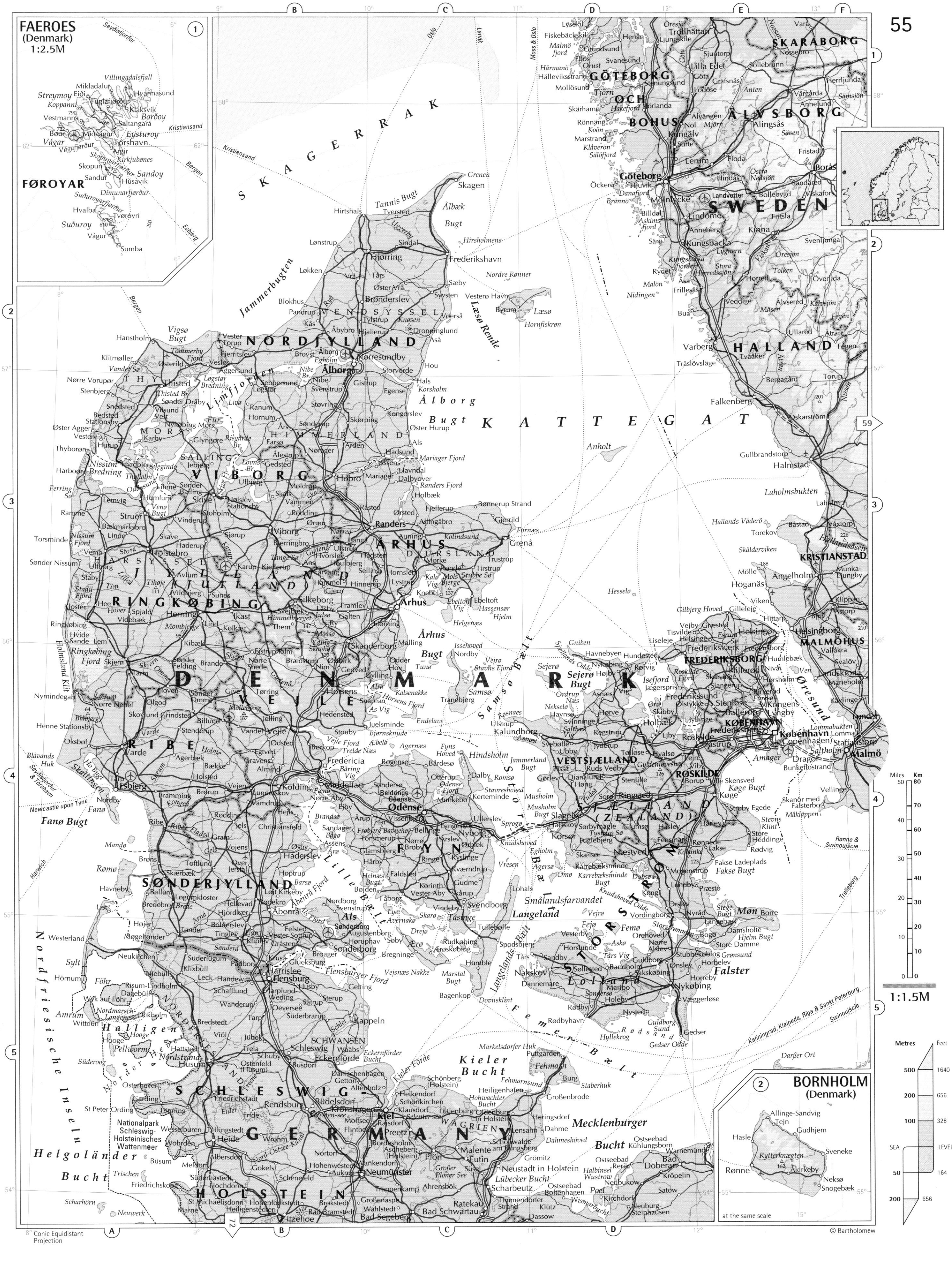
FAEROES
(Denmark)
1:2.5M
FØROYAR
Streymoy
Vágar
Eysturoy
Tórshavn
Sandoy
Suðuroy
BORNHOLM
(Denmark)
Rønne
Nexø
at the same scale
SKAGERRAK
KATTEGAT
DENMARK
SWEDEN
GERMANY
NORDJYLLAND
VIBORG
ÅRHUS
RINGKØBING
VEJLE
RIBE
SØNDERJYLLAND
FYN
VESTSJÆLLAND
FREDERIKSBORG
KØBENHAVN
ROSKILDE
STORSTRØM
SCHLESWIG-HOLSTEIN
GÖTEBORG OCH BOHUS
ÄLVSBORG
HALLAND
SKARABORG
KRISTIANSTAD
MALMÖHUS
JYLLAND (JUTLAND)
SJÆLLAND (ZEALAND)
Lolland
Falster
Møn
Langeland
Als
Samsø
Anholt
Læsø
Fehmarn
Sylt
Föhr
Amrum
København (Copenhagen)
Århus
Odense
Ålborg
Esbjerg
Randers
Kolding
Vejle
Horsens
Herning
Silkeborg
Fredericia
Viborg
Helsingør
Roskilde
Næstved
Svendborg
Skagen
Frederikshavn
Hjørring
Göteborg
Malmö
Helsingborg
Halmstad
Kiel
Flensburg
Schleswig
Neumünster
Jammerbugten
Limfjorden
Ålborg Bugt
Lillebælt
Storebælt
Øresund
Femer Bælt
Kieler Bucht
Mecklenburger Bucht
Helgoländer Bucht
Nordfriesische Inseln
Conic Equidistant Projection
© Bartholomew
1:1.5M
Miles
Km
Metres
Feet
SEA LEVEL

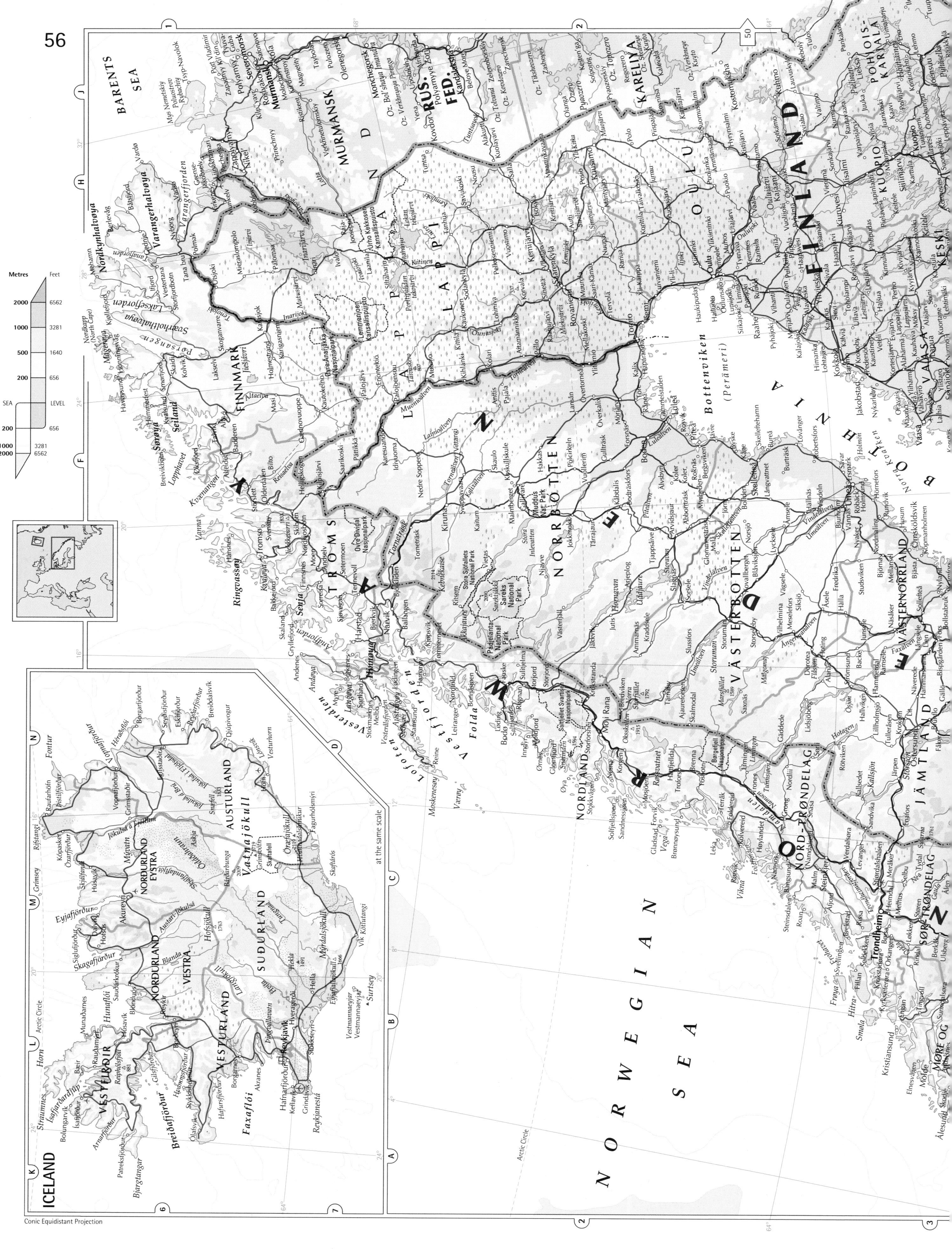
Metres
Feet
2000
6562
1000
3281
500
1640
200
656
SEA
LEVEL
200
656
1000
3281
2000
6562
BARENTS SEA
NORWEGIAN SEA
FINNMARK
TROMS
NORDLAND
NORD-TRØNDELAG
SØR-TRØNDELAG
MØRE OG
NORRBOTTEN
VÄSTERBOTTEN
VÄSTERNORRLAND
JÄMTLAND
LAPPI
OULU
VAASA
KUOPIO
POHJOIS-KARJALA
FINLAND
MURMANSK
KARELIYA
RUS. FED.
Bottenviken
(Perämeri)
Vestfjorden
Lofoten
Vesterålen
ICELAND
VESTFIRÐIR
NORÐURLAND VESTRA
NORÐURLAND EYSTRA
AUSTURLAND
SUÐURLAND
VESTURLAND
Vatnajökull
Faxaflói
Breiðafjörður
Reykjavík
at the same scale
Arctic Circle
Conic Equidistant Projection

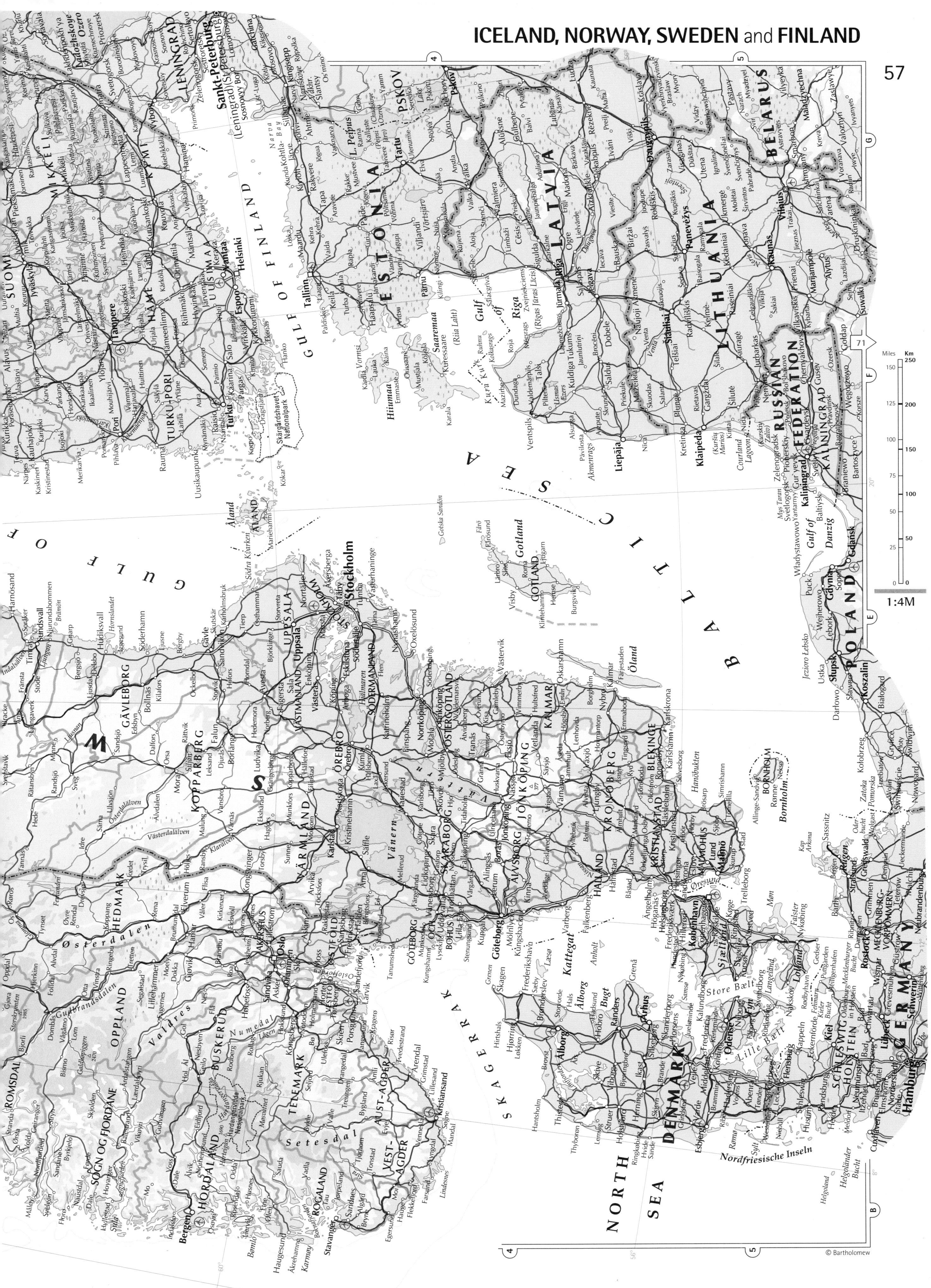

GULF OF FINLAND
GULF OF BOTHNIA
BALTIC SEA
SKAGERRAK
Kattegat
NORTH SEA
Gulf of Riga
Gulf of Danzig
ESTONIA
LATVIA
LITHUANIA
BELARUS
RUSSIAN FEDERATION
POLAND
GERMANY
DENMARK
SUOMI
Stockholm
Oslo
Helsinki
Tallinn
Riga
Vilnius
København
Sankt-Peterburg
Gotland
Öland
Bornholm
Åland
Saaremaa
Hiiumaa
Vänern
Vättern
1:4M
Miles
Km
© Bartholomew

NORWAY
DENMARK
NORTH SEA
SKAGERRAK
KATTEGAT
SOGN OG FJORDANE
HORDALAND
OPPLAND
HEDMARK
BUSKERUD
AKERSHUS
OSLO
ØSTFOLD
VESTFOLD
TELEMARK
ROGALAND
AUST-AGDER
VEST-AGDER
GÖTEBORG OCH BOHUS
NORDJYLLAND
VIBORG
ÅRHUS
RINGKØBING
VEJLE
RIBE
FYN
VESTSJÆLLAND
JYLLAND
Bergen
Stavanger
Oslo
Kristiansand
Drammen
Lillehammer
Hamar
Skien
Larvik
Arendal
Fredrikstad
Sarpsborg
Göteborg
Ålborg
Århus
Esbjerg
Odense
Randers
Viborg
Frederikshavn
Skagen
Hirtshals
Herning
Horsens
Kolding
Fredericia
Vejle
Silkeborg
Holstebro
Skive
Hardangervidda
Jotunheimen Nasjonalpark
Jostedalsbreen Nasjonalpark
Hardangervidda Nasjonalpark
Sognefjorden
Hardangerfjorden
Jammerbugten
Tannis Bugt
Ålbæk Bugt
Ålborg Bugt
Århus Bugt
Limfjorden
Oslofjorden
Mjøsa
Lindesnes
Læsø
Anholt
Samsø
Tórshavn
Lerwick
Newcastle upon Tyne
Amsterdam
Metres
Feet
2000
6562
1500
4921
1000
3281
500
1640
200
656
100
328
SEA
LEVEL
50
164
200
656
Conic Equidistant Projection
A
B
C
D
1
2
3
4
55

GULF OF BOTHNIA
FINLAND
ÅLAND
SWEDEN
KOPPARBERG
GÄVLEBORG
UPPSALA
VÄRMLAND
VÄSTMANLAND
STOCKHOLM
Stockholm
ÖREBRO
SÖDERMANLAND
SKARABORG
ÖSTERGOTLAND
ÄLVSBORG
JÖNKÖPING
KALMAR
HALLAND
KRONOBERG
BLEKINGE
KRISTIANSTAD
MALMÖHUS
GOTLAND
Gotland
Öland
VÄNERN
VÄTTERN
Mälaren
Hjälmaren
Gotska Sandön
Gotska Sandön Nationalpark
Uppsala
Gävle
Falun
Karlstad
Örebro
Västerås
Norrköping
Linköping
Jönköping
Växjö
Kalmar
Karlskrona
Halmstad
Helsingborg
Malmö
Lund
Visby
København
Södra Kvarken
Hanöbukten
BALTIC SEA
Miles
Km
1:2M
© Bartholomew

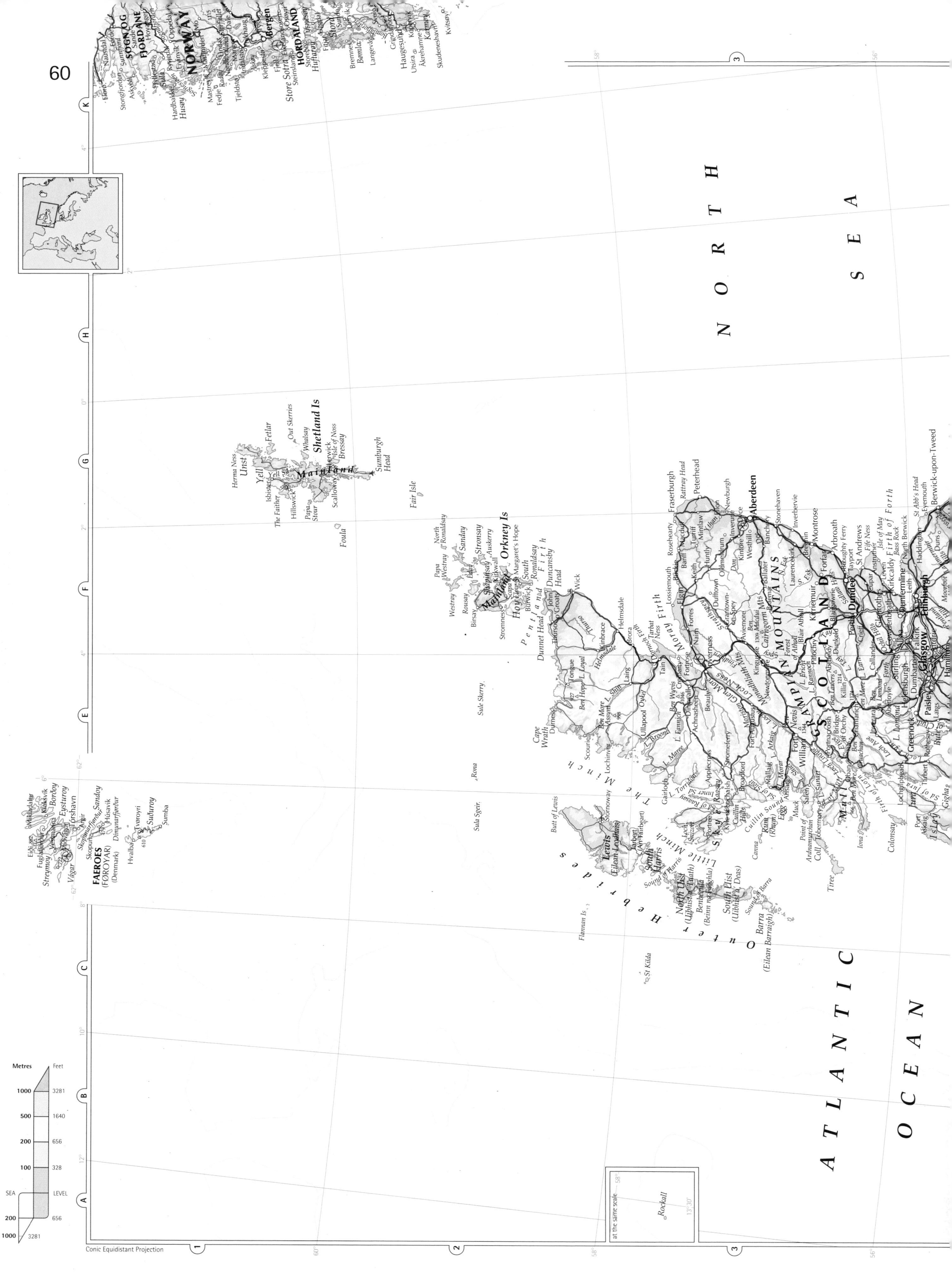
NORTH SEA
ATLANTIC OCEAN
NORWAY
SOGN OG FJORDANE
HORDALAND
Bergen
Haugesund
Stord
Karmøy
Shetland Is
Unst
Yell
Mainland
Lerwick
Sumburgh Head
Fair Isle
Foula
Orkney Is
Kirkwall
Hoy
Stromness
Pentland Firth
Dunnet Head
Duncansby Head
John o' Groats
Thurso
Wick
Cape Wrath
Sule Skerry
Rona
Sula Sgeir
Butt of Lewis
Lewis (Eilean Leodhais)
Stornoway
Harris
North Uist
Benbecula
South Uist
Barra
Outer Hebrides
The Minch
Little Minch
Flannan Is
St Kilda
Skye
Mull
Colonsay
Jura
Islay
Tiree
Coll
Rum
Eigg
Canna
Muck
Moray Firth
Inverness
Aberdeen
Peterhead
Fraserburgh
GRAMPIAN MOUNTAINS
SCOTLAND
Dundee
Perth
Edinburgh
Glasgow
Paisley
Greenock
Stirling
Falkirk
Kirkcaldy
Dunfermline
Firth of Forth
St Andrews
Montrose
Arbroath
Berwick-upon-Tweed
Fort William
Ben Nevis
Oban
Ullapool
Loch Ness
Cairngorm Mts
FAEROES (FØROYAR) (Denmark)
Tórshavn
Streymoy
Eysturoy
Vágar
Sandoy
Suðuroy
Rockall
at the same scale
Metres
Feet
1000
3281
500
1640
200
656
100
328
SEA
LEVEL
200
656
1000
3281
Conic Equidistant Projection

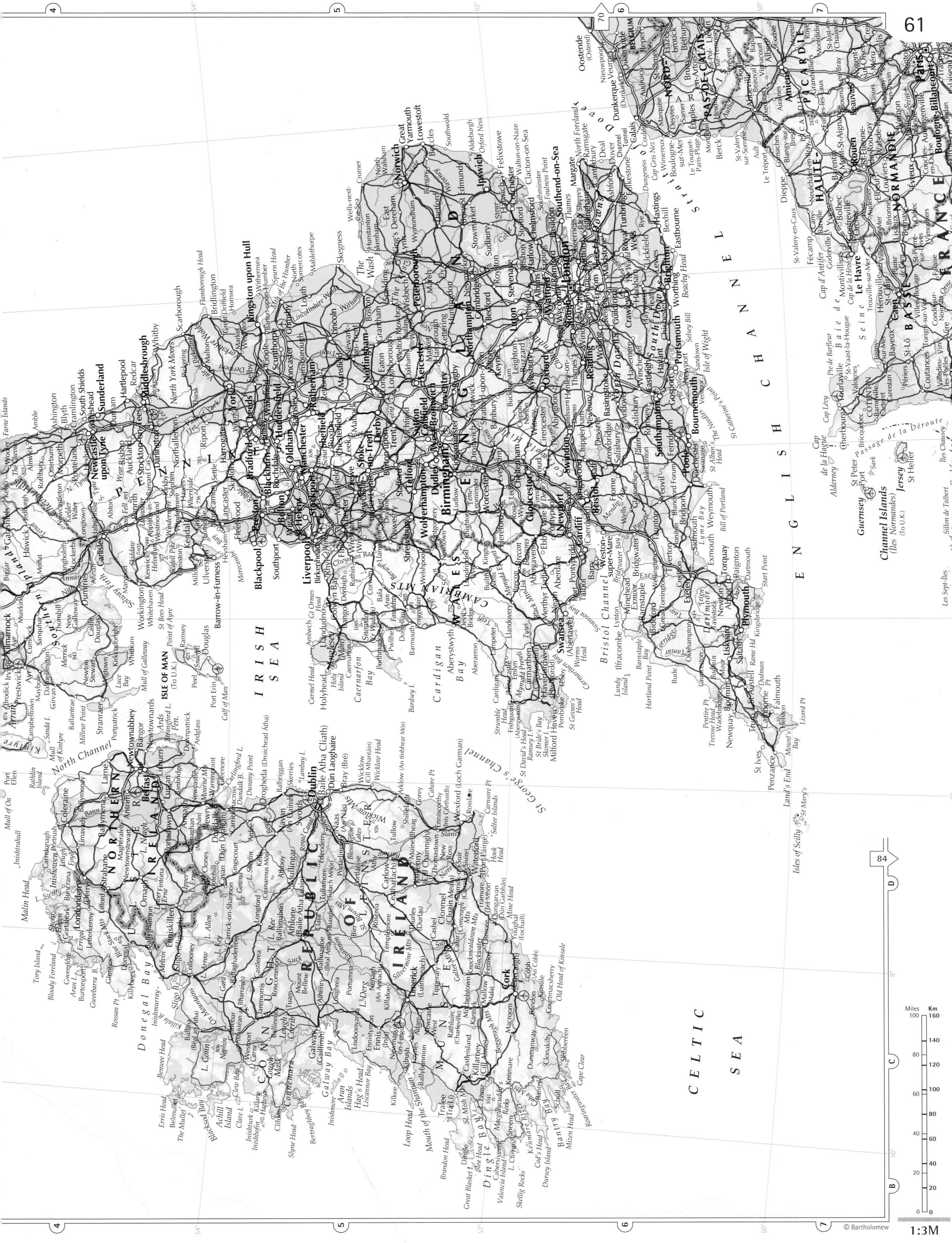
IRISH SEA
CELTIC SEA
ENGLISH CHANNEL
NORTHERN IRELAND
REPUBLIC OF IRELAND
ISLE OF MAN (To U.K.)
Channel Islands (Îles Normandes) (To U.K.)
FRANCE
CAMBRIAN MTS
Bristol Channel
St George's Channel
North Channel
Cardigan Bay
Donegal Bay
Galway Bay
Dublin
Belfast
Cork
Birmingham
Liverpool
Manchester
Cardiff
Swansea
Plymouth
Southampton
Portsmouth
Brighton
London
Oxford
Norwich
Ipswich
Leeds
Sheffield
Nottingham
Leicester
Coventry
Bristol
Kingston upon Hull
Middlesbrough
Sunderland
Newcastle upon Tyne
Carlisle
Blackpool
Preston
Paris
Rouen
Le Havre
Caen
Amiens
Miles
Km
1:3M
© Bartholomew

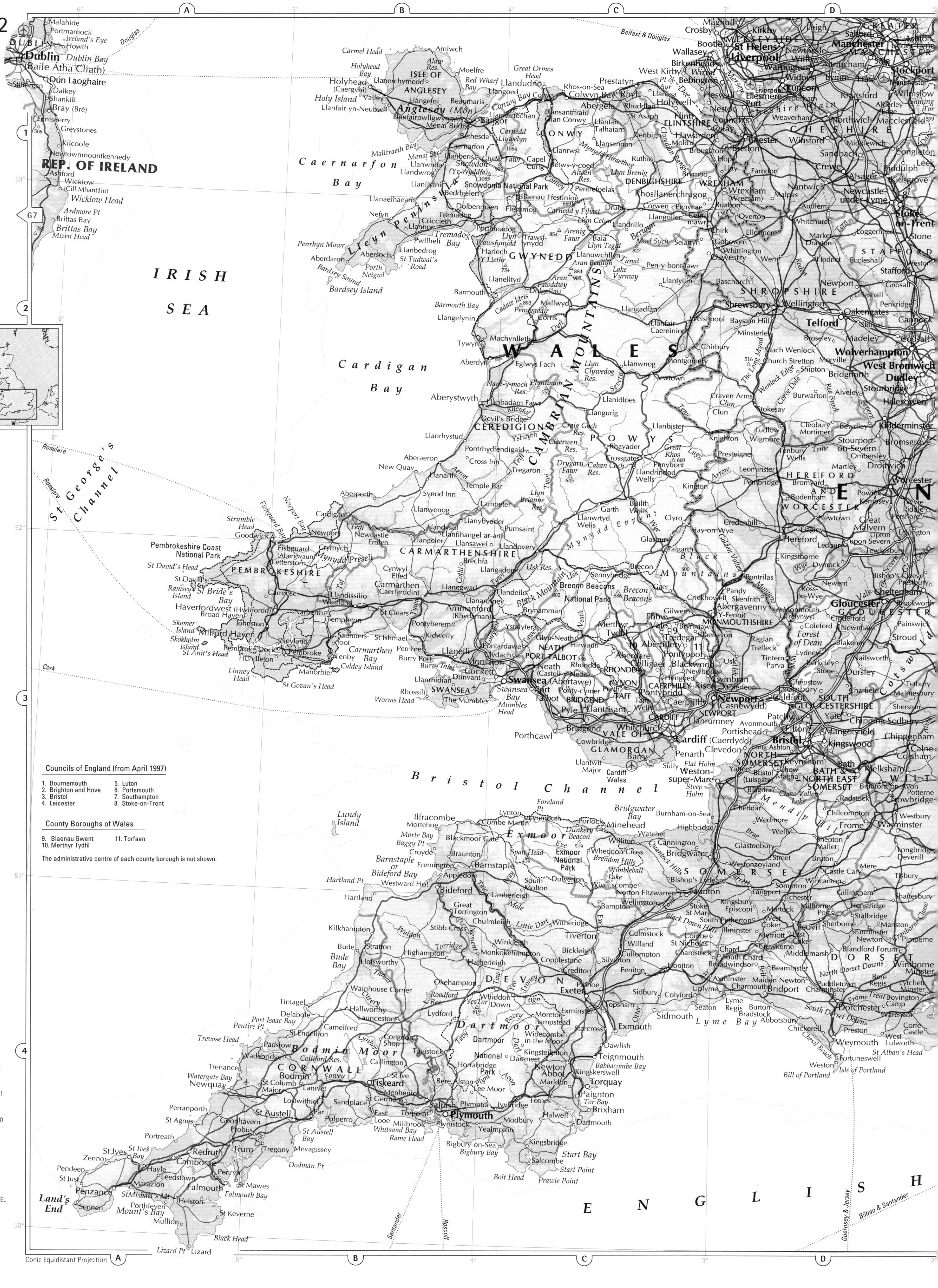
IRISH SEA
REP. OF IRELAND
WALES
Cardigan Bay
Caernarfon Bay
St George's Channel
Bristol Channel
ENGLISH
CAMBRIAN MOUNTAINS
Pembrokeshire Coast National Park
Snowdonia National Park
Brecon Beacons National Park
Exmoor National Park
Dartmoor
Bodmin Moor
ISLE OF ANGLESEY
GWYNEDD
CONWY
DENBIGHSHIRE
FLINTSHIRE
WREXHAM
CEREDIGION
POWYS
PEMBROKESHIRE
CARMARTHENSHIRE
SWANSEA
NEATH PORT TALBOT
BRIDGEND
RHONDDA CYNON TAFF
CAERPHILLY
MONMOUTHSHIRE
NEWPORT
CARDIFF
VALE OF GLAMORGAN
CHESHIRE
SHROPSHIRE
HEREFORD AND WORCESTER
GLOUCESTERSHIRE
SOUTH GLOUCESTERSHIRE
NORTH SOMERSET
BATH & NORTH EAST SOMERSET
SOMERSET
DEVON
CORNWALL
DORSET
Dublin (Baile Átha Cliath)
Cardiff (Caerdydd)
Swansea (Abertawe)
Newport (Casnewydd)
Bristol
Plymouth
Exeter
Liverpool
Manchester
Councils of England (from April 1997)
1. Bournemouth
2. Brighton and Hove
3. Bristol
4. Leicester
5. Luton
6. Portsmouth
7. Southampton
8. Stoke-on-Trent
County Boroughs of Wales
9. Blaenau Gwent
10. Merthyr Tydfil
11. Torfaen
The administrative centre of each county borough is not shown.
Metres
Feet
1000
3281
500
1640
200
656
100
328
SEA
LEVEL
50
164
Conic Equidistant Projection

N O R T H
S E A
C H A N N E L
Strait of Dover
The Wash
Thames
North Downs
South Downs
The Weald
The Fens
Lincolnshire Wolds
Vale of White Horse
Salisbury Plain
Isle of Wight
SOUTH YORKSHIRE
DERBYSHIRE
NOTTINGHAMSHIRE
LINCOLNSHIRE
LEICESTERSHIRE
RUTLAND
NORFOLK
CAMBRIDGESHIRE
NORTHAMPTONSHIRE
WARWICKSHIRE
SUFFOLK
BEDFORDSHIRE
BUCKINGHAMSHIRE
HERTFORDSHIRE
OXFORDSHIRE
ESSEX
BERKSHIRE
HAMPSHIRE
SURREY
KENT
WEST SUSSEX
EAST SUSSEX
WEST MIDLANDS
GREATER LONDON
ENGLAND
London
Birmingham
Sheffield
Nottingham
Leicester
Coventry
Derby
Lincoln
Peterborough
Cambridge
Norwich
Ipswich
Colchester
Oxford
Reading
Luton
Southampton
Portsmouth
Bournemouth
Brighton
Southend-on-Sea
Great Yarmouth
Lowestoft
Dover
Folkestone
Hastings
Margate
Ramsgate
Canterbury
Maidstone
Chelmsford
Swindon
Salisbury
Winchester
FRANCE
Calais
Boulogne-sur-Mer
Cap Gris Nez
Cap Blanc Nez
Dunkerque
Oostende
Vlissingen
Hoek van Holland
Zeebrugge
Hamburg
Esbjerg
Göteborg
Cherbourg
Dieppe
St-Malo
Caen & Le Havre
1 Isles of Scilly
Land's End
Penzance
St Ives
Mount's Bay
St Mary's
Hugh Town
Bryher
Tresco
St Martin's
St Agnes
at the same scale
2 CHANNEL ISLANDS
(ÎLES NORMANDES)
(To United Kingdom)
Alderney
Guernsey
St Peter Port
Sark
Herm
Jersey
St Helier
Passage de la Déroute
Cap de la Hague
at the same scale
Miles
Km
1:1.2M
© Bartholomew

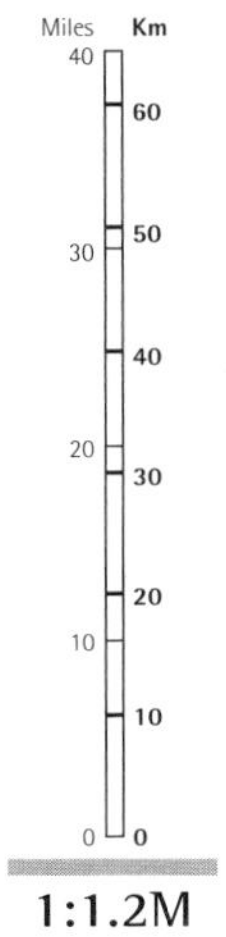

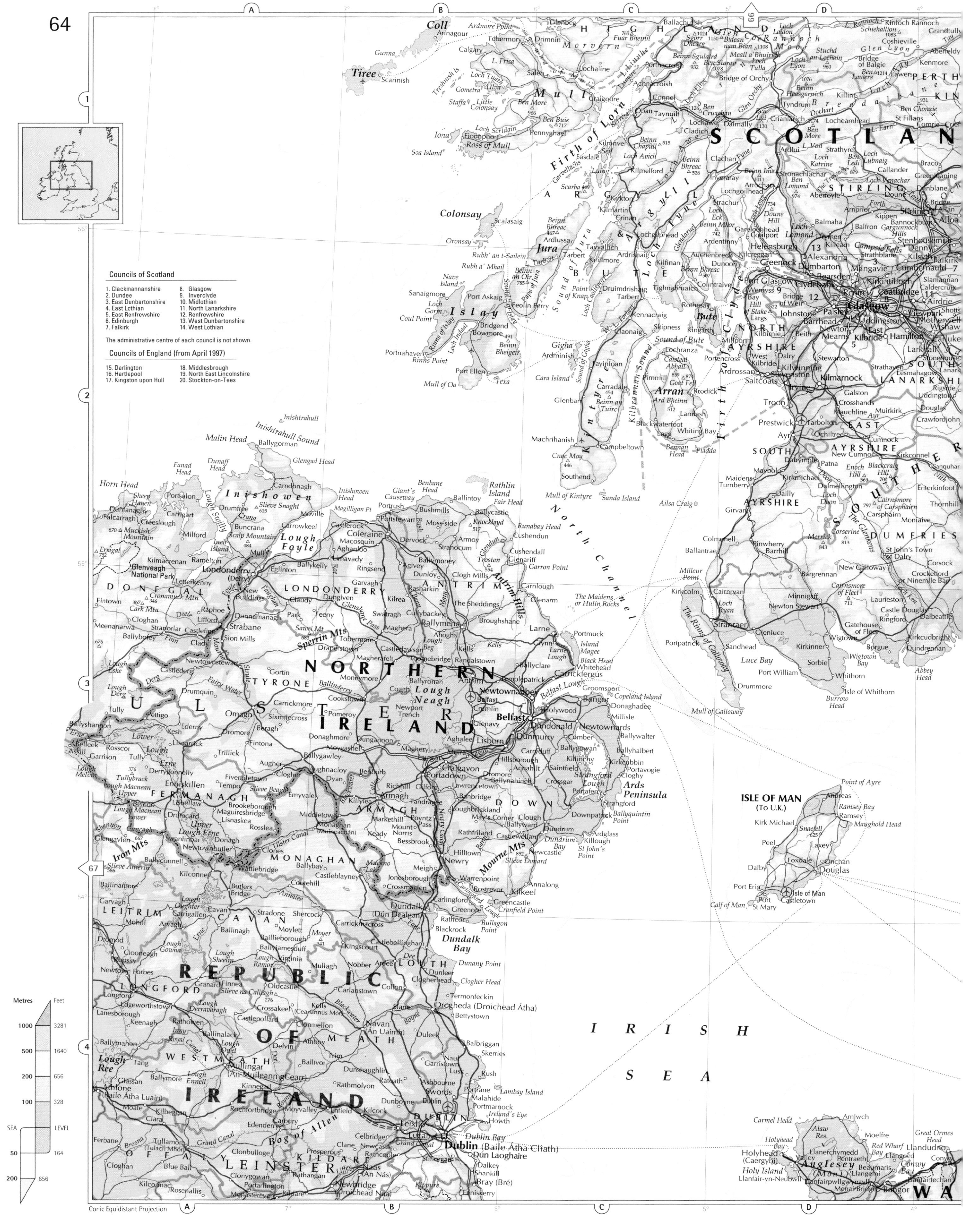
Councils of Scotland
1. Clackmannanshire
2. Dundee
3. East Dunbartonshire
4. East Lothian
5. East Renfrewshire
6. Edinburgh
7. Falkirk
8. Glasgow
9. Inverclyde
10. Midlothian
11. North Lanarkshire
12. Renfrewshire
13. West Dunbartonshire
14. West Lothian
The administrative centre of each council is not shown.
Councils of England (from April 1997)
15. Darlington
16. Hartlepool
17. Kingston upon Hull
18. Middlesbrough
19. North East Lincolnshire
20. Stockton-on-Tees
Metres
Feet
1000
3281
500
1640
200
656
100
328
SEA
LEVEL
50
164
200
656
SCOTLAN
NORTHERN IRELAND
REPUBLIC OF IRELAND
ULSTER
LEINSTER
ISLE OF MAN
(To U.K.)
IRISH SEA
North Channel
Firth of Lorn
Firth of Clyde
Sound of Jura
Kilbrannan Sound
Inishowen
Lough Foyle
Lough Neagh
Sperrin Mts
Antrim Hills
Mourne Mts
Ards Peninsula
Dundalk Bay
Bog of Allen
Iron Mts
Coll
Tiree
Mull
Iona
Colonsay
Jura
Islay
Gigha
Arran
Bute
Kintyre
Rathlin Island
Anglesey
Holy Island
Glasgow
Paisley
Greenock
Kilmarnock
Ayr
Oban
Campbeltown
Stranraer
Belfast
Londonderry
(Derry)
Armagh
Newry
Lisburn
Dundalk
Drogheda (Droichead Átha)
Dublin (Baile Átha Cliath)
Dún Laoghaire
Douglas
Holyhead
(Caergybi)
Bangor
DONEGAL
LONDONDERRY
ANTRIM
TYRONE
FERMANAGH
ARMAGH
DOWN
MONAGHAN
CAVAN
LEITRIM
LONGFORD
LOUTH
MEATH
WESTMEATH
OFFALY
KILDARE
DUBLIN
ARGYLL & BUTE
STIRLING
NORTH AYRSHIRE
EAST AYRSHIRE
SOUTH AYRSHIRE
SOUTH LANARKSHIRE
DUMFRIES
PERTH
67
66

N O R T H
S E A
Firth of Forth
Firth of Tay
Solway Firth
Mouth of the Humber
ANGUS
FIFE
SCOTTISH BORDERS
UPLANDS
NORTHUMBERLAND
TYNE AND WEAR
DURHAM
CUMBRIA
NORTH YORKSHIRE
EAST RIDING OF YORKSHIRE
WEST YORKSHIRE
SOUTH YORKSHIRE
LANCASHIRE
MERSEYSIDE
GREATER MANCHESTER
CHESHIRE
DERBYSHIRE
NOTTINGHAMSHIRE
NORTH LINCOLNSHIRE
LINCOLNSHIRE
ENGLAND
PENNINES
Cheviot Hills
Lake District National Park
Yorkshire Dales National Park
North York Moors National Park
Northumberland National Park
Peak District National Park
Dundee
Perth
St Andrews
Kirkcaldy
Dunfermline
Edinburgh
Dunbar
Berwick-upon-Tweed
Galashiels
Hawick
Carlisle
Newcastle upon Tyne
Gateshead
Sunderland
Durham
Hartlepool
Middlesbrough
Darlington
Whitby
Scarborough
York
Harrogate
Leeds
Bradford
Kingston upon Hull
Grimsby
Scunthorpe
Doncaster
Sheffield
Rotherham
Huddersfield
Wakefield
Oldham
Bolton
Manchester
Stockport
Liverpool
St Helens
Warrington
Preston
Blackburn
Blackpool
Lancaster
Kendal
Barrow-in-Furness
Dumfries
Lincoln
Chesterfield
Chester
Stavanger & Bergen
Göteborg
Esbjerg
Hamburg
Rotterdam & Zeebrugge
Miles
Km
© Bartholomew
1:1.2M

SCOTLAND

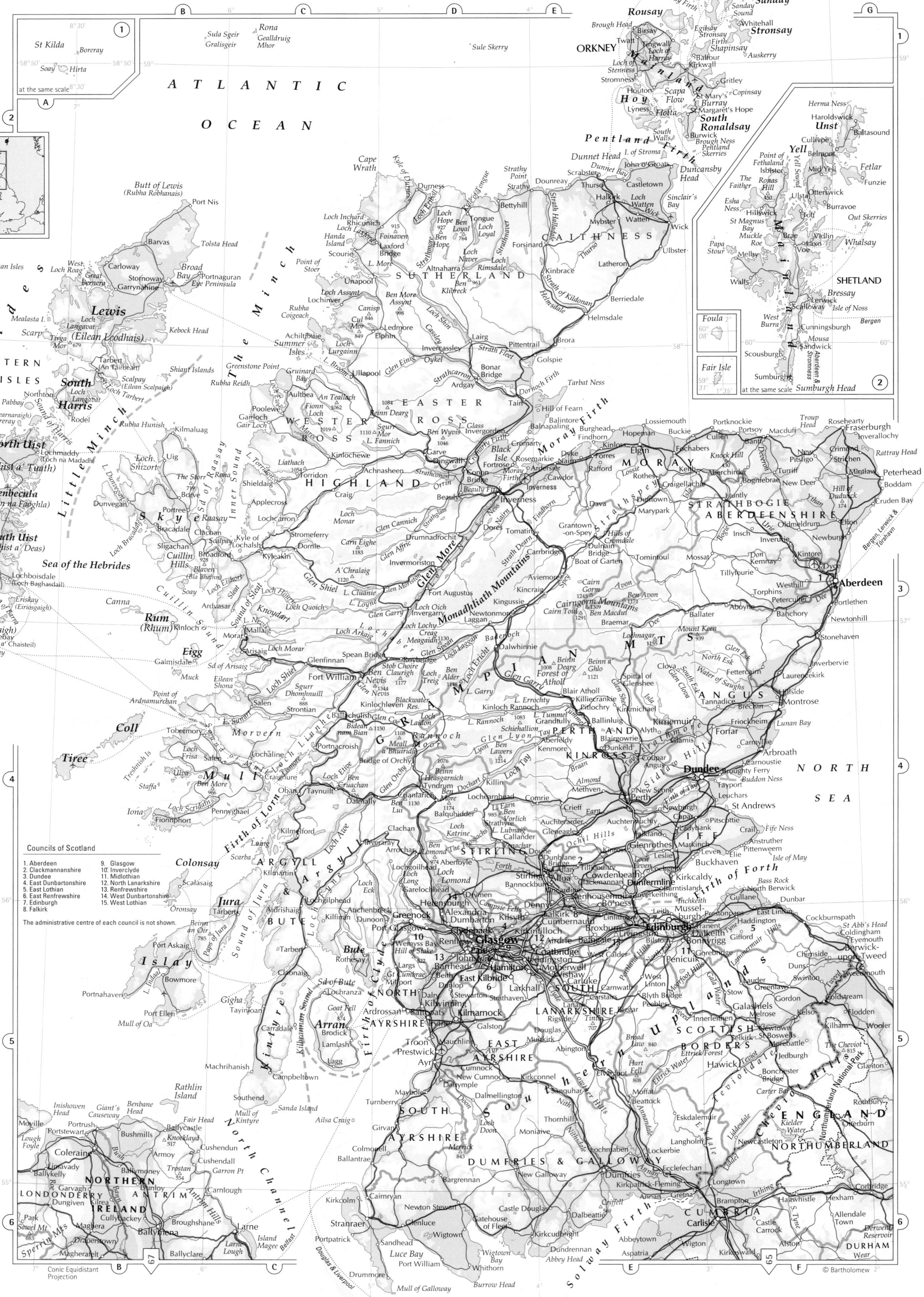

ATLANTIC OCEAN
NORTH SEA
ORKNEY
SHETLAND
WESTERN ISLES
HIGHLAND
MORAY
ABERDEENSHIRE
ANGUS
PERTH AND KINROSS
ARGYLL & BUTE
STIRLING
FIFE
SCOTTISH BORDERS
EAST AYRSHIRE
SOUTH AYRSHIRE
NORTH AYRSHIRE
SOUTH LANARKSHIRE
DUMFRIES & GALLOWAY
NORTHUMBERLAND
CUMBRIA
DURHAM
ENGLAND
NORTHERN IRELAND
LONDONDERRY
ANTRIM
Outer Hebrides
The Minch
Little Minch
Sea of the Hebrides
Inner Sound
Pentland Firth
Moray Firth
Firth of Forth
Firth of Clyde
Firth of Lorn
North Channel
Solway Firth
GRAMPIAN MTS
Southern Uplands
Cheviot Hills
Aberdeen
Dundee
Edinburgh
Glasgow
Inverness
Perth
Stirling
Fort William
Oban
Ayr
Dumfries
Carlisle
Kirkwall
Lerwick
Stornoway
Wick
Thurso
Lewis
Harris
North Uist
South Uist
Benbecula
Barra
Skye
Rum
Eigg
Coll
Tiree
Mull
Colonsay
Jura
Islay
Arran
Bute
Kintyre
Hoy
Mainland
Unst
Yell
Fair Isle
Foula
St Kilda
1
2
Councils of Scotland
1. Aberdeen
2. Clackmannanshire
3. Dundee
4. East Dunbartonshire
5. East Lothian
6. East Renfrewshire
7. Edinburgh
8. Falkirk
9. Glasgow
10. Inverclyde
11. Midlothian
12. North Lanarkshire
13. Renfrewshire
14. West Dunbartonshire
15. West Lothian
The administrative centre of each council is not shown.
Miles
Km
1:1.5M
Metres
Feet
SEA LEVEL
at the same scale
Conic Equidistant Projection
© Bartholomew

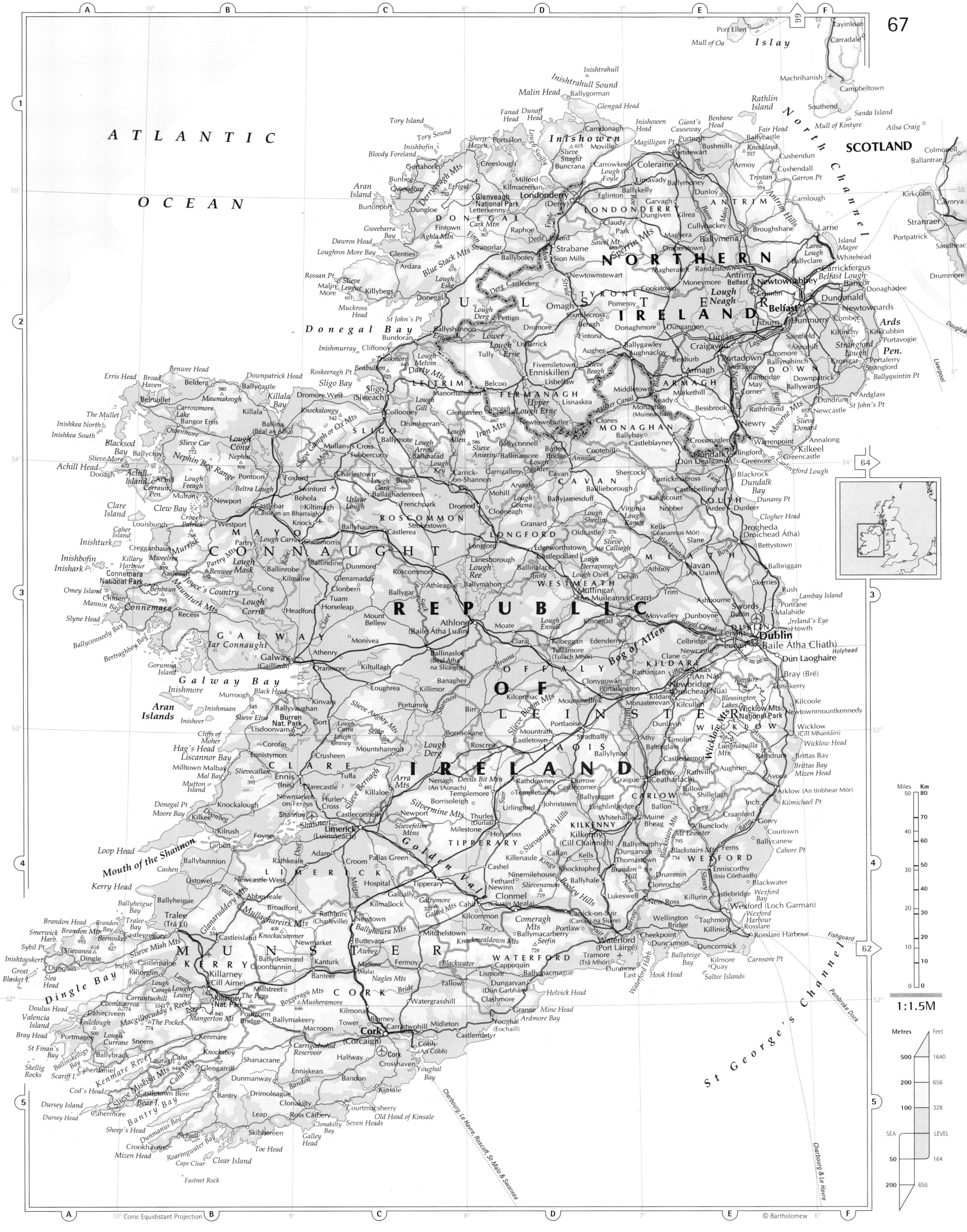

ATLANTIC
OCEAN
NORTHERN IRELAND
REPUBLIC OF IRELAND
SCOTLAND
ULSTER
CONNAUGHT
LEINSTER
MUNSTER
North Channel
St George's Channel
Donegal Bay
Galway Bay
Dingle Bay
Bantry Bay
Islay
Port Ellen
Mull of Oa
Tayinloan
Carradale
Machrihanish
Campbeltown
Southend
Sanda Island
Mull of Kintyre
Ailsa Craig
Colmonell
Ballantrae
Kirkcolm
Stranraer
Portpatrick
Sandhead
Drummore
Inishtrahull
Inishtrahull Sound
Malin Head
Ballygorman
Glengad Head
Fanad Head
Dunaff Head
Tory Island
Tory Sound
Inishbofin
Bloody Foreland
Inishowen
Inishowen Head
Carndonagh
Moville
Buncrana
Slieve Snaght
Lough Swilly
Lough Foyle
Rathlin Island
Giant's Causeway
Benbane Head
Fair Head
Ballycastle
Knocklayd
Cushendun
Cushendall
Garron Pt
Portrush
Portstewart
Bushmills
Coleraine
Limavady
Ballymoney
Armoy
Ballykelly
Magilligan Pt
Londonderry (Derry)
LONDONDERRY
ANTRIM
Antrim Hills
Eglinton
Dungiven
Garvagh
Kilrea
Dunloy
Cullybackey
Carnlough
Broughshane
Larne
Ballymena
Claudy
Park
Sawel Mt
Sperrin Mts
Maghera
Draperstown
Magherafelt
Randalstown
Antrim
Islandmagee
Larne Lough
Ballyclare
Whitehead
Carrickfergus
Belfast Lough
Newtownabbey
Bangor
Donaghadee
Belfast
Dundonald
Newtownards
Comber
Ards Pen.
Kirkcubbin
Portavogie
Killinchy
Strangford
Strangford Lough
Portaferry
Ballyquintin Pt
Lough Neagh
Moneymore
Cookstown
Crumlin
Lisburn
Dunmurry
Saintfield
Ballynahinch
Downpatrick
Dundrum
Ballyward
Newcastle
Ardglass
St John's Pt
DOWN
Lurgan
Craigavon
Portadown
Tandragee
Banbridge
Armagh
ARMAGH
Markethill
Middletown
Keady
Bessbrook
Newry
Rathfriland
Mourne Mts
Slieve Donard
Warrenpoint
Kilkeel
Annalong
Greencastle
Greenore
Carlingford
Carlingford Lough
Crossmaglen
Dundalk (Dún Dealgan)
Dundalk Bay
Blackrock
Dunany Pt
Clogher Head
Drogheda (Droichead Átha)
Bettystown
Balbriggan
Skerries
Rush
Lambay Island
Portrane
Malahide
Swords
Ireland's Eye
Howth
Dublin (Baile Átha Cliath)
Dún Laoghaire
Bray (Bré)
Enniskerry
Kilcoole
Newtownmountkennedy
Wicklow (Cill Mhantáin)
Wicklow Head
Brittas Bay
Mizen Head
Arklow (An tInbhear Mór)
Kilmichael Pt
Gorey
Courtown
Ballycanew
Cahore Pt
Wexford (Loch Garman)
Wexford Harbour
Rosslare
Rosslare Harbour
Carnsore Pt
Kilmore Quay
Saltee Islands
Hook Head
Waterford (Port Láirge)
Tramore (Trá Mhór)
Dunmore East
Dungarvan (Dún Garbhán)
Helvick Head
Youghal (Eochaill)
Youghal Bay
Ardmore Bay
Mine Head
Cork (Corcaigh)
Cóbh (An Cóbh)
Kinsale
Old Head of Kinsale
Courtmacsherry
Seven Heads
Clonakilty
Ross Carbery
Skibbereen
Galley Head
Toe Head
Baltimore
Clear Island
Cape Clear
Fastnet Rock
Mizen Head
Crookhaven
Schull
Roaringwater Bay
Dunmanus Bay
Sheep's Head
Bantry
Glengarriff
Bere I.
Castletown Bere
Dursey Island
Dursey Head
Cod's Head
Kenmare
Kenmare River
Sneem
Caha Mts
Bray Head
Valencia Island
Portmagee
Cahirciveen
Skellig Rocks
Scariff I.
Ballinskelligs Bay
Macgillycuddy's Reeks
Carrantuohill
Killarney (Cill Airne)
Killarney Nat. Park
Mangerton Mt
Dingle
Slea Head
Great Blasket I.
Inishtooskert
Sybil Pt
Smerwick Harb.
Brandon Head
Brandon Mtn
Brandon Bay
Tralee (Trá Lí)
Tralee Bay
Castlegregory
Castlemaine
Castleisland
Slieve Mish Mts
Ballyheigue
Kerry Head
Listowel
Ballybunnion
Tarbert
Mouth of the Shannon
Loop Head
Kilrush
Kilkee
Doonbeg
Moore Bay
Donegal Pt
Mutton Island
Mal Bay
Milltown Malbay
Liscannor Bay
Hag's Head
Cliffs of Moher
Ennistymon
Lisdoonvarna
Burren Nat. Park
Ballyvaughan
Black Head
Aran Islands
Inishmore
Inishmaan
Inisheer
Gorumna Island
Galway (Gaillimh)
Oranmore
Athenry
Ennis (Inis)
Shannon
Limerick (Luimneach)
Newcastle West
Abbeyfeale
Rathkeale
Adare
Croom
Kilmallock
Charleville (Ráth Luirc)
Mitchelstown
Fermoy
Mallow (Mala)
Kanturk
Millstreet
Macroom
Bandon
Dunmanway
Clonmel (Cluain Meala)
Cahir
Tipperary
Cashel
Thurles (Durlas)
Nenagh (An tAonach)
Roscrea
Templemore
Kilkenny (Cill Chainnigh)
Carlow (Ceatharlach)
Athy
Portlaoise
Tullamore (Tulach Mhór)
Athlone (Baile Átha Luain)
Mullingar (An Muileann gCearr)
Navan (An Uaimh)
Longford
Roscommon
Ballinasloe (Béal Átha na Sluaighe)
Castlebar (Caisleán an Bharraigh)
Westport
Ballina (Béal an Átha)
Sligo (Sligeach)
Donegal
Letterkenny
Strabane
Omagh
Enniskillen
Monaghan (Muineachán)
Cavan
Carrick-on-Shannon
Clifden
Connemara
Connemara National Park
Achill Island
Achill Head
Clare Island
Clew Bay
Croagh Patrick
Blacksod Bay
Belmullet
Erris Head
Inishkea North
Inishkea South
Killala Bay
Benwee Head
Downpatrick Head
Glenveagh National Park
Errigal
Derryveagh Mts
Blue Stack Mts
Slieve League
Aran Island
Burtonport
Dungloe
Gweebarra Bay
Dawros Head
Loughros More Bay
Rossan Pt
Malin More
Killybegs
Muckross Head
St John's Pt
Bundoran
Ballyshannon
Lough Derg
Lower Lough Erne
Upper Lough Erne
Lough Ree
Lough Derg
Lough Corrib
Lough Mask
Lough Conn
Bog of Allen
Slieve Bloom Mts
Wicklow Mts
Wicklow Mts National Park
Lugnaquilla Mtn
Blackstairs Mts
Mt Leinster
Comeragh Mts
Knockmealdown Mts
Galtymore
Galtee Mts
Golden Vale
Silvermine Mts
Slieve Aughty Mts
Nagles Mts
Boggeragh Mts
Mullaghareirk Mts
Glanaruddery Mts
DONEGAL
TYRONE
FERMANAGH
MONAGHAN
CAVAN
LEITRIM
SLIGO
MAYO
ROSCOMMON
LONGFORD
GALWAY
WESTMEATH
MEATH
LOUTH
OFFALY
KILDARE
LAOIS
WICKLOW
CARLOW
KILKENNY
WEXFORD
CLARE
TIPPERARY
LIMERICK
KERRY
CORK
WATERFORD
Holyhead
Liverpool
Douglas
Fishguard
Pembroke Dock
Cherbourg & Le Havre
Cherbourg, Le Havre, Roscoff, St-Malo & Swansea
64
62
66
1:1.5M
Miles
Km
Metres
Feet
SEA LEVEL
Conic Equidistant Projection
© Bartholomew

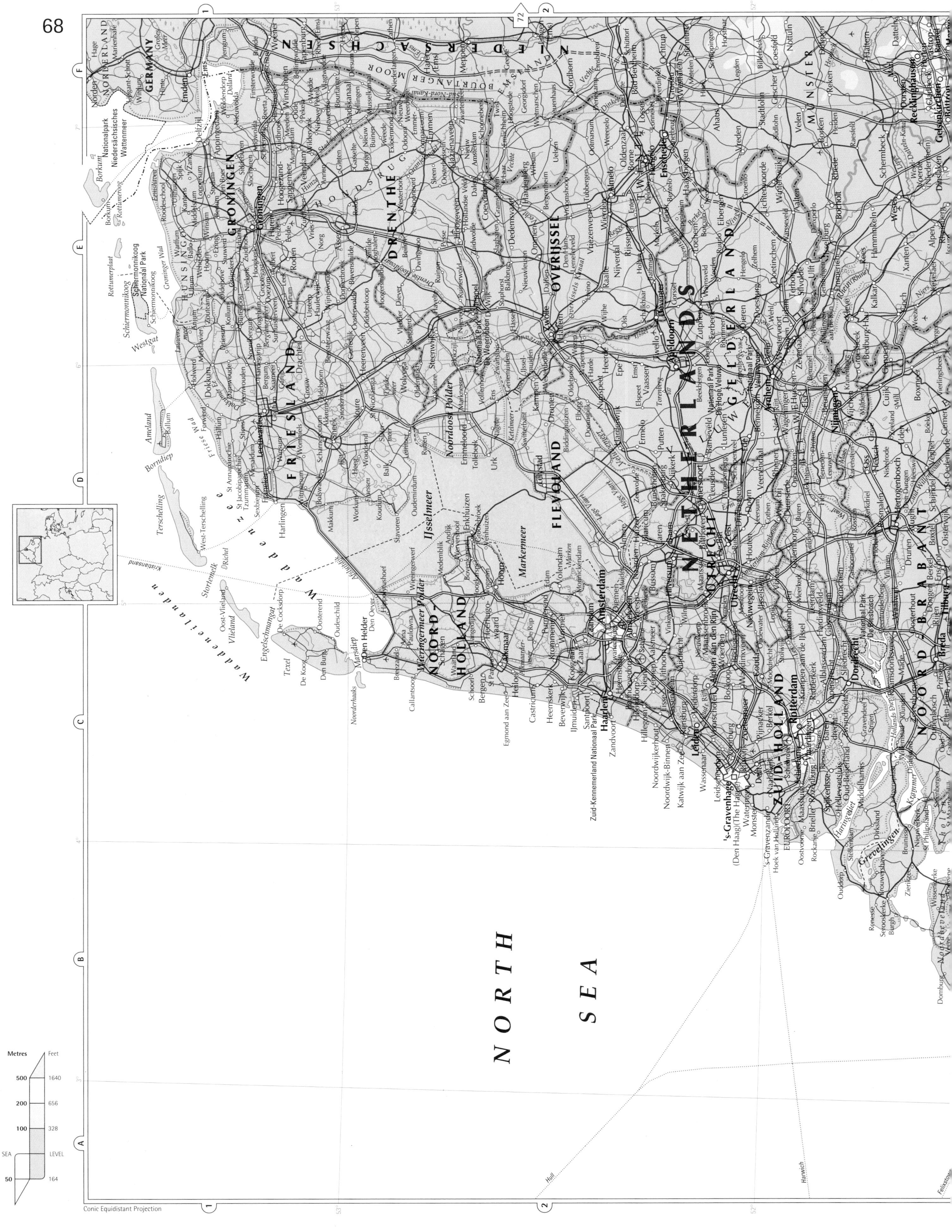

Conic Equidistant Projection

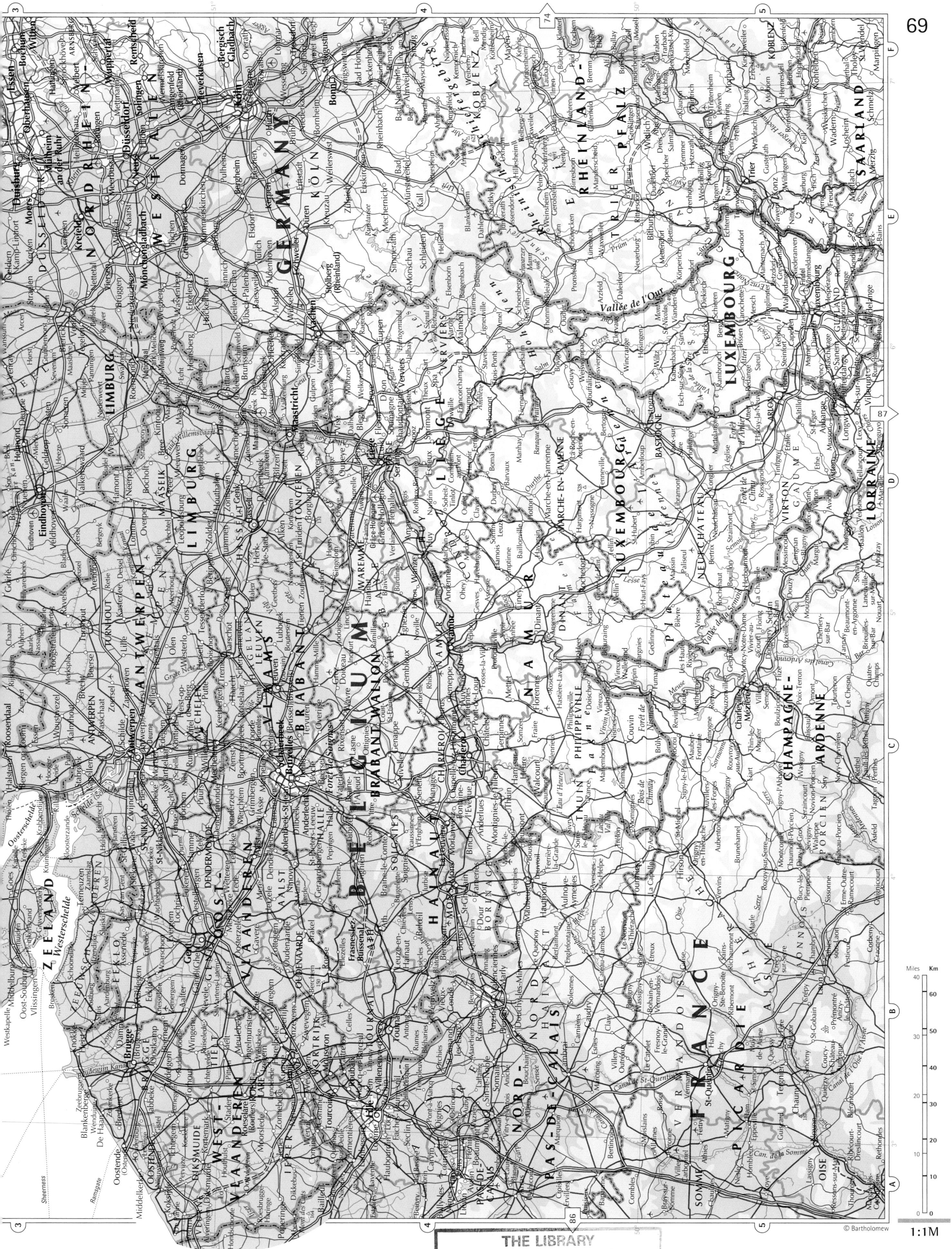

1:1M

© Bartholomew

THE LIBRARY
GUILDFORD COLLEGE

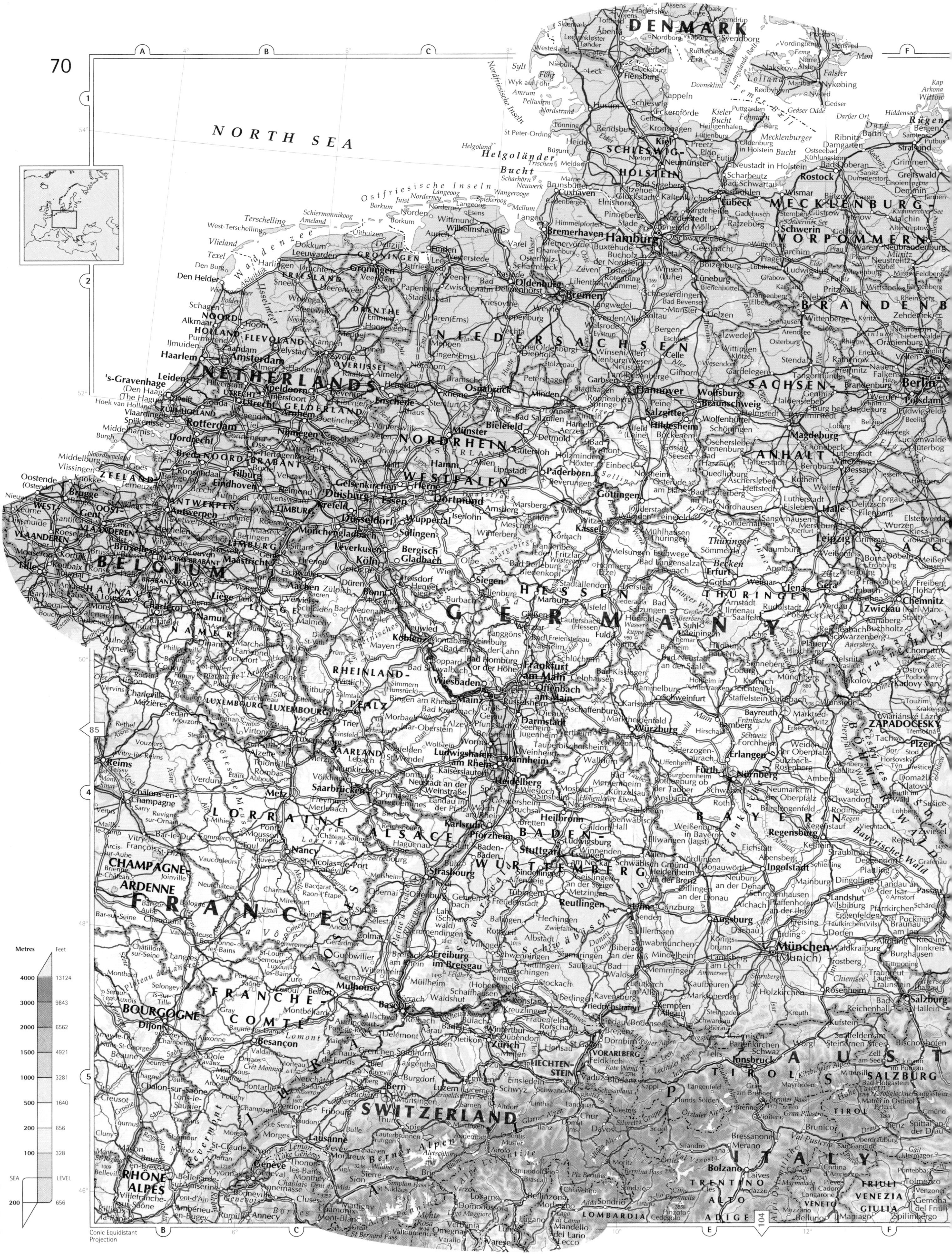
DENMARK
NORTH SEA
NETHERLANDS
BELGIUM
GERMANY
FRANCE
SWITZERLAND
LIECHTENSTEIN
AUSTRIA
ITALY
LUXEMBOURG
SCHLESWIG-HOLSTEIN
MECKLENBURG-VORPOMMERN
NIEDERSACHSEN
BRANDENBURG
SACHSEN-ANHALT
NORDRHEIN-WESTFALEN
HESSEN
THÜRINGEN
SACHSEN
RHEINLAND-PFALZ
SAARLAND
BADEN-WÜRTTEMBERG
BAYERN
LORRAINE
ALSACE
CHAMPAGNE-ARDENNE
FRANCHE-COMTÉ
BOURGOGNE
RHÔNE-ALPES
ZAPADOČESKÝ
TIROL
VORARLBERG
SALZBURG
TRENTINO ALTO ADIGE
LOMBARDIA
FRIULI VENEZIA GIULIA
VENETO
Ostfriesische Inseln
Nordfriesische Inseln
Helgoländer Bucht
Waddenzee
Amsterdam
Berlin
Hamburg
Bremen
Hannover
Köln
Frankfurt am Main
Stuttgart
München (Munich)
Zürich
Bern
Strasbourg
Bruxelles
Luxembourg
Metz
Nancy
Reims
Dijon
Genève
Lausanne
Innsbruck
Praha
Conic Equidistant Projection
Metres
Feet
4000
13124
3000
9843
2000
6562
1500
4921
1000
3281
500
1640
200
656
100
328
SEA
LEVEL
200
656
85
104

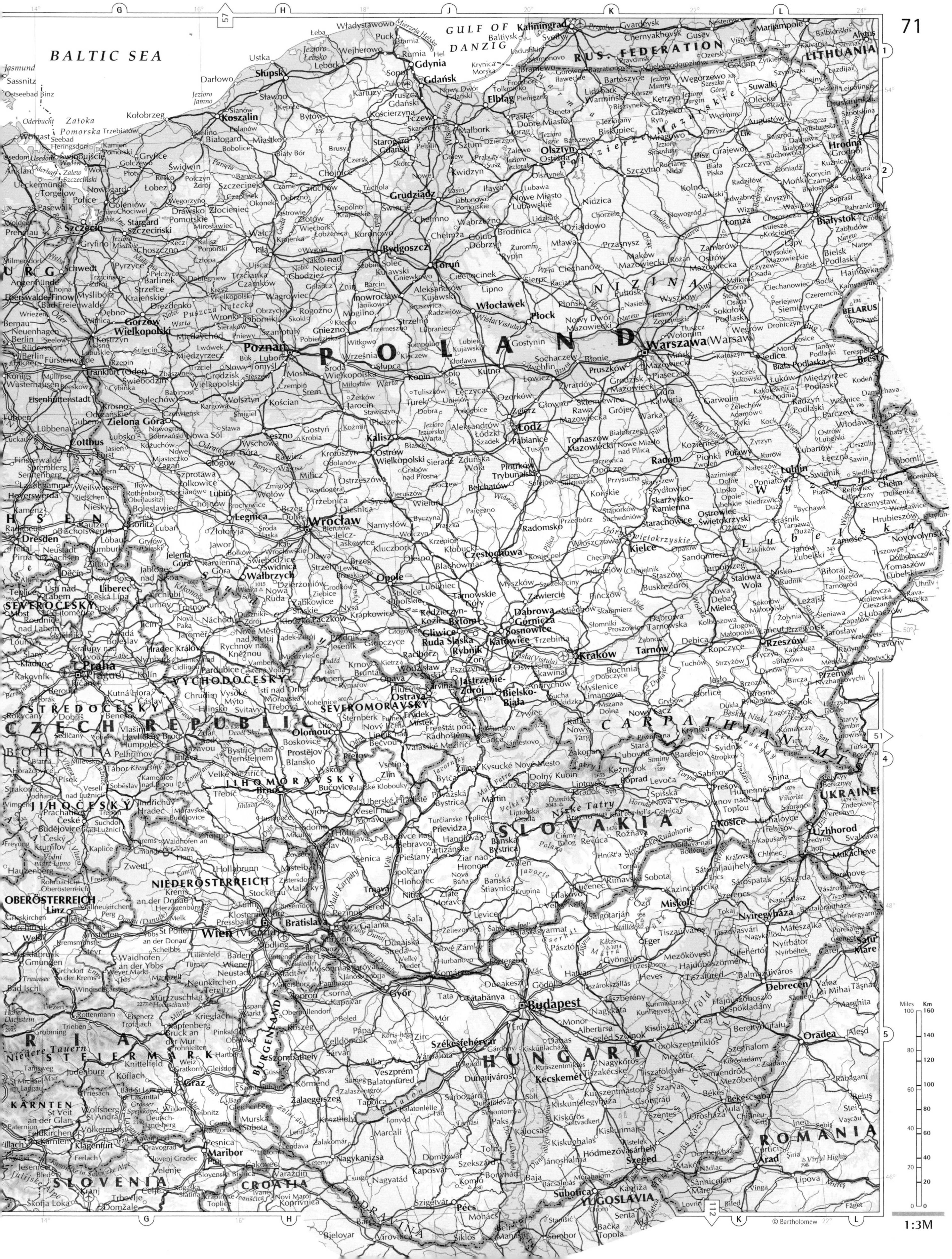
BALTIC SEA
GULF OF DANZIG
RUS. FEDERATION
LITHUANIA
BELARUS
POLAND
CZECH REPUBLIC
SLOVAKIA
HUNGARY
UKRAINE
ROMANIA
SLOVENIA
CROATIA
YUGOSLAVIA
CARPATHIAN MTS
Kaliningrad
Gdańsk
Gdynia
Szczecin
Koszalin
Słupsk
Elbląg
Olsztyn
Bydgoszcz
Toruń
Grudziądz
Białystok
Poznań
Warszawa (Warsaw)
Łódź
Wrocław
Opole
Częstochowa
Katowice
Kraków
Kielce
Radom
Lublin
Rzeszów
Tarnów
Praha (Prague)
Dresden
Brno
Olomouc
Ostrava
Bratislava
Wien (Vienna)
Linz
Graz
Maribor
Košice
Uzhhorod
Budapest
Debrecen
Miskolc
Szeged
Pécs
Győr
Kecskemét
Oradea
Arad
Subotica
© Bartholomew
1:3M
Miles
Km

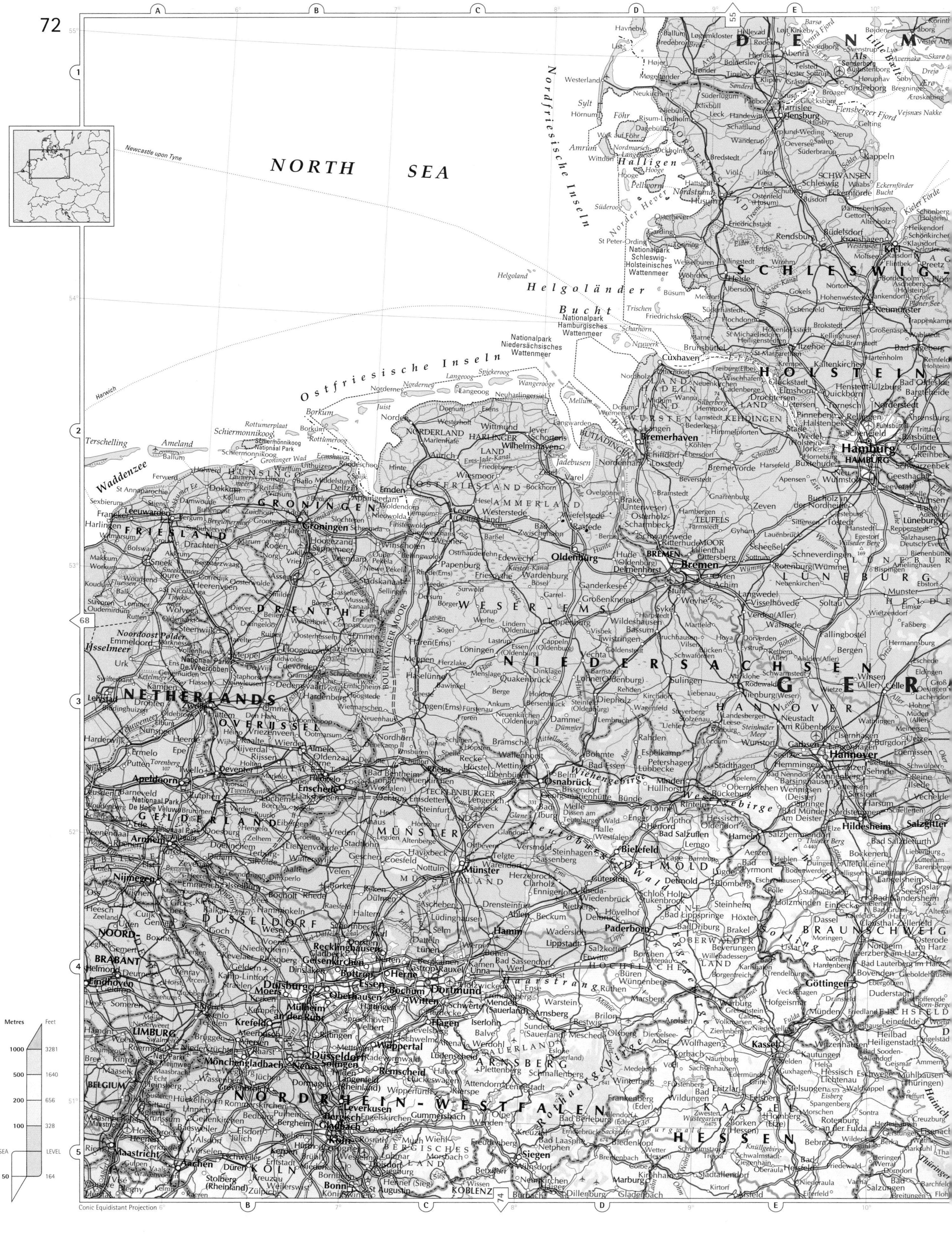
NORTH SEA
DENMARK
SCHLESWIG-HOLSTEIN
NIEDERSACHSEN
NETHERLANDS
NORDRHEIN-WESTFALEN
HESSEN
GERMANY
BELGIUM
Nordfriesische Inseln
Ostfriesische Inseln
Helgoländer Bucht
Waddenzee
Ijsselmeer
Hamburg
Bremen
Bremerhaven
Hannover
Kiel
Flensburg
Groningen
Leeuwarden
Osnabrück
Münster
Bielefeld
Dortmund
Essen
Duisburg
Düsseldorf
Köln
Bonn
Aachen
Maastricht
Kassel
Göttingen
Hildesheim
Oldenburg
Emden
Wilhelmshaven
Cuxhaven
Lüneburg
Paderborn
Siegen
Marburg
Enschede
Arnhem
Nijmegen
Eindhoven
Apeldoorn
Zwolle
Newcastle upon Tyne
Harwich
Metres
Feet
1000
3281
500
1640
200
656
100
328
SEA
LEVEL
50
164
Conic Equidistant Projection

BALTIC SEA
Bornholm (Denmark)
Mecklenburger Bucht
Kieler Bucht
Lolland
Falster
Møn
Rügen
Zatoka Pomorska
Oderhaff
MECKLENBURG-VORPOMMERN
BRANDENBURG
SACHSEN-ANHALT
SACHSEN
THÜRINGEN
POLAND
CZECH REPUBLIC
Rostock
Stralsund
Greifswald
Schwerin
Lübeck
Wismar
Neubrandenburg
Szczecin
Berlin
Potsdam
Brandenburg
Magdeburg
Halle
Leipzig
Dresden
Chemnitz
Cottbus
Frankfurt (Oder)
Gorzów Wielkopolski
Zielona Góra
Koszalin
Wolfsburg
Braunschweig
Erfurt
Weimar
Jena
Gera
Görlitz
Liberec
Miles
Km

1:1.5M

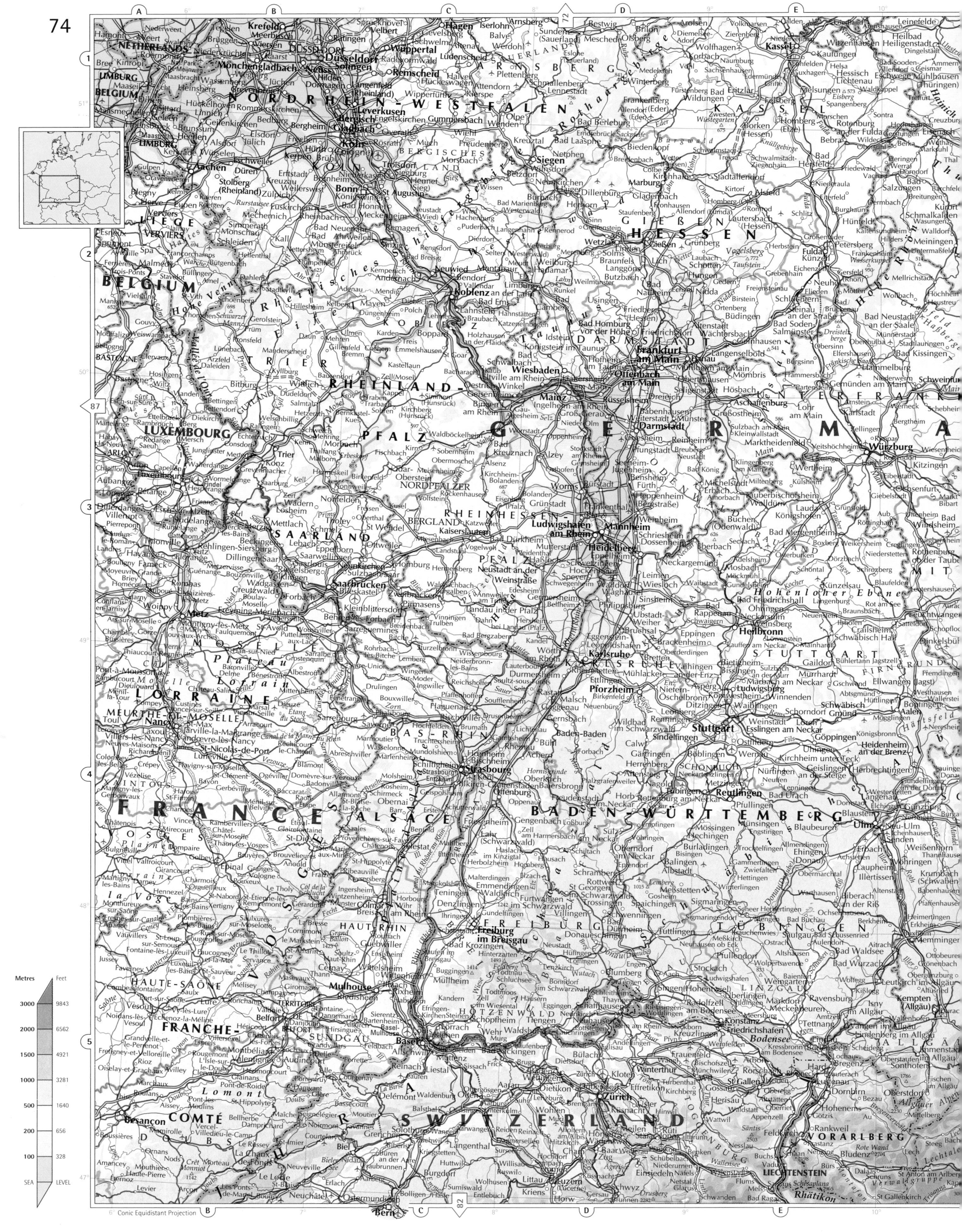
NORDRHEIN-WESTFALEN
HESSEN
RHEINLAND-PFALZ
SAARLAND
BADEN-WÜRTTEMBERG
GERMANY
FRANCE
LORRAINE
ALSACE
FRANCHE-COMTÉ
SWITZERLAND
BELGIUM
NETHERLANDS
LUXEMBOURG
LIECHTENSTEIN
VORARLBERG
Düsseldorf
Köln
Bonn
Koblenz
Frankfurt am Main
Wiesbaden
Mainz
Mannheim
Heidelberg
Karlsruhe
Stuttgart
Strasbourg
Metz
Nancy
Saarbrücken
Luxembourg
Basel
Zürich
Bern
Freiburg im Breisgau
Würzburg
Kassel
Metres
Feet
3000
2000
1500
1000
500
200
100
SEA
9843
6562
4921
3281
1640
656
328
LEVEL
87
72
82
Conic Equidistant Projection

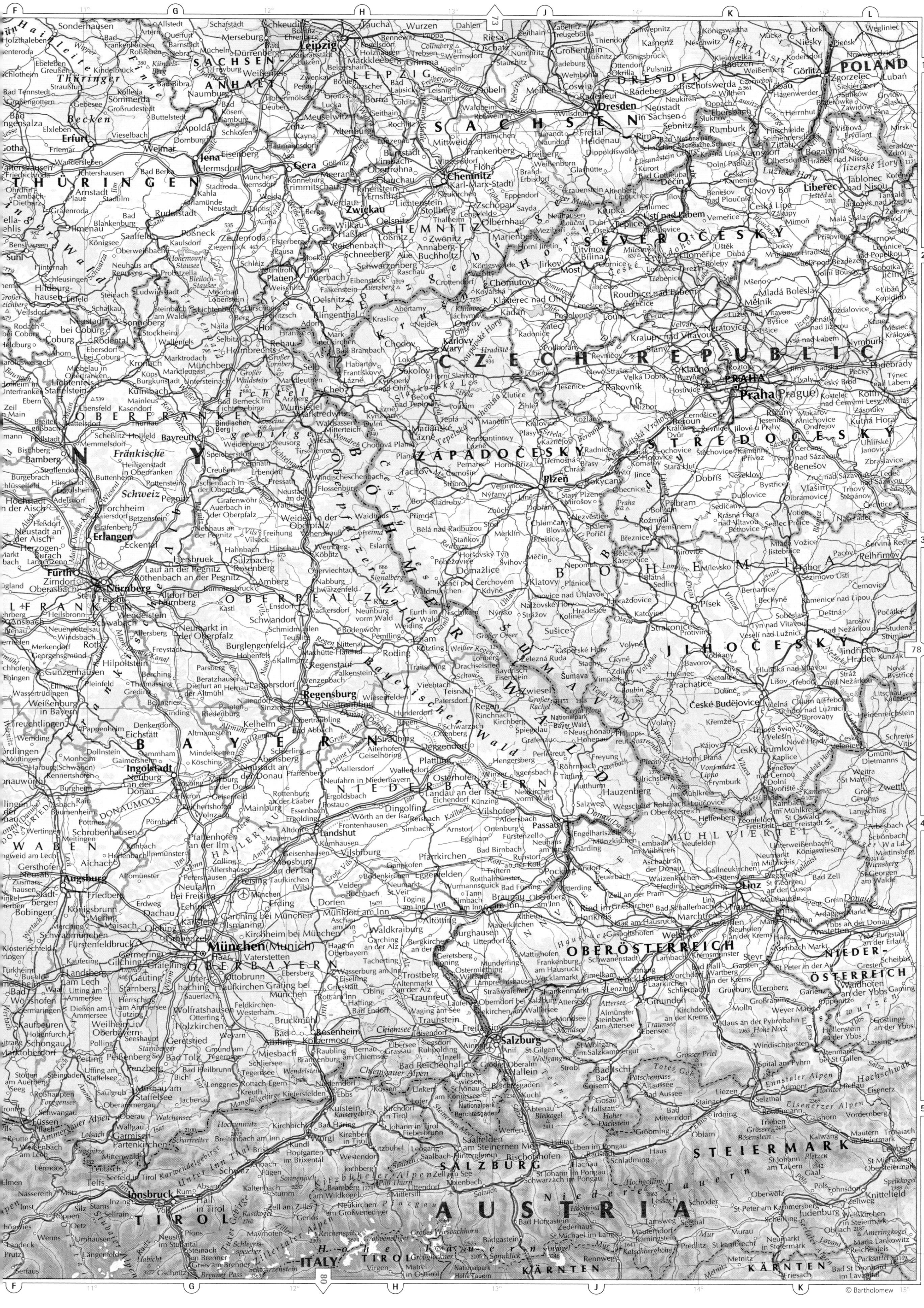
POLAND
CZECH REPUBLIC
AUSTRIA
ITALY
SACHSEN
SACHSEN-ANHALT
THÜRINGEN
BAYERN
OBERFRANKEN
OBERPFALZ
NIEDERBAYERN
OBERBAYERN
SEVEROČESKÝ
ZÁPADOČESKÝ
STŘEDOČESKÝ
JIHOČESKÝ
BOHEMIA
OBERÖSTERREICH
NIEDER-ÖSTERREICH
STEIERMARK
SALZBURG
TIROL
KÄRNTEN
Leipzig
Dresden
Chemnitz
Zwickau
Plauen
Erfurt
Weimar
Jena
Gera
Praha (Prague)
Plzeň
Nürnberg
Erlangen
Bamberg
Bayreuth
Regensburg
Ingolstadt
Augsburg
München (Munich)
Landshut
Passau
Linz
Salzburg
Innsbruck
Liberec
Ústí nad Labem
České Budějovice
Karlovy Vary
F
G
H
J
K
L
1
2
3
4
5
73
78
80
11°
12°
13°
14°
15°
51°
50°
49°
48°
47°
© Bartholomew

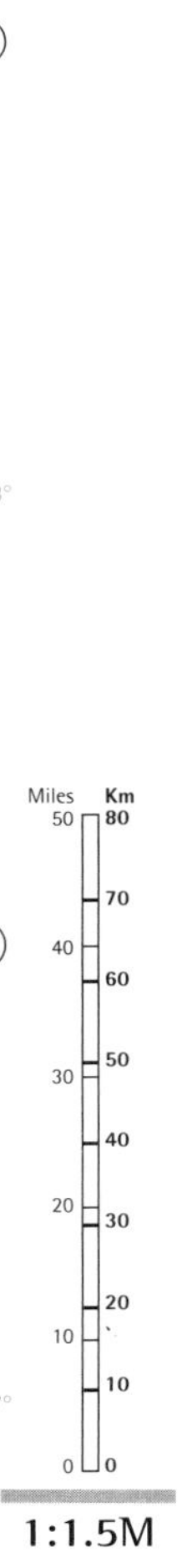
Miles
Km
50
40
30
20
10
0
80
70
60
50
40
30
20
10
0

1:1.5M

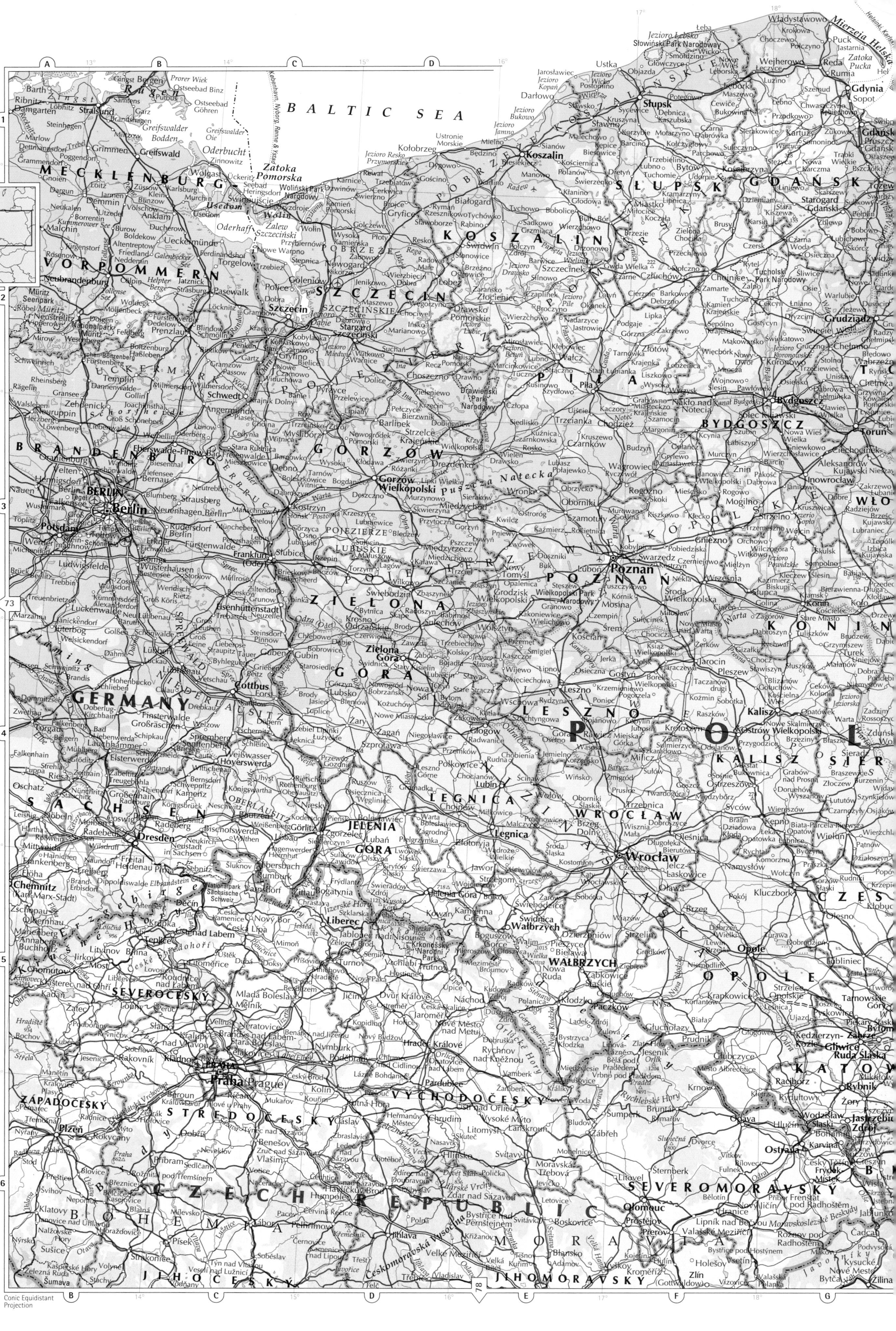
BALTIC SEA
MECKLENBURG-
VORPOMMERN
BRANDENBURG
GERMANY
SACHSEN
POLAND
CZECH REPUBLIC
BOHEMIA
MORAVIA
SZCZECIN
KOSZALIN
SŁUPSK
GDAŃSK
PIŁA
GORZÓW
ZIELONA GÓRA
POZNAŃ
BYDGOSZCZ
LESZNO
KALISZ
KONIN
LEGNICA
JELENIA GÓRA
WROCŁAW
WAŁBRZYCH
OPOLE
SEVEROČESKÝ
ZÁPADOČESKÝ
STŘEDOČESKÝ
VÝCHODOČESKÝ
JIHOČESKÝ
JIHOMORAVSKÝ
SEVEROMORAVSKÝ
Berlin
Szczecin
Poznań
Wrocław
Dresden
Praha
Gdynia
Bydgoszcz
Toruń
Opole
Ostrava
Olomouc
Liberec
Plzeň
Cottbus
Frankfurt (Oder)
Zielona Góra
Gorzów Wielkopolski
Koszalin
Słupsk
Legnica
Kalisz
Hradec Králové
Pardubice
Jihlava
Chemnitz (Karl-Marx-Stadt)
Zatoka Pomorska
Zalew Szczeciński
Rügen
Usedom
Wolin
Mierzeja Helska
Zatoka Pucka
73
78
A B C D
B C D E F G
1 2 3 4 5 6
13° 14° 15° 16° 17° 18°
54° 53° 52° 51° 50°
Conic Equidistant Projection

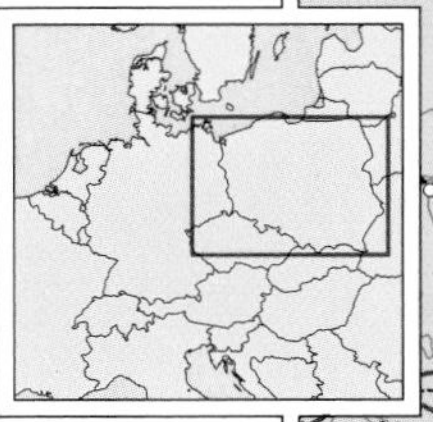

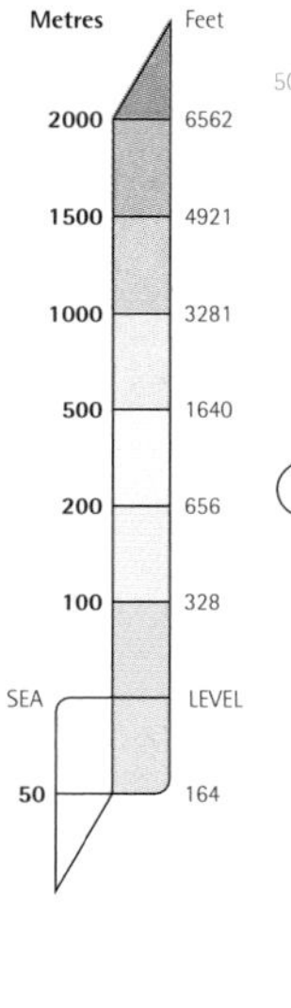
Metres
Feet
2000 6562
1500 4921
1000 3281
500 1640
200 656
100 328
SEA LEVEL
50 164

POLAND

GULF OF DANZIG

RUSSIAN FEDERATION

LITHUANIA

BELARUS

UKRAINE

SLOVAKIA

ELBLĄG

OLSZTYN

SUWAŁKI

ŁOMŻA

BIAŁYSTOK

HRODNA

CIECHANÓW

OSTROŁĘKA

PŁOCK

WARSZAWA

SIEDLCE

BIAŁA PODLASKA

BREST

SKIERNIEWICE

ŁÓDŹ

RADOM

LUBLIN

CHEŁM

VOLYNS'K

PIOTRKÓW

KIELCE

TARNOBRZEG

ZAMOŚĆ

RZESZÓW

PRZEMYŚL

L'VIV

KRAKÓW

TARNÓW

NOWY SĄCZ

KROSNO

CARPATHIAN MTS

Kaliningrad · Elbląg · Olsztyn · Suwałki · Białystok · Hrodna · Warszawa (Warsaw) · Płock · Włocławek · Łódź · Radom · Siedlce · Brest · Lublin · Chełm · Kielce · Częstochowa · Katowice · Kraków · Tarnów · Rzeszów · Przemyśl · L'viv (L'vov) · Kovel' · Lida

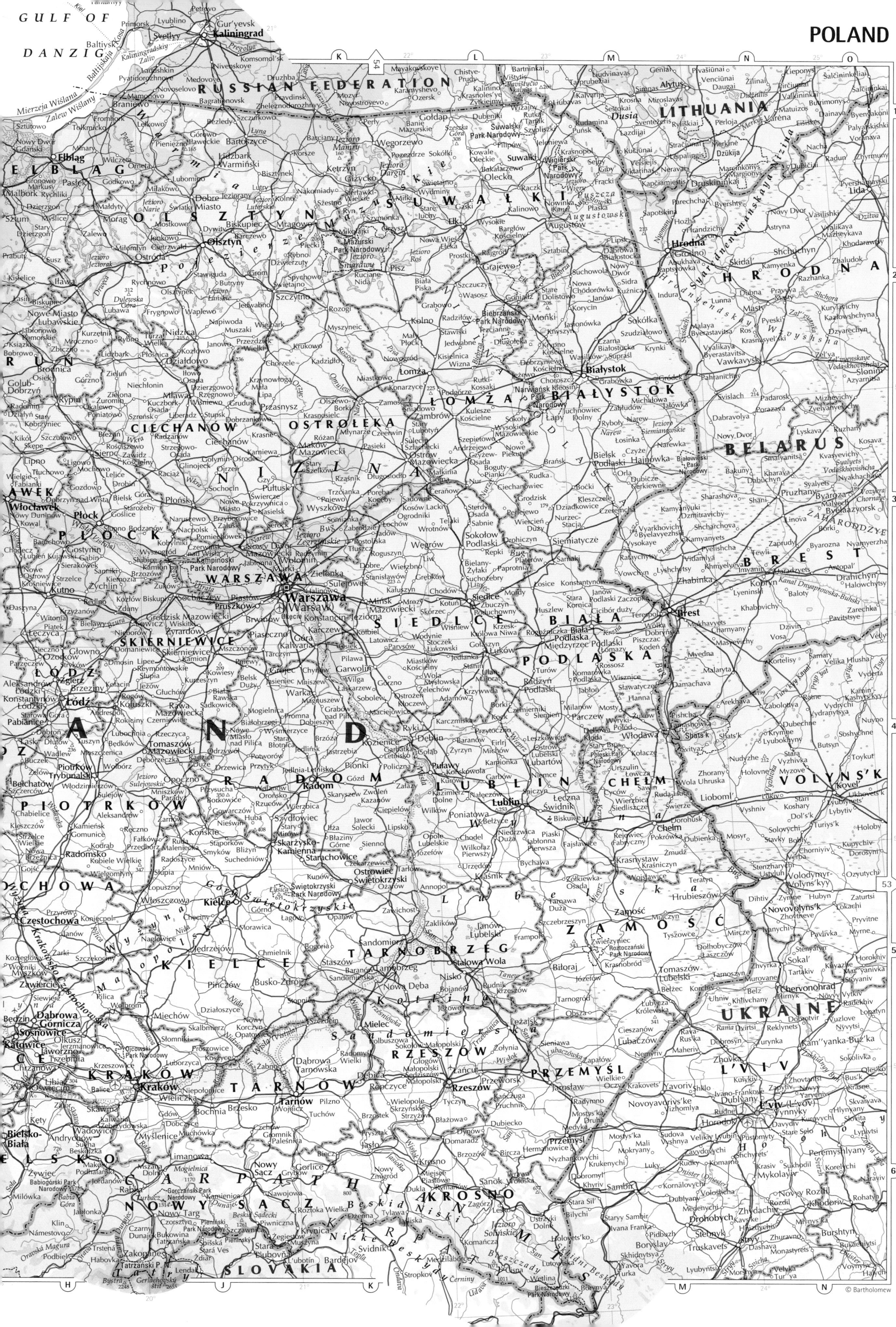

Miles / Km

1:1.8M

© Bartholomew

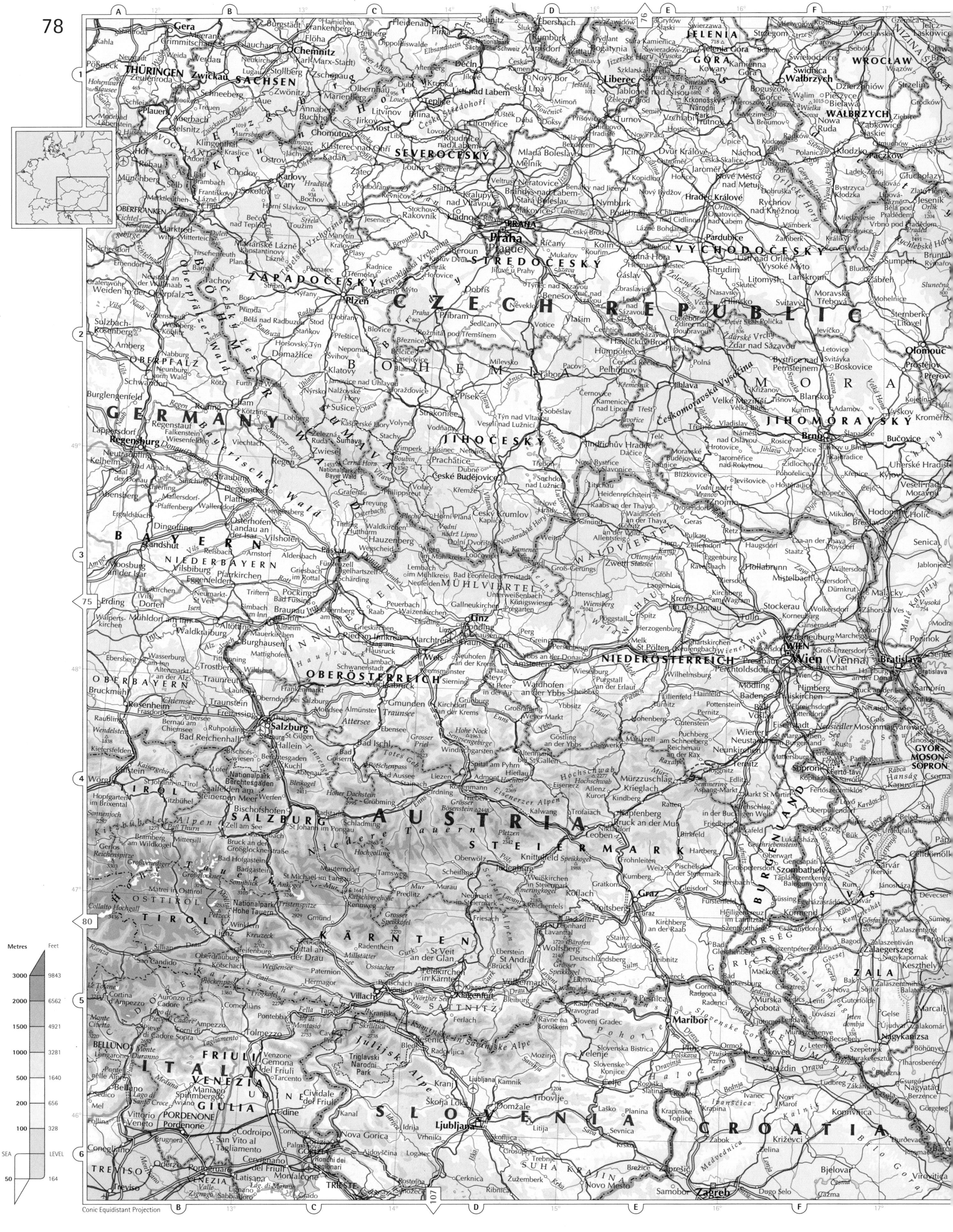

Conic Equidistant Projection

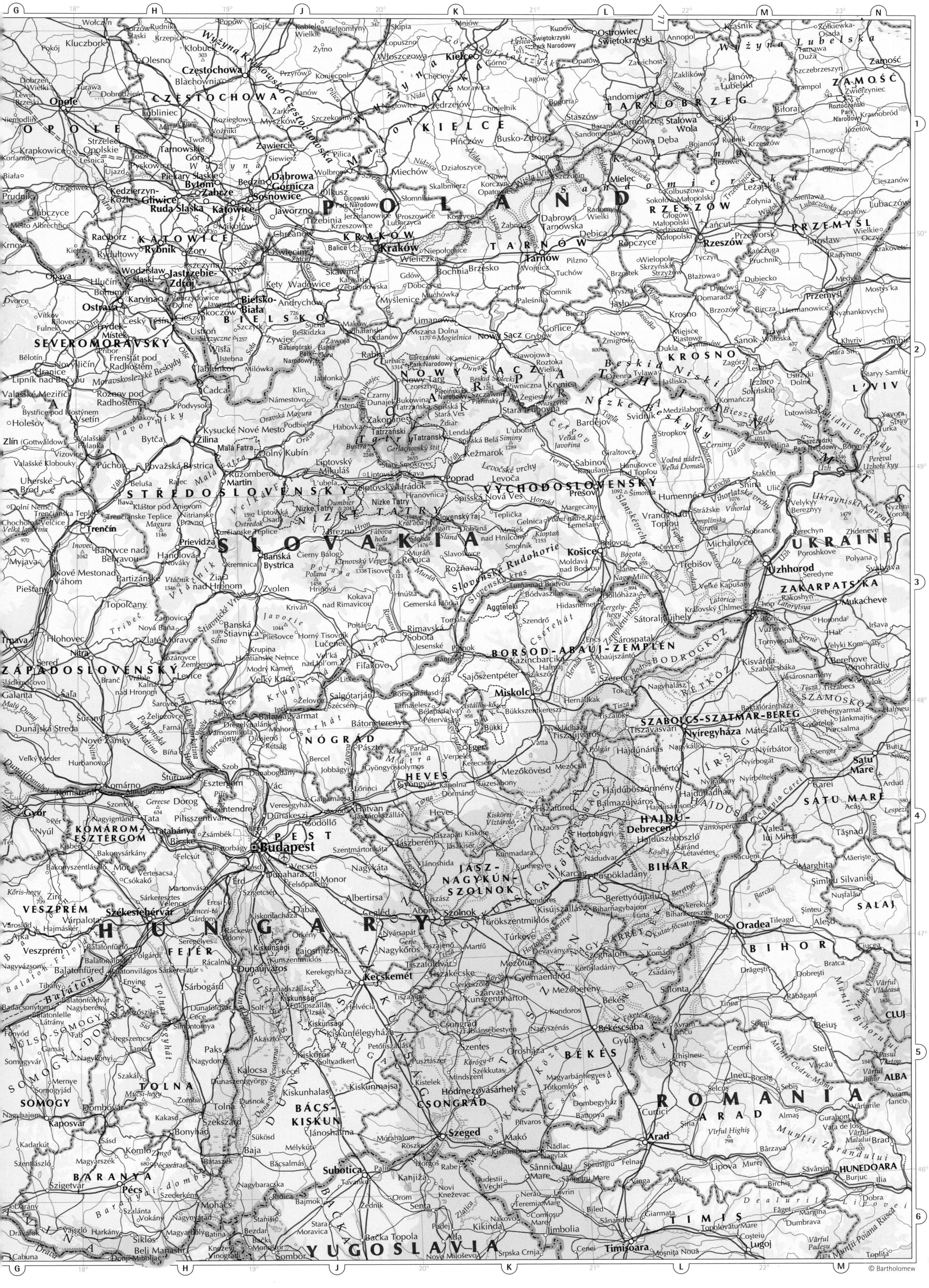
POLAND
SLOVAKIA
HUNGARY
ROMANIA
UKRAINE
YUGOSLAVIA
OPOLE
CZĘSTOCHOWA
KATOWICE
BIELSKO
KIELCE
TARNOBRZEG
KRAKÓW
TARNÓW
RZESZÓW
PRZEMYŚL
NOWY SĄCZ
KROSNO
ZAMOŚĆ
L'VIV
ZAKARPATS'KA
SEVEROMORAVSKÝ
STŘEDOSLOVENSKÝ
VÝCHODOSLOVENSKÝ
ZÁPADOSLOVENSKÝ
BORSOD-ABAÚJ-ZEMPLÉN
SZABOLCS-SZATMÁR-BEREG
NÓGRÁD
HEVES
PEST
KOMÁROM-ESZTERGOM
VESZPRÉM
FEJÉR
JÁSZ-NAGYKUN-SZOLNOK
HAJDÚ-BIHAR
BÉKÉS
CSONGRÁD
BÁCS-KISKUN
TOLNA
SOMOGY
BARANYA
SATU MARE
SALAJ
BIHOR
ARAD
TIMIS
HUNEDOARA
ALBA
CLUJ
Budapest
Kraków
Katowice
Košice
Miskolc
Debrecen
Szeged
Pécs
Győr
Oradea
Arad
Timişoara
Uzhhorod
Rzeszów
Ostrava
Kielce
Częstochowa
Opole
Tarnów
Žilina
Nyíregyháza
Kecskemét
Székesfehérvár
Szolnok
Subotica
Tatry
Nízke Tatry
Slovenské Rudohorie
Balaton
Mátra
Bükk
18°
19°
20°
21°
22°
23°
50°
49°
48°
47°
46°
G
H
J
K
L
M
N
1
2
3
4
5
6
77
© Bartholomew

Miles 60 45 30 15 0
Km 90 75 60 45 30 15 0

1:1.8M

GERMANY
ITALY
SWITZERLAND
LIECHTENSTEIN
BAYERN
OBERBAYERN
NIEDERBAYERN
OBERPFALZ
MITTELFRANKEN
SCHWABEN
BADEN-WÜRTTEMBERG
TIROL
VORARLBERG
SALZBURG
TRENTINO ALTO ADIGE
FRIULI VENEZIA GIULIA
LOMBARDIA
München (Munich)
Augsburg
Regensburg
Ingolstadt
Ulm
Innsbruck
Salzburg
Bolzano
Trento
Bodensee
Metres
Feet
4000
13124
3000
9843
2000
6562
1500
4921
1000
3281
500
1640
200
656
100
328
SEA
LEVEL
50
164
Conic Equidistant Projection

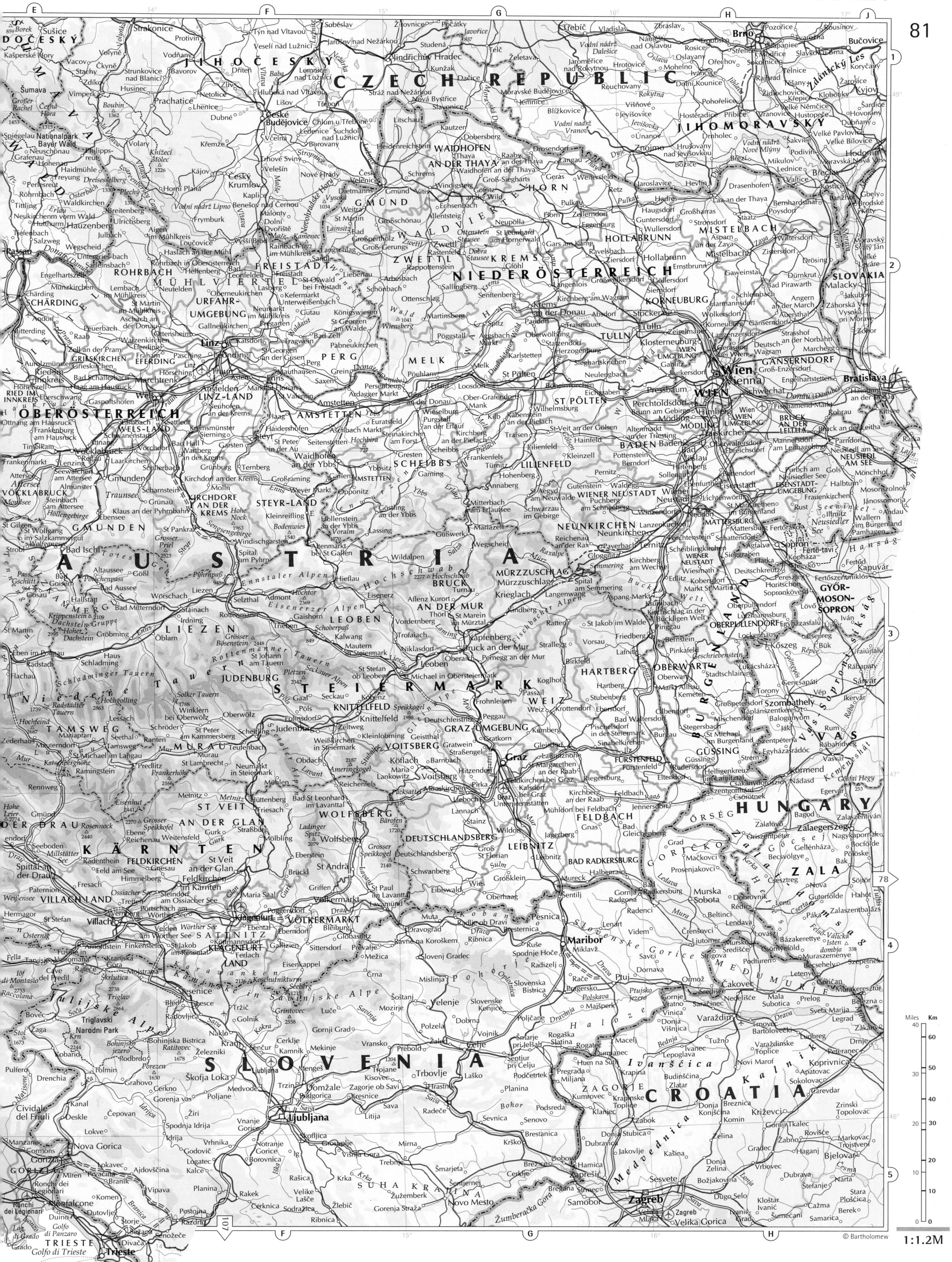
CZECH REPUBLIC
AUSTRIA
SLOVENIA
CROATIA
HUNGARY
SLOVAKIA
JIHOČESKÝ
JIHOMORAVSKÝ
NIEDERÖSTERREICH
OBERÖSTERREICH
STEIERMARK
KÄRNTEN
BURGENLAND
Wien (Vienna)
Bratislava
Graz
Linz
Klagenfurt
Ljubljana
Zagreb
Maribor
Brno
Trieste
Villach
St Pölten
Sopron
Szombathely
Zalaegerszeg
Miles
Km
© Bartholomew

1:1.2M

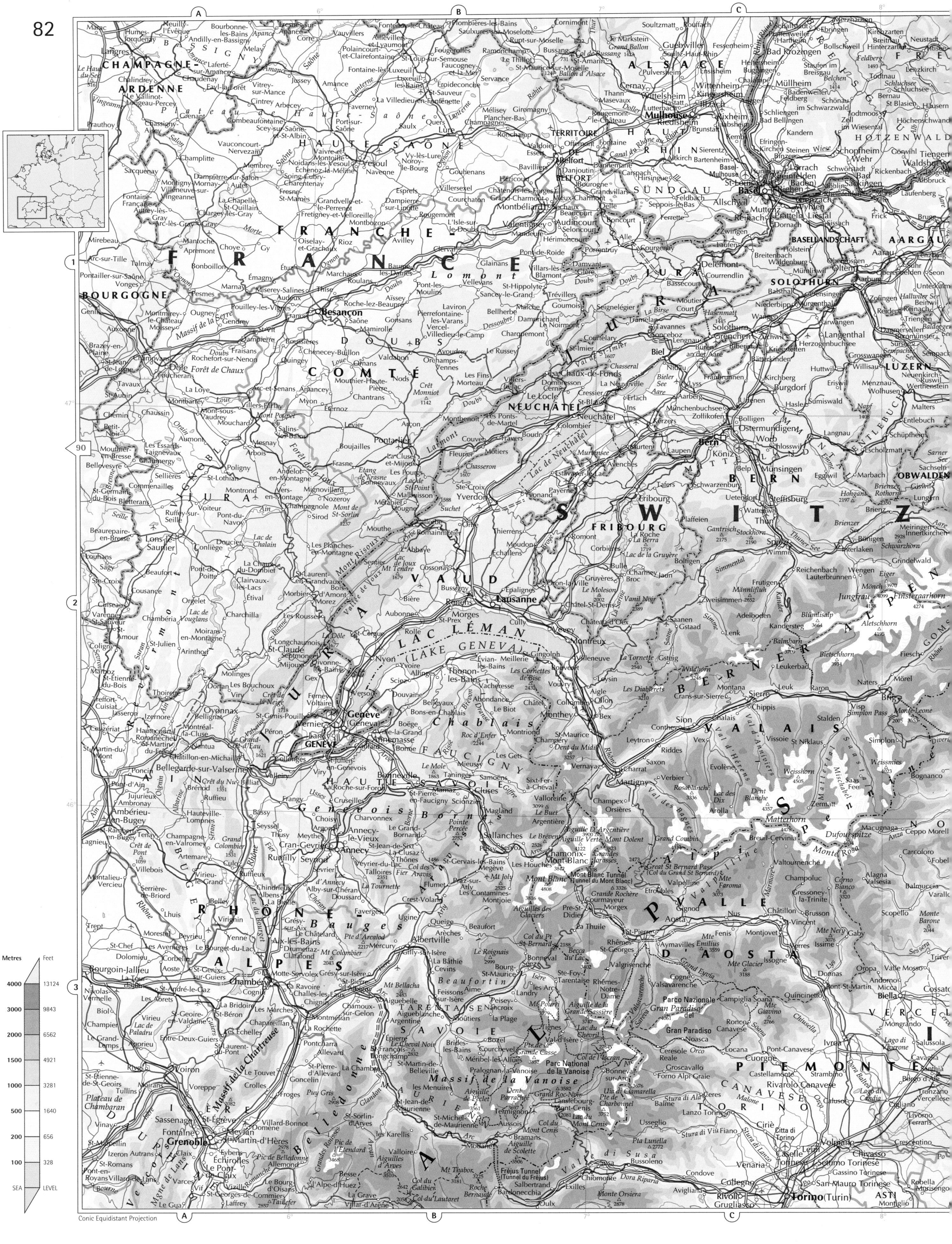

Conic Equidistant Projection

GERMANY
BADEN-WÜRTTEMBERG
BAYERN
SCHWABEN
OBERBAYERN
Bodensee
THURGAU
SCHAFFHAUSEN
ZÜRICH
Zürich
Konstanz
Friedrichshafen
ST GALLEN
St Gallen
APPENZELL
A-R
I-R
VORARLBERG
LIECHTENSTEIN
Vaduz
Bregenz
Feldkirch
Innsbruck
INNSBRUCK
TIROL
AUSTRIA
LANDECK
IMST
REUTTE
BREGENZ
BLUDENZ
Allgäuer Alpen
Lechtaler Alpen
Ötztaler Alpen
Silvretta Gruppe
Rhätikon
SCHWYZ
GLARUS
ZUG
Luzern (Lucerne)
NIDWALDEN
To OBWALDEN
URI
SWITZERLAND
GRAUBÜNDEN
Davos
Chur
St Moritz
Swiss National Park
TICINO
Bellinzona
Lugano
Locarno
ALPS
Lepontine Alpi
Glarner Alpen
BOLZANO
Merano
TRENTINO
ALTO ADIGE
Trento
SONDRIO
Sondrio
Alpi Orobie
BERGAMO
Bergamo
BRESCIA
Brescia
COMO
Como
VARESE
Varese
LOMBARDIA
ITALY
Milano (Milan)
MILANO
Monza
Novara
PAVIA
Pavia
CREMONA
Cremona
MANTOVA
Mantova (Mantua)
VERONA
Verona
VENETO
Lago di Garda
Lago di Como
Lago Maggiore
Piacenza
ALESSANDRIA
Vercelli
Lodi
Parco Nazionale dello Stelvio
Miles
Km
© Bartholomew

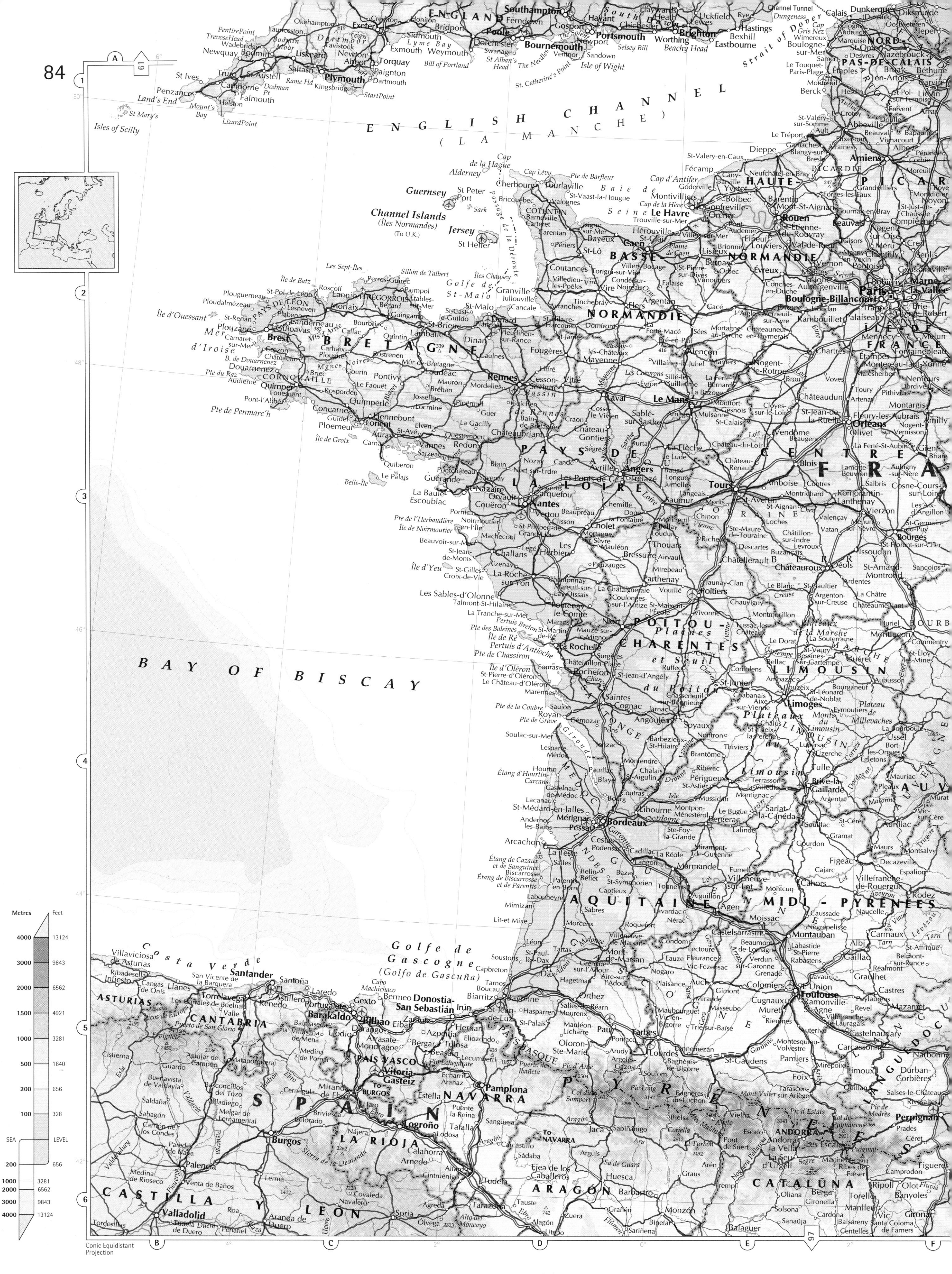
ENGLAND
ENGLISH CHANNEL
(LA MANCHE)
Strait of Dover
Channel Tunnel
Isles of Scilly
Land's End
Plymouth
Southampton
Portsmouth
Brighton
Bournemouth
Channel Islands
(Îles Normandes)
(To U.K.)
Guernsey
Jersey
Alderney
NORD-PAS-DE-CALAIS
PICARDIE
HAUTE-NORMANDIE
BASSE-NORMANDIE
BRETAGNE
PAYS DE LA LOIRE
CENTRE
ÎLE-DE-FRANCE
POITOU-CHARENTES
LIMOUSIN
AQUITAINE
MIDI-PYRÉNÉES
LANGUEDOC
FRANCE
Paris
Le Havre
Rouen
Caen
Rennes
Brest
Nantes
Angers
Le Mans
Tours
Orléans
Poitiers
Limoges
Bordeaux
Toulouse
Perpignan
BAY OF BISCAY
Golfe de Gascogne
(Golfo de Gascuña)
Costa Verde
SPAIN
ASTURIAS
CANTABRIA
PAIS VASCO
NAVARRA
LA RIOJA
ARAGÓN
CATALUÑA
CASTILLA Y LEÓN
ANDORRA
PYRÉNÉES
Santander
Bilbao
Donostia-San Sebastián
Vitoria-Gasteiz
Pamplona
Burgos
Logroño
Valladolid
Huesca
Metres
Feet
4000
13124
3000
9843
2000
6562
1500
4921
1000
3281
500
1640
200
656
100
328
SEA
LEVEL
Conic Equidistant
Projection
A
B
C
D
E
F
1
2
3
4
5
6
61
97

BELGIUM
LUXEMBOURG
LORRAINE
ALSACE
CHAMPAGNE-ARDENNE
BOURGOGNE
FRANCHE-COMTÉ
RHÔNE-ALPES
PROVENCE-ALPES-CÔTE-D'AZUR
ROUSSILLON
MASSIF CENTRAL
RHEINLAND-PFALZ
SAARLAND
BADEN-WÜRTTEMBERG
BAYERN
GERMANY
SWITZERLAND
AUSTRIA
TIROL
CZECH REP.
LIECHTENSTEIN
ITALY
LOMBARDIA
PIEMONTE
VALLE D'AOSTA
LIGURIA
EMILIA-ROMAGNA
VENETO
TRENTINO ALTO ADIGE
TOSCANA
MONACO
CORSE (CORSICA) (France)
LIGURIAN SEA
Golfo di Genova
Golfe du Lion
Miles
Km
© Bartholomew

1:3M

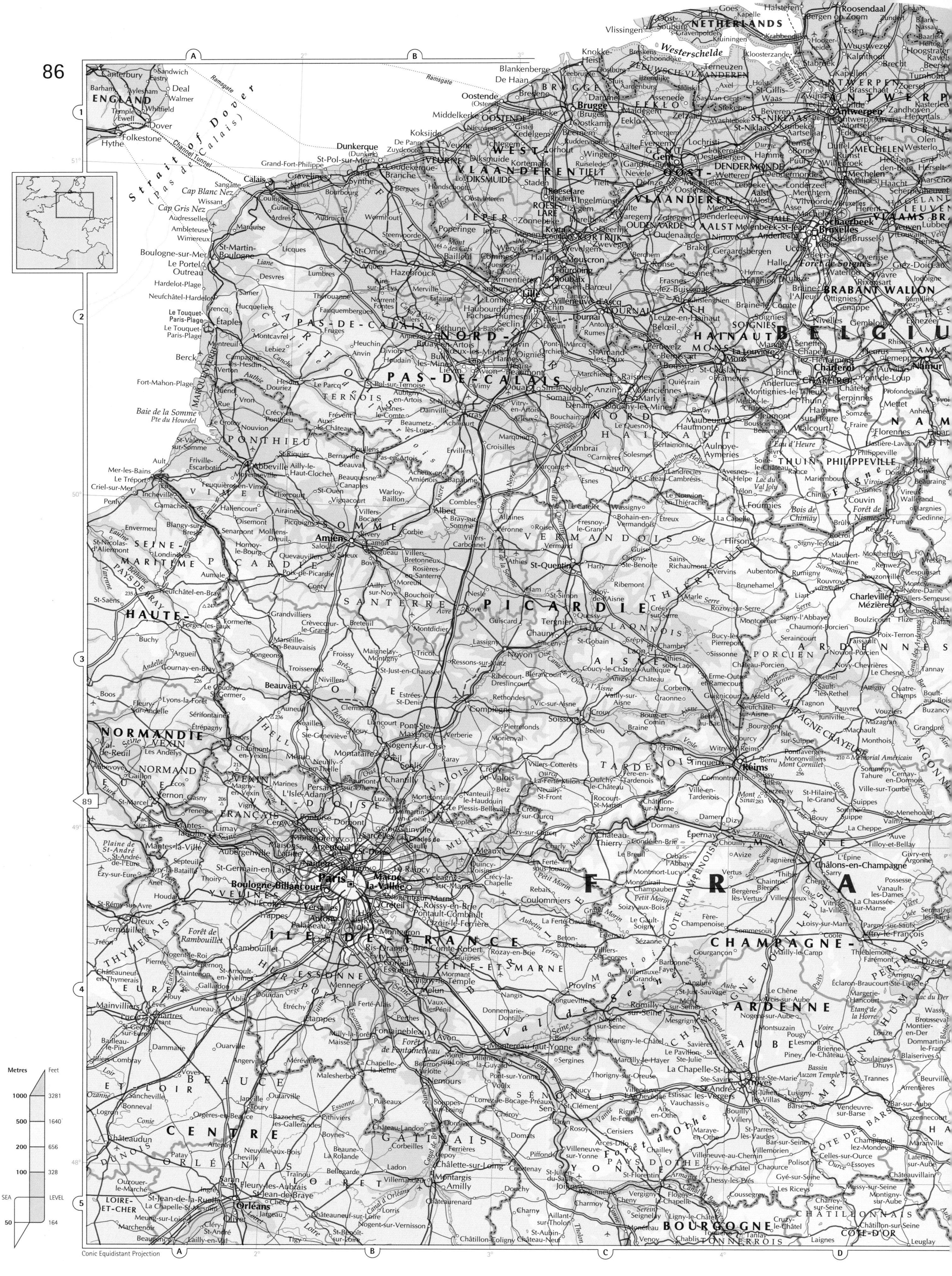
ENGLAND
Strait of Dover
(Pas de Calais)
Channel Tunnel
NETHERLANDS
Westerschelde
ZEEUWSCH-VLAANDEREN
BRUGGE
WEST-VLAANDEREN
OOST-VLAANDEREN
ANTWERPEN
VLAAMS BRABANT
BRABANT WALLON
HAINAUT
BELGIUM
NAMUR
NORD-PAS-DE-CALAIS
PAS-DE-CALAIS
NORD
PICARDIE
SOMME
AISNE
OISE
SEINE-MARITIME
HAUTE-NORMANDIE
EURE
VAL-D'OISE
ÎLE-DE-FRANCE
YVELINES
ESSONNE
SEINE-ET-MARNE
EURE-ET-LOIR
CENTRE
LOIRET
LOIR-ET-CHER
YONNE
BOURGOGNE
CÔTE-D'OR
AUBE
MARNE
CHAMPAGNE-ARDENNE
ARDENNES
FRANCE
Paris
Lille
Amiens
Reims
Orléans
Troyes
Châlons-en-Champagne
Bruxelles (Brussels)
Antwerpen (Antwerp)
Gent
Brugge
Calais
Dunkerque (Dunkirk)
Boulogne-sur-Mer
Beauvais
Rouen
Chartres
Metres
Feet
1000
3281
500
1640
200
656
100
328
SEA LEVEL
50
164
A
B
C
D
1
2
3
4
5
89
Conic Equidistant Projection

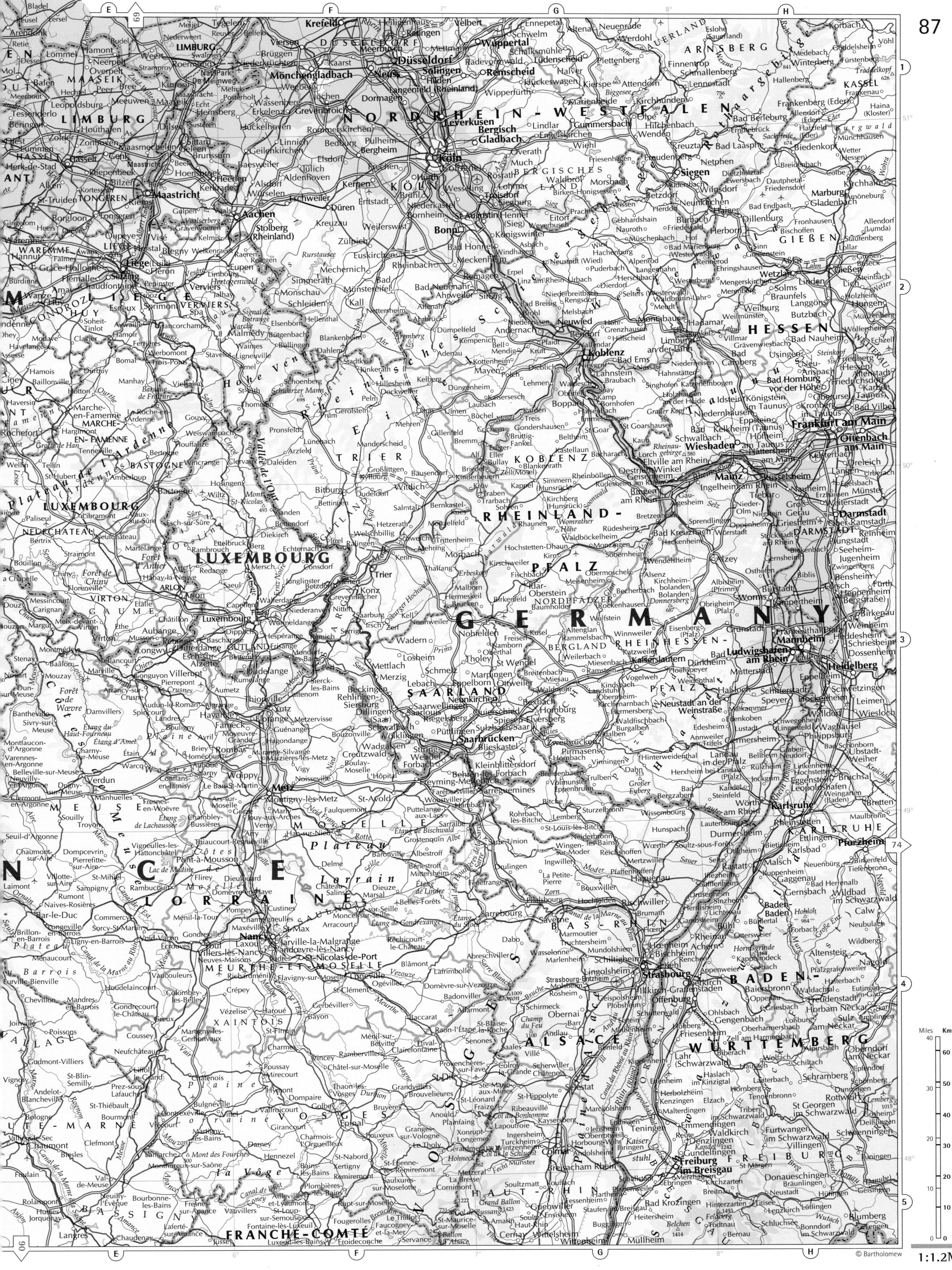
GERMANY
NORDRHEIN-WESTFALEN
RHEINLAND-PFALZ
SAARLAND
HESSEN
BADEN-WÜRTTEMBERG
LUXEMBOURG
LORRAINE
ALSACE
FRANCHE-COMTÉ
LIMBURG
LIÈGE
MOSELLE
MEUSE
MEURTHE-ET-MOSELLE
VOSGES
BAS-RHIN
HAUT-RHIN
Düsseldorf
Köln
Bonn
Aachen
Koblenz
Trier
Saarbrücken
Mainz
Wiesbaden
Frankfurt am Main
Darmstadt
Mannheim
Heidelberg
Karlsruhe
Strasbourg
Metz
Nancy
Colmar
Freiburg im Breisgau
Liège
Maastricht
Luxembourg
Kassel
Marburg
Gießen
Siegen
Kaiserslautern
Ludwigshafen am Rhein
Épinal
Chaumont
Langres
Bar-le-Duc
Verdun
Miles
Km
© Bartholomew
1:1.2M

ENGLISH CHANNEL
(LA MANCHE)
Alderney
Guernsey
Sark
Jersey
CHANNEL ISLANDS
(ÎLES NORMANDES)
(To United Kingdom)
St Peter Port
St Helier
Passage de la Déroute
Cap de la Hague
Cherbourg
Octeville
Équerdreville-Hainneville
Valognes
COTENTIN
Les Minquiers
Îles Chausey
Granville
Golfe de St-Malo
Cap Fréhel
St-Malo
Dinard
Baie du Mont St-Michel
Les Sept-Îles
Les Triagoz
Île de Batz
Roscoff
Morlaix
Lannion
TRÉGORROIS
Perros-Guirec
Paimpol
Guingamp
St-Brieuc
Baie de St-Brieuc
Lamballe
Dinan
PAYS DE LÉON
Île d'Ouessant
Passage du Fromveur
Île Molène
Île de Beniguet
Pte de St-Mathieu
Brest
Landerneau
Guipavas
Le Relecq-Kerhuon
Plougastel-Daoulas
Goulet de Brest
Presq. de Crozon
Crozon
Camaret-sur-Mer
Pte de Penhir
Mer d'Iroise
Cap de la Chèvre
Baie de Douarnenez
Douarnenez
Île de Sein
Pte du Raz
Audierne
CORNOUAILLE
Quimper
Concarneau
Quimperlé
Pte de Penmarc'h
Îles de Glénan
Monts d'Arrée
FINISTÈRE
CÔTES-D'ARMOR
BRETAGNE
MORBIHAN
Landes de Lanvaux
Montagnes Noires
Pontivy
Loudéac
Lac de Guerlédan
Lorient
Île de Groix
Hennebont
Auray
Vannes
Carnac
Quiberon
Presq. de Quiberon
Passage de la Teignouse
Belle-Île
Le Palais
Île de Houat
Île de Hœdic
Presq. de Rhuys
ILLE-ET-VILAINE
Rennes
Bassin de Rennes
Fougères
Vitré
Redon
Châteaubriant
LOIRE-ATLANTIQUE
GRANDE BRIÈRE
Guérande
La Baule
St-Nazaire
Loire
Nantes
Rezé
St-Sébastien
PAYS DE RETZ
Lac de Grand-Lieu
Pte de St-Gildas
Baie de Bourgneuf
Île de Noirmoutier
Noirmoutier-en-l'Île
Challans
Marais Breton
Île d'Yeu
Port-Joinville
St-Gilles-Croix-de-Vie
VENDÉE
La Roche-sur-Yon
BOCAGE VENDÉEN
BAY OF BISCAY
Cork & Rosslare
Cork
Plymouth
Weymouth
Portsmouth
Metres
Feet
200
656
100
328
SEA
LEVEL
50
164
200
656
Conic Equidistant Projection

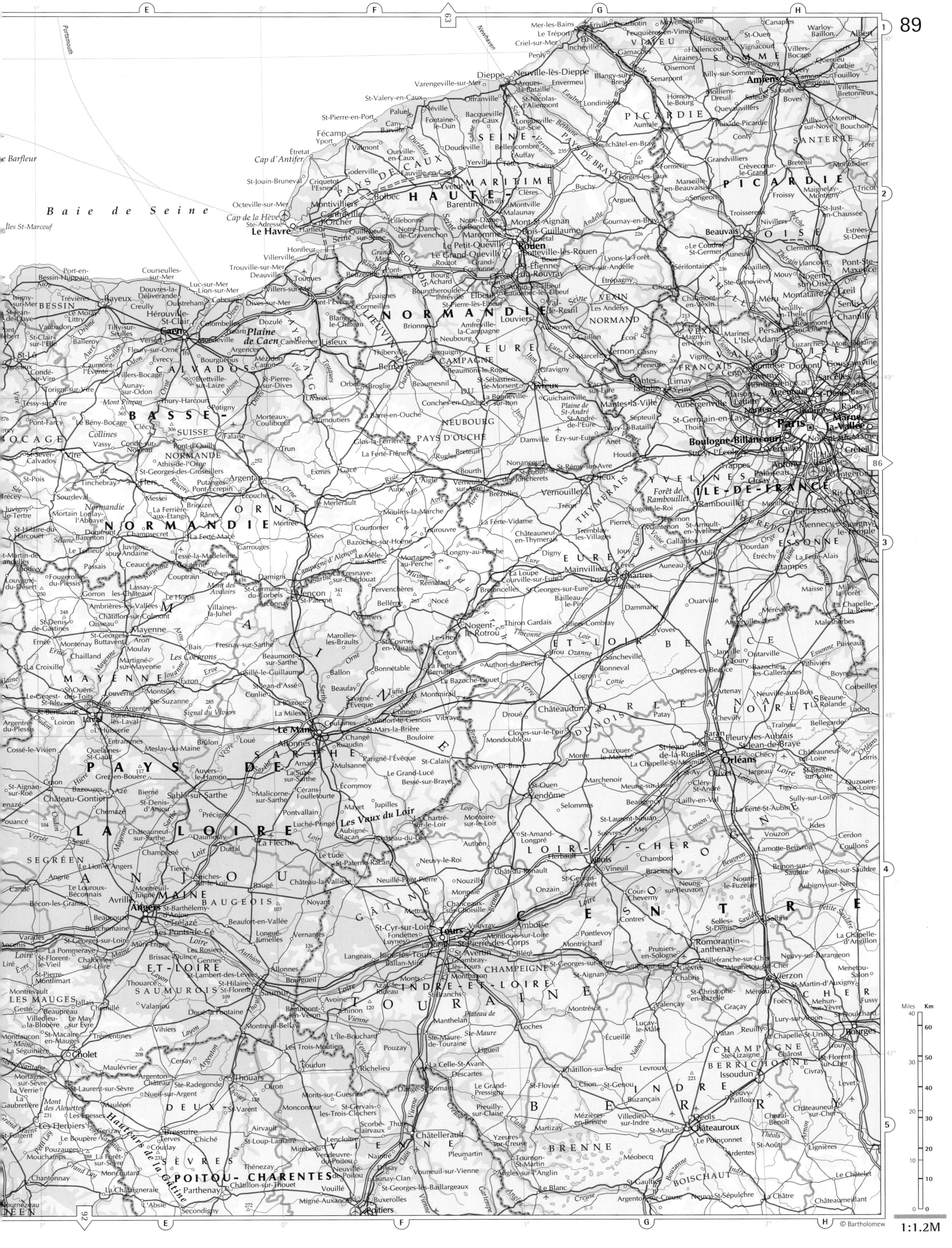
HAUTE-NORMANDIE
BASSE-NORMANDIE
PICARDIE
ILE-DE-FRANCE
CENTRE
PAYS DE LA LOIRE
POITOU-CHARENTES
SEINE-MARITIME
SOMME
OISE
CALVADOS
EURE
ORNE
MAYENNE
SARTHE
EURE-ET-LOIR
LOIR-ET-CHER
INDRE-ET-LOIRE
MAINE-ET-LOIRE
DEUX-SÈVRES
VIENNE
INDRE
CHER
LOIRET
YVELINES
ESSONNE
VAL D'OISE
Baie de Seine
Paris
Rouen
Le Havre
Caen
Amiens
Beauvais
Évreux
Chartres
Orléans
Le Mans
Laval
Alençon
Tours
Blois
Angers
Saumur
Cholet
Poitiers
Châteauroux
Bourges
Vierzon
Dieppe
Bayeux
Lisieux
Versailles
Châtellerault
Vendôme
Châteaudun
© Bartholomew
Miles
Km

1:1.2M

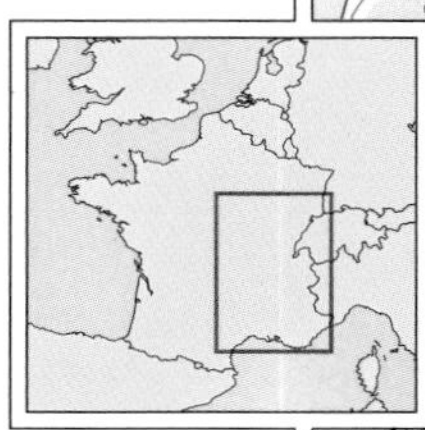

Metres	Feet
4000	13124
3000	9843
2000	6562
1500	4921
1000	3281
500	1640
200	656
100	328
SEA	LEVEL
50	164
200	656
1000	3281

Conic Equidistant Projection

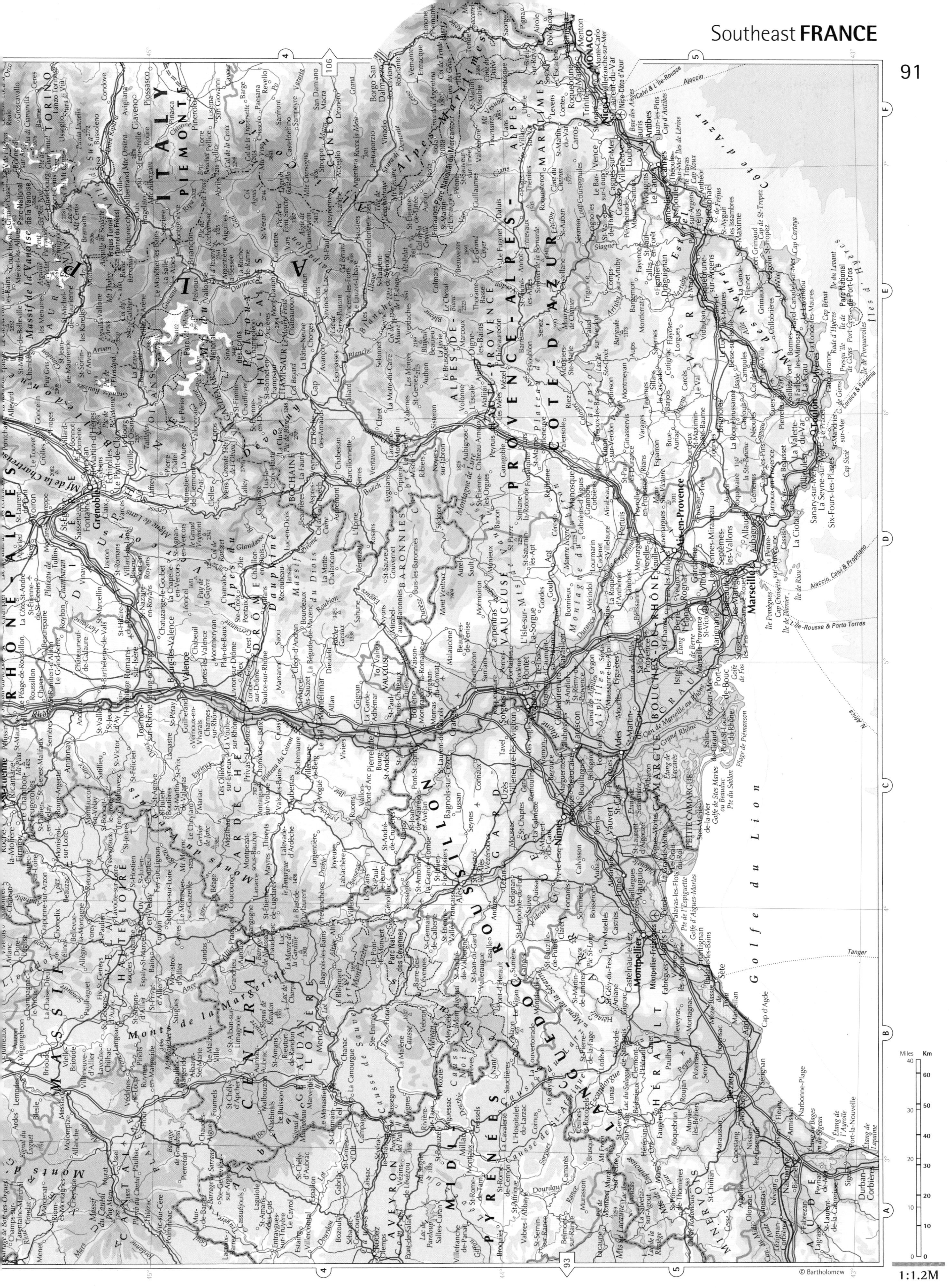

© Bartholomew

1:1.2M

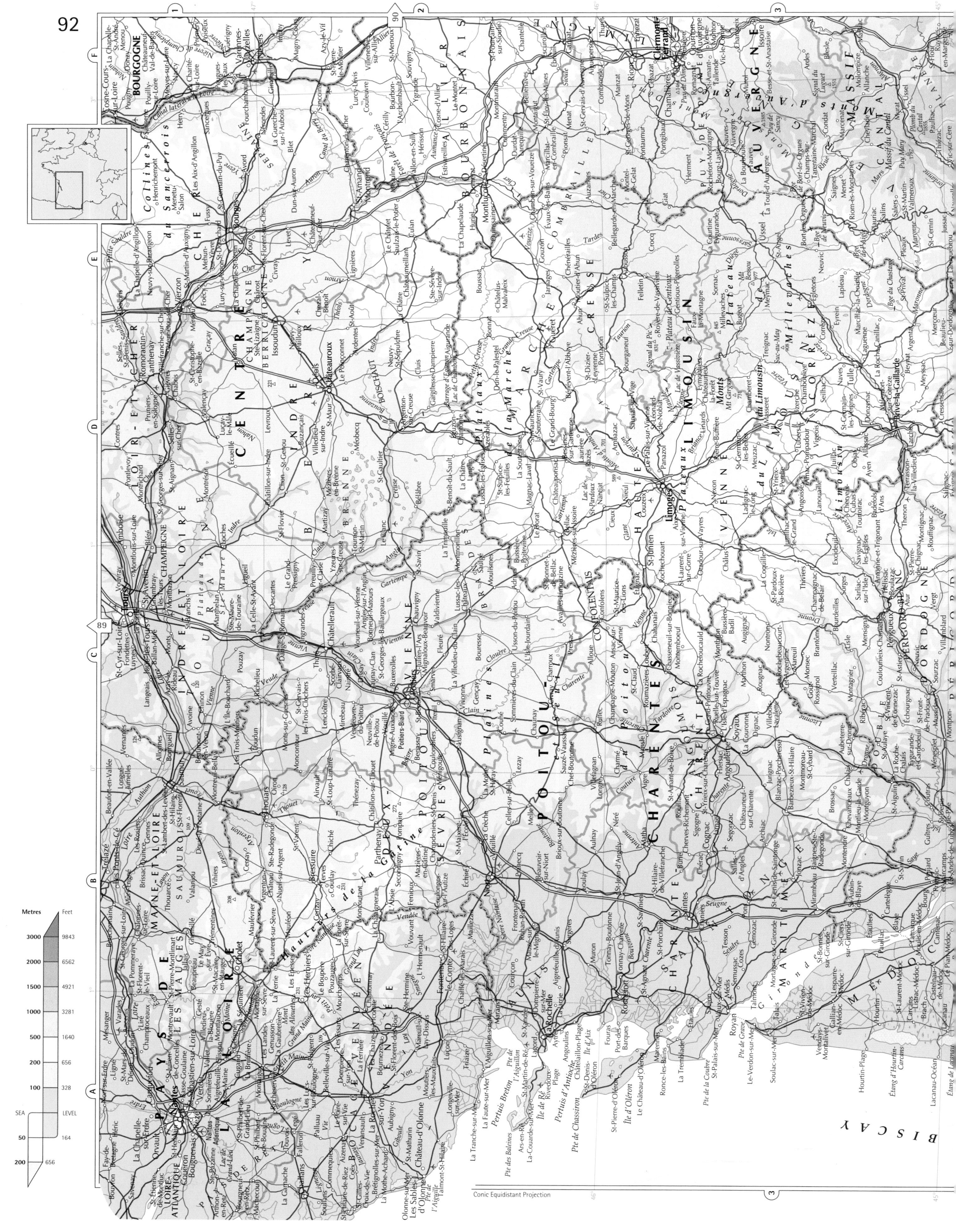
Metres
Feet
3000
9843
2000
6562
1500
4921
1000
3281
500
1640
200
656
100
328
SEA
LEVEL
50
164
200
656
BOURGOGNE
CENTRE
POITOU-CHARENTES
LIMOUSIN
AUVERGNE
PAYS DE LA LOIRE
Nantes
Tours
Poitiers
Limoges
Clermont-Ferrand
La Rochelle
Angoulême
Niort
Châteauroux
Bourges
Cholet
Saumur
Rochefort
Saintes
Cognac
Périgueux
Brive-la-Gaillarde
Tulle
Guéret
Montluçon
Vierzon
Issoudun
Châtellerault
Royan
Île de Ré
Île d'Oléron
BISCAY
89
90
Conic Equidistant Projection

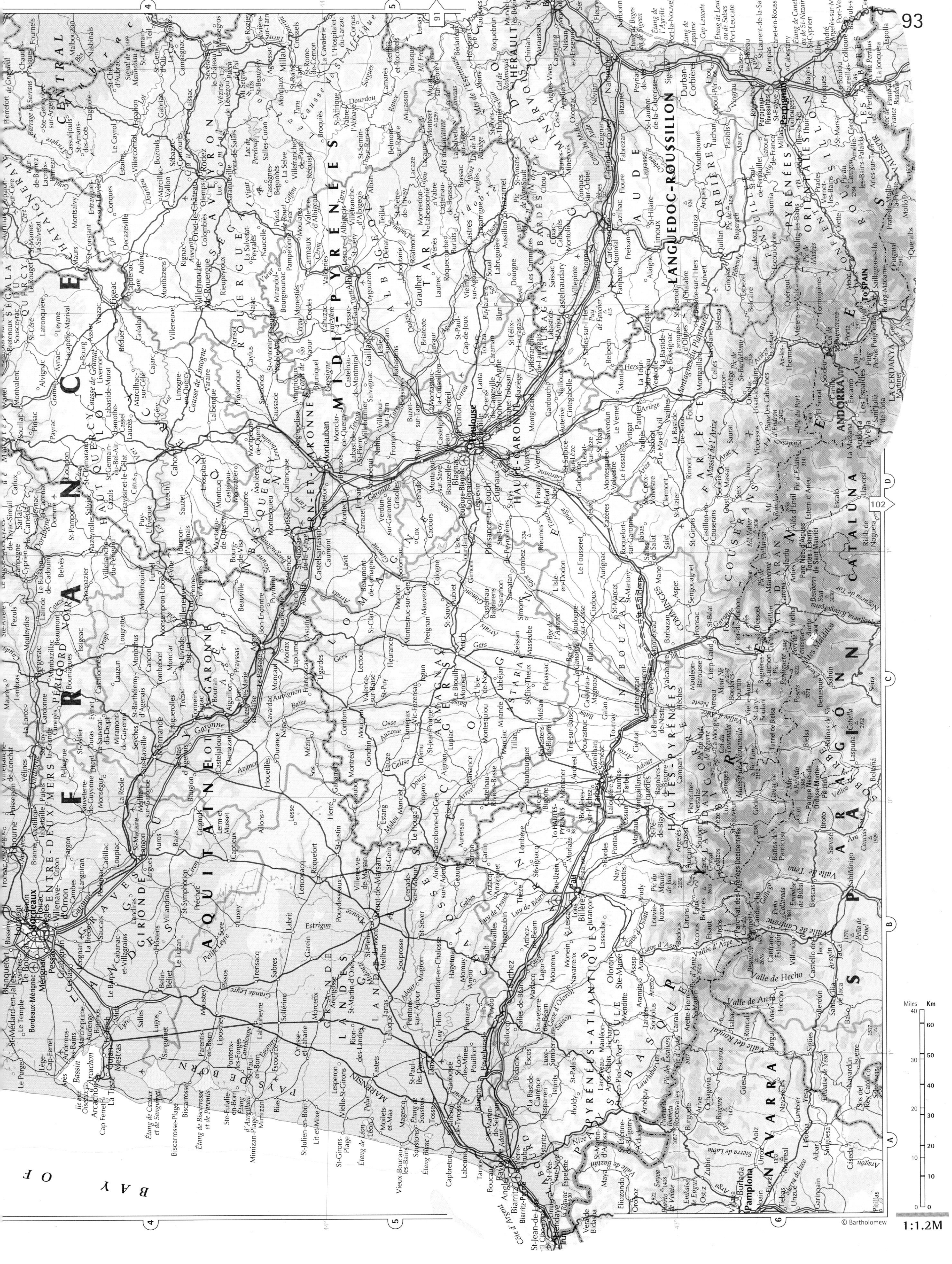
FRANCE
MIDI-PYRÉNÉES
LANGUEDOC-ROUSSILLON
AQUITAINE
ANDORRA
NAVARRA
ARAGÓN
CATALUNA
PYRÉNÉES-ATLANTIQUES
HAUTES-PYRÉNÉES
HAUTE-GARONNE
Toulouse
Bordeaux
Perpignan
Pamplona
BAY OF
Miles
Km
1:1.2M
© Bartholomew

A
B
C
D
E
F
REPUBLIC OF IRELAND
Cork
Wexford
Waterford
St George's Channel
WALES
ENGLAND
Birmingham
Wolverhampton
Derby
Nottingham
Lincoln
Leicester
Norwich
Great Yarmouth
Northampton
Gloucester
Cambridge
Luton
Swansea
Cardiff
Newport
Bristol
Bristol Channel
Reading
London
Southend-on-Sea
Margate
Bournemouth
Southampton
Brighton
Dover
Exeter
Plymouth
Portsmouth
Penzance
Land's End
Isles of Scilly
I. of Wight
English Channel
Strait of Dover
Hamburg
Lübeck
Schwerin
Szczecin
Bremerhaven
Bremen
Groningen
Oldenburg
Den Helder
Haarlem
NETHERLANDS
Amsterdam
'S-Gravenhage
(Den Haag)(The Hague)
Rotterdam
Utrecht
Arnhem
Berlin
Hannover
Wolfsburg
Potsdam
Magdeburg
Osnabrück
Münster
Salzgitter
Cottbus
Göttingen
Halle
Leipzig
Dresden
Dortmund
Essen
Düsseldorf
Kassel
Erfurt
Jena
Gera
Chemnitz
Zwickau
Köln
(Cologne)
Bonn
GERMANY
Antwerpen
Brugge
Bruxelles
BELGIUM
Lille
Calais
Dunkerque
Charleroi
Koblenz
Frankfurt am Main
Offenbach
Praha
(Prague)
Plzeň
CZECH
LUX.
Luxembourg
Mainz
Würzburg
Bamberg
Bayreuth
Erlangen
Nürnberg
Mannheim
Heidelberg
Ludwigshafen am Rhein
Saarbrücken
Karlsruhe
Pforzheim
Stuttgart
Regensburg
Metz
Nancy
Strasbourg
Ulm
Augsburg
Landshut
Passau
München
(Munich)
Freiburg im Breisgau
Mulhouse
Salzburg
Innsbruck
Basel
Zürich
Bern
LIECH.
SWITZERLAND
AUSTR
Lausanne
Genève
(Geneva)
Cherbourg
Le Havre
Rouen
Caen
Amiens
Reims
Abbeville
Dieppe
Channel Islands
(Îles Normandes)
(To U.K.)
Guernsey
Jersey
Île d'Ouessant
Brest
St-Malo
St-Brieuc
Rennes
Quimper
Lorient
Vannes
Laval
Le Mans
Alençon
Chartres
Versailles
Paris
Évreux
Orléans
Angers
Tours
Blois
Nantes
St-Nazaire
FRANCE
Dijon
Besançon
Troyes
Bay of Biscay
La Roche-sur-Yon
Poitiers
Niort
La Rochelle
Limoges
Clermont Ferrand
Vichy
Moulins
Lyon
St-Étienne
Grenoble
Annecy
Chambéry
Bordeaux
Périgueux
Angoulême
Brive-la-Gaillarde
Massif Central
Le-Puy-en-Velay
Valence
Montélimar
Avignon
Nîmes
Montpellier
Béziers
Toulouse
Carcassonne
Agen
Montauban
Albi
Rodez
Marseille
Aix-en-Provence
Toulon
Nice
Cannes
MONACO
Monte-Carlo
Golfe du Lion
Narbonne
Perpignan
Pau
Tarbes
Bayonne
Golfe de Gascogne
(Golfe de Gascuña)
Milano
(Milan)
Torino
(Turin)
Genova
(Genoa)
Bergamo
Brescia
Verona
Vicenza
Padova
(Padua)
Venezia
(Venice)
Trieste
Ljubljana
SLOVENIA
Bolzano
Trento
Novara
Pavia
Parma
Modena
Bologna
Ferrara
Ravenna
Rimini
SAN MARINO
Forlì
Firenze
(Florence)
La Spezia
Pisa
Livorno
Ancona
Perugia
Arezzo
Grosseto
ITALY
Terni
Pescara
Viterbo
Civitavecchia
Roma
(Rome)
Latina
Napoli (Naples)
Salerno
Golfo di Salerno
Benevento
Golfo di Genova
Ligurian Sea
Corse
(Corsica)
(France)
Bastia
Calvi
Ajaccio
Bonifacio
Strait of Bonifacio
Sardegna
(Sardinia)
(Italy)
Sassari
Olbia
Nuoro
Oristano
Iglesias
Cagliari
C. Carbonara
C. Spartivento
Tyrrhenian Sea
A Coruña
Cabo Fisterra
(Cape Finisterre)
Santiago
Lugo
Oviedo
Gijón
Cordillera Cantábrica
(Cantabrian Mountains)
Santander
Bilbao
Vitoria-Gasteiz
Donostia-San Sebastián
Pamplona
Pyrenees
ANDORRA
Andorra la Vella
Pontevedra
Vigo
Ourense
Ponferrada
León
Burgos
Logroño
Miranda de Ebro
Palencia
Valladolid
Zamora
Salamanca
Soria
Zaragoza
Lleida
Sabadell
Girona
Figueres
Barcelona
Tarragona
Porto
Braga
Bragança
Douro
PORTUGAL
Coimbra
Guarda
Ciudad Rodrigo
Covilhã
Ávila
Segovia
Madrid
Guadalajara
Alcalá de Henares
SPAIN
Calatayud
Tortosa
Castelló de la Plana
Lisboa
(Lisbon)
Setúbal
Sines
Portalegre
Plasencia
Tajo (Tagus)
Talavera de la Reina
Toledo
Aranjuez
Mérida
Badajoz
Évora
Beja
Villanueva de la Serena
Puertollano
Ciudad Real
Valdepeñas
Villarrobledo
Albacete
Sagunto
Valencia
Golfo de Valencia
Gandía
Sierra Morena
Córdoba
(Cordova)
Andújar
Linares
Jaén
Alicante
Elche
Murcia
Lorca
Cartagena
Sevilla
(Seville)
Huelva
Faro
Lagos
Cabo de São Vicente
(Cape St Vincent)
Écija
Antequera
Granada
Guadix
Sa Nevada
Mulhacén
Almería
Adra
Málaga
Cádiz
Jerez de la Frontera
Algeciras
Gibraltar (U.K.)
Strait of Gibraltar
Ceuta (Sp.)
Palma de Mallorca
Menorca
Mahón
Manacor
Mallorca
Islas Baleares
(Balearic Islands)
Eivissa
(Ibiza)
Formentera
MEDITERRANEAN
Tanger
(Tangier)
Tétouan
(Tetuán)
Larache
Ksar el Kebir
Chaouèn
Al Hoceima
Melilla (Sp.)
Nador
Kénitra
Rabat
Casablanca
El Jadida
Settat
Khouribga
Meknès
Fès (Fez)
Sidi Kacem
Taza
Oujda
Taourirt
Moyen Atlas
Azrou
MOROCCO
Oued Zem
Khenifra
Kasba Tadla
Beni Mellal
HAUT ATLAS
(HIGH ATLAS)
Er Rachidia
Bouârfa
Figuig
Ouarzazate
Abadla
Béchar
Hammada du Drâa
Oran
Mostaganem
Relizane
Mascara
Beni-Saf
Ghazaouet
Sidi Bel Abbès
Tlemcen
Tiaret
Hauts Plateaux
Saïda
Mecheria
El Bayadh
Aïn Sefra
Alger
(Algiers)
Blida
Ech Chélif
Tizi Ouzou
Bejaïa
Skikda
Annaba
Constantine
Sétif
Guelma
Souk Ahras
El Eulma
Batna
Khenchela
Tébessa
Biskra
Chott el Hodna
Bou Saâda
Djelfa
Saharien Atlas
Laghouat
El Meghaïer
Chott Melrhir
Touggourt
El Oued
Ghardaïa
Ouargla
Hassi Messaoud
Grand Erg Occidental
Grand Erg Oriental
Beni-Abbès
ALGERIA
El Goléa
Timimoun
El Homr
Tabelbala
Ksabi
Sbaa
Adrar
Erg Iguidi
Plateau du Tademaït
(Tademaït Plateau)
Plateau du Tinrhert
Bordj Messaouda
Bordj Omar Driss
In Aménas
In Salah
Reggane
El Eglab
Chenachane
TUNISIA
Tunis
Bizerte
Menzel Bourguiba
Béja
Jendouba
Nabeul
Golfe de Hammamet
Kairouan
Sousse
M'Saken
Sbeïtla
Kasserine
Sfax
Gafsa
G. de Gabès
Gabès
Tozeur
Chott el Jerid
Zarzis
Medenine
C. Bon
Sicilian Channel
Isola di Pantelleria (Italy)
MALTA
Valletta
Sicilia
(Sicily)
Isole Lipari
Palermo
Trapani
Marsala
Caltanissetta
Agrigento
Gela
Ragusa
Tarābulus
(Tripoli)
Zuwārah
Al Khums
Gharyān
Banī Walīd
Mizdah
TRIPOLITANIA
Ghadāmis
Darāj
Al Hamādah al Hamrā
Idhān Awbārī
Metres
Feet
4000
13124
3000
9843
2000
6562
1000
3281
500
1640
200
656
SEA
LEVEL
200
656
1000
3281
2000
6562
3000
9843
4000
13124
5000
16409
Lambert Conformal Conic Projection
121

POLAND
BELARUS
UKRAINE
RUSSIAN FEDERATION
SLOVAKIA
HUNGARY
ROMANIA
MOLDOVA (MOLDAVIA)
CROATIA
BOSNIA-HERZEGOVINA
YUGOSLAVIA
BULGARIA
MACEDONIA (F.Y.R.O.M.)
ALBANIA
GREECE
TURKEY
GEORGIA
SYRIA
CYPRUS
LEBANON
ISRAEL
WEST BANK
JORDAN
SAUDI ARABIA
EGYPT
LIBYA
GAZA
BLACK SEA
(CHERNOYE MORE)
(KARA DENIZ)
Sea of Azov
Adriatic Sea
Ionian Sea
Aegean Sea
RED SEA
Warszawa (Warsaw)
Kyyiv (Kiev)
Minsk
Budapest
Wien (Vienna)
Bratislava
Bucureşti (Bucharest)
Beograd (Belgrade)
Sofiya (Sofia)
Skopje
Tiranë (Tirana)
Athina (Athens)
İstanbul
Ankara
Izmir
Odesa (Odessa)
Chişinău (Kishinev)
Kharkiv (Khar'kov)
Donets'k
Rostov-na-Donu
Lefkosia (Nicosia)
Beirut (Beyrouth)
Dimashq (Damascus)
Halab (Aleppo)
Tel Aviv-Yafo (Jaffa)
Jerusalem (Yerushalayim)
'Ammān
Alexandria (El Iskandarîya)
Cairo (El Qâhira)
El Gîza
Port Said (Bûr Sa'îd)
Banghāzī
Khalīj Surt (Gulf of Sirte)
Kriti (Crete)
Rodos (Rhodes)
Western Desert
Eastern Desert
SINAI
Libyan Plateau
Qattara Depression
Great Sand Sea
Calanscio Sand Sea
CYRENAICA
AS SARIR
Anadolu Dağları
Toros Dağları
Carpathian Mts
Stara Planina
Miles
Km
1:9M
© Bartholomew

BAY OF BISCAY
(MAR CANTÁBRICO)
ATLANTIC
OCEAN
GOLFO DE CÁDIZ
Costa Verde
Costa del Sol
Costa de la Luz
CORDILLERA CANTÁBRICA
CANTABRIAN MOUNTAINS
GALICIA
ASTURIAS
CANTABRIA
CASTILLA Y LEÓN
EXTREMADURA
CASTILLA-LA MANCHA
ANDALUCÍA
SIERRA MORENA
SPAIN
PORTUGAL
MINHO
TRÁS-OS-MONTES
BEIRA ALTA
BEIRA BAIXA
BEIRA LITORAL
MADRID
MOROCCO
A Coruña
Ferrol
Lugo
Santiago
Pontevedra
Ourense
Vigo
Oviedo
Gijón
Avilés
Santander
Burgos
León
Ponferrada
Palencia
Valladolid
Zamora
Salamanca
Segovia
Ávila
Madrid
Móstoles
Alcalá de Henares
Fuenlabrada
Toledo
Talavera de la Reina
Cáceres
Badajoz
Mérida
Ciudad Real
Puertollano
Córdoba
Jaén
Granada
Sevilla
Huelva
Cádiz
Jeréz de la Frontera
Málaga
Marbella
Algeciras
Gibraltar (U.K.)
Strait of Gibraltar
Tarifa
Ceuta (Spain)
Tanger (Tangier)
Tétouan (Tetuán)
Viana do Castelo
Braga
Vila Real
Bragança
Porto
Aveiro
Viseu
Guarda
Coimbra
Castelo Branco
Leiria
Santarém
Lisboa (Lisbon)
Portalegre
Setúbal
Évora
Beja
Faro
Cabo Fisterra (Cape Finisterre)
Cabo de São Vicente (Cape St Vincent)
Cabo Trafalgar
MADEIRA ISLANDS (Portugal)
Porto Santo
Ilha da Madeira
Funchal
Ilhas Desertas
Deserta Grande
Bugio
Metres
Feet
SEA LEVEL
at the same scale
Conic Equidistant Projection

Golfe de Gascogne
(Golfo de Gascuña)
AQUITAINE
MIDI-PYRÉNÉES
FRANCE
LANGUEDOC-ROUSSILLON
Golfe du Lion
PAÍS VASCO
NAVARRA
LA RIOJA
ARAGÓN
CATALUÑA
VALENCIA
MURCIA
LA MANCHA
PYRENEES
ANDORRA
Toulouse
Montpellier
Marseille
Perpignan
Bilbao
Donostia-San Sebastián
Vitoria-Gasteiz
Pamplona
Logroño
Zaragoza
Lleida
Barcelona
Tarragona
Castelló de la Plana
Valencia
Golfo de Valencia
Alicante
Elche
Murcia
Cartagena
Albacete
Cuenca
Teruel
Almería
Costa Brava
Costa Dorada
Costa del Azahar
Costa Blanca
MENORCA
MALLORCA
Palma de Mallorca
Mahón
EIVISSA
(IBIZA)
Formentera
ISLAS BALEARES
(BALEARIC ISLANDS)
MEDITERRANEAN SEA
ALGERIA
Melilla (Spain)
Beni-Saf
Ghazaouet
Nador
CANARY ISLANDS
(Spain)
ISLAS CANARIAS
La Palma
Tenerife
Sta Cruz de Tenerife
San Cristóbal de la Laguna
La Gomera
El Hierro
Gran Canaria
Las Palmas de Gran Canaria
Fuerteventura
Puerto del Rosario
Lanzarote
Arrecife
Alegranza
Graciosa
at the same scale
© Bartholomew
Miles
Km
1:3M

BAY OF
(MAR CANT
ATLANTIC
OCEAN
PORTUGAL
GALICIA
ASTURI
CORDILLERA CANTÁ
CANTABRIAN MOU
LA CORUÑA
LUGO
ORENSE
PONTEVEDRA
LEÓ
ZAMORA
SALAMANCA
EXTREMADURA
CÁCERES
VIANA DO CASTELO
BRAGA
PORTO
VILA REAL
BRAGANÇA
AVEIRO
VISEU
GUARDA
COIMBRA
CASTELO BRANCO
LEIRIA
SANTARÉM
BERGANTIÑOS
AS MARIÑAS
EL BIERZO
MARAGATERÍA
SANABRIA
SAYAGO
TIERRA DEL PAN
TIERRA DEL VINO
ABADENGO
LAS HURDES
A LIMIA
LA VERA
CAMPO
BABIA
A Coruña
Ferrol
Santiago
Santiago de Compostela
Lugo
Ourense
Pontevedra
Vigo
Oviedo
Gijón
Avilés
León
Ponferrada
Astorga
Zamora
Salamanca
Bragança
Chaves
Braga
Guimarães
Porto
Vila Nova de Gaia
Matosinhos
Aveiro
Viseu
Guarda
Coimbra
Figueira da Foz
Leiria
Castelo Branco
Covilhã
Plasencia
Coria
Ciudad-Rodrigo
Benavente
Cabo Ortegal
Cabo Fisterra
(Cape Finisterre)
Cabo Touriñán
Cabo de Peñas
Cabo Mondego
Serra da Estrela
Sierra de la Cabrera
Sierra de la Culebra
Serra de Montemuro
Serra do Caramulo
Sierra de Gata
Montes de León
Miño
Douro
Duero
Tajo
Tejo
Parque Nacional da Peneda Gerês
Metres
Feet
2000
6562
1500
4921
1000
3281
500
1640
200
656
100
328
SEA
LEVEL
50
164
200
656
1000
3281
2000
6562
Conic Equidistant
Projection
100

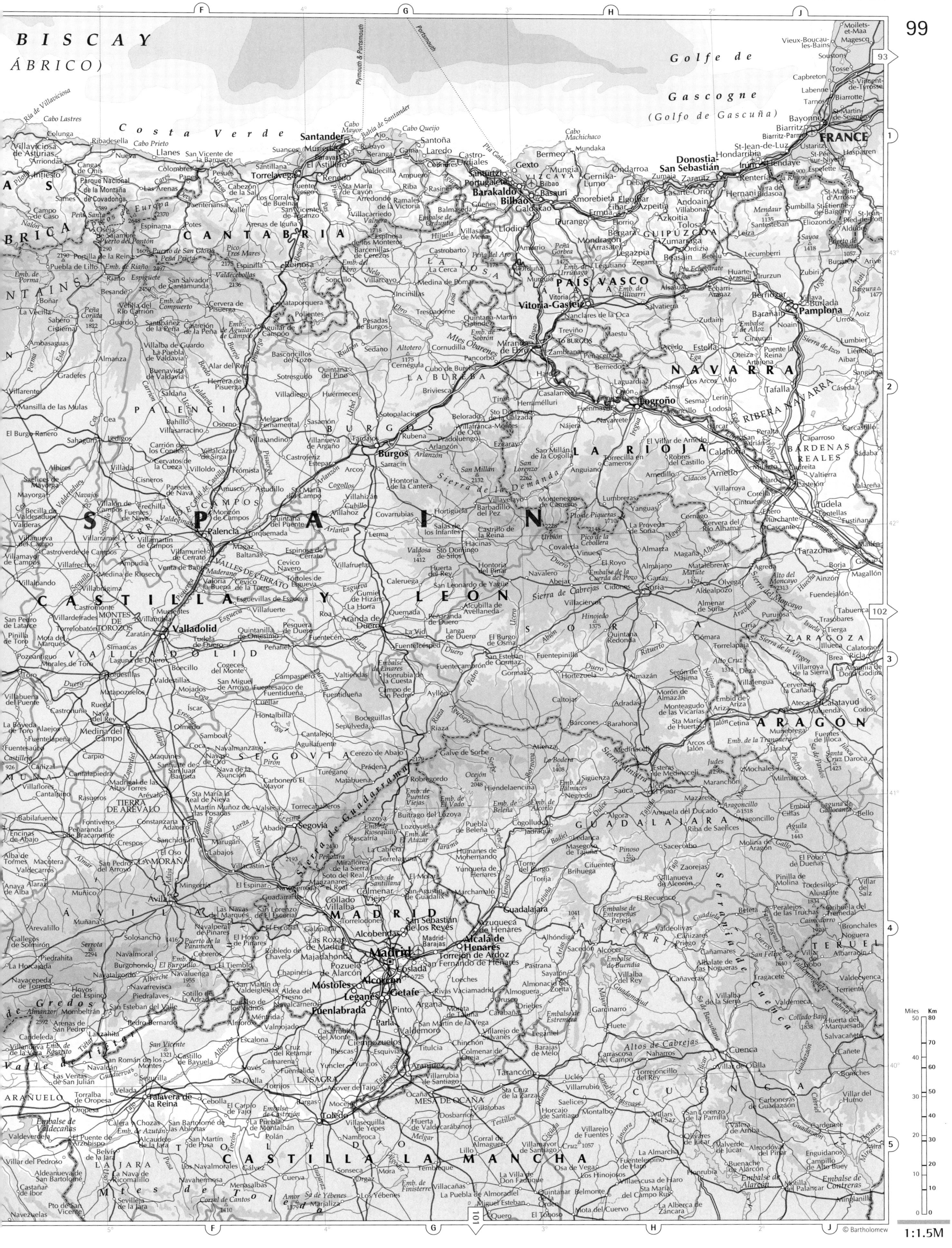
BISCAY
ÁBRICO)
Golfe de Gascogne
(Golfo de Gascuña)
Costa Verde
FRANCE
CANTABRIA
PAÍS VASCO
NAVARRA
LA RIOJA
SPAIN
CASTILLA Y LEÓN
PALENCIA
BURGOS
VALLADOLID
SORIA
SEGOVIA
ÁVILA
MADRID
GUADALAJARA
ARAGÓN
ZARAGOZA
TERUEL
CUENCA
TOLEDO
CASTILLA LA MANCHA
Santander
Bilbao
Vitoria-Gasteiz
Donostia-San Sebastián
Pamplona
Logroño
Burgos
Palencia
Valladolid
Soria
Segovia
Ávila
Madrid
Guadalajara
Toledo
Talavera de la Reina
Cuenca
Bayonne
Sierra de Guadarrama
Sierra de la Demanda
Serranía de Cuenca
RIBERA NAVARRA
BARDENAS REALES
Miles
Km
© Bartholomew
1:1.5M

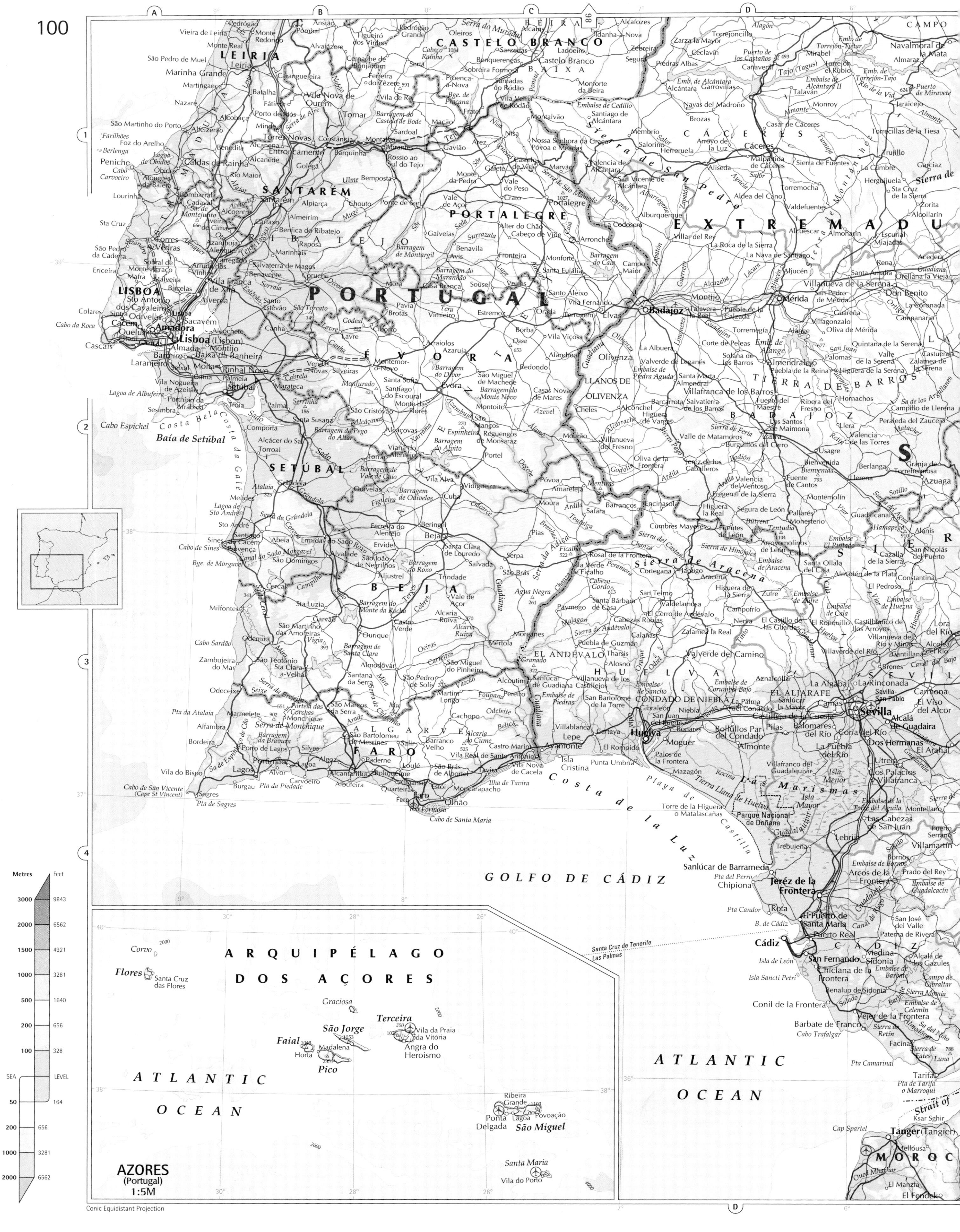

PORTUGAL
LEIRIA
CASTELO BRANCO
BEIRA BAIXA
SANTARÉM
RIBATEJO
PORTALEGRE
LISBOA
ÉVORA
ALENTEJO
SETÚBAL
BEJA
ALGARVE
FARO
CÁCERES
EXTREMADURA
BADAJOZ
HUELVA
SEVILLA
CÁDIZ
MOROC
Lisboa (Lisbon)
Setúbal
Badajoz
Mérida
Cáceres
Huelva
Sevilla
Cádiz
Jeréz de la Frontera
Tanger (Tangier)
Baía de Setúbal
Costa de la Luz
GOLFO DE CÁDIZ
ATLANTIC OCEAN
Strait of
LLANOS DE OLIVENZA
EL ANDEVALO
EL ALJARAFE
CONDADO DE NIEBLA
TIERRA DE BARROS
Sierra de Aracena
Sierra de San Pedro
Las Marismas
Parque Nacional de Doñana
ARQUIPÉLAGO DOS AÇORES
Corvo
Flores
Santa Cruz das Flores
Graciosa
Terceira
São Jorge
Faial
Horta
Pico
Angra do Heroismo
Vila da Praia da Vitória
Ponta Delgada
São Miguel
Santa Maria
Vila do Porto
AZORES
(Portugal)
1:5M
Metres
Feet
3000
9843
2000
6562
1500
4921
1000
3281
500
1640
200
656
100
328
SEA
LEVEL
50
164
200
656
1000
3281
2000
6562

CASTILLA-LA MANCHA
ANDALUCÍA
SPAIN
MURCIA
TOLEDO
CIUDAD REAL
ALBACETE
CUENCA
CÓRDOBA
JAÉN
GRANADA
ALMERÍA
MÁLAGA
MEDITERRANEAN SEA
Costa del Sol
Sierra Nevada
Sierra Morena
Montes de Toledo
CAMPO DE CALATRAVA
CAMPO DE MONTIEL
VALLE DE ALCUDIA
Toledo
Talavera de la Reina
Ciudad Real
Puertollano
Valdepeñas
Albacete
Hellín
Linares
Jaén
Córdoba (Cordova)
Granada
Almería
Málaga
Marbella
Motril
Lorca
Águilas
Baza
Guadix
Úbeda
Baeza
La Línea de la Concepción
Gibraltar (U.K.)
Algeciras
Ceuta (Spain)
Tétouan
Estepona
Fuengirola
Torremolinos
Benalmádena
Vélez-Málaga
El Ejido
Roquetas de Mar
Golfo de Almería
Cabo de Gata
Isla de Alborán (Spain)
Parque Nacional de las Tablas de Daimiel
Lagunas de Ruidera
Mulhacén 3481
Sète
Melilla
GIBRALTAR
(United Kingdom)
1:75 000
The Rock
Bay of Gibraltar
(Bahía de Algeciras)
Gibraltar Harbour
North Mole
Detached Mole
South Mole
MOORISH CASTLE (RUINS)
KING'S BASTION
GOVT. HO.
Runway
Eastern Beach
Catalan Bay
Sandy Bay
Europa Point
Little Bay
Rosia
Buena Vista
Windmill Hill Flats
Middle Hill
Signal Hill
Cable Car
Mt Misery
Summit 426
Alameda Gardens
Dock Yard
St Abb's Head
Miles
Km

Metres
Feet
3000
9843
2000
6562
1500
4921
1000
3281
500
1640
200
656
100
328
SEA
LEVEL
50
164
200
656
1000
3281
2000
6562
Conic Equidistant
Projection
F R A N C E
AQUITAINE
MIDI-PYRÉNÉES
LANGUEDOC-ROUSSILLON
HAUTE-GARONNE
HAUTES-PYRÉNÉES
PYRÉNÉES-ORIENTALES
PAIS VASCO
NAVARRA
LA RIOJA
ARAGÓN
CATALUÑA
CASTILLA Y LEÓN
S P A I N
ANDORRA
Donostia-San Sebastián
Pamplona
Logroño
Zaragoza
Lleida
Barcelona
L'Hospitalet de Llobregat
Sta Coloma de Gramanet
Badalona
Sabadell
Terrassa
Mataró
Tarragona
Reus
Girona
Perpignan
Narbonne
Béziers
Pau
Tarbes
Bayonne
Biarritz
Costa Dorada
Costa Brava
Golf de Sant Jordi
Golf de Roses
Cap de Creus
Cap Cerbère
93
99

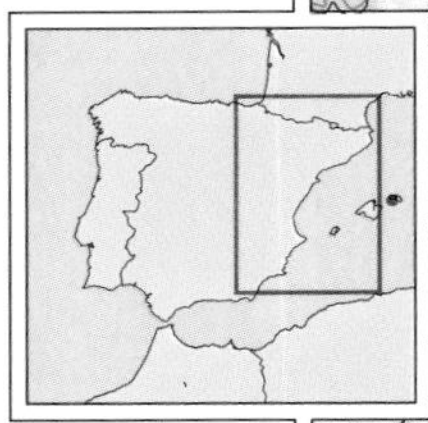

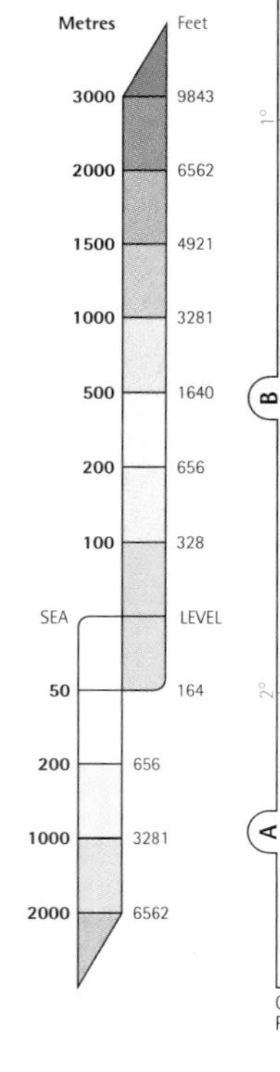

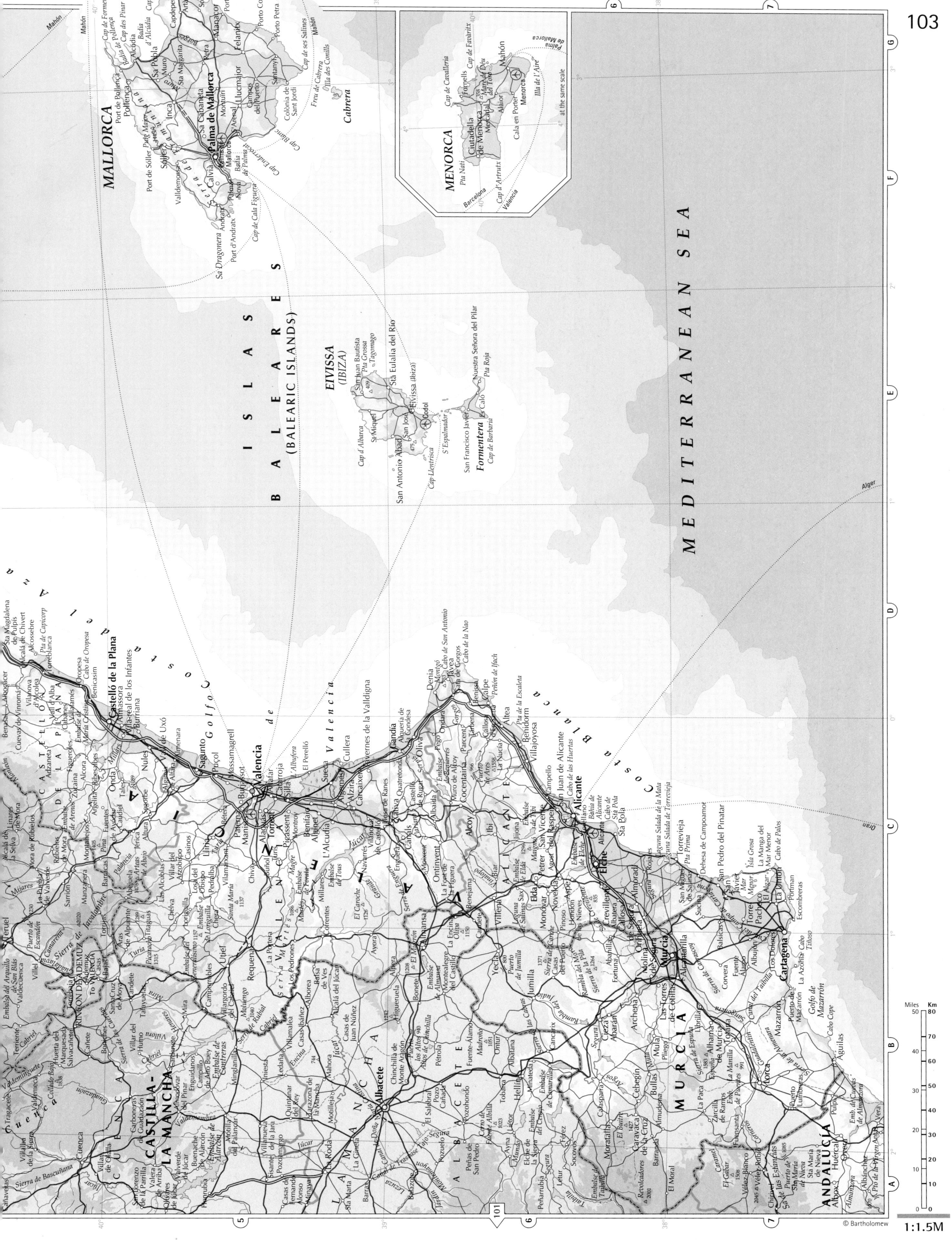
MALLORCA
Palma de Mallorca
MENORCA
Mahón
Ciutadella de Menorca
EIVISSA (IBIZA)
Eivissa (Ibiza)
Formentera
Cabrera
ISLAS BALEARES (BALEARIC ISLANDS)
MEDITERRANEAN SEA
Costa del Azahar
Costa Blanca
Golfo de Valencia
Castelló de la Plana
Valencia
Alicante
Elche
Murcia
Cartagena
Albacete
Cuenca
Teruel
Lorca
Sagunto
Benidorm
Gandía
Denia
Requena
Almansa
Orihuela
Torrevieja
CASTILLA-LA MANCHA
MURCIA
ANDALUCÍA
at the same scale
Miles
Km
1:1.5M

© Bartholomew

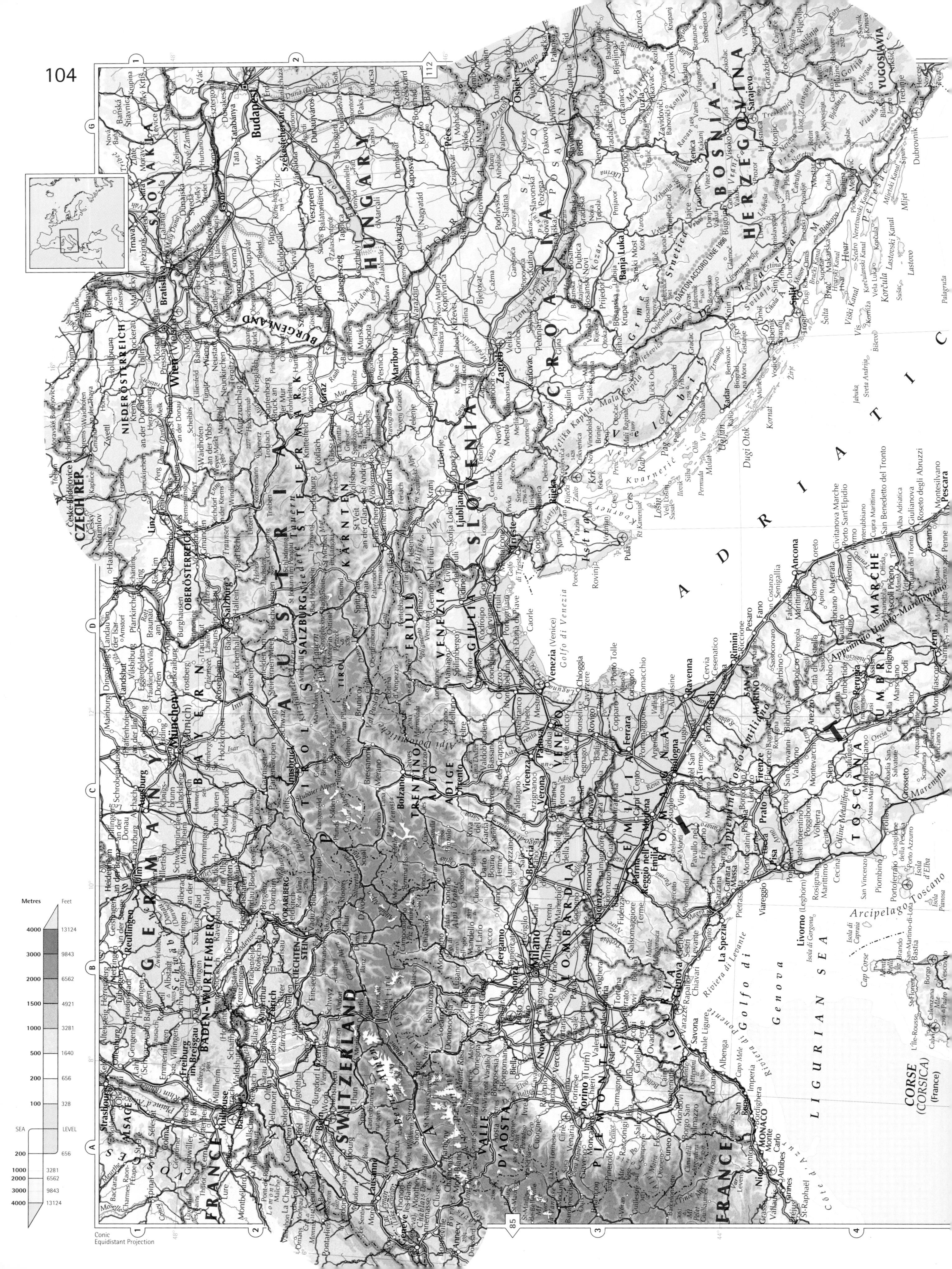
Metres
Feet
4000
13124
3000
9843
2000
6562
1500
4921
1000
3281
500
1640
200
656
100
328
SEA
LEVEL
200
656
1000
3281
2000
6562
3000
9843
4000
13124
Conic Equidistant Projection
GERMANY
FRANCE
SWITZERLAND
LIECHTENSTEIN
AUSTRIA
ITALY
SLOVENIA
CROATIA
HUNGARY
SLOVAKIA
CZECH REP.
BOSNIA-HERZEGOVINA
YUGOSLAVIA
MONACO
CORSE (CORSICA) (France)
ADRIATIC
LIGURIAN SEA
Golfo di Genova
DAYTON ACCORD LINE 1995

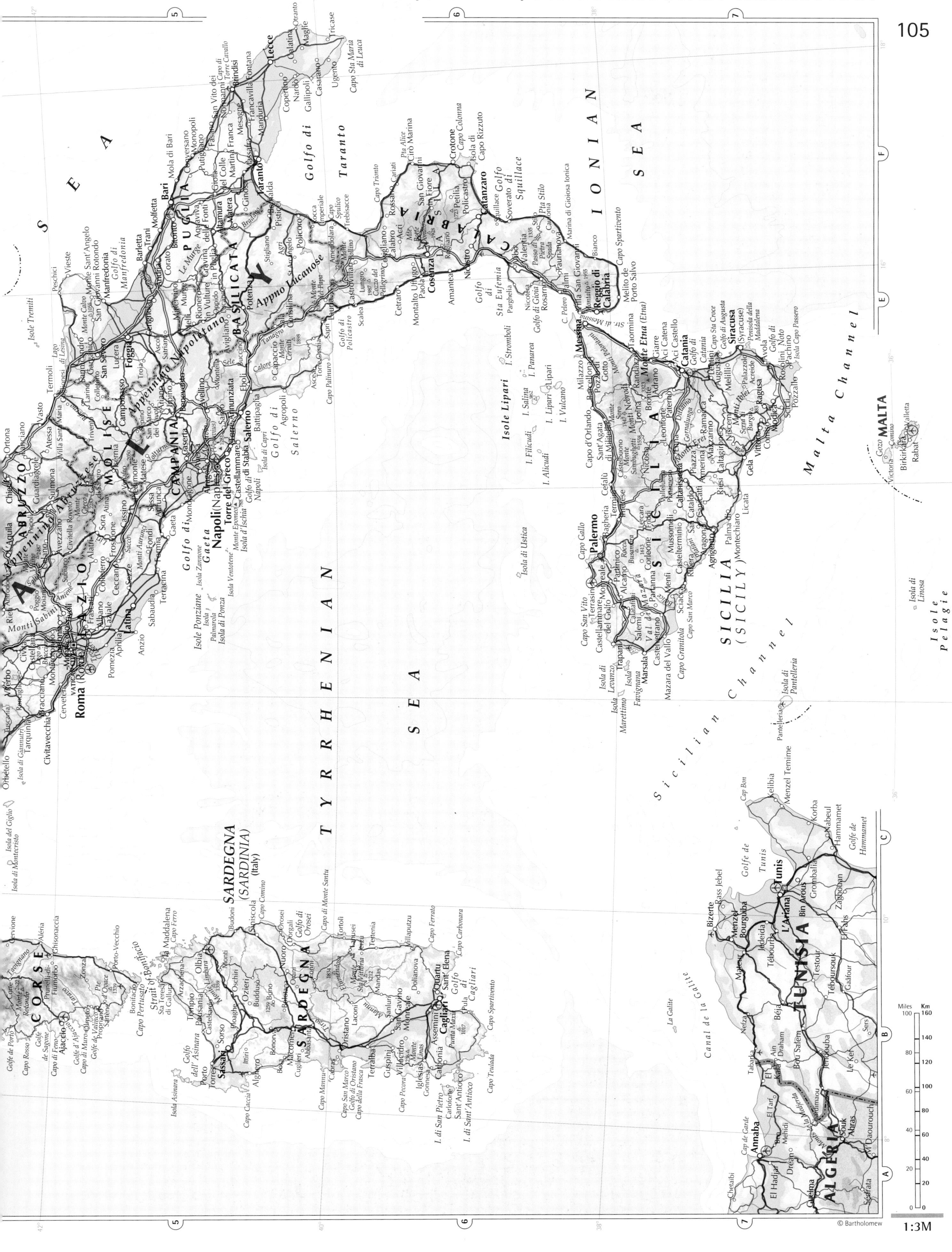
TYRRHENIAN SEA
IONIAN SEA
Malta Channel
Sicilian Channel
Canal de la Galite
Golfo di Taranto
Golfo di Squillace
Golfo di Salerno
Golfo di Gaeta
Golfo di Cagliari
Golfe de Tunis
Golfe de Hammamet
SICILIA (SICILY)
SARDEGNA (SARDINIA) (Italy)
CORSE
TUNISIA
ALGERIA
MALTA
CALABRIA
BASILICATA
PUGLIA
CAMPANIA
MOLISE
ABRUZZO
LAZIO
Roma (Rome)
Napoli (Naples)
Palermo
Catania
Messina
Siracusa (Syracuse)
Reggio di Calabria
Cagliari
Sassari
Bari
Taranto
Lecce
Brindisi
Foggia
Salerno
Cosenza
Catanzaro
Crotone
Tunis
Bizerte
Annaba
Ajaccio
Valletta
Monte Etna (Etna)
Isole Lipari
Isole Pelagie
Isola di Pantelleria
Isola di Ustica
Isole Tremiti
Strait of Bonifacio
Miles
Km
© Bartholomew
1:3M

SWITZERLAND
FRANCE
ITALIA
LIGURIAN SEA
Golfo di Genova
Riviera di Ponente
Riviera di Levante
Côte d'Azur
LAC LÉMAN (LAKE GENEVA)
JURA
FRANCHE-COMTÉ
RHÔNE-ALPES
PROVENCE-ALPES-CÔTE D'AZUR
VALLE D'AOSTA
PIEMONTE
LOMBARDIA
LIGURIA
LIECHTENSTEIN
VORARLBERG
BERNER ALPEN
Alpi Pennine
Alpi Cozie
Alpes Maritimes
Bodensee
Milano (Milan)
Torino (Turin)
Genova (Genoa)
Zürich
Bern
Basel
Lausanne
Genève (Geneva)
Besançon
Nice
MONACO
Livorno (Leghorn)
Metres
Feet
4000
13124
3000
9843
2000
6562
1500
4921
1000
3281
500
1640
200
656
100
328
SEA
LEVEL
50
164
200
656
1000
3281
Conic Equidistant Projection

AUSTRIA
SLOVENIA
CROATIA
ADRIATIC SEA
Golfo di Venezia
Golfo di Trieste
TIROL
STEIERMARK
KÄRNTEN
SALZBURG
TRENTINO
ALTO ADIGE
FRIULI VENEZIA GIULIA
VENETO
EMILIA ROMAGNA
TOSCANA
MARCHE
SAN MARINO
Istra
Venezia (Venice)
Trieste
Ljubljana
Rijeka
Bologna
Firenze (Florence)
Padova (Padua)
Verona
Ancona
Rimini
Ravenna
Ferrara
Innsbruck
Klagenfurt
Bolzano
Trento
Udine
Miles
Km
© Bartholomew

1:1.5M

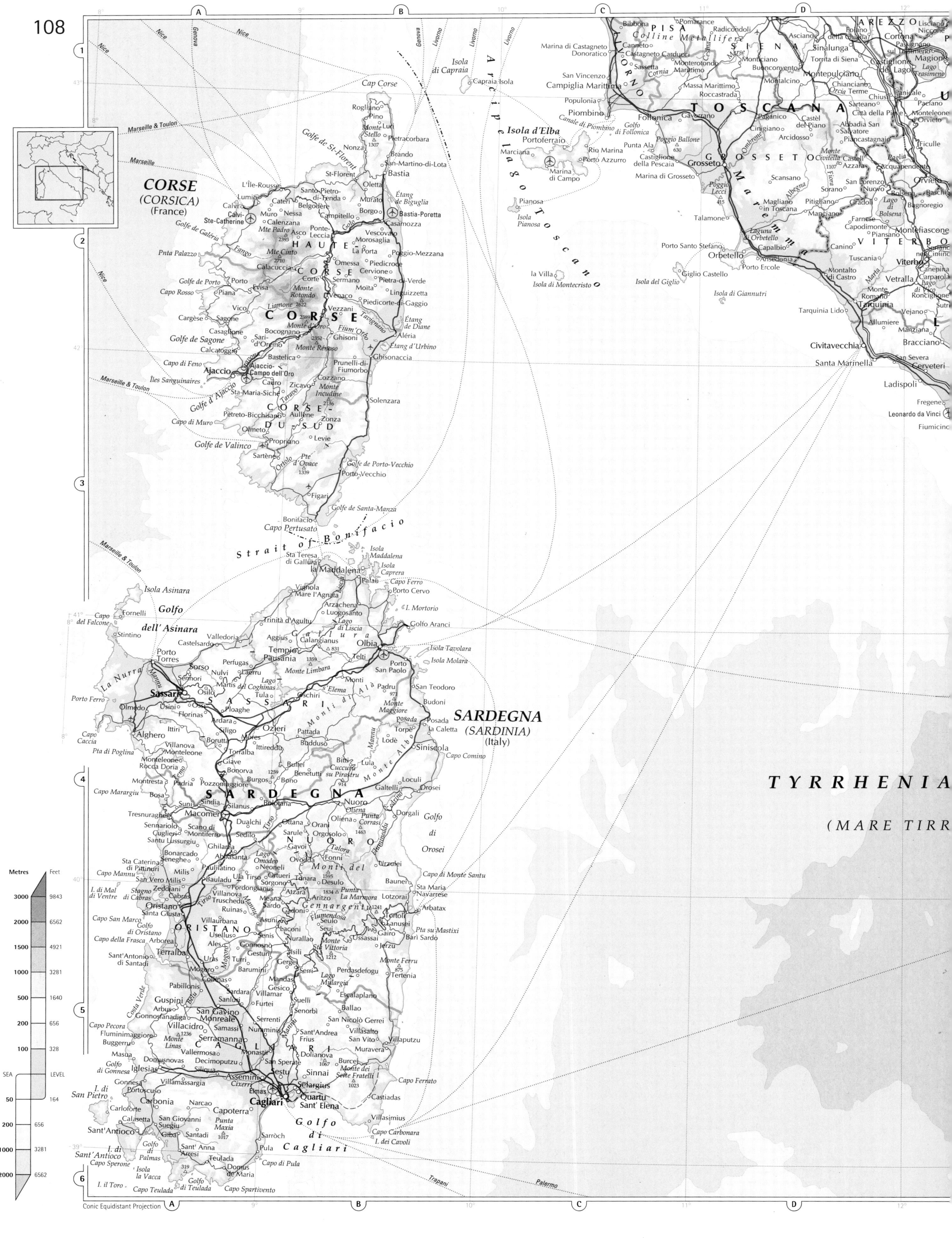

CORSE
(CORSICA)
(France)
HAUTE-CORSE
CORSE
CORSE-DU-SUD
SARDEGNA
(SARDINIA)
(Italy)
SASSARI
NUORO
ORISTANO
CAGLIARI
TOSCANA
PISA
SIENA
LIVORNO
GROSSETO
VITERBO
AREZZO
TYRRHENIA
(MARE TIRR
Arcipelago Toscano
Strait of Bonifacio
Cap Corse
Bastia
Ajaccio
Calvi
Corte
Porto-Vecchio
Bonifacio
Propriano
Sartène
Monte Cinto
Monte Rotondo
Golfe de St-Florent
Golfe de Porto
Golfe de Sagone
Golfe d'Ajaccio
Golfe de Valinco
Isola d'Elba
Portoferraio
Isola di Capraia
Isola Pianosa
Isola di Montecristo
Isola del Giglio
Isola di Giannutri
Piombino
Follonica
Grosseto
Orbetello
Civitavecchia
Santa Marinella
Ladispoli
Tarquinia
Viterbo
Bracciano
Montepulciano
Siena
Leonardo da Vinci
Fiumicino
Maremma
Colline Metallifere
Isola Asinara
Golfo dell' Asinara
La Maddalena
Olbia
Golfo Aranci
Sassari
Porto Torres
Alghero
Tempio Pausania
Ozieri
Siniscola
Nuoro
Macomer
Oristano
Golfo di Orosei
Gennargentu
Iglesias
Carbonia
Cagliari
Golfo di Cagliari
Villacidro
Sant'Antioco
I. di San Pietro
Capo Spartivento
Capo Teulada
Capo Carbonara
Metres
Feet
3000
9843
2000
6562
1500
4921
1000
3281
500
1640
200
656
100
328
SEA
LEVEL
50
164
Conic Equidistant Projection

CROATIA
ADRIATIC SEA
MARCHE
ABRUZZO
MOLISE
CAMPANIA
PUGLIA
BASILICATA
CALABRIA
Perugia
Roma (Rome)
Pescara
Chieti
L'Aquila
Teramo
Ascoli Piceno
Latina
Frosinone
Isernia
Campobasso
Foggia
Caserta
Benevento
Napoli (Naples)
Avellino
Salerno
Potenza
Matera
Cosenza
Termoli
Manfredonia
Barletta
Golfo di Gaeta
Golfo di Napoli
Golfo di Salerno
Golfo di Policastro
Golfo di Manfredonia
Isole Ponziane
Isola d'Ischia
Isole Tremiti
Vesuvio
Palagruža
Vis
Hvar
Miles
Km
1:1.5M
© Bartholomew

TYRRHENIAN SEA
(MARE TIRRENO)
SICILIA
(SICILY)
SICILIAN CHANNEL
TUNISIA
Cap Bon
Kelibia
Golfo di Gaeta
Isole Ponziane
Isola Palmarola
Isola di Ponza
Ponza
Isola Zannone
Parco Nazionale del Circeo
Isola Ventotene
Napoli (Naples)
Vesuvio
Torre del Greco
Isola d'Ischia
Golfo di Napoli
Castellammare di Stabia
Sorrento
Massa Lubrense
Anacapri
Capri
Isola di Capri
Golfo di Salerno
Salerno
Agropoli
Battipaglia
Caserta
Aversa
Pozzuoli
Procida
Ischia
Gaeta
Formia
Terracina
Latina
Fondi
Isola di Ustica
Ustica
Isole Lipari
Isola Alicudi
Isola Filicudi
Isola Salina
Isola Lipari
Lipari
Isola Vulcano
Palermo
Golfo di Palermo
Golfo di Castellammare
Golfo di Termini Imerese
Capo San Vito
Capo Gallo
Capo Zafferano
Trapani
Erice
Marsala
Isola di Levanzo
Isola Marettimo
Isola Favignana
Mazara del Vallo
Castelvetrano
Capo Granitola
Sciacca
Capo San Marco
Agrigento
Porto Empedocle
Palma di Montechiaro
Licata
Gela
Golfo di Gela
Caltanissetta
Enna
Cefalù
Termini Imerese
Corleone
Madonie
Monti Nebrodi
Capo d'Orlando
Caltagirone
Vittoria
Comiso
Ragusa
Modica
Scicli
Pozzallo
Isola di Pantelleria
Pantelleria
Linosa
Metres
Feet
SEA LEVEL
Conic Equidistant Projection

ADRIATIC SEA
Strait of Otranto
Golfo di Taranto
IONIAN SEA
Golfo di Policastro
Golfo di Sta Eufemia
Golfo di Squillace
Golfo di Gioia
Golfo di Catania
Golfo di Augusta
Golfo di Noto
PUGLIA
BASILICATA
CALABRIA
BARI
TARANTO
BRINDISI
LECCE
MATERA
POTENZA
COSENZA
CATANZARO
REGGIO DI CALABRIA
FOGGIA
SALERNO
Bari
Taranto
Brindisi
Lecce
Potenza
Matera
Cosenza
Catanzaro
Crotone
Reggio di Calabria
Messina
Catania
Siracusa
Barletta
Trani
Andria
Molfetta
Altamura
Gallipoli
Otranto
Capo Sta Maria di Leuca
Capo Spartivento
Capo Colonna
Capo Rizzuto
Capo Vaticano
Pta Stilo
Monte Etna (Etna)
Isola Stromboli
MALTA and GOZO
1:500 000
Gozo
MALTA
MEDITERRANEAN SEA
Victoria
Valletta
Sliema
Mdina
Rabat
Marsaskala
Marsaxlokk
Zejtun
Birzebbuga
Mellieha
St Paul's Bay
Filfla
Comino
N. Comino Chan.
S. Comino Chan.
Miles
Km
1:1.5M
© Bartholomew

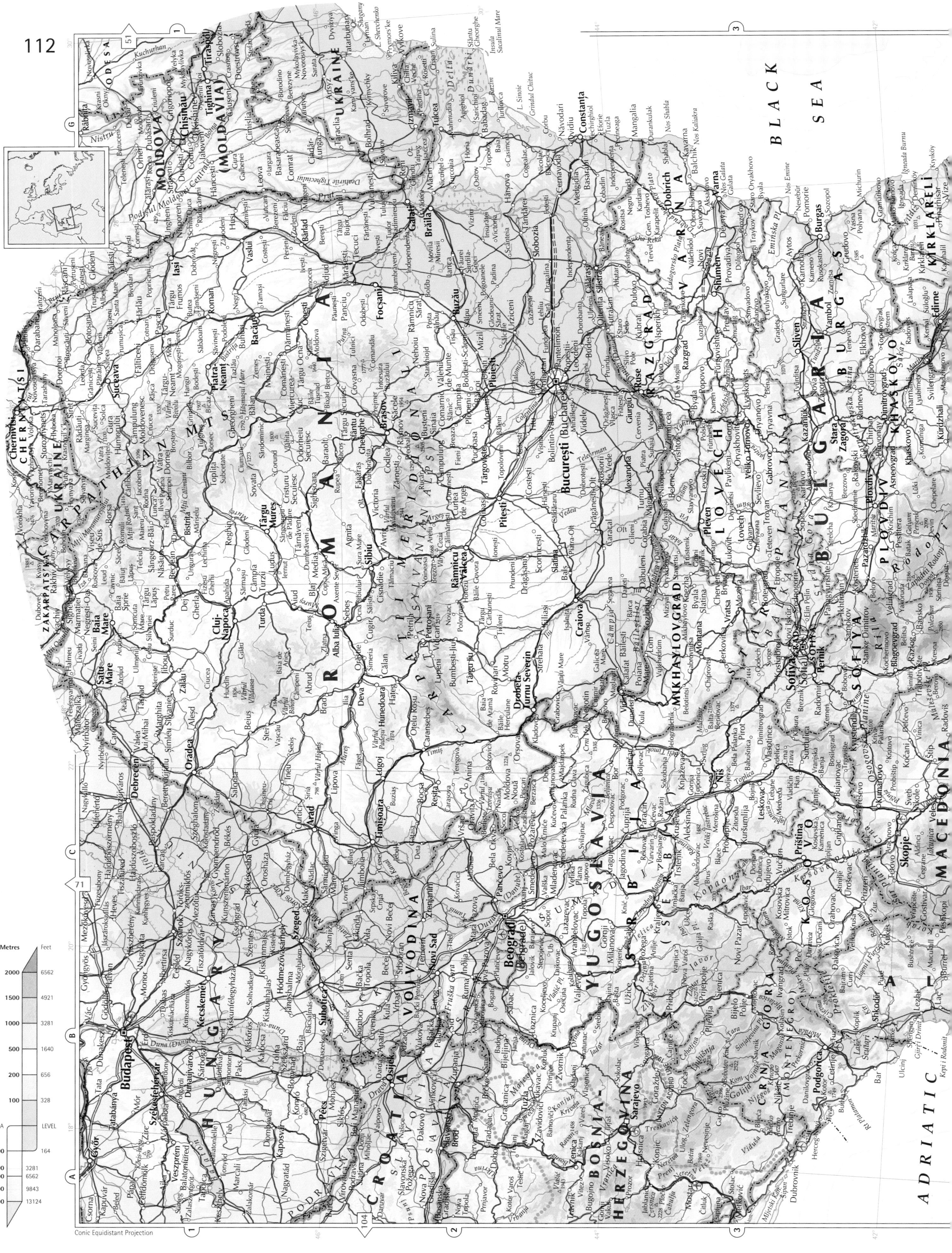
ROMANIA
BULGARIA
HUNGARY
YUGOSLAVIA
SERBIA
KOSOVO
MACEDONIA
CROATIA
BOSNIA-HERZEGOVINA
CRNA GORA (MONTENEGRO)
VOJVODINA
MOLDOVA (MOLDAVIA)
UKRAINE
BLACK SEA
ADRIATIC
București (Bucharest)
Beograd (Belgrade)
Budapest
Sofiya (Sofia)
Sarajevo
Skopje
Chișinău
Metres
Feet
SEA LEVEL
Conic Equidistant Projection

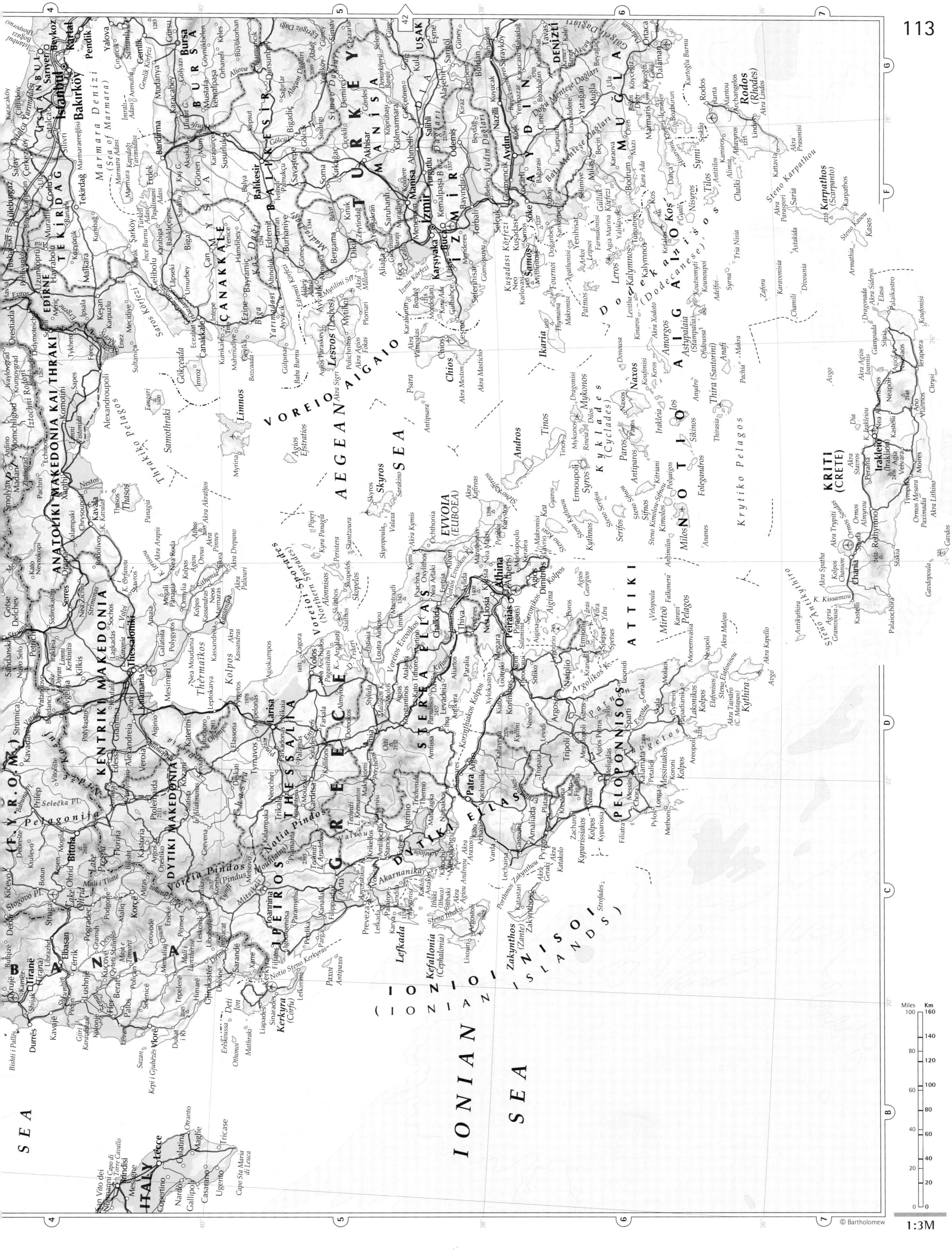
AEGEAN SEA
IONIAN SEA
VOREIO AIGAIO
KRITI (CRETE)
PELOPONNISOS
ATTIKI
STEREA ELLAS
THESSALIA
IPEIROS
KENTRIKI MAKEDONIA
DYTIKI MAKEDONIA
ANATOLIKI MAKEDONIA KAI THRAKI
IONIOI NISOI (IONIAN ISLANDS)
GREECE
TURKEY
ITALY
(F.Y.R.O.M.)
Athina (Athens)
Thessaloniki
Izmir
Bursa
Istanbul
Tiranë
Lecce
Brindisi
Kerkyra (Corfu)
Rodos (Rhodes)
Karpathos
Kykladês (Cyclades)
Dodekanisos (Dodecanese)
Lesvos (Lesbos)
Limnos
Evvoia (Euboea)
Chania
Irakleio
Patra
Larisa
Ioannina
Kalamata
Samos
Chios
Ikaria
Naxos
Tinos
Andros
Skyros
Kefallonia (Cephalonia)
Zakynthos (Zante)
Lefkada
Miles
Km
© Bartholomew
1:3M

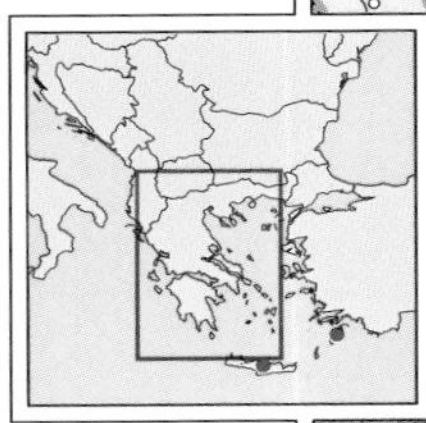

BULGARIA
SOFIYA
PLOVDIV
KHASKOVO
MACEDONIA (F.Y.R.O.M.)
ALBANIA
ANATOLIKI MAKEDONIA KAI THRAKI
KENTRIKI MAKEDONIA
DYTIKI MAKEDONIA
THESSALIA
IPEIROS
STEREA ELLAS
VOREIO AIGAIO
AEGEAN SEA
Thermaïkos Kolpos
Thrakiko Pelagos
Thessaloniki
Larisa
Ioannina
Kerkyra (Corfu)
Limnos
Thasos
Samothraki
Skyros
Lefkada
Tiranë (Tirana)
Vorea Pindos
Notia Pindos
Voreioi Sporades (Northern Sporades)
Conic Equidistant Projection

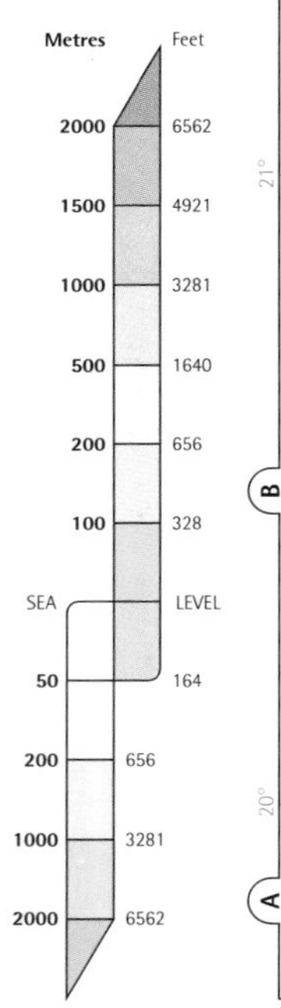
Metres
Feet
2000
6562
1500
4921
1000
3281
500
1640
200
656
100
328
SEA
LEVEL
50
164
200
656
1000
3281
2000
6562

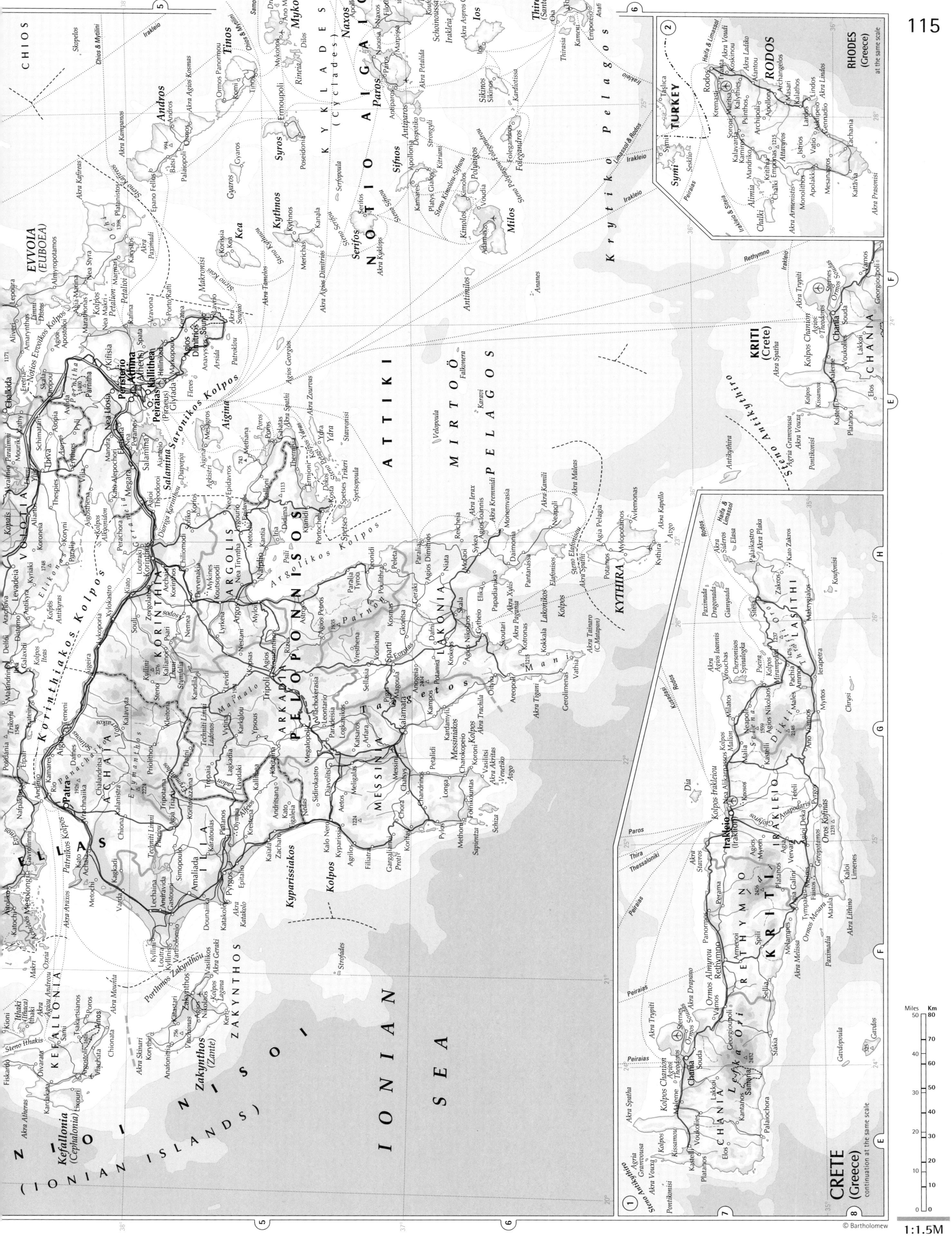
IONIAN SEA
IONIOI NISOI (IONIAN ISLANDS)
PELOPONNISOS
ATTIKI
MIRTOÖ PELAGOS
NOTIO AIGAIO
KYKLADES (Cyclades)
Krytiko Pelagos
EVVOIA (EUBOEA)
CHIOS
Korinthiakos Kolpos
Saronikos Kolpos
Athina (Athens)
Peiraias (Piraeus)
Patra
Kalamata
Korinthos
Sparti
Tripoli
Pyrgos
ACHAIA
ILIA
KORINTHIA
ARGOLIS
ARKADIA
MESSINIA
LAKONIA
KEFALLONIA
ZAKYNTHOS
Kefallonia (Cephalonia)
Zakynthos (Zante)
Kyparissiakos Kolpos
KYTHIRA
Andros
Tinos
Mykonos
Naxos
Paros
Syros
Kea
Kythnos
Serifos
Sifnos
Milos
Ios
Thira (Santorini)
CRETE (Greece)
continuation at the same scale
KRITI (Crete)
Irakleio (Iraklion)
Chania
Rethymno
CHANIA
RETHYMNO
IRAKLEIO
LASITHI
RHODES (Greece)
at the same scale
RODOS
TURKEY
Miles
Km
1:1.5M
© Bartholomew

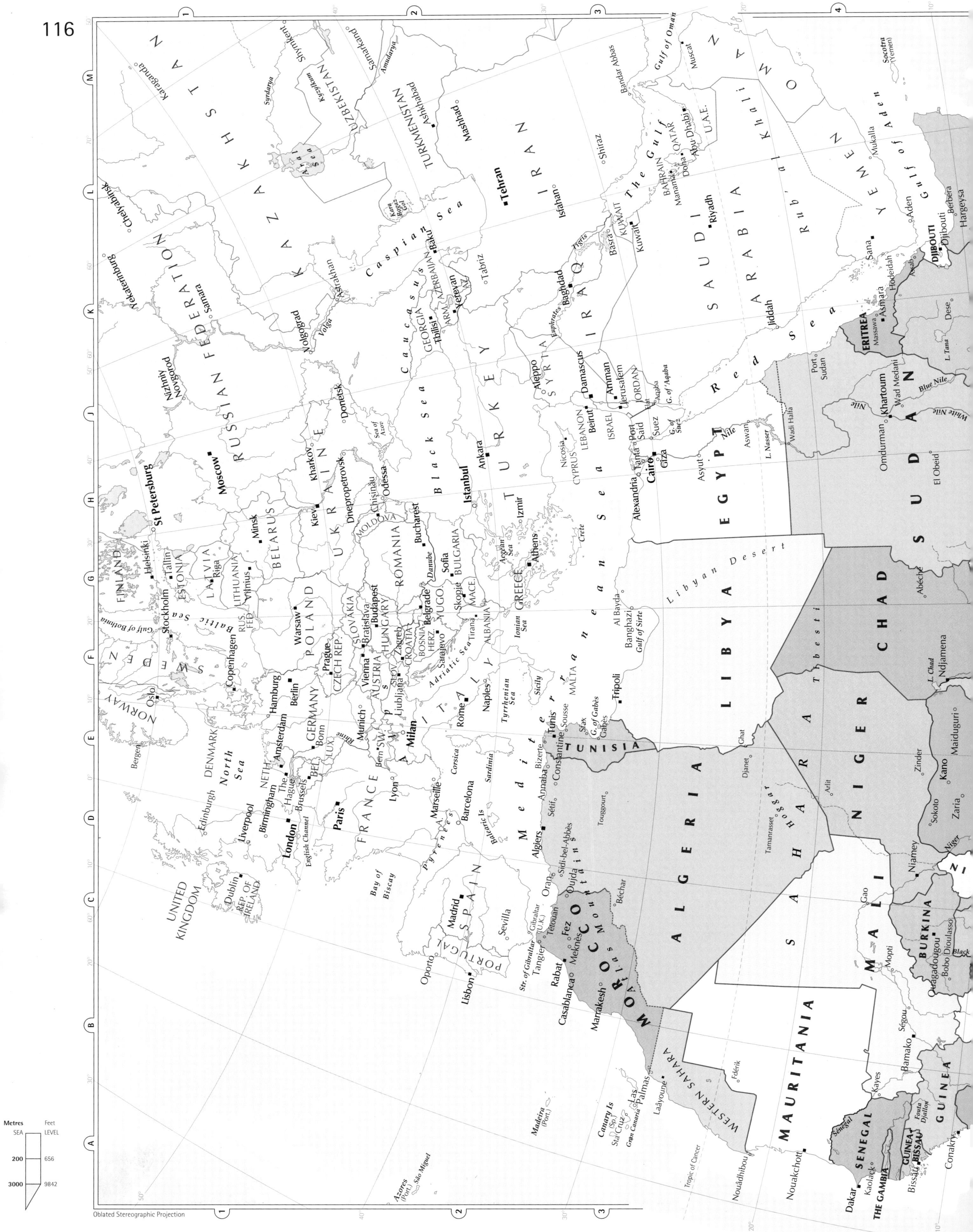

Oblated Stereographic Projection

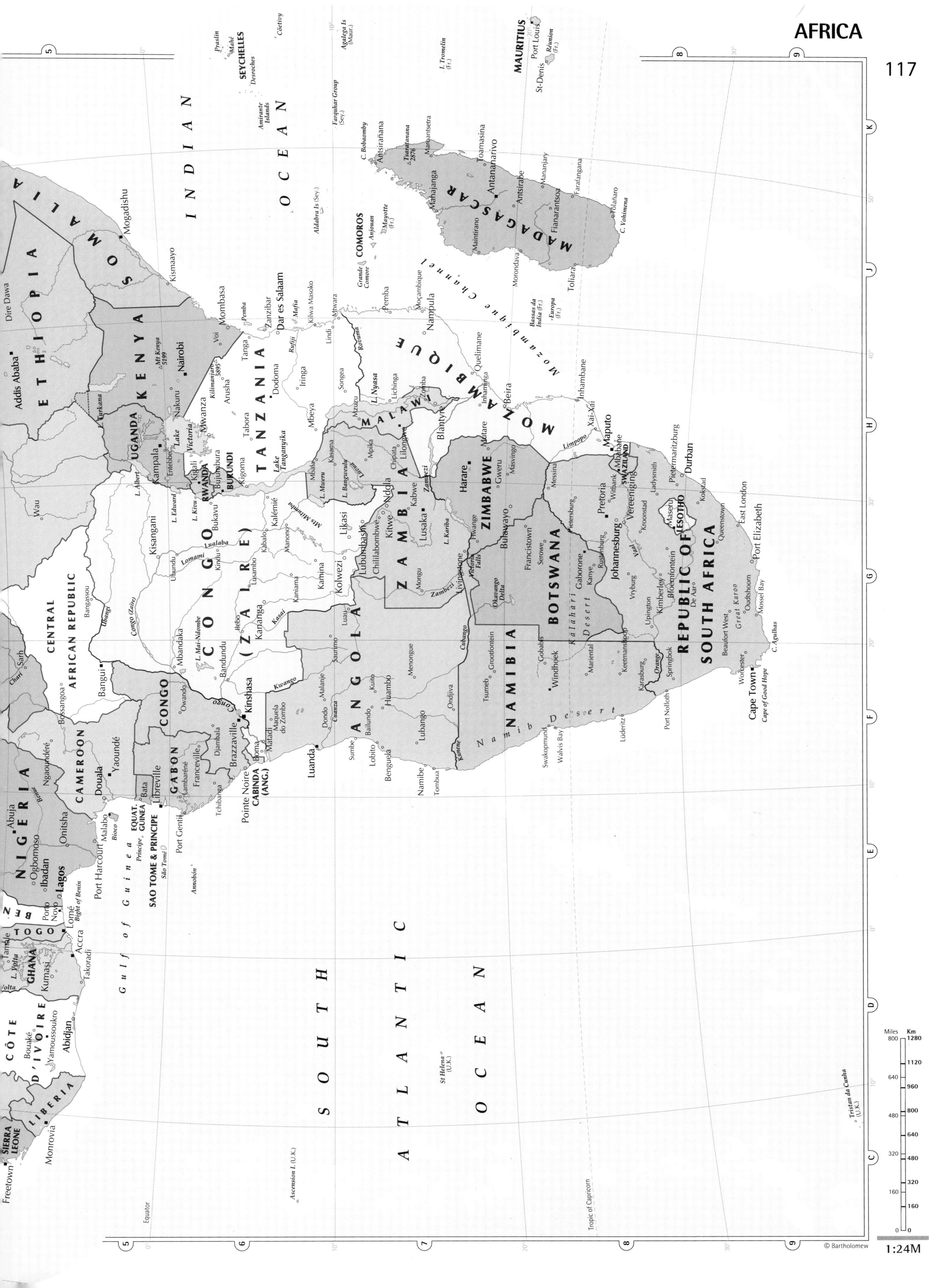
ETHIOPIA
SOMALIA
KENYA
UGANDA
RWANDA
BURUNDI
TANZANIA
CONGO (ZAIRE)
CONGO
GABON
CAMEROON
CENTRAL AFRICAN REPUBLIC
NIGERIA
BENIN
TOGO
GHANA
CÔTE D'IVOIRE
LIBERIA
SIERRA LEONE
EQUAT. GUINEA
SAO TOME & PRINCIPE
CABINDA (ANG.)
ANGOLA
ZAMBIA
MALAWI
MOZAMBIQUE
ZIMBABWE
BOTSWANA
NAMIBIA
REPUBLIC OF SOUTH AFRICA
LESOTHO
SWAZILAND
MADAGASCAR
COMOROS
MAURITIUS
SEYCHELLES
INDIAN OCEAN
SOUTH ATLANTIC OCEAN
Gulf of Guinea
Mozambique Channel
Kalahari Desert
Namib Desert
Addis Ababa
Dire Dawa
Mogadishu
Kismayo
Nairobi
Mombasa
Kampala
Kigali
Bujumbura
Dodoma
Dar es Salaam
Zanzibar
Kinshasa
Brazzaville
Libreville
Yaoundé
Douala
Bangui
Abuja
Lagos
Ibadan
Accra
Lomé
Porto Novo
Abidjan
Yamoussoukro
Monrovia
Freetown
Luanda
Lusaka
Lilongwe
Harare
Maputo
Mbabane
Maseru
Gaborone
Windhoek
Pretoria
Johannesburg
Durban
Cape Town
Port Elizabeth
East London
Bloemfontein
Antananarivo
Port Louis
St-Denis
Réunion (Fr.)
Equator
Tropic of Capricorn
St Helena (U.K.)
Ascension I. (U.K.)
Tristan da Cunha (U.K.)
Miles
Km
1:24M
© Bartholomew

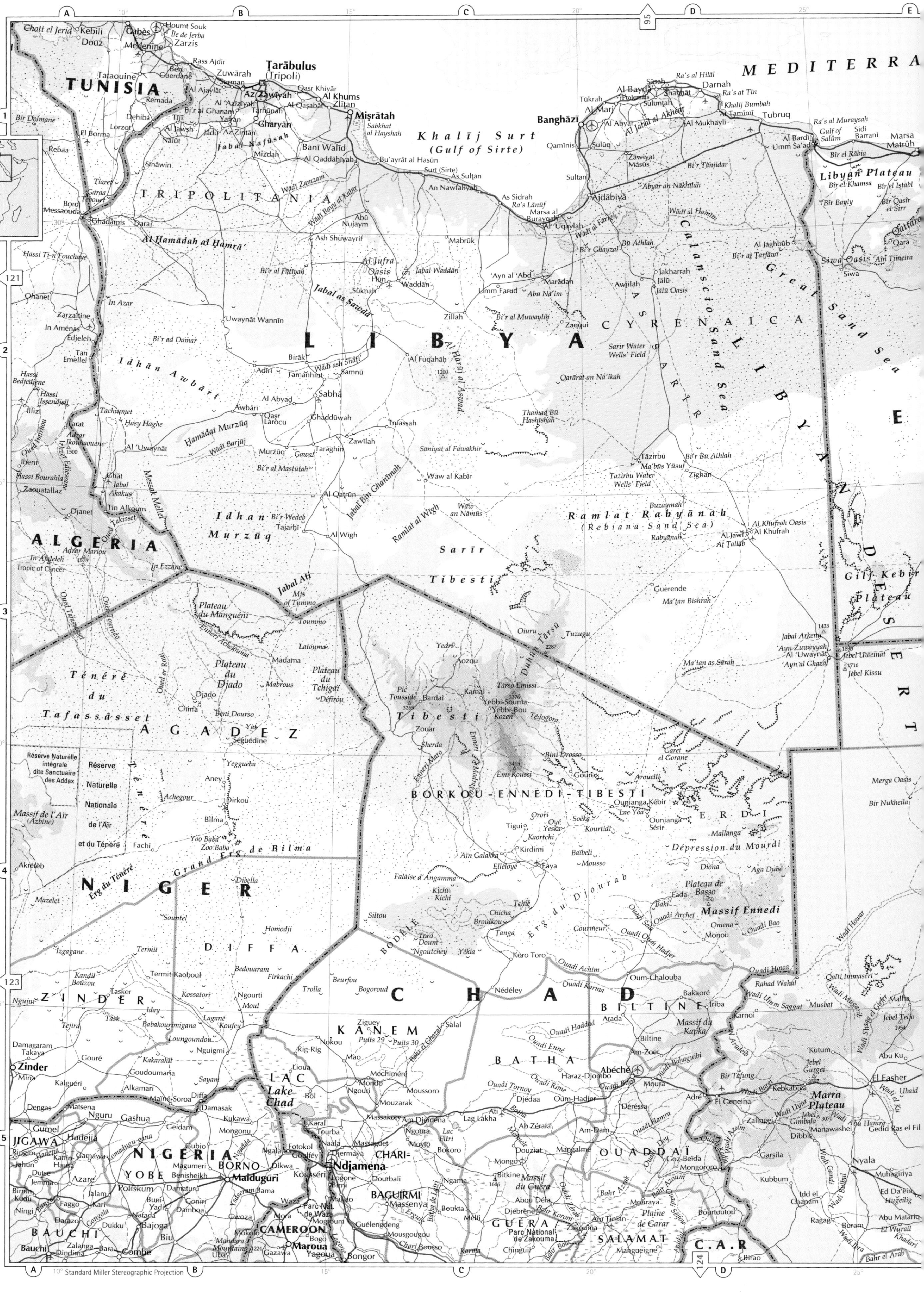

MEDITERRA
TUNISIA
LIBYA
ALGERIA
NIGER
CHAD
NIGERIA
CAMEROON
C.A.R
Ṭarābulus (Tripoli)
Banghāzī
Miṣrātah
Khalīj Surt (Gulf of Sirte)
TRIPOLITANIA
CYRENAICA
Al Ḥamādah al Ḥamrā'
Idhān Awbārī
Idhān Murzūq
Ramlat Rabyānah (Rebiana Sand Sea)
Calanscio Sand Sea
Great Sand Sea
Libyan Plateau
LIBYAN DESERT
Gilf Kebir Plateau
Sarīr Tibesti
Tibesti
BORKOU-ENNEDI-TIBESTI
Emi Koussi
AGADEZ
Ténéré du Tafassâsset
Grand Erg de Bilma
Erg du Ténéré
Massif de l'Aïr (Azbine)
Réserve Naturelle intégrale dite Sanctuaire des Addax
Réserve Naturelle Nationale de l'Aïr et du Ténéré
DIFFA
ZINDER
Zinder
KANEM
BATHA
BILTINE
Abéché
OUADDAÏ
GUÉRA
SALAMAT
BAGUIRMI
CHARI-BAGUIRMI
Ndjamena
Lake Chad
LAC
BORNO
Maiduguri
YOBE
JIGAWA
BAUCHI
Bauchi
Maroua
Massif Ennedi
Erg du Djourab
Dépression du Mourdi
Marra Plateau
El Fasher
Nyala
Fezzan
Sabhā
Ghadāmis
Ajdābiyā
Tubruq
Darnah
Al Khufrah
Jabal al Akhḍar
Jabal Nafūsah
Tropic of Cancer
Standard Miller Stereographic Projection

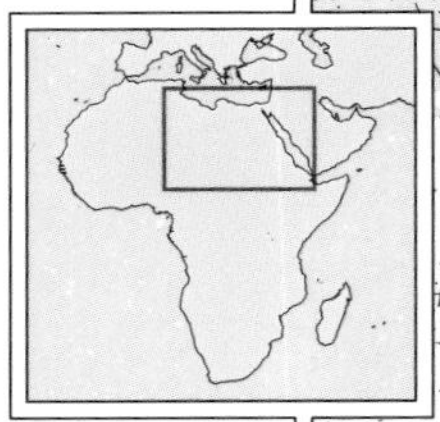

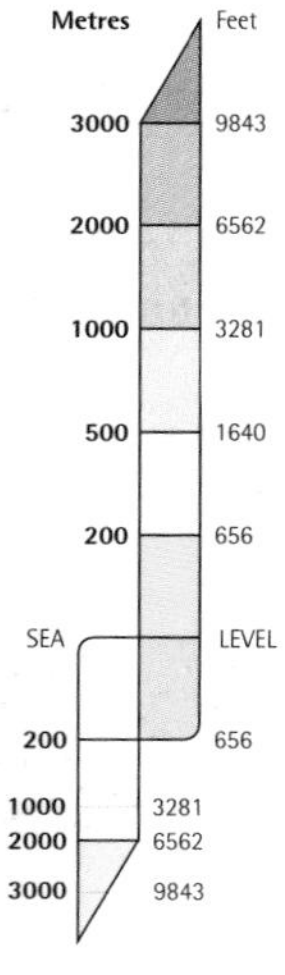

Metres
Feet
3000
9843
2000
6562
1000
3281
500
1640
200
656
SEA
LEVEL

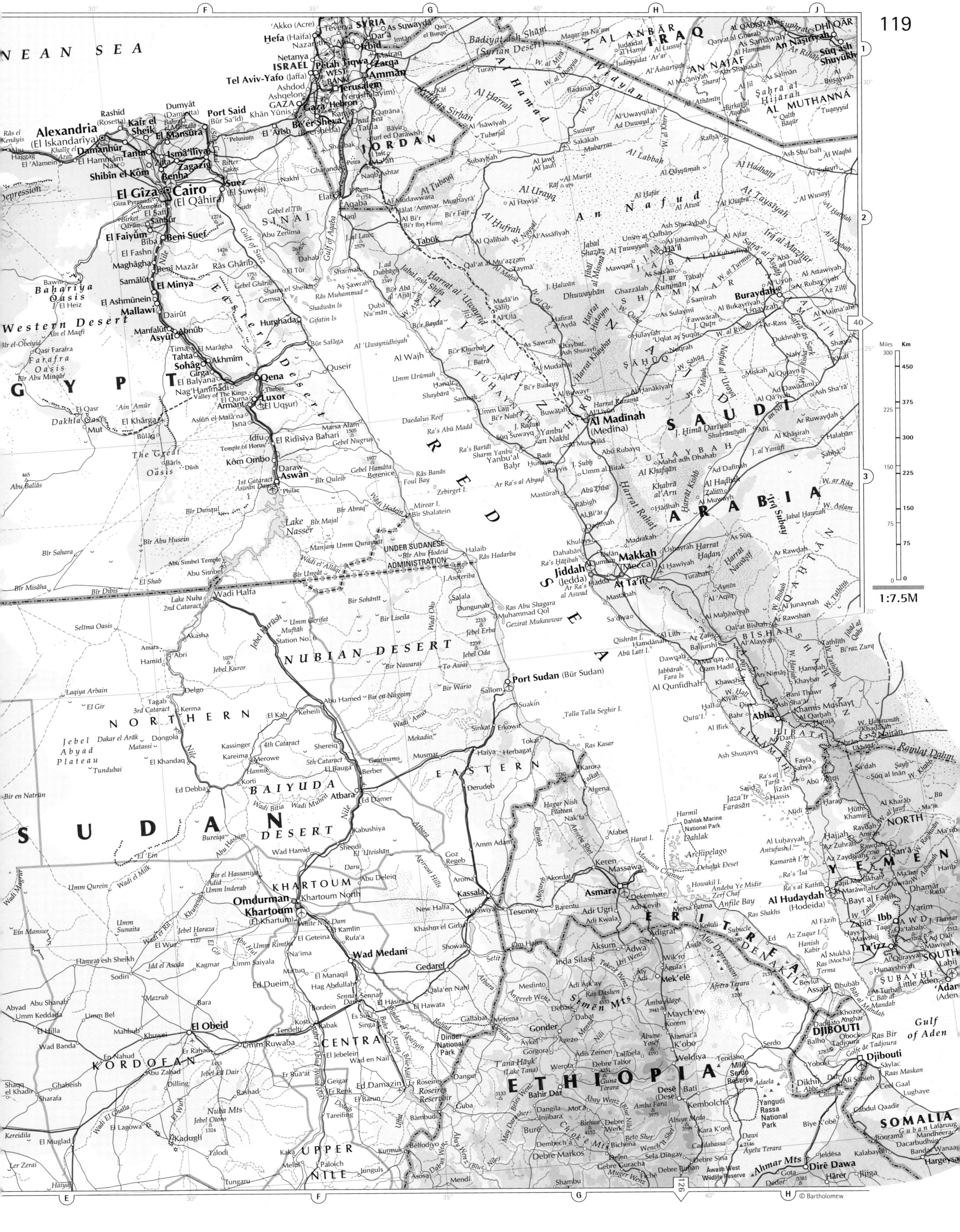
MEDITERRANEAN SEA
SYRIA
IRAQ
ISRAEL
JORDAN
WEST BANK
GAZA
EGYPT
SUDAN
SAUDI ARABIA
ERITREA
ETHIOPIA
DJIBOUTI
SOMALIA
NORTH YEMEN
SOUTH YEMEN
RED SEA
Gulf of Aden
Gulf of Suez
Gulf of Aqaba
SINAI
Western Desert
Eastern Desert
NUBIAN DESERT
BAIYUDA DESERT
NORTHERN
EASTERN
KHARTOUM
CENTRAL
KORDOFAN
UPPER NILE
HIJAZ
NAJD
An Nafud
AL ANBĀR
AN NAJAF
AL MUTHANNĀ
Bādiyat ash Shām (Syrian Desert)
Al Hamad
UNDER SUDANESE ADMINISTRATION
Alexandria (El Iskandarîya)
Port Said (Bûr Sa'îd)
Cairo (El Qâhira)
El Gîza
Suez (El Suweis)
Tel Aviv-Yafo (Jaffa)
Jerusalem (Yerushalayim)
'Ammān
Hefa (Haifa)
Beer Sheva (Beersheba)
Tabūk
Al Madīnah (Medina)
Makkah (Mecca)
Jiddah (Jedda)
At Ṭā'if
Port Sudan (Būr Sudan)
Wadi Halfa
Lake Nasser
Aswân
Luxor (El Uqsur)
Asyût
Atbara
Omdurman
Khartoum (El Khartum)
Khartoum North
Wad Medani
El Obeid
Kassala
Asmara
Massawa
Gonder
T'ana Hāyk' (Lake Tana)
Dessē (Dese)
Dirē Dawa
Djibouti
Ṣan'ā'
Al Hudaydah (Hodeida)
Ta'izz
'Adan (Aden)
Abhā
Hā'il
Buraydah
An Nāṣirīyah
Dahlak Archipelago
Jebel Abyad Plateau
Ethiopian Highlands
1:7.5M
Miles
Km
© Bartholomew

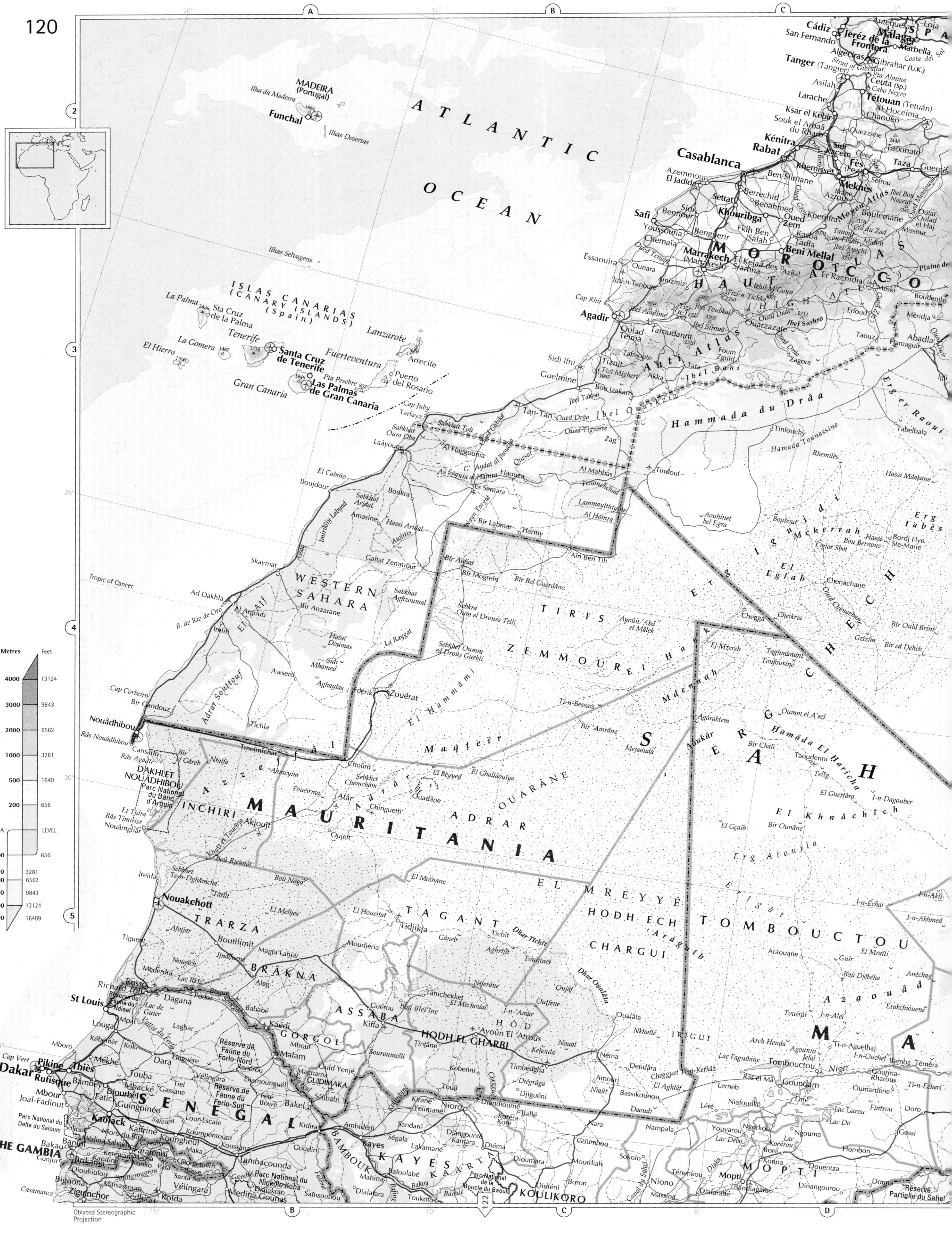
ATLANTIC OCEAN
MADEIRA (Portugal)
Ilha da Madeira
Funchal
Ilhas Desertas
Ilhas Selvagens
ISLAS CANARIAS (CANARY ISLANDS) (Spain)
La Palma
Sta Cruz de la Palma
Tenerife
La Gomera
El Hierro
Santa Cruz de Tenerife
Lanzarote
Arrecife
Fuerteventura
Puerto del Rosario
Gran Canaria
Las Palmas de Gran Canaria
MOROCCO
Cádiz
Jerez de la Frontera
Málaga
San Fernando
Algeciras
Gibraltar (U.K.)
Tanger (Tangier)
Strait of Gibraltar
Ceuta (Sp.)
Tétouan (Tetuán)
Asilah
Larache
Ksar el Kebir
Al Hoceima
Chaouen
Kénitra
Rabat
Casablanca
Azemmour
El Jadida
Sidi Kacem
Fès (Fez)
Meknès
Taza
Khemisset
Ben Slimane
Berrechid
Settat
Khouribga
Safi
Youssoufia
Chemaia
Marrakech (Marrakesh)
Essaouira
Beni Mellal
Kasba Tadla
Fkih Ben Salah
Oued Zem
Khenifra
Moyen Atlas
Haut Atlas
Er Rachidia
Ouarzazate
Agadir
Cap Rhir
Taroudannt
Anti Atlas
Tiznit
Sidi Ifni
Guelmine
Tan-Tan
Cap Juby
Tarfaya
Tata
Zagora
Jbel Ouarkziz
Hammada du Drâa
Tindouf
Tabelbala
WESTERN SAHARA
Laâyoune
Boujdour
Es Semara
Ad Dakhla
Tropic of Cancer
Bir Anzarane
Cap Corbeiro
Bir Gandouz
Nouâdhibou
Râs Nouâdhibou
MAURITANIA
TIRIS ZEMMOUR
Zouérat
Fdérik
DAKHLET NOUÂDHIBOU
Parc National du Banc d'Arguin
INCHIRI
Akjoujt
ADRAR
Atâr
Chinguetti
Ouadâne
Nouakchott
TRARZA
TAGANT
Tidjikja
BRÂKNA
Aleg
ASSABA
Kiffa
GORGOL
Kaédi
HODH EL GHARBI
Ayoûn El Atroûs
HODH ECH CHARGUI
Néma
Oualâta
Rosso
St Louis
Dakar
Thiès
Rufisque
Mbour
Kaolack
SENEGAL
THE GAMBIA
Banjul
Ziguinchor
Tambacounda
Kayes
Nioro
Bamako
KOULIKORO
Tombouctou
TOMBOUCTOU
Taoudenni
Araouane
Mopti
MOPTI
Gao
Metres
Feet
SEA
LEVEL
Oblated Stereographic Projection

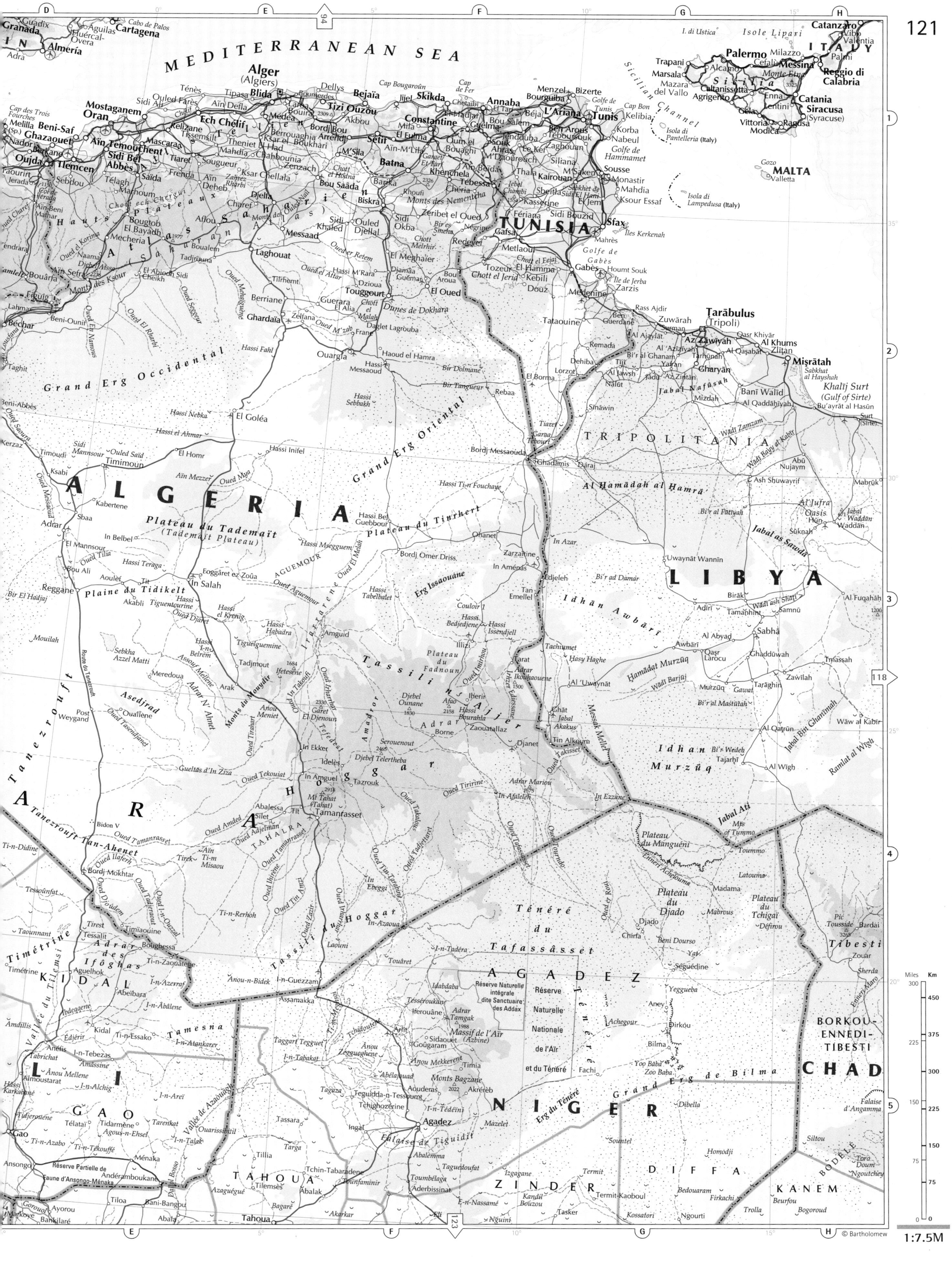
MEDITERRANEAN SEA
Alger
(Algiers)
Oran
Constantine
Annaba
Tunis
TUNISIA
Sfax
Palermo
Messina
Catania
Siracusa
(Syracuse)
ITALY
MALTA
Valletta
Sicilian Channel
Ṭarābulus
(Tripoli)
Miṣrātah
Khalīj Surt
(Gulf of Sirte)
TRIPOLITANIA
ALGERIA
LIBYA
Grand Erg Occidental
Grand Erg Oriental
Plateau du Tademaït
(Tademaït Plateau)
Plateau du Tinrhert
Al Ḥamādah al Ḥamrā'
Idhān Awbārī
Idhān Murzūq
Sabhā
Tassili n'Ajjer
Ahaggar
Tamanrasset
Tanezrouft
Ténéré
AGADEZ
Réserve Naturelle intégrale dite Sanctuaire des Addax
Réserve Naturelle Nationale de l'Aïr et du Ténéré
Massif de l'Aïr
(Azbine)
Agadez
NIGER
CHAD
BORKOU-ENNEDI-TIBESTI
Tibesti
KANEM
DIFFA
ZINDER
TAHOUA
GAO
KIDAL
Adrar des Ifôghas
Gao
Erg de Bilma
Grand Erg de Bilma
Plateau du Djado
Plateau du Manguéni
Plateau du Tchigaï
Pic Toussidé
3265
Miles
Km
1:7.5M
© Bartholomew

WESTERN SAHARA
MAURITANIA
TIRIS ZEMMOUR
INCHIRI
ADRAR
TRARZA
BRÂKNA
TAGANT
ASSABA
GORGOL
GUIDIMAKA
HODH ECH CHARGUI
HODH EL GHARBI
DAKHLET NOUÂDHIBOU
Nouâdhibou
Nouakchott
St Louis
Dakar
SENEGAL
THE GAMBIA
Banjul
GUINEA-BISSAU
Bissau
GUINEA
Conakry
SIERRA LEONE
Freetown
LIBERIA
Monrovia
CÔTE D'IVOIRE
Abidjan
Yamoussoukro
MALI
Bamako
KAYES
KOULIKORO
SÉGOU
SIKASSO
MOPTI
TOMBOUCTOU
BURKINA
Ouagadougou
GHANA
Accra
ATLANTIC OCEAN
CAPE VERDE
Praia
Metres
Feet
4000
13124
3000
9843
2000
6562
1000
3281
500
1640
200
656
SEA
LEVEL
200
656
1000
3281
2000
6562
3000
9843
4000
13123
at the same scale
Oblated Stereographic Projection

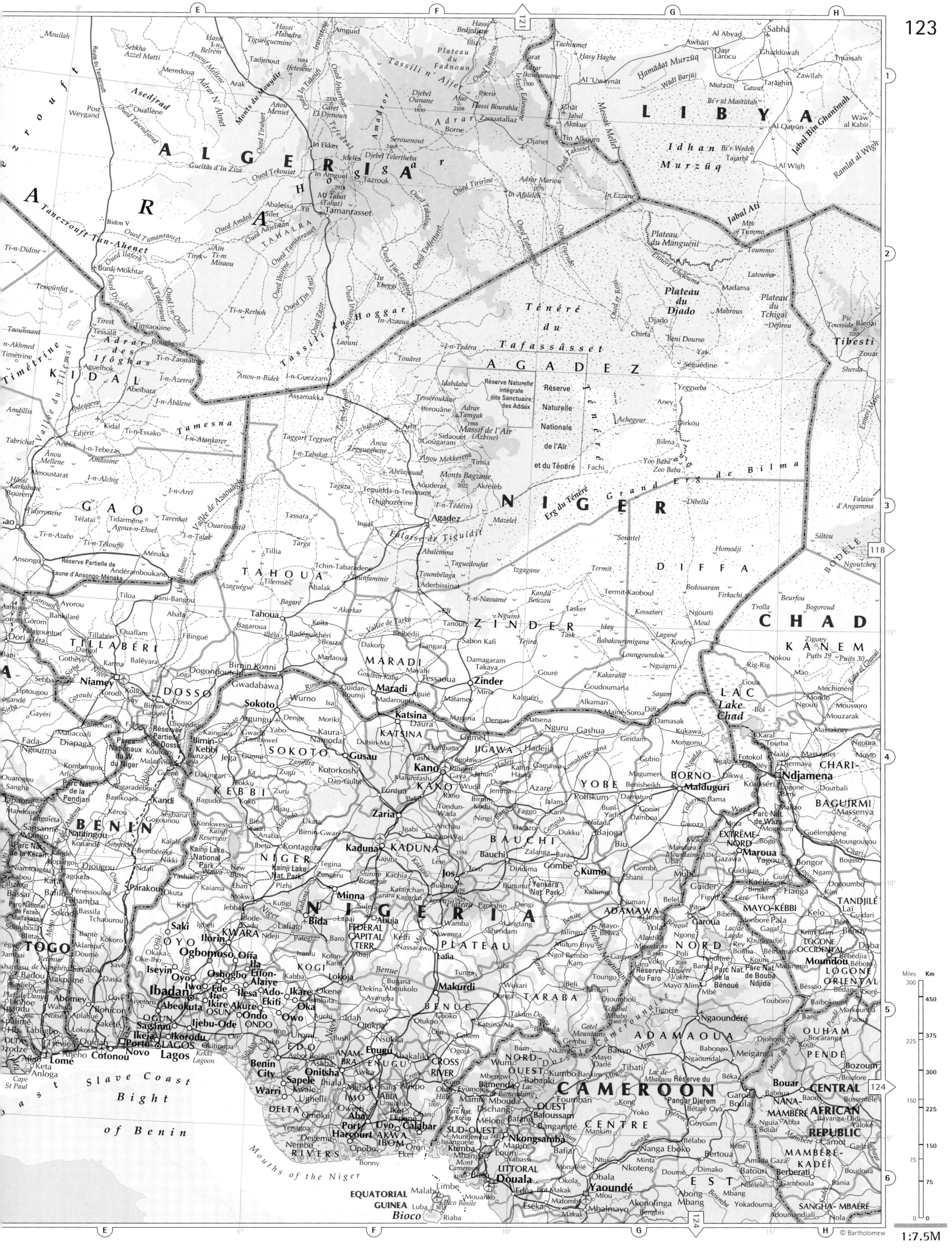
ALGERIA
LIBYA
NIGER
CHAD
NIGERIA
BENIN
TOGO
CAMEROON
CENTRAL AFRICAN REPUBLIC
EQUATORIAL GUINEA
AGADEZ
DIFFA
ZINDER
MARADI
TAHOUA
TILLABÉRI
DOSSO
KIDAL
GAO
Ahaggar
Tassili n' Ajjer
Tassili du Hoggar
Ténéré du Tafassâsset
Massif de l'Aïr
Grand Erg de Bilma
Erg du Ténéré
Plateau du Djado
Tibesti
Lac Chad
Lake Chad
KANEM
BAGUIRMI
Tamanrasset
Agadez
Tahoua
Niamey
Maradi
Zinder
Sokoto
Katsina
Kano
Kaduna
Zaria
Jos
Bauchi
Maiduguri
Ndjamena
Maroua
Garoua
Ngaoundéré
Yaoundé
Douala
Lagos
Ibadan
Abeokuta
Porto-Novo
Cotonou
Lomé
Benin City
Enugu
Port Harcourt
Calabar
Makurdi
Lokoja
Abuja
Ilorin
Ogbomoso
Parakou
Kandi
Moundou
Bouar
Slave Coast
Bight of Benin
Mouths of the Niger
Bioco
Malabo
Réserve Naturelle intégrale dite Sanctuaire des Addax
Réserve Naturelle Nationale de l'Aïr et du Ténéré
Miles
Km
© Bartholomew

1:7.5M

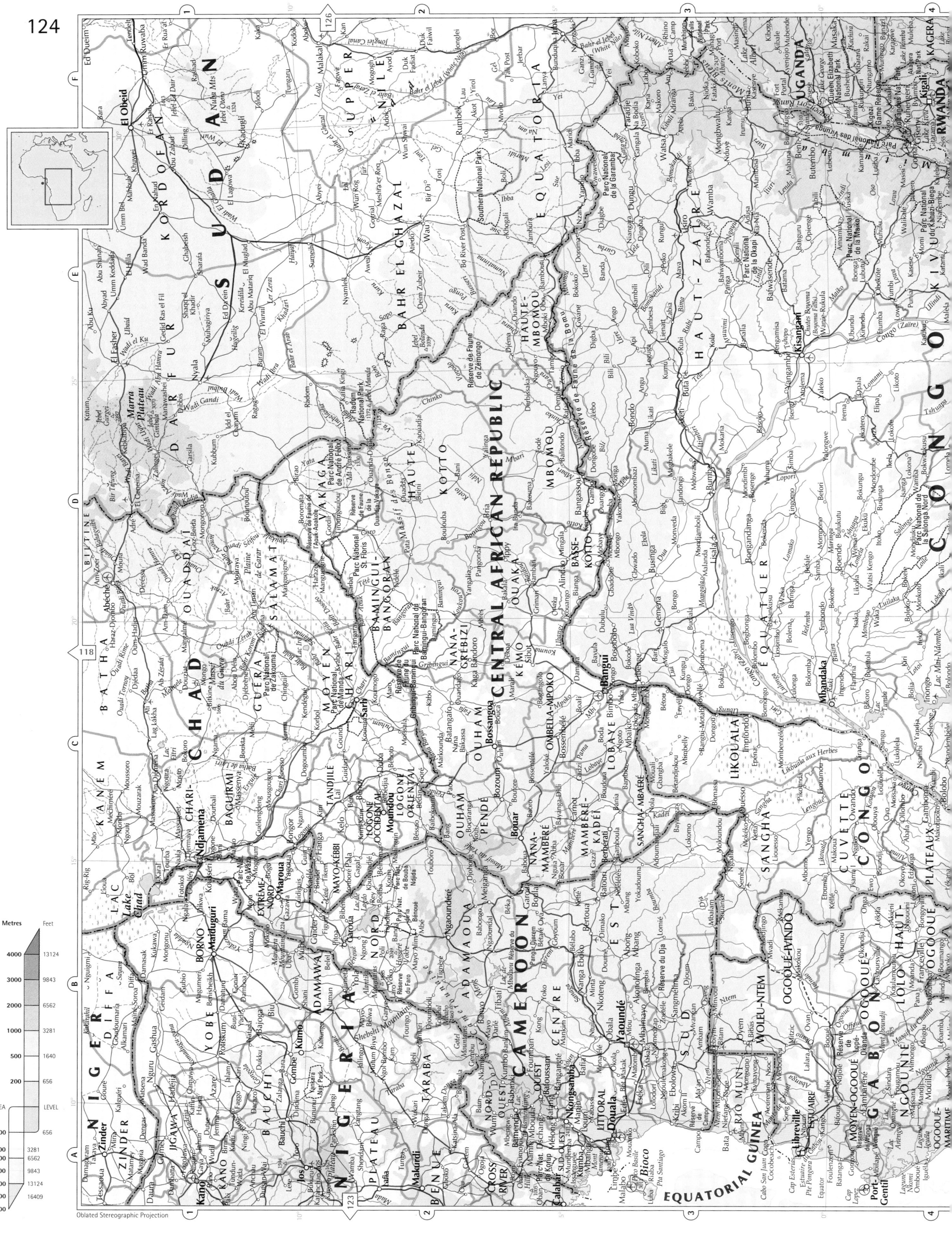
SUDAN
CHAD
CENTRAL AFRICAN REPUBLIC
CAMEROON
NIGERIA
NIGER
CONGO
GABON
EQUATORIAL GUINEA
UGANDA
RWANDA
HAUT-ZAÏRE
EQUATEUR
KORDOFAN
DARFUR
BAHR EL GHAZAL
EQUATORIA
Ndjamena
Bangui
Yaoundé
Douala
Libreville
Kisangani
Mbandaka
El Obeid
Abéché
Sarh
Moundou
Maiduguri
Kano
Zinder
Jos
Makurdi
Bioco
Metres
Feet
Oblated Stereographic Projection

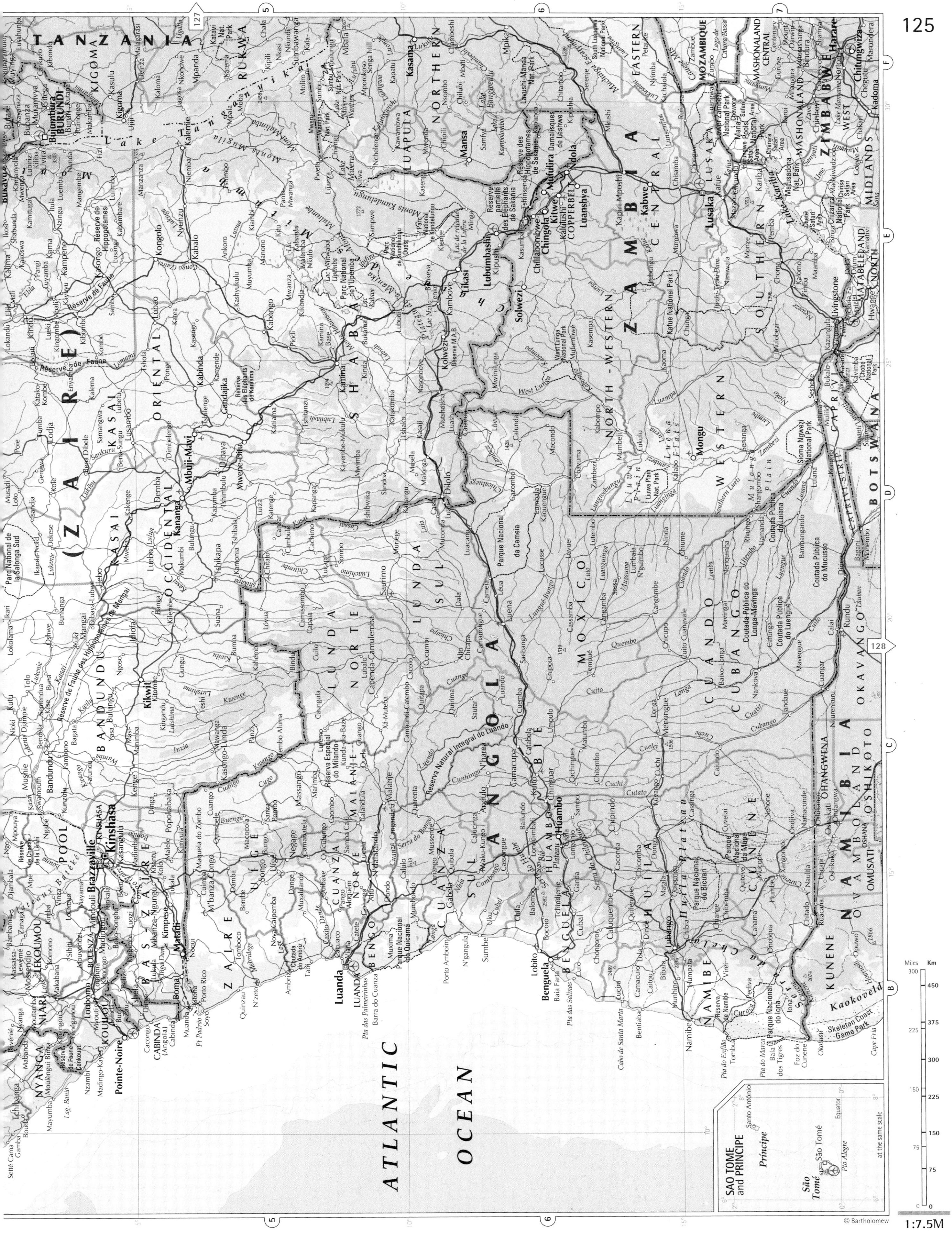
TANZANIA
BURUNDI
Bujumbura
ZAIRE
ZAMBIA
ANGOLA
NAMIBIA
BOTSWANA
ZIMBABWE
MOZAMBIQUE
CONGO
CABINDA (Angola)
Kinshasa
Brazzaville
Pointe-Noire
Luanda
Lusaka
Harare
Lubumbashi
Kananga
Mbuji-Mayi
Kisangani
Huambo
Benguela
Lobito
Lubango
Namibe
Ndola
Kitwe
Livingstone
Kasama
Mansa
Mongu
Solwezi
Kolwezi
Likasi
Kalemie
Kigoma
Matadi
Kikwit
Luena
Menongue
Rundu
Saurimo
Malanje
ATLANTIC
OCEAN
SAO TOME and PRINCIPE
Príncipe
São Tomé
Equator
at the same scale
Miles
Km
1:7.5M
© Bartholomew

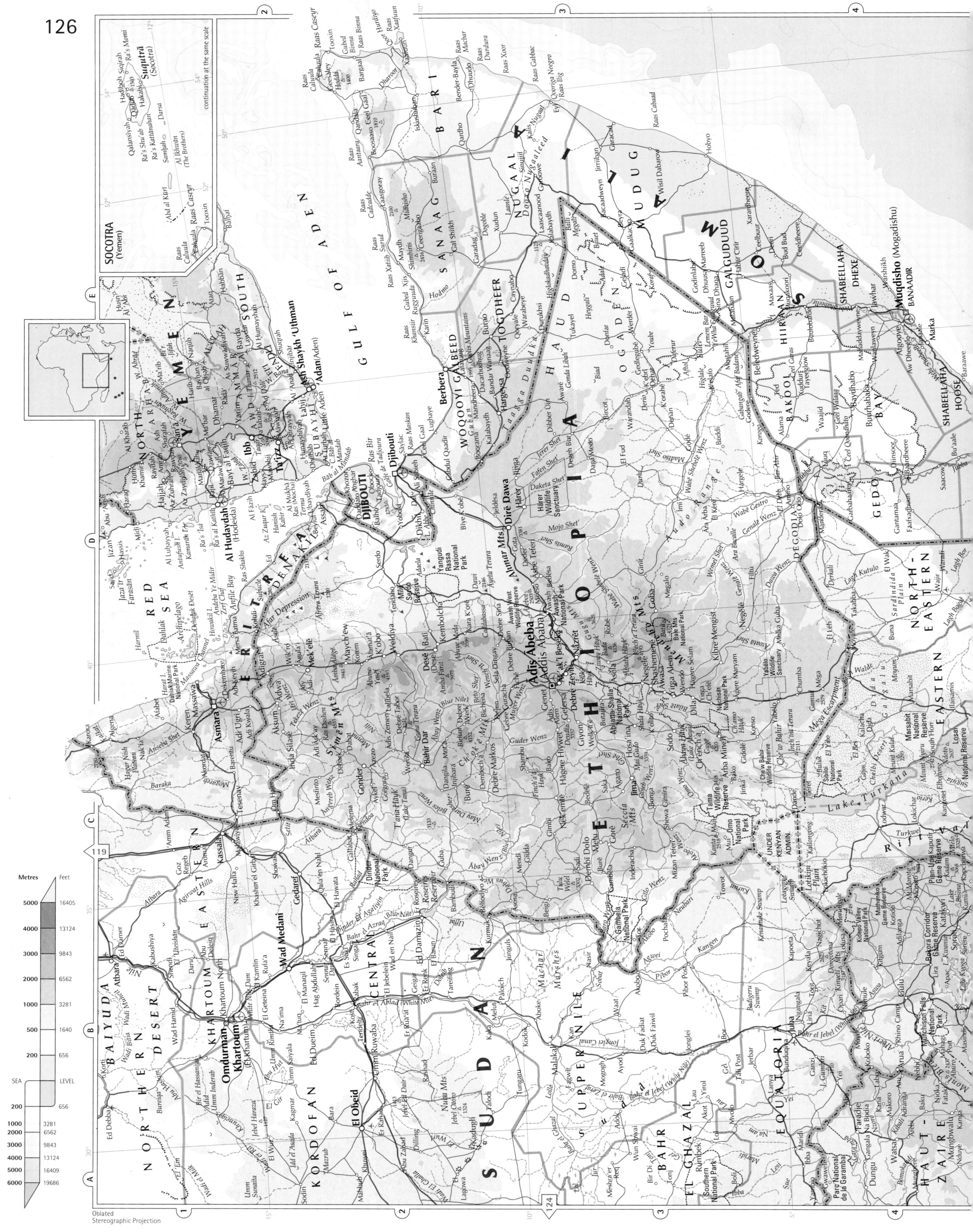
SOCOTRA (Yemen)
Suquṭrā (Socotra)
continuation at the same scale
GULF OF ADEN
RED SEA
NORTH YEMEN
SOUTH YEMEN
DJIBOUTI
ERITREA
ETHIOPIA
SOMALIA
SUDAN
NORTHERN DESERT
KHARTOUM
EASTERN
KORDOFAN
CENTRAL
UPPER NILE
BAHR EL GHAZAL
EQUATORIA
HAUT-ZAIRE
NORTH-EASTERN
EASTERN
OGADEN
HAUD
MUDUG
GALGUDUUD
BARI
SANAAG
TOGDHEER
NUGAAL
WOQOOYI GALBEED
BAKOOL
HIIRAAN
GEDO
BAY
SHABEELLAHA DHEXE
SHABEELLAHA HOOSE
BANAADIR
Ādis Ābeba (Addis Ababa)
Asmara
Djibouti
Berbera
Hargeysa
Muqdisho (Mogadishu)
Khartoum (El Khartum)
Omdurman
Wad Medani
El Obeid
Juba
Dirē Dawa
Bahir Dar
Gonder
Mek'elē
'Adan (Aden)
San'a
Al Hudaydah (Hodeida)
Ta'izz
Kassala
Gedaref
Lake Turkana
T'ana Hāyk' (Lake Tana)
Metres
Feet
SEA LEVEL
Oblated Stereographic Projection
119
124

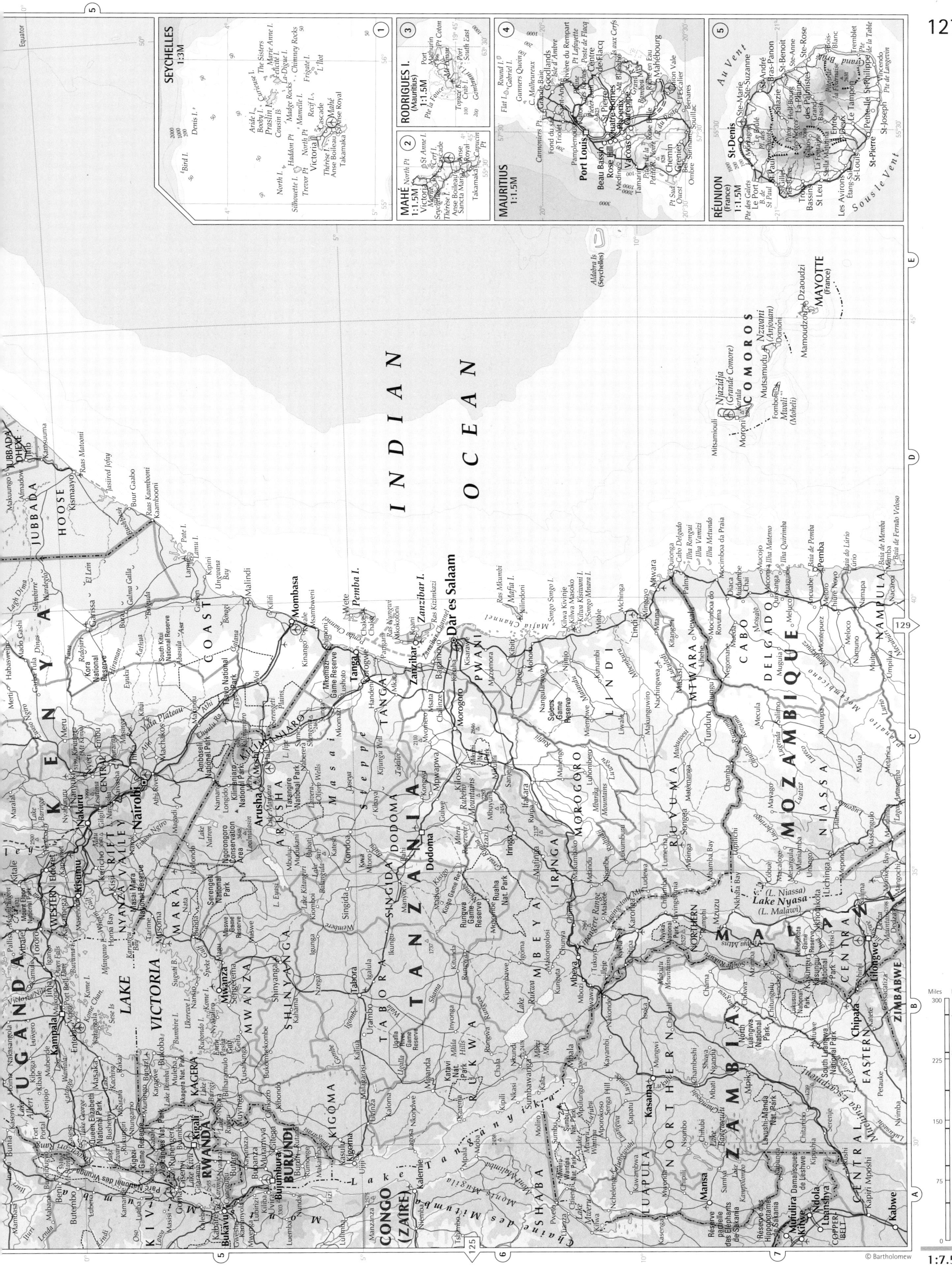
INDIAN OCEAN
TANZANIA
KENYA
UGANDA
RWANDA
BURUNDI
MOZAMBIQUE
ZAMBIA
MALAWI
ZIMBABWE
CONGO (ZAIRE)
COMOROS
MAYOTTE (France)
LAKE VICTORIA
Lake Nyasa (L. Niassa) (L. Malawi)
Dar es Salaam
Nairobi
Mombasa
Dodoma
Zanzibar
Kampala
Lilongwe
Kigali
Bujumbura
Moroni
Aldabra Is (Seychelles)
SEYCHELLES 1:3M
MAHÉ 1:1.5M
RODRIGUES I. (Mauritius) 1:1.5M
MAURITIUS 1:1.5M
RÉUNION (France) 1:1.5M
Port Louis
St-Denis
Victoria
Miles
Km
© Bartholomew
1:7.5M

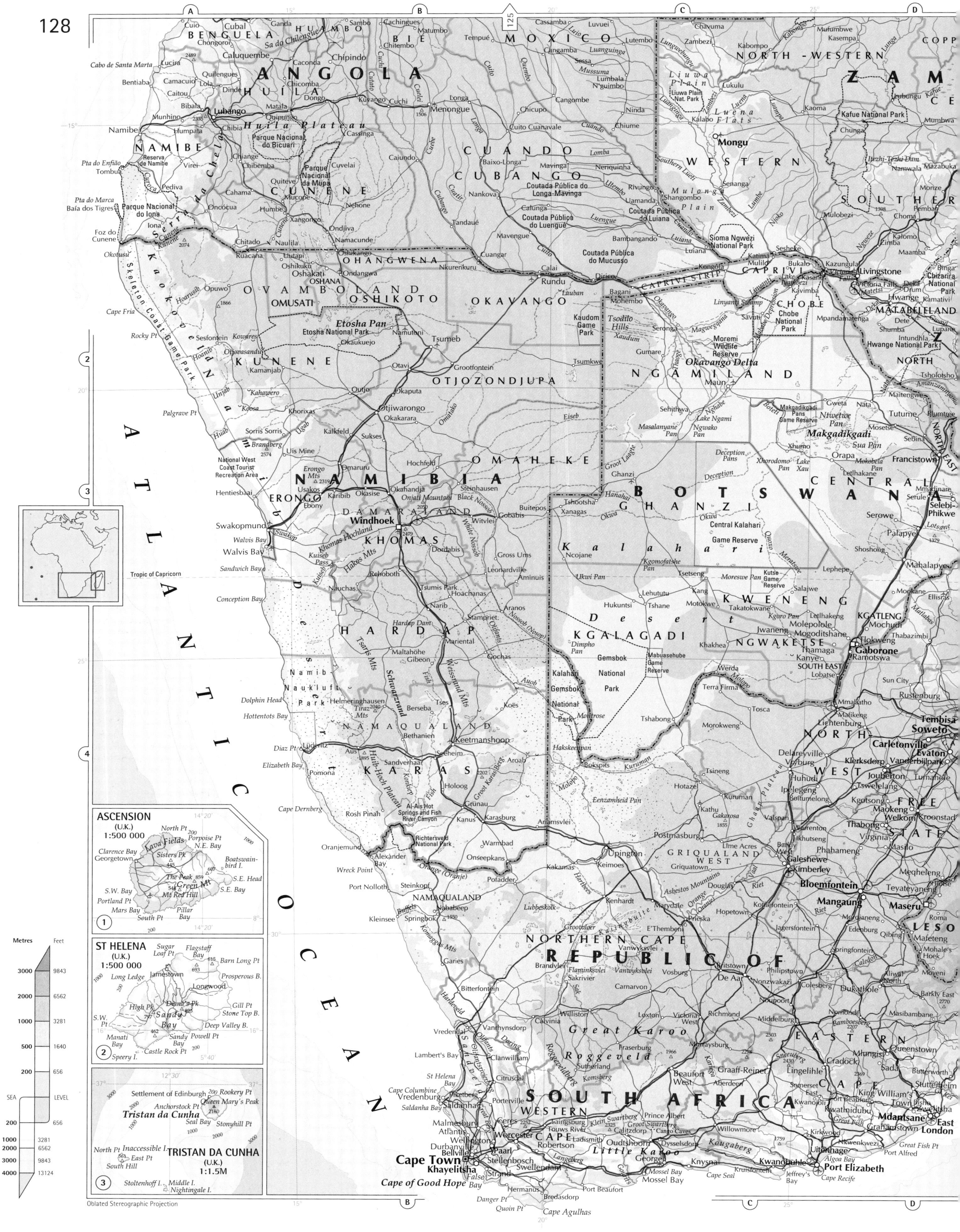
A
B
C
D
125
15°
20°
25°
ANGOLA
BENGUELA
HUÍLA
MOXICO
HUAMBO
BIÉ
Cuio
Cubal
Ganda
Sambo
Cachingues
Matumbo
Tempué
Cassamba
Luvuei
Chavuma
Zambezi
Kabompo
Mufumbwe
Kasempa
Chongoroi
Caluquembe
Chipindo
Lutembo
Cangamba
Cabo de Santa Marta
Lucira
Caconda
Chitembo
Quilengues
Bentiaba
Camacuio
Lola
Chicomba
Caitou
Dinde
Dongo
Bibala
Lubango
Matala
Kuvango
Cuchi
Longa
Menongue
Chicupo
Cangombe
Nindá
Namibe
Munhino
Humpata
Chibia
Huila Plateau
Parque Nacional do Bicuari
Cassinga
Cuito Cuanavale
Chiume
NAMIBE
Reserva de Namibe
Pta do Enfião
Tombua
Virei
Chiange
Chibemba
Cuvelai
Parque Nacional da Mupa
Cajundo
CUANDO CUBANGO
Baixo-Longa
Mavinga
Neriquinha
Coutada Pública do Longa-Mavinga
Pta do Marca
Baía dos Tigres
Parque Nacional do Iona
Cahama
Oncócua
Quiteve
Mucope
CUNENE
Humbe
Nehone
Nankova
Rivungo
Uamanda
Coutada Pública do Luiana
Iona
Xangongo
Ondjiva
Tandaué
Calunga
Coutada Pública do Luengue
Foz do Cunene
Namacunde
Mavengue
Bambangando
Luiana
Chitado
Naulila
Ruacana
Okotusu
Oshikango
Cuangar
Coutada Pública do Mucusso
Dirico
Calai
Rundu
NORTH-WESTERN
ZAMBIA
Liuwa Plain
Liuwa Plain Nat. Park
Lukulu
Luena Flats
Kalabo
Kaoma
Kafue National Park
Mumbwa
Mongu
WESTERN
Senanga
Shangombo
Mulonga Plain
Sioma Ngwezi National Park
SOUTHERN
Mulobezi
Kalomo
Choma
Livingstone
Kazungula
Victoria Falls
Hwange
Hwange National Park
MATABELELAND NORTH
Sesheke
Katima Mulilo
Kongola
CAPRIVI
CAPRIVI STRIP
Bagani
Mohembo
OHANGWENA
Oshakati
Ondangwa
OSHANA
OMUSATI
OSHIKOTO
OVAMBOLAND
Nkurenkuru
OKAVANGO
Kaudom Game Park
Tsodilo Hills
Seronga
CHOBE
Chobe National Park
Linyanti Swamp
Savuti
Kavimba
Moremi Wildlife Reserve
Okavango Delta
Skeleton Coast Game Park
Kaokoveld
Opuwo
Cape Fria
Etosha Pan
Etosha National Park
Namutoni
Okaukuejo
Tsumeb
Rocky Pt
Sesfontein
Kowares
KUNENE
Kamanjab
Otavi
Grootfontein
Tsumkwe
Gumare
NGAMILAND
Maun
Outjo
Okaputa
OTJOZONDJUPA
Otjiwarongo
Okakarara
Palgrave Pt
Khorixas
Lake Ngami
Sehithwa
Makgadikgadi Pans Game Reserve
Gweta
Nata
Makgadikgadi
Ntwetwe Pan
Sua Pan
Francistown
Sorris Sorris
Brandberg
Uis Mine
Kalkfeld
Sukses
National West Coast Tourist Recreation Area
Erongo Mts
Omaruru
Hochfeld
OMAHEKE
Ghanzi
Deception Pans
Orapa
Serowe
Palapye
Selebi-Phikwe
CENTRAL
BOTSWANA
GHANZI
Hentiesbaai
NAMIBIA
ERONGO
Usakos
Karibib
Okasise
Okahandja
Steinhausen
DAMARALAND
Windhoek
KHOMAS
Gobabis
Buitepos
Tshootsha
Xanagas
Central Kalahari Game Reserve
Swakopmund
Walvis Bay
Tropic of Capricorn
Sandwich Bay
Kalahari
Dordabis
Gross Ums
Leonardville
Aminuis
Ncojane
Rehoboth
Mahalapye
Conception Bay
Nauchas
Tsumis Park
Hoachanas
Tsetseng
Lehututu
Hukuntsi
Tshane
Kang
KWENENG
Molepolole
KGATLENG
Mochudi
ATLANTIC OCEAN
HARDAP
Mariental
Stampriet
Aranos
Desert
KGALAGADI
Jwaneng
Mogoditshane
Gaborone
Ramotswa
NGWAKETSE
Thamaga
Kanye
SOUTH EAST
Lobatse
Maltahöhe
Gibeon
Gochas
Namib-Naukluft Park
Helmeringhausen
Gemsbok National Park
Kalahari Gemsbok National Park
Mabuasehube Game Reserve
Werda
Terra Firma
Sun City
Rustenburg
Dolphin Head
Berseba
Tses
Koës
Tshabong
Tosca
Mmabatho
Mafikeng
Lichtenburg
Hottentots Bay
NAMAQUALAND
Bethanien
Keetmanshoop
Morokweng
NORTH-WEST
Carletonville
Soweto
Tembisa
Evaton
Diaz Pt
Lüderitz
Aus
Seeheim
Aroab
Hakskeenpan
Bokspits
Delareyville
Vryburg
Klerksdorp
Vanderbijlpark
Elizabeth Bay
Pomona
KARAS
Hunts Plateau
Holoog
Tsineng
Huhudi
Ipelegeng
Jouberton
Cape Dernberg
Rosh Pinah
Grünau
Karasburg
Ariamsvlei
Kuruman
Hotazel
Kathu
Valspan
Welkom
Kroonstad
FREE STATE
ASCENSION (U.K.) 1:500 000
North Pt
Porpoise Pt
Lava Fields
N.E. Bay
Clarence Bay
Georgetown
Sisters Pk
Boatswain-bird I.
The Peak
Green Mt
S.E. Head
S.W. Bay
Mt Red Hill
S.E. Bay
Portland Pt
Mars Bay
Pillar Bay
South Pt
Oranjemund
Alexander Bay
Richtersveld National Park
Warmbad
Onseepkans
Upington
Keimoes
Postmasburg
GRIQUALAND WEST
Galeshewe
Kimberley
Bloemfontein
Mangaung
Maseru
LESOTHO
Wreck Point
Port Nolloth
Steinkopf
Pofadder
Kakamas
Kenhardt
Douglas
Prieska
Hopetown
Koffiefontein
Jagersfontein
Metres
Feet
3000
9843
2000
6562
1000
3281
500
1640
200
656
SEA
LEVEL
4000
13124
ST HELENA (U.K.) 1:500 000
Sugar Loaf Pt
Flagstaff Bay
Barn Long Pt
Long Ledge
Jamestown
Prosperous B.
Longwood
High Pk
Diana's Pk
Gill Pt
Stone Top B.
Sandy Bay
Deep Valley B.
Manati Bay
Powell Pt
Castle Rock Pt
Speery I.
Kleinsee
Springbok
NAMAQUALAND
Nababeep
Garies
NORTHERN CAPE
REPUBLIC OF SOUTH AFRICA
Brandvlei
Vanwyksvlei
Vosburg
Britstown
De Aar
Philipstown
Colesberg
Aliwal North
Carnarvon
Bitterfontein
Williston
Loxton
Victoria West
Richmond
Middelburg
Vredendal
Vanrhynsdorp
Calvinia
Great Karoo
Murraysburg
Graaff-Reinet
Cradock
Queenstown
EASTERN CAPE
Lambert's Bay
Clanwilliam
Roggeveld
Fraserburg
Sutherland
Beaufort West
Aberdeen
St Helena Bay
Cape Columbine
Vredenburg
Saldanha Bay
Citrusdal
Porterville
WESTERN CAPE
Settlement of Edinburgh
Rookery Pt
Anchorstock Pt
Queen Mary's Peak
Tristan da Cunha
Seal Bay
Stonyhill Pt
North Pt
Inaccessible I.
East Pt
South Hill
TRISTAN DA CUNHA (U.K.) 1:1.5M
Stoltenhoff I.
Middle I.
Nightingale I.
Malmesbury
Atlantis
Wellington
Durbanville
Bellville
Cape Town
Khayelitsha
Paarl
Stellenbosch
Worcester
Robertson
Swellendam
Ceres
Laingsburg
Prince Albert
Oudtshoorn
Little Karoo
George
Knysna
Mossel Bay
Willowmore
Uitenhage
Port Elizabeth
Algoa Bay
Cape Recife
Jeffrey's Bay
Kwanobuhle
King William's Town
Mdantsane
East London
Grahamstown
Port Alfred
Cape of Good Hope
False Bay
Strand
Hermanus
Bredasdorp
Danger Pt
Quoin Pt
Cape Agulhas
Port Beaufort
Oblated Stereographic Projection

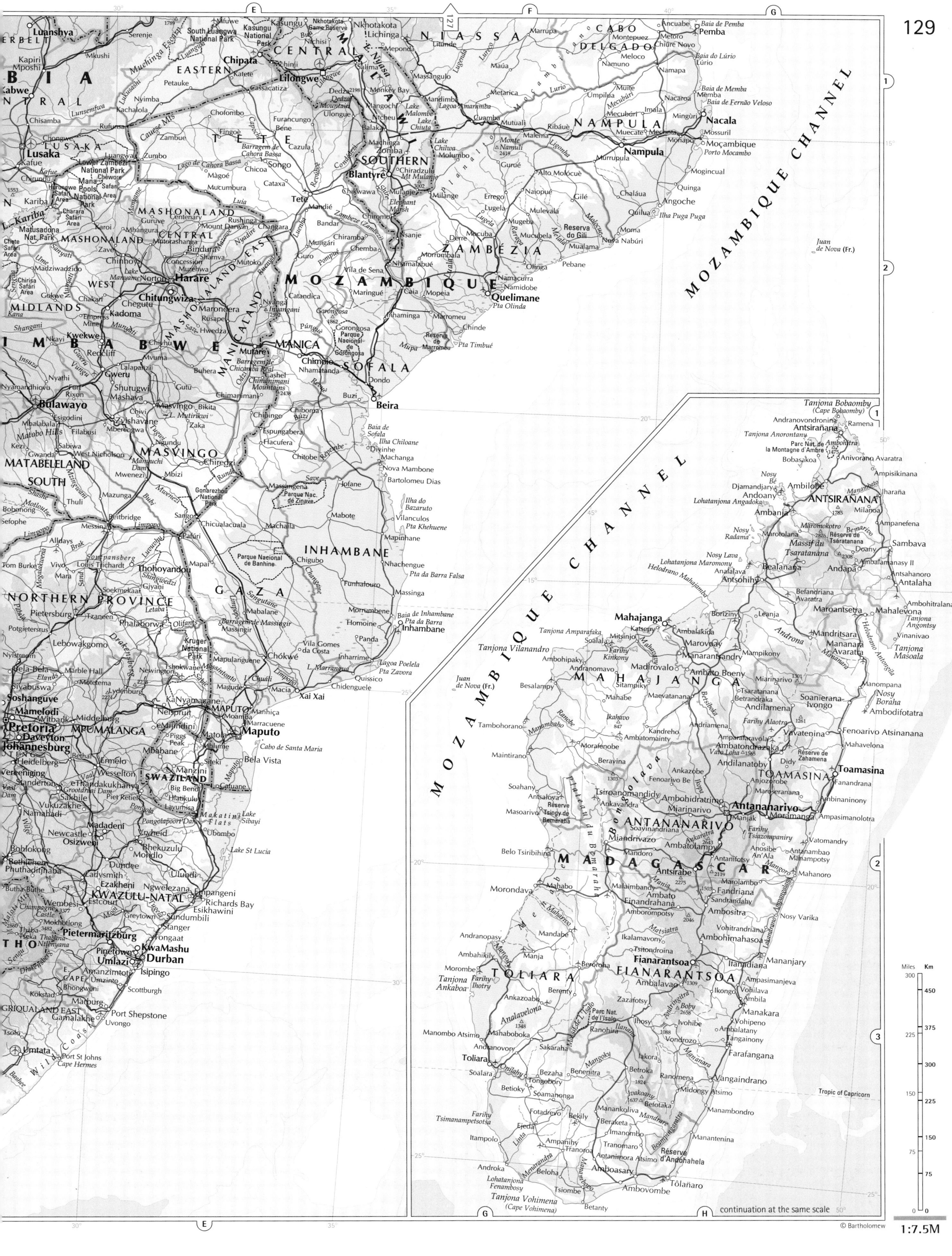
MOZAMBIQUE
MALAWI
ZIMBABWE
MADAGASCAR
SWAZILAND
MOZAMBIQUE CHANNEL
NIASSA
CABO DELGADO
NAMPULA
ZAMBÉZIA
TETE
MANICA
SOFALA
INHAMBANE
GAZA
MASHONALAND
MANICALAND
MASVINGO
MIDLANDS
MATABELELAND SOUTH
NORTHERN PROVINCE
MPUMALANGA
KWAZULU-NATAL
MAHAJANGA
ANTSIRAÑANA
TOAMASINA
ANTANANARIVO
FIANARANTSOA
TOLIARA
Lusaka
Harare
Lilongwe
Blantyre
Bulawayo
Beira
Quelimane
Nampula
Nacala
Pemba
Tete
Chimoio
Mutare
Maputo
Xai Xai
Inhambane
Pretoria
Johannesburg
Durban
Pietermaritzburg
Richards Bay
Mahajanga
Antsirañana
Toamasina
Antananarivo
Antsirabe
Fianarantsoa
Toliara
Tôlañaro
Juan de Nova (Fr.)
Tropic of Capricorn
continuation at the same scale
Miles
Km
1:7.5M
© Bartholomew

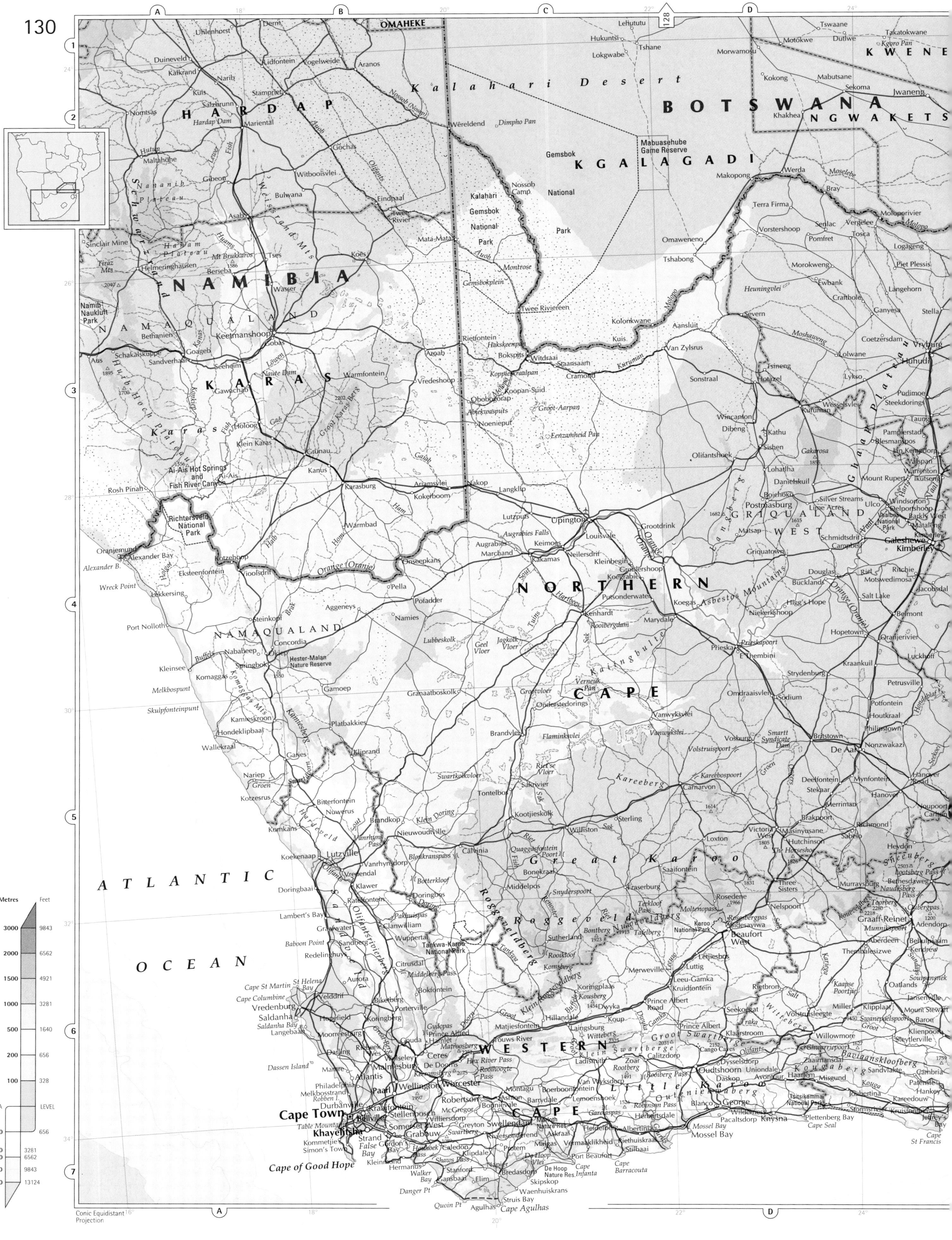
OMAHEKE
128
KWENE
BOTSWANA
NGWAKETSE
Kalahari Desert
HARDAP
Hardap Dam
Mariental
KGALAGADI
Mabuasehube Game Reserve
Gemsbok National Park
Kalahari Gemsbok National Park
NAMIBIA
NAMAQUALAND
Keetmanshoop
KARAS
Ai-Ais Hot Springs and Fish River Canyon
Richtersveld National Park
Orange (Oranje)
Upington
NORTHERN
CAPE
GRIQUALAND WEST
Kimberley
Asbestos Mountains
Great Karoo
Roggeveld
ATLANTIC
OCEAN
WESTERN
CAPE
Little Karoo
Beaufort West
Cape Town
Khayelitsha
Bellville
Stellenbosch
Worcester
George
Knysna
Mossel Bay
Cape of Good Hope
Cape Agulhas
Metres
Feet
3000
9843
2000
6562
1500
4921
1000
3281
500
1640
200
656
100
328
SEA
LEVEL
200
656
1000
3281
2000
6562
3000
9843
4000
13124
Conic Equidistant Projection

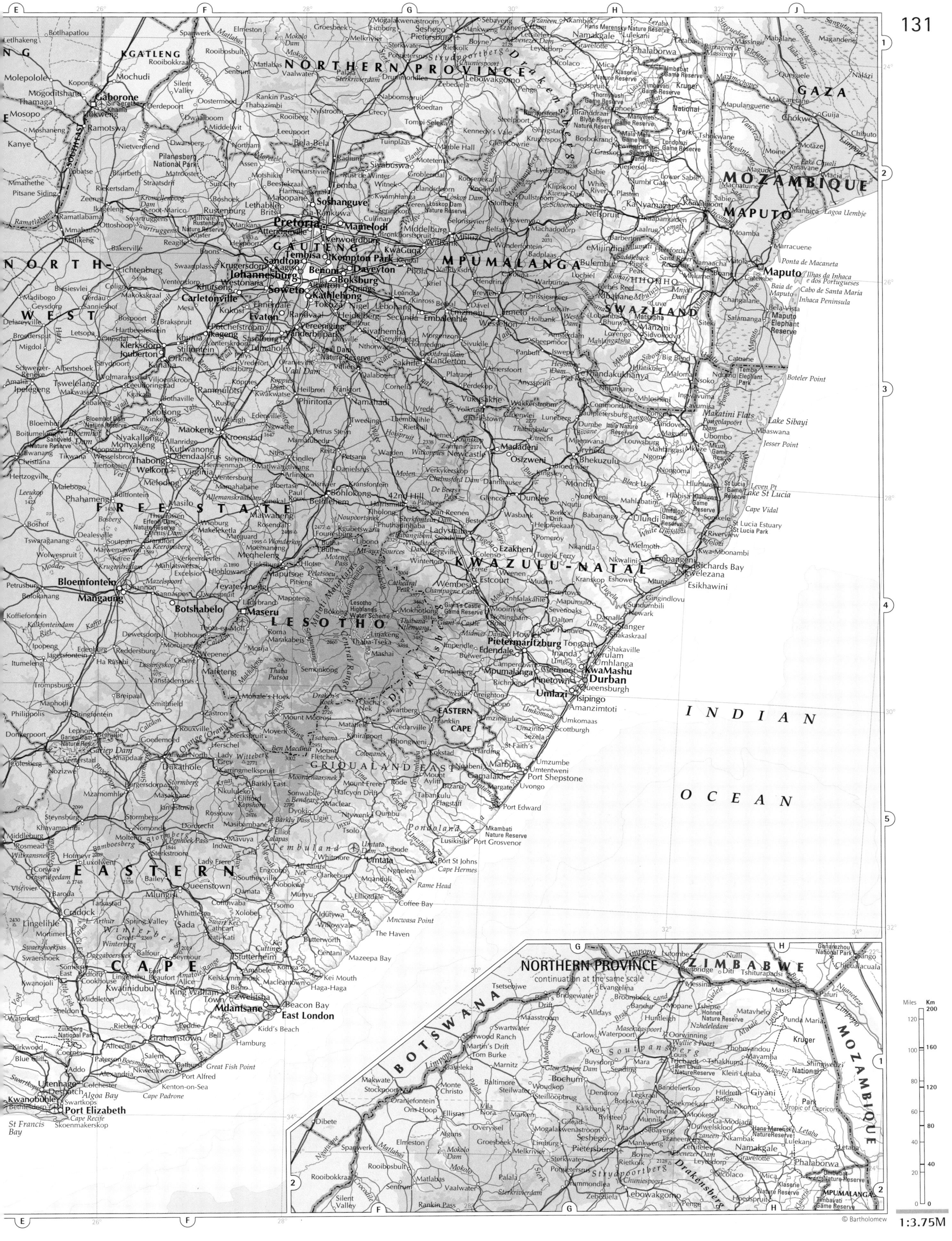
NORTHERN PROVINCE
MPUMALANGA
GAUTENG
NORTH-WEST
FREE STATE
KWAZULU-NATAL
LESOTHO
EASTERN CAPE
SWAZILAND
MOZAMBIQUE
MAPUTO
GAZA
KGATLENG
INDIAN OCEAN
Pretoria
Johannesburg
Soweto
Bloemfontein
Mangaung
Maseru
Pietermaritzburg
Durban
Maputo
Gaborone
East London
Port Elizabeth
Mbabane
Nelspruit
Pietersburg
Umtata
Kimberley
Queenstown
Grahamstown
Richards Bay
Port Shepstone
Drakensberg
NORTHERN PROVINCE
continuation at the same scale
BOTSWANA
ZIMBABWE
MOZAMBIQUE
MPUMALANGA
Miles
Km
© Bartholomew
1:3.75M

Metres SEA / Feet LEVEL
200 — 656
3000 — 9843

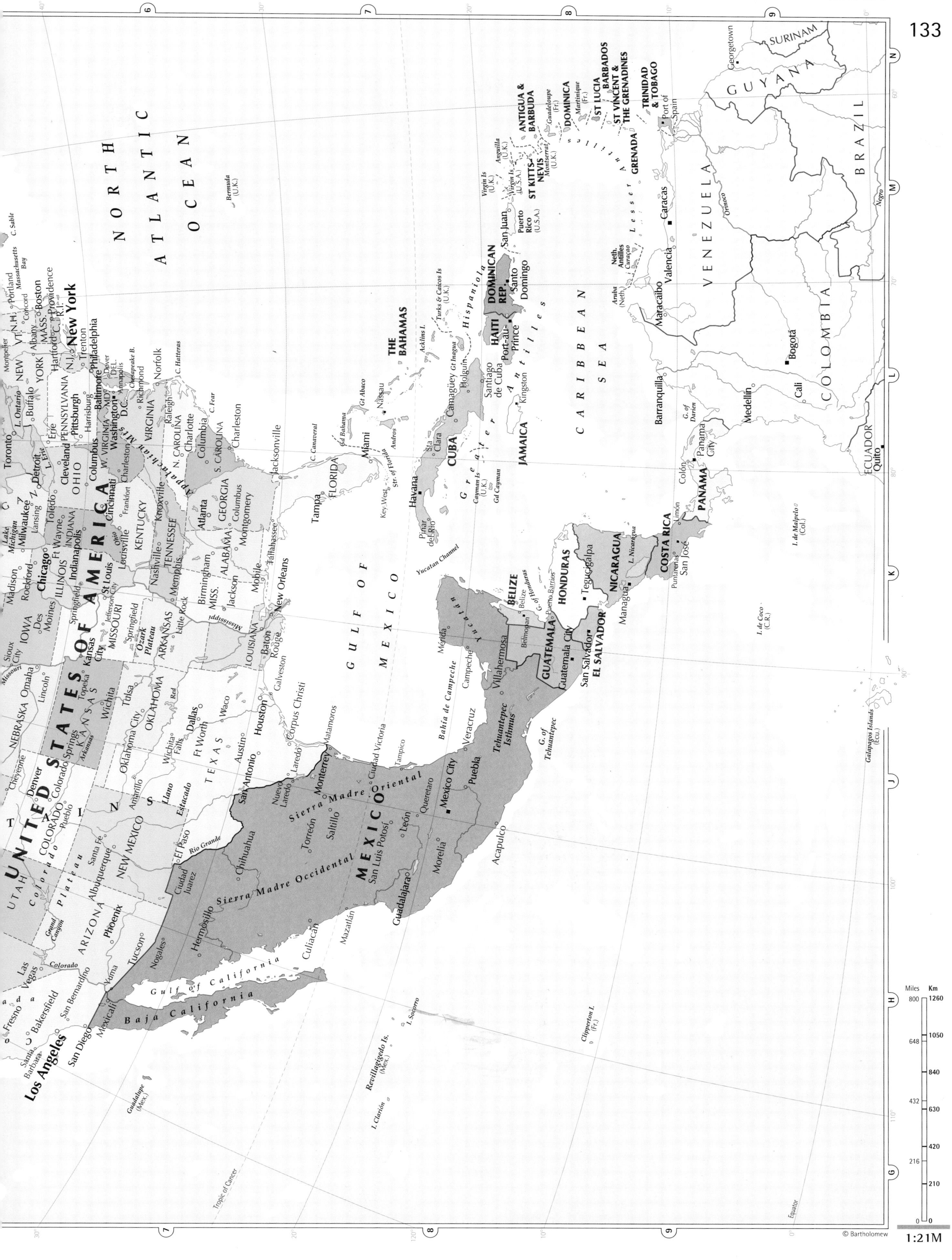
NORTH ATLANTIC OCEAN
UNITED STATES OF AMERICA
MEXICO
GULF OF MEXICO
CARIBBEAN SEA
THE BAHAMAS
CUBA
HAITI
DOMINICAN REP.
JAMAICA
BELIZE
GUATEMALA
HONDURAS
EL SALVADOR
NICARAGUA
COSTA RICA
PANAMA
VENEZUELA
COLOMBIA
GUYANA
SURINAM
BRAZIL
ECUADOR
ANTIGUA & BARBUDA
DOMINICA
ST LUCIA
BARBADOS
ST VINCENT & THE GRENADINES
GRENADA
TRINIDAD & TOBAGO
ST KITTS-NEVIS
Puerto Rico (U.S.A.)
Bermuda (U.K.)
Greater Antilles
Lesser Antilles
Hispaniola
Gulf of California
Baja California
Sierra Madre Occidental
Sierra Madre Oriental
Yucatán
Yucatan Channel
Bahía de Campeche
Tehuantepec Isthmus
Appalachian Mts
Rio Grande
Mississippi
Tropic of Cancer
Equator
New York
Philadelphia
Washington D.C.
Chicago
Houston
Dallas
Los Angeles
San Diego
Miami
Havana
Mexico City
Guadalajara
Monterrey
Caracas
Bogotá
Quito
Panama City
Kingston
Port-au-Prince
Santo Domingo
San Juan
Port of Spain
Georgetown
Managua
Tegucigalpa
San Salvador
Guatemala City
Belmopan
San José
Nassau
Miles
800
648
432
216
0
Km
1260
1050
840
630
420
210
0
© Bartholomew
1:21M

ARCTIC OCEAN
BERING SEA
Chukchi Sea
Bering Strait
BEAUFORT SEA
GULF OF ALASKA
PACIFIC OCEAN
RUSSIAN FEDERATION
U.S.A.
ALASKA
CANADA
YUKON TERRITORY
NORTHWEST TE
BRITISH COLUMBIA
ALBERTA
SASKATCHEWAN
MANI
WASHINGTON
OREGON
IDAHO
MONTANA
WYOMING
NORTH DAKOTA
SOUTH DAKOTA
NEBRASKA
NEVADA
CALIFORNIA
UTAH
COLORADO
Brooks Range
Alaska Range
Aleutian Range
Aleutian Islands
Kuskokwim Mts
Mackenzie Mountains
ROCKY MOUNTAINS
Coast Mountains
Cassiar Mountains
Banks Island
Victoria Island
Melville Island
Great Bear Lake
Great Slave Lake
Lake Athabasca
Anchorage
Fairbanks
Whitehorse
Yellowknife
Edmonton
Calgary
Vancouver
Victoria
Seattle
Tacoma
Spokane
Portland
Salem
Eugene
Boise
Salt Lake City
Reno
Sacramento
San Francisco
San Jose
Stockton
Saskatoon
Regina
Winnipeg
Billings
Cheyenne
Fargo
Sioux Falls
Chamberlin Trimetric Projection

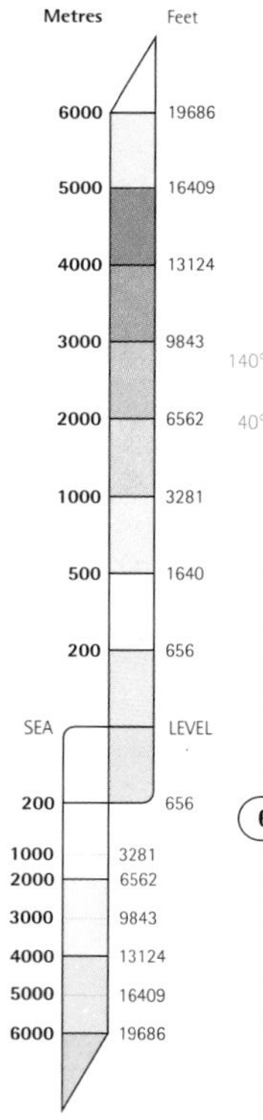
Metres
Feet
6000
19686
5000
16409
4000
13124
3000
9843
2000
6562
1000
3281
500
1640
200
656
SEA
LEVEL
200
656

GREENLAND SEA
GREENLAND (KALAALLIT NUNAAT) (Denmark)
Peary Land
Lincoln Sea
Ellesmere Island
Nares Strait
Kane Basin
Devon Island
BAFFIN BAY
BAFFIN ISLAND
DAVIS STRAIT
Denmark Strait
ICELAND
Reykjavík
Jan Mayen (Norway)
Melville Peninsula
Foxe Basin
Foxe Peninsula
Southampton Island
Hudson Strait
Péninsule d'Ungava
Ungava Bay
Labrador Sea
ATLANTIC OCEAN
HUDSON BAY
James Bay
NEWFOUNDLAND
LABRADOR
QUÉBEC
ONTARIO
MANITOBA
MINNESOTA
MICHIGAN
WISCONSIN
IOWA
ILLINOIS
OHIO
PENNSYLVANIA
NEW YORK
MAINE
NEW BRUNSWICK
NOVA SCOTIA
PRINCE EDWARD ISLAND
Gulf of St Lawrence
Cabot Strait
Lake Superior
Lake Michigan
Lake Huron
Lake Erie
Lake Ontario
Montréal
Québec
Ottawa
Toronto
Halifax
St John's
Chicago
Detroit
Cleveland
Buffalo
Boston
New York
Thunder Bay
Sudbury
Iqaluit
Nuuk (Godthåb)
Churchill
Miles
Km
© Bartholomew
1:15M

YUKON TERRITORY
MACKENZIE MOUNTAINS
Selwyn Mountains
Franklin Mountains
Great Bear Lake
Great Slave Lake
ALASKA
Alexander Archipelago
COAST MOUNTAINS
BRITISH COLUMBIA
ROCKY MOUNTAINS
ALBERTA
Queen Charlotte Islands
Queen Charlotte Sound
Hecate Strait
Vancouver Island
PACIFIC OCEAN
WASHINGTON
IDAHO
Fraser Plateau
Whitehorse
Prince George
Kamloops
Vancouver
Victoria
Edmonton
Calgary
Kelowna
Prince Rupert
Dawson Creek
Fort St John
Fort Nelson
Yellowknife
Metres
Feet
6000
19686
5000
16409
4000
13124
3000
9843
2000
6562
1000
3281
500
1640
200
656
SEA
LEVEL
Transverse Mercator Projection
152

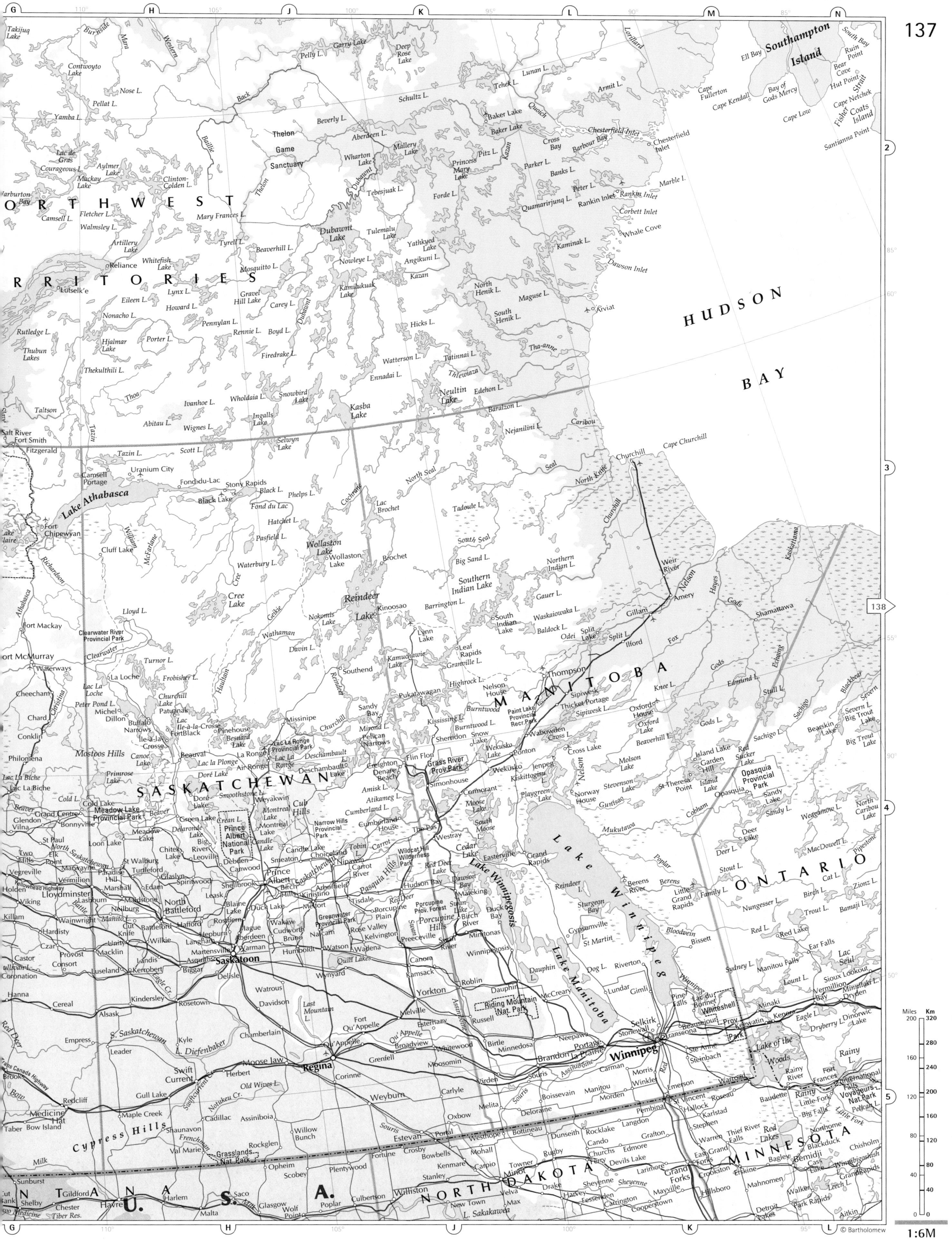
NORTHWEST TERRITORIES
HUDSON BAY
MANITOBA
SASKATCHEWAN
ONTARIO
MINNESOTA
NORTH DAKOTA
MONTANA
U. S. A.
Southampton Island
Coats Island
Thelon Game Sanctuary
Lake Athabasca
Reindeer Lake
Wollaston Lake
Southern Indian Lake
Lake Winnipeg
Lake Winnipegosis
Lake Manitoba
Cedar Lake
Lake of the Woods
Dubawnt Lake
Kasba Lake
Nueltin Lake
Baker Lake
Chesterfield Inlet
Rankin Inlet
Whale Cove
Arviat
Churchill
Cape Churchill
Thompson
Gillam
Flin Flon
The Pas
Uranium City
Fort Chipewyan
Fort McMurray
Lloydminster
North Battleford
Prince Albert
Saskatoon
Regina
Moose Jaw
Swift Current
Medicine Hat
Yorkton
Brandon
Portage la Prairie
Winnipeg
Selkirk
Dauphin
Kenora
Dryden
Fort Frances
Grand Forks
Minot
Williston
Estevan
Weyburn
Riding Mountain Nat. Park
Prince Albert National Park
Grasslands Nat. Park
Voyageurs Nat. Park
Cypress Hills
Miles
Km
1:6M
© Bartholomew

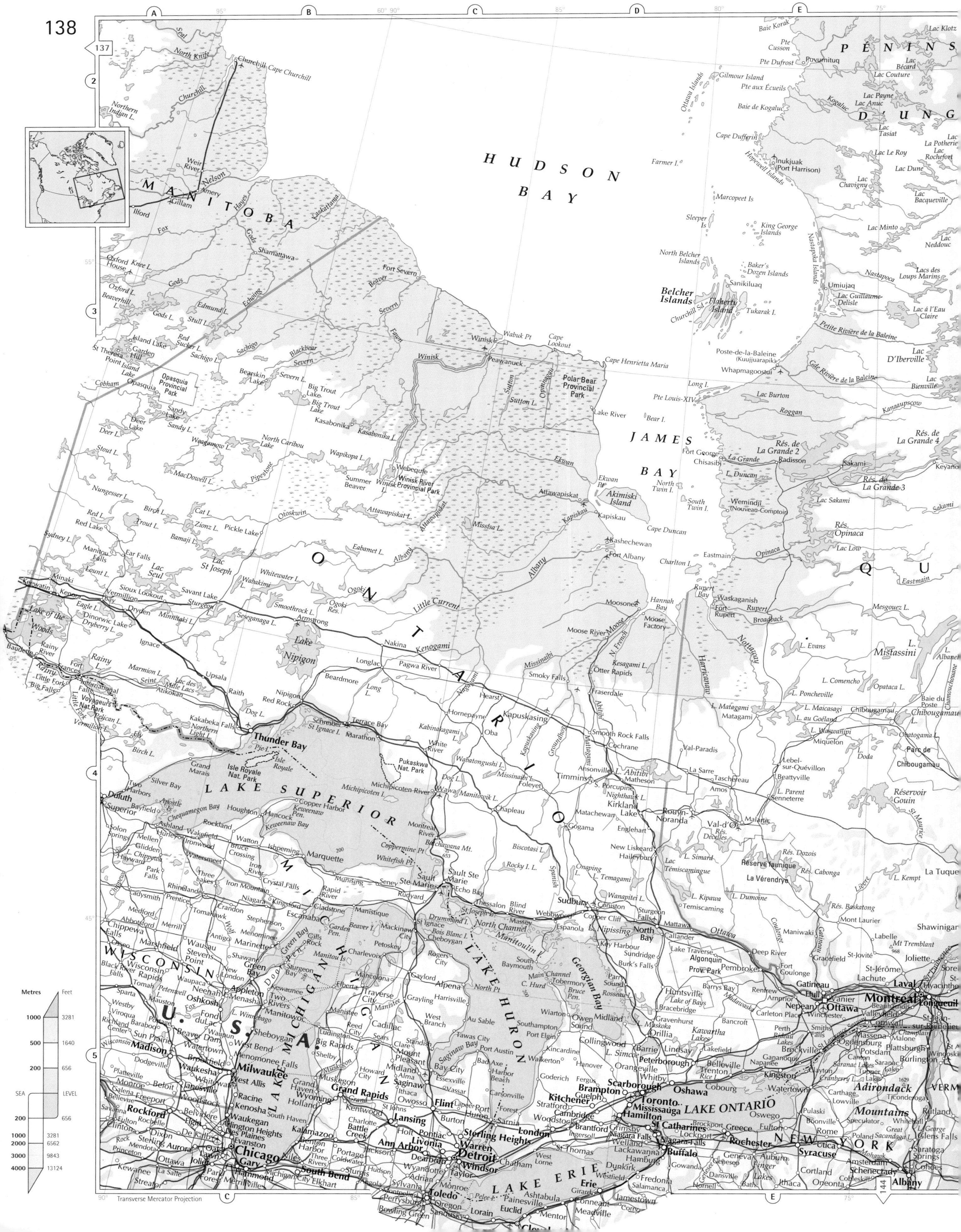
137
HUDSON BAY
JAMES BAY
MANITOBA
ONTARIO
LAKE SUPERIOR
MICHIGAN
LAKE MICHIGAN
LAKE HURON
LAKE ERIE
LAKE ONTARIO
WISCONSIN
U. S. A.
NEW YORK
PÉNINSULE D'UNGAVA
QU
Churchill
Cape Churchill
North Knife
Seal
Northern Indian L.
Weir River
Nelson
Amery
Gillam
Ilford
Fox
Hayes
Gods
Shamattawa
Kaskattama
Oxford House
Knee L.
Oxford L.
Beaverhill L.
Gods L.
Edmund L.
Echoing
Stull L.
Fort Severn
Beaver
Severn
Fawn
Winisk
Wabuk Pt
Cape Lookout
Peawanuck
Cape Henrietta Maria
Polar Bear Provincial Park
Sutton L.
Opinnagau
Island Lake
Red Sucker L.
Sachigo L.
Sachigo
Garden Hill
St Theresa Point
Island Lake
Cobham
Opasquia
Opasquia Provincial Park
Blackbear
Bearskin Lake
Severn L.
Big Trout Lake
Kasabonika
Kasabonika L.
Sandy Lake
Sandy L.
Deer Lake
Deer L.
Weagamow L.
North Caribou Lake
Wapikopa L.
Webequie
Winisk River Provincial Park
Summer Beaver
Stout L.
MacDowell L.
Pipestone
Nungesser L.
Birch L.
Cat L.
Red L.
Red Lake
Trout L.
Zionz L.
Pickle Lake
Otoskwin
Attawapiskat L.
Attawapiskat
Missisa L.
Ekwan
Ekwan Pt
Akimiski Island
Kapiskau
Cape Duncan
Kashechewan
Fort Albany
Albany
Eabamet L.
Sydney L.
Bamaji L.
Manitou Falls
Ear Falls
Lac Seul
Lac St Joseph
Lount L.
Minaki
Keewatin
Kenora
Vermillion Bay
Sioux Lookout
Savant Lake
Whitewater L.
Wabakimi L.
Ogoki
Ogoki Res.
Eagle L.
Dinorwic Lake
Dryden
Dryberry L.
Minnitaki L.
Sturgeon
Lake of the Woods
Seseganaga L.
Smoothrock L.
Armstrong
Little Current
Kenogami
Nakina
Longlac
Pagwa River
Lake Nipigon
Ignace
Rainy River
Baudette
Rainy L.
Fort Frances
International Falls
Little Fork
Big Falls
Marmion L.
Seine
Lac des Mille Lacs
Atikokan
Upsala
Raith
Beardmore
Long L.
Nipigon
Red Rock
Dog L.
Kakabeka Falls
Northern Light L.
Thunder Bay
Voyageurs Nat. Park
Pelican L.
Vermilion L.
Birch L.
Schreiber
St Ignace I.
Terrace Bay
Marathon
Pie I.
Isle Royale
Isle Royale Nat. Park
Grand Marais
Two Harbors
Silver Bay
Duluth
Superior
Apostle Is
Bayfield
Chequamegon Bay
Houghton
Copper Harbor
Keweenaw Pen.
Keweenaw Bay
Hancock
Michipicoten I.
Michipicoten River
Wawa
Pukaskwa Nat. Park
Dog L.
White River
Hornepayne
Hearst
Kabinakagami L.
Oba
Kapuskasing
Wabatongushi L.
Missinaibi L.
Foleyet
Chapleau
Manitowik L.
Missinaibi
Smoky Falls
Otter Rapids
Fraserdale
Kesagami L.
Moosonee
Moose River
Moose Factory
Hannah Bay
Abitibi
Mattagami
Groundhog
Smooth Rock Falls
Cochrane
Timmins
Ansonville
L. Abitibi
Matheson
S. Porcupine
Nighthawk L.
Kirkland Lake
Matachewan
Gogama
Englehart
New Liskeard
Haileybury
Rouyn-Noranda
Val-d'Or
Malartic
Amos
La Sarre
Taschereau
Val-Paradis
Monfreal River
Batchawana Mt.
653
Coppermine Pt
Whitefish Pt
Sault Ste Marie
Rocky I. L.
Biscotasi L.
Spanish
Onaping L.
Temagami
Sudbury
Coniston
Copper Cliff
Wanapitei L.
Sturgeon Falls
Nipissing
North Bay
Mattawa
Callander
Espanola
Massey
Blind River
Thessalon
Echo Bay
Ste Marie
Seney
Munising
Marquette
Ishpeming
Crystal Falls
Iron River
Iron Mountain
Rudyard
Rapid River
Gladstone
Escanaba
Manistique
Beaver I.
Garden Pen.
Mackinaw City
St Ignace
Drummond I.
St Joseph I.
Bois Blanc I.
Cheboygan
North Channel
Manitoulin I.
South Baymouth
Georgian Bay
Parry Sound
Tobermory
Bruce Pen.
Key Harbour
Sundridge
Burk's Falls
Huntsville
Lake of Bays
Bracebridge
Gravenhurst
Orillia
Owen Sound
Wiarton
Midland
Southampton
Port Elgin
Kincardine
Walkerton
Goderich
Hanover
Collingwood
Barrie
L. Simcoe
Orangeville
Lindsay
Peterborough
Kawartha Lakes
Belleville
Trenton
Cobourg
Oshawa
Whitby
Scarborough
Toronto
Mississauga
Brampton
Guelph
Kitchener
Stratford
Cambridge
Hamilton
Woodstock
Brantford
London
Ingersoll
St Catharines
Grimsby
Niagara Falls
Welland
Sarnia
St Thomas
Chatham
West Lorne
Windsor
Detroit
Warren
Sterling Heights
Port Huron
Pontiac
Livonia
Ann Arbor
Toledo
Dearborn
Wyandotte
Monroe
Sandusky
Lorain
Cleveland
Euclid
Painesville
Ashtabula
Erie
Mentor
Conneaut
Meadville
Jamestown
Dunkirk
Buffalo
Lackawanna
Hamburg
Lockport
Rochester
Greece
Brockport
Geneva
Auburn
Syracuse
Oswego
Fulton
Utica
Rome
Ithaca
Cortland
Oneonta
Schenectady
Albany
Saratoga Springs
Glens Falls
Lake George
Adirondack Mountains
Ticonderoga
Plattsburgh
Burlington
Kingston
Watertown
Gananoque
Brockville
Ogdensburg
Massena
Potsdam
Malone
Cornwall
Valleyfield
Winchester
Ottawa
Hull
Nepean
Vanier
Gatineau
Montréal
Laval
Longueuil
St-Jérôme
Lachute
Joliette
Shawinigan
Mont Tremblant
968
Labelle
Mont Laurier
Maniwaki
Pembroke
Renfrew
Arnprior
Carleton Place
Perth
Smiths Falls
Deep River
Fort Coulonge
Algonquin Prov. Park
Lake Traverse
Barrys Bay
Bancroft
Témiscaming
L. Kipawa
Lac Témiscamingue
L. Simard
Rés. Decelles
Rés. Dozois
Réserve Faunique La Vérendrye
Rés. Cabonga
L. Dumoine
Rés. Baskatong
Gouin Réservoir
Senneterre
L. Parent
Lebel-sur-Quévillon
Beattyville
Chibougamau
Chapais
Miquelon
L. Waswanipi
L. Matagami
Matagami
L. Poncheville
L. Comencho
L. Evans
L. Mistassini
Nottaway
Harricana
Rupert Bay
Waskaganish
Fort Rupert
Broadback
Eastmain
Opinaca
Rés. Opinaca
Lac Low
Wemindji
Lac Sakami
Rés. de La Grande 3
Rés. de La Grande 2
Radisson
Chisasibi
Fort George
La Grande
L. Duncan
Lac Burton
Roggan
Kanaaupscow
Rés. de La Grande 4
Lac Bienville
Lac D'Iberville
Grde Rivière de la Baleine
Petite Rivière de la Baleine
Whapmagoostui
Poste-de-la-Baleine (Kuujjuarapik)
Long I.
Pte Louis-XIV
Bear I.
North Twin I.
South Twin I.
Charlton I.
Belcher Islands
Flaherty Island
Sanikiluaq
Churchill Sd
Tukarak I.
Baker's Dozen Islands
North Belcher Islands
King George Islands
Sleeper Is
Marcopeet Is
Nastapoka Islands
Nastapoca
Umiujaq
Lac Guillaume-Delisle
Lac à l'Eau Claire
Lacs des Loups Marins
Lac Minto
Lac Bacqueville
Lac Chavigny
Lac Dune
Lac Le Roy
Lac La Potherie
Lac Rochefort
Lac Tasiat
Lac Payne
Lac Anuc
Lac Couture
Lac Bécard
Lac Klotz
Kogaluc
Baie de Kogaluc
Inukjuak (Port Harrison)
Hopewell Islands
Cape Dufferin
Farmer I.
Ottawa Islands
Gilmour Island
Pte aux Écueils
Puvurnituq
Pte Dufrost
Pte Cusson
Baie Korak
Transverse Mercator Projection
144
Metres
Feet
1000
3281
500
1640
200
656
SEA LEVEL
2000
6562
3000
9843
4000
13124

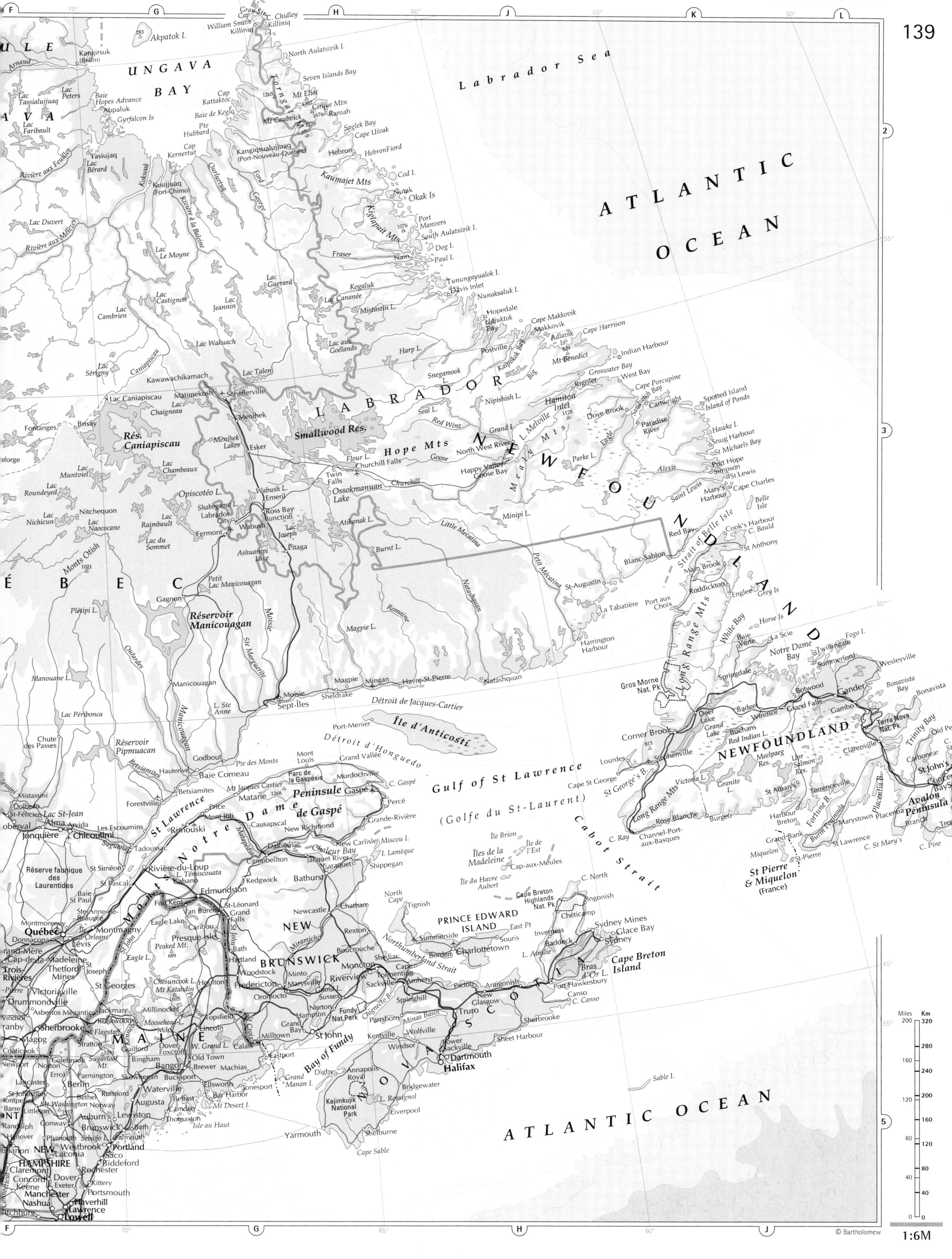
UNGAVA BAY
Labrador Sea
ATLANTIC OCEAN
LABRADOR
NEWFOUNDLAND
QUÉBEC
Gulf of St Lawrence
(Golfe du St-Laurent)
Cabot Strait
Détroit de Jacques-Cartier
Détroit d'Honguedo
Île d'Anticosti
Akpatok I.
Kangirsuk (Bellin)
William Smith
Killiniq
C. Chidley
North Aulatsivik I.
Seven Islands Bay
Torngat Mts
Mt Eliot
Cirque Mtn
Ramah
Mt Caubvick
Saglek Bay
Cape Uivak
Hebron
HebronFiord
Kangiqsualujjuaq (Port-Nouveau-Québec)
Kaumajet Mts
Cod I.
Nutak
Okak Is
Kiglapait Mts
Port Manvers
South Aulatsivik I.
Dog I.
Paul I.
Nain
Fraser
Kuujjuaq (Fort-Chimo)
Lac Duvert
Rivière aux Mélèzes
Rivière aux Feuilles
Lac Bérard
Tasiujaq
Lac Faribault
Aupaluk
Gyrfalcon Is
Lac Le Moyne
Lac Guerard
Lac Castignon
Lac Jeannin
Lac Cambrien
Kogaluk
Lac Cananée
Mistastin L.
Tunungayualok I.
Davis Inlet
Nunaksaluk I.
Hopedale
Cape Makkovik
Makkovik
Adlavik Is
Cape Harrison
Mt Benedict
Indian Harbour
Groswater Bay
West Bay
Rigolet
Cape Porcupine
Sandwich Bay
Cartwright
Spotted Island
Island of Ponds
Hamilton Inlet
Lac Wakuach
Lac aux Goélands
Harp L.
Postville
Snegamook L.
Nipishish L.
Seal L.
Red Wine
Grand L.
L. Melville
Mealy Mts
Doye Brook
Paradise River
Hawke I.
Snug Harbour
St Michaels Bay
Port Hope Simpson
St Lewis
Alexis
Saint Lewis
Mary's Harbour
Cape Charles
Belle Isle
Kawawachikamach
Lac Talon
Schefferville
Matimekosh
Lac Caniapiscau
Lac Chaigneau
Menihek
Brisay
Fontanges
Rés. Caniapiscau
Menihek Lakes
Esker
Smallwood Res.
Hope Mts
North West River
Happy Valley-Goose Bay
Churchill Falls
Flour L.
Goose
Parke L.
Twin Falls
Ossokmanuan Lake
Churchill
Lac Muntviel
Lac Chambeaux
Lac Roundeyed
Opiscotéo L.
Wabush L.
Emeril
Nitchequon
Lac Nichicun
Lac Naocoane
Shabogamo L.
Labrador City
Wabush
Ross Bay Junction
Lac Joseph
Lac Raimbault
Fermont
Lac du Sommet
Atikonak L.
Minipi L.
Little Mecatina
Red Bay
Cook's Harbour
C. Bauld
St Anthony
Strait of Belle Isle
Monts Otish
Ashuanipi Lake
Pitaga
Burnt L.
Blanc-Sablon
Main Brook
Petit Mécatina
St-Augustin
Natashquan
Roddickton
Englee
Grey Is
Petit Lac Manicouagan
Gagnon
Réservoir Manicouagan
Moisie
Romaine
Magpie L.
La Tabatière
Port aux Choix
Horse Is
White Bay
Plétipi L.
Harrington Harbour
Baie Verte
La Scie
Fogo I.
Notre Dame Bay
Twillingate
Summerford
Wesleyville
Long Range Mts
Ste Marguerite
Outardes
Manouane L.
Manicouagan
Magpie
Mingan
Havre-St-Pierre
Natashquan
Gros Morne Nat. Pk
Springdale
Botwood
Gander
Bonavista Bay
Bonavista
Moisie
Sept-Îles
Sheldrake
L. Ste Anne
Lac Péribonca
Deer Lake
Badger
Windsor
Grand Falls
Gambo
Terra Nova Nat. Pk
Trinity Bay
Old Perlican
Port-Menier
Chute des Passes
Réservoir Pipmuacan
Betsiamites
Corner Brook
Grand Lake
Buchans
Red Indian L.
NEWFOUNDLAND
Clarenville
Carbonear
C. St Francis
Pouch Cove
St John's
Conception Bay South
Godbout
Pte des Monts
Mont Louis
Grand Vallée
Murdochville
Baie Comeau
Hauterive
Parc de la Gaspésie
C. Gaspé
Gaspé
Percé
Lourdes
Stephenville
Meelpaeg Res.
Upr Salmon Res.
St George's B.
Cape St George
Mt Jacques Cartier
Matane
Peninsule de Gaspé
Mistassini
St-Félicien
Lac St-Jean
Roberval
Alma
Arvida
Jonquière
Chicoutimi
Saguenay
Les Escoumins
Forestville
St Lawrence
Price
Mont Joli
Rimouski
Causapscal
Grande-Rivière
New Richmond
Victoria L.
Granite L.
Long Range Mts
Rose Blanche
Channel-Port-aux-Basques
C. Ray
Burgeo
St Alban's
Terrenceville
Fortune B.
Burin Peninsula
Placentia B.
Placentia
Marystown
Harbour Breton
Grand Bank
St Lawrence
C. St Mary's
Avalon Peninsula
Branch
Trepassey
C. Pine
C. Race
Miquelon
St-Pierre
St Pierre & Miquelon (France)
Île Brion
Îles de la Madeleine
Île de l'Est
Cap-aux-Meules
Île du Havre Aubert
Tadoussac
Notre Dame
Matapedia
Dalhousie
New Carlisle
Miscou I.
Chaleur Bay
I. Lamèque
Shippegan
Campbellton
Jacquet River
Caraquet
Bathurst
Réserve faunique des Laurentides
St Siméon
Rivière-du-Loup
L. Témiscouata
Cabano
St Pascal
Kedgwick
Baie St Paul
Edmundston
Ste-Anne-de-Beaupré
St-Léonard
Grand Falls
Fort Kent
Van Buren
Montmorency
Québec
Donnacona
Île d'Orléans
Montmagny
Lévis
Eagle Lake
Caribou
Presque Isle
Peaked Mt.
Newcastle
NEW BRUNSWICK
Miramichi
Chatham
North Cape
Tignish
PRINCE EDWARD ISLAND
East Pt
Summerside
Charlottetown
Souris
Borden
Northumberland Strait
C. North
Cape Breton Highlands Nat. Pk
Ingonish
Chéticamp
Sydney Mines
Glace Bay
Sydney
Inverness
Baddeck
L. Ainslie
Bras d'Or L.
Cape Breton Island
Port Hawkesbury
Canso
C. Canso
Grand-Mère
Cap-de-la-Madeleine
Trois-Rivières
Thetford Mines
St Joseph
St Georges
Victoriaville
Drummondville
Asbestos
Mégantic
Sherbrooke
Magog
Coaticook
Newport
Granby
Jackman
Eagle L.
Bath
Hartland
Woodstock
Houlton
Chesuncook L.
Mt Katahdin
Millinocket
Moosehead L.
Milo
Rockwood
Flagstaff
Stratton
MAINE
Dover Foxcroft
Guilford
Bingham
Rexton
Bouctouche
Shediac
Moncton
Riverview
Minto
Marysville
Fredericton
Oromocto
Sussex
Grand L.
Hampton
Norton
St John
Grand Bay
Fundy Nat. Park
Chignecto B.
Cape Tormentine
Sackville
Amherst
Springhill
Parrsboro
Minas Basin
Pictou
Antigonish
New Glasgow
Truro
NOVA SCOTIA
Sherbrooke
Sheet Harbour
Wolfville
Kentville
Windsor
Lower Sackville
Dartmouth
Halifax
Bay of Fundy
Topsfield
Lincoln
W. Grand L.
Calais
St Croix
Milltown
Eastport
Old Town
Bangor
Brewer
Machias
Colebrook
Norton
Errol
Sugarloaf Mt.
Skowhegan
Bucksport
Farmington
Lancaster
Berlin
Waterville
Rumford
Bethel
Ellsworth
Jonesport
Grand Manan I.
Digby
Annapolis Royal
Bridgewater
Kejimkujik National Park
L. Rossignol
Liverpool
Belfast
Bar Harbor
Mt Desert I.
Camden
Augusta
St Johnsbury
Montpelier
Barre
Littleton
Mt Washington
Norway
Auburn
Lewiston
Conway
Thomaston
Isle au Haut
Randolph
Brunswick
Bath
Hanover
Lebanon
Plymouth
Sebago L.
Falmouth
Portland
Westbrook
NEW HAMPSHIRE
Laconia
Saco
Biddeford
Claremont
Concord
Dover
Rochester
Exeter
Kittery
Keene
Manchester
Portsmouth
Nashua
Haverhill
Lawrence
Lowell
Fitchburg
Yarmouth
Shelburne
Cape Sable
Sable I.
Miles
Km
1:6M
© Bartholomew

LAKE SUPERIOR
LAKE MICHIGAN
LAKE HURON
LAKE ERIE
Georgian Bay
North Channel
Lake Nipigon
WISCONSIN
MICHIGAN
ONTARIO
CANADA
Thunder Bay
Isle Royale
Isle Royale National Park
Pukaskwa National Park
Lake Superior National Park
Pictured Rocks National Lakeshore
Sleeping Bear Dunes National Seashore
Manitoulin I.
Fathom Five National Marine Park
Bruce Peninsula National Park
Killarney National Park
Point Pelee National Park
Sault Ste Marie
Sudbury
Timmins
Kapuskasing
Marquette
Escanaba
Green Bay
Milwaukee
Chicago
Grand Rapids
Lansing
Flint
Saginaw
Detroit
Windsor
Toledo
London
Sarnia
Kitchener
Guelph
Owen Sound
Conic Equidistant Projection
Metres
Feet
1500
4921
1000
3281
500
1640
200
656
100
328
SEA
LEVEL
200
656

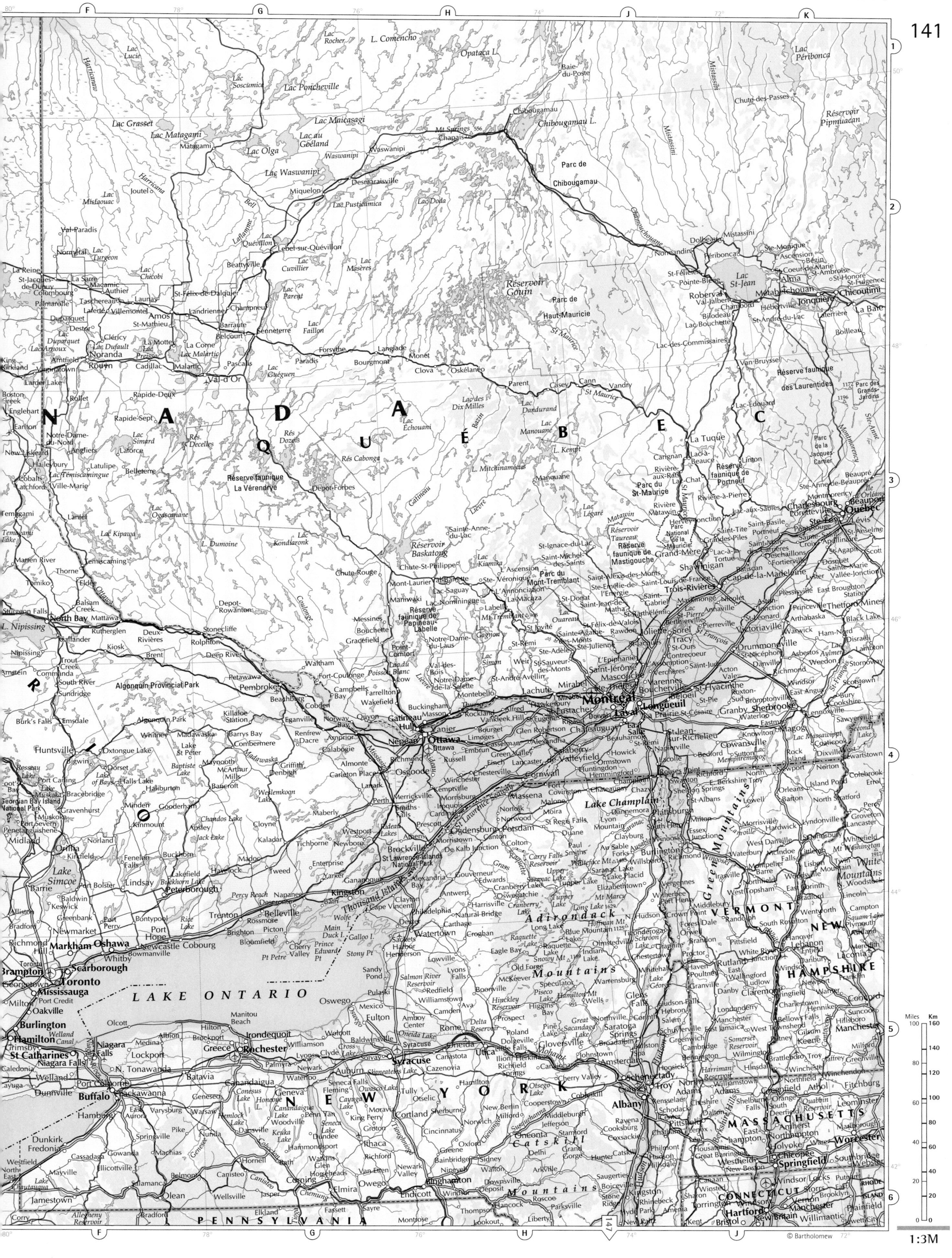
Q U É B E C
O N T A R I O
N E W Y O R K
VERMONT
NEW HAMPSHIRE
MASSACHUSETTS
CONNECTICUT
PENNSYLVANIA
LAKE ONTARIO
Lake Champlain
Réservoir Gouin
Parc de Chibougamau
Parc de Haut-Mauricie
Réserve faunique La Vérendrye
Réserve faunique des Laurentides
Algonquin Provincial Park
Adirondack Mountains
Green Mountains
Catskill Mountains
Montréal
Ottawa
Québec
Toronto
Trois-Rivières
Sherbrooke
Syracuse
Rochester
Buffalo
Albany
Springfield
Hartford
Miles
Km
© Bartholomew

1:3M

PACIFIC OCEAN
CANADA
BRITISH COLUMBIA
ALBERTA
SASKATCHEWAN
MANITOBA
WASHINGTON
OREGON
IDAHO
MONTANA
NORTH DAKOTA
SOUTH DAKOTA
WYOMING
NEBRASKA
NEVADA
UTAH
COLORADO
KANSAS
CALIFORNIA
ARIZONA
NEW MEXICO
OKLAHOMA
TEXAS
MEXICO
BAJA CALIFORNIA NORTE
BAJA CALIFORNIA SUR
SONORA
CHIHUAHUA
COAHUILA
NUEVO LEÓN
SINALOA
DURANGO
ROCKY MOUNTAINS
Sierra Nevada
Cascade Range
Coast Ranges
Great Basin
Colorado Plateau
Columbia Plateau
Snake River Plain
Sierra Madre Occidental
Golfo de California
Baja California
Bolson de Mapimí
Edwards Plateau
Llano Estacado
Smoky Hills
Edmonton
Calgary
Vancouver
Victoria
Seattle
Tacoma
Spokane
Portland
Salem
Eugene
Boise
Great Falls
Helena
Billings
Salt Lake City
Ogden
Provo
Reno
Sacramento
San Francisco
Oakland
San Jose
Fresno
Las Vegas
Los Angeles
Long Beach
San Diego
Tijuana
Mexicali
Phoenix
Tucson
Albuquerque
Santa Fe
El Paso
Ciudad Juárez
Denver
Aurora
Colorado Springs
Cheyenne
Chihuahua
Hermosillo
Culiacán
Monterrey
Saltillo
Torreón
San Antonio
Austin
Lubbock
Amarillo
Oklahoma City
Regina
Saskatoon
Winnipeg
Metres
Feet
4000 13124
3000 9843
2000 6562
1000 3281
500 1640
200 656
SEA LEVEL
200 656
1000 3281
2000 6562
3000 9843
4000 13124
5000 16409
Lambert Conformal Conic Projection
134
156

CANADA
ONTARIO
QUÉBEC
NEW BRUNSWICK
NOVA SCOTIA
PRINCE EDWARD I.
James Bay
Lake Nipigon
LAKE SUPERIOR
LAKE MICHIGAN
LAKE HURON
Lake Ontario
Lake Erie
Georgian Bay
Bay of Fundy
Gulf of St Lawrence
MINNESOTA
WISCONSIN
MICHIGAN
IOWA
ILLINOIS
INDIANA
OHIO
PENNSYLVANIA
NEW YORK
VERMONT
NEW HAMP.
MAINE
MASS.
CONN.
R.I.
NEW JERSEY
MARYLAND
DELAWARE
WEST VIRGINIA
VIRGINIA
KENTUCKY
TENNESSEE
NORTH CAROLINA
SOUTH CAROLINA
GEORGIA
FLORIDA
ALABAMA
MISSISSIPPI
LOUISIANA
ARKANSAS
MISSOURI
KANSAS
Ozark Plateau
Appalachian Mountains
Blue Ridge
Coastal Plain
ATLANTIC OCEAN
GULF OF MEXICO
THE BAHAMAS
Straits of Florida
Winnipeg
Thunder Bay
Duluth
Minneapolis
St Paul
Milwaukee
Madison
Chicago
Detroit
Toledo
Cleveland
Columbus
Cincinnati
Indianapolis
St Louis
Kansas City
Des Moines
Omaha
Toronto
Hamilton
Buffalo
Rochester
Syracuse
Ottawa
Montréal
Québec
Boston
Providence
Hartford
New Haven
Bridgeport
New York
Newark
Philadelphia
Baltimore
Washington D.C.
Pittsburgh
Richmond
Norfolk
Virginia Beach
Louisville
Nashville
Memphis
Knoxville
Chattanooga
Charlotte
Greensboro
Raleigh
Atlanta
Birmingham
Montgomery
Jackson
New Orleans
Baton Rouge
Shreveport
Little Rock
Tulsa
Dallas
Fort Worth
Houston
Galveston
Corpus Christi
Matamoros
Savannah
Charleston
Jacksonville
Tallahassee
Orlando
Tampa
St Petersburg
Miami
Fort Lauderdale
Hollywood
West Palm Beach
Key West
Nassau
Freeport
Andros
Cape Hatteras
Cape Cod
Cape Canaveral
Cape Sable
© Bartholomew
Miles
Km
1:10M

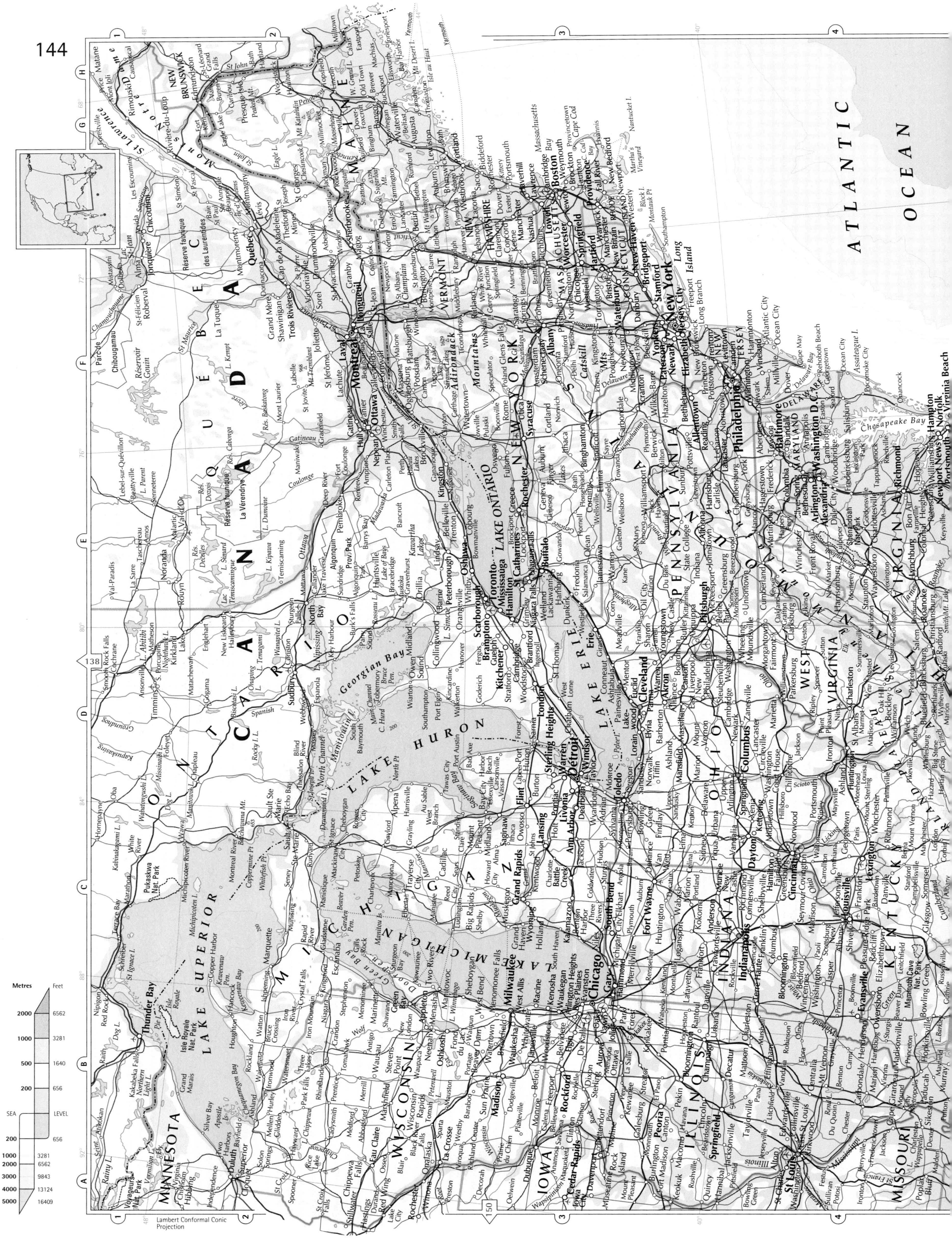
ATLANTIC
OCEAN
CANADA
ONTARIO
QUÉBEC
MAINE
NEW BRUNSWICK
NEW YORK
PENNSYLVANIA
OHIO
INDIANA
ILLINOIS
MICHIGAN
WISCONSIN
MINNESOTA
IOWA
MISSOURI
KENTUCKY
WEST VIRGINIA
VIRGINIA
MARYLAND
NEW JERSEY
VERMONT
NEW HAMPSHIRE
MASSACHUSETTS
CONNECTICUT
RHODE ISLAND
LAKE SUPERIOR
LAKE MICHIGAN
LAKE HURON
LAKE ERIE
LAKE ONTARIO
Georgian Bay
Long Island
Chesapeake Bay
Toronto
Montréal
Ottawa
Québec
Boston
New York
Philadelphia
Baltimore
Washington D.C.
Pittsburgh
Cleveland
Detroit
Chicago
Milwaukee
Indianapolis
Cincinnati
Columbus
Buffalo
St Louis
Thunder Bay
Metres
Feet
2000
6562
1000
3281
500
1640
200
656
SEA
LEVEL
200
656
1000
3281
2000
6562
3000
9843
4000
13124
5000
16409
138
150
Lambert Conformal Conic Projection

BERMUDA
(United Kingdom)
1:500 000
NEW PROVIDENCE
(The Bahamas)
1:600 000
PUERTO RICO and VIRGIN ISLANDS
1:3M
VIRGIN ISLANDS (U.K.)
VIRGIN ISLANDS (U.S.A.)
THE BAHAMAS
GULF OF MEXICO
Straits of Florida
TENNESSEE
NORTH CAROLINA
SOUTH CAROLINA
GEORGIA
ALABAMA
MISSISSIPPI
FLORIDA
Miles
Km

1:6M

© Bartholomew

CANADA
ONTARIO
MICHIGAN
OHIO
PENNSYLVANIA
NEW
WEST VIRGINIA
VIRGINIA
KENTUCKY
TENNESSEE
MAR
LAKE HURON
LAKE ERIE
LAKE ONTARIO
Georgian Bay
Saginaw Bay
Lake Simcoe
APPALACHIAN MOUNTAINS
ALLEGHENY MOUNTAINS
BLUE RIDGE
Toronto
Detroit
Cleveland
Columbus
Pittsburgh
Buffalo
Cincinnati
Washington D.C.
Baltimore
Richmond
Toledo
Dayton
Akron
Lansing
Flint
Hamilton
Rochester
Harrisburg
Charleston
Roanoke
Lynchburg
Erie
Windsor
London
Kitchener
Metres
Feet
1500
4921
1000
3281
500
1640
200
656
100
328
SEA
LEVEL
200
656
1000
3281
2000
6562
3000
9843
149
141
Lambert Conformal Conic Projection

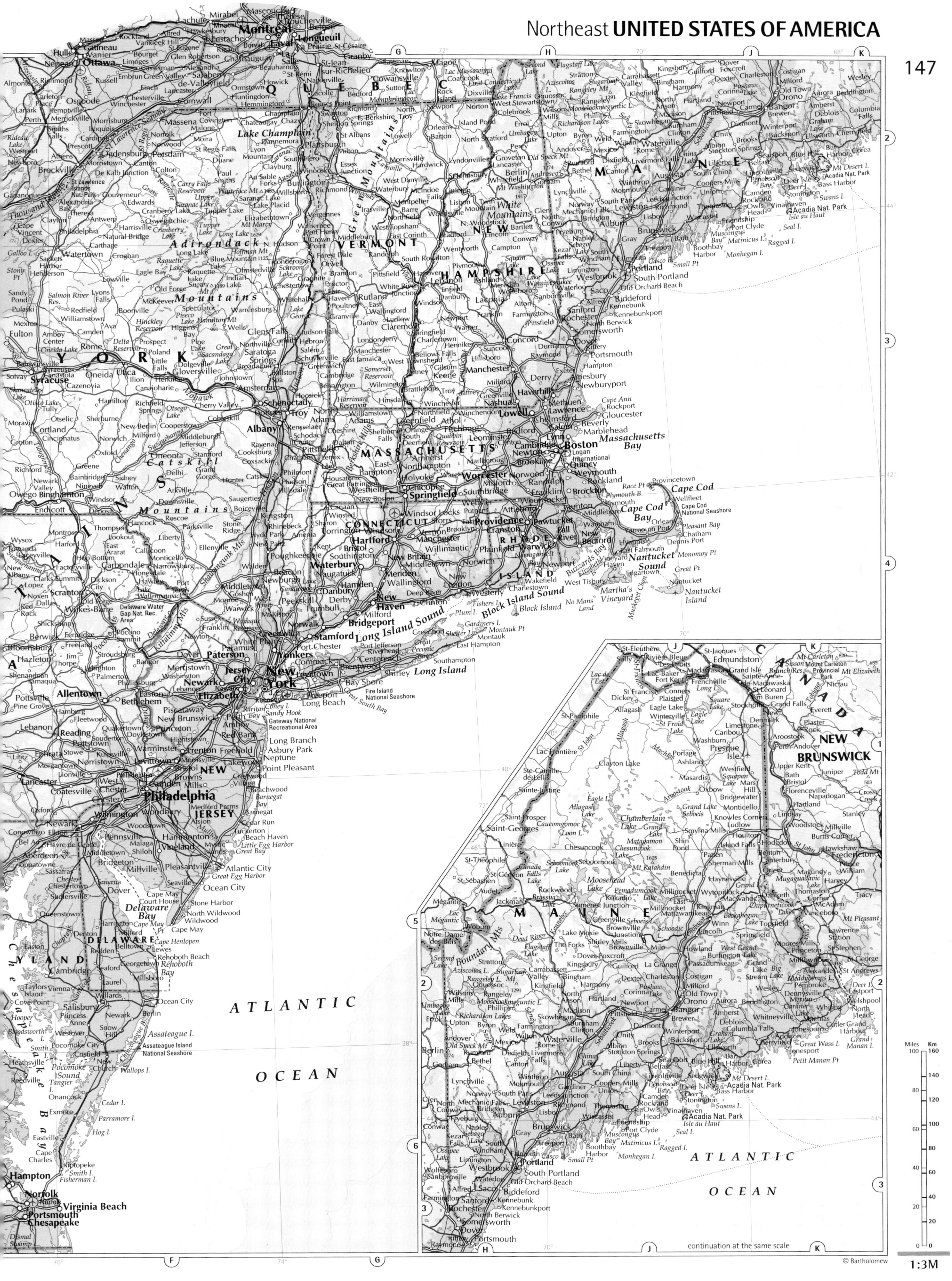
QUEBEC
NEW YORK
VERMONT
NEW HAMPSHIRE
MAINE
MASSACHUSETTS
CONNECTICUT
RHODE ISLAND
NEW JERSEY
DELAWARE
MARYLAND
CANADA
NEW BRUNSWICK
Adirondack Mountains
Catskill Mountains
White Mountains
Green Mountains
Lake Champlain
Massachusetts Bay
Cape Cod Bay
Cape Cod
Nantucket Sound
Long Island Sound
Block Island Sound
Long Island
Delaware Bay
Chesapeake Bay
ATLANTIC OCEAN
Montréal
Ottawa
Boston
New York
Philadelphia
Albany
Hartford
Providence
Portland
Augusta
Concord
Trenton
continuation at the same scale
Miles
Km
1:3M
© Bartholomew

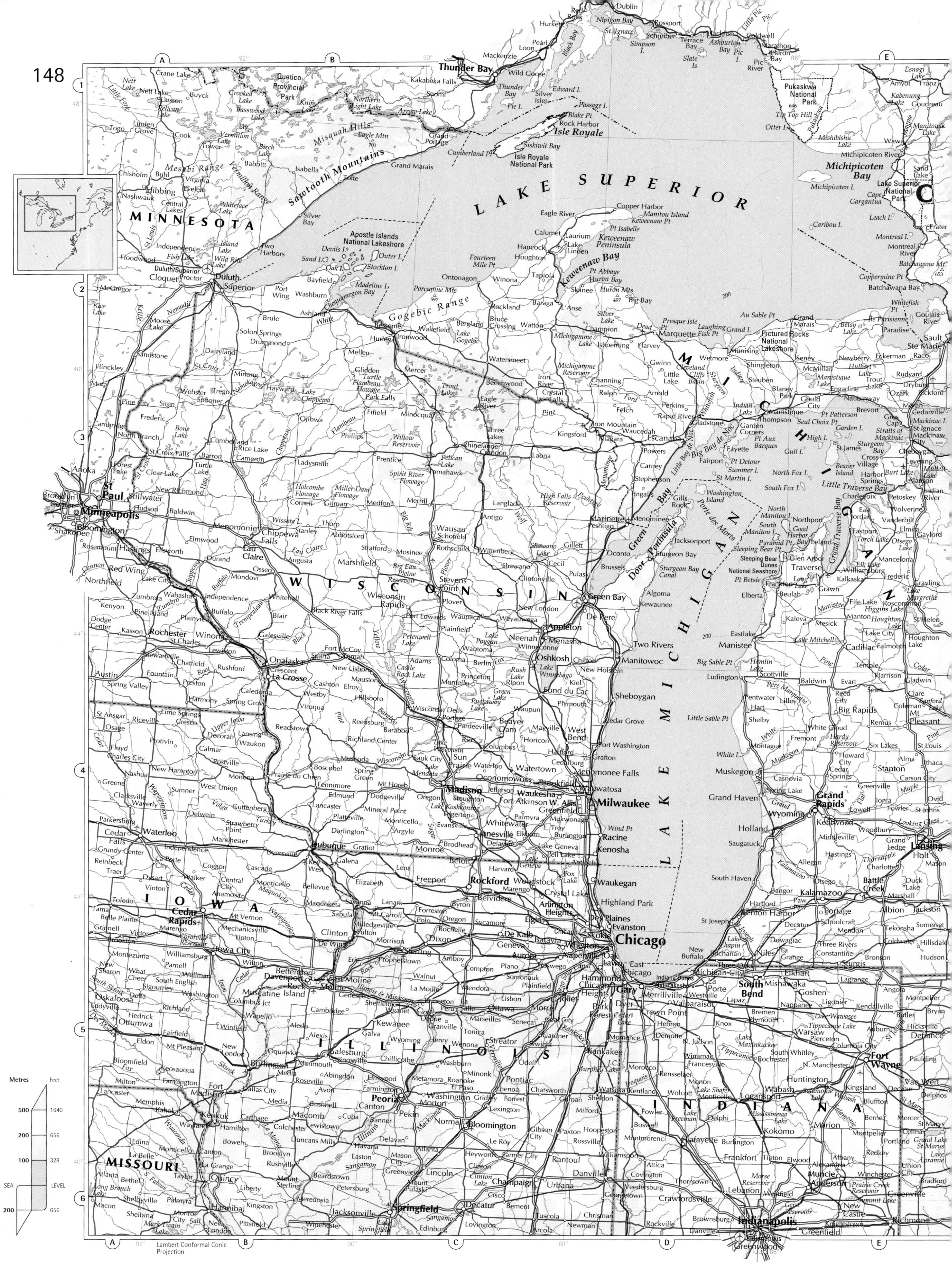
LAKE SUPERIOR
LAKE MICHIGAN
MINNESOTA
WISCONSIN
MICHIGAN
IOWA
ILLINOIS
INDIANA
MISSOURI
Isle Royale
Isle Royale National Park
Apostle Islands National Lakeshore
Pictured Rocks National Lakeshore
Sleeping Bear Dunes National Seashore
Pukaskwa National Park
Lake Superior Provincial Park
Quetico Provincial Park
Keweenaw Peninsula
Keweenaw Bay
Green Bay
Grand Traverse Bay
Michipicoten Bay
Thunder Bay
Duluth
Superior
St Paul
Minneapolis
Rochester
Eau Claire
La Crosse
Madison
Milwaukee
Racine
Kenosha
Green Bay
Appleton
Oshkosh
Sheboygan
Marquette
Sault Ste Marie
Traverse City
Grand Rapids
Lansing
Kalamazoo
South Bend
Fort Wayne
Indianapolis
Chicago
Gary
Joliet
Rockford
Peoria
Bloomington
Champaign
Springfield
Decatur
Dubuque
Davenport
Cedar Rapids
Iowa City
Waterloo
Quincy
Hannibal
Metres
Feet
500
1640
200
656
100
328
SEA
LEVEL
200
656
A
B
C
D
E
1
2
3
4
5
6
92°
90°
88°
86°
48°
46°
44°
42°
40°
Lambert Conformal Conic Projection

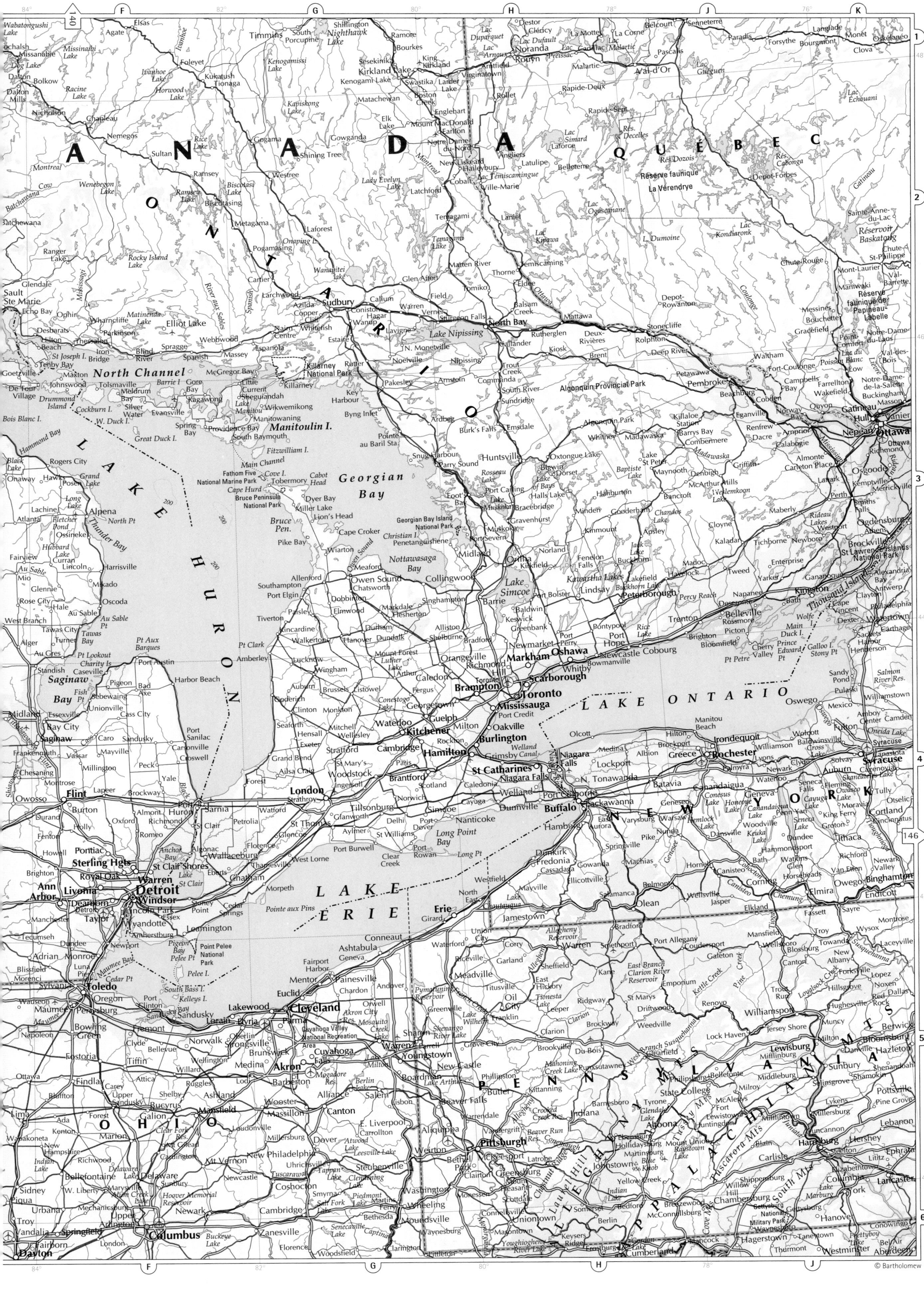
CANADA
ONTARIO
QUÉBEC
NEW YORK
PENNSYLVANIA
OHIO
APPALACHIAN MTS
ALLEGHENY MTS
LAKE HURON
LAKE ONTARIO
LAKE ERIE
Georgian Bay
North Channel
Manitoulin I.
Saginaw Bay
Lake Nipissing
Lake Simcoe
Algonquin Provincial Park
Réserve faunique La Vérendrye
Sudbury
North Bay
Ottawa
Toronto
Mississauga
Hamilton
Kitchener
London
Buffalo
Rochester
Syracuse
Detroit
Windsor
Toledo
Cleveland
Akron
Erie
Pittsburgh
Columbus
Kingston
Peterborough
Oshawa
Barrie
Sault Ste Marie
Flint
Saginaw
Harrisburg
Altoona
State College
Youngstown
Canton
Mansfield
Dayton
Binghamton
Elmira
Ithaca
Williamsport
Lancaster
Miles
Km
© Bartholomew

1:3M

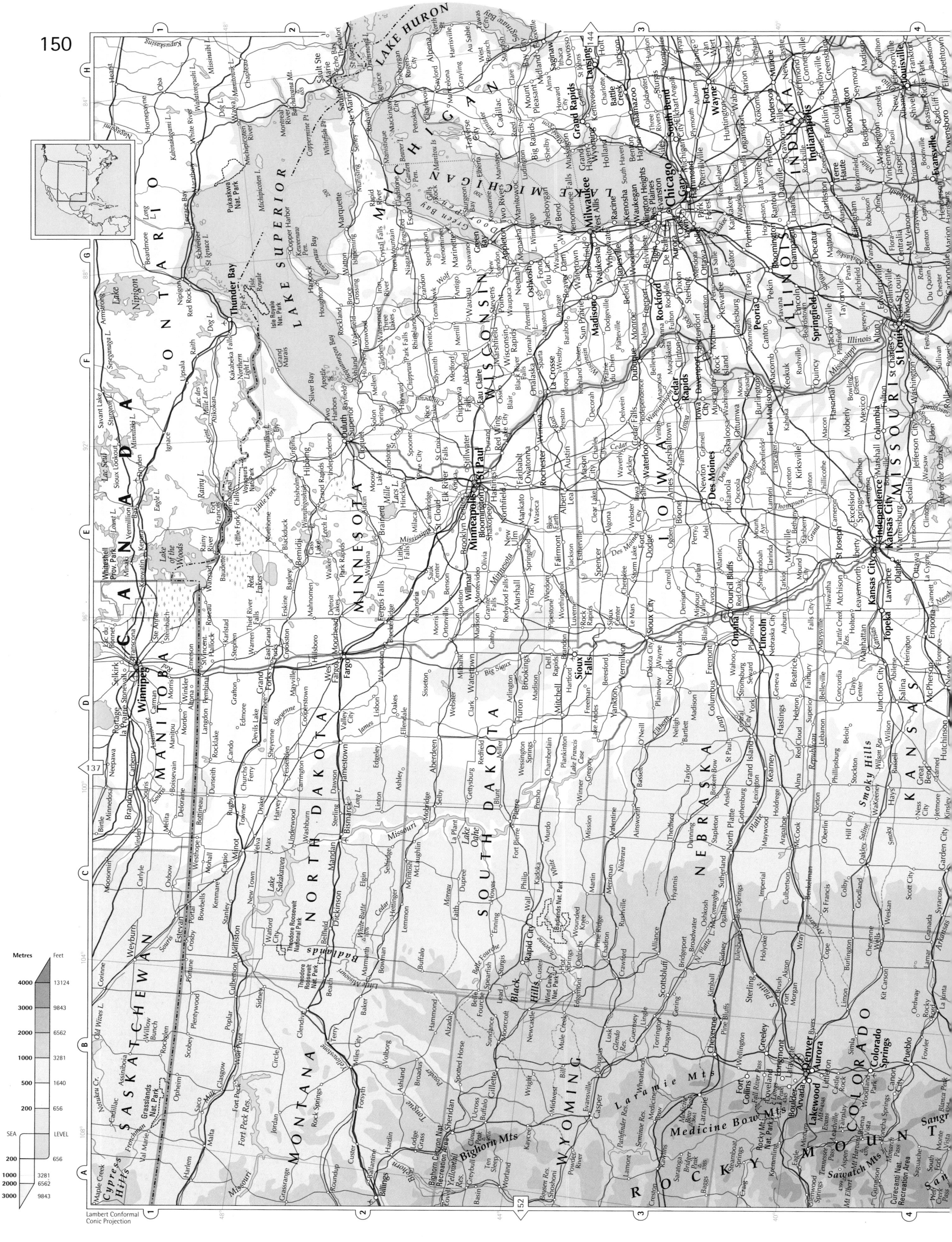
CANADA
ONTARIO
MANITOBA
SASKATCHEWAN
LAKE SUPERIOR
LAKE MICHIGAN
LAKE HURON
MINNESOTA
WISCONSIN
MICHIGAN
ILLINOIS
INDIANA
IOWA
MISSOURI
NORTH DAKOTA
SOUTH DAKOTA
NEBRASKA
KANSAS
MONTANA
WYOMING
COLORADO
ROCKY MOUNTAINS
Metres
Feet
4000
13124
3000
9843
2000
6562
1000
3281
500
1640
200
656
SEA
LEVEL
200
656
1000
3281
2000
6562
3000
9843
137
144
152
Lambert Conformal
Conic Projection

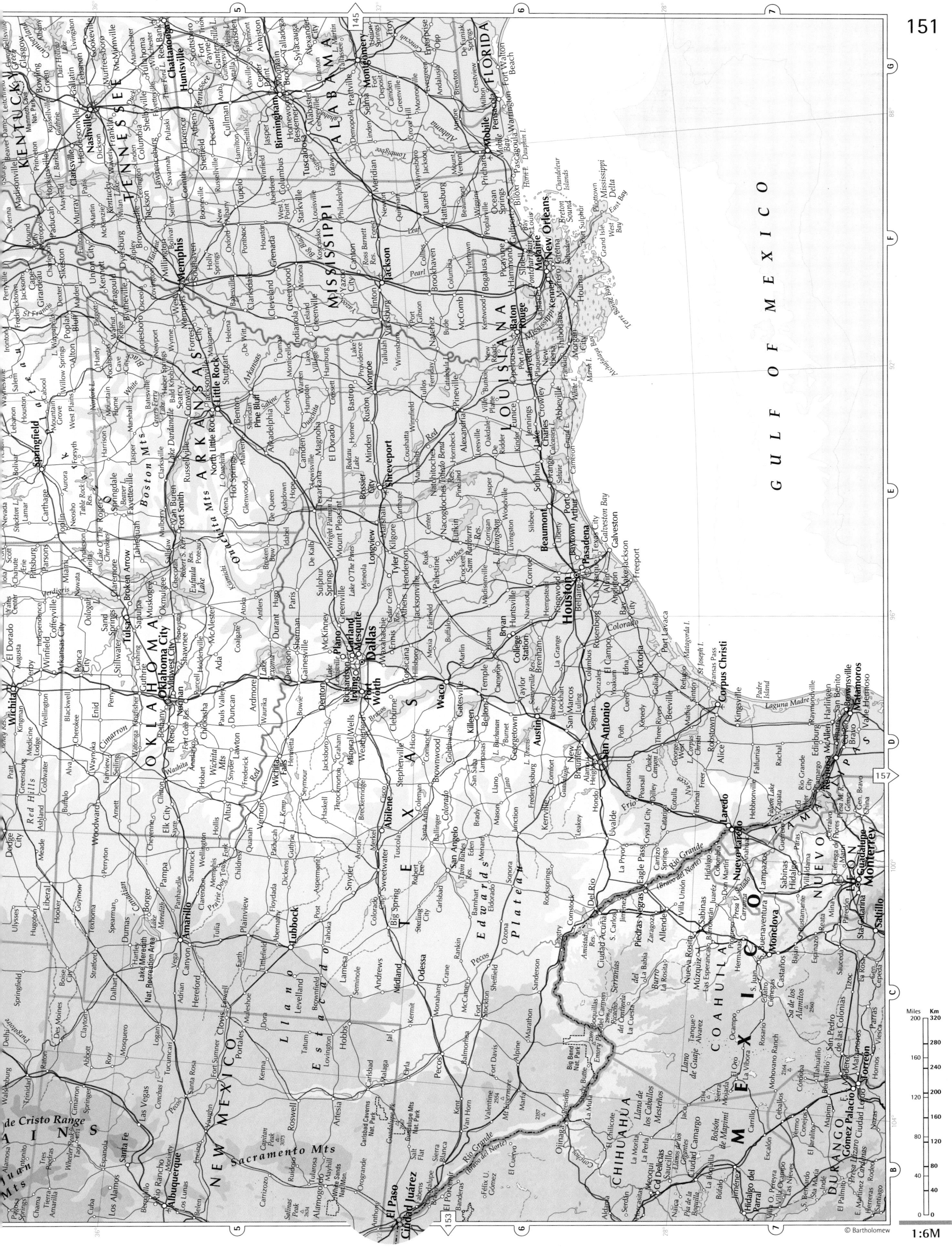
KENTUCKY
TENNESSEE
ALABAMA
FLORIDA
MISSISSIPPI
ARKANSAS
LOUISIANA
OKLAHOMA
TEXAS
NEW MEXICO
MEXICO
COAHUILA
CHIHUAHUA
NUEVO LEON
TAMAULIPAS
DURANGO
GULF OF MEXICO
Nashville
Memphis
New Orleans
Houston
Dallas
San Antonio
Oklahoma City
Albuquerque
El Paso
Ciudad Juárez
Monterrey
Miles
Km
1:6M
© Bartholomew

Metres
Feet
4000
13124
3000
9841
2000
6562
1000
3281
500
1640
200
656
SEA
LEVEL
200
656
1000
3281
2000
6562
3000
9843
4000
13124
5000
16409
C A N A D A
U N I T E D S T A T E S
R O C K Y M O U N T A I N S
O C E A N
ALBERTA
SASKATCHEWAN
BRITISH COLUMBIA
WASHINGTON
OREGON
IDAHO
MONTANA
WYOMING
NORTH DAKOTA
SOUTH DAKOTA
NEBRASKA
COAST MOUNTAINS
Vancouver Island
Seattle
Portland
Spokane
Boise
Calgary
Regina
Saskatoon
Salt Lake City
Denver
Sacramento
Lambert Conformal Conic Projection

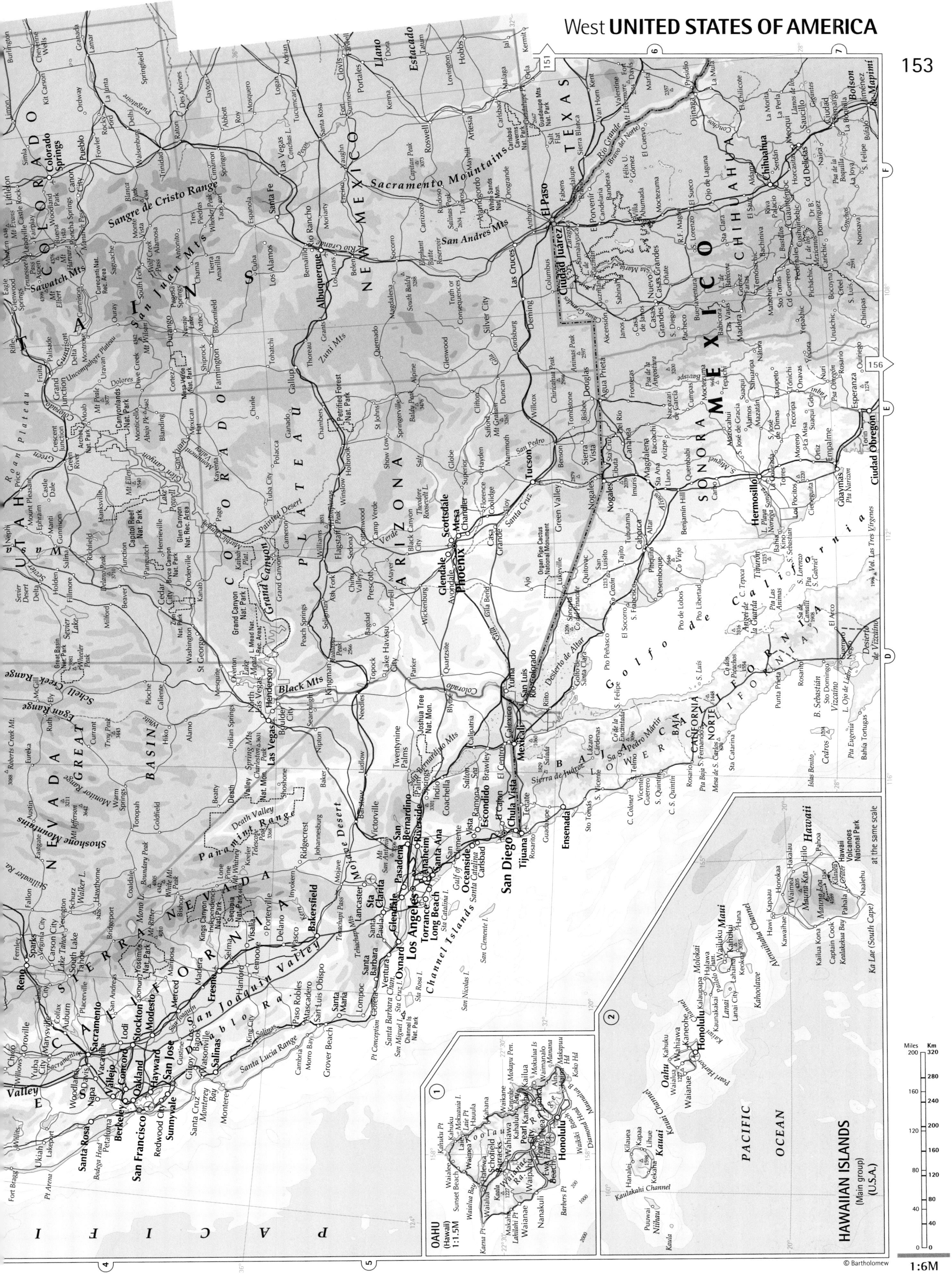
UTAH
COLORADO
NEW MEXICO
ARIZONA
NEVADA
CALIFORNIA
TEXAS
SONORA
CHIHUAHUA
BAJA CALIFORNIA NORTE
MEXICO
Golfo de California
PACIFIC OCEAN
HAWAIIAN ISLANDS (Main group) (U.S.A.) at the same scale
OAHU (Hawaii) 1:1.5M
Miles
Km

© Bartholomew

1:6M

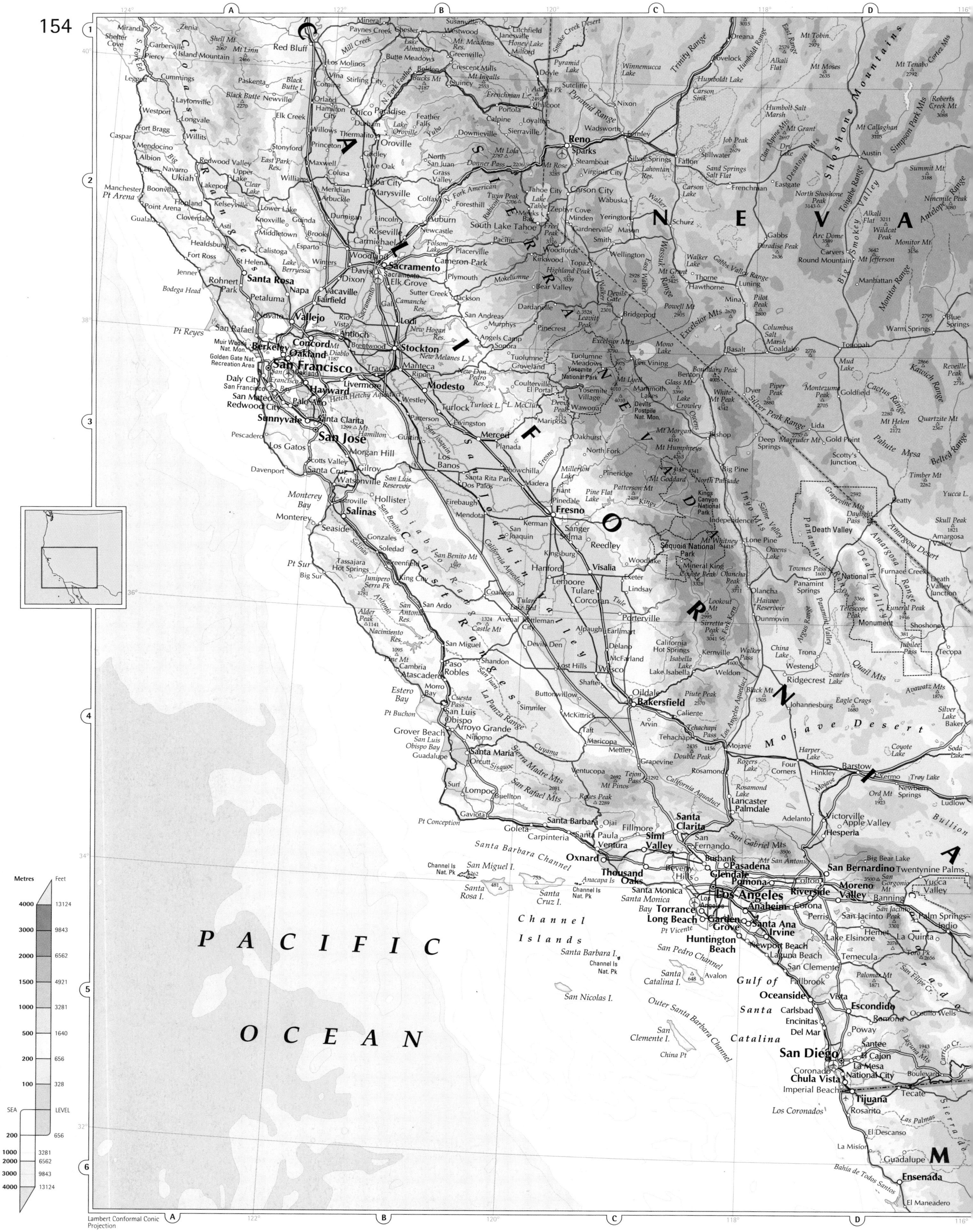
CALIFORNIA
NEVADA
SIERRA NEVADA
PACIFIC OCEAN
Channel Islands
Gulf of Santa Catalina
Mojave Desert
San Francisco
Oakland
Berkeley
Concord
Vallejo
Hayward
Daly City
San Mateo
Redwood City
Palo Alto
Sunnyvale
Santa Clarita
San Jose
Los Gatos
Santa Cruz
Gilroy
Watsonville
Salinas
Monterey
Seaside
Hollister
Sacramento
Stockton
Modesto
Merced
Fresno
Visalia
Hanford
Tulare
Bakersfield
Reno
Sparks
Carson City
Red Bluff
Chico
Oroville
Santa Rosa
Petaluma
Napa
Ukiah
Fort Bragg
Eureka
Santa Barbara
Ventura
Oxnard
Thousand Oaks
Simi Valley
Santa Clarita
Lancaster
Palmdale
Los Angeles
Pasadena
Glendale
Burbank
Pomona
Long Beach
Torrance
Anaheim
Santa Ana
Irvine
Garden Grove
Huntington Beach
Newport Beach
Riverside
San Bernardino
Moreno Valley
Palm Springs
Oceanside
Escondido
San Diego
Chula Vista
National City
El Cajon
Tijuana
Ensenada
Tecate
Rosarito
Barstow
Victorville
Hesperia
Death Valley
Bishop
Lone Pine
Tonopah
Hawthorne
Fallon
Paso Robles
San Luis Obispo
Santa Maria
Lompoc
Pt Conception
Pt Reyes
Pt Sur
Monterey Bay
San Pablo Bay
Santa Barbara Channel
San Pedro Channel
San Miguel I.
Santa Rosa I.
Santa Cruz I.
Anacapa Is
Santa Barbara I.
Santa Catalina I.
San Nicolas I.
San Clemente I.
Mt Whitney 4418
Yosemite National Park
Kings Canyon National Park
Sequoia National Park
Lake Tahoe
Mono Lake
Coast Ranges
Diablo Range
San Joaquin Valley
Sierra Madre Mts
Shoshone Mountains
Inyo Mts
Metres
Feet
4000 13124
3000 9843
2000 6562
1500 4921
1000 3281
500 1640
200 656
100 328
SEA LEVEL
200 656
1000 3281
2000 6562
3000 9843
4000 13124
Lambert Conformal Conic Projection

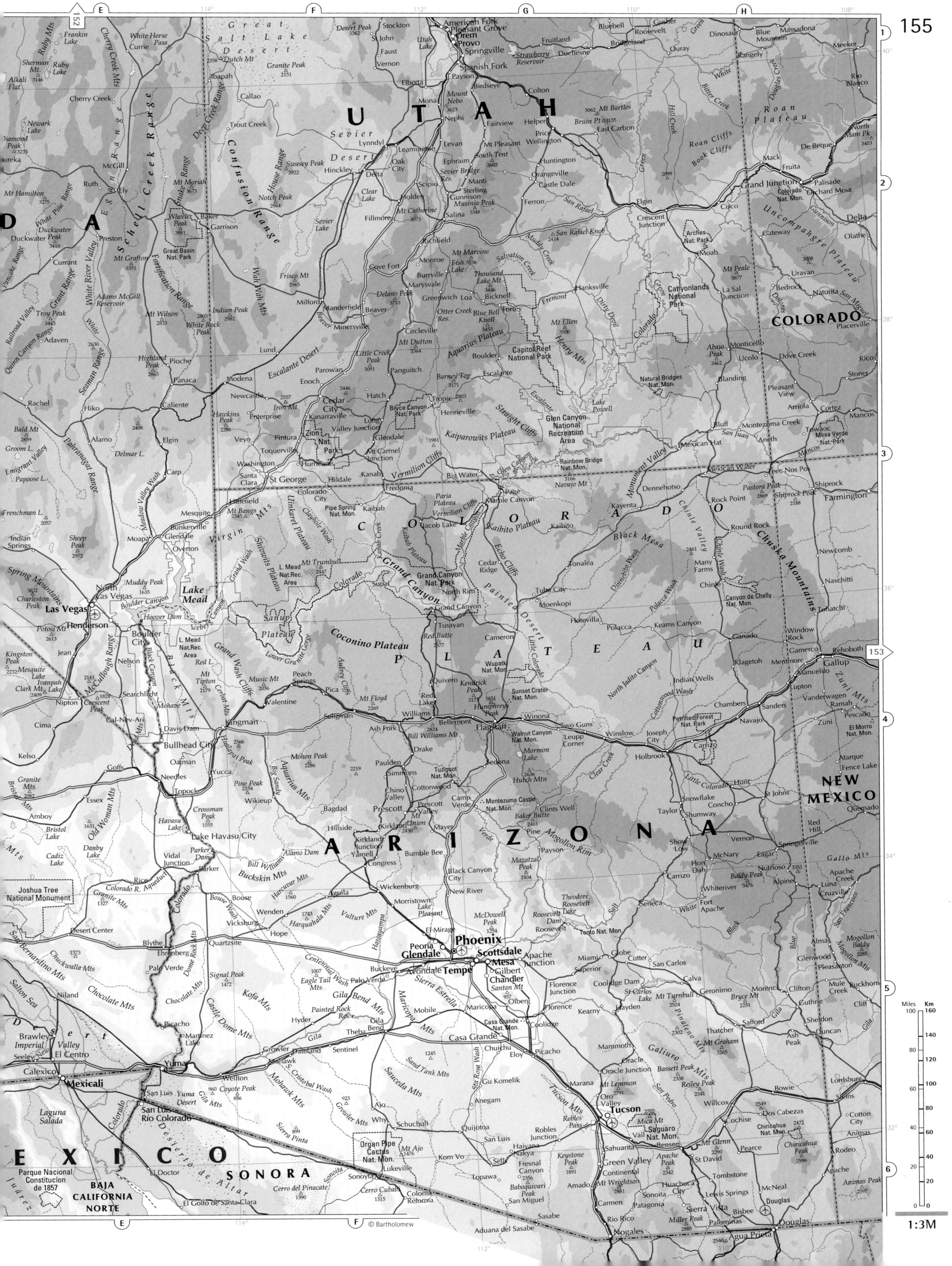
UTAH
COLORADO
ARIZONA
NEW MEXICO
MEXICO
SONORA
BAJA CALIFORNIA NORTE
COLORADO PLATEAU
Great Salt Lake Desert
Sevier Desert
Confusion Range
Escalante Desert
Provo
Orem
Springville
Spanish Fork
Nephi
Delta
Richfield
Cedar City
St George
Kanab
Moab
Canyonlands National Park
Capitol Reef National Park
Glen Canyon National Recreation Area
Lake Powell
Grand Junction
Uncompahgre Plateau
Durango
Farmington
Gallup
Chuska Mountains
Black Mesa
Kayenta
Monument Valley
Grand Canyon
Grand Canyon Nat. Park
Kaibab Plateau
Coconino Plateau
Painted Desert
Lake Mead
Las Vegas
Henderson
Boulder City
Kingman
Bullhead City
Needles
Lake Havasu City
Flagstaff
Williams
Sedona
Prescott
Winslow
Holbrook
Mogollon Rim
Payson
Show Low
Springerville
Wickenburg
Phoenix
Glendale
Scottsdale
Tempe
Mesa
Chandler
Casa Grande
Gila Bend
Yuma
El Centro
Mexicali
Tucson
Nogales
Douglas
Agua Prieta
Sierra Vista
Tombstone
Bisbee
Willcox
Safford
Lordsburg
Salton Sea
Joshua Tree National Monument
Organ Pipe Cactus Nat. Mon.
Parque Nacional Constitucion de 1857
San Luis Río Colorado
© Bartholomew
1:3M
Miles
Km

ARIZONA
NEW MEXICO
UNITE
SONORA
CHIHUAHUA
COAHUILA
SINALOA
DURANGO
ZACATECAS
NAYARIT
JALISCO
AGS
MEX
BAJA CALIFORNIA NORTE
BAJA CALIFORNIA SUR
GOLFO DE CALIFORNIA
SIERRA MADRE OCCIDENTAL
PACIFIC
Tijuana
Chula Vista
Mexicali
Calexico
Yuma
San Luis Río Colorado
Ensenada
Tucson
Nogales
El Paso
Ciudad Juárez
Hermosillo
Guaymas
Ciudad Obregón
Navojoa
Los Mochis
Culiacán
Mazatlán
Chihuahua
Cd Delicias
Durango
Torreón
Gómez Palacio
Zacatecas
Aguascalientes
Tepic
Guadalajara
Colima
Uruapan
Hidalgo del Parral
La Paz
Santa Rosalía
Islas Revillagigedo (Mexico)
I. Clarión
I. Socorro
I. Roca Partida
I. S. Benedicto
at the same scale
Guadalupe (Mex.)
Golfo de Honduras
HONDURAS
Tegucigalpa
San Pedro Sula
La Ceiba
EL SALVADOR
San Salvador
San Miguel
NICARAGUA
Managua
León
Granada
Lago de Nicaragua
COSTA RICA
San José
Limón
PANAMA
Panamá
Colón
David
CARIBBEAN SEA
PACIFIC OCEAN
COSTA DE MOSQUITOS
MOSQUITIA
Golfo de Panamá
Metres
Feet
4000
13124
3000
9843
2000
6562
1000
3281
500
1640
200
656
SEA
LEVEL
200
656
1000
3281
2000
6562
3000
9843
4000
13124
5000
16409
6000
19686
continuation at the same scale
Lambert Conformal Conic Projection

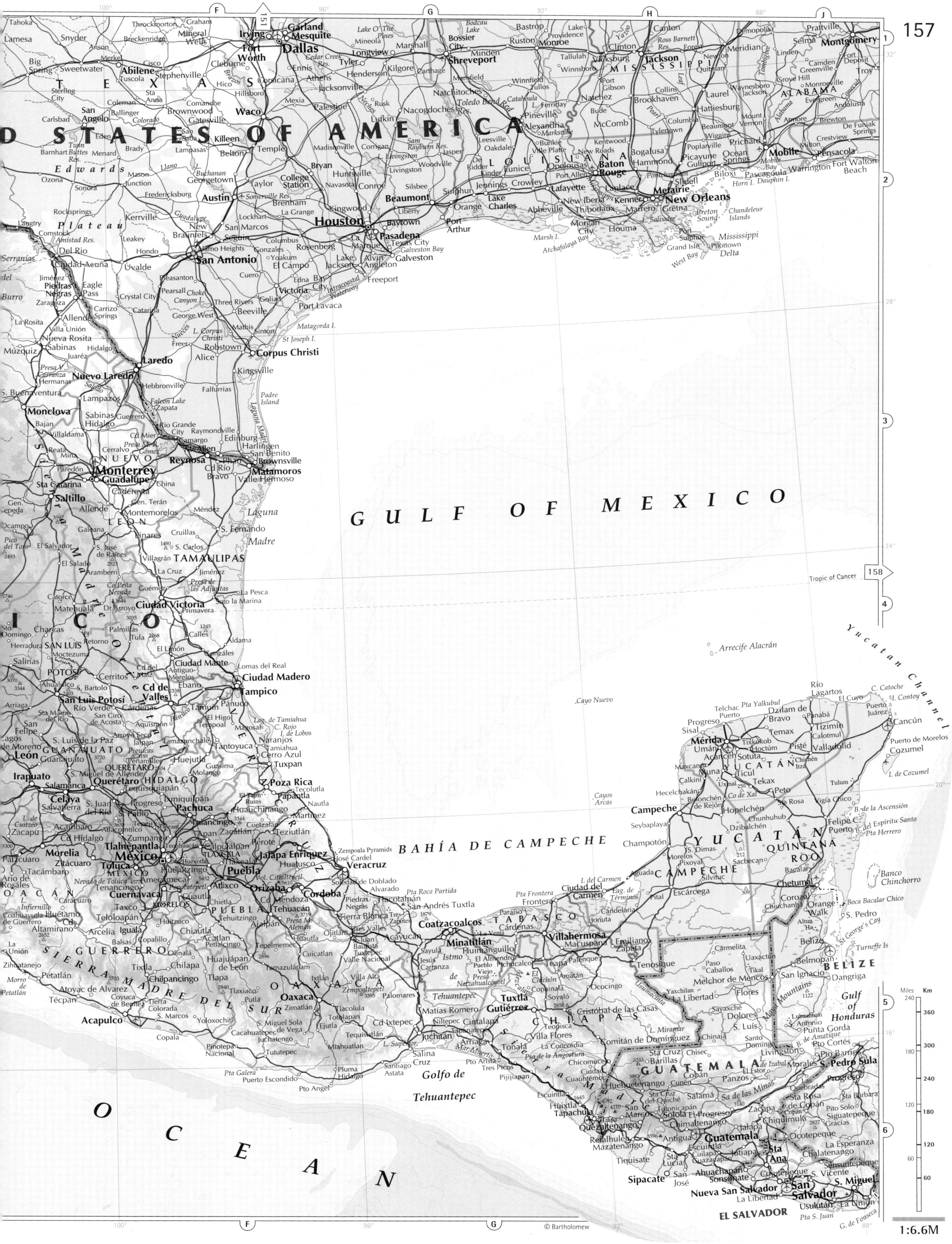
UNITED STATES OF AMERICA
TEXAS
LOUISIANA
MISSISSIPPI
ALABAMA
GULF OF MEXICO
BAHÍA DE CAMPECHE
Golfo de Tehuantepec
OCEAN
SIERRA MADRE DEL SUR
Edwards Plateau
Yucatan Channel
Tropic of Cancer
Dallas
Fort Worth
Shreveport
Jackson
Montgomery
Austin
Houston
San Antonio
Baton Rouge
New Orleans
Mobile
Pensacola
Corpus Christi
Galveston
Beaumont
Laredo
Nuevo Laredo
Monterrey
Saltillo
Matamoros
Brownsville
Reynosa
Ciudad Victoria
Tampico
Ciudad Madero
San Luis Potosí
León
Querétaro
Pachuca
México
Toluca
Puebla
Veracruz
Jalapa Enríquez
Cuernavaca
Acapulco
Oaxaca
Coatzacoalcos
Villahermosa
Campeche
Mérida
Cancún
Cozumel
Chetumal
Belize
Belmopan
Tuxtla Gutiérrez
Tapachula
Quezaltenango
Guatemala
San Pedro Sula
San Salvador
NUEVO LEÓN
TAMAULIPAS
SAN LUIS POTOSÍ
GUANAJUATO
QUERÉTARO
HIDALGO
MÉXICO
MORELOS
TLAXCALA
PUEBLA
VERACRUZ
GUERRERO
OAXACA
TABASCO
CHIAPAS
CAMPECHE
YUCATÁN
QUINTANA ROO
BELIZE
GUATEMALA
EL SALVADOR
Gulf of Honduras
Arrecife Alacrán
Cayo Nuevo
Cayos Arcas
Banco Chinchorro
158
151
1:6.6M
© Bartholomew

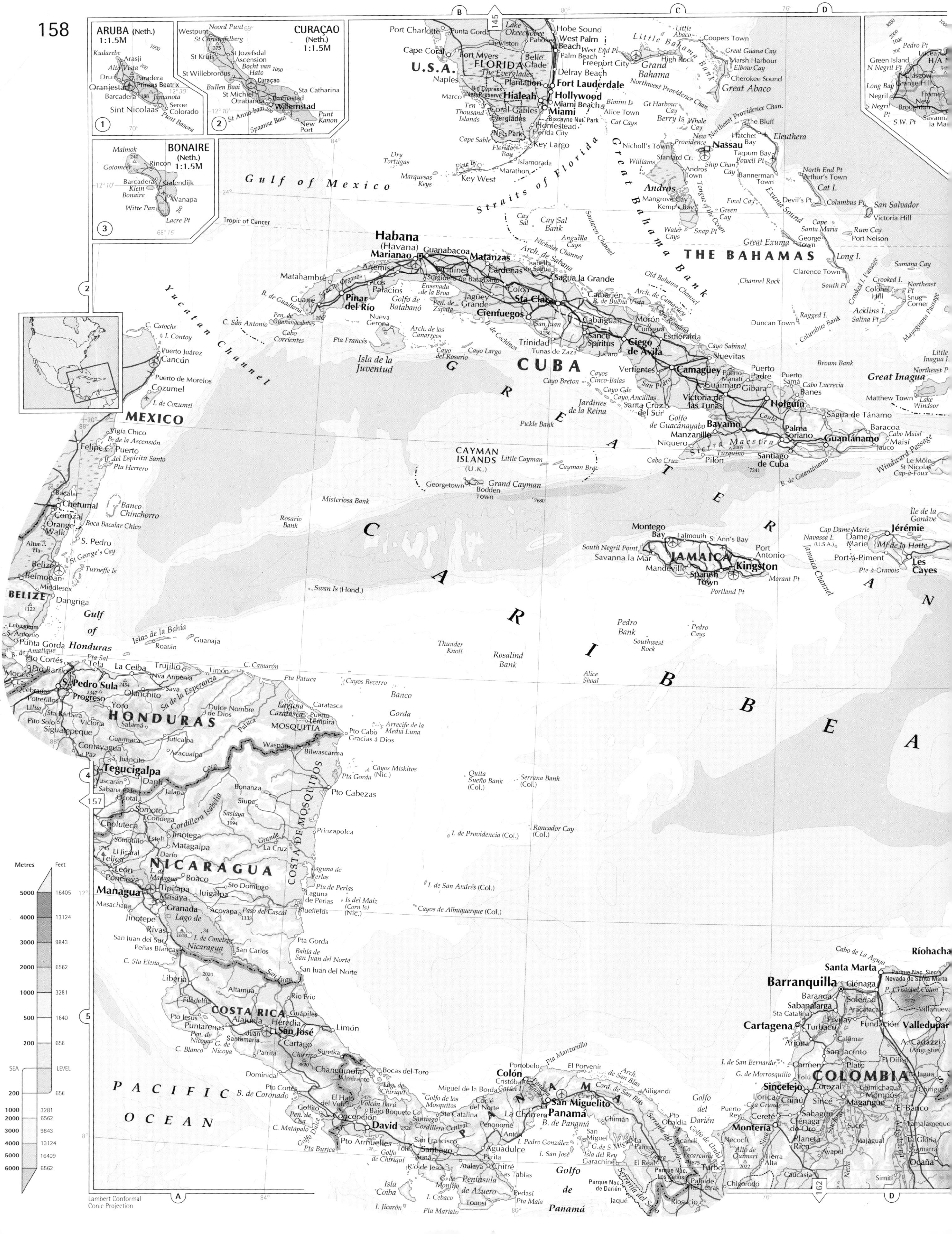
ARUBA (Neth.)
1:1.5M
Oranjestad
Sint Nicolaas
CURAÇAO (Neth.)
1:1.5M
Willemstad
BONAIRE (Neth.)
1:1.5M
Kralendijk
Gulf of Mexico
Tropic of Cancer
Straits of Florida
U.S.A.
FLORIDA
The Everglades
Miami
Hialeah
Hollywood
Fort Lauderdale
West Palm Beach
Key West
Naples
Cape Coral
THE BAHAMAS
Grand Bahama
Freeport City
Great Abaco
Nassau
Andros
Eleuthera
Great Bahama Bank
Exuma Sound
Cat I.
San Salvador
Long I.
Crooked I.
Acklins I.
Great Inagua
Habana (Havana)
Marianao
Matanzas
Pinar del Río
Cienfuegos
Sta Clara
Sancti Spíritus
Ciego de Avila
Camagüey
Holguín
Bayamo
Santiago de Cuba
Guantánamo
CUBA
Isla de la Juventud
Yucatan Channel
MEXICO
Cancún
Cozumel
Chetumal
BELIZE
Belmopan
Gulf of Honduras
CAYMAN ISLANDS (U.K.)
Grand Cayman
Georgetown
Little Cayman
Cayman Brac
JAMAICA
Kingston
Montego Bay
Spanish Town
Jamaica Channel
Windward Passage
Jérémie
Les Cayes
GREATER
CARIBBEAN
Pedro Bank
Rosalind Bank
HONDURAS
Tegucigalpa
San Pedro Sula
La Ceiba
MOSQUITIA
NICARAGUA
Managua
León
Granada
Lago de Nicaragua
COSTA DE MOSQUITOS
Bluefields
COSTA RICA
San José
Limón
PANAMA
Panama
Colón
David
Golfo de Panamá
PACIFIC OCEAN
COLOMBIA
Barranquilla
Cartagena
Santa Marta
Montería
Sincelejo
Valledupar
Ríohacha
Metres
Feet
5000
4000
3000
2000
1000
500
200
SEA LEVEL
6000
16405
13124
9843
6562
3281
1640
656
16409
Lambert Conformal Conic Projection

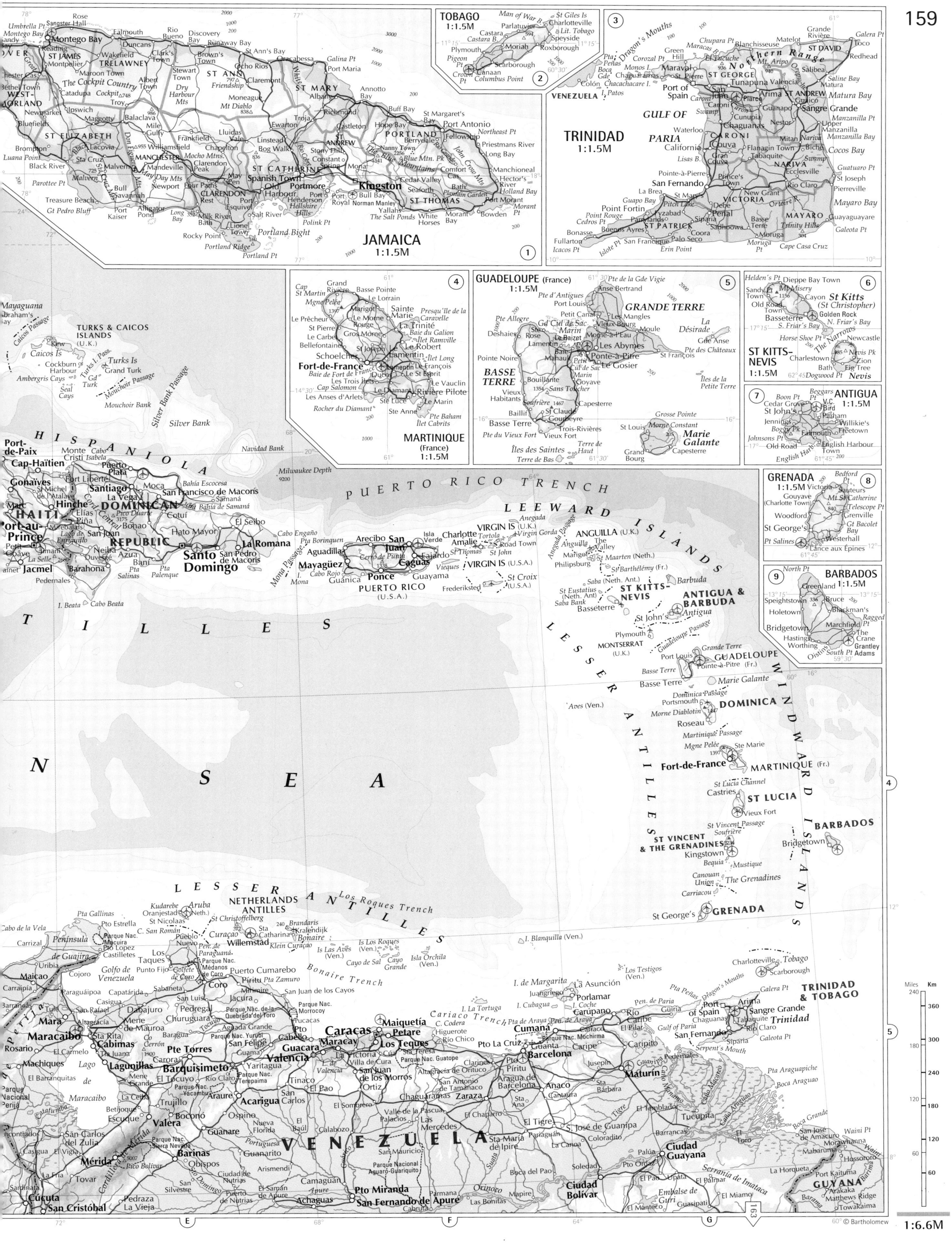

JAMAICA
1:1.5M
TOBAGO
1:1.5M
TRINIDAD
1:1.5M
GULF OF PARIA
VENEZUELA
MARTINIQUE
(France)
1:1.5M
GUADELOUPE (France)
1:1.5M
GRANDE TERRE
BASSE TERRE
ST KITTS-NEVIS
1:1.5M
ANTIGUA
1:1.5M
GRENADA
1:1.5M
BARBADOS
1:1.5M
TURKS & CAICOS ISLANDS (U.K.)
HISPANIOLA
HAITI
DOMINICAN REPUBLIC
Port-au-Prince
Santo Domingo
PUERTO RICO (U.S.A.)
PUERTO RICO TRENCH
LEEWARD ISLANDS
LESSER ANTILLES
WINDWARD ISLANDS
VIRGIN IS (U.K.)
VIRGIN IS (U.S.A.)
ANGUILLA (U.K.)
ST KITTS-NEVIS
ANTIGUA & BARBUDA
MONTSERRAT (U.K.)
GUADELOUPE (Fr.)
DOMINICA
MARTINIQUE (Fr.)
ST LUCIA
ST VINCENT & THE GRENADINES
BARBADOS
GRENADA
TRINIDAD & TOBAGO
NETHERLANDS ANTILLES
Aruba (Neth.)
Curaçao
Bonaire
A N T I L L E S
N S E A
Caracas
VENEZUELA
Maracaibo
Lago de Maracaibo
Barquisimeto
Valencia
Barcelona
Cumaná
Maturín
Ciudad Guayana
Ciudad Bolívar
GUYANA
Miles
Km
© Bartholomew

1:6.6M

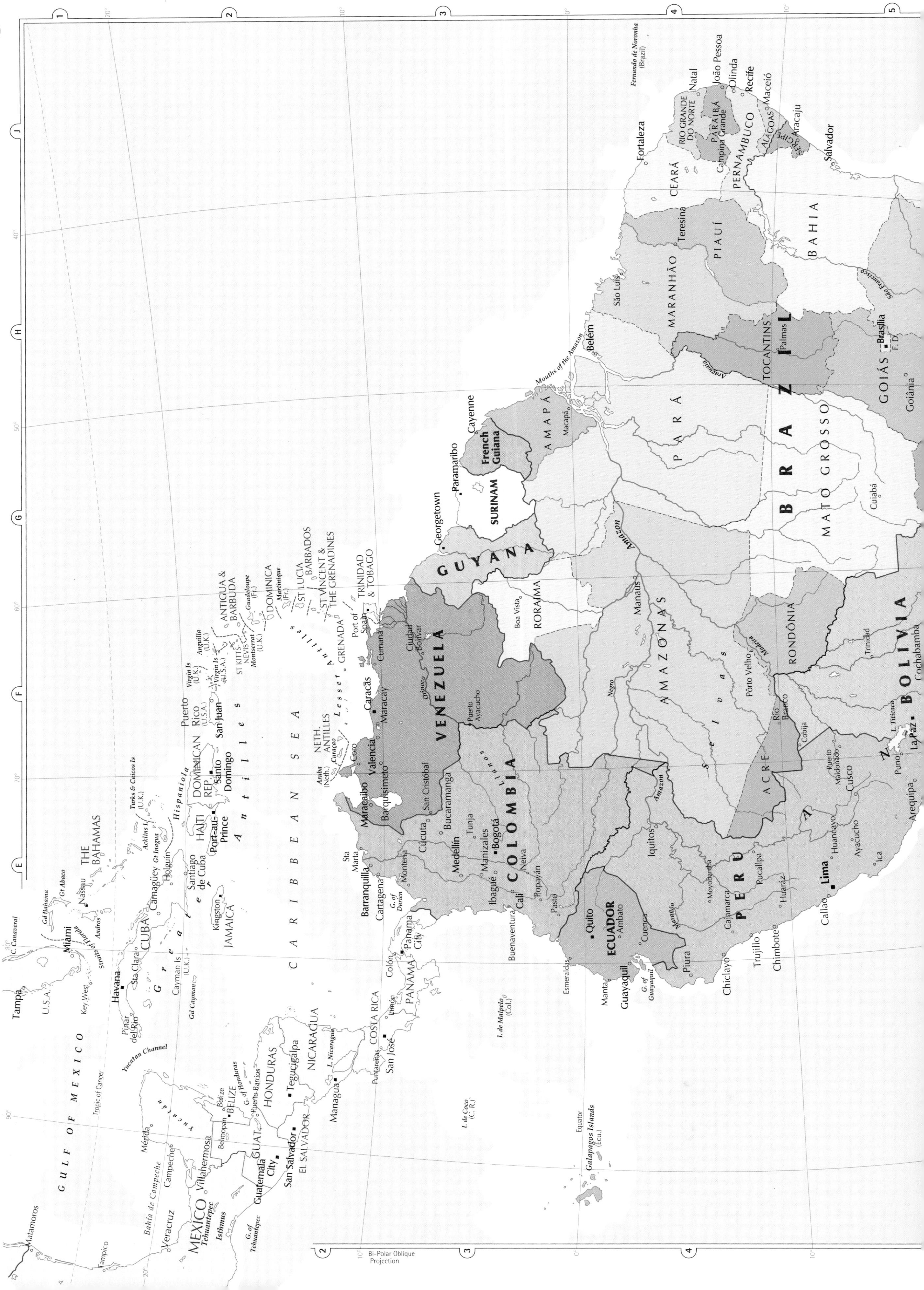
GULF OF MEXICO
CARIBBEAN SEA
Greater Antilles
Lesser Antilles
MEXICO
U.S.A.
THE BAHAMAS
CUBA
JAMAICA
HAITI
DOMINICAN REP.
Puerto Rico (U.S.A.)
BELIZE
GUAT.
HONDURAS
EL SALVADOR
NICARAGUA
COSTA RICA
PANAMA
VENEZUELA
COLOMBIA
ECUADOR
PERU
BOLIVIA
BRAZIL
GUYANA
SURINAM
French Guiana
TRINIDAD & TOBAGO
BARBADOS
GRENADA
ST LUCIA
ST VINCENT & THE GRENADINES
DOMINICA
ANTIGUA & BARBUDA
ST KITTS-NEVIS
NETH. ANTILLES
AMAZONAS
PARÁ
MATO GROSSO
GOIÁS
BAHIA
MARANHÃO
PIAUÍ
CEARÁ
PERNAMBUCO
TOCANTINS
RONDÔNIA
ACRE
RORAIMA
AMAPÁ
Selvas
Mouths of the Amazon
Amazon
Galapagos Islands (Ecu.)
Equator
Tropic of Cancer
Yucatan Channel
Straits of Florida
Tampa
Miami
Havana
Nassau
Kingston
Port-au-Prince
Santo Domingo
San Juan
Caracas
Maracaibo
Bogotá
Medellín
Cali
Quito
Guayaquil
Lima
La Paz
Manaus
Belém
Fortaleza
Recife
Salvador
Brasília
Georgetown
Paramaribo
Cayenne
Panama City
Managua
Tegucigalpa
San Salvador
Guatemala City
San José
Metres
Feet
SEA LEVEL
200
656
3000
9843
Bi-Polar Oblique Projection

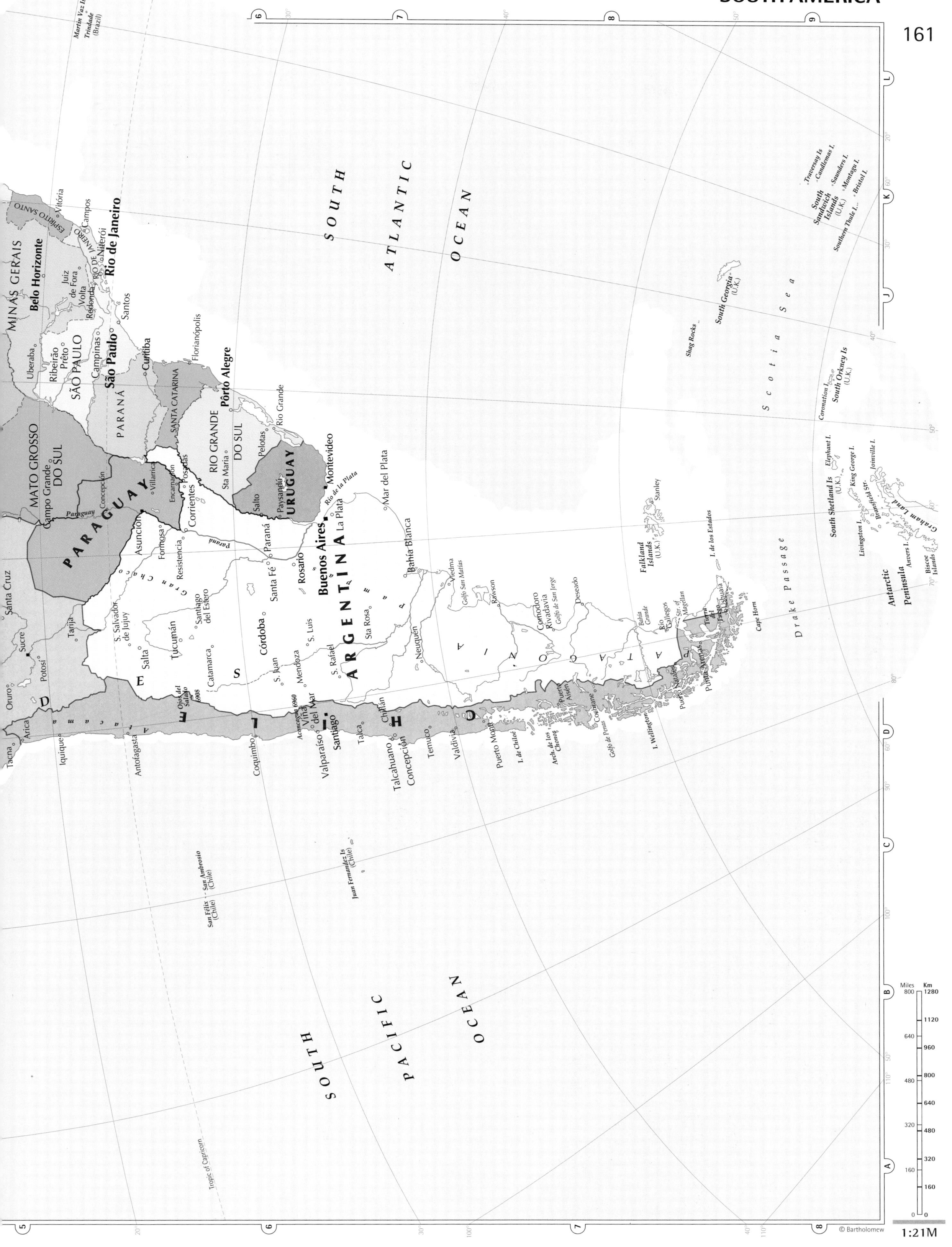
SOUTH ATLANTIC OCEAN
SOUTH PACIFIC OCEAN
PARAGUAY
URUGUAY
ARGENTINA
CHILE
PATAGONIA
MINAS GERAIS
SÃO PAULO
PARANÁ
SANTA CATARINA
RIO GRANDE DO SUL
MATO GROSSO DO SUL
ESPIRITO SANTO
RIO DE JANEIRO
Belo Horizonte
Rio de Janeiro
São Paulo
Curitiba
Pôrto Alegre
Montevideo
Buenos Aires
La Plata
Rosario
Córdoba
Mendoza
Santiago
Valparaíso
Asunción
Corrientes
Posadas
Tucumán
Salta
Bahía Blanca
Mar del Plata
Concepción
Talcahuano
Temuco
Valdivia
Puerto Montt
Antofagasta
Iquique
Arica
Tacna
Sucre
Potosí
Santa Cruz
Oruro
Tarija
Coquimbo
Comodoro Rivadavia
Río Gallegos
Punta Arenas
Ushuaia
Tierra del Fuego
Str. of Magellan
Cape Horn
Drake Passage
Falkland Islands (U.K.)
Stanley
South Georgia (U.K.)
Shag Rocks
Scotia Sea
South Orkney Is (U.K.)
Coronation I.
South Shetland Is (U.K.)
Elephant I.
King George I.
Livingston I.
Joinville I.
Bransfield Str.
Antarctic Peninsula
Graham Land
Anvers I.
Biscoe Islands
South Sandwich Islands (U.K.)
Traversay Is
Candlemas I.
Saunders I.
Montagu I.
Bristol I.
Southern Thule I.
Martin Vaz Is
Trindade (Brazil)
Juan Fernández Is (Chile)
San Félix - San Ambrosio (Chile)
Tropic of Capricorn
Aconcagua 6960
Ojos del Salado 6908
I. de Chiloé
I. Wellington
I. de los Estados
Miles
Km
1:21M
© Bartholomew

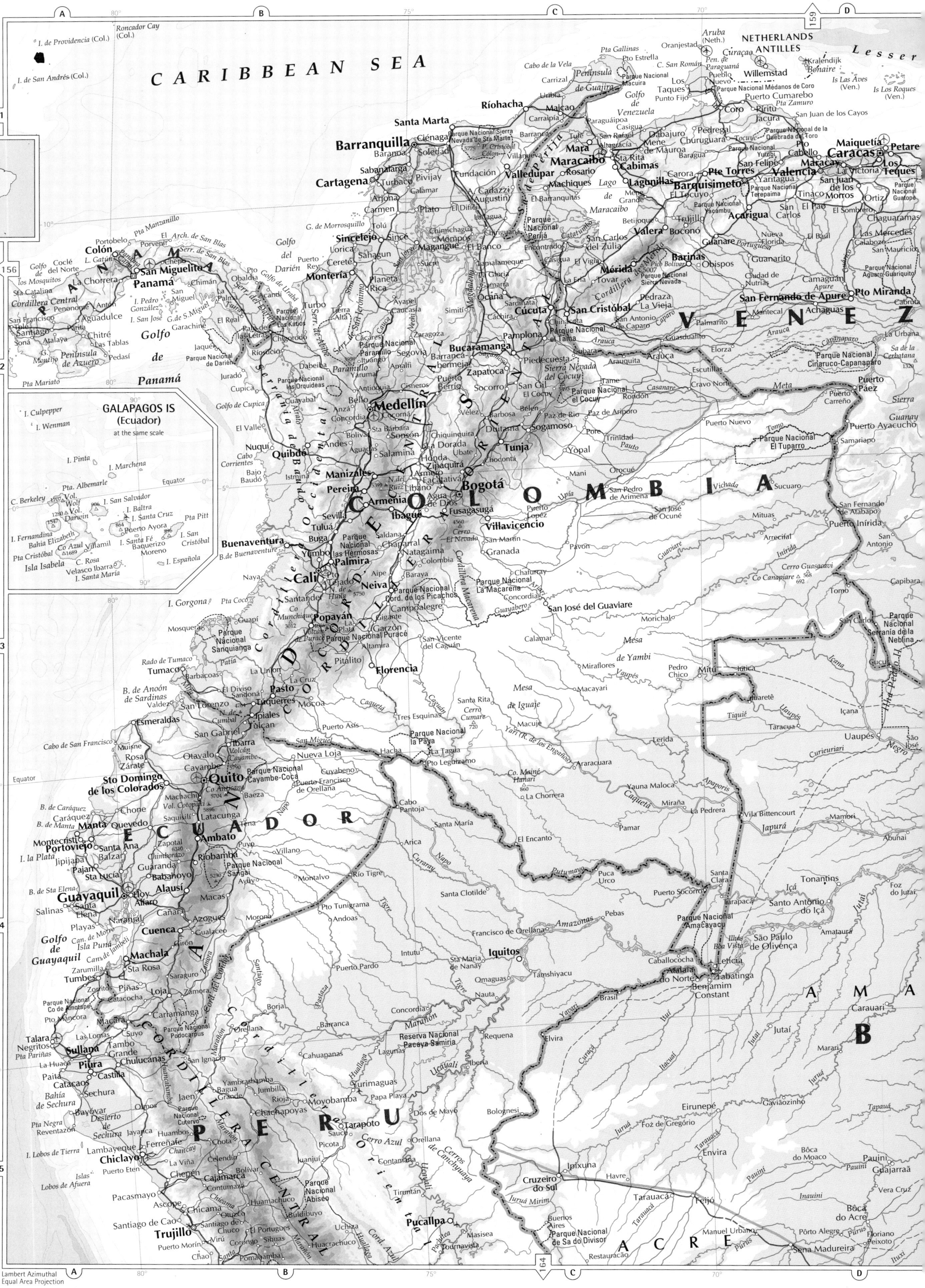

Metres / Feet: 5000 16409; 4000 13124; 3000 9843; 2000 6562; 1000 3281; 500 1640; 200 656; SEA LEVEL; 200 656; 1000 3281; 2000 6562; 3000 9843; 4000 13124; 5000 16409; 6000 19686

Lambert Azimuthal
Equal Area Projection

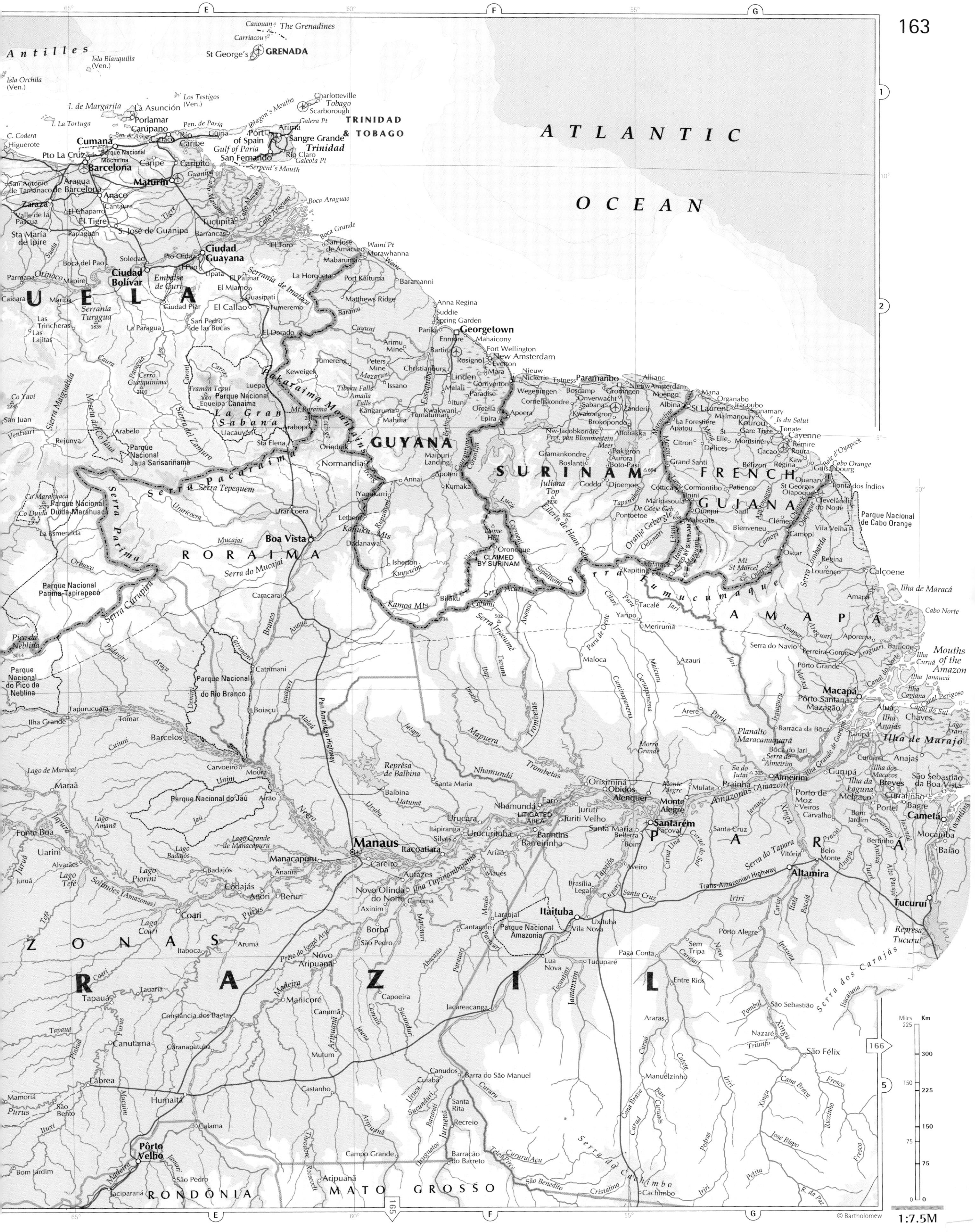
ATLANTIC
OCEAN
GUYANA
SURINAM
FRENCH
GUIANA
RORAIMA
AMAPÁ
PARÁ
BRAZIL
ZONAS
RONDÔNIA
MATO GROSSO
TRINIDAD & TOBAGO
GRENADA
Antilles
The Grenadines
St George's
Isla Blanquilla (Ven.)
Isla Orchila (Ven.)
I. de Margarita
La Asunción
Los Testigos (Ven.)
Charlotteville
Tobago
Scarborough
Porlamar
Carúpano
Cumaná
Port of Spain
Sangre Grande
Trinidad
Arima
Gulf of Paria
San Fernando
Serpent's Mouth
Pto La Cruz
Barcelona
Maturín
Anaco
Zaraza
El Tigre
Tucupita
Boca Grande
Ciudad Guayana
Ciudad Bolívar
Orinoco
El Callao
Tumeremo
Serranía de Imataca
Guasipati
El Dorado
Ciudad Piar
Matthews Ridge
Port Kaituma
Anna Regina
Georgetown
New Amsterdam
Fort Wellington
Linden
Bartica
Pakaraima Mountains
Parque Nacional Canaima
La Gran Sabana
Mt Roraima 2810
Sta Elena
Orinduik
Annai
Lethem
Boa Vista
Kanuku Mts
Serra Pacaraima
Serra Parima
Serra do Mucajaí
Caracaraí
Kamoa Mts
Paramaribo
Nieuw Nickerie
Nieuw Amsterdam
Moengo
Albina
St Laurent
Mana
Zanderij
Brokopondo
Afobakka
Juliana Top 1230
Goddo
Djoemoe
Pontoetoe
Oranje Gebergte
Kourou
Cayenne
Îles du Salut
Régina
Saül
Ouanary
St Georges
Oiapoque
Cabo Orange
Parque Nacional de Cabo Orange
Serra Tumucumaque
Mitaraca
Serra Acarí
Calçoene
Ilha de Maracá
Cabo Norte
Macapá
Mouths of the Amazon
Ilha de Marajó
Chaves
Almeirim
Prainha
Monte Alegre
Santarém
Alenquer
Óbidos
Oriximiná
Parintins
Itacoatiara
Manaus
Manacapuru
Coari
Tefé
Codajás
Borba
Itaituba
Altamira
Tucuruí
Cametá
Breves
Gurupá
Porto de Moz
Vitória
Trans-Amazonian Highway
Pan American Highway
Amazonas (Amazon)
Solimões (Amazonas)
Negro
Branco
Madeira
Tapajós
Xingu
Trombetas
Nhamundá
Jari
Represa de Balbina
Parque Nacional do Jaú
Parque Nacional do Pico da Neblina
Pico da Neblina 3014
Parque Nacional Parima-Tapirapecó
Parque Nacional do Rio Branco
Parque Nacional Amazonia
Barcelos
Carvoeiro
Moura
Novo Aripuanã
Manicoré
Humaitá
Lábrea
Pôrto Velho
Jacareacanga
Canutama
Tapauá
São Félix
Serra dos Carajás
Serra do Cachimbo
Cachimbo
LITIGATED AREA
CLAIMED BY SURINAM

Miles
Km
1:7.5M
© Bartholomew

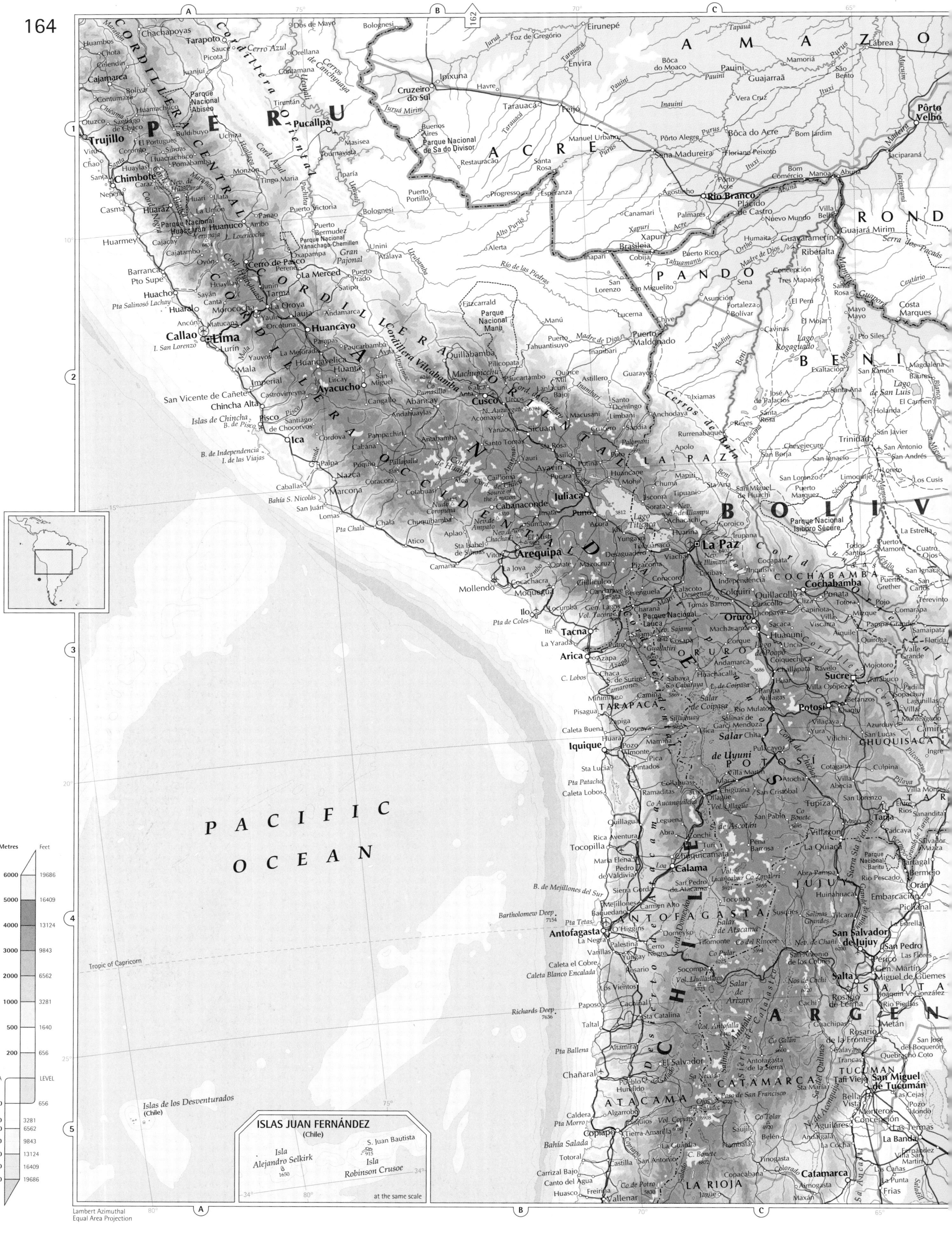
PERU
ACRE
PANDO
BENI
LA PAZ
COCHABAMBA
ORURO
POTOSÍ
CHUQUISACA
TARAPACÁ
ANTOFAGASTA
ATACAMA
JUJUY
SALTA
TUCUMÁN
CATAMARCA
LA RIOJA
CHILE
PACIFIC OCEAN
Lima
Callao
Trujillo
Chimbote
Huancayo
Ayacucho
Cusco
Arequipa
Juliaca
Puno
La Paz
Cochabamba
Oruro
Sucre
Potosí
Arica
Tacna
Iquique
Antofagasta
Calama
Copiapó
Salta
San Salvador de Jujuy
San Miguel de Tucumán
Catamarca
Rio Branco
Pôrto Velho
Cruzeiro do Sul
Pucallpa
Tropic of Capricorn
Bartholomew Deep 7154
Richards Deep 7636
Islas de los Desventurados (Chile)
ISLAS JUAN FERNÁNDEZ (Chile)
Isla Alejandro Selkirk
Isla Robinson Crusoe
S. Juan Bautista
at the same scale
Metres
Feet
6000 19686
5000 16409
4000 13124
3000 9843
2000 6562
1000 3281
500 1640
200 656
SEA LEVEL
200 656
Lambert Azimuthal Equal Area Projection

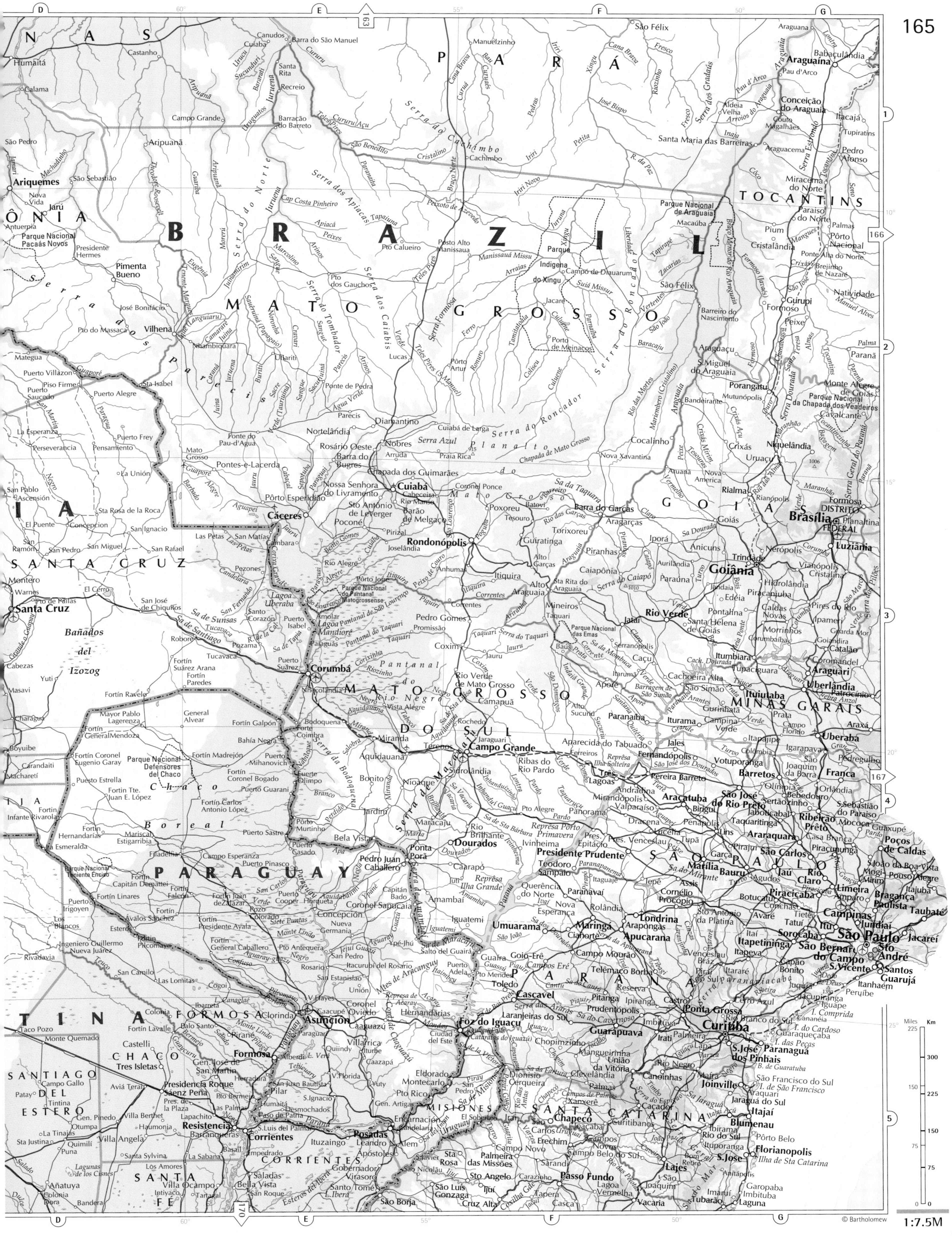
BRAZIL
PARÁ
MATO GROSSO
TOCANTINS
GOIÁS
MATO GROSSO DO SUL
MINAS GARAIS
SÃO PAULO
PARANÁ
SANTA CATARINA
PARAGUAY
SANTA CRUZ
Bañados del Izozog
Chaco Boreal
CHACO
FORMOSA
SANTIAGO DEL ESTERO
SANTA FE
CORRIENTES
MISIONES
Brasília
DISTRITO FEDERAL
Goiânia
Cuiabá
Campo Grande
Corumbá
Santa Cruz
Asunción
São Paulo
Curitiba
Florianópolis
Campinas
Londrina
Uberlândia
Uberaba
Ribeirão Prêto
Araguaína
Rondonópolis
Dourados
Cáceres
Vilhena
Ariquemes
Foz do Iguaçu
Posadas
Corrientes
Resistencia
Formosa
Encarnación
Ciudad del Este
Pedro Juan Caballero
Concepción
Ponta Grossa
Joinville
Blumenau
Chapecó
Passo Fundo
Santos
Sorocaba
Bauru
Marília
Presidente Prudente
Araraquara
São Carlos
Piracicaba
Jundiaí
Cascavel
Maringá
Guarapuava
Lajes
Parque Nacional de Araguaia
Parque Indígena do Xingu
Parque Nacional da Chapada dos Veadeiros
Parque Nacional das Emas
Parque Nacional do Pantanal Matogrossense
Parque Nacional Pacaás Novos
Parque Nacional Defensores del Chaco
Pantanal
Serra do Roncador
Serra dos Parecis
Serra do Cachimbo
Planalto do Mato Grosso
Chapada de Mato Grosso
Serra da Bodoquena
Serra de Maracaju
Miles
Km
225
300
150
225
75
150
75
0
0
1:7.5M
© Bartholomew

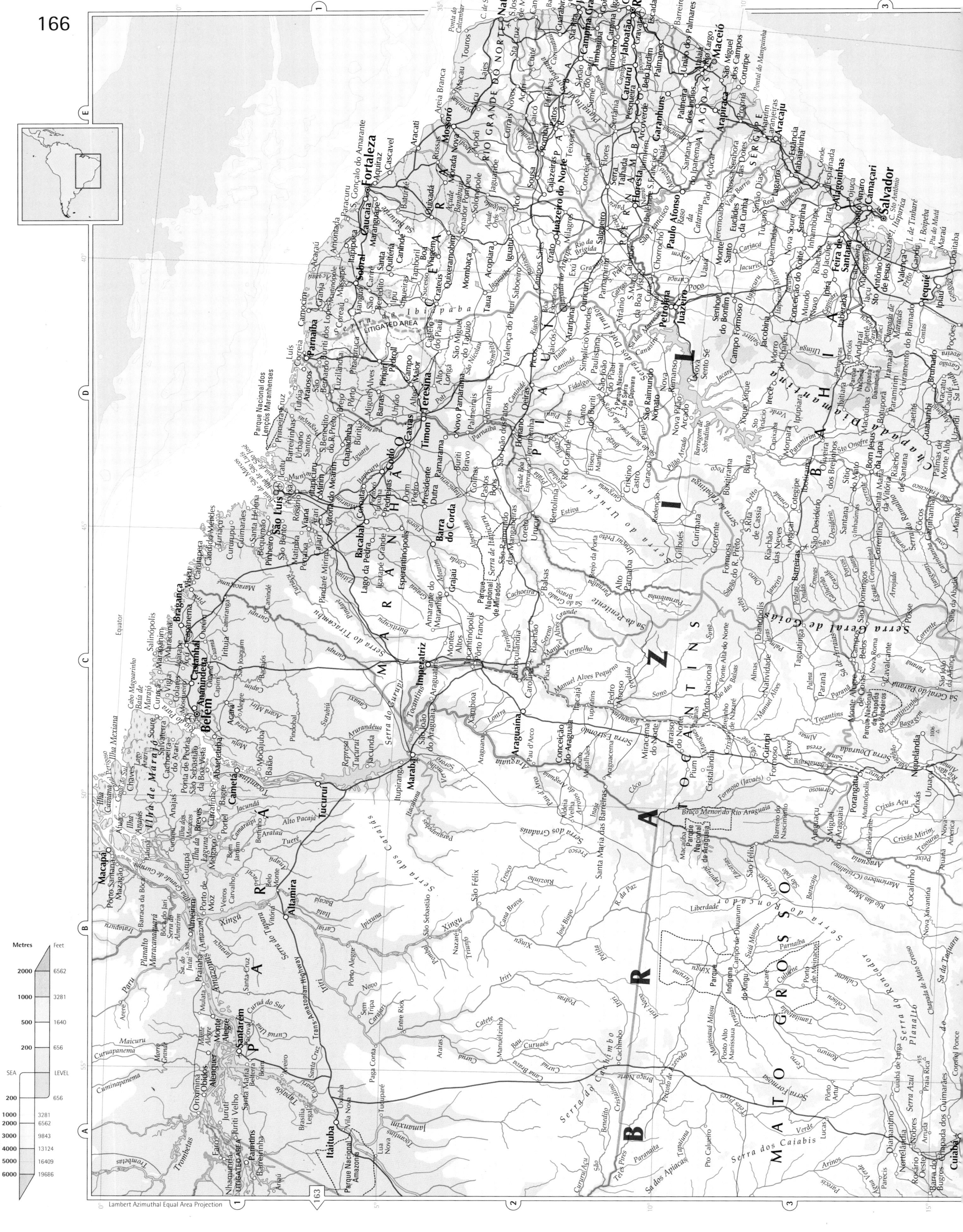
Metres
Feet
2000
6562
1000
3281
500
1640
200
656
SEA
LEVEL
200
656
1000
3281
2000
6562
3000
9843
4000
13124
5000
16409
6000
19686
Lambert Azimuthal Equal Area Projection
BRAZIL
PARÁ
MARANHÃO
PIAUÍ
CEARÁ
RIO GRANDE DO NORTE
PARAÍBA
PERNAMBUCO
ALAGOAS
SERGIPE
BAHIA
TOCANTINS
MATO GROSSO
Belém
São Luís
Teresina
Fortaleza
Natal
João Pessoa
Recife
Maceió
Aracaju
Salvador
Cuiabá
Equator
Serra Geral de Goiás
Chapada Diamantina
LITIGATED AREA

163

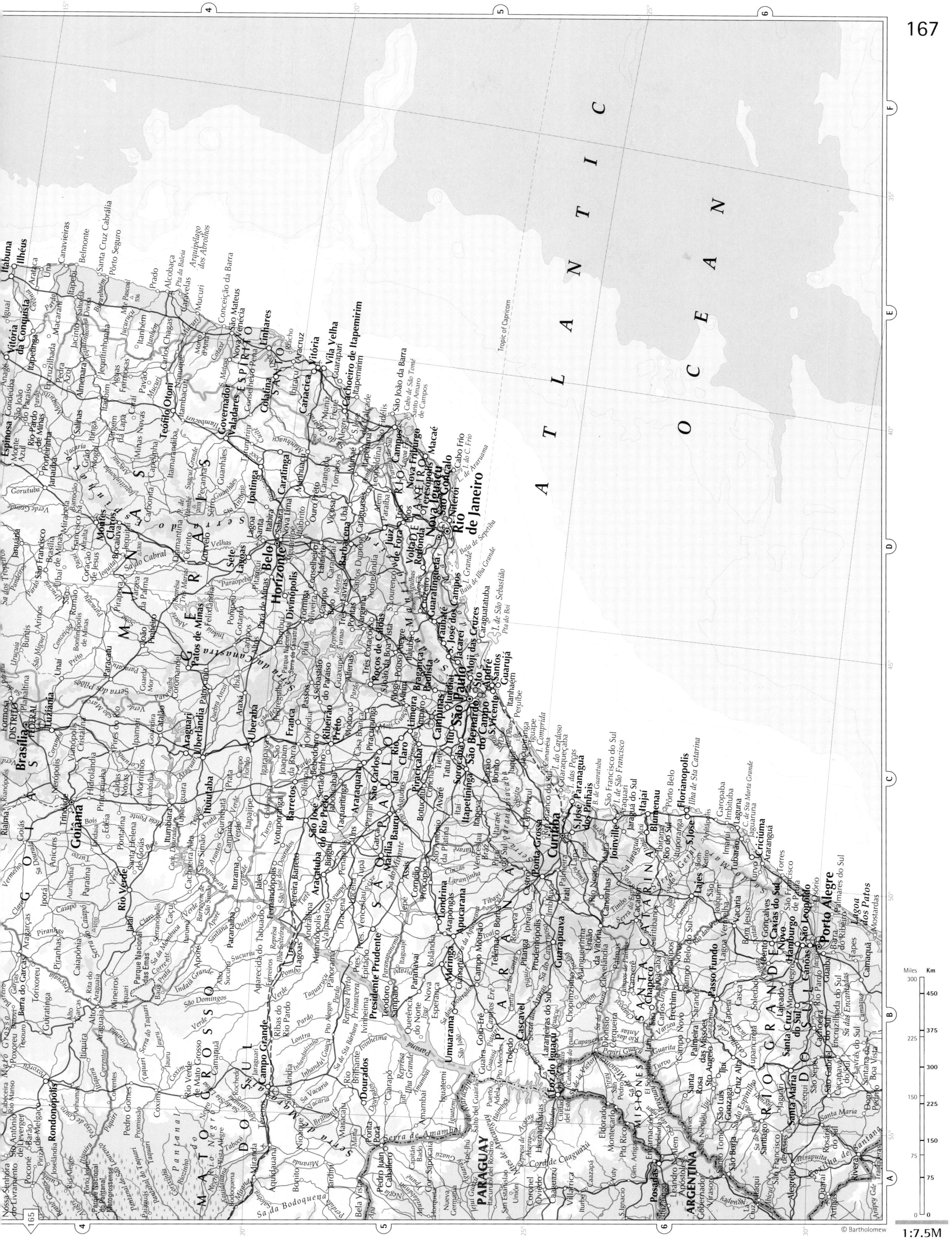
ATLANTIC OCEAN
Tropic of Capricorn
Rio de Janeiro
São Paulo
Belo Horizonte
Brasília
Curitiba
Porto Alegre
Florianópolis
Vitória
Goiânia
MINAS GERAIS
SÃO PAULO
PARANÁ
SANTA CATARINA
RIO GRANDE DO SUL
MATO GROSSO DO SUL
ESPÍRITO SANTO
RIO DE JANEIRO
PARAGUAY
ARGENTINA
Miles
Km
165

© Bartholomew

1:7.5M

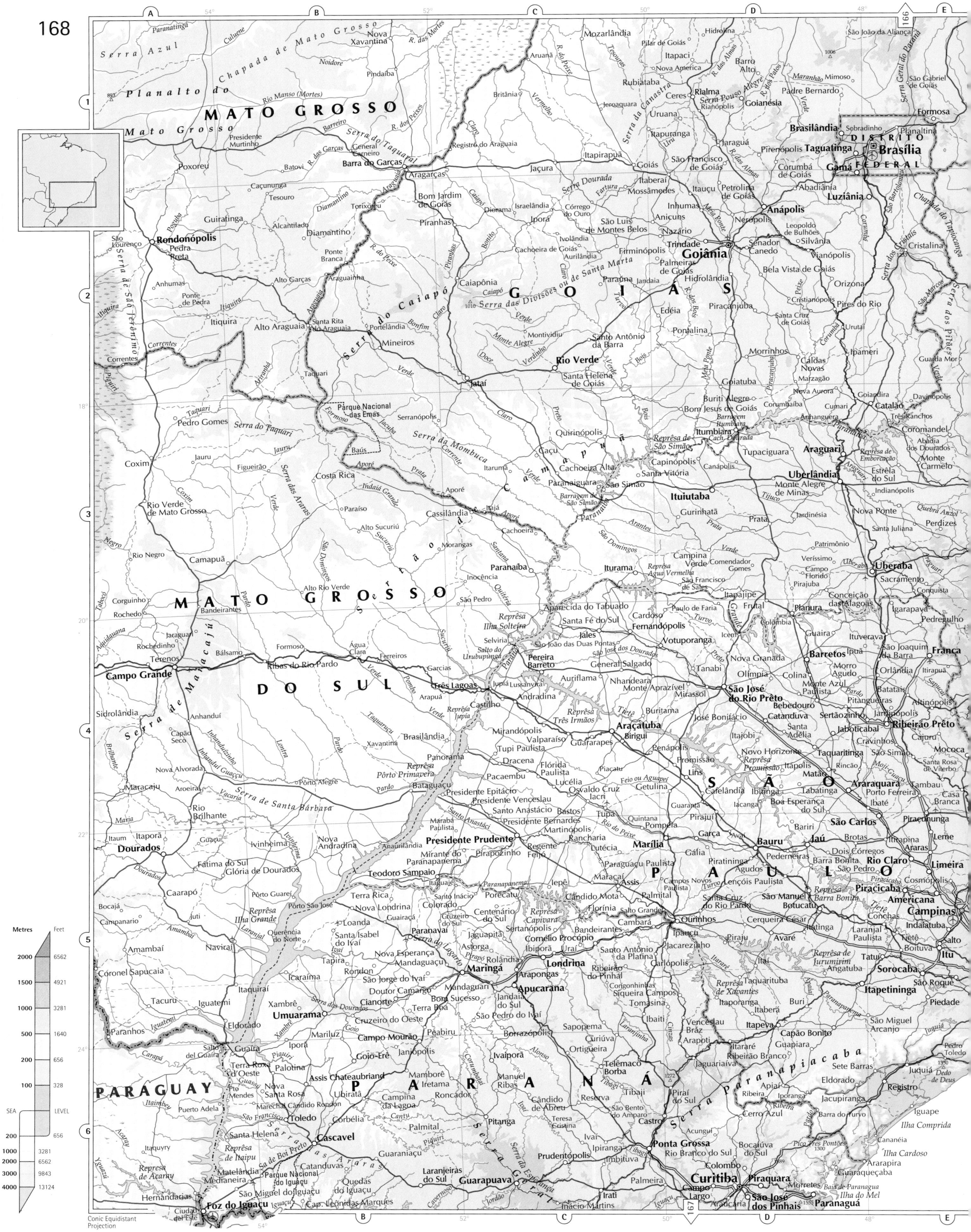
MATO GROSSO
MATO GROSSO DO SUL
GOIÁS
SÃO PAULO
PARANÁ
PARAGUAY
DISTRITO FEDERAL
Brasília
Goiânia
Anápolis
Uberlândia
Uberaba
Campo Grande
Ribeirão Prêto
Campinas
Curitiba
Ponta Grossa
Londrina
Maringá
Presidente Prudente
Bauru
São José do Rio Prêto
Rondonópolis
Dourados
Cascavel
Foz do Iguaçu
Paranaguá
Sorocaba
Três Lagoas
Rio Verde
Jataí
Itumbiara
Araguari
Catalão
Araçatuba
Marília
Guarapuava
Planalto do Mato Grosso
Chapada de Mato Grosso
Serra do Caiapó
Serra da Mombuca
Serra de Maracajú
Serra Geral
Serra Paranapiacaba
Serra de Santa Bárbara
Represa de Itaipu
Represa Três Irmãos
Represa Capivara
Parque Nacional das Emas
Parque Nacional do Iguaçu
Ilha Comprida
Ilha do Mel
Metres
Feet
2000
6562
1500
4921
1000
3281
500
1640
200
656
100
328
SEA
LEVEL
3000
9843
4000
13124
Conic Equidistant Projection
A
B
C
D
E
1
2
3
4
5
6
54°
52°
50°
48°
166
167

F
G
H
J
46°
44°
42°
40°
3
4
5
6
16°
18°
20°
22°
24°
B A H I A
M I N A S
G E R A I S
ESPÍRITO
SANTO
RIO DE JANEIRO
ATLANTIC
OCEAN
Tropic of Capricorn
Serra de Santa Maria
Serra dos Tropeiros
Serra do Espinhaço
Chapadão de Santa Maria
Serra do Rio Prêto
Serra da Canastra
Serra do Cabral
Serra Negra
Serra do Chifre
Serra dos Aimorés
Planalto do Brasil
Serra da Mantiqueira
Serra do Mar
Serra da Cana Brava
Represa Três Marias
Represa Furnas
Represa Peixoto
Parque Nacional da Serra da Canastra
Pico da Bandeira
Pico de Itambé
Pico das Agulhas Negras
Arquipélago dos Abrolhos
Ilha Cacumba
Cabo de São Tomé
Cabo Frio
Ilha do Cabo Frio
Baía de Guanabara
Baía de Sepetiba
Restinga de Marambaia
Ilha Grande
Ilha de São Sebastião
Ilha dos Buzios
Pta do Boi
Manga
Matias Cardoso
Itacarambi
Januária
Janaúba
Porteirinha
Espinosa
Monte Azul
Vitória da Conquista
Itabuna
Ilhéus
Canavieiras
Belmonte
Santa Cruz Cabrália
Pôrto Seguro
Prado
Alcobaça
Caravelas
Nova Viçosa
Mucuri
Itapetinga
Pirapora
Buritizeiro
Montes Claros
Bocaiúva
Salinas
Almenara
Araçuaí
Teófilo Otoni
Paracatu
Unaí
João Pinheiro
Patos de Minas
Curvelo
Diamantina
Governador Valadares
Conceição da Barra
São Mateus
Linhares
Colatina
Aracruz
Serra
Cariacica
Vitória
Vila Velha
Guarapari
Cachoeiro de Itapemirim
Itapemirim
Sete Lagoas
Coronel Fabriciano
Ipatinga
Caratinga
Ribeirão das Neves
Contagem
Belo Horizonte
Sabará
Betim
Divinópolis
Formiga
Manhuaçu
Ouro Prêto
Conselheiro Lafaiete
Barbacena
São João del Rei
Lavras
Muriaé
Cataguases
Juiz de Fora
Campos
São João da Barra
Poços de Caldas
Varginha
Três Corações
Pouso Alegre
Itajubá
Mogi-Guaçu
Volta Redonda
Barra Mansa
Resende
Petrópolis
Teresópolis
Nova Friburgo
Macaé
Duque de Caxias
Nova Iguaçu
Rio de Janeiro
Niterói
São Gonçalo
Itaboraí
Araruama
Cabo Frio
Guaratinguetá
Taubaté
Pindamonhangaba
São José dos Campos
Jacareí
Bragança Paulista
Jundiaí
Osasco
São Paulo
Santo André
Cubatão
Santos
Guarujá
Praia Grande
Ubatuba
Caraguatatuba
Ilhabela
São Sebastião
Mongaguá
Itanhaém
Miles
Km
0
20
40
60
80
100
120
160
200

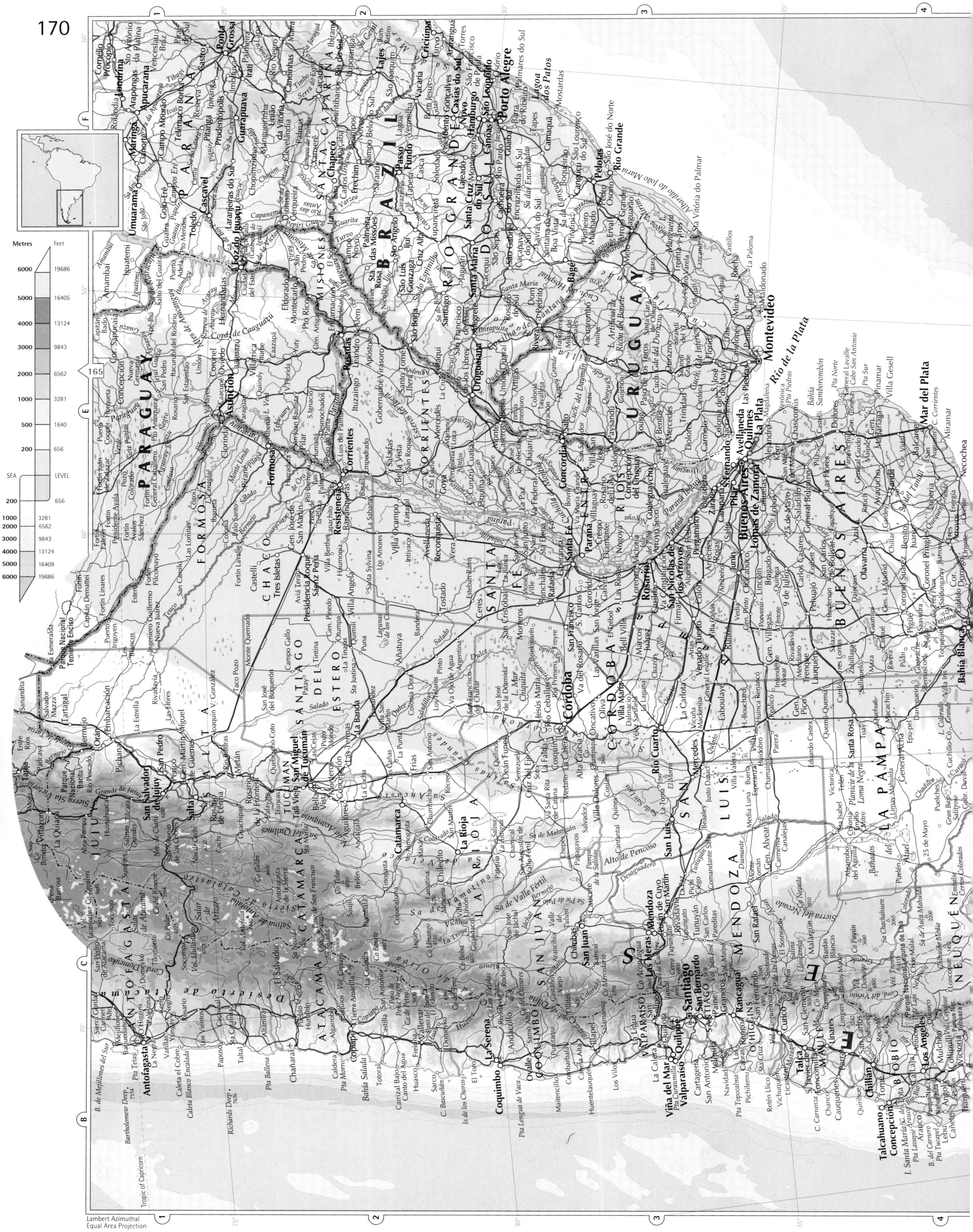

Metres Feet
6000 19686
5000 16405
4000 13124
3000 9843
2000 6562
1000 3281
500 1640
200 656
SEA LEVEL
200 656
1000 3281
2000 6562
3000 9843
4000 13124
5000 16409
6000 19686
165
PARAGUAY
BRAZIL
URUGUAY
PARANÁ
SANTA CATARINA
RIO GRANDE DO SUL
MISIONES
CORRIENTES
ENTRE RIOS
SANTA FÉ
CHACO
FORMOSA
SANTIAGO DEL ESTERO
TUCUMAN
SALTA
JUJUY
CATAMARCA
LA RIOJA
SAN JUAN
CÓRDOBA
SAN LUIS
MENDOZA
LA PAMPA
BUENOS AIRES
NEUQUÉN
ANTOFAGASTA
ATACAMA
COQUIMBO
VALPARAISO
SANTIAGO
O'HIGGINS
MAULE
BIOBÍO
Asunción
Montevideo
Buenos Aires
Córdoba
Rosario
Santiago
Porto Alegre
Río de la Plata
Tropic of Capricorn
Lambert Azimuthal
Equal Area Projection

SOUTH ATLANTIC OCEAN
ARGENTINA
CHILE
RIO NEGRO
CHUBUT
SANTA CRUZ
AISEN
LOS LAGOS
LA ARAUCANIA
MAGALLANES & ANTARTICA CHILENA
TIERRA DEL FUEGO
FALKLAND ISLANDS
(ISLAS MALVINAS)
(U.K.)
West Falkland
East Falkland
Stanley
SOUTH GEORGIA
(U.K.)
Grytviken
at the same scale
Bahía Blanca
Golfo San Matías
Golfo de San Jorge
Comodoro Rivadavia
Río Gallegos
Punta Arenas
Ushuaia
Puerto Montt
Valdivia
Osorno
Temuco
Neuquén
Rawson
Trelew
Puerto Madryn
Península Valdés
Estrecho de Magallanes
Isla Grande de Tierra del Fuego
Isla de Chiloé
Archipiélago de los Chonos
Golfo de Penas
Isla Wellington
Archipiélago de la Reina Adelaida
Cabo de Hornos
(C. Horn)
Is Hermite
Miles
Km
© Bartholomew
1:7.5M

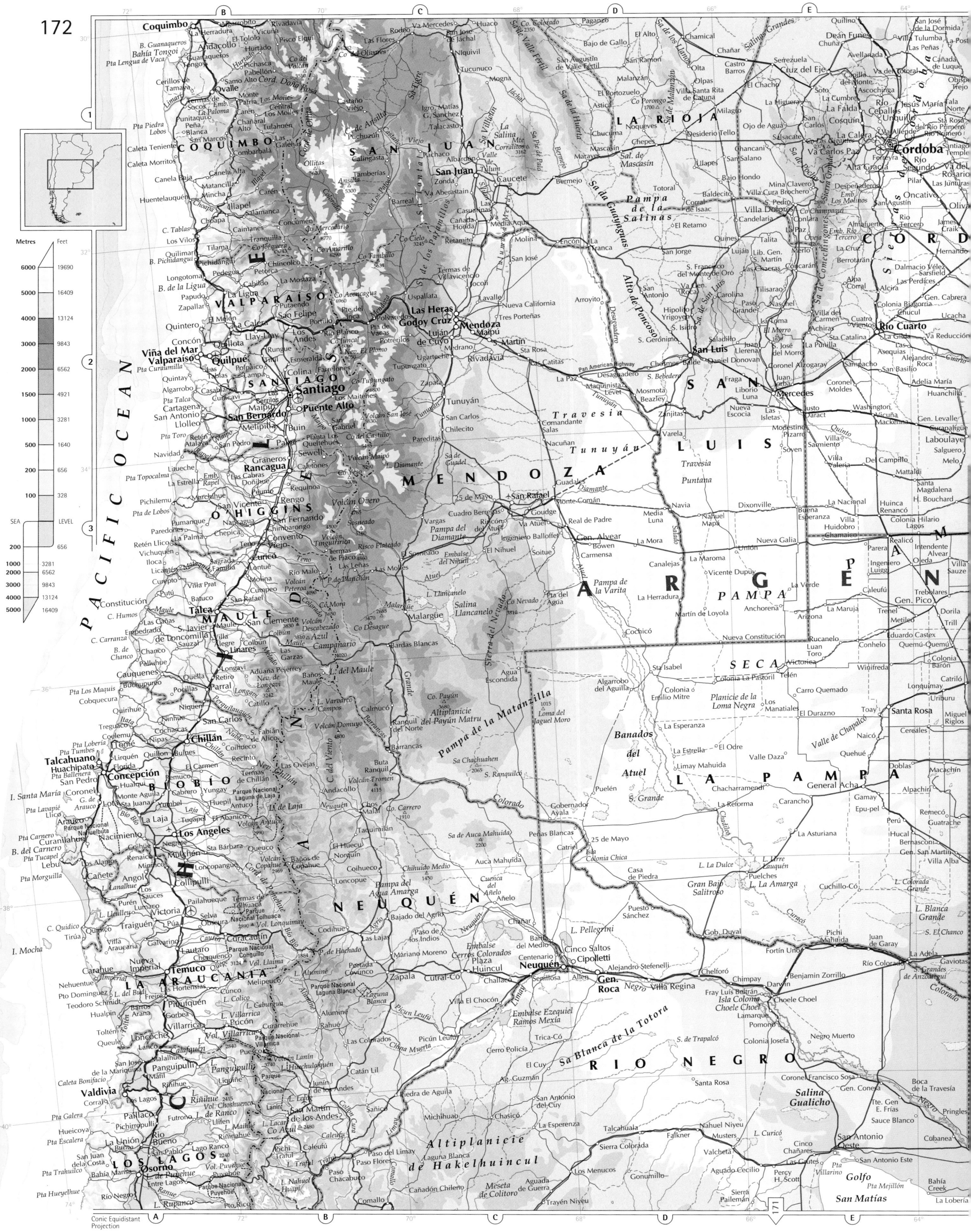
PACIFIC OCEAN
Metres
Feet
6000 19690
5000 16409
4000 13124
3000 9843
2000 6562
1500 4921
1000 3281
500 1640
200 656
100 328
SEA LEVEL
200 656
1000 3281
2000 6562
3000 9843
4000 13124
5000 16409
COQUIMBO
VALPARAÍSO
SANTIAGO
O'HIGGINS
MAULE
BIOBÍO
LA ARAUCANÍA
LOS LAGOS
SAN JUAN
LA RIOJA
MENDOZA
SAN LUIS
NEUQUÉN
LA PAMPA
RIO NEGRO
CÓRDOBA
ARGENTINA
CHILE
ANDES
Coquimbo
La Serena
Ovalle
Illapel
Viña del Mar
Valparaíso
Quilpué
Santiago
Puente Alto
San Bernardo
Rancagua
San Fernando
Curicó
Talca
Linares
Chillán
Talcahuano
Concepción
Los Angeles
Temuco
Valdivia
Osorno
San Juan
Mendoza
Godoy Cruz
Las Heras
Luján de Cuyo
San Rafael
San Luis
Mercedes
Córdoba
Río Cuarto
Santa Rosa
General Acha
Neuquén
Cipolletti
Gen. Roca
Villa Regina
Choele Choel
Viedma
San Antonio Oeste
Golfo San Matías
Pampa de la Matanzilla
Altiplanicie del Payún Matru
Altiplanicie de Hakelhuincul
Pampa de las Salinas
Travesia Puntana
Travesia Tunuyán
Salinas Grandes
Salina Gualicho
Co Aconcagua 6960
Co Tupungato 6800
Co Mercedario 6770
Volcán San José
Volcán Maipo
Co Payún 3680
Volcán Lanín 3740
Volcán Domuyo 4800
Colorado
Negro
Limay
Conic Equidistant Projection
A
B
C
D
E
1
2
3

171

ATLANTIC
OCEAN
Bahía Samborombón
Río de la Plata
Bahía Blanca
Bahía Anegada
Delta del R.Colorado
Delta del Paraná
BUENOS AIRES
SANTA FE
ENTRE RÍOS
URUGUAY
BRAZIL
ARTIGAS
SALTO
PAYSANDÚ
RIVERA
TACUAREMBÓ
CERRO LARGO
RIO NEGRO
DURAZNO
TREINTA-Y-TRES
SORIANO
FLORES
FLORIDA
LAVALLEJA
ROCHA
COLONIA
S. JOSÉ
CANELONES
MALDONADO
Buenos Aires
Montevideo
Rosario
Santa Fe
Paraná
La Plata
Mar del Plata
Bahía Blanca
Concordia
Salto
Viedma
Necochea
Tandil
Olavarría
Azul
Miles
Km
1:3.75M
© Bartholomew

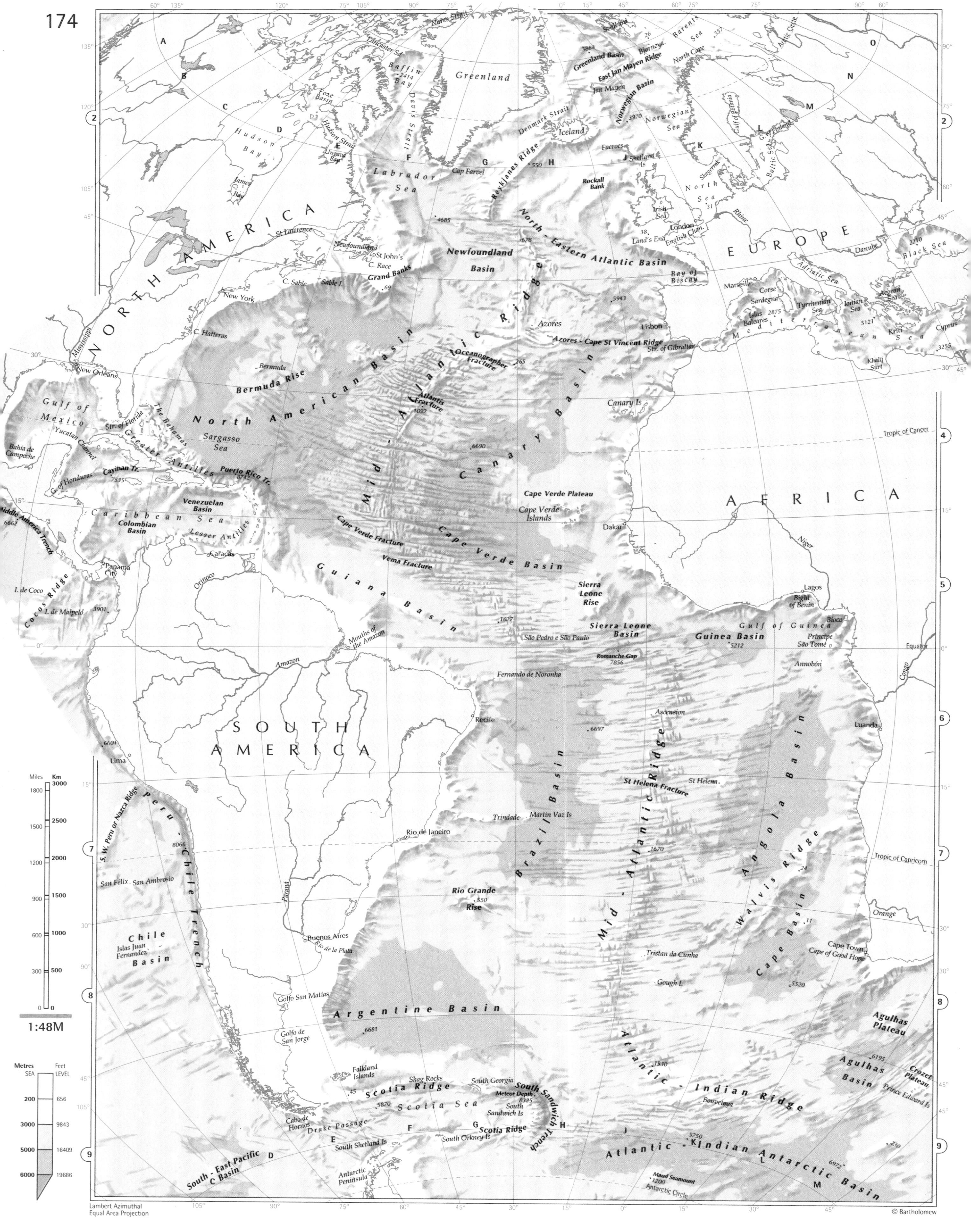
NORTH AMERICA
SOUTH AMERICA
EUROPE
AFRICA
Greenland
Iceland
Baffin Bay
Davis Strait
Nares Strait
Lancaster Sd
Foxe Basin
Hudson Strait
Hudson Bay
James Bay
Labrador Sea
Cap Farvel
Denmark Strait
Reykjanes Ridge
Greenland Basin
East Jan Mayen Ridge
Jan Mayen
Norwegian Basin
Norwegian Sea
Barents Sea
Bjørnøya
Svalbard
North Cape
Arctic Circle
Faeroes
Shetland Is
Rockall Bank
North Sea
Skagerrak
Gulf of Bothnia
G. of Finland
Baltic Sea
Irish Sea
London
Land's End
English Chan.
Rhine
Danube
Black Sea
North - Eastern Atlantic Basin
Newfoundland Basin
Newfoundland
St John's
C. Race
Grand Banks
St Lawrence
C. Sable
Sable I.
New York
C. Hatteras
Mississippi
New Orleans
Bay of Biscay
Azores
Lisbon
Azores - Cape St Vincent Ridge
Str. of Gibraltar
Marseille
Corse
Sardegna
Islas Baleares
Tyrrhenian Sea
Ionian Sea
Adriatic Sea
Aegean Sea
Mediterranean Sea
Kriti
Cyprus
Khalij Surt
Bermuda
Bermuda Rise
North American Basin
Mid - Atlantic Ridge
Oceanographer Fracture
Atlantis Fracture
Canary Basin
Canary Is
Tropic of Cancer
Gulf of Mexico
Str. of Florida
The Bahamas
Yucatan Channel
Bahía de Campeche
Greater Antilles
Sargasso Sea
Cayman Tr.
G. of Honduras
Puerto Rico Tr.
Caribbean Sea
Venezuelan Basin
Colombian Basin
Lesser Antilles
Middle America Trench
Caracas
Panama City
I. de Coco
Cocos Ridge
I. de Malpelo
Cape Verde Plateau
Cape Verde Islands
Dakar
Niger
Cape Verde Fracture
Cape Verde Basin
Vema Fracture
Guiana Basin
Orinoco
Sierra Leone Rise
Sierra Leone Basin
Lagos
Bight of Benin
Gulf of Guinea
Bioco
Príncipe
São Tomé
Guinea Basin
São Pedro e São Paulo
Romanche Gap
Mouths of the Amazon
Amazon
Equator
Annobón
Congo
Fernando de Noronha
Ascension
Recife
Luanda
Lima
St Helena Fracture
St Helena
Brazil Basin
Angola Basin
Trindade
Martin Vaz Is
Rio de Janeiro
Tropic of Capricorn
Peru - Chile Trench
S.W. Peru or Nazca Ridge
San Félix
San Ambrosio
Walvis Ridge
Rio Grande Rise
Paraná
Orange
Chile Basin
Islas Juan Fernández
Buenos Aires
Río de la Plata
Tristan da Cunha
Gough I.
Cape Basin
Cape Town
Cape of Good Hope
Golfo San Matías
Argentine Basin
Golfo de San Jorge
Agulhas Plateau
Agulhas Basin
Crozet Plateau
Prince Edward Is
Falkland Islands
Shag Rocks
South Georgia
Scotia Ridge
Scotia Sea
Meteor Depth
South Sandwich Is
South Sandwich Trench
Atlantic - Indian Ridge
Bouvetøya
Cabo de Hornos
Drake Passage
South Orkney Is
South Shetland Is
Antarctic Peninsula
South - East Pacific Basin
Atlantic - Indian Antarctic Basin
Maud Seamount
Antarctic Circle
Miles
Km
1:48M
Metres
Feet
SEA LEVEL

Lambert Azimuthal
Equal Area Projection

© Bartholomew

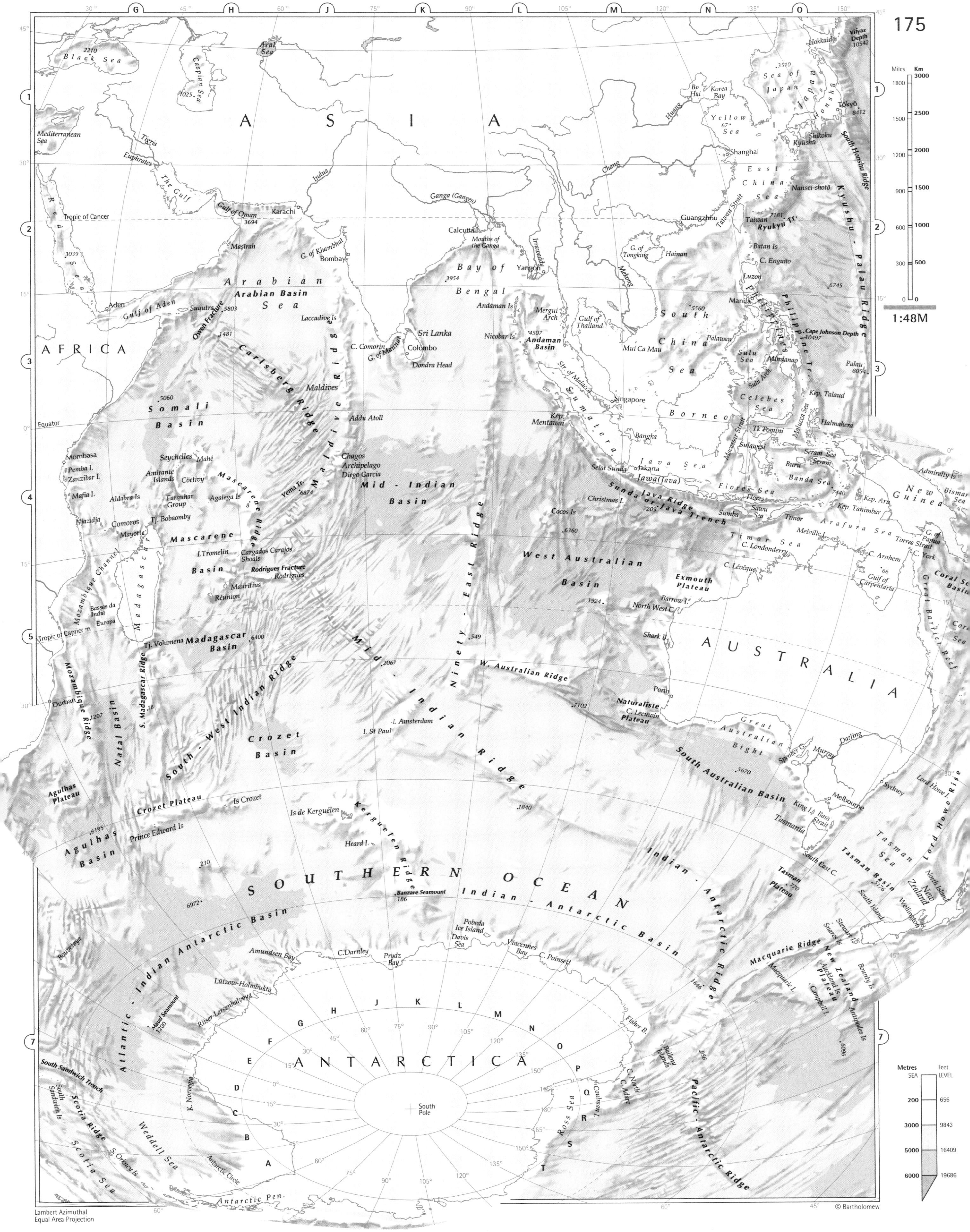
ASIA
AFRICA
AUSTRALIA
ANTARCTICA
SOUTHERN OCEAN
Black Sea
Caspian Sea
Aral Sea
Mediterranean Sea
Red Sea
The Gulf
Gulf of Oman
Gulf of Aden
Arabian Sea
Arabian Basin
Bay of Bengal
Andaman Basin
South China Sea
Sea of Japan
Yellow Sea
East China Sea
Java Sea
Timor Sea
Arafura Sea
Coral Sea
Tasman Sea
Somali Basin
Mascarene Basin
Madagascar Basin
Natal Basin
Crozet Basin
Agulhas Basin
Mid - Indian Basin
West Australian Basin
South Australian Basin
Indian - Antarctic Basin
Atlantic - Indian Antarctic Basin
Carlsberg Ridge
Maldive Ridge
Mascarene Ridge
Ninety - East Ridge
Mid - Indian Ridge
South - West Indian Ridge
Kerguelen Ridge
Indian - Antarctic Ridge
Pacific - Antarctic Ridge
Sunda or Java Trench
Java Ridge
W. Australian Ridge
Exmouth Plateau
Naturaliste Plateau
Crozet Plateau
Agulhas Plateau
Tasman Plateau
Scotia Ridge
Scotia Sea
Weddell Sea
Ross Sea
Madagascar
Sri Lanka
Maldives
Tropic of Cancer
Equator
Tropic of Capricorn
Antarctic Circle
South Pole
Miles
Km
1:48M
Metres
Feet
SEA LEVEL
200
656
3000
9843
5000
16409
6000
19686

Lambert Azimuthal Equal Area Projection

© Bartholomew

ASIA
AUSTRALIA
MICRONESIA
MELANESIA
POLYNESIA
Sea of Okhotsk
Sea of Japan
Yellow Sea
East China Sea
South China Sea
Bay of Bengal
Sulu Sea
Celebes Sea
Java Sea
Banda Sea
Flores Sea
Sawu Sea
Timor Sea
Arafura Sea
Coral Sea
Tasman Sea
Bering Sea
Chukchi Sea
Ross Sea
Bismarck Sea
Solomon Sea
Seram Sea
Molucca Sea
Great Australian Bight
Gulf of Carpentaria
Gulf of Thailand
Great Barrier Reef
Kuril Trench
Aleutian Trench
Aleutian Islands
Emperor Seamount Chain
Japan Tr.
Ryukyu Tr.
Philippine Tr.
Marianas Tr.
Marianas Ridge
Kyushu - Palau Ridge
South Honshu Ridge
Yap Tr.
Palau Tr.
Mid - Pacific Mountains
Hawaiian Islands
Hawaiian Ridge
Magellan Seamounts
Caroline Islands
W. Caroline Basin
E. Caroline Basin
Kapingamarangi Rise
Marshall Islands
Coral Sea Basin
South Fiji Basin
Lord Howe Rise
Norfolk Island Ridge
Norfolk Island Trough
Tonga Tr.
Kermadec Tr.
Tasman Basin
Chatham Rise
New Zealand Plateau
Macquarie Ridge
Tasman Plateau
South Australian Basin
Naturaliste Plateau
W. Australian Ridge
West Australian Basin
Exmouth Plateau
Ninety - East Ridge
Mid - Indian Basin
Mid - Indian Ridge
Java Ridge
Sunda or Java Trench
Indian - Antarctic Ridge
Indian - Antarctic Basin
Andaman Basin
Vityaz Depth 10542
Ramapo Deep 10374
Challenger Deep 11022
Cape Johnson Depth 10497
Horizon Depth 10882
Planet Deep 9140
South Pacific
Equator
Tropic of Cancer
Tropic of Capricorn
Arctic Circle
Antarctic Circle
Sumatera
Borneo
Jawa (Java)
Sulawesi
New Guinea
Philippines
Japan
Honshu
Kyushu
Shikoku
Hokkaido
Ostrov Sakhalin
Taiwan
Hainan
Sri Lanka
Tasmania
New Zealand
North Island
South Island
Nouvelle Calédonie
Vanuatu
Fiji
Tonga
Samoa
Tuvalu
Kiribati
Tokelau
Solomon Islands
Lord Howe I.
Norfolk I.
Kermadec Is
Chatham Is
Macquarie I.
Campbell I.
Auckland Is
Bounty Is
Antipodes Is
Balleny Islands
Tōkyō
Shanghai
Guangzhou
Singapore
Jakarta
Manila
Brisbane
Sydney
Melbourne
Auckland
Wellington
Port Moresby
Murray
Darling
Mekong
Chang
Huang
Irrawaddy
Ganga (Ganges)
Argun
Guam
Saipan
Rota
Yap
Palau
Chuuk
Pohnpei
Kosrae
Bikini
Enewetak
Kwajalein
Majuro
Nauru
Wake I.
Johnston I.
Midway Is
Kure Atoll
Christmas I.
Cocos Is
Lambert Azimuthal Equal Area Projection
Metres
SEA
Feet
LEVEL
200
656
3000
9843
5000
16409
6000
19686

Pt Barrow
Mackenzie
Hudson Bay
James Bay
Newfoundland
Sable I.
C. Sable
Gulf of Alaska
Kodiak I.
Alexander Archipelago
Queen Charlotte Islands
Vancouver Island
Vancouver
Columbia
Missouri
New York
C. Hatteras
Bermuda
Bermuda Rise
North American Basin
Mid-Atlantic Ridge
Atlantis Fracture
NORTH AMERICA
Mendocino Seascarp
C. Mendocino
San Francisco
Colorado
Mississippi
New Orleans
Grande
Erben Tablemount
Los Angeles
Murray Seascarp
Guadalupe
Golfo de California
Gulf of Mexico
Str. of Florida
The Bahamas
Greater Antilles
Puerto Rico Tr.
Molokai Fracture Zone
Kauai
Oahu
Maui
Hawaii
Yucatan Channel
Bahía de Campeche
Cayman Tr.
G. of Honduras
Venezuelan Basin
Caribbean Sea
Cape Verde Fracture
Vema Fracture
Is Revillagigedo
I. Clarión
I. Socorro
East Pacific Rise
G. de Tehuantepec
Tehuantepec Ridge
Middle America Trench
Clarion Fracture Zone
Lesser Antilles
Colombian Basin
Caracas
Guiana Basin
Clipperton Fracture Zone
Clipperton I.
Orinoco
Panama City
I. de Coco
Cocos Ridge
I. de Malpelo
Tabuaeran
Kiritimati
Jarvis I.
Islas Galápagos
Carnegie Ridge
G. de Guayaquil
Mouths of the Amazon
Amazon
Malden I.
Starbuck I.
Tongareva
Caroline I.
Nuku Hiva
Is Marquises
Hiva Oa
Flint I.
SOUTH AMERICA
Is du Roi Georges
Îles de Désappointement
Is Tuamotu
Fenua Ura
Raiatea
Tahiti
Raroia
Anaa
Hao
Is de la Société
Hervey Is
Lima
Peru-Chile Trench
Rarotonga
Mangaia
Îles Maria
Hérèhérètué
Îles Duc de Gloucester
Mururoa
Groupe Actéon
Tubuai
Raivavae
Is Tubuai
Is Gambier
Henderson I.
Pitcairn I.
Ducie I.
Rapa
Peru Basin
S. W. Peru or Nazca Ridge
East Pacific Ridge
Easter Island Fracture Zone
Easter I.
I. Sala y Gómez
San Félix
San Ambrosio
South-West Pacific Basin
Challenger Fracture Zone
Chile Basin
Is Juan Fernández
Robinson Crusoe
Rio de Janeiro
Paraná
Santiago
Pacific-Antarctic Ridge
Eltanin Fracture Zone
Buenos Aires
Río de la Plata
Golfo San Matías
Golfo de San Jorge
South-East Pacific Basin
Argentine Basin
Cabo de Hornos
Drake Passage
Scotia Sea
Scotia Ridge
Falkland Islands
Amundsen Sea
Peter I Øy
Antarctic Peninsula
South Shetland Is
© Bartholomew
Miles
Km
1:48M

NORTH AMERICA
ARCTIC OCEAN
ASIA
EUROPE
Greenland
(Kalaallit Nunaat)
Hudson Bay
Baffin Island
Baffin Bay
Baffin Basin
Davis Strait
Labrador Sea
Hudson Strait
Foxe Basin
Victoria Island
Banks Island
Queen Elizabeth Islands
Parry Islands
Ellesmere Island
Melville Island
Prince Patrick Island
Beaufort Sea
Canada Basin
Mendeleyev Ridge
Makarov Basin
Lomonosov (Harris) Ridge
North Pole
Amundsen Basin
Arctic-Mid Ocean Ridge
Nansen Basin
Wandel Sea
Greenland Sea
Greenland Basin
Norwegian Sea
Norwegian Basin
Denmark Strait
Iceland
Jan Mayen
East Jan Mayen Ridge
Svalbard
Barents Sea
Chukchi Sea
East Siberian Sea
Laptev Sea
Karskoye More
Novaya Zemlya
Severnaya Zemlya
Zemlya Frantsa-Iosifa
(Franz Josef Land)
Bering Sea
Gulf of Alaska
Aleutian Trench
Aleutian Islands
Alaska Pen.
Anchorage
Yukon
Mackenzie
Great Bear L.
Great Slave L.
Lake Athabasca
Lake Winnipeg
Inuvik
Barrow
average minimum extent of sea ice
average maximum extent of drift ice
Arctic Circle
Murmansk
Arkhangel'sk
Salekhard
Dudinka
Yenisey
Lena
Kolyma
Indigirka
Ob'
Pechora
Tromsø
Bergen
Reykjavik
North Sea
Baltic Sea
Gulf of Bothnia
G. of Finland
Ladozhskoye Oz.
Oz. Onezhskoye
Miles
Km
1:24M
Metres
Feet
SEA LEVEL
200
656
3000
9843
5000
16409
6000
19686
JAN MAYEN
(Norway)
1:2.5M
Haakon VII Topp
2277
Nordkapp
Sörkapp
Rudolftoppen
BEAR I.
(Svalbard)
1:2.5M
Kapp Duner
Kapp Kåre
Miseryfjellet
Stappen
Tunheim
SVALBARD
(Norway)
1:10M
Spitsbergen
Nordaustlandet
Kvitøya
Longyearbyen
Barentsøya
Edgeøya
Ny-Ålesund
Newtontoppen
1717
Erik Eriksenstretet
Olgastretet
Storfjorden
Sveagruva
Barentsburg
Bellsund
K. Melchers
K. Platen
Polar Stereographic Projection
© Bartholomew

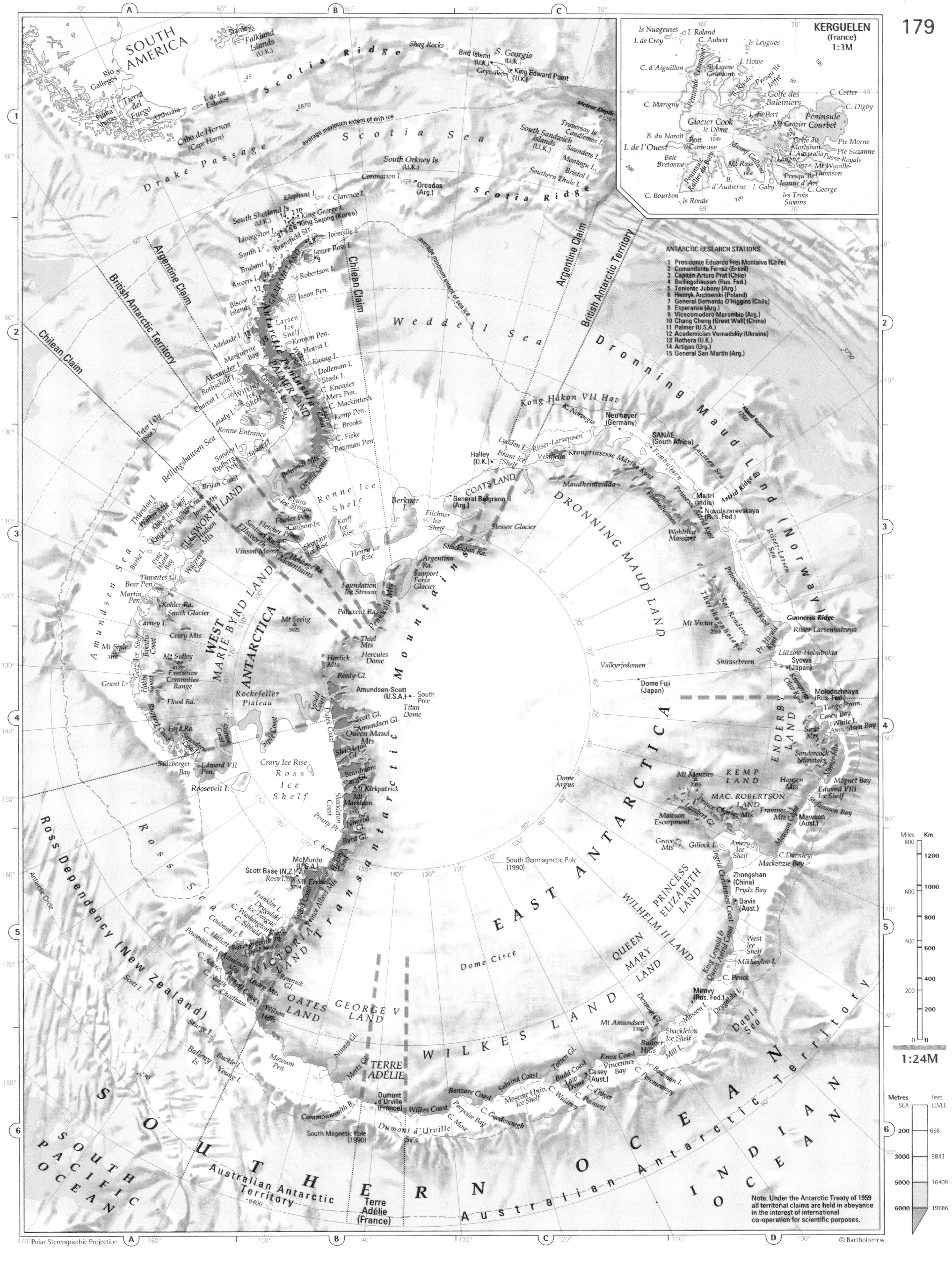

KERGUELEN
(France)
1:3M
ANTARCTIC RESEARCH STATIONS
1 Presidente Eduardo Frei Montalva (Chile)
2 Comandante Ferraz (Brazil)
3 Capitán Arturo Prat (Chile)
4 Bellingshausen (Rus. Fed.)
5 Teniente Jubany (Arg.)
6 Henryk Arctowski (Poland)
7 General Bernardo O'Higgins (Chile)
8 Esperanza (Arg.)
9 Vicecomodoro Marambio (Arg.)
10 Chang Cheng (Great Wall) (China)
11 Palmer (U.S.A.)
12 Academician Vernadskiy (Ukraine)
13 Rothera (U.K.)
14 Artigas (Urg.)
15 General San Martin (Arg.)
SOUTH AMERICA
Falkland Islands (U.K.)
Scotia Ridge
Scotia Sea
Drake Passage
S. Georgia (U.K.)
South Sandwich Islands (U.K.)
South Orkney Is (U.K.)
South Shetland Is
Weddell Sea
Dronning Maud Land (Norway)
DRONNING MAUD LAND
Argentine Claim
British Antarctic Territory
Chilean Claim
Ronne Ice Shelf
Bellingshausen Sea
Amundsen Sea
WEST ANTARCTICA
MARIE BYRD LAND
ELLSWORTH LAND
PALMER LAND
Transantarctic Mountains
Ross Ice Shelf
Ross Sea
Ross Dependency (New Zealand)
EAST ANTARCTICA
ENDERBY LAND
KEMP LAND
MAC. ROBERTSON LAND
PRINCESS ELIZABETH LAND
WILHELM II LAND
QUEEN MARY LAND
WILKES LAND
GEORGE V LAND
OATES LAND
VICTORIA LAND
TERRE ADÉLIE
Amundsen-Scott (U.S.A.)
South Pole
McMurdo (U.S.A.)
Scott Base (N.Z.)
Mt Erebus
Vinson Massif
Dome Argus
Dome Circe
Dome Fuji (Japan)
South Geomagnetic Pole (1990)
South Magnetic Pole (1990)
Davis Sea
SOUTHERN OCEAN
SOUTH PACIFIC OCEAN
INDIAN OCEAN
Australian Antarctic Territory
Terre Adélie (France)
Miles
Km
1:24M
Metres
Feet
SEA LEVEL
Note: Under the Antarctic Treaty of 1959 all territorial claims are held in abeyance in the interest of international co-operation for scientific purposes.
Polar Stereographic Projection
© Bartholomew

THE INDEX INCLUDES the names on the maps in the ATLAS of the WORLD section. The names are indexed to the largest scale map on which they appear, and can be located using the grid reference letters and numbers around the map frame. Names on insets have a symbol: □, followed by the inset number.

Abbreviations used to describe features in the index, and for country names in the index, are explained on the right. Abbreviations used in feature names on the maps, and within feature names in the index, are explained on pages 82 and 83 of the Introduction to the Atlas.

A.C.T.	Australian Capital Territory
b.	bay
B.C.	British Columbia
Bos.-Herz.	Bosnia-Herzegovina
c.	cape
chan.	channel
div.	division
est.	estuary
g.	gulf
gl.	glacier
h.	hill, hills
i., I.	island
is, Is	islands
l.	lake
lag.	lagoon
mt.	mountain
mts	mountains
N.	North
nat. park.	national park
N.W.T.	Northwest Territories
pen.	peninsula
plat.	plateau
P.N.G.	Papua New Guinea
pt	point
r.	river
reg.	region
Rep.	Republic
res.	reserve
resr	reservoir
Rus. Fed.	Russian Federation
S.	South
Str.	Strait
Terr.	Territory
U.A.E.	United Arab Emirates
U.K.	United Kingdom
U.S.A.	United States of America
v.	valley

A

86 B2 Aa r. France
83 E1 Aach r. Germany
74 D5 Aach Germany
74 B2 Aachen Germany
83 D1 Aadorf Switzerland
74 F4 Aalen Germany
68 C2 Aalsmeer Netherlands
69 B4 Aalst div. *Oost-Vlaanderen* Belgium
69 C4 Aalst Belgium
68 E3 Aalten Netherlands
69 B3 Aalter Belgium
130 D3 Aansluit South Africa
82 D1 Aarau Switzerland
82 C1 Aarberg Switzerland
82 C1 Aarburg Switzerland
69 B3 Aardenburg Netherlands
82 D1 Aare r. Switzerland
82 D1 Aargau div. Switzerland
69 C4 Aarschot Belgium
69 C3 Aartselaar Belgium
82 C1 Aarwangen Switzerland
67 B3 Aasleagh Rep. of Ireland
32 C1 Aba China
123 F5 Aba Nigeria
124 F3 Aba Congo(Zaire)
119 H2 Abā ad Dūd Saudi Arabia
163 F5 Abacaxis r. Brazil
39 B3 Abādān Iran
39 C3 Abādeh Iran
98 D4 Abadengo reg. Spain
99 F4 Abades Spain
168 E3 Abadia dos Dourados Brazil
168 D2 Abadiânia Brazil
98 C1 Abadín Spain
120 D2 Abadla Algeria
169 F3 Abaeté r. Brazil
169 F3 Abaeté Brazil
166 C1 Abaetetuba Brazil
31 F2 Abagaytuy Rus. Fed.
31 E4 Abag Qi China
98 B1 A Baiuca Spain
123 F5 Abaji Nigeria
153 E4 Abajo Pk summit *Utah* U.S.A.
123 F5 Abakaliki Nigeria
47 L2 Abakan r. Rus. Fed.
47 M2 Abakan Rus. Fed.
47 L2 Abakanskiy Khrebet mountain range Rus. Fed.
124 C4 Abala Congo
123 E4 Abala Niger
123 F3 Abalak Niger
123 F3 Abalemma well Niger
121 E4 Abalessa Algeria
39 C3 Āb Anbār Iran
164 B2 Abancay Peru
124 B3 Abanga r. Gabon
103 B6 Abanilla Spain
103 B6 Abarán Spain
39 C3 Abarqū Iran
98 C2 A Barrela Spain
28 K1 Abashiri Japan
28 K2 Abashiri-gawa r. Japan
28 K2 Abashiri-ko l. Japan
28 K1 Abashiri-wan b. Japan
127 C5 Abasula waterhole Kenya
47 H1 Abatskiy Rus. Fed.
6 □1 Abau P.N.G.
79 L3 Abaújszántó Hungary
47 H3 Abay Kazakhstan
126 C3 Ābaya Hāyk' l. Ethiopia
Ābay Wenz *see* Blue Nile
47 M2 Abaza Rus. Fed.
124 C2 Abba Central African Rep.
108 D2 Abbadia San Salvatore Italy
39 D2 Abbāsābād Iran
108 A4 Abbasanta *Sardegna* Italy
148 C2 Abbaye, Pt pt *Michigan* U.S.A.
59 E4 Abbekås Sweden
126 D2 Abbe, L. l. Djibouti/Ethiopia
151 E6 Abbeville *Louisiana* U.S.A.
145 D5 Abbeville *S. Carolina* U.S.A.
86 A2 Abbeville France
67 B4 Abbeyfeale Rep. of Ireland
66 E6 Abbey Head headland *Scotland* U.K.
15 F2 Abbey Peak h. *Queensland* Australia
65 E3 Abbeytown *England* U.K.
106 C3 Abbiategrasso Italy
56 E2 Abborrträsk Sweden
179 A3 Abbot Ice Shelf ice feature Antarctica
15 F4 Abbot, Mt mt. *Queensland* Australia
62 D4 Abbotsbury *England* U.K.
136 E5 Abbotsford *B.C.* Canada
148 B3 Abbotsford *Wisconsin* U.S.A.
63 F3 Abbots Langley *England* U.K.
153 F4 Abbott *New Mexico* U.S.A.
36 C2 Abbottabad Pakistan
42 D2 'Abd al 'Azīz, J. h. Syria
126 □ 'Abd al Kūrī i. *Socotra* Yemen
50 J4 Abdi Rus. Fed.
39 D2 Abdolabād Iran
39 D1 Abdollāhābād Iran
39 C2 Abdollāhābād Iran
46 D2 Abdulino Rus. Fed.
118 D5 Abéché Chad
39 D3 Āb-e Garm Iran
123 E3 Abeïbara well Mali
99 H3 Abejar Spain
103 C5 Abejuela Spain
123 F5 Abejukolo Nigeria
100 B2 Abela Portugal
123 F3 Abélajouad well Niger
69 A4 Abele Belgium
9 D4 Abel Tasman National Park nat. park New Zealand
122 D5 Abengourou Côte d'Ivoire
101 F2 Abenójar Spain
55 B4 Åbenrå Denmark
55 B4 Åbenrå Fjord inlet Denmark
75 G4 Abens r. Germany
75 G4 Abensberg Germany
123 E5 Abeokuta Nigeria
62 B2 Aberaeron *Wales* U.K.
66 F3 Aberchirder *Scotland* U.K.
62 C3 Aberdare *Wales* U.K.
62 B2 Aberdaron *Wales* U.K.
147 E5 Aberdeen *Maryland* U.S.A.
151 F5 Aberdeen *Mississippi* U.S.A.
13 G3 Aberdeen *New South Wales* Australia
137 H4 Aberdeen *Saskatchewan* Canada
66 F3 Aberdeen *Scotland* U.K.
150 D2 Aberdeen *S. Dakota* U.S.A.
152 B2 Aberdeen *Washington* U.S.A.
27 □ Aberdeen *Hong Kong* China
130 E6 Aberdeen South Africa
66 F3 Aberdeen, div. *Scotland* U.K.
137 J2 Aberdeen Lake l. *N.W.T.* Canada
66 F3 Aberdeenshire div. *Scotland* U.K.
62 B2 Aberdyfi *Wales* U.K.
66 E4 Aberfeldy *Scotland* U.K.
65 G4 Aberford *England* U.K.
66 D4 Aberfoyle *Scotland* U.K.
62 C3 Abergavenny *Wales* U.K.
62 C1 Abergele *Wales* U.K.
Abergwaun *see* Fishguard
65 F1 Aberlady *Scotland* U.K.
151 C5 Abernathy *Texas* U.S.A.
65 E1 Abernethy *Scotland* U.K.
62 B2 Aberporth *Wales* U.K.
62 B2 Abersoch *Wales* U.K.
75 H2 Abertamy Czech Rep.
Abertawe *see* Swansea
62 C3 Abertillery *Wales* U.K.
65 E1 Aberuthven *Scotland* U.K.
62 B2 Aberystwyth *Wales* U.K.
107 E4 Abetone Italy
119 H4 Abhā Saudi Arabia
39 B1 Abhar r. Iran
39 B1 Abhar Iran
54 D2 Abia Estonia
123 F5 Abia div. Nigeria
126 C3 Ābīata Hāyk' l. Ethiopia
39 B2 Ab-i Bazuft r. Iran
122 D5 Abidjan Côte d'Ivoire
102 C2 Abiego Spain
130 C3 Abiekwasputs salt pan South Africa
39 G2 Ab-i-Istada l. Afghanistan
126 C3 Abijatta-Shalla National Park nat. park Ethiopia
39 D2 Ab-i-Kavir salt flat Iran
29 H6 Abiko Japan
150 D4 Abilene *Kansas* U.S.A.
151 D5 Abilene *Texas* U.S.A.
63 E3 Abingdon *England* U.K.
148 B5 Abingdon *Illinois* U.S.A.
146 C6 Abingdon *Virginia* U.S.A.
66 E5 Abington *Scotland* U.K.
15 G3 Abington Reef reef *Coral Sea Islands Terr.* Pacific Ocean
51 F6 Abinsk Rus. Fed.
99 H3 Abión r. Spain
39 E2 Ab-i-Rahuk Afghanistan
39 F1 Ab-i-Safed r. Afghanistan
164 A1 Abiseo, Parque Nacional nat. park Peru
137 H2 Abitau Lake l. *N.W.T.* Canada
140 E2 Abitibi r. *Ontario* Canada
140 E2 Abitibi Canyon Dam dam *Ontario* Canada
140 E2 Abitibi, Lake l. *Ontario/Québec* Canada
51 G7 Abkhazia div. Georgia
Abkhazskaya Respublika *see* Abkhazia
101 H3 Abla Spain
89 G3 Ablis France
12 C1 Abminga *S. Australia* Australia
119 F2 Abnûb Egypt
122 D5 Aboisso Côte d'Ivoire
126 B3 Aboke Sudan
123 E5 Abomey Benin
36 C3 Abonar India
90 E2 Abondance France
124 B3 Abong Mbang Cameroon
79 K4 Abony Hungary
122 D5 Abooso Ghana
23 A4 Aborlan Philippines
124 C1 Abou Déia Chad
42 F1 Abovyan Armenia
66 F3 Aboyne *Scotland* U.K.
Abqaiq *see* Buqayq
164 C4 Abra Chile
126 E1 Abrād, W. watercourse Yemen
159 D2 Abraham's Bay The Bahamas
100 B1 Abrantes Portugal
170 C1 Abra Pampa Argentina
98 C4 Abravezes Portugal
169 G4 Abre Campo Brazil
98 C3 Abreiro Portugal
87 G4 Abreschviller France
119 F3 'Abri Sudan
91 E4 Abriès France
173 K3 Abril, 19 de Uruguay
112 D1 Abrud Romania
54 C2 Abruka i. Estonia
109 F2 Abruzzo div. Italy
109 F3 Abruzzo, Parco Nazionale d' nat. park Italy
80 C3 Absam Austria
152 E2 Absaroka Range mountain range *Montana/Wyoming* U.S.A.
81 G2 Absdorf Austria
41 H1 Abşeron Yarımdası pen. Azerbaijan
75 J5 Abtenau Austria
74 E4 Abtsgmünd Germany
28 C6 Abu Japan
43 D2 Abū aḍ Ḍuhūr Syria
39 B4 Abū'Alī i. Saudi Arabia
39 C4 Abual Jirab i. U.A.E.
43 D5 Abu 'Amūd, W. watercourse Jordan
119 H4 Abū 'Arīsh Saudi Arabia
43 C4 Abu 'Aweigîla well Egypt
119 E3 Abu Ballûs h. Egypt
119 F4 Abu Deleiq Sudan
39 C4 Abu Dhabi U.A.E.
119 G3 Abū Ḍībā' Saudi Arabia
43 B5 Abu Durba Egypt
43 B5 Abu Hâd, W. watercourse Egypt
43 D3 Abu Hafrah, W. watercourse Jordan
119 E1 Abu Haggag Egypt
43 D4 Abū Hallūfa, J. h. Jordan
119 F4 Abu Hamed Sudan
119 F4 Abu Hashim watercourse Sudan
119 F5 Abu Hut watercourse Sudan
123 F5 Abuja Nigeria
43 A4 Abu Kebîr Egypt
77 N2 Abukhava Belarus
118 E5 Abu Ku Sudan
29 H5 Abukuma-gawa r. Japan
29 H5 Abukuma-kochi plat. Japan
119 G4 Abū Latt I. i. Saudi Arabia
124 E1 Abu Matariq Sudan
124 D3 Abumombazi Congo(Zaire)
39 C4 Abū Mūsá i. U.A.E.
164 C1 Abunã r. Bolivia
164 C1 Abunã Brazil
162 D4 Abunai Brazil
118 C2 Abū Nā'im well Libya
126 C2 Ābune Yosēf mt. Ethiopia
118 C1 Abū Nujaym Libya
43 D2 Abū Qa'ţūr Syria
43 A6 Abu Qurqâs Egypt
124 F3 Aburo mt. Congo(Zaire)
36 C4 Abu Road India
119 G3 Abū Rubayq Saudi Arabia
43 B5 Abu Rudeis Egypt
43 D5 Abu Sallah watercourse Saudi Arabia
119 E5 Abu Shanab Sudan
119 F3 Abu Simbel Egypt
119 F3 Abu Simbel Temple Egypt
42 F4 Abū Şukhayr Iraq
9 C5 Abut Head headland New Zealand
43 D5 Abū Ujayyijāt well Saudi Arabia
126 C2 Abuye Meda mt. Ethiopia
23 C4 Abuyog Philippines
119 E5 Abu Zabad Sudan
Abū Ẓabī *see* Abu Dhabi
119 F2 Abu Zenîma Egypt
59 F3 Åby Sweden
119 E5 Abyad Sudan
119 E4 Abyad Plateau, Jebel plat. Sudan
118 D1 Abyār an Nākhīlah well Libya
43 C5 Abyār Banī Murr well Saudi Arabia
55 B2 Åbybro Denmark
16 B4 Abydos *Western Australia* Australia
124 E2 Abyei Sudan
118 C5 Ab Zérafa Chad
147 J2 Acadia Nat. Park nat. park *Maine* U.S.A.
157 E4 Acambaro Mexico
157 H4 Acancéh Mexico
162 B2 Acandí Colombia
98 B2 A Cañiza Spain
156 D4 Acaponeta Mexico
157 F5 Acapulco Mexico
166 C1 Acará r. Brazil
166 C1 Acará Brazil
166 C1 Acará Miri r. Brazil
166 D1 Acaraú r. Brazil
166 D1 Acaraú Brazil
165 E5 Acaray r. Paraguay
169 F1 Acari r. Brazil
166 E2 Acarí Brazil
162 D2 Acarigua Venezuela
79 M4 Acâş Romania
110 D5 Acate *Sicilia* Italy
157 F5 Acatlan Mexico
157 G5 Acayucán Mexico
109 H3 Accadia Italy
91 E4 Acceglio Italy
109 J4 Accettura Italy
109 H4 Acciaroli Italy
93 B6 Accous France
122 D5 Accra Ghana
65 F4 Accrington *England* U.K.
109 F2 Accumoli Italy
173 G2 Aceba Argentina
100 E1 Acedera Spain
99 H2 Acedo Spain
173 K1 Aceguá Brazil
109 H4 Acerenza Italy
109 H4 Acerno Italy
109 G4 Acerra Italy
80 C3 Ach r. Germany
80 D2 Ach Austria
164 C3 Achacachi Bolivia
162 D2 Achaguas Venezuela
115 C4 Achaïa div. Greece
36 D5 Achalpur India
38 B2 Achampet India
173 J2 Achar Uruguay
45 T3 Achayvayam Rus. Fed.
123 G3 Achegour well Niger
115 C4 Acheloös r. Greece
31 H3 Acheng China
80 C3 Achensee l. Austria
74 D4 Achern Germany
86 B2 Acheux-en-Amiénois France
86 B2 Achicourt France
51 H6 Achikulak Rus. Fed.
67 B3 Achill Rep. of Ireland
114 D4 Achilleio Greece
67 A3 Achill Head headland Rep. of Ireland
67 A3 Achill Island i. Rep. of Ireland
66 C2 Achiltibuie *Scotland* U.K.
72 E2 Achim Germany
45 L4 Achinsk Rus. Fed.
172 E2 Achiras Argentina
47 G4 Achisay Kazakhstan
46 E1 Achit Rus. Fed.
114 E1 Achladochori Greece
64 C1 Achnacroish *Scotland* U.K.
66 C3 Achnasheen *Scotland* U.K.
43 B2 Achno Cyprus
66 C3 A'Chralaig mt. *Scotland* U.K.
80 D2 Achslach Germany
74 E4 Achstetten Germany
111 E5 Aci Castello *Sicilia* Italy
111 E5 Aci Catena *Sicilia* Italy
42 B2 Acıpayam Turkey
111 E5 Acireale *Sicilia* Italy
150 E3 Ackley *Iowa* U.S.A.
158 D2 Acklins I. i. The Bahamas
63 H2 Acle *England* U.K.
90 B2 Acolin r. France
164 B2 Acomayo Peru
172 B2 Aconcagua, Co mt. Argentina
170 C2 Aconquija, Nevado de mountain range Argentina
166 E2 Acopiara Brazil
164 C3 Acora Peru
100 □ Açores, Arquipélago dos is Portugal
131 H2 Acornhoek South Africa
98 B1 A Coruña Spain
156 J7 Acoyapa Nicaragua
110 D4 Acquacalda Italy
107 G5 Acqualagna Italy
83 F3 Acquanegra sul Chiese Italy
108 D2 Acquapendente Italy
83 D2 Acquarossa Switzerland
109 F2 Acquasanta Terme Italy
109 E2 Acquasparta Italy
109 F2 Acquaviva Picena Italy
110 D4 Acquedolci *Sicilia* Italy
106 C4 Acqui Terme Italy
12 C3 Acraman, L. salt flat *S. Australia* Australia
164 B1 Acre div. Brazil
164 C2 Acre r. Brazil
Acre *see* 'Akko
111 F3 Acri Italy
98 C2 A Cruz de Incio Spain
A.C.T. div. *see* Australian Capital Territory
141 J4 Acton Vale *Québec* Canada
166 E2 Açu Brazil
166 E2 Açude Banabuiu resr Brazil
166 D2 Açude Boa Esperança resr Brazil
166 E2 Açude Orós resr Brazil
168 D6 Acungui Brazil
124 B3 Acurenam Equatorial Guinea
146 B4 Ada *Ohio* U.S.A.
151 D5 Ada *Oklahoma* U.S.A.
29 □2 Ada Japan
79 K6 Ada Yugoslavia
23 □2 Adacao *Guam* Pacific Ocean
126 D2 Adaela well Ethiopia
99 F3 Adaja r. Spain
126 E3 Adale well Ethiopia
Adalia *see* Antalya
124 B2 Adamaoua div. Cameroon
115 F6 Adamas Greece
123 G5 Adamawa div. Nigeria
80 B4 Adamello mt. Italy
13 G4 Adaminaby *New South Wales* Australia
171 E7 Adam, Mt h. Falkland Is.
78 F2 Adamov Czech Rep.
46 F2 Adamovka Rus. Fed.
77 L4 Adamów Poland
147 G3 Adams *Massachusetts* U.S.A.
148 C4 Adams *Wisconsin* U.S.A.
38 B4 Adam's Bridge reef India/Sri Lanka
8 □1 Adams I. i. *Auckland Is* New Zealand
136 F4 Adams L. l. *B.C.* Canada
155 E2 Adams McGill Reservoir resr *Nevada* U.S.A.
9 E4 Adams, Mt h. New Zealand
136 C3 Adams Mt. mt. *Alaska* U.S.A.
152 B2 Adams, Mt mt. *Washington* U.S.A.
9 C5 Adams, Mt mt. New Zealand
154 B2 Adams Peak mt. *California* U.S.A.
38 C5 Adam's Pk Sri Lanka
7 □14 Adam's Rock rock *Pitcairn I.* Pacific Ocean
7 □14 Adamstown *Pitcairn I.* Pacific Ocean
101 F2 Adamuz Spain
126 D2 'Adan Yemen
43 C1 Adana div. Turkey
42 C2 Adana Turkey
99 F4 Adanero Spain
22 D2 Adang, Tk b. Indonesia
98 C4 Adão Portugal
67 C4 Adare Rep. of Ireland
179 A5 Adare, C. c. Antarctica
15 F5 Adavale *Queensland* Australia
155 E2 Adaven *Nevada* U.S.A.
54 D3 Ādaži Latvia
106 D3 Adda r. Italy
124 D2 Adda watercourse Central African Rep./Sudan
119 H3 Ad Dafīnah Saudi Arabia
41 G4 Ad Dahnā reg. Saudi Arabia
120 A4 Ad Dakhla *Western Sahara*
126 D2 Aḍ Ḍāli' Yemen
39 B4 Ad Dammām Saudi Arabia
119 H4 Ad Darb Saudi Arabia
119 H3 Ad Dawādimī Saudi Arabia
Ad Dawhah *see* Doha
43 D2 Ad Daww plain Syria
123 F3 Addax, Réserve Naturelle intégrale dite Sanctuaire des res. Niger
63 E2 Adderbury *England* U.K.
41 G5 Ad Dir'īyah Saudi Arabia
147 K2 Addison *Maine* U.S.A.
42 F4 Ad Dīwānīyah Iraq
63 F3 Addlestone *England* U.K.
131 E6 Addo South Africa
175 J4 Addu Atoll atoll Maldives
43 D2 Ad Duraykīsh Syria
119 H1 Ad Duwayd well Saudi Arabia
145 D6 Adel *Georgia* U.S.A.
150 E3 Adel *Iowa* U.S.A.
12 D3 Adelaide *S. Australia* Australia
145 □2 Adelaide The Bahamas
179 B2 Adelaide I i. Antarctica
14 B2 Adelaide River *Northern Terr.* Australia
154 D4 Adelanto *California* U.S.A.
82 C2 Adelboden Switzerland
114 E3 Adelfi i. Greece
111 F1 Adelfia Italy
113 F6 Adelfoi i. Greece
172 E2 Adelia María Argentina
75 F3 Adelsdorf Germany
74 E3 Adelsheim Germany
103 B4 Ademuz Spain
Aden *see* 'Adan
74 B2 Adenau Germany
72 F2 Adendorf Germany
130 E6 Adendorp South Africa
41 G7 Aden, Gulf of g. Somalia/Yemen
123 F3 Aderbissinat Niger
126 D1 Adhanah, W. watercourse Yemen
39 C4 Adh Dhayd U.A.E.
21 K7 Adi i. Indonesia
126 C2 Ādī Ārk'ay Ethiopia
100 C3 Adiça, Serra da h. Portugal
119 F4 'Adid Umm Inderab well Sudan
107 G3 Adige r. Italy
126 C2 Ādīgrat Ethiopia
126 C2 Adi Keyih Eritrea
126 C2 Adi Kwala Eritrea
38 B2 Adilabad India
126 B4 Adilanga Uganda
42 E2 Adilcevaz Turkey
152 B3 Adin *California* U.S.A.
118 B2 Adīrī Libya
147 F2 Adirondack Mountains mountain range *New York* U.S.A.
126 C3 Ādīs Ābeba Ethiopia
126 C3 Ādīs Alem Ethiopia
126 C2 Ādīs Zemen Ethiopia
126 C2 Adi Ugri Eritrea
42 D2 Adıyaman Turkey
112 F1 Adjud Romania
145 □3 Adjuntas Puerto Rico
157 F4 Adjuntas, Presa de las resr Mexico
139 J3 Adlavik Islands is *Newfoundland* Canada
51 F7 Adler Rus. Fed.
83 D1 Adliswil Switzerland
16 D2 Admiralty Gulf b. *Western Australia* Australia
16 D2 Admiralty Gulf Abor. Reserve res. *Western Australia* Australia
135 K2 Admiralty Inlet inlet *N.W.T.* Canada
10 □4 Admiralty Is is *Lord Howe I.* Pacific Ocean
136 C3 Admiralty Island i. *Alaska* U.S.A.
136 C3 Admiralty Island Nat. Monument *Alaska* U.S.A.
6 □1 Admiralty Islands is P.N.G.
179 A5 Admiralty Mts mountain range Antarctica
81 F3 Admont Austria
123 F5 Ado-Ekiti Nigeria
126 B3 Adok Sudan
173 G5 Adolfo Gon. Chaves Argentina
6 □6 Adolphus Reef reef Fiji
38 B3 Adoni India
79 H4 Adony Hungary
75 H2 Adorf Germany
124 C3 Adoumandjali Central African Rep.
93 A5 Adour r. France
101 H4 Adra r. Spain
101 G4 Adra Spain
99 H3 Adradas Spain
124 F3 Adranga Congo(Zaire)
110 D5 Adrano *Sicilia* Italy
120 B4 Adrar div. Mauritania
120 B4 Adrâr h. Mauritania
121 F4 Adrar mts Algeria
121 D3 Adrar Algeria
123 E3 Adrar des Ifôghas reg. Mali
121 F3 Adrar Ikouhaouene mt. Algeria
121 F4 Adrar Mariou mt. Algeria
121 E3 Adrar N'Ahnet mts Algeria
120 A4 Adrar Souttouf mts *Western Sahara*
123 F3 Adrar Tamgak mt. Niger
43 B1 Adras D. mt. Turkey
39 E2 Adraskand r. Afghanistan
118 D5 Adré Chad
107 G3 Adria Italy
149 E5 Adrian *Michigan* U.S.A.
151 C5 Adrian *Texas* U.S.A.
95 F3 Adriatic Sea sea Mediterranean Sea
92 C2 Adriers France
155 G6 Aduana del Sasabe Mexico
172 B4 Aduana Pejerrey Chile
68 E1 Aduard Netherlands
83 E2 Adula Gruppe mt. Switzerland
54 E3 Aduliena Latvia
38 B4 Adur India
124 E3 Adusa Congo(Zaire)
126 C2 Ādwa Ethiopia
45 P3 Adycha r. Rus. Fed.
51 F6 Adygeya div. Rus. Fed.
51 F6 Adygeysk Rus. Fed.
51 H6 Adyk Rus. Fed.
103 C4 Adzaneta Spain
53 E2 Adzhamka Ukraine
Adzharskaya Respublika *see* Ajaria
122 D5 Adzopé Côte d'Ivoire
55 C4 Æbelø i. Denmark
114 F3 Aegean Sea sea Greece/Turkey
54 D2 Aegna i. Estonia
54 D2 Aegvidu Estonia
55 C5 Ærø i. Denmark
62 B2 Aeron r. *Wales* U.K.
55 C5 Ærøskøbing Denmark
72 E3 Aerzen Germany
98 B2 A Estrada Spain
114 C2 Aetos *Dytiki Makedonia* Greece
115 C5 Aetos *Peloponnisos* Greece
7 □11 Afaahiti *French Polynesia* Pacific Ocean
126 C1 Afabet Eritrea
126 D3 Afaf Badane well Ethiopia
Afal watercourse *see* 'Ifāl, W.
115 □ Afantou Greece
121 F3 Afao mt. Algeria
126 D2 Afar Depression depression Eritrea/Ethiopia
7 □11 Afareaitu *French Polynesia* Pacific Ocean
88 C4 Aff r. France
122 D5 Afféri Côte d'Ivoire
80 B2 Affing Germany
163 F2 Affobakka Surinam
83 D1 Affoltern am Albis Switzerland
18 H6 Afghanistan country Asia
126 E4 Afgooye Somalia
131 F1 Afguns South Africa
7 □12 Afiamalu Western Samoa
119 H3 'Afīf Saudi Arabia
98 B3 Afife Portugal
123 F5 Afikpo Nigeria
52 B1 Afim'ino Rus. Fed.
56 C3 Åfjord Norway
123 E5 Aflao Ghana
81 G3 Aflenz Kurort Austria
121 E2 Aflou Algeria
127 D4 Afmadow Somalia
134 C4 Afognak I. i. *Alaska* U.S.A.
120 A5 Afojjar well Mauritania
98 C1 A Fonsagrada Spain
169 H4 Afonso Cláudio Brazil
98 C2 A Forxa Spain
58 C2 Åfoss Norway
109 G4 Afragola France
166 D2 Afrânio Brazil
126 D2 Āfrēra Terara mt. Ethiopia
56 J2 Afrikanda Rus. Fed.
43 D1 'Afrīn Syria
43 D1 'Afrīn r. Syria/Turkey
42 D2 Afşin Turkey
68 D2 Afsluitdijk dam Netherlands
126 D3 Aftol well Ethiopia
152 E3 Afton *Wyoming* U.S.A.
166 B1 Afuá Brazil
43 C3 'Afula Israel
42 B2 Afyon Turkey
31 E2 Aga r. Rus. Fed.
43 A4 Aga Egypt
75 H2 Aga Germany
31 E2 Aga Rus. Fed.
123 F2 Agadez div. Niger
123 F3 Agadez Niger
120 C2 Agadir Morocco
118 D4 Aga Dubé well Chad
47 H3 Agadyr' Kazakhstan
117 K7 Agalega Islands is Seychelles
23 □2 Agana *Guam* Pacific Ocean
36 D5 Agar India
122 C2 Agâraktem well Mali
126 C3 Āgaro Ethiopia
37 G5 Agartala India
58 D1 Agåsen h. Norway
38 A2 Agashi India
23 □2 Agat *Guam* Pacific Ocean
149 F2 Agate *Ontario* Canada
47G3 Agat, G. h. Kazakhstan
113 F6 Agathonisi i. Greece
35 D8 Agatti i. India
123 F5 Agbor Bojiboji Nigeria
122 D5 Agboville Côte d'Ivoire
42 F1 Ağcabädi Azerbaijan
42 F1 Agdaş Azerbaijan
Agdash *see* Agdaş
91 B5 Agde France
Agdzhabedi *see* Ağcabädi
93 C4 Agen France
93 C4 Agenais reg. France
29 G5 Ageo Japan
102 D2 Àger Spain
55 A4 Agerbæk Denmark
126 C3 Āgere Maryam Ethiopia
74 D5 Ägerisee l. Switzerland
55 C4 Agernæs pt Denmark
55 D4 Agersø i. Denmark
52 C2 Ageyevo Rus. Fed.
81 H3 Ágfalva Hungary
130 B4 Aggeneys South Africa
74 C2 Agger r. Germany
55 B2 Aggersund Denmark
108 B4 Aggius *Sardegna* Italy
81 G2 Aggsbach Markt Austria
79 K3 Aggteleki nat. park Hungary
172 C5 Ag. Guzmán Argentina
64 B3 Aghalee *Northern Ireland* U.K.
64 B2 Aghanloo *Northern Ireland* U.K.
120 B4 Aghaylas well *Western Sahara*
36 D1 Aghil Pass pass China
67 C2 Aghla Mountain h. Rep. of Ireland
120 C5 Aghrîjît well Mauritania
114 E4 Agia Anna Greece
115 F7 Agia Galini Greece
115 F4 Agia Marina *Attiki* Greece
113 F6 Agia Marina *Notio Aigiao* Greece
115 D6 Agia Pelagia Greece
115 C5 Agia Triada Greece
115 G7 Agia Vervara Greece
112 G2 Agighiol Romania
42 D2 Ağin Turkey
30 E2 Aginskiy-Buryatskiy Avt. Okr. Rus. Fed.
30 E2 Aginskoye Rus. Fed.
114 C3 Agiofyllo Greece
115 E4 Agioi Apostoloi Greece
115 F7 Agioi Deka Greece
114 C3 Agioi Theodoroi *Dytiki Makedonia* Greece
115 E5 Agioi Theodoroi *Pelopónnisos* Greece
114 D3 Agiokampos Greece
114 F2 Agion Oros div. Greece
114 G2 Agios Charalampos Greece
115 E5 Agios Dimitrios *Attiki* Greece
114 D2 Agios Dimitrios *Kentriki Makedonia* Greece
115 D6 Agios Dimitrios *Peloponnisos* Greece
114 G3 Agios Efstratios i. Greece
114 F3 Agios Efstratios Greece
115 E5 Agios Georgios i. Greece
114 C4 Agios Georgios *Stereá Ellás* Greece
115 D6 Agios Ioannis Greece
115 D5 Agios Konstantinos *Peloponnisos* Greece
114 D4 Agios Konstantinos *Stereá Ellás* Greece
115 G7 Agios Myron Greece
115 B5 Agios Nikolaos *Ionioi Nisoi* Greece
114 B3 Agios Nikolaos *Ípeiros* Greece
114 E2 Agios Nikolaos *Kentriki Makedonia* Greece
115 G7 Agios Nikolaos *Kríti* Greece
115 D6 Agios Nikolaos *Peloponnisos* Greece
114 C4 Agios Nikolaos *Stereá Ellás* Greece
113 E5 Agios Paraskevi Greece
115 D5 Agios Petros Greece
115 E7 Agios Theodoros i. Greece
110 D5 Agira *Sicilia* Italy

119 G4 **Agirwat Hills h.** Sudan
64 B2 **Agivey** *Northern Ireland* U.K.
115 E5 **Agkistri i.** Greece
93 E6 **Agly r.** France
114 C3 **Agnantero** Greece
89 D2 **Agneaux** France
12 B1 **Agnes, Mt h.** *S. Australia* Australia
122 D5 **Agnibilékrou** Côte d'Ivoire
112 E2 **Agnita** Romania
107 F3 **Agno r.** Italy
83 D2 **Agno** Switzerland
109 G3 **Agnone** Italy
106 C3 **Agogna r.** Italy
122 D5 **Agogo** Ghana
98 B2 **A Golada** Spain
122 D5 **Agona Swedru** Ghana
99 H2 **Agoncillo** Spain
88 D2 **Agon-Coutainville** France
30 B5 **Agong** China
107 G2 **Agordo** Italy
103 C6 **Agost** Spain
164 C1 **Agostinho** Brazil
173 F4 **Agosto, 17 de** Argentina
173 F4 **Agosto, 30 de** Argentina
122 D3 **Agounni Jefal well** Mali
123 E3 **Agous-n-Ehsel well** Mali
93 D5 **Agout r.** France
36 D4 **Agra** India
173 H2 **Agraciada** Uruguay
114 C3 **Agrafiotis r.** Greece
51 H7 **Agrakhanskiy Poluostrov** Rus. Fed.
102 E3 **Agramunt** Spain
83 E3 **Agrate Brianza** Italy
102 B3 **Agreda** Spain
111 F2 **Agri r.** Italy
42 E2 **Ağri** Turkey
115 E7 **Agria Gramvousa i.** Greece
110 C5 **Agrigento div.** Italy
110 C5 **Agrigento** *Sicilia* Italy
21 M3 **Agrihan i.** *Northern Mariana Is* Pacific Ocean
115 C5 **Agrilos** Greece
114 C4 **Agrinio** Greece
172 B5 **Agrio r.** Argentina
114 E3 **Agriovotano** Greece
109 G4 **Agropoli** Italy
46 D1 **Agryz** Rus. Fed.
156 E4 **Ags div.** Mexico
42 G1 **Ağsu** Azerbaijan
169 G2 **Água Boa** Brazil
156 D4 **Agua Brava, L. lag.** Mexico
168 B4 **Água Clara** Brazil
157 H5 **Aguada** Mexico
172 C6 **Aguada de Guerra** Argentina
159 E5 **Aguada Grande** Venezuela
162 B2 **Aguadas** Colombia
162 C3 **Agua de Dios** Colombia
145 □3 **Aguadilla** Puerto Rico
172 E6 **Aguado Cecilio** Argentina
156 K7 **Aguadulce** Panama
101 F3 **Aguadulce** Spain
172 C4 **Agua Escondida** Argentina
100 C3 **Agua Negra h.** Portugal
165 E3 **Aguapei r.** Brazil
170 E2 **Aguapey r.** Argentina
156 C2 **Agua Prieta** Mexico
165 E4 **Aguaray Guazú r.** Paraguay
165 E4 **Aguaray-guazu r.** Paraguay
98 B3 **A Guardia** Spain
162 D2 **Aguaro-Guariquito, Parque Nacional nat. park** Venezuela
101 H3 **Aguas r.** Spain
102 C2 **Aguas** Spain
156 E4 **Aguascalientes** Mexico
169 H2 **Águas Formosas** Brazil
100 E2 **Agua, Sierra del h.** Spain
169 H1 **Águas Vermelhas** Brazil
102 C3 **Aguasvivas r.** Spain
165 E2 **Água Verde r.** Brazil
102 C4 **Aguaviva** Spain
102 F3 **Agudes, Les mt.** Spain
98 C2 **A Gudiña** Spain
101 F2 **Agudo** Spain
168 D5 **Agudos** Brazil
98 D4 **Águeda r.** Spain
98 B4 **Águeda** Portugal
123 E3 **Aguelhok** Mali
121 E3 **Aguemour reg.** Algeria
99 G1 **Agüera r.** Spain
91 B4 **Aguessac** France
107 H5 **Agugliano** Italy
98 C4 **Aguiar da Beira** Portugal
123 F4 **Aguié** Niger
98 B4 **Aguieira, Barragem de resr** Portugal
102 B4 **Aguila mt.** Spain
155 F5 **Aguila** *Arizona* U.S.A.
99 F3 **Aguilafuente** Spain
99 F2 **Aguilar de Campóo** Spain
99 F2 **Aguilar de Campóo, Emb. de resr** Spain
101 F3 **Aguilar de la Frontera** Spain
170 C2 **Aguilares** Argentina
103 B7 **Águilas** Spain
23 B4 **Aguisan** Philippines
99 G3 **Aguisejo r.** Spain
145 □3 **Agujereada, Pta pt** Puerto Rico
126 C2 **Āgula'i** Ethiopia
130 C7 **Agulhas** South Africa
175 F7 **Agulhas Basin sea feature** Indian Ocean
130 C7 **Agulhas, Cape c.** South Africa
169 F5 **Agulhas Negras, Pico das mt.** Brazil
175 F6 **Agulhas Plateau sea feature** Indian Ocean
22 C4 **Agung, G. volcano** Indonesia
23 C4 **Agusan r.** Philippines
23 B4 **Agutaya** Philippines
51 D7 **Ağva** Turkey
126 B3 **Agwei r.** Sudan
29 □2 **Aha** Japan
123 E5 **Ahamasu** Ghana
42 F2 **Ahar** Iran
9 C5 **Ahaura r.** New Zealand
9 C5 **Ahaura** New Zealand
72 C3 **Ahaus** Germany
7 □10 **Ahé i.** *French Polynesia* Pacific Ocean
8 F3 **Ahimanawa Ra. mountain range** New Zealand
8 D1 **Ahipara** New Zealand
8 D1 **Ahipara Bay b.** New Zealand
43 B1 **Ahırlı** Turkey
54 E2 **Ahja r.** Estonia
134 B4 **Ahklun Mts** *Alaska* U.S.A.
42 E2 **Ahlat** Turkey
73 K2 **Ahlbeck** Germany
72 E3 **Ahlden (Aller)** Germany
72 C4 **Ahlen** Germany
36 C5 **Ahmadabad** India
39 D3 **Ahmadī** Iran
38 A2 **Ahmadnagar** India
36 B3 **Ahmadpur East** Pakistan
36 B3 **Ahmadpur Sial** Pakistan
126 D3 **Ahmar Mountains mountain range** Ethiopia
113 F5 **Ahmetli** Turkey
120 B4 **Aḥmeyim well** Mauritania
64 B3 **Ahoghill** *Northern Ireland* U.K.
36 C4 **Ahore** India
75 F2 **Ahorn** Germany
80 C3 **Ahornspitze mt.** Austria
74 B2 **Ahr r.** Germany
74 B2 **Ahrbrück** Germany
73 F1 **Ahrensbök** Germany
72 F2 **Ahrensburg** Germany
73 J3 **Ahrensfelde** Germany
73 H1 **Ahrenshagen** Germany
57 G3 **Ähtäri** Finland
54 E2 **Ahtme** Estonia
157 H6 **Ahuachapán** El Salvador
157 E4 **Ahualulco** Mexico
92 E2 **Ahun** France
7 □10 **Ahunui i.** *French Polynesia* Pacific Ocean
9 B6 **Ahuriri r.** New Zealand
59 F4 **Åhus** Sweden
39 B3 **Ahvāz** Iran
36 C5 **Ahwa** India
Ahwāz *see* **Ahvāz**
130 A3 **Ai-Ais** Namibia
128 B4 **Ai-Ais Hot Springs and Fish River Canyon res.** Namibia
114 C2 **Aiani** Greece
115 E5 **Aianteio** Greece
30 D4 **Aibag Gol r.** China
102 B2 **Aibar** Spain
28 J2 **Aibetsu** Japan
145 □3 **Aibonito** Puerto Rico
75 G4 **Aichach** Germany
29 F6 **Aichi div.** Japan
83 F1 **Aichstetten** Germany
28 E6 **Aida** Japan
110 D5 **Aidone** *Sicilia* Italy
153 □1 **Aiea** *Hawaii* U.S.A.
111 F3 **Aiello Calabro** Italy
115 D4 **Aigeira** Greece
114 G1 **Aigeiros** Greece
81 E2 **Aigen im Mühlkreis** Austria
43 C2 **Aigialousa** Cyprus
115 E5 **Aigina i.** Greece
115 E5 **Aigina** Greece
114 D2 **Aiginio** Greece
115 D4 **Aigio** Greece
82 B2 **Aigle** Switzerland
92 E3 **Aigle, Barrage de l' dam** France
91 E4 **Aigle de Chambeyron mt.** France
91 E4 **Aiglun** France
93 C5 **Aignan** France
90 C1 **Aignay-le-Duc** France
115 E4 **Aigosthena** Greece
91 B4 **Aigoual, Mont mt.** France
92 C3 **Aigre** France
92 B2 **Aigrefeuille-d'Aunis** France
88 D4 **Aigrefeuille-sur-Maine** France
173 K3 **Aiguá** Uruguay
102 F3 **Aiguafreda** Spain
90 E3 **Aiguebelle** France
82 B3 **Aigueblanche** France
90 B2 **Aigueperse** France
91 D4 **Aigues r.** France
91 C5 **Aigues-Mortes** France
91 B5 **Aigues-Mortes, Golfe d' b.** France
102 D2 **Aigües Tortes i Estany de St Maurici, Parque Nacional d' nat. park** Spain
93 E5 **Aigues-Vives** France
91 B3 **Aiguilhe** France
82 C3 **Aiguille d'Argentière mt.** France/Switzerland
90 E3 **Aiguille de la Grande Sassière mt.** France
91 E3 **Aiguille de Peclet mt.** France
91 E3 **Aiguille de Scolette mt.** France/Italy
92 A2 **Aiguille, Pte de l' pt** France
91 E4 **Aiguilles** France
91 E3 **Aiguilles d'Arves mountain range** France
90 E3 **Aiguilles des Glaciers mt.** France
90 E3 **Aiguille Verte mt.** France
93 C4 **Aiguillon** France
179 □ **Aiguillon, C. d' c.** *Kerguelen* Indian Ocean
92 A2 **Aiguillon, Pte de l' pt** France
92 D2 **Aigurande** France
31 H2 **Aihui** China
29 G4 **Aikawa** Japan
145 D5 **Aiken** *S. Carolina* U.S.A.
32 C3 **Ailao Shan mountain range** China
156 L7 **Ailigandi** Panama
90 B1 **Aillant-sur-Tholon** France
91 E5 **Aille r.** France
87 F5 **Aillevillers-et-Lyaumont** France
86 A2 **Ailly-le-Haut-Clocher** France
86 B3 **Ailly-sur-Noye** France
89 H2 **Ailly-sur-Somme** France
66 C5 **Ailsa Craig i.** *Scotland* U.K.
140 E5 **Ailsa Craig** *Ontario* Canada
91 C5 **Aimargues** France
90 E3 **Aime** France
22 E4 **Aimere** Indonesia
170 C2 **Aimogasta** Argentina
169 H3 **Aimorés** Brazil
169 H3 **Aimorés, Sa dos h.** Brazil
90 D2 **Ain div.** *Rhône-Alpes* France
90 D2 **Ain r.** France
119 F2 **'Ain 'Amûr spring** Egypt
121 F1 **Aïn Beïda** Algeria
121 D2 **Aïn Beni Mathar** Morocco
120 C3 **'Aïn Ben Tili** Mauritania
121 E1 **Aïn Defla** Algeria
121 E2 **Aïn Deheb** Algeria
43 B5 **Ain el Bâgha well** Egypt
43 C5 **'Ain el Furtâga well** Egypt
119 E2 **Aîn el Maqfi spring** Egypt
80 D4 **Ainet** Austria
118 C4 **Aïn Galakka spring** Chad
24 A2 **Ainggyi** Myanmar
121 E3 **Aïn Mezzer well** Algeria
121 F1 **Aïn-M'Lila** Algeria
115 B4 **Ainos nat. park** Greece
75 H5 **Ainring** Germany
102 D2 **Ainsa** Spain
121 D2 **Aïn Sefra** Algeria
139 H4 **Ainslie, Lake l.** *Nova Scotia* Canada
43 B5 **Ain Sukhna** Egypt
150 D3 **Ainsworth** *Nebraska* U.S.A.
121 D1 **Aïn Temouchent** Algeria
118 E2 **'Aîn Timeira spring** Egypt
121 E4 **Aïn Ti-m Misaou well** Algeria
102 B3 **Ainzón** Spain
162 B3 **Aipe** Colombia
164 C3 **Aiquile** Bolivia
25 D7 **Air i.** Indonesia
23 □1 **Airai** Palau
89 G2 **Airaines** France
163 E4 **Airão** Brazil
136 G4 **Airdrie** *Alberta* Canada
66 E5 **Airdrie** *Scotland* U.K.
86 D3 **Aire r.** France
103 □ **Aire, Illa de l' i.** Spain
100 B1 **Aire, Serra de mountain range** Portugal
93 B5 **Aire-sur-l'Adour** France
86 B2 **Aire-sur-la-Lys** France
123 G3 **Aïr et du Ténéré, Rés. Naturelle Nat. de l' res.** Niger
135 L3 **Air Force I. i.** *N.W.T.* Canada
30 D4 **Airgin Sum** China
22 B2 **Airhitam r.** Indonesia
22 B2 **Airhitam, Tk b.** Indonesia
54 C1 **Airisto Erstan b.** Finland
91 F5 **Airole** Italy
83 D2 **Airolo** Switzerland
137 H3 **Air Ronge** *Saskatchewan* Canada
92 B2 **Airvault** France
75 F3 **Aisch r.** Germany
171 B6 **Aisen div.** Chile
171 B6 **Aisén, Pto** Chile
31 G5 **Ai Shan h.** China
136 B2 **Aishihik** *Yukon Terr.* Canada
136 B2 **Aishihik Lake l.** *Yukon Terr.* Canada
80 B2 **Aislingen** Germany
86 C3 **Aisne div.** *Picardie* France
86 C3 **Aisne r.** France
121 D2 **Aïssa, Djebel mt.** Algeria
90 E1 **Aïssey** France
90 C1 **Aisy-sur-Armançon** France
56 G2 **Aitamännikkö** Finland
6 □1 **Aitape** P.N.G.
80 D2 **Aiterach r.** Germany
75 H4 **Aiterhofen** Germany
150 E2 **Aitkin** *Minnesota* U.S.A.
114 C4 **Aitolia Kai Akarnania div.** Greece
115 C4 **Aitoliko** Greece
102 D3 **Aitona** Spain
74 F5 **Aitrach** Germany
75 F5 **Aitrang** Germany
5 L6 **Aitutaki i.** *Cook Islands* Pacific Ocean
112 D1 **Aiud** Romania
54 E3 **Aiviekste r.** Latvia
23 □1 **Aiwokako Passage chan.** Palau
90 B2 **Aix r.** France
86 C4 **Aix-en-Othe** France
91 D5 **Aix-en-Provence** *Bouches-du-Rhône* France
92 D3 **Aixe-sur-Vienne** France
92 A2 **Aix, Île d' i.** France
90 D3 **Aix-les-Bains** France
126 C2 **Āīy Ādī** Ethiopia
136 D3 **Aiyansh** *B.C.* Canada
37 F5 **Aiyar Res.** India
123 E5 **Aiyetoro** Nigeria
37 H5 **Aizawl** India
92 A2 **Aizenay** France
54 D3 **Aizkraukle** Latvia
54 B3 **Aizpute** Latvia
29 G5 **Aizutakada** Japan
29 G5 **Aizu-wakamatsu** Japan
42 F2 **'Ajab Shīr** Iran
108 A3 **Ajaccio** *Corse* France
108 A3 **Ajaccio-Campo dell'Oro airport** *Corse* France
36 E4 **Ajaigarh** India
119 H2 **Ajā, J. mts** Saudi Arabia
157 F5 **Ajalpán** Mexico
17 A5 **Ajana** *Western Australia* Australia
36 C5 **Ajanta** India
Ajanta Range h. *see* **Sahyadriparvat or Ajanta Range**
123 F5 **Ajaokuta** Nigeria
51 G7 **Ajaria** Georgia
56 D2 **Ajaureforsen** Sweden
9 D5 **Ajax, Mt mt.** New Zealand
23 □2 **Ajayan Bay b.** *Guam* Pacific Ocean
118 D1 **Ajdābiyā** Libya
81 E5 **Ajdovščina** Slovenia
a-Jiddét gravel area *see* **Jiddat al Ḥarāsīs**
28 H3 **Ajigasawa** Japan
37 G4 **Ājimganj** India
79 G4 **Ajka** Hungary
39 C4 **Ajman** U.A.E.
36 C4 **Ajmer** India
155 F5 **Ajo** *Arizona* U.S.A.
99 G1 **Ajo** Spain
82 B1 **Ajoie reg.** Switzerland
155 F5 **Ajo, Mt mt.** *Arizona* U.S.A.
23 B4 **Ajuy** Philippines
28 J2 **Akabira** Japan
121 E3 **Akabli** Algeria
29 G5 **Akadomari** Japan
29 G4 **Aka-gawa r.** Japan
127 B5 **Akagera National Park nat. park** Rwanda
126 C3 **Āk'ak'ī Beseka** Ethiopia
118 B3 **Akakus, Jabal mts** Libya
38 B2 **Akalkot** India
28 K2 **Akan** Japan
28 K2 **Akan National Park** Japan
43 B2 **Akanthou** Cyprus
28 D7 **Akaoka** Japan
29 □2 **Akarie-Ue** Japan
123 F3 **Akarkar well** Niger
114 B4 **Akarnanika mountain range** Greece
9 D5 **Akaroa** New Zealand
9 D5 **Akaroa Har harbour** New Zealand
37 H4 **Akas reg.** India
119 F3 **Akasha** Sudan
79 J5 **Akasztó** Hungary
47 H3 **Akbakay** Kazakhstan
47 J3 **Akbalyk** Kazakhstan
36 E4 **Akbarpur** India
37 E4 **Akbarpur** India
46 F3 **Akbasty** Kazakhstan
47 H5 **Akbaytal** Tajikistan
47 H5 **Akbaytal P. pass** Tajikistan
121 E1 **Akbou** Algeria
46 E2 **Akbulak** Rus. Fed.
42 D2 **Akçadağ** Turkey
42 D2 **Akçakale** Turkey
42 B1 **Akçakoca** Turkey
43 D1 **Akçakoyunlu** Turkey
113 G6 **Akçay r.** Turkey
46 E4 **Akchakaya, Vpadina depression** Turkmenistan
47 H3 **Akchatau** Kazakhstan
113 G5 **Akdağ mt.** Turkey
42 C2 **Akdağmadeni** Turkey
65 F2 **Akeld** *England* U.K.
73 H4 **Aken** Germany
58 B2 **Åkernes** Norway
59 H2 **Åkersberga** Sweden
58 D1 **Akershus div.** Norway
124 D3 **Aketi** Congo(Zaire)
46 E5 **Akhal div.** Turkmenistan
51 G7 **Akhalk'alak'i** Georgia
51 G7 **Akhalts'ikhe** Georgia
41 J5 **Akhḍar, Jabal mountain range** Oman
43 D5 **Akhḍar, W. al watercourse** Saudi Arabia
42 A2 **Akhisar** Turkey
119 F2 **Akhmîm** Egypt
36 C2 **Akhnoor** India
Akhsu *see* **Ağsu**
52 G4 **Akhtuba** Rus. Fed.
51 H5 **Akhtubinsk** Rus. Fed.
51 H7 **Akhty** Rus. Fed.
39 B2 **Ākhvoreh-ye Bālā** Iran
28 D7 **Aki** Japan
124 B4 **Akiéni** Gabon
31 E1 **Akima** Rus. Fed.
138 D3 **Akimiski Island i.** *N.W.T.* Canada
42 C2 **Akıncı Br. pt** Turkey
55 □2 **Åkirkeby** Denmark
29 H4 **Akita div.** Japan
29 H4 **Akita** Japan
120 B5 **Akjoujt** Mauritania
120 C3 **Akka** Morocco
46 F3 **Akkabak** Kazakhstan
56 E2 **Akkajaure l.** Sweden
47 G3 **Akkanse** Kazakhstan
28 K2 **Akkeshi** Japan
28 K2 **Akkeshi-ko l.** Japan
28 K2 **Akkeshi-wan b.** Japan
43 C3 **'Akko** Israel
46 C3 **Akkol'** Kazakhstan
47 H4 **Akkol'** Kazakhstan
68 D1 **Akkrum** Netherlands
42 D1 **Akkuş** Turkey
46 D3 **Akkystau** Kazakhstan
123 E5 **Aklampa** Benin
36 D4 **Aklera** India
54 C3 **Akmenė** Lithuania
54 B3 **Akmenrags pt** Latvia
36 D1 **Akmeqit** China
47 H2 **Akmola div.** Kazakhstan
47 H2 **Akmola** Kazakhstan
54 D3 **Aknīste** Latvia
28 E6 **Akō** Japan
126 B3 **Akobo r.** Ethiopia/Sudan
126 B3 **Akobo** Sudan
36 D5 **Akola** India
124 B3 **Akom II** Cameroon
124 B3 **Akonolinga** Cameroon
126 C1 **Akordat** Eritrea
42 C2 **Akören** Turkey
36 D5 **Akot** India
126 B3 **Akot** Sudan
122 D5 **Akoupé** Côte d'Ivoire
139 G1 **Akpatok Island i.** *Québec* Canada
43 B1 **Akpınar** Turkey
47 J4 **Akqi** China
114 D2 **Akra Acherada pt** Greece
114 G3 **Akra Agia Eirinis pt** Greece
115 F5 **Akra Agios Dimitrios pt** Greece
113 F5 **Akra Agios Fokas pt** Greece
115 G7 **Akra Agios Ioannis pt** Greece
115 G5 **Akra Agios Kosmas pt** Greece
115 B4 **Akra Agiou Andreou pt** Greece
114 F2 **Akra Akrathos pt** Greece
115 C6 **Akra Akritas pt** Greece
114 F2 **Akra Arapis pt** Greece
115 C4 **Akra Araxos pt** Greece
115 □ **Akra Armenistis pt** Greece
114 B3 **Akra Asprokavos pt** Greece
115 G6 **Akra Aspros Gremnos pt** Greece
115 B4 **Akra Atheras pt** Greece
114 B4 **Akra Dafnoudi pt** Greece
114 D3 **Akra Dermatas pt** Greece
43 D1 **Akrād, Jabal al mountain range** Syria
114 B4 **Akra Doukato pt** Greece
115 F7 **Akra Drapano pt** Greece
114 E3 **Akra Drepano pt** Greece
114 D2 **Akra Epanomi pt** Greece
114 F3 **Akra Erimitis pt** Greece
58 B2 **Akrafjorden inlet** Norway
114 E3 **Akra Gerakas pt** Greece
115 B5 **Akra Geraki pt** Greece
114 E3 **Akra Gourouni pt** Greece
115 E6 **Akra Ierax i.** Greece
115 E4 **Akraifnio** Greece
43 C2 **Akra, Jabal mt.** Syria/Turkey
115 F4 **Akra Kafireas pt** Greece
115 E6 **Akra Kamili i.** Greece
115 F4 **Akra Kampanos pt** Greece
115 E6 **Akra Kapello pt** Greece
114 F4 **Akra Kartsino pt** Greece
114 E3 **Akra Kassandras pt** Greece
115 C5 **Akra Katakolo pt** Greece
114 F2 **Akra Kefalas pt** Greece
114 G2 **Akra Kipos pt** Greece
115 E6 **Akra Kremmidi i.** Greece
115 F5 **Akra Kyklops pt** Greece
114 F4 **Akra Kymis pt** Greece
114 F3 **Akra Kyra pt** Greece
115 □ **Akra Ladiko pt** Greece
115 □ **Akra Lindos pt** Greece
114 F4 **Akra Lithari pt** Greece
115 F8 **Akra Lithino pt** Greece
115 E6 **Akra Maleas pt** Greece
113 F5 **Akra Maleas pt** Greece
113 E5 **Akra Masticho pt** Greece
115 F7 **Akra Melissa pt** Greece
113 E5 **Akra Meston pt** Greece
115 B4 **Akra Mounta pt** Greece
114 G3 **Akra Mourtzeflos pt** Greece
56 L6 **Akranes** Iceland
135 Q3 **Akranes** Iceland
114 F4 **Akra Ochthonia pt** Greece
114 F4 **Akra Oros pt** Greece
115 D6 **Akra Pagania pt** Greece
114 E3 **Akra Paliouri pt** Greece
113 F7 **Akra Paraspori pt** Greece
115 F5 **Akra Paximadi pt** Greece
115 G6 **Akra Petalida pt** Greece
114 F2 **Akra Pinnes pt** Greece
114 G2 **Akra Plaka pt** Greece
115 H7 **Akra Plaka pt** Greece
114 D3 **Akra Platamonas pt** Greece
115 □ **Akra Prasonisi pt** Greece
114 E2 **Akra Pyrgos pt** Greece
114 F2 **Akra Pyrgos pt** Greece
114 E2 **Akra Rigas pt** Greece
114 F2 **Akra Salonikos pt** Greece
114 E4 **Akra Sarakiniko pt** Greece
115 H7 **Akra Sideros pt** Greece
113 E5 **Akra Sigri pt** Greece
115 B5 **Akra Skinari pt** Greece
115 F5 **Akra Sounio pt** Greece
115 E7 **Akra Spatha pt** Greece
115 E5 **Akra Spathi pt** Greece
115 D6 **Akra Spathi pt** Greece
114 E3 **Akra Stavros pt** Greece
115 F7 **Akra Stavros pt** Greece
114 F2 **Akra Stavros Babouras pt** Greece
115 D6 **Akra Tainaro pt** Greece
115 F5 **Akra Tamelos pt** Greece
114 G3 **Akra Tigani pt** Greece
115 D6 **Akra Tigani pt** Greece
115 D6 **Akra Trachila pt** Greece
114 F3 **Akra Trypiti pt** Greece
115 F7 **Akra Trypiti pt** Greece
113 F5 **Akra Vamvakas pt** Greece
115 □ **Akra Voudi pt** Greece
115 E7 **Akra Vouxa pt** Greece
113 F6 **Akra Xodoto pt** Greece
115 D6 **Akra Xylis pt** Greece
115 E5 **Akra Zourvas pt** Greece
58 A2 **Åkrehamne** Norway
123 F3 **Akrérèb** Niger
39 F2 **Ak Robat P. pass** Afghanistan
152 G3 **Akron** *Colorado* U.S.A.
146 C4 **Akron** *Ohio* U.S.A.
146 C4 **Akron City Reservoir resr** *Ohio* U.S.A.
43 B2 **Akrotirion B. b.** Cyprus
36 D2 **Aksai Chin reg.** *Jammu and Kashmir*
113 G4 **Aksakal** Turkey
112 F3 **Aksakovo** Bulgaria
42 C2 **Aksaray** Turkey
51 F6 **Aksay** Rus. Fed.
36 D2 **Aksayqin Hu l.** China/Jammu and Kashmir
42 B2 **Akşehir** Turkey
42 B2 **Akseki** Turkey
39 C3 **Aks-e Rostam r.** Iran
30 E2 **Aksha** Rus. Fed.
46 F3 **Akshiganak** Kazakhstan
47 J4 **Akshiy** Kazakhstan
47 K4 **Aksu r.** China
47 J3 **Aksu r.** Kazakhstan
42 B2 **Aksu r.** Turkey
47 K4 **Aksu** China
47 H2 **Aksu** Kazakhstan
47 J3 **Aksu** Kazakhstan
47 K3 **Aksuat** Kazakhstan
46 F2 **Aksuat** Kazakhstan
47 H3 **Aksu-Ayuly** Kazakhstan
47 H4 **Aksuek** Kazakhstan
126 C2 **Āksum** Ethiopia
47 G4 **Aksumbe** Kazakhstan
42 E2 **Aktas Dāgh mt.** Turkey
46 D4 **Aktau** Kazakhstan
47 H2 **Aktau** Kazakhstan
47 H3 **Aktau** Kazakhstan
47 J5 **Akto** China
47 H3 **Aktogay** Kazakhstan
47 J3 **Aktogay** Kazakhstan
54 F5 **Aktsyabrski** Belarus
47 G3 **Aktuma** Kazakhstan
46 E3 **Aktumsyk** Kazakhstan
46 E2 **Aktyubinsk** Kazakhstan
46 E3 **Aktyubinsk div.** Kazakhstan
135 L3 **Akulivik** *Québec* Canada
28 C7 **Akune** Japan
123 F5 **Akure** Nigeria
56 M6 **Akureyri** Iceland
134 B4 **Akutan** *Alaska* U.S.A.
123 F6 **Akwa Ibom div.** Nigeria
123 F5 **Akwanga** Nigeria
37 G1 **Akxokesay** China
Akyab *see* **Sittwe**
43 C1 **Akyatan Gölü l.** Turkey
47 H3 **Akzhal** Kazakhstan
47 G4 **Akzhaykyn, Oz. salt lake** Kazakhstan
58 C1 **Ål** Norway
107 F3 **Ala** Italy
39 B4 **Al 'Abā** Saudi Arabia
145 C5 **Alabama div.** U.S.A.
145 C6 **Alabama r.** *Alabama* U.S.A.
145 C5 **Alabaster** *Alabama* U.S.A.
23 B3 **Alabat i.** Philippines
118 B2 **Al Abyaḍ** Libya
118 D1 **Al Abyār** Libya
42 C1 **Alaca** Turkey
42 D2 **Alacahan** Turkey
42 C1 **Alaçam** Turkey
113 G5 **Alaçam Dağları mountain range** Turkey
114 G1 **Aladag mt.** Bulgaria
42 C2 **Ala Dağ mts** Turkey
52 E2 **Alad'ino** Rus. Fed.
99 E3 **Alaejos** Spain
Alagez mt. *see* **Aragats Lerr**
42 F1 **Alagir** Rus. Fed.
106 B3 **Alagna Valsesia** Italy
91 B3 **Alagnon r.** France
166 E2 **Alagoas div.** Brazil
166 E3 **Alagoinhas** Brazil
98 D5 **Alagón r.** Spain
102 B3 **Alagón** Spain
56 F3 **Alahärmä** Finland
42 F4 **Al Ahmadī** Kuwait
93 E5 **Alaigne** France
103 □ **Alaior** Spain
47 H5 **Alai Range mountain range** Asia
56 F3 **Alajärvi** Finland
118 B1 **Al Ajaylāt** Libya
119 H2 **Al Ajfar** Saudi Arabia
156 J7 **Alajuela** Costa Rica
43 D5 **Al Akhḍar** Saudi Arabia
43 A1 **Alakır r.** Turkey
47 K3 **Alakol', Oz. salt lake** Kazakhstan
50 D1 **Alakurtti** Rus. Fed.
163 E4 **Alalaú r.** Brazil
119 H4 **Al'Alayyah** Saudi Arabia
126 D4 **Alama** Somalia
21 M3 **Alamagan i.** *Northern Mariana Is* Pacific Ocean
42 F4 **Al 'Amārah** Iraq
126 C2 **Ālamat'ā** Ethiopia
37 H3 **Alamdo** China
101 F3 **Alameda** Spain
101 F2 **Alamillo** Spain
23 A2 **Alaminos** Philippines
156 E3 **Alamítos, Sa de los mt.** Mexico
100 C2 **Álamo r.** Portugal
155 E3 **Alamo** *Nevada* U.S.A.
155 F4 **Alamo Dam dam** *Arizona* U.S.A.
153 F5 **Alamogordo** *New Mexico* U.S.A.
151 D6 **Alamo Heights** *Texas* U.S.A.
108 B4 **Alà, Monti di mountain range** *Sardegna* Italy
153 E6 **Alamos** *Sonora* Mexico
156 C3 **Alamos** *Sonora* Mexico
173 F4 **Alamos** Argentina
153 F4 **Alamosa** *Colorado* U.S.A.
38 B3 **Alampur** India
107 J3 **Alan** Croatia
126 D2 **Al 'Anad** Yemen
56 D2 **Alanäs** Sweden
42 E3 **Al Anbār div.** Iraq
57 F3 **Åland div.** Finland
57 E3 **Åland i.** Finland
73 G3 **Aland r.** Germany
42 F2 **Aland r.** Iran
38 B2 **Aland** India
43 D2 **Al Andarīn** Syria
100 C2 **Alandroal** Portugal
25 C7 **Alang Besar i.** Indonesia
100 D2 **Alange** Spain
100 D2 **Alange, Emb. de resr** Spain
100 E2 **Alanís** Spain
148 E3 **Alanson** *Michigan* U.S.A.
124 B2 **Alantika Mountains mountain range** Cameroon/Nigeria
42 C2 **Alanya** Turkey
Alappuzha *see* **Alleppey**
119 H3 **Al 'Aqīq** Saudi Arabia
103 C5 **Alaquàs** Spain
42 D3 **Al Arak oasis** Syria
99 E4 **Alaraz** Spain
99 F2 **Alar del Rey** Spain
120 A4 **Al Argoub** *Western Sahara*
119 J2 **Al Arṭāwīyah** Saudi Arabia
22 D4 **Alas** Indonesia
42 B2 **Alaşehir** Turkey
42 E4 **Al'Āshūrīyah well** Iraq
134 C3 **Alaska div.** U.S.A.
134 D4 **Alaska, Gulf of g.** U.S.A.
136 E3 **Alaska Highway** Canada/U.S.A.
134 B4 **Alaska Peninsula pen.** U.S.A.
134 C3 **Alaska Range mountain range** U.S.A.
119 G2 **Al'Assāfīyah** Saudi Arabia
106 C4 **Alassio** Italy
54 C1 **Alastaro** Finland
41 G2 **Älät** Azerbaijan
46 F5 **Alat** Uzbekistan
Alataw Shankou pass *see* **Dzungarian Gate**
42 E4 **Al 'Athāmīn h.** Iraq
109 F3 **Alatri** Italy
119 H2 **Al Atwā' well** Saudi Arabia
52 G2 **Alatyr' r.** Rus. Fed.
52 H2 **Alatyr'** Rus. Fed.
162 B4 **Alausí** Ecuador
99 H2 **Álava div.** Spain
42 F1 **Alaverdi** Armenia
39 B2 **'Alavī** Iran
56 G2 **Alavieska** Finland
57 F3 **Alavus** Finland
24 B1 **Alawbum** Myanmar
12 E3 **Alawoona** *S. Australia* Australia
62 B1 **Alaw Res. resr** *Wales* U.K.
52 H3 **Alay r.** Rus. Fed.
47 H4 **Alaykuu** Kyrgyzstan
51 H7 **Alazani r.** Azerbaijan/Georgia
42 F3 **Al 'Azīzīyah** Iraq
118 B1 **Al 'Azīzīyah** Libya
82 D1 **Alb r.** Germany
79 M5 **Alba div.** Romania
106 C4 **Alba** Italy
109 F2 **Alba Adriatica** Italy
43 D1 **Al Bāb** Syria
103 B6 **Albacete div.** *Castilla - La Mancha* Spain
103 B5 **Albacete** *Albacete* Spain
12 E3 **Albacutya, L. l.** *Victoria* Australia
43 C5 **Al Bad'** Saudi Arabia
96 D2 **Alba de Tormes** Spain
42 F4 **Al Bādiyah al Janūbīyah h.** Iraq
55 C2 **Ålbæk Bugt b.** Denmark
47 L2 **Al'bagan, G. mt.** Rus. Fed.
43 C2 **Al Bahlūlīyah** Syria
103 C6 **Albaida** Spain
112 D1 **Alba Iulia** Romania
101 H2 **Albaladejo** Spain
102 C3 **Albalate de Arzobispo** Spain
102 D3 **Albalate de Cinca** Spain
99 H4 **Albalate de las Nogueras** Spain
93 E5 **Alban** France
101 H3 **Albánchez** Spain
138 F3 **Albanel, L. l.** *Québec* Canada
48 G4 **Albania country** Europe
109 J4 **Albano di Lucania** Italy
109 E3 **Albano Laziale** Italy
138 C3 **Albany r.** *Ontario* Canada
145 C6 **Albany** *Georgia* U.S.A.
148 E5 **Albany** *Indiana* U.S.A.
144 C4 **Albany** *Kentucky* U.S.A.
147 G3 **Albany** *New York* U.S.A.
152 B2 **Albany** *Oregon* U.S.A.
17 B7 **Albany** *Western Australia* Australia
159 □1 **Albany** Jamaica
103 E5 **Albarca, Cap d' pt** Spain
170 F3 **Albardão do João Maria coastal area** Brazil
118 E1 **Al Bardī** Libya
172 C1 **Albardón** Argentina
91 B4 **Albaret-Ste-Marie** France
90 D3 **Albarine r.** France
91 C5 **Albaron** France
102 B4 **Albarracín** Spain
100 D1 **Albarragena r.** Spain
42 F4 **Al Başrah div.** Iraq
42 F4 **Al Başrah** Iraq
103 B6 **Albatana** Spain
103 C6 **Albatera** Spain
15 E2 **Albatross Bay b.** *Queensland* Australia
9 □3 **Albatross Pt pt** *Antipodes Is* New Zealand
8 E3 **Albatross Pt pt** New Zealand
118 D1 **Al Bayḍā'** Libya
126 E2 **Al Bayda** Yemen
82 D1 **Albbruck** Germany
87 F4 **Albe r.** France
108 D2 **Albegna r.** Italy
102 D3 **Albelda** Spain
162 □ **Albemarle, Pta pt** *Galapagos Is* Ecuador
145 E5 **Albemarle Sd chan.** *N. Carolina* U.S.A.
106 C4 **Albenga** Italy
90 D3 **Albens** France
99 F4 **Alberche r.** Spain
165 E5 **Alberdi** Paraguay
12 C1 **Alberga watercourse** *S. Australia* Australia
12 C1 **Alberga** *S. Australia* Australia
59 G2 **Ålberga** Sweden
98 B4 **Albergaria-a-Velha** Portugal
106 A3 **Albergian, Monte mt.** Italy
111 G2 **Alberobello** Italy
107 G3 **Alberoni** Italy
72 E1 **Albersdorf** Germany
14 D3 **Albert r.** *Queensland* Australia
86 B3 **Albert** France
136 F4 **Alberta div.** Canada
146 E6 **Alberta** *Virginia* U.S.A.
136 F4 **Alberta, Mt mt.** *Alberta* Canada
173 G3 **Alberti** Argentina
130 C7 **Albertinia** South Africa
79 J4 **Albertirsa** Hungary
69 D3 **Albert Kanaal canal** Belgium
12 D3 **Albert, L. l.** *S. Australia* Australia
127 B4 **Albert, Lake l.** Uganda/Congo(Zaire)
150 E3 **Albert Lea** *Minnesota* U.S.A.
126 B4 **Albert Nile r.** Sudan/Uganda
171 B7 **Alberto de Agostini, Parque Nacional nat. park** Chile
131 G3 **Alberton** South Africa
131 E3 **Albertshoek** South Africa
159 □1 **Albert Town** Jamaica
90 E3 **Albertville** France
112 F1 **Albeşti** Romania
87 F4 **Albestroff** France
93 E5 **Albi** France
119 G3 **Al Bi'ār** Saudi Arabia
111 F3 **Albidona** Italy
93 D5 **Albigeois reg.** France
107 F3 **Albignasego** Italy
163 G2 **Albina** Surinam
106 D3 **Albino** Italy
154 A2 **Albion** *California* U.S.A.
147 J2 **Albion** *Maine* U.S.A.
148 E4 **Albion** *Michigan* U.S.A.
146 D3 **Albion** *New York* U.S.A.
119 G2 **Al Bi'r** Saudi Arabia
99 E2 **Albires** Spain
119 H4 **Al Birk** Saudi Arabia
87 H3 **Albisheim (Pfrimm)** Germany
106 C4 **Albisola Superiore** Italy
68 C3 **Alblasserdam** Netherlands
103 D4 **Albocácer** Spain
101 H3 **Alboloduy** Spain
108 B4 **Albo, Monte mountain range** *Sardegna* Italy
101 G5 **Alborán, Isla de i.** Spain
103 B5 **Alborea** Spain
55 B2 **Ålborg** Denmark
55 C3 **Ålborg Bugt b.** Denmark
101 H3 **Albox** Spain
136 F4 **Albreda** *B.C.* Canada
15 F4 **Albro** *Queensland* Australia
74 E4 **Albstadt** Germany
39 B4 **Al Budayyi** Bahrain
100 B3 **Albufeira** Portugal
100 A2 **Albufeira, Lagoa de lag.** Portugal
103 B7 **Albujón** Spain
42 E3 **Āl Bū Kamāl** Syria
119 H2 **Al Bukayrīyah** Saudi Arabia
83 E2 **Albula r.** Switzerland
83 E2 **Albula Alpen mountain range** Switzerland
101 G4 **Albuñol** Spain
153 F5 **Albuquerque** *New Mexico* U.S.A.
43 D2 **Al Burayj** Syria
41 J5 **Al Buraymī** Oman
109 H4 **Alburno, Monte mt.** Italy
100 D1 **Alburquerque** Spain
13 F4 **Albury** *New South Wales* Australia
42 D4 **Al Busayṭā' plain** Saudi Arabia
42 F4 **Al Buşayyah** Iraq
119 G3 **Al Buwayr** Saudi Arabia
90 E3 **Alby-sur-Chéran** France
164 B3 **Alca** Peru
100 B2 **Alcácer do Sal** Portugal
100 B2 **Alcáçovas r.** Portugal
100 B2 **Alcáçovas** Portugal
98 C5 **Alcafozes** Portugal
98 C5 **Alcains** Portugal
103 D4 **Alcalá de Chivert** Spain
100 E3 **Alcalá de Guadaira** Spain
102 C2 **Alcalá de Gurrea** Spain
99 G4 **Alcalá de Henares** Spain
103 C4 **Alcalá de la Selva** Spain
103 B5 **Alcalá del Júcar** Spain
100 E4 **Alcalá de los Gazules** Spain
101 E4 **Alcalá del Valle** Spain
101 G3 **Alcalá la Real** Spain
110 B5 **Alcamo** *Sicilia* Italy
102 C3 **Alcanadre r.** Spain
102 D4 **Alcanar** Spain
100 B1 **Alcanede** Portugal
100 B1 **Alcanena** Portugal
98 D3 **Alcañices** Spain
102 C3 **Alcañiz** Spain
100 D1 **Alcántara** Spain
100 B3 **Alcantarilha** Portugal
103 B7 **Alcantarilla** Spain
168 B2 **Alcantilado** Brazil
101 F2 **Alcaracejos** Spain
101 H2 **Alcaraz** Spain
101 H2 **Alcaraz, Sierra de mountain range** Spain
100 C3 **Alcaria do Cume h.** Portugal
100 C3 **Alcaria Ruiva h.** Portugal
100 C3 **Alcaria Ruiva** Portugal
100 C2 **Alcarrache r.** Portugal/Spain
102 D3 **Alcarràs** Spain
101 F3 **Alcaudete** Spain
99 F5 **Alcaudete de la Jara** Spain
100 D2 **Alcazaba r.** Spain
101 G1 **Alcázar de San Juan** Spain
63 E2 **Alcester** *England* U.K.
51 F5 **Alchevs'k** Ukraine
172 E2 **Alcira** Argentina
101 F1 **Alcoba** Spain
169 J2 **Alcobaça** Brazil
100 B1 **Alcobaça** Portugal

99 G4 **Alcobendas** Spain
99 H4 **Alcocer** Spain
100 B2 **Alcochete** Portugal
100 B1 **Alcoentre** Portugal
101 F3 **Alcolea** Spain
102 D3 **Alcolea de Cinca** Spain
99 H3 **Alcolea del Pinar** Spain
100 E3 **Alcolea del Río** Spain
100 E1 **Alcollarín** Spain
100 C2 **Alconchel** Spain
103 C4 **Alcora** Spain
99 G4 **Alcorcón** Spain
102 C4 **Alcorisa** Spain
99 H3 **Alcorlo, Emb. de resr** Spain
100 C1 **Alcorneo r.** Portugal/Spain
173 G2 **Alcorta** Argentina
103 D4 **Alcossebre** Spain
100 C3 **Alcoutim** Portugal
102 E3 **Alcover** Spain
103 C6 **Alcoy** Spain
102 C3 **Alcubierre** Spain
99 G3 **Alcubilla de Avellaneda** Spain
101 F2 **Alcudia r.** Spain
103 G5 **Alcúdia** Spain
101 G3 **Alcudia de Guadix** Spain
101 F2 **Alcudia, Sierra de mountain range** Spain
101 F2 **Alcudia, Valle de reg.** Spain
100 D1 **Alcuéscar** Spain
117 J6 **Aldabra Islands is** Seychelles
42 F3 **Al Daghghārah** Iraq
156 D2 **Aldama** *Chihuahua* Mexico
157 F4 **Aldama** *Tamaulipas* Mexico
45 P3 **Aldan r.** Rus. Fed.
45 O4 **Aldan** Rus. Fed.
65 H4 **Aldbrough** *England* U.K.
63 H2 **Alde r.** *England* U.K.
98 D3 **Aldeadávila de la Ribera** Spain
100 D1 **Aldea del Cano** Spain
99 F4 **Aldea del Fresno** Spain
101 G2 **Aldea del Rey** Spain
99 H3 **Aldealpozo** Spain
98 E4 **Aldeanueva del Camino** Spain
101 E1 **Aldeanueva de San Bartolomé** Spain
98 E3 **Aldearrodrigo** Spain
63 H2 **Aldeburgh** *England* U.K.
98 C4 **Aldeia de João Pires** Portugal
166 B2 **Aldeia Velha** Brazil
69 E4 **Aldenhoven** Germany
83 G3 **Aldeno** Italy
63 E4 **Alderholt** *England* U.K.
62 D1 **Alderley Edge** *England* U.K.
8 F2 **Aldermen Is, The is** New Zealand
63 □2 **Alderney i.** Channel Is.
154 B4 **Alder Peak summit** *California* U.S.A.
75 J4 **Aldersbach** Germany
63 F3 **Aldershot** *England* U.K.
146 C6 **Alderson** *W. Virginia* U.S.A.
112 C4 **Aldinci** Macedonia
65 E3 **Aldingham** *England* U.K.
80 C3 **Aldrans** Austria
93 A5 **Aldudes** France
148 B5 **Aledo** *Illinois* U.S.A.
120 B5 **Aleg** Mauritania
97 □ **Alegranza i.** *Canary Is* Spain
165 E3 **Alegre r.** Brazil
169 H4 **Alegre** *Espírito Santo* Brazil
167 C1 **Alegre** *Pará* Brazil
166 B1 **Alegre, Monte h.** Brazil
168 C2 **Alegre, Monte r.** Brazil
125 □ **Alegre, Pto pt** Sao Tome and Principe
167 A6 **Alegrete** Brazil
173 K2 **Alejandro Gallinal** Uruguay
172 F2 **Alejandro Roca** Argentina
172 D5 **Alejandro Stefenelli** Argentina
50 E2 **Alekhovshchina** Rus. Fed.
46 D4 **Aleksandra Bekovicha-Cherkassogo, Zaliv bay** Kazakhstan
52 E3 **Aleksandro-Nevskiy** Rus. Fed.
52 D1 **Aleksandrov** Rus. Fed.
112 C3 **Aleksandrovac** Yugoslavia
51 J5 **Aleksandrov Gay** Rus. Fed.
112 E3 **Aleksandrovo** Bulgaria
27 Q1 **Aleksandrovo-Sakhalinskiy** Rus. Fed.
51 H6 **Aleksandrovskoye** Rus. Fed.
77 H4 **Aleksandrów** Poland
76 G3 **Aleksandrów Kujawski** Poland
77 H4 **Aleksandrów Łódzki** Poland
47 L3 **Alekseyevka** Kazakhstan
47 H2 **Alekseyevka** Kazakhstan
47 G2 **Alekseyevka** Kazakhstan
47 J2 **Alekseyevka** Kazakhstan
51 F5 **Alekseyevka** Rus. Fed.
53 G1 **Alekseyevka** Rus. Fed.
52 H3 **Alekseyevka** Rus. Fed.
52 F4 **Alekseyevka** Rus. Fed.
52 E5 **Aleksin** Rus. Fed.
112 C3 **Aleksinac** Yugoslavia
52 D2 **Aleksino-Shatur** Rus. Fed.
59 G3 **Ålem** Sweden
157 F5 **Alemán, Presa, M. resr** Mexico
124 B4 **Alèmbé** Gabon
169 G4 **Além Paraíba** Brazil
56 C3 **Ålen** Norway
89 F3 **Alençon** France
90 B2 **Alène r.** France
100 A1 **Alenquer r.** Portugal
166 B1 **Alenquer** Brazil
100 B1 **Alenquer** Portugal
100 C2 **Alentejo reg.** Portugal
153 □2 **Alenuihaha Channel chan.** *Hawaii* U.S.A.
122 D5 **Alépé** Côte d'Ivoire
Aleppo *see* **Ḩalab**
108 B2 **Aléria** *Corse* France
135 M1 **Alert** *N.W.T.* Canada
164 B2 **Alerta** Peru
136 D4 **Alert Bay** *B.C.* Canada
108 A5 **Ales** *Sardegna* Italy
91 C4 **Alès** France
79 M4 **Aleşd** Romania
106 C4 **Alessandria div.** *Piemonte* Italy
106 C4 **Alessandria** *Alessandria* Italy
110 C5 **Alessandria della Rocca** *Sicilia* Italy
111 H3 **Alessano** Italy
55 B3 **Ålestrup** Denmark
56 B3 **Ålesund** Norway
82 C2 **Aletschhorn mt.** Switzerland
134 B4 **Aleutian Islands** *Alaska* U.S.A.
134 C4 **Aleutian Range mountain range** *Alaska* U.S.A.
178 D1 **Aleutian Trench sea feature** Pacific Ocean
45 R4 **Alevina, M. c.** Rus. Fed.
Alevisik *see* **Samandağı**
147 K2 **Alexander** *Maine* U.S.A.
134 E4 **Alexander Archipelago is** *Alaska* U.S.A.
130 A4 **Alexander B. b.** Namibia/South Africa
130 A4 **Alexander Bay** South Africa
145 C5 **Alexander City** *Alabama* U.S.A.
179 A2 **Alexander I. i.** Antarctica
14 E3 **Alexandra r.** *Queensland* Australia
13 F4 **Alexandra** *Victoria* Australia
9 B6 **Alexandra** New Zealand
171 □ **Alexandra, C. c.** *S. Georgia* Atlantic Ocean
114 D2 **Alexandreia** Greece
Alexandretta *see* **İskenderun**
148 E5 **Alexandria** *Indiana* U.S.A.
151 E6 **Alexandria** *Louisiana* U.S.A.
150 E2 **Alexandria** *Minnesota* U.S.A.
14 D3 **Alexandria** *Northern Terr.* Australia
141 H4 **Alexandria** *Ontario* Canada
66 D5 **Alexandria** *Scotland* U.K.
146 E5 **Alexandria** *Virginia* U.S.A.
119 E1 **Alexandria** Egypt
112 E3 **Alexandria** Romania
131 F6 **Alexandria** South Africa
147 E2 **Alexandria Bay** *New York* U.S.A.
12 D3 **Alexandrina, L. l.** *S. Australia* Australia
113 E4 **Alexandroupoli** Greece
139 J3 **Alexis r.** *Newfoundland* Canada
148 B5 **Alexis** *Illinois* U.S.A.
136 E4 **Alexis Creek** *B.C.* Canada
47 K2 **Aley r.** Rus. Fed.
43 C3 **'Āley** Lebanon
47 K2 **Aleysk** Rus. Fed.
74 C2 **Alf** Germany
103 C5 **Alfafar** Spain
98 D4 **Alfaiates** Portugal
102 C3 **Alfajarín** Spain
102 C4 **Alfambra r.** Spain
103 B3 **Alfambra** Portugal
102 B4 **Alfambra** Spain
98 D3 **Alfândéga da Fé** Portugal
102 D3 **Alfántega** Spain
98 B4 **Alfarelos** Portugal
102 B2 **Alfaro** Spain
102 D3 **Alfarràs** Spain
42 F4 **Al Farwānīyah** Kuwait
112 F3 **Alfatar** Bulgaria
42 E3 **Al Fatḩah** Iraq
42 G4 **Al Fāw** Iraq
126 D2 **Al Fāzih** Yemen
80 A2 **Alfdorf** Germany
109 G3 **Alfedena** Italy
115 C5 **Alfeios r.** Greece
100 A1 **Alfeizerão** Portugal
72 E4 **Alfeld (Leine)** Germany
169 F4 **Alfenas** Brazil
79 K4 **Alföld plain** Hungary
107 G4 **Alfonsine** Italy
63 G1 **Alford** *England* U.K.
147 H3 **Alfred** *Maine* U.S.A.
141 H4 **Alfred** *Ontario* Canada
169 H4 **Alfredo Chaves** Brazil
63 E1 **Alfreton** *England* U.K.
42 G4 **Al Fuḩayḩīl** Kuwait
39 D4 **Al-Fujayrah** U.A.E.
118 C2 **Al Fuqahā'** Libya
46 E3 **Alga** Kazakhstan
46 D2 **Algabas** Kazakhstan
58 A2 **Algård** Norway
101 F3 **Algarinejo** Spain
173 F5 **Algarroba** Argentina
172 B1 **Algarrobito** Chile
170 B2 **Algarrobo** *Atacama* Chile
172 B2 **Algarrobo** *Valparaiso* Chile
172 D4 **Algarrobo del Aguilla** Argentina
173 F6 **Algarrobo, S. del salt pan** Argentina
100 B3 **Algarve reg.** Portugal
52 E3 **Algasovo** Rus. Fed.
101 E4 **Algeciras** Spain
Algeciras, Bahía de b. *see* **Gibraltar, Bay of**
103 C5 **Algemesí** Spain
126 C1 **Algena** Eritrea
149 E3 **Alger** *Michigan* U.S.A.
121 E1 **Alger** Algeria
116 D3 **Algeria country** Africa
42 F4 **Al Ghammas** Iraq
41 H6 **Al Ghayḑah** Yemen
108 A4 **Alghero** *Sardegna* Italy
59 F3 **Älghult** Sweden
Algiers *see* **Alger**
103 C5 **Algimia de Alfara** Spain
103 C5 **Alginet** Spain
131 F6 **Algoa Bay b.** South Africa
101 E4 **Algodonales** Spain
99 G5 **Algodor r.** Spain
148 D3 **Algoma** *Wisconsin* U.S.A.
150 E3 **Algona** *Iowa* U.S.A.
149 F4 **Algonac** *Michigan* U.S.A.
141 F4 **Algonquin Park** *Ontario* Canada
141 F4 **Algonquin Provincial Park res.** *Ontario* Canada
99 H4 **Algora** Spain
173 J2 **Algorta** Uruguay
98 D3 **Algoso** Portugal
100 B3 **Algoz** Portugal
87 F3 **Algrange** France
24 A4 **Alguada Reef reef** Myanmar
102 D3 **Alguaire** Spain
119 H3 **Al Hadbah reg.** Saudi Arabia
39 B4 **Al Ḩadd** Bahrain
119 H2 **Al Ḩadhālīl plat.** Saudi Arabia
43 D2 **Al Ḩadīdīyah** Syria
42 E3 **Al Ḩadīthah** Iraq
43 D4 **Al Ḩadīthah** Saudi Arabia
42 E3 **Al Ḩaḑr** Iraq
119 H2 **Al Ḩafār well** Saudi Arabia
120 B3 **Al Haggounia** *Western Sahara*
101 G3 **Alhama r.** Spain
99 H3 **Alhama r.** Spain
42 D3 **Al Hamad plain** Jordan/Saudi Arabia
118 B2 **Al Ḩamādah al Ḩamrā' plat.** Libya
101 H4 **Alhama de Almería** Spain
101 G3 **Alhama de Granada** Spain
103 B7 **Alhama de Murcia** Spain
101 G2 **Alhambra** Spain
43 C2 **Al Ḩamīdīyah** Syria
101 H4 **Alhamilla, Sierra h.** Spain
42 F4 **Al Ḩammām well** Iraq
120 C3 **Al Hamra watercourse** *Western Sahara*
43 D2 **Al Ḩamrāt** Syria
119 H3 **Al Ḩanākīyah** Saudi Arabia
119 J2 **Al Ḩanbalī plain** Saudi Arabia
119 G1 **Al Ḩarrah h.** Saudi Arabia
118 C2 **Al Harūj al Aswad mountain range** Libya
42 E2 **Al Ḩasakah** Syria
42 F3 **Al Hāshimīyah** Iraq
119 J2 **Al Ḩatīfah plain** Saudi Arabia
101 F4 **Alhaurín de la Torre** Spain
119 H3 **Al Ḩawīyah** Saudi Arabia
119 G2 **Al Hawja'** Saudi Arabia
42 F3 **Al Ḩayy** Iraq
43 D5 **Al Hazm** Saudi Arabia
42 F3 **Al Ḩillah** Iraq
39 B4 **Al Ḩinnāh** Saudi Arabia
43 D4 **Al Ḩinw mt.** Saudi Arabia
43 C5 **Al Ḩismā plain** Saudi Arabia
120 D1 **Al Hoceima** Morocco
96 E5 **Al Hoceima, Baie d' b.** Morocco
99 H4 **Alhóndiga** Spain
126 D2 **Al Hudaydah** Yemen
119 G2 **Al Ḩufrah reg.** Saudi Arabia
39 B4 **Al Hufuf** Saudi Arabia
43 C5 **Al Ḩumayḑah** Saudi Arabia
126 E2 **Al Ḩumayshah** Yemen
39 B4 **Al Ḩunayy** Saudi Arabia
43 D2 **Al Ḩuwayz** Syria
111 E4 **Alì** *Sicilia* Italy
36 D2 **Ali** China
110 C5 **Alia** *Sicilia* Italy
101 E1 **Alía** Spain
39 E3 **'Alīābād** Iran
39 C1 **Alīābad** Iran
39 C1 **Alīābād** Iran
39 C3 **Alīābad** Iran
102 C4 **Aliaga** Spain
42 A2 **Aliağa** Turkey
114 D2 **Aliakmonas r.** Greece
42 F3 **'Alī al Gharbī** Iraq
109 J4 **Aliano** Italy
115 E4 **Aliartos** Greece
38 A2 **Alībāg** India
36 B4 **Ali Bandar** Pakistan
42 G2 **Äli Bayramlı** Azerbaijan
113 F5 **Alibey Adası i.** Turkey
123 E4 **Alibori r.** Benin
112 C2 **Alibunar** Yugoslavia
103 C6 **Alicante airport** Spain
103 C6 **Alicante div.** *Valencia* Spain
103 C6 **Alicante** *Alicante* Spain
103 C6 **Alicante, Bahía de b.** Spain
15 E2 **Alice r.** *Queensland* Australia
15 F4 **Alice watercourse** *Queensland* Australia
15 F4 **Alice** *Queensland* Australia
151 D7 **Alice** *Texas* U.S.A.
131 F6 **Alice** South Africa
136 D3 **Alice Arm** *B.C.* Canada
131 F6 **Alicedale** South Africa
111 G3 **Alice, Punta pt** Italy
158 C3 **Alice Shoal sea feature** Caribbean
14 C4 **Alice Springs** *Northern Terr.* Australia
158 C1 **Alice Town** The Bahamas
47 H5 **Alichur** Tajikistan
173 F1 **Alicia** Argentina
23 B5 **Alicia** Philippines
15 E4 **Alick Cr. r.** *Queensland* Australia
110 D4 **Alicudi, Isola i.** Italy
103 C3 **Alicún de Ortega** Spain
109 G3 **Alife** Italy
36 D4 **Aligarh** India
98 C3 **Alijó** Portugal
126 □ **Al Ikhwān is** *Socotra* Yemen
52 H2 **Alikovo** Rus. Fed.
124 C4 **Alima r.** Congo
110 D5 **Alimena** *Sicilia* Italy
115 □ **Alimia i.** Greece
98 C2 **A Limia reg.** Spain
124 D2 **Alindao** Central African Rep.
22 D2 **Alindau** Indonesia
39 G2 **Alinghar r.** Afghanistan
59 E3 **Alingsås** Sweden
113 G5 **Aliova r.** Turkey
37 G4 **Alipur Duar** India
146 C4 **Aliquippa** *Pennsylvania* U.S.A.
126 D2 **Ali Sabieh** Djibouti
43 D4 **'Al 'Īsāwīyah** Saudi Arabia
100 D1 **Aliseda** Spain
153 E6 **Alisos r.** Mexico
98 D3 **Aliste r.** Spain
111 E4 **Alì Terme** *Sicilia* Italy
115 F4 **Aliveri** Greece
131 F5 **Aliwal North** South Africa
136 G4 **Alix** *Alberta* Canada
36 B2 **Alizai** Pakistan
118 D1 **Al Jabal al Akhḑar mts** Libya
39 B4 **Al Jāfūrah desert** Saudi Arabia
118 D2 **Al Jaghbūb** Libya
42 F4 **Al Jahrah** Kuwait
39 B4 **Al Jamalīyah** Qatar
Al Jauf *see* **Al Jawf**
118 D3 **Al Jawf** Libya
42 D4 **Al Jawf** Saudi Arabia
118 B1 **Al Jawsh** Libya
42 E3 **Al Jazīrah reg.** Iraq/Syria
39 B4 **Al Jībān reg.** Saudi Arabia
42 F4 **Al Jil well** Iraq
119 H2 **Al Jilh escarpment** Saudi Arabia
39 B4 **Al Jishshah** Saudi Arabia
119 H2 **Al Jithāmīyah** Saudi Arabia
39 B4 **Al Jubayl** Saudi Arabia
100 D1 **Aljucén r.** Spain
100 D1 **Aljucén** Spain
118 C2 **Al Jufra Oasis oasis** Libya
119 G3 **Al Jumūm** Saudi Arabia
119 H3 **Al Junaynah** Saudi Arabia
39 B4 **Al Jurayd i.** Saudi Arabia
100 B3 **Aljustrel** Portugal
43 D3 **Al Juwayf depression** Syria
43 D5 **Al Kabid waterhole** Jordan
154 D2 **Alkali Flat salt flat** *Nevada* U.S.A.
154 D1 **Alkali Flat salt flat** *Nevada* U.S.A.
155 E1 **Alkali Flat salt flat** *Nevada* U.S.A.
123 G4 **Alkamari** Niger
69 D4 **Alken** Belgium
41 J5 **Al Khābūrah** Oman
119 H2 **Al Khaḑrā' well** Saudi Arabia
119 H3 **Al Khafqān salt pan** Saudi Arabia
42 F3 **Al Khālis** Iraq
126 D1 **Al Kharāb** Yemen
39 D4 **Al Khaşab** Oman
119 H3 **Al Khāşirah** Saudi Arabia
39 B4 **Al Khawr** Qatar
39 B4 **Al Khişāh well** Saudi Arabia
118 D3 **Al Khufrah** Libya
118 D3 **Al Khufrah Oasis oasis** Libya
118 B1 **Al Khums** Libya
43 C3 **Al Khushnīyah** Syria
39 B4 **Al Kir'ānah** Qatar
43 D3 **Al Kiswah** Syria
68 C2 **Alkmaar** Netherlands
68 C2 **Alkmaardermeer l.** Netherlands
42 F3 **Al Kūfah** Iraq
119 H2 **Al Kuhayfīyah** Saudi Arabia
42 F3 **Al Kumayt** Iraq
42 F3 **Al Kūt** Iraq
42 F4 **Al Kuwayt** Kuwait
119 H2 **Al Labbah plain** Saudi Arabia
42 C3 **Al Lādhiqīyah** Syria
147 J1 **Allagash r.** *Maine* U.S.A.
147 J1 **Allagash** *Maine* U.S.A.
147 J1 **Allagash Lake l.** *Maine* U.S.A.
37 E4 **Allahabad** India
86 B3 **Allaines** France
88 C4 **Allaire** France
43 D3 **Al Lajā lava** Syria
45 P3 **Allakh-Yun'** Rus. Fed.
91 C4 **Allan** France
92 E3 **Allanche** France
24 A3 **Allanmyo** Myanmar
131 F3 **Allanridge** South Africa
52 D1 **Allariz** Spain
87 G4 **Allarmont** France
92 D3 **Allassac** France
91 D5 **Allauch** France
131 G1 **Alldays** South Africa
82 C1 **Alle** Switzerland
148 E4 **Allegan** *Michigan* U.S.A.
107 G2 **Alleghe** Italy
146 D4 **Allegheny r.** *Pennsylvania* U.S.A.
146 C6 **Allegheny Mountains mountain range** U.S.A.
146 D4 **Allegheny Reservoir resr** *New York/Pennsylvania* U.S.A.
91 B3 **Allègre** France
159 □5 **Allègre, Pte pt** *Guadeloupe* Caribbean
91 D5 **Alleins** France
131 F4 **Allemanskraaldam resr** South Africa
82 B3 **Allemond** France
172 D5 **Allen** Argentina
145 D5 **Allendale** *S. Carolina* U.S.A.
65 F3 **Allendale Town** *England* U.K.
157 E2 **Allende** *Coahuila* Mexico
157 E3 **Allende** *Nuevo León* Mexico
72 D4 **Allendorf (Eder)** Germany
74 D2 **Allendorf (Lumda)** Germany
140 E4 **Allenford** *Ontario* Canada
65 F3 **Allenheads** *England* U.K.
67 C2 **Allen, Lough l.** Rep. of Ireland
9 A7 **Allen, Mt h.** New Zealand
83 E1 **Allensbach** Germany
147 F4 **Allentown** *Pennsylvania* U.S.A.
81 G2 **Allentsteig** Austria
38 B4 **Alleppey** India
102 C4 **Allepuz** Spain
72 F3 **Aller r.** Germany
90 C2 **Allerey-sur-Saône** France
75 G3 **Allersberg** Germany
75 G4 **Allershausen** Germany
91 E3 **Allevard** France
91 C4 **Allex** France
74 F5 **Allgäu reg.** Germany
80 B3 **Allgäuer Alpen mountain range** Austria/Germany
59 F3 **Allgunnen l.** Sweden
163 G2 **Allianc** Surinam
150 C3 **Alliance** *Nebraska* U.S.A.
146 C4 **Alliance** *Ohio* U.S.A.
90 B2 **Allier div.** *Auvergne* France
90 B2 **Allier r.** France
159 □1 **Alligator Pond** Jamaica
55 C3 **Allingåbro** Denmark
82 B2 **Allinges** France
55 □2 **Allinge-Sandvig** Denmark
147 F4 **Alliston** *Ontario* Canada
119 H3 **Al Līth** Saudi Arabia
74 E4 **Allmendingen** Germany
99 H2 **Allo** Spain
66 E4 **Alloa** *Scotland* U.K.
89 F4 **Allonnes** *Maine-et-Loire* France
89 F4 **Allonnes** *Sarthe* France
93 B4 **Allons** France
15 H5 **Allora** *Queensland* Australia
92 C2 **Alloue** France
131 G5 **All Saints Nek pass** South Africa
82 C1 **Allschwil** Switzerland
73 G4 **Allstedt** Germany
22 D3 **Allu** Indonesia
126 D1 **Al Luḩayyah** Yemen
108 D2 **Allumiere** Italy
38 C3 **Allur** India
38 C3 **Alluru Kottapatnam** India
42 E4 **Al Lussuf well** Iraq
90 B1 **Alluy** France
148 E4 **Alma** *Michigan* U.S.A.
150 D3 **Alma** *Nebraska* U.S.A.
155 H5 **Alma** *New Mexico* U.S.A.
141 K2 **Alma** *Québec* Canada
Alma Ata *see* **Almaty**
42 E4 **Al Ma'ānīyah** Iraq
102 D3 **Almacelles** Spain
100 A2 **Almada** Portugal
43 D5 **Al Madāfi' plat.** Saudi Arabia
126 D1 **Al Maḑāyā** Saudi Arabia
15 F3 **Almaden** *Queensland* Australia
101 F2 **Almadén** Spain
100 D3 **Almadén de la Plata** Spain
169 J1 **Almadina** Brazil
119 G3 **Al Madīnah** Saudi Arabia
172 E2 **Almafuerte** Argentina
101 G2 **Almagro** Spain
119 H3 **Al Maḩāwiyah** Saudi Arabia
120 C3 **Al Mahbas** *Western Sahara*
119 G2 **Al Maḩiā depression** Saudi Arabia
99 H3 **Almajano** Spain
119 J2 **Al Majma'ah** Saudi Arabia
39 B4 **Al Malsūnīyah reg.** Saudi Arabia
47 G4 **Almalyk** Uzbekistan
39 B4 **Al Manāmah** Bahrain
154 B1 **Almanor, Lake l.** *California* U.S.A.
103 B6 **Almansa** Spain
100 B3 **Almansil** Portugal
99 E2 **Almanza** Spain
99 E4 **Almanzor mt.** Spain
101 H3 **Almanzora r.** Spain
119 H4 **Al Ma'qaş** Saudi Arabia
42 F4 **Al Ma'qil** Iraq
99 F4 **Almar r.** Spain
126 D2 **Al Marāwi'ah** Yemen
98 E5 **Almaraz** Spain
101 E3 **Almargen** Spain
118 D1 **Al Marj** Libya
99 H3 **Almarza** Spain
166 C3 **Almas r.** Brazil
166 C3 **Almas** Brazil
79 M5 **Almaş** Romania
79 H4 **Almásfüzitő** Hungary
168 D1 **Almas, R. das r.** Brazil
103 C5 **Almassora** Spain
47 J4 **Almaty div.** Kazakhstan
47 J4 **Almaty** Kazakhstan
42 E2 **Al Mawşil** Iraq
99 H3 **Almazán** Spain
45 N3 **Almaznyy** Rus. Fed.
101 H2 **Almedina** Spain
103 C5 **Almedinilla** Spain
98 D4 **Almeida** Portugal
98 D3 **Almeida de Sayago** Spain
166 B1 **Almeirim** Brazil
100 B1 **Almeirim** Portugal
68 E2 **Almelo** Netherlands
169 H2 **Almenara** Brazil
103 C5 **Almenara** Spain
101 H2 **Almenaras mt.** Spain
103 B7 **Almenara, Sierra de la h.** Spain
99 H3 **Almenar de Soria** Spain
100 D2 **Almendral** Spain
100 D2 **Almendralejo** Spain
68 D2 **Almere** Netherlands
101 H4 **Almería airport** Spain
101 H3 **Almería div.** *Andalucia* Spain
101 H4 **Almería** *Almeria* Spain
101 H4 **Almería, Golfo de b.** Spain
101 H4 **Almerimar** Spain
46 D2 **Al'met'yevsk** Rus. Fed.
59 F3 **Älmhult** Sweden
101 G4 **Almijara, Sierra de mountain range** Spain
101 E5 **Almina, Pta pt** *Ceuta* Spain
55 B4 **Almind** Denmark
171 C7 **Almirantazgo, S. del chan.** Chile
156 K7 **Almirante** Panama
39 B3 **Al Mish'āb** Saudi Arabia
42 D3 **Al Mismīyah** Syria
100 E4 **Almodôvar r.** Spain
100 B3 **Almodôvar** Portugal
101 F2 **Almodóvar del Campo** Spain
103 B5 **Almodóvar del Pinar** Spain
101 F4 **Almogía** Spain
99 H4 **Almoguera** Spain
100 D1 **Almoharín** Spain
99 H4 **Almonacid del Zorita** Spain
66 E4 **Almond r.** *Scotland* U.K.
149 F4 **Almont** *Michigan* U.S.A.
100 D1 **Almonte r.** Spain
141 G4 **Almonte** *Ontario* Canada
100 D3 **Almonte** Spain
36 D3 **Almora** India
103 C6 **Almoradí** Spain
99 F4 **Almorox** Spain
100 B1 **Almoster r.** Portugal
123 E3 **Almoustarat** Mali
59 H2 **Älmsta** Sweden
39 B4 **Al Mubarrez** Saudi Arabia
119 G2 **Al Mudarraj** Saudi Arabia
42 C4 **Al Mudawwara** Jordan
103 B6 **Almudema** Spain
102 C2 **Almudévar** Spain
39 B4 **Al Muharraq** Bahrain
43 D5 **Al Muḩtaṭab depression** Saudi Arabia
41 G7 **Al Mukallā** Yemen
126 D2 **Al Mukhā** Yemen
118 D1 **Al Mukhaylī** Libya
101 G4 **Almuñécar** Spain
59 H2 **Almunge** Sweden
81 E3 **Almünster** Austria
42 F3 **Al Muqdādīyah** Iraq
101 G2 **Almuradiel** Spain
100 C1 **Almuro r.** Portugal
119 G2 **Al Murūt well** Saudi Arabia
119 G3 **Al Musayjīd** Saudi Arabia
42 F3 **Al Musayyib** Iraq
42 F4 **Al Muthannā div.** Iraq
119 H3 **Al Muwayh** Saudi Arabia
59 G3 **Almvik** Sweden
115 F4 **Almyropotamos** Greece
113 D5 **Almyros** Greece
153 □1 **Alna Haina** *Hawaii* U.S.A.
65 G2 **Alnwick** *England* U.K.
54 D3 **Aloja** Latvia
54 F3 **Alolya r.** Rus. Fed.
24 A2 **Alon** Myanmar
37 H3 **Along** India
30 G2 **Alongshan** China
114 E3 **Alonnisos i.** Greece
114 E3 **Alonnisos** Greece
168 C6 **Alonso r.** Brazil
21 H8 **Alor i.** Indonesia
101 F4 **Álora** Spain
25 C6 **Alor Setar** Malaysia
102 E2 **Alós d'Ensil** Spain
100 C3 **Alosno** Spain
Alost *see* **Aalst**
36 C5 **Alot** India
6 □1 **Alotau** P.N.G.
92 B2 **Alouettes, Mont des h.** France
90 C1 **Aloxe-Corton** France
17 E5 **Aloysius, Mt mt.** *Western Australia* Australia
101 F4 **Alozaina** Spain
102 E2 **Alp** Spain
172 F4 **Alpachiri** Argentina
172 E2 **Alpa Corral** Argentina
154 C4 **Alpaugh** *California* U.S.A.
98 C4 **Alpedrinha** Portugal
68 E3 **Alpen** Germany
149 F3 **Alpena** *Michigan* U.S.A.
87 G2 **Alpenrod** Germany
103 B6 **Alpera** Spain
166 C2 **Alpercatas r.** Brazil
91 E4 **Alpes-de-Haute-Provence div.** France
91 D4 **Alpes du Dauphiné mts** France
91 F5 **Alpes-Maritimes div.** France
91 E4 **Alpes Maritimes mountain range** France/Italy
15 F4 **Alpha** *Queensland* Australia
69 C3 **Alphen** Netherlands
68 C2 **Alphen aan den Rijn** Netherlands
106 E4 **Alpi Apuane mountain range** Italy
100 B1 **Alpiarça** Portugal
106 A4 **Alpi Cozie mountain range** France/Italy
107 F2 **Alpi Dolomitiche mountain range** Italy
83 D2 **Alpi Lepontine mountain range** Italy/Switzerland
91 C5 **Alpilles h.** France
155 H5 **Alpine** *Arizona* U.S.A.
151 C6 **Alpine** *Texas* U.S.A.
152 E3 **Alpine** *Wyoming* U.S.A.
169 E4 **Alpinópolis** Brazil
106 D2 **Alpi Orobie mountain range** Italy
82 C3 **Alpi Pennine mountain range** Italy/Switzerland
87 H4 **Alpirsbach** Germany
83 D2 **Alpnach** Switzerland
94 E2 **Alps** Europe
41 G6 **Al Qa'āmīyāt reg.** Saudi Arabia
118 C1 **Al Qaddāḩīyah** Libya
42 F4 **Al Qādisīyah div.** Iraq
43 D2 **Al Qadmūs** Syria
119 H3 **Al Qā'īyah** Saudi Arabia
119 G2 **Al Qalībah** Saudi Arabia
42 E2 **Al Qāmishlī** Syria
119 H4 **Al Qarḩah** Saudi Arabia
43 D4 **Al Qarqar** Saudi Arabia
43 D2 **Al Qaryatayn** Syria
118 B1 **Al Qaşabāt** Libya
39 B4 **Al Qaţīf** Saudi Arabia
41 G6 **Al Qaţn** Yemen
118 B3 **Al Qaţrūn** Libya
119 H2 **Al Qāyşūmah well** Saudi Arabia
103 C6 **Alquería de la Condesa** Spain
43 C3 **Al Qunayţirah div.** Syria
43 C3 **Al Qunayţirah** Syria
119 H4 **Al Qunfidhah** Saudi Arabia
119 H3 **Al Qurayn** Saudi Arabia
126 D2 **Al Qurayyah** Yemen
42 F4 **Al Qurnah** Iraq
43 D2 **Al 'Quşayr** Syria
43 D3 **Al Quţayfah** Syria
63 E2 **Alrewas** *England* U.K.
55 C4 **Alrø i.** Denmark
14 D3 **Alroy Downs** *Northern Terr.* Australia
55 B4 **Als i.** Denmark
55 C3 **Als** Denmark
87 G4 **Alsace div.** France
62 D1 **Alsager** *England* U.K.
137 H4 **Alsask** *Saskatchewan* Canada
99 H2 **Alsasua** Spain
74 B2 **Alsdorf** Germany
74 C3 **Alsenz** Germany
74 E2 **Alsfeld** Germany
55 B4 **Als Fjord inlet** Denmark
52 G3 **Al'shanka** Rus. Fed.
173 H2 **Alsina** Argentina
73 G4 **Alsleben** Germany
59 E3 **Alsterbro** Sweden
65 F3 **Alston** *England* U.K.
54 B3 **Alsunga** Latvia
54 E3 **Alsviķi** Latvia
56 F1 **Alta** Norway
83 G2 **Altacroce, Monte mt.** Italy
56 F1 **Altaelva r.** Norway
172 E1 **Alta Gracia** Argentina
162 C1 **Altagracia** Venezuela
159 F5 **Altagracia de Orituco** Venezuela
26 E2 **Altai Mountains mountain range** Asia
145 D6 **Altamaha r.** *Georgia* U.S.A.
166 B1 **Altamira** Brazil
170 C2 **Altamira** Chile
162 B3 **Altamira** Colombia
156 J7 **Altamira** Costa Rica
173 H3 **Altamirano** Argentina
101 E1 **Altamira, Sierra de mountain range** Spain
102 F2 **Alt Amporda reg.** Spain
9 B6 **Alta, Mt mt.** New Zealand
109 J4 **Altamura** France
30 D2 **Altan** Rus. Fed.
30 C3 **Altanbulag** Mongolia
30 C2 **Altanbulag** Mongolia
156 C2 **Altar** Mexico
156 D3 **Altata** Mexico
81 E3 **Altaussee** Austria
109 G4 **Altavilla Irpina** Italy
109 H4 **Altavilla Silentina** Italy
146 D6 **Altavista** *Virginia* U.S.A.
47 L3 **Altay** China
30 A3 **Altay** Mongolia
47 L2 **Altay, Respublika div.** Rus. Fed.
47 L2 **Altayskiy** Rus. Fed.
47 K2 **Altayskiy Kray div.** Rus. Fed.
75 H4 **Altdorf** Germany
83 D2 **Altdorf** Switzerland
75 G3 **Altdorf bei Nürnberg** Germany
103 C6 **Altea** Spain
73 J1 **Altefähr** Germany
56 F1 **Alteidet** Norway
72 C4 **Altena** Germany
69 E4 **Altenahr** Germany
72 F4 **Altenau** Germany
75 J2 **Altenberg** Germany
72 C3 **Altenberge** Germany
75 H2 **Altenburg** Germany
87 G3 **Altenglan** Germany
72 F1 **Altenholz** Germany
73 J1 **Altenkirchen** Germany
75 H4 **Altenmarkt an der Alz** Germany
81 G2 **Altenmarkt an der Triesting** Austria
81 F3 **Altenmarkt bei St Gallen** Austria
73 F2 **Altenmedingen** Germany
80 B2 **Altenmünster** Germany
37 H1 **Altenqoke** China
74 F4 **Altenstadt** *Baden-Württemberg* Germany
83 F1 **Altenstadt** *Bayern* Germany
74 D2 **Altenstadt** *Hessen* Germany
74 D4 **Altensteig** Germany
73 J2 **Altentreptow** Germany
73 K3 **Alte Oder r.** Germany
100 C1 **Alter do Chão** Portugal
80 D2 **Altfraunhofen** Germany
80 E2 **Altheim** Austria
91 B4 **Altier r.** France
91 B4 **Altier** France
39 G2 **Altimur P. pass** Afghanistan
113 F5 **Altınoluk** Turkey
168 E4 **Altinópolis** Brazil
113 F5 **Altınova** Turkey
42 B2 **Altıntaş** Turkey
172 C6 **Altiplanicie de Hakelhuincul plat.** Argentina
172 C4 **Altiplanicie del Payún Matru plat.** Argentina
164 C3 **Altiplano plain** Bolivia
83 G2 **Altissima, l' mt.** Austria/Italy
90 F1 **Altkirch** France
75 G4 **Altmannstein** Germany
73 G3 **Altmark reg.** Germany
75 G4 **Altmühl r.** Germany
66 D2 **Altnaharra** *Scotland* U.K.
173 F2 **Alto Alegre** Argentina
168 B2 **Alto Araguaia** Brazil
125 C6 **Alto Chicapa** Angola
99 H3 **Alto Cruz mt.** Spain
102 B3 **Alto del Moncayo mt.** Spain
172 D2 **Alto de Pencoso h.** Argentina
158 C5 **Alto de Quimari mt.** Colombia
101 G3 **Alto de San Juan mt.** Spain
110 C4 **Altofonte** *Sicilia* Italy
168 B2 **Alto Garças** Brazil
166 D2 **Alto Longá** Brazil
129 F2 **Alto Molócuè** Mozambique
111 F3 **Altomonte** Italy
75 G4 **Altomünster** Germany
63 F3 **Alton** *England* U.K.
144 B4 **Alton** *Illinois* U.S.A.
151 F4 **Alton** *Missouri* U.S.A.
147 H3 **Alton** *New Hampshire* U.S.A.
150 D1 **Altona** *Manitoba* Canada
12 D1 **Alton Downs** *S. Australia* Australia
146 D4 **Altoona** *Pennsylvania* U.S.A.
166 B1 **Alto Pacajá r.** Brazil
166 C2 **Alto Parnaíba** Brazil
107 E5 **Altopascio** Italy
164 B2 **Alto Purús r.** Peru
98 C3 **Alto Rabagão, Barragem do resr** Portugal
169 G4 **Alto Rio Doce** Brazil
168 B3 **Alto Rio Verde** Brazil
102 D3 **Altorricón** Spain
166 D2 **Altos** Brazil
99 H4 **Altos de Cabrejas mountain range** Spain
103 B6 **Altos de Chinchilla mountain range** Spain
173 F1 **Altos de Chipión** Argentina
168 B3 **Alto Sucuriú** Brazil
99 G2 **Altotero mt.** Spain
75 H4 **Altötting** Germany
158 □1 **Alto Vista h.** *Aruba* Caribbean
69 E5 **Altrich** Germany
65 F4 **Altrincham** *England* U.K.
73 H3 **Alt Ruppin** Germany
74 E5 **Altshausen** Germany
83 E1 **Altstätten** Switzerland
52 B3 **Altukhovo** Rus. Fed.
157 H5 **Altun Ha** Belize
26 E4 **Altun Shan mountain range** China
103 C5 **Altura** Spain
152 B3 **Alturas** *California* U.S.A.
151 D5 **Altus** *Oklahoma* U.S.A.
74 F5 **Altusried** Germany
46 F3 **Altynasar** Kazakhstan
53 E1 **Altynivka** Ukraine
52 H2 **Altyshevo** Rus. Fed.
54 D2 **Alu** Estonia
42 D1 **Alucra** Turkey
54 E3 **Alūksne** Latvia
119 G2 **Al 'Ulā** Saudi Arabia
126 E2 **Al'ulah reg.** Yemen
146 B4 **Alum Creek Lake l.** *Ohio* U.S.A.
172 B5 **Aluminé r.** Argentina
172 B5 **Aluminé** Argentina
172 B5 **Aluminé, L. l.** Argentina
59 H1 **Alunda** Sweden
51 E6 **Alupka** Ukraine
118 C1 **Al 'Uqaylah** Libya
39 B4 **Al 'Uqayr** Saudi Arabia
119 G2 **Al Urayq desert** Saudi Arabia
51 E6 **Alushta** Ukraine
102 B4 **Alustante** Spain
43 D5 **Al Uthaylī** Saudi Arabia
39 B4 **Al 'Uthmānīyah** Saudi Arabia
118 D3 **Al 'Uwaynāt** Libya
118 B2 **Al 'Uwaynāt** Libya
119 G2 **Al 'Uwaynidhīyah i.** Saudi Arabia
119 H1 **Al 'Uwayqīlah** Saudi Arabia
119 H2 **Al 'Uyūn** Saudi Arabia
119 G3 **Al 'Uyūn** Saudi Arabia
98 B4 **Alva r.** Portugal
151 D4 **Alva** *Oklahoma* U.S.A.
98 B5 **Alvaiázere** Portugal
100 B3 **Alvalade** Portugal
83 E2 **Alvaneu** Switzerland
59 E3 **Älvängen** Sweden
157 G5 **Alvarado** Mexico
163 E4 **Alvarães** Brazil
98 B4 **Alvares** Portugal
173 G2 **Alvarez** Argentina
56 C3 **Alvdal** Norway
59 F1 **Älvdalen** Sweden
98 B1 **Alvedro airport** Spain
62 D2 **Alveley** *England* U.K.
100 A2 **Alverca** Portugal
69 A3 **Alveringem** Belgium
59 F3 **Alvesta** Sweden
93 D4 **Alvignac** France
58 B1 **Ålvik** Norway
151 E6 **Alvin** *Texas* U.S.A.
169 G4 **Alvinópolis** Brazil
100 C2 **Alvito, Barragem do resr** Portugal
59 G1 **Älvkarleby** Sweden

100 B3 Alvor Portugal
58 A1 Alvøy i. Norway
59 E2 Älvsborg div. Sweden
56 F2 Älvsbyn Sweden
59 E3 Älvsered Sweden
119 G2 Al Wajh Saudi Arabia
39 B4 Al Wakrah Qatar
39 B4 Al Wannān Saudi Arabia
119 J2 Al Waqbá well Saudi Arabia
36 D4 Alwar India
38 B4 Alwaye India
62 C1 Alwen Res. resr *Wales* U.K.
42 E4 Al Widyān desert Iraq/Saudi Arabia
118 B3 Al Wīgh Libya
119 H2 Al Wusayṭ well Saudi Arabia
30 B5 Alxa Youqi China
30 C5 Alxa Zuoqi China
14 D2 Alyangula *Northern Terr.* Australia
114 F2 Alyki Greece
114 C3 Alyki Greece
66 E4 Alyth *Scotland* U.K.
54 D4 Alytus Lithuania
75 H4 Alz r. Germany
152 F2 Alzada *Montana* U.S.A.
173 H4 Alzaga Argentina
83 E3 Alzano Lombardo Italy
69 E5 Alzette r. Luxembourg
74 D3 Alzey Germany
103 C5 Alzira Spain
91 B5 Alzon France
93 E5 Alzonne France
131 F6 Amabele South Africa
162 C4 Amacayacu, Parque Nacional nat. park Colombia
124 C3 Amada Gaza Central African Rep.
14 B5 Amadeus, Lake salt flat *Northern Terr.* Australia
42 E2 Amādīyah Iraq
135 M3 Amadjuak Lake l. *N.W.T.* Canada
155 G6 Amado *Arizona* U.S.A.
100 A2 Amadora Portugal
121 F4 Amadror plain Algeria
55 E4 Amager i. Denmark
28 C7 Amagi Japan
69 C5 Amagne France
163 F2 Amaila Falls waterfall Guyana
28 C7 Amakusa-Kami-shima i. Japan
28 B7 Amakusa-nada b. Japan
28 C7 Amakusa-Shimo-shima i. Japan
59 E2 Åmål Sweden
38 C2 Amalapuram India
162 B2 Amalfi Colombia
109 G4 Amalfi Italy
131 E3 Amalia South Africa
115 C5 Amaliada Greece
36 C5 Amalner India
21 L7 Amamapare Indonesia
168 A5 Amambaí r. Brazil
168 A5 Amambaí Brazil
27 N6 Amami-guntō is Japan
27 N6 Amami-Ōshima i. Japan
124 E4 Amamula Congo(Zaire)
163 E4 Amanã, Lago l. Brazil
90 D1 Amance r. France
82 B1 Amance France
90 E1 Amancey France
109 F2 Amandola Italy
46 E3 Amangel'dy Kazakhstan
47 G2 Amangel'dy Kazakhstan
47 K4 Amankol China
59 G2 Åmänningen l. Sweden
111 F3 Amantea Italy
7 □10 Amanu i. *French Polynesia* Pacific Ocean
128 D2 Amanzamnyama r. Zimbabwe
131 H5 Amanzimtoti South Africa
163 G3 Amapá div. Brazil
163 G3 Amapá Brazil
163 G3 Amapari r. Brazil
119 F3 Amara Sudan
129 F1 Amaramba, Lagoa l. Mozambique
166 D2 Amarante Brazil
166 C2 Amarante do Maranhão Brazil
114 C3 Amaranto Greece
24 B2 Amarapura Myanmar
30 C3 Amardalay Mongolia
100 C2 Amareleja Portugal
98 B3 Amares Portugal
172 E5 Amarga, L. La l. Argentina
154 D3 Amargosa Desert desert *Nevada* U.S.A.
154 D3 Amargosa Range mts *California* U.S.A.
154 D3 Amargosa Valley *Nevada* U.S.A.
101 G1 Amarguillo r. Spain
54 D2 Ämari Estonia
151 C5 Amarillo *Texas* U.S.A.
172 B2 Amarillo, Co mt. Argentina
109 G2 Amaro, Monte mt. Italy
36 E4 Amarpatan India
115 E4 Amarynthos Greece
109 F3 Amaseno Italy
120 B3 Amasine *Western Sahara*
42 C1 Amasra Turkey
123 E3 Amâssine well Mali
42 C1 Amasya Turkey
157 G5 Amatán Mexico
162 D4 Amataurá Brazil
156 H6 Amatique, B. de b. Guatemala
156 D4 Amatlán de Cañas Mexico
111 F4 Amato r. Italy
131 F6 Amatole Range mountain range South Africa
109 F2 Amatrice Italy
69 D4 Amay Belgium
31 G1 Amazar r. Rus. Fed.
Amazon r. *see* Amazonas
164 B3 Amazon, Source of the river source Peru
163 D4 Amazonas div. Brazil
163 G4 Amazonas r. South America
166 A1 Amazonia, Parque Nacional nat. park Brazil
163 G3 Amazon, Mouths of the river mouth Brazil
36 C2 Amb Pakistan
126 C2 Āmba Ālagē mt. Ethiopia
38 A2 Ambad India
126 C2 Amba Farit mt. Ethiopia
36 D4 Ambah India
129 G3 Ambahikily Madagascar
38 B2 Ambajogai India
36 D3 Ambala India
129 H2 Ambalakida Madagascar
129 H1 Ambalamanasy II Madagascar
38 C5 Ambalangoda Sri Lanka
129 H3 Ambalatany Madagascar
129 H3 Ambalavao Madagascar
14 C4 Ambalindum *Northern Terr.* Australia
124 B3 Ambam Cameroon
129 H1 Ambanja Madagascar
39 D3 Ambar Iran
22 B3 Ambarawa Indonesia
45 S3 Ambarchik Rus. Fed.
50 E1 Ambarnyy Rus. Fed.
99 E2 Ambasaguas Spain
38 B4 Ambasamudram India
15 F5 Ambathala *Queensland* Australia
162 B4 Ambato Ecuador
129 H2 Ambato Boeny Madagascar
129 H3 Ambato Finandrahana Madagascar
129 H2 Ambatolampy Madagascar
129 H2 Ambatomainty Madagascar
129 H2 Ambatondrazaka Madagascar
92 D3 Ambazac France
92 D3 Ambazac, Monts d' h. France
75 G3 Amberg Germany
63 E1 Ambergate *England* U.K.
159 E2 Ambergris Cays is *Turks and Caicos Is* Caribbean
90 D3 Ambérieu-en-Bugey France
140 E4 Amberley *Ontario* Canada
9 D5 Amberley New Zealand
69 D4 Amberloup Belgium
90 B3 Ambert France
122 B4 Ambidédi Mali
90 B2 Ambierle France
37 E5 Ambikapur India
129 H3 Ambila Madagascar
129 H1 Ambilobe Madagascar
129 H2 Ambinaninony Madagascar
136 C3 Ambition, Mt mt. *B.C.* Canada
65 G2 Amble *England* U.K.
65 F3 Ambleside *England* U.K.
86 A2 Ambleteuse France
69 D4 Amblève r. Belgium
164 A2 Ambo Peru
129 H3 Amboasary Madagascar
129 H2 Ambodifotatra Madagascar
129 H2 Ambohidratrimo Madagascar
129 H3 Ambohimahasoa Madagascar
129 G2 Ambohipaky Madagascar
129 H1 Ambohitra mt. Madagascar
129 H2 Ambohitralanana Madagascar
Amboina *see* Ambon
89 F4 Amboise France
21 J7 Ambon i. Indonesia
88 C4 Ambon France
21 J7 Ambon Indonesia
129 H3 Amborompotsy Madagascar
127 C5 Amboseli National Park nat. park Kenya
129 H3 Ambositra Madagascar
129 H3 Ambovombe Madagascar
155 E4 Amboy *California* U.S.A.
148 C5 Amboy *Illinois* U.S.A.
147 F3 Amboy Center *New York* U.S.A.
127 □4 Ambre, Isle d' i. Mauritius
89 E3 Ambrières-les-Vallées France
125 B5 Ambriz Angola
90 D2 Ambronay France
6 □2 Ambrym i. Vanuatu
22 C3 Ambunten Indonesia
38 B3 Ambur India
118 D5 Am-Dam Chad
44 H3 Amderma Rus. Fed.
123 D3 Amdillis well Mali
118 C5 Am Djéména Chad
37 G2 Amdo China
156 D4 Ameca Mexico
157 F5 Amecameca Mexico
173 F3 Ameghino Argentina
69 E4 Amel Belgium
68 D1 Ameland i. Netherlands
109 E2 Amelia Italy
146 E6 Amelia Court House *Virginia* U.S.A.
93 E6 Amélie-les-Bains-Palalda France
72 F2 Amelinghausen Germany
111 F3 Amendolara Italy
111 E4 Amendolea r. Italy
147 G4 Amenia *New York* U.S.A.
102 F2 Amer Spain
80 D3 Amerang Germany
168 E5 Americana Brazil
152 D3 American Falls *Idaho* U.S.A.
152 D3 American Falls Res. resr *Idaho* U.S.A.
155 G1 American Fork *Utah* U.S.A.
5 L6 American Samoa territory Pacific Ocean
145 C5 Americus *Georgia* U.S.A.
81 F3 Ameringkogel mt. Austria
103 G5 Amer, Pta de n' pt Spain
68 D2 Amersfoort Netherlands
131 G3 Amersfoort South Africa
63 F3 Amersham *England* U.K.
137 L3 Amery *Manitoba* Canada
179 D5 Amery Ice Shelf ice feature Antarctica
150 E3 Ames *Iowa* U.S.A.
63 E3 Amesbury *England* U.K.
147 H3 Amesbury *Massachusetts* U.S.A.
36 C4 Amet India
37 E4 Amethi India
114 D4 Amfikleia Greece
114 C4 Amfilochia Greece
114 E2 Amfipoli Greece
114 D4 Amfissa Greece
89 F2 Amfreville-la-Campagne France
45 P3 Amga Rus. Fed.
27 P2 Amgu China
121 F3 Amguid Algeria
45 P4 Amgun' r. Rus. Fed.
147 J2 Amherst *Maine* U.S.A.
147 G3 Amherst *Massachusetts* U.S.A.
139 H4 Amherst *Nova Scotia* Canada
146 D6 Amherst *Virginia* U.S.A.
Amherst *see* Kyaikkami
140 D5 Amherstburg *Ontario* Canada
16 D3 Amherst, Mt h. *Western Australia* Australia
43 C2 Amicun Lebanon
86 B3 Amiens *Somme* France
42 E3 Amij, Wādī watercourse Iraq
43 D1 Amik Ovası marsh Turkey
86 B5 Amilly France
39 C3 'Amīnābād Iran
38 A4 Amindivi Islands is India
126 D4 Amino Ethiopia
28 E6 Amino Japan
128 B3 Aminuis Namibia
Amirabad *see* Fūlād Maïalleh
42 F3 Amīrābād Iran
117 K6 Amirante Islands is Seychelles
39 E3 Amir Chah Pakistan
137 J4 Amisk L. l. *Saskatchewan* Canada
151 C6 Amistad Res. resr Mexico/U.S.A.
120 C2 Amizmiz Morocco
36 D5 Amla *Madhya Pradesh* India
36 D5 Amla *Madhya Pradesh* India
123 E5 Amlamé Togo
37 F4 Amlekhganj Nepal
58 C2 Åmli Norway
62 B1 Amlwch *Wales* U.K.
119 G4 'Amm Adam Sudan
42 C4 'Ammān Jordan
62 C3 Ammanford *Wales* U.K.
56 H2 Ämmänsaari Finland
126 E2 'Ammār reg. Yemen
56 E2 Ammarnäs Sweden
14 C4 Ammaroo *Northern Terr.* Australia
75 F5 Ammer r. Germany
80 B3 Ammergauer Alpen mountain range Austria/Germany
72 C2 Ammerland reg. Germany
72 F4 Ammern Germany
75 G4 Ammersee l. Germany
43 B2 Ammochostos Cyprus
43 B2 Ammochostos Bay b. Cyprus
114 B3 Ammotopos Greece
Amne Machin Range mountain range *see* A'nyêmaqên Shan
32 C4 Amo r. China
36 C5 Amod India
39 C1 Amol Iran
165 E3 Amolar Brazil
114 E2 Amoliani i. Greece
52 B4 Amon' Rus. Fed.
87 H2 Amöneburg Germany
166 E1 Amontada Brazil
101 F1 Amor mt. Spain
74 E3 Amorbach Germany
99 H1 Amorebieta Spain
113 E6 Amorgos i. Greece
141 F2 Amos *Québec* Canada
58 C2 Åmot Norway
59 G1 Åmot Sweden
59 E2 Åmotfors Sweden
93 B5 Amou France
120 C5 Amourj Mauritania
Amoy *see* Xiamen
22 C2 Ampah Indonesia
129 H1 Ampanefena Madagascar
129 G3 Ampanihy Madagascar
129 H2 Amparafaka, Tanjona c. Madagascar
129 H2 Amparafaravola Madagascar
38 C5 Amparai India
169 E5 Amparo Brazil
129 H3 Ampasimanjeva Madagascar
129 H2 Ampasimanolotra Madagascar
164 B3 Ampato, Nevado de mt. Peru
114 D3 Ampelonas Greece
22 D4 Ampenan Indonesia
75 G4 Amper r. Germany
107 G2 Ampezzo Italy
80 D2 Ampfing Germany
22 E2 Ampibaku Indonesia
129 H1 Ampisikinana Madagascar
90 C3 Amplepuis France
111 F3 Ampollino, Lago l. Italy
102 D4 Amposta Spain
63 F2 Ampthill *England* U.K.
99 F3 Ampudia Spain
99 G1 Ampuero Spain
126 D1 Amrān Yemen
36 D5 Amravati India
36 B5 Amreli India
36 B4 Amri Pakistan
37 H4 Amring India
83 E1 Amriswil Switzerland
36 C3 Amritsar India
36 D3 Amroha India
72 D1 Amrum i. Germany
56 E2 Åmsele Sweden
68 C2 Amstelveen Netherlands
147 F3 Amsterdam *New York* U.S.A.
68 C2 Amsterdam Netherlands
131 H3 Amsterdam South Africa
175 K6 Amsterdam, Île i. Indian Ocean
68 D2 Amsterdam-Rijnkanaal canal Netherlands
81 F2 Amstetten div. Austria
81 F2 Amstetten Austria
80 A2 Amstetten Germany
124 D1 Am Timan Chad
74 E5 Amtzell Germany
46 F4 Amudar'ya r. Turkmenistan/Uzbekistan
135 J2 Amund Ringnes I. i. *N.W.T.* Canada
178 C4 Amundsen Basin sea feature Arctic Ocean
179 D4 Amundsen Bay b. Antarctica
179 B4 Amundsen Gl. gl. Antarctica
134 F2 Amundsen Gulf g. *N.W.T.* Canada
179 C5 Amundsen, Mt mt. Antarctica
179 B4 Amundsen-Scott U.S.A. Base Antarctica
179 A3 Amundsen Sea sea Antarctica
59 F1 Amungen l. Sweden
22 C2 Amuntai Indonesia
Amur r. *see* Heilong
27 P1 Amur r. Rus. Fed.
99 H1 Amurrio Spain
27 P1 Amursk Rus. Fed.
31 J3 Amurzet Rus. Fed.
99 F2 Amusco Spain
114 B4 Amvrakikos Kolpos b. Greece
51 F6 Amvrosiyivka Ukraine
114 C2 Amyntaio Greece
140 C2 Amyot *Ontario* Canada
118 D5 Am-Zoer Chad
24 A3 An Myanmar
113 F4 Ana r. Turkey
7 □10 Anaa i. *French Polynesia* Pacific Ocean
123 E4 Anaba Nigeria
22 E2 Anabanua Indonesia
45 N2 Anabar r. Rus. Fed.
45 N2 Anabarskiy Zaliv b. Rus. Fed.
154 C4 Anacapa Is is *California* U.S.A.
109 G4 Anacapri Italy
163 E2 Anaco Venezuela
152 D2 Anaconda *Montana* U.S.A.
152 B1 Anacortes *Washington* U.S.A.
151 D5 Anadarko *Oklahoma* U.S.A.
98 B4 Anadia Portugal
42 D1 Anadolu Dağları mountain range Turkey
45 T3 Anadyr' r. Rus. Fed.
45 T3 Anadyr' Rus. Fed.
Anadyrskiy Khrebet mountain range *see* Chukotskiy Khrebet
134 A3 Anadyrskiy Zaliv b. Rus. Fed.
113 E6 Anafi i. Greece
115 B5 Anafonitria Greece
97 □ Anaga, Pta de pt *Canary Is* Spain
169 H1 Anagé Brazil
109 F3 Anagni Italy
42 E3 'Ānah Iraq
154 D5 Anaheim *California* U.S.A.
136 D4 Anahim Lake *B.C.* Canada
151 C7 Anáhuac Mexico
38 B4 Anaimalai Hills mts India
38 B4 Anai Mudi Pk mt. India
166 C1 Anajás Brazil
166 B1 Anajás, Ilha i. Brazil
38 C2 Anakapalle India
129 H1 Analalava Madagascar
129 G3 Analavelona mts Madagascar
163 E4 Anamã Brazil
123 F5 Anambra div. Nigeria
148 B4 Anamosa *Iowa* U.S.A.
163 F3 Anamu r. Brazil
42 C2 Anamur Turkey
42 C2 Anamur Br. pt Turkey
28 E7 Anan Japan
36 C5 Anand India
37 F5 Ānandapur India
37 F5 Anandpur r. India
115 F6 Ananes i. Greece
166 C1 Ananindeua Brazil
38 B3 Anantapur India
36 C2 Anantnag India
53 C3 Anan'yiv Ukraine
51 F6 Anapa Rus. Fed.
111 E5 Anapo r. *Sicilia* Italy
115 G7 Anapodaris r. Greece
168 D2 Anápolis Brazil
166 B1 Anapú r. Brazil
39 C3 Anār Iran
39 C2 Anārak Iran
39 B2 Anarbar r. Iran
39 E2 Anardara Afghanistan
10 □3 Anare Station *Macquarie I.* Pacific Ocean
114 C2 Anargyroi Greece
145 □3 Añasco Puerto Rico
21 M3 Anatahan i. *Northern Mariana Is* Pacific Ocean
114 B3 Anatoli Greece
42 B2 Anatolia reg. Turkey
114 C4 Anatolichis Frangista Greece
114 E1 Anatoliki Makedonia kai Thraki div. Greece
114 C2 Anatoliko Greece
6 □2 Anatom i. Vanuatu
170 D2 Añatuya Argentina
163 E3 Anauá r. Brazil
168 B5 Anaurilândia Brazil
114 D3 Anavra Greece
115 E5 Anavyssos Greece
99 E4 Anaya de Alba Spain
Anaypazari *see* Gülnar
43 D5 Anaz mts Saudi Arabia
39 B1 Anbūh Iran
31 H5 Anbyon North Korea
98 D2 Ancares, Serra dos mountain range Spain
170 C2 Ancasti, Sa mountain range Argentina
91 B4 Ance r. France
88 D4 Ancenis France
123 F4 Anchau Nigeria
169 H4 Anchieta Brazil
171 B7 Ancho, Can. chan. Chile
164 C2 Anchodaya Bolivia
134 D3 Anchorage *Alaska* U.S.A.
149 F4 Anchor Bay b. *Michigan* U.S.A.
172 E3 Anchorena Argentina
128 □3 Anchorstock Pt pt *Tristan da Cunha* Atlantic Ocean
An Cóbh *see* Cóbh
173 G3 Ancón Argentina
164 A2 Ancón Peru
107 H5 Ancona div. *Marche* Italy
107 H5 Ancona *Ancona* Italy
86 B2 Ancre r. France
65 F2 Ancroft *England* U.K.
127 C7 Ancuabe Mozambique
171 B5 Ancud Chile
171 B5 Ancud, G. de g. Chile
90 C1 Ancy-le-Franc France
31 H3 Anda China
Anda *see* Daqing
172 B4 Andacollo Argentina
172 B1 Andacollo Chile
14 C5 Andado *Northern Terr.* Australia
164 B2 Andahuaylas Peru
170 C2 Andalgalá Argentina
56 B3 Åndalsnes Norway
101 F3 Andalucía div. Spain
151 G6 Andalusia *Alabama* U.S.A.
25 A5 Andaman & Nicobar Islands div. India
175 L3 Andaman Basin sea feature
25 A4 Andaman Islands is *Andaman and Nicobar Is* India
25 A5 Andaman Sea sea Asia
164 C3 Andamarca Bolivia
164 B2 Andamarca Peru
12 D2 Andamooka Australia
91 C3 Andance France
129 H1 Andapa Madagascar
36 B2 Andarab reg. Afghanistan
39 G2 Andarāb Afghanistan
166 D3 Andaraí Brazil
101 H4 Andarax r. Spain
81 J3 Andau Austria
126 D2 Andeba YeMīdir Zerf Chaf pt Eritrea
83 E2 Andeer Switzerland
83 D1 Andelfingen Switzerland
89 G2 Andelle r. France
87 E4 Andelot-Blancheville France
90 D2 Andelot-en-Montagne France
56 E1 Andenes Norway
69 D4 Andenne Belgium
123 E3 Andéramboukane Mali
69 C4 Anderlecht Belgium
69 C4 Anderlues Belgium
83 D2 Andermatt Switzerland
74 C2 Andernach Germany
93 A4 Andernos-les-Bains France
59 G1 Andersbo Sweden
59 E4 Anderslöv Sweden
134 F3 Anderson r. *N.W.T.* Canada
134 D3 Anderson *Alaska* U.S.A.
148 E5 Anderson *Indiana* U.S.A.
151 E4 Anderson *Missouri* U.S.A.
145 D5 Anderson *S. Carolina* U.S.A.
173 G3 Anderson Argentina
13 F5 Anderson B. b. *Tasmania* Australia
160 E5 Andes mountain range South America
162 B2 Andes Colombia
150 D3 Andes, Lake *S. Dakota* U.S.A.
100 C3 Andévalo, Sierra de h. Spain
56 E1 Andfjorden chan. Norway
38 B2 Andhra Pradesh div. India
68 D2 Andijk Netherlands
129 H2 Andilamena Madagascar
129 H2 Andilanatoby Madagascar
82 A1 Andilly-en-Bassigny France
39 B2 Andīmeshk Iran
47 K5 Andirlangar China
115 C4 Andirrio Greece
51 H7 Andiyskoye Koysu r. Rus. Fed.
47 H4 Andizhan Uzbekistan
39 F1 Andkhui r. Afghanistan
39 F1 Andkhvoy Afghanistan
87 G4 Andlau r. France
87 G4 Andlau France
99 H1 Andoain Spain
129 H1 Andoany Madagascar
162 B4 Andoas Peru
129 H3 Andohahela, Réserve d' res. Madagascar
38 B2 Andol India
87 G4 Andolsheim France
31 J5 Andong South Korea
15 E2 Andoom *Queensland* Australia
81 E2 Andorf Austria
82 D3 Andorno Micca Italy
48 F4 Andorra country Europe
102 C4 Andorra Spain
93 D6 Andorra la Vella Andorra
63 E3 Andover *England* U.K.
147 H2 Andover *Maine* U.S.A.
146 C4 Andover *Ohio* U.S.A.
56 D1 Andøya i. Norway
91 C3 Andrable r. France
169 E5 Andradas Brazil
168 C4 Andradina Brazil
129 H2 Andranomavo Madagascar
129 G3 Andranopasy Madagascar
129 H1 Andranovondronina Madagascar
129 G3 Andranovory Madagascar
103 F5 Andratx Spain
115 C5 Andravida Greece
132 A4 Andreanof Is *Alaska* U.S.A.
52 A1 Andreapol' Rus. Fed.
64 D3 Andreas Isle of Man
124 D2 Andre Felix, Parc National de nat. park Central African Rep.
169 H1 André Fernandes Brazil
169 F4 Andrelândia Brazil
169 F3 Andrequicé Brazil
173 J2 Andresito Uruguay
77 H4 Andrespol Poland
93 C5 Andrest France
151 C5 Andrews *Texas* U.S.A.
47 K3 Andreyevka Kazakhstan
52 G2 Andreyevka Rus. Fed.
52 E2 Andreyevo Rus. Fed.
52 A3 Andreykovichi Rus. Fed.
90 C3 Andrézieux-Bouthéon France
109 J3 Andria Italy
129 H2 Andriamena Madagascar
129 H3 Andringitra mts Madagascar
115 C5 Andritsana Greece
53 G3 Andrivka Ukraine
53 G2 Andriyivka *Kharkiv* Ukraine
53 G3 Andriyivka *Zaporizhzhya* Ukraine
129 G4 Androka Madagascar
129 H2 Androna reg. Madagascar
52 D1 Androniki Rus. Fed.
115 F5 Andros i. Greece
158 C1 Andros i. The Bahamas
115 F5 Andros Greece
147 H2 Androscoggin r. U.S.A.
158 C1 Andros Town The Bahamas
38 A4 Āndrott i. India
53 C1 Andrushivka Ukraine
53 C2 Andrushky Ukraine
77 H6 Andrychów Poland
77 L3 Andrzejewo Poland
56 E1 Andselv Norway
101 F2 Andújar Spain
125 C6 Andulo Angola
91 B4 Anduze France
122 D3 Anéchag well Mali
123 E3 Anéfis Mali
145 □3 Anegada i. *Virgin Is* Caribbean
173 F6 Anegada, Bahía b. Argentina
159 G3 Anegada Passage chan. *Virgin Is* Caribbean
155 F5 Anegam *Arizona* U.S.A.
123 E5 Aného Togo
172 C5 Añelo Argentina
124 A4 Anengué, Lac l. Gabon
53 C3 Anenii Noi Moldova
89 G3 Anet France
155 H3 Aneth *Utah* U.S.A.
102 D2 Aneto mt. Spain
123 G3 Aney Niger
126 D2 Anfile Bay b. Eritrea
83 F3 Anfo Italy
33 F3 Anfu China
129 H1 Angadoka, Lohatanjona pt Madagascar
14 B2 Angalarri r. *Northern Terr.* Australia
31 G3 Ang'angxi China
45 L4 Angara r. Rus. Fed.
123 E4 Angaradébou Benin
30 B1 Angarsk Rus. Fed.
14 C5 Angas Downs *Northern Terr.* Australia
16 E4 Angas Ra. h. *Western Australia* Australia
23 B3 Angat Philippines
168 D5 Angatuba Brazil
23 □1 Angaur i. Palau
57 D3 Ånge Sweden
156 B2 Angel de la Guarda i. Mexico
23 B3 Angeles Philippines
6 □2 Angelghowhat Vanuatu
59 E3 Ängelholm Sweden
173 G1 Angelica Argentina
15 F5 Angellala Cr. r. *Queensland* Australia
114 C4 Angelokastro Greece
157 F6 Angel, Pto Mexico
154 B2 Angels Camp *California* U.S.A.
83 D3 Angera Italy
126 C2 Āngereb Wenz r. Ethiopia
56 E2 Ångermanälven r. Sweden
73 K2 Angermünde Germany
81 H2 Angern an der March Austria
89 E4 Angers *Maine-et-Loire* France
86 B4 Angerville France
91 F5 Anges, Baie des b. France
107 G5 Anghiari Italy
166 D3 Angical Brazil
137 K2 Angikuni Lake l. *N.W.T.* Canada
25 C4 Angkor Cambodia
9 A7 Anglem, Mt mt. New Zealand
93 E5 Anglès France
102 F3 Anglès Spain
62 B1 Anglesey, Isle of div. *Wales* U.K.
62 B1 Anglesey i. *Wales* U.K.
92 C2 Angles-sur-l'Anglin France
93 A5 Anglet France
151 E6 Angleton *Texas* U.S.A.
141 F3 Angliers *Québec* Canada
92 C2 Anglin r. France
86 C4 Anglure France
Angmagssalik *see* Tasiilaq
63 F4 Angmering *England* U.K.
25 □ Ang Mo Kio Singapore
124 E3 Ango Congo(Zaire)
129 F2 Angoche Mozambique
39 D4 Angohrān Iran
92 D3 Angoisse France
172 A4 Angol Chile
117 F7 Angola country Africa
148 E5 Angola *Indiana* U.S.A.
174 K7 Angola Basin sea feature Atlantic Ocean
129 H2 Agontsy, Tanjona c. Madagascar
157 G6 Angostura, Psa de la resr Mexico
156 C2 Angostura, Psa de la resr Mexico
173 L3 Angosturas Uruguay
92 C3 Angoulême France
92 A2 Angoulins France
92 C3 Angoumois reg. France
100 □ Angra do Heroismo *Azores* Portugal
169 F5 Angra dos Reis Brazil
47 H4 Angren Uzbekistan
89 E4 Angrie France
25 C4 Ang Thong Thailand
124 D3 Angu Congo(Zaire)
31 G3 Anguang China
102 C2 Angüés Spain
99 H2 Anguiano Spain
133 M8 Anguilla territory Caribbean
158 C2 Anguilla Cays is The Bahamas
107 F3 Anguillara Veneta Italy
30 E4 Anguli Nur l. China
31 E5 Anguo China
66 F4 Angus div. *Scotland* U.K.
168 A4 Anhanduí Brazil
168 D3 Anhanguera Brazil
69 C4 Anhée Belgium
55 D3 Anholt i. Denmark
33 E2 Anhua China
33 G1 Anhui div. China
168 A2 Anhumas Brazil
Anhwei *see* Anhui
91 B5 Aniane France
69 B4 Aniche France
168 D2 Anicuns Brazil
109 F3 Aniene r. Italy
93 B6 Anie, Pic d' mt. France
80 E3 Anif Austria
31 G1 Anikino Rus. Fed.
50 G3 Anikovo Rus. Fed.
155 H6 Animas *New Mexico* U.S.A.
155 H6 Animas Peak summit *New Mexico* U.S.A.
156 B2 Animas, Pta Las pt Mexico
59 E2 Ånimmen l. Sweden
24 B4 Anin Myanmar
112 C2 Anina Romania
167 C6 Anitápolis Brazil
27 Q2 Aniva, Mys c. Rus. Fed.
129 H1 Anivorano Avaratra Madagascar
6 □2 Aniwa i. Vanuatu
86 C3 Anizy-le-Château France
129 H2 Anjafy mt. Madagascar
54 E1 Anjalankoski Finland
38 B4 Anjengo India
33 G2 Anji China
36 D5 Anji India
29 F6 Anjō Japan
39 D2 Anjoman Iran
89 E4 Anjou reg. France
Anjouan i. *see* Nzwani
129 H2 Anjozorobe Madagascar
31 H5 Anjŭ North Korea
68 E1 Anjum Netherlands
129 G3 Ankaboa, Tanjona pt Madagascar
33 E1 Ankang China
42 C2 Ankara Turkey
107 H3 Ankaran Slovenia
129 H2 Ankaratra mts Madagascar
129 H2 Ankavandra Madagascar
129 G3 Ankazoabo Madagascar
129 H2 Ankazobe Madagascar
25 E4 An Khê Vietnam
73 J2 Anklam Germany
36 C5 Ankleshwar India
80 E3 Ankogel mt. Austria
125 E5 Ankoro Congo(Zaire)
52 D1 An'kovo Rus. Fed.
123 F5 Ankpa Nigeria
72 C3 Ankum Germany
65 H4 Anlaby *England* U.K.
80 C2 Anlauter r. Germany
90 B2 Anlezy France
123 E5 Anloga Ghana
32 D3 Anlong China
25 D4 Ânlong Vêng Cambodia
33 F2 Anlu China
An Muileann gCearr *see* Mullingar
31 H5 Anmyŏn Do i. South Korea
51 G5 Anna Rus. Fed.
121 F1 Annaba Algeria
81 G3 Annaberg Austria
75 J2 Annaberg-Buchholtz Germany
43 D4 An Nabk Saudi Arabia
42 D3 An Nabk Syria
119 H2 An Nafūd desert Saudi Arabia
67 E2 Annahilt *Northern Ireland* U.K.
163 F3 Annai Guyana
42 E4 An Najaf div. Iraq
42 F4 An Najaf Iraq
29 G5 Annaka Japan
146 E5 Anna, Lake l. *Virginia* U.S.A.
67 D2 Annalee r. Rep. of Ireland
67 F2 Annalong *Northern Ireland* U.K.
24 D3 Annam reg. Vietnam
43 C5 An Na'mī well Saudi Arabia
66 E5 Annan r. *Scotland* U.K.
66 E6 Annan *Scotland* U.K.
66 E5 Annandale v. *Scotland* U.K.
68 C2 Anna Paulowna Netherlands
171 A6 Anna Pink, Bahía b. Chile
16 C3 Anna Plains *Western Australia* Australia
146 E5 Annapolis *Maryland* U.S.A.
139 G5 Annapolis Royal *Nova Scotia* Canada
37 E3 Annapurna mt. Nepal
39 B4 An Naqīrah well Saudi Arabia
149 F4 Ann Arbor *Michigan* U.S.A.
163 F2 Anna Regina Guyana
An Nás *see* Naas
42 F4 An Nāṣirīyah Iraq
141 J3 Annaville *Québec* Canada
118 C1 An Nawfalīyah Libya
147 H3 Ann, Cape headland *Massachusetts* U.S.A.
17 B5 Annean, L. salt flat *Western Australia* Australia
59 E3 Anneberg Sweden
90 E3 Annecy France
90 E3 Annecy, Lac d' l. France
90 E3 Annecy-le-Vieux France
59 E3 Annelund Sweden
90 E2 Annemasse France
68 E1 Annen Netherlands
136 C4 Annette I. i. *Alaska* U.S.A.
86 B2 Annezin France
145 □1 Annie's Bay b. Bermuda
54 E2 Annikvere Estonia
119 H4 An Nimāṣ Saudi Arabia
32 C3 Anning r. China
32 C3 Anning China
52 E3 Annino Rus. Fed.
145 C5 Anniston *Alabama* U.S.A.
174 K6 Annobón i. Equatorial Guinea
91 C3 Annonay France
77 K5 Annopol Poland
91 E5 Annot France
159 □1 Annotto Bay Jamaica
39 B4 An Nu'ayrīyah Saudi Arabia
74 C3 Annweiler am Trifels Germany
114 C4 Ano Agios Vlasios Greece
115 D6 Anogeia Greece
148 A3 Anoka *Minnesota* U.S.A.
114 E3 Ano Lechonia Greece
115 G5 Ano Mera Greece
162 B3 Anoón de Sardinas, B. de b. Colombia
52 E2 Anopino Rus. Fed.
114 E1 Ano Poroïa Greece
69 C5 Anor France
163 E4 Anori Brazil
129 H1 Anorontany, Tanjona headland Madagascar
129 H2 Anosibe An'Ala Madagascar
87 F4 Anould France
123 F3 Anou Mekkerene watercourse Niger
123 E3 Ânou Mellene well Mali
121 E4 Anou Meniet well Algeria
121 E5 Anou-n-Bidek well Algeria
123 F3 Ânou Zegguegheme well Niger
99 G5 Añover de Tajo Spain
115 G7 Ano Viannos Greece
33 E4 Anpu China
33 E4 Anpu Gang China
33 G2 Anqing China
31 F5 Anqiu China
99 H4 Anquela del Ducado Spain
33 F3 Anren China
69 D4 Ans Belgium
55 B3 Ans Denmark
92 C3 Ansac-sur-Vienne France
30 D5 Ansai China
75 F3 Ansbach Germany
90 C3 Anse France
126 C1 Anseba Shet watercourse Eritrea
159 □5 Anse Bertrand *Guadeloupe* Caribbean
127 □2 Anse Boileau Seychelles
88 A4 Anse de Benodet b. France
88 B4 Anse de Pouldu b. France
108 D2 Ansedonia Italy
69 C4 Anseremme Belgium
127 □2 Anse Royal Seychelles
81 F2 Ansfelden Austria
31 G4 Anshan China
32 D3 Anshun China
98 B5 Ansião Portugal
172 C1 Ansilta mt. Argentina
172 C1 Ansilta, C. de mountain range Argentina
173 K1 Ansina Uruguay
150 D3 Ansley *Nebraska* U.S.A.
102 C2 Ansó Spain
151 D5 Anson *Texas* U.S.A.
11 □1 Anson B. b. *Norfolk I.* Pacific Ocean
14 B2 Anson B. b. *Northern Terr.* Australia
123 E3 Ansongo Mali
123 E3 Ansongo-Ménaka, Réserve Partielle de Faune d' res. Mali

140 E2 Ansonville Ontario Canada
102 C2 Ansó, Valle de reg. Spain
146 C5 Ansted W. Virginia U.S.A.
54 E3 Anstla Estonia
66 F4 Anstruther Scotland U.K.
63 H2 Ant r. England U.K.
36 D4 Anta India
164 B2 Anta Peru
164 B2 Antabamba Peru
An Tairbeart see Tarbet
42 D2 Antakya Turkey
129 H1 Antalaha Madagascar
42 B2 Antalya Turkey
42 B2 Antalya Körfezi g. Turkey
129 H2 Antanambao Manampotsy Madagascar
129 H2 Antananarivo div. Madagascar
129 H2 Antananarivo Madagascar
129 H2 Antanifotsy Madagascar
129 H3 Antanimora Atsimo Madagascar
An tAonach see Nenagh
179 B2 Antarctic Peninsula pen. Antarctica
167 B6 Antas r. Brazil
101 J3 Antas r. Spain
98 B3 Antas Portugal
103 B7 Antas Spain
167 B6 Antas, R. das r. Brazil
66 C3 An Teallach mt. Scotland U.K.
154 D2 Antelope Range mts Nevada U.S.A.
59 E2 Anten l. Sweden
92 B3 Antenne r. France
101 F3 Antequera Spain
91 E5 Anthéor France
80 E3 Anthering Austria
114 D4 Anthili Greece
153 F5 Anthony New Mexico U.S.A.
14 C3 Anthony Lagoon Northern Terr. Australia
120 C3 Anti Atlas mountain range Morocco
91 F5 Antibes France
91 F5 Antibes, Cap d' pt France
139 H4 Anticosti, Île d' i. Québec Canada
89 F2 Antifer, Cap d' pt France
148 C3 Antigo Wisconsin U.S.A.
139 H4 Antigonish Nova Scotia Canada
114 C2 Antigonos Greece
159 □7 Antigua i. Antigua and Barbuda Caribbean
97 □ Antigua Canary Is Spain
157 H6 Antigua Guatemala
133 M8 Antigua and Barbuda country Caribbean
159 □5 Antigues, Pte d' pt Guadeloupe Caribbean
157 F4 Antiguo-Morelos Mexico
115 D4 Antikyra Greece
115 E7 Antikythira i. Greece
Anti-Lebanon mountain range see Sharqi, Jebel esh
111 E5 Antillo Sicilia Italy
115 F6 Antimilos i. Greece
An tInbhear Mór see Arklow
154 B3 Antioch California U.S.A.
148 C4 Antioch Illinois U.S.A.
Antioch see Antakya
162 B2 Antioquia Colombia
115 G5 Antiparos i. Greece
115 G5 Antiparos Greece
114 B3 Antipaxoi i. Greece
9 □3 Antipodes I. i. Antipodes Is New Zealand
113 E5 Antipsara i. Greece
162 B4 Antisana, Co volcano Ecuador
113 F6 Antitilos i. Greece
151 E5 Antlers Oklahoma U.S.A.
164 C4 Antofagasta div. Chile
164 B4 Antofagasta Chile
170 C2 Antofagasta de la Sierra Argentina
170 C2 Antofalla, Vol. volcano Argentina
69 B4 Antoing Belgium
156 K7 Antón Panama
53 B2 Antoniny Ukraine
154 B3 Antonio r. California U.S.A.
166 D3 Antônio r. Brazil
169 G4 Antônio Carlos Brazil
171 C6 Antonio de Biedma Argentina
169 G3 Antônio Dias Brazil
165 E4 Antônio João Paraguay
153 F4 Antonito Colorado U.S.A.
53 C2 Antoniv Ukraine
53 E1 Antonivka Chernihivs'ka Oblast' Ukraine
53 E3 Antonivka Khersons'ka Oblast' Ukraine
92 C3 Antonne-et-Trigonant France
86 B4 Antony France
77 N3 Antopal' Belarus
91 C4 Antraigues-sur-Volane France
88 D3 Antrain France
67 E2 Antrim div. Northern Ireland U.K.
67 E2 Antrim Northern Ireland U.K.
67 E2 Antrim Hills h. Northern Ireland U.K.
16 E3 Antrim Plateau plat. Western Australia Australia
109 F2 Antrodoco Italy
50 G3 Antropovo Rus. Fed.
129 H1 Antsahanoro Madagascar
129 G2 Antsalova Madagascar
129 H2 Antsirabe Madagascar
129 H1 Antsirañana div. Madagascar
129 H1 Antsirañana Madagascar
129 H1 Antsohihy Madagascar
56 F2 Anttis Sweden
57 G3 Anttola Finland
31 J4 Antu China
172 B4 Antuco Chile
165 D2 Antuerpia Brazil
126 D1 Antufush I. i. Yemen
147 F2 Antwerp New York U.S.A.
Antwerp see Antwerpen
69 C3 Antwerpen div. Antwerpen Belgium
69 C3 Antwerpen div. Belgium
69 C3 Antwerpen Belgium
An Uaimh see Navan
7 □10 Anuanu Raro i. French Polynesia Pacific Ocean
138 E2 Anuc, Lac l. Québec Canada
37 F5 Anugul India
36 C3 Anupgarh India
38 C1 Anuppur India
38 C4 Anuradhapura Sri Lanka
39 C4 Anveh Iran
Anvers see Antwerpen
179 B2 Anvers I. i. Antarctica
86 B2 Anvin France
26 G3 Anxi China
33 G3 Anxi China
32 D2 An Xian China
33 F2 Anxiang China
31 E5 Anxin China
12 C3 Anxious Bay b. S. Australia Australia
122 D5 Anyama Côte d'Ivoire
30 E5 Anyang China
31 H5 Anyang South Korea
22 A3 Anyar Indonesia
113 E6 Anydro i. Greece
32 B1 A'nyêmaqên Shan mountain range China
33 F2 Anyi China
54 D4 Anykščiai Lithuania
131 H3 Anysspruit South Africa
33 F3 Anyuan Jiangxi China
33 F3 Anyuan Jiangxi China
32 D2 Anyue China
45 S3 Anyuy, Mal. r. Rus. Fed.
45 S3 Anyuysk Rus. Fed.
106 C3 Anza r. Italy
162 B2 Anzá Colombia
30 E5 Anze China
69 B4 Anzegem Belgium
44 K4 Anzhero-Sudzhensk Rus. Fed.
109 H4 Anzi Italy
124 D4 Anzi Congo(Zaire)
86 C2 Anzin France
80 C2 Anzing Germany
109 E3 Anzio Italy
172 F5 Anzoategui, S. Grandes salt pan Argentina
101 F3 Anzur r. Spain
6 □2 Aoba i. Vanuatu
25 B5 Ao Ban Don b. Thailand
31 F4 Aohan Qi China
102 B2 Aoiz Spain
28 H3 Aomori div. Japan
28 H3 Aomori Japan
7 □11 Aorai mt. French Polynesia Pacific Ocean
Aoraki, Mt mt. see Cook, Mt
9 E4 Aorangi Mts mts New Zealand
8 D4 Aorere r. New Zealand
25 B5 Ao Sawi b. Thailand
106 B3 Aosta Italy
106 B3 Aosta, Valle d' div. Italy
90 D3 Aoste France
123 F3 Aouderas Niger
120 C3 Aouhinet bel Egra well Algeria
124 D1 Aoukalé r. Central African Rep./Chad
124 D2 Aouk-Aoakole, Réserve de Faune de l' res. Central African Rep.
120 C4 Aoukâr reg. Mali/Mauritania
121 E3 Aoulef Algeria
120 C2 Aoulime, Jbel mt. Morocco
28 E6 Aoya Japan
118 C3 Aozou Chad
165 E4 Apa r. Brazil
126 B4 Apac Uganda
155 H6 Apache Arizona U.S.A.
155 H5 Apache Creek New Mexico U.S.A.
155 G5 Apache Junction Arizona U.S.A.
155 G6 Apache Peak summit Arizona U.S.A.
112 D1 Apahida Romania
168 D5 Apaiaí r. Brazil
145 C6 Apalachee Bay b. Florida U.S.A.
145 C6 Apalachicola Florida U.S.A.
157 F5 Apan Mexico
87 E5 Apance r. France
162 D4 Apaporis r. Colombia
168 C4 Aparecida do Tabuado Brazil
9 B6 Aparima r. New Zealand
23 B2 Aparri Philippines
22 D2 Apar, Tk b. Indonesia
54 D3 Apaščia r. Lithuania
7 □10 Apataki i. French Polynesia Pacific Ocean
112 B2 Apatin Yugoslavia
44 E3 Apatity Rus. Fed.
163 G2 Apatou French Guiana
81 H4 Apatovac Croatia
156 E5 Apatzingán Mexico
54 E3 Ape Latvia
107 G5 Apecchio Italy
68 D2 Apeldoorn Netherlands
72 E3 Apelern Germany
72 C2 Apen Germany
72 E2 Apensen Germany
36 E3 Api mt. Nepal
124 E3 Api Congo(Zaire)
7 □12 Apia Western Samoa
165 E2 Apiacá r. Brazil
168 D6 Apiaí Brazil
6 □1 Apio Solomon Is.
107 H5 Apiro Italy
8 E3 Apiti New Zealand
123 E5 Aplahoué Benin
164 B3 Aplao Peru
166 E2 Apodi r. Brazil
166 E2 Apodi Brazil
163 F2 Apoera Surinam
115 □ Apolakkia Greece
73 G4 Apolda Germany
13 E4 Apollo Bay Victoria Australia
115 G5 Apollon Greece
115 □ Apollona Greece
115 F6 Apollonia Greece
164 C2 Apolo Bolivia
23 C5 Apo, Mt volcano Philippines
98 C1 A Pontenova Spain
145 D6 Apopka, L. l. Florida U.S.A.
168 C3 Aporé r. Brazil
168 C3 Aporé Brazil
163 G3 Aporema Brazil
144 B2 Apostle Is is Michigan U.S.A.
148 B2 Apostle Islands National Lakeshore res. Wisconsin U.S.A.
170 E2 Apóstoles Argentina
43 C2 Apostolos Andreas, C. headland Cyprus
53 E3 Apostolove Ukraine
163 F3 Apoteri Guyana
146 B6 Appalachia Virginia U.S.A.
146 C6 Appalachian Mountains mountain range U.S.A.
94 E3 Appennino mountain range Italy
109 F2 Appennino Abruzzese mountain range Italy
109 H4 Appennino Lucano mountain range Italy
109 G3 Appennino Napoletano mountain range Italy
107 E4 Appennino Tosco-Emiliano mts Italy
109 E1 Appennino Umbro-Marchigiano mountain range Italy
87 G4 Appenweier Germany
83 E1 Appenzell Switzerland
83 E1 Appenzell-Ausserrhoden div. Switzerland
83 E1 Appenzell-Innerrhoden div. Switzerland
107 F2 Appiano sulla Strada del Vino Italy
107 H5 Appignano Italy
68 E1 Appingedam Netherlands
65 F3 Appleby-in-Westmorland England U.K.
63 E2 Appleby Magna England U.K.
66 C3 Applecross Scotland U.K.
62 B3 Appledore England U.K.
63 G3 Appledore England U.K.
150 D2 Appleton Minnesota U.S.A.
148 C3 Appleton Wisconsin U.S.A.
154 D4 Apple Valley California U.S.A.
59 J1 Äppolö Finland
146 D6 Appomattox Virginia U.S.A.
91 D3 Apprieu France
163 G3 Approuague r. French Guiana
23 □2 Apra Harb. harbour Guam Pacific Ocean
23 □2 Apra Heights Guam Pacific Ocean
52 C2 Aprelevka Rus. Fed.
82 A1 Apremont France
106 E2 Aprica Italy
111 F3 Aprigliano Italy
109 E3 Aprilia Italy
37 H3 Aprunyi India
114 D2 Apsalos Greece
51 F6 Apsheronsk Rus. Fed.
141 F4 Apsley Ontario Canada
14 B1 Apsley Str. chan. Northern Terr. Australia
91 D5 Apt France
168 C5 Apucarana Brazil
23 A4 Apurahuan Philippines
162 D2 Apure r. Venezuela
164 B2 Apurimac r. Peru
42 C4 'Aqaba Jordan
43 C6 Aqaba, Gulf of g. Africa/Asia
43 C5 'Aqaba, W. el watercourse Egypt
39 C1 Aqbana Iran
39 F1 Āqchah Afghanistan
39 C2 Āqdā Iran
42 F2 Aqdoghmish r. Iran
119 G2 Aqla well Saudi Arabia
37 G1 Aqqikkol Hu salt lake China
43 D4 'Aqran h. Saudi Arabia
155 F4 Aquarius Mts mts Arizona U.S.A.
155 G3 Aquarius Plateau plat. Utah U.S.A.
111 F2 Aquaviva delle Fonti Italy
165 E4 Aquidabán mi r. Paraguay
165 E3 Aquidauana r. Brazil
167 A5 Aquidauana Brazil
156 E5 Aquila Mexico
109 F3 Aquino Italy
166 E1 Aquiraz Brazil
157 F4 Aquismón Mexico
93 B4 Aquitaine div. France
102 C2 Ara r. Spain
37 F4 Ara India
126 D3 Āra Ārba Ethiopia
145 C5 Arab Alabama U.S.A.
39 F3 Arab Afghanistan
39 D2 'Arabābād Iran
126 D3 Ara Bacalle well Ethiopia
163 E3 Arabelo Venezuela
175 J3 Arabian Basin sea feature Indian Ocean
175 J2 Arabian Sea sea Indian Ocean
163 E2 Arabopó Venezuela
93 D6 Arac r. France
42 C1 Araç Turkey
163 E3 Araça r. Brazil
166 E3 Aracaju Brazil
165 E4 Aracangy, Mtes de h. Paraguay
158 D5 Aracataca Colombia
166 E1 Aracati Brazil
166 D3 Aracatu Brazil
168 C4 Araçatuba Brazil
100 D3 Aracena Spain
171 B7 Aracena, I. i. Chile
100 D3 Aracena, Sierrra de h. Spain
115 D4 Arachova Greece
114 C3 Arachthos r. Greece
112 C3 Aračinovo Macedonia
169 H3 Aracruz Brazil
169 G2 Araçuaí r. Brazil
169 G2 Araçuaí Brazil
79 L5 Arad div. Romania
43 C4 'Arad Israel
79 L5 Arad Romania
118 D5 Arada Chad
98 B4 Arada, Sa de mountain range Portugal
100 B3 Arade r. Portugal
21 K8 Arafura Sea sea Australia/Indonesia
168 B1 Aragarças Brazil
42 F1 Aragats Lerr mt. Armenia
29 G5 Ara-gawa r. Japan
102 C3 Aragón div. Spain
102 B2 Aragón r. Spain
110 C5 Aragona Sicilia Italy
99 H4 Aragoncillo mt. Spain
99 H4 Aragoncillo Spain
166 C2 Araguacema Brazil
166 C3 Araguaçu Brazil
163 E2 Aragua de Barcelona Venezuela
166 C2 Araguaia r. Brazil
166 B3 Araguaia, Parque Nacional de nat. park Brazil
166 C2 Araguaína Brazil
168 B2 Araguainha Brazil
166 C2 Araguana Brazil
159 G5 Araguapiche, Pta pt Venezuela
168 D3 Araguari r. Brazil
163 G3 Araguari r. Amapá Brazil
168 D3 Araguari Brazil
166 C2 Araguatins Brazil
120 C5 Arâguîb reg. Mali/Mauritania
51 H7 Aragvi r. Georgia
29 G5 Arai Japan
43 C4 Araif el Naga, G. h. Egypt
166 D1 Araiosos Brazil
121 E3 Arak Algeria
39 B2 Arāk Iran
23 □1 Arakabesan i. Palau
159 G6 Arakaka Guyana
24 A3 Arakan div. Myanmar
24 A3 Arakan Yoma mountain range Myanmar
29 □2 Arakawa Japan
8 G3 Arakihi h. New Zealand
38 B3 Arakkonam India
Araks r. see Araz
Araks r. see Aras
46 E3 Aral Sea salt lake Kazakhstan
46 F3 Aral'sk Kazakhstan
Aral'skoye More salt lake see Aral Sea
46 D3 Aralsor, Oz. salt lake Kazakhstan
46 C3 Aralsor, Ozero l. Kazakhstan
46 F3 Aralsul'fat Kazakhstan
15 F4 Aramac Queensland Australia
15 F4 Aramac Cr. watercourse Queensland Australia
98 B2 A Ramallosa Spain
157 F3 Aramberri Mexico
6 □1 Aramia r. P.N.G.
93 B5 Aramits France
91 C5 Aramon France
38 B1 Aran r. India
59 E1 Äran r. Sweden
101 G3 Arana, Sierra mountain range Spain
62 C2 Aran Benllyn h. Wales U.K.
170 C3 Arancibia Argentina
99 G3 Aranda de Duero Spain
112 C2 Aranđelovac Yugoslavia
62 C2 Aran Fawddwy h. Wales U.K.
38 B3 Arani India
67 C1 Aran Island i. Rep. of Ireland
67 B3 Aran Islands is Rep. of Ireland
114 A2 Aranitas Albania
99 G4 Aranjuez Spain
128 B3 Aranos Namibia
151 D7 Aransas Pass Texas U.S.A.
168 C3 Arantes r. Brazil
28 C7 Arao Japan
122 D3 Araouane Mali
150 D3 Arapahoe Nebraska U.S.A.
9 E4 Arapawa Island i. New Zealand
173 J1 Arapey Grande r. Uruguay
166 E2 Arapiraca Brazil
42 D2 Arapkir Turkey
168 C5 Arapongas Brazil
168 D6 Arapoti Brazil
37 F4 A Rapti Doon r. Nepal
168 B4 Arapuá Brazil
8 E3 Arapuni New Zealand
167 C6 Araquari Brazil
42 E4 'Ar'ar Saudi Arabia
162 C4 Araracuara Colombia
167 C6 Araranguá Brazil
168 D6 Ararapira Brazil
168 D4 Araraquara Brazil
166 B2 Araras Pará Brazil
168 E5 Araras São Paulo Brazil
13 E4 Ararat Victoria Australia
42 F2 Ararat Armenia
Ararat, Mt mt. see Büyük Ağri
166 D1 Arari Brazil
37 F4 Araria India
166 C1 Arari, Lago l. Brazil
166 D2 Araripina Brazil
169 G5 Araruama Brazil
169 G5 Araruama, Lago de lag. Brazil
167 D5 Araruama, L. de lag. Brazil
42 E4 'Ar'ar, Wādī watercourse Iraq/Saudi Arabia
42 E2 Aras r. Turkey
103 B5 Aras de Alpuente Spain
30 C2 Ar Asgat Mongolia
158 □1 Arasji Aruba Caribbean
169 J1 Arataca Brazil
166 B1 Arataú r. Brazil
162 D2 Arauca r. Venezuela
162 C2 Arauca Colombia
168 D6 Araucária Brazil
172 A4 Arauco Chile
172 A4 Arauco, G. de b. Chile
162 C2 Arauquita Colombia
159 E5 Araure Venezuela
54 D2 Aravete Estonia
99 J3 Araviana r. Spain
90 E3 Aravis mts France
114 D2 Aravissos Greece
6 □1 Arawa P.N.G.
8 F3 Arawhana mt. New Zealand
167 C4 Araxá Minas Gerais Brazil
169 E3 Araxá Minas Gerais Brazil
163 E1 Araya, Pen. de pen. Venezuela
159 F5 Araya, Pta de pt Venezuela
42 F2 Araz r. Azerbaijan/Iran
29 □2 Ara-zaki c. Japan
98 B4 Arazede Portugal
102 B3 Arba r. Spain
102 B2 Arba de Luesia r. Spain
31 F2 Arbagar Rus. Fed.
126 C3 Ārba Minch Ethiopia
42 F3 Arbat Iraq
108 B5 Arbatax Sardegna Italy
50 J3 Arbazh Rus. Fed.
82 A1 Arbecey France
52 G3 Arbekovo Rus. Fed.
80 B1 Arberg Germany
81 F2 Arbesbach Austria
42 F2 Arbīl div. Iraq
42 F2 Arbīl Iraq
59 F2 Arboga Sweden
90 D2 Arbois France
173 G4 Arboledas Argentina
173 K2 Arbolito Uruguay
83 E1 Arbon Switzerland
108 A5 Arborea Sardegna Italy
137 J4 Arborfield Saskatchewan Canada
106 C3 Arborio Italy
66 F4 Arbroath Scotland U.K.
102 F3 Arbúcies Spain
154 A2 Arbuckle California U.S.A.
108 A5 Arbus Sardegna Italy
53 D3 Arbuzynka Ukraine
91 D5 Arc r. Provence-Alpes-Côte d'Azur France
91 E3 Arc r. Rhône-Alpes France
93 A4 Arcachon France
145 D7 Arcadia Florida U.S.A.
90 E3 Arcalod, Pte d' mt. France
152 A3 Arcata California U.S.A.
154 D2 Arc Dome summit Nevada U.S.A.
109 F3 Arce Italy
157 E5 Arcelia Mexico
69 E3 Arcen Netherlands
86 C4 Arces-Dilo France
82 A1 Arc-et-Senans France
107 G5 Arcevia Italy
115 D5 Archaia Korinthos Greece
Archangel see Arkhangel'sk
115 □ Archangelos Greece
103 B6 Archena Spain
15 E2 Archer r. Queensland Australia
15 E2 Archer Bend Nat. Park Queensland Australia
155 H2 Arches Nat. Park nat. park Utah U.S.A.
122 D3 Arch Henda well Mali
92 B3 Archiac France
101 F3 Archidona Spain
7 □10 Archipel de la Société is French Polynesia Pacific Ocean
7 □10 Archipel des Tuamotu is French Polynesia Pacific Ocean
171 B7 Archipiélago de la Reina Adelaida is Chile
171 A6 Archipiélago de los Chonos is Chile
156 L7 Archipiélago de San Blas is Panama
115 □ Archipoli Greece
108 D2 Arcidosso Italy
108 B1 Arcipelago Toscano is Italy
86 D4 Arcis-sur-Aube France
12 C1 Arckaringa watercourse S. Australia Australia
82 A1 Arc-lès-Gray France
152 D3 Arco Idaho U.S.A.
107 E3 Arco Italy
98 C3 Arco de Baúlhe Portugal
148 C6 Arcola Illinois U.S.A.
90 E2 Arçon France
90 C2 Arconce r. France
89 F3 Arconnay France
169 F4 Arcos Brazil
99 G2 Arcos Spain
99 H3 Arcos de Jalón Spain
100 E4 Arcos de la Frontera Spain
98 B3 Arcos de Valdevez Portugal
166 E2 Arcoverde Brazil
98 B3 Arcozelo Portugal
90 D1 Arc-sur-Tille France
135 K2 Arctic Bay N.W.T. Canada
134 B2 Arctic Ocean ocean
134 E3 Arctic Red r. N.W.T. Canada
179 B2 Arctowski Poland Base Antarctica
102 D2 Arcusa Spain
106 D4 Arda r. Italy
39 B1 Ardabīl div. Iran
42 G2 Ardabīl Iran
81 F2 Ardagger Markt Austria
42 E1 Ardahan Turkey
39 C2 Ardakān Iran
39 B3 Ardal Iran
43 D3 Arḍ al Karā' lava Syria
58 B2 Årdalsknapen h. Norway
58 B1 Årdalstangen Norway
108 A4 Ardara Sardegna Italy
67 C2 Ardara Rep. of Ireland
112 F4 Ardas r. Greece
52 F2 Ardatov Rus. Fed.
52 H2 Ardatov Rus. Fed.
140 E4 Ardbeg Ontario Canada
64 C2 Ard Bheinn h. Scotland U.K.
109 E3 Ardea Italy
91 C4 Ardèche div. Rhône-Alpes France
91 C4 Ardèche r. France
67 E3 Ardee Rep. of Ireland
55 B3 Arden Denmark
86 D3 Ardennes div. Champagne-Ardenne France
Ardennes plat. see Plateau de l'Ardenne
86 D3 Ardennes r. France
92 D2 Ardentes France
64 D1 Ardentinny Scotland U.K.
66 D3 Ardersier Scotland U.K.
91 B3 Ardes France
39 C2 Ardestān Iran
83 F2 Ardez Switzerland
66 D3 Ardgay Scotland U.K.
64 C5 Ardglass Rep. of Ireland
67 F2 Ardglass Northern Ireland U.K.
43 D4 Ardh es Suwwān desert Jordan
100 C2 Ardila r. Portugal
114 G1 Ardino Bulgaria
13 F3 Ardlethan New South Wales Australia
64 D1 Ardlui Scotland U.K.
64 C1 Ardlussa Scotland U.K.
64 C2 Ardminish Scotland U.K.
151 D5 Ardmore Oklahoma U.S.A.
67 D5 Ardmore Bay b. Rep. of Ireland
64 B1 Ardmore Point pt Scotland U.K.
62 A2 Ardmore Point pt Rep. of Ireland
66 B4 Ardnamurchan, Point of pt Scotland U.K.
111 F4 Ardore Italy
86 A2 Ardres France
66 C4 Ardrishaig Scotland U.K.
12 D3 Ardrossan S. Australia Australia
66 D5 Ardrossan Scotland U.K.
67 F2 Ards Peninsula pen. Rep. of Ireland
79 M4 Ardud Romania
112 D1 Ardusat Romania
66 C3 Ardvasar Scotland U.K.
169 E4 Areado Brazil
124 E3 Arebi Congo(Zaire)
82 B3 Arèches France
145 □3 Arecibo Puerto Rico
173 H3 Areco r. Argentina
52 D1 Arefino Rus. Fed.
112 E2 Arefu Romania
166 E1 Areia Branca Brazil
23 □1 Arekalong Peninsula pen. Palau
77 M4 Arekhava Belarus
58 D2 Aremark Norway
69 E4 Aremberg h. Germany
102 D2 Arén Spain
23 B4 Arena reef Philippines
171 B6 Arenales, Co mt. Chile
154 A2 Arena, Pt pt California U.S.A.
156 C4 Arena, Pta pt Mexico
99 F1 Arenas de Iguña Spain
101 G4 Arenas del Rey Spain
99 E4 Arenas de San Pedro Spain
173 G3 Arenaza Argentina
58 C2 Arendal Norway
69 D3 Arendonk Belgium
73 G3 Arendsee Germany
93 B4 Arengosse France
62 C2 Arenig Fawr h. Wales U.K.
101 F2 Arenosillo r. Spain
72 E4 Arenshausen Germany
102 F3 Arenys de Mar Spain
106 C4 Arenzano Italy
115 D6 Areopoli Greece
164 B3 Arequipa Peru
173 G2 Arequlto Argentina
166 B1 Arere Brazil
93 A4 Arès France
102 C4 Ares del Maestre Spain
93 B5 Arette France
93 B6 Arette-Pierre-St-Martin France
99 E4 Arevalillo Spain
99 F3 Arévalo Spain
173 K2 Arevalo Uruguay
100 C1 Arez Portugal
107 F5 Arezzo div. Toscana Italy
107 F5 Arezzo Arezzo Italy
42 D4 'Arfajah well Saudi Arabia
115 D5 Arfara Greece
102 B2 Arga r. Spain
30 D3 Argalant Mongolia
114 E3 Argalasti Greece
100 E2 Argallanes, Sierra de los h. Spain
101 G1 Argamasilla de Alba Spain
101 F2 Argamasilla de Calatrava Spain
99 G4 Argana Spain
98 B4 Arganil Portugal
23 B4 Argao Philippines
52 H3 Argash Rus. Fed.
30 C3 Argatay Mongolia
109 F3 Argatone, Monte mt. Italy
46 F1 Argayash Rus. Fed.
106 D3 Argegno Italy
93 B5 Argelés-Gazost France
93 F6 Argelès-sur-Mer France
93 E5 Argeliers France
103 C4 Argelita Spain
74 E5 Argen r. Germany
83 E1 Argenbühl Germany
89 E2 Argences France
91 E5 Argens r. France
107 F4 Argenta Italy
89 E3 Argentan France
92 D3 Argentat France
102 B4 Argente Spain
106 A4 Argentera Italy
106 B4 Argentera, Cima dell' mt. Italy
86 B4 Argenteuil France
90 E3 Argentière France
161 F7 Argentina country South America
170 D2 Argentina Argentina
173 J4 Argentina, L. La l. Argentina
179 B3 Argentina Ra. mountain range Antarctica
82 B3 Argentine France
174 G8 Argentine Basin sea feature Atlantic Ocean
171 B7 Argentino, Lago l. Argentina
89 E4 Argenton r. France
92 B2 Argenton-Château France
92 D2 Argenton-sur-Creuse France
89 E3 Argentre France
89 D3 Argentré-du-Plessis France
89 H4 Argent-sur-Sauldre France
101 H3 Argerín mt. Spain
112 E2 Argeș r. Romania
39 F3 Arghandab r. Afghanistan
39 F3 Arghastan r. Afghanistan
55 □1 Argir Faeroes
115 D5 Argolikos Kolpos b. Greece
115 D5 Argolis div. Greece
90 E3 Argonay France
86 D3 Argonne reg. France
22 C3 Argopuro, G. volcano Indonesia
6 □7 Argo Reefs reef Fiji
103 B6 Argos r. Spain
115 D5 Argos Greece
114 C2 Argos Orestiko Greece
115 B4 Argostoli Greece
88 D3 Argouges France
89 G2 Argueil France
101 H2 Arguellite Spain
88 C3 Arguenon r. France
102 C2 Arguís Spain
31 G2 Argun' r. China/Rus. Fed.
51 H7 Argun r. Georgia/Rus. Fed.
51 H7 Argun Rus. Fed.
123 E4 Argungu Nigeria
31 F2 Argunsk Rus. Fed.
31 F2 Argunskiy Khr. mountain range Rus. Fed.
154 D4 Argus Range mts California U.S.A.
30 B3 Arguut Mongolia
148 C4 Argyle Wisconsin U.S.A.
16 E3 Argyle, Lake l. Western Australia Australia
66 C4 Argyll reg. Scotland U.K.
66 C4 Argyll and Bute div. Scotland U.K.
114 A3 Argyrades Greece
126 E1 Arḥab reg. Yemen
30 B3 Arhangay div. Mongolia
31 G4 Ar Horqin Qi China
59 G3 Århult Sweden
55 C3 Århus div. Denmark
55 C3 Århus Århus Denmark
55 C3 Århus Bugt b. Denmark
8 E3 Aria New Zealand
28 C7 Ariake-kai b. Japan
111 F3 Ariamacina, Lago di l. Italy
128 B4 Ariamsvlei Namibia
109 H3 Ariano Irpino Italy
162 C3 Ariari r. Colombia
173 F2 Arias Argentina
35 D10 Ari Atoll atoll Maldives
166 A1 Ariaú Brazil
122 D4 Aribinda Burkina
164 B3 Arica Chile
162 B4 Arica Peru
28 E6 Arida Japan
17 C7 Arid, C. c. Western Australia Australia
127 □1 Aride I. i. Seychelles
93 D6 Ariège div. Midi-Pyrénées France
93 D5 Ariège r. France
173 H4 Ariel Argentina
30 B2 Arigiyn Gol r. Mongolia
152 G4 Arikaree r. Colorado U.S.A.
112 C3 Arilje Yugoslavia
159 □3 Arima Trinidad and Tobago
163 F2 Arimu Mine Guyana
64 B1 Arinagour Scotland U.K.
102 C3 Ariño Spain
165 E2 Arinos r. Brazil
169 E1 Arinos Minas Gerais Brazil
90 D2 Arinthod France
157 E5 Ario de Rosáles Mexico
54 C4 Ariogala Lithuania
159 □3 Aripo, Mt h. Trinidad Trinidad and Tobago
163 E5 Aripuanã r. Brazil
165 D1 Aripuanã Brazil
165 D1 Ariquemes Brazil
168 B2 Ariranhá r. Brazil
66 C4 Arisaig Scotland U.K.
66 C4 Arisaig, Sound of chan. Scotland U.K.
43 B4 'Arîsh, W. el watercourse Egypt
159 E5 Arismendi Venezuela
157 G6 Arista, Pto Mexico
136 D4 Aristazabal I. i. B.C. Canada
171 C6 Aristizábal, C. pt Argentina
108 B5 Aritzo Sardegna Italy
102 B2 Arive Spain
Arixang see Wenquan
99 H3 Ariza Spain
93 D5 Arize r. France
155 G4 Arizona div. U.S.A.
172 E3 Arizona Argentina
156 C2 Arizpe Mexico
59 E2 Årjäng Sweden
22 C3 Arjasa Indonesia
56 E2 Arjeplog Sweden
162 B1 Arjona Colombia
101 F3 Arjona Spain
22 C3 Arjuna, G. volcano Indonesia
52 F4 Arkadak Rus. Fed.
151 E5 Arkadelphia Arkansas U.S.A.
115 D5 Arkadia div. Greece
66 C4 Arkaig, Loch l. Scotland U.K.
47 G2 Arkalyk Kazakhstan
151 E5 Arkansas div. U.S.A.
151 F5 Arkansas r. Arkansas U.S.A.
151 D4 Arkansas City Kansas U.S.A.
37 G1 Arkatag Shan mountain range China
59 F3 Arkelstorp Sweden
118 D3 Arkenu, Jabal mt. Libya
50 F2 Arkhangel'sk div. Rus. Fed.
50 G1 Arkhangel'sk Rus. Fed.
52 C3 Arkhangel'skoye Rus. Fed.
53 E3 Arkhanhel's'ke Ukraine
31 J2 Arkhara r. Rus. Fed.
31 J2 Arkhara Rus. Fed.
45 L2 Arkhipelag Nordenshel'da is Rus. Fed.
52 E1 Arkhipovka Rus. Fed.
114 E4 Arkitsa Greece
67 E4 Arklow Rep. of Ireland
59 G2 Arkö i. Sweden
113 F6 Arkoi i. Greece
73 J1 Arkona, Kap headland Germany
59 G2 Årkosund Sweden
114 B4 Arkoudi i. Greece
44 J1 Arkticheskogo Instituta, O-va is Rus. Fed.
147 F3 Arkville New York U.S.A.
91 B3 Arlanc France
59 G2 Arlanda airport Sweden
99 G2 Arlanza r. Spain
99 G2 Arlanzón r. Spain
99 G2 Arlanzón Spain
99 H4 Arlas r. Spain
80 B3 Arlbergpaß pass Austria
91 C5 Arles France
93 E6 Arles-sur-Tech France
86 C2 Arleux France
123 E4 Arli Burkina
152 B2 Arlington Oregon U.S.A.
150 D2 Arlington S. Dakota U.S.A.
146 E5 Arlington Virginia U.S.A.
131 F4 Arlington South Africa
148 D4 Arlington Heights Illinois U.S.A.
123 F3 Arlit Niger
69 D5 Arlon div. Luxembourg Belgium
69 D5 Arlon Belgium
90 E3 Arly r. France
65 E2 Armadale Scotland U.K.
23 C5 Armadores i. Indonesia
Armageddon see Tel Megiddo
67 E2 Armagh div. Northern Ireland U.K.
67 E2 Armagh Northern Ireland U.K.
93 C5 Armagnac reg. France
98 C3 Armamar Portugal
45 R4 Arman' Rus. Fed.
86 C4 Armance r. France
90 C1 Armançon r. France
119 F2 Armant Egypt
113 F7 Armathia i. Greece
51 G6 Armavir Rus. Fed.
18 F5 Armenia country Asia
162 B3 Armenia Colombia
83 D3 Armeno Italy
115 F7 Armenoi Greece
86 B2 Armentières France
162 C3 Armero Colombia
111 E5 Armi, Capo dell' c. Italy
13 G2 Armidale New South Wales Australia
101 G3 Armilla Spain
173 G2 Arminda Argentina
91 B5 Armissan France
137 L2 Armit Lake l. N.W.T. Canada
47 G1 Armizonskoye Rus. Fed.
36 E5 Armori India
136 B3 Armour, Mt mt. Canada/U.S.A.
67 E1 Armoy Northern Ireland U.K.
14 B3 Armstrong r. Northern Terr. Australia
136 F4 Armstrong B.C. Canada
140 A1 Armstrong Ontario Canada
173 G2 Armstrong Argentina

151 D4 **Augusta** *Kansas* U.S.A.
147 J2 **Augusta** *Maine* U.S.A.
111 E5 **Augusta** *Sicilia* Italy
17 A7 **Augusta** *Western Australia* Australia
148 B3 **Augusta** *Wisconsin* U.S.A.
111 E5 **Augusta, Golfo di b.** *Sicilia* Italy
55 B5 **Augustenborg** Denmark
162 C1 **Augustin Cadazzi** Colombia
169 F3 **Augusto de Lima** Brazil
77 L2 **Augustów** Poland
16 D2 **Augustus I. i.** *Western Australia* Australia
17 B5 **Augustus, Mt mt.** *Western Australia* Australia
80 C2 **Au in der Hallertau** Germany
87 E5 **Aujon r.** France
72 E1 **Aukrug** Germany
54 C4 **Aukštelkai** Lithuania
16 C4 **Auld, L. salt flat** *Western Australia* Australia
74 E5 **Aulendorf** Germany
109 H4 **Auletta** Italy
106 D4 **Aulla** Italy
108 B3 **Aullène** *Corse* France
92 B2 **Aulnay** France
88 B3 **Aulne r.** France
86 C2 **Aulnoye-Aymeries** France
86 A2 **Ault** France
66 C3 **Aultbea** *Scotland* U.K.
75 G2 **Auma** Germany
89 G2 **Aumale** France
92 E2 **Aumance r.** France
87 E3 **Aumetz** France
90 D2 **Aumont** France
91 B4 **Aumont-Aubrac** France
90 B1 **Aunay-en-Bazois** France
89 E2 **Aunay-sur-Odon** France
89 G3 **Auneau** France
86 B3 **Auneuil** France
55 C3 **Auning** Denmark
92 A2 **Aunis reg.** France
7 □13 **Aunuu i.** *American Samoa* Pacific Ocean
130 B2 **Auob r.** Namibia/South Africa
139 G2 **Aupaluk** *Québec* Canada
91 E5 **Aups** France
25 D7 **Aur i.** Malaysia
54 C1 **Aura** Finland
74 F3 **Aurach** Germany
80 D3 **Aurach bei Kitzbühel** Austria
36 D4 **Auraiya** India
37 F4 **Aurangabad** India
38 A2 **Aurangābād** India
88 C4 **Auray** France
58 C1 **Aurdal** Norway
89 E2 **Aure r.** France
91 C3 **Aurec-sur-Loire** France
93 C5 **Aureilhan** France
91 D4 **Aurel** France
93 B5 **Aurensan** France
93 C6 **Aure, Vallée d' v.** France
72 C2 **Aurich** Germany
168 C4 **Auriflama** Brazil
93 C5 **Aurignac** France
168 C2 **Aurilândia** Brazil
93 E4 **Aurillac** France
91 D5 **Auriol** France
22 B2 **Aurkuning** Indonesia
58 B1 **Aurlandsfjorden inlet** Norway
81 E2 **Aurolzmünster** Austria
92 E2 **Auron r.** France
91 E4 **Auron** France
107 G2 **Auronzo di Cadore** Italy
152 F4 **Aurora** *Colorado* U.S.A.
148 C5 **Aurora** *Illinois* U.S.A.
146 A5 **Aurora** *Indiana* U.S.A.
147 J2 **Aurora** *Maine* U.S.A.
151 E4 **Aurora** *Missouri* U.S.A.
23 B5 **Aurora** Philippines
130 B6 **Aurora** South Africa
163 F3 **Aurora** Surinam
93 B4 **Auros** France
91 B4 **Auroux** France
15 E2 **Aurukun** *Queensland* Australia
109 F3 **Aurunci, Monti mts** Italy
128 B4 **Aus** Namibia
149 E3 **Au Sable r.** *Michigan* U.S.A.
147 G2 **Ausable r.** *New York* U.S.A.
149 F3 **Au Sable** *Michigan* U.S.A.
147 G2 **Ausable Forks** *New York* U.S.A.
148 D2 **Au Sable Pt pt** *Michigan* U.S.A.
149 F3 **Au Sable Pt pt** *Michigan* U.S.A.
107 H3 **Ausa-Corno** Italy
66 F1 **Auskerry i.** *Scotland* U.K.
109 F3 **Ausonia** Italy
93 E5 **Aussillon** France
82 B3 **Aussois** France
58 B2 **Aust-Agder div.** Norway
56 M6 **Austari-Jökulsá r.** Iceland
148 A4 **Austin** *Minnesota* U.S.A.
154 D2 **Austin** *Nevada* U.S.A.
151 D6 **Austin** *Texas* U.S.A.
17 B5 **Austin, L. salt flat** *Western Australia* Australia
14 D4 **Austral Downs** *Northern Terr.* Australia
4 C7 **Australia country**
179 □ **Australia, I. i.** *Kerguelen* Indian Ocean
179 C6 **Australian Antarctic Territory reg.** Antarctica
13 G3 **Australian Capital Territory div.** Australia
58 A1 **Austrheim** Norway
48 G4 **Austria country** Europe
56 D1 **Austvågøy i.** Norway
163 F4 **Autazes** Brazil
93 D5 **Auterive** France
82 A1 **Autet** France
86 A2 **Authie r.** France
141 F2 **Authier** *Québec* Canada
89 E4 **Authion r.** France
89 F4 **Authon** *Centre* France
91 E4 **Authon** *Provence - Alpes - Côte-d'Azur* France
89 F3 **Authon-du-Perche** France
156 D5 **Autlán** Mexico
82 A3 **Autrans** France
90 D1 **Autrey-lès-Gray** France
56 G2 **Autti** Finland
90 C2 **Autun** France
90 C2 **Autunois reg.** France
86 D3 **Auve** France
69 C4 **Auvelais** Belgium
90 B3 **Auvergne div.** France
92 E4 **Auvergne reg.** France
92 E3 **Auvergne, Monts d' mountain range** France
89 E4 **Auvers-le-Hamon** France
92 D3 **Auvézère r.** France
93 C4 **Auvignon r.** France
93 C4 **Auvillar** France
69 C5 **Auvillers-les-Forges** France
90 B1 **Auxerre** France
90 B1 **Auxerrois reg.** France
86 B2 **Auxi-le-Château** France
90 C1 **Auxois reg.** France
90 D1 **Auxonne** France
90 C2 **Auxy** France
92 E2 **Auzances** France
164 B2 **Auzangate, Nevado mt.** Peru
92 E3 **Auze r.** France
91 B3 **Auzon** France
93 C5 **Auzoue r.** France
147 F3 **Ava** *New York* U.S.A.
59 J1 **Åva** Finland
24 A2 **Ava** Myanmar
168 D5 **Avaí** Brazil
92 C2 **Availles-Limouzine** France
90 B1 **Avallon** France
89 E3 **Avaloirs, Mont des h.** France
154 C5 **Avalon** *California* U.S.A.
139 K4 **Avalon Peninsula pen.** *Newfoundland* Canada
170 E2 **Avalos r.** Argentina
42 F2 **Avān** Iran
98 B4 **Avanca** Portugal
93 C4 **Avance r.** France
91 E4 **Avançon** France
42 C2 **Avanos** Turkey
168 D5 **Avaré** Brazil
42 F2 **Āvārsīn** Iran
51 H7 **Avarskoye Koysu r.** Rus. Fed.
154 D4 **Avawatz Mts mts** *California* U.S.A.
39 E2 **Avaz** Iran
114 F2 **Avdira** Greece
53 G2 **Avdiyivka** Ukraine
98 B3 **Ave r.** Portugal
98 D2 **A Veiga** Spain
100 B1 **Aveiras de Cima** Portugal
98 B4 **Aveiro div.** Portugal
166 A1 **Aveiro** Brazil
98 B4 **Aveiro** Portugal
39 B2 **Āvej** Iran
69 B4 **Avelgem** Belgium
109 G4 **Avella** Italy
172 E1 **Avellanada** *Cordoba* Argentina
173 H3 **Avellaneda** *Buenos Aires* Argentina
170 E2 **Avellaneda** *Santa Fé* Argentina
109 G4 **Avellino div.** *Campania* Italy
109 G4 **Avellino** *Avellino* Italy
88 B4 **Aven r.** France
154 B3 **Avenal** *California* U.S.A.
82 C2 **Avenches** Switzerland
90 B2 **Avermes** France
55 C4 **Avernakø i.** Denmark
83 E2 **Avers** Switzerland
109 G4 **Aversa** Italy
159 G4 **Aves i.** Venezuela
86 B2 **Avesnes-le-Comte** France
86 C2 **Avesnes-sur-Helpe** France
59 G1 **Avesta** Sweden
93 E4 **Aveyron div.** *Midi-Pyrénées* France
93 E4 **Aveyron r.** France
109 F2 **Avezzano** Italy
113 E7 **Avgo i.** Greece
115 C6 **Avgo i.** Greece
115 E6 **Avgo i.** Greece
107 G2 **Aviano** Italy
170 D2 **Aviá Terai** Argentina
64 C1 **Avich, Loch l.** *Scotland* U.K.
66 E3 **Aviemore** *Scotland* U.K.
106 B3 **Avigliana** Italy
109 H4 **Avigliano** Italy
91 C5 **Avignon** France
99 F4 **Ávila div.** *Castilla y León* Spain
99 F4 **Ávila** *Ávila* Spain
98 E1 **Avilés** Spain
90 E1 **Avilley** France
98 B1 **Aviño** Spain
54 E2 **Avinurme** Estonia
102 E3 **Avinyó** Spain
107 E3 **Avio** Italy
86 B2 **Avion** France
69 D5 **Avioth** France
100 C1 **Avis** Portugal
107 F2 **Avisio r.** Italy
38 C5 **Avissawella** Sri Lanka
86 D4 **Avize** France
115 E6 **Avlemonas** Greece
115 E4 **Avlida** Greece
114 A3 **Avliotes** Greece
114 F4 **Avlonari** Greece
55 A3 **Avlum** Denmark
50 H2 **Avnyugskiy** Rus. Fed.
13 E4 **Avoca r.** *Victoria* Australia
150 E3 **Avoca** *Iowa* U.S.A.
13 F5 **Avoca** *Tasmania* Australia
13 E4 **Avoca** *Victoria* Australia
67 E4 **Avoca** Rep. of Ireland
54 D3 **Avoci** Latvia
89 F4 **Avoine** France
111 E6 **Avola** *Sicilia* Italy
63 E3 **Avon r.** *England* U.K.
62 C4 **Avon r.** *England* U.K.
62 D3 **Avon r.** *England* U.K.
66 E3 **Avon r.** *Scotland* U.K.
17 B6 **Avon r.** *Western Australia* Australia
148 B5 **Avon** *Illinois* U.S.A.
86 B4 **Avon** France
155 F5 **Avondale** *Arizona* U.S.A.
14 D3 **Avon Downs** *Northern Terr.* Australia
15 F4 **Avon Downs** *Queensland* Australia
67 E4 **Avonmore r.** Rep. of Ireland
62 D3 **Avonmouth** *England* U.K.
145 D7 **Avon Park** *Florida* U.S.A.
130 D6 **Avontuur** South Africa
92 E1 **Avord** France
82 B1 **Avoudrey** France
79 M5 **Avram Iancu** *Alba* Romania
79 L5 **Avram Iancu** *Bihor* Romania
88 D3 **Avranches** France
89 F3 **Avre r.** France
86 B3 **Avre r.** *Picardie* France
112 E2 **Avrig** Romania
87 E3 **Avril** France
89 E4 **Avrillé** France
6 □1 **Avuavu** Solomon Is.
29 □2 **Awa** Japan
43 D3 **A'waj r.** Syria
28 E6 **Awaji-shima i.** Japan
8 E3 **Awakino** New Zealand
39 B4 **Awālī** Bahrain
22 D4 **Awang** Indonesia
69 D4 **Awans** Belgium
8 D1 **Awanui** New Zealand
22 C3 **Awarawar, Tg pt** Indonesia
126 D3 **Āwarē** Ethiopia
9 B6 **Awarua Pt pt** New Zealand
126 C3 **Āwasa** Ethiopia
126 D3 **Āwash** Ethiopia
29 G4 **Awa-shima i.** Japan
126 D3 **Āwash National Park nat. park** Ethiopia
126 D3 **Āwash West Wildlife Reserve res.** Ethiopia
47 K4 **Awat** China
126 C3 **Āwatā Shet' watercourse** Ethiopia
9 D4 **Awatere r.** New Zealand
118 B2 **Awbārī** Libya
67 C4 **Awbeg r.** Rep. of Ireland
126 D2 **Awd reg.** Yemen
126 D4 **Aw Dheegle** Somalia
124 E2 **Aweil** Sudan
66 C4 **Awe, Loch l.** *Scotland* U.K.
118 D2 **Awjilah** Libya
123 F5 **Awka** Nigeria
120 B3 **Awlitis watercourse** *Western Sahara*
22 E2 **Awo r.** Indonesia
120 B4 **Awserd** *Western Sahara*
80 C3 **Axams** Austria
93 E6 **Axat** France
62 C4 **Axe r.** *England* U.K.
69 B3 **Axel** Netherlands
135 J2 **Axel Heiberg Island i.** *N.W.T.* Canada
112 E1 **Axente Sever** Romania
122 D6 **Axim** Ghana
163 F4 **Axinim** Brazil
114 D2 **Axios r.** Greece
166 D1 **Axixa** Brazil
93 D6 **Ax-les-Thermes** France
59 G1 **Axmar** Sweden
62 D4 **Axminster** *England* U.K.
46 E1 **Ay r.** Rus. Fed.
86 D3 **Ay** France
29 E6 **Ayabe** Japan
120 D2 **Ayachi, Jbel mt.** Morocco
173 H4 **Ayacucho** Argentina
164 B2 **Ayacucho** Peru
24 A2 **Ayadaw** Myanmar
47 J3 **Ayaguz watercourse** Kazakhstan
47 K3 **Ayaguz** Kazakhstan
46 F4 **Ayakagytma, Vpadina depression** Uzbekistan
47 G4 **Ayakkuduk** Uzbekistan
26 E4 **Ayakkum Hu salt lake** China
122 D5 **Ayamé, Lac d' l.** Côte d'Ivoire
100 C3 **Ayamonte** Spain
45 P4 **Ayan** Rus. Fed.
42 C1 **Ayancık** Turkey
31 H5 **Ayang** North Korea
123 F5 **Ayangba** Nigeria
162 B2 **Ayapel** Colombia
164 B2 **Ayaviri** Peru
39 G1 **Āybak** Afghanistan
46 C3 **Aybas** Kazakhstan
65 G3 **Aycliffe** *England* U.K.
51 F5 **Aydar r.** Rus. Fed.
47 G4 **Aydarkul', Ozero l.** Uzbekistan
113 F6 **Aydin div.** Turkey
42 A2 **Aydın** Turkey
43 B1 **Aydıncık** Turkey
113 F5 **Aydın Dağları mountain range** Turkey
43 C1 **Aydos Dağı mt.** Turkey
126 D2 **Āyelu Terara mt.** Ethiopia
92 D3 **Ayen** France
102 C2 **Ayerbe** Spain
25 □ **Ayer Chawan, P. i.** Singapore
25 □ **Ayer Merbau, P. i.** Singapore
14 B5 **Ayers Rock h.** *Northern Terr.* Australia
80 C3 **Aying** Germany
126 C2 **Āykel** Ethiopia
46 F2 **Ayke, Oz. l.** Kazakhstan
45 N3 **Aykhal** Rus. Fed.
50 J2 **Aykino** Rus. Fed.
63 F3 **Aylesbury** *England* U.K.
9 D5 **Aylesbury** New Zealand
63 H3 **Aylesham** *England* U.K.
146 E6 **Aylett** *Virginia* U.S.A.
99 G3 **Ayllón** Spain
140 E5 **Aylmer** *Ontario* Canada
141 K4 **Aylmer, Lac l.** *Québec* Canada
137 H2 **Aylmer Lake l.** *N.W.T.* Canada
63 H2 **Aylsham** *England* U.K.
82 C3 **Aymavilles** Italy
164 B2 **Ayna** Peru
101 H2 **Ayna** Spain
93 D4 **Aynac** France
39 B3 **'Ayn al 'Abd well** Saudi Arabia
118 C2 **'Ayn al 'Abd** Libya
43 D4 **'Ayn al Baidā'** Saudi Arabia
118 D3 **'Ayn al Ghazāl spring** Libya
47 G5 **Ayní** Tajikistan
119 H3 **'Aynīn well** Saudi Arabia
42 D2 **'Ayn 'Īsá** Syria
43 C5 **'Aynūnah** Saudi Arabia
118 D3 **'Ayn Zuwayyah spring** Libya
126 B3 **Ayod** Sudan
45 S3 **Ayon, O. i.** Rus. Fed.
103 B5 **Ayora** Spain
123 E4 **Ayorou** Niger
120 C4 **'Ayoûn 'Abd el Mâlek well** Mauritania
120 C5 **'Ayoûn El 'Atroûs** Mauritania
66 D5 **Ayr r.** *Scotland* U.K.
15 F3 **Ayr** *Queensland* Australia
66 D5 **Ayr** *Scotland* U.K.
43 B1 **Ayrancı** Turkey
64 D3 **Ayre, Point of pt** Isle of Man
65 G3 **Aysgarth** *England* U.K.
80 B2 **Aystetten** Germany
112 F3 **Aytos** Bulgaria
92 A2 **Aytré** France
100 D1 **Ayuela r.** Spain
25 C4 **Ayutthaya** Thailand
162 B4 **Ayuy** Ecuador
52 G3 **Ayva r.** Rus. Fed.
42 A2 **Ayvacık** Turkey
42 A2 **Ayvalık** Turkey
69 D4 **Aywaille** Belgium
156 J6 **Azacualpa** Honduras
123 E3 **Azaguégué well** Niger
102 C3 **Azaila** Spain
29 □2 **Azama** Japan
100 C2 **Azambuja r.** Portugal
100 B1 **Azambuja** Portugal
37 E4 **Azamgarh** India
102 D3 **Azanúy** Spain
122 D3 **Azaouâd reg.** Mali
123 E3 **Azaouagh, Vallée de watercourse** Mali/Niger
164 C3 **Azapa r.** Chile
164 B3 **Azapa** Chile
39 A1 **Āzarān** Iran
42 F2 **Azarbayjan-e Gharbi div.** Iran
39 A1 **Āzarbāyjān-e Shargi div.** Iran
123 G4 **Azare** Nigeria
100 C2 **Azaruja** Portugal
54 F5 **Azarychy** Belarus
163 G3 **Azauri** Brazil
89 F4 **Azay-le-Rideau** France
43 D1 **A'zāz** Syria
Azbine mts *see* **Massif de l'Aïr**
42 C1 **Azdavay** Turkey
89 E4 **Azé** France
120 C2 **Azemmour** Morocco
92 D2 **Azerables** France
18 F5 **Azerbaijan country** Asia
90 C2 **Azergues r.** France
173 K1 **Azevedo Sodré** Brazil
100 C2 **Azevel r.** Portugal
126 C2 **Āzezo** Ethiopia
42 F2 **Āzghān** Iran
46 F4 **Azhar** Kazakhstan
47 L2 **Azhu-Tayga, G. mt.** Rus. Fed.
120 C2 **Azilal** Morocco
140 E3 **Azilda** *Ontario* Canada
147 H2 **Aziscohos Lake l.** *Maine* U.S.A.
39 D3 **'Azīzābād** Iran
99 H1 **Azkoitia** Spain
119 G2 **Azlam, W. watercourse** Saudi Arabia
100 D3 **Aznalcóllar** Spain
162 B4 **Azogues** Ecuador
50 H1 **Azopol'ye** Rus. Fed.
Azores is *see* **Açores, Arquipélago dos**
174 H3 **Azores - Cape St Vincent Ridge sea feature** Atlantic Ocean
51 F6 **Azov** Rus. Fed.
51 E6 **Azov, Sea of sea** Asia/Europe
Azovskoye More sea *see* **Azov, Sea of**
99 H1 **Azpeitia** Spain
120 C2 **Azrou** Morocco
153 F4 **Aztec** *New Mexico* U.S.A.
159 E3 **Azua** Dominican Rep.
100 E2 **Azuaga** Spain
102 C3 **Azuara** Spain
28 B7 **Azūchi-Ō-shima i.** Japan
101 G2 **Azuer r.** Spain
156 K8 **Azuero, Península de pen.** Panama
173 H4 **Azul r.** Argentina
172 B3 **Azul volcano** Chile
173 H4 **Azul** Argentina
172 B6 **Azul, C. mt.** Argentina
162 B5 **Azul, Cerro h.** Peru
162 □ **Azul, Co volcano** *Galapagos Is* Ecuador
164 A1 **Azul, Cord. mountain range** Peru
29 H5 **Azuma-san volcano** Japan
99 G4 **Azuqueca de Henares** Spain
164 D4 **Azurduy** Bolivia
99 F5 **Azután, Emb. de resr** Spain
77 O2 **Azyarnitsa** Belarus
90 B2 **Azy-le-Vif** France
77 N2 **Azyory** Belarus
43 D3 **Az Zabadānī** Syria
119 H4 **Aẓ Ẓafīr** Saudi Arabia
39 B4 **Aẓ Ẓahrān** Saudi Arabia
107 G3 **Azzano Decimo** Italy
118 B1 **Az Zāwīyah** Libya
126 D1 **Az Zaydīyah** Yemen
120 A4 **Azzeffâl h.** Mauritania
119 H2 **Az Zilfī** Saudi Arabia
118 B1 **Az Zintān** Libya
83 F3 **Azzone** Italy
42 F4 **Az Zubayr** Iraq
126 D1 **Az Zuhrah** Yemen
126 D2 **Az Zuqur I. i.** Yemen

B

32 D2 **Ba r.** China
6 □8 **Ba r.** Fiji
6 □8 **Ba** Fiji
6 □2 **Baâba i.** *New Caledonia* Pacific Ocean
22 D1 **Baai r.** Indonesia
43 D2 **Ba'albek** Lebanon
87 E3 **Baâlon** France
43 C3 **Baaqline** Lebanon
87 H4 **Baar reg.** Germany
83 D1 **Baar** Switzerland
126 D4 **Baardheere** Somalia
69 C3 **Baarle-Hertog** Belgium
69 C3 **Baarle-Nassau** Netherlands
68 D2 **Baarn** Netherlands
36 D4 **Bab** India
81 F1 **Baba h.** Czech Rep.
120 B5 **Bababé** Mauritania
113 F5 **Baba Burnu pt** Turkey
166 C2 **Babaçulândia** Brazil
112 G2 **Babadag** Romania
113 G6 **Babadağ** Turkey
39 D1 **Babadurmaz** Turkmenistan
113 F4 **Babaeski** Turkey
162 B4 **Babahoyo** Ecuador
37 E3 **Babai r.** Nepal
36 D5 **Babai** India
30 C4 **Babai Gaxun** China
23 C5 **Babak** Philippines
39 C2 **Bābā Khalāl** Iran
123 G4 **Babakourimigana well** Niger
39 F2 **Bābā, Kūh-e mountain range** Afghanistan
126 D2 **Bāb al Mandab str.** Asia
126 D2 **Bāb al Mandab, C. c.** Yemen
22 D2 **Babana** Indonesia
131 H4 **Babanango** South Africa
131 G4 **Babangiboni mt.** South Africa
124 B2 **Babanki** Cameroon
43 D2 **Bābannā** Syria
32 D4 **Babao** China
114 C2 **Baba Planina mountain range** Greece/Macedonia
21 J8 **Babar i.** Indonesia
127 C5 **Babati** Tanzania
50 E3 **Babayevo** Rus. Fed.
51 H7 **Babayurt** Rus. Fed.
62 C4 **Babbacombe Bay b.** *England* U.K.
148 B2 **Babbitt** *Minnesota* U.S.A.
23 □1 **Babelthuap i.** Palau
74 F4 **Babenhausen** *Baden-Württemberg* Germany
74 D3 **Babenhausen** *Hessen* Germany
36 E4 **Baberu** India
52 F2 **Babeyevo** Rus. Fed.
98 D1 **Babia reg.** Spain
77 H6 **Babia Góra mt.** Poland
76 G3 **Babiak** Poland
32 C4 **Babian r.** China
156 C2 **Babicora** Mexico
156 D2 **Babícora, L. de salt lake** Mexico
42 F3 **Bābil div.** Iraq
99 E4 **Babilafuente** Spain
76 D3 **Babimost** Poland
15 F3 **Babinda** *Queensland* Australia
136 D4 **Babine Lake l.** *B.C.* Canada
77 H6 **Babiogórski Park Narodowy nat. park** Poland
21 K7 **Babo** Indonesia
44 G6 **Bābol** Iran
124 E3 **Babonde** Congo(Zaire)
124 B2 **Babongo** Cameroon
130 B6 **Baboon Pt pt** South Africa
155 G6 **Baboquivari Peak summit** *Arizona* U.S.A.
124 B2 **Baboua** Central African Rep.
54 F5 **Babruysk** Belarus
31 K2 **Babstovo** Rus. Fed.
54 C4 **Babtai** Lithuania
36 B4 **Babuhri** India
114 C1 **Babuna Planina mountain range** Macedonia
112 D3 **Babušnica** Yugoslavia
23 B2 **Babuyan i.** Philippines
23 A4 **Babuyan** Philippines
23 B2 **Babuyan Channel chan.** Philippines
23 B2 **Babuyan Islands is** Philippines
42 F3 **Babylon** Iraq
52 B2 **Babynino** Rus. Fed.
126 E3 **Bacaadweyn** Somalia
166 D1 **Bacabal** Brazil
166 B1 **Bacajá r.** Brazil
157 H5 **Bacalar** Mexico
21 J7 **Bacan i.** Indonesia
23 B2 **Bacarra** Philippines
112 F1 **Bacău** Romania
87 F4 **Baccarat** France
107 F3 **Bacchiglione r.** Italy
13 F4 **Bacchus Marsh** *Victoria* Australia
106 C2 **Baceno** Italy
24 D2 **Băc Giang** Vietnam
24 D2 **Băc Giang** Vietnam
80 B3 **Bach** Austria
31 K2 **Bacha** China
74 C2 **Bacharach** Germany
80 B2 **Bachhagel** Germany
153 F6 **Bachiniva** Mexico
47 J5 **Bachu** China
47 J5 **Bachu Liuchang** China
137 J1 **Back r.** *N.W.T.* Canada
79 J5 **Bačka reg.** Hungary/Yugoslavia
112 B2 **Bačka Palanka** Yugoslavia
79 J6 **Bačka Topola** Yugoslavia
136 D2 **Backbone Ranges mountain range** *N.W.T.* Canada
56 E3 **Backe** Sweden
59 E2 **Bäckefors** Sweden
59 F2 **Bäckhammar** Sweden
79 H6 **Bački Monoštor** Yugoslavia
112 B2 **Bački Petrovac** Yugoslavia
12 D3 **Backstairs Pass. chan.** *S. Australia* Australia
24 D2 **Bac Lac** Vietnam
25 D5 **Bac Liêu** Vietnam
156 C2 **Bacoachi** Mexico
109 G4 **Bacoli** Italy
23 B4 **Bacolod** Philippines
23 B3 **Baco, Mt mt.** Philippines
24 D2 **Băc Quang** Vietnam
89 F2 **Bacqueville-en-Caux** France
138 F2 **Bacqueville, Lac l.** *Québec* Canada
79 J5 **Bácsalmás** Hungary
79 J5 **Bács-Kiskun div.** Hungary
73 L3 **Baczyna** Poland
25 B5 **Bada i.** Myanmar
126 C3 **Bada mt.** Ethiopia
30 D2 **Bada** Rus. Fed.
75 H4 **Bad Abbach** Germany
79 G5 **Badacsonytomaj** Hungary
38 A4 **Badagara** India
75 H5 **Bad Aibling** Germany
30 B4 **Badain Jaran Shamo desert** China
163 E4 **Badajós** *Amazonas* Brazil
166 C1 **Badajós** *Pará* Brazil
163 E4 **Badajós, Lago l.** Brazil
100 D2 **Badajoz div.** *Extremadura* Spain
100 D2 **Badajoz** *Badajoz* Spain
102 F3 **Badalona** Spain
38 A3 **Badami** India
119 H1 **Badanah** Saudi Arabia
Badaojiang *see* **Hunjiang**
36 D3 **Badarīnāth** India
37 H4 **Badarpur** India
81 E3 **Bad Aussee** Austria
149 F4 **Bad Axe** *Michigan* U.S.A.
82 C1 **Bad Bellingen** Germany
72 C3 **Bad Bentheim** Germany
74 C3 **Bad Bergzabern** Germany
75 G2 **Bad Berka** Germany
72 D4 **Bad Berleburg** Germany
75 G2 **Bad Berneck im Fichtelgebirge** Germany
73 F2 **Bad Bevensen** Germany
73 G4 **Bad Bibra** Germany
75 J4 **Bad Birnbach** Germany
75 G2 **Bad Blankenburg** Germany
75 H2 **Bad Brambach** Germany
72 E2 **Bad Bramstedt** Germany
74 C2 **Bad Breisig** Germany
74 E2 **Bad Brückenau** Germany
74 E4 **Bad Buchau** Germany
74 D2 **Bad Camberg** Germany
139 H4 **Baddeck** *Nova Scotia* Canada
56 F1 **Badderen** Norway
39 F3 **Baddo watercourse** Pakistan
73 G1 **Bad Doberan** Germany
72 E4 **Bad Driburg** Germany
73 H4 **Bad Düben** Germany
74 D3 **Bad Dürkheim** Germany
73 H4 **Bad Dürrenberg** Germany
74 D4 **Bad Dürrheim** Germany
92 D3 **Badefols-d'Ans** France
123 F4 **Badéguichéri** Niger
74 C2 **Bad Ems** Germany
81 H3 **Baden div.** Austria
81 H2 **Baden** Austria
83 D1 **Baden** Switzerland
74 D4 **Baden-Baden** Germany
87 H2 **Bad Endbach** Germany
75 H5 **Bad Endorf** Germany
66 D4 **Badenoch reg.** *Scotland* U.K.
82 C1 **Badenweiler** Germany
74 D4 **Baden-Württemberg div.** Germany
107 H3 **Baderna** Croatia
72 D3 **Bad Essen** Germany
80 D3 **Bad Feilnbach** Germany
73 G4 **Bad Frankenhausen** Germany
73 K3 **Bad Freienwalde** Germany
74 E3 **Bad Friedrichshall** Germany
75 J4 **Bad Füssing** Germany
72 F4 **Bad Gandersheim** Germany
80 E3 **Badgastein** Austria
139 J4 **Badger** *Newfoundland* Canada
81 G4 **Bad Gleichenberg** Austria
81 E3 **Bad Goisern** Austria
81 F2 **Bad Großpertholz** Austria
72 F4 **Bad Grund (Harz)** Germany
81 F2 **Bad Hall** Austria
80 D3 **Bad Häring** Austria
73 F4 **Bad Harzburg** Germany
75 G5 **Bad Heilbrunn** Germany
87 H4 **Bad Herrenalb** Germany
74 E2 **Bad Hersfeld** Germany
68 C2 **Badhoevedorp** Netherlands
80 E3 **Bad Hofgastein** Austria
74 D2 **Bad Homburg vor der Höhe** Germany
74 C2 **Bad Honnef** Germany
107 F2 **Badia** Italy
103 G5 **Badia d'Alcúdia b.** Spain
103 F5 **Badia de Palma b.** Spain
103 G5 **Badia de Pollença b.** Spain
107 F3 **Badia Polesine** Italy
72 D3 **Bad Iburg** Germany
99 H4 **Badiel r.** Spain
126 B3 **Badigeru Swamp** Sudan
36 B4 **Badin** Pakistan
156 D3 **Badiraguato** Mexico
81 E3 **Bad Ischl** Austria
42 D3 **Bādiyat ash Shām desert** Asia
72 E4 **Bad Karlshafen** Germany
74 F2 **Bad Kissingen** Germany
73 G2 **Bad Kleinen** Germany
74 E3 **Bad König** Germany
73 G4 **Bad Kösen** Germany
74 C3 **Bad Kreuznach** Germany
74 C5 **Bad Krozingen** Germany
74 D2 **Bad Laasphe** Germany
150 C2 **Badlands reg.** *N. Dakota* U.S.A.
150 C3 **Badlands Nat. Park** *S. Dakota* U.S.A.
73 F4 **Bad Langensalza** Germany
73 H4 **Bad Lausick** Germany
72 F4 **Bad Lauterberg im Harz** Germany
81 F2 **Bad Leonfelden** Austria
73 J4 **Bad Liebenwerda** Germany
72 D4 **Bad Lippspringe** Germany
74 C2 **Bad Marienberg (Westerwald)** Germany
74 E3 **Bad Mergentheim** Germany
81 E3 **Bad Mitterndorf** Austria
72 E3 **Bad Münder am Deister** Germany
74 B2 **Bad Münstereifel** Germany
73 K4 **Bad Muskau** Germany
74 D2 **Bad Nauheim** Germany
72 E3 **Bad Nenndorf** Germany
74 C2 **Bad Neuenahr-Ahrweiler** Germany
74 F2 **Bad Neustadt an der Saale** Germany
36 C4 **Badnor** India
101 F3 **Badolatosa** Spain
72 F2 **Bad Oldesloe** Germany
33 E2 **Badong** China
25 D5 **Ba Đông** Vietnam
87 F4 **Badonviller** France
123 E5 **Badou** Togo
46 C5 **Bädovan Burnu pt** Azerbaijan
112 B2 **Badovinci** Yugoslavia
81 H2 **Bad Pirawarth** Austria
131 H2 **Badplass** South Africa
72 E4 **Bad Pyrmont** Germany
81 G4 **Bad Radkersburg div.** Austria
81 H4 **Bad Radkersburg** Austria
83 E1 **Bad Ragaz** Switzerland
42 F3 **Badrah** Iraq
74 E3 **Bad Rappenau** Germany
75 H5 **Bad Reichenhall** Germany
119 G3 **Badr Ḩunayn** Saudi Arabia
36 D3 **Badrinath Peaks mts** India
73 K3 **Bad Saarow-Pieskow** Germany
73 F4 **Bad Sachsa** Germany
82 C1 **Bad Säckingen** Germany
81 F4 **Bad St Leonhard im Lavanttal** Austria
72 F3 **Bad Salzdetfurth** Germany
72 D3 **Bad Salzuflen** Germany
74 F2 **Bad Salzungen** Germany
72 D4 **Bad Sassendorf** Germany
81 E2 **Bad Schallerbach** Austria
75 K2 **Bad Schandau** Germany
73 H4 **Bad Schmiedeberg** Germany
87 H3 **Bad Schönborn** Germany
74 E4 **Bad Schussenried** Germany
74 D2 **Bad Schwalbach** Germany
73 F2 **Bad Schwartau** Germany
72 F2 **Bad Segeberg** Germany
74 E2 **Bad Soden-Salmünster** Germany
72 E4 **Bad Sooden-Allendorf** Germany
75 F1 **Bad Tennstedt** Germany
75 G5 **Bad Tölz** Germany
11 H1 **Badu I. i.** *Queensland* Australia
38 C5 **Badulla** Sri Lanka
74 E4 **Bad Urach** Germany
87 H2 **Bad Vilbel** Germany
81 H3 **Bad Vöslau** Austria
74 E5 **Bad Waldsee** Germany
81 H3 **Bad Waltersdorf** Austria
72 E4 **Bad Wildungen** Germany
73 G3 **Bad Wilsnack** Germany
74 F3 **Bad Windsheim** Germany
75 F5 **Bad Wörishofen** Germany
74 E5 **Bad Wurzach** Germany
81 F2 **Bad Zell** Austria
31 K2 **Badzhal** Rus. Fed.
72 D2 **Bad Zwischenahn** Germany
56 L6 **Bæir** Iceland
55 B4 **Bække** Denmark
55 A3 **Bækmarksbro** Denmark
69 D4 **Baelen** Belgium
101 F3 **Baena** Spain
72 B5 **Baesweiler** Germany
162 B4 **Baeza** Ecuador
101 G3 **Baeza** Spain
124 B2 **Bafang** Cameroon
122 B4 **Bafatá** Guinea-Bissau
36 C2 **Baffa** Pakistan
178 A3 **Baffin Basin sea feature** Atlantic Ocean
135 M2 **Baffin Bay sea** Canada/Greenland
135 L2 **Baffin Island i.** *N.W.T.* Canada
124 B3 **Bafia** Cameroon
123 E5 **Bafilo** Togo
122 B4 **Bafing r.** Guinea/Mali
122 B4 **Bafing, Parc National du nat. park** Mali
43 D1 **Bafliyun** Syria
68 E1 **Baflo** Netherlands
122 B4 **Bafoulabé** Mali
124 B2 **Bafoussam** Cameroon
39 C3 **Bāfq** Iran
42 C1 **Bafra** Turkey
42 D1 **Bafra Burun pt** Turkey
39 D3 **Bāft** Iran
124 E3 **Bafwamboma** Congo(Zaire)
124 E3 **Bafwasende** Congo(Zaire)
166 C3 **Bagagem r.** Brazil
37 F4 **Bagaha** India
111 E4 **Bagaladi** Italy
38 A2 **Bagalkot** India
127 C6 **Bagamoyo** Tanzania
25 C7 **Bagan Datuk** Malaysia
128 C2 **Bagani** Namibia
23 B5 **Baganian Peninsula pen.** Philippines
25 C6 **Bagan Serai** Malaysia
25 C7 **Bagansiapiapi** Indonesia
113 F6 **Bağarası** Turkey
123 F3 **Bagaré well** Niger
123 E4 **Bagaroua** Niger
125 C4 **Bagata** Congo(Zaire)
32 B1 **Bag Belqer** China
155 F4 **Bagdad** *Arizona* U.S.A.
173 K1 **Bagé** Brazil
90 C2 **Bâgé-le-Châtel** France
55 C5 **Bagenkop** Denmark
102 E3 **Bages reg.** Spain
93 E6 **Bages** France
59 F2 **Baggå** Sweden
152 F3 **Baggs** *Wyoming* U.S.A.
62 B3 **Baggy Point pt** *England* U.K.
36 C5 **Bagh** India
Bagh a' Chaisteil *see* **Castlebay**
39 F3 **Baghak** Pakistan
Baghasdail, Loch *see* **Lochboisdale**
42 F3 **Baghdād** Iraq
39 B3 **Bāgh-e Malek** Iran
110 C4 **Bagheria** *Sicilia* Italy
39 D3 **Bāghīn** Iran
39 G1 **Baghlān** Afghanistan
39 F2 **Baghrān** Afghanistan
150 E2 **Bagley** *Minnesota* U.S.A.
37 E3 **Baglung** Nepal
107 F4 **Bagnacavallo** Italy
111 E4 **Bagnara Calabra** Italy
80 E5 **Bagnaria Arsa** Italy
106 C4 **Bagnasco** Italy
93 C5 **Bagnères-de-Bigorre** France
93 C6 **Bagnères-de-Luchon** France
107 E4 **Bagni di Lucca** Italy
106 D2 **Bagni di Masino** Italy
107 E2 **Bagni di Rabbi** Italy
107 F5 **Bagno di Romagna** Italy
109 G3 **Bagnoli del Trigno** Italy
109 H4 **Bagnoli Irpino** Italy
106 E3 **Bagnolo Mella** Italy
83 F3 **Bagnolo San Vito** Italy
91 B4 **Bagnols-les-Bains** France
91 C4 **Bagnols-sur-Cèze** France
106 E4 **Bagnone** Italy
108 E2 **Bagnoregio** Italy
37 F4 **Bagnuiti r.** Nepal
30 D5 **Bag Nur l.** China
55 B4 **Bågø i.** Denmark
Bago *see* **Pegu**
23 B4 **Bago** Philippines
78 F5 **Bagod** Hungary
122 C4 **Bagoé r.** Côte d'Ivoire/Mali
106 E3 **Bagolino** Italy
54 B4 **Bagrationovsk** Rus. Fed.
Bagrax Hu l. *see* **Bosten Hu**
166 B1 **Bagre** Brazil
162 B5 **Bagua Grande** Peru
123 E4 **Bagudo** Nigeria
23 B2 **Bagulo** Philippines
123 F3 **Bagzane, Monts mt.** Niger
37 E4 **Bahadurganj** Nepal
36 D3 **Bahadurgarh** India
Bahāmabād *see* **Rafsanjān**
133 L7 **Bahamas, The country** Caribbean
159 □4 **Baham, Pte pt** *Martinique* Caribbean
37 G4 **Baharampur** India
36 B4 **Bahardipur** Pakistan

119 E2 Bahariya Oasis oasis Egypt
25 C7 Bahau Malaysia
22 C2 Bahaur Indonesia
36 C3 Bahawalnagar Pakistan
36 B3 Bahawalpur Pakistan
42 D2 Bahçe Turkey
36 D3 Baheri India
127 C6 Bahi Tanzania
169 H1 Bahia div. Brazil
173 F5 Bahía Blanca Argentina
171 C6 Bahía Bustamante Argentina
172 F6 Bahía Creek Argentina
7 □15 Bahia Cumberland b. *Juan Fernandez Is* Chile
162 □ Bahia Elizabeth b. *Galapagos Is* Ecuador
156 J5 Bahía, Islas de la is Honduras
156 C2 Bahía Kino Mexico
171 C6 Bahía Laura Argentina
172 A6 Bahía Mansa Chile
165 E4 Bahía Negra Paraguay
173 F6 Bahía San Blas Argentina
99 F2 Bahíllo Spain
126 C2 Bahir Dar Ethiopia
39 B3 Bahmanyārī ye Pā'īn Iran
119 H4 Bahr Saudi Arabia
43 A4 Bahra el Burullus lag. Egypt
43 A4 Bahra el Manzala lag. Egypt
37 E4 Bahraich India
18 G7 Bahrain country Asia
39 B4 Bahrain, Gulf of g. Asia
37 E4 Bahramghat India
39 D3 Bahrāmjerd Iran
124 D2 Bahr Aouk r. Central African Rep./Chad
43 D2 Bahrat Hims resr Syria
118 D5 Bahr Azoum watercourse Chad
118 D5 Bahr Azrak watercourse Chad
124 C2 Bahr Dosséo r. Chad
126 B2 Bahr el Abiad r. Sudan/Uganda
124 E1 Bahr el Arab watercourse Sudan
119 F5 Bahr el Azraq r. Ethiopia/Sudan
124 E2 Bahr El Ghazal div. Sudan
118 C5 Bahr el Ghazal r. Chad
124 E2 Bahr el Ghazal r. Sudan
126 B3 Bahr el Jebel r. Sudan/Uganda
Bahr el Nîl r. see Nile
126 B3 Bahr el Zeraf r. Sudan
124 C2 Bahr Kéita r. Chad
124 C1 Bahr Korom watercourse Chad
36 D4 Bahror India
124 C2 Bahr Salamat r. Chad
43 D3 Bahr Şayqal l. Syria
43 A5 Bahr Yûsef r. Egypt
39 E4 Bāhū Kālāt Iran
33 F1 Bai r. China
112 G2 Baia Romania
112 D2 Baia de Aramă Romania
112 D1 Baia de Arieş Romania
166 F2 Baía de Traição Brazil
125 B7 Baía dos Tigres Angola
125 B6 Baia Farta Angola
112 D1 Baia Mare Romania
166 C1 Baião Brazil
106 B5 Baiardo Italy
112 D1 Baia Sprie Romania
39 C2 Baiazeh Iran
118 D4 Baïbeli well Chad
124 C2 Baïbokoum Chad
47 K4 Baicheng China
31 G3 Baicheng China
112 E2 Băicoi Romania
124 D2 Baïdou r. Central African Rep.
139 G4 Baie Comeau *Québec* Canada
141 J1 Baie du Poste *Québec* Canada
159 □5 Baie-Mahault b. *Guadeloupe* Caribbean
74 E5 Baienfurt Germany
74 D4 Baiersbronn Germany
75 G3 Baiersdorf Germany
139 F4 Baie Saint Paul *Québec* Canada
139 J4 Baie Verte *Newfoundland* Canada
92 B3 Baignes-Ste-Radegonde France
90 C1 Baigneux-les-Juifs France
173 G3 Baigorrita Argentina
31 F5 Baigou r. China
102 B2 Baigura mt. Spain
32 B3 Baihanchang China
36 E5 Baihar India
33 E1 Baihe China
31 J4 Baihe China
42 E3 Baiji Iraq
47 L3 Baijiantan China
36 D2 Baijnath India
36 D3 Baijnath India
Baikal, Lake l. see Baykal, Ozero
Baile Átha Cliath see Dublin
Baile Átha Luain see Athlone
112 E2 Băile Govora Romania
112 D2 Băile Herculane Romania
101 G2 Bailén Spain
112 D2 Băileşti Romania
112 E1 Băile Tuşnad Romania
131 F5 Bailey South Africa
17 C6 Bailey R. h. *Western Australia* Australia
163 G3 Bailique Brazil
91 C5 Baillargues France
89 G3 Bailleau-le-Pin France
86 B2 Bailleul France
137 H2 Baillie r. *N.W.T.* Canada
67 E3 Baillieborough Rep. of Ireland
159 □5 Baillif *Guadeloupe* Caribbean
69 D4 Baillonville Belgium
93 B6 Bailo Spain
32 C1 Bailong r. China
125 C6 Bailundo Angola
32 C1 Baima China
65 H4 Bain r. *England* U.K.
37 G3 Bainang China
145 C6 Bainbridge *Georgia* U.S.A.
147 F3 Bainbridge *New York* U.S.A.
88 D4 Bain-de-Bretagne France
83 E1 Baindt Germany
159 D3 Bainet Haiti
37 G3 Baingoin China
91 B3 Bains France
131 G1 Bain's Drift Botswana
87 F4 Bains-les-Bains France
88 C4 Bains-sur-Oust France
65 H4 Bainton *England* U.K.
98 B1 Baio Grande Spain
98 B2 Baiona Spain
31 H3 Baiquan China
37 E2 Bairab Co l. China
37 F4 Bairagnia India
134 B3 Baird Mountains mountain range *Alaska* U.S.A.
4 J4 Bairiki Kiribati
31 F4 Bairing Qiao China
31 F4 Bairin Youqi China
31 F4 Bairin Zuoqi China
47 G4 Bairkum Kazakhstan
13 F4 Bairnsdale *Victoria* Australia
42 D4 Bā'ir, Wādī watercourse Jordan
89 E3 Bais France
23 B4 Bais Philippines
93 C4 Baïse r. France
32 E2 Baisha China
33 F3 Baisha China
33 E5 Baisha China
31 H4 Baishan China
32 D1 Baishui r. China
107 E4 Baiso Italy
54 C4 Baisogala Lithuania
33 G3 Baisong Guan pass China
24 D3 Bai Thương Vietnam
31 F4 Baitle r. China
112 E1 Băiuţ Romania
91 C4 Baix France
100 A2 Baixa da Banheira Portugal
102 D4 Baix Ebre reg. Spain
31 G4 Baixingt China
169 H3 Baixo Guandu Brazil
125 C7 Baixo-Longa Angola
30 C5 Baiyin China
32 B2 Baiyü China
119 F4 Baiyuda Desert desert Sudan
79 H5 Baja Hungary
156 B2 Baja California pen. Mexico
156 B2 Baja California Norte div. Mexico
156 B3 Baja California Sur div. Mexico
172 B5 Bajada del Agrio Argentina
157 E3 Bajan Mexico
36 E3 Bajang Nepal
7 □16 Baja, Pta pt *Easter I.* Chile
156 A2 Baja, Pta pt Mexico
36 B2 Bajaur reg. Pakistan
21 H8 Bajawa Indonesia
37 G5 Baj Baj India
39 D1 Bājgīrān Iran
126 D2 Bājil Yemen
112 B3 Bajina Bašta Yugoslavia
37 G4 Bajitpur Bangladesh
79 J6 Bajmok Yugoslavia
162 B2 Bajo Baudó Colombia
156 K7 Bajo Boquete Panama
172 D1 Bajo de Gallo Argentina
123 G4 Bajoga Nigeria
171 C6 Bajo Grande Argentina
172 E1 Bajo Hondo Argentina
112 B3 Bajram Curri Albania
78 F5 Bak Hungary
22 C2 Baka, Bukit mt. Indonesia
46 E2 Bakal Rus. Fed.
124 D2 Bakala Central African Rep.
77 L1 Bakałarzewo Poland
47 J4 Bakanas Kazakhstan
118 D4 Bakaoré Chad
107 J3 Bakar Croatia
122 A4 Bakau The Gambia
22 D2 Bakaucengal Indonesia
53 E1 Bakayivka Ukraine
122 B4 Bakel Senegal
154 D4 Baker *California* U.S.A.
152 F2 Baker *Montana* U.S.A.
155 E2 Baker *Nevada* U.S.A.
152 C2 Baker *Oregon* U.S.A.
155 G4 Baker Butte summit *Arizona* U.S.A.
136 C3 Baker I. i. *Alaska* U.S.A.
5 K4 Baker I. i. Pacific Ocean
137 K2 Baker Lake l. *N.W.T.* Canada
137 K2 Baker Lake *N.W.T.* Canada
152 B1 Baker, Mt volcano *Washington* U.S.A.
138 E2 Baker's Dozen Islands is *N.W.T.* Canada
154 C4 Bakersfield *California* U.S.A.
131 F2 Bakerville South Africa
25 D4 Bâ Kêv Cambodia
43 B2 Bakhany Rus. Fed.
46 E5 Bakharden Turkmenistan
46 E5 Bakhardok Turkmenistan
39 E2 Bākharz mountain range Iran
36 B4 Bakhasar India
51 E6 Bakhchysaray Ukraine
31 J2 Bakhirevo Rus. Fed.
53 E1 Bakhmach Ukraine
52 B1 Bakhmutovo Rus. Fed.
39 B2 Bakhtiari Country reg. Iran
37 F4 Bakhtiyarpur India
47 K3 Bakhty Kazakhstan
52 F2 Bakhtyzino Rus. Fed.
118 D4 Baki well Chad
42 G1 Bakı Azerbaijan
42 G2 Bakı Komissarı, 26 Azerbaijan
113 F5 Bakır r. Turkey
42 B1 Bakırköy Turkey
56 E1 Bakkejord Norway
122 C5 Bako Côte d'Ivoire
126 C3 Bako Ethiopia
126 C3 Bako Ethiopia
79 G4 Bakony mts Hungary
79 H4 Bakonysárkány Hungary
79 G4 Bakonyszentlászló Hungary
126 D4 Bakool div. Somalia
124 D2 Bakouma Central African Rep.
124 B4 Bakoumba Gabon
122 B4 Bakoy r. Mali
51 G7 Baksan Rus. Fed.
79 M3 Baktalórántháza Hungary
Baku see Bakı
124 F3 Baku Congo(Zaire)
22 A1 Bakung i. Indonesia
77 N3 Bakuny Belarus
52 G3 Bakur r. Rus. Fed.
51 G7 Bakuriani Georgia
52 G3 Bakury Rus. Fed.
179 A4 Bakutis Coast coastal area Antarctica
Baku see Bakı
62 C2 Bala *Wales* U.K.
42 C2 Balâ Turkey
23 A5 Balabac i. Philippines
23 A4 Balabac Philippines
23 A5 Balabac Strait str. Malaysia/Philippines
131 J1 Bala-Bala r. Mozambique
22 D2 Balabalangan, Kep. atolls Indonesia
52 C2 Balabanovo Rus. Fed.
6 □2 Balabio i. *New Caledonia* Pacific Ocean
159 □1 Balaclava Jamaica
39 B3 Bālādeh Iran
39 B1 Baladeh Iran
36 E5 Balaghat India
38 A2 Balaghat Range h. India
102 D3 Balaguer Spain
39 D3 Bālā Ḥowz Iran
22 B1 Balaiberkuak Indonesia
22 B1 Balaikarangan Indonesia
22 B2 Balairiam Indonesia
129 E1 Balaka Malawi
52 F1 Balakhna Rus. Fed.
52 D1 Balakirevo Rus. Fed.
12 D3 Balaklava *S. Australia* Australia
51 E6 Balaklava Ukraine
53 G2 Balakliya Ukraine
51 H4 Balakovo Rus. Fed.
Bala Lake l. see Tegid, Llyn
23 A5 Balambangan i. Malaysia
39 E2 Bālā Morghāb Afghanistan
86 D3 Balan France
36 E4 Bālān India
112 E1 Bălan Romania
52 G4 Balanda r. Rus. Fed.
113 G6 Balan Dağı mt. Turkey
23 B3 Balanga Philippines
127 C5 Balangida, Lake l. Tanzania
37 E5 Balāngīr India
38 C5 Balangoda Sri Lanka
91 B5 Balaruc-les-Bains France
22 E2 Balase r. Indonesia
52 C2 Balashikha Rus. Fed.
51 G5 Balashov Rus. Fed.
38 A1 Balasinor India
79 J3 Balassagyarmat Hungary
79 G5 Balaton l. Hungary
79 H4 Balatonalmádi Hungary
78 G5 Balatonberény Hungary
79 G5 Balatonfelvidék h. Hungary
79 G5 Balatonföldvár Hungary
79 G5 Balatonfüred Hungary
79 H4 Balatonfőzfő Hungary
79 G5 Balatonlelle Hungary
79 H5 Balatonvilágos Hungary
101 H2 Balazote Spain
65 E1 Balbeggie *Scotland* U.K.
54 C4 Balbieriškis Lithuania
90 C3 Balbigny France
163 F4 Balbina Brazil
67 E3 Balbriggan Rep. of Ireland
12 D2 Balcanoona *S. Australia* Australia
173 H4 Balcarce Argentina
112 G3 Balchik Bulgaria
9 B7 Balclutha New Zealand
172 D2 Balde Argentina
172 E1 Baldecito Argentina
82 D1 Baldegger See l. Switzerland
65 F3 Balderhead Res. resr *England* U.K.
63 F1 Balderton *England* U.K.
17 B7 Bald Hd headland *Western Australia* Australia
169 G3 Baldim Brazil
151 F5 Bald Knob *Arkansas* U.S.A.
155 E3 Bald Mt mt. *Nevada* U.S.A.
63 F3 Baldock *England* U.K.
137 K3 Baldock Lake l. *Manitoba* Canada
63 G4 Baldslow *England* U.K.
114 A1 Baldushk Albania
145 D6 Baldwin *Florida* U.S.A.
148 E4 Baldwin *Michigan* U.S.A.
141 F4 Baldwin *Ontario* Canada
148 A3 Baldwin *Wisconsin* U.S.A.
147 E3 Baldwinsville *New York* U.S.A.
155 H5 Baldy Peak mt. *Arizona* U.S.A.
30 D2 Bal'dzhikan Rus. Fed.
107 H3 Bale Croatia
122 B4 Baléa Mali
94 D4 Baleares, Islas is Spain
Balearic Islands is see Baleares, Islas
22 C1 Baleh r. Malaysia
92 A2 Baleines, Pte des pt France
126 C3 Bale Mts National Park nat. park Ethiopia
69 D3 Balen Belgium
112 E2 Băleni Romania
23 B3 Baler Philippines
23 B3 Baler Bay b. Philippines
101 H4 Balerma Spain
37 F5 Bāleshwar India
58 B1 Balestrand Norway
110 C4 Balestrate *Sicilia* Italy
31 F2 Baley Rus. Fed.
123 E4 Baléyara Niger
15 F4 Balfe's Creek *Queensland* Australia
66 F1 Balfour *Scotland* U.K.
9 B6 Balfour New Zealand
131 G3 Balfour South Africa
131 F6 Balfour South Africa
64 D1 Balfron *Scotland* U.K.
30 A3 Balgatay Mongolia
30 A2 Balgazin Rus. Fed.
16 D4 Balgo Mission *Western Australia* Australia
127 C5 Balguda well Kenya
47 L4 Balguntay China
126 E2 Bālḥaf Yemen
126 D2 Balho Djibouti
22 C4 Bali div. Indonesia
22 C3 Bali i. Indonesia
36 C4 Bali India
77 H5 Balice airport Poland
20 C6 Balige Indonesia
37 E5 Baliguda India
31 F4 Balihan China
43 C1 Balık r. Turkey
113 F5 Balıkesir div. Turkey
42 A2 Balıkesir Turkey
42 D2 Balīkh r. Syria/Turkey
113 F4 Balıklıçeşme Turkey
22 D2 Balikpapan Indonesia
22 D2 Balikpapan, Tk b. Indonesia
23 A5 Balimbing Philippines
38 C2 Balimila Reservoir resr India
6 □1 Balimo P.N.G.
31 G2 Balin China
59 G2 Bälinge Sweden
74 D4 Balingen Germany
23 B2 Balintang Channel chan. Philippines
66 E3 Balintore *Scotland* U.K.
23 C3 Bali Sea g. Indonesia
124 D2 Balitondo Central African Rep.
23 B5 Baliungan i. Philippines
119 H4 Baljurshī Saudi Arabia
68 D2 Balk Netherlands
39 C1 Balkan div. Turkmenistan
Balkan Mts mts see Stara Planina
47 G2 Balkashino Kazakhstan
68 E2 Balkbrug Netherlands
39 F1 Balkh Afghanistan
39 F1 Balkhab r. Afghanistan
47 H3 Balkhash Kazakhstan
47 H3 Balkhash, Ozero l. Kazakhstan
51 H6 Balkuduk Kazakhstan
66 C4 Ballachulish *Scotland* U.K.
17 C7 Balladonia *Western Australia* Australia
67 C3 Ballaghaderreen Rep. of Ireland
56 E1 Ballangen Norway
89 F4 Ballan-Miré France
152 E2 Ballantine *Montana* U.S.A.
66 D5 Ballantrae *Scotland* U.K.
108 B5 Ballao *Sardegna* Italy
13 E4 Ballarat *Victoria* Australia
17 C6 Ballard, L. salt flat *Western Australia* Australia
38 B2 Ballarpur India
66 E3 Ballater *Scotland* U.K.
122 C3 Ballé Mali
170 B2 Ballena, Pta pt Chile
172 A4 Ballenera, Punta pt Chile
73 G4 Ballenstedt Germany
179 A6 Balleny Is is Antarctica
89 E2 Balleroy France
55 E4 Ballerup Denmark
173 F2 Ballesteros Argentina
37 F4 Ballia India
126 E3 Balli Megali well Ethiopia
13 H2 Ballina *New South Wales* Australia
67 B2 Ballina Rep. of Ireland
67 C2 Ballinafad Rep. of Ireland
67 A4 Ballinagh Rep. of Ireland
67 D3 Ballinalack Rep. of Ireland
67 D2 Ballinamore Rep. of Ireland
67 C3 Ballinasloe Rep. of Ireland
64 B3 Ballinderry r. *Northern Ireland* U.K.
67 C3 Ballindine Rep. of Ireland
151 D6 Ballinger *Texas* U.S.A.
66 E4 Ballinluig *Scotland* U.K.
67 B3 Ballinrobe Rep. of Ireland
67 A5 Ballinskelligs Bay b. Rep. of Ireland
64 B2 Ballintoy *Northern Ireland* U.K.
64 B4 Ballivor Rep. of Ireland
102 D3 Ballobar Spain
89 F3 Ballon France
67 E4 Ballon Rep. of Ireland
90 E1 Ballon d'Alsace mt. France
10 □4 Ball's Pyramid i. *Lord Howe I.* Pacific Ocean
147 G3 Ballston Spa *New York* U.S.A.
55 A4 Ballum Denmark
68 D1 Ballum Netherlands
67 E2 Ballybay Rep. of Ireland
67 D2 Ballybofey Rep. of Ireland
67 A5 Ballybrack Rep. of Ireland
67 B4 Ballybunnion Rep. of Ireland
67 E4 Ballycanew Rep. of Ireland
67 E1 Ballycastle *Northern Ireland* U.K.
67 B2 Ballycastle Rep. of Ireland
67 F2 Ballyclare *Northern Ireland* U.K.
67 A3 Ballyconneely Bay b. Rep. of Ireland
67 D2 Ballyconnell Rep. of Ireland
67 B2 Ballycroy Rep. of Ireland
67 B4 Ballydesmond Rep. of Ireland
67 C3 Ballygar Rep. of Ireland
67 D2 Ballygawley *Northern Ireland* U.K.
67 D1 Ballygorman Rep. of Ireland
64 C3 Ballygowan *Northern Ireland* U.K.
64 C3 Ballyhalbert *Northern Ireland* U.K.
67 D4 Ballyhale Rep. of Ireland
67 C3 Ballyhaunis Rep. of Ireland
67 B4 Ballyheigue Rep. of Ireland
67 B4 Ballyheigue Bay b. Rep. of Ireland
67 D4 Ballyhoura Mts h. Rep. of Ireland
67 D3 Ballyjamesduff Rep. of Ireland
67 D1 Ballykelly *Northern Ireland* U.K.
67 D4 Ballylynan Rep. of Ireland
67 D4 Ballymacarberry Rep. of Ireland
67 D4 Ballymacmague Rep. of Ireland
67 D3 Ballymahon Rep. of Ireland
67 B5 Ballymakeery Rep. of Ireland
67 E2 Ballymena *Northern Ireland* U.K.
67 E1 Ballymoney *Northern Ireland* U.K.
64 A4 Ballymore Rep. of Ireland
67 C2 Ballymote Rep. of Ireland
67 E4 Ballymurphy Rep. of Ireland
67 F2 Ballynahinch *Northern Ireland* U.K.
67 F2 Ballyquintin Point pt Rep. of Ireland
67 D4 Ballyragget Rep. of Ireland
64 B3 Ballyronan *Northern Ireland* U.K.
67 C2 Ballyshannon Rep. of Ireland
67 E4 Ballyteige Bay b. Rep. of Ireland
67 B3 Ballyvaughan Rep. of Ireland
64 C3 Ballywalter *Northern Ireland* U.K.
67 E2 Ballyward *Northern Ireland* U.K.
171 B6 Balmaceda Chile
64 D1 Balmaha *Scotland* U.K.
66 A3 Balmartin *Scotland* U.K.
99 G1 Balmaseda Spain
79 L4 Balmazújváros Hungary
106 B3 Balme Italy
Balmer see Barmer
82 C2 Balmhorn mt. Switzerland
12 E4 Balmoral *Victoria* Australia
151 C6 Balmorhea *Texas* U.S.A.
82 D3 Balmuccia Italy
66 D3 Balnapaling *Scotland* U.K.
173 F1 Balnearia Argentina
173 F6 Balneario Massini Argentina
173 H5 Balneario Orense Argentina
173 G5 Balneario Oriente Argentina
36 A3 Balochistān div. Pakistan
36 E5 Balod India
37 E5 Baloda Bazar India
78 F4 Balogunyom Hungary
22 A2 Balok, Tk b. Indonesia
125 B6 Balombo Angola
15 G6 Balonne r. *Queensland* Australia
36 C4 Balotra India
77 N3 Baloty Belarus
37 F4 Balpahari Res. resr India
66 D4 Balquhidder *Scotland* U.K.
37 E4 Balrampur India
13 E3 Balranald *New South Wales* Australia
112 E2 Balş Romania
103 B5 Balsa de Ves Spain
141 F3 Balsam Creek *Ontario* Canada
168 B4 Bálsamo Brazil
102 E3 Balsareny Spain
156 E5 Balsas r. Mexico
166 C2 Balsas Brazil
157 F5 Balsas Mexico
103 C7 Balsicas Spain
109 F3 Balsorano Italy
59 G2 Bålsta Sweden
82 C1 Balsthal Switzerland
53 C3 Balta Ukraine
112 D3 Balta Berilovac Yugoslavia
99 F3 Baltanás Spain
173 J1 Baltasar Brum Uruguay
50 J3 Baltasi Rus. Fed.
66 □2 Baltasound *Scotland* U.K.
52 H3 Baltay Rus. Fed.
53 B3 Bălţi Moldova
48 G3 Baltic Sea g. Europe
77 H1 Baltiskaja Kosa spit Rus. Fed.
43 A4 Balṭîm Egypt
146 E5 Baltimore *Maryland* U.S.A.
131 G1 Baltimore South Africa
54 E3 Baltinava Latvia
67 E4 Baltinglass Rep. of Ireland
36 C2 Baltistan reg. Jammu and Kashmir
54 A4 Baltiysk Rus. Fed.
59 H2 Baltora Sweden
162 □ Baltra, I. i. *Galapagos Is* Ecuador
37 H4 Balu India
39 D3 Baluch Ab well Iran
Baluchistan div. see Balochistān
22 C2 Baluran, G. mt. Indonesia
37 G4 Balurghat India
112 F1 Băluşeni Romania
23 C5 Balut i. Philippines
74 C2 Balve Germany
54 E3 Balvi Latvia
54 E3 Balvu l. Latvia
16 D4 Balwina Abor. Reserve res. *Western Australia* Australia
113 F5 Balya Turkey
30 D2 Balyaga Rus. Fed.
47 J4 Balykchy Kyrgyzstan
47 L2 Balyksa Rus. Fed.
46 D3 Balykshi Kazakhstan
30 A2 Balyktyg-Khem r. Rus. Fed.
53 B2 Balyn Ukraine
162 B4 Balzar Ecuador
83 E1 Balzers Liechtenstein
30 E2 Bal'zino Rus. Fed.
39 D1 Bām Iran
39 D3 Bam Iran
32 D3 Bama China
123 G4 Bama Nigeria
15 E1 Bamaga *Queensland* Australia
138 B3 Bamaji L. l. *Ontario* Canada
122 C4 Bamako Mali
122 D3 Bamba Mali
125 B4 Bambama Congo
23 B2 Bambang Philippines
125 D7 Bambangando Angola
124 D2 Bambari Central African Rep.
145 D5 Bamberg *S. Carolina* U.S.A.
75 F3 Bamberg Germany
124 E3 Bambesa Congo(Zaire)
122 A4 Bambey Senegal
124 E3 Bambili Congo(Zaire)
124 C3 Bambio Central African Rep.
131 F5 Bamboesberg mts South Africa
122 B4 Bambouk reg. Mali
127 □4 Bambou Mts h. Mauritius
124 E2 Bambouti Central African Rep.
126 B2 Bambudi Ethiopia
169 F4 Bambuí Brazil
65 G2 Bamburgh *England* U.K.
32 B2 Bamda China
124 B2 Bamenda Cameroon
124 B2 Bamendjing, Lac de l. Cameroon
39 F2 Bāmīān Afghanistan
31 H4 Bamiancheng China
124 C2 Bamingui r. Central African Rep.
124 D2 Bamingui Central African Rep.
124 D2 Bamingui-Bangoran div. Central African Rep.
124 C2 Bamingui-Bangoran, Parc National du nat. park Central African Rep.
24 C4 Bamnet Narong Thailand
39 E4 Bam Posht reg. Iran
39 E4 Bam Posht, Kūh-e mountain range Iran
62 C4 Bampton *England* U.K.
63 E3 Bampton *England* U.K.
39 D4 Bampūr watercourse Iran
39 E4 Bampūr Iran
39 E2 Bamrūd Iran
126 E4 Banaadir div. Somalia
4 H5 Banaba i. Kiribati
173 K2 Bañado de Medina Uruguay
172 D4 Banados del Atuel marsh Argentina
165 D3 Bañados del Izozog swamp Bolivia
67 D3 Banagher Rep. of Ireland
124 E3 Banalia Congo(Zaire)
122 C4 Banamba Mali
15 G5 Banana *Queensland* Australia
25 A6 Bananga *Andaman and Nicobar Is* India
38 D2 Bānapur India
25 C4 Ban Aranyaprathet Thailand
113 F4 Banarlı Turkey
36 D4 Banas r. India
126 E2 Bana, W. watercourse Yemen
22 D3 Banawaya i. Indonesia
42 B2 Banaz Turkey
24 C3 Ban Ban Laos
37 H3 Banbar China
25 C6 Ban Betong Thailand
67 E2 Banbridge *Northern Ireland* U.K.
25 C4 Ban Bua Chum Thailand
24 C4 Ban Bua Yai Thailand
63 E2 Banbury *England* U.K.
24 C2 Ban Cang Vietnam
120 A4 Banc d'Arguin, Parc National du nat. park Mauritania
24 C3 Ban Channabot Thailand
24 B3 Ban Chiang Dao Thailand
66 F3 Banchory *Scotland* U.K.
157 J5 Banco Chinchorro is Mexico
158 B4 Banco Gorda sand bank Honduras
23 A5 Bancoran i. Philippines
141 G4 Bancroft *Ontario* Canada
39 D2 Band Iran
124 B2 Banda Cameroon
36 E4 Banda India
124 E3 Banda Congo(Zaire)
20 C5 Banda Aceh Indonesia
36 B2 Banda Daud Shah Pakistan
29 H5 Bandai-Asahi National Park Japan
122 B5 Bandajuma Sierra Leone
58 C2 Bandak l. Norway
122 D5 Bandama r. Côte d'Ivoire
122 C5 Bandama Blanc r. Côte d'Ivoire
39 E3 Bandān Iran
39 E3 Bandān Kūh mountain range Iran
Bandar see Machilipatnam
129 E2 Bandar Mozambique
22 A3 Bandaragung Indonesia
37 H5 Bandarban Bangladesh
39 D4 Bāndār-e Abbās Iran
39 B1 Bandar-e Anzalī Iran
39 B3 Bandar-e Deylam Iran
39 C4 Bandar-e Khoemir Iran
39 C4 Bandar-e Lengeh Iran
39 C4 Bandar-e Māqām Iran
39 B3 Bandar-e Ma'shur Iran
Bandar-e Pahlavi see Bandar-e Anzalī
39 B3 Bandar-e Rīg Iran
Bandar-e Shāhpūr see Bandar Khomeynī
39 C1 Bandar-e Torkeman Iran
39 B3 Bandar Khomeynī Iran
25 D6 Bandar Labuan Malaysia
36 D3 Bandarpunch mt. India
20 F6 Bandar Seri Begawan Brunei
126 D3 Bandar Wanaag Somalia
21 J8 Banda Sea g. Indonesia
39 D4 Band Bonī Iran
98 C2 Bande Spain
39 C4 Band-e Chārak Iran
169 H1 Bandeira Brazil
166 B3 Bandeirante Brazil
168 A3 Bandeirantes *Mato Grosso do Sul* Brazil
168 C5 Bandeirantes *São Paulo* Brazil
169 H4 Bandeiras, Pico de mt. Brazil
131 G1 Bandelierkop South Africa
39 C4 Band-e Moghūyeh Iran
170 D2 Bandera Argentina
156 D2 Banderas Mexico
156 D4 Banderas, Bahía de b. Mexico
39 C2 Band-e Sar Qom Iran
55 D5 Bandholm Denmark
36 C4 Bandi r. *Rajasthan* India
36 C4 Bandi r. *Rajasthan* India
38 C2 Bandia r. India
122 D4 Bandiagara Mali
39 F2 Band-i-Amir r. Afghanistan
39 E2 Band-i-Baba mountain range Afghanistan
36 D4 Bandikui India
36 C2 Bandipur India
37 F4 Bandipur Nepal
42 B1 Bandırma Turkey
39 E2 Band-i-Turkestan mountain range Afghanistan
67 B5 Bandon r. Rep. of Ireland
67 C5 Bandon Rep. of Ireland
Ban Don see Surat Thani
125 C4 Bandundu div. Congo(Zaire)
125 C4 Bandundu Congo(Zaire)
22 A3 Bandung Indonesia
131 G1 Bandur South Africa
17 C5 Bandya *Western Australia* Australia
112 F2 Băneasa Romania
42 F3 Bāneh Iran
158 D2 Banes Cuba
136 F4 Banff *Alberta* Canada
66 F3 Banff *Scotland* U.K.
136 F4 Banff National Park nat. park *Alberta* Canada
122 D4 Banfora Burkina
124 C2 Bang Central African Rep.
23 C5 Banga Philippines
125 D5 Banga Congo(Zaire)
23 C5 Bangai Point pt Philippines
38 B3 Bangalore India
124 B2 Bangangté Cameroon
37 G5 Bangaon India
23 B2 Bangar Philippines
124 D3 Bangassou Central African Rep.
37 E2 Bangdag Co salt lake China
21 H7 Banggai Indonesia
25 E6 Banggi i. Malaysia
118 D1 Banghāzī Libya
22 C3 Bangil Indonesia
22 A2 Bangka i. Indonesia
22 C2 Bangkal Indonesia
22 C3 Bangkalan Indonesia
22 E1 Bangkir Indonesia
37 G3 Bangkog Co l. China
25 C4 Bangkok Thailand
25 C4 Bangkok, Bight of b. Thailand
22 D4 Bangkulua Indonesia
18 K7 Bangladesh country Asia
32 B4 Bangma Shan mountain range China
122 C5 Bangolo Côte d'Ivoire
36 D2 Bangong Co l. China
147 J2 Bangor *Maine* U.S.A.
148 D4 Bangor *Michigan* U.S.A.
67 F2 Bangor *Northern Ireland* U.K.
147 F4 Bangor *Pennsylvania* U.S.A.
62 B1 Bangor *Wales* U.K.
124 C2 Bangoran r. Central African Rep.
67 B2 Bangor Erris Rep. of Ireland
22 D2 Bangsalsepulun Indonesia
25 B5 Bang Saphan Yai Thailand
155 F3 Bangs, Mt mt. *Arizona* U.S.A.
56 C2 Bangsund Norway
23 B2 Bangued Philippines
124 C3 Bangui Central African Rep.
23 B2 Bangui Philippines
124 C3 Bangui-Motaba Congo
124 E3 Banguru Congo(Zaire)
125 E6 Bangweulu, Lake l. Zambia
25 C6 Ban Hat Yai Thailand
129 E3 Banhine, Parque Nacional de nat. park Mozambique
24 C3 Ban Hin Heup Laos
24 C2 Ban Houayxay Laos
25 B6 Ban Hua Hin Thailand
122 C4 Bani r. Mali
123 D4 Bani Burkina
124 D2 Bani Central African Rep.
159 E3 Baní Dominican Rep.
124 C3 Bania Central African Rep.
123 E3 Bani-Bangou Niger
76 C2 Banie Poland
77 L1 Banie Mazurskie Poland
122 C4 Banifing r. Mali
120 C3 Bani, Jbel ridge Morocco
123 E4 Banikoara Benin
125 B4 Banio, Lag. lag. Gabon
146 D6 Banister r. *Virginia* U.S.A.
119 H4 Banī Thawr Saudi Arabia
118 B1 Banī Walīd Libya
43 C3 Bāniyās Syria
43 C3 Bāniyās Syria
104 F3 Banja Luka Bos.-Herz.
36 D3 Banjar India
22 C2 Banjarbaru Indonesia
22 C2 Banjarmasin Indonesia
122 A4 Banjul The Gambia
37 F4 Banka India
14 C3 Banka Banka *Northern Terr.* Australia
25 D4 Ban Kadian Laos
25 B6 Ban Kantang Thailand
38 A3 Bankapur India
122 D4 Bankass Mali
65 E1 Bankfoot *Scotland* U.K.
25 B4 Ban Khao Yoi Thailand
24 D3 Ban Khemmarat Thailand
25 C4 Ban Khlung Thailand
25 B5 Ban Khok Kloi Thailand
24 B3 Ban Khun Yuam Thailand
37 F5 Banki India
123 E4 Bankilaré Niger
124 B2 Bankim Cameroon
122 B4 Banko Guinea
22 D3 Bankobankoang i. Indonesia
136 C4 Banks I. i. *B.C.* Canada
134 F2 Banks Island i. *N.W.T.* Canada
6 □2 Banks Islands is Vanuatu
152 C2 Banks L. l. *Washington* U.S.A.
137 L2 Banks Lake l. *N.W.T.* Canada
9 D5 Banks Peninsula pen. New Zealand
13 G5 Banks Strait chan. *Tasmania* Australia
25 B4 Ban Kui Nua Thailand
37 F5 Bankura India
24 B3 Ban Mae La Luang Thailand
24 B3 Ban Mae Sariang Thailand
24 B3 Ban Mae Sot Thailand
24 B3 Ban Mae Thalop Thailand
24 A1 Banmauk Myanmar
36 B2 Banmi Pakistan
24 C3 Ban Mouang Laos
24 C4 Ban Muang Phon Thailand
67 E2 Bann r. *Northern Ireland* U.K.
67 E4 Bann r. Rep. of Ireland
24 D3 Ban Na Kae Thailand
24 D3 Ban Nakham Laos
88 B4 Bannalec France
24 C3 Ban Na Noi Thailand
25 B5 Ban Na San Thailand
25 C6 Ban Na Thawi Thailand
90 A1 Bannay France
148 C5 Banner *Illinois* U.S.A.
158 C1 Bannerman Town The Bahamas
154 D5 Banning *California* U.S.A.
66 E4 Bannockburn *Scotland* U.K.
24 B3 Ban Noi Myanmar
91 D4 Banon France
122 B4 Banora Guinea
172 B4 Baños de Copahue Chile
98 C2 Baños de Molgas Spain
98 E4 Baños de Montemayor Spain
102 C2 Baños de Panticosa Spain
172 B4 Baños Maule Chile

79 H3 Bánovce nad Bebravou Slovakia
104 G3 Banoviči Bos.-Herz.
Banow see Andarāb
24 C3 Ban Pak-Leng Laos
25 C5 Ban Pak Phanang Thailand
25 C4 Ban Pak Thong Chai Thailand
24 D3 Ban Phaeng Thailand
24 C4 Ban Phai Thailand
25 C4 Ban Phanat Nikhom Thailand
24 D4 Ban Phon Laos
24 C3 Ban Phon Thong Thailand
24 B4 Banphot Phisai Thailand
24 B3 Ban Phran Katai Thailand
Ban Pla Soi see Chon Buri
25 B4 Ban Pong Thailand
24 C3 Ban Pua Thailand
79 K3 Bánréve Hungary
24 B3 Ban Saraphi Thailand
25 C4 Ban Sattahip Thailand
25 B5 Ban Sawi Thailand
37 E4 Bansi India
25 B5 Ban Sichon Thailand
25 C4 Ban Si Racha Thailand
79 J3 Banská Bystrica Slovakia
79 H3 Banská Štiavnica Slovakia
112 D4 Bansko Bulgaria
24 B3 Ban Sop Prap Thailand
24 B3 Ban Sut Ta Thailand
38 B2 Banswada India
36 C5 Banswara India
22 D3 Bantaeng Indonesia
24 C4 Ban Ta Khli Thailand
25 B5 Ban Takua Pa Thailand
10 □1 Bantam Cocos Is Indian Ocean
24 C3 Ban Taviang Laos
23 B4 Bantayan i. Philippines
123 E5 Bantè Benin
67 C4 Banteer Rep. of Ireland
25 B5 Ban Tha Chang Thailand
24 B2 Ban Tha Don Thailand
25 B5 Ban Thai Muang Thailand
25 B5 Ban Tha Kham Thailand
24 B3 Ban Tha Song Yang Thailand
24 C4 Ban Tha Tako Thailand
24 C4 Ban Tha Tum Thailand
24 D3 Ban Tha Uthen Thailand
87 E3 Bantheville France
25 B4 Ban Thung Luang Thailand
23 B3 Banton i. Philippines
24 D3 Ban Tôp Laos
67 B5 Bantry Rep. of Ireland
67 B5 Bantry Bay b. Rep. of Ireland
22 B3 Bantul Indonesia
38 A3 Bantval India
24 C3 Ban Woen Laos
25 D4 Ban Xepian Laos
24 C3 Ban Yang Talat Thailand
124 B2 Banyo Cameroon
102 F2 Banyoles Spain
22 A2 Banyuasin r. Indonesia
93 F6 Banyuls-sur-Mer France
22 C4 Banyuwangi Indonesia
6 □1 Banz P.N.G.
179 C6 Banzare Coast coastal area Antarctica
175 K7 Banzare Seamount sea feature Indian Ocean
73 G2 Banzkow Germany
Ba'oan see Shenzhen
30 B6 Bao'an China
31 E5 Baoding China
33 F1 Baofeng China
24 D2 Bao Hà Vietnam
32 D1 Baoji China
32 D1 Baoji China
33 E2 Baojing China
33 E2 Baokang China
25 D5 Bao Lôc Vietnam
31 K3 Baoqing China
124 C2 Baoro Central African Rep.
32 B3 Baoshan China
30 D4 Baotou China
122 C4 Baoulé r. Kayes/Koulikoro Mali
122 C4 Baoulé r. Sikasso Mali
32 C2 Baoxing China
33 G1 Baoying China
36 C4 Bap India
38 C3 Bapatla India
86 B2 Bapaume France
141 F4 Baptiste Lake l. Ontario Canada
39 C2 Baqam Iran
37 H2 Baqêm China
37 H3 Baqên China
43 C5 Bāqir, J. mt. Jordan
42 F3 Ba'qūbah Iraq
164 C4 Baquedano Chile
162 □ Baquerizo Moreno Galapagos Is Ecuador
86 D3 Bar r. France
30 C2 Bar Rus. Fed.
53 B2 Bar Ukraine
112 B3 Bar Yugoslavia
37 E4 Bara India
123 G4 Bara Nigeria
119 F5 Bara Sudan
126 D4 Baraawe Somalia
22 C2 Barabai Indonesia
36 E4 Bara Banki India
47 J1 Barabinsk Rus. Fed.
47 J2 Barabinskaya Step' plain Rus. Fed.
126 D4 Bar Abir well Ethiopia
148 B4 Baraboo r. Wisconsin U.S.A.
148 C4 Baraboo Wisconsin U.S.A.
166 B3 Baracaju r. Brazil
Baracaldo see Barakaldo
158 D2 Baracoa Cuba
43 D3 Barada r. Syria
43 D2 Baradah Syria
173 H2 Baradero Argentina
13 G2 Baradine r. New South Wales Australia
13 G2 Baradine New South Wales Australia
148 C2 Baraga Michigan U.S.A.
37 E5 Baragarh India
162 D1 Baragua Venezuela
159 E3 Barahona Dominican Rep.
99 H3 Barahona Spain
37 H4 Barail Range mountain range India
99 H4 Barajas de Melo Spain
112 C2 Barajevo Yugoslavia
37 H4 Barak r. India
39 G1 Barak Afghanistan
Barak see Kargamiş
126 C1 Baraka watercourse Eritrea/Sudan
99 H1 Barakaldo Spain
39 G2 Barakī Barak Afghanistan
37 F5 Bārākot India
52 D2 Barakovo Rus. Fed.
47 G2 Barakpay Kazakhstan
15 G5 Baralaba Queensland Australia
36 D2 Bara Lacha Pass pass India
98 C2 Baralla Spain
42 E3 Baŗ al Milḩ l. Iraq
137 K3 Baralzon Lake l. Manitoba Canada
163 F2 Barama r. Guyana
163 F2 Baramanni Guyana
38 A2 Baramati India
15 G5 Barambah r. Queensland Australia
36 C2 Baramula Jammu and Kashmir
36 A4 Baran r. Pakistan
36 D4 Baran India
102 B2 Barañain Spain
54 E5 Baranavichy Belarus
122 D4 Barani Burkina
45 S3 Baranikha Rus. Fed.
53 B1 Baranivka Ukraine
39 E2 Bārān, Kūh-e mountain range Iran
162 C1 Baranoa Colombia
109 F4 Barano d'Ischia Italy
136 B3 Baranof Island i. Alaska U.S.A.
52 H3 Baranovka Rus. Fed.
77 L4 Baranów Poland
77 K5 Baranów Sandomierska Poland
79 H5 Baranya div. Hungary
79 H6 Baranyai-dombság h. Hungary
167 A4 Barão de Melgaço Brazil
112 E1 Baraolt Romania
122 C4 Baraouéli Mali
69 D4 Baraque de Fraiture h. Belgium
93 E4 Baraqueville France
163 F5 Bararati r. Brazil
52 F2 Barashevo Rus. Fed.
12 D3 Baratta S. Australia Australia
36 D3 Baraut India
54 F4 Baravukha Belarus
162 B3 Baraya Colombia
169 G4 Barbacena Brazil
162 B3 Barbacoas Colombia
99 G2 Barbadillo del Pez Spain
165 E3 Barbado r. Brazil
133 N8 Barbados country Caribbean
107 J3 Barban Croatia
140 B2 Barbara Lake l. Ontario Canada
43 B5 Barbar, G. el mt. Egypt
103 E6 Barbaria, Cap de pt Spain
102 D2 Barbastro Spain
107 J4 Barbat Croatia
100 E4 Barbate r. Spain
100 E4 Barbate de Franco Spain
93 C5 Barbazan France
107 F4 Barberino di Mugello Italy
140 E2 Barber's Bay Ontario Canada
153 □1 Barbers Pt pt Hawaii U.S.A.
146 C4 Barberton Ohio U.S.A.
131 H2 Barberton South Africa
92 B3 Barbezieux-St-Hilaire France
86 C4 Barbonne-Fayel France
162 C2 Barbosa Colombia
137 L2 Barbour Bay b. N.W.T. Canada
146 B6 Barbourville Kentucky U.S.A.
23 B4 Barboza Philippines
159 G3 Barbuda i. Antigua and Barbuda Caribbean
73 G4 Barby Germany
112 D3 Bârca Romania
98 D3 Barca de Alva Portugal
158 □1 Barcadera Aruba Caribbean
158 □3 Barcadera Bonaire Netherlands Ant.
15 F4 Barcaldine Queensland Australia
100 D2 Barcarrota Spain
79 M4 Barcău r. Romania
111 E4 Barcellona Pozzo di Gotto Sicilia Italy
102 F3 Barcelona airport Spain
102 E3 Barcelona div. Spain
102 F3 Barcelona Barcelona Spain
163 E1 Barcelona Venezuela
145 □3 Barceloneta Puerto Rico
93 B5 Barcelonne-du-Gers France
91 E4 Barcelonnette France
163 E4 Barcelos Brazil
98 B3 Barcelos Portugal
99 G1 Barcenillas de Cerezos Spain
74 F2 Barchfeld Germany
77 K1 Barciany Poland
91 D4 Barcillonnette France
76 F3 Barcin Poland
76 E1 Barcino Poland
122 C6 Barclayville Liberia
99 H3 Barcones Spain
15 E5 Barcoo watercourse Queensland Australia
Barcoo Creek watercourse see Cooper Cr.
78 G6 Barcs Hungary
77 J2 Barczewo Poland
42 F1 Bärdä Azerbaijan
172 C5 Barda del Medio Argentina
118 C3 Bardai Chad
56 M6 Bárðarbunga mt. Iceland
172 C3 Bardas Blancas Argentina
37 F5 Barddhamān India
79 L2 Bardejov Slovakia
102 B2 Bárdenas Reales reg. Spain
55 C4 Bårdesø Denmark
39 B4 Bardestān Iran
37 E4 Bardi India
106 D4 Bardi Italy
106 C4 Bardineto Italy
90 C1 Bard, Montagne de h. France
63 F1 Bardney England U.K.
107 E3 Bardolino Italy
25 D4 Bar Đôn Vietnam
106 A3 Bardonecchia Italy
62 B2 Bardsey Island i. Wales U.K.
62 B2 Bardsey Sound chan. Wales U.K.
144 C4 Bardstown Kentucky U.S.A.
146 B5 Bardwell Ohio U.S.A.
93 C6 Barèges France
36 D3 Bareilly India
13 F3 Barellan New South Wales Australia
73 F2 Barendorf Germany
68 C3 Barendrecht Netherlands
89 F2 Barentin France
89 E3 Barenton France
178 □3 Barentsburg Svalbard Arctic Ocean
178 □3 Barentsøya i. Svalbard Arctic Ocean
44 E2 Barents Sea sea Arctic Ocean
126 C1 Barentu Eritrea
88 D2 Barfleur France
88 D2 Barfleur, Pte de pt France
36 E3 Barga China
106 E4 Barga Italy
126 F2 Bargaal Somalia
15 H5 Bargara Queensland Australia
99 F5 Bargas Spain
106 B4 Barge Italy
91 E5 Bargemon France
83 F3 Barghe Italy
36 D5 Bargi India
77 L2 Bargłów Kościelny Poland
66 D5 Bargrennan Scotland U.K.
72 F2 Bargteheide Germany
93 C4 Barguelonne r. France
37 G5 Barguna Bangladesh
37 E4 Barhalganj India
63 H3 Barham England U.K.
147 J2 Bar Harbor Maine U.S.A.
109 J3 Bari div. Puglia Italy
126 F2 Bari div. Somalia
111 F1 Bari Bari Italy
36 D4 Bari India
124 C3 Bari Congo(Zaire)
25 D5 Ba Ria Vietnam
121 F1 Barika Algeria
39 G2 Barikot Afghanistan
37 E3 Barikot Nepal
159 H6 Barima r. Guyana
162 C2 Barinas Venezuela
124 D3 Baringa Congo(Zaire)
127 C4 Baringo, L. l. Kenya
55 B4 Båring Vig b. Denmark
111 F1 Bari Palese airport Italy
168 D5 Bariri Brazil
119 F3 Bârîs Egypt
37 G5 Barisal Bangladesh
108 B5 Barì Sardo Sardegna Italy
109 F2 Barisciano Italy
22 C2 Barito r. Indonesia
170 D1 Baritu, Parque Nacional nat. park Argentina
91 C4 Barjac France
91 E5 Barjaude mt. France
91 E5 Barjols France
32 C2 Barkam China
39 B3 Barkan, Ra's-e pt Iran
54 E3 Barkava Latvia
136 E4 Barkerville B.C. Canada
36 B3 Barkhan Pakistan
37 F4 Barki Saraiya India
144 C4 Barkley, L. l. Kentucky U.S.A.
136 D5 Barkley Sd inlet B.C. Canada
14 D4 Barkly Downs Queensland Australia
131 F5 Barkly East South Africa
131 F5 Barkly Pass South Africa
14 D3 Barkly Tableland reg. Northern Terr. Australia
130 E4 Barkly West South Africa
26 F3 Barkol China
76 F2 Barkowo Poland
39 D3 Barkūh Iran
63 G2 Barkway England U.K.
112 F1 Bârlad Romania
73 G3 Barleben Germany
87 E4 Bar-le-Duc France
17 B6 Barlee, L. salt flat Western Australia Australia
17 B4 Barlee Ra. h. Western Australia Australia
109 J3 Barletta Italy
63 G2 Barley England U.K.
76 D3 Barlinek Poland
13 F3 Barmedman New South Wales Australia
36 B4 Barmer India
12 E3 Barmera S. Australia Australia
62 B2 Barmouth Wales U.K.
62 B2 Barmouth Bay b. Wales U.K.
36 C5 Barnagar India
36 C3 Barnala India
65 G3 Barnard Castle England U.K.
13 F2 Barnato New South Wales Australia
78 B2 Bärnau Germany
47 K2 Barnaul Rus. Fed.
81 G3 Barnbach Austria
73 G3 Barneberg Germany
147 F5 Barnegat New Jersey U.S.A.
147 F5 Barnegat Bay b. New Jersey U.S.A.
146 D4 Barnesboro Pennsylvania U.S.A.
135 L2 Barnes Icecap ice cap N.W.T. Canada
63 F3 Barnet England U.K.
68 D2 Barneveld Netherlands
88 D2 Barneville-Carteret France
73 H3 Barnewitz Germany
155 G3 Barney Top mt. Utah U.S.A.
151 C6 Barnhart Texas U.S.A.
128 □2 Barn Long Pt pt St Helena Atlantic Ocean
65 F4 Barnoldswick England U.K.
76 C3 Barnowko Poland
65 G4 Barnsley England U.K.
73 G4 Barnstädt Germany
62 B3 Barnstaple England U.K.
62 B3 Barnstaple Bay b. England U.K.
72 D3 Barnstorf Germany
72 E4 Barntrup Germany
145 D5 Barnwell S. Carolina U.S.A.
123 F5 Baro Nigeria
Baroda see Vadodara
131 E5 Baroda South Africa
130 E6 Baroe South Africa
81 F4 Bärofen mt. Austria
106 C3 Barone, Monte mt. Italy
32 B2 Barong China
91 D4 Baronnies reg. France
17 D4 Barons Ra. h. Western Australia Australia
87 F4 Baronville France
126 B3 Baro Wenz r. Ethiopia
37 H4 Barpathar India
37 G4 Barpeta India
43 D5 Barqā 'Damaj well Saudi Arabia
43 C5 Barqa, G. mt. Egypt
148 D3 Barques, Pt Aux pt Michigan U.S.A.
149 F3 Barques, Pt Aux pt Michigan U.S.A.
162 D1 Barquisimeto Venezuela
87 G4 Barr France
66 A4 Barra i. Scotland U.K.
166 D3 Barra Brazil
13 G2 Barraba New South Wales Australia
168 D5 Barra Bonita Brazil
166 B1 Barraca da Bôca Brazil
165 E1 Barracão do Barreto Brazil
103 C4 Barracas Spain
130 C7 Barracouta, Cape headland South Africa
169 E6 Barra de Santos inlet Brazil
169 H3 Barra de São Francisco Brazil
169 G5 Barra de São João Brazil
166 A4 Barra do Bugres Brazil
166 C2 Barra do Corda Brazil
125 B5 Barra do Cuanza Angola
168 B1 Barra do Garças Brazil
169 G5 Barra do Piraí Brazil
173 J1 Barra do Quaraí Brazil
167 B7 Barra do Ribeiro Brazil
163 F5 Barra do São Manuel Brazil
168 D6 Barra do Turvo Brazil
129 F3 Barra Falsa, Pta da pt Mozambique
110 D5 Barrafranca Sicilia Italy
169 G4 Barra Longa Brazil
169 F5 Barra Mansa Brazil
162 B4 Barranca Peru
164 A2 Barranca Peru
162 C2 Barranca-bermeja Colombia
172 B4 Barrancas r. Argentina
170 E3 Barrancas r. Corrientes Argentina
172 C4 Barrancas Neuquen Argentina
173 G2 Barrancas Santa Fe Argentina
162 C1 Barrancas Colombia
163 E2 Barrancas Venezuela
100 D2 Barrancos Portugal
100 C3 Barranco Velho Portugal
103 B6 Barranda Spain
170 E2 Barranqueras Argentina
162 C1 Barranquilla Colombia
129 F3 Barra, Pta da pt Mozambique
166 D1 Barras Brazil
66 A3 Barra, Sound of chan. Scotland U.K.
141 G2 Barraute Québec Canada
101 H1 Barrax Spain
147 G2 Barre Vermont U.S.A.
172 C1 Barreal Argentina
91 B4 Barre-des-Cévennes France
166 D3 Barreiras Brazil
166 A1 Barreirinha Brazil
166 D1 Barreirinhas Brazil
168 B1 Barreiro r. Brazil
100 A2 Barreiro Portugal
166 B3 Barreiro do Nascimento Brazil
166 E2 Barreiros Brazil
91 E5 Barrême France
25 A4 Barren I. i. Andaman and Nicobar Is India
168 D4 Barretos Brazil
16 D3 Barrett, Mt h. Western Australia Australia
136 G4 Barrhead Alberta Canada
66 D5 Barrhead Scotland U.K.
64 D2 Barrhill Scotland U.K.
141 F4 Barrie Ontario Canada
98 B2 Barrié de la Maza, Emb. de resr Spain
140 D4 Barrie I i. Ontario Canada
8 E2 Barrier, Cape c. New Zealand
136 E4 Barrière B.C. Canada
13 E2 Barrier Range h. New South Wales Australia
137 J3 Barrington Lake l. Manitoba Canada
13 G3 Barrington, Mt mt. New South Wales Australia
168 D1 Barro Alto Brazil
169 G2 Barrocão Brazil
148 B3 Barron Wisconsin U.S.A.
15 F3 Barron Falls waterfall Queensland Australia
172 A5 Barros Arana Chile
169 G4 Barroso Brazil
151 C7 Barroterán Mexico
67 D4 Barrow r. Rep. of Ireland
134 C2 Barrow Alaska U.S.A.
173 G5 Barrow Argentina
14 C2 Barrow, C. c. Northern Terr. Australia
14 C4 Barrow Creek Northern Terr. Australia
16 A4 Barrow I. i. Western Australia Australia
65 E3 Barrow-in-Furness England U.K.
17 D5 Barrow Ra. h. Western Australia Australia
135 J2 Barrow Strait str. N.W.T. Canada
17 C5 Barr Smith Ra. h. Western Australia Australia
98 D3 Barruecopardo Spain
62 C3 Barry Wales U.K.
130 C6 Barrydale South Africa
141 G4 Barrys Bay Ontario Canada
46 E3 Barsa-Kel'mes, O. i. Kazakhstan
36 C3 Barsalpur India
112 E1 Bârsana Romania
72 F2 Barsbüttel Germany
47 J3 Barshatas Kazakhstan
38 A2 Barsi India
36 D5 Barsi lakli India
72 E3 Barsinghausen Germany
55 B4 Barsø i. Denmark
72 C2 Barßel Germany
154 D4 Barstow California U.S.A.
54 B3 Barstyčiai Lithuania
52 C2 Barsuki Rus. Fed.
86 D4 Bar-sur-Aube France
86 D4 Bar-sur-Seine France
90 F1 Bartenheim France
73 H1 Barth Germany
80 A3 Bartholomäberg Austria
164 B4 Bartholomew Deep depth Chile
163 F2 Bartica Guyana
42 C1 Bartın Turkey
15 F3 Bartle Frere, Mt mt. Queensland Australia
155 G2 Bartles, Mt mt. Utah U.S.A.
150 D3 Bartlett Nebraska U.S.A.
147 H2 Bartlett New Hampshire U.S.A.
136 F2 Bartlett Lake l. N.W.T. Canada
77 M1 Bartninkai Lithuania
129 F3 Bartolomeu Dias Mozambique
147 G2 Barton Vermont U.S.A.
65 H4 Barton-upon-Humber England U.K.
77 J1 Bartoszyce Poland
77 H3 Baruchowo Poland
108 B5 Barumini Sardegna Italy
22 C4 Barung i. Indonesia
73 J3 Baruth Germany
30 C2 Baruunharaa Mongolia
30 C4 Baruunsuu Mongolia
30 E3 Baruun Urt Mongolia
66 B2 Barvas Scotland U.K.
69 D4 Barvaux Belgium
53 G2 Barvinkove Ukraine
36 D5 Barwah India
36 C3 Barwala India
36 C5 Barwani India
36 D4 Barwa Sagar India
76 E2 Barwice Poland
13 G2 Barwon r. New South Wales Australia
52 B2 Baryatino Rus. Fed.
76 F4 Barycz r. Poland
54 F4 Barysaw Belarus
52 H3 Barysh r. Rus. Fed.
52 H3 Barysh Rus. Fed.
53 D1 Baryshivka Ukraine
79 M5 Bârzava Romania
106 D3 Barzio Italy
39 B2 Barzūk Iran
39 C4 Basaidu Iran
170 E2 Basail Argentina
15 F3 Basalt r. Queensland Australia
154 C2 Basalt Nevada U.S.A.
27 □ Basalt I. i. Hong Kong China
124 C3 Basankusu Congo(Zaire)
38 B2 Basar India
53 C3 Basarabeasca Moldova
112 G2 Basarabi Romania
99 H1 Basauri Spain
173 H2 Basavilbaso Argentina
102 F2 Bàscara Spain
69 D5 Bascharage Luxembourg
108 E2 Baschi Italy
62 D2 Baschurch England U.K.
23 B1 Basco Philippines
99 G2 Basconcillos del Tozo Spain
99 H4 Bascuñana, Sa de mountain range Spain
170 B2 Bascuñán, C. c. Chile
69 B4 Basècles Belgium
82 C1 Basel Switzerland
83 G2 Baselga di Pinè Italy
82 C1 Basellandschaft div. Switzerland
90 F1 Basel-Mulhouse airport France
111 F2 Basentello r. Italy
111 F2 Basento r. Italy
148 B1 Basewood Lake l. Minnesota U.S.A.
39 D4 Bashākerd, Kūhhā-ye mountain range Iran
136 G4 Bashaw Alberta Canada
131 G6 Bashee r. South Africa
39 G2 Bashgul r. Afghanistan
46 E1 Bashkortostan div. Rus. Fed.
52 F3 Bashmakovo Rus. Fed.
39 B3 Bāsht Iran
53 E3 Bashtanka Ukraine
37 F5 Basia India
23 B5 Basilan i. Philippines
23 B5 Basilan Strait chan. Philippines
63 G3 Basildon England U.K.
107 H2 Basiliano Italy
109 H4 Basilicata div. Italy
111 E4 Basiluzzo, Isola i. Italy
152 E2 Basin Wyoming U.S.A.
63 E3 Basingstoke England U.K.
37 G5 Basirhat India
107 J4 Baška Croatia
147 K2 Baskahegan Lake l. Maine U.S.A.
52 B2 Baskakovka Rus. Fed.
42 F2 Başkale Turkey
141 H3 Baskatong, Réservoir resr Québec Canada
43 B1 Başköy Turkey
Basle see Basel
63 E1 Baslow England U.K.
22 A2 Baso i. Indonesia
36 D5 Basoda India
83 D2 Basodino mt. Italy/Switzerland
124 D3 Basoko Congo(Zaire)
Basque Country div. see País Vasco
93 D4 Bas Quercy reg. France
Basra see Al Başrah
87 G4 Bas-Rhin div. France
107 F3 Bassano del Grappa Italy
123 E5 Bassar Togo
117 J8 Bassas da India is Indian Ocean
82 C1 Bassecourt Switzerland
88 D4 Basse-Goulaine France
24 A4 Bassein r. Myanmar
24 A3 Bassein Myanmar
124 D3 Basse-Kotto div. Central African Rep.
69 D4 Bassenge Belgium
89 E3 Basse-Normandie div. France
93 B4 Bassens France
65 E3 Bassenthwaite Lake l. England U.K.
159 □4 Basse Pointe Martinique Caribbean
122 B4 Basse Santa Su The Gambia
159 □5 Basse Terre i. Guadeloupe Caribbean
159 □5 Basse Terre Guadeloupe Caribbean
159 □6 Basseterre St Kitts-Nevis Caribbean
159 □3 Basse Terre Trinidad and Tobago
150 D3 Bassett Nebraska U.S.A.
155 G5 Bassett Peak summit Arizona U.S.A.
147 J2 Bass Harbor Maine U.S.A.
87 E5 Bassigny reg. France
120 C5 Bassikounou Mauritania
123 E5 Bassila Benin
86 D4 Bassin Auzon Temple resr France
93 A4 Bassin d'Arcachon inlet France
88 D3 Bassin de Rennes basin France
91 B5 Bassin de Thau lag. France
66 F4 Bass Rock i. Scotland U.K.
13 F4 Bass Strait str. Australia
72 D3 Bassum Germany
82 A3 Bassy France
59 E3 Båstad Sweden
39 C4 Bastak Iran
42 F2 Bastānābād Iran
109 E2 Bastardo Italy
108 B2 Bastelica Corse France
70 E3 Bastheim Germany
37 E4 Basti India
108 B2 Bastia Corse France
109 E1 Bastia Italy
108 B2 Bastia-Poretta airport Corse France
166 E2 Bastioes r. Brazil
69 D5 Bastogne div. Luxembourg Belgium
69 D4 Bastogne Belgium
168 C4 Bastos Brazil
151 F5 Bastrop Louisiana U.S.A.
151 D6 Bastrop Texas U.S.A.
59 F1 Basttjärn Sweden
39 F4 Basul r. Pakistan
Basuo see Dongfang
22 A2 Basu, Tg pt Indonesia
125 B5 Bas-Zaire div. Congo(Zaire)
124 A3 Bata Equatorial Guinea
158 B2 Batabanó, Golfo de b. Cuba
23 B2 Batac Philippines
45 P3 Batagay Rus. Fed.
45 P3 Batagay-Alyta Rus. Fed.
30 B1 Batagol Rus. Fed.
168 B4 Bataguaçu Brazil
112 E4 Batak Bulgaria
22 C3 Batakan Indonesia
36 C3 Batala India
100 B1 Batalha Portugal
22 A1 Batam i. Indonesia
124 E3 Batama Congo(Zaire)
45 O3 Batamay Rus. Fed.
46 E2 Batamshinskiy Kazakhstan
23 B1 Batan i. Philippines
32 B2 Batang China
124 A4 Batanga Gabon
124 C2 Batangafo Central African Rep.
23 B3 Batangas Philippines
22 2 Batanghari r. Indonesia
23 B1 Batan Islands is Philippines
79 H5 Bátaszék Hungary
168 E4 Batatais Brazil
148 C5 Batavia Illinois U.S.A.
146 D3 Batavia New York U.S.A.
52 A3 Batayeva Rus. Fed.
51 F6 Bataysk Rus. Fed.
140 C3 Batchawana r. Ontario Canada
140 C3 Batchawana Bay Ontario Canada
138 D4 Batchawana Mt. h. Ontario Canada
14 B2 Batchelor Northern Terr. Australia
140 C3 Batchewana Ontario Canada
140 C3 Batchewana Mt mt. Ontario Canada
25 C4 Bătdâmbâng Cambodia
102 D3 Batea Spain
13 G3 Batemans Bay New South Wales Australia
29 □2 Baten Japan
11 □1 Bates, Mt h. Norfolk I. Pacific Ocean
17 C5 Bates Ra. h. Western Australia Australia
151 F5 Batesville Arkansas U.S.A.
151 F5 Batesville Mississippi U.S.A.
50 D3 Batetskiy Rus. Fed.
62 D3 Bath England U.K.
147 J3 Bath Maine U.S.A.
139 G4 Bath New Brunswick Canada
146 E3 Bath New York U.S.A.
141 G4 Bath Ontario Canada
159 □6 Bath St Kitts-Nevis Caribbean
118 C5 Batha div. Chad
118 C5 Batha watercourse Chad
124 C1 Batha de Laïri watercourse Chad
62 D3 Bath and North East Somerset div. England U.K.
66 E5 Bathgate Scotland U.K.
36 C3 Bathinda India
68 E2 Bathmen Netherlands
139 G4 Bathurst New Brunswick Canada
13 G3 Bathurst New South Wales Australia
173 G4 Bathurst Argentina
131 F6 Bathurst South Africa
14 B1 Bathurst I. i. Northern Terr. Australia
135 J2 Bathurst I. i. N.W.T. Canada
14 B1 Bathurst I. Abor. Land res. Northern Terr. Australia
134 H3 Bathurst Inlet inlet N.W.T. Canada
134 H3 Bathurst Inlet N.W.T. Canada
126 C2 Batī Ethiopia
122 D5 Batié Burkina
22 E2 Batikala, Tg pt Indonesia
6 □8 Batiki i. Fiji
113 F6 Batı Menteşe Dağları mountain range Turkey
79 H6 Batina Croatia
141 J3 Batiscan Québec Canada
39 C2 Bāţlāq-e Gavkhūnī salt marsh Iran
65 G4 Batley England U.K.
13 G3 Batlow New South Wales Australia
42 E2 Batman Turkey
52 F1 Batmany Rus. Fed.
121 F1 Batna Algeria
151 F6 Baton Rouge Louisiana U.S.A.
79 J3 Bátonyterenye Hungary
156 D3 Batopilas Mexico
124 B3 Batouri Cameroon
168 B1 Batovi Brazil
119 G2 Batrā, J. mt. Saudi Arabia
43 C5 Batrā, J. el mt. Jordan
43 C2 Batroûn Lebanon
56 H1 Båtsfjord Norway
115 F5 Batsi Greece
30 A2 Bat-Sot Rus. Fed.
82 C1 Bätterkinden Switzerland
36 C3 Batti India
38 C5 Batticaloa Sri Lanka
25 A5 Batti Malv i. Andaman and Nicobar Is India
109 G4 Battipaglia Italy
137 G4 Battle r. Alberta Canada
63 G4 Battle England U.K.
148 E4 Battle Creek Michigan U.S.A.
137 H4 Battleford Saskatchewan Canada
152 C3 Battle Mountain Nevada U.S.A.
79 L5 Battonya Hungary
36 C1 Battura Gl. gl. Jammu and Kashmir
126 C3 Batu mt. Ethiopia
22 C1 Batuayau, Bukit mt. Indonesia
22 A2 Batubetumbang Indonesia
172 B3 Batuco Chile
22 C1 Batuesambang, Bukit mt. Indonesia
25 C6 Batu Gajah Malaysia
22 C4 Batukau, G. volcano Indonesia
23 C5 Batulaki Philippines
22 D4 Batulanteh mt. Indonesia
22 C2 Batulicin Indonesia
22 C1 Batulilangmebang, G. mt. Indonesia
Batum see Bat'umi
51 G7 Bat'umi Georgia
25 C7 Batu Pahat Malaysia
20 C7 Batu, P.P. is Indonesia
25 C6 Batu Puteh, Gunung mt. Malaysia
22 A3 Baturaja Indonesia
22 B3 Baturetno Indonesia
166 E1 Baturité Brazil
166 E1 Baturite, Sa h. Brazil
53 E1 Baturyn Ukraine
52 H2 Batyrevo Rus. Fed.
88 A3 Batz, Île de i. France
88 C4 Batz-sur-Mer France
6 □8 Bau i. Fiji
166 B2 Bau r. Brazil
21 H8 Baubau Indonesia
123 G4 Bauchi div. Nigeria
123 F4 Bauchi Nigeria
88 B4 Baud France
37 F5 Bauda India
150 E1 Baudette Minnesota U.S.A.
83 D2 Bauen Switzerland
10 □3 Bauer Bay b. Macquarie I. Pacific Ocean
126 E3 Bauet well Ethiopia
89 E4 Baugé France
89 E4 Baugeois reg. France
90 E3 Bauges mts France
15 G5 Bauhinia Downs Queensland Australia
108 A4 Bauladu Sardegna Italy
74 E3 Bauland reg. Germany
139 K3 Bauld, C. headland Newfoundland Canada
90 E1 Baume-les-Dames France
87 G3 Baumholder Germany
75 F2 Baunach r. Germany
108 B4 Baunei Sardegna Italy
164 D2 Baures Bolivia
168 D5 Bauru Brazil
168 B3 Baús Brazil
74 B2 Bausendorf Germany
54 D3 Bauska Latvia
73 K4 Bautzen Germany
Bavaria div. see Bayern
86 C2 Bavay France
59 G2 Båven l. Sweden
106 C3 Baveno Italy
130 D6 Baviaanskloofberg mts South Africa
82 B1 Bavilliers France
156 C2 Bavispe r. Mexico
52 D1 Bavleny Rus. Fed.
46 D2 Bavly Rus. Fed.
81 F1 Bavorov Czech Rep.
124 C3 Bavula Congo(Zaire)
24 A2 Baw Myanmar
22 B2 Bawal i. Indonesia
22 B2 Bawang, Tg pt Indonesia
63 H2 Bawdeswell England U.K.
24 B2 Bawdwin Myanmar
22 C3 Bawean i. Indonesia
72 C3 Bawinkel Germany
119 E2 Bawiti Egypt
122 D4 Bawku Ghana
24 B3 Bawlake Myanmar
32 C2 Bawolung China
32 C1 Baxi China
32 D2 Ba Xian China
31 F5 Ba Xian China
145 D6 Baxley Georgia U.S.A.
32 B2 Baxoi China
126 D4 Bay div. Somalia
Bay see Baicheng
158 C2 Bayamo Cuba
145 □3 Bayamón Puerto Rico
31 H3 Bayan China
22 D4 Bayan Indonesia
30 D2 Bayan Mongolia
30 B3 Bayan Mongolia
36 D4 Bayana India
47 J2 Bayanaul Kazakhstan
30 D3 Bayanbulag Hentiy Mongolia
30 A3 Bayanbulag Bayan-Hongor Mongolia
30 D3 Bayandelger Mongolia
124 C3 Bayanga Central African Rep.
124 C2 Bayanga-Didi Central African Rep.
30 B2 Bayangol Rus. Fed.
32 A1 Bayan Har Shan mountain range China
32 B1 Bayan Har Shankou pass China
30 A3 Bayan- Hongor div. Mongolia
30 B3 Bayanhongor Mongolia
30 B3 Bayanhushuu Mongolia
30 C4 Bayan Mod China
30 D4 Bayan Obo China
30 E3 Bayan-Ovoo Mongolia
31 G3 Bayan Qagan China
30 A3 Bayansayr Mongolia
47 K4 Bayansumküre China
31 F2 Bayan Ta China
99 H2 Bayas r. Spain
30 E3 Bayasgalant Mongolia
42 B2 Bayat Turkey

39 C3 Bayāẕ Iran
23 C4 Baybay Philippines
42 E1 Bayburt Turkey
149 F4 Bay City Michigan U.S.A.
151 D6 Bay City Texas U.S.A.
44 H3 Baydaratskaya Guba b. Rus. Fed.
126 D4 Baydhabo Somalia
30 A3 Baydrag Gol r. Mongolia
75 J3 Bayerisch Eisenstein Germany
75 H3 Bayerischer Wald mountain range Germany
75 G4 Bayern div. Germany
83 G1 Bayersoien Germany
75 J4 Bayer Wald, Nationalpark nat. park Germany
89 E2 Bayeux France
47 K2 Bayevo Rus. Fed.
148 B2 Bayfield Wisconsin U.S.A.
46 E3 Bayganin Kazakhstan
173 J2 Baygorria, Lago Artificial de resr Uruguay
126 E2 Bayḩan al Qişab Yemen
113 F5 Bayındır Turkey
42 D4 Bāyir Jordan
47 H4 Baykadam Kazakhstan
30 C2 Baykal Rus. Fed.
30 C1 Baykal, Ozero l. Rus. Fed.
30 C2 Baykal'sk Rus. Fed.
47 G3 Baykonur Kazakhstan
47 J5 Baykurt China
23 B3 Bay, Laguna de lag. Philippines
46 E2 Baymak Rus. Fed.
8 F3 Bay of Plenty div. New Zealand
23 B2 Bayombong Philippines
87 F4 Bayon France
93 A5 Bayonne France
23 B4 Bayo Point pt Philippines
162 A5 Bayóvar Peru
46 F5 Bayramaly Turkmenistan
42 A2 Bayramiç Turkey
122 D4 Bay, Réserve de res. Mali
75 G3 Bayreuth Germany
151 F6 Bay St Louis Mississippi U.S.A.
119 H4 Baysh watercourse Saudi Arabia
147 G4 Bay Shore New York U.S.A.
62 D2 Bayston Hill England U.K.
47 G5 Baysun Uzbekistan
126 D2 Bayt al Faqīh Yemen
151 E6 Baytown Texas U.S.A.
22 A2 Bayunglincir Indonesia
8 F3 Bay View New Zealand
101 H3 Baza r. Spain
101 H3 Baza Spain
81 H4 Bázakerettye Hungary
53 B2 Bazaliya Ukraine
53 C1 Bazar Ukraine
39 B1 Bāzār-e Māsāl Iran
52 H3 Bazarnaya Ken'sha Rus. Fed.
52 H3 Bazarnyy Karabulak Rus. Fed.
52 H3 Bazarnyy Syzgan Rus. Fed.
46 D3 Bazartobe Kazakhstan
129 F3 Bazaruto, Ilha do i. Mozambique
93 B4 Bazas France
101 H3 Baza, Sierra de mountain range Spain
39 F4 Bazdar Pakistan
69 C5 Bazeilles France
32 D2 Bazhong China
93 D5 Baziège France
141 H3 Bazin r. Québec Canada
39 E4 Bazman Iran
39 E3 Bazmān, Kūh-e mt. Iran
90 B1 Bazoches France
86 B4 Bazoches-les-Gallerandes France
89 F3 Bazoches-sur-Hoëne France
90 B1 Bazois reg. France
89 E4 Bazouges France
93 A5 Baztán, Valle de v. France/Spain
107 F4 Bazzano Italy
179 □ B. d'Audierne b. Kerguelen Indian Ocean
25 D5 Be r. Vietnam
150 C2 Beach N. Dakota U.S.A.
141 G4 Beachburg Ontario Canada
147 F5 Beach Haven New Jersey U.S.A.
12 E4 Beachport S. Australia Australia
147 F5 Beachwood New Jersey U.S.A.
63 G4 Beachy Head headland England U.K.
147 G4 Beacon New York U.S.A.
17 B6 Beacon Western Australia Australia
131 F6 Beacon Bay South Africa
27 □ Beacon Hill h. Hong Kong China
63 F3 Beaconsfield England U.K.
13 F5 Beaconsfield Tasmania Australia
65 G2 Beadnell Bay b. England U.K.
16 C3 Beagle Bay Abor. Reserve res. Western Australia Australia
14 B2 Beagle Gulf b. Northern Terr. Australia
129 H1 Bealanana Madagascar
Béal an Átha see Ballina
Béal Átha na Sluaighe see Ballinasloe
62 D4 Beaminster England U.K.
129 H3 Beampingaratra mts Madagascar
146 B6 Bean Station Tennessee U.S.A.
152 E3 Bear r. Idaho U.S.A.
137 N2 Bear Cove b. N.W.T. Canada
140 B2 Beardmore Ontario Canada
179 B4 Beardmore Gl. gl. Antarctica
15 G5 Beardmore Res. resr Queensland Australia
148 B5 Beardstown Illinois U.S.A.
138 D3 Bear Island i. N.W.T. Canada
Bear Island i. see Bjørnøya
67 B5 Bear Island i. Rep. of Ireland
98 B2 Beariz Spain
152 E3 Bear L. l. Idaho/Utah U.S.A.
136 D3 Bear Lake B.C. Canada
36 D5 Bearma r. India
93 B5 Béarn reg. France
152 E1 Bear Paw Mt. mt. Montana U.S.A.
179 A3 Bear Pen. pen. Antarctica
64 D2 Bearsden Scotland U.K.
138 B3 Bearskin Lake Ontario Canada
154 B2 Bear Valley California U.S.A.
99 H1 Beasain Spain
159 E3 Beata, Cabo c. Dominican Rep.
159 E3 Beata, I. i. Dominican Rep.
150 D3 Beatrice Nebraska U.S.A.
14 D2 Beatrice, C. c. Northern Terr. Australia
66 E5 Beattock Scotland U.K.
136 E3 Beatton r. B.C. Canada
136 E3 Beatton River B.C. Canada
154 D3 Beatty Nevada U.S.A.
141 G2 Beattyville Québec Canada
127 □4 Beau Bassin Mauritius
91 C5 Beaucaire France
89 G3 Beauce reg. France
171 E7 Beauchene I. i. Falkland Is.
90 E1 Beaucourt France
89 E4 Beaucouzé France
15 H5 Beaudesert Queensland Australia
89 F3 Beaufay France
90 D2 Beaufort Franche-Comté France
90 E3 Beaufort Rhône-Alpes France
145 D5 Beaufort S. Carolina U.S.A.
13 E4 Beaufort Victoria Australia
43 C3 Beaufort Castle Lebanon
89 E4 Beaufort-en-Vallée France
90 E3 Beaufortin mts France
134 D2 Beaufort Sea sea Canada/U.S.A.
130 D6 Beaufort West South Africa
89 G4 Beaugency France
141 J4 Beauharnois Québec Canada
91 E4 Beaujeu Provence - Alpes - Côte-d'Azur France
90 C2 Beaujeu Rhône-Alpes France
90 C2 Beaujolais, Monts du mts France
92 D4 Beaulieu-sur-Dordogne France
90 B2 Beaulon France
66 D3 Beauly Scotland U.K.
66 D3 Beauly Firth est. Scotland U.K.
62 B1 Beaumaris Wales U.K.
91 D4 Beaumes-de-Venise France
89 F2 Beaumesnil France
86 B2 Beaumetz-lès-Loges France
93 C4 Beaumont Aquitaine France
151 F6 Beaumont Mississippi U.S.A.
146 B5 Beaumont Ohio U.S.A.
88 D2 Beaumont Picardie France
151 E6 Beaumont Texas U.S.A.
69 C4 Beaumont Belgium
9 B6 Beaumont New Zealand
93 C5 Beaumont-de-Lomagne France
69 D5 Beaumont-en-Argonne France
89 F4 Beaumont-en-Véron France
89 F2 Beaumont-le-Roger France
86 B3 Beaumont-sur-Oise France
89 F3 Beaumont-sur-Sarthe France
90 C1 Beaune France
86 B4 Beaune-La Rolande France
141 K3 Beauport Québec Canada
6 □2 Beaupré i. New Caledonia Pacific Ocean
141 K3 Beaupré Québec Canada
89 E4 Beaupréau France
86 B2 Beauquesne France
69 C4 Beauraing Belgium
91 D3 Beaurepaire France
90 D2 Beaurepaire-en-Bresse France
91 D4 Beaurières France
137 K4 Beausejour Manitoba Canada
6 □2 Beautemps i. New Caledonia Pacific Ocean
69 B5 Beautor France
86 B3 Beauvais France
137 H3 Beauval Saskatchewan Canada
86 B2 Beauval France
91 E4 Beauvezer France
93 C4 Beauville France
88 C5 Beauvoir-sur-Mer France
92 B2 Beauvoir-sur-Niort France
91 C3 Beauzac France
93 D5 Beauzelle France
136 H4 Beaver r. Alberta Canada
136 D2 Beaver r. B.C./Yukon Canada
138 C2 Beaver r. Ontario Canada
155 F2 Beaver r. Utah U.S.A.
155 F2 Beaver Utah U.S.A.
136 A2 Beaver Creek Yukon Terr. Canada
144 C4 Beaver Dam Kentucky U.S.A.
148 C4 Beaver Dam Wisconsin U.S.A.
146 C4 Beaver Falls Pennsylvania U.S.A.
152 D2 Beaverhead Mts mountain range Montana U.S.A.
137 K4 Beaverhill L. l. Manitoba Canada
137 J2 Beaverhill L. l. N.W.T. Canada
148 E3 Beaver Island i. Michigan U.S.A.
151 E4 Beaver L. resr Arkansas U.S.A.
136 F3 Beaverlodge Alberta Canada
146 D4 Beaver Run Reservoir resr Pennsylvania U.S.A.
36 C4 Beawar India
172 D2 Beazley Argentina
172 D2 Bebedero, S. salt pan Argentina
124 C2 Bébédjia Chad
168 D4 Bebedouro Brazil
73 G3 Bebertal Germany
65 E4 Bebington England U.K.
124 C2 Béboto Chad
74 E2 Bebra Germany
138 F1 Bécard, Lac l. Québec Canada
90 E3 Becca du Lac mt. France
63 H2 Beccles England U.K.
83 G3 Becco di Filadonna mt. Italy
98 E4 Becedas Spain
112 B2 Bečej Yugoslavia
98 C2 Becerreá Spain
121 D2 Béchar Algeria
134 C4 Becharof L. l. Alaska U.S.A.
87 G3 Becherbach Germany
88 D3 Bécherel France
75 F3 Bechhofen Germany
75 K3 Bechyně Czech Rep.
99 E2 Becilla de Valderaduey Spain
113 F6 Beçin Turkey
74 B3 Beckingen Germany
65 H4 Beckingham England U.K.
146 C6 Beckley W. Virginia U.S.A.
72 D4 Beckum Germany
112 E1 Beclean Romania
89 E4 Bécon-les-Granits France
78 B1 Bečov nad Teplou Czech Rep.
78 F5 Becsehely Hungary
81 H4 Becsvölgye Hungary
65 G3 Bedale England U.K.
124 C2 Bédan Chad
91 B5 Bédarieux France
74 B2 Bedburg Germany
68 E3 Bedburg-Hau Germany
62 B1 Beddgelert Wales U.K.
63 G4 Beddingham England U.K.
147 J2 Beddington Maine U.S.A.
126 C3 Bedelē Ethiopia
47 J4 Bedel Pass pass China/Kyrgyzstan
72 D2 Bederkesa Germany
126 D3 Bedēsa Ethiopia
63 F2 Bedford England U.K.
144 C4 Bedford Indiana U.S.A.
147 H3 Bedford Massachusetts U.S.A.
146 D4 Bedford Pennsylvania U.S.A.
141 J4 Bedford Québec Canada
146 D6 Bedford Virginia U.S.A.
131 F6 Bedford South Africa
15 F2 Bedford, C. c. Queensland Australia
63 F2 Bedford Level reg. England U.K.
159 □8 Bedford Pt pt Grenada Caribbean
63 F2 Bedfordshire div. England U.K.
77 H4 Będków Poland
65 G2 Bedlington England U.K.
77 H3 Bedlno Poland
101 G3 Bedmar Spain
78 F5 Bednja r. Croatia
52 F3 Bednodem'yanovsk Rus. Fed.
25 □ Bedok Singapore
25 □ Bedok Res. resr Singapore
80 C4 Bedollo Italy
106 D4 Bedonia Italy
123 G3 Bedouaram well Niger
14 D5 Bedourie Queensland Australia
93 B5 Bedous France
155 H2 Bedrock Colorado U.S.A.
55 A3 Bedsted Stationsby Denmark
93 D4 Béduer France
68 E1 Bedum Netherlands
63 E2 Bedworth England U.K.
77 H5 Będzin Poland
76 D1 Będzino Poland
15 F5 Beechal Cr. watercourse Queensland Australia
146 B5 Beech Fork Lake l. W. Virginia U.S.A.
148 C2 Beechwood Michigan U.S.A.
13 G3 Beecroft Pen. pen. New South Wales Australia
68 D3 Beek Gelderland Netherlands
69 D4 Beek Limburg Netherlands
69 D3 Beek Noord-Brabant Netherlands
68 D2 Beekbergen Netherlands
73 H3 Beelitz Germany
15 H5 Beenleigh Queensland Australia
67 A4 Beenoskee h. Rep. of Ireland
73 J2 Beenz Germany
17 B6 Beeringgnurding, Mt h. Western Australia Australia
43 C4 Beer Menuha Israel
69 B3 Beernem Belgium
43 C5 Beer Ora Israel
69 C3 Beerse Belgium
69 C4 Beersel Belgium
Beersheba see Be'ér Sheva'
43 C4 Be'ér Sheva' Israel
68 F1 Beerta Netherlands
73 K3 Beeskow Germany
131 F2 Beestekraal South Africa
14 C3 Beetaloo Northern Terr. Australia
68 E1 Beetsterzwaag Netherlands
73 G3 Beetzendorf Germany
73 H3 Beetzsee l. Germany
151 D6 Beeville Texas U.S.A.
124 D3 Befale Congo(Zaire)
129 H2 Befandriana Avaratra Madagascar
124 D3 Befori Congo(Zaire)
129 H3 Befotaka Madagascar
13 G4 Bega New South Wales Australia
37 G5 Begamganj Bangladesh
88 B3 Bégard France
112 C2 Begejski Kanal canal Romania/Yugoslavia
159 □7 Beggars Pt pt Antigua and Barbuda Caribbean
101 G3 Begíjar Spain
141 K2 Bégin Québec Canada
93 B4 Bègles France
64 B3 Beg, Lough l. Northern Ireland U.K.
58 D1 Begna r. Norway
58 C1 Begndal Norway
114 D1 Begnište Macedonia
122 D5 Begoro Ghana
52 H3 Beguch Rus. Fed.
36 C4 Begun India
102 G3 Begur Spain
102 G3 Begur, Cap de pt Spain
37 F4 Begusarai India
39 D2 Behābād Iran
39 B3 Behbehān Iran
37 G1 Behleg China
136 C3 Behm Canal inlet Alaska U.S.A.
179 B3 Behrendt Mts mts Antarctica
87 F3 Behren-lès-Forbach France
39 C1 Behshahr Iran
39 F2 Behsūd Afghanistan
130 E6 Behulpsaam South Africa
33 F4 Bei r. China
31 H2 Bei'an China
32 D1 Beiba China
32 D2 Beibei China
32 D2 Beichuan China
126 B3 Beigi Ethiopia
33 E4 Beihai China
31 F4 Beijing div. China
31 F5 Beijing China
68 E2 Beilen Netherlands
33 E4 Beiliu China
75 G3 Beilngries Germany
124 C2 Béinamar Chad
66 E4 Beinn a' Ghlo mt. Scotland U.K.
66 B5 Beinn an Oir h. Scotland U.K.
64 C2 Beinn an Tuirc h. Scotland U.K.
64 B2 Beinn Bheigeir h. Scotland U.K.
64 C2 Beinn Bhreac h. Scotland U.K.
64 C1 Beinn Bhreac h. Scotland U.K.
64 C1 Beinn Chapull h. Scotland U.K.
66 E4 Beinn Dearg mt. Scotland U.K.
66 D3 Beinn Dearg mt. Scotland U.K.
66 D4 Beinn Heasgarnich mt. Scotland U.K.
64 D1 Beinn Ime mt. Scotland U.K.
64 C1 Beinn Mhor h. Scotland U.K.
Beinn na Faoghla i. see Benbecula
64 C1 Beinn Sgulaird mt. Scotland U.K.
82 D1 Beinwil Switzerland
31 G4 Beipiao China
129 E2 Beira Mozambique
98 C4 Beira Alta reg. Portugal
98 C5 Beira Baixa reg. Portugal
98 B4 Beira Litoral reg. Portugal
33 F1 Beiru r. China
43 C3 Beirut Lebanon
30 A4 Beishan China
131 H1 Beitbridge Zimbabwe
66 D5 Beith Scotland U.K.
79 M5 Beiuş Romania
31 G4 Beizhen China
100 B3 Beja div. Portugal
100 C2 Beja Portugal
121 F1 Béja Tunisia
121 F1 Bejaïa Algeria
114 A2 Bejar Albania
98 E4 Béjar Spain
39 D2 Bejestān Iran
36 B3 Beji r. Pakistan
124 B2 Béka Cameroon
22 A3 Bekasi Indonesia
46 D4 Bekdash Turkmenistan
79 L5 Békés div. Hungary
79 L5 Békés Hungary
79 L5 Békéscsaba Hungary
53 E3 Bekhtery Ukraine
129 H3 Bekily Madagascar
28 K2 Bekkai Japan
30 E2 Beklemishevo Rus. Fed.
52 F3 Bekovo Rus. Fed.
122 D5 Bekyem Ghana
37 E4 Bela India
36 A4 Bela Pakistan
131 G2 Bela-Bela South Africa
124 B3 Bélabo Cameroon
92 D2 Bélâbre France
112 C2 Bela Crkva Yugoslavia
47 K2 Bel'agach Kazakhstan
88 C3 Bel Air h. France
147 E5 Bel Air Maryland U.S.A.
101 E2 Belalcázar Spain
78 B2 Bělá nad Radbuzou Czech Rep.
112 D3 Bela Palanka Yugoslavia
79 K3 Bélapátfalva Hungary
78 D1 Bělá pod Bezdězem Czech Rep.
78 G1 Bělá pod Pradědem Czech Rep.
13 F3 Belaraboon New South Wales Australia
49 H3 Belarus country Europe
114 D1 Belasica mts Bulgaria/Macedonia
52 G1 Belasovka Rus. Fed.
167 A5 Bela Vista Brazil
129 E4 Bela Vista Mozambique
168 D2 Bela Vista de Goiás Brazil
45 T3 Belaya r. Rus. Fed.
53 F1 Belaya Rus. Fed.
52 A3 Belaya Berezka Rus. Fed.
51 G6 Belaya Glina Rus. Fed.
51 G5 Belaya Kalitva Rus. Fed.
50 J3 Belaya Kholunitsa Rus. Fed.
22 C1 Belayan r. Indonesia
52 G1 Belbazh Rus. Fed.
123 F4 Belbédji Niger
106 C4 Belbo r. Italy
93 D6 Belcaire France
77 H4 Bełchatów Poland
82 C1 Belchen mt. Germany
146 B6 Belcher Kentucky U.S.A.
135 L4 Belcher Islands is N.W.T. Canada
39 F2 Belchiragh Afghanistan
102 C3 Belchite Spain
78 C2 Bělčice Czech Rep.
67 D2 Belcoo Northern Ireland U.K.
141 G2 Belcourt Québec Canada
154 B1 Belden California U.S.A.
67 B2 Belderg Rep. of Ireland
55 C4 Beldringe-Odense airport Denmark
46 D2 Belebey Rus. Fed.
78 G4 Beled Hungary
126 E4 Beledweyne Somalia
122 C5 Belefuanai Liberia
107 J4 Belej Croatia
46 D5 Belek Turkmenistan
123 G5 Belel Nigeria
166 C1 Belém Brazil
166 E2 Belém de S. Francisco Brazil
153 F5 Belen New Mexico U.S.A.
170 C2 Belén Argentina
162 C2 Belen Colombia
173 J1 Belén Uruguay
99 G4 Beleña, Emb. de resr Spain
173 J1 Belén, Cuch. de h. Uruguay
112 E3 Belene Bulgaria
53 G1 Belenikhino Rus. Fed.
93 D6 Bélesta France
126 C2 Beles Wenz r. Ethiopia
46 E4 Beleuli Uzbekistan
47 G3 Beleutty r. Kazakhstan
52 C3 Belev Rus. Fed.
113 F5 Belevi Turkey
78 F5 Belezna Hungary
67 E2 Belfast airport Northern Ireland U.K.
147 J2 Belfast Maine U.S.A.
67 F2 Belfast Northern Ireland U.K.
9 D5 Belfast New Zealand
131 H2 Belfast South Africa
67 F2 Belfast Lough inlet Northern Ireland U.K.
69 E3 Belfeld Netherlands
150 C2 Belfield N. Dakota U.S.A.
126 B2 Bēlfodiyo Ethiopia
65 G2 Belford England U.K.
90 E1 Belfort France
90 E1 Belfort, Territoire de div. France
38 A3 Belgaum India
52 G4 Belgaza r. Rus. Fed.
73 J4 Belgern Germany
73 H4 Belgershain Germany
106 D3 Belgioioso Italy
48 F3 Belgium country Europe
108 B2 Belgodère Corse France
53 G1 Belgorod div. Rus. Fed.
53 G1 Belgorod Rus. Fed.
152 E2 Belgrade Montana U.S.A.
Belgrade see Beograd
122 B4 Béli Guinea-Bissau
123 G5 Beli Nigeria
102 E3 Belianes Spain
110 B5 Belice r. Sicilia Italy
100 C3 Beliche r. Portugal
112 C3 Beli Drim r. Albania/Yugoslavia
112 F3 Beli Lom r. Bulgaria
79 H6 Beli Manastir Croatia
93 B4 Belin-Béliet France
52 F3 Belinskiy Rus. Fed.
22 A2 Belinyu Indonesia
112 D3 Beli Timok r. Yugoslavia
112 D4 Belitsa Bulgaria
53 F1 Belitsa Rus. Fed.
22 B2 Belitung i. Indonesia
133 K8 Belize country Central America
125 B4 Belize Cabinda Angola
157 H5 Belize Belize
163 G3 Bélizon French Guiana
112 C2 Beljanica mt. Yugoslavia
45 P2 Bel'kovskiy, O. i. Rus. Fed.
141 G2 Bell r. Québec Canada
15 G5 Bell Queensland Australia
69 F4 Bell Germany
131 F6 Bell South Africa
109 H4 Bella Italy
136 D4 Bella Bella B.C. Canada
92 D2 Bellac France
90 E3 Bellacha, Mont mt. France
136 D4 Bella Coola B.C. Canada
106 D3 Bellagio Italy
151 E6 Bellaire Texas U.S.A.
106 D2 Bellano Italy
109 F2 Bellante Italy
107 G4 Bellaria Italy
38 B3 Bellary India
13 G2 Bellata New South Wales Australia
173 J1 Bella Unión Uruguay
170 E2 Bella Vista Corrientes Argentina
171 B7 Bella Vista Santa Cruz Argentina
170 C2 Bella Vista Tucumán Argentina
13 H2 Bellbrook New South Wales Australia
15 G4 Bell Cay reef Queensland Australia
102 D3 Bellclaire d'Urgell Spain
91 D3 Belledonne mts France
91 D3 Belledonne, Pic de mt. France
64 A3 Belleek Northern Ireland U.K.
159 □4 Bellefontaine Martinique Caribbean
146 B4 Bellefontaine Ohio U.S.A.
146 E4 Bellefonte Pennsylvania U.S.A.
150 C2 Belle Fourche r. S. Dakota U.S.A.
150 C2 Belle Fourche S. Dakota U.S.A.
86 B5 Bellegarde Centre France
91 C5 Bellegarde Languedoc-Roussillon France
92 E3 Bellegarde-en-Marche France
90 D2 Bellegarde-sur-Valserine France
145 D7 Belle Glade Florida U.S.A.
88 B4 Belle-Île i. France
139 K3 Belle Isle i. Newfoundland Canada
88 B3 Belle-Isle-en-Terre France
139 J3 Belle Isle, Strait of str. Newfoundland Canada
89 F3 Bellême France
155 G4 Bellemont Arizona U.S.A.
90 B2 Bellenaves France
89 G2 Bellencombre France
148 A5 Belle Plaine Iowa U.S.A.
90 B2 Bellerive-sur-Allier France
87 F4 Belles-Forêts France
141 F3 Belleterre Québec Canada
86 C3 Belleu France
82 B2 Bellevaux France
90 D2 Bellevesvre France
150 D4 Belleville Kansas U.S.A.
141 G4 Belleville Ontario Canada
90 C2 Belleville France
87 E3 Belleville-sur-Meuse France
92 A2 Belleville-sur-Vie France
152 D3 Bellevue Idaho U.S.A.
148 B4 Bellevue Iowa U.S.A.
146 B4 Bellevue Ohio U.S.A.
152 B2 Bellevue Washington U.S.A.
91 B3 Bellevue-la-Montagne France
90 D3 Belley France
74 D3 Bellheim Germany
90 E1 Bellherbe France
90 D2 Bellignat France
Bellin see Kangirsuk
55 C4 Bellinge Denmark
13 H2 Bellingen New South Wales Australia
65 F2 Bellingham England U.K.
152 B1 Bellingham Washington U.S.A.
179 B2 Bellingshausen Rus. Fed. Base South Shetland Islands Antarctica
179 A3 Bellingshausen Sea sea Antarctica
68 F1 Bellingwolde Netherlands
106 C3 Bellinzago Novarese Italy
83 E2 Bellinzona Switzerland
102 D3 Bell-Lloc d'Urgell Spain
162 B2 Bello Colombia
102 B4 Bello Spain
93 B5 Bellocq France
147 G3 Bellows Falls Vermont U.S.A.
36 B3 Bellpat Pakistan
102 E3 Bellpuig d'Urgell Spain
178 □3 Bellsund inlet Svalbard Arctic Ocean
147 F5 Belltown Delaware U.S.A.
107 F2 Belluno div. Veneto Italy
107 G2 Belluno Italy
38 B3 Belluru India
173 F2 Bell Ville Argentina
130 B6 Bellville South Africa
72 D3 Belm Germany
101 E2 Bélmez Spain
101 G3 Bélmez de la Moraleda Spain
146 D3 Belmont New York U.S.A.
66 □2 Belmont Scotland U.K.
130 E4 Belmont South Africa
90 C2 Belmont-de-la-Loire France
98 D1 Belmonte Asturias Spain
101 H1 Belmonte Castilla - La Mancha Spain
169 J1 Belmonte Brazil
98 C4 Belmonte Portugal
93 E5 Belmont-sur-Rance France
157 H5 Belmopan Belize
15 E3 Belmore Cr. r. Queensland Australia
67 B2 Belmullet Rep. of Ireland
169 H1 Belo Campo Brazil
141 J4 Beloeil Québec Canada
69 B4 Belœil Belgium
31 J2 Belogorsk Rus. Fed.
112 D3 Belogradchik Bulgaria
129 H3 Beloha Madagascar
169 G3 Belo Horizonte Brazil
150 D4 Beloit Kansas U.S.A.
148 C4 Beloit Wisconsin U.S.A.
166 E2 Belo Jardim Brazil
47 K2 Belokurikha Rus. Fed.
127 □4 Bel Ombre Mauritius
166 B1 Belo Monte Brazil
50 E1 Belomorsk Rus. Fed.
37 G5 Belonia India
52 D2 Beloomut Rus. Fed.
52 D2 Beloozerskiy Rus. Fed.
22 E2 Belopa Indonesia
99 G2 Belorado Spain
51 F6 Belorechensk Rus. Fed.
42 C2 Belören Turkey
46 E2 Beloretsk Rus. Fed.
Belorussia see Belarus
79 G2 Bělotín Czech Rep.
112 D3 Belotintsi Bulgaria
129 G2 Belo Tsiribihina Madagascar
47 K2 Belousovka Kazakhstan
52 C2 Belousovo Rus. Fed.
112 D3 Belovo Bulgaria
47 L2 Belovo Rus. Fed.
52 H2 Belovod'ye Rus. Fed.
50 F1 Beloye Rus. Fed.
44 E3 Beloye More g. Rus. Fed.
50 F1 Beloye More Rus. Fed.
50 F2 Beloye, Ozero l. Rus. Fed.
50 F2 Belozersk Rus. Fed.
82 C2 Belp Switzerland
110 D5 Belpasso Sicilia Italy
93 D5 Belpech France
63 E1 Belper England U.K.
146 C5 Belpre Ohio U.S.A.
65 G2 Belsay England U.K.
114 A2 Belsh Albania
77 J4 Belsk Duży Poland
52 E2 Bel'skoye Rus. Fed.
152 E2 Belt Montana U.S.A.
12 D2 Beltana S. Australia Australia
154 D3 Belted Range mts Nevada U.S.A.
166 B1 Belterra Brazil
30 A2 Beltes Gol r. Mongolia
87 G2 Beltheim Germany
81 H4 Beltinci Slovenia
151 D6 Belton Texas U.S.A.
67 B3 Beltra Lough l. Rep. of Ireland
108 A5 Belu r. Sardegna Italy
38 A3 Belur India
23 A5 Beluran Malaysia
79 H2 Beluša Slovakia
111 E3 Belvedere Marittimo Italy
93 D4 Belvès France
148 C4 Belvidere Illinois U.S.A.
99 F5 Belvís de la Jara Spain
15 F4 Belyando r. Queensland Australia
47 G4 Belye Vody Kazakhstan
50 H3 Belyshevo Rus. Fed.
52 A2 Belyy Rus. Fed.
52 B3 Belyye Berega Rus. Fed.
52 C1 Belyy Gorodok Rus. Fed.
44 H2 Belyy, O. i. Rus. Fed.
88 B4 Belz France
77 N5 Belz Ukraine
77 M5 Bełżec Poland
73 H3 Belzig Germany
77 L4 Bełżyce Poland
129 G2 Bemaraha, Plateau du plat. Madagascar
129 H1 Bemarivo r. Madagascar
125 B5 Bembe Angola
123 E4 Bembéréké Benin
101 E2 Bembézar r. Spain
98 D2 Bembibre Spain
63 E4 Bembridge England U.K.
148 C6 Bement Illinois U.S.A.
150 E2 Bemidji Minnesota U.S.A.
68 D3 Bemmel Netherlands
100 B1 Bemposta Portugal
65 H3 Bempton England U.K.
122 D4 Béna Burkina
102 D2 Benabarre Spain
125 D4 Bena Dibele Congo(Zaire)
22 C2 Benagin Indonesia
101 H4 Benahadux Spain
120 C2 Benahmed Morocco
66 D4 Ben Alder mt. Scotland U.K.
13 F4 Benalla Victoria Australia
101 F4 Benalmádena Spain
101 G3 Benalúa de Guadix Spain
101 G3 Benalúa de las Villas Spain
100 E4 Benalup de Sidonia Spain
101 F4 Benamargosa Spain
101 H3 Benamaurel Spain
127 □4 Benares Mauritius
121 G1 Ben Arous Tunisia
103 C4 Benasal Spain
102 D2 Benasque Spain
92 C2 Benassay France
125 D4 Bena-Sungu Congo(Zaire)
91 E5 Bénat, Cap c. France
78 D1 Benátky nad Jizerou Czech Rep.
100 B2 Benavente Portugal
98 E2 Benavente Spain
98 E2 Benavides de Orbigo Spain
100 C1 Benavila Portugal
66 E3 Ben Avon mt. Scotland U.K.
67 E1 Benbane Head headland Northern Ireland U.K.
67 B3 Benbaun h. Rep. of Ireland
66 A3 Benbecula i. Scotland U.K.
64 C1 Ben Buie h. Scotland U.K.
67 C2 Benbulben h. Rep. of Ireland
67 E2 Benburb Northern Ireland U.K.
64 E1 Ben Chonzie mt. Scotland U.K.
66 C4 Ben Cruachan mt. Scotland U.K.
17 B6 Bencubbin Western Australia Australia
152 B2 Bend Oregon U.S.A.
131 G5 Bendearg mt. South Africa
125 C4 Bendela Congo(Zaire)
13 G2 Bendemeer New South Wales Australia
126 F3 Bender-Bayla Somalia
13 F4 Bendigo Victoria Australia
13 G4 Bendoc Victoria Australia
74 C2 Bendorf Germany
54 C3 Bēne Latvia
129 E2 Bene Mozambique
68 D3 Beneden-Leeuwen Netherlands
147 J2 Benedicta Maine U.S.A.
80 C3 Benediktbeuren Germany
100 B1 Benedita Portugal
103 C6 Benejama Spain
129 H3 Benenitra Madagascar
78 D2 Benešov Czech Rep.
81 F2 Benešov nad Černou Czech Rep.
75 K2 Benešov nad Ploučnicí Czech Rep.
87 F4 Bénestroff France
108 B4 Benetutti Sardegna Italy
92 D2 Bénévent-l'Abbaye France
109 G3 Benevento div. Campania Italy
109 G3 Benevento Benevento Italy
87 G4 Benfeld France
100 B1 Benfica do Ribatejo Portugal
33 G1 Beng r. China
37 G5 Bengal, Bay of sea Asia
124 E3 Bengamisa Congo(Zaire)
124 B3 Bengbis Cameroon
33 G1 Bengbu China
25 C7 Bengkalis Indonesia
22 B1 Bengkayang Indonesia
22 A3 Bengkulu div. Indonesia
20 D7 Bengkulu Indonesia
22 D2 Bengkung Indonesia
125 B5 Bengo div. Angola
59 E2 Bengtsfors Sweden
125 B6 Benguela div. Angola
125 B6 Benguela Angola
121 G2 Ben Guerdane Tunisia
120 C2 Benguerir Morocco
43 A4 Benha Egypt
66 D2 Ben Hope mt. Scotland U.K.
164 D2 Beni div. Bolivia
164 C2 Beni r. Bolivia
124 E3 Beni Congo(Zaire)
121 D2 Beni-Abbès Algeria
96 D5 Beni Boufrah Morocco
102 D4 Benicarló Spain
103 D4 Benicasim Spain
103 C6 Benidorm Spain
123 G2 Ben Dourso well Niger
103 C5 Benifaio Spain
88 A3 Beniguet, Île de i. France
43 A6 Beni Hasan Egypt
119 F2 Benî Mazâr Egypt
120 C2 Beni Mellal Morocco
117 E5 Benin country Africa
123 F5 Benin r. Nigeria
123 E5 Benin, Bight of g. Africa
123 F5 Benin City Nigeria
121 D2 Beni-Ounif Algeria
121 D1 Beni-Saf Algeria
123 G4 Benisheikh Nigeria
103 D6 Benissa Spain
43 A5 Beni Suef Egypt
156 B2 Benito, Islas is Mexico
173 H4 Benito Juárez Argentina
23 B2 Benito Soliven Philippines
114 A3 Benitses Greece
162 D4 Benjamim Constant Brazil
156 C2 Benjamín Hill Mexico
171 B5 Benjamin, I. i. Chile
172 E5 Benjamín Zorrillo Argentina
21 K8 Benjina Indonesia
28 H2 Benkei-misaki pt Japan
150 C3 Benkelman Nebraska U.S.A.
83 E1 Benken Switzerland
66 D2 Ben Klibreck mt. Scotland U.K.
104 E3 Benkovac Croatia
131 G1 Ben Lavin Nature Reserve res. South Africa
66 D4 Ben Lawers mt. Scotland U.K.
64 D1 Ben Ledi h. Scotland U.K.
13 G2 Ben Lomond mt. New South Wales Australia
66 D4 Ben Lomond mt. Scotland U.K.
13 F5 Ben Lomond Nat. Park nat. park Tasmania Australia
66 D2 Ben Loyal h. Scotland U.K.

66 D4 Ben Lui mt. Scotland U.K.
131 F5 Ben Macdhui mt. Lesotho
66 E3 Ben Macdui mt. Scotland U.K.
66 D4 Ben More mt. Scotland U.K.
66 B4 Ben More mt. Scotland U.K.
66 D2 Ben More Assynt mt. Scotland U.K.
9 C6 Benmore, L. l. New Zealand
9 C6 Benmore Pk mt. New Zealand
64 C2 Bennan Head headland Scotland U.K.
68 D2 Bennekom Netherlands
45 Q2 Bennetta, O. i. Rus. Fed.
8 □1 Bennett, C. c. Auckland Is New Zealand
66 C4 Ben Nevis mt. Scotland U.K.
73 H4 Bennewitz Germany
147 G3 Bennington Vermont U.S.A.
88 A4 Bénodet France
9 B6 Ben Ohau Ra. mountain range New Zealand
131 G3 Benoni South Africa
124 B2 Bénoué r. Cameroon
124 B2 Bénoué, Parc National de la nat. park Cameroon
124 C2 Bénoy Chad
98 C5 Benquerenças Portugal
75 F2 Benshausen Germany
74 D3 Bensheim Germany
120 C2 Ben Slimane Morocco
155 G6 Benson Arizona U.S.A.
150 E2 Benson Minnesota U.S.A.
122 B5 Bensonville Liberia
64 C1 Ben Starav mt. Scotland U.K.
39 D4 Bent Iran
25 C6 Benta Seberang Malaysia
146 D6 Bent Creek Virginia U.S.A.
68 E2 Bentelo Netherlands
22 E3 Benteng Indonesia
125 B6 Bentiaba Angola
96 E5 Ben Tieb Morocco
14 D3 Bentinck I. i. Queensland Australia
25 B5 Bentinck I. i. Myanmar
43 C3 Bent Jbail Lebanon
65 G4 Bentley England U.K.
165 E3 Bento Gomes r. Brazil
167 B6 Bento Gonçalves Brazil
151 E5 Benton Arkansas U.S.A.
154 C3 Benton California U.S.A.
144 B4 Benton Illinois U.S.A.
147 K2 Benton New Brunswick Canada
148 D4 Benton Harbor Michigan U.S.A.
25 D5 Bên Tre Vietnam
25 C7 Bentung Malaysia
73 H1 Bentwisch Germany
22 A1 Benua i. Indonesia
123 F5 Benue div. Nigeria
123 F5 Benue r. Nigeria
66 D4 Ben Vorlich mt. Scotland U.K.
67 B3 Benwee h. Rep. of Ireland
67 B2 Benwee Head headland Rep. of Ireland
66 D3 Ben Wyvis mt. Scotland U.K.
31 G4 Benxi China
31 H4 Benxi China
23 C5 Beo Indonesia
112 C2 Beograd Yugoslavia
37 E5 Beohari India
122 C5 Béoumi Côte d'Ivoire
32 D3 Bepian r. China
28 C7 Beppu Japan
28 C7 Beppu-wan b. Japan
6 □8 Beqa i. Fiji
6 □8 Beqa Barrier Reef reef Fiji
159 G4 Bequia i. St Vincent
166 D1 Bequimão Brazil
173 G2 Berabevú Argentina
36 C4 Berach r. India
67 D2 Beragh Northern Ireland U.K.
129 H3 Beraketa Madagascar
124 C3 Bérandjokou Congo
99 G1 Beranga Spain
139 G2 Bérard, Lac l. Québec Canada
36 D5 Berasia India
114 A2 Berat Albania
93 D5 Bérat France
22 D2 Beratus, G. mt. Indonesia
75 G3 Beratzhausen Germany
129 H2 Beravina Madagascar
173 H3 Berazategui Argentina
119 F4 Berber Sudan
126 E2 Berbera Somalia
124 C3 Bérberati Central African Rep.
163 F3 Berbice r. Guyana
79 J4 Bercel Hungary
106 D4 Berceto Italy
69 B4 Berchem Belgium
75 G3 Berching Germany
75 J5 Berchtesgaden Germany
80 D3 Berchtesgadener Alpen mts Germany
75 H5 Berchtesgaden, Nationalpark nat. park Germany
86 A2 Berck France
53 G3 Berda r. Ukraine
45 O3 Berdigestyakh Rus. Fed.
47 K2 Berdsk Rus. Fed.
98 D1 Berducedo Spain
93 B6 Berdún Spain
53 G3 Berdyans'k Ukraine
53 G3 Berdyans'ka Kosa spit Ukraine
53 G3 Berdyans'ka Zatoka b. Ukraine
53 C2 Berdychiv Ukraine
124 C2 Béré Chad
146 A6 Berea Kentucky U.S.A.
62 B4 Bere Alston England U.K.
53 A2 Berehomet Ukraine
79 M3 Berehove Ukraine
6 □1 Bereina P.N.G.
81 H5 Berek Croatia
53 G2 Bereka r. Ukraine
53 G2 Bereka Ukraine
122 D5 Berekum Ghana
52 D1 Berendeyevo Rus. Fed.
164 C3 Berenguela Bolivia
119 G3 Berenice Egypt
137 K4 Berens r. Manitoba Canada
137 K4 Berens River Manitoba Canada
129 H3 Berenty Madagascar
62 D4 Bere Regis England U.K.
150 D3 Beresford S. Dakota U.S.A.
53 A1 Berestechko Ukraine
112 F1 Bereşti Romania
53 E1 Berestivka Ukraine
53 G3 Berestove Dnipropetrovs'ka Oblast' Ukraine
53 G2 Berestove Kharkivs'ka Oblast' Ukraine
53 F2 Berestoven'ka Ukraine
53 A1 Berestyane Ukraine
79 L4 Berettyó r. Hungary
79 L4 Berettyóújfalu Hungary
53 D1 Berezan' Ukraine
53 D3 Berezanka Ukraine
53 B1 Berezdiv Ukraine
112 G1 Berezeni Romania
53 A2 Berezhany Ukraine
53 E1 Berezivka Chernihivs'ka Oblast' Ukraine
53 E3 Berezivka Kirovohrads'ka Oblast' Ukraine
53 D3 Berezivka Odes'ka Oblast' Ukraine
53 B2 Berezivka Zhytomyrs'ka Oblast' Ukraine
53 C1 Berezivka Zhytomyrs'ka Oblast' Ukraine
53 D1 Berezna Ukraine
53 B1 Berezne Ukraine
53 E3 Bereznehuvate Ukraine
50 G2 Bereznik Rus. Fed.
44 G4 Berezniki Rus. Fed.
52 G3 Berezovka Rus. Fed.
31 H2 Berezovka Rus. Fed.
44 H3 Berezovo Rus. Fed.
53 C3 Berezyne Ukraine
80 C3 Berg Bayern Germany
75 G2 Berg Bayern Germany
69 E4 Berg Nordrhein-Westfalen Germany
80 E4 Berg Austria
69 E5 Berg Luxembourg
69 D4 Berg Netherlands
73 G4 Berga Sachsen-Anhalt Germany
75 H2 Berga Thüringen Germany
102 E2 Berga Spain
55 E3 Bergagård Sweden
42 A2 Bergama Turkey
106 D3 Bergamo div. Lombardia Italy
106 D3 Bergamo Bergamo Italy
102 C4 Bergantes r. Spain
98 B1 Bergantiños reg. Spain
99 H1 Bergara Spain
83 E1 Bergatreute Germany
59 G1 Bergby Sweden
72 C3 Berge Germany
102 E2 Bergeda reg. Spain
80 D3 Bergen Bayern Germany
68 E3 Bergen Limburg Netherlands
73 J1 Bergen Mecklenburg-Vorpommern Germany
72 E3 Bergen Niedersachsen Germany
68 C2 Bergen Noord-Holland Netherlands
58 A1 Bergen Norway
73 F3 Bergen (Dumme) Germany
69 C3 Bergen op Zoom Netherlands
68 E2 Bergentheim Netherlands
93 C4 Bergerac France
86 D4 Bergères-lès-Vertus France
69 D3 Bergeyk Netherlands
80 C2 Bergheim Bayern Germany
74 B2 Bergheim Nordrhein-Westfalen Germany
74 C2 Bergisches Land reg. Germany
74 C2 Bergisch Gladbach Germany
72 C4 Bergkamen Germany
80 C2 Bergkirchen Germany
148 C2 Bergland Michigan U.S.A.
58 A1 Bergsbukken mt. Norway
59 H2 Bergshamra Sweden
57 E3 Bergsjö Sweden
59 F2 Bergs slussar Sweden
56 F2 Bergsviken Sweden
74 F3 Bergtheim Germany
86 B2 Bergues France
68 E1 Bergum Netherlands
68 E1 Bergumermeer l. Netherlands
83 E2 Bergün Switzerland
131 G4 Bergville South Africa
30 D3 Berh Mongolia
22 A2 Berikat, Tg pt Indonesia
169 G2 Berilo Brazil
45 S4 Beringa, O. i. Rus. Fed.
17 B5 Beringarra Western Australia Australia
100 C2 Beringel Portugal
69 D3 Beringen Belgium
45 T3 Beringovskiy Rus. Fed.
134 A4 Bering Sea sea Pacific Ocean
134 A3 Bering Strait str. Rus. Fed./U.S.A.
39 D4 Berīzak Iran
53 D3 Berizky Ukraine
101 H4 Berja Spain
74 F2 Berka Germany
56 C3 Berkåk Norway
121 D2 Berkane Morocco
68 E2 Berkel r. Germany/Netherlands
68 C3 Berkel Netherlands
68 D3 Berkel-Enschot Netherlands
154 A3 Berkeley California U.S.A.
62 D3 Berkeley England U.K.
162 □ Berkeley, C. c. Galapagos Is Ecuador
146 D5 Berkeley Springs W. Virginia U.S.A.
74 F4 Berkheim Germany
179 B3 Berkner I. i. Antarctica
112 D3 Berkovitsa Bulgaria
63 E3 Berkshire div. England U.K.
63 E3 Berkshire Downs h. England U.K.
141 J5 Berkshire Hills h. Massachusetts U.S.A.
86 C2 Berlaimont France
100 E2 Berlanga Spain
100 A1 Berlenga i. Portugal
56 H1 Berlevåg Norway
73 J3 Berlin div. Germany
73 J3 Berlin Berlin Germany
147 F5 Berlin Maryland U.S.A.
147 H2 Berlin New Hampshire U.S.A.
146 D5 Berlin Pennsylvania U.S.A.
148 C4 Berlin Wisconsin U.S.A.
146 C4 Berlin Lake l. Ohio U.S.A.
112 C2 Berlişte Romania
83 E1 Bermatingen Germany
173 F6 Bermeja, Pta pt Argentina
101 E4 Bermeja, Sierra mountain range Spain
156 E3 Bermejíllo Mexico
172 D1 Bermejo r. Argentina
170 E2 Bermejo r. Chaco/Formosa Argentina
172 D1 Bermejo Argentina
164 D4 Bermejo Bolivia
173 G5 Bermejo, I. i. Argentina
170 E2 Bermejo, Pto Argentina
99 H1 Bermeo Spain
98 D3 Bermillo de Sayago Spain
174 E3 Bermuda i. Atlantic Ocean
174 E3 Bermuda Rise sea feature Atlantic Ocean
82 C2 Bern div. Switzerland
82 C2 Bern Bern Switzerland
173 J1 Bernabé Rivera Uruguay
111 F2 Bernalda Italy
153 F5 Bernalillo New Mexico U.S.A.
91 E5 Bernarde, Sommet de la mt. France
171 B6 Bernardo O'Higgins, Parque Nacional nat. park Chile
75 K3 Bernartice Czech Rep.
172 F4 Bernasconi Argentina
82 D1 Bernau Baden-Württemberg Germany
73 J3 Bernau Brandenburg Germany
75 H5 Bernau am Chiemsee Germany
86 B2 Bernaville France
89 F2 Bernay France
83 F1 Bernbeuren Germany
73 G4 Bernburg Germany
81 H3 Berndorf Austria
148 E5 Berne Indiana U.S.A.
72 D2 Berne Germany
99 H2 Bernedo Spain
82 C2 Berner Alpen mts Switzerland
66 A3 Berneray i. Scotland U.K.
66 A4 Berneray i. Scotland U.K.
98 E2 Bernesga r. Spain
81 H2 Bernhardsthal Austria
135 K2 Bernier Bay b. N.W.T. Canada
17 A5 Bernier I. i. Western Australia Australia
83 F2 Bernina Pass pass Switzerland
91 C5 Bernis France
69 B4 Bernissart Belgium
74 C3 Bernkastel-Kues Germany
73 K4 Bernsdorf Germany
81 H3 Bernstein Austria
82 D1 Beromünster Switzerland
129 H3 Beroroha Madagascar
78 D2 Beroun Czech Rep.
78 C2 Berounka r. Czech Rep.
112 D4 Berovo Macedonia
107 F4 Berra Italy
82 C2 Berra, La mt. Switzerland
120 C2 Berrechid Morocco
91 D5 Berre-l'Étang France
12 E3 Berri S. Australia Australia
121 E2 Berriane Algeria
66 E2 Berriedale Scotland U.K.
88 B3 Berrien France
13 F3 Berrigan New South Wales Australia
102 B2 Berriozar Spain
172 E2 Berrotarán Argentina
121 E1 Berrouaghia Algeria
86 D3 Berru France
92 D2 Berry reg. France
13 G3 Berry New South Wales Australia
86 C3 Berry-au-Bac France
159 □1 Berrydale Jamaica
154 A2 Berryessa, Lake l. California U.S.A.
158 C1 Berry Is. is The Bahamas
128 B4 Berseba Namibia
72 C3 Bersenbrück Germany
53 C2 Bershad' Ukraine
107 E3 Bersone Italy
25 C6 Bertam Malaysia
141 J3 Berthierville Québec Canada
69 A4 Bertincourt France
166 B1 Bertinho Brazil
107 G4 Bertinoro Italy
69 D4 Bertogne Belgium
166 D2 Bertolinía Brazil
169 H2 Bertópolis Brazil
124 B3 Bertoua Cameroon
67 B3 Bertraghboy Bay b. Rep. of Ireland
69 D5 Bertrix Belgium
107 G4 Bertuzzi, Valle lag. Italy
4 J5 Beru i. Kiribati
46 F4 Beruni Uzbekistan
163 E4 Beruri Brazil
147 E4 Berwick Pennsylvania U.S.A.
65 F2 Berwick-upon-Tweed England U.K.
62 C2 Berwyn h. Wales U.K.
136 F3 Berwyn Alberta Canada
53 E3 Beryslav Ukraine
112 C2 Berzasca Romania
54 C4 Beržė r. Lithuania
78 G5 Berzence Hungary
54 E3 Bērzpils Latvia
54 E3 Bērzuane Latvia
91 B4 Bès r. France
129 G2 Besalampy Madagascar
102 F2 Besalú Spain
90 E1 Besançon Doubs France
99 F2 Besande Spain
22 C2 Besar, G. mt. Indonesia
99 F1 Besaya r. Spain
46 E3 Besbay Kazakhstan
90 B2 Besbre r. France
52 C4 Besedino Rus. Fed.
47 H4 Besharyk Uzbekistan
47 G5 Beshkent Uzbekistan
39 C3 Beshneh Iran
102 D2 Besiberri Sud mt. Spain
77 K6 Beskid Niski h. Poland
77 J6 Beskid Sądecki mountain range Poland
43 A1 Beskonak Turkey
137 H3 Besnard Lake l. Saskatchewan Canada
42 D2 Besni Turkey
83 D3 Besozzo Italy
124 C2 Béssao Chad
90 B2 Bessay-sur-Allier France
67 E2 Bessbrook Northern Ireland U.K.
82 B3 Besse France
92 E3 Besse-et-St-Anastaise France
91 C4 Bessèges France
145 C5 Bessemer Alabama U.S.A.
148 B2 Bessemer Michigan U.S.A.
90 C3 Bessenay France
89 F4 Bessé-sur-Braye France
91 E5 Besse-sur-Issole France
93 D5 Bessières France
89 E2 Bessin reg. France
92 D2 Bessines-sur-Gartempe France
52 G3 Bessonovka Rus. Fed.
92 E3 Bessou, Mont h. France
69 D3 Best Netherlands
47 J3 Bestamak Kazakhstan
46 E3 Bestamak Kazakhstan
73 J3 Bestensee Germany
131 G4 Besters South Africa
47 H2 Bestobe Kazakhstan
50 G2 Bestuzhevo Rus. Fed.
72 D4 Bestwig Germany
14 C2 Beswick Abor. Land res. Northern Terr. Australia
129 H3 Betanty Madagascar
164 C3 Betanzos Bolivia
98 B1 Betanzos Spain
124 B2 Bétaré Oya Cameroon
102 B1 Betelu Spain
103 C5 Bétera Spain
99 H4 Beteta Spain
43 C4 Bet Guvrin Israel
131 G3 Bethal South Africa
128 B4 Bethanien Namibia
150 E3 Bethany Missouri U.S.A.
151 D5 Bethany Oklahoma U.S.A.
134 B3 Bethel Alaska U.S.A.
147 H2 Bethel Maine U.S.A.
148 A6 Bethel Missouri U.S.A.
146 A5 Bethel Ohio U.S.A.
146 D4 Bethel Park Pennsylvania U.S.A.
159 □1 Bethel Town Jamaica
146 E5 Bethesda Maryland U.S.A.
146 C4 Bethesda Ohio U.S.A.
62 B1 Bethesda Wales U.K.
130 E5 Bethesdaweg South Africa
147 F4 Bethlehem Pennsylvania U.S.A.
43 C4 Bethlehem West Bank
131 G4 Bethlehem South Africa
131 E6 Bethlesdorp South Africa
131 E5 Bethulie South Africa
89 G2 Béthune r. France
86 B2 Béthune France
162 C2 Betijoque Venezuela
169 F3 Betim Brazil
129 G3 Betioky Madagascar
52 A2 Betlitsa Rus. Fed.
86 C4 Beton-Bazoches France
22 B1 Betong Malaysia
14 E5 Betoota Queensland Australia
126 C2 Beto Shet' r. Ethiopia
124 C3 Bétou Congo
47 H3 Betpak-Dala plain Kazakhstan
47 H3 Betpak-Dala Kazakhstan
129 H2 Betrandraka Madagascar
129 H3 Betroka Madagascar
43 C3 Bet She'an Israel
139 G4 Betsiamites r. Québec Canada
139 G4 Betsiamites Québec Canada
129 H2 Betsiboka r. Madagascar
148 D3 Betsie, Pt pt Michigan U.S.A.
148 E2 Betsy Lake l. Michigan U.S.A.
69 E5 Bettembourg Luxembourg
148 B5 Bettendorf Iowa U.S.A.
69 E5 Bettendorf Luxembourg
37 F4 Bettiah India
74 B3 Bettingen Germany
59 G2 Bettna Sweden
106 D4 Bettola Italy
88 D3 Betton France
109 E1 Bettona Italy
66 D2 Bettyhill Scotland U.K.
67 E3 Bettystown Rep. of Ireland
36 D5 Betul India
68 D3 Betuwe reg. Netherlands
36 D4 Betwa r. India
62 C1 Betws-y-coed Wales U.K.
86 B3 Betz France
74 C2 Betzdorf Germany
69 E5 Betzdorf Luxembourg
75 G3 Betzenstein Germany
83 F1 Betzigau Germany
148 D3 Beulah Michigan U.S.A.
63 G3 Beult r. England U.K.
68 D3 Beuningen Netherlands
118 C4 Beurfou well Chad
86 D4 Beurville France
69 B4 Beuvrages France
90 B1 Beuvron r. France
89 G4 Beuvron r. Centre France
69 A4 Beuvry France
89 F2 Beuzeville France
109 E2 Bevagna Italy
69 C3 Beveren Belgium
65 H4 Beverley England U.K.
17 B7 Beverley Western Australia Australia
15 G4 Beverley Group is Queensland Australia
147 H3 Beverly Massachusetts U.S.A.
146 C5 Beverly Ohio U.S.A.
154 C4 Beverly Hills California U.S.A.
137 J2 Beverly Lake l. N.W.T. Canada
72 D2 Beverstedt Germany
72 E4 Beverungen Germany
68 C2 Beverwijk Netherlands
62 D2 Bewdley England U.K.
63 G3 Bewl Water resr England U.K.
82 C2 Bex Switzerland
87 G3 Bexbach Germany
63 G4 Bexhill England U.K.
113 G6 Beyağaç Turkey
39 A2 Beyānlū Iran
113 G5 Beydağ Turkey
42 B2 Bey Dağları mountain range Turkey
42 B1 Beykoz Turkey
122 C5 Beyla Guinea
126 D2 Beylul Eritrea
93 D4 Beynac-et-Cazenac France
92 D3 Beynat France
46 E3 Beyneu Kazakhstan
42 B1 Beypazarı Turkey
38 A4 Beypore India
126 E3 Beyra Somalia
Beyrouth see Beirut
42 B2 Beyşehir Turkey
42 B2 Beyşehir Gölü l. Turkey
51 F6 Beysug r. Rus. Fed.
31 H1 Beytonovo Rus. Fed.
91 D4 Bez r. France
129 G3 Bezaha Madagascar
39 D2 Bezameh Iran
80 A3 Bezau Austria
50 J3 Bezbozhnik Rus. Fed.
79 H6 Bezdan Yugoslavia
52 H2 Bezdna r. Rus. Fed.
90 D1 Bèze France
54 F3 Bezhanitskaya Vozvyshennost' reg. Rus. Fed.
54 F3 Bezhanitsy Rus. Fed.
52 C1 Bezhetsk Rus. Fed.
52 C1 Bezhetskiy Verkh. h. Rus. Fed.
91 B5 Béziers France
77 J1 Bezledy Poland
91 C5 Bezouce France
Bezwada see Vijayawada
173 F5 B. Falsa b. Argentina
172 B1 B. Guanaqueros b. Chile
36 B4 Bhabhar India
37 E4 Bhabua India
36 D4 Bhadaura India
37 F4 Bhadgaon Nepal
37 E4 Bhadohi India
38 C2 Bhadrachalam India
Bhādrachalam Road Sta. see Kottagudem
37 F5 Bhadrakh India
38 A3 Bhadra Reservoir resr India
38 A3 Bhadravati India
36 A3 Bhag Pakistan
36 D2 Bhaga r. India
37 F4 Bhagalpur India
36 D5 Bhainsdehi India
37 G4 Bhairab Bazar Bangladesh
36 B3 Bhakkar Pakistan
38 B2 Bhalki India
24 B1 Bhamo Myanmar
38 C2 Bhamragarh India
36 D4 Bhander India
38 D2 Bhanjanagar India
36 C4 Bhanpura India
36 D5 Bhanrer Range India
36 D4 Bharatpur India
39 E4 Bhari r. Pakistan
36 D4 Bharthana India
36 C5 Bharuch India
37 E5 Bhatapara India
Bhatarsaigh i. see Vatersay
38 A3 Bhatkal India
Bhatnair see Hanumangarh
37 G5 Bhatpara India
38 B4 Bhavani r. India
38 B4 Bhavani India
36 C5 Bhavnagar India
36 C3 Bhawana Pakistan
38 C2 Bhawanipatna India
131 H3 Bhekuzulu South Africa
37 E3 Bheri r. Nepal
36 C4 Bhildi India
36 C4 Bhilwara India
38 B2 Bhima r. India
38 C2 Bhīmavaram India
37 F4 Bhimnagar India
36 D4 Bhind India
37 E4 Bhinga India
36 C4 Bhinmal India
36 D3 Bhiwani India
37 F4 Bhojpur Nepal
37 G5 Bhola Bangladesh
38 B2 Bhongir India
131 G5 Bhongweni South Africa
36 D5 Bhopal India
38 C2 Bhopalpatnam India
38 A2 Bhor India
37 F5 Bhuban India
37 F5 Bhubaneshwar India
36 B5 Bhuj India
24 B3 Bhumiphol Dam dam Thailand
131 H3 Bhunya Swaziland
36 C5 Bhusawal India
18 K7 Bhutan country Asia
36 B4 Bhuttewala India
39 D4 Bīabān mountain range Iran
126 D3 Biad well Ethiopia
36 C2 Biafo Gl. gl. Pakistan
21 L7 Biak i. Indonesia
21 L7 Biak Indonesia
76 F5 Biała Poland
77 L2 Biała Piska Poland
77 M4 Biała Podlaska div. Poland
77 M3 Biała Podlaska Poland
77 J4 Biała Rawska Poland
77 J4 Białobrzegi Poland
76 D2 Białogard Poland
77 M3 Białowieski Park Narodowy nat. park Poland
76 E2 Biały Bór Poland
77 M2 Białystok div. Poland
77 M2 Białystok Poland
110 D5 Biancavilla Sicilia Italy
111 F4 Bianco Italy
83 D3 Biandrate Italy
124 D3 Bianga Central African Rep.
122 C5 Biankouma Côte d'Ivoire
122 D5 Bianouan Côte d'Ivoire
103 C6 Biar Spain
39 C1 Bīārjmand Iran
93 A5 Biarritz France
93 A5 Biarritz-Parme airport France
93 A5 Biarrotte France
93 D4 Biars-sur-Cère France
93 A4 Bias France
83 D2 Biasca Switzerland
173 J1 Biassini Uruguay
76 G4 Biata-Parcela Pierwsza Poland
79 H4 Biatorbágy Hungary
43 A5 Biba Egypt
28 H2 Bibai Japan
125 B6 Bibala Angola
124 B3 Bibas Gabon
13 G4 Bibbenluke New South Wales Australia
107 F5 Bibbiena Italy
107 E5 Bibbona Italy
124 B2 Bibémi Cameroon
87 H4 Biberach Germany
74 E4 Biberach an der Riß Germany
80 B2 Biberbach Germany
82 C1 Biberist Switzerland
122 D5 Bibiani Ghana
107 H3 Bibione Italy
37 G4 Bibiyana r. Bangladesh
87 H3 Biblis Germany
Biblos see Jbail
53 A2 Bibrka Ukraine
63 E3 Bibury England U.K.
169 G4 Bicas Brazil
112 F1 Bicaz Romania
109 H3 Biccari Italy
63 E3 Bicester England U.K.
159 □3 Biche Trinidad and Tobago
137 G4 Biche, Lac La l. Alberta Canada
126 C2 Bichena Ethiopia
13 G5 Bicheno Tasmania Australia
75 G5 Bichl Germany
30 C2 Bichura Rus. Fed.
87 H3 Bickenbach Germany
14 D2 Bickerton I. i. Northern Terr. Australia
62 C4 Bickleigh England U.K.
155 G2 Bicknell Utah U.S.A.
79 H4 Bicske Hungary
125 B7 Bicuari, Parque Nacional do nat. park Angola
123 F5 Bida Nigeria
93 A5 Bidache France
23 A5 Bidadari, Tg pt Malaysia
39 C3 Bida Khabit Iran
38 B2 Bidar India
147 H3 Biddeford Maine U.S.A.
68 D2 Biddinghuizen Netherlands
62 D1 Biddulph England U.K.
66 C4 Bidean nam Bian mt. Scotland U.K.
62 B3 Bideford England U.K.
Bideford Bay b. see Barnstaple Bay
121 E4 Bidon V Algeria
79 L3 Bidovce Slovakia
31 J3 Bidzhan Rus. Fed.
31 J2 Bidzhar r. Rus. Fed.
125 C6 Bié div. Angola
77 L2 Biebrza r. Poland
77 L2 Biebrzański Park Narodowy nat. park Poland
77 K6 Biecz Poland
74 D2 Biedenkopf Germany
102 C2 Biel Spain
82 C1 Biel Switzerland
77 L3 Bielany-Żyłaki Poland
76 E5 Bielawa Poland
77 H3 Bielawy Poland
72 D3 Bielefeld Germany
80 B4 Bielerhöhe pass Austria
82 C1 Bieler See l. Switzerland
76 C2 Bielice Poland
106 C3 Biella Italy
102 D2 Bielsa Spain
77 H3 Bielsk Poland
77 H6 Bielsko div. Poland
77 H6 Bielsko-Biała Poland
77 M3 Bielsk Podlaski Poland
72 F2 Bienenbüttel Germany
25 D5 Biên Hoa Vietnam
76 D4 Bieniów Poland
90 D2 Bienne r. France
Bienne see Biel
163 G3 Bienveneu French Guiana
100 D2 Bienvenida h. Spain
100 D2 Bienvenida Spain
138 F2 Bienville, Lac l. Québec Canada
125 C6 Bié Plateau plat. Angola
82 B2 Bière Switzerland
89 E4 Bierné France
76 F4 Bierutów Poland
76 G3 Bierzwienna-Długa Poland
76 D2 Bierzwnik Poland
68 C3 Biesbosch, Nationaal Park de Netherlands
102 C2 Biescas Spain
73 J3 Biesenthal Germany
76 E1 Biesiekierz Poland
131 E3 Biesiesvlei South Africa
87 E4 Biesles France
76 E1 Biesowice Poland
77 L6 Bieszczady mts Poland
77 L6 Bieszczadzki Park Narodowy nat. park Poland
87 H4 Bietigheim Germany
74 E4 Bietigheim-Bissingen Germany
73 J2 Bietikow Germany
82 C2 Bietschhorn mt. Switzerland
69 D5 Bièvre Belgium
77 H3 Bieżuń Poland
109 G3 Biferno r. Italy
124 B4 Bifoun Gabon
28 J1 Bifuka Japan
154 A2 Big r. California U.S.A.
139 J3 Big r. Newfoundland Canada
42 A1 Biga Turkey
42 B2 Bigadiç Turkey
173 G2 Bigand Argentina
93 B4 Biganos France
113 F5 Biga Yarımadası pen. Turkey
6 □2 Big B. b. Vanuatu
9 B6 Big Bay b. New Zealand
148 D2 Big Bay Michigan U.S.A.
148 D3 Big Bay de Noc b. Michigan U.S.A.
154 D4 Big Bear Lake California U.S.A.
152 E2 Big Belt Mts mountain range Montana U.S.A.
131 H3 Big Bend Swaziland
151 C6 Big Bend Nat. Park Texas U.S.A.
151 F5 Big Black r. Mississippi U.S.A.
62 C4 Bigbury Bay b. England U.K.
62 C4 Bigbury-on-Sea England U.K.
145 D7 Big Cypress Nat. Preserve nat. park Florida U.S.A.
148 C3 Big Eau Pleine Reservoir resr Wisconsin U.S.A.
30 A3 Biger Nuur salt lake Mongolia
137 L5 Big Falls Minnesota U.S.A.
137 H4 Biggar Saskatchewan Canada
66 E5 Biggar Scotland U.K.
16 D2 Bigge I. i. Western Australia Australia
15 H5 Biggenden Queensland Australia
136 B3 Bigger, Mt mt. B.C. Canada
87 G1 Biggesee l. Germany
63 F2 Biggleswade England U.K.
152 D2 Big Hole r. Montana U.S.A.
152 F2 Bighorn r. Montana U.S.A.
152 E2 Bighorn Canyon Nat. Recreation Area nat. park Montana U.S.A.
152 F2 Bighorn Mts mountain range Wyoming U.S.A.
145 F7 Bight, The The Bahamas
135 L3 Big I. i. N.W.T. Canada
136 F2 Big I. i. N.W.T. Canada
124 D3 Bigi Congo(Zaire)
52 D3 Bigil'dino Rus. Fed.
147 K2 Big Lake l. Maine U.S.A.
88 C4 Bignan France
83 D2 Bignasco Switzerland
122 A4 Bignona Senegal
93 B6 Bigorre reg. France
146 D6 Big Otter r. Virginia U.S.A.
154 C3 Big Pine California U.S.A.
148 E4 Big Rapids Michigan U.S.A.
148 C3 Big Rib r. Wisconsin U.S.A.
137 H4 Big River Saskatchewan Canada
148 D3 Big Sable Pt pt Michigan U.S.A.
136 C2 Big Salmon r. Yukon Terr. Canada
137 K3 Big Sand Lake l. Manitoba Canada
155 F4 Big Sandy r. Arizona U.S.A.
150 D2 Big Sioux r. S. Dakota U.S.A.
154 D2 Big Smokey Valley v. Nevada U.S.A.
151 C5 Big Spring Texas U.S.A.
150 C3 Big Springs Nebraska U.S.A.
146 B6 Big Stone Gap Virginia U.S.A.
154 B3 Big Sur California U.S.A.
152 E2 Big Timber Montana U.S.A.
138 C3 Big Trout Lake l. Ontario Canada
138 C3 Big Trout Lake Ontario Canada
155 G3 Big Water Utah U.S.A.
141 F4 Bigwin Ontario Canada
104 E3 Bihać Bos.-Herz.
37 F4 Bihar India
37 F4 Bihariganj India
79 L4 Biharkeresztes Hungary
79 L4 Biharnagybajom Hungary
37 F4 Bihar Sharif India
79 M5 Bihor div. Romania
28 K2 Bihoro Japan
79 M5 Bihorului, Munţii mountain range Romania
37 H4 Bihpuriagaon India
122 A4 Bijagós, Arquipélago dos is Guinea-Bissau
36 C4 Bijainagar India
36 D4 Bijaipur India
38 A2 Bijapur India
39 A2 Bījār Iran
38 C2 Bijārpur India
36 D4 Bijawar India
104 G3 Bijeljina Bos.-Herz.
112 B3 Bijelo Polje Yugoslavia
32 B3 Bijiang China
32 D3 Bijie China
39 D4 Bījnābād Iran
37 G4 Bijni India
36 D3 Bijnor India
36 B3 Bijnot Pakistan
36 C3 Bikaner India
46 F3 Bikbauli Kazakhstan
31 K3 Bikin Rus. Fed.
4 H4 Bikini i. Marshall Is
129 E3 Bikita Zimbabwe
124 C4 Bikoro Congo(Zaire)
32 D1 Bikou China
23 C4 Bilaa Pt pt Philippines
36 C4 Bilara India
43 D2 Bil'ās, J. al mountain range Syria
37 E5 Bilaspur India
42 G2 Biläsuvar Azerbaijan
126 C3 Bilatē Shet' r. Ethiopia
53 D2 Bila Tserkva Ukraine
25 B4 Bilauktaung Range mountain range Myanmar/Thailand
99 H1 Bilbao airport Spain
99 H1 Bilbao Vizcaya Spain
43 A4 Bilbeis Egypt
112 E1 Bilbor Romania
30 D2 Bil'chir Rus. Fed.
104 G4 Bileća Bos.-Herz.
42 B1 Bilecik Turkey
104 G4 Bilečko Jezero resr Bos.-Herz.
79 K6 Biled Romania
53 G2 Bilen'ke Donets'ka Oblast' Ukraine
53 F3 Bilen'ke Zaporiz'ka Oblast' Ukraine
127 B5 Bilharamulo Tanzania
53 D3 Bilhorod-Dnistrovs'kyy Ukraine
124 D3 Bili r. Congo(Zaire)
124 E3 Bili Congo(Zaire)
45 S3 Bilibino Rus. Fed.
24 B3 Bilin Myanmar
78 C1 Bílina Czech Rep.
23 C4 Biliran i. Philippines
114 B2 Bilisht Albania
152 F3 Bill Wyoming U.S.A.
17 A5 Billabalong Western Australia Australia
Billabong r. see Moulamein
55 D2 Billdal Sweden
68 F3 Billerbeck Germany
93 B5 Billère France
63 G3 Billericay England U.K.
82 A2 Billiat France
16 D3 Billiluna Western Australia Australia
65 G3 Billingham England U.K.
63 F1 Billinghay England U.K.
152 E2 Billings Montana U.S.A.
59 E2 Billingsfors Sweden
63 F3 Billingshurst England U.K.
62 D4 Bill of Portland headland England U.K.
90 B3 Billom France
55 B4 Billund Denmark
155 F4 Bill Williams r. Arizona U.S.A.
155 F4 Bill Williams Mt mt. Arizona U.S.A.
90 B2 Billy France
123 G3 Bilma Niger
141 J2 Bilodeau Québec Canada
15 G5 Biloela Queensland Australia
78 F5 Bilo Gora h. Croatia
51 E6 Bilohirs'k Ukraine
53 B1 Bilohir"ya Ukraine
53 B2 Bilohorodka Ukraine
163 F3 Biloku Guyana
38 B2 Biloli India
53 F1 Bilopillya Ukraine
77 L5 Biłoraj Poland
53 G3 Bilosarays'ka Kosa spit Ukraine
53 B1 Bilotyn Ukraine
79 H2 Bílovec Czech Rep.
51 F5 Bilovods'k Ukraine
145 B6 Biloxi Mississippi U.S.A.
53 E3 Bilozerka Ukraine
53 G2 Bilozers'ke Ukraine
14 D5 Bilpa Morea Claypan salt flat Queensland Australia
53 F1 Bil's'k Ukraine

80 E1 **Bodenmais** Germany
83 E1 **Bodensee l.** Germany/Switzerland
73 F3 **Bodenteich** Germany
72 E4 **Bodenwerder** Germany
81 F3 **Bodenwies mt.** Austria
75 H3 **Bodenwöhr** Germany
99 H3 **Bodera, La mt.** Spain
123 E5 **Bode-Sadu** Nigeria
112 F1 **Bodești** Romania
38 B2 **Bodhan** India
38 B4 **Bodinayakkanur** India
100 D2 **Bodión r.** Spain
83 E1 **Bodman** Germany
62 B4 **Bodmin** England U.K.
62 B4 **Bodmin Moor reg.** England U.K.
83 E1 **Bodnegg** Germany
56 D2 **Bodø** Norway
83 E1 **Bodolz** Germany
167 A4 **Bodoquena** Brazil
79 L3 **Bodrog r.** Hungary
79 L3 **Bodrogköz reg.** Hungary
42 A2 **Bodrum** Turkey
56 F2 **Bodträskfors** Sweden
79 K3 **Bódvaszilas** Hungary
77 J3 **Bodzanów** Poland
99 F3 **Boecillo** Spain
99 F2 **Boedo r.** Spain
90 E2 **Boëge** France
68 D3 **Boekel** Netherlands
90 C3 **Boën** France
124 D4 **Boende** Congo(Zaire)
25 D4 **Bœng Lvea** Cambodia
130 C6 **Boerboonfontein** South Africa
131 F6 **Boesmans r.** South Africa
98 D2 **Boeza r.** Spain
122 B4 **Boffa** Guinea
37 H3 **Boga** India
98 D4 **Bogajo** Spain
24 A3 **Bogale** Myanmar
151 F6 **Bogalusa** Louisiana U.S.A.
13 F3 **Bogan r.** New South Wales Australia
123 D4 **Bogandé** Burkina
13 F3 **Bogan Gate** New South Wales Australia
124 C2 **Bogangolo** Central African Rep.
15 F4 **Bogantungan** Queensland Australia
112 B2 **Bogatić** Yugoslavia
75 G5 **Bogatynia** Poland
42 C2 **Boğazlıyan** Turkey
37 F3 **Bogcang Zangbo r.** China
124 C3 **Bogbonga** Congo(Zaire)
114 D1 **Bogdanci** Macedonia
76 D3 **Bogdaniec** Poland
26 E3 **Bogda Shan mountain range** China
75 H4 **Bogen** Germany
55 C4 **Bogense** Denmark
15 G6 **Boggabilla** Queensland Australia
13 G2 **Boggabri** New South Wales Australia
67 B4 **Boggeragh Mts h.** Rep. of Ireland
17 B4 **Boggola h.** Western Australia Australia
159 □7 **Boggy Pk mt.** Antigua and Barbuda Caribbean
6 □1 **Bogia** P.N.G.
66 F3 **Bogie r.** Scotland U.K.
82 D2 **Bognanco** Italy
66 F3 **Bogniebrae** Scotland U.K.
63 F4 **Bognor Regis** England U.K.
124 B1 **Bogo** Cameroon
55 E5 **Bogø** Denmark
23 C4 **Bogo** Philippines
67 D3 **Bog of Allen reg.** Rep. of Ireland
52 E1 **Bogolyubovo** Rus. Fed.
52 A2 **Bogolyubovo** Rus. Fed.
13 F4 **Bogong, Mt mt.** Victoria Australia
22 A3 **Bogor** Indonesia
77 K5 **Bogoria** Poland
52 D3 **Bogoroditsk** Rus. Fed.
52 B3 **Bogoroditskoye** Rus. Fed.
52 F1 **Bogorodsk** Rus. Fed.
50 J3 **Bogorodskoye** Rus. Fed.
118 C4 **Bogoroud well** Chad
79 L3 **Bogota h.** Slovakia
162 C3 **Bogotá** Colombia
37 G4 **Bogra** Bangladesh
59 E1 **Bograngen** Sweden
45 L4 **Boguchany** Rus. Fed.
51 G5 **Boguchar** Rus. Fed.
120 B5 **Bogué** Mauritania
43 D1 **Böğürtlen** Turkey
76 E5 **Boguszów-Gorce** Poland
77 L3 **Boguty-Pianki** Poland
159 □1 **Bog Walk** Jamaica
22 C1 **Boh r.** Indonesia
31 F5 **Bo Hai g.** China
31 E5 **Bohai Haixia chan.** China
86 C3 **Bohain-en-Vermandois** France
31 F5 **Bohai Wan b.** China
83 A3 **Bohars** France
112 E1 **Bohdan** Ukraine
81 G2 **Böheimkirchen** Austria
78 C2 **Bohemia div.** Czech Rep.
123 E5 **Bohicon** Benin
81 E4 **Bohinjska Bistrica** Slovenia
81 E4 **Bohinjsko Jezero l.** Slovenia
54 E4 **Bohinskaye, Vozyera l.** Belarus
73 H4 **Böhlen** Germany
73 H4 **Böhlitz-Ehrenberg** Germany
131 G4 **Bohlokong** South Africa
72 E3 **Böhme r.** Germany
75 H3 **Böhmer Wald mts** Germany
72 D3 **Bohmte** Germany
53 F1 **Bohodukhiv** Ukraine
23 C4 **Bohol i.** Philippines
67 B3 **Bohola** Rep. of Ireland
23 C4 **Bohol Sea sea** Philippines
23 B4 **Bohol Str. chan.** Philippines
78 G5 **Böhönye** Hungary
81 G4 **Bohor mt.** Slovenia
53 A2 **Bohorodchany** Ukraine
30 D3 **Böhöt** Mongolia
79 H2 **Bohumín** Czech Rep.
53 D2 **Bohuslav** Ukraine
75 J3 **Bohutín** Czech Rep.
163 E4 **Boiaçu** Brazil
147 F4 **Boiceville** New York U.S.A.
130 D4 **Boichoko** South Africa
141 K2 **Boileau** Québec Canada
16 C3 **Boileau, C. c.** Western Australia Australia
166 A1 **Boim** Brazil
24 A2 **Boinu r.** Myanmar
166 E3 **Boipeba, I. i.** Brazil
168 B6 **Boi Preto, Sa de h.** Brazil
98 B2 **Boiro** Spain
168 C3 **Bois r.** Brazil
127 □5 **Bois Blanc** Réunion Indian Ocean
149 E3 **Bois Blanc I. i.** Michigan U.S.A.
92 D2 **Boischaut reg.** France
82 B2 **Bois-d'Amont** France
69 C4 **Bois de Chimay woodland** Belgium
152 C3 **Boise** Idaho U.S.A.
151 C4 **Boise City** Oklahoma U.S.A.
89 G2 **Bois-Guillaume** France
90 B3 **Bois-Noirs h.** France
91 C5 **Boisseron** France
137 J5 **Boissevain** Manitoba Canada
107 G2 **Boite r.** Italy
131 E3 **Boitumelong** South Africa
168 E5 **Boituva** Brazil
73 J2 **Boitzenburg** Germany
92 C2 **Boivre r.** France
73 F2 **Boize r.** Germany
73 F2 **Boizenburg** Germany
76 D4 **Bojadła** Poland
109 G3 **Bojano** Italy
77 K5 **Bojanów** Poland
76 E4 **Bojanowo** Poland
55 C4 **Bøjden** Denmark
23 B2 **Bojeador, Cape c.** Philippines
112 C3 **Bojnik** Yugoslavia
39 D1 **Bojnūrd** Iran
22 B3 **Bojonegoro** Indonesia
22 A3 **Bojong** Indonesia
37 G1 **Bokadaban Feng mt.** China
37 H4 **Bokajan** India
124 C3 **Bokala** Congo(Zaire)
37 F5 **Bokaro** India
124 C4 **Bokatola** Congo(Zaire)
122 B4 **Boké** Guinea
124 D4 **Bokele** Congo(Zaire)
124 D3 **Bokenda** Congo(Zaire)
130 B6 **Bokfontein** South Africa
13 F2 **Bokhara r.** New South Wales Australia
52 E3 **Bokino** Rus. Fed.
58 A2 **Boknafjorden chan.** Norway
125 B4 **Boko** Congo
124 C3 **Bokode** Congo(Zaire)
124 E3 **Bokondo** Congo(Zaire)
Bokombayevskoye see **Bökönbaev**
47 J4 **Bökönbaev** Kyrgyzstan
131 G4 **Bokong** Lesotho
126 B4 **Bokora Corridor Game Reserve res.** Uganda
118 C5 **Bokoro** Chad
125 B4 **Boko-Songho** Congo
124 D4 **Bokote** Congo(Zaire)
52 G1 **Bokovaya** Rus. Fed.
51 G5 **Bokovskaya** Rus. Fed.
25 B5 **Bokpyin** Myanmar
131 G3 **Boksburg** South Africa
50 E3 **Boksitogorsk** Rus. Fed.
128 C4 **Bokspits** Botswana
124 D4 **Bokungu** Congo(Zaire)
124 D4 **Bokwankusu** Congo(Zaire)
118 B5 **Bol** Chad
124 C1 **Bola, Bahr watercourse** Chad
125 D4 **Bolaiti** Congo(Zaire)
122 A4 **Bolama** Guinea-Bissau
124 E2 **Bolanda, Jebel mt.** Sudan
74 D3 **Bolanden** Germany
106 D4 **Bolano** Italy
23 □2 **Bolanos h.** Guam Pacific Ocean
156 E4 **Bolaños** Mexico
101 G2 **Bolaños de Calatrava** Spain
36 A3 **Bolan Pass** Pakistan
89 F2 **Bolbec** France
39 B3 **Boldajī** Iran
73 J2 **Boldekow** Germany
55 B5 **Bolderslev** Denmark
112 F2 **Boldești-Scăeni** Romania
52 G3 **Boldovo** Rus. Fed.
64 E4 **Boldre** England U.K.
112 F2 **Boldu** Romania
47 K4 **Bole** China
122 D5 **Bole** Ghana
124 C4 **Boleko** Congo(Zaire)
124 C3 **Bolena** Congo(Zaire)
76 D4 **Bolesławiec** Poland
76 C3 **Boleszkowice** Poland
50 J4 **Bolgar** Rus. Fed.
122 D4 **Bolgatanga** Ghana
53 C3 **Bolhrad** Ukraine
31 H2 **Boli** China
124 E2 **Boli** Sudan
124 C4 **Bolia** Congo(Zaire)
57 E3 **Boliden** Sweden
23 A2 **Bolinao** Philippines
112 E2 **Bolintin-Vale** Romania
100 B3 **Boliqueime** Portugal
151 E4 **Bolivar** Missouri U.S.A.
145 B5 **Bolivar** Tennessee U.S.A.
164 C2 **Bolívar** Bolivia
162 B3 **Bolívar** Colombia
162 B5 **Bolívar** Peru
160 F5 **Bolivia country** South America
112 D3 **Boljevac** Yugoslavia
42 C2 **Bolkar Dağları mountain range** Turkey
58 C2 **Bolkesjø** Norway
52 C3 **Bolkhov** Rus. Fed.
140 D2 **Bolkow** Ontario Canada
76 E5 **Bolków** Poland
9 □3 **Bollans I. i.** Antipodes Is New Zealand
59 E3 **Bollebygd** Sweden
91 C4 **Bollène** France
82 C2 **Bolligen** Switzerland
57 E3 **Bollnäs** Sweden
15 F6 **Bollon** Queensland Australia
82 C1 **Bollschweil** Germany
56 E3 **Bollstabruk** Sweden
100 D3 **Bollullos Par del Condado** Spain
59 E3 **Bolmen l.** Sweden
51 H7 **Bolnisi** Georgia
124 C4 **Bolobo** Congo(Zaire)
107 F4 **Bologna div.** Emilia-Romagna Italy
107 F4 **Bologna** Bologna Italy
87 E4 **Bologne** France
162 C5 **Bolognesi** Peru
50 E3 **Bologoye** Rus. Fed.
131 E4 **Bolokanang** South Africa
52 C2 **Bolokhovo** Rus. Fed.
124 C3 **Bolomba** Congo(Zaire)
124 C3 **Bolombo** Congo(Zaire)
157 H4 **Bolonchén de Rejón** Mexico
124 C4 **Bolondo** Congo(Zaire)
23 B5 **Bolong** Philippines
108 A4 **Bolotana** Sardegna Italy
47 K1 **Bolotnoye** Rus. Fed.
25 D4 **Bolovens, Plateau des plat.** Laos
170 C2 **Bolsa, Co mt.** Argentina
108 D2 **Bolsena** Italy
108 D2 **Bolsena, Lago di l.** Italy
54 B4 **Bol'shakovo** Rus. Fed.
52 G2 **Bol'shaya Arya** Rus. Fed.
52 D3 **Bol'shaya Bereyka** Rus. Fed.
46 D2 **Bol'shaya Glushitsa,** Rus. Fed.
56 J2 **Bol'shaya Imandra, Oz. l.** Rus. Fed.
52 H2 **Bol'shaya Kandarat'** Rus. Fed.
50 H3 **Bol'shaya Kokshaga r.** Rus. Fed.
52 E3 **Bol'shaya Lipovitsa** Rus. Fed.
51 G6 **Bol'shaya Martinovka** Rus. Fed.
51 G6 **Bol'shaya Orlovka** Rus. Fed.
50 J1 **Bol'shaya Pyssa** Rus. Fed.
52 H2 **Bol'shaya Tsivil' r.** Rus. Fed.
46 E1 **Bol'shaya Usa** Rus. Fed.
52 H2 **Bol'shaya Vladimirovka** Kazakhstan
52 G3 **Bol'shaya Yelan'** Rus. Fed.
52 G2 **Bol'shaya Yelkhovka** Rus. Fed.
47 J2 **Bol'shegrivskoye** Rus. Fed.
47 K3 **Bol'shenarymskoye** Kazakhstan
47 H1 **Bol'sherech'ye** Rus. Fed.
53 G1 **Bol'shetroitskoye** Rus. Fed.
45 M2 **Bolshevik, O. i.** Rus. Fed.
52 H2 **Bol'shiye Algashi** Rus. Fed.
52 G2 **Bol'shiye Berezniki** Rus. Fed.
50 H2 **Bol'shiye Chirki** Rus. Fed.
50 F1 **Bol'shiye Kozly** Rus. Fed.
52 C3 **Bol'shiye Medvedki** Rus. Fed.
52 E3 **Bol'shiye Mozhary** Rus. Fed.
52 H3 **Bol'shiye Ozerki** Rus. Fed.
51 H6 **Bol'shoy Altsyn, Oz. l.** Rus. Fed.
45 S3 **Bol'shoy Aluy r.** Rus. Fed.
45 N2 **Bol'shoy Begichev, O. i.** Rus. Fed.
54 F1 **Bol'shoy Berezovyy, O. i.** Rus. Fed.
52 A2 **Bol'shoye Beresnevo** Rus. Fed.
52 G2 **Bol'shoye Boldino** Rus. Fed.
30 C2 **Bol'shoye Goloustnoye** Rus. Fed.
53 G1 **Bol'shoye Gorodishche** Rus. Fed.
52 G2 **Bol'shoye Mares'yevo** Rus. Fed.
52 D1 **Bol'shoye Mikhaylovskoye** Rus. Fed.
52 G2 **Bol'shoye Murashkino** Rus. Fed.
52 D3 **Bol'shoye Popovo** Rus. Fed.
52 D1 **Bol'shoye Selo** Rus. Fed.
52 F3 **Bol'shoye Sheremet'yevo** Rus. Fed.
53 F1 **Bol'shoye Soldatskoye** Rus. Fed.
54 F2 **Bol'shoye Sremleniye** Rus. Fed.
54 F2 **Bol'shoye Stremleniye** Rus. Fed.
30 D1 **Bol'shoye Yeravnoye, Ozero l.** Rus. Fed.
51 J5 **Bol'shoy Irgiz r.** Rus. Fed.
Bol'shoy Kavkaz mountain range see **Caucasus**
52 D3 **Bol'shoy Khomutets** Rus. Fed.
50 H3 **Bol'shoy Kundysh r.** Rus. Fed.
52 H2 **Bol'shoy Kuvay** Rus. Fed.
30 C1 **Bol'shoy Lug** Rus. Fed.
45 P2 **Bol'shoy Lyakhovskiy, O. i.** Rus. Fed.
51 J5 **Bol'shoy Uzen' r.** Rus. Fed.
52 G3 **Bol'shoy V'yas** Rus. Fed.
156 D3 **Bolson de Mapimí desert** Mexico
63 E1 **Bolsover** England U.K.
68 D1 **Bolsward** Netherlands
102 D2 **Boltaña** Spain
62 C4 **Bolt Head headland** England U.K.
82 C2 **Boltigen** Switzerland
65 F4 **Bolton** England U.K.
146 B6 **Bolton** Virginia U.S.A.
52 A2 **Boltutino** Rus. Fed.
52 F2 **Boltyshka** Ukraine
42 B1 **Bolu** Turkey
56 L6 **Bolungarvík** Iceland
37 H1 **Boluntay** China
33 F4 **Boluo** China
52 B3 **Bolva r.** Rus. Fed.
42 B2 **Bolvadin** Turkey
107 F2 **Bolzano div.** Trentino Alto Adige Italy
107 F2 **Bolzano** Bolzano Italy
125 B5 **Boma** Congo(Zaire)
13 G3 **Bomaderry** New South Wales Australia
69 D4 **Bomal** Belgium
124 C3 **Bomassa** Congo
13 G4 **Bombala** New South Wales Australia
100 A1 **Bombarral** Portugal
Bombay see **Mumbai**
21 K7 **Bomberai Peninsula pen.** Indonesia
125 C5 **Bombo r.** Congo(Zaire)
124 C3 **Bomboma** Congo(Zaire)
169 F3 **Bom Despacho** Brazil
37 H4 **Bomdila** India
43 A2 **Bomi** China
122 B5 **Bomi Hills h.** Liberia
124 E3 **Bomili** Congo(Zaire)
164 C1 **Bom Comércio** Brazil
166 B1 **Bom Jardim** Pará Brazil
168 B2 **Bom Jardim de Goiás** Brazil
167 B6 **Bom Jesus** Brazil
166 D2 **Bom Jesus da Gurgueia, Sa do h.** Brazil
166 D3 **Bom Jesus da Lapa** Brazil
168 D3 **Bom Jesus de Goiás** Brazil
169 H4 **Bom Jesus do Itabapoana** Brazil
58 A2 **Bomlafjorden chan.** Norway
58 A2 **Bømlo i.** Norway
124 E3 **Bomokandi r.** Congo(Zaire)
124 C3 **Bomongo** Congo(Zaire)
93 E6 **Bompas** France
167 C6 **Bom Retiro** Brazil
169 F4 **Bom Sucesso** Minas Gerais Brazil
168 C5 **Bom Sucesso** Paraná Brazil
124 D3 **Bomu, Réserve de Faune de la res.** Congo(Zaire)
42 F2 **Bonāb** Iran
83 E2 **Bonaduz** Switzerland
146 E6 **Bon Air** Virginia U.S.A.
158 □3 **Bonaire i.** Netherlands Ant.
156 J6 **Bonanza** Nicaragua
159 E3 **Bonao** Dominican Rep.
16 D2 **Bonaparte Archipelago is** Western Australia Australia
99 E2 **Boñar** Spain
66 D3 **Bonar Bridge** Scotland U.K.
108 A4 **Bonarcado** Sardegna Italy
100 D3 **Bonares** Spain
159 □3 **Bonasse** Trinidad and Tobago
106 D4 **Bonassola** Italy
139 K4 **Bonavista** Newfoundland Canada
139 K4 **Bonavista Bay b.** Newfoundland Canada
90 D1 **Bonboillon** France
12 C2 **Bon Bon** S. Australia Australia
121 G1 **Bon, Cap c.** Tunisia
89 E3 **Bonchamp-lès-Laval** France
66 F5 **Bonchester Bridge** Scotland U.K.
82 C1 **Boncourt** Switzerland
52 F3 **Bondari** Rus. Fed.
107 F4 **Bondeno** Italy
124 D3 **Bondo** Congo(Zaire)
23 B3 **Bondoc Pen pen.** Philippines
22 D4 **Bondokodi** Indonesia
122 D5 **Bondoukou** Côte d'Ivoire
122 D4 **Bondoukui** Burkina
22 C3 **Bondowoso** Indonesia
145 □2 **Bonefish Pond l.** The Bahamas
130 C5 **Bonekraal** South Africa
148 A3 **Bone Lake l.** Wisconsin U.S.A.
72 C4 **Bönen** Germany
93 C4 **Bon-Encontre** France
22 E3 **Bonerate i.** Indonesia
22 E3 **Bonerate** Indonesia
22 E3 **Bonerate, Kep. is** Indonesia
66 E4 **Bo'ness** Scotland U.K.
103 B6 **Bonete** Spain
170 C2 **Bonete, Co mt.** Argentina
164 C4 **Bonete, Co mt.** Bolivia
168 B2 **Bonfim r.** Brazil
169 F4 **Bonfim** Brazil
169 F2 **Bonfinópolis de Minas** Brazil
126 C3 **Bonga** Ethiopia
23 B3 **Bongabong** Philippines
37 G4 **Bongaigaon** India
124 D3 **Bongandanga** Congo(Zaire)
23 A5 **Bongao** Philippines
37 G3 **Bong Co salt lake** China
122 B5 **Bong Mts h.** Liberia
23 B5 **Bongo i.** Philippines
124 D3 **Bongo** Congo(Zaire)
129 H2 **Bongolava mts** Madagascar
124 C1 **Bongor** Chad
125 C5 **Bongo, Serra do mts** Angola
122 D5 **Bongouanou** Côte d'Ivoire
124 B4 **Bongoville** Gabon
25 E4 **Bông Sơn** Vietnam
103 B5 **Boniches** Spain
108 B3 **Bonifacio** Corse France
82 C2 **Bönigen** Switzerland
Bonin Is is see **Ogasawara-shoto**
168 C2 **Bonito r.** Brazil
167 A5 **Bonito** Mato Grosso do Sul Brazil
169 F1 **Bonito** Minas Gerais Brazil
74 C2 **Bonn** Germany
56 D2 **Bonnåsjøen** Norway
92 D2 **Bonnat** France
74 D5 **Bonndorf im Schwarzwald** Germany
91 E4 **Bonne r.** France
82 B2 **Bonne** France
152 C1 **Bonners Ferry** Idaho U.S.A.
55 C3 **Bønnerup Strand** Denmark
89 F3 **Bonnétable** France
92 C2 **Bonneuil-Matours** France
89 G3 **Bonneval** Centre France
82 B3 **Bonneval** Rhône-Alpes France
91 F3 **Bonneval-sur-Arc** France
82 B2 **Bonnevaux** France
90 E2 **Bonneville** France
12 E4 **Bonney, L. l.** S. Australia Australia
17 B6 **Bonnie Rock** Western Australia Australia
91 D5 **Bonnieux** France
130 C6 **Bonnievale** South Africa
123 F6 **Bonny** Nigeria
66 E5 **Bonnyrigg** Scotland U.K.
90 A1 **Bonny-sur-Loire** France
137 G4 **Bonnyville** Alberta Canada
108 B4 **Bono** Sardegna Italy
23 A4 **Bonobono** Philippines
28 C8 **Bōno-misaki pt** Japan
25 D5 **Bonom Mhai mt.** Vietnam
108 A4 **Bonorva** Sardegna Italy
122 D5 **Bonoua** Côte d'Ivoire
90 E2 **Bons-en-Chablais** France
13 G2 **Bonshaw** New South Wales Australia
22 D1 **Bontang** Indonesia
130 C6 **Bontberg mt.** South Africa
122 B5 **Bonthe** Sierra Leone
23 B2 **Bontoc** Philippines
22 E3 **Bontomatane** Indonesia
22 D3 **Bontosunggu** Indonesia
79 H5 **Bonyhád** Hungary
14 B4 **Bonython Ra. h.** Northern Terr. Australia
59 H2 **Boo** Sweden
127 □1 **Booby I. i.** Seychelles
69 C3 **Booischot** Belgium
12 C2 **Bookabie** S. Australia Australia
155 H2 **Book Cliffs cliff** Utah U.S.A.
122 C5 **Boola** Guinea
13 E3 **Boolaboolka L. l.** New South Wales Australia
12 D3 **Booleroo Centre** S. Australia Australia
67 D4 **Booley Hills h.** Rep. of Ireland
13 F3 **Booligal** New South Wales Australia
13 G2 **Boomi** New South Wales Australia
15 H5 **Boonah** Queensland Australia
150 E3 **Boone** Iowa U.S.A.
145 D4 **Boone** N. Carolina U.S.A.
146 B6 **Boone Lake l.** Tennessee U.S.A.
146 B6 **Booneville** Kentucky U.S.A.
151 F5 **Booneville** Mississippi U.S.A.
159 □7 **Boon Pt pt** Antigua and Barbuda Caribbean
131 F2 **Boons** South Africa
30 A3 **Böön Tsagaan Nuur salt lake** Mongolia
154 A2 **Boonville** California U.S.A.
144 C4 **Boonville** Indiana U.S.A.
150 E4 **Boonville** Missouri U.S.A.
147 F3 **Boonville** New York U.S.A.
126 D3 **Boorama** Somalia
13 F3 **Booroorban** New South Wales Australia
13 G3 **Boorowa** New South Wales Australia
69 C4 **Boortmeerbeek** Belgium
89 G2 **Boos** France
126 E2 **Boosaaso** Somalia
147 J3 **Boothbay Harbor** Maine U.S.A.
135 K3 **Boothia, Gulf of g.** N.W.T. Canada
135 J2 **Boothia Peninsula pen.** N.W.T. Canada
65 F4 **Bootle** England U.K.
124 B4 **Booué** Gabon
74 F4 **Bopfingen** Germany
74 C2 **Boppard** Germany
170 F3 **Boquerão** Brazil
167 A6 **Boquerão, Sa do h.** Brazil
156 D3 **Boquilla, Psa de la resr** Mexico
156 E2 **Boquillas del Carmen** Mexico
78 B2 **Bor** Czech Rep.
52 G1 **Bor** Rus. Fed.
126 B3 **Bor** Sudan
42 C2 **Bor** Turkey
112 D2 **Bor** Yugoslavia
7 □10 **Bora-Bora i.** French Polynesia Pacific Ocean
127 C5 **Boragi waterhole** Kenya
152 D2 **Borah Peak summit** Idaho U.S.A.
59 E3 **Borås** Sweden
39 B3 **Borāzjān** Iran
163 F4 **Borba** Brazil
32 B1 **Borba** China
100 C2 **Borba** Portugal
98 D4 **Borbollón, Emb. del resr** Spain
72 D4 **Borchen** Germany
179 B5 **Borchgrevink Coast coastal area** Antarctica
42 E1 **Borçka** Turkey
68 E2 **Borculo** Netherlands
12 D3 **Borda, C. c.** S. Australia Australia
93 B4 **Bordeaux** Gironde France
93 B4 **Bordeaux-Mérignac airport** France
119 F5 **Bordein** Sudan
100 B3 **Bordeira** Portugal
139 H4 **Borden** Prince Edward I. Canada
17 B7 **Borden** Western Australia Australia
134 G2 **Borden I. i.** N.W.T. Canada
135 K2 **Borden Peninsula pen.** N.W.T. Canada
93 C6 **Bordères-Louron** France
93 C5 **Bordères-sur-l'Échez** France
12 E4 **Bordertown** S. Australia Australia
93 B5 **Bordes** France
72 F1 **Bordesholm** Germany
56 L6 **Borðeyri** Iceland
106 D5 **Bordighera** Italy
110 B5 **Bordino r.** Sicilia Italy
121 E1 **Bordj Bou Arréridj** Algeria
120 D3 **Bordj Flye Ste-Marie** Algeria
121 F2 **Bordj Messaouda** Algeria
121 E4 **Bordj Mokhtar** Algeria
121 F3 **Bordj Omer Driss** Algeria
55 □1 **Borðoy i.** Faeroes
122 D3 **Boré** Mali
81 E1 **Borek h.** Czech Rep.
76 F4 **Borek Wielkopolski** Poland
59 F2 **Boren l.** Sweden
59 F2 **Borensberg** Sweden
66 A3 **Boreray i.** Scotland U.K.
66 □1 **Boreray i.** U.K.
69 E5 **Borg** Germany
56 N6 **Borgarfjörður** Iceland
56 L6 **Borgarnes** Iceland
56 D2 **Børgefjell nat. park** Norway
72 E4 **Borgentreich** Germany
151 C5 **Borger** Texas U.S.A.
72 C3 **Börger** Germany
68 E2 **Borger** Netherlands
103 G5 **Borges r.** Spain
106 B4 **Borghetto d'Arroscia** Italy
59 G3 **Borgholm** Sweden
111 F4 **Borgia** Italy
69 D4 **Borgloon** Belgium
108 B2 **Borgo** Corse France
107 E5 **Borgo a Mozzano** Italy
82 D3 **Borgo d'Ale** Italy
83 F3 **Borgoforte** Italy
106 C3 **Borgomanero** Italy
106 D3 **Borgonovo Val Tidone** Italy
107 G5 **Borgo Pace** Italy
107 F4 **Borgo Panigale airport** Italy
106 B4 **Borgo San Dalmazzo** Italy
107 F5 **Borgo San Lorenzo** Italy
106 C3 **Borgosesia** Italy
106 D4 **Borgo Val di Taro** Italy
107 F2 **Borgo Valsugana** Italy
83 D3 **Borgo Vercelli** Italy
64 D3 **Borgue** Scotland U.K.
58 B1 **Borgund** Norway
58 B2 **Borhaug** Norway
52 B3 **Borilovo** Rus. Fed.
69 B4 **Borinage reg.** Belgium
159 F3 **Borinquen, Pta pt** Puerto Rico
52 D3 **Borinskoye** Rus. Fed.
51 G5 **Borisoglebsk** Rus. Fed.
52 D1 **Borisoglebskiy** Rus. Fed.
53 G1 **Borisovka** Rus. Fed.
52 C2 **Borisovo** Rus. Fed.
50 F3 **Borisovo-Sudskoye** Rus. Fed.
124 E2 **Bo River Post** Sudan
129 H2 **Boriziny** Madagascar
162 B4 **Borja** Peru
102 B3 **Borja** Spain
39 B3 **Borj-e Chīn** Iran
51 G7 **Borjomi** Georgia
54 F4 **Borkavichy** Belarus
72 B4 **Borken** Germany
56 E1 **Borkenes** Norway
72 E4 **Borken (Hessen)** Germany
72 E4 **Borken (Hessen)** Germany
77 N3 **Borki** Belarus
77 L4 **Borki** Poland
55 B4 **Børkop** Denmark
118 C4 **Borkou-Ennedi-Tibesti div.** Chad
77 J4 **Borkowice** Poland
72 B2 **Borkum i.** Germany
72 B2 **Borkum** Germany
59 F1 **Borlänge** Sweden
91 E5 **Bormes-les-Mimosas** France
106 C4 **Bormida r.** Italy
106 C4 **Bormida Spigno r.** Italy
106 C4 **Bormido Millesimo r.** Italy
106 E2 **Bormio** Italy
73 H4 **Borna** Germany
73 H1 **Born am Darß** Germany
72 F4 **Born-Berge h.** Germany
68 D1 **Borndiep chan.** Netherlands
90 E3 **Borne r.** France
121 F4 **Borne** Algeria
68 E2 **Borne** Netherlands
69 C3 **Bornem** Belgium
22 B1 **Borneo** Asia
90 E3 **Bornes mts** France
98 D3 **Bornes** Portugal
74 B2 **Bornheim** Germany
87 G2 **Bornhofen** Germany
55 □2 **Bornholm i.** Denmark
123 G4 **Borno div.** Nigeria
100 E4 **Bornos** Spain
99 H3 **Bornova r.** Spain
42 A2 **Bornova** Turkey
124 D2 **Boro watercourse** Sudan
23 B4 **Borocay i.** Philippines
44 K3 **Borodino** Rus. Fed.
53 C3 **Borodino** Ukraine
54 F1 **Borodinskoye** Rus. Fed.
53 C1 **Borodyanka** Ukraine
45 P3 **Borogontsy** Rus. Fed.
47 K4 **Borohoro Shan mountain range** China
52 D1 **Borok** Rus. Fed.
52 C1 **Borok-Sulezhskiy** Rus. Fed.
124 D1 **Boromata** Central African Rep.
53 F1 **Boromlya r.** Ukraine
53 F1 **Boromlya** Ukraine
122 D4 **Boromo** Burkina
122 C4 **Boron** Mali
23 C4 **Borongan** Philippines
15 G5 **Bororen** Queensland Australia
122 C5 **Borotou** Côte d'Ivoire
65 G3 **Boroughbridge** England U.K.
53 G2 **Borova** Kharkivs'ka Oblast' Ukraine
53 D1 **Borova** Kyyivs'ka Oblast' Ukraine
81 F2 **Borovany** Czech Rep.
54 G2 **Borovichi** Novgorod Rus. Fed.
81 F5 **Borovnica** Slovenia
50 J3 **Borovoy** Rus. Fed.
50 K2 **Borovoy** Rus. Fed.
50 E1 **Borovoy** Rus. Fed.
47 H2 **Borovoye** Kazakhstan
52 C2 **Borovsk** Rus. Fed.
47 G1 **Borovskiy** Rus. Fed.
46 F2 **Borovskoy** Kazakhstan
169 F3 **Borrachudo r.** Brazil
168 C5 **Borrazópolis** Brazil
59 F4 **Borrby** Sweden
55 E5 **Borre** Denmark
73 H2 **Borrentin** Germany
67 C4 **Borrisokane** Rep. of Ireland
67 D4 **Borrisoleigh** Rep. of Ireland
14 D3 **Borroloola** Northern Terr. Australia
59 G2 **Börrum** Sweden
79 L4 **Bors** Romania
56 C3 **Børsa** Norway
112 E1 **Borșa** Romania
112 E1 **Borsec** Romania
114 A2 **Borsh** Albania
52 E4 **Borshchevskiye Peski** Rus. Fed.
53 B2 **Borshchiv** Ukraine
30 D2 **Borshchovochnyy Khrebet mountain range** Rus. Fed.
79 L3 **Borsod-Abaúj-Zemplén div.** Hungary
79 K3 **Borsodnádasd** Hungary
47 K4 **Bortala r.** China
92 E3 **Bort-les-Orgues** France
92 E3 **Bort-les-Orgues, Barrage de dam** France
39 B3 **Borūjen** Iran
39 B2 **Borūjerd** Iran
30 A4 **Bor Ul Shan mountain range** China
55 D4 **Borup** Denmark
108 A4 **Borutta** Sardegna Italy
66 B3 **Borve** Scotland U.K.
77 K6 **Borynya** Ukraine
77 M6 **Boryslav** Ukraine
53 D1 **Boryspil'** Ukraine
53 E1 **Borzenka r.** Ukraine
Borzhomi see **Borjomi**
53 E1 **Borzna** Ukraine
106 D4 **Borzonasca** Italy
79 H4 **Börzsöny h.** Hungary
31 E2 **Borzya r.** Rus. Fed.
31 F2 **Borzya** Rus. Fed.
108 A4 **Bosa** Sardegna Italy
47 H3 **Bosaga** Kazakhstan
104 F3 **Bosanska Dubica** Bos.-Herz.
104 F3 **Bosanska Gradiška** Bos.-Herz.
104 F3 **Bosanska Kostajnica** Bos.-Herz.
104 F3 **Bosanska Krupa** Bos.-Herz.
104 F3 **Bosanski Novi** Bos.-Herz.
104 F3 **Bosanski Petrovac** Bos.-Herz.
104 F3 **Bosansko Grahovo** Bos.-Herz.
131 F4 **Bosberg mt.** South Africa
131 H2 **Bosbokrand** South Africa
163 F2 **Boscamp** Surinam
173 H4 **Bosch** Argentina
148 B4 **Boscobel** Wisconsin U.S.A.
107 F3 **Bosco Chiesanuova** Italy
32 D4 **Bose** China
72 C2 **Bösel** Germany
124 D3 **Bosenge** Congo(Zaire)
63 F4 **Bosham** England U.K.
131 F2 **Boshoek** South Africa
131 E4 **Boshof** South Africa
39 D2 **Boshruyeh** Iran
112 D3 **Bosilegrad** Yugoslavia
68 C2 **Boskoop** Netherlands
78 F2 **Boskovice** Czech Rep.
163 F3 **Boslanti** Surinam
104 F3 **Bosna r.** Bos.-Herz.
48 G4 **Bosnia-Herzegovina country** Europe
112 C3 **Bošnjane** Yugoslavia
124 C3 **Bosobolo** Congo(Zaire)
29 H6 **Bōsō-hantō pen.** Japan
131 F3 **Bospoort** South Africa
Bosporus str. see **İstanbul Boğazı**
124 C2 **Bossangoa** Central African Rep.
124 C2 **Bossembélé** Central African Rep.
124 C2 **Bossentélé** Central African Rep.
151 E5 **Bossier City** Louisiana U.S.A.
106 C4 **Bossolasco** Italy
122 D4 **Bossora** Burkina
102 D2 **Bòssost** Spain
37 F1 **Bostan** China
36 A3 **Bostan** Pakistan
51 J5 **Bostandyk** Kazakhstan
26 E3 **Bosten Hu l.** China
63 F2 **Boston** England U.K.
147 H3 **Boston** Massachusetts U.S.A.
12 C3 **Boston B. b.** S. Australia Australia
141 F2 **Boston Creek** Ontario Canada
147 H3 **Boston-Logan International airport** Massachusetts U.S.A.
151 E5 **Boston Mts mts** Arkansas U.S.A.
65 G4 **Boston Spa** England U.K.
148 D5 **Boswell** Indiana U.S.A.
36 B5 **Botad** India
13 G3 **Botany B. b.** New South Wales Australia
98 B4 **Botão** Portugal
131 J3 **Boteler Point pt** South Africa
128 C3 **Boteti r.** Botswana
112 E3 **Botev mt.** Bulgaria
112 D3 **Botevgrad** Bulgaria
131 F3 **Bothaville** South Africa
65 E3 **Bothel** England U.K.
13 F5 **Bothwell** Tasmania Australia
98 C3 **Boticas** Portugal
104 G4 **Botin mt.** Bos.-Herz.
53 F3 **Botiyeve** Ukraine
51 H5 **Botkul', Ozero l.** Rus. Fed.
131 E1 **Botlhapatlou** Botswana
131 G1 **Botlokwa** South Africa
124 B3 **Bot Makak** Cameroon
53 C3 **Botna r.** Moldova
163 F3 **Boto-Pasi** Surinam
112 F1 **Botoșani** Romania
31 F5 **Botou** China
24 D3 **Bồ Trach** Vietnam
111 F4 **Botricello** Italy
131 F4 **Botshabelo** South Africa
117 G8 **Botswana country** Africa
111 F3 **Botte Donato, Monte mt.** Italy
56 F2 **Bottenviken g.** Finland/Sweden
130 B5 **Botterkloof pass** South Africa
65 H4 **Bottesford** England U.K.
150 C1 **Bottineau** N. Dakota U.S.A.
59 E3 **Bottnaryd** Sweden
72 B4 **Bottrop** Germany
168 D5 **Botucatu** Brazil
114 B1 **Botun** Macedonia
166 D3 **Botuporã** Brazil
139 K4 **Botwood** Newfoundland Canada
122 C5 **Bouaflé** Côte d'Ivoire
96 D5 **Bou Ahmed** Morocco
122 C5 **Bouaké** Côte d'Ivoire
121 E2 **Boualem** Algeria
121 D3 **Bou Ali** Algeria
122 C5 **Bouandougou** Côte d'Ivoire
124 C2 **Bouar** Central African Rep.
121 D2 **Bouârfa** Morocco
121 F2 **Bou Aroua** Algeria
124 B2 **Bouba Ndjida, Parc National de nat. park** Cameroon
78 C2 **Boubín mt.** Czech Rep.
120 B5 **Boû Bleï'ine well** Mauritania
120 C3 **Boubout well** Algeria
124 C2 **Bouca** Central African Rep.
93 A5 **Boucau** France
14 C2 **Boucaut B. b.** Northern Terr. Australia
86 C2 **Bouchain** France
89 E4 **Bouchemaine** France
141 J4 **Boucherville** Québec Canada
91 D5 **Bouches-du-Rhône div.** France
141 H3 **Bouchette** Québec Canada
86 B3 **Bouchoir** France
122 C4 **Boucle du Baoulé, Parc National de la nat. park** Mali
139 H4 **Bouctouche** New Brunswick Canada
125 B4 **Bouda** Gabon
120 D2 **Boudenib** Morocco
69 B3 **Boudewijn Kanaal canal** Belgium
96 E5 **Boudinar** Morocco

13 G3 **Broken B. b.** *New South Wales* Australia
150 D3 **Broken Bow** *Nebraska* U.S.A.
151 E5 **Broken Bow** *Oklahoma* U.S.A.
12 E2 **Broken Hill** *New South Wales* Australia
163 F2 **Brokopondo** Surinam
72 E2 **Brokstedt** Germany
110 D4 **Brolo** *Sicilia* Italy
73 F3 **Brome** Germany
63 G3 **Bromley** *England* U.K.
59 G2 **Bromma airport** Sweden
59 E2 **Brommo i.** Sweden
159 □1 **Brompton** Jamaica
141 K4 **Bromptonville** *Québec* Canada
59 G3 **Brömsebro** Sweden
62 D2 **Bromsgrove** *England* U.K.
62 D2 **Bromyard** *England* U.K.
90 C3 **Bron** France
102 B4 **Bronchales** Spain
55 B2 **Brønderslev** Denmark
122 D5 **Brong-Ahafo div.** Ghana
106 D3 **Broni** Italy
131 G2 **Bronkhorstspruit** South Africa
56 D2 **Brønnøysund** Norway
55 A4 **Brøns** Denmark
148 E5 **Bronson** *Michigan* U.S.A.
110 D5 **Bronte** *Sicilia* Italy
53 B1 **Bronyts'ka Huta** Ukraine
83 E3 **Bronzone, Monte mt.** Italy
63 H2 **Brooke** *England* U.K.
64 A3 **Brookeborough** *Northern Ireland* U.K.
23 A4 **Brooke's Point** Philippines
148 C4 **Brookfield** *Wisconsin* U.S.A.
151 F6 **Brookhaven** *Mississippi* U.S.A.
152 A3 **Brookings** *Oregon* U.S.A.
150 D2 **Brookings** *S. Dakota* U.S.A.
147 H3 **Brookline** *Massachusetts* U.S.A.
148 B5 **Brooklyn** *Illinois* U.S.A.
148 A5 **Brooklyn** *Iowa* U.S.A.
148 A3 **Brooklyn Center** *Minnesota* U.S.A.
146 D6 **Brookneal** *Virginia* U.S.A.
137 G4 **Brooks** *Alberta* Canada
154 A2 **Brooks** *California* U.S.A.
147 J2 **Brooks** *Maine* U.S.A.
179 B3 **Brooks, C. c.** Antarctica
134 C3 **Brooks Range mountain range** *Alaska* U.S.A.
145 D6 **Brooksville** *Florida* U.S.A.
17 B7 **Brookton** *Western Australia* Australia
146 D4 **Brookville** *Pennsylvania* U.S.A.
131 G1 **Broombeek** South Africa
16 C3 **Broome** *Western Australia* Australia
17 B7 **Broome Hill** *Western Australia* Australia
66 C3 **Broom, Loch inlet** *Scotland* U.K.
88 C3 **Broons** France
93 E4 **Broquiès** France
66 E2 **Brora** *Scotland* U.K.
55 B4 **Brørup** Denmark
59 F4 **Brösarp** Sweden
112 F1 **Broscăuți** Romania
62 D2 **Broseley** *England* U.K.
67 D3 **Brosna r.** Rep. of Ireland
92 B3 **Brossac** France
112 E1 **Broșteni** Romania
168 D5 **Brotas** Brazil
100 B2 **Brotas** Portugal
25 A5 **Brothers i.** *Andaman and Nicobar Is* India
152 B3 **Brothers** *Oregon* U.S.A.
Brothers, The is *see* **Al Ikhwān**
27 □ **Brothers, The is** *Hong Kong* China
93 B6 **Broto** Spain
59 H2 **Brottby** Sweden
65 H3 **Brotton** *England* U.K.
89 G3 **Brou** France
65 F3 **Brough** *England* U.K.
65 H4 **Brough** *England* U.K.
66 E1 **Brough Head headland** *Scotland* U.K.
66 F2 **Brough Ness pt** *Scotland* U.K.
67 E2 **Broughshane** *Northern Ireland* U.K.
12 D3 **Broughton r.** *S. Australia* Australia
65 E2 **Broughton** *Scotland* U.K.
62 D1 **Broughton** *Wales* U.K.
8 □3 **Broughton I. i.** *Snares Is* New Zealand
135 M3 **Broughton Island** *N.W.T.* Canada
66 F4 **Broughty Ferry** *Scotland* U.K.
118 C4 **Broulkou well** Chad
78 F1 **Broumov** Czech Rep.
86 D4 **Brousseval** France
87 F4 **Brouvelieures** France
68 B3 **Brouwershaven** Netherlands
53 D1 **Brovary** Ukraine
55 B2 **Brovst** Denmark
158 D2 **Brown Bank sea feature** The Bahamas
151 C5 **Brownfield** *Texas* U.S.A.
63 E2 **Brownhills** *England* U.K.
152 D1 **Browning** *Montana* U.S.A.
17 B6 **Brown, L. salt flat** *Western Australia* Australia
12 D3 **Brown, Mt mt.** *S. Australia* Australia
12 C3 **Brown, Pt headland** *S. Australia* Australia
148 D6 **Brownsburg** *Indiana* U.S.A.
147 F5 **Browns Mills** *New Jersey* U.S.A.
159 □1 **Brown's Town** Jamaica
145 B5 **Brownsville** *Tennessee* U.S.A.
151 D7 **Brownsville** *Texas* U.S.A.
147 J2 **Brownville** *Maine* U.S.A.
147 J2 **Brownville Junction** *Maine* U.S.A.
151 D6 **Brownwood** *Texas* U.S.A.
16 C2 **Browse I. i.** *Western Australia* Australia
66 E5 **Broxburn** *Scotland* U.K.
82 B2 **Broye r.** Switzerland
100 D1 **Brozas** Spain
114 B2 **Brozdovec** Albania
54 F5 **Brozha** Belarus
83 F3 **Brozzo** Italy
86 B2 **Bruay-en-Artois** France
159 □9 **Bruce** *Barbados* Caribbean
9 B5 **Bruce Bay b.** New Zealand
148 C2 **Bruce Crossing** *Michigan* U.S.A.
16 B4 **Bruce, Mt mt.** *Western Australia* Australia
140 E4 **Bruce Pen. pen.** *Ontario* Canada
140 E4 **Bruce Peninsula National Park nat. park** *Ontario* Canada
17 B6 **Bruce Rock** *Western Australia* Australia
87 G4 **Bruche r.** France
72 E3 **Bruchhausen-Vilsen** Germany
74 D3 **Bruchsal** Germany
73 H3 **Brück** Germany
80 D3 **Bruck an der Großglocknerstraße** Austria
81 H2 **Bruck an der Leitha div.** Austria
81 H2 **Bruck an der Leitha** Austria
81 G3 **Bruck an der Mur div.** Austria
81 G3 **Bruck an der Mur** Austria
69 F5 **Brücken** Germany
81 F4 **Brückl** Austria
75 G5 **Bruckmühl** Germany
111 E5 **Brucoli** *Sicilia* Italy
76 G3 **Brudzew** Poland
62 D3 **Brue r.** *England* U.K.
91 D5 **Brue-Auriac** France
69 B4 **Brugelette** Belgium
Bruges *see* **Brugge**
82 D1 **Brugg** Switzerland
69 B3 **Brugge div.** *West-Vlaanderen* Belgium
69 B3 **Brugge** *Brugge* Belgium
72 B4 **Brüggen** Germany
107 G3 **Brugnera** Italy
74 B2 **Brühl** Germany
68 C3 **Bruinisse** Netherlands
155 G2 **Bruin Pt summit** *Utah* U.S.A.
37 H3 **Bruint** India
130 A2 **Brukkaros, Mt mt.** Namibia
43 B4 **Brûk, W. el watercourse** Egypt
148 B2 **Brule** *Wisconsin* U.S.A.
89 E4 **Brûlon** France
69 C5 **Brûly** Belgium
169 F4 **Brumadinho** Brazil
166 D3 **Brumado** Brazil
87 G4 **Brumath** France
68 E2 **Brummen** Netherlands
58 D1 **Brumunddal** Norway
73 G3 **Brunau** Germany
152 D3 **Bruneau r.** *Idaho* U.S.A.
152 D3 **Bruneau** *Idaho* U.S.A.
86 D3 **Brunehamel** France
19 N9 **Brunei country** Asia
14 C3 **Brunette Downs** *Northern Terr.* Australia
56 D3 **Brunflo** Sweden
107 F2 **Brunico** Italy
93 D4 **Bruniquel** France
59 G2 **Brunna** Sweden
81 H2 **Brunn am Gebirge** Austria
83 D2 **Brunnen** Switzerland
9 C5 **Brunner, L. l.** New Zealand
137 H4 **Bruno** *Saskatchewan* Canada
59 E2 **Brunsberg** Sweden
72 E2 **Brunsbüttel** Germany
69 D4 **Brunssum** Netherlands
82 C1 **Brunstatt** France
145 D6 **Brunswick** *Georgia* U.S.A.
147 J3 **Brunswick** *Maine* U.S.A.
146 C4 **Brunswick** *Ohio* U.S.A.
16 D2 **Brunswick Bay b.** *Western Australia* Australia
17 A7 **Brunswick Jct.** *Western Australia* Australia
140 D2 **Brunswick Lake l.** *Ontario* Canada
171 B7 **Brunswick, Península de pen.** Chile
78 G2 **Bruntál** Czech Rep.
179 C3 **Brunt Ice Shelf ice feature** Antarctica
13 F5 **Bruny I. i.** *Tasmania* Australia
112 C3 **Brus** Yugoslavia
58 A2 **Brusand** Norway
50 G2 **Brusenets** Rus. Fed.
152 G3 **Brush** *Colorado* U.S.A.
83 F2 **Brusio** Switzerland
93 E5 **Brusque** France
Brussel *see* **Bruxelles**
140 E5 **Brussels** *Ontario* Canada
148 D3 **Brussels** *Wisconsin* U.S.A.
Brussels *see* **Bruxelles**
106 B3 **Brusson** Italy
73 K2 **Brüssow** Germany
76 F2 **Brusy** Poland
53 C1 **Brusyliv** Ukraine
13 F4 **Bruthen** *Victoria* Australia
62 D3 **Bruton** *England* U.K.
87 G2 **Bruttig-Fankel** Germany
86 D2 **Bruxelles airport** Belgium
69 C4 **Bruxelles** *Brabant* Belgium
87 F4 **Bruyères** France
88 D3 **Bruz** France
59 F3 **Bruzaholm** Sweden
111 F4 **Bruzzano, Capo c.** Italy
77 J3 **Brwinów** Poland
146 A4 **Bryan** *Ohio* U.S.A.
151 D6 **Bryan** *Texas* U.S.A.
179 A3 **Bryan Coast coastal area** Antarctica
12 D3 **Bryan, Mt h.** *S. Australia* Australia
52 A3 **Bryansk div.** Rus. Fed.
52 B3 **Bryansk** Rus. Fed.
51 H6 **Bryanskoye** Rus. Fed.
155 F3 **Bryce Canyon Nat. Park nat. park** *Utah* U.S.A.
155 H5 **Bryce Mt mt.** *Arizona* U.S.A.
63 □1 **Bryher i.** *England* U.K.
53 E3 **Brylivka** Ukraine
62 C1 **Brymbo** *Wales* U.K.
62 C3 **Brynamman** *Wales* U.K.
58 A2 **Bryne** Norway
62 C3 **Brynmawr** *Wales* U.K.
51 F6 **Bryukhovetskaya** Rus. Fed.
76 F5 **Brzeg** Poland
76 E4 **Brzeg Dolny** Poland
76 G3 **Brześc Kujawski** Poland
77 J6 **Brzesko** Poland
76 E2 **Brzezie** Poland
76 G4 **Brzeziny** *Kalisz* Poland
77 H4 **Brzeziny** *Skierniewice* Poland
73 L4 **Brzeźnica** Poland
76 D2 **Brzeźno** Poland
77 K6 **Brzostek** Poland
77 K4 **Brzóza** Poland
77 L6 **Brzozów** *Krosno* Poland
77 J3 **Brzozów** *Plock* Poland
119 J4 **Bū well** Yemen
127 B7 **Bua r.** Malawi
6 □6 **Bua** Fiji
59 E3 **Bua** Sweden
126 D4 **Bu'aale** Somalia
6 □1 **Buala** Solomon Is.
98 B4 **Buarcos** Portugal
10 D1 **Bua, Tg pt** Indonesia
118 D2 **Bū Athlah well** Libya
118 C1 **Bu'ayrāt al Hasūn** Libya
122 A4 **Buba** Guinea-Bissau
127 A5 **Bubanza** Burundi
111 □ **Bubaqra** Malta
122 A4 **Bubaque** Guinea-Bissau
129 E3 **Bubi r.** Zimbabwe
42 G4 **Būbīyān I. i.** Kuwait
88 B4 **Bubry** France
23 B5 **Bubuan i.** Philippines
65 H4 **Bubwith** *England* U.K.
6 □6 **Buca** Fiji
113 F5 **Buca** Turkey
42 B2 **Bucak** Turkey
43 B1 **Bucakkışla** Turkey
162 C2 **Bucaramanga** Colombia
23 C4 **Bucas Grande i.** Philippines
16 C3 **Buccaneer Archipelago is** *Western Australia* Australia
109 G2 **Bucchianico** Italy
109 H4 **Buccino** Italy
100 A2 **Bucelas** Portugal
80 B2 **Buch** Germany
53 A2 **Buchach** Ukraine
13 G4 **Buchan** *Victoria* Australia
148 D5 **Buchanan** *Michigan* U.S.A.
146 D6 **Buchanan** *Virginia* U.S.A.
122 B5 **Buchanan** Liberia
151 D6 **Buchanan, L. l.** *Texas* U.S.A.
15 F4 **Buchanan, L. salt flat** *Queensland* Australia
17 C5 **Buchanan, L. salt flat** *Western Australia* Australia
135 L2 **Buchan Gulf b.** *N.W.T.* Canada
139 J4 **Buchans** *Newfoundland* Canada
Bucharest *see* **București**
75 H4 **Buchbach** Germany
80 A3 **Buchboden** Austria
69 F4 **Büchel** Germany
73 F2 **Büchen** Germany
74 E3 **Buchen (Odenwald)** Germany
73 H2 **Buchholz** Germany
75 F4 **Buchloe** Germany
72 E2 **Bucholz in der Nordheide** Germany
83 E1 **Buchs** Switzerland
172 A4 **Buchupureo** Chile
89 G2 **Buchy** France
114 B2 **Buçimas** Albania
107 F5 **Bucine** Italy
13 F2 **Buckambool Mt h.** *New South Wales* Australia
72 E3 **Bückeburg** Germany
72 E3 **Bücken** Germany
155 F5 **Buckeye** *Arizona* U.S.A.
146 B5 **Buckeye Lake l.** *Ohio* U.S.A.
146 C5 **Buckhannon r.** *W. Virginia* U.S.A.
146 C5 **Buckhannon** *W. Virginia* U.S.A.
66 E4 **Buckhaven** *Scotland* U.K.
155 H5 **Buckhorn** *New Mexico* U.S.A.
141 F4 **Buckhorn** *Ontario* Canada
146 B6 **Buckhorn Lake l.** *Kentucky* U.S.A.
141 F4 **Buckhorn Lake l.** *Ontario* Canada
66 F3 **Buckie** *Scotland* U.K.
63 F3 **Buckingham** *England* U.K.
141 H4 **Buckingham** *Québec* Canada
146 D6 **Buckingham** *Virginia* U.S.A.
14 C2 **Buckingham B. b.** *Northern Terr.* Australia
63 F3 **Buckinghamshire div.** *England* U.K.
130 D4 **Bucklands** South Africa
15 G5 **Buckland Tableland reg.** *Queensland* Australia
179 A6 **Buckle I. i.** Antarctica
10 □3 **Buckles Bay b.** *Macquarie I.* Pacific Ocean
14 D4 **Buckley watercourse** *Queensland* Australia
81 G3 **Bucklige Welt h.** Austria
Buckner Bay b. *see* **Nagagusuku-wan**
155 F4 **Buckskin Mts mts** *Arizona* U.S.A.
154 B2 **Bucks Mt mt.** *California* U.S.A.
147 J2 **Bucksport** *Maine* U.S.A.
73 H3 **Bückwitz** Germany
78 G2 **Bučovice** Czech Rep.
125 B4 **Buco-Zau** *Cabinda* Angola
112 E2 **București** Romania
86 C3 **Bucy-lès-Pierrepont** France
146 B4 **Bucyrus** *Ohio* U.S.A.
77 H4 **Buczek** Poland
52 B3 **Buda** Rus. Fed.
102 D4 **Buda, Illa de i.** Spain
114 C1 **Budakovo** Macedonia
24 A2 **Budalin** Myanmar
79 J4 **Budapest** Hungary
36 D3 **Budaun** India
126 E4 **Bud Bud** Somalia
179 C6 **Budd Coast coastal area** Antarctica
126 D3 **Buddi** Ethiopia
66 F4 **Buddon Ness pt** *Scotland* U.K.
108 B4 **Buddusò** *Sardegna* Italy
62 B4 **Bude** *England* U.K.
151 F6 **Bude** *Mississippi* U.S.A.
62 B4 **Bude Bay b.** *England* U.K.
69 D3 **Budel** Netherlands
72 E1 **Büdelsdorf** Germany
51 H6 **Budennovsk** Rus. Fed.
112 F2 **Budești** Romania
36 B4 **Budhapur** Pakistan
43 B5 **Budhîya, G. mountain range** Egypt
36 C3 **Budhlada** India
172 A5 **Budi, L. del l.** Chile
74 E2 **Büdingen** Germany
81 H4 **Budinšćina** Croatia
124 C3 **Budjala** Congo(Zaire)
36 D5 **Budni** India
50 E3 **Budogoshch'** Rus. Fed.
80 D4 **Budoia** Italy
37 H2 **Budongquan** China
108 B4 **Budoni** *Sardegna* Italy
107 F4 **Budrio** Italy
112 B3 **Budva** Yugoslavia
76 E3 **Budzyń** Poland
124 A3 **Buea** Cameroon
91 D4 **Buëch r.** France
58 A1 **Buefjorden b.** Norway
154 B4 **Buellton** *California* U.S.A.
99 H5 **Buenache de Alarcón** Spain
172 E3 **Buena Esperanza** Argentina
162 B3 **Buenaventura** Colombia
156 D2 **Buenaventura** Mexico
162 B3 **Buenaventure, B. de b.** Colombia
153 F4 **Buena Vista** *Colorado* U.S.A.
146 D6 **Buena Vista** *Virginia* U.S.A.
101 □ **Buena Vista** Gibraltar
158 C2 **Buena Vista, B. de b.** Cuba
99 F2 **Buenavista de Valdavia** Spain
125 C5 **Buenga r.** Angola
172 A6 **Bueno r.** Chile
169 F2 **Buenópolis** Brazil
173 G4 **Buenos Aires div.** Argentina
173 H3 **Buenos Aires** Argentina
164 B1 **Buenos Aires** Brazil
171 B6 **Buenos Aires, L. l.** Argentina/Chile
159 □3 **Buenos Ayres** Trinidad and Tobago
171 C6 **Buen Pasto** Argentina
171 C7 **Buen Tiempo, C. headland** Argentina
169 J1 **Buerarema** Brazil
90 E2 **Buet, Le mt.** France
98 B2 **Bueu** Spain
156 D3 **Búfalo** Mexico
136 G3 **Buffalo r.** *Alberta* Canada
148 B3 **Buffalo r.** *Wisconsin* U.S.A.
146 D3 **Buffalo** *New York* U.S.A.
151 D4 **Buffalo** *Oklahoma* U.S.A.
150 C2 **Buffalo** *S. Dakota* U.S.A.
151 D6 **Buffalo** *Texas* U.S.A.
148 B3 **Buffalo** *Wisconsin* U.S.A.
152 F2 **Buffalo** *Wyoming* U.S.A.
136 F3 **Buffalo Head Hills h.** *Yukon Terr.* Canada
136 F2 **Buffalo Lake l.** *N.W.T.* Canada
137 H3 **Buffalo Narrows** *Saskatchewan* Canada
159 □1 **Buff Bay** Jamaica
130 C6 **Buffels r.** South Africa
131 H3 **Buffels r.** South Africa
130 A4 **Buffels watercourse** South Africa
145 D5 **Buford** *Georgia* U.S.A.
112 E2 **Buftea** Romania
77 K3 **Bug r.** Europe
162 B3 **Buga** Colombia
79 J5 **Bugac reg.** Hungary
123 F5 **Bugana** Nigeria
30 C2 **Bugant** Mongolia
93 E6 **Bugarach, Pic de mt.** France
92 D3 **Bugeat** France
22 B3 **Bugel, Tg pt** Indonesia
90 D3 **Bugey reg.** France
108 A5 **Buggerru** *Sardegna* Italy
74 C5 **Buggingen** Germany
111 □ **Bugibba** Malta
96 □ **Bugio i.** *Madeira* Portugal
104 F3 **Bugojno** Bos.-Herz.
44 F3 **Bugrino** Rus. Fed.
23 A4 **Bugsuk i.** Philippines
31 G2 **Bugt** China
23 B2 **Buguey** Philippines
30 C1 **Bugul'deyka** Rus. Fed.
46 D2 **Bugul'ma** Rus. Fed.
46 F3 **Bugun'** Kazakhstan
Bügür *see* **Luntai**
46 D2 **Buguruslan** Rus. Fed.
30 A5 **Buh r.** China
39 C3 **Būhābād** Iran
113 G6 **Buharkent** Turkey
42 C3 **Buḩayrat al Asad resr** Syria
43 D3 **Buhayrat al Hījānah l.** Syria
42 E3 **Buḩayrat ath Tharthār l.** Iraq
129 E2 **Buhera** Zimbabwe
23 B3 **Buhi** Philippines
152 D3 **Buhl** *Idaho* U.S.A.
148 A2 **Buhl** *Minnesota* U.S.A.
74 D4 **Bühl** Germany
87 H4 **Bühlertal** Germany
74 E3 **Bühlertann** Germany
42 E2 **Bühtan r.** Turkey
127 C6 **Buhu r.** Tanzania
112 F1 **Buhuși** Romania
107 H2 **Buia** Italy
62 C2 **Builth Wells** *Wales* U.K.
172 B2 **Buin** Chile
6 □1 **Buin** P.N.G.
122 D5 **Bui National Park nat. park** Ghana
50 J4 **Buinsk** Rus. Fed.
52 H2 **Buinsk** Rus. Fed.
39 B2 **Bu'in Zahrā** Iran
31 F3 **Buir Nur l.** Mongolia
91 D4 **Buis-les-Baronnies** France
68 E1 **Buitenpost** Netherlands
128 B3 **Buitepos** Namibia
99 G4 **Buitrago del Lozoya** Spain
101 F3 **Bujalance** Spain
112 C3 **Bujanovac** Yugoslavia
102 C3 **Bujaraloz** Spain
107 H3 **Buje** Croatia
112 E3 **Bujoru** Romania
127 A5 **Bujumbura** Burundi
78 F4 **Bük** Hungary
76 E3 **Buk** Poland
31 F1 **Bukachacha** Rus. Fed.
77 N6 **Bukachivtsi** Ukraine
6 □1 **Buka I. i.** P.N.G.
128 C2 **Bukalo** Namibia
125 E5 **Bukama** Congo(Zaire)
52 B3 **Bukan'** Rus. Fed.
39 C3 **Būkand** Iran
125 E4 **Bukavu** Congo(Zaire)
46 F5 **Bukhara** Uzbekistan
47 K3 **Bukhtarminskoye Vdkhr. resr** Kazakhstan
23 C6 **Bukide i.** Indonesia
25 □ **Bukit Batok** Singapore
25 C7 **Bukit Fraser** Malaysia
22 C2 **Bukitlidi** Indonesia
25 □ **Bukit Panjang** Singapore
25 □ **Bukit Timah** Singapore
20 D7 **Bukittinggi** Indonesia
79 K3 **Bükk mts** Hungary
43 C4 **Bukka, J. el mt.** Jordan
79 K3 **Bukki nat. park** Hungary
79 K3 **Bükkszentkereszt** Hungary
127 B5 **Bukoba** Tanzania
127 B5 **Bukombekombe** Tanzania
54 D4 **Bukonys** Lithuania
114 C2 **Bukovo** Macedonia
73 L3 **Bukowiec h.** Poland
76 F1 **Bukowina** Poland
77 J6 **Bukowina Tatrzańska** Poland
76 G4 **Bukownica** Poland
52 D2 **Bukrino** Rus. Fed.
25 □ **Bukum, P. i.** Singapore
123 F5 **Bukuru** Nigeria
22 A2 **Buku, Tg pt** Indonesia
53 D2 **Buky** Ukraine
21 K7 **Bula** Indonesia
83 D1 **Bülach** Switzerland
30 D2 **Bulag** Mongolia
30 C2 **Bulagtay** Mongolia
13 H3 **Bulahdelal** *New South Wales* Australia
23 B3 **Bulan** Philippines
42 D1 **Bulancak** Turkey
36 D3 **Bulandshahr** India
42 E2 **Bulanık** Turkey
119 F2 **Bûlâq** Egypt
129 D3 **Bulawayo** Zimbabwe
47 H2 **Bulayevo** Kazakhstan
114 B2 **Bulçar** Albania
42 B2 **Buldan** Turkey
36 D5 **Buldana** India
164 A1 **Buldibuyo** Peru
126 D3 **Bulei well** Ethiopia
131 H2 **Bulembu** Swaziland
63 E3 **Bulford** *England* U.K.
30 B2 **Bulgan div.** Mongolia
30 B2 **Bulgan** *Bulgan* Mongolia
30 B2 **Bulgan** *Hövsgöl* Mongolia
30 B3 **Bulgan** *Ömnögovĭ* Mongolia
49 H4 **Bulgaria country** Europe
87 E4 **Bulgnéville** France
63 E2 **Bulkington** *England* U.K.
64 B4 **Bullagon Point pt** Rep. of Ireland
101 F1 **Bullaque r.** Spain
103 B6 **Bullas** Spain
69 F4 **Bullay** Germany
159 □1 **Bull Bay** Jamaica
82 C2 **Bulle** Switzerland
158 □2 **Bullen Baai b.** *Curaçao* Netherlands Ant.
9 D4 **Buller r.** New Zealand
13 F4 **Buller, Mt mt.** *Victoria* Australia
155 E4 **Bullhead City** *Arizona* U.S.A.
69 E4 **Büllingen** Belgium
154 D4 **Bullion Mts mts** *California* U.S.A.
15 E6 **Bulloo watercourse** *Queensland* Australia
15 E6 **Bulloo Downs** *Queensland* Australia
15 E6 **Bulloo L. salt flat** *Queensland* Australia
8 □2 **Bull Rock i.** *Campbell I.* New Zealand
8 E4 **Bulls** New Zealand
159 □1 **Bull Savannah** Jamaica
86 B2 **Bully-les-Mines** France
172 A4 **Bulnes** Chile
25 □ **Buloh, P. i.** Singapore
6 □1 **Bulolo** P.N.G.
114 B1 **Bulqizë** Albania
108 B4 **Bultei** *Sardegna* Italy
131 F4 **Bultfontein** South Africa
23 C5 **Buluan** Philippines
22 E3 **Bulubulu** Indonesia
126 C4 **Buluk well** Kenya
22 E3 **Bulukumba** Indonesia
124 D4 **Bulukutu** Congo(Zaire)
45 O2 **Bulun** Rus. Fed.
125 C4 **Bulungu** *Bandundu* Congo(Zaire)
125 D5 **Bulungu** *Kasai-Occidental* Congo(Zaire)
47 G5 **Bulungur** Uzbekistan
23 C3 **Bulusan** Philippines
130 B2 **Bulwana** Namibia
131 G4 **Bulwer** South Africa
124 B2 **Bum** Cameroon
125 C5 **Bumba** *Bandundu* Congo(Zaire)
124 D3 **Bumba** *Équateur* Congo(Zaire)
30 C3 **Bumbat** Mongolia
30 C4 **Bumbat Sum** China
112 D2 **Bumbești-Jiu** Romania
127 B5 **Bumbire I. i.** Tanzania
155 F4 **Bumble Bee** *Arizona* U.S.A.
23 A5 **Bum-Bum i.** Malaysia
24 B1 **Bumhkang** Myanmar
126 C4 **Buna** Kenya
125 C4 **Buna** Congo(Zaire)
127 B5 **Bunazi** Tanzania
67 C1 **Bunbeg** Rep. of Ireland
17 A7 **Bunbury** *Western Australia* Australia
67 E4 **Bunclody** Rep. of Ireland
67 D1 **Buncrana** Rep. of Ireland
127 B5 **Bunda** Tanzania
15 H5 **Bundaberg** *Queensland* Australia
15 F6 **Bundaleer** *Queensland* Australia
13 G2 **Bundarra** *New South Wales* Australia
68 F1 **Bunde** Germany
72 D3 **Bünde** Germany
14 C4 **Bundey watercourse** *Northern Terr.* Australia
36 C4 **Bundi** India
127 B4 **Bundibugyo** Uganda
67 C2 **Bundoran** Rep. of Ireland
37 F5 **Bundu** India
126 B3 **Bunduqiya** Sudan
123 F4 **Bunga watercourse** Nigeria
63 H2 **Bungay** *England* U.K.
24 C4 **Bung Boraphet l.** Thailand
13 G3 **Bungendore** *New South Wales* Australia
179 C6 **Bunger Hills h.** Antarctica
15 G5 **Bungil Cr. r.** *Queensland* Australia
16 E3 **Bungle Bungle Nat. Park nat. park** *Western Australia* Australia
125 C5 **Bungo** Angola
28 D7 **Bungo-suidō chan.** Japan
28 C7 **Bungo-takada** Japan
124 F3 **Bunia** Congo(Zaire)
125 D4 **Bunianga** Congo(Zaire)
123 G4 **Buni-Yadi** Nigeria
36 C2 **Bunji** *Jammu and Kashmir*
55 E4 **Bunkeflostrand** Sweden
15 H4 **Bunker Group atolls** *Queensland* Australia
155 E3 **Bunkerville** *Nevada* U.S.A.
125 E6 **Bunkeya** Congo(Zaire)
151 E6 **Bunkie** *Louisiana* U.S.A.
145 D6 **Bunnell** *Florida* U.S.A.
68 D2 **Bunnik** Netherlands
103 C5 **Buñol** Spain
68 D2 **Bunschoten-Spakenburg** Netherlands
22 C2 **Buntok** Indonesia
22 C2 **Buntokecil** Indonesia
123 F5 **Bununu** Nigeria
42 C2 **Bünyan** Turkey
23 A6 **Bunyu i.** Indonesia
123 E4 **Bunza** Nigeria
104 F3 **Buoač** Bos.-Herz.
83 D2 **Buochs** Switzerland
39 B3 **Bu ol Kheyr** Iran
109 H4 **Buonabitacolo** Italy
108 D1 **Buonconvento** Italy
25 E4 **Buôn Hô** Vietnam
25 E4 **Buôn Mê Thuôt** Vietnam
39 B4 **Buqayq** Saudi Arabia
127 C5 **Bura** Kenya
126 E2 **Buraan** Somalia
124 E1 **Buram** Sudan
47 L3 **Buran** Kazakhstan
36 E3 **Burang** China
169 J2 **Buranhaém r.** Brazil
169 H2 **Buranhaém** Brazil
107 G5 **Burano r.** Italy
126 E3 **Burao** Somalia
43 D3 **Burāq** Syria
52 H3 **Burasy** Rus. Fed.
23 C4 **Burauen** Philippines
119 H2 **Buraydah** Saudi Arabia
74 D2 **Burbach** Germany
63 E3 **Burbage** *England* U.K.
102 B3 **Burbáguena** Spain
154 C4 **Burbank** *California* U.S.A.
108 B5 **Burcei** *Sardegna* Italy
13 F3 **Burcher** *New South Wales* Australia
15 F4 **Burdekin r.** *Queensland* Australia
15 F4 **Burdekin Falls waterfall** *Queensland* Australia
69 D4 **Burdinne** Belgium
43 A1 **Burdur div.** Turkey
42 B2 **Burdur** Turkey
63 H2 **Bure r.** *England* U.K.
126 C2 **Burē** Ethiopia
126 B3 **Burē** Ethiopia
56 F2 **Bureå** Sweden
119 F4 **Bureiqa well** Sudan
31 K2 **Bureiskiy Khrebet mountain range** Rus. Fed.
99 F2 **Burejo r.** Spain
98 C1 **Burela, Cabo pt** Spain
72 D4 **Büren** Germany
68 D3 **Buren** Netherlands
82 C1 **Büren an der Aare** Switzerland
30 A2 **Buren-Khem** Rus. Fed.
30 D3 **Bürentsogt** Mongolia
91 D4 **Bure, Pic de mt.** France
31 J2 **Bureya r.** Rus. Fed.
31 J2 **Bureya** Rus. Fed.
63 E3 **Burford** *England* U.K.
73 K4 **Burg** *Brandenburg* Germany
73 G1 **Burg** *Sachsen-Anhalt* Germany
112 F3 **Burgas div.** Bulgaria
112 F3 **Burgas** Bulgaria
81 H3 **Burgau** Austria
74 F4 **Burgau** Germany
100 B3 **Burgau** Portugal
145 E5 **Burgaw** *N. Carolina* U.S.A.
73 G3 **Burg bei Magdeburg** Germany
83 F1 **Burgberg im Allgäu** Germany
74 F3 **Burgbernheim** Germany
72 F3 **Burgdorf** Germany
82 C1 **Burgdorf** Switzerland
75 F3 **Burgebrach** Germany
81 H3 **Burgenland div.** Austria
139 J4 **Burgeo** *Newfoundland* Canada
131 F5 **Burgersdorp** South Africa
131 H2 **Burgersfort** South Africa
17 C6 **Burges, Mt h.** *Western Australia* Australia
63 F4 **Burgess Hill** *England* U.K.
68 B3 **Burgh** Netherlands
74 E2 **Burghaun** Germany
75 H4 **Burghausen** Germany
66 E3 **Burghead** *Scotland* U.K.
75 G4 **Burgheim** Germany
63 G1 **Burgh le Marsh** *England* U.K.
110 C5 **Burgio** *Sicilia* Italy
75 H4 **Burgkirchen an der Alz** Germany
75 G2 **Burgkunstadt** Germany
83 E1 **Bürglen** Switzerland
75 H3 **Burglengenfeld** Germany
99 F4 **Burgohondo** Spain
99 G2 **Burgos div.** Spain
99 G2 **Burgos** *Burgos* Spain
108 A4 **Burgos** *Sardegna* Italy
74 E2 **Burgsinn** Germany
75 H2 **Burgstädt** Germany
73 J2 **Burg Stargand** Germany
59 H3 **Burgsvik** Sweden
102 B2 **Burguete** Spain
102 B2 **Burgui** Spain
100 D2 **Burguillos del Cerro** Spain
Burgundy div. *see* **Bourgogne**
74 D2 **Burgwald forest** Germany
26 G4 **Burhan Budai Shan mountain range** China
42 A2 **Burhaniye** Turkey
36 D5 **Burhanpur** India
37 E5 **Burhar-Dhanpuri** India
37 F4 **Burhi Gandak r.** India
168 D5 **Buri** Brazil
23 B3 **Burias i.** Philippines
23 B3 **Burias Pass. chan.** Philippines
46 E2 **Buribay** Rus. Fed.
156 K7 **Burica, Pta pt** Costa Rica
92 B3 **Burie** France
127 B5 **Burigi, Lake l.** Tanzania
139 J4 **Burin Peninsula pen.** *Newfoundland* Canada
25 C4 **Buriram** Thailand
168 C4 **Buritama** Brazil
165 E2 **Buriti r.** Brazil
166 D1 **Buriti** Brazil
168 D3 **Buriti Alegre** Brazil
166 D2 **Buriti Bravo** Brazil
166 C2 **Buriticupu r.** Brazil
166 D1 **Buriti dos Lopes** Brazil
166 D3 **Buritirama** Brazil
169 E1 **Buritis** Brazil
169 F2 **Buritizeiro** Brazil
114 A1 **Burizanë** Albania
36 A3 **Burj** Pakistan
103 C5 **Burjassot** Spain
79 M6 **Burjuc** Romania
80 B1 **Burk** Germany
14 D4 **Burke watercourse** *Queensland* Australia
179 A3 **Burke I. i.** Antarctica
9 C6 **Burke Pass** New Zealand
14 D3 **Burketown** *Queensland* Australia
116 D4 **Burkina country** Africa
141 F4 **Burk's Falls** *Ontario* Canada
47 J2 **Burla r.** Rus. Fed.
47 J2 **Burla** Rus. Fed.
102 B2 **Burlada** Spain
74 E4 **Burladingen** Germany
93 E5 **Burlats** France
15 E4 **Burleigh** *Queensland* Australia
152 D3 **Burley** *Idaho* U.S.A.
46 D2 **Burlin** Kazakhstan
153 G4 **Burlington** *Colorado* U.S.A.
148 D5 **Burlington** *Indiana* U.S.A.
148 B5 **Burlington** *Iowa* U.S.A.
147 J2 **Burlington** *Maine* U.S.A.
141 F5 **Burlington** *Ontario* Canada
147 G2 **Burlington** *Vermont* U.S.A.
148 C4 **Burlington** *Wisconsin* U.S.A.
Burma *see* **Myanmar**
52 E3 **Burminka** Rus. Fed.
151 D6 **Burnet** *Texas* U.S.A.
15 H5 **Burnett r.** *Queensland* Australia
152 B3 **Burney** *California* U.S.A.
63 F3 **Burnham** *England* U.K.
147 J2 **Burnham** *Maine* U.S.A.
63 G3 **Burnham-on-Crouch** *England* U.K.
62 D3 **Burnham-on-Sea** *England* U.K.
13 F5 **Burnie** *Tasmania* Australia
65 H3 **Burniston** *England* U.K.
65 F4 **Burnley** *England* U.K.
47 H4 **Burnoye** Kazakhstan
152 C3 **Burns** *Oregon* U.S.A.
137 H1 **Burnside r.** *N.W.T.* Canada
17 C5 **Burnside, L. salt flat** *Western Australia* Australia
134 F4 **Burns Lake** *B.C.* Canada
146 C5 **Burnsville Lake l.** *W. Virginia* U.S.A.
145 F7 **Burnt Ground** The Bahamas
66 E4 **Burntisland** *Scotland* U.K.
139 H3 **Burnt Lake l.** *Labrador/Québec* Canada
11 □1 **Burnt Pine** *Norfolk I.* Pacific Ocean
137 K3 **Burntwood r.** *Manitoba* Canada
63 E2 **Burntwood Green** *England* U.K.
137 J3 **Burnt Wood Lake l.** *Manitoba* Canada
106 C3 **Buronzo** Italy
73 J2 **Burow** Germany
47 L3 **Burqin** China
12 D3 **Burra** *S. Australia* Australia
66 □2 **Burravoe** *Scotland* U.K.
66 F2 **Burray i.** *Scotland* U.K.
112 C4 **Burrel** Albania
13 G3 **Burrendong Reservoir resr** *New South Wales* Australia
13 G2 **Burren Jct.** *New South Wales* Australia
67 B3 **Burren National Park nat. park** Rep. of Ireland
103 C5 **Burriana** Spain
13 G3 **Burrinjuck** *New South Wales* Australia
13 G3 **Burrinjuck Reservoir resr** *New South Wales* Australia
146 B5 **Burr Oak Reservoir resr** *Ohio* U.S.A.
66 D6 **Burrow Head headland** *Scotland* U.K.
14 B2 **Burrundie** *Northern Terr.* Australia
155 G2 **Burrville** *Utah* U.S.A.
62 B3 **Burry Inlet inlet** *Wales* U.K.
62 B3 **Burry Port** *Wales* U.K.
80 A3 **Bürs** Austria
113 G4 **Bursa div.** Turkey
42 B1 **Bursa** Turkey
119 F2 **Bûr Safâga** Egypt
Bûr Sa'îd *see* **Port Said**
65 F4 **Burscough Bridge** *England* U.K.
53 A2 **Burshtyn** Ukraine
74 D3 **Bürstadt** Germany
Būr Sudan *see* **Port Sudan**
43 B5 **Bûr Taufiq** Egypt
80 B2 **Burtenbach** Germany
148 E3 **Burt Lake l.** *Michigan* U.S.A.
54 D3 **Burtnieku l.** Latvia
63 E4 **Burton** *England* U.K.
149 F4 **Burton** *Michigan* U.S.A.
62 D4 **Burton Bradstock** *England* U.K.
65 F3 **Burton-in-Kendal** *England* U.K.
138 E3 **Burton, Lac l.** *Québec* Canada
63 F2 **Burton Latimer** *England* U.K.
67 C2 **Burtonport** Rep. of Ireland
63 E2 **Burton upon Trent** *England* U.K.
56 F2 **Burträsk** Sweden
147 K1 **Burtts Corner** *New Brunswick* Canada
13 E3 **Burtundy** *New South Wales* Australia
21 J7 **Buru i.** Indonesia
Burultokay *see* **Fuhai**
117 G6 **Burundi country** Africa
127 A5 **Bururi** Burundi
62 D2 **Burwarton** *England* U.K.
63 G4 **Burwash** *England* U.K.
136 B2 **Burwash Landing** *Yukon Terr.* Canada
63 G2 **Burwell** *England* U.K.
66 F2 **Burwick** *Scotland* U.K.
65 F4 **Bury** *England* U.K.
141 K4 **Bury** *Québec* Canada
30 B2 **Buryatiya div.** Rus. Fed.
53 E1 **Buryn'** Ukraine
46 D3 **Burynshyk** Kazakhstan
63 G2 **Bury St Edmunds** *England* U.K.
76 G4 **Burzenin** Poland
36 C2 **Burzil Pass pass** Jammu & Kashmir
106 C4 **Busalla** Italy
106 E4 **Busana** Italy
124 D4 **Busanga** Congo(Zaire)
106 B4 **Busca** Italy
72 E1 **Busdorf** Germany

114 C1 Buševa Planina mountain range Macedonia
67 E1 Bush r. Northern Ireland U.K.
53 C2 Busha Ukraine
127 D5 Bushbush r. Kenya/Somalia
53 B1 Bushcha Ukraine
39 B3 Būshehr div. Iran
39 B3 Būshehr Iran
37 E2 Bushêngcaka China
127 B5 Bushenyi Uganda
Bushire see Būshehr
67 E1 Bushmills Northern Ireland U.K.
148 B5 Bushnell Illinois U.S.A.
112 C4 Bushtricë Albania
31 F1 Bushuley Rus. Fed.
69 B4 Busigny France
124 D3 Businga Congo(Zaire)
25 □ Busing, P. i. Singapore
124 C4 Busira r. Congo(Zaire)
53 A2 Bus'k Ukraine
58 C1 Buskerud div. Norway
77 J5 Busko-Zdrój Poland
43 D3 Buşrá ash Shām Syria
82 B1 Bussang France
31 H2 Busse Rus. Fed.
17 A7 Busselton Western Australia Australia
124 E2 Busseri watercourse Sudan
106 E3 Busseto Italy
92 C3 Bussière-Badil France
92 C2 Bussière-Poitevine France
82 B2 Bussigny Switzerland
109 F2 Bussi sul Tirino Italy
83 F3 Bussolengo Italy
82 C3 Bussoleno Italy
68 D2 Bussum Netherlands
90 C1 Bussy-le-Grand France
151 C7 Bustamante Mexico
171 C6 Bustamante, B. b. Argentina
112 E2 Buşteni Romania
156 D2 Bustillos, L. l. Mexico
106 C3 Busto Arsizio Italy
98 D1 Busto, Cabo pt Spain
23 A3 Busuanga i. Philippines
23 A3 Busuanga Philippines
72 D1 Büsum Germany
80 E4 But r. Italy
124 D3 Buta Congo(Zaire)
126 C3 Butajīra Ethiopia
25 B6 Butang Group is Thailand
172 C4 Buta Ranquil Argentina
127 A5 Butare Rwanda
66 C5 Bute i. Scotland U.K.
112 F1 Butea Romania
136 D4 Butedale B.C. Canada
136 D4 Bute In. inlet B.C. Canada
124 E3 Butembo Congo(Zaire)
110 D5 Butera Sicilia Italy
66 C5 Bute, Sound of chan. Scotland U.K.
69 E4 Bütgenbach Belgium
131 G4 Butha-Buthe Lesotho
24 A2 Buthidaung Myanmar
79 M4 Butiz Romania
72 D2 Butjadingen reg. Germany
148 E5 Butler Indiana U.S.A.
146 D4 Butler Pennsylvania U.S.A.
67 D2 Butlers Bridge Rep. of Ireland
21 H8 Buton i. Indonesia
53 G1 Butovo Rus. Fed.
73 H2 Bütow Germany
100 D2 Butrera mt. Spain
77 O1 Butrimonys Lithuania
77 J2 Butryny Poland
83 E1 Bütschwil Switzerland
77 N4 Butsyn Ukraine
152 D2 Butte Montana U.S.A.
73 G4 Buttelstedt Germany
154 B1 Butte Meadows California U.S.A.
75 G3 Buttenheim Germany
65 E3 Buttermere England U.K.
25 C6 Butterworth Malaysia
131 G6 Butterworth South Africa
67 C4 Buttevant Rep. of Ireland
136 D5 Buttle L. l. B.C. Canada
66 B2 Butt of Lewis headland Scotland U.K.
135 M3 Button Is is Newfoundland Canada
154 C4 Buttonwillow California U.S.A.
17 C7 Butty Hd pt Western Australia Australia
23 C4 Butuan Philippines
53 C3 Butuceni Moldova
32 C3 Butuo China
52 G2 Buturlino Rus. Fed.
51 G5 Buturlinovka Rus. Fed.
37 E4 Butwal Nepal
52 E2 Butylitsy Rus. Fed.
74 D2 Butzbach Germany
73 G2 Bützow Germany
126 E4 Buulobarde Somalia
127 D5 Buur Gaabo Somalia
126 D4 Buurhabaka Somalia
126 B4 Buvuma I. i. Uganda
43 C5 Buwārah, J. mt. Saudi Arabia
119 G3 Buwāṭah Saudi Arabia
37 F4 Buxar India
92 C2 Buxerolles France
74 F5 Buxheim Germany
63 G4 Buxted England U.K.
72 E2 Buxtehude Germany
63 E1 Buxton England U.K.
90 C2 Buxy France
50 G3 Buy Rus. Fed.
30 D3 Buyant Mongolia
30 A3 Buyant Mongolia
30 A3 Buyant Gol r. Mongolia
30 C3 Buyant-Ovoo Mongolia
30 D3 Buyant-Uhaa Mongolia
148 A1 Buyck Minnesota U.S.A.
51 H7 Buynaksk Rus. Fed.
122 C5 Buyo, Lac de l. Côte d'Ivoire
131 G1 Buysdorp South Africa
32 C4 Buyuan r. China
42 E2 Büyük Ağri mt. Turkey
43 B1 Büyük Egri D. mt. Turkey
113 F4 Büyükkarıştıran Turkey
113 G6 Büyükmenderes r. Turkey
113 G5 Büyükorhan Turkey
31 G4 Buyun Shan mt. China
46 D4 Buzachi, Pov. pen. Kazakhstan
92 D2 Buzançais France
86 D3 Buzancy France
112 F2 Buzău Romania
118 D3 Buzaymah oasis Libya
28 C7 Buzen Japan
107 H3 Buzet Croatia
93 C4 Buzet-sur-Baïse France
93 D5 Buzet-sur-Tarn France
52 E2 Buzha r. Rus. Fed.
129 E3 Búzi r. Mozambique
129 E2 Buzi Mozambique
112 C2 Buziaş Romania
169 H5 Buzios, Cabo dos headland Brazil
169 F5 Buzios, Ilha dos i. Brazil
52 G3 Buzovlevo Rus. Fed.
51 G5 Buzuluk r. Rus. Fed.
46 D2 Buzuluk Rus. Fed.
147 H4 Buzzards Bay b. Massachusetts U.S.A.
6 □1 Bwagaoia P.N.G.
54 F4 Byahoml' Belarus
37 G4 Byakar Bhutan
112 F3 Byala Burgas Bulgaria
112 E3 Byala Razgrad Bulgaria
112 D3 Byala Slatina Bulgaria
114 G1 Byal Izvor Bulgaria
50 D4 Byalynichy Belarus
134 H2 Byam Martin I. i. N.W.T. Canada
54 E4 Byarezina r. Belarus
77 N3 Byaroza Belarus
54 D5 Byarozawka Belarus
77 N3 Byarozna Belarus
77 L4 Bychawa Poland
52 E3 Bychki Rus. Fed.
76 G4 Byczyna Poland
76 F2 Bydgoszcz div. Poland
76 G2 Bydgoszcz Poland
77 O3 Byelaazyorsk Belarus
77 M3 Byelavyezhski Belarus
54 E4 Byel'ki Belarus
77 O1 Byenyakoni Belarus
54 F5 Byerazino Belarus
54 E5 Byeraznyaki Belarus
152 F4 Byers Colorado U.S.A.
77 N2 Byershty Belarus
54 F4 Byeshankovichy Belarus
63 E2 Byfield England U.K.
58 C1 Bygdin l. Norway
58 B2 Bygland Norway
58 B2 Byglandsfjord Norway
58 B2 Byglandsfjorden l. Norway
58 A1 Bygstad Norway
73 K4 Byhleguhre Germany
50 D4 Bykhaw Belarus
58 B2 Bykle Norway
58 B2 Bykleheiane reg. Norway
51 H5 Bykovo Rus. Fed.
135 L2 Bylot Island i. N.W.T. Canada
131 G1 Bylsteel South Africa
140 E4 Byng Inlet Ontario Canada
179 B5 Byrd Gl. gl. Antarctica
31 F2 Byrka Rus. Fed.
58 B2 Byrkjedal Norway
56 B3 Byrkjelo Norway
58 A1 Byrknesøy i. Norway
53 E1 Byrlivka Ukraine
13 F2 Byrock New South Wales Australia
148 C4 Byron Illinois U.S.A.
147 H2 Byron Maine U.S.A.
13 H2 Byron Bay New South Wales Australia
13 H2 Byron, C. headland New South Wales Australia
55 C2 Byrum Denmark
52 A3 Byryne Ukraine
53 C1 Byshiv Ukraine
75 K2 Byšice Czech Rep.
56 F2 Byske Sweden
79 J2 Bystrá mt. Slovakia
75 K3 Bystřice Czech Rep.
78 F2 Bystřice nad Pernštejnem Czech Rep.
79 G2 Bystřice pod Hostýnem Czech Rep.
30 D2 Bystrinskiy Golets, G. mt. Rus. Fed.
76 E5 Bystrzyca Kłodzka Poland
78 F1 Bystrzyckie, Góry mountain range Czech Rep./Poland
45 P3 Bytantay r. Rus. Fed.
79 H2 Bytča Slovakia
76 D3 Bytnica Poland
76 G5 Bytom Poland
76 D4 Bytom Odrzański Poland
52 B3 Bytosh' Rus. Fed.
76 F1 Bytów Poland
127 B5 Byumba Rwanda
46 E5 Byuzmeyin Turkmenistan
59 G3 Byxelkrok Sweden
77 J3 Bzura r. Poland

C

165 E5 Caacupé Paraguay
165 E5 Caaguazú Paraguay
125 C6 Caála Angola
168 A5 Caarapó Brazil
169 H1 Caatiba Brazil
169 F2 Caatinga Brazil
165 E5 Caazapá Paraguay
165 E3 Cabaçal r. Brazil
158 C2 Cabaiguán Cuba
164 A2 Caballas Peru
162 C4 Caballococha Peru
156 D2 Caballos Mesteños, Llano de los plain Mexico
164 B2 Cabana Peru
93 B4 Cabanac-et-Villagrains France
164 B3 Cabanaconde Peru
98 E1 Cabañaquinta Spain
101 H3 Cabañas mt. Spain
23 B3 Cabanatuan Philippines
62 C2 Caban Coch Res. resr Wales U.K.
103 D4 Cabanes Spain
139 G4 Cabano Québec Canada
107 J3 Čabar Croatia
164 C3 Cabaraya, Co mt. Bolivia
93 E5 Cabardès reg. France
126 D2 Cabdul Qaadir Somalia
167 A4 Cabeceira Rio Manso Brazil
98 C3 Cabeceiras de Basto Portugal
100 C1 Cabeço de Vide Portugal
98 C5 Cabeço Rainha mt. Portugal
166 F2 Cabedelo Brazil
106 D4 Cabella Ligure Italy
93 E6 Cabestany France
101 G2 Cabeza de Buey mt. Spain
101 E2 Cabeza del Buey Spain
101 F2 Cabezarados Spain
165 D3 Cabezas Bolivia
145 □3 Cabezas de San Juan pt Puerto Rico
100 C3 Cabezas Rubias Spain
100 C3 Cabezo Gordo h. Spain
99 F1 Cabezón de la Sal Spain
98 E4 Cabezuela del Valle Spain
173 G5 Cabildo Argentina
172 B2 Cabildo Chile
162 C1 Cabimas Venezuela
125 B5 Cabinda div. Angola
125 B5 Cabinda Cabinda Angola
152 C1 Cabinet Mts mountain range Montana U.S.A.
23 B5 Cabingan i. Philippines
145 □2 Cable Beach The Bahamas
171 C6 Cabo Blanco Argentina
101 H4 Cabo de Gata, Sierra del h. Spain
127 C7 Cabo Delgado div. Mozambique
169 G5 Cabo Frio Brazil
169 H5 Cabo Frio, Ilha do c. Brazil
141 G3 Cabonga, Réservoir resr Québec Canada
151 E4 Cabool Missouri U.S.A.
15 H5 Caboolture Queensland Australia
163 G3 Cabo Orange, Parque Nacional de nat. park Brazil
162 B4 Cabo Pantoja Peru
Cabora Bassa Dam dam see Cahora Bassa, Barragem de
171 C5 Cabo Raso Argentina
156 B2 Caborca Mexico
145 □3 Cabo Rojo Puerto Rico
140 E4 Cabot Head pt Ontario Canada
139 J4 Cabot Strait str. Newfoundland/Nova Scotia Canada
89 E2 Cabourg France
101 F3 Cabra r. Spain
101 F3 Cabra Spain
101 G3 Cabra del Santo Cristo Spain
108 A5 Cabras Sardegna Italy
103 B6 Cabras, Sierra de mountain range Spain
99 H3 Cabrejas, Sierra de mountain range Spain
100 B2 Cabrela r. Portugal
103 F5 Cabrera i. Spain
101 J3 Cabrera, Sierra mountain range Spain
98 D2 Cabrera, Sierra de la mountain range Spain
172 A4 Cabrero Chile
103 B5 Cabriel r. Spain
91 D5 Cabrières-d'Aigues France
98 D4 Cabrillas Spain
159 □4 Cabrits, Îlet i. Martinique Caribbean
166 E2 Cabrobó Brazil
162 D2 Cabruta Venezuela
23 B2 Cabugao Philippines
104 F4 Čabulja mt. Bos.-Herz.
79 G6 Cabuna Croatia
172 B5 Caburgua, L. l. Chile
98 D2 Cacabelos Spain
167 B6 Caçador Brazil
157 F5 Cacahuatepec Mexico
112 C3 Čačak Yugoslavia
163 G3 Cacao French Guiana
169 F5 Caçapava Brazil
167 B7 Caçapava do Sul Brazil
146 D5 Cacapon r. W. Virginia U.S.A.
162 B2 Cácares Colombia
110 C5 Caccamo Sicilia Italy
108 A4 Caccia, Capo pt Sardegna Italy
111 F3 Caccuri Italy
100 A2 Cacém Portugal
167 B6 Cacequi Brazil
100 D1 Cáceres div. Spain
100 D1 Cáceres Cáceres Spain
165 E3 Cáceres Brazil
173 H4 Cachari Argentina
152 D3 Cache Peak summit Idaho U.S.A.
122 A4 Cacheu Guinea-Bissau
170 C2 Cachi Argentina
166 B2 Cachimbo Brazil
125 D5 Cachimo Angola
164 C4 Cachinal Chile
125 C6 Cachingues Angola
162 C2 Cáchira Colombia
166 C2 Cachoeira r. Brazil
166 E3 Cachoeira Bahia Brazil
168 C3 Cachoeira Mato Grosso do Sul Brazil
168 C3 Cachoeira Alta Brazil
168 C2 Cachoeira de Goiás Brazil
166 C1 Cachoeira do Arari Brazil
167 B7 Cachoeira do Sul Brazil
169 F5 Cachoeira Paulista Brazil
169 G5 Cachoeiras de Macacu Brazil
169 H4 Cachoeiro de Itapemirim Brazil
100 C3 Cachopo Portugal
101 G3 Cacín r. Spain
122 A4 Cacine Guinea-Bissau
125 C6 Cacolo Angola
125 C6 Caconda Angola
125 B5 Cacongo Cabinda Angola
154 D3 Cactus Range mts Nevada U.S.A.
168 C3 Caçu Brazil
125 B5 Cacuaco Angola
166 D3 Caculé Brazil
169 J2 Cacumba, Ilha i. Brazil
168 B2 Caçununga Brazil
62 B2 Cadair Idris h. Wales U.K.
99 F4 Cadalso de los Vidrios Spain
100 A1 Cadaval Portugal
79 H2 Čadca Slovakia
126 D2 Caddabassa I. Ethiopia
107 E4 Cadelbosco di Sopra Italy
72 E2 Cadenberge Germany
91 D5 Cadenet France
157 E3 Cadereyta Mexico
12 C2 Cadibarrawirracanna, L. salt flat S. Australia Australia
23 B3 Cadig Mts mountain range Philippines
148 E3 Cadillac Michigan U.S.A.
141 F2 Cadillac Québec Canada
137 H5 Cadillac Saskatchewan Canada
93 B4 Cadillac France
100 E4 Cádiz div. Spain
100 D4 Cádiz Spain
23 B4 Cadiz Philippines
100 D4 Cádiz, B. de b. Spain
100 C4 Cádiz, Golfo de g. Spain
155 E4 Cadiz Lake l. California U.S.A.
136 F4 Cadomin Canada
107 G2 Cadore reg. Italy
93 D5 Cadours France
17 B6 Cadoux Western Australia Australia
102 B2 Cadreita Spain
89 E2 Caen Calvados France
Caerdydd see Cardiff
Caerfyrddin see Carmarthen
Caergybi see Holyhead
62 D3 Caerleon Wales U.K.
62 B1 Caernarfon Wales U.K.
62 B1 Caernarfon Bay b. Wales U.K.
62 C3 Caerphilly div. Wales U.K.
62 C3 Caerphilly Wales U.K.
146 B5 Caesar Creek Lake l. Ohio U.S.A.
43 C3 Caesarea Israel
166 D3 Caetité Brazil
170 C2 Cafayate Argentina
168 D4 Cafelândia Brazil
163 F3 Cafuini r. Brazil
23 B4 Cagayan i. Philippines
23 B2 Cagayan r. Philippines
23 C4 Cagayan de Oro Philippines
23 B4 Cagayan Islands is Philippines
107 G5 Cagli Italy
108 A5 Cagliari div. Sardegna Italy
108 B5 Cagliari Sardegna Italy
108 B5 Cagliari, Golfo di b. Sardegna Italy
109 H3 Cagnano Varano Italy
91 F5 Cagnes-sur-Mer France
162 C3 Caguán r. Colombia
145 □3 Caguas Puerto Rico
67 B5 Caha h. Rep. of Ireland
145 C5 Cahaba r. Alabama U.S.A.
125 B7 Cahama Angola
67 B5 Caha Mts h. Rep. of Ireland
67 A3 Caher Island i. Rep. of Ireland
67 A5 Cahermore Rep. of Ireland
67 D4 Cahir Rep. of Ireland
67 A5 Cahirciveen Rep. of Ireland
129 E2 Cahora Bassa, Barragem de dam Mozambique
129 E2 Cahora Bassa, Lago de resr. Mozambique
67 E4 Cahore Point pt Rep. of Ireland
93 D4 Cahors France
162 B5 Cahuapanas Peru
53 C3 Cahul Moldova
93 D5 Cahuzac-sur-Vère France
100 C1 Caia r. Portugal
129 F2 Caia Mozambique
100 C1 Caia, Barragem do resr Portugal
125 D6 Caianda Angola
168 C2 Caiapó r. Brazil
168 C2 Caiapônia Brazil
158 C2 Caibarién Cuba
25 D5 Cai Be Vietnam
163 D2 Caicara Venezuela
166 E2 Caicó Brazil
159 D2 Caicos Is is Turks and Caicos Is Caribbean
159 D2 Caicos Passage chan. The Bahamas/Turks and Caicos Is Caribbean
164 B3 Cailloma Peru
172 B1 Caimanes Chile
23 A3 Caiman Point pt Philippines
102 B4 Caimodorro mt. Spain
25 D5 Cai Nước Vietnam
66 E3 Cairn Gorm mt. Scotland U.K.
66 E3 Cairngorm Mts mountain range Scotland U.K.
66 C6 Cairnryan Scotland U.K.
15 F3 Cairns Queensland Australia
64 D2 Cairnsmore of Carsphairn h. Scotland U.K.
64 D3 Cairnsmore of Fleet h. Scotland U.K.
66 E3 Cairn Toul mt. Scotland U.K.
145 C6 Cairo Georgia U.S.A.
43 A4 Cairo Egypt
106 C4 Cairo Montenotte Italy
Caisléan an Bharraigh see Castlebar
64 C2 Caisteal Abhail h. Scotland U.K.
63 H2 Caister-on-Sea England U.K.
65 H4 Caistor England U.K.
66 E2 Caithness reg. Scotland U.K.
125 B6 Caitou Angola
125 C7 Caiundo Angola
15 F6 Caiwarro Queensland Australia
33 G2 Caizi Hu l. China
164 A2 Cajacay Peru
145 □3 Caja de Muertos, I. i. Puerto Rico
162 B5 Cajamarca Peru
93 D4 Cajarc France
166 C1 Cajari Brazil
164 A2 Cajatambo Peru
166 E2 Cajàzeiras Brazil
112 B3 Čajetina Yugoslavia
23 B3 Cajidiocan Philippines
104 G4 Čajniče Bos.-Herz.
168 E4 Cajuru Brazil
30 A5 Caka China
30 A5 Caka Yanhu salt lake China
43 A1 Çakırlar Turkey
43 C1 Çakit r. Turkey
78 F5 Čakovec Croatia
42 B2 Çal Turkey
165 E3 Cal, R. de la r. Bolivia
100 D3 Cala r. Spain
131 F5 Cala South Africa
100 D3 Cala Spain
123 F6 Calabar Nigeria
141 G4 Calabogie Ontario Canada
162 D2 Calabozo Venezuela
111 F4 Calabria div. Italy
111 E4 Calabria, Parco Nazionale della nat. park Italy
101 F4 Calaburra, Punta de pt Spain
102 D3 Calaceite Spain
164 C3 Calacoto Bolivia
108 B2 Calacuccia Corse France
103 □ Cala en Porter Spain
102 E3 Calaf Spain
112 D3 Calafat Romania
171 B7 Calafate Argentina
103 F5 Cala Figuera, Cap de pt Spain
172 A5 Calafquén, L. l. Chile
23 B3 Calagua Islands is Philippines
102 B2 Calahorra Spain
125 C7 Calai Angola
147 K2 Calais Maine U.S.A.
86 A2 Calais France
170 C2 Calalasteo, Sierra de mountain range Argentina
107 G2 Calalzo di Cadore Italy
165 D1 Calama Brazil
164 C4 Calama Chile
162 C1 Calamar Bolívar Colombia
162 C3 Calamar Guaviare Colombia
23 A3 Calamian Group is Philippines
102 B4 Calamocha Spain
112 D2 Călan Romania
100 D3 Calañas Spain
83 E2 Calancasca r. Switzerland
102 C4 Calanda Spain
125 C5 Calandula Angola
108 B4 Calangianus Sardegna Italy
118 D2 Calanscio Sand Sea desert Libya
23 B3 Calapan Philippines
131 F5 Calapas pass South Africa
101 H3 Calar Alta mt. Spain
53 C3 Călăraşi Moldova
112 F2 Călăraşi Romania
101 H2 Calar del Mundo mountain range Spain
110 D5 Calascibetta Sicilia Italy
108 A5 Calasetta Sardegna Italy
103 B6 Calasparra Spain
110 B5 Calatafimi Sicilia Italy
102 B3 Calatayud Spain
102 B3 Calatorao Spain
73 J4 Calau Germany
23 B3 Calauag Philippines
110 D4 Calavà, Capo c. Sicilia Italy
23 B3 Calavite, Cape c. Philippines
23 B2 Calayan i. Philippines
23 C3 Calbayog Philippines
73 G4 Calbe Germany
23 C4 Calbiga Philippines
171 B5 Calbuco Chile
164 B2 Calca Peru
166 E1 Calcanhar, Ponta do pt Brazil
151 E6 Calcasieu L. l. Louisiana U.S.A.
108 A2 Calcatoggio Corse France
83 E3 Calcio Italy
163 G3 Calçoene Brazil
37 G5 Calcutta India
112 E2 Căldăraru Romania
83 G2 Caldaro, Lago di l. Italy
83 G2 Caldaro sulla Strada del Vino Italy
100 A1 Caldas da Rainha Portugal
98 B3 Caldas de Vizela Portugal
168 D2 Caldas Novas Brazil
100 B3 Caldeirão, Serra de mountain range Portugal
72 E4 Calden Germany
170 B2 Caldera Chile
64 E2 Caldercruix Scotland U.K.
101 G1 Calderina, Sierra de la mountain range Spain
15 F5 Caldervale Queensland Australia
102 F3 Caldes de Montbui Spain
65 E3 Caldew r. England U.K.
62 B3 Caldey Island i. Wales U.K.
62 D3 Caldicot Wales U.K.
42 E2 Çaldıran Turkey
83 G2 Caldonazzo Italy
107 F2 Caldonazzo, Lago di l. Italy
152 C3 Caldwell Idaho U.S.A.
131 F5 Caledon r. Lesotho/South Africa
140 E5 Caledon Ontario Canada
130 B7 Caledon South Africa
14 D2 Caledon B. b. Northern Terr. Australia
148 B4 Caledonia Minnesota U.S.A.
141 F5 Caledonia Ontario Canada
102 F3 Calella Spain
15 G4 Calen Queensland Australia
108 A2 Calenzana Corse France
156 E4 Calera Mexico
99 E5 Calera y Chozas Spain
99 G3 Caleruega Spain
164 B4 Caleta Blanco Encalada b. Chile
172 A5 Caleta Bonifacio pt Chile
164 B3 Caleta Buena Chile
171 B7 Caleta Clarencia Chile
171 C7 Caleta Coig inlet Argentina
164 B4 Caleta el Cobre Chile
171 C7 Caleta Josefina Chile
164 B4 Caleta Lobos Chile
172 B1 Caleta Morritos Chile
171 C6 Caleta Olivia Argentina
172 B1 Caleta Teniente Chile
172 B3 Caletones Chile
172 B6 Caleufu r. Argentina
172 B6 Caleufú Neuquen Argentina
172 E3 Caleufú Pampas Argentina
155 E5 Calexico California U.S.A.
64 D3 Calf of Man i. Isle of Man
65 F3 Calf, The h. England U.K.
136 G4 Calgary Alberta Canada
64 B1 Calgary Scotland U.K.
96 □ Calheta Madeira Portugal
145 C5 Calhoun Georgia U.S.A.
162 B3 Cali Colombia
23 C4 Calicoan i. Philippines
38 A4 Calicut India
154 C4 Caliente California U.S.A.
155 E3 Caliente Nevada U.S.A.
154 B3 California div. U.S.A.
159 □3 California Trinidad and Tobago
154 B3 California Aqueduct canal California U.S.A.
156 B2 California, Golfo de g. Mexico
154 C4 California Hot Springs California U.S.A.
42 G2 Calilabad Azerbaijan
112 E2 Călimăneşti Romania
172 C1 Calingasta Argentina
153 D5 Calipatria California U.S.A.
154 A2 Calistoga California U.S.A.
109 H4 Calitri Italy
130 C6 Calitzdorp South Africa
106 C4 Calizzano Italy
157 H4 Calkiní Mexico
12 E2 Callabonna Cr. watercourse S. Australia Australia
12 D2 Callabonna, L. salt flat S. Australia Australia
88 B3 Callac France
154 D2 Callaghan, Mt mt. Nevada U.S.A.
145 D6 Callahan Florida U.S.A.
64 B3 Callan r. Northern Ireland U.K.
67 D4 Callan Rep. of Ireland
141 F3 Callander Ontario Canada
66 D4 Callander Scotland U.K.
68 C2 Callantsoog Netherlands
155 F2 Callao Utah U.S.A.
164 A2 Callao Peru
91 E5 Callas France
157 F4 Calles Mexico
147 F4 Callicoon New York U.S.A.
15 G5 Callide Queensland Australia
62 B4 Callington England U.K.
15 G5 Calliope Queensland Australia
103 C6 Callosa d'En Sarrià Spain
103 C6 Callosa de Segura Spain
140 E3 Callum Ontario Canada
136 G4 Calmar Alberta Canada
148 B4 Calmar Iowa U.S.A.
172 C4 Calmucó Argentina
62 D3 Calne England U.K.
155 E4 Cal-Nev-Ari Nevada U.S.A.
106 D3 Calolziocorte Italy
145 D7 Caloosahatchee r. Florida U.S.A.
109 G3 Calore r. Italy
111 E2 Calore r. Campania Italy
157 H4 Calotmul Mexico
15 H5 Caloundra Queensland Australia
103 D6 Calpe Spain
43 A1 Çalpınar Turkey
154 B2 Calpine California U.S.A.
157 F5 Calpulálpan Mexico
140 C2 Calstock Ontario Canada
110 C5 Caltabellotta Sicilia Italy
110 D5 Caltagirone r. Sicilia Italy
110 D5 Caltagirone Sicilia Italy
110 D5 Caltanissetta div. Italy
110 C5 Caltanissetta i. Sicilia Italy
110 C5 Caltavuturo Sicilia Italy
99 H3 Caltojar Spain
125 C6 Calucinga Angola
90 C3 Caluire-et-Cuire France
125 B5 Calulo Angola
148 C2 Calumet Michigan U.S.A.
125 D6 Calunda Angola
125 C7 Calunga Angola
125 B6 Caluquembe Angola
23 B4 Calusa i. Philippines
82 C3 Caluso Italy
126 F2 Caluula Somalia
155 G5 Calva Arizona U.S.A.
89 E2 Calvados div. France
98 B4 Calvão Portugal
109 H4 Calvello Italy
14 D3 Calvert r. Northern Terr. Australia
14 D3 Calvert Hills Northern Terr. Australia
136 D4 Calvert I. i. B.C. Canada
17 C4 Calvert Ra. h. Western Australia Australia
108 A2 Calvi Corse France
103 F5 Calvià Spain
156 E4 Calvillo Mexico
130 B5 Calvinia South Africa
91 C5 Calvisson France
108 A2 Calvi-Ste-Catherine airport Corse France
98 E4 Calvitero mt. Spain
109 H3 Calvo, Monte mt. Italy
73 G3 Calvörde Germany
98 C3 Calvos Spain
74 D4 Calw Germany
101 G2 Calzada de Calatrava Spain
98 E3 Calzada de Valdunciel Spain
63 G2 Cam r. England U.K.
125 C5 Camabatela Angola
169 J1 Camacã Brazil
166 E3 Camaçari Brazil
154 B2 Camache Reservoir resr California U.S.A.
156 E3 Camacho Mexico
125 B6 Camacuio Angola
125 C6 Camacupa Angola
162 D2 Camaguán Venezuela
158 C2 Camagüey Cuba
158 C2 Camagüey, Arch. de is Cuba
25 C6 Camah, Gunung mt. Malaysia
106 E5 Camaiore Italy
163 F5 Camaiú r. Brazil
Çamalan see Gülek
156 B2 Camalli, Sa de mt. Mexico
164 B3 Camana Peru
125 D6 Camanongue Angola
168 A3 Camapuã Brazil
167 B7 Camaquã r. Brazil
167 B7 Camaquã Brazil
96 □ Câmara de Lobos Madeira Portugal
166 B1 Camaraipi r. Brazil
165 E2 Camararé r. Brazil
103 B4 Camarena r. Spain
99 F4 Camarena Spain
93 E5 Camarès France
88 A3 Camaret-sur-Mer France
157 F3 Camargo Mexico
91 C5 Camargue reg. France
102 C4 Camarillas Spain
100 E4 Camarinal, Pta pt Spain
98 A1 Camariñas Spain
158 A4 Camarón, C. c. Honduras
156 D4 Camaronero, L. del lag. Mexico
164 C3 Camarones r. Chile
171 C5 Camarones Argentina
171 C5 Camarones, Bahía b. Argentina
98 D2 Camarzana de Tera Spain
152 B2 Camas Washington U.S.A.
100 D3 Camas Spain
110 C5 Camastra Sicilia Italy
25 D5 Ca Mau Vietnam
98 B2 Cambados Spain
168 C5 Cambará Brazil
165 E3 Cambara Brazil
Cambay see Khambhat
Cambay, Gulf of g. see Khambhat, Gulf of
63 F3 Camberley England U.K.
93 B4 Cambes France
19 M8 Cambodia country Asia
125 B6 Cambongo r. Angola
62 A4 Camborne England U.K.
86 C2 Cambrai France
98 B1 Cambre Spain
89 F2 Cambremer France
154 B4 Cambria California U.S.A.
130 E6 Cambria South Africa
62 C2 Cambrian Mountains mountain range Wales U.K.
63 G2 Cambridge England U.K.
148 B5 Cambridge Illinois U.S.A.
147 E5 Cambridge Maryland U.S.A.
147 H3 Cambridge Massachusetts U.S.A.
148 A3 Cambridge Minnesota U.S.A.
147 G3 Cambridge New York U.S.A.
146 C4 Cambridge Ohio U.S.A.
140 E5 Cambridge Ontario Canada
8 E2 Cambridge New Zealand
134 H3 Cambridge Bay N.W.T. Canada
16 E2 Cambridge Gulf b. Western Australia Australia
63 F2 Cambridgeshire div. England U.K.
139 G2 Cambrien, Lac l. Québec Canada
102 E3 Cambrils de Mar Spain
69 A4 Cambrin France
169 E5 Cambuí Brazil
125 D5 Cambulo Angola
125 C6 Cambundi-Catembo Angola
169 F4 Cambuquira Brazil
73 G4 Camburg Germany
145 C5 Camden Alabama U.S.A.
147 J2 Camden Maine U.S.A.
147 F5 Camden New Jersey U.S.A.
13 G3 Camden New South Wales Australia
147 F3 Camden New York U.S.A.
145 D5 Camden S. Carolina U.S.A.
171 B7 Camden, Is i. Chile
16 D2 Camden Sd chan. Western Australia Australia
125 D6 Cameia Angola
125 D6 Cameia, Parque Nacional da nat. park Angola
62 B4 Camelford England U.K.
53 C2 Camenca Moldova
107 H5 Camerano Italy
83 D3 Cameri Italy
109 F1 Camerino Italy
155 G4 Cameron Arizona U.S.A.
151 E6 Cameron Louisiana U.S.A.
150 E4 Cameron Missouri U.S.A.
151 D6 Cameron Texas U.S.A.
148 B3 Cameron Wisconsin U.S.A.
140 A2 Cameron Falls Ontario Canada
25 C6 Cameron Highlands Malaysia
136 F3 Cameron Hills h. Yukon Terr. Canada
9 A7 Cameron Mts mts New Zealand
154 B2 Cameron Park California U.S.A.
117 F5 Cameroon country Africa
109 H4 Camerota Italy
124 A3 Cameroun, Mont mt. Cameroon
173 J4 Camet Argentina
166 C1 Cametá Brazil
23 C4 Camiguin i. Philippines
23 B2 Camiguin i. Philippines
23 B3 Camiling Philippines
145 C6 Camilla Georgia U.S.A.
164 C3 Camiña Chile
98 B3 Caminha Portugal
98 D4 Caminomorisco Spain
102 B4 Caminreal Spain
166 C1 Camiranga Brazil
164 D4 Camiri Bolivia
125 D5 Camissombo Angola
43 C1 Çamlıyayla Turkey
110 C5 Cammarata Sicilia Italy
110 C5 Cammarata, Monte mt. Sicilia Italy
156 C3 Camoa Mexico
166 D1 Camocim Brazil
106 D4 Camogli Italy
86 B3 Camon France
14 D3 Camooweal Queensland Australia
163 G3 Camopi r. French Guiana
163 G3 Camopi Brazil
88 C3 Camors France
25 A5 Camorta i. Andaman and Nicobar Is India
23 C4 Camotes Sea g. Philippines
109 H4 Campagna Italy
91 B4 Campagnac France
109 E2 Campagnano di Roma Italy
93 C4 Campagne France
89 F3 Campagne d'Alençon plain France
86 A2 Campagne-lès-Hesdin France
173 J1 Campamento Uruguay
93 C5 Campan France
173 H3 Campana Argentina
111 F3 Campana Italy
173 J3 Campana Uruguay
171 A6 Campana, I. i. Chile
172 B3 Campanario mt. Argentina/Chile
168 A5 Campanario Brazil
169 H3 Campanário Brazil
100 E2 Campanario Spain
169 F4 Campanha Brazil
109 G3 Campania div. Italy
136 D4 Campania I. i. B.C. Canada
99 F3 Campaspero Spain
130 D4 Campbell South Africa
9 E4 Campbell, Cape c. New Zealand
25 B5 Campbell I. i. Myanmar
8 □2 Campbell I. i. New Zealand
36 C2 Campbellpore Pakistan
136 D4 Campbell River B.C. Canada

146 B4 Cedar Pt pt Ohio U.S.A.
148 B5 Cedar Rapids Iowa U.S.A.
155 G3 Cedar Ridge Arizona U.S.A.
147 F5 Cedar Run New Jersey U.S.A.
148 E4 Cedar Springs Michigan U.S.A.
140 D5 Cedar Springs Ontario Canada
145 C5 Cedartown Georgia U.S.A.
159 □1 Cedar Valley Jamaica
148 E3 Cedarville Michigan U.S.A.
131 G5 Cedarville South Africa
106 E2 Cedegolo Italy
98 B1 Cedeira h. Spain
98 B1 Cedeira Spain
102 C4 Cedrillas Spain
108 B4 Cedrino r. Sardegna Italy
156 B2 Cedros i. Mexico
159 □3 Cedros Pt pt Trinidad Trinidad and Tobago
12 C3 Ceduna S. Australia Australia
76 C3 Cedynia Poland
98 A2 Cée Spain
126 E4 Ceelbuur Somalia
126 E4 Ceeldheere Somalia
126 F2 Ceel Gaal Bari Somalia
126 D2 Ceel Gaal Woqooyi Galbeed Somalia
126 D4 Ceel Garas well Somalia
126 D4 Ceel Qoondhato well Somalia
126 D4 Ceel Walaaq well Somalia
126 E2 Ceerigaabo Somalia
110 D4 Cefalù Sicilia Italy
62 C2 Cefn-mawr Wales U.K.
99 F3 Cega r. Spain
107 G3 Ceggia Italy
79 J4 Cegléd Hungary
111 G2 Ceglie Messapica Italy
112 C4 Čegrane Macedonia
103 B6 Cehegín Spain
32 D3 Ceheng China
112 B3 Čehotina r. Yugoslavia
112 D1 Cehu Silvaniei Romania
145 □3 Ceiba Puerto Rico
173 H2 Ceibas Argentina
91 B5 Ceilhes-et-Rocozels France
98 B4 Ceira r. Portugal
78 F3 Čejč Czech Rep.
76 G2 Cekcyn Poland
42 C1 Çekerek Turkey
76 G4 Ceków-Kolonia Poland
25 C6 Celah, Gunung mt. Malaysia
78 D1 Čelákovice Czech Rep.
109 F2 Celano Italy
98 C2 Celanova Spain
157 E4 Celaya Mexico
67 E3 Celbridge Rep. of Ireland
Celebes i. see Sulawesi
21 H6 Celebes Sea sea Indonesia/Philippines
162 B5 Celendín Peru
146 A4 Celina Ohio U.S.A.
81 G4 Celje Slovenia
78 G4 Celldömölk Hungary
72 F3 Celle Niedersachsen Germany
69 B4 Celles Belgium
93 D6 Celles France
92 B2 Celles-sur-Belle France
86 D4 Celles-sur-Ource France
80 D4 Cellina r. Italy
111 G2 Cellino San Marco Italy
109 H3 Celone r. Italy
114 C1 Čelopeci Macedonia
98 C4 Celorico da Beira Portugal
98 B3 Celorico de Basto Portugal
61 D6 Celtic Sea Rep. of Ireland/U.K.
62 C2 Celyn, Llyn l. Wales U.K.
107 F2 Cembra Italy
79 K6 Cenei Romania
99 H2 Cenicero Spain
106 D4 Ceno r. Italy
93 B4 Cenon France
22 D2 Cenrana Philippines
131 G6 Centani South Africa
102 F3 Centelles Spain
172 C5 Centenario Argentina
168 C5 Centenário do Sul Brazil
129 E2 Centenary Zimbabwe
155 F5 Centennial Wash r. Arizona U.S.A.
151 E6 Center Texas U.S.A.
147 G4 Centereach New York U.S.A.
145 C5 Center Point Alabama U.S.A.
146 B5 Centerville Ohio U.S.A.
107 F4 Cento Italy
128 D3 Central div. Botswana
122 D5 Central div. Ghana
127 C5 Central div. Kenya
127 B7 Central div. Malawi
119 F5 Central div. Sudan
125 E6 Central div. Zambia
117 F5 Central African Republic country Africa
16 E4 Central Australia Aboriginal Reserve res. Western Australia Australia
17 E5 Central Australia Aboriginal Reserve (Warburton) res. Western Australia Australia
36 A3 Central Brahui Ra. mountain range Pakistan
148 B4 Central City Iowa U.S.A.
150 D3 Central City Nebraska U.S.A.
162 B3 Central, Cord. mountain range Colombia
159 E3 Central, Cord. mountain range Dominican Rep.
164 C3 Central, Cordillera mountain range Bolivia
156 K7 Central, Cordillera mountain range Panama
164 A1 Central, Cordillera mountain range Peru
23 B2 Central, Cordillera mountain range Philippines
169 H3 Central de Minas Brazil
14 B4 Central Desert Aboriginal Land res. Northern Terr. Australia
27 □ Central District Hong Kong China
144 B4 Centralia Illinois U.S.A.
152 B2 Centralia Washington U.S.A.
128 C3 Central Kalahari Game Reserve res. Botswana
148 A2 Central Lakes Minnesota U.S.A.
172 B1 Central Los Molles Chile
39 E4 Central Makran Range mountain range Pakistan
14 C4 Central Mt Stuart h. Northern Terr. Australia
14 B4 Central Mt Wedge mt. Northern Terr. Australia
152 B3 Central Point Oregon U.S.A.
6 □1 Central Ra. mountain range P.N.G.
131 G4 Central Range mountain range Lesotho
124 B2 Centre div. Cameroon
89 G4 Centre div. France
127 □4 Centre de Flacq Mauritius
9 A7 Centre I. i. New Zealand
145 C5 Centreville Alabama U.S.A.
173 L2 Centurión Uruguay
110 D5 Centuripe Sicilia Italy
33 E4 Cenxi China
93 D4 Céou r. France
109 G2 Cepagatti Italy
Cephalonia i. see Kefallonia
81 E4 Čepovan Slovenia
86 B4 Cepoy France
106 B5 Ceppo, Monte mt. Italy
82 D3 Ceppo Morelli Italy
109 F3 Ceprano Italy
77 L3 Cerańow Poland
89 F4 Cérans-Foulletourte France
109 H4 Ceraso Italy
162 D2 Cerbatana, Sa de la mt. Venezuela
155 E4 Cerbat Mts mts Arizona U.S.A.
93 F6 Cerbère France
102 G2 Cerbère, Cap pt France/Spain
100 B3 Cercal Portugal
100 B3 Cercal, Sa do mountain range Portugal
75 K3 Čerčany Czech Rep.
98 B2 Cercedo Spain
110 C5 Cerda Sicilia Italy
102 F3 Cerdanyola del Vallès Spain
89 H4 Cerdon France
93 E4 Cère r. France
107 F3 Cerea Italy
137 G4 Cereal Alberta Canada
172 F4 Cereales Argentina
62 B2 Ceredigion div. Wales U.K.
107 F3 Ceregnano Italy
88 D3 Cérences France
170 D2 Ceres Argentina
168 D1 Ceres Brazil
106 B3 Ceres Italy
130 B6 Ceres South Africa
106 B3 Ceresole Reale Italy
91 D5 Céreste France
93 E6 Céret France
162 B2 Cereté Colombia
99 G3 Cerezo de Abajo Spain
127 □2 Cerf I. i. Seychelles
127 □4 Cerfs, Is aux is Mauritius
79 L2 Čergov mts Slovakia
86 B3 Cergy France
109 H3 Cerignola Italy
42 C2 Çerikli Turkey
172 B1 Cerillos de Tamaya Chile
92 E2 Cérilly France
111 F3 Cerisano Italy
86 C4 Cerisiers France
88 D2 Cerisy-la-Salle France
92 B2 Cerizay France
51 E7 Çerkeş Turkey
113 G4 Çerkezköy Turkey
81 G5 Cerklje Slovenia
81 F4 Cerklje Slovenia
81 F5 Cerknica Slovenia
81 E4 Cerkno Slovenia
76 D1 Cerkwica Poland
79 L5 Cermei Romania
42 D2 Çermik Turkey
98 B5 Cernache de Bonjardim Portugal
98 D3 Cernadilla, Emb. de resr Spain
78 C3 Černá Hora mt. Czech Rep.
112 G2 Cernavodă Romania
90 F1 Cernay France
86 D3 Cernay-en-Dormois France
75 J2 Černčice Czech Rep.
99 G2 Cernégula Spain
82 B1 Cernier Switzerland
79 M2 Černiny h. Slovakia
106 D3 Cernobbio Italy
75 K3 Černošice Czech Rep.
75 H3 Černošín Czech Rep.
78 D2 Černovice Czech Rep.
93 D4 Cérou r. France
107 J3 Cerovlje Croatia
168 D5 Cerqueira César Brazil
98 D4 Cerralbo Spain
157 F3 Cerralvo Mexico
99 F3 Cerrato, Valles de v. Spain
114 A1 Cërrik Albania
173 K1 Cerrillada Uruguay
157 E4 Cerritos Mexico
157 F4 Cerro Azul Brazil
168 D6 Cerro Azul Brazil
173 K2 Cerro Chato Uruguay
162 A4 Cerro de Amotape, Parque Nacional nat. park Peru
164 A2 Cerro de Pasco Peru
101 G4 Cerrón mt. Spain
159 E5 Cerrón, Co mt. Venezuela
170 C1 Cerro Negro Chile
172 C5 Cerro Policía Argentina
164 C2 Cerros de Bala mountain range Bolivia
162 C5 Cerros de Canchyuaya h. Peru
89 E4 Cersay France
109 J4 Cersosimo Italy
107 F5 Certaldo Italy
106 D3 Certosa di Pavia Italy
109 H3 Cervaro r. Italy
109 H4 Cervati, Monte mt. Italy
99 F2 Cervatos de la Cueza Spain
78 F1 Červená Voda Czech Rep.
112 E3 Cervenia Romania
102 E3 Cervera Spain
102 B3 Cervera de la Cañada Spain
102 B2 Cervera del Río Alhama Spain
99 F2 Cervera de Pisuerga Spain
108 E3 Cerveteri Italy
107 G4 Cervia Italy
107 H3 Cervignano del Friuli Italy
107 F2 Cervina, Punta mt. Italy
109 G3 Cervinara Italy
78 E2 Červiná Řečice Czech Rep.
108 B2 Cervione Corse France
106 C3 Cervo r. Italy
106 C5 Cervo Italy
98 C1 Cervo Spain
111 F3 Cerzeto Italy
106 D3 Cesano Boscone Italy
83 E3 Cesano Maderno Italy
110 D5 Cesarò Sicilia Italy
107 G4 Cesena Italy
107 G4 Cesenatico Italy
108 D1 Cesina r. Italy
54 D3 Cēsis Latvia
78 D1 Česká Kamenice Czech Rep.
78 D1 Česká Lípa Czech Rep.
78 F1 Česká Skalice Czech Rep.
78 D3 České Budějovice Czech Rep.
78 C1 České Středohoří h. Czech Rep.
81 F2 České Velenice Czech Rep.
78 E2 Českomoravská Vysočina reg. Czech Rep.
78 D1 Český Brod Czech Rep.
78 D3 Český Krumlov Czech Rep.
78 B2 Český Les mts Czech Rep./Germany
79 H2 Český Těšín Czech Rep.
78 F6 Česma r. Croatia
42 A2 Çeşme Turkey
93 E5 Cesse r. France
13 G3 Cessnock New South Wales Australia
88 D3 Cesson-Sévigné France
93 B4 Cestas France
122 C5 Cestos r. Liberia
54 E3 Cesvaine Latvia
112 D2 Cetate Romania
104 F4 Cetina r. Croatia
102 B3 Cetina Spain
112 B3 Cetinje Yugoslavia
83 F2 Ceto Italy
89 F3 Ceton France
111 E3 Cetraro Italy
101 E5 Ceuta Spain
106 C4 Ceva Italy
107 E2 Cevedale, Monte mt. Italy
91 B5 Cévennes mts France
91 B4 Cévennes, Parc National des nat. park France
99 F3 Cevico de la Torre Spain
99 F3 Cevico Navero Spain
90 E3 Cevins France
83 D2 Cevio Switzerland
43 A1 Cevizli Turkey
76 F1 Cewice Poland
42 D2 Ceyhan r. Turkey
42 C2 Ceyhan Turkey
42 D2 Ceylanpinar Turkey
90 D2 Ceyzériat France
91 B4 Cèze r. France
39 E1 Chaacha Turkmenistan
52 G3 Chaadayevka Rus. Fed.
52 F2 Chaadayevo Rus. Fed.
69 C3 Chaam Netherlands
92 C3 Chabanais France
173 G2 Chabas Argentina
91 D4 Chabestan France
91 D4 Chabeuil France
77 H4 Chabielice Poland
90 E2 Chablais mts France
90 B1 Chablis France
91 D4 Chabre ridge France
90 B3 Chabreloche France
89 G4 Chabris France
164 B3 Chaca Chile
173 G3 Chacabuco Argentina
159 □3 Chacachacare I. i. Trinidad Trinidad and Tobago
171 B5 Chacao Chile
170 C4 Chachahuen, Sa mt. Argentina
164 B3 Chachani, Nevado de mt. Peru
162 B5 Chachapoyas Peru
172 E4 Chacharramendi Argentina
51 D4 Chachersk Belarus
25 C4 Chachoengsao Thailand
36 B4 Chachro Pakistan
172 C4 Chachuahen, Sa mt. Argentina
170 D2 Chaco div. Argentina
165 E4 Chaco Boreal reg. Paraguay
136 C4 Chacon, C. c. Alaska U.S.A.
116 F4 Chad country Africa
26 F1 Chadan Rus. Fed.
172 D4 Chadileo r. Argentina
118 B5 Chad, Lake l. Africa
150 C3 Chadron Nebraska U.S.A.
24 B3 Chae Hom Thailand
47 H4 Chaek Kyrgyzstan
31 H5 Chaeryŏng North Korea
162 C3 Chafurray Colombia
39 F3 Chagai Pakistan
39 E3 Chagai Hills mountain range Afghanistan/Pakistan
47 J2 Chagan Kazakhstan
37 F2 Chagdo Kangri China
39 F2 Chaghcharān Afghanistan
47 G2 Chaglinka r. Kazakhstan
90 C2 Chagny France
50 E3 Chagoda Rus. Fed.
175 J4 Chagos Archipelago is British Indian Ocean Territory
31 J1 Chagoyan Rus. Fed.
46 E3 Chagrayskoye Plato plat. Kazakhstan
159 □3 Chaguanas Trinidad and Tobago
159 □3 Chaguaramas Trinidad and Tobago
162 D2 Chaguaramas Venezuela
46 E4 Chagyl Turkmenistan
37 G3 Cha'gyüngoinba China
39 E3 Chahah Burjal Afghanistan
39 D2 Chāh Ākhvor Iran
39 B2 Chahār Maḩāll va Bakhtīārī div. Iran
39 D2 Chahār Takāb Iran
39 C2 Chāh Badam Iran
39 E4 Chāh Bahār Iran
121 E1 Chahbounia Algeria
39 E1 Chahchaheh Iran
39 D2 Chāh-e Kavīr well Iran
39 C2 Chāh-e Khorāsān well Iran
39 D2 Chāh-e Khoshāb Iran
39 C2 Chāh-e Malek well Iran
39 D3 Chāh-e Malek Iran
39 C2 Chāh-e Mirzā well Iran
39 C2 Chāh-e Mūjān well Iran
39 C2 Chāh-e Nūklok well Iran
39 C2 Chāh-e Nūklok Iran
39 C3 Chāh-e Qeyşar well Iran
39 C2 Chāh-e Qobād well Iran
39 C3 Chāh-e Rāh Iran
39 D3 Chāh-e-Raḩmān well Iran
39 C2 Chāh-e Shur well Iran
39 C2 Chāh-e Shūr Iran
39 C3 Chāh-e Ţāqestān well Iran
39 C2 Chah Haji Abdulla well Iran
39 C3 Chāh Ḩaqq Iran
39 G1 Chah-i-Ab Afghanistan
42 F3 Chah-i-Shurkh Iraq
39 C2 Chāh Pās well Iran
39 B3 Chāh Rūstā'ī Iran
39 E3 Chah Sandan Pakistan
127 D7 Chai Mozambique
37 F5 Chāībāsa India
139 G3 Chaigneau, Lac l. Québec Canada
63 F4 Chailey England U.K.
89 E3 Chailland France
92 A2 Chaillé-les-Marais France
86 C4 Chailley France
123 E4 Chaîne de l'Atakora mountain range Benin
125 E6 Chaine des Mitumba mountain range Congo(Zaire)
86 D4 Chaintrix-Bierges France
25 C4 Chai Si r. Thailand
171 B5 Chaitén Chile
27 □ Chai Wan Hong Kong China
25 B5 Chaiya Thailand
24 C4 Chaiyaphum Thailand
173 J1 Chajarí Argentina
129 D2 Chakari Zimbabwe
36 C2 Chakdarra Pakistan
127 C6 Chake Chake Tanzania
39 E3 Chakhānsūr Afghanistan
36 A4 Chakku Pakistan
36 C1 Chakmaktin L. l. Afghanistan
37 F5 Chakradharpur India
36 C2 Chakwal Pakistan
164 B3 Chala Peru
127 B6 Chala Tanzania
93 E6 Chalabre France
90 D2 Chalain, Lac de l. France
92 C3 Chalais France
82 C2 Chalais Switzerland
102 D3 Chalamera Spain
90 D2 Chalamont France
82 C1 Chalampé France
115 C4 Chalandritsa Greece
39 F2 Chalap Dalan mountain range Afghanistan
164 B3 Chala, Pta pt Peru
90 C2 Chalaronne r. France
156 H6 Chalatenango El Salvador
129 F2 Chaláua Mozambique
32 B1 Chalaxung China
126 C4 Chalbi Desert desert Kenya
63 E4 Chale England U.K.
86 B4 Châlette-sur-Loing France
139 G4 Chaleur Bay inlet New Brunswick Canada
171 B6 Chalía r. Argentina
82 A1 Chalindrey France
33 F3 Chaling China
127 C6 Chalinze Tanzania
36 C5 Chalisgaon India
115 □ Chalki i. Greece
114 D3 Chalki Thessalia Greece
115 E4 Chalkida Greece
114 E2 Chalkidiki div. Greece
114 D2 Chalkidona Greece
47 J4 Chalkudysu Kazakhstan
9 A7 Chalky Inlet inlet New Zealand
172 C5 Challacó Argentina
92 A2 Challans France
164 C3 Challapata Bolivia
176 E5 Challenger Deep depth Pacific Ocean
177 M8 Challenger Fracture Zone sea feature Pacific Ocean
82 A3 Challes-les-Eaux France
152 D2 Challis Idaho U.S.A.
89 E4 Challones-sur-Loire France
50 F1 Chal'mny Varre Rus. Fed.
37 G5 Chalna India
90 C1 Chaloire r. France
86 D4 Châlons-en-Champagne France
90 C2 Chalon-sur-Saône France
93 B5 Chalosse reg. France
36 C1 Chalt Jammu and Kashmir
31 H4 Chaluhe China
92 C3 Châlus France
39 B1 Chālūs Iran
75 H3 Cham Germany
83 D1 Cham Switzerland
153 F4 Chama New Mexico U.S.A.
127 B7 Chama Zambia
172 E3 Chamaico Argentina
90 B3 Chamalières France
91 D4 Chamaloc France
36 A3 Chaman Pakistan
39 D1 Chaman Bid Iran
75 H3 Chamb r. Germany
36 D2 Chamba India
127 C7 Chamba Tanzania
36 D4 Chambal r. India
139 G3 Chambeaux, Lac l. Québec Canada
92 D3 Chamberet France
90 D2 Chambéria France
16 D3 Chamberlain r. Western Australia Australia
137 H4 Chamberlain Saskatchewan Canada
150 D3 Chamberlain S. Dakota U.S.A.
173 J2 Chamberlain Uruguay
147 J1 Chamberlain Lake l. Maine U.S.A.
155 H4 Chambers Arizona U.S.A.
146 E5 Chambersburg Pennsylvania U.S.A.
90 D3 Chambéry France
127 B7 Chambeshi r. Zambia
127 B7 Chambeshi Zambia
121 F1 Chambi, Jebel mt. Tunisia
87 E3 Chambley-Bussières France
92 D2 Chambon, Lac de l. France
92 E2 Chambon-sur-Voueize France
141 J2 Chambord Québec Canada
89 G4 Chambord France
92 D3 Chamboulive France
89 F4 Chambray-lès-Tours France
86 C3 Chambry France
39 B2 Cham-e Ḩannā Iran
90 C1 Chamesson France
39 B3 Cham-e Zeydun Iran
172 D1 Chamical Argentina
113 F7 Chamili i. Greece
37 F4 Chamlang mt. Nepal
25 C5 Châmnar Cambodia
126 C3 Ch'amo Hāyk' l. Ethiopia
36 D3 Chamoli India
90 E3 Chamonix-Mont-Blanc France
141 J2 Chamouchouane r. Québec Canada
90 E3 Chamoux-sur-Gelon France
37 E5 Champa India
92 C3 Champagnac-de-Belair France
91 B3 Champagnac-le-Vieux France
136 B2 Champagne Yukon Terr. Canada
86 D4 Champagne-Ardenne div. France
89 G4 Champagne Berrichonne reg. France
131 G4 Champagne Castle mt. South Africa
86 D3 Champagne Crayeuse reg. France
90 D3 Champagne-en-Valromey France
86 D4 Champagne Humide reg. France
92 C3 Champagne-Mouton France
86 D4 Champagne Pouilleuse reg. France
90 E1 Champagney France
90 D2 Champagnole France
148 C5 Champaign Illinois U.S.A.
172 E1 Champaqui, Co mt. Argentina
25 D4 Champasak Laos
86 C4 Champaubert France
92 B2 Champdeniers-St-Denis France
87 G4 Champ du Feu mt. France
89 F4 Champeigne reg. France
90 B3 Champeix France
82 B2 Champéry Switzerland
82 C2 Champex Switzerland
37 H5 Champhai India
91 D3 Champier France
89 E4 Champigné France
87 F4 Champigneulles France
86 D4 Champignol-lez-Mondeville France
148 D2 Champion Michigan U.S.A.
147 G2 Champlain New York U.S.A.
147 G2 Champlain, L. l. Canada/U.S.A.
90 D1 Champlitte France
141 G2 Champneuf Québec Canada
91 E4 Champoléon France
106 B3 Champoluc Italy
157 H5 Champotón Mexico
91 E4 Champsaur reg. France
89 E3 Champsecret France
92 E3 Champs-sur-Tarentaine-Marchal France
90 B1 Champs-sur-Yonne France
88 D4 Champtoceaux France
82 A1 Champvans France
38 B4 Chamrajnagar India
52 H2 Chamzinka Rus. Fed.
52 G2 Chamzinka Rus. Fed.
25 C6 Chana Thailand
36 D2 Chanab r. India
166 C3 Chanabrava r. Brazil
91 B4 Chanac France
173 H1 Chañar Entre Rios Argentina
172 E1 Chañar La Rioja Argentina
172 C5 Chañar Neuquen Argentina
170 B2 Chañaral Chile
172 B1 Chañaral Alto Chile
39 D1 Chanārān Iran
173 F2 Chañar Ladeado Argentina
Chança see Chanza
91 C3 Chanas France
172 E1 Chancani Argentina
162 B5 Chancay r. Peru
90 C1 Chanceaux France
89 F4 Chanceaux-sur-Choisille France
172 A3 Chanco Chile
172 A3 Chanco, B. de b. Chile
Chanda see Chandrapur
134 D3 Chandalar r. Alaska U.S.A.
37 E5 Chandarpur India
36 D3 Chandausi India
37 F5 Chandbali India
151 F6 Chandeleur Islands is Louisiana U.S.A.
36 D4 Chanderi India
36 E5 Chandia India
36 D3 Chandigarh India
155 G5 Chandler Arizona U.S.A.
30 A2 Chandmany Mongolia
141 G4 Chandos Lake l. Ontario Canada
37 G5 Chandpur Bangladesh
36 D3 Chandpur India
37 H5 Chandraghana Bangladesh
38 B2 Chandrapur India
115 C6 Chandrinos Greece
36 D5 Chandur India
32 G2 Chang r. China
131 J3 Changalane Mozambique
129 E3 Changane r. Mozambique
129 E2 Changara Mozambique
31 H4 Changbai Shan mts China
32 E5 Changcheng China
179 B1 Chang Cheng (Great Wall) China Base South Shetland Islands Antarctica
31 H4 Changchun China
31 G5 Changdao China
33 E2 Changde China
89 E3 Changé Mayenne France
89 F4 Changé Sarthe France
33 G1 Changfeng China
31 J5 Changgi Gap pt South Korea
31 G5 Changhai China
31 H6 Changhang South Korea
33 F2 Chang Hu l. China
33 E5 Changhua r. China
33 H3 Chang-hua Taiwan
25 □ Changi airport Singapore
25 □ Changi Singapore
33 E5 Changjiang China
33 H2 Changjiang Kou river mouth China
31 H4 Changjin North Korea
33 G3 Changle China
31 F5 Changli China
31 G3 Changling China
30 C5 Changliushui China
36 D2 Changlung Jammu and Kashmir
33 F3 Changning China
28 B6 Ch'angnyŏng South Korea
31 F4 Changping China
31 F5 Changqing China
31 H5 Changsan-got pt North Korea
33 F2 Changsha China
33 G2 Changshan China
31 G5 Changshan Qundao is China
32 D2 Changshou China
33 F2 Changshoujie China
33 H2 Changshu China
32 D3 Changshun China
31 H6 Changsŏng South Korea
33 G3 Changtai China
33 G3 Changting China
31 J3 Changting China
31 H4 Changtu China
156 K7 Changuinola Panama
31 J6 Ch'angwŏn South Korea
32 D1 Changwu China
33 G2 Changxing China
31 G5 Changxing Dao i. China
33 E2 Changyang China
31 F5 Changyi China
33 F1 Changyuan China
30 E5 Changzhi China
33 G2 Changzhou China
30 E6 Changzi China
170 C1 Chañi, Nevado de mt. Argentina
115 E7 Chania div. Greece
115 F7 Chania Greece
92 B3 Chaniers France
114 E2 Chaniotis Greece
31 H4 Chanjin r. North Korea
30 C6 Chankou China
38 B3 Channapatna India
154 C5 Channel Islands is California U.S.A.
63 □2 Channel Islands is English Channel
154 B5 Channel Is Nat. Park nat. park California U.S.A.
139 J4 Channel-Port-aux-Basques Newfoundland Canada
17 B7 Channel Pt pt Western Australia Australia
158 C2 Channel Rock i. The Bahamas
63 H3 Channel Tunnel tunnel France/U.K.
148 C2 Channing Michigan U.S.A.
98 C2 Chantada Spain
90 B2 Chantelle France
88 D3 Chantepie France
25 C4 Chanthaburi Thailand
86 B3 Chantilly France
92 A2 Chantonnay France
82 B1 Chantrans France
25 A5 Chanumla Andaman and Nicobar Is India
151 E4 Chanute Kansas U.S.A.
47 J1 Chany Rus. Fed.
47 J2 Chany, Oz. salt lake Rus. Fed.
100 C3 Chanza r. Portugal/Spain
164 A1 Chao Peru
98 C1 Chao Spain
33 G2 Chao Hu l. China
25 C4 Chao Phraya r. Thailand
31 G3 Chaor r. China
31 G2 Chaor China
120 C1 Chaouèn Morocco
86 D4 Chaource France
32 A1 Chaowula Shan mts China
33 G2 Chao Xian China
33 G4 Chaoyang China
31 G4 Chaoyang China
31 G2 Chaozhong China
33 G4 Chaozhou China
166 D3 Chapada de Maracás reg. Brazil
168 B1 Chapada de Mato Grosso plat. Brazil
166 D3 Chapada Diamantina plat. Brazil
166 D3 Chapada Diamantina, Parque Nacional nat. park Brazil
166 D2 Chapada do Araripe reg. Brazil
166 A4 Chapada dos Guimarães Brazil
166 C3 Chapada dos Veadeiros, Parque Nacional da nat. park Brazil
168 E2 Chapada do Tapiocanga mts Brazil
169 F1 Chapadão de Santa Maria reg. Brazil
166 D1 Chapadinha Brazil
141 H2 Chapais Québec Canada
156 E4 Chapala Mexico
156 E4 Chapala, L. de l. Mexico
172 E4 Chapalcó, Valle de v. Argentina
173 H4 Chapaleofú Argentina
90 D3 Chapareillan France
162 B3 Chaparral Colombia
46 D2 Chapayev Kazakhstan
53 F2 Chapayeve Ukraine
53 E2 Chapayevka Ukraine
50 J4 Chapayevsk Rus. Fed.
47 H2 Chapayevskoye Kazakhstan
167 B6 Chapecó r. Brazil
167 B6 Chapecó Brazil
63 E1 Chapel-en-le-Frith England U.K.
65 F3 Chapelfell Top h. England U.K.
145 E5 Chapel Hill N. Carolina U.S.A.
69 C4 Chapelle-lez-Herlaimont Belgium
159 □1 Chapelton Jamaica
65 G4 Chapeltown England U.K.
173 J1 Chapicuy Uruguay
99 F4 Chapinería Spain
148 D5 Chapin, Lake l. Michigan U.S.A.
140 D3 Chapleau Ontario Canada
53 E1 Chapliyivka Ukraine
52 D3 Chaplygin Rus. Fed.
53 G2 Chaplyne Ukraine
53 E3 Chaplynka Ukraine
146 B6 Chapmanville W. Virginia U.S.A.
50 F1 Chapoma Rus. Fed.
13 F5 Chappell Is is Tasmania Australia
39 F2 Chapri P. pass Afghanistan
173 G2 Chapuy Argentina
164 C3 Chaqui Bolivia
36 D2 Char India
165 D3 Charagua Bolivia
36 B5 Charakra Doi India
164 C3 Charana Bolivia
129 D2 Charara Safari Area res. Zimbabwe
114 C2 Charavgi Greece
90 C2 Charbonnat France
91 F3 Charbonnel, Pte de mt. France
157 E4 Charcas Mexico
90 D2 Charchilla France
37 H3 Char Chu r. China
179 A2 Charcot I. i. Antarctica
137 G3 Chard Alberta Canada
62 D4 Chard England U.K.
47 G4 Chardara Kazakhstan
146 C4 Chardon Ohio U.S.A.
62 D4 Chardstock England U.K.
46 F5 Chardzhev Turkmenistan
121 E2 Charef Algeria
92 C3 Charente div. Poitou-Charentes France
92 B3 Charente r. France
92 B3 Charente-Maritime div. France
92 E2 Charenton-du-Cher France
89 F2 Charentonne r. France
62 D3 Charfield England U.K.
82 A1 Chargey-lès-Gray France
124 C2 Chari r. Cameroon/Chad
39 D3 Chārī Iran
124 C1 Chari-Baguirmi div. Chad
39 G2 Chārīkār Afghanistan
150 E3 Chariton r. Iowa U.S.A.
149 F3 Charity Is i. Michigan U.S.A.
36 D4 Charkhari India
63 E3 Charlbury England U.K.
69 C4 Charleroi div. Hainaut Belgium
69 C4 Charleroi Charleroi Belgium
141 K3 Charlesbourg Québec Canada
148 A4 Charles City Iowa U.S.A.
86 B3 Charles de Gaulle airport France
151 E6 Charles, Lake Louisiana U.S.A.
17 C7 Charles Pk h. Western Australia Australia
144 B4 Charleston Illinois U.S.A.
147 J2 Charleston Maine U.S.A.
151 F4 Charleston Missouri U.S.A.
145 E5 Charleston S. Carolina U.S.A.
146 C5 Charleston W. Virginia U.S.A.
9 C4 Charleston New Zealand
155 E3 Charleston Peak summit Nevada U.S.A.
147 G3 Charlestown New Hampshire U.S.A.
147 H4 Charlestown Rhode Island U.S.A.
159 □6 Charlestown St Kitts-Nevis Caribbean
146 E5 Charles Town W. Virginia U.S.A.
67 C3 Charlestown Rep. of Ireland
131 G3 Charlestown South Africa
15 F5 Charleville Queensland Australia
Charleville see Rathluirc
86 D3 Charleville-Mézières France
148 E3 Charlevoix Michigan U.S.A.
136 E3 Charlie Lake B.C. Canada
90 C2 Charlieu France
148 E4 Charlotte Michigan U.S.A.
145 D5 Charlotte N. Carolina U.S.A.
145 □3 Charlotte Amalie Virgin Is Caribbean
25 D6 Charlotte Bank sand bank Vietnam
145 D7 Charlotte Harbor b. Florida U.S.A.
59 E2 Charlottenberg Sweden
146 D5 Charlottesville Virginia U.S.A.
Charlotte Town see Gouyave
139 H4 Charlottetown Prince Edward I. Canada
159 □2 Charlotteville Tobago Trinidad and Tobago
13 E4 Charlton Victoria Australia
138 E3 Charlton I. i. N.W.T. Canada
86 C4 Charly France
92 C3 Charmé France
87 F4 Charmes France
91 C4 Charmes-sur-Rhône France
82 C2 Charmey Switzerland
62 D4 Charminster England U.K.
87 F4 Charmois-l'Orgueilleux France
62 D4 Charmouth England U.K.
86 C5 Charmoy France
16 D3 Charnley r. Western Australia Australia
90 B1 Charny France
77 N4 Charnyany Belarus
87 E3 Charny-sur-Meuse France
115 C6 Charokopeio Greece
90 C2 Charollais reg. France
90 C2 Charolles France
92 E2 Chârost France
50 F2 Charozero Rus. Fed.
91 B4 Charpal, Lac de l. France
82 B1 Charquemont France
82 C2 Charrat Switzerland
86 D5 Charrey-sur-Seine France
92 C2 Charroux France
36 B2 Charsadda Pakistan
39 F1 Charshanga Turkmenistan
47 K3 Charsk Kazakhstan
54 F4 Charstsvyatskaye, Vozyera l. Belarus
15 F4 Charters Towers Queensland Australia
89 G3 Chartres France
88 D3 Chartres-de-Bretagne France

164 B2 Coracora Peru
140 E1 Coral Ontario Canada
145 D7 Coral Gables Florida U.S.A.
135 K3 Coral Harbour N.W.T. Canada
145 □2 Coral Harbour The Bahamas
176 F7 Coral Sea sea Pacific Ocean
176 E6 Coral Sea Basin sea feature Pacific Ocean
4 G6 Coral Sea Islands Territory div. Pacific Ocean
148 B5 Coralville Reservoir resr Iowa U.S.A.
13 E4 Corangamite, L. l. Victoria Australia
163 F3 Corantijn r. Surinam
109 J3 Corato Italy
88 B3 Coray France
102 C4 Corbalán Spain
86 B4 Corbeil-Essonnes France
86 B4 Corbeilles France
120 A4 Corbeiro, Cap pt Western Sahara
168 B6 Corbélia Brazil
90 D3 Corbelin France
86 C3 Corbeny France
173 G3 Corbett Argentina
137 L2 Corbett Inlet inlet N.W.T. Canada
86 B3 Corbie France
93 E6 Corbières reg. France
91 D5 Corbières France
82 C2 Corbières Switzerland
98 B1 Corbigny France
146 A6 Corbin Kentucky U.S.A.
101 E3 Corbones r. Spain
65 F3 Corbridge England U.K.
112 G2 Corbu Romania
63 F2 Corby England U.K.
102 G3 Corça Spain
Corcaigh see Cork
90 D1 Corcelles-lès-Cîteaux France
109 E2 Corchiano Italy
101 H1 Córcoles r. Spain
154 C3 Corcoran California U.S.A.
171 B5 Corcovado Argentina
171 B5 Corcovado, G. de chan. Chile
171 B5 Corcovado, V. volcano Chile
98 A2 Corcubión Spain
166 C2 Corda r. Brazil
169 G5 Cordeiro Brazil
145 D6 Cordele Georgia U.S.A.
80 D5 Cordenòns Italy
93 D4 Cordes France
165 E5 Cordillera de Caaguazú h. Paraguay
162 C3 Cordillera de los Picachos, Parque Nacional nat. park Colombia
172 B4 Cordillera de Pemehue mountain range Chile
23 B4 Cordilleras Range mountain range Philippines
12 E1 Cordillo Downs S. Australia Australia
169 F3 Cordisburgo Brazil
172 F2 Córdoba div. Argentina
101 F2 Córdoba div. Spain
101 F3 Córdoba Córdoba Spain
171 C5 Córdoba Argentina
172 E1 Córdoba Argentina
157 F5 Córdoba Mexico
165 E3 Córdoba Mexico
101 F3 Córdoba, Sierra de h. Spain
170 D3 Cordoba, Sierras de mountain range Argentina
173 K2 Cordobes r. Uruguay
134 D3 Cordova Alaska U.S.A.
Cordova see Córdoba
164 A2 Cordova Peru
136 C4 Cordova Bay b. Alaska U.S.A.
147 K2 Corea Maine U.S.A.
166 D1 Coreaú Brazil
14 E4 Corella r. Queensland Australia
102 B2 Corella Spain
14 C3 Corella L. salt flat Northern Terr. Australia
62 D4 Corfe Castle England U.K.
15 E4 Corfield Queensland Australia
109 F2 Corfinio Italy
Corfu i. see Kerkyra
98 C3 Corgo r. Portugal
168 A3 Corguinho Brazil
109 E3 Cori Italy
98 D5 Coria Spain
100 D3 Coria del Río Spain
111 F3 Corigliano Calabro Italy
107 H5 Corinaldo Italy
15 G3 Coringa Is is Coral Sea Islands Terr. Pacific Ocean
147 J2 Corinna Maine U.S.A.
13 F5 Corinna Tasmania Australia
137 J4 Corinne Saskatchewan Canada
151 F5 Corinth Mississippi U.S.A.
147 G3 Corinth New York U.S.A.
169 F3 Corinto Brazil
101 E4 Coripe Spain
165 E3 Corixa Grande r. Bolivia
165 E3 Corixinha r. Brazil
67 C5 Cork airport Rep. of Ireland
67 C4 Cork div. Rep. of Ireland
67 C5 Cork Rep. of Ireland
88 B3 Corlay France
110 C5 Corleone Sicilia Italy
109 J4 Corleto Perticara Italy
42 A1 Çorlu Turkey
90 C2 Cormatin France
89 F2 Cormeilles France
107 H3 Cormons Italy
163 G3 Cormontibo French Guiana
86 D3 Cormontreuil France
23 □1 Cormoran Reef reef Palau
137 J4 Cormorant Manitoba Canada
109 H3 Cornacchia, Monte mt. Italy
99 H2 Cornago Spain
131 G3 Cornelia South Africa
168 C5 Cornélio Procópio Brazil
163 F2 Corneliskondre Surinam
148 B3 Cornell Wisconsin U.S.A.
102 F3 Cornellá de Llobregat Spain
98 D1 Cornellana Spain
139 J4 Corner Brook Newfoundland Canada
13 F4 Corner Inlet b. Victoria Australia
103 B7 Corneros r. Spain
53 C3 Cornești Moldova
82 B2 Cornettes de Bise, Les mts France/Switzerland
107 F3 Cornetto mt. Italy
108 C1 Cornia r. Italy
106 E4 Corniglio Italy
86 D3 Cornillet, Mont h. France
87 F5 Cornimont France
154 A2 Corning California U.S.A.
146 E3 Corning New York U.S.A.
Corn Is i. see Maíz, Is del
108 B3 Corno Bianco mt. Italy
83 F2 Corno dei Tre Signori mt. Italy
83 F2 Corno di Campo mt. Italy/Switzerland
109 F2 Corno, Monte mt. Italy
88 A3 Cornouaille reg. France
107 G3 Cornuda Italy
99 G2 Cornudilla Spain
91 B5 Cornus France
62 B4 Cornwall div. England U.K.
141 H4 Cornwall Ontario Canada
135 J2 Cornwall I. i. N.W.T. Canada
135 J2 Cornwallis I. i. N.W.T. Canada
12 D3 Corny Pt pt S. Australia Australia
162 D1 Coro Venezuela
169 G3 Coroaci Brazil
166 D1 Coroatá Brazil
164 C3 Corocoro Bolivia
67 B4 Corofin Rep. of Ireland
164 C3 Coroico Bolivia
168 E3 Coromandel Brazil
38 C4 Coromandel Coast coastal area India
8 E2 Coromandel Peninsula pen. New Zealand
8 E2 Coromandel Range h. New Zealand
23 B3 Coron Philippines
102 B4 Corona r. Portugal
154 D5 Corona California U.S.A.
12 E2 Corona New South Wales Australia
154 D5 Coronado California U.S.A.
156 K7 Coronado, B. de b. Panama
171 B5 Coronados, G. de los inlet Chile
137 G4 Coronation Alberta Canada
134 G3 Coronation Gulf b. N.W.T. Canada
179 B1 Coronation I. i. S. Orkney Is Atlantic Ocean
16 D2 Coronation Is is Western Australia Australia
136 C3 Coronation Island i. Alaska U.S.A.
23 B4 Coron Bay b. Philippines
173 G1 Coronda Argentina
172 A4 Coronel Chile
172 E2 Coronel Alzogaray Argentina
173 H3 Coronel Brandsen Argentina
173 G5 Coronel Dorrego Argentina
169 G3 Coronel Fabriciano Brazil
172 E6 Coronel Francisco Sosa Argentina
172 E2 Coronel Moldes Argentina
169 G2 Coronel Murta Brazil
165 E5 Coronel Oviedo Paraguay
166 B4 Coronel Ponce Brazil
173 G4 Coronel Pringles Argentina
168 A5 Coronel Sapucaia Brazil
173 G4 Coronel Suárez Argentina
173 J4 Coronel Vidal Argentina
164 A1 Corongo Peru
173 K1 Coronilla Uruguay
114 B2 Çorovodë Albania
13 F3 Corowa New South Wales Australia
157 H5 Corozal Belize
158 D5 Corozal Colombia
159 □3 Corozal Pt pt Trinidad Trinidad and Tobago
91 D4 Corps France
151 D7 Corpus Christi Texas U.S.A.
151 D6 Corpus Christi, L. l. Texas U.S.A.
164 C3 Corque Bolivia
172 A5 Corral Chile
99 G5 Corral de Almaguer Spain
173 F2 Corral de Bustos Argentina
101 F1 Corral de Cantos mt. Spain
172 D1 Corral de Isaac Argentina
97 □ Corralejo Canary Is Spain
172 D1 Corralitos, Mte mt. Argentina
108 B4 Corrasi, Punta mt. Sardegna Italy
67 B3 Corraun Peninsula pen. Rep. of Ireland
82 A1 Corre France
107 E4 Correggio Italy
168 C2 Córrego do Ouro Brazil
169 G3 Córrego Novo Brazil
168 C3 Corrente r. Brazil
166 D3 Corrente r. Brazil
166 C3 Corrente r. Goiás Brazil
166 C3 Corrente Brazil
169 G3 Corrente Grande r. Brazil
167 B4 Correntes r. Brazil
168 A2 Correntes Brazil
Correntina r. see Éguas
166 D3 Correntina Brazil
92 D3 Corrèze div. Limousin France
92 D3 Corrèze r. France
92 D3 Corrèze France
67 B3 Corrib, Lough l. Rep. of Ireland
107 H5 Corridonia Italy
170 E2 Corrientes div. Argentina
170 E2 Corrientes r. Argentina
170 E2 Corrientes Argentina
173 J5 Corrientes, C. c. Argentina
156 D4 Corrientes, C. c. Mexico
162 B2 Corrientes, Cabo pt Colombia
158 A2 Corrientes, Cabo pt Cuba
151 E6 Corrigan Texas U.S.A.
17 B7 Corrigin Western Australia Australia
62 C2 Corris Wales U.K.
163 F2 Corriverton Guyana
146 D4 Corry Pennsylvania U.S.A.
13 F4 Corryong Victoria Australia
106 B4 Corsaglia r. Italy
108 B2 Corse div. France
108 A2 Corse i. France
108 B1 Corse, Cap c. Corse France
108 A3 Corse-du-Sud div. Corse France
64 D2 Corserine h. Scotland U.K.
62 D3 Corsham England U.K.
Corsica i. see Corse
151 D5 Corsicana Texas U.S.A.
106 D3 Corsico Italy
64 E2 Corsock Scotland U.K.
Cort Adelaer, Kap headland see Kangeq
108 B2 Corte Corse France
100 D2 Corte de Peleas Spain
98 B2 Cortegada Spain
100 D3 Cortegana Spain
106 C4 Cortemilia Italy
83 F2 Corteno Golgi Italy
106 D3 Corteolona Italy
102 C4 Cortes de Aragón Spain
101 H3 Cortes de Baza Spain
155 H3 Cortez Colorado U.S.A.
154 D1 Cortez Mts mts Nevada U.S.A.
102 D3 Cortiella r. Spain
101 F1 Cortijo de Arriba Spain
101 H2 Cortijos Nuevos Spain
107 G2 Cortina d'Ampezzo Italy
147 E3 Cortland New York U.S.A.
107 F3 Corto, Lago del l. Italy
63 H2 Corton England U.K.
107 F5 Cortona Italy
100 B2 Coruche Portugal
42 E1 Çoruh r. Turkey
42 C1 Çorum Turkey
168 D2 Corumbá r. Brazil
165 E3 Corumbá Brazil
168 D1 Corumbá de Goiás Brazil
168 D3 Corumbaíba Brazil
168 C6 Corumbataí r. Brazil
169 J2 Corumbaú, Pta pt Brazil
112 E1 Corund Romania
166 E3 Coruripe Brazil
152 B2 Corvallis Oregon U.S.A.
107 F2 Corvara in Badia Italy
62 D2 Corve Dale v. England U.K.
103 B7 Corvera Spain
100 □ Corvo i. Azores Portugal
62 C2 Corwen Wales U.K.
102 B4 Cosa Spain
156 D3 Cosalá Mexico
164 C3 Cosapa Bolivia
164 C3 Coscaya Chile
111 F3 Coscile r. Italy
111 F3 Cosenza div. Calabria Italy
111 F3 Cosenza Cosenza Italy
64 E1 Coshieville Scotland U.K.
146 C4 Coshocton Ohio U.S.A.
99 G4 Coslada Spain
168 E5 Cosmópolis Brazil
92 E1 Cosne-Cours-sur-Loire France
92 E2 Cosne-d'Allier France
172 E1 Cosquín Argentina
106 C3 Cossato Italy
89 E4 Cossé-le-Vivien France
89 G4 Cosson r. France
82 B2 Cossonay Switzerland
100 A2 Costa Bela coastal area Portugal
103 C6 Costa Blanca coastal area Spain
102 G3 Costa Brava coastal area France/Spain
100 B2 Costa da Galé coastal area Portugal
102 D4 Costa de Fora coastal area Spain
100 C3 Costa de la Luz reg. Spain
103 C5 Costa del Azahar coastal area Spain
101 F4 Costa del Sol coastal area Spain
156 K6 Costa de Mosquitos reg. Nicaragua
102 F3 Costa Dorada coastal area Spain
173 G2 Costa Grande Argentina
164 D2 Costa Marques Brazil
165 E2 Costa Pinheiro, Cap r. Brazil
133 K8 Costa Rica country Central America
168 B3 Costa Rica Brazil
156 D3 Costa Rica Mexico
108 A5 Costa Verde coastal area Sardegna Italy
99 F1 Costa Verde reg. Spain
79 L6 Coşteiu Romania
53 B3 Costești Moldova
112 F1 Costești Romania
147 J2 Costigan Maine U.S.A.
106 C4 Costigliole d'Asti Italy
73 H4 Coswig Sachsen-Anhalt Germany
73 J4 Coswig Sachsen Germany
23 C5 Cotabato Philippines
164 C4 Cotagaita Bolivia
164 B3 Cotahuasi Peru
169 H3 Cotaxé r. Brazil
86 C4 Côte Champenoise reg. France
93 A5 Côte d'Argent reg. France
91 F5 Côte d'Azur reg. France
86 D4 Côte des Bars reg. France
117 D5 Côte d'Ivoire country Africa
90 C1 Côte-d'Or div. France
90 C2 Côte d'Or reg. France
166 D3 Cotegipe Brazil
136 C3 Cote, Mt mt. Alaska U.S.A.
88 D2 Cotentin pen. France
88 C2 Côtes-d'Armor div. France
87 E3 Côtes de Meuse ridge France
87 E4 Côtes de Moselle reg. France
112 E2 Cotești Romania
68 D2 Cothen Netherlands
62 B3 Cothi r. Wales U.K.
102 D2 Cotiella mt. Spain
91 E5 Cotignac France
163 E3 Cotingo r. Brazil
53 C3 Cotiujeni Moldova
53 C3 Cotiujenii Mici Moldova
112 F1 Cotnari Romania
123 E5 Cotonou Benin
127 □3 Coton, Pt pt Rodrigues I. Mauritius
162 B4 Cotopaxi, Vol. volcano Ecuador
111 F3 Cotronei Italy
62 D3 Cotswold Hills h. England U.K.
152 B3 Cottage Grove Oregon U.S.A.
109 E2 Cottanello Italy
73 K4 Cottbus Germany
38 B3 Cotteliar r. India
63 G2 Cottenham England U.K.
179 □ Cotter, C. c. Kerguelen Indian Ocean
63 F2 Cottesmore England U.K.
163 G3 Cottica Surinam
155 H5 Cotton City New Mexico U.S.A.
155 F4 Cottonwood Arizona U.S.A.
155 G4 Cottonwood Wash r. Arizona U.S.A.
159 E3 Cotuí Dominican Rep.
151 D6 Cotulla Texas U.S.A.
91 B3 Coubon France
92 A3 Coubre, Pte de la pt France
90 C2 Couches France
91 B4 Coucouron France
86 C3 Coucy-le-Château-Auffrique France
86 B1 Coudekerque-Branche France
146 D4 Coudersport Pennsylvania U.S.A.
12 D4 Couëdic, C. de c. S. Australia Australia
88 D4 Couëron France
88 D3 Couesnon r. France
92 C2 Couhé France
93 E6 Couiza France
89 F3 Coulaines France
90 B1 Coulanges-la-Vineuse France
90 B1 Coulanges-sur-Yonne France
92 E2 Couleuvre France
89 H4 Coullons France
179 B1 Coulman I. i. Antarctica
90 C1 Coulmier-le-Sec France
86 A2 Coulogne France
121 F3 Couloir 1 well Algeria
92 C2 Coulombiers France
86 C4 Coulommiers France
91 D5 Coulon r. France
141 G3 Coulonge r. Québec Canada
92 B2 Coulonges-sur-l'Autize France
92 C3 Coulounieix-Chamiers France
64 B2 Coul Point pt Scotland U.K.
64 D1 Coulport Scotland U.K.
154 B3 Coulterville California U.S.A.
152 C2 Council Idaho U.S.A.
150 E3 Council Bluffs Iowa U.S.A.
66 E4 Coupar Angus Scotland U.K.
89 E3 Couptrain France
137 G2 Courageous Lake l. N.W.T. Canada
163 F3 Courantyne r. Guyana
179 □ Courbet, Péninsule pen. Kerguelen Indian Ocean
82 B1 Courchaton France
91 E3 Courchevel France
89 G4 Cour-Cheverny France
92 B2 Courçon France
86 D3 Courcy France
82 C1 Courgenay Switzerland
54 B4 Courland Lagoon lag. Lithuania/Rus. Fed.
92 B2 Courlay France
82 B3 Courmayeur Italy
90 B3 Cournon-d'Auvergne France
90 B3 Courpière France
8 □2 Courrejolles Pt pt Campbell I. New Zealand
82 C1 Courrendlin Switzerland
69 A4 Courrières France
91 B5 Coursan France
91 F5 Coursegoules France
89 E2 Courseulles-sur-Mer France
90 B1 Courson-les-Carrières France
82 C1 Court Switzerland
82 C1 Courtelary Switzerland
136 E5 Courtenay B.C. Canada
86 C4 Courtenay France
91 C4 Courthézon France
67 C5 Courtmacsherry Rep. of Ireland
89 F3 Courtomer France
67 E4 Courtown Rep. of Ireland
Courtrai see Kortrijk
69 C4 Court-St-Étienne Belgium
89 G3 Courville-sur-Eure France
82 A2 Cousance France
93 C6 Couserans reg. France
151 E5 Coushatta Louisiana U.S.A.
90 C1 Cousin r. France
127 □1 Cousin Is is Seychelles
86 D5 Coussegrey France
87 E4 Coussey France
125 B5 Coutada do Ambriz res. Angola
125 D7 Coutada Pública do Longa-Mavinga res. Angola
125 D7 Coutada Pública do Luengué res. Angola
125 D7 Coutada Pública do Luiana res. Angola
125 D7 Coutada Pública do Mucusso res. Angola
88 D2 Coutances France
89 E3 Couterne France
169 G3 Couto de Magalhães de Minas Brazil
166 C2 Couto Magalhães Brazil
92 B3 Coutras France
92 B3 Couture r. France
138 E2 Couture, Lac l. Québec Canada
159 □3 Couva Trinidad and Tobago
82 B2 Couvet Switzerland
69 C4 Couvin Belgium
93 C4 Couze r. France
92 D3 Couzeix France
99 H3 Covaleda Spain
99 G2 Covarrubias Spain
112 F2 Covasna Romania
123 E5 Covè Benin
155 F2 Cove Fort Utah U.S.A.
140 E4 Cove I. i. Ontario Canada
173 H3 Covelo Argentina
146 E5 Cove Mts h. Pennsylvania U.S.A.
63 E2 Coventry England U.K.
147 E5 Cove Point Maryland U.S.A.
65 G3 Cover r. England U.K.
98 C4 Covilhã Portugal
145 D5 Covington Georgia U.S.A.
148 D5 Covington Indiana U.S.A.
146 A5 Covington Kentucky U.S.A.
145 B5 Covington Tennessee U.S.A.
146 D6 Covington Virginia U.S.A.
140 D3 Cow r. Ontario Canada
13 F3 Cowal, L. l. New South Wales Australia
17 C6 Cowan, L. salt flat Western Australia Australia
141 J4 Cowansville Québec Canada
32 B1 Cowargarze China
62 C3 Cowbridge Wales U.K.
17 B6 Cowcowing Lakes salt flat Western Australia Australia
66 E4 Cowdenbeath Scotland U.K.
12 D3 Cowell S. Australia Australia
63 E4 Cowes England U.K.
13 F4 Cowes Victoria Australia
63 F4 Cowfold England U.K.
65 F3 Cow Green Res. resr England U.K.
15 F5 Cowley Queensland Australia
146 D5 Cowpasture r. Virginia U.S.A.
13 G3 Cowra New South Wales Australia
93 D5 Cox France
166 D3 Coxá r. Brazil
173 K1 Coxilha de Santana h. Brazil/Uruguay
167 B6 Coxilha Grande hills Brazil
168 A3 Coxim r. Brazil
168 A3 Coxim Brazil
14 C2 Cox R. r. Northern Terr. Australia
147 G3 Coxsackie New York U.S.A.
37 G5 Cox's Bazar Bangladesh
65 G3 Coxwold England U.K.
122 B5 Coyah Guinea
171 C7 Coy Aike Argentina
154 D4 Coyote Lake l. California U.S.A.
155 E5 Coyote Peak summit Arizona U.S.A.
154 C3 Coyote Peak summit California U.S.A.
156 C3 Coyote, Pta pt Mexico
156 D4 Coyotitán Mexico
157 E5 Coyuca de Benitez Mexico
92 B3 Cozes France
37 F2 Cozhê China
153 D6 Cozón, Co mt. Mexico
157 J4 Cozumel Mexico
157 J4 Cozumel, I. de i. Mexico
108 B3 Cozzano Corse France
111 F3 Cozzo del Pellegrino mt. Italy
67 E4 Craanford Rep. of Ireland
15 E1 Crab I. i. Queensland Australia
127 □3 Crab I. i. Rodrigues I. Mauritius
13 G3 Craboon New South Wales Australia
88 B4 Crach France
15 G5 Cracow Queensland Australia
13 F5 Cradle Mountain Lake St Clair Nat. Park nat. park Tasmania Australia
12 D2 Cradock S. Australia Australia
131 E6 Cradock South Africa
8 E2 Cradock Channel chan. New Zealand
83 F3 Craffaro r. Italy
130 E3 Crafthole South Africa
136 C3 Craig Alaska U.S.A.
152 F3 Craig Colorado U.S.A.
66 C3 Craig Scotland U.K.
67 E2 Craigavon Northern Ireland U.K.
66 E3 Craigellachie Scotland U.K.
62 C2 Craig Goch Res. resr Wales U.K.
13 F4 Craigieburn Victoria Australia
66 C4 Craignure Scotland U.K.
146 D5 Craigsville Virginia U.S.A.
66 F4 Crail Scotland U.K.
74 F3 Crailsheim Germany
112 D2 Craiova Romania
65 G2 Cramlington England U.K.
130 C3 Cramond South Africa
64 A2 Crana r. Rep. of Ireland
147 F2 Cranberry L. l. New York U.S.A.
147 F2 Cranberry Lake New York U.S.A.
62 D4 Cranborne Chase forest England U.K.
13 F4 Cranbourne Victoria Australia
136 F5 Cranbrook B.C. Canada
17 B7 Cranbrook Western Australia Australia
148 C3 Crandon Wisconsin U.S.A.
152 C3 Crane Oregon U.S.A.
151 C6 Crane Texas U.S.A.
148 A1 Crane Lake Minnesota U.S.A.
159 □9 Crane, The Barbados Caribbean
64 B3 Cranfield Point pt Northern Ireland U.K.
90 E3 Cran-Gevrier France
63 F3 Cranleigh England U.K.
82 C2 Crans-sur-Sierre Switzerland
147 H4 Cranston Rhode Island U.S.A.
89 E4 Craon France
86 C3 Craonne France
91 B3 Craponne-sur-Arzon France
179 B4 Crary Ice Rise ice feature Antarctica
179 A4 Crary Mts mts Antarctica
79 M4 Crasna r. Romania
53 C3 Crasnoe Moldova
152 B3 Crater L. l. Oregon U.S.A.
152 B3 Crater Lake Nat. Pk Oregon U.S.A.
152 D3 Craters of the Moon Nat. Mon. nat. park Idaho U.S.A.
166 D2 Crateús Brazil
111 F3 Crati r. Italy
166 E2 Crato Brazil
100 C1 Crato Portugal
91 C5 Crau reg. France
90 B1 Cravant France
166 E2 Cravari r. Brazil
62 D2 Craven Arms England U.K.
168 E4 Cravinhos Brazil
162 C2 Cravo Norte Colombia
150 C3 Crawford Nebraska U.S.A.
64 E2 Crawfordjohn Scotland U.K.
148 D5 Crawfordsville Indiana U.S.A.
145 C6 Crawfordville Florida U.S.A.
63 F3 Crawley England U.K.
145 □1 Crawl, The pt Bermuda
152 E2 Crazy Mts mountain range Montana U.S.A.
66 D4 Creag Meagaidh mt. Scotland U.K.
88 D2 Créances France
90 C1 Créancey France
137 H4 Crean L. l. Saskatchewan Canada
90 C2 Crêches-sur-Saône France
131 G2 Crecy South Africa
86 A2 Crécy-en-Ponthieu France
86 B4 Crécy-la-Chapelle France
86 C3 Crécy-sur-Serre France
62 D2 Credenhill England U.K.
62 C4 Crediton England U.K.
137 H3 Cree r. Saskatchewan Canada
156 D3 Creel Mexico
137 H3 Cree Lake l. Saskatchewan Canada
67 D1 Creeslough Rep. of Ireland
67 B3 Cregganbaun Rep. of Ireland
74 F3 Creglingen Germany
137 J4 Creighton Saskatchewan Canada
131 G5 Creighton South Africa
86 B3 Creil France
91 B4 Creissels France
106 D3 Crema Italy
90 D3 Crémieu France
73 F3 Cremlingen Germany
106 E3 Cremona div. Lombardia Italy
106 E3 Cremona Cremona Italy
81 H4 Črenšovci Slovenia
93 B4 Créon France
87 E4 Crépey France
86 C3 Crépy France
86 B3 Crépy-en-Valois France
107 J4 Cres i. Croatia
107 J4 Cres Croatia
152 A3 Crescent City California U.S.A.
27 □ Crescent I. i. Hong Kong China
106 C3 Crescentino Italy
155 H2 Crescent Junction Utah U.S.A.
154 B1 Crescent Mills California U.S.A.
155 E4 Crescent Peak summit Nevada U.S.A.
148 A4 Cresco Iowa U.S.A.
173 G2 Crespo Argentina
99 F4 Crespos Spain
92 D3 Cressensac France
82 C1 Cressier Switzerland
14 C3 Cresswell watercourse Northern Terr. Australia
91 D4 Crest France
136 F5 Creston B.C. Canada
150 E3 Creston Iowa U.S.A.
152 F3 Creston Wyoming U.S.A.
145 C6 Crestview Florida U.S.A.
90 E3 Crest-Voland France
147 F5 Crestwood Village New Jersey U.S.A.
63 E1 Creswell England U.K.
13 E4 Creswick Victoria Australia
80 D4 Creta Forata, Mte mt. Italy
90 D2 Crêt de la Neige mt. France
90 D3 Crêt de Pont mt. France
90 D2 Crêt du Nu mt. France
Crete i. see Kriti
86 B4 Créteil France
90 E1 Crêt Monniot mt. France
102 D4 Creu de Santos, La mt. Spain
89 E2 Creully France
102 G2 Creus, Cap de pt Spain
92 E2 Creuse div. Limousin France
92 C2 Creuse r. France
75 G3 Creußen Germany
87 F3 Creutzwald France
72 F4 Creuzburg Germany
107 F4 Crevalcore Italy
86 B3 Crèvecœur-le-Grand France
103 C6 Crevillente Spain
103 C6 Crevillente, Sa de mountain range Spain
106 C2 Crevoladossola Italy
62 D1 Crewe England U.K.
146 D6 Crewe Virginia U.S.A.
62 D4 Crewkerne England U.K.
66 D4 Crianlarich Scotland U.K.
62 B2 Criccieth Wales U.K.
167 C6 Criciúma Brazil
62 C3 Crickhowell Wales U.K.
53 C3 Cricova Moldova
66 E4 Crieff Scotland U.K.
89 G1 Criel-sur-Mer France
66 E6 Criffell h. Scotland U.K.
107 J3 Crikvenica Croatia
Crimea pen. see Krym
75 H2 Crimmitschau Germany
66 G3 Crimond Scotland U.K.
64 C1 Crinan Scotland U.K.
89 F2 Criquetot-l'Esneval France
112 G2 Crișan Romania
147 F6 Crisfield Maryland U.S.A.
106 B4 Crissolo Italy
166 C3 Cristalândia Brazil
168 E2 Cristalina Brazil
163 F5 Cristalino r. Brazil
Cristalino r. see Mariembero
80 D4 Cristallo mt. Italy
124 B3 Cristal, Monts de mountain range Equatorial Guinea/Gabon
168 D2 Cristianópolis Brazil
166 D2 Cristino Castro Brazil
156 L7 Cristóbal Panama
162 C1 Cristóbal Colón, P. mt. Colombia
162 □ Cristóbal, Pta pt Galapagos Is Ecuador
106 C4 Cristoforo Colombo airport Italy
112 E1 Cristuru Secuiesc Romania
53 C3 Criuleni Moldova
73 G2 Crivitz Germany
166 C3 Crixás r. Brazil
166 C3 Crixás Brazil
166 C3 Crixás Açu r. Brazil
166 B3 Crixás Mirim r. Brazil
114 C1 Crna r. Macedonia
81 F4 Črna Slovenia
112 B3 Crna Gora div. Yugoslavia
112 C3 Crna Gora mts Macedonia/Yugoslavia
112 D3 Crna Trava Yugoslavia
112 D2 Crni Vrh mt. Yugoslavia
104 E3 Črnomelj Slovenia
67 B3 Croagh Patrick h. Rep. of Ireland
13 G4 Croajingolong Nat. Park nat. park Victoria Australia
48 G4 Croatia country Europe
107 F2 Croce, Monte mt. Italy
64 E2 Crocketford Scotland U.K.
151 E6 Crockett Texas U.S.A.
131 F5 Crocodile r. South Africa
92 E3 Crocq France
107 G2 Croda dei Toni mt. Italy
107 G2 Croda Rossa mt. Italy
106 C2 Crodo Italy
147 F3 Croghan New York U.S.A.
91 D5 Croisette, Cap c. France
88 C4 Croisic, Pte de pt France
86 B2 Croisilles France
14 C1 Croker I. i. Northern Terr. Australia
91 D3 Crolles France
66 D3 Cromarty Scotland U.K.
66 D3 Cromarty Firth est. Scotland U.K.
66 E3 Cromdale, Hills of h. Scotland U.K.
63 H2 Cromer England U.K.
9 B6 Cromwell New Zealand
9 C5 Cronadun New Zealand
64 A3 Cronamuck Mtn h. Rep. of Ireland
91 B3 Cronce r. France
65 G3 Crook England U.K.
146 D4 Crooked Creek Reservoir resr Pennsylvania U.S.A.
27 □ Crooked I. i. Hong Kong China
158 D2 Crooked I. i. The Bahamas
158 D2 Crooked I. Passage chan. The Bahamas
148 B1 Crooked Lake l. Canada/U.S.A.
65 F2 Crookham England U.K.
67 B5 Crookhaven Rep. of Ireland
150 D2 Crookston Minnesota U.S.A.
13 G3 Crookwell New South Wales Australia
67 C4 Croom Rep. of Ireland
111 F3 Cropalati Italy
111 F4 Cropani Italy
13 G2 Croppa Cr. New South Wales Australia
15 E2 Crosbie r. Queensland Australia
65 E4 Crosby England U.K.
137 J5 Crosby N. Dakota U.S.A.
123 F5 Cross r. Nigeria
64 A4 Crossakeel Rep. of Ireland
137 L2 Cross Bay b. N.W.T. Canada
65 E3 Crosscanonby England U.K.
145 D6 Cross City Florida U.S.A.
147 K1 Cross Creek New Brunswick Canada
151 E5 Crossett Arkansas U.S.A.
65 F3 Cross Fell h. England U.K.
67 F2 Crossgar Northern Ireland U.K.
62 C2 Crossgates Wales U.K.
64 D2 Crosshands Scotland U.K.
67 C5 Crosshaven Rep. of Ireland
62 B2 Cross Inn Wales U.K.
137 K4 Cross Lake l. Manitoba Canada
146 E3 Cross Lake l. New York U.S.A.
137 K4 Cross Lake Manitoba Canada
9 D5 Crossley, Mt mt. New Zealand
67 E2 Crossmaglen Northern Ireland U.K.
155 E4 Crossman Peak summit Arizona U.S.A.
123 F5 Cross River div. Nigeria
136 B3 Cross Sound chan. Alaska U.S.A.
148 E3 Cross Village Michigan U.S.A.
145 C5 Crossville Tennessee U.S.A.
149 F4 Croswell Michigan U.S.A.
111 G3 Crotone Italy
91 E4 Crots France
75 H2 Crottendorf Germany
173 G4 Crotto Argentina
63 G3 Crouch r. England U.K.
86 C3 Crouy France
86 C3 Crouy-sur-Ourcq France
13 F2 Crowal watercourse New South Wales Australia
63 G3 Crowborough England U.K.
13 F2 Crowl watercourse New South Wales Australia
63 F2 Crowland England U.K.
65 H4 Crowle England U.K.
151 E6 Crowley Louisiana U.S.A.
154 C3 Crowley, Lake l. California U.S.A.
148 D5 Crown Point Indiana U.S.A.
147 G3 Crown Point New York U.S.A.
179 D4 Crown Prince Olav Coast coastal area Antarctica
179 C3 Crown Princess Martha Coast coastal area Antarctica
159 □2 Crown Pt pt Tobago Trinidad and Tobago
15 H5 Crows Nest Queensland Australia
136 G5 Crowsnest Pass Alberta Canada
62 B3 Croyde England U.K.
63 F3 Croydon England U.K.
15 E3 Croydon Queensland Australia
179 □ Croy, I. de i. Kerguelen Indian Ocean
175 H6 Crozet Basin sea feature Indian Ocean
175 H7 Crozet, Îles is Indian Ocean
175 G6 Crozet Plateau sea feature Indian Ocean
134 F2 Crozier Chan. chan. N.W.T. Canada
179 □ Crozier, Mt h. Kerguelen Indian Ocean
88 A3 Crozon France
88 A3 Crozon, Presqu'île de pen. France
91 C4 Cruas France
112 E1 Crucea Romania
164 B2 Crucero Peru
66 G3 Cruden Bay Scotland U.K.
157 F3 Cruillas Mexico
67 E2 Crumlin Northern Ireland U.K.
65 E3 Crummock Water l. England U.K.
90 E2 Cruseilles France
67 C4 Crusheen Rep. of Ireland

87 E3 Crusnes r. France
99 H5 Cruz mt. Spain
173 G2 Cruz Alta Argentina
167 B6 Cruz Alta Brazil
145 □3 Cruz Bay Virgin Is Caribbean
158 C3 Cruz, Cabo c. Cuba
172 E1 Cruz del Eje Argentina
169 F5 Cruzeiro Brazil
168 B5 Cruzeiro do Oeste Brazil
164 B1 Cruzeiro do Sul Acre Brazil
168 B5 Cruzeiro do Sul Paraná Brazil
155 H5 Cruzville New Mexico U.S.A.
90 C1 Cruzy-le-Châtel France
112 B2 Crvenka Yugoslavia
62 B3 Crymych Wales U.K.
136 E3 Crysdale, Mt mt. B.C. Canada
12 D3 Crystal Brook S. Australia Australia
151 D6 Crystal City Texas U.S.A.
148 C2 Crystal Falls Michigan U.S.A.
148 C4 Crystal Lake Illinois U.S.A.
78 F5 Csákánydoroszió Hungary
79 K5 Csanádi-hát h. Hungary
79 M4 Csenger Hungary
81 H3 Csepreg Hungary
79 K3 Cserehát mts Hungary
79 J4 Cserhát h. Hungary
79 K5 Cserkeszőlő Hungary
78 F5 Cserta r. Hungary
78 F5 Csesztreg Hungary
79 H4 Csókakő Hungary
79 K5 Csongrád div. Hungary
79 K5 Csongrád Hungary
78 G4 Csorna Hungary
81 H4 Csörnyeföld Hungary
81 H4 Csörötnek Hungary
78 G5 Csurgó Hungary
173 F5 Cta. Brightman inlet Argentina
98 D2 Cua r. Spain
159 F5 Cúa Venezuela
98 E4 Cuacos de Yuste Spain
171 C5 Cuadrada, Sierra h. Argentina
172 C3 Cuadro Berregas Argentina
98 C3 Cualedro Spain
25 D5 Cua Lon r. Vietnam
129 F1 Cuamba Mozambique
125 D7 Cuando r. Angola
125 C7 Cuando Cubango div. Angola
125 C7 Cuangar Angola
125 C5 Cuango r. Angola
125 C5 Cuango Lunda Norte Angola
125 C5 Cuango Uíge Angola
125 C5 Cuanza r. Angola
125 C5 Cuanza Norte div. Angola
125 C6 Cuanza Sul div. Angola
173 J1 Cuareim r. Brazil/Uruguay
173 J1 Cuaro r. Uruguay
172 F2 Cuarto r. Argentina
125 C7 Cuatir r. Angola
156 E3 Cuatro Ciénegas Mexico
164 D3 Cuatro Ojos Bolivia
172 E2 Cuatro Vientos Argentina
156 D2 Cuauhtémoc Mexico
157 F5 Cuautla Mexico
162 B2 Cuayabal Colombia
133 L8 Cuba country Caribbean
148 B5 Cuba Illinois U.S.A.
153 F4 Cuba New Mexico U.S.A.
100 C2 Cuba Portugal
155 F6 Cubabi, Cerro summit Mexico
159 F5 Cubagua, I. i. Venezuela
125 B6 Cubal r. Angola
125 B6 Cubal Angola
172 F6 Cubanea Argentina
125 C7 Cubango r. Angola/Namibia
162 C2 Cubara Colombia
169 E5 Cubatão Brazil
102 D3 Cubells Spain
137 J4 Cub Hills h. Saskatchewan Canada
101 G3 Cubillas r. Spain
99 G2 Cubillo r. Spain
99 G2 Cubo de Bureba Spain
42 C1 Çubuk Turkey
92 B4 Cubzac-les-Ponts France
108 B4 Cuccuru su Pirastru h. Sardegna Italy
125 C6 Cuchi r. Angola
125 C6 Cuchi Angola
173 K2 Cuchilla h. Uruguay
173 K2 Cuchilla Caraghuatá Uruguay
173 J2 Cuchilla de Haedo h. Uruguay
170 E3 Cuchilla del Daymán h. Uruguay
173 H1 Cuchilla de Montiel h. Argentina
173 J2 Cuchilla de Peralta Uruguay
170 E3 Cuchilla Grande h. Uruguay
170 E3 Cuchilla Grande del Durazno h. Uruguay
170 E3 Cuchilla Grande Inferior h. Uruguay
173 J1 Cuchilla Negra h. Brazil/Uruguay
172 E5 Cuchillo-Có Argentina
63 F3 Cuckfield England U.K.
63 G4 Cuckmere r. England U.K.
146 E6 Cuckoo Virginia U.S.A.
162 D3 Cucuí Brazil
125 C6 Cucumbi Angola
162 C2 Cúcuta Colombia
102 C3 Cucutas mt. Spain
38 B4 Cuddalore India
38 B3 Cuddapah India
98 D1 Cudillero Spain
137 H4 Cudworth Saskatchewan Canada
17 B5 Cue Western Australia Australia
125 C7 Cuebe r. Angola
125 C6 Cuelei r. Angola
99 F3 Cuéllar Spain
125 C6 Cuemba Angola
101 H1 Cuenca div. Castilla - La Mancha Spain
162 B4 Cuenca Ecuador
99 H4 Cuenca Spain
172 C5 Cuenca del Añelo reg. Argentina
156 E3 Cuencamé Mexico
103 B5 Cuerdas, Sierra de las mountain range Spain
157 F5 Cuernavaca Mexico
151 D6 Cuero Texas U.S.A.
91 E5 Cuers France
101 F1 Cuerva Spain
102 B4 Cuervo r. Spain
154 B4 Cuesta Pass pass California U.S.A.
157 F4 Cuetzalán Mexico
101 E4 Cuevas del Becerro Spain
101 H3 Cuevas del Campo Spain
103 D4 Cuevas de Vinromá Spain
88 D4 Cugand France
91 D5 Cuges-les-Pins France
112 D2 Cugir Romania
108 A4 Cuglieri Sardegna Italy
93 D5 Cugnaux France
125 C5 Cugo r. Angola
165 E3 Cuiabá r. Brazil
163 F5 Cuiaba Brazil
166 A4 Cuiabá Brazil
166 A3 Cuiabá de Larga Brazil
157 F5 Cuicatlan Mexico
7 □16 Cuidado, Pta pt Easter I. Chile
68 D3 Cuijk Netherlands
157 H6 Cuilapa Guatemala
66 B3 Cuillin Hills mts Scotland U.K.
66 B3 Cuillin Sound chan. Scotland U.K.
125 C5 Cuilo Angola
31 J3 Cuiluan China
125 B5 Cuimba Angola
125 B6 Cuio Angola
90 D2 Cuiseaux France
90 C2 Cuisery France
169 H3 Cuité r. Brazil
166 E2 Cuité Brazil
125 C7 Cuito r. Angola
125 C7 Cuito Cuanavale Angola
157 E5 Cuitzeo, L. de l. Mexico
163 E4 Cuiuni r. Brazil
112 D2 Cujmir Romania
25 C6 Cukai Malaysia
114 B3 Çukë Albania
42 E2 Çukurca Turkey
92 E2 Culan France
24 E4 Cu Lao Cham i. Vietnam
24 E4 Cu Lao Re i. Vietnam
25 E5 Cu Lao Thu i. Vietnam
152 F1 Culbertson Montana U.S.A.
150 C3 Culbertson Nebraska U.S.A.
13 F3 Culcairn New South Wales Australia
145 □3 Culebra, Isla de i. Puerto Rico
98 D3 Culebra, Sierra de la mountain range Spain
68 D3 Culemborg Netherlands
42 F2 Culfa Azerbaijan
13 F2 Culgoa r. New South Wales Australia
156 D3 Culiacán Mexico
156 D3 Culiacancito Mexico
23 A4 Culion i. Philippines
23 A4 Culion Philippines
166 B3 Culiseiu r. Brazil
101 H3 Cullar r. Spain
101 H3 Cúllar-Baza Spain
66 F3 Cullen Scotland U.K.
15 E1 Cullen Pt pt Queensland Australia
103 C5 Cullera Spain
131 G2 Cullinan South Africa
66 □2 Cullivoe Scotland U.K.
145 C5 Cullman Alabama U.S.A.
62 C4 Cullompton England U.K.
42 E2 Çullu Turkey
82 B2 Cully Switzerland
67 E2 Cullybackey Northern Ireland U.K.
66 C2 Cul Mor h. Scotland U.K.
62 C4 Culmstock England U.K.
90 D3 Culoz France
146 D5 Culpeper Virginia U.S.A.
162 □ Culpepper, I. i. Galapagos Is Ecuador
164 D4 Culpina Bolivia
166 B3 Culuena r. Brazil
166 B3 Culuene r. Brazil
9 D5 Culverden New Zealand
17 D7 Culver, Pt pt Western Australia Australia
163 E1 Cumaná Venezuela
162 C3 Cumare, Cerro h. Colombia
168 D3 Cumari Brazil
162 B3 Cumbal, Nevado de mt. Colombia
144 C4 Cumberland r. Kentucky U.S.A.
146 D5 Cumberland Maryland U.S.A.
148 A3 Cumberland Wisconsin U.S.A.
Cumberland, Cape c. see Nahoï, Cap
137 J4 Cumberland House Saskatchewan Canada
15 G4 Cumberland Is is Queensland Australia
137 J4 Cumberland Lake l. Saskatchewan Canada
146 B6 Cumberland Mtn mountain range Kentucky/Tennessee U.S.A.
135 M3 Cumberland Peninsula pen. N.W.T. Canada
144 C4 Cumberland Plateau plat. U.S.A.
148 C2 Cumberland Pt pt Michigan U.S.A.
135 M3 Cumberland Sound chan. N.W.T. Canada
66 E5 Cumbernauld Scotland U.K.
100 D2 Cumbres Mayores Spain
65 F3 Cumbria div. England U.K.
163 F3 Cuminapanema r. Brazil
73 G2 Cumlosen Germany
154 A2 Cummings California U.S.A.
12 C3 Cummins S. Australia Australia
66 D5 Cumnock Scotland U.K.
156 C2 Cumpas Mexico
172 B3 Cumpeo Chile
42 C2 Çumra Turkey
156 C2 Cumuripa Mexico
169 J2 Cumuruxatiba Brazil
158 C2 Cunagua Cuba
173 K1 Cuñapiru r. Uruguay
67 D2 Cuncagh h. Rep. of Ireland/U.K.
172 A5 Cunco Chile
17 B6 Cunderdin Western Australia Australia
93 C4 Cunegès France
157 H6 Cunén Guatemala
125 C7 Cunene div. Angola
125 B7 Cunene r. Angola
106 B4 Cuneo div. Piemonte Italy
106 B4 Cuneo Cuneo Italy
25 E4 Cung Sơn Vietnam
125 C6 Cunhinga r. Angola
53 C3 Cunicea Moldova
90 B3 Cunlhat France
15 F6 Cunnamulla Queensland Australia
66 □2 Cunningsburgh Scotland U.K.
98 B2 Cuntis Spain
159 □3 Cunupia Trinidad and Tobago
106 B3 Cuorgnè Italy
66 E4 Cupar Scotland U.K.
166 A1 Cupari r. Brazil
53 B2 Cupcina Moldova
162 B2 Cupica Colombia
162 B2 Cupica, Golfo de b. Colombia
109 F1 Cupra Marittima Italy
112 C3 Ćuprija Yugoslavia
93 D5 Cuq-Toulza France
162 C5 Curaçá r. Brazil
166 E2 Curaçá r. Brazil
166 E2 Curaçá Brazil
158 □2 Curaçao airport Curaçao Netherlands Ant.
158 □2 Curaçao i. Netherlands Ant.
172 B5 Curacautín Chile
172 B2 Curacaví Chile
172 E5 Curacó r. Argentina
173 F4 Cura Malal, Sa de mt. Argentina
172 A4 Curanilahue Chile
172 F3 Curapaligüe Argentina
162 C4 Curaray r. Peru
172 B5 Curarrehue Chile
173 F3 Curarú Argentina
172 B2 Curaumilla, Punta pt Chile
90 B1 Cure r. France
153 F4 Curecanti Nat. Rec. Area res. Colorado U.S.A.
127 □4 Curepipe Mauritius
172 A3 Curepto Chile
172 B3 Curicó Chile
172 E6 Curicó, L. l. Argentina
162 D4 Curieuriari r. Brazil
127 □1 Curieuse I. i. Seychelles
166 D3 Curimata Brazil
166 E2 Curimataú r. Brazil
168 D6 Curitiba Brazil
167 B6 Curitibanos Brazil
168 C6 Curiúva Brazil
12 D2 Curnamona S. Australia Australia
125 B7 Curoca r. Angola
106 D4 Curone r. Italy
83 F2 Curon Venosta Italy
166 E2 Currais Novos Brazil
166 C1 Curralinho Brazil
122 □ Curral Velho Cape Verde
149 F3 Curran Michigan U.S.A.
67 A5 Currane, Lough l. Rep. of Ireland
155 E2 Currant Nevada U.S.A.
15 E5 Currawilla Queensland Australia
145 E7 Current The Bahamas
155 E1 Currie Nevada U.S.A.
13 E4 Currie Tasmania Australia
112 E2 Curtea de Argeș Romania
79 L5 Curtici Romania
173 J2 Curtina Uruguay
15 H5 Curtis Channel chan. Queensland Australia
13 F4 Curtis Group is Tasmania Australia
8 □4 Curtis I. i. Kermadec Is New Zealand
15 G4 Curtis I. i. Queensland Australia
166 B2 Curuá r. Brazil
166 B1 Curuá do Sul r. Brazil
166 B2 Curuaés r. Brazil
163 G3 Curuá, Ilha i. Brazil
163 G4 Curuapanema r. Brazil
166 B1 Curuá Una r. Brazil
166 C1 Curuçá Brazil
166 B1 Curumu Brazil
163 F5 Cururu r. Brazil
163 F5 Cururu Açu r. Brazil
166 D1 Cururupu Brazil
170 E2 Curuzú Cuatiá Argentina
169 F3 Curvelo Brazil
164 B2 Cusco Peru
67 E1 Cushendall Northern Ireland U.K.
67 E1 Cushendun Northern Ireland U.K.
151 D4 Cushing Oklahoma U.S.A.
156 D2 Cusihuiráchic Mexico
106 E4 Cusna, Monte mt. Italy
90 B2 Cusset France
145 C5 Cusseta Georgia U.S.A.
148 A1 Cusson Minnesota U.S.A.
138 E1 Cusson, Pte pt Québec Canada
152 F2 Custer Montana U.S.A.
150 C3 Custer S. Dakota U.S.A.
87 F4 Custines France
125 C6 Cutato r. Angola
152 D1 Cut Bank Montana U.S.A.
162 B5 Cutervo, Parque Nacional nat. park Peru
145 C6 Cuthbert Georgia U.S.A.
137 H4 Cut Knife Saskatchewan Canada
147 K2 Cutler Maine U.S.A.
145 D7 Cutler Ridge Florida U.S.A.
172 C5 Cutral-Co Argentina
67 C3 Cutra, Lough l. Rep. of Ireland
111 F3 Cutro Italy
111 H2 Cutrofiano Italy
37 F5 Cuttack India
155 G5 Cutter Arizona U.S.A.
125 C7 Cuvelai Angola
124 C4 Cuvette div. Congo
17 A5 Cuvier, C. headland Western Australia Australia
141 G2 Cuvillier, Lac l. Québec Canada
93 E5 Cuxac-Cabardès France
72 D2 Cuxhaven Niedersachsen Germany
162 B4 Cuyabeno Ecuador
146 C4 Cuyahoga Falls Ohio U.S.A.
146 C4 Cuyahoga Valley National Recreation Area res. Ohio U.S.A.
154 C4 Cuyama r. California U.S.A.
23 B3 Cuyapo Philippines
23 B4 Cuyo i. Philippines
23 B4 Cuyo Philippines
23 B4 Cuyo East Pass. chan. Philippines
23 B4 Cuyo Islands is Philippines
23 B4 Cuyo West Pass. chan. Philippines
163 F2 Cuyuni r. Guyana
Cuzco see Cusco
101 F2 Cuzna r. Spain
104 F4 Čvrsnica mts Bos.-Herz.
62 C3 Cwmbran Wales U.K.
127 A5 Cyangugu Rwanda
76 C3 Cybinka Poland
Cyclades is see Kyklades
77 M4 Cyców Poland
Cydweli see Kidwelly
146 A5 Cynthiana Kentucky U.S.A.
62 B3 Cynwyl Elfed Wales U.K.
137 G5 Cypress Hills mountain range Saskatchewan Canada
18 E6 Cyprus country Asia
118 D2 Cyrenaica reg. Libya
76 E2 Czaplinek Poland
137 G4 Czar Alberta Canada
77 M2 Czarna Białostocka Poland
76 F1 Czarna Dąbrówka Poland
76 G2 Czarna Woda Poland
76 E2 Czarne Poland
76 E3 Czarnków Poland
76 G4 Czarnożyły Poland
77 H6 Czarny Dunajec r. Poland
77 H6 Czarny Dunajec Poland
77 J6 Czchów Poland
48 G4 Czech Republic country Europe
77 K3 Czeerwin Poland
77 K4 Czekarzewice Poland
77 L4 Czemierniki Poland
76 E3 Czempiń Poland
77 M3 Czeremcha Poland
73 L4 Czerna Mała r. Poland
73 L4 Czerna Wielka r. Poland
76 F2 Czernica r. Poland
76 F4 Czernica Poland
76 F3 Czerniejewo Poland
77 J4 Czerniewice Poland
76 F2 Czersk Poland
76 D3 Czerwieńsk Poland
77 J3 Czerwińsk nad Wisłą Poland
77 H5 Częstochowa div. Poland
77 H5 Częstochowa Poland
76 E2 Człopa Poland
76 F2 Człuchów Poland
73 K4 Czorneboh h. Germany
77 J6 Czorsztyn Poland
77 M3 Czyże Poland
77 L3 Czyżew-Osada Poland

D

31 H3 Da'an China
43 D4 Dab'a Jordan
162 C1 Dabajuro Venezuela
122 D5 Dabakala Côte d'Ivoire
30 B5 Daban Shan mountain range China
79 J4 Dabas Hungary
32 E1 Daba Shan mountain range China
126 C2 Dabat Ethiopia
122 B4 Dabatou Guinea
Dabba see Daocheng
162 B2 Dabeiba Colombia
24 B3 Dabein Myanmar
73 G2 Dabel Germany
36 C5 Dabhoi India
38 A2 Dabhol India
76 G3 Dąbie Konin Poland
76 D3 Dąbie Zielona Góra Poland
33 F2 Dabie Shan mountain range China
43 D5 Dabl, W. watercourse Saudi Arabia
87 G4 Dabo France
36 D4 Daboh India
122 B4 Dabola Guinea
122 D5 Dabou Côte d'Ivoire
36 D4 Dabra India
77 N3 Dabravolya Belarus
76 C3 Dąbroszyn Gorzow Poland
76 G3 Dąbroszyn Konin Poland
76 F3 Dąbrowa Poland
77 M2 Dąbrowa Białostocka Poland
76 G2 Dąbrowa Chełmińska Poland
77 H5 Dąbrowa Górnicza Poland
77 J5 Dąbrowa Tarnowska Poland
33 G3 Dabu China
77 N3 Dabuchyn Belarus
112 E3 Dăbuleni Romania
126 B2 Dabus Wenz r. Ethiopia
126 D3 Dacarbudhug Somalia
75 G4 Dachau Germany
80 C2 Dachauer Moos marsh Germany
30 B5 Dachechang China
38 B2 Dachepalle India
81 E3 Dachstein Gruppe mts Austria
78 E2 Dačice Czech Rep.
141 G4 Dacre Ontario Canada
163 F3 Dadanawa Guyana
126 D2 Daddato Djibouti
145 D6 Dade City Florida U.S.A.
36 A3 Dadhar Pakistan
93 D5 Dadou r. France
36 C5 Dadra India
36 C5 Dadra and Nagar Haveli div. India
32 C2 Dadu r. China
36 A4 Dadu Pakistan
25 D5 Đa Dung r. Vietnam
119 G3 Daedalus Reef reef Saudi Arabia
23 B3 Daet Philippines
32 D3 Dafang China
43 C5 Dafdaf, J. mt. Saudi Arabia
33 H1 Dafeng China
126 D3 Daferur well Ethiopia
37 H4 Dafla Hills mountain range India
115 C4 Dafnes Greece
114 F2 Dafni Agion Oros Greece
115 D5 Dafni Dytiki Ellas Greece
115 D6 Dafni Peloponnisos Greece
126 D3 Daga Medo Ethiopia
122 A3 Dagana Senegal
32 C1 Dagcanglhamo China
54 E3 Dagda Latvia
72 D1 Dagebüll Germany
51 H6 Dagestan div. Rus. Fed.
46 C4 Dagestan Rus. Fed.
131 E6 Daggaboersnek pass South Africa
9 A6 Dagg Sd inlet New Zealand
121 F2 Daglet Lagrouba Algeria
82 C1 Dagmersellen Switzerland
31 G5 Dagu r. China
32 C3 Daguan China
27 □ D'Aguilar Peak h. Hong Kong China
23 B2 Dagupan Philippines
37 H1 Dagur China
Dagxoi see Yidun
37 G3 Dagzê China
37 F3 Dagzê Co salt lake China
37 G3 Dagzhuka China
119 F2 Dahab Egypt
119 G3 Dahabān Saudi Arabia
38 A2 Dahanu India
30 D4 Dahei r. China
31 J3 Daheiding Shan mt. China
33 G3 Daheng China
31 K3 Dahezhen China
31 F3 Da Hinggan Ling mts. China
126 D1 Dahlak Archipelago is Eritrea
126 C1 Dahlak Marine National Park nat. park Eritrea
74 B2 Dahlem Germany
73 J4 Dahlen Germany
73 F2 Dahlenburg Germany
73 J4 Dahlener Heide heath Germany
111 □ Dahlet Qorrot b. Malta
73 J4 Dahme r. Germany
73 J4 Dahme Brandenburg Germany
73 G1 Dahme Schleswig-Holstein Germany
73 G1 Dahmeshöved headland Germany
74 C3 Dahn Germany
36 C5 Dāhod India
36 D2 Dahongliutan China/Jammu and Kashmir
73 F3 Dähre Germany
42 E2 Dahūk div. Iraq
42 E2 Dahūk Iraq
31 H4 Dahuofang Sk. resr China
30 E4 Dai Hai l. China
22 A2 Daik Indonesia
24 B3 Daik-u Myanmar
31 E3 Dailamin Sum China
37 E3 Dailekh Nepal
64 D2 Dailly Scotland U.K.
39 D2 Daim Iran
28 D5 Daimanji-san h. Japan
101 G1 Daimiel Spain
115 D6 Daimonia Greece
77 N1 Dainava Lithuania
29 F6 Dainichiga-take volcano Japan
32 B1 Dainkog China
32 B1 Dainkognubma China
15 F3 Daintree Nat. Park Queensland Australia
86 B2 Dainville France
29 F6 Daiō Japan
29 F6 Daiō-zaki pt Japan
173 G4 Daireaux Argentina
Dairen see Dalian
119 F2 Dairūt Egypt
148 A2 Dairyland Wisconsin U.S.A.
28 D6 Daisen volcano Japan
33 H2 Daishan China
4 E2 Daito-jima is Japan
30 E5 Dai Xian China
33 G3 Daiyun Shan mountain range China
14 D4 Dajarra Queensland Australia
32 C2 Dajin Chuan r. China
30 B5 Dajing China
37 H1 Da Juh China
122 D5 Daka r. Ghana
122 A4 Dakar Senegal
119 E4 Dakar el Arāk well Sudan
37 G3 Dakelangsi China
126 D3 Daketa Shet' watercourse Ethiopia
37 G5 Dakhin Shahbaz-pur I. i. Bangladesh
119 E2 Dakhla Oasis oasis Egypt
120 A4 Dakhlet Nouâdhibou div. Mauritania
123 E4 Dakingari Nigeria
25 D4 Dak Kon Vietnam
25 A6 Dakoank Andaman and Nicobar Is India
54 F5 Dakol'ka r. Belarus
122 C4 Dakoro Burkina
123 F4 Dakoro Niger
150 D3 Dakota City Nebraska U.S.A.
112 C3 Đakovica Yugoslavia
104 G3 Đakovo Croatia
31 H1 Daktuy Rus. Fed.
126 D2 Dal well Djibouti
125 D6 Dala Angola
80 B3 Dalaas Austria
122 B4 Dalaba Guinea
30 D4 Dalad Qi China
31 F4 Dalai Nur l. China
43 B5 Dalal, G. mt. Egypt
59 G1 Dalälven r. Sweden
30 E4 Dalamamiao China
42 B2 Dalaman r. Turkey
42 B2 Dalaman Turkey
30 C4 Dalandzadgad Mongolia
23 B4 Dalanganem Islands is Philippines
4 J4 Dalap-Uliga-Dorrit Marshall Islands
59 H2 Dalarö Sweden
25 E5 Đa Lat Vietnam
30 B4 Dalay Mongolia
39 F3 Dalbandin Pakistan
66 E6 Dalbeattie Scotland U.K.
59 E2 Dalbosjön l. Sweden
15 G5 Dalby Queensland Australia
55 C4 Dalby Denmark
64 D3 Dalby Isle of Man
59 E4 Dalby Sweden
55 C3 Dalbyover Denmark
58 A1 Dale Hordaland Norway
58 A1 Dale Sogn og Fjordane Norway
146 E5 Dale City Virginia U.S.A.
151 G4 Dale Hollow Lake l. Kentucky/Tennessee U.S.A.
74 B2 Daleiden Germany
68 E2 Dalen Netherlands
58 B2 Dalen Norway
24 A3 Dalet Myanmar
24 A2 Daletme Myanmar
59 F1 Dalfors Sweden
68 E2 Dalfsen Netherlands
39 D4 Dalgān Iran
17 B5 Dalgaranger, Mt h. Western Australia Australia
65 E1 Dalgety Bay Scotland U.K.
151 C4 Dalhart Texas U.S.A.
69 D4 Dalhem Belgium
139 G4 Dalhousie New Brunswick Canada
33 E1 Dali Shaanxi China
32 C3 Dali Yunnan China
31 G5 Dalian China
32 C2 Daliang Shan mountain range China
31 G4 Dalin China
31 F4 Daling r. China
31 H4 Dalizi China
66 E5 Dalkeith Scotland U.K.
64 B4 Dalkey Rep. of Ireland
37 F4 Dālkola India
15 H5 Dallarnil Queensland Australia
147 F4 Dallas Pennsylvania U.S.A.
151 D5 Dallas Texas U.S.A.
148 B5 Dallas City Illinois U.S.A.
152 B2 Dalles, The Oregon U.S.A.
136 C4 Dall I. i. Alaska U.S.A.
123 E3 Dallol Bosso watercourse Mali/Niger
39 C4 Dalmā i. U.A.E.
104 F4 Dalmacija reg. Croatia
172 F2 Dalmacio Vélez Sarsfield Argentina
66 D4 Dalmally Scotland U.K.
36 E4 Dalman India
46 F1 Dalmatovo Rus. Fed.
66 D5 Dalmellington Scotland U.K.
106 D3 Dalmine Italy
31 K3 Dal'nerechensk Rus. Fed.
52 G2 Dal'neye Konstantinovo Rus. Fed.
122 C5 Daloa Côte d'Ivoire
32 D3 Dalou Shan mountain range China
66 D5 Dalry Scotland U.K.
66 D5 Dalrymple Scotland U.K.
15 F4 Dalrymple, L. l. Queensland Australia
15 G4 Dalrymple, Mt mt. Queensland Australia
54 C1 Dalsbruk Finland
65 F3 Dalston England U.K.
37 F4 Daltenganj India
145 C5 Dalton Georgia U.S.A.
147 G3 Dalton Massachusetts U.S.A.
140 C2 Dalton Ontario Canada
131 H4 Dalton South Africa
65 E3 Dalton-in-Furness England U.K.
140 C2 Dalton Mills Ontario Canada
91 E4 Daluis France
32 C4 Da Luo China
23 B2 Dalupiri i. Philippines
56 M6 Dalvík Iceland
66 D4 Dalwhinnie Scotland U.K.
14 B2 Daly r. Northern Terr. Australia
154 A3 Daly City California U.S.A.
54 E4 Dalyokiya Belarus
14 B2 Daly River Abor. Land res. Northern Terr. Australia
14 C3 Daly Waters Northern Terr. Australia
77 M4 Damachava Belarus
123 F4 Damagaram Takaya Niger
125 E6 Damalisques de Leshwe res. Congo(Zaire)
36 C5 Daman India
36 C5 Damān and Diu Div. India
54 D5 Damanava Belarus
43 A4 Damanhûr Egypt
39 B2 Damaq Iran
31 E4 Damaqun Shan mountain range China
21 J8 Damar i. Indonesia
23 C6 Damar Indonesia
124 C3 Damara Central African Rep.
128 B3 Damaraland reg. Namibia
123 G4 Damasak Nigeria
Damascus see Dimashq
114 D3 Damasi Greece
114 C2 Damaskina Greece
76 F3 Damasławek Poland
170 B3 Damas, P. de las Argentina/Chile
123 G4 Damaturu Nigeria
39 C2 Damāvand mt. Iran
39 C2 Damavand Iran
93 C4 Damazan France
125 C5 Damba Angola
123 E5 Dambai Ghana
123 F4 Dambatta Nigeria
123 G4 Damboa Nigeria
38 C5 Dambulla Sri Lanka
158 D3 Dame Marie Haiti
158 D3 Dame Marie, Cap c. Haiti
86 C3 Damery France
39 C1 Damghan Iran
Damietta see Dumyât
89 F3 Damigni France
31 E5 Daming China
43 C3 Dāmiya Jordan
32 A1 Damjong China
89 G3 Dammarie France
86 B3 Dammartin-en-Goële France
83 D2 Dammastock mt. Switzerland
69 B3 Damme Belgium
72 D3 Damme Germany
36 D5 Damoh India
122 D5 Damongo Ghana
22 D1 Dampelas, Tg pt Indonesia
16 B4 Dampier Western Australia Australia
16 B4 Dampier Arch. is Western Australia Australia
90 D1 Dampierre France
82 B1 Dampierre-sur-Linotte France
90 D1 Dampierre-sur-Salon France
6 □1 Dampier Strait chan. P.N.G.
22 C4 Dampit Indonesia
90 E1 Damprichard France
Damqoq Kanbab r. see Maquan
37 H2 Dam Qu r. China
37 H3 Damroh India
55 E5 Damsholte Denmark
82 B1 Damvant Switzerland
89 G3 Damville France
87 E3 Damvillers France
68 E1 Damwoude Netherlands
37 G3 Damxung China
37 E3 Dana Nepal
101 G2 Dañador r. Spain
55 D2 Danafjord chan. Sweden
122 C5 Danané Côte d'Ivoire
24 E3 Đa Năng Vietnam
23 C4 Danao Philippines
22 E2 Danau Poso l. Indonesia
32 C2 Danba China
147 G4 Danbury Connecticut U.S.A.
147 H3 Danbury New Hampshire U.S.A.
147 G3 Danby Vermont U.S.A.
155 E4 Danby Lake l. California U.S.A.
33 F1 Dancheng China
17 A6 Dandaragan Western Australia Australia
125 B5 Dande r. Angola
126 C4 Dande Ethiopia
36 E3 Dandel'dhura Nepal
38 A3 Dandeli India
13 F4 Dandenong Victoria Australia
31 H4 Dandong China
141 H3 Dandurand, Lac l. Québec Canada
62 D1 Dane r. England U.K.
135 Q2 Daneborg Greenland
112 D3 Daneți Romania
33 E1 Danfeng China
147 K2 Danforth Maine U.S.A.
33 F4 Dangan Liedao is China
31 J3 Dangbizhen Rus. Fed.
32 D1 Dangchang China
125 C5 Dange Angola
176 J6 Danger Islands is Cook Islands Pacific Ocean
130 B7 Danger Pt pt South Africa
92 C2 Dangé-St-Romain France
47 G5 Danghara Tajikistan
126 C2 Dangila Ethiopia
Dangla Shan mountain range see Tanggula Shan
37 G3 Dangqên China
157 H5 Dangriga Belize
33 G1 Dangshan China
33 G2 Dangtu China
123 F4 Dan-Gulbi Nigeria
126 C2 Dangur Ethiopia
33 E2 Dangyang China
152 E3 Daniel Wyoming U.S.A.
172 D2 Daniel Donovan Argentina
130 D4 Danielskuil South Africa
131 G3 Danielsrus South Africa
50 G3 Danilov Rus. Fed.
112 B3 Danilovgrad Yugoslavia
51 H5 Danilovka Rus. Fed.
52 G3 Danilovka Rus. Fed.
50 F3 Danilovskaya Vozvyshennost' Rus. Fed.
30 D5 Daning China
72 F1 Dänischenhagen Germany
33 E1 Danjiangkou Sk. resr China
28 B7 Danjo-guntō is Japan
90 E1 Danjoutin France
36 D2 Dankhar India
52 D3 Dankov Rus. Fed.
32 C2 Danleng China
156 J6 Danlí Honduras
122 C5 Dan, Mts des mts Côte d'Ivoire
Dannebrogsø i. see Qillak
55 D5 Dannemare Denmark
90 F1 Dannemarie France
147 G2 Dannemora New York U.S.A.
73 G2 Dannenberg (Elbe) Germany
73 J2 Dannenwalde Germany
8 F4 Dannevirke New Zealand
131 H4 Dannhauser South Africa
122 D4 Dano Burkina
24 C3 Dan Sai Thailand
58 C2 Dansevalheia h. Norway
146 E3 Dansville New York U.S.A.
36 C4 Danta India
38 C2 Dantewara India
Dantu see Zhenjiang
Danube r. Austria/Germany see Donau
Danube r. Bulgaria/Romania see Dunav
Danube r. Czech Rep. see Dunaj
Danube r. Hungary see Duna
Danube r. Romania see Dunărea
24 A3 Danubyu Myanmar
22 C1 Danumparai Indonesia
148 D5 Danville Illinois U.S.A.
148 D6 Danville Indiana U.S.A.
144 C4 Danville Kentucky U.S.A.
149 J5 Danville Pennsylvania U.S.A.
141 J4 Danville Québec Canada
146 D6 Danville Virginia U.S.A.
33 E5 Dan Xian China
33 G2 Danyang China
32 D3 Danzhai China
77 H1 Danzig, Gulf of g. Poland/Rus. Fed.
98 C4 Dão r. Portugal
23 B4 Dao Philippines
24 D2 Đao Bach Long Vi i. Vietnam
24 D2 Đao Cai Bâu i. Vietnam
24 D2 Đao Cat Ba i. Vietnam
32 C2 Daocheng China
25 C5 Đao Phu Quôc i. Vietnam
30 B5 Daotanghe China
25 C5 Đao Thô Chư i. Vietnam
120 C5 Daoudi well Mauritania
122 D5 Daoukro Côte d'Ivoire
25 C5 Đao Vây i. Vietnam
33 E3 Dao Xian China
32 D2 Daozhen China
23 C4 Dapa Philippines
123 E4 Dapaong Togo
37 H4 Daphabum mt. India
43 B4 Daphnae Egypt
23 B4 Dapiak, Mt mt. Philippines
23 B4 Dapitan Philippines
26 G4 Da Qaidam China
31 H3 Daqing China
30 D4 Daqing Shan mountain range China
39 C2 Daqq-e Dombūn Iran
42 F3 Dāqūq Iraq
33 H2 Daqu Shan i. China
122 A3 Dara Senegal
43 D3 Dar'ā div. Syria
43 D3 Dar'a Syria
39 C3 Dārāb Iran
36 B3 Daraban Pakistan
112 F1 Darabani Romania
54 F5 Darahanava Belarus
118 B1 Daraj Libya
39 C3 Dārākūyeh Iran

41 H3 Dārān Iran
79 G6 Darány Hungary
47 H3 Darat Kazakhstan
112 C3 Daravica mt. Yugoslavia
119 F3 Daraw Egypt
123 G4 Darazo Nigeria
39 D3 Darband Iran
36 B1 Darband Pakistan
54 B3 Darbėnai Lithuania
96 D5 Dar Ben Karricha el Behri Morocco
37 F4 Darbhanga India
32 B1 Darcang China
96 D5 Dar Chaoui Morocco
104 G3 Darda Croatia
154 C2 Dardanelle California U.S.A.
151 E5 Dardanelle, Lake l. Arkansas U.S.A.
Dardanelles str. see Çanakkale Boğazı
73 F4 Dardesheim Germany
Dardo see Kangding
42 D2 Darende Turkey
127 C6 Dar es Salaam Tanzania
9 D5 Darfield New Zealand
106 E3 Darfo Boario Terme Italy
118 D4 Darfur div. Sudan
36 B2 Dargai Pakistan
46 F4 Dargan-Ata Turkmenistan
8 D1 Dargaville New Zealand
13 F4 Dargo Victoria Australia
123 E4 Dargol Niger
73 H2 Dargun Germany
30 C2 Darhan Mongolia
30 D4 Darhan Muminggan Lianheqi China
145 D6 Darien Georgia U.S.A.
162 B2 Darién, Golfo del g. Colombia
156 L8 Darién, Parque Nacional de nat. park Panama
47 H3 Dar'inskiy Kazakhstan
156 J6 Darío Nicaragua
37 G4 Dārjiling India
17 B7 Darkan Western Australia Australia
32 B1 Darlag China
13 E3 Darling r. New South Wales Australia
130 B6 Darling South Africa
15 G5 Darling Downs reg. Queensland Australia
17 B7 Darling Range h. Western Australia Australia
65 G3 Darlington div. England U.K.
65 G3 Darlington England U.K.
148 B4 Darlington Wisconsin U.S.A.
13 F3 Darlington Point New South Wales Australia
17 C5 Darlot, L. salt flat Western Australia Australia
76 E1 Darłowo Poland
112 F1 Dărmănești Romania
36 E3 Darma Pass pass China/India
38 B2 Darmaraopet India
39 D3 Dar Mazār Iran
74 D2 Darmstadt div. Hessen Germany
74 D3 Darmstadt Darmstadt Germany
38 A2 Darna r. India
118 D1 Darnah Libya
131 H4 Darnall South Africa
89 G2 Darnétal France
87 F4 Darney France
13 E3 Darnick New South Wales Australia
134 F3 Darnley Bay b. N.W.T. Canada
179 D5 Darnley, C. c. Antarctica
102 B3 Daroca Spain
47 H5 Daroot-Korgan Kyrgyzstan
50 G3 Darovka Rus. Fed.
50 H3 Darovskoy Rus. Fed.
98 B3 Darque Portugal
15 E4 Darr watercourse Queensland Australia
173 F4 Darregueira Argentina
39 D2 Darreh Bīd Iran
39 D1 Darreh Gaz Iran
39 G2 Darri-i-Shikar r. Afghanistan
126 □ Darsa i. Socotra Yemen
38 B3 Darsi India
73 H1 Darß pen. Germany
73 H1 Darßer Ort c. Germany
62 C4 Dart r. England U.K.
63 G3 Dartford England U.K.
62 C4 Dartmeet England U.K.
62 B4 Dartmoor reg. England U.K.
12 E4 Dartmoor Victoria Australia
62 C4 Dartmoor National Park England U.K.
62 C4 Dartmouth England U.K.
139 H5 Dartmouth Nova Scotia Canada
15 F5 Dartmouth, L. salt flat Queensland Australia
65 G4 Darton England U.K.
67 C2 Darty Mts h. Rep. of Ireland
119 F4 Daru waterhole Sudan
6 □1 Daru P.N.G.
122 B5 Daru Sierra Leone
37 G3 Darum Tso l. China
104 F3 Daruvar Croatia
46 E4 Darvaza Turkmenistan
39 B3 Darvīsla Iran
39 F3 Darwazgai Afghanistan
65 F4 Darwen England U.K.
39 F3 Darweshan Afghanistan
14 B2 Darwin Northern Terr. Australia
172 E5 Darwin Argentina
171 E7 Darwin Falkland Is.
171 C7 Darwin, Mte mt. Chile
162 □ Darwin, Vol. volcano Galapagos Is Ecuador
39 C3 Daryācheh-ye Bakhtegan salt lake Iran
39 C3 Daryācheh-ye Mahārlū salt lake Iran
39 B2 Daryācheh-ye Namak salt flat Iran
42 F2 Daryācheh-ye Orūmīyeh salt lake Iran
39 E3 Daryacheh-ye Sīstan marsh Afghanistan
39 C3 Daryacheh-ye Tashk salt lake Iran
39 D3 Dārzīn Iran
39 C4 Dās i. U.A.E.
77 N6 Dashava Ukraine
30 E2 Dashbalbar Mongolia
33 E2 Dashennongjia mt. China
53 C2 Dashiv Ukraine
31 G3 Dashizhai China
Dashkesan see Daşkäsän
46 E4 Dashkhovuz div. Turkmenistan
46 E4 Dashkhovuz Turkmenistan
39 E4 Dasht r. Pakistan
39 D1 Dasht Iran
39 D3 Dasht Āb Iran
39 E2 Dasht-e-Daqq-e-Tundi depression Afghanistan
39 C2 Dasht-e-Kavir salt flat Iran
39 D2 Dasht-e-Lut desert Iran
39 E2 Dasht-e-Naomid plain Afghanistan/Iran
39 B3 Dasht-e Palang r. Iran
39 F3 Dasht-i-Arbu Lut desert Afghanistan
39 E4 Dashtiari Iran
39 E3 Dasht-i-Margo desert Afghanistan
30 C5 Dashuikeng China
30 C5 Dashuitou China
80 C2 Dasing Germany
36 C2 Daska Pakistan
42 F1 Daşkäsän Azerbaijan
130 D6 Daskop South Africa
36 C1 Daspar mt. Pakistan
123 E5 Dassa Benin
72 E4 Dassel Germany
130 B6 Dassen Island i. South Africa
73 F2 Dassow Germany
39 D2 Dastgardān Iran
31 J4 Da Suifen He r. China
36 C3 Dasuya India
131 G3 Dasville South Africa
77 H3 Daszyna Poland
22 C1 Datadian Indonesia
42 A2 Datça Turkey
28 H2 Date Japan
155 F5 Dateland Arizona U.S.A.
36 D4 Datia India
33 G3 Datian China
30 A5 Datong r. China
30 B5 Datong China
30 E4 Datong China
31 H3 Datong China
30 A5 Datong Shan mountain range China
72 C4 Datteln Germany
22 B1 Datu i. Indonesia
22 A2 Datuk, Tg pt Indonesia
23 C5 Datu Piang Philippines
22 B1 Datu, Tg c. Indonesia/Malaysia
36 B2 Daud Khel Pakistan
37 F4 Daudnagar India
50 C3 Dauga r. Latvia
77 N1 Daugai Lithuania
54 D4 Daugailiai Lithuania
54 D3 Daugava r. Europe
54 E4 Daugavpils Latvia
39 F1 Daulatabad Afghanistan
Daulatabad see Malāyer
89 E4 Daumeray France
74 B2 Daun Germany
38 A2 Daund India
25 B4 Daung Kyun i. Myanmar
24 A2 Daungyu r. Myanmar
137 J4 Dauphin Manitoba Canada
91 D3 Dauphiné reg. France
151 F6 Dauphin I. i. Alabama U.S.A.
137 K4 Dauphin L. l. Manitoba Canada
123 F4 Daura Nigeria
17 A5 Daurie Cr. r. Western Australia Australia
31 F2 Dauriya Rus. Fed.
30 D2 Daurskiy Khrebet mountain range Rus. Fed.
36 D4 Dausa India
87 H2 Dautphetal-Friedensdorf Germany
66 E3 Dava Scotland U.K.
42 G1 Däväçi Azerbaijan
38 A3 Davangere India
23 C5 Davao Philippines
23 C5 Davao Gulf b. Philippines
39 E4 Dāvar Panāh Iran
39 D1 Dāvarzan Iran
131 G3 Davel South Africa
154 A3 Davenport California U.S.A.
148 B5 Davenport Iowa U.S.A.
15 E5 Davenport Downs Queensland Australia
14 B4 Davenport, Mt h. Northern Terr. Australia
14 C4 Davenport Ra. h. Northern Terr. Australia
63 E2 Daventry England U.K.
131 G3 Daveyton South Africa
156 K7 David Panama
137 H4 Davidson Saskatchewan Canada
12 B1 Davies, Mt mt. S. Australia Australia
137 J3 Davin Lake l. Saskatchewan Canada
168 E3 Davinópolis Brazil
179 D5 Davis Australia Base Antarctica
154 B2 Davis California U.S.A.
155 E4 Davis Dam Arizona U.S.A.
139 H2 Davis Inlet Newfoundland Canada
179 D5 Davis Sea sea Antarctica
135 N3 Davis Strait str. Canada/Greenland
46 D2 Davlekanovo Rus. Fed.
114 D4 Davlia Greece
83 E2 Davos Graubünden Switzerland
77 N6 Davydiv Ukraine
53 E3 Davydiv Brid Ukraine
52 D1 Davydovo Rus. Fed.
30 A4 Dawan China
20 D4 Dawa Wenz r. Ethiopia
37 F3 Dawaxung China
32 C2 Dawe China
Dawei see Tavoy
39 B4 Dawhat Salwah b. Qatar/Saudi Arabia
126 D2 Dawi well Ethiopia
62 C4 Dawlish England U.K.
53 C1 Dawlyady Belarus
24 B3 Dawna Range mountain range Myanmar/Thailand
41 H6 Dawqah Oman
119 H4 Dawqah Saudi Arabia
126 D2 Dawrān Yemen
67 C2 Dawros Head headland Rep. of Ireland
15 G5 Dawson r. Queensland Australia
145 C6 Dawson Georgia U.S.A.
150 D2 Dawson N. Dakota U.S.A.
134 E3 Dawson Yukon Terr. Canada
137 J4 Dawson Bay b. Manitoba Canada
136 E3 Dawson Creek B.C. Canada
137 L2 Dawson Inlet inlet N.W.T. Canada
136 B2 Dawson Range mountain range N.W.T. Canada
32 C2 Dawu China
33 F2 Dawu China
Dawukou see Shizuishan
93 A5 Dax France
32 D2 Daxian China
32 D4 Daxin China
31 F5 Daxing China
32 C2 Daxue Shan mountain range China
37 H4 Dayang r. India
31 H2 Dayangshu China
47 L3 Dayan Nuur l. Mongolia
32 C3 Dayao China
33 E4 Dayao Shan mountain range China
33 F2 Daye China
32 C2 Dayi China
154 D3 Daylight Pass pass Nevada U.S.A.
173 J1 Daymán r. Uruguay
173 J1 Daymán Uruguay
173 J1 Dayman, Cuch. del h. Uruguay
33 E2 Dayong China
43 D2 Dayr 'Aṭīyah Syria
42 E3 Dayr az Zawr Syria
146 A5 Dayton Ohio U.S.A.
145 C5 Dayton Tennessee U.S.A.
152 C2 Dayton Washington U.S.A.
145 D6 Daytona Beach Florida U.S.A.
33 F3 Dayu China
22 C2 Dayu Indonesia
33 F3 Dayu Ling mountain range China
31 F5 Da Yunhe canal Hebei China
33 G1 Da Yunhe r. Jiangsu China
152 C2 Dayville Oregon U.S.A.
28 C7 Dazaifu Japan
32 D2 Dazhu China
32 D2 Dazu China
130 D5 De Aar South Africa
148 D2 Dead r. Michigan U.S.A.
145 F7 Deadman's Cay The Bahamas
155 E4 Dead Mts mts Nevada U.S.A.
147 H2 Dead River r. Maine U.S.A.
43 C4 Dead Sea salt lake Israel/Jordan
63 H3 Deal England U.K.
131 E4 Dealesville South Africa
79 M6 Dealurile Lipovei mountain range Romania
53 C3 Dealurile Prenistrului h. Moldova
53 C3 Dealurile Tigheciului h. Moldova
136 D4 Dean r. B.C. Canada
33 F2 De'an China
62 D3 Dean, Forest of forest England U.K.
172 E1 Deán Funes Argentina
65 F1 Dean Water r. Scotland U.K.
149 F4 Dearborn Michigan U.S.A.
136 D3 Dease r. B.C. Canada
134 F3 Dease Arm b. N.W.T. Canada
136 C3 Dease Lake B.C. Canada
134 H3 Dease Strait chan. N.W.T. Canada
154 D3 Death Valley v. California U.S.A.
154 D3 Death Valley Junction California U.S.A.
154 D3 Death Valley National Monument nat. park California U.S.A.
89 F2 Deauville France
99 H1 Deba Spain
22 B1 Debak Malaysia
33 D4 Debao China
114 B1 Debar Macedonia
126 C2 Debark Ethiopia
114 B1 Debarsko Ezero l. Macedonia
137 H4 Debden Saskatchewan Canada
159 □3 Debe Trinidad and Tobago
131 G4 De Beers Pass pass South Africa
63 H2 Deben r. England U.K.
63 H2 Debenham England U.K.
155 H2 De Beque Colorado U.S.A.
77 K5 Dębica Poland
68 D2 De Bilt Netherlands
45 R3 Debin Rus. Fed.
77 K4 Dęblin Poland
147 J2 Deblois Maine U.S.A.
76 F1 Dębnica Kaszubska Poland
76 C3 Dębno Poland
122 D3 Débo, Lac l. Mali
17 B6 Deborah, L. salt flat Western Australia Australia
77 J4 Dęborzeczka Poland
77 M4 Dębowa Kłoda Poland
126 C3 Debre Birhan Ethiopia
79 L4 Debrecen Hungary
126 C2 Debre Markos Ethiopia
126 C3 Debre Sīna Ethiopia
114 C1 Debrešte Macedonia
126 C2 Debre Tabor Ethiopia
126 C2 Debre Werk' Ethiopia
126 C3 Debre Zeyit Ethiopia
76 F2 Debrzno Poland
112 C3 Dečani Yugoslavia
145 C5 Decatur Alabama U.S.A.
145 C5 Decatur Georgia U.S.A.
148 C6 Decatur Illinois U.S.A.
148 E5 Decatur Indiana U.S.A.
148 E4 Decatur Michigan U.S.A.
93 E4 Decazeville France
141 G3 Decelles, Réservoir resr Québec Canada
128 C3 Deception watercourse Botswana
128 C3 Deception Pans salt pan Botswana
32 C3 Dechang China
108 A5 Decimomannu Sardegna Italy
78 D1 Děčín Czech Rep.
90 C3 Décines-Charpieu France
90 B2 Decize France
68 C1 De Cocksdorp Netherlands
111 F3 Decollatura Italy
148 B4 Decorah Iowa U.S.A.
63 E3 Deddington England U.K.
23 □2 Dededo Guam Pacific Ocean
73 F3 Dedeleben Germany
73 J2 Dedelow Germany
68 E2 Dedemsvaart Netherlands
126 D3 Deder Ethiopia
52 D2 Dedinovo Rus. Fed.
171 B5 Dedo, Co mt. Chile
168 E6 Dedo de Deus mt. Brazil
130 B6 De Doorns South Africa
51 H7 Dedoplis Tsqaro Georgia
122 D4 Dédougou Burkina
53 F3 Dedovichi Rus. Fed.
31 H2 Dedu China
129 E1 Dedza Malawi
129 E1 Dedza Mountain mt. Malawi
62 C1 Dee est. England/Wales U.K.
62 D2 Dee r. England/Wales U.K.
66 F3 Dee r. Scotland U.K.
64 B4 Dee r. Rep. of Ireland
36 D4 Deeg India
67 C4 Deel r. Rep. of Ireland
64 A4 Deel r. Westmeath Rep. of Ireland
67 D2 Deele r. Rep. of Ireland
130 D5 Deelfontein South Africa
27 □ Deep Bay b. Hong Kong China
146 D5 Deep Creek Lake l. Maryland U.S.A.
155 F2 Deep Creek Range mts Utah U.S.A.
147 G4 Deep River Connecticut U.S.A.
141 G3 Deep River Ontario Canada
137 K1 Deep Rose Lake l. N.W.T. Canada
154 D3 Deep Springs California U.S.A.
128 □2 Deep Valley B. b. St Helena Atlantic Ocean
13 G2 Deepwater New South Wales Australia
146 B5 Deer Creek Lake l. Ohio U.S.A.
147 J2 Deer I. i. Maine U.S.A.
147 K2 Deer I. i. New Brunswick Canada
126 E4 Deeri Somalia
17 E5 Deering, Mt mt. Western Australia Australia
147 J2 Deer Isle Maine U.S.A.
138 B3 Deer L. l. Ontario Canada
139 J4 Deer Lake Newfoundland Canada
138 B3 Deer Lake Ontario Canada
69 B4 Deerlijk Belgium
152 D2 Deer Lodge Montana U.S.A.
165 D4 Defensores del Chaco, Parque Nacional nat. park Paraguay
173 H5 Defferrari Argentina
146 A4 Defiance Ohio U.S.A.
123 G2 Défirou well Niger
145 C6 De Funiak Springs Florida U.S.A.
98 D2 Degaña Spain
80 D4 Degano r. Italy
32 B2 Dêgê China
100 C2 Degebe r. Portugal
59 F4 Degeberga Sweden
126 D3 Degeh Bur Ethiopia
123 F6 Degema Nigeria
37 G3 Dêgên China
59 F2 Degerfors Sweden
75 H4 Deggendorf Germany
106 C4 Dego Italy
126 D4 Degodia reg. Ethiopia
163 G3 De Goeje Geb h. Surinam
16 C4 De Grey r. Western Australia Australia
16 B4 De Grey Western Australia Australia
52 E3 Degtyanka Rus. Fed.
69 B3 De Haan Belgium
39 C3 Dehaj Iran
39 E3 Dehak Iran
39 E4 Dehak Iran
126 D1 Dehalak Desēt i. Eritrea
Deh Barez see Rudan
39 C3 Deh Bīd Iran
39 B3 Deh-Dasht Iran
39 B3 Dehdez Iran
39 B3 Deh-e Khalīfeh Iran
103 C7 Dehesa de Campoamor Spain
39 A2 Dehgolān Iran
121 G2 Dehiba Tunisia
38 B5 Dehiwala-Mount Lavinia Sri Lanka
39 C4 Dehküyeh Iran
39 A2 Dehlonān Iran
130 C7 De Hoop Vlei l. South Africa
36 D3 Dehra Dun India
37 F4 Dehri India
39 D3 Deh Salm Iran
39 D3 Deh Sard Iran
39 E3 Deh Shū Afghanistan
33 G3 Dehua China
31 H3 Dehui China
101 G3 Deifontes Spain
124 E2 Deim Zubeir Sudan
69 B4 Deinze Belgium
Deir-ez-Zor see Dayr az Zawr
87 H4 Deißlingen Germany
112 D1 Dej Romania
59 E2 Deje Sweden
126 C2 Dejen Ethiopia
32 E2 Dejiang China
128 D2 Deka r. Zimbabwe
128 D2 Deka Drum Zimbabwe
148 C5 De Kalb Illinois U.S.A.
151 E5 De Kalb Texas U.S.A.
147 F2 De Kalb Junction New York U.S.A.
107 H3 Dekani Slovenia
27 Q1 De-Kastri Rus. Fed.
126 C1 Dekemhare Eritrea
125 D4 Dekese Congo(Zaire)
123 F5 Dekina Nigeria
124 C2 Dékoa Central African Rep.
68 C1 De Koog Netherlands
62 B4 Delabole England U.K.
173 G4 De la Garma Argentina
154 C4 Delano California U.S.A.
155 F2 Delano Peak summit Utah U.S.A.
39 E2 Delārām Afghanistan
131 E3 Delareyville South Africa
137 H4 Delaronde Lake l. Saskatchewan Canada
59 E3 Delary Sweden
148 C5 Delavan Illinois U.S.A.
148 C4 Delavan Wisconsin U.S.A.
147 F5 Delaware div. U.S.A.
147 F4 Delaware r. New York U.S.A.
146 B4 Delaware Ohio U.S.A.
147 F5 Delaware Bay b. U.S.A.
146 B4 Delaware Lake l. Ohio U.S.A.
147 F4 Delaware Water Gap National Recreational Area res. U.S.A.
72 D4 Delbrück Germany
172 E3 Del Campillo Argentina
112 D4 Delčevo Macedonia
68 E2 Delden Netherlands
13 G4 Delegate New South Wales Australia
82 C1 Delémont Switzerland
59 J1 Delet Teili b. Finland
169 E4 Delfinópolis Brazil
115 D4 Delfoi Greece
68 C2 Delft Netherlands
38 B4 Delft I. i. Sri Lanka
68 E1 Delfzijl Netherlands
127 D7 Delgado, Cabo pt Mozambique
30 A2 Delger Mörön r. Mongolia
119 F3 Delgo Sudan
153 F4 Delhi Colorado U.S.A.
147 F3 Delhi New York U.S.A.
140 E5 Delhi Ontario Canada
36 D3 Delhi India
22 A3 Deli i. Indonesia
110 B5 Delia r. Sicilia Italy
110 C5 Delia Sicilia Italy
42 C1 Delice r. Turkey
163 G3 Délices French Guiana
109 H3 Deliceto Italy
39 B2 Delījān Iran
11 □ Delimara Pt pt Malta
136 E1 Déljne N.W.T. Canada
26 G4 Delingha China
137 H4 Delisle Saskatchewan Canada
73 H4 Delitzsch Germany
80 E4 Dellach Austria
90 F1 Delle France
72 E4 Delligsen Germany
83 F3 Dello Italy
150 D3 Dell Rapids S. Dakota U.S.A.
121 E1 Dellys Algeria
154 D5 Del Mar California U.S.A.
155 E3 Delmar L. l. Nevada U.S.A.
87 F4 Delme France
72 D2 Delmenhorst Niedersachsen Germany
107 J3 Delnice Croatia
45 R2 De-Longa, O-va i. Rus. Fed.
134 B3 De Long Mts mountain range Alaska U.S.A.
137 J5 Deloraine Manitoba Canada
13 F5 Deloraine Tasmania Australia
148 D5 Delphi Indiana U.S.A.
146 A4 Delphos Ohio U.S.A.
130 E4 Delportshoop South Africa
145 D7 Delray Beach Florida U.S.A.
151 C6 Del Rio Texas U.S.A.
153 E6 Del Río Mexico
57 E3 Delsbo Sweden
123 F5 Delta div. Nigeria
155 H2 Delta Colorado U.S.A.
148 A5 Delta Iowa U.S.A.
155 F2 Delta Utah U.S.A.
173 H3 Delta del Paraná delta Argentina
173 F5 Delta del R. Colorado delta Argentina
15 E3 Delta Downs Queensland Australia
112 G2 Delta Dunării delta Romania
122 A4 Delta du Saloum, Parc National du nat. park Senegal
134 D3 Delta Junction Alaska U.S.A.
147 F3 Delta Reservoir resr New York U.S.A.
145 D6 Deltona Florida U.S.A.
13 G2 Delungra New South Wales Australia
68 F2 De Lutte Netherlands
173 G3 Del Valle Argentina
67 D3 Delvin Rep. of Ireland
114 B3 Delvinaki Greece
114 B3 Delvinë Albania
53 A2 Delyatyn Ukraine
46 E2 Dema r. Rus. Fed.
99 G2 Demanda, Sierra de la mountain range Spain
125 D5 Demba Congo(Zaire)
54 D4 Dembava Lithuania
126 C2 Dembech'a Ethiopia
124 D2 Dembia Central African Rep.
126 B3 Dembī Dolo Ethiopia
69 C4 Demer r. Belgium
50 D4 Demidov Rus. Fed.
52 E2 Demidovo Rus. Fed.
153 F5 Deming New Mexico U.S.A.
163 E4 Demini r. Brazil
42 B2 Demirci Turkey
114 C1 Demir Hisar Macedonia
113 G5 Demirköprü Barajı resr Turkey
112 F4 Demirköy Turkey
73 J2 Demmin Germany
145 C5 Demopolis Alabama U.S.A.
148 D5 Demotte Indiana U.S.A.
20 D7 Dempo, G. volcano Indonesia
17 C7 Dempster, Pt pt Western Australia Australia
36 D2 Dêmqog Jammu and Kashmir
93 C5 Dému France
53 G2 Demuryne Ukraine
52 A2 Demyakhi Rus. Fed.
50 H2 Dem'yanovo Rus. Fed.
50 E3 Demyansk Rus. Fed.
53 A1 Demydivka Ukraine
86 C2 Denain France
126 D2 Denakil reg. Eritrea
126 D3 Denan Ethiopia
137 J4 Denare Beach Saskatchewan Canada
93 E5 Dénat France
47 G5 Denau Uzbekistan
141 G4 Denbigh Ontario Canada
62 C1 Denbigh Wales U.K.
62 C1 Denbighshire div. Wales U.K.
68 C1 Den Burg Netherlands
24 C3 Den Chai Thailand
22 A2 Dendang Indonesia
120 C5 Dendâra Mauritania
69 C4 Denderleeuw Belgium
69 B3 Dendermonde div. Oost-Vlaanderen Belgium
69 C3 Dendermonde Belgium
126 C3 Dendi mt. Ethiopia
69 B4 Dendre r. Belgium
131 G1 Dendron South Africa
68 D3 Den Dungen Netherlands
68 F2 Denekamp Netherlands
123 F4 Dengas Niger
123 F4 Denge Nigeria
123 F5 Dengi Nigeria
30 C4 Dengkou China
32 A2 Dêngqên China
33 F1 Deng Xian China
Den Haag see 's-Gravenhage
17 A5 Denham Western Australia Australia
68 E2 Den Ham Netherlands
8 □4 Denham B. b. Kermadec Is New Zealand
14 D3 Denham I. i. Queensland Australia
15 F4 Denham Ra. mountain range Queensland Australia
17 A5 Denham Sound chan. Western Australia Australia
68 C2 Den Helder Netherlands
65 F2 Denholm Scotland U.K.
103 D6 Denia Spain
12 C3 Denial B. b. S. Australia Australia
13 F3 Deniliquin New South Wales Australia
152 C3 Denio Nevada U.S.A.
127 □1 Denis I. i. Seychelles
150 E3 Denison Iowa U.S.A.
151 D5 Denison Texas U.S.A.
16 E3 Denison Plains plain Western Australia Australia
113 G6 Denizli div. Turkey
42 B2 Denizli Turkey
75 G4 Denkendorf Germany
83 E1 Denkingen Germany
83 F1 Denklingen Germany
13 G3 Denman New South Wales Australia
179 C5 Denman Glacier gl. Antarctica
48 F3 Denmark country Europe
17 B7 Denmark Western Australia Australia
135 Q3 Denmark Strait str. Greenland/Iceland
155 H3 Dennehotso Arizona U.S.A.
147 H4 Dennis Port Massachusetts U.S.A.
66 E4 Denny Scotland U.K.
147 K2 Dennysville Maine U.S.A.
68 D2 Den Oever Netherlands
22 C4 Denpasar Indonesia
82 C2 Dent Blanche mt. Switzerland
82 B2 Dent du Midi mt. Switzerland
8 □2 Dent I. i. Campbell I. New Zealand
147 F5 Denton Maryland U.S.A.
151 D5 Denton Texas U.S.A.
91 E3 Dent Parrachée mt. France
6 □1 D'Entrecasteaux Islands is P.N.G.
17 A7 D'Entrecasteaux, Pt pt Western Australia Australia
152 F4 Denver Colorado U.S.A.
74 C4 Denzlingen Germany
36 D3 Deoband India
37 E5 Deogarh mt. India
36 C4 Deogarh India
37 F5 Deogarh India
37 F4 Deoghar India
92 D2 Déols France
36 D5 Deori India
37 E4 Deoria India
36 C2 Deosai, Plains of plain Pakistan
37 E5 Deosil India
69 A3 De Panne Belgium
68 D3 De Peel reg. Netherlands
148 C3 De Pere Wisconsin U.S.A.
147 F3 Deposit New York U.S.A.
141 G3 Depot-Forbes Québec Canada
141 G3 Depot-Rowanton Québec Canada
118 D4 Dépression du Mourdi depression Chad
148 C5 Depue Illinois U.S.A.
45 P3 Deputatskiy Rus. Fed.
32 B2 Dêqên China
33 H2 Deqing China
33 E4 Deqing China
33 G3 Deqiu China
151 E5 De Queen Arkansas U.S.A.
36 B3 Dera Bugti Pakistan
36 B3 Dera Ghazi Khan Pakistan
36 B3 Dera Ismail Khan Pakistan
36 B3 Derajat reg. Pakistan
36 B3 Derawar Fort Pakistan
53 B1 Derazhne Ukraine
53 B2 Derazhnya Ukraine
51 J7 Derbent Rus. Fed.
113 G5 Derbent Turkey
47 G5 Derbent Uzbekistan
124 D2 Derbissaka Central African Rep.
147 G4 Derby Connecticut U.S.A.
63 E2 Derby div. England U.K.
63 E2 Derby England U.K.
151 D4 Derby Kansas U.S.A.
16 C3 Derby Western Australia Australia
63 E1 Derbyshire div. England U.K.
131 F2 Derdepoort South Africa
73 F4 Derenburg Germany
118 D5 Dérésa Chad
67 D2 Derg r. Northern Ireland U.K.
51 J5 Dergachi Rus. Fed.
67 D2 Derg, Lough l. Rep. of Ireland
67 C4 Derg, Lough l. Rep. of Ireland
53 G1 Derhachi Ukraine
151 E6 De Ridder Louisiana U.S.A.
68 C2 De Rijp Netherlands
42 E2 Derik Turkey
42 C2 Derinkuyu Turkey
126 D3 Derito well Ethiopia
53 E2 Deriyivka Ukraine
126 D4 Derkali well Kenya
51 F5 Derkul r. Rus. Fed.
86 D4 Der, Lac du l. France
130 B1 Derm Namibia
72 F4 Dermbach Germany
128 B4 Dernberg, Cape c. Namibia
53 A1 Derno Ukraine
32 B2 Dêrong China
67 D3 Derravaragh, Lough l. Rep. of Ireland
129 F2 Derre Mozambique
67 E4 Derry r. Rep. of Ireland
147 H3 Derry New Hampshire U.S.A.
Derry see Londonderry
64 A3 Derrygonnelly Northern Ireland U.K.
67 C2 Derryveagh Mts h. Rep. of Ireland
63 G2 Dersingham England U.K.
30 B4 Derstei China
72 C3 Dersum Germany
119 G4 Derudeb Sudan
109 E2 Deruta Italy
88 D4 Derval France
115 D5 Dervenakia Greece
104 F3 Derventa Bos.-Herz.
83 E2 Dervio Italy
114 B3 Derviziana Greece
64 B2 Dervock Northern Ireland U.K.
65 H3 Derwent r. England U.K.
13 F5 Derwent r. Tasmania Australia
65 G3 Derwent Res. resr England U.K.
65 G4 Derwent Res. resr England U.K.
65 E3 Derwent Water l. England U.K.
52 B1 Derza r. Rus. Fed.
47 G2 Derzhavinsk Kazakhstan
172 D2 Desaguadero r. Argentina
164 C3 Desaguadero r. Bolivia
172 D2 Desaguadero Argentina
164 C3 Desaguadero Peru
172 C3 Desague, Co mt. Argentina
83 D3 Desana Italy
7 □10 Désappointement, Îles de islands French Polynesia Pacific Ocean
154 D2 Desatoya Mts mts Nevada U.S.A.
140 D3 Desbarats Ontario Canada
134 F3 Des Bois, Lac l. N.W.T. Canada
98 D4 Descargamaría Spain
92 C2 Descartes France
141 J3 Deschaillons Québec Canada
137 H3 Deschambault L. l. Saskatchewan Canada
137 J4 Deschambault Lake Saskatchewan Canada
152 B2 Deschutes r. Oregon U.S.A.
126 C2 Desē Ethiopia
171 C6 Deseado r. Argentina
171 C6 Deseado Argentina
145 □3 Desecheo, I. i. Puerto Rico
156 B2 Desemboque Mexico
171 C6 Desengaño, Pta pt Argentina
107 E3 Desenzano del Garda Italy
141 G4 Deseronto Ontario Canada
96 □ Deserta Grande i. Madeira Portugal
96 □ Desertas, Ilhas is Madeira Portugal
155 E5 Desert Center California U.S.A.
92 E2 Désertines France
155 F1 Desert Peak summit Utah U.S.A.
101 G2 Desfiladero de Despeñaperros pass Spain
159 □5 Deshaies Guadeloupe Caribbean
114 A2 Dëshiran Albania
36 C4 Deshnok India
172 D1 Desiderio Tello Argentina
156 B2 Desierto de Altar desert Mexico
170 C2 Desierto de Atacama desert Chile
102 C3 Desierto de Calanda reg. Spain
162 A5 Desierto de Sechura desert Peru
156 B3 Desierto de Vizcaíno desert Mexico
106 D3 Desio Italy
114 C3 Deskati Greece
81 E4 Deskle Slovenia
136 G3 Desmarais Alberta Canada
141 G2 Desmaraisville Québec Canada
165 E5 Desmochados Paraguay
148 A5 Des Moines r. Iowa U.S.A.
150 E3 Des Moines Iowa U.S.A.
153 G4 Des Moines New Mexico U.S.A.
52 A3 Desna r. Rus. Fed.
53 D1 Desna Ukraine
52 A2 Desnogorsk Rus. Fed.
171 B5 Desnudo, Co mt. Argentina
171 A7 Desolación, I. i. Chile
23 C4 Desolation Point pt Philippines
131 E6 Despatch South Africa
172 E1 Despeñaderos Argentina
148 D4 Des Plaines Illinois U.S.A.
115 F6 Despotiko i. Greece
112 C2 Despotovac Yugoslavia
117 K6 Desroches i. Seychelles
73 H4 Dessau Sachsen-Anhalt Germany
69 D3 Dessel Belgium
90 E1 Dessoubre r. France
69 B3 Destelbergen Belgium
75 K3 Deštná Czech Rep.
141 F2 Destor Québec Canada
12 D3 D'Estrees B. b. S. Australia Australia
98 D2 Destriana Spain
136 B2 Destruction Bay Yukon Terr. Canada
108 B4 Desulo Sardegna Italy
86 A2 Desvres France
76 D3 Deszczno Poland
112 C2 Deta Romania
136 G2 Detah N.W.T. Canada
52 C2 Detchino Rus. Fed.
128 D2 Dete Zimbabwe
114 A3 Deti Jon b. Albania/Greece
112 B3 Detinja r. Yugoslavia
72 D4 Detmold div. Germany
72 D4 Detmold Nordrhein-Westfalen Germany
148 D3 Detour, Pt pt Michigan U.S.A.
149 F3 De Tour Village Michigan U.S.A.
149 F4 Detroit airport Michigan U.S.A.
149 F4 Detroit Michigan U.S.A.

139 H4 Détroit de Jacques-Cartier chan. Québec Canada
139 G4 Détroit d'Honguedo chan. Québec Canada
150 E2 Detroit Lakes Minnesota U.S.A.
73 H1 Dettmannsdorf Germany
13 G3 Deua Nat. Park nat. park New South Wales Australia
73 H4 Deuben Germany
69 C3 Deurne airport Belgium
69 D3 Deurne Netherlands
72 F2 Deutsch Evern Germany
81 G3 Deutschfeistritz Austria
73 H3 Deutschhof Germany
81 H3 Deutschkreutz Austria
81 G4 Deutschlandsberg div. Austria
81 G4 Deutschlandsberg Austria
81 H2 Deutsch-Wagram Austria
141 F3 Deux-Rivières Ontario Canada
92 B2 Deux-Sèvres div. France
99 F1 Deva r. Spain
112 D2 Deva Romania
38 B2 Devarkonda India
79 K4 Dévaványa Hungary
78 G4 Devecser Hungary
42 C2 Develi Turkey
68 E2 Deventer Netherlands
83 D2 Devero r. Italy
66 F3 Deveron r. Scotland U.K.
78 F2 Devét Skal h. Czech Rep.
36 B4 Devikot India
9 D4 Devil River Pk mt. New Zealand
67 D4 Devils Bit Mt. h. Rep. of Ireland
62 C2 Devil's Bridge Wales U.K.
154 C4 Devils Den California U.S.A.
154 C2 Devils Gate pass California U.S.A.
148 B2 Devils I. i. Wisconsin U.S.A.
150 D1 Devils Lake N. Dakota U.S.A.
136 C3 Devil's Paw mt. Canada/U.S.A.
154 C3 Devils Peak summit California U.S.A.
154 C3 Devils Postpile National Monument nat. park California U.S.A.
158 D1 Devil's Pt The Bahamas
112 E4 Devin Bulgaria
63 E3 Devizes England U.K.
36 C4 Devli India
112 F3 Devnya Bulgaria
113 C4 Devoll r. Albania
91 D4 Dévoluy mts France
62 C4 Devon div. England U.K.
63 F1 Devon r. England U.K.
65 E1 Devon r. Scotland U.K.
136 G4 Devon Alberta Canada
135 J2 Devon Island i. N.W.T. Canada
13 F5 Devonport Tasmania Australia
173 F1 Devoto Argentina
42 C1 Devrek Turkey
42 C1 Devrekâni Turkey
42 C1 Devrez r. Turkey
38 A2 Devrukh India
22 D3 Dewakang Besar i. Indonesia
37 G4 Dewangiri Bhutan
36 D5 Dewas India
131 F4 Dewetsdorp South Africa
146 B6 Dewey Lake l. Kentucky U.S.A.
68 E2 De Wijk Netherlands
151 F5 De Witt Arkansas U.S.A.
148 B5 De Witt Iowa U.S.A.
65 G4 Dewsbury England U.K.
33 G2 Dexing China
147 J2 Dexter Maine U.S.A.
151 F4 Dexter Missouri U.S.A.
147 E2 Dexter New York U.S.A.
32 D2 Deyang China
12 B2 Dey-Dey L. salt flat S. Australia Australia
39 D2 Deyhuk Iran
46 F5 Deynau Turkmenistan
21 L8 Deyong, Tg pt Indonesia
39 B4 Deyyer Iran
98 B2 Deza r. Spain
99 H3 Deza Spain
39 B2 Dezfül Iran
39 B3 Dez Gerd Iran
31 F5 Dezhou China
83 F2 Dezzo r. Italy
Dhahran see Az Zahrān
37 G5 Dhaka Bangladesh
37 F5 Dhalbhum reg. India
37 G4 Dhaleswari r. Bangladesh
37 H4 Dhaleswari r. India
126 D2 Dhamar Yemen
37 F5 Dhāmara India
36 C5 Dhamnod India
36 D3 Dhampur India
37 E5 Dhamtari India
36 B3 Dhana Sar Pakistan
37 F5 Dhanbad India
36 C5 Dhandhuka India
36 E3 Dhangarhi Nepal
37 E3 Dhang Ra. mountain range Nepal
37 F5 Dhankuta Nepal
36 C5 Dhar India
37 F4 Dharan Bazar Nepal
38 B4 Dharapuram India
36 B5 Dhari India
38 B3 Dharmapuri India
38 B3 Dharmavaram India
37 E5 Dharmjaygarh India
36 D2 Dharmshala India
126 F2 Dharoor watercourse Somalia
120 C5 Dhar Oualâta h. Mauritania
120 C5 Dhar Tîchît h. Mauritania
38 A3 Dhārwād India
36 D2 Dharwas India
36 B5 Dhasa India
36 D4 Dhasan r. India
37 E3 Dhaulagiri mt. Nepal
36 D4 Dhaulpur India
36 C4 Dhebar L. l. India
37 H4 Dhekiajuli India
37 F5 Dhenkanal India
42 C4 Dhībān Jordan
37 H4 Dhing India
42 F4 Dhī Qār div. Iraq
38 B3 Dhone India
36 B5 Dhoraji India
36 B5 Dhrangadhra India
126 D2 Dhubāb Yemen
36 C5 Dhule India
37 F4 Dhulian India
37 F4 Dhunche Nepal
126 F3 Dhuudo Somalia
126 E3 Dhuusa Marreeb Somalia
119 G2 Dhuwaybān basin Saudi Arabia
115 G7 Dia i. Greece
91 F4 Diable, Cime du mt. France
82 C2 Diablerets, Les mts Switzerland
159 □1 Diablo, Mt h. Jamaica
154 B3 Diablo, Mt mt. California U.S.A.
154 B3 Diablo Range mts California U.S.A.
127 C7 Diaca Mozambique
122 C4 Diafarabé Mali
124 E3 Diagbe Congo(Zaire)
122 D4 Diaka r. Mali
122 B4 Dialafara Mali
122 B4 Dialakoto Senegal
122 D4 Diallassagou Mali
172 D3 Diamante r. Argentina
173 G2 Diamante Argentina
111 E3 Diamante Italy
172 C3 Diamante, L. l. Argentina
14 D5 Diamantina watercourse Queensland Australia
169 G3 Diamantina Brazil
15 E4 Diamantina Lakes Queensland Australia
168 B2 Diamantino r. Brazil
168 B2 Diamantino Mato Grosso Brazil
166 A3 Diamantino Mato Grosso Brazil
37 G5 Diamond Harb. India
153 □1 Diamond Head headland Hawaii U.S.A.
15 G3 Diamond Islets is Coral Sea Islands Terr. Pacific Ocean
155 E2 Diamond Peak summit Nevada U.S.A.
122 B3 Diamounguél Senegal
55 D4 Dianalund Denmark
128 □2 Diana's Pk h. St Helena Atlantic Ocean
33 E4 Dianbai China
32 B3 Diancang Shan mt China
32 C3 Dian Chi l. China
122 C3 Diandioumé Mali
15 G2 Diane Bank sand bank Coral Sea Islands Terr. Pacific Ocean
122 C4 Diangounté Kamara Mali
32 D2 Dianjiang China
106 C5 Diano Marina Italy
166 C3 Dianópolis Brazil
122 C5 Dianra Côte d'Ivoire
31 J3 Diaoling China
123 E4 Diapaga Burkina
115 E5 Diaporioi i. Greece
114 E2 Diaporos i. Greece
114 E3 Diavlos Pelagonisou chan. Greece
114 E3 Diavlos Skiathou chan. Greece
115 C5 Diavolitsi Greece
25 A4 Diavolo, Mt h. Andaman and Nicobar Is India
173 G2 Diaz Argentina
128 B4 Diaz Pt pt Namibia
37 H4 Dibang r. India
125 D5 Dibaya Congo(Zaire)
125 C4 Dibaya-Lubwe Congo(Zaire)
126 D3 Dibber Uin Ethiopia
118 D5 Dibbis Sudan
123 G3 Dibella well Niger
130 D3 Dibeng South Africa
138 F2 D'Iberville, Lac l. Québec Canada
131 F1 Dibete Botswana
37 H4 Dibrugarh India
151 C5 Dickens Texas U.S.A.
147 J1 Dickey Maine U.S.A.
150 C2 Dickinson N. Dakota U.S.A.
8 □1 Dick, Mt h. Auckland Is New Zealand
145 C4 Dickson Tennessee U.S.A.
147 F4 Dickson City Pennsylvania U.S.A.
42 E2 Dicle r. Iraq/Turkey
107 F5 Dicomano Italy
126 C4 Dida Galgalu reg. Kenya
68 E3 Didam Netherlands
63 E3 Didcot England U.K.
54 E4 Didiasalis Lithuania
23 B2 Didicas i. Philippines
122 C4 Didiéni Mali
115 E5 Didima Greece
53 C1 Didivshchyna Ukraine
36 C4 Didwana India
129 H2 Didy Madagascar
113 F4 Didymoteicho Greece
77 N1 Didžiulis l. Lithuania
91 D4 Die France
74 C2 Dieblich Germany
122 D4 Diébougou Burkina
85 J2 Dieburg Germany
80 B2 Diedorf Germany
137 H4 Diefenbaker, L. l. Saskatchewan Canada
92 E3 Diège r. France
171 A7 Diego de Almagro, I. i. Chile
173 F3 Diego de Alvear Argentina
175 J4 Diego Garcia i. British Indian Ocean Territory
120 C5 Diégrâga well Mauritania
122 C5 Diéké Guinea
69 E5 Diekirch Luxembourg
83 D1 Dielsdorf Switzerland
122 C4 Diéma Mali
122 A4 Diembéreng Senegal
72 E4 Diemel r. Germany
72 D4 Diemelsee-Adorf Germany
68 C2 Diemen Netherlands
24 C2 Điện Biên Vietnam
24 D3 Điện Châu Vietnam
25 E4 Điện Khanh Vietnam
54 D3 Dienvidsuseja r. Latvia
69 D4 Diepenbeek Belgium
68 E2 Diepenheim Netherlands
72 D3 Diepholz Germany
89 G2 Dieppe France
159 □6 Dieppe Bay Town St Kitts-Nevis Caribbean
74 C2 Dierdorf Germany
68 E2 Dieren Netherlands
30 C5 Di'er Nonchang Qu r. China
31 H3 Di'er Songhua r. China
73 F3 Diesdorf Germany
73 H4 Dieskau Germany
75 G5 Dießen am Ammersee Germany
83 D1 Diessenhofen Switzerland
69 D4 Diest Belgium
80 B2 Dietenheim Germany
75 G3 Dietfurt an der Altmühl Germany
83 D1 Dietikon Switzerland
81 F2 Dietmanns Austria
83 F1 Dietmannsried Germany
87 H2 Dietzhölztal-Ewersbach Germany
91 D4 Dieulefit France
87 F4 Dieulouard France
87 F4 Dieuze France
68 E2 Diever Netherlands
101 G3 Diezma Spain
123 G3 Diffa div. Niger
123 G4 Diffa Niger
69 D5 Differdange Luxembourg
Difuntios, L. de los see Negra, L.
38 D2 Digapahandi India
124 E3 Digba Congo(Zaire)
37 H4 Digboi India
139 G5 Digby Nova Scotia Canada
179 □ Digby, C. c. Kerguelen Indian Ocean
37 F5 Digha India
92 C3 Dignac France
80 D4 Dignano Italy
91 E4 Digne-les-Bains France
89 G3 Digny France
90 B2 Digoin France
23 C5 Digos Philippines
36 D5 Digras India
36 B4 Digri Pakistan
21 M8 Digul r. Indonesia
122 D5 Digya National Park nat. park Ghana
37 H3 Dihang r. India
77 N5 Dihtiv Ukraine
53 E1 Dihtyari Ukraine
126 D4 Diinsoor Somalia
69 C4 Dijle r. Belgium
90 D1 Dijon Côte-d'Or France
90 D1 Dijon-Longvic airport France
126 D2 Dikhil Djibouti
42 A2 Dikili Turkey
43 A4 Dîkirnis Egypt
69 A4 Dikkebus Belgium
51 H7 Diklosmta mt. Rus. Fed.
122 C5 Dikodougou Côte d'Ivoire
69 A3 Diksmuide div. Belgium
69 A3 Diksmuide Belgium
44 K2 Dikson Rus. Fed.
115 G7 Dikti mt. Greece
123 G4 Dikwa Nigeria
126 C3 Dīla Ethiopia
101 G3 Dilar r. Spain
39 D3 Dilaram Iran
69 C4 Dilbeek Belgium
21 J8 Dili Indonesia
125 D4 Dili Congo(Zaire)
25 A5 Diligent Str. chan. Andaman and Nicobar Is India
42 F1 Dilijan Armenia
25 E5 Di Linh Vietnam
9 D5 Dillon Cone mt. New Zealand
Dilizhan see Dilijan
74 D2 Dillenburg Germany
151 D6 Dilley Texas U.S.A.
119 E5 Dilling Sudan
80 B2 Dillingen an der Donau Germany
74 B3 Dillingen (Saar) Germany
134 C4 Dillingham Alaska U.S.A.
152 D2 Dillon Montana U.S.A.
137 H3 Dillon Saskatchewan Canada
145 E5 Dillon S. Carolina U.S.A.
125 D6 Dilolo Congo(Zaire)
115 G5 Dilos i. Greece
69 D3 Dilsen Belgium
123 B3 Dimako Cameroon
37 H4 Dimapur India
83 F2 Dimaro Italy
43 D3 Dimashq div. Syria
43 D3 Dimashq Syria
125 D5 Dimbelenge Congo(Zaire)
122 D5 Dimbokro Côte d'Ivoire
13 E4 Dimboola Victoria Australia
15 F3 Dimbulah Queensland Australia
114 E2 Dimitritsi Greece
112 E3 Dimitrovgrad Bulgaria
50 J4 Dimitrovgrad Rus. Fed.
112 D3 Dimitrovgrad Yugoslavia
43 C4 Dimona Israel
128 C3 Dimpho Pan salt pan Botswana
55 □1 Dimunarfjørður chan. Faeroes
23 C4 Dinagat i. Philippines
23 C4 Dinagat Sound chan. Philippines
37 G4 Dinajpur Bangladesh
88 C3 Dinan France
122 D4 Dinangourou Mali
69 C4 Dinant div. Namur Belgium
69 C4 Dinant Belgium
37 F4 Dinapur India
42 B2 Dinar Turkey
104 F3 Dinara mountain range Croatia
88 C3 Dinard France
39 B3 Dīnār, Kūh-e mt. Iran
127 C4 Dinas well Kenya
125 B6 Dinde Angola
119 F5 Dinder r. Ethiopia/Sudan
119 G5 Dinder National Park nat. park Sudan
38 B4 Dindigul India
123 G4 Dindima Nigeria
36 E5 Dindori India
88 A3 Dinéault France
43 B1 Dinek Turkey
125 C5 Dinga Congo(Zaire)
36 B2 Dinga Pakistan
124 E3 Dingba Congo(Zaire)
30 C5 Dingbian China
125 B5 Dinge Cabinda Angola
88 D3 Dingé France
72 F4 Dingelstädt Germany
73 F4 Dingelstedt am Huy Germany
33 H2 Dinghai China
37 F4 Dingla Nepal
67 A4 Dingle Rep. of Ireland
67 A4 Dingle Bay b. Rep. of Ireland
111 □ Dingli Malta
33 F3 Dingnan China
15 G4 Dingo Queensland Australia
75 H4 Dingolfing Germany
23 B2 Dingras Philippines
33 F1 Dingtao China
122 B4 Dinguiraye Guinea
66 D3 Dingwall Scotland U.K.
32 D1 Dingxi China
31 E5 Ding Xian China
30 A4 Dingxin China
31 E5 Dingxing China
33 G1 Dingyuan China
31 G5 Dingzi Gang inlet China
37 G4 Dinhata India
24 D2 Dinh Lâp Vietnam
68 E2 Dinkel r. Netherlands
74 F3 Dinkelsbühl Germany
75 F4 Dinkelscherben Germany
72 D3 Dinklage Germany
155 G3 Dinnebito Wash r. Arizona U.S.A.
37 F3 Dinngyê China
137 L5 Dinorwic Lake Minnesota U.S.A.
155 H1 Dinosaur Colorado U.S.A.
152 E3 Dinosaur Nat. Mon. nat. park Colorado U.S.A.
72 B4 Dinslaken Nordrhein-Westfalen Germany
68 C3 Dinteloord Netherlands
22 A3 Dinteladas Indonesia
68 E3 Dinxperlo Netherlands
122 C4 Dioïla Mali
122 C5 Dion r. Guinea
118 D4 Diona well Chad
169 G3 Dionísio Brazil
167 B6 Dionísio Cerqueira Brazil
168 C2 Diorama Brazil
115 E5 Dioriga Korinthou b. Greece
79 H4 Diósd Hungary
79 J4 Diósjenő Hungary
90 B2 Diou France
122 A4 Diouloulou Senegal
122 C4 Dioumara Mali
122 E4 Dioundiou Niger
122 A4 Diourbel Senegal
37 H4 Diphu India
36 B4 Diplo Pakistan
23 B4 Dipolog Philippines
114 F1 Dipotama Greece
69 E5 Dippach Luxembourg
75 J2 Dippoldiswalde Germany
9 B6 Dipton New Zealand
41 M2 Dir Pakistan
122 D3 Diré Mali
15 E2 Direction, C. c. Queensland Australia
10 □1 Direction I. i. Cocos Is Indian Ocean
126 D3 Dirē Dawa Ethiopia
114 E4 Dirfys mts Greece
125 D7 Dirico Angola
110 D5 Dirillo r. Sicilia Italy
17 A5 Dirk Hartog I. i. Western Australia Australia
123 G3 Dirkou Niger
68 C3 Dirksland Netherlands
15 G6 Dirranbandi Queensland Australia
119 H4 Dirs Saudi Arabia
155 G2 Dirty Devil r. Utah U.S.A.
36 C1 Disa India
159 □1 Disappointment, C. c. S. Georgia Atlantic Ocean
152 A2 Disappointment, C. c. Washington U.S.A.
8 □1 Disappointment I. i. Auckland Is New Zealand
Disappointment Is is see Désappointement, Îles de
17 C4 Disappointment, L. salt flat Western Australia Australia
13 G4 Disaster B. b. New South Wales Australia
12 E4 Discovery Bay b. Australia
27 □ Discovery Bay b. Hong Kong China
159 □1 Discovery Bay Jamaica
83 D2 Disentis Muster Switzerland
106 D2 Disgrazia, Monte mt. Italy
Disko i. see Qeqertarsuaq
Disko Bugt b. see Qeqertarsuup Tunua
147 E6 Dismal Swamp swamp N. Carolina U.S.A.
111 H2 Diso Italy
69 D4 Dison Belgium
37 G4 Dispur India
141 K4 Disraëli Québec Canada
63 H2 Diss England U.K.
92 C2 Dissay France
72 D3 Dissen am Teutoburger Wald Germany
122 D4 Dissin Burkina
65 E3 Distington England U.K.
115 D4 Distomo Greece
114 C2 Distrato Greece
168 E1 Distrito Federal div. Brazil
43 A4 Disûq Egypt
23 B4 Dit i. Philippines
131 H1 Diti Zimbabwe
110 D5 Dittaino r. Sicilia Italy
74 E4 Ditzingen Germany
23 C4 Diuata Mts mountain range Philippines
23 C4 Diuata Pt pt Philippines
81 E5 Divača Slovenia
39 A2 Divāndarreh Iran
115 B4 Divarata Greece
125 B4 Divénié Congo
106 C2 Diveria r. Italy
89 F2 Dives r. France
89 E2 Dives-sur-Mer France
52 F2 Diveyevo Rus. Fed.
Divichi see Däväçi
111 E4 Divieto Sicilia Italy
23 B2 Divilacan Bay b. Philippines
129 E3 Divinhe Mozambique
169 F4 Divinópolis Brazil
86 B2 Divion France
51 G6 Divnoye Rus. Fed.
122 C5 Divo Côte d'Ivoire
90 E2 Divonne-les-Bains France
100 B2 Divor r. Portugal
100 C2 Divor, Barragem do resr Portugal
113 F7 Divounia i. Greece
42 D2 Divriği Turkey
36 A4 Diwana Pakistan
122 D6 Dixcove Ghana
147 H2 Dixfield Maine U.S.A.
82 C2 Dix, Lac des l. Switzerland
141 H3 Dix Milles, Lac des l. Québec Canada
147 J2 Dixmont Maine U.S.A.
154 B2 Dixon California U.S.A.
148 C5 Dixon Illinois U.S.A.
136 C4 Dixon Entrance chan. Canada/U.S.A.
136 F3 Dixonville Alberta Canada
172 E3 Dixonville Argentina
141 K4 Dixville Québec Canada
42 D2 Diyadin Turkey
42 F3 Diyālá div. Iraq
42 E2 Diyarbakır Turkey
Dizak see Dāvar Panāh
39 C2 Diz Chah Iran
86 C3 Dizy France
69 C5 Dizy-le-Gros France
124 B3 Dja r. Cameroon
123 G2 Djado Niger
121 F2 Djamâa Algeria
129 H1 Djamandjary Madagascar
125 B4 Djambala Congo
125 C4 Djampie Congo(Zaire)
121 F4 Djanet Algeria
124 B3 Dja, Réserve du res. Cameroon
6 □1 Djaul I. i. P.N.G.
124 C1 Djébrène Chad
118 C5 Djédaa Chad
121 F2 Djelfa Algeria
124 E2 Djéma Central African Rep.
122 D4 Djenné Mali
124 B2 Djerem r. Cameroon
124 C1 Djermaya Chad
122 D4 Djibo Burkina
116 J4 Djibouti country Africa
126 D2 Djibouti Djibouti
120 C5 Djiguéni Mauritania
163 F3 Djoemoe Surinam
124 B2 Djohong Cameroon
123 E5 Djougou Benin
124 B3 Djoum Cameroon
124 B2 Djoumboli Cameroon
56 N6 Djúpivogur Iceland
59 G3 Djupvik Sweden
59 F1 Djurås Sweden
55 C3 Djursland reg. Denmark
77 L2 Długołęka Białystok Poland
76 F4 Długołęka Wrocław Poland
77 K3 Długosiodło Poland
77 H4 Dłutów Poland
22 C2 D Melintang l. Indonesia
47 L2 Dmitriyevka Rus. Fed.
52 B3 Dmitriyev-L'govskiy Rus. Fed.
30 B1 Dmitriyevskiy Rus. Fed.
52 C2 Dmitriyevskoye Rus. Fed.
52 C1 Dmitrov Rus. Fed.
52 A3 Dmitrovo Rus. Fed.
52 D2 Dmitrovskiy Pogost Rus. Fed.
52 B3 Dmitrovsk-Orlovskiy Rus. Fed.
52 D3 Dmitryashevka Rus. Fed.
77 H4 Dmosin Poland
53 E1 Dmytrivka Chernihiv Ukraine
53 F3 Dmytrivka Dnipropetrovs'k Ukraine
53 E3 Dmytrivka Kherson Ukraine
53 G3 Dmytrivka Zaporizhzhya Ukraine
52 A2 Dnepr r. Rus. Fed.
52 A2 Dneprovskoye Rus. Fed.
53 C3 Dnestrovsc Moldova
Dnieper r. Belarus see Dnyapro
Dnieper r. Rus. Fed. see Dnepr
Dnieper r. Ukraine see Dnipro
Dniester r. see Dnister
53 E1 Dnipro r. Ukraine
53 F2 Dniprodzerzhyns'k Ukraine
53 F2 Dniprodzerzhyns'ke Vodoskhovyshche resr Ukraine
53 F2 Dnipropetrovs'k div. Ukraine
53 F2 Dnipropetrovs'k Ukraine
53 F3 Dniprorudne Ukraine
53 F2 Dniprovs'ke Ukraine
53 F2 Dniprovs'ke Vodoskhovyshche resr Ukraine
53 D3 Dniprovs'kyy Lyman est. Ukraine
77 M6 Dnister r. Ukraine
54 F3 Dno Rus. Fed.
50 D4 Dnyapro r. Belarus
39 F2 Doabi Mekh-i-Zarin Afghanistan
22 D3 Doangdoangan Besar i. Indonesia
22 D3 Doangdoangan Kecil i. Indonesia
129 H1 Doany Madagascar
124 C2 Doba Chad
37 G3 Doba China
107 G2 Dobbiaco Italy
140 E4 Dobbinton Ontario Canada
77 J6 Dobczyce Poland
54 C3 Dobele Latvia
73 J4 Döbeln Germany
73 J4 Doberlug-Kirchhain Germany
73 K4 Döbern Germany
81 G2 Dobersberg Austria
76 D3 Dobiegniew Poland
77 K4 Dobieszyn Poland
172 E4 Doblas Argentina
21 K8 Dobo Indonesia
104 G3 Doboj Bos.-Herz.
81 G5 Dobova Slovenia
76 G4 Dobra Konin Poland
76 D2 Dobra Szczecin Poland
76 C2 Dobra Szczecin Poland
79 M6 Dobra Romania
78 C2 Dobřany Czech Rep.
81 G2 Dobra Stausee l. Austria
77 K3 Dobre Siedlce Poland
76 G3 Dobre Włocławek Poland
77 J2 Dobre Miasto Poland
114 B2 Dobrenj Albania
114 D1 Dobrešinci Macedonia
79 M5 Dobrești Romania
112 F3 Dobrich Bulgaria
52 E3 Dobrinka Rus. Fed.
78 D2 Dobříš Czech Rep.
73 H3 Dobritz Germany
81 G4 Dobrna Slovenia
76 G5 Dobrodzień Poland
77 L6 Dobromyl' Ukraine
77 H4 Dobroń Poland
53 G2 Dobropillya Ukraine
77 M5 Dobrosyn Ukraine
76 F4 Dobroszyce Poland
112 E2 Dobroteşti Romania
77 N5 Dobrotvir Ukraine
112 F1 Dobrovăț Romania
53 D2 Dobrovelychkivka Ukraine
81 H4 Dobrovnik Slovenia
54 C4 Dobrovol'sk Rus. Fed.
52 D3 Dobroye Rus. Fed.
112 F3 Dobrudzhansko Plato plat. Bulgaria
114 C1 Dobruševo Macedonia
78 F1 Dobruška Czech Rep.
77 J3 Dobrzankowo Poland
73 L2 Dobrzany Poland
76 F5 Dobrzeń Wielki Poland
77 M2 Dobrzyniewo Kościelne Poland
77 H3 Dobrzyń nad Wisłą Poland
79 K3 Dobšiná Slovakia
23 A5 Doc Can reef Philippines
168 C2 Doce r. Brazil
169 H3 Doce r. Brazil
66 D4 Dochart r. Scotland U.K.
63 G2 Docking England U.K.
69 E4 Dockweiler Germany
153 F6 Doctor B. Domínguez Mexico
36 C2 Doda India
141 H2 Doda, Lac l. Québec Canada
36 B3 Dodapur Pakistan
38 B3 Dod Ballapur India
Dodecanese is see Dodekanisos
113 F6 Dodekanisos is Greece
152 C2 Dodge Washington U.S.A.
148 A3 Dodge Center Minnesota U.S.A.
151 C4 Dodge City Kansas U.S.A.
148 B4 Dodgeville Wisconsin U.S.A.
107 F3 Dodici, Cima mt. Italy
62 B4 Dodman Point pt England U.K.
127 C6 Dodoma div. Tanzania
127 C6 Dodoma Tanzania
114 B3 Dodoni Greece
68 E2 Doesburg Netherlands
68 E3 Doetinchem Netherlands
68 E1 Doezum Netherlands
21 J7 Dofa Indonesia
37 G2 Dogai Coring salt lake China
113 F6 Doğanbey Turkey
42 D2 Doğanşehir Turkey
136 E4 Dog Creek B.C. Canada
37 G3 Dogên Co salt lake China
82 D1 Dogern Germany
139 H2 Dog Island i. Newfoundland Canada
137 K4 Dog L. l. Manitoba Canada
140 A2 Dog Lake l. Ontario Canada
140 C2 Dog Lake l. Ontario Canada
106 B4 Dogliani Italy
28 D5 Dōgo i. Japan
126 E3 Dogoble well Somalia
123 E4 Dogondoutchi Niger
124 C1 Dogoumbo Chad
30 D6 Dōgo-yama mt. Japan
42 F2 Doğubeyazıt Turkey
113 G6 Doğu Menteşe Dağları mountain range Turkey
159 □6 Dogwood Pt pt St Kitts-Nevis Caribbean
37 G3 Do'gyaling China
39 B4 Doha Qatar
Doha see Ad Dawhah
Dohad see Dāhod
37 H5 Dohazar Bangladesh
37 G3 Doilungdêqên China
24 B3 Doi Saket Thailand
69 C4 Doische Belgium
168 D5 Dois Córregos Brazil
114 D1 Dojran, Lake l. Greece/Macedonia
Dojransko Ezero l. see Dojran, Lake
58 D1 Dokka Norway
68 D1 Dokkum Netherlands
68 D1 Dokkumer Ee r. Netherlands
115 E5 Dokos i. Greece
36 B4 Dokri Pakistan
54 E4 Dokshytsy Belarus
78 D1 Doksy Czech Rep.
28 L1 Dokuchayeva,M. pt Rus. Fed.
46 F2 Dokuchayevka Kazakhstan
53 G3 Dokuchayevs'k Ukraine
122 D3 Do, Lac l. Mali
21 L8 Dolak, P. i. Indonesia
171 C5 Dolavón Argentina
141 J2 Dolbeau Québec Canada
62 B2 Dolbenmaen Wales U.K.
106 B5 Dolceacqua Italy
88 D3 Dol-de-Bretagne France
90 D1 Dole France
126 B2 Doleib watercourse Sudan
82 B2 Dôle, La mt. Switzerland
114 C1 Dolenci Macedonia
107 J3 Dolenja vas Slovenia
82 C3 Dolent, Mont mt. France/Italy
62 C2 Dolgellau Wales U.K.
73 J2 Dolgen Germany
147 F3 Dolgeville New York U.S.A.
53 F1 Dolgiye Budy Rus. Fed.
52 D3 Dolgorukovo Rus. Fed.
52 C3 Dolgoye Rus. Fed.
77 N5 Dolhobyczów Poland
108 B5 Dolianova Sardegna Italy
76 D2 Dolice Poland
27 Q2 Dolinsk Rus. Fed.
112 C3 Doljevac Yugoslavia
65 E1 Dollar Scotland U.K.
179 B2 Dolleman I. i. Antarctica
90 F1 Dollern r. France
75 G4 Dollnstein Germany
75 L2 Dolní Bousov Czech Rep.
78 D3 Dolní Dvořiště Czech Rep.
81 H1 Dolní Kounice Czech Rep.
79 G3 Dolní Němčí Czech Rep.
75 K2 Dolní Podluží Czech Rep.
79 J2 Dolný Kubín Slovakia
107 G3 Dolo Italy
82 A3 Dolomieu France
107 F2 Dolomiti Bellunesi, delle Parco Nazionale nat. park Italy
Dolonnur see Duolon
126 D4 Dolo Odo Ethiopia
30 C3 Doloon Mongolia
155 H2 Dolores r. Colorado U.S.A.
173 J4 Dolores Argentina
157 H5 Dolores Guatemala
173 H2 Dolores Uruguay
134 G3 Dolphin and Union Str. chan. N.W.T. Canada
171 E7 Dolphin, C. c. Falkland Is.
128 A4 Dolphin Head headland Namibia
80 D4 Dölsach Austria
76 F4 Dolsk Poland
77 N4 Dol's'k Ukraine
24 D3 Đô Lương Vietnam
51 B5 Dolyna Ukraine
53 E2 Dolyns'ka Ukraine
53 C3 Dolyns'ke Ukraine
111 F3 Domanico Italy
77 H3 Domaniewice Poland
53 D3 Domanivka Ukraine
37 G4 Domar Bangladesh
36 E2 Domar China
77 K6 Domaradz Poland
83 E2 Domat Ems Switzerland
86 C4 Domats France
78 B2 Domažlice Czech Rep.
32 A1 Domba China
57 C3 Dombås Norway
79 L5 Dombegyház Hungary
90 C2 Dombes reg. France
79 H5 Dombóvár Hungary
82 B1 Dombresson Switzerland
68 B3 Domburg Netherlands
169 G3 Dom Cavati Brazil
179 C4 Dome Argus ice feature Antarctica
179 C5 Dome Circe ice feature Antarctica
136 E4 Dome Creek B.C. Canada
80 D4 Domegge di Cadore Italy
163 F3 Dome Hill h. Guyana
54 C4 Domeikava Lithuania
Domel I. i. see Letsok-aw Kyun
92 E3 Dôme, Monts mts France
90 D3 Domène France
136 D2 Dome Pk summit N.W.T. Canada
92 E2 Domérat France
155 E5 Dome Rock Mts mts Arizona U.S.A.
87 E4 Domèvre-en-Haye France
87 F4 Domèvre-sur-Vezouze France
164 C4 Domeyko Antofagasta Chile
170 B2 Domeyko Atacama Chile
164 C4 Domeyko, Cord. mountain range Chile
89 E3 Domfront France
169 H4 Domingos Martins Brazil
133 M8 Dominica country Caribbean
156 K7 Dominical Costa Rica
133 L8 Dominican Republic country Caribbean
159 G4 Dominica Passage chan. Dominica/Guadeloupe
135 L3 Dominion, C. headland N.W.T. Canada
73 G2 Dömitz Germany
86 D4 Dommartin-le-Franc France
93 D4 Domme France
69 D3 Dommel r. Netherlands
73 H4 Dommitzsch Germany
30 E2 Domna Rus. Fed.
112 F2 Domneşti Romania
25 D4 Dom Noi, L. r. Thailand
126 E3 Domo Ethiopia
52 C2 Domodedovo Rus. Fed.
106 C2 Domodossola Italy
114 D3 Domokos Greece
127 D7 Domoni Comoros
86 B3 Domont France
87 E4 Dompaire France
87 E4 Dompcevrin France
173 K1 Dom Pedrito Brazil
166 D2 Dom Pedro Brazil
90 B2 Dompierre-sur-Besbre France
92 A2 Dompierre-sur-Mer France
92 A2 Dompierre-sur-Yon France
22 D4 Dompu Indonesia
108 A6 Domus de Maria Sardegna Italy
108 A5 Domusnovas Sardegna Italy
15 G6 Domville, Mt h. Queensland Australia
81 F4 Domžale Slovenia
66 F3 Don r. Scotland U.K.
88 D4 Don r. France
38 B2 Don r. India
44 F5 Don r. Rus. Fed.
156 C3 Don Mexico
64 A3 Donagh Northern Ireland U.K.
67 F2 Donaghadee Northern Ireland U.K.
67 E2 Donaghmore Northern Ireland U.K.
13 E4 Donald Victoria Australia
101 F3 Doña Mencía Spain
100 D4 Doñana, Parque Nacional de nat. park Spain
172 B1 Doña Rosa, Cord. mountain range Chile
81 H2 Donau r. Austria/Germany
74 D5 Donaueschingen Germany
75 G4 Donaumoos reg. Germany
75 F4 Donauried reg. Germany
80 D1 Donaustauf Germany
75 F4 Donauwörth Germany
100 E2 Don Benito Spain
65 G4 Doncaster England U.K.
86 D3 Donchery France
125 B5 Dondo Angola
129 E2 Dondo Mozambique
23 B4 Dondonay i. Philippines
22 E1 Dondo, Tg pt Indonesia
38 C5 Dondra Head c. Sri Lanka
53 B2 Dondușeni Moldova
67 C2 Donegal div. Rep. of Ireland
67 C2 Donegal Rep. of Ireland
67 C2 Donegal Bay g. Rep. of Ireland
67 B4 Donegal Point pt Rep. of Ireland
53 G3 Donets'k div. Ukraine
53 G3 Donets'k Ukraine
51 F5 Donets'kyy Kryazh ridge Rus. Fed./Ukraine
126 E3 Donfar Ethiopia
159 □1 Don Figuerero Mts mts Jamaica
32 D1 Dong r. China
30 B4 Dong r. China
123 G5 Donga r. Cameroon/Nigeria
123 G5 Donga Nigeria
33 E3 Dong'an China
17 A6 Dongara Western Australia Australia
36 E5 Dongargarh India
32 C3 Dongchuan China
37 F2 Dongco China
24 D2 Đông Đăng Vietnam
31 F5 Dong'e China
68 C3 Dongen Netherlands
88 C4 Donges France
32 E5 Dongfang China
31 K3 Dongfanghong China
31 H4 Dongfeng China
33 F1 Dongfeng China
22 D2 Donggala Indonesia
32 B1 Donggi Cona l. China
31 H5 Donggou China
33 F3 Donggu China
33 F4 Dongguan China
31 F5 Dongguang China

24 D3 Đông Ha Vietnam
33 G1 Donghai China
33 E4 Donghai Dao China
24 D3 Đông Hôi Vietnam
31 J3 Dongjingcheng China
37 H3 Dongjug China
22 D2 Dongkait, Tg pt Indonesia
21 H6 Dongkalang Indonesia
33 E3 Dongkou China
37 G4 Dongkya La India
32 D3 Donglan China
30 B5 Dongle China
31 G4 Dongliao r. China
31 G3 Dongminzhutun China
31 J4 Dongning China
125 C6 Dongo Angola
106 D2 Dongo Italy
124 C3 Dongo Congo(Zaire)
124 D3 Dongobe Congo(Zaire)
119 F4 Dongola Sudan
126 B4 Dongotona Mts mt. Sudan
124 C3 Dongou Congo
24 C3 Dong Phraya Fai mountain range Thailand
25 C4 Dong Phraya Yen escarpment Thailand
31 F6 Dongping China
33 F4 Dongping China
37 G3 Dongqiao China
33 G4 Dongshan China
33 G4 Dongshan Dao i. China
30 D5 Dongsheng China
33 H1 Dongtai r. China
33 H1 Dongtai China
33 F2 Dongting Hu l. China
33 H3 Dongtou China
31 F3 Dong Ujimqin Qi China
33 G2 Dongxiang China
30 B6 Dongxiangzu China
32 D4 Dongxing China
33 H2 Dongyang China
31 F5 Dongying China
30 B5 Dongzhen China
33 G2 Dongzhi China
172 B3 Doñihue Chile
98 E4 Doñinos de Salamanca Spain
112 C3 Donja Dubnica Yugoslavia
81 H4 Donja Konjšćina Croatia
81 G5 Donja Stubica Croatia
81 H4 Donja Višnjica Croatia
81 H5 Donja Zelina Croatia
136 B2 Donjek r. *Yukon Terr.* Canada
79 H6 Donji Miholjac Croatia
112 D2 Donji Milanovac Yugoslavia
104 F3 Donji Vakuf Bos.-Herz.
68 E1 Donkerbroek Netherlands
131 E5 Donkerpoort South Africa
37 G5 Donmanick Is. is Bangladesh
151 C7 Don Martín Mexico
139 F4 Donnacona *Québec* Canada
110 D6 Donnalucata *Sicilia* Italy
82 C3 Donnas Italy
136 F3 Donnelly *Alberta* Canada
8 D1 Donnellys Crossing New Zealand
86 C4 Donnemarie-Dontilly France
154 B2 Donner Pass pass *California* U.S.A.
87 G3 Donnersberg h. Germany
17 A7 Donnybrook *Western Australia* Australia
87 G4 Donon mt. France
102 B1 Donostia-San Sebastián *Guipúzcoa* Spain
113 E6 Donousa i. Greece
53 G3 Dons'ke Ukraine
50 F4 Donskoy Rus. Fed.
52 D3 Donskoye Rus. Fed.
51 G6 Donskoye Rus. Fed.
23 B3 Donsol Philippines
88 D3 Donville-les-Bains France
80 A2 Donzdorf Germany
107 G4 Donzella, Isola della i. Italy
92 D3 Donzenac France
90 B1 Donzy France
67 A3 Dooagh Rep. of Ireland
16 B4 Dooleena h. *Western Australia* Australia
14 D3 Doomadgee *Queensland* Australia
14 D3 Doomadgee Abor. Land res. *Queensland* Australia
66 D5 Doon r. *Scotland* U.K.
67 B4 Doonbeg r. Rep. of Ireland
66 D5 Doon, Loch l. *Scotland* U.K.
130 B6 Doorn r. South Africa
68 D2 Doorn Netherlands
68 D3 Doornspijk Netherlands
148 D3 Door Peninsula pen. *Michigan* U.S.A.
126 E3 Dooxo Nugaaleed v. Somalia
32 C1 Do Qu r. China
39 E3 Dor watercourse Afghanistan
52 B2 Dor Rus. Fed.
153 G5 Dora *New Mexico* U.S.A.
106 B3 Dora Baltea r. Italy
16 C4 Dora, L. salt flat *Western Australia* Australia
106 B3 Dora Riparia r. Italy
Dorbiljin *see* Emin
31 H3 Dorbod China
Dorbod Qi *see* Siziwang Qi
62 D4 Dorchester *England* U.K.
128 B3 Dordabis Namibia
86 B4 Dordives France
92 C3 Dordogne div. *Aquitaine* France
93 C4 Dordogne r. France
68 C3 Dordrecht Netherlands
131 F5 Dordrecht South Africa
90 B3 Dore r. France
137 H4 Doré L. l. *Saskatchewan* Canada
137 H4 Doré Lake *Saskatchewan* Canada
91 B3 Dore-l'Église France
92 E3 Dore, Monts mts France
66 D3 Dores *Scotland* U.K.
169 F3 Dores do Indaiá Brazil
75 H4 Dorfen Germany
80 E3 Dorfgastein Austria
73 G2 Dorf Mecklenburg Germany
108 B4 Dorgali *Sardegna* Italy
39 F3 Dori r. Afghanistan
123 D4 Dori Burkina
172 F3 Dorila Argentina
130 B6 Doring r. South Africa
130 B5 Doringbaai South Africa
130 B5 Doringbos South Africa
63 F3 Dorking *England* U.K.
122 D5 Dormaa-Ahenkro Ghana
72 B4 Dormagen *Nordrhein-Westfalen* Germany
79 K4 Dormánd Hungary
86 C3 Dormans France
31 K3 Dormidontovka Rus. Fed.
82 C1 Dornach Switzerland
81 G4 Dornava Slovenia
83 E1 Dornbirn div. Austria
80 A3 Dornbirn Austria
73 G4 Dornburg Germany
74 F2 Dorndorf Germany
90 B2 Dornes France
30 D3 Dorngovĭ div. Mongolia
66 C3 Dornie *Scotland* U.K.
83 D3 Dorno Italy
66 D3 Dornoch Firth est. *Scotland* U.K.
31 E3 Dornod div. Mongolia
74 E4 Dornstadt Germany
72 C2 Dornum Germany
122 D3 Doro Mali
112 F2 Dorobanţu Romania
52 C3 Dorobino Rus. Fed.
79 H4 Dorog Hungary
52 A2 Dorogobuzh Rus. Fed.
50 H1 Dorogorskoye Rus. Fed.
52 G1 Dorogucha Rus. Fed.
112 F1 Dorohoi Romania
77 M4 Dorohusk Poland
52 C2 Dorokhovo Rus. Fed.
39 D2 Dorokhsh Iran
26 F2 Dorööö Nuur salt lake Mongolia
77 N5 Dorosyni Ukraine
56 F2 Dorotea Sweden
68 F2 Dörpen Germany
17 A5 Dorre I. i. *Western Australia* Australia
13 H2 Dorrigo *New South Wales* Australia
152 B3 Dorris *California* U.S.A.
124 B2 Dorsale Camerounaise slope Cameroon/Nigeria
62 D4 Dorset div. *England* U.K.
141 F4 Dorset *Ontario* Canada
72 B4 Dorsten *Nordrhein-Westfalen* Germany
90 D2 Dortan France
72 C4 Dortmund Germany
72 C4 Dortmund-Ems-Kanal canal Germany
146 B6 Dorton *Kentucky* U.S.A.
43 D1 Dörtyol Turkey
76 G4 Doruchów Poland
72 D2 Dorum Germany
124 E3 Doruma Congo(Zaire)
39 D2 Dorūneh Iran
141 J4 Dorval *Québec* Canada
72 F3 Dörverden Germany
73 J2 Dörzbach Germany
31 F2 Dosatuy Rus. Fed.
171 C5 Dos Bahías, C. c. Argentina
99 G5 Dosbarrios Spain
155 H5 Dos Cabezas *Arizona* U.S.A.
52 F2 Doschatoye Rus. Fed.
162 B5 Dos de Mayo Peru
101 E3 Dos Hermanas Spain
24 D2 Đo Son Vietnam
154 B3 Dos Palos *California* U.S.A.
112 D4 Dospat r. Bulgaria
112 E4 Dospat Bulgaria
141 K3 Dosquet *Québec* Canada
73 H2 Dosse r. Germany
74 D3 Dossenheim Germany
123 F4 Dosso div. Niger
123 E4 Dosso Niger
46 D3 Dossor Kazakhstan
123 E4 Dosso, Réserve Partielle de res. Niger
145 C6 Dothan *Alabama* U.S.A.
83 D1 Döttingen Switzerland
86 C2 Douai France
124 A3 Douala Cameroon
88 A3 Douarnenez France
88 A3 Douarnenez, Baie de b. France
92 C3 Double reg. France
27 Double I. i. *Hong Kong* China
15 H5 Double Island Pt pt *Queensland* Australia
154 C4 Double Peak summit *California* U.S.A.
15 F3 Double Pt pt *Queensland* Australia
78 E2 Doubrava r. Czech Rep.
90 E1 Doubs div. France
90 D2 Doubs r. France/Switzerland
9 A6 Doubtful Sound inlet New Zealand
8 D1 Doubtless Bay b. New Zealand
86 C5 Douchy France
86 C2 Douchy-les-Mines France
90 D2 Doucier France
89 F2 Doudeville France
89 E4 Doué-la Fontaine France
122 D4 Douentza Mali
9 A7 Doughboy Bay b. New Zealand
155 H6 Douglas airport *Arizona* U.S.A.
136 C3 Douglas *Alaska* U.S.A.
155 H6 Douglas *Arizona* U.S.A.
145 D6 Douglas *Georgia* U.S.A.
66 E5 Douglas *Scotland* U.K.
152 F3 Douglas *Wyoming* U.S.A.
64 D3 Douglas Isle of Man
130 D4 Douglas South Africa
136 D4 Douglas Chan. chan. *B.C.* Canada
12 D2 Douglas Cr. watercourse *S. Australia* Australia
155 H2 Douglas Creek r. *Colorado* U.S.A.
86 B2 Doullens France
67 A5 Doulus Head headland Rep. of Ireland
123 E5 Doumè Benin
124 B3 Doumé Cameroon
124 D2 Douna Mali
115 C5 Dounaiika Greece
66 D4 Doune *Scotland* U.K.
64 D1 Doune Hill h. *Scotland* U.K.
66 E2 Dounreay *Scotland* U.K.
75 J2 Doupovské Hory mts Czech Rep.
69 B4 Dour Belgium
167 B4 Dourada, Cach. waterfall Brazil
168 D3 Dourada, Cach. waterfall Brazil
168 A5 Dourados r. Brazil
168 A5 Dourados Brazil
124 C1 Dourbali Chad
91 B4 Dourbie r. France
86 B4 Dourdan France
93 E5 Dourdou r. France
93 E5 Dourgne France
86 A2 Douriez France
98 C3 Douro r. Portugal
90 E3 Doussard France
168 B5 Doutor Camargo Brazil
82 B2 Douvaine France
88 D2 Douve r. France
89 E2 Douvres-la-Délivrande France
91 C3 Doux r. France
121 F2 Douz Tunisia
93 B5 Douze r. France
118 C5 Douziat Chad
87 E3 Douzy France
53 C1 Dovbysh Ukraine
63 E1 Dove r. *England* U.K.
63 H2 Dove r. *England* U.K.
65 H3 Dove r. *England* U.K.
139 J3 Dove Brook *Newfoundland* Canada
155 H3 Dove Creek *Colorado* U.S.A.
147 F5 Dover *Delaware* U.S.A.
63 H3 Dover *England* U.K.
147 H3 Dover *New Hampshire* U.S.A.
147 F4 Dover *New Jersey* U.S.A.
146 C4 Dover *Ohio* U.S.A.
13 F5 Dover *Tasmania* Australia
147 J2 Dover-Foxcroft *Maine* U.S.A.
17 D7 Dover, Pt pt *Western Australia* Australia
42 F3 Doveyrīch r. Iran/Iraq
53 A1 Dovhoshyyi Ukraine
55 C5 Dovnsklint cliff Denmark
47 J2 Dovol'noye Rus. Fed.
148 D5 Dowagiac *Michigan* U.S.A.
39 C3 Dow Chāhī Iran
39 D1 Dowgha'ī Iran
39 C2 Dow Kūh mt. Iran
39 E2 Dowlatābād Afghanistan
39 F1 Dowlatābād Afghanistan
39 C3 Dowlatābād Iran
39 E1 Dowlatābād Iran
39 D3 Dowlatābād Iran
39 D1 Dowlatābād Iran
39 C3 Dowlatābād Iran
39 F2 Dowl at Yār Afghanistan
67 E2 Down div. *Northern Ireland* U.K.
63 G2 Downham Market *England* U.K.
154 B2 Downieville *California* U.S.A.
67 F2 Downpatrick *Northern Ireland* U.K.
67 B2 Downpatrick Head headland Rep. of Ireland
147 F3 Downsville *New York* U.S.A.
63 E4 Downton *England* U.K.
39 B2 Dow Rūd Iran
39 D3 Dowsārī Iran
39 G2 Dowshī Afghanistan
154 B1 Doyle *California* U.S.A.
173 H2 Doyle Argentina
147 F4 Doylestown *Pennsylvania* U.S.A.
112 E3 Doyrentsi Bulgaria
39 D3 Dozdān r. Iran
28 D5 Dōzen i. Japan
141 G3 Dozois, Réservoir resr *Québec* Canada
89 E2 Dozulé France
53 E2 Drabiv Ukraine
53 D2 Drabivka Ukraine
91 D4 Drac r. France
168 C4 Dracena Brazil
52 E2 Drachevo Rus. Fed.
75 J3 Drachselsried Germany
68 E1 Drachten Netherlands
112 F2 Dragalina Romania
112 F2 Drăgăneşti-Olt Romania
112 E2 Drăgăneşti-Vlaşca Romania
112 E2 Drăgăşani Romania
79 M5 Drăgeşti Romania
115 H7 Dragonada i. Greece
109 G3 Dragoni Italy
115 G5 Dragonisi i. Greece
159 Dragon's Mouths str. Trinidad and Tobago/Venezuela
55 E4 Dragør Denmark
114 C2 Dragoš Macedonia
57 F3 Dragsfjärd Finland
91 E5 Draguignan France
112 F1 Drăguşeni Romania
77 O3 Drahichyn Belarus
155 F4 Drake *Arizona* U.S.A.
137 J5 Drake *N. Dakota* U.S.A.
131 G5 Drakensberg mountain range Lesotho/South Africa
131 H2 Drakensberg mountain range South Africa
131 G5 Draken's Rock mt. South Africa
179 A1 Drake Passage str. Antarctica
114 F1 Drama div. Greece
114 F1 Drama Greece
58 D2 Drammen Norway
58 D2 Dramsfjorden inlet Norway
58 C2 Drangedal Norway
90 E2 Dranse r. France
72 E4 Dransfeld Germany
67 E2 Draperstown *Northern Ireland* U.K.
36 C2 Dras India
36 C1 Drasan Pakistan
81 H2 Drasenhofen Austria
81 F4 Drau r. Austria
78 E5 Drava r. Croatia/Hungary
79 G6 Drávafok Hungary
78 F5 Dravinja r. Slovenia
114 E2 Draviskos Greece
81 G4 Dravograd Slovenia
76 D3 Drawa r. Poland
76 D2 Drawieński Park Narodowy nat. park Poland
76 D2 Drawno Poland
76 E3 Drawsko Poland
76 D2 Drawsko Pomorskie Poland
136 G4 Drayton Valley *Alberta* Canada
105 A7 Dréan Algeria
73 K4 Drebkau Germany
90 C1 Drée r. France
79 J3 Drégelypalánk Hungary
74 D2 Dreieich Germany
69 E5 Dreis Germany
87 G4 Dreisam r. Germany
81 E2 Dreisesselberg mt. Germany
74 E2 Dreistelzberge h. Germany
80 C3 Dreitorspitze mt. Germany
55 C5 Drejø i. Denmark
107 H2 Drenchia Italy
114 B2 Drenovë Albania
72 C4 Drensteinfurt Germany
68 E2 Drenthe div. Netherlands
68 E2 Drentse Hoofdvaart canal Netherlands
114 C2 Drepano Greece
76 B4 Dresden airport Germany
73 J4 Dresden Germany
102 D4 Dreta de l'Ebre, La delta Spain
54 F4 Dretun' Belarus
76 E2 Dretyń Poland
89 G3 Dreux France
56 D3 Drevsjø Norway
73 H3 Drewitz Germany
73 H2 Drewitzer See l. Germany
76 D3 Drezdenko Poland
32 B2 Dri China
54 E3 Driceni Latvia
54 E4 Dridža l. Latvia
68 D2 Driebergen Netherlands
99 G4 Driebes Spain
68 E1 Driesum Netherlands
63 E3 Driffield *England* U.K.
140 E2 Driftwood *Ontario* Canada
146 D4 Driftwood *Pennsylvania* U.S.A.
53 D1 Drimaylivka Ukraine
64 C1 Drimnin *Scotland* U.K.
67 B5 Drimoleague Rep. of Ireland
112 B2 Drina r. Bos.-Herz./Yugoslavia
113 C4 Drino r. Albania
81 F1 Dřítež Czech Rep.
81 H2 Drnholec Czech Rep.
104 F4 Drniš Croatia
81 H4 Drnje Croatia
83 F3 Dro Italy
58 D2 Drøbak Norway
112 D2 Drobeta-Turnu Severin Romania
91 C4 Drobie r. France
77 H3 Drobin Poland
53 B2 Drochia Moldova
72 E2 Drochtersen Germany
68 E1 Drogeham Netherlands
67 E3 Drogheda Rep. of Ireland
77 L3 Drohiczyn Poland
77 M6 Drohobych Ukraine
Droichead Átha *see* Drogheda
Droichead Nua *see* Newbridge
62 D2 Droitwich *England* U.K.
37 G4 Drokung India
91 D4 Drôme div. France
89 E2 Drôme r. *Basse-Normandie* France
91 D4 Drôme r. *Rhône-Alpes* France
73 F3 Drömling reg. Germany
67 D3 Dromod Rep. of Ireland
67 E2 Dromore *Northern Ireland* U.K.
67 D2 Dromore *Northern Ireland* U.K.
67 C2 Dromore West Rep. of Ireland
106 B4 Dronero Italy
63 E1 Dronfield *England* U.K.
92 C3 Dronne r. France
135 Q2 Dronning Louise Land reg. Greenland
55 C2 Dronninglund Denmark
179 C3 Dronning Maud Land reg. Antarctica
68 D2 Dronten Netherlands
92 C4 Dropt r. France
81 G2 Drosendorf Austria
36 B2 Drosh Pakistan
81 H2 Drösing Austria
52 C3 Droskovo Rus. Fed.
114 C2 Drosopigi *Dytiki Makedonia* Greece
114 C3 Drosopigi *Ipeiros* Greece
89 G3 Droué France
30 E2 Drovyanaya Rus. Fed.
140 B1 Drowning r. *Ontario* Canada
53 B1 Drozdyn' Ukraine
6 Drua Drua i. Fiji
62 C2 Druid *Wales* U.K.
158 Druif *Aruba* Caribbean
64 C2 Druimdrishaig *Scotland* U.K.
37 H3 Druk La China
54 E4 Drūkšiai l. Belarus/Lithuania
87 G4 Drulingen France
64 A3 Drumcard *Northern Ireland* U.K.
90 D3 Drumettaz-Clarafond France
64 A2 Drumfree Rep. of Ireland
136 G4 Drumheller *Alberta* Canada
67 C2 Drumkeeran Rep. of Ireland
67 E4 Drummin Rep. of Ireland
152 D2 Drummond *Montana* U.S.A.
148 B2 Drummond *Wisconsin* U.S.A.
149 F3 Drummond Island i. *Michigan* U.S.A.
131 G2 Drummondlea South Africa
14 D3 Drummond, Mt h. *Northern Terr.* Australia
15 F4 Drummond Range h. *Queensland* Australia
141 J4 Drummondville *Québec* Canada
66 D6 Drummore *Scotland* U.K.
66 D3 Drumnadrochit *Scotland* U.K.
64 A3 Drumquin *Northern Ireland* U.K.
68 D3 Drunen Netherlands
83 D1 Drusberg mt. Switzerland
87 G4 Drusenheim France
54 D5 Druskininkai Lithuania
54 D3 Drusti Latvia
68 D3 Druten Netherlands
54 E4 Druya Belarus
90 B1 Druyes-les-Belles-Fontaines France
77 K1 Druzhba Rus. Fed.
52 A3 Druzhba Ukraine
53 F3 Druzhbivka Ukraine
45 Q3 Druzhina Rus. Fed.
53 G2 Druzhkivka Ukraine
54 G2 Druzhnaya Gorka Rus. Fed.
77 H2 Drwęca r. Poland
112 E3 Dryanovo Bulgaria
52 D3 Dryazgi Rus. Fed.
136 B3 Dry Bay b. *Alaska* U.S.A.
137 L5 Dryberry L. l. *Ontario* Canada
148 E2 Dryburg *Michigan* U.S.A.
138 B4 Dryden *Ontario* Canada
179 D5 Drygalski I. i. Antarctica
179 B5 Drygalski Ice Tongue ice feature Antarctica
62 C2 Drygarn Fawr h. *Wales* U.K.
159 Dry Harbour Mts mts Jamaica
154 D2 Dry Lake l. *Nevada* U.S.A.
66 D4 Drymen *Scotland* U.K.
54 F4 Drysa r. Belarus
16 D2 Drysdale r. *Western Australia* Australia
14 C1 Drysdale I. i. *Northern Terr.* Australia
16 D2 Drysdale River Nat. Park nat. park *Western Australia* Australia
158 B1 Dry Tortugas is *Florida* U.S.A.
76 G2 Dryzcim Poland
76 G3 Drzewce Poland
77 J4 Drzewica Poland
76 E2 Drzonowo Poland
124 B2 Dschang Cameroon
33 E1 Du r. China
124 D3 Dua r. Congo(Zaire)
39 B2 Dūāb r. Iran
108 A4 Dualchi *Sardegna* Italy
32 E4 Du'an China
147 F2 Duane *New York* U.S.A.
15 G4 Duaringa *Queensland* Australia
37 G4 Duars reg. India
78 D1 Dubá Czech Rep.
119 G2 Dubā Saudi Arabia
39 C4 Dubai U.A.E.
53 C3 Dubăsari Moldova
53 C3 Dubău Moldova
137 J2 Dubawnt r. *N.W.T.* Canada
137 J2 Dubawnt Lake l. *N.W.T.* Canada
Dubayy *see* Dubai
119 G2 Dubbāgh, J. ad mt. Saudi Arabia
43 C6 Dubbagh, J. ad mt. Saudi Arabia
13 G3 Dubbo *New South Wales* Australia
77 N4 Dubechne Ukraine
73 H4 Düben Germany
83 D1 Dübendorf Switzerland
73 H4 Dübener Heide forest Germany
77 L1 Dubeniki Poland
52 H2 Dubenki Rus. Fed.
52 D1 Dubets Rus. Fed.
78 C1 Dubí Czech Rep.
77 N1 Dubičiai Lithuania
77 M3 Dubicze Cerkiewne Poland
77 L6 Dubiecko Poland
77 M4 Dubienka Poland
54 D4 Dubingiai Lithuania
52 H4 Dubki Rus. Fed.
67 E3 Dublin div. Rep. of Ireland
145 D5 Dublin *Georgia* U.S.A.
140 B2 Dublin *Ontario* Canada
67 E3 Dublin Rep. of Ireland
64 B4 Dublin Bay b. Rep. of Ireland
75 K3 Dublovice Czech Rep.
77 M6 Dublyany Ukraine
77 N6 Dublyany Ukraine
54 E3 Dubna r. Latvia
52 C1 Dubna r. Rus. Fed.
77 N2 Dubna Belarus
52 C2 Dubna Rus. Fed.
52 C1 Dubna Rus. Fed.
81 J2 Dubňany Czech Rep.
78 D3 Dubné Czech Rep.
53 A1 Dubno Ukraine
152 D2 Dubois *Idaho* U.S.A.
146 D4 Du Bois *Pennsylvania* U.S.A.
152 E3 Dubois *Wyoming* U.S.A.
52 C3 Dubovaya Roshcha Rus. Fed.
112 D1 Dubove Ukraine
53 F2 Dubovi Hryady Ukraine
53 D3 Dubovka Rus. Fed.
51 H5 Dubovka Rus. Fed.
51 G5 Dubovka Rus. Fed.
51 G6 Dubovskoye Rus. Fed.
53 E1 Dubov"yazivka Ukraine
81 H5 Dubrava Croatia
81 G5 Dubrava Croatia
122 B5 Dubréka Guinea
53 B1 Dubrivka Ukraine
52 A3 Dubrovka Rus. Fed.
52 F3 Dubrovki Rus. Fed.
104 G4 Dubrovnik Croatia
53 B1 Dubrovytsya Ukraine
50 D4 Dubrowna Belarus
124 D3 Dubulu Congo(Zaire)
148 B4 Dubuque *Iowa* U.S.A.
53 D2 Dubynove Ukraine
54 C4 Dubysa r. Lithuania
7 Duc de Gloucester, Îles is *French Polynesia* Pacific Ocean
88 D3 Ducey France
33 G2 Duchang China
73 J2 Ducherow Germany
155 G1 Duchesne *Utah* U.S.A.
14 D4 Duchess *Queensland* Australia
177 L7 Ducie Island i. *Pitcairn Islands* Pacific Ocean
145 C5 Duck r. *Tennessee* U.S.A.
137 J4 Duck Bay *Manitoba* Canada
16 B4 Duck Cr. r. *Western Australia* Australia
148 E4 Duck Lake *Michigan* U.S.A.
137 H4 Duck Lake *Saskatchewan* Canada
155 E2 Duckwater *Nevada* U.S.A.
155 E2 Duckwater Peak summit *Nevada* U.S.A.
159 Ducos *Martinique* Caribbean
25 E4 Đưc Pho Vietnam
25 E5 Đưc Trong Vietnam
53 D3 Duchhany Ukraine
69 E5 Dudelange Luxembourg
74 B3 Dudeldorf Germany
72 F4 Duderstadt Germany
79 K5 Dudeştii Vechi Romania
37 E4 Dudhi India
37 G4 Dudhnai India
36 E3 Dudhwa India
44 K3 Dudinka Rus. Fed.
62 D2 Dudley *England* U.K.
38 B2 Dudna r. India
52 B3 Dudorovskiy Rus. Fed.
66 F3 Dudwick, Hill of h. *Scotland* U.K.
122 C5 Duékoué Côte d'Ivoire
98 D2 Duerna r. Spain
98 D3 Duero r. Spain
107 F3 Dueville Italy
141 F2 Dufault, Lac l. *Québec* Canada
179 B4 Dufek Coast coastal area Antarctica
69 C3 Duffel Belgium
138 E2 Dufferin, Cape headland *Québec* Canada
146 B6 Duffield *Virginia* U.S.A.
4 H5 Duff Is is Solomon Is.
66 E3 Dufftown *Scotland* U.K.
82 C3 Dufourspitze summit Italy/Switzerland
138 E1 Dufrost, Pte pt *Québec* Canada
43 D5 Dughdash mountain range Saudi Arabia
104 E4 Dugi Otok i. Croatia
104 F4 Dugi Rat Croatia
52 C2 Dugna Rus. Fed.
87 E3 Dugny-sur-Meuse France
104 F4 Dugopolje Croatia
78 F6 Dugo Selo Croatia
30 D5 Dugui Qarag China
118 C3 Duhūn Tārsū mts Chad/Libya
163 D3 Duida, Co mt. Venezuela
162 D3 Duida-Marahuaca, Parque Nacional nat. park Venezuela
15 E2 Duifken Pt pt *Queensland* Australia
130 A1 Duineveld Namibia
72 E3 Duingen Germany
107 H3 Duino Italy
72 B4 Duisburg Germany
162 C2 Duitama Colombia
68 E3 Duiven Netherlands
131 H1 Duiwelskloof South Africa
45 R3 Dukat Rus. Fed.
131 F5 Dukathole South Africa
113 B4 Dukat i Ri Albania
136 C4 Duke I. i. *Alaska* U.S.A.
Duke of Gloucester Is is *see* Duc de Gloucester, Îles
126 B3 Duk Fadiat Sudan
126 B3 Duk Faiwil Sudan
39 B4 Dukhān Qatar
119 H2 Dukhnah Saudi Arabia
52 A2 Dukhovshchina Rus. Fed.
36 B3 Duki Pakistan
123 G4 Dukku Nigeria
77 K6 Dukla Poland
32 C3 Dukou China
54 E4 Dūkštas Lithuania
30 C2 Dulaanhaan Mongolia
26 G4 Dulan China
170 D2 Dulce r. Argentina
99 H4 Dulce r. Spain
156 K7 Dulce, Golfo b. Costa Rica
156 J6 Dulce Nombre de Dios Honduras
30 E2 Dul'durga Rus. Fed.
64 B4 Duleek Rep. of Ireland
112 F3 Dŭlgopol Bulgaria
15 E1 Dulhunty r. *Queensland* Australia
37 E2 Dulishi Hu salt lake China
37 H4 Dullabchara India
131 H2 Dullstroom South Africa
72 C4 Dülmen Germany
66 E3 Dulnain Bridge *Scotland* U.K.
112 F3 Dulovo Bulgaria
148 A2 Duluth *Minnesota* U.S.A.
148 A2 Duluth/Superior airport *Minnesota* U.S.A.
62 C3 Dulverton *England* U.K.
52 E1 Dulyapino Rus. Fed.
42 D3 Dūmā Syria
23 B4 Dumaguete Philippines
25 C7 Dumai Indonesia
23 B4 Dumaran i. Philippines
13 G2 Dumaresq r. *New South Wales* Australia
151 F5 Dumas *Arkansas* U.S.A.
151 C5 Dumas *Texas* U.S.A.
43 D3 Ḑumayr Syria
43 D3 Ḑumayr, J. mountain range Syria
66 D5 Dumbarton *Scotland* U.K.
66 D4 Dumbarton and Clydebank div. *Scotland* U.K.
131 H3 Dumbe South Africa
6 Dumbéa *New Caledonia* Pacific Ocean
79 J3 Ďumbier mt. Slovakia
79 M6 Dumbrava Romania
112 E1 Dumbrăveni *Sibiu* Romania
112 F2 Dumbrăveni *Vrancea* Romania
112 E2 Dumbrăviţa Romania
98 A1 Dumbría Spain
36 D2 Dumchele India
22 A1 Dumdum i. Indonesia
37 H4 Dum Duma India
88 C4 Dumet, Île i. France
66 E5 Dumfries *Scotland* U.K.
66 E5 Dumfries and Galloway div. *Scotland* U.K.
52 B3 Duminichi Rus. Fed.
112 F1 Dumitra Romania
37 F4 Dumka India
72 D3 Dümmer l. Germany
73 H2 Dummerstorf Germany
141 G3 Dumoine, L. l. *Québec* Canada
179 Dumont d'Urville France Base Antarctica
179 B6 Dumont d'Urville Sea sea Antarctica
74 B2 Dümpelfeld Germany
43 A4 Dumyāt Egypt
72 F4 Dün ridge Germany
79 H5 Duna r. Hungary
79 J4 Dunabogdány Hungary
67 D1 Dunaff Head headland Rep. of Ireland
79 H5 Dunaföldvár Hungary
79 J4 Dunaharaszti Hungary
112 B1 Dunaj r. Hungary
77 J5 Dunajec r. Poland
79 G4 Dunajská Streda Slovakia
79 J4 Dunakeszi Hungary
13 F5 Dunalley *Tasmania* Australia
67 E3 Dunany Point pt Rep. of Ireland
112 E3 Dunărea r. Romania
112 B1 Dunaszekcső Hungary
79 H5 Dunaszentgyörgy Hungary
79 J5 Duna-Tisza Köze reg. Hungary
79 H5 Dunaújváros Hungary
112 F3 Dunav r. Bulgaria/Romania
79 J5 Duna-völgyi-főcsatorna canal Hungary
112 D3 Dunavtsi Bulgaria
53 B2 Dunayivtsi *Khmel'nyts'kyy* Ukraine
53 B2 Dunayivtsi *Khmel'nyts'kyy* Ukraine
9 C6 Dunback New Zealand
15 E3 Dunbar *Queensland* Australia
66 F4 Dunbar *Scotland* U.K.
66 E4 Dunblane *Scotland* U.K.
67 E3 Dunboyne Rep. of Ireland
155 H5 Duncan *Arizona* U.S.A.
136 E5 Duncan *B.C.* Canada
151 D5 Duncan *Oklahoma* U.S.A.
138 D3 Duncan, Cape c. *Ontario* Canada
138 E3 Duncan, L. l. *Québec* Canada
146 E4 Duncannon *Pennsylvania* U.S.A.
67 E4 Duncannon Rep. of Ireland
25 A5 Duncan Passage chan. *Andaman and Nicobar Is* India
159 Duncans Jamaica
66 E2 Duncansby Head headland *Scotland* U.K.
148 B5 Duncans Mills *Illinois* U.S.A.
158 D2 Duncan Town The Bahamas
63 E2 Dunchurch *England* U.K.
67 E4 Duncormick Rep. of Ireland
54 C3 Dundaga Latvia
146 E5 Dundalk *Maryland* U.S.A.
140 E4 Dundalk *Ontario* Canada
67 E2 Dundalk Rep. of Ireland
67 E3 Dundalk Bay b. Rep. of Ireland
Dundas *see* Uummannaq
136 C4 Dundas I. i. *B.C.* Canada
17 C7 Dundas, L. salt flat *Western Australia* Australia
14 B1 Dundas Str. chan. *Northern Terr.* Australia
30 D3 Dundbürd Mongolia
Dún Dealgan *see* Dundalk
149 F5 Dundee *Michigan* U.S.A.
146 E3 Dundee *New York* U.S.A.
66 F4 Dundee *Scotland* U.K.
131 H4 Dundee South Africa
66 E4 Dundee div. *Scotland* U.K.
30 C3 Dundgovĭ div. Mongolia
67 F2 Dundonald *Northern Ireland* U.K.
15 F5 Dundoo *Queensland* Australia
66 E6 Dundrennan *Scotland* U.K.
67 F2 Dundrum *Northern Ireland* U.K.
64 C3 Dundrum Bay b. *Northern Ireland* U.K.
37 E4 Dundwa Ra. mountain range Nepal
145 D6 Dunedin *Florida* U.S.A.
9 C6 Dunedin New Zealand
138 F2 Dune, Lac l. *Québec* Canada
47 J3 Dunenbay Kazakhstan
121 F2 Dunes de Dokhara sand dunes Algeria
64 A2 Dunfanaghy Rep. of Ireland
66 E4 Dunfermline *Scotland* U.K.
67 E2 Dungannon *Northern Ireland* U.K.
Dún Garbhán *see* Dungarvan
36 C3 Dungargarh India
36 C5 Dungarpur India
67 D4 Dungarvan Rep. of Ireland
80 D2 Dungau reg. Germany
63 G4 Dungeness headland *England* U.K.
171 C7 Dungeness, Pta pt Argentina
74 C2 Düngenheim Germany
67 E2 Dungiven *Northern Ireland* U.K.
67 C2 Dungloe Rep. of Ireland
13 G3 Dungog *New South Wales* Australia
124 E3 Dungu Congo(Zaire)
25 C6 Dungun Malaysia
119 G3 Dungunab Sudan
63 F1 Dunholme *England* U.K.
31 J4 Dunhua China
26 F3 Dunhuang China
66 E4 Dunkeld *Scotland* U.K.
81 G2 Dunkelsteiner Wald forest Austria
86 B1 Dunkerque France
62 C3 Dunkery Beacon h. *England* U.K.
146 D3 Dunkirk *New York* U.S.A.
Dunkirk *see* Dunkerque
122 D5 Dunkwa Ghana
67 E3 Dún Laoghaire Rep. of Ireland
67 E3 Dunlavin Rep. of Ireland
67 E3 Dunleer Rep. of Ireland
92 D2 Dun-le-Palestel France
66 D5 Dunlop *Scotland* U.K.
67 E1 Dunloy *Northern Ireland* U.K.
67 B5 Dunmanus Bay b. Rep. of Ireland
67 B5 Dunmanway Rep. of Ireland
14 C3 Dunmarra *Northern Terr.* Australia

E

8 □1 Enderby I. i. Auckland Is New Zealand
179 D4 Enderby Land reg. Antarctica
103 F5 Enderrocat, Cap pt Spain
147 E3 Endicott New York U.S.A.
136 C3 Endicott Arm inlet Alaska U.S.A.
134 C3 Endicott Mts mountain range Alaska U.S.A.
83 E3 Endine, Lago di l. Italy
87 G4 Endingen Germany
93 D6 Endron, Pique d' mt. France
17 A6 Eneabba Western Australia Australia
58 D2 Enebakk Norway
47 J4 Energeticheskiy Kazakhstan
46 E2 Energetik Rus. Fed.
173 H5 Energía Argentina
53 F3 Enerhodar Ukraine
42 A1 Enez Turkey
98 B2 Enfesta Spain
125 B7 Enfião, Pta do pt Angola
63 F3 Enfield England U.K.
147 G3 Enfield New Hampshire U.S.A.
64 B4 Enfield Rep. of Ireland
148 E2 Engadine Michigan U.S.A.
56 C3 Engan Norway
159 E3 Engaño, Cabo pt Dominican Rep.
23 B2 Engaño, Cape c. Philippines
Engaños, R. de los r. see Yari
28 J1 Engaru Japan
131 G5 Engcobo South Africa
83 D2 Engelberg Switzerland
81 H2 Engelhartstetten Austria
81 E2 Engelhartszell Austria
52 H4 Engel's Rus. Fed.
68 C1 Engelschmangat chan. Netherlands
73 H4 Engelsdorf Germany
74 C2 Engelskirchen Germany
74 D5 Engen Germany
169 G2 Engenheiro Navarro Brazil
12 C2 Engenina watercourse S. Australia Australia
72 D3 Enger Germany
20 D8 Enggano i. Indonesia
69 C4 Enghien Belgium
69 D4 Engis Belgium
22 B1 Engkilili Malaysia
61 F5 England div. U.K.
139 J3 Englee Newfoundland Canada
69 B4 Englefontaine France
145 F5 Englehard N. Carolina U.S.A.
141 F3 Englehart Ontario Canada
62 C4 English Channel str. France/U.K.
14 D1 English Company's Is., The is Northern Terr. Australia
159 □7 English Harbour b. Antigua and Barbuda Caribbean
159 □7 English Harbour Town Antigua and Barbuda Caribbean
50 E1 Engozero Rus. Fed.
74 E4 Engstingen Germany
103 C6 Enguera Spain
103 C6 Enguera, Serra de mountain range Spain
103 B5 Enguidanos Spain
54 C3 Engure Latvia
54 C3 Engures Ezers l. Latvia
51 G7 Enguri r. Georgia
43 C4 'En Hazeva Israel
131 H4 Enhlalakahle South Africa
151 D4 Enid Oklahoma U.S.A.
114 D3 Enipefs r. Greece
28 H2 Eniwa Japan
45 Q4 Enkan, M. pt Rus. Fed.
68 D2 Enkhuizen Netherlands
59 J1 Enklinge Finland
59 G2 Enköping Sweden
163 F2 Enmore Guyana
110 D5 Enna div. Sicilia Italy
83 E3 Enna r. Italy
110 D5 Enna Sicilia Italy
137 J2 Ennadai Lake l. N.W.T. Canada
119 E5 En Nahud Sudan
123 F3 E-n-Nassamé well Niger
67 D3 Ennell, Lough l. Rep. of Ireland
87 G1 Ennepetal Germany
131 F3 Ennerdale South Africa
65 E3 Ennerdale Water l. England U.K.
123 G2 Enneri Achelouma watercourse Niger
118 C4 Enneri Maro watercourse Chad
118 C3 Enneri Modragué watercourse Chad
90 B3 Ennezat France
13 F2 Enngonia New South Wales Australia
72 D4 Ennigerloh Germany
150 C2 Enning S. Dakota U.S.A.
152 E2 Ennis Montana U.S.A.
151 D5 Ennis Texas U.S.A.
67 C4 Ennis Rep. of Ireland
67 E4 Enniscorthy Rep. of Ireland
67 C5 Enniskean Rep. of Ireland
67 E3 Enniskerry Rep. of Ireland
67 D2 Enniskillen Northern Ireland U.K.
67 B4 Ennistymon Rep. of Ireland
43 C3 Enn Nâqoûra Lebanon
81 F3 Enns r. Austria
81 F2 Enns Austria
81 F3 Ennstaler Alpen mts Austria
56 H3 Eno Finland
155 F3 Enoch Utah U.S.A.
64 D2 Enoch Hill h. Scotland U.K.
22 A2 Enok Indonesia
56 F1 Enontekiö Finland
33 F4 Enping China
22 D2 Enrekang Indonesia
23 B2 Enrile Philippines
159 E3 Enriquillo, Lago de l. Dominican Rep.
68 D2 Ens Netherlands
13 F4 Ensay Victoria Australia
68 E2 Enschede Netherlands
75 G3 Ensdorf Germany
72 D4 Ense Germany
173 J3 Ensenada Argentina
156 A2 Ensenada Mexico
145 □3 Ensenada Puerto Rico
158 B2 Ensenada de la Broa b. Cuba
101 F4 Ensenada de Marbella b. Spain
33 E2 Enshi China
90 F1 Ensisheim France
127 B4 Entebbe Uganda
68 E2 Enter Netherlands
64 E2 Enterkinfoot Scotland U.K.
145 C6 Enterprise Alabama U.S.A.
136 F2 Enterprise N.W.T. Canada
141 G4 Enterprise Ontario Canada
152 C2 Enterprise Oregon U.S.A.
155 F3 Enterprise Utah U.S.A.
101 H4 Entinas, Pta de las pt Spain
82 C2 Entlebuch reg. Switzerland
82 D2 Entlebuch Switzerland
106 B4 Entracque Italy
85 G4 Entraigues-sur-Sorgues France
90 B1 Entrains-sur-Nohain France
89 E4 Entrammes France
136 F4 Entrance Alberta Canada
91 E4 Entraunes France
93 E4 Entraygues-sur-Truyère France
127 □5 Entre-Deux Réunion Indian Ocean
82 A3 Entre-Deux-Guiers France
93 B4 Entre-deux-Mers reg. France
172 A6 Entre Lagos Chile
173 H1 Entre Ríos div. Argentina
164 D4 Entre Rios Bolivia
166 B2 Entre Rios Brazil
169 F4 Entre Rios de Minas Brazil
91 E5 Entrevaux France
100 B1 Entroncamento Portugal
123 F5 Enugu div. Nigeria
123 F5 Enugu Nigeria
134 A3 Enurmino Rus. Fed.
89 G2 Envermeu France
164 B1 Envira Brazil
125 D4 Enyamba Congo(Zaire)
124 C3 Enyéllé Congo
79 H5 Enying Hungary
9 C5 Enys, Mt mt. New Zealand
74 D4 Enz r. Germany
106 E4 Enza r. Italy
29 G6 Enzan Japan
6 □2 Eo i. New Caledonia Pacific Ocean
98 C1 Eo r. Spain
Eochaill see Youghal
89 F2 Épaignes France
82 B2 Epalignes Switzerland
115 F5 Epano Fellos Greece
114 D2 Epanomi Greece
68 D2 Epe Netherlands
173 F4 Epecuén, L. l. Argentina
124 C3 Epéna Congo
86 C3 Épernay France
89 G3 Épernon France
74 D4 Epfendorf Germany
155 G2 Ephraim Utah U.S.A.
147 E4 Ephrata Pennsylvania U.S.A.
152 C2 Ephrata Washington U.S.A.
6 □2 Epi i. Vanuatu
115 E5 Epidavros Greece
91 E3 Épierre France
90 C2 Épinac France
87 F4 Épinal France
163 F2 Epira Guyana
90 B1 Epiry France
43 B2 Episkopi Cyprus
43 B2 Episkopi B. b. Cyprus
115 C5 Epitalio Greece
109 F4 Epomeo, Monte h. Italy
74 B3 Eppelborn Germany
74 D3 Eppelheim Germany
87 G3 Eppenbrunn Germany
75 J2 Eppendorf Germany
69 B5 Eppeville France
63 G3 Epping England U.K.
74 D3 Eppingen Germany
87 H2 Eppstein Germany
63 F3 Epsom England U.K.
114 C2 Eptachori Greece
89 G2 Epte r. France
172 E4 Epu-pel Argentina
65 H4 Epworth England U.K.
39 C3 Eqlīd Iran
124 D3 Équateur div. Congo(Zaire)
126 B3 Equatoria div. Sudan
117 E5 Equatorial Guinea country Africa
163 E2 Equeipa Venezuela
88 D2 Équerdreville-Hainneville France
107 E5 Era r. Italy
15 F5 Erac Cr. watercourse Queensland Australia
107 G3 Eraclea Italy
122 D3 Erakchiouene well Mali
23 A4 Eran Philippines
36 C5 Erandol India
115 D4 Erateini Greece
114 C2 Eratyra Greece
106 D3 Erba Italy
42 D1 Erbaa Turkey
74 E4 Erbach Baden-Württemberg Germany
74 E3 Erbach Hessen Germany
119 G3 Erba, Jebel mt. Sudan
75 H3 Erbendorf Germany
74 C3 Erbeskopf h. Germany
88 D4 Erbray France
42 E2 Erçek Turkey
42 E2 Erciş Turkey
42 C2 Erciyes Daği mt. Turkey
79 H4 Ercsi Hungary
79 H4 Érd Hungary
31 H4 Erdao r. China
37 H2 Erdaogou China
42 A1 Erdek Turkey
43 C1 Erdemli Turkey
30 C2 Erdenet Mongolia
30 A2 Erdenet Mongolia
30 C4 Erdenetsogt Mongolia
88 B4 Erdeven France
118 D4 Erdi reg. Chad
75 G4 Erding Germany
80 C2 Erdinger Moos marsh Germany
88 D4 Erdre r. France
75 G4 Erdweg Germany
179 B5 Erebus, Mt mt. Antarctica
42 F4 Erech Iraq
167 B6 Erechim Brazil
31 E2 Ereentsav Mongolia
42 C2 Ereğli Konya Turkey
42 B1 Ereğli Zonguldak Turkey
113 B5 Ereikoussa i. Greece
110 D5 Erei, Monti mts Sicilia Italy
30 E4 Erenhot China
39 D2 Eresk Iran
99 F3 Eresma r. Spain
115 E4 Eretria Greece
Erevan see Yerevan
173 G2 Erézcano Argentina
72 E1 Erfde Germany
131 F4 Erfenis Dam resr South Africa
131 F4 Erfenis Dam Nature Reserve res. South Africa
120 D2 Erfoud Morocco
74 B2 Erftstadt Germany
75 G2 Erfurt Germany
42 D2 Ergani Turkey
122 C2 Erg Atouila sand dunes Mali
120 C4 'Erg Chech sand dunes Algeria/Mali
118 C4 Erg du Djourab sand dunes Chad
123 G3 Erg du Ténéré sand dunes Niger
30 D4 Ergel Mongolia
42 A1 Ergene r. Turkey
120 D2 Erg er Raoui sand dunes Algeria
120 D3 Erg labès sand dunes Algeria
120 C3 Erg Iguidi sand dunes Algeria/Mauritania
121 F3 Erg Issaouane sand dunes Algeria
54 D3 Ērgļi Latvia
75 H4 Ergolding Germany
75 H4 Ergoldsbach Germany
88 A3 Ergué-Gabéric France
124 C1 Erguig r. Chad
Ergun r. see Argun'
31 G2 Ergun Yougi China
31 G2 Ergun Zuoqi China
32 C3 Er Hai l. China
31 H4 Erhulai China
98 E2 Eria r. Spain
66 D2 Eriboll, Loch inlet Scotland U.K.
110 B4 Erice Sicilia Italy
100 A2 Ericeira Portugal
65 E1 Ericht r. Scotland U.K.
66 D4 Ericht, Loch l. Scotland U.K.
148 B5 Erie Illinois U.S.A.
151 E4 Erie Kansas U.S.A.
146 C3 Erie Pennsylvania U.S.A.
149 F5 Erie, Lake l. Canada/U.S.A.
122 C3 'Erîgât sand dunes Mali
178 □3 Erik Eriksenstretet str. Svalbard Arctic Ocean
59 F3 Eriksmåla Sweden
101 E2 Erillas h. Spain
28 J2 Erimo Japan
28 J3 Erimo-misaki c. Japan
80 E2 Ering Germany
12 C1 Eringa S. Australia Australia
59 F3 Eringsboda Sweden
159 □3 Erin Point pt Trinidad Trinidad and Tobago
66 A3 Eriskay i. Scotland U.K.
83 E1 Eriskirch Germany
82 C1 Eriswil Switzerland
116 H4 Eritrea country Africa
69 E3 Erkelenz Germany
59 H2 Erken l. Sweden
74 F4 Erkheim Germany
73 J3 Erkner Germany
119 G4 Erkowit Sudan
80 D3 Erl Austria
102 C2 Erla Spain
82 C1 Erlach Switzerland
75 G3 Erlangen Germany
81 E2 Erlau r. Germany
81 G3 Erlauf r. Austria
81 G2 Erlauf Austria
14 C5 Erldunda Northern Terr. Australia
106 C4 Erli Italy
31 J4 Erlong Shan mt. China
31 H4 Erlongshan Sk. resr China
30 E2 Ermana, Khr. mountain range Rus. Fed.
68 D2 Ermelo Netherlands
131 G3 Ermelo South Africa
43 B1 Ermenek r. Turkey
42 C2 Ermenek Turkey
98 B3 Ermesinde Portugal
100 B2 Ermidas do Sado Portugal
115 E5 Ermioni Greece
115 F5 Ermoupoli Greece
73 G4 Ermsleben Germany
99 H1 Ermua Spain
38 B4 Ernakulam India
74 D2 Erndtebrück Germany
67 C2 Erne r. Rep. of Ireland/U.K.
89 E3 Ernée r. France
89 E3 Ernée France
17 C5 Ernest Giles Ra. h. Western Australia Australia
9 A7 Ernest Is is New Zealand
81 H2 Ernstbrunn Austria
69 E5 Ernz Noire r. Luxembourg
38 B4 Erode India
15 E5 Eromanga Queensland Australia
128 A3 Erongo div. Namibia
128 B3 Erongo Mts mts Namibia
69 F4 Erpel Germany
120 D2 Er Rachidia Morocco
119 F5 Er Rahad Sudan
129 F2 Errego Mozambique
126 B2 Er Renk Sudan
67 C1 Errigal h. Rep. of Ireland
67 A2 Erris Head headland Rep. of Ireland
66 D4 Errochty, Loch l. Scotland U.K.
147 H2 Errol New Hampshire U.S.A.
6 □2 Erromango i. Vanuatu
Erronan i. see Futuna
126 B2 Er Roseires Sudan
119 F5 Er Rua'at Sudan
43 D3 Er Ruseifa Jordan
114 B2 Ersekë Albania
150 D2 Erskine Minnesota U.S.A.
56 F3 Ersmark Sweden
87 G4 Erstein France
52 E4 Ertil' Rus. Fed.
47 L3 Ertix r. China
69 B3 Ertvelde Belgium
12 D2 Erudina S. Australia Australia
42 E2 Eruh Turkey
173 L2 Erval Brazil
169 G4 Ervália Brazil
89 E3 Erve r. France
100 B3 Ervidel Portugal
86 B2 Ervillers France
86 C4 Ervy-le-Châtel France
146 D5 Erwin W. Virginia U.S.A.
72 D4 Erwitte Germany
73 G3 Erxleben Germany
115 C5 Erymanthos mts Greece
115 C5 Erymanthos r. Greece
115 E4 Erythres Greece
32 B3 Eryuan China
75 J2 Erzgebirge mountain range Czech Rep./Germany
31 H2 Erzhan China
87 H3 Erzhausen Germany
30 A2 Erzin Rus. Fed.
43 D1 Erzin Turkey
42 D2 Erzincan Turkey
42 E2 Erzurum Turkey
54 C4 Eržvilkas Lithuania
6 □1 Esa-ala P.N.G.
28 H3 Esan-misaki pt Japan
111 F3 Esaro r. Italy
29 H4 Esashi Japan
28 H3 Esashi Japan
28 J1 Esashi Japan
28 D7 Esawasaki Japan
55 A4 Esbjerg Denmark
166 E2 Escada Brazil
98 C2 Escairón Spain
155 G3 Escalante r. Utah U.S.A.
155 G3 Escalante Utah U.S.A.
155 F3 Escalante Desert desert Utah U.S.A.
108 B5 Escalaplano Sardegna Italy
172 A6 Escalera, Punta pt Chile
103 C6 Escaleta, Pta de la pt Spain
93 A5 Escaliers, Pic des mt. France
103 E6 Es Caló Spain
102 E2 Escaló Spain
156 D3 Escalón Mexico
99 F4 Escalona Spain
98 C5 Escalos de Cima Portugal
148 D3 Escanaba Michigan U.S.A.
91 B5 Escandorgue ridge France
101 F3 Escañuela Spain
157 H5 Escárcega Mexico
102 B2 Escaroz Spain
23 B2 Escarpada Point pt Philippines
102 C3 Escatrón Spain
86 C2 Escaut r. France
80 B3 Eschach r. Germany
72 F3 Eschede Germany
83 D1 Eschenbach Switzerland
75 G3 Eschenbach in der Oberpfalz Germany
72 E4 Eschershausen Germany
83 G2 Eschio r. Italy
75 H3 Eschlkam Germany
82 C2 Escholzmatt Switzerland
69 D5 Esch-sur-Alzette Luxembourg
69 D5 Esch-sur-Sûre Luxembourg
72 F4 Eschwege Germany
74 B2 Eschweiler Germany
159 E3 Escocesa, Bahía b. Caribbean
98 B2 Escodelo, Pta pt Spain
164 C3 Escoma Bolivia
103 C7 Escombreras Spain
154 D5 Escondido California U.S.A.
102 C4 Escorihuela Spain
93 A5 Escos France
93 E6 Escouloubre France
93 A4 Escource r. France
93 A4 Escource France
91 E5 Escragnolles France
156 D4 Escuinapa Mexico
157 H6 Escuintla Guatemala
157 G6 Escuintla Mexico
159 E5 Escuque Venezuela
100 E1 Escurial Spain
102 C4 Escuriza r. Spain
90 B2 Escurolles France
169 E2 Escurso r. Brazil
162 C2 Escutillas Colombia
124 B3 Eséka Cameroon
39 C1 Esenguly Turkmenistan
72 C2 Esens Germany
102 D2 Ésera r. Spain
39 B2 Eşfahan div. Iran
39 B2 Eşfahan Iran
39 C3 Esfandāran Iran
39 B3 Esfarjan Iran
99 F3 Esgueva r. Spain
99 F3 Esguevillas de Esgueva Spain
66 □2 Esha Ness headland Scotland U.K.
46 E5 Eshāqābād Iran
39 C4 Eshkanān Iran
131 H4 Eshowe South Africa
43 C4 Esh Sharā reg. Jordan
39 B2 Eshtehārd Iran
129 D3 Esigodini Zimbabwe
131 J4 Esikhawini South Africa
107 H5 Esino r. Italy
13 F5 Esk r. Tasmania Australia
15 H5 Esk Queensland Australia
39 B2 Eskandarī Iran
66 F5 Eskdale v. Scotland U.K.
8 F3 Eskdale New Zealand
66 E5 Eskdalemuir Scotland U.K.
67 C2 Eske, Lough l. Rep. of Ireland
139 G3 Esker Newfoundland Canada
53 G2 Eskhar Ukraine
56 N6 Eskifjörður Iceland
59 G2 Eskilstuna Sweden
42 C1 Eskipazar Turkey
42 B2 Eskişehir Turkey
59 G1 Eskön i. Sweden
98 E2 Esla r. Spain
42 F3 Eslamābād e Gharb Iran
75 H3 Eslarn Germany
72 D4 Eslohe (Sauerland) Germany
59 E4 Eslöv Sweden
42 B2 Eşme Turkey
172 B2 Esmeralda Chile
158 C2 Esmeralda Cuba
171 A6 Esmeralda, I. i. Chile
162 B3 Esmeraldas Ecuador
98 B4 Esmoriz Portugal
140 B1 Esnagami lake l. Ontario Canada
140 C2 Esnagi Lake l. Ontario Canada
86 C2 Esnes France
69 D4 Esneux Belgium
39 E4 Espakeh Iran
93 E4 Espalion France
91 B3 Espaly-St-Marcel France
153 F4 Espanola New Mexico U.S.A.
140 E3 Espanola Ontario Canada
162 □ Española, I. i. Galapagos Is Ecuador
102 E3 Esparraguera Spain
91 D5 Esparron France
101 E3 Esparteros, Sierra de h. Spain
173 F4 Espartillar Argentina
154 A2 Esparto California U.S.A.
98 D4 Espeja Spain
101 F3 Espejo Spain
93 A5 Espelette France
72 D3 Espelkamp Germany
101 G2 Espelúy Spain
17 C7 Esperance Western Australia Australia
17 C7 Esperance B. b. Western Australia Australia
8 □4 Espérance Rock, L' i. Kermadec Is New Zealand
166 D1 Esperantinópolis Brazil
179 B2 Esperanza Argentina Base Antarctica
171 B7 Esperanza Santa Cruz Argentina
173 G1 Esperanza Santa Fé Argentina
156 C3 Esperanza Mexico
164 B1 Esperanza Peru
23 C4 Esperanza Philippines
145 □3 Esperanza Puerto Rico
173 J2 Esperanza Uruguay
156 J6 Esperanza, Sa de la mountain range Honduras
109 F3 Esperia Italy
93 E6 Espezel France
100 A2 Espichel, Cabo headland Portugal
101 F2 Espiel Spain
173 G4 Espigas Argentina
99 F2 Espigüete mt. Spain
91 C5 Espiguette, Pointe de l' pt France
102 D4 Espina, L' mt. Spain
99 F1 Espinama Spain
91 E4 Espinasses France
151 C7 Espinazo Mexico
100 B3 Espinhaço de Cão, Sa de mountain range Portugal
100 C2 Espinheira h. Portugal
98 B3 Espinho Portugal
167 B6 Espinilho, Sa do h. Brazil
99 F1 Espinilla Spain
169 G1 Espinosa Brazil
99 G3 Espinosa de Cerrato Spain
99 G1 Espinosa de los Monteros Spain
93 E5 Espinouse, Monts de l' mts France
169 H3 Espírito Santo div. Brazil
23 B2 Espiritu Philippines
6 □2 Espíritu Santo i. Vanuatu
157 J5 Espíritu Santo, B. del b. Mexico
156 C3 Espíritu Sto i. Mexico
166 E3 Esplanada Brazil
102 G2 Espolla Spain
57 G3 Espoo Finland
98 B3 Esposende Portugal
90 E1 Esprels France
103 B7 Espuña mt. Spain
103 B7 Espuña, Sierra de mountain range Spain
129 E3 Espungabera Mozambique
171 B5 Esquel Argentina
136 E5 Esquimalt B.C. Canada
170 E3 Esquina Argentina
99 G4 Esquivias Spain
55 E3 Esrum Sø l. Denmark
43 D3 Es Samrā Jordan
23 C5 Essang Indonesia
120 C2 Essaouira Morocco
120 B3 Es Semara Western Sahara
69 C3 Essen Belgium
72 C4 Essen Germany
75 H4 Essenbach Germany
17 C5 Essendon, Mt h. Western Australia Australia
72 C3 Essen (Oldenburg) Germany
163 F2 Essequibo r. Guyana
90 E1 Essert France
63 G3 Essex div. England U.K.
155 E4 Essex California U.S.A.
140 D5 Essex Ontario Canada
147 G2 Essex Junction Vermont U.S.A.
149 F4 Essexville Michigan U.S.A.
74 E4 Esslingen am Neckar Germany
45 R4 Esso Rus. Fed.
86 B4 Essonne div. Île-de-France France
86 B4 Essonne r. France
86 D4 Essoyes France
54 E2 Essu Estonia
119 F5 Es Suki Sudan
124 B3 Est div. Cameroon
98 C1 Estaca de Bares, Pta da pt Spain
173 H1 Estacas Argentina
101 G2 Estación de Baeza Spain
171 D7 Estados, I. de los i. Argentina
39 C3 Eşţahbānāt Iran
93 E4 Estaing France
140 E3 Estaire Ontario Canada
86 B2 Estaires France
166 E3 Estância Brazil
171 C7 Estancia Camerón Chile
101 H3 Estancias, Sierra de las mountain range Spain
93 B5 Estang France
98 B4 Estarreja Portugal
93 D6 Estats, Pic d' mt. France/Spain
82 B2 Estavayer-le-Lac Switzerland
131 G4 Estcourt South Africa
171 C7 Est. de Le Maire chan. Argentina
72 E2 Este r. Germany
107 F3 Este Italy
102 C3 Esteban mt. Spain
170 D2 Esteban Rams Argentina
98 B3 Estela Portugal
156 J6 Estelí Nicaragua
99 H2 Estella Spain
101 F1 Estena r. Spain
101 F3 Estepa Spain
99 G2 Estepar Spain
101 E4 Estepona Spain
145 □3 Este, Pta pt Puerto Rico
173 K3 Este, Punta del pt Uruguay
101 F2 Esteras r. Spain
99 H3 Esteras de Medinaceli Spain
91 E5 Esterel reg. France
83 G1 Estergebirge mountain range Germany
137 J4 Esterhazy Saskatchewan Canada
124 A3 Esterias, Cap pt Gabon
86 C4 Esternay France
154 B4 Estero Bay b. California U.S.A.
91 E5 Esteron r. Italy
165 D4 Esteros Paraguay
170 E2 Esteros del Iberá marsh Argentina
102 E2 Esterri d'Aneu Spain
137 J5 Estevan Saskatchewan Canada
100 B2 Estêvão r. Portugal
150 E3 Estherville Iowa U.S.A.
139 H4 Est, Île de l' i. Québec Canada
145 D5 Estill S. Carolina U.S.A.
86 C4 Estissac France
166 D2 Estiva r. Brazil
169 E5 Estiva Brazil
92 E2 Estivareilles France
147 J1 Est, Lac de l' l. Québec Canada
100 C3 Estói Portugal
166 D2 Estolado r. Brazil
49 H3 Estonia country Europe
100 A2 Estoril Lisboa Portugal
91 E5 Estoublon France
86 B3 Estrées-St-Denis France
169 F3 Estrêla do Indaiá Brazil
168 E3 Estrêla do Sul Brazil
98 C4 Estrela, Serra da mountain range Portugal
101 G2 Estrella mt. Spain
100 A1 Estremadura reg. Portugal
100 C2 Estremoz Portugal
93 B4 Estrigon r. France
124 B3 Estuaire div. Gabon
124 A3 Estuaire du Gabon est. Gabon
79 H4 Esztergom Hungary
88 C3 Étables-sur-Mer France
12 D2 Etadunna S. Australia Australia
92 C3 Étagnac France
36 D4 Etah India
87 E3 Étain France
69 D5 Etalle Belgium
86 B4 Étampes France
12 D1 Etamunbanie, L. salt flat S. Australia Australia
88 C4 Etang au Duc l. France
93 A5 Étang Blanc l. France
87 E3 Étang d'Amel l. France
93 A4 Étang d'Aureilhan l. France
91 B5 Étang de Bages en de Sigean lag. France
91 D5 Étang de Berre lag. France
108 B2 Étang de Biguglia lag. Corse France
93 A4 Étang de Biscarrosse et de Parentis l. France
87 F4 Étang de Bischwald l. France
93 F6 Étang de Canet ou de St-Nazaire lag. France
93 A4 Étang de Cazaux et de Sanguinet l. France
108 B2 Étang de Diane lag. Corse France
90 E2 Etang de Frasne l. France
87 F4 Étang de Gondrexange l. France
92 A4 Étang de Lacanau l. France
87 E3 Étang de Lachaussée l. France
86 D4 Étang de la Horre l. France
91 B5 Étang de Lapalme lag. France
91 B5 Étang de l'Ayrolle lag. France
93 A5 Étang de Léon l. France
93 F6 Étang de Leucate ou de Salses l. France
87 F4 Étang de Lindre l. France
91 C5 Étang de Scamandre lag. France
93 A5 Étang de Soustons l. France
91 C5 Étang de Vaccarès lag. France
90 B1 Étang de Vaux l. France
92 A3 Étang d'Hourtin-Carcans l. France
87 E3 Étang du Haut-Fourneau l. France
108 B2 Étang d'Urbino lag. Corse France
87 F4 Étang du Stock l. France
127 □5 Étang Salé Réunion Indian Ocean
86 A2 Étaples France
92 A3 Étaules France
92 B3 Étauliers France
36 D4 Etawah India
88 B4 Étel France
59 J1 Etelä-Vartsala Finland
91 E3 Etendard, Pic de l' mt. France
90 E1 Éternoz France
131 H3 eThandakukhanya South Africa
69 D5 Ethe Belgium
17 C4 Ethel Creek Western Australia Australia
6 □8 Ethel Reefs reef Fiji
130 D4 E'Thembini South Africa
15 E3 Etheridge r. Queensland Australia
117 H5 Ethiopia country Africa
42 C2 Etimesğut Turkey
90 D2 Étival France
87 F4 Étival-Clairefontaine France
66 C4 Etive, Loch inlet Scotland U.K.
90 C1 Étivey France
58 C1 Etna r. Norway
111 E5 Etna, Monte volcano Sicilia Italy
58 A2 Etne Norway
136 C3 Etolin I. i. Alaska U.S.A.
15 G4 Eton Queensland Australia
128 B2 Etosha National Park nat. park Namibia
128 B2 Etosha Pan salt pan Namibia
124 B3 Etoumbi Congo
86 B4 Étréchy France
89 G2 Étrépagny France
89 F2 Étretat France
86 C3 Étreux France
112 E3 Etropole Bulgaria
82 C3 Etroubles Italy
93 B6 Etsaut France
38 B4 Ettaiyapuram India
69 E5 Ettelbruck Luxembourg
74 C4 Ettenheim Germany
68 C3 Etten-Leur Netherlands
120 A5 Et Tîdra i. Mauritania
63 E2 Ettington England U.K.
74 D4 Ettlingen Germany
65 E2 Ettrick Scotland U.K.
66 F5 Ettrick Forest forest Scotland U.K.
66 E5 Ettrick Water r. Scotland U.K.
75 F4 Ettringen Germany
124 E4 Etumba Congo(Zaire)
90 D1 Étuz France
63 E2 Etwall England U.K.
156 D4 Etzatlán Mexico
89 G1 Eu France
6 □4 'Eua i. Tonga
13 F3 Euabalong New South Wales Australia
6 □4 'Eua Iki i. Tonga
6 □3 Euakafa i. Tonga
Euboea i. see Evvoia
17 E6 Eucla Western Australia Australia
146 C4 Euclid Ohio U.S.A.
166 E3 Euclides da Cunha Brazil
13 G4 Eucumbene, L. l. New South Wales Australia
12 D3 Eudunda S. Australia Australia
145 C6 Eufaula Alabama U.S.A.
151 E5 Eufaula Lake resr Oklahoma U.S.A.
152 B2 Eugene Oregon U.S.A.
165 E2 Eugênia r. Brazil
156 B3 Eugenia, Pta c. Mexico
13 G3 Eugowra New South Wales Australia
15 F6 Eulo Queensland Australia
98 C1 Eume r. Spain
13 G2 Eumungerie New South Wales Australia
15 G4 Eungella Nat. Park nat. park Queensland Australia
151 E6 Eunice Louisiana U.S.A.
69 E4 Eupen Belgium
42 F4 Euphrates r. Iraq
54 C1 Eura Finland
81 F2 Euratsfeld Austria
89 G2 Eure div. Haute-Normandie France
89 G2 Eure r. France
89 G3 Eure-et-Loir div. France
152 A3 Eureka California U.S.A.
152 D1 Eureka Montana U.S.A.
155 E2 Eureka Nevada U.S.A.
169 J2 Euriápolis Brazil
12 E2 Eurinilla watercourse S. Australia Australia
12 E2 Euriowie New South Wales Australia
13 F4 Euroa Victoria Australia
15 G5 Eurombah Queensland Australia
15 G5 Eurombah Cr. r. Queensland Australia
175 G5 Europa, Île i. Indian Ocean
99 E1 Europa, Picos de mountain range Spain
101 □ Europa Point headland Gibraltar
68 C3 Europoort Netherlands
87 E4 Eurville-Bienville France
74 B2 Euskirchen Germany
13 E3 Euston New South Wales Australia
136 D4 Eustuk Lake l. B.C. Canada
145 C5 Eutaw Alabama U.S.A.
73 F1 Eutin Germany
87 H4 Eutingen im Gäu Germany
73 H4 Eutzsch Germany
14 C3 Eva Downs Northern Terr. Australia
131 G1 Evangelina South Africa
145 □1 Evans Bay Bermuda
136 F4 Evansburg Alberta Canada
13 H2 Evans Head New South Wales Australia
179 B3 Evans Ice Stream ice feature Antarctica
138 E3 Evans, L. l. Québec Canada
153 F4 Evans, Mt mt. Colorado U.S.A.
152 D2 Evans, Mt mt. Montana U.S.A.
135 K3 Evans Strait chan. N.W.T. Canada
148 D4 Evanston Illinois U.S.A.
152 E3 Evanston Wyoming U.S.A.
144 C4 Evansville Indiana U.S.A.
140 D4 Evansville Ontario Canada
148 C4 Evansville Wisconsin U.S.A.
152 F3 Evansville Wyoming U.S.A.
148 E4 Evart Michigan U.S.A.
131 F3 Evaton South Africa
92 E2 Évaux-les-Bains France
39 C4 Evaz Iran
148 A2 Eveleth Minnesota U.S.A.
45 R3 Evensk Rus. Fed.
9 □1 Eveque, Cape L' c. Chatham Is New Zealand
12 C2 Everard, L. salt flat S. Australia Australia
12 C1 Everard, Mt mt. S. Australia Australia
12 C1 Everard Park S. Australia Australia
12 C1 Everard Range h. S. Australia Australia
37 F4 Everest, Mt mt. China
147 K1 Everett New Brunswick Canada
152 B1 Everett Washington U.S.A.
69 B3 Evergem Belgium
145 D7 Everglades Nat. Park Florida U.S.A.
145 D7 Everglades, The swamp Florida U.S.A.
151 G6 Evergreen Alabama U.S.A.
163 F2 Everton Guyana
59 E1 Evertsberg Sweden
63 E2 Evesham England U.K.
15 E4 Evesham Queensland Australia
63 E2 Evesham, Vale of v. England U.K.
90 E2 Évian-les-Bains France
56 F3 Evijärvi Finland
124 B3 Evinayong Equatorial Guinea
115 C4 Evinos r. Greece
108 A2 Evisa Corse France
58 B2 Evje Norway
82 C2 Evolène Switzerland
100 C2 Évora div. Portugal
100 C2 Évora Portugal
27 P1 Evoron, Ozero l. Rus. Fed.
114 D2 Evosmo Greece
88 D3 Évran France

89 D4 Èvre r. France
89 E2 Évrecy France
89 G2 Évreux France
89 E3 Évron France
113 F4 Evros r. Greece/Turkey
115 D5 Evrotas r. Greece
86 B4 Évry France
114 C3 Evrytania div. Greece
114 E4 Evvoia div. Greece
115 F4 Evvoia i. Greece
153 □1 Ewa Beach *Hawaii* U.S.A.
159 □1 Ewarton Jamaica
127 C5 Ewaso Ngiro r. Kenya
130 D3 Ewbank South Africa
66 C3 Ewe, Loch inlet *Scotland* U.K.
31 F2 Ewenkizu Zizhiqi China
8 □1 Ewing I. i. *Auckland Is* New Zealand
179 B2 Ewing I. i. Antarctica
124 B4 Ewo Congo
164 C2 Exaltación Bolivia
131 F4 Excelsior South Africa
154 C2 Excelsior Mt mt. *California* U.S.A.
154 C2 Excelsior Mts mts *Nevada* U.S.A.
150 E4 Excelsior Springs *Missouri* U.S.A.
92 D3 Excideuil France
62 C4 Exe r. *England* U.K.
179 A4 Executive Committee Range mountain range Antarctica
154 C3 Exeter *California* U.S.A.
62 C4 Exeter *England* U.K.
147 H3 Exeter *New Hampshire* U.S.A.
13 G3 Exeter *New South Wales* Australia
140 E5 Exeter *Ontario* Canada
82 B3 Exilles Italy
89 F3 Exmes France
62 C4 Exminster *England* U.K.
62 C3 Exmoor reg. *England* U.K.
62 C3 Exmoor National Park nat. park *England* U.K.
147 F6 Exmore *Virginia* U.S.A.
62 C4 Exmouth *England* U.K.
16 A4 Exmouth *Western Australia* Australia
16 A4 Exmouth Gulf b. *Western Australia* Australia
175 M5 Exmouth Plateau sea feature Indian Ocean
114 C1 Exochi Greece
15 G5 Expedition Range mountain range *Queensland* Australia
6 □7 Exploring Is is Fiji
100 D1 Extremadura div. Spain
124 B1 Extrême-Nord div. Cameroon
98 B3 Extremo Portugal
166 E2 Exú Brazil
158 C1 Exuma Sound chan. The Bahamas
124 D4 Eyangu Congo(Zaire)
127 B5 Eyasi, Lake salt lake Tanzania
91 D3 Eybens France
63 H2 Eye *England* U.K.
63 F2 Eye *England* U.K.
66 F5 Eyemouth *Scotland* U.K.
66 B2 Eye Peninsula pen. *Scotland* U.K.
91 D4 Eygues r. France
91 D4 Eyguians France
91 D5 Eyguières France
92 E3 Eygurande France
92 E3 Eygurande-et-Gardedeuil France
56 M6 Eyjafjörður b. Iceland
126 E3 Eyl Somalia
93 C4 Eymet France
92 D3 Eymoutiers France
Eynihal *see* Kale
39 C2 Eyn or Rashid Iran
63 E3 Eynsham *England* U.K.
93 B4 Eyre r. France
14 D5 Eyre Cr. watercourse *Queensland* Australia
92 D3 Eyrein France
9 B6 Eyre Mountains mountain range New Zealand
12 D2 Eyre (North), Lake salt flat *S. Australia* Australia
12 C3 Eyre Peninsula pen. *S. Australia* Australia
12 D2 Eyre (South), L. salt flat *S. Australia* Australia
91 C4 Eyrieux r. France
93 B4 Eysines France
72 E3 Eystrup Germany
55 □1 Eysturoy i. Faeroes
127 C5 Eyuku waterhole Kenya
124 A2 Eyumojok Cameroon
131 H4 Ezakheni South Africa
99 H2 Ezcaray Spain
91 F5 Èze France
50 J2 Ezhva Rus. Fed.
42 A2 Ezine Turkey
68 E1 Ezinge Netherlands
89 G3 Ézy-sur-Eure France

F

7 □11 Faaa *French Polynesia* Pacific Ocean
35 D9 Faadhippolhu Atoll atoll Maldives
126 D4 Faafxadhuun Somalia
7 □10 Faaite i. *French Polynesia* Pacific Ocean
7 □11 Faaone *French Polynesia* Pacific Ocean
93 D5 Fabas France
151 B6 Fabens *Texas* U.S.A.
136 F2 Faber Lake l. *N.W.T.* Canada
25 □ Faber, Mt h. Singapore
98 D2 Fabero Spain
77 H3 Fabianki Poland
79 K5 Fábiánsebestyén Hungary
55 C4 Fåborg Denmark
79 J3 Fabova hoľa mt. Slovakia
91 B5 Fabrègues France
93 E5 Fabrezan France
107 G5 Fabriano Italy
101 H2 Fábricas de San Juan de Alcaraz Spain
111 F4 Fabrizia Italy
162 C3 Facatativá Colombia
86 C2 Faches-Thumesnil France
123 G3 Fachi Niger
100 E4 Facinas Spain
15 G4 Facing I. i. *Queensland* Australia
23 □2 Facpi Pt pt *Guam* Pacific Ocean
147 F4 Factoryville *Pennsylvania* U.S.A.
171 B6 Facundo Argentina
118 D4 Fada Chad
123 E4 Fada-Ngourma Burkina
126 E2 Fadli reg. Yemen
55 B4 Fænø i. Denmark
107 F4 Faenza Italy
Færingehavn *see* Kangerluarsoruseq
55 □1 Faeroes is Atlantic Ocean
109 H3 Faeto Italy
6 □4 Fafa i. Tonga
124 C2 Fafa r. Central African Rep.
21 K7 Fafanlap Indonesia
98 B3 Fafe Portugal
126 D3 Fafen Shet' watercourse Ethiopia
7 □12 Fagaloa Bay b. Western Samoa
7 □12 Fagamalo Western Samoa
112 E2 Făgăraş Romania
59 F3 Fågelfors Sweden
59 F3 Fagerhult Sweden
58 C1 Fagernes Norway
59 F2 Fagersta Sweden
79 M6 Făget Romania
107 F4 Faggeta, Monte la mt. Italy
123 F4 Faggo Nigeria
111 F3 Fagnano Castello Italy
171 C7 Fagnano, L. l. Argentina
69 C4 Fagne reg. Belgium
86 D4 Fagnières France
122 D3 Faguibine, Lac l. Mali
56 M7 Fagurhólsmýri Iceland
126 B3 Fagwir Sudan
39 D3 Fahraj Iran
100 □ Faial i. *Azores* Portugal
96 □ Faial *Madeira* Portugal
109 G3 Faicchio Italy
69 F4 Faid Germany
83 D2 Faido Switzerland
141 G2 Faillon, Lac l. *Québec* Canada
69 D4 Faimes Belgium
153 J3 Fairbanks *Alaska* U.S.A.
146 B5 Fairborn *Ohio* U.S.A.
150 D3 Fairbury *Nebraska* U.S.A.
146 E5 Fairfax *Virginia* U.S.A.
154 A2 Fairfield *California* U.S.A.
148 B5 Fairfield *Iowa* U.S.A.
146 A5 Fairfield *Ohio* U.S.A.
151 D6 Fairfield *Texas* U.S.A.
147 G3 Fair Haven *Vermont* U.S.A.
67 E1 Fair Head headland *Northern Ireland* U.K.
23 A4 Fairie Queen sand bank Philippines
66 □1 Fair Isle i. *Scotland* U.K.
63 G4 Fairlight *England* U.K.
15 F2 Fairlight *Queensland* Australia
150 E3 Fairmont *Minnesota* U.S.A.
146 C5 Fairmont *W. Virginia* U.S.A.
153 F4 Fairplay *Colorado* U.S.A.
148 D3 Fairport *Michigan* U.S.A.
146 C4 Fairport Harbor *Ohio* U.S.A.
136 F3 Fairview *Alberta* Canada
149 E3 Fairview *Michigan* U.S.A.
151 D4 Fairview *Oklahoma* U.S.A.
15 F2 Fairview *Queensland* Australia
155 G2 Fairview *Utah* U.S.A.
27 □ Fairview Park *Hong Kong* China
136 B3 Fairweather, Cape c. *Alaska* U.S.A.
136 B3 Fairweather, Mt mt. *Alaska/British Columbia* Canada/U.S.A.
64 A3 Fairy Water r. *Northern Ireland* U.K.
21 M5 Fais i. Fed. States of Micronesia
36 C3 Faisalabad Pakistan
86 D3 Faissault France
115 F7 Faistos Greece
150 C2 Faith *S. Dakota* U.S.A.
66 □2 Faither, The pt *Scotland* U.K.
37 E4 Faizabad India
145 □3 Fajardo Puerto Rico
77 L4 Fajsławice Poland
7 □10 Fakaina i. *French Polynesia* Pacific Ocean
6 □3 Fakalele i. Tonga
5 K5 Fakaofo i. *Tokelau* Pacific Ocean
7 □10 Fakarava i. *French Polynesia* Pacific Ocean
63 G2 Fakenham *England* U.K.
56 D3 Fåker Sweden
21 K7 Fakfak Indonesia
37 G3 Fakhrabad Iran
55 E4 Fakse Denmark
55 E4 Fakse Bugt b. Denmark
55 E4 Fakse Ladeplads Denmark
31 G4 Faku China
62 B4 Fal r. *England* U.K.
122 B5 Falaba Sierra Leone
123 E4 Falagountou Burkina
89 E3 Falaise France
118 C4 Falaise d'Angamma cliff Chad
122 D4 Falaise de Bandiagara escarpment Mali
122 D4 Falaise de Banfora escarpment Burkina
123 F3 Falaise de Tiguidit escarpment Niger
37 G4 Falakata India
24 A2 Falam Myanmar
39 B2 Falavarjan Iran
107 F2 Falcade Italy
64 A2 Falcarragh Rep. of Ireland
112 G1 Fălciu Romania
107 F5 Falco, Monte mt. Italy
Falcon i. *see* Fonuafo'ou
110 D5 Falconara *Sicilia* Italy
107 H5 Falconara Marittima Italy
111 E4 Falcone *Sicilia* Italy
108 A4 Falcone, Capo del pt *Sardegna* Italy
151 D7 Falcon Lake l. Mexico/U.S.A.
55 C4 Faldsled Denmark
7 □12 Falealupo Western Samoa
7 □12 Faleasiu Western Samoa
7 □12 Falelima Western Samoa
122 B4 Falémé r. Mali/Senegal
50 J3 Falenki Rus. Fed.
7 □12 Falerai Western Samoa
111 F3 Falerna Italy
53 B3 Făleşti Moldova
7 □12 Faleula Western Samoa
151 D7 Falfurrias *Texas* U.S.A.
136 F3 Falher *Alberta* Canada
126 C1 Falkat r. Eritrea
73 J4 Falkenberg Germany
59 E3 Falkenberg Sweden
73 H2 Falkenhagen Germany
76 A4 Falkenhain Germany
73 J3 Falkensee Germany
75 H3 Falkenstein *Bayern* Germany
75 H2 Falkenstein *Sachsen* Germany
66 E5 Falkirk div. *Scotland* U.K.
66 E5 Falkirk *Scotland* U.K.
66 E4 Falkland *Scotland* U.K.
171 E7 Falkland Islands is Atlantic Ocean
171 D7 Falkland Sound chan. Falkland Is.
172 D6 Falkner Argentina
115 E6 Falkonera i. Greece
59 E2 Falköping Sweden
77 J4 Fałków Poland
154 D5 Fallbrook *California* U.S.A.
92 A2 Falleron France
92 E3 Fallingbostel Germany
154 C2 Fallon *Nevada* U.S.A.
147 H4 Fall River *Massachusetts* U.S.A.
152 F3 Fall River Pass *Colorado* U.S.A.
150 E3 Falls City *Nebraska* U.S.A.
59 E1 Falltorp Sweden
123 E4 Falmey Niger
159 □7 Falmouth *Antigua and Barbuda* Caribbean
62 A4 Falmouth *England* U.K.
146 A5 Falmouth *Kentucky* U.S.A.
147 H3 Falmouth *Maine* U.S.A.
148 E3 Falmouth *Michigan* U.S.A.
159 □1 Falmouth Jamaica
62 A4 Falmouth Bay b. *England* U.K.
130 B7 False Bay b. South Africa
102 D3 Falset Spain
55 E5 Falster i. Denmark
62 F2 Falstone *England* U.K.
112 F1 Fălticeni Romania
59 F1 Falun Sweden
80 D4 Falzarego, Passo di pass Italy
Famagusta *see* Ammochostos
170 C2 Famatina Argentina
170 C2 Famatina, Sa de mountain range Argentina
125 C4 Fambono Congo(Zaire)
87 F3 Fameck France
69 C4 Famenne v. Belgium
137 K4 Family L. l. *Manitoba* Canada
122 C4 Fana Mali
67 D1 Fanad Head Rep. of Ireland
129 H2 Fanambana Madagascar
112 C4 Fanari Greece
33 G2 Fanchang China
129 H3 Fandriana Madagascar
67 E3 Fane r. Rep. of Ireland
24 B3 Fang Thailand
7 □10 Fangatau i. *French Polynesia* Pacific Ocean
6 □4 Fanga Uta lag. Tonga
33 F1 Fangcheng China
32 E4 Fangcheng China
32 E2 Fangdou Shan mountain range China
33 H4 Fang-liao Taiwan
59 G2 Fångo i. Sweden
108 A2 Fango r. *Corse* France
30 D5 Fangshan China
33 H4 Fangshan Taiwan
33 E1 Fang Xian China
31 J3 Fangzheng China
55 F3 Fanipal' Belarus
93 E5 Fanjeaux France
27 □ Fanling *Hong Kong* China
66 C3 Fannich, Loch l. *Scotland* U.K.
39 D4 Fannūj Iran
55 A4 Fanø i. Denmark
107 H5 Fano Italy
55 A4 Fanø Bugt b. Denmark
33 H3 Fanshan China
30 E5 Fanshi China
24 C2 Fan Si Pan mt. Vietnam
59 F2 Fanthyttan Sweden
31 E6 Fan Xian China
46 F5 Farab Turkmenistan
122 B4 Faraba Mali
124 E3 Faradje Congo(Zaire)
129 H3 Farafangana Madagascar
122 A4 Farafenni The Gambia
119 E2 Farafra Oasis oasis Egypt
39 C3 Farāgheh Iran
39 F2 Farāh Afghanistan
39 E2 Farah Rud r. Afghanistan
39 G2 Farakhulm Afghanistan
21 M2 Farallon de Pajaros i. *Northern Mariana Is* Pacific Ocean
122 B4 Faranah Guinea
109 G2 Fara San Martino Italy
59 G3 Fårbo Sweden
83 G1 Farchant Germany
69 C4 Farciennes Belgium
109 J4 Fardella Italy
101 G3 Fardes r. Spain
87 F3 Farébersviller France
63 E4 Fareham *England* U.K.
8 D4 Farewell, Cape c. New Zealand
8 D4 Farewell Spit spit New Zealand
150 D2 Fargo *N. Dakota* U.S.A.
93 B4 Fargues France
150 E2 Faribault *Minnesota* U.S.A.
139 F2 Faribault, Lac l. *Québec* Canada
36 D3 Faridabad India
36 C3 Faridkot India
37 G5 Faridpur Bangladesh
36 D3 Faridpur India
129 H2 Farihy Alaotra l. Madagascar
129 G3 Farihy Ihotry l. Madagascar
129 H2 Farihy Kinkony l. Madagascar
129 H2 Farihy Tsiazompaniry l. Madagascar
129 G3 Farihy Tsimanampetsotsa l. Madagascar
100 A1 Farilhões i. Portugal
39 D2 Farīmān Iran
63 E3 Faringdon *England* U.K.
166 C2 Farinha r. Brazil
43 A4 Fâriskûr Egypt
98 D3 Fariza de Sayago Spain
59 G3 Färjestaden Sweden
114 D3 Farkadhon Greece
47 G5 Farkhor Tajikistan
113 F6 Farmakonisi i. Greece
148 C5 Farmer City *Illinois* U.S.A.
138 D2 Farmer Island i. *N.W.T.* Canada
136 E3 Farmington *B.C.* Canada
148 B5 Farmington *Illinois* U.S.A.
148 B5 Farmington *Iowa* U.S.A.
147 H2 Farmington *Maine* U.S.A.
147 H3 Farmington *New Hampshire* U.S.A.
155 H3 Farmington *New Mexico* U.S.A.
152 E3 Farmington *Utah* U.S.A.
136 D4 Far Mt. mt. *B.C.* Canada
146 D6 Farmville *Virginia* U.S.A.
79 H3 Farná Slovakia
59 F2 Färna Sweden
59 F1 Färnäs Sweden
63 F3 Farnborough *England* U.K.
62 D1 Farndon *England* U.K.
59 G1 Färnebo-fjärden l. Sweden
65 G2 Farne Islands is *England* U.K.
108 D2 Farnese Italy
63 F3 Farnham *England* U.K.
136 F4 Farnham, Mt mt. *B.C.* Canada
73 G4 Farnstädt Germany
100 C3 Faro airport Portugal
100 B3 Faro div. Portugal
59 H3 Fårö i. Sweden
100 C3 Faro Portugal
136 C2 Faro *Yukon Terr.* Canada
173 G5 Faro Argentina
166 A1 Faro Brazil
106 B3 Faroma, Monte mt. Italy
124 B2 Faro, Réserve du res. Cameroon
98 C2 Faro, Serra do mountain range Spain
59 H3 Fårösund Sweden
117 K7 Farquhar Group is Seychelles
15 E5 Farrars Cr. watercourse *Queensland* Australia
39 C3 Farrāshband Iran
146 C4 Farrell *Pennsylvania* U.S.A.
141 H4 Farrellton *Québec* Canada
172 B2 Farrelones Chile
58 C2 Farris l. Norway
39 D2 Farrokhī Iran
Farrukhabad *see* Fatehgarh
39 C3 Fārs div. Iran
39 C2 Farsakh Iran
114 D3 Farsala Greece
39 E2 Fārsī Afghanistan
55 B3 Farsø Denmark
152 E3 Farson *Wyoming* U.S.A.
58 B2 Farsund Norway
112 F2 Fărţăneşti Romania
168 C2 Fartura r. Brazil
167 B6 Fartura, Sa da mountain range Brazil
55 B3 Fårvang Denmark
Farvel, Kap c. *see* Uummannarsuaq
151 C5 Farwell *Texas* U.S.A.
39 C3 Fasā Iran
111 G2 Fasano Italy
72 F3 Faßberg Germany
146 E4 Fassett *Pennsylvania* U.S.A.
53 C1 Fastiv Ukraine
53 E1 Fastivtsi Ukraine
67 B5 Fastnet Rock i. Rep. of Ireland
124 F3 Fataki Congo(Zaire)
36 C3 Fatehabad India
36 D4 Fatehgarh India
36 C4 Fatehjang Pakistan
36 C4 Fatehnagar India
36 E4 Fatehpur India
36 E4 Fatehpur India
36 C4 Fatehpur India
36 B3 Fatehpur Pakistan
36 D4 Fatehpur Sikri India
100 E4 Fates, Sierra de mountain range Spain
52 B3 Fateyevka Rus. Fed.
52 B3 Fatezh Rus. Fed.
39 C3 Fathābād Iran
140 E4 Fathom Five National Marine Park nat. park *Ontario* Canada
122 A4 Fatick Senegal
100 B1 Fátima *Santarém* Portugal
168 A5 Fátima do Sul Brazil
6 □3 Fatumanga i. Tonga
125 C4 Fatundu Congo(Zaire)
90 E2 Faucigny reg. France
90 E1 Faucogney-et-la-Mer France
91 B5 Faugères France
64 A3 Faughan r. *Northern Ireland* U.K.
93 C4 Fauguerolles France
65 E2 Fauldhouse *Scotland* U.K.
73 H2 Faulenrost Germany
87 F3 Faulquemont France
86 B2 Fauquembergues France
140 D2 Fauquier *Ontario* Canada
17 A5 Faure I. i. *Western Australia* Australia
112 F2 Făurei Romania
56 D2 Fauske Norway
155 F1 Faust *Utah* U.S.A.
173 H2 Faustino M. Parera Argentina
89 F2 Fauville-en-Caux France
92 D3 Faux-la-Montagne France
98 C3 Favaios Portugal
107 G5 Favalto, Monte mt. Italy
110 C5 Favara *Sicilia* Italy
103 □ Favàritx, Cap de pt Spain
90 E3 Faverges France
90 E1 Faverney France
63 G3 Faversham *England* U.K.
110 B5 Favignana *Sicilia* Italy
110 B5 Favignana, Isola i. *Sicilia* Italy
136 G4 Fawcett *Alberta* Canada
63 E4 Fawley *England* U.K.
138 C3 Fawn r. *Ontario* Canada
119 H2 Fawwārah Saudi Arabia
56 K6 Faxaflói b. Iceland
56 E3 Faxälven r. Sweden
32 C3 Faxian Hu l. China
118 C4 Faya Chad
88 D4 Fay-de-Bretagne France
91 E5 Fayence France
148 D3 Fayette *Michigan* U.S.A.
151 E4 Fayetteville *Arkansas* U.S.A.
145 E5 Fayetteville *N. Carolina* U.S.A.
145 C5 Fayetteville *Tennessee* U.S.A.
119 H4 Fayfā Saudi Arabia
43 B4 Fāyid Egypt
42 G4 Faylakah i. Kuwait
90 D1 Fayl-la-Forêt France
102 D3 Fayón Spain
91 C4 Fay-sur-Lignon France
43 D5 Fazair al Ghrazi watercourse Saudi Arabia
107 H4 Fažana Croatia
123 E5 Fazao Malfakassa, Parc National de nat. park Togo
63 E2 Fazeley *England* U.K.
36 C3 Fazilka India
36 B3 Fazilpur Pakistan
39 B4 Fazrān, J. h. Saudi Arabia
120 B4 Fdérik Mauritania
67 B4 Feale r. Rep. of Ireland
145 E5 Fear, Cape c. *N. Carolina* U.S.A.
154 B2 Feather Falls *California* U.S.A.
9 E4 Featherston New Zealand
13 F4 Feathertop, Mt mt. *Victoria* Australia
89 F2 Fécamp France
87 G4 Fecht r. France
173 J1 Federación Argentina
123 F5 Federal Capital Territory div. Nigeria
58 A1 Fedje Norway
46 D2 Fedorovka Kazakhstan
46 F2 Fedorovka Kazakhstan
47 J2 Fedorovka Kazakhstan
53 F3 Fedotova Kosa spit Ukraine
67 B3 Feeagh, Lough l. Rep. of Ireland
64 A3 Feeny *Northern Ireland* U.K.
59 E3 Fegen l. Sweden
59 E3 Fegen Sweden
79 M4 Fehérgyarmat Hungary
73 G1 Fehmarn i. Germany
73 F1 Fehmarnsund chan. Germany
169 H5 Feia, Lagoa lag. Brazil
33 G2 Feidong China
69 B4 Feignies France
33 H1 Feihuanghe Kou river mouth China
164 B1 Feijó Brazil
8 E4 Feilding New Zealand
75 G2 Feilitzsch Germany
168 C4 Feio ou Aguapei r. Brazil
166 E3 Feira de Santana Brazil
98 C1 Feira do Monte Spain
43 B5 Feirān well Egypt
43 B5 Feirān, W. watercourse Egypt
90 E3 Feissons-sur-Isère France
33 G2 Feixi China
33 G1 Fei Xian China
79 H4 Fejér div. Hungary
55 D5 Fejø i. Denmark
42 C2 Feke Turkey
79 L5 Fekete-Körös r. Hungary
103 G5 Felanitx Spain
148 D3 Felch *Michigan* U.S.A.
79 H4 Felcsút Hungary
83 G1 Feldafing Germany
81 E4 Feld am See Austria
81 G4 Feldbach div. Austria
81 G4 Feldbach Austria
90 F1 Feldbach France
74 D5 Feldberg mt. Germany
82 C1 Feldberg *Baden-Württemberg* Germany
73 J2 Feldberg *Mecklenburg-Vorpommern* Germany
80 A3 Feldkirch div. Austria
80 A3 Feldkirch Austria
81 E4 Feldkirchen div. Austria
81 G3 Feldkirchen bei Graz Austria
81 F4 Feldkirchen in Kärnten Austria
75 G5 Feldkirchen-Westerham Germany
112 E1 Feldru Romania
6 □3 Feletoa Tonga
98 B3 Felgueiras Portugal
173 H1 Feliciano r. Argentina
127 □1 Félicité I. i. Seychelles
35 D10 Felidu Atoll atoll Maldives
91 B3 Félines France
157 H5 Felipe C. Puerto Mexico
169 F3 Felixlândia Brazil
63 H3 Felixstowe *England* U.K.
156 D2 Félix U. Gómez Mexico
106 C4 Felizzano Italy
69 E5 Fell Germany
107 H2 Fella r. Italy
92 E3 Felletin France
59 F2 Fellingsbro Sweden
159 □1 Fellowship Jamaica
79 L5 Felnac Romania
72 E4 Felsberg Germany
79 J4 Felsőpakony Hungary
81 H4 Felső-Válicka r. Hungary
55 B5 Felsted Denmark
107 F2 Feltre Italy
166 C3 Femeas r. Brazil
73 F1 Femer Bælt str. Denmark/Germany
111 F3 Femminamorta, Monte mt. Italy
55 D5 Femø i. Denmark
58 D2 Femsjøen l. Norway
57 C3 Femunden l. Norway
30 D5 Fen r. China
129 G4 Fenambosy, Lohatanjona pt Madagascar
155 H4 Fence Lake *New Mexico* U.S.A.
141 F4 Fenelon Falls *Ontario* Canada
Fener Br. c. *see* Karataş Br.
106 B3 Fenestrelle Italy
87 G4 Fénétrange France
53 D1 Fenevychi Ukraine
114 G2 Fengari mt. Greece
31 H4 Fengcheng China
33 F2 Fengcheng China
32 D2 Fengdu China
32 D3 Fenggang China
33 H2 Fenghua China
33 E3 Fenghuang China
32 E2 Fengjie China
33 E4 Fengkai China
33 H4 Fenglin Taiwan
31 F5 Fengnan China
31 F4 Fengning China
32 B3 Fengqing China
33 F1 Fengqiu China
31 F5 Fengrun China
32 D3 Fengshan China
33 G4 Fengshun China
33 G1 Fengtai China
32 D1 Feng Xian China
33 F2 Fengxin China
33 G1 Fengyang China
30 E4 Fengzhen China
37 G5 Feni Bangladesh
6 □1 Feni Is is P.N.G.
92 B2 Fenioux France
106 B3 Fenis Italy
62 C4 Feniton *England* U.K.
148 B4 Fennimore *Wisconsin* U.S.A.
129 H2 Fenoarivo Atsinanana Madagascar
129 H2 Fenoarivo Be Madagascar
108 A3 Feno, Capo di pt *Corse* France
93 E6 Fenouillet reg. France
58 A1 Fensfjorden chan. Norway
55 D4 Fensmark Denmark
63 F2 Fens, The reg. *England* U.K.
149 F4 Fenton *Michigan* U.S.A.
177 J7 Fenua Ura is *French Polynesia* Pacific Ocean
65 G2 Fenwick *England* U.K.
30 D5 Fenxi China
30 D5 Fenyang China
51 E6 Feodosiya Ukraine
66 B2 Feolin Ferry *Scotland* U.K.
69 C4 Fépin France
64 A4 Ferbane Rep. of Ireland
121 F1 Fer, Cap de headland Algeria
111 F4 Ferdinandea Italy
73 J2 Ferdinandshof Germany
39 D2 Ferdows Iran
86 C4 Fère-Champenoise France
86 C3 Fère-en-Tardenois France
88 C4 Férel France
109 E2 Ferentillo Italy
109 F3 Ferentino Italy
113 F4 Feres Greece
103 B6 Férez Spain
47 H4 Fergana Uzbekistan
Fergana Range mountain range *see* Fergana Too Tizmegi
47 H4 Fergana Too Tizmegi mountain range Kyrgyzstan
140 E5 Fergus *Ontario* Canada
150 D2 Fergus Falls *Minnesota* U.S.A.
6 □1 Fergusson I. i. P.N.G.
121 F2 Fériana Tunisia
100 D2 Feria, Sierra de h. Spain
122 C5 Ferkessédougou Côte d'Ivoire
110 D5 Ferla *Sicilia* Italy
81 F4 Ferlach Austria
140 A1 Ferland *Ontario* Canada
122 B3 Ferlo-Nord, Réserve de Faune du res. Senegal
122 B4 Ferlo Sud, Réserve de Faune du res. Senegal
122 A3 Ferlo, Vallée du watercourse Senegal
67 D2 Fermanagh div. *Northern Ireland* U.K.
107 G5 Fermignano Italy
109 F1 Fermo Italy
139 G3 Fermont *Québec* Canada
98 D3 Fermoselle Spain
67 C4 Fermoy Rep. of Ireland
101 G1 Fernáncaballero Spain
170 D2 Fernández Argentina
145 D6 Fernandina Beach *Florida* U.S.A.
162 □ Fernandina, I. i. *Galapagos Is* Ecuador
171 B7 Fernando de Magallanes, Parque Nacional nat. park Chile
174 G6 Fernando de Noronha i. Atlantic Ocean
168 C4 Fernandópolis Brazil
169 F2 Fernão Dias Brazil
129 G1 Fernão Veloso, Baia de b. Mozambique
152 B1 Ferndale *Washington* U.S.A.
63 E4 Ferndown *England* U.K.
90 E2 Ferney-Voltaire France
156 C2 Fernie *B.C.* Canada
154 C2 Fernley *Nevada* U.S.A.
80 B3 Fernpaß Austria
147 F4 Fernridge *Pennsylvania* U.S.A.
67 E4 Ferns Rep. of Ireland
152 C2 Fernwood *Idaho* U.S.A.
111 F4 Ferrandina Italy
107 F4 Ferrara div. *Emilia-Romagna* Italy
107 F4 Ferrara *Ferrara* Italy
108 B5 Ferrato, Capo pt *Sardegna* Italy
109 G3 Ferrazzano Italy
98 C1 Ferreira Spain
100 B2 Ferreira do Alentejo Portugal
100 B1 Ferreira do Zêzere Portugal
163 G3 Ferreira-Gomes Brazil
168 B4 Ferreiros Brazil
162 B5 Ferreñafe Peru
102 B3 Ferreruela de Huerva Spain
90 F1 Ferrette France
172 E1 Ferreyra Argentina
151 F6 Ferriday *Louisiana* U.S.A.
106 D4 Ferriere Italy
69 C4 Ferrière-la-Grande France
69 D4 Ferrières Belgium
86 B4 Ferrières France
55 A3 Ferring Sø l. Denmark
166 B3 Ferro r. Brazil
108 B3 Ferro, Capo pt *Sardegna* Italy
98 B1 Ferrol Spain
155 G2 Ferron *Utah* U.S.A.
169 G3 Ferros Brazil
108 B5 Ferru, Monte h. *Sardegna* Italy
103 G5 Ferrutx, Cap pt Spain
65 G3 Ferryhill *England* U.K.
78 F4 Fertő l. Austria/Hungary
81 H3 Fertőd Hungary
78 F4 Fertőrákos Hungary
78 F4 Fertőszentmiklós Hungary
78 F4 Fertő-tavi nat. park Hungary
68 D1 Ferwerd Netherlands
52 C2 Ferzikovo Rus. Fed.
120 D2 Fès Morocco
125 C5 Feshi Congo(Zaire)
137 K5 Fessenden *N. Dakota* U.S.A.
87 G5 Fessenheim France
69 B5 Festieux France
150 F4 Festus *Missouri* U.S.A.
122 B4 Fété Bowé Senegal
112 F2 Feteşti Romania
66 □2 Fethaland, Point of pt *Scotland* U.K.
67 D4 Fethard Rep. of Ireland
42 B2 Fethiye Turkey
66 □2 Fetlar i. *Scotland* U.K.
66 F4 Fettercairn *Scotland* U.K.
75 G3 Feucht Germany
74 F3 Feuchtwangen Germany
89 G1 Feuquières-en-Vimeu France
90 C3 Feurs France
43 D1 Fevzipaşa Turkey
39 G1 Feyzābād Afghanistan
39 D2 Feyzābād Iran
Fez *see* Fès
62 C2 Ffestiniog *Wales* U.K.
170 C2 Fiambalá Argentina
109 F2 Fiamignano Italy
122 D4 Fian Ghana
129 H3 Fianarantsoa div. Madagascar
129 H3 Fianarantsoa Madagascar
124 C2 Fianga Chad
82 C3 Fiano Italy
109 E2 Fiano Romano Italy
100 C3 Ficalho h. Portugal
126 C3 Fichē Ethiopia
75 H2 Fichtelgebirge h. Germany
75 H3 Fichtelnaab r. Germany
131 F4 Ficksburg South Africa
108 E2 Ficulle Italy
166 D2 Fidalgo r. Brazil
106 E4 Fidenza Italy
58 B2 Fidjeland Norway
80 D3 Fieberbrunn Austria
136 F4 Field *B.C.* Canada
140 E3 Field *Ontario* Canada
14 C2 Field I. i. *Northern Terr.* Australia
112 E2 Fieni Romania
90 D3 Fier r. France
113 B4 Fier Albania
107 F2 Fiera di Primiero Italy
14 D3 Fiery Cr. r. *Queensland* Australia
82 D2 Fiesch Switzerland
66 F4 Fife div. *Scotland* U.K.
148 E3 Fife Lake *Michigan* U.S.A.
66 F4 Fife Ness pt *Scotland* U.K.
13 F3 Fifield *New South Wales* Australia
148 B3 Fifield *Wisconsin* U.S.A.
119 F4 5th Cataract rapids Sudan
91 E5 Figanières France
108 B3 Figari *Corse* France
93 E4 Figeac France
59 G3 Figeholm Sweden
159 □6 Fig Tree *St Kitts-Nevis* Caribbean
100 B2 Figueira r. Portugal
98 B4 Figueira da Foz Portugal
98 D4 Figueira de Castelo Rodrigo Portugal
168 B3 Figueirão Brazil
100 C1 Figueiró r. Portugal
98 B5 Figueiró dos Vinhos Portugal
102 F2 Figueres Spain
103 C4 Figueroles Spain
121 D2 Figuig Morocco
124 B2 Figuil Cameroon
43 D5 Fiha al 'Ināb reg. Saudi Arabia
126 E2 Fi'i reg. Yemen
4 J6 Fiji country Pacific Ocean
101 H3 Filabres, Sa de los mountain range Spain
129 D3 Filabusi Zimbabwe
156 J7 Filadelfia Costa Rica
111 F4 Filadelfia Italy
165 D4 Filadélfia Paraguay
79 J3 Fiľakovo Slovakia
122 C4 Filamana Mali
179 B3 Filchner Ice Shelf ice feature Antarctica
109 F3 Filettino Italy
65 H3 Filey *England* U.K.
112 D2 Filiaşi Romania
114 B3 Filiates Greece
115 C5 Filiatra Greece
110 D4 Filicudi, Isola i. Italy
110 D4 Filicudi Porto Italy
123 E4 Filingué Niger
52 F2 Filinskoye Rus. Fed.
114 G2 Filiouri r. Greece
77 L1 Filipów Poland
114 B3 Filippiada Greece
114 F2 Filippoi Greece
59 F2 Filipstad Sweden
83 E2 Filisur Switzerland
56 C3 Fillan Norway
154 C4 Fillmore *California* U.S.A.
155 F2 Fillmore *Utah* U.S.A.
114 C2 Filotas Greece
115 G5 Filoti Greece
107 H5 Filottrano Italy
74 E4 Fils r. Germany
62 D3 Filton *England* U.K.
126 D3 Filtu Ethiopia
156 E3 F. I. Madero Mexico
179 C3 Fimbulheimen mountain range Antarctica
179 C3 Fimbulisen ice feature Antarctica
110 D4 Finale *Sicilia* Italy
107 F4 Finale Emilia Italy
106 C4 Finale Ligure Italy
141 H4 Finch *Ontario* Canada
126 C3 Finch'a'ā Hayk' l. Ethiopia
69 E5 Findel airport Luxembourg
66 E3 Findhorn r. *Scotland* U.K.
66 E3 Findhorn *Scotland* U.K.
43 C1 Fındıkpınarı Turkey
146 B4 Findlay *Ohio* U.S.A.
63 F4 Findon *England* U.K.
13 G5 Fingal *Tasmania* Australia
138 E5 Finger Lakes lake *New York* U.S.A.
129 E2 Fingoè Mozambique
93 D5 Finhan France

12 E4 Frances S. Australia Australia
93 C4 Francescas France
136 D2 Frances Lake l. Yukon Terr. Canada
136 D2 Frances Lake Yukon Terr. Canada
158 B2 Francés, Pta pt Cuba
148 D5 Francesville Indiana U.S.A.
124 B4 Franceville Gabon
90 E1 Franche-Comté div. France
150 D3 Francis Case, Lake l. S. Dakota U.S.A.
162 C4 Francisco de Orellana Peru
156 D3 Francisco I. Madero Mexico
169 G2 Francisco Sá Brazil
147 H2 Francis, Lake l. New Hampshire U.S.A.
128 D3 Francistown Botswana
169 E5 Franco da Rocha Brazil
110 D5 Francofonte Sicilia Italy
136 D4 Francois Lake l. B.C. Canada
102 E3 Francolí r. Spain
69 D4 Francorchamps Belgium
152 E3 Francs Peak summit Wyoming U.S.A.
121 F2 Frane Algeria
68 D1 Franeker Netherlands
90 D2 Frangy France
87 H1 Frankenau Germany
75 J2 Frankenberg Germany
72 D4 Frankenberg (Eder) Germany
81 E2 Frankenburg am Hausruck Austria
81 G3 Frankenfels Austria
74 F2 Frankenheim Germany
81 E3 Frankenmarkt Austria
149 F4 Frankenmuth Michigan U.S.A.
74 D3 Frankenthal (Pfalz) Germany
75 G2 Frankenwald forest Germany
159 □1 Frankfield Jamaica
148 D5 Frankfort Indiana U.S.A.
144 C4 Frankfort Kentucky U.S.A.
148 D3 Frankfort Michigan U.S.A.
131 G3 Frankfort South Africa
87 H2 Frankfurt am Main airport Germany
74 D2 Frankfurt am Main Hessen Germany
73 K3 Frankfurt (Oder) Germany
155 E1 Franklin Lake l. Nevada U.S.A.
75 F4 Frankische Alb h. Germany
74 E2 Fränkische Saale r. Germany
75 G3 Fränkische Schweiz reg. Germany
17 B7 Frankland r. Western Australia Australia
152 E3 Franklin Idaho U.S.A.
144 C4 Franklin Indiana U.S.A.
151 F6 Franklin Louisiana U.S.A.
147 H3 Franklin Massachusetts U.S.A.
145 D5 Franklin N. Carolina U.S.A.
147 H3 Franklin New Hampshire U.S.A.
147 F4 Franklin New Jersey U.S.A.
146 D4 Franklin Pennsylvania U.S.A.
145 C5 Franklin Tennessee U.S.A.
146 E6 Franklin Virginia U.S.A.
146 D5 Franklin W. Virginia U.S.A.
131 G5 Franklin South Africa
134 F2 Franklin Bay b. N.W.T. Canada
152 C1 Franklin D. Roosevelt Lake l. Washington U.S.A.
12 D3 Franklin Harb. harbour S. Australia Australia
179 B5 Franklin I. i. Antarctica
136 E2 Franklin Mountains mountain range N.W.T. Canada
9 A6 Franklin Mts mts New Zealand
13 F5 Franklin Sd chan. Tasmania Australia
135 J2 Franklin Str. chan. N.W.T. Canada
90 D1 Franois France
56 E3 Fränsta Sweden
78 B1 Františkovy Lázně Czech Rep.
140 C2 Franz Ontario Canada
9 C5 Franz Josef Glacier New Zealand
Franz Josef Land is see Zemlya Frantsa-Iosifa
108 A5 Frasca, Capo della pt Sardegna Italy
83 G3 Frascati Italy
111 F3 Frascineto Italy
80 D3 Frasdorf Germany
136 E4 Fraser r. B.C. Canada
139 H2 Fraser r. Newfoundland Canada
130 C5 Fraserburg South Africa
66 F3 Fraserburgh Scotland U.K.
140 E2 Fraserdale Ontario Canada
15 H5 Fraser I. i. Queensland Australia
15 H5 Fraser I. Nat. Park Queensland Australia
136 E4 Fraser Lake B.C. Canada
17 B5 Fraser, Mt h. Western Australia Australia
136 E4 Fraser Plateau plat. B.C. Canada
8 F3 Frasertown New Zealand
90 E2 Frasne France
69 B4 Frasnes-lez-Buissenal Belgium
107 E4 Frassinoro Italy
80 A3 Frastanz Austria
100 C1 Fratel Portugal
110 D5 Fratello r. Sicilia Italy
140 C3 Frater Ontario Canada
112 E3 Frăţeşti Romania
107 F3 Fratta r. Italy
82 C1 Fraubrunnen Switzerland
83 D1 Frauenfeld Switzerland
81 H3 Frauenkirchen Austria
75 J2 Frauenstein Germany
80 D2 Fraunberg Germany
173 H2 Fray Bentos Uruguay
172 E5 Fray Luis Beltrán Argentina
173 K3 Fray Marcos Uruguay
93 D4 Frayssinet-le-Gélat France
98 B3 Freamunde Portugal
74 B2 Frechen Germany
99 F2 Frechilla Spain
91 B5 Frech, Mt mt. France
65 F4 Freckleton England U.K.
55 E4 Fredensborg Denmark
148 E3 Frederic Michigan U.S.A.
148 A3 Frederic Wisconsin U.S.A.
55 B4 Fredericia Denmark
17 B5 Frederick r. Western Australia Australia
146 E5 Frederick Maryland U.S.A.
151 D5 Frederick Oklahoma U.S.A.
135 Q1 Frederick E. Hyde Fjord inlet Greenland
15 H4 Frederick Reef reef Coral Sea Islands Terr. Pacific Ocean
151 D6 Fredericksburg Texas U.S.A.
146 E5 Fredericksburg Virginia U.S.A.
136 C3 Frederick Sound chan. Alaska U.S.A.
151 F4 Fredericktown Missouri U.S.A.
139 G4 Fredericton New Brunswick Canada
55 E4 Frederiksberg Denmark
55 E4 Frederiksberg div. Denmark
Frederikshåb see Paamiut
55 C2 Frederikshavn Denmark
55 E4 Frederikssund Denmark
145 □3 Frederiksted Virgin Is Caribbean
159 F3 Frederiksted Virgin Is Caribbean
55 E4 Frederiksværk Denmark
73 J3 Fredersdorf Germany
155 F3 Fredonia Arizona U.S.A.
146 D3 Fredonia New York U.S.A.
56 E2 Fredrika Sweden
59 F1 Fredriksberg Sweden
58 D2 Fredrikstad Norway
147 F4 Freehold New Jersey U.S.A.
147 F4 Freeland Pennsylvania U.S.A.
12 D2 Freeling Heights mt. S. Australia Australia
14 C4 Freeling, Mt mt. Northern Terr. Australia
154 C2 Freel Peak summit California U.S.A.
150 D3 Freeman S. Dakota U.S.A.
148 D5 Freeman, Lake l. Indiana U.S.A.
148 B5 Freeport Illinois U.S.A.
147 H3 Freeport Maine U.S.A.
147 G4 Freeport New York U.S.A.
151 E6 Freeport Texas U.S.A.
158 C1 Freeport City The Bahamas
151 D7 Freer Texas U.S.A.
131 F4 Free State div. South Africa
159 □7 Freetown Antigua and Barbuda Caribbean
122 B5 Freetown Sierra Leone
100 D2 Fregenal de la Sierra Spain
108 E3 Fregene Italy
88 C3 Fréhel France
88 C3 Fréhel, Cap pt France
75 J2 Freiberg Germany
74 D5 Freiburg div. Germany
72 E2 Freiburg (Elbe) Germany
75 J2 Freiberger Mulde r. Germany
74 C4 Freiburg im Breisgau Germany
74 E2 Freiensteinau Germany
75 G3 Freihung Germany
169 H3 Frei Inocêncio Brazil
75 H5 Freilassing Germany
172 A5 Freire Chile
170 B2 Freirina Chile
74 C3 Freisen Germany
75 G4 Freising Germany
81 F2 Freistadt div. Austria
81 F2 Freistadt Austria
75 J2 Freital Germany
98 C4 Freixedas Portugal
98 B3 Freixo Portugal
98 D3 Freixo de Espada à Cinta Portugal
91 E5 Fréjus France
91 E5 Fréjus, G. de b. France
91 E3 Fréjus Tunnel France/Italy
58 A1 Frekhaug Norway
17 A7 Fremantle Western Australia Australia
74 F4 Fremdingen Germany
62 B3 Fremington England U.K.
155 G2 Fremont r. Utah U.S.A.
148 E4 Fremont Michigan U.S.A.
150 D3 Fremont Nebraska U.S.A.
146 B4 Fremont Ohio U.S.A.
146 B6 Frenchburg Kentucky U.S.A.
146 C4 French Creek r. Pennsylvania U.S.A.
160 G3 French Guiana territory South America
13 F4 French I. i. Victoria Australia
137 H5 Frenchman r. Canada/U.S.A.
154 C2 Frenchman Nevada U.S.A.
13 F5 Frenchman Cap mt. Tasmania Australia
154 B2 Frenchman L. l. California U.S.A.
155 E3 Frenchman L. l. Nevada U.S.A.
67 C3 Frenchpark Rep. of Ireland
9 D4 French Pass New Zealand
5 N6 French Polynesia territory Pacific Ocean
3 French Southern and Antarctic Lands territory Indian Ocean
147 J1 Frenchville Maine U.S.A.
86 A2 Frencq France
121 E1 Frenda Algeria
89 G2 Freneuse France
79 H2 Frenštát pod Radhoštěm Czech Rep.
109 G2 Frentani, Monti dei mts Italy
131 G4 Frere South Africa
72 C3 Freren Germany
81 E4 Fresach Austria
122 C5 Fresco Côte d'Ivoire
166 B2 Fresco r. Brazil
63 E4 Freshwater England U.K.
155 G6 Fresnal Canyon Arizona U.S.A.
89 F3 Fresnay-sur-Sarthe France
101 G2 Fresnedas r. Spain
87 E3 Fresnes-en-Woëvre France
87 E5 Fresnes-sur-Apance France
82 A1 Fresne-St-Mamès France
156 E4 Fresnillo Mexico
154 C3 Fresno r. California U.S.A.
154 C3 Fresno California U.S.A.
98 E4 Fresno Alhándiga Spain
98 E3 Fresno de la Ribera Spain
98 E3 Fresno de Sayago Spain
86 C3 Fresnoy-le-Grand France
63 H2 Fressingfield England U.K.
58 B1 Fresvikbreen mt. Norway
90 D1 Fretigney-et-Velloreille France
97 H3 Freu, Cap des pt Spain
103 F5 Freu de Cabrera chan. Spain
74 C2 Freudenberg Germany
69 E5 Freudenburg Germany
74 D4 Freudenstadt Germany
86 B2 Frévent France
14 C3 Frewena Northern Terr. Australia
73 G4 Freyburg Germany
17 A5 Freycinet Est. b. Western Australia Australia
13 G5 Freycinet Nat. Park nat. park Tasmania Australia
73 H2 Freyenstein Germany
87 F3 Freyming-Merlebach France
173 F1 Freyre Argentina
75 G3 Freystadt Germany
75 J4 Freyung Germany
122 B4 Fria Guinea
128 A2 Fria, Cape c. Namibia
154 C3 Friant California U.S.A.
170 D2 Frias Argentina
82 C2 Fribourg div. Switzerland
82 C2 Fribourg Switzerland
82 D1 Frick Switzerland
83 E1 Frickingen Germany
65 H3 Fridaythorpe England U.K.
81 H3 Friedberg Austria
75 F4 Friedberg Germany
74 D2 Friedberg (Hessen) Germany
72 C2 Friedeburg Germany
74 E2 Friedewald Hessen Germany
87 G2 Friedewald Rheinland-Pfalz Germany
73 K3 Friedland Brandenburg Germany
73 J2 Friedland Mecklenburg-Vorpommern Germany
72 E4 Friedland Niedersachsen Germany
75 F2 Friedrichroda Germany
74 D2 Friedrichsdorf Germany
74 E5 Friedrichshafen Germany
72 D1 Friedrichskoog Germany
73 G2 Friedrichsruhe Germany
72 E1 Friedrichstadt Germany
73 J2 Friedrichswalde Germany
75 F2 Friemar Germany
159 □1 Friendship h. Jamaica
147 J3 Friendship Maine U.S.A.
81 F4 Friesach Austria
73 H3 Friesack Germany
87 G2 Friesenhagen Germany
74 C4 Friesenheim Germany
83 F1 Friesenried Germany
68 D1 Friese Wad tidal flats Netherlands
68 D1 Friesland div. Netherlands
72 C2 Friesoythe Germany
127 □ Frigate I. i. Seychelles
107 E4 Frignano reg. Italy
59 E3 Frillesås Sweden
59 F3 Frinnaryd Sweden
63 H3 Frinton-on-Sea England U.K.
151 D6 Frio r. Texas U.S.A.
66 F4 Friockheim Scotland U.K.
98 C1 Friol Spain
66 B4 Frisa, Loch l. Scotland U.K.
69 E5 Frisange Luxembourg
155 F2 Frisco Mt mt. Utah U.S.A.
59 E3 Fristad Sweden
59 E3 Fritsla Sweden
72 E4 Fritzlar Germany
107 G2 Friuli - Venezia Giulia div. Italy
89 G1 Friville-Escarbotin France
135 M3 Frobisher Bay b. N.W.T. Canada
137 H3 Frobisher Lake l. Saskatchewan Canada
55 C4 Frøbjerg Bavnehøj h. Denmark
80 B4 Frodolfo r. Italy
62 D1 Frodsham England U.K.
91 D3 Froges France
63 F3 Frogmore England U.K.
56 C3 Frohavet b. Norway
70 F3 Frohburg Germany
81 G3 Frohnleiten Austria
90 E1 Froideconche France
86 B3 Froissy France
58 C2 Froland Norway
52 F1 Frolishchi Rus. Fed.
51 G5 Frolovo Rus. Fed.
52 F2 Frolovskaya Rus. Fed.
77 H1 Frombork Poland
62 D4 Frome r. England U.K.
12 D2 Frome watercourse S. Australia Australia
62 D3 Frome England U.K.
159 □1 Frome Jamaica
12 D2 Frome Downs S. Australia Australia
12 D2 Frome, Lake salt flat S. Australia Australia
99 F2 Frómista Spain
72 C4 Fröndenberg Germany
74 D2 Fronhausen Germany
93 B4 Fronsac Aquitaine France
93 C6 Fronsac Midi-Pyrénées France
100 C1 Fronteira Portugal
92 B2 Frontenay-Rohan-Rohan France
75 H4 Frontenhausen Germany
97 □ Frontera Canary Is Spain
157 G5 Frontera Mexico
157 G5 Frontera, Pta pt Mexico
156 C2 Fronteras Mexico
91 B5 Frontignan France
93 D5 Fronton France
146 D5 Front Royal Virginia U.S.A.
109 F3 Frosinone div. Lazio Italy
109 F3 Frosinone Italy
109 G3 Frosolone Italy
146 D5 Frostburg Maryland U.S.A.
59 F2 Frövi Sweden
56 C3 Frøya i. Norway
86 B2 Fruges France
155 H2 Fruita Colorado U.S.A.
155 G1 Fruitland Utah U.S.A.
52 D2 Fruktovaya Rus. Fed.
112 F1 Frumuşica Romania
53 F3 Frunze Kherson Ukraine
53 F3 Frunze Kherson Ukraine
47 H4 Frunze Kyrgyzstan
Frunze see Bishkek
53 C3 Frunzivka Ukraine
112 B2 Fruška Gora h. Yugoslavia
168 D4 Frutal Brazil
82 C2 Frutigen Switzerland
79 H2 Frýdek-Místek Czech Rep.
78 E1 Frýdlant Czech Rep.
147 H2 Fryeburg Maine U.S.A.
77 J2 Frygnowo Poland
81 F2 Frymburk Czech Rep.
77 K6 Frysztak Poland
114 D4 Fthiotis div. Greece
32 D1 Fu r. China
6 □4 Fua'amotu Tonga
6 □3 Fuamotu i. Tonga
33 G3 Fu'an China
64 C1 Fuar Bheinn h. Scotland U.K.
107 E5 Fucecchio Italy
83 F1 Fuchstal Germany
28 D6 Fuchū Japan
33 E3 Fuchuan China
29 H3 Fudai Japan
66 A3 Fuday i. Scotland U.K.
33 G3 Fude China
33 H3 Fuding China
101 F2 Fuencaliente Spain
102 B3 Fuendejalón Spain
101 F4 Fuengirola Spain
99 G4 Fuenlabrada Spain
99 H2 Fuenmayor Spain
99 F4 Fuensalida Spain
103 B7 Fuensanta Spain
103 B7 Fuente Álamo Spain
103 B6 Fuente-Álamo Spain
103 B6 Fuente Albilla, Cerro de mt. Spain
99 G3 Fuentecambrón Spain
99 G3 Fuentecén Spain
100 D2 Fuente de Cantos Spain
100 D2 Fuente del Maestre Spain
101 F3 Fuente de Piedra Spain
101 F3 Fuente de Piedra, Laguna de l. Spain
101 G1 Fuente el Fresno Spain
98 D4 Fuenteguinaldo Spain
99 E3 Fuentelapeña Spain
99 G3 Fuentelcésped Spain
101 H1 Fuentelespino de Haro Spain
101 E2 Fuente Obejuna Spain
101 E3 Fuente Palmera Spain
99 H3 Fuentepinilla Spain
102 C3 Fuenterodos Spain
99 E3 Fuentesaúco Spain
99 F3 Fuentesaúco de Fuentidueña Spain
103 C4 Fuentes de Ayódar Spain
102 C3 Fuentes de Ebro Spain
102 B3 Fuentes de Jiloca Spain
100 D2 Fuentes de León Spain
99 F2 Fuentes de Nava Spain
98 D4 Fuentes de Oñoro Spain
102 D4 Fuentespalda Spain
100 D1 Fuentes, Sierra de Spain
99 G3 Fuentidueña Spain
171 B7 Fuerte Bulnes Chile
101 G3 Fuerte del Rey Spain
165 E4 Fuerte Olimpo Paraguay
97 □ Fuerteventura i. Canary Is Spain
23 B2 Fuga i. Philippines
80 C3 Fügen Austria
55 □1 Fuglafjørður Faeroes
55 D4 Fuglebjerg Denmark
32 B3 Fugong China
33 F1 Fugou China
30 D5 Fugu China
47 L3 Fuhai China
72 F2 Fuhlsbüttel airport Germany
73 H4 Fuhne r. Germany
Fujairah see Al Fujayrah
29 G6 Fuji Japan
33 G3 Fujian div. China
29 G6 Fujieda Japan
29 G6 Fuji-Hakone-Izu National Park Japan
31 J3 Fujin China
29 G6 Fujinomiya Japan
28 H3 Fujisaki Japan
29 G6 Fuji-san volcano Japan
29 G6 Fujiyoshida Japan
42 A4 Fûka Egypt
28 J2 Fukagawa Japan
28 G3 Fukaura Japan
Fukien see Fujian
29 E6 Fukuchiyama Japan
28 B7 Fukue Japan
28 B7 Fukue-jima i. Japan
29 F6 Fukui div. Japan
29 F5 Fukui Japan
28 C7 Fukuoka div. Japan
28 C7 Fukuoka Japan
29 H5 Fukushima div. Japan
29 H5 Fukushima Japan
28 H3 Fukushima Japan
28 C8 Fukuyama Japan
122 A4 Fulacunda Guinea-Bissau
72 C1 Fūlād Maïalleh Iran
6 □7 Fulaga i. Fiji
72 E4 Fulda r. Germany
74 E2 Fulda Hessen Germany
65 G4 Fulford England U.K.
63 F3 Fulham England U.K.
33 G1 Fuliji China
32 D1 Fuling China
159 □3 Fullarton Trinidad and Tobago
137 M2 Fullerton, Cape headland N.W.T. Canada
79 G2 Fulnek Czech Rep.
79 J5 Fülöpszállás Hungary
80 C3 Fulpmes Austria
148 B5 Fulton Illinois U.S.A.
144 B4 Fulton Kentucky U.S.A.
150 F4 Fulton Missouri U.S.A.
147 E3 Fulton New York U.S.A.
173 H4 Fulton Argentina
86 D3 Fumay France
93 C4 Fumel France
29 H6 Funabashi Japan
4 J5 Funafuti i. Tuvalu
96 □ Funchal Madeira Portugal
162 C1 Fundación Colombia
169 H3 Fundão Brazil
98 C4 Fundão Portugal
156 C3 Fundición Mexico
112 F2 Fundulea Romania
80 B3 Fundusfeiler mt. Austria
139 G5 Fundy, Bay of b. New Brunswick/Nova Scotia Canada
139 G4 Fundy Nat. Park nat. park New Brunswick Canada
154 D3 Funeral Peak summit California U.S.A.
129 E3 Funhalouro Mozambique
32 D4 Funing China
33 G1 Funing China
33 E1 Funiu Shan mountain range China
123 F4 Funtua Nigeria
66 □2 Funzie Scotland U.K.
30 E5 Fuping China
33 G3 Fuqing China
32 D3 Fuquan China
55 B3 Fur i. Denmark
129 E1 Furancungo Mozambique
28 J2 Furano Japan
28 K2 Füren-ko l. Japan
55 E4 Furesø l. Denmark
39 C3 Fürg Iran
59 H3 Furilden i. Sweden
83 D2 Furkapass Switzerland
43 C2 Furmanov Rus. Fed.
47 H4 Furmanovka Kazakhstan
46 C3 Furmanovo Kazakhstan
154 D3 Furnace Creek California U.S.A.
13 G5 Furneaux Group is Tasmania Australia
43 D2 Furqlus Syria
72 C3 Fürstenau Germany
73 J2 Fürstenberg Brandenburg Germany
72 D4 Fürstenberg Nordrhein-Westfalen Germany
81 G3 Fürstenfeld div. Austria
81 H3 Fürstenfeld Austria
75 G4 Fürstenfeldbruck Germany
73 K3 Fürstenwalde Germany
73 J2 Fürstenwerder Germany
75 J4 Fürstenzell Germany
79 L4 Furta Hungary
59 E2 Furtan Sweden
108 A5 Furtei Sardegna Italy
75 F3 Fürth Bayern Germany
74 D3 Fürth Hessen Germany
75 H3 Furth im Wald Germany
74 D4 Furtwangen im Schwarzwald Germany
28 H2 Furubira Japan
59 F1 Furudal Sweden
29 F5 Furukawa Japan
29 H4 Furukawa Japan
135 K3 Fury and Hecla Strait str. N.W.T. Canada
162 C3 Fusagasugá Colombia
110 F3 Fuscaldo Italy
114 B2 Fushë-Bardhe Albania
114 A1 Fushë-Krujë Albania
31 G4 Fushun China
32 D2 Fushun China
107 H2 Fusine in Valromana Italy
31 H4 Fusong China
75 F5 Füssen Germany
89 H4 Fussy France
102 B2 Fustiñana Spain
32 D4 Fusui China
28 C7 Futago-san volcano Japan
171 B5 Futaleufú Chile
107 F4 Futa, Passo della pass Italy
29 □1 Futatsu-ne is Japan
29 □2 Futemma Japan
112 B2 Futog Yugoslavia
172 A6 Futrono Chile
29 G6 Futtsu Japan
6 □2 Futuna i. Vanuatu
33 G3 Futun Xi r. China
91 D5 Fuveau France
30 D6 Fu Xian China
Fuxian see Wafangdian
31 G4 Fuxin China
29 G4 Fuya Japan
31 E5 Fuyang r. China
33 G2 Fuyang China
33 F1 Fuyang China
31 H3 Fuyu China
31 K2 Fuyuan China
32 D3 Fuyuan China
26 E2 Fuyun China
79 K4 Füzesabony Hungary
33 G3 Fuzhou Fujian China
33 G3 Fuzhou Jiangxi China
107 J3 Fužine Croatia
55 C4 Fyn i. Denmark
64 D1 Fyne r. Scotland U.K.
66 C5 Fyne, Loch inlet Scotland U.K.
55 C4 Fyns Hoved headland Denmark
58 C2 Fyresdal Norway
58 C2 Fyresvatn l. Norway
59 G1 Fyrisån r. Sweden
114 C4 Fyteies Greece
159 □3 Fyzabad Trinidad and Tobago

G

105 B7 Gaâfour Tunisia
81 F3 Gaal Austria
126 E3 Gaalkacyo Somalia
130 B3 Gab watercourse Namibia
126 D3 Gabangab well Ethiopia
93 C5 Gabarret France
93 B5 Gabas r. France
154 D2 Gabbs Nevada U.S.A.
154 C2 Gabbs Valley Range mts Nevada U.S.A.
125 B6 Gabela Angola
121 G2 Gabès Tunisia
121 G2 Gabès, Golfe de g. Tunisia
101 G3 Gabia la Grande Spain
107 G5 Gabicce Mare Italy
77 H3 Gąbin Poland
8 G3 Gable End Foreland headland New Zealand
81 H2 Gablitz Austria
13 G4 Gabo I. i. Victoria Australia
117 F6 Gabon country Africa
128 D3 Gaborone Botswana
173 G2 Gaboto Argentina
93 E4 Gabriac France
127 □4 Gabriel I. i. Mauritius
39 D4 Gābrīk watercourse Iran
39 D4 Gābrīk Iran
112 D3 Gabrovnitsa Bulgaria
112 E3 Gabrovo Bulgaria
122 B4 Gabú Guinea-Bissau
106 B3 Gaby Italy
179 □ Gaby, I. i. Kerguelen Indian Ocean
89 F3 Gacé France
39 B1 Gach Sār Iran
104 G4 Gacko Bos.-Herz.
38 A3 Gadag India
56 D2 Gäddede Sweden
32 B1 Gadê China
73 G2 Gadebusch Germany
80 C4 Gadera r. Italy
36 B5 Gadhra India
83 D2 Gadmen Switzerland
108 B5 Gadoni Sardegna Italy
101 H4 Gádor Spain
101 H4 Gádor, Sierra de mountain range Spain
36 B4 Gadra Pakistan
145 C5 Gadsden Alabama U.S.A.
38 B2 Gadwal India
124 C3 Gadzi Central African Rep.
56 F1 Gædnovuoppe Norway
62 C3 Gaer Wales U.K.
112 E2 Găeşti Romania
109 F3 Gaeta Italy
109 F3 Gaeta, Golfo di g. Italy
98 B4 Gafanha da Nazare Portugal
4 F4 Gaferut i. Fed. States of Micronesia
100 C1 Gáfete Portugal
145 D5 Gaffney S. Carolina U.S.A.
121 F2 Gafsa Tunisia
124 C2 Gagal Chad
52 B2 Gagarin Rus. Fed.
47 G4 Gagarin Uzbekistan
74 D4 Gaggenau Germany
111 E5 Gaggi Sicilia Italy
107 E4 Gaggio Montano Italy
52 G2 Gagino Rus. Fed.
110 D5 Gagliano Castelferrato Sicilia Italy
111 H3 Gagliano del Capo Italy
122 C5 Gagnoa Côte d'Ivoire
139 G3 Gagnon Québec Canada
141 H3 Gagnon, Lac l. Québec Canada
51 G7 Gagra Georgia
102 E3 Gaià r. Spain
130 B3 Gaiab r. Namibia
37 G4 Gaibanda Bangladesh
80 D4 Gail r. Austria
74 E4 Gaildorf Germany
83 D1 Gailingen Germany
93 D5 Gaillac France
90 E2 Gaillard France
Gaillimh see Galway
89 G2 Gaillon France
171 C5 Gaimán Argentina
75 G4 Gaimersheim Germany
145 D6 Gainesville Florida U.S.A.
145 D5 Gainesville Georgia U.S.A.
151 D5 Gainesville Texas U.S.A.
65 H4 Gainsborough England U.K.
17 B7 Gairdner r. Western Australia Australia
12 C2 Gairdner, Lake salt flat S. Australia Australia
66 C3 Gair Loch inlet Scotland U.K.
66 C3 Gairloch Scotland U.K.
108 B5 Gairo Sardegna Italy
83 E1 Gais Switzerland
81 F3 Gaishorn Austria
31 G4 Gai Xian China
38 C2 Gajapatinagaram India
36 A4 Gajar Pakistan
78 F3 Gajary Slovakia
126 C4 Gajos well Kenya
130 D3 Gakarosa mt. South Africa
123 F5 Gakem Nigeria
36 C1 Gakuch Jammu and Kashmir
37 G3 Gala China
46 F5 Galaasiya Uzbekistan
43 A5 Galâla el Baharîya, G. el plat. Egypt
43 A5 Galâla el Qiblîya, G. el plat. Egypt
93 C5 Galan France
127 C5 Galana r. Kenya
170 C2 Galán, Co mt. Argentina
39 C1 Galand Iran
79 G3 Galanta Slovakia
23 □1 Galap Palau
99 G4 Galapagar Spain
162 □ Galápagos, Islas is Ecuador
66 F5 Galashiels Scotland U.K.
112 F3 Galata Bulgaria
115 E5 Galatas Greece
53 B Galaţi div. Romania
112 F2 Galaţi Romania
111 H2 Galatina Italy
114 C2 Galatini Greece
114 E2 Galatista Greece
111 H2 Galatone Italy
66 F5 Gala Water r. Scotland U.K.
146 C6 Galax Virginia U.S.A.
115 D4 Galaxidi Greece
67 C4 Galbally Rep. of Ireland
15 E3 Galbraith Queensland Australia
99 H1 Galdakao Spain
97 □ Gáldar Canary Is Spain
57 C3 Galdhøpiggen summit Norway
157 E3 Galeana Mexico
99 G1 Galea, Pta pt Spain
39 C4 Galeh Dār Iran
148 B4 Galena Illinois U.S.A.
73 J2 Galenbecker See l. Germany
159 □3 Galeota Pt pt Trinidad Trinidad and Tobago
101 H3 Galera r. Spain
101 H3 Galera Spain
159 □3 Galera Pt pt Trinidad Trinidad and Tobago
157 F6 Galera, Pta pt Mexico
172 A5 Galera, Punta headland Chile
148 B5 Galesburg Illinois U.S.A.
130 E4 Galeshewe South Africa
148 B3 Galesville Wisconsin U.S.A.
146 E4 Galeton Pennsylvania U.S.A.
127 □5 Galets, Pte des pt Réunion Indian Ocean
79 J4 Galgamácsa Hungary
126 E3 Galguduud div. Somalia
166 C3 Galheirão r. Brazil
51 G7 Gali Georgia
168 D5 Gália Brazil
112 D2 Galicea Mare Romania
50 G3 Galich Rus. Fed.
50 G3 Galichskaya Vozvyshennost' h. Rus. Fed.
98 B2 Galicia div. Spain
114 B2 Galičica mountain range Macedonia
114 B1 Galičica nat. park Macedonia
15 F4 Galilee, L. salt flat Queensland Australia
Galilee, Sea of l. see Tiberias, L.
169 H3 Galiléia Brazil
106 E5 Galileo airport Italy
83 E1 Galinakopf mt. Austria/Liechtenstein
159 □1 Galina Pt pt Jamaica
146 B4 Galion Ohio U.S.A.
159 □4 Galion, Baie du b. Martinique Caribbean
114 C1 Galište Ezero l. Macedonia
98 D5 Galisteo Spain
52 C3 Galitsa Rus. Fed.
155 G5 Galiuro Mts mts Arizona U.S.A.
119 G5 Gallabat Sudan
106 C3 Gallarate Italy
89 G3 Gallardon France
152 E2 Gallatin r. Montana U.S.A.
145 C4 Gallatin Tennessee U.S.A.
38 C5 Galle Sri Lanka
102 C2 Gállego r. Spain
171 B7 Gallegos r. Argentina
99 E4 Gallegos de Solmirón Spain
67 C5 Galley Head headland Rep. of Ireland
92 B3 Gallian-en-Médoc France
106 C3 Galliate Italy
102 E2 Gallina Pelada mt. Spain
162 C1 Gallinas, Pta pt Colombia
107 F3 Gallio Italy
111 H2 Gallipoli Italy
146 B5 Gallipolis Ohio U.S.A.
56 F2 Gällivare Sweden
81 F4 Gallizien Austria
81 F2 Gallneukirchen Austria
99 J4 Gallo r. Spain
56 D3 Gällö Sweden
102 B4 Gallocanta, Laguna de l. Spain
110 C4 Gallo, Capo c. Sicilia Italy
147 E3 Gallo I. i. New York U.S.A.
106 E2 Gallo, Lago di l. Italy
155 H4 Gallo Mts mts New Mexico U.S.A.
9 □3 Galloway, Mt h. Antipodes Is New Zealand
66 D6 Galloway, Mull of c. Scotland U.K.
59 E3 Gällstad Sweden
155 H4 Gallup New Mexico U.S.A.
102 B3 Gallur Spain
108 B4 Gallura reg. Sardegna Italy
47 G5 Gallyaaral Uzbekistan
127 D5 Galma Galla waterhole Kenya
66 B4 Galmisdale Scotland U.K.
13 G3 Galong New South Wales Australia
38 C5 Gal Oya r. Sri Lanka
38 C4 Galoya Sri Lanka
126 E2 Gal Shiikh Somalia
66 D5 Galston Scotland U.K.
154 B2 Galt California U.S.A.
120 B3 Galtat Zemmour Western Sahara
67 C4 Galtee Mountains h. Rep. of Ireland
108 B4 Galtelli Sardegna Italy
59 G2 Galten l. Sweden
55 B3 Galten Denmark
58 D1 Galterud Norway
80 B4 Galtür Austria
67 C4 Galtymore h. Rep. of Ireland
39 D2 Galūgāh-e Āsīyeh Iran
148 B5 Galva Illinois U.S.A.
172 A5 Galvarino Chile
99 G3 Galve de Sorbe Spain
100 C1 Galveias Portugal
151 E6 Galveston Texas U.S.A.
151 E6 Galveston Bay b. Texas U.S.A.
173 G2 Galvez Argentina
101 F1 Gálvez Spain
37 E3 Galwa Nepal
67 B3 Galway div. Rep. of Ireland
67 B3 Galway Rep. of Ireland
67 B3 Galway Bay g. Rep. of Ireland
24 D2 Gâm r. Vietnam
168 D2 Gamá Brazil
99 G1 Gama Spain
89 G2 Gamaches France
29 F6 Gamagōri Japan
173 F6 Gama, I. i. Argentina
131 H5 Gamalakhe South Africa
162 C2 Gamarra Colombia
79 G5 Gamás Hungary
123 G4 Gamawa Nigeria
172 E4 Gamay Argentina
37 G3 Gamba China
125 A4 Gamba Gabon
122 D4 Gambaga Ghana
106 E3 Gambara Italy
111 E4 Gambarie Italy
126 B3 Gambēla Ethiopia
126 B3 Gambela National Park nat. park Ethiopia
134 A3 Gambell Alaska U.S.A.
107 G4 Gambettola Italy
122 A4 Gambia r. The Gambia
116 C4 Gambia, The country Africa
122 B4 Gambie r. Senegal
14 B1 Gambier, C. c. Northern Terr. Australia
5 O7 Gambier, Îles is French Polynesia Pacific Ocean
12 D3 Gambier Is is S. Australia Australia
145 □2 Gambier Village The Bahamas
139 K4 Gambo Newfoundland Canada
124 D3 Gambo Central African Rep.
106 C3 Gambolò Italy
124 C4 Gamboma Congo
15 E3 Gamboola Queensland Australia
124 C3 Gamboula Central African Rep.
87 G4 Gambsheim France
155 H4 Gamerco New Mexico U.S.A.
81 G3 Gaming Austria
130 C6 Gamka r. South Africa
59 G3 Gamleby Sweden

119 F4 Gammams well Sudan
56 F2 Gammelstaden Sweden
74 E4 Gammertingen Germany
12 D2 Gammon Ranges Nat. Park nat. park S. Australia Australia
131 H1 Ga-Modjadji South Africa
130 B4 Gamoep South Africa
98 E1 Gamonal mt. Spain
38 C5 Gampola Sri Lanka
83 E1 Gams Switzerland
32 B2 Gamtog China
126 C4 Gamud mt. Ethiopia
33 F3 Gan r. China
31 H2 Gan r. China
32 C1 Gana China
155 H4 Ganado Arizona U.S.A.
91 D4 Ganagobie France
141 G4 Gananoque Ontario Canada
39 B3 Ganāveh Iran
42 F1 Gäncä Azerbaijan
32 E5 Gancheng China
Gand see Gent
125 B6 Ganda Angola
22 D2 Gandadiwata, Bukit mt. Indonesia
37 G3 Gandaingoin China
125 D5 Gandajika Congo(Zaire)
98 B1 Gándara Galicia Spain
98 B1 Gándara Galicia Spain
36 B3 Gandari Mt. mt. Pakistan
36 A3 Gandava Pakistan
139 K4 Gander Newfoundland Canada
72 D2 Ganderkesee Germany
102 D3 Gandesa Spain
36 C5 Gandevi India
36 B5 Gāndhīdhām India
36 C5 Gāndhinagar India
36 C4 Gāndhi Sāgar resr India
103 C6 Gandia Spain
106 D3 Gandino Italy
39 E3 Gand-i-Zureh depression Afghanistan
166 E3 Gandu Brazil
Gandzha see Gäncä
120 B5 Gâneb well Mauritania
36 F4 Ganga r. India
38 C5 Ganga r. Sri Lanka
124 E3 Gangala Na Bodia Congo(Zaire)
37 G5 Ganga, Mouths of the river mouth Bangladesh
171 C5 Gangán Argentina
36 C3 Ganganagar India
36 C4 Gangapur India
36 D4 Gangapur India
123 F4 Gangara Niger
24 A2 Gangaw Myanmar
38 B3 Gangawati India
24 B1 Gangaw Range mountain range Myanmar
30 B5 Gangca China
37 E3 Gangdisê Shan mountain range China
Ganges r. see Ganga
91 B5 Ganges France
110 D5 Gangi r. Sicilia Italy
110 D5 Gangi Sicilia Italy
75 H4 Gangkofen Germany
36 D3 Gangotri mt. India
37 G4 Gangtok India
32 D1 Gangu China
38 D2 Ganjam India
39 B3 Ganjgān Iran
31 E3 Ganjur Sum China
32 C2 Ganluo China
13 F3 Ganmain New South Wales Australia
31 G3 Gannan China
90 B2 Gannat France
152 E3 Gannett Peak summit Wyoming U.S.A.
53 B1 Gannopil' Ukraine
36 C5 Ganora India
30 D5 Ganquan China
130 B7 Gansbaai South Africa
81 H2 Gänserndorf div. Austria
81 H2 Gänserndorf Austria
69 C4 Ganshoren Belgium
30 B5 Gansu div. China
126 D4 Gantamaa Somalia
30 C5 Gantang China
12 D4 Gantheaume, C. headland S. Australia Australia
51 G7 Gant'iadi Georgia
82 C2 Gantrisch mt. Switzerland
22 B2 Gantung Indonesia
37 F4 Ganwan India
33 F3 Gan Xian China
123 G5 Ganye Nigeria
130 E3 Ganyesa South Africa
33 G1 Ganyu China
46 C3 Ganyushkino Kazakhstan
33 F3 Ganzhou China
126 B4 Ganzi Sudan
73 H2 Ganzlin Germany
123 E3 Gao div. Mali
123 D3 Gao Mali
33 F2 Gao'an China
31 E5 Gaocheng China
33 G2 Gaochun China
33 G2 Gaohebu China
30 B5 Gaolan China
32 B3 Gaoligong Shan mountain range China
31 F5 Gaomi China
33 E3 Gaomutang China
30 E6 Gaoping China
31 F5 Gaoqing China
30 A5 Gaotai China
31 F5 Gaotang China
30 D4 Gaotouyao China
122 D4 Gaoua Burkina
122 B4 Gaoual Guinea
32 D2 Gao Xian China
Gaoxiong see Kao-hsiung
31 E5 Gaoyang China
31 E5 Gaoyi China
33 G1 Gaoyou China
33 G1 Gaoyou Hu l. China
33 E4 Gaozhou China
91 E4 Gap France
23 B3 Gapan Philippines
91 D5 Gapeau r. France
36 E2 Gar China
121 F2 Garaa Tebourt well Tunisia
126 E3 Garacad Somalia
156 L7 Garachiné Panama
126 E3 Garadag Somalia
121 F1 Garaet Et Tarf salt pan Algeria
39 E3 Garagheh Iran
109 J4 Garaguso Italy
13 G2 Garah New South Wales Australia
122 C4 Garalo Mali
67 C3 Gara, Lough l. Rep. of Ireland
124 E3 Garamba r. Congo(Zaire)
124 E3 Garamba, Parc National de la nat. park Congo(Zaire)
166 E2 Garanhuns Brazil
131 F2 Ga-Rankuwa South Africa
169 E2 Garapuava Brazil
124 D2 Garba Central African Rep.
126 D4 Garbahaarey Somalia
77 K4 Garbatka-Letnisko Poland
127 C4 Garba Tula Kenya
101 F1 Garbayuela Spain
154 A1 Garberville California U.S.A.
77 L4 Garbów Poland
72 E3 Garbsen Niedersachsen Germany
168 D5 Garça Brazil
166 D2 Garças r. Brazil
168 B1 Garças, R. das r. Brazil
75 H4 Garching an der Alz Germany
75 G4 Garching bei München Germany
102 D3 Garcia Spain
168 B4 Garcias Brazil
130 C6 Garciaspas pass South Africa
100 E1 Garciaz Spain
99 H4 Garcinarro Spain
37 G2 Garco China
91 C4 Gard div. Languedoc-Roussillon France
91 C5 Gard r. France
107 E3 Garda Italy
107 E3 Garda, Lago di l. Italy
91 D5 Gardanne France
105 A7 Garde, Cap de c. Algeria
76 G2 Gardeja Poland
73 G3 Gardelegen Germany
80 C4 Gardena r. Italy
150 C4 Garden City Kansas U.S.A.
148 D3 Garden Corners Michigan U.S.A.
154 C5 Garden Grove California U.S.A.
137 L4 Garden Hill Manitoba Canada
148 E3 Garden I. i. Michigan U.S.A.
144 C2 Garden Pen. pen. Michigan U.S.A.
173 H4 Gardey Argentina
39 G2 Gardēz Afghanistan
114 C4 Gardiki Greece
147 J2 Gardiner Maine U.S.A.
152 E2 Gardiner Montana U.S.A.
140 E2 Gardiner Ontario Canada
147 G4 Gardiners I. i. New York U.S.A.
72 D1 Garding Germany
148 C5 Gardner Illinois U.S.A.
147 K2 Gardner Lake l. Maine U.S.A.
176 H4 Gardner Pinnacles is Hawaii U.S.A.
154 C2 Gardnerville Nevada U.S.A.
83 F3 Gardone Riviera Italy
106 E3 Gardone Val Trompia Italy
93 C4 Gardonne France
79 H4 Gárdony Hungary
93 D5 Gardouch France
59 E4 Gårdstånga Sweden
93 B4 Garein France
66 D4 Garelochhead Scotland U.K.
91 E5 Garéoult France
104 F3 Garešnica Croatia
106 C4 Garessio Italy
121 F4 Garet El Djenoun mt. Algeria
118 D3 Garet el Gorane depression Chad
163 G3 Gare Tigre French Guiana
65 G4 Garforth England U.K.
115 C5 Gargalianoi Greece
101 E1 Gargáligas r. Spain
92 D3 Gargan, Mont h. France
140 C3 Gargantua, Cape c. Ontario Canada
83 G2 Gargazzone Italy
92 D2 Gargilesse-Dampierre France
107 E3 Gargnano Italy
64 D1 Gargunnock Hills h. Scotland U.K.
Gargunsa see Gar
54 B4 Gargždai Lithuania
36 D5 Garhakota India
36 E5 Garhchiroli India
39 F3 Garhi Khairo Pakistan
36 D4 Garhi Malehra India
136 E5 Garibaldi, Mt mt. B.C. Canada
136 E5 Garibaldi Prov. Park nat. park B.C. Canada
131 E5 Gariep Dam dam South Africa
131 E5 Gariep Dam Nature Reserve res. South Africa
130 A5 Garies South Africa
109 F3 Garigliano r. Italy
68 D1 Garijp Netherlands
93 A6 Garinoain Spain
127 C5 Garissa Kenya
54 D3 Garkalne Latvia
146 D4 Garland Pennsylvania U.S.A.
151 D5 Garland Texas U.S.A.
106 C3 Garlasco Italy
83 E3 Garlate, Lago di l. Italy
81 F3 Garlenz Austria
54 C4 Garliava Lithuania
93 B5 Garlin France
39 D1 Garmeh Iran
75 G5 Garmisch-Partenkirchen Germany
39 C2 Garmsar Iran
39 E3 Garmsel reg. Afghanistan
150 E4 Garnett Kansas U.S.A.
13 E3 Garnpung Lake l. New South Wales Australia
37 G4 Gāro Hills India
102 D2 Garona r. Spain
93 B4 Garonne r. France
91 C5 Garons France
126 E3 Garoowe Somalia
167 C6 Garopaba Brazil
123 G4 Garoua Cameroon
124 B2 Garoua Boulai Cameroon
122 D3 Garou, Lac l. Mali
98 E2 Garrafe de Torio Spain
99 H3 Garray Spain
173 F4 Garré Argentina
72 D3 Garrel Germany
91 B5 Garrigues reg. France
64 A3 Garrison Northern Ireland U.K.
155 E2 Garrison Utah U.S.A.
64 B4 Garristown Rep. of Ireland
67 F1 Garron Pt pt Northern Ireland U.K.
100 D1 Garrovillas Spain
101 J3 Garrucha Spain
102 C4 Garrucha, Sierra de la mountain range Spain
36 A3 Garruk Pakistan
137 J1 Garry Lake l. N.W.T. Canada
66 D4 Garry, Loch l. Scotland U.K.
66 B2 Garrynahine Scotland U.K.
81 G2 Gars am Kamp Austria
59 F1 Garsås Sweden
127 D5 Garsen Kenya
118 D5 Garsila Sudan
65 F4 Garstang England U.K.
81 F2 Garsten Austria
Gartar see Qianning
92 C2 Gartempe r. France
62 C2 Garth Wales U.K.
Gartok see Garyarsa
73 G2 Gartow Germany
74 D4 Gärtringen Germany
73 K2 Gartz Germany
23 □1 Garusuun Palau
22 A3 Garut Indonesia
67 E2 Garvagh Northern Ireland U.K.
64 A4 Garvagh Rep. of Ireland
65 F2 Garvald Scotland U.K.
100 B3 Garvão Portugal
66 D3 Garve Scotland U.K.
64 C1 Garvellachs i. Scotland U.K.
9 B6 Garvie Mts mts New Zealand
37 E4 Garwa India
77 K4 Garwolin Poland
148 D5 Gary Indiana U.S.A.
36 E3 Garyarsa China
32 B2 Garyi China
28 D6 Garyū-zan mt. Japan
73 J1 Garz Germany
36 E2 Gar Zangbo r. China
32 B2 Garzê China
162 B3 Garzón Colombia
173 K3 Garzón, L. l. Uruguay
80 B4 Gaschurn Austria
93 B5 Gascogne reg. France
99 H1 Gascogne, Golfe de g. France/Spain
150 E4 Gasconade r. Missouri U.S.A.
17 A5 Gascoyne r. Western Australia Australia
17 A5 Gascoyne Junction Western Australia Australia
17 B5 Gascoyne, Mt h. Western Australia Australia
Gascuña, Golfo de g. see Gascogne, Golfe de
131 F1 Gaseleka South Africa
36 D2 Gasherbrum mt. China/Jammu and Kashmir
39 E4 Gasht Iran
124 D4 Gashua Nigeria
39 D2 Gask Iran
77 L2 Gąski Poland
89 G2 Gasny France
139 H4 Gaspé Québec Canada
139 H4 Gaspé, C. c. Québec Canada
139 G4 Gaspé, Péninsule de pen. Québec Canada
139 G4 Gaspésie, Parc de la nat. park Québec Canada
81 E2 Gaspoltshofen Austria
29 H4 Gassan volcano Japan
122 A4 Gassane Senegal
68 E2 Gasselte Netherlands
106 B3 Gassino Torinese Italy
80 B3 Gasteiner Tal v. Austria
99 H2 Gasteiz-Vitoria Spain
145 D5 Gastonia N. Carolina U.S.A.
115 C5 Gastouni Greece
171 C5 Gastre Argentina
98 D4 Gata Spain
43 B2 Gata, C. c. Cyprus
101 H4 Gata, Cabo de c. Spain
103 D6 Gata de Gorgos Spain
72 C2 Gătaia Romania
98 D4 Gata, Sierra de mountain range Spain
92 G2 Gatchina Rus. Fed.
146 B6 Gate City Virginia U.S.A.
66 D6 Gatehouse of Fleet Scotland U.K.
65 G3 Gateshead England U.K.
151 D6 Gatesville Texas U.S.A.
155 H2 Gateway Colorado U.S.A.
147 F4 Gateway National Recreational Area res. New Jersey U.S.A.
86 B4 Gâtinais reg. France
89 F4 Gâtine reg. France
141 H3 Gatineau r. Québec Canada
141 H4 Gatineau Québec Canada
39 C3 Gatrūyeh Iran
107 G4 Gatteo a Mare Italy
106 C3 Gattinara Italy
15 H5 Gatton Queensland Australia
156 K7 Gatún L. l. Panama
39 B2 Gatvand Iran
63 F3 Gatwick airport England U.K.
6 □8 Gau i. Fiji
73 D3 Gau-Algesheim Germany
69 B5 Gauchy France
101 E4 Gaucín Spain
137 K3 Gauer Lake l. Manitoba Canada
54 D3 Gauja r. Latvia
56 C3 Gaula r. Norway
146 C5 Gauley Bridge W. Virginia U.S.A.
69 D5 Gaume reg. Belgium
58 B2 Gaupefjellet mt. Norway
58 B1 Gaupne Norway
37 F5 Gaurella India
58 C2 Gausta mt. Norway
131 F2 Gauteng div. South Africa
75 G4 Gauting Germany
102 C3 Gautizalema r. Spain
39 F2 Gauzan Afghanistan
102 F3 Gavà Spain
83 F3 Gavardo Italy
93 B6 Gavarnie France
39 E4 Gavāter Iran
39 C4 Gāvbandī Iran
39 C4 Gāvbūs, Kūh-e mountain range Iran
115 F8 Gavdopoula i. Greece
115 F8 Gavdos i. Greece
93 B5 Gave r. France
93 B5 Gave d'Aspe r. France
93 B5 Gave d'Oloron r. France
93 B5 Gave d'Ossau r. France
42 F3 Gaveh r. Iran
69 B4 Gavere Belgium
106 C4 Gavi Italy
166 D3 Gavião r. Brazil
100 C1 Gavião Portugal
162 D5 Gaviãozinho Brazil
154 B4 Gaviota California U.S.A.
172 F5 Gaviotas Argentina
106 C3 Gavirate Italy
39 D3 Gāv Koshī Iran
59 G1 Gävle Sweden
59 G1 Gävleborg div. Sweden
59 G1 Gävlebukten b. Sweden
108 B4 Gavoi Sardegna Italy
108 C2 Gavorrano Italy
88 D3 Gavray France
52 F3 Gavrilovka Vtoraya Rus. Fed.
52 E1 Gavrilov Posad Rus. Fed.
52 D1 Gavrilov-Yam Rus. Fed.
115 C4 Gavrolimni Greece
54 E3 Gavry Rus. Fed.
130 A3 Gawachab Namibia
24 B1 Gawai Myanmar
118 B2 Gawat well Libya
81 H2 Gaweinstal Austria
12 D3 Gawler S. Australia Australia
12 C3 Gawler Ranges h. S. Australia Australia
30 B4 Gaxun Nur salt lake China
46 E2 Gay Rus. Fed.
31 J4 Gaya r. China
37 F4 Gaya India
123 E4 Gaya Niger
123 F4 Gaya Nigeria
36 C2 Gayal Gah Pakistan
22 C3 Gayam Indonesia
120 B3 G'Aydat al Jhoucha ridge Western Sahara
123 E4 Gayéri Burkina
148 E3 Gaylord Michigan U.S.A.
15 G5 Gayndah Queensland Australia
52 C1 Gaynovo Rus. Fed.
114 E1 Gaytaninovo Bulgaria
50 F3 Gayutino Rus. Fed.
129 E3 Gaza div. Mozambique
43 C4 Gaza territory Asia
43 C4 Gaza Gaza
46 F4 Gaz-Achak Turkmenistan
39 D3 Gazak Iran
47 G4 Gazalkent Uzbekistan
46 E5 Gazandzhyk Turkmenistan
124 B1 Gazawa Cameroon
43 D1 Gaziantep div. Turkey
42 D2 Gaziantep Turkey
39 E2 Gazīk Iran
31 F2 Gazimur r. Rus. Fed.
30 D2 Gazimuro-Ononskiy Khrebet mountain range Rus. Fed.
31 F2 Gazimurskiy Khr. mountain range Rus. Fed.
31 F2 Gazimurskiy Zavod Rus. Fed.
42 C2 Gazipaşa Turkey
46 F4 Gazli Uzbekistan
39 D4 Gaz Māhū Iran
114 E1 Gazoros Greece
39 D3 Gaz Šāleḥ Iran
83 G3 Gazzo Veronese Italy
107 E3 Gazzuolo Italy
122 C5 Gbaaka Liberia
124 D3 Gbadolite Congo(Zaire)
122 B5 Gbangbatok Sierra Leone
122 C5 Gbarnga Liberia
122 C5 Gbatala Liberia
81 J2 Gbely Slovakia
123 F5 Gboko Nigeria
124 D3 Gbwado Congo(Zaire)
76 G1 Gdańsk div. Poland
76 G1 Gdańsk Poland
54 F2 Gdov Rus. Fed.
77 J6 Gdów Poland
76 G1 Gdynia Poland
66 C1 Gealldruig Mhor i. Scotland U.K.
93 B5 Geaune France
73 F4 Gebesee Germany
87 G2 Gebhardshain Germany
43 A1 Gebiz Turkey
126 C3 Gebre Guracha Ethiopia
119 G5 Gedaref Sudan
63 F2 Geddington England U.K.
74 B2 Gedern Germany
118 E5 Gedid Ras el Fil Sudan
69 C5 Gedinne Belgium
42 A2 Gediz r. Turkey
42 B2 Gediz Turkey
126 D3 Gedlegubē Ethiopia
63 G2 Gedney Drove End England U.K.
56 H1 Gednje Norway
126 D4 Gedo div. Somalia
93 C6 Gèdre France
55 D5 Gedser Denmark
55 D5 Gedser Odde pt Denmark
55 B3 Gedsted Denmark
55 B4 Gedved Denmark
13 F4 Geelong Victoria Australia
17 A6 Geelvink Channel chan. Western Australia Australia
130 C4 Geel Vloer l. South Africa
69 D4 Geer r. Belgium
68 C3 Geertruidenberg Netherlands
126 F2 Geesaley Somalia
72 C3 Geeste Germany
72 F2 Geesthacht Germany
69 D4 Geetbets Belgium
126 C3 Gefersa Ethiopia
114 A2 Gegai Albania
54 D4 Gegužinė Lithuania
36 E2 Gê'gyai China
33 G2 Ge Hu l. China
123 G4 Geidam Nigeria
126 B2 Geigar Sudan
137 J3 Geikie r. Saskatchewan Canada
140 A1 Geikie I. i. Ontario Canada
15 E2 Geikie Ra. h. Queensland Australia
74 B2 Geilenkirchen Germany
58 C1 Geilo Norway
56 B3 Geiranger Norway
75 H4 Geiselhöring Germany
75 G4 Geisenfeld Germany
75 H4 Geisenhausen Germany
74 C3 Geisenheim Germany
83 D1 Geisingen Germany
74 E4 Geislingen an der Steige Germany
72 F4 Geismar Germany
87 G4 Geispolsheim France
148 E6 Geist Reservoir resr Indiana U.S.A.
81 G3 Geistthal Austria
127 B5 Geita Tanzania
73 H4 Geithain Germany
32 C4 Gejiu China
126 B3 Gel r. Bahr el Ghazal/Equatoria Sudan
124 E2 Gel watercourse Sudan
110 D5 Gela r. Sicilia Italy
110 D5 Gela Sicilia Italy
126 E3 Geladī Ethiopia
110 D5 Gela, Golfo di g. Sicilia Italy
22 B2 Gelam i. Indonesia
25 C6 Gelang, Tanjung pt Malaysia
91 F4 Gélas, Cime du mt. France/Italy
68 E2 Gelderland div. Netherlands
68 D3 Geldermalsen Netherlands
72 B4 Geldern Germany
69 D3 Geldrop Netherlands
69 D4 Geleen Netherlands
51 F6 Gelendzhik Rus. Fed.
54 C4 Gelgaudiškis Lithuania
42 A1 Gelibolu Turkey
113 F4 Gelibolu Yarımadası pen. Turkey
93 C5 Gelise r. France
81 H4 Gellénháza Hungary
62 C3 Gelligaer Wales U.K.
39 D2 Gelmord Iran
74 E2 Gelnhausen Germany
79 K3 Gelnica Slovakia
55 B4 Gels r. Denmark
102 C3 Gelsa Spain
78 G5 Gelse Hungary
72 C4 Gelsenkirchen Germany
72 E1 Gelting Germany
25 C7 Gemas Malaysia
69 C4 Gembloux Belgium
123 G5 Gembu Nigeria
23 C5 Gemeh Indonesia
124 C3 Gemena Congo(Zaire)
91 D5 Gémenos France
42 C2 Gemerek Turkey
79 K3 Gemerská Hôrka Slovakia
68 D3 Gemert Netherlands
42 B1 Gemlik Turkey
113 G4 Gemlik Körfezi b. Turkey
107 H2 Gemona del Friuli Italy
92 B3 Gémozac France
119 F2 Gemsa Egypt
128 C4 Gemsbok National Park nat. park Botswana
130 C3 Gemsbokplein well South Africa
74 E2 Gemünden am Main Germany
31 G2 Gen r. China
101 E4 Genal r. Spain
126 D3 Genalē Wenz r. Ethiopia
69 C4 Genappe Belgium
109 E3 Genazzano Italy
92 C2 Gençay France
78 F4 Gencsapáti Hungary
171 B7 Gendarme Barreto Argentina
126 C2 Gendoa r. Ethiopia
90 D1 Gendrey France
68 E3 Gendringen Netherlands
68 E2 Genemuiden Netherlands
172 E4 General Acha Argentina
173 G4 General Alvear Buenos Aires Argentina
172 D3 General Alvear Mendoza Argentina
173 G3 General Arenales Argentina
165 E5 General Artigas Paraguay
173 H3 General Belgrano Argentina
179 B3 General Belgrano II Argentina Base Antarctica
179 B2 General Bernardo O'Higgins Chile Base Antarctica
151 D7 General Bravo Mexico
172 F2 General Cabrera Argentina
173 H1 General Campos Argentina
168 B1 General Carneiro Brazil
171 B6 General Carrera, L. l. Chile
157 F3 General Cepeda Mexico
173 J4 General Conesa Buenos Aires Argentina
172 E6 General Conesa Rio Negro Argentina
173 F5 General D. Cerri Argentina
173 L2 General Enrique Martinez Uruguay
173 H2 General Galarza Argentina
173 H4 General Guido Argentina
173 J4 General J. Madariaga Argentina
170 E2 General José de San Martin Argentina
164 C3 General Lagos Chile
173 G4 General La Madrid Argentina
173 H3 General Las Heras Argentina
173 J4 General Lavalle Argentina
172 F3 General Levalle Argentina
23 C4 General Luna Philippines
23 C4 General MacArthur Philippines
170 D1 General Martin Miguel de Güemes Argentina
173 G3 General O'Brien Argentina
171 B5 General Paz, L. l. Argentina/Chile
172 F3 General Pico Argentina
170 D2 General Pinedo Argentina
173 G3 General Pinto Argentina
173 J4 General Pirán Argentina
172 D5 General Roca Argentina
168 C4 General Salgado Brazil
172 F4 General San Martín Argentina
173 H3 General San Martin Argentina
179 B2 General San Martín Argentina Base Antarctica
23 C5 General Santos Philippines
157 F3 General Terán Mexico
112 F3 General Toshevo Bulgaria
173 G3 General Viamonte Argentina
173 F3 General Villegas Argentina
146 D3 Genesee r. New York U.S.A.
148 B5 Geneseo Illinois U.S.A.
146 E3 Geneseo New York U.S.A.
126 C3 Genet Ethiopia
148 C5 Geneva Illinois U.S.A.
150 D3 Geneva Nebraska U.S.A.
146 E3 Geneva New York U.S.A.
146 C4 Geneva Ohio U.S.A.
Geneva see Genève
148 C4 Geneva, Lake l. Wisconsin U.S.A.
82 B2 Genève div. Switzerland
82 B2 Genève Genève Switzerland
90 E2 Genevois mts France
107 G5 Genga Italy
74 D4 Gengenbach Germany
32 B4 Gengma China
125 D4 Gengwa Congo(Zaire)
77 M1 Geniai Lithuania
140 E2 Genier Ontario Canada
101 E3 Genil r. Spain
114 F1 Genisea Greece
69 D4 Genk Limburg Belgium
28 B7 Genkai-nada b. Japan
90 D1 Genlis France
115 □ Gennadio Greece
108 B5 Gennargentu, Monti del mountain range Sardegna Italy
68 D3 Gennep Netherlands
89 E4 Gennes France
171 B5 Genoa r. Argentina
13 G4 Genoa Victoria Australia
Genoa see Genova
106 B4 Genola Italy
91 B4 Génolhac France
106 C4 Genova div. Liguria Italy
106 C4 Genova Genova Italy
106 C4 Genova, Golfo di g. Italy
69 B3 Gent div. Oost-Vlaanderen Belgium
69 B3 Gent Gent Belgium
22 C3 Genteng i. Indonesia
22 A3 Genteng Indonesia
73 H3 Genthin Germany
92 D3 Gentioux-Pigerolles France
109 J4 Genzano di Lucania Italy
109 E3 Genzano di Roma Italy
17 A7 Geographe Bay b. Western Australia Australia
17 A5 Geographe Channel chan. Western Australia Australia
139 G2 George r. Québec Canada
16 B4 George r. Western Australia Australia
130 D6 George South Africa
179 □ George, C. c. Kerguelen Indian Ocean
14 B4 George Gills Ra. mountain range Northern Terr. Australia
145 D6 George, L. l. Florida U.S.A.
147 G3 George, L. l. New York U.S.A.
13 G3 George, L. l. New South Wales Australia
12 D4 George, L. l. S. Australia Australia
16 C4 George, L. salt flat Western Australia Australia
127 B4 George, Lake l. Uganda
75 G3 Georgensgmünd Germany
73 F5 Georgenthal Germany
9 A6 George Sd inlet New Zealand
128 □1 Georgetown Ascension Atlantic Ocean
158 B3 Georgetown Cayman Is Caribbean
147 F5 Georgetown Delaware U.S.A.
148 D6 Georgetown Illinois U.S.A.
144 C4 Georgetown Kentucky U.S.A.
146 B5 Georgetown Ohio U.S.A.
141 F5 Georgetown Ontario Canada
15 E3 Georgetown Queensland Australia
145 E5 Georgetown S. Carolina U.S.A.
15 F9 George Town Tasmania Australia
151 D6 Georgetown Texas U.S.A.
163 F2 Georgetown Guyana
25 C6 George Town Malaysia
158 D2 George Town The Bahamas
122 B4 Georgetown The Gambia
179 B2 George VI Sd chan. Antarctica
179 B5 George V Land reg. Antarctica
151 D6 George West Texas U.S.A.
118 E4 Georgia country Asia
145 D5 Georgia div. U.S.A.
140 E4 Georgian Bay l. Ontario Canada
141 F4 Georgian Bay Island National Park nat. park Ontario Canada
14 D4 Georgina watercourse Queensland Australia
115 F7 Georgioupoli Greece
112 F3 Georgi Traykov Bulgaria
47 H4 Georgiyevka Kazakhstan
47 K3 Georgiyevka Kazakhstan
51 G6 Georgiyevsk Rus. Fed.
50 H3 Georgiyevskoye Rus. Fed.
68 F2 Georgsdorf Germany
72 D3 Georgsmarienhütte Germany
102 E2 Ger Spain
75 H2 Gera Germany
69 B4 Geraardsbergen Belgium
111 F4 Gerace Italy
110 D5 Geraci Siculo Italy
115 D6 Geraki Greece
9 C6 Geraldine New Zealand
140 B2 Geraldton Ontario Canada
17 A6 Geraldton Western Australia Australia
115 D5 Geraneia mts Greece
43 C4 Gerar watercourse Israel
87 F4 Gérardmer France
81 G2 Geras Austria
81 H2 Gerasdorf bei Wien Austria
39 C4 Gerāsh Iran
87 F4 Gerbéviller France
91 C4 Gerbier de Jonc mt. France
73 G4 Gerbstedt Germany
42 E2 Gercüş Turkey
131 F3 Gerdau South Africa
79 H4 Gerecse mt. Hungary
42 C1 Gerede r. Turkey
42 C1 Gerede Turkey
39 F3 Gereshk Afghanistan
98 C3 Gerês, Serra do mountain range Portugal
80 D2 Geretsberg Austria
75 G5 Geretsried Germany
101 H3 Gérgal Spain
108 B5 Gergei Sardegna Italy
79 L3 Gergely-hegy mt. Hungary
122 B5 Gerihun Sierra Leone
25 C6 Gerik Malaysia
39 D2 Gerīmenj Iran
150 C3 Gering Nebraska U.S.A.
79 J4 Gerje r. Hungary
152 C3 Gerlach Nevada U.S.A.
79 K2 Gerlachovský štít mt. Slovakia
80 C3 Gerlos Austria
80 D3 Gerlospaß pass Austria
173 F3 Germania Argentina
135 Q2 Germania Land reg. Greenland
136 E3 Germansen Landing B.C. Canada
146 E5 Germantown Maryland U.S.A.
48 F3 Germany country Europe
75 F5 Germaringen Germany
113 F6 Germencik Turkey
75 G4 Germering Germany
74 D3 Germersheim Germany
99 H1 Gernika-Lumo Spain
73 G4 Gernrode Germany
74 D4 Gernsbach Germany
74 D3 Gernsheim Germany
29 F6 Gero Japan
106 D2 Gerola Alta Italy
115 D6 Gerolimenas Greece
74 B2 Gerolstein Germany
Gerona see Girona
155 G5 Geronimo Arizona U.S.A.
115 F7 Geropotamos r. Greece
107 J3 Gerovo Croatia
69 C4 Gerpinnes Belgium
93 C5 Gers div. Midi-Pyrénées France
93 C5 Gers r. France
83 D1 Gersau Switzerland
74 E2 Gersfeld (Rhön) Germany
73 J4 Gerste r. Germany
80 B2 Gerstetten Germany
75 F4 Gersthofen Germany
74 F2 Gerstungen Germany
73 J2 Gerswalde Germany
91 D4 Gervanne r. France
73 G3 Gerwisch Germany
90 B3 Gerzat France
37 F2 Gêrzê China
42 C1 Gerze Turkey
58 D2 Gesäter Sweden
72 C4 Gescher Germany
81 H3 Geschriebenstein h. Austria
108 B5 Gesico Sardegna Italy
86 D3 Gespunsart France
173 G1 Gessler Argentina
106 B4 Gesso r. Italy
89 D4 Gesté France
108 B5 Gesturi Sardegna Italy
32 B1 Gesu China
109 H3 Gesualdo Italy
59 F1 Gesunda Sweden
69 D4 Gesves Belgium
59 H1 Geta Finland
99 G4 Getafe Spain
39 C2 Getcheh, Kūh-e h. Iran
69 D4 Gete r. Belgium
92 A1 Gétigné France
72 E1 Gettorf Germany
146 E5 Gettysburg Pennsylvania U.S.A.
150 D2 Gettysburg S. Dakota U.S.A.
146 E5 Gettysburg National Military Park res. Pennsylvania U.S.A.
32 D3 Getu r. China
168 D4 Getulina Brazil
179 A4 Getz Ice Shelf ice feature Antarctica
69 D4 Geul r. Netherlands
13 G3 Geurie New South Wales Australia
42 E4 Gevaş Turkey
91 B4 Gévaudan reg. France
72 C4 Gevelsberg Germany
88 D3 Gevezé France
114 D1 Gevgelija Macedonia
90 C1 Gevrey-Chambertin France
90 E2 Gex France
99 H1 Gexto Spain
Gey see Nikshahr
43 A1 Geydik D. mts Turkey
43 B1 Geyik Dağ mt. Turkey
113 F5 Geyikli Turkey
25 □ Geylang Singapore
131 E3 Geysdorp South Africa
42 B1 Geyve Turkey
114 B1 Gezavesh Albania
33 E2 Gezhouba China
119 G3 Gezirat Mukawwar i. Sudan
81 G2 Gföhl Austria
130 D3 Ghaap Plateau plat. South Africa
43 D3 Ghabāghib Syria
119 E5 Ghabeish Sudan
43 D4 Ghadaf, W. el watercourse Jordan
118 A1 Ghadāmis Libya
118 B2 Ghaddūwah Libya
43 D3 Ghadīr Minqār l. Syria
39 C1 Ghaem Shahr Iran
47 G4 Ghafurov Tajikistan
37 E4 Ghaghara r. India
37 F5 Ghaghra India
111 □ Ghajn Tuffieha Bay b. Malta
117 D5 Ghana country Africa
39 C4 Ghanādah, Rās pt U.A.E.
36 C4 Ghanliala India
128 C3 Ghanzi div. Botswana
128 C3 Ghanzi Botswana
42 C4 Gharandal Jordan
121 E2 Ghardaïa Algeria
119 F2 Ghârib, Gebel mt. Egypt
36 A4 Gharo Pakistan
39 B4 Ghār, Ras al pt Saudi Arabia
118 B1 Gharyān Libya
118 B2 Ghāt Libya
36 E4 Ghatampur India
121 D1 Ghazaouet Algeria
36 D3 Ghaziabad India
37 E4 Ghazipur India
36 A3 Ghazluna Pakistan
39 G2 Ghazni r. Afghanistan
39 G2 Ghaznī Afghanistan
39 F2 Ghazoor Afghanistan
119 H2 Ghazzālah Saudi Arabia
106 E3 Ghedi Italy
53 B Ghelinta Romania

Ghent *see* **Gent**
112 E1 **Gheorgheni** Romania
112 D1 **Gherla** Romania
108 A4 **Ghilarza** *Sardegna* Italy
39 F3 **Ghilzai reg.** Afghanistan
86 C2 **Ghislenghien** Belgium
108 B2 **Ghisonaccia** *Corse* France
108 B2 **Ghisoni** *Corse* France
39 F2 **Ghizao** Afghanistan
36 C1 **Ghizar** Pakistan
38 A2 **Ghod r.** India
36 B4 **Ghotāru** India
36 B4 **Ghotki** Pakistan
39 C3 **Ghōwrī** Iran
42 E3 **Ghudāf, Wādī al watercourse** Iraq
38 B2 **Ghugus** India
43 D2 **Ghunthur** Syria
39 E2 **Ghurian** Afghanistan
130 D6 **Ghwarriepoort pass** South Africa
25 D5 **Gia Đinh** Vietnam
114 A3 **Giannades** Greece
114 D2 **Giannitsa** Greece
108 D2 **Giannutri, Isola di i.** Italy
131 G4 **Giant's Castle mt.** South Africa
131 G4 **Giant's Castle Game Reserve res.** South Africa
67 E1 **Giant's Causeway** *Northern Ireland* U.K.
22 C4 **Gianyar** Indonesia
115 H7 **Gianysada i.** Greece
25 D5 **Gia Rai** Vietnam
111 E5 **Giardini-Naxos** *Sicilia* Italy
79 L6 **Giarmata** Romania
111 E5 **Giarre** *Sicilia* Italy
92 E3 **Giat** France
108 A4 **Giave** *Sardegna* Italy
106 B3 **Giaveno** Italy
82 C3 **Giavino, Monte mt.** Italy
108 A5 **Giba** *Sardegna* Italy
158 C2 **Gibara** Cuba
16 D3 **Gibb River** *Western Australia* Australia
145 □1 **Gibb's Hill h.** Bermuda
43 B5 **Gibeil** Egypt
110 B5 **Gibellina Nuova** *Sicilia* Italy
128 B4 **Gibeon** Namibia
126 C3 **Gībē Shet' r.** Ethiopia
92 A2 **Giboule r.** France
100 D3 **Gibraleón** Spain
48 E5 **Gibraltar territory** Europe
101 □ **Gibraltar, Bay of b.** Gibraltar/Spain
100 E5 **Gibraltar, Strait of str.** Morocco/Spain
148 C5 **Gibson City** *Illinois* U.S.A.
17 C5 **Gibson Desert desert** *Western Australia* Australia
77 M1 **Giby** Poland
30 A3 **Gichgeniyn Nuruu mountain range** Mongolia
126 C3 **Gidda** Ethiopia
38 B3 **Giddalur** India
43 B4 **Giddi, G. el h.** Egypt
126 C3 **Gīdolē** Ethiopia
74 E3 **Giebelstadt** Germany
72 F4 **Gieboldehausen** Germany
77 H4 **Gieczno** Poland
90 A1 **Gien** France
80 B2 **Giengen an der Brenz** Germany
91 E5 **Giens, G. de b.** France
74 D2 **Gießen div.** *Hessen* Germany
74 D2 **Gießen** Germany
68 E1 **Gieten** Netherlands
77 J2 **Gietrzwałd** Poland
89 G4 **Gièvres** France
119 F2 **Gifatin Is i.** Egypt
66 F5 **Gifford** *Scotland* U.K.
93 E4 **Giffou r.** France
90 E2 **Giffre r.** France
73 F3 **Gifhorn** Germany
136 F3 **Gift Lake** *Alberta* Canada
29 F6 **Gifu div.** Japan
29 F6 **Gifu** Japan
51 G6 **Gigant** Rus. Fed.
162 B3 **Gigante** Colombia
172 E1 **Gigantes, Co Los mt.** Argentina
151 B7 **Gigantes, Llanos de los plain** Mexico
66 C5 **Gigha i.** *Scotland* U.K.
64 C2 **Gigha, Sound of chan.** *Scotland* U.K.
108 C2 **Giglio Castello** Italy
108 C2 **Giglio, Isola del i.** Italy
91 B5 **Gignac** France
106 B3 **Gignod** Italy
98 E1 **Gijón** Spain
93 E5 **Gijou r.** France
155 F5 **Gila r.** *Arizona* U.S.A.
155 F5 **Gila Bend** *Arizona* U.S.A.
155 F5 **Gila Bend Mts mts** *Arizona* U.S.A.
155 E5 **Gila Mts mts** *Arizona* U.S.A.
39 B1 **Gīlān div.** Iran
42 F3 **Gilan Garb** Iran
112 D1 **Gilău** Romania
42 G1 **Gilazi** Azerbaijan
15 E3 **Gilbert r.** *Queensland* Australia
155 G5 **Gilbert** *Arizona* U.S.A.
146 C6 **Gilbert** *W. Virginia* U.S.A.
173 H2 **Gilbert** Argentina
4 J5 **Gilbert Islands is** Kiribati
15 E3 **Gilbert Ra. mountain range** *Queensland* Australia
15 E3 **Gilbert River** *Queensland* Australia
55 E3 **Gilbjerg Hoved pt** Denmark
166 C2 **Gilbués** Brazil
39 D2 **Gil Chashmeh** Iran
75 G4 **Gilching** Germany
152 E1 **Gildford** *Montana* U.S.A.
129 F2 **Gilé** Mozambique
43 C3 **Gilead reg.** Jordan
131 G1 **Gilead** South Africa
14 B3 **Giles Cr. r.** *Northern Terr.* Australia
17B6 **Giles, L. salt flat** *Western Australia* Australia
118 E3 **Gilf Kebir Plateau plat.** Egypt
64 B3 **Gilford** *Northern Ireland* U.K.
136 D4 **Gilford I. i.** *B.C.* Canada
13 G2 **Gilgandra** *New South Wales* Australia
127 C5 **Gilgil** Kenya
13 G2 **Gil Gil Cr. r.** *New South Wales* Australia
36 C1 **Gilgit r.** Pakistan
36 C2 **Gilgit** *Jammu and Kashmir*
13 F3 **Gilgunnia** *New South Wales* Australia
136 D4 **Gil I. i.** *B.C.* Canada
22 C4 **Gilimanuk** Indonesia
Gılındire *see* **Aydıncık**
129 F2 **Gili, Reserva do res.** Mozambique
137 L3 **Gillam** *Manitoba* Canada
55 E3 **Gilleleje** Denmark
74 B2 **Gillenfeld** Germany
17 D5 **Gillen, L. salt flat** *Western Australia* Australia
12 D3 **Gilles, L. salt flat** *S. Australia* Australia
9 B5 **Gillespies Pt pt** New Zealand
148 C3 **Gillett** *Wisconsin* U.S.A.
152 F2 **Gillette** *Wyoming* U.S.A.
15 E4 **Gilliat** *Queensland* Australia
63 G3 **Gillingham** *England* U.K.
62 D3 **Gillingham** *England* U.K.
65 G3 **Gilling West** *England* U.K.
67 C2 **Gill, Lough l.** Rep. of Ireland
179 D5 **Gillock I. i.** Antarctica
128 □2 **Gill Pt pt** *St Helena* Atlantic Ocean
148 D3 **Gills Rock** *Wisconsin* U.S.A.
90 E3 **Gilly-sur-Isère** France
148 D5 **Gilman** *Illinois* U.S.A.
148 B3 **Gilman** *Wisconsin* U.S.A.
138 E2 **Gilmour Island i.** *N.W.T.* Canada
126 B3 **Gīlo Wenz r.** Ethiopia
154 B3 **Gilroy** *California* U.S.A.
56 L6 **Gilsfjörður b.** Iceland
65 F3 **Gilsland** *England* U.K.
147 G3 **Gilsum** *New Hampshire* U.S.A.
6 □1 **Giluwe, Mt mt.** P.N.G.
62 C3 **Gilwern** *Wales* U.K.
68 C3 **Gilze** Netherlands
118 D5 **Gimbala, Jebel mt.** Sudan
126 C3 **Gīmbī** Ethiopia
137 K4 **Gimli** *Manitoba* Canada
59 H1 **Gimo** Sweden
93 C5 **Gimonde, Barrage de la dam** France
93 C5 **Gimone r.** France
93 C5 **Gimont** France
90 B2 **Gimouille** France
91 D5 **Ginasservis** France
15 G4 **Gindie** *Queensland* Australia
43 B4 **Gineifa** Egypt
91 A5 **Ginestas** France
38 C5 **Gin Ganga r.** Sri Lanka
38 B3 **Gingee** India
69 D4 **Gingelom** Belgium
15 G5 **Gin Gin** *Queensland* Australia
17 A6 **Gingin** *Western Australia* Australia
131 H4 **Gingindlovu** South Africa
73 J1 **Gingst** Germany
126 D3 **Gīnīr** Ethiopia
54 C4 **Ginkūnai** Lithuania
93 E6 **Ginoles** France
111 F2 **Ginosa** Italy
111 E4 **Ginostra** Italy
128 D5 **Ginsberg** South Africa
29 □2 **Ginowan** Japan
115 G7 **Giofyros r.** Greece
109 F3 **Gioia dei Marsi** Italy
111 F2 **Gioia del Colle** Italy
111 E4 **Gioia, Golfo di b.** Italy
111 E4 **Gioia Tauro** Italy
111 F4 **Gioiosa Ionica** Italy
110 D4 **Gioiosa Marea** *Sicilia* Italy
83 D2 **Giornico** Switzerland
114 F3 **Gioura i.** Greece
83 F2 **Gioveretto mt.** Italy
83 F2 **Gioveretto, Lago di l.** Italy
109 J3 **Giovinazzo** Italy
13 F4 **Gippsland reg.** *Victoria* Australia
36 B4 **Girab** India
79 L2 **Giraltovce** Slovakia
87 F4 **Girancourt** France
146 C3 **Girard** *Pennsylvania* U.S.A.
43 B5 **Girâ, W. watercourse** Egypt
36 B3 **Girdao** Pakistan
39 F4 **Girdar Dhor r.** Pakistan
39 E3 **Girdi** Iran
39 D4 **Gireh, Kūh-e mt.** Iran
42 D1 **Giresun** Turkey
36 B5 **Gir Forest forest** India
119 F2 **Girga** Egypt
124 C3 **Giri r.** Congo(Zaire)
37 F4 **Girīdīh** India
111 F4 **Girifalco** Italy
13 F2 **Girilambone** *New South Wales* Australia
36 C5 **Girna r.** India
90 E1 **Giromagny** France
162 B4 **Girón** Ecuador
102 F2 **Girona div.** *Catalunya* Spain
102 F3 **Girona** Spain
93 B4 **Gironde div.** *Aquitaine* France
92 B3 **Gironde est.** France
173 G3 **Girondo** Argentina
102 E2 **Gironella** Spain
93 D5 **Girou r.** France
66 D5 **Girvan** *Scotland* U.K.
50 E2 **Girvas** Rus. Fed.
31 F2 **Giryunino, Nizh.** Rus. Fed.
8 F3 **Gisborne div.** New Zealand
8 G3 **Gisborne** New Zealand
136 E4 **Giscome** *B.C.* Canada
127 A5 **Gisenyi** Rwanda
59 E3 **Gislaved** Sweden
89 G2 **Gisors** France
47 G5 **Gissar Range mountain range** Tajikistan/Uzbekistan
109 G2 **Gissi** Italy
59 F2 **Gisslarbo** Sweden
69 A3 **Gistel** Belgium
55 B3 **Gistrup** Denmark
82 D2 **Giswil** Switzerland
127 A5 **Gitarama** Rwanda
127 A5 **Gitega** Burundi
58 D1 **Gitvola h.** Norway
83 E2 **Giubiasco** Switzerland
109 G4 **Giugliano in Campania** Italy
109 F3 **Giuliano di Roma** Italy
109 F2 **Giulianova** Italy
112 E3 **Giurgiu** Romania
55 B4 **Give** Denmark
86 D2 **Givet** France
90 C3 **Givors** France
69 C4 **Givry** Belgium
90 C2 **Givry** France
86 D4 **Givry-en-Argonne** France
131 H1 **Giyani** South Africa
126 C3 **Giyon** Ethiopia
43 A4 **Gizai** Egypt
76 F3 **Gizałki** Poland
119 F2 **Giza Pyramids** Egypt
46 F4 **Gizhduvan** Uzbekistan
45 S3 **Gizhiga** Rus. Fed.
6 □1 **Gizo** Solomon Is.
77 K1 **Giżycko** Poland
111 F4 **Gizzeria** Italy
55 B3 **Gjern** Denmark
55 C3 **Gjerrild** Denmark
58 C2 **Gjerstad** Norway
112 B4 **Gjiri i Drinit b.** Albania
113 B4 **Gjiri i Karavastasë b.** Albania
114 B2 **Gjirokastër** Albania
135 J3 **Gjoa Haven** *N.W.T.* Canada
56 C3 **Gjøra** Norway
58 D1 **Gjøvik** Norway
114 D4 **Gkiona mts** Greece
115 D5 **Gkoritsa** Greece
139 J4 **Glace Bay** *Nova Scotia* Canada
136 B3 **Glacier B. b.** *Alaska* U.S.A.
136 B3 **Glacier Bay National Park and Preserve** *Alaska* U.S.A.
179 □ **Glacier Cook gl.** *Kerguelen* Indian Ocean
82 C3 **Glacier, Monte mt.** Italy
136 F4 **Glacier Nat. Park** *B.C.* Canada
152 D1 **Glacier Nat. Park** *Montana* U.S.A.
152 B1 **Glacier Peak volcano** *Washington* U.S.A.
72 B4 **Gladbeck** *Nordrhein-Westfalen* Germany
74 D2 **Gladenbach** Germany
56 D2 **Gladstad** Norway
148 D3 **Gladstone** *Michigan* U.S.A.
15 G4 **Gladstone** *Queensland* Australia
12 D3 **Gladstone** *S. Australia* Australia
13 G5 **Gladstone** *Tasmania* Australia
148 E4 **Gladwin** *Michigan* U.S.A.
90 E1 **Glainans** France
66 E4 **Glamis** *Scotland* U.K.
104 F3 **Glamoč** Bos.-Herz.
62 C3 **Glamorgan, Vale of div.** *Wales* U.K.
55 C4 **Glamsbjerg** Denmark
74 C3 **Glan r.** Austria/Germany
23 C5 **Glan** Philippines
67 B4 **Glanaruddery Mts h.** Rep. of Ireland
91 D4 **Glandage** France
91 D4 **Glandasse mt.** France
91 E3 **Glandon r.** France
72 D3 **Glandorf** Germany
92 D3 **Glane r.** France
72 C3 **Glane r.** Germany
68 E2 **Glanerbrug** Netherlands
65 G2 **Glanton** *England* U.K.
140 E5 **Glanworth** *Ontario* Canada
83 D2 **Glarner Alpen mountain range** Switzerland
83 D2 **Glärnisch mts** Switzerland
83 E2 **Glarus div.** Switzerland
83 E1 **Glarus** Switzerland
62 C2 **Glasbury** *Wales* U.K.
59 E2 **Glasfjorden l.** Sweden
144 C4 **Glasgow** *Kentucky* U.S.A.
152 F1 **Glasgow** *Montana* U.S.A.
66 D5 **Glasgow** *Scotland* U.K.
146 D6 **Glasgow** *Virginia* U.S.A.
159 □1 **Glasgow** Jamaica
66 D5 **Glasgow, div.** *Scotland* U.K.
75 J2 **Glashütte** Germany
137 H4 **Glaslyn** *Saskatchewan* Canada
64 A4 **Glassan** Rep. of Ireland
66 D3 **Glass, Loch l.** *Scotland* U.K.
154 C3 **Glass Mt mt.** *California* U.S.A.
62 D3 **Glastonbury** *England* U.K.
83 D1 **Glatt r.** Switzerland
75 H2 **Glauchau** Germany
52 E3 **Glazok** Rus. Fed.
44 G4 **Glazov** Rus. Fed.
52 C3 **Glazunovka** Rus. Fed.
73 G4 **Gleina** Germany
81 G3 **Gleinalpe mt.** Austria
81 G3 **Gleisdorf** Austria
147 H2 **Glen** *New Hampshire* U.S.A.
66 D3 **Glen Affric v.** *Scotland* U.K.
140 E3 **Glen Afton** *Ontario* Canada
8 E2 **Glen Afton** New Zealand
134 D3 **Glenallen** *Alaska* U.S.A.
131 G1 **Glen Alpine Dam dam** South Africa
67 C3 **Glenamaddy** Rep. of Ireland
88 A4 **Glénan, Îles is** France
148 E3 **Glen Arbor** *Michigan* U.S.A.
64 B2 **Glenariff** *Northern Ireland* U.K.
64 C3 **Glenarm** *Northern Ireland* U.K.
64 B3 **Glenavy** *Northern Ireland* U.K.
9 C6 **Glenavy** New Zealand
64 C2 **Glenbarr** *Scotland* U.K.
64 C1 **Glenbeg** *Scotland* U.K.
66 D3 **Glen Cannich v.** *Scotland* U.K.
153 E4 **Glen Canyon gorge** *Utah* U.S.A.
155 G3 **Glen Canyon National Recreation Area res.** *Utah* U.S.A.
66 E4 **Glen Clova v.** *Scotland* U.K.
66 C4 **Glen Coe v.** *Scotland* U.K.
140 E5 **Glencoe** *Ontario* Canada
131 H4 **Glencoe** South Africa
131 G2 **Glen Cowrie** South Africa
155 F5 **Glendale** *Arizona* U.S.A.
154 C4 **Glendale** *California* U.S.A.
155 E3 **Glendale** *Nevada* U.S.A.
140 C3 **Glendale** *Ontario* Canada
155 F3 **Glendale** *Utah* U.S.A.
146 D4 **Glendale Lake l.** *Pennsylvania* U.S.A.
64 C1 **Glendaruel v.** *Scotland* U.K.
152 F2 **Glendive** *Montana* U.S.A.
137 G4 **Glendon** *Alberta* Canada
152 F3 **Glendo Res. l.** *Wyoming* U.S.A.
64 B2 **Glendun r.** Rep. of Ireland
66 E4 **Gleneagles** *Scotland* U.K.
66 D3 **Glen Einig v.** *Scotland* U.K.
12 E4 **Glenelg r.** *Victoria* Australia
66 F4 **Glen Esk v.** *Scotland* U.K.
66 C4 **Glenfinnan** *Scotland* U.K.
67 D1 **Glengad Head headland** Rep. of Ireland
67 B5 **Glengarriff** Rep. of Ireland
66 D4 **Glen Garry v.** *Scotland* U.K.
66 C3 **Glen Garry v.** *Scotland* U.K.
17 B5 **Glengarry Ra. h.** *Western Australia* Australia
67 D2 **Glengavlen** Rep. of Ireland
14 D5 **Glengyle** *Queensland* Australia
13 G2 **Glen Innes** *New South Wales* Australia
64 D2 **Glenkens, The v.** *Scotland* U.K.
66 D6 **Glenluce** *Scotland* U.K.
66 D4 **Glen Lyon v.** *Scotland* U.K.
66 D3 **Glen More v.** *Scotland* U.K.
15 G5 **Glenmorgan** *Queensland* Australia
66 D3 **Glen Moriston v.** *Scotland* U.K.
66 C4 **Glen Nevis v.** *Scotland* U.K.
149 F3 **Glennie** *Michigan* U.S.A.
155 G6 **Glenn, Mt mt.** *Arizona* U.S.A.
146 E6 **Glenns** *Virginia* U.S.A.
136 C3 **Glenora** *B.C.* Canada
66 D4 **Glen Orchy v.** *Scotland* U.K.
15 E3 **Glenore** *Queensland* Australia
14 D4 **Glenormiston** *Queensland* Australia
141 H4 **Glen Robertson** *Ontario* Canada
66 E4 **Glenrothes** *Scotland* U.K.
147 G3 **Glens Falls** *New York* U.S.A.
64 B3 **Glenshane Pass pass** *Northern Ireland* U.K.
66 E4 **Glen Shee v.** *Scotland* U.K.
66 C3 **Glen Shiel v.** *Scotland* U.K.
66 D4 **Glen Spean v.** *Scotland* U.K.
67 C2 **Glenties** Rep. of Ireland
67 D1 **Glenveagh National Park** Rep. of Ireland
146 C5 **Glenville** *W. Virginia* U.S.A.
151 E5 **Glenwood** *Arkansas* U.S.A.
155 H5 **Glenwood** *New Mexico* U.S.A.
153 F4 **Glenwood Springs** *Colorado* U.S.A.
90 E1 **Glère** France
83 D2 **Gletsch** Switzerland
73 H1 **Glewitz** Germany
148 B2 **Glidden** *Wisconsin* U.S.A.
104 F3 **Glina** Croatia
72 F2 **Glinde** Germany
52 B3 **Glinishchevo** Rus. Fed.
53 B3 **Glinjeni** Moldova
52 A2 **Glinka** Rus. Fed.
77 J3 **Glinojeck** Poland
63 F2 **Glinton** *England* U.K.
59 H2 **Glissingö i.** Sweden
76 G5 **Gliwice** Poland
81 F4 **Globasnitz** Austria
155 G5 **Globe** *Arizona* U.S.A.
114 B1 **Globočica Ezero l.** Macedonia
112 F2 **Glodeanu-Sărat** Romania
53 B3 **Glodeni** Moldova
112 E1 **Glodeni** Romania
76 E2 **Głodowa** Poland
81 G3 **Gloggnitz** Austria
83 E2 **Glogn r.** Switzerland
112 C3 **Glogovac** Yugoslavia
76 E4 **Głogów** Poland
76 F5 **Głogówek** Poland
77 K5 **Głogów Małopolski** Poland
56 D2 **Glomfjord** Norway
58 D2 **Glomma l.** Norway
58 D1 **Glomma r.** Norway
56 E2 **Glommersträsk** Sweden
75 G4 **Glonn r.** Germany
80 C3 **Glonn** Germany
107 E2 **Glorenza** Italy
168 A5 **Glória de Dourados** Brazil
89 F3 **Glos-la-Ferrière** France
114 E3 **Glossa** Greece
65 G4 **Glossop** *England* U.K.
52 H3 **Glotovka** Rus. Fed.
62 D3 **Gloucester** *England* U.K.
147 H3 **Gloucester** *Massachusetts* U.S.A.
13 G2 **Gloucester** *New South Wales* Australia
146 E6 **Gloucester** *Virginia* U.S.A.
6 □1 **Gloucester** P.N.G.
62 D3 **Gloucestershire div.** *England* U.K.
62 D3 **Gloucester, Vale of v.** *England* U.K.
147 F3 **Gloversville** *New York* U.S.A.
76 F1 **Główczyce** Poland
73 J1 **Glowe** Germany
73 H3 **Glöwen** Germany
77 H4 **Głowno** Poland
76 F5 **Głubczyce** Poland
51 G5 **Glubokiy** Rus. Fed.
51 G6 **Glubokiy** Rus. Fed.
47 K2 **Glubokoye** Kazakhstan
54 F3 **Glubokoye** Rus. Fed.
54 F1 **Glubokoye, Oz. l.** Rus. Fed.
76 F5 **Głuchołazy** Poland
77 J4 **Głuchów** Poland
72 E1 **Glücksburg** Germany
72 E2 **Glückstadt** Germany
52 F2 **Glukhovo** Rus. Fed.
55 D4 **Glumsø** Denmark
65 G4 **Glusburn** *England* U.K.
53 F1 **Glushkovo** Rus. Fed.
76 E5 **Głuszyca** Poland
47 G2 **Glyadyanskoye** Rus. Fed.
62 B1 **Glyder Fawr mt.** *Wales* U.K.
114 D4 **Glyfa** Greece
115 E5 **Glyfada** Greece
114 B3 **Glyki** Greece
55 A3 **Glyngøre** Denmark
64 C3 **Glynn** *Northern Ireland* U.K.
62 C3 **Glyn-Neath** *Wales* U.K.
51 H5 **Gmelinka** Rus. Fed.
81 F2 **Gmünd div.** Austria
81 E4 **Gmünd** *Kärnten* Austria
81 F2 **Gmünd** *Niederösterreich* Austria
75 G5 **Gmund am Tegernsee** Germany
81 E3 **Gmunden div.** Austria
81 E3 **Gmunden** Austria
57 E3 **Gnarp** Sweden
72 E2 **Gnarrenburg** Germany
81 G4 **Gnas** Austria
81 E4 **Gnesau** Austria
59 G2 **Gnesta** Sweden
55 D3 **Gniben pt** Denmark
76 G2 **Gniew** Poland
76 G3 **Gniewkowo** Poland
76 F3 **Gniezno** Poland
59 H3 **Gnisvärd** Sweden
112 C3 **Gnjilane** Yugoslavia
107 G4 **Gnocchetta** Italy
73 H2 **Gnoien** Germany
62 D2 **Gnosall** *England* U.K.
38 A3 **Goa div.** India
38 A3 **Goa** India
130 A3 **Goageb** Namibia
13 G4 **Goalen Head headland** *New South Wales* Australia
37 G4 **Goalpara** India
22 D4 **Goang** Indonesia
122 D5 **Goaso** Ghana
66 C5 **Goat Fell h.** *Scotland* U.K.
126 D3 **Goba** Ethiopia
128 B3 **Gobabis** Namibia
130 B3 **Gobas** Namibia
172 C4 **Gobernador Ayala** Argentina
173 G1 **Gobernador Crespo** Argentina
172 D5 **Gobernador Duval** Argentina
171 B6 **Gobernador Gregores** Argentina
173 G1 **Gobernador Racedo** Argentina
173 G3 **Gobernador Ugarte** Argentina
170 E2 **Gobernador Virasoro** Argentina
30 B3 **Gobi desert** Mongolia
52 A3 **Gobiki** Rus. Fed.
28 E7 **Gobō** Japan
62 C2 **Gobowen** *England* U.K.
72 B4 **Goch** Germany
128 B3 **Gochas** Namibia
25 D5 **Go Công** Vietnam
78 F5 **Göcsej h.** Hungary
63 F3 **Godalming** *England* U.K.
38 C2 **Godavari r.** India
38 C2 **Godavari, Mouths of the river mouth** India
139 G4 **Godbout** *Québec* Canada
37 F4 **Godda** India
154 C3 **Goddard, Mt mt.** *California* U.S.A.
87 H1 **Goddelsheim** Germany
163 F3 **Goddo** Surinam
126 D3 **Godé** Ethiopia
100 B2 **Godeal h.** Portugal
112 D3 **Godech** Bulgaria
43 A1 **Gödene** Turkey
126 D4 **Godere** Ethiopia
140 E5 **Goderich** *Ontario* Canada
89 F2 **Goderville** France
36 C5 **Godhra** India
106 D4 **Godiasco** Italy
126 E3 **Godinlabe** Somalia
77 H1 **Godkowo** Poland
63 F2 **Godmanchester** *England* U.K.
100 C2 **Godolín r.** Portugal/Spain
79 J4 **Gödöllő** Hungary
81 F5 **Godovič** Slovenia
173 G2 **Godoy** Argentina
172 C2 **Godoy Cruz** Argentina
137 L3 **Gods r.** *Manitoba* Canada
137 L4 **Gods Lake l.** *Manitoba* Canada
137 M2 **Gods Mercy, Bay of b.** *N.W.T.* Canada
Godthåb *see* **Nuuk**
36 C4 **Godwar reg.** India
Godwin-Austen, Mt mt. *see* **K2, Mt**
52 H3 **Godyaykino** Rus. Fed.
131 F5 **Goedemoed** South Africa
141 G2 **Goéland, Lac au l.** *Québec* Canada
139 H2 **Goélands, Lac aux l.** *Québec* Canada
69 B3 **Goes** Netherlands
149 E2 **Goetzville** *Michigan* U.S.A.
155 E4 **Goffs** *California* U.S.A.
51 G6 **Gofitskoye** Rus. Fed.
81 G2 **Göfritz an der Wild** Austria
140 E3 **Gogama** *Ontario* Canada
28 D6 **Gō-gawa r.** Japan
148 C2 **Gogebic, Lake l.** *Michigan* U.S.A.
148 C2 **Gogebic Range h.** *Michigan* U.S.A.
16 D3 **Gogo** *Western Australia* Australia
123 E4 **Gogounou** Benin
Gogra r. *see* **Ghaghara**
124 E2 **Gogrial** Sudan
36 D4 **Gohad** India
166 F2 **Goiana** Brazil
168 D3 **Goiandira** Brazil
168 D1 **Goianésia** Brazil
168 D2 **Goiânia** Brazil
168 C2 **Goiás div.** Brazil
168 C1 **Goiás** Brazil
168 D3 **Goiatuba** Brazil
23 □1 **Goikul** Palau
32 B2 **Goinxab** China
168 B5 **Goio r.** Brazil
168 B6 **Goio-Erê** Brazil
69 D3 **Goirle** Netherlands
98 B4 **Góis** Portugal
107 E3 **Goito** Italy
126 C3 **Gojeb Wenz r.** Ethiopia
29 H4 **Gojōme** Japan
36 C3 **Gojra** Pakistan
77 H4 **Gojść** Poland
38 A2 **Gokak** India
28 C7 **Gokase-gawa r.** Japan
43 B1 **Gök Çay r.** Turkey
42 A1 **Gökçeada i.** Turkey
113 G5 **Gökçeören** Turkey
43 B1 **Gökdere r.** Turkey
72 E1 **Gokels** Germany
37 G3 **Gokhar La** China
42 C1 **Gökirmak r.** Turkey
39 E4 **Gokprosh Hills mountain range** Pakistan
43 B1 **Göksu r.** Turkey
42 D2 **Göksun** Turkey
129 D2 **Gokwe** Zimbabwe
58 C1 **Gol** Norway
78 G5 **Gola** Croatia
36 E3 **Gola** India
77 K4 **Gołąb** Poland
37 H4 **Golaghat** India
76 F3 **Gołańcz** Poland
39 D4 **Golāshkerd** Iran
77 L4 **Gołaszyn** Poland
39 G2 **Golbahār** Afghanistan
42 D2 **Gölbaşi** Turkey
87 F4 **Golbey** France
44 K2 **Gol'chikha** Rus. Fed.
113 G5 **Gölcük r.** Turkey
113 G5 **Gölcük** *Balıkesir* Turkey
42 B1 **Gölcük** *Kocaeli* Turkey
76 C2 **Golczewo** Poland
83 E1 **Goldach** Switzerland
77 L1 **Gołdap** Poland
73 H2 **Goldberg** Germany
122 D6 **Gold Coast coastal area** Ghana
15 H6 **Gold Coast** *Queensland* Australia
136 F4 **Golden** *B.C.* Canada
8 D4 **Golden Bay b.** New Zealand
73 F4 **Goldene Aue reg.** Germany
154 A3 **Golden Gate National Recreation Area nat. park** *California* U.S.A.
136 D5 **Golden Hinde mt.** *B.C.* Canada
159 □6 **Golden Rock airport** *St Kitts-Nevis* Caribbean
72 D3 **Goldenstedt** Germany
67 C4 **Golden Vale lowland** Rep. of Ireland
62 D2 **Golden Valley v.** *England* U.K.
154 D3 **Goldfield** *Nevada* U.S.A.
154 D3 **Gold Point** *Nevada* U.S.A.
145 E5 **Goldsboro** *N. Carolina* U.S.A.
16 B4 **Goldsworthy** *Western Australia* Australia
151 D6 **Goldthwaite** *Texas* U.S.A.
42 E1 **Göle** Turkey
100 B1 **Golegã** Portugal
76 C2 **Goleniów** Poland
39 E2 **Golestān** Afghanistan
39 C3 **Golestānak** Iran
154 C4 **Goleta** *California* U.S.A.
30 C1 **Golets-Davydov, G. mt.** Rus. Fed.
93 C4 **Golfech** France
108 E3 **Golfe d'Ajaccio b.** France
179 □ **Golfe de Baleiniers b.** *Kerguelen* Indian Ocean
108 A2 **Golfe de Galéria b.** *Corse* France
179 □ **Golfe de Morbihan b.** *Kerguelen* Indian Ocean
108 A2 **Golfe de Porto b.** *Corse* France
108 B3 **Golfe de Porto-Vecchio b.** *Corse* France
108 A2 **Golfe de Sagone b.** *Corse* France
108 B3 **Golfe de Santa-Manza b.** *Corse* France
108 A3 **Golfe de Valinco b.** *Corse* France
159 E5 **Golfete de Coro b.** Venezuela
156 K7 **Golfito** Costa Rica
108 B4 **Golfo Aranci** *Sardegna* Italy
113 G6 **Gölgeli Dağlari mountain range** Turkey
107 J4 **Goli i.** Croatia
151 D6 **Goliad** *Texas* U.S.A.
112 B3 **Golija mountain range** Yugoslavia
112 C3 **Golija Planina mts** Yugoslavia
76 G3 **Golina** Poland
31 G3 **Golin Baixing** China
52 G3 **Golitsyno** Rus. Fed.
52 C2 **Golitsyno** Rus. Fed.
42 D1 **Gölköy** Turkey
81 H2 **Göllersdorf** Austria
73 J2 **Gollin** Germany
73 J2 **Gollmitz** Germany
113 F5 **Gölmarmara** Turkey
73 J3 **Golmberg h.** Germany
37 H1 **Golmud r.** China
37 H1 **Golmud** China
81 F4 **Golnik** Slovenia
23 B3 **Golo i.** Philippines
108 B2 **Golo r.** *Corse* France
52 E2 **Golobino** Rus. Fed.
101 E1 **Golondrinos, Sierra de los mountain range** Spain
52 E2 **Golovanovo** Rus. Fed.
52 G3 **Golovinshchino** Rus. Fed.
28 K2 **Golovnino** Rus. Fed.
39 B2 **Golpāyegān** Iran
98 E3 **Golpejas** Spain
81 H3 **Gols** Austria
81 G2 **Gölsen r.** Austria
66 E3 **Golspie** *Scotland* U.K.
73 J4 **Golßen** Germany
52 G3 **Gol'tsovka** Rus. Fed.
77 H2 **Golub-Dobrzyń** Poland
47 H2 **Golubovka** Kazakhstan
76 F4 **Gołuchów** Poland
52 C3 **Golun'** Rus. Fed.
125 B5 **Golungo Alto** Angola
39 E2 **Gol Vardeh** Iran
112 E3 **Golyama Zhelyazna** Bulgaria
112 E4 **Golyam Persenk mt.** Bulgaria
113 G4 **Gölyazı** Turkey
77 J3 **Gołymin-Ośrodec** Poland
47 G1 **Golyshmanovo** Rus. Fed.
73 H3 **Golzow** Germany
124 E4 **Goma** Congo(Zaire)
37 G3 **Gomang Co l.** China
99 H3 **Gómara** Spain
114 E2 **Gomati** Greece
25 □ **Gombak, Bukit h.** Singapore
127 B5 **Gombe r.** Tanzania
123 G4 **Gombe** Nigeria
123 G4 **Gombi** Nigeria
127 □3 **Gombrani I. i.** *Rodrigues I.* Mauritius
113 F5 **Gömeç** Turkey
98 E3 **Gomecello** Spain
97 □ **Gomera, La i.** *Canary Is* Spain
64 B1 **Gometra i.** *Scotland* U.K.
156 D2 **Gomez Farias** Mexico
156 E3 **Gómez Palacio** Mexico
157 F3 **Gómez, Presa M. R. resr** Mexico
39 C1 **Gomīshān** Iran
73 G3 **Gommern** Germany
37 F2 **Gomo** China
37 F2 **Gomo Co salt lake** China
82 D2 **Goms reg.** Switzerland
77 H4 **Gomunice** Poland
39 D1 **Gonābād** Iran
Gonabad *see* **Jūymand**
159 D3 **Gonaïves** Haiti
129 E3 **Gonarezhou National Park nat. park** Zimbabwe
158 D3 **Gonâve, Île de la i.** Haiti
39 C1 **Gonbad-e Kavus** Iran
91 D3 **Goncelin** France
37 E4 **Gonda** India
36 B5 **Gondal** India
126 E3 **Gonda Libah well** Ethiopia
126 C2 **Gonder** Ethiopia
87 G2 **Gondershausen** Germany
36 E5 **Gondia** India
98 B3 **Gondomar** Portugal
98 B2 **Gondomar** Spain
87 E4 **Gondrecourt-le-Château** France
87 E4 **Gondreville** France
93 C5 **Gondrin** France
42 A1 **Gönen** Turkey
89 F2 **Gonfreville-l'Orcher** France
33 F2 **Gong'an** China
37 H3 **Gongbo'gyamda** China
33 E3 **Gongcheng** China
37 G3 **Gonggar** China
32 C2 **Gongga Shan mt.** China
30 B5 **Gonghe** China
30 E4 **Gonghui** China
47 K4 **Gongliu** China
166 E3 **Gongogi r.** Brazil
123 G4 **Gongola r.** Nigeria
13 F2 **Gongolgon** *New South Wales* Australia
124 A4 **Gongoué** Gabon
32 B3 **Gongshan** China
32 C3 **Gongwang Shan mountain range** China
33 F1 **Gong Xian** China
32 D2 **Gong Xian** China
77 L2 **Goniądz** Poland
123 G4 **Goniri** Nigeria
32 B2 **Gonjo** China
108 A5 **Gonnesa** *Sardegna* Italy
108 A5 **Gonnesa, Golfo di b.** *Sardegna* Italy
108 A5 **Gonnosfanadiga** *Sardegna* Italy
108 A5 **Gonnosnò** *Sardegna* Italy
28 H3 **Gonohe** Japan
28 B7 **Gōnoura** Japan
82 B1 **Gonsans** France
172 D6 **Gonumillo** Argentina
154 B3 **Gonzales** *California* U.S.A.
151 D6 **Gonzales** *Texas* U.S.A.
157 F4 **Gonzáles** Mexico
172 F3 **Gonzáles Moreno** Argentina
146 E6 **Goochland** *Virginia* U.S.A.
179 C6 **Goodenough, C. c.** Antarctica
6 □1 **Goodenough I. i.** P.N.G.
141 F4 **Gooderham** *Ontario* Canada
148 E3 **Good Harbor Bay b.** *Michigan* U.S.A.
130 B7 **Good Hope, Cape of c.** South Africa
152 D3 **Gooding** *Idaho* U.S.A.
150 C4 **Goodland** *Kansas* U.S.A.
127 □4 **Goodlands** Mauritius
13 F2 **Goodooga** *New South Wales* Australia
62 B2 **Goodwick** *Wales* U.K.
65 H4 **Goole** *England* U.K.
13 F3 **Goolgowi** *New South Wales* Australia
126 E3 **Goolis Mountains mts** Somalia
12 D3 **Goolwa** *S. Australia* Australia
17 B6 **Goomalling** *Western Australia* Australia
13 F2 **Goombalie** *New South Wales* Australia
15 H5 **Goomeri** *Queensland* Australia
15 G6 **Goondiwindi** *Queensland* Australia
17 C6 **Goongarrie, L. salt flat** *Western Australia* Australia
62 A4 **Goonhavern** *England* U.K.
68 E2 **Goor** Netherlands
139 H3 **Goose r.** *Newfoundland* Canada
171 E7 **Goose Green** Falkland Is.
152 B3 **Goose L. l.** *California/Oregon* U.S.A.
38 B3 **Gooty** India
37 F4 **Gopālganj** India
74 E4 **Göppingen** Germany
101 G3 **Gor r.** Spain
76 E4 **Góra** *Leszno* Poland
77 J3 **Góra** *Płock* Poland
51 H7 **Gora Bazardyuzi mt.** Rus. Fed.
Goradiz *see* **Horadiz**
77 K4 **Góra Kalwaria** Poland
37 E4 **Gorakhpur** India
27 Q1 **Gora Lopatina mt.** Rus. Fed.
27 P2 **Gora Medvezh'ya mt.** China/Rus. Fed.
27 P2 **Gora Tardoki-Yani mt.** Rus. Fed.
73 L2 **Gorawino** Poland
104 G4 **Goražde** Bos.-Herz.
52 C3 **Gorbachevo** Rus. Fed.
52 F1 **Gorbatov** Rus. Fed.
172 A5 **Gorbea** Chile
173 H3 **Gorchs** Argentina
77 J6 **Gorczański Park Narodowy nat. park** Poland
145 E7 **Gorda Cay i.** The Bahamas
156 K6 **Gorda, Pta pt** Nicaragua
156 K7 **Gorda, Pta** Nicaragua
101 F3 **Gorda, Sierra mountain range** Spain
91 D5 **Gordes** France
42 B2 **Gördes** Turkey
124 D2 **Gordil** Central African Rep.
13 F5 **Gordon r.** *Tasmania* Australia
66 F5 **Gordon** *Scotland* U.K.
14 B1 **Gordon B. b.** *Northern Terr.* Australia
16 E3 **Gordon Downs** *Western Australia* Australia
13 F5 **Gordon, L. l.** *Tasmania* Australia
136 G2 **Gordon Lake l.** *N.W.T.* Canada
146 D5 **Gordon Lake l.** *Pennsylvania* U.S.A.
130 B7 **Gordon's Bay** South Africa
146 D5 **Gordonsville** *Virginia* U.S.A.
15 F3 **Gordonvale** *Queensland* Australia
124 C2 **Goré** Chad
126 C3 **Gorē** Ethiopia
9 B7 **Gore** New Zealand
140 D4 **Gore Bay** *Ontario* Canada
66 E5 **Gorebridge** *Scotland* U.K.
52 C2 **Gorelki** Rus. Fed.
52 E3 **Goreloye** Rus. Fed.
81 G5 **Gorenja Straža** Slovenia

88 B4 Hennebont France
74 C2 Hennef (Sieg) Germany
131 F3 Hennenman South Africa
55 A4 Henne Stationsby Denmark
87 F4 Hennezel France
73 J3 Hennigsdorf Berlin Germany
147 H3 Henniker New Hampshire U.S.A.
58 C2 Hennseid Norway
92 E1 Henrichemont France
151 D5 Henrietta Texas U.S.A.
138 D2 Henrietta Maria, Cape c. Ontario Canada
155 G3 Henrieville Utah U.S.A.
148 C5 Henry Illinois U.S.A.
179 B3 Henry Ice Rise ice feature Antarctica
135 M3 Henry Kater, C. headland N.W.T. Canada
25 A4 Henry Lawrence I. i. Andaman and Nicobar Is India
155 G2 Henry Mts mts Utah U.S.A.
140 E5 Hensall Ontario Canada
72 E2 Henstedt-Ulzburg Germany
62 D4 Henstridge England U.K.
128 A3 Hentiesbaai Namibia
30 D3 Hentiy div. Mongolia
29 □2 Hentona Japan
13 F3 Henty New South Wales Australia
24 A3 Henzada Myanmar
29 □2 Henza-jima i. Japan
137 H4 Hepburn Saskatchewan Canada
33 F3 Heping China
74 D3 Heppenheim (Bergstraße) Germany
33 E4 Hepu China
30 D5 Hequ China
56 N6 Héraðsflói b. Iceland
42 D3 Heraklia Syria
15 G3 Herald Cays atolls Coral Sea Islands Terr. Pacific Ocean
8 □4 Herald Islets is Kermadec Is New Zealand
8 E3 Herangi h. New Zealand
39 E2 Herāt Afghanistan
91 B5 Hérault div. Languedoc-Roussillon France
91 B5 Hérault r. France
119 G4 Herbagat Sudan
91 D3 Herbasse r. France
89 G4 Herbault France
15 F3 Herbert r. Queensland Australia
137 H4 Herbert Saskatchewan Canada
9 C6 Herbert New Zealand
25 A5 Herbertabad Andaman and Nicobar Is India
14 D4 Herbert Downs Queensland Australia
74 E4 Herbertingen Germany
15 F3 Herberton Queensland Australia
130 C7 Herbertsdale South Africa
69 D5 Herbeumont Belgium
88 C4 Herbignac France
74 C4 Herbolzheim Germany
74 D2 Herborn Germany
74 F4 Herbrechtingen Germany
74 E2 Herbstein Germany
112 B3 Herceg-Novi Yugoslavia
179 B4 Hercules Dome ice feature Antarctica
72 C4 Herdecke Germany
87 G2 Herdorf Germany
156 J7 Heredia Costa Rica
62 D2 Hereford England U.K.
151 C5 Hereford Texas U.S.A.
173 F3 Hereford Argentina
62 D2 Hereford and Worcester div. England U.K.
131 H2 Herefords Swaziland
58 C2 Herefoss Norway
7 □10 Héréhérétué i. French Polynesia Pacific Ocean
8 D1 Herekino New Zealand
101 G1 Herencia Spain
69 C4 Herent Belgium
69 C3 Herentals Belgium
91 B5 Hérépian France
72 D3 Herford Germany
100 E1 Herguijuela Spain
88 D4 Héric France
90 E1 Héricourt France
90 E1 Hérimoncourt France
74 F2 Heringen (Werra) Germany
73 G1 Heringsdorf Germany
150 D4 Herington Kansas U.S.A.
9 B6 Heriot New Zealand
83 E1 Herisau Switzerland
92 E1 Hérisson France
179 B3 Heritage Ra. mountain range Antarctica
69 D4 Herk r. Belgium
69 D4 Herk-de-Stad Belgium
147 F3 Herkimer New York U.S.A.
31 E2 Herlen r. China
30 D3 Herlen Mongolia
Herlen Gol r. see Kerulen
72 F4 Herleshausen Germany
63 □2 Herm i. Channel Is.
80 E4 Hermagor div. Austria
81 E4 Hermagor Austria
53 B2 Hermakivka Ukraine
157 E3 Hermanas Mexico
66 □2 Herma Ness headland Scotland U.K.
14 C4 Hermannsburg Northern Terr. Australia
72 F3 Hermannsburg Germany
77 L6 Hermanowice Poland
58 B1 Hermansverk Norway
130 B7 Hermanus South Africa
78 E2 Heřmanův Městec Czech Rep.
43 D2 Hermel Lebanon
92 E3 Herment France
74 C3 Hermersberg Germany
131 G5 Hermes, Cape c. South Africa
74 B3 Hermeskeil Germany
13 F2 Hermidale New South Wales Australia
97 □ Hermigua Canary Is Spain
152 C2 Hermiston Oregon U.S.A.
171 C7 Hermite, Is is Chile
Hermon, Mt mt. see Shaykh, Jabal esh
162 B3 Hermosas, Parque Nacional las nat. park Colombia
156 C2 Hermosillo Mexico
75 G2 Hermsdorf Germany
79 L3 Hernád r. Hungary
79 K3 Hernádkak Hungary
165 F5 Hernandarias Paraguay
173 G2 Hernández Argentina
172 F2 Hernando Argentina
102 B1 Hernani Spain
69 C4 Herne Belgium
72 C4 Herne Germany
63 H3 Herne Bay England U.K.
55 A3 Herning Denmark
69 D4 Héron Belgium
140 B2 Heron Bay Ontario Canada
89 E2 Hérouville-St-Clair France
78 G4 Herpenyő r. Hungary
170 E2 Herradura Argentina
157 E4 Herradura Mexico
99 G2 Herramélluri Spain
93 B5 Herré France
74 D4 Herrenberg Germany
102 B3 Herrera mt. Spain
101 F3 Herrera Spain
101 E1 Herrera del Duque Spain
102 B3 Herrera de los Navarros Spain
99 F2 Herrera de Pisuerga Spain
156 D3 Herreras Mexico
173 G4 Herrera Vegas Argentina
157 J5 Herrero, Pta pt Mexico
100 D1 Herreruela Spain
13 F5 Herrick Tasmania Australia
75 F3 Herrieden Germany
87 G4 Herrlisheim France
59 E2 Herrljunda Sweden
73 K4 Herrnhut Germany
75 G5 Herrsching am Ammersee Germany
59 H3 Herrvik Sweden
92 E1 Herry France
93 D5 Hers r. France
75 G3 Hersbruck Germany
87 G2 Herschbach Germany
131 F5 Herschel South Africa
69 C3 Herselt Belgium
146 E4 Hershey Pennsylvania U.S.A.
69 D4 Herstal Belgium
63 G4 Herstmonceux England U.K.
72 C4 Herten Germany
63 F3 Hertford England U.K.
63 F3 Hertfordshire div. England U.K.
69 E4 Hertogenwald forest Belgium
131 E4 Hertzogville South Africa
98 E4 Hervás Spain
69 D4 Herve Belgium
15 H5 Hervey B. b. Queensland Australia
15 H5 Hervey Bay Queensland Australia
177 J7 Hervey Islands is Cook Is Pacific Ocean
141 J3 Hervey-Jonction Québec Canada
15 F3 Hervey Ra. mountain range Queensland Australia
74 D3 Herxheim bei Landau (Pfalz) Germany
73 H3 Herzberg Brandenburg Germany
73 J4 Herzberg Brandenburg Germany
72 F4 Herzberg am Harz Germany
72 D4 Herzebrock-Clarholz Germany
69 B4 Herzele Belgium
72 C3 Herzlake Germany
43 C3 Herzliyya Israel
75 F3 Herzogenaurach Germany
82 C1 Herzogenbuchsee Switzerland
81 G2 Herzogenburg Austria
73 H2 Herzsprung Germany
69 C4 Hesbaye reg. Belgium
86 B2 Hesdin France
72 C2 Hesel Germany
24 E2 Heshan China
33 F2 Heshengqiao China
30 D6 Heshui China
30 E5 Heshun China
69 E5 Hespérange Luxembourg
154 D4 Hesperia California U.S.A.
136 C2 Hess r. Yukon Terr. Canada
75 F3 Heßdorf Germany
80 B1 Hesselberg h. Germany
55 D3 Hesselø i. Denmark
74 E2 Hessen div. Germany
72 E4 Hessisch Lichtenau Germany
72 E3 Hessisch Oldendorf Germany
130 B4 Hester-Malan Nature Reserve res. South Africa
62 C1 Heswall England U.K.
24 C2 Het r. Laos
154 B3 Hetch Hetchy Aqueduct canal California U.S.A.
81 H4 Hetés h. Hungary
33 E4 Hetou China
80 C2 Hettens-hausen Germany
74 E4 Hettingen Germany
150 C2 Hettinger N. Dakota U.S.A.
65 F3 Hetton England U.K.
73 G4 Hettstedt Germany
74 B3 Hetzerath Germany
68 F3 Heubach r. Germany
86 B2 Heuchin France
130 D3 Heuningvlei salt pan South Africa
74 F2 Heustreu Germany
89 F2 Hève, Cap de la pt France
79 K4 Heves div. Hungary
79 K4 Heves Hungary
81 H2 Hevlín Czech Rep.
80 B3 Hexenkopf mt. Austria
65 F3 Hexham England U.K.
33 E3 He Xian China
33 G2 He Xian China
30 B5 Hexibao China
32 F4 Hexigten Qi China
130 B6 Hex River Pass South Africa
33 E1 Heyang China
39 C3 Ḩeydarābād Iran
39 G2 Ḩeydarābād Iran
130 E5 Heydon South Africa
126 E3 Heygali well Ethiopia
90 D3 Heyrieux France
65 F3 Heysham England U.K.
131 H3 Heyshope Dam dam South Africa
65 F4 Heywood England U.K.
12 E4 Heywood Victoria Australia
148 C5 Heyworth Illinois U.S.A.
33 F1 Heze China
32 D3 Hezhang China
32 C1 Hezheng China
32 C1 Hezuozhen China
131 H3 Hhohho reg. Swaziland
157 H5 Hialeah Florida U.S.A.
150 E4 Hiawatha Kansas U.S.A.
119 H4 Hibata reg. Saudi Arabia
148 A2 Hibbing Minnesota U.S.A.
13 F5 Hibbs, Pt headland Tasmania Australia
16 C2 Hibernia Reef reef Australia
28 C6 Hibiki-nada b. Japan
63 H2 Hickling Broad l. England U.K.
145 D5 Hickory N. Carolina U.S.A.
8 G2 Hicks Bay New Zealand
137 K2 Hicks L. l. N.W.T. Canada
146 A4 Hicksville Ohio U.S.A.
151 D5 Hico Texas U.S.A.
28 J2 Hidaka Japan
28 J2 Hidaka-sanmyaku mountain range Japan
157 F4 Hidalgo div. Mexico
157 F3 Hidalgo Coahuila Mexico
156 D3 Hidalgo del Parral Mexico
156 C3 Hidalgo, Psa M. resr Mexico
79 L3 Hidasnémeti Hungary
73 J1 Hiddensee i. Germany
15 F3 Hidden Valley Queensland Australia
168 D2 Hidrolândia Brazil
168 D1 Hidrolina Brazil
81 F3 Hieflau Austria
99 H3 Hiendelaencina Spain
6 □2 Hienghène New Caledonia Pacific Ocean
89 E4 Hière r. France
92 B3 Hiersac France
28 D6 Higashi-Hiroshima Japan
29 □1 Higashi-iwa is Japan
29 G6 Higashi-izu Japan
29 H4 Higashine Japan
29 □2 Higashi-Onna Japan
29 E6 Higashi-ōsaka Japan
28 B7 Higashi-suidō chan. Japan
147 F3 Higgins Bay New York U.S.A.
148 E3 Higgins Lake l. Michigan U.S.A.
130 D4 Higg's Hope South Africa
63 F2 Higham Ferrers England U.K.
62 B4 Highampton England U.K.
High Atlas mountain range see Haut Atlas
62 D3 Highbridge England U.K.
63 E3 Highclere England U.K.
152 B3 High Desert desert Oregon U.S.A.
148 C3 High Falls Reservoir resr Wisconsin U.S.A.
65 F3 High Hesket England U.K.
148 E3 High I. i. Michigan U.S.A.
8 □3 High I. i. Snares Is New Zealand
27 □ High Island Res. resr Hong Kong China
66 C3 Highland div. Scotland U.K.
148 D4 Highland Park Illinois U.S.A.
154 C2 Highland Peak summit California U.S.A.
155 E3 Highland Peak summit Nevada U.S.A.
136 F3 High Level Alberta Canada
65 G4 High Peak h. England U.K.
128 □2 High Pk h. St Helena Atlantic Ocean
145 E5 High Point N. Carolina U.S.A.
136 F3 High Prairie Alberta Canada
136 G4 High River Alberta Canada
158 C1 High Rock The Bahamas
137 J3 Highrock Lake l. Manitoba Canada
13 F5 High Rocky Pt headland Tasmania Australia
65 F3 High Seat h. England U.K.
147 F4 Hightstown New Jersey U.S.A.
63 E3 Highworth England U.K.
63 F3 High Wycombe England U.K.
126 D3 Higlale well Ethiopia
126 E3 Higlokadhacday well Somalia
100 E2 Higuera de la Serena Spain
100 D3 Higuera de la Sierra Spain
100 D2 Higuera de Vargas Spain
156 C3 Higuera de Zaragoza Mexico
100 D2 Higuera La Real Spain
145 □3 Higuero, Pta pt Puerto Rico
163 D1 Higuerote Venezuela
103 B6 Higueruela Spain
43 A4 Hihya Egypt
126 E4 Hiiraan div. Somalia
54 C2 Hiiumaa i. Estonia
102 C3 Híjar Spain
119 G2 Ḩijāz reg. Saudi Arabia
99 G1 Híjuela r. Spain
28 C7 Hikari Japan
155 E3 Hiko Nevada U.S.A.
29 F6 Hikone Japan
7 □10 Hikuéru i. French Polynesia Pacific Ocean
8 G2 Hikurangi mt. New Zealand
8 E1 Hikurangi New Zealand
8 G2 Hikutaia New Zealand
87 H2 Hilchenbach Germany
155 F3 Hildale Utah U.S.A.
75 F2 Hildburghausen Germany
72 B4 Hilden Germany
74 F2 Hilders Germany
72 E3 Hildesheim Germany
131 H1 Hildreth Ridge South Africa
80 C2 Hilgertshausen Germany
37 G4 Hili Bangladesh
130 C6 Hillandale South Africa
179 B5 Hillary Coast coastal area Antarctica
150 D4 Hill City Kansas U.S.A.
155 H2 Hill Creek r. Utah U.S.A.
68 C2 Hillegom Netherlands
55 E4 Hillerød Denmark
74 B2 Hillesheim Germany
15 F3 Hillgrove Queensland Australia
66 E3 Hill of Fearn Scotland U.K.
150 D2 Hillsboro N. Dakota U.S.A.
147 H3 Hillsboro New Hampshire U.S.A.
146 B5 Hillsboro Ohio U.S.A.
151 D5 Hillsboro Texas U.S.A.
148 B4 Hillsboro Wisconsin U.S.A.
146 C5 Hillsboro W. Virginia U.S.A.
64 B3 Hillsborough Northern Ireland U.K.
15 G4 Hillsborough, C. c. Queensland Australia
87 G2 Hillscheid Germany
148 E5 Hillsdale Michigan U.S.A.
147 G3 Hillsdale New York U.S.A.
146 E4 Hillsgrove Pennsylvania U.S.A.
155 F4 Hillside Arizona U.S.A.
66 F4 Hillside Scotland U.K.
140 C2 Hillsport Ontario Canada
13 F3 Hillston New South Wales Australia
146 C6 Hillsville Virginia U.S.A.
66 □2 Hillswick Scotland U.K.
64 B3 Hilltown Northern Ireland U.K.
153 □2 Hilo Hawaii U.S.A.
75 G3 Hilpoltstein Germany
65 E3 Hilpsford Point pt England U.K.
146 E3 Hilton New York U.S.A.
140 D3 Hilton Beach Ontario Canada
145 D5 Hilton Head Island S. Carolina U.S.A.
42 D2 Hilvan Turkey
68 D3 Hilvarenbeek Netherlands
68 D2 Hilversum Netherlands
36 D3 Himachal Pradesh India
119 H3 Ḩimā Ḑarīyah, J. mt. Saudi Arabia
36 D2 Himalaya mountain range Asia
37 F3 Himalchul mt. Nepal
56 F2 Himanka Finland
114 A2 Himarë Albania
36 C5 Himatnagar India
81 H2 Himberg Austria
28 E6 Himeji Japan
29 H4 Himekami-dake mt. Japan
29 F6 Hime-shima i. Japan
29 G4 Hime-zaki pt Japan
29 F5 Himi Japan
81 F4 Himmelberg Austria
55 B3 Himmelbjerget h. Denmark
72 E2 Himmelpforten Germany
55 B3 Himmerland reg. Denmark
43 D2 Ḩimş div. Syria
43 D2 Ḩimş Syria
28 C7 Hinagu Japan
23 C4 Hinatuan Philippines
159 D3 Hinche Haiti
15 F3 Hinchinbrook I. i. Queensland Australia
63 E2 Hinckley England U.K.
148 A2 Hinckley Minnesota U.S.A.
155 F2 Hinckley Utah U.S.A.
147 F3 Hinckley Reservoir resr New York U.S.A.
125 B4 Hinda Congo
36 D3 Hindan r. India
59 E3 Hindås Sweden
36 D4 Hindaun India
83 F1 Hindelang Germany
65 H3 Hinderwell England U.K.
63 E2 Hindhead England U.K.
65 F4 Hindley England U.K.
146 B6 Hindman Kentucky U.S.A.
12 E4 Hindmarsh, L. l. Victoria Australia
37 F5 Hindola India
9 C6 Hinds New Zealand
55 C4 Hindsholm pen. Denmark
39 G2 Hindu Kush mountain range Asia
38 B3 Hindupur India
43 C5 Hind, W. al watercourse Saudi Arabia
136 F3 Hines Creek Alberta Canada
145 D6 Hinesville Georgia U.S.A.
36 D5 Hinganghat India
39 F4 Hinglaj Pakistan
Hingol r. see Girdar Dhor
38 B2 Hingoli India
42 E2 Hınıs Turkey
154 D4 Hinkley California U.S.A.
55 C3 Hinnerup Denmark
56 D1 Hinnøya i. Norway
28 D6 Hino Japan
23 B4 Hinobaan Philippines
100 D3 Hinojales, Sierra de h. Spain
101 H3 Hinojares Spain
99 H3 Hinojedo mt. Spain
173 G4 Hinojo Argentina
98 D4 Hinojosa de Duero Spain
101 E2 Hinojosa del Duque Spain
28 C7 Hinokage Japan
28 D6 Hino-misaki pt Japan
147 G3 Hinsdale New Hampshire U.S.A.
59 G1 Hinsen i. Sweden
72 C2 Hinte Germany
80 C3 Hinteres Sonnenwendjoch mt. Austria
75 F2 Hinternah Germany
83 E2 Hinterrhein r. Switzerland
83 E2 Hinterrhein Switzerland
80 E3 Hintersee Austria
87 G3 Hinterweidenthal Germany
74 D5 Hinterzarten Germany
136 F4 Hinton Alberta Canada
146 C6 Hinton W. Virginia U.S.A.
83 D1 Hinwil Switzerland
93 B5 Hinx France
172 D2 Hipolito Yrigoyen Argentina
80 C3 Hippach Austria
68 C2 Hippolytushoef Netherlands
125 C4 Hippopotames de Mangai, Réserve de Faune des res. Congo(Zaire)
125 E6 Hippopotames de Sakania, Réserve des res. Congo(Zaire)
125 E4 Hippopotames, Réserve de res. Congo(Zaire)
42 F2 Hirabit Dağ mt. Turkey
28 B7 Hirado Japan
28 B7 Hirado-shima i. Japan
37 E5 Hirakud Reservoir resr India
127 C5 Hiraman watercourse Kenya
36 D4 Hirapur India
28 D6 Hirata Japan
29 G6 Hiratsuka Japan
122 C5 Hiré-Watta Côte d'Ivoire
77 N5 Hirnyk Ukraine
28 J2 Hiroo Japan
28 H3 Hirosaki Japan
28 D6 Hiroshima div. Japan
28 D6 Hiroshima Japan
75 G3 Hirschaid Germany
75 G3 Hirschau Germany
80 C3 Hirschberg mt. Germany
75 G2 Hirschberg Germany
75 K2 Hirschfelde Germany
55 C2 Hirsholmene is Denmark
90 F1 Hirsingue France
53 F3 Hirsivka Ukraine
53 D2 Hirs'kyy Tikych r. Ukraine
86 D3 Hirson France
66 □1 Hirta i. Scotland U.K.
81 H3 Hirtenberg Austria
55 B2 Hirtshals Denmark
62 C3 Hirwaun Wales U.K.
28 B7 Hisaka-jima i. Japan
42 C1 Hisarönü Turkey
113 F6 Hisarönü Körfezi b. Turkey
47 G5 Hisor Tajikistan
159 E2 Hispaniola i. Caribbean
36 C1 Hispur Gl gl. Pakistan
36 C3 Hissar India
63 G2 Histon England U.K.
37 F4 Hisua India
43 D2 Hisyah Syria
42 E3 Hīt Iraq
28 C7 Hita Japan
29 H5 Hitachi Japan
29 H5 Hitachi-ōta Japan
63 F3 Hitchin England U.K.
7 □11 Hitiaa French Polynesia Pacific Ocean
28 C7 Hitoyoshi Japan
56 C3 Hitra i. Norway
55 E3 Hittarp Sweden
80 A3 Hittisau Austria
73 G2 Hitzacker Germany
81 G3 Hitzendorf Austria
83 D1 Hitzkirch Switzerland
6 □2 Hiu i. Vanuatu
29 G5 Hiuchiga-take volcano Japan
28 D6 Hiuchi-nada b. Japan
177 K6 Hiva Oa i. French Polynesia Pacific Ocean
136 E4 Hixon B.C. Canada
43 C4 Hiyon watercourse Israel
42 E2 Hizan Turkey
55 C2 Hjallerup Denmark
59 F2 Hjälmaren l. Sweden
137 H2 Hjalmar Lake l. N.W.T. Canada
59 F3 Hjältevad Sweden
58 C2 Hjartdal Norway
58 C2 Hjartdøld r. Norway
58 A1 Hjellestad Norway
55 C3 Hjelm i. Denmark
55 E5 Hjelm Bugt b. Denmark
58 B2 Hjelmeland Norway
58 A1 Hjeltefjorden chan. Norway
56 C3 Hjerkinn Norway
59 F2 Hjo Sweden
55 B4 Hjordkær Denmark
55 C2 Hjørring Denmark
59 G3 Hjorted Sweden
59 F2 Hjortkvarn Sweden
58 D3 Hjuvik Sweden
24 B2 Hkok r. Myanmar
24 B1 Hkring Bum mt. Myanmar
131 H4 Hlabisa South Africa
24 A3 Hlaing r. Myanmar
37 F3 Hlako Kangri mt. China
131 H3 Hlatikulu Swaziland
53 A3 Hlazove Ukraine
24 B3 Hlegu Myanmar
78 E2 Hlinsko Czech Rep.
53 E2 Hlobyne Ukraine
131 F4 Hlohlowane South Africa
79 G3 Hlohovec Slovakia
131 G4 Hlotse Lesotho
81 F1 Hluboká nad Vltavou Czech Rep.
79 H2 Hlučín Czech Rep.
131 J4 Hluhluwe South Africa
131 J4 Hluhluwe Game Reserve res. South Africa
53 E1 Hlukhiv Ukraine
24 B2 Hlung-Tan Myanmar
54 F5 Hlusha Belarus
53 B1 Hlushkavichy Belarus
54 F5 Hlusk Belarus
53 D2 Hlyboka Ukraine
54 E4 Hlybokaye Belarus
53 E2 Hlyns'k Ukraine
77 N6 Hlynyany Ukraine
53 C2 Hnivan' Ukraine
77 N6 Hnizdychiv Ukraine
79 J3 Hnúšťa Slovakia
53 C1 Hnylytsya Ukraine
53 B2 Hnylyy Tikych r. Ukraine
123 E5 Ho Ghana
24 D2 Hoa Binh Vietnam
128 B3 Hoachanas Namibia
128 A2 Hoanib watercourse Namibia
128 A2 Hoarusib watercourse Namibia
151 D5 Hobart Oklahoma U.S.A.
13 F5 Hobart Tasmania Australia
153 G5 Hobbs New Mexico U.S.A.
179 A4 Hobbs Coast coastal area Antarctica
145 D7 Hobe Sound Florida U.S.A.
131 F4 Hobhouse South Africa
47 L3 Hoboksar China
Hobot Xar Qi see Xianghuang Qi
55 B3 Hobro Denmark
55 A4 Ho Bugt inlet Denmark
59 H3 Hoburg Sweden
59 H3 Hoburgen pt Sweden
126 E3 Hobyo Somalia
74 E3 Höchberg Germany
81 F2 Hochbira h. Austria
72 E1 Hochdonn Germany
83 D1 Hochdorf Switzerland
82 D1 Höchenschwand Germany
80 C4 Hochfeiler mt. Austria/Italy
81 E3 Hochfeind mt. Austria
128 B3 Hochfeld Namibia
87 G4 Hochfelden France
72 D4 Hochfläche reg. Germany
Hochgall mt see Collalto
81 E3 Hochgolling mt. Austria
74 F2 Hochheim Germany
25 D5 Hô Chi Minh Vietnam
81 F3 Hochschwab mountain range Austria
81 G3 Hochschwab mt. Austria
87 G3 Hochspeyer Germany
80 A3 Höchst Austria
75 F3 Höchstadt an der Aisch Germany
87 G3 Hochstetten-Dhaun Germany
80 A2 Hochsträß reg. Germany
81 F3 Hochtor mt. Austria
80 C3 Hochunnutz mt. Austria
83 E2 Hochwang mt. Switzerland
74 D3 Hockenheim Germany
146 B5 Hocking r. Ohio U.S.A.
157 H4 Hoctúm Mexico
120 C5 Ḥōḍ reg. Mauritania
126 F2 Hodda mt. Somalia
65 F4 Hodder r. England U.K.
63 F3 Hoddesdon England U.K.
Hodeida see Al Hudaydah
147 K1 Hodgdon Maine U.S.A.
120 C5 Hodh Ech Chargui div. Mauritania
120 C5 Hodh El Gharbi div. Mauritania
79 K5 Hódmezővásárhely Hungary
126 E2 Hodmo watercourse Somalia
62 D2 Hodnet England U.K.
78 G3 Hodonín Czech Rep.
30 A2 Hödrögö Mongolia
88 C4 Hœdic, Île de i. France
131 H2 Hoedspruit South Africa
68 C3 Hoek van Holland Netherlands
87 G4 Hœnheim France
69 D4 Hoensbroek Netherlands
87 G4 Hœrdt France
31 J4 Hoeryŏng North Korea
69 D4 Hoeselt Belgium
31 H5 Hoeyang North Korea
75 G2 Hof Bayern Germany
87 H2 Hof Rheinland-Pfalz Germany
83 F1 Höfen Austria
141 H5 Hoffman Mt mt. New York U.S.A.
72 E4 Hofgeismar Germany
74 D2 Hofheim am Taunus Germany
75 F2 Hofheim in Unterfranken Germany
131 E5 Hofmeyr South Africa
56 N6 Höfn Iceland
59 G1 Hofors Sweden
56 M6 Hofsjökull ice cap Iceland
56 M6 Hofsós Iceland
28 C6 Hōfu Japan
Hofuf see Al Hufuf
59 E3 Höganäs Sweden
15 F5 Hoganthulla Cr. r. Queensland Australia
14 D4 Hogarth, Mt h. Northern Terr. Australia
59 G1 Högbacka Sweden
68 D2 Hoge Vaart canal Netherlands
68 D2 Hoge Veluwe, Nationaal Park De Netherlands
121 E4 Hoggar plat. Algeria
147 F6 Hog I. i. Virginia U.S.A.
59 E2 Högsäter Sweden
59 G3 Högsby Sweden
59 F2 Högsjö Sweden
87 G4 Hohberg Germany
81 E4 Hohe Leier mt. Austria
80 E4 Hohe Leiten mt. Austria
80 B2 Hohen-altheim Germany
75 J4 Hohenau Germany
81 G3 Hohenberg Austria
73 J4 Hohenbucko Germany
80 A3 Hohenems Austria
75 G3 Hohenfels Germany
75 F2 Hohenfurch Germany
72 E2 Hohenlockstedt Germany
74 E3 Hohenloher Ebene plain Germany
73 H4 Hohenmölsen Germany
73 H3 Hohennauen Germany
81 F3 Hohe Nock mt. Austria
83 G1 Hohenpeißenberg Germany
73 K3 Hohensaaten Germany
75 H2 Hohenstein-Ernstthal Germany
73 H2 Hohen Wangelin Germany
80 C2 Hohenwart Germany
75 G2 Hohenwarte-Stausee resr Germany
72 E1 Hohenwestedt Germany
81 E2 Hohenzell Austria
81 E3 Hoher Dachstein mt. Austria
74 E2 Hoher Rhön mountain range Germany
80 B3 Hoher Ifen mt. Austria/Germany
80 D3 Hohe Tauern mountain range Austria
80 D3 Hohe Tauern, Nationalpark nat. park Austria
69 E4 Hohe Venn moorland Belgium
82 C2 Hohgant mt. Switzerland
30 D4 Hohhot China
87 H4 Hohloh h. Germany
72 F3 Hohne Germany
87 G4 Hohneck mt. France
123 E5 Hohoe Ghana
28 C6 Hōhoku Japan
53 E2 Hoholeve Ukraine
53 D1 Hoholiv Ukraine
53 F3 Hoholivka Ukraine
87 G2 Höhr-Grenzhausen Germany
73 F1 Hohwachter Bucht b. Germany
37 G2 Hoh Xil Hu salt lake China
37 G2 Hoh Xil Shan mountain range China
24 E4 Hôi An Vietnam
127 B4 Hoima Uganda
24 D2 Hôi Xuân Vietnam
37 H4 Hojai India
55 D4 Højby Denmark
55 A5 Højer Denmark
28 D7 Hōjo Japan
55 B3 Højslev Stationsby Denmark
32 B4 Hok r. Myanmar
59 F3 Hok Sweden
Hokang see Hegang
59 G3 Hökhallen b. Sweden
59 H1 Hökhuvud Sweden
8 D1 Hokianga Harbour harbour New Zealand
29 G5 Hōki-gawa r. Japan
9 C5 Hokitika New Zealand
28 J2 Hokkaidō div. Japan
28 J2 Hokkaidō i. Japan
58 C2 Hokksund Norway
39 D1 Hokmābād Iran
9 B6 Hokonui Hills h. New Zealand
42 F1 Hoktemberyan Armenia
29 F6 Hokuriku Tunnel tunnel Japan
58 C1 Hol Norway
38 B3 Holalkere India
164 D2 Holanda Bolivia
53 E3 Hola Prystan' Ukraine
55 C3 Holbæk Århus Denmark
55 D4 Holbæk Vestsjælland Denmark
131 H3 Holbank South Africa
63 G2 Holbeach England U.K.
63 F2 Holbeach Marsh marsh England U.K.
15 G3 Holborne I. i. Queensland Australia
155 G4 Holbrook Arizona U.S.A.
13 F3 Holbrook New South Wales Australia
148 B3 Holcombe Flowage resr Wisconsin U.S.A.
137 G4 Holden Alberta Canada
155 F2 Holden Utah U.S.A.
151 D5 Holdenville Oklahoma U.S.A.
65 H4 Holderness pen. England U.K.
72 D3 Holdorf Germany
150 D3 Holdrege Nebraska U.S.A.
55 D5 Holeby Denmark
38 B3 Hole Narsipur India
79 G2 Holešov Czech Rep.
159 □9 Holetown Barbados Caribbean
130 A4 Holgat watercourse South Africa
158 C2 Holguín Cuba
78 G3 Holíč Slovakia
59 E1 Höljan r. Sweden
59 E1 Höljes Sweden
81 H2 Hollabrunn div. Austria
81 H2 Hollabrunn Austria
148 D4 Holland Michigan U.S.A.
159 □1 Holland Bay b. Jamaica
63 F2 Holland Fen reg. England U.K.
63 H3 Holland-on-Sea England U.K.
68 C3 Hollands Diep est. Netherlands
68 E2 Hollandse Veld Netherlands
69 D5 Hollange Belgium
75 G4 Hollenbach Germany
81 E3 Höllengebirge h. Austria
81 F3 Hollenstein an der Ybbs Austria
63 H2 Hollesley Bay b. England U.K.
75 G3 Hollfeld Germany
146 D4 Hollidaysburg Pennsylvania U.S.A.
63 G4 Hollington England U.K.
136 C3 Hollis Alaska U.S.A.
151 D5 Hollis Oklahoma U.S.A.
154 B3 Hollister California U.S.A.
79 L3 Hollóháza Hungary
54 D1 Hollola Finland
149 F4 Holly Michigan U.S.A.
151 F5 Holly Springs Mississippi U.S.A.
145 D7 Hollywood Florida U.S.A.
134 G2 Holman N.W.T. Canada
55 B4 Holme r. Denmark
131 G3 Holmedene South Africa
65 H4 Holme-on-Spalding-Moor England U.K.
15 F3 Holmes Reef reef Coral Sea Islands Terr. Pacific Ocean
58 D2 Holmestrand Vestfold Norway
56 G1 Holmestrand Finnmark Norway
65 G4 Holmfirth England U.K.
56 F3 Holmön i. Sweden
59 F3 Holmsjö Sweden
55 A4 Holmsland Klit spit Denmark
135 N2 Holms Ø i. Greenland
59 G1 Holmsveden Sweden
53 A1 Holoby Ukraine
53 A2 Holohory h. Ukraine
43 C3 Holon Israel
6 □3 Holonga Tonga
128 B3 Holoog Namibia
53 D2 Holovanivs'k Ukraine
77 L6 Holovets'ko Ukraine
53 E2 Holovkivka Ukraine
77 N4 Holovne Ukraine
53 C1 Holovyne Ukraine
15 E2 Holroyd r. Queensland Australia
58 B1 Holskarvatnet l. Norway
58 A1 Holsnøy i. Norway
131 G3 Holspruit r. South Africa
55 A3 Holstebro Denmark
55 A4 Holsted Denmark
82 C1 Hölstein Switzerland
Holsteinsborg see Sisimiut
145 D4 Holston r. Tennessee U.S.A.
146 C6 Holston Lake l. Tennessee U.S.A.
62 B4 Holsworthy England U.K.
63 H2 Holt England U.K.
148 E4 Holt Michigan U.S.A.
68 E2 Holten Netherlands
150 E4 Holton Kansas U.S.A.
53 F2 Holubivka Ukraine
68 D1 Holwerd Netherlands
67 D4 Holycross Rep. of Ireland
62 B1 Holyhead Wales U.K.
62 B1 Holyhead Bay b. Wales U.K.
65 G2 Holy Island i. England U.K.
62 B1 Holy Island i. Wales U.K.
152 G3 Holyoke Colorado U.S.A.
147 G3 Holyoke Massachusetts U.S.A.
62 C1 Holywell Wales U.K.
64 C3 Holywood Northern Ireland U.K.
73 H4 Holzhausen Germany
74 C2 Holzhausen an der Haide Germany
80 B2 Holzheim Bayern Germany
80 B2 Holzheim Bayern Germany
87 H2 Holzheim Hessen Germany
75 G5 Holzkirchen Germany
72 E4 Holzminden Germany
73 F4 Holzthaleben Germany
72 C4 Holzwickede Germany
130 B4 Hom watercourse Namibia
127 B5 Homa Bay Kenya
24 A1 Homalin Myanmar

39 B2 Homâyunshahr Iran
72 E4 Homberg (Efze) Germany
74 D2 Homberg (Ohm) Germany
69 A5 Hombleux France
122 D3 Hombori Mali
74 C3 Homburg Germany
135 M3 Home Bay b. N.W.T. Canada
87 E3 Homécourt France
15 F3 Home Hill Queensland Australia
10 1 Home I. i. Cocos Is Indian Ocean
98 B3 Homem r. Portugal
134 C4 Homer Alaska U.S.A.
151 E5 Homer Louisiana U.S.A.
63 H2 Homersfield England U.K.
145 D6 Homerville Georgia U.S.A.
114 B1 Homesh Albania
145 D7 Homestead Florida U.S.A.
15 F4 Homestead Queensland Australia
145 C5 Homewood Alabama U.S.A.
38 B2 Homnabad India
112 F1 Homocea Romania
123 G3 Homodji well Niger
129 F3 Homoine Mozambique
23 C4 Homonhon pt Philippines
Homs see Ḥimş
54 F5 Homyel' div. Belarus
51 D4 Homyel' Homyel'skaya Voblasts' Belarus
38 A3 Honavar India
42 B2 Honaz Turkey
28 J2 Honbetsu Japan
53 D1 Honcharivs'ke Ukraine
162 C2 Honda Colombia
23 A4 Honda Bay b. Philippines
155 H4 Hon Dah Arizona U.S.A.
102 B1 Hondarribia Spain
130 E5 Hondeblaf r. South Africa
130 A5 Hondeklipbaai South Africa
30 D4 Hondlon Ju China
151 D6 Hondo Texas U.S.A.
28 C7 Hondo Japan
103 C6 Hondón de las Nieves Spain
86 B2 Hondschoote France
68 E1 Hondsrug reg. Netherlands
133 K8 Honduras country Central America
157 H5 Honduras, Gulf of g. Mexico
58 D1 Hønefoss Norway
147 F4 Honesdale Pennsylvania U.S.A.
154 B1 Honey Lake l. California U.S.A.
8 2 Honey, Mt h. Campbell I. New Zealand
147 E3 Honeyoye Lake l. New York U.S.A.
89 F2 Honfleur France
33 F1 Hong r. China
55 D4 Høng Denmark
33 F2 Hong'an China
31 H5 Hongch'ŏn South Korea
24 D2 Hông Gai Vietnam
33 F4 Honghai Wan b. China
32 C4 Honghe China
33 F2 Honghu China
33 E3 Hongjiang China
27 Hong Kong div. China
27 Hong Kong Island i. Hong Kong China
30 D5 Hongliu r. China
30 A4 Hongliu Daquan well China
30 A4 Hongliugou China
30 A4 Hongliujing China
30 B5 Hongliuyuan China
25 D5 Hông Ngự Vietnam
30 E3 Hongor China
30 E3 Hongor Mongolia
24 D2 Hong or Red River, Mouths of the river mouth Vietnam
33 E5 Hongqizhen China
30 C5 Hongshansi China
31 H4 Hongshi China
32 D3 Hongshui r. China
30 D5 Hongtong China
29 E7 Hongū Japan
31 H4 Hongwŏn North Korea
31 G3 Hongxing China
32 C1 Hongyuan China
33 G1 Hongze China
33 G1 Hongze Hu l. China
6 1 Honiara Solomon Is.
62 C4 Honiton England U.K.
29 H4 Honjō Japan
57 F3 Honkajoki Finland
29 G6 Honkawane Japan
25 D5 Hon Khoai i. Vietnam
65 G4 Honley England U.K.
25 E4 Hon Lơn i. Vietnam
24 D3 Hon Mê i. Vietnam
38 A3 Honnali India
131 H1 Honnet Nature Reserve res. South Africa
56 G1 Honningsvåg Norway
153 2 Honokaa Hawaii U.S.A.
153 1 Honolulu Hawaii U.S.A.
73 J3 Hönow Germany
25 D5 Hon Rai i. Vietnam
99 H5 Honrubia Spain
99 G3 Honrubia de la Cuesta Spain
28 D6 Honshū i. Japan
99 F3 Hontalbilla Spain
79 H3 Hontianske Nemce Slovakia
99 G2 Hontoria de la Cantera Spain
99 G3 Hontoria del Pinar Spain
152 B2 Hood, Mt volcano Oregon U.S.A.
17 B7 Hood Pt pt Western Australia Australia
68 C2 Hoofddorp Netherlands
72 D1 Hooge i. Germany
72 D1 Hooge Germany
69 C3 Hoogerheide Netherlands
68 E2 Hoogersmilde Netherlands
68 E2 Hoogeveen Netherlands
68 E1 Hoogezand-Sappemeer Netherlands
68 E2 Hooghalen Netherlands
68 D2 Hoogkarspel Netherlands
68 E1 Hoogkerk Netherlands
72 B3 Hoogstede Germany
69 C3 Hoogstraten Belgium
63 F3 Hook England U.K.
151 C4 Hooker Oklahoma U.S.A.
14 B3 Hooker Creek Abor. Reserve res. Northern Terr. Australia
67 E4 Hook Head headland Rep. of Ireland
15 G4 Hook I. i. Queensland Australia
Hook of Holland see Hoek van Holland
15 G3 Hook Rf reef Queensland Australia
136 B3 Hoonah Alaska U.S.A.
134 B3 Hooper Bay Alaska U.S.A.
147 E5 Hooper I. i. Maryland U.S.A.
148 D5 Hoopeston Illinois U.S.A.
131 E3 Hoopstad South Africa
59 E4 Höör Sweden
68 D2 Hoorn Netherlands
176 H6 Hoorn, Îles de Wallis & Futuna Pacific Ocean
147 G3 Hoosick New York U.S.A.
155 E3 Hoover Dam dam Arizona U.S.A.
146 B4 Hoover Memorial Reservoir resr Ohio U.S.A.
30 B3 Höövör Mongolia
42 E1 Hopa Turkey
147 F4 Hop Bottom Pennsylvania U.S.A.
9 D5 Hope r. New Zealand
155 F5 Hope Arizona U.S.A.
151 E5 Hope Arkansas U.S.A.
142 B2 Hope B.C. Canada
62 C1 Hope Wales U.K.
159 1 Hope Bay Jamaica
139 J2 Hopedale Newfoundland Canada
130 B6 Hopefield South Africa
12 D2 Hope, L. salt flat S. Australia Australia
17 C7 Hope, L. salt flat Western Australia Australia
157 H5 Hopelchén Mexico
66 D2 Hope, Loch l. Scotland U.K.
66 E3 Hopeman Scotland U.K.
139 H3 Hope Mountains mountain range Newfoundland Canada
44 D2 Hopen i. Svalbard Arctic Ocean
9 D4 Hope Saddle pass New Zealand
139 G2 Hopes Advance, Baie h. Québec Canada
13 E3 Hopetoun Victoria Australia
17 C7 Hopetoun Western Australia Australia
130 E4 Hopetown South Africa
15 F2 Hope Vale Queensland Australia
146 E6 Hopewell Virginia U.S.A.
138 E2 Hopewell Islands is N.W.T. Canada
80 D3 Hopfgarten im Brixental Austria
24 B1 Hopin Myanmar
13 E4 Hopkins r. Victoria Australia
17 E5 Hopkins, L. salt flat Western Australia Australia
144 C4 Hopkinsville Kentucky U.S.A.
154 A2 Hopland California U.S.A.
24 B2 Hopong Myanmar
69 F5 Hoppstädten Germany
63 H2 Hopton England U.K.
55 B4 Hoptrup Denmark
152 B2 Hoquiam Washington U.S.A.
32 C1 Hor China
42 F2 Horadiz Azerbaijan
63 G4 Horam England U.K.
33 G3 'Hora Mohila Bel'mak h. Ukraine
42 E1 Horasan Turkey
78 C2 Horažďovice Czech Rep.
74 D4 Horb am Neckar Germany
55 E5 Horbelev Denmark
87 G4 Horbourg-Wihr France
83 E1 Hörbranz Austria
59 E4 Hörby Sweden
101 F1 Horcajo de los Montes Spain
99 H5 Horcajo de Santiago Spain
156 D2 Horcasitas Mexico
58 B2 Horda Norway
58 A1 Hordaland div. Norway
53 B3 Horeşti Moldova
112 D2 Horezu Romania
83 D1 Horgen Switzerland
83 E1 Horgenzell Germany
30 A2 Horgo Mongolia
30 J5 Horgoš Yugoslavia
53 A2 Horhany r. Ukraine
30 C4 Hörh Uul mts Mongolia
112 G2 Horia Romania
78 E1 Hořice Czech Rep.
148 C4 Horicon Wisconsin U.S.A.
30 D4 Horinger China
30 H3 Horitschon Austria
30 B3 Horiult Mongolia
176 H7 Horizon Depth depth Pacific Ocean
73 K4 Horka Germany
50 D4 Horki Belarus
63 F3 Horley England U.K.
179 B4 Horlick Mts mts Antarctica
51 F5 Horlivka Ukraine
39 E3 Hormak Iran
39 D4 Hormoz i. Iran
39 D4 Hormozgan div. Iran
39 D4 Hormuz, Strait of str. Iran/Oman
56 L6 Horn c. Iceland
80 E2 Horn div. Austria
136 F2 Horn r. N.W.T. Canada
80 E2 Horn Austria
59 F3 Horn Sweden
100 D2 Hornachos Spain
101 E3 Hornachuelos Spain
79 K3 Hornád r. Slovakia
56 F2 Hornavan l. Sweden
87 G3 Hornbach Germany
151 E6 Hornbeck Louisiana U.S.A.
74 D4 Hornberg Germany
73 F3 Hornburg Germany
65 F3 Hornby England U.K.
Horn, C. c. see Hornos, Cabo de
63 F1 Horncastle England U.K.
59 G1 Horndal Sweden
63 G4 Horndean England U.K.
72 E2 Horneburg Germany
56 E3 Hörnefors Sweden
146 E3 Hornell New York U.S.A.
140 C2 Hornepayne Ontario Canada
55 D2 Hornfiskrøn i. Denmark
67 C1 Horn Head headland Rep. of Ireland
145 B6 Horn I. i. Mississippi U.S.A.
15 E1 Horn I. i. Queensland Australia
75 J2 Horní Bříza Czech Rep.
75 J2 Horní Jiřetín Czech Rep.
55 C3 Hørning Denmark
78 D3 Horní Planá Czech Rep.
74 D4 Hornisgrinde mt. Germany
78 B1 Horní Slavkov Czech Rep.
58 B2 Hornnes Norway
157 F4 Hornos Mexico
101 H2 Hornos Spain
171 C7 Hornos, Cabo de c. Chile
171 C7 Hornos, Parque Nacional de nat. park Chile
53 E3 Hornostayivka Ukraine
89 G2 Hornoy-le-Bourg France
65 H4 Hornsea England U.K.
57 E3 Hornslandet pen. Sweden
55 C3 Hornslet Denmark
59 G3 Hornsviken l. Sweden
58 B3 Hornum Denmark
72 D1 Hörnum Germany
79 J3 Horný Tisovník Slovakia
53 A2 Horodenka Ukraine
53 E1 Horodets' Ukraine
53 D1 Horodnya Ukraine
53 B1 Horodnytsya Ukraine
53 B2 Horodok Khmel'nyts'kyy Ukraine
77 M6 Horodok L'viv Ukraine
53 D2 Horodyshche Ukraine
28 J1 Horokanai Japan
53 A1 Horokhiv Ukraine
79 M3 Horonda Ukraine
28 H1 Horonobe Japan
28 J2 Horoshiri-dake mt. Japan
78 C2 Hořovice Czech Rep.
31 G4 Horqin Shadi reg. China
31 G3 Horqin Youyi Qianqi China
31 G3 Horqin Youyi Zhongqi China
31 G4 Horqin Zuoyi Houqi China
31 G3 Horqin Zuoyi Zhongqi China
165 E4 Horqueta Paraguay
62 B4 Horrabridge England U.K.
55 D5 Horreby Denmark
59 E3 Horred Sweden
17 A6 Horrocks Western Australia Australia
37 G3 Horru China
10 1 Horsburgh I. i. Cocos Is Indian Ocean
81 F2 Hörsching Austria
136 E4 Horsefly B.C. Canada
146 E3 Horseheads New York U.S.A.
139 J3 Horse Is is Newfoundland Canada
67 C3 Horseleap Rep. of Ireland
55 B4 Horsens Denmark
55 C4 Horsens Fjord inlet Denmark
152 C3 Horseshoe Bend Idaho U.S.A.
159 6 Horse Shoe Pt pt St Kitts-Nevis Caribbean
130 D5 Horseshoe, The mt. South Africa
65 G4 Horsforth England U.K.
63 F3 Horsham England U.K.
13 E4 Horsham Victoria Australia
55 E4 Hørsholm Denmark
55 D5 Horslunde Denmark
78 B2 Horšovský Týn Czech Rep.
69 E3 Horst Netherlands
73 G3 Hörstel Germany
72 C3 Horstmar Germany
100 Horta Azores Portugal
58 D2 Horten Norway
99 H3 Hortezuela Spain
99 G2 Hortigüela Spain
79 L4 Hortobágy reg. Hungary
79 K4 Hortobágy-Berettyó canal Hungary
79 L4 Hortobágyi nat. park Hungary
55 B5 Høruphav Denmark
119 F3 Horus, Temple of Egypt
55 D4 Hørve Denmark
59 F3 Hörvik Sweden
83 D1 Horw Switzerland
65 F4 Horwich England U.K.
140 D2 Horwood Lake l. Ontario Canada
53 B1 Horyn' r. Ukraine
37 H2 Ho Sai Hu salt lake China
126 C3 Hosa'ina Ethiopia
74 E2 Hösbach Germany
38 B3 Hosdurga India
39 B2 Ḥoseynābād Iran
39 A2 Ḥoseynābād Iran
39 B3 Ḥoseynīyeh Iran
39 E4 Hoshab Pakistan
36 D5 Hoshangabad India
53 B1 Hoshcha Ukraine
36 C3 Hoshiarpur India
47 L3 Hoshööt Mongolia
30 B2 Hoshööt Mongolia
69 E4 Hosingen Luxembourg
6 1 Hoskins P.N.G.
38 B3 Hospet India
67 C4 Hospital Rep. of Ireland
173 K2 Hospital, Cuch. del h. Uruguay
124 B2 Hosséré Vokre mt. Cameroon
83 E1 Hoßkirch Germany
159 H5 Hossororo Guyana
102 F3 Hostalric Spain
171 C7 Hoste, I. i. Chile
93 B4 Hostens France
78 F3 Hostěradice Czech Rep.
78 E1 Hostinné Czech Rep.
75 K2 Hostivice Czech Rep.
56 D3 Hotagen r. Sweden
47 K5 Hotan watercourse China
36 E1 Hotan China
130 D3 Hotazel South Africa
155 G4 Hotevilla Arizona U.S.A.
17 B7 Hotham r. Western Australia Australia
14 B2 Hotham, C. c. Northern Terr. Australia
13 F4 Hotham, Mt mt. Victoria Australia
56 E2 Hoting Sweden
151 E5 Hot Springs Arkansas U.S.A.
150 C3 Hot Springs S. Dakota U.S.A.
136 F1 Hottah Lake l. N.W.T. Canada
128 A4 Hottentots Bay b. Namibia
69 D4 Hotton Belgium
74 D5 Hotzenwald reg. Germany
55 C2 Hou Denmark
6 2 Houaïlu New Caledonia Pacific Ocean
88 C4 Houat, Île de i. France
86 B2 Houdain France
89 G3 Houdan France
87 E4 Houdelaincourt France
93 C4 Houeillès France
69 D4 Houffalize Belgium
25 Hougang Singapore
148 C2 Houghton Michigan U.S.A.
148 E3 Houghton Lake l. Michigan U.S.A.
148 E3 Houghton Lake Michigan U.S.A.
65 G3 Houghton le Spring England U.K.
63 F3 Houghton Regis England U.K.
130 B7 Houhoek Pass pass South Africa
55 B3 Houlbjerg Denmark
147 K1 Houlton Maine U.S.A.
6 3 Houma i. Tonga
151 F6 Houma Louisiana U.S.A.
30 D6 Houma China
6 4 Houma Tonga
6 4 Houma Tonga
6 4 Houma Toloa pt Tonga
121 G2 Houmt Souk Tunisia
122 D4 Houndé Burkina
86 A2 Hourdel, Pte du pt France
66 C3 Hourn, Loch inlet Scotland U.K.
92 A3 Hourtin France
92 A3 Hourtin-Plage France
147 G3 Housatonic Massachusetts U.S.A.
155 F2 House Range mts Utah U.S.A.
136 D4 Houston B.C. Canada
151 F5 Houston Mississippi U.S.A.
151 F4 Houston Missouri U.S.A.
151 E6 Houston Texas U.S.A.
68 D2 Houten Netherlands
69 D3 Houthalen Belgium
69 A4 Houthulst Belgium
130 E5 Houtkraal South Africa
17 A6 Houtman Abrolhos is Western Australia Australia
66 E2 Houton Scotland U.K.
59 J1 Houtskär Finland
55 C4 Hov Denmark
58 D1 Hov Norway
59 F2 Hova Sweden
30 B3 Hovd Mongolia
26 F2 Hovd Mongolia
58 C2 Hovdefjell h. Norway
58 B2 Hovden Norway
63 F4 Hove England U.K.
72 D4 Hövelhof Germany
55 A4 Hoven Denmark
55 A3 Hover r. Denmark
63 H2 Hoveton England U.K.
39 B3 Hoveyzeh Iran
65 H3 Hovingham England U.K.
59 F3 Hovmantorp Sweden
81 H2 Hovorany Czech Rep.
30 A2 Hövsgöl div. Mongolia
30 D4 Hövsgöl Mongolia
30 B2 Hövsgöl Nuur l. Mongolia
53 F2 Hovtva r. Ukraine
53 E2 Hovtva Ukraine
30 B4 Hövüün Mongolia
126 D1 Howakil I. i. Eritrea
15 H5 Howard Queensland Australia
148 E4 Howard City Michigan U.S.A.
14 C2 Howard I. i. Northern Terr. Australia
137 H2 Howard Lake l. N.W.T. Canada
65 H4 Howden England U.K.
13 G4 Howe, C. headland Victoria Australia
179 Howe, I. i. Kerguelen Indian Ocean
149 F4 Howell Michigan U.S.A.
150 C2 Howes S. Dakota U.S.A.
141 J4 Howick Québec Canada
131 H4 Howick South Africa
12 D1 Howitt, L. salt flat S. Australia Australia
13 F4 Howitt, Mt mt. Victoria Australia
147 J2 Howland Maine U.S.A.
176 H5 Howland I. Pacific Ocean
176 E3 Howth Rep. of Ireland
39 D2 Ḥowz well Iran
39 C2 Ḥowz-e Dūmatu Iran
39 D3 Ḥowz-e Panj Iran
39 D2 Ḥowz-i-Khan well Iran
72 E4 Höxter Germany
66 E2 Hoy i. Scotland U.K.
72 E3 Hoya Germany
58 B1 Høyanger Norway
73 K4 Hoyerswerda Germany
56 D2 Høylandet Norway
140 E2 Hoyle Ontario Canada
73 G4 Hoym Germany
98 D4 Hoyos Spain
99 E4 Hoyos del Espino Spain
56 H3 Höytiäinen l. Finland
42 D2 Hozat Turkey
101 F4 Hozgarganta r. Spain
77 M2 Hozha Belarus
Hpa-an see Pa-an
78 E1 Hradec Králové Czech Rep.
75 K2 Hrádek nad Nisou Czech Rep.
75 J3 Hradešice Czech Rep.
78 C1 Hradiště h. Czech Rep.
53 E2 Hradyz'k Ukraine
77 M2 Hrandzichy Belarus
79 G2 Hranice Severomoravský Czech Rep.
75 H2 Hranice Západočeský Czech Rep.
53 C1 Hranitne Ukraine
79 K3 Hranovnica Slovakia
104 G4 Hrasnica Bos.-Herz.
81 G4 Hrastnik Slovenia
42 F1 Hrazdan Armenia
53 E1 Hrebinka Ukraine
53 D2 Hrebinky Ukraine
52 A3 Hrem"yach Ukraine
53 E3 Hreyhove Ukraine
79 J3 Hriňová Slovakia
53 C2 Hristovaia Moldova
77 O2 Hrodna div. Belarus
77 M2 Hrodna Belarus
77 M2 Hrodnyendskaye Wzvyshsha reg. Belarus
79 H4 Hron r. Slovakia
78 F2 Hrotovice Czech Rep.
77 M5 Hrubieszów Poland
53 F1 Hrun' r. Ukraine
53 F1 Hrun' Ukraine
53 G2 Hrushuvakha Ukraine
81 H2 Hrušovany nad Jevišovkou Czech Rep.
53 E1 Hryhorivka Chernihiv Ukraine
53 E3 Hryhorivka Kherson Ukraine
53 B2 Hrymayliv Ukraine
53 A3 Hrynyava Ukraine
53 C2 Hryshkivtsi Ukraine
53 B2 Hrytsiv Ukraine
24 B2 Hsenwi Myanmar
24 B2 Hsi-hkip Myanmar
24 B2 Hsi-hseng Myanmar
33 G4 Hsi-hsu-p'ing Hsü i. Taiwan
33 H3 Hsin-chu Taiwan
24 B2 Hsipaw Myanmar
33 H3 Hsüeh Shan mt. Taiwan
33 G3 Hua'an China
128 A3 Huab watercourse Namibia
164 C3 Huachacalla Bolivia
30 D5 Huachi China
172 A4 Huachipato Chile
164 A2 Huacho Peru
31 J3 Huachuan China
155 G6 Huachuca City Arizona U.S.A.
172 C1 Huaco Argentina
164 A1 Huacrachuco Peru
30 E4 Huade China
31 H4 Huadian China
7 10 Huahine i. French Polynesia Pacific Ocean
33 F1 Huai r. China
30 E4 Huai'an China
33 G1 Huai'an China
33 G1 Huaibei China
33 F1 Huaibin China
31 H4 Huaidezhen China
33 E3 Huaihua China
33 F4 Huaiji China
33 F4 Huailai China
24 C3 Huai Luang r. Thailand
33 G1 Huainan China
33 G2 Huaining China
30 E5 Huairen China
33 F2 Huaiyang China
33 G1 Huaiyin China
32 E3 Huaiyuan China
33 G1 Huaiyuan China
32 D1 Huajialing China
157 F5 Huajuápan de León Mexico
21 J8 Huaki Indonesia
155 F4 Hualapai Peak summit Arizona U.S.A.
33 H3 Hua-lien Taiwan
162 B5 Huallaga r. Peru
30 B5 Hualong China
172 A5 Hualpin Chile
172 A4 Hualqui Chile
164 A1 Huamachuco Peru
125 C6 Huambo div. Angola
125 C6 Huambo Angola
162 B5 Huambos Peru
130 A2 Huams watercourse Namibia
33 C5 Huan r. China
31 J3 Huanan China
162 B5 Huancabamba r. Peru
171 C5 Huancache, Sa mountain range Argentina
164 C3 Huancane Peru
164 A2 Huancavelica Peru
164 A2 Huancayo Peru
172 F2 Huanchilla Argentina
31 F5 Huang r. China
30 B5 Huangcheng China
33 F1 Huangchuan China
33 F2 Huanggang China
Huang Hai sea see Yellow Sea
31 F5 Huanghe Kou river mouth China
32 A1 Huanghetan China
31 F5 Huanghua China
33 H1 Huangjiajian China
30 D6 Huangling China
32 E5 Huangliu China
33 F2 Huangmei China
31 H4 Huangnihe China
33 F2 Huangpi China
32 D3 Huangping China
30 E4 Huangqi Hai l. China
33 F2 Huangshajie China
33 G2 Huang Shan mt. China
33 G2 Huangshan China
33 F2 Huangshi China
33 G2 Huang Shui r. China
30 C5 Huangtu Gaoyuan mountain range China
173 G4 Huanguelén Argentina
31 G5 Huang Xian China
33 H2 Huangyan China
30 B5 Huangyuan China
32 E3 Huanjiang China
31 H4 Huanren China
164 B2 Huanta Peru
31 F5 Huantai China
164 A1 Huanuco Peru
164 C3 Huanuni Bolivia
30 C5 Huan Xian China
164 B2 Huanzo, Cord. de mountain range Peru
32 C3 Huaping China
33 H3 Hua-p'ing Hsü i. Taiwan
164 C3 Huar Bolivia
164 C4 Huara Chile
164 A2 Huaral Peru
164 A1 Huaráz Peru
164 A1 Huari Peru
164 C3 Huarina Bolivia
164 A2 Huarmey Peru
33 F2 Huarong China
102 B2 Huarte-Araquil Spain
164 A1 Huascaran, Nevado de mt. Peru
164 A1 Huascarán, Parque Nacional nat. park Peru
170 B2 Huasco r. Chile
170 B2 Huasco Chile
33 E1 Hua Shan mt. China
31 B1 Huashixia China
156 C3 Huatabampo Mexico
32 D1 Huating China
157 F5 Huatusco Mexico
157 F4 Huauchinango Mexico
157 F5 Huautla Mexico
30 E6 Hua Xian China
33 E1 Hua Xian China
164 A2 Huayhuash, Cord. mountain range Peru
164 A1 Huaylas Peru
164 A2 Huayllay Peru
33 F2 Huayuan China
32 D2 Huayuan China
33 E4 Huazhou China
77 J4 Huba Poland
149 F3 Hubbard Lake l. Michigan U.S.A.
136 B2 Hubbard, Mt mt. Alaska/Yukon Territory Canada/U.S.A.
139 G2 Hubbard, Pointe headland Québec Canada
33 E2 Hubei div. China
38 A3 Hubli India
77 N5 Hubyn Ukraine
53 F2 Hubynykha Ukraine
172 E4 Hucal Argentina
31 H4 Huch'ang North Korea
72 B4 Hückelhoven Germany
72 C4 Hückeswagen Germany
63 E1 Hucknall England U.K.
86 A2 Hucqueliers France
65 G4 Huddersfield England U.K.
59 G2 Huddinge Sweden
146 B6 Huddy Kentucky U.S.A.
72 D2 Hude (Oldenburg) Germany
31 G2 Huder China
57 E3 Hudiksvall Sweden
144 F3 Hudson r. New York U.S.A.
148 E5 Hudson Michigan U.S.A.
147 G3 Hudson New York U.S.A.
148 A3 Hudson Wisconsin U.S.A.
138 D2 Hudson Bay sea Canada
137 J4 Hudson Bay Saskatchewan Canada
147 G3 Hudson Falls New York U.S.A.
135 Q2 Hudson Land reg. Greenland
179 A3 Hudson Mts mts Antarctica
136 E3 Hudson's Hope B.C. Canada
135 L3 Hudson Strait str. Québec/N.W.T. Canada
24 D3 Huê Vietnam
98 D4 Huebra r. Spain
102 B3 Huecha r. Spain
171 B5 Huechucuicui, Pta pt Chile
172 B5 Huechulafquén, L. l. Argentina
112 D1 Huedin Romania
157 H6 Huehuetenango Guatemala
156 D3 Huehueto, Co mt. Mexico
172 A6 Hueicoya Chile
157 F5 Huejotzingo Mexico
157 F4 Huejutla Mexico
101 G3 Huélago Spain
88 B3 Huelgoat France
101 G3 Huelma Spain
100 D3 Huelva div. Andalucia Spain
100 D3 Huelva r. Spain
100 D3 Huelva Spain
172 B1 Huentelauquén Chile
172 B4 Huepil Chile
103 B7 Huércal-Overa Spain
99 G2 Huérmeces Spain
103 B4 Huerta del Marquesada Spain
99 G3 Huerta del Rey Spain
99 G5 Huerta de Valdecarábanos Spain
172 D1 Huerta, Sa de la mountain range Argentina
103 C6 Huertas, Cabo de las pt Spain
102 C3 Huerva r. Spain
101 G3 Huesa Spain
102 C2 Huesca div. Aragón Spain
102 C2 Huesca Spain
101 H3 Huéscar Spain
157 E5 Huétamo Mexico
99 H4 Huete Spain
101 G3 Huétor-Tájar Spain
101 G3 Huétor-Vega Spain
157 F5 Huexotla Mexico
172 A6 Hueyelhue, Punta pt Chile
100 E3 Huezna r. Spain
74 D5 Hüfingen Germany
58 A1 Huftarøy i. Norway
124 E1 Hugeitig pool Sudan
14 C5 Hugh watercourse Northern Terr. Australia
15 F4 Hughenden Queensland Australia
173 G2 Hughes Argentina
146 E4 Hughesville Pennsylvania U.S.A.
63 1 Hugh Town England U.K.
37 F5 Hugli inlet India
37 G5 Hugli-Chunchura India
151 E5 Hugo Oklahoma U.S.A.
151 C4 Hugoton Kansas U.S.A.
30 E5 Huguan China
Huhehot see Hohhot
130 E3 Huhudi South Africa
33 G3 Hui'an China
30 C5 Hui'anbu China
8 F3 Huiarau Range mountain range New Zealand
128 B4 Huib-Hoch Plateau Namibia
33 F3 Huichang China
31 H4 Huich'ŏn North Korea
33 F4 Huidong China
32 C3 Huidong China
31 H4 Huifa r. China
31 F2 Huihe China
33 F1 Huiji r. China
125 B6 Huíla div. Angola
33 G4 Huilai China
162 B3 Huila, Nevado de mt. Colombia
125 C7 Huila Plateau plat. Angola
32 C3 Huili China
157 G5 Huimanguillo Mexico
31 F5 Huimin China
170 C1 Huinahuaca Argentina
31 H4 Huinan China
172 E3 Huinca Renancó Argentina
30 C6 Huining China
80 B2 Huisheim Germany
32 D3 Huishui China
89 F3 Huisne r. France
68 D3 Huissen Netherlands
37 G2 Huiten Nur l. China
33 E3 Huitong China
57 F3 Huittinen Finland
157 F5 Huitzuco Mexico
33 F1 Hui Xian China
32 D1 Hui Xian China
157 G6 Huixtla Mexico
Huiyang see Huizhou
32 C3 Huize China
68 D2 Huizen Netherlands
33 F4 Huizhou China
30 C3 Hujirt Mongolia
24 B1 Hukawng Valley v. Myanmar
33 G2 Hukou China
128 C3 Hukuntsi Botswana
31 H3 Hulan r. China
31 H3 Hulan China
31 G3 Hulan Ergi China
119 H2 Ḥulayfah Saudi Arabia
148 E2 Hulbert Lake l. Michigan U.S.A.
39 A2 Hulilan Iran
31 G3 Hulin r. China
31 K3 Hulin China
78 G2 Hulín Czech Rep.
Hulin Rocks is see Maidens, The
141 H4 Hull Québec Canada
72 D3 Hüllhorst Germany
54 C2 Hulo Estonia
69 C3 Hulst Netherlands
59 F3 Hultsfred Sweden
31 G4 Huludao China
Hulun see Hailar
31 F2 Hulun Nur l. China
53 G3 Hulyaypole Ukraine
31 G1 Huma r. China
31 H2 Huma China
145 3 Humacao Puerto Rico
164 C2 Humaita Bolivia
165 D1 Humaitá Brazil
165 E5 Humaitá Paraguay
99 G4 Humanes de Mohernando Spain
125 B7 Humbe Angola
65 H4 Humber, Mouth of the river mouth England U.K.
65 H4 Humberside airport England U.K.
125 B6 Humbe, Serra do mts Angola
55 C5 Humble Denmark
152 C3 Humboldt r. Nevada U.S.A.
137 H4 Humboldt Saskatchewan Canada
173 G1 Humboldt Argentina
152 A3 Humboldt Bay b. California U.S.A.
154 C1 Humboldt Lake l. Nevada U.S.A.
6 2 Humboldt, Mt mt. New Caledonia Pacific Ocean
154 C1 Humboldt Range mts Nevada U.S.A.
154 D2 Humbolt Salt Marsh marsh Nevada U.S.A.
15 F5 Humeburn Queensland Australia
173 G4 Humeda plain Argentina
39 D4 Hümedān Iran
33 F4 Hu Men chan. China
79 L3 Humenné Slovakia
13 F3 Hume Res. resr New South Wales Australia
87 E5 Humes-Jorquenay France
55 E4 Humlebæk Denmark
55 A3 Humlum Denmark
59 G2 Hummelsta Sweden
9 C6 Hummock h. New Zealand
81 G4 Hum na Sutli Croatia
172 A3 Humos, C. headland Chile
125 B7 Humpata Angola
154 C3 Humphreys, Mt mt. California U.S.A.
155 G4 Humphreys Peak summit Arizona U.S.A.
78 E2 Humpolec Czech Rep.
54 C1 Humppila Finland
65 F2 Humshaugh England U.K.
31 J4 Hun r. China
31 H4 Hun r. China
118 C2 Hūn Libya
56 L6 Húnaflói b. Iceland
33 E3 Hunan div. China
126 D2 Ḥunayshīyah Yemen
31 J4 Hunchun China
73 H4 Hundeluft Germany
75 H4 Hunderdorf Germany
55 D4 Hundested Denmark
62 B3 Hundleton Wales U.K.
136 E4 100 Mile House B.C. Canada
79 M5 Hunedoara div. Romania
112 D2 Hunedoara Romania
74 E2 Hünfeld Germany
6 3 Hunga i. Tonga
6 5 Hunga Ha'apai i. Tonga
48 G4 Hungary country Europe
6 5 Hunga Tonga i. Tonga
74 D2 Hungen Germany
63 E3 Hungerford England U.K.
15 F6 Hungerford Queensland Australia
31 H5 Hŭngnam North Korea
152 D1 Hungry Horse Res. resr Montana U.S.A.
27 Hung Shui Kiu Hong Kong China
24 D2 Hưng Yên Vietnam
90 F1 Huningue France
31 H4 Hunjiang China
65 H3 Hunmanby England U.K.
59 F2 Hunn l. Sweden
58 D2 Hunnebostrand Sweden
68 E1 Hunsingo reg. Netherlands
87 G4 Hunspach France
63 G2 Hunstanton England U.K.
38 B3 Hunsur India
155 H4 Hunt Arizona U.S.A.
140 E2 Hunta Ontario Canada
72 D2 Hunte r. Germany
13 G3 Hunter r. New South Wales Australia
9 B6 Hunter r. New Zealand
147 F3 Hunter New York U.S.A.
136 D4 Hunter I. i. B.C. Canada
176 G7 Hunter I. i. New Caledonia Pacific Ocean
13 F5 Hunter I. i. Tasmania Australia
13 F5 Hunter Is is Tasmania Australia
24 A3 Hunter's Bay b. Myanmar
9 C6 Hunters Hills, The h. New Zealand
63 F2 Huntingdon England U.K.
146 E4 Huntingdon Pennsylvania U.S.A.
141 H4 Huntingdon Québec Canada
148 E5 Huntington Indiana U.S.A.
155 G2 Huntington Utah U.S.A.
146 B5 Huntington W. Virginia U.S.A.
154 D5 Huntington Beach California U.S.A.
131 G1 Huntleigh South Africa
66 F3 Huntly Scotland U.K.
8 E2 Huntly New Zealand
145 C5 Huntsville Alabama U.S.A.
141 F4 Huntsville Ontario Canada
151 E6 Huntsville Texas U.S.A.
30 E5 Hunyuan China
47 H5 Hunza reg. Jammu and Kashmir
36 C1 Hunza Pakistan

68 E1 Hunze r. Netherlands
47 K4 Huocheng China
33 F1 Huojia China
31 G3 Huolin r. China
31 H2 Huolongmen China
6 □2 Huon i. New Caledonia Pacific Ocean
24 D3 Hương Khê Vietnam
24 D3 Hương Thuy Vietnam
6 □1 Huon Peninsula pen. P.N.G.
13 F5 Huonville Tasmania Australia
33 G1 Huoqiu China
33 G2 Huo Shan mt. China
33 G2 Huoshan China
33 H4 Huo-shao Tao i. Taiwan
30 D5 Huo Xian China
53 F2 Hupalivka Ukraine
Hupeh see Hubei
43 D1 Hupnik r. Turkey
39 D3 Ḥūr Iran
79 H4 Hurbanovo Slovakia
58 D1 Hurdalssjøen l. Norway
140 E4 Hurd, Cape headland Ontario Canada
10 □3 Hurd Pt pt Macquarie I. Pacific Ocean
30 C4 Hure Jadgai China
30 B2 Hüremt Mongolia
89 H3 Hurepoix reg. France
31 G4 Hure Qi China
119 F2 Hurghada Egypt
92 E2 Huriel France
53 E2 Hurivka Ukraine
140 A2 Hurkett Ontario Canada
67 C4 Hurler's Cross Rep. of Ireland
148 B2 Hurley Wisconsin U.S.A.
150 D2 Huron S. Dakota U.S.A.
148 C2 Huron Bay b. Michigan U.S.A.
149 F3 Huron, Lake l. Canada/U.S.A.
148 D2 Huron Mts h. Michigan U.S.A.
155 F3 Hurricane Utah U.S.A.
63 E3 Hursley England U.K.
63 G3 Hurst Green England U.K.
63 F4 Hurstpierpoint England U.K.
172 B1 Hurtado r. Chile
172 B1 Hurtado Chile
74 B2 Hürth Germany
22 C1 Hurung, G. mt. Indonesia
129 D2 Hurungwe Safari Area res. Zimbabwe
9 D5 Hurunui r. New Zealand
55 A3 Hurup Denmark
36 B3 Husain Nika Pakistan
53 G3 Husarka Ukraine
56 L6 Húsavík Norðurland eystra Iceland
56 M6 Húsavík Vestfirðir Iceland
55 □1 Húsavik Faeroes
63 E2 Husbands Bosworth England U.K.
72 E1 Husby Germany
59 G1 Husby Sweden
112 G1 Huși Romania
78 C2 Husinec Czech Rep.
59 F3 Huskvarna Sweden
134 C3 Huslia Alaska U.S.A.
43 C3 Husn Jordan
126 E1 Ḩusn Āl 'Abr Yemen
58 A2 Husnes Norway
58 A1 Husøy i. Norway
37 F4 Hussainabad India
78 F3 Hustopeče Czech Rep.
72 E1 Husum Germany
56 E3 Husum Sweden
53 B2 Husyatyn Ukraine
77 L3 Huszlew Poland
30 B2 Hutag Mongolia
39 D3 Hūtak Iran
150 D4 Hutchinson Kansas U.S.A.
130 D5 Hutchinson South Africa
155 G4 Hutch Mtn mt. Arizona U.S.A.
126 D1 Ḩūth Yemen
24 B3 Huthi Myanmar
31 K3 Hutou China
137 N2 Hut Point pt N.W.T. Canada
80 E3 Hüttau Austria
81 F4 Hüttenberg Austria
75 J4 Hutthurm Germany
80 A2 Hüttisheim Germany
74 F4 Hüttlingen Germany
15 G5 Hutton, Mt h. Queensland Australia
65 G3 Hutton Rudby England U.K.
146 D5 Huttonsville W. Virginia U.S.A.
80 E3 Hüttschlag Austria
82 C1 Huttwil Switzerland
47 L4 Hutubi China
30 E5 Hutuo r. China
130 A2 Hutup watercourse Namibia
53 F1 Huty Ukraine
35 D10 Huvadu Atoll atoll Maldives
32 E1 Hu Xian China
9 B6 Huxley, Mt mt. New Zealand
69 D4 Huy div. Belgium
69 D4 Huy Belgium
31 G2 Huzhong China
33 H2 Huzhou China
30 B5 Huzhu China
55 □1 Hvalba Faeroes
58 D2 Hvaler i. Norway
55 D4 Hvalsø Denmark
56 L6 Hvammsfjörður b. Iceland
56 M7 Hvannadalshnúkur mt. Iceland
55 □1 Hvannasund Faeroes
104 F4 Hvar i. Croatia
109 J1 Hvar Croatia
51 E6 Hvardiys'ke Ukraine
104 F4 Hvarski Kanal chan. Croatia
56 L6 Hveragerði Iceland
55 A3 Hvidbjerg Denmark
55 A3 Hvide Sande Denmark
56 L6 Hvíta r. Iceland
58 C2 Hvittingfoss Norway
53 A2 Hvizdets' Ukraine
55 B3 Hvorslev Denmark
53 E1 Hvyntove Ukraine
128 D2 Hwange Zimbabwe
128 D2 Hwange National Park nat. park Zimbabwe
129 E2 Hwedza Zimbabwe
Hwlffordd see Haverfordwest
29 □2 Hyakuna Japan
147 H4 Hyannis Massachusetts U.S.A.
150 C3 Hyannis Nebraska U.S.A.
26 F2 Hyargas Nuur salt lake Mongolia
136 C3 Hydaburg Alaska U.S.A.
9 C6 Hyde New Zealand
146 B6 Hyden Kentucky U.S.A.
17 B7 Hyden Western Australia Australia
147 G4 Hyde Park New York U.S.A.
155 F5 Hyder Arizona U.S.A.
38 B2 Hyderabad India
36 B4 Hyderabad Pakistan
91 E5 Hyères France
91 E Hyères, Îles d' is France
54 E4 Hyermanavichy Belarus
31 J4 Hyesan North Korea
136 D2 Hyland r. Yukon Terr. Canada
58 B2 Hylestad Norway
55 D5 Hyllekrog i. Denmark
58 A1 Hyllestad Norway
59 E3 Hyltebruk Sweden
87 F4 Hymont France
28 E6 Hyōgo div. Japan
28 E6 Hyōnosen mt. Japan
56 H2 Hyrynsalmi Finland
114 A2 Hysgjokaj Albania
136 F3 Hythe Alberta Canada
63 E4 Hythe England U.K.
63 H3 Hythe England U.K.
59 G1 Hyttön Sweden
28 C7 Hyūga Japan
57 G3 Hyvinkää Finland

I

168 D4 Iacanga Brazil
112 E1 Iacobeni Romania
168 C4 Iacri Brazil
166 D3 Iaçu Brazil
129 H3 Iakora Madagascar
112 F2 Ialomița r. Romania
53 C3 Ialoveni Moldova
112 F2 Ianca Romania
169 G3 Iapu Brazil
67 B3 Iar Connaught reg. Rep. of Ireland
53 C3 Iargara Moldova
112 F1 Iași Romania
23 A3 Iba Philippines
123 E5 Ibadan Nigeria
162 B3 Ibagué Colombia
168 C5 Ibaiti Brazil
155 F1 Ibapah Utah U.S.A.
112 C3 Ibar r. Yugoslavia
28 D6 Ibara Japan
29 H5 Ibaraki div. Japan
173 K1 Ibare Brazil
162 B3 Ibarra Ecuador
170 E2 Ibarreta Argentina
168 E4 Ibaté Brazil
126 D2 Ibb Yemen
124 E2 Ibba watercourse Sudan
124 E3 Ibba Sudan
72 C3 Ibbenbüren Germany
123 E3 Ibdeqqene watercourse Mali
170 E2 Iberá, L. l. Argentina
162 C5 Iberia Peru
123 F4 Ibeto Nigeria
123 F5 Ibi Nigeria
103 C6 Ibi Spain
169 E3 Ibiá Brazil
169 F2 Ibiaí Brazil
98 D2 Ibias r. Spain
169 J1 Ibicaraí Brazil
167 A6 Ibicuí r. Brazil
169 J1 Ibicuí Brazil
173 K1 Ibicuí da Cruz r. Brazil
91 C4 Ibie r. France
166 E2 Ibimirim Brazil
168 C5 Ibiporã Brazil
169 H3 Ibiraçu Brazil
167 C6 Ibirama Brazil
169 H2 Ibiranhém Brazil
167 A6 Ibirapuita r. Brazil
166 D3 Ibitiara Brazil
168 D4 Ibitinga Brazil
Ibiza i. see Eivissa
Ibiza see Eivissa
110 D5 Iblei, Monti mts Sicilia Italy
124 E4 Ibonga Congo(Zaire)
166 D3 Ibotirama Brazil
124 B4 Iboundji, Mont mt. Gabon
41 J5 Ibrā' Oman
52 H2 Ibresi Rus. Fed.
41 J5 Ibrī Oman
43 A5 Ibshawâi Egypt
63 E2 Ibstock England U.K.
29 □2 Ibu Japan
23 B1 Ibuhos i. Philippines
28 C8 Ibusuki Japan
162 D4 Içá r. Brazil
164 A2 Ica Peru
159 □3 Icacos Pt pt Trinidad Trinidad and Tobago
162 D3 Içana r. Brazil
162 D3 Içana Brazil
168 B5 Icaraíma Brazil
166 D1 Icatu Brazil
155 E3 Iceberg Canyon Nevada U.S.A.
43 B1 İçel div. Turkey
42 C2 İçel Turkey
48 C2 Iceland country Europe
168 D4 Icem Brazil
38 A2 Ichalkaranji India
52 G2 Ichalki Rus. Fed.
38 D2 Ichchapuram India
74 F4 Ichenhausen Germany
28 C7 Ichifusa-yama mt. Japan
29 H6 Ichihara Japan
164 D3 Ichilo r. Bolivia
29 F6 Ichinomiya Japan
29 H4 Ichinoseki Japan
53 E1 Ichnya Ukraine
31 H5 Ich'ŏn South Korea
69 B3 Ichtegem Belgium
75 F2 Ichtershausen Germany
80 C3 Icking Germany
63 G4 Icklesham England U.K.
63 G2 Icklingham England U.K.
113 G6 İçmeler Turkey
166 E2 Icó Brazil
97 □ Icod de Los Vinos Canary Is Spain
169 H4 Iconha Brazil
136 B3 Icy Pt pt Alaska U.S.A.
136 B3 Icy Strait chan. Alaska U.S.A.
123 F3 Idabdaba well Niger
151 E5 Idabel Oklahoma U.S.A.
123 F5 Idah Nigeria
152 D2 Idaho div. U.S.A.
152 D3 Idaho City Idaho U.S.A.
152 D3 Idaho Falls Idaho U.S.A.
43 C2 Idaidet Ghazir Lebanon
43 B2 Idalion Cyprus
9 C6 Ida, Mt mt. New Zealand
98 C5 Idanha-a-Nova Portugal
74 C3 Idar-Oberstein Germany
69 F5 Idarwald forest Germany
123 G4 Iday well Niger
119 E5 Idd el Asoda well Sudan
124 D1 Idd el Chanam Sudan
58 D2 Idefjorden inlet Norway/Sweden
121 F4 Idelès Algeria
30 A2 Ider Mongolia
30 A2 Ideriyn Gol r. Mongolia
119 F3 Idfu Egypt
118 B2 Idhān Awbārī desert Libya
118 B3 Idhan Murzūq desert Libya
115 F7 Idi mts Greece
107 F4 Idice r. Italy
125 C4 Idiofa Congo(Zaire)
134 C3 Iditarod Alaska U.S.A.
56 F1 Idivuoma Sweden
43 D2 Idlib div. Syria
43 D2 Idlib Syria
52 G4 Idolga r. Rus. Fed.
57 D3 Idre Sweden
81 F4 Idrija Slovenia
81 E4 Idrijca r. Slovenia
47 M2 Idrinskoye Rus. Fed.
54 F3 Idritsa Rus. Fed.
106 E3 Idro Italy
83 F3 Idro, Lago d' l. Italy
74 D2 Idstein Germany
131 G6 Idutywa South Africa
54 D3 Iecava Latvia
29 □2 Ie-jima i. Japan
168 C5 Iepê Brazil
69 A4 Ieper div. Belgium
69 A4 Ieper Belgium
115 G7 Ierapetra Greece
112 E1 Iermut Romania
29 □2 Ie-suido str. Japan
127 C6 Ifakara Tanzania
43 C5 'Ifāl, W. watercourse Saudi Arabia
129 H3 Ifanadiana Madagascar
123 E5 Ife Nigeria
123 F3 Iferouâne Niger
121 E3 Ifetesene mt. Algeria
83 G1 Iffeldorf Germany
87 H4 Iffezheim Germany
15 E3 Iffley Queensland Australia
56 G1 Ifjord Norway
123 F5 Ifon Nigeria
120 C2 Ifrane Morocco
89 E2 Ifs France
81 F5 Ig Slovenia
29 F6 Iga Japan
123 F4 Igabi Nigeria
127 B6 Igalula Tanzania
20 F6 Igan Malaysia
127 B4 Iganga Uganda
166 F2 Igaraçu Brazil
168 E4 Igarapava Brazil
166 C1 Igarape Açú Brazil
166 D1 Igarapé Grande Brazil
44 K3 Igarka Rus. Fed.
173 F5 Igarzabal Argentina
38 A2 Igatpuri India
123 E5 Igbeti Nigeria
42 F2 Iğdır Turkey
75 J4 Iggensbach Germany
56 E3 Iggesund Sweden
59 G1 Iggön i. Sweden
83 E2 Igis Switzerland
108 A5 Iglesias Sardegna Italy
120 D2 Igli Algeria
80 B2 Igling Germany
135 K3 Igloolik N.W.T. Canada
43 B5 'Igma, Gebel el plat. Egypt
138 B4 Ignace Ontario Canada
156 D2 Ignacio Zaragosa Mexico
54 E4 Ignalina Lithuania
31 G1 Ignashino Rus. Fed.
42 B1 İğneada Turkey
112 G4 İğneada Burnu pt Turkey
25 A5 Ignoitijala Andaman and Nicobar Is India
90 C1 Ignon r. France
127 B6 Igoma Tanzania
127 B5 Igombe r. Tanzania
90 C1 Igornay France
114 B3 Igoumenitsa Greece
98 B2 Igrexario Spain
44 H3 Igrim Rus. Fed.
167 B6 Iguaçu r. Brazil
170 F2 Iguaçu Falls waterfall Argentina/Brazil
168 B6 Iguaçu, Parque Nacional do nat. park Argentina
169 H1 Iguaí Brazil
157 F5 Iguala Mexico
102 E3 Igualada Spain
168 E6 Iguape Brazil
166 D1 Iguará r. Brazil
167 D5 Iguarapé Brazil
169 F4 Iguatama Brazil
168 A5 Iguatemi r. Brazil
168 A5 Iguatemi Brazil
166 E2 Iguatu Brazil
124 A4 Iguéla Gabon
98 D2 Igueña Spain
127 B5 Igunga Tanzania
129 H1 Iharaña Madagascar
78 G5 Iharosberény Hungary
30 C4 Ihbulag Mongolia
121 F3 Iherir Algeria
30 C3 Ihhayrhan Mongolia
123 F5 Ihiala Nigeria
43 A5 Ihnâsya el Madîna Egypt
93 A5 Iholdy France
129 H3 Ihosy Madagascar
74 C4 Ihringen Germany
30 C2 Ihsuuj Mongolia
31 G4 Ih Tal China
29 F6 Iida Japan
29 G5 Iide-san mt. Japan
56 H1 Iijärvi l. Finland
56 G2 Iijoki r. Finland
56 G3 Iisalmi Finland
54 E1 Iitti Finland
29 G5 Iiyama Japan
28 C7 Iizuka Japan
123 E5 Ijebu-Ode Nigeria
68 D1 IJlst Netherlands
68 C2 IJmuiden Netherlands
120 B5 Ijnâouene well Mauritania
68 D2 IJssel r. Netherlands
68 D2 IJsselmeer l. Netherlands
68 D2 IJsselmuiden Netherlands
68 D2 IJsselstein Netherlands
167 B6 Ijuí r. Brazil
167 B6 Ijuí Brazil
69 B3 IJzendijke Netherlands
69 A3 Ijzer r. Belgium
57 F3 Ikaalinen Finland
131 F2 Ikageleng South Africa
131 F3 Ikageng South Africa
129 H2 Ikahavo h. Madagascar
129 H3 Ikalamavony Madagascar
124 D4 Ikali Congo(Zaire)
9 C5 Ikamatua New Zealand
125 D4 Ikanda-Nord Congo(Zaire)
123 F5 Ikare Nigeria
125 C4 Ikari Congo(Zaire)
113 F6 Ikaria i. Greece
55 B3 Ikast Denmark
28 J2 Ikeda Japan
29 □2 Ikei-jima i. Japan
123 E5 Ikeja Nigeria
124 D4 Ikela Congo(Zaire)
124 C3 Ikelemba r. Congo(Zaire)
78 F4 Ikervár Hungary
112 D3 Ikhtiman Bulgaria
130 E4 Ikhutseng South Africa
28 B7 Iki i. Japan
51 H6 Iki-Burul Rus. Fed.
127 B5 Ikimba, Lake l. Tanzania
123 E5 Ikire Nigeria
28 B7 Iki-suidō chan. Japan
54 D3 Ikla Estonia
123 F5 Ikom Nigeria
129 H3 Ikongo Madagascar
129 H2 Ikopa r. Madagascar
123 E5 Ikorodu Nigeria
125 E4 Ikosi Congo(Zaire)
123 F5 Ikot Ekpene Nigeria
51 H6 Ikryanoye Rus. Fed.
127 B6 Ikungu Tanzania
28 E6 Ikuno Japan
53 A1 Ikva r. Ukraine
123 E5 Ila Nigeria
23 B2 Ilagan Philippines
126 C4 Ilaisamis Kenya
39 A2 Īlām div. Iran
42 F3 Īlām Iran
37 F4 Ilam Nepal
33 H3 I'lan Taiwan
129 H3 Ilanana r. Madagascar
73 K3 Ilanka r. Poland
83 E2 Ilanz Switzerland
53 F2 Ilarionove Ukraine
79 H3 Ilava Slovakia
77 H2 Iława Poland
39 D3 Ilazārān, Kūh-e mt. Iran
62 D4 Ilchester England U.K.
137 H3 Île-à-la-Crosse Saskatchewan Canada
137 H3 Île-à-la-Crosse, Lac l. Saskatchewan Canada
125 D4 Ilebo Congo(Zaire)
86 B4 Île-de-France div. France
127 B6 Ileje Tanzania
46 E2 Ilek r. Rus. Fed.
46 D2 Ilek Rus. Fed.
126 C4 Ileret Kenya
123 E5 Ilesa Nigeria
46 C1 Ilet' r. Rus. Fed.
73 F4 Ilfeld Germany
63 G3 Ilford England U.K.
137 K3 Ilford Manitoba Canada
62 B3 Ilfracombe England U.K.
15 F4 Ilfracombe Queensland Australia
42 C1 Ilgaz Turkey
42 B2 Ilgın Turkey
169 F5 Ilhabela Brazil
163 D4 Ilha Grande Brazil
169 F5 Ilha Grande, Baía da b. Brazil
98 B4 Ílhavo Portugal
169 J1 Ilhéus Brazil
122 □ Ilhéus Secos ou do Rombo i. Cape Verde
115 C5 Ilia div. Greece
79 M6 Ilia Romania
134 C4 Iliamna Lake l. Alaska U.S.A.
42 D2 İliç Turkey
47 G4 Il'ich Kazakhstan
Il'ichevsk see Şärur
23 C4 Iligan Philippines
23 C4 Iligan Bay b. Philippines
104 G4 Ilijaš Bos.-Herz.
30 E2 Il'inskiy Rus. Fed.
52 C1 Il'inskoye Rus. Fed.
52 D1 Il'inskoye Rus. Fed.
52 B3 Il'inskoye Rus. Fed.
52 D1 Il'inskoye-Khovanskoye Rus. Fed.
52 G1 Il'insko-Zaborskoye Rus. Fed.
147 F3 Ilion New York U.S.A.
107 J3 Ilirska Bistrica Slovenia
38 B3 Ilkal India
63 E2 Ilkeston England U.K.
52 E2 Il'kino Rus. Fed.
65 G4 Ilkley England U.K.
111 □ Il-Kullana pt Malta
87 G4 Ill r. France
164 C3 Illampu, Nevado de mt. Bolivia
23 B5 Illana Bay b. Philippines
172 B1 Illapel r. Chile
172 B1 Illapel Chile
101 H4 Illar Spain
83 G3 Illasi r. Italy
12 C1 Illbillee, Mt h. S. Australia Australia
88 D3 Ille r. France
88 D3 Ille-et-Vilaine div. France
123 F4 Illéla Niger
74 F4 Iller r. Germany
74 F4 Illertissen Germany
99 G4 Illescas Spain
173 K2 Illescas Uruguay
93 E6 Ille-sur-Têt France
53 D3 Illichivs'k Ukraine
89 G3 Illiers-Combray France
164 C3 Illimani, Nevado de mt. Bolivia
53 D3 Illinka Ukraine
148 C5 Illinois div. U.S.A.
148 C5 Illinois r. Illinois U.S.A.
148 B5 Illinois and Mississippi Canal canal Illinois U.S.A.
53 C2 Illintsi Ukraine
121 F3 Illizi Algeria
87 G4 Illkirch-Graffenstaden France
83 E1 Illmensee Germany
81 H3 Illmitz Austria
101 G3 Íllora Spain
102 B3 Illueca Spain
90 F1 Illzach France
75 G4 Ilm r. Bayern Germany
73 G5 Ilm r. Thüringen Germany
73 F2 Ilmenau r. Germany
75 F2 Ilmenau Germany
50 D3 Il'men', Ozero l. Rus. Fed.
62 D4 Ilminster England U.K.
75 G4 Ilmmünster Germany
164 B3 Ilo Peru
23 A4 Iloc i. Philippines
172 A3 Iloca Chile
23 B4 Iloilo Philippines
56 H3 Ilomantsi Finland
123 E5 Ilorin Nigeria
51 F6 Ilovays'k Ukraine
107 J4 Ilovik i. Croatia
51 H5 Ilovlya r. Rus. Fed.
51 G5 Ilovlya Rus. Fed.
76 D4 Iłowa Poland
77 J2 Iłowo Osada Poland
45 S3 Il'pyrskiy Rus. Fed.
111 □ Il Qala Ta San Blas b. Malta
72 F3 Ilsede Germany
73 F4 Ilsenburg Germany
74 E3 Ilshofen Germany
51 F6 Il'skiy Rus. Fed.
54 E4 Ilūkste Latvia
135 N3 Ilulissat Greenland
123 F5 Ilushi Nigeria
54 E4 Il'ya Belarus
46 E4 Il'yaly Turkmenistan
52 F1 Il'ya-Vysokovo Rus. Fed.
75 J4 Ilz r. Germany
81 G3 Ilz Austria
77 K4 Iłża Poland
28 D6 Imabari Japan
163 F3 Imabú r. Brazil
29 G5 Imaichi Japan
29 F6 Imajō Japan
129 F1 Imala Mozambique
56 J2 Imandra Rus. Fed.
44 E3 Imandra, Ozero l. Rus. Fed.
129 H3 Imanombo Madagascar
170 E2 Iman, Sa del h. Argentina
28 B7 Imari Japan
167 C6 Imaruí Brazil
164 B3 Imata Peru
114 D2 Imathia div. Greece
57 H3 Imatra Finland
54 D2 Imavere Estonia
29 F6 Imazu Japan
167 C6 Imbituba Brazil
168 C6 Imbituva Brazil
50 G3 imeni Babushkina Rus. Fed.
46 F5 imeni Chapayeva Turkmenistan
53 F1 imeni Karla Libknekhta Rus. Fed
50 H3 imeni M.I. Kalinina Rus. Fed.
52 G2 imeni Stepana Razina Rus. Fed.
imeni 26 Bakinskikh Komissarov see Bakı Komissarı, 26
52 E2 imeni Vorovskogo Rus. Fed.
53 F2 Imeny Lenina, Ozero l. Ukraine
126 D3 Īmī Ethiopia
120 C2 Imi-n-Tanoute Morocco
120 B3 Imirikliy Labyad reg. Western Sahara
Imishli see İmişli
42 G2 İmişli Azerbaijan
31 H6 Imja Do i. South Korea
120 A4 Imlili Western Sahara
83 D1 Immendingen Germany
83 E1 Immenstaad am Bodensee Germany
74 F5 Immenstadt im Allgäu Germany
65 H4 Immingham England U.K.
123 F5 Imo div. Nigeria
123 F5 Imo r. Nigeria
107 F4 Imola Italy
104 F4 Imotski Croatia
131 G4 Impendle South Africa
166 C2 Imperatriz Brazil
106 B5 Imperia div. Liguria Italy
106 C5 Imperia Italy
172 A5 Imperial r. Chile
150 C3 Imperial Nebraska U.S.A.
164 A2 Imperial Peru
154 D5 Imperial Beach California U.S.A.
155 E5 Imperial Valley v. California U.S.A.
16 B3 Imperieuse Reef Western Australia Australia
124 C3 Impfondo Congo
37 H4 Imphal India
90 B2 Imphy France
107 F5 Impruneta Italy
113 G4 İmralı Adası i. Turkey
113 E4 İmroz Turkey
80 B3 Imst div. Austria
80 B3 Imst Austria
42 D3 Imtān Syria
156 C2 Imuris Mexico
23 A4 Imuruan Bay b. Philippines
77 N3 Imyanin Belarus
52 G2 Imza r. Rus. Fed.
96 E5 Imzouren Morocco
76 C2 Ina r. Poland
29 F6 Ina Japan
123 E3 I-n-Âbâlene well Mali
128 □3 Inaccessible I. i. Tristan da Cunha Atlantic Ocean
168 C6 Inácio Martins Brazil
121 F4 In Afaleleh well Algeria
29 G5 Ina-gawa r. Japan
166 B2 Inaja r. Brazil
166 E2 Inajá Brazil
123 D3 I-n-Akhmed well Mali
122 D2 I-n-Akli well Mali
123 E3 I-n-Alchig well Mali
122 D3 I-n-Aleï well Mali
120 C5 I-n-'Amar well Mauritania
164 B2 Inambari r. Peru
164 C2 Inambari Peru
121 F3 In Aménas Algeria
121 F4 In Amguel Algeria
131 H4 Inanda South Africa
9 C4 Inangahua Junction New Zealand
21 K7 Inanwatan Indonesia
164 C2 Iñapari Peru
23 □2 Inarajan Guam Pacific Ocean
123 E3 I-n-Areï well Mali
56 G1 Inari Finland
56 G1 Inarijärvi l. Finland
56 G1 Inarijoki r. Finland
123 E3 I-n-Atankarer well Mali
162 D5 Inauini r. Brazil
29 H5 Inawashiro-ko l. Japan
123 F2 In-Azaoua well Niger
118 B2 In Azar well Libya
29 F6 Inazawa Japan
123 E3 I-n-Azerraf well Mali
121 E3 In Belbel Algeria
103 F5 Inca Spain
113 F4 İnce Burnu pt Turkey
42 C1 İnce Burun headland Turkey
42 C2 Incekum Burun pt Turkey
67 B4 Inch Kerry Rep. of Ireland
67 E4 Inch Wicklow Rep. of Ireland
66 C2 Inchard, Loch b. Scotland U.K.
89 G1 Incheville France
126 C4 Inch'īnī Terara mt. Ethiopia
120 A5 Inchiri div. Mauritania
64 A2 Inch Island i. Rep. of Ireland
66 E4 Inchkeith i. Scotland U.K.
31 H5 Inch'ŏn South Korea
99 G2 Incinillas Spain
107 F5 Incisa in Val d'Arno Italy
131 J2 Incomati r. Mozambique
69 C4 Incourt Belgium
66 B5 Indaal, Loch inlet Scotland U.K.
122 D2 I-n-Dagouber well Mali
169 F3 Indaiá r. Brazil
168 B3 Indaiá Grande r. Brazil
168 E5 Indaiatuba Brazil
57 E3 Indalsälven r. Sweden
58 A1 Indalstø Norway
126 C2 Inda Silasē Ethiopia
24 B2 Indaw Myanmar
24 B1 Indawgyi, L. l. Myanmar
156 D3 Indé Mexico
154 C3 Independence California U.S.A.
148 B4 Independence Iowa U.S.A.
151 E4 Independence Kansas U.S.A.
148 A2 Independence Minnesota U.S.A.
150 E4 Independence Missouri U.S.A.
146 C6 Independence Virginia U.S.A.
148 B3 Independence Wisconsin U.S.A.
135 P1 Independence Fj. inlet Greenland
152 C3 Independence Mts mountain range Nevada U.S.A.
164 C3 Independencia Bolivia
164 A2 Independencia, B. de b. Peru
112 F2 Independența Călărași Romania
112 G3 Independența Constanța Romania
112 F2 Independența Galați Romania
126 C3 Inderacha Ethiopia
46 D3 Inderborskiy Kazakhstan
46 D3 Inder, Oz. salt lake Kazakhstan
38 B2 Indi India
18 J7 India country Asia
148 D2 Indian r. Michigan U.S.A.
148 D5 Indiana div. U.S.A.
146 D4 Indiana Pennsylvania U.S.A.
148 D5 Indiana Dunes National Lakeshore res. Indiana U.S.A.
175 O7 Indian-Antarctic Ridge sea feature Pacific Ocean
148 D6 Indianapolis airport Indiana U.S.A.
148 D6 Indianapolis Indiana U.S.A.
139 J3 Indian Harbour Newfoundland Canada
148 D3 Indian Lake l. Michigan U.S.A.
146 B4 Indian Lake l. Ohio U.S.A.
146 D4 Indian Lake l. Pennsylvania U.S.A.
147 F3 Indian Lake New York U.S.A.
150 E3 Indianola Iowa U.S.A.
151 F5 Indianola Mississippi U.S.A.
168 E3 Indianópolis Brazil
155 F2 Indian Peak summit Utah U.S.A.
148 E3 Indian River Michigan U.S.A.
155 E3 Indian Springs Nevada U.S.A.
155 G4 Indian Wells Arizona U.S.A.
166 B3 Indigena Do Xingu, Parque nat. park Brazil
45 Q2 Indigirka r. Rus. Fed.
112 C2 Inđija Yugoslavia
136 F2 Indin Lake l. N.W.T. Canada
154 D5 Indio California U.S.A.
173 G5 Indio Rico Argentina
19 N10 Indonesia country Asia
36 C5 Indore India
22 B3 Indramayu Indonesia
22 B3 Indramayu, Tg pt Indonesia
38 C2 Indravati r. India
92 D2 Indre div. Centre France
92 D1 Indre r. France
58 A1 Indre Arna Norway
89 F4 Indre-et-Loire div. France
Indur see Nizamabad
77 M2 Indura Belarus
36 B4 Indus r. Pakistan
36 A4 Indus, Mouths of the river mouth Pakistan
131 F5 Indwe r. South Africa
131 F5 Indwe South Africa
121 F4 In Ebeggi well Algeria
42 C1 İnebolu Turkey
122 D2 I-n-Échaï well Mali
42 B1 İnegöl Turkey
121 F4 In Ekker Algeria
22 E4 Inerie volcano Indonesia
79 L5 Ineu Romania
146 B6 Inez Kentucky U.S.A.
121 G4 In Ezzane well Algeria
130 C7 Infanta, Cape headland South Africa
157 E5 Infiernillo, L. l. Mexico
99 E1 Infiesto Spain
54 D1 Ingå Finland
50 E1 Inga Rus. Fed.
24 A3 Ingabu Myanmar
123 F3 Ingal Niger
148 D3 Ingalls Michigan U.S.A.
137 J2 Ingalls Lake l. N.W.T. Canada
154 B2 Ingalls, Mt mt. California U.S.A.
47 H1 Ingaly Rus. Fed.
63 G3 Ingatestone England U.K.
59 F3 Ingatorp Sweden
74 D3 Ingelheim am Rhein Germany
69 B4 Ingelmunster Belgium
124 C4 Ingende Congo(Zaire)
172 D3 Ingeniero Balloffet Argentina
170 D1 Ingeniero Guillermo Nueva Juárez Argentina
171 C5 Ingeniero Jacobacci Argentina
172 E3 Ingeniero Luiggi Argentina
172 C1 Ingeniero Matías G. Sanchez Argentina
97 □ Ingenio Canary Is Spain
87 G4 Ingersheim France
140 E5 Ingersoll Ontario Canada
30 B2 Ingettolgoy Mongolia
15 F3 Ingham Queensland Australia
65 F3 Ingleborough h. England U.K.
135 L2 Inglefield Land reg. Greenland
65 F3 Ingleton England U.K.
15 G6 Inglewood Queensland Australia
13 E4 Inglewood Victoria Australia
8 E3 Inglewood New Zealand
65 F3 Inglewood Forest forest England U.K.
30 E2 Ingoda r. Rus. Fed.
63 G1 Ingoldmells England U.K.
75 G4 Ingolstadt Germany
139 H4 Ingonish Nova Scotia Canada
37 G4 Ingrāj Bāzār India
92 C2 Ingrandes France
136 F2 Ingray Lake l. N.W.T. Canada
164 D4 Ingre Bolivia
89 G4 Ingré France
179 D5 Ingrid Christensen Coast coastal area Antarctica
121 F5 I-n-Guezzam Algeria
88 B4 Inguiniel France
Inguri r. see Enguri
51 H7 Ingushetiya div. Rus. Fed.
131 J3 Ingwavuma South Africa
87 G4 Ingwiller France
131 J3 Inhaca e dos Portugueses, Ilhas da is Mozambique
131 J3 Inhaca Peninsula pen. Mozambique
129 E3 Inhambane div. Mozambique
129 F3 Inhambane Mozambique
129 F3 Inhambane, Baia de b. Mozambique
166 E3 Inhambupe Brazil
129 F2 Inhaminga Mozambique
168 A4 Inhanduízinho r. Brazil
169 G3 Inhapim Brazil
129 F3 Inharrime Mozambique
166 D3 Inhaúmas Brazil
169 H1 Inhobim Brazil
53 E3 Inhul r. Ukraine
53 E3 Inhulets' r. Ukraine
53 E3 Inhulets' Ukraine
168 D2 Inhumas Brazil
103 B5 Iniesta Spain
169 F3 Inimutaba Brazil
163 G3 Inini French Guiana
59 J1 Iniö Finland
162 D3 Inírida r. Colombia
Inis see Ennis
Inis Córthaidh see Enniscorthy
67 A3 Inishark i. Rep. of Ireland
67 A3 Inishbofin i. Rep. of Ireland
67 C1 Inishbofin Rep. of Ireland
67 B3 Inisheer i. Rep. of Ireland
67 A2 Inishkea North i. Rep. of Ireland
67 A2 Inishkea South i. Rep. of Ireland
67 B3 Inishmaan i. Rep. of Ireland
67 B3 Inishmore i. Rep. of Ireland
67 C2 Inishmurray i. Rep. of Ireland
67 D1 Inishowen pen. Rep. of Ireland
67 E1 Inishowen Head headland Rep. of Ireland
67 A4 Inishtooskert i. Rep. of Ireland
67 D1 Inishtrahull i. Rep. of Ireland
67 D1 Inishtrahull Sound chan. Rep. of Ireland
67 A3 Inishturk i. Rep. of Ireland
31 F3 Injgan Sum China
126 C2 Injibara Ethiopia
15 G5 Injune Queensland Australia
15 E3 Inkerman Queensland Australia
39 E1 Inkylap Turkmenistan
9 D5 Inland Kaikoura Range mountain range New Zealand
24 B2 Inle, L. l. Myanmar
80 D2 Inn r. Europe
12 E1 Innamincka S. Australia Australia
56 D2 Inndyr Norway
66 E5 Innerleithen Scotland U.K.
Inner Mongolian Aut. Region div. see Nei Mongol Zizhiqu
66 C3 Inner Sound chan. Scotland U.K.
82 D2 Innertkirchen Switzerland
80 D4 Innervillgraten Austria
15 F3 Innisfail Queensland Australia
31 J2 Innokent'yevka Rus. Fed.
28 D6 Innoshima Japan
80 C3 Innsbruck div. Austria
80 C3 Innsbruck Austria
81 E2 Innviertel reg. Austria
67 D3 Inny r. Rep. of Ireland
168 C3 Inocência Brazil
124 C4 Inongo Congo(Zaire)
122 D3 I-n-Ouchef well Mali
79 H3 Inovec mt. Slovakia
76 G3 Inowrocław Poland
164 C3 Inquisivi Bolivia
82 C1 Ins Switzerland
121 E3 In Salah Algeria
52 G2 Insar r. Rus. Fed.
52 G3 Insar Rus. Fed.
66 F3 Insch Scotland U.K.
17 A5 Inscription, C. c. Western Australia Australia
24 B3 Insein Myanmar
76 D2 Ińsko Poland
112 G2 Insula Sacalinul Mare i. Romania
112 F2 Însurăței Romania
129 D2 Insuza r. Zimbabwe
44 H3 Inta Rus. Fed.
123 F3 I-n-Tabakat well Niger
123 F2 I-n-Tadéra well Niger
123 E3 I-n-Talak well Mali
123 E3 I-n-Tebezas Mali
123 F3 I-n-Tédéïni well Niger
172 F3 Intendente Alvear Argentina
113 F4 İntepe Turkey
82 C2 Interlaken Switzerland

J

82 B2 **Joux, Vallée de v.** Switzerland
89 G3 **Jouy** France
87 F3 **Jouy-aux-Arches** France
37 H4 **Jowai** India
67 B3 **Joyce's Country reg.** Rep. of Ireland
91 C4 **Joyeuse** France
77 K4 **Józefów** *Lublin* Poland
77 M5 **Józefów** *Zamość* Poland
120 A5 **Jreïda** Mauritania
156 E3 **Juan Aldama** Mexico
173 G3 **Juan B. Alberdi** Argentina
31 E6 **Juancheng** China
173 J4 **Juancho** Argentina
152 A1 **Juan de Fuca, Str. of chan.** *Washington* U.S.A.
172 E5 **Juan de Garay** Argentina
129 G2 **Juan de Nova i.** Indian Ocean
173 G4 **Juan E. Barra** Argentina
177 O8 **Juan Fernández, Islas is** Chile
159 G5 **Juangriego** Venezuela
172 E2 **Juan Jorba** Argentina
173 H2 **Juan Jorge** Argentina
173 F3 **Juan José Paso** Argentina
162 B5 **Juanjuí** Peru
56 H3 **Juankoski** Finland
91 F5 **Juan-les-Pins** France
173 J3 **Juan. L. Lacaze** Uruguay
172 E2 **Juan Llerena** Argentina
173 H5 **Juan N. Fernández** Argentina
156 J7 **Juan Santamaria airport** Costa Rica
157 E3 **Juaréz** Mexico
156 A1 **Juárez, Sierra de mountain range** Mexico
166 D2 **Juàzeiro** Brazil
166 E2 **Juàzeiro do Norte** Brazil
122 C5 **Juazohn** Liberia
37 E5 **Juba** India
126 B4 **Juba** Sudan
126 D4 **Jubba r.** Somalia
127 D4 **Jubbada Dhexe div.** Somalia
127 D4 **Jubbada Hoose div.** Somalia
72 E1 **Jübek** Germany
17 D6 **Jubilee L. salt flat** *Western Australia* Australia
154 D4 **Jubilee Pass pass** *California* U.S.A.
173 H1 **Jubileo** Argentina
120 B3 **Juby, Cap pt** Morocco
103 C5 **Júcar r.** Spain
158 C2 **Jucaro** Cuba
157 F5 **Juchatengo** Mexico
72 B4 **Jüchen** Germany
156 E4 **Juchipila** Mexico
157 G5 **Juchitán** Mexico
156 D4 **Juchitlán** Mexico
77 M2 **Juchnowiec Dolny** Poland
169 J2 **Jucuruçu** Brazil
169 J2 **Jucuruçu r.** Brazil
42 E4 **Judaidat al Hamir** Iraq
42 E4 **Judayyidat 'Ar'ar well** Iraq
81 F3 **Judenburg div.** Austria
81 F3 **Judenburg** Austria
99 H3 **Judes mt.** Spain
101 G2 **Juego de Bolos mt.** Spain
55 C4 **Juelsminde** Denmark
162 J2 **Juerana** Brazil
88 C3 **Jugon-les-Lacs** France
30 D5 **Juh** China
119 G2 **Juhaynah reg.** Saudi Arabia
31 G4 **Juhua Dao i.** China
156 J6 **Juigalpa** Nicaragua
92 D3 **Juillac** France
165 E2 **Juina r.** Brazil
165 E2 **Juinamirim r.** Brazil
86 B4 **Juine r.** France
72 C2 **Juist i.** Germany
169 G4 **Juiz de Fora** Brazil
90 D2 **Jujurieux** France
170 C1 **Jujuy div.** Argentina
164 C4 **Julaca** Bolivia
58 D1 **Julassa r.** Norway
81 E2 **Julbach** Austria
152 G3 **Julesburg** *Colorado* U.S.A.
164 C3 **Juli** Peru
164 B3 **Juliaca** Peru
15 E4 **Julia Cr. r.** *Queensland* Australia
15 E4 **Julia Cr.** *Queensland* Australia
69 D3 **Juliana Kanaal canal** Netherlands
163 F3 **Juliana Top summit** Surinam
Julianehåb *see* **Qaqortoq**
74 B2 **Jülich** Germany
90 C2 **Julien, Mont h.** France
81 E4 **Julijske Alpe mts** Slovenia
173 G4 **Julio, 16 de** Argentina
173 G3 **Julio, 9 de** Argentina
14 D4 **Julius, Lake l.** *Queensland* Australia
88 D3 **Jullouville** France
55 B3 **Julsø l.** Denmark
32 B1 **Jumanggoin** China
162 B5 **Jumbilla** Peru
91 B3 **Jumeaux** France
92 D3 **Jumilhac-le-Grand** France
103 B6 **Jumilla** Spain
37 E3 **Jumla** Nepal
43 C4 **Jum Suwwāna mt.** Jordan
36 B5 **Junagadh** India
38 C2 **Junagarh** India
33 G1 **Junan** China
31 F3 **Jun Bulen** China
170 B3 **Juncal mt.** Chile
172 B2 **Juncal, Co mt.** Argentina/Chile
173 F6 **Juncal, L. l.** Argentina
145 □3 **Juncos** Puerto Rico
151 D6 **Junction** *Texas* U.S.A.
153 D4 **Junction** *Utah* U.S.A.
14 C1 **Junction B. b.** *Northern Terr.* Australia
150 D4 **Junction City** *Kansas* U.S.A.
15 E5 **Jundah** *Queensland* Australia
169 E5 **Jundiaí** Brazil
136 C3 **Juneau** *Alaska* U.S.A.
102 D3 **Juneda** Spain
16 C3 **Jün el Khudr b.** Lebanon
82 C2 **Jungfrau mt.** Switzerland
47 L3 **Junggar Pendi basin** China
69 E5 **Junglinster** Luxembourg
36 A4 **Jungshahi** Pakistan
126 B2 **Junguls** Sudan
146 E4 **Juniata r.** *Pennsylvania* U.S.A.
173 G3 **Junin** Argentina
164 A2 **Junin** Peru
172 B5 **Junín de los Andes** Argentina
147 K1 **Juniper** *New Brunswick* Canada
154 B3 **Junipero Serro Peak summit** *California* U.S.A.
29 H3 **Jūnisho reg.** Japan
86 D3 **Juniville** France
69 E4 **Jünkerath** Germany
32 D2 **Junlian** China
38 A2 **Junnar** India
56 E3 **Junsele** Sweden
33 G2 **Junshan Hu l.** China
152 C3 **Juntura** *Oregon* U.S.A.
33 E1 **Jun Xian** China
32 B1 **Ju'nyunggoin** China
54 B4 **Juodkrantė** Lithuania
54 D3 **Juodupe** Lithuania
54 D4 **Juostinikai** Lithuania
54 D4 **Juozapinės kalnas h.** Lithuania
169 H3 **Juparanã, Lagoa l.** Brazil
168 C4 **Jupiá** Brazil
89 F4 **Jupilles** France
69 D4 **Juprelle** Belgium
168 E6 **Juquiá r.** Brazil
168 E6 **Juquiá** Brazil
124 E2 **Jur r.** Sudan
90 D2 **Jura div.** France
82 C1 **Jura div.** Switzerland
66 C4 **Jura i.** *Scotland* U.K.
82 A2 **Jura mountain range** France/Switzerland
166 D3 **Jurací** Brazil
162 B2 **Juradó** Colombia
169 G2 **Juramento** Brazil
93 B5 **Jurançon** France
66 C5 **Jura, Sound of chan.** *Scotland* U.K.
57 F5 **Jurbarkas** Lithuania
69 B4 **Jurbise** Belgium
42 C4 **Jurf ed Darāwīsh** Jordan
73 H2 **Jürgenstorf** Germany
31 G3 **Jurh** China
31 G3 **Jurhe** China
37 G2 **Jurhen Ul Shan mountain range** China
54 D2 **Jüri** Estonia
92 B3 **Jurignac** France
112 G2 **Jurilovca** Romania
166 A1 **Juriti Velho** Brazil
107 J4 **Jurjevo** Croatia
54 C3 **Jūrmala** Latvia
59 J1 **Jurmo** Finland
56 G2 **Jurmu** Finland
33 G2 **Jurong** China
25 □ **Jurong** Singapore
162 D5 **Juruá r.** Brazil
163 D4 **Juruá** Brazil
162 C5 **Juruá Mirim r.** Brazil
165 E1 **Juruena r.** Brazil
166 B3 **Juruna r.** Brazil
166 A1 **Juruti** Brazil
57 F3 **Jurva** Finland
28 H3 **Jūsan-ko l.** Japan
159 G5 **Jusepín** Venezuela
43 D2 **Jūsīyah** Syria
92 E4 **Jussac** France
54 C2 **Jussarö i.** Finland
90 D1 **Jussey** France
173 F2 **Justiniano Posse** Argentina
172 E2 **Justo Daract** Argentina
162 D5 **Jutaí r.** Brazil
162 D5 **Jutaí** *Amazonas* Brazil
166 B1 **Jutai, Sa do h.** Brazil
73 J4 **Jüterbog** Germany
168 A5 **Juti** Brazil
157 H6 **Jutiapa** Guatemala
157 J6 **Juticalpa** Honduras
56 E2 **Jutis** Sweden
Jutland pen. *see* **Jylland**
76 E2 **Jutrosin** Poland
56 H3 **Juuka** Finland
54 E1 **Juurikorpi** Finland
57 G3 **Juva** Finland
158 B2 **Juventud, Isla de la i.** Cuba
89 D3 **Juvigny-le-Tertre** France
89 E3 **Juvigny-sous-Andaine** France
39 E3 **Juwain** Afghanistan
22 B3 **Juwana** Indonesia
31 F6 **Ju Xian** China
30 B4 **Juyan** China
33 G1 **Juye** China
39 D2 **Jūymand** Iran
39 C3 **Jūyom** Iran
86 D4 **Juzennecourt** France
128 C3 **Jwaneng** Botswana
55 D4 **Jyderup** Denmark
55 A3 **Jylland pen.** Denmark
55 E4 **Jyllinge** Denmark
57 G3 **Jyväskylä** Finland
57 G3 **Jyväskylän mlk** Finland

K

36 D2 **K2 mt.** China/Jammu and Kashmir
31 H5 **Ka i.** North Korea
123 E4 **Ka r.** Nigeria
46 E5 **Kaakhka** Turkmenistan
153 □1 **Kaala mt.** *Hawaii* U.S.A.
6 □2 **Kaala-Gomen** *New Caledonia* Pacific Ocean
131 H2 **Kaalrug** South Africa
127 D5 **Kaambooni** Kenya
130 D6 **Kaapse Poortjie pass** South Africa
57 F3 **Kaarina** Finland
73 G2 **Kaarßen** Germany
72 B4 **Kaarst** Germany
122 C4 **Kaarta reg.** Mali
56 H3 **Kaavi** Finland
Kaba *see* **Habahe**
21 H8 **Kabaena i.** Indonesia
46 F5 **Kabakly** Turkmenistan
122 B5 **Kabala** Sierra Leone
127 A5 **Kabale** Uganda
125 E5 **Kabalo** Congo(Zaire)
125 E5 **Kabamba, Lac l.** Congo(Zaire)
125 E4 **Kabambare** Congo(Zaire)
125 D6 **Kabangu** Congo(Zaire)
30 C2 **Kabansk** Rus. Fed.
6 □7 **Kabara i.** Fiji
51 G7 **Kabardino-Balkariya div.** Rus. Fed.
124 E4 **Kabare** Congo(Zaire)
28 B7 **Kaba-shima i.** Japan
57 F2 **Kåbdalis** Sweden
28 D6 **Kabe** Japan
140 C2 **Kabenung Lake l.** *Ontario* Canada
121 E3 **Kabertene** Algeria
140 C2 **Kabinakagami r.** *Ontario* Canada
140 C2 **Kabinakagami Lake l.** *Ontario* Canada
125 D5 **Kabinda** Congo(Zaire)
54 D2 **Kabli** Estonia
124 C2 **Kabo** Central African Rep.
125 D6 **Kabompo r.** Zambia
125 D6 **Kabompo** Zambia
22 B1 **Kabong** Malaysia
125 E5 **Kabongo** Congo(Zaire)
123 E5 **Kabou** Togo
39 E2 **Kabūdeh** Iran
39 D1 **Kabūd Gonbad** Iran
39 B2 **Kabūd Rāhang** Iran
23 B2 **Kabugao** Philippines
39 G2 **Kabul r.** Afghanistan
39 G2 **Kābul** Afghanistan
125 E6 **Kabunda** Congo(Zaire)
22 B4 **Kabunduk** Indonesia
23 C6 **Kaburuang i.** Indonesia
119 F4 **Kabushiya** Sudan
125 E6 **Kabwe** Zambia
125 E5 **Kabwe, Lac l.** Congo(Zaire)
46 F2 **Kabyrga r.** Kazakhstan
112 C3 **Kačanik** Yugoslavia
39 E3 **Kacha Kuh mountain range** Iran/Pakistan
51 H5 **Kachalinskaya** Rus. Fed.
36 B5 **Kachchh, Gulf of b.** India
36 A3 **Kachh** Pakistan
123 F5 **Kachia** Nigeria
24 B1 **Kachin State div.** Myanmar
127 B5 **Kachira, Lake l.** Uganda
47 J2 **Kachiry** Kazakhstan
26 J1 **Kachug** Rus. Fed.
42 E1 **Kackar Daği mt.** Turkey
76 E2 **Kaczory** Poland
52 H3 **Kadada r.** Rus. Fed.
24 B3 **Kadaingti** Myanmar
38 B4 **Kadaiyanallur** India
126 B4 **Kadam mt.** Uganda
78 C1 **Kadaň** Czech Rep.
39 F3 **Kadanai r.** Afghanistan/Pakistan
25 B4 **Kadan Kyun i.** Myanmar
22 C3 **Kadapongan i.** Indonesia
79 G5 **Kadarkút** Hungary
36 D4 **Kadaura** India
6 □7 **Kadavu i.** Fiji
6 □8 **Kadavu Passage chan.** Fiji
31 F2 **Kadaya** Rus. Fed.
124 C3 **Kadéï r.** Central African Rep.
29 □2 **Kadena** Japan
42 F3 **Kādhimain** Iraq
36 C5 **Kadi** India
42 B1 **Kadıköy** Turkey
12 D3 **Kadina** *S. Australia* Australia
42 C2 **Kadınhanı** Turkey
122 C4 **Kadiolo** Mali
122 B4 **Kadiondola, Mt mt.** Guinea
38 B3 **Kadiri** India
42 D2 **Kadirli** Turkey
123 E5 **Kadjebi** Ghana
35 D8 **Kadmat i.** India
50 G3 **Kadnikov** Rus. Fed.
150 C3 **Kadoka** *S. Dakota* U.S.A.
52 F2 **Kadom** Rus. Fed.
129 D2 **Kadoma** Zimbabwe
24 A4 **Kadonkani** Myanmar
52 G1 **Kadoshkino** Rus. Fed.
24 B2 **Kadu** Myanmar
126 B3 **Kadugli** Sudan
124 E1 **Kaduna div.** Nigeria
123 F4 **Kaduna r.** Nigeria
123 F4 **Kaduna** Nigeria
32 B2 **Kadusam mt.** China
50 F3 **Kaduy** Rus. Fed.
38 A2 **Kadwa r.** India
52 H2 **Kadyshevo** Rus. Fed.
50 G3 **Kadyy** Rus. Fed.
Kadzhi-Say *see* **Kajy-Say**
77 K2 **Kadzidło** Poland
31 H5 **Kaechon** North Korea
122 B3 **Kaédi** Mauritania
124 B1 **Kaélé** Cameroon
153 □2 **Kaena Pt pt** *Hawaii* U.S.A.
8 D1 **Kaeo** New Zealand
31 H5 **Kaesŏng** North Korea
119 G3 **Kāf** Saudi Arabia
125 D5 **Kafakumba** Congo(Zaire)
123 F5 **Kafanchan** Nigeria
123 G4 **Kaffin-Hausa** Nigeria
131 F4 **Kaffir r.** South Africa
122 A4 **Kaffrine** Senegal
124 D2 **Kafia Kingi** Sudan
43 D2 **Kafr Buhum** Syria
119 F1 **Kafr el Sheik** Egypt
43 A4 **Kafr Sa'd** Egypt
126 B4 **Kafu r.** Uganda
125 E7 **Kafue r.** Zambia
125 E7 **Kafue** Zambia
125 E6 **Kafue National Park nat. park** Zambia
29 F5 **Kaga** Japan
124 C2 **Kaga Bandoro** Central African Rep.
36 C2 **Kagan** Pakistan
46 F5 **Kagan** Uzbekistan
32 C1 **Kagang** China
123 F5 **Kagarko** Nigeria
28 E6 **Kagawa div.** Japan
140 D4 **Kagawong** *Ontario* Canada
56 F2 **Kåge** Sweden
127 B5 **Kagera div.** Tanzania
59 E4 **Kågeröd** Sweden
59 G3 **Kaggebo** Sweden
140 B2 **Kagiano Lake l.** *Ontario* Canada
131 F3 **Kagiso** South Africa
42 E1 **Kağızman** Turkey
115 C4 **Kagkadi** Greece
119 F5 **Kagmar** Sudan
123 F5 **Kagoro** Nigeria
28 C8 **Kagoshima div.** Japan
28 C8 **Kagoshima** Japan
28 C8 **Kagoshima-wan b.** Japan
30 A2 **Kagzhirba** Rus. Fed.
39 B2 **Kahak** Iran
43 C6 **Kahala, W. al watercourse** Saudi Arabia
153 □1 **Kahaluu** *Hawaii* U.S.A.
127 B5 **Kahama** Tanzania
36 B3 **Kahan** Pakistan
153 □1 **Kahana** *Hawaii* U.S.A.
53 D2 **Kaharlyk** Ukraine
128 A3 **Kahawero watercourse** Namibia
22 C2 **Kahayan r.** Indonesia
125 C5 **Kahemba** Congo(Zaire)
9 A6 **Kaherekoau Mts mts** New Zealand
75 G2 **Kahla** Germany
Kahnu *see* **Kahnūj**
39 D4 **Kahnūj** Iran
148 B5 **Kahoka** *Missouri* U.S.A.
153 □2 **Kahoolawe i.** *Hawaii* U.S.A.
42 D2 **Kahraman Maraş** Turkey
36 B3 **Kahror** Pakistan
42 D2 **Kahta** Turkey
9 □1 **Kahuitara Pt pt** *Chatham Is* New Zealand
153 □1 **Kahuku** *Hawaii* U.S.A.
153 □1 **Kahuku Pt pt** *Hawaii* U.S.A.
153 □2 **Kahului** *Hawaii* U.S.A.
39 D3 **Kahurak** Iran
8 D4 **Kahurangi Point pt** New Zealand
124 E4 **Kahuzi-Biega, Parc National du nat. park** Congo(Zaire)
115 C5 **Kaïafa** Greece
123 E5 **Kaiama** Nigeria
6 □1 **Kaiapit** P.N.G.
9 D5 **Kaiapoi** New Zealand
155 F3 **Kaibab** *Arizona* U.S.A.
153 D4 **Kaibab Plat. plat.** *Arizona* U.S.A.
28 E6 **Kaibara** Japan
21 K8 **Kai Besar i.** Indonesia
155 G3 **Kaibito** *Arizona* U.S.A.
155 G3 **Kaibito Plateau plat.** *Arizona* U.S.A.
47 K4 **Kaidu r.** China
33 F1 **Kaifeng** China
33 F1 **Kaifeng** China
8 D1 **Kaihu** New Zealand
33 G2 **Kaihua** China
130 C4 **Kaiingbulte reg.** South Africa
32 D2 **Kaijiang** China
21 K8 **Kai Kecil i.** Indonesia
9 D5 **Kaikohe** New Zealand
9 D5 **Kaikoura** New Zealand
9 D5 **Kaikoura Peninsula pen.** New Zealand
27 □ **Kai Kung Leng h.** *Hong Kong* China
122 B5 **Kailahun** Sierra Leone
Kailas mt. *see* **Kangrinboqê Feng**
Kailas Range mountain range *see* **Gangdisê Shan**
37 G4 **Kailāshahr** India
32 D3 **Kaili** China
126 C4 **Kailongong waterhole** Kenya
31 G4 **Kailu** China
153 □1 **Kailua** *Hawaii* U.S.A.
153 □2 **Kailua Kona** *Hawaii* U.S.A.
8 E2 **Kaimai Range h.** New Zealand
21 K7 **Kaimana** Indonesia
8 E3 **Kaimanawa Mountains mountain range** New Zealand
32 A1 **Kaimar** China
36 D4 **Kaimganj** India
37 E4 **Kaimur Range h.** India
54 C2 **Käina** Estonia
29 E6 **Kainan** Japan
28 E7 **Kainan** Japan
24 A2 **Kaing** Myanmar
123 E4 **Kaingiwa** Nigeria
123 E4 **Kainji Lake National Park nat. park** Nigeria
123 F5 **Kainji Lake Nat. Park nat. park** Nigeria
123 E4 **Kainji Reservoir resr** Nigeria
38 D1 **Kaintarāgarh** India
8 E2 **Kaipara Harbour harbour** New Zealand
155 G3 **Kaiparowits Plateau plat.** *Utah* U.S.A.
33 F4 **Kaiping** China
139 J3 **Kaipokok Bay inlet** *Newfoundland* Canada
36 D3 **Kairana** India
121 G1 **Kairouan** Tunisia
80 D3 **Kaisergebirge mts** Austria
69 F4 **Kaisersesch** Germany
74 C3 **Kaiserslautern** Germany
87 G4 **Kaiserstuhl h.** Germany
31 J4 **Kaishantun** China
80 B2 **Kaisheim** Germany
54 D4 **Kaišiadorys** Lithuania
8 D1 **Kaitaia** New Zealand
9 B7 **Kaitangata** New Zealand
8 F3 **Kaitawa** New Zealand
36 D3 **Kaithal** India
22 A2 **Kait, Tg pt** Indonesia
56 F2 **Kaitum** Sweden
21 J8 **Kaiwatu** Indonesia
153 □2 **Kaiwi Channel chan.** *Hawaii* U.S.A.
32 E2 **Kai Xian** China
32 D3 **Kaiyang** China
32 C4 **Kaiyuan** China
31 H4 **Kaiyuan** China
56 G2 **Kajaani** Finland
14 E4 **Kajabbi** *Queensland* Australia
39 F2 **Kajaki** Afghanistan
22 E3 **Kajang** Indonesia
25 C7 **Kajang** Malaysia
36 B3 **Kajanpur** Pakistan
81 F2 **Kájov** Czech Rep.
39 F2 **Kajrān** Afghanistan
123 F4 **Kajuru** Nigeria
47 J4 **Kajy-Say** Kyrgyzstan
126 B2 **Kaka** Sudan
138 C4 **Kakabeka Falls** *Ontario* Canada
14 C2 **Kakadu Nat. Park nat. park** *Northern Terr.* Australia
130 C4 **Kakamas** South Africa
127 B4 **Kakamega** Kenya
29 F6 **Kakamigahara** Japan
25 A5 **Kakana** *Andaman and Nicobar Is* India
104 G3 **Kakanj** Bos.-Herz.
9 C6 **Kakanui Mts mts** New Zealand
123 G4 **Kakarahil well** Niger
8 E3 **Kakaramea** New Zealand
79 H5 **Kakasd** Hungary
122 B5 **Kakata** Liberia
8 E3 **Kakatahi** New Zealand
37 H4 **Kakching** India
136 C3 **Kake** *Alaska* U.S.A.
28 D6 **Kake** Japan
29 G6 **Kakegawa** Japan
125 D4 **Kakenge** Congo(Zaire)
73 G3 **Kakerbeck** Germany
Kakhi *see* **Qax**
53 E3 **Kakhovka** Ukraine
53 E3 **Kakhovs'ke Vodoskhovyshche resr** Ukraine
39 B3 **Kākī** Iran
38 C2 **Kākināda** India
136 F2 **Kakisa r.** *N.W.T.* Canada
136 F2 **Kakisa** *N.W.T.* Canada
136 F2 **Kakisa Lake l.** *N.W.T.* Canada
54 B3 **Kākišķe** Latvia
28 E6 **Kakogawa** Japan
71 L3 **Kąkolewnica Wschodnia** Poland
36 E4 **Kakori** India
125 E4 **Kakoswa** Congo(Zaire)
122 D5 **Kakpin** Côte d'Ivoire
36 D4 **Kakrala** India
122 B4 **Kakrima r.** Guinea
114 B2 **Kakrukë** Albania
134 D2 **Kaktovik** *Alaska* U.S.A.
29 H5 **Kakuda** Japan
136 F4 **Kakwa r.** *Alberta* Canada
36 B3 **Kala** Pakistan
127 B6 **Kala** Tanzania
Kalaallit Nunaat terr. *see* **Greenland**
36 B2 **Kalabagh** Pakistan
21 H8 **Kalabahi** Indonesia
25 A3 **Kalabakan** Malaysia
126 E3 **Kalabaydh** *Nugaal* Somalia
126 D3 **Kalabaydh** *Woqooyi Galbeed* Somalia
12 E2 **Kalabity** *S. Australia* Australia
125 D6 **Kalabo** Zambia
51 G5 **Kalach** Rus. Fed.
39 F2 **Kalacha** Afghanistan
126 C4 **Kalacha Dida** Kenya
47 H2 **Kalachinsk** Rus. Fed.
51 G5 **Kalach-na-Donu** Rus. Fed.
24 A2 **Kaladan r.** India/Myanmar
141 G4 **Kaladar** *Ontario* Canada
153 □2 **Ka Lae c.** *Hawaii* U.S.A.
22 E2 **Kalaena r.** Indonesia
24 B2 **Kalagwe** Myanmar
128 C3 **Kalahari Desert desert** Africa
130 C2 **Kalahari Gemsbok National Park nat. park** South Africa
46 F5 **Kala-I-Mor** Turkmenistan
56 G2 **Kalajoki r.** Finland
56 F2 **Kalajoki** Finland
123 F4 **Kalalé** Benin
36 C2 **Kalam** Pakistan
114 D2 **Kalamaria** Greece
115 D5 **Kalamata** Greece
148 D4 **Kalamazoo r.** *Michigan* U.S.A.
148 E4 **Kalamazoo** *Michigan* U.S.A.
22 C3 **Kalambau i.** Indonesia
114 B4 **Kalamos i.** Greece
114 F2 **Kalamoto** Greece
114 F3 **Kalampaka** Greece
114 F1 **Kalampaki** Greece
122 C4 **Kalana** Mali
36 C3 **Kalanaur** India
53 E3 **Kalanchak** Ukraine
39 E3 **Kalandi** Pakistan
114 E3 **Kalandra** Greece
127 B5 **Kalangala** Uganda
31 F2 **Kalanguy** Rus. Fed.
115 C4 **Kalanistra** Greece
17 B6 **Kalannie** *Western Australia* Australia
36 C3 **Kalanwali** India
22 E3 **Kalao i.** Indonesia
23 C5 **Kalaong** Philippines
38 C4 **Kala Oya r.** Sri Lanka
22 A2 **Kalapa** Indonesia
39 E4 **Kalar watercourse** Iran
42 F3 **Kalār** Iraq
52 F1 **Kalashnikovo** Rus. Fed.
Kalāt *see* **Kabūd Gonbad**
36 A3 **Kalat** Pakistan
115 □ **Kalathos** Greece
6 □4 **Kalau i.** Tonga
153 □2 **Kalaupapa** *Hawaii* U.S.A.
51 G6 **Kalaus r.** Rus. Fed.
115 □ **Kalavarda** Greece
115 D4 **Kalavryta** Greece
24 B2 **Kalaw** Myanmar
76 D3 **Kaława** Poland
17 A5 **Kalbarri** *Western Australia* Australia
17 A5 **Kalbarri Nat. Park nat. park** *Western Australia* Australia
73 G3 **Kalbe** Germany
39 D2 **Kalbū** Iran
81 F5 **Kalce** Slovenia
53 G3 **Kal'chyk r.** Ukraine
58 B1 **Kaldafjellet mt.** Norway
113 G6 **Kale** *Denizli* Turkey
42 A2 **Kale** Turkey
43 A1 **Kaleardı Br. pt** Turkey
42 C1 **Kalecik** Turkey
72 F4 **Kalefeld** Germany
124 E4 **Kalehe** Congo(Zaire)
24 A3 **Kaleindaung inlet** Myanmar
125 D4 **Kalema** Congo(Zaire)
125 E5 **Kalemie** Congo(Zaire)
24 A2 **Kalemyo** Myanmar
114 B3 **Kalentzi** Greece
148 D3 **Kaleva** *Michigan* U.S.A.
56 H2 **Kalevala** Rus. Fed.
24 A2 **Kalewa** Myanmar
42 F2 **Kaleybar** Iran
31 F2 **Kalga** Rus. Fed.
17 B7 **Kalgan r.** *Western Australia* Australia
Kalgan *see* **Zhangjiakou**
17 C6 **Kalgoorlie** *Western Australia* Australia
123 G4 **Kalguéri** Niger
36 E3 **Kali r.** India
104 E3 **Kali** Croatia
22 A2 **Kalianda** Indonesia
115 D5 **Kalianoi** Greece
23 B4 **Kalibo** Philippines
37 E4 **Kali Gadaki r.** Nepal
52 D3 **Kalikino** Rus. Fed.
125 E4 **Kalima** Congo(Zaire)
22 C2 **Kalimantan reg.** Indonesia
22 B2 **Kalimantan Barat div.** Indonesia
22 C2 **Kalimantan Selatan div.** Indonesia
22 C2 **Kalimantan Tengah div.** Indonesia
22 D1 **Kalimantan Timur div.** Indonesia
37 G4 **Kālimpang** India
36 D3 **Kali Nadi r.** India
38 A3 **Kalinadi r.** India
46 E4 **Kalinin** Turkmenistan
54 B4 **Kaliningrad div.** Rus. Fed.
54 B4 **Kaliningrad** Rus. Fed.
77 J1 **Kaliningradskiy Zaliv b.** Rus. Fed.
Kalinino *see* **Tashir**
77 L1 **Kalinino** Rus. Fed.
52 H2 **Kalinino** Rus. Fed.
51 H5 **Kalininsk** Rus. Fed.
51 F6 **Kalininskaya** Rus. Fed.
53 E3 **Kalinins'ke** Ukraine
51 D4 **Kalinkavichy** Belarus
46 E3 **Kalinovka** Kazakhstan
52 B4 **Kalinovka** Rus. Fed.
77 L2 **Kalinowo** Poland
126 E3 **Kalis** Somalia
36 D5 **Kali Sindh r.** India
152 D1 **Kalispell** *Montana* U.S.A.
76 F4 **Kalisz div.** Poland
76 G4 **Kalisz** Poland
76 D2 **Kalisz Pomorski** Poland
51 F5 **Kalitva r.** Rus. Fed.
127 B6 **Kaliua** Tanzania
56 F2 **Kalix** Sweden
56 F2 **Kalixälven r.** Sweden
53 G3 **Kal'ka r.** Ukraine
36 D3 **Kalka** India
42 B2 **Kalkan** Turkey
72 B4 **Kalkar** Germany
12 D1 **Kalkaringi** *Northern Terr.* Australia
148 E3 **Kalkaska** *Michigan* U.S.A.
131 G1 **Kalkbank** South Africa
128 B3 **Kalkfeld** Namibia
131 E4 **Kalkfonteindam dam** South Africa
130 A2 **Kalkrand** Namibia
74 B2 **Kall** Germany
12 D1 **Kallakoopah Cr. watercourse** *S. Australia* Australia
59 E2 **Kållandsö i.** Sweden
25 □ **Kallang** Singapore
54 E2 **Kallaste** Estonia
56 G3 **Kallavesi l.** Finland
59 E2 **Kålleboda** Sweden
114 D4 **Kallidromo mts** Greece
114 C3 **Kallifoni** Greece
115 E5 **Kallithea** *Athina* Greece
115 C5 **Kallithea** *Peloponnisos* Greece
75 G3 **Kallmünz** Germany
115 E5 **Kalloni** Greece
56 D3 **Kallsedet** Sweden
56 D3 **Kallsjön l.** Sweden
52 E1 **Kalmanka** Rus. Fed.
59 G3 **Kalmar div.** Sweden
59 G3 **Kalmar** Sweden
59 G3 **Kalmarsund chan.** Sweden
51 F6 **Kal'mius r.** Ukraine
69 C3 **Kalmthout** Belgium
39 D1 **Kalmūkh Qal'eh** Iran
38 C5 **Kalmunai** Sri Lanka
51 H6 **Kalmykiya div.** Rus. Fed.
46 D3 **Kalmykovo** Kazakhstan
79 H3 **Kalná nad Hronom** Slovakia
54 C3 **Kalnciems** Latvia
37 G4 **Kalni r.** Bangladesh
78 F5 **Kalnik mountain range** Croatia
79 H5 **Kalocsa** Hungary
115 F8 **Kaloi Limenes** Greece
36 C5 **Kalol** India
23 C6 **Kaloma i.** Indonesia
127 B6 **Kaloma** Tanzania
125 E7 **Kalomo** Zambia
136 D4 **Kalone Pk summit** *B.C.* Canada
114 C2 **Kaloneri** Greece
115 C5 **Kalo Nero** Greece
43 B2 **Kalopanagiotis** Cyprus
55 C3 **Kalø Vig b.** Denmark
36 D3 **Kalpa** India
114 B3 **Kalpakio** Greece
38 A4 **Kalpeni i.** India
47 J4 **Kalpin** China
80 D4 **Kals am Großglockner** Austria
81 G4 **Kalsdorf bei Graz** Austria
55 C4 **Kalsenakke pt** Denmark
134 C3 **Kaltag** *Alaska* U.S.A.
47 L2 **Kaltan** Rus. Fed.
54 D4 **Kaltanėnai** Lithuania
83 E1 **Kaltbrunn** Switzerland
80 C3 **Kaltenbach** Austria
72 E2 **Kaltenkirchen** Germany
74 F2 **Kaltensundheim** Germany
123 G5 **Kaltungo** Nigeria
36 C3 **Kalu** India
52 B2 **Kaluga div.** Rus. Fed.
52 C2 **Kaluga** Rus. Fed.
52 F3 **Kalugino** Rus. Fed.
53 E3 **Kaluha** Ukraine
22 D3 **Kalukalukuang i.** Indonesia
22 D2 **Kaluku** Indonesia
125 E6 **Kalulushi** Zambia
16 D2 **Kalumburu** *Western Australia* Australia
16 D2 **Kalumburu Abor. Land Reserve res.** *Western Australia* Australia
55 D4 **Kalundborg** Denmark
125 E5 **Kalungwishi r.** Zambia
36 B2 **Kalur Kot** Pakistan
53 A2 **Kalush** Ukraine
77 K3 **Kałuszyn** Poland
38 B5 **Kalutara** Sri Lanka
54 C4 **Kalvarija** Lithuania
56 F3 **Kälviä** Finland
59 E3 **Kalvsjön l.** Sweden
81 F3 **Kalwang** Austria
77 H6 **Kalwaria Zebrzydowska** Poland
38 A2 **Kalyan** India
52 C1 **Kalyazin** Rus. Fed.
113 F6 **Kalymnos i.** Greece
113 F6 **Kalymnos** Greece
53 D1 **Kalynivka** *Kyyiv* Ukraine
53 C2 **Kalynivka** *Vinnytsya* Ukraine
53 D1 **Kalyta** Ukraine
115 □ **Kalythies** Greece
115 F2 **Kalyves** Greece
114 C4 **Kalyvia** Greece
123 G5 **Kam** Nigeria
50 K3 **Kama r.** Rus. Fed.
24 A3 **Kama** Myanmar
125 E4 **Kama** Congo(Zaire)
29 H4 **Kamaishi** Japan
29 □1 **Kama-iwa i.** Japan
29 G6 **Kamakura** Japan
122 B5 **Kamakwie** Sierra Leone
118 C3 **Kamal** Chad
36 C3 **Kamalia** Pakistan
24 B3 **Kamamaung** Myanmar
36 D4 **Kaman** India
42 C2 **Kaman** Turkey
124 E4 **Kamande** Congo(Zaire)
128 A2 **Kamanjab** Namibia
125 E4 **Kamanyola** Congo(Zaire)
126 E1 **Kamaran** Yemen
126 D1 **Kamarān I. i.** Yemen
39 F2 **Kamard reg.** Afghanistan
38 B2 **Kamareddi** India
115 C4 **Kamares** *Dytiki Ellas* Greece
115 F6 **Kamares** *Notio Aigiao* Greece
114 G2 **Kamariotissa** Greece
39 E4 **Kamarod** Pakistan
122 B5 **Kamaron** Sierra Leone
53 D1 **Kamaryn** Belarus
47 G5 **Kamashi** Uzbekistan
128 D2 **Kamativi** Zimbabwe
24 B1 **Kambaiti** Myanmar
17 C6 **Kambalda** *Western Australia* Australia
38 B4 **Kambam** India
22 B4 **Kambangan i.** Indonesia
46 D1 **Kambarka** Rus. Fed.
47 K4 **Kamberdi** China
122 B5 **Kambia** Sierra Leone
10 □1 **Kambling I. i.** *Cocos Is* Indian Ocean
31 J4 **Kambo Ho mt.** North Korea
125 E6 **Kambove** Congo(Zaire)
22 E2 **Kambuno, Bukit mt.** Indonesia
45 S4 **Kamchatka pen.** Rus. Fed.
45 R4 **Kamchatka r.** Rus. Fed.
39 G2 **Kamdesh** Afghanistan
51 J5 **Kamelik r.** Rus. Fed.
112 E3 **Kamen** Bulgaria
72 C4 **Kamen** Germany
125 D5 **Kamende** Congo(Zaire)
78 D3 **Kamenec mt.** Czech Rep.
115 G6 **Kameni i.** Greece
114 B2 **Kamenicë** Albania
78 E2 **Kamenice nad Lipou** Czech Rep.
107 H4 **Kamenjak, Rt pt** Croatia
46 D2 **Kamenka** Kazakhstan
50 H1 **Kamenka** Rus. Fed.
54 F1 **Kamenka** Rus. Fed.
52 E3 **Kamenka** Rus. Fed.
52 B3 **Kamenka** Rus. Fed.
52 G1 **Kamenka** Rus. Fed.
51 F5 **Kamenka** Rus. Fed.
52 G3 **Kamenka** Rus. Fed.
52 A2 **Kamenka** Rus. Fed.
47 K2 **Kamen'-na-Obi** Rus. Fed.
52 D1 **Kamenniki** Rus. Fed.
54 F1 **Kamennogorsk** Rus. Fed.
75 K3 **Kamenný Přívoz** Czech Rep.
112 F3 **Kameno** Bulgaria
51 G6 **Kamenolomni** Rus. Fed.
31 K3 **Kamen'-Rybolov** Rus. Fed.
45 S3 **Kamenskoye** Rus. Fed.
52 D3 **Kamenskoye** Rus. Fed.
51 G5 **Kamensk-Shakhtinskiy** Rus. Fed.
46 F1 **Kamensk-Ural'skiy** Rus. Fed.
73 K4 **Kamenz** Germany
52 E1 **Kameshkovo** Rus. Fed.
36 D3 **Kamet mt.** China
114 A1 **Kamëz** Albania
28 B6 **Kamiagata** Japan
77 J6 **Kamienica** Poland
76 F2 **Kamień Krajeński** Poland
76 E5 **Kamienna Góra** Poland
76 C2 **Kamień Pomorski** Poland
77 H4 **Kamieńsk** Poland
130 B5 **Kamiesberg mountain range** South Africa
130 A5 **Kamieskroon** South Africa
28 J2 **Kamikawa** Japan
28 B8 **Kami-Koshiki-jima i.** Japan
14 E3 **Kamileroi** *Queensland* Australia
137 J2 **Kamilukuak Lake l.** *N.W.T.* Canada
125 D5 **Kamina** Congo(Zaire)
125 E5 **Kamina Base** Congo(Zaire)
137 L2 **Kaminak Lake l.** *N.W.T.* Canada
53 A1 **Kamin'-Kashyrs'kyy** Ukraine
28 H3 **Kaminokuni** Japan
29 H4 **Kaminoyama** Japan
81 F4 **Kaminške in Savinjske Alpe mountain range** Slovenia
52 E1 **Kaminskiy** Rus. Fed.
29 F5 **Kamioka** Japan
77 J4 **Kamion** *Skierniewice* Poland
77 J3 **Kamion** *Skierniewice* Poland
77 L4 **Kamionka** Poland
115 □ **Kamiros** Greece
28 J2 **Kamishihoro** Japan
28 B6 **Kamitsushima** Japan
125 E4 **Kamituga** Congo(Zaire)
29 □2 **Kamiyama-jima i.** Japan
37 H4 **Kamjong** India
37 F4 **Kamla r.** India
47 L2 **Kamlak** Rus. Fed.
136 E4 **Kamloops** *B.C.* Canada
80 B2 **Kammel r.** Germany
78 D5 **Kamnik** Slovenia
29 G5 **Kamo** Japan
8 E1 **Kamo** New Zealand
163 F3 **Kamoa Mts mts** Guyana
28 H2 **Kamoenai** Japan
29 H6 **Kamogawa** Japan
36 C3 **Kamoke** Pakistan
125 D5 **Kamonia** Congo(Zaire)
81 G2 **Kamp r.** Austria
87 G2 **Kamp** Germany
127 B4 **Kampala** Uganda
25 C6 **Kampar** Malaysia
54 C3 **Kamparkalns h.** Latvia
68 D2 **Kampen** Netherlands
125 E4 **Kampene** Congo(Zaire)
24 B3 **Kamphaeng Phet** Thailand
77 J3 **Kampinoski Park Narodowy nat. park** Poland
38 B3 **Kampli** India
72 B4 **Kamp-Lintfort** Germany
125 E6 **Kampolombo, Lake l.** Zambia
25 D5 **Kâmpóng Cham** Cambodia
25 D4 **Kâmpóng Chhnăng** Cambodia
25 D4 **Kâmpóng Khleăng** Cambodia
Kâmpóng Saôm *see* **Sihanoukville**
25 D5 **Kâmpóng Spoe** Cambodia
25 D4 **Kâmpóng Thum** Cambodia
25 D5 **Kâmpóng Tranch** Cambodia
115 D6 **Kampos** Greece
25 D5 **Kâmpôt** Cambodia
122 D4 **Kampti** Burkina
Kampuchea *see* **Cambodia**
137 J4 **Kamsack** *Saskatchewan* Canada
122 B4 **Kamsar** Guinea
50 J4 **Kamskoye Ust'ye** Rus. Fed.
44 G4 **Kamskoye Vdkhr. resr** Rus. Fed.
127 D4 **Kamsuuma** Somalia
137 J3 **Kamuchawie Lake l.** *Manitoba* Canada

127 B4 Kamuli Uganda
114 C3 Kamvounia mountain range Greece
53 B1 Kam"yane Rivne Ukraine
53 F1 Kam"yane Sumy Ukraine
53 B2 Kam"yanets'-Podil's'kyy Ukraine
53 E2 Kam"yanka Cherkasy Ukraine
53 G2 Kam"yanka Kharkiv Ukraine
53 D3 Kam"yanka Odesa Ukraine
53 A1 Kam"yanka-Buz'ka Ukraine
53 F3 Kam"yanka-Dniprovs'ka Ukraine
112 G2 Kam"yans'ke Ukraine
77 M3 Kamyanyets Belarus
77 M3 Kamyanyuki Belarus
53 B1 Kam"yanyy Brid Ukraine
53 D3 Kam"yanyy Mist Ukraine
42 F3 Kāmyārān Iran
54 F4 Kamyen' Belarus
77 N2 Kamyenka Belarus
51 F6 Kamyshevatskaya Rus. Fed.
51 H5 Kamyshin Rus. Fed.
46 F3 Kamyshlybash Kazakhstan
46 F3 Kamyslybas, Oz. l. Kazakhstan
51 J6 Kamyzyak Rus. Fed.
39 D4 Kamzar Oman
126 B3 Kan Sudan
129 D2 Kana r. Zimbabwe
124 F3 Kana Congo(Zaire)
138 F3 Kanaaupscow r. Québec Canada
155 F3 Kanab Utah U.S.A.
155 F3 Kanab Creek r. Arizona U.S.A.
6 □6 Kanacea i. Fiji
29 G6 Kanagawa div. Japan
36 A3 Kanak Pakistan
81 E4 Kanal Slovenia
115 F5 Kanala Greece
77 M2 Kanał Augustowski canal Poland
76 F2 Kanał Bydgoski canal Poland
77 N3 Kanal Dnyaprowska-Buhski canal Belarus
114 B3 Kanali Greece
114 B3 Kanallaki Greece
76 E4 Kanał Obry canal Poland
107 J3 Kanal Srednja Vrata chan. Croatia
107 J3 Kanal Vela Vrata chan. Croatia
77 M4 Kanał Wieprz-Krzna canal Poland
131 F3 Kanana South Africa
125 D5 Kananga Congo(Zaire)
13 G3 Kanangra Nat. Park nat. park New South Wales Australia
155 F3 Kanarraville Utah U.S.A.
130 A3 Kanas watercourse Namibia
52 H2 Kanash Rus. Fed.
146 C5 Kanawha r. W. Virginia U.S.A.
29 F6 Kanayama Japan
29 F5 Kanazawa Japan
29 F5 Kanazu Japan
24 A2 Kanbalu Myanmar
25 B4 Kanchanaburi Thailand
38 B3 Kanchipuram India
77 L6 Kańczuga Poland
36 A3 Kand mt. Pakistan
39 F3 Kandahār Afghanistan
56 J2 Kandalaksha Rus. Fed.
50 E1 Kandalakshskiy Zaliv g. Rus. Fed.
22 C2 Kandangan Indonesia
54 C3 Kandava Latvia
123 E5 Kandé Togo
87 H4 Kandel mt. Germany
74 D3 Kandel Germany
73 J1 Kandelin Germany
82 C2 Kander r. Switzerland
74 C5 Kandern Germany
82 C2 Kandersteg Switzerland
36 B3 Kandhkot Pakistan
36 B2 Kandhura Pakistan
123 E4 Kandi Benin
36 A3 Kandi Pakistan
36 B4 Kandiaro Pakistan
115 D5 Kandila Peloponnisos Greece
114 B4 Kandila Stereá Ellás Greece
123 G3 Kandil Bouzou well Niger
114 E4 Kandilio mts Greece
42 B1 Kandıra Turkey
36 B5 Kandla India
13 G3 Kandos New South Wales Australia
129 H2 Kandreho Madagascar
6 □1 Kandrian P.N.G.
38 B3 Kandukur India
38 C5 Kandy Sri Lanka
146 D4 Kane Pennsylvania U.S.A.
135 M2 Kane Basin b. Canada/Greenland
39 C4 Kaneh watercourse Iran
118 C5 Kanem div. Chad
153 □1 Kaneohe Hawaii U.S.A.
153 □1 Kaneohe Bay b. Hawaii U.S.A.
50 F1 Kanevka Rus. Fed.
51 F6 Kanevskaya Rus. Fed.
29 H4 Kaneyama Japan
128 C3 Kang Botswana
37 G5 Kanga r. Bangladesh
124 F3 Kanga Congo(Zaire)
135 N3 Kangaatsiaq Greenland
122 C4 Kangaba Mali
42 D2 Kangal Turkey
39 D4 Kangān Iran
39 C4 Kangan Iran
25 C6 Kangar Malaysia
12 D3 Kangaroo I. i. S. Australia Australia
163 F2 Kangaruma Guyana
57 H3 Kangaslampi Finland
56 G3 Kangasniemi Finland
39 A2 Kangāvar Iran
31 E4 Kangbao China
37 G4 Kangchenjunga mt. Nepal
32 C2 Kangding China
31 H5 Kangdong North Korea
22 C3 Kangean i. Indonesia
22 C3 Kangean, Kep. is Indonesia
126 B3 Kangen r. Sudan
135 O3 Kangeq headland Greenland
135 N3 Kangerluarsoruseq Greenland
135 P3 Kangerlussuaq inlet Greenland
135 N3 Kangerlussuaq Greenland
135 N2 Kangersuatsiaq Greenland
135 P3 Kangertittivatsiaq inlet Greenland
126 C4 Kangetet Kenya
31 H4 Kanggye North Korea
135 Q2 Kangikajik c. Greenland
31 F1 Kangil Rus. Fed.
139 G2 Kangiqsualujjuaq Québec Canada
135 L3 Kangiqsujuaq Québec Canada
139 G1 Kangirsuk Québec Canada
28 A6 Kangjon South Korea
32 C1 Kangle China
Kang-ma see Kangmar
37 F3 Kangmar China
37 G3 Kangmar China
31 J5 Kangnŭng South Korea
124 B3 Kango Gabon
29 □1 Kangoku-iwa i. Japan
31 G4 Kangping China
36 D2 Kangra India
37 H3 Kangri Karpo Pass India
37 E3 Kangrinboqê Feng mt. China
37 H4 Kangto mt. China
37 F2 Kangtog China
32 D1 Kang Xian China
36 D1 Kangxiwar China
24 A3 Kangyidaung Myanmar
38 B1 Kanhan r. India
37 E4 Kanhar r. India
122 C5 Kani Côte d'Ivoire
24 A2 Kani Myanmar
125 D5 Kaniama Congo(Zaire)
9 C5 Kaniere New Zealand
9 C5 Kaniere, L. l. New Zealand
122 A4 Kanifing The Gambia
38 B3 Kanigiri India
36 B2 Kaniguram Pakistan
44 F3 Kanin Nos Rus. Fed.
44 F3 Kanin Nos, M. c. Rus. Fed.
44 F3 Kanin, P-ov pen. Rus. Fed.
83 E1 Kanisfluh mt. Austria
28 H3 Kanita Japan
53 D2 Kaniv Ukraine
12 E4 Kaniva Victoria Australia
79 K5 Kanjiža Yugoslavia
56 F3 Kankaanpää Finland
148 C5 Kankakee r. Illinois U.S.A.
148 D5 Kankakee Illinois U.S.A.
122 C4 Kankan Guinea
122 C5 Kankan, Réserve Naturelle de res. Guinea
37 E5 Kanker India
38 C4 Kankesanturai Sri Lanka
36 C1 Kankhun P. pass Afghanistan/Pakistan
25 B5 Kanmaw Kyun i. Myanmar
59 E3 Kånna Sweden
36 D4 Kannanj India
145 D5 Kannapolis N. Carolina U.S.A.
Kanniya Kumari c. see Comorin, Cape
38 B4 Kanniyakumari India
36 D5 Kannod India
56 G3 Kannonkoski Finland
Kannur see Cannanore
56 F3 Kannus Finland
54 E1 Kannuskoski Finland
123 F4 Kano div. Nigeria
28 C6 Kano Japan
123 F4 Kano Nigeria
28 D6 Kan-onji Japan
22 C1 Kanowit Malaysia
28 C8 Kanoya Japan
36 E4 Kanpur India
36 B3 Kanpur Pakistan
36 A4 Kanrach reg. Pakistan
150 D4 Kansas div. U.S.A.
150 D4 Kansas r. Kansas U.S.A.
150 E4 Kansas City Kansas U.S.A.
150 E4 Kansas City Missouri U.S.A.
45 L4 Kansk Rus. Fed.
Kansu div. see Gansu
47 J5 Kansu China
47 H4 Kant Kyrgyzstan
126 C3 Kanta mt. Ethiopia
115 E7 Kantanos Greece
25 D4 Kantaralak Thailand
123 E4 Kantchari Burkina
51 F5 Kantemirovka Rus. Fed.
68 E1 Kantens Netherlands
37 F5 Kānthi India
37 F4 Kanti India
115 D5 Kantia Greece
176 H6 Kanton Island i. Kiribati
29 G6 Kanto-sanchi mountain range Japan
67 C4 Kanturk Rep. of Ireland
163 F3 Kanuku Mts mts Guyana
29 G5 Kanuma Japan
128 B4 Kanus Namibia
6 □1 Kanuwe r. P.N.G.
131 H2 KaNyamazane South Africa
128 D3 Kanye Botswana
52 A2 Kanyutino Rus. Fed.
6 □5 Kao i. Tonga
25 C5 Kaôh Kŏng i. Cambodia
25 C5 Kaôh Rŭng i. Cambodia
33 H4 Kao-hsiung Taiwan
25 C5 Kaôh Smăch i. Cambodia
128 A2 Kaokoveld plat. Namibia
122 A4 Kaolack Senegal
125 D6 Kaoma Zambia
118 C4 Kaortchi well Chad
124 D2 Kaouadja Central African Rep.
153 □2 Kapaa Hawaii U.S.A.
153 □2 Kapaau Hawaii U.S.A.
47 J3 Kapal Kazakhstan
125 D5 Kapanga Congo(Zaire)
127 B6 Kapatu Zambia
47 J4 Kapchagay Kazakhstan
47 J4 Kapchagayskoye Vdkhr. resr Kazakhstan
126 B4 Kapchorwa Uganda
77 M2 Kapčiamiestis Lithuania
69 B3 Kapelle Netherlands
69 C3 Kapellen Belgium
59 H2 Kapellskär Sweden
81 G3 Kapfenberg Austria
37 H4 Kapili r. India
176 F5 Kapingamarangi Rise sea feature Pacific Ocean
36 B3 Kapip Pakistan
125 E6 Kapiri Mposhi Zambia
135 N3 Kapisigdlit Greenland
138 D3 Kapiskau r. Ontario Canada
138 D3 Kapiskau Ontario Canada
140 E3 Kapiskong Lake l. Ontario Canada
22 C1 Kapit Malaysia
53 D2 Kapitanivka Ukraine
8 E4 Kapiti I. i. New Zealand
163 F3 Kapiting Brazil
78 D3 Kaplice Czech Rep.
25 B5 Kapoe Thailand
126 B4 Kapoeta Sudan
79 K4 Kápolna Hungary
8 E3 Kaponga New Zealand
79 G5 Kaposvár Hungary
131 H2 Kappamuiden South Africa
39 E4 Kappar Pakistan
178 □2 Kapp Duner c. Bjørnøya Arctic Ocean
74 C3 Kappel Germany
72 E1 Kappeln Germany
87 H4 Kappelrodeck Germany
59 H3 Kappelshamnsviken b. Sweden
178 □2 Kapp Kåre c. Bjørnøya Arctic Ocean
80 B3 Kappl Austria
178 □3 Kapp Platen c. Svalbard Arctic Ocean
69 B3 Kaprijke Belgium
127 C4 Kapsabet Kenya
31 J4 Kapsan North Korea
115 D5 Kapsas Greece
114 C2 Kapshticë Albania
31 F2 Kaptsegaytuy Rus. Fed.
77 M2 Kaptsyowka Belarus
22 B1 Kapuas r. Kalimantan Barat Indonesia
22 C2 Kapuas r. Kalimantan Tengah Indonesia
12 D3 Kapunda S. Australia Australia
36 C4 Kapūriya India
36 C3 Kapurthala India
79 L2 Kapušany Slovakia
140 D2 Kapuskasing r. Ontario Canada
140 D2 Kapuskasing Ontario Canada
51 H5 Kapustin Yar Rus. Fed.
53 D1 Kapustyntsi Ukraine
13 G2 Kaputar mt. New South Wales Australia
126 C4 Kaputir Kenya
78 G4 Kapuvár Hungary
54 E5 Kapyl' Belarus
52 A2 Kapyrevshchina Rus. Fed.
42 E2 Kara r. Turkey
123 E5 Kara Togo
113 F6 Kara Ada i. Turkey
113 F5 Kara Ada i. Turkey
47 H4 Kara-Balta Kyrgyzstan
52 D1 Karabanovo Rus. Fed.
46 F5 Karabekaul Turkmenistan
42 A1 Karabiga Turkey
46 D4 Kara-Bogaz-Gol Turkmenistan
42 C1 Karabük Turkey
52 E2 Karabukhino Rus. Fed.
47 J4 Karabulak Kazakhstan
47 K3 Karabulak Kazakhstan
47 J3 Karabulakskaya Kazakhstan
113 F5 Karaburun Turkey
46 F3 Karabutak Kazakhstan
113 G4 Karacabey Turkey
42 B1 Karacaköy Turkey
42 D2 Karacalı Dağlari mt. Turkey
43 B1 Karaçal T. mt. Turkey
113 G6 Karacasu Turkey
51 G7 Karachayevo-Cherkesiya div. Rus. Fed.
51 G7 Karachayevsk Rus. Fed.
52 B3 Karachev Rus. Fed.
36 A4 Karachi Pakistan
38 A2 Karad India
42 C2 Kara Dağ mt. Turkey
47 H4 Kara-Darya r. Kyrgyzstan
Kara Deniz sea see Black Sea
122 D5 Karaga Ghana
47 H3 Karaganda Kazakhstan
47 J3 Karagayly Kazakhstan
45 S4 Karaginskiy, O. i. Rus. Fed.
45 S4 Karaginskiy Zaliv b. Rus. Fed.
46 D4 Karagiye, Vpadina depression Kazakhstan
127 B5 Karagwe Tanzania
112 F4 Karahalil Turkey
113 G6 Karahisar Turkey
38 B4 Kāraikāl India
38 B4 Karaikkudi India
47 K3 Kara Irtysh r. Kazakhstan
42 C2 Karaisalı Turkey
39 B2 Karaj Iran
42 C4 Karak Jordan
46 E5 Kara Kala Turkmenistan
46 E4 Karakalpakiya Uzbekistan
47 J5 Karakax r. China
23 C5 Karakelong i. Indonesia
23 C6 Karakitang i. Indonesia
Karaklis see Vanadzor
42 E2 Karakoçan Turkey
47 G3 Karakoin, Oz. salt lake Kazakhstan
46 D3 Karakol' Kazakhstan
47 H4 Kara-Köl Kyrgyzstan
47 J4 Karakol Kyrgyzstan
36 D2 Karakoram Pass pass China/Jammu and Kashmir
36 C1 Karakoram Range mountain range Asia
126 C2 Kara K'orē Ethiopia
31 E2 Karaksar Rus. Fed.
46 F5 Karakul' Uzbekistan
47 H5 Karakul', Ozero l. Tajikistan
124 B1 Karal Chad
54 B2 Karala Estonia
22 D2 Karama r. Indonesia
43 B1 Karaman div. Turkey
42 C2 Karaman Turkey
47 K3 Karamay China
54 F3 Karamayshevo Rus. Fed.
47 H5 Karambar Pass pass Afghanistan/Pakistan
22 D2 Karambu Indonesia
9 D4 Karamea New Zealand
9 C4 Karamea Bight b. New Zealand
9 D4 Karamea River r. New Zealand
39 F1 Karamet-Niyaz Turkmenistan
22 C3 Karamian i. Indonesia
37 F1 Karamiran China
37 F1 Karamiran Shankou pass China
77 L1 Karamyshevo Rus. Fed.
39 B4 Karān i. Saudi Arabia
39 G1 Karan r. Afghanistan
42 F3 Karand Iran
22 A2 Karangagung Indonesia
22 A3 Karangan Indonesia
22 C4 Karangasem Indonesia
22 B4 Karangbolong, Tg pt Indonesia
22 D2 Karang, Tg pt Indonesia
38 B2 Karanja r. India
36 D5 Karanja India
37 F5 Karanjia India
47 J2 Karaoba Kazakhstan
113 F6 Karaova Turkey
47 H3 Karaoy Kazakhstan
112 F3 Karapelit Bulgaria
42 C2 Karapınar Turkey
113 G5 Karapürçek Turkey
128 B4 Karas div. Namibia
130 A3 Karas mts Namibia
37 E1 Karasay China
47 J4 Kara-Say Kyrgyzstan
128 B4 Karasburg Namibia
Kara Sea sea see Karskoye More
52 D1 Karash Rus. Fed.
56 G1 Karasjok Norway
47 H2 Karasu r. Kazakhstan
43 D1 Karasu r. Turkey
46 F2 Karasu Kazakhstan
47 G2 Karasu Kazakhstan
51 D7 Karasu Turkey
47 K2 Karasuk r. Rus. Fed.
47 J2 Karasuk Rus. Fed.
47 H4 Kara-Suu Kyrgyzstan
53 A1 Karasyn Ukraine
39 E2 Karāt Iran
47 L3 Karatan Kazakhstan
42 C2 Karataş Turkey
43 C1 Karataş Br. c. Turkey
47 H4 Karatau Kazakhstan
47 G4 Karatau, Khr. mountain range Kazakhstan
36 E2 Karatax Shan mountain range China
25 B5 Karathuri Myanmar
38 B4 Karativu i. Sri Lanka
46 D3 Karatobe Kazakhstan
47 J3 Karatol r. Kazakhstan
46 D3 Karaton Kazakhstan
115 C5 Karatoulas Greece
37 G4 Karatoya r. Bangladesh
28 B7 Karatsu Japan
23 C5 Karatung i. Indonesia
47 G2 Karaturgay r. Kazakhstan
47 J3 Karaul Kazakhstan
36 D4 Karauli India
46 E4 Karauzyak Uzbekistan
47 H4 Karavan Kyrgyzstan
115 E6 Karavi i. Greece
113 F7 Karavonisia i. Greece
43 B2 Karavostasi Cyprus
22 A3 Karawang Indonesia
81 F4 Karawanken mountain range Austria
Karaxahar r. see Kaidu
52 F4 Karay r. Rus. Fed.
47 K4 Karayulgan China
47 H3 Karazhal Kazakhstan
46 E4 Karazhar Uzbekistan
47 H3 Karazhingil Kazakhstan
42 E3 Karbalā' div. Iraq
42 F3 Karbalā' Iraq
87 H2 Karben Germany
47 J3 Karbushevka Kazakhstan
55 A3 Karby Denmark
79 K4 Karcag Hungary
77 K3 Karczew Poland
77 L4 Karczmiska Poland
115 B4 Kardakata Greece
112 G3 Kardam Bulgaria
115 D6 Kardamyli Greece
74 C2 Karden Germany
115 G6 Kardiotissa i. Greece
114 C3 Karditsa div. Greece
114 C3 Karditsa Greece
54 C2 Kärdla Estonia
78 F4 Kardos-ér r. Hungary
52 A2 Kardymovo Rus. Fed.
131 F4 Karee South Africa
130 C5 Kareeberg mts South Africa
130 D5 Kareebospoort pass South Africa
130 E6 Kareedouw South Africa
119 F4 Kareima Sudan
36 D5 Kareli India
54 E5 Karelichy Belarus
50 D1 Kareliya div. Rus. Fed.
50 E1 Karel'skiy Bereg coastal area Rus. Fed.
127 B6 Karema Tanzania
36 D4 Karera India
56 F1 Karesuando Sweden
39 E4 Kārevāndar Iran
51 H7 Kargalinskaya Rus. Fed.
46 E2 Kargalinskoye Kazakhstan
43 D1 Kargamiş Turkey
46 F1 Kargapol'ye Rus. Fed.
47 K1 Kargat r. Rus. Fed.
47 K1 Kargat Rus. Fed.
Karghalik see Yecheng
51 E7 Kargı Turkey
36 D2 Kargil Jammu and Kashmir
52 H3 Kargino Rus. Fed.
50 F2 Kargopol' Rus. Fed.
76 D3 Kargowa Poland
59 G1 Karholmsbruk Sweden
123 G4 Kari Nigeria
52 E3 Karian Rus. Fed.
114 E2 Kariani Greece
129 D2 Kariba Zimbabwe
129 D2 Kariba, Lake l. Zambia/Zimbabwe
28 G2 Kariba-yama volcano Japan
128 B3 Karibib Namibia
130 D6 Kariega watercourse South Africa
56 G1 Karigasniemi Finland
57 F3 Karijoki Finland
28 J2 Karikachi Pass pass Japan
8 D1 Karikari, Cape c. New Zealand
39 C2 Karīmābād Iran
22 B2 Karimata i. Indonesia
22 B2 Karimata, P.P. is Indonesia
39 B2 Karim Khanch Iran
38 B2 Karimnagar India
22 B3 Karimunjawa i. Indonesia
22 B3 Karimunjawa, P.P. is Indonesia
126 E2 Karin Somalia
54 C1 Karinainen Finland
54 C1 Karis Finland
39 D2 Karit Iran
115 D5 Karitaina Greece
114 D2 Karitsa Greece
29 F6 Kariya Japan
38 A2 Karjat India
37 F5 Karkai r. India
38 A3 Karkal India
115 D5 Karkalou Greece
47 J3 Karkaralinsk Kazakhstan
6 □1 Karkar I. i. P.N.G.
39 B3 Karkheh r. Iran
39 D4 Kārkīn Dar Iran
51 E6 Karkinits'ka Zatoka g. Ukraine
54 D1 Karkkila Finland
57 G3 Kärkölä Finland
59 J2 Karlby Finland
76 D1 Karlino Poland
42 E2 Karlıova Turkey
53 F2 Karlivka Ukraine
47 H5 Karl Marks mt. Tajikistan
Karl-Marx-Stadt see Chemnitz
104 E3 Karlovac Croatia
112 E3 Karlovo Bulgaria
78 B1 Karlovy Vary Czech Rep.
87 H4 Karlsbad Germany
59 F2 Karlsborg Sweden
73 J2 Karlsburg Germany
75 G4 Karlsfeld Germany
59 F3 Karlshamn Sweden
80 C2 Karlshuld Germany
59 F2 Karlskoga Sweden
75 G4 Karlskron Germany
59 F3 Karlskrona Sweden
74 D4 Karlsruhe div. Baden-Württemberg Germany
74 D3 Karlsruhe Karlsruhe Germany
150 D1 Karlstad Minnesota U.S.A.
59 E2 Karlstad Sweden
74 E3 Karlstadt Germany
81 G2 Karlstetten Austria
124 C1 Karma r. Chad
51 D4 Karma Belarus
123 E4 Karma Niger
38 A2 Karmala India
52 B2 Karmanovo Rus. Fed.
58 A2 Karmøy i. Norway
37 H5 Karnafuli Reservoir resr Bangladesh
36 D3 Karnal India
37 E3 Karnali r. Nepal
36 D3 Karnaprayag India
38 A3 Karnataka div. India
76 D1 Karnice Poland
77 J3 Karniewa Poland
80 D4 Karnische Alpen mountain range Austria
112 F3 Karnobat Bulgaria
118 D4 Karnoi Sudan
58 D2 Kärnsjön l. Sweden
81 E4 Kärnten div. Austria
36 A4 Karodi Pakistan
129 D2 Karoi Zimbabwe
107 H3 Karojba Croatia
6 □6 Karoko Fiji
24 B4 Karokpi Myanmar
37 G3 Karo La China
37 H4 Karong India
127 B6 Karonga Malawi
127 A5 Karonje mt. Rwanda
130 D6 Karoo National Park nat. park South Africa
12 D3 Karoonda S. Australia Australia
36 B3 Karor Pakistan
126 C1 Karora Eritrea
22 D2 Karossa Indonesia
22 D4 Karossa, Tg pt Indonesia
73 H2 Karow Germany
113 F7 Karpathos i. Greece
113 F7 Karpathos Greece
77 K6 Karpaty mountain range Poland/Slovakia
114 C4 Karpenisi Greece
114 E1 Karperi Greece
114 C3 Karpero Greece
50 H1 Karpogory Rus. Fed.
43 A1 Karpuz r. Turkey
113 F6 Karpuzlu Aydın Turkey
113 F4 Karpuzlu Edirne Turkey
53 B1 Karpylivka Ukraine
16 B4 Karratha Western Australia Australia
55 D4 Karrebæksminde Denmark
55 D4 Karrebæksminde Bugt b. Denmark
131 F5 Karringmelkspruit South Africa
39 E2 Karrukh Afghanistan
39 E1 Karrychirla Turkmenistan
42 E1 Kars Turkey
56 G3 Kärsämäki Finland
54 E3 Karsava Latvia
46 D4 Karshi Turkmenistan
47 G5 Karshi Uzbekistan
76 F2 Karsin Poland
113 F5 Karşıyaka Turkey
44 J2 Karskoye More sea Rus. Fed.
73 G2 Karstädt Germany
56 G3 Karstula Finland
52 H2 Karsun Rus. Fed.
42 B1 Kartal Turkey
127 D7 Kartala crater Comoros
46 F2 Kartaly Rus. Fed.
50 K1 Kartayel' Rus. Fed.
54 B4 Kartena Lithuania
56 G3 Karttula Finland
76 G1 Kartuzy Poland
15 E3 Karumba Queensland Australia
39 B3 Kārūn r. Iran
127 B5 Karungu Bay b. Kenya
22 D4 Karuni Indonesia
55 B3 Karup r. Denmark
55 B3 Karup Denmark
38 B4 Karur India
57 F3 Karvia Finland
57 F3 Karvianjoki r. Finland
79 H2 Karviná Czech Rep.
114 B3 Karvounari Greece
38 A3 Karwar India
80 C3 Karwendelgebirge mts Austria
114 B4 Karya Greece
114 F2 Karyes Greece
30 E2 Karymskoye Rus. Fed.
115 F4 Karystos Greece
52 G3 Karzhimant Rus. Fed.
55 B2 Kås Denmark
138 C3 Kasabonika Ontario Canada
138 C3 Kasabonika Lake l. Ontario Canada
125 C4 Kasai r. Congo(Zaire)
28 E6 Kasai Japan
125 D5 Kasai Occidental div. Congo(Zaire)
125 D5 Kasai Oriental div. Congo(Zaire)
125 D6 Kasaji Congo(Zaire)
29 H5 Kasama Japan
127 B7 Kasama Zambia
47 G5 Kasan Uzbekistan
128 D2 Kasane Botswana
125 C4 Kasangulu Congo(Zaire)
47 H4 Kasansay Uzbekistan
38 A3 Kasaragod India
54 C2 Kasari r. Estonia
137 J2 Kasba Lake l. N.W.T. Canada
120 C2 Kasba Tadla Morocco
28 C8 Kaseda Japan
78 C2 Kasejovice Czech Rep.
125 E6 Kasempa Zambia
75 G2 Kasendorf Germany
125 E6 Kasenga Congo(Zaire)
125 E5 Kasengu Congo(Zaire)
124 F3 Kasenye Congo(Zaire)
127 B4 Kasese Uganda
124 E4 Kasese Congo(Zaire)
36 D4 Kasganj India
39 B2 Kāshān Iran
51 G5 Kashary Rus. Fed.
138 D3 Kashechewan Ontario Canada
Kashgar see Kashi
47 J5 Kashi China
29 E6 Kashihara Japan
28 C7 Kashima Japan
29 H5 Kashima-nada b. Japan
52 C1 Kashin Rus. Fed.
52 C1 Kashinka r. Rus. Fed.
54 E3 Kashino Rus. Fed.
36 D3 Kashipur India
52 D2 Kashira Rus. Fed.
51 F5 Kashirskoye Rus. Fed.
29 G5 Kashiwazaki Japan
47 H3 Kashkanteniz Kazakhstan
50 F1 Kashkarantsy Rus. Fed.
53 G3 Kashlahach r. Ukraine
52 F3 Kashma r. Rus. Fed.
39 D2 Kāshmar Iran
Kashmir territory see Jammu and Kashmir
36 B3 Kashmor Pakistan
39 G2 Kashmund reg. Afghanistan
125 E5 Kashyukulu Congo(Zaire)
37 E4 Kasia India
52 A3 Kasilovo Rus. Fed.
22 D2 Kasimbar Indonesia
52 E2 Kasimov Rus. Fed.
81 H5 Kašina Croatia
144 B4 Kaskaskia r. Illinois U.S.A.
137 L3 Kaskattama r. Manitoba Canada
47 J4 Kaskelen Kazakhstan
57 F3 Kaskinen Finland
46 F1 Kasli Rus. Fed.
22 C2 Kasongan Indonesia
125 E4 Kasongo Congo(Zaire)
125 C5 Kasongo-Lunda Congo(Zaire)
113 F7 Kasos i. Greece
114 G3 Kaspakas Greece
78 C2 Kašperské Hory Czech Rep.
51 H7 Kaspi Georgia
51 H7 Kaspiysk Rus. Fed.
Kaspiyskoye More sea see Caspian Sea
54 C2 Kassaare Laht b. Estonia
119 G4 Kassala Sudan
114 E2 Kassandra pen. Greece
114 E2 Kassandreia Greece
72 E4 Kassel div. Hessen Germany
72 E4 Kassel Kassel Germany
121 F1 Kasserine Tunisia
119 F4 Kassinger Sudan
114 A3 Kassiopi Greece
148 A3 Kasson Minnesota U.S.A.
114 B3 Kassopi Greece
42 C1 Kastamonu Turkey
114 D2 Kastania Kentriki Makedonia Greece
114 C3 Kastania Thessalia Greece
74 C2 Kastellaun Germany
115 E7 Kastelli Kriti Greece
115 G7 Kastelli Kriti Greece
69 C3 Kasterlee Belgium
80 D2 Kastl Bayern Germany
75 G3 Kastl Bayern Germany
59 G3 Kastlösa Sweden
114 C2 Kastoria div. Greece
114 C2 Kastoria Greece
52 D4 Kastornoye Rus. Fed.
114 B4 Kastos i. Greece
114 B3 Kastrosykia Greece
28 C7 Kasuga Japan
29 F6 Kasugai Japan
124 E4 Kasuku Congo(Zaire)
127 B5 Kasulu Tanzania
125 E6 Kasumbalesa Congo(Zaire)
28 E6 Kasumi Japan
29 H5 Kasumiga-ura l. Japan
51 J7 Kasumkent Rus. Fed.
127 B7 Kasungu Malawi
127 B7 Kasungu National Park nat. park Malawi
36 C3 Kasur Pakistan
76 E4 Kaszczor Poland
147 J2 Katahdin, Mt mt. Maine U.S.A.
36 D2 Kataklik Jammu and Kashmir
125 D4 Katako-Kombe Congo(Zaire)
115 C5 Katakolo Greece
126 B4 Katakwi Uganda
36 D5 Katangi India
17 B7 Katanning Western Australia Australia
124 E4 Katanti Congo(Zaire)
115 B5 Katastari Greece
127 B6 Katavi National Park nat. park Tanzania
46 E2 Katav Ivanovsk Rus. Fed.
39 G2 Katawaz Afghanistan
46 F1 Kataysk Rus. Fed.
25 A6 Katchall i. Andaman and Nicobar Is India
125 E5 Katea Congo(Zaire)
125 D5 Katenge Congo(Zaire)
114 D2 Katerini Greece
53 D2 Katerynopil' Ukraine
127 C5 Katesh Tanzania
136 C3 Kate's Needle mt. Alaska/British Columbia Canada/U.S.A.
127 B7 Katete Zambia
37 E5 Katghora India
24 B1 Katha Myanmar
43 B5 Katherîna, G. mt. Egypt
14 C2 Katherine r. Northern Terr. Australia
14 C2 Katherine Northern Terr. Australia
15 E4 Katherine Cr. watercourse Queensland Australia
14 C2 Katherine Gorge Nat. Park nat. park Northern Terr. Australia
36 B5 Kathiawar India
43 B4 Kathîb el Henu h. Egypt
43 B4 Kathîb el Makhâzin sand dunes Egypt
38 C4 Kathiraveli Sri Lanka
131 G3 Kathlehong South Africa
73 K4 Kathlow Germany
37 F4 Kathmandu Nepal
130 D3 Kathu South Africa
127 C5 Kathua watercourse Kenya
36 C2 Kathua India
122 C4 Kati Mali
37 F4 Katihar India
8 E2 Katikati New Zealand
131 F6 Kati-Kati South Africa
7 □16 Katiki h. Easter I. Chile
128 C2 Katima Mulilo Namibia
122 C5 Katiola Côte d'Ivoire
7 □10 Katiu i. French Polynesia Pacific Ocean
115 C4 Kato Achaïa Greece
115 E4 Kato Alepochori Greece
115 C4 Katochi Greece
115 C5 Kato Figaleia Greece
115 G6 Kato Koufonisi i. Greece
36 D5 Katol India
114 C4 Kato Makrinou Greece
114 E1 Kato Nevrokopi Greece
25 □ Katong Singapore
127 B4 Katonga r. Uganda
114 D3 Kato Olympos mt. Greece
13 G3 Katoomba New South Wales Australia
114 D4 Kato Tithorea Greece
114 C4 Katouna Greece
75 J3 Katovice Czech Rep.
114 E1 Kato Vrontou Greece
76 G5 Katowice div. Poland
77 H5 Katowice Poland
37 G5 Katoya India
115 H7 Kato Zakros Greece
59 G2 Katrineholm Sweden
66 D4 Katrine, Loch l. Scotland U.K.
115 D5 Katsaros Greece
81 E3 Katschberghöhe pass Austria
81 F2 Katsdorf Austria
129 H2 Katsepy Madagascar
123 F4 Katsina div. Nigeria
123 F4 Katsina Nigeria
123 F5 Katsina-Ala Nigeria
28 B7 Katsumoto Japan
29 □2 Katsuren-zaki c. Japan
29 H5 Katsuta Japan
29 H6 Katsuura Japan
28 D6 Katsuyama Japan
29 F5 Katsuyama Japan
139 G2 Kattaktoc, Cap headland Québec Canada
47 G5 Kattakurgan Uzbekistan
115 □ Kattavia Greece
140 E2 Kattawagami Lake l. Ontario Canada
59 F1 Kattbo Sweden
55 C3 Kattegat str. Denmark/Sweden
59 E2 Kättilstorp Sweden
47 L2 Katun' r. Rus. Fed.
52 F1 Katunki Rus. Fed.
47 L2 Katunskiy Khrebet mountain range Rus. Fed.
36 B3 Katuri Pakistan
68 C2 Katwijk aan Zee Netherlands
76 E4 Kąty Wrocławskie Poland
74 C2 Katzenelnbogen Germany
74 C3 Katzweiler Germany
153 □2 Kauai i. Hawaii U.S.A.
153 □2 Kauai Channel chan. Hawaii U.S.A.
74 C2 Kaub Germany
128 C2 Kaudom Game Park res. Namibia
7 □10 Kauehi i. French Polynesia Pacific Ocean
75 F5 Kaufbeuren Germany
75 F4 Kaufering Germany
72 E4 Kaufungen Germany
57 F3 Kauhajoki Finland
56 F3 Kauhava Finland
24 B1 Kaukkwè Hills mountain range Myanmar
56 G2 Kaukonen Finland
54 E2 Kauksi Estonia
7 □10 Kaukura i. French Polynesia Pacific Ocean
153 □2 Kaula i. Hawaii U.S.A.
153 □2 Kaulakahi Channel chan. Hawaii U.S.A.
75 G2 Kaulsdorf Germany
139 H2 Kaumajet Mts mountain range Newfoundland Canada
153 □2 Kaunakakai Hawaii U.S.A.
54 C4 Kaunas Lithuania
54 E3 Kaunata Latvia
46 D4 Kaundy, Vpadina depression Kazakhstan
80 B4 Kaunertal v. Austria
58 B1 Kaupanger Norway
123 F4 Kaura-Namoda Nigeria
27 □ Kau Sai Chau i. Hong Kong China
56 F3 Kaustinen Finland
69 E5 Kautenbach Luxembourg
56 F1 Kautokeino Norway
81 G2 Kautzen Austria
25 B5 Kau-ye Kyun i. Myanmar
114 D1 Kavadarci Macedonia
113 B4 Kavajë Albania
113 F4 Kavak Çanakkale Turkey
42 C1 Kavak Samsun Turkey
113 G6 Kavaklıdere Turkey
114 F1 Kavala div. Greece
114 F2 Kavala Kavála Greece
38 C3 Kavali India
39 C3 Kavār Iran
35 D8 Kavaratti i. India
112 G3 Kavarna Bulgaria
54 D4 Kavarskas Lithuania
52 A2 Kavel'shchino Rus. Fed.
73 H2 Kavelstorf Germany
122 B4 Kavendou, Mt mt. Guinea
38 B4 Kāveri r. India
52 E2 Kaverino Rus. Fed.
6 □1 Kavieng P.N.G.
128 C2 Kavimba Botswana
39 C3 Kavīr salt flat Iran
39 C2 Kavir salt flat Iran
39 D2 Kavīr-e Namak salt flat Iran
39 B2 Kavir e Namak-e Mīqhān salt flat Iran
55 F4 Kävlinge Sweden
114 B3 Kavos Greece
77 M6 Kavs'ke Ukraine
46 D3 Kavzshanbas Kazakhstan
163 G3 Kaw French Guiana
29 H4 Kawabe Japan
29 G6 Kawagoe Japan
29 G6 Kawaguchi Japan
29 H4 Kawai Japan
153 □2 Kawaihae Hawaii U.S.A.
28 D6 Kawajiri Japan
8 E1 Kawakawa New Zealand
125 E5 Kawambwa Zambia
28 C7 Kawaminami Japan
29 E6 Kawanishi Japan
138 E5 Kawartha Lakes lakes Ontario Canada
27 P4 Kawasaki Japan
28 C6 Kawashiri-misaki pt Japan
28 H3 Kawauchi Japan
8 E2 Kawau I. i. New Zealand
28 C7 Kawaura Japan

139 G2 Kawawachikamach Québec Canada
8 F3 Kaweka mt. New Zealand
8 F3 Kawerau New Zealand
8 E3 Kawhia New Zealand
8 E3 Kawhia Harbour harbour New Zealand
154 D3 Kawich Range mts Nevada U.S.A.
22 D4 Kawinda Indonesia
24 B3 Kawkareik Myanmar
24 A2 Kawlin Myanmar
24 B3 Kawludo Myanmar
25 B4 Kawmapyin Myanmar
24 B2 Kawngmeum Myanmar
25 B5 Kawthaung Myanmar
47 K4 Kax r. China
47 J5 Kaxgar r. China
37 E1 Kaxtax Shan mountain range China
122 D4 Kaya Burkina
24 B3 Kayah State div. Myanmar
45 M2 Kayak Rus. Fed.
127 B6 Kayambi Zambia
22 C2 Kayan r. Kalimantan Barat Indonesia
22 C1 Kayan r. Kalimantan Timur Indonesia
127 A5 Kayanaza Burundi
23 □1 Kayangel Islands is Palau
23 □1 Kayangel Passage chan. Palau
38 B4 Kayankulam India
47 G2 Kaybagar, Oz. l. Kazakhstan
152 F3 Kaycee Wyoming U.S.A.
125 D5 Kayembe-Mukulu Congo(Zaire)
155 G3 Kayenta Arizona U.S.A.
122 B4 Kayes div. Mali
122 B4 Kayes Mali
46 F2 Kayga Kazakhstan
24 B3 Kayin State div. Myanmar
75 H2 Kayna Germany
47 J3 Kaynar Kazakhstan
42 D2 Kaynar Turkey
29 □2 Kayo Japan
51 H5 Kaysatskoye Rus. Fed.
42 C2 Kayseri Turkey
87 G4 Kaysersberg France
22 E3 Kayuadi i. Indonesia
22 A2 Kayuagung Indonesia
125 E4 Kayuyu Congo(Zaire)
44 K3 Kayyerkan Rus. Fed.
52 D3 Kazachka Rus. Fed.
45 P2 Kazach'ye Rus. Fed.
Kazakh see Qazax
47 H3 Kazakhskiy reg. Kazakhstan
46 D4 Kazakhskiy Zaliv b. Kazakhstan
18 G5 Kazakhstan country Asia
52 D3 Kazaki Rus. Fed.
46 F4 Kazalinsk Kazakhstan
137 K2 Kazan r. N.W.T. Canada
50 J4 Kazan' Rus. Fed.
42 C2 Kazancı Turkey
46 C1 Kazanka r. Rus. Fed.
53 E3 Kazanka Ukraine
112 E3 Kazanlŭk Bulgaria
31 E2 Kazanovo Rus. Fed.
77 K4 Kazanów Poland
21 M1 Kazan-rettō is Japan
51 G5 Kazanskaya Rus. Fed.
52 G3 Kazarka Rus. Fed.
47 H4 Kazarman Kyrgyzstan
51 H7 Kazbek mt. Georgia
113 F5 Kaz Dağı mts Turkey
39 B3 Kāzerūn Iran
50 J2 Kazhim Rus. Fed.
39 E4 Kazhmak r. Pakistan
53 F3 Kazhovs'kyy Mahistral'nyy Kanal canal Ukraine
Kazi Magomed see Qazımämmäd
76 G3 Kazimierz Biskupi Poland
77 K4 Kazimierz Dolne Poland
79 K3 Kazincbarcika Hungary
53 G1 Kazinka Rus. Fed.
77 O2 Kazlowshchyna Belarus
54 C4 Kazlų Rūda Lithuania
76 E3 Kaźmierz Poland
39 E4 Kazmīr Iran
75 J3 Kaznějov Czech Rep.
29 G5 Kazo Japan
46 C3 Kaztalovka Kazakhstan
125 D5 Kazumba Congo(Zaire)
125 E7 Kazungula Zambia
29 H3 Kazuno Japan
54 F4 Kazyany Belarus
44 H3 Kazymskiy Mys Rus. Fed.
76 F3 Kcynia Poland
75 J3 Kdyně Czech Rep.
115 F5 Kea i. Greece
115 F5 Kea Greece
67 E2 Keady Northern Ireland U.K.
153 □2 Kealakekua Bay b. Hawaii U.S.A.
155 G4 Keams Canyon Arizona U.S.A.
Kéamu i. see Anatom
150 D3 Kearney Nebraska U.S.A.
155 G5 Kearny Arizona U.S.A.
42 D2 Keban Turkey
42 D2 Keban Barajı dam Turkey
22 B2 Kebatu i. Indonesia
123 E4 Kebbi div. Nigeria
122 A3 Kébémèr Senegal
121 F2 Kebili Tunisia
43 D2 Kebīr r. Lebanon/Syria
118 D5 Kebkabiya Sudan
56 E2 Kebnekaise mt. Sweden
66 B2 Kebock Head headland Scotland U.K.
126 D3 K'ebrī Dehar Ethiopia
22 B3 Kebumen Indonesia
79 J5 Kecel Hungary
39 E4 Kech reg. Pakistan
126 C3 K'ech'a Terara mt. Ethiopia
136 D3 Kechika r. B.C. Canada
114 F1 Kechrokampos Greece
79 J5 Kecskemét Hungary
25 C6 Kedah div. Malaysia
54 C4 Kėdainiai Lithuania
36 D3 Kedarnath India
36 D3 Kedarnath Pk. mt. India
139 G4 Kedgwick New Brunswick Canada
22 C3 Kediri Indonesia
31 H3 Kedong China
122 B4 Kédougou Senegal
22 B3 Kedungwuni Indonesia
50 K1 Kedva r. Rus. Fed.
50 K1 Kedvavom Rus. Fed.
76 G5 Kędzierzyn-Koźle Poland
136 D2 Keele r. Yukon Terr. Canada
136 C2 Keele Pk summit Yukon Terr. Canada
153 C4 Keeler California U.S.A.
64 A4 Keenagh Rep. of Ireland
23 A5 Keenapusan i. Philippines
147 G3 Keene New Hampshire U.S.A.
14 B2 Keep r. Northern Terr. Australia
69 C4 Keerbergen Belgium
130 B6 Keeromsberg mt. South Africa
131 F4 Keeromsberg mt. South Africa
15 E2 Keer-weer, C. c. Queensland Australia
128 B4 Keetmanshoop Namibia
137 L5 Keewatin Minnesota U.S.A.
138 B4 Keewatin Ontario Canada
115 B4 Kefallonia div. Greece
115 B4 Kefallonia i. Greece
113 F6 Kefalos Greece
21 H8 Kefamenanu Indonesia
Keferdiz see Sakçagöze
81 F2 Kefermarkt Austria
123 F5 Keffi Nigeria
56 L6 Keflavík Iceland
38 C5 Kegalla Sri Lanka
47 J4 Kegen' Kazakhstan
46 E4 Kegeyli Uzbekistan
139 G2 Keglo, Baie de b. Québec Canada
51 H6 Kegul'ta Rus. Fed.
63 E2 Kegworth England U.K.
119 F4 Keheili Sudan
74 C4 Kehl Germany
69 E5 Kehlen Luxembourg
120 C5 Kehoula well Mauritania
54 D2 Kehra Estonia
69 F4 Kehrig Germany
24 B2 Kehsi Mansam Myanmar
54 D2 Kehtna Estonia
53 F2 Kehychivka Ukraine
131 F6 Kei Cuttings pass South Africa
65 G4 Keighley England U.K.
54 D2 Keila Estonia
64 C2 Keillmore Scotland U.K.
130 C4 Keimoes South Africa
131 G6 Kei Mouth South Africa
131 F6 Keiskama r. South Africa
131 F6 Keiskammahoek South Africa
123 F4 Keïta Niger
56 G3 Keitele l. Finland
56 G3 Keitele Finland
12 E4 Keith S. Australia Australia
66 F3 Keith Scotland U.K.
136 E1 Keith Arm b. N.W.T. Canada
6 □8 Keiyasi Fiji
139 G5 Kejimkujik National Park nat. park Nova Scotia Canada
153 □2 Kekaha Hawaii U.S.A.
54 D3 Ķekava Latvia
9 E5 Kekerengu New Zealand
79 K4 Kékes mt. Hungary
123 E5 Kekki Lagoon lag. Nigeria
23 □1 Keklau Palau
36 C4 Kekri India
126 D3 K'elafo Ethiopia
35 D9 Kelai i. Maldives
30 D5 Kelan China
25 C7 Kelang Malaysia
25 C6 Kelantan div. Malaysia
74 B2 Kelberg Germany
73 G4 Kelbra Germany
114 B2 Këlcyrë Albania
113 G5 Keles Turkey
79 L4 Keleti-főcsatorna canal Hungary
75 G4 Kelheim Germany
121 G1 Kelibia Tunisia
39 F1 Kelif Turkmenistan
46 F5 Kelifskiy Uzboy marsh Turkmenistan
87 H2 Kelkheim (Taunus) Germany
42 D1 Kelkit r. Turkey
42 D1 Kelkit Turkey
74 B3 Kell Germany
114 C2 Kella Greece
124 B4 Kéllé Congo
17 B6 Kellerberrin Western Australia Australia
136 E2 Keller Lake l. N.W.T. Canada
47 G2 Kellerovka Kazakhstan
134 F2 Kellett, Cape headland N.W.T. Canada
146 B4 Kelleys I. i. Ohio U.S.A.
72 E2 Kellinghusen Germany
80 B2 Kellmünz an der Iller Germany
152 C2 Kellogg Idaho U.S.A.
64 B3 Kells r. Northern Ireland U.K.
64 B3 Kells Northern Ireland U.K.
67 D4 Kells Waterford Rep. of Ireland
67 E3 Kells Rep. of Ireland
136 D1 Kelly Lake l. N.W.T. Canada
54 C4 Kelmė Lithuania
53 B2 Kel'mentsi Ukraine
69 E4 Kelmis Belgium
124 C2 Kelo Chad
136 F5 Kelowna B.C. Canada
136 D4 Kelsey Bay B.C. Canada
154 A2 Kelseyville California U.S.A.
155 E4 Kelso California U.S.A.
66 F5 Kelso Scotland U.K.
152 B2 Kelso Washington U.S.A.
87 H2 Kelsterbach Germany
25 C7 Keluang Malaysia
63 G3 Kelvedon England U.K.
137 J4 Kelvington Saskatchewan Canada
140 A2 Kelvin I. i. Ontario Canada
114 E2 Kelyfos i. Greece
50 E1 Kem' r. Rus. Fed.
50 E1 Kem' Rus. Fed.
42 D2 Kemah Turkey
112 F4 Kemal Turkey
42 D2 Kemaliye Turkey
42 A2 Kemalpaşa Turkey
136 D4 Kemano B.C. Canada
124 D3 Kemba Central African Rep.
22 B1 Kembayan Indonesia
124 D3 Kembé Central African Rep.
73 H4 Kemberg Germany
126 C2 Kembolcha Ethiopia
82 C1 Kembs France
78 F4 Kemeneshát h. Hungary
42 B2 Kemer Antalya Turkey
42 B2 Kemer Muğla Turkey
113 G6 Kemer Barajı resr Turkey
47 L2 Kemerovo Rus. Fed.
47 L1 Kemerovo Rus. Fed.
81 H3 Kemeten Austria
56 G2 Kemi Finland
56 G2 Kemijärvi l. Finland
56 G2 Kemijärvi Finland
56 G2 Kemijoki r. Finland
52 G2 Kemlya Rus. Fed.
152 E3 Kemmerer Wyoming U.S.A.
75 G3 Kemnath Germany
66 F3 Kemnay Scotland U.K.
73 J1 Kemnitz Germany
124 C2 Kémo div. Central African Rep.
56 G2 Kempele Finland
69 C3 Kempen reg. Belgium
72 B4 Kempen Germany
74 C2 Kempenich Germany
69 D3 Kempisch Kanaal canal Belgium
151 D5 Kemp, L. l. Texas U.S.A.
179 D4 Kemp Land reg. Antarctica
179 B2 Kemp Pen. pen. Antarctica
158 C1 Kemp's Bay The Bahamas
62 D2 Kempsey England U.K.
13 H2 Kempsey New South Wales Australia
63 F2 Kempston England U.K.
74 F5 Kempten (Allgäu) Germany
141 H3 Kempt, L. l. Québec Canada
131 G3 Kempton Park South Africa
141 H4 Kemptville Ontario Canada
22 B3 Kemujan i. Indonesia
36 E4 Ken r. India
134 C3 Kenai Alaska U.S.A.
134 C4 Kenai Mts mountain range Alaska U.S.A.
126 B3 Kenamuke Swamp swamp Sudan
39 C3 Keñāreh Iran
39 E2 Kenar-e-Kapeh Afghanistan
65 F3 Kendal England U.K.
22 B3 Kendal Indonesia
131 G3 Kendal South Africa
15 E2 Kendall r. Queensland Australia
13 H2 Kendall New South Wales Australia
137 M2 Kendall, Cape headland N.W.T. Canada
9 D4 Kendall, Mt mt. New Zealand
148 E5 Kendallville Indiana U.S.A.
22 A3 Kendang, G. volcano Indonesia
21 H7 Kendari Indonesia
22 B2 Kendawangan Indonesia
124 C1 Kendégué Chad
79 K4 Kenderes Hungary
37 F5 Kendrāparha India
130 E6 Kendrew South Africa
152 C2 Kendrick Idaho U.S.A.
155 G4 Kendrick Peak summit Arizona U.S.A.
37 F5 Kendujhargarh India
47 H4 Kendyktas mountain range Kazakhstan
151 D6 Kenedy Texas U.S.A.
131 G5 Keneka r. South Africa
122 B5 Kenema Sierra Leone
46 E4 Keneurgench Turkmenistan
125 C4 Kenge Congo(Zaire)
24 B2 Keng Hkam Myanmar
24 B2 Keng Lon Myanmar
24 B2 Keng Tawng Myanmar
24 B2 Kengtung Myanmar
130 C4 Kenhardt South Africa
122 B4 Kéniéba Mali
63 E2 Kenilworth England U.K.
120 C2 Kénitra Morocco
31 F5 Kenli China
64 D2 Ken, Loch l. Scotland U.K.
150 C1 Kenmare N. Dakota U.S.A.
67 B5 Kenmare Rep. of Ireland
67 A5 Kenmare River inlet Rep. of Ireland
66 E4 Kenmore Scotland U.K.
74 B3 Kenn Germany
153 G5 Kenna New Mexico U.S.A.
64 C2 Kennacraig Scotland U.K.
147 J2 Kennebec r. Maine U.S.A.
147 H3 Kennebunk Maine U.S.A.
147 H3 Kennebunkport Maine U.S.A.
15 F2 Kennedy r. Queensland Australia
17 A5 Kennedy Ra. h. Western Australia Australia
131 H2 Kennedy's Vale South Africa
151 F6 Kenner Louisiana U.S.A.
63 E3 Kennet r. England U.K.
17 B4 Kenneth Ra. h. Western Australia Australia
151 F4 Kennett Missouri U.S.A.
152 C2 Kennewick Washington U.S.A.
136 B2 Keno Yukon Terr. Canada
140 C1 Kenogami r. Ontario Canada
140 E2 Kenogami Lake Ontario Canada
140 E2 Kenogamissi Lake l. Ontario Canada
138 B4 Kenora Ontario Canada
148 D4 Kenosha Wisconsin U.S.A.
50 F2 Kenozero, Ozero l. Rus. Fed.
63 G3 Kent div. England U.K.
65 F3 Kent r. England U.K.
147 G4 Kent Connecticut U.S.A.
151 B6 Kent Texas U.S.A.
152 B2 Kent Washington U.S.A.
47 G4 Kentau Kazakhstan
13 F4 Kent Group is Tasmania Australia
148 D5 Kentland Indiana U.S.A.
146 B4 Kenton Ohio U.S.A.
131 F6 Kenton-on-Sea South Africa
114 D2 Kentriki Makedonia div. Greece
114 D1 Kentriko Greece
146 A6 Kentucky div. U.S.A.
145 B4 Kentucky Lake l. Kentucky/Tennessee U.S.A.
63 G3 Kent, Vale of v. England U.K.
139 H4 Kentville Nova Scotia Canada
151 F6 Kentwood Louisiana U.S.A.
148 E4 Kentwood Michigan U.S.A.
117 H5 Kenya country Africa
148 A3 Kenyon Minnesota U.S.A.
179 B2 Kenyon Pen. pen. Antarctica
47 H3 Kenzharyk Kazakhstan
87 G4 Kenzingen Germany
153 □2 Keokea Hawaii U.S.A.
148 B5 Keokuk Iowa U.S.A.
24 D3 Keo Neua, Col de pass Laos/Vietnam
148 B5 Keosauqua Iowa U.S.A.
76 E1 Kępice Poland
113 B4 Kepi i Gjuhëzës pt Albania
112 B4 Kepi i Rodonit pt Albania
50 G1 Kepina Rus. Fed.
76 F4 Kępno Poland
15 G4 Keppel B. b. Queensland Australia
25 □ Keppel Harbour chan. Singapore
113 G5 Kepsut Turkey
25 D7 Kepulauan Anambas is Indonesia
21 K8 Kepulauan Aru is Indonesia
21 J8 Kepulauan Babar is Indonesia
22 A1 Kepulauan Badas i. Indonesia
21 J7 Kepulauan Banda is Indonesia
21 H7 Kepulauan Banggai is Indonesia
21 J8 Kepulauan Barat Daya is Indonesia
21 K8 Kepulauan Kai is Indonesia
23 C5 Kepulauan Karkaralong is Indonesia
22 C3 Kepulauan Laut Kecil is Indonesia
21 J8 Kepulauan Leti is Indonesia
22 A2 Kepulauan Lingga is Indonesia
20 C7 Kepulauan Mentawai is Indonesia
23 C5 Kepulauan Nanusa is Indonesia
25 D7 Kepulauan Natuna is Indonesia
22 A1 Kepulauan Riau is Indonesia
23 C6 Kepulauan Sangir is Indonesia
21 J8 Kepulauan Sermata is Indonesia
21 H8 Kepulauan Solor is Indonesia
21 J7 Kepulauan Sula is Indonesia
23 C5 Kepulauan Talaud is Indonesia
22 A1 Kepulauan Tambelan is Indonesia
21 K8 Kepulauan Tanimbar is Indonesia
21 H7 Kepulauan Togian is Indonesia
21 H8 Kepulauan Tukangbesi is Indonesia
21 K7 Kepulauan Watubela is Indonesia
21 H8 Kepulauaun Alor is Indonesia
39 D3 Kerāh Iran
38 A4 Kerala div. India
114 B3 Keramitsa Greece
114 F2 Keramoti Greece
13 E3 Kerang Victoria Australia
123 E4 Kéran, Parc National de la nat. park Togo
114 B3 Kerasona Greece
115 E5 Keratea Greece
16 B3 Keraudren, C. c. Western Australia Australia
57 G3 Kerava Finland
51 F6 Kerch Ukraine
50 K2 Kerchem'ya Rus. Fed.
114 E2 Kerdylio mts Greece
79 K4 Kerecsend Hungary
124 E1 Kereidila pool Sudan
79 J5 Kerekegyháza Hungary
6 □1 Kerema P.N.G.
136 F5 Keremeos B.C. Canada
42 C1 Kerempe Burun pt Turkey
126 C1 Keren Eritrea
8 E2 Kerepehi New Zealand
122 A4 Kerewan The Gambia
39 D1 Kergeli Turkmenistan
179 □ Kerguélen, Îles is Indian Ocean
175 J7 Kerguelen Ridge sea feature Indian Ocean
115 B5 Keri Greece
127 C5 Kericho Kenya
22 C1 Kerihun mt. Indonesia
8 D1 Kerikeri New Zealand
57 H3 Kerimäki Finland
20 D7 Kerinci, G. volcano Indonesia
126 C4 Kerio watercourse Kenya
47 K5 Keriya r. China
Keriya see Yutian
37 E2 Keriya Shankou China
78 F5 Kerka r. Hungary
68 D3 Kerkdriel Netherlands
72 B4 Kerken Germany
121 G2 Kerkenah, Îles is Tunisia
47 G5 Kerki Turkmenistan
39 F1 Kerkichi Turkmenistan
114 D1 Kerkini mts Greece
114 E1 Kerkini Greece
69 E4 Kerkrade Netherlands
114 A3 Kerkyra div. Greece
114 A3 Kerkyra i. Greece
114 A3 Kerkyra Greece
88 A3 Kerlouan France
119 F4 Kerma Sudan
8 □4 Kermadec Is is New Zealand
176 H8 Kermadec Tr. sea feature Pacific Ocean
39 D3 Kermān div. Iran
154 B3 Kerman California U.S.A.
39 D3 Kermān Iran
39 D3 Kermān Desert desert Iran
39 A2 Kermānshāh Iran
39 C3 Kermānshāhān Iran
52 F3 Kermis' Rus. Fed.
151 C6 Kermit Texas U.S.A.
153 C5 Kern r. California U.S.A.
139 G2 Kernertut, Cap pt Québec Canada
154 C4 Kernville California U.S.A.
115 G6 Keros i. Greece
50 K2 Keros Rus. Fed.
123 E4 Kérou Benin
122 C5 Kérouané Guinea
74 B2 Kerpen Germany
179 B5 Kerr, C. c. Antarctica
64 C1 Kerrera i. Scotland U.K.
137 H4 Kerrobert Saskatchewan Canada
151 D6 Kerrville Texas U.S.A.
67 B4 Kerry div. Rep. of Ireland
67 B4 Kerry Hd headland Rep. of Ireland
59 G1 Kerstinbo Sweden
25 C6 Kerteh Malaysia
55 C4 Kerteminde Denmark
Kerulen r. see Herlen
30 E3 Kerulen r. Mongolia
43 B2 Keryneia Cyprus
121 D3 Kerzaz Algeria
82 C2 Kerzers Switzerland
52 G2 Kerzhemok Rus. Fed.
52 G1 Kerzhenets r. Rus. Fed.
52 G1 Kerzhenets Rus. Fed.
140 E1 Kesagami Lake l. Ontario Canada
57 H3 Kesälahti Finland
42 A1 Keşan Turkey
125 C4 Kese Congo(Zaire)
29 H4 Kesennuma Japan
64 A3 Kesh Northern Ireland U.K.
31 H2 Keshan China
39 G1 Keshem Afghanistan
39 F1 Keshendeh-ye Bala Afghanistan
36 B5 Keshod India
36 D4 Keshorai Patan India
39 B2 Keshvar Iran
42 C2 Kèskin Turkey
56 G3 Keski Suomi div. Finland
52 C1 Kesova Gora Rus. Fed.
80 B2 Kessel r. Germany
63 H2 Kessingland England U.K.
50 D1 Kesten'ga Rus. Fed.
56 G2 Kestilä Finland
65 E3 Keswick England U.K.
141 F4 Keswick Ontario Canada
78 G5 Keszthely Hungary
123 E5 Keta Ghana
25 □ Ketam, P. i. Singapore
22 C3 Ketapang Indonesia
22 B2 Ketapang Indonesia
136 C3 Ketchikan Alaska U.S.A.
142 D3 Ketchum Idaho U.S.A.
68 D2 Ketelmeer l. Netherlands
36 A4 Keti Bandar Pakistan
47 K4 Ketmen', Khr. mountain range China/Kazakhstan
53 E3 Ketrysanivka Ukraine
77 K1 Kętrzyn Poland
124 C3 Ketta Congo
124 B3 Kétté Cameroon
63 F2 Kettering England U.K.
146 A5 Kettering Ohio U.S.A.
80 B2 Kettershausen Germany
136 F5 Kettle r. B.C. Canada
148 A2 Kettle r. Minnesota U.S.A.
146 E4 Kettle Creek r. Pennsylvania U.S.A.
154 C3 Kettleman City California U.S.A.
152 C1 Kettle River Ra. mountain range Washington U.S.A.
65 F3 Kettlewell England U.K.
22 B1 Ketungau r. Indonesia
77 H6 Kęty Poland
73 J4 Ketzerbach r. Germany
73 H3 Ketzin Germany
146 E3 Keuka Lake l. New York U.S.A.
56 G3 Keuruu Finland
52 F3 Kevdo-Vershina Rus. Fed.
72 B4 Kevelaer Germany
159 D2 Kew Turks and Caicos Is Caribbean
148 C5 Kewanee Illinois U.S.A.
148 D3 Kewaunee Wisconsin U.S.A.
148 C2 Keweenaw Bay b. Michigan U.S.A.
148 C2 Keweenaw Peninsula pen. Michigan U.S.A.
148 D2 Keweenaw Pt pt Michigan U.S.A.
163 E2 Keweigek Guyana
126 B4 Keyala Sudan
138 F3 Keyano Québec Canada
140 E4 Key Harbour Ontario Canada
31 G2 Keyihe China
145 D7 Key Largo Florida U.S.A.
67 C2 Key, Lough l. Rep. of Ireland
63 F4 Keymer England U.K.
62 D3 Keynsham England U.K.
146 D5 Keyser W. Virginia U.S.A.
146 D5 Keysers Ridge Maryland U.S.A.
155 G6 Keystone Peak summit Arizona U.S.A.
146 D6 Keysville Virginia U.S.A.
9 A6 Key, The New Zealand
145 D7 Key West Florida U.S.A.
148 B4 Key West Iowa U.S.A.
147 H3 Kezar Falls Maine U.S.A.
129 D3 Kezi Zimbabwe
79 K2 Kežmarok Slovakia
131 F3 Kgakala South Africa
128 C3 Kgalagadi div. Botswana
128 D3 Kgatleng div. Botswana
128 C3 Kgomofatshe Pan salt pan Botswana
128 C3 Kgoro Pan salt pan Botswana
131 F3 Kgotsong South Africa
131 G4 Kgubetswana South Africa
31 K2 Khabarovsk div. Rus. Fed.
31 K2 Khabarovsk Rus. Fed.
47 J2 Khabary Rus. Fed.
119 H4 Khabb, W. watercourse Yemen
Khabis see Shahdāb
77 N3 Khabovichy Belarus
119 H3 Khabrā al'Arn salt pan Saudi Arabia
43 D3 Khabrat Abu al Ḩusain reg. Jordan
43 D5 Khabrat Umm ar Raqabah l. Saudi Arabia
42 E3 Khabur r. Syria
Khachmas see Xaçmaz
119 H4 Khaḑārah Saudi Arabia
124 E1 Khadari watercourse Sudan
51 F6 Khadyzhensk Rus. Fed.
36 E4 Khaga India
37 F4 Khagaria India
37 G5 Khagrachbari Bangladesh
36 E5 Khairagarh India
36 B3 Khairgarh Pakistan
36 C3 Khaïrpur Pakistan
36 B4 Khairpur Pakistan
36 D4 Khairthal India
36 B2 Khajuri Kach Pakistan
47 M2 Khakasiya Rus. Fed.
52 G1 Khakhaly Rus. Fed.
128 C3 Khakhea Botswana
39 F2 Khakīr Afghanistan
39 F3 Khak-rēz Afghanistan
39 F3 Khakriz reg. Afghanistan
46 F5 Khalach Turkmenistan
39 B3 Khalafabād Iran
39 B2 Khalajestan reg. Iran
39 C2 Khalidabad Iran
36 A3 Khalifat mt. Pakistan
43 A4 Khalîg Abu Qîr b. Egypt
119 E1 Khalîg el 'Arab b. Egypt
43 B4 Khalig el Tîna b. Egypt
118 D1 Khalīj Bumbah b. Libya
118 C1 Khalīj Surt g. Libya
39 D2 Khalilabad Iran
46 C5 Khalkhāl Iran
38 D2 Khallikot India
54 F4 Khalopyenichy Belarus
30 B2 Khamar-Daban, Khrebet mountain range Rus. Fed.
36 C5 Khambhat India
36 B6 Khambhat, Gulf of b. India
36 D5 Khamgaon India
126 D1 Khamir Yemen
43 D5 Khamīsah Saudi Arabia
119 H4 Khamis Mushayţ Saudi Arabia
24 D3 Khamkkeut Laos
38 C2 Khammam India
45 O3 Khampa Rus. Fed.
45 N3 Khamra Rus. Fed.
43 B4 Khamsa Egypt
39 A1 Khamseh reg. Iran
39 G2 Khan Afghanistan
39 G1 Khānābād Afghanistan
42 E3 Khān al Baghdādī Iraq
38 A3 Khanapur India
42 F2 Khānaqāh Iran
42 F3 Khānaqīn Iraq
43 D4 Khān az Zabīb Jordan
47 H5 Khanbari P. pass Jammu and Kashmir
36 C4 Khandela India
36 B2 Khand P. pass Afghanistan/Pakistan
36 C1 Khandud Afghanistan
36 D5 Khandwa India
45 P3 Khandyga Rus. Fed.
36 B3 Khanewal Pakistan
25 E4 Khanh Dương Vietnam
52 C2 Khanino Rus. Fed.
39 C3 Khanīyak Iran
31 K3 Khanka, Lake l. China/Rus. Fed.
36 D3 Khanna India
36 B3 Khanpur Pakistan
43 D2 Khān Shaykhūn Syria
47 H4 Khantau Kazakhstan
45 L3 Khantayskoye, Ozero l. Rus. Fed.
Khan Tengri mt. see Hantengri Feng
44 H3 Khanty-Mansiysk Rus. Fed.
43 C4 Khān Yūnis Gaza
25 B5 Khao Chum Thong Thailand
25 B5 Khao Lang Kha Toek mt. Thailand
25 B5 Khao Luang mt. Thailand
25 C4 Khao Sai Dao Tai mt. Thailand
36 D5 Khapa India
39 B2 Khar r. Iran
51 H6 Kharabali Rus. Fed.
37 F5 Kharagpur India
30 D2 Kharagun Rus. Fed.
30 B2 Khara-Khuzhar Rus. Fed.
39 D1 Kharakī Iran
39 D3 Khārān r. Iran
36 A3 Kharan Pakistan
39 C2 Kharānáq Iran
Kharari see Abu Road
77 N3 Kharava Belarus
43 B6 Kharâza, G. el mt. Egypt
38 A2 Khardi India
36 D2 Khardung La pass India
39 E2 Kharez Ilias Afghanistan
39 B3 Khārg Is is Iran
36 C5 Khargon India
36 C4 Khari r. Rajasthan India
36 C4 Khari r. Rajasthan India
36 C2 Kharian Pakistan
37 E5 Khariar India
43 B4 Kharîm, G. h. Egypt
53 G2 Kharkiv div. Ukraine
53 G2 Kharkiv Ukraine
Khar'kov see Kharkiv
57 H3 Kharlu Rus. Fed.
112 E4 Kharmanli Bulgaria
39 G2 Kharoti reg. Afghanistan
50 G3 Kharovsk Rus. Fed.
37 E5 Kharsia India
119 F4 Khartoum div. Sudan
119 F4 Khartoum Sudan
119 F4 Khartoum North Sudan
51 H7 Khasavyurt Rus. Fed.
39 E3 Khash Afghanistan
39 E3 Khāsh Iran
39 E3 Khash Desert desert Afghanistan
119 G5 Khashm el Girba Sudan
39 E3 Khash Rud r. Afghanistan
51 G7 Khashuri Georgia
37 G4 Khāsi Hills India
112 E3 Khaskovo div. Bulgaria
112 E4 Khaskovo Bulgaria
45 M2 Khatanga Rus. Fed.
43 B4 Khatmia Pass pass Egypt
120 A5 Khatt et Toueïrja watercourse Mauritania
39 C3 Khātūnābād Iran
45 T3 Khatyrka Rus. Fed.
52 D4 Khava r. Rus. Fed.
47 G4 Khavast Uzbekistan
36 B5 Khavda India
39 G2 Khawak P. pass Afghanistan
39 D4 Khawr Fakkan U.A.E.
25 B4 Khawsa Myanmar
119 H4 Khawsh Saudi Arabia
131 E5 Khayamnandi South Africa
119 G2 Khaybar Saudi Arabia
119 H4 Khaybar Saudi Arabia
47 H5 Khaydarken Kyrgyzstan
130 B7 Khayelitsha South Africa
46 F4 Khazarasp Uzbekistan
42 E2 Khāzir r. Iraq
24 D3 Khê Bo Vietnam
38 A2 Khed India
36 C4 Khedbrahma India
39 D2 Khedrî Iran
129 F3 Khehuene, Pta pt Mozambique
36 E3 Khela India
120 C2 Khemisset Morocco
121 F1 Khenchela Algeria
120 C2 Khenifra Morocco
39 C3 Kherāmeh Iran
39 B2 Khersan r. Iran
53 E3 Kherson div. Ukraine
53 E3 Kherson Ukraine
51 E6 Khersones, Mys pt Ukraine
45 L2 Kheta r. Rus. Fed.
39 C3 Kheyrābād Iran
39 C1 Khezerābād Iran
36 D4 Khilchipur India
30 C2 Khilok r. Rus. Fed.
30 D2 Khilok Rus. Fed.
52 C2 Khimki Rus. Fed.
42 D3 Khirbat Isrīyah Syria
42 E4 Khirr, Wādī al watercourse Saudi Arabia
112 E3 Khisarya Bulgaria
36 D2 Khitai P. pass China/Jammu and Kashmir
52 E3 Khitrovo Rus. Fed.
46 F4 Khiva Uzbekistan
42 F2 Khīyāv Iran
57 H3 Khiytola Rus. Fed.
52 B2 Khlepen' Rus. Fed.
52 D3 Khlevnoye Rus. Fed.
77 M5 Khlivchany Ukraine
52 D3 Khmelinets Rus. Fed.
52 A2 Khmelita Rus. Fed.
53 E1 Khmeliv Ukraine
53 B2 Khmel'nyts'kyy div. Ukraine
53 B2 Khmel'nyts'kyy Ukraine
53 B2 Khmil'nyk Ukraine
77 M3 Khmyelyeva Belarus
52 E3 Khobotovo Rus. Fed.
42 F2 Khodā Afarīn Iran
77 O2 Khodarawtsy Belarus
53 A2 Khodoriv Ukraine
53 C1 Khodorkiv Ukraine
46 E4 Khodzheyli Uzbekistan
124 E2 Khogali Sudan
36 A3 Khojak P. pass Pakistan
52 F1 Khokhloma Rus. Fed.
51 F5 Khokhol'skiy Rus. Fed.
36 D2 Khoksar India
39 F1 Kholm Afghanistan
50 D3 Kholm Rus. Fed.
52 B3 Kholmechi Rus. Fed.
50 G1 Kholmogory Rus. Fed.
27 Q2 Kholmsk Rus. Fed.
53 E1 Kholmy Ukraine
52 A2 Kholm-Zhirkovskiy Rus. Fed.
30 B2 Kholtoson Rus. Fed.
52 E1 Kholuy Rus. Fed.
128 B3 Khomas div. Namibia
128 B3 Khomas Hochland reg. Namibia
39 B2 Khomeyn Iran
53 B2 Khomora r. Ukraine
52 B4 Khomutovka Rus. Fed.
52 C3 Khomutovo Rus. Fed.
39 B2 Khondāb Iran
51 G7 Khoni Georgia
39 C4 Khonj Iran
37 H4 Khonsa India
45 Q3 Khonuu Rus. Fed.
52 F3 Khoper r. Saratov Rus. Fed.
51 G5 Khoper r. Volgograd Rus. Fed.
45 P5 Khor r. Rus. Fed.
31 K3 Khor Rus. Fed.
36 B4 Khora Pakistan
39 D2 Khorāsan div. Iran
37 F5 Khordha India
39 B4 Khor Duweihin b. Saudi Arabia/U.A.E.
30 D1 Khorinsk Rus. Fed.
128 A3 Khorixas Namibia
52 D2 Khorlovo Rus. Fed.
53 E2 Khorol r. Ukraine
31 K3 Khorol Rus. Fed.
53 E2 Khorol Ukraine
53 G2 Khoroshe Ukraine
53 A2 Khorostkiv Ukraine
39 B2 Khorramābād Iran
47 H5 Khorugh Tajikistan
39 D2 Khosf Iran
51 H6 Khosheutovo Rus. Fed.
39 B3 Khosravī Iran
36 A3 Khost Pakistan
52 C3 Khotetovo Rus. Fed.
53 F1 Khotin' Ukraine
52 C1 Khot'kovo Rus. Fed.
52 B3 Khot'kovo Rus. Fed.
53 F1 Khotmyzhsk Rus. Fed.
52 A3 Khotsimsk Rus. Fed.
53 D2 Khots'ky Ukraine
52 B3 Khotynets Rus. Fed.
120 C2 Khouribga Morocco
37 G4 Khowai India
39 C3 Khowrjān Iran
39 G2 Khowst Afghanistan
53 C1 Khoyniki Belarus
126 D2 Khozor Anghar Djibouti
53 E2 Khrestyteleve Ukraine
24 A2 Khreum Myanmar
37 G4 Khri r. India
50 H2 Khristoforovo Rus. Fed.
46 E2 Khromtau Kazakhstan
53 E3 Khrystoforivka Ukraine
53 C2 Khrystynivka Ukraine
131 G4 Khubelu r. Lesotho
30 D2 Khudan r. Rus. Fed.
Khudat see Xudat
36 A4 Khude Hills mountain range Pakistan
30 D2 Khudunskiy Khr. mountain range Rus. Fed.
119 H3 Khuff Saudi Arabia
130 C3 Khuis Botswana
47 G4 Khŭjand Tajikistan
25 D4 Khu Khan Thailand
53 F1 Khukhra Ukraine
119 G3 Khulays Saudi Arabia
51 H6 Khulkhuta Rus. Fed.
39 F2 Khulm r. Afghanistan
37 G5 Khulna Bangladesh
37 G5 Khulna Bangladesh
131 F3 Khuma South Africa
43 D2 Khunayzīr, J. al mountain range Syria
119 F4 Khuneiqa watercourse Sudan
36 C1 Khunjerab Pass pass China/Jammu and Kashmir
39 B2 Khunsar Iran
37 F5 Khunti India
39 D2 Khūr Iran
36 D4 Khurai India
39 C4 Khūran chan. Iran
36 D3 Khurja India
39 E2 Khurmalik Afghanistan
36 C2 Khushab Pakistan
39 D3 Khushk Rud Iran
43 D5 Khush Shah, W. el watercourse Jordan
39 E2 Khuspas Afghanistan
51 B5 Khust Ukraine
51 G6 Khutorskoy Rus. Fed.
131 F3 Khutsong South Africa
119 E5 Khuwei Sudan
36 A4 Khuzdar Pakistan
39 B3 Khūzestān div. Iran
39 E2 Khvāf Iran
42 F2 Khvājeh Iran
51 J4 Khvalynsk Rus. Fed.
52 B2 Khvashchevka Rus. Fed.
52 B3 Khvastovichi Rus. Fed.
52 H3 Khvatovka Rus. Fed.
39 C2 Khvor Iran
39 D2 Khvord Nārvan Iran
39 B3 Khvormūj Iran
52 E3 Khvorostyanka Rus. Fed.
42 F2 Khvoy Iran

50 E3 **Khvoynaya** Rus. Fed.
25 B4 **Khwae Noi r.** Thailand
39 E3 **Khwaja Ali** Afghanistan
36 A3 **Khwaja Amran mt.** Pakistan
39 G1 **Khwaja Muhammad Ra. mountain range** Afghanistan
36 B2 **Khyber Pass pass** Afghanistan/Pakistan
77 L6 **Khyriv** Ukraine
6 □6 **Kia i.** Fiji
13 G3 **Kiama** *New South Wales* Australia
23 C5 **Kiamba** Philippines
125 E5 **Kiambi** Congo(Zaire)
151 E5 **Kiamichi r.** *Oklahoma* U.S.A.
141 H3 **Kiamika, Lac l.** *Québec* Canada
Kiangsu *see* **Jiangsu**
56 H2 **Kiantajärvi l.** Finland
39 C1 **Kiāseh** Iran
115 D4 **Kiato** Greece
55 A3 **Kibæk** Denmark
127 C6 **Kibaha** Tanzania
127 B4 **Kibale** Uganda
124 E3 **Kibali r.** Congo(Zaire)
125 B4 **Kibangou** Congo
36 D2 **Kibar** India
23 C5 **Kibawe** Philippines
127 C6 **Kibaya** Tanzania
127 C6 **Kibiti** Tanzania
127 B4 **Kiboga** Uganda
125 E4 **Kibombo** Congo(Zaire)
127 B5 **Kibondo** Tanzania
126 C3 **Kibre Mengist** Ethiopia
114 B1 **Kičevo** Macedonia
36 D3 **Kichha** India
118 C4 **Kichi-Kichi well** Chad
50 H3 **Kichmengskiy Gorodok** Rus. Fed.
123 E3 **Kidal div.** Mali
123 E3 **Kidal** Mali
62 D2 **Kidderminster** *England* U.K.
131 F6 **Kidd's Beach** South Africa
126 B4 **Kidepo Valley National Park nat. park** Uganda
122 B4 **Kidira** Senegal
63 E3 **Kidlington** *England* U.K.
36 D2 **Kidmang** India
8 F3 **Kidnappers, Cape c.** New Zealand
62 D1 **Kidsgrove** *England* U.K.
43 C5 **Kid, W. watercourse** Egypt
62 B3 **Kidwelly** *Wales* U.K.
75 H5 **Kiefersfelden** Germany
148 C4 **Kiel** *Wisconsin* U.S.A.
72 F1 **Kiel** Germany
77 J5 **Kielce div.** Poland
77 J5 **Kielce** Poland
65 F2 **Kielder Water resr** *England* U.K.
69 C3 **Kieldrecht** Belgium
73 F1 **Kieler Bucht b.** Germany
72 F1 **Kieler Förde g.** Germany
77 H3 **Kiemozia** Poland
125 E6 **Kienge** Congo(Zaire)
131 H2 **Kiepersol** South Africa
72 C4 **Kierspe** Germany
76 G5 **Kietrz** Poland
73 K3 **Kietz** Germany
Kiev *see* **Kyyiv**
120 B5 **Kiffa** Mauritania
115 E4 **Kifisia** Greece
114 D4 **Kifisos r.** Greece
42 F3 **Kifrī** Iraq
127 B5 **Kigali** Rwanda
124 E4 **Kigezi Game Reserve res.** Uganda
42 E2 **Kiğı** Turkey
139 H2 **Kiglapait Mts mountain range** *Newfoundland* Canada
122 C4 **Kignan** Mali
127 B5 **Kigoma div.** Tanzania
127 A5 **Kigoma** Tanzania
56 F2 **Kihlanki** Finland
57 F3 **Kihniö** Finland
54 C2 **Kihnu i.** Estonia
59 J1 **Kihti Skiftet chan.** Finland
47 H3 **Kiik** Kazakhstan
56 G2 **Kiiminki** Finland
29 F6 **Kii-nagashima** Japan
28 C8 **Kiire** Japan
29 E6 **Kii-sanchi mountain range** Japan
28 E7 **Kii-suidō chan.** Japan
29 □2 **Kijoka** Japan
127 C6 **Kijungu Well well** Tanzania
54 F2 **Kikerino** Rus. Fed.
79 K6 **Kikinda** Yugoslavia
39 E4 **Kikki** Pakistan
52 H1 **Kiknur** Rus. Fed.
28 H3 **Kikonai** Japan
125 E5 **Kikondja** Congo(Zaire)
6 □1 **Kikori r.** P.N.G.
6 □1 **Kikori** P.N.G.
76 D2 **Kikorze** Poland
78 H3 **Kikót** Poland
28 C7 **Kikuchi** Japan
51 G5 **Kikvidze** Rus. Fed.
125 C5 **Kikwit** Congo(Zaire)
59 E2 **Kil** Sweden
56 E3 **Kilafors** Sweden
38 B4 **Kilakkarai** India
36 D2 **Kilar** India
153 □2 **Kilauea** *Hawaii* U.S.A.
153 □2 **Kilauea Crater crater** *Hawaii* U.S.A.
81 G2 **Kilb** Austria
43 B1 **Kılbasan** Turkey
67 D3 **Kilbeggan** Rep. of Ireland
64 D2 **Kilbirnie** *Scotland* U.K.
66 C5 **Kilbrannan Sound chan.** *Scotland* U.K.
83 D1 **Kilchberg** Switzerland
53 F2 **Kil'chen' r.** Ukraine
31 J4 **Kilchu** North Korea
64 B4 **Kilcock** Rep. of Ireland
67 D4 **Kilcommon** Rep. of Ireland
64 A3 **Kilconney** Rep. of Ireland
67 E3 **Kilcoole** Rep. of Ireland
67 D3 **Kilcormac** Rep. of Ireland
15 H5 **Kilcoy** *Queensland* Australia
64 D2 **Kilcreggan** *Scotland* U.K.
67 E3 **Kilcullen** Rep. of Ireland
67 E3 **Kildare div.** Rep. of Ireland
67 E3 **Kildare** Rep. of Ireland
56 J1 **Kil'dinstroy** Rus. Fed.
52 H1 **Kilemary** Rus. Fed.
125 C5 **Kilembe** Congo(Zaire)
66 C5 **Kilfinan** *Scotland* U.K.
151 E5 **Kilgore** *Texas* U.S.A.
14 C3 **Kilgour r.** *Northern Terr.* Australia
65 F2 **Kilham** *England* U.K.
125 E4 **Kiliba** Congo(Zaire)
127 C5 **Kilifi** Kenya
127 C5 **Kilimanjaro div.** Tanzania
127 C5 **Kilimanjaro mt.** Tanzania
127 C5 **Kilimanjaro National Park nat. park** Tanzania
6 □1 **Kilinailau Is is** P.N.G.
127 C6 **Kilindoni** Tanzania
54 D2 **Kilingi-Nõmme** Estonia
42 D2 **Kilis** Turkey
112 G2 **Kiliya** Ukraine
67 B4 **Kilkee** Rep. of Ireland
67 F2 **Kilkeel** *Northern Ireland* U.K.
67 D4 **Kilkenny div.** Rep. of Ireland
67 D4 **Kilkenny** Rep. of Ireland
62 B4 **Kilkhampton** *England* U.K.
114 D1 **Kilkis div.** Greece
114 D2 **Kilkis** Greece
15 H5 **Kilkivan** *Queensland* Australia
67 B2 **Killala** Rep. of Ireland
67 B2 **Killala Bay b.** Rep. of Ireland
140 E2 **Killala Lake l.** *Ontario* Canada
67 C4 **Killaloe** Rep. of Ireland
141 G4 **Killaloe Station** *Ontario* Canada
137 G4 **Killam** *Alberta* Canada
140 E4 **Killarney** *Ontario* Canada
15 H6 **Killarney** *Queensland* Australia
67 B4 **Killarney** Rep. of Ireland
145 □2 **Killarney, Lake l.** The Bahamas
140 E3 **Killarney National Park nat. park** *Ontario* Canada
67 B4 **Killarney National Park nat. park** Rep. of Ireland
67 B3 **Killary Harbour harbour** Rep. of Ireland
64 D1 **Killearn** *Scotland* U.K.
151 D6 **Killeen** *Texas* U.S.A.
67 D4 **Killenaule** Rep. of Ireland
66 E4 **Killiecrankie** *Scotland* U.K.
67 C3 **Killimor** Rep. of Ireland
66 D4 **Killin** *Scotland* U.K.
67 F2 **Killinchy** *Northern Ireland* U.K.
67 E4 **Killinick** Rep. of Ireland
139 H1 **Killiniq** *Québec* Canada
139 H1 **Killiniq Island i.** *Newfoundland* Canada
67 B4 **Killorglin** Rep. of Ireland
64 C3 **Killough** *Northern Ireland* U.K.
67 E4 **Killurin** Rep. of Ireland
67 C2 **Killybegs** Rep. of Ireland
64 B3 **Killylea** *Northern Ireland* U.K.
67 D1 **Kilmacrenan** Rep. of Ireland
67 B3 **Kilmaine** Rep. of Ireland
67 C4 **Kilmallock** Rep. of Ireland
66 B3 **Kilmaluag** *Scotland* U.K.
66 D5 **Kilmarnock** *Scotland* U.K.
66 C4 **Kilmartin** *Scotland* U.K.
66 C4 **Kilmelford** *Scotland* U.K.
50 J3 **Kil'mez' r.** Rus. Fed.
67 E4 **Kilmichael Point pt** Rep. of Ireland
67 C5 **Kilmona** Rep. of Ireland
13 F4 **Kilmore** *Victoria* Australia
67 E4 **Kilmore Quay** Rep. of Ireland
64 C1 **Kilninver** *Scotland* U.K.
127 C6 **Kilosa** Tanzania
56 F1 **Kilpisjärvi** Finland
56 J1 **Kilp"yavr** Rus. Fed.
67 E2 **Kilrea** *Northern Ireland* U.K.
67 B4 **Kilrush** Rep. of Ireland
66 D5 **Kilsyth** *Scotland* U.K.
67 C3 **Kiltimagh** Rep. of Ireland
38 A4 **Kilttān i.** India
67 C3 **Kiltullagh** Rep. of Ireland
39 B3 **Kīlūr Karīm** Iran
125 E5 **Kilwa** Congo(Zaire)
127 C6 **Kilwa Kisiwani i.** Tanzania
127 C6 **Kilwa Kivinje** Tanzania
127 C6 **Kilwa Masoko** Tanzania
66 D5 **Kilwinning** *Scotland* U.K.
Kilyazi *see* **Gilazi**
124 C2 **Kim** Chad
127 C6 **Kimambi** Tanzania
125 B4 **Kimba** Congo
150 C3 **Kimball** *Nebraska* U.S.A.
6 □1 **Kimbe** P.N.G.
136 F5 **Kimberley** *B.C.* Canada
131 E4 **Kimberley** South Africa
130 E4 **Kimberley airport** South Africa
16 D3 **Kimberley Downs** *Western Australia* Australia
16 D3 **Kimberley Plateau plat.** *Western Australia* Australia
8 E4 **Kimbolton** New Zealand
31 J4 **Kimch'aek** North Korea
31 J5 **Kimch'ŏn** South Korea
28 B6 **Kimhae** South Korea
57 F3 **Kimito** Finland
31 H6 **Kimje** South Korea
114 F1 **Kimmeria** Greece
28 H2 **Kimobetsu** Japan
115 F6 **Kimolos i.** Greece
115 F6 **Kimolos** Greece
125 B4 **Kimongo** Congo
52 D3 **Kimovsk** Rus. Fed.
122 D4 **Kimparana** Mali
125 B5 **Kimpese** Congo(Zaire)
29 G4 **Kimpoku-san mt.** Japan
52 C1 **Kimry** Rus. Fed.
125 C5 **Kimvula** Congo(Zaire)
50 H1 **Kimzha** Rus. Fed.
29 □2 **Kin** Japan
29 □2 **Kina** Japan
23 A5 **Kinabalu, G. mt.** Malaysia
23 A5 **Kinabatangan r.** Malaysia
127 C5 **Kinango** Kenya
113 F6 **Kinaros i.** Greece
142 C1 **Kinbasket Lake l.** *B.C.* Canada
66 E2 **Kinbrace** *Scotland* U.K.
140 E4 **Kincardine** *Ontario* Canada
66 E4 **Kincardine** *Scotland* U.K.
24 B1 **Kinchang** Myanmar
136 D3 **Kincolith** *B.C.* Canada
66 E3 **Kincraig** *Scotland* U.K.
125 E5 **Kinda** Congo(Zaire)
24 A2 **Kindat** Myanmar
81 G3 **Kindberg** Austria
73 G4 **Kindelbrück** Germany
151 E6 **Kinder** *Louisiana* U.S.A.
69 F4 **Kinderbeuern** Germany
65 G4 **Kinder Scout h.** *England* U.K.
137 H4 **Kindersley** *Saskatchewan* Canada
122 B4 **Kindia** Guinea
75 G4 **Kinding** Germany
87 G3 **Kindsbach** Germany
125 E4 **Kindu** Congo(Zaire)
46 D2 **Kinel'** Rus. Fed.
46 D2 **Kinel'-Cherkasy** Rus. Fed.
52 F1 **Kineshma** Rus. Fed.
15 F4 **King r.** *Northern Terr.* Australia
13 F5 **King r.** *Tasmania* Australia
125 C5 **Kingandu** Congo(Zaire)
15 G5 **Kingaroy** *Queensland* Australia
64 C2 **Kingarth** *Scotland* U.K.
154 B3 **King City** *California* U.S.A.
14 D5 **King Cr. watercourse** *Queensland* Australia
16 D2 **King Edward r.** *Western Australia* Australia
179 C1 **King Edward Point U.K. Base** Antarctica
82 C1 **Kingersheim** France
146 E3 **King Ferry** *New York* U.S.A.
147 H2 **Kingfield** *Maine* U.S.A.
151 D5 **Kingfisher** *Oklahoma* U.S.A.
171 D7 **King George B. b.** Falkland Is.
179 B1 **King George I. i.** *S. Shetland Is* Antarctica
138 E2 **King George Islands is** *N.W.T.* Canada
17 B7 **King George Sound b.** *Western Australia* Australia
16 C4 **King Hill h.** *Western Australia* Australia
136 D4 **King I. i.** *B.C.* Canada
13 F4 **King I. i.** *Tasmania* Australia
King I. i. *see* **Kadan Kyun**
125 B4 **Kingimbi** Congo(Zaire)
54 F2 **Kingisepp** Rus. Fed.
Kingissepa *see* **Kuressaare**
141 F2 **King Kirkland** *Ontario* Canada
179 D5 **King Leopold and Queen Astrid Coast coastal area** Antarctica
16 D3 **King Leopold Ranges h.** *Western Australia* Australia
155 E4 **Kingman** *Arizona* U.S.A.
151 D4 **Kingman** *Kansas* U.S.A.
147 J2 **Kingman** *Maine* U.S.A.
136 D3 **King Mtn mt.** *B.C.* Canada
125 E4 **Kingombe Mbali** Congo(Zaire)
12 C2 **Kingoonya** *S. Australia* Australia
179 A3 **King Pen. pen.** Antarctica
10 □4 **King Pt pt** *Lord Howe I.* Pacific Ocean
36 B3 **Kingri** Pakistan
154 C3 **Kings r.** *California* U.S.A.
67 D4 **Kings r.** Rep. of Ireland
62 C4 **Kingsbridge** *England* U.K.
154 C3 **Kingsburg** *California* U.S.A.
147 J2 **Kingsbury** *Maine* U.S.A.
62 D4 **Kingsbury Episcopi** *England* U.K.
154 C3 **Kings Canyon National Park nat. park** *California* U.S.A.
63 E3 **Kingsclere** *England* U.K.
12 D3 **Kingscote** *S. Australia* Australia
67 E3 **Kingscourt** Rep. of Ireland
179 B2 **King Sejong Korea Base** *South Shetland Islands* Antarctica
148 C3 **Kingsford** *Michigan* U.S.A.
62 C4 **Kingskerswell** *England* U.K.
145 D6 **Kingsland** *Georgia* U.S.A.
148 E5 **Kingsland** *Indiana* U.S.A.
131 H3 **Kingsley** South Africa
63 G2 **King's Lynn** *England* U.K.
63 G3 **Kingsnorth** *England* U.K.
16 C3 **King Sound b.** *Western Australia* Australia
152 E3 **Kings Peak summit** *Utah* U.S.A.
146 B6 **Kingsport** *Tennessee* U.S.A.
62 C4 **Kingsteignton** *England* U.K.
62 D3 **Kingsthorne** *England* U.K.
148 B6 **Kingston** *Illinois* U.S.A.
147 F4 **Kingston** *New York* U.S.A.
11 □1 **Kingston** *Norfolk I.* Pacific Ocean
141 G4 **Kingston** *Ontario* Canada
13 F5 **Kingston** *Tasmania* Australia
159 □1 **Kingston** Jamaica
9 B6 **Kingston** New Zealand
63 E3 **Kingston Bagpuize** *England* U.K.
155 E4 **Kingston Peak summit** *California* U.S.A.
12 D4 **Kingston S.E.** *S. Australia* Australia
65 H4 **Kingston upon Hull div.** *England* U.K.
65 H4 **Kingston upon Hull** *England* U.K.
63 F3 **Kingston upon Thames** *England* U.K.
159 G4 **Kingstown** St Vincent
151 D7 **Kingsville** *Texas* U.S.A.
62 D3 **Kingswood** *England* U.K.
63 E3 **King's Worthy** *England* U.K.
62 C2 **Kington** *England* U.K.
66 D3 **Kingussie** *Scotland* U.K.
135 J3 **King William I. i.** *N.W.T.* Canada
131 F6 **King William's Town** South Africa
151 E6 **Kingwood** *Texas* U.S.A.
146 D5 **Kingwood** *W. Virginia* U.S.A.
113 F5 **Kınık** Turkey
131 G5 **Kinirapoort** South Africa
137 J4 **Kinistino** *Saskatchewan* Canada
53 G3 **Kinka r.** Ukraine
125 B4 **Kinkala** Congo
29 H4 **Kinka-san i.** Japan
136 B3 **Kinleith** New Zealand
66 B3 **Kinloch** *Scotland* U.K.
9 B6 **Kinloch** New Zealand
66 C4 **Kinlochewe** *Scotland* U.K.
66 D4 **Kinlochleven** *Scotland* U.K.
66 D4 **Kinloch Rannoch** *Scotland* U.K.
66 E3 **Kinloss** *Scotland* U.K.
24 A3 **Kinmaw** Myanmar
29 □2 **Kin-misaki c.** Japan
141 F4 **Kinmount** *Ontario* Canada
59 E3 **Kinna** Sweden
67 D3 **Kinnegad** Rep. of Ireland
59 E2 **Kinneviken b.** Sweden
38 C4 **Kinniyai** Sri Lanka
56 G3 **Kinnula** Finland
29 E6 **Kino-kawa r.** Japan
137 J3 **Kinoosao** *Saskatchewan* Canada
69 D3 **Kinrooi** Belgium
66 E4 **Kinross** *Scotland* U.K.
131 G3 **Kinross** South Africa
67 C5 **Kinsale** Rep. of Ireland
58 B1 **Kinsarvik** Norway
125 C4 **Kinshasa div.** Congo(Zaire)
125 C4 **Kinshasa** Congo(Zaire)
150 D4 **Kinsley** *Kansas* U.S.A.
145 E5 **Kinston** *N. Carolina* U.S.A.
54 B4 **Kintai** Lithuania
22 C4 **Kintamali** Indonesia
122 D5 **Kintampo** Ghana
122 C4 **Kintinian** Guinea
22 C2 **Kintop** Indonesia
66 F3 **Kintore** *Scotland* U.K.
12 B1 **Kintore, Mt mt.** *S. Australia* Australia
14 B4 **Kintore Ra. h.** *Northern Terr.* Australia
66 C5 **Kintyre pen.** *Scotland* U.K.
66 C5 **Kintyre, Mull of headland** *Scotland* U.K.
24 A2 **Kinu** Myanmar
136 F3 **Kinuso** *Alberta* Canada
67 C3 **Kinvara** Rep. of Ireland
29 □2 **Kin-wan b.** Japan
126 B4 **Kinyeti mt.** Sudan
74 C4 **Kinzig r.** Germany
127 B5 **Kiomboi** Tanzania
115 B4 **Kioni** Greece
141 F3 **Kiosk** *Ontario* Canada
141 F3 **Kipawa, Lac l.** *Québec* Canada
127 B6 **Kipembawe** Tanzania
54 F2 **Kipen'** Rus. Fed.
127 B6 **Kipengere Range mountain range** Tanzania
127 B6 **Kipili** Tanzania
127 D5 **Kipini** Kenya
114 C3 **Kipoureio** Greece
64 D1 **Kippen** *Scotland* U.K.
87 G4 **Kippenheim** Germany
64 B4 **Kippure h.** Rep. of Ireland
53 D1 **Kipti** Ukraine
147 F6 **Kiptopeke** *Virginia* U.S.A.
125 E6 **Kipushi** Congo(Zaire)
125 E6 **Kipushia** Congo(Zaire)
112 B3 **Kir r.** Albania
6 □1 **Kirakira** Solomon Is.
43 B1 **Kıraman** Turkey
38 C2 **Kirandul** India
122 B3 **Kirané** Mali
54 F5 **Kiraws k** Belarus
113 G5 **Kiraz** Turkey
54 C2 **Kirbla** Estonia
80 E4 **Kirchbach** Austria
82 C1 **Kirchberg** *Bern* Switzerland
83 E1 **Kirchberg** *St Gallen* Switzerland
75 J4 **Kirchberg** Germany
81 G2 **Kirchberg am Wagram** Austria
81 G3 **Kirchberg am Wechsel** Austria
81 G2 **Kirchberg an der Pielach** Austria
81 G4 **Kirchberg an der Raab** Austria
74 C3 **Kirchberg (Hunsrück)** Germany
80 D3 **Kirchberg in Tirol** Austria
80 D3 **Kirchbichl** Austria
73 G2 **Kirchdorf** *Mecklenburg-Vorpommern* Germany
72 D3 **Kirchdorf** *Niedersachsen* Germany
81 F3 **Kirchdorf an der Krems div.** Austria
81 F3 **Kirchdorf an der Krems** Austria
80 D3 **Kirchdorf in Tirol** Austria
74 D2 **Kirchhain** Germany
75 G4 **Kirchheim bei München** Germany
74 D3 **Kirchheim-bolanden** Germany
74 E4 **Kirchheim unter Teck** Germany
87 H1 **Kirchhundem** Germany
80 D2 **Kirchroth** Germany
81 H3 **Kirchschlag in der Buckligen Welt** Austria
82 C1 **Kirchzarten** Germany
118 C4 **Kirdimi** Chad
45 M4 **Kirensk** Rus. Fed.
53 G2 **Kireyevsk** Rus. Fed.
52 B3 **Kireykovo** Rus. Fed.
Kirghizia *see* **Kyrgyzstan**
47 H4 **Kirghiz Range mountain range** Asia
Kirgizskiy Khrebet mountain range *see* **Kirghiz Range**
124 C4 **Kiri** Congo(Zaire)
4 J4 **Kiribati country** Pacific Ocean
42 D2 **Kırıkhan** Turkey
42 C2 **Kırıkkale** Turkey
50 F3 **Kirillov** Rus. Fed.
52 F3 **Kirillovo** Rus. Fed.
52 G1 **Kirillovo** Rus. Fed.
54 F1 **Kirillovskoye** Rus. Fed.
127 C5 **Kirinyaga mt.** Kenya
36 B3 **Kiri Shamozai** Pakistan
50 E3 **Kirishi** Rus. Fed.
28 C8 **Kirishima-yama volcano** Japan
177 J5 **Kiritimati i.** Kiribati
42 A2 **Kırkağaç** Turkey
65 E3 **Kirkbean** *Scotland* U.K.
39 A1 **Kirk Bulāg D. mt.** Iran
65 F4 **Kirkby** *England* U.K.
65 F3 **Kirkby Lonsdale** *England* U.K.
65 H3 **Kirkbymoorside** *England* U.K.
65 F3 **Kirkby Stephen** *England* U.K.
66 E4 **Kirkcaldy** *Scotland* U.K.
66 C6 **Kirkcolm** *Scotland* U.K.
66 E5 **Kirkconnel** *Scotland* U.K.
67 F2 **Kirkcubbin** *Northern Ireland* U.K.
66 D6 **Kirkcudbright** *Scotland* U.K.
59 E1 **Kirkenær** Norway
56 H1 **Kirkenes** Norway
141 F4 **Kirkfield** *Ontario* Canada
65 F4 **Kirkham** *England* U.K.
64 D3 **Kirkinner** *Scotland* U.K.
66 D5 **Kirkintilloch** *Scotland* U.K.
55 □1 **Kirkjubønes pt** Faeroes
57 G3 **Kirkkonummi** Finland
155 F4 **Kirkland** *Arizona* U.S.A.
155 F4 **Kirkland Junction** *Arizona* U.S.A.
140 E2 **Kirkland Lake** *Ontario* Canada
112 F4 **Kırklareli div.** Turkey
42 A1 **Kırklareli** Turkey
112 F4 **Kırklareli Barajı resr** Turkey
9 C6 **Kirkliston Range mountain range** New Zealand
64 D2 **Kirkmichael** *Scotland* U.K.
66 E4 **Kirkmichael** *Scotland* U.K.
64 D3 **Kirk Michael** Isle of Man
65 F3 **Kirkoswald** *England* U.K.
66 E5 **Kirkpatrick-Fleming** *Scotland* U.K.
179 B4 **Kirkpatrick, Mt mt.** Antarctica
150 E3 **Kirksville** *Missouri* U.S.A.
64 C1 **Kirkton** *Scotland* U.K.
42 F3 **Kirkūk** Iraq
66 F2 **Kirkwall** *Scotland* U.K.
154 B2 **Kirkwood** *California* U.S.A.
150 F4 **Kirkwood** *Missouri* U.S.A.
131 E6 **Kirkwood** South Africa
43 C1 **Kırmıt** Turkey
74 C3 **Kirn** Germany
Kirobasi *see* **Mağara**
50 J3 **Kirov div.** Rus. Fed.
47 H4 **Kirov** Kyrgyzstan
52 B2 **Kirov** Rus. Fed.
Kirovabad *see* **Gäncä**
53 E2 **Kirove** *Kirovohrad* Ukraine
53 F3 **Kirove** *Zaporizhzhya* Ukraine
46 D2 **Kirovo** Kazakhstan
46 F1 **Kirovo** Rus. Fed.
50 J3 **Kirovo-Chepetsk** Rus. Fed.
53 E2 **Kirovohrad div.** Ukraine
53 E2 **Kirovohrad** Ukraine
50 D3 **Kirovsk** Rus. Fed.
39 E1 **Kirovsk** Turkmenistan
47 J4 **Kirovskiy** Kazakhstan
31 K3 **Kirovskiy** Rus. Fed.
39 G1 **Kirovskiy** Tajikistan
66 E4 **Kirriemuir** *Scotland* U.K.
50 K3 **Kirs** Rus. Fed.
52 F3 **Kirsanov** Rus. Fed.
69 F5 **Kirschweiler** Germany
42 C2 **Kırşehir** Turkey
36 A4 **Kirthar Range mountain range** Pakistan
65 H4 **Kirton in Lindsey** *England* U.K.
74 E2 **Kirtorf** Germany
56 F2 **Kiruna** Sweden
124 E4 **Kirundu** Congo(Zaire)
52 H2 **Kirya r.** Rus. Fed.
52 H2 **Kirya** Rus. Fed.
29 G5 **Kiryū** Japan
52 D1 **Kirzhach** Rus. Fed.
52 G2 **Kirzhemany** Rus. Fed.
59 F3 **Kisa** Sweden
29 G4 **Kisakata** Japan
124 E3 **Kisangani** Congo(Zaire)
125 C5 **Kisantu** Congo(Zaire)
25 B7 **Kisaran** Indonesia
127 C6 **Kisarawe** Tanzania
79 H4 **Kisbér** Hungary
47 L2 **Kiselevsk** Rus. Fed.
37 F4 **Kishanganj** India
36 B4 **Kishangarh** India
36 C4 **Kishangarh** India
36 C2 **Kishen Ganga r.** India
Kishinev *see* **Chişinău**
29 E6 **Kishiwada** Japan
52 F2 **Kishma r.** Rus. Fed.
37 G4 **Kishorganj** Bangladesh
36 C2 **Kishtwar** India
123 E5 **Kisi** Nigeria
77 H2 **Kisielice** Poland
77 L2 **Kisielnica** Poland
127 B6 **Kisigo r.** Tanzania
127 B5 **Kisii** Kenya
137 K4 **Kiskittogisu L. l.** *Manitoba* Canada
54 C1 **Kisko** Finland
79 K4 **Kisköre** Hungary
79 K4 **Kiskörei-Víztároló resr** Hungary
79 J5 **Kiskőrös** Hungary
79 J5 **Kiskunfélegyháza** Hungary
79 J5 **Kiskunhalas** Hungary
79 J4 **Kiskunlacháza** Hungary
79 J5 **Kiskunmajsa** Hungary
79 J5 **Kiskunság reg.** Hungary
79 J5 **Kiskunsági nat. park** Hungary
51 G7 **Kislovodsk** Rus. Fed.
127 D5 **Kismaayo** Somalia
29 F6 **Kiso-gawa r.** Japan
127 A5 **Kisoro** Uganda
29 F6 **Kiso-sanmyaku mountain range** Japan
81 F4 **Kisovec** Slovenia
Kisseraing I. i. *see* **Kanmaw Kyun**
122 B5 **Kissidougou** Guinea
145 D6 **Kissimmee** *Florida* U.S.A.
145 D7 **Kissimmee, L. l.** *Florida* U.S.A.
80 B2 **Kissing** Germany
137 J3 **Kississing L. l.** *Manitoba* Canada
74 E5 **Kißlegg** Germany
118 E3 **Kissu, Jebel mt.** Sudan
104 E4 **Kistanje** Croatia
79 J5 **Kistelek** Hungary
52 F3 **Kistendey** Rus. Fed.
Kistna r. *see* **Krishna**
79 K4 **Kisújszállás** Hungary
127 B5 **Kisumu** Kenya
79 M3 **Kisvárda** Hungary
76 F3 **Kiszkowo** Poland
79 K5 **Kiszombor** Hungary
126 B4 **Kit r.** Sudan
122 C4 **Kita** Mali
47 G5 **Kitab** Uzbekistan
28 C7 **Kitagawa** Japan
28 G2 **Kitahiyama** Japan
29 H5 **Kitaibaraki** Japan
29 H4 **Kitakami** Japan
29 H4 **Kitakami-gawa r.** Japan
28 C7 **Kitakata** Japan
29 G5 **Kitakata** Japan
28 C7 **Kita-Kyūshū** Japan
127 C4 **Kitale** Kenya
28 J2 **Kitami** Japan
28 J1 **Kitami-sanchi mountain range** Japan
127 C7 **Kitangari** Tanzania
127 B5 **Kitangiri, Lake l.** Tanzania
29 □1 **Kitano-hana c.** Japan
153 G4 **Kit Carson** *Colorado* U.S.A.
140 E5 **Kitchener** *Ontario* Canada
57 H3 **Kitee** Finland
126 B4 **Kitgum** Uganda
36 D3 **Kither** India
140 D2 **Kitigan** *Ontario* Canada
136 D4 **Kitimat** *B.C.* Canada
56 G2 **Kitinen r.** Finland
125 C5 **Kitombe** Congo(Zaire)
125 B5 **Kitona** Congo(Zaire)
52 E1 **Kitovo** Rus. Fed.
30 B1 **Kitoyskiye Gol'tsy mountain range** Rus. Fed.
115 F6 **Kitriani i.** Greece
114 D2 **Kitros** Greece
53 A2 **Kitsman'** Ukraine
28 C7 **Kitsuki** Japan
12 D2 **Kittakittaooloo, L. salt flat** *S. Australia* Australia
146 D4 **Kittanning** *Pennsylvania* U.S.A.
147 F4 **Kittatinny Mts h.** *New Jersey* U.S.A.
147 H3 **Kittery** *Maine* U.S.A.
56 G2 **Kittilä** Finland
81 J2 **Kittsee** Austria
145 F4 **Kitty Hawk** *N. Carolina* U.S.A.
125 E5 **Kitu** Congo(Zaire)
127 C5 **Kitui** Kenya
127 B6 **Kitunda** Tanzania
136 D3 **Kitwanga** *B.C.* Canada
125 E6 **Kitwe** Zambia
80 D3 **Kitzbüheler Alpen mts** Austria
80 D3 **Kitzbühel div.** Austria
80 D3 **Kitzbühel** Austria
74 F3 **Kitzingen** Germany
73 H4 **Kitzscher** Germany
56 G3 **Kiuruvesi** Finland
52 C1 **Kivertsi** Rus. Fed.
53 A1 **Kivertsi** Ukraine
56 G3 **Kivijärvi** Finland
54 E2 **Kiviõli** Estonia
54 D2 **Kivi-Vigala** Estonia
53 G2 **Kivsharivka** Ukraine
124 E4 **Kivu div.** Congo(Zaire)
127 A5 **Kivu, Lake l.** Congo(Zaire)/Rwanda
29 □2 **Kiyan** Japan
29 □2 **Kiyan-zaki c.** Japan
119 H4 **Kiyāt** Saudi Arabia
47 H2 **Kiyevka** Kazakhstan
52 C2 **Kiyevskiy** Rus. Fed.
112 G4 **Kıyıköy** Turkey
47 G2 **Kiyma** Kazakhstan
44 G4 **Kizel** Rus. Fed.
50 H2 **Kizema** Rus. Fed.
30 D2 **Kizha** Rus. Fed.
30 D2 **Kizhinga** Rus. Fed.
127 B6 **Kizigo Game Reserve res.** Tanzania
47 K4 **Kizil** China
43 B1 **Kızılalan** Turkey
43 A1 **Kızılcadağ** Turkey
43 C1 **Kızılcahamam** Turkey
43 D1 **Kızıldağ mt.** Turkey
42 C2 **Kızılırmak r.** Turkey
42 B2 **Kızılkaya** Turkey
46 E2 **Kizil'skoye** Rus. Fed.
51 H7 **Kizil"yurt** Rus. Fed.
42 E2 **Kızıltepe** Turkey
51 H7 **Kizlyar** Rus. Fed.
51 H6 **Kizlyarskiy Zaliv b.** Rus. Fed.
46 D5 **Kizyl-Atrek** Turkmenistan
39 F1 **Kizylayak** Turkmenistan
36 D2 **Kizyl Jilga** China/Jammu and Kashmir
55 B3 **Kjellerup** Denmark
56 G1 **Kjøllefjord** Norway
56 E1 **Kjøpsvik** Norway
130 D6 **Klaarstroom** South Africa
59 E1 **Klacken h.** Sweden
104 G3 **Kladanj** Bos.-Herz.
73 G3 **Klöden** Germany
78 D1 **Kladno** Czech Rep.
112 D2 **Kladovo** Yugoslavia
75 H3 **Kladruby** Czech Rep.
78 D5 **Klagenfurt airport** Austria
81 F4 **Klagenfurt** Austria
81 F4 **Klagenfurt Land div.** Austria
155 H4 **Klagetoh** *Arizona* U.S.A.
54 B4 **Klaipėda** Lithuania
55 □1 **Klaksvík** Faeroes
152 B3 **Klamath r.** *California* U.S.A.
152 B3 **Klamath Falls** *Oregon* U.S.A.
152 B3 **Klamath Mts mts** *California* U.S.A.
22 D1 **Klampo** Indonesia
107 J3 **Klana** Croatia
76 E1 **Klanino** Poland
81 G4 **Klanjec** Croatia
59 E1 **Klarälven r.** Sweden
131 H2 **Klaserie r.** South Africa
131 H2 **Klaserie Nature Reserve res.** South Africa
59 E2 **Klässbol** Sweden
78 C1 **Klášterec nad Ohří** Czech Rep.
79 H3 **Kláštor pod Znievom** Slovakia
22 B3 **Klaten** Indonesia
78 C2 **Klatovy** Czech Rep.
81 F3 **Klaus an der Pyhrnbahn** Austria
72 F1 **Klausdorf** Germany
69 E5 **Klausen** Germany
54 C4 **Klausučiai** Lithuania
51 D1 **Klavdiyevo-Tarasove** Ukraine
130 B5 **Klawer** South Africa
136 C3 **Klawock** *Alaska* U.S.A.
68 E2 **Klazienaveen** Netherlands
76 E2 **Kłębowiec** Poland
76 F3 **Klecko** Poland
76 G3 **Kleczew** Poland
136 E4 **Kleena Kleene** *B.C.* Canada
43 C2 **Kleides Is i.** Cyprus
114 D2 **Kleidi** Greece
130 C4 **Kleinbegin** South Africa
74 C3 **Kleinblittersdorf** Germany
158 □3 **Klein Bonaire i.** *Bonaire* Netherlands Ant.
73 J2 **Klein Bünzow** Germany
159 E5 **Klein Curaçao i.** Netherlands Ant.
130 B5 **Klein Doring r.** South Africa
73 J4 **Kleine Elster r.** Germany
75 H4 **Kleine Laaber r.** Germany
73 J1 **Kleiner Jasmunder Bodden b.** Germany
80 C3 **Kleiner Solstein mt.** Austria
73 K3 **Kleine Spree r.** Germany
80 D4 **Kleine Vils r.** Germany
130 B3 **Klein Karas** Namibia
131 H1 **Klein Letaba r.** South Africa
131 H1 **Klein Letaba** South Africa
81 F3 **Kleinlobming** Austria
73 J3 **Kleinmachnow** Germany
130 B7 **Kleinmond** South Africa
81 F3 **Kleinreifling** Austria
130 C6 **Klein Roggeveldberg mountain range** South Africa
130 A4 **Kleinsee** South Africa
130 C6 **Klein Swartberg mts** South Africa
131 F4 **Klein-Vet r.** South Africa
74 E3 **Kleinwallstadt** Germany
73 K4 **Kleinwelka** Germany
81 G3 **Kleinzell** Austria
114 C2 **Kleisoura** Greece
115 D5 **Kleitoria** Greece
104 F3 **Klekovača mt.** Bos.-Herz.
53 C2 **Klembivka** Ukraine
136 D4 **Klemtu** *B.C.* Canada
75 H3 **Klenčí pod Čerchovem** Czech Rep.
79 J3 **Klenovský Vepor mt.** Slovakia
77 M2 **Kleosin** Poland
114 C1 **Klepa mt.** Macedonia
58 A2 **Kleppe** Norway
58 A1 **Kleppestø** Norway
131 F3 **Klerksdorp** South Africa
53 B1 **Klesiv** Ukraine
77 M3 **Kleszczele** Poland
77 H4 **Kleszczów** Poland
52 A3 **Kletnya** Rus. Fed.
51 G5 **Kletskiy** Rus. Fed.
83 D1 **Klettgau reg.** Germany/Switzerland
53 A1 **Klevan'** Ukraine
72 B4 **Kleve** Germany
31 F2 **Klichka** Rus. Fed.
130 E6 **Klienpoort** South Africa
73 H3 **Klietz** Germany
52 C1 **Klimatino** Rus. Fed.
50 D4 **Klimavichy** Belarus
112 F3 **Kliment** Bulgaria
51 E4 **Klimovo** Rus. Fed.
52 C2 **Klimovsk** Rus. Fed.
52 E2 **Klimov Zavod** Rus. Fed.
52 C1 **Klin** Rus. Fed.
79 J2 **Klin** Slovakia
112 C3 **Klina r.** Yugoslavia
136 D4 **Klinaklini r.** *B.C.* Canada
74 E3 **Klingenberg am Main** Germany
75 H2 **Klingenthal** Germany
22 B1 **Klingkang Ra. mountain range** Malaysia
73 H2 **Klink** Germany
78 C1 **Klínovec mt.** Czech Rep.
59 H3 **Klintehamn** Sweden
51 J5 **Klintsovka** Rus. Fed.
51 E4 **Klintsy** Rus. Fed.
131 G3 **Klip r.** South Africa
130 B7 **Klipdale** South Africa
55 B5 **Kliplev** Denmark
55 F3 **Klippan** Sweden
130 E6 **Klipplaat** South Africa
130 B5 **Kliprand** South Africa
131 H2 **Klipskool** South Africa
112 D3 **Klisura** Yugoslavia
55 A2 **Klitmøller** Denmark
73 K4 **Klitten** Germany
72 D1 **Klixbüll** Germany
104 F3 **Ključ** Bos.-Herz.
6 □6 **Kloa i.** Fiji
81 H2 **Klobouky** Czech Rep.
76 G5 **Kłobuck** Poland
77 K4 **Kłoczew** Poland
76 D3 **Kłodawa** *Gorzów* Poland
76 G3 **Kłodawa** *Konin* Poland
76 E5 **Kłodzko** *Wałbrzych* Poland
58 D1 **Kløfta** Norway
69 C3 **Kloosterzande** Netherlands
79 K3 **Klopťaň mt.** Slovakia
81 H5 **Kloštar Ivanić** Croatia
55 A3 **Kloster** Denmark
75 F4 **Klosterlechfeld** Germany
73 G4 **Klostermansfeld** Germany
81 H2 **Klosterneuburg** Austria
83 E2 **Klosters** Switzerland
73 K3 **Klosterwasser r.** Germany
83 D1 **Kloten** Switzerland
74 F4 **Klotten** Germany
73 G3 **Klötze** Germany
138 F1 **Klotz, Lac l.** *Québec* Canada
140 C2 **Klotz Lake Provincial Park res.** *Ontario* Canada
136 A2 **Kluane Game Sanctuary res.** *Yukon Terr.* Canada
136 B2 **Kluane Lake l.** *Yukon Terr.* Canada
136 B2 **Kluane National Park nat. park** *Yukon Terr.* Canada
22 B2 **Kluang, Tg pt** Indonesia
76 G5 **Kluczbork** Poland
22 D2 **Klumpang, Tk b.** Indonesia
68 C3 **Klundert** Netherlands
36 B4 **Klupro** Pakistan
73 G2 **Klütz** Germany
52 D2 **Klyaz'ma r.** Rus. Fed.
54 E5 **Klyetsk** Belarus
53 F2 **Klymivka** Ukraine
45 S4 **Klyuchevskaya Sopka volcano** Rus. Fed.
45 S4 **Klyuchi** Rus. Fed.
52 H4 **Klyuchi** Rus. Fed.
31 H2 **Klyuchi** Rus. Fed.
52 F2 **Klyuchishchi** Rus. Fed.
131 F5 **Knapdaar** South Africa
64 C2 **Knap, Point of pt** *Scotland* U.K.
59 E3 **Knäred** Sweden
65 G3 **Knaresborough** *England* U.K.
59 F1 **Knästen h.** Sweden
55 C3 **Knebel** Denmark
137 L3 **Knee Lake l.** *Manitoba* Canada
69 B3 **Knesselare** Belgium
107 J3 **Knežak** Slovenia
79 H6 **Kneževi Vinogradi** Croatia
112 D3 **Knezha** Bulgaria
112 C3 **Knić** Yugoslavia
148 B1 **Knife Lake l.** Canada/U.S.A.
136 D4 **Knight In. inlet** *B.C.* Canada
62 C2 **Knighton** *Wales* U.K.
148 E6 **Knightstown** *Indiana* U.S.A.
104 F3 **Knin** Croatia
59 F3 **Knislinge** Sweden
81 F3 **Knittelfeld div.** Austria
81 F3 **Knittelfeld** Austria
59 G2 **Knivsta** Sweden
81 F2 **Knížecí stolec mt.** Czech Rep.
112 D3 **Knjaževac** Yugoslavia

17 A6 **Knobby Head headland** *Western Australia* Australia
67 C3 **Knock** Rep. of Ireland
67 B5 **Knockaboy h.** Rep. of Ireland
67 B4 **Knockacummer h.** Rep. of Ireland
67 C2 **Knockalongy h.** Rep. of Ireland
67 B4 **Knockalough** Rep. of Ireland
66 F3 **Knock Hill h.** *Scotland* U.K.
67 E1 **Knocklayd h.** *Northern Ireland* U.K.
67 C4 **Knockmealdown Mts h.** Rep. of Ireland
67 D4 **Knocktopher** Rep. of Ireland
69 B3 **Knokke-Heist** Belgium
55 C2 **Knøsen h.** Denmark
115 G7 **Knosos** Greece
65 G4 **Knottingley** *England* U.K.
63 E2 **Knowle** *England* U.K.
179 B2 **Knowles, C. c.** Antarctica
147 J1 **Knowles Corner** *Maine* U.S.A.
141 J4 **Knowlton** *Québec* Canada
148 D5 **Knox** *Indiana* U.S.A.
136 C4 **Knox, C. c.** *B.C.* Canada
179 C6 **Knox Coast coastal area** Antarctica
154 A2 **Knoxville** *California* U.S.A.
148 B5 **Knoxville** *Illinois* U.S.A.
145 D4 **Knoxville** *Tennessee* U.S.A.
66 C3 **Knoydart reg.** *Scotland* U.K.
135 M1 **Knud Rasmussen Land reg.** Greenland
55 C4 **Knudshoved headland** Denmark
55 D4 **Knudshoved Odde pen.** Denmark
74 E2 **Knüllgebirge h.** Germany
59 H2 **Knutby** Sweden
62 D1 **Knutsford** *England* U.K.
52 G2 **Knyaginino** Rus. Fed.
53 E3 **Knyaze-Hryhorivka** Ukraine
77 N5 **Knyazhe** Ukraine
52 C1 **Knyazhikha** Rus. Fed.
130 D7 **Knysna** South Africa
77 L2 **Knyszyn** Poland
127 C6 **Koani** Tanzania
Koartac *see* **Quaqtaq**
22 A2 **Koba** Indonesia
55 E4 **Kobanke h.** Denmark
81 G4 **Kobansko mountain range** Slovenia
81 E4 **Kobarid** Slovenia
28 C8 **Kobayashi** Japan
56 H1 **Kobbfoss** Rus. Fed.
29 E6 **Kōbe** Japan
53 F2 **Kobelyaky** Ukraine
55 E4 **København div.** Denmark
55 E4 **København** Denmark
120 C5 **Kobenni** Mauritania
81 F3 **Kobenz** Austria
80 E2 **Kobernaußer Wald forest** Austria
81 H3 **Kobersdorf** Austria
77 H4 **Kobiele Wielkie** Poland
83 E1 **Koblach** Austria
74 C2 **Koblenz div.** *Rheinland-Pfalz* Germany
74 C2 **Koblenz** *Koblenz* Germany
53 D3 **Kobleve** Ukraine
126 C2 **K'obo** Ethiopia
37 H4 **Kobo** India
126 B4 **Koboko** Uganda
50 J3 **Kobra** Rus. Fed.
21 K8 **Kobroör i.** Indonesia
77 N3 **Kobryn** Belarus
51 G7 **K'obulet'i** Georgia
52 F3 **Kobyaki** Rus. Fed.
76 C2 **Kobylanka** Poland
76 F4 **Kobylin** Poland
76 F3 **Kobylnica** Poland
77 J3 **Kobylniki** Poland
112 D4 **Kočani** Macedonia
113 F6 **Koçarlı** Turkey
112 B2 **Koceljevo** Yugoslavia
107 J3 **Kočevje** Slovenia
107 J3 **Kočevska Reka** Slovenia
25 C4 **Ko Chang i.** Thailand
31 J6 **Kōch'ang** South Korea
37 G4 **Koch Bihār** India
52 G2 **Kochelayevo** Rus. Fed.
80 C3 **Kochelsee l.** Germany
47 K1 **Kochenevo** Rus. Fed.
74 E3 **Kocher r.** Germany
53 F2 **Kocherezhky** Ukraine
112 D3 **Kocherinovo** Bulgaria
53 C1 **Kocheriv** Ukraine
52 G4 **Kochetovka** Rus. Fed.
52 E3 **Kochetovka** Rus. Fed.
28 D7 **Kōchi div.** Japan
Kochi *see* **Cochin**
28 D7 **Kōchi** Japan
29 ᵖ2 **Kochinada** Japan
47 K2 **Kochki** Rus. Fed.
47 J4 **Kochkor** Kyrgyzstan
52 G2 **Kochkurovo** Rus. Fed.
51 H6 **Kochubey** Rus. Fed.
51 G6 **Kochubeyevskoye** Rus. Fed.
114 F4 **Kochylas h.** Greece
77 L4 **Kock** Poland
76 F2 **Koczała** Poland
38 B4 **Kodaikanal** India
53 D1 **Kodaky** Ukraine
38 D2 **Kodala** India
37 F4 **Kodari** Nepal
37 F4 **Kodarma** India
77 M4 **Kodeń** Poland
73 K4 **Kodersdorf** Germany
134 C4 **Kodiak** *Alaska* U.S.A.
134 C4 **Kodiak Island i.** *Alaska* U.S.A.
50 F2 **Kodino** Rus. Fed.
54 B1 **Kodisjoki** Finland
126 B3 **Kodok** Sudan
28 H3 **Kodomari-misaki pt** Japan
51 G7 **Kodori r.** Georgia
53 C1 **Kodra** Ukraine
77 H4 **Kodrąb** Poland
53 C3 **Kodyma r.** Ukraine
53 C2 **Kodyma** Ukraine
113 E4 **Kodzhaele mt.** Bulgaria/Greece
130 D4 **Koegas** South Africa
130 C4 **Koegrabie** South Africa
69 A3 **Koekelare** Belgium
130 B5 **Koekenaap** South Africa
37 E4 **Koel r.** India
37 F5 **Koel, S. r.** India
128 B4 **Koës** Namibia
155 F5 **Kofa Mts mts** *Arizona* U.S.A.
112 F4 **Kofçaz** Turkey
80 D2 **Köfering** Germany
131 E4 **Koffiefontein** South Africa
81 G3 **Köflach** Austria
122 D5 **Koforidua** Ghana
29 G6 **Kōfu** Japan
138 E2 **Kogaluc r.** *Québec* Canada
138 E2 **Kogaluc, Baie de b.** *Québec* Canada
139 H2 **Kogaluk r.** *Newfoundland* Canada
55 E4 **Køge** Denmark
55 E4 **Køge Bugt b.** Denmark
123 F5 **Kogi div.** Nigeria
81 G3 **Koglhof** Austria
122 B4 **Kogon r.** Guinea
28 A6 **Kogŭm do i.** South Korea
28 C6 **Kogushi** Japan
36 A4 **Kohan** Pakistan
36 B2 **Kohat** Pakistan
39 F2 **Koh-i-Hisar mountain range** Afghanistan
54 D2 **Kohila** Estonia
37 H4 **Kohima** India
39 F2 **Koh-i-Mazar mt.** Afghanistan
36 A4 **Koh-i-Patandar mt.** Pakistan
39 F2 **Koh-i-Sangan mt.** Afghanistan
39 G2 **Kohistan reg.** Afghanistan
36 C2 **Kohistan reg.** Pakistan
39 E3 **Koh-i-Sultan mt.** Pakistan
39 B3 **Kohkīlūyeh va Būyer Ahmadī div.** Iran
72 D2 **Köhlen** Germany
179 A3 **Kohler Ra. mountain range** Antarctica
36 B3 **Kohlu** Pakistan
39 E2 **Kohsan** Afghanistan
54 E2 **Kohtla-Järve** Estonia
8 E2 **Kohukohunui h.** New Zealand
31 H6 **Kohŭng** South Korea
9 C6 **Kohurau mt.** New Zealand
29 G5 **Koide** Japan
136 A2 **Koidern** *Yukon Terr.* Canada
25 A5 **Koihoa** *Andaman and Nicobar Is* India
38 B3 **Koilkuntla** India
114 F2 **Koinyra i.** Greece
42 F2 **Koi Sanjaq** Iraq
31 J6 **Kŏje do i.** South Korea
78 G2 **Kojetín** Czech Rep.
29 G7 **Ko-jima i.** Japan
28 G3 **Ko-jima i.** Japan
17 B7 **Kojonup** *Western Australia* Australia
24 B3 **Kok r.** Thailand
147 J2 **Kokadjo** *Maine* U.S.A.
46 F3 **Kokalaat** Kazakhstan
47 H4 **Kokand** Uzbekistan
57 F4 **Kökar** Finland
59 J2 **Kökarsfjärden b.** Finland
79 J3 **Kokava nad Rimavicou** Slovakia
39 G1 **Kokcha r.** Afghanistan
57 F3 **Kokemäenjoki r.** Finland
130 B4 **Kokerboom** Namibia
126 C3 **K'ok' Hāyk' l.** Ethiopia
52 E1 **Kokhma** Rus. Fed.
122 A3 **Koki** Senegal
115 D6 **Kokkala** Greece
38 C4 **Kokkilai** Sri Lanka
56 F3 **Kokkola** Finland
47 L3 **Kok Kuduk well** China
54 D3 **Koknese** Latvia
123 E4 **Koko** Nigeria
122 C4 **Kokofata** Mali
153 ᵖ1 **Koko Hd headland** *Hawaii* U.S.A.
148 D5 **Kokomo** *Indiana* U.S.A.
130 D2 **Kokong** Botswana
28 C7 **Kokonoe** Japan
52 B3 **Kokorevka** Rus. Fed.
123 E5 **Kokoro** Benin
131 F3 **Kokosi** South Africa
122 B4 **Kokou mt.** Guinea
47 K3 **Kokpekty** Kazakhstan
74 F4 **Kokra r.** Slovenia
47 G4 **Koksaray** Kazakhstan
47 J4 **Kokshaal-Tau mountain range** China/Kyrgyzstan
47 G2 **Kokshetau** Kazakhstan
47 G2 **Kokshetau div.** Kazakhstan
69 A3 **Koksijde** Belgium
139 G2 **Koksoak r.** *Québec* Canada
131 G5 **Kokstad** South Africa
56 D2 **Koksuranda** Norway
47 J4 **Koktal** Kazakhstan
46 C3 **Kokterek** Kazakhstan
Koktokay *see* **Fuyun**
28 C8 **Kokubu** Japan
25 C5 **Ko Kut i.** Thailand
31 F1 **Kokuy** Rus. Fed.
56 J1 **Kola** Rus. Fed.
Kolab r. *see* **Sābari**
36 A4 **Kolachi r.** Pakistan
76 F3 **Kołacin** Poland
77 M4 **Kołacze** Poland
36 C2 **Kolahoi mt.** India
21 H7 **Kolaka** Indonesia
25 B6 **Ko Lanta i.** Thailand
25 B6 **Ko Lanta** Thailand
Kola Peninsula pen. *see* **Kolskiy Poluostrov**
38 C2 **Kolar** India
38 B3 **Kolar** India
36 D4 **Kolaras** India
38 B3 **Kolar Gold Fields** India
56 F2 **Kolari** Finland
112 B3 **Kolašin** Yugoslavia
36 C4 **Kolayat** India
59 G2 **Kolbäck** Sweden
76 C2 **Kołbaskowo** Poland
75 H5 **Kolbermoor** Germany
77 K3 **Kołbiel** Poland
58 D2 **Kolbotn** Norway
77 K5 **Kolbuszowa** Poland
52 D1 **Kol'chugino** Rus. Fed.
76 F1 **Kołczygłowy** Poland
73 L3 **Kołczyn** Poland
122 B4 **Kolda** Senegal
113 F5 **Koldere** Turkey
55 B4 **Kolding** Denmark
124 E3 **Kole** *Haute-Zaïre* Congo(Zaire)
125 D4 **Kole** *Kasai-Oriental* Congo(Zaire)
56 F2 **Koler** Sweden
54 D2 **Kolga-Jaani** Estonia
44 F3 **Kolguyev, O. i.** Rus. Fed.
37 F5 **Kolhan** India
38 A2 **Kolhapur** India
25 B6 **Ko Libong i.** Thailand
122 B3 **Kolimbiné watercourse** Mali/Mauritania
78 E1 **Kolín** Czech Rep.
55 C3 **Kolindsund reclaimed land** Denmark
75 J3 **Kolinec** Czech Rep.
126 C3 **K'olīto** Ethiopia
54 C2 **Kõljala** Estonia
55 B3 **Kølkær** Denmark
54 C3 **Kolkasrags pt** Latvia
47 G5 **Kolkhozobod** Tajikistan
73 K4 **Kolkwitz** Germany
53 A1 **Kolky** Ukraine
Kollam *see* **Quilon**
75 H4 **Kollbach r.** Germany
73 G4 **Kölleda** Germany
38 B3 **Kollegal** India
38 C2 **Kolleru L. l.** India
123 E4 **Kollo** Niger
68 E1 **Kollum** Netherlands
74 B2 **Köln div.** *Nordrhein-Westfalen* Germany
74 B2 **Köln** *Köln* Germany
77 K2 **Kolno** *Łomża* Poland
77 J2 **Kolno** *Olsztyn* Poland
76 G3 **Koło** Poland
125 B5 **Kolo** Congo(Zaire)
6 ᵖ3 **Kolo i.** Tonga
52 E1 **Kolob** Rus. Fed.
76 D1 **Kołobrzeg** *Koszalin* Poland
53 A2 **Kolodne** Ukraine
50 H3 **Kologriv** Rus. Fed.
52 G4 **Kologrivovka** Rus. Fed.
122 C4 **Kolokani** Mali
52 D1 **Koloksha r.** Rus. Fed.
53 F2 **Kolomak r.** Ukraine
53 F2 **Kolomak** Ukraine
6 ᵖ1 **Kolombangara i.** Solomon Is.
52 D2 **Kolomna** Rus. Fed.
53 A2 **Kolomyya** Ukraine
122 C4 **Kolondiéba** Mali
22 E2 **Kolonedale** Indonesia
6 ᵖ4 **Kolonga** Tonga
113 B4 **Kolonjë** Albania
130 C3 **Kolonkwane** Botswana
53 F2 **Kolontayiv** Ukraine
47 H1 **Kolosovka** Rus. Fed.
6 ᵖ4 **Kolovai** Tonga
46 D2 **Kolovertnoye** Kazakhstan
52 E2 **Kolp'** Rus. Fed.
44 K4 **Kolpashevo** Rus. Fed.
52 C3 **Kolpny** Rus. Fed.
114 E2 **Kolpos Agiou Orous b.** Greece
115 E4 **Kolpos Alkyonidon b.** Greece
115 D4 **Kolpos Antikyras b.** Greece
115 E7 **Kolpos Chanion b.** Greece
115 E5 **Kolpos Ierissou b.** Greece
115 G7 **Kolpos Irakleiou b.** Greece
115 D4 **Kolpos Iteas b.** Greece
114 E2 **Kolpos Kassandras b.** Greece
114 F2 **Kolpos Kavalas b.** Greece
115 E7 **Kolpos Kissamou b.** Greece
115 B5 **Kolpos Lagana b.** Greece
115 G7 **Kolpos Malion b.** Greece
115 G7 **Kolpos Mirampelou b.** Greece
114 E2 **Kolpos Orfanou b.** Greece
115 F4 **Kolpos Petalion b.** Greece
114 G3 **Kolpos Pournias b.** Greece
114 D2 **Kolpos Thessalonikis b.** Greece
115 E5 **Kolpos Ydras chan.** Greece
44 E3 **Kolskiy Poluostrov pen.** Rus. Fed.
76 D4 **Kolsko** Poland
59 F2 **Kolsva** Sweden
52 G3 **Koltovskoye** Rus. Fed.
112 B2 **Kolubara r.** Yugoslavia
126 D2 **Koluli** Eritrea
35 D10 **Kolumadulu Atoll atoll** Maldives
77 H4 **Koluszki** Poland
52 G2 **Kolutton** Kazakhstan
38 A2 **Kolvan** India
56 C2 **Kolvereid** Norway
56 G1 **Kolvik** Norway
50 E1 **Kolvitskoye, Ozero l.** Rus. Fed.
39 F4 **Kolwa reg.** Pakistan
125 E6 **Kolwezi** Congo(Zaire)
52 D3 **Kolybel'skoye** Rus. Fed.
45 R3 **Kolyma r.** Rus. Fed.
45 R3 **Kolymskaya Nizmennost lowland** Rus. Fed.
45 S3 **Kolymskiy, Khrebet mountain range** Rus. Fed.
52 G3 **Kolyshley r.** Rus. Fed.
52 G3 **Kolyshley** Rus. Fed.
47 K1 **Kolyvan'** Rus. Fed.
79 L4 **Komádi** Hungary
123 G4 **Komadugu-gana watercourse** Nigeria
29 F6 **Komagane** Japan
28 H2 **Komaga-take volcano** Japan
130 A4 **Komaggas** South Africa
130 A4 **Komaggas Mts mts** South Africa
77 L6 **Komańcza** Poland
45 S4 **Komandorskiye Ostrova is** Rus. Fed.
114 C2 **Komanos** Greece
52 B3 **Komarichi** Rus. Fed.
53 B2 **Komariv** Ukraine
79 H4 **Komárno** Slovakia
77 M6 **Komarno** Ukraine
79 H4 **Komárom** Hungary
79 H4 **Komárom-Esztergom div.** Hungary
75 J3 **Komárov** Czech Rep.
53 A1 **Komarove** Ukraine
77 L4 **Komarówka Podlaska** Poland
131 H3 **Komati r.** Swaziland
131 H2 **Komatipoort** South Africa
29 F5 **Komatsu** Japan
28 E6 **Komatsushima** Japan
125 E4 **Kombe** Congo(Zaire)
122 D4 **Kombissiri** Burkina
123 E4 **Kombongou** Burkina
37 H3 **Komdi mt.** India
23 ᵖ1 **Komebail Lagoon lag.** Palau
127 B5 **Kome Channel chan.** Uganda
127 B5 **Kome I. i.** Uganda
127 B5 **Kome Island i.** Tanzania
81 E5 **Komen** Slovenia
22 A2 **Komering r.** Indonesia
131 F6 **Komga** South Africa
50 J2 **Komi div.** Rus. Fed.
115 G5 **Komi** Greece
81 H4 **Komin** Croatia
28 H3 **Kominternivs'ke** Ukraine
53 D3 **Kominternivs'ke** Ukraine
109 J1 **Komiža** Croatia
130 B5 **Komkans** South Africa
79 H5 **Komló** Hungary
114 C3 **Kommeno** Greece
130 B7 **Kommetjie** South Africa
47 L2 **Kommunar** Rus. Fed.
52 E1 **Kommunar** Rus. Fed.
22 D4 **Komodo i.** Indonesia
122 C5 **Komodou** Guinea
122 D5 **Komoé r.** Côte d'Ivoire
119 F3 **Kôm Ombo** Egypt
125 B4 **Komono** Congo
29 G5 **Komoro** Japan
76 G4 **Komorzno** Poland
114 F4 **Komotini** Greece
53 E2 **Kompaniyivka** Ukraine
114 C3 **Kompoti** Greece
130 C6 **Komsberg mts** South Africa
46 F2 **Komsomolets** Kazakhstan
45 M1 **Komsomolets, O. i.** Rus. Fed.
52 E1 **Komsomol'sk** Rus. Fed.
77 J1 **Komsomol'sk** Rus. Fed.
46 F5 **Komsomol'sk** Turkmenistan
53 E2 **Komsomol's'k** Ukraine
53 G2 **Komsomol's'ke** Ukraine
52 G2 **Komsomol'skiy** Rus. Fed.
27 P1 **Komsomol'sk-na-Amure** Rus. Fed.
46 E4 **Komsomol'sk-na-Ustyurte** Uzbekistan
46 F2 **Komsomol'skoye** Kazakhstan
52 H2 **Komsomol'skoye** Rus. Fed.
30 D1 **Komsomol'skoye** Rus. Fed.
112 E4 **Komuniga** Bulgaria
51 G7 **Kömürlü** Turkey
155 F6 **Kom Vo** *Arizona* U.S.A.
112 B3 **Kom Vojnik mts** Yugoslavia
53 E1 **Komyshnya** Ukraine
53 F3 **Komyshuvakha** Ukraine
37 E4 **Kon** India
52 C1 **Konakovo** Rus. Fed.
37 F6 **Konārka** India
37 F5 **Konar Res.** India
39 B3 **Konār Takhteh Dālakī** Iran
77 L2 **Konarzyce** Poland
36 D4 **Konch** India
36 C2 **Kondagaon** India
122 B5 **Kondembaia** Sierra Leone
141 G3 **Kondiaronk, Lac l.** *Québec* Canada
17 B7 **Kondinin** *Western Australia* Australia
127 C5 **Kondoa** Tanzania
52 G3 **Kondol'** Rus. Fed.
50 E2 **Kondopoga** Rus. Fed.
79 K5 **Kondoros** Hungary
54 F1 **Kondrat'yevo** Rus. Fed.
52 B2 **Kondrovo** Rus. Fed.
39 G1 **Kondūz** Afghanistan
6 ᵖ2 **Koné** *New Caledonia* Pacific Ocean
114 D1 **Konečka Planina mts** Macedonia
124 B2 **Kong** Cameroon
55 D4 **Køng** Denmark
135 P3 **Kong Christian IX Land reg.** Greenland
135 Q2 **Kong Christian X Land reg.** Greenland
55 A4 **Kongeå r.** Denmark
55 E4 **Kongens Lyngby** Denmark
55 C3 **Kongerslev** Denmark
135 Q2 **Kong Frederik VIII Land reg.** Greenland
135 O3 **Kong Frederik VI Kyst coastal area** Greenland
179 C2 **Kong Håkon VII Hav sea** Antarctica
44 D2 **Kong Karl's Land is** *Svalbard* Arctic Ocean
22 D1 **Kongkemul mt.** Indonesia
128 C2 **Kongola** Namibia
125 E5 **Kongolo** Congo(Zaire)
135 Q2 **Kong Oscar Fjord inlet** Greenland
122 D4 **Kongoussi** Burkina
58 C2 **Kongsberg** Norway
59 E1 **Kongsvinger** Norway
25 D4 **Kông, T. r.** Cambodia
47 J5 **Kongur Shan mt.** China
127 C6 **Kongwa** Tanzania
135 Q2 **Kong Wilhelm Land reg.** Greenland
77 H5 **Koniecpol** Poland
74 F4 **Königsbronn** Germany
73 J4 **Königsbrück** Germany
75 F4 **Königsbrunn** Germany
80 C3 **Königsdorf** Germany
75 G2 **Königsee** Germany
73 F3 **Königslutter am Elm** Germany
80 D3 **Königssee l.** Germany
80 D3 **Königssee** Germany
74 D2 **Königstein im Taunus** Germany
75 J2 **Königswalde** Germany
73 K4 **Königswartha** Germany
81 F2 **Königswiesen** Austria
74 C2 **Königswinter** Germany
73 J3 **Königs Wusterhausen** Germany
76 G3 **Konin div.** Poland
76 G3 **Konin** Poland
114 B3 **Konispol** Albania
114 B2 **Konitsa** Greece
82 C2 **Köniz** Switzerland
104 F4 **Konjic** Bos.-Herz.
104 G3 **Konjuh mts** Bos.-Herz.
128 B4 **Konkiep watercourse** Namibia
52 D3 **Kon'-Kolodez'** Rus. Fed.
123 E4 **Konkwesso** Nigeria
122 D4 **Konna** Mali
73 G4 **Könnern** Germany
56 G3 **Konnevesi** Finland
122 D5 **Konongo** Ghana
53 E1 **Kononivka** Ukraine
50 G2 **Konosha** Rus. Fed.
29 G5 **Kōnosu** Japan
53 E1 **Konotop** Ukraine
25 E4 **Kon Plong** Vietnam
23 ᵖ1 **Konrei** Palau
77 J4 **Końskie** Poland
77 L4 **Końskowola** Poland
126 C3 **Konso** Ethiopia
77 K3 **Konstancin-Jeziorna** Poland
31 H2 **Konstantinovka** Rus. Fed.
52 D1 **Konstantinovo** Rus. Fed.
51 G6 **Konstantinovsk** Rus. Fed.
52 D1 **Konstantinovskiy** Rus. Fed.
78 B2 **Konstantinovy Lázně** Czech Rep.
77 M3 **Konstantynów** Poland
77 H4 **Konstantynów Łódzki** Poland
74 E5 **Konstanz** Germany
123 F4 **Kontagora** Nigeria
24 B2 **Kontha** Myanmar
114 G3 **Kontias** Greece
69 C3 **Kontich** Belgium
56 H3 **Kontiolahti** Finland
114 G3 **Kontopouli** Greece
115 C5 **Kontovazaina** Greece
56 G2 **Konttila** Finland
25 D4 **Kon Tum** Vietnam
25 E4 **Kontum, Plateau du plat.** Vietnam
50 G1 **Konushin, Mys pt** Rus. Fed.
54 D2 **Konuverve r.** Estonia
43 B1 **Konya div.** Turkey
42 C2 **Konya** Turkey
52 B4 **Konyshevka** Rus. Fed.
74 B3 **Konz** Germany
68 C2 **Koog aan de Zaan** Netherlands
17 C6 **Kookynie** *Western Australia* Australia
153 ᵖ1 **Koolau Range mountain range** *Hawaii* U.S.A.
14 D5 **Koolivoo, L. salt flat** *Queensland* Australia
17 B6 **Koolyanobbing** *Western Australia* Australia
13 F3 **Koondrook** *Victoria* Australia
54 D2 **Koonga** Estonia
12 C2 **Koonibba** *S. Australia* Australia
146 D5 **Koon Lake l.** *Pennsylvania* U.S.A.
130 C3 **Koopan-Suid** South Africa
13 G3 **Koorawatha** *New South Wales* Australia
17 B6 **Koorda** *Western Australia* Australia
54 D3 **Koorküla** Estonia
73 J1 **Koos i.** Germany
128 A3 **Koosa waterhole** Namibia
54 E2 **Koosa** Estonia
152 C2 **Kooskia** *Idaho* U.S.A.
136 F5 **Kootenay r.** Canada/U.S.A.
136 F5 **Kootenay L. l.** *B.C.* Canada
136 F4 **Kootenay Nat. Park nat. park** *B.C.* Canada
130 C5 **Kootjieskolk** South Africa
115 E4 **Kopaïs l.** Greece
112 C3 **Kopaonik mountain range** Yugoslavia
38 A2 **Kopargaon** India
123 E5 **Kopargo** Benin
56 M6 **Kópasker** Iceland
53 B2 **Kopayhorod** Ukraine
47 J3 **Kopbirlik** Kazakhstan
107 H3 **Koper** Slovenia
58 A2 **Kopervik** Norway
46 E5 **Kopet Dag, Khrebet mountain range** Turkmenistan
46 F1 **Kopeysk** Rus. Fed.
25 C5 **Ko Phangan i.** Thailand
78 F4 **Kópháza** Hungary
25 B5 **Ko Phra Thong i.** Thailand
25 B6 **Ko Phuket i.** Thailand
78 E1 **Kopidlno** Czech Rep.
59 G2 **Köping** Sweden
112 B3 **Koplik** Albania
56 E3 **Köpmanholmen** Sweden
131 E2 **Kopong** Botswana
52 B2 **Koporikha** Rus. Fed.
54 F2 **Kopor'ye** Rus. Fed.
38 B3 **Koppal** India
57 C3 **Koppang** Norway
55 ᵖ1 **Koppanni h.** Faeroes
59 F1 **Kopparberg div.** Sweden
59 F2 **Kopparberg** Sweden
131 F3 **Koppies** South Africa
131 F3 **Koppies Dam dam** South Africa
130 C3 **Koppieskraalpan salt pan** South Africa
59 E2 **Koppom** Sweden
78 F5 **Koprivnica** Croatia
42 B2 **Köprü r.** Turkey
113 G5 **Köprübaşı** Turkey
131 F5 **Kopshorn mt.** South Africa
54 D2 **Kõpu** Estonia
53 A2 **Kopychyntsi** Ukraine
39 B3 **Kor watercourse** Iran
112 C4 **Korab mountain range** Albania/Macedonia
52 E3 **Korablino** Rus. Fed.
126 E3 **K'orahē** Ethiopia
126 D3 **K'orahē** Ethiopia
36 A4 **Korak** Pakistan
138 E1 **Korak, Baie b.** *Québec* Canada
127 C5 **Kora National Reserve res.** Kenya
38 B2 **Korangal** India
36 A4 **Korangi** Pakistan
39 G1 **Korān va Monjan** Afghanistan
38 C2 **Koraput** India
122 D3 **Korarou, Lac l.** Mali
Korat *see* **Nakhon Ratchasima**
37 E5 **Korba** India
121 G1 **Korba** Tunisia
72 D4 **Korbach** Germany
124 C2 **Korbol** Chad
25 C6 **Korbu, Gunung mt.** Malaysia
114 B2 **Korçë** *Korçë* Albania
77 M5 **Korchiv** Ukraine
53 B2 **Korchivka** Ukraine
104 F4 **Korčula i.** Croatia
104 F4 **Korčula** Croatia
104 F4 **Korčulanski Kanal chan.** Croatia
69 E5 **Kordel** Germany
39 A2 **Kördestan div.** Iran
39 C1 **Kord Kūy** Iran
119 E5 **Kordofan div.** Sudan
39 E4 **Kords reg.** Iran
39 C3 **Kord Sheykh** Iran
31 G5 **Korea Bay g.** China/North Korea
28 B6 **Korea Strait str.** Japan/South Korea
122 D4 **Koréba** Burkina
38 A2 **Koregaon** India
77 N6 **Korelychi** Ukraine
126 C2 **Korem** Ethiopia
51 G7 **Koren' r.** Rus. Fed.
53 E1 **Korenevo** Rus. Fed.
75 L2 **Kořenov** Czech Rep.
51 F6 **Korenovsk** Rus. Fed.
122 C3 **Koréra-Koré** Mali
53 B1 **Korets'** Ukraine
53 E3 **Korf** Rus. Fed.
76 F5 **Korfantów** Poland
42 B1 **Körfez** Turkey
179 B3 **Korff Ice Rise ice feature** Antarctica
115 E5 **Korfos** Greece
37 F1 **Korgan** China
56 D2 **Korgen** Norway
122 C5 **Korhogo** Côte d'Ivoire
54 E1 **Koria** Finland
36 B5 **Kori Creek r.** India
115 C5 **Korifasi** Greece
130 B6 **Koringberg** South Africa
130 C6 **Koringplaas** South Africa
114 D2 **Korinos** Greece
55 C4 **Korinth** Denmark
115 D5 **Korinthia div.** Greece
114 D4 **Korinthiakos Kolpos chan.** Greece
115 D5 **Korinthos** Greece
79 G4 **Kőris-hegy mt.** Hungary
114 C2 **Korisos** Greece
115 F5 **Korissia** Greece
29 H5 **Kōriyama** Japan
46 F2 **Korkino** Rus. Fed.
42 B2 **Korkuteli** Turkey
47 L4 **Korla** China
52 H1 **Korlyaki** Rus. Fed.
43 B2 **Kormakitis, C. c.** Cyprus
78 F4 **Körmend** Hungary
47 H1 **Kormilovka** Rus. Fed.
77 M6 **Kornalovychi** Ukraine
104 E4 **Kornati i.** Croatia
81 H2 **Korneuburg div.** Austria
81 H2 **Korneuburg** Austria
47 G2 **Korneyevka** Kazakhstan
51 J5 **Korneyevka** Rus. Fed.
76 F3 **Kórnik** Poland
114 G3 **Kornos** Greece
58 D2 **Kornsjø** Norway
74 E4 **Kornwestheim** Germany
53 C1 **Kornyn** Ukraine
122 D4 **Koro** Mali
6 ᵖ8 **Koro i.** Fiji
6 ᵖ8 **Koroba mt.** Fiji
52 A2 **Korobets** Rus. Fed.
53 G1 **Korocha** Rus. Fed.
42 B1 **Köroğlu Tepesi mt.** Turkey
126 D4 **Korogo well** Ethiopia
127 C6 **Korogwe** Tanzania
79 K5 **Kórógy-ér r.** Hungary
13 E4 **Koroit** *Victoria* Australia
6 ᵖ8 **Korolevu** Fiji
6 ᵖ8 **Korolevu** Fiji
107 J4 **Koromačno** Croatia
115 D4 **Koroneia** Greece
13 E4 **Korong Vale** *Victoria* Australia
115 C6 **Koroni** Greece
114 E2 **Koronia, L. l.** Greece
114 B3 **Koronisia** Greece
114 E2 **Koronouda** Greece
76 F2 **Koronowo** Poland
53 E1 **Korop** Ukraine
23 ᵖ1 **Koror** Palau
23 ᵖ1 **Koror i.** Palau
79 K5 **Körös r.** Hungary
6 ᵖ6 **Koro Sea sea** Fiji
79 L5 **Körösladány** Hungary
53 C1 **Korosten'** Ukraine
53 C1 **Korostyshiv** Ukraine
79 L5 **Körös-vidék reg.** Hungary
6 ᵖ6 **Korotasere** Fiji
52 H1 **Korotni** Rus. Fed.
118 C4 **Koro Toro** Chad
6 ᵖ1 **Korovou** Solomon Is.
53 E1 **Korovyntsi** Ukraine
6 ᵖ8 **Koroyanitu mt.** Fiji
52 D1 **Korozhechna r.** Rus. Fed.
69 E5 **Körperich** Germany
57 G3 **Korpilahti** Finland
57 F3 **Korpo** Finland
27 Q2 **Korsakov** Rus. Fed.
52 C3 **Korsakovo** Rus. Fed.
59 F3 **Korsberga** Sweden
55 C3 **Korsholm i.** Denmark
52 A3 **Korsiki** Rus. Fed.
56 F3 **Korsnäs** Finland
55 D4 **Korsør** Denmark
53 D2 **Korsun'-Shevchenkivs'kyy** Ukraine
77 K1 **Korsze** Poland
77 N4 **Kortelisy** Ukraine
69 B3 **Kortemark** Belgium
56 F3 **Kortesjärvi** Finland
69 D4 **Kortessem** Belgium
68 B3 **Kortgene** Netherlands
119 F4 **Korti** Sudan
50 J2 **Kortkeros** Rus. Fed.
69 B4 **Kortrijk div.** *West-Vlaanderen* Belgium
69 B4 **Kortrijk** Belgium
50 G3 **Kortsovo** Rus. Fed.
124 A2 **Korup, Parc National de nat. park** Cameroon
56 G2 **Korvala** Finland
36 D4 **Korwai** India
45 R4 **Koryakskaya Sopka volcano** Rus. Fed.
45 S3 **Koryakskiy Khrebet mountain range** Rus. Fed.
50 H2 **Koryazhma** Rus. Fed.
81 J1 **Koryčany** Czech Rep.
77 M2 **Korycin** Poland
114 D4 **Koryni** Greece
115 B5 **Korythi** Greece
53 E1 **Koryukivka** Ukraine
76 E4 **Korzeńsko** Poland
52 H2 **Korzhevka** Rus. Fed.
76 E1 **Korzybie** Poland
113 F6 **Kos i.** Greece
113 F6 **Kos** *Kos* Greece
51 E6 **Kosa Arabats'ka Strilka spit** Ukraine
53 D1 **Kosachivka** Ukraine
25 C5 **Ko Samui i.** Thailand
77 O3 **Kosava** Belarus
52 C2 **Kosaya Gora** Rus. Fed.
46 D3 **Koschagyl** Kazakhstan
75 G4 **Kösching** Germany
81 F4 **Koschutnikturm mt.** Austria/Slovenia
76 E3 **Kościan** Poland
76 G3 **Kościelec** Poland
76 G4 **Kościelna Wieś** Poland
76 E1 **Kościernica** Poland
76 F1 **Kościerzyna** Poland
151 F5 **Kosciusko** *Mississippi* U.S.A.
136 C3 **Kosciusko I. i.** *Alaska* U.S.A.
13 G4 **Kosciusko, Mt mt.** *New South Wales* Australia
13 G4 **Kosciusko National Park nat. park** *New South Wales* Australia
54 D2 **Kose** Estonia
42 D1 **Köse Dağı mt.** Turkey
79 L4 **Kösély r.** Hungary
59 E3 **Kösen l.** Sweden
38 B2 **Kosgi** India
26 E2 **Kosh-Agach** Rus. Fed.
53 E1 **Koshary** Ukraine
28 B8 **Koshikijima-rettō is** Japan
28 B8 **Koshiki-kaikyō chan.** Japan
28 K2 **Koshimizu** Japan
39 E2 **Koshkak** Iran
39 E2 **Koshk-e-Kohneh** Afghanistan
50 J4 **Koshki** Rus. Fed.
148 C4 **Koshkoning, Lake l.** *Wisconsin* U.S.A.
53 B2 **Koshlyaky** Ukraine
53 F2 **Koshmanivka** Ukraine
46 D4 **Koshoba** Turkmenistan
29 G5 **Kōshoku** Japan
36 D3 **Kosi r.** India
36 D4 **Kosi** India
79 L3 **Košice** Slovakia
38 B3 **Kosigi** India
46 E2 **Kos-Istek** Kazakhstan
53 A2 **Kosiv** Ukraine
53 E2 **Kosivka** Ukraine
112 B3 **Kosjerić** Yugoslavia
113 G6 **Köşk** Turkey
54 C1 **Koski** Finland
52 A2 **Koski** Rus. Fed.
115 ᵖ **Koskinou** Greece
52 C2 **Koskol'** Kazakhstan
47 J4 **Koskuduk** Kazakhstan
56 F2 **Koskullskule** Sweden
50 J2 **Koslan** Rus. Fed.
115 D5 **Kosmas** Greece
52 E1 **Kosmynino** Rus. Fed.
31 J5 **Kosŏng** North Korea
52 C3 **Kosorzha** Rus. Fed.
112 C3 **Kosovo div.** Yugoslavia
112 C3 **Kosovo Polje plain** Yugoslavia
112 C3 **Kosovska Kamenica** Yugoslavia
112 C3 **Kosovska Mitrovica** Yugoslavia
77 L3 **Kosów Lacki** Poland
4 H4 **Kosrae i.** Fed. States of Micronesia
47 J5 **Kosrap** China
123 G3 **Kossatori well** Niger
73 J4 **Koßdorf** Germany
75 G3 **Kösseine h.** Germany
80 D3 **Kössen** Austria
23 ᵖ1 **Kossol Passage chan.** Palau
23 ᵖ1 **Kossol Reef reef** Palau
122 C5 **Kossou, Lac de l.** Côte d'Ivoire
115 E5 **Kosta** Greece
114 B3 **Kostakioi** Greece
75 K3 **Kostelec nad Černými Lesy** Czech Rep.
112 D3 **Kostenets** Bulgaria
131 F2 **Koster** South Africa
52 D2 **Kosterevo** Rus. Fed.
119 F5 **Kosti** Sudan
81 H2 **Kostice** Czech Rep.
112 D3 **Kostinbrod** Bulgaria
44 K3 **Kostino** Rus. Fed.
112 C2 **Kostolac** Yugoslavia
76 E4 **Kostomłoty** Poland
56 H2 **Kostomuksha** Rus. Fed.
53 B1 **Kostopil'** Ukraine
50 G3 **Kostroma div.** Rus. Fed.
50 G3 **Kostroma r.** Rus. Fed.
52 E1 **Kostroma** Rus. Fed.
76 C3 **Kostrzyn** *Gorzow* Poland
76 F3 **Kostrzyn** *Poznań* Poland
51 F5 **Kostyantynivka** *Donets'k* Ukraine
53 F2 **Kostyantynivka** *Kharkiv* Ukraine
53 F3 **Kostyantynivka** *Zaporizhzhya* Ukraine
52 A2 **Kostyri** Rus. Fed.
76 E2 **Koszalin div.** Poland
76 E1 **Koszalin** Poland
78 F4 **Kőszeg** Hungary
77 J5 **Koszyce** Poland
36 C4 **Kota** India
37 E5 **Kota** India
22 A3 **Kotaagung** Indonesia
22 B2 **Kotabaru** Indonesia
22 D2 **Kotabaru** Indonesia
22 C2 **Kotabesi** Indonesia
25 C6 **Kota Bharu** Malaysia
22 A3 **Kotabumi** Indonesia
36 B3 **Kot Addu** Pakistan
20 G5 **Kota Kinabalu** Malaysia
25 B5 **Ko Tao i.** Thailand
38 C2 **Kotapārh** India
114 C2 **Kotas** Greece
25 C7 **Kota Tinggi** Malaysia
36 B4 **Kot Diji** Pakistan
36 D3 **Kotdwara** India
50 J3 **Kotel'nich** Rus. Fed.
51 G6 **Kotel'nikovo** Rus. Fed.
45 P2 **Kotel'nyy, O. i.** Rus. Fed.
53 F1 **Kotel'va** Ukraine
38 C2 **Kotgar** India
36 D3 **Kotgarh** India
73 G4 **Köthen** Germany
36 E4 **Kothi** India
126 B4 **Kotido** Uganda
36 C3 **Kot Kapura** India
76 E4 **Kotla** Poland
50 H2 **Kotlas** Rus. Fed.
134 B3 **Kotlik** *Alaska* U.S.A.
77 K5 **Kotlina Sandomierska basin** Poland
56 M7 **Kötlutangi pt** Iceland
54 F2 **Kotly** Rus. Fed.
123 F5 **Koton-Karifi** Nigeria
112 B3 **Kotor** Yugoslavia
123 F4 **Kotorkoshi** Nigeria
104 F3 **Kotor Varoš** Bos.-Herz.
122 D5 **Kotouba** Côte d'Ivoire
51 H5 **Kotovo** Rus. Fed.
52 F4 **Kotovras** Rus. Fed.
52 E3 **Kotovsk** Rus. Fed.
53 C3 **Kotovs'k** Ukraine
36 D4 **Kot Putli** India
38 C1 **Kotri r.** India
36 B4 **Kotri** Pakistan
115 D6 **Kotronas** Greece
36 A5 **Kot Sarae** Pakistan
80 E4 **Kötschach** Austria
53 D1 **Kotsyubyns'ke** Ukraine
38 C2 **Kottagudem** India
38 B4 **Kottarakara** India
38 B4 **Kottayam** India
38 B5 **Kotte** Sri Lanka
69 F4 **Kottenheim** Germany
81 F4 **Köttmannsdorf** Austria
124 D2 **Kotto r.** Central African Rep.
38 B3 **Kotturu** India
6 ᵖ5 **Kotu i.** Tonga
6 ᵖ5 **Kotu Group is** Tonga
77 L3 **Kotuń** Poland
45 M3 **Kotuy r.** Rus. Fed.
80 B2 **Kötz** Germany
134 B3 **Kotzebue** *Alaska* U.S.A.
134 B3 **Kotzebue Sound b.** *Alaska* U.S.A.
130 A4 **Kotzehoop** Namibia
130 A5 **Kotzesrus** South Africa
75 H3 **Kötzting** Germany
123 E4 **Kouandé** Benin
124 D3 **Kouango** Central African Rep.
122 B4 **Koubia** Guinea
122 D4 **Koudougou** Burkina
68 D2 **Koudum** Netherlands
130 D6 **Koueveldberg mts** South Africa

L

66 D4 Laidon, Loch l. Scotland U.K.
153 □1 Laie Hawaii U.S.A.
153 □1 Laie Pt pt Hawaii U.S.A.
33 E2 Laifeng China
69 C5 Laifour France
89 F3 L'Aigle France
102 C4 La Iglesuela del Cid Spain
90 C1 Laignes France
106 C5 Laigueglia Italy
92 A2 L'Aiguillon-sur-Mer France
56 F3 Laihia Finland
24 B2 Lai-hka Myanmar
24 B2 Lai-Hsak Myanmar
89 G4 Lailly-en-Val France
37 H4 Laimakuri India
6 □2 Laimbélé, Mt h. Vanuatu
87 E4 Laimont France
106 D3 Lainate Italy
130 C6 Laingsburg South Africa
56 F2 Lainioälven r. Sweden
81 F2 Lainsitz r. Austria
66 D2 Lairg Scotland U.K.
93 E4 Laissac France
57 F3 Laitila Finland
127 C5 Laivera well Tanzania
107 F2 Laives Italy
31 F5 Laiwu China
31 G5 Laixi China
31 G5 Laiyang China
31 E5 Laiyuan China
89 E2 Laize r. France
31 F5 Laizhou Wan b. China
89 E2 Laizon r. France
172 A4 Laja r. Chile
158 D5 La Jagua Colombia
172 B4 Laja, L. de l. Chile
14 B3 Lajamanu Northern Terr. Australia
102 D4 La Jana Spain
51 G7 Lajanurpekhi Georgia
101 F1 La Jara reg. Spain
92 A2 La Jarrie France
91 E4 La Javie France
167 B6 Lajeado Brazil
166 E2 Lajes Rio Grande do Norte Brazil
167 B6 Lajes Santa Catarina Brazil
169 H4 Lajinha Brazil
112 C2 Lajkovac Yugoslavia
102 F2 La Jonquera Spain
79 J4 Lajosmizse Hungary
156 D3 La Joya Mexico
164 B3 La Joya Peru
78 G4 Lajta r. Austria/Hungary
162 C2 La Jugua Colombia
153 G4 La Junta Colorado U.S.A.
122 C4 Lakamané Mali
129 H3 Lakandrano Ampangalana canal Madagascar
52 E2 Lakash Rus. Fed.
152 E2 Lake Wyoming U.S.A.
8 E4 Lake Alice New Zealand
6 □7 Lakeba i. Fiji
6 □7 Lakeba Passage chan. Fiji
13 F3 Lake Cargelligo New South Wales Australia
152 B1 Lake Chelan Nat. Recreation Area res. Washington U.S.A.
145 D6 Lake City Florida U.S.A.
148 E3 Lake City Michigan U.S.A.
148 A3 Lake City Minnesota U.S.A.
145 E5 Lake City S. Carolina U.S.A.
65 E3 Lake District National Park nat. park England U.K.
154 D5 Lake Elsinore California U.S.A.
12 D2 Lake Eyre Nat. Park nat. park S. Australia Australia
141 F4 Lakefield Ontario Canada
15 F2 Lakefield Queensland Australia
15 F2 Lakefield Nat. Park nat. park Queensland Australia
148 C4 Lake Geneva Wisconsin U.S.A.
17 B7 Lake Grace Western Australia Australia
135 L3 Lake Harbour N.W.T. Canada
155 E4 Lake Havasu City Arizona U.S.A.
154 C4 Lake Isabella California U.S.A.
17 B7 Lake King Western Australia Australia
145 D6 Lakeland Florida U.S.A.
15 F2 Lakeland Queensland Australia
148 C2 Lake Linden Michigan U.S.A.
136 F4 Lake Louise Alberta Canada
14 B4 Lake Mackay Aboriginal Land res. Northern Terr. Australia
17 A5 Lake MacLeod Western Australia Australia
155 E4 Lake Mead Nat. Rec. Area, res. Arizona U.S.A.
147 J2 Lake Moxie Maine U.S.A.
14 D4 Lake Nash Northern Terr. Australia
63 G2 Lakenheath England U.K.
141 F4 Lake of Bays l. Ontario Canada
152 B2 Lake Oswego Oregon U.S.A.
9 B5 Lake Paringa New Zealand
147 G2 Lake Placid New York U.S.A.
154 A2 Lakeport California U.S.A.
9 C6 Lake Pukaki New Zealand
138 D3 Lake River Ontario Canada
141 F4 Lake St Peter Ontario Canada
13 G4 Lakes Entrance Victoria Australia
140 C3 Lake Superior National Park nat. park Ontario Canada
9 C6 Lake Tekapo New Zealand
138 E4 Lake Traverse Ontario Canada
152 B3 Lakeview Oregon U.S.A.
152 F4 Lakewood Colorado U.S.A.
147 F4 Lakewood New Jersey U.S.A.
146 C4 Lakewood Ohio U.S.A.
145 D7 Lake Worth Florida U.S.A.
57 H3 Lakhdenpokh'ya Rus. Fed.
36 D4 Lakheri India
36 E4 Lakhimpur India
36 D5 Lakhnadon India
36 B5 Lakhpat India
52 D1 Lakinsk Rus. Fed.
114 B3 Lakka Greece
36 B2 Lakki Pakistan
115 E7 Lakkoi Greece
114 G2 Lakkoma Greece
58 A2 Lakksvelafjellet h. Norway
22 E4 Lakohembi Indonesia
115 D6 Lakonia div. Greece
115 D6 Lakonikos Kolpos b. Greece
122 C5 Lakota Côte d'Ivoire
56 G1 Laksefjorden chan. Norway
56 G1 Lakselv Norway
38 A4 Lakshadweep div. India
37 G5 Laksham Bangladesh
38 B2 Lakshettipet India
37 G5 Lakshmikantapur India
23 B5 Lala Philippines
37 H4 Lalaghat India
173 F2 La Laguna Argentina
172 A4 La Laja Chile
6 □3 Lalalomei Bank reef Tonga
101 E3 La Lantejuela Spain
129 E2 Lalapanzi Zimbabwe
112 F4 Lalapaşa Turkey
124 B3 Lalara Gabon
93 D4 Lalbenque France
103 C5 L'Albufera l. Spain
103 C5 L'Alcudia Spain
15 G4 Laleham Queensland Australia
73 H2 Lalendorf Germany
91 C4 Lalevade-d'Ardèche France
39 B2 Lālī Iran
126 C2 Lalībela Ethiopia
157 H6 La Libertad El Salvador
157 H5 La Libertad Guatemala
92 B3 La Ligua Chile
31 H3 Lalin r. China
31 H3 Lalin China
98 B2 Lalín Spain
93 C4 Lalinde France
101 E4 La Línea de la Concepción Spain
36 D4 Lalitpur India
36 D3 Lalkua India
69 B4 Lallaing France
91 D4 Lalley France
23 B2 Lal-Lo Philippines
37 G4 Lalmanir Hat Bangladesh
173 F6 La Lobería Argentina
137 H3 La Loche Saskatchewan Canada
137 H3 La Loche, Lac l. Saskatchewan Canada
7 □12 Lalomanu Western Samoa
91 E5 La Londe-les-Maures France
99 H2 La Losa reg. Spain
93 C5 Laloubère France
173 H3 La Louisa Argentina
89 G3 La Loupe France
91 C3 Lalouvesc France
69 C4 La Louvière Hainaut Belgium
82 A1 La Loye France
83 B1 l'Alpe-d'Huez France
50 H2 Lal'sk Rus. Fed.
36 D4 Lalsot India
101 E3 La Luisiana Spain
93 B5 Laluque France
37 H5 Lama Bangladesh
141 H3 La Macaza Québec Canada
90 B2 La Machine France
108 B3 la Maddalena Sardegna Italy
23 A5 Lamag Malaysia
98 E2 La Magdalena Spain
24 B4 Lamaing Myanmar
91 B4 La Malène France
101 H1 La Mancha reg. Spain
103 C7 La Manga del Mar Menor Spain
153 G4 Lamar Colorado U.S.A.
151 E4 Lamar Missouri U.S.A.
87 E4 Lamarche France
39 C4 Lamard Iran
108 B5 La Marmora, Punta mt. Sardegna Italy
172 D3 La Maroma Argentina
151 E6 La Marque Texas U.S.A.
172 E5 Lamarque Argentina
92 B3 Lamarque France
172 E3 La Maruja Argentina
43 C1 Lamas r. Turkey
93 D6 La Massana Andorra
91 C4 Lamastre France
81 E2 Lambach Austria
88 C3 Lamballe France
124 B4 Lambaréné Gabon
162 B5 Lambayeque Peru
67 E3 Lambay Island i. Rep. of Ireland
22 C2 Lambeng Indonesia
86 C2 Lambersart France
16 B4 Lambert, C. headland Western Australia Australia
179 D4 Lambert Gl. gl. Antarctica
130 B6 Lambert's Bay South Africa
91 D5 Lambesc France
36 C3 Lambi India
59 F1 Lamborn Sweden
63 E3 Lambourn England U.K.
63 E3 Lambourn Downs h. England U.K.
69 B4 Lambres-lez-Douai France
106 D3 Lambro r. Italy
141 K4 Lambton Québec Canada
24 D4 Lam Chi r. Thailand
98 C3 Lamego Portugal
164 B2 La Mejorada Peru
6 □2 Lamen Vanuatu
159 □5 Lamentin Guadeloupe Caribbean
159 □4 Lamentin Martinique Caribbean
139 H4 Lamèque, I. i. New Brunswick Canada
164 A2 La Merced Peru
12 E3 Lameroo S. Australia Australia
154 D5 La Mesa California U.S.A.
151 C5 Lamesa Texas U.S.A.
102 D4 L'Ametlla de Mar Spain
111 F4 Lamezia Italy
114 D4 Lamia Greece
89 F3 La Milesse France
81 G3 Laming r. Austria
15 H6 Lamington Nat. Park nat. park Queensland Australia
153 E6 La Misa Mexico
154 D5 La Misión Mexico
23 B5 Lamitan Philippines
66 C5 Lamlash Scotland U.K.
27 □ Lamma I. i. Hong Kong China
120 C3 Lammaylthiyine watercourse Western Sahara
65 F2 Lammer Law h. Scotland U.K.
9 B6 Lammerlaw Ra. mountain range New Zealand
9 B6 Lammerlaw Top mt. New Zealand
66 F5 Lammermuir Hills h. Scotland U.K.
59 F3 Lammhult Sweden
54 D1 Lammi Häme Finland
57 G3 Lammi Finland
52 E2 Lammijärv chan. Estonia/Rus. Fed.
37 F3 Lamna La pass China
147 G2 Lamoille r. Vermont U.S.A.
148 C5 La Moille Illinois U.S.A.
148 B5 La Moine r. Illinois U.S.A.
91 E5 La Môle France
80 C4 Lamon Italy
23 B3 Lamon Bay b. Philippines
107 G4 Lamone r. Italy
22 C3 Lamongan Indonesia
93 C6 La Mongie France
150 E3 Lamoni Iowa U.S.A.
90 B3 La Monnerie-le-Montel France
152 F3 Lamont Wyoming U.S.A.
127 □5 La Montagne Réunion Indian Ocean
172 D3 La Mora Argentina
99 F4 La Moraña reg. Spain
151 B6 La Morita Mexico
172 B2 La Mostaza Chile
92 A2 La Mothe-Achard France
93 D4 Lamothe-Cassel France
92 B2 La Mothe-St-Héray France
141 F2 La Motte Québec Canada
89 H4 Lamotte-Beuvron France
91 D4 La Motte-Chalancon France
91 E4 La Motte-du-Caire France
90 D3 La Motte-Servolex France
172 B2 Lampa Chile
24 C3 Lam Pao Res. resr Thailand
151 D6 Lampasas Texas U.S.A.
88 A3 Lampaul France
157 E3 Lampazos Mexico
105 D7 Lampedusa, Isola di i. Italy
58 C2 Lampeland Norway
87 H3 Lampertheim Germany
62 B2 Lampeter Wales U.K.
25 C4 Lam Plai Mat r. Thailand
50 H1 Lampozhnya Rus. Fed.
80 D3 Lamprechtshausen Austria
22 A3 Lampung div. Indonesia
52 D3 Lamskoye Rus. Fed.
72 F4 Lamspringe Germany
72 E2 Lamstedt Germany
27 □ Lam Tin Hong Kong China
127 D5 Lamu Kenya
24 A3 Lamu Myanmar
102 B3 La Muela Spain
127 D5 Lamu I. i. Kenya
156 D2 La Mula Mexico
91 D4 La Mure France
90 C2 Lamure-sur-Azergues France
15 G4 Lana Queensland Australia
107 F2 Lana Italy
172 E3 La Nacional Argentina
153 □2 Lanai i. Hawaii U.S.A.
153 □2 Lanai City Hawaii U.S.A.
102 C3 Lanaja Spain
69 D4 Lanaken Belgium
172 A4 Lanalhue, L. l. Chile
23 C5 Lanao, Lake l. Philippines
91 C4 Lanarce France
148 C4 Lanark Illinois U.S.A.
141 G4 Lanark Ontario Canada
65 E2 Lanark Scotland U.K.
23 A5 Lanas Malaysia
101 F1 La Nava de Ricomalillo Spain
100 D1 La Nava de Santiago Spain
25 B5 Lanbi Kyun i. Myanmar
32 B2 Lancang r. China
32 B4 Lancang China
32 C4 Lancang Jiang r. China
65 F4 Lancashire div. England U.K.
65 F4 Lancashire Plain lowland England U.K.
154 C4 Lancaster California U.S.A.
65 F3 Lancaster England U.K.
148 A5 Lancaster Missouri U.S.A.
147 H2 Lancaster New Hampshire U.S.A.
146 B5 Lancaster Ohio U.S.A.
141 H4 Lancaster Ontario Canada
147 E4 Lancaster Pennsylvania U.S.A.
145 D5 Lancaster S. Carolina U.S.A.
148 B4 Lancaster Wisconsin U.S.A.
65 F4 Lancaster Canal canal England U.K.
135 K2 Lancaster Sound str. N.W.T. Canada
159 □8 Lance aux Épines Grenada Caribbean
17 A6 Lancelin Western Australia Australia
65 G3 Lanchester England U.K.
Lanchow see Lanzhou
109 G2 Lanciano Italy
172 A5 Lanco Chile
31 G5 Lancun China
77 L5 Łańcut Poland
82 B2 Lancy Switzerland
22 B1 Landak r. Indonesia
75 H4 Landau an der Isar Germany
74 D3 Landau in der Pfalz Germany
80 B3 Landeck div. Austria
80 B3 Landeck Austria
88 A3 Landéda France
52 F1 Landekh r. Rus. Fed.
88 B3 Landeleau France
69 D4 Landen Belgium
14 C4 Lander watercourse Northern Terr. Australia
152 E3 Lander Wyoming U.S.A.
88 A3 Landerneau France
93 B5 Landes div. Aquitaine France
93 B4 Landes reg. France
72 E3 Landesbergen Germany
88 C4 Landes de Lanvaux reg. France
88 C3 Landes du Mené reg. France
173 F2 Landeta Argentina
103 B5 Landete Spain
88 B4 Landévant France
25 A4 Landfall I. i. Andaman and Nicobar Is India
63 H3 Landguard Point pt England U.K.
72 D2 Land Hadeln reg. Germany
36 B2 Landi Kotal Pakistan
93 B4 Landiras France
137 H4 Landis Saskatchewan Canada
88 A3 Landivisiau France
89 D3 Landivy France
72 E2 Land Kehdingen reg. Germany
17 B5 Landor Western Australia Australia
91 B4 Landos France
83 E2 Landquart r. Switzerland
83 E2 Landquart Switzerland
86 C3 Landrecies France
87 E3 Landres France
141 G2 Landrienne Québec Canada
98 C1 Landro r. Spain
82 B3 Landry France
75 F4 Landsberg am Lech Germany
15 F4 Landsborough Cr. watercourse Queensland Australia
62 A4 Land's End pt England U.K.
75 H4 Landshut Germany
59 E4 Landskrona Sweden
74 C3 Landstuhl Germany
59 E3 Landvetter airport Sweden
72 D2 Land Wursten reg. Germany
173 H4 La Negra Argentina
164 B4 La Negra Chile
67 D3 Lanesborough Rep. of Ireland
88 B4 Lanester France
82 C1 La Neuveville Switzerland
69 D5 Laneuville-sur-Meuse France
55 B3 Langå Denmark
33 E4 La'nga Co l. China
99 G3 Langa de Duero Spain
32 E1 Langan China
36 C1 Langar Afghanistan
39 C3 Langar Iran
81 G2 Langau Austria
66 B2 Langavat, Loch l. Scotland U.K.
130 D4 Langberg mts South Africa
150 D1 Langdon N. Dakota U.S.A.
10 □3 Langdon Pt pt Macquarie I. Pacific Ocean
80 E1 Langdorf Germany
91 B3 Langeac France
89 F4 Langeais France
130 B6 Langebaan South Africa
55 E5 Langebæk Denmark
128 C5 Langeberg mts South Africa
68 C2 Langedijk Netherlands
130 E3 Langehorn South Africa
55 C4 Langeland i. Denmark
55 C5 Langelands Bælt chan. Denmark
57 G3 Längelmäki Finland
57 G3 Längelmävesi l. Finland
72 F4 Langelsheim Germany
87 H3 Langen Hessen Germany
72 D2 Langen Niedersachsen Germany
83 E1 Langenargen Germany
74 F4 Langenau Germany
74 E3 Langenburg Germany
80 B3 Längenfeld Austria
72 B4 Langenfeld (Rheinland) Germany
72 E3 Langenhagen Germany
74 C2 Langenhahn Germany
81 G2 Langenlois Austria
74 E2 Langenselbold Germany
82 C1 Langenthal Switzerland
81 G3 Langenwang Austria
73 G3 Langenweddingen Germany
75 F3 Langenzenn Germany
81 H2 Langenzersdorf Austria
72 C2 Langeoog i. Germany
72 C2 Langeoog Germany
73 J3 Langer Berg h. Germany
55 C4 Langeskov Denmark
58 C2 Langesund Norway
58 A2 Langevåg Norway
127 □5 Langevin, Pointe de pt Réunion Indian Ocean
37 H3 Langgar China
74 D2 Langgöns Germany
59 G2 Långhalsen l. Sweden
137 H4 Langham Saskatchewan Canada
106 E4 Langhirano Italy
66 F5 Langholm Scotland U.K.
56 L6 Langjökull ice cap Iceland
25 B6 Langkawi i. Kedah Malaysia
130 C4 Langklip South Africa
23 A5 Langkon Malaysia
141 H2 Langlade Québec Canada
148 C3 Langlade Wisconsin U.S.A.
15 F5 Langlo watercourse Queensland Australia
15 F5 Langlo Crossing Queensland Australia
Langmusi see Dagcanglhamo
82 C2 Langnau Switzerland
91 B4 Langogne France
93 B4 Langoiran France
58 G1 Langön i. Sweden
93 B4 Langon France
88 B3 Langonnet France
56 D1 Langøya i. Norway
37 F3 Langphu mt. China
62 D3 Langport England U.K.
33 G3 Langqi China
80 D2 Langquaid Germany
98 E1 Langreo Spain
90 D1 Langres France
36 D1 Langru China
20 D6 Langsa Indonesia
81 F2 Langschlag Austria
56 E3 Långsele Sweden
30 C4 Lang Shan mountain range China
30 C4 Langshan China
59 G1 Långshyttan Sweden
24 D2 Lang Sơn Vietnam
65 F3 Langstrothdale Chase reg. England U.K.
69 E5 Langsur Germany
123 F5 Langtang Nigeria
24 B1 Langtao Myanmar
65 H3 Langtoft England U.K.
31 G3 Langtoutun China
151 C6 Langtry Texas U.S.A.
93 D5 Languedoc reg. France
91 B5 Languedoc-Roussillon div. France
88 C3 Langueux France
Languiaru r. see Iquê
88 B4 Languidic France
56 F2 Långvattnet Sweden
72 D2 Langwarden Germany
65 F3 Langwathby England U.K.
72 E3 Langwedel Germany
75 F4 Langweid am Lech Germany
33 G2 Langxi China
32 D2 Langzhong China
141 F3 Laniel Québec Canada
137 H4 Lanigan Saskatchewan Canada
153 □1 Lanikai Hawaii U.S.A.
172 B5 Lanín, Parque Nacional nat. park Argentina
171 B4 Lanín, V. volcano Argentina
62 B4 Lanivet England U.K.
53 B2 Lanivtsi Ukraine
22 B1 Lanjak, Bukit mt. Malaysia
33 F1 Lankao China
42 G2 Länkäran Azerbaijan
164 B2 Lanlacuni Bajo Peru
88 B3 Lanmeur France
59 F2 Lanna Sweden
81 G4 Lannach Austria
93 C5 Lannemezan France
93 C5 Lannepax France
88 A3 Lannilis France
88 B3 Lannion France
141 H3 L'Annonciation Québec Canada
86 C2 Lannoy France
102 D3 La Noguera reg. Spain
102 E3 L'Anoia r. Spain
102 E3 L'Anoia Spain
156 D4 La Noria Mexico
92 D3 Lanouaille France
56 F2 Lansån Sweden
148 C2 L'Anse Michigan U.S.A.
136 C2 Lansing r. Yukon Terr. Canada
148 B4 Lansing Iowa U.S.A.
148 E4 Lansing Michigan U.S.A.
78 F2 Lanškroun Czech Rep.
91 E3 Lanslebourg-Mont-Cenis France
91 D4 Lans, Montagne de mts France
93 D5 Lanta France
33 F4 Lantau I. i. Hong Kong China
27 □ Lantau Island i. Hong Kong China
27 □ Lantau Peak h. Hong Kong China
90 E1 Lanterne r. France
91 F5 Lantosque France
90 B2 Lanty France
114 E2 Lantzas, L. l. Greece
103 C6 La Nucía Spain
108 A4 La Nurra reg. Sardegna Italy
173 H3 Lanús Argentina
108 B5 Lanusei Sardegna Italy
23 C4 Lanuza Bay b. Philippines
88 A3 Lanvéoc France
88 C3 Lanvollon France
31 H3 Lanxi China
33 G2 Lanxi China
126 B3 Lanya Sudan
33 H4 Lan Yü i. Taiwan
73 G2 Lanz Germany
99 F4 Lanzahita Spain
97 □ Lanzarote i. Canary Is Spain
81 H3 Lanzenkirchen Austria
81 E2 Lanžhot Czech Rep.
30 B5 Lanzhou China
31 G3 Lanzijing China
106 B3 Lanzo Torinese Italy
111 E3 Lao r. Italy
23 B2 Laoag Philippines
23 C3 Laoang Philippines
32 B4 Laobie Shan mountain range China
24 C2 Lao Cai Vietnam
31 G4 Laoha r. China
33 E1 Laohekou China
31 G5 Laohutun China
67 D4 Laois div. Rep. of Ireland
97 □ La Oliva Canary Is Spain
86 C3 Laon France
148 C3 Laona Wisconsin U.S.A.
86 C3 Laonnois reg. France
97 □ La Orotava Canary Is Spain
164 A2 La Oroya Peru
19 M8 Laos country Asia
31 G5 Laoshan China
31 J4 Laotougou China
121 F4 Laouni well Algeria
93 E5 Laouzas, Lac de l. France
Laowohi see Khardung La
30 B4 Laoximiao China
31 J4 Laoye Ling mountain range China
31 H3 Laoye Ling mountain range China
167 C6 Lapa Brazil
23 B5 Lapac i. Philippines
103 B7 La Paca Spain
90 B2 La Pacaudière France
170 E2 Lapachito Argentina
123 F5 Lapai Nigeria
90 B2 Lapalisse France
172 B3 La Palma Chile
156 L7 La Palma Panama
100 D3 La Palma del Condado Spain
173 K2 La Paloma Durazno Uruguay
173 K3 La Paloma Rocha Uruguay
172 B1 La Paloma, Emb. resr Chile
91 E5 La Palud-sur-Verdon France
172 D4 La Pampa div. Argentina
154 B4 La Panza Range, mts California U.S.A.
173 F1 La Para Argentina
163 E2 La Paragua Venezuela
23 A5 Laparan i. Philippines
114 A2 Lapardha Albania
164 C2 La Paz div. Bolivia
172 E2 La Paz Córdoba Argentina
173 H1 La Paz Entre Ríos Argentina
148 D5 Lapaz Indiana U.S.A.
172 D2 La Paz Mendoza Argentina
164 C3 La Paz Bolivia
156 J6 La Paz Honduras
156 C3 La Paz Mexico
173 J3 La Paz Uruguay
162 D4 La Pedrera Colombia
173 K3 La Pedrera Uruguay
149 F4 Lapeer Michigan U.S.A.
171 C1 La Pelada Argentina
171 B6 La Peninsular Argentina
91 D5 La Penne-sur-Huveaune France
156 D2 La Perla Mexico
7 □16 La Pérouse, Bahía b. Easter I. Chile
27 Q2 La Pérouse Strait str. Japan/Rus. Fed.
157 F4 La Pesca Mexico
87 G4 La Petite-Pierre France
173 G1 La Picada Argentina
156 E4 La Piedad Mexico
152 B3 La Pine Oregon U.S.A.
23 C3 Lapinig Philippines
54 E1 Lapinjärvi Finland
56 G3 Lapinlahti Finland
43 B2 Lapithos Cyprus
110 C5 La Pizzuta mt. Sicilia Italy
151 F6 Laplace Louisiana U.S.A.
90 E3 La Plagne France
127 □5 La Plaine des Palmistes Réunion Indian Ocean
150 C2 La Plant S. Dakota U.S.A.
173 J3 La Plata Argentina
162 B3 La Plata Colombia
173 F2 La Playosa Argentina
92 E3 Lapleau France
93 C4 Laplume France
54 C3 Lapmežciems Latvia
102 D2 La Pobla de Segur Spain
102 E3 La Pola de Gordón Spain
50 G1 Lapominka Rus. Fed.
89 E4 La Pommeraye France
108 B2 La Porta Corse France
148 D5 La Porte Indiana U.S.A.
148 A4 La Porte City Iowa U.S.A.
103 B5 La Portera Spain
172 F1 La Posta Argentina
87 G4 Lapoutroie France
112 C2 Lapovo Yugoslavia
56 F3 Lappajärvi l. Finland
56 F3 Lappajärvi Finland
59 F2 Lappe Sweden
57 H3 Lappeenranta Finland
75 H3 Lappersdorf Germany
56 G2 Lappi div. Finland
54 B1 Lappi Turku-Pori Finland
44 D3 Lappland reg. Europe
59 J1 Lappo Finland
54 C2 Lappohja Finland
141 J4 La Prairie Québec Canada
173 G4 Laprida Argentina
173 G4 La Primavera Argentina
99 H2 La Proveda de Soria Spain
151 D6 La Pryor Texas U.S.A.
113 F4 Lâpseki Turkey
Laptev Sea see More Laptevykh
56 F3 Lapua Finland
101 G1 La Puebla de Almoradiel Spain
101 E3 La Puebla de Cazalla Spain
101 E3 La Puebla de los Infantes Spain
100 D3 La Puebla del Río Spain
99 F5 La Puebla de Montalbán Spain
99 F2 La Puebla de Valdavia Spain
103 C4 La Puebla de Valverde Spain
173 F1 La Puerta Argentina
101 H2 La Puerta de Segura Spain
23 B4 Lapu-Lapu Philippines
172 E2 La Punilla Argentina
83 E2 La Punt Switzerland
170 D2 La Punta Argentina
112 E1 Lăpuş Romania
77 L3 Łapy Poland
119 E3 Laqiya Arbain well Sudan
170 C1 La Quiaca Argentina
109 F2 L'Aquila div. Abruzzo Italy
109 F2 L'Aquila Italy
154 D5 La Quinta California U.S.A.
39 C4 Lār Iran
122 D5 Larabanga Ghana
98 B1 Laracha Spain
120 C1 Larache Morocco
91 D4 Laragne-Montéglin France
39 D4 Lārak i. Iran
101 F3 La Rambla Spain
152 F3 Laramie Wyoming U.S.A.
152 F3 Laramie Mts mountain range Wyoming U.S.A.
Laranda see Karaman
168 A5 Laranjal r. Brazil
163 F4 Laranjal Brazil
168 E5 Laranjal Paulista Brazil
166 E3 Laranjeiras Brazil
168 B6 Laranjeiras do Sul Brazil
100 A2 Laranjeiro Portugal
168 C5 Laranjinha r. Brazil
21 H8 Larantuka Indonesia
21 K8 Larat i. Indonesia
90 D3 La Ravoire France
120 B4 La Raygat reg. Western Sahara
121 E1 Larba Algeria
90 C3 L'Arbresle France
59 H3 Lärbro Sweden
93 A5 Larceveau-Arros-Cibits France
92 D3 Larche Limousin France
91 E4 Larche Provence-Alpes-Côte-d'Azur France
140 E3 Larchwood Ontario Canada
88 C3 L'Arcouest, Pte de pt France
107 E3 Lardaro Italy
141 F2 Larder Lake Ontario Canada
115 □ Lardos Greece
151 D7 Laredo Texas U.S.A.
99 G1 Laredo Spain
172 D4 La Reforma Argentina
141 F2 La Reine Québec Canada
68 D2 Laren Netherlands
93 B4 La Réole France
91 C4 Largentière France
91 E4 l'Argentière la-Bessée France
145 D7 Largo Florida U.S.A.
173 K2 Largo, Cerro div. Uruguay
65 F1 Largoward Scotland U.K.
66 D5 Largs Scotland U.K.
42 F2 Lārī Iran
121 G1 L'Ariana Tunisia
22 D2 Lariang r. Indonesia
22 D2 Lariang Indonesia
173 H3 La Rica Argentina
91 C3 La Ricamarie France
89 F4 La Riche France
137 K5 Larimore N. Dakota U.S.A.
100 E3 La Rinconada Spain
109 G3 Larino Italy
172 D1 La Rioja div. Argentina
99 H2 La Rioja div. Spain
170 C2 La Rioja Argentina
54 G1 Larionovo Rus. Fed.
114 D3 Larisa div. Greece
114 D3 Larisa Greece
39 D4 Laristan reg. Iran
36 B4 Larkana Pakistan
66 E5 Larkhall Scotland U.K.
63 G2 Larling England U.K.
82 B2 Larmont mt. France/Switzerland
88 B4 Larmor-Plage France
43 B2 Larnaca Bay b. Cyprus
43 B2 Larnaka Cyprus
67 F2 Larne Northern Ireland U.K.
150 D4 Larned Kansas U.S.A.
67 F2 Larne Lough l. Northern Ireland U.K.
124 B2 Laro Cameroon
98 E2 La Robla Spain
100 D1 La Roca de la Sierra Spain
82 C2 La Roche Switzerland
92 C3 La Rochebeaucourt-et-Argentine France
88 C4 La Roche-Bernard France
92 D3 La Roche-Canillac France
92 C3 La Roche-Chalais France
91 E4 La Roche-de-Rame France
88 B3 La Roche-Derrien France
91 D4 La Roche-des-Arnauds France
69 D4 La Roche-en-Ardenne Belgium
92 C3 La Rochefoucauld France
92 A2 La Rochelle France
90 E2 La Roche-sur-Foron France
92 A2 La Roche-sur-Yon France
91 E3 La Rochette France
69 E5 Larochette Luxembourg
101 H1 La Roda Spain
101 F3 La Roda de Andalucía Spain
159 E3 La Romana Dominican Rep.
22 E2 Larompong Indonesia
137 H3 La Ronge Saskatchewan Canada
92 E4 Laroquebrou France
91 D5 La Roquebrussanne France
91 D5 La Roque-d'Anthéron France
93 D6 Laroque-d'Olmes France
151 C7 La Rosa Mexico
157 E2 La Rosita Mexico
93 B5 Larrau France
93 D5 Larrazet France
14 C2 Larrimah Northern Terr. Australia
173 H2 Larroque Argentina
179 B2 Larsen Ice Shelf ice feature Antarctica
56 F3 Larsmo Finland
93 B6 Laruns France
58 D2 Larvik Norway
53 G3 Laryne Ukraine
83 F2 Lasà Italy
170 E2 La Sabana Argentina
99 F4 La Sagra reg. Spain
103 C5 Las Alcublas Spain
172 C1 La Salina salt pan Argentina
155 H2 La Sal Junction Utah U.S.A.
148 C5 La Salle Illinois U.S.A.
141 J4 La Salle Québec Canada
91 B4 Lasalle France
91 E4 La Salle les Alpes France
93 E4 La Salvetat-Peyralès France
93 E5 La Salvetat-sur-Agout France
99 F1 Las Arenas Spain
173 K2 Las Arenas Uruguay
173 J4 Las Armas Argentina
141 F2 La Sarre Québec Canada
99 H1 Lasarte-Orio Spain
172 F2 Las Asequias Argentina
93 C4 La Sauvetat-du-Dropt France
162 D1 Las Aves, Is is Venezuela
173 G2 Las Bandurrias Argentina
81 F2 Lasberg Austria
159 F6 Las Bonitas Venezuela
55 B3 Låsby Denmark
100 E4 Las Cabezas de San Juan Spain
172 B3 Las Cabras Chile
170 C2 Las Cañas Argentina
172 A3 Las Cañas Chile
172 C1 Las Casuarinas Argentina
172 C2 Las Catitas Argentina
170 D2 Las Cejas Argentina
141 H3 L'Ascension Québec Canada
141 K2 L'Ascension Québec Canada
172 E2 Las Chacras Argentina
139 J4 La Scie Newfoundland Canada
172 B5 Las Colorados Argentina
153 F5 Las Cruces New Mexico U.S.A.
102 D2 Lascuarre Spain
89 E4 La Séguinière France
159 D3 La Selle mt. Haiti
93 E4 La Selve France
102 D4 La Sènia Spain
101 E2 La Serena reg. Spain
170 B2 La Serena Chile
151 C7 Las Esperancas Mexico
102 E2 La Seu d'Urgell Spain
91 D5 La Seyne-sur-Mer France
173 H4 Las Flores Buenos Aires Argentina
172 C1 Las Flores San Juan Argentina

13 F4 Leongatha Victoria Australia
115 D5 Leonidi Greece
100 D4 León, Isla de i. Spain
98 D2 León, Montes de mountain range Spain
17 C6 Leonora Western Australia Australia
173 J1 León, Paso del pass Brazil
115 D5 Leontario Greece
16 D3 Leopold r. Western Australia Australia
169 G4 Leopoldina Brazil
69 B3 Leopold Kanaal canal Belgium
168 D2 Leopoldo de Bulhões Brazil
69 D3 Leopoldsburg Belgium
87 G4 Leopoldskanal canal Germany
112 F1 Leorda Romania
53 C3 Leova Moldova
137 H4 Leoville Saskatchewan Canada
88 B4 Le Palais France
92 D3 Le Palais-sur-Vienne France
22 A2 Lepar i. Indonesia
86 B2 Le Parcq France
93 C4 Le Passage France
86 C4 Le Pavillon-Ste-Julie France
100 C3 Lepe Spain
91 C3 Le Péage-de-Roussillon France
114 C4 Lepenou Greece
91 D4 Le Périer France
93 E6 Le Perthus France
89 G2 Le Petit-Quevilly France
128 D3 Lephepe Botswana
131 E5 Lephoi South Africa
92 B4 Le Pian-Médoc France
86 D4 L'Épine Champagne-Ardenne France
91 D4 L'Épine Provence - Alpes - Côte-d'Azur France
33 G2 Leping China
141 J4 L'Épiphanie Québec Canada
86 B3 Le Plessis-Belleville France
91 D4 Le Poët France
81 H4 Lepoglava Croatia
92 D2 Le Poinçonnet France
92 A2 Le Poiré-sur-Vie France
91 D3 Le Pont-de-Claix France
91 B4 Le Pont-de-Monvert France
91 C5 Le Pontet France
93 A4 Le Porge France
127 □5 Le Port Réunion Indian Ocean
86 A2 Le Portel France
112 C3 Leposavić Yugoslavia
88 C4 Le Pouliguen France
115 F4 Lepoura Greece
91 C4 Le Pouzin France
56 G3 Leppävirta Finland
91 E5 Le Pradet France
47 J3 Lepsy Kazakhstan
114 D2 Leptokarya Greece
91 B3 Le-Puy-en-Velay France
86 C2 Le Quesnoy France
110 H2 Lequile Italy
86 B4 Le Raincy France
159 □5 Le Raizet airport Guadeloupe Caribbean
110 C5 Lercara Friddi Sicilia Italy
124 B2 Léré Chad
90 A1 Léré France
123 F4 Lere Nigeria
88 A3 Le Relecq-Kerhuon France
98 B2 Lérez r. Spain
106 D4 Lerici Italy
162 C4 Lerida Colombia
Lérida see Lleida
42 G2 Lerik Azerbaijan
102 B2 Lerin Spain
91 F5 Lérins, Îles de is France
99 G2 Lerma Spain
93 B4 Lerm-et Musset France
51 G6 Lermontov Rus. Fed.
31 K3 Lermontovka Rus. Fed.
80 B3 Lermoos Austria
122 D3 Lerneb Mali
159 □4 Le Robert Martinique Caribbean
90 E3 Le Roignais mt. France
113 F6 Leros i. Greece
93 E4 Le Rouget France
148 C5 Le Roy Illinois U.S.A.
91 B4 Le Rozier France
59 E3 Lerum Sweden
90 E1 Le Russey France
66 □2 Lerwick Scotland U.K.
124 E1 Ler Zerai well Sudan
93 C6 Lés Spain
83 D3 Lesa Italy
90 D3 Les Abrets France
159 □5 Les Abymes Guadeloupe Caribbean
159 □4 Le St Esprit Martinique Caribbean
92 E1 Les Aix-d'Angillon France
93 E6 les Albères reg. France
89 G2 Les Andelys France
91 C5 Les Angles France
114 B1 Lešani Macedonia
159 □4 Les Anses d'Arlets Martinique Caribbean
90 E3 Les Arcs France
127 C5 Lesatima mt. Kenya
82 A3 Les Avenières France
127 □5 Les Avirons Réunion Indian Ocean
102 D3 Les Borges Blanques Spain
Lesbos i. see Lesvos
90 D2 Les Bouchoux France
65 G2 Lesbury England U.K.
93 D6 Les Cabannes France
102 G2 L'Escala Spain
91 E4 L'Escale France
127 □4 L'Escalier Mauritius
93 E5 Les Cammazes France
93 B5 Lescar France
91 F5 L'Escarène France
158 D3 Les Cayes Haiti
81 F4 Lesce Slovenia
89 E3 Les Coëvrons h. France
82 B3 Les Contamines-Montjoie France
93 E5 Lescure-d'Albigeois France
111 F3 Lese r. Italy
91 D3 Les Échelles France
88 D4 Le Sel-de-Bretagne France
82 B2 Le Sentier Switzerland
92 B2 Les Epesses France
93 D6 Les Escaldes Andorra
139 G4 Les Escoumins Québec Canada
90 D2 Les Essards-Taignevaux France
92 A2 Les Essarts France
147 J1 Les Étroits Québec Canada
93 D4 Les Eyzies-de-Tayac-Sireuil France
90 E1 Les Fins France
82 B2 Les Fourgs France
90 E2 Les Gets France
32 C2 Leshan China
69 C5 Les Hautes-Rivières France
92 A2 Les Herbiers France
82 B3 Les Houches France
50 H1 Leshukonskoye Rus. Fed.
124 E2 Lesi watercourse Sudan
6 □6 Lesiaceva Pt pt Fiji
106 D4 Lesima, Monte mt. Italy
109 H3 Lesina Italy
109 H3 Lesina, Lago di lag. Italy
91 E5 les Issambres France
59 F2 Lesjöfors Sweden
91 E3 les Karellis France
77 L6 Lesko Poland
112 C3 Leskovac Yugoslavia
114 B2 Leskovik Albania
53 E2 Les'ky Ukraine
92 A2 Les Landes-Genusson France
66 E4 Leslie Scotland U.K.
92 A2 Les Lucs-sur-Boulogne France
64 E2 Lesmahagow Scotland U.K.
159 □5 Les Mangles Guadeloupe Caribbean
90 E3 Les Marches France
91 B5 Les Matelles France
89 E4 Les Mauges reg. France
91 D4 Les Mées France
91 E3 les Menuires France
88 C3 Les Minquiers is Channel Is.
86 D4 Lesmont France
73 L4 Leśna Poland
52 D1 Lesnaya Polyana Rus. Fed.
88 A3 Lesneven France
76 G5 Leśnica Poland
73 L4 Leśniów Wielki Poland
52 E2 Lesnoy Rus. Fed.
50 K3 Lesnoy Rus. Fed.
50 E3 Lesnoye Rus. Fed.
54 F1 Lesnoy, O. i. Rus. Fed.
52 F2 Lesogorsk Rus. Fed.
54 F1 Lesogorskiy Rus. Fed.
91 C4 Les Ollières-sur-Eyrieux France
44 L4 Lesosibirsk Rus. Fed.
117 G8 Lesotho country Africa
131 G4 Lesotho Highlands Water Scheme Lesotho
31 K3 Lesozavodsk Rus. Fed.
92 B3 Lesparre-Médoc France
91 D5 Les Pennes-Mirabeau France
93 A5 Lesperon France
79 N4 Lespezi h. Romania
88 D2 Les Pieux France
90 E2 Les Planches-en-Montagne France
89 E4 Les Ponts-de-Cé France
82 B1 Les Ponts-de-Martel Switzerland
86 D5 Les Riceys France
89 E4 Les Rosiers France
90 E2 Les Rousses France
92 A2 Les Sables-d'Olonne France
81 E3 Lessach Austria
88 D2 Lessay France
69 D4 Lesse r. Belgium
159 G3 Lesser Antilles is Caribbean
Lesser Caucasus mountain range see Malyy Kavkaz
136 F3 Lesser Slave Lake l. Yukon Terr. Canada
136 G3 Lesser Slave Lake Provincial Park nat. park Alberta Canada
86 C2 Lessines Belgium
131 F4 Lessingskop mt. South Africa
83 G3 Lessini, Monti mts Italy
88 D4 Les Sorinières France
91 E4 Les Thuiles France
93 G3 Lestijärvi l. Finland
56 G3 Lestijärvi Finland
159 □4 Les Trois Îlets is Martinique Caribbean
89 F4 Les Trois-Moutiers France
179 □ les Trois Swains is Kerguelen Indian Ocean
16 D2 Lesueur I. i. Western Australia Australia
17 A6 Lesueur, Mt h. Western Australia Australia
91 C4 Les Vans France
91 B4 Les Vignes France
114 G3 Lesvos div. Greece
113 E5 Lesvos i. Greece
73 L2 Leszczyn Poland
77 L4 Leszkowice Poland
76 E4 Leszno div. Poland
76 E4 Leszno Poland
76 D4 Leszno Górne Poland
131 H1 Letaba r. South Africa
131 H1 Letaba South Africa
59 F2 Letälven r. Sweden
127 □5 Le Tampon Réunion Indian Ocean
79 L4 Létavértes Hungary
63 F3 Letchworth England U.K.
93 A4 Le Teich France
91 C4 Le Teil France
89 E3 Le Teilleul France
93 B4 Le Temple France
78 F5 Letenye Hungary
36 D4 Leteri India
131 F2 Lethabile South Africa
24 A2 Letha Range mountain range Myanmar
136 G5 Lethbridge Alberta Canada
89 F3 Le Theil France
163 F3 Lethem Guyana
87 F5 Le Thillot France
87 F4 Le Tholy France
91 C5 Le Thor France
162 D4 Leticia Colombia
51 F5 Leting China
109 G3 Letino Italy
130 D6 Letjiesbos South Africa
128 D3 Letlhakane Botswana
128 D3 Letlhakeng Botswana
50 F1 Letniy Navolok Rus. Fed.
52 F1 Letnyaya Baza Rus. Fed.
80 D4 Le Tofane mt. Italy
111 E5 Letoianni Sicilia Italy
86 A2 Le Touquet-Paris-Plage airport France
86 A2 Le Touquet-Paris-Plage France
91 D3 Le Touvet France
78 F2 Letovice Czech Rep.
24 A3 Letpadan Myanmar
91 E5 le Trayas France
89 G1 Le Tréport France
73 K3 Letschin Germany
131 H1 Letsitele South Africa
25 B5 Letsok-aw Kyun i. Myanmar
131 E3 Letsopa South Africa
67 D2 Letterkenny Rep. of Ireland
62 B3 Letterston Wales U.K.
25 D7 Letung Indonesia
101 H2 Letur Spain
93 B4 Le Tuzan France
53 B2 Letychiv Ukraine
73 G3 Letzlingen Germany
125 D6 Léua Angola
93 F6 Leucate, Cap pt France
66 F4 Leuchars Scotland U.K.
112 E1 Leud Romania
90 C1 Leuglay France
82 C2 Leuk Switzerland
82 C2 Leukerbad Switzerland
73 H4 Leuna Germany
50 G1 Leunovo Rus. Fed.
155 G4 Leupp Corner Arizona U.S.A.
15 G4 Leura Queensland Australia
68 D2 Leusden Netherlands
80 C3 Leutasch Austria
74 F3 Leutershausen Germany
74 F5 Leutkirch im Allgäu Germany
69 C4 Leuven div. Belgium
69 C4 Leuven Belgium
69 B4 Leuze-en-Hainaut Belgium
115 D4 Levadeia Greece
91 E5 Le Val France
90 D1 Le Vallinot-Longeau-Percey France
155 G2 Levan Utah U.S.A.
113 B4 Levan Albania
56 C3 Levanger Norway
91 E5 Levant, Île du i. France
106 D4 Levanto Italy
110 B5 Levanzo Sicilia Italy
110 B4 Levanzo, Isola di i. Sicilia Italy
51 H7 Levashi Rus. Fed.
159 □4 Le Vauclin Martinique Caribbean
151 C5 Levelland Texas U.S.A.
9 C6 Levels New Zealand
65 H4 Leven England U.K.
66 F4 Leven Scotland U.K.
66 E4 Leven, Loch l. Scotland U.K.
131 J3 Leven Pt pt South Africa
65 F3 Levens England U.K.
91 F5 Levens France
16 C3 Lévêque, C. c. Western Australia Australia
111 H2 Leverano Italy
92 A3 Le-Verdon-sur-Mer France
148 E3 Levering Michigan U.S.A.
72 B4 Leverkusen Germany
93 D5 Le Vernet France
89 G3 Lèves France
92 E2 Levet France
93 E4 Lévézou mts France
79 H3 Levice Slovakia
107 F2 Levico Terme Italy
115 D5 Levidi Greece
108 B3 Levie Corse France
92 E2 Levier France
91 B5 Le Vigan France
8 E4 Levin New Zealand
141 K3 Lévis Québec Canada
113 F6 Levitha i. Greece
147 G4 Levittown New York U.S.A.
147 F4 Levittown Pennsylvania U.S.A.
79 K2 Levoča Slovakia
79 K2 Levočské vrchy mountain range Slovakia
92 D2 Levroux France
112 E3 Levski Bulgaria
52 D3 Lev Tolstoy Rus. Fed.
6 □8 Levuka Fiji
114 E1 Levunovo Bulgaria
88 D2 Lévy, Cap pt France
22 D4 Lewa Indonesia
24 B3 Lewe Myanmar
130 A2 Lewer watercourse Namibia
147 F5 Lewes Delaware U.S.A.
63 G4 Lewes England U.K.
76 F5 Lewin Brzeski Poland
66 B2 Lewis i. Scotland U.K.
146 E4 Lewisburg Pennsylvania U.S.A.
146 C6 Lewisburg W. Virginia U.S.A.
9 D5 Lewis Pass pass New Zealand
16 E4 Lewis Ra. h. Western Australia Australia
152 D1 Lewis Range mountain range Montana U.S.A.
145 C5 Lewis Smith, L. l. Alabama U.S.A.
155 G6 Lewis Springs Arizona U.S.A.
152 C2 Lewiston Idaho U.S.A.
147 H2 Lewiston Maine U.S.A.
140 C4 Lewiston Michigan U.S.A.
148 B4 Lewiston Minnesota U.S.A.
148 B5 Lewistown Illinois U.S.A.
152 E2 Lewistown Montana U.S.A.
146 E4 Lewistown Pennsylvania U.S.A.
151 E5 Lewisville Arkansas U.S.A.
151 D5 Lewisville, Lake l. Texas U.S.A.
148 C5 Lexington Illinois U.S.A.
144 C4 Lexington Kentucky U.S.A.
150 E4 Lexington Missouri U.S.A.
145 D5 Lexington N. Carolina U.S.A.
150 D3 Lexington Nebraska U.S.A.
145 B5 Lexington Tennessee U.S.A.
146 D6 Lexington Virginia U.S.A.
146 E5 Lexington Park Maryland U.S.A.
69 D5 Lexy France
65 G3 Leyburn England U.K.
131 H1 Leydsdorp South Africa
32 D3 Leye China
179 □ Leygues, Is is Kerguelen Indian Ocean
65 F4 Leyland England U.K.
93 D4 Leyme France
82 C2 Leysin Switzerland
23 C4 Leyte i. Philippines
23 C4 Leyte Gulf g. Philippines
82 C2 Leytron Switzerland
77 L5 Leżajsk Poland
91 C4 Lézan France
93 D5 Lézat-sur-Lèze France
92 B2 Lezay France
93 D5 Lèze r. France
84 B4 Lezhë Albania
32 D2 Lezhi China
52 E1 Lezhnevo Rus. Fed.
93 E5 Lézignan-Corbières France
90 B3 Lezoux France
101 H2 Lezuza r. Spain
101 H2 Lezuza Spain
52 B4 L'gov Rus. Fed.
37 H3 Lhari China
37 G4 Lhasa Tibet China
86 B4 L'Hay-les-Roses France
37 F3 Lhazê China
37 F3 Lhazhong China
81 F1 Lhenice Czech Rep.
88 C4 l'Herbaudière, Pte de pt France
92 B2 L'Hermenault France
88 D3 L'Hermitage France
87 F3 L'Hôpital France
20 C5 Lhokseumawe Indonesia
32 A2 Lhorong China
93 D4 Lhospitalet France
102 D4 L'Hospitalet de l'Infant Spain
102 F3 L'Hospitalet de Llobregat Spain
91 B5 L'Hospitalet-du-Larzac France
102 D4 L'Hostal del Alls Spain
82 A3 Lhuis France
89 E3 L'Huisserie France
37 H3 Lhünzê China
37 G3 Lhünzhub China
33 E3 Li r. China
128 C2 Liambezi, Lake l. Namibia
108 A2 Liamone r. Corse France
33 G3 Liancheng China
86 B3 Liancourt France
Liancourt Rocks is see Tok-tō
86 A2 Liane r. France
23 C4 Lianga Philippines
23 C4 Lianga Bay b. Philippines
33 F2 Liangaz Hu l. China
30 E4 Liangcheng China
32 D1 Liangdang China
32 D1 Lianghekou China
32 D2 Liangping China
22 C1 Liangpran, Bukit mt. Indonesia
31 E6 Liangshan China
33 E4 Liangtian China
32 C3 Liangwang Shan mountain range China
30 D5 Liangzhen China
33 F3 Lianhua China
33 F4 Lianhua Shan mountain range China
33 G3 Lianjiang China
33 E4 Lianjiang China
33 E3 Liannan China
114 D4 Lianokladi Greece
33 F3 Lianping China
33 E3 Lianshan China
33 G1 Lianshui China
25 C4 Liant, C. c. Thailand
33 F3 Lian Xian China
31 G1 Lianyin China
33 E3 Lianyuan China
33 G1 Lianyungang China
33 G1 Lianyungang China
Lianzhou see Hepu
31 J3 Lianzhushan China
31 G4 Liao r. China
31 E5 Liaocheng China
31 G4 Liaodong Bandao pen. China
31 G4 Liaodong Wan b. China
31 G4 Liaoning div. China
31 G4 Liaoyang China
31 H4 Liaoyuan China
31 G4 Liaozhong China
114 A3 Liapades Greece
36 B2 Liaqatabad Pakistan
136 E2 Liard r. B.C./N.W.T. Canada
136 D3 Liard River B.C. Canada
36 A4 Liari Pakistan
86 D3 Liart France
66 C3 Liathach mt. Scotland U.K.
59 F3 Liatorp Sweden
75 L2 Libáň Czech Rep.
43 C3 Liban, Jebel mountain range Lebanon
173 G4 Libano Argentina
162 B3 Líbano Colombia
101 E4 Libar, Sierra de mountain range Spain
152 D1 Libby Montana U.S.A.
78 C1 Libčeves Czech Rep.
124 C3 Libenge Congo(Zaire)
77 J2 Liberadz Poland
151 C4 Liberal Kansas U.S.A.
166 B3 Liberdade r. Brazil
169 F5 Liberdade Minas Gerais Brazil
78 E1 Liberec Czech Rep.
117 D5 Liberia country Africa
156 J7 Liberia Costa Rica
173 J3 Libertad Uruguay
172 E1 Libertador General San Martín Argentina
156 B2 Libertad, Pto Mexico
131 F4 Libertase South Africa
148 B6 Liberty Illinois U.S.A.
147 J2 Liberty Maine U.S.A.
150 E4 Liberty Missouri U.S.A.
147 F4 Liberty New York U.S.A.
151 E6 Liberty Texas U.S.A.
77 H5 Libiąż Poland
69 D5 Libin Belgium
23 B3 Libmanan Philippines
32 D3 Libo China
131 G5 Libode South Africa
114 B2 Libohovë Albania
131 G4 Libono Lesotho
172 E2 Liborio Luna Argentina
75 K2 Libouchec Czech Rep.
93 B4 Libourne France
69 D5 Libramont Belgium
114 B1 Librazhd Albania
124 A3 Libreville Gabon
103 B7 Librilla Spain
23 C5 Libuganon r. Philippines
116 F3 Libya country Africa
118 D2 Libyan Desert desert Egypt/Libya
118 E1 Libyan Plateau plat. Egypt
164 C4 Licancabur, Vol. volcano Chile
172 A3 Licantén Chile
110 C5 Licata Sicilia Italy
106 E4 Licciana Nardi Italy
42 E2 Lice Turkey
74 D2 Lich Germany
114 D4 Lichas pen. Greece
30 E5 Licheng China
63 E2 Lichfield England U.K.
127 C7 Lichinga Mozambique
70 E3 Lichte Germany
74 D4 Lichtenau Baden-Württemberg Germany
75 F3 Lichtenau Bayern Germany
72 D4 Lichtenau Nordrhein-Westfalen Germany
72 G2 Lichtenberg Germany
131 F3 Lichtenburg South Africa
75 G2 Lichtenfels Germany
75 H2 Lichtenstein Germany
68 E3 Lichtenvoorde Netherlands
81 H3 Lichtenwörth Austria
69 B3 Lichtervelde Belgium
33 E2 Lichuan China
33 G3 Lichuan China
169 G1 Licinio de Almeida Brazil
146 B5 Licking r. Kentucky U.S.A.
104 E3 Lički Osik Croatia
86 A2 Licques France
154 D3 Lida Nevada U.S.A.
77 O2 Lida Belarus
59 E2 Lidan r. Sweden
65 F2 Liddel r. England/Scotland U.K.
66 F5 Liddesdale v. Scotland U.K.
130 B2 Lidfontein Namibia
59 E3 Lidhult Sweden
59 H2 Lidingö Sweden
59 E2 Lidköping Sweden
107 G3 Lido Italy
107 G4 Lido Adriano Italy
107 G4 Lido di Classe Italy
107 G3 Lido di Jesolo Italy
111 F2 Lido di Metaponto Italy
109 E3 Lido di Ostia Italy
107 G4 Lido di Spina Italy
56 D2 Lidsjöberg Sweden
54 E3 Lidumnieki Latvia
77 H2 Lidzbark Poland
77 J1 Lidzbark Warmiński Poland
81 F2 Liebenau Austria
72 E3 Liebenau Germany
72 F3 Liebenburg Germany
73 J3 Liebenwalde Germany
73 K4 Lieberose Germany
14 B4 Liebig, Mt mt. Northern Terr. Australia
81 G4 Lieboch Austria
48 F4 Liechtenstein country Europe
102 B2 Liédena Spain
69 D4 Liège div. Belgium
69 D4 Liège Belgium
56 H3 Lieksa Finland
54 C3 Lielupe r. Latvia
54 D3 Lielvārde Latvia
56 E3 Lien Sweden
124 E3 Lienart Congo(Zaire)
80 D4 Lienz div. Austria
80 D4 Lienz Austria
54 B3 Liepāja Latvia
73 J2 Liepen Germany
54 E3 Liepna Latvia
77 N1 Lieponys Lithuania
69 C3 Lier Belgium
90 C1 Liernais France
69 D4 Lierneux Belgium
58 A2 Liervik Norway
81 F3 Liesing r. Austria
82 C1 Liestal Switzerland
54 C1 Lieto Finland
103 B6 Liétor Spain
89 F2 Lieuvin reg. France
86 B2 Liévin France
141 H3 Lièvre r. Québec Canada
81 F3 Liezen div. Austria
81 F3 Liezen Austria
124 D3 Lifanga Congo(Zaire)
67 E3 Liffey r. Rep. of Ireland
87 E4 Liffol-le-Grand France
67 D2 Lifford Rep. of Ireland
88 D3 Liffré France
171 C5 Lifi Mahuida mt. Argentina
6 □2 Lifou i. New Caledonia Pacific Ocean
6 □5 Lifuka i. Tonga
23 B3 Ligao Philippines
93 C4 Ligardes France
57 G4 Ligatne Latvia
13 F2 Lightning Ridge New South Wales Australia
107 H3 Lignano Sabbiadoro Italy
88 D4 Ligné France
92 A2 Ligneron r. France
69 E4 Ligneuville Belgium
92 E2 Lignières France
91 C4 Lignon r. Auvergne France
90 B3 Lignon r. Rhône-Alpes France
87 E4 Ligny-en-Barrois France
90 B1 Ligny-le-Châtel France
129 F2 Ligonha r. Mozambique
148 E5 Ligonier Indiana U.S.A.
77 H3 Ligowo Poland
172 B2 Ligua, B. de la b. Chile
89 F4 Ligueil France
156 C3 Ligui Mexico
106 C4 Liguria div. Italy
106 C5 Ligurian Sea sea France/Italy
127 C7 Lihehe Tanzania
6 □1 Lihir Group is P.N.G.
55 A3 Lihme Denmark
15 G3 Lihou Reef & Cays reef Coral Sea Islands Terr. Pacific Ocean
153 □2 Lihue Hawaii U.S.A.
54 C2 Lihula Estonia
32 C3 Lijiang China
31 F5 Lijin China
125 E6 Likasi Congo(Zaire)
124 D3 Likati r. Congo(Zaire)
124 D3 Likati Congo(Zaire)
136 E4 Likely B.C. Canada
59 E1 Likenäs Sweden
52 B1 Likhoslavl' Rus. Fed.
124 D4 Likolia Congo(Zaire)
124 D4 Likoto Congo(Zaire)
124 C3 Likouala div. Congo
124 C3 Likouala r. Congo
124 C3 Likouala aux Herbes r. Congo
22 B1 Liku Indonesia
6 □8 Likuri Harb. b. Fiji
89 F4 L'Île-Bouchard France
108 A2 L'Île-Rousse Corse France
81 G3 Lilienfeld div. Austria
81 G2 Lilienfeld Austria
72 D2 Lilienthal Germany
33 F3 Liling China
36 C2 Lilla Pakistan
59 E2 Lilla Edet Sweden
59 H3 Lilla Karlsö i. Sweden
86 C2 Lille Nord France
69 C3 Lille Belgium
55 A3 Lilleå r. Denmark
55 B4 Lille Bælt chan. Denmark
89 F2 Lillebonne France
58 D1 Lillehammer Norway
86 C2 Lille-Lesquin airport France
86 B2 Lillers France
58 C2 Lillesand Norway
62 D2 Lilleshall England U.K.
55 E4 Lille Skensved Denmark
58 D2 Lillestrøm Norway
148 E4 Lilley Michigan U.S.A.
56 D3 Lillholmsjö Sweden
17 D5 Lillian, Pt h. Western Australia Australia
65 F2 Lilliesleaf Scotland U.K.
101 G1 Lillo Spain
136 E4 Lillooet r. B.C. Canada
136 E4 Lillooet B.C. Canada
37 H4 Lilong India
129 E1 Lilongwe r. Malawi
127 B7 Lilongwe Malawi
127 □1 L'Ilot i. Seychelles
23 B4 Liloy Philippines
171 B5 Lilpela, P. pass Argentina/Chile
13 F5 Lilydale Tasmania Australia
152 D2 Lima Montana U.S.A.
146 A4 Lima Ohio U.S.A.
173 H3 Lima Argentina
164 A2 Lima Peru
169 G4 Lima Duarte Brazil
90 B3 Limagne reg. France
39 D4 Līmah Oman
Lima Is is see Wanshan Qundao
51 H6 Liman Rus. Fed.
22 B3 Liman, G. mt. Indonesia
77 J6 Limanowa Poland
172 B1 Limarí r. Chile
37 E2 Lima Ringma Tso l. China
22 A1 Limas Indonesia
Limassol see Lemesos
67 E1 Limavady Northern Ireland U.K.
172 C5 Limay r. Argentina
89 G2 Limay France
172 D4 Limay Mahuida Argentina
75 H2 Limbach-Oberfrohna Germany
164 C2 Limbani Peru
108 B4 Limbara, Monte mountain range Sardegna Italy
54 D3 Limbaži Latvia
124 A3 Limbe Cameroon
69 D4 Limbourg Belgium
22 C2 Limbungan Indonesia
69 D3 Limburg div. Belgium
69 D3 Limburg div. Netherlands
131 G1 Limburg South Africa
74 D2 Limburg an der Lahn Germany
25 □ Lim Chu Kang h. Singapore
25 □ Lim Chu Kang Singapore
130 D4 Lime Acres South Africa
59 E1 Limedsforsen Sweden
9 B7 Limehills New Zealand
168 E5 Limeira Brazil
114 F2 Limenaria Greece
67 B4 Limerick div. Rep. of Ireland
67 C4 Limerick Rep. of Ireland
148 A4 Lime Springs Iowa U.S.A.
147 K1 Limestone Maine U.S.A.
55 A3 Limfjorden chan. Denmark
98 C2 Limia r. Spain
56 D2 Limingen l. Norway
56 D2 Limingen Nord-Trøndelag Norway
147 H3 Limington Maine U.S.A.
56 G2 Liminka Finland
14 D2 Limmen Bight b. Northern Terr. Australia
14 C3 Limmen Bight R. r. Northern Terr. Australia
114 E4 Limni Greece
114 C2 Limni Aliakmonas l. Greece
114 C4 Limni Amvrakia l. Greece
115 F4 Limni Distos l. Greece
Limni Doïranis l. see Dojran, Lake
114 B3 Limni Ioanninon l. Greece
114 C2 Limni Kastorias l. Greece
114 E1 Limni Kerkinitis l. Greece
114 C4 Limni Lysimachia l. Greece
114 C2 Limni Mikri Prespa l. Greece
114 C4 Limni Ozeros l. Greece
114 D2 Limni Sfikia resr Greece
115 D5 Limni Stymfalia l. Greece
114 C4 Limni Trichonida l. Greece
114 G1 Limni Vistonida lag. Greece
114 B4 Limni Voulkaria l. Greece
115 E4 Limni Yliki l. Greece
114 G3 Limnos i. Greece
166 E2 Limoeiro Brazil
92 D3 Limoges Haute-Vienne France
141 H4 Limoges Ontario Canada
93 D4 Limogne-en-Quercy France
153 G4 Limon Colorado U.S.A.
156 K7 Limón Costa Rica
156 J6 Limón Honduras
106 B4 Limone Piemonte Italy
107 E3 Limone sul Garda Italy
100 D2 Limonetes r. Spain
127 □3 Limon, Mt h. Rodrigues I. Mauritius
164 D3 Limoquije Bolivia
92 D3 Limousin div. France
92 D3 Limousin reg. France
92 D3 Limousin, Monts du h. France
93 E5 Limoux France
129 E3 Limpopo r. Africa
33 E3 Limu China
114 B1 Lin Albania
131 G4 Linakeng Lesotho
56 H1 Linakhamari Rus. Fed.
33 G2 Lin'an China
23 A4 Linapacan i. Philippines
23 A4 Linapacan Strait chan. Philippines
92 D3 Linards France
172 B3 Linares Chile
157 F3 Linares Mexico
101 G2 Linares Spain
103 C4 Linares de Mora Spain
98 E4 Linares de Riofrío Spain
114 F4 Linaria Greece
108 A5 Linas, Monte mt. Sardegna Italy
106 D3 Linate airport Italy
32 C4 Lincang China
69 D4 Lincent Belgium
30 E5 Lincheng China
33 G3 Linchuan China
154 B2 Lincoln California U.S.A.
63 F1 Lincoln England U.K.
148 C5 Lincoln Illinois U.S.A.
147 J2 Lincoln Maine U.S.A.
149 F3 Lincoln Michigan U.S.A.
150 D3 Lincoln Nebraska U.S.A.
147 H2 Lincoln New Hampshire U.S.A.
173 G3 Lincoln Argentina
9 D5 Lincoln New Zealand
152 A2 Lincoln City Oregon U.S.A.
149 F4 Lincoln Park Michigan U.S.A.
135 M1 Lincoln Sea sea Canada/Greenland
63 F1 Lincolnshire div. England U.K.
65 H4 Lincolnshire Wolds reg. England U.K.
147 J2 Lincolnville Maine U.S.A.
55 A3 Lind Denmark
52 F1 Linda r. Rus. Fed.
52 G1 Linda Rus. Fed.
58 A1 Lindas Norway
166 D3 Linda, Sa h. Brazil
73 H3 Lindau Germany
74 E5 Lindau (Bodensee) Germany
55 A3 Linde Denmark
145 C5 Linden Alabama U.S.A.
145 C5 Linden Tennessee U.S.A.
74 D2 Linden Germany
163 F2 Linden Guyana
74 E5 Lindenberg im Allgäu Germany
148 A2 Linden Grove Minnesota U.S.A.
135 O3 Lindenow Fjord inlet Greenland
72 C3 Lindern (Oldenburg) Germany
59 E4 Linderödsåsen h. Sweden
17 B7 Lindesay, Mt h. Western Australia Australia
59 F2 Lindesberg Sweden
58 B2 Lindesnes c. Norway
127 C6 Lindi div. Tanzania
124 E4 Lindi r. Congo(Zaire)
127 C6 Lindi Tanzania
31 H3 Lindian China
Lindisfarne i. see Holy Island
87 G1 Lindlar Germany
131 F3 Lindley South Africa
58 E3 Lindome Sweden
165 E4 Lindo, Monte r. Paraguay
65 E1 Lindores Scotland U.K.
115 □ Lindos Greece
154 C3 Lindsay California U.S.A.
147 K1 Lindsay New Brunswick Canada
141 F4 Lindsay Ontario Canada
59 G3 Lindsdal Sweden
75 J3 Líně Czech Rep.
5 M5 Line Islands is Pacific Ocean
47 K2 Linevo Rus. Fed.
30 D5 Linfen China
38 A3 Linganamakki Reservoir resr India
33 E5 Lingao China
23 B2 Lingayen Philippines
23 B2 Lingayen Gulf b. Philippines
33 E1 Lingbao China
33 G1 Lingbi China
30 E6 Lingchuan China
33 E3 Lingchuan China
131 F6 Lingelethu South Africa
131 E6 Lingelihle South Africa
72 C3 Lingen (Ems) Germany
87 H3 Lingenfeld Germany
63 F3 Lingfield England U.K.
22 A2 Lingga i. Indonesia
22 B1 Lingga Malaysia
23 C4 Lingig Philippines
152 F3 Lingle Wyoming U.S.A.
87 G4 Lingolsheim France
124 D3 Lingomo Congo(Zaire)
30 E5 Lingqiu China
33 E4 Lingshan China
31 G6 Lingshan Dao i. China
30 D5 Lingshi China
33 E5 Lingshui China
38 B2 Lingsugur India
32 D1 Lingtai China
32 E5 Lingtou China
111 E5 Linguaglossa Sicilia Italy
122 A3 Linguère Senegal
33 E3 Lingui China
108 B2 Linguizzetta Corse France
30 C5 Lingwu China
33 F5 Ling Xian China
31 F4 Lingyuan China
32 D3 Lingyun China
36 D2 Lingzi Thang Plains plain China/Jammu and Kashmir
33 H2 Linhai China
169 H3 Linhares Brazil
24 D3 Linh Cam Vietnam
30 C4 Linhe China
147 H1 Linière Québec Canada
76 G1 Liniewo Poland
31 H4 Linjiang China
87 H3 Linkenheim-Hochstetten Germany
59 F2 Linköping Sweden
31 J3 Linkou China
54 C3 Linkuva Lithuania
33 E2 Linli China
65 E5 Linlithgow Scotland U.K.
62 A3 Linney Head headland Wales U.K.
66 C4 Linnhe, Loch est. Scotland U.K.
74 B2 Linnich Germany
154 A1 Linn, Mt mt. California U.S.A.
105 D7 Linosa, Isola di i. Italy
77 N3 Linova Belarus
31 E5 Linqing China
31 F5 Linqu China
33 F1 Linquan China
33 F1 Linru China
168 D4 Lins Brazil
33 G1 Linshu China
32 D2 Linshui China
159 □1 Linstead Jamaica
129 G3 Linta r. Madagascar
32 C1 Lintan China
32 C1 Lintao China
83 E1 Linth r. Switzerland
83 E2 Linthal Switzerland
150 C2 Linton N. Dakota U.S.A.
141 J3 Linton Québec Canada
33 E1 Lintong China

77 L6 Lutowiska Poland
77 J1 Lutry Poland
137 G2 Łutselk'e N.W.T. Canada
125 C5 Lutshima r. Congo(Zaire)
53 A1 Luts'k Ukraine
72 F4 Lutter am Barenberge Germany
82 C1 Lutterbach France
63 E2 Lutterworth England U.K.
130 D6 Luttig South Africa
76 G4 Lututów Poland
73 H4 Lützen Germany
81 H3 Lutzmannsburg Austria
73 G2 Lützow Germany
179 D4 Lützow-Holmbukta b. Antarctica
130 C4 Lutzputs South Africa
130 B5 Lutzville South Africa
23 B5 Luuk Philippines
57 G3 Luumäki Finland
126 D4 Luuq Somalia
131 H3 Luve Swaziland
150 D3 Luverne Minnesota U.S.A.
125 E5 Luvua r. Congo(Zaire)
125 D6 Luvuei Angola
131 H1 Luvuvhu r. South Africa
127 C6 Luwegu r. Tanzania
127 B4 Luwero Uganda
21 H7 Luwuk Indonesia
48 F4 Luxembourg country Europe
69 D4 Luxembourg div. Belgium
69 E5 Luxembourg Luxembourg
93 A5 Luxe-Sumberraute France
90 E1 Luxeuil-les-Bains France
93 B4 Luxey France
33 E2 Luxi China
32 B3 Luxi China
32 C3 Luxi China
131 E5 Luxolweni South Africa
119 F2 Luxor Egypt
93 B5 Luy r. France
125 E4 Luyamba Congo(Zaire)
93 B5 Luy de Béarn r. France
93 B5 Luy de France r. France
33 F1 Luyi China
89 F4 Luynes France
169 F3 Luz Brazil
50 J2 Luza r. Rus. Fed.
50 H2 Luza Rus. Fed.
86 B3 Luzarches France
93 D4 Luzech France
75 K2 Lužec nad Vltavou Czech Rep.
93 D6 Luzenac France
82 D1 Luzern div. Switzerland
83 D1 Luzern Luzern Switzerland
33 E3 Luzhai China
32 D3 Luzhi China
32 D2 Luzhou China
168 E2 Luziânia Brazil
78 D1 Lužické Hory mts Czech Rep.
166 D1 Luzilândia Brazil
76 G1 Luzino Poland
54 B3 Lūžņas Latvia
78 D2 Lužnice r. Czech Rep.
23 B3 Luzon i. Philippines
23 B1 Luzon Strait str. Philippines
93 C6 Luz-St-Sauveur France
90 B2 Luzy France
111 F3 Luzzi Italy
53 B1 L'va r. Ukraine
52 C2 L'va Tolstogo Rus. Fed.
53 A1 L'viv div. Ukraine
53 A2 L'viv Ukraine
L'vov see L'viv
52 C2 L'vovskiy Rus. Fed.
76 E3 Lwówek Poland
76 D4 Lwówek Śląski Poland
54 F2 Lyady Rus. Fed.
54 E5 Lyakhavichy Belarus
52 E2 Lyakhi Rus. Fed.
45 Q2 Lyakhovskiy, O. Mal. i. Rus. Fed.
136 G5 Lyall, Mt mt. Alberta Canada
Lyallpur see Faisalabad
52 G2 Lyambir' Rus. Fed.
50 F1 Lyamtsa Rus. Fed.
53 E2 Lyashivka Ukraine
112 E3 Lyaskovets Bulgaria
77 M3 Lyasnaya r. Belarus
77 N4 Lybytiv Ukraine
76 B2 Lychen-Boitzenberg res. Germany
53 F2 Lychkove Ukraine
43 A1 Lycia reg. Turkey
56 E2 Lycksele Sweden
63 G4 Lydd England U.K.
179 C3 Lyddan I. i. Antarctica
131 H2 Lydenburg South Africa
62 B4 Lydford England U.K.
113 G5 Lydia reg. Turkey
62 D3 Lydney England U.K.
55 A4 Lydum r. Denmark
53 C1 Lyel'chytsy Belarus
14 B4 Lyell Brown, Mt h. Northern Terr. Australia
136 C4 Lyell I. i. B.C. Canada
154 C3 Lyell, Mt mt. California U.S.A.
77 N3 Lyeninski Belarus
54 F4 Lyepyel' Belarus
145 □2 Lyford Cay The Bahamas
59 E3 Lygnern l. Sweden
115 E5 Lygourio Greece
53 G2 Lyhivka Ukraine
146 E4 Lykens Pennsylvania U.S.A.
53 D1 Lykhachiv Ukraine
53 E2 Lykhivka Ukraine
115 D4 Lykoporia Greece
130 E3 Lykso South Africa
152 E3 Lyman Wyoming U.S.A.
112 G2 Lyman Ukraine
53 C3 Lymans'ke Ukraine
62 D4 Lyme Bay b. England U.K.
62 D4 Lyme Regis England U.K.
63 E4 Lymington England U.K.
65 F4 Lymm England U.K.
77 J1 Łyna r. Poland
146 D6 Lynchburg Virginia U.S.A.
147 H2 Lynchville Maine U.S.A.
15 E3 Lynd r. Queensland Australia
63 E4 Lyndhurst England U.K.
15 F3 Lyndhurst Queensland Australia
12 D2 Lyndhurst S. Australia Australia
15 F3 Lynd Junction, The Queensland Australia
17 A4 Lyndon r. Western Australia Australia
147 G2 Lyndonville Vermont U.S.A.
65 F2 Lyne r. England U.K.
63 E3 Lyneham England U.K.
66 E2 Lyness Scotland U.K.
58 B2 Lyngdal Norway
58 B2 Lyngna l. Norway
62 B4 Lynher r. England U.K.
16 C2 Lynher Reef reef Western Australia Australia
62 C3 Lynmouth England U.K.
147 H3 Lynn Massachusetts U.S.A.
136 B3 Lynn Canal chan. Alaska U.S.A.
155 F2 Lynndyl Utah U.S.A.
137 J3 Lynn Lake Manitoba Canada
53 F1 Lynove Ukraine
53 E1 Lynovytsya Ukraine
62 C3 Lynton England U.K.
54 E4 Lyntupy Belarus
137 H2 Lynx Lake l. N.W.T. Canada
55 C4 Lyø i. Denmark
66 D4 Lyon r. Scotland U.K.
90 C3 Lyon Rhône France
64 D1 Lyon, Loch l. Scotland U.K.
147 G2 Lyon Mountain New York U.S.A.
90 C3 Lyonnais, Monts du reg. France
17 A5 Lyons r. Western Australia Australia
145 D5 Lyons Georgia U.S.A.
146 E3 Lyons New York U.S.A.
12 C2 Lyons S. Australia Australia
90 D3 Lyon/Satolas airport France
147 F3 Lyons Falls New York U.S.A.
89 G2 Lyons-la-Forêt France
50 D4 Lyozna Belarus
77 N6 Lypivtsi Ukraine
53 C1 Lypnyky Ukraine
53 E1 Lypova Dolyna Ukraine
53 C2 Lypovets' Ukraine
53 G1 Lyptsi Ukraine
59 F2 Lyrestad Sweden
115 D5 Lyrkeia Greece
86 B2 Lys r. France
82 C3 Lys r. Italy
53 D2 Lysa Hora Ukraine
75 K2 Lysá nad Labem Czech Rep.
58 B2 Lysefjorden inlet Norway
58 D2 Lysekil Sweden
77 M3 Lyshchytsy Belarus
77 J5 Łysica h. Poland
77 N3 Lyskava Belarus
52 G1 Lyskovo Rus. Fed.
76 G2 Łysomice Poland
82 C1 Lyss Switzerland
141 K3 Lyster Québec Canada
55 C3 Lystrup Denmark
59 E1 Lysvik Sweden
53 D2 Lysyanka Ukraine
51 F5 Lysychans'k Ukraine
52 G4 Lysyye Gory Rus. Fed.
62 D4 Lytchett Minster England U.K.
65 E4 Lytham St Anne's England U.K.
52 C2 Lytkarino Rus. Fed.
9 D5 Lyttelton New Zealand
136 E4 Lytton B.C. Canada
54 F5 Lyuban' Belarus
53 B2 Lyubar Ukraine
53 D3 Lyubashivka Ukraine
52 B3 Lyubazh Rus. Fed.
54 E5 Lyubcha Belarus
53 D1 Lyubech Ukraine
52 C2 Lyubertsy Rus. Fed.
53 A1 Lyubeshiv Ukraine
50 G3 Lyubim Rus. Fed.
112 E4 Lyubimets Bulgaria
52 D3 Lyubimovka Rus. Fed.
47 H1 Lyubinskiy Rus. Fed.
77 J1 Lyublino Rus. Fed.
77 N4 Lyublynets' Ukraine
52 B3 Lyubokhna Rus. Fed.
77 N4 Lyubokhyny Ukraine
53 F2 Lyubotyn Ukraine
54 E5 Lyubyacha Belarus
53 G3 Lyubymivka Ukraine
77 M6 Lyubyntsi Ukraine
50 E3 Lyubytino Rus. Fed.
52 B3 Lyudinovo Rus. Fed.
52 H1 Lyul'pany Rus. Fed.
112 F3 Lyulyakovo Bulgaria
52 G1 Lyunda r. Rus. Fed.
53 F1 Lyutens'ki Budyshchyna Ukraine
54 E3 Lža r. Latvia
54 F3 L'zha r. Rus. Fed.

M

35 D9 Maalosmadulu Atoll atoll Maldives
125 E7 Maamba Zambia
124 B3 Ma'an Cameroon
42 C4 Ma'ān Jordan
56 G3 Maaninka Finland
56 H2 Maaninkavaara Finland
33 G2 Ma'anshan China
30 C3 Maanyt Mongolia
30 B2 Maanyt Mongolia
54 D2 Maardu Estonia
42 D3 Ma'arrat an Nu'mān Syria
68 D2 Maarssen Netherlands
68 D2 Maarssenbroek Netherlands
68 D3 Maas r. Netherlands
69 D3 Maasbracht Netherlands
69 E3 Maasbree Netherlands
69 D3 Maaseik div. Limburg Belgium
69 D3 Maaseik Belgium
23 C4 Maasin Philippines
69 D4 Maasmechelen Belgium
68 C3 Maassluis Netherlands
131 G1 Maasstroom South Africa
69 D4 Maastricht Netherlands
13 F5 Maatsuyker Is is Tasmania Australia
128 C2 Mababe Depression Botswana
23 B3 Mabalacat Philippines
129 E3 Mabalane Mozambique
124 E3 Mabana Congo(Zaire)
125 B4 Mabanda Gabon
126 D2 Ma'bar Yemen
163 F2 Mabaruma Guyana
24 B2 Mabein Myanmar
141 G4 Maberly Ontario Canada
32 C2 Mabian China
65 J4 Mablethorpe England U.K.
90 C2 Mably France
131 G2 Mabopane South Africa
129 E3 Mabote Mozambique
125 D6 M.A.B., Réserve res. Congo(Zaire)
123 G2 Mabrous well Niger
118 C2 Mabrūk Libya
128 C4 Mabuasehube Game Reserve res. Botswana
23 B1 Mabudis i. Philippines
29 □2 Mabuni Japan
118 D2 Ma'būs Yūsuf oasis Libya
130 D2 Mabutsane Botswana
172 F4 Macachín Argentina
166 B1 Macacos, Ilha dos i. Brazil
147 K2 McAdam New Brunswick Canada
169 H5 Macaé Brazil
23 C4 Macajalar Bay b. Philippines
151 E5 McAlester Oklahoma U.S.A.
146 E4 McAlevys Fort Pennsylvania U.S.A.
13 G3 McAlister mt. New South Wales Australia
13 F4 Macalister r. Victoria Australia
151 D7 McAllen Texas U.S.A.
127 C7 Macaloge Mozambique
134 H3 MacAlpine Lake l. N.W.T. Canada
141 F2 Macamic Québec Canada
171 B6 Macá, Mt mt. Chile
100 C1 Mação Portugal
166 B1 Macapá Brazil
Macar see Gebiz
162 B4 Macará Ecuador
169 H1 Macarani Brazil
162 C3 Macarena, Cordillera mountain range Colombia
162 C3 Macarena, Parque Nacional La nat. park Colombia
14 D3 McArthur r. Northern Terr. Australia
146 B5 McArthur Ohio U.S.A.
12 E4 Macarthur Victoria Australia
141 G4 McArthur Mills Ontario Canada
136 B2 McArthur Wildlife Sanctuary res. Yukon Terr. Canada
98 D3 Maçãs r. Portugal/Spain
162 B4 Macas Ecuador
22 D2 Macassar Strait str. Indonesia
19 N7 Macau territory Asia
166 E2 Macau Brazil
166 B3 Macaúba Brazil
166 D3 Macaúbas Brazil
8 □4 Macauley I. i. Kermadec Is New Zealand
162 C3 Macayari Colombia
136 E4 McBride B.C. Canada
152 C2 McCall Idaho U.S.A.
151 C6 McCamey Texas U.S.A.
152 D3 McCammon Idaho U.S.A.
131 J2 Maccaretane Mozambique
136 C4 McCauley I. i. B.C. Canada
62 D1 Macclesfield England U.K.
134 H2 McClintock Channel chan. N.W.T. Canada
16 D3 McClintock Ra. h. Western Australia Australia
14 C1 McCluer I. i. Northern Terr. Australia
154 B3 McClure, L. l. California U.S.A.
134 F2 McClure Strait str. N.W.T. Canada
151 F6 McComb Mississippi U.S.A.
150 C3 McConaughy, L. l. Nebraska U.S.A.
146 E5 McConnellsburg Pennsylvania U.S.A.
146 C5 McConnelsville Ohio U.S.A.
150 C3 McCook Nebraska U.S.A.
137 K4 McCreary Manitoba Canada
155 E4 McCullough Range mts Nevada U.S.A.
136 D3 McDame B.C. Canada
152 C3 McDermitt Nevada U.S.A.
140 A2 Macdiarmid Ontario Canada
16 E4 Macdonald, L. salt flat Western Australia Australia
152 D2 McDonald Peak summit Montana U.S.A.
8 □4 Macdonald Rock i. Kermadec Is New Zealand
14 C4 Macdonnell Ranges mountain range Northern Terr. Australia
138 B3 MacDowell L. l. Ontario Canada
155 G5 McDowell Peak summit Arizona U.S.A.
66 F3 Macduff Scotland U.K.
98 C2 Maceda Spain
98 D3 Macedo de Cavaleiros Portugal
13 F4 Macedon mt. Victoria Australia
49 H4 Macedonia country Europe
166 E2 Maceió Brazil
81 G4 Macelj Croatia
122 C5 Macenta Guinea
107 H5 Macerata div. Marche Italy
107 H5 Macerata Italy
154 C4 McFarland California U.S.A.
137 H3 McFarlane r. Saskatchewan Canada
12 D3 Macfarlane, L. salt flat S. Australia Australia
9 B5 McFarlane, Mt mt. New Zealand
155 E2 McGill Nevada U.S.A.
67 B5 Macgillycuddy's Reeks mountain range Rep. of Ireland
134 C3 McGrath Alaska U.S.A.
136 E4 McGregor r. B.C. Canada
148 A2 McGregor Minnesota U.S.A.
130 B6 McGregor South Africa
140 E3 McGregor Bay Ontario Canada
15 E5 McGregor Ra. h. Queensland Australia
152 D2 McGuire, Mt mt. Idaho U.S.A.
36 A3 Mach Pakistan
169 H2 Machacalis Brazil
164 C3 Machacamarca Bolivia
162 B4 Machachi Ecuador
165 D1 Machadinho r. Brazil
169 F4 Machado Brazil
131 H2 Machadodorp South Africa
129 E3 Machaila Mozambique
127 C5 Machakos Kenya
162 B4 Machala Ecuador
129 E3 Machanga Mozambique
165 D4 Machareti Bolivia
126 B3 Machar Marshes marsh Sudan
14 D5 Machattie, L. salt flat Queensland Australia
131 J2 Machatuine Mozambique
86 D3 Machault France
92 A2 Machecoul France
69 C4 Machelen Belgium
33 F2 Macheng China
38 B2 Macherla India
101 F1 Machero mt. Spain
38 C2 Māchhakund Dam dam India
37 E4 Machhlishahr India
147 J1 Machias r. Maine U.S.A.
147 K2 Machias Maine U.S.A.
146 D3 Machias New York U.S.A.
99 H1 Machichaco, Cabo pt Spain
96 □ Machico Madeira Portugal
38 C2 Machilipatnam India
129 F2 Machinga Malawi
162 C1 Machiques Venezuela
66 C5 Machrihanish Scotland U.K.
53 F2 Machukhy Ukraine
164 B2 Machupicchu mt. Peru
62 C2 Machynlleth Wales U.K.
129 E4 Macia Mozambique
77 K4 Maciejowice Poland
15 E2 McIlwraith Ra. h. Queensland Australia
112 G2 Măcin Romania
147 G2 McIndoe Falls Vermont U.S.A.
150 C2 McIntosh S. Dakota U.S.A.
Macintyre r. see Barwon
155 H2 Mack Colorado U.S.A.
152 D2 Mackay Idaho U.S.A.
15 G4 Mackay Queensland Australia
137 G2 Mackay Lake l. N.W.T. Canada
140 B2 McKay Lake l. Ontario Canada
16 E4 Mackay, Lake salt flat Western Australia Australia
16 C4 McKay Ra. h. Western Australia Australia
176 H6 McKean Island i. Kiribati
146 A6 McKee Kentucky U.S.A.
146 D4 McKeesport Pennsylvania U.S.A.
147 F3 McKeever New York U.S.A.
134 F3 Mackenzie r. N.W.T. Canada
15 G4 Mackenzie r. Queensland Australia
136 E3 Mackenzie B.C. Canada
140 A2 Mackenzie Ontario Canada
145 B4 McKenzie Tennessee U.S.A.
134 E3 Mackenzie Bay b. Yukon Terr. Canada
179 D5 Mackenzie Bay b. Antarctica
136 F2 Mackenzie Bison Sanctuary res. N.W.T. Canada
134 G2 Mackenzie King I. i. N.W.T. Canada
136 C2 Mackenzie Mountains mountain range N.W.T. Canada
9 B6 McKerrow, L. l. New Zealand
Mackillop, L. salt flat see Yamma Yamma, L.
148 E3 Mackinac I. i. Michigan U.S.A.
148 E3 Mackinac, Straits of chan. Michigan U.S.A.
148 C5 Mackinaw r. Illinois U.S.A.
148 E3 Mackinaw City Michigan U.S.A.
15 E4 McKinlay r. Queensland Australia
15 E4 McKinlay Queensland Australia
151 D5 McKinney Texas U.S.A.
179 B2 Mackintosh, C. c. Antarctica
17 D5 Mackintosh Ra. h. Western Australia Australia
154 C4 McKittrick California U.S.A.
137 H4 Macklin Saskatchewan Canada
81 H4 Mačkovci Slovenia
13 H2 Macksville New South Wales Australia
150 C2 McLaughlin S. Dakota U.S.A.
13 H2 Maclean New South Wales Australia
131 F6 Macleantown South Africa
131 G5 Maclear South Africa
13 H2 Macleay r. New South Wales Australia
136 F3 McLennan Alberta Canada
136 F4 McLeod r. Alberta Canada
17 A5 Macleod, Lake l. Western Australia Australia
136 E3 McLeod Lake B.C. Canada
152 B3 McLoughlin, Mt mt. Oregon U.S.A.
136 C2 Macmillan r. Yukon Terr. Canada
148 E2 McMillan Michigan U.S.A.
152 B2 McMinnville Oregon U.S.A.
145 C5 McMinnville Tennessee U.S.A.
179 B5 McMurdo U.S.A. Base Antarctica
155 H4 McNary Arizona U.S.A.
136 F4 McNaughton Lake l. B.C. Canada
155 H6 McNeal Arizona U.S.A.
64 A3 Macnean Lower, Lough l. Northern Ireland U.K.
64 A3 Macnean Upper, Lough l. Rep. of Ireland/U.K.
125 C5 Macocola Angola
148 B5 Macomb Illinois U.S.A.
108 A4 Macomer Sardegna Italy
127 D7 Macomia Mozambique
145 D5 Macon Georgia U.S.A.
148 A6 Macon Missouri U.S.A.
90 C2 Mâcon Saône-et-Loire France
125 D6 Macondo Angola
90 C2 Mâconnais reg. France
64 B2 Macosquin Northern Ireland U.K.
99 E4 Macotera Spain
150 D4 McPherson Kansas U.S.A.
13 H2 McPherson Ra. mountain range New South Wales Australia
13 F2 Macquarie r. New South Wales Australia
13 F5 Macquarie r. Tasmania Australia
13 F5 Macquarie Harb. harbour Tasmania Australia
10 □3 Macquarie Island i. Pacific Ocean
13 G3 Macquarie, L. b. New South Wales Australia
13 F2 Macquarie Marshes marsh New South Wales Australia
13 G3 Macquarie Mt mt. New South Wales Australia
175 P7 Macquarie Ridge sea feature Pacific Ocean
136 B2 McQuesten r. Yukon Terr. Canada
145 D5 McRae Georgia U.S.A.
16 B4 McRae, Mt mt. Western Australia Australia
25 □ MacRitchie Res. resr Singapore
179 D4 Mac. Robertson Land reg. Antarctica
67 C5 Macroom Rep. of Ireland
6 □6 Macuata-i-wai i. Fiji
106 B3 Macugnaga Italy
162 C1 Macuira, Parque Nacional nat. park Colombia
162 C3 Macuje Colombia
112 C4 Macukull Albania
12 D1 Macumba watercourse S. Australia Australia
164 B2 Macusani Peru
157 G5 Macuspana Mexico
156 C3 Macuzari, Psa resr Mexico
112 B2 Mačvanska Mitrovica Yugoslavia
136 E1 McVicar Arm b. N.W.T. Canada
147 J2 Macwahoc Maine U.S.A.
123 F5 Mada r. Nigeria
42 C4 Mādabā Jordan
131 H3 Madadeni South Africa
117 J8 Madagascar country Africa
175 H5 Madagascar Basin sea feature Indian Ocean
119 G2 Madā'in Şāliḩ Saudi Arabia
38 B3 Madakasira India
23 □1 Madalai Palau
100 □ Madalena Azores Portugal
123 G2 Madama Niger
113 E4 Madan Bulgaria
38 B3 Madanapalle India
6 □1 Madang P.N.G.
123 F4 Madaoua Niger
37 G5 Madaripur Bangladesh
123 F4 Madarounfa Niger
141 G4 Madawaska r. Ontario Canada
147 J1 Madawaska Maine U.S.A.
141 G4 Madawaska Ontario Canada
24 B2 Madaya Myanmar
52 G2 Madayevo Rus. Fed.
108 B3 Maddalena, Isola i. Sardegna Italy
109 G3 Maddaloni Italy
68 C3 Made Netherlands
163 E5 Madeira r. Brazil
96 □ Madeira, Ilha da i. Atlantic Ocean
139 H4 Madeleine, Îles de la is Québec Canada
90 B2 Madeleine, Monts de la mts France
62 D2 Madeley England U.K.
148 B2 Madeline I. i. Wisconsin U.S.A.
42 D2 Maden Turkey
154 B3 Madera California U.S.A.
156 C2 Madera Mexico
99 F3 Madero r. Spain
80 B3 Madererspitze mt. Austria
38 A3 Madgaon India
127 □1 Madge Rocks i. Seychelles
37 F4 Madhepura India
38 C2 Madhira India
37 F4 Madhubani India
37 F4 Madhupur India
36 D5 Madhya Pradesh India
131 E3 Madibogo South Africa
38 A3 Madikeri India
125 C5 Madimba Congo(Zaire)
122 C5 Madinani Côte d'Ivoire
87 E4 Madine, Lac de l. France
125 B4 Madingo-Kayes Congo
125 B4 Madingou Congo
124 C2 Madingrin Cameroon
164 C2 Madini r. Bolivia
129 H2 Madirovalo Madagascar
134 G5 Madison r. Montana U.S.A.
144 C4 Madison Indiana U.S.A.
147 J2 Madison Maine U.S.A.
150 D2 Madison Minnesota U.S.A.
150 D3 Madison Nebraska U.S.A.
150 D2 Madison S. Dakota U.S.A.
148 C4 Madison Wisconsin U.S.A.
146 C5 Madison W. Virginia U.S.A.
144 C4 Madisonville Kentucky U.S.A.
151 E6 Madisonville Texas U.S.A.
126 D3 Madīso Shet' watercourse Ethiopia
22 E4 Madita Indonesia
22 B3 Madiun Indonesia
124 B3 Madjingo Gabon
17 C5 Madley, Mt h. Western Australia Australia
54 D3 Madliena Latvia
141 G4 Madoc Ontario Canada
127 C4 Mado Gashi Kenya
32 B1 Madoi China
87 F4 Madon r. France
54 E3 Madona Latvia
110 C5 Madonie mts Sicilia Italy
107 E2 Madonna di Campiglio Italy
36 B4 Madpura India
113 F5 Madra Dağı mountain range Turkey
119 G3 Madrakah Saudi Arabia
152 B2 Madras Oregon U.S.A.
38 C3 Madras India
Madras see Chennai
169 F4 Madre de Deus de Minas Brazil
164 C2 Madre de Dios r. Bolivia/Peru
171 A7 Madre de Dios, I. i. Chile
151 D7 Madre, Laguna lag. Texas U.S.A.
157 F3 Madre, Laguna lag. Mexico
93 E6 Madrès, Pic de mt. France
99 G4 Madrid div. Spain
99 G4 Madrid Madrid Spain
23 C4 Madrid Philippines
99 G4 Madrid-Barajas airport Spain
23 B4 Madridejos Philippines
101 G1 Madridejos Spain
99 F3 Madrigal de las Altas Torres Spain
83 E2 Madrisahorn mt. Austria/Switzerland
101 F2 Madrona, Sierra mountain range Spain
103 B6 Madroño mt. Spain
38 C2 Madugula India
22 C3 Madura i. Indonesia
17 D6 Madura Western Australia Australia
38 B4 Madurai India
37 E4 Madwas India
36 C2 Madyan Pakistan
127 B6 Madyo Tanzania
51 H7 Madzhalis Rus. Fed.
112 E4 Madzharovo Bulgaria
129 D2 Madziwadzido Zimbabwe
29 G5 Maebashi Japan
24 B3 Mae Hong Son Thailand
29 □2 Mae-jima i. Japan
25 B4 Mae Khlong r. Thailand
24 B3 Mae Lao r. Thailand
88 B3 Maël-Carhaix France
24 B3 Mae Li r. Thailand
102 D3 Maella Spain
24 C3 Mae Nam Ing r. Thailand
24 C4 Mae Nam Mun r. Thailand
24 C3 Mae Nam Nan r. Thailand
24 C3 Mae Nam Pa Sak r. Thailand
24 B3 Mae Nam Ping r. Thailand
24 C3 Mae Nam Song Khram r. Thailand
24 B3 Mae Nam Wang r. Thailand
24 B3 Mae Nam Yom r. Thailand
24 B3 Mae Rim Thailand
79 M4 Măerişte Romania
158 C2 Maestra, Sierra mountain range Cuba
101 E3 Maestre h. Spain
99 H2 Maestu Spain
129 H2 Maevatanana Madagascar
6 □2 Maéwa i. Vanuatu
24 B3 Mae Yuam r. Myanmar/Thailand
137 J4 Mafeking Manitoba Canada
131 F4 Mafeteng Lesotho
127 C6 Mafia Channel chan. Tanzania
127 C6 Mafia I. i. Tanzania
131 E2 Mafikeng South Africa
172 A5 Máfil Chile
127 C6 Mafinga Tanzania
167 C6 Mafra Brazil
100 A2 Mafra Portugal
42 D3 Mafraq Jordan
45 R4 Magadan Rus. Fed.
127 C5 Magadi Kenya
171 B7 Magallanes, Estrecho de chan. Chile
171 B7 Magallanes & Antartica Chilena div. Chile
102 B3 Magallón Spain
99 H3 Magaña Spain
131 J1 Magandene Mozambique
162 C2 Magangue Colombia
112 B3 Maganik mt. Yugoslavia
42 C2 Mağara Turkey
123 F4 Magaria Niger
29 □2 Magari-zaki c. Japan
Magas see Zābolī
23 B2 Magat r. Philippines
99 F3 Magaz Spain
124 D3 Magbakele Congo(Zaire)
122 B5 Magburaka Sierra Leone
31 H1 Magdagachi Rus. Fed.
162 C2 Magdalena r. Colombia
153 F5 Magdalena New Mexico U.S.A.
173 J3 Magdalena Argentina
164 D2 Magdalena Bolivia
156 C2 Magdalena Mexico
156 C3 Magdalena, B. Mexico
156 B3 Magdalena, I. i. Mexico
171 B5 Magdalena, Isla i. Chile
23 A5 Magdaleno, Mt mt. Malaysia
73 G3 Magdeburg Germany
15 G3 Magdelaine Cays atoll Coral Sea Islands Terr. Pacific Ocean
22 B3 Magelang Indonesia
176 F4 Magellan Seamounts sea feature Pacific Ocean
106 C3 Magenta Italy
17 B7 Magenta, L. salt flat Western Australia Australia
56 G1 Magerøya i. Norway
93 A5 Magescq France
83 D2 Maggia r. Switzerland
83 D2 Maggia Switzerland
173 F2 Maggiolo Argentina
106 D4 Maggiorasca, Monte mt. Italy
106 C3 Maggiore, Lago l. Italy
108 B4 Maggiore, Monte h. Sardegna Italy
159 □1 Maggotty Jamaica
119 F2 Maghâgha Egypt
43 C5 Maghā'ir Shu'ayb Saudi Arabia
120 B5 Maghama Mauritania
43 B4 Maghâra, G. h. Egypt
67 E2 Maghera Northern Ireland U.K.
67 E2 Magherafelt Northern Ireland U.K.
64 B3 Maghery Northern Ireland U.K.
65 F4 Maghull England U.K.
67 E1 Magilligan Point pt Northern Ireland U.K.
101 G3 Mágina, Sierra mountain range Spain
108 E1 Magione Italy
104 G3 Maglaj Bos.-Herz.
82 B2 Magland France
112 D2 Maglavit Romania
109 F2 Magliano de'Marsi Italy
108 D2 Magliano in Toscana Italy
109 E2 Magliano Sabina Italy
112 B3 Maglić mt. Bos.-Herz./Yugoslavia
111 H2 Maglie Italy
152 D3 Magna Utah U.S.A.
92 D2 Magnac-Laval France
110 B6 Magna Grande h. Italy
111 E5 Magna Grande mt. Sicilia Italy
179 D4 Magnet Bay b. Antarctica
15 F3 Magnetic I. i. Queensland Australia
56 J1 Magnetity Rus. Fed.
52 B3 Magnitnyy Rus. Fed.
46 E2 Magnitogorsk Rus. Fed.
151 E5 Magnolia Arkansas U.S.A.
59 E2 Magnor Norway
77 K4 Magnuszew Poland
90 B2 Magny-Cours France
89 G2 Magny-en-Vexin France
114 D3 Magnysia div. Greece
6 □6 Mago i. Fiji
129 E2 Màgoé Mozambique
141 J4 Magog Québec Canada
157 F4 Magosal Mexico
115 D5 Magoula Greece
140 C2 Magpie r. Ontario Canada
139 H3 Magpie Québec Canada
139 H3 Magpie L. l. Québec Canada
148 E1 Magpie Lake l. Ontario Canada
106 D4 Magra r. Italy
136 G5 Magrath Alberta Canada
103 C5 Magre r. Spain
154 D3 Magruder Mt mt. Nevada U.S.A.
120 B5 Magṭa' Laḥjar Mauritania
127 B5 Magu Tanzania
32 D4 Maguan China
166 C1 Maguarinho, Cabo pt Brazil
129 E4 Magude Mozambique
131 H3 Magudu South Africa
64 A3 Maguiresbridge Northern Ireland U.K.
123 G4 Magumeri Nigeria
147 K2 Magundy New Brunswick Canada
79 H3 Magura mt. Slovakia
137 K2 Maguse Lake l. N.W.T. Canada
Magway see Magwe
24 A2 Magwe div. Myanmar
24 A2 Magwe Myanmar
128 C2 Magwegqana r. Botswana
79 K5 Magyarbánhegyes Hungary
79 H6 Magyarbóly Hungary
79 H5 Magyarszék Hungary
24 A2 Magyichaung Myanmar
42 F2 Mahābād Iran
38 A2 Mahabaleshwar India
Mahabalipuram see Māmallapuram
129 H2 Mahabe Madagascar
37 F4 Mahabharat Range mountain range Nepal
129 G3 Mahabo Madagascar
129 G3 Mahaboboka Madagascar
38 A2 Mahad India
126 E4 Mahaddayweyne Somalia
36 D5 Mahadeo Hills India
7 □11 Mahaena French Polynesia Pacific Ocean
124 F3 Mahagi Port Congo(Zaire)
163 F2 Mahaicony Guyana
36 C3 Mahajan India
129 H2 Mahajanga div. Madagascar
129 H2 Mahajanga Madagascar
22 D2 Mahakam r. Indonesia
128 D3 Mahalapye Botswana
129 H2 Mahalevona Madagascar
39 B2 Mahallāt Iran
36 D3 Maham India
22 C4 Mahameru, G. volcano Indonesia
39 D3 Mahān Iran
37 F5 Mahanadi r. India
129 H2 Mahanoro Madagascar
37 F4 Maharajganj India
37 E4 Maharajganj India
38 A2 Maharashtra div. India
129 G3 Maharivo r. Madagascar
37 E5 Mahasamund India
24 C3 Maha Sarakham Thailand
43 C5 Mahasham, W. el watercourse Egypt
43 B5 Mahash, W. watercourse Egypt
129 H2 Mahavavy r. Madagascar
129 H2 Mahavelona Madagascar
38 C5 Mahaweli Ganga r. Sri Lanka
24 D3 Mahaxai Laos
119 E5 Mahbub Sudan
38 C2 Mahbubabad India
38 B2 Mahbubnagar India
119 H3 Mahd adh Dhahab Saudi Arabia
39 C4 Maḥdah Oman
53 F2 Mahdalynivka Ukraine
163 F2 Mahdia Guyana
121 G1 Mahdia Tunisia
127 □4 Mahébourg Mauritius
127 □1 Mahé i. Seychelles
38 D2 Mahendragiri mt. India
127 C6 Mahenge Tanzania
9 C6 Maheno New Zealand
77 M5 Maheriv Ukraine
36 C5 Mahesāna India
36 C5 Maheshwar India
36 D4 Mahgawan India
36 C5 Mahi r. India
39 E3 Māhī watercourse Iran
8 F3 Mahia Peninsula pen. New Zealand
98 D3 Mahide Spain
54 F5 Mahilyow div. Belarus
50 D4 Mahilyow Belarus
7 □11 Mahina French Polynesia Pacific Ocean
122 B4 Mahina Mali
9 B6 Mahinerangi, L. l. New Zealand
38 C5 Mahiyangana Sri Lanka
131 H4 Mahlabatini South Africa
24 A2 Mahlaing Myanmar
131 H3 Mahlangasi South Africa
131 H3 Mahlangatsha h. Swaziland
131 F4 Mahlatswetsa South Africa
74 C4 Mahlberg Germany
73 G3 Mahlsdorf Germany
39 G2 Maḥmūd-e'Erāqī Afghanistan
112 G2 Mahmudia Romania

59 G1 Månkarbo Sweden
150 E2 Mankato *Minnesota* U.S.A.
36 B3 Mankera Pakistan
124 B2 Mankim Cameroon
53 D2 Man'kivka Ukraine
122 C5 Mankono Côte d'Ivoire
38 C4 Mankulam Sri Lanka
131 G1 Mankweng South Africa
24 B1 Manlc Myanmar
81 G2 Manle Austria
102 F3 Manlleu Spain
36 C5 Manmad India
14 C2 Mann r. *Northern Terr.* Australia
24 B2 Man Na Myanmar
12 D3 Mannahill *S. Australia* Australia
38 B4 Mannar Sri Lanka
38 B4 Mannar, Gulf of g. India/Sri Lanka
83 D1 Männedorf Switzerland
58 B3 Mannefjorden b. Norway
81 H3 Mannersdorf am Leithagebirge Austria
38 B3 Manneru r. India
74 D3 Mannheim Germany
67 A3 Mannin Bay b. Rep. of Ireland
13 G2 Manning r. *New South Wales* Australia
136 F3 Manning *Alberta* Canada
145 D5 Manning *S. Carolina* U.S.A.
63 H3 Manningtree *England* U.K.
82 C2 Männlifluh mt. Switzerland
12 B1 Mann Ranges mountain range *S. Australia* Australia
108 A4 Mannu r. *Sardegna* Italy
108 A5 Mannu r. *Sardegna* Italy
108 B4 Mannu r. *Sardegna* Italy
108 B5 Mannu r. *Sardegna* Italy
108 A4 Mannu, Capo pt *Sardegna* Italy
12 D3 Mannum *S. Australia* Australia
122 B5 Mano r. Liberia/Sierra Leone
122 B5 Mano Sierra Leone
164 C1 Manoa Bolivia
159 □2 Man of War B. b. *Tobago* Trinidad and Tobago
36 D4 Manohar Thana India
21 K7 Manokwari Indonesia
112 E1 Manoleasa Romania
129 G3 Manombo Atsimo Madagascar
129 H2 Manompana Madagascar
125 E5 Manono Congo(Zaire)
109 G2 Manoppello Italy
62 B3 Manorbier *Wales* U.K.
67 C2 Manorhamilton Rep. of Ireland
122 B5 Mano River Liberia
25 B5 Manoron Myanmar
91 D5 Manosque France
141 H3 Manouane *Québec* Canada
141 H3 Manouane, Lac l. *Québec* Canada
76 E1 Manowo Poland
24 B2 Man Pan Myanmar
31 H4 Manp'o North Korea
176 H6 Manra i. Kiribati
102 E3 Manresa Spain
36 C3 Mānsa India
125 E6 Mansa Zambia
122 A4 Mansabá Guinea-Bissau
122 A4 Mansa Konko The Gambia
73 K3 Manschnow Germany
36 C2 Mansehra Pakistan
135 K3 Mansel I. i. *N.W.T.* Canada
73 G4 Mansfeld Germany
63 E1 Mansfield *England* U.K.
151 E5 Mansfield *Louisiana* U.S.A.
146 B4 Mansfield *Ohio* U.S.A.
146 E4 Mansfield *Pennsylvania* U.S.A.
13 F4 Mansfield *Victoria* Australia
63 E1 Mansfield Woodhouse *England* U.K.
24 A1 Mansi Myanmar
99 E2 Mansilla de las Mulas Spain
92 C3 Mansle France
122 A4 Mansôa Guinea-Bissau
136 E3 Manson Creek *B.C.* Canada
62 D4 Manston *England* U.K.
162 A4 Manta Ecuador
162 A4 Manta, B. de b. Ecuador
31 J4 Mantapsan mt. North Korea
154 B3 Manteca *California* U.S.A.
162 D2 Mantecal Venezuela
98 C4 Manteigas Portugal
169 H3 Mantena Brazil
145 F5 Manteo *N. Carolina* U.S.A.
69 E5 Manternach Luxembourg
89 G3 Mantes-la-Jolie France
89 G3 Mantes-la-Ville France
38 B2 Manthani India
89 F4 Manthelan France
155 G2 Manti *Utah* U.S.A.
90 D1 Mantoche France
148 E3 Manton *Michigan* U.S.A.
114 E4 Mantoudi Greece
107 E3 Mantova div. *Lombardia* Italy
107 E3 Mantova *Mantova* Italy
57 G3 Mäntsälä Finland
57 G3 Mänttä Finland
Mantua *see* Mantova
15 F5 Mantuan Downs *Queensland* Australia
53 G1 Manturovo Rus. Fed.
50 H3 Manturovo Rus. Fed.
57 G3 Mäntyharju Finland
56 G2 Mäntyjärvi Finland
164 B2 Manú Peru
7 □13 Manua Is is *American Samoa* Pacific Ocean
166 C3 Manuel Alves r. Brazil
166 C2 Manuel Alves Grande r. Brazil
166 C2 Manuel Alves Pequeno r. Brazil
155 H4 Manuelito *New Mexico* U.S.A.
173 J3 Manuel J. Cobo Argentina
168 C6 Manuel Ribas Brazil
171 B7 Manuel Rodriguez, I. i. Chile
164 C1 Manuel Urbano Brazil
166 B2 Manuelzinho Brazil
7 □10 Manuhangi i. *French Polynesia* Pacific Ocean
21 H7 Manui i. Indonesia
39 D4 Manūjān Iran
23 B4 Manukan Philippines
8 E2 Manukau New Zealand
8 E2 Manukau Harbour harbour New Zealand
23 A5 Manuk Manka i. Philippines
12 D3 Manunda watercourse *S. Australia* Australia
164 B2 Manu, Parque Nacional nat. park Peru
6 □1 Manus I. i. P.N.G.
38 B3 Manvi India
129 E2 Manyame r. Mozambique/Zimbabwe
129 E2 Manyame, Lake l. Zimbabwe
127 C5 Manyara, Lake salt lake Tanzania
113 F4 Manyas Turkey
51 G6 Manych-Gudilo, Ozero l. Rus. Fed.
131 H2 Manyeleti Game Reserve res. South Africa
155 H3 Many Farms *Arizona* U.S.A.
53 B2 Manykivtsi Ukraine
127 B6 Manyoni Tanzania
129 E3 Manyuchi Dam dam Zimbabwe
36 B2 Manzai Pakistan
Manzala, L. lag. *see* Bahra el Manzala
101 G1 Manzanares Spain
99 G4 Manzanares el Real Spain
103 C4 Manzanera Spain
159 □3 Manzanilla Bay b. *Trinidad* Trinidad and Tobago
159 □3 Manzanilla Pt pt *Trinidad* Trinidad and Tobago
158 C2 Manzanillo Cuba
156 D5 Manzanillo Mexico
156 L7 Manzanillo, Pta pt Panama
81 E5 Manzano Italy
125 E5 Manzanza Congo(Zaire)
39 B2 Manzariyeh Iran
92 E3 Manzat France
31 F2 Manzhouli China
108 E2 Manziana Italy
43 D4 Manzil Jordan
131 H3 Manzini Swaziland
118 C5 Mao Chad
Maó *see* Mahón
30 C5 Maojiachuan China
131 F3 Maokeng South Africa
30 B5 Maomao Shan mt. China
33 E4 Maoming China
27 □ Ma On Shan h. *Hong Kong* China
32 C3 Maotou Shan mt. China
129 E3 Mapai Mozambique
37 E3 Mapam Yumco l. China
22 E2 Mapane Indonesia
131 E5 Maphodi South Africa
156 E3 Mapimí Mexico
23 A5 Mapin i. Philippines
129 F3 Mapinhane Mozambique
163 E2 Mapire Venezuela
164 C3 Mapiri Bolivia
148 E4 Maple r. *Michigan* U.S.A.
137 H5 Maple Creek *Saskatchewan* Canada
15 E1 Mapoon *Queensland* Australia
15 E2 Mapoon Abor. Reserve res. *Queensland* Australia
22 A1 Mapor i. Indonesia
131 F4 Mapoteng Lesotho
6 □1 Maprik P.N.G.
163 F4 Mapuera r. Brazil
129 E3 Mapulanguene Mozambique
131 H4 Mapumulo South Africa
129 E4 Maputo div. Mozambique
129 E4 Maputo r. Mozambique/South Africa
129 E4 Maputo Mozambique
131 J3 Maputo, Baia de b. Mozambique
131 J3 Maputo Elephant Reserve res. Mozambique
131 F4 Maputsoe Lesotho
42 D4 Maqar an Na'am well Iraq
114 B1 Maqellarë Albania
32 C1 Maqên China
32 B1 Maqên Gangri mt. China
47 L4 Maqiao China
43 C5 Maqla, J. al mt. Saudi Arabia
43 C5 Maqnā Saudi Arabia
120 B4 Maqteïr reg. Mauritania
32 C1 Maqu China
37 E3 Maquan r. China
23 C3 Maqueda Channel chan. Philippines
125 C5 Maquela do Zombo Angola
171 C5 Maquinchao r. Argentina
171 C5 Maquinchao Argentina
172 D2 Maquinista Levet Argentina
172 A4 Maquis, Punta Los pt Chile
148 B4 Maquoketa r. *Iowa* U.S.A.
148 B4 Maquoketa *Iowa* U.S.A.
58 C1 Mår r. Norway
36 A4 Mar r. Pakistan
127 B5 Mara div. Tanzania
137 H1 Mara r. *N.W.T.* Canada
163 F2 Mara Guyana
37 E5 Māra India
131 G1 Mara South Africa
162 C1 Mara Venezuela
7 □11 Maraa *French Polynesia* Pacific Ocean
163 D4 Maraã Brazil
166 C2 Maraba Brazil
168 C5 Marabá Paulista Brazil
22 C3 Marabatua is Indonesia
15 F4 Maraboon, L. resr *Queensland* Australia
82 A1 Marac France
163 G3 Maracá r. Brazil
166 C1 Maracaçumé r. Brazil
168 C5 Maracaí Brazil
162 C1 Maracaibo Venezuela
162 C2 Maracaibo, Lago de l. Venezuela
163 D4 Maracaí, Lago de l. Brazil
163 G3 Maracá, Ilha de i. Brazil
168 A4 Maracaju Brazil
165 E4 Maracaju, Sa de h. Paraguay
166 C1 Maracanã Brazil
159 □3 Maracas B. b. *Trinidad* Trinidad and Tobago
162 D1 Maracay Venezuela
54 F4 Marachkova Belarus
118 C2 Marādah Libya
123 F4 Maradi div. Niger
123 F4 Maradi Niger
98 D2 Maragatería reg. Spain
42 F2 Marāgheh Iran
166 E3 Maragogipe Brazil
23 B3 Maragondon Philippines
163 D3 Marahuaca, Co mt. Venezuela
88 C5 Marais Breton marsh France
166 C1 Marajó, Baía de est. Brazil
166 B1 Marajó, Ilha de i. Brazil
131 G4 Marakabeis Lesotho
59 G1 Maråkersbotten b. Sweden
38 B3 Marakkanam India
127 C4 Maralal Kenya
124 C2 Marali Central African Rep.
12 B2 Maralinga *S. Australia* Australia
6 □1 Maramasike i. Solomon Is.
23 C5 Marampit i. Indonesia
25 C7 Maran Malaysia
155 G5 Marana *Arizona* U.S.A.
99 H3 Maranchón Spain
42 F2 Marand Iran
107 E4 Maranello Italy
25 C6 Marang Malaysia
25 B5 Marang Myanmar
87 F3 Marange-Silvange France
166 E1 Maranguape Brazil
166 C1 Maranhão div. Brazil
166 C3 Maranhão r. Brazil
100 C1 Maranhão, Barragem do resr Portugal
15 G5 Maranoa r. *Queensland* Australia
109 G4 Marano di Napoli Italy
107 H3 Marano, Laguna di lag. Italy
162 B4 Marañón r. Peru
92 B2 Marans France
86 D4 Maranville France
98 C3 Marão mt. Portugal
122 C5 Maraoué r. Côte d'Ivoire
122 C5 Maraoue, Parc National de la nat. park Côte d'Ivoire
166 C1 Marapanim Brazil
108 A4 Marargiu, Capo pt *Sardegna* Italy
162 D5 Marari Brazil
9 A6 Mararoa r. New Zealand
173 L2 Marasco Brazil
22 D3 Marasende i. Indonesia
112 F2 Mărășești Romania
111 E3 Maratea Italy
100 B2 Marateca Portugal
145 D7 Marathon *Florida* U.S.A.
140 B2 Marathon *Ontario* Canada
151 C6 Marathon *Texas* U.S.A.
115 C4 Marathonas Greece
166 E3 Maraú Brazil
22 B2 Marau Indonesia
91 B5 Maraussan France
159 □3 Maraval Trinidad and Tobago
23 C4 Marawi Philippines
74 C4 Maraye-en-Othe France
172 D1 Marayes Argentina
62 A4 Marazion *England* U.K.
82 C1 Marbach Switzerland
74 E4 Marbach am Neckar Germany
101 F4 Marbella Spain
16 B4 Marble Bar *Western Australia* Australia
155 G3 Marble Canyon gorge *Arizona* U.S.A.
155 G3 Marble Canyon *Arizona* U.S.A.
131 G2 Marble Hall South Africa
147 H3 Marblehead *Massachusetts* U.S.A.
137 L2 Marble I. i. *N.W.T.* Canada
90 D2 Marboz France
36 C2 Marbul Pass pass India
74 D2 Marburg Germany
131 H5 Marburg South Africa
146 E5 Marburg, Lake l. *Pennsylvania* U.S.A.
78 G5 Marcali Hungary
107 H4 Marčana Croatia
125 B7 Marca, Pta do pt Angola
107 E3 Marcaria Italy
173 G1 Marcelino Escalada Argentina
92 E3 Marcenat France
81 H2 March r. Austria/Slovakia
63 G2 March *England* U.K.
36 E3 Marcha India
99 G4 Marchamalo Spain
130 C4 Marchand South Africa
90 E1 Marchaux France
107 G5 Marche div. Italy
92 D2 Marche reg. France
69 D4 Marche-en-Famenne div. *Luxembourg* Belgium
69 D4 Marche-en-Famenne Belgium
81 H2 Marchegg Austria
101 E3 Marchena Spain
162 □ Marchena, I. i. *Galapagos Is* Ecuador
89 G4 Marchenoir France
93 B4 Marcheprime France
159 □9 Marchfield *Barbados* Caribbean
86 C2 Marchiennes France
172 B3 Marchihue Chile
69 D4 Marchin Belgium
63 E2 Marchington *England* U.K.
173 G3 Mar Chiquita l. Argentina
173 J4 Mar Chiquita Argentina
173 J4 Mar Chiquita, L. l. *Buenos Aires* Argentina
173 F1 Mar Chiquita, L. l. *Cordoba* Argentina
81 F2 Marchtrenk Austria
93 C5 Marciac France
108 C2 Marciana Italy
54 E3 Mārciena Latvia
90 C2 Marcigny France
93 D4 Marcilhac-sur-Célé France
92 E3 Marcillac-la-Croisille France
93 E4 Marcillac-Vallon France
92 E2 Marcillat-en-Combraille France
86 C4 Marcilly-le-Hayer France
77 N1 Marcinkonys Lithuania
76 E2 Marcinkowice Poland
86 A2 Marck France
87 G4 Marckolsheim France
145 D7 Marco *Florida* U.S.A.
98 B3 Marco de Canaveses Portugal
86 C2 Marcoing France
165 E2 Marcolino r. Brazil
164 A3 Marcona Peru
138 E2 Marcopeet Islands is *Québec* Canada
107 G3 Marco Polo airport Italy
173 F2 Marcos Juárez Argentina
91 E4 Marcoux France
86 C2 Marcq-en-Barœul France
147 G2 Marcy, Mt mt. *New York* U.S.A.
36 C2 Mardan Pakistan
173 J4 Mar de Ajó Argentina
173 J4 Mar del Plata Argentina
16 A4 Mardie *Western Australia* Australia
42 E2 Mardin Turkey
30 B3 Mardzad Mongolia
6 □2 Maré i. *New Caledonia* Pacific Ocean
90 C3 Mare r. France
107 F2 Marebbe Italy
107 G5 Marecchia r. Italy
168 A6 Marechal Cândido Rondon Brazil
103 □ Mare de Déu del Toro h. Spain
15 F3 Mareeba *Queensland* Australia
66 C3 Maree, Loch l. *Scotland* U.K.
108 D2 Maremma reg. Italy
148 C4 Marengo *Illinois* U.S.A.
148 A5 Marengo *Iowa* U.S.A.
92 A3 Marennes France
93 A5 Marensin reg. France
111 G2 Mare Piccolo b. Italy
63 G4 Maresfield *England* U.K.
Mare Tirreno sea *see* Tyrrhenian Sea
110 B5 Marettimo *Sicilia* Italy
110 B5 Marettimo, Isola i. *Sicilia* Italy
92 C3 Mareuil France
92 A2 Mareuil-sur-Lay-Dissais France
52 A1 Marevo Rus. Fed.
151 B6 Marfa *Texas* U.S.A.
111 □ Marfa Pt pt Malta
111 □ Marfa Rge ridge Malta
37 F2 Margai Caka salt lake China
16 D3 Margaret r. *Western Australia* Australia
12 D2 Margaret watercourse *S. Australia* Australia
17 A7 Margaret River *Western Australia* Australia
163 E1 Margarita, I. de i. Venezuela
63 H3 Margate *England* U.K.
131 H5 Margate South Africa
79 L3 Margecany Slovakia
91 B3 Margeride, Monts de la mts France
86 D4 Margerie-Hancourt France
37 H4 Margherita India
109 J3 Margherita di Savoia Italy
79 M4 Marghita Romania
47 H4 Margilan Uzbekistan
79 M6 Margina Romania
112 E1 Marginea Romania
77 N2 Margionys Lithuania
69 A5 Margny-lès-Compiègne France
76 F3 Margonin Poland
23 B5 Margosatubig Philippines
140 C4 Margrethe, Lake l. *Michigan* U.S.A.
136 E4 Marguerite *B.C.* Canada
179 B2 Marguerite Bay b. Antarctica
91 C5 Marguerittes France
87 E3 Margut France
37 G3 Margyang China
53 F3 Marhanets' Ukraine
173 K1 Marhinote Uruguay
121 D2 Marhoum Algeria
24 B1 Mari Myanmar
168 A4 Maria r. Brazil
91 C4 Mariac France
156 D4 María Cleofas, I. i. Mexico
164 C4 María Elena Chile
173 G1 Mariá Eugenia Argentina
55 B3 Mariager Denmark
55 C3 Mariager Fjord inlet Denmark
14 C2 Maria I. i. *Northern Terr.* Australia
13 G5 Maria I. i. *Tasmania* Australia
173 H4 María Ignacia Argentina
177 J7 Maria, Îles is *French Polynesia* Pacific Ocean
81 G3 Maria Lankowitz Austria
156 D4 María Madre, I. i. Mexico
156 D4 María Magdalena, I. i. Mexico
15 G4 Marian *Queensland* Australia
169 G4 Mariana Brazil
158 B2 Marianao Cuba
176 E4 Marianas Ridge sea feature Pacific Ocean
176 E5 Marianas Tr. sea feature Pacific Ocean
37 H4 Mariani India
136 F2 Marian Lake l. *N.W.T.* Canada
151 F5 Marianna *Arkansas* U.S.A.
145 C6 Marianna *Florida* U.S.A.
59 F3 Mariannelund Sweden
83 E3 Mariano Comense Italy
170 E2 Mariano Loza Argentina
172 B5 Mariano Moreno Argentina
173 G4 Mariano Unzué Argentina
76 D2 Marianowo Poland
78 B2 Mariánské Lázně Czech Rep.
81 E3 Mariapfarr Austria
81 F4 Maria Saal Austria
101 H3 María, Sierra de mountain range Spain
156 D4 Marías, Islas is Mexico
156 K8 Mariato, Pta pt Panama
8 D1 Maria van Diemen, Cape c. New Zealand
81 G3 Mariazell Austria
126 E1 Ma'rib Yemen
55 D5 Maribo Denmark
81 G4 Maribor Slovenia
131 F2 Marico r. South Africa
155 F5 Maricopa *Arizona* U.S.A.
154 C4 Maricopa *California* U.S.A.
155 F5 Maricopa Mts mts *Arizona* U.S.A.
124 E2 Maridi watercourse Sudan
124 E3 Maridi Sudan
127 □1 Marie Anne I. i. Seychelles
179 A4 Marie Byrd Land reg. Antarctica
59 G2 Mariefred Sweden
159 □5 Marie Galante i. *Guadeloupe* Caribbean
57 E3 Mariehamn Finland
59 E4 Marieholm Sweden
52 H1 Mari-El div. Rus. Fed.
166 B3 Mariembero r. Brazil
69 C4 Mariembourg Belgium
75 J2 Marienberg Germany
72 C2 Marienhafe Germany
87 G1 Marienheide Germany
128 B3 Mariental Namibia
59 E2 Mariestad Sweden
145 C5 Marietta *Georgia* U.S.A.
146 C5 Marietta *Ohio* U.S.A.
109 G4 Marigliano Italy
91 D5 Marignane France
88 D2 Marigny France
179 □ Marigny, C. c. *Kerguelen* Indian Ocean
86 C4 Marigny-le-Châtel France
159 G3 Marigot *Guadeloupe* Caribbean
159 □4 Marigot *Martinique* Caribbean
54 C4 Marijampolė Lithuania
131 F2 Marikana South Africa
114 E1 Marikostinovo Bulgaria
168 D5 Marília Brazil
16 B4 Marillana *Western Australia* Australia
168 B6 Mariluz Brazil
163 F4 Marimari r. Brazil
125 C5 Marimba Angola
22 C2 Marimun Indonesia
151 C7 Marin Mexico
98 B2 Marín Spain
109 H4 Marina di Camerota Italy
108 C2 Marina di Campo Italy
108 C1 Marina di Castagneto Donoratico Italy
111 F2 Marina di Ginosa Italy
111 F4 Marina di Gioiosa Ionica Italy
108 C2 Marina di Grosseto Italy
111 H3 Marina di Leuca Italy
111 H3 Marina di Novaglie Italy
111 G2 Marina di Pulsano Italy
110 D6 Marina di Ragusa *Sicilia* Italy
107 G4 Marina di Ravenna Italy
54 F5 Mar"ina Horka Belarus
101 F3 Marinaleda Spain
107 G4 Marina Romea Italy
23 B3 Marinduque i. Philippines
110 B5 Marinella *Sicilia* Italy
110 C5 Marineo *Sicilia* Italy
89 G2 Marines France
148 D3 Marinette *Wisconsin* U.S.A.
124 D3 Maringa r. Congo(Zaire)
168 C5 Maringá Brazil
129 E2 Maringué Mozambique
90 B3 Maringues France
98 B4 Marinha das Ondas Portugal
98 B5 Marinha Grande Portugal
100 B1 Marinhais Portugal
144 B4 Marion *Illinois* U.S.A.
148 E5 Marion *Indiana* U.S.A.
147 K2 Marion *Maine* U.S.A.
146 B4 Marion *Ohio* U.S.A.
145 E5 Marion *S. Carolina* U.S.A.
146 C6 Marion *Virginia* U.S.A.
14 D4 Marion Downs *Queensland* Australia
145 D5 Marion, L. l. *S. Carolina* U.S.A.
15 H3 Marion Reef reef *Coral Sea Islands Terr.* Pacific Ocean
114 C2 Mariovo reg. Macedonia
163 D2 Maripa Venezuela
163 G3 Maripasoula French Guiana
154 C3 Mariposa *California* U.S.A.
173 K3 Mariscala Uruguay
165 D4 Mariscal Estigarribia Paraguay
112 E1 Mărişelu Romania
112 E3 Maritsa r. Bulgaria
115 □ Maritsa Greece
50 J3 Mari Turek Rus. Fed.
53 G3 Mariupol' Ukraine
42 F3 Marīvān Iran
101 G1 Marjaliza Spain
54 D2 Märjamaa Estonia
Marjan *see* Wazi Khwa
43 C3 Marjayoûn Lebanon
126 D4 Marka Somalia
47 L3 Markakol', Oz. l. Kazakhstan
122 C4 Markala Mali
32 B2 Markam China
38 B3 Markapur India
59 E3 Markaryd Sweden
39 B2 Markazī div. Iran
140 E4 Markdale *Ontario* Canada
74 E5 Markdorf Germany
68 E2 Markelo Netherlands
73 G1 Markelsdorfer Huk pt Germany
68 D2 Marken i. Netherlands
131 G1 Marken South Africa
68 D2 Markermeer l. Netherlands
63 F2 Market Deeping *England* U.K.
62 D2 Market Drayton *England* U.K.
63 F2 Market Harborough *England* U.K.
67 E2 Markethill *Northern Ireland* U.K.
65 H4 Market Rasen *England* U.K.
65 H4 Market Weighton *England* U.K.
45 O3 Markha r. Rus. Fed.
141 F5 Markham *Ontario* Canada
179 B4 Markham, Mt mt. Antarctica
77 K3 Marki Poland
66 E4 Markinch *Scotland* U.K.
73 J3 Märkisch Buchholz Germany
47 J5 Markit China
73 H4 Markkleeberg Germany
80 D2 Marklkofen Germany
72 E3 Marklohe Germany
68 D2 Marknesse Netherlands
75 H2 Markneukirchen Germany
115 E5 Markopoulo Greece
124 C2 Markounda Central African Rep.
81 H5 Markovac Trojstveni Croatia
114 E1 Markovi Kladentsi mt. Bulgaria
53 F1 Markovo Rus. Fed.
45 T3 Markovo Rus. Fed.
52 E1 Markovo Rus. Fed.
123 E4 Markoye Burkina
73 H4 Markranstädt Germany
52 H4 Marks Rus. Fed.
74 F2 Marksuhl Germany
81 H3 Markt Allhau Austria
74 F3 Markt Bibart Germany
75 F3 Markt Erlbach Germany
74 E3 Marktheidenfeld Germany
80 C2 Markt Indersdorf Germany
75 G2 Marktleugast Germany
75 H2 Marktleuthen Germany
75 F5 Marktoberdorf Germany
75 H2 Marktredwitz Germany
83 F1 Markt Rettenbach Germany
75 G2 Marktrodach Germany
81 F2 Markt St Florian Austria
81 H3 Markt St Martin Austria
80 C2 Markt Schwaben Germany
148 B6 Mark Twain Lake l. *Missouri* U.S.A.
80 B2 Markt Wald Germany
72 C4 Marl Germany
12 C1 Marla *S. Australia* Australia
9 D4 Marlborough div. New Zealand
63 E3 Marlborough *England* U.K.
147 H3 Marlborough *Massachusetts* U.S.A.
15 G4 Marlborough *Queensland* Australia
63 E3 Marlborough Downs h. *England* U.K.
62 C4 Marldon *England* U.K.
86 C3 Marle France
87 G4 Marlenheim France
90 D2 Marlieux France
151 D6 Marlin *Texas* U.S.A.
146 C5 Marlinton *W. Virginia* U.S.A.
13 G4 Marlo *Victoria* Australia
130 C7 Marloth Nature Reserve South Africa
63 F3 Marlow *England* U.K.
73 H1 Marlow Germany
87 F3 Marly *Lorraine* France
86 C2 Marly *Nord-Pas-de-Calais* France
93 C4 Marmande France
114 D4 Marmara Greece
113 F4 Marmara Turkey
42 B1 Marmara Denizi sea Turkey
113 F4 Marmaraereğlisi Turkey
Marmara, Sea of sea *see* Marmara Denizi
115 F4 Marmari Greece
42 B2 Marmaris Turkey
150 C2 Marmarth *N. Dakota* U.S.A.
100 B3 Marmelete Portugal
103 C7 Mar Menor lag. Spain
146 C5 Marmet *W. Virginia* U.S.A.
138 B4 Marmion L. l. *Ontario* Canada
17 C6 Marmion, Lake salt pan *Western Australia* Australia
83 F3 Marmirolo Italy
107 F2 Marmolada mt. Italy
101 F2 Marmolejo Spain
82 C3 Marmore r. Italy
87 G4 Marmoutier France
157 G5 Mar Muerto l. Mexico
90 D1 Marnay France
90 E2 Marnaz France
86 D3 Marne div. *Champagne-Ardenne* France
86 C3 Marne r. France
72 E2 Marne Germany
86 B4 Marne-la-Vallée France
73 G2 Marnitz Germany
131 G1 Marnitz South Africa
124 C2 Maro Chad
129 H2 Maroantsetra Madagascar
169 J2 Maroba r. Brazil
7 □10 Marokau i. *French Polynesia* Pacific Ocean
36 D2 Marol *Jammu and Kashmir*
129 H3 Marolambo Madagascar
75 F2 Maroldsweisach Germany
89 F3 Marolles-les-Braults France
89 G2 Maromme France
129 H1 Maromokotro mt. Madagascar
129 H1 Maromony, Lohatanjona headland Madagascar
129 E2 Marondera Zimbabwe
163 G3 Maroni r. French Guiana
92 E3 Maronne r. France
15 H5 Maroochydore *Queensland* Australia
159 □1 Maroon Town Jamaica
22 D3 Maros Indonesia
129 H2 Maroseranana Madagascar
79 K5 Maros-Körös Köze plain Hungary
107 F3 Marostica Italy
5 N7 Marotiri is *French Polynesia* Pacific Ocean
129 H1 Marotolana Madagascar
124 B1 Maroua Cameroon
88 C3 Maroué France
163 G3 Marouini r. French Guiana
129 H2 Marovoay Madagascar
163 G2 Marowijne r. Surinam
69 F5 Marpingen Germany
115 G5 Marpissa Greece
65 F4 Marple *England* U.K.
42 E3 Marqādah Syria
32 C1 Mar Qu r. China
131 F4 Marquard South Africa
86 A2 Marquenterre reg. France
Marquesas Islands is *see* Marquises, Îles
145 D7 Marquesas Keys is *Florida* U.S.A.
148 D2 Marquette *Michigan* U.S.A.
86 C2 Marquion France
86 A2 Marquise France
177 K6 Marquises, Îles is *French Polynesia* Pacific Ocean
13 F2 Marra r. *New South Wales* Australia
129 E4 Marracuene Mozambique
120 C2 Marrakech Morocco
Marrakesh *see* Marrakech
129 E3 Marrangua, L. l. Mozambique
118 D5 Marra Plateau plat. Sudan
13 F5 Marrawah *Tasmania* Australia
166 D2 Marrecas, Sa das h. Brazil
12 D2 Marree *S. Australia* Australia
151 F6 Marrero *Louisiana* U.S.A.
129 F2 Marromeu Mozambique
129 F2 Marromeu, Reserva de res. Mozambique
127 C7 Marrupa Mozambique
92 E3 Mars r. France
119 F2 Marsa Alam Egypt
118 C1 Marsa al Burayqah Libya
126 C4 Marsabit Kenya
126 C4 Marsabit National Reserve res. Kenya
90 B3 Marsac-en-Livradois France
88 D4 Marsac-sur-Don France
43 C5 Marsa Dahab b. Egypt
106 D4 Marsaglia Italy
87 F4 Marsal France
110 B5 Marsala *Trapani* Italy
111 □ Marsalforn Malta
118 E1 Marsa Matrûh Egypt
90 C1 Marsannay-la-Côte France
91 C4 Marsanne France
111 □ Marsaskala Malta
122 A4 Marsassoum Senegal
111 □ Marsaxlokk Malta
111 □ Marsaxlokk B. b. Malta
128 □1 Mars Bay b. *Ascension* Atlantic Ocean
72 D4 Marsberg Germany
109 E2 Marsciano Italy
13 F3 Marsden *New South Wales* Australia
68 C2 Marsdiep chan. Netherlands
91 B5 Marseillan France
91 D5 Marseille *Bouches-du-Rhône* France
89 G2 Marseille-en-Beauvaisis France
91 D5 Marseille-Provence airport France
148 C5 Marseilles *Illinois* U.S.A.
56 D2 Marsfjället mt. Sweden
14 D4 Marshall watercourse *Northern Terr.* Australia
151 E5 Marshall *Arkansas* U.S.A.
144 C4 Marshall *Illinois* U.S.A.
148 E4 Marshall *Michigan* U.S.A.
150 E2 Marshall *Minnesota* U.S.A.
150 E4 Marshall *Missouri* U.S.A.
137 H4 Marshall *Saskatchewan* Canada
151 E5 Marshall *Texas* U.S.A.
122 B5 Marshall Liberia
13 F4 Marshall B. b. *Tasmania* Australia
4 H3 Marshall Islands country Pacific Ocean
140 B1 Marshall Lake l. *Ontario* Canada
150 E3 Marshalltown *Iowa* U.S.A.
54 F3 Marshavitsy Rus. Fed.
148 B3 Marshfield *Wisconsin* U.S.A.
158 C1 Marsh Harbour The Bahamas
147 K1 Mars Hill *Maine* U.S.A.
151 F6 Marsh Island i. *Louisiana* U.S.A.
136 C2 Marsh Lake l. *Yukon Terr.* Canada
63 G2 Marsh, The reg. *England* U.K.
109 H4 Marsico Nuovo Italy
152 C3 Marsing *Idaho* U.S.A.
93 E5 Marssac-sur-Tarn France
59 G2 Märsta Sweden
55 C5 Marstal Denmark
55 C5 Marstal Bugt b. Denmark
83 E1 Märstetten Switzerland
58 D3 Marstrand Sweden
37 F3 Marsyangdi r. Nepal
108 D2 Marta r. Italy
24 B3 Martaban Myanmar
24 B3 Martaban, Gulf of g. Myanmar
59 F1 Mårtanberg Sweden
111 H2 Martano Italy
22 A3 Martapura Indonesia
22 C2 Martapura Indonesia
93 D4 Martel France
69 D5 Martelange Belgium
107 G3 Martellago Italy
83 F2 Martello Italy
141 F3 Marten River *Ontario* Canada
137 H4 Martensville *Saskatchewan* Canada
103 C5 Martés mt. Spain
103 B5 Martés, Serra mountain range Spain
72 E3 Martfeld Germany
79 K4 Martfo Hungary
147 H4 Martha's Vineyard i. *Massachusetts* U.S.A.
92 C3 Marthon France
88 D4 Martigné-Ferchaud France
89 E3 Martigné-sur-Mayenne France
82 C2 Martigny Switzerland
87 E4 Martigny-les-Bains France
87 E4 Martigny-les-Gerbonvaux France
101 E5 Martil Morocco
100 C3 Martim Longo Portugal
102 C3 Martín r. Spain
150 C3 Martin *S. Dakota* U.S.A.
145 B4 Martin *Tennessee* U.S.A.
79 H2 Martin Slovakia
111 G2 Martina Franca Italy
173 H3 Martín Chico Uruguay
173 H4 Martin Colman Argentina
101 F3 Martín de la Jara Spain
172 D3 Martín de Loyola Argentina
102 E2 Martinet Spain
157 F4 Martínez Mexico
155 E5 Martinez Lake *Arizona* U.S.A.
100 B1 Martingança Portugal
173 H3 Martín García, I. i. Argentina
169 F3 Martinho Campos Brazil
133 M8 Martinique territory Caribbean

159 G4 Martinique Passage chan. Dominica/Martinique
145 C5 Martin, L. l. Alabama U.S.A.
99 F3 Martín Muñoz de las Posadas Spain
114 E4 Martino Greece
166 D1 Martinópole Brazil
168 C5 Martinópolis Brazil
179 A3 Martin Pen. pen. Antarctica
9 A6 Martins Bay b. New Zealand
81 G2 Martinsberg Austria
146 D4 Martinsburg Pennsylvania U.S.A.
146 E5 Martinsburg W. Virginia U.S.A.
107 J4 Martinšćica Croatia
131 F1 Martin's Drift South Africa
146 C4 Martins Ferry Ohio U.S.A.
146 D6 Martinsville Virginia U.S.A.
174 H7 Martin Vas, Ilhas is Atlantic Ocean
108 A4 Martis Sardegna Italy
92 D2 Martizay France
62 D2 Martley England U.K.
62 D4 Martock England U.K.
8 E4 Marton New Zealand
79 H4 Martonvásar Hungary
102 E3 Martorell Spain
101 G3 Martos Spain
136 F2 Martre, Lac la l. N.W.T. Canada
54 C1 Marttila Finland
46 E2 Martuk Kazakhstan
53 C1 Martynovychi Ukraine
39 E2 Maruchak Afghanistan
23 A5 Marudu, Tk b. Malaysia
28 D6 Marugame Japan
99 F4 Marugán Spain
9 D5 Maruia r. New Zealand
166 E3 Maruim Brazil
173 F1 Marull Argentina
68 E1 Marum Netherlands
6 □2 Marum, Mt mt. Vanuatu
36 B4 Marusthali reg. India
7 □10 Marutéa i. French Polynesia Pacific Ocean
100 C1 Marvão Portugal
39 C3 Marvast Iran
91 B4 Marvejols France
87 E3 Marville France
155 G2 Marvine, Mt mt. Utah U.S.A.
36 C4 Marwar Jct India
137 G4 Marwayne Alberta Canada
46 F5 Mary div. Turkmenistan
14 B2 Mary r. Northern Terr. Australia
46 F5 Mary Turkmenistan
77 N5 Mar"yanivka Volyn Ukraine
53 G3 Mar"yanivka Zaporizhzhya Ukraine
53 B1 Mar"yanivka Zhytomyr Ukraine
47 H2 Mar'yanovka Rus. Fed.
15 H5 Maryborough Queensland Australia
13 E4 Maryborough Victoria Australia
130 D4 Marydale South Africa
52 H3 Mar'yevka Rus. Fed.
137 H2 Mary Frances Lake l. N.W.T. Canada
53 G3 Mar"yinka Ukraine
147 E5 Maryland div. U.S.A.
112 E1 Marynychi Ukraine
66 E3 Maryport Scotland U.K.
65 E3 Maryport England U.K.
139 J3 Mary's Harbour Newfoundland Canada
139 K4 Marystown Newfoundland Canada
155 F2 Marysvale Utah U.S.A.
154 B2 Marysville California U.S.A.
150 D4 Marysville Kansas U.S.A.
139 G4 Marysville New Brunswick Canada
146 B4 Marysville Ohio U.S.A.
15 F3 Maryvale Queensland Australia
150 E3 Maryville Missouri U.S.A.
107 F4 Marzabotto Italy
168 D2 Marzagão Brazil
73 H3 Marzahna Germany
73 H3 Marzahne Germany
111 E6 Marzamemi Sicilia Italy
80 C2 Marzling Germany
43 A4 Masabb Dumyât river mouth Egypt
43 A4 Masabb Rashîd river mouth Egypt
156 J7 Masachapa Nicaragua
42 D3 Maşâf Syria
127 B5 Masai Mara National Reserve res. Kenya
127 C5 Masai Steppe plain Tanzania
127 B5 Masaka Uganda
131 F5 Masakhane South Africa
128 C3 Masalanyane Pan salt pan Botswana
22 C3 Masalembu Besar i. Indonesia
22 C3 Masalembu Kecil i. Indonesia
42 G2 Masallı Azerbaijan
22 E2 Masamba mt. Indonesia
22 E2 Masamba Indonesia
31 J6 Masan South Korea
147 J1 Masardis Maine U.S.A.
115 □ Masari Greece
127 C7 Masasi Tanzania
165 D3 Masavi Bolivia
156 J7 Masaya Nicaragua
23 B3 Masbate i. Philippines
23 B3 Masbate Philippines
111 E5 Mascalucia Sicilia Italy
121 E1 Mascara Algeria
175 H5 Mascarene Basin sea feature Indian Ocean
175 J4 Mascarene Ridge sea feature Indian Ocean
172 D1 Mascasín Argentina
169 J1 Mascote Brazil
141 J4 Mascouche Québec Canada
102 C4 Mas de las Matas Spain
99 H4 Masegoso de Tajuña Spain
131 G1 Masekwaspoort pass South Africa
59 E3 Mäsen l. Sweden
127 B4 Maseno Kenya
83 D2 Masera Italy
80 D5 Maserada sul Piave Italy
141 G2 Masères, Lac l. Québec Canada
131 F4 Maseru Lesotho
90 E1 Masevaux France
58 A1 Masfjorden Norway
131 G4 Mashai Lesotho
65 G3 Masham England U.K.
32 E4 Mashan China
129 E3 Mashava Zimbabwe
36 D2 Masherbrum mt. Pakistan
39 D1 Mashhad Iran
36 C4 Mashi r. India
28 H2 Mashike Japan
53 F2 Mashivka Ukraine
39 D3 Mashīz Iran
39 E4 Mashket r. Pakistan
39 E3 Mashki Chah Pakistan
39 E4 Mãshkīd r. Iran
129 E2 Mashonaland Central div. Zimbabwe
129 E2 Mashonaland East div. Zimbabwe
129 D2 Mashonaland West div. Zimbabwe
Mashtagi see Maştağa
28 K2 Mashū-ko l. Japan
56 F1 Masi Norway
156 C3 Masiáca Mexico
131 F5 Masibambane South Africa
98 B2 Maside Spain
131 F4 Masilo South Africa
125 C4 Masi-Manimba Congo(Zaire)
22 D2 Masimbu Indonesia
126 B4 Masindi Uganda
127 C5 Masinga Res. resr Kenya
23 A3 Masinloc Philippines
83 E2 Masino r. Italy
130 D5 Masinyusane South Africa
41 J5 Maşīrah i. Oman
41 J6 Maşīrah, Gulf of b. Oman
164 B1 Masisea Peru
131 H1 Masisi South Africa
124 E4 Masisi Congo(Zaire)
39 B3 Masjed Soleymān Iran
42 D2 Maskanah Syria
141 J3 Maskinongé Québec Canada
67 B3 Mask, Lough l. Rep. of Ireland
54 C1 Masku Finland
39 D4 Maskūtān Iran
93 B5 Maslacq France
79 L5 Maşloc Romania
53 G1 Maslova Pristan' Rus. Fed.
39 F3 Maslti Pakistan
47 K2 Maslyanino Rus. Fed.
98 C1 Masma r. Spain
80 C4 Maso r. Italy
129 J2 Masoala, Tanjona c. Madagascar
129 G2 Masoarivo Madagascar
173 K1 Masoller Uruguay
148 E4 Mason Michigan U.S.A.
154 C2 Mason Nevada U.S.A.
151 D6 Mason Texas U.S.A.
9 A7 Mason Bay b. New Zealand
148 C5 Mason City Illinois U.S.A.
150 E3 Mason City Iowa U.S.A.
146 D5 Masontown Pennsylvania U.S.A.
41 J5 Masqaţ Oman
106 E4 Massa Italy
147 G3 Massachusetts div. U.S.A.
147 H3 Massachusetts Bay b. U.S.A.
106 E5 Massaciuccoli, Lago di l. Italy
155 H1 Massadona Colorado U.S.A.
106 D4 Massa e Carrara div. Italy
111 G2 Massafra Italy
124 C1 Massaguet Chad
124 C1 Massakory Chad
109 G4 Massa Lubrense Italy
103 C5 Massamagrell Spain
108 C1 Massa Marittimo Italy
109 E2 Massa Martana Italy
129 B4 Massana Gabon
129 E3 Massangena Mozambique
125 C5 Massango Angola
127 C7 Massangulo Mozambique
166 D1 Massapê Brazil
106 E5 Massarosa Italy
125 B4 Massassa-Lewémé Congo
93 D6 Massat France
126 C1 Massawa Eritrea
126 C1 Massawa Channel chan. Eritrea
141 K4 Massawippi, Lac l. Québec Canada
147 F2 Massena New York U.S.A.
124 C1 Massenya Chad
92 D3 Masseret France
136 C4 Masset B.C. Canada
93 C5 Masseube France
140 D3 Massey Ontario Canada
91 B3 Massiac France
91 B3 Massif Central mts France
122 B4 Massif de Banko mt. Guinea
91 D3 Massif de la Chartreuse mountain range France
158 D3 Massif de la Hotte mountain range Haiti
123 F3 Massif de l'Aïr mts Niger
93 D6 Massif de l'Arize mt. France
90 D1 Massif de la Serre h. France
91 E3 Massif de la Vanoise mts France
129 H3 Massif de L'Isalo mts Madagascar
93 C6 Massif de Néouvielle mts France
124 D2 Massif des Bongo mts Central African Rep.
91 E5 Massif des Maures reg. France
92 E3 Massif du Cantal mts France
124 B4 Massif du Chaillu mts Gabon
91 D4 Massif du Diois mts France
124 C1 Massif du Guéra mts Chad
118 D5 Massif du Kapka mts Chad
91 E4 Massif du Pelvoux mts France
122 B4 Massif du Tamgué mts Guinea
129 H1 Massif du Tsaratanana mts Madagascar
124 C2 Massif du Yadé mts Central African Rep.
118 D4 Massif Ennedi mts Chad
179 □ Massif Galliéni mts Kerguelen Indian Ocean
122 C4 Massigui Mali
146 C4 Massillon Ohio U.S.A.
122 C4 Massina Mali
80 D2 Massing Germany
129 F3 Massinga Mozambique
129 E3 Massingir Mozambique
129 E3 Massingir, Barragem de resr Mozambique
129 E3 Massintonto r. Mozambique/South Africa
141 H4 Masson Québec Canada
179 D5 Masson I. i. Antarctica
119 G3 Mastābah Saudi Arabia
42 G1 Maştağa Azerbaijan
47 G5 Mastchoh Tajikistan
46 D3 Masteksay Kazakhstan
9 E4 Masterton New Zealand
145 E7 Mastic Point The Bahamas
141 J3 Mastigouche, Réserve faunique de res. Québec Canada
108 B5 Mastixi, Pta su pt Sardegna Italy
58 A1 Mastrevik Norway
36 C1 Mastuj Pakistan
36 A3 Mastung Pakistan
119 G3 Mastūrah Saudi Arabia
77 N2 Masty Belarus
108 A5 Masua Sardegna Italy
28 C6 Masuda Japan
Masulipatam see Machilipatnam
129 E3 Masvingo div. Zimbabwe
129 E3 Masvingo Zimbabwe
127 B5 Maswe Tanzania
127 B5 Maswe Game Reserve res. Tanzania
77 M4 Masyevichy Belarus
76 F1 Maszewo Słupsk Poland
76 D2 Maszewo Szczecin Poland
8 G2 Mata r. New Zealand
24 B1 Mata Myanmar
126 E3 Matabaan Somalia
128 D2 Matabeleland North div. Zimbabwe
129 D3 Matabeleland South div. Zimbabwe
37 G4 Matabhanga India
99 E2 Matabuena Spain
100 E2 Matachel r. Spain
140 E3 Matachewan Ontario Canada
153 F6 Matachic Mexico
125 B5 Matadi Congo(Zaire)
156 J6 Matagalpa Nicaragua
141 G2 Matagami Québec Canada
141 F2 Matagami, Lac l. Québec Canada
151 D6 Matagorda I. i. Texas U.S.A.
158 B2 Matahambre Cuba
43 A5 Maţâî Egypt
7 □11 Mataiea French Polynesia Pacific Ocean
7 □10 Mataiva i. French Polynesia Pacific Ocean
25 D7 Matak i. Indonesia
8 F2 Matakana Island i. New Zealand
125 C6 Matala Angola
115 F8 Matala Greece
38 C5 Matale Sri Lanka
99 H3 Matalebreras Spain
130 E4 Mataleng South Africa
122 B3 Matam Senegal
8 E2 Matamata New Zealand
130 C2 Mata-Mata South Africa
123 F4 Matamey Niger
156 E3 Matamoros Coahuila Mexico
157 F3 Matamoros Tamaulipas Mexico
23 B5 Matanal Point pt Philippines
118 D3 Ma'tan as Sārah well Libya
118 D3 Ma'ţan Bishrah well Libya
172 B1 Matancilla Chile
127 C7 Matandu r. Tanzania
139 G4 Matane Québec Canada
158 B2 Matanzas Cuba
168 D4 Matão Brazil
173 J1 Mataojo Uruguay
156 K7 Matapalo, C. c. Costa Rica
Matapan, C. c. see Akra Tainaro
76 G5 Mata Panew r. Poland
139 G4 Matapédia r. Québec Canada
99 F2 Mataporquera Spain
99 F3 Matapozuelos Spain
172 B3 Mataquito r. Chile
38 C5 Matara Sri Lanka
114 C4 Mataragka Dytiki Ellas Greece
114 D3 Mataragka Thessalia Greece
22 D4 Mataram Indonesia
14 C2 Mataranka Northern Terr. Australia
102 F3 Mataró Spain
102 D3 Matarraña r. Spain
22 C3 Matasiri i. Indonesia
119 E4 Matassi well Sudan
131 G5 Matatiele South Africa
7 □13 Matatula, C. c. American Samoa Pacific Ocean
9 B7 Mataura r. New Zealand
9 B7 Mataura New Zealand
7 □12 Matautu Western Samoa
6 □3 Mata'utuliki i. Tonga
7 □12 Matavanu Crater crater Western Samoa
7 □16 Mataveri Easter I. Chile
131 H1 Matavhelo South Africa
8 F3 Matawai New Zealand
141 J3 Matawin r. Québec Canada
165 D2 Mategua Bolivia
157 E4 Matehuala Mexico
168 B6 Matelândia Brazil
111 H5 Matelica Italy
159 □3 Matelot Trinidad and Tobago
127 C7 Matemanga Tanzania
127 D7 Matemo, Ilha i. Mozambique
109 J4 Matera div. Basilicata Italy
109 J4 Matera Matera Italy
109 G3 Matese, Monti del mts Italy
79 M4 Mátészalka Hungary
128 D2 Matetsi r. Zimbabwe
105 B7 Mateur Tunisia
98 C3 Mateus Portugal
169 F3 Mateus Leme Brazil
92 B3 Matha France
126 B4 Matheniko Game Reserve res. Uganda
140 E2 Matheson Ontario Canada
151 D6 Mathis Texas U.S.A.
113 B5 Mathraki i. Greece
36 D4 Mathura India
23 C5 Mati Philippines
123 E4 Matiacoali Burkina
37 G4 Matiali India
33 F3 Matianxu China
36 B4 Matiari Pakistan
169 G4 Matias Barbosa Brazil
169 G1 Matias Cardoso Brazil
157 G5 Matías Romero Mexico
88 C3 Matignon France
69 B5 Matigny France
139 G3 Matimekosh Newfoundland Canada
140 D3 Matinenda Lake l. Ontario Canada
166 C1 Matinha Brazil
147 J3 Matinicus I. i. Maine U.S.A.
111 H2 Matino Italy
7 □11 Matiti French Polynesia Pacific Ocean
130 C6 Matjiesfontein South Africa
37 G5 Matla r. India
131 F1 Matlabas r. South Africa
131 F2 Matlabas South Africa
63 E1 Matlock England U.K.
131 F3 Matlwangtlwang South Africa
129 D3 Matobo Hills mts Zimbabwe
166 A3 Mato Grosso div. Brazil
165 E3 Mato Grosso Brazil
168 A3 Mato Grosso do Sul div. Brazil
129 E4 Matola Mozambique
124 B3 Matomb Cameroon
98 B3 Matosinhos Portugal
90 C2 Matour France
169 G1 Mato Verde Brazil
169 F3 Matozinhos Brazil
79 J4 Mátra mts Hungary
41 J5 Maţraḩ Oman
58 A1 Matre Norway
80 D3 Matrei in Osttirol Austria
130 B6 Matroosberg mt. South Africa
131 F2 Matroosster South Africa
122 B5 Matru Sierra Leone
130 D4 Matsap South Africa
131 H3 Matsapha Swaziland
123 G4 Matsena Nigeria
51 F7 Matsesta Rus. Fed.
129 H3 Matsiatra r. Madagascar
28 D6 Matsue Japan
28 H3 Matsumae Japan
29 F5 Matsumoto Japan
29 F6 Matsusaka Japan
33 G3 Matsu Tao i. Taiwan
28 B7 Matsuura Japan
28 D7 Matsuyama Japan
140 E2 Mattagami r. Ontario Canada
172 E3 Mattaldi Argentina
141 F3 Mattawa Ontario Canada
147 J2 Mattawamkeag Maine U.S.A.
152 D3 Matterhorn mt. Nevada U.S.A.
82 C3 Matterhorn mt. Italy/Switzerland
81 H3 Mattersburg div. Austria
81 H3 Mattersburg Austria
82 C2 Mattertal v. Switzerland
163 E2 Matthews Ridge Guyana
158 D2 Matthew Town The Bahamas
140 D2 Mattice Ontario Canada
80 E2 Mattighofen Austria
109 J3 Mattinata Italy
29 F5 Mattō Japan
144 B4 Mattoon Illinois U.S.A.
Matturai see Matara
164 A2 Matucana Peru
38 C5 Matugama Sri Lanka
77 N1 Matuizos Lithuania
6 □7 Matuku i. Fiji
107 J3 Matulji Croatia
125 C6 Matumbo Angola
Matun see Khowst
119 F5 Ma'tuq Sudan
159 □3 Matura Trinidad and Tobago
159 □3 Matura Bay b. Trinidad Trinidad and Tobago
163 E2 Maturín Venezuela
129 D2 Matusadona National Park nat. park Zimbabwe
99 H3 Matute mt. Spain
169 F3 Matutina Brazil
23 C5 Matutuang i. Indonesia
52 H1 Matvinur Rus. Fed.
53 D3 Matviyivka Mykolayiv Ukraine
53 F3 Matviyivka Zaporizhzhya Ukraine
131 F4 Matwabeng South Africa
52 E3 Matyra r. Rus. Fed.
52 D3 Matyrskiy Rus. Fed.
52 D3 Matyrskoye Vdkhr. resr Rus. Fed.
127 C5 Mau mt. Kenya
37 E4 Mau India
36 D4 Mau India
127 C7 Maúa Mozambique
37 E4 Mau Aimma India
102 D2 Mauberme, Pic de mt. Spain
86 D3 Maubert-Fontaine France
86 C2 Maubeuge France
24 B1 Ma-ubin Myanmar
93 C5 Maubourguet France
66 D5 Mauchline Scotland U.K.
36 E4 Maudaha India
13 F3 Maude New South Wales Australia
179 C3 Maudheimvidda mountain range Antarctica
17 A4 Maud, Pt pt Western Australia Australia
179 D2 Maud Seamount sea feature Antarctica
80 E2 Mauerkirchen Austria
75 G4 Mauern Germany
83 F1 Mauerstetten Germany
163 F4 Maués r. Brazil
163 F4 Maués Brazil
37 E4 Mauganj India
64 D3 Maughold Head headland Isle of Man
21 M2 Maug Islands is Northern Mariana Is Pacific Ocean
91 C5 Mauguio France
153 □2 Maui i. Hawaii U.S.A.
5 M7 Mauke i. Cook Islands Pacific Ocean
24 A2 Maukkadaw Myanmar
87 H4 Maulbronn Germany
92 D3 Maulde r. France
172 B3 Maule div. Chile
172 A3 Maule r. Chile
172 B3 Maule Chile
172 B4 Maule, L. del l. Chile
92 B2 Mauléon France
93 C6 Mauléon-Barousse France
93 B5 Mauléon-Licharre France
89 E4 Maulévrier France
171 B5 Maullín Chile
37 G4 Maulvi-Bazar Bangladesh
67 B2 Maumakeogh h. Rep. of Ireland
149 E5 Maumee r. Ohio U.S.A.
146 B4 Maumee Ohio U.S.A.
149 F5 Maumee Bay b. Michigan/Ohio U.S.A.
21 H8 Maumere Indonesia
67 B3 Maumturk Mts h. Rep. of Ireland
128 C2 Maun Botswana
153 □2 Mauna Kea volcano Hawaii U.S.A.
153 □2 Mauna Loa volcano Hawaii U.S.A.
153 □1 Maunalua B. b. Hawaii U.S.A.
8 F3 Maungahaumi mt. New Zealand
8 F3 Maungapohatu mt. New Zealand
8 F3 Maungataniwha mt. New Zealand
8 E1 Maungatapere New Zealand
8 E2 Maungaturoto New Zealand
24 A2 Maungdaw Myanmar
25 B4 Maungmagan Is is Myanmar
25 B4 Maungmagon Myanmar
134 F3 Maunoir, Lac l. N.W.T. Canada
36 D4 Mau Rampur India
88 D4 Maure-de-Bretagne France
93 E6 Maureillas-las-Illas France
93 C4 Maurens France
164 C3 Mauri r. Bolivia
92 E3 Mauriac France
12 B2 Maurice, L. salt flat S. Australia Australia
141 J3 Mauricie, Parc National de la nat. park Québec Canada
91 E3 Maurienne reg. France
116 C4 Mauritania country Africa
117 K7 Mauritius country Indian Ocean
109 G3 Mauro, Monte mt. Italy
88 C3 Mauron France
98 C3 Mauros mt. Spain
93 E4 Maurs France
93 E6 Maury France
91 C5 Maussanne-les-Alpilles France
148 B4 Mauston Wisconsin U.S.A.
81 E3 Mauterndorf Austria
81 F3 Mautern in Steiermark Austria
81 F2 Mauthausen Austria
80 D4 Mauthen Austria
93 C5 Mauvezin France
92 B2 Mauzé-sur-le-Mignon France
124 E3 Mava Congo(Zaire)
127 C7 Mavago Mozambique
131 H1 Mavamba South Africa
125 C7 Mavengue Angola
125 D7 Mavinga Angola
114 C2 Mavrochori Greece
114 C3 Mavrommati Greece
114 E2 Mavrothalassa Greece
114 D3 Mavrovouni mts Greece
131 F5 Mavuya South Africa
36 D3 Mawana India
125 B4 Mawanga Congo(Zaire)
32 B4 Ma Wang Dui China
25 B5 Mawdaung Pass pass Myanmar/Thailand
8 G3 Mawhai Pt pt New Zealand
24 B1 Mawhun Myanmar
126 D2 Māwiyah Yemen
24 B2 Mawkmai Myanmar
24 A2 Mawlaik Myanmar
Mawlamyine see Moulmein
37 G4 Mawphlang India
119 H2 Mawqaq Saudi Arabia
126 D2 Mawshij Yemen
179 D4 Mawson Australia Base Antarctica
179 D5 Mawson Coast coastal area Antarctica
179 D4 Mawson Escarpment escarpment Antarctica
179 B6 Mawson Pen. pen. Antarctica
25 B5 Maw Taung mt. Myanmar
150 C2 Max N. Dakota U.S.A.
126 E4 Maxaas Somalia
170 C2 Maxán Argentina
157 H4 Maxcanú Mexico
87 F4 Maxéville France
75 H3 Maxhütte-Haidhof Germany
108 A5 Maxia, Punta mt. Sardegna Italy
148 D5 Maxinkuckee, Lake l. Indiana U.S.A.
56 F3 Maxmo Finland
149 F2 Maxton Michigan U.S.A.
154 A2 Maxwell California U.S.A.
15 G4 Maxwelton Queensland Australia
45 P4 Maya r. Rus. Fed.
22 B2 Maya i. Indonesia
93 A5 Maya Spain
53 F2 Mayachka Ukraine
42 E3 Mayādīn Syria
159 D2 Mayaguana i. The Bahamas
158 D2 Mayaguana Passage chan. The Bahamas
145 □3 Mayagüez Puerto Rico
123 F4 Mayahi Niger
77 L1 Mayakovskoye Rus. Fed.
125 B4 Mayama Congo
39 C1 Mayamey Iran
157 H5 Maya Mountains mountain range Belize
32 D1 Mayan China
33 E3 Mayang China
159 □3 Mayaro div. Trinidad Trinidad and Tobago
29 G4 Maya-san mt. Japan
66 D5 Maybole Scotland U.K.
126 C2 Maych'ew Ethiopia
52 E1 Maydakovo Rus. Fed.
43 D1 Maydān Ikbis Turkey
126 C2 May Darashet' r. Ethiopia
39 G2 Maydā Shahr Afghanistan
159 □1 May Day Mts mts Jamaica
126 E2 Maydh Somalia
74 C2 Mayen Germany
89 E3 Mayenne div. Pays de la Loire France
89 E4 Mayenne r. France
89 E3 Mayenne France
155 F4 Mayer Arizona U.S.A.
136 F4 Mayerthorpe Alberta Canada
89 F4 Mayet France
53 F4 Mayevo Rus. Fed.
144 B4 Mayfield Kentucky U.S.A.
9 C5 Mayfield New Zealand
30 B3 Mayhan Mongolia
153 F5 Mayhill New Mexico U.S.A.
31 J3 Mayi r. China
66 F4 May, Isle of i. Scotland U.K.
47 J2 Maykain Kazakhstan
47 J3 Maykamys Kazakhstan
51 G6 Maykop Rus. Fed.
46 F3 Maylibash Kazakhstan
47 H4 Mayly-Say Kyrgyzstan
47 L2 Mayma Rus. Fed.
24 B2 Maymyo Myanmar
50 H4 Mayna Rus. Fed.
15 E4 Mayne watercourse Queensland Australia
38 A2 Mayni India
141 G4 Maynooth Ontario Canada
67 B3 Mayo div. Rep. of Ireland
171 B6 Mayo r. Argentina
136 B2 Mayo Yukon Terr. Canada
173 G3 Mayo, 25 de Buenos Aires Argentina
172 D4 Mayo, 25 de La Pampa Argentina
172 C3 Mayo, 25 de Mendoza Argentina
173 J3 Mayo, 25 de Uruguay
124 B2 Mayo Alim Cameroon
23 C5 Mayo Bay b. Philippines
123 G5 Mayo-Belwa Nigeria
124 B2 Mayo Darlé Cameroon
124 B2 Mayo-Kébbi div. Chad
124 B4 Mayoko Congo
136 B2 Mayo Lake l. Yukon Terr. Canada
164 C2 Mayo Mayo Bolivia
23 B3 Mayon volcano Philippines
99 H4 Mayor r. Castilla-La Mancha Spain
99 H3 Mayor r. León/La Rioja Spain
173 F5 Mayor Buratovich Argentina
99 G1 Mayor, Cabo c. Spain
99 F4 Mayorga Spain
8 F2 Mayor I. i. New Zealand
159 □3 Mayoro Bay b. Trinidad Trinidad and Tobago
165 D3 Mayor Pablo Lagerenza Paraguay
127 E7 Mayotte terr. Africa
159 □1 May Pen Jamaica
23 B2 Mayraira Point pt Philippines
91 C4 Mayres France
80 C3 Mayrhofen Austria
42 F4 Maysān div. Iraq
69 F4 Mayschoß Germany
67 E2 May's Corner Northern Ireland U.K.
52 H1 Mayskiy Rus. Fed.
53 G1 Mayskiy Rus. Fed.
27 N1 Mayskiy Rus. Fed.
146 B5 Maysville Kentucky U.S.A.
125 B4 Mayumba Gabon
37 E3 Mayum La pass China
38 B4 Mayuram India
149 F4 Mayville Michigan U.S.A.
150 D2 Mayville N. Dakota U.S.A.
146 D3 Mayville New York U.S.A.
148 C4 Mayville Wisconsin U.S.A.
150 C3 Maywood Nebraska U.S.A.
45 P3 Mayya Rus. Fed.
173 F4 Maza Argentina
125 E7 Mazabuka Zambia
166 B1 Mazagão Brazil
100 C3 Mazagón Spain
93 E5 Mazamet France
93 D3 Mazan France
38 C1 Mazar China
43 C4 Mazār Jordan
110 B5 Mazara del Vallo Sicilia Italy
39 F1 Mazār-e Sharīf Afghanistan
99 H4 Mazarete Spain
171 C6 Mazarredo Argentina
103 B7 Mazarrón Spain
103 B7 Mazarrón, Golfo de b. Spain
163 F2 Mazaruni r. Guyana
47 K5 Mazartagh mt. China
156 C2 Mazatán Mexico
157 H6 Mazatenango Guatemala
156 D4 Mazatlán Mexico
155 G4 Mazatzal Peak summit Arizona U.S.A.
131 G6 Mazeepa Bay South Africa
54 C3 Mažeikiai Lithuania
123 F3 Mazelet well Niger
131 F4 Mazelspoort l. South Africa
93 D4 Mazeyrolles France
46 D3 Mazhambet Kazakhstan
113 F6 Mazı Turkey
92 B2 Mazières-en-Gâtine France
131 J2 Mazimechopes r. Mozambique
54 C3 Mazirbe Latvia
156 C2 Mazocahui Mexico
164 C3 Mazocruz Peru
127 C6 Mazomora Tanzania
127 E2 Mazowe r. Zimbabwe
43 C4 Mazra Jordan
119 E5 Mazrub well Sudan
54 D3 Mazsalaca Latvia
114 C1 Mažučište Macedonia
129 D3 Mazunga Zimbabwe
77 K1 Mazurski Kanal canal Poland/Rus. Fed.
77 K2 Mazurski Park Narodowy nat. park Poland
51 D4 Mazyr Belarus
110 D5 Mazzarino Sicilia Italy
110 D5 Mazzarrone Sicilia Italy
131 H3 Mbabane Swaziland
122 A4 Mbacké Senegal
122 D5 Mbahiakro Côte d'Ivoire
124 C3 Mbaïki Central African Rep.
124 B2 Mbakaou, Lac de l. Cameroon
127 B6 Mbala Zambia
129 D3 Mbalabala Zimbabwe
124 B3 Mbalam Cameroon
127 B4 Mbale Uganda
124 B3 Mbalmayo Cameroon
124 B2 Mbam r. Cameroon
127 B7 Mbamba Bay Tanzania
124 C4 Mbandaka Congo(Zaire)
124 B3 Mbang Cameroon
124 A3 Mbanga Cameroon
125 B5 M'banza Congo Angola
125 B5 Mbanza-Ngungu Congo(Zaire)
127 B5 Mbarara Uganda
124 D3 Mbari r. Central African Rep.
127 C6 Mbarika Mountains mts Tanzania
131 J3 Mbaswana South Africa
124 C3 Mbata Central African Rep.
127 B7 Mbati Zambia
122 D5 Mbatto Côte d'Ivoire
124 B2 Mbé Cameroon
127 C6 Mbemkuru r. Tanzania
124 B2 Mbengwi Cameroon
124 B2 Mbenqué Côte d'Ivoire
129 D3 Mberengwa Zimbabwe
127 B6 Mbeya div. Tanzania
127 B6 Mbeya Tanzania
124 C3 Mbi r. Central African Rep.
124 B4 Mbigou Gabon
124 A4 Mbilapé Gabon
124 B4 Mbinda Congo
127 C7 Mbinga Tanzania
124 A3 Mbini Equatorial Guinea
129 E3 Mbizi Zimbabwe
127 B6 Mbizi Mts mts Tanzania
124 E2 Mboki Central African Rep.
124 B3 Mbomo Congo
124 D2 Mbomou div. Central African Rep.
124 D3 Mbomou r. Central African Rep.
114 B2 Mborje Albania
122 A3 Mboro Senegal
124 B2 Mbouda Cameroon
122 A4 Mbour Senegal
120 B5 Mbout Mauritania
124 C2 Mbrès Central African Rep.
125 D5 Mbuji-Mayi Congo(Zaire)
127 C5 Mbulu Tanzania
131 H3 Mbuluzi r. Swaziland
127 C6 Mbuyuni Tanzania
120 D3 Mcherrah reg. Algeria
127 C6 Mchinga Tanzania
127 B7 Mchinji Malawi
127 B6 Mdandu Tanzania
131 F6 Mdantsane South Africa
121 F1 M'Daourouch Algeria
120 C4 Mdennah reg. Mali/Mauritania
111 □ Mdina Malta
101 E5 Mdiq Morocco
140 D2 Mead Ontario Canada
151 C4 Meade Kansas U.S.A.
98 B3 Meadela Portugal
155 E3 Mead, Lake l. Arizona/Nevada U.S.A.
137 H4 Meadow Lake Saskatchewan Canada
137 H4 Meadow Lake Provincial Park nat. park Saskatchewan Canada
155 E3 Meadow Valley Wash r. Nevada U.S.A.
146 C4 Meadville Pennsylvania U.S.A.
140 E4 Meaford Ontario Canada
28 K2 Meaken-dake volcano Japan
66 A2 Mealasta Island i. Scotland U.K.
98 B4 Mealhada Portugal
66 D4 Meall a'Bhuiridh mt. Scotland U.K.
139 J3 Mealy Mountains mountain range Newfoundland Canada
39 E1 Meana Turkmenistan
108 B5 Meana Sardo Sardegna Italy
15 G5 Meandarra Queensland Australia
136 F3 Meander River Alberta Canada
23 C5 Meares i. Indonesia
166 D1 Mearim r. Brazil
63 E2 Mease r. England U.K.
63 E2 Measham England U.K.
67 E3 Meath div. Rep. of Ireland
92 E2 Meaulne France
86 B4 Meaux France
125 B5 Mebridege r. Angola
Mecca see Makkah
147 H2 Mechanic Falls Maine U.S.A.
146 B4 Mechanicsburg Ohio U.S.A.
148 B5 Mechanicsville Iowa U.S.A.
69 C3 Mechelen div. Antwerpen Belgium
69 C3 Mechelen Mechelen Belgium
121 D2 Mecheria Algeria
74 B2 Mechernich Germany
118 C5 Mechimeré Chad
173 H5 Mechongue Argentina
73 L2 Mechowo Poland
113 F4 Mecidiye Turkey
75 J3 Měčín Czech Rep.
101 G4 Mecina-Bombarón Spain
42 C1 Mecitözü Turkey
74 E5 Meckenbeuren Germany
74 C2 Meckenheim Germany
73 G1 Mecklenburger Bucht b. Germany
73 G2 Mecklenburgische Seenplatte reg. Germany
73 H2 Mecklenburg-Vorpommern div. Germany
129 F1 Meconta Mozambique
129 F1 Mecubúri r. Mozambique
129 F1 Mecubúri Mozambique
127 C7 Mecula Mozambique
98 C2 Meda mt. Spain
16 D3 Meda r. Western Australia Australia

98 C4 **Meda** Portugal
38 B2 **Medak** India
22 D4 **Medang i.** Indonesia
20 C6 **Medan** Indonesia
170 C3 **Medano** Argentina
173 H2 **Médanos** *Entre Ríos* Argentina
173 F5 **Médanos** Argentina
171 C6 **Médanosa, Pta pt** Argentina
162 D1 **Médanos de Coro, Parque Nacional nat. park** Venezuela
38 C4 **Medawachchiya** Sri Lanka
38 B2 **Medchal** India
147 K2 **Meddybemps L. l.** *Maine* U.S.A.
106 C3 **Mede** Italy
121 E1 **Médéa** Algeria
72 D4 **Medebach** Germany
169 H2 **Medeiros Neto** Brazil
98 C4 **Medelim** Portugal
162 B2 **Medellín** Colombia
68 D2 **Medemblik** Netherlands
63 E1 **Meden r.** *England* U.K.
121 G2 **Medenine** Tunisia
77 M6 **Medenychi** Ukraine
120 A5 **Mederdra** Mauritania
43 C1 **Medetsiz T. mt.** Turkey
152 B3 **Medford** *Oregon* U.S.A.
148 B3 **Medford** *Wisconsin* U.S.A.
147 F5 **Medford Farms** *New Jersey* U.S.A.
112 G2 **Medgidia** Romania
148 B5 **Media** *Illinois* U.S.A.
172 D3 **Media Luna** Argentina
102 C3 **Mediana** Spain
101 J4 **Mediana Naranja, Pta de la headland** Spain
168 A6 **Medianeira** Brazil
112 E1 **Mediaș** Romania
152 C2 **Medical Lake** *Washington* U.S.A.
107 F4 **Medicina** Italy
152 F3 **Medicine Bow** *Wyoming* U.S.A.
152 F3 **Medicine Bow Mts mountain range** *Wyoming* U.S.A.
152 F3 **Medicine Bow Peak summit** *Wyoming* U.S.A.
137 G4 **Medicine Hat** *Alberta* Canada
151 D4 **Medicine Lodge** *Kansas* U.S.A.
146 D3 **Medina** *New York* U.S.A.
146 C4 **Medina** *Ohio* U.S.A.
169 H2 **Medina** Brazil
Medina *see* **Al Madīnah**
99 H3 **Medinaceli** Spain
99 F3 **Medina del Campo** Spain
99 G2 **Medina de Pomar** Spain
99 E3 **Medina de Rioseco** Spain
122 B4 **Medina Gounas** Senegal
122 A4 **Médina Sabakh** Senegal
100 E4 **Medina-Sidonia** Spain
127 □4 **Medine** Mauritius
37 F5 **Medinīpur** India
92 B3 **Médis** France
94 D4 **Mediterranean Sea sea**
105 A7 **Medjerda, Monts de la mts** Algeria
46 E2 **Mednogorsk** Rus. Fed.
52 B1 **Mednoye** Rus. Fed.
176 G2 **Mednyy, Ostrov i.** Rus. Fed.
92 B3 **Médoc reg.** France
124 B3 **Médouneu** Gabon
77 J1 **Medovoye** Rus. Fed.
172 C2 **Medrano** Argentina
Medu Kongkar *see* **Maizhokunggar**
107 H4 **Medulin** Croatia
78 F5 **Medumurje reg.** Croatia
107 G3 **Meduna r.** Italy
80 D4 **Meduno** Italy
107 G3 **Medveda** Yugoslavia
52 H1 **Medvedevo** Rus. Fed.
52 C1 **Medveditsa r.** *Tver'* Rus. Fed.
51 H5 **Medveditsa r.** *Volgograd* Rus. Fed.
78 E6 **Medvednica mts** Croatia
50 J3 **Medvedok** Rus. Fed.
53 G1 **Medvenka** Rus. Fed.
45 S2 **Medvezh'i, O-va is** Rus. Fed.
50 E2 **Medvezh'yegorsk** Rus. Fed.
81 F4 **Medvode** Slovenia
63 G3 **Medway r.** *England* U.K.
10 □2 **Medwin Pt pt** *Christmas I.* Indian Ocean
52 H2 **Medyana** Rus. Fed.
77 L6 **Medyka** Poland
52 B2 **Medyn'** Rus. Fed.
53 B2 **Medzhybizh** Ukraine
79 L2 **Medzilaborce** Slovakia
17 A5 **Meeberrie** *Western Australia* Australia
68 E1 **Meeden** Netherlands
17 B5 **Meekatharra** *Western Australia* Australia
155 H1 **Meeker** *Colorado* U.S.A.
154 B2 **Meeks Bay** *California* U.S.A.
139 J4 **Meelpaeg Res. resr** *Newfoundland* Canada
64 A3 **Meenanarwa** Rep. of Ireland
75 H2 **Meerane** Germany
54 E2 **Meerapalu** Estonia
72 B4 **Meerbusch** Germany
69 D3 **Meerhout** Belgium
68 C3 **Meerkerk** Netherlands
74 E5 **Meersburg** Germany
69 D4 **Meerssen** Netherlands
36 D3 **Meerut** India
152 E2 **Meeteetse** *Wyoming* U.S.A.
69 D3 **Meeuwen** Belgium
126 C4 **Mēga** Ethiopia
126 C4 **Mega Escarpment escarpment** Ethiopia/Kenya
114 C3 **Megala Kalyvia** Greece
114 E2 **Megali Panagia** Greece
126 D3 **Megalo** Ethiopia
114 C3 **Megalochori** Greece
115 D5 **Megalopoli** Greece
114 B4 **Meganisi i.** Greece
139 F4 **Mégantic** *Québec* Canada
115 E5 **Megara** Greece
30 B1 **Meget** Rus. Fed.
82 B3 **Megève** France
37 G4 **Meghalaya** India
37 F5 **Meghāsani mt.** India
56 G1 **Mehamn** Norway
36 A4 **Mehar** Pakistan
17 B4 **Meharry, Mt mt.** *Western Australia* Australia
59 G1 **Mehedeby** Sweden
36 D5 **Mehekar** India
37 G5 **Meherpur** Bangladesh
146 E6 **Meherrin r.** *Virginia* U.S.A.
7 □10 **Mehetia i.** *French Polynesia* Pacific Ocean
37 E4 **Mehndawal** India
42 F2 **Mehrābān** Iran
39 C4 **Mehrān watercourse** Iran
42 F3 **Mehrān** Iraq
74 B2 **Mehren** Germany
74 B3 **Mehring** Germany
39 C3 **Mehriz** Iran
39 G2 **Mehtar Lām** Afghanistan
89 H4 **Mehun-sur-Yèvre** France
33 F3 **Mei r.** China
168 D3 **Meia Ponte r.** Brazil
124 B2 **Meiganga** Cameroon
64 B3 **Meigh** *Northern Ireland* U.K.
135 J2 **Meighen I. i.** *N.W.T.* Canada
32 C2 **Meigu** China
69 D3 **Meijel** Netherlands
91 E3 **Meije, La mt.** France
69 D3 **Meijnweg, Nationaal Park De** Netherlands
65 E1 **Meikleour** *Scotland* U.K.
65 F2 **Meikle Says Law h.** *Scotland* U.K.
24 A2 **Meiktila** Myanmar
83 D1 **Meilen** Switzerland
93 B5 **Meilhan** France
93 C4 **Meilhan-sur-Garonne** France
88 D3 **Meillac** France
90 E2 **Meillerie** France
Meilü *see* **Wuchuan**
98 C4 **Meimoa** Portugal
106 C3 **Meina** Italy
73 F3 **Meine** Germany
72 F3 **Meinersen** Germany
74 F2 **Meiningen** Germany
98 C1 **Meira** Spain
98 C1 **Meira, Serra de mountain range** Spain
82 D2 **Meiringen** Switzerland
74 C3 **Meisenheim** Germany
32 C2 **Meishan** China
73 J4 **Meißen** Germany
87 G4 **Meißenheim** Germany
32 D3 **Meitan** China
75 F4 **Meitingen** Germany
69 D5 **Meix-devant-Virton** Belgium
31 J3 **Meixi** China
32 D1 **Mei Xian** China
Mei Xian *see* **Meizhou**
33 G3 **Meizhou** China
36 C4 **Mej r.** India
120 C4 **Mejaouda well** Mauritania
170 C2 **Mejicana mt.** Argentina
164 B4 **Mejillones** Chile
164 B4 **Mejillones del Sur, B. de b.** Chile
172 E6 **Mejillón, Punta pt** Argentina
119 G4 **Mekadio well** Sudan
124 B3 **Mékambo** Gabon
126 C2 **Mek'elē** Ethiopia
122 A3 **Mékhé** Senegal
36 B3 **Mekhtar** Pakistan
81 F4 **Mekinje** Slovenia
120 C2 **Meknès** Morocco
Mekong r. *see* **Mènam Khong**
25 D6 **Mekong, Mouths of the river mouth** Vietnam
107 G2 **Mel** Italy
172 B3 **Melado r.** Chile
25 C7 **Melaka div.** Malaysia
25 C7 **Melaka** Malaysia
129 F2 **Melala r.** Mozambique
22 A2 **Melalo, Tg pt** Indonesia
115 F7 **Melampes** Greece
176 F6 **Melanesia is** Pacific Ocean
114 C2 **Melanthi** Greece
22 C2 **Melawi r.** Indonesia
82 A1 **Melay** France
63 G2 **Melbourn** *England* U.K.
145 D6 **Melbourne** *Florida* U.S.A.
13 F4 **Melbourne** *Victoria* Australia
66 □2 **Melby** *Scotland* U.K.
178 □3 **Melchers, Kapp c.** *Svalbard* Arctic Ocean
157 H5 **Melchor de Mencos** Guatemala
171 B6 **Melchor, I. i.** Chile
107 G4 **Meldola** Italy
72 E1 **Meldorf** Germany
140 D4 **Meldrum Bay** *Ontario* Canada
106 C4 **Mele** Italy
106 C5 **Mele, Capo pt** Italy
106 D3 **Melegnano** Italy
23 □1 **Melekeiok** Palau
52 E1 **Melekhovo** Rus. Fed.
111 H2 **Melendugno** Italy
52 E2 **Melenki** Rus. Fed.
88 D3 **Melesse** France
46 E2 **Meleuz** Rus. Fed.
124 C1 **Mélfi** Chad
109 H4 **Melfi** Italy
137 J4 **Melfort** *Saskatchewan* Canada
166 B1 **Melgaço** Brazil
98 B2 **Melgaço** Portugal
101 G1 **Melgar r.** Spain
99 F2 **Melgar de Fernamental** Spain
98 D3 **Melgar de Tera** Spain
88 B4 **Melgven** France
56 C3 **Melhus** Norway
22 B2 **Meliau** Indonesia
63 E3 **Melick** Netherlands
98 C2 **Melide** Spain
100 B2 **Melides** Portugal
115 C5 **Meligalas** Greece
114 D2 **Meliki** Greece
168 D6 **Mel, Ilha do i.** Brazil
121 D1 **Melilla** Spain
111 E5 **Melilli** *Sicilia* Italy
171 B5 **Melimoyu, Mte mt.** Chile
9 B6 **Melina, Mt mt.** New Zealand
173 G2 **Melincué** Argentina
173 G2 **Melincué, L. l.** Argentina
53 F2 **Melioratyvne** Ukraine
172 B5 **Melipeuco** Chile
172 B2 **Melipilla** Chile
90 E1 **Mélisey** France
137 J5 **Melita** *Manitoba* Canada
114 C2 **Meliti** Greece
111 E5 **Melito di Porto Salvo** Italy
53 F3 **Melitopol'** Ukraine
114 D3 **Melivoia** Greece
81 G2 **Melk div.** Austria
81 G2 **Melk r.** Austria
81 G2 **Melk** Austria
126 C4 **Melka Guba** Ethiopia
130 A4 **Melkbospunt pt** South Africa
130 B6 **Melkbosstrand** South Africa
47 H3 **Melkosopochnik reg.** Kazakhstan
131 G1 **Melkrivier** South Africa
62 D3 **Melksham** *England* U.K.
106 E3 **Mella r.** Italy
88 B4 **Mellac** France
56 G2 **Mellakoski** Finland
59 E2 **Mellan Fryken l.** Sweden
56 E3 **Mellansel** Sweden
92 B2 **Melle** France
72 D3 **Melle** Germany
148 B2 **Mellen** *Wisconsin* U.S.A.
59 E2 **Mellerud** Sweden
111 □ **Mellieha** Malta
111 □ **Mellieha Bay b.** Malta
54 C1 **Melliliä** Finland
171 B6 **Mellizo Sur, C. mt.** Chile
100 E5 **Mellousa** Morocco
74 F2 **Mellrichstadt** Germany
72 D2 **Mellum i.** Germany
118 C5 **Melmele watercourse** Chad
131 H4 **Melmoth** South Africa
114 E1 **Melnik** Bulgaria
78 D1 **Mělník** Czech Rep.
54 F1 **Mel'nikovo** Rus. Fed.
172 F3 **Melo** Argentina
173 K2 **Melo** Uruguay
127 C7 **Meloco** Mozambique
131 F4 **Meloding** South Africa
51 H1 **Melogorskoye** Rus. Fed.
22 E4 **Melolo** Indonesia
124 A2 **Mélong** Cameroon
66 F5 **Melrose** *Scotland* U.K.
83 E1 **Mels** Switzerland
87 G2 **Melsbach** Germany
72 E4 **Melsungen** Germany
23 A5 **Melta, Mt mt.** Malaysia
65 G4 **Meltham** *England* U.K.
63 F2 **Melton Mowbray** *England* U.K.
52 G2 **Mel'tsany** Rus. Fed.
22 B1 **Meluan** Malaysia
127 C7 **Meluco** Mozambique
86 B4 **Melun** France
126 B2 **Melut** Sudan
137 J4 **Melville** *Saskatchewan* Canada
14 D2 **Melville B. b.** *Northern Terr.* Australia
135 M2 **Melville Bugt b.** Greenland
15 F2 **Melville, C. c.** *Queensland* Australia
23 A5 **Melville, C. c.** Philippines
14 B1 **Melville I. i.** *Northern Terr.* Australia
14 B1 **Melville I. Abor. Land res.** *Northern Terr.* Australia
134 G2 **Melville Island i.** *N.W.T.* Canada
139 J3 **Melville, Lake l.** *Newfoundland* Canada
135 K3 **Melville Peninsula pen.** *N.W.T.* Canada
67 C2 **Melvin, Lough l.** Rep. of Ireland
79 J5 **Mélykút** Hungary
45 T3 **Melyuveyem** Rus. Fed.
106 D3 **Melzo** Italy
114 A2 **Memaliaj** Albania
37 E2 **Mêmar Co salt lake** China
129 G1 **Memba** Mozambique
129 G1 **Memba, Baia de b.** Mozambique
21 L7 **Memberamo r.** Indonesia
22 D4 **Memboro** Indonesia
90 D1 **Membrey** France
100 C1 **Membrio** Spain
131 G3 **Memel** South Africa
54 D3 **Memel's r.** Lithuania
75 F3 **Memmelsdorf** Germany
74 F5 **Memmingen** Germany
80 B3 **Memmingerberg** Germany
86 D3 **Mémorial Américain h.** France
22 B1 **Mempawah** Indonesia
148 A5 **Memphis** *Missouri* U.S.A.
145 B5 **Memphis** *Tennessee* U.S.A.
151 C5 **Memphis** *Texas* U.S.A.
119 F2 **Memphis** Egypt
141 J4 **Memphrémagog, Lac l.** *Québec* Canada
28 J2 **Memuro-dake mt.** Japan
151 E5 **Mena** *Arkansas* U.S.A.
53 E1 **Mena** Ukraine
129 G3 **Menabe mts** Madagascar
173 J2 **Menafra** Uruguay
106 D2 **Menaggio** Italy
83 G3 **Menago r.** Italy
62 B1 **Menai Bridge** *Wales* U.K.
62 B1 **Menai Strait chan.** *Wales* U.K.
123 E3 **Ménaka** Mali
68 D1 **Menaldum** Netherlands
24 C3 **Mènam Khong r.** Asia
129 G4 **Menarandra r.** Madagascar
151 D6 **Menard** *Texas* U.S.A.
101 F1 **Menasalbas** Spain
148 C3 **Menasha** *Wisconsin* U.S.A.
92 E2 **Menat** France
87 E4 **Menaucourt** France
101 G3 **Mencal mt.** Spain
22 A2 **Mendanau i.** Indonesia
169 G3 **Mendanha** Brazil
22 A1 **Mendarik i.** Indonesia
102 B1 **Mendaur mt.** Spain
22 C2 **Mendawai r.** Indonesia
22 C2 **Mendawai** Indonesia
91 B4 **Mende** France
126 C3 **Mendebo Mountains mountain range** Ethiopia
136 C3 **Mendenhall Glacier gl.** *Alaska* U.S.A.
114 D3 **Mendenitsa** Greece
72 C4 **Menden (Sauerland)** Germany
113 F5 **Menderes** Turkey
157 F3 **Méndez** Mexico
126 C3 **Mendī** Ethiopia
6 □1 **Mendi** P.N.G.
74 C2 **Mendig** Germany
62 D3 **Mendip Hills h.** *England* U.K.
93 B5 **Menditte** France
173 K2 **Mendizabal** Uruguay
154 A2 **Mendocino** *California* U.S.A.
152 A3 **Mendocino, C. c.** *California* U.S.A.
177 K3 **Mendocino Seascarp sea feature** Pacific Ocean
110 C5 **Mendola r.** *Sicilia* Italy
148 E4 **Mendon** *Michigan* U.S.A.
154 B3 **Mendota** *California* U.S.A.
148 C5 **Mendota** *Illinois* U.S.A.
148 C4 **Mendota, Lake l.** *Wisconsin* U.S.A.
172 C3 **Mendoza div.** Argentina
172 C2 **Mendoza r.** Argentina
172 C2 **Mendoza** Argentina
83 D3 **Mendrisio** Switzerland
88 C3 **Ménéac** France
162 C1 **Mene de Mauroa** Venezuela
106 D4 **Menegosa, Monte mt.** Italy
162 C2 **Mene Grande** Venezuela
42 A2 **Menemen** Turkey
69 B4 **Menen** Belgium
92 C3 **Ménesplet** France
92 E3 **Menet** France
89 H4 **Menetou-Salon** France
88 B3 **Menez Bré h.** France
88 A3 **Menez Hom h.** France
110 B5 **Menfi** *Sicilia* Italy
124 B2 **Meng r.** Cameroon
33 G1 **Mengcheng** China
74 E4 **Mengen** Germany
51 E7 **Mengen** Turkey
87 H2 **Mengerskirchen** Germany
81 F4 **Mengeš** Slovenia
22 A3 **Menggala** Indonesia
32 C4 **Menghai** China
101 G3 **Mengíbar** Spain
22 C2 **Mengkatip** Indonesia
80 D2 **Mengkofen** Germany
22 E2 **Mengkoka, G. mt.** Indonesia
32 C4 **Mengla** China
32 B4 **Menglian** China
32 E3 **Mengshan** China
31 F6 **Mengyin** China
32 C4 **Mengzi** China
62 B4 **Menheniot** *England* U.K.
114 C3 **Menidi** Greece
92 B2 **Ménigoute** France
139 G3 **Menihek** *Newfoundland* Canada
139 G3 **Menihek Lakes lakes** *Newfoundland* Canada
87 E4 **Ménil-la-Tour** France
87 F4 **Ménil-sur-Belvitte** France
Menin *see* **Menen**
13 E3 **Menindee** *New South Wales* Australia
13 E3 **Menindee L. l.** *New South Wales* Australia
12 D3 **Meningie** *S. Australia* Australia
45 O3 **Menkere** Rus. Fed.
114 B2 **Menkulas** Albania
126 C2 **Menna r.** Ethiopia
86 B4 **Mennecy** France
89 G4 **Mennetou-sur-Cher** France
114 E1 **Menoikio mts** Greece
148 D3 **Menominee r.** *Wisconsin* U.S.A.
148 D3 **Menominee** *Michigan* U.S.A.
148 C4 **Menomonee Falls** *Wisconsin* U.S.A.
148 B3 **Menomonie** *Wisconsin* U.S.A.
125 C6 **Menongue** Angola
103 □ **Menorca airport** Spain
103 □ **Menorca i.** *Islas Baleares* Spain
90 B1 **Menou** France
91 D4 **Mens** France
23 A6 **Mensalong** Indonesia
92 C3 **Mensignac** France
72 C3 **Menslage** Germany
109 E2 **Mentana** Italy
22 C2 **Mentaya r.** Indonesia
25 C7 **Mentekab** Malaysia
73 F4 **Menteroda** Germany
100 C2 **Mentiras h.** Portugal
101 H2 **Mentiras mt.** Spain
155 H4 **Mentmore** *New Mexico* U.S.A.
22 A2 **Mentok** Indonesia
91 F5 **Menton** France
146 C4 **Mentor** *Ohio* U.S.A.
99 F4 **Méntrida** Spain
22 C2 **Menukung** Indonesia
22 E1 **Menunu** Indonesia
52 G2 **Menya r.** Rus. Fed.
22 D1 **Menyapa, G. mt.** Indonesia
30 B5 **Menyuan** China
30 D2 **Menza r.** Rus. Fed.
30 D2 **Menza** Rus. Fed.
121 F1 **Menzel Bourguiba** Tunisia
105 C7 **Menzel Temime** Tunisia
17 C6 **Menzies** *Western Australia* Australia
179 D4 **Menzies, Mt mt.** Antarctica
82 D1 **Menznau** Switzerland
92 D2 **Méobecq** France
107 G3 **Meolo** Italy
156 D2 **Meoqui** Mexico
127 B7 **Meponda** Mozambique
68 E2 **Meppel** Netherlands
72 C3 **Meppen** Germany
131 F4 **Meqheleng** South Africa
102 D3 **Mequinenza** Spain
89 G4 **Mer** France
106 D2 **Mera r.** Italy
50 G3 **Mera r.** Rus. Fed.
107 J4 **Merag** Croatia
22 D1 **Merah** Indonesia
42 D3 **Merak** Indonesia
56 C3 **Meråker** Norway
150 F4 **Meramec r.** *Missouri* U.S.A.
107 F2 **Merano** Italy
106 D3 **Merate** Italy
131 E2 **Meratswe r.** Botswana
21 M8 **Merauke** Indonesia
13 E3 **Merbein** *Victoria* Australia
69 C4 **Merbes-le-Château** Belgium
100 D3 **Mercadal** Spain
91 E4 **Mercantour, Parc National du nat. park** France
107 G5 **Mercatino Conca** Italy
109 G4 **Mercato San Severino** Italy
154 B3 **Merced** *California* U.S.A.
172 B1 **Mercedario, Co mt.** Argentina
173 H3 **Mercedes** *Buenos Aires* Argentina
172 E2 **Mercedes** *San Luis* Argentina
170 E2 **Mercedes** Argentina
173 H2 **Mercedes** Uruguay
146 A4 **Mercer** *Ohio* U.S.A.
148 B2 **Mercer** *Wisconsin* U.S.A.
169 G4 **Mercês** Brazil
75 F4 **Merching** Germany
69 C4 **Merchtem** Belgium
43 C1 **Mercimek** Turkey
92 D3 **Mercœur** France
109 G4 **Mercogliano** Italy
82 B3 **Mercury** France
8 E2 **Mercury Islands is** New Zealand
135 M3 **Mercy, C. headland** *N.W.T.* Canada
88 A3 **Mer d'Iroise g.** France
88 C3 **Merdrignac** France
62 D3 **Mere** *England* U.K.
69 B4 **Mere** Belgium
89 H4 **Méreau** France
147 H3 **Meredith** *New Hampshire* U.S.A.
171 D7 **Meredith, C. c.** Falkland Is.
151 C5 **Meredith, Lake l.** *Texas* U.S.A.
151 C5 **Meredith Nat. Recreation Area, Lake res.** *Texas* U.S.A.
148 B6 **Meredosia** *Illinois* U.S.A.
121 E3 **Meredoua** Algeria
53 G2 **Merefa** Ukraine
6 □2 **Mere Lava i.** Vanuatu
69 B4 **Merelbeke** Belgium
74 D2 **Merenberg** Germany
93 D6 **Mérens-les-Vals** France
86 B4 **Méréville** France
118 E4 **Merga Oasis oasis** Sudan
106 C3 **Mergozzo** Italy
25 B4 **Mergui** Myanmar
25 B5 **Mergui Archipelago is** Myanmar
12 E3 **Meribah** *S. Australia* Australia
91 E3 **Méribel-les-Allues** France
113 F4 **Meriç r.** Greece/Turkey
113 F4 **Meriç** Turkey
115 F5 **Merichas** Greece
157 H4 **Mérida** Mexico
100 D2 **Mérida** Spain
162 C2 **Mérida** Venezuela
162 C2 **Mérida, Cordillera de mountain range** Venezuela
147 G4 **Meriden** *Connecticut* U.S.A.
154 B2 **Meridian** *California* U.S.A.
151 F5 **Meridian** *Mississippi* U.S.A.
170 D4 **Meridiano** Argentina
120 D2 **Mèridja** Algeria
6 □2 **Merig i.** Vanuatu
93 B4 **Mérignac** France
56 G2 **Merijärvi** Finland
57 F3 **Merikarvia** Finland
15 G4 **Merinda** *Queensland* Australia
91 D5 **Mérindol** France
71 C4 **Mering** Germany
12 E3 **Meringur** *Victoria* Australia
163 G3 **Merirumã** Brazil
15 G5 **Merivale r.** *Queensland* Australia
23 □2 **Merizo** *Guam* Pacific Ocean
47 H4 **Merke** Kazakhstan
151 C5 **Merkel** *Texas* U.S.A.
75 F3 **Merkendorf** Germany
77 N1 **Merkinė** Lithuania
75 J3 **Merklín** Czech Rep.
72 C3 **Merklingen** Germany
69 C3 **Merksplas** Belgium
54 D4 **Merkys r.** Lithuania
89 G1 **Mer-les-Bains** France
88 B4 **Merlevenez** France
25 □ **Merlimau, P. i.** Singapore
53 F1 **Merlo r.** Ukraine
172 E2 **Merlo** Argentina
15 E2 **Merluna** *Queensland* Australia
16 B3 **Mermaid Reef reef** *Western Australia* Australia
79 G5 **Mernye** Hungary
89 B1 **Mero r.** Spain
112 C3 **Merošina** Yugoslavia
119 F4 **Merowe** Sudan
17 B6 **Merredin** *Western Australia* Australia
66 D5 **Merrick h.** *Scotland* U.K.
141 H4 **Merrickville** *Ontario* Canada
148 C3 **Merrill** *Wisconsin* U.S.A.
148 D5 **Merrillville** *Indiana* U.S.A.
150 C3 **Merriman** *Nebraska* U.S.A.
130 D5 **Merriman** South Africa
62 D4 **Merriott** *England* U.K.
136 E4 **Merritt** *B.C.* Canada
145 D6 **Merritt Island** *Florida* U.S.A.
13 G2 **Merrygoen** *New South Wales* Australia
126 D2 **Mersa Fatma** Eritrea
69 E5 **Mersch** Luxembourg
108 D1 **Merse r.** Italy
73 G4 **Merseburg** Germany
65 F4 **Mersey est.** *England* U.K.
65 E4 **Merseyside div.** *England* U.K.
Mersin *see* **İçel**
25 C7 **Mersing** Malaysia
54 C3 **Mērsrags** Latvia
36 C4 **Merta** India
109 F3 **Merta, la mt.** Italy
69 E5 **Mertert** Luxembourg
62 C3 **Merthyr Tydfil div.** *Wales* U.K.
62 C3 **Merthyr Tydfil** *Wales* U.K.
127 C4 **Merti** Kenya
80 B2 **Mertingen** Germany
100 C3 **Mértola** Portugal
179 B6 **Mertz Gl. gl.** Antarctica
87 G4 **Mertzwiller** France
127 C5 **Meru crater** Tanzania
86 B3 **Méru** France
127 C4 **Meru** Kenya
39 E3 **Meruí** Pakistan
23 A5 **Merutai** Malaysia
Merv *see* **Mary**
90 D2 **Mervans** France
86 B2 **Merville** France
130 C6 **Merweville** South Africa
86 C4 **Méry-sur-Seine** France
82 C1 **Merzhausen** Germany
42 C1 **Merzifon** Turkey
74 B3 **Merzig** Germany
179 B2 **Merz Pen. pen.** Antarctica
102 A3 **Mesa r.** Spain
155 G5 **Mesa** *Arizona* U.S.A.
131 F3 **Mesa** South Africa
148 A2 **Mesabi Range h.** *Minnesota* U.S.A.
162 C3 **Mesa de Iguaje h.** Colombia
99 G5 **Mesa de Ocaña reg.** Spain
153 D6 **Mesa de S. Carlos h.** Mexico
162 C3 **Mesa de Yambi h.** Colombia
111 G2 **Mesagne** Italy
115 E5 **Mesagros** Greece
115 □ **Mesanagros** Greece
22 A1 **Mesanak i.** Indonesia
88 D4 **Mésanger** France
98 C3 **Mesão Frio** Portugal
155 H3 **Mesa Verde Nat. Park nat. park** *Colorado* U.S.A.
171 C5 **Mesa Volcánica de Somuncurá plat.** Argentina
72 D4 **Meschede** Germany
56 E2 **Meselefors** Sweden
172 C6 **Meseta de Colitoro plat.** Argentina
163 E2 **Meseta del Co Jáua plat.** Venezuela
171 C5 **Meseta de Montemayor plat.** Argentina
126 C2 **Mesfinto** Ethiopia
138 F3 **Mesgouez L. l.** *Québec* Canada
86 C4 **Mesgrigny** France
52 D2 **Meshcherskaya Nizmennost' lowland** Rus. Fed.
52 B2 **Meshchovsk** Rus. Fed.
50 J2 **Meshchura** Rus. Fed.
Meshed *see* **Mashhad**
39 D1 **Meshkān** Iran
124 E2 **Meshra'er Req** Sudan
148 E3 **Mesick** *Michigan* U.S.A.
104 F4 **Mesihovina** Bos.-Herz.
111 F4 **Mesima r.** Italy
114 E2 **Mesimeri** Greece
120 D2 **Meski** Morocco
89 E4 **Meslay-du-Maine** France
82 A2 **Mesnay** France
83 E2 **Mesocco** Switzerland
114 C3 **Mesochora** Greece
107 G4 **Mesola** Italy
115 C4 **Mesolongi** Greece
98 B1 **Mesón do Vento** Spain
114 A3 **Mesongi** Greece
42 E3 **Mesopotamia reg.** Iraq
114 C2 **Mesopotamia** Greece
114 B3 **Mesopotamo** Greece
111 F3 **Mesoraca** Italy
169 G3 **Mesquita** Brazil
155 E3 **Mesquite** *Nevada* U.S.A.
151 D5 **Mesquite** *Texas* U.S.A.
155 E4 **Mesquite Lake l.** *California* U.S.A.
121 E2 **Messaad** Algeria
88 D4 **Messac** France
118 B2 **Messak Mellet h.** Libya
127 C7 **Messalo r.** Mozambique
73 G3 **Meßdorf** Germany
89 E3 **Messei** France
110 D5 **Messina div.** *Sicilia* Italy
111 E4 **Messina** *Sicilia* Italy
131 H1 **Messina** South Africa
87 E3 **Messincourt** France
141 G3 **Messines** *Québec* Canada
115 D5 **Messini** Greece
115 C5 **Messinia div.** Greece
115 D6 **Messiniakos Kolpos b.** Greece
74 E5 **Meßkirch** Germany
74 D4 **Meßstetten** Germany
114 E1 **Mesta r.** Bulgaria
101 H2 **Mesta r.** Spain
75 L2 **Městec Králové** Czech Rep.
135 Q2 **Mesters Vig** Greenland
73 G2 **Mestlin** Germany
79 G1 **Město Albrechtice** Czech Rep.
107 G3 **Mestre** Italy
22 A2 **Mesuji r.** Indonesia
92 E1 **Mesves-sur-Loire** France
90 C2 **Mesvres** France
90 C2 **Mesvrin r.** France
162 D2 **Meta r.** Colombia/Venezuela
141 K2 **Métabetchouan** *Québec* Canada
90 E2 **Métabief** France
140 E3 **Metagama** *Ontario* Canada
114 E2 **Metagkitsi** Greece
135 L3 **Meta Incognita Pen. pen.** *N.W.T.* Canada
151 F6 **Metairie** *Louisiana* U.S.A.
148 C5 **Metamora** *Illinois* U.S.A.
170 D2 **Metán** Argentina
22 C2 **Metangai** Indonesia
127 B7 **Metangula** Mozambique
129 F1 **Metarica** Mozambique
107 G5 **Metauro r.** Italy
68 F2 **Metelen** Germany
126 C2 **Metema** Ethiopia
114 C3 **Meteora** Greece
174 H9 **Meteor Depth depth** Atlantic Ocean
115 E5 **Methana** Greece
63 F1 **Metheringham** *England* U.K.
115 C6 **Methoni** Greece
147 H3 **Methuen** *Massachusetts* U.S.A.
66 E4 **Methven** *Scotland* U.K.
63 G2 **Methwold** *England* U.K.
172 F3 **Metileo** Argentina
104 F4 **Metković** Croatia
136 C3 **Metlakatla** *Alaska* U.S.A.
121 F2 **Metlaoui** Tunisia
104 E3 **Metlika** Slovenia
81 F4 **Metnitz r.** Austria
81 F4 **Metnitz** Austria
115 C4 **Metochi** *Dytiki Ellas* Greece
115 D5 **Metochi** *Peloponnisos* Greece
127 C7 **Metoro** Mozambique
22 A3 **Metro** Indonesia
144 B4 **Metropolis** *Illinois* U.S.A.
68 E1 **Metslawier** Netherlands
114 C3 **Metsovo** Greece
80 D2 **Metten** Germany
69 E5 **Mettendorf** Germany
69 C4 **Mettet** Belgium
72 C3 **Mettingen** Germany
74 B3 **Mettlach** Germany
154 C4 **Mettler** *California* U.S.A.
72 B4 **Mettmann** Germany
89 F4 **Mettray** France
38 B4 **Mettur** India
126 C3 **Metu** Ethiopia
127 D7 **Metundo, Ilha i.** Mozambique
87 F3 **Metz** *Moselle* France
87 G4 **Metzeral** France
87 F3 **Metzervisse** France
74 E4 **Metzingen** Germany
88 C3 **Meu r.** France
74 C2 **Meudt** Germany
69 B4 **Meulebeke** Belgium
89 G4 **Meung-sur-Loire** France
87 F4 **Meurthe r.** France
87 F4 **Meurthe-et-Moselle div.** France
87 E3 **Meuse div.** France
69 C5 **Meuse r.** Belgium/France
73 H4 **Meuselwitz** Germany
92 D3 **Meuzac** France
90 C1 **Meuzin r.** France
62 B4 **Mevagissey** *England* U.K.
32 C1 **Mêwa** China
65 G4 **Mexborough** *England* U.K.
151 D6 **Mexia** *Texas* U.S.A.
166 C1 **Mexiana, Ilha i.** Brazil
156 B1 **Mexicali** Mexico
155 H3 **Mexican Hat** *Utah* U.S.A.
153 F6 **Mexicanos, L. de los l.** Mexico
155 H3 **Mexican Water** *Arizona* U.S.A.
133 H7 **Mexico country** Central America
157 F5 **México div.** Mexico
147 H2 **Mexico** *Maine* U.S.A.
150 F4 **Mexico** *Missouri* U.S.A.
147 E3 **Mexico** *New York* U.S.A.
157 F5 **México** Mexico
157 G3 **Mexico, Gulf of g.** Mexico/U.S.A.
90 D3 **Meximieux** France
39 C2 **Meybod** Iran
73 H2 **Meyenburg** Germany
91 D3 **Meylan** France
92 E3 **Meymac** France
39 F2 **Meymaneh** Afghanistan
39 B2 **Meymeh** Iran
42 F3 **Meymeh r.** Iran
45 T3 **Meynypil'gyno** Rus. Fed.
91 D5 **Meyrargues** France
91 E4 **Meyronnes** France
91 B4 **Meyrueis** France
92 D3 **Meyssac** France
90 E3 **Meythet** France
90 C3 **Meyzieu** France
43 C4 **Mezada** Israel
157 G5 **Mezcalapa r.** Mexico
112 D3 **Mezdra** Bulgaria
91 B5 **Mèze** France
91 E4 **Mézel** France
44 F3 **Mezen' r.** Rus. Fed.
50 H1 **Mezen'** Rus. Fed.
91 C4 **Mézenc, Mt mt.** France
50 G1 **Mezenskaya Guba g.** Rus. Fed.
52 A1 **Mezha r.** Rus. Fed.
47 L2 **Mezhdurechensk** Rus. Fed.
50 J2 **Mezhdurechensk** Rus. Fed.
44 G2 **Mezhdusharskiy, O. i.** Rus. Fed.
53 G2 **Mezhova** Ukraine
75 J2 **Meziboří** Czech Rep.
81 F4 **Mežica** Slovenia
89 E2 **Mézidon-Canon** France
92 D2 **Mézières-en-Brenne** France
92 C2 **Mézières-sur-Issoire** France
91 C4 **Mézilhac** France
90 B1 **Mézilles** France
78 F1 **Mezimĕstí** Czech Rep.
93 C4 **Mézin** France
98 C4 **Mezio** Portugal
79 L5 **Mezőberény** Hungary
79 L4 **Mezőcsát** Hungary
79 K4 **Mezőkövesd** Hungary
79 H5 **Mezőszilas** Hungary
79 K5 **Mezőtúr** Hungary
102 C4 **Mezquita de Jarque** Spain
156 D4 **Mezquital r.** Mexico
156 D4 **Mezquital** Mexico
156 E4 **Mezquitic** Mexico
54 E3 **Mežvidi** Latvia
107 E2 **Mezzana** Italy
107 F2 **Mezzano** Italy
83 G2 **Mezzocorona** Italy
110 C5 **Mezzojuso** *Sicilia* Italy
106 D2 **Mezzola, Lago di l.** Italy
83 E2 **Mezzoldo** Italy
107 F2 **Mezzolombardo** Italy
127 B5 **Mfangano I. i.** Kenya
124 B3 **Mfou** Cameroon
127 B7 **Mfuwe** Zambia
111 □ **Mgarr** Malta
123 F5 **Mgbidi** Nigeria
52 A3 **Mglin** Rus. Fed.
131 F5 **Mgwali r.** South Africa
129 E2 **Mhangura** Zimbabwe
38 A2 **Mhasvad** India
131 H3 **Mhlosheni** Swaziland
131 H3 **Mhlume** Swaziland
131 G2 **Mhluzi** South Africa
36 C5 **Mhow** India
31 F5 **Mi r.** China
24 A2 **Mi r.** Myanmar
77 M5 **Miączyn** Poland
157 F5 **Miahuatlan** Mexico
100 E1 **Miajadas** Spain
155 G5 **Miami** *Arizona* U.S.A.
145 D7 **Miami** *Florida* U.S.A.
151 E4 **Miami** *Oklahoma* U.S.A.
145 D7 **Miami Beach** *Florida* U.S.A.
39 B3 **Mīān Āb** Iran
39 D1 **Miānābād** Iran
39 E4 **Mianaz** Pakistan
30 A6 **Miancaowan** China
33 E1 **Mianchi** China
39 C2 **Miāndarreh** Iran
39 D1 **Miāndasht** Iran
42 F2 **Miandowāb** Iran
129 H2 **Miandrivazo** Madagascar
31 G2 **Mianduhe** China
39 A1 **Mīāneh** Iran
23 C5 **Miangas i.** Philippines
36 A4 **Miani Hor b.** Pakistan
39 F2 **Mianjoi** Afghanistan
36 B2 **Mian Kalai** Pakistan
32 C3 **Mianmian Shan mountain range** China
32 C2 **Mianning** China
36 B2 **Mianwali** Pakistan
32 D1 **Mian Xian** China
33 F2 **Mianyang** China
32 D2 **Mianyang** China
32 D2 **Mianzhu** China
31 G5 **Miao Dao i.** China
31 G5 **Miaodao Qundao is** China
47 K3 **Miao'ergou** China
33 H3 **Miaoli** Taiwan
129 H2 **Miarinarivo** *Antananarivo* Madagascar
129 H2 **Miarinarivo** *Toamasina* Madagascar
76 F2 **Miasteczko Krajeńskie** Poland
76 E1 **Miastko** Poland
77 K4 **Miastków Kościelny** Poland
77 K2 **Miastkowo** Poland
131 H2 **Mica** South Africa
173 G5 **Micaela Cascallares** Argentina

155 G5 **Mica Mt** mt. *Arizona* U.S.A.
32 D1 **Micang Shan** mountain range China
50 J1 **Michaichmon'** Rus. Fed.
79 L3 **Michalovce** Slovakia
77 M2 **Michałowa** Poland
137 H3 **Michel** *Saskatchewan* Canada
75 G2 **Michelau in Oberfranken** Germany
74 E3 **Michelstadt** Germany
73 J3 **Michendorf** Germany
148 C2 **Michigamme Lake** l. *Michigan* U.S.A.
148 C2 **Michigamme Reservoir** resr *Michigan* U.S.A.
148 D2 **Michigan** div. U.S.A.
148 D5 **Michigan City** *Indiana* U.S.A.
148 D4 **Michigan, Lake** l. U.S.A.
172 C6 **Michihuao** Argentina
140 C3 **Michipicoten Bay** b. *Ontario* Canada
140 C3 **Michipicoten I.** i. *Ontario* Canada
140 C3 **Michipicoten River** *Ontario* Canada
156 E5 **Michoacán** div. Mexico
77 L4 **Michów** Poland
112 F3 **Michurin** Bulgaria
52 E3 **Michurinsk** Rus. Fed.
124 B3 **Micomeseng** Equatorial Guinea
176 E5 **Micronesia** is Pacific Ocean
4 G4 **Micronesia, Federated States of** country Pacific Ocean
25 D7 **Midai** i. Indonesia
174 G4 **Mid-Atlantic Ridge** sea feature Atlantic Ocean
130 B6 **Middelberg Pass** pass South Africa
131 E5 **Middelburg** *Eastern Cape* South Africa
131 G2 **Middelburg** *Mpumalanga* South Africa
69 B3 **Middelburg** Netherlands
55 B4 **Middelfart** Denmark
68 C3 **Middelharnis** Netherlands
69 A3 **Middelkerke** Belgium
130 C5 **Middelpos** South Africa
68 E1 **Middelstum** Netherlands
131 F2 **Middelwit** South Africa
152 C3 **Middle Alkali Lake** l. *Nevada* U.S.A.
174 C5 **Middle America Trench** sea feature Pacific Ocean
25 A4 **Middle Andaman** i. *Andaman and Nicobar Is* India
147 H4 **Middleboro** *Massachusetts* U.S.A.
146 E4 **Middleburg** *Pennsylvania* U.S.A.
147 F3 **Middleburgh** *New York* U.S.A.
147 G2 **Middlebury** *Vermont* U.S.A.
15 E3 **Middle Cr.** r. *Queensland* Australia
65 G3 **Middleham** *England* U.K.
101 □ **Middle Hill** h. Gibraltar
128 □3 **Middle I.** i. *Tristan da Cunha* Atlantic Ocean
Middle Level lowland *see* **Bedford Level**
9 C6 **Middlemarch** New Zealand
62 D4 **Middlemarsh** *England* U.K.
146 B6 **Middlesboro** *Kentucky* U.S.A.
65 G3 **Middlesbrough** *England* U.K.
65 G3 **Middlesbrough** div *England* U.K.
158 A3 **Middlesex** Belize
65 F4 **Middleton** *England* U.K.
15 E4 **Middleton** *Queensland* Australia
131 E6 **Middleton** South Africa
63 E2 **Middleton Cheney** *England* U.K.
63 F4 **Middleton-on-Sea** *England* U.K.
65 G3 **Middleton St George** *England* U.K.
154 A2 **Middletown** *California* U.S.A.
147 G4 **Middletown** *Connecticut* U.S.A.
147 F5 **Middletown** *Delaware* U.S.A.
147 F4 **Middletown** *New York* U.S.A.
67 E2 **Middletown** *Northern Ireland* U.K.
146 A5 **Middletown** *Ohio* U.S.A.
148 E4 **Middleville** *Michigan* U.S.A.
62 D1 **Middlewich** *England* U.K.
9 B6 **Mid Dome** mt. New Zealand
120 D2 **Midelt** Morocco
126 E2 **Midhisho** well Somalia
63 F4 **Midhurst** *England* U.K.
126 D1 **Mīdī** Yemen
93 C6 **Midi de Bigorre, Pic du** mt. France
175 K4 **Mid-Indian Basin** sea feature Indian Ocean
175 K6 **Mid-Indian Ridge** sea feature Indian Ocean
93 D5 **Midi-Pyrénées** div. France
149 E4 **Midland** *Michigan* U.S.A.
141 F4 **Midland** *Ontario* Canada
151 C5 **Midland** *Texas* U.S.A.
129 D2 **Midlands** div. Zimbabwe
67 C5 **Midleton** Rep. of Ireland
66 E5 **Midlothian** div. *Scotland* U.K.
72 D2 **Midlum** Germany
131 H4 **Midmar Dam** dam South Africa
129 H3 **Midongy Atsimo** Madagascar
28 C7 **Midori-k** r. Japan
93 B5 **Midou** r. France
93 B5 **Midouze** r. France
176 F4 **Mid-Pacific Mountains** sea feature Pacific Ocean
32 C3 **Midu** China
55 □1 **Miðvágur** Faeroes
Midway *see* **Thamarīt**
176 H4 **Midway Islands** is Pacific Ocean
152 F3 **Midwest** *Wyoming* U.S.A.
151 D5 **Midwest City** *Oklahoma* U.S.A.
68 F1 **Midwolda** Netherlands
42 E2 **Midyat** Turkey
66 □2 **Mid Yell** *Scotland* U.K.
112 D3 **Midzhur** mt. Bulgaria/Yugoslavia
29 F6 **Mie** div. Japan
28 C7 **Mie** Japan
77 J5 **Miechów** Poland
76 D3 **Miedzichowo** Poland
76 F4 **Międzybórz** Poland
76 D3 **Międzychód** Poland
76 E4 **Międzylesie** Poland
77 L4 **Międzyrzec Podlaski** Poland
76 D3 **Międzyrzecz** Poland
76 C2 **Międzyzdroje** *Szczecin* Poland
57 G3 **Miehikkälä** Finland
77 K6 **Miejsce Piastowe** Poland
76 E4 **Miejska-Górka** Poland
56 G2 **Miekojärvi** l. Finland
93 C5 **Miélan** France
77 K5 **Mielec** Poland
76 E1 **Mielno** Poland
76 F3 **Mielżyn** Poland
127 C6 **Miembwe** Tanzania
80 B3 **Mieminger Gebirge** mountain range Austria
59 F3 **Mien** l. Sweden
13 F5 **Miena** *Tasmania* Australia
33 H3 **Mien-hua Hsü** i. Taiwan
56 G1 **Mieraslompolo** Finland
112 E1 **Miercurea-Ciuc** Romania
98 E1 **Mieres** Spain
69 D3 **Mierlo** Netherlands
76 E5 **Mieroszów** Poland
76 G1 **Mierzeja Helska** pen. Poland
77 H1 **Mierzeja Wiślana** spit Poland
87 G3 **Miesau** Germany
75 G5 **Miesbach** Germany
76 F3 **Mieścisko** Poland
74 C3 **Miesenbach** Germany
126 D3 **Mī'ēso** Ethiopia
73 G3 **Mieste** Germany
76 C3 **Mieszkowice** Poland
80 A2 **Mietingen** Germany
54 B1 **Mietoinen** Finland
82 B2 **Mieussy** France
146 E4 **Mifflinburg** *Pennsylvania* U.S.A.
146 E4 **Mifflintown** *Pennsylvania* U.S.A.
32 D1 **Migang Shan** mt. China
131 E3 **Migdol** South Africa
86 C5 **Migennes** France
39 D3 **Mighān** Iran
37 H3 **Miging** India
107 F4 **Migliarino** Italy
109 J4 **Miglionica** Italy
92 C2 **Mignaloux-Beauvoir** France
92 C2 **Migné-Auxances** France
82 B2 **Mignovillard** France
166 D1 **Miguel Alves** Brazil
156 E3 **Miguel Auza** Mexico
156 K7 **Miguel de la Borda** Panama
101 G1 **Miguel Esteban** Spain
173 J3 **Miguelete** Uruguay
172 F4 **Miguel Riglos** Argentina
25 B4 **Migyaunglaung** Myanmar
24 A3 **Migyaunye** Myanmar
112 E2 **Mihăileşti** Romania
42 B2 **Mihalıççık** Turkey
28 D6 **Mihara** Japan
29 G6 **Mihara-yama** volcano Japan
43 C1 **Mihmandar** Turkey
103 C4 **Mijares** r. Spain
101 F4 **Mijas** Spain
101 F4 **Mijas, Sierra de** mountain range Spain
68 C2 **Mijdrecht** Netherlands
90 E2 **Mijoux** France
149 F3 **Mikado** *Michigan* U.S.A.
28 H2 **Mikasa** Japan
29 F6 **Mikawa-wan** b. Japan
54 E5 **Mikhanavichy** Belarus
50 F4 **Mikhaylov** Rus. Fed.
112 D3 **Mikhaylovgrad** div. Bulgaria
179 D5 **Mikhaylov I.** i. Antarctica
47 J2 **Mikhaylovka** Kazakhstan
47 H4 **Mikhaylovka** Kazakhstan
52 B3 **Mikhaylovka** Rus. Fed.
51 G5 **Mikhaylovka** Rus. Fed.
30 D2 **Mikhaylovka** Rus. Fed.
112 D3 **Mikhaylovo** Bulgaria
52 F1 **Mikhaylovo** Rus. Fed.
46 E1 **Mikhaylovsk** Rus. Fed.
47 J2 **Mikhaylovskiy** Rus. Fed.
52 G1 **Mikhaylovskoye** Rus. Fed.
52 C2 **Mikhnevo** Rus. Fed.
28 E6 **Miki** Japan
37 H4 **Mikir Hills** mountain range India
56 G3 **Mikkeli** div. Finland
57 G3 **Mikkeli** Finland
56 G3 **Mikkelin mlk** Finland
136 G3 **Mikkwa** r. *Alberta* Canada
55 □1 **Mikladalur** Faeroes
81 G4 **Miklavž** Slovenia
77 K2 **Mikołajki** Poland
76 G5 **Mikołów** Poland
114 E2 **Mikra Volvi** Greece
76 F4 **Mikstat** Poland
75 L3 **Mikuláš** Czech Rep.
78 F3 **Mikulov** Czech Rep.
127 C6 **Mikumi** Tanzania
127 C6 **Mikumi National Park** nat. park Tanzania
50 J2 **Mikun'** Rus. Fed.
29 G5 **Mikuni-sammyaku** mountain range Japan
29 G7 **Mikura-jima** i. Japan
121 F1 **Mila** Algeria
150 E2 **Milaca** *Minnesota* U.S.A.
35 D9 **Miladhunmadulu Atoll** atoll Maldives
166 E2 **Milagres** Brazil
172 E1 **Milagro** Argentina
102 B2 **Milagro** Spain
77 J1 **Miłakowo** Poland
145 B5 **Milan** *Tennessee* U.S.A.
Milan *see* **Milano**
125 C5 **Milando, Reserva Especial do** res. Angola
12 D3 **Milang** *S. Australia* Australia
129 F2 **Milange** Mozambique
106 D3 **Milano** div. *Lombardia* Italy
106 D3 **Milano** *Milano* Italy
129 H1 **Milanoa** Madagascar
106 C3 **Milano Malpensa** airport Italy
77 L4 **Milanów** Poland
42 A2 **Milas** Turkey
115 G7 **Milatos** Greece
111 E4 **Milazzo** *Sicilia* Italy
111 E4 **Milazzo, Capo di** c. *Sicilia* Italy
111 E4 **Milazzo, Golfo di** b. *Sicilia* Italy
150 D2 **Milbank** *S. Dakota* U.S.A.
62 D4 **Milborne Port** *England* U.K.
63 G2 **Mildenhall** *England* U.K.
13 E3 **Mildura** *Victoria* Australia
32 C4 **Mile** China
159 □1 **Mile Gully** Jamaica
43 B4 **Mileiz, W. el** watercourse Egypt
110 C5 **Milena** *Sicilia* Italy
15 G5 **Miles** *Queensland* Australia
152 F2 **Miles City** *Montana* U.S.A.
126 D2 **Mīlē Serdo Reserve** res. Ethiopia
75 J2 **Milešovka** h. Czech Rep.
67 C4 **Milestone** Rep. of Ireland
111 F4 **Mileto** Italy
109 G3 **Miletto, Monte** mt. Italy
17 B5 **Mileura** *Western Australia* Australia
78 D2 **Milevsko** Czech Rep.
52 B3 **Mileyevo** Rus. Fed.
100 B3 **Milfontes** Portugal
154 B1 **Milford** *California* U.S.A.
147 G4 **Milford** *Connecticut* U.S.A.
147 F5 **Milford** *Delaware* U.S.A.
148 D5 **Milford** *Illinois* U.S.A.
147 J2 **Milford** *Maine* U.S.A.
147 H3 **Milford** *Massachusetts* U.S.A.
147 H3 **Milford** *New Hampshire* U.S.A.
147 F3 **Milford** *New York* U.S.A.
155 F2 **Milford** *Utah* U.S.A.
67 D1 **Milford** Rep. of Ireland
62 A3 **Milford Haven** *Wales* U.K.
9 A6 **Milford Sound** inlet New Zealand
9 A6 **Milford Sound** New Zealand
15 E3 **Milgarra** *Queensland* Australia
17 B5 **Milgun** *Western Australia* Australia
98 D3 **Milhão** Portugal
91 C5 **Milhaud** France
76 F4 **Milicz** Poland
17 B6 **Miling** *Western Australia* Australia
108 A4 **Milis** *Sardegna* Italy
110 D5 **Militello in Val di Catania** *Sicilia* Italy
81 G4 **Miljana** Croatia
152 F1 **Milk** r. Canada/U.S.A.
77 K2 **Miłki** Poland
45 R4 **Mil'kovo** Rus. Fed.
76 E4 **Miłkowice** Poland
159 □1 **Milk River Bath** Jamaica
68 D3 **Mill** Netherlands
15 F3 **Millaa Millaa** *Queensland* Australia
103 C5 **Millares** Spain
103 C5 **Millárs** r. Spain
145 □2 **Millars** The Bahamas
93 E6 **Millas** France
91 B4 **Millau** France
62 B4 **Millbrook** *England* U.K.
154 B1 **Mill Creek** r. *California* U.S.A.
145 D5 **Milledgeville** *Georgia* U.S.A.
148 C5 **Milledgeville** *Illinois* U.S.A.
150 E2 **Mille Lacs L.** l. *Minnesota* U.S.A.
138 B4 **Mille Lacs, Lac des** l. *Ontario* Canada
150 D2 **Miller** *S. Dakota* U.S.A.
130 D6 **Miller** South Africa
148 B3 **Miller Dam Flowage** resr *Wisconsin* U.S.A.
140 E4 **Miller Lake** *Ontario* Canada
51 G5 **Millerovo** Rus. Fed.
155 G6 **Miller Peak** summit *Arizona* U.S.A.
146 C4 **Millersburg** *Ohio* U.S.A.
146 E4 **Millersburg** *Pennsylvania* U.S.A.
9 B6 **Millers Flat** New Zealand
146 E6 **Millers Tavern** *Virginia* U.S.A.
154 C3 **Millerton Lake** l. *California* U.S.A.
64 C2 **Milleur Point** pt *Scotland* U.K.
92 E3 **Millevaches** France
179 C6 **Mill I.** i. Antarctica
12 E4 **Millicent** *S. Australia* Australia
68 E3 **Millingen aan de Rijn** Netherlands
149 F4 **Millington** *Michigan* U.S.A.
145 B5 **Millington** *Tennessee* U.S.A.
147 J2 **Millinocket** *Maine* U.S.A.
64 C3 **Millisle** *Northern Ireland* U.K.
15 G5 **Millmerran** *Queensland* Australia
65 E3 **Millom** *England* U.K.
66 D5 **Millport** *Scotland* U.K.
147 F5 **Millsboro** *Delaware* U.S.A.
15 E4 **Mills Cr.** watercourse *Queensland* Australia
136 F2 **Mills Lake** l. *N.W.T.* Canada
81 E4 **Millstätter See** l. Austria
146 C5 **Milltown** *W. Virginia* U.S.A.
67 B4 **Milltown** Rep. of Ireland
139 G4 **Milltown** *New Brunswick* Canada
67 B4 **Milltown Malbay** Rep. of Ireland
15 E3 **Millungera** *Queensland* Australia
131 F2 **Millvale** South Africa
147 K1 **Millville** *New Brunswick* Canada
147 F5 **Millville** *New Jersey* U.S.A.
86 B4 **Milly-la-Forêt** France
17 B5 **Milly Milly** *Western Australia* Australia
102 B3 **Milmarcos** Spain
73 J2 **Milmersdorf** Germany
65 E1 **Milnathort** *Scotland* U.K.
135 Q2 **Milne Land** i. Greenland
64 D2 **Milngavie** *Scotland* U.K.
65 F3 **Milnthorpe** *England* U.K.
122 C5 **Milo** r. Guinea
147 J2 **Milo** *Maine* U.S.A.
111 E5 **Milo** *Sicilia* Italy
76 E2 **Miłocice** Poland
77 H2 **Miłomłyn** Poland
115 F6 **Milos** i. Greece
52 D3 **Miloslavskoye** Rus. Fed.
76 F3 **Miłosław** Poland
53 G1 **Milove** Ukraine
77 H6 **Milówka** Poland
13 E2 **Milparinka** *New South Wales* Australia
146 E4 **Milroy** *Pennsylvania* U.S.A.
80 D1 **Miltach** Germany
75 G3 **Miltenberg** Germany
151 G6 **Milton** *Florida* U.S.A.
145 C6 **Milton** *Florida* U.S.A.
148 A5 **Milton** *Iowa* U.S.A.
13 G3 **Milton** *New South Wales* Australia
141 F5 **Milton** *Ontario* Canada
146 E4 **Milton** *Pennsylvania* U.S.A.
147 G2 **Milton** *Vermont* U.S.A.
9 B7 **Milton** New Zealand
152 C2 **Milton-Freewater** *Oregon* U.S.A.
63 F2 **Milton Keynes** div. *England* U.K.
63 F2 **Milton Keynes** *England* U.K.
146 C4 **Milton, Lake** l. *Ohio* U.S.A.
73 J1 **Miltzow** Germany
33 F2 **Miluo** China
148 D4 **Milwaukee** *Wisconsin* U.S.A.
159 E3 **Milwaukee Depth** depth Caribbean
46 F3 **Mily** Kazakhstan
51 G5 **Milyutinskaya** Rus. Fed.
124 C3 **Mimbelly** Congo
93 A4 **Mimizan** France
93 A4 **Mimizan-Plage** France
78 D1 **Mimoň** Czech Rep.
124 B4 **Mimongo** Gabon
168 D1 **Mimoso** Brazil
169 H4 **Mimoso do Sul** Brazil
28 E6 **Mimuroyama** mt. Japan
32 C2 **Min** r. China
154 C2 **Mina** *Nevada* U.S.A.
157 E3 **Mina** Mexico
39 D4 **Mīnāb** Iran
36 B3 **Mina Bazar** Pakistan
172 C1 **Mina Clavero** Argentina
21 H6 **Minahasa Semenanjung** pen. Indonesia
138 B3 **Minaki** *Ontario* Canada
28 C7 **Minamata** Japan
29 F6 **Minami Alps National Park** nat. park Japan
20 D6 **Minas** Indonesia
173 K3 **Minas** Uruguay
42 G4 **Mīnā'Sa'ūd** Kuwait
139 H4 **Minas Basin** b. *Nova Scotia* Canada
173 K1 **Minas de Corrales** Uruguay
169 F2 **Minas Gerais** div. Brazil
169 G2 **Minas Novas** Brazil
157 H6 **Minas, Sa de las** mountain range Guatemala
103 B6 **Minateda** Spain
157 G5 **Minatitlán** Mexico
101 H1 **Minaya** Spain
24 A2 **Minbu** Myanmar
24 A2 **Minbya** Myanmar
172 B1 **Mincha** Chile
171 B5 **Minchinmávida** volcano Chile
65 E2 **Minch Moor** h. *Scotland* U.K.
66 C3 **Minch, The** str. *Scotland* U.K.
107 E3 **Mincio** r. Italy
42 F2 **Mincivan** Azerbaijan
23 C5 **Mindanao** i. Philippines
24 A2 **Mindat Sakan** Myanmar
100 B1 **Minde** Portugal
74 F4 **Mindel** r. Germany
75 F4 **Mindelheim** Germany
122 □ **Mindelo** Cape Verde
75 G4 **Mindelstetten** Germany
151 E5 **Minden** *Louisiana* U.S.A.
154 C2 **Minden** *Nevada* U.S.A.
141 F4 **Minden** *Ontario* Canada
72 D3 **Minden** Germany
24 A3 **Mindon** Myanmar
13 E3 **Mindona L.** l. *New South Wales* Australia
23 B3 **Mindoro** i. Philippines
23 B3 **Mindoro Strait** str. Philippines
125 B4 **Mindouli** Congo
79 K5 **Mindszent** Hungary
169 F4 **Minduri** Brazil
Mindzhivan *see* **Mincivan**
28 C6 **Mine** Japan
67 D5 **Mine Head** headland Rep. of Ireland
62 C3 **Minehead** *England* U.K.
168 B2 **Mineiros** Brazil
151 E5 **Mineola** *Texas* U.S.A.
154 B1 **Mineral** *California* U.S.A.
154 C3 **Mineral King** *California* U.S.A.
51 G6 **Mineral'nyye Vody** Rus. Fed.
148 B4 **Mineral Point** *Wisconsin* U.S.A.
151 D5 **Mineral Wells** *Texas* U.S.A.
107 F4 **Minerbio** Italy
155 F2 **Minersville** *Utah* U.S.A.
109 J3 **Minervino Murge** Italy
93 E5 **Minervois** reg. France
31 F1 **Minfeng** China
125 E6 **Minga** Congo(Zaire)
42 F1 **Mingäçevir** Azerbaijan
42 F1 **Mingäçevir Su Anbarı** resr Azerbaijan
124 D2 **Mingala** Central African Rep.
139 H3 **Mingan** *Québec* Canada
111 E2 **Mingardo** r. Italy
Mingechaur *see* **Mingäçevir**
Mingechaurskoye Vdkhr. l. *see* **Mingäçevir Su Anbarı**
15 F3 **Mingela** *Queensland* Australia
17 A6 **Mingenew** *Western Australia* Australia
14 D4 **Mingera Cr.** watercourse *Queensland* Australia
33 F1 **Minggang** China
24 A2 **Mingin** Myanmar
24 A1 **Mingin Range** mountain range Myanmar
47 H4 **Ming-Kush** Kyrgyzstan
103 B5 **Minglanilla** Spain
99 F4 **Mingorria** Spain
127 C7 **Mingoyo** Tanzania
31 H3 **Mingshui** China
36 C1 **Mingteke** China
66 A4 **Mingulay** i. *Scotland* U.K.
129 G1 **Minguri** Mozambique
33 G3 **Mingxi** China
30 B5 **Minhe** China
24 A3 **Minhla** Myanmar
24 A3 **Minhla** Myanmar
98 B3 **Minho** reg. Portugal
38 A4 **Minicoy** i. India
17 C6 **Minigwal, L.** salt flat *Western Australia* Australia
54 B4 **Minija** r. Lithuania
17 A4 **Minilya** r. *Western Australia* Australia
17 A4 **Minilya** *Western Australia* Australia
164 C3 **Miñimiñe** Chile
172 A4 **Mininco** Chile
122 C4 **Minintan** Côte d'Ivoire
139 H3 **Minipi Lake** l. *Newfoundland* Canada
99 H3 **Ministra, Sierra** mountain range Spain
137 J4 **Minitonas** *Manitoba* Canada
Min-Kush *see* **Ming-Kush**
12 D3 **Minlaton** *S. Australia* Australia
30 B5 **Minle** China
123 F5 **Minna** Nigeria
29 □2 **Minna-jima** i. Japan
56 D3 **Minne** Sweden
148 A3 **Minneapolis** *Minnesota* U.S.A.
137 K4 **Minnedosa** *Manitoba* Canada
148 A2 **Minnesota** div. U.S.A.
143 G3 **Minnesota** r. U.S.A.
58 D1 **Minnesund** Norway
17 A4 **Minnie Creek** *Western Australia* Australia
64 D3 **Minnigaff** *Scotland* U.K.
12 C3 **Minnipa** *S. Australia* Australia
138 B4 **Minnitaki L.** l. *Ontario* Canada
98 B3 **Miño** r. Portugal/Spain
29 G6 **Minobu** Japan
148 C3 **Minocqua** *Wisconsin* U.S.A.
173 H1 **Miñones** Argentina
148 B2 **Minong** *Wisconsin* U.S.A.
148 C5 **Minonk** *Illinois* U.S.A.
Minorca i. *see* **Menorca**
150 C1 **Minot** *N. Dakota* U.S.A.
30 B5 **Minqin** China
33 G3 **Minqing** China
32 C1 **Min Shan** mountain range China
24 A1 **Minsin** Myanmar
54 E5 **Minsk** div. Belarus
54 E5 **Minsk** Belarus
77 K3 **Mińsk Mazowiecki** Poland
62 D2 **Minsterley** *England* U.K.
124 B3 **Minta** Cameroon
36 C1 **Mintaka P.** pass China/Jammu and Kashmir
66 G3 **Mintlaw** *Scotland* U.K.
139 G4 **Minto** *New Brunswick* Canada
134 G2 **Minto Inlet** inlet *N.W.T.* Canada
138 F2 **Minto, Lac** l. *Québec* Canada
153 F4 **Minturn** *Colorado* U.S.A.
109 F3 **Minturno** Italy
106 E4 **Minucciano** Italy
43 A4 **Minûf** Egypt
47 M2 **Minusinsk** Rus. Fed.
83 D2 **Minusio** Switzerland
37 H3 **Minutang** India
124 B3 **Minvoul** Gabon
32 D1 **Min Xian** China
43 A4 **Minya el Qamh** Egypt
Minya Konka mt. *see* **Gongga Shan**
46 E1 **Minyar** Rus. Fed.
24 A2 **Minywa** Myanmar
37 H4 **Minzong** India
149 E3 **Mio** *Michigan* U.S.A.
90 C3 **Mionnay** France
93 B4 **Mios** France
139 J4 **Miquelon** i. *St-Pierre and Miquelon* Canada
141 G2 **Miquelon** *Québec* Canada
54 E5 **Mir** Belarus
162 B3 **Mira** r. Colombia
100 B3 **Mira** r. Portugal
103 B5 **Mira** r. Spain
107 G3 **Mira** Italy
98 B4 **Mira** Portugal
103 B5 **Mira** Spain
39 E3 **Mirabad** Afghanistan
91 D5 **Mirabeau** France
141 H4 **Mirabel airport** *Québec* Canada
141 H4 **Mirabel** *Québec* Canada
91 D5 **Mirabel** Spain
169 F2 **Mirabela** Brazil
91 D4 **Mirabel-aux-Baronnies** France
109 H3 **Mirabella Eclano** Italy
169 G4 **Miracema** Brazil
166 C2 **Miracema** Brazil
165 G1 **Miracema do Norte** Brazil
166 C2 **Mirador, Parque Nacional de** nat. park Brazil
162 C3 **Miraflores** Colombia
99 G4 **Miraflores de la Sierra** Spain
169 G4 **Miraí** Brazil
169 G2 **Miralta** Brazil
173 J5 **Miramar** *Buenos Aires* Argentina
173 F1 **Miramar** *Cordoba* Argentina
107 G4 **Miramare** Italy
157 H5 **Miramar, L.** l. Mexico
85 G5 **Miramas** France
93 B4 **Mirambeau** France
102 C4 **Mirambel** Spain
143 N2 **Miramichi** r. *New Brunswick* Canada
93 C4 **Miramont-de-Guyenne** France
36 B2 **Miram Shah** Pakistan
162 C4 **Miraña** Colombia
165 E4 **Miranda** r. Brazil
154 A1 **Miranda** *California* U.S.A.
167 A5 **Miranda** Brazil
99 H2 **Miranda de Ebro** Spain
98 E4 **Miranda del Castañar** Spain
98 B4 **Miranda do Corvo** Portugal
98 D3 **Miranda do Douro** Portugal
93 C5 **Mirande** France
98 C3 **Mirandela** Portugal
107 F4 **Mirandola** Italy
93 E4 **Mirandol-Bourgnounac** France
168 C4 **Mirandópolis** Brazil
107 G3 **Mirano** Italy
168 C5 **Mirante do Paranapanema** Brazil
167 B5 **Mirante, Sa do** h. Brazil
112 B5 **Miras** Albania
168 D4 **Mirassol** Brazil
42 E4 **Mirā', Wādī al** watercourse Iraq/Saudi Arabia
39 G2 **Mir Bacheh Kowt** Afghanistan
41 H6 **Mirbāţ** Oman
77 M5 **Mircze** Poland
119 G3 **Mirear I.** i. Egypt
159 D3 **Mirebalais** Haiti
90 D1 **Mirebeau** *Bourgogne* France
92 C2 **Mirebeau** *Poitou-Charentes* France
87 F4 **Mirecourt** France
81 E5 **Miren** Slovenia
93 D5 **Mirepoix** France
20 F6 **Miri** Malaysia
123 F4 **Miria** Niger
38 B2 **Mirialguda** India
159 E5 **Mirimire** Venezuela
170 F3 **Mirim, Lagoa** l. Brazil
170 E2 **Miriñay** r. Argentina
39 E3 **Mīrjāveh** Iran
104 D3 **Mirna** r. Croatia
81 G5 **Mirna** Slovenia
179 D5 **Mirnyy** Rus. Fed. Base Antarctica
45 N3 **Mirnyy** Rus. Fed.
50 G2 **Mirnyy** Rus. Fed.
137 J3 **Mirond L.** l. *Saskatchewan* Canada
77 M1 **Miroslavas** Lithuania
76 E2 **Mirosławiec** Poland
75 J3 **Mirošov** Czech Rep.
75 K3 **Mirovice** Czech Rep.
73 H2 **Mirow** Germany
36 C2 **Mirpur** Pakistan
36 B4 **Mirpur Khas** Pakistan
36 A4 **Mirpur Sakro** Pakistan
136 G4 **Mirror** *Alberta* Canada
47 L4 **Mirsali** China
27 □ **Mirs Bay** b. *Hong Kong* China
39 D4 **Mir Shahdād** Iran
75 L2 **Mirsk** Poland
15 F4 **Mirtna** *Queensland* Australia
111 F3 **Mirto Crosia** Italy
115 E6 **Mirtoö Pelagos** sea Greece
36 C1 **Mir Wali** Jammu and Kashmir
31 J6 **Miryang** South Korea
46 F5 **Mirzachirla** Turkmenistan
37 E4 **Mirzapur** India
28 D7 **Misaki** Japan
29 H6 **Misaki** Japan
47 K5 **Misalay** China
29 □2 **Misato** Japan
28 H3 **Misawa** Japan
82 C2 **Mischabel** mts Switzerland
81 H3 **Mischendorf** Austria
139 H4 **Miscou I.** i. *New Brunswick* Canada
109 G4 **Miseno, Capo** c. Italy
90 D1 **Miserey-Salines** France
178 □2 **Miseryfjellet** h. *Bjørnøya* Arctic Ocean
101 □ **Misery, Mt** h. Gibraltar
159 □6 **Misery, Mt** mt. *St Kitts-Nevis* Caribbean
36 C1 **Misgar** Pakistan
130 D6 **Misgund** South Africa
25 A6 **Misha** *Andaman and Nicobar Is* India
31 J3 **Mishan** China
39 B4 **Mishāsh al Hādī** well Saudi Arabia
39 B4 **Mishāsh'Uwayr** well Saudi Arabia
148 D5 **Mishawaka** *Indiana* U.S.A.
52 D2 **Misheronskiy** Rus. Fed.
140 C2 **Mishibishu Lake** l. *Ontario* Canada
28 C6 **Mi-shima** i. Japan
29 G6 **Mishima** Japan
46 E1 **Mishkino** Rus. Fed.
37 H3 **Mishmi Hills** mountain range India
110 C4 **Misilmeri** *Sicilia* Italy
6 □1 **Misima I.** i. P.N.G.
170 F2 **Misiones** div. Argentina
170 F2 **Misiones, Sa de** h. Argentina
171 C7 **Misión Fagnano** Argentina
43 C1 **Misis Dağ** h. Turkey
119 H3 **Miskah** Saudi Arabia
79 K3 **Miskolc** Hungary
81 G4 **Mislinja** Slovenia
119 H2 **Mismā, Jibāl al** mountain range Saudi Arabia
91 D4 **Mison** France
21 J7 **Misoöl** i. Indonesia
148 B2 **Misquah Hills** h. *Minnesota* U.S.A.
118 C1 **Mişrātah** Libya
36 E4 **Misrikh** India
140 C2 **Missanabie** *Ontario* Canada
109 J4 **Missanello** Italy
140 D1 **Missinaibi** r. *Ontario* Canada
140 D2 **Missinaibi Lake** l. *Ontario* Canada
137 J3 **Missinipe** *Saskatchewan* Canada
15 E2 **Mission** r. *Queensland* Australia
136 E5 **Mission** *B.C.* Canada
150 C3 **Mission** *S. Dakota* U.S.A.
138 D3 **Missisa L.** l. *Ontario* Canada
140 D3 **Mississagi** r. *Ontario* Canada
141 F5 **Mississauga** *Ontario* Canada
148 E5 **Mississinewa Lake** l. *Indiana* U.S.A.
151 F5 **Mississippi** div. U.S.A.
151 F6 **Mississippi** r. *Illinois* U.S.A.
141 G4 **Mississippi** r. *Ontario* Canada
151 F6 **Mississippi Delta** delta *Louisiana* U.S.A.
152 D2 **Missoula** *Montana* U.S.A.
120 D2 **Missour** Morocco
148 A6 **Missouri** div. U.S.A.
150 C2 **Missouri** r. *S. Dakota* U.S.A.
150 E3 **Missouri Valley** *Iowa* U.S.A.
15 F4 **Mistake Cr.** r. *Queensland* Australia
141 F2 **Mistaouac, Lac** l. *Québec* Canada
141 J1 **Mistassibi** r. *Québec* Canada
139 F4 **Mistassini** r. *Québec* Canada
141 J2 **Mistassini** *Québec* Canada
138 F3 **Mistassini, L.** l. *Québec* Canada
139 H2 **Mistastin Lake** l. *Newfoundland* Canada
81 H2 **Mistelbach** div. Austria
81 H2 **Mistelbach** Austria
111 E5 **Misterbianco** *Sicilia* Italy
158 B3 **Misteriosa Bank** sand bank Caribbean
173 F1 **Mistolar, L.** l. Argentina
110 D5 **Mistretta** *Sicilia* Italy
136 C3 **Misty Fjords National Monument** res. *Alaska* U.S.A.
28 C6 **Misumi** Japan
28 C7 **Misumi** Japan
107 G2 **Misurina** Italy
159 □3 **Mitan** Trinidad and Tobago
59 E1 **Mitandersfors** Sweden
156 D4 **Mita, Pta de** headland Mexico
163 G3 **Mitaraca** h. Surinam
13 H2 **Mitchell** r. *New South Wales* Australia
15 E2 **Mitchell** r. *Queensland* Australia
13 F4 **Mitchell** r. *Victoria* Australia
140 E5 **Mitchell** *Ontario* Canada
15 F5 **Mitchell** *Queensland* Australia
150 D3 **Mitchell** *S. Dakota* U.S.A.
148 E3 **Mitchell, Lake** l. *Michigan* U.S.A.
145 D5 **Mitchell, Mt** mt. *N. Carolina* U.S.A.
14 B1 **Mitchell Pt** pt *Northern Terr.* Australia
67 C4 **Mitchelstown** Rep. of Ireland
141 H3 **Mitchinamécus, Lake** l. *Québec* Canada
43 A4 **Mīt Ghamr** Egypt
36 B3 **Mithankot** Pakistan
36 C2 **Mitha Tiwana** Pakistan
36 B4 **Mithi** Pakistan
52 A2 **Mitishkovo** Rus. Fed.
136 C3 **Mitkof I.** i. *Alaska* U.S.A.
29 H5 **Mito** Japan
28 C6 **Mitō** Japan
127 C6 **Mitole** Tanzania
8 E4 **Mitre** mt. New Zealand
4 J6 **Mitre Island** i. Solomon Is.
114 C3 **Mitropoli** Greece
114 E1 **Mitrousi** Greece
127 D7 **Mitsamiouli** Comoros
114 B3 **Mitsikeli** mt. Greece
129 H2 **Mitsinjo** Madagascar
28 J2 **Mitsuishi** Japan
29 G5 **Mitsuke** Japan
28 B6 **Mitsushima** Japan
13 F4 **Mitta Mitta** *Victoria* Australia
80 B4 **Mittelberg** *Tirol* Austria
80 B3 **Mittelberg** *Vorarlberg* Austria
75 F3 **Mittelfranken** div. Germany
82 C2 **Mittelland** reg. Switzerland
72 D3 **Mittelland kanal** canal Germany
75 G5 **Mittenwald** Germany
73 J2 **Mittenwalde** Germany
81 G3 **Mitterbach am Erlaufsee** Austria
81 E2 **Mitterding** Austria
87 H4 **Mittersheim** France
80 D3 **Mittersill** Austria
75 H3 **Mitterteich** Germany
75 H2 **Mittweida** Germany
162 C3 **Mitú** Colombia
162 D3 **Mituas** Colombia
124 E4 **Mitumba, Monts** mountain range Congo(Zaire)
54 C4 **Mituva** r. Lithuania
125 E5 **Mitwaba** Congo(Zaire)
124 B3 **Mitzic** Gabon
Miughalaigh i. *see* **Mingulay**
29 G6 **Miura** Japan
29 F6 **Miya-gawa** r. Japan
29 H4 **Miyagi** div. Japan
29 □2 **Miyagi** Japan
29 □2 **Miyagusuku-jima** i. Japan
42 D3 **Miyah, Wādī el** watercourse Syria
119 H3 **Miyah, W. al** watercourse Saudi Arabia
28 C7 **Miyaji** Japan
29 G6 **Miyake-jima** i. Japan
29 H4 **Miyako** Japan
28 C8 **Miyakonojō** Japan
32 C2 **Miyaluo** China
46 D3 **Miyaly** Kazakhstan
36 B5 **Miyāni** India
28 C7 **Miyazaki** div. Japan
28 C8 **Miyazaki** Japan
29 E6 **Miyazu** Japan
29 E6 **Miyazu-wan** b. Japan
32 C3 **Miyi** China
28 D6 **Miyoshi** Japan
31 F4 **Miyun** China
31 F4 **Miyun Sk.** resr China
39 F2 **Mīzānī** Afghanistan
126 C3 **Mīzan Teferī** Ethiopia
118 B1 **Mizdah** Libya
67 B5 **Mizen Head** headland Rep. of Ireland
67 E4 **Mizen Head** headland Rep. of Ireland
77 O3 **Mizhevichy** Belarus
30 D5 **Mizhi** China
112 F2 **Mizil** Romania
112 D3 **Miziya** Bulgaria
53 B1 **Mizoch** Ukraine
24 A2 **Mizoram** div. India
43 C4 **Mizpe Ramon** Israel
164 C3 **Mizque** Bolivia
29 H4 **Mizusawa** Japan
59 F2 **Mjölby** Sweden
58 B2 **Mjølfell** Norway
58 D2 **Mjøndalen** Norway
59 E3 **Mjörn** l. Sweden
58 D1 **Mjøsa** l. Norway
131 H5 **Mkambati Nature Reserve** res. South Africa
127 C6 **Mkata** Tanzania
131 H3 **Mkhondvo** r. Swaziland
127 C6 **Mkokotoni** Tanzania
127 C5 **Mkomazi** Tanzania
127 C5 **Mkomazi Game Reserve** res. Tanzania
125 E6 **Mkushi** Zambia
131 J3 **Mkuze** r. South Africa
131 J3 **Mkuze** South Africa
131 J3 **Mkuzi Game Reserve** res. South Africa
75 D1 **Mladá Boleslav** Czech Rep.
75 K3 **Mladá Vožice** Czech Rep.
112 C2 **Mladenovac** Yugoslavia
127 B6 **Mlala Hills** h. Tanzania
131 H3 **Mlaula** r. Swaziland
112 C2 **Mlava** r. Yugoslavia
77 J2 **Mława** Poland
104 F4 **Mljet** i. Croatia

104 F4 Mljetski Kanal chan. Croatia
77 H1 Mlnary Poland
131 H2 Mlumati r. Swaziland
131 F5 Mlungisi South Africa
77 K3 Młynarze Poland
53 A1 Mlyniv Ukraine
77 N6 Mlynys'ka Ukraine
131 E2 Mmabatho South Africa
128 D3 Mmadinare Botswana
131 E2 Mmathethe Botswana
131 G6 Mncwasa Point pt South Africa
75 K3 Mnichovice Czech Rep.
78 D1 Mnichovo Hradiště Czech Rep.
77 J4 Mniów Poland
79 K3 Mníšek nad Hnilcom Slovakia
77 K4 Mniszew Poland
77 J4 Mniszków Poland
131 H3 Mnjoli Dam dam Swaziland
58 A1 Mo Norway
43 C4 Moab reg. Jordan
155 H2 Moab *Utah* U.S.A.
124 B4 Moabi Gabon
11 H1 Moa I. i. *Queensland* Australia
6 □7 Moala i. Fiji
39 C2 Mo'alla Iran
129 E4 Moamba Mozambique
98 B2 Moaña Spain
124 B4 Moanda Gabon
155 E3 Moapa *Nevada* U.S.A.
67 D3 Moate Rep. of Ireland
125 E5 Moba Congo(Zaire)
29 H6 Mobara Japan
124 D3 Mobaye Central African Rep.
124 D3 Mobayi-Mbongo Congo(Zaire)
150 E4 Moberly *Missouri* U.S.A.
140 C2 Mobert *Ontario* Canada
145 B6 Mobile *Alabama* U.S.A.
155 F5 Mobile *Arizona* U.S.A.
145 B6 Mobile Bay b. *Alabama* U.S.A.
150 C2 Mobridge *S. Dakota* U.S.A.
Mobutu, Lake l. *see* Albert, Lake
124 D3 Mobwasa Congo(Zaire)
159 E3 Moca Dominican Rep.
166 C1 Mocajuba Brazil
129 G2 Moçambique Mozambique
24 D2 Môc Châu Vietnam
6 □7 Moce i. Fiji
99 G5 Mocejón Spain
52 F1 Mocha r. Rus. Fed.
Mocha *see* Al Mukhā
172 A5 Mocha, I. i. Chile
102 B3 Mochales Spain
163 E1 Mochirma, Parque Nacional nat. park Venezuela
159 □1 Mocho Mts mts Jamaica
77 H3 Mochowo Poland
128 D3 Mochudi Botswana
127 D7 Mocimboa da Praia Mozambique
127 C7 Mocimboa do Rovuma Mozambique
59 F3 Möckeln l. Sweden
73 G3 Möckern Germany
74 E3 Möckmühl Germany
73 H4 Mockrehna Germany
162 B3 Mocoa Colombia
168 E4 Mococa Brazil
173 H1 Mocoretá r. Argentina
156 D2 Moctezuma *Chihuahua* Mexico
157 E4 Moctezuma *San Luis Potosí* Mexico
156 C2 Moctezuma *Sonora* Mexico
129 F2 Mocuba Mozambique
91 E3 Modane France
36 C5 Modasa India
69 D4 Modave Belgium
62 C4 Modbury *England* U.K.
131 E4 Modder r. South Africa
107 E4 Modena div. *Emilia-Romagna* Italy
107 E4 Modena *Modena* Italy
155 F3 Modena *Utah* U.S.A.
87 G4 Moder r. France
172 E3 Modestino Pizarro Argentina
154 B3 Modesto *California* U.S.A.
110 D6 Modica *Ragusa* Italy
107 F4 Modigliana Italy
81 H2 Mödling div. Austria
81 H2 Mödling Austria
30 D3 Modot Mongolia
78 G3 Modra Slovakia
104 G3 Modriča Bos.-Herz.
81 H1 Modřice Czech Rep.
79 J3 Modrý Kameň Slovakia
111 F1 Modugno Italy
32 B2 Modung China
13 F4 Moe *Victoria* Australia
8 E2 Moehau h. New Zealand
88 B4 Moëlan-sur-Mer France
62 B1 Moelfre *Wales* U.K.
62 C2 Moel Sych h. *Wales* U.K.
58 D1 Moely Norway
131 F4 Moemaneng South Africa
56 E1 Moen Norway
80 C4 Moena Italy
163 G2 Moengo Surinam
155 G3 Moenkopi *Arizona* U.S.A.
9 C6 Moeraki Pt pt New Zealand
69 B3 Moerbeke Belgium
8 E1 Moerewa New Zealand
72 B4 Moers Germany
83 E2 Moesa r. Switzerland
66 E5 Moffat *Scotland* U.K.
98 D3 Mofreita Portugal
36 C3 Moga India
Mogadishu *see* Muqdisho
146 C4 Mogadore Reservoir resr *Ohio* U.S.A.
98 D3 Mogadouro Portugal
98 D3 Mogadouro, Sa de mountain range Portugal
131 G1 Mogalakwena r. South Africa
131 G1 Mogalakwenastroom South Africa
124 C3 Mogalo Congo(Zaire)
29 G4 Mogami-gawa r. Japan
126 C1 Mogareb watercourse Eritrea
24 B1 Mogaung Myanmar
31 K2 Mogdy Rus. Fed.
55 A5 Møgeltønder Denmark
55 D4 Mogenstrup Denmark
74 E4 Mögglingen Germany
77 J6 Mogielnica mt. *Nowy Sacz* Poland
77 J4 Mogielnica *Radom* Poland
169 E5 Mogi-Guaçu Brazil
114 C1 Mogila Macedonia
76 F3 Mogilno Poland
167 C5 Mogi-Mirim Brazil
129 G2 Mogincual Mozambique
169 J2 Mogiquiçaba Brazil
109 F1 Mogliano Italy
107 G3 Mogliano Veneto Italy
172 C1 Mogna Argentina
27 L1 Mogocha Rus. Fed.
128 D3 Mogoditshane Botswana
126 B3 Mogogh Sudan
24 B2 Mogok Myanmar
155 H5 Mogollon Baldy mt. *New Mexico* U.S.A.
155 H5 Mogollon Mts mts *New Mexico* U.S.A.
155 G4 Mogollon Rim plat. *Arizona* U.S.A.
108 A5 Mogoro r. *Sardegna* Italy
108 A5 Mogoro *Sardegna* Italy
112 F1 Mogoșești-Siret Romania
31 E2 Mogoytuy Rus. Fed.
124 C1 Mogroum Chad
100 D3 Moguer Spain
31 G3 Moguqi China
30 E2 Mogzon Rus. Fed.
79 H6 Mohács Hungary
8 F3 Mohaka r. New Zealand
131 F5 Mohale's Hoek Lesotho
137 J5 Mohall *N. Dakota* U.S.A.
39 D2 Mohammad Iran
Moḩammadābād *see* Darreh Gaz
36 E3 Mohan r. India
36 D4 Mohana India
37 G4 Mohanganj Bangladesh
155 E4 Mohave, L. l. *Nevada* U.S.A.
147 F3 Mohawk r. *New York* U.S.A.
155 F5 Mohawk *Arizona* U.S.A.
155 F5 Mohawk Mts mts *Arizona* U.S.A.
31 G1 Mohe China
Moheli i. *see* Mwali
78 F2 Mohelnice Czech Rep.
81 H1 Mohelno Czech Rep.
128 C2 Mohembo Botswana
67 D3 Mohill Rep. of Ireland
82 C1 Möhlin Switzerland
72 D4 Möhne r. Germany
164 C3 Moho Peru
155 F4 Mohon Peak summit *Arizona* U.S.A.
79 J4 Mohora Hungary
127 C6 Mohoro Tanzania
151 C7 Mohovano Ranch Mexico
53 F1 Mohrytsya Ukraine
53 B2 Mohyliv Podil's'kyy Ukraine
58 B2 Moi Norway
102 F3 Moià Spain
93 A5 Moilets-et-Maa France
98 C4 Moimenta da Beira Portugal
36 E3 Moincêr China
6 □2 Moindou *New Caledonia* Pacific Ocean
89 D4 Moine r. France
131 J2 Moine Mozambique
112 F1 Moinești Romania
90 C3 Moingt France
147 F2 Moira *New York* U.S.A.
64 B3 Moira *Northern Ireland* U.K.
56 D2 Mo i Rana Norway
37 H4 Moirang India
91 D3 Moirans France
90 D2 Moirans-en-Montagne France
93 C4 Moirax France
115 F7 Moires Greece
173 K1 Moirones Uruguay
57 G4 Mõisaküla Estonia
88 D4 Moisdon-la-Rivière France
173 G1 Moisés Ville Argentina
139 G3 Moisie r. *Québec* Canada
139 G3 Moisie *Québec* Canada
69 A5 Moislains France
93 D4 Moissac France
124 C2 Moïssala Chad
82 A1 Moissey France
108 B2 Moïta *Corse* France
100 B2 Moita Portugal
103 C6 Moixent Spain
59 H2 Möja i. Sweden
101 J3 Mojácar Spain
99 F3 Mojados Spain
154 D4 Mojave r. *California* U.S.A.
154 C4 Mojave *California* U.S.A.
154 D4 Mojave Desert desert *California* U.S.A.
32 C4 Mojiang China
167 C5 Moji das Cruzes Brazil
168 E4 Moji-Guaçu r. Brazil
28 C7 Mojikō Japan
112 B3 Mojkovac Yugoslavia
164 C4 Mojo Bolivia
22 C3 Mojokerto Indonesia
101 G3 Mojón Alto mt. Spain
126 D3 Mojo Shet' r. Ethiopia
164 C3 Mojotoro Bolivia
81 E4 Mojstrana Slovenia
166 C1 Moju r. Brazil
29 H5 Mōka Japan
8 E3 Mokai New Zealand
37 F4 Mokāma India
153 □1 Mokapu Pen. pen. *Hawaii* U.S.A.
124 D3 Mokaria Congo(Zaire)
8 E3 Mokau r. New Zealand
8 E3 Mokau New Zealand
124 C3 Mokéko Congo
154 B2 Mokelumne r. *California* U.S.A.
131 G4 Mokhotlong Lesotho
52 C3 Mokhovoye Rus. Fed.
45 O3 Mokhsogollokh Rus. Fed.
53 B1 Mokiyivtsi Ukraine
128 D3 Mokobela Pan salt pan Botswana
8 E1 Mokohinau Is is New Zealand
37 H4 Mokokchung India
131 F2 Mokolo r. South Africa
124 B1 Mokolo Cameroon
131 F1 Mokolo Dam dam South Africa
31 H6 Mokp'o South Korea
112 C3 Mokra Gora mts Yugoslavia
53 D2 Mokra Kalyhirka Ukraine
112 B3 Mokra Planina mts Yugoslavia
52 F3 Mokraya Panda r. Rus. Fed.
51 H5 Mokrous Rus. Fed.
52 C3 Mokroye Rus. Fed.
52 F3 Mokryy Karay r. Rus. Fed.
52 E2 Moksha r. Rus. Fed.
52 G3 Mokshan Rus. Fed.
56 G3 Möksy Finland
153 □1 Mokuauia I. i. *Hawaii* U.S.A.
153 □1 Mokulua Is is *Hawaii* U.S.A.
53 B1 Mokvyn Ukraine
123 F5 Mokwa Nigeria
69 D3 Mol Belgium
111 G1 Mola di Bari Italy
157 F4 Molango Mexico
115 D6 Molaoi Greece
108 B4 Molara, Isola i. *Sardegna* Italy
98 C3 Molares Portugal
107 J4 Molat i. Croatia
81 F4 Mölbling Austria
62 C1 Mold *Wales* U.K.
79 L3 Moldava nad Bodvou Slovakia
Moldavia *see* Moldova
56 B3 Molde Norway
56 D2 Moldjord Norway
49 H4 Moldova country Europe
112 C2 Moldova Nouă Romania
112 G1 Moldovei Centrale, Podișul reg. Moldova
53 B2 Moldovei de Nord, Podișul plat. Moldova
55 B3 Møldrup Denmark
62 C4 Mole r. *England* U.K.
24 B1 Mole Chaung r. Myanmar
90 E2 Mole, Le mt. France
131 G4 Molen r. South Africa
122 D5 Mole National Park nat. park Ghana
69 C4 Molenbeek-St-Jean Belgium
88 A3 Molène, Île i. France
128 D3 Molepolole Botswana
54 D4 Molėtai Lithuania
109 J3 Molfetta Italy
72 F1 Molfsee Germany
93 D4 Molières France
172 C2 Molina Argentina
172 B3 Molina Chile
102 B4 Molina de Aragón Spain
103 B6 Molina de Segura Spain
83 F3 Molina di Ledro Italy
148 B5 Moline *Illinois* U.S.A.
107 F4 Molinella Italy
90 B2 Molinet France
90 D2 Molinges France
80 C4 Molini di Tures Italy
173 G2 Molino Doll Argentina
172 E1 Molinos, Emb. Los resr Argentina
102 F3 Molins de Rei Spain
125 F5 Moliro Congo(Zaire)
109 G3 Molise div. Italy
109 H4 Moliterno Italy
93 E6 Molitg-les-Bains France
59 E2 Molkom Sweden
80 D4 Möll r. Austria
114 B2 Mollas Albania
59 E3 Mölle Sweden
55 B4 Møllebjerg h. Denmark
59 F3 Möllefjorden b. Sweden
73 J2 Möllenbeck Germany
164 B3 Mollendo Peru
73 H2 Möllenhagen Germany
17 B6 Mollerin, L. salt flat *Western Australia* Australia
102 D3 Mollerussa Spain
102 F3 Mollet del Vallès Spain
86 B3 Molliens-Dreuil France
83 E1 Mollis Switzerland
81 F3 Molln Austria
73 F2 Mölln Germany
93 E6 Molló Spain
55 D1 Mollösund Sweden
78 B4 Mölltal v. Austria
59 F2 Mölltorp Sweden
59 E3 Mölnlycke Sweden
53 F3 Molochans'k Ukraine
53 F3 Molochna r. Ukraine
50 F3 Molochnoye Rus. Fed.
56 J1 Molochnyy Rus. Fed.
53 F3 Molochnyy Lyman est. Ukraine
129 F2 Molocue r. Mozambique
179 D4 Molodezhnaya Rus. Fed. Base Antarctica
53 E2 Molodizhne Ukraine
52 A1 Molodoy Tud Rus. Fed.
153 □2 Molokai i. *Hawaii* U.S.A.
177 K4 Molokai Fracture Zone sea feature Pacific Ocean
50 J3 Moloma r. Rus. Fed.
91 B3 Molompize France
13 G3 Molong *New South Wales* Australia
130 C3 Molopo watercourse Botswana/South Africa
130 E2 Moloporivier South Africa
114 D4 Molos Greece
124 C3 Moloundou Cameroon
53 C3 Molovata Moldova
90 C1 Moloy France
55 C3 Mols Bjerge h. Denmark
87 G4 Molsheim France
137 K4 Molson L. l. *Manitoba* Canada
131 F5 Molteno South Africa
130 D6 Moltenopass pass South Africa
Moluccas is *see* Maluku
21 J6 Molucca Sea g. Indonesia
103 B5 Moluengo mt. Spain
129 F2 Molumbo Mozambique
107 E2 Molveno Italy
83 F2 Molveno, Lago di l. Italy
129 F2 Moma Mozambique
13 E2 Momba *New South Wales* Australia
166 E2 Mombaça Brazil
127 C5 Mombasa Kenya
99 E4 Mombeltrán Spain
124 C3 Mombenzélé Congo(Zaire)
37 H4 Mombi New India
55 A3 Mombjerge h. Denmark
124 C4 Momboyo r. Congo(Zaire)
74 E2 Mömbris Germany
98 D2 Mombuey Spain
114 G1 Momchilgrad Bulgaria
148 D5 Momence *Illinois* U.S.A.
124 E4 Momi Congo(Zaire)
100 E4 Momia, Sierra mountain range Spain
69 C4 Momignies Belgium
106 C3 Momo Italy
23 B3 Mompog Pass. chan. Philippines
124 D3 Mompono Congo(Zaire)
162 C2 Mompós Colombia
93 B5 Momuy France
Môn i. *see* Anglesey
55 E4 Møn i. Denmark
24 B3 Mon Myanmar
155 G2 Mona *Utah* U.S.A.
159 □1 Mona Jamaica
101 G3 Monachil r. Spain
66 A3 Monach Is is *Scotland* U.K.
66 A3 Monach, Sound of chan. *Scotland* U.K.
91 F5 Monaco country Europe
66 D3 Monadhliath Mts mountain range *Scotland* U.K.
67 D2 Monaghan div. Rep. of Ireland
67 E2 Monaghan Rep. of Ireland
151 C6 Monahans *Texas* U.S.A.
159 F3 Mona, I. i. Puerto Rico
159 E3 Mona Passage chan. Dominican Rep.
129 G1 Monapo Mozambique
136 D4 Monarch Mt. mt. *B.C.* Canada
153 F4 Monarch Pass pass *Colorado* U.S.A.
66 C3 Monar, Loch l. *Scotland* U.K.
136 F4 Monashee Mts mountain range *B.C.* Canada
111 F4 Monasterace Italy
67 D3 Monasterevan Rep. of Ireland
108 B5 Monastir *Sardegna* Italy
121 G1 Monastir Tunisia
114 B4 Monastiraki Greece
77 N6 Monastyrets' Ukraine
53 C2 Monastyryshche Ukraine
53 A2 Monastyrys'ka Ukraine
124 B3 Monatélé Cameroon
6 □8 Monavatu mt. Fiji
93 C4 Monbahus France
93 C4 Monbazillac France
93 D5 Monbéqui France
28 J1 Monbetsu Japan
28 J2 Monbetsu Japan
124 B2 Monboré Cameroon
106 B3 Moncalieri Italy
98 D2 Moncalvo mt. Spain
106 C3 Moncalvo Italy
98 B2 Monção Portugal
100 C3 Moncarapacho Portugal
93 C4 Moncaut France
102 B3 Moncayo, Sierra del mountain range Spain
87 F4 Moncel-sur-Seille France
82 D2 Mönch mt. Switzerland
56 J2 Monchegorsk Rus. Fed.
72 B4 Mönchengladbach Germany
81 H3 Mönchhof Austria
100 B3 Monchique Portugal
100 B3 Monchique, Serra de mountain range Portugal
145 E5 Moncks Corner *S. Carolina* U.S.A.
93 C4 Monclar France
93 D5 Monclar-de-Quercy France
157 E3 Monclova Mexico
88 C3 Moncontour *Bretagne* France
92 B2 Moncontour *Poitou-Charentes* France
92 B2 Moncoutant France
139 H4 Moncton *New Brunswick* Canada
101 F4 Monda Spain
107 G5 Mondavio Italy
165 E5 Monday r. Paraguay
98 C4 Mondego r. Portugal
98 B4 Mondego, Cabo pt Portugal
110 C4 Mondello *Sicilia* Italy
89 E2 Mondeville France
124 D3 Mondimbi Congo(Zaire)
98 C3 Mondim de Basto Portugal
124 D3 Mondjamboli Congo(Zaire)
124 D4 Mondjuku Congo(Zaire)
131 H3 Mondlo South Africa
118 C5 Mondo Chad
107 H5 Mondolfo Italy
124 D4 Mondombe Congo(Zaire)
98 C1 Mondoñedo Spain
69 E5 Mondorf-les-Bains Luxembourg
89 F4 Mondoubleau France
148 B3 Mondovi *Wisconsin* U.S.A.
106 B4 Mondovì Italy
91 C4 Mondragon France
99 H1 Mondragón Spain
109 F3 Mondragone Italy
81 E3 Mondsee l. Austria
80 E3 Mondsee Austria
30 B2 Mondy Rus. Fed.
159 □1 Moneague Jamaica
106 D4 Moneglia Italy
102 C3 Monegrillo Spain
93 B5 Monein France
115 E6 Monemvasia Greece
27 P2 Moneron, Ostrov i. Rus. Fed.
146 D4 Monessen *Pennsylvania* U.S.A.
100 D2 Monesterio Spain
91 D4 Monestier-de-Clermont France
93 E4 Monestiés France
141 H2 Monet *Québec* Canada
90 B1 Monéteau France
67 E2 Moneymore *Northern Ireland* U.K.
107 H3 Monfalcone Italy
93 C4 Monflanquin France
93 C5 Monfort France
100 C1 Monforte Portugal
98 C2 Monforte Spain
100 C1 Monforte da Beira Portugal
106 B4 Monforte d'Alba Italy
98 D4 Monfortinho Portugal
100 B2 Monfurado mt. Portugal
124 D3 Monga Congo(Zaire)
169 E6 Mongaguá Brazil
124 D3 Mongala r. Congo(Zaire)
124 F3 Mongbwalu Congo(Zaire)
24 D2 Mông Cai Vietnam
17 B6 Mongers Lake salt flat *Western Australia* Australia
91 E4 Monges, Les mt. France
Monggolküre *see* Zhaosu
31 F2 Monggon Qulu China
24 B2 Mong Hang Myanmar
107 F4 Monghidoro Italy
24 B2 Mong Hpayak Myanmar
24 B2 Mong Hsat Myanmar
24 B2 Mong Hsu Myanmar
24 B2 Mong Kung Myanmar
24 B2 Mong Lang Myanmar
24 C2 Mong Lin Myanmar
24 C2 Mong Loi Myanmar
24 B2 Mong Ma Myanmar
24 B3 Mong Mau Myanmar
24 B2 Mong Nai Myanmar
24 B2 Mong Nawng Myanmar
118 C5 Mongo Chad
19 L5 Mongolia country Asia
124 B3 Mongomo Equatorial Guinea
123 G4 Mongonu Nigeria
36 C2 Mongora Pakistan
118 D5 Mongororo Chad
124 C3 Mongoumba Central African Rep.
24 B2 Mong Pan Myanmar
24 B2 Mong Pat Myanmar
24 B2 Mong Ping Myanmar
24 B2 Mong Pu Myanmar
24 B2 Mong Pu-awn Myanmar
82 D3 Mongrando Italy
24 B2 Mong Ton Myanmar
125 D7 Mongu Zambia
107 G2 Monguelfo Italy
24 C2 Mong Un Myanmar
24 B2 Mong Yai Myanmar
24 B2 Mong Yang Myanmar
24 C2 Mong Yawng Myanmar
24 B2 Mong Yu Myanmar
147 J3 Monhegan I. i. *Maine* U.S.A.
75 F4 Monheim Germany
114 F2 Moni Agiou Dionysiou Greece
66 E5 Moniaive *Scotland* U.K.
114 F2 Moni Chiliandariou Greece
91 D4 Monieux France
173 G1 Monigotes Argentina
114 F2 Moni Iviron Greece
114 F2 Moni Megistis Lavras Greece
114 F2 Moni Simonos Petras Greece
91 B4 Monistrol-d'Allier France
91 C3 Monistrol-sur-Loire France
154 D2 Monitor Mt mt. *Nevada* U.S.A.
154 D2 Monitor Range mts *Nevada* U.S.A.
114 F2 Moni Vatopediou Greece
67 C3 Monivea Rep. of Ireland
169 F3 Monjolos Brazil
129 F1 Monkey Bay Malawi
77 L2 Mońki Poland
14 E5 Monkira *Queensland* Australia
62 B4 Monkokehampton *England* U.K.
124 D4 Monkoto Congo(Zaire)
140 E5 Monkton *Ontario* Canada
103 C4 Monleón r. Spain
148 B5 Monmouth *Illinois* U.S.A.
147 H2 Monmouth *Maine* U.S.A.
62 D3 Monmouth *Wales* U.K.
136 E4 Monmouth Mt. mt. *B.C.* Canada
62 C3 Monmouthshire div. *Wales* U.K.
89 F4 Monnaie France
68 D2 Monnickendam Netherlands
62 D3 Monnow r. *England/Wales* U.K.
123 E5 Mono r. Benin/Togo
154 C3 Mono Lake l. *California* U.S.A.
115 □ Monolithos Greece
147 H4 Monomoy Pt pt *Massachusetts* U.S.A.
148 D5 Monon *Indiana* U.S.A.
148 B4 Monona *Iowa* U.S.A.
111 G2 Monopoli Italy
79 J4 Monor Hungary
146 C5 Monorgahela r. *Pennsylvania* U.S.A.
159 □3 Monos I. i. *Trinidad* Trinidad and Tobago
118 D4 Monou Chad
103 C6 Monóvar Spain
93 C4 Monpazier France
101 H1 Monreal r. Spain
93 A6 Monreal Spain
102 B4 Monreal del Campo Spain
110 C4 Monreale *Sicilia* Italy
151 E5 Monroe *Louisiana* U.S.A.
149 F5 Monroe *Michigan* U.S.A.
145 D5 Monroe *N. Carolina* U.S.A.
147 F4 Monroe *New York* U.S.A.
155 F2 Monroe *Utah* U.S.A.
148 C4 Monroe *Wisconsin* U.S.A.
148 B6 Monroe City *Missouri* U.S.A.
145 C6 Monroeville *Alabama* U.S.A.
122 B5 Monrovia Liberia
100 D1 Monroy Spain
102 C4 Monroyo Spain
69 B4 Mons div. *Hainaut* Belgium
69 B4 Mons *Mons* Belgium
93 E5 Mons France
173 J4 Monsalvo Argentina
74 B2 Monschau Germany
92 C3 Monsec France
93 C4 Monségur France
107 F3 Monselice Italy
93 C4 Monsempron-Libos France
90 C2 Monsols France
68 C2 Monster Netherlands
107 E5 Monsummano Terme Italy
74 C2 Montabaur Germany
91 B5 Montady France
80 A3 Montafon v. Austria
91 B5 Montagnac France
107 F3 Montagnana Italy
93 B4 Montagne France
129 H1 Montagne d'Ambre, Parc National de la nat. park Madagascar
92 C3 Montagrier France
130 C6 Montagu South Africa
148 D4 Montague *Michigan* U.S.A.
17 B5 Montague Ra. h. *Western Australia* Australia
16 D2 Montague Sd b. *Western Australia* Australia
179 C1 Montagu I. i. *S. Sandwich Is* Atlantic Ocean
92 A2 Montaigu France
93 D4 Montaigu-de-Quercy France
92 E2 Montaigut France
93 D5 Montaigut-sur-Save France
102 C4 Montalbán Spain
111 E4 Montalbano Elicona *Sicilia* Italy
109 J4 Montalbano Jonico Italy
99 H5 Montalbo Spain
108 D1 Montalcino Italy
98 C3 Montalegre Portugal
90 D3 Montalieu-Vercieu France
111 E4 Montalto mt. Italy
108 D2 Montalto di Castro Italy
111 F3 Montalto Uffugo Italy
100 C1 Montalvão Portugal
162 B4 Montalvo Ecuador
100 B1 Montalvo Portugal
98 E3 Montamarta Spain
152 E2 Montana div. U.S.A.
112 D3 Montana Bulgaria
82 C2 Montana Switzerland
99 E1 Montaña de Covadonga, Parque Nacional de la nat. park Spain
100 D1 Montánchez, Sierra de mountain range Spain
103 C4 Montanejos Spain
93 B5 Montaner France
169 H3 Montanha Brazil
109 H4 Montano Antilia Italy
100 B1 Montargil, Barragem de resr Portugal
86 B5 Montargis France
93 E5 Montaset, Pic de mt. France
93 D5 Montastruc-la-Conseillère France
86 B3 Montataire France
88 C3 Montauban *Bretagne* France
93 D4 Montauban *Midi-Pyrénées* France
147 G4 Montauk *New York* U.S.A.
147 H4 Montauk Pt pt *New York* U.S.A.
93 B5 Montaut *Aquitaine* France
93 D5 Montaut *Midi-Pyrénées* France
90 C1 Montbard France
90 D1 Montbarrey France
93 E4 Montbazens France
89 F4 Montbazon France
90 E1 Montbéliard France
90 E2 Montbenoît France
93 D4 Montbeton France
102 E3 Montblanc Spain
106 A3 Mont Blanc mt. France/Italy
127 □4 Mont Blanche Mauritius
90 E3 Mont Blanc Tunnel France/Italy
82 B1 Montbozon France
90 C3 Montbrison France
92 C3 Montbron France
86 A2 Montcavrel France
90 C2 Montceau-les-Mines France
90 C2 Montcenis France
91 E3 Mont Cenis, Lac du l. France
90 C2 Montchanin France
86 D3 Montcornet France
93 D4 Montcuq France
86 D3 Montcy-Notre-Dame France
91 B5 Montdardier France
91 E4 Mont-Dauphin France
93 B5 Mont-de-Marsan France
86 B3 Montdidier France
111 E3 Montea mt. Italy
164 D3 Monteagudo Bolivia
99 H3 Monteagudo de las Vicarías Spain
172 A4 Monte Aguila Chile
166 B1 Monte Alegre Brazil
166 C3 Monte Alegre de Goiás Brazil
103 B6 Montealegre del Castillo Spain
168 D3 Monte Alegre de Minas Brazil
168 D4 Monte Aprazível Brazil
169 G1 Monte Azul Brazil
168 D4 Monte Azul Paulista Brazil
141 H4 Montebello *Québec* Canada
111 E5 Montebello Ionico Italy
16 A4 Monte Bello Is is *Western Australia* Australia
107 G3 Montebelluna Italy
88 D2 Montebourg France
173 F2 Monte Buey Argentina
170 F2 Montecarlo Argentina
106 B5 Monte-Carlo Monaco
168 E3 Monte Carmelo Brazil
173 J1 Monte Caseros Argentina
109 E2 Montecastrilli Italy
107 E5 Montecatini Terme Italy
106 E4 Montecchio Emilia Italy
107 F3 Montecchio Maggiore Italy
93 D5 Montech France
131 F1 Monte Christo South Africa
109 G3 Montecilfone Italy
172 D3 Monte Comán Argentina
109 J4 Monte Cotugna, Lago di l. Italy
107 G2 Montecreale Valcellina Italy
159 E3 Monte Cristi Dominican Rep.
162 A4 Montecristi Ecuador
108 C2 Montecristo, Isola di i. Italy
100 B3 Monte da Rocha, Barragem do resr Portugal
100 C2 Monte das Flores Portugal
171 C7 Monte Dinero Argentina
109 E2 Montefalco Italy
109 H3 Montefalcone di Val Fortore Italy
107 G5 Montefelcino Italy
107 G5 Montefeltro reg. Italy
108 E2 Montefiascone Italy
109 F1 Montefiore dell'Aso Italy
107 E4 Montefiorino Italy
109 F2 Montefortino Italy
101 F3 Montefrío Spain
109 J4 Montegiordano Italy
109 F1 Montegiorgio Italy
159 □1 Montego Bay b. Jamaica
159 □1 Montego Bay Jamaica
107 H5 Montegranaro Italy
107 F3 Montegrotto Terme Italy
173 G5 Monte Hermoso Argentina
98 D4 Montehermoso Spain
101 E4 Montejaque Spain
14 B3 Montejinnie *Northern Terr.* Australia
100 A1 Montejunto, Serra de h. Portugal
92 E3 Montel-de-Gelat France
173 F4 Monte, L. del l. Argentina
109 H3 Monteleone di Puglia Italy
109 E2 Monteleone di Spoleto Italy
108 E2 Monteleone d'Orvieto Italy
108 A4 Monteleone Rocca Doria *Sardegna* Italy
110 C4 Montelepre *Sicilia* Italy
91 C4 Montélimar France
170 E2 Monte Lindo r. Argentina
109 H4 Montella Italy
100 E3 Montellano Spain
148 C4 Montello *Wisconsin* U.S.A.
107 H5 Montelupone Italy
110 C5 Montemaggiore Belsito *Sicilia* Italy
173 F2 Monte Maíz Argentina
109 H4 Montemarano Italy
101 H2 Montemayon r. Spain
92 C3 Montemboeuf France
111 G2 Montemesola Italy
100 D2 Montemolín Spain
109 F2 Montemonaco Italy
157 F3 Montemorelos Mexico
100 B2 Montemor-o-Novo Portugal
98 B4 Montemor-o-Velho Portugal
107 F5 Montemurlo Italy
98 B3 Montemuro, Serra de mountain range Portugal
89 E3 Montenay France
92 B3 Montendre France
167 B6 Montenegro Brazil
Montenegro div. *see* Crna Gora
99 H2 Montenegro de Cameros Spain
109 G3 Montenero di Bisaccia Italy
100 C2 Monte Novo, Barragem do resr Portugal
172 B1 Monte Patria Chile
107 H5 Monte Porzio Italy
127 C7 Montepuez r. Mozambique
127 C7 Montepuez Mozambique
108 D1 Montepulciano Italy
170 D2 Monte Quemado Argentina
107 G5 Monterchi Italy
98 B5 Monte Real Portugal
109 F2 Montereale Italy
86 B4 Montereau-faut-Yonne France
98 B5 Monte Redondo Portugal
154 B3 Monterey *California* U.S.A.
146 D5 Monterey *Virginia* U.S.A.
154 B3 Monterey Bay b. *California* U.S.A.
162 B2 Montería Colombia
107 F5 Monteriggioni Italy
165 D3 Montero Bolivia
108 D2 Monte Romano Italy
170 C2 Monteros Argentina
82 C3 Monte Rosa mt. Italy/Switzerland
109 E2 Monterosi Italy
106 D4 Monterosso al Mare Italy
110 D5 Monterosso Almo *Sicilia* Italy
109 E2 Monterotondo Italy
108 C1 Monterotondo Marittimo Italy
157 E3 Monterrey Mexico
98 C2 Monterroso Spain
101 E2 Monterrubio de la Serena Spain
109 F1 Monterubbiano Italy
166 C2 Montes Altos Brazil
111 H3 Montesano Salentino Italy
109 H4 Montesano sulla Marcellana Italy
107 F5 Monte San Savino Italy
109 H3 Monte Sant'Angelo Italy
166 E3 Monte Santo Brazil
169 E4 Monte Santo de Minas Brazil
108 B4 Monte Santu, Capo di pt *Sardegna* Italy
107 H5 Monte San Vito Italy
109 G3 Montesarchio Italy
111 F2 Montescaglioso Italy
169 G2 Montes Claros Brazil
107 E5 Montescudaio Italy
101 F1 Montes de Toledo mountain range Spain
109 G2 Montesilvano Italy
102 D2 Montes Malditos mountain range Spain
93 D4 Montesquieu France
93 D5 Montesquieu-Volvestre France
93 C5 Montesquiou France
93 C5 Montestruc-sur-Gers France
107 F5 Montevarchi Italy
109 H3 Monteverde Italy
150 E2 Montevideo *Minnesota* U.S.A.
173 J3 Montevideo Uruguay
153 F4 Monte Vista *Colorado* U.S.A.
148 A5 Montezuma *Iowa* U.S.A.
155 G4 Montezuma Castle National Monument nat. park *Arizona* U.S.A.
155 H3 Montezuma Creek *Utah* U.S.A.
154 D3 Montezuma Peak summit *Nevada* U.S.A.
89 D4 Montfaucon France
87 E3 Montfaucon-d'Argonne France
91 C3 Montfaucon-en-Velay France
91 E5 Montferrat France
68 C2 Montfoort Netherlands
88 D3 Montfort France
93 B5 Montfort-en-Chalosse France
89 F3 Montfort-le-Gesnois France
93 D6 Montgaillard *Midi-Pyrénées* France
93 C5 Montgaillard *Midi-Pyrénées* France
91 E4 Montgenèvre France
86 B4 Montgeron France
93 D5 Montgiscard France
103 D6 Montgó h. Spain
145 C5 Montgomery *Alabama* U.S.A.
62 C2 Montgomery *Wales* U.K.
92 B3 Montguyon France
86 D3 Monthermé France
82 B2 Monthey Switzerland
86 D3 Monthois France
87 E4 Monthureux-sur-Saône France
108 B4 Monti *Sardegna* Italy
107 G3 Monticano r. Italy
106 D3 Monticelli d'Ongina Italy
151 F5 Monticello *Arkansas* U.S.A.
145 D6 Monticello *Florida* U.S.A.
148 D5 Monticello *Indiana* U.S.A.
148 B4 Monticello *Iowa* U.S.A.
147 K1 Monticello *Maine* U.S.A.
148 B5 Monticello *Missouri* U.S.A.
147 F4 Monticello *New York* U.S.A.
155 H3 Monticello *Utah* U.S.A.

124 E2 Mvolo Sudan
127 C6 Mvomero Tanzania
125 B4 Mvouti Congo
129 E2 Mvuma Zimbabwe
127 D7 Mwali i. Comoros
127 B5 Mwanza div. Tanzania
127 B5 Mwanza Tanzania
125 E5 Mwanza Congo(Zaire)
67 B3 Mweelrea h. Rep. of Ireland
125 D4 Mweka Congo(Zaire)
125 E6 Mwenda Zambia
125 D5 Mwene-Ditu Congo(Zaire)
129 E3 Mwenezi r. Zimbabwe
129 E3 Mwenezi Zimbabwe
125 E4 Mwenga Congo(Zaire)
125 E5 Mweru, Lake l. Zambia
125 E5 Mweru Wantipa, Lake l. Zambia
125 E5 Mweru Wantipa Nat. Park nat. park Zambia
125 D5 Mwimba Congo(Zaire)
125 D6 Mwinilunga Zambia
54 E4 Myadzyel Belarus
24 A2 Myaing Myanmar
36 B4 Myājlār India
53 B1 M"yakoty Ukraine
13 H3 Myall L. l. *New South Wales* Australia
24 A3 Myanaung Myanmar
19 L7 Myanmar country Asia
52 B2 Myatlevo Rus. Fed.
24 A3 Myaungmya Myanmar
24 B3 Myawadi Thailand
66 E2 Mybster *Scotland* U.K.
24 A2 Myebon Myanmar
77 M4 Myedna Belarus
24 A2 Myedu Myanmar
24 A2 Myingyan Myanmar
24 B2 Myinkyado Myanmar
25 B4 Myinmoletkat mt. Myanmar
24 A2 Myinmu Myanmar
24 B1 Myitkyina Myanmar
24 B2 Myitson Myanmar
25 B4 Myitta Myanmar
37 H5 Myittha r. Myanmar
24 B2 Myittha Myanmar
79 G3 Myjava Slovakia
53 F3 Mykhaylivka *Zaporizhzhya* Ukraine
53 F3 Mykhaylivka *Zaporizhzhya* Ukraine
53 D1 Mykhaylo-Kotsyubyns'ke Ukraine
114 F1 Myki Greece
115 D5 Mykines Greece
53 E3 Mykolayiv div. Ukraine
77 M6 Mykolayiv *L'viv* Ukraine
53 E3 Mykolayiv *Mykolayiv* Ukraine
53 F3 Mykolayivka *Dnipropetrovs'k* Ukraine
53 F3 Mykolayivka *Kherson* Ukraine
53 D3 Mykolayivka *Odesa* Ukraine
53 C3 Mykolayivka-Novorosiys'ka Ukraine
115 G5 Mykonos i. Greece
115 G5 Mykonos Greece
54 E1 Myllykoski Finland
115 D5 Myloi Greece
115 D6 Mylopotamos Greece
37 G4 Mymensingh Bangladesh
54 C1 Mynämäki Finland
130 D5 Mynfontein South Africa
62 C2 Mynydd Eppynt h. *Wales* U.K.
62 C1 Mynydd Hiraethog h. *Wales* U.K.
62 B3 Mynydd Preseli h. *Wales* U.K.
24 A2 Myohaung Myanmar
24 B2 Myohla Myanmar
29 G5 Myōkō-san volcano Japan
82 A1 Myon France
31 J4 Myonggan North Korea
54 E4 Myory Belarus
24 A2 Myothit Myanmar
56 M7 Mýrdalsjökull ice cap Iceland
56 D1 Myre Norway
56 F2 Myrheden Sweden
53 E2 Myrhorod Ukraine
114 G3 Myrina Greece
53 E2 Myrivs'ke Ukraine
53 G3 Myrne *Donets'k* Ukraine
53 E3 Myrne *Kherson* Ukraine
53 D1 Myrne *Kyyiv* Ukraine
77 N5 Myrne *Volyn* Ukraine
53 G2 Myronivka *Kharkiv* Ukraine
53 D2 Myronivka *Kyyiv* Ukraine
53 B1 Myropil' Ukraine
53 F3 Myrove Ukraine
54 D1 Myrskylä Finland
145 E5 Myrtle Beach *S. Carolina* U.S.A.
152 A3 Myrtle Point *Oregon* U.S.A.
115 G7 Myrtos Greece
134 A3 Mys Chukotskiy c. Rus. Fed.
134 A3 Mys Dezhneva c. Rus. Fed.
58 D2 Mysen Norway
31 J4 Mys Gamova c. Rus. Fed.
52 D1 Myshkin Rus. Fed.
113 F5 Mysıa reg. Turkey
46 F4 Mys Karatobe pt Kazakhstan
47 L2 Myski Rus. Fed.
73 K3 Myśla r. Poland
77 H6 Myślenice Poland
76 C3 Myślibórz Poland
77 H2 Myślice Poland
56 J1 Mys Nemetskiy c. Rus. Fed.
38 B3 Mysore India
46 D4 Mys Peschanyy pt Kazakhstan
46 D4 Mys Sagyndyk pt Kazakhstan
46 D4 Mys Sengiri pt Kazakhstan
45 T3 Mys Shmidta Rus. Fed.
46 D4 Mys Suz pt Kazakhstan
54 A4 Mys Taran pt Rus. Fed.
27 Q2 Mys Terpeniya Rus. Fed.
147 F5 Mystic Islands *New Jersey* U.S.A.
46 C4 Mys Tyub-Karagan headland Kazakhstan
77 H5 Myszków Poland
77 K2 Myszyneic Poland
52 F1 Myt Rus. Fed.
25 D5 My Tho Vietnam
114 B4 Mytikas Greece
113 F5 Mytilini Greece
113 F6 Mytilinioi Greece
113 F5 Mytilini Strait chan. Greece/Turkey
52 C2 Mytishchi Rus. Fed.
78 C2 Mýto Czech Rep.
56 M6 Mývatn l. Iceland
77 N4 Myzove Ukraine
131 F5 Mzamomhle South Africa
75 H3 Mže r. Czech Rep.
127 B7 Mzimba Malawi
129 D3 Mzingwani r. Zimbabwe
127 B7 Mzuzu Malawi

N

75 G3 Naab r. Germany
124 C1 Naala Chad
68 C3 Naaldwijk Netherlands
153 □2 Naalehu *Hawaii* U.S.A.
124 E2 Na'am watercourse Sudan
121 D2 Naama Algeria
57 F3 Naantali Finland
68 D2 Naarden Netherlands
67 E3 Naas Rep. of Ireland
24 B1 Naba Myanmar
130 A4 Nababeep South Africa
98 B5 Nabão r. Portugal
38 C2 Nabarangapur India
29 F6 Nabari Japan
23 B4 Nabas Philippines
43 C3 Nabatiyet et Tahta Lebanon
6 □6 Nabavatu Fiji
75 H3 Nabburg Germany
127 C5 Naberera Tanzania
52 D4 Naberezhnoye Rus. Fed.
46 D1 Naberezhnyye Chelny Rus. Fed.
121 G1 Nabeul Tunisia
36 D3 Nabha India
39 D3 Nabīd Iran
165 E4 Nabileque r. Brazil
21 L7 Nabire Indonesia
43 C3 Nablus *West Bank*
122 D4 Nabolo Ghana
131 G2 Naboomspruit South Africa
6 □8 Naboutini Fiji
6 □6 Nabouwalu Fiji
43 C5 Nabq Egypt
36 D2 Nabra r. India
25 B4 Nabule Myanmar
129 G1 Nacala Mozambique
156 J6 Nacaome Honduras
129 F1 Nacaroa Mozambique
78 D2 Načeradec Czech Rep.
77 N1 Nacha Belarus
152 B2 Naches *Washington* U.S.A.
127 C7 Nachingwea Tanzania
36 B4 Nāchna India
78 F1 Náchod Czech Rep.
6 □8 Nacilau Pt pt Fiji
101 H3 Nacimiento r. Spain
172 A4 Nacimiento Chile
154 B4 Nacimiento Reservoir resr *California* U.S.A.
151 E6 Nacogdoches *Texas* U.S.A.
156 C2 Nacozari de García Mexico
77 J3 Nacpolsk Poland
172 D3 Nacuñan Argentina
Nada *see* Dan Xian
29 G5 Nadachi Japan
6 □8 Nadarivatu Fiji
76 E2 Nadarzyce Poland
81 H4 Nádasd Hungary
63 E3 Nadder r. *England* U.K.
6 □8 Nadi Fiji
36 C5 Nadiad India
6 □8 Nadi B. b. Fiji
39 C3 Nadīk Iran
79 K5 Nădlac Romania
121 D1 Nador Morocco
6 □8 Nadrau Plateau plat. Fiji
79 L4 Nádudvar Hungary
111 □ Nadur Malta
6 □6 Naduri Fiji
111 □ Nadur Tower Malta
53 A2 Nadvirna Ukraine
50 E2 Nadvoitsy Rus. Fed.
44 J3 Nadym Rus. Fed.
36 C4 Naenwa India
55 D4 Næstved Denmark
123 G4 Nafada Nigeria
83 E1 Näfels Switzerland
115 C4 Nafpaktos Greece
115 D5 Nafplio Greece
42 F3 Naft r. Iraq
39 B3 Naft-e Safīd Iran
42 F3 Naft Khanen Iraq
42 F3 Naft Shahr Iran
119 H2 Nafud al 'Urayq sand dunes Saudi Arabia
118 B1 Nafūsah, Jabal h. Libya
119 H2 Nafy Saudi Arabia
23 B3 Naga Philippines
140 C2 Nagagami r. *Ontario* Canada
140 C2 Nagagami Lake l. *Ontario* Canada
140 C2 Nagagamisis Lake l. *Ontario* Canada
140 C2 Nagagamisis Provincial Park res. *Ontario* Canada
29 □2 Nagagusuku-wan b. *Okinawa* Japan
28 D7 Nagahama Japan
29 F6 Nagahama Japan
37 H4 Naga Hills mountain range India
29 H4 Nagai Japan
37 H4 Nagaland India
29 □2 Nagannu-jima i. Japan
29 F5 Nagano div. Japan
29 G5 Nagano Japan
29 G5 Nagaoka Japan
37 H4 Nagaon India
38 B4 Nagappattinam India
36 D2 Nagar India
36 D4 Nagar India
38 B2 Nāgārjuna Sāgar Reservoir resr India
36 B4 Nagar Parkar Pakistan
37 G3 Nagarzê China
28 B7 Nagasaki div. Japan
28 B7 Nagasaki Japan
28 C7 Naga-shima i. Japan
28 D7 Naga-shima i. Japan
28 C7 Nagashima Japan
28 C6 Nagato Japan
36 C4 Nagaur India
38 C2 Nagavali r. India
37 G2 Nag, Co salt lake China
36 C5 Nagda India
68 D2 Nagele Netherlands
38 B4 Nagercoil India
39 F4 Nagha Kalat Pakistan
119 F2 Nag 'Hammâdi Egypt
126 B4 Nagichot Sudan
36 D3 Nagina India
67 C4 Nagles Mts h. Rep. of Ireland
77 J5 Nagłowice Poland
37 E3 Nagma Nepal
29 □2 Nago Japan
36 E4 Nagod India
74 D4 Nagold r. Germany
74 D4 Nagold Germany
32 A2 Nagong Chu r. China
Nagorno-Karabakh div. *see* Qarabağ
50 J3 Nagorsk Rus. Fed.
52 D1 Nagor'ye Rus. Fed.
30 A2 Nagor'ye Sangilen mountain range Rus. Fed.
107 E3 Nago-Torbole Italy
29 □2 Nago-wan b. Japan
29 F6 Nagoya Japan
36 D5 Nagpur India
37 H3 Nagqu China
54 B1 Nagu Finland
145 □3 Naguabo Puerto Rico
23 C3 Nagumbuaya Point pt Philippines
44 F1 Nagurskoye Rus. Fed.
78 G5 Nagyatád Hungary
79 G5 Nagybajom Hungary
79 H5 Nagybaracska Hungary
79 H5 Nagyberény Hungary
79 H5 Nagydorog Hungary
79 L3 Nagyhalász Hungary
79 H4 Nagyigmánd Hungary
79 L4 Nagykálló Hungary
78 G5 Nagykanizsa Hungary
78 G5 Nagykapornak Hungary
79 J4 Nagykáta Hungary
79 L4 Nagykereki Hungary
79 H5 Nagykónyi Hungary
79 J4 Nagykőrös Hungary
79 K4 Nagykunság reg. Hungary
79 K5 Nagylak Hungary
79 L3 Nagy-Milic mt. Hungary/Slovakia
79 H6 Nagynyárád Hungary
79 L4 Nagy-Sárrét reg. Hungary
79 K5 Nagyszénás Hungary
79 G5 Nagyvázsony Hungary
29 □2 Naha Japan
39 E4 Nahang r. Iran/Pakistan
136 E2 Nahanni Butte *N.W.T.* Canada
136 D2 Nahanni National Park nat. park *N.W.T.* Canada
43 C3 Naharayim Israel
43 C3 Nahariyya Israel
99 H4 Naharros Spain
39 B2 Nahāvand Iran
74 C3 Nahe r. Germany
6 □2 Nahoï, Cap c. Vanuatu
89 G4 Nahon r. France
43 D1 Nahr Sājūr r. Syria/Turkey
172 A4 Nahuelbuta, Parque Nacional nat. park Chile
172 B6 Nahuel Huapí, L. l. Argentina
171 B5 Nahuel Huapi, Parque Nacional nat. park Argentina
172 D3 Nahuel Mapá Argentina
172 D6 Nahuel Niyeu Argentina
173 J4 Nahuel Rucá Argentina
145 D6 Nahunta *Georgia* U.S.A.
39 F1 Naibabad Afghanistan
156 D3 Naica Mexico
172 E4 Naicó Argentina
112 C2 Naidăş Romania
6 □6 Naidi Fiji
24 B1 Nai Ga Myanmar
6 □8 Naigani i. Fiji
37 H2 Naij Tal China
75 G2 Naila Germany
93 D5 Nailloux France
6 □6 Nailotha Pk h. Fiji
62 D3 Nailsworth *England* U.K.
119 F5 Na'ima Sudan
31 G4 Naiman Qi China
139 H2 Nain *Newfoundland* Canada
39 C2 Nā'īn Iran
36 D3 Naini Tal India
36 E5 Nainpur India
92 C2 Naintré France
129 F2 Naiopué Mozambique
6 □8 Nairai i. Fiji
66 D3 Nairn r. *Scotland* U.K.
66 E3 Nairn *Scotland* U.K.
140 E3 Nairn Centre *Ontario* Canada
127 C5 Nairobi Kenya
54 D2 Naissaar i. Estonia
6 □6 Naituaba i. Fiji
Nai-tung *see* Nêdong
127 C5 Naivasha Kenya
127 C5 Naivasha, L. l. Kenya
87 E4 Naives-Rosières France
31 H4 Naizishan China
93 D4 Najac France
39 B2 Najafābād Iran
119 H2 Najd reg. Saudi Arabia
99 H2 Nájera Spain
36 D3 Najibabad India
99 H3 Nájima r. Spain
31 J4 Najin North Korea
119 H4 Najrān Saudi Arabia
28 A6 Naju South Korea
28 B7 Nakadōri-shima i. Japan
29 H5 Naka-gawa r. Japan
28 E7 Naka-gawa r. Japan
28 J1 Nakagawa Japan
29 □2 Nakagusuku-wan b. Japan
28 C7 Nakama Japan
122 D4 Nakambe watercourse Burkina/Ghana
28 D7 Nakamura Japan
45 M3 Nakanno Rus. Fed.
29 G5 Nakano Japan
28 D5 Nakano-shima i. Japan
28 D6 Nakanoumi lag. Japan
29 □2 Nakaoshi Japan
127 B4 Nakasangola Uganda
28 H3 Nakasato Japan
28 J2 Nakasatsunai Japan
28 K2 Nakashibetsu Japan
28 C7 Nakatsu Japan
29 F6 Nakatsugawa Japan
126 C1 Nak'fa Eritrea
Nakhichevan' *see* Naxçıvan
119 F2 Nakhl Egypt
27 O3 Nakhodka Rus. Fed.
37 H4 Nakhola India
25 C4 Nakhon Nayok Thailand
25 C4 Nakhon Pathom Thailand
25 C4 Nakhon Ratchasima Thailand
25 B5 Nakhon Si Thammarat Thailand
24 C3 Nakhon Thai Thailand
36 B5 Nakhtarana India
136 C3 Nakina *B.C.* Canada
140 B1 Nakina *Ontario* Canada
81 F4 Naklo Slovenia
76 F2 Nakło nad Notecią Poland
134 C4 Naknek *Alaska* U.S.A.
36 C3 Nakodar India
77 K1 Nakomiady Poland
127 B6 Nakonde Zambia
130 B4 Nakop Namibia
54 C3 Nākotne Latvia
79 K6 Nakovo Yugoslavia
55 D5 Nakskov Denmark
31 J6 Naktong r. South Korea
127 C5 Nakuru Kenya
136 F4 Nakusp *B.C.* Canada
39 F4 Nal r. Pakistan
36 A4 Nal Pakistan
30 C3 Nalayh Mongolia
131 J2 Nalázi Mozambique
37 G4 Nalbari India
51 G7 Nal'chik Rus. Fed.
36 D3 Naldera India
38 B2 Naldurg India
77 L4 Nałęczów Poland
122 D4 Nalerigu Ghana
38 B2 Nalgonda India
37 F4 Nalhati India
38 B3 Nallamala Hills h. India
42 B1 Nallıhan Turkey
99 E1 Nalón r. Spain
118 B1 Nālūt Libya
78 C2 Nalžovské Hory Czech Rep.
131 J2 Namaacha Mozambique
6 □8 Namacu Fiji
125 C7 Namacunde Angola
129 F2 Namacurra Mozambique
131 G3 Namahadi South Africa
23 □1 Namai Bay b. Palau
131 H1 Namakgale South Africa
39 D3 Namakzar-e Shadad salt flat Iran
22 A2 Namang Indonesia
127 C5 Namanga Kenya
47 H4 Namangan Uzbekistan
6 □8 Namanu-i-Ra i. Fiji
127 C7 Namapa Mozambique
128 B4 Namaqualand reg. Namibia
130 A4 Namaqualand reg. South Africa
6 □1 Namatanai P.N.G.
24 C2 Nam Beng r. Laos
37 H4 Nambol India
69 F5 Namborn Germany
15 H5 Nambour *Queensland* Australia
99 G5 Nambroca Spain
13 H2 Nambucca Heads *New South Wales* Australia
25 D5 Năm Căn Vietnam
37 H3 Namcha Barwa mt. China
37 F4 Namche Bazar Nepal
31 H5 Namch'ŏn North Korea
37 G3 Nam Co salt lake China
56 D2 Namdalen v. Norway
56 C2 Namdalseid Norway
24 D2 Nam Đinh Vietnam
59 H2 Nämdö i. Sweden
148 B3 Namekagon r. *Wisconsin* U.S.A.
23 □1 Namelakl Passage chan. Palau
6 □8 Namena Barrier Reef reef Fiji
6 □8 Namenalala i. Fiji
78 F2 Náměšť nad Oslavou Czech Rep.
79 J2 Námestovo Slovakia
31 J6 Namhae Do i. South Korea
24 B2 Nam Hka r. Myanmar
24 B2 Namhkam Myanmar
24 B2 Nam Hsin r. Myanmar
128 A3 Namib Desert desert Namibia
125 B7 Namibe div. Angola
125 B7 Namibe Angola
125 B7 Namibe, Reserva de res. Angola
117 F8 Namibia country Africa
128 B4 Namib-Naukluft Park res. Namibia
129 F2 Namidobe Mozambique
29 H5 Namie Japan
130 B4 Namies South Africa
24 C3 Nam Khan r. Laos
24 B2 Namlan Myanmar
24 B2 Namlang r. Myanmar
21 J7 Namlea Indonesia
24 C3 Nam Lik r. Laos
24 C2 Nam Loi r. Myanmar
Nam Mao r. *see* Shweli
24 B3 Nammekon Myanmar
24 C2 Nam Na r. China/Vietnam
24 C3 Nam Ngum r. Laos
13 G2 Namoi r. *New South Wales* Australia
6 □8 Namosi Pks mts Fiji
24 C2 Nam Ou r. Laos
136 F3 Nampa *Alberta* Canada
152 C3 Nampa *Idaho* U.S.A.
122 C3 Nampala Mali
24 C3 Nam Pat Thailand
24 C3 Nam Phong Thailand
31 H5 Namp'o North Korea
129 F1 Nampula div. Mozambique
129 F2 Nampula Mozambique
37 G2 Namru Co salt lake China
37 H4 Namrup India
24 B1 Namsai Myanmar
24 D3 Nam Sam r. Laos/Vietnam
37 E3 Namsê La Nepal
56 D2 Namsen r. Norway
37 H4 Namsi India
56 C2 Namsos Norway
24 B2 Nam Teng r. Myanmar
24 C2 Nam Tha r. Laos
24 B3 Namtok Myanmar
25 B4 Nam Tok Thailand
24 B2 Namton Myanmar
45 O3 Namtsy Rus. Fed.
24 B2 Namtu Myanmar
6 □7 Namuka-i-lau i. Fiji
129 F2 Namuli, Monte mt. Mozambique
127 C7 Namuno Mozambique
69 C4 Namur div. *Namur* Belgium
69 C4 Namur div. *Wallonia* Belgium
69 C4 Namur *Namur* Belgium
128 B2 Namutoni Namibia
125 E7 Namwala Zambia
31 H6 Namwŏn South Korea
24 B1 Namya Ra Myanmar
24 B2 Nam Yi Tu r. Myanmar
76 F4 Namysłów Poland
124 C2 Nana Bakassa Central African Rep.
124 C2 Nana Barya r. Central African Rep./Chad
124 C2 Nana-Grébizi div. Central African Rep.
136 E5 Nanaimo *B.C.* Canada
153 □1 Nanakuli *Hawaii* U.S.A.
124 C2 Nana-Mambéré div. Central African Rep.
33 G3 Nan'an China
15 H5 Nanango *Queensland* Australia
130 A2 Nananib Plateau plat. Namibia
29 F5 Nanao Japan
29 F5 Nanao-wan b. Japan
29 F5 Nanatsu-shima i. Japan
32 D2 Nanbu China
172 B3 Nancagua Chile
31 J3 Nancha China
33 F2 Nanchang China
33 F2 Nanchang China
33 G3 Nancheng China
32 D2 Nanchong China
32 D2 Nanchuan China
99 H2 Nanclares de la Oca Spain
25 A6 Nancowry i. *Andaman and Nicobar Is* India
87 F4 Nancy *Meurthe-et-Moselle* France
36 E3 Nanda Devi mt. India
36 E3 Nanda Kot mt. India
32 D3 Nandan China
28 E6 Nandan Japan
38 B2 Nānded India
13 G2 Nandewar Range mountain range *New South Wales* Australia
36 C5 Nandgaon India
Nandi *see* Nadi
32 B4 Nanding r. China/Myanmar
69 D4 Nandrin Belgium
33 E5 Nandu r. China
36 C5 Nandurbar India
38 B3 Nandyal India
33 G3 Nanfeng China
33 E4 Nanfeng China
124 B3 Nanga Eboko Cameroon
22 C1 Nangahbunut Indonesia
22 B2 Nangah Dedai Indonesia
22 C1 Nangahembaloh Indonesia
22 B1 Nangahkantuk Indonesia
22 C2 Nangahkemangai Indonesia
22 B1 Nangahketungau Indonesia
22 B1 Nangah Merakai Indonesia
22 B2 Nangahpinoh Indonesia
22 C1 Nangahtempuai Indonesia
31 J4 Nangang Shan mts China
36 C2 Nanga Parbat mt. *Jammu and Kashmir*
22 B2 Nangatayap Indonesia
25 B5 Nangin Myanmar
86 C4 Nangis France
31 H5 Nangnim Sanmaek mountain range South Korea
28 C8 Nangō Japan
31 E5 Nangong China
32 B1 Nangqên China
127 C6 Nangulangwa Tanzania
37 H3 Nang Xian China
32 C3 Nanhua China
30 A5 Nanhua China
33 H2 Nanhui China
39 G2 Nani Afghanistan
38 B3 Nanjangud India
32 C3 Nanjian China
32 D1 Nanjiang China
33 G3 Nanjing China
33 G1 Nanjing China
32 B4 Nanka r. China
33 F3 Nankang China
Nanking *see* Nanjing
28 D7 Nankoku Japan
125 C7 Nankova Angola
31 E5 Nanle China
32 B4 Nanlei r. China
33 E3 Nan Ling mountain range China
33 G2 Nanling China
33 E4 Nanliu r. China
32 E4 Nanning China
159 □1 Nanny Town Jamaica
135 O3 Nanortalik Greenland
32 D3 Nanpan r. China
37 E4 Nanpara India
31 G4 Nanpiao China
32 D1 Nanping China
33 G3 Nanping China
33 G3 Nanri Dao i. China
99 F1 Nansa r. Spain
27 N6 Nansei-shotō is Japan
175 N2 Nansei-shotō Trench sea feature Pacific Ocean
135 O1 Nansen Land reg. Greenland
135 J1 Nansen Sound chan. *N.W.T.* Canada
127 B5 Nansio Tanzania
91 B4 Nant France
86 B4 Nanterre France
88 D4 Nantes *Loire-Atlantique* France
88 D4 Nantes Atlantique airport France
86 B3 Nanteuil-le-Haudouin France
38 C4 Nanthi Kadal lag. Sri Lanka
92 D2 Nantiat France
22 A3 Nanti, Bukit mt. Indonesia
147 F5 Nanticoke r. *Maryland* U.S.A.
140 E5 Nanticoke *Ontario* Canada
136 G4 Nanton *Alberta* Canada
33 H1 Nantong China
33 H2 Nantong China
33 H4 Nant'ou Taiwan
90 D2 Nantua France
147 H4 Nantucket *Massachusetts* U.S.A.
147 H4 Nantucket I. i. *Massachusetts* U.S.A.
147 H4 Nantucket Sound b. *Massachusetts* U.S.A.
62 D1 Nantwich *England* U.K.
62 C2 Nant-y-moch Res. resr *Wales* U.K.
6 □8 Nanukuloa Fiji
6 □6 Nanuku Passage chan. Fiji
6 □6 Nanuku Reef reef Fiji
4 J5 Nanumanga i. Tuvalu
176 G6 Nanumea i. Tuvalu
169 H2 Nanuque Brazil
17 A4 Nanutarra Roadhouse *Western Australia* Australia
32 D2 Nanxi China
33 F2 Nan Xian China
33 F3 Nanxiong China
33 F1 Nanyang China
29 H4 Nanyō Japan
127 C5 Nanyuki Kenya
31 H4 Nanzamu China
33 E2 Nanzhang China
33 F1 Nanzhao China
103 D6 Nao, Cabo de la headland Spain
139 F3 Naococane, Lac l. *Québec* Canada
37 G4 Naogaon Bangladesh
36 C2 Naoshera India
115 G5 Naousa Greece
33 E4 Naozhou Dao China
154 A2 Napa *California* U.S.A.
147 K1 Napadogan *New Brunswick* Canada
173 H4 Napaleofú Argentina
134 C3 Napamute *Alaska* U.S.A.
141 G4 Napanee *Ontario* Canada
36 C4 Napasar India
135 N3 Napasoq Greenland
148 C5 Naperville *Illinois* U.S.A.
82 C1 Napf mt. Switzerland
8 F3 Napier New Zealand
130 B7 Napier South Africa
16 D2 Napier Broome B. b. *Western Australia* Australia
179 D4 Napier Mts mountain range Antarctica
14 C2 Napier Pen. pen. *Northern Terr.* Australia
141 J4 Napierville *Québec* Canada
77 J2 Napiwoda Poland
145 D7 Naples *Florida* U.S.A.
147 H3 Naples *Maine* U.S.A.
Naples *see* Napoli
162 C4 Napo r. Ecuador/Peru
32 D4 Napo China
146 A4 Napoleon *Ohio* U.S.A.
109 G4 Napoli div. *Campania* Italy
109 G4 Napoli *Napoli* Italy
109 G4 Napoli, Golfo di b. Italy
173 F5 Naposta r. Argentina
173 F5 Naposta *Buenos Aires* Argentina
148 E5 Nappanee *Indiana* U.S.A.
7 □10 Napuka i. *French Polynesia* Pacific Ocean
42 C4 Naqb Ashtar Jordan
43 B5 Naqb Malha mt. Egypt
126 E2 Naqūb Yemen
29 E6 Nara div. Japan
52 C2 Nara r. Rus. Fed.
29 E6 Nara Japan
122 C3 Nara Mali
54 E4 Narach Belarus
12 E4 Naracoorte *S. Australia* Australia
13 F3 Naradhan *New South Wales* Australia
38 C2 Narainpur India
30 E2 Naranbulag Mongolia
162 B4 Naranjal Ecuador
156 C3 Naranjo Mexico
157 F4 Naranjos Mexico
28 B7 Narao Japan
38 D2 Narasannapeta India
38 C2 Narasapatnam, Pt pt India
38 C2 Narasapur India
38 C2 Narasaraopet India
30 E2 Narasun Rus. Fed.
25 C6 Narathiwat Thailand
37 G5 Narayanganj Bangladesh
38 A2 Narayangaon India
37 F4 Narayanghat Nepal
77 N6 Narayiv Ukraine
Narbada r. *see* Narmada
62 B3 Narberth *Wales* U.K.
91 B5 Narbonne France
91 B5 Narbonne-Plage France
63 E2 Narborough *England* U.K.
63 G2 Narborough *England* U.K.
108 A5 Narcao *Sardegna* Italy
98 D1 Narcea r. Spain
25 A4 Narcondam I. i. *Andaman and Nicobar Is* India
90 B1 Narcy France
39 C1 Nardin Iran
111 H2 Nardò Italy
173 G1 Nare Argentina
36 B3 Narechi r. Pakistan
17 B7 Narembeen *Western Australia* Australia
135 L2 Nares Strait str. Canada/Greenland
77 J3 Narew r. Poland
77 M3 Narew Poland
77 M3 Narewka Poland
39 F3 Nari r. Pakistan
128 B3 Narib Namibia
130 A5 Nariep South Africa
51 H6 Narimanov Rus. Fed.
47 K3 Narimskiy Khr. mountain range Kazakhstan
39 G1 Narin Afghanistan
29 H6 Narita Japan
159 □3 Nariva div. *Trinidad* Trinidad and Tobago
159 □3 Nariva Swamp swamp *Trinidad* Trinidad and Tobago
156 C3 Narizon, Pta pt Mexico
37 F4 Narkatiaganj India
43 D1 Narlı Turkey
36 C5 Narmada r. India
36 D3 Narnaul India
109 E2 Narni Italy
110 C5 Naro r. *Sicilia* Italy
110 C5 Naro *Sicilia* Italy
53 C1 Narodychi Ukraine
52 C2 Naro-Fominsk Rus. Fed.
127 C5 Narok Kenya
13 G4 Narooma *New South Wales* Australia
52 F3 Narovchat Rus. Fed.
53 C1 Narowlya Belarus
57 F3 Närpes Finland
13 G2 Narrabri *New South Wales* Australia
147 H4 Narragansett Bay b. *Rhode Island* U.S.A.
13 F2 Narran r. *New South Wales* Australia
13 F3 Narrandera *New South Wales* Australia
13 F2 Narran L. l. *New South Wales* Australia
17 B7 Narrogin *Western Australia* Australia
13 G3 Narromine *New South Wales* Australia
137 J4 Narrow Hills Provincial Park *Saskatchewan* Canada
146 C6 Narrows *Virginia* U.S.A.
147 F4 Narrowsburg *Pennsylvania* U.S.A.
159 □6 Narrows, The chan. *St Kitts-Nevis* Caribbean
132 O3 Narsarsuaq Greenland
36 D5 Narsimhapur India
37 G5 Narsingdi Bangladesh
36 D5 Narsinghgarh India
38 C2 Narsipatnam India
31 E4 Nart China
30 C2 Nart Mongolia
81 H5 Narta Croatia
91 E5 Nartuby r. France
52 G2 Naruksovo Rus. Fed.
77 J3 Naruszewo Poland
28 E6 Naruto Japan
54 E2 Narva r. Estonia/Rus. Fed.
54 E2 Narva Bay b. Estonia/Rus. Fed.
23 B2 Narvacan Philippines
56 E1 Narvik Norway
54 F2 Narvskoye Vdkhr. resr Rus. Fed.
36 D3 Narwana India
36 D4 Narwar India
77 L2 Narwiańsk Park Narodowy nat. park Poland
44 G3 Nar'yan Mar Rus. Fed.
47 J4 Naryn div. Kyrgyzstan
47 H4 Naryn r. Kyrgyzstan
47 J4 Naryn Kyrgyzstan
30 A2 Naryn Rus. Fed.
52 B3 Naryshkino Rus. Fed.
59 F1 Nås Sweden
56 E3 Näsåker Sweden
112 E1 Năsăud Romania
78 E2 Nasavrky Czech Rep.
91 B4 Nasbinals France
172 E2 Naschel Argentina
155 H3 Naschitti *New Mexico* U.S.A.
9 C6 Naseby New Zealand
148 A4 Nashua *Iowa* U.S.A.
147 H3 Nashua *New Hampshire* U.S.A.
145 C4 Nashville *Tennessee* U.S.A.
148 A2 Nashwauk *Minnesota* U.S.A.
42 D3 Nasib Syria
104 G3 Našice Croatia
77 J3 Nasielsk Poland
57 F3 Näsijärvi l. Finland
36 C5 Nasik India
22 B1 Nasilat Indonesia
126 B3 Nasir Sudan
Nasirabad *see* Mymensingh
36 C4 Nasirabad India
36 B3 Nasirabad Pakistan
37 F4 Nasmganj India
110 D4 Naso *Sicilia* Italy
125 E6 Nasondoye Congo(Zaire)
6 □6 Nasorolevu mt. Fiji
Nasosnyy *see* Hacı Zeynalabdin
119 F1 Nasr Egypt
39 B2 Naşrābād Iran
39 D2 Naşrābād Iran
43 D3 Naşrānī, J. an mountain range Syria
Nasratabad *see* Zābol
42 F3 Nasrīān-e-Pā'īn Iran
136 D3 Nass r. *B.C.* Canada
123 F5 Nassarawa Nigeria
145 □2 Nassau airport The Bahamas
176 J6 Nassau i. *Cook Is* Pacific Ocean
15 E2 Nassau r. *Queensland* Australia
87 G2 Nassau Germany
145 □2 Nassau The Bahamas
171 C7 Nassau, B. de b. Chile
145 □2 Nassau Village The Bahamas
80 B3 Nassereith Austria
119 F3 Nasser, Lake resr Egypt
59 F3 Nässjö Sweden
69 D4 Nassogne Belgium
138 E2 Nastapoca r. *Québec* Canada
138 E2 Nastapoka Islands is *N.W.T.* Canada
54 D1 Nastola Finland
29 G5 Nasu-dake volcano Japan
23 B3 Nasugbu Philippines
59 F3 Näsum Sweden
50 D3 Nasva Rus. Fed.
128 D2 Nata watercourse Botswana/Zimbabwe
128 D3 Nata Botswana
127 B5 Nata Tanzania
162 B3 Natagaima Colombia
166 E2 Natal Brazil
Natal div. *see* Kwazulu-Natal
175 G6 Natal Basin sea feature Indian Ocean
39 B2 Naţanz Iran
139 H3 Natashquan r. *Québec* Canada
139 H3 Natashquan *Québec* Canada
151 F6 Natchez *Mississippi* U.S.A.
151 E6 Natchitoches *Louisiana* U.S.A.
82 C2 Naters Switzerland
6 □6 Natewa Bay b. Fiji
13 F4 Nathalia *Victoria* Australia
36 C4 Nathdwara India
12 E4 Natimuk *Victoria* Australia
154 D5 National City *California* U.S.A.
8 E3 National Park New Zealand
128 A3 National West Coast Tourist Recreation Area res. Namibia
103 □ Nati, Pta pt Spain
81 E4 Natisone r. Italy
123 E4 Natitingou Benin
169 H4 Natividade *Rio de Janeiro* Brazil
166 C3 Natividade *Tocantins* Brazil
24 A2 Natogyi Myanmar
156 C2 Nátora Mexico
29 H4 Natori Japan
127 C5 Natron, Lake salt lake Tanzania
29 H5 Natsui-gawa r. Japan
24 A3 Nattalin Myanmar
59 H2 Nåttarö i. Sweden
80 B2 Nattheim Germany

145 C5 **Newnan** *Georgia* U.S.A.
62 D3 **Newnham** *England* U.K.
13 F5 **New Norfolk** *Tasmania* Australia
151 F6 **New Orleans** *Louisiana* U.S.A.
147 F4 **New Paltz** *New York* U.S.A.
146 C4 **New Philadelphia** *Ohio* U.S.A.
66 F3 **New Pitsligo** *Scotland* U.K.
8 E3 **New Plymouth** New Zealand
32 C3 **Newport div.** *Wales* U.K.
151 F5 **Newport** *Arkansas* U.S.A.
158 □2 **New Port** *Curaçao* Netherlands Ant.
62 D2 **Newport** *England* U.K.
63 E4 **Newport** *England* U.K.
63 G3 **Newport** *England* U.K.
146 A5 **Newport** *Kentucky* U.S.A.
147 J2 **Newport** *Maine* U.S.A.
67 B3 **Newport** *Mayo* Rep. of Ireland
149 F5 **Newport** *Michigan* U.S.A.
147 G3 **Newport** *New Hampshire* U.S.A.
152 A2 **Newport** *Oregon* U.S.A.
147 H4 **Newport** *Rhode Island* U.S.A.
67 C4 **Newport** *Tipperary* Rep. of Ireland
147 G2 **Newport** *Vermont* U.S.A.
62 B2 **Newport** *Wales* U.K.
62 C3 **Newport** *Wales* U.K.
152 C1 **Newport** *Washington* U.S.A.
159 □1 **Newport** Jamaica
62 B2 **Newport Bay b.** *Wales* U.K.
154 D5 **Newport Beach** *California* U.S.A.
146 E6 **Newport News** *Virginia* U.S.A.
65 F1 **Newport-on-Tay** *Scotland* U.K.
63 F2 **Newport Pagnell** *England* U.K.
64 B3 **Newport Trench** *Northern Ireland* U.K.
145 □2 **New Providence i.** The Bahamas
62 A4 **Newquay** *England* U.K.
62 B2 **New Quay** *Wales* U.K.
139 G4 **New Richmond** *Québec* Canada
148 A3 **New Richmond** *Wisconsin* U.S.A.
155 F5 **New River** *Arizona* U.S.A.
151 F6 **New Roads** *Louisiana* U.S.A.
63 G4 **New Romney** *England* U.K.
67 E4 **New Ross** Rep. of Ireland
67 E2 **Newry** *Northern Ireland* U.K.
67 E2 **Newry Canal canal** *Northern Ireland* U.K.
66 E4 **New Scone** *Scotland* U.K.
148 A5 **New Sharon** *Iowa* U.S.A.
New Siberia Islands *see* **Novosibirskiye Ostrova**
145 D6 **New Smyrna Beach** *Florida* U.S.A.
13 F3 **New South Wales div.** Australia
27 □ **New Territories reg.** *Hong Kong* China
65 F4 **Newton** *England* U.K.
150 E3 **Newton** *Iowa* U.S.A.
150 D4 **Newton** *Kansas* U.S.A.
147 H3 **Newton** *Massachusetts* U.S.A.
151 F5 **Newton** *Mississippi* U.S.A.
147 F4 **Newton** *New Jersey* U.S.A.
62 C4 **Newton Abbot** *England* U.K.
66 F3 **Newtonhill** *Scotland* U.K.
65 F4 **Newton-le-Willows** *England* U.K.
64 D2 **Newton Mearns** *Scotland* U.K.
66 D3 **Newtonmore** *Scotland* U.K.
66 D6 **Newton Stewart** *Scotland* U.K.
178 □3 **Newtontoppen mt.** *Svalbard* Arctic Ocean
62 D2 **Newtown** *England* U.K.
150 C1 **New Town** *N. Dakota* U.S.A.
62 C2 **Newtown** *Wales* U.K.
67 C4 **Newtown** Rep. of Ireland
67 F2 **Newtownabbey** *Northern Ireland* U.K.
67 F2 **Newtownards** *Northern Ireland* U.K.
67 D2 **Newtownbutler** *Northern Ireland* U.K.
64 A4 **Newtown Forbes** Rep. of Ireland
67 E3 **Newtownmountkennedy** Rep. of Ireland
66 F5 **Newtown St Boswells** *Scotland* U.K.
67 D2 **Newtownstewart** *Northern Ireland* U.K.
150 E2 **New Ulm** *Minnesota* U.S.A.
154 A2 **Newville** *California* U.S.A.
136 E5 **New Westminster** *B.C.* Canada
147 E3 **New York div.** *New York* U.S.A.
147 G4 **New York** *New York* U.S.A.
147 G4 **New York-John F. Kennedy airport** *New York* U.S.A.
147 F4 **New York-Newark airport** *New Jersey* U.S.A.
4 J9 **New Zealand country** Australasia
175 Q7 **New Zealand Plateau sea feature** Pacific Ocean
92 D3 **Nexon** France
50 G3 **Neya r.** Rus. Fed.
50 G3 **Neya** Rus. Fed.
39 C2 **Neyestānak** Iran
62 B3 **Neyland** *Wales* U.K.
39 C3 **Neyrīz** Iran
39 D1 **Neyshābūr** Iran
38 B4 **Neyyattinkara** India
140 B2 **Nezah** *Ontario* Canada
78 D2 **Nežárka r.** Czech Rep.
53 G1 **Nezhegol' r.** Rus. Fed.
52 F1 **Nezhitino** Rus. Fed.
75 J3 **Nezvěstice** Czech Rep.
53 A2 **Nezvys'ko** Ukraine
22 B1 **Ngabang** Indonesia
125 C4 **Ngabé** Congo
25 B4 **Nga Chong, Kh. mt.** Myanmar/Thailand
123 G4 **Ngadda watercourse** Nigeria
22 D4 **Ngadubolu** Indonesia
24 B1 **Ngagahtawng** Myanmar
123 G4 **Ngala** Nigeria
23 C6 **Ngalipaëng** Indonesia
22 E4 **Ngalu** Indonesia
124 C1 **Ngam** Chad
124 C1 **Ngama** Chad
23 □1 **Ngamegei Passage chan.** Palau
128 C3 **Ngami, Lake l.** Botswana
128 C2 **Ngamiland div.** Botswana
37 F3 **Ngamring** China
126 B4 **Ngangala** Sudan
37 E3 **Ngangla Ringco salt lake** China
37 E2 **Nganglong Kangri mountain range** China
36 E2 **Nganglong Kangri mt.** China
125 B6 **N'gangula** Angola
37 F3 **Ngangzê Co salt lake** China
22 B3 **Nganjuk** Indonesia
24 B3 **Ngao** Thailand
124 B2 **Ngaoundal** Cameroon
124 B2 **Ngaoundéré** Cameroon
37 H5 **Ngape** Myanmar
24 A3 **Ngaputaw** Myanmar
127 B5 **Ngara** Tanzania
22 A3 **Ngaras** Indonesia
23 □1 **Ngardmau** Palau
23 □1 **Ngardmau Bay b.** Palau
23 □1 **Ngardololok** Palau
23 □1 **Ngaregur i.** Palau
8 E2 **Ngaruawahia** New Zealand
8 F3 **Ngaruroro r.** New Zealand
8 E2 **Ngatea** New Zealand
23 □1 **Ngateguil, Pt pt** Palau
24 A3 **Ngathainggyaung** Myanmar
8 E3 **Ngauruhoe, Mt volcano** New Zealand
Ngawa *see* **Aba**
22 B3 **Ngawi** Indonesia
124 E3 **Ngayu r.** Congo(Zaire)
124 B3 **Ngbala** Congo
23 □1 **Ngemelis Is is** Palau
23 □1 **Ngeregong i.** Palau
23 □1 **Ngergoi i.** Palau
23 □1 **Ngesebus i.** Palau
6 □1 **Nggatokae i.** Solomon Is.
6 □6 **Nggele Levu i.** Fiji
128 C3 **Nghabe r.** Botswana
24 C3 **Ngiap r.** Laos
125 C4 **Ngo** Congo
23 □1 **Ngobasangel i.** Palau
25 D4 **Ngoc Linh mt.** Vietnam
37 F3 **Ngoin, Co l.** China
124 C4 **Ngoko** Congo
123 G5 **Ngol Bembo** Nigeria
131 H3 **Ngome** South Africa
124 B3 **Ngomedzap** Cameroon
32 A1 **Ngom Qu r.** China
124 B2 **Ngong** Cameroon
37 F2 **Ngoqumaima** China
32 B1 **Ngoring** China
32 B1 **Ngoring Hu l.** China
122 D3 **Ngorkou** Mali
127 C5 **Ngorongoro Conservation Area res.** Tanzania
125 C4 **Ngoso** Congo(Zaire)
124 C3 **Ngoto** Central African Rep.
131 F2 **Ngotwane r.** Botswana
124 B3 **Ngoulémakong** Cameroon
122 D3 **Ngouma** Mali
124 B4 **Ngounié div.** Gabon
124 B4 **Ngounié r.** Gabon
124 B4 **Ngouoni** Gabon
124 C1 **Ngoura** Chad
118 C5 **Ngouri** Chad
123 G3 **Ngourti** Niger
118 C4 **Ngoutchey well** Chad
124 E2 **Ngouyo** Central African Rep.
131 G5 **Ngqeleni** South Africa
124 B2 **Nguia Bouar** Central African Rep.
123 G4 **Nguigmi** Niger
123 F3 **Nguini well** Niger
21 L5 **Ngulu i.** Fed. States of Micronesia
6 □2 **Nguna i.** Vanuatu
129 E3 **Ngundu** Zimbabwe
22 C4 **Ngunut** Indonesia
123 G4 **Nguru** Nigeria
24 D2 **Nguy ên Binh** Vietnam
128 C3 **Ngwaketse div.** Botswana
128 C3 **Ngwako Pan salt pan** Botswana
131 F3 **Ngwathe** South Africa
131 H4 **Ngwelezana** South Africa
125 E7 **Ngweze r.** Zambia
129 F3 **Nhachengue** Mozambique
24 D3 **Nhac Son** Vietnam
129 F2 **Nhamalabué** Mozambique
129 E2 **Nhamatanda** Mozambique
165 E2 **Nhambiquara** Brazil
163 F4 **Nhamundá r.** Brazil
166 A1 **Nhamundá** Brazil
168 C4 **Nhandeara** Brazil
125 C6 **N'harea** Angola
25 E4 **Nha Trang** Vietnam
165 E3 **Nhecolândia** Brazil
125 B6 **Nhia r.** Angola
12 E4 **Nhill** *Victoria* Australia
131 H3 **Nhlangano** Swaziland
24 D2 **Nho Quan** Vietnam
14 D2 **Nhulunbuy** *Northern Terr.* Australia
124 E4 **Niabembe** Congo(Zaire)
137 J4 **Niacam** *Saskatchewan* Canada
122 D3 **Niafounké** Mali
148 D3 **Niagara** *Wisconsin* U.S.A.
146 D3 **Niagara Falls** *New York* U.S.A.
141 F5 **Niagara Falls** *Ontario* Canada
149 H4 **Niagara River r.** Canada/U.S.A.
123 E4 **Niagassola** Guinea
122 C4 **Niagouelé, Mt du h.** Guinea
36 D2 **Niagzu** China/Jammu and Kashmir
122 C5 **Niakaramandougou** Côte d'Ivoire
123 E4 **Niamey** Niger
23 C5 **Niampak** Indonesia
123 E5 **Niamtougou** Togo
122 C5 **Niandan r.** Guinea
122 C4 **Niandankoro** Guinea
124 E3 **Niangara** Congo(Zaire)
122 D4 **Niangoloko** Burkina
124 E3 **Nia-Nia** Congo(Zaire)
31 G3 **Nianzishan** China
125 B4 **Niari div.** Congo
20 C6 **Nias i.** Indonesia
127 C7 **Niassa div.** Mozambique
Niassa, L. l. *see* **Nyasa, Lake**
115 D6 **Niata** Greece
53 B3 **Nibe** Denmark
55 B2 **Nibe Bredning b.** Denmark
54 B3 **Nīca** Latvia
133 K8 **Nicaragua country** Central America
156 J7 **Nicaragua, Lago de l.** Nicaragua
111 F4 **Nicastro** Italy
91 F5 **Nice** France
91 F5 **Nice-Côte d'Azur airport** France
106 B3 **Nichelino** Italy
139 F3 **Nichicun, Lac l.** *Québec* Canada
28 C6 **Nichihara** Japan
28 C8 **Nichinan** Japan
37 E4 **Nichlaul** India
158 B2 **Nicholas Channel chan.** The Bahamas/Cuba
158 C1 **Nicholl's Town** The Bahamas
14 D3 **Nicholson r.** *Queensland* Australia
140 D3 **Nicholson** *Ontario* Canada
16 E3 **Nicholson** *Western Australia* Australia
17 B5 **Nicholson Ra. h.** *Western Australia* Australia
25 A5 **Nicobar Islands is** *Andaman and Nicobar Is* India
112 G2 **Nicolae Bălcescu** Romania
173 F5 **Nicolás Levalle** Argentina
141 J3 **Nicolet** *Québec* Canada
110 D5 **Nicoletti, Lago l.** *Sicilia* Italy
111 E5 **Nicolosi** *Sicilia* Italy
110 D5 **Nicosia** *Sicilia* Italy
Nicosia *see* **Lefkosia**
111 E4 **Nicotera** Italy
156 J7 **Nicoya, G. de b.** Mexico
156 J7 **Nicoya, Pen. de pen.** Costa Rica
147 K1 **Nictau** *New Brunswick* Canada
112 G2 **Niculițel** Romania
77 J5 **Nida r.** Poland
54 B4 **Nida** Lithuania
82 C1 **Nidau** Switzerland
65 G4 **Nidd r.** *England* U.K.
74 E2 **Nidda** Germany
74 E2 **Nidder r.** Germany
65 G3 **Nidderdale v.** *England* U.K.
58 D3 **Nidingen i.** Sweden
83 D2 **Nidwalden div.** Switzerland
114 C2 **Nidže mt.** Greece/Macedonia
77 J5 **Nidzica r.** Poland
77 J2 **Nidzica** Poland
100 D3 **Niebla** Spain
77 J3 **Nieborów** Poland
72 D1 **Niebüll** Germany
77 J2 **Niechłonin** Poland
73 L1 **Niechorze** Poland
87 F3 **Nied r.** France
69 E5 **Niederanven** Luxembourg
74 E2 **Niederaula** Germany
75 H4 **Niederbayern div.** Germany
82 C1 **Niederbipp** Switzerland
87 G2 **Niederbreitbach** Germany
81 E3 **Niedere Tauern mts** Austria
74 C2 **Niederkassel** Germany
72 B4 **Niederkrüchten** Germany
68 F2 **Niederlangen** Germany
73 J4 **Niederlausitz reg.** Germany
80 D3 **Niederndorf** Austria
87 H2 **Niederneisen** Germany
87 H2 **Niedernhausen** Germany
80 D3 **Niedernsill** Austria
73 H4 **Nieder-Olm** Germany
81 G2 **Niederösterreich div.** Austria
72 D3 **Niedersachsen div.** Germany
72 C2 **Niedersächsiches Wattenmeer, Nationalpark nat. park** Germany
74 E3 **Niederstetten** Germany
83 E1 **Niederurnen** Switzerland
72 E4 **Niedervellmar** Germany
80 D2 **Niederviehbach** Germany
72 D4 **Niederwerrn** Germany
69 F4 **Niederzissen** Germany
77 L4 **Niedrzwica Duża** Poland
124 B3 **Niefang** Equatorial Guinea
74 D4 **Niefern-Öschelbronn** Germany
76 D4 **Niegosławice** Poland
68 E1 **Niekerk** Netherlands
130 D4 **Niekerkshoop** South Africa
69 C3 **Niel** Belgium
131 H1 **Nielele r.** South Africa
125 E5 **Niemba** Congo(Zaire)
77 L4 **Niemce** Poland
73 H3 **Niemegk** Germany
76 F5 **Niemodlin** Poland
76 G4 **Niemysłów** Poland
122 C4 **Niéna** Mali
73 G4 **Nienburg** Germany
72 E3 **Nienburg (Weser)** Germany
122 C5 **Niénokoué, Mt h.** Côte d'Ivoire
77 J5 **Niepołomice** Poland
69 A4 **Nieppe** France
72 B4 **Niers r.** Germany
87 H3 **Nierstein** Germany
73 K4 **Niesky** Germany
77 J4 **Nieświń** Poland
76 G3 **Nieszawa** Poland
131 F2 **Nietverdiend** South Africa
92 D3 **Nieul** France
68 E2 **Nieuw Amsterdam** Netherlands
163 F2 **Nieuw Amsterdam** Surinam
68 E2 **Nieuw Buinen** Netherlands
68 D2 **Nieuwegein** Netherlands
68 E1 **Nieuwe Pekela** Netherlands
68 C3 **Nieuwerkerk** Netherlands
68 F1 **Nieuweschans** Netherlands
163 F3 **Nieuw-Jacobkondre** Surinam
68 C2 **Nieuwkopp** Netherlands
68 E2 **Nieuwleusen** Netherlands
163 F2 **Nieuw Nickerie** Surinam
68 E1 **Nieuwolda** Netherlands
130 B5 **Nieuwoudtville** South Africa
69 A3 **Nieuwpoort** Belgium
68 C2 **Nieuw Vennep** Netherlands
68 E2 **Nieuw-Weerdinge** Netherlands
87 G2 **Nievern** Germany
97 □ **Nieves, Pico de las mt.** *Canary Is* Spain
90 B1 **Nièvre div.** *Bourgogne* France
90 B1 **Nièvre r.** France
90 B1 **Nièvre de Champlemy r.** France
69 D4 **Niewerkerken** Belgium
42 C2 **Niğde** Turkey
131 G3 **Nigel** South Africa
116 E4 **Niger country** Africa
123 F4 **Niger div.** Nigeria
122 F5 **Niger r.** Africa
117 E5 **Nigeria country** Africa
123 F6 **Niger, Mouths of the river mouth** Nigeria
122 B5 **Niger, Source of the** Guinea
9 B6 **Nightcaps** New Zealand
140 E2 **Nighthawk Lake l.** *Ontario* Canada
128 □3 **Nightingale I. i.** *Tristan da Cunha* Atlantic Ocean
98 B2 **Nigrán** Spain
114 E2 **Nigrita** Greece
29 H5 **Nihonmatsu** Japan
29 G5 **Niigata div.** Japan
29 G5 **Niigata** Japan
28 D7 **Niihama** Japan
153 □2 **Niihau i.** *Hawaii* U.S.A.
29 G6 **Nii-jima i.** Japan
28 J2 **Niikappu** Japan
28 D6 **Niimi** Japan
29 G5 **Niitsu** Japan
101 H4 **Nijar** Spain
120 C5 **Nijerâne well** Mauritania
68 E2 **Nijeveen** Netherlands
68 D2 **Nijkerk** Netherlands
69 C3 **Nijlen** Belgium
68 D3 **Nijmegen** Netherlands
68 E2 **Nijverdal** Netherlands
114 D3 **Nikaia** Greece
56 H1 **Nikel'** Rus. Fed.
114 C2 **Niki** Greece
51 F5 **Nikitovka** Rus. Fed.
123 E5 **Nikki** Benin
29 G5 **Nikkō Nat. Park** Japan
81 G3 **Niklasdorf** Austria
114 C1 **Nikodin** Macedonia
47 G2 **Nikolayevka** Kazakhstan
46 F2 **Nikolayevka** Rus. Fed.
52 H3 **Nikolayevka** Rus. Fed.
31 K2 **Nikolayevka** Rus. Fed.
51 H5 **Nikolayevsk** Rus. Fed.
45 Q4 **Nikolayevsk-na-Amure** Rus. Fed.
50 H3 **Nikol'sk** Rus. Fed.
52 H3 **Nikol'sk** Rus. Fed.
50 G3 **Nikol'skiy** Rus. Fed.
45 S4 **Nikol'skoye** Rus. Fed.
112 E3 **Nikopol** Bulgaria
53 F3 **Nikopol'** Ukraine
114 B3 **Nikopoli** Greece
39 B1 **Nik Pey** Iran
42 D1 **Niksar** Turkey
39 E4 **Nikshahr** Iran
112 B3 **Nikšić** Yugoslavia
176 H6 **Nikumaroro i.** Kiribati
176 G6 **Nikunau i.** Kiribati
36 C2 **Nila** Pakistan
37 F5 **Nilagiri** India
155 E5 **Niland** *California* U.S.A.
35 D10 **Nilande Atoll atoll** Maldives
36 D3 **Nilang** India
38 B2 **Nilanga** India
119 F2 **Nile r.** Africa
148 D5 **Niles** *Michigan* U.S.A.
38 A3 **Nileswaram** India
38 B4 **Nilgiri Hills mts** India
126 C2 **Nil r.** Ethiopia
39 F2 **Nil P. pass** Afghanistan
56 H3 **Nilsiä** Finland
157 G5 **Niltepec** Mexico
55 B4 **Nim** Denmark
36 C4 **Nimach** India
36 C4 **Nimbahera** India
122 C5 **Nimba, Monts mt.** Côte d'Ivoire
Nimbhera *see* **Nimbahera**
91 C5 **Nîmes** *Gard* France
13 G4 **Nimmitabel** *New South Wales* Australia
179 B4 **Nimrod Gl. gl.** Antarctica
126 B4 **Nimule** Sudan
42 E3 **Nīnawá div.** Iraq
125 D6 **Ninda** Angola
15 G6 **Nindigully** *Queensland* Australia
35 D9 **Nine Degree Channel chan.** India
Nine Mile Bar *see* **Crocketford**
67 D4 **Ninemilehouse** Rep. of Ireland
154 D2 **Ninemile Peak summit** *Nevada* U.S.A.
27 □ **Ninepin Group is** *Hong Kong* China
175 K5 **Ninety-East Ridge sea feature** Indian Ocean
13 F4 **Ninety Mile Beach beach** *Victoria* Australia
8 D1 **Ninety Mile Beach beach** New Zealand
147 F3 **Nineveh** *New York* U.S.A.
42 E2 **Nineveh** Iraq
171 D5 **Ninfas, Pta pt** Argentina
31 J3 **Ning'an** China
33 H2 **Ningbo** China
31 F4 **Ningcheng** China
33 G3 **Ningde** China
33 F3 **Ningdu** China
33 F3 **Ninggang** China
33 G2 **Ningguo** China
33 H2 **Ninghai** China
31 F5 **Ninghe** China
33 G3 **Ninghua** China
123 F4 **Ningi** Nigeria
32 B2 **Ningjing Shan mountain range** China
32 C3 **Ninglang** China
33 F1 **Ningling** China
32 D4 **Ningming** China
32 C3 **Ningnan** China
32 D1 **Ningqiang** China
32 E1 **Ningshan** China
Ningsia div. *see* **Ningxia**
30 E5 **Ningwu** China
30 C5 **Ningxia div.** China
32 D1 **Ning Xian** China
33 F2 **Ningxiang** China
31 F6 **Ningyang** China
33 E3 **Ningyuan** China
24 D2 **Ninh Binh** Vietnam
25 E4 **Ninh Hoa** Vietnam
172 A4 **Ninhue** Chile
6 □5 **Niniva i.** Tonga
179 B6 **Ninnis Gl. gl.** Antarctica
29 H3 **Ninohe** Japan
100 E4 **Niño, Sa del mountain range** Spain
69 C4 **Ninove** Belgium
171 B6 **Ninualac, Can. chan.** Chile
167 A5 **Nioaque** Brazil
150 C3 **Niobrara r.** *Nebraska* U.S.A.
124 F3 **Nioka** Congo(Zaire)
125 C4 **Nioki** Congo(Zaire)
37 H4 **Nioko** India
122 B4 **Niokolo Koba, Parc National du nat. park** Senegal
122 C4 **Niono** Mali
122 C3 **Nioro** Mali
122 A4 **Nioro du Rip** Senegal
92 B2 **Niort** France
120 C5 **Nioût well** Mauritania
6 □1 **Nipa** P.N.G.
38 A2 **Nipani** India
172 A4 **Ñipas** Chile
137 J4 **Nipawin** *Saskatchewan* Canada
137 J4 **Nipawin Provincial Park nat. park** *Saskatchewan* Canada
140 A2 **Nipigon** *Ontario* Canada
140 A2 **Nipigon Bay b.** *Ontario* Canada
140 A2 **Nipigon, Lake l.** *Ontario* Canada
139 H3 **Nipishish Lake l.** *Newfoundland* Canada
141 F3 **Nipissing** *Ontario* Canada
141 F3 **Nipissing, L. l.** *Ontario* Canada
154 B4 **Nipomo** *California* U.S.A.
Nippon Hai sea *see* **Japan, Sea of**
155 E4 **Nipton** *California* U.S.A.
166 C3 **Niquelândia** Brazil
172 B4 **Niquen** Chile
158 C2 **Niquero** Cuba
172 C1 **Niquivil** Argentina
42 F2 **Nir** Iran
38 A2 **Nira r.** India
29 G6 **Nirasaki** Japan
119 H3 **Nīr, J. an h.** Saudi Arabia
38 B2 **Nirmal** India
37 F4 **Nirmali** India
38 B2 **Nirmal Range h.** India
112 C3 **Niš** Yugoslavia
100 C1 **Nisa r.** Portugal
100 C1 **Nisa** Portugal
110 D5 **Niscemi** *Sicilia* Italy
28 H2 **Niseko** Japan
Nīshāpūr *see* **Neyshābūr**
29 G5 **Nishiaizu** Japan
28 K2 **Nishibetsu-gawa r.** Japan
28 C8 **Nishikata** Japan
29 H4 **Nishikawa** Japan
28 E6 **Nishino-shima i.** Japan
28 D5 **Nishino-shima i.** Japan
28 B7 **Nishi-Sonogi-hantō pen.** Japan
28 B6 **Nishi-suidō chan.** South Korea
28 E6 **Nishiwaki** Japan
77 L5 **Nisko** Poland
136 B2 **Nisling r.** *Yukon Terr.* Canada
69 C4 **Nismes** Belgium
53 C3 **Nisporeni** Moldova
59 E3 **Nissafors** Sweden
59 E3 **Nissan r.** Sweden
91 B5 **Nissan-lez-Enserune** France
58 C2 **Nisser l.** Norway
55 A3 **Nissum Bredning b.** Denmark
55 A3 **Nissum Fjord lag.** Denmark
68 D3 **Nistelrode** Netherlands
53 C3 **Nistru r.** Moldova
136 C2 **Nisutlin r.** *Yukon Terr.* Canada
113 F6 **Nisyros i.** Greece
39 B4 **Niţā** Saudi Arabia
139 F3 **Nitchequon** *Québec* Canada
169 G5 **Niterói** Brazil
66 E5 **Nith r.** *Scotland* U.K.
66 E5 **Nithsdale v.** *Scotland* U.K.
79 H4 **Nitra r.** Slovakia
79 H3 **Nitra** Slovakia
79 H3 **Nitrianske Pravno** Slovakia
146 C5 **Nitro** *W. Virginia* U.S.A.
90 B1 **Nitry** France
58 D1 **Nittedal** Norway
69 E5 **Nittel** Germany
75 H3 **Nittenau** Germany
75 G3 **Nittendorf** Germany
6 □4 **Niu' Aunofo pt** Tonga
5 L6 **Niue i.** Pacific Ocean
176 G6 **Niulakita i.** Tuvalu
32 C3 **Niulan r.** China
4 J5 **Niutao i.** Tuvalu
31 G4 **Niuzhuang** China
55 E4 **Nivå** Denmark
56 G3 **Nivala** Finland
93 A5 **Nive r.** France
15 F5 **Nive watercourse** *Queensland* Australia
15 F5 **Nive Downs** *Queensland* Australia
69 C4 **Nivelles div.** Belgium
69 C4 **Nivelles** Belgium
77 J1 **Nivenskoye** Rus. Fed.
90 B1 **Nivernais reg.** France
88 C4 **Nivillac** France
86 B3 **Nivillers** France
90 D3 **Nivolas-Vermelle** France
50 K2 **Nivshera** Rus. Fed.
36 C4 **Niwāi** India
154 C2 **Nixon** *Nevada* U.S.A.
47 K5 **Niya r.** China
Niya *see* **Minfeng**
28 D7 **Niyodo-gawa r.** Japan
22 B1 **Niyut, G. mt.** Indonesia
38 B2 **Nizamabad** India
38 B2 **Nizam Sagar l.** India
75 K3 **Nižbor** Czech Rep.
46 D1 **Nizhnekamsk** Rus. Fed.
46 D1 **Nizhnekamskoye Vdkhr. resr** Rus. Fed.
45 S3 **Nizhnekolymsk** Rus. Fed.
45 L4 **Nizhneudinsk** Rus. Fed.
44 J3 **Nizhnevartovsk** Rus. Fed.
45 P2 **Nizhneyansk** Rus. Fed.
51 G5 **Nizhniy Chir** Rus. Fed.
52 F3 **Nizhniy Lomov** Rus. Fed.
50 G3 **Nizhniy Novgorod div.** Rus. Fed.
50 G3 **Nizhniy Novgorod** Rus. Fed.
50 K2 **Nizhniy Odes** Rus. Fed.
52 F3 **Nizhniy Shibryay** Rus. Fed.
52 G3 **Nizhniy Shkaft** Rus. Fed.
44 G4 **Nizhniy Tagil** Rus. Fed.
31 E2 **Nizhniy Tsasuchey** Rus. Fed.
50 H3 **Nizhniy Yenangsk** Rus. Fed.
50 H1 **Nizhnyaya Mola** Rus. Fed.
47 H1 **Nizhnyaya Omka** Rus. Fed.
31 F2 **Nizhnyaya Shakhtama** Rus. Fed.
50 G1 **Nizhnyaya Zolotitsa** Rus. Fed.
53 D1 **Nizhyn** Ukraine
77 J3 **Nizina reg.** Poland
77 L2 **Nizina Podlaska reg.** Poland
76 F4 **Nizina Śląska reg.** Poland
76 F4 **Nizina Wielkopolska reg.** Poland
43 D1 **Nizip r.** Turkey
42 D2 **Nizip** Turkey
79 L2 **Nízke Beskydy reg.** Slovakia
79 J3 **Nízke Tatry mts** Slovakia
79 J3 **Nízke Tatry nat. park** Slovakia
106 C4 **Nizza Monferrato** Italy
56 E2 **Njavve** Sweden
127 D7 **Njazidja i.** Comoros
112 B3 **Njegoš mts** Yugoslavia
127 C6 **Njinjo** Tanzania
107 J3 **Njivice** Croatia
125 D7 **Njoko r.** Zambia
127 B6 **Njombe r.** Tanzania
127 B6 **Njombe** Tanzania
57 E3 **Njurundabommen** Sweden
131 H1 **Nkambak** South Africa
124 B2 **Nkambe** Cameroon
131 H4 **Nkandla** South Africa
127 B6 **Nkasi** Tanzania
122 D5 **Nkawkaw** Ghana
129 D2 **Nkayi** Zimbabwe
120 C5 **Nkhaïlé well** Mauritania
127 B7 **Nkhata Bay** Malawi
127 B7 **Nkhotakota** Malawi
127 B7 **Nkhotakota Game Reserve res.** Malawi
131 H1 **Nkomo** South Africa
127 B6 **Nkondwe** Tanzania
124 A3 **Nkongsamba** Cameroon
122 D5 **Nkoranza** Ghana
124 B3 **Nkoteng** Cameroon
131 F5 **Nkululeko** South Africa
127 B6 **Nkundi** Tanzania
128 B2 **Nkurenkuru** Namibia
131 H4 **Nkwalini** South Africa
131 F6 **Nkwenkwezi** South Africa
24 B1 **Nmai Hka r.** Myanmar
37 H4 **Noa Dihing r.** India
86 B3 **Noailles** France
102 B2 **Noain** Spain
37 G5 **Noakhali** Bangladesh
37 F5 **Noamundi** India
82 C3 **Noasca** Italy
67 E3 **Nobber** Rep. of Ireland
28 C7 **Nobeoka** Japan
131 F5 **Nobokwe** South Africa
28 H2 **Noboribetsu** Japan
166 A3 **Nobres** Brazil
15 E5 **Noccundra** *Queensland* Australia
107 E2 **Noce r.** Italy
89 F3 **Nocé** France
109 G4 **Nocera Inferiore** Italy
111 F3 **Nocera Terinese** Italy
109 E1 **Nocera Umbra** Italy
106 E4 **Noceto** Italy
111 G2 **Noci** Italy
110 D5 **Nociara r.** *Sicilia* Italy
111 H2 **Nociglia** Italy
15 E5 **Nockatunga** *Queensland* Australia
58 B2 **Nodeland** Norway
90 E1 **Nods** France
93 D5 **Noé** France
140 E5 **Noelville** *Ontario* Canada
130 C3 **Noenieput** South Africa
173 F2 **Noetinger** Argentina
86 B2 **Nœux-les-Mines** France
156 C2 **Nogales** Mexico
83 G3 **Nogara** Italy
93 B5 **Nogaro** France
28 C7 **Nōgata** Japan
89 G3 **Nogent-le-Roi** France
89 F3 **Nogent-le-Rotrou** France
86 D4 **Nogent-sur-Aube** France
86 B4 **Nogent-sur-Marne** France
86 B3 **Nogent-sur-Oise** France
86 C4 **Nogent-sur-Seine** France
90 A1 **Nogent-sur-Vernisson** France
59 F3 **Nogersund** Sweden
52 D2 **Noginsk** Rus. Fed.
45 L3 **Noginsky** Rus. Fed.
15 G5 **Nogo r.** *Queensland* Australia
15 F6 **Nogo r.** *Queensland* Australia
29 F6 **Nōgōhaku-san mt.** Japan
173 H2 **Nogoya r.** Argentina
173 H2 **Nogoyá** Argentina
79 J4 **Nógrád div.** Hungary
102 B4 **Noguera** Spain
93 C6 **Noguera de Tor r.** Spain
102 E2 **Noguera Pallaresa r.** Spain
102 D2 **Noguera Ribagorçana r.** Spain
31 J5 **Nogwak-san mt.** South Korea
90 B1 **Nohain r.** France
36 C3 **Nohar** India
28 H3 **Noheji** Japan
74 C3 **Nohfelden** Germany
93 D5 **Nohic** France
98 B2 **Noia** Spain
90 E1 **Noidans-lès-Vesoul** France
168 B1 **Noidore r.** Brazil
93 E5 **Noire, Montagne mts** France
159 □5 **Noire, Pointe pt** *Guadeloupe* Caribbean
96 E5 **Noire, Pte pt** Morocco
88 B3 **Noires, Montagnes h.** France
90 B3 **Noirétable** France
88 C4 **Noirmoutier-en-l'Île** France
88 C5 **Noirmoutier, Île de i.** France
87 F3 **Noisseville** France
29 G6 **Nojima-zaki c.** Japan
36 C4 **Nokha** India
39 E3 **Nok Kundi** Pakistan
137 J3 **Nokomis Lake l.** *Saskatchewan* Canada
118 B5 **Nokou** Chad
37 G4 **Nokrek Pk. mt.** India
59 E3 **Nol** Sweden
124 C3 **Nola** Central African Rep.
109 G4 **Nola** Italy
90 C2 **Nolay** France
50 J3 **Nolinsk** Rus. Fed.
28 C8 **Noma-misaki pt** Japan
147 H4 **No Mans Land i.** *Massachusetts* U.S.A.
134 B3 **Nome** *Alaska* U.S.A.
30 C4 **Nomgon** Mongolia
28 D6 **Nōmi-jima i.** Japan
4 G4 **Nomoi Islands is** Fed. States of Micronesia
131 F5 **Nomonde** South Africa
28 B7 **Nomo-zaki pt** Japan
130 A2 **Nomtsas** Namibia
6 □5 **Nomuka i.** Tonga
6 □5 **Nomuka Group is** Tonga
6 □5 **Nomuka Iki i.** Tonga
50 G3 **Nomzha** Rus. Fed.
137 H2 **Nonacho Lake l.** *N.W.T.* Canada
89 G3 **Nonancourt** France
131 H4 **Nondweni** South Africa
106 B4 **None** Italy
31 H3 **Nong'an** China
24 D3 **Nông Hèt** Laos
25 C4 **Nong Hong** Thailand
24 C3 **Nong Khai** Thailand
131 H3 **Nongoma** South Africa
37 G4 **Nongstoin** India
Nonni r. *see* **Nen**
12 D3 **Nonning** *S. Australia* Australia
74 B3 **Nonnweiler** Germany
156 D3 **Nonoava** Mexico
176 G6 **Nonouti i.** Kiribati
31 H5 **Nonsan** South Korea
25 C4 **Nonthaburi** Thailand
92 C3 **Nontron** France
108 B2 **Nonza** *Corse* France
130 E5 **Nonzwakazi** South Africa
54 E2 **Nõo** Estonia
17 B5 **Nookawarra** *Western Australia* Australia
12 D1 **Noolyeanna L. salt flat** *S. Australia* Australia
15 F6 **Noorama Cr. watercourse** *Queensland* Australia
68 E1 **Noordbergum** Netherlands
68 B3 **Noordbeveland i.** Netherlands
68 C3 **Noord-Brabant div.** Netherlands
68 C2 **Noorderhaaks i.** Netherlands
68 C2 **Noord-Holland div.** Netherlands
68 D2 **Noordoost Polder reclaimed land** Netherlands
158 □2 **Noord Punt pt** *Curaçao* Netherlands Ant.
68 C2 **Noordwijk-Binnen** Netherlands
68 C2 **Noordwijkerhout** Netherlands
136 D5 **Nootka I. i.** *B.C.* Canada
172 D1 **Noqueves** Argentina
125 B5 **Nóqui** Angola
59 F2 **Nora** Sweden
55 B3 **Norager** Denmark
47 G5 **Norak** Tajikistan
23 C5 **Norala** Philippines
59 F1 **Norberg** Sweden
109 F2 **Norcia** Italy
124 B2 **Nord div.** Cameroon
86 C2 **Nord div.** France
135 R1 **Nord** Greenland
58 C2 **Nordagutu** Norway
44 D2 **Nordaustlandet i.** *Svalbard* Arctic Ocean
55 B4 **Nordborg** Denmark
55 C4 **Nordby** *Århus* Denmark
55 A4 **Nordby** *Ribe* Denmark
72 C2 **Norden** Germany
72 D2 **Nordenham** Germany
72 D1 **Norder Hever chan.** Germany
72 C2 **Norderland reg.** Germany
72 C2 **Norderney i.** Germany
72 C2 **Norderney** Germany
72 F2 **Norderstedt** Germany
57 B3 **Nordfjordeid** Norway
56 D2 **Nordfold** Norway
72 D1 **Nordfriesische Inseln is** Germany
72 D1 **Nordfriesland reg.** Germany
73 F4 **Nordhausen** Germany
72 D2 **Nordholz** Germany
58 A1 **Nordhordland reg.** Norway
72 C3 **Nordhorn** Germany
58 A2 **Nordhuglo** Norway
55 B2 **Nordjylland div.** Denmark
178 □2 **Nordkapp c.** *Bjørnøya* Arctic Ocean
178 □1 **Nordkapp c.** *Jan Mayen* Arctic Ocean
178 □3 **Nordkapp c.** *Svalbard* Arctic Ocean
56 G1 **Nordkapp c.** Norway
56 E1 **Nordkjosbotn** Norway
56 H1 **Nordkynhalvøya i.** Norway
56 D2 **Nordland div.** Norway
56 D2 **Nordlii** Norway
75 F4 **Nördlingen** Germany
56 E3 **Nordmaling** Sweden
58 B1 **Nordmannslågen l.** Norway
72 D1 **Nordmarsch-Langeness i.** Germany
72 E1 **Nord-Ostsee-Kanal canal** Germany
124 B2 **Nord-Ouest div.** Cameroon
86 B2 **Nord - Pas-de-Calais div.** France
74 C3 **Nordpfälzer Bergland reg.** Germany
55 C2 **Nordre Rønner i.** Denmark
135 N3 **Nordre Strømfjord inlet** Greenland

72 C4 Nordrhein-Westfalen div. Germany
72 E3 Nordstemmen Germany
72 D1 Nordstrand i. Germany
56 C2 Nord-Trøndelag div. Norway
59 M6 Norðurland Eystra div. Iceland
56 L6 Norðurland Vestra div. Iceland
45 N2 Nordvik Rus. Fed.
67 D4 Nore r. Rep. of Ireland
54 C4 Noreikiškės Lithuania
93 E5 Nore, Pic de mt. France
58 C1 Noresund Norway
147 E6 Norfolk airport Virginia U.S.A.
63 G2 Norfolk div. England U.K.
150 D3 Norfolk Nebraska U.S.A.
147 F2 Norfolk New York U.S.A.
11 □1 Norfolk I. i. Pacific Ocean
176 G7 Norfolk Island Ridge sea feature Pacific Ocean
176 F7 Norfolk Island Trough sea feature Pacific Ocean
151 E4 Norfork L. l. Arkansas/Missouri U.S.A.
68 E1 Norg Netherlands
58 B1 Norheimsund Norway
29 F5 Norikura-dake volcano Japan
44 K3 Noril'sk Rus. Fed.
52 A3 Norino Rus. Fed.
141 F4 Norland Ontario Canada
109 E3 Norma Italy
148 C5 Normal Illinois U.S.A.
15 E3 Norman r. Queensland Australia
151 D5 Norman Oklahoma U.S.A.
15 F2 Normanby r. Queensland Australia
6 □1 Normanby I. i. P.N.G.
15 G4 Normanby Ra. h. Queensland Australia
Normandes, Îles is see Channel Islands
163 F3 Normandia Brazil
141 J2 Normandin Québec Canada
145 □3 Norman I. i. Virgin Is Caribbean
8 □1 Norman Inlet inlet Auckland Is New Zealand
145 D5 Norman, L. l. N. Carolina U.S.A.
159 □1 Norman Manley airport Jamaica
15 E3 Normanton Queensland Australia
136 D1 Norman Wells N.W.T. Canada
141 F2 Normétal Québec Canada
165 E2 Noronha r. Brazil
82 B1 Noroy-le-Bourg France
172 B4 Norquín Argentina
171 B5 Norquinco Argentina
56 F3 Norra Kvarken str. Finland/Sweden
56 D2 Norra Storfjället mts Sweden
59 F1 Norr Barken l. Sweden
56 E2 Norrbotten div. Sweden
55 B3 Nørreå r. Denmark
55 B4 Nørre Åby Denmark
55 D5 Nørre Alslev Denmark
55 B4 Nørre Broby Denmark
55 A4 Nørre Nebel Denmark
86 B2 Norrent-Fontes France
55 B4 Nørre Snede Denmark
55 B2 Nørresundby Denmark
55 A3 Nørre Vorupør Denmark
59 F3 Norrhult-Klavreström Sweden
140 C2 Norris Ontario Canada
146 B6 Norris Lake l. Tennessee U.S.A.
147 F4 Norristown Pennsylvania U.S.A.
59 G2 Norrköping Sweden
59 H2 Norrpada is Sweden
59 G1 Norrsundet Sweden
59 H2 Norrtälje Sweden
17 C7 Norseman Western Australia Australia
8 F4 Norsewood New Zealand
59 F2 Norsholm Sweden
58 C2 Norsjø l. Norway
56 E2 Norsjö Sweden
6 □2 Norsup Vanuatu
7 □16 Norte, Cabo c. Easter I. Chile
163 G3 Norte, Cabo pt Brazil
166 A3 Nortelândia Brazil
72 E4 Nörten-Hardenberg Germany
173 J4 Norte, Pta pt Argentina
171 D5 Norte, Pta pt Argentina
147 G3 North Adams Massachusetts U.S.A.
65 G3 Northallerton England U.K.
17 B6 Northam Western Australia Australia
131 F2 Northam South Africa
174 F4 North American Basin sea feature Atlantic Ocean
63 F2 Northampton England U.K.
147 G3 Northampton Massachusetts U.S.A.
17 A6 Northampton Western Australia Australia
15 F5 Northampton Downs Queensland Australia
63 E2 Northamptonshire div. England U.K.
25 A4 North Andaman i. Andaman and Nicobar Is India
146 E5 North Anna r. Virginia U.S.A.
147 J2 North Anson Maine U.S.A.
136 G2 North Arm b. N.W.T. Canada
6 □7 North Astrolabe Reef reef Fiji
145 D5 North Augusta S. Carolina U.S.A.
139 H2 North Aulatsivik Island i. Newfoundland Canada
66 D5 North Ayrshire div. Scotland U.K.
63 E4 North Baddesley England U.K.
23 A4 North Balabac Strait chan. Philippines
137 H4 North Battleford Saskatchewan Canada
141 F3 North Bay Ontario Canada
138 E2 North Belcher Islands is N.W.T. Canada
152 A3 North Bend Oregon U.S.A.
147 H3 North Berwick Maine U.S.A.
66 F4 North Berwick Scotland U.K.
148 A3 North Branch Minnesota U.S.A.
9 □3 North C. c. Antipodes Is New Zealand
139 H4 North, C. c. Nova Scotia Canada
171 □ North C. c. S. Georgia Atlantic Ocean
179 A5 North, C. c. Antarctica
8 D1 North Cape c. New Zealand
139 H4 North Cape pt Prince Edward I. Canada
138 B3 North Caribou Lake l. Ontario Canada
145 D5 North Carolina div. U.S.A.
152 B1 North Cascades Nat. Park Washington U.S.A.
65 H4 North Cave England U.K.
145 □2 North Cay i. The Bahamas
140 D3 North Channel chan. Ontario Canada
66 C5 North Channel str. Northern Ireland/Scotland U.K.
17 B7 Northcliffe Western Australia Australia
111 □ North Comino Chan. chan. Malta
147 H2 North Conway New Hampshire U.S.A.
150 C2 North Dakota div. U.S.A.
62 D4 North Dorset Downs h. England U.K.
63 E3 North Downs h. England U.K.
128 D3 North East div. Botswana
146 D3 North East Pennsylvania U.S.A.
128 □1 North East Bay b. Ascension Atlantic Ocean
126 D4 North-Eastern div. Kenya
174 H2 North-Eastern Atlantic Basin sea feature Atlantic Ocean
8 □2 North East Harb. inlet Campbell I. New Zealand
8 □3 North East Island i. Snares Is New Zealand
65 H4 North East Lincolnshire div. England U.K.
10 □2 North East Point pt Christmas I. Indian Ocean
159 □1 Northeast Point pt Jamaica
158 D2 Northeast Point pt The Bahamas
158 D2 Northeast Point pt The Bahamas
158 C1 Northeast Providence Chan. chan. The Bahamas
72 E4 Northeim Germany
158 D1 North End Pt pt The Bahamas
23 □1 North Entrance chan. Palau
122 D5 Northern div. Ghana
127 B7 Northern div. Malawi
122 B5 Northern div. Sierra Leone
119 E4 Northern div. Sudan
127 B7 Northern div. Zambia
36 C1 Northern Areas div. Pakistan
130 C4 Northern Cape div. South Africa
137 K3 Northern Indian Lake l. Manitoba Canada
67 □ Northern Ireland div. U.K.
138 B4 Northern Light L. l. Ontario Canada
4 F3 Northern Mariana Islands territory Pacific Ocean
10 □2 Northern Plateau plat. Christmas I. Indian Ocean
131 G2 Northern Province div. South Africa
159 □3 Northern Range mountain range Trinidad Trinidad and Tobago
Northern Sporades is see Voreioi Sporades
14 C3 Northern Territory div. Australia
Northern Transvaal see Northern Province
66 E5 North Esk r. Scotland U.K.
66 F4 North Esk r. Scotland U.K.
147 G3 Northfield Massachusetts U.S.A.
148 A3 Northfield Minnesota U.S.A.
147 G2 Northfield Vermont U.S.A.
63 H3 North Foreland c. England U.K.
154 C3 North Fork California U.S.A.
154 B2 North Fork American r. California U.S.A.
154 B2 North Fork Feather r. California U.S.A.
148 E3 North Fox I. i. Michigan U.S.A.
140 E1 North French r. Ontario Canada
159 □6 North Friar's Bay b. St Kitts-Nevis Caribbean
65 H3 North Grimston England U.K.
8 E2 North Head headland New Zealand
10 □3 North Head pt Macquarie I. Pacific Ocean
147 K2 North Head New Brunswick Canada
137 K2 North Henik Lake l. N.W.T. Canada
147 G3 North Hudson New York U.S.A.
63 F1 North Hykeham England U.K.
10 □4 North I. i. Lord Howe I. Pacific Ocean
127 □1 North I. i. Seychelles
23 B1 North Is i. Philippines
8 E3 North Island i. New Zealand
23 B4 North Islet reef Philippines
155 G4 North Jadito Canyon Arizona U.S.A.
148 D5 North Judson Indiana U.S.A.
10 □1 North Keeling I. i. Cocos Is Indian Ocean
137 K3 North Knife r. Manitoba Canada
19 O5 North Korea country Asia
37 H4 North Lakhimpur India
66 E5 North Lanarkshire div. Scotland U.K.
8 E1 Northland div. New Zealand
155 E3 North Las Vegas Nevada U.S.A.
65 H4 North Lincolnshire div. England U.K.
151 E5 North Little Rock Arkansas U.S.A.
127 B7 North Luangwa National Park nat. park Zambia
155 H2 North Mam Peak summit Colorado U.S.A.
148 E5 North Manchester Indiana U.S.A.
148 D3 North Manitou I. i. Michigan U.S.A.
140 E3 North Monetville Ontario Canada
136 D2 North Nahanni r. N.W.T. Canada
159 □1 North Negril Pt pt Jamaica
137 L5 Northome Minnesota U.S.A.
154 C3 North Palisade summit California U.S.A.
150 C3 North Platte r. Nebraska U.S.A.
150 C3 North Platte Nebraska U.S.A.
27 □ North Point Hong Kong China
128 □1 North Point pt Ascension Atlantic Ocean
159 □9 North Point pt Barbados Caribbean
144 D2 North Point pt Michigan U.S.A.
13 F4 North Point pt Tasmania Australia
128 □3 North Point pt Tristan da Cunha Atlantic Ocean
127 □2 North Point pt Seychelles
148 E3 Northport Michigan U.S.A.
8 □3 North Promontory pt Snares Is New Zealand
25 A4 North Reef I. i. Andaman and Nicobar Is India
155 F3 North Rim Arizona U.S.A.
66 F1 North Ronaldsay i. Scotland U.K.
66 F1 North Ronaldsay Firth chan. Scotland U.K.
154 B2 North San Juan California U.S.A.
137 G4 North Saskatchewan r. Alberta Canada
48 F3 North Sea sea Europe
137 J3 North Seal r. Manitoba Canada
25 A5 North Sentinel I. i. Andaman and Nicobar Is India
65 G2 North Shields England U.K.
154 D2 North Shoshone Peak summit Nevada U.S.A.
65 J4 North Somercotes England U.K.
62 D3 North Somerset div. England U.K.
66 F1 North Sound, The chan. Scotland U.K.
15 H5 North Stradbroke I. i. Queensland Australia
147 H2 North Stratford New Hampshire U.S.A.
65 G2 North Sunderland England U.K.
8 E3 North Taranaki Bight b. New Zealand
136 F4 North Thompson r. B.C. Canada
63 E3 North Tidworth England U.K.
66 A3 Northton Scotland U.K.
146 D3 North Tonawanda New York U.S.A.
36 D3 North Tons r. India
9 A7 North Trap reef New Zealand
147 G2 North Troy Vermont U.S.A.
138 D3 North Twin I. i. N.W.T. Canada
65 F2 North Tyne r. England U.K.
66 A3 North Uist i. Scotland U.K.
65 F2 Northumberland div. England U.K.
15 G4 Northumberland Is is Queensland Australia
65 F2 Northumberland National Park England U.K.
139 H4 Northumberland Strait chan. Canada
136 E5 North Vancouver B.C. Canada
147 F3 Northville New York U.S.A.
63 H2 North Walsham England U.K.
131 E3 North-West div. South Africa
8 □2 North West B. b. Campbell I. New Zealand
8 □1 North West C. c. Auckland Is New Zealand
16 A4 North West C. c. Western Australia Australia
125 D6 North-Western div. Zambia
36 C2 North West Frontier Pakistan
10 □2 North West Point pt Christmas I. Indian Ocean
158 C1 Northwest Providence Chan. chan. The Bahamas
139 J3 North West River Newfoundland Canada
134 H3 Northwest Territories div. N.W.T. Canada
62 D1 Northwich England U.K.
147 F5 North Wildwood New Jersey U.S.A.
147 H2 North Woodstock New Hampshire U.S.A.
65 H3 North York Moors reg. England U.K.
65 H3 North York Moors National Park England U.K.
65 G3 North Yorkshire div. England U.K.
65 H3 Norton England U.K.
150 D4 Norton Kansas U.S.A.
139 G4 Norton New Brunswick Canada
147 H2 Norton Vermont U.S.A.
146 B6 Norton Virginia U.S.A.
129 E2 Norton Zimbabwe
62 C3 Norton Fitzwarren England U.K.
134 B3 Norton Sound b. Alaska U.S.A.
72 E1 Nortorf Germany
88 D4 Nort-sur-Erdre France
173 G3 Norumbega Argentina
179 C2 Norvegia, C. c. Antarctica
147 G4 Norwalk Connecticut U.S.A.
146 B4 Norwalk Ohio U.S.A.
48 F2 Norway country Europe
147 H2 Norway Maine U.S.A.
141 G4 Norway Bay Québec Canada
137 K4 Norway House Manitoba Canada
178 B5 Norwegian Basin sea feature Atlantic Ocean
135 J2 Norwegian Bay b. N.W.T. Canada
178 B5 Norwegian Sea sea Atlantic Ocean
63 H2 Norwich airport England U.K.
147 G4 Norwich Connecticut U.S.A.
63 H2 Norwich England U.K.
147 F3 Norwich New York U.S.A.
140 E5 Norwich Ontario Canada
147 H3 Norwood Massachusetts U.S.A.
147 F2 Norwood New York U.S.A.
146 A5 Norwood Ohio U.S.A.
28 K2 Nosapu-misaki pt Japan
170 C1 Nos de Cachi mt. Argentina
137 H1 Nose Lake l. N.W.T. Canada
112 F3 Nos Emine pt Bulgaria
112 F3 Nos Galata pt Bulgaria
28 H1 Noshappu-misaki headland Japan
29 G3 Noshiro Japan
50 J2 Noshul' Rus. Fed.
53 D1 Nosivka Ukraine
112 G3 Nos Kaliakra pt Bulgaria
53 B2 Noskivtsi Ukraine
Nosop r. see Nossob
52 G1 Nosovaya Rus. Fed.
39 D3 Noșratābād Iran
55 E1 Nossan r. Sweden
100 C1 Nossa Senhora da Graça Póvoa e Meadas Portugal
166 E3 Nossa Senhora das Dores Brazil
167 A4 Nossa Senhora do Livramento Brazil
59 E2 Nossebro Sweden
73 J4 Nossen Germany
73 H2 Nossendorf Germany
112 G3 Nos Shabla pt Bulgaria
66 □2 Noss, Isle of i. Scotland U.K.
130 B2 Nossob r. Africa
130 C2 Nossob Camp South Africa
122 C4 Nossombougou Mali
129 H1 Nosy Bé i. Madagascar
129 H2 Nosy Boraha i. Madagascar
129 H1 Nosy Lava i. Madagascar
129 H1 Nosy Radama i. Madagascar
129 H3 Nosy Varika Madagascar
109 F2 Notaresco Italy
155 F2 Notch Peak summit Utah U.S.A.
76 D3 Noteć r. Poland
114 D1 Notia Greece
114 C3 Notia Pindos mountain range Greece
115 F5 Notio Aigaio div. Greece
115 E4 Notios Evvoïkos Kolpos chan. Greece
114 B3 Notio Steno Kerkyras chan. Greece
111 E6 Noto Sicilia Italy
29 F5 Noto Japan
58 C2 Notodden Norway
111 E6 Noto, Golfo di g. Sicilia Italy
29 F5 Noto-hantō pen. Japan
29 F5 Noto-jima i. Japan
28 K1 Notoro-ko l. Japan
81 F5 Notranje Gorice Slovenia
139 K4 Notre Dame Bay b. Newfoundland Canada
89 G2 Notre-Dame-de-Bondeville France
89 F2 Notre-Dame-de-Gravenchon France
141 H4 Notre-Dame-de-la-Salette Québec Canada
88 C5 Notre-Dame-de-Monts France
147 H2 Notre-Dame-des-Bois Québec Canada
141 H3 Notre-Dame-du-Laus Québec Canada
141 F3 Notre-Dame-du-Nord Québec Canada
139 G4 Notre Dame, Monts mountain range Québec Canada
123 E5 Notsé Togo
28 K2 Notsuke-saki pt Japan
28 K2 Notsuke-suidō chan. Japan
140 E4 Nottawasaga Bay b. Ontario Canada
138 E3 Nottaway r. Québec Canada
63 E2 Nottingham England U.K.
131 H4 Nottingham Road South Africa
63 E1 Nottinghamshire div. England U.K.
146 E6 Nottoway r. Virginia U.S.A.
72 C4 Nottuln Germany
137 H5 Notukeu Cr. r. Saskatchewan Canada
120 A4 Nouâdhibou Mauritania
120 A5 Nouakchott Mauritania
120 C5 Noual well Mauritania
120 A5 Nouâmghâr Mauritania
89 H4 Nouan-le-Fuzelier France
87 E3 Nouart France
24 D4 Nouei Vietnam
120 A5 Noueïch well Mauritania
6 □2 Nouméa New Caledonia Pacific Ocean
124 B3 Noun r. Cameroon
122 D4 Nouna Burkina
130 E5 Noupoort South Africa
131 G4 Noupoortsnek pass South Africa
56 H2 Nousu Finland
Nouveau-Comptoir see Wemindji
Nouvelle Calédonie territory see New Caledonia
86 A2 Nouvion France
89 F4 Nouzilly France
86 D3 Nouzonville France
47 G4 Nov Tajikistan
54 C2 Nõva Estonia
78 F5 Nova Hungary
169 H4 Nova Almeida Brazil
168 A4 Nova Alvorada Brazil
168 D1 Nova America Brazil
168 B5 Nova Andradina Brazil
51 F5 Nova Astrakhan' Ukraine
168 D3 Nova Aurora Brazil
79 H3 Nová Baňa Slovakia
53 C1 Nova Borova Ukraine
78 E2 Nová Bystřice Czech Rep.
125 B5 Nova Caipemba Angola
114 C1 Novaci Macedonia
112 D2 Novaci Romania
169 G3 Nova Era Brazil
168 B5 Nova Esperança Brazil
107 G5 Novafeltria Italy
169 G5 Nova Friburgo Brazil
81 E5 Nova Gorica Slovenia
104 F3 Nova Gradiška Croatia
168 D4 Nova Granada Brazil
169 G5 Nova Iguaçu Brazil
53 E3 Nova Kakhovka Ukraine
79 H3 Nováky Slovakia
107 F2 Nova Levante Italy
169 G3 Nova Lima Brazil
107 J4 Novalja Croatia
168 B5 Nova Londrina Brazil
54 F4 Novalukoml' Belarus
129 F3 Nova Mambone Mozambique
53 E3 Nova Mayachka Ukraine
129 F2 Nova Nabúri Mozambique
53 D3 Nova Odesa Ukraine
78 E1 Nová Paka Czech Rep.
112 C2 Nova Pazova Yugoslavia
166 D2 Nova Pilão Arcado Brazil
168 E3 Nova Ponte Brazil
53 D2 Nova Praha Ukraine
106 C2 Novara div. Piemonte Italy
106 C3 Novara Novara Italy
166 D2 Nova Remanso Brazil
169 E4 Nova Resende Brazil
166 C3 Nova Roma Brazil
168 B6 Nova Santa Rosa Brazil
139 H5 Nova Scotia div. Canada
166 D2 Nova Sento Sé Brazil
169 F3 Nova Serrana Brazil
109 J4 Nova Siri Italy
53 F1 Nova Sloboda Ukraine
166 E3 Nova Soure Brazil
106 D2 Novate Mezzola Italy
154 A2 Novato California U.S.A.
104 F3 Nova Topola Bos.-Herz.
53 B2 Nova Ushytsya Ukraine
112 B3 Nova Varoš Yugoslavia
169 H3 Nova Venécia Brazil
169 J2 Nova Viçosa Brazil
165 D2 Nova Vida Brazil
53 F2 Nova Vodolaha Ukraine
168 B1 Nova Xavantina Brazil
52 H3 Novaya Bekshanka Rus. Fed.
46 C3 Novaya Kazanka Kazakhstan
50 E2 Novaya Ladoga Rus. Fed.
52 E3 Novaya Lyada Rus. Fed.
45 R2 Novaya Sibir', O. i. Rus. Fed.
44 G2 Novaya Zemlya i. Rus. Fed.
112 E3 Nova Zagora Bulgaria
53 E3 Nova Zbur"yivka Ukraine
53 E2 Nove Ukraine
78 D3 Nové Hrady Czech Rep.
103 C6 Novelda Spain
107 F4 Novellara Italy
78 F1 Nové Město nad Metuj Czech Rep.
79 G3 Nové Mesto nad Váhom Slovakia
99 F4 Novés Spain
75 J2 Nové Strašecí Czech Rep.
79 H4 Nové Zámky Slovakia
50 J3 Novgorod div. Rus. Fed.
50 D3 Novgorod Rus. Fed.
53 E2 Novhorodka Ukraine
52 A4 Novhorod-Sivers'kyy Ukraine
112 C2 Novi Bečej Yugoslavia
53 C1 Novi Bilokorovychi Ukraine
53 D1 Novi Borovychi Ukraine
53 A1 Novi Chervyshcha Ukraine
107 E4 Novi di Modena Italy
107 H3 Novigrad Croatia
112 D3 Novi Iskŭr Bulgaria
79 K5 Novi Kneževac Yugoslavia
106 C4 Novi Ligure Italy
69 C4 Noville Belgium
78 F5 Novi Marof Croatia
53 E1 Novi Mlyny Ukraine
86 D3 Novion-Porcien France
112 F3 Novi Pazar Bulgaria
112 C3 Novi Pazar Yugoslavia
112 B2 Novi Sad Yugoslavia
53 F2 Novi Sanzhary Ukraine
107 J3 Novi Vinodolski Croatia
52 E1 Novki Rus. Fed.
52 G1 Novlyanka Rus. Fed.
166 B1 Novo r. Brazil
51 G6 Novoaleksandrovsk Rus. Fed.
52 B2 Novoaleksandrovskiy Rus. Fed.
46 E2 Novoalekseyevka Kazakhstan
47 K2 Novoaltaysk Rus. Fed.
53 G5 Novoanninskiy Rus. Fed.
163 E5 Novo Aripuanã Brazil
53 D2 Novoarkhanhel's'k Ukraine
51 F6 Novoazovs'k Ukraine
53 F3 Novobohdanivka Ukraine
52 E3 Novobokino Rus. Fed.
52 H1 Novocheboksarsk Rus. Fed.
51 G6 Novocherkassk Rus. Fed.
169 H2 Novo Cruzeiro Brazil
53 F3 Novodanylivka Ukraine
52 F2 Novodmitriyevka Rus. Fed.
53 B2 Novodnistrovs'k Ukraine
47 H2 Novodolinka Kazakhstan
53 G2 Novodonets'ke Ukraine
52 B2 Novodugino Rus. Fed.
50 G1 Novodvinsk Rus. Fed.
53 C2 Novofastiv Ukraine
31 H2 Novogeorgiyevka Rus. Fed.
52 B3 Novognezdilovo Rus. Fed.
52 C2 Novogurovskiy Rus. Fed.
167 B6 Novo Hamburgo Brazil
168 D4 Novo Horizonte Brazil
53 E3 Novohradivka Ukraine
78 D3 Novohradské Hory mts Czech Rep.
53 B1 Novohrad-Volyns'kyy Ukraine
53 G2 Novohrodivka Ukraine
30 D2 Novoil'insk Rus. Fed.
53 F3 Novoivanivka Ukraine
52 D4 Novokastornoye Rus. Fed.
46 F3 Novokazalinsk Kazakhstan
54 F4 Novokhovansk Rus. Fed.
31 J2 Novokiyevskiy Uval Rus. Fed.
51 G6 Novokubansk Rus. Fed.
50 J4 Novokuybyshevsk Rus. Fed.
47 L2 Novokuznetsk Rus. Fed.
53 E3 Novokyyivka Ukraine
179 D3 Novolazarevskaya Rus. Fed. Base Antarctica
45 M2 Novoletov'ye Rus. Fed.
53 F2 Novomar"yivka Ukraine
81 G5 Novo mesto Slovenia
104 E3 Novo Mesto Slovenia
52 D2 Novomichurinsk Rus. Fed.
51 F6 Novomikhaylovskiy Rus. Fed.
79 K6 Novo Miloševo Yugoslavia
50 F4 Novomoskovsk Rus. Fed.
53 F2 Novomoskovs'k Ukraine
53 F3 Novomykhaylivka Ukraine
53 F3 Novomykolayivka Ukraine
53 D2 Novomyrhorod Ukraine
53 E3 Novonatalivka Ukraine
51 G5 Novonikolayevskiy Rus. Fed.
51 H5 Novonikol'skoye Rus. Fed.
53 F3 Novooleksiyivka Ukraine
163 F4 Novo Olinda do Norte Brazil
46 E2 Novoorsk Rus. Fed.
53 E1 Novoorzhyts'ke Ukraine
53 C1 Novoozeryanka Ukraine
166 D2 Novo Parnarama Brazil
53 D3 Novopavlivka Ukraine
30 D2 Novopavlovka Rus. Fed.
52 E1 Novopistsovo Rus. Fed.
53 F2 Novopokrovka Ukraine
51 G6 Novopokrovskaya Rus. Fed.
52 F4 Novopokrovskoye Rus. Fed.
53 E3 Novopoltavka Ukraine
52 D3 Novopolyan'ye Rus. Fed.
51 F5 Novopskov Ukraine
31 J1 Novorossiyka Rus. Fed.
51 F6 Novorossiysk Rus. Fed.
45 M2 Novorybnoye Rus. Fed.
54 F3 Novorzhev Rus. Fed.
53 C3 Novoselivka Ukraine
52 F2 Novoselki Rus. Fed.
114 D1 Novo Selo Macedonia
77 J1 Novoselovo Rus. Fed.
54 F2 Novosel'ye Rus. Fed.
53 B2 Novoselytsya Ukraine
46 D2 Novosergiyevka Rus. Fed.
51 F6 Novoshakhtinsk Rus. Fed.
47 K2 Novosibirsk Rus. Fed.
47 K1 Novosibirsk Rus. Fed.
45 P2 Novosibirskiye Ostrova is Rus. Fed.
52 C3 Novosil' Rus. Fed.
52 D4 Novosil'skoye Rus. Fed.
46 F1 Novosineglazovskiy Rus. Fed.
50 D3 Novosokol'niki Rus. Fed.
77 K1 Novostroyevo Rus. Fed.
46 E2 Novotroitsk Rus. Fed.
47 H4 Novotroitskoye Kazakhstan
52 A3 Novotroitskoye Rus. Fed.
52 G2 Novotroitskoye Rus. Fed.
53 F3 Novotroyits'ke Ukraine
53 D2 Novoukrayinka Kirovohrad Ukraine
53 A1 Novoukrayinka Rivne Ukraine
51 J5 Novouzensk Rus. Fed.
53 F3 Novovasylivka Ukraine
53 A1 Novovolyns'k Ukraine
51 F5 Novovoronezh Rus. Fed.
53 E3 Novovorontsovka Ukraine
52 F1 Novovyazniki Rus. Fed.
77 M6 Novoyavorivs'ke Ukraine
52 D3 Novoye Dubovoye Rus. Fed.
52 E1 Novoye Leushino Rus. Fed.
52 E3 Novoyur'yevo Rus. Fed.
52 C1 Novozavidovskiy Rus. Fed.
53 C2 Novozhyvotiv Ukraine
51 D4 Novozybkov Rus. Fed.
78 D1 Nový Bor Czech Rep.
78 E1 Nový Bydžov Czech Rep.
86 D3 Novy-Chevrières France
77 N2 Novy Dvor Hrodna Belarus
77 N3 Novy Dvor Hrodna Belarus
79 G2 Nový Jičín Czech Rep.
45 M2 Novyy Rus. Fed.
53 E3 Novyy Buh Ukraine
53 D1 Novyy Bykiv Ukraine
52 H2 Novyye Aybesi Rus. Fed.
52 H3 Novyye Burasy Rus. Fed.
52 A3 Novyye Ivaytenki Rus. Fed.
52 D1 Novyy Nekouz Rus. Fed.
53 G1 Novyy Oskol Rus. Fed.
44 J3 Novyy Port Rus. Fed.
77 N6 Novyy Rozdil Ukraine
52 C3 Novyy Sinets Rus. Fed.
53 E2 Novyystarodub Ukraine
50 J3 Novyy Tor"yal Rus. Fed.
44 J3 Novyy Urengoy Rus. Fed.
31 K2 Novyy Urgal Rus. Fed.
46 D4 Novyy Uzen' Kazakhstan
77 N5 Novyy Vytkiv Ukraine
77 N6 Novyy Yarychiv Ukraine
39 C3 Now Iran
77 H4 Nowa Brzeźnica Poland
77 M2 Nowa Chodorówka Poland
77 K5 Nowa Dęba Poland
76 G1 Nowa Karczma Poland
76 E5 Nowa Ruda Poland
76 D4 Nowa Sól Poland
151 E4 Nowata Oklahoma U.S.A.
77 L2 Nowa Wieś Ełcka Poland
76 G3 Nowa Wieś Wielka Poland
39 B2 Nowbarān Iran
76 G2 Nowe Poland
76 C2 Nowe Czarnowo Poland
77 J4 Nowe Miasło nad Pilicą Poland
76 D4 Nowe Miasteczko Poland
77 J3 Nowe Miasto Poland
77 H2 Nowe Miasto Lubawskie Poland
76 F3 Nowe Miasto nad Wartą Poland
77 H3 Nowe Ostrowy Poland
77 L3 Nowe Piekuty Poland
76 F4 Nowe Skalmierzyce Poland
76 C2 Nowe Warpno Poland
76 F1 Nowe Wieś Lęborska Poland
36 D4 Nowgong India
Nowgong see Nagaon
77 L2 Nowinka Poland
42 G2 Nowjeh Deh Iran
39 C1 Now Kharegan Iran
137 J2 Nowleye Lake l. N.W.T. Canada
76 D2 Nowogard Poland
77 K2 Nowogród Poland
76 D4 Nowogród Bobrzański Poland
76 D3 Nowogródek Pomorski Poland
73 L4 Nowogrodziec Poland
13 G3 Nowra New South Wales Australia
42 G2 Nowshahr Iran
39 B1 Now Shahr Iran
36 C2 Nowshera Pakistan
77 H3 Nowy Duninów Poland
77 M2 Nowy Dwór Białystok Poland
76 F2 Nowy Dwór Toruń Poland
77 H1 Nowy Dwór Gdański Poland
77 J3 Nowy Dwór Mazowiecki Poland
77 J5 Nowy Korczyn Poland
77 J6 Nowy Sącz div. Poland
77 J6 Nowy Sącz Poland
77 J6 Nowy Targ Poland
76 E3 Nowy Tomyśl Poland
77 K6 Nowy Żmigród Poland
147 E4 Noxen Pennsylvania U.S.A.
44 J3 Noyabr'sk Rus. Fed.
88 C3 Noyal-Pontivy France
89 F4 Noyant France
90 B1 Noyers France
91 D4 Noyers-sur-Jabron France
136 C3 Noyes I. i. Alaska U.S.A.
86 B3 Noyon France
88 D4 Nozay France
90 E2 Nozeroy France
131 E5 Nozizwe South Africa
83 F3 Nozza r. Italy
131 H5 Nqabeni South Africa
131 H4 Nqutu South Africa
124 C4 Nsambi Congo(Zaire)
129 F2 Nsanje Malawi
122 D5 Nsawam Ghana
124 B3 Nsoc Equatorial Guinea
131 H3 Nsoko Swaziland
125 E6 Nsombo Zambia
122 D5 Nsuatre Ghana
123 F5 Nsukka Nigeria
120 A4 Ntalfa well Mauritania
124 C4 Ntandembele Congo(Zaire)
129 E1 Ntcheu Malawi
127 B7 Ntchisi Malawi
124 B3 Ntem r. Africa
131 F3 Ntha South Africa
131 G3 Nthorwane South Africa
124 A3 Ntoum Gabon
124 B3 Ntui Cameroon
127 B5 Ntungamo Uganda
128 D3 Ntwetwe Pan salt pan Botswana
131 G5 Ntywenka South Africa
32 B3 Nu r. China
179 □ Nuageuses, Is is Kerguelen Indian Ocean
131 H1 Nuaneteze r. Mozambique
6 □3 Nuapapu i. Tonga
41 J5 Nu'aym reg. Oman
119 F3 Nuba, Lake l. Sudan
126 B2 Nuba Mountains mts Sudan
119 F3 Nubian Desert desert Sudan
172 B4 Nuble r. Chile
98 E1 Nubledo Spain
30 D4 Nüden Mongolia
164 B3 Nudo Coropuna mt. Peru
77 N4 Nudyzhe Ukraine
151 D6 Nueces r. Texas U.S.A.
92 B2 Nueil-sur-Argent France
69 D3 Nuenen Netherlands
103 E6 Nuestra Señora del Pilar Spain
99 F1 Nueva Spain
156 J6 Nueva Armenia Honduras
172 C2 Nueva California Argentina
172 D3 Nueva Constitución Argentina
172 E2 Nueva Escocia Argentina
162 D2 Nueva Florida Venezuela
172 E3 Nueva Galia Argentina
165 E4 Nueva Germania Paraguay
158 B2 Nueva Gerona Cuba
173 J3 Nueva Helvecia Uruguay
171 C7 Nueva, I. i. Chile
172 A5 Nueva Imperial Chile
162 B3 Nueva Loja Ecuador
171 B5 Nueva Lubecka Argentina
173 H2 Nueva Palmira Uruguay
157 E3 Nueva Rosita Mexico
157 H6 Nueva San Salvador El Salvador
158 C2 Nuevitas Cuba
173 H2 Nuevo Berlín Uruguay
156 D2 Nuevo Casas Grandes Mexico
171 D5 Nuevo, G. g. Argentina
156 D3 Nuevo Ideal Mexico
157 F3 Nuevo Laredo Mexico
157 F3 Nuevo Leon div. Mexico
164 C2 Nuevo Mundo Bolivia
126 E3 Nugaal div. Somalia
126 E3 Nugaal watercourse Somalia
9 B7 Nugget Pt pt New Zealand
119 F3 Nugrus, Gebel mt. Egypt
6 □1 Nuguria Is is P.N.G.
8 F3 Nuhaka New Zealand
176 G6 Nui i. Tuvalu
54 D2 Nuia Estonia
54 F1 Nuijamaa Finland
90 C1 Nuits France

90 C1 **Nuits-St-Georges** France
12 C3 **Nukey Bluff h.** *S. Australia* Australia
6 □4 **Nuku i.** Tonga
6 □4 **Nuku'alofa** Tonga
6 □6 **Nukubasaga reef** Fiji
176 G6 **Nukufetau i.** Tuvalu
177 K6 **Nuku Hiva i.** *French Polynesia* Pacific Ocean
176 G6 **Nukulaelae i.** Tuvalu
6 □1 **Nukumanu Is is** P.N.G.
5 K5 **Nukunono atoll** *Tokelau* Pacific Ocean
46 E4 **Nukus** Uzbekistan
103 C5 **Nules** Spain
16 C4 **Nullagine r.** *Western Australia* Australia
16 C4 **Nullagine** *Western Australia* Australia
12 B2 **Nullarbor** *S. Australia* Australia
12 B2 **Nullarbor Nat. Park nat. park** *S. Australia* Australia
12 B2 **Nullarbor Plain plain** Australia
131 H1 **Nulli** Zimbabwe
31 F4 **Nulu'erhu Shan mountain range** China
108 A4 **Nulvi** *Sardegna* Italy
119 G2 **Nu'mān i.** Saudi Arabia
123 G5 **Numan** Nigeria
107 H5 **Numana** Italy
29 G5 **Numata** Japan
28 H2 **Numata** Japan
124 E2 **Numatinna watercourse** Sudan
29 G6 **Numazu** Japan
131 H2 **Numbi Gate** South Africa
14 C2 **Numbulwar** *Northern Terr.* Australia
58 C1 **Numedal v.** Norway
21 K7 **Numfor i.** Indonesia
31 H3 **Numin r.** China
54 D1 **Nummela** Finland
13 F4 **Numurkah** *Victoria* Australia
139 H2 **Nunaksaluk Island i.** *Newfoundland* Canada
135 O3 **Nunarsuit i.** Greenland
137 M2 **Nunavut reg.** *N.W.T.* Canada
73 J4 **Nünchritz** Germany
146 E3 **Nunda** *New York* U.S.A.
125 E4 **Nunda** Congo(Zaire)
13 G2 **Nundle** *New South Wales* Australia
63 E2 **Nuneaton** *England* U.K.
138 B3 **Nungesser L. l.** *Ontario* Canada
31 F3 **Nungnain Sum** China
134 B4 **Nunivak I.** *Alaska* U.S.A.
36 D2 **Nunkun mt.** India
134 A3 **Nunligran** Rus. Fed.
98 D4 **Nuñomoral** Spain
73 J3 **Nunsdorf** Germany
68 D2 **Nunspeet** Netherlands
31 G2 **Nuomin r.** China
108 B4 **Nuoro div.** *Sardegna* Italy
108 B4 **Nuoro** *Sardegna* Italy
119 H2 **Nuqrah** Saudi Arabia
162 B2 **Nuquí** Colombia
36 E1 **Nur** China
77 L3 **Nur** Poland
47 H2 **Nura r.** Kazakhstan
47 H3 **Nura** Kazakhstan
39 B3 **Nurābād** Iran
46 C5 **Nūrābād** Iran
108 B5 **Nurallao** *Sardegna* Italy
108 B5 **Nuraminis** *Sardegna* Italy
47 G4 **Nurata** Uzbekistan
47 G4 **Nuratau, Khr. mountain range** Uzbekistan
43 D1 **Nur Dağları mountain range** Turkey
106 D4 **Nure r.** Italy
Nuremberg *see* **Nürnberg**
39 G2 **Nūr Gal** Afghanistan
36 A3 **Nūr Gamma** Pakistan
156 C2 **Nuri** Mexico
39 G2 **Nuristan reg.** Afghanistan
22 B2 **Nuri, Tk b.** Indonesia
36 D2 **Nurla** India
50 J4 **Nurlat** Rus. Fed.
56 H3 **Nurmes** Finland
54 D1 **Nurmijärvi** Finland
56 F3 **Nurmo** Finland
75 G3 **Nürnberg** Germany
36 B3 **Nurpur** Pakistan
13 F2 **Nurri, Mt h.** *New South Wales* Australia
74 E4 **Nürtingen** Germany
37 H1 **Nur Turu** China
77 L3 **Nurzec r.** Poland
77 M3 **Nurzec-Stacja** Poland
82 C3 **Nus** Italy
22 D4 **Nusa Tenggara Barat div.** Indonesia
22 D4 **Nusa Tenggara Timur div.** Indonesia
42 E2 **Nusaybin** Turkey
43 D2 **Nuşayrīyah, Jabal al mountain range** Syria
79 M4 **Nuşfalău** Romania
32 B3 **Nu Shan mountain range** China
36 A3 **Nushki** Pakistan
80 D3 **Nußdorf am Inn** Germany
139 H2 **Nutak** *Newfoundland* Canada
69 D4 **Nuth** Netherlands
155 H5 **Nutrioso** *Arizona* U.S.A.
36 B3 **Nuttal** Pakistan
14 C2 **Nutwood Downs** *Northern Terr.* Australia
135 N3 **Nuuk** Greenland
56 G2 **Nuupas** Finland
7 □11 **Nuupéré, Pte pt** *French Polynesia* Pacific Ocean
135 N2 **Nuussuaq pen.** Greenland
135 N2 **Nuussuaq** Greenland
7 □13 **Nuuuli** *American Samoa* Pacific Ocean
38 C5 **Nuwara Eliya** Sri Lanka
43 C5 **Nuweiba el Muzeina** Egypt
130 B5 **Nuwerus** South Africa
130 C6 **Nuweveldberg mts** South Africa
52 G2 **Nuya r.** Rus. Fed.
77 N4 **Nuyno** Ukraine
12 C3 **Nuyts Arch. is** *S. Australia* Australia
17 B7 **Nuyts, Pt pt** *Western Australia* Australia
83 E1 **Nüziders** Austria
17 B7 **Nyabing** *Western Australia* Australia
129 E2 **Nyadire r.** Zimbabwe
44 H3 **Nyagan'** Rus. Fed.
Nyagquka *see* **Yajiang**
Nyagrong *see* **Xinlong**
127 C4 **Nyahururu** Kenya
13 E3 **Nyah West** *Victoria* Australia
37 G3 **Nyainqêntanglha Feng mt.** China
37 G3 **Nyainqêntanglha Shan mountain range** China
37 H2 **Nyainrong** China
127 B5 **Nyakaliro** Tanzania
131 F3 **Nyakallong** South Africa
56 E3 **Nyaker** Sweden
77 O3 **Nyakhachava** Belarus
118 D5 **Nyala** Sudan
37 F3 **Nyalam** China
178 □3 **Ny-Ålesund** *Svalbard* Arctic Ocean
129 D2 **Nyamandhiovu** Zimbabwe
124 E2 **Nyamlell** Sudan
77 O3 **Nyamyerzha** Belarus
52 G2 **Nyandoma** Rus. Fed.
50 F2 **Nyandomskiy Vozvyshennost' h.** Rus. Fed.
125 B4 **Nyanga div.** Gabon
125 B4 **Nyanga** Congo
129 E2 **Nyanga** Zimbabwe
37 G3 **Nyang Qu r.** China
122 D5 **Nyankpala** Ghana
127 B5 **Nyanza div.** Kenya
127 A5 **Nyanza** Rwanda
22 D1 **Nyapa, G. mt.** Indonesia
79 J4 **Nyársapát** Hungary
127 B6 **Nyasa, Lake l.** Africa
54 E5 **Nyasvizh** Belarus
129 D2 **Nyathi** Zimbabwe
24 B3 **Nyaunglebin** Myanmar
24 A2 **Nyaungu** Myanmar
46 E1 **Nyazepetrovsk** Rus. Fed.
59 F2 **Nybble** Sweden
59 E1 **Nybergsund** Norway
55 C4 **Nyborg** Denmark
56 H1 **Nyborg** Norway
59 F3 **Nybro** Sweden
135 N1 **Nyeboe Land reg.** Greenland
54 E5 **Nyeharelaye** Belarus
79 K4 **Nyékládháza** Hungary
37 G3 **Nyêmo** China
Nyenchen Tanglha Range mountain range *see* **Nyainqêntanglha Shan**
127 C5 **Nyeri** Kenya
54 F4 **Nyeshcharda, Vozyera l.** Belarus
59 F1 **Nyhammar** Sweden
127 B7 **Nyika National Park nat. park** Malawi
37 F3 **Nyima** China
127 B7 **Nyimba** Zambia
37 H3 **Nyingchi** China
79 L4 **Nyíradony** Hungary
79 M4 **Nyírbátor** Hungary
79 M4 **Nyírbéltek** Hungary
79 M4 **Nyírbogát** Hungary
79 L4 **Nyíregyháza** Hungary
79 L4 **Nyírség reg.** Hungary
56 F3 **Nykarleby** Finland
55 D5 **Nykøbing** Denmark
55 A3 **Nykøbing Mors** Denmark
55 D4 **Nykøbing Sjælland** Denmark
59 G2 **Nyköping** Sweden
59 G1 **Nykrogen** Sweden
59 F2 **Nykroppa** Sweden
59 G2 **Nykvarn** Sweden
59 F2 **Nykyrke** Sweden
56 E3 **Nyland** Sweden
131 G2 **Nylstroom** South Africa
13 F3 **Nymagee** *New South Wales* Australia
13 H2 **Nymboida r.** *New South Wales* Australia
78 E1 **Nymburk** Czech Rep.
114 A3 **Nymfes** Greece
55 A4 **Nymindegab** Denmark
59 G2 **Nynäshamn** Sweden
13 F2 **Nyngan** *New South Wales* Australia
54 C5 **Nyoman r.** Belarus/Lithuania
54 E5 **Nyomanskaya Nizina lowland** Belarus
82 B2 **Nyon** Switzerland
36 F4 **Nyonni Ri mt.** China
91 D4 **Nyons** France
55 D4 **Nyråd** Denmark
78 C2 **Nýřany** Czech Rep.
78 C2 **Nýrsko** Czech Rep.
76 F5 **Nysa** Poland
76 F5 **Nysa Kłodzka r.** Poland
73 K4 **Nysa Łużycka r.** Germany/Poland
59 E2 **Nysäter** Sweden
55 D5 **Nysted** Denmark
58 C1 **Nystølfjell mt.** Norway
50 J2 **Nyuchpas** Rus. Fed.
29 G4 **Nyūdō-zaki pt** Japan
50 H2 **Nyukhcha** Rus. Fed.
50 H2 **Nyuksenitsa** Rus. Fed.
79 G4 **Nyúl** Hungary
125 E5 **Nyunzu** Congo(Zaire)
45 N3 **Nyurba** Rus. Fed.
50 J2 **Nyuvchim** Rus. Fed.
77 N5 **Nyvytsi** Ukraine
77 L6 **Nyzhankovychi** Ukraine
53 F3 **Nyzhni Sirohozy** Ukraine
53 F3 **Nyzhni Torhayi** Ukraine
79 N3 **Nyzhni Vorota** Ukraine
53 F1 **Nyzhnya Syrovatka** Ukraine
53 F1 **Nyzy** Ukraine
125 B4 **Nzambi** Congo
124 E3 **Nzara** Sudan
122 C5 **Nzébéla** Guinea
127 B5 **Nzega** Tanzania
125 B5 **N'zeto** Angola
131 H1 **Nzhelele Dam dam** South Africa
122 D5 **Nzi r.** Côte d'Ivoire
125 E6 **Nzilo, Lac l.** Congo(Zaire)
125 E4 **Nzingu** Congo(Zaire)
124 B4 **Nzoia r.** Kenya
124 E3 **Nzoro r.** Congo(Zaire)
127 D7 **Nzwani i.** Comoro

O

63 E2 **Oadby** *England* U.K.
150 C2 **Oahe, Lake l.** *S. Dakota* U.S.A.
153 □1 **Oahu i.** *Hawaii* U.S.A.
12 E3 **Oakbank** *S. Australia* Australia
155 F2 **Oak City** *Utah* U.S.A.
151 E6 **Oakdale** *Louisiana* U.S.A.
62 D2 **Oakengates** *England* U.K.
150 D2 **Oakes** *N. Dakota* U.S.A.
15 G5 **Oakey** *Queensland* Australia
63 F2 **Oakham** *England* U.K.
152 B1 **Oak Harbor** *Washington* U.S.A.
146 C6 **Oak Hill** *W. Virginia* U.S.A.
154 C3 **Oakhurst** *California* U.S.A.
148 B2 **Oak I. i.** *Wisconsin* U.S.A.
154 A3 **Oakland airport** *California* U.S.A.
154 A3 **Oakland** *California* U.S.A.
146 D5 **Oakland** *Maryland* U.S.A.
150 D3 **Oakland** *Nebraska* U.S.A.
152 B2 **Oakland** *Oregon* U.S.A.
148 D5 **Oak Lawn** *Illinois* U.S.A.
150 C4 **Oakley** *Kansas* U.S.A.
16 C4 **Oakover r.** *Western Australia* Australia
152 B3 **Oakridge** *Oregon* U.S.A.
145 C4 **Oak Ridge** *Tennessee* U.S.A.
13 D3 **Oakura** New Zealand
141 F5 **Oakville** *Ontario* Canada
9 C6 **Oamaru** New Zealand
66 B5 **Oa, Mull of headland** *Scotland* U.K.
9 D5 **Oaro** New Zealand
23 B3 **Oas** Philippines
28 D6 **Ōasa** Japan
152 D3 **Oasis** *Nevada* U.S.A.
43 D3 **Oasis of Rhube oasis** Syria
179 B5 **Oates Land reg.** Antarctica
13 F5 **Oatlands** *Tasmania* Australia
130 E6 **Oatlands** South Africa
155 E4 **Oatman** *Arizona* U.S.A.
157 F5 **Oaxaca div.** Mexico
157 F5 **Oaxaca** Mexico
49 O3 **Ob' r.** Rus. Fed.
140 C2 **Oba** *Ontario* Canada
140 C2 **Obakamiga Lake l.** *Ontario* Canada
54 F4 **Obal' r.** Belarus
54 F4 **Obal'** *Vitsyebskaya Voblasts'* Belarus
124 B3 **Obala** Cameroon
140 C2 **Oba Lake l.** *Ontario* Canada
29 E6 **Obama** Japan
66 C4 **Oban** *Scotland* U.K.
123 F5 **Oban** Nigeria
29 H4 **Obanazawa** Japan
123 F5 **Oban Hills mt.** Nigeria
98 D2 **O Barco** Spain
99 G2 **Obarenes, Mtes mountain range** Spain
138 F4 **Obatogama L. l.** *Québec* Canada
81 F3 **Obdach** Austria
75 J3 **Obecnice** Czech Rep.
136 F4 **Obed** *Alberta* Canada
54 D4 **Obeliai** Lithuania
9 B6 **Obelisk mt.** New Zealand
81 G3 **Oberaich** Austria
81 E3 **Oberalm** Austria
83 D2 **Oberalpstock mt.** Switzerland
75 G5 **Oberammergau** Germany
75 F3 **Oberasbach** Germany
75 G5 **Oberau** Germany
72 E5 **Oberaula** Germany
75 G4 **Oberbayern div.** Germany
74 D3 **Oberderdingen** Germany
80 D4 **Oberdrauburg** Austria
83 E1 **Oberegg** Switzerland
83 E2 **Ober Engadin reg.** Switzerland
82 D1 **Oberentfelden** Switzerland
80 A3 **Oberessendorf** Germany
87 G2 **Oberfell** Germany
75 G2 **Oberfranken div.** Germany
82 C1 **Obergösgen** Switzerland
81 G2 **Ober-Grafendorf** Austria
74 F5 **Obergünzburg** Germany
80 C4 **Obergurgl** Austria
81 G4 **Oberhaag** Austria
87 H4 **Oberharmersbach** Germany
73 F4 **Oberharz nat. park** Germany
72 B4 **Oberhausen** Germany
83 F1 **Oberjoch Paß pass** Austria/Germany
74 D4 **Oberkirch** Germany
80 B2 **Oberkochen** Germany
73 K4 **Oberlausitz reg.** Germany
150 C4 **Oberlin** *Kansas* U.S.A.
146 B4 **Oberlin** *Ohio* U.S.A.
74 E4 **Obermarchtal** Germany
74 C3 **Obermoschel** Germany
90 F2 **Obernai** France
75 J4 **Obernberg am Inn** Austria
74 D4 **Oberndorf am Neckar** Germany
80 D3 **Oberndorf bei Salzburg** Austria
81 F2 **Oberneukirchen** Austria
87 G3 **Obernheim-Kirchenarnbach** Germany
72 E3 **Obernkirchen** Germany
81 E2 **Oberösterreich div.** Austria
75 G3 **Oberpfalz div.** Germany
75 H3 **Oberpfälzer Wald mts** Germany
81 H3 **Oberpullendorf div.** Austria
81 H3 **Oberpullendorf** Austria
87 H3 **Ober-Ramstadt** Germany
83 E1 **Oberreute** Germany
83 E1 **Oberriet** Switzerland
87 G4 **Oberrot** Germany
80 D2 **Oberschneiding** Germany
83 D1 **Obersiggenthal** Switzerland
74 E2 **Obersinn** Germany
74 F5 **Oberstaufen** Germany
74 F5 **Oberstdorf** Germany
83 E1 **Oberteuringen** Germany
74 C3 **Oberthal** Germany
74 E5 **Oberthulba** Germany
75 H4 **Obertraubling** Germany
80 E3 **Obertrum am See** Austria
74 D2 **Obertshausen** Germany
53 A2 **Obertyn** Ukraine
73 J2 **Oberueckersee l.** Germany
87 H2 **Oberursel (Taunus)** Germany
80 E4 **Obervellach** Austria
75 H3 **Oberviechtach** Germany
83 D2 **Oberwald** Switzerland
72 E4 **Oberwälder Land reg.** Germany
81 H3 **Oberwaltersdorf** Austria
81 H3 **Oberwart div.** Austria
81 H3 **Oberwart** Austria
75 G2 **Oberweißbach** Germany
81 G2 **Oberwölbling** Austria
81 F3 **Oberwölz** Austria
52 B4 **Obesta r.** Rus. Fed.
21 J7 **Obi i.** Indonesia
166 A1 **Óbidos** Brazil
100 A1 **Óbidos** Portugal
100 A1 **Óbidos, Lagoa de lag.** Portugal
47 G5 **Obigarm** Tajikistan
29 J2 **Obihiro** Japan
51 H6 **Obil'noye** Rus. Fed.
75 H4 **Obing** Germany
28 H1 **Obira** Japan
162 C2 **Obispos** Venezuela
172 F1 **Obispo Trejo** Argentina
92 D3 **Objat** France
76 F3 **Objazda** Poland
81 E3 **Öblarn** Austria
51 G5 **Oblivskaya** Rus. Fed.
31 J2 **Obluch'ye** Rus. Fed.
52 C2 **Obninsk** Rus. Fed.
124 E2 **Obo** Central African Rep.
30 B5 **Obo** China
130 C3 **Obobogorap** South Africa
126 D2 **Obock** Djibouti
124 E4 **Obokote** Congo(Zaire)
98 C2 **O Bolo** Spain
53 E2 **Obolon'** Ukraine
76 E3 **Oborniki** Poland
76 E4 **Oborniki Śląskie** Poland
124 C4 **Obouya** Congo
53 G1 **Oboyan'** Rus. Fed.
50 G2 **Obozerskiy** Rus. Fed.
76 G2 **Obra r.** Poland
37 E4 **Obra** India
156 C3 **Obregón, Psa resr** Mexico
87 H3 **Obrigheim (Pfalz)** Germany
75 J2 **Obrnice** Czech Rep.
112 F3 **Obrochishte** Bulgaria
107 J3 **Obrov** Slovenia
76 E3 **Obrzycko** Poland
10 □4 **Observatory Rock i.** *Lord Howe I.* Pacific Ocean
46 D2 **Obshchiy Syrt h.** Rus. Fed.
44 J3 **Obskaya Guba chan.** Rus. Fed.
77 L5 **Obsza** Poland
53 E1 **Obtove** Ukraine
123 D5 **Obuasi** Ghana
53 D1 **Obukhiv** Ukraine
82 D2 **Obwalden div.** Switzerland
50 J2 **Ob"yachevo** Rus. Fed.
53 G3 **Obytichna Kosa spit** Ukraine
53 F3 **Obytichna Zakota b.** Ukraine
52 F1 **Obzherikha** Rus. Fed.
98 C1 **O Cádabo** Spain
145 D6 **Ocala** *Florida* U.S.A.
156 E3 **Ocampo** *Coahuila* Mexico
156 E3 **Ocampo** *Coahuila* Mexico
162 C2 **Ocaña** Colombia
99 G5 **Ocaña** Spain
98 B2 **O Castelo** Spain
107 F4 **Occhiobello** Italy
109 G3 **Occhito, Lago di l.** Italy
164 C3 **Occidental, Cord. mountain range** Chile
162 B3 **Occidental, Cordillera mountain range** Colombia
164 A2 **Occidental, Cordillera mountain range** Peru
83 D3 **Occimiano** Italy
136 B3 **Ocean Cape pt** *Alaska* U.S.A.
147 F5 **Ocean City** *Maryland* U.S.A.
147 F5 **Ocean City** *New Jersey* U.S.A.
136 D4 **Ocean Falls** *B.C.* Canada
174 G3 **Oceanographer Fracture sea feature** Atlantic Ocean
154 D5 **Oceanside** *California* U.S.A.
151 F6 **Ocean Springs** *Mississippi* U.S.A.
99 G3 **Ocejón mt.** Spain
93 A6 **Ochagavía** Spain
53 D3 **Ochakiv** Ukraine
51 G7 **Och'amch'ire** Georgia
115 F4 **Ochi mt.** Greece
28 D6 **Ōchi** Japan
28 K2 **Ochiishi-misaki pt** Japan
66 E4 **Ochil Hills h.** *Scotland* U.K.
64 D2 **Ochiltree** *Scotland* U.K.
52 A3 **Ochkyne** Ukraine
159 □1 **Ocho Rios** Jamaica
74 F3 **Ochsenfurt** Germany
74 E4 **Ochsenhausen** Germany
68 D3 **Ochten** Netherlands
114 F4 **Ochthonia** Greece
72 C3 **Ochtrup** Germany
59 G1 **Ockelbo** Sweden
58 D3 **Öckerö** Sweden
72 D1 **Ockholm** Germany
112 D2 **Ocna Sibiului** Romania
53 B2 **Ocniţa** Moldova
157 G5 **Ococingo** Mexico
148 C4 **Oconomowoc** *Wisconsin* U.S.A.
148 D3 **Oconto** *Wisconsin* U.S.A.
98 B2 **O Convento** Spain
98 C2 **O Corgo** Spain
156 J6 **Ocotal** Nicaragua
156 H6 **Ocotepeque** Honduras
154 D5 **Ocotillo Wells** *California* U.S.A.
156 E4 **Ocotlán** Mexico
98 C5 **Ocreza r.** Portugal
90 D2 **Octeville** France
89 F2 **Octeville-sur-Mer** France
October Revolution Island i. *see* **Oktyabr'skiy Revolyutsii, Ostrov**
122 D5 **Oda** Ghana
28 D6 **Ōda** Japan
56 M6 **Ódáðahraun lava** Iceland
119 G3 **Oda, Jebel mt.** Sudan
29 H3 **Ōdate** Japan
29 G6 **Odawara** Japan
58 B1 **Odda** Norway
55 C4 **Odder** Denmark
55 A3 **Oddesund chan.** Denmark
100 C2 **Odearce r.** Portugal
100 B3 **Odeceixe** Portugal
137 K3 **Odei r.** *Manitoba* Canada
100 C3 **Odeleite r.** Portugal
148 C5 **Odell** *Illinois* U.S.A.
80 C2 **Odelzhausen** Germany
100 B3 **Odemira** Portugal
42 A2 **Ödemiş** Turkey
131 F3 **Odendaalsrus** South Africa
59 F2 **Odensbacken** Sweden
55 C4 **Odense** Denmark
55 C4 **Odense Fjord b.** Denmark
74 D3 **Odenwald reg.** Germany
Oder r. *see* **Odra**
73 K3 **Oderberg** Germany
73 K3 **Oderbruch reg.** Germany
73 K1 **Oderbucht b.** Germany
73 K2 **Oderhaff b.** Germany
73 J3 **Oder-Havel-Kanal canal** Germany
107 G3 **Oderzo** Italy
53 C3 **Odesa div.** Ukraine
51 D6 **Odesa** Ukraine
59 F2 **Ödeshog** Sweden
151 C6 **Odessa** *Texas* U.S.A.
47 H2 **Odesskoye** Rus. Fed.
88 B3 **Odet r.** France
100 D3 **Odiel r.** Spain
122 C5 **Odienné** Côte d'Ivoire
52 C2 **Odintsovo** Rus. Fed.
100 B2 **Odivelas** *Beja* Portugal
100 A2 **Odivelas** *Lisboa* Portugal
100 B2 **Odivelas, Barragem de resr** Portugal
112 F2 **Odobeşti** Romania
76 F4 **Odolanów** Poland
89 E2 **Odon r.** France
25 D5 **Ŏdôngk** Cambodia
68 E2 **Odoorn** Netherlands
112 E1 **Odorheiu Secuiesc** Romania
52 C3 **Odoyev** Rus. Fed.
76 C2 **Odra r.** Germany/Poland
44 C4 **Odra r.** Poland
77 J4 **Odrzywół** Poland
55 B4 **Ødsted** Denmark
112 B2 **Odžaci** Yugoslavia
129 E2 **Odzi r.** Zimbabwe
73 F3 **Oebisfelde** Germany
100 C3 **Oeiras r.** Portugal
166 D2 **Oeiras** Brazil
100 A2 **Oeiras** Portugal
163 G3 **Oelemari r.** Surinam
150 C3 **Oelrichs** *S. Dakota* U.S.A.
75 H2 **Oelsnitz** *Sachsen* Germany
148 B4 **Oelwein** *Iowa* U.S.A.
5 P7 **Oeno atoll** *Pitcairn Islands* Pacific Ocean
14 C2 **Oenpelli** *Northern Terr.* Australia
82 C1 **Oensingen** Switzerland
69 D5 **Oesling h.** Luxembourg
74 C2 **Oestrich-Winkel** Germany
80 B2 **Oettingen in Bayern** Germany
80 B3 **Oetz** Austria
72 E1 **Oeversee** Germany
42 E1 **Of** Turkey
109 H3 **Ofanto r.** Italy
43 C4 **Ofaqim** Israel
131 H2 **Ofcolaco** South Africa
123 E5 **Offa** Nigeria
67 D3 **Offaly div.** Rep. of Ireland
83 E3 **Offanengo** Italy
82 B1 **Offemont** France
87 D2 **Offenbach am Main** Germany
75 H4 **Offenberg** Germany
74 C4 **Offenburg** Germany
80 B2 **Offingen** Germany
124 B4 **Offoué r.** Gabon
89 G2 **Offranville** France
113 F6 **Ofidoussa i.** Greece
123 E5 **Ofiki r.** Nigeria
6 □5 **Ofolanga i.** Tonga
7 □13 **Ofu i.** *American Samoa* Pacific Ocean
6 □3 **Ofu i.** Tonga
29 H4 **Ōfunato** Japan
28 H2 **Ofuyu-misaki pt** Japan
22 C1 **Oga r.** Indonesia
29 G4 **Oga** Japan
29 H4 **Ogachi** Japan
126 E3 **Ogadēn reg.** Ethiopia
29 G4 **Oga-hantō pen.** Japan
29 F6 **Ōgaki** Japan
150 C3 **Ogallala** *Nebraska* U.S.A.
22 A2 **Ogan r.** Indonesia
59 E1 **Ogan r.** Sweden
21 M1 **Ogasawara-shotō is** Japan
141 F3 **Ogascanane, Lac l.** *Québec* Canada
29 H5 **Ōgawa** Japan
28 H3 **Ogawara-ko l.** Japan
123 E5 **Ogbomoso** Nigeria
150 E3 **Ogden** *Iowa* U.S.A.
152 E3 **Ogden** *Utah* U.S.A.
136 C3 **Ogden, Mt mt.** *B.C.* Canada
147 F2 **Ogdensburg** *New York* U.S.A.
6 □7 **Ogea i.** Fiji
87 F4 **Ogéviller** France
58 C2 **Ogge l.** Norway
106 D3 **Oggiono** Italy
29 G5 **Ogi** Japan
52 H1 **Ogibnoye** Rus. Fed.
134 E3 **Ogilvie r.** *N.W.T.* Canada
29 □2 **Ogimi** Japan
120 D3 **Oglat Sbot well** Algeria
145 C5 **Oglethorpe, Mt mt.** *Georgia* U.S.A.
109 H4 **Ogliastro Cilento** Italy
109 D5 **Ogliastro, Lago di l.** *Sicilia* Italy
106 E3 **Oglio r.** Italy
15 G4 **Ogmore** *Queensland* Australia
90 D1 **Ognon r.** France
22 D1 **Ogoamas, G. mt.** Indonesia
123 F5 **Ogoja** Nigeria
138 C3 **Ogoki r.** *Ontario* Canada
138 C3 **Ogoki Res. resr** *Ontario* Canada
124 B4 **Ogooué r.** Gabon
124 B3 **Ogooué-Ivindo div.** Gabon
124 B4 **Ogooué-Lolo div.** Gabon
124 A4 **Ogooué-Maritime div.** Gabon
28 C7 **Ogōri** Japan
28 C6 **Ogōri** Japan
54 D3 **Ogre r.** Latvia
54 D3 **Ogre** Latvia
114 B2 **Ogren** Albania
76 G3 **Ogrodniki** Poland
98 B2 **O Grove** Spain
104 E3 **Ogulin** Croatia
123 E5 **Ogun div.** Nigeria
123 E5 **Ogun r.** Nigeria
46 D5 **Ogurchinskiy, O. i.** Turkmenistan
42 F1 **Oğuz** Azerbaijan
43 D1 **Oğuzeli** Turkey
123 F5 **Ohafia** Nigeria
9 A6 **Ohai** New Zealand
8 E3 **Ohakune** New Zealand
101 H3 **Ohanes** Spain
121 F3 **Ohanet** Algeria
128 B2 **Ohangwena div.** Namibia
28 H3 **Ōhata** Japan
8 E4 **Ohau** New Zealand
9 B6 **Ohau, L. l.** New Zealand
8 E2 **Ohaupo** New Zealand
80 E2 **Ohe r.** Germany
69 D4 **Ohey** Belgium
172 B3 **O'Higgins div.** Chile
164 B4 **O'Higgins** Chile
7 □16 **O'Higgins, C. c.** *Easter I.* Chile
171 B6 **O'Higgins, L. l.** Argentina
146 B4 **Ohio div.** U.S.A.
144 C4 **Ohio r.** *Indiana* U.S.A.
53 F2 **Ohiyivka** Ukraine
87 G4 **Ohlsbach** Germany
74 D2 **Ohm r.** Germany
83 D1 **Öhningen** Germany
6 □4 **Ohonua** Tonga
75 F2 **Ohrdruf** Germany
78 C1 **Ohře r.** Czech Rep.
70 E2 **Ohre r.** Germany
114 B1 **Ohrid** Macedonia
114 B1 **Ohrid, Lake l.** Albania/Macedonia
Ohridsko Ezero l. *see* **Ohrid, Lake**
131 H2 **Ohrigstad** South Africa
74 E3 **Öhringen** Germany
8 E3 **Ohura** New Zealand
115 G6 **Oia** Greece
98 B4 **Oiã** Portugal
163 G3 **Oiapoque r.** Brazil
163 G3 **Oiapoque** Brazil
66 D3 **Oich, Loch l.** *Scotland* U.K.
37 H3 **Oiga** China
86 B2 **Oignies** France
90 D2 **Oignin r.** France
146 D4 **Oil City** *Pennsylvania* U.S.A.
154 C4 **Oildale** *California* U.S.A.
32 B2 **Oi Qu r.** China
28 H3 **Oirase-gawa r.** Japan
92 B2 **Oiron** France
69 D3 **Oirschot** Netherlands
91 E3 **Oisans reg.** France
86 B3 **Oise div.** *Picardie* France
86 B3 **Oise r.** France
93 A4 **Oiseaux, Île aux i.** France
90 D1 **Oiselay-et-Grachaux** France
89 G2 **Oisemont** France
89 E3 **Oisseau** France
89 G2 **Oissel** France
68 D3 **Oisterwijk** Netherlands
159 □9 **Oistins** *Barbados* Caribbean
28 C7 **Ōita div.** Japan
28 C7 **Ōita** Japan
98 B2 **Oitavén r.** Spain
114 D4 **Oiti mt.** Greece
114 D4 **Oiti nat. park** Greece
54 D1 **Oitti** Finland
115 D6 **Oitylo** Greece
118 C3 **Oiuru well** Libya
28 H2 **Oiwake** Japan
154 C4 **Ojai** *California* U.S.A.
101 G2 **Ojailén r.** Spain
77 H5 **Ojcowski Park Narodowy nat. park** Poland
59 E1 **Öje** Sweden
172 E3 **Ojeda** Argentina
59 E1 **Öjen l.** Sweden
148 B3 **Ojibwa** *Wisconsin* U.S.A.
28 B7 **Ojika-jima i.** Japan
156 D2 **Ojinaga** Mexico
157 F5 **Ojitlán** Mexico
29 G5 **Ojiya** Japan
172 E1 **Ojo de Agua** Argentina
170 D2 **Ojo de Agua, Va** Argentina
156 D2 **Ojo de Laguna** Mexico
156 B3 **Ojo de Liebre, L. b.** Mexico
170 C2 **Ojos del Salado mt.** Argentina
77 J3 **Ojrzeń** Poland
123 F5 **Oju** Nigeria
52 F1 **Oka r.** Rus. Fed.
123 F5 **Oka** Nigeria
128 B3 **Okahandja** Namibia
8 E3 **Okahukura** New Zealand
8 D1 **Okaihau** New Zealand
123 E5 **Okaka** Nigeria
128 B3 **Okakarara** Namibia
139 H2 **Okak Islands is** *Newfoundland* Canada
77 H2 **Okalewo** Poland
136 F5 **Okanagan Falls** *B.C.* Canada
136 F4 **Okanagan Lake l.** *B.C.* Canada
124 B3 **Okano r.** Gabon
152 C1 **Okanogan r.** Canada/U.S.A.
136 F5 **Okanogan** *Washington* U.S.A.
152 B1 **Okanogan Range mountain range** *Washington* U.S.A.
124 E3 **Okapi, Parc National de la nat. park** Congo(Zaire)
128 B3 **Okaputa** Namibia
36 C3 **Okara** Pakistan
46 D5 **Okarem** Turkmenistan
9 C5 **Okarito Lagoon lag.** New Zealand
128 B3 **Okasise** Namibia
128 B2 **Okaukuejo** Namibia
128 B2 **Okavango div.** Namibia
128 C2 **Okavango r.** Botswana/Namibia
128 C2 **Okavango Delta swamp** Botswana
28 C7 **Ōkawa** Japan
29 G5 **Ō-kawa-gawa r.** Japan
9 □1 **Okawa Pt pt** *Chatham Is* New Zealand
29 G5 **Okaya** Japan
28 D6 **Okayama div.** Japan
28 D6 **Okayama** Japan
29 F6 **Okazaki** Japan
77 J3 **Okęcie airport** Poland
145 D7 **Okeechobee** *Florida* U.S.A.
145 D7 **Okeechobee, L. l.** *Florida* U.S.A.
145 D6 **Okefenokee Swamp swamp** *Georgia* U.S.A.
62 B4 **Okehampton** *England* U.K.
123 E5 **Oke-Iho** Nigeria
62 B4 **Okement r.** *England* U.K.
123 F5 **Okene** Nigeria
72 F3 **Oker r.** Germany
36 B5 **Okha** India
45 Q4 **Okha** Rus. Fed.
37 F4 **Okhaldhunga** Nepal
36 B5 **Okha Rann** India
52 C4 **Okhochevka** Rus. Fed.
52 D1 **Okhotino** Rus. Fed.
45 Q3 **Okhotka r.** Rus. Fed.
45 Q4 **Okhotsk** Rus. Fed.
45 Q4 **Okhotskoye More sea** Rus. Fed.
Okhotsk, Sea of sea *see* **Okhotskoye More**
53 F1 **Okhtyrka** Ukraine
130 A4 **Okiep** South Africa
27 N6 **Okinawa i.** Japan
29 □2 **Okinawa** Japan
27 N6 **Okinawa-guntō is** Japan
28 D7 **Okino-shima i.** Japan
28 C6 **Okino-shima i.** Japan
28 D5 **Oki-shotō i.** Japan
123 E5 **Okitipupa** Nigeria
24 A3 **Okkan** Myanmar
151 D5 **Oklahoma div.** U.S.A.
151 D5 **Oklahoma City** *Oklahoma* U.S.A.
151 D5 **Okmulgee** *Oklahoma* U.S.A.
124 B3 **Okola** Cameroon
124 B4 **Okondja** Gabon
76 E2 **Okonek** Poland
136 G4 **Okotoks** *Alberta* Canada
128 A2 **Okotusu well** Namibia
52 A2 **Okovskiy Les forest** Rus. Fed.
124 C4 **Okoyo** Congo
55 A4 **Oksbøl** Denmark
56 F1 **Øksfjord** Norway
52 E3 **Oksko- Donskaya Ravnina plain** Rus. Fed.
50 F2 **Oksovskiy** Rus. Fed.
56 D2 **Oksskolten inlet** Greenland
47 H5 **Oksu r.** Tajikistan
Oktemberyan *see* **Hoktemberyan**
24 B3 **Oktwin** Myanmar
52 C1 **Oktyabr'** Rus. Fed.
46 E3 **Oktyabr'sk** Kazakhstan
52 F1 **Oktyabr'skaya** Rus. Fed.
46 D2 **Oktyabr'skiy** Rus. Fed.
52 D2 **Oktyabr'skiy** Rus. Fed.
52 G1 **Oktyabr'skiy** Rus. Fed.
45 R4 **Oktyabr'skiy** Rus. Fed.
52 E1 **Oktyabr'skiy** Rus. Fed.
50 H3 **Oktyabr'skiy** Rus. Fed.
51 G6 **Oktyabr'skiy** Rus. Fed.
50 G2 **Oktyabr'skiy** Rus. Fed.
53 G1 **Oktyabr'skiy** Rus. Fed.
47 G2 **Oktyabr'skoye** Kazakhstan
44 H3 **Oktyabr'skoye** Rus. Fed.
45 L2 **Oktyabr'skoy Revolyutsii, O. i.** Rus. Fed.
29 □2 **Oku** Japan
104 F3 **Okučani** Croatia
28 C7 **Ōkuchi** Japan
50 E3 **Okulovka** Rus. Fed.
28 G2 **Okushiri-kaikyō chan.** Japan
28 G2 **Okushiri-tō i.** Japan
123 E5 **Okuta** Nigeria
29 E6 **Okutango-hantō pen.** Japan
128 C3 **Okwa watercourse** Botswana/Namibia
56 L6 **Ólafsvík** Iceland
54 C3 **Olaine** Latvia
154 C3 **Olancha** *California* U.S.A.
154 C3 **Olancha Peak summit** *California* U.S.A.
156 J6 **Olanchito** Honduras
59 G3 **Öland i.** Sweden
56 H3 **Olanga** Rus. Fed.
91 E4 **Olan, Pic d' mt.** France
155 H2 **Olathe** *Colorado* U.S.A.
150 E4 **Olathe** *Kansas* U.S.A.
173 G4 **Olavarría** Argentina
76 F5 **Oława** Poland
81 H3 **Olbendorf** Austria
155 G5 **Olberg** *Arizona* U.S.A.
75 J2 **Olbernhau** Germany
75 K2 **Olbersdorf** Germany
108 B4 **Olbia** *Sardegna* Italy
75 K3 **Olbramovice** Czech Rep.
75 G3 **Olching** Germany
146 D3 **Olcott** *New York* U.S.A.
158 C2 **Old Bahama Channel chan.** The Bahamas/Cuba
38 C2 **Old Bastar** India
67 D3 **Oldcastle** Rep. of Ireland
15 G4 **Old Cork** *Queensland* Australia
134 E3 **Old Crow** *Yukon Terr.* Canada
68 E2 **Oldeberkoop** Netherlands
68 D1 **Oldeboorn** Netherlands
68 D2 **Oldebroek** Netherlands
68 E1 **Oldehove** Netherlands
68 D2 **Oldemarkt** Netherlands
72 D2 **Oldenburg** *Niedersachsen* Germany
73 F1 **Oldenburg in Holstein** Germany
68 E2 **Oldenzaal** Netherlands
56 F1 **Olderdalen** Norway
147 F3 **Old Forge** *New York* U.S.A.
147 F4 **Old Forge** *Pennsylvania* U.S.A.
145 □2 **Old Fort** The Bahamas
145 □2 **Old Fort Pt pt** The Bahamas
65 F4 **Oldham** *England* U.K.
159 □1 **Old Harbour** Jamaica
67 C5 **Old Head of Kinsale headland** Rep. of Ireland
63 G1 **Old Leake** *England* U.K.
136 G4 **Oldman r.** *Alberta* Canada
65 E3 **Old Man of Coniston, The h.** *England* U.K.
66 F3 **Oldmeldrum** *Scotland* U.K.
147 H3 **Old Orchard Beach** *Maine* U.S.A.
139 K4 **Old Perlican** *Newfoundland* Canada
159 □7 **Old Road** *Antigua and Barbuda* Caribbean
159 □6 **Old Road Town** *St Kitts-Nevis* Caribbean
136 G4 **Olds** *Alberta* Canada
147 J2 **Old Town** *Maine* U.S.A.
137 H4 **Old Wives L. l.** *Saskatchewan* Canada
155 E4 **Old Woman Mts mts** *California* U.S.A.
30 B2 **Öldziyt** Mongolia
30 D3 **Öldziyt** Mongolia
146 D3 **Olean** *New York* U.S.A.
77 L1 **Olecko** Poland
106 C3 **Oleggio** Italy
98 C5 **Oleiros** Portugal
45 O3 **Olekminsk** Rus. Fed.
53 E1 **Oleksandrivka** *Chernihiv* Ukraine
53 G2 **Oleksandrivka** *Donets'k* Ukraine

53 E2 Oleksandrivka Kirovohrad Ukraine
53 D2 Oleksandrivka Kirovohrad Ukraine
53 D3 Oleksandrivka Mykolayiv Ukraine
53 E2 Oleksandriya Kirovohrad Ukraine
53 B1 Oleksandriya Rivne Ukraine
53 E3 Oleksiyivka Ukraine
50 H1 Olema Rus. Fed.
93 E4 Olemps France
69 C3 Olen Belgium
58 A2 Ølen Norway
56 J1 Olenegorsk Rus. Fed.
45 M3 Olenek r. Rus. Fed.
45 N3 Olenek Rus. Fed.
52 A1 Olenino Rus. Fed.
50 E1 Olenitsa Rus. Fed.
53 G3 Olenivka Ukraine
30 E2 Olentuy Rus. Fed.
47 H2 Olenty r. Kazakhstan
92 A3 Oléron, Île d' i. France
102 E3 Olesa de Montserrat Spain
53 F1 Oleshnya Ukraine
53 A2 Oles'ko Ukraine
76 F4 Oleśnica Poland
76 G5 Olesno Poland
108 B2 Oletta Corse France
93 E6 Olette France
53 B1 Olevs'k Ukraine
141 G2 Olga, Lac l. Québec Canada
14 B5 Olga, Mt mt. Northern Terr. Australia
178 □3 Olgastretet str. Svalbard Arctic Ocean
83 E3 Olginate Italy
55 A4 Ølgod Denmark
100 C3 Olhão Portugal
102 E2 Oliana Spain
107 J4 Olib i. Croatia
108 B4 Oliena r. Sardegna Italy
108 B4 Oliena Sardegna Italy
102 C3 Oliete Spain
130 B5 Olifants r. South Africa
130 D3 Olifantshoek South Africa
130 B6 Olifantsrivierberg mts South Africa
173 K2 Olimar Chico r. Uruguay
173 K2 Olimar Grande r. Uruguay
168 D4 Olímpia Brazil
157 F5 Olinalá Mexico
166 F2 Olinda Brazil
129 F2 Olinda, Pta pt Mozambique
129 F2 Olinga Mozambique
15 E4 Olio Queensland Australia
103 B6 Oliva mt. Spain
172 F2 Oliva Argentina
103 C6 Oliva Spain
170 C2 Oliva, Cord. de mountain range Chile
100 D2 Oliva de la Frontera Spain
100 D2 Oliva de Mérida Spain
172 C1 Olivares, Co del mt. Chile
99 H5 Olivares de Júcar Spain
146 B5 Olive Hill Kentucky U.S.A.
169 F4 Oliveira Brazil
98 B4 Oliveira de Azeméis Portugal
98 B4 Oliveira de Frades Portugal
98 B4 Oliveira do Bairro Portugal
98 B3 Oliveira do Douro Portugal
98 C4 Oliveira do Hospital Portugal
166 D3 Oliveira dos Brejinhos Brazil
100 C2 Olivenza r. Portugal/Spain
100 C2 Olivenza Spain
173 G2 Oliveros Argentina
89 G4 Olivet France
150 E2 Olivia Minnesota U.S.A.
9 B6 Olivine Range mountain range New Zealand
83 D2 Olivone Switzerland
127 C5 Oljoro Wells well Tanzania
58 B1 Øljuvatnet l. Norway
52 E3 Ol'khi Rus. Fed.
51 F5 Ol'khovatka Rus. Fed.
52 D3 Ol'khovets Rus. Fed.
51 H5 Ol'khovka Rus. Fed.
77 H5 Olkusz Poland
164 C4 Ollagüe Chile
164 C4 Ollagüe, Vol. volcano Bolivia
90 B3 Olliergues France
91 D5 Ollioules France
172 B1 Ollita, Cord. de mountain range Argentina
172 B1 Ollitas mt. Argentina
124 C4 Ollombo Congo
82 C2 Ollon Switzerland
108 A4 Olmedo Sardegna Italy
99 F3 Olmedo Spain
108 A3 Olmeto Corse France
173 F2 Olmos Argentina
162 B5 Olmos Peru
147 G3 Olmstedville New York U.S.A.
63 F2 Olney England U.K.
144 C4 Olney Illinois U.S.A.
59 F3 Olofström Sweden
78 G2 Olomouc Czech Rep.
50 E2 Olonets Rus. Fed.
23 B3 Olongapo Philippines
22 C2 Olongliko Indonesia
92 A2 Olonne-sur-Mer France
93 E5 Olonzac France
93 B5 Oloron-Ste-Marie France
7 □13 Olosega i. American Samoa Pacific Ocean
102 F2 Olot Spain
31 E2 Olovyannaya Rus. Fed.
36 C5 Olpad India
172 D1 Olpas Argentina
72 C4 Olpe Germany
80 C3 Olperer mt. Austria
59 E2 Olsätter Sweden
72 D4 Olsberg Germany
79 H2 Olše r. Czech Rep.
53 G1 Ol'shanka Rus. Fed.
53 D3 Ol'shans'ke Ukraine
68 E2 Olst Netherlands
55 E4 Ølstykke Denmark
77 K2 Olszewo-Borki Poland
77 J2 Olsztyn div. Poland
77 J2 Olsztyn Olsztyn Poland
77 J2 Olsztynek Poland
76 D4 Olszyna Poland
112 E2 Olt r. Romania
172 D1 Olta Argentina
58 B2 Oltedal Norway
82 C1 Olten Switzerland
112 F2 Oltenița Romania
112 F2 Oltina Romania
42 E1 Oltu Turkey
101 H3 Olula del Río Spain
23 B5 Olutanga i. Philippines
102 B3 Ólvega Spain
101 E4 Olvera Spain
53 A1 Olyka Ukraine
52 C3 Olym r. Rus. Fed.
152 B2 Olympia Washington U.S.A.
115 C5 Olympia Greece
114 E2 Olympias Greece
152 A2 Olympic Nat. Park Washington U.S.A.
152 B2 Olympic Nat. Park nat. park Washington U.S.A.
114 D2 Olympos mt. Greece
114 E4 Olympos mts Greece
114 D2 Olympos nat. park Greece
43 B2 Olympus mt. Cyprus
152 B2 Olympus, Mt mt. Washington U.S.A.
114 E2 Olynthos Greece
53 D1 Olyshivka Ukraine
45 S3 Olyutorskiy Rus. Fed.
45 T4 Olyutorskiy, M. c. Rus. Fed.
45 S3 Olyutorskiy Zaliv b. Rus. Fed.
47 J1 Om' r. Rus. Fed.
50 H1 Oma r. Rus. Fed.
37 E2 Oma China
28 H3 Ōma Japan
50 H1 Oma Rus. Fed.
29 F5 Ōmachi Japan
29 G6 Omae-zaki pt Japan
29 H4 Ōmagari Japan
67 D2 Omagh Northern Ireland U.K.
162 C4 Omaguas Peru
150 E3 Omaha Nebraska U.S.A.
128 B3 Omaheke div. Namibia
152 C1 Omak Washington U.S.A.
51 H7 Omalo Georgia
18 G8 Oman country Asia
41 J4 Oman, Gulf of g. Asia
23 □1 Omaok Palau
9 B6 Omarama New Zealand
128 B3 Omaruru Namibia
128 B3 Omatako watercourse Namibia
164 B3 Omate Peru
130 D2 Omaweneno Botswana
28 H3 Ōma-zaki c. Japan
Omba i. see Aoba
124 C2 Ombella-Mpoko div. Central African Rep.
62 D2 Ombersley England U.K.
58 A2 Ombo i. Norway
124 A4 Omboué Gabon
108 D2 Ombrone r. Italy
37 F3 Ombu China
173 J2 Ombúes de Lavalle Uruguay
130 D5 Omdraaisvlei South Africa
119 F4 Omdurman Sudan
29 G6 Ōme Japan
106 C3 Omegna Italy
53 E2 Omel'nyk Ukraine
118 D4 Omena well Chad
13 F4 Omeo Victoria Australia
108 B2 Omessa Corse France
156 J7 Ometepe, I. de i. Nicaragua
67 A3 Omey Island i. Rep. of Ireland
126 C2 Om Hajer Eritrea
39 B3 Omīdīyeh Iran
29 F6 Ōmihachiman Japan
Omilo see Omalo
136 D3 Omineca Mountains mountain range B.C. Canada
104 F4 Omiš Croatia
107 J3 Omišalj Croatia
29 G6 Ōmiya Japan
136 C3 Ommaney, Cape headland Alaska U.S.A.
55 A4 Omme r. Denmark
68 E2 Ommen Netherlands
30 B4 Ömnögovĭ div. Mongolia
55 D4 Omø i. Denmark
108 B4 Omodeo, Lago l. Sardegna Italy
123 F5 Omoku Nigeria
45 S2 Omolon r. Rus. Fed.
126 C3 Omo National Park nat. park Ethiopia
29 H4 Omono-gawa r. Japan
69 C5 Omont France
126 C3 Omo Wenz r. Ethiopia
47 H2 Omsk div. Rus. Fed.
47 H2 Omsk Rus. Fed.
45 R3 Omsukchan Rus. Fed.
28 J1 Ōmū Japan
77 K2 Omulew r. Poland
28 B7 Ōmura Japan
28 B7 Ōmura-wan b. Japan
112 F3 Omurtag Bulgaria
128 A2 Omusati div. Namibia
47 G1 Omutinskiy Rus. Fed.
50 K3 Omutninsk Rus. Fed.
140 E1 Onakawana Ontario Canada
148 B4 Onalaska Wisconsin U.S.A.
140 B1 Onaman lake l. Ontario Canada
147 F6 Onancock Virginia U.S.A.
22 D2 Onang Philippines
124 B4 Onangué, Lac l. Gabon
140 E3 Onaping Lake l. Ontario Canada
156 D2 Oñate Mexico
156 C2 Onavas Mexico
149 E3 Onaway Michigan U.S.A.
28 J2 Onbetsu Japan
25 B4 Onbingwin Myanmar
172 F1 Oncativo Argentina
64 D3 Onchan Isle of Man
125 B7 Oncócua Angola
103 C5 Onda Spain
103 D6 Ondara Spain
99 H1 Ondarroa Spain
166 C3 Ondas r. Brazil
79 L3 Ondava r. Slovakia
130 C5 Onderstedorings South Africa
125 C7 Ondjiva Angola
123 F5 Ondo div. Nigeria
123 E5 Ondo Nigeria
30 D3 Öndörhaan Mongolia
31 G3 Ondor Had China
30 E2 Öndörhushuu Mongolia
30 C4 Ondor Mod China
30 E4 Ondor Sum China
75 K3 Ondřejov Czech Rep.
15 F2 One & a Half Mile Opening chan. Queensland Australia
35 D10 One and Half Degree Channel chan. Maldives
6 □7 Oneata i. Fiji
50 F2 Onega r. Rus. Fed.
50 F2 Onega Rus. Fed.
Onega, Lake l. see Onezhskoye Ozero
147 F3 Oneida New York U.S.A.
147 F3 Oneida L. l. New York U.S.A.
150 D3 O'Neill Nebraska U.S.A.
45 R5 Onekotan, O. i. Rus. Fed.
147 F3 Oneonta New York U.S.A.
8 E2 Oneroa New Zealand
93 A4 Onesse-et-Laharie France
112 F1 Onești Romania
93 E4 Onet-le-Château France
6 □4 Onevai i. Tonga
50 E1 Onezhskaya Guba g. Rus. Fed.
50 E2 Onezhskoye Ozero l. Rus. Fed.
37 E5 Ong r. India
124 B4 Onga Gabon
8 F3 Ongaonga New Zealand
130 D5 Ongers watercourse South Africa
17 B7 Ongerup Western Australia Australia
30 B3 Ongi Mongolia
30 B3 Ongiyn Gol watercourse Mongolia
31 H5 Ongjin North Korea
31 F4 Ongniud Qi China
38 C3 Ongole India
30 B3 Ongon Mongolia
47 L2 Onguday Rus. Fed.
51 G7 Oni Georgia
129 G3 Onilahy r. Madagascar
123 F5 Onitsha Nigeria
128 B3 Onjati Mountain mt. Namibia
29 □2 Onna Japan
29 □2 Onna-dake h. Japan
69 B4 Onnaing France
6 □7 Ono i. Fiji
29 H5 Ono Japan
29 F6 Ōno Japan
28 H3 Ōno Japan
28 C7 Onoda Japan
176 H7 Ono-i-Lau i. Fiji
28 D6 Onomichi Japan
31 E2 Onon r. Mongolia/Rus. Fed.
30 D2 Onon Mongolia
176 G6 Onotoa i. Kiribati
136 G4 Onoway Alberta Canada
130 B4 Onseepkans South Africa
131 F1 Ons Hoop South Africa
98 B2 Ons, Illa de i. Spain
55 D5 Ønslev Denmark
16 A4 Onslow Western Australia Australia
145 E5 Onslow Bay b. N. Carolina U.S.A.
31 J4 Onsong North Korea
68 F1 Onstwedde Netherlands
29 F6 Ontake-san volcano Japan
138 B3 Ontario div. Canada
152 C2 Ontario Oregon U.S.A.
149 H4 Ontario, Lake l. Canada/U.S.A.
102 D3 Ontiñena Spain
103 C6 Ontinyent Spain
148 C2 Ontonagon Michigan U.S.A.
6 □1 Ontong Java Atoll atoll Solomon Is.
103 B6 Ontur Spain
53 E2 Onufriyivka Ukraine
163 F2 Onverwacht Surinam
89 G4 Onzain France
98 E2 Onzonilla Spain
12 C1 Oodnadatta S. Australia Australia
126 E3 Oodweyne Somalia
12 B2 Ooldea S. Australia Australia
151 E4 Oologah L. resr Oklahoma U.S.A.
68 C3 Ooltgensplaat Netherlands
14 C4 Ooratippra r. Northern Terr. Australia
15 E4 Oorindi Queensland Australia
131 G1 Oorwinning South Africa
69 B3 Oostburg Netherlands
69 A3 Oostende div. West-Vlaanderen Belgium
69 A3 Oostende Oostende Belgium
68 C1 Oosterend Netherlands
68 E2 Oosterhesseln Netherlands
68 C3 Oosterhout Netherlands
131 F2 Oostermoed South Africa
69 C3 Oosterschelde est. Netherlands
68 E2 Oosterwolde Netherlands
69 B4 Oosterzele Belgium
69 C2 Oosthuizen Netherlands
69 B3 Oostkamp Belgium
69 B3 Oost-Souburg Netherlands
69 B4 Oost-Vlaanderen div. Belgium
69 A4 Oostvleteren Belgium
68 D1 Oost-Vlieland Netherlands
68 C3 Oostvoorne Netherlands
68 E2 Ootmarsum Netherlands
136 D4 Ootsa Lake l. B.C. Canada
136 D4 Ootsa Lake B.C. Canada
146 E5 Opal Virginia U.S.A.
124 D4 Opala Congo(Zaire)
76 E3 Opalenica Poland
126 B4 Opari Sudan
50 J3 Oparino Rus. Fed.
140 D2 Opasatika r. Ontario Canada
140 D2 Opasatika Ontario Canada
140 D2 Opasatika Lake l. Ontario Canada
138 B3 Opasquia Ontario Canada
138 B3 Opasquia Provincial Park Ontario Canada
141 H1 Opataca L. l. Québec Canada
107 J3 Opatija Croatia
78 E1 Opatovice nad Labem Czech Rep.
76 G4 Opatów Kalisz Poland
77 K5 Opatów Tarnobrzeg Poland
76 G4 Opatówek Poland
77 J5 Opatowiec Poland
79 G2 Opava Czech Rep.
145 C5 Opelika Alabama U.S.A.
151 E6 Opelousas Louisiana U.S.A.
83 E1 Opfenbach Germany
69 D3 Opglabbeek Belgium
152 F1 Opheim Montana U.S.A.
68 D3 Opheusden Netherlands
140 D3 Ophir Ontario Canada
124 E3 Opienge Congo(Zaire)
9 C6 Opihi r. New Zealand
138 E3 Opinaca r. Québec Canada
138 E3 Opinaca, Réservoir resr Québec Canada
138 D3 Opinnagau r. Ontario Canada
139 G3 Opiscotéo L. l. Québec Canada
53 F2 Opishnya Ukraine
81 G4 Oplotnica r. Slovenia
123 F6 Opobo Nigeria
54 F3 Opochka Rus. Fed.
77 J4 Opoczno Poland
76 F5 Opole div. Poland
76 F5 Opole Poland
77 K4 Opole Lubelskie Poland
46 D3 Opornyy Kazakhstan
Oporto see Porto
8 F3 Opotiki New Zealand
93 E6 Opoul-Périllos France
145 C6 Opp Alabama U.S.A.
73 K4 Oppach Germany
57 C3 Oppdal Norway
83 G3 Oppeano Italy
59 F2 Oppeby Sweden
58 A1 Oppedal Norway
74 D4 Oppenau Germany
74 D3 Oppenheim Germany
109 H4 Oppido Lucano Italy
111 E4 Oppido Mamertina Italy
58 D1 Oppkuven h. Norway
58 C1 Oppland div. Norway
81 F3 Opponitz Austria
107 H3 Oprtalj Croatia
8 D3 Opunake New Zealand
128 A2 Opuwo Namibia
46 D3 Opytnoye Kazakhstan
148 B5 Oquawka Illinois U.S.A.
147 H2 Oquossoc Maine U.S.A.
107 F2 Ora Italy
159 □1 Oracabessa Jamaica
155 G5 Oracle Arizona U.S.A.
155 G5 Oracle Junction Arizona U.S.A.
100 C2 Orada Portugal
79 L4 Oradea Romania
92 C3 Oradour-sur-Vayres France
56 M6 Öræfajökull ice cap Iceland
112 C3 Orahovac Yugoslavia
36 D4 Orai India
90 D2 Orain r. France
121 D1 Oran Algeria
170 D1 Orán Argentina
53 D1 Orane Ukraine
25 D4 O Rang Cambodia
37 H3 Orang China
130 B4 Orange r. Namibia/South Africa
147 G3 Orange Massachusetts U.S.A.
13 G3 Orange New South Wales Australia
151 E6 Orange Texas U.S.A.
146 D5 Orange Virginia U.S.A.
91 C4 Orange France
145 D5 Orangeburg S. Carolina U.S.A.
163 G3 Orange, Cabo pt Brazil
Orange Free State see Free State
140 E5 Orangeville Ontario Canada
155 G2 Orangeville Utah U.S.A.
157 H5 Orange Walk Belize
122 A4 Orango, Ilha de i. Guinea-Bissau
108 B4 Orani Sardegna Italy
23 B3 Orani Philippines
73 J3 Oranienburg Germany
Oranje r. see Orange
131 F1 Oranjefontein South Africa
163 F3 Oranje Gebergte h. Surinam
68 E2 Oranjekanaal canal Netherlands
128 B4 Oranjemund Namibia
130 E4 Oranjerivier South Africa
158 □1 Oranjestad Aruba Caribbean
131 G3 Oranjeville South Africa
67 C3 Oranmore Rep. of Ireland
128 D3 Orapa Botswana
100 D3 Oraque r. Spain
23 C3 Oras Philippines
112 D2 Orăștie Romania
53 C2 Orativ Ukraine
79 J2 Orava r. Slovakia
56 F3 Oravais Finland
112 C2 Oravița Romania
79 J2 Oravská Magura mts Slovakia
9 A7 Orawia New Zealand
91 B5 Orb r. France
106 C4 Orba r. Italy
98 B3 Orbacém Portugal
36 E2 Orba Co l. China
55 C4 Ørbæk Denmark
86 C4 Orbais-l'Abbaye France
106 B3 Orbassano Italy
82 B2 Orbe r. Switzerland
82 B2 Orbe Switzerland
89 F2 Orbec France
108 D2 Orbetello Italy
108 D2 Orbetello, Laguna di lag. Italy
93 E5 Orbieu r. France
98 E2 Orbigo r. Spain
13 G4 Orbost Victoria Australia
59 G1 Örbyhus Sweden
179 B1 Orcadas Argentina Base South Orkney Islands Atlantic Ocean
101 H2 Orcera Spain
101 H3 Orce, Sierra de mountain range Spain
82 B1 Orchamps-Vennes France
155 H2 Orchard Mesa Colorado U.S.A.
86 C2 Orchies France
163 D1 Orchila, Isla i. Venezuela
76 G3 Orchowo Poland
108 D1 Orcia r. Italy
91 E4 Orcières France
106 B3 Orco r. Italy
164 A2 Orcotuna Peru
154 B4 Orcutt California U.S.A.
16 E3 Ord r. Western Australia Australia
153 D4 Orderville Utah U.S.A.
98 B1 Ordes Spain
102 D2 Ordesa-Monte-Perdido, Parque Nacional de nat. park Spain
99 H1 Ordizia Spain
16 D3 Ord, Mt h. Western Australia Australia
154 D4 Ord Mt mt. California U.S.A.
173 F2 Ordoñez Argentina
55 D4 Ordrup Næs pt Denmark
42 D1 Ordu Turkey
Ordu see Yayladaği
42 F2 Ordubad Azerbaijan
99 H2 Orduña Spain
153 G4 Ordway Colorado U.S.A.
47 K2 Ordynskoye Rus. Fed.
46 F2 Ordzhonikidze Kazakhstan
Ordzhonikidze see Vladikavkaz
53 F3 Ordzhonikidze Ukraine
123 E5 Ore Nigeria
163 F2 Orealla Guyana
154 C1 Oreana Nevada U.S.A.
59 F2 Örebro div. Sweden
59 F2 Örebro Sweden
81 H1 Ořechov Czech Rep.
54 G2 Oredezh r. Rus. Fed.
152 B3 Oregon div. U.S.A.
148 C4 Oregon Illinois U.S.A.
146 B4 Oregon Ohio U.S.A.
148 C4 Oregon Wisconsin U.S.A.
152 B2 Oregon City Oregon U.S.A.
59 H1 Öregrund Sweden
59 H1 Öregrundsgrepen b. Sweden
55 D5 Orehoved Denmark
52 F2 Orekhovets Rus. Fed.
54 F2 Orekhovno Rus. Fed.
52 D2 Orekhovo-Zuyevo Rus. Fed.
52 C3 Orel div. Rus. Fed.
53 F2 Orel' r. Ukraine
52 C3 Orel Rus. Fed.
114 E1 Orelek mt. Bulgaria
162 B4 Orellana Peru
162 B5 Orellana Peru
100 E1 Orellana la Vieja Spain
155 G1 Orem Utah U.S.A.
42 B2 Ören Turkey
46 E2 Orenburg div. Rus. Fed.
46 E2 Orenburg Rus. Fed.
69 E5 Orenhofen Germany
98 C2 Orense div. Spain
173 H5 Orense Argentina
Orense Spain see Ourense
114 E4 Oreoi Greece
9 A7 Orepuki New Zealand
53 B1 Orepy Ukraine
59 E3 Öresjön l. Sweden
58 D2 Öreskilsälven r. Sweden
113 F4 Orestiada Greece
55 E4 Øresund str. Denmark
9 B7 Oreti r. New Zealand
8 E2 Orewa New Zealand
69 D4 Oreye Belgium
63 H2 Orford England U.K.
13 F5 Orford Tasmania Australia
63 H2 Orford Ness spit England U.K.
163 G2 Organabo French Guiana
158 B2 Organos, Sierra de los h. Cuba
155 F5 Organ Pipe Cactus National Monument nat. park Arizona U.S.A.
102 E2 Organyà Spain
101 G1 Orgaz Spain
86 B4 Orge r. France
90 D2 Orgelet France
89 G3 Orgères-en-Beauce France
107 F3 Orgiano Italy
30 A2 Orgil Mongolia
101 G4 Orgiva Spain
91 D5 Orgon France
108 B4 Orgosolo Sardegna Italy
52 E1 Orgtrud Rus. Fed.
113 G5 Orhaneli Turkey
51 D7 Orhangazi Turkey
53 C3 Orhei Moldova
30 B2 Orhon Gol r. Mongolia
30 C2 Orhontuul Mongolia
102 B2 Orhy, Pic d' mt. France/Spain
111 G2 Oria Italy
101 H3 Oria Spain
50 J3 Orichi Rus. Fed.
147 K2 Orient Maine U.S.A.
164 C3 Oriental, Cordillera mountain range Bolivia
162 B3 Oriental, Cordillera mountain range Colombia
162 B4 Oriental, Cordillera mountain range Ecuador/Peru
164 B2 Oriental, Cordillera mountain range Peru
140 A2 Orient Bay Ontario Canada
173 G5 Oriente Argentina
69 C5 Origny-en-Thiérache France
86 C3 Origny-Ste-Benoite France
103 C6 Orihuela Spain
102 B4 Orihuela del Tremedal Spain
53 F3 Orikhiv Ukraine
53 G2 Oril'ka r. Ukraine
53 G2 Oril'ka Ukraine
141 F4 Orillia Ontario Canada
57 G3 Orimattila Finland
163 E3 Orinduik Guyana
163 D2 Orinoco r. Colombia/Venezuela
109 J4 Oriolo Italy
54 C1 Oripää Finland
37 F5 Orissa India
54 C2 Orissaare Estonia
108 A5 Oristano div. Sardegna Italy
108 A5 Oristano Sardegna Italy
108 A5 Oristano, Golfo di b. Sardegna Italy
78 F5 Őriszentpéter Hungary
57 G3 Orivesi Finland
50 D2 Orivesi l. Finland
166 A1 Oriximiná Brazil
157 F5 Orizaba Mexico
168 D2 Orizona Brazil
56 C3 Orkanger Norway
59 E3 Örkelljunga Sweden
79 J4 Örkény Hungary
56 C3 Orkla r. Norway
66 E1 Orkney div. Scotland U.K.
131 F3 Orkney South Africa
151 C6 Orla Texas U.S.A.
77 M3 Orla Poland
75 G2 Orlamünde Germany
154 A2 Orland California U.S.A.
168 E4 Orlândia Brazil
145 D6 Orlando Florida U.S.A.
89 G3 Orléanais reg. France
89 G4 Orléans Loiret France
147 J4 Orleans Massachusetts U.S.A.
147 G2 Orleans Vermont U.S.A.
141 K3 Orléans, Île d' i. Québec Canada
59 F2 Orlen l. Sweden
78 E1 Orlice r. Czech Rep.
78 F1 Orlické Hory mountain range Czech Rep.
78 G1 Orlík mt. Czech Rep.
53 E1 Orlivka Chernihiv Ukraine
53 G3 Orlivka Zaporizhzhya Ukraine
50 J3 Orlov Rus. Fed.
51 J5 Orlov Gay Rus. Fed.
52 D4 Orlovo Rus. Fed.
31 E2 Orlovskiy Rus. Fed.
51 G6 Orlovskiy Rus. Fed.
86 B4 Orly airport France
39 F4 Ormara Pakistan
39 F4 Ormara, Ras headland Pakistan
59 F3 Ormaryd Sweden
65 F2 Ormiston Scotland U.K.
23 C4 Ormoc Philippines
145 D6 Ormond Beach Florida U.S.A.
115 F5 Ormos Greece
115 F7 Ormos Almyrou b. Greece
114 F4 Ormos Kymis b. Greece
115 F7 Ormos Mesara b. Greece
114 G3 Ormos Moudrou b. Greece
115 G5 Ormos Panormou Greece
115 F7 Ormos Soudas b. Greece
114 G2 Ormos Vistonias b. Greece
81 H4 Ormož Slovenia
65 F4 Ormskirk England U.K.
141 J4 Ormstown Québec Canada
58 C1 Ormtjernkampen Nasjonalpark nat. park Norway
114 E2 Ormylia Greece
87 E4 Ornain r. France
90 E1 Ornans France
83 D3 Ornavasso Italy
89 F3 Orne div. Basse-Normandie France
89 E2 Orne r. France
56 D2 Ørnes Norway
77 J1 Orneta Poland
59 H2 Ornö i. Sweden
93 D6 Ornolac-Ussat-les-Bains France
56 E3 Örnsköldsvik Sweden
55 D4 Orø i. Denmark
54 C2 Örö i. Finland
162 C3 Orocué Colombia
122 D4 Orodara Burkina
152 C2 Orofino Idaho U.S.A.
30 B3 Orog Nuur salt lake Mongolia
153 F5 Orogrande New Mexico U.S.A.
7 □11 Orohena mt. French Polynesia Pacific Ocean
107 F3 Orolo r. Italy
79 J6 Orom Yugoslavia
139 G4 Oromocto New Brunswick Canada
108 B2 Oro, Monte d' mt. Corse France
43 C4 Oron Israel
123 F6 Oron Nigeria
176 H6 Orona i. Kiribati
82 B2 Oron-la-Ville Switzerland
147 J2 Orono Maine U.S.A.
163 F3 Oronoque Guyana
93 A5 Oronoz Spain
66 B4 Oronsay i. Scotland U.K.
77 J4 Orońsko Poland
Orontes r. see 'Āṣī
106 B3 Oropa Italy
99 E5 Oropesa Extremadura Spain
103 D4 Oropesa Valencia Spain
103 D4 Oropesa, Cabo de headland Spain
159 □3 Oropuche r. Trinidad Trinidad and Tobago
31 G2 Oroqen Zizhiqi China
23 B4 Oroquieta Philippines
118 C4 Orori well Chad
170 E2 Oro, Río de r. Argentina
108 B4 Orosei Sardegna Italy
108 B4 Orosei, Golfo di b. Sardegna Italy
79 K5 Orosháza Hungary
115 G8 Oros Kofinas mt. Greece
23 □2 Orote Pen. pen. Guam Pacific Ocean
45 R3 Orotukan Rus. Fed.
155 G5 Oro Valley Arizona U.S.A.
154 B2 Oroville California U.S.A.
152 C1 Oroville Washington U.S.A.
154 B2 Oroville, Lake l. California U.S.A.
91 D4 Orpierre France
31 G2 Orqohan China
162 B2 Orquideas, Parque Nacional las nat. park Colombia
54 E1 Orrengrund i. Finland
66 D3 Orrin r. Scotland U.K.
58 D1 Orrkjølen h. Norway
12 D3 Orroroo S. Australia Australia
59 F1 Orsa Sweden
59 F1 Orsasjön l. Sweden
86 B4 Orsay France
59 G2 Örsbacken b. Sweden
78 F5 Őrség reg. Hungary
50 D4 Orsha Belarus
52 C1 Orsha Rus. Fed.
52 H1 Orshanka Rus. Fed.
106 B3 Orsiera, Monte mt. Italy
82 C2 Orsières Switzerland
59 F3 Örsjö Sweden
46 E2 Orsk Rus. Fed.
59 H1 Örskär i. Sweden
55 D4 Orslev Denmark
112 D2 Orșova Romania
56 B3 Ørsta Norway
55 C3 Ørsted Denmark
59 G2 Örsundaän r. Sweden
59 G2 Örsundsbro Sweden
113 G6 Ortaca Turkey
106 C3 Orta, Lago d' l. Italy
109 H3 Orta Nova Italy
109 E2 Orte Italy
98 C1 Ortegal, Cabo c. Spain
74 C4 Ortenau reg. Germany
74 E2 Ortenberg Germany
75 J4 Ortenburg Germany
93 B5 Orthez France
164 C2 Ortho r. Bolivia
114 C3 Orthovouni Greece
100 E2 Ortiga r. Spain
168 C6 Ortigueira Brazil
98 C1 Ortigueira Spain
107 F2 Ortisei Italy
156 C2 Ortiz Mexico
162 D2 Ortiz Venezuela
107 E2 Ortles mt. Italy
159 □3 Ortoire R. r. Trinidad Trinidad and Tobago
108 A3 Ortolo r. Corse France
65 F3 Orton England U.K.
109 G2 Ortona Italy
150 D2 Ortonville Minnesota U.S.A.
73 J4 Ortrand Germany
108 A4 Ortueri Sardegna Italy
72 F3 Örtze r. Germany
23 □1 Orukuizu i. Palau
45 O3 Orulgan, Khrebet mountain range Rus. Fed.
55 B3 Ørum Denmark
122 D5 Orumbo Boka h. Côte d'Ivoire
42 F2 Orūmīyeh Iran
164 C3 Oruro div. Bolivia
164 C3 Oruro Bolivia
93 G4 Orusco Spain
55 D1 Orust i. Sweden
98 C4 Orvalho Portugal
88 D4 Orvault France
108 E2 Orvieto Italy
179 B3 Orville Coast coastal area Antarctica
114 E1 Orvilos mts Greece
109 E2 Orvinio Italy
146 C4 Orwell Ohio U.S.A.
147 G3 Orwell Vermont U.S.A.
31 F2 Orxon Gol r. China
112 D3 Oryakhovo Bulgaria
53 B2 Orynyn Ukraine
53 E2 Orzhytsya r. Ukraine
53 E2 Orzhytsya Ukraine
106 D3 Orzinuovi Italy
77 K2 Orzyc r. Poland
77 K2 Orzysz Poland
57 C3 Os Norway
101 H1 Osa de Vega Spain
150 E4 Osage r. Missouri U.S.A.
148 A4 Osage Iowa U.S.A.
29 E6 Ōsaka div. Japan
29 E6 Ōsaka Japan
47 H2 Osakarovka Kazakhstan
156 K7 Osa, Pen. de pen. Costa Rica
169 E5 Osasco Brazil
69 E5 Osburger Hochwald forest Germany
55 B4 Øsby Denmark
59 E3 Osby Sweden
163 G3 Oscar French Guiana
151 F5 Osceola Arkansas U.S.A.
150 E3 Osceola Iowa U.S.A.
73 J4 Oschatz Germany
73 G3 Oschersleben Germany
108 B4 Oschiri Sardegna Italy
149 F3 Oscoda Michigan U.S.A.
112 B2 Osečina Yugoslavia
98 B3 O Seixo Spain
99 E1 Oseja de Sajambre Spain
75 J2 Osek Czech Rep.
102 C3 Osera Spain
76 E4 Osetno Poland
52 D2 Osetr r. Rus. Fed.
28 B7 Ōse-zaki pt Japan
141 H4 Osgoode Ontario Canada
47 H4 Osh div. Kyrgyzstan
47 H4 Osh Kyrgyzstan
47 H1 Osha r. Rus. Fed.
128 B2 Oshakati Namibia
28 H2 Oshamanbe Japan
128 B2 Oshana div. Namibia
141 F5 Oshawa Ontario Canada
29 H4 Oshika Japan
29 H4 Oshika-hantō pen. Japan
128 B2 Oshikango Namibia
128 B2 Oshikoto div. Namibia
28 G3 Ō-shima i. Japan
28 C7 Ō-shima i. Japan
29 G6 Ō-Shima i. Japan
29 E7 Ō-shima i. Japan
28 H2 Oshima-hantō pen. Japan
150 C3 Oshkosh Nebraska U.S.A.
148 C3 Oshkosh Wisconsin U.S.A.
41 G2 Oshnovīyeh Iran
123 E5 Oshogbo Nigeria
125 C4 Oshwe Congo(Zaire)
76 G2 Osie Poland
76 G2 Osieczna Gdansk Poland
76 E4 Osieczna Leszno Poland
76 D4 Osiecznica Poland
77 K4 Osiek Siedlce Poland
77 H2 Osiek Toruń Poland
76 G2 Osielsko Poland
95 G2 Osijek Croatia
108 A4 Osilo Sardegna Italy
107 H5 Osimo Italy
73 L2 Osina Poland
47 L2 Osinniki Rus. Fed.
83 E3 Osio Sotto Italy
36 C4 Osiyān India
131 H3 Osizweni South Africa
76 G4 Osjaków Poland
104 F3 Osječenica mts Bos.-Herz.
56 D3 Ösjön l. Sweden
148 A5 Oskaloosa Iowa U.S.A.
59 G3 Oskarshamn Sweden
59 E3 Oskarström Sweden
141 H2 Oskélanéo Québec Canada
53 G1 Oskol r. Rus. Fed.
59 G1 Oslättfors Sweden
78 F2 Oslava r. Czech Rep.
81 H1 Oslavany Czech Rep.
58 D2 Oslo div. Norway
58 D2 Oslo Norway
23 B4 Oslob Philippines
58 D2 Oslofjorden inlet Norway
38 B2 Osmānābād India
42 C1 Osmancık Turkey
42 D2 Osmaniye Turkey
54 F2 Os'mino Rus. Fed.
59 G2 Ösmo Sweden
54 C2 Osmussaar i. Estonia
72 D3 Osnabrück Germany
76 C3 Osno Lubuskie Poland
124 E4 Oso r. Congo(Zaire)
112 D3 Osogovske Planine mountain range Bulgaria/Macedonia
107 H2 Osoppo Italy
107 J4 Osor Croatia
167 B6 Osório Brazil
172 A6 Osorno Chile
99 F2 Osorno Spain
171 B5 Osorno, Vol. volcano Chile
136 F5 Osoyoos B.C. Canada
58 A1 Osøyri Norway
159 E5 Ospino Venezuela
106 E3 Ospitaletto Italy
15 F2 Osprey Reef reef Coral Sea Islands Terr. Pacific Ocean
68 D3 Oss Netherlands
100 C2 Ossa h. Portugal
114 D3 Ossa mt. Greece
101 H2 Ossa de Montiel Spain
13 F5 Ossa, Mt mt. Tasmania Australia

P

98 E2 Pozuelo del Páramo Spain
98 D4 Pozuelo de Zarzón Spain
80 C4 Pozza di Fasso Italy
110 D6 Pozzallo *Sicilia* Italy
108 A4 Pozzomaggiore *Sardegna* Italy
109 G4 Pozzuoli Italy
80 E5 Pozzuolo del Friuli Italy
122 D5 Pra r. Ghana
52 E2 Pra r. Rus. Fed.
22 A2 Prabumulih Indonesia
77 H2 Prabuty Poland
100 C1 Pracana, Barragem de resr Portugal
78 D2 Prachatice Czech Rep.
25 C4 Prachin Buri Thailand
87 G2 Pracht Germany
25 B5 Prachuap Khiri Khan Thailand
80 D1 Prackenbach Germany
166 B1 Pracuí r. Brazil
98 C1 Pradairo mt. Spain
78 G1 Praděd mt. Czech Rep.
91 B4 Pradelles France
99 G3 Prádena Spain
93 E6 Prades France
169 J2 Prado Brazil
100 E4 Prado del Rey Spain
99 G2 Pradoluengo Spain
55 E4 Præstø Denmark
91 E3 Pragelato Italy
81 G4 Pragersko Slovenia
Prague *see* Praha
78 D1 Praha div. Czech Rep.
78 C2 Praha h. Czech Rep.
78 D1 Praha Czech Rep.
92 B2 Prahecq France
122 □ Praia Cape Verde
111 E3 Praia a Mare Italy
98 B4 Praia da Tocha Portugal
98 B4 Praia de Mira Portugal
169 E6 Praia Grande Brazil
166 A3 Praia Rica Brazil
166 B1 Prainha Brazil
15 F4 Prairie *Queensland* Australia
148 E5 Prairie Creek Reservoir resr *Indiana* U.S.A.
151 C5 Prairie Dog Town Fork r. *Texas* U.S.A.
148 B4 Prairie du Chien *Wisconsin* U.S.A.
25 C4 Prakhon Chai Thailand
82 B3 Pralognan-la-Vanoise France
81 E2 Pram r. Austria
114 C3 Pramanta Greece
25 B4 Pran r. Thailand
54 D2 Prangli i. Estonia
38 B2 Pranhita r. India
81 F3 Prankerhöhe mt. Austria
20 C6 Prapat Indonesia
25 D4 Prasat Preăh Vihear Thailand
127 □1 Praslin I. i. Seychelles
114 F4 Prasouda i. Greece
76 G4 Praszka Poland
171 B6 Prat i. Chile
168 D3 Prata r. *Goiás* Brazil
168 B3 Prata r. *Minas Gerais* Brazil
169 E2 Prata r. *Minas Gerais* Brazil
166 D2 Prata r. *Piauí* Brazil
168 D3 Prata *Minas Gerais* Brazil
36 C4 Pratapgarh India
102 D4 Prat de Comte Spain
169 E3 Pratinha Brazil
107 F5 Prato Italy
107 E2 Prato allo Stelvio Italy
109 F2 Pratola Peligna Italy
102 F2 Prats de Lluçanes Spain
93 E6 Prats-de-Mollo-la-Preste France
151 D4 Pratt *Kansas* U.S.A.
82 C1 Pratteln Switzerland
83 E2 Prättigau reg. Switzerland
151 G5 Prattville *Alabama* U.S.A.
90 D1 Prauthoy France
38 A2 Pravara r. India
52 F1 Pravdinsk Rus. Fed.
54 B4 Pravdinsk Rus. Fed.
53 E3 Pravdyne Ukraine
98 D1 Pravia Spain
77 N2 Pravyya Masty Belarus
62 C4 Prawle Point pt *England* U.K.
22 D4 Praya Indonesia
93 C4 Prayssas France
54 F4 Prazaroki Belarus
90 E3 Praz-sur-Arly France
25 D4 Preăh Vihear Cambodia
81 G4 Prebold Slovenia
93 B4 Préchac France
52 A2 Prechistoye Rus. Fed.
89 E4 Précigné France
90 C1 Précy-sous-Thil France
107 F2 Predazzo Italy
112 E2 Predeal Romania
81 E3 Predlitz Austria
137 J4 Preeceville *Saskatchewan* Canada
89 E3 Pré-en-Pail France
72 F1 Preetz Germany
107 G3 Preganziòl Italy
81 F2 Pregarten Austria
54 B4 Pregolya r. Rus. Fed.
81 G4 Pregrada Croatia
166 D1 Preguiças r. Brazil
93 C5 Preignan France
54 E3 Preiļi Latvia
141 F2 Preissac, Lac l. *Québec* Canada
93 E5 Preixan France
112 E2 Prejmer Romania
112 B3 Prekornica mts Yugoslavia
25 D5 Prêk Tnaôt l. Cambodia
81 H4 Prelog Croatia
78 E1 Přelouč Czech Rep.
107 H4 Premantura Croatia
90 B1 Prémery France
83 D2 Premia Italy
102 F3 Premià de Mar Spain
73 H3 Premnitz Germany
69 B5 Prémontré France
104 F4 Prenj mts Bos.-Herz.
148 B3 Prentice *Wisconsin* U.S.A.
73 J2 Prenzlau Germany
53 F3 Preobrazhenka Ukraine
25 A4 Preparis I. i. *Cocos Is* Indian Ocean
25 A4 Preparis North Channel chan. *Cocos Is* Indian Ocean
25 A4 Preparis South Channel chan. *Cocos Is* Indian Ocean
90 B2 Préporché France
78 G2 Přerov Czech Rep.
107 E2 Presanella, Cima mt. Italy
155 F4 Prescott *Arizona* U.S.A.
141 H4 Prescott *Ontario* Canada
155 F4 Prescott Valley *Arizona* U.S.A.
9 A7 Preservation Inlet inlet New Zealand
112 C3 Preševo Yugoslavia
150 C3 Presho *S. Dakota* U.S.A.
111 H3 Presicce Italy
170 D2 Presidencia Roque Sáenz Peña Argentina
168 C5 Presidente Bernardes Brazil
170 E2 Presidente de la Plaza Argentina
166 D2 Presidente Dutra Brazil
168 B4 Presidente Epitácio Brazil
165 D2 Presidente Hermes Brazil
169 H1 Presidente Jânio Quadros Brazil
169 F3 Presidente Juscelino Brazil
168 B1 Presidente Murtinho Brazil
169 E3 Presidente Olegário Brazil
168 C5 Presidente Prudente Brazil
171 B6 Presidente Rios, L. l. Chile
168 C4 Presidente Venceslau Brazil
151 B6 Presidio *Texas* U.S.A.
112 F3 Preslav Bulgaria
47 G2 Presnogorkovka Kazakhstan
47 G2 Presnovka Kazakhstan
79 L3 Prešov Slovakia
114 C2 Prespa, Lake l. Europe
Prespansko Ezero l. *see* Prespa, Lake
114 C2 Prespes nat. park Greece
147 K1 Presque Isle *Maine* U.S.A.
148 D2 Presque Isle Pt pt *Michigan* U.S.A.
91 E5 Presqu'île de Giens pen. France
159 □4 Presqu'Île de la Caravelle pen. *Martinique* Caribbean
7 □11 Presqu'île de Taiarapu pen. *French Polynesia* Pacific Ocean
179 □ Presqu'île Jeanne d'Arc pen. *Kerguelen* Indian Ocean
179 □ Presqu'île Joffre pen. *Kerguelen* Indian Ocean
92 C2 Pressac France
75 G3 Pressath Germany
81 H2 Pressbaum Austria
62 C1 Prestatyn *Wales* U.K.
62 D3 Prestbury *England* U.K.
106 A3 Pre-St-Didier Italy
122 D5 Prestea Ghana
58 D2 Prestebakke Norway
62 C2 Presteigne *Wales* U.K.
78 C2 Přeštice Czech Rep.
62 D4 Preston *England* U.K.
65 F4 Preston *England* U.K.
152 E3 Preston *Idaho* U.S.A.
148 A4 Preston *Minnesota* U.S.A.
151 E4 Preston *Missouri* U.S.A.
155 E2 Preston *Nevada* U.S.A.
65 F2 Preston *Scotland* U.K.
16 B4 Preston, C. c. *Western Australia* Australia
66 F5 Prestonpans *Scotland* U.K.
146 B6 Prestonsburg *Kentucky* U.S.A.
66 D5 Prestwick *Scotland* U.K.
166 D3 Prêto r. *Bahia* Brazil
166 E3 Prêto r. *Bahia* Brazil
168 C3 Prêto r. *Goiás* Brazil
169 E2 Prêto r. *Minas Gerais* Brazil
168 D4 Preto r. *São Paulo* Brazil
163 E5 Prêto do Igapó Acu r. Brazil
131 G2 Pretoria South Africa
146 E5 Prettyboy Lake l. *Maryland* U.S.A.
73 G3 Pretzier Germany
73 H4 Pretzsch Germany
92 C2 Preuilly-sur-Claise France
81 F4 Prevalje Slovenia
91 B4 Prévenchères France
114 B3 Preveza div. Greece
114 B4 Preveza Greece
25 D5 Prey Vêng Cambodia
107 J3 Prezid Croatia
87 E4 Prez-sous-Lafauche France
31 K2 Priamurskiy Rus. Fed.
98 D2 Priaranza del Bierzo Spain
31 F2 Priargunsk Rus. Fed.
81 H2 Přibice Czech Rep.
134 A4 Pribilof Islands *Alaska* U.S.A.
112 B3 Priboj Yugoslavia
79 H2 Příbor Czech Rep.
78 D2 Příbram Czech Rep.
78 E2 Přibyslav Czech Rep.
139 G4 Price *Québec* Canada
155 G2 Price *Utah* U.S.A.
136 D4 Price I. i. *B.C.* Canada
145 B6 Prichard *Alabama* U.S.A.
99 H4 Priego Spain
101 F3 Priego de Córdoba Spain
54 B3 Priekule Latvia
54 B4 Priekulė Lithuania
54 D3 Priekuļi Latvia
54 C4 Prienai Lithuania
80 D3 Prien am Chiemsee Germany
130 D4 Prieska South Africa
130 D4 Prieskapoort pass South Africa
152 C1 Priest L. l. *Idaho* U.S.A.
159 □1 Priestmans River Jamaica
152 C1 Priest River *Idaho* U.S.A.
156 B2 Prieta, Punta Mexico
99 F1 Prieto, Cabo pt Spain
156 D3 Prieto, Cerro Mexico
79 H3 Prievidza Slovakia
92 B3 Prignac-et-Marcamps France
73 H2 Prignitz reg. Germany
52 A3 Prigor'ye Rus. Fed.
47 L2 Priiskovyy Rus. Fed.
31 F2 Priiskovyy Rus. Fed.
104 F3 Prijedor Bos.-Herz.
112 B3 Prijepolje Yugoslavia
46 C4 Prikaspiyskaya Nizmennost' lowland Kazakhstan/Rus. Fed.
114 C1 Prilep Macedonia
103 C7 Prima, Pta pt Spain
157 F4 Primavera Mexico
78 B2 Přimda Czech Rep.
166 D1 Primeira Cruz Brazil
88 B3 Primel, Pte de pt France
173 F1 Primero r. Argentina
13 F5 Prime Seal I. i. *Tasmania* Australia
107 F3 Primolano Italy
51 H5 Primorsk Rus. Fed.
54 F1 Primorsk Rus. Fed.
77 J1 Primorsk Rus. Fed.
31 J4 Primorskiy Rus. Fed.
51 F6 Primorsko-Akhtarsk Rus. Fed.
137 H3 Primrose Lake l. *Saskatchewan* Canada
74 B3 Prims r. Germany
137 H4 Prince Albert *Saskatchewan* Canada
130 D6 Prince Albert South Africa
179 B5 Prince Albert Mts mts Antarctica
137 H4 Prince Albert National Park nat. park *Saskatchewan* Canada
134 G2 Prince Albert Peninsula pen. *N.W.T.* Canada
130 C6 Prince Albert Road South Africa
134 G2 Prince Albert Sound chan. *N.W.T.* Canada
134 F2 Prince Alfred, C. c. *N.W.T.* Canada
130 B6 Prince Alfred Hamlet South Africa
135 L3 Prince Charles Island i. *N.W.T.* Canada
179 D4 Prince Charles Mts mts Antarctica
139 H4 Prince Edward Island div. Canada
175 G7 Prince Edward Islands is Indian Ocean
141 G5 Prince Edward Pt pt *Ontario* Canada
146 E5 Prince Frederick *Maryland* U.S.A.
136 E4 Prince George *B.C.* Canada
134 H2 Prince Gustaf Adolf Sea chan. *N.W.T.* Canada
134 B3 Prince of Wales, Cape c. *Alaska* U.S.A.
15 E1 Prince of Wales I. i. *Queensland* Australia
136 C3 Prince of Wales Island i. *Alaska* U.S.A.
135 J2 Prince of Wales Island i. *N.W.T.* Canada
134 G2 Prince of Wales Strait chan. *N.W.T.* Canada
134 F2 Prince Patrick I. i. *N.W.T.* Canada
16 D2 Prince Regent r. *Western Australia* Australia
135 J2 Prince Regent Inlet chan. *N.W.T.* Canada
136 C4 Prince Rupert *B.C.* Canada
63 F3 Princes Risborough *England* U.K.
147 F5 Princess Anne *Maryland* U.S.A.
179 D3 Princess Astrid Coast coastal area Antarctica
15 E2 Princess Charlotte Bay b. *Queensland* Australia
179 D5 Princess Elizabeth Land reg. Antarctica
137 K2 Princess Mary Lake l. *N.W.T.* Canada
16 D2 Princess May Ra. h. *Western Australia* Australia
17 C5 Princess Ra. h. *Western Australia* Australia
179 D3 Princess Ragnhild Coast coastal area Antarctica
136 D4 Princess Royal I. i. *B.C.* Canada
159 □3 Prince's Town *Trinidad* Trinidad and Tobago
136 E5 Princeton *B.C.* Canada
154 A2 Princeton *California* U.S.A.
148 C5 Princeton *Illinois* U.S.A.
144 C4 Princeton *Indiana* U.S.A.
144 C4 Princeton *Kentucky* U.S.A.
147 K2 Princeton *Maine* U.S.A.
150 E3 Princeton *Missouri* U.S.A.
147 F4 Princeton *New Jersey* U.S.A.
148 C4 Princeton *Wisconsin* U.S.A.
146 C6 Princeton *W. Virginia* U.S.A.
141 K3 Princeville *Québec* Canada
147 K2 Prince William *New Brunswick* Canada
134 D3 Prince William Sound b. *Alaska* U.S.A.
125 □ Príncipe i. Sao Tome and Principe
152 B2 Prineville *Oregon* U.S.A.
172 F6 Pringles Argentina
68 C3 Prinsenbeek Netherlands
158 □1 Prinses Beatrix airport *Aruba* Caribbean
179 D4 Prins Harald Kyst coastal area Antarctica
44 B2 Prins Karls Forland i. *Svalbard* Arctic Ocean
156 K6 Prinzapolca Nicaragua
115 D5 Priolithos Greece
10 □3 Prion Lake l. *Macquarie I.* Pacific Ocean
98 B1 Prior, Cabo pt Spain
47 K3 Priozerny Kazakhstan
54 G1 Priozersk Rus. Fed.
Pripet r. *see* Pryp"yat
56 H1 Prirechnyy Rus. Fed.
78 E1 Přišovice Czech Rep.
53 G1 Pristen' Rus. Fed.
112 C3 Priština *Kosovo* Yugoslavia
73 H3 Pritzerbe Germany
73 G2 Pritzier Germany
73 H2 Pritzwalk Germany
91 C4 Privas France
109 F3 Priverno Italy
104 E3 Privlaka Croatia
52 B2 Privokzal'nyy Rus. Fed.
52 E1 Privolzhsk Rus. Fed.
52 G4 Privolzhskaya Vozvyshennost' reg. Rus. Fed.
52 H4 Privolzhskiy Rus. Fed.
112 C3 Prizren Yugoslavia
110 C5 Prizzi *Sicilia* Italy
104 F3 Prnjavor Bos.-Herz.
98 D2 Proba Spain
112 D3 Probištip Macedonia
22 C3 Probolinggo Indonesia
75 G2 Probstzella Germany
62 B4 Probus *England* U.K.
76 E4 Prochowice Poland
109 G4 Procida Italy
148 A2 Proctor *Minnesota* U.S.A.
147 G3 Proctor *Vermont* U.S.A.
98 C5 Proenca-a-Nova Portugal
163 F3 Professor van Blommestein Meer resr Surinam
69 C4 Profondeville Belgium
83 F3 Progno r. Italy
114 A2 Progonat Albania
151 C7 Progreso *Coahuila* Mexico
157 F4 Progreso *Hidalgo* Mexico
157 H4 Progreso *Yucatán* Mexico
173 G1 Progreso Argentina
156 J6 Progreso Honduras
31 J2 Progress Rus. Fed.
164 B1 Progresso Brazil
51 H7 Prokhladnyy Rus. Fed.
53 G1 Prokhorovka Rus. Fed.
53 E1 Prokhory Ukraine
112 B3 Prokletije mountain range Albania/Yugoslavia
114 E4 Prokopi Greece
47 L2 Prokop'yevsk Rus. Fed.
112 C3 Prokuplje Yugoslavia
50 D3 Proletariy Rus. Fed.
51 G6 Proletarsk Rus. Fed.
52 C2 Proletarskiy Rus. Fed.
53 F1 Proletarskiy Rus. Fed.
45 P2 Proliv Dmitriya Lapteva chan. Rus. Fed.
44 G3 Proliv Karskiye Vorota chan. Rus. Fed.
45 T2 Proliv Longa chan. Rus. Fed.
44 G2 Proliv Matochkin Shar chan. Rus. Fed.
45 L2 Proliv Vil'kitskogo str. Rus. Fed.
Prome *see* Pyè
167 A4 Promissão *Mato Grosso do Sul* Brazil
168 D4 Promissão *São Paulo* Brazil
77 J4 Promna Poland
109 H3 Promontorio del Gargano plat. Italy
114 E3 Promyri Greece
47 K2 Promyshlennaya Rus. Fed.
50 G3 Pronino Rus. Fed.
74 B2 Pronsfeld Germany
52 D2 Pronsk Rus. Fed.
52 E2 Pronya r. Rus. Fed.
134 F4 Prophet r. *B.C.* Canada
136 E3 Prophet River *B.C.* Canada
148 C5 Prophetstown *Illinois* U.S.A.
166 E3 Propriá Brazil
108 A3 Propriano *Corse* France
73 J1 Prorer Wiek b. Germany
81 H4 Prosenjakovci Slovenia
15 G4 Proserpine *Queensland* Australia
114 G2 Proskynites Greece
76 F3 Prosna r. Poland
114 E1 Prosotsani Greece
147 F3 Prospect *New York* U.S.A.
23 C4 Prosperidad Philippines
64 B4 Prosperous Rep. of Ireland
128 □2 Prosperous B. b. *St Helena* Atlantic Ocean
109 F3 Prossedi Italy
78 G2 Prostějov Czech Rep.
77 L2 Prostki Poland
15 G5 Proston *Queensland* Australia
47 H3 Prostornoye Kazakhstan
53 F2 Prosyane Ukraine
77 J5 Proszowice Poland
130 C7 Protem South Africa
115 C5 Proti i. Greece
148 A4 Protivin *Iowa* U.S.A.
81 F1 Protivín Czech Rep.
53 G2 Protopopivka Ukraine
52 C2 Protva r. Rus. Fed.
52 C2 Protva Rus. Fed.
52 C2 Protvino Rus. Fed.
73 J3 Prötzel Germany
112 F3 Provadiya Bulgaria
Prøven *see* Kangersuatsiaq
100 B3 Provença Portugal
91 E5 Provence-Alpes-Côte-d'Azur div. France
87 G4 Provenchères-sur-Fave France
147 H4 Providence *Rhode Island* U.S.A.
140 D4 Providence Bay *Ontario* Canada
9 A7 Providence, Cape c. New Zealand
151 F5 Providence, Lake *Louisiana* U.S.A.
156 K6 Providencia, I. de i. Colombia
134 A3 Provideniya Rus. Fed.
147 H3 Provincetown *Massachusetts* U.S.A.
86 C4 Provins France
155 G1 Provo *Utah* U.S.A.
137 G4 Provost *Alberta* Canada
104 F4 Prozor Bos.-Herz.
114 B1 Prrenjas Albania
122 D5 Pru r. Ghana
51 D6 Prubiynyy, Mys pt Ukraine
77 L6 Pruchnik Poland
112 E2 Prudeni Romania
168 C6 Prudentópolis Brazil
134 D2 Prudhoe Bay *Alaska* U.S.A.
15 G4 Prudhoe I. i. *Queensland* Australia
76 F5 Prudnik Poland
53 G1 Prudyanka Ukraine
74 B2 Prüm r. Germany
74 B2 Prüm Germany
112 F2 Prundu Romania
108 B2 Prunelli-di-Fiumorbo *Corse* France
89 G4 Pruniers-en-Sologne France
76 E4 Prusice Poland
76 G1 Pruszcz Gdański Poland
77 J3 Pruszków Poland
112 G1 Prut r. Europe
80 B3 Prutz Austria
77 N3 Pruzhany Belarus
81 E5 Prvačina Slovenia
107 J4 Prvić i. Croatia
52 B4 Pryamitsyno Rus. Fed.
53 F3 Pryazovs'ke Ukraine
179 D5 Prydz Bay b. Antarctica
53 G1 Prykolotne Ukraine
53 E1 Pryluky Ukraine
53 G3 Prymors'k Ukraine
53 E3 Prymors'ke *Kherson* Ukraine
112 G2 Prymors'ke *Odesa* Ukraine
53 D1 Pryp"yat r. Europe
53 D1 Pryp"yat' Ukraine
51 C4 Prypyats' r. Belarus
53 F3 Pryshyb Ukraine
53 A1 Pryvitne Ukraine
77 J2 Przasnysz Poland
76 F2 Przechlewo Poland
77 H4 Przedbórz Poland
76 G3 Przedecz Poland
76 D2 Przelewice Poland
76 E3 Przemęt Poland
76 D4 Przemków Poland
77 L5 Przemyśl div. Poland
77 L6 Przemyśl Poland
77 L5 Przeworsk Poland
76 C4 Przewóz Poland
77 J2 Przezdzięk Wielki Poland
Przheval'sk *see* Karakol
76 G1 Przodkowo Poland
76 C2 Przybiernów Poland
77 J3 Przyborowice Poland
76 F4 Przygodzice Poland
77 H5 Przyrów Poland
77 J4 Przysucha Poland
76 D3 Przytoczna Poland
77 L4 Przytoczno Poland
77 J4 Przytyk Poland
114 E4 Psachna Greece
113 E5 Psara i. Greece
114 C2 Psarades Greece
115 D5 Psari Greece
114 F3 Psathoura i. Greece
51 G6 Psebay Rus. Fed.
115 G7 Pseira i. Greece
53 F1 Psel r. Rus. Fed.
53 G1 Pselets Rus. Fed.
51 F6 Pshekha r. Rus. Fed.
51 F6 Pshish r. Rus. Fed.
115 D5 Psili i. Greece
115 □ Psinthos Greece
50 D3 Pskov div. Rus. Fed.
54 F3 Pskov Rus. Fed.
54 F2 Pskova r. Rus. Fed.
54 E2 Pskov, Lake l. Estonia/Rus. Fed.
104 F3 Psunj mts Croatia
76 D3 Pszczew Poland
76 G1 Pszczółki Poland
76 G6 Pszczyna Poland
114 D3 Pteleos Greece
114 C2 Ptolemaïda Greece
118 D1 Ptolemais Libya
54 F5 Ptsich r. Belarus
81 G4 Ptuj Slovenia
81 G4 Ptujsko jezero l. Slovenia
30 C6 Pu r. China
22 A2 Pu r. Indonesia
172 A5 Púa Chile
173 F4 Puán Argentina
32 D3 Pu'an China
31 H6 Puan South Korea
7 □12 Puapua Western Samoa
7 □12 Puava, C. c. Western Samoa
33 E4 Pubei China
164 B1 Pucallpa Peru
164 B3 Pucará r. Peru
164 B3 Pucara Peru
162 C4 Puca Urco Peru
81 G3 Puchberg am Schneeberg Austria
33 E1 Pucheng China
33 G3 Pucheng China
52 F1 Puchezh Rus. Fed.
80 C2 Puchheim Germany
31 H5 Puch'ŏn South Korea
79 H2 Púchov Slovakia
172 C1 Puchuzúh Argentina
112 E2 Pucioasa Romania
76 G1 Puck Poland
148 C4 Puckaway Lake l. *Wisconsin* U.S.A.
103 C5 Puçol Spain
172 B5 Pucón Chile
Pudai watercourse *see* Dor
39 C2 Pūdanū Iran
56 G2 Pudasjärvi Finland
62 D4 Puddletown *England* U.K.
74 C2 Puderbach Germany
130 E3 Pudimoe South Africa
50 F2 Pudozh Rus. Fed.
65 G4 Pudsey *England* U.K.
Puduchcheri *see* Pondicherry
38 B4 Pudukkottai India
157 F5 Puebla div. Mexico
157 F5 Puebla Mexico
173 G1 Puebla Brugo Argentina
99 G4 Puebla de Beleña Spain
101 H3 Puebla de Don Fadrique Spain
101 F1 Puebla de Don Rodrigo Spain
100 C3 Puebla de Guzmán Spain
100 D2 Puebla de la Calzada Spain
100 D2 Puebla de la Reina Spain
98 B2 Puebla del Caramiñal Spain
99 E1 Puebla de Lillo Spain
101 H2 Puebla del Príncipe Spain
98 D2 Puebla de Sanabria Spain
98 C2 Puebla de San Xulián Spain
98 C2 Puebla de Trives Spain
153 F4 Pueblo *Colorado* U.S.A.
173 H1 Pueblo Arrúa Argentina
170 B2 Pueblo Hundido Chile
173 F2 Pueblo Italiano Argentina
173 H1 Pueblo Libertador Argentina
173 G1 Pueblo Marini Argentina
162 D1 Pueblo Nuevo Venezuela
157 G5 Pueblo Viejo Mexico
93 E4 Puech del Pal mt. France
93 E4 Puech de Rouet h. France
172 E5 Puelches Argentina
172 D4 Puelén Argentina
172 B2 Puente Alto Chile
98 D2 Puente de Domingo Flórez Spain
101 H2 Puente de Génave Spain
98 E4 Puente del Congosto Spain
172 C2 Puente del Inca Argentina
102 D2 Puente de Montañana Spain
101 F3 Puente-Genil Spain
102 B2 Puente la Reina Spain
99 F1 Puentenansa Spain
99 G3 Puentes Viejas, Emb. de resr Spain
162 D1 Puente Torres Venezuela
99 G1 Puente Viesgo Spain
32 C4 Pu'er China
165 F4 Puerto Adela Paraguay
165 D2 Puerto Alegre Bolivia
165 E4 Puerto Antequera Paraguay
156 K7 Puerto Armuelles Panama
162 B3 Puerto Asís Colombia
162 D2 Puerto Ayacucho Venezuela
162 □ Puerto Ayora *Galapagos Is* Ecuador
157 H6 Puerto Barrios Guatemala
173 F5 Puerto Belgrano Argentina
164 B2 Puerto Bermudez Peru
162 C2 Puerto Berrío Colombia
162 D1 Puerto Cabello Venezuela
156 K6 Puerto Cabezas Nicaragua
156 K6 Puerto Cabo Gracias á Dios Nicaragua
166 A3 Puerto Calueiro Brazil
162 D2 Puerto Carreño Colombia
165 E4 Puerto Casado Paraguay
171 B5 Puerto Cisnes Chile
171 C7 Puerto Coig Argentina
173 H2 Puerto Constanza Argentina
165 E4 Puerto Cooper Paraguay
156 K7 Puerto Cortés Costa Rica
156 J6 Puerto Cortés Honduras
156 C3 Puerto Cortés Mexico
162 D1 Puerto Cumarebo Venezuela
101 H3 Puerto de Almaciles pass Spain
103 C6 Puerto de Ares pass Spain
98 E4 Puerto de Béjar Spain
102 C4 Puerto de Cabrillas pass Spain
103 C4 Puerto de Escandón pass Spain
102 B1 Puerto de Ibañeta pass Spain
103 B6 Puerto de Jumilla pass Spain
97 □ Puerto de la Cruz *Canary Is* Spain
97 □ Puerto de la Estaca *Canary Is* Spain
99 F4 Puerto de la Paramera pass Spain
101 G3 Puerto de la Ragua pass Spain
101 H3 Puerto de la Vírgen pass Spain
98 D2 Puerto del Manzanal pass Spain
98 D5 Puerto de los Castaños pass Spain
101 H2 Puerto de los Pocicos pass Spain
99 E1 Puerto del Pontón pass Spain
101 F2 Puerto del Rayo pass Spain
97 □ Puerto del Rosario *Canary Is* Spain
101 E4 Puerto del Viento pass Spain
103 B7 Puerto de Mazarrón Spain
102 B4 Puerto de Minguez pass Spain
100 E1 Puerto de Miravete pass Spain
157 J4 Puerto de Morelos Mexico
101 F2 Puerto de Niefla pass Spain
159 E5 Puerto de Nutrias Venezuela
165 D3 Puerto de Pailas Bolivia
98 E1 Puerto de Pajares pass Spain
99 F1 Puerto de San Glorio pass Spain
101 H3 Puerto de Santa María de Nieva pass Spain
101 E1 Puerto de San Vicente Spain
101 G3 Puerto de Tiscar pass Spain
93 A5 Puerto de Velate pass Spain
165 D2 Puerto do Massaca Brazil
172 A5 Puerto Dominguez Chile
165 E2 Puerto dos Gauchos Brazil
157 F6 Puerto Escondido Mexico
162 C1 Puerto Estrella Colombia
162 B5 Puerto Eten Peru
162 B4 Puerto Francisco de Orellana Ecuador
165 D2 Puerto Frey Bolivia
164 D3 Puerto Grether Bolivia
165 E4 Puerto Guarani Paraguay
173 H2 Puerto Ibicuy Argentina
173 F5 Puerto Ingeniero White Argentina
162 D3 Puerto Inírida Colombia
170 D1 Puerto Irigoyen Argentina
165 E3 Puerto Isabel Bolivia
156 J7 Puerto Jesus Costa Rica
157 J4 Puerto Juárez Mexico
163 E1 Puerto La Cruz Venezuela
101 G1 Puerto Lápice Spain
162 C4 Puerto Leguizamo Colombia
156 K6 Puerto Lempira Honduras
101 F2 Puertollano Spain
171 D5 Puerto Lobos Argentina
162 C3 Puerto Lopéz Colombia
159 E5 Puerto Lopez Castilletes Colombia
103 B6 Puerto los Altos pass Spain
103 B7 Puerto Lumbreras Spain
171 C5 Puerto Madryn Argentina
164 C2 Puerto Maldonado Peru
164 D3 Puerto Mamoré Bolivia
158 C2 Puerto Manatí Cuba
162 A4 Puerto Máncora Peru
164 C3 Puerto Marquez Bolivia
165 F4 Puerto Mendes Paraguay
165 E4 Puerto Mihanovich Paraguay
162 D2 Puerto Miranda Venezuela
171 B5 Puerto Montt Chile
162 B5 Puerto Morín Peru
171 B7 Puerto Natáles Chile
162 D2 Puerto Nuevo Colombia
156 L7 Puerto Obaldia Panama
163 E2 Puerto Ordaz Venezuela
158 C2 Puerto Padre Cuba
162 D2 Puerto Páez Venezuela
162 B4 Puerto Pardo Peru
165 E4 Puerto Pinasco Paraguay
171 D5 Puerto Pirámides Argentina
159 F5 Puerto Píritu Venezuela
159 E3 Puerto Plata Dominican Rep.
164 B1 Puerto Portillo Peru
164 B2 Puerto Prado Peru
23 A4 Puerto Princesa Philippines
100 D4 Puerto Real Spain
162 B2 Puerto Rey Colombia
133 M8 Puerto Rico territory Caribbean
164 C2 Puerto Rico Bolivia
172 A6 Puerto Rico Chile
159 F3 Puerto Rico Trench sea feature Caribbean
173 H2 Puerto Ruiz Argentina
158 D2 Puerto Samá Cuba
171 C7 Puerto Santa Cruz inlet Argentina
165 E4 Puerto Sastre Paraguay
165 D2 Puerto Saucedo Bolivia
100 E4 Puerto Serrano Spain
164 D2 Puerto Siles Bolivia
162 C4 Puerto Socorro Peru
165 E3 Puerto Suárez Bolivia
164 A2 Puerto Supe Peru
164 B2 Puerto Tahuantisuyo Peru
162 B3 Puerto Tejado Colombia
162 B4 Puerto Tunigrama Peru
164 A1 Puerto Victoria Peru
165 D2 Puerto Villazon Bolivia
171 C6 Puerto Visser Argentina
172 B5 Puesco Chile
165 D4 Puesto Estrella Paraguay
172 D5 Puesto Sánchez Argentina
7 □11 Pueu *French Polynesia* Pacific Ocean
51 J4 Pugachev Rus. Fed.
36 C3 Pugal India
129 F2 Puga Puga, Ilha i. Mozambique
32 C3 Puge China
22 C4 Puger Indonesia
91 E5 Puget-sur-Argens France
91 E5 Puget-Théniers France
91 E5 Puget-Ville France
109 H3 Puglia div. Italy
109 J3 Pugnochiuso Italy
22 A3 Pugung, G. mt. Indonesia
39 C4 Pūhāl-e Khamīr, Kuh-e mountain range Iran
7 □16 Puhi h. *Easter I.* Chile
54 E2 Puhja Estonia
102 E2 Puigcerdà Spain
103 F5 Puig Major mt. Spain
102 F2 Puigmal mt. France/Spain
102 E2 Puig Pedrós mt. Spain
102 E3 Puig-reig Spain
27 □ Pui O Wan b. *Hong Kong* China
90 B1 Puisaye reg. France
86 B4 Puiseaux France
69 A4 Puisieux France
93 B4 Puisseguin France
86 D4 Puits r. France
118 C5 Puits 29 well Chad
118 C5 Puits 30 well Chad
93 E6 Puivert France
122 B5 Pujehun Sierra Leone
33 G2 Pujiang China
93 B4 Pujols France
9 C6 Pukaki, L. l. New Zealand
5 O6 Pukapuka atoll *French Polynesia* Pacific Ocean
140 C2 Pukaskwa r. *Ontario* Canada
140 C2 Pukaskwa National Park nat. park *Ontario* Canada
137 J3 Pukatawagan *Manitoba* Canada
59 F3 Pukavik Sweden
59 F3 Pukaviksbukten b. Sweden
31 J4 Pukch'ŏng North Korea
112 B3 Pukë Albania
8 G2 Pukeamara mt. New Zealand
8 E2 Pukekohe New Zealand
9 D5 Puketeraki Ra. mountain range New Zealand
8 F4 Puketoi Range h. New Zealand
9 C6 Pukeuri Junction New Zealand
54 D1 Pukkila Finland
50 G2 Puksoozero Rus. Fed.
107 H4 Pula airport Croatia
107 H4 Pula Croatia
108 B5 Pula *Sardegna* Italy
108 B6 Pula, Capo di pt *Sardegna* Italy
164 C4 Pulacayo Bolivia
31 G5 Pulandian Wan b. China
23 C4 Pulangi r. Philippines
22 C2 Pulangpisau Indonesia
164 C4 Pular, Co mt. Chile
22 E3 Pulasi i. Indonesia
147 E3 Pulaski *New York* U.S.A.
145 C5 Pulaski *Tennessee* U.S.A.
146 C6 Pulaski *Virginia* U.S.A.
148 C3 Pulaski *Wisconsin* U.S.A.
22 A2 Pulaukijang Indonesia
77 K4 Puławy Poland
63 F4 Pulborough *England* U.K.
107 H2 Pulfero Italy
72 B4 Pulheim Germany
38 C3 Pulicat L. b. India
38 B3 Pulivendla India
38 B4 Puliyangudi India
81 H2 Pulkau r. Austria
81 G2 Pulkau Austria
56 G2 Pulkkila Finland
152 C2 Pullman *Washington* U.S.A.
56 J1 Pulozero Rus. Fed.
103 B7 Pulpí Spain
156 C3 Púlpito, Pta pt Mexico
111 G2 Pulsano Italy
73 J4 Pulsnitz r. Germany
73 K4 Pulsnitz Germany
77 K3 Pułtusk Poland
37 E1 Pulu China
42 D2 Pülümür Turkey
23 C5 Pulutan Indonesia
82 C1 Pulversheim France
172 B3 Pumanque Chile
164 B2 Pumasillo, Co mt. Peru
37 G3 Puma Yumco l. China
62 C2 Pumsaint *Wales* U.K.
170 D2 Puna Argentina
7 □11 Punaauia *French Polynesia* Pacific Ocean
162 A4 Puná, Isla i. Ecuador
37 G4 Punakha Bhutan
107 J3 Punat Croatia
164 C3 Punata Bolivia
36 C2 Punch India
136 E4 Punchaw *B.C.* Canada
37 G3 Püncogling China
131 H1 Punda Maria South Africa
36 D3 Pundri India
38 A2 Pune India
25 □ Punggol Singapore
31 J4 P'ungsan North Korea
129 E2 Púnguè r. Mozambique
80 B4 Puni r. Italy
124 E4 Punia Congo(Zaire)
33 G4 Puning China
172 B1 Punitaqui Chile
36 C3 Punjab India
36 B3 Punjab, The Pakistan
54 C1 Punkalaidun Finland
36 D2 Punmah Gl. gl. China/Jammu and Kashmir
164 B3 Puno Peru
77 M1 Puńsk Poland
108 C2 Punta Ala Italy
173 G5 Punta Alta Argentina

171 B7 Punta Arenas Chile
145 □3 Punta, Cerro de mt. Puerto Rico
172 C3 Punta del Agua Argentina
173 K3 Punta del Este Uruguay
171 D5 Punta Delgada Argentina
171 C7 Punta Delgada Chile
172 C2 Punta de Vacas Argentina
145 D7 Punta Gorda *Florida* U.S.A.
156 H5 Punta Gorda Belize
107 J4 Punta Križa Croatia
97 □ Puntallana *Canary Is* Spain
171 D5 Punta Norte Argentina
156 J7 Puntarenas Costa Rica
107 G3 Punta Sabbioni Italy
100 D3 Punta Umbría Spain
158 □1 Punt Basora pt *Aruba* Caribbean
158 □2 Punt Kanon pt *Curaçao* Netherlands Ant.
162 C1 Punto Fijo Venezuela
146 D4 Punxsutawney *Pennsylvania* U.S.A.
56 G2 Puokio Finland
56 G2 Puolanka Finland
33 F2 Puqi China
164 B2 Puquio Peru
170 C2 Puquios Chile
44 J3 Pur r. Rus. Fed.
39 D4 Pūr Iran
162 B3 Puracé, Parque Nacional nat. park Colombia
36 E3 Puranpur India
6 □1 Purari r. P.N.G.
81 H3 Purbach am Neusiedler See Austria
22 B3 Purbalingga Indonesia
151 D5 Purcell *Oklahoma* U.S.A.
136 F4 Purcell Mts mountain range *B.C.* Canada
37 E2 Pur Co l. China
52 F2 Purdoshki Rus. Fed.
172 A5 Purén Chile
153 G4 Purgatoire r. *Colorado* U.S.A.
81 G2 Purgstall an der Erlauf Austria
37 F6 Puri India
54 D2 Purita r. Estonia
81 H2 Purkersdorf Austria
68 C2 Purmerend Netherlands
36 D5 Purna r. *Maharashtra* India
36 D6 Purna r. *Maharashtra* India
37 F4 Pūrnia India
171 B5 Purranque Chile
102 B3 Purujosa Spain
22 C2 Purukcahu Indonesia
37 F5 Puruliya India
101 G3 Purullena Spain
163 E4 Purus r. Brazil
57 H3 Puruvesi l. Finland
112 E3 Pŭrvomay Bulgaria
22 A3 Purwakarta Indonesia
22 B3 Purwareja Indonesia
22 B3 Purwodadi Indonesia
22 B3 Purwoketto Indonesia
31 J4 Puryŏng North Korea
99 F5 Pusa r. Spain
54 E3 Puša Latvia
22 B1 Pusa Malaysia
38 B2 Pusad India
31 J6 Pusan South Korea
22 B1 Pusatdamai Indonesia
147 J2 Pushaw Lake l. *Maine* U.S.A.
53 D1 Pushcha-Vodytsya Ukraine
52 C2 Pushchino Rus. Fed.
50 H2 Pushemskiy Rus. Fed.
54 G2 Pushkin Rus. Fed.
Pushkino *see* Biläsuvar
51 H5 Pushkino Rus. Fed.
52 C1 Pushkino Rus. Fed.
54 F3 Pushkinskiye Gory Rus. Fed.
39 E3 Pusht-i-Rud reg. Afghanistan
83 E3 Pusiano, Lago di l. Italy
102 C2 Pusilibro mt. Spain
79 L4 Püspökladány Hungary
141 G2 Pusticamica, Lac l. *Québec* Canada
77 M6 Pustomyty Ukraine
54 F3 Pustoshka Rus. Fed.
77 M2 Puszcza Augustowska forest Poland
76 D3 Puszcza Natecka forest Poland
76 E3 Puszczykowo Poland
79 J5 Pusztaszer Hungary
172 B2 Putaendo Chile
89 E3 Putanges-Pont-Écrepin France
24 B1 Putao Myanmar
8 E3 Putaruru New Zealand
73 J1 Putbus Germany
33 G3 Putian China
111 G2 Putignano Italy
52 C3 Putimets Rus. Fed.
164 C2 Putina Peru
22 B2 Puting, Tg pt Indonesia
50 H3 Putilovo Rus. Fed.
157 F5 Putla Mexico
39 F3 Putla Khan Afghanistan
73 H2 Putlitz Germany
112 F2 Putna r. Romania
147 H4 Putnam *Connecticut* U.S.A.
147 G3 Putney *Vermont* U.S.A.
79 K3 Putnok Hungary
164 C3 Putre Chile
130 C4 Putsonderwater South Africa
38 B4 Puttalam Sri Lanka
38 B4 Puttalam Lagoon Sri Lanka
69 C3 Putte Belgium
69 C3 Putte Netherlands
87 F3 Puttelange-aux-Lacs France
68 D2 Putten Netherlands
73 G1 Puttgarden Germany
87 F3 Püttlingen Germany
172 A3 Putú Chile
162 C4 Putumayo r. Colombia/Peru
42 D2 Pütürge Turkey
22 C1 Putusibau Indonesia
52 E2 Putyatino Rus. Fed.
53 A3 Putyla Ukraine
53 E1 Putyvl' Ukraine
57 H3 Puumala Finland
69 C3 Puurs Belgium
153 □2 Puuwai *Hawaii* U.S.A.
138 E1 Puvurnituq *Québec* Canada
30 D5 Pu Xian China
152 B2 Puyallup *Washington* U.S.A.
31 E6 Puyang China
92 F3 Puy-de-Dôme div. France
92 E3 Puy de Dôme mt. France
93 D5 Puy de Faucher h. France
91 D4 Puy de la Gagère mt. France
92 E3 Puy de Sancy mt. France
172 A6 Puyehue Chile
172 A6 Puyehue, L. de l. Chile
172 A6 Puyehue, Parque Nacional nat. park Chile
172 A6 Puyehue, Vol. volcano Chile
93 E5 Puygouzon France
91 E3 Puy Gris mt. France
93 D4 Puylaroque France
93 E5 Puylaurens France
93 D4 Puy-L'Évêque France
92 E3 Puy Mary mt. France
93 C4 Puymirol France
162 B4 Puyo Ecuador
93 B5 Puyôo France
9 A7 Puysegur Pt pt New Zealand
50 K2 Puzla Rus. Fed.
127 C6 Pwani div. Tanzania
125 E5 Pweto Congo(Zaire)
62 B2 Pwllheli *Wales* U.K.
50 F1 Pyalitsa Rus. Fed.
50 E2 Pyal'ma Rus. Fed.
24 A3 Pyalo Myanmar
24 A4 Pyamalaw r. Myanmar
52 G2 P'yana r. Rus. Fed.
47 G5 Pyandzh r. Afghanistan/Tajikistan
50 D1 Pyaozero, Ozero l. Rus. Fed.
56 H2 Pyaozerskiy Rus. Fed.
24 A3 Pyapon Myanmar
44 K2 Pyasina r. Rus. Fed.
77 J1 Pyatidorozhnoye Rus. Fed.
51 G6 Pyatigorsk Rus. Fed.
53 C1 P"yatka Ukraine
53 G1 Pyatnitskoye Rus. Fed.
52 C2 Pyatovskiy Rus. Fed.
53 E2 P"yatykhatky Ukraine
24 B2 Pyawbwe Myanmar
24 A3 Pyè Myanmar
77 M3 Pyelishcha Belarus
9 B7 Pye, Mt h. New Zealand
77 O2 Pyershamayski Belarus
77 N2 Pyeski Belarus
51 D4 Pyetrykaw Belarus
54 C1 Pyhäjärvi l. Finland
56 G3 Pyhäjärvi Finland
56 G2 Pyhäjoki r. Finland
56 G2 Pyhäjoki Finland
54 E1 Pyhältö Finland
56 G2 Pyhäntä Finland
54 B1 Pyhäranta Finland
56 H3 Pyhäselkä l. Finland
81 F3 Pyhrnpaß pass Austria
24 A2 Pyingaing Myanmar
24 B3 Pyinmana Myanmar
62 C3 Pyle *Wales* U.K.
115 E4 Pyli *Stereá Ellás* Greece
114 C3 Pyli *Thessalia* Greece
44 K3 Pyl'karamo Rus. Fed.
115 C6 Pylos Greece
146 C4 Pymatuning Reservoir resr *Pennsylvania* U.S.A.
31 H5 Pyŏksŏng North Korea
31 H4 Pyŏktong North Korea
31 H5 P'yŏnggang North Korea
31 H5 P'yŏngsong North Korea
31 H5 P'yŏngt'aek South Korea
31 H5 P'yŏngyang North Korea
80 D3 Pyramidenspitze mt. Austria
13 F4 Pyramid Hill *Victoria* Australia
9 □1 Pyramid I. i. *Chatham Is* New Zealand
154 C1 Pyramid Lake l. *Nevada* U.S.A.
148 E3 Pyramid Pt pt *Michigan* U.S.A.
154 C2 Pyramid Range mts *Nevada* U.S.A.
93 A5 Pyrenees mountain range France
93 B5 Pyrénées-Atlantiques div. France
93 B6 Pyrénées Occidentales, Parc National des nat. park France/Spain
93 E6 Pyrénées-Orientales div. France
114 D3 Pyrgetos Greece
114 F1 Pyrgoi Greece
115 C5 Pyrgos *Dytiki Ellas* Greece
114 D2 Pyrgos *Kentriki Makedonia* Greece
115 G7 Pyrgos *Kriti* Greece
53 C1 Pyrizhky Ukraine
53 E2 Pyrohy Ukraine
53 E1 Pyryatyn Ukraine
76 C2 Pyrzyce Poland
50 H3 Pyshchug Rus. Fed.
46 F1 Pyshma r. Rus. Fed.
46 F1 Pyshma Rus. Fed.
76 G5 Pyskowice Poland
54 E3 Pytalovo Rus. Fed.
24 B3 Pyu Myanmar
114 E4 Pyxaria mt. Greece

Q

135 M2 Qaanaaq Greenland
43 D4 Qā 'Aẕamān Saudi Arabia
43 C3 Qabatiya Israel
37 H3 Qabnag China
131 G5 Qacha's Nek Lesotho
119 G3 Qaḑīmah Saudi Arabia
42 F3 Qādir Karam Iraq
42 E3 Qadissiya Dam dam Iraq
126 □ Qādub *Socotra* Yemen
43 D4 Qā'el Hafīra salt flat Jordan
43 D4 Qa'el Jinz salt flat Jordan
43 D4 Qa'el 'Umarī salt flat Jordan
114 A2 Qafa e Gllavës pass Albania
114 B2 Qafa e Zvezdës pass Albania
114 B2 Qafzez Albania
31 F2 Qagan China
30 C4 Qagan Ders China
31 H3 Qagan Nur l. China
30 E4 Qagan Nur l. *Nei Mongol Zizhiqu* China
31 E4 Qagan Nur resr China
30 A5 Qagan Nur China
30 D5 Qagan Nur China
30 E4 Qagan Nur China
31 F3 Qagan Qulut China
30 E4 Qagan Teg China
37 H2 Qagan Tohoi China
31 E4 Qagan Us China
37 H3 Qagbasêrag China
37 E2 Qagcaka China
Qagchêng *see* Xiangcheng
135 O3 Qagssimiut Greenland
30 E4 Qahar Youyi Qianqi China
30 E4 Qahar Youyi Zhongqi China
119 H2 Qahd, W. watercourse Saudi Arabia
119 H4 Qahr, Jibāl al h. Saudi Arabia
119 H3 Qaḩţān reg. Saudi Arabia
26 F4 Qaidam Pendi basin China
39 F1 Qaisar r. Afghanistan
39 F2 Qaisar Afghanistan
36 E1 Qakar China
43 D3 Qa Khanna reg. Jordan
131 G3 Qalabotjha South Africa
119 F5 Qala'en Nahl Sudan
47 H5 Qal'aikhum Tajikistan
126 □ Qalansīyah *Socotra* Yemen
39 F2 Qala Shinia Takht Afghanistan
39 F2 Qalāt Afghanistan
43 D2 Qal'at al Ḩiṣn Syria
43 D2 Qal'at al Ḩiṣn Syria
43 C2 Qal'at al Marqab Syria
119 G2 Qal'at al Mu'aẓẓam Saudi Arabia
42 E3 Qal'at as Sālihīyah Syria
43 C4 Qalat at Hasel Jordan
119 H3 Qal'at Bīshah Saudi Arabia
42 F4 Qal'at Sālih Iraq
39 E2 Qala Vali Afghanistan
39 A2 Qal'eh Safid Iran
39 E2 Qal 'eh-ve Now Afghanistan
39 F3 Qal 'eh-ye Bost Afghanistan
42 F4 Qalīb Bāqūr well Iraq
118 E4 Qalti Immaseri well Sudan
43 A4 Qalyûb Egypt
32 B1 Qamalung China
131 F5 Qamata South Africa
36 B4 Qambar Pakistan
32 B2 Qamdo China
6 □6 Qamea i. Fiji
119 H4 Qam Hadīl Saudi Arabia
118 C1 Qamīnis Libya
36 B3 Qamruddin Karez Pakistan
39 B2 Qamşar Iran
126 E2 Qandala Somalia
31 E4 Qangdin Sum China
39 C1 Qapan Iran
47 K4 Qapqal China
118 E2 Qara Egypt
43 C3 Qaraaoun Lebanon
42 F2 Qarabağ div. Azerbaijan
39 B2 Qara Chai r. Iran
39 G2 Qarah Bāgh Afghanistan
118 C2 Qarārat an Nā'ikah depression Libya
126 E3 Qardho Somalia
42 F3 Qareh Su r. Iran
37 H1 Qarhan China
Qarkilik *see* Ruoqiang
43 B5 Qarn el Kabsh, G. mt. Egypt
Qarqan *see* Qiemo
39 F1 Qarqīn Afghanistan
43 C2 Qartaba Lebanon
42 F4 Qaryat al Gharab Iraq
39 A4 Qaryat al Ulyā Saudi Arabia
39 A4 Qaryat as Sufla Saudi Arabia
39 D2 Qasamī Iran
39 E2 Qasa Murg mountain range Afghanistan
39 D2 Qāsemābād Iran
43 D5 Qa 'Sharawrā' salt pan Saudi Arabia
39 B3 Qash Qai reg. Iran
135 N3 Qasigiannguit Greenland
119 H2 Qasīm reg. Saudi Arabia
43 D2 Qasr al Ḩayr Syria
42 E3 Qasr al Khubbāz Iraq
42 G4 Qaşr aş Şabīyah Kuwait
42 D4 Qasr el Azraq Jordan
42 D3 Qasr el Burqu Jordan
43 D4 Qasr el Kharana Jordan
39 E4 Qaşr-e-Qand Iran
119 E2 Qasr Farafra Egypt
118 B1 Qasr Khiyār Libya
118 B2 Qaşr Larocu Libya
126 D2 Qa'tabah Yemen
43 D4 Qatafa, W. watercourse Jordan
42 D3 Qaţanā Syria
18 G8 Qatar country Asia
39 D1 Qatlish Iran
43 D1 Qaţma Syria
47 H5 Qatorkŭhi Darvoz mountain range Tajikistan
47 H5 Qatorkŭhi Yazgulom mountain range Tajikistan
47 G5 Qatorkŭhi Zarafshon mountain range Tajikistan
42 D4 Qatrāna Jordan
43 A5 Qaţrâni, Gebel escarpment Egypt
119 E2 Qattâra Depression depression Egypt
119 G2 Qā', W. al watercourse Saudi Arabia
42 F1 Qax Azerbaijan
39 D2 Qāyen Iran
42 E3 Qayyarah Iraq
42 F2 Qazangöldag mt. Armenia
42 F1 Qazax Azerbaijan
36 B4 Qazi Ahmad Pakistan
42 G1 Qazımämmäd Azerbaijan
39 B1 Qazvīn Iran
30 B4 Qeh China
6 □6 Qeleni Fiji
30 E3 Qelin Ul China
119 F2 Qena Egypt
114 A2 Qeparo Albania
135 N3 Qeqertarsuatsiaat Greenland
135 N3 Qeqertarsuatsiaq i. Greenland
135 N3 Qeqertarsuup Tunua b. Greenland
39 C4 Qeshm i. Iran
39 D4 Qeshm Iran
39 B1 Qeydār Iran
39 C4 Qeys i. Iran
42 G2 Qezel Owzan r. Iran
43 C4 Qeẕi'ot Israel
32 D1 Qian r. China
31 F5 Qian'an China
31 H3 Qian'an China
33 E3 Qiancheng China
33 G1 Qiang r. China
31 H3 Qian Gorlos China
33 F2 Qianjiang China
32 E2 Qianjiang China
31 K3 Qianjin China
32 C2 Qianning China
31 G3 Qianqihao China
31 G4 Qian Shan mountain range China
47 K4 Qianshanlaoba China
31 F4 Qianxi China
32 D3 Qianxi China
32 E1 Qian Xian China
32 D1 Qianyang China
33 E3 Qianyang China
33 G2 Qianyang China
30 E5 Qiaocun China
32 C3 Qiaojia China
131 F4 Qibing South Africa
33 H2 Qidong China
33 F3 Qidong China
32 A1 Qidukou China
26 E4 Qiemo China
31 F5 Qihe China
32 D2 Qijiang China
34 H2 Qijiaojing China
39 E4 Qila Ladgasht Pakistan
31 F4 Qilaotu Shan mountain range China
39 E3 Qila Safed Pakistan
36 B3 Qila Saifullah Pakistan
30 B5 Qilian China
30 A5 Qilian Shan mountain range China
30 A5 Qilian Shan mt. China
135 P3 Qillak i. Greenland
33 G2 Qimen China
30 E6 Qin r. China
32 D1 Qin'an China
33 E2 Qing r. China
31 H4 Qing r. China
31 H3 Qing'an China
31 G4 Qingchengzi China
32 D1 Qingchuan China
31 G5 Qingdao China
31 H3 Qinggang China
30 A5 Qinghai div. China
34 K3 Qinghai Hu salt lake China
30 A5 Qinghai Nanshan mountain range China
30 D5 Qingjian China
33 F2 Qingjiang China
33 G1 Qingjiang China
33 G3 Qingliu China
31 F5 Qinglong r. China
31 F4 Qinglong China
32 D3 Qinglong China
33 E4 Qingping China
33 H2 Qingpu China
30 B5 Qingshizui China
32 D1 Qingshui China
30 A5 Qingshui China
30 D5 Qingshuihe China
32 B1 Qingshuihe China
47 K4 Qingshuihezi China
33 H2 Qingtian China
31 F5 Qing Xian China
30 E5 Qingxu China
30 C5 Qingyang China
33 G2 Qingyang China
33 G3 Qingyuan China
33 F4 Qingyuan China
31 H4 Qingyuan China
31 F5 Qinhuangdao China
32 D1 Qin Ling mountain range China
30 E6 Qinshui China
30 C5 Qintongxia China
30 E5 Qin Xian China
33 F1 Qinyang China
30 E5 Qinyuan China
32 E4 Qinzhou China
32 E4 Qinzhou Wan b. China
33 E5 Qionghai China
32 C2 Qionglai China
32 C2 Qionglai Shan mountain range China
33 E5 Qiongshan China
33 E5 Qiongzhong China
33 E4 Qiongzhou Haixia China
32 D1 Qipan Guan pass China
31 G1 Qiqian China
31 G3 Qiqihar China
39 C3 Qīr Iran
36 E1 Qira China
43 C4 Qiryat Gat Israel
32 E4 Qisha China
43 C3 Qishon r. Israel
119 G3 Qishrān I. i. Saudi Arabia
43 D4 Qitab ash Shāmah crater Saudi Arabia
31 J3 Qitaihe China
32 D3 Qiubei China
33 F2 Qiujin China
31 G5 Qixia China
30 E6 Qi Xian China
30 E5 Qi Xian China
31 K3 Qixing r. China
33 E3 Qiyang China
30 C5 Qiying China
33 E5 Qizhou Liedao China
Qogir Feng mt. *see* K2, Mt
30 C4 Qog Qi China
39 A1 Qojūr Iran
39 B2 Qom Iran
32 A2 Qomdo China
39 B2 Qomishēh Iran
Qomolangma Feng mt. *see* Everest, Mt
37 G3 Qonggyai China
30 D4 Qongi China
126 F2 Qoor Hurdiyo b. Somalia
126 E3 Qooriga Neegro b. Somalia
Qoqek *see* Tacheng
111 □ Qormi Malta
43 D2 Qornet es Saouda mt. Lebanon
39 A2 Qorveh Iran
126 E3 Qoryale Somalia
42 E2 Qosh Tepe Iraq
39 D4 Qoţbābād Iran
42 F2 Qotūr Iran
32 D2 Qu r. China
147 G3 Quabbin Reservoir resr *Massachusetts* U.S.A.
130 C5 Quaggasfontein Poort pass South Africa
154 D4 Quail Mts mts *California* U.S.A.
17 B7 Quairading *Western Australia* Australia
72 C3 Quakenbrück Germany
147 F4 Quakertown *Pennsylvania* U.S.A.
137 K2 Quamarirjunq Lake l. *N.W.T.* Canada
13 F2 Quambone *New South Wales* Australia
14 E4 Quamby *Queensland* Australia
151 D5 Quanah *Texas* U.S.A.
33 E1 Quanbao Shan mt. China
25 E4 Quang Ngai Vietnam
24 D3 Quang Tri Vietnam
24 D2 Quang Yen Vietnam
33 F3 Quannan China
62 C3 Quantock Hills h. *England* U.K.
33 E3 Quanzhou China
33 G3 Quanzhou China
137 J4 Qu'Appelle r. *Saskatchewan* Canada
137 J4 Qu'Appelle *Saskatchewan* Canada
135 M3 Quaqtaq *Québec* Canada
173 J1 Quaraí Brazil
125 C6 Quarenta Angola
83 D3 Quarona Italy
90 B1 Quarré-les-Tombes France
27 □ Quarry Bay *Hong Kong* China
100 B3 Quarteira Portugal
83 E1 Quarten Switzerland
108 B5 Quartu Sant'Elena *Sardegna* Italy
154 D3 Quartzite Mt mt. *Nevada* U.S.A.
155 E5 Quartzsite *Arizona* U.S.A.
127 □4 Quatre Bornes Mauritius
86 D3 Quatre-Champs France
103 C6 Quatretonda Spain
136 D4 Quatsino Sound inlet Canada
42 G1 Quba Azerbaijan
39 D1 Quchan Iran
13 G3 Queanbeyan *New South Wales* Australia
141 G3 Québec div. Canada
141 K3 Québec *Québec* Canada
168 E3 Quebra Anzol r. Brazil
173 J1 Quebracho Uruguay
170 D2 Quebracho Coto Argentina
162 D1 Quebrada del Toro, Parque Nacional de la nat. park Venezuela
145 □3 Quebradillas Puerto Rico
171 B5 Quedal, C. pt Chile
168 B6 Quedas do Iguaçu Brazil
73 G4 Quedlinburg Germany
136 E4 Queen Bess, Mt mt. *B.C.* Canada
63 G3 Queenborough *England* U.K.
136 C4 Queen Charlotte *B.C.* Canada
171 D7 Queen Charlotte B. b. Falkland Is.
136 C4 Queen Charlotte Islands is *B.C.* Canada
9 E4 Queen Charlotte Sd chan. New Zealand
136 D4 Queen Charlotte Sound chan. Canada
136 D4 Queen Charlotte Str. chan. *B.C.* Canada
134 H2 Queen Elizabeth Islands is *N.W.T.* Canada
127 B5 Queen Elizabeth National Park nat. park Uganda
179 C5 Queen Mary Land reg. Antarctica
128 □3 Queen Mary's Peak mt. *Tristan da Cunha* Atlantic Ocean
134 H3 Queen Maud Gulf b. *N.W.T.* Canada
Queen Maud Land reg. *see* Dronning Maud Land
179 B4 Queen Maud Mts mts Antarctica
131 H4 Queensburgh South Africa
135 J2 Queens Chan. chan. *N.W.T.* Canada
14 B2 Queens Channel chan. *Northern Terr.* Australia
13 F4 Queenscliff *Victoria* Australia
15 F4 Queensland div. Australia
147 E5 Queenstown *Maryland* U.S.A.
13 F5 Queenstown *Tasmania* Australia
9 B6 Queenstown New Zealand
25 □ Queenstown Singapore
131 F5 Queenstown South Africa
152 A2 Queets *Washington* U.S.A.
173 J2 Queguay Grande r. Uruguay
131 J2 Queguele Mozambique
172 E4 Quehué Argentina
82 B3 Queige France
99 G1 Queijo, Cabo pt Spain
171 B5 Queilén Chile
166 E3 Queimadas Brazil
125 C5 Quela Angola
89 E4 Quelaines-St-Gault France
129 F2 Quelimane Mozambique
172 A4 Quella Chile
171 B5 Quellón Chile
Quelpart I. i. *see* Cheju Do
100 A2 Queluz *Lisboa* Portugal
99 G3 Quemada Spain
155 H4 Quemado *New Mexico* U.S.A.
125 C6 Quembo r. Angola
171 B5 Quemchi Chile
Quemoy *see* Chinmen
172 F4 Quemú-Quemú Argentina
86 A2 Quend France
172 A5 Quepe r. Chile
173 H5 Quequén Grande r. Argentina
102 F2 Queralbs Spain
93 D4 Quercy reg. France
168 B5 Querência do Norte Brazil
157 F4 Querétaro div. Mexico
157 E4 Querétaro Mexico
73 G4 Querfurt Germany
93 E6 Quérigut France
80 C5 Quero Italy
101 G1 Quero Spain
156 C2 Querobabi Mexico
89 H2 Querrieu France
82 B1 Quers France
101 G3 Quesada Spain
120 B3 Quesat watercourse *Western Sahara*
33 F1 Queshan China
136 E4 Quesnel r. *B.C.* Canada
136 E4 Quesnel *B.C.* Canada
136 E4 Quesnel L. l. *B.C.* Canada
86 C2 Quesnoy-sur-Deûle France
88 C3 Quessoy France
86 C3 Quessy France
88 C4 Questembert France
148 B1 Quetico Provincial Park res. *Ontario* Canada
36 A3 Quetta Pakistan
88 D2 Quettehou France
172 B4 Queuco Chile
171 B5 Queulat, Parque Nacional nat. park Chile
172 A5 Queule Chile
86 B3 Quevauvillers France
162 B4 Quevedo Ecuador
88 B4 Quéven France
141 G2 Quévillon, Lac l. *Québec* Canada
157 H6 Quezaltenango Guatemala
23 A4 Quezon Philippines
23 B3 Quezon City Philippines
126 D1 Quflat al 'Udhr Yemen
31 F6 Qufu China
125 B6 Quibala Angola
125 B5 Quibaxe Angola
162 B2 Quibdó Colombia
88 B4 Quiberon France
88 B4 Quiberon, Baie de b. France
88 B4 Quiberon, Presqu'île de pen. France
125 B5 Quiçama, Parque Nacional do nat. park Angola
24 D3 Qui Châu Vietnam
72 E2 Quickborn Germany
125 C5 Quiculungo Angola
172 A5 Quidico Chile
172 A5 Quidico, C. c. Chile
87 G3 Quierschied Germany
69 B5 Quierzy France
69 B4 Quiévrain Belgium
165 E5 Quiindy Paraguay
155 F5 Quijotoa *Arizona* U.S.A.
171 B5 Quilán, C. c. Chile
173 G4 Quilco Argentina
125 B6 Quilengues Angola
172 B2 Quilimarí Chile
172 E1 Quilino Argentina
164 B2 Quillabamba Peru
164 C3 Quillacollo Bolivia
164 C4 Quillagua Chile
47 G5 Quillai Chimtargha mt. Tajikistan
93 E6 Quillan France
89 F2 Quillebeuf-sur-Seine France
137 J4 Quill Lakes lakes *Saskatchewan* Canada
172 A4 Quillon Chile
172 B2 Quillota Chile
173 H3 Quilmes Argentina
170 C2 Quilmes, Sa del mountain range Argentina
38 B4 Quilon India
15 F5 Quilpie *Queensland* Australia
172 B2 Quilpué Chile
129 F2 Quilua Mozambique
125 C5 Quimbele Angola
170 D2 Quimilí Argentina
88 A3 Quimper France
88 B4 Quimperlé France
164 B2 Quince Mil Peru
106 B3 Quincinetto Italy
154 B2 Quincy *California* U.S.A.
145 C6 Quincy *Florida* U.S.A.
148 B6 Quincy *Illinois* U.S.A.
147 H3 Quincy *Massachusetts* U.S.A.
86 B4 Quincy-Voisins France
172 E2 Quines Argentina
88 D2 Quinéville France
129 G2 Quinga Mozambique
90 D1 Quingey France
122 A4 Quinhámel Guinea-Bissau
25 E4 Qui Nhơn Vietnam
173 G4 Quiñihual Argentina
155 E3 Quinn Canyon Range mts *Nevada* U.S.A.
91 E5 Quinson France
92 E2 Quinssaines France
168 C5 Quintana Brazil
100 E2 Quintana de la Serena Spain
98 D2 Quintana del Castillo Spain
99 G2 Quintana del Pino Spain
99 F2 Quintana del Puente Spain
99 G2 Quintana-Martín Galíndez Spain
101 G1 Quintanar de la Orden Spain
103 B5 Quintanar del Rey Spain
99 H3 Quintana Redonda Spain
157 H5 Quintana Roo div. Mexico
98 D3 Quintanilha Portugal
99 F3 Quintanilla de Omesimo Spain
172 B2 Quintay Chile
172 B2 Quintero Chile
88 C3 Quintin France
172 E3 Quinto r. Argentina
102 C3 Quinto Spain
106 E3 Quinzano d'Oglio Italy
125 B5 Quinzau Angola
127 D7 Quionga Mozambique
125 B6 Quipungo Angola
172 A4 Quirihue Chile
125 C6 Quirima Angola
127 D7 Quirimba, Ilha i. Mozambique
13 G2 Quirindi *New South Wales* Australia
168 C3 Quirinópolis Brazil
173 G3 Quiroga Argentina
164 C3 Quiroga Bolivia
98 C2 Quiroga Spain
173 L2 Quiroga, Punta pt Uruguay
91 C5 Quissac France
127 D7 Quissanga Mozambique
129 E3 Quissico Mozambique
125 C6 Quitapa Angola
158 B4 Quita Sueño Bank sea feature Colombia
168 C3 Quitéria r. Brazil
125 C7 Quiteve Angola
145 D6 Quitman *Georgia* U.S.A.
145 B5 Quitman *Mississippi* U.S.A.
162 B4 Quito Ecuador
153 D6 Quitovac Mexico
155 F4 Quivero *Arizona* U.S.A.
166 E1 Quixadá Brazil
166 E2 Quixeramobim Brazil
33 F3 Qujiang China
33 E4 Qujie China
32 C3 Qujing China
114 B1 Qukës Albania
47 H5 Qullai Garmo mt. Tajikistan
32 A1 Qumar r. China
32 A1 Qumarlêb China
37 H2 Qumarrabdün China
37 H2 Qumaryan China
131 G5 Qumbu South Africa
32 B2 Qu'nyido China
137 L2 Quoich r. *N.W.T.* Canada
66 C3 Quoich, Loch l. *Scotland* U.K.
14 B2 Quoin I. i. *Northern Terr.* Australia
130 B7 Quoin Pt pt South Africa
37 E2 Quong Muztag mt. China
12 D3 Quorn *S. Australia* Australia
128 C3 Quoxo r. Botswana
Quqên *see* Jinchuan
43 D5 Qurayyah Saudi Arabia
47 G5 Qŭrghonteppa Tajikistan
139 G2 Qurlurtuq r. *Québec* Canada
Qurlurtuuq *see* Coppermine
42 G1 Qusar Azerbaijan
119 F2 Quseir Egypt
42 F2 Qūshchi Iran
33 E2 Qutang Xia r. China
131 F5 Quthing r. Lesotho
39 B2 Qūtīābād Iran
119 H2 Quţn, J. h. Saudi Arabia
119 H4 Qutū' I. i. Saudi Arabia
43 D1 Quwayq r. Syria
30 C5 Quwu Shan mountain range China
Qu Xian *see* Quzhou
32 D2 Qu Xian China
37 G3 Qüxü China
24 D3 Quynh Luu Vietnam
24 C2 Quynh Nhai Vietnam
141 G4 Quyon *Québec* Canada
33 G2 Quzhou China
31 E5 Quzhou China
51 H7 Qvareli Georgia
Qyteti Stalin *see* Kuçovë

R

81 H4 Raab r. Austria
81 E2 Raab Austria
81 G2 Raabs an der Thaya Austria
56 G2 Raahe Finland
56 H3 Rääkkylä Finland
68 E2 Raalte Netherlands
68 C3 Raamsdonksveer Netherlands
56 G2 Raanujärvi Finland
22 C3 Raas i. Indonesia
126 E2 Raas Aantaara pt Somalia
66 B3 Raasay i. *Scotland* U.K.
66 B3 Raasay, Sound of chan. *Scotland* U.K.
126 F2 Raas Binna pt Somalia
126 E3 Raas Cabaad pt Somalia
126 E2 Raas Cadcadde pt Somalia
126 F2 Raas Caluula pt Somalia
126 F2 Raas Caseyr c. Somalia
126 F3 Raas Durdura pt Somalia
126 F3 Raas Gabbac pt Somalia
126 E3 Raas Ilig pt Somalia
127 D5 Raas Kaambooni pt Somalia
126 E2 Raas Khansiir pt Somalia
126 F3 Raas Macbar pt Somalia
126 D2 Raas Maskan pt Somalia
127 D5 Raas Matooni pt Somalia
126 E2 Raas Surud pt Somalia
126 F2 Raas Xaafuun pt Somalia
126 E2 Raas Xatiib pt Somalia
126 F3 Raas Xoor pt Somalia
107 J4 Rab i. Croatia
107 J4 Rab Croatia
78 F4 Rába r. Hungary
77 J5 Raba r. Poland
22 D4 Raba Indonesia
107 J3 Rabac Croatia
98 C3 Rabaçal r. Portugal/Spain
98 C1 Rábade Spain
79 M5 Răbăgani Romania
81 H3 Rábahidvég Hungary
119 F5 Rabak Sudan
36 E2 Rabang China
81 H3 Rábapaty Hungary
93 D5 Rabastens France
93 C5 Rabastens-de-Bigorre France
111 □ Rabat Malta
120 C2 Rabat Morocco
39 D2 Rabāt-e Kamah Iran
6 □1 Rabaul P.N.G.
58 D2 Rabbalshede Sweden
107 F4 Rabbi r. Italy
136 D3 Rabbit r. *B.C.* Canada
78 G4 Rábca r. Hungary
79 K5 Rabe Yugoslavia
81 G2 Rabenstein an der Pielach Austria
6 □6 Rabi i. Fiji
119 G3 Rābigh Saudi Arabia
76 D2 Rąbino Poland
83 E2 Rabiusa r. Switzerland
77 H6 Rabka Poland
Rabkob *see* Dharmjaygarh
37 G5 Rabnabad Is. is Bangladesh
53 C3 Râbniţa Moldova
50 E1 Rabocheostrovsk Rus. Fed.
39 D3 Rābor Iran
52 G1 Rabotki Rus. Fed.
118 D3 Rabyānah oasis Libya
111 H3 Racale Italy
79 H4 Rácalmás Hungary
110 C5 Racalmuto *Sicilia* Italy
81 E4 Raccolana r. Italy
106 B4 Racconigi Italy
146 B5 Raccoon Creek r. *Ohio* U.S.A.
81 G4 Rače Slovenia

139 K4 **Race, C.** c. *Newfoundland* Canada
147 H3 **Race Pt** pt *Massachusetts* U.S.A.
151 D7 **Rachal** *Texas* U.S.A.
155 E3 **Rachel** *Nevada* U.S.A.
52 C1 **Rachevo** Rus. Fed.
25 D5 **Rach Gia** Vietnam
77 J3 **Raciąż** Poland
76 G5 **Racibórz** Poland
73 K2 **Racimierz** Poland
148 D4 **Racine** *Wisconsin* U.S.A.
140 D2 **Racine Lake** l. *Ontario* Canada
79 H4 **Ráckeve** Hungary
148 E2 **Raco** *Michigan* U.S.A.
112 E1 **Racoș** Romania
77 L2 **Raczki** Poland
59 E1 **Råda** Sweden
126 D2 **Radā'** Yemen
54 E4 **Radashkovichy** Belarus
112 E1 **Rădăuți** Romania
78 C2 **Radbuza** r. Czech Rep.
52 C1 **Radchenko** Rus. Fed.
144 C4 **Radcliff** *Kentucky* U.S.A.
31 J2 **Radde** Rus. Fed.
110 D5 **Raddusa** *Sicilia* Italy
58 D2 **Rade** Norway
73 J4 **Radeberg** Germany
73 J4 **Radebeul** Germany
73 J4 **Radeburg** Germany
81 G4 **Radeče** Slovenia
91 E5 **Rade d'Hyères** harbour France
53 A1 **Radekhiv** Ukraine
81 H4 **Radenci** Slovenia
81 E4 **Radenthein** Austria
72 C4 **Radevormwald** Germany
76 E1 **Radew** r. Poland
146 C6 **Radford** *Virginia* U.S.A.
36 B5 **Radhanpur** India
107 F5 **Radicondoli** Italy
52 H4 **Radishchevo** Rus. Fed.
138 E3 **Radisson** *Québec* Canada
52 B3 **Raditsa-Krylovka** Rus. Fed.
131 G2 **Radium** South Africa
136 F4 **Radium Hot Springs** *B.C.* Canada
81 G4 **Radizelj** Slovenia
53 G1 **Rad'kovka** Rus. Fed.
76 E5 **Radków** Poland
81 G4 **Radlje ob Dravi** Slovenia
112 E3 **Radnevo** Bulgaria
78 C2 **Radnice** Czech Rep.
162 B3 **Rado de Tumaco** inlet Colombia
74 D5 **Radolfzell am Bodensee** Germany
77 K4 **Radom** div. Poland
77 K4 **Radom** Poland
124 D2 **Radom** Sudan
77 H2 **Radomin** Poland
114 E1 **Radomir** mt. Bulgaria/Greece
112 D3 **Radomir** Bulgaria
53 E1 **Radomka** Ukraine
124 D2 **Radom National Park** nat. park Sudan
77 H4 **Radomsko** Poland
53 C1 **Radomyshl'** Ukraine
77 K5 **Radomyśl Wielki** Poland
75 J2 **Radonice** Czech Rep.
77 J4 **Radoszyce** Poland
76 D3 **Radoszyn** Poland
112 F4 **Radovets** Bulgaria
112 D4 **Radoviš** Macedonia
52 D2 **Radovitskiy** Rus. Fed.
81 F4 **Radovljica** Slovenia
76 D2 **Radowo Małe** Poland
58 A1 **Radøy** i. Norway
81 E3 **Radstadt** Austria
80 E3 **Radstädter Tauern** mts Austria
81 E3 **Radstädter Tauern** pass Austria
62 D3 **Radstock** *England* U.K.
12 C3 **Radstock, C.** headland *S. Australia* Australia
112 F1 **Răducăneni** Romania
53 D1 **Radul'** Ukraine
77 N1 **Radun'** Belarus
53 E3 **Radushne** Ukraine
54 C4 **Radviliškis** Lithuania
119 G3 **Raḍwá, J.** mt. Saudi Arabia
76 D4 **Radwanice** Poland
77 L6 **Radymno** Poland
53 A1 **Radyvyliv** *Rivne* Ukraine
53 C1 **Radyvyliv** *Zhytomyr* Ukraine
77 J3 **Radzanów** Poland
77 J4 **Radzice Duże** Poland
76 G3 **Radziejów** Poland
73 K3 **Radzików** Poland
77 L2 **Radziłów** Poland
77 K3 **Radzymin** Poland
76 G2 **Radzyń Chełminski** Poland
77 L4 **Radzyń Podlaski** Poland
36 E4 **Rae Bareli** India
136 F2 **Rae-Edzo** *N.W.T.* Canada
7 □10 **Raeffsky, Îles** is *French Polynesia* Pacific Ocean
136 F2 **Rae Lakes** *N.W.T.* Canada
69 E4 **Raeren** Belgium
72 B4 **Raesfeld** Germany
17 C6 **Raeside, Lake** salt flat *Western Australia* Australia
8 E3 **Raetihi** New Zealand
119 G2 **Rāf** h. Saudi Arabia
173 G1 **Rafaela** Argentina
173 G3 **Rafael Obligado** Argentina
43 C4 **Rafah** *Gaza*
124 D3 **Rafaï** Central African Rep.
53 B1 **Rafalivka** Ukraine
110 C5 **Raffadali** *Sicilia* Italy
66 E3 **Rafford** *Scotland* U.K.
119 H2 **Rafḥā** Saudi Arabia
115 F4 **Rafina** Greece
59 E1 **Råforsen** Sweden
39 D3 **Rafsanjān** Iran
124 E2 **Raga** Sudan
124 D1 **Ragag** Sudan
54 D3 **Ragana** Latvia
23 C5 **Ragang, Mt** volcano Philippines
23 B3 **Ragay Gulf** b. Philippines
73 H2 **Rägelin** Germany
147 J3 **Ragged I.** i. *Maine* U.S.A.
158 D2 **Ragged I.** i. The Bahamas
17 C7 **Ragged, Mt** h. *Western Australia* Australia
159 □9 **Ragged Pt** pt *Barbados* Caribbean
36 D4 **Rāghogarh** India
126 D1 **Raghwān, W.** watercourse Yemen
62 D3 **Raglan** *Wales* U.K.
8 E2 **Raglan** New Zealand
73 H3 **Ragösen** Germany
73 H4 **Raguhn** Germany
110 D6 **Ragusa** div. *Sicilia* Italy
110 D6 **Ragusa** *Sicilia* Italy
32 C1 **Ra'gyagoinba** China
21 H7 **Raha** Indonesia
95 K1 **Rahachow** Belarus
119 G5 **Rahad** r. Sudan
118 D4 **Rahad Wahal** well Sudan
Rahaeng *see* **Tak**
72 D3 **Rahden** Germany
42 E3 **Raḥḥālīyah** Iraq
38 A2 **Rahimatpur** India
36 B3 **Rahimyar Khan** Pakistan
90 E1 **Rahin** r. France
39 B2 **Rāhjerd** Iran
8 D3 **Rahotu** New Zealand
172 B5 **Rahue** Argentina
38 A2 **Rahuri** India
39 E2 **Rahzanak** Afghanistan
7 □10 **Raiatea** i. *French Polynesia* Pacific Ocean
Raibu i. *see* **Air**
38 B2 **Raichur** India
37 G4 **Raiganj** India
37 E5 **Raigarh** India
6 □3 **Raihifahifa** i. Tonga
155 E2 **Railroad Valley** v. *Nevada* U.S.A.
37 G5 **Raimangal** r. Bangladesh
139 G3 **Raimbault, Lac** l. *Québec* Canada
75 F4 **Rain** Germany
81 F2 **Rainbach im Mühlkreis** Austria
155 G3 **Rainbow Bridge Nat. Mon.** nat. park *Utah* U.S.A.
136 F3 **Rainbow Lake** *Alberta* Canada
15 F1 **Raine Entrance** chan. *Queensland* Australia
15 E1 **Raine I.** i. *Queensland* Australia
146 C6 **Rainelle** *W. Virginia* U.S.A.
152 B2 **Rainier, Mt** volcano *Washington* U.S.A.
36 B4 **Raini N.** r. Pakistan
138 B4 **Rainy** r. *Minnesota* U.S.A.
143 H2 **Rainy Lake** l. Canada/U.S.A.
138 B4 **Rainy River** *Ontario* Canada
36 C4 **Raipur** India
37 E5 **Raipur** India
37 F5 **Rairangpur** India
72 F1 **Raisdorf** Germany
36 D5 **Raisen** India
36 C3 **Raisinghnagar** India
57 F3 **Raisio** Finland
110 C4 **Raisi, Pta** pt *Sicilia* Italy
86 C2 **Raismes** France
80 C1 **Raitenbuch** Germany
177 K7 **Raivavae** i. *French Polynesia* Pacific Ocean
36 C3 **Raiwind** Pakistan
54 E2 **Raja** Estonia
22 A3 **Rajabasa, G.** volcano Indonesia
37 F5 **Rajagangapur** India
38 C2 **Rajahmundry** India
56 H1 **Raja-Jooseppi** Finland
36 D4 **Rajakhera** India
36 C4 **Rajaldesar** India
54 D1 **Rajamäki** Finland
38 B3 **Rajampet** India
22 C1 **Rajang** r. Malaysia
36 B3 **Rajanpur** Pakistan
38 B4 **Rajapalaiyam** India
38 A2 **Rajapur** India
36 C4 **Rajasthan** India
37 G5 **Rajbari** Bangladesh
79 H2 **Rajec** Slovakia
36 D4 **Rajgarh** India
36 C3 **Rajgarh** India
77 L2 **Rajgród** Poland
81 H1 **Rajhrad** Czech Rep.
78 F2 **Rajhradice** Czech Rep.
22 A2 **Rajik** Indonesia
37 E5 **Rajim** India
78 G3 **Rajka** Hungary
36 B5 **Rajkot** India
37 F4 **Rajmahal** India
37 F4 **Rajmahal Hills** h. India
36 E5 **Raj Nandgaon** India
36 C5 **Rajpipla** India
36 C4 **Rajsamand** India
37 G4 **Rajshahi** div. Bangladesh
37 G4 **Rajshahi** Bangladesh
38 B2 **Rajura** India
37 F3 **Raka** China
5 L5 **Rakahanga** atoll *Cook Islands* Pacific Ocean
127 B5 **Rakai** Uganda
9 C5 **Rakaia** r. New Zealand
39 B4 **Rakan, Ra's** pt Qatar
36 C1 **Rakaposhi** mt. Pakistan
37 G3 **Raka Zangbo** r. China
31 J5 **Rakdong** r. South Korea
81 F5 **Rakek** Slovenia
112 E1 **Rakhiv** Ukraine
53 E3 **Rakhmanivka** Ukraine
36 B3 **Rakhni** Pakistan
39 F4 **Rakhshan** r. Pakistan
6 □8 **Rakiraki** Fiji
22 B3 **Rakit** i. Indonesia
53 F1 **Rakitnoye** Rus. Fed.
54 E2 **Rakke** Estonia
58 D2 **Rakkestad** Norway
36 B3 **Rakni** r. Pakistan
76 F3 **Rakoniewice** Poland
79 M3 **Rakoshyn** Ukraine
78 C1 **Rakovník** Czech Rep.
112 E3 **Rakovski** Bulgaria
52 E3 **Raksha** Rus. Fed.
58 D1 **Rakskiftet** h. Norway
40 D3 **Rakusha** Kazakhstan
54 E2 **Rakvere** Estonia
145 E5 **Raleigh** *N. Carolina* U.S.A.
4 H4 **Ralik Chain** is Marshall Islands
74 B3 **Ralingen** Germany
22 D3 **Ralla** Indonesia
179 □ **Rallier du Baty, Péninsule** pen. *Kerguelen* Indian Ocean
148 D2 **Ralph** *Michigan* U.S.A.
136 E2 **Ram** r. *N.W.T.* Canada
43 C5 **Ram** Jordan
77 M5 **Rama** r. Ukraine
43 C3 **Rama** Israel
110 D5 **Ramacca** *Sicilia* Italy
164 C4 **Ramaditas** Chile
139 H2 **Ramah** *Newfoundland* Canada
155 H4 **Ramah** *New Mexico* U.S.A.
99 G1 **Ramales de la Victoria** Spain
173 G2 **Ramallo** Argentina
38 B3 **Ramanagaram** India
38 B4 **Ramanathapuram** India
37 E5 **Ramanuj Ganj** India
52 A3 **Ramasukha** Rus. Fed.
131 E2 **Ramatlabama** r. Botswana/South Africa
131 E2 **Ramatlabama** Botswana
87 F4 **Rambervillers** France
103 B6 **Rambla del Judío** r. Spain
103 B6 **Rambla del Moro** r. Spain
89 G3 **Rambouillet** France
69 D5 **Rambrouch** Luxembourg
87 E4 **Rambucourt** France
6 □1 **Rambutyo I.** i. P.N.G.
38 A3 **Ramdurg** India
37 F4 **Ramechhap** Nepal
62 B4 **Rame Head** headland *England* U.K.
131 G5 **Rame Head** pt South Africa
64 A2 **Ramelton** Rep. of Ireland
129 H1 **Ramena** Madagascar
52 D2 **Ramenki** Rus. Fed.
52 D2 **Ramenskoye** Rus. Fed.
52 C1 **Rameshki** Rus. Fed.
38 B4 **Rameswaram** India
36 D3 **Ramganga** r. India
37 G5 **Ramgarh** Bangladesh
36 B4 **Ramgarh** India
37 F5 **Ramgarh** India
39 G2 **Ramgul** reg. Afghanistan
39 B3 **Rāmhormoz** Iran
69 C4 **Ramillies** Belgium
81 E3 **Ramingstein** Austria
126 D3 **Ramis Shet'** r. Ethiopia
42 C4 **Ram, Jebel** mt. Jordan
43 C4 **Ramla** Israel
118 C3 **Ramlat al Wigh** sand dunes Libya
119 H4 **Ramlat Dahm** sand dunes Saudi Arabia/Yemen
118 D3 **Ramlat Rabyānah** desert Libya
55 A3 **Ramme** Denmark
87 G3 **Rammelsbach** Germany
80 B2 **Rammingen** Germany
131 F3 **Rammulotsi** South Africa
Ramnad *see* **Ramanathapuram**
36 C2 **Ramnagar** India
36 D3 **Ramnagar** India
59 G2 **Ramnäs** Sweden
112 F2 **Râmnicu Sărat** Romania
112 E2 **Râmnicu Vâlcea** Romania
52 D4 **Ramon'** Rus. Fed.
154 D5 **Ramona** *California* U.S.A.
82 B1 **Ramonchamp** France
173 K2 **Ramón Trigo** Uruguay
93 D5 **Ramonville-St-Agne** France
140 E2 **Ramore** *Ontario* Canada
67 D3 **Ramor, Lough** l. Rep. of Ireland
83 F2 **Ramosch** Switzerland
128 D3 **Ramotswa** Botswana
65 E3 **Rampside** *England* U.K.
36 D3 **Rampur** India
36 D3 **Rampur** India
36 D3 **Rampur** India
36 C4 **Rampura** India
Rampur Boalia *see* **Rajshahi**
37 F4 **Rampur Hat** India
24 A3 **Ramree** Myanmar
24 A3 **Ramree I.** i. Myanmar
59 F2 **Ramsberg** Sweden
63 F4 **Ramsbottom** *England* U.K.
56 E3 **Ramsele** Sweden
83 D1 **Ramsen** Switzerland
63 F2 **Ramsey** *England* U.K.
140 D3 **Ramsey** *Ontario* Canada
64 D3 **Ramsey** Isle of Man
64 D3 **Ramsey Bay** b. Isle of Man
62 A3 **Ramsey Island** i. *Wales* U.K.
140 D3 **Ramsey Lake** l. *Ontario* Canada
63 H3 **Ramsgate** *England* U.K.
37 G4 **Ramshai Hat** India
87 G3 **Ramstein** Germany
36 D5 **Ramtek** India
43 C4 **Ramtha** Jordan
6 □1 **Ramu** r. P.N.G.
159 □4 **Ramville, Îlet** i. *Martinique* Caribbean
54 D4 **Ramygala** Lithuania
52 F3 **Ramza** Rus. Fed.
98 D1 **Rañadoiro, Sierra de** mountain range Spain
37 G5 **Ranaghat** India
22 E4 **Ranakah, P.** mt. Indonesia
36 C5 **Ranapur** India
23 A5 **Ranau** Malaysia
22 A3 **Ranau, D.** l. Indonesia
172 B3 **Rancagua** Chile
88 C3 **Rance** r. *Bretagne* France
93 E5 **Rance** r. *Midi-Pyrénées* France
69 C4 **Rance** Belgium
168 C5 **Rancharia** Brazil
37 F5 **Ranchi** India
173 H3 **Ranchos** Argentina
172 A6 **Ranco, L. de** l. Chile
13 F3 **Rand** *New South Wales* Australia
67 E2 **Randalstown** *Northern Ireland* U.K.
90 B2 **Randan** France
110 D5 **Randazzo** *Sicilia* Italy
55 C3 **Randers** Denmark
55 C3 **Randers Fjord** inlet Denmark
147 H3 **Randolph** *Massachusetts* U.S.A.
147 G3 **Randolph** *Vermont* U.S.A.
73 K2 **Randow** r. Germany
58 D1 **Randsfjorden** l. Norway
56 D3 **Randsjö** Sweden
131 G3 **Randvaal** South Africa
56 F2 **Råneå** Sweden
122 B3 **Ranérou** Senegal
89 E3 **Ranes** France
9 C6 **Ranfurly** New Zealand
25 C6 **Rangae** Thailand
37 G4 **Rangamati** Bangladesh
37 H4 **Rangapara North** India
22 D2 **Rangas, Tg** pt Indonesia
22 D2 **Rangas, Tg** pt Indonesia
9 □1 **Rangatira I.** i. *Chatham Is* New Zealand
8 D1 **Rangaunu Bay** b. New Zealand
147 H2 **Rangeley** *Maine* U.S.A.
147 H2 **Rangeley Lake** l. *Maine* U.S.A.
155 H1 **Rangely** *Colorado* U.S.A.
140 D3 **Ranger Lake** *Ontario* Canada
37 G4 **Rangia Patharughat** India
9 D5 **Rangiora** New Zealand
8 F2 **Rangipoua** mt. New Zealand
7 □10 **Rangiroa** i. *French Polynesia* Pacific Ocean
8 F3 **Rangitaiki** r. New Zealand
9 C5 **Rangitata** r. New Zealand
8 E4 **Rangitikei** r. New Zealand
8 D4 **Rangitoto Is** is New Zealand
22 A3 **Rangkasbitung** Indonesia
47 H5 **Rangkŭl** Tajikistan
24 B3 **Rangoon** r. Myanmar
Rangoon *see* **Yangon**
37 G4 **Rangpur** Bangladesh
25 C7 **Rangsang** i. Indonesia
73 J3 **Rangsdorf** Germany
38 A3 **Ranibennur** India
37 F5 **Raniganj** India
37 E5 **Ranijula Pk** mt. India
36 D3 **Ranikhet** India
36 B4 **Ranipur** Pakistan
36 C4 **Raniwara** India
14 D4 **Ranken** watercourse *Northern Terr.* Australia
151 C6 **Rankin** *Texas* U.S.A.
137 L2 **Rankin Inlet** inlet *N.W.T.* Canada
137 L2 **Rankin Inlet** *N.W.T.* Canada
131 F2 **Rankin Pass** South Africa
13 F3 **Rankin's Springs** *New South Wales* Australia
80 A3 **Rankweil** Austria
54 E2 **Ranna** Estonia
15 G5 **Rannes** *Queensland* Australia
66 D4 **Rannoch, L.** l. *Scotland* U.K.
66 D4 **Rannoch Moor** moorland *Scotland* U.K.
36 B4 **Rann of Kachchh** marsh India
123 F4 **Rano** Nigeria
129 G2 **Ranobe** r. Madagascar
129 H3 **Ranohira** Madagascar
7 □16 **Rano Kito** h. *Easter I.* Chile
129 H3 **Ranomena** Madagascar
6 □2 **Ranon** Vanuatu
25 B5 **Ranong** Thailand
6 □1 **Ranongga** i. Solomon Is.
7 □16 **Rano Raraku** h. *Easter I.* Chile
25 C6 **Ranot** Thailand
52 D3 **Ranova** r. Rus. Fed.
172 C4 **Ranquilcó, S.** salt pan Argentina
172 C4 **Ranquil del Norte** Argentina
39 B2 **Rānsa** Iran
59 E1 **Ransby** Sweden
21 K7 **Ransiki** Indonesia
56 H3 **Rantasalmi** Finland
22 C2 **Rantau** Indonesia
22 C2 **Rantaupanjang** Indonesia
20 D6 **Rantauprapat** Indonesia
22 D2 **Rantemario, G.** mt. Indonesia
81 F3 **Ranten** Austria
22 D2 **Rantepao** Indonesia
148 C5 **Rantoul** *Illinois* U.S.A.
52 B1 **Rantsevo** Rus. Fed.
56 G2 **Rantsila** Finland
56 G2 **Ranua** Finland
172 A6 **Ranue** r. Chile
55 B3 **Ranum** Denmark
112 B4 **Ranxë** Albania
42 F2 **Rānya** Iraq
31 K3 **Raohe** China
87 F4 **Raon-l'Étape** France
33 G4 **Raoping** China
8 □4 **Raoul I.** i. *Kermadec Is* New Zealand
177 K7 **Rapa** i. *French Polynesia* Pacific Ocean
106 D4 **Rapallo** Italy
36 B5 **Rapar** India
39 D4 **Rapch** watercourse Iran
172 B2 **Rapel** r. Chile
172 B3 **Rapel, Emb.** resr Chile
67 D2 **Raphoe** Rep. of Ireland
146 E5 **Rapidan** r. *Virginia* U.S.A.
12 D3 **Rapid Bay** *S. Australia* Australia
150 C2 **Rapid City** *S. Dakota* U.S.A.
141 F3 **Rapide-Deux** *Québec* Canada
141 F3 **Rapide-Sept** *Québec* Canada
148 D3 **Rapid River** *Michigan* U.S.A.
54 E2 **Räpina** Estonia
54 D2 **Rapla** Estonia
109 H4 **Rapolla** Italy
100 B1 **Raposa** Portugal
146 E5 **Rappahannock** r. *Virginia* U.S.A.
22 D2 **Rappang** Indonesia
83 D1 **Rapperswil** Switzerland
81 G2 **Rappottenstein** Austria
37 E4 **Rapti** r. India
36 B5 **Rapur** India
23 C3 **Rapurapu** i. Philippines
147 F2 **Raquette** r. *New York* U.S.A.
147 F3 **Raquette Lake** l. *New York* U.S.A.
147 F3 **Raquette Lake** *New York* U.S.A.
129 F2 **Raraga** r. Mozambique
7 □10 **Raraka** i. *French Polynesia* Pacific Ocean
86 B3 **Raray** France
147 F4 **Raritan Bay** b. *New Jersey* U.S.A.
7 □10 **Raroia** atoll *French Polynesia* Pacific Ocean
82 C2 **Raron** Switzerland
177 J7 **Rarotonga** i. *Cook Islands* Pacific Ocean
119 G3 **Ra's Abū Madd** headland Saudi Arabia
119 G3 **Ras Abu Shagara** pt Sudan
120 A4 **Râs Agâdîr** pt Mauritania
42 A4 **Râs 'Alam el Rûm** c. Egypt
43 C2 **Ra's al Basīṭ** c. Syria
118 D1 **Ra's al Hilāl** pt Libya
126 D2 **Ra's al Kathīb** pt Yemen
39 C4 **Ra's al Khaymah** U.A.E.
118 E1 **Ra's al Muraysah** pt Libya
43 C5 **Ras al Qaṣbah** pt Saudi Arabia
173 F6 **Rasa, Pta** pt Argentina
119 H4 **Ra's aṭ Ṭarfā** pt Saudi Arabia
118 D1 **Ra's at Tīn** pt Libya
119 G3 **Râs Banâs** pt Egypt
119 G3 **Ra's Barīdī** headland Saudi Arabia
126 D2 **Ras Bir** pt Djibouti
43 B4 **Râs Burûn** pt Egypt
112 F1 **Râșca** Romania
99 G4 **Rascafría** Spain
53 B3 **Rășcani** Moldova
75 H2 **Raschau** Germany
126 C2 **Ras Dashen** mt. Ethiopia
43 B5 **Râs Dib** pt Egypt
54 C4 **Raseiniai** Lithuania
43 A4 **Râs el Barr** pt Egypt
43 B5 **Râs el Gineina** mt. Egypt
119 E1 **Râs el Kenâyis** pt Egypt
122 D3 **Râs el Mâ** Mali
43 C5 **Râs el Nafas** mt. Egypt
43 B5 **Râs el Sudr** pt Egypt
119 F2 **Râs Ghârib** Egypt
30 C3 **Rashaant** Mongolia
126 B2 **Rashad** Sudan
119 G3 **Râs Hadarba** pt Sudan
43 C4 **Rashādīya** Jordan
64 B3 **Rasharkin** *Northern Ireland* U.K.
119 G3 **Ra's Ḥāṭibah** pt Saudi Arabia
119 F1 **Rashîd** Egypt
39 F3 **Rashid Qala** Afghanistan
53 E1 **Rashivka** Ukraine
39 C2 **Rashm** Iran
39 B1 **Rasht** Iran
43 C2 **Ras Ibn Hāni'** pt Syria
81 F5 **Rašica** Slovenia
111 □ **Ras Id-Dawwara** pt Malta
111 □ **Ras il-Irqieqa** pt Malta
111 □ **Ras il-Dwejra** pt Malta
111 □ **Ras il-Qala** pt Malta
111 □ **Ras il-Qammieh** pt Malta
111 □ **Ras il-Wahx** pt Malta
111 □ **Ras il-Wardija** pt Malta
112 C3 **Rasina** r. Yugoslavia
99 G1 **Rasines** Spain
38 B4 **Rasipuram** India
111 □ **Ras ir-Raheb** pt Malta
126 D1 **Ra's 'Īsá** pt Yemen
39 E4 **Rāsk** Iran
112 C3 **Raška** Yugoslavia
47 J5 **Raskam** mountain range China
119 G4 **Ras Kasar** pt Sudan
126 □ **Ra's Kattānahan** pt *Socotra* Yemen
127 C6 **Ras Kizimkazi** pt Tanzania
39 F3 **Raskoh** mountain range Pakistan
36 A3 **Ras Koh** mt. Pakistan
118 C1 **Ra's Lānūf** pt Libya
43 B5 **Râs Mal'ab** pt Egypt
43 B5 **Râs Matarma** Egypt
127 C6 **Ras Mkumbi** pt Tanzania
126 □ **Ra's Momi** pt *Socotra* Yemen
119 F2 **Râs Muhammad** c. Egypt
135 J3 **Rasmussen Basin** b. *N.W.T.* Canada
120 A4 **Râs Nouâdhibou** c. *Western Sahara*
112 E2 **Râșnov** Romania
127 C6 **Ras Nungwi** pt Tanzania
171 C5 **Raso, C.** pt Argentina
166 E2 **Raso da Catarina** reg. Brazil
17 D6 **Rason L.** salt flat *Western Australia* Australia
54 F4 **Rasony** Belarus
42 A4 **Râs Qattâra** Egypt
102 D3 **Rasquera** Spain
37 E4 **Rasra** India
43 B5 **Râs Ruahmi** pt Egypt
121 G2 **Ras Ajdir** Tunisia
111 □ **Ras San Dimitri** pt Malta
126 D2 **Ras Shakhs** pt Eritrea
126 □ **Ra's Shu'ab** pt *Socotra* Yemen
43 B5 **Râs Shukheir** Egypt
105 C7 **Rass Jebel** Tunisia
52 E3 **Rasskazovo** Rus. Fed.
39 B4 **Ras Tannurah** Saudi Arabia
96 D5 **Ras Targa** Morocco
74 D4 **Rastatt** Germany
55 B3 **Råsted** Denmark
72 D2 **Rastede** Germany
81 G2 **Rastenfeld** Austria
126 D2 **Ras Terma** pt Eritrea
120 A5 **Râs Timirist** pt Mauritania
80 C3 **Rastkogel** mt. Austria
73 G2 **Rastow** Germany
99 E3 **Rasueros** Spain
39 C4 **Rasūl** watercourse Iran
43 B6 **Râs Umm 'Omeiyid** h. Egypt
59 F2 **Råsvalen** l. Sweden
76 F4 **Raszków** Poland
52 C4 **Rat'** r. Rus. Fed.
4 J3 **Ratak Chain** is Marshall Islands
36 C3 **Ratangarh** India
56 D3 **Rätansbyn** Sweden
77 M3 **Rataychytsy** Belarus
25 B4 **Rat Buri** Thailand
54 D3 **Ratchino** Rus. Fed.
81 E4 **Rateče** Slovenia
73 F2 **Ratekau** Germany
130 B5 **Ratelfontein** South Africa
36 D4 **Rath** India
67 E3 **Rathangan** Rep. of Ireland
64 B4 **Rathcoole** Rep. of Ireland
64 B4 **Rathcor** Rep. of Ireland
67 D4 **Rathdowney** Rep. of Ireland
67 E4 **Rathdrum** Rep. of Ireland
24 A2 **Rathedaung** Myanmar
73 H3 **Rathenow** Germany
67 E2 **Rathfriland** *Northern Ireland* U.K.
67 C4 **Rathkeale** Rep. of Ireland
67 E1 **Rathlin Island** i. *Northern Ireland* U.K.
67 C4 **Rathluirc** Rep. of Ireland
64 B4 **Rathmolyon** Rep. of Ireland
64 A4 **Rathowen** Rep. of Ireland
67 E4 **Rathvilly** Rep. of Ireland
72 B4 **Ratingen** Germany
81 F4 **Ratitovec** mt. Slovenia
36 C3 **Ratiya** India
36 C5 **Ratlam** India
38 A2 **Ratnagiri** India
38 C5 **Ratnapura** Sri Lanka
53 A1 **Ratne** Ukraine
64 B4 **Ratoath** Rep. of Ireland
36 B4 **Rato Dero** Pakistan
153 F4 **Raton** *New Mexico* U.S.A.
75 F2 **Rattelsdorf** Germany
81 G3 **Ratten** Austria
80 C3 **Rattenberg** Austria
65 E1 **Rattray** *Scotland* U.K.
66 G3 **Rattray Head** headland *Scotland* U.K.
59 F1 **Rättvik** Sweden
73 F2 **Ratzeburg** Germany
73 G3 **Rätzlingen** Germany
136 C3 **Ratz, Mt** mt. *B.C.* Canada
25 C7 **Raub** Malaysia
75 H5 **Raubling** Germany
173 H4 **Rauch** Argentina
58 C1 **Raudbergskarvet** mt. Norway
42 F4 **Raudhatain** Kuwait
54 C4 **Raudondvaris** Lithuania
56 N6 **Raufarhöfn** Iceland
8 G2 **Raukumara** mt. New Zealand
8 F3 **Raukumara Range** mountain range New Zealand
169 G4 **Raul Soares** Brazil
57 F3 **Rauma** Finland
9 E4 **Raumati** New Zealand
54 D3 **Rauna** Latvia
58 B1 **Raundalselvi** r. Norway
63 F2 **Raunds** *England* U.K.
22 C4 **Raung, G.** volcano Indonesia
8 E3 **Raurimu** New Zealand
80 D3 **Rauris** Austria
37 F5 **Raurkela** India
28 K1 **Rausu** Japan
53 B3 **Răut** r. Moldova
56 H3 **Rautavaara** Finland
57 H3 **Rautjärvi** Finland
107 G2 **Ràut, Monte** mt. Italy
7 □10 **Ravahéré** i. *French Polynesia* Pacific Ocean
152 D2 **Ravalli** *Montana* U.S.A.
104 G3 **Ravan** mt. Bos.-Herz.
39 D4 **Rāvang** Iran
42 F3 **Ravānsar** Iran
110 C5 **Ravanusa** *Sicilia* Italy
39 D3 **Rāvar** Iran
77 M5 **Rava-Rus'ka** Ukraine
109 G4 **Ravello** Italy
164 C3 **Ravelo** Bolivia
69 C3 **Ravels** Belgium
81 G2 **Ravelsbach** Austria
59 F3 **Rävemåla** Sweden
147 G3 **Ravena** *New York* U.S.A.
65 E3 **Ravenglass** *England* U.K.
107 F4 **Ravenna** div. Italy
107 G4 **Ravenna** Italy
74 E5 **Ravensburg** Germany
15 F3 **Ravenshoe** *Queensland* Australia
68 D3 **Ravenstein** Netherlands
17 C7 **Ravensthorpe** *Western Australia* Australia
15 F4 **Ravenswood** *Queensland* Australia
146 C5 **Ravenswood** *W. Virginia* U.S.A.
36 C3 **Ravi** r. Pakistan
93 E5 **Raviège, Lac de la** l. France
107 J3 **Ravna Gora** Croatia
81 F4 **Ravne na Koroškem** Slovenia
46 F5 **Ravnina** Turkmenistan
47 G3 **Ravnina Dar'yalyktakyr** plain Kazakhstan
135 Q3 **Ravn, Kap** pt Greenland
46 E4 **Ravshan** Uzbekistan
42 E3 **Rāwah** Iraq
5 K5 **Rawaki** i. Kiribati
36 C2 **Rawalpindi** Pakistan
77 J4 **Rawa Mazowiecka** Poland
42 F2 **Rawāndiz** Iraq
36 C3 **Rawatsar** India
126 D1 **Rawḍah** Yemen
141 J3 **Rawdon** *Québec* Canada
43 D5 **Rawghah** watercourse Saudi Arabia
76 E4 **Rawicz** Poland
146 D5 **Rawley Springs** *Virginia* U.S.A.
17 D6 **Rawlinna** *Western Australia* Australia
152 F3 **Rawlins** *Wyoming* U.S.A.
17 D5 **Rawlinson, Mt** h. *Western Australia* Australia
17 E5 **Rawlinson Ra.** h. *Western Australia* Australia
173 G3 **Rawson** *Buenos Aires* Argentina
171 D5 **Rawson** *Chubut* Argentina
65 F4 **Rawtenstall** *England* U.K.
32 B2 **Rawu** China
81 G3 **Raxalpe** mts Austria
37 F4 **Raxaul** India
22 B2 **Raya, Bukit** mt. *Kalimantan Barat/Kalimantan Tengah* Indonesia
22 C2 **Raya, Bukit** mt. *Kalimantan Barat* Indonesia
38 B3 **Rayachoti** India
38 B3 **Rayadurg** India
38 C2 **Rāyagarha** India
139 J4 **Ray, C.** headland *Newfoundland* Canada
31 J2 **Raychikhinsk** Rus. Fed.
126 D1 **Raydah** Yemen
46 D2 **Rayevskiy** Rus. Fed.
63 G3 **Rayleigh** *England* U.K.
136 G5 **Raymond** *Alberta* Canada
147 H3 **Raymond** *New Hampshire* U.S.A.
152 B2 **Raymond** *Washington* U.S.A.
151 D7 **Raymondville** *Texas* U.S.A.
91 E5 **Rayol-Canadel-sur-Mer** France
25 C4 **Rayong** Thailand
146 D4 **Raystown Lake** l. *Pennsylvania* U.S.A.
43 D5 **Rayth al Khayl** watercourse Saudi Arabia
119 G3 **Rayyis** Saudi Arabia
39 B2 **Razan** Iran
112 C3 **Ražanj** Yugoslavia
Razdan *see* **Hrazdan**
31 J4 **Razdol'noye** Rus. Fed.
30 B1 **Razdol'ye** Rus. Fed.
81 F5 **Razdrto** Slovenia
39 B2 **Razeh** Iran
92 D2 **Razès** France
112 E3 **Razgrad** div. Bulgaria
112 F3 **Razgrad** Bulgaria
77 N2 **Razhanka** Belarus
112 G2 **Razim, L.** lag. Romania
112 D4 **Razlog** Bulgaria
36 B2 **Razmak** Pakistan
54 E3 **Rāznas** r. Latvia
88 A3 **Raz, Pte du** pt France
53 G1 **Razumnoye** Rus. Fed.
62 D2 **Rea Brook** r. *England* U.K.
63 F3 **Reading** *England* U.K.
147 F4 **Reading** *Pennsylvania* U.S.A.
159 □1 **Reading** Jamaica
148 B4 **Readstown** *Wisconsin* U.S.A.
131 F2 **Reagile** South Africa
166 E3 **Real** r. Brazil
173 H4 **Real Audiencia** Argentina
164 C3 **Real, Cord.** mts Bolivia
172 D3 **Real de Padre** Argentina
101 E4 **Reales** mt. Spain
172 E3 **Realicó** Argentina
93 E5 **Réalmont** France
25 C4 **Reăng Kesei** Cambodia
157 E3 **Reata** Mexico
121 F2 **Rebaa** Algeria
86 C4 **Rebais** France
17 C6 **Rebecca, L.** salt flat *Western Australia* Australia
69 C4 **Rebecq** Belgium
93 E6 **Rébenty** r. France
Rebiana Sand Sea desert *see* **Ramlat Rabyānah**
76 G1 **Rębiechowo** airport Poland
173 K3 **Reboledo** Uruguay
101 F2 **Rebollera** mt. Spain
98 C3 **Rebordelo** Portugal
28 H1 **Rebun-suidō** chan. Japan
28 H1 **Rebun-tō** i. Japan
173 G4 **Recalde** Argentina
107 H5 **Recanati** Italy
53 C3 **Recea** Moldova
67 B3 **Recess** Rep. of Ireland
90 C1 **Recey-sur-Ource** France
17 C7 **Recherche, Archipelago of the** is *Western Australia* Australia
87 F4 **Réchicourt-le-Château** France
36 C3 **Rechna Doab** lowland Pakistan
69 E4 **Recht** Belgium
51 D4 **Rechytsa** Belarus
6 □2 **Récif de la Gazelle** reef *New Caledonia* Pacific Ocean
6 □2 **Récif des Français** reef *New Caledonia* Pacific Ocean
6 □2 **Récif Durand** reef *New Caledonia* Pacific Ocean
166 F2 **Recife** Brazil
131 E7 **Recife, Cape** c. South Africa
127 □1 **Recif I.** i. Seychelles
6 □2 **Récif Petrie** reef *New Caledonia* Pacific Ocean
6 □2 **Récifs de l'Astrolabe** reef *New Caledonia* Pacific Ocean
6 □2 **Récifs d'Entrecasteaux** reef *New Caledonia* Pacific Ocean
172 B4 **Recinto** Chile
72 C3 **Recke** Germany
72 C4 **Recklinghausen** Germany
73 H1 **Recknitz** r. Germany
107 F3 **Recoaro Terme** Italy
170 E2 **Reconquista** Argentina
91 D4 **Recoubeau-Jansac** France
165 E1 **Recreio** *Mato Grosso* Brazil
169 G4 **Recreio** *Minas Gerais* Brazil
170 C2 **Recreo** *Catamarca* Argentina
173 G1 **Recreo** *Santa Fé* Argentina
76 D2 **Recz** Poland
77 H4 **Ręczno** Poland
151 E6 **Red** r. *Louisiana* U.S.A.
137 K5 **Red** r. Canada/U.S.A.
76 G1 **Reda** Poland
58 D1 **Redalen** Norway
25 C6 **Redang** i. Malaysia
69 D5 **Redange** Luxembourg
147 F4 **Red Bank** *New Jersey* U.S.A.
145 C5 **Red Bank** *Tennessee* U.S.A.
139 J3 **Red Bay** *Newfoundland* Canada
154 A1 **Red Bluff** *California* U.S.A.
155 F4 **Red Butte** summit *Arizona* U.S.A.
65 G3 **Redcar** *England* U.K.
65 G3 **Redcar and Cleveland** div. *England* U.K.
137 G4 **Redcliff** *Alberta* Canada
129 D2 **Redcliff** Zimbabwe
15 H5 **Redcliffe** *Queensland* Australia
17 C6 **Redcliffe, Mt** h. *Western Australia* Australia
13 E3 **Red Cliffs** *Victoria* Australia
150 D3 **Red Cloud** *Nebraska* U.S.A.
137 G4 **Red Deer** r. *Alberta* Canada
137 J4 **Red Deer** r. *Saskatchewan* Canada
136 G4 **Red Deer** *Alberta* Canada
137 J4 **Red Deer L.** l. *Manitoba* Canada
147 F5 **Redden** *Delaware* U.S.A.
131 F4 **Reddersburg** South Africa
152 B3 **Redding** *California* U.S.A.
63 E2 **Redditch** *England* U.K.
65 F2 **Rede** r. *England* U.K.
73 G2 **Redefin** Germany
130 B6 **Redelinghuys** South Africa
166 D2 **Redenção** Brazil
121 F2 **Redeyef** Tunisia
147 F3 **Redfield** *New York* U.S.A.
150 D2 **Redfield** *S. Dakota* U.S.A.
159 □3 **Redhead** Trinidad and Tobago
63 F3 **Redhill** *England* U.K.
155 H4 **Red Hill** *New Mexico* U.S.A.
12 D3 **Redhill** *S. Australia* Australia
128 □1 **Red Hill, Mt** h. *Ascension* Atlantic Ocean
151 D4 **Red Hills** h. *Kansas* U.S.A.
78 F5 **Rédics** Hungary
139 J4 **Red Indian L.** l. *Newfoundland* Canada
148 E5 **Redkey** *Indiana* U.S.A.
52 C1 **Redkino** Rus. Fed.
138 B3 **Red L.** l. *Ontario* Canada
155 E4 **Red L.** l. *Arizona* U.S.A.
138 B3 **Red Lake** *Ontario* Canada
150 E1 **Red Lakes** lakes *Minnesota* U.S.A.
152 E2 **Red Lodge** *Montana* U.S.A.
63 E4 **Redlynch** *England* U.K.
152 B2 **Redmond** *Oregon* U.S.A.
75 G3 **Rednitz** r. Germany
150 E3 **Red Oak** *Iowa* U.S.A.
127 C5 **Redojari** waterhole Kenya
88 C4 **Redon** France
98 B2 **Redondela** Spain
100 C2 **Redondo** Portugal
Red River r. *see* **Song Hông**
140 A2 **Red Rock** *Ontario* Canada

147 E4 Red Rock Pennsylvania U.S.A.
17 D7 Red Rocks Pt pt Western Australia Australia
62 A4 Redruth England U.K.
119 G3 Red Sea sea Africa/Asia
136 D2 Redstone r. N.W.T. Canada
136 E4 Redstone B.C. Canada
137 L4 Red Sucker L. l. Manitoba Canada
Red Volta r. see Nazinon
136 G4 Redwater Alberta Canada
62 B1 Red Wharf Bay b. Wales U.K.
139 H3 Red Wine r. Newfoundland Canada
148 A3 Red Wing Minnesota U.S.A.
154 A3 Redwood City California U.S.A.
150 E2 Redwood Falls Minnesota U.S.A.
152 B3 Redwood Nat. Park California U.S.A.
154 A2 Redwood Valley California U.S.A.
148 E4 Reed City Michigan U.S.A.
154 C3 Reedley California U.S.A.
148 C4 Reedsburg Wisconsin U.S.A.
152 A3 Reedsport Oregon U.S.A.
147 E6 Reedville Virginia U.S.A.
179 B4 Reedy Gl. gl. Antarctica
Reef Islands is see Rowa
9 C5 Reefton New Zealand
67 D3 Ree, Lough l. Rep. of Ireland
72 B4 Rees Germany
73 G2 Reetz Germany
42 D2 Refahiye Turkey
43 D3 Refa'i, T. mt. Jordan/Syria
171 B5 Refugio i. Chile
151 D6 Refugio Texas U.S.A.
76 D2 Rega r. Poland
110 D5 Regalbuto Sicilia Italy
81 E3 Regau Austria
75 H3 Regen r. Germany
75 J4 Regen Germany
169 J3 Regência Brazil
75 H3 Regensburg Germany
83 D1 Regensdorf Switzerland
75 H3 Regenstauf Germany
168 C5 Regente Feijó Brazil
121 E3 Reggane Algeria
68 E2 Regge r. Netherlands
107 F5 Reggello Italy
111 E4 Reggio di Calabria div. Italy
111 E4 Reggio di Calabria Italy
107 E4 Reggio Emilia div. Italy
107 E4 Reggiolo Italy
107 E4 Reggio nell'Emilia Italy
112 E1 Reghin Romania
137 J4 Regina Saskatchewan Canada
163 G3 Regina Brazil
163 G3 Régina French Guiana
39 F3 Registan reg. Afghanistan
168 E6 Registro Brazil
168 C1 Registro do Araguaia Brazil
59 F2 Regna Sweden
56 H2 Regozero Rus. Fed.
55 D4 Regstrup Denmark
98 B2 Reguengo Spain
100 C2 Reguengos de Monsaraz Portugal
75 H2 Rehau Germany
72 E3 Rehburg Germany
72 D3 Rehden Germany
36 D5 Rehli India
80 B2 Rehling Germany
74 B3 Rehlingen-Siersburg Germany
75 J2 Řehlovice Czech Rep.
73 G2 Rehna Germany
155 H4 Rehoboth New Mexico U.S.A.
128 B3 Rehoboth Namibia
147 F5 Rehoboth Bay b. Delaware U.S.A.
147 F5 Rehoboth Beach Delaware U.S.A.
43 C4 Rehovot Israel
115 E6 Reicheia Greece
81 G3 Reichenau an der Rax Austria
75 H2 Reichenbach Germany
82 C2 Reichenbach Switzerland
81 F3 Reichenfels Austria
80 D3 Reichenspitze mt. Austria
75 G4 Reichertshofen Germany
87 G4 Reichshoffen France
82 C1 Reiden Switzerland
6 □7 Reid Reef reef Fiji
145 E4 Reidsville N. Carolina U.S.A.
63 F3 Reigate England U.K.
92 A2 Ré, Île de i. France
155 G5 Reiley Peak summit Arizona U.S.A.
91 D5 Reillanne France
86 D3 Reims Marne France
82 D1 Reinach Aargau Switzerland
82 C1 Reinach Basel Switzerland
148 A4 Reinbeck Iowa U.S.A.
72 F2 Reinbek Germany
137 J3 Reindeer r. Saskatchewan Canada
137 K4 Reindeer I. i. Manitoba Canada
137 J3 Reindeer Lake l. Saskatchewan Canada
56 D2 Reine Norway
58 C1 Reineskarvet mt. Norway
72 F2 Reinfeld (Holstein) Germany
8 D1 Reinga, Cape c. New Zealand
74 D3 Reinheim Germany
99 F2 Reinosa Spain
90 C3 Reins r. France
69 E5 Reinsfeld Germany
58 B2 Reinsnosi mt. Norway
58 D1 Reinsvoll Norway
56 L2 Reipholsfjöll mt. Iceland
56 F1 Reisaelva r. Norway
75 H4 Reisbach Germany
80 D2 Reischach Germany
56 G3 Reisjärvi Finland
72 B2 Reitdiep r. Netherlands
110D5 Reitano Sicilia Italy
131 G3 Reitz South Africa
131 F3 Reitzburg South Africa
59 F2 Rejmyre Sweden
77 M4 Rejowiec Fabryczny Poland
163 D3 Rejunya Venezuela
72 C4 Reken Germany
36 A3 Rekgwash Pakistan
28 J2 Rekifune-gawa r. Japan
77 N5 Reklynets' Ukraine
112 C3 Rekovac Yugoslavia
58 C1 Reksjåeggi mt. Norway
137 H2 Reliance N.W.T. Canada
121 E1 Relizane Algeria
72 E2 Rellingen Germany
121 G2 Remada Tunisia
74 C2 Remagen Germany
89 F3 Rémalard France
9 □3 Remarkable Arch arch Antipodes Is New Zealand
12 D3 Remarkable, Mt mt. S. Australia Australia
22 B3 Rembang Indonesia
77 F2 Remecó Argentina
98 A2 Remedios, Pta dos pt Spain
39 D4 Remeshk Iran
69 E5 Remich Luxembourg
163 G3 Rémire French Guiana
87 F4 Remiremont France
36 D2 Remo Gl. gl. India
102 B3 Remolinos Spain
51 G6 Remontnoye Rus. Fed.
91 C5 Remoulins France
22 A1 Rempang i. Indonesia
74 E5 Rems r. Germany
72 C4 Remscheid Germany
88 C4 Remungol France
148 E4 Remus Michigan U.S.A.
91 D4 Rémuzat France
32 E1 Ren r. China
58 D1 Rena r. Norway
58 D1 Rena Norway
100 E1 Rena Spain
172 A4 Renaico Chile
90 B2 Renaison France
37 B2 Renapur India
89 D4 Renazé France
87 H4 Renchen Germany
107 F3 Rende Italy
144 B4 Rend L. l. Illinois U.S.A.
6 □1 Rendova i. Solomon Is.
72 E1 Rendsburg Germany
99 G1 Renedo Spain
82 B2 Renens Switzerland
68 B3 Renesse Netherlands
141 G4 Renfrew Ontario Canada
66 D5 Renfrew Scotland U.K.
66 D5 Renfrewshire div. Scotland U.K.
172 B3 Rengo Chile
72 C2 Rengsdorf Germany
33 F2 Renheji China
33 F3 Renhua China
32 D3 Renhuai China
53 C3 Reni Ukraine
54 D1 Renko Finland
Renland reg. see Tuttut Nunaat
12 E3 Renmark S. Australia Australia
31 H3 Renmin China
6 □1 Rennell i. Solomon Is.
74 D2 Rennerod Germany
75 G4 Rennertshofen Germany
88 D3 Rennes Ille-et-Vilaine France
58 A2 Rennesøy i. Norway
179 B5 Rennick Gl. gl. Antarctica
137 H2 Rennie Lake l. N.W.T. Canada
74 D4 Renningen Germany
81 E3 Rennweg Austria
107 F4 Reno r. Italy
154 C2 Reno Nevada U.S.A.
107 F2 Renò Italy
108 B2 Rénoso, Monte mt. Corse France
130 C6 Renoster r. South Africa
131 F3 Renoster r. South Africa
146 E4 Renovo Pennsylvania U.S.A.
31 F5 Renqiu China
32 D2 Renshou China
148 D5 Rensselaer Indiana U.S.A.
147 G3 Rensselaer New York U.S.A.
102 B1 Rentería Spain
115 C4 Rentina Greece
152 B2 Renton Washington U.S.A.
37 E4 Renukut India
86 D3 Renwez France
9 D4 Renwick New Zealand
122 D4 Réo Burkina
22 E4 Reo Indonesia
78 F4 Répce r. Hungary
129 E3 Repembe r. Mozambique
77 L3 Repki Poland
54 F2 Repolka Rus. Fed.
8 F3 Reporoa New Zealand
72 F2 Reppenstedt Germany
168 C3 Represa Agua Vermelha resr Brazil
168 D5 Represa Barra Bonita resr Brazil
168 C5 Represa Capivara resr Brazil
165 E5 Represa de Acaray resr Paraguay
163 F4 Represa de Balbina resr Brazil
168 E3 Represa de Emborcação resr Brazil
168 A6 Represa de Itaipu resr Brazil
168 D5 Represa de Jurumirim resr Brazil
168 D3 Represa de São Simão resr Brazil
168 D5 Represa de Xavantes resr Brazil
169 E4 Represa Furnas resr Brazil
168 B5 Represa Ilha Grande resr Brazil
168 C4 Represa Ilha Solteira resr Brazil
168 C4 Represa Jupiá resr Brazil
169 E4 Represa Peixoto resr Brazil
168 B4 Represa Pôrto Primavera resr Brazil
168 D4 Represa Promissão resr Brazil
168 C4 Represa Três Irmãos resr Brazil
169 F3 Represa Três Marias resr Brazil
166 C1 Represa Tucuruí Brazil
152 C1 Republic Washington U.S.A.
150 D3 Republican r. Nebraska U.S.A.
15 G4 Repulse B. b. Queensland Australia
135 K3 Repulse Bay N.W.T. Canada
162 C5 Requena Peru
103 B5 Requena Spain
172 B3 Requinoa Chile
93 E4 Réquista France
42 D1 Reşadiye Turkey
22 A3 Resag, G. mt. Indonesia
114 C1 Resen Macedonia
169 F5 Resende Brazil
98 C3 Resende Portugal
168 C6 Reserva Brazil
52 F1 Reshetikha Rus. Fed.
52 C1 Reshetnikovo Rus. Fed.
53 F2 Reshetylivka Ukraine
52 F1 Reshma Rus. Fed.
39 D1 Reshteh-ye Esfarayen mountain range Iran
107 E2 Resia, Lago di l. Italy
80 B4 Resia, Passo di pass Austria/Italy
170 E2 Resistencia Argentina
112 C2 Reşiţa Romania
76 D2 Resko Poland
135 J2 Resolute N.W.T. Canada
135 M3 Resolution Island i. N.W.T. Canada
9 A6 Resolution Island i. New Zealand
169 H3 Resplendor Brazil
52 B2 Ressa r. Rus. Fed.
52 B3 Resseta r. Rus. Fed.
86 B3 Ressons-sur-Matz France
159 □1 Rest Jamaica
164 B1 Restauracão Brazil
101 E5 Restinga Morocco
169 G5 Restinga de Marambaia beach Brazil
65 F2 Reston Scotland U.K.
110 D5 Resuttano Sicilia Italy
53 E1 Ret' r. Ukraine
157 H6 Retalhuleu Guatemala
172 C2 Retamito Argentina
25 □ Retan Laut, P. i. Singapore
172 B2 Retén Atalaya Chile
172 A3 Retén Llico Chile
123 E5 Retenue de Nangbéto res. Togo
63 F1 Retford England U.K.
86 D3 Rethel France
72 E3 Rethem (Aller) Germany
86 B3 Rethondes France
115 F7 Rethymno div. Greece
115 F7 Rethymno Greece
69 D3 Retie Belgium
88 D4 Retiers France
100 D2 Retín r. Spain
100 E4 Retín, Sierra de mountain range Spain
172 B4 Retiro Chile
79 L3 Rétköz reg. Hungary
91 C3 Retournac France
79 J4 Rétság Hungary
83 F1 Rettenberg Germany
102 B4 Retuerta mt. Spain
81 G2 Retz Austria
73 H3 Reuden Germany
89 H4 Reuilly France
117 K8 Réunion i. Indian Ocean
102 E3 Reus Spain
69 D3 Reusel Netherlands
83 D1 Reuss r. Switzerland
53 F1 Reut r. Rus. Fed.
87 G4 Reute Germany
73 H2 Reuterstadt Stavenhagen Germany
74 E4 Reutlingen Germany
80 B3 Reutte div. Austria
80 B3 Reutte Austria
69 E3 Reuver Netherlands
46 E1 Revda Rus. Fed.
154 D3 Reveille Peak summit Nevada U.S.A.
93 E5 Revel France
37 F4 Revelganj India
91 F4 Revello Italy
136 F4 Revelstoke B.C. Canada
162 A5 Reventazón Peru
90 D2 Revermont reg. France
85 G2 Revigny-sur-Ornain France
136 C3 Revillagigedo I. i. Alaska U.S.A.
156 □ Revillagigedo, Islas is Mexico
86 D3 Revin France
43 C4 Revivim Israel
52 B3 Revna r. Rus. Fed.
75 K3 Řevnice Czech Rep.
78 C1 Řevničov Czech Rep.
107 F2 Revò Italy
101 H2 Revolcadores mt. Spain
129 E2 Revúboè r. Mozambique
79 K3 Revúca Slovakia
129 E2 Revuè r. Mozambique
52 C2 Revyakino Rus. Fed.
6 □8 Rewa r. Fiji
37 E4 Rewa India
76 D1 Rewal Poland
36 D3 Rewari India
152 E3 Rexburg Idaho U.S.A.
139 H4 Rexton New Brunswick Canada
53 C1 Reya Ukraine
124 B2 Rey Bouba Cameroon
56 N6 Reyðarfjörður b. Iceland
164 C2 Reyes Bolivia
154 C4 Reyes Peak summit California U.S.A.
43 D1 Reyhanlı Turkey
156 L7 Rey, Isla del i. Panama
56 L6 Reykir Iceland
174 H2 Reykjanes Ridge sea feature Atlantic Ocean
56 L7 Reykjanestá pt Iceland
56 L6 Reykjavík Iceland
14 C4 Reynolds Ra. mountain range Northern Terr. Australia
157 F3 Reynosa Mexico
90 D2 Reyssouze r. France
88 D4 Rezé France
54 E3 Rēzekne r. Latvia
54 E3 Rēzekne Latvia
106 E3 Rezzato Italy
156 D2 R.F. Magón Mexico
112 D2 Rgotina Yugoslavia
83 E1 Rhätikon mts Switzerland
87 G3 Rhaunen Germany
62 C2 Rhayader Wales U.K.
72 D4 Rheda-Wiedenbrück Germany
72 B4 Rhede Germany
72 C2 Rhede (Ems) Germany
62 E2 Rheidol r. Wales U.K.
68 E3 Rhein r. Germany/Switzerland
74 C4 Rheinau Germany
87 G2 Rheinaugebirge h. Germany
74 B2 Rheinbach Germany
74 B4 Rheinberg Germany
87 G3 Rheinböllen Germany
69 F4 Rheinbreitbach Germany
72 C3 Rheine Germany
83 E1 Rheineck Switzerland
82 C1 Rheinfelden Switzerland
82 C1 Rheinfelden (Baden) Germany
74 C3 Rheinhessen-Pfalz div. Germany
74 B2 Rheinisches Schiefergebirge h. Germany
74 C3 Rheinland-Pfalz div. Germany
73 H2 Rheinsberg Germany
74 D4 Rheinstetten Germany
83 E2 Rheinwaldhorn mt. Switzerland
106 B3 Rhêmes-Notre-Dame Italy
82 C3 Rhêmes-St-Georges Italy
120 D3 Rhemilès well Algeria
68 D3 Rhenen Netherlands
66 D2 Rhiconich Scotland U.K.
74 C5 Rhin r. France
Rhine r. Germany/Switzerland see Rhein
Rhine r. France see Rhin
Rhine r. Netherlands see Rijn
147 G4 Rhinebeck New York U.S.A.
148 C3 Rhinelander Wisconsin U.S.A.
73 H3 Rhinkanal canal Germany
73 H3 Rhinluch marsh Germany
126 B4 Rhino Camp Uganda
73 H3 Rhinow Germany
73 H3 Rhinowes Berge h. Germany
120 C2 Rhir, Cap pt Morocco
69 C4 Rhisnes Belgium
106 D3 Rho Italy
147 H4 Rhode Island div. U.S.A.
Rhodes i. see Rodos
152 D2 Rhodes Pk summit Idaho U.S.A.
62 C3 Rhondda Wales U.K.
62 C3 Rhondda Cynon Taff div. Wales U.K.
90 C3 Rhône div. France
91 C5 Rhône r. France/Switzerland
91 D3 Rhône-Alpes div. France
68 C3 Rhoon Netherlands
80 D3 Rhordorf Germany
62 C1 Rhosllanerchrugog Wales U.K.
62 C1 Rhos-on-Sea Wales U.K.
62 B3 Rhossili Wales U.K.
121 F1 Rhoufi Algeria
62 C1 Rhuddlan Wales U.K.
92 E3 Rhue r. France
Rhum i. see Rum
102 B1 Rhune, La h. Spain
88 C4 Rhuys, Presqu'île de pen. France
Rhydaman see Ammanford
62 C1 Rhyl Wales U.K.
124 A3 Riaba Equatorial Guinea
111 F4 Riace Italy
166 C2 Riachão Brazil
166 D3 Riachão das Neves Brazil
166 E3 Riachão do Jacuípe Brazil
166 D2 Riacho r. Brazil
169 H3 Riacho Brazil
166 D3 Riacho de Santana Brazil
169 G1 Riacho dos Machados Brazil
173 F6 Riachos, I. de los i. Argentina
171 D5 Riachos, Is de los i. Argentina
98 B2 Ria de Arousa est. Spain
98 B4 Ria de Aveiro est. Portugal
98 E1 Ría de Avilés inlet Spain
98 B1 Ría de Betanzos est. Spain
98 A2 Ría de Corcubión b. Spain
98 A2 Ría de Corme e Laxe b. Spain
98 A1 Ría de Lires b. Spain
98 A2 Ría de Muros e Noia est. Spain
98 D1 Ría de Navia inlet Spain
98 B2 Ría de Pontevedra est. Spain
98 B2 Ría de Vigo est. Spain
99 E1 Ría de Villaviciosa inlet Spain
98 C1 Ría de Viveiro est. Spain
100 C4 Ría Formosa lag. Portugal
88 D4 Riaillé France
98 B2 Rial Spain
102 E2 Rialb de Noguera Spain
168 D1 Rialma Brazil
22 B2 Riam Indonesia
22 C2 Riamkanan, D. l. Indonesia
99 F2 Riaño Spain
168 D1 Rianópolis Brazil
91 D5 Rians France
101 G3 Riansáres r. Spain
88 B4 Riantec France
98 B2 Rianxo Spain
36 C2 Riasi India
22 A1 Riau div. Indonesia
99 G3 Riaza r. Spain
99 G3 Riaza Spain
99 G1 Riba Spain
98 B2 Ribadavia Spain
98 D2 Ribadelago Spain
98 C1 Ribadeo Spain
99 H4 Riba de Saelices Spain
99 E1 Ribadesella Spain
168 B4 Ribas do Rio Pardo Brazil
39 G1 Ribat Afghanistan
100 B1 Ribatejo reg. Portugal
129 F1 Ribáuè Mozambique
63 E1 Ribble r. England U.K.
65 F3 Ribblesdale reg. England U.K.
55 A4 Ribe div. Denmark
55 A4 Ribe r. Denmark
55 A4 Ribe Denmark
87 G4 Ribeauvillé France
86 B3 Ribécourt-Dreslincourt France
168 D6 Ribeira r. Brazil
168 D6 Ribeira Brazil
98 B3 Ribeira Portugal
96 □ Ribeira Brava Madeira Portugal
96 C3 Ribeira de Pena Portugal
100 □ Ribeira Grande Azores Portugal
168 D6 Ribeirão Branco Brazil
169 F3 Ribeirão das Neves Brazil
168 C5 Ribeirão do Pinhal Brazil
168 E4 Ribeirão Prêto Brazil
86 C3 Ribemont France
110 C5 Ribera Sicilia Italy
92 C3 Ribérac France
100 D2 Ribera del Fresno Spain
164 C2 Riberalta Bolivia
102 B2 Ribera Navarra reg. Spain
103 C4 Ribesalbes Spain
102 F2 Ribes de Freser Spain
91 D4 Ribiers France
81 F5 Ribnica Slovenia
81 G4 Ribnica Slovenia
73 H1 Ribnitz-Damgarten Germany
164 C4 Rica Aventura Chile
111 E4 Ricadi Italy
78 D2 Říčany Czech Rep.
107 G3 Riccia Italy
107 G4 Riccione Italy
155 E4 Rice California U.S.A.
148 A2 Rice Lake l. Minnesota U.S.A.
140 D3 Rice Lake l. Ontario Canada
148 B3 Rice Lake Wisconsin U.S.A.
148 A5 Riceville Iowa U.S.A.
146 D4 Riceville Pennsylvania U.S.A.
87 F4 Richardménil France
131 J4 Richards Bay South Africa
170 B2 Richards Deep depth Pacific Ocean
137 G3 Richardson r. Alberta Canada
151 D5 Richardson Texas U.S.A.
147 H2 Richardson Lakes l. Maine U.S.A.
134 E3 Richardson Mts mountain range N.W.T. Canada
9 B6 Richardson Mts mountain range New Zealand
6 □3 Richards Patches reef Tonga
122 A3 Richard Toll Senegal
127 □4 Riche en Eau Mauritius
68 D1 Richel i. Netherlands
89 F4 Richelieu France
152 E3 Richfield Utah U.S.A.
147 F3 Richfield Springs New York U.S.A.
147 E3 Richford New York U.S.A.
147 G2 Richford Vermont U.S.A.
64 B3 Richhill Northern Ireland U.K.
148 B5 Richland Iowa U.S.A.
148 B4 Richland Center Wisconsin U.S.A.
146 C6 Richlands Virginia U.S.A.
146 E6 Richmond airport Virginia U.S.A.
65 G3 Richmond England U.K.
148 E6 Richmond Indiana U.S.A.
146 A6 Richmond Kentucky U.S.A.
131 H4 Richmond KwaZulu-Natal South Africa
147 J2 Richmond Maine U.S.A.
149 F4 Richmond Michigan U.S.A.
13 G3 Richmond New South Wales Australia
130 D5 Richmond Northern Cape South Africa
141 H4 Richmond Ontario Canada
141 J4 Richmond Québec Canada
15 E4 Richmond Queensland Australia
147 G2 Richmond Vermont U.S.A.
146 E6 Richmond Virginia U.S.A.
159 □1 Richmond Jamaica
9 D4 Richmond New Zealand
141 F5 Richmond Hill Ontario Canada
9 D4 Richmond, Mt mt. New Zealand
13 H2 Richmond Ra. h. New South Wales Australia
9 D4 Richmond Range mountain range New Zealand
73 H1 Richtenberg Germany
130 A4 Richtersveld National Park nat. park South Africa
83 D1 Richterswil Switzerland
148 B4 Richwood Ohio U.S.A.
146 C5 Richwood W. Virginia U.S.A.
82 C1 Rickenbach Germany
102 B3 Ricla Spain
155 H3 Rico Colorado U.S.A.
98 E3 Ricobayo, Emb. de resr Spain
170 E2 Rico, Pto Argentina
68 C3 Ridderkerk Netherlands
82 C2 Riddes Switzerland
14 C4 Riddock, Mt mt. Northern Terr. Australia
141 H4 Rideau r. Ontario Canada
141 G4 Rideau Lakes l. Ontario Canada
154 D4 Ridgecrest California U.S.A.
146 D4 Ridgway Pennsylvania U.S.A.
79 J5 Ridica Yugoslavia
22 A3 Ridingan, Bukit mt. Indonesia
137 J4 Riding Mountain Nat. Park nat. park Manitoba Canada
131 F6 Riebeek-Oos South Africa
130 B6 Riebeek Wes South Africa
88 B4 Riec-sur-Belon France
80 C2 Ried Germany
83 F1 Riedbergerhorn mt. Germany
75 G4 Riedenburg Germany
81 E2 Ried im Innkreis div. Austria
81 E2 Ried im Innkreis Austria
80 B3 Ried im Oberinntal Austria
90 F1 Riedisheim France
74 B3 Riegelsberg Germany
81 G3 Riegersburg Austria
82 C1 Riehen Switzerland
131 F2 Riekertsdam South Africa
83 D1 Rielasingen-Worblingen Germany
69 D4 Riemst Belgium
58 B2 Rienshornhei mt. Norway
107 G2 Rienza r. Italy
73 J4 Riesa Germany
171 B7 Riesco, Isla i. Chile
110 D5 Riesi Sicilia Italy
73 G4 Riestedt Germany
130 E4 Riet r. South Africa
130 C5 Riet r. South Africa
54 B4 Rietavas Lithuania
72 D4 Rietberg Germany
130 D6 Rietbron South Africa
131 G2 Rietfontein South Africa
130 C7 Riethuiskraal South Africa
109 E2 Rieti div. Lazio Italy
109 E2 Rieti Italy
131 G2 Rietkolk South Africa
131 G3 Rietkuil South Africa
73 K4 Rietschen Germany
130 C5 Riet se Vloer salt pan South Africa
80 C3 Rietz Austria
93 D5 Rieumes France
93 E4 Rieupeyroux France
91 B4 Rieutort-de-Randon France
88 C4 Rieux Bretagne France
93 D5 Rieux Midi-Pyrénées France
91 E5 Riez France
153 F4 Rifle Colorado U.S.A.
56 M6 Rifstangi pt Iceland
127 C5 Rift Valley div. Kenya
37 H3 Riga India
54 D3 Rīga Latvia
54 C3 Riga, Gulf of g. Estonia/Latvia
114 D3 Rigaio Greece
39 D3 Rīgān Iran
Rīgas Jūras Līcis see Riga, Gulf of
141 H4 Rigaud Québec Canada
152 C2 Riggins Idaho U.S.A.
93 E4 Rignac France
109 E2 Rignano Flaminio Italy
86 C4 Rigny-le-Ferron France
90 C2 Rigny-sur-Arroux France
139 J3 Rigolet Newfoundland Canada
118 B5 Rig-Rig Chad
66 E5 Rigside Scotland U.K.
39 D2 Rīgū Iran
37 E5 Rihand r. India
Riia Laht see Riga, Gulf of
57 G3 Riihimäki Finland
179 D4 Riiser-Larsenhalvøya pen. Antarctica
179 C3 Riiser-Larsenisen pen. Antarctica
179 D3 Riiser-Larsen Sea sea Antarctica
54 D2 Riisipere Estonia
153 D5 Riito Mexico
123 F4 Rijau Nigeria
107 J3 Riječki Zaliv b. Croatia
107 J3 Rijeka airport Croatia
107 J3 Rijeka Croatia
68 C3 Rijn r. Netherlands
69 D3 Rijen Netherlands
68 C2 Rijnsburg Netherlands
69 C3 Rijsbergen Netherlands
68 E2 Rijssen Netherlands
68 C2 Rijswijk Netherlands
119 H3 Rikā, W. ar watercourse Saudi Arabia
28 J2 Rikubetsu Japan
29 H4 Rikuzen-takata Japan
112 D3 Rila mts Bulgaria
152 C3 Riley Oregon U.S.A.
69 C3 Rilland Netherlands
90 C3 Rillieux-la-Pape France
102 C4 Rillo Spain
123 F4 Rima watercourse Niger/Nigeria
119 H2 Rimah, W. al watercourse Saudi Arabia
5 M7 Rimatara i. French Polynesia Pacific Ocean
22 A2 Rimau r. Indonesia
79 J3 Rimava r. Slovakia
79 K3 Rimavská Sobota Slovakia
136 G4 Rimbey Alberta Canada
59 H2 Rimbo Sweden
59 F3 Rimforsa Sweden
107 G4 Rimini Italy
69 C5 Rimogne France
93 D6 Rimont France
139 G4 Rimouski Québec Canada
74 E3 Rimpar Germany
66 D2 Rimsdale, Loch l. Scotland U.K.
37 G3 Rinbung China
22 D4 Rinca i. Indonesia
168 D4 Rincão Brazil
75 J4 Rinchnach Germany
158 □3 Rincon Bonaire Netherlands Ant.
145 □3 Rincon Puerto Rico
101 F1 Rinconada, Sierra de la mountain range Spain
164 C4 Rincon, Co del mt. Chile
103 B4 Rincon de Ademuz reg. Spain
172 C3 Rincón del Atuel Argentina
101 F4 Rincón de la Victoria Spain
170 E3 Rincón del Bonete, L. Artificial de resr Uruguay
173 J2 Rincón de Palacio Uruguay
156 E4 Rincón de Romos Mexico
56 C3 Rindal Norway
115 G5 Rineia i. Greece
110 D4 Rinella Italy
13 F5 Ringarooma B. b. Tasmania Australia
59 G2 Ringarum Sweden
36 C4 Rīngas India
37 G2 Ring Co salt lake China
55 C4 Ringe Denmark
57 C3 Ringebu Norway
83 E2 Ringelspitz mt. Switzerland
64 D3 Ringford Scotland U.K.
6 □6 Ringgold Isles is Fiji
24 B1 Ringhkung Myanmar
123 F4 Ringim Nigeria
55 A3 Ringkøbing div. Denmark
55 A3 Ringkøbing Denmark
55 A4 Ringkøbing Fjord lag. Denmark
63 G4 Ringmer England U.K.
64 B2 Ringsend Northern Ireland U.K.
59 E4 Ringsjön l. Sweden
59 G2 Ringsön i. Sweden
58 D1 Ringsrudåsen h. Norway
55 D4 Ringsted Denmark
56 E2 Ringvassøy i. Norway
63 E4 Ringwood England U.K.
172 A5 Riñihue Chile
172 A5 Riñihue, L. l. Chile
172 A6 Riñinahué Chile
22 D4 Rinjani, G. volcano Indonesia
59 F4 Rinkaby Sweden
64 C3 Rinns of Galloway, The pen. Scotland U.K.
64 B2 Rinns of Islay pen. Scotland U.K.
64 B2 Rinns Point pt Scotland U.K.
72 E3 Rinteln Germany
148 C4 Rio Wisconsin U.S.A.
115 C4 Rio Greece
167 A4 Rio Alegre Brazil
162 B4 Riobamba Ecuador
155 H2 Rio Blanco Colorado U.S.A.
172 B2 Río Blanco Chile
169 G5 Rio Bonito Brazil
164 C2 Rio Branco Brazil
173 L2 Río Branco Uruguay
168 D6 Rio Branco do Sul Brazil
163 E3 Rio Branco, Parque Nacional do nat. park Brazil
168 A4 Rio Brilhante Brazil
172 A6 Río Bueno Chile
159 □1 Rio Bueno Jamaica
163 E1 Río Caribe Venezuela
169 G4 Rio Casca Brazil
172 E1 Río Ceballos Argentina
159 F5 Río Chico Venezuela
168 E5 Rio Claro Brazil
159 G5 Rio Claro Trinidad and Tobago
159 E5 Río Claro Venezuela
159 □1 Rio Cobre r. Jamaica
172 E5 Río Colorado Argentina
122 B4 Rio Corubal r. Guinea-Bissau
172 E2 Río Cuarto Argentina
166 C3 Rio das Balsas r. Brazil
169 F4 Rio das Mortes r. Brazil
166 B3 Rio das Mortes r. Brazil
169 G5 Rio de Janeiro div. Brazil
169 G5 Rio de Janeiro Brazil
156 K8 Río de Jesús Panama
173 J3 Río de la Plata est. Argentina/Uruguay
164 B2 Río de las Piedras r. Peru
100 E1 Río de la Vid r. Spain
98 D3 Rio de Onor Portugal
120 A4 Río de Oro, B. de b. Western Sahara
166 C1 Rio do Para r. Brazil
168 C5 Rio do Peixe r. Brazil
167 C6 Rio do Sul Brazil
156 K7 Río Frio Costa Rica
98 D3 Riofrío de Aliste Spain
171 C7 Río Gallegos Argentina
122 B4 Rio Gêba r. Guinea-Bissau/Senegal
101 F4 Riogordo Spain
159 □1 Rio Grande r. Jamaica
156 D2 Rio Grande r. Mexico/U.S.A.
156 J6 Río Grande r. Nicaragua
166 D2 Rio Grande r. Piauí Brazil
170 F3 Rio Grande Rio Grande do Sul Brazil
171 C7 Río Grande Argentina
156 E4 Río Grande Mexico
151 D7 Rio Grande City Texas U.S.A.
156 D4 Río Grande de Santiago r. Mexico
166 E2 Rio Grande do Norte div. Brazil
167 B6 Rio Grande do Sul div. Brazil
174 G8 Rio Grande Rise sea feature Atlantic Ocean
162 C1 Riohacha Colombia
162 B5 Rioja Peru
157 H4 Río Lagartos Mexico
166 E2 Rio Largo Brazil
107 F4 Riolo Terme Italy
90 B3 Riom France
100 B1 Rio Maior Portugal
172 B3 Río Malo Chile
168 B1 Rio Manso r. Brazil
108 C2 Rio Marina Italy
92 E3 Riom-ès-Montagnes France
164 C3 Río Mulatos Bolivia
124 B3 Río Muni reg. Equatorial Guinea
93 B5 Rion-des-Landes France
172 D5 Río Negro div. Argentina
173 J2 Río Negro div. Uruguay
168 A3 Rio Negro Mato Grosso do Sul Brazil
167 C6 Rio Negro Paraná Brazil
172 A6 Río Negro Chile
98 D2 Rionegro del Puente Spain
109 H4 Rionero in Vulture Italy
51 G7 Rioni r. Georgia
169 G4 Rio Novo Brazil
169 H4 Rio Novo do Sul Brazil
167 B6 Rio Pardo Brazil
169 G1 Rio Pardo de Minas Brazil
170 D1 Río Pescado Argentina
170 D2 Río Piedras Argentina
169 G4 Rio Pomba Brazil
169 G5 Rio Prêto Brazil
172 F1 Río Primero Argentina
153 F5 Rio Rancho New Mexico U.S.A.
155 G6 Rio Rico Arizona U.S.A.
98 C3 Riós Spain
98 E2 Rioseco de Tapia Spain
172 F1 Río Segundo Argentina
99 G4 Riosequillo, Emb. de resr Spain
162 B2 Ríosucio Colombia
173 H2 Río Tala Argentina
172 E2 Río Tercero Argentina
172 E2 Río Tercero, Emb. resr Argentina
162 B4 Río Tigre Ecuador
98 B3 Rio Tinto Portugal
23 A4 Rio Tuba Philippines
91 D5 Riou, Île de i. France
168 C2 Rio Verde Brazil
171 B7 Río Verde Chile
157 F4 Río Verde Mexico
168 A3 Rio Verde de Mato Grosso Brazil
154 B2 Rio Vista California U.S.A.
90 E1 Rioz France
165 E3 Riozinho r. Brazil
166 B2 Riozinho r. Brazil
106 A4 Ripa r. Italy
112 C2 Ripanj Yugoslavia
107 E5 Riparbella Italy
109 F2 Ripatransone Italy
107 H5 Ripe Italy
53 D1 Ripky Ukraine
65 G3 Ripley England U.K.
63 E1 Ripley England U.K.
146 B5 Ripley Ohio U.S.A.
145 B5 Ripley Tennessee U.S.A.
146 C5 Ripley W. Virginia U.S.A.
102 F2 Ripoll Spain
102 F2 Ripolles reg. Spain
154 B3 Ripon California U.S.A.
65 G3 Ripon England U.K.
148 C4 Ripon Wisconsin U.S.A.
111 E5 Riposto Sicilia Italy
62 C3 Risca Wales U.K.
93 B5 Riscle France
172 C3 Risco Plateado mt. Argentina

8 F3 Rotorua, L. l. New Zealand
69 C4 Rotselaar Belgium
80 D4 Rotsteinberg mt. Austria
75 J4 Rott r. Germany
83 F1 Rott Germany
75 G5 Rottach-Egern Germany
75 H5 Rott am Inn Germany
87 F4 Rotte r. France
80 C1 Röttenbach Germany
83 F1 Rottenbuch Germany
74 D4 Rottenburg am Neckar Germany
75 H4 Rottenburg an der Laaber Germany
74 F3 Rottendorf Germany
81 F3 Rottenmann Austria
81 F3 Rottenmanner Tauern mts Austria
68 C3 Rotterdam Netherlands
75 J4 Rotthalmünster Germany
74 E3 Röttingham Germany
73 F4 Rottleberode Germany
59 E1 Rottnan r. Sweden
59 F3 Rottnen l. Sweden
59 E2 Rottneros Sweden
17 A7 Rottnest I. i. Western Australia Australia
83 E3 Rottofreno Italy
68 E1 Rottumeroog i. Netherlands
68 E1 Rottumerplaat i. Netherlands
74 D4 Rottweil Germany
176 G6 Rotuma i. Fiji
56 D3 Rötviken Sweden
75 H3 Rötz Germany
86 C2 Roubaix France
93 D6 Rouch, Mt mt. France/Spain
81 H1 Rouchovany Czech Rep.
78 D1 Roudnice nad Labem Czech Rep.
89 G2 Rouen Seine-et-Marne France
93 E4 Rouergue reg. France
87 G5 Rouffach France
92 C3 Rouffignac France
54 E3 Rõuge Estonia
88 D4 Rougé France
90 E1 Rougemont France
90 E1 Rougemont-le-Château France
9 B6 Rough Ridge ridge New Zealand
92 C3 Rougnac France
92 B3 Rouillac France
91 B5 Roujan France
°0 E1 Roulans France
Roulers see Roeselare
92 C3 Roumazières-Loubert France
89 F2 Roumois reg. France
139 F3 Roundeyed, Lac l. Québec Canada
65 G3 Round Hill h. England U.K.
127 □3 Round I. i. Rodrigues I. Mauritius
154 D2 Round Mountain Nevada U.S.A.
13 H2 Round Mt mt. New South Wales Australia
155 H3 Round Rock Arizona U.S.A.
152 E2 Roundup Montana U.S.A.
31 J2 Rouny Rus. Fed.
163 G3 Roura French Guiana
91 F3 Roure Italy
66 E1 Rousay i. Scotland U.K.
147 G2 Rouses Point New York U.S.A.
81 H1 Rousínov Czech Rep.
93 E6 Roussillon reg. France
91 C3 Roussillon Rhône-Alpes France
Routh Bank sand bank see Seahorse Bank
89 F2 Routot France
89 E3 Rouvre r. France
86 D3 Rouvroy-sur-Audry France
91 E5 Roux, Cap c. France
131 F5 Rouxville South Africa
90 B1 Rouy France
141 F2 Rouyn-Noranda Québec Canada
56 G2 Rovaniemi Finland
83 D3 Rovasenda r. Italy
106 E3 Rovato Italy
51 F5 Roven'ki Rus. Fed.
83 F3 Roverbella Italy
83 E2 Roveredo Switzerland
107 F3 Rovereto Italy
73 H1 Rövershagen Germany
109 E2 Roviano Italy
25 D4 Rôviĕng Tbong Cambodia
107 F3 Rovigo div. Italy
107 F3 Rovigo Italy
112 D2 Rovinari Romania
107 H3 Rovinj Croatia
81 H5 Rovišće Croatia
51 H5 Rovnoye Rus. Fed.
127 C7 Rovuma r. Mozambique
76 C3 Rów Poland
6 □2 Rowa is Vanuatu
39 B2 Row'ān Iran
13 G2 Rowena New South Wales Australia
16 B3 Rowley Shoals sand bank Western Australia Australia
23 B4 Roxas Philippines
23 B3 Roxas Philippines
23 B2 Roxas Philippines
23 B4 Roxas Philippines
23 A4 Roxas Philippines
145 E4 Roxboro N. Carolina U.S.A.
159 □2 Roxborough Tobago Trinidad and Tobago
14 D4 Roxborough Downs Queensland Australia
9 B6 Roxburgh New Zealand
15 E2 Roxby Nat. Park nat. park Queensland Australia
59 F2 Roxen l. Sweden
100 B3 Roxo r. Portugal
100 B3 Roxo, Barragem do resr Portugal
122 A4 Roxo, Cabo pt Senegal
141 J4 Roxton-Sud Québec Canada
153 F4 Roy New Mexico U.S.A.
106 B5 Roya r. France/Italy
67 E3 Royal Canal canal Rep. of Ireland
148 C1 Royale, Isle i. Michigan U.S.A.
149 F4 Royal Oak Michigan U.S.A.
92 A3 Royan France
91 D3 Roybon France
66 D4 Roybridge Scotland U.K.
86 B3 Roye France
92 D3 Royère-de-Vassivière France
53 D1 Royishche Ukraine
58 D2 Røyken Norway
138 E2 Roy, Lac Le l. Québec Canada
63 F2 Royston England U.K.
65 F4 Royton England U.K.
112 C3 Rožaj Yugoslavia
77 K3 Różan Poland
76 D3 Różanki Poland
86 B4 Rozay-en-Brie France
75 L2 Rožďalovice Czech Rep.
77 N6 Rozdil Ukraine
53 D3 Rozdil'na Ukraine
51 E6 Rozdol'ne Ukraine
68 C3 Rozenburg Netherlands
47 H2 Rozhdestvenka Kazakhstan
52 C1 Rozhdestveno Rus. Fed.
52 C1 Rozhdestveno Rus. Fed.
50 H3 Rozhdestvenskoye Rus. Fed.
52 H1 Rozhentsovo Rus. Fed.
53 A2 Rozhniv Ukraine
53 C1 Rozhnivka Ukraine
53 A1 Rozhyshche Ukraine
53 G3 Rozivka Ukraine
78 C2 Rožmitál pod Třemšínem Czech Rep.
79 K3 Rožňava Slovakia
79 H2 Rožnov pod Radhoštěm Czech Rep.
77 K2 Rozoga r. Poland
77 K2 Rozogi Poland
86 D3 Rozoy-sur-Serre France
77 M5 Roztoczański Park Narodowy nat. park Poland
77 J6 Roztoka Wielka Poland
75 K2 Roztoky Czech Rep.
106 D3 Rozzano Italy
52 F3 Rtishchevo Rus. Fed.
98 C4 Rua Portugal
62 C2 Ruabon Wales U.K.
127 B6 Ruaha National Park nat. park Tanzania
8 E3 Ruapehu, Mt volcano New Zealand
9 B7 Ruapuke I. i. New Zealand
8 F3 Ruarine Range mountain range New Zealand
9 C5 Ruatapu New Zealand
8 G2 Ruatoria New Zealand
89 F4 Ruaudin France
41 G6 Rub al Khālī desert Saudi Arabia
53 F3 Rubanivka Ukraine
107 F3 Rubano Italy
99 G1 Rubayo Spain
127 C6 Rubeho Mountains mts Tanzania
169 G2 Rubelita Brazil
99 G2 Rubena Spain
28 J2 Rubeshibe Japan
66 C2 Rubha Coigeach pt Scotland U.K.
66 B3 Rubha Hunish pt Scotland U.K.
64 B2 Rubh a'Mhail pt Scotland U.K.
64 B2 Rubh' an t-Sailein pt Scotland U.K.
66 C3 Rubha Reidh pt Scotland U.K.
Rubha Robhanais headland see Butt of Lewis
124 E3 Rubi r. Congo(Zaire)
124 E3 Rubi Congo(Zaire)
103 B5 Rubial, Serra de mountain range Spain
168 D1 Rubiataba Brazil
154 B2 Rubicon r. California U.S.A.
103 C4 Rubielos de Mora Spain
51 F5 Rubizhne Ukraine
127 B5 Rubondo Island i. Tanzania
53 G2 Rubtsi Ukraine
47 K2 Rubtsovsk Rus. Fed.
134 C3 Ruby Alaska U.S.A.
155 E1 Ruby Lake l. Nevada U.S.A.
155 E1 Ruby Mountains mts Nevada U.S.A.
172 E4 Rucanelo Argentina
112 E2 Rucăr Romania
33 F3 Rucheng China
50 G1 Ruch'i Rus. Fed.
77 K2 Ruciane-Nida Poland
73 J4 Rückersdorf Germany
146 D5 Ruckersville Virginia U.S.A.
59 G3 Ruda Sweden
77 M4 Ruda-Huta Poland
16 C4 Rudall watercourse Western Australia Australia
16 C4 Rudall River Nat. Park nat. park Western Australia Australia
77 J4 Ruda Maleniecka Poland
77 M1 Rudamina Lithuania
39 D4 Rudan Iran
37 E4 Rudarpur India
76 G5 Ruda Śląska Poland
37 E4 Rudauli India
39 E3 Rudbar Afghanistan
69 B3 Ruddervoorde Belgium
39 D1 Rūd-e Kāl-Shūr r. Iran
73 J1 Ruden i. Germany
81 H3 Rudersdorf Austria
73 J3 Rüdersdorf Berlin Germany
87 G3 Rüdesheim Germany
87 G3 Rüdesheim am Rhein Germany
39 D3 Rūd-e Shur watercourse Iran
39 F2 Rud-i Musa Qala r. Afghanistan
54 D4 Rūdiškės Lithuania
53 E1 Rudivka Ukraine
77 L3 Rudka Poland
55 C5 Rudkøbing Denmark
77 M6 Rudky Ukraine
76 E4 Rudna Poland
112 C2 Rudna Glava Yugoslavia
28 K1 Rudnaya Rus. Fed.
27 P3 Rudnaya Pristan' China
77 M6 Rudne Ukraine
50 K3 Rudnichnyy Rus. Fed.
77 L5 Rudnik Poland
76 G4 Rudniki Poland
52 G2 Rudnya r. Rus. Fed.
50 D4 Rudnya Rus. Fed.
51 H5 Rudnya Rus. Fed.
53 B1 Rudnya-Ivanivs'ka Ukraine
53 C2 Rudnytsya Ukraine
46 F2 Rudnyy Kazakhstan
44 G1 Rudolfa, O. i. Rus. Fed.
178 □1 Rudolftoppen h. Jan Mayen Arctic Ocean
75 G2 Rudolstadt Germany
33 H1 Rudong China
52 F3 Rudovka Rus. Fed.
114 F1 Rudozem Bulgaria
99 G2 Rudrón r. Spain
39 B1 Rūdsar Iran
58 C2 Rudsgrendi Norway
55 D4 Ruds Vedby Denmark
148 E2 Rudyard Michigan U.S.A.
54 E5 Rudzyensk Belarus
86 A2 Rue France
101 E1 Ruecas r. Spain
99 F3 Rueda Spain
102 B3 Rueda de Jalón Spain
92 C3 Ruelle-sur-Touvre France
129 E2 Ruenya r. Zimbabwe
80 C3 Ruetz r. Austria
119 F5 Rufa'a Sudan
111 H3 Ruffano Italy
92 C2 Ruffec France
82 A2 Ruffey-sur-Seille France
90 D2 Ruffieu France
90 D3 Ruffieux France
145 □3 Ruffing Pt pt Virgin Is Caribbean
127 C6 Rufiji r. Tanzania
173 F3 Rufino Argentina
122 A4 Rufisque Senegal
125 E7 Rufunsa Zambia
54 E3 Rugāji Latvia
33 H1 Rugao China
73 G2 Rugberg h. Germany
63 F2 Rugby England U.K.
150 C1 Rugby N. Dakota U.S.A.
63 E2 Rugeley England U.K.
73 J1 Rügen i. Germany
146 B4 Ruggles Ohio U.S.A.
75 F3 Rügland Germany
89 F3 Rugles France
127 A5 Ruhengeri Rwanda
73 J4 Ruhland Germany
54 C3 Ruhnu i. Estonia
75 H5 Ruhpolding Germany
72 B4 Ruhr r. Germany
75 J4 Ruhstorf an der Rott Germany
127 C6 Ruhudji r. Tanzania
33 H3 Rui'an China
33 F2 Ruichang China
33 E1 Ruicheng China
101 H2 Ruidera Spain
153 F5 Ruidoso New Mexico U.S.A.
33 F3 Ruijin China
32 B3 Ruili China
108 A5 Ruinas Sardegna Italy
68 E2 Ruinen Netherlands
68 E2 Ruinerwold Netherlands
137 N2 Ruin Point pt N.W.T. Canada
127 C6 Ruipa Tanzania
69 B3 Ruiselede Belgium
156 D4 Ruiz Mexico
162 B3 Ruiz, Nevado de volcano Colombia
54 D3 Rūjiena Latvia
39 B4 Rukbah well Saudi Arabia
124 C4 Ruki r. Congo(Zaire)
58 B1 Ruklenuten mt. Norway
37 E3 Rukumkot Nepal
127 A5 Rukungiri Uganda
6 □6 Rukuruku B. b. Fiji
127 B6 Rukwa div. Tanzania
127 B6 Rukwa, Lake l. Tanzania
39 D4 Rūl Qadnah U.A.E.
16 D2 Rulhieres, C. c. Western Australia Australia
87 H3 Rülzheim Germany
66 B3 Rum i. Scotland U.K.
80 C3 Rum Austria
78 F4 Rum Hungary
39 D2 Rūm Iran
112 B2 Ruma Yugoslavia
14 C5 Rumbalara Northern Terr. Australia
124 E2 Rumbek Sudan
101 G2 Rumblar r. Spain
78 D1 Rumburk Czech Rep.
158 D2 Rum Cay i. The Bahamas
69 E5 Rumelange Luxembourg
69 B4 Rumes Belgium
147 H2 Rumford Maine U.S.A.
76 G1 Rumia Poland
86 D3 Rumigny France
90 D3 Rumilly France
14 B2 Rum Jungle Northern Terr. Australia
119 H2 Rummān, J. ar mts Saudi Arabia
28 H2 Rumoi Japan
127 A5 Rumonge Burundi
87 E4 Rumont France
127 B7 Rumphi Malawi
69 C3 Rumst Belgium
15 F3 Rumula Queensland Australia
64 B2 Runabay Head Northern Ireland U.K.
33 F1 Runan China
9 C5 Runanga New Zealand
159 □1 Runaway Bay Jamaica
8 F2 Runaway, Cape c. New Zealand
65 F4 Runcorn England U.K.
129 E3 Runde r. Zimbabwe
128 B2 Rundu Namibia
56 E3 Rundvik Sweden
22 C2 Rungan r. Indonesia
124 E3 Rungu Congo(Zaire)
172 B2 Rungue Chile
127 B6 Rungwa r. Tanzania
127 B6 Rungwa Rukwa Tanzania
127 B6 Rungwa Singida Tanzania
127 B6 Rungwa Game Reserve res. Tanzania
33 G1 Runheji China
74 D2 Runkel Germany
59 F1 Runn l. Sweden
59 G3 Runnö i. Sweden
17 C4 Runton Ra. h. Western Australia Australia
32 C1 Ru'nying China
56 H3 Ruokolahti Finland
91 C4 Ruoms France
26 E4 Ruoqiang China
30 A4 Ruo Shui r. China
54 E1 Ruotsinpyhtää Finland
107 J3 Rupa Croatia
37 H4 Rupa India
172 A6 Rupanco, L. l. Chile
13 E4 Rupanyup Victoria Australia
112 E1 Rupea Romania
138 E3 Rupert r. Québec Canada
152 D3 Rupert Idaho U.S.A.
138 E3 Rupert Bay b. Québec Canada
179 A4 Ruppert Coast coastal area Antarctica
87 F5 Rupt-sur-Moselle France
163 F3 Rupununi r. Guyana
164 C2 Rurrenabaque Bolivia
74 B2 Rurstausee l. Germany
5 M7 Rurutu i. French Polynesia Pacific Ocean
101 H1 Rus r. Spain
129 E2 Rusape Zimbabwe
112 E1 Ruscova Romania
112 E3 Ruse Bulgaria
81 G4 Ruše Slovenia
37 F4 Rusera India
67 E3 Rush Rep. of Ireland
31 G5 Rushan China
63 F2 Rushden England U.K.
148 B4 Rushford Minnesota U.S.A.
129 E2 Rushinga Zimbabwe
148 C4 Rush Lake l. Wisconsin U.S.A.
37 H3 Rushon India
148 B5 Rushville Illinois U.S.A.
150 C3 Rushville Nebraska U.S.A.
76 E2 Rusinowo Poland
151 E6 Rusk Texas U.S.A.
59 F3 Rusken l. Sweden
145 D7 Ruskin Florida U.S.A.
54 B4 Rusnė Lithuania
112 F3 Rusokastro Bulgaria
54 E3 Rušona Latvia
54 C2 Russarö i. Finland
166 E1 Russas Brazil
150 D4 Russell Kansas U.S.A.
137 J4 Russell Manitoba Canada
141 H4 Russell Ontario Canada
8 E1 Russell New Zealand
136 F2 Russel Lake l. N.W.T. Canada
135 J2 Russell I. i. N.W.T. Canada
6 □1 Russell Is is Solomon Is.
17 C7 Russell Ra. h. Western Australia Australia
145 C4 Russellville Alabama U.S.A.
151 E5 Russellville Arkansas U.S.A.
144 C4 Russellville Kentucky U.S.A.
74 D3 Rüsselsheim Germany
107 G4 Russi Italy
49 K2 Russian Federation country Asia/Europe
52 C3 Russkiy Brod Rus. Fed.
52 H3 Russkiy Kameshkir Rus. Fed.
45 Q2 Russkoye Ust'ye Rus. Fed.
81 H3 Rust Austria
51 H7 Rust'avi Georgia
52 G1 Rustay Rus. Fed.
131 G2 Rust de Winter South Africa
131 F2 Rustenburg South Africa
131 F2 Rustenburg Nature Reserve res. South Africa
58 B2 Rustfjellheii mt. Norway
131 F3 Rustig South Africa
151 E5 Ruston Louisiana U.S.A.
82 D1 Ruswil Switzerland
76 D4 Ruszów Poland
127 A5 Rutana Burundi
101 F3 Rute Spain
22 E4 Ruteng Indonesia
155 E2 Ruth Nevada U.S.A.
72 D4 Rüthen Germany
141 F3 Rutherglen Ontario Canada
62 C1 Ruthin Wales U.K.
83 D1 Rüti Switzerland
111 G1 Rutigliano Italy
109 H4 Rutino Italy
52 H1 Rutka r. Rus. Fed.
77 L1 Rutka-Tartak Poland
77 L2 Rutki-Kossaki Poland
63 F2 Rutland div. England U.K.
147 G3 Rutland Vermont U.S.A.
25 A5 Rutland I. i. Andaman and Nicobar Is India
15 E2 Rutland Plains Queensland Australia
63 F2 Rutland Water resr England U.K.
137 G2 Rutledge Lake l. N.W.T. Canada
36 D2 Rutog China
68 D2 Rutten Netherlands
140 E3 Rutter Ontario Canada
51 H7 Rutul Rus. Fed.
56 G2 Ruukki Finland
68 E2 Ruurlo Netherlands
39 D4 Ru'us al Jibāl mts Oman
109 J3 Ruvo di Puglia Italy
127 C7 Ruvuma div. Tanzania
127 C7 Ruvuma r. Tanzania
43 A5 Ruwayān, W. el depression Egypt
42 D3 Ruwayshid, Wādī watercourse Jordan
43 C5 Ruweijil pt Saudi Arabia
39 C4 Ruweis U.A.E.
43 D5 Ruweita, W. watercourse Jordan
127 A5 Ruwenzori Range mountain range Uganda/Congo(Zaire)
91 B3 Ruynes-en-Margeride France
33 F3 Ruyuan China
52 C2 Ruza r. Rus. Fed.
52 C2 Ruza Rus. Fed.
47 G2 Ruzayevka Kazakhstan
52 G2 Ruzayevka Rus. Fed.
77 N3 Ruzhany Belarus
52 B3 Ruzhnoye Rus. Fed.
53 C2 Ruzhyn Ukraine
79 J2 Ružomberok Slovakia
78 D1 Ruzyně airport Czech Rep.
107 H3 Rvignano Italy
117 G6 Rwanda country Africa
Rwenzori Range mountain range see Ruwenzori Range
127 B5 Rweru, Lake l. Burundi
55 B3 Ry Denmark
55 B2 Ryå r. Denmark
39 C1 Ryābād Iran
54 F1 Ryabovo Rus. Fed.
50 H2 Ryadovo Rus. Fed.
64 C3 Ryan, Loch b. Scotland U.K.
53 F3 Ryas'ke Ukraine
53 D3 Ryasnopil' Ukraine
50 F4 Ryazan' div. Rus. Fed.
50 F4 Ryazan' Rus. Fed.
52 F3 Ryazanka Rus. Fed.
52 D2 Ryazanovskiy Rus. Fed.
52 D1 Ryazantsevo Rus. Fed.
52 E3 Ryazhsk Rus. Fed.
Rybach'ye see Ysyk-Köl Canada
50 F3 Rybinskoye Vdkhr. resr. Rus. Fed.
52 F2 Rybkino Rus. Fed.
76 G5 Rybnik Poland
77 H2 Rybno Ciechanow Poland
77 K2 Rybno Olsztyn Poland
50 F4 Rybnoye Rus. Fed.
77 M3 Ryboły Poland
78 G1 Rychlebské Hory h. Czech Rep.
77 H2 Rychliki Poland
78 F1 Rychnov nad Kněžnou Czech Rep.
77 J2 Rychnowo Poland
76 F4 Rychtal Poland
76 G3 Rychwał Poland
54 E4 Rychy, Vozyera l. Belarus/Lithuania
73 J1 Ryck r. Germany
136 F3 Rycroft Alberta Canada
76 E3 Ryczywół Poland
59 F3 Ryd Sweden
59 F3 Rydaholm Sweden
179 B3 Rydberg Pen. pen. Antarctica
63 E4 Ryde England U.K.
55 E2 Rydet Sweden
53 A2 Rydomyl' Ukraine
59 F3 Rydsnäs Sweden
76 G5 Rydułtowy Poland
76 E4 Rydzyna Poland
65 G3 Rye r. England U.K.
63 G4 Rye England U.K.
63 G4 Rye Bay b. England U.K.
58 A2 Ryfylke reg. Norway
58 C2 Rykene Norway
53 B1 Rykhal's'ke Ukraine
53 B2 Rykhta Ukraine
77 K4 Ryki Poland
77 N1 Rykiškiai Lithuania
52 B4 Ryl'sk Rus. Fed.
13 G3 Rylstone New South Wales Australia
76 D2 Rymań Poland
77 K6 Rymanów Poland
78 G2 Rýmařov Czech Rep.
54 B1 Rymättylä Finland
77 K2 Ryn Poland
46 C3 Ryn-Peski desert Kazakhstan
76 G2 Ryńsk Poland
29 H4 Ryōri-zaki pt Japan
29 G4 Ryōtsu Japan
77 H2 Rypin Poland
52 B3 Ryshkovo Rus. Fed.
58 A1 Rysjedal Norway
55 C4 Ryslinge Denmark
76 F2 Rytel Poland
55 □2 Rytterknægten h. Denmark
52 A3 Ryukhovo Rus. Fed.
Ryukyu Islands is see Nansei-shoto
114 B1 Ržanovo Macedonia
77 K3 Rząśnik Poland
77 J4 Rzeczyca Poland
77 J2 Rzęgnowo Poland
76 C3 Rzepin Poland
76 D2 Rzesznikowo Poland
77 K5 Rzeszów div. Poland
77 L5 Rzeszów Poland
52 F3 Rzhaksa Rus. Fed.
52 B1 Rzhev Rus. Fed.
53 D2 Rzhyshchiv Ukraine
77 J4 Rzuców Poland

S

39 D2 Sa'ābād Iran
126 D4 Saacow Somalia
43 D5 Sa'ada al Barsa mountain range Saudi Arabia
39 C3 Sa'ādatābād Fārs Iran
39 C3 Sa'ādatābād Hormozgān Iran
39 C3 Sa'ādatābād Kermān Iran
130 C5 Saaifontein South Africa
80 D3 Saalach r. Austria
80 C2 Saal an der Donau Germany
80 C3 Saalbach-Hinterglemm Austria
73 G4 Saale r. Germany
73 H1 Saaler Bodden inlet Germany
87 G4 Saales France
75 G2 Saalfeld Germany
80 D3 Saalfelden am Steinernen Meer Austria
89 F2 Saâne r. France
82 C2 Saane r. Switzerland
82 C2 Saanen Switzerland
74 B3 Saar r. Germany
74 B3 Saarbrücken Germany
74 B3 Saarburg Germany
54 C3 Sääre Estonia
54 E2 Saare Estonia
54 C2 Saaremaa i. Estonia
56 G2 Saarenkylä Finland
69 E5 Saargau reg. Germany
56 G3 Saarijärvi Finland
56 G2 Saari-Kämä Finland
56 F1 Saarikoski Finland
74 B3 Saarland div. Germany
74 B3 Saarlouis Germany
74 B3 Saarwellingen Germany
82 C2 Saas Fee Switzerland
82 C2 Saastal v. Switzerland
42 G2 Saatli Azerbaijan
Saatly see Saatli
54 C3 Säätse Estonia
173 F4 Saavedra Argentina
159 G3 Saba i. Netherlands Ant.
43 B4 Saba'a Egypt
159 G3 Saba Bank sea feature Caribbean
42 D3 Şab' Ābār Syria
112 B2 Šabac Yugoslavia
102 F3 Sabadell Spain
29 F5 Sabae Japan
23 A5 Sabah div. Malaysia
25 C7 Sabak Malaysia
22 D3 Sabalana i. Indonesia
22 D3 Sabalana, Kep. is Indonesia
36 D4 Sabalgarh India
163 F2 Sabana Surinam
158 B2 Sabana, Arch. de is Cuba
156 J6 Sabana Gde Honduras
162 C1 Sabanalarga Colombia
159 E5 Sabaneta Venezuela
22 E2 Sabang Indonesia
22 D1 Sabang Indonesia
112 F1 Săbăoani Romania
169 G3 Sabará Brazil
93 D5 Sabarat France
38 C2 Sābari r. India
36 C5 Sabarmati r. India
22 D3 Sabaru i. Indonesia
43 C3 Sabastiya Israel
109 G4 Sabato r. Italy
109 F3 Sabaudia Italy
109 F3 Sabaudia, Lago di lag. Italy
164 C3 Sabaya Bolivia
106 E4 Sabbionetta Italy
39 D2 Sabeh Iran
130 D5 Sabelo South Africa
99 E2 Sabero Spain
118 B2 Sabhā Libya
119 H3 Şabḩā' Saudi Arabia
36 D4 Sabi r. India
131 J2 Sabie r. Mozambique/South Africa
131 J2 Sabie Mozambique
131 H2 Sabie South Africa
131 H2 Sabie Sand Game Res. res. South Africa
54 C3 Sabile Latvia
156 D2 Sabinal Mexico
102 C2 Sabiñánigo Spain
101 H4 Sabinar, Pta del mt. Spain
157 E3 Sabinas Mexico
157 E3 Sabinas Hidalgo Mexico
151 E6 Sabine L. l. Louisiana/Texas U.S.A.
109 E2 Sabini, Monti mts Italy
169 G3 Sabinópolis Brazil
79 L2 Sabinov Slovakia
101 G2 Sabiote Spain
129 D3 Sabiwa Zimbabwe
120 B4 Sabkhat Aghzoumal salt flat Western Sahara
118 C1 Sabkhat al Hayshah salt pan Libya
43 D2 Sabkhat al Jabbūl salt flat Syria
43 D2 Sabkhat al Marāghah salt flat Syria
120 B3 Sabkhat Aridal salt pan Western Sahara
120 B3 Sabkhat Oum Dba salt pan Western Sahara
120 B3 Sabkhat Tah salt pan Morocco
43 B4 Sabkhet el Bardawīl lag. Egypt
23 B3 Sablayan Philippines
139 G5 Sable, Cape c. Nova Scotia Canada
145 D7 Sable, Cape c. Florida U.S.A.
139 J5 Sable I. i. Nova Scotia Canada
6 □2 Sable, Î. de i. New Caledonia Pacific Ocean
89 E4 Sablé-sur-Sarthe France
91 C5 Sablon, Pointe du pt France
77 L3 Sabnie Poland
166 E2 Saboeiro Brazil
123 F4 Sabon Kafi Niger
122 D4 Sabou Burkina
93 B4 Sabres France
179 C6 Sabrina Coast coastal area Antarctica
98 C3 Sabrosa Portugal
23 B1 Sabtang i. Philippines
98 C4 Sabugal Portugal
148 B4 Sabula Iowa U.S.A.
22 E2 Sabulu Indonesia
119 H4 Şabyā Saudi Arabia
Sabzawar see Shindand
39 D1 Sabzevār Iran
Sabzvārān see Jiroft
103 F5 Sa Cabaneta Spain
164 C3 Sacaca Bolivia
173 F1 Sacanta Argentina
100 A2 Sacavém Portugal
157 F5 Sacbecan Mexico
91 F4 Saccarel, Mt mt. France/Italy
109 F3 Sacco r. Italy
99 H4 Sacecorbo Spain
99 H4 Sacedón Spain
112 E1 Săcel Romania
112 E2 Săcele Romania
125 C6 Sachanga Angola
138 B3 Sachigo r. Ontario Canada
138 B3 Sachigo L. l. Ontario Canada
36 C5 Sachin India
28 B6 Sach'ŏn South Korea
36 D2 Sach P. pass India
82 D2 Sachseln Switzerland
73 J4 Sachsen div. Germany
73 G3 Sachsen-Anhalt div. Germany
72 E4 Sachsenhausen Germany
134 F2 Sachs Harbour N.W.T. Canada
75 K2 Sächsische Schweiz, Nationalpark nat. park Germany
107 G3 Sacile Italy
147 E3 Sackets Harbor New York U.S.A.
74 D2 Sackpfeife h. Germany
139 H4 Sackville New Brunswick Canada
147 H3 Saco Maine U.S.A.
152 F1 Saco Montana U.S.A.
23 B5 Sacol i. Philippines
82 A1 Sacquenay France
154 B2 Sacramento airport California U.S.A.
154 B2 Sacramento r. California U.S.A.
154 B2 Sacramento California U.S.A.
168 E3 Sacramento Brazil
153 F5 Sacramento Mts mountain range New Mexico U.S.A.
152 B3 Sacramento Valley v. California U.S.A.
101 G4 Sacratif, Cabo pt Spain
165 E2 Sacre r. Brazil
79 M4 Săcueni Romania
165 E2 Sacuriuiná r. Brazil
131 F6 Sada South Africa
98 B1 Sada Spain
102 B2 Sádaba Spain
39 B3 Sa'dabad Iran
42 D3 Şadad Syria
119 H4 Şa'dah Yemen
39 B4 Sada, J. as h. Saudi Arabia
28 D7 Sada-misaki pt Japan
25 C6 Sadao Thailand
36 B2 Sadda Pakistan
131 H2 Saddleback pass South Africa
15 F2 Saddle Hill h. Queensland Australia
Saddle I. i. see Mota Lava
25 A4 Saddle Peak summit Andaman and Nicobar Is India
25 D5 Sa Dec Vietnam
37 H3 Sadêng China
36 D3 Sadhaura India
159 □3 Sadhoowa Trinidad and Tobago
126 C3 Sadi Ethiopia
39 D4 Sadīj watercourse Iran
36 B3 Sadiqabad Pakistan
36 C1 Sad Istragh mt. Afghanistan/Pakistan
37 H4 Sadiya India
119 G3 Sa'diya Saudi Arabia
39 C4 Sa'diyyat i. U.A.E.
39 D1 Sad-Kharv Iran
77 J4 Sadkowice Poland
76 E2 Sadkowo Poland
76 G2 Sadlinki Poland
100 B2 Sado r. Portugal
29 G4 Sadoga-shima i. Japan
51 H7 Sadon Rus. Fed.
22 B1 Sadong r. Malaysia
51 H6 Sadovoye Rus. Fed.
77 K3 Sadowne Poland
103 F5 Sa Dragonera i. Spain
36 C4 Sadri India
75 K2 Sadská Czech Rep.
43 C4 Sadūt Egypt
55 C2 Sæby Denmark
99 H5 Saelices Spain
99 E2 Saelices de Mayorga Spain
72 C3 Saerbeck Germany
69 D5 Saeul Luxembourg
43 D3 Safa lava Syria
Safad see Zefat
100 C2 Safara Portugal
7 □12 Safata B. b. Western Samoa
42 F4 Safayal Maqūf well Iraq
47 H5 Safed Khirs mts Afghanistan
39 G2 Safed Koh mountain range Afghanistan/Pakistan
59 E2 Säffle Sweden
155 H5 Safford Arizona U.S.A.
88 D4 Saffré France
63 G2 Saffron Walden England U.K.
43 C4 Safi Jordan
120 C2 Safi Morocco
39 C2 Safid Ab Iran
39 E3 Safidabeh Iran
39 B2 Safid Dasht Iran
39 E2 Safid Sagak Iran
169 G3 Safiras, Sa de mts Brazil
42 D3 Şāfītā Syria
56 J1 Safonovo Rus. Fed.
52 A2 Safonovo Rus. Fed.
50 J1 Safonovo Rus. Fed.
7 □12 Safotu Western Samoa
119 H2 Safrā' al Asyāḩ escarpment Saudi Arabia
119 H2 Safrā' as Sark escarpment Saudi Arabia
42 C1 Safranbolu Turkey
7 □12 Safune Western Samoa
42 F4 Safwān Iraq
37 F3 Saga China
28 C7 Saga div. Japan
28 C7 Saga Japan
46 F3 Saga Kazakhstan
29 H4 Sagae Japan
24 A2 Sagaing div. Myanmar
24 A2 Sagaing Myanmar
29 G6 Sagamihara Japan
29 G6 Sagami-nada g. Japan
29 G6 Sagami-wan b. Japan
162 C2 Sagamoso r. Colombia
123 E5 Sagamu Nigeria
140 D2 Saganash Lake l. Ontario Canada
47 J4 Sagankuduk China
25 B4 Saganthit Kyun i. Myanmar
36 D5 Sagar India
38 B2 Sagar India
38 A3 Sagar India
Sagaredzho see Sagarejo
51 H7 Sagarejo Georgia
37 G5 Sagar I. i. India
45 O2 Sagastyr Rus. Fed.
37 F4 Sagauli India
59 F1 Sågen Sweden
39 C2 Saghand Iran
39 E2 Saghar Afghanistan
114 B3 Sagiada Greece
38 B3 Sagileru r. India
149 F4 Saginaw Michigan U.S.A.
149 F4 Saginaw Bay b. Michigan U.S.A.
113 G5 Sağırlar Turkey
46 D3 Sagiz r. Kazakhstan
46 D3 Sagiz Kazakhstan
122 C5 Sagleipie Liberia
139 H2 Saglek Bay b. Newfoundland Canada
108 A2 Sagone Corse France
101 H3 Sagra mt. Spain
172 B3 Sagrada Familia Chile
100 B3 Sagres Portugal
100 B4 Sagres, Pta de pt Portugal
30 A3 Sagsay watercourse Mongolia
24 A2 Sagu Myanmar
153 F4 Saguache Colorado U.S.A.
158 D2 Sagua de Tánamo Cuba
158 B2 Sagua la Grande Cuba
155 G5 Saguaro National Monument nat. park Arizona U.S.A.
139 F4 Saguenay r. Québec Canada
103 C5 Sagunto Spain
58 A2 Sagvåg Norway
36 C5 Sagwara India
82 A2 Sagy France
43 D4 Sahāb Jordan
42 G2 Şahağac Azerbaijan
162 B2 Sahagun Colombia
99 E2 Sahagún Spain
120 C4 Sahara desert Africa
43 C5 Sahara, G. mt. Egypt
Saharan Atlas mountain range see Atlas Saharien
36 D3 Saharanpur India
37 F4 Saharsa India
36 D3 Sahaswan India
42 F2 Şahbuz Azerbaijan
43 B5 Saheira, W. el watercourse Egypt
122 D4 Sahel, Réserve partielle du res. Burkina
37 F4 Sahibganj India
36 C3 Sahiwal Pakistan
36 C3 Sahiwal Pakistan
39 D2 Sahlābād Iran
42 F3 Şaḩneh Iran

42 F4 Şaḩrā al Ḩijārah reg. Iraq
43 A5 Sahra Esh Sharqiya desert Egypt
156 C2 Sahuaripa Mexico
155 G6 Sahuarita Arizona U.S.A.
156 E4 Sahuayo Mexico
93 C6 Sahún Spain
91 D4 Sahune France
119 H2 Şāḩūq reg. Saudi Arabia
119 H2 Şāhūq, W. watercourse Saudi Arabia
25 E4 Sa Huynh Vietnam
79 H3 Šahy Slovakia
Sahyadri mountain range see Western Ghats
36 C5 Sahyadriparvat h. India
43 D2 Sahyūn Syria
37 E4 Sai r. India
25 C6 Sai Buri r. Thailand
25 C6 Sai Buri Thailand
121 E2 Saïda Algeria
43 C3 Saïda Lebanon
39 C3 Sa'īdābād Iran
39 E4 Sa'īdī Iran
37 G4 Saidpur Bangladesh
37 E4 Saidpur India
92 E3 Saignes France
28 D5 Saigō Japan
Saigon see Hô Chi Minh
37 H5 Saiha India
30 B4 Saihan Toroi China
28 D7 Saijō Japan
28 C7 Saiki Japan
27 □ Sai Kung Hong Kong China
36 C5 Sailana India
93 E6 Saillagouse-Llo France
91 D4 Saillans France
57 H3 Saimaa l. Finland
42 D2 Saimbeyli Turkey
39 C3 Sā'īn Iran
156 E4 Sain Alto Mexico
39 E3 Saindak Pakistan
42 F2 Sa'īndezh Iran
Saīn Qal'eh see Sa'īndezh
122 B4 Saïnsoubou Senegal
86 C3 Sains-Richaumont France
66 F5 St Abb's Head headland Scotland U.K.
101 □ St Abb's Head headland Gibraltar
81 G3 St Aegyd am Neuwalde Austria
93 E5 St-Affrique France
141 K3 St-Agapit Québec Canada
109 G3 St Agata de' Goti Italy
111 F4 St Agata del Bianco Italy
111 E3 St Agata di Esaro Italy
90 B2 St-Agnan France
91 D4 St-Agnan-en-Vercors France
92 B3 St-Agnant France
63 □1 St Agnes i. England U.K.
62 A4 St Agnes England U.K.
91 C3 St-Agrève France
102 F2 St Agustí de Lluçanès Spain
89 G4 St-Aignan France
89 D4 St-Aignan-sur-Roë France
92 B3 St-Aigulin France
90 C2 St-Albain France
63 F3 St Albans England U.K.
139 J4 St Alban's Newfoundland Canada
147 G2 St Albans Vermont U.S.A.
146 C5 St Albans W. Virginia U.S.A.
62 D4 St Alban's Head headland England U.K.
91 B4 St-Alban-sur-Limagnole France
136 G4 St Albert Alberta Canada
141 J3 Saint-Alexis-des-Monts Québec Canada
90 B1 St-Amand-en-Puisaye France
86 C2 St-Amand-les-Eaux France
89 G4 St-Amand-Longpré France
92 E2 St-Amand-Montrond France
91 B4 St-Amans France
93 E4 St-Amans-des-Cots France
93 E5 St-Amans-Soult France
92 C3 St-Amant-de-Boixe France
90 B3 St-Amant-Roche-Savine France
90 B3 St-Amant-Tallende France
87 G5 St-Amarin France
141 K2 St-Ambroise Québec Canada
91 C4 St-Ambroix France
90 D2 St-Amour France
91 C5 St-Andiol France
81 F4 St Andrä Austria
93 E6 St-André Languedoc-Roussillon France
91 F5 St-André Provence-Alpes-Côte-d'Azur France
127 □5 St-André Réunion Indian Ocean
127 □4 Saint-André Mauritius
111 F4 St Andrea Apostolo dello Ionio Italy
73 F4 St Andreasberg Germany
141 H4 St-André-Avellin Québec Canada
91 C4 St-André-de-Cruzières France
92 B4 St-André-de-Cubzac France
89 G3 St-André-de-l'Eure France
91 B5 St-André-de-Sangonis France
91 B4 St-André-de-Valborgne France
141 K2 St-André-du-Lac Québec Canada
90 D3 St-André-le-Gaz France
91 E5 St-André-les-Alpes France
86 D4 St-André-les-Vergers France
89 G3 St-André, Plaine de plain France
159 □3 St Andrew div. Trinidad Trinidad and Tobago
159 □1 St Andrew div. Jamaica
147 K2 St Andrews New Brunswick Canada
66 F4 St Andrews Scotland U.K.
92 E3 St-Angel France
159 □1 St Ann div. Jamaica
158 □2 St Anna'-baai b. Curaçao Netherlands Ant.
68 D1 St Annaparochie Netherlands
63 □2 St Anne Alderney Channel Is.
127 □2 St Anne I. i. Seychelles
159 □1 St Ann's Bay Jamaica
62 A3 St Ann's Head headland Wales U.K.
141 K3 St-Anselme Québec Canada
148 A4 St Ansgar Iowa U.S.A.
90 B3 St-Anthème France
152 E3 St Anthony Idaho U.S.A.
139 J3 St Anthony Newfoundland Canada
43 B5 St Anthony, Mon. of Egypt
80 B3 St Anton am Arlberg Austria
93 D4 St-Antonin-Noble-Val France
92 D2 St-Août France
141 K3 Saint-Apollinaire Québec Canada
90 D1 St-Apollinaire France
109 J4 St Arcangelo Italy
91 B3 St-Arcons-d'Allier France
13 E4 St Arnaud Victoria Australia
9 D5 St Arnaud Range mountain range New Zealand
89 G3 St-Arnoult-en-Yvelines France
62 C1 St Asaph Wales U.K.
93 C4 St-Astier Aquitaine France
92 C3 St-Astier Aquitaine France
91 E5 St-Auban France
82 A1 St-Aubin France
90 B1 St-Aubin-Château-Neuf France
88 D3 St-Aubin-d'Aubigné France
92 B3 St-Aubin-de-Blaye France
88 D3 St-Aubin-du-Cormier France
89 G2 St-Aubin-lès-Elbeuf France
139 J3 St-Augustin Québec Canada
74 C2 St Augustin Germany
145 D6 St Augustine Florida U.S.A.
92 C3 St-Aulaye France
62 B4 St Austell England U.K.
62 B4 St Austell Bay b. England U.K.
62 C4 St-Avé France
89 F4 St-Avertin France
87 F3 St-Avold France
89 G4 St-Ay France
91 E5 St-Aygulf France
141 J3 St-Barthélémi Québec Canada
159 G3 St Barthélemy i. Guadeloupe Caribbean
93 D6 St-Barthélemy, Pic de mt. France
93 C4 St-Barthélemy-d'Agenais France
89 E4 St-Barthélemy-d'Anjou France
91 C3 St-Barthélemy-de-Vals France
141 K3 Saint-Basile Québec Canada
9 B6 St Bathans, Mt mt. New Zealand
91 B5 St-Bauzille-de-Putois France
93 C6 St-Béat France
93 E4 St-Beauzély France
65 E3 St Bees England U.K.
65 E3 St Bees Head headland England U.K.
91 B1 St-Benin-d'Azy France
127 □5 St-Benoît Réunion Indian Ocean
92 C2 St-Benoît France
93 E5 St-Benoît France
92 D2 St-Benoît-du-Sault France
86 B5 St-Benoît-sur-Loire France
90 D3 St-Béron France
89 E3 St-Berthevin France
82 B1 St-Blaise Switzerland
87 G4 St-Blaise-la-Roche France
82 D1 St Blasien Germany
87 E4 St-Blin-Semilly France
92 C2 St-Bonnet-de-Bellac France
90 C2 St-Bonnet-de-Joux France
91 E4 St-Bonnet-en-Champsaur France
91 C3 St-Bonnet-le-Château France
91 C3 St-Bonnet-le-Froid France
92 B3 St-Bonnet-sur-Gironde France
89 F4 St-Branchs France
63 □2 St Brelade Jersey Channel Is.
88 C4 St-Brevin-les-Pins France
88 D3 St-Brice-en-Coglès France
62 A3 St Bride's Bay b. Wales U.K.
88 C3 St-Brieuc France
88 C3 St-Brieuc, Baie de b. France
90 B1 St-Bris-le-Vineux France
90 C1 St-Brisson France
89 F4 St-Calais France
155 G5 St Carlos Lake l. Arizona U.S.A.
88 C3 St-Cast-le-Guildo France
141 F5 St Catharines Ontario Canada
145 □1 St Catharine's Pt pt Bermuda
159 □1 St Catherine div. Jamaica
43 B5 St Catherine, Mon. of Egypt
159 □8 St Catherine, Mt h. Grenada Caribbean
145 D6 St Catherines I. i. Georgia U.S.A.
63 E4 St Catherine's Point pt England U.K.
102 F3 St Celoni Spain
93 D4 St-Céré France
82 B2 St-Cergue Switzerland
92 E3 St-Cernin France
141 J4 St-Césaire Québec Canada
93 D4 St-Chamarand France
91 D5 St-Chamas France
85 G4 St-Chamond France
91 C5 St-Chaptes France
152 E3 St Charles Idaho U.S.A.
146 E5 St Charles Maryland U.S.A.
148 A4 St Charles Minnesota U.S.A.
150 F4 St Charles Missouri U.S.A.
82 A3 St-Chef France
91 B4 St-Chély-d'Apcher France
93 E4 St-Chély-d'Aubrac France
93 E5 St-Chinian France
158 □2 St Christoffelberg h. Curaçao Netherlands Ant.
91 C4 St-Christol-lès-Alès France
89 G4 St-Christophe-en-Bazelle France
St Christopher see Fig Tree
St Christopher i. see St Kitts
92 B3 St-Ciers-sur-Gironde France
149 F4 St Clair Michigan U.S.A.
91 C3 St-Clair-du-Rhône France
140 D5 St Clair, Lake l. Ontario Canada
149 F4 St Clair Shores Michigan U.S.A.
89 D2 St-Clair-sur-l'Elle France
93 C5 St-Clar France
92 C3 St-Claud France
159 □5 St Claude Guadeloupe Caribbean
90 D2 St-Claude France
62 B3 St Clears Wales U.K.
86 C4 St-Clément Bourgogne France
63 □2 St Clement Jersey Channel Is.
87 F4 St-Clément Lorraine France
150 E2 St Cloud Minnesota U.S.A.
141 K2 St-Coeur-de-Marie Québec Canada
62 B4 St Columb Major England U.K.
92 E4 St-Constant France
89 F3 St-Cosme-en-Vairais France
159 F3 St Croix i. Virgin Is Caribbean
139 G4 St Croix r. New Brunswick Canada
148 A2 St Croix r. Wisconsin U.S.A.
148 A3 St Croix Falls Wisconsin U.S.A.
145 □3 St Croix I. i. Virgin Is Caribbean
93 D4 St-Cyprien Aquitaine France
93 F6 St-Cyprien Provence-Alpes-Côte-d'Azur France
86 B4 St-Cyr-l'École France
89 F4 St-Cyr-sur-Loire France
91 D5 St-Cyr-sur-Mer France
159 □3 St David div. Trinidad Trinidad and Tobago
155 G6 St David Arizona U.S.A.
62 A3 St David's Wales U.K.
62 A3 St David's Head headland Wales U.K.
145 □1 St David's Island i. Bermuda
127 □5 St-Denis Réunion Indian Ocean
86 B4 St-Denis France
117 K8 St-Denis Mauritius
89 E4 St-Denis-d'Anjou France
89 E3 St-Denis-de-Gastines France
92 B4 St-Denis-de-Pile France
92 A2 St-Denis-d'Oléron France
91 C3 St-Didier-en-Velay France
87 F4 St-Dié France
90 B3 St-Dier-d'Auvergne France
86 D4 St-Dizier France
92 D2 St-Dizier-Leyrenne France
88 C4 St-Dolay France
141 H3 St-Donat Québec Canada
91 H3 St-Doulchard France
141 H4 Ste-Adèle Québec Canada
89 F2 Ste-Adresse France
141 H3 Sainte-Agathe-des-Monts Québec Canada
93 C4 Ste-Alvère France
141 K3 Ste-Anne r. Québec Canada
137 K5 Ste Anne Manitoba Canada
159 □4 Ste Anne Martinique Caribbean
127 □5 Ste-Anne Réunion Indian Ocean
141 K3 Ste-Anne-de-Beaupré Québec Canada
147 J1 Sainte-Anne-de-Madawaska New Brunswick Canada
141 H3 Sainte-Anne-du-Lac Québec Canada
139 G3 Ste Anne, L. l. Québec Canada
91 D5 Ste-Baume, la mt. France
93 C4 Ste-Bazeille France
147 H1 Ste-Camille-de-Lellis Québec Canada
90 D2 Ste-Croix Bourgogne France
141 K3 Sainte-Croix Québec Canada
91 D4 Ste-Croix Rhône-Alpes France
82 B2 Ste-Croix Switzerland
91 E5 Ste-Croix, Lac de l. France
93 D5 Ste-Croix-Volvestre France
141 J3 Ste-Emélie-de-l'Energie Québec Canada
91 B4 Ste-Enimie France
93 A4 Ste-Eulalie-en-Born France
141 K3 Ste-Foy Québec Canada
93 D5 Ste-Foy-de-Peyrolières France
93 C4 Ste-Foy-la-Grande France
90 C3 Ste-Foy-l'Argentière France
90 C3 Ste-Foy-lès-Lyon France
90 E3 Ste-Foy-Tarentaise France
86 B3 Ste-Geneviève France
93 E4 Ste-Geneviève-sur-Argence France
91 D3 St-Égrève France
92 A2 Ste-Hermine France
141 J4 Ste-Julienne Québec Canada
147 H1 Sainte-Justine Québec Canada
147 J1 Ste-Éleuthère Québec Canada
134 D4 St Elias, C. c. Alaska U.S.A.
136 B2 St Elias Mountains mountain range Yukon Terr. Canada
163 G3 St Elie French Guiana
93 C4 Ste-Livrade-sur-Lot France
93 C5 St-Élix-Theux France
159 □1 St Elizabeth div. Jamaica
89 H4 Ste-Lizaigne France
92 E2 St-Éloy-les-Mines France
159 □4 Ste Luce Martinique Caribbean
139 G3 Ste Marguerite r. Québec Canada
159 □4 Sainte Marie Martinique Caribbean
141 K3 Sainte-Marie Québec Canada
127 □5 Ste-Marie Réunion Indian Ocean
87 G4 Ste-Marie-aux-Mines France
89 F4 Ste-Maure-de-Touraine France
89 F4 Ste-Maure, Plateau de plat. France
91 E5 Ste-Maxime France
86 D3 Ste-Menehould France
88 D2 Ste-Mère-Église France
141 K2 Ste-Monique Québec Canada
62 B4 St Endellion England U.K.
88 D4 Ste-Pazanne France
92 B2 Ste-Radegonde France
86 C3 St Erme-Outre-et-Ramecourt France
159 □5 Ste Rose Guadeloupe Caribbean
127 □5 Ste-Rose Réunion Indian Ocean
92 B3 Saintes France
90 C1 Ste-Sabine France
86 D4 Ste-Savine France
92 E2 Ste-Sévère-sur-Indre France
159 □5 Saintes, Îles des is Guadeloupe Caribbean
91 C5 Stes-Maries-de-la-Mer France
91 C5 Stes Maries ou Beauduc, Golfe de b. France
93 E6 St-Estève France
127 □5 Ste-Suzanne Réunion Indian Ocean
89 E3 Ste-Suzanne France
141 J4 Ste-Thérèse Québec Canada
91 C3 St-Étienne Loire France
93 A5 St-Étienne-de-Baïgorry France
91 B4 St-Étienne-de-Lugdarès France
88 D4 St-Étienne-de-Montluc France
91 D3 St-Étienne-de-St-Geoirs France
91 E4 St-Étienne-de-Tinée France
90 D2 St-Étienne-du-Bois France
89 G2 St-Étienne-du-Rouvray France
91 D4 St-Étienne-en-Dévoluy France
91 D4 St-Étienne-les-Orgues France
87 F4 St-Étienne-lès-Remiremont France
91 B4 St-Étienne-Vallée-Française France
111 E4 St Eufemia d'Aspromonte Italy
141 H4 St Eugene Ontario Canada
141 J4 St-Eustache Québec Canada
159 G3 St Eustatius i. Netherlands Ant.
141 H3 Ste-Véronique Québec Canada
91 D5 Ste-Victoire, Montagne mt. France
131 H5 St Faith's South Africa
90 B1 St-Fargeau France
141 J2 St-Félicien Québec Canada
91 C3 St-Félicien France
102 F3 St Feliu Sasserra Spain
141 F2 St-Félix-de-Dalquier Québec Canada
141 J3 St-Félix-de-Valois Québec Canada
93 D5 St-Félix-Lauragais France
67 F2 Saintfield Northern Ireland U.K.
64 D1 St Fillans Scotland U.K.
67 A5 St Finan's Bay b. Rep. of Ireland
87 F4 St-Firmin Lorraine France
91 E4 St-Firmin Provence-Alpes-Côte-d'Azur France
108 B2 St-Florent Corse France
92 A2 St-Florent-des-Bois France
108 B2 St-Florent, Golfe de b. Corse France
86 C4 St-Florentin France
89 D4 St-Florent-le-Vieil France
92 E2 St-Florent-sur-Cher France
124 D2 St Floris, Parc National nat. park Central African Rep.
91 B3 St-Flour France
92 D2 St-Flovier France
151 F4 St Francis r. Missouri U.S.A.
147 J1 St Francis r. Canada/U.S.A.
150 C4 St Francis Kansas U.S.A.
147 J1 St Francis Maine U.S.A.
131 E7 St Francis Bay b. South Africa
139 K4 St Francis, C. c. Newfoundland Canada
130 E7 St Francis, C. c. South Africa
141 J3 St-François r. Québec Canada
159 □5 St François Guadeloupe Caribbean
82 B3 St-François-Longchamp France
147 J1 St Froid Lake l. Maine U.S.A.
92 C3 St-Front-de-Pradoux France
141 K2 St-Fulgence Québec Canada
92 A2 St-Fulgent France
141 J3 Saint-Gabriel Québec Canada
83 E1 St Gallen div. Switzerland
83 E1 St Gallen St Gallen Switzerland
80 A3 St Gallenkirch Austria
90 C3 St-Galmier France
93 C5 St-Gaudens France
92 D2 St-Gaultier France
147 H2 St-Gédéon Québec Canada
93 B5 St-Gein France
91 B5 St-Gély-du-Fesc France
91 C3 St-Genest-Malifaux France
90 C2 St-Gengoux-le-National France
91 E4 St-Geniez France
93 E4 St-Geniez-d'Olt France
92 B3 St-Genis-de-Saintonge France
82 B2 St-Genis-Pouilly France
90 D3 St-Genix-sur-Guiers France
92 D2 St-Genou France
82 A3 St-Geoire-en-Valdaine France
159 □3 St George div. Trinidad Trinidad and Tobago
134 B4 St George Alaska U.S.A.
147 K2 St George New Brunswick Canada
15 G6 St George Queensland Australia
145 D5 St George S. Carolina U.S.A.
155 F3 St George Utah U.S.A.
145 □1 St George Bermuda
6 □1 St George, C. pt P.N.G.
134 A4 St George I. i. Alaska U.S.A.
145 C6 St George I. i. Florida U.S.A.
81 F2 St Georgen am Walde Austria
81 F2 St Georgen an der Gusen Austria
74 D4 St Georgen im Schwarzwald Germany
152 A3 St George, Pt pt California U.S.A.
16 D3 St George Ra. h. Western Australia Australia
159 □8 St George's Grenada Caribbean
139 F4 St Georges Québec Canada
163 G3 St Georges French Guiana
139 J4 St George's B. b. Newfoundland Canada
89 E3 St-Georges-Buttavent France
157 J5 St George's Cay i. Belize
6 □1 St George's Channel chan. P.N.G.
67 E5 St George's Channel chan. Rep. of Ireland/U.K.
91 B3 St-Georges-d'Aurac France
82 A3 St-Georges-de-Commiers France
92 B3 St-Georges-de-Mons France
89 E3 St-Georges-des-Groseillers France
90 B3 St-Georges-en-Couzan France
145 □1 St George's Island i. Bermuda
92 C2 St-Georges-lès-Baillargeaux France
90 B1 St-Georges-sur-Baulche France
89 G4 St-Georges-sur-Cher France
89 G3 St-Georges-sur-Eure France
89 E4 St-Georges-sur-Loire France
90 B2 St-Gérand-le-Puy France
90 B2 St-Germain-Chassenay France
91 B4 St-Germain-de-Calberte France
90 B2 St-Germain-des-Fossés France
93 D4 St-Germain-du-Bel-Air France
90 D2 St-Germain-du-Bois France
89 F3 St-Germain-du-Corbeis France
90 C2 St-Germain-du-Plain France
92 E1 St-Germain-du-Puy France
91 B4 St-Germain-du-Teil France
86 B4 St-Germain-en-Laye France
90 C3 St-Germain-Laval France
92 D3 St-Germain-les-Belles France
92 D3 St-Germain-les-Vergnes France
90 B3 St-Germain-l'Herm France
62 B4 St Germans England U.K.
92 E2 St-Gervais-d'Auvergne France
89 G4 St-Gervais-la-Forêt France
90 E3 St-Gervais-les-Bains France
92 C2 St-Gervais-les-Trois-Clochers France
91 B5 St-Gervais-sur-Mare France
93 D4 St-Géry France
69 B4 St-Ghislain Belgium
88 C4 St-Gildas-des-Bois France
88 C4 St-Gildas, Pte de pt France
159 □2 St Giles Is i. Tobago Trinidad and Tobago
81 E3 St Gilgen Austria
91 C5 St-Gilles France
92 A2 St-Gilles-Croix-de-Vie France
127 □5 St-Gilles-les-Bains Réunion Indian Ocean
69 C3 St-Gillis-Waas Belgium
90 E2 St-Gingolph France
93 D6 St-Girons France
93 A5 St-Girons-Plage France
74 C2 St Goar Germany
87 G2 St Goarshausen Germany
86 C3 St-Gobain France
62 B3 St Govan's Head headland Wales U.K.
88 D3 St-Grégoire France
90 B2 St-Haon-le-Châtel France
148 E3 St Helen Michigan U.S.A.
174 J7 St Helena i. Atlantic Ocean
154 A2 St Helena California U.S.A.
130 B6 St Helena Bay b. South Africa
174 J6 St Helena Fracture sea feature Atlantic Ocean
65 F4 St Helens England U.K.
152 B2 St Helens Oregon U.S.A.
13 G5 St Helens Tasmania Australia
152 B2 St Helens, Mt volcano Washington U.S.A.
13 G5 St Helens Pt pt Tasmania Australia
63 □2 St Helier Jersey Channel Is.
88 D4 St-Herblain France
93 E5 St-Hilaire France
92 A2 St-Hilaire-de-Riez France
92 B2 St-Hilaire-des-Loges France
92 B3 St-Hilaire-de-Villefranche France
89 D3 St-Hilaire-du-Harcouët France
91 D3 St-Hilaire-du-Rosier France
90 B2 St-Hilaire-Fontaine France
86 D3 St-Hilaire-le-Grand France
89 E4 St-Hilaire-St-Florent France
102 F3 St Hilari Sacalm Spain
87 G4 St-Hippolyte Alsace France
90 E1 St-Hippolyte Franche-Comté France
91 B5 St-Hippolyte-du-Fort France
141 K2 St-Honoré Québec Canada
91 C3 St-Hostien France
69 D4 St-Hubert Belgium
141 J4 St-Hyacinthe Québec Canada
148 E3 St Ignace Michigan U.S.A.
141 J3 St-Ignace-du-Lac Québec Canada
140 A2 St Ignace I. i. Ontario Canada
82 B1 St-Imier Switzerland
82 B1 St-Imier, Val de v. Switzerland
62 B3 St Ishmael Wales U.K.
62 B4 St Ive England U.K.
63 F2 St Ives England U.K.
62 A4 St Ives England U.K.
62 A4 St Ives Bay b. England U.K.
68 D1 St Jacobiparochie Netherlands
147 J1 St-Jacques New Brunswick Canada
141 J4 St-Jacques Québec Canada
141 F2 St-Jacques-de-Dupuy Québec Canada
88 D3 St-Jacques-de-la-Lande France
81 F4 St Jakob im Rosental Austria
81 G3 St Jakob im Walde Austria
159 □1 St James div. Jamaica
148 E3 St James Michigan U.S.A.
88 D3 St-James France
136 C4 St James, Cape pt B.C. Canada
69 C3 St Jansteen Netherlands
93 D5 St-Jean France
88 C4 St-Jean-Brévelay France
92 B3 St-Jean-d'Angély France
89 F3 St-Jean-d'Assé France
90 D3 St-Jean-de-Bournay France
89 G4 St-Jean-de-Braye France
89 D2 St-Jean-de-Daye France
89 G4 St-Jean-de-la-Ruelle France
90 D1 St-Jean-de-Losne France
93 A5 St-Jean-de-Luz France
141 J3 Saint-Jean-de-Matha Québec Canada
91 C4 St-Jean-de-Mauréjols-et-Avéjan France
91 E3 St-Jean-de-Maurienne France
88 C5 St-Jean-de-Monts France
90 E3 St-Jean-de-Sixt France
91 B4 St-Jean-du-Gard France
141 J2 St-Jean, Lac l. Québec Canada
93 A5 St-Jean-Pied-de-Port France
93 C5 St-Jean-Poutge France
141 J4 St-Jean-sur-Richelieu Québec Canada
141 H4 Saint-Jérôme Québec Canada
91 C3 St-Jeure-d'Ay France
91 C3 St-Jeures France
88 C4 St-Joachim France
152 C2 St Joe r. Idaho U.S.A.
81 F3 St Johann am Tauern Austria
80 E3 St Johann im Pongau Austria
80 D3 St Johann in Tirol Austria
159 F3 St John i. Virgin Is Caribbean
147 K2 St John r. Canada/U.S.A.
122 C5 St John r. Liberia
63 □2 St John Jersey Channel Is.
139 G4 St John New Brunswick Canada
155 F1 St John Utah U.S.A.
145 □3 St John I. i. Virgin Is Caribbean
145 D6 St Johns r. Florida U.S.A.
159 □7 St John's Antigua and Barbuda Caribbean
155 H4 St Johns Arizona U.S.A.
148 E4 St Johns Michigan U.S.A.
139 K4 St John's Newfoundland Canada
147 H2 St Johnsbury Vermont U.S.A.
65 F3 St John's Chapel England U.K.
67 C2 St John's Point pt Rep. of Ireland
67 F2 St John's Point pt Rep. of Ireland
64 D2 St John's Town of Dalry Scotland U.K.
93 D5 St-Jory France
148 D4 St Joseph r. Michigan U.S.A.
148 E5 St Joseph r. Ohio U.S.A.
159 □4 St Joseph Martinique Caribbean
148 D4 St Joseph Michigan U.S.A.
150 E4 St Joseph Missouri U.S.A.
139 F4 St Joseph Québec Canada
127 □5 St-Joseph Réunion Indian Ocean
159 □3 St Joseph Trinidad and Tobago
140 D3 St Joseph I. i. Ontario Canada
151 D7 St Joseph I. i. Texas U.S.A.
138 B3 St Joseph, Lac l. Ontario Canada
89 F2 St-Jouin-Bruneval France
141 H3 St Jovité Québec Canada
158 □2 St Jozefsdal Curaçao Netherlands Ant.
141 J4 Saint-Jude Québec Canada
93 E5 St-Juéry France
111 □ St Julian's Malta
90 D2 St-Julien France
91 C4 St-Julien-Boutières France
91 C3 St-Julien-Chapteuil France
88 D4 St-Julien-de-Concelles France
88 D4 St-Julien-de-Vouvantes France
86 C4 St-Julien-du-Sault France
93 A4 St-Julien-en-Born France
90 E2 St-Julien-en-Genevois France
92 C2 St-Julien-l'Ars France
91 C4 St-Julien-les-Rosiers France
86 D4 St-Julien-les-Villas France
90 D2 St-Julien-sur-Reyssouze France
92 C3 St-Junien France
62 A4 St Just England U.K.
91 C4 St Just France
86 B3 St-Just-en-Chaussée France
90 B3 St-Just-en-Chevalet France
93 B5 St-Justin France
86 C4 St-Just-Sauvage France
90 C3 St-Just-St-Rambert France
62 A4 St Keverne England U.K.
66 □1 St Kilda is Scotland U.K.
159 □6 St Kitts i. St Kitts-Nevis Caribbean
133 M8 St Kitts-Nevis country Caribbean
158 □2 St Kruis Curaçao Netherlands Ant.
89 E4 St-Lambert-des-Levées France
81 F3 St Lambrecht Austria
179 □ St Lanne Gramont, I. i. Kerguelen Indian Ocean
93 C6 St-Lary-Soulan France
163 G2 St Laurent French Guiana
69 A4 St-Laurent-Blangy France
91 C5 St-Laurent-d'Aigouze France
91 C4 St-Laurent-de-Carnols France
90 C3 St-Laurent-de-Chamousset France
93 E5 St-Laurent-de-la-Cabrerisse France
93 E6 St-Laurent-de-la-Salanque France
93 C5 St-Laurent-de-Neste France
91 D3 St-Laurent-du-Pont France
91 F5 St-Laurent-du-Var France
91 E4 St-Laurent-du-Verdon France
90 D2 St-Laurent-en-Grandvaux France
92 B3 St-Laurent-Médoc France
89 G4 St-Laurent-Nouan France
92 C3 St-Laurent-sur-Gorre France
92 B2 St-Laurent-sur-Sèvre France
139 G4 St Lawrence chan. Québec Canada
139 K4 St Lawrence Newfoundland Canada
15 G4 St Lawrence Queensland Australia
139 H4 St Lawrence, Gulf of g. Canada/U.S.A.
134 B3 St Lawrence I. i. Alaska U.S.A.
141 H4 St Lawrence Islands National Park nat. park Ontario Canada
147 F2 St Lawrence River chan. Canada/U.S.A.
69 D5 St-Léger Belgium
90 C2 St-Léger-sous-Beuvray France
90 C2 St-Léger-sur-Dheune France
139 G4 St-Léonard New Brunswick Canada
141 J3 St-Léonard Québec Canada
87 F4 St-Léonard France
92 D3 St-Léonard-de-Noblat France
63 E4 St Leonards England U.K.
81 G2 St Leonhard am Hornerwald Austria
80 B3 St Leonhard im Pitztal Austria
127 □5 St-Leu Réunion Indian Ocean
139 J3 Saint Lewis r. Newfoundland Canada
139 J3 St Lewis Newfoundland Canada
93 D5 St-Lizier France
89 D2 St-Lô France
93 A5 St-Lon-les-Mines France
90 D2 St-Lothian France
148 A2 St Louis r. Minnesota U.S.A.
159 □5 St Louis Guadeloupe Caribbean
148 E4 St Louis Michigan U.S.A.
150 F4 St Louis Missouri U.S.A.
127 □5 St-Louis Réunion Indian Ocean
82 C1 St-Louis France
122 A3 St Louis Senegal
141 J3 Saint-Louis-de-France Québec Canada
87 G4 St-Louis-lès-Bitche France
92 B2 St-Loup-Lamairé France
91 B5 St-Loup, Pic h. France

80 D4 San Maddalena Vallalta Italy
98 C2 San Mamede, Serra do mountain range Spain
173 H4 San Manuel Argentina
107 E4 San Marcello Pistoiese Italy
110 C5 San Marco, Capo c. Sicilia Italy
108 A5 San Marco, Capo pt Sardegna Italy
109 G3 San Marco dei Cavoti Italy
109 H3 San Marco in Lamis Italy
151 D6 San Marcos Texas U.S.A.
172 B1 San Marcos Chile
157 H6 San Marcos Guatemala
157 F5 San Marcos Mexico
107 G5 San Marino country Europe
107 G5 San Marino San Marino
165 D2 San Martín r. Bolivia
172 C2 San Martín Argentina
170 C2 San Martín Argentina
162 C3 San Martín Colombia
99 G4 San Martín de la Vega Spain
172 B6 San Martín de los Andes Argentina
99 F5 San Martín de Pusa Spain
99 F4 San Martín de Valdeiglesias Spain
171 B6 San Martín, L. l. Argentina/Chile
83 G3 San Martino Buon Albergo Italy
107 F2 San Martino di Castrozza Italy
108 B2 San-Martino-di-Lota Corse France
83 G2 San Martino in Passiria Italy
154 A3 San Mateo California U.S.A.
102 C3 San Mateo de Gállego Spain
165 E3 San Matías Bolivia
171 D5 San Matías, Golfo g. Argentina
162 D2 San Mauricio Venezuela
109 J4 San Mauro Forte Italy
82 C3 San Mauro Torinese Italy
33 H2 Sanmen China
109 H3 San Menaio Italy
33 H2 Sanmen Wan b. China
33 E1 Sanmenxia China
155 H2 San Miguel r. Colorado U.S.A.
164 D2 San Miguel r. Bolivia
162 B3 San Miguel r. Colombia
156 C2 San Miguel r. Mexico
155 G6 San Miguel Arizona U.S.A.
154 B4 San Miguel California U.S.A.
165 D3 San Miguel Bolivia
156 H6 San Miguel El Salvador
156 L7 San Miguel Panama
164 B2 San Miguel Peru
23 B3 San Miguel Bay b. Philippines
157 E4 San Miguel de Allende Mexico
99 F3 San Miguel de Arroyo Spain
164 C3 San Miguel de Huachi Bolivia
173 H3 San Miguel del Monte Argentina
103 C7 San Miguel de Salinas Spain
170 C2 San Miguel de Tucumán Argentina
166 B3 San Miguel do Araguaia Brazil
156 L7 San Miguel, G. de b. Panama
154 B4 San Miguel I. i. California U.S.A.
23 A5 San Miguel Is. is Philippines
164 C2 San Miguelito Bolivia
156 L7 San Miguelito Panama
157 F5 San Miguel Sola de Vega Mexico
99 G2 San Millán mt. Spain
99 H2 San Millán de la Cogolla Spain
33 G3 Sanming China
107 E5 San Miniato Italy
23 B3 San Narciso Philippines
131 F4 Sannaspos South Africa
111 □ Sannat Malta
106 C3 Sannazzaro de'Burgondi Italy
36 A3 Sanni Pakistan
109 H3 Sannicandro Garganico Italy
111 H2 Sannicola Italy
111 F3 San Nicola dell'Alto Italy
173 G2 San Nicolás de los Arroyos Argentina
100 E2 San Nicolás del Puerto Spain
97 □ San Nicolás de Tolentino Canary Is Spain
154 C5 San Nicolas I. i. California U.S.A.
79 K5 Sânnicolau Mare Romania
108 B5 San Nicolò Gerrei Sardegna Italy
131 E3 Sannieshof South Africa
77 H3 Sanniki Poland
122 C5 Sanniquellie Liberia
29 H3 Sannohe Japan
77 L6 Sanok Poland
164 C4 San Pablo Potosí Bolivia
165 D3 San Pablo Santa Cruz Bolivia
172 A6 San Pablo Chile
157 F4 San Pablo Mexico
23 B3 San Pablo Philippines
83 G2 San Pancrazio Italy
111 G2 San Pancrazio Salentino Italy
83 F3 San Paolo, Isola i. Italy
155 G5 San Pedro r. Arizona U.S.A.
158 C2 San Pedro r. Cuba
172 A4 San Pedro Biobío Chile
173 H2 San Pedro Buenos Aires Argentina
170 D1 San Pedro Jujuy Argentina
170 F2 San Pedro Misiones Argentina
172 B2 San Pedro Santiago Chile
172 E1 San Pedro Argentina
157 J5 San Pedro Belize
165 D3 San Pedro Bolivia
122 C6 San-Pédro Côte d'Ivoire
156 C4 San Pedro Mexico
165 E4 San Pedro Paraguay
23 B3 San Pedro Philippines
154 C5 San Pedro Channel California U.S.A.
101 F4 San Pedro de Alcántara Spain
162 C3 San Pedro de Arimena Colombia
164 C4 San Pedro de Atacama Chile
99 F4 San Pedro del Arroyo Spain
163 E2 San Pedro de las Bocas Venezuela
156 E3 San Pedro de las Colonias Mexico
99 E3 San Pedro de Latarce Spain
103 C7 San Pedro del Pinatar Spain
159 E3 San Pedro de Macorís Dominican Rep.
100 D2 San Pedro de Mérida Spain
100 C1 San Pedro, Sierra de mountain range Spain
156 H6 San Pedro Sula Honduras
106 D3 San Pellegrino Terme Italy
79 K5 Sânpetru Mare Romania
110 D4 San Piero Patti Italy
111 E4 San Pietro Italy
107 E3 San Pietro in Cariano Italy
107 F4 San Pietro in Casale Italy
108 A5 San Pietro, Isola di i. Sardegna Italy
111 H2 San Pietro Vernotico Italy
106 E4 San Polo d'Enza Italy
42 G1 Sanqaçal Azerbaijan
66 E5 Sanquhar Scotland U.K.
162 B3 Sanquianga, Parque Nacional nat. park Colombia
102 D3 San Quílez mt. Spain
156 B2 San Quintín Mexico
156 A2 San Quintín, C. c. Mexico
155 G2 San Rafael r. Utah U.S.A.
154 A3 San Rafael California U.S.A.
172 C3 San Rafael Argentina
165 D3 San Rafael Bolivia
172 B3 San Rafael Chile
162 C1 San Rafael Venezuela
155 G2 San Rafael Knob summit Utah U.S.A.
154 C4 San Rafael Mts mts California U.S.A.
164 D2 San Ramón Beni Bolivia
165 D3 San Ramón Santa Cruz Bolivia
172 D1 San Ramon Argentina
173 K3 San Ramon Uruguay
106 B5 San Remo Italy
173 G5 San Román Argentina
162 C1 San Román, C. c. Venezuela
99 F4 San Román de los Montes Spain
101 E4 San Roque Andalucía Spain
98 B1 San Roque Galicia Spain
170 E2 San Roque Argentina
109 H4 San Rufo Italy
151 D6 San Saba Texas U.S.A.
172 E1 San Salano Argentina
122 B4 Sansalé Guinea
158 D1 San Salvador i. The Bahamas
173 J2 San Salvador r. Uruguay
173 H1 San Salvador Argentina
156 H6 San Salvador El Salvador
99 F2 San Salvador de Cantamunda Spain
170 C1 San Salvador de Jujuy Argentina
162 □ San Salvador, I. i. Galapagos Is Ecuador
106 C4 San Salvatore Monferrato Italy
109 G2 San Salvo Italy
122 C4 Sansanding Mali
123 E4 Sansanné-Mango Togo
36 D5 Sansar India
98 B2 San Sebastián h. Spain
156 B2 San Sebastián i. Mexico
San Sebastián see Donostia-San Sebastián
171 C7 San Sebastián Argentina
145 □3 San Sebastián Puerto Rico
171 C7 San Sebastián, B. de b. Argentina
97 □ San Sebastián de la Gomera Canary Is Spain
99 G4 San Sebastián de los Reyes Spain
107 G5 Sansepolcro Italy
108 D2 San Severa Italy
107 H5 San Severino Marche Italy
109 H3 San Severo Italy
33 H3 Sansha China
33 F4 Sanshui China
159 E5 San Silvestre Venezuela
104 F3 Sanski Most Bos.-Herz.
99 H2 San Soain Spain
111 F3 San Sosti Italy
108 B5 San Sperate Sardegna Italy
159 □5 Sans Toucher mt. Guadeloupe Caribbean
32 E3 Sansui China
25 D4 San, T. r. Cambodia
112 E1 Şanţ Romania
164 A1 Santa r. Peru
164 A1 Santa Peru
168 D4 Santa Adélia Brazil
100 D1 Santa Amalia Spain
154 D5 Santa Ana California U.S.A.
164 C3 Sta Ana Bolivia
164 C2 Santa Ana Bolivia
162 A4 Santa Ana Ecuador
157 H6 Sta Ana El Salvador
156 C2 Santa Ana Mexico
159 F5 Sta Ana Venezuela
173 H2 Sta Anita Argentina
151 D6 Santa Anna Texas U.S.A.
101 H3 Santa Bárbara mt. Spain
154 C4 Santa Barbara California U.S.A.
169 G3 Santa Bárbara Brazil
172 A4 Sta Bárbara Chile
162 B2 Sta Bárbara Colombia
156 H6 Sta Bárbara Honduras
156 D3 Santa Bárbara Mexico
102 D4 Sta Bárbara Spain
159 G5 Sta Bárbara Venezuela
154 B4 Santa Barbara Channel chan. California U.S.A.
100 C3 Santa Bárbara de Casa Spain
154 C5 Santa Barbara I. i. California U.S.A.
167 B5 Sta Bárbara, Sa de h. Brazil
173 J2 Santa Bernardina Uruguay
156 C3 Sta Catalina i. Mexico
172 E2 Sta Catalina Argentina
170 C2 Sta Catalina Chile
158 D5 Sta Catalina Colombia
156 K7 Sta Catalina Panama
98 B1 Santa Catalina de Armada Spain
154 D5 Santa Catalina, Gulf of b. California U.S.A.
154 C5 Santa Catalina I. i. California U.S.A.
167 B6 Santa Catarina div. Brazil
156 B2 Sta Catarina Baja California Mexico
157 E3 Sta Catarina Nuevo León Mexico
167 C6 Sta Catarina, Ilha de i. Brazil
108 A4 Sta Caterina di Pittinuri Sardegna Italy
110 D5 Sta Caterina Villarmosa Sicilia Italy
158 □2 Sta Catharina Curaçao Netherlands Ant.
111 H2 Sta Cesarea Terme Italy
102 C2 Santa Cilia de Jaca Spain
7 □15 Santa Clara i. Juan Fernandez Is Chile
154 B3 Santa Clara California U.S.A.
155 F3 Santa Clara Utah U.S.A.
162 D4 Santa Clara Colombia
158 C2 Sta Clara Cuba
156 D2 Sta Clara Mexico
100 B3 Santa Clara-a-Velha Portugal
100 B3 Santa Clara, Barragem de resr. Portugal
100 C3 Santa Clara de Louredo Portugal
173 K2 Santa Clara de Olimar Uruguay
173 G1 Sta Clara de Saguier Argentina
154 C4 Santa Clarita California U.S.A.
162 C4 Santa Clotilde Peru
102 F3 Sta Coloma de Farners Spain
102 F3 Sta Coloma de Gramanet Spain
102 E3 Santa Coloma de Queralt Spain
98 D2 Santa Colomba de Somoza Spain
98 B4 Santa Comba Dão Portugal
98 E2 Santa Cristina de la Polvorosa Spain
110 D6 Sta Croce Camerina Sicilia Italy
111 E5 Sta Croce, Capo c. Sicilia Italy
107 E5 Santa Croce sull'Arno Italy
171 B6 Santa Cruz div. Argentina
165 D3 Santa Cruz div. Bolivia
102 B3 Santa Cruz mt. Spain
153 E5 Santa Cruz r. Arizona U.S.A.
171 C7 Santa Cruz r. Argentina
166 A1 Santa Cruz r. Brazil
154 A3 Santa Cruz California U.S.A.
166 B1 Santa Cruz Pará Brazil
165 D3 Santa Cruz Bolivia
166 E2 Sta Cruz Brazil
170 B3 Sta Cruz Chile
159 □1 Sta Cruz Jamaica
156 C2 Sta Cruz Mexico
23 B3 Santa Cruz Philippines
23 A3 Sta Cruz Philippines
23 B2 Santa Cruz Philippines
100 A1 Sta Cruz Portugal
157 H6 Sta Cruz Barillas Guatemala
169 J2 Santa Cruz Cabrália Brazil
100 □ Santa Cruz das Flores Azores Portugal
168 D2 Santa Cruz de Goiás Brazil
97 □ Sta Cruz de la Palma Canary Is Spain
100 E1 Santa Cruz de la Sierra Spain
99 G5 Santa Cruz de la Zarza Spain
157 H6 Sta Cruz del Quiché Guatemala
99 F4 Santa Cruz del Retamar Spain
158 C2 Santa Cruz del Sur Cuba
103 B5 Santa Cruz de Moya Spain
101 G2 Santa Cruz de Mudela Spain
97 □ Sta Cruz de Tenerife Canary Is Spain
168 D5 Santa Cruz do Rio Pardo Brazil
167 B6 Santa Cruz do Sul Brazil
154 C4 Santa Cruz I. i. California U.S.A.
162 □ Santa Cruz, I. i. Galapagos Is Ecuador
176 G6 Santa Cruz Is is Solomon Is.
159 □1 Sta Cruz Mts mts Jamaica
171 C7 Santa Cruz, Pto Argentina
108 A5 Santadi Sardegna Italy
111 E3 Sta Domenica Talao Italy
110 D5 Sta Domenica Vittoria Sicilia Italy
173 H1 Sta Elena Argentina
162 A4 Santa Elena Ecuador
163 E3 Sta Elena Venezuela
162 A4 Sta Elena, B. de b. Ecuador
156 J7 Sta Elena, C. headland Costa Rica
101 F3 Santaella Spain
173 F2 Sta Eufemia Argentina
101 F2 Santa Eufemia Spain
111 F4 Sta Eufemia, Golfo di g. Italy
98 B2 Santa Eugenia Spain
100 C1 Santa Eulália Portugal
102 B4 Santa Eulalia Spain
103 E6 Sta Eulalia del Rio Spain
173 G1 Santa Fé div. Argentina
153 F5 Santa Fe New Mexico U.S.A.
173 G1 Santa Fé Argentina
101 G3 Santa Fe Spain
169 F2 Santa Fé de Minas Brazil
168 C4 Santa Fé do Sul Brazil
162 □ Santa Fé, I. i. Galapagos Is Ecuador
110 D4 Sant'Agata di Militello Sicilia Italy
156 C4 Sta Genovéva mt. Mexico
108 A5 Santa Giusta Sardegna Italy
80 D4 Santa Giustina Italy
166 C1 Santa Helena Maranhão Brazil
168 A6 Santa Helena Paraná Brazil
168 C2 Santa Helena de Goiás Brazil
32 D2 Santai China
171 B7 Santa Inés, Isla i. Chile
6 □1 Santa Isabel i. Solomon Is.
172 D4 Sta Isabel Argentina
173 G2 Santa Isabel Argentina
165 D2 Sta Isabel Brazil
145 □3 Santa Isabel Puerto Rico
164 B3 Sta Isabel de Sihuas Peru
168 B5 Santa Isabel do Ivaí Brazil
172 A4 Sta Juana Chile
168 E3 Santa Juliana Brazil
170 D2 Sta Justina Argentina
102 D2 Sta Liestra y San Quílez Spain
36 B5 Santalpur India
107 E5 Santa Luce Italy
170 E2 Sta Lucia Argentina
164 B4 Sta Lucia Chile
162 B4 Sta Lucia Ecuador
157 H6 Sta Lucia Guatemala
173 J3 Sta Lucia Uruguay
111 E4 Sta Lucia del Mela Sicilia Italy
97 □ Sta Lucía de Tirajana Canary Is Spain
173 F2 Sta Lucia, L. l. Argentina
153 B4 Santa Lucia Range mountain range California U.S.A.
167 B4 Sta Luísa, Sa de h. Brazil
122 □ Santa Luzia i. Cape Verde
100 B3 Santa Luzia Portugal
172 F3 Sta Magdalena Argentina
103 D4 Santa Magdalena de Pulpis Spain
112 F1 Santa Mare Romania
102 E3 Sta Margarida de Montbui Spain
156 C3 Sta Margarita i. Mexico
103 G5 Sta Margarita Spain
110 C5 Sta Margherita di Belice Sicilia Italy
106 D4 Sta Margherita Ligure Italy
100 □ Santa Maria i. Azores Portugal
103 C5 Santa María mt. Spain
169 E1 Santa Maria r. Brazil
173 K1 Santa Maria r. Brazil
153 F6 Sta María r. Mexico
164 F4 Santa Maria Amazonas Brazil
154 B4 Santa Maria California U.S.A.
166 B1 Santa Maria Pará Brazil
167 B6 Santa Maria Rio Grande do Sul Brazil
170 C2 Sta María Argentina
122 □ Santa Maria Cape Verde
156 D3 Sta María Mexico
162 C4 Santa Maria Peru
83 F2 Santa Maria Switzerland
173 K3 Santa Maria, C. c. Uruguay
100 C4 Santa Maria, Cabo de c. Portugal
129 E4 Santa Maria, Cabo de pt Mozambique
109 G3 Sta Maria Capua Vetere Italy
166 E2 Santa Maria da Boa Vista Brazil
98 B4 Santa Maria da Feira Portugal
166 C2 Santa Maria das Barreiras Brazil
166 D3 Santa Maria da Vitória Brazil
99 G1 Santa María de Cayón Spain
99 H3 Sta María de Huertas Spain
163 D2 Sta María de Ipire Venezuela
99 G2 Santa María del Campo Spain
101 H1 Santa María del Campo Rus Spain
111 E3 Sta Maria del Cedro Italy
98 E2 Santa María del Páramo Spain
157 E4 Sta María del Río Mexico
162 C4 Sta María de Nanay Peru
103 B7 Santa María de Nieva Spain
109 G4 Sta Maria di Castellabate Italy
111 H3 Sta Maria di Leuca, Capo c. Italy
169 H2 Santa Maria do Salto Brazil
169 G3 Santa Maria do Suaçuí Brazil
162 □ Santa María, I. i. Galapagos Is Ecuador
172 A4 Santa María, I. i. Chile
6 □2 Santa Maria I. i. Vanuatu
99 F3 Sta María la Real de Nieva Spain
169 G4 Santa Maria Madalena Brazil
106 C2 Sta Maria Maggiore Italy
108 B5 Sta Maria Navarrese Sardegna Italy
83 E2 Santa Maria Rezzonico Italy
108 A3 Santa-Maria-Siché Corse France
158 D2 Sta Marie, Cape c. The Bahamas
110 D4 Sta Marina Salina Italy
108 D2 Santa Marinella Italy
101 H1 Santa Marta Castilla - La Mancha Spain
100 D2 Santa Marta Extremadura Spain
162 C1 Santa Marta Colombia
125 B6 Santa Marta, Cabo de c. Angola
98 C3 Santa Marta de Penaguião Portugal
98 E4 Santa Marta de Tormes Spain
167 C6 Sta Marta Grande, C. de Brazil
154 C4 Santa Monica California U.S.A.
154 C5 Santa Monica Bay b. California U.S.A.
22 D2 Santan Indonesia
168 C3 Santana r. Brazil
166 D3 Santana Bahia Brazil
167 B7 Santana da Boa Vista Brazil
100 B3 Santana da Serra Portugal
166 E2 Santana do Ipanema Brazil
173 K1 Santana do Livramento Brazil
109 G4 Sant'Anastasia Italy
162 B3 Santander Colombia
99 G1 Santander Spain
99 G1 Santander, Bahía de b. Spain
108 B5 Sant' Andrea Frius Sardegna Italy
111 G2 Sant'Andrea, Isola i. Italy
109 H4 Sant'Angelo a Fasanella Italy
109 H4 Sant'Angelo dei Lombardi Italy
110 D4 Sant'Angelo di Brolo Sicilia Italy
107 G5 Sant' Angelo in Lizzola Italy
106 D3 Sant Angelo Lodigiano Italy
110 B5 Sta Ninfa Sicilia Italy
155 G5 Santan Mt mt. Arizona U.S.A.
108 A5 Sant' Anna Arresi Sardegna Italy
108 A5 Sant' Antioco Sardegna Italy
108 A5 Sant' Antioco, Isola di i. Sardegna Italy
108 A5 Sant' Antonio di Santadi Sardegna Italy
103 G5 Santanyi Spain
99 F4 Santa Olalla Spain
100 D3 Santa Olalla del Cala Spain
111 E5 Sta Panagia, Capo c. Sicilia Italy
154 C4 Santa Paula California U.S.A.
103 C6 Sta Pola Spain
103 C6 Santa Pola, Cabo de pt Spain
166 D1 Santa Quitéria Brazil
107 G4 Santarcangelo di Romagna Italy
173 F3 Sta Regina Argentina
100 B1 Santarém div. Portugal
100 B1 Santarém Santarém Portugal
166 B1 Santarém Brazil
158 C2 Santaren Channel chan. The Bahamas
23 □2 Santa Rita Guam Pacific Ocean
166 F2 Sta Rita Brazil
165 E1 Santa Rita Brazil
162 C3 Santa Rita Colombia
162 C1 Sta Rita Venezuela
166 D3 Santa Rita de Cassia Brazil
168 B2 Santa Rita do Araguaia Brazil
169 F5 Santa Rita do Sapucaí Brazil
154 B3 Santa Rita Park California U.S.A.
164 B1 Santa Rosa Acre Brazil
164 C2 Santa Rosa Beni Bolivia
164 C2 Santa Rosa Beni Bolivia
154 A2 Santa Rosa California U.S.A.
172 E4 Santa Rosa La Pampa Argentina
153 F5 Santa Rosa New Mexico U.S.A.
167 B6 Santa Rosa Rio Grande do Sul Brazil
172 D6 Santa Rosa Río Negro Argentina
172 C2 Sta Rosa Argentina
162 B4 Sta Rosa Ecuador
157 H5 Sta Rosa Mexico
164 B2 Sta Rosa Peru
156 H6 Sta Rosa de Copán Honduras
165 D3 Sta Rosa de la Roca Bolivia
172 F1 Sta Rosa del Río Primero Argentina
168 E4 Santa Rosa de Viterbo Brazil
154 B5 Santa Rosa I. i. California U.S.A.
156 B3 Sta Rosalía Mexico
152 C3 Sta Rosa Ra. mountain range Nevada U.S.A.
155 G5 Santa Rosa Wash r. Arizona U.S.A.
109 H4 Sant'Arsenio Italy
111 F3 Sta Severina Italy
107 F5 Santa Sofia Italy
100 B2 Santa Sofia Portugal
100 B2 Santa Susana Portugal
170 D2 Santa Sylvina Argentina
166 C3 Santa Teresa r. Brazil
14 C5 Santa Teresa Northern Terr. Australia
173 G2 Sta Teresa Argentina
169 H3 Santa Teresa Brazil
159 F5 Sta Teresa Venezuela
108 B3 Sta Teresa di Gallura Sardegna Italy
111 E5 Sta Teresa di Riva Sicilia Italy
98 E4 Sta Teresa, Embalse de resr Spain
173 J4 Sta Teresita Argentina
170 C1 Sta Victoria, Sierra mountain range Argentina
168 C3 Santa Vitória Brazil
173 L2 Sta Vitória do Palmar Brazil
108 B5 Sta Vittoria, Monte mt. Sardegna Italy
102 F3 Sant Boix de Llobregat Spain
102 D4 Sant Carles de la Ràpita Spain
88 A3 Santec France
145 E5 Santee r. S. Carolina U.S.A.
154 D5 Santee California U.S.A.
109 G3 Sant' Elia a Pianisi Italy
156 A2 San Telmo Mexico
100 D3 San Telmo Spain
156 E5 San Telmo, Pta pt Mexico
107 H5 Sant Elpidio a Mare Italy
108 B4 San Teodoro Sardegna Italy
111 F2 Santeramo in Colle Italy
107 F4 Santerno r. Italy
86 B3 Santerre reg. France
102 B1 Santesteban Spain
102 G3 Sant Feliu de Guíxols Spain
102 F2 Sant Feliu de Palterols Spain
106 C3 Santhià Italy
172 B2 Santiago div. Chile
162 B4 Santiago r. Peru
156 C4 Santiago Baja California Sur Mexico
156 D3 Santiago Durango Mexico
167 B6 Santiago Brazil
172 B2 Santiago Chile
159 E3 Santiago Dominican Rep.
156 K7 Santiago Panama
23 B2 Santiago Philippines
98 B2 Santiago Spain
157 G5 Santiago Astata Mexico
171 A7 Santiago, C. headland Chile
156 K7 Santiago, Co mt. Panama
100 C1 Santiago de Alcántara Spain
101 F3 Santiago de Calatrava Spain
162 B5 Santiago de Cao Peru
164 A2 Santiago de Chocorvos Peru
164 A1 Santiago de Chuco Peru
98 B2 Santiago de Compostela airport Spain
158 D2 Santiago de Cuba Cuba
101 H2 Santiago de la Espada Spain
170 D2 Santiago del Estero div. Argentina
100 B2 Santiago do Cacém Portugal
100 B2 Santiago do Escoural Portugal
156 D4 Santiago Ixcuintla Mexico
124 A3 Santiago, Pta pt Equatorial Guinea
165 E3 Santiago, Sa de h. Bolivia
172 F1 Santiago Temple Argentina
156 D3 Santiaguillo, L. de l. Mexico
137 N2 Santianna Point pt N.W.T. Canada
99 F2 Santibáñez de la Peña Spain
98 E4 Santibáñez de la Sierra Spain
98 D2 Santibáñez de Vidriales Spain
22 E1 Santigi Indonesia
99 F1 Santillana Spain
99 G4 Santillana, Emb. de resr Spain
83 E1 Säntis mt. Switzerland
101 G2 Santisteban del Puerto Spain
99 F3 Santiuste de San Juan Bautista Spain
102 D4 Sant Jordi, Golf de g. Spain
93 D6 Sant Julià de Lòria Andorra
102 E2 Sant Llorenç de Morunys Spain
100 C2 Santo Aleixo Portugal
166 E3 Santo Amaro Brazil
169 H4 Santo Amaro de Campos Brazil
168 C4 Santo Anastácio r. Brazil
168 C4 Santo Anastácio Brazil
169 E5 Santo André Brazil
100 B2 Santo André Portugal
100 B2 Santo André, Lagoa de lag. Portugal
167 B6 Sto Angelo Brazil
122 □ Santo Antão i. Cape Verde
169 G3 Sto Antônio r. Brazil
166 E3 Sto Antônio, C. c. Brazil
125 □ Santo António Sao Tome and Principe
168 C2 Santo Antônio da Barra Brazil
168 C5 Santo Antônio da Platina Brazil
166 E3 Santo Antônio de Jesus Brazil
167 A4 Sto Antônio de Leverger Brazil
169 G4 Santo Antônio de Pádua Brazil
162 D4 Santo Antônio do Içá Brazil
169 H2 Santo Antônio do Jacinto Brazil
169 F4 Santo Antônio do Monte Brazil
100 A2 Sto Antonio dos Cavaleiros Portugal
169 J2 Santo Antônio, Pta pt Brazil
165 E3 Santo Corazón Bolivia
107 G2 Santo Croce, Lago di l. Italy
159 E5 Sto Domingo r. Venezuela
156 B2 Sto Domingo Baja California Mexico
156 C3 Sto Domingo Baja California Sur Mexico
97 □ Sto Domingo Canary Is Spain
157 E4 Sto Domingo San Luis Potosí Mexico
159 E3 Santo Domingo Dominican Rep.
157 H6 Santo Domingo Guatemala
156 J6 Sto Domingo Nicaragua
164 C2 Santo Domingo Peru
99 H2 Sto Domingo de la Calzada Spain
162 B4 Sto Domingo de los Colorados Ecuador
99 G3 Santo Domingo de Silos Spain
100 B2 Santo Estêvão Portugal
169 F3 Santo Hipólito Brazil
168 C5 Santo Inácio Brazil
166 D3 Sto Inácio Brazil
73 L3 Santok Poland
99 G1 Santoña Spain
166 D3 Sto Onofre r. Brazil
108 B2 Santo-Pietro-di-Tenda Corse France
Santorini i. see Thira
169 E5 Santos Brazil
169 G4 Santos Dumont Brazil
101 E2 Santos, Sierra de los h. Spain
106 D4 Sto Stefano d'Aveto Italy
80 D4 Santo Stefano di Cadore Italy
110 D4 Sto Stefano di Camastra Sicilia Italy
106 D4 Sto Stefano di Magra Italy
80 D5 Santo Stino di Livenza Italy
98 B3 Sto Tirso Portugal
156 A2 Sto Tomás Baja California Mexico
156 D2 Sto Tomás Chihuahua Mexico
156 J6 Sto Tomás Nicaragua
164 B2 Santo Tomás Peru
170 E2 Santo Tomé Corrientes Argentina
173 G1 Santo Tomé Santa Fé Argentina
101 G2 Santo Tomé Spain
98 E3 Santovenia Spain
68 C2 Santpoort Netherlands
108 A4 Santu Lussurgiu Sardegna Italy
99 G1 Santurtzi Spain
155 F3 Sanup Plateau plat. Arizona U.S.A.
171 B6 San Valentín, Co mt. Chile
109 E2 San Venanzo Italy
80 D5 San Vendemiano Italy
108 A4 San Vero Milis Sardegna Italy
99 F4 San Vicente mt. Spain
173 H3 San Vicente Buenos Aires Argentina
173 G1 San Vicente Santa Fe Argentina
172 B3 San Vicente Chile
156 H6 San Vicente El Salvador
156 A2 San Vicente Mexico
23 B2 San Vicente Philippines
100 C1 San Vicente de Alcántara Spain
164 A2 San Vicente de Cañete Peru
99 F1 San Vicente de la Barquera Spain
162 C3 San Vicente del Caguán Colombia
103 C6 San Vicente del Raspeig Spain
99 G1 San Vicente de Toranzo Spain
173 H1 San Victor Argentina
111 E4 San Vincenzo Sicilia Italy
108 C1 San Vincenzo Italy
108 B5 San Vito Sardegna Italy
107 G3 San Vito al Tagliamento Italy
110 B4 San Vito, Capo c. Sicilia Italy
109 G2 San Vito Chietino Italy
111 G2 San Vito dei Normanni Italy
110 B4 San Vito lo Capo Sicilia Italy
109 E3 San Vito Romano Italy
109 F1 San Vittoria in Matenano Italy
38 A1 Sanwer India
98 B2 Sanxenxo Spain
33 E5 Sanya China
129 D2 Sanyati r. Zimbabwe
33 E1 Sanyuan China
109 H4 Sanza Italy
125 C5 Sanza Pombo Angola
168 E2 São Bartolomeu r. Brazil
100 B3 São Bartolomeu de Messines Portugal
163 F5 São Benedito r. Brazil
166 D1 São Benedito Brazil
164 C1 São Bento Amazonas Brazil
166 D1 São Bento Maranhão Brazil
168 C6 São Bento do Amparo Brazil
166 D1 São Bernardo Brazil
167 C5 São Bernardo do Campo Brazil
167 A6 São Borja Brazil
100 C3 São Brás Portugal
100 C3 São Brás de Alportel Portugal
167 B6 São Carlos Santa Catarina Brazil
168 E5 São Carlos São Paulo Brazil
100 B2 São Cristóvão Portugal
166 D3 São Desidério r. Brazil
166 D3 São Desidério Brazil
168 E3 São Domingos r. Goiás Brazil
168 B3 São Domingos r. Mato Grosso do Sul Brazil
169 E1 São Domingos r. Minas Gerais Brazil
166 C3 São Domingos Brazil
100 B3 São Domingos Portugal
166 B3 São Félix Mato Grosso Brazil
166 B2 São Félix Pará Brazil
98 B3 São Félix da Marinha Portugal
169 H4 São Fidélis Brazil
122 □ São Filipe Cape Verde
166 E2 São Francisco r. Brazil
168 A6 São Francisco r. Paraná Brazil
169 F1 São Francisco Minas Gerais Brazil
167 A6 São Francisco de Assis Brazil
168 D1 São Francisco de Goiás Brazil
167 B6 São Francisco de Paula Brazil
168 D3 São Francisco de Sales Brazil
167 C6 São Francisco do Sul Brazil
167 C6 São Francisco, I. de i. Brazil
173 K1 São Gabriel Brazil
169 H3 São Gabriel da Palha Brazil
168 E1 São Gabriel de Goiás Brazil
169 G5 São Gonçalo Brazil
169 F5 São Gonçalo do Abaeté Brazil
166 E1 São Gonçalo do Amarante Brazil
169 F4 São Gonçalo do Sapucaí Brazil
169 E3 São Gotardo Brazil
166 B3 São João r. Mato Grosso Brazil
167 B5 São João r. Paraná Brazil
168 E1 São João da Aliança Brazil
169 H4 São João da Barra Brazil
169 E4 São João da Boa Vista Brazil
98 B4 São João da Madeira Portugal
98 C3 São João da Pesqueira Portugal

137 K2 Schultz Lake l. N.W.T. Canada
73 K3 Schulzendorf Germany
73 J3 Schulzendorf bei Eichwalde Germany
82 D2 Schüpfheim Switzerland
154 C2 Schurz Nevada U.S.A.
74 E5 Schussen r. Germany
80 C2 Schutter r. Germany
74 C4 Schutterwald Germany
72 C3 Schüttorf Germany
147 G3 Schuylerville New York U.S.A.
73 H2 Schwaan Germany
75 G3 Schwabach Germany
75 F4 Schwaben div. Germany
80 C2 Schwabhausan Germany
74 E4 Schwäbische Alb mts Germany
74 E4 Schwäbisch Gmünd Germany
74 E3 Schwäbisch Hall Germany
75 F4 Schwabmünchen Germany
72 D3 Schwaförden Germany
74 E3 Schwaigern Germany
87 F3 Schwalbach Germany
74 E2 Schwalmstadt-Treysa Germany
74 E2 Schwalmstadt-Ziegenhain Germany
81 G4 Schwanberg Austria
83 E1 Schwanden Switzerland
75 H3 Schwandorf Germany
73 G4 Schwanebeck Germany
81 E2 Schwanenstadt Austria
72 D2 Schwanewede Germany
75 F5 Schwangau Germany
72 E1 Schwansen reg. Germany
72 E3 Schwarmstedt Germany
73 H2 Schwarz Germany
75 G2 Schwarza r. Germany
75 H4 Schwarzach Germany
80 E3 Schwarzach im Pongau Austria
81 G3 Schwarzau im Gebirge Austria
73 J4 Schwarze Elster r. Germany
75 G3 Schwarze Laber r. Germany
72 F2 Schwarzenbek Germany
75 H2 Schwarzenberg Germany
82 C2 Schwarzenburg Switzerland
75 H3 Schwarzenfeld Germany
80 C3 Schwarzenstein mt. Austria/Italy
74 B2 Schwarzer Mann h. Germany
75 H3 Schwarzer Regen r. Germany
73 K4 Schwarzer Schöps r. Germany
73 J4 Schwarzheide Germany
83 G1 Schwarzhorn mt. Austria
82 D2 Schwarzhorn mt. Switzerland
128 B4 Schwarzrand mts Namibia
74 D4 Schwarzwald mts Germany
80 C3 Schwaz div. Austria
80 C3 Schwaz Austria
81 H2 Schwechat Austria
73 K2 Schwedt Germany
74 D3 Schwegenheim Germany
74 B3 Schweich Germany
74 F2 Schweinfurt Germany
73 J4 Schweinitz Germany
73 H2 Schweinrich Germany
131 E3 Schweizer-Reneke South Africa
72 C4 Schwelm Germany
80 C3 Schwendau Austria
80 A2 Schwendi Germany
74 D4 Schwenningen Germany
73 J4 Schwepnitz Germany
73 G2 Schwerin Germany
73 G2 Schweriner See l. Germany
72 C4 Schwerte Germany
74 D3 Schwetzingen Germany
73 J2 Schwichtenberg Germany
73 K3 Schwielochsee l. Germany
72 E2 Schwinge r. Germany
82 C1 Schwörstadt Germany
72 F3 Schwülper Germany
83 D1 Schwyz div. Switzerland
83 D1 Schwyz Schwyz Switzerland
110 C5 Sciacca Sicilia Italy
110 D6 Scicli Sicilia Italy
89 G2 Scie r. France
82 B2 Sciez France
111 E4 Scilla Italy
63 □1 Scilly, Isles of is England U.K.
76 E4 Ścinawa Poland
80 C2 Scionzier France
146 B5 Scioto r. Ohio U.S.A.
155 F2 Scipio Utah U.S.A.
152 F1 Scobey Montana U.S.A.
110 D6 Scoglitti Sicilia Italy
63 H2 Scole England U.K.
13 G3 Scone New South Wales Australia
106 C3 Scopello Italy
92 C2 Scorbé-Clairvaux France
111 E4 Scordia, Monte mt. Italy
110 D5 Scordia Sicilia Italy
135 Q2 Scoresby Land reg. Greenland
135 Q2 Scoresby Sund chan. Greenland
Scoresbysund see Ittoqqortoormiit
88 B4 Scorff r. France
112 E2 Scornicești Romania
107 G3 Scorzè Italy
65 G3 Scotch Corner England U.K.
179 B1 Scotia Ridge sea feature Atlantic Ocean
174 G9 Scotia Sea sea Atlantic Ocean
60 E3 Scotland div. U.K.
140 E5 Scotland Ontario Canada
141 K4 Scotstown Québec Canada
141 K3 Scott Québec Canada
179 B5 Scott Base N.Z. Base Antarctica
131 H5 Scottburgh South Africa
136 D4 Scott, C. c. B.C. Canada
14 B2 Scott, C. c. Northern Terr. Australia
150 C4 Scott City Kansas U.S.A.
179 B5 Scott Coast coastal area Antarctica
146 D4 Scottdale Pennsylvania U.S.A.
179 B4 Scott Gl. gl. Antarctica
179 A5 Scott I. i. Antarctica
135 L2 Scott Inlet inlet N.W.T. Canada
66 F5 Scottish Borders div. Scotland U.K.
137 H3 Scott Lake l. Saskatchewan Canada
179 D4 Scott Mts mountain range Antarctica
8 D1 Scott Pt pt New Zealand
16 C2 Scott Reef reef Western Australia Australia
150 C3 Scottsbluff Nebraska U.S.A.
145 C5 Scottsboro Alabama U.S.A.
144 C4 Scottsburg Indiana U.S.A.
153 E5 Scottsdale Arizona U.S.A.
13 F5 Scottsdale Tasmania Australia
154 A3 Scotts Valley California U.S.A.
148 D4 Scottville Michigan U.S.A.
154 D3 Scotty's Junction Nevada U.S.A.
66 C2 Scourie Scotland U.K.
66 □2 Scousburgh Scotland U.K.
66 E2 Scrabster Scotland U.K.
147 F4 Scranton Pennsylvania U.S.A.
66 B4 Scridain, Loch inlet Scotland U.K.
65 H4 Scunthorpe England U.K.
83 F2 Scuol Switzerland
112 B3 Scutari, Lake l. Albania/Yugoslavia
17 B6 Seabrook, L. salt flat Western Australia Australia
147 F5 Seaford Delaware U.S.A.
63 G4 Seaford England U.K.
140 E5 Seaforth Ontario Canada
15 G4 Seaforth Queensland Australia
159 □1 Seaforth Jamaica
23 A4 Seahorse Bank sand bank Philippines
137 K3 Seal r. Manitoba Canada
13 E3 Sea Lake Victoria Australia
128 □3 Seal Bay b. Tristan da Cunha Atlantic Ocean
130 D7 Seal, Cape c. South Africa
159 E2 Seal Cays is Turks and Caicos Is Caribbean
147 J3 Seal I. i. Maine U.S.A.
141 J3 Seal Lake l. Newfoundland Canada
155 E3 Seaman Range mts Nevada U.S.A.
65 H3 Seamer England U.K.
155 E4 Searchlight Nevada U.S.A.
151 F5 Searcy Arkansas U.S.A.
154 D4 Searles Lake l. California U.S.A.
148 E4 Sears Michigan U.S.A.
147 J2 Searsport Maine U.S.A.
63 E3 Seascale England U.K.
154 B3 Seaside California U.S.A.
152 B2 Seaside Oregon U.S.A.
62 C4 Seaton England U.K.
65 E3 Seaton England U.K.
65 G2 Seaton Delaval England U.K.
152 B2 Seattle Washington U.S.A.
63 E4 Seaview England U.K.
15 F3 Seaview Ra. mountain range Queensland Australia
147 F5 Seaville New Jersey U.S.A.
9 D5 Seaward Kaikoura Ra. mountain range New Zealand
147 H3 Sebago Lake l. Maine U.S.A.
22 D2 Sebakung Indonesia
22 C2 Sebangan, Tk b. Indonesia
22 A1 Sebangka i. Indonesia
156 B2 Sebastián Vizcaíno, Bahía b. Mexico
147 J2 Sebasticook r. Maine U.S.A.
23 A5 Sebatik i. Indonesia
131 G1 Sebayeng South Africa
93 E4 Sébazac-Concourès France
123 E4 Sebba Burkina
55 B3 Sebbersund Denmark
121 D2 Sebdou Algeria
122 C4 Sébékoro Mali
112 D2 Sebeș Romania
22 A3 Sebesi i. Indonesia
149 F4 Sebewaing Michigan U.S.A.
54 F3 Sebezh Rus. Fed.
128 D3 Sebina Botswana
42 D1 Şebin Karahisar Turkey
79 M5 Sebiș Romania
121 E3 Sebkha Azzel Matti salt pan Algeria
120 B4 Sebkhet Chemchâm salt lake Mauritania
121 G1 Sebkhet de Sidi El Hani salt pan Tunisia
120 B4 Sebkhet Oumm ed Drous Guebli salt lake Mauritania
120 A5 Sebkhet Te-n-Dghâmcha salt marsh Mauritania
120 B3 Sebkra Oum el Drouss Telli salt flat Mauritania
75 K2 Sebnitz Germany
147 J2 Seboeis Lake l. Maine U.S.A.
147 J2 Seboomook Maine U.S.A.
147 J2 Seboomook Lake l. Maine U.S.A.
145 D7 Sebring Florida U.S.A.
22 D2 Sebuku i. Indonesia
22 B1 Sebuyau Malaysia
106 E4 Secchia r. Italy
126 C3 Seccia Mts mts Ethiopia
52 G2 Sechenovo Rus. Fed.
162 A5 Sechura Peru
162 A5 Sechura, Bahía de b. Peru
74 E3 Seckach Germany
81 F3 Seckau Austria
81 F3 Seckauer Alpen mts Austria
86 C2 Seclin France
102 D4 Seco r. Spain
119 F3 2nd Cataract rapids Sudan
122 D6 Secondi Ghana
92 B2 Secondigny France
147 H2 Second Lake l. New Hampshire U.S.A.
15 E2 2nd Three Mile Opening chan. Queensland Australia
140 C5 Second Lake l. Michigan U.S.A.
79 L3 Sečovce Slovakia
9 A6 Secretary Island i. New Zealand
131 G3 Secunda South Africa
38 B2 Secunderabad India
164 C3 Sécure r. Bolivia
79 K5 Secusigiu Romania
100 C1 Seda r. Portugal
54 D3 Seda Latvia
54 C3 Seda Lithuania
150 E4 Sedalia Missouri U.S.A.
38 B2 Sedam India
12 D3 Sedan S. Australia Australia
86 D3 Sedan France
99 G2 Sedano Spain
65 F3 Sedbergh England U.K.
9 E4 Seddon New Zealand
9 C4 Seddonville New Zealand
42 A1 Seddülbahir Turkey
43 C4 Sede Boqer Israel
39 D2 Sedeh Iran
91 D4 Séderon France
43 C4 Sederot Israel
65 G3 Sedgefield England U.K.
147 J2 Sedgwick Maine U.S.A.
122 A4 Sédhiou Senegal
107 G2 Sedico Italy
108 A4 Sedilo Sardegna Italy
78 D2 Sedlčany Czech Rep.
75 K3 Sedlec Prčice Czech Rep.
75 J3 Sedlice Czech Rep.
53 A1 Sedlyshche Ukraine
53 D1 Sedniv Ukraine
43 C4 Sedom Israel
155 G4 Sedona Arizona U.S.A.
105 A7 Sédrata Algeria
22 D1 Sedulang Indonesia
54 C4 Šeduva Lithuania
77 K5 Sędziszów Małopolski Poland
89 D3 Sée r. France
87 H4 Seebach Germany
72 E4 Seebad Heringsdorf Germany
81 F4 Seeberg pass Austria/Slovenia
81 E4 Seeboden Austria
80 D3 Seebruck Germany
73 F2 Seedorf Germany
80 C2 Seefeld Germany
80 C3 Seefeld in Tirol Austria
67 D4 Seefin h. Rep. of Ireland
75 F5 Seeg Germany
73 J2 Seehausen Brandenburg Germany
73 G3 Seehausen Sachsen-Anhalt Germany
83 G1 Seehausen am Staffelsee Germany
128 B4 Seeheim Namibia
74 D3 Seeheim-Jugenheim Germany
80 E3 Seekirchen am Wallersee Austria
130 D6 Seekoegat South Africa
130 E5 Seekoei r. South Africa
155 E5 Seeley California U.S.A.
179 B3 Seelig, Mt mt. Antarctica
73 K3 Seelow Germany
72 E3 Seelze Germany
83 D1 Seerücken v. Switzerland
89 F3 Sées France
72 F4 Seesen Germany
75 G5 Seeshaupt Germany
83 F1 Seetaler Alpen mountain range Austria
81 E3 Seethal Austria
72 F2 Seevetal Germany
81 E3 Seewalchen am Attersee Austria
81 H3 Seewinkel marsh Austria
90 E3 Sées France
122 B5 Sefadu Sierra Leone
113 F5 Seferihisar Turkey
39 B2 Sefīd Dasht Iran
129 D3 Sefophe Botswana
120 D2 Sefrou Morocco
93 E4 Ségala reg. France
122 B4 Ségala Mali
93 E4 Ségala du Quercy reg. France
58 D1 Segalstad Norway
23 A5 Segama r. Malaysia
25 D7 Segamat Malaysia
96 E5 Segangane Morocco
112 D2 Şegarcea Romania
102 E3 Segarra reg. Spain
123 E4 Ségbana Benin
22 D3 Segeri Indonesia
59 G2 Segersäng Sweden
50 E2 Segezha Rus. Fed.
39 G1 Seghnān Afghanistan
88 B3 Séglien France
83 E2 Segl, Lago da l. Switzerland
109 F3 Segni Italy
92 B3 Segonzac France
102 C3 Segorbe Spain
122 C4 Ségou div. Mali
122 C4 Ségou Mali
99 F3 Segovia div. Castilla y León Spain
162 C2 Segovia Colombia
99 F4 Segovia Spain
50 E2 Segozerskoye, Oz. l. Rus. Fed.
102 D3 Segre r. Spain
89 E4 Segré France
89 E4 Segréen reg. France
102 D3 Segrià reg. Spain
123 G2 Séguédine Niger
122 C5 Séguéla Côte d'Ivoire
122 C5 Séguélon Côte d'Ivoire
173 G2 Seguí Argentina
151 D6 Seguin Texas U.S.A.
173 F1 Segundo r. Argentina
103 C6 Segura r. Spain
98 D5 Segura Portugal
101 H2 Segura de la Sierra Spain
100 D2 Segura de León Spain
102 C4 Segura de los Baños Spain
101 H2 Segura, Sierra de mountain range Spain
99 F4 Segurilla Spain
128 C3 Sehithwa Botswana
72 E3 Sehnde Germany
36 D5 Sehore India
36 A4 Sehwan Pakistan
98 C4 Seia Portugal
88 D4 Seiche r. France
89 E4 Seiches-sur-le-Loir France
75 K2 Seifhennersdorf Germany
90 B1 Seignelay France
82 B1 Seignelégier Switzerland
93 E4 Seignes, Mt mt. France
24 A2 Seikpyu Myanmar
64 C1 Seil i. Scotland U.K.
56 F1 Seiland i. Norway
92 D3 Seilhac France
151 D4 Seiling Oklahoma U.S.A.
90 D2 Seille r. Bourgogne/Franche-Comté France
87 F4 Seille r. Lorraine France
69 D4 Seilles Belgium
56 F3 Seinäjoki Finland
138 B4 Seine r. Ontario Canada
89 F2 Seine r. France
89 E2 Seine, Baie de b. France
86 B4 Seine-et-Marne div. France
89 F2 Seine-Maritime div. France
86 C4 Seine, Val de v. France
112 D1 Seini Romania
88 A3 Sein, Île de i. France
22 C2 Seipinang Indonesia
93 C6 Seira Spain
93 C5 Seissan France
81 F2 Seitenstetten Austria
93 D6 Seix France
100 A2 Seixal Portugal
100 B3 Seixe r. Portugal
55 D4 Sejerø i. Denmark
55 D4 Sejerø Bugt b. Denmark
77 M1 Sejny Poland
22 B1 Sekadau Indonesia
22 A2 Sekanak, Tk b. Indonesia
23 A6 Sekatak Bengara Indonesia
22 A2 Sekayu Indonesia
29 F6 Seki Japan
130 D2 Sekoma Botswana
52 G3 Sekretarka Rus. Fed.
39 E3 Sekūheh Iran
22 B1 Sekura Indonesia
126 C3 Sela Dingay Ethiopia
152 B2 Selah Washington U.S.A.
22 B1 Selakau Indonesia
25 C7 Selangor div. Malaysia
108 B5 Selargius Sardegna Italy
21 K8 Selaru i. Indonesia
22 D4 Selat Alas chan. Indonesia
22 C3 Selatan, Tg pt Indonesia
22 C4 Selat Bali chan. Indonesia
22 A2 Selat Bangka chan. Indonesia
22 A2 Selat Berhala chan. Indonesia
21 K7 Selat Dampir chan. Indonesia
22 A2 Selat Gaspar chan. Indonesia
25 □ Selat Johor chan. Malaysia/Singapore
25 □ Selat Jurong chan. Singapore
22 B2 Selat Karimata str. Indonesia
22 C2 Selat Laut chan. Indonesia
22 C4 Selat Lombok chan. Indonesia
22 C3 Selat Madura chan. Indonesia
25 □ Selat Pandan chan. Singapore
22 E3 Selat Salayar chan. Indonesia
22 D4 Selat Sape chan. Indonesia
22 D4 Selat Sumba chan. Indonesia
22 A3 Selat Sunda chan. Indonesia
62 C2 Selattyn England U.K.
21 L7 Selat Yapen chan. Indonesia
134 B3 Selawik Alaska U.S.A.
75 H2 Selb Germany
56 C3 Selbekken Norway
80 D3 Selbhorn mt. Austria
75 G2 Selbitz Germany
58 A2 Selbjørnsfjorden chan. Norway
56 C3 Selbu Norway
65 G4 Selby England U.K.
150 C2 Selby S. Dakota U.S.A.
107 J3 Selce Croatia
113 F6 Selçuk Turkey
79 L5 Seleuș Romania
109 H4 Sele r. Italy
128 D3 Selebi-Phikwe Botswana
114 C1 Selečka Planina mountain range Macedonia
108 B4 s 'Elema r. Sardegna Italy
115 G7 Selena mt. Greece
113 G5 Selendi Turkey
30 C2 Selenduma Rus. Fed.
30 C1 Seleng r. Rus. Fed.
30 C2 Selenge div. Mongolia
30 B2 Selenge Mongolia
124 C4 Selenge Congo(Zaire)
30 C2 Selenge Mörön r. Mongolia
30 C2 Selenginsk Rus. Fed.
113 B4 Selenicë Albania
72 F1 Selenter See l. Germany
87 G4 Sélestat France
25 □ Seletar Singapore
25 □ Seletar, P. i. Singapore
25 □ Seletar Res. resr Singapore
47 H2 Seletinskoye Kazakhstan
47 H2 Selety r. Kazakhstan
47 H2 Seletyteniz, Oz. salt lake Kazakhstan
Seleucia see Silifke
Seleucia Piera see Samandağı
54 F1 Seleznevo Rus. Fed.
150 C2 Selfridge N. Dakota U.S.A.
50 J2 Selib Rus. Fed.
120 B5 Sélibabi Mauritania
52 B3 Selichnya Rus. Fed.
74 D2 Seligenstadt Germany
52 A1 Seliger, Oz. l. Rus. Fed.
155 F4 Seligman Arizona U.S.A.
119 E3 Selîma Oasis oasis Sudan
22 C1 Selimbau Indonesia
113 F6 Selimiye Muğla Turkey
43 A1 Selimiye Turkey
122 C4 Sélingué, Lac de l. Mali
115 D4 Selinous r. Greece
149 J5 Selinsgrove Pennsylvania U.S.A.
52 A1 Selishche Rus. Fed.
52 F2 Selishchi Rus. Fed.
51 H6 Selitrennoye Rus. Fed.
52 A1 Selizharovo Rus. Fed.
58 C2 Seljord Norway
58 C2 Seljordsvatnet l. Norway
73 G4 Selke r. Germany
137 K4 Selkirk Manitoba Canada
66 F5 Selkirk Scotland U.K.
136 F4 Selkirk Mountains mountain range B.C. Canada
65 E3 Sellafield England U.K.
109 E2 Sellano Italy
115 D5 Sellasia Greece
89 G4 Selles-St-Denis France
89 G4 Selles-sur-Cher France
115 F7 Sellia Greece
111 F4 Sellia Marina Italy
90 D2 Sellières France
63 G3 Sellindge England U.K.
55 C3 Selling Denmark
68 F2 Sellingen Netherlands
Sellore I. i. see Saganthit Kyun
80 C3 Sellrain Austria
155 G6 Sells Arizona U.S.A.
72 C4 Selm Germany
145 C5 Selma Alabama U.S.A.
154 C3 Selma California U.S.A.
145 B5 Selmer Tennessee U.S.A.
73 F2 Selmsdorf Germany
89 G4 Selommes France
82 B1 Seloncourt France
22 D4 Selong Indonesia
90 D1 Selongey France
91 E4 Selonnet France
131 G2 Selonsrivier South Africa
122 B4 Sélouma Guinea
127 C6 Selous Game Reserve res. Tanzania
39 E3 Selseleh-ye-Pīr Shūrān mountain range Iran
65 F3 Selset Res. resr England U.K.
63 F4 Selsey England U.K.
63 F4 Selsey Bill headland England U.K.
74 C2 Selters (Westerwald) Germany
52 B3 Sel'tso Bryansk Rus. Fed.
52 B3 Sel'tso Bryansk Rus. Fed.
87 H4 Seltz France
89 E3 Selune r. France
102 B2 Selva mt. Spain
102 F3 Selva reg. Spain
111 G2 Selva Italy
172 A5 Selva Oscura Chile
168 C4 Selviria Brazil
137 J3 Selwyn Lake l. N.W.T. Canada
136 C2 Selwyn Mountains mountain range Yukon Terr. Canada
14 D4 Selwyn Range h. Queensland Australia
53 A3 Selyatyn Ukraine
53 G2 Selydove Ukraine
74 D3 Selz r. Germany
81 F3 Selzthal Austria
113 B4 Seman r. Albania
22 A3 Semangka, Tk b. Indonesia
22 B3 Semarang Indonesia
22 B1 Sematan Malaysia
22 C2 Semayang, D. l. Indonesia
23 A6 Sembakung r. Indonesia
25 □ Sembawang Singapore
124 B3 Sembé Congo
93 C5 Séméac France
22 C4 Semenanjung Blambangan pen. Indonesia
125 C4 Semendua Congo(Zaire)
52 D1 Semendyayevo Rus. Fed.
51 E4 Semenivka Chernihiv Ukraine
53 E2 Semenivka Poltava Ukraine
50 H3 Semenov Rus. Fed.
50 H3 Semenovo Rus. Fed.
52 D1 Semibratovo Rus. Fed.
50 G3 Semigorodnyaya Rus. Fed.
52 G3 Semiley Rus. Fed.
52 F2 Semilovo Rus. Fed.
52 D4 Semiluki Rus. Fed.
78 E1 Semily Czech Rep.
111 E4 Seminara Italy
90 D2 Semine r. France
152 F3 Seminoe Res. resr Wyoming U.S.A.
151 C5 Seminole Texas U.S.A.
145 C6 Seminole, L. l. Georgia/Florida U.S.A.
47 L2 Seminskiy Khrebet mountain range Rus. Fed.
52 E2 Semion Rus. Fed.
46 F2 Semiozernoye Kazakhstan
30 D2 Semiozer'ye Rus. Fed.
47 J3 Semipalatinsk div. Kazakhstan
47 K2 Semipalatinsk Kazakhstan
23 B3 Semirara i. Philippines
23 B4 Semirara Islands is Philippines
39 B3 Semīrom Iran
22 B1 Semitau Indonesia
47 J2 Semiyarka Kazakhstan
47 H2 Semiz-Bugu Kazakhstan
73 F3 Semmenstedt Germany
81 G3 Semmering pass Austria
39 C2 Semnān div. Iran
39 C2 Semnān Iran
30 B5 Semnyi China
69 D5 Semois r. Belgium
69 C5 Semois, Vallée de la v. Belgium/France
131 G4 Semonkong Lesotho
82 D1 Sempach Switzerland
82 D1 Sempacher See l. Switzerland
23 A5 Semporna Malaysia
22 C4 Sempu i. Indonesia
166 B1 Sem Tripa Brazil
52 A3 Semtsy Rus. Fed.
90 C1 Semur-en-Auxois France
90 C2 Semur-en-Brionnais France
92 B3 Semussac France
50 H1 Semzha Rus. Fed.
164 C2 Sena Bolivia
79 L3 Seňa Slovakia
102 C3 Sena Spain
168 D2 Senador Canedo Brazil
166 E2 Senador Pompeu Brazil
22 B3 Senaja Malaysia
107 E2 Senales Italy
164 C1 Sena Madureira Brazil
38 C5 Senanayake Samudra l. Sri Lanka
125 D7 Senanga Zambia
22 B1 Senaning Indonesia
92 B3 Senarpont France
91 D5 Sénas France
53 E1 Šencha Ukraine
81 F4 Šenčur Slovenia
29 H4 Sendai Japan
28 C8 Sendai Japan
28 C8 Sendai-gawa r. Japan
74 F4 Senden Germany
98 D3 Sendim Portugal
131 G1 Sending South Africa
32 A2 Sêndo China
88 C4 Séné France
25 C7 Senebui, Tanjung pt Indonesia
78 G3 Senec Slovakia
155 G5 Seneca Arizona U.S.A.
148 C5 Seneca Illinois U.S.A.
152 C2 Seneca Oregon U.S.A.
146 E3 Seneca Falls New York U.S.A.
146 E3 Seneca Lake l. New York U.S.A.
146 D5 Seneca Rocks W. Virginia U.S.A.
146 C5 Senecaville Lake l. Ohio U.S.A.
69 C4 Seneffe Belgium
116 C4 Senegal country Africa
122 B3 Sénégal r. Mauritania/Senegal
108 A4 Seneghe Sardegna Italy
131 F4 Senekal South Africa
148 E2 Seney Michigan U.S.A.
91 E5 Senez France
81 G2 Senftenberg Austria
73 K4 Senftenberg Germany
127 B6 Senga Hill Zambia
36 D4 Sengar r. India
22 D1 Sengata Indonesia
80 C1 Sengenthal Germany
127 B5 Sengerema Tanzania
50 J4 Sengiley Rus. Fed.
111 □ Senglea Malta
93 C6 Sengouagnet France
81 F3 Sengsengebirge mts Austria
171 B6 Senguerr r. Argentina
129 D2 Sengwa r. Zimbabwe
166 D3 Senhor do Bonfim Brazil
78 G3 Senica Slovakia
107 H5 Senigallia Italy
172 C5 Senillosa Argentina
107 F4 Senio r. Italy
108 A5 Senis Sardegna Italy
109 J4 Senise Italy
107 J4 Senj Croatia
56 E1 Senja i. Norway
122 C5 Senko Guinea
53 G2 Sen'kove Ukraine
36 D2 Senku India
130 D2 Senlac South Africa
86 B3 Senlis France
25 D4 Senmonorom Cambodia
29 E6 Sennan Japan
119 F5 Sennar Sudan
119 F5 Sennar Dam dam Sudan
108 A4 Sennariolo Sardegna Italy
72 D4 Senne reg. Germany
90 C2 Sennecey-le-Grand France
62 A4 Sennen England U.K.
141 G2 Senneterre Québec Canada
108 A4 Sennori Sardegna Italy
52 H3 Sennoy Rus. Fed.
83 E1 Sennwald Switzerland
62 C3 Sennybridge Wales U.K.
86 C4 Sénonais reg. France
87 F4 Senones France
171 B7 Seno Otway b. Chile
108 B5 Senorbì Sardegna Italy
91 B3 Senouire r. France
81 G4 Senovo Slovenia
81 F5 Senožeče Slovenia
131 F3 Senqu r. Lesotho
131 G4 Senqunyane r. Lesotho
86 C4 Sens France
86 C2 Sensée r. France
156 H6 Sensuntepeque El Salvador
79 K6 Senta Yugoslavia
102 D2 Sentenada Spain
81 G4 Šentilj Slovenia
155 F5 Sentinel Arizona U.S.A.
136 E3 Sentinel Pk summit B.C. Canada
179 B3 Sentinel Ra. mountain range Antarctica
81 G5 Šentjernej Slovenia
81 G4 Šentjur pri Celju Slovenia
25 □ Sentosa i. Singapore
131 F2 Sentrum South Africa
22 D1 Senyiur Indonesia
42 E2 Şenyurt Turkey
28 D7 Sen-zaki pt Japan
28 C6 Senzaki Japan
82 D1 Seon Switzerland
36 D5 Seoni India
37 E5 Seorinarayan India
Seoul see Sŏul
93 C4 Séoune r. France
22 C3 Sepanjang i. Indonesia
8 D4 Separation Pt pt New Zealand
22 D1 Sepasu Indonesia
22 B1 Sepauk Indonesia
167 D5 Sepetiba, Baía de b. Brazil
39 B3 Sepīdān Iran
6 □1 Sepik r. P.N.G.
22 D1 Sepinang Indonesia
109 G3 Sepino Italy
76 F2 Sępólno Krajeńskie Poland
165 E3 Sepotuba r. Brazil
82 C1 Seppois-le-Bas France
92 E2 Septaine reg. France
91 D5 Septèmes-les-Vallons France
89 G3 Septeuil France
93 D4 Septfonds France
139 G3 Sept-Îles Québec Canada
88 B3 Sept-Îles, Les is France
82 A2 Septmoncel France
99 G3 Sepúlveda Spain
22 A3 Seputih r. Indonesia
107 G2 Sequals Italy
173 J1 Sequeira Uruguay
98 D4 Sequeros Spain
99 E3 Sequillo r. Spain
154 C3 Sequoia National Park nat. park California U.S.A.
51 G5 Serafimovich Rus. Fed.
86 D3 Seraincourt France
69 D4 Seraing Belgium
39 E1 Serakhs Turkmenistan
21 J7 Seram i. Indonesia
21 J7 Seram Sea g. Indonesia
90 D3 Séran r. France
22 A3 Serang Indonesia
25 □ Serangoon Harbour harbour Singapore
25 □ Serangoon, P. i. Singapore
91 B5 Séranne, Montagne de la ridge France
91 E5 Séranon France
25 E7 Serasan i. Indonesia
106 E5 Seravezza Italy
25 E7 Seraya i. Indonesia
25 □ Seraya, P. i. Singapore
43 B5 Serbâl, G. mt. Egypt
Serbia div. see Srbija
106 E4 Serchio r. Italy
156 D2 Serdán Mexico
126 D2 Serdo Ethiopia
52 G3 Serdoba r. Rus. Fed.
52 G3 Serdobsk Rus. Fed.
47 K3 Serebryansk Kazakhstan
52 D2 Serebryanyye Prudy Rus. Fed.
79 G3 Sered' Slovakia
52 E1 Sereda Rus. Fed.
52 B2 Seredeyskiy Rus. Fed.
54 F2 Seredka Rus. Fed.
52 D2 Serednikovo Rus. Fed.
52 B3 Seredyna-Buda Ukraine
79 M3 Seredyne Ukraine
42 C2 Şereflikoçhisar Turkey
79 H4 Seregélyes Hungary
106 D3 Seregno Italy
90 B1 Serein r. France
25 C7 Seremban Malaysia
127 B5 Serengeti National Park nat. park Tanzania
127 C5 Serengeti Plains plain Kenya
127 B7 Serenje Zambia
166 C2 Sereno r. Brazil
88 C4 Sérent France
126 B4 Serere Uganda
53 A2 Seret r. Ukraine
52 F2 Serezha r. Rus. Fed.
80 B3 Serfaus Austria
115 F5 Serfopoula i. Greece
52 G2 Sergach Rus. Fed.
30 E2 Sergelen Mongolia
30 D3 Sergelen Mongolia
47 G2 Sergeyevka Kazakhstan
86 C4 Sergines France
166 E3 Sergipe div. Brazil
114 G2 Sergitsi i. Greece
51 G6 Sergiyevka Rus. Fed.
52 D1 Sergiyev Posad Rus. Fed.
46 D2 Sergiyevsk Rus. Fed.
52 C3 Sergiyevskoye Orel Rus. Fed.
52 D3 Sergiyevskoye Lipetsk Rus. Fed.
Sergiyevskoye see Sergiyevka
83 E3 Sergnano Italy
53 E1 Serhiyivka Chernihivs'ka Oblast' Ukraine
53 D3 Serhiyivka Odes'ka Oblast' Ukraine
53 D3 Serhiyivka Odes'ka Oblast' Ukraine
20 F6 Seria Brunei
22 B1 Serian Malaysia
83 E3 Seriate Italy
89 G2 Sérifontaine France
115 F5 Serifos i. Greece
115 F5 Serifos Greece
91 B5 Sérignan France
91 C4 Sérignan-du-Comtat France
139 G2 Sérigny, Lac l. Québec Canada
42 B2 Serik Turkey
47 J5 Serikbuya China
16 C2 Seringapatam Reef reef Western Australia Australia
131 G2 Seringkop South Africa
109 G4 Serino Italy
106 D3 Serio r. Italy
12 D2 Serle, Mt h. S. Australia Australia
86 D4 Sermaize-les-Bains France
108 B2 Sermano Corse France
107 F4 Sermide Italy
109 F3 Sermoneta Italy
54 D3 Sērmūkši Latvia
98 C4 Sernancelhe Portugal
79 M3 Serne r. Ukraine
50 J3 Sernur Rus. Fed.
46 F5 Sernyy Zavod Turkmenistan
77 K3 Serock Poland
158 □1 Seroe Colorado Aruba Caribbean
51 H6 Seroglazovka Rus. Fed.
101 H3 Serón Spain
99 H3 Serón de Nájima Spain
128 C2 Seronga Botswana
68 B3 Serooskerke Netherlands
102 D3 Seròs Spain
121 F4 Serouenout well Algeria
44 H4 Serov Rus. Fed.
128 D3 Serowe Botswana
100 C3 Serpa Portugal
12 B2 Serpentine Lakes salt flat S. Australia Australia
163 E2 Serpent's Mouth chan. Venezuela
52 B2 Serpeysk Rus. Fed.
103 C6 Serpis r. Spain
53 C3 Serpneve Ukraine
52 E3 Serpovoye Rus. Fed.
52 C2 Serpukhov Rus. Fed.
89 F2 Serquigny France
169 H4 Serra Brazil
163 F3 Serra Acari h. Guyana
168 A1 Serra Azul h. Brazil
169 E1 Serra Bonita Brazil
109 H3 Serracapriola Italy
163 E3 Serra Curupira mountain range Brazil
167 B5 Serra da Apucarana h. Brazil
169 F5 Serra da Bocaina, Parque Nacional da nat. park Brazil
167 A5 Serra da Bodoquena h. Brazil
169 H2 Serra da Cana Brava h. Brazil
168 C1 Serra da Canastra mts Brazil
169 E4 Serra da Canastra, Parque Nacional da nat. park Brazil
168 C6 Serra da Esperança mountain range Brazil
167 D4 Serra da Espinhaco mountain range Brazil
166 D1 Serra da Ibiapaba h. Brazil
169 F5 Serra da Mantiqueira mountain range Brazil
168 B3 Serra da Mombuca h. Brazil
168 B3 Serra das Araras h. Brazil
168 B6 Serra das Araras mountain range Brazil
169 F1 Serra das Araras Brazil
168 C2 Serra das Divisões ou de Santa Marta mountain range Brazil
166 D3 Serra da Tabatinga h. Brazil
165 E4 Serra de Amambaí h. Brazil/Paraguay

28 D6 Shimane-hantō pen. Japan
31 H1 Shimanovsk Rus. Fed.
126 E2 Shimbiris mt. Somalia
127 D4 Shimbirre waterhole Kenya
33 E2 Shimen China
32 C2 Shimian China
29 G6 Shimizu Japan
36 D3 Shimla India
29 G6 Shimoda Japan
29 G5 Shimodate Japan
38 A3 Shimoga India
28 H3 Shimokita-hantō pen. Japan
28 B8 Shimo-Koshiki-jima i. Japan
127 C5 Shimoni Kenya
28 C7 Shimonoseki Japan
52 F2 Shimorskoye Rus. Fed.
36 C1 Shimshal Jammu and Kashmir
50 D3 Shimsk Rus. Fed.
33 E4 Shinan China
29 G5 Shinano-gawa r. Japan
39 E2 Shindand Afghanistan
63 F3 Shinfield *England* U.K.
24 B1 Shingbwiyang Myanmar
24 B1 Shing-gai Myanmar
36 B3 Shinghar Pakistan
36 C1 Shinghshal P. pass Pakistan
148 D2 Shingleton *Michigan* U.S.A.
27 □ Shing Mun Res. resr *Hong Kong* China
36 D2 Shingo P. pass India
47 K3 Shingozha Kazakhstan
29 F7 Shingū Japan
131 H1 Shingwedzi r. South Africa
131 H1 Shingwedzi South Africa
62 D1 Shining Tor h. *England* U.K.
140 E3 Shining Tree *Ontario* Canada
28 D6 Shinji-ko l. Japan
29 H4 Shinjō Japan
39 F3 Shīnkāy Afghanistan
66 D2 Shin, Loch l. *Scotland* U.K.
29 F5 Shinminato Japan
28 C6 Shin-nanyō Japan
147 J1 Shin Pond *Maine* U.S.A.
43 D2 Shinshār Syria
28 J2 Shintoku Japan
127 B5 Shinyanga div. Tanzania
127 B5 Shinyanga Tanzania
29 H4 Shiogama Japan
29 F5 Shiojiri Japan
29 E7 Shiono-misaki c. Japan
29 H5 Shioya-zaki pt Japan
158 C1 Ship Chan Cay i. The Bahamas
52 D1 Shipilovo Rus. Fed.
32 C4 Shiping China
36 D3 Shipki Pass pass China/India
65 G4 Shipley *England* U.K.
139 H4 Shippegan *New Brunswick* Canada
146 E4 Shippensburg *Pennsylvania* U.S.A.
155 H3 Shiprock *New Mexico* U.S.A.
155 H3 Shiprock Peak summit *New Mexico* U.S.A.
63 E2 Shipston on Stour *England* U.K.
62 D2 Shipton *England* U.K.
33 H2 Shipu China
47 K2 Shipunovo Rus. Fed.
32 E3 Shiqian China
36 E2 Shiquan r. China
32 E1 Shiquan China
Shiquanhe *see* Ali
32 E1 Shiquan Sk. resr China
47 M2 Shira Rus. Fed.
29 E7 Shirahama Japan
28 H3 Shirakami-misaki pt Japan
29 H5 Shirakawa Japan
29 F5 Shirakawa Japan
29 G5 Shirane-san volcano Japan
28 K2 Shiranuka Japan
28 H2 Shiraoi Japan
179 D4 Shirasebreen gl. Antarctica
179 A4 Shirase Coast coastal area Antarctica
28 J2 Shirataki Japan
39 C3 Shīrāz Iran
43 A4 Shirbîn Egypt
129 E2 Shire r. Malawi
30 E3 Shireet Mongolia
28 K2 Shiretoko-hantō pen. Japan
28 K1 Shiretoko-misaki c. Japan
46 F4 Shirikrabat Kazakhstan
36 A3 Shirinab r. Pakistan
52 F3 Shiringushi Rus. Fed.
28 H3 Shiriya-zaki c. Japan
46 E3 Shirkala reg. Kazakhstan
147 G4 Shirley *New York* U.S.A.
147 J2 Shirley Mills *Maine* U.S.A.
29 H5 Shiroishi Japan
29 G5 Shirone Japan
123 F5 Shiroro Reservoir resr Nigeria
29 F6 Shirotori Japan
36 C5 Shirpur India
30 A4 Shirten Hōloy Gobi desert China
39 D1 Shīrvān Iran
31 H2 Shisanzhan China
33 F2 Shishou China
33 G2 Shitai China
33 H2 Shitang China
29 F6 Shitara Japan
42 E3 Shithāthah Iraq
36 B4 Shiv India
144 C4 Shively *Kentucky* U.S.A.
36 D4 Shivpuri India
43 C4 Shivta Israel
155 F3 Shivwits Plateau plat. *Arizona* U.S.A.
39 G1 Shiwal l. Afghanistan
32 D4 Shiwan Dashan mountain range China
127 B7 Shiwa Ngandu Zambia
33 F3 Shixing China
33 E1 Shiyan China
32 E2 Shizhu China
32 C3 Shizong China
29 H4 Shizugawa Japan
30 C5 Shizuishan China
29 G6 Shizuoka div. Japan
29 G6 Shizuoka Japan
42 E1 Shkhara mt. Rus. Fed.
77 M6 Shklo Ukraine
50 D4 Shklow Belarus
112 B3 Shkodër *Shkodër* Albania
113 B4 Shkumbin r. Albania
53 G1 Shlyakhovo Rus. Fed.
45 L1 Shmidta, O. i. Rus. Fed.
15 G4 Shoalwater B. b. *Queensland* Australia
28 D6 Shōbara Japan
28 E6 Shōdo-shima i. Japan
29 F5 Shō-gawa r. Japan
46 E5 Shoghlābād Iran
28 H2 Shokanbetsu-dake mt. Japan
50 E1 Shomba r. Rus. Fed.
46 E3 Shomishkol' Kazakhstan
50 J2 Shomvukva Rus. Fed.
37 G4 Shongar Bhutan
43 A4 Shôni Egypt
52 D1 Shopsha Rus. Fed.
36 D2 Shor India
38 B4 Shoranur India
36 A4 Shorap Pakistan
39 F3 Shorawak reg. Afghanistan
46 E4 Shor Barsa-Kel'mes salt marsh Uzbekistan
63 F4 Shoreham-by-Sea *England* U.K.
36 C3 Shorkot Pakistan
6 □1 Shortland Is is Solomon Is.
28 H1 Shosanbetsu Japan
52 B1 Shosha r. Rus. Fed.
152 E2 Shoshone r. *Wyoming* U.S.A.
154 D4 Shoshone *California* U.S.A.
152 D3 Shoshone *Idaho* U.S.A.
152 E2 Shoshone L. l. *Wyoming* U.S.A.
153 C4 Shoshone Mts mountain range *Nevada* U.S.A.
128 D3 Shoshong Botswana
152 E3 Shoshoni *Wyoming* U.S.A.
53 E1 Shostka Ukraine
64 E2 Shotts *Scotland* U.K.
31 F5 Shouguang China
33 G3 Shouning China
33 G1 Shou Xian China
30 E5 Shouyang China
32 E1 Shouyang Shan mt. China
37 E3 Shovo Tso salt lake China
119 G5 Showak Sudan
155 G4 Show Low *Arizona* U.S.A.
44 F3 Shoyna Rus. Fed.
52 E4 Shpikulovo Rus. Fed.
53 D2 Shpola Ukraine
53 C2 Shpykiv Ukraine
53 E1 Shramkivka Ukraine
151 E5 Shreveport *Louisiana* U.S.A.
62 D2 Shrewsbury *England* U.K.
38 A2 Shrigonda India
36 B4 Shri Mohangarh India
63 E3 Shrivenham *England* U.K.
62 D2 Shropshire div. *England* U.K.
114 B2 Shtërmen Albania
33 G1 Shu r. China
32 C3 Shuangbai China
31 H3 Shuangcheng China
32 D2 Shuanghechang China
31 J2 Shuanghedagang Rus. Fed.
32 B4 Shuangjiang China
31 G4 Shuangliao China
33 E3 Shuangpai China
31 H4 Shuangyang China
31 J3 Shuangyashan China
46 E3 Shubarkuduk Kazakhstan
46 E3 Shubarshi Kazakhstan
43 D2 Shubayṭ, J. ash h. Syria
52 G2 Shubino Rus. Fed.
119 H3 Shubrāmīyah well Saudi Arabia
33 G2 Shucheng China
37 H4 Shuganu India
52 H2 Shugurovo Rus. Fed.
Shuicheng *see* Liupanshui
33 G3 Shuiji China
30 B5 Shuiquanzi China
32 C2 Shuituo r. China
36 D5 Shujalpur India
39 B3 Shūl watercourse Iran
31 H3 Shulan China
47 J5 Shule China
52 E3 Shul'gino Rus. Fed.
31 E5 Shulu China
134 C4 Shumagin Islands is *Alaska* U.S.A.
53 G1 Shumakovo Rus. Fed.
46 E4 Shumanay Uzbekistan
28 J1 Shumarinai-ko l. Japan
128 D2 Shumba Zimbabwe
112 F3 Shumen Bulgaria
52 H2 Shumerlya Rus. Fed.
46 F1 Shumikha Rus. Fed.
54 F4 Shumilina Belarus
53 B1 Shums'k Ukraine
155 G4 Shumway *Arizona* U.S.A.
50 E4 Shumyachi Rus. Fed.
43 C4 Shuna Jordan
33 G3 Shunchang China
33 F4 Shunde China
52 E1 Shunga Rus. Fed.
134 C3 Shungrak *Alaska* U.S.A.
31 F4 Shunyi China
32 D4 Shuolong China
30 E5 Shuo Xian China
36 C2 Shupiyan India
126 E2 Shuqrah Yemen
39 C3 Shūr r. *Fars/Būshehr* Iran
39 C3 Shūr r. *Fars/Hormozgān* Iran
39 C4 Shūr r. *Fars/Hormozgān* Iran
39 C3 Shūr r. *Kermān* Iran
39 D2 Shur r. *Khorāsān* Iran
39 D2 Shur r. *Khorāsān* Iran
39 C4 Shūr watercourse Iran
39 D3 Shūr Āb r. Iran
39 C2 Shūrāb Iran
39 B2 Shūr Āb Iran
39 B2 Shurâb Iran
39 D2 Shūrāb Iran
47 G5 Shurchi Uzbekistan
39 D3 Shūr Gaz Iran
29 □2 Shuri Japan
39 C3 Shūrjestān Iran
50 J3 Shurma Rus. Fed.
129 E2 Shurugwi Zimbabwe
39 E3 Shusf Iran
39 B2 Shūsh Iran
Shusha *see* Şuşa
114 B1 Shushicë Albania
50 G3 Shushkodom Rus. Fed.
39 B2 Shushtar Iran
52 B4 Shustovo Rus. Fed.
136 F4 Shuswap L. l. *B.C.* Canada
39 F2 Shutar Khun P. pass Afghanistan
52 G2 Shuvary Rus. Fed.
52 E1 Shuya Rus. Fed.
33 G1 Shuyang China
24 A3 Shwebandaw Myanmar
24 A2 Shwebo Myanmar
24 A3 Shwedaung Myanmar
24 A1 Shwedwin Myanmar
24 B3 Shwegun Myanmar
24 B3 Shwegyin Myanmar
24 B2 Shweli r. Myanmar
24 B2 Shweudaung mt. Myanmar
53 B2 Shybena Ukraine
47 G4 Shymkent Kazakhstan
36 D2 Shyok r. India
53 G2 Shypuvate Ukraine
53 E3 Shyroke *Dnipropetrovs'k* Ukraine
53 F2 Shyroke *Dnipropetrovs'k* Ukraine
53 D3 Shyrokolanivka Ukraine
53 D3 Shyryayeve Ukraine
53 F2 Shyshaky Ukraine
54 E5 Shyshchytsy Belarus
21 K8 Sia Indonesia
36 D2 Siachen Gl. gl. *Jammu and Kashmir*
91 E5 Siagne r. France
39 E4 Siahan Range mountain range Pakistan
42 F2 Sīah Chashmeh Iran
39 F2 Siah Koh mountain range Afghanistan
39 C2 Sīāh Kūh mountain range Iran
39 F3 Siah Sang P. pass Afghanistan
36 C2 Sialkot Pakistan
Sian *see* Xi'an
76 E1 Sianów Poland
25 D7 Siantan i. Indonesia
39 E3 Sīāreh Iran
23 C4 Siargao i. Philippines
23 B5 Siasi i. Philippines
23 B5 Siasi Philippines
114 C2 Siatista Greece
23 B4 Siaton Philippines
54 C4 Šiauliai Lithuania
Siazan' *see* Siyäzän
39 E4 Sib Iran
111 F3 Sibari Italy
47 L3 Sibati China
23 B4 Sibay i. Philippines
46 E2 Sibay Rus. Fed.
131 J3 Sibayi, Lake l. South Africa
179 B5 Sibbald, C. c. Antarctica
104 E4 Šibenik Croatia
18 L3 Siberia reg. Rus. Fed.
20 C7 Siberut i. Indonesia
36 A3 Sibi Pakistan
126 C4 Sibiloi National Park nat. park Kenya
125 B4 Sibiti Congo
112 E2 Sibiu Romania
63 G3 Sible Hedingham *England* U.K.
22 E1 Siboa Indonesia
20 C6 Sibolga Indonesia
22 E1 Siboluton Indonesia
131 H3 Sibowe r. Swaziland
37 H4 Sibsagar India
63 G1 Sibsey *England* U.K.
20 F6 Sibu Malaysia
23 B5 Sibuco Philippines
23 B5 Sibuguey r. Philippines
23 B5 Sibuguey Bay b. Philippines
124 C2 Sibut Central African Rep.
23 A5 Sibutu i. Philippines
23 A5 Sibutu Passage chan. Philippines
23 B3 Sibuyan i. Philippines
23 B3 Sibuyan Sea sea Philippines
23 B2 Sicapoo mt. Philippines
12 D2 Siccus watercourse *S. Australia* Australia
32 C2 Sichuan div. China
32 D2 Sichuan Pendi basin China
91 D5 Sicié, Cap c. France
110 C5 Sicilia div. *Sicilia* Italy
110 B5 Sicilia i. Italy
110 B5 Sicilian Channel chan. Italy/Tunisia
Sicily i. *see* Sicilia
164 B2 Sicuani Peru
110 C5 Siculiana *Sicilia* Italy
112 B2 Šid Yugoslavia
123 F3 Sidaouet Niger
114 A3 Sidari Greece
62 C4 Sidbury *England* U.K.
63 G3 Sidcup *England* U.K.
68 E1 Siddeburen Netherlands
36 C5 Siddhapur India
38 B2 Siddipet India
Side *see* Selimiye
122 D4 Sidéradougou Burkina
111 F4 Siderno Italy
130 D6 Sidesaviwa South Africa
37 E4 Sidhi India
121 E1 Sidi Ali Algeria
118 E1 Sidi Barrani Egypt
121 D1 Sidi Bel Abbès Algeria
120 C2 Sidi Bennour Morocco
121 F1 Sidi Bouzid Tunisia
120 B3 Sidi Ifni Morocco
120 C2 Sidi Kacem Morocco
121 E2 Sidi Khaled Algeria
122 C4 Sidikila Guinea
121 D3 Sidi Mannsour well Algeria
120 B4 Sidi Mhamed well *Western Sahara*
121 F2 Sidi Okba Algeria
114 E1 Sidirokastro *Kentriki Makedonia* Greece
115 C5 Sidirokastro *Peloponnisos* Greece
43 A4 Sidi Sâlim Egypt
66 E4 Sidlaw Hills h. *Scotland* U.K.
63 G4 Sidley *England* U.K.
179 A4 Sidley, Mt mt. Antarctica
62 C4 Sidmouth *England* U.K.
136 E5 Sidney *B.C.* Canada
152 F2 Sidney *Montana* U.S.A.
150 C3 Sidney *Nebraska* U.S.A.
147 F3 Sidney *New York* U.S.A.
146 A4 Sidney *Ohio* U.S.A.
145 D5 Sidney Lanier, L. l. *Georgia* U.S.A.
122 C4 Sido Mali
22 E1 Sidoan Indonesia
22 C3 Sidoarjo Indonesia
93 E5 Sidobre reg. France
24 A2 Sidoktaya Myanmar
Sidon *see* Saïda
77 M2 Sidra Poland
168 A4 Sidrolândia Brazil
131 H3 Sidvokodvo Swaziland
73 L4 Siecieborzyce Poland
77 L3 Siedlce div. Poland
77 L3 Siedlce Poland
73 L2 Siedlice Poland
76 E3 Siedlisko Poland
77 M4 Siedliszcze Poland
74 C2 Sieg r. Germany
74 C2 Siegburg Germany
74 D2 Siegen Germany
80 C2 Siegenburg Germany
81 H3 Sieggraben Austria
81 H2 Sieghartskirchen Austria
75 H5 Siegsdorf Germany
76 D4 Siekierczyn Poland
77 L3 Siemiatycze Poland
77 L4 Siemień Poland
25 C4 Siĕmréab Cambodia
73 L1 Siemyśl Poland
107 F5 Siena div. *Toscana* Italy
107 F5 Siena *Siena* Italy
77 L5 Sieniawa Poland
88 D3 Sienne r. France
77 K4 Sienno Poland
76 G4 Sieradz div. Poland
76 G4 Sieradz Poland
76 E3 Sieraków Poland
77 H3 Sierakówek Poland
76 F1 Sierakowice Poland
87 F3 Sierck-les-Bains France
90 F1 Sierentz France
81 H2 Sierndorf Austria
81 F2 Sierning Austria
77 H3 Sierpc Poland
151 B6 Sierra Blanca *Texas* U.S.A.
173 G4 Sierra Chica Argentina
172 D6 Sierra Colorada Argentina
102 C2 Sierra de Luna Spain
163 E2 Sierra del Zamuro mountain range Venezuela
162 C2 Sierra de Perija mountain range Venezuela
101 F3 Sierra de Yeguas Spain
155 F5 Sierra Estrella mts *Arizona* U.S.A.
164 C4 Sierra Gorda Chile
172 E1 Sierra Grande mountain range Argentina
171 C5 Sierra Grande Argentina
162 D2 Sierra Guanay mts Venezuela
117 C5 Sierra Leone country Africa
174 H5 Sierra Leone Basin sea feature Atlantic Ocean
174 H5 Sierra Leone Rise sea feature Atlantic Ocean
157 G5 Sierra Madre mountain range Mexico
23 B2 Sierra Madre mt. Philippines
157 E5 Sierra Madre del Sur mountain range Mexico
154 C4 Sierra Madre Mts mts *California* U.S.A.
156 C2 Sierra Madre Occidental mountain range Mexico
157 E3 Sierra Madre Oriental mountain range Mexico
163 D2 Sierra Maigualida mountain range Venezuela
156 E3 Sierra Mojada Mexico
170 C2 Sierra Nevada mt. Argentina
153 B4 Sierra Nevada mountain range *California* U.S.A.
162 C2 Sierra Nevada del Cocuy mt. Colombia
162 C1 Sierra Nevada de Santa Marta nat. park Colombia
162 C2 Sierra Nevada, Parque Nacional nat. park Venezuela
172 E6 Sierra Pailemán Argentina
155 F5 Sierra Pinta summit *Arizona* U.S.A.
171 D5 Sierra, Pta pt Argentina
154 B2 Sierraville *California* U.S.A.
155 G6 Sierra Vista *Arizona* U.S.A.
156 B3 Sierra Vizcaíno mountain range Mexico
82 C2 Sierre Switzerland
54 D4 Siesartis r. Lithuania
165 E4 Siete Puntas r. Paraguay
73 H2 Sietow Germany
107 F5 Sieve r. Italy
73 H3 Sieversdorf Germany
56 G3 Sievi Finland
77 H5 Siewierz Poland
32 D4 Sifang Ling mountain range China
31 H3 Sifangtai China
59 F1 Sifferbo Sweden
115 F5 Sifnos i. Greece
6 □8 Sigatoka r. Fiji
6 □8 Sigatoka Fiji
93 E5 Sigean France
111 □ Siggiewi Malta
112 D1 Sighetu Marmației Romania
112 E1 Sighișoara Romania
107 G5 Sigillo Italy
25 □ Siglap Singapore
35 J9 Sigli Indonesia
56 M6 Siglufjörður Iceland
23 B4 Sigma Philippines
74 E4 Sigmaringen Germany
74 E4 Sigmaringendorf Germany
107 F5 Signa Italy
75 H3 Signalberg h. Germany
69 E4 Signal de Botrange h. Belgium
91 B4 Signal de Mailhebiau mt. France
91 B4 Signal de Randon mt. France
92 E3 Signal du Luguet mt. France
92 D3 Signal du Pic h. France
89 E3 Signal du Viviers h. France
101 □ Signal Hill h. Gibraltar
155 E5 Signal Peak summit *Arizona* U.S.A.
59 H1 Signilskär i. Finland
179 B1 Signy U.K. Base *South Orkney Islands* Atlantic Ocean
86 D3 Signy-L'Abbaye France
86 D3 Signy-le-Petit France
92 B3 Sigogne France
148 A5 Sigourney *Iowa* U.S.A.
52 A1 Sig, Oz. l. Rus. Fed.
59 G2 Sigtuna Sweden
156 J6 Siguatepeque Honduras
99 H3 Sigüenza Spain
102 B2 Sigües Spain
122 C4 Siguiri Guinea
54 D3 Sigulda Latvia
25 C5 Sihanoukville Cambodia
83 D1 Sihlsee l. Switzerland
33 G1 Sihong China
36 E5 Sihora India
164 A1 Sihuas Peru
33 F4 Sihui China
56 G2 Siikajoki Finland
56 G3 Siilinjärvi Finland
42 E2 Siirt Turkey
20 D7 Sijunjung Indonesia
36 B5 Sika India
136 E3 Sikanni Chief r. *B.C.* Canada
136 E3 Sikanni Chief *B.C.* Canada
36 C4 Sikar India
39 G2 Sikaram mt. Afghanistan
122 C4 Sikasso div. Mali
122 C4 Sikasso Mali
24 B2 Sikaw Myanmar
114 E2 Sikea Greece
151 F4 Sikeston *Missouri* U.S.A.
27 P3 Sikhote-Alin mountain range China/Rus. Fed.
115 G6 Sikinos i. Greece
115 G6 Sikinos Greece
37 G4 Sikkim div. India
79 H6 Siklós Hungary
56 E2 Siksjö Sweden
23 A5 Sikuati Malaysia
98 C2 Sil r. Spain
23 C4 Silago Philippines
54 C4 Šilalė Lithuania
107 E2 Silandro Italy
22 B1 Silantek, G. h. Indonesia/Malaysia
108 A4 Silanus *Sardegna* Italy
23 B4 Silay Philippines
107 J4 Silba i. Croatia
107 J4 Silbanski Kanal chan. Croatia
72 E2 Silberberg h. Germany
37 H4 Silchar India
58 B1 Sildefjorden chan. Norway
54 E4 Silene Latvia
83 D2 Silenen Switzerland
69 C4 Silenrieux Belgium
131 F2 Silent Valley South Africa
38 C2 Sileru r. India
101 H2 Siles Spain
121 E4 Silet Algeria
36 E3 Silgarhi Nepal
37 H4 Silghat India
127 □1 Silhouette I. i. Seychelles
121 F1 Siliana Tunisia
42 C2 Silifke Turkey
108 A4 Siligo *Sardegna* Italy
37 G3 Siling Co salt lake China
36 D4 Silipur India
108 A5 Siliqua *Sardegna* Italy
7 □12 Silisili mt. Western Samoa
Silistat *see* Bozkır
112 E2 Siliștea Nouă Romania
112 F2 Silistra Bulgaria
113 G4 Silivri Turkey
59 F1 Siljan l. Sweden
58 C2 Siljan Norway
55 B3 Silkeborg Denmark
80 C3 Sill r. Austria
103 C5 Silla Spain
164 C3 Sillajhuay mt. Chile
54 E2 Sillamäe Estonia
91 E5 Sillans la Cascade France
107 F4 Sillaro r. Italy
98 B2 Silleda Spain
89 E3 Sillé-le-Guillaume France
86 D3 Sillery France
80 D4 Sillian Austria
36 C5 Sillod India
88 B3 Sillon de Talbert pen. France
65 E3 Silloth *England* U.K.
76 E2 Silnowo Poland
37 G3 Silong China
102 F3 Sils Spain
83 E2 Sils Switzerland
151 E6 Silsbee *Texas* U.S.A.
56 G1 Siltaharju Finland
54 E1 Siltakylä Finland
118 C4 Siltou well Chad
22 B1 Siluas Indonesia
123 F5 Siluko r. Nigeria
123 F5 Siluko Nigeria
39 E4 Sīlūp r. Iran
54 B4 Šilutė Lithuania
169 G5 Silva Jardim Brazil
42 E2 Silvan Turkey
168 D2 Silvânia Brazil
83 E2 Silvaplana Switzerland
83 E2 Silvaplaner See l. Switzerland
98 C4 Silvares Portugal
36 C5 Silvassa India
100 B2 Silveiras Portugal
159 E2 Silver Bank sea feature *Turks and Caicos Is* Caribbean
159 E2 Silver Bank Passage chan. *Turks and Caicos Is* Caribbean
148 B2 Silver Bay *Minnesota* U.S.A.
153 E5 Silver City *New Mexico* U.S.A.
140 A2 Silver Islet *Ontario* Canada
154 D4 Silver Lake l. *California* U.S.A.
148 D2 Silver Lake l. *Michigan* U.S.A.
152 B3 Silver Lake *Oregon* U.S.A.
67 C4 Silvermine Mts h. Rep. of Ireland
154 D3 Silver Peak Range mts *Nevada* U.S.A.
146 E5 Silver Spring *Maryland* U.S.A.
154 C2 Silver Springs *Nevada* U.S.A.
63 E2 Silverstone *England* U.K.
130 D4 Silver Streams South Africa
62 C4 Silverton *England* U.K.
12 E2 Silverton *New South Wales* Australia
140 D4 Silver Water *Ontario* Canada
100 B3 Silves *Faro* Portugal
163 F4 Silves Brazil
109 G2 Silvi Italy
157 H5 Silvituc Mexico
83 F2 Silvretta Gruppe mountain range Switzerland
80 B3 Silz Austria
46 E2 Sim r. Rus. Fed.
46 E2 Sim Rus. Fed.
52 D1 Sima Rus. Fed.
99 F3 Simancas Spain
22 B1 Simanggang Malaysia
53 C1 Simanichy Belarus
114 E2 Simantra Greece
32 C4 Simao China
166 E3 Simão Dias Brazil
23 B3 Simara i. Philippines
141 F3 Simard, Lac l. *Québec* Canada
42 F3 Sīmareh r. Iran
37 F4 Simaria India
42 B2 Simav Turkey
113 G5 Simav Dağları mountain range Turkey
124 D3 Simba Congo(Zaire)
75 H4 Simbach Germany
75 J4 Simbach am Inn Germany
111 F4 Simbario Italy
Simbirsk *see* Ul'yanovsk
Simbor i. *see* Pānikoita
140 E5 Simcoe *Ontario* Canada
141 F4 Simcoe, Lake l. *Ontario* Canada
37 F5 Simdega India
126 C2 Simēn Mountains mountain range Ethiopia
111 F4 Simeri r. Italy
112 D2 Simeria Romania
110 D5 Simeto r. *Sicilia* Italy
20 C6 Simeuluë i. Indonesia
51 E6 Simferopol' Ukraine
91 D5 Simiane-la-Rotonde France
37 E3 Simikot Nepal
83 F2 Similaun mt. Austria/Italy
79 K2 Siminy mt. Slovakia
162 C2 Simití Colombia
112 D4 Simitli Bulgaria
154 C4 Simi Valley *California* U.S.A.
153 F4 Simla *Colorado* U.S.A.
79 M4 Şimleu Silvaniei Romania
82 C2 Simme r. Switzerland
82 C2 Simmental v. Switzerland
74 B2 Simmerath Germany
74 C3 Simmern (Hunsrück) Germany
154 C4 Simmler *California* U.S.A.
155 F4 Simmons *Arizona* U.S.A.
145 F7 Simms The Bahamas
145 □2 Simms Pt pt The Bahamas
54 C4 Simnas Lithuania
56 G2 Simojärvi l. Finland
136 F4 Simonette r. *Alberta* Canada
137 J4 Simonhouse *Manitoba* Canada
79 L3 Šimonka mt. Slovakia
141 H4 Simon, Lac l. *Québec* Canada
59 G2 Simonstorp Sweden
130 B7 Simon's Town South Africa
79 H5 Simontornya Hungary
115 C5 Simopoulo Greece
93 C5 Simorre France
114 C4 Simos Greece
22 A2 Simpang Indonesia
69 D4 Simpelveld Netherlands
166 D2 Simplício Mendes Brazil
82 D2 Simplon Switzerland
82 D2 Simplon Pass pass Switzerland
171 B6 Simpson r. Chile
14 D5 Simpson Desert desert *Northern Terr.* Australia
12 D1 Simpson Desert Conservation Park res. *S. Australia* Australia
14 D5 Simpson Desert Nat. Park nat. park *Queensland* Australia
17 D5 Simpson Hill h. *Western Australia* Australia
140 B2 Simpson I. i. *Ontario* Canada
154 D2 Simpson Park Mts mts *Nevada* U.S.A.
59 F4 Simrishamn Sweden
22 B1 Simunjan Malaysia
23 A5 Simunul i. Philippines
45 R5 Simushir, O. i. Rus. Fed.
38 A2 Sina r. India
81 G3 Sinabelkirchen Austria
126 E3 Sina Dhaqa Somalia
43 C6 Sināfir i. Saudi Arabia
119 F2 Sinai pen. Egypt
112 E2 Sinaia Romania
86 D3 Sinai, Mont h. France
Sinai, Mount mt *see* Katherîna, G.
42 E2 Şınak Turkey
156 C3 Sinaloa div. Mexico
108 D1 Sinalunga Italy
32 E3 Sinan China
31 H5 Sinanju North Korea
46 F1 Sinara r. Rus. Fed.
114 A3 Sinarades Greece
118 B1 Sīnāwin Libya
24 A3 Sinbaungwe Myanmar
24 B1 Sinbo Myanmar
24 A2 Sinbyugyun Myanmar
42 D2 Sincan Turkey
162 B2 Sincé Colombia
162 B2 Sincelejo Colombia
86 C3 Sinceny France
145 D5 Sinclair, L. l. *Georgia* U.S.A.
136 E4 Sinclair Mills *B.C.* Canada
130 A2 Sinclair Mine Namibia
66 E2 Sinclair's Bay b. *Scotland* U.K.
36 D4 Sind r. India
Sind *see* Thul
55 C2 Sindal Denmark
23 B4 Sindañgan Philippines
22 A3 Sindangbarang Indonesia
124 B4 Sindara Gabon
36 B4 Sindari India
74 D4 Sindelfingen Germany
38 B2 Sindgi India
36 B4 Sindh Pakistan
38 B3 Sindhnur India
54 D2 Sindi Estonia
108 A4 Sindia *Sardegna* Italy
113 G5 Sındırgı Turkey
38 B2 Sindkhed India
36 C5 Sindkheda India
50 J2 Sindor Rus. Fed.
114 D2 Sindos Greece
37 F5 Sindri India
36 B3 Sind Sagar Doab lowland Pakistan
50 J3 Sinegor'ye Rus. Fed.
123 E4 Sinendé Benin
100 B3 Sines Portugal
100 B3 Sines, Cabo de pt Portugal
56 G2 Sinettä Finland
52 B3 Sinezerki Rus. Fed.
122 C5 Sinfra Côte d'Ivoire
24 B2 Sing Myanmar
119 F5 Singa Sudan
36 E3 Singahi India
32 B4 Singaingmyo Myanmar
31 H4 Sin'galp'a China
36 D2 Singa P. pass India
19 M9 Singapore country Asia
25 C7 Singapore Singapore
22 A1 Singapore, Str. of chan. Indonesia/Singapore
22 C4 Singaraja Indonesia
25 C4 Sing Buri Thailand
74 D5 Singen (Hohentwiel) Germany
140 E4 Singhampton *Ontario* Canada
87 G2 Singhofen Germany
127 B6 Singida div. Tanzania
127 B5 Singida Tanzania
24 A1 Singkaling Hkamti Myanmar
22 E3 Singkang Indonesia
22 B1 Singkawang Indonesia
22 A2 Singkep i. Indonesia
13 G3 Singleton *New South Wales* Australia
14 B4 Singleton, Mt h. *Northern Terr.* Australia
17 B6 Singleton, Mt h. *Western Australia* Australia
59 H1 Singö i. Sweden
36 C4 Singoli India
Singora *see* Songkhla
24 A2 Singu Myanmar
131 J1 Singuedeze r. Mozambique
112 E2 Singureni Romania
22 D2 Sinio, G. mt. Indonesia
108 B4 Siniscola *Sardegna* Italy
104 F4 Sinj Croatia
22 E3 Sinjai Indonesia
112 B3 Sinjajevina Planina mountain range Yugoslavia
42 E2 Sinjār Iraq
42 E2 Sinjār, Jabal mt. Iraq
119 G4 Sinkat Sudan
Sinkiang Uighur Aut. Region div. *see* Xinjiang Uygur Zizhiqu
86 C2 Sin-le-Noble France
31 H5 Sinmi i. North Korea
74 D2 Sinn Germany
108 B5 Sinnai *Sardegna* Italy
163 G2 Sinnamary French Guiana
43 B5 Sinn Bishr, G. h. Egypt
Sinneh *see* Sanandaj
111 F2 Sinni r. Italy
43 A5 Sinnûris Egypt
112 G2 Sinoie, L. lag. Romania
54 E3 Sinole Latvia
42 C1 Sinop Turkey
31 J4 Sinp'o North Korea
31 H5 Sinp'yŏng North Korea
83 D1 Sins Switzerland
31 H5 Sinsang North Korea
74 D3 Sinsheim Germany
22 B1 Sintang Indonesia
79 M4 Şinteu Romania
158 □1 Sint Nicolaas *Aruba* Caribbean
151 D6 Sinton *Texas* U.S.A.
100 A2 Sintra *Lisboa* Portugal
162 B2 Sinú r. Colombia
31 H5 Sinŭiju North Korea
126 E3 Sinujiif Somalia
54 F3 Sinyaya r. Rus. Fed.
87 H4 Sinzheim Germany
74 C2 Sinzig Germany
75 H4 Sinzing Germany
79 H5 Sió r. Hungary
102 D3 Sió r. Spain
23 B5 Siocon Philippines
125 D7 Sioma Ngwezi National Park nat. park Zambia
82 C2 Sion Switzerland
67 D2 Sion Mills *Northern Ireland* U.K.
90 B2 Sioule r. France
150 D3 Sioux Center *Iowa* U.S.A.
150 D3 Sioux City *Iowa* U.S.A.
150 D3 Sioux Falls *S. Dakota* U.S.A.
138 B3 Sioux Lookout *Ontario* Canada
157 H6 Sipacate Guatemala
23 B4 Sipalay Philippines
163 F3 Sipaliwini r. Surinam
104 F4 Šipan i. Croatia
22 B1 Sipang, Tg pt Malaysia
159 □3 Siparia Trinidad and Tobago
24 B2 Sipein Myanmar
31 H4 Siping China
137 K3 Sipiwesk *Manitoba* Canada
137 K3 Sipiwesk L. l. *Manitoba* Canada
179 B4 Siple Coast coastal area Antarctica
179 A4 Siple, Mt mt. Antarctica
83 E1 Sipplingen Germany
36 C5 Sipra r. India
145 C5 Sipsey r. *Alabama* U.S.A.
20 C7 Sipura i. Indonesia
126 □ Siqirah *Socotra* Yemen
168 D5 Siqueira Campos Brazil
23 B4 Siquijor i. Philippines
23 B4 Siquijor Philippines
39 G4 Sir r. Pakistan
58 B2 Sira r. Norway
38 B3 Sira India
58 B2 Sira Norway
39 C4 Şīr Abū Nu'āyr i. U.A.E.
91 E4 Sirac mt. France
111 E5 Siracusa reg. *Sicilia* Italy
111 E5 Siracusa *Sicilia* Italy
37 G4 Sirajganj Bangladesh
136 E4 Sir Alexander, Mt mt. *B.C.* Canada
92 E4 Siran France
36 A4 Siranda L. l. Pakistan
123 E4 Sirba r. Burkina/Niger
39 C4 Şīr Banī Yās i. U.A.E.
58 B2 Sirdalsvatn l. Norway
14 D2 Sir Edward Pellew Group is *Northern Terr.* Australia
122 B5 Sirekude Sierra Leone
148 A3 Siren *Wisconsin* U.S.A.
112 F1 Siret Romania
39 E4 Sīrgān Iran
16 D2 Sir Graham Moore Is is *Western Australia* Australia
36 D3 Sirhind India
79 L5 Şiria Romania
24 C3 Siri Kit Dam dam Thailand
36 B3 Siritoi r. Pakistan
39 C3 Sīrīz Iran
136 D2 Sir James McBrien, Mt mt. *N.W.T.* Canada
39 C3 Sīrjan salt flat Iran
Sirjan *see* Sa'īdābād
12 D3 Sir Joseph Bank's Group is *S. Australia* Australia
39 D4 Sirk Iran
107 E3 Sirmione Italy
83 E1 Sirnach Switzerland

90 E2 Sirod France
38 C2 Sironcha India
36 D4 Sironj India
120 C2 Siroua, Jbel mt. Morocco
38 B2 Sirpur India
154 C4 Sirretta Peak summit *California* U.S.A.
36 C3 Sirsa *Haryana* India
37 E4 Sirsa *Uttar Pradesh* India
136 F4 Sir Sanford, Mt mt. *B.C.* Canada
131 F2 Sir Seretse Khama airport Botswana
36 D3 Sirsi *Uttar Pradesh* India
38 A3 Sirsi *Karnataka* India
38 B2 Sirsilla India
Sirte *see* Surt
Sirte, Gulf of g. *see* Khalīj Surt
12 B1 Sir Thomas, Mt h. *S. Australia* Australia
101 E2 Siruela Spain
38 A2 Sirur India
54 D4 Širvintos Lithuania
42 F3 Sīrwān r. Iraq
136 F4 Sir Wilfred Laurier, Mt mt. *B.C.* Canada
15 E2 Sir William Thompson Range h. *Queensland* Australia
Sis *see* Kozan
104 F3 Sisak Croatia
25 D4 Sisaket Thailand
39 B3 Sīsakht Iran
157 H4 Sisal Mexico
101 H1 Sisante Spain
98 B1 Sisargas, Illas is Spain
130 D3 Sishen South Africa
42 F2 Sisian Armenia
122 D4 Sisili r. Burkina/Ghana
135 N3 Sisimiut Greenland
148 C2 Siskiwit Bay b. *Michigan* U.S.A.
25 C4 Sisŏphŏn Cambodia
154 B4 Sisquoc r. *California* U.S.A.
82 C1 Sissach Switzerland
150 D2 Sisseton *S. Dakota* U.S.A.
147 K1 Sisson Branch Reservoir resr *New Brunswick* Canada
86 C3 Sissonne France
39 E3 Sistan reg. Iran
39 E3 Sīstān va Balūchestān div. Iran
91 D4 Sisteron France
25 A5 Sisters i. *Andaman and Nicobar Is* India
128 □1 Sisters Pk h. *Ascension* Atlantic Ocean
9 □1 Sisters, The is *Chatham Is* New Zealand
127 □1 Sisters, The is Seychelles
37 F4 Sitamarhi India
36 C5 Sitamau India
129 H2 Sitampiky Madagascar
23 A5 Sitangkai Philippines
36 E4 Sitapur India
115 H7 Siteia Greece
131 H3 Siteki Swaziland
102 E3 Sitges Spain
114 E2 Sithonia pen. Greece
169 E1 Sítio da Abadia Brazil
166 D3 Sítio do Mato Brazil
136 B3 Sitka *Alaska* U.S.A.
37 E4 Sitlaha India
112 C3 Sitnica r. Yugoslavia
79 H3 Sitno mt. Slovakia
54 F2 Sitnya r. Rus. Fed.
24 B3 Sittang r. Myanmar
69 D4 Sittard Netherlands
24 A1 Sittaung Myanmar
72 E2 Sittensen Germany
83 E1 Sitter r. Germany
81 F4 Sittersdorf Austria
63 G3 Sittingbourne *England* U.K.
24 A2 Sittwe Myanmar
22 C3 Situbondo Indonesia
73 H4 Sitzenroda Germany
27 □ Siu A Chau i. *Hong Kong* China
7 □12 Siumu Western Samoa
156 J6 Siuna Nicaragua
54 D1 Siuntio Finland
37 F5 Siuri India
38 B4 Sivaganga India
38 B4 Sivakasi India
31 H1 Sivaki Rus. Fed.
39 C3 Sivand Iran
42 D2 Sivas Turkey
42 B2 Sivaslı Turkey
42 D2 Siverek Turkey
54 G2 Siverskiy Rus. Fed.
52 F2 Sivin' r. Rus. Fed.
52 G2 Sivin' Rus. Fed.
42 B2 Sivrihisar Turkey
69 C4 Sivry Belgium
87 E3 Sivry-sur-Meuse France
131 G3 Sivukile South Africa
118 E2 Siwa Egypt
22 E2 Siwa Indonesia
36 D3 Siwalik Range mountain range India
37 F4 Siwan India
36 C4 Siwana India
118 E2 Siwa Oasis oasis Egypt
91 D5 Six-Fours-les-Plages France
33 G1 Si Xian China
30 A5 Sixin China
148 E4 Six Lakes *Michigan* U.S.A.
67 D2 Sixmilecross *Northern Ireland* U.K.
90 E2 Sixt-Fer-à-Cheval France
131 G2 Siyabuswa South Africa
33 G1 Siyang China
131 G3 Siyathemba South Africa
42 G1 Siyäzän Azerbaijan
30 D4 Siyitang China
39 C2 Sīyunī Iran
100 A1 Sizandro r. Portugal
31 H2 Sizhan China
30 A2 Sizim Rus. Fed.
30 D4 Siziwang Qi China
88 A3 Sizun France
55 D4 Sjælland i. Denmark
55 D4 Sjællands Odde pen. Denmark
112 C3 Sjenica Yugoslavia
59 E4 Sjöbo Sweden
55 B3 Sjørup Denmark
59 E2 Sjötorp Sweden
56 E1 Sjøvegan Norway
59 F3 Sjunnen Sweden
55 E1 Sjuntorp Sweden
53 E3 Skadovs'k Ukraine
55 D4 Skælsør Denmark
55 A4 Skærbæk Denmark
135 R2 Skærfjorden inlet Greenland
59 E4 Skævinge Denmark
56 M6 Skaftafell nat. park Iceland
56 M7 Skaftárós b. Iceland
55 C2 Skagen Denmark
59 F2 Skagern l. Sweden
58 C3 Skagerrak str. Denmark/Norway
152 B1 Skagit r. Canada/U.S.A.
136 B3 Skagway *Alaska* U.S.A.
56 G1 Skaidi Norway
54 D4 Skaidiškės Lithuania
115 D6 Skala Greece
56 E1 Skaland Norway
115 E4 Skala Oropou Greece
53 B2 Skala-Podil's'ka Ukraine
53 A2 Skalat Ukraine
77 J5 Skalbmierz Poland
59 E3 Skälderviken b. Sweden
55 A4 Skallingen pen. Denmark
56 D2 Skalmodal Sweden
114 F1 Skaloti Greece
55 B3 Skals r. Denmark
55 B3 Skals Denmark
55 B3 Skanderborg Denmark
147 E3 Skaneateles Lake l. *New York* U.S.A.
148 C2 Skanee *Michigan* U.S.A.
59 E4 Skåne-Tranås Sweden
59 F2 Skänninge Sweden
59 E4 Skanör med Falsterbo Sweden
114 F3 Skantzoura i. Greece
76 D3 Skąpe Poland
59 E2 Skara Sweden
59 E2 Skaraborg div. Sweden
107 J4 Škarda i. Croatia
15 E1 Skardon r. *Queensland* Australia
36 C2 Skardu *Jammu and Kashmir*
58 B2 Skare Norway
59 J2 Skärgårdshavet Nationalpark nat. park Finland
55 D2 Skärhamn Sweden
58 D1 Skarnes Norway
55 C4 Skarø i. Denmark
59 G1 Skärplinge Sweden
76 G1 Skarszewy Poland
55 C4 Skårup Denmark
77 K4 Skaryszew Poland
53 B2 Skarzhyntsi Ukraine
77 J4 Skarżysko-Kamienna Poland
59 E1 Skasbegert h. Norway
59 E2 Skattkärr Sweden
59 F1 Skattungbyn Sweden
54 C4 Skaudvilė Lithuania
56 F2 Skaulo Sweden
54 E3 Škaune Latvia
55 A3 Skave Denmark
77 H6 Skawa r. Poland
77 H6 Skawina Poland
120 A4 Skaymat *Western Sahara*
59 H2 Skebobruk Sweden
59 F3 Skede Sweden
59 F2 Skedevi Sweden
58 D2 Skee Sweden
136 D3 Skeena r. *B.C.* Canada
136 D3 Skeena Mountains mountain range *B.C.* Canada
56 M6 Skegafjörður b. Iceland
63 G1 Skegness *England* U.K.
128 A2 Skeleton Coast Game Park res. Namibia
56 F2 Skellefteå Sweden
56 E2 Skellefteälven r. Sweden
56 F2 Skelleftehamn Sweden
67 A5 Skellig Rocks i. Rep. of Ireland
65 F4 Skelmersdale *England* U.K.
62 D3 Skenfrith *Wales* U.K.
77 H3 Skępe Poland
67 E3 Skerries Rep. of Ireland
77 L6 Skhidni Beskydy mountain range Poland/Ukraine
77 M6 Skhidnytsya Ukraine
58 D2 Ski Norway
114 E3 Skiathos i. Greece
114 E3 Skiathos Greece
67 B5 Skibbereen Rep. of Ireland
55 D4 Skibby Denmark
56 F1 Skibotn Norway
77 N2 Skidal' Belarus
65 E3 Skiddaw mt. *England* U.K.
54 D4 Skiemonys Lithuania
58 C2 Skien Norway
77 J3 Skierniewice div. Poland
77 J4 Skierniewice Poland
121 F1 Skikda Algeria
59 F3 Skillingaryd Sweden
59 F2 Skinnskatteberg Sweden
36 D2 Skio India
64 C2 Skipness *Scotland* U.K.
65 H4 Skipsea *England* U.K.
130 C7 Skipskop South Africa
65 F4 Skipton *England* U.K.
13 E4 Skipton *Victoria* Australia
55 B3 Skive Denmark
55 B3 Skive Fjord b. Denmark
56 M6 Skjálfandafljót r. Iceland
56 M6 Skjálfandi b. Iceland
58 D2 Skjeberg Norway
58 D1 Skjellbreidfjellet mt. Norway
58 B2 Skjerkeknuten mt. Norway
55 A4 Skjern r. Denmark
55 A4 Skjern Denmark
57 B3 Skjolden Norway
114 D3 Sklithro Greece
52 C1 Sknyatino Rus. Fed.
59 H1 Skoby Sweden
76 G6 Skoczów Poland
56 B3 Skodje Norway
131 E7 Skoenmakerskop South Africa
81 F4 Škofja Loka Slovenia
81 F5 Škofljica Slovenia
59 G1 Skog Sweden
56 G1 Skoganvarre Norway
59 G2 Skogstorp Sweden
62 A3 Skokholm Island i. *Wales* U.K.
76 F3 Skoki Poland
148 D4 Skokie *Illinois* U.S.A.
58 C2 Skollenborg Norway
59 F2 Sköllersta Sweden
62 A3 Skomer Island i. *Wales* U.K.
131 F3 Skoonspruit r. South Africa
115 G4 Skopelos i. Greece
114 E3 Skopelos i. Greece
114 E3 Skopelos *Thessalia* Greece
114 E3 Skopelou, D. chan. Greece
114 G3 Skopia h. Greece
52 D3 Skopin Rus. Fed.
112 C4 Skopje Macedonia
55 □1 Skopun Faeroes
55 □1 Skopunarfjørður chan. Faeroes
76 G2 Skórcz Poland
58 C2 Skornetten h. Norway
53 G1 Skorodnoye Rus. Fed.
52 D1 Skoropuskovskiy Rus. Fed.
55 B3 Skørping Denmark
77 L3 Skórzec Poland
59 E2 Skotterud Norway
114 E1 Skoutari *Kentriki Makedonia* Greece
115 D6 Skoutari *Peloponnisos* Greece
59 E2 Skövde Sweden
55 A4 Skovlund Denmark
27 M1 Skovorodino Rus. Fed.
147 J2 Skowhegan *Maine* U.S.A.
114 D1 Skra Greece
59 F1 Skräddrabo Sweden
58 D1 Skreia Norway
58 C2 Skrimfjell h. Norway
54 D3 Skrīveri Latvia
81 E4 Škrlutica mt. Slovenia
54 C3 Skrunda Latvia
76 G6 Skrzyczne mt. Poland
58 A2 Skudeneshavn Norway
136 B2 Skukum, Mt mt. *Yukon Terr.* Canada
154 D3 Skull Peak summit *Nevada* U.S.A.
130 A5 Skulpfonteinpunt pt South Africa
76 G3 Skulsk Poland
59 E2 Skultorp Sweden
59 G2 Skultuna Sweden
148 B5 Skunk r. *Iowa* U.S.A.
54 B3 Skuodas Lithuania
59 E4 Skurup Sweden
78 E2 Skuteč Czech Rep.
59 G1 Skutskär Sweden
77 N6 Skvaryava Ukraine
53 C2 Skvyra Ukraine
76 D3 Skwierzyna Poland
114 D2 Skydra Greece
66 B3 Skye i. *Scotland* U.K.
58 B2 Skykula h. Norway
114 F4 Skyropoula i. Greece
114 F4 Skyros i. Greece
114 F4 Skyros Greece
179 B3 Skytrain Ice Rise ice feature Antarctica
54 E4 Slabodka Belarus
79 G3 Sládkovičovo Slovakia
55 D4 Slagelse Denmark
68 E2 Slagharen Netherlands
56 E2 Slagnäs Sweden
64 E2 Slamannan *Scotland* U.K.
22 B3 Slamet, G. volcano Indonesia
79 K3 Slaná r. Slovakia
67 E3 Slane Rep. of Ireland
79 L3 Slanec Slovakia
67 E4 Slaney r. Rep. of Ireland
55 E4 Slangerup Denmark
112 E2 Slănic Romania
112 F1 Slănic Moldova Romania
79 L3 Slanskévrchy mountain range Slovakia
54 F2 Slantsy Rus. Fed.
78 D1 Slaný Czech Rep.
54 C4 Slapaberžė Lithuania
78 F2 Šlapanice Czech Rep.
51 G5 Slashchevskaya Rus. Fed.
52 G4 Slastukha Rus. Fed.
59 G2 Slätbaken inlet Sweden
140 B2 Slate Is is *Ontario* Canada
112 E2 Slatina Romania
114 B1 Slatino Macedonia
53 G1 Slatyne Ukraine
137 G2 Slave r. *N.W.T.* Canada
123 E5 Slave Coast coastal area Africa
136 G3 Slave Lake *Alberta* Canada
47 J2 Slavgorod Rus. Fed.
53 F2 Slavhorod *Dnipropetrovs'k* Ukraine
53 F1 Slavhorod *Sumy* Ukraine
54 F3 Slavkovichi Rus. Fed.
75 H2 Slavkovský Les h. Czech Rep.
78 F2 Slavkov u Brna Czech Rep.
52 C1 Slavnoye Rus. Fed.
78 E3 Slavonice Czech Rep.
104 F3 Slavonija reg. Croatia
104 F3 Slavonska Požega Croatia
104 G3 Slavonski Brod Croatia
79 K3 Slavošovce Slovakia
53 B1 Slavuta Ukraine
53 D1 Slavutych Ukraine
47 G4 Slavyanka Kazakhstan
31 J4 Slavyanka Rus. Fed.
112 E3 Slavyanovo Bulgaria
51 F6 Slavyansk-na-Kubani Rus. Fed.
76 E4 Sława Poland
77 M4 Sławatycze Poland
76 E1 Sławno Poland
76 D2 Sławoborze Poland
76 E1 Sławsko Poland
63 F2 Sleaford *England* U.K.
12 C3 Sleaford B. b. *S. Australia* Australia
67 A4 Slea Head headland Rep. of Ireland
66 C3 Sleat pen. *Scotland* U.K.
66 C3 Sleat, Sound of chan. *Scotland* U.K.
68 E2 Sleen Netherlands
138 E2 Sleeper Islands is *N.W.T.* Canada
148 D3 Sleeping Bear Dunes National Seashore res. *Michigan* U.S.A.
148 D3 Sleeping Bear Pt pt *Michigan* U.S.A.
65 H3 Sleights *England* U.K.
51 H7 Sleptsovskaya Rus. Fed.
76 F2 Ślesin *Bydgoszcz* Poland
76 G3 Ślesin *Konin* Poland
179 C3 Slessor Glacier gl. Antarctica
151 F6 Slidell *Louisiana* U.S.A.
68 C3 Sliedrecht Netherlands
111 □ Sliema Malta
67 A4 Slievanea h. Rep. of Ireland
67 D2 Slieve Anierin h. Rep. of Ireland
67 D4 Slieveardagh Hills h. Rep. of Ireland
67 C3 Slieve Aughty Mts h. Rep. of Ireland
67 D2 Slieve Beagh h. Rep. of Ireland/U.K.
67 C4 Slieve Bernagh h. Rep. of Ireland
67 D3 Slieve Bloom Mts h. Rep. of Ireland
67 B4 Slievecallan h. Rep. of Ireland
67 B2 Slieve Car h. Rep. of Ireland
67 F2 Slieve Donard h. *Northern Ireland* U.K.
67 B3 Slieve Elva h. Rep. of Ireland
67 C4 Slievefelim Mts h. Rep. of Ireland
67 B2 Slieve Gamph h. Rep. of Ireland
67 C2 Slieve League h. Rep. of Ireland
67 B4 Slieve Mish Mts h. Rep. of Ireland
67 A5 Slieve Miskish Mts h. Rep. of Ireland
67 A2 Slieve More h. Rep. of Ireland
67 D3 Slieve na Calliagh h. Rep. of Ireland
67 D4 Slievenamon h. Rep. of Ireland
67 D1 Slieve Snaght mt. Rep. of Ireland
66 B3 Sligachan *Scotland* U.K.
Sligeach *see* Sligo
67 C2 Sligo div. Rep. of Ireland
67 C2 Sligo Rep. of Ireland
67 C2 Sligo Bay b. Rep. of Ireland
63 F3 Slinfold *England* U.K.
68 E2 Slinge r. Netherlands
59 H3 Slite Sweden
112 F3 Sliven Bulgaria
112 F3 Slivo Pole Bulgaria
76 G2 Śliwice Poland
53 C3 Slobidka Ukraine
50 H2 Sloboda Rus. Fed.
50 J2 Slobodchikovo Rus. Fed.
52 B2 Slobodka Rus. Fed.
50 J3 Slobodskoy Rus. Fed.
53 C3 Slobozia Moldova
112 F2 Slobozia Romania
136 F5 Slocan *B.C.* Canada
68 E1 Slochteren Netherlands
77 J5 Słomniki Poland
77 O2 Slonim Belarus
53 G1 Slonovka Rus. Fed.
76 D2 Słonowice Poland
76 C3 Słońsk Poland
68 D2 Slotermeer l. Netherlands
6 □1 Slot, The chan. Solomon Is.
63 F3 Slough *England* U.K.
52 A4 Slout Ukraine
48 G4 Slovakia country Europe
53 C1 Slovechne Ukraine
48 G4 Slovenia country Europe
81 G4 Slovenj Gradec Slovenia
81 G4 Slovenska Bistrica Slovenia
81 G4 Slovenske Gorice h. Slovenia
81 G4 Slovenske Konjice Slovenia
79 K3 Slovenské Rudohorie mountain range Slovakia
79 K3 Slovenský kras mountain range Slovakia
79 K3 Slovenský raj nat. park Slovakia
77 N6 Slovita Ukraine
53 G2 Slov"yanohirs'k Ukraine
53 G2 Slov"yans'k Ukraine
53 C1 Slovyechna r. Belarus
76 F1 Słowiński Park Narodoway nat. park Poland
77 H3 Słubice *Płock* Poland
76 C3 Słubice *Zielona Gora* Poland
54 E5 Sluch r. Belarus
53 B1 Sluch r. Ukraine
83 F2 Sluderno Italy
69 B3 Sluis Netherlands
69 B3 Sluiskil Netherlands
78 D1 Šluknov Czech Rep.
78 G2 Slunečná h. Czech Rep.
104 E3 Slunj Croatia
76 F3 Słupca Poland
77 J4 Słupia *Kielce* Poland
77 H4 Słupia *Skierniewice* Poland
77 H3 Słupno Poland
76 F1 Słupsk div. Poland
76 F1 Słupsk Poland
56 E2 Slussfors Sweden
76 G4 Słuszków Poland
54 E5 Slutsk Belarus
54 C4 Šlyna r. Lithuania
67 A3 Slyne Head headland Rep. of Ireland
30 B2 Slyudyanka Rus. Fed.
92 B2 Smagne r. France
55 D4 Smålandsfarvandet chan. Denmark
59 E3 Smälandsstenar Sweden
147 J3 Small Pt pt *Maine* U.S.A.
139 H3 Smallwood Reservoir resr *Newfoundland* Canada
77 N3 Smalyanitsa Belarus
54 F4 Smalyavichy Belarus
54 E4 Smarhon' Belarus
81 G4 Šmarje pri Jelšah Slovenia
81 G5 Šmarjeta Slovenia
130 D5 Smartt Syndicate Dam resr South Africa
92 C2 Smarves France
137 J4 Smeaton *Saskatchewan* Canada
75 L2 Smědá r. Czech Rep.
112 C2 Smederevo Yugoslavia
112 C2 Smederevska Palanka Yugoslavia
59 F1 Smedjebacken Sweden
112 F2 Smeeni Romania
67 A4 Smerwick Harbour harbour Rep. of Ireland
146 D4 Smethport *Pennsylvania* U.S.A.
31 K2 Smidovich Rus. Fed.
76 E3 Śmigiel Poland
53 D2 Smila Ukraine
54 F5 Smilavichy Belarus
68 E2 Smilde Netherlands
53 E1 Smile Ukraine
54 D3 Smiltene Latvia
52 G2 Smirnovo Rus. Fed.
146 C6 Smith r. *Virginia* U.S.A.
136 G3 Smith *Alberta* Canada
154 C2 Smith *Nevada* U.S.A.
173 G3 Smith Argentina
134 F3 Smith Arm b. *N.W.T.* Canada
136 D4 Smithers *B.C.* Canada
145 E5 Smithfield *N. Carolina* U.S.A.
152 E3 Smithfield *Utah* U.S.A.
131 F5 Smithfield South Africa
179 A3 Smith Glacier gl. Antarctica
25 A4 Smith I. i. *Andaman and Nicobar Is* India
147 E5 Smith I. i. *Maryland* U.S.A.
179 B2 Smith I. i. *S. Shetland Is* Antarctica
147 F6 Smith I. i. *Virginia* U.S.A.
146 D6 Smith Mountain Lake l. *Virginia* U.S.A.
136 D3 Smith River *B.C.* Canada
141 G4 Smiths Falls *Ontario* Canada
135 L2 Smith Sound str. Canada/Greenland
13 F5 Smithton *Tasmania* Australia
154 C1 Smoke Creek Desert desert *Nevada* U.S.A.
136 F4 Smoky r. *Alberta* Canada
150 C4 Smoky r. *Kansas* U.S.A.
12 C3 Smoky Bay *S. Australia* Australia
13 H2 Smoky C. headland *New South Wales* Australia
140 D1 Smoky Falls *Ontario* Canada
150 D4 Smoky Hills h. *Kansas* U.S.A.
136 G4 Smoky Lake *Alberta* Canada
56 B3 Smøla i. Norway
76 F1 Smołdzino Poland
52 A2 Smolensk div. Rus. Fed.
52 A2 Smolensk Rus. Fed.
52 A2 Smolenskaya Vozvyshennost' h. Rus. Fed.
47 K2 Smolenskoye Rus. Fed.
114 B2 Smolikas mt. Greece
52 F1 Smolino Rus. Fed.
59 E2 Smolmark Sweden
79 K3 Smolník Slovakia
113 E4 Smolyan Bulgaria
140 E2 Smooth Rock Falls *Ontario* Canada
138 C3 Smoothrock L. l. *Ontario* Canada
137 H4 Smoothstone Lake l. *Saskatchewan* Canada
56 G1 Smørfjord Norway
53 B2 Smotrych Ukraine
112 F3 Smyadovo Bulgaria
59 E4 Smygehamn Sweden
53 A1 Smyha Ukraine
77 J4 Smyków Poland
179 B3 Smyley I. i. Antarctica
147 F5 Smyrna *Delaware* U.S.A.
145 C5 Smyrna *Georgia* U.S.A.
146 C4 Smyrna *Ohio* U.S.A.
147 J1 Smyrna Mills *Maine* U.S.A.
53 G3 Smyrnove Ukraine
64 D3 Snaefell h. Isle of Man
56 N6 Snæfell mt. Iceland
136 A2 Snag *Yukon Terr.* Canada
65 H3 Snainton *England* U.K.
65 G4 Snaith *England* U.K.
152 D3 Snake r. *Idaho* U.S.A.
155 E2 Snake Range mts *Nevada* U.S.A.
152 D3 Snake River Plain plain *Idaho* U.S.A.
158 C2 Snap Pt pt The Bahamas
55 C4 Snaptun Denmark
136 G2 Snare Lake *N.W.T.* Canada
8 □3 Snares Is is New Zealand
56 D2 Snasa Norway
55 A3 Snedsted Denmark
68 D1 Sneek Netherlands
68 D1 Sneekermeer l. Netherlands
67 B5 Sneem Rep. of Ireland
130 E5 Sneeuberg mts South Africa
139 H3 Snegamook Lake l. *Newfoundland* Canada
54 B3 Snēpele Latvia
59 H1 Snesslinge Sweden
63 G2 Snettisham *England* U.K.
55 A4 Sneum r. Denmark
44 K3 Snezhnogorsk Rus. Fed.
107 J3 Snežnik mt. Slovenia
77 K2 Śniadowo Poland
76 D5 Sniežka mt. Czech Rep./Poland
53 E3 Snihurivka Ukraine
79 M3 Snina Slovakia
66 B3 Snizort, Loch b. *Scotland* U.K.
58 B2 Snjoheii mt. Norway
55 □2 Snogebæk Denmark
152 B2 Snohomish *Washington* U.S.A.
58 B2 Snønuten mt. Norway
152 B2 Snoqualmie Pass pass *Washington* U.S.A.
56 D2 Snøtinden mt. Norway
53 D1 Snov r. Ukraine
52 D3 Snova r. Rus. Fed.
54 E5 Snow Belarus
137 J2 Snowbird Lake l. *N.W.T.* Canada
62 B1 Snowdon mt. *Wales* U.K.
9 B6 Snowdon mt. New Zealand
62 B1 Snowdonia National Park *Wales* U.K.
155 G4 Snowflake *Arizona* U.S.A.
147 F5 Snow Hill *Maryland* U.S.A.
145 E5 Snow Hill *N. Carolina* U.S.A.
137 J4 Snow Lake *Manitoba* Canada
12 D3 Snowtown *S. Australia* Australia
152 D3 Snowville *Utah* U.S.A.
13 G4 Snowy r. *Victoria* Australia
141 H5 Snowy Mt mt. *New York* U.S.A.
13 G4 Snowy Mts mountain range *New South Wales* Australia
54 E4 Snudy, Vozyera l. Belarus
158 D2 Snug Corner The Bahamas
139 J3 Snug Harbour *Newfoundland* Canada
140 E4 Snug Harbour *Ontario* Canada
25 D4 Snuŏl Cambodia
53 A2 Snyatyn Ukraine
151 D5 Snyder *Oklahoma* U.S.A.
151 C5 Snyder *Texas* U.S.A.
130 C5 Snyderspoort pass South Africa
129 G2 Soahany Madagascar
64 B1 Soa Island i. *Scotland* U.K.
98 B3 Soajo Portugal
9 A6 Soaker, Mt mt. New Zealand
129 H2 Soalala Madagascar
129 G3 Soalara Madagascar
98 B3 Soalhães Portugal
129 G3 Soamanonga Madagascar
82 C3 Soana r. Italy
129 H2 Soanierana-Ivongo Madagascar
28 A6 Soan kundo i. South Korea
107 F3 Soave Italy
129 H2 Soavinandriana Madagascar
66 B3 Soay i. *Scotland* U.K.
66 □1 Soay i. *Scotland* U.K.
126 B3 Sobat r. Sudan
74 C3 Sobernheim Germany
78 D2 Soběslav Czech Rep.
21 M7 Sobger r. Indonesia
77 K4 Sobolew Poland
28 C7 Sobo-san mt. Japan
76 E5 Sobótka Poland
75 L2 Sobotka Czech Rep.
76 F4 Sobótka Poland
168 E1 Sobradinho Brazil
166 D3 Sobradinho, Barragem de resr Brazil
166 D1 Sobral Brazil
100 A1 Sobral de Monte Agraço Portugal
79 M3 Sobrance Slovakia
102 D2 Sobrarbe reg. Spain
98 C5 Sobreira Formosa Portugal
99 G2 Sobrón, Emb. de resr Spain
55 C5 Søby Denmark
53 E1 Sobych Ukraine
81 E4 Soča r. Slovenia
173 K3 Soca Uruguay
77 J3 Sochaczew Poland
90 E1 Sochaux France
51 F7 Sochi Rus. Fed.
77 J3 Sochocin Poland
114 E2 Sochos Greece
Society Islands is *see* Archipel de la Société
112 C2 Socol Romania
164 C4 Socompa Chile
153 F5 Socorro *New Mexico* U.S.A.
169 E5 Socorro Brazil
162 C2 Socorro Colombia
156 □ Socorro, I. i. Mexico
Socotra i. *see* Suqutrā
103 B6 Socovos Spain
25 D5 Soc Trăng Vietnam
101 H1 Socuéllamos Spain
154 D4 Soda Lake l. *California* U.S.A.
56 G2 Sodankylä Finland
36 D2 Soda Plains plain China/Jammu and Kashmir
152 E3 Soda Springs *Idaho* U.S.A.
59 G3 Söderåkra Sweden
59 H1 Söderboda Sweden
59 H2 Söderby-Karl Sweden
59 G1 Söderfors Sweden
57 E3 Söderhamn Sweden
59 G2 Söderköping Sweden
59 G2 Södermanland div. Sweden
59 G2 Södertälje Sweden
119 E5 Sodiri Sudan
130 D5 Sodium South Africa
126 C3 Sodo Ethiopia
57 E3 Södra Kvarken str. Finland/Sweden
81 F5 Sodražica Slovenia
118 D4 Soéka well Chad
131 G1 Soekmekaar South Africa
54 C2 Soela Väin chan. Estonia
72 D4 Soest Germany
68 D2 Soest Netherlands
72 C3 Soeste r. Germany
114 D3 Sofades Greece
129 E2 Sofala div. Mozambique
129 E3 Sofala, Baia de b. Mozambique
Sofia *see* Sofiya
115 E5 Sofiko Greece
52 F4 Sof'ino Rus. Fed.
112 D3 Sofiya div. Bulgaria
112 D3 Sofiya Bulgaria
53 E2 Sofiyivka Ukraine
56 H2 Sofporog Rus. Fed.
52 C1 Sofrino Rus. Fed.
162 C2 Sogamoso Colombia
31 K2 Sogda Rus. Fed.
72 C3 Sögel Germany
58 B1 Sogndalsfjøra Norway
58 B2 Søgne Norway
58 A1 Sognefjorden inlet Norway
58 A1 Sognesjøen chan. Norway
58 A1 Sogn og Fjordane div. Norway
23 C4 Sogod Philippines
30 B4 Sogo Nur l. China
50 H2 Sogra Rus. Fed.
32 C1 Sogruma China
37 H3 Sog Xian China
119 F2 Sohâg Egypt
36 D5 Sohagpur India
63 G2 Soham *England* U.K.
36 C2 Sohan r. Pakistan
6 □1 Sohano P.N.G.
69 D4 Soheit-Tinlot Belgium
37 E5 Sohela India
36 D3 Sohna India
74 C3 Sohren Germany
69 C4 Soignies div. Belgium
69 C4 Soignies Belgium
32 B2 Soila China
79 M5 Şoimi Romania
82 A1 Soing-Cubry-Charentenay France
56 G3 Soini Finland
86 D2 Soire-le-Château France
86 C3 Soissons France
172 D3 Soitue Argentina
86 C4 Soizy-aux-Bois France
28 D6 Sōja Japan
36 C4 Sojat India
23 B4 Sojoton Point pt Philippines
78 F5 Söjtör Hungary
46 D2 Sok r. Rus. Fed.
53 A1 Sokal' Ukraine
31 J5 Sokch'o South Korea
42 A2 Söke Turkey
47 H5 Sokh Tajikistan
30 D2 Sokhondo, G. mt. Rus. Fed.
51 G7 Sokhumi Georgia
112 C3 Sokobanja Yugoslavia
123 E5 Sokodé Togo
27 □ Soko Islands is *Hong Kong* China
50 G3 Sokol Rus. Fed.
104 G4 Sokolac Bos.-Herz.
53 D2 Sokolivka *Cherkasy* Ukraine
77 N5 Sokolivka *L'viv* Ukraine
77 M2 Sokółka Poland
77 L1 Sokółki Poland
81 H1 Sokolnice Czech Rep.
52 B1 Sokol'niki Rus. Fed.
52 D2 Sokol'niki Rus. Fed.
122 C4 Sokolo Mali
53 F3 Sokolohirne Ukraine
78 B1 Sokolov Czech Rep.
81 H4 Sokolovac Croatia
52 G4 Sokolovyy Rus. Fed.
77 L5 Sokołów Małopolski Poland
77 L3 Sokołow Podlaski Poland
52 F1 Sokol'skoye Rus. Fed.
77 L3 Sokoły Poland
122 A4 Sokone Senegal
29 □2 Sokoniya Japan
123 F4 Sokoto div. Nigeria
123 E4 Sokoto watercourse Nigeria
123 F4 Sokoto Nigeria
52 G4 Sokur Rus. Fed.
53 B2 Sokyryany Ukraine
77 H6 Soła r. Poland
173 H2 Sola Argentina
36 D3 Solan India
100 D2 Solana de los Barros Spain
101 F2 Solana del Pino Spain
9 A7 Solander I. i. New Zealand
58 C1 Sølandsfjellet mt. Norway
173 H4 Solanet Argentina
110 B4 Solanto, Pta di pt *Sicilia* Italy
38 A2 Solāpur India
111 E5 Solarino *Sicilia* Italy
112 E1 Solca Romania
83 F2 Solda r. Italy
83 F2 Solda Italy
53 C3 Şoldăneşti Moldova
80 C4 Sölden Austria
93 D6 Soldeu Andorra
76 G2 Solec Kujawski Poland
154 B3 Soledad *California* U.S.A.
173 G1 Soledad Argentina
162 C1 Soledad Colombia
163 E2 Soledad Venezuela
157 F5 Soledad de Doblado Mexico
167 B6 Soledade Brazil
51 G6 Solenoye Rus. Fed.
63 E4 Solent, The str. *England* U.K.
108 B3 Solenzara *Corse* France
107 F3 Solesino Italy
86 C2 Solesmes France
111 H2 Soleto Italy
93 B4 Solférino France
83 F3 Solferino Italy
56 D2 Solfjellsjøen Norway
59 F3 Solgen l. Sweden
50 G2 Solginskiy Rus. Fed.
42 E2 Solhan Turkey
107 E4 Soliera Italy
50 G3 Soligalich Rus. Fed.
91 B4 Solignac-sur-Loire France
80 D5 Soligo r. Italy
63 E2 Solihull *England* U.K.
44 G4 Solikamsk Rus. Fed.
46 D2 Sol'-Iletsk Rus. Fed.
163 E4 Solimões r. Brazil
72 C4 Solingen Germany
173 K3 Solís Uruguay
173 K3 Solís de Mataojo Uruguay
81 F3 Solker Tauern pass Austria
59 E2 Sollebrunn Sweden
56 E3 Sollefteå Sweden
81 H3 Sollenau Austria
59 G2 Sollentuna Sweden
103 F5 Sóller Spain
59 F1 Sollerön Sweden
55 D5 Søllested Denmark
73 H4 Söllichau Germany
91 E5 Solliès-Pont France
72 E4 Solling h. Germany
74 D2 Solms Germany
52 C1 Solnechnogorsk Rus. Fed.
53 G1 Solntsevo Rus. Fed.
22 B3 Solo r. Indonesia
53 B2 Solobkivtsi Ukraine
109 G4 Solofra Italy
89 G4 Sologne reg. France
157 H6 Sololá Guatemala
93 C5 Solomiac France
53 B2 Solomna Ukraine
4 H5 Solomon Islands country Pacific Ocean
6 □1 Solomon Sea sea P.N.G./Solomon Is.
31 G3 Solon China
53 G2 Solona r. Ukraine
46 F3 Solonchak Ghalkarteniz salt marsh Kazakhstan
46 E4 Solonchak Goklenkuy salt lake Turkmenistan
46 D4 Solonchak Kendyrlisor salt lake Kazakhstan
46 E5 Solonchakovyye Vpadiny Unguz salt flat Turkmenistan
46 E4 Solonchak Shorkozakhly depression Turkmenistan
53 F2 Solone Ukraine
52 E1 Solonitsa r. Rus. Fed.
166 E2 Solonópole Brazil
148 B2 Solon Springs *Wisconsin* U.S.A.
58 D1 Solør reg. Norway
99 F4 Solosancho Spain
54 F3 Solot" r. Rus. Fed.
52 D2 Solotcha Rus. Fed.
82 C1 Solothurn div. Switzerland
82 C1 Solothurn Switzerland
53 A2 Solotvyn Ukraine
50 E1 Solovetskiye Ostrova is Rus. Fed.
52 E3 Solovoye Rus. Fed.
77 N4 Solovychi Ukraine
31 E2 Solov'yevsk Rus. Fed.
102 E3 Solsona Spain
58 A1 Solsvik Norway
79 J5 Solt Hungary
104 F4 Šolta i. Croatia
39 B3 Solţānābād Iran
39 B2 Soltānābād Iran
39 D2 Solţānābād Iran
39 D1 Soltānābād Iran
42 F3 Solţanqolī Iran
72 E3 Soltau Germany
79 J5 Solti-síkság reg. Hungary
50 D3 Sol'tsy Rus. Fed.
79 J5 Soltvadkert Hungary
147 E3 Solvay *New York* U.S.A.
59 F3 Sölvesborg Sweden
50 H2 Sol'vychegodsk Rus. Fed.
66 E6 Solway Firth est. *England/Scotland* U.K.
125 E6 Solwezi Zambia

29 H5 Sōma Japan
42 A2 Soma Turkey
86 C2 Somain France
117 J5 Somalia country Africa
175 H3 Somali Basin sea feature Indian Ocean
122 D5 Somanya Ghana
90 C1 Sombernon France
125 D5 Sombo Angola
79 J6 Sombor Yugoslavia
69 C4 Sombreffe Belgium
156 E4 Sombrerete Mexico
171 C7 Sombrero Chile
25 A6 Sombrero Channel chan. *Andaman and Nicobar Is* India
36 C4 Somdari India
69 D3 Someren Netherlands
147 J2 Somerest Junction *Maine* U.S.A.
57 F3 Somero Finland
62 C3 Somerset div. *England* U.K.
144 C4 Somerset *Kentucky* U.S.A.
148 E4 Somerset *Michigan* U.S.A.
146 D5 Somerset *Pennsylvania* U.S.A.
145 □1 Somerset Bermuda
131 E6 Somerset East South Africa
135 J2 Somerset Island i. *N.W.T.* Canada
145 □1 Somerset Island i. Bermuda
147 G3 Somerset Reservoir resr *Vermont* U.S.A.
130 B7 Somerset West South Africa
147 H3 Somersworth *New Hampshire* U.S.A.
62 D3 Somerton *England* U.K.
151 D6 Somerville Res. resr *Texas* U.S.A.
112 D1 Someș r. Romania
9 □1 Somes, Pt pt *Chatham Is* New Zealand
77 K3 Somianka Poland
131 J4 Somkele South Africa
83 F3 Sommacampagna Italy
106 C3 Somma Lombardo Italy
110 C5 Sommatino *Sicilia* Italy
86 B3 Somme div. *Picardie* France
90 B2 Somme r. *Bourgogne* France
86 A2 Somme r. *Picardie* France
86 A2 Somme, Baie de la b. France
69 D4 Somme-Leuze Belgium
59 F2 Sommen l. Sweden
59 F2 Sommen Sweden
86 D3 Sommepy-Tahure France
73 G4 Sömmerda Germany
86 D4 Somme-Soude r. France
86 D4 Sommesous France
86 D3 Somme-Suippe France
139 G3 Sommet, Lac du l. *Québec* Canada
91 C5 Sommières France
92 C2 Sommières-du-Clain France
36 B5 Somnath India
79 G5 Somogy div. Hungary
79 G5 Somogyi-dombsag reg. Hungary
79 G5 Somogyjád Hungary
79 G5 Somogyvár Hungary
148 C5 Somonauk *Illinois* U.S.A.
76 G1 Somonino Poland
6 □6 Somosomo Fiji
6 □6 Somosomo Str. chan. Fiji
156 J6 Somotillo Nicaragua
156 J6 Somoto Nicaragua
52 C3 Somovo Rus. Fed.
52 D4 Somovo Rus. Fed.
52 B3 Somovo Rus. Fed.
54 E2 Sompa Estonia
76 G3 Sompolno Poland
69 C4 Somzée Belgium
37 E4 Son r. India
69 D3 Son Netherlands
58 D2 Son Norway
156 K8 Soná Panama
47 H3 Sonaly Kazakhstan
37 G5 Sonamura India
37 E5 Sonapur India
36 D4 Sonar r. India
37 H4 Sonari India
82 C1 Sonceboz Switzerland
31 H5 Sŏnch'ŏn North Korea
99 G2 Soncillo Spain
106 D3 Soncino Italy
106 E2 Sondalo Italy
58 C2 Søndeled Norway
55 B5 Sønderå r. Denmark
55 A3 Sønder Balling Denmark
55 B5 Sønderborg airport Denmark
55 B5 Sønderborg Denmark
55 A3 Sønder Dråby Denmark
55 A4 Sønder Felding Denmark
73 F4 Sonderhausen Germany
55 A4 Sønderjylland div. Denmark
55 A3 Sønder Nissum Denmark
55 A4 Sønder Omme Denmark
55 D5 Sondersø l. Denmark
55 C4 Søndersø Denmark
55 B3 Sønderup Denmark
106 D2 Sondrio div. *Lombardia* Italy
106 D2 Sondrio Italy
38 B2 Sonepet India
124 B3 Song Gabon
36 B5 Songad India
33 F2 Songbu China
25 E4 Sông Cau Vietnam
24 D3 Song Con r. Vietnam
24 C2 Sông Đa r. Vietnam
25 E4 Sông Đa Răng r. Vietnam
127 C7 Songea Tanzania
89 G2 Songeons France
58 B2 Songevatnet l. Norway
25 D5 Song Hâu Giang r. Vietnam
24 D2 Sông Hông r. Vietnam
31 J3 Songhua r. China
31 H4 Songhua Hu resr China
31 H3 Songhua Jiang China
33 H2 Songjiang China
28 A6 Songjŏng South Korea
32 D2 Songkan China
25 C6 Songkhla Thailand
31 F4 Song Ling mountain range China
31 G3 Songling China
24 B2 Songlong Myanmar
24 D2 Sông Ma r. Laos/Vietnam
32 C3 Songming China
31 H5 Sŏngnam South Korea
31 H5 Songnim North Korea
125 B5 Songo Angola
129 E2 Songo Mozambique
127 C6 Songo Mnara I. i. Tanzania
127 C6 Songo Songo I. i. Tanzania
32 C1 Songpan China
25 D5 Song Saigon r. Vietnam
37 G4 Songsak India
33 E2 Songtao China
33 G3 Songxi China
33 F1 Song Xian China
33 E2 Songzi China
25 E4 Sơn Ha Vietnam
30 E4 Sonid Youqi China
30 E4 Sonid Zuoqi China
36 D3 Sonīpat India
56 G3 Sonkajärvi Finland
52 C1 Sonkovo Rus. Fed.
24 C2 Sơn La Vietnam
36 A4 Sonmiani Pakistan
36 A4 Sonmiani Bay b. Pakistan
80 D3 Sonnblick mt. Austria
75 G2 Sonneberg Germany
80 D3 Sonnenjoch mt. Austria
73 J4 Sonnewalde Germany
109 F3 Sonnino Italy
166 C2 Sono r. Brazil
169 F2 Sono r. Brazil
155 F6 Sonoita r. Mexico
155 G6 Sonoita *Arizona* U.S.A.
156 C2 Sonora div. Mexico
156 C2 Sonora r. Mexico
154 B3 Sonora *California* U.S.A.
151 C6 Sonora *Texas* U.S.A.
155 F6 Sonoyta Mexico
39 A2 Sonqor Iran
101 G1 Sonseca Spain
103 G5 Son Servera Spain
162 B2 Sonsón Colombia
157 H6 Sonsonate El Salvador
130 D3 Sonstraal South Africa
24 D2 Sơn Tây Vietnam
80 B2 Sontheim Germany
80 B2 Sontheim an der Brenz Germany
74 F5 Sonthofen Germany
72 E4 Sontra Germany
131 G5 Sonwabile South Africa
Soochow *see* Suzhou
87 G3 Soonwald forest Germany
164 D3 Sopachuy Bolivia
173 J1 Sopas r. Uruguay
102 D2 Sopeira Spain
124 E2 Sopo watercourse Sudan
112 E3 Sopot Bulgaria
76 G1 Sopot Poland
112 C2 Sopot Yugoslavia
78 F4 Sopron Hungary
81 H3 Sopronkövesd Hungary
47 H4 Sopu-Korgon Kyrgyzstan
36 C2 Sopur India
93 E5 Sor r. France
100 B1 Sôr r. Portugal
98 C1 Sor r. Spain
109 F3 Sora Italy
38 D2 Sorada India
57 E3 Soråker Sweden
31 J5 Sŏraksan mt. South Korea
108 D2 Sorano Italy
164 C3 Sorata Bolivia
58 B2 Sør-Audnedal Norway
59 F1 Sör Barken l. Sweden
101 H3 Sorbas Spain
99 G4 Sorbe r. Spain
64 D3 Sorbie *Scotland* U.K.
90 C3 Sorbiers France
58 C1 Sørbølfjellet mt. Norway
55 D4 Sørbymagle Denmark
87 E4 Sorcy-St-Martin France
46 E3 Sor Donyztau l. Kazakhstan
93 B4 Sore France
141 J3 Sorel *Québec* Canada
13 F5 Sorell *Tasmania* Australia
13 F5 Sorell L. l. *Tasmania* Australia
43 C4 Soreq r. Israel
106 D3 Soresina Italy
58 B1 Sørfjorden inlet Norway
92 C3 Sorges France
108 B4 Sorgono *Sardegna* Italy
93 E5 Sorgues r. France
91 C4 Sorgues France
43 C1 Sorgun r. Turkey
42 C2 Sorgun Turkey
99 H3 Soria div. Spain
99 H3 Soria Spain
173 H2 Soriano div. Uruguay
173 H2 Soriano Uruguay
111 F4 Soriano Calabro Italy
108 E2 Soriano nel Cimino *Sardegna* Italy
101 G2 Sorihuela del Gaudalimar Spain
178 □1 Sörkapp c. *Jan Mayen* Arctic Ocean
44 C2 Sørkappøya i. *Svalbard* Arctic Ocean
46 D4 Sor Kaydak l. Kazakhstan
39 C2 Sorkheh Iran
39 C2 Sorkh, Kūh-e mountain range Iran
56 D2 Sørli Norway
46 D3 Sor Mertvyy Kultuk l. Kazakhstan
58 D1 Sør-Mesna l. Norway
86 D3 Sormonne r. France
92 E3 Sornac France
55 D4 Sorø Denmark
37 F5 Soro India
53 C2 Soroca Moldova
168 E5 Sorocaba Brazil
52 C3 Sorochinka Rus. Fed.
46 D2 Sorochinsk Rus. Fed.
21 M5 Sorol i. Fed. States of Micronesia
110 D5 Soro, Monte mt. *Sicilia* Italy
21 K7 Sorong Indonesia
115 □ Soroni Greece
166 C2 Sororó r. Brazil
126 B4 Soroti Uganda
56 F1 Sørøya i. Norway
100 B2 Sorraia r. Portugal
56 E1 Sorreisa Norway
13 F4 Sorrento *Victoria* Australia
109 G4 Sorrento Italy
128 A3 Sorris Sorris Namibia
179 D3 Sør-Rondane mts Antarctica
56 E2 Sorsele Sweden
47 M2 Sorsk Rus. Fed.
108 A4 Sorso *Sardegna* Italy
23 C3 Sorsogon Philippines
102 E2 Sort Spain
57 H3 Sortavala Rus. Fed.
111 E5 Sortino *Sicilia* Italy
56 D1 Sortland Norway
50 J2 Sortopolovskaya Rus. Fed.
56 C3 Sør-Trøndelag div. Norway
59 G2 Sorunda Sweden
Sõrve Väin chan. *see* Kura Kurk
50 J3 Sorvizhi Rus. Fed.
93 C4 Sos France
31 H5 Sŏsan South Korea
114 D2 Sosandra Greece
141 G1 Soscumica, Lac l. *Québec* Canada
59 E3 Sösdala Sweden
102 B2 Sos del Rey Católico Spain
52 F3 Sosedka Rus. Fed.
52 B2 Sosenskiy Rus. Fed.
131 G2 Soshanguve South Africa
77 N4 Soshychne Ukraine
52 B3 Soskovo Rus. Fed.
52 D3 Sosna r. Rus. Fed.
172 B3 Sosneado mt. Argentina
76 F4 Sośnie Poland
53 A1 Sosnivka Ukraine
50 K2 Sosnogorsk Rus. Fed.
53 B1 Sosnove Ukraine
52 G2 Sosnovka Rus. Fed.
52 E3 Sosnovka Rus. Fed.
52 F3 Sosnovka Rus. Fed.
50 G1 Sosnovka Rus. Fed.
50 H2 Sosnovka Rus. Fed.
52 H1 Sosnovka Rus. Fed.
52 H2 Sosnovka Rus. Fed.
54 G1 Sosnovo Rus. Fed.
52 H3 Sosnovoborsk Rus. Fed.
52 G3 Sosnovoborskoye Rus. Fed.
30 D1 Sosnovo-Ozerskoye Rus. Fed.
52 F2 Sosnovskoye Rus. Fed.
54 F2 Sosnovyy Bor Rus. Fed.
77 H5 Sosnowice Poland
54 E5 Sosny Belarus
53 E1 Sosnytsya Ukraine
91 F5 Sospel France
81 G4 Šoštanj Slovenia
29 □2 Sosu Japan
51 F6 Sosyka r. Rus. Fed.
123 E4 Sota r. Benin
100 E2 Sotillo r. Spain
99 F4 Sotillo de la Adrada Spain
56 H2 Sotkamo Finland
52 E2 Sotnitsyno Rus. Fed.
172 E1 Soto Argentina
98 D1 Soto Spain
99 G4 Soto del Real Spain
157 F4 Soto la Marina Mexico
99 G2 Sotopalacios Spain
123 E5 Sotouboua Togo
99 F2 Sotresgudo Spain
98 E1 Sotrondio Spain
59 F2 Sottern l. Sweden
89 G2 Sotteville-lès-Rouen France
72 E2 Sottrum Germany
59 J1 Sottunga Finland
101 H1 Sotuélamos Spain
157 H4 Sotuta Mexico
93 E5 Soual France
124 B3 Souanké Congo
122 C5 Soubré Côte d'Ivoire
86 C4 Soucy France
115 F7 Souda Greece
14 D4 Soudan *Northern Terr.* Australia
88 D4 Soudan France
147 F4 Souderton *Pennsylvania* U.S.A.
93 D6 Soueix France
87 G4 Soufflenheim France
113 F4 Soufli Greece
159 □5 Soufrière volcano *Guadeloupe* Caribbean
159 G4 Soufrière volcano St Vincent
122 B4 Souguéta Guinea
121 E1 Sougueur Algeria
93 D4 Souillac France
127 □4 Souillac Mauritius
87 E3 Souilly France
121 F1 Souk Ahras Algeria
120 C2 Souk el Arbaâ du Rharb Morocco
96 D5 Souk el Had el Rharbia Morocco
96 C5 Souk Khemis du Sahel Morocco
101 E5 Souk Tleta Taghramet Morocco
96 D5 Souk-Tnine-de-Sidi-el-Yamani Morocco
31 H5 Sŏul South Korea
92 A3 Soulac-sur-Mer France
86 D4 Soulaines-Dhuys France
93 B5 Soule reg. France
115 D5 Souli Greece
92 A2 Soullans France
88 D2 Soulles r. France
93 B6 Soulom France
90 F1 Soultz-Haut-Rhin France
87 G5 Soultzmatt France
87 G4 Soultz-sous-Forêts France
69 D4 Soumagne Belgium
25 A4 Sound I. i. *Andaman and Nicobar Is* India
122 A4 Soungrougrou r. Senegal
115 F5 Sounio nat. park Greece
123 G3 Sountel well Niger
86 B4 Souppes-sur-Loing France
93 B5 Souprosse France
43 C3 Soûr Lebanon
131 G4 Sources, Mt-aux- mt. Lesotho
89 E3 Sourdeval France
166 C1 Soure Brazil
98 B4 Soure Portugal
137 J5 Souris r. Canada/U.S.A.
137 J5 Souris *Manitoba* Canada
139 H4 Souris *Prince Edward I.* Canada
93 E6 Sournia France
120 B5 Souroumelli well Mauritania
92 C3 Sourzac France
98 B3 Sousa r. Portugal
166 E2 Sousa Brazil
93 E4 Sousceyrac France
100 C2 Sousel Portugal
121 G1 Sousse Tunisia
93 A5 Soustons France
130 B5 Sout r. *Western Cape* South Africa
130 C4 Sout watercourse *Northern Cape* South Africa
117 G9 South Africa, Republic of country Africa
14 C2 South Alligator r. *Northern Terr.* Australia
63 E2 Southam *England* U.K.
63 E4 Southampton div. *England* U.K.
63 E4 Southampton *England* U.K.
147 G4 Southampton *New York* U.S.A.
140 E4 Southampton *Ontario* Canada
137 M2 Southampton Island i. *N.W.T.* Canada
25 A5 South Andaman i. *Andaman and Nicobar Is* India
146 E6 South Anna r. *Virginia* U.S.A.
65 G4 South Anston *England* U.K.
161 □ South Atlantic Ocean Atlantic Ocean
139 H2 South Aulatsivik Island i. *Newfoundland* Canada
12 C2 South Australia div. Australia
175 N6 South Australian Basin sea feature Indian Ocean
151 F5 Southaven *Mississippi* U.S.A.
66 D5 South Ayrshire div. *Scotland* U.K.
153 F5 South Baldy mt. *New Mexico* U.S.A.
65 G3 South Bank *England* U.K.
146 B4 South Bass I. i. *Ohio* U.S.A.
137 N2 South Bay b. *N.W.T.* Canada
140 D4 South Baymouth *Ontario* Canada
148 D5 South Bend *Indiana* U.S.A.
152 B2 South Bend *Washington* U.S.A.
145 E7 South Bight chan. The Bahamas
63 G3 Southborough *England* U.K.
146 D6 South Boston *Virginia* U.S.A.
147 G3 Southbridge *Massachusetts* U.S.A.
9 D5 Southbridge New Zealand
South Cape c. *see* Ka Lae
6 □6 South Cape c. Fiji
145 D5 South Carolina div. U.S.A.
65 H4 South Cave *England* U.K.
62 D4 South Chard *England* U.K.
147 J2 South China *Maine* U.S.A.
20 F3 South China Sea sea Pacific Ocean
111 □ South Comino Chan. chan. Malta
150 C2 South Dakota div. U.S.A.
147 G3 South Deerfield *Massachusetts* U.S.A.
62 D4 South Dorset Downs h. *England* U.K.
63 F4 South Downs h. *England* U.K.
131 E2 South East div. Botswana
128 □1 South East Bay b. *Ascension* Atlantic Ocean
13 F5 South East C. c. *Tasmania* Australia
8 □2 South East Harb. inlet *Campbell I.* New Zealand
128 □1 South East Head headland *Ascension* Atlantic Ocean
17 C7 South East Is is *Western Australia* Australia
174 C9 South-East Pacific Basin sea feature Pacific Ocean
10 □3 South East Reef reef *Macquarie I.* Pacific Ocean
10 □4 South East Rock i. *Lord Howe I.* Pacific Ocean
137 J3 Southend *Saskatchewan* Canada
66 C5 Southend *Scotland* U.K.
63 G3 Southend-on-Sea *England* U.K.
148 A5 South English *Iowa* U.S.A.
129 F2 Southern div. Malawi
122 B5 Southern div. Sierra Leone
125 E7 Southern div. Zambia
9 C5 Southern Alps mountain range New Zealand
17 B6 Southern Cross *Western Australia* Australia
137 K3 Southern Indian Lake l. *Manitoba* Canada
125 D7 Southern Lueti r. Angola/Zambia
124 E2 Southern National Park nat. park Sudan
179 A1 Southern Ocean ocean
145 E5 Southern Pines *N. Carolina* U.S.A.
179 C1 Southern Thule I. i. *S. Sandwich Is* Atlantic Ocean
66 D5 Southern Uplands h. *Scotland* U.K.
63 G2 Southery *England* U.K.
66 E4 South Esk r. *Scotland* U.K.
16 D4 South Esk Tableland reg. *Western Australia* Australia
131 F5 Southeyville South Africa
148 B6 South Fabius r. *Missouri* U.S.A.
153 F4 South Fork *Colorado* U.S.A.
154 A2 South Fork Eel r. *California* U.S.A.
154 C4 South Fork Kern r. *California* U.S.A.
146 D5 South Fork South Branch r. *W. Virginia* U.S.A.
148 E3 South Fox I. i. *Michigan* U.S.A.
159 □6 South Friar's Bay b. *St Kitts-Nevis* Caribbean
179 C5 South Geomagnetic Pole Antarctica
171 □ South Georgia i. Atlantic Ocean
62 D3 South Gloucestershire div. *England* U.K.
66 B3 South Harris i. *Scotland* U.K.
63 F4 South Harting *England* U.K.
37 G5 South Hatia I. i. Bangladesh
148 D4 South Haven *Michigan* U.S.A.
137 K2 South Henik Lake l. *N.W.T.* Canada
147 G2 South Hero *Vermont* U.S.A.
128 □3 South Hill h. *Tristan da Cunha* Atlantic Ocean
146 D6 South Hill *Virginia* U.S.A.
175 O2 South Honshu Ridge sea feature Pacific Ocean
126 C4 South Horr Kenya
137 K3 South Indian Lake *Manitoba* Canada
147 G4 Southington *Connecticut* U.S.A.
10 □1 South Island i. *Cocos Is* Indian Ocean
9 C6 South Island i. New Zealand
9 □3 South Islet i. *Antipodes Is* New Zealand
23 A4 South Islet reef Philippines
65 G4 South Kirkby *England* U.K.
127 C5 South Kitui National Reserve res. Kenya
19 O6 South Korea country Asia
154 B2 South Lake Tahoe *California* U.S.A.
66 E5 South Lanarkshire div. *Scotland* U.K.
9 A6 Southland div. New Zealand
127 B7 South Luangwa National Park nat. park Zambia
175 G6 South Madagascar Ridge sea feature Indian Ocean
179 B6 South Magnetic Pole Antarctica
148 D3 South Manitou I. i. *Michigan* U.S.A.
145 D7 South Miami *Florida* U.S.A.
63 G3 Southminster *England* U.K.
62 C3 South Molton *England* U.K.
137 J4 South Moose L. l. *Manitoba* Canada
146 E5 South Mts h. *Pennsylvania* U.S.A.
136 D2 South Nahanni r. *N.W.T.* Canada
159 □1 South Negril Pt pt Jamaica
63 G3 South Ockendon *England* U.K.
179 B1 South Orkney Is is Atlantic Ocean
51 G7 South Ossetia reg. Georgia
5 N8 South Pacific Ocean ocean
147 H2 South Paris *Maine* U.S.A.
62 D4 South Petherton *England* U.K.
152 G3 South Platte r. *Colorado* U.S.A.
179 B4 South Pole Antarctica
140 E2 South Porcupine *Ontario* Canada
65 E4 Southport *England* U.K.
147 H3 South Portland *Maine* U.S.A.
8 □3 South Promontory pt *Snares Is* New Zealand
128 □1 South Pt pt *Ascension* Atlantic Ocean
159 □9 South Pt pt *Barbados* Caribbean
158 D2 South Pt pt The Bahamas
141 F4 South River *Ontario* Canada
66 F2 South Ronaldsay i. *Scotland* U.K.
147 G3 South Royalton *Vermont* U.S.A.
127 B7 South Rukuru r. Malawi
179 C1 South Sandwich Islands is Atlantic Ocean
174 H9 South Sandwich Trench sea feature Atlantic Ocean
137 H4 South Saskatchewan r. *Saskatchewan* Canada
137 K3 South Seal r. *Manitoba* Canada
179 B2 South Shetland Is is Antarctica
65 G2 South Shields *England* U.K.
65 H4 South Skirlaugh *England* U.K.
148 A5 South Skunk r. *Iowa* U.S.A.
8 E3 South Taranaki Bight b. New Zealand
155 G2 South Tent summit *Utah* U.S.A.
37 E4 South Tons r. India
138 E3 South Twin I. i. *N.W.T.* Canada
65 F3 South Tyne r. *England* U.K.
66 A3 South Uist i. *Scotland* U.K.
66 E2 South Walls pen. *Scotland* U.K.
63 F1 Southwell *England* U.K.
14 D3 South Wellesley Is is *Queensland* Australia
128 □1 South West Bay b. *Ascension* Atlantic Ocean
145 □2 South West Bay b. The Bahamas
8 □1 South West C. c. *Auckland Is* New Zealand
13 F5 South West C. headland *Tasmania* Australia
9 A7 South West Cape c. New Zealand
145 □3 South West Cape *Virgin Is* Caribbean
175 H6 South-West Indian Ridge sea feature Indian Ocean
15 G3 South West I. i. *Coral Sea Islands Terr.* Pacific Ocean
13 F5 South West Nat. Park nat. park *Tasmania* Australia
174 D7 South-West Peru Ridge sea feature Pacific Ocean
10 □3 South West Pt pt *Macquarie I.* Pacific Ocean
128 □2 South West Pt pt *St Helena* Atlantic Ocean
159 □1 South-West Pt pt Jamaica
158 C3 Southwest Rock i. Caribbean
148 E5 South Whitley *Indiana* U.S.A.
147 H3 South Windham *Maine* U.S.A.
63 H2 Southwold *England* U.K.
63 G3 South Woodham Ferrers *England* U.K.
63 G2 South Wootton *England* U.K.
65 G4 South Yorkshire div. *England* U.K.
98 D4 Souto Portugal
131 F4 Soutpan South Africa
131 G1 Soutpansberg mountain range South Africa
130 E6 Soutpansnek pass South Africa
90 B2 Souvigny France
58 B1 Sovarnuten mt. Norway
112 E1 Sovata Romania
172 E3 Soven Argentina
111 F4 Soverato Italy
43 B2 Sovereign Base Area (Akrotiri) Cyprus
43 B2 Sovereign Base Area (Dhekelia) Cyprus
111 F3 Soveria Mannelli Italy
50 B4 Sovetsk Rus. Fed.
50 J3 Sovetsk Rus. Fed.
52 C3 Sovetsk Rus. Fed.
27 Q2 Sovetskaya Gavan' Rus. Fed.
44 H3 Sovetskiy Rus. Fed.
54 F1 Sovetskiy Rus. Fed.
50 J3 Sovetskiy Rus. Fed.
51 H7 Sovetskoye Rus. Fed.
52 H2 Sovetskoye Rus. Fed.
52 H4 Sovetskoye Rus. Fed.
6 □8 Sovi B. b. Fiji
50 G1 Sovpol'ye Rus. Fed.
51 E6 Sovyets'kyy Ukraine
131 F3 Soweto South Africa
39 D3 Sowghān Iran
73 K2 Sowno Poland
157 G5 Soyaló Mexico
28 H1 Sōya-misaki c. Japan
50 G1 Soyana r. Rus. Fed.
92 C3 Soyaux France
28 H1 Sōya-wan b. Japan
125 B5 Soyo Angola
51 D4 Sozh r. Belarus
52 A2 Sozh r. Rus. Fed.
50 K3 Sozimskiy Rus. Fed.
112 F3 Sozopol Bulgaria
69 D4 Spa Belgium
158 □2 Spaanse Baai b. *Curaçao* Netherlands Ant.
179 B3 Spaatz I. i. Antarctica
111 E4 Spadafora *Sicilia* Italy
74 D4 Spaichingen Germany
48 E4 Spain country Europe
63 F2 Spalding *England* U.K.
12 D3 Spalding *S. Australia* Australia
75 J3 Spálené Poříčí Czech Rep.
80 B1 Spalt Germany
72 E4 Spangenberg Germany
62 C3 Span Head h. *England* U.K.
140 E3 Spanish r. *Ontario* Canada
140 D3 Spanish *Ontario* Canada
155 G1 Spanish Fork *Utah* U.S.A.
145 □1 Spanish Pt pt Bermuda
145 □3 Spanish Town *Virgin Is* Caribbean
159 □1 Spanish Town Jamaica
131 F1 Spanwerk South Africa
109 G3 Sparanise Italy
154 C2 Sparks *Nevada* U.S.A.
59 G2 Sparreholm Sweden
146 C6 Sparta *N. Carolina* U.S.A.
148 B4 Sparta *Wisconsin* U.S.A.
145 D5 Spartanburg *S. Carolina* U.S.A.
100 E5 Spartel, Cap c. Morocco
115 D5 Sparti Greece
111 F5 Spartivento, Capo c. Italy
108 A6 Spartivento, Capo pt *Sardegna* Italy
114 C4 Sparto Greece
136 G5 Sparwood *B.C.* Canada
52 B2 Spas-Demensk Rus. Fed.
52 E2 Spas-Klepiki Rus. Fed.
53 E2 Spasove Ukraine
50 E2 Spasskaya Guba Rus. Fed.
31 K3 Spassk-Dal'niy Rus. Fed.
52 G2 Spasskoye Rus. Fed.
52 E2 Spassk-Ryazanskiy Rus. Fed.
52 C1 Spas-Ugol Rus. Fed.
115 E5 Spata Greece
136 D3 Spatsizi Plateau Wilderness Provincial Park res. *B.C.* Canada
87 G2 Spay Germany
66 D4 Spean Bridge *Scotland* U.K.
150 C2 Spearfish *S. Dakota* U.S.A.
151 C4 Spearman *Texas* U.S.A.
147 F3 Speculator *New York* U.S.A.
128 □2 Speery I. i. *St Helena* Atlantic Ocean
69 E5 Speicher Germany
75 G3 Speichersdorf Germany
159 □9 Speightstown *Barbados* Caribbean
81 G3 Speikkogel mt. Austria
127 B5 Speke Gulf b. Tanzania
72 C3 Spelle Germany
109 E2 Spello Italy
152 D2 Spencer *Idaho* U.S.A.
150 E3 Spencer *Iowa* U.S.A.
146 C5 Spencer *W. Virginia* U.S.A.
12 D3 Spencer, C. headland *S. Australia* Australia
136 B3 Spencer, Cape c. *Alaska* U.S.A.
12 D3 Spencer Gulf est. *S. Australia* Australia
136 E4 Spences Bridge *B.C.* Canada
65 G3 Spennymoor *England* U.K.
9 D5 Spenser Mts mountain range New Zealand
114 C4 Spercheios r. Greece
58 E1 Sperillen l. Norway
110 D5 Sperlinga *Sicilia* Italy
109 F3 Sperlonga Italy
108 A6 Sperone, Capo pt *Sardegna* Italy
67 D2 Sperrin Mountains h. *Northern Ireland* U.K.
146 D5 Sperryville *Virginia* U.S.A.
74 E3 Spessart reg. Germany
115 E5 Spetses i. Greece
115 E5 Spetses Greece
115 E5 Spetsopoula i. Greece
66 E3 Spey r. *Scotland* U.K.
74 D3 Speyer Germany
159 □2 Speyside *Tobago* Trinidad and Tobago
36 A3 Spezand Pakistan
88 B3 Spézet France
111 F3 Spezzano Albanese Italy
111 F3 Spezzano della Sila Italy
77 L4 Spiczyn Poland
75 J4 Spiegelau Germany
72 C2 Spiekeroog i. Germany
87 G3 Spiesen-Elversberg Germany
82 C2 Spiez Switzerland
68 E1 Spijk Netherlands
68 C3 Spijkenisse Netherlands
115 F7 Spili Greece
107 G2 Spilimbergo Italy
63 G1 Spilsby *England* U.K.
109 J4 Spinazzola Italy
39 F3 Spīn Būldak Afghanistan
87 E3 Spincourt France
36 B3 Spintangi Pakistan
36 B2 Spinwam Pakistan
136 F3 Spirit River *Alberta* Canada
148 C3 Spirit River Flowage resr *Wisconsin* U.S.A.
137 H4 Spiritwood *Saskatchewan* Canada
52 B1 Spirovo Rus. Fed.
39 F2 Spirsang P. pass Afghanistan
79 K2 Spišská Belá Slovakia
79 K3 Spišská Nová Ves Slovakia
79 K2 Spišská Stará Ves Slovakia
81 F3 Spital am Pyhrn Austria
81 G3 Spital am Semmering Austria
36 D2 Spiti r. India
178 □3 Spitsbergen i. *Svalbard* Arctic Ocean
80 E4 Spittal an der Drau div. Austria
81 E4 Spittal an der Drau Austria
66 E4 Spittal of Glenshee *Scotland* U.K.
81 G2 Spitz Austria
80 D4 Spitzkofel mt. Austria
83 E1 Spitzmeilen mt. Switzerland
55 A3 Spjald Denmark
104 F4 Split Croatia
137 K3 Split Lake l. *Manitoba* Canada
137 K3 Split Lake *Manitoba* Canada
83 E2 Spluga, Passo dello pass Italy/Switzerland
83 E2 Splügen Switzerland
53 C2 Spodakhy Ukraine
81 F4 Spodnja Idrija Slovenia
81 G4 Spodnje Hoče Slovenia
55 C5 Spodsbjerg Denmark
65 G4 Spofforth *England* U.K.
152 C2 Spokane *Washington* U.S.A.
80 B4 Spöl r. Italy
109 E2 Spoleto Italy
83 F2 Spondigna Italy
25 D4 Spong Cambodia
148 B3 Spooner *Wisconsin* U.S.A.
73 G2 Spornitz Germany
152 F2 Spotted Horse *Wyoming* U.S.A.
139 J3 Spotted Island *Newfoundland* Canada
140 D3 Spragge *Ontario* Canada
136 E4 Spranger, Mt mt. *B.C.* Canada
20 F5 Spratly Islands is South China Sea
152 C2 Spray *Oregon* U.S.A.
104 G3 Spreča r. Bos.-Herz.
73 K3 Spree r. Germany
73 J3 Spreewald reg. Germany
83 D1 Spreitenbach Switzerland
73 K4 Spremberg Germany
87 G3 Sprendlingen Germany
107 G3 Spresiano Italy
69 D4 Sprimont Belgium
140 D4 Spring Bay *Ontario* Canada
130 A4 Springbok South Africa
14 D3 Spring Cr. r. *Northern Terr.* Australia
14 E4 Spring Cr. watercourse *Queensland* Australia
9 D4 Spring Creek New Zealand
151 E4 Springdale *Arkansas* U.S.A.
139 J4 Springdale *Newfoundland* Canada
72 E3 Springe Germany
153 F4 Springer *New Mexico* U.S.A.
155 H4 Springerville *Arizona* U.S.A.
153 G4 Springfield *Colorado* U.S.A.
148 C6 Springfield *Illinois* U.S.A.
147 J2 Springfield *Maine* U.S.A.
147 G3 Springfield *Massachusetts* U.S.A.
150 E2 Springfield *Minnesota* U.S.A.
151 E4 Springfield *Missouri* U.S.A.
146 B5 Springfield *Ohio* U.S.A.
152 B2 Springfield *Oregon* U.S.A.
147 G3 Springfield *Vermont* U.S.A.
146 D5 Springfield *W. Virginia* U.S.A.
9 C5 Springfield New Zealand
148 C6 Springfield, Lake l. *Illinois* U.S.A.
131 E5 Springfontein South Africa
163 F2 Spring Garden Guyana
148 B4 Spring Green *Wisconsin* U.S.A.
148 B4 Spring Grove *Minnesota* U.S.A.
145 D6 Spring Hill *Florida* U.S.A.
139 H4 Springhill *Nova Scotia* Canada
148 D4 Spring Lake *Michigan* U.S.A.
155 E3 Spring Mountains mts *Nevada* U.S.A.
131 G3 Springs South Africa
9 D5 Springs Junction New Zealand
141 H2 Springs, Mt h. *Québec* Canada
15 G5 Springsure *Queensland* Australia
14 E4 Springvale *Queensland* Australia
148 A4 Spring Valley *Minnesota* U.S.A.
131 F6 Spring Valley South Africa
146 D3 Springville *New York* U.S.A.
155 G1 Springville *Utah* U.S.A.
72 C4 Sprockhövel Germany
55 C4 Sprogø i. Denmark
63 H2 Sprowston *England* U.K.
136 G4 Spruce Grove *Alberta* Canada
146 D5 Spruce Knob-Seneca Rocks National Recreation Area res. *W. Virginia* U.S.A.

152 D3 Spruce Mt. mt. Nevada U.S.A.
111 F3 Spulico, Capo c. Italy
65 J4 Spurn Head c. England U.K.
136 E5 Spuzzum B.C. Canada
77 K2 Spychowo Poland
136 E5 Squamish B.C. Canada
147 H3 Squam Lake l. New Hampshire U.S.A.
147 J1 Squapan Lake l. Maine U.S.A.
147 J1 Square Lake l. Maine U.S.A.
111 F4 Squillace Italy
111 F4 Squillace, Golfo di g. Italy
111 H2 Squinzano Italy
17 D5 Squires, Mt h. Western Australia Australia
22 B3 Sragen Indonesia
112 C3 Srbija div. Yugoslavia
112 B2 Srbobran Yugoslavia
25 C5 Srê Âmběl Cambodia
104 G3 Srebrenica Bos.-Herz.
45 R4 Sredinnyy Khrebet mountain range Rus. Fed.
81 H4 Središče Slovenia
112 F3 Sredishte Bulgaria
112 D3 Sredna Gora mountain range Bulgaria
31 H2 Srednebelaya Rus. Fed.
45 R3 Srednekolymsk Rus. Fed.
52 C2 Sredne-Russkaya Vozvyshennost' reg. Rus. Fed.
45 M3 Sredne-Sibirskoye Ploskogor'ye plat. Rus. Fed.
50 D1 Sredneye Kuyto, Oz. l. Rus. Fed.
112 E3 Srednogorie Bulgaria
51 H5 Srednyaya Akhtuba Rus. Fed.
112 B2 Srem reg. Yugoslavia
76 F3 Śrem Poland
25 D4 Srêpok, T. r. Cambodia
31 F1 Sretensk Rus. Fed.
53 E1 Sribne Ukraine
38 C3 Sriharikota I. i. India
38 D2 Srikakulam India
38 B3 Sri Kālahasti India
18 K9 Sri Lanka country Asia
36 C2 Srinagar Jammu and Kashmir
36 D3 Srinagar Uttar Pradesh India
38 B4 Srirangam India
24 C3 Sri Thep Thailand
38 B4 Srivaikuntam India
38 A2 Srivardhan India
38 B4 Srivilliputtur India
104 F3 Srnetica mts Bos.-Herz.
76 E4 Środa Śląska Poland
76 F3 Środa Wielkopolska Poland
79 K6 Srpska Crnja Yugoslavia
38 C2 Srungavarapukota India
52 D3 Sselki Rus. Fed.
130 C3 Staansaam South Africa
15 E3 Staaten r. Queensland Australia
15 E3 Staaten River Nat. Park nat. park Queensland Australia
81 H2 Staatz Austria
73 G1 Staberhuk c. Germany
69 C3 Stabroek Belgium
55 A3 Staby Denmark
78 C2 Stachy Czech Rep.
72 E2 Stade Germany
69 B4 Staden Belgium
55 A3 Stadil Fjord lag. Denmark
68 E1 Stadskanaal canal Netherlands
68 E2 Stadskanaal Netherlands
74 E2 Stadtallendorf Germany
75 F4 Stadtbergen Germany
72 E3 Stadthagen Germany
75 G2 Stadtilm Germany
74 B2 Stadtkyll Germany
74 F2 Stadtlauringen Germany
72 B4 Stadtlohn Germany
72 E4 Stadtoldendorf Germany
75 G2 Stadtroda Germany
81 H3 Stadtschlaining Austria
83 D1 Stäfa Switzerland
66 B4 Staffa i. Scotland U.K.
55 F4 Staffanstorp Sweden
83 G1 Staffelsee l. Germany
75 F2 Staffelstein Germany
106 D4 Staffora r. Italy
62 D2 Stafford England U.K.
146 E5 Stafford Virginia U.S.A.
62 D2 Staffordshire div. England U.K.
22 D2 Stagen Indonesia
108 A5 Stagno di Cabras l. Sardegna Italy
54 D3 Staicele Latvia
81 F3 Stainach Austria
65 G3 Staindrop England U.K.
63 F3 Staines England U.K.
81 G4 Stainz Austria
111 F6 Staiti Italy
79 M2 Stakčín Slovakia
66 D5 Stake, Hill of h. Scotland U.K.
51 F5 Stakhanov Ukraine
62 D4 Stalbridge England U.K.
82 C2 Stalden Switzerland
63 H2 Stalham England U.K.
58 B1 Stalheim Norway
Stalingrad see Volgograd
136 E3 Stalin, Mt mt. B.C. Canada
59 G2 Stallarholmen Sweden
59 F2 Ställdalen Sweden
77 L5 Stalowa Wola Poland
112 F2 Stâlpu Romania
147 G4 Stamford Connecticut U.S.A.
63 F2 Stamford England U.K.
147 F3 Stamford New York U.S.A.
15 E4 Stamford Queensland Australia
65 H4 Stamford Bridge England U.K.
65 G2 Stamfordham England U.K.
75 G4 Stammham Germany
Stampalia i. see Astypalaia
128 B3 Stampriet Namibia
80 B3 Stams Austria
56 D1 Stamsund Norway
150 E3 Stanberry Missouri U.S.A.
131 G3 Standerton South Africa
65 F4 Standish England U.K.
149 F4 Standish Michigan U.S.A.
144 C4 Stanford Kentucky U.S.A.
130 B7 Stanford South Africa
59 H3 Stånga Sweden
59 F3 Stångån r. Sweden
131 H4 Stanger South Africa
65 F3 Stanhope England U.K.
158 C1 Staniard Ck The Bahamas
112 G1 Stănilești Romania
77 L4 Stanin Poland
112 B2 Stanišić Yugoslavia
53 E3 Stanislav Ukraine
77 K3 Stanisławów Poland
112 D3 Stanke Dimitrov Bulgaria
78 C2 Staňkov Czech Rep.
65 G3 Stanley England U.K.
152 D2 Stanley Idaho U.S.A.
150 C1 Stanley N. Dakota U.S.A.
147 K1 Stanley New Brunswick Canada
65 E1 Stanley Scotland U.K.
13 F5 Stanley Tasmania Australia
148 B3 Stanley Wisconsin U.S.A.
171 E7 Stanley Falkland Is.
27 □ Stanley Hong Kong China
13 E5 Stanley, Mt h. Tasmania Australia
126 A4 Stanley, Mt mt. Uganda/Congo(Zaire)
38 B4 Stanley Reservoir resr India
65 G2 Stannington England U.K.
114 C4 Stanos Greece
45 R3 Stanovaya Rus. Fed.
47 H1 Stanovka Rus. Fed.
52 D3 Stanovoye Rus. Fed.
45 N4 Stanovoye Nagor'ye mts Rus. Fed.
45 O4 Stanovoy Khrebet mountain range Rus. Fed.
52 C3 Stanovoy Kolodez' Rus. Fed.
83 D2 Stans Switzerland
16 E4 Stansmore Ra. h. Western Australia Australia
63 G3 Stansted airport England U.K.
63 G3 Stansted Mountfitchet England U.K.
15 G6 Stanthorpe Queensland Australia
63 G2 Stanton England U.K.
146 B6 Stanton Kentucky U.S.A.
148 E4 Stanton Michigan U.S.A.
52 D3 Stantsiya Babarykino Rus. Fed.
80 B3 Stanzach Austria
68 E2 Staphorst Netherlands
63 G3 Staplehurst England U.K.
150 C3 Stapleton Nebraska U.S.A.
77 J4 Stąporków Poland
178 □2 Stappen c. Bjørnøya Arctic Ocean
52 B3 Star' Rus. Fed.
53 D1 Stara Basan' Ukraine
77 J4 Stara Błotnica Poland
77 K4 Starachowice Poland
75 K3 Stará Huť Czech Rep.
78 E1 Stara Kamienica Poland
76 G2 Stara Kiszewa Poland
77 L3 Stara Kornica Poland
76 E2 Stara Łubianka Poland
79 K2 Stará Ľubovňa Slovakia
79 J6 Stara Moravica Yugoslavia
107 J4 Stara Novalja Croatia
112 C2 Stara Pazova Yugoslavia
112 D3 Stara Planina mountain range Bulgaria/Yugoslavia
81 H5 Stara Pološćica Croatia
76 C3 Stara Rudnica Poland
76 C1 Stara Sil' Ukraine
53 B2 Stara Synyava Ukraine
53 B2 Stara Ushytsya Ukraine
114 C1 Staravina Macedonia
53 A1 Stara Vyzhivka Ukraine
52 H1 Staraya Rudka Rus. Fed.
50 D3 Staraya Russa Rus. Fed.
50 J4 Staraya Tumba Rus. Fed.
52 E1 Staraya Vichuga Rus. Fed.
112 E3 Stara Zagora Bulgaria
5 M5 Starbuck Island i. Kiribati
53 G3 Starchenkove Ukraine
112 F2 Starchiojd Romania
62 C4 Starcross England U.K.
76 C2 Stare Czarnowo Poland
76 D2 Stare Dąbrowa Poland
77 L2 Stare Dolistowo Poland
77 L2 Stare Juchy Poland
76 G3 Stare Miasto Poland
77 N6 Stare Selo Ukraine
76 E4 Stare Strącze Poland
76 D2 Stargard Szczeciński Szczecin Poland
77 N4 Stari Koshary Ukraine
52 B1 Staritsa Rus. Fed.
145 D6 Starke Florida U.S.A.
9 □1 Star Keys is Chatham Is New Zealand
151 F5 Starkville Mississippi U.S.A.
75 G5 Starnberg Germany
75 G5 Starnberger See l. Germany
47 K2 Staroaleyskoye Rus. Fed.
51 F5 Starobil's'k Ukraine
54 E5 Starobyn Belarus
52 A3 Starodub Rus. Fed.
73 L2 Starogard Poland
76 G2 Starogard Gdański Poland
53 B2 Starokostyantyniv Ukraine
53 C3 Starokozache Ukraine
52 D2 Staroletovo Rus. Fed.
51 F6 Starominskaya Rus. Fed.
53 G3 Staromlynivka Ukraine
112 F3 Staro Oryakhovo Bulgaria
53 G1 Starooskol'skoye Vdkhr. resr Rus. Fed.
112 F3 Staro Selo Bulgaria
52 E3 Staroseslavino Rus. Fed.
76 C4 Starosiedle Poland
46 E2 Starosubkhangulovo Rus. Fed.
53 F2 Starovirivka Ukraine
77 H4 Starowa Góra Poland
52 H2 Staroye Drozhzhanoye Rus. Fed.
52 A2 Staroye Istomino Rus. Fed.
52 G2 Staroye Shaygovo Rus. Fed.
52 G2 Staroye-Sindrovo Rus. Fed.
52 G3 Staroye Slavkino Rus. Fed.
52 E3 Staroyur'yevo Rus. Fed.
77 H3 Starożeby Poland
52 D2 Starozhilovo Rus. Fed.
62 C4 Start Bay b. England U.K.
62 C4 Start Point pt England U.K.
77 M4 Stary Brus Poland
77 H2 Stary Dzierzgoń Poland
76 D4 Stary Kisielin Poland
77 H3 Stary Kobrzyniec Poland
77 K3 Stary Lubotyń Poland
77 K4 Stary Mirów Poland
75 J3 Starý Plzenec Czech Rep.
79 K2 Starý Smokovec Slovakia
77 K3 Stary Szelków Poland
53 G1 Starytsya Ukraine
54 F5 Staryya Darohi Belarus
31 E2 Staryy Chindant Rus. Fed.
52 H3 Staryy Chirchim Rus. Fed.
52 H2 Staryye Aybesi Rus. Fed.
53 G3 Staryy Krym Ukraine
31 F1 Staryy Olov Rus. Fed.
53 G1 Staryy Oskol Rus. Fed.
53 B2 Staryy Ostropil' Ukraine
77 L6 Staryy Sambir Ukraine
73 G4 Staßfurt Germany
77 K5 Staszów Poland
146 E4 State College Pennsylvania U.S.A.
145 D5 Statesboro Georgia U.S.A.
145 D5 Statesville N. Carolina U.S.A.
58 C2 Stathelle Norway
119 F3 Station No. 6 Sudan
82 G2 Statzendorf Austria
73 J4 Stauchitz Germany
74 D2 Staufenberg Germany
74 C5 Staufen im Breisgau Germany
80 B2 Staufersberg h. Germany
146 D5 Staunton Virginia U.S.A.
83 F2 Stausee Gepatsch l. Austria
80 D3 Stausee Mooserboden l. Austria
58 A2 Stavanger Norway
63 E1 Staveley England U.K.
69 D4 Stavelot Belgium
112 E3 Stavertsi Bulgaria
53 D3 Stavkove Ukraine
77 N4 Stavky Ukraine
55 C4 Stavns Fjord b. Denmark
68 D2 Stavoren Netherlands
55 C4 Stavreshoved headland Denmark
115 E5 Stavronisi i. Greece
51 G6 Stavropol' Rus. Fed.
51 G6 Stavropol' div. Rus. Fed.
51 G6 Stavropol'skaya Vovyshennost' reg. Rus. Fed.
114 E2 Stavros Greece
114 F1 Stavroupoli Greece
59 H2 Stavsnäs Sweden
53 D2 Stavyshche Ukraine
15 E4 Stawell r. Queensland Australia
13 E4 Stawell Victoria Australia
77 J2 Stawiguda Poland
77 L2 Stawiski Poland
76 G4 Stawiszyn Poland
53 B3 Stayki Rus. Fed.
131 G4 Steadville South Africa
154 C2 Steamboat Nevada U.S.A.
152 F3 Steamboat Springs Colorado U.S.A.
114 B1 Steblevë Albania
53 D2 Stebliv Ukraine
77 M6 Stebnyk Ukraine
111 F4 Steccato Italy
75 K3 Štěchovice Czech Rep.
83 D1 Steckborn Switzerland
68 E1 Stedum Netherlands
80 D3 Steeg Austria
130 E3 Steekdorings South Africa
140 B2 Steel r. Ontario Canada
179 B2 Steele I. i. Antarctica
131 F2 Steelpoort r. South Africa
131 H2 Steelpoort South Africa
11 □1 Steel's Pt pt Norfolk I. Pacific Ocean
146 E4 Steelton Pennsylvania U.S.A.
68 C3 Steenbergen Netherlands
131 H2 Steenkampsberg mts South Africa
136 F3 Steen River Alberta Canada
152 C3 Steens Mt. mt. Oregon U.S.A.
135 N2 Steenstrup Gletscher gl. Greenland
86 B2 Steenvoorde France
68 E2 Steenwijk Netherlands
62 C3 Steep Holm i. England U.K.
65 G4 Steeton England U.K.
81 H5 Štefanje Croatia
179 D4 Stefansson Bay b. Antarctica
134 H2 Stefansson I. i. N.W.T. Canada
53 C3 Ştefan Vodă Moldova
82 C2 Steffisburg Switzerland
52 D3 Stegalovka Rus. Fed.
55 E5 Stege Bugt b. Denmark
81 H3 Stegersbach Austria
68 E2 Steggerda Netherlands
79 M5 Stei Romania
81 G3 Steiermark div. Austria
74 F3 Steigerwald forest Germany
131 G1 Steilloopbrug South Africa
131 G1 Steilwater South Africa
75 G3 Stein Germany
69 D4 Stein Netherlands
82 C1 Stein Switzerland
83 D1 Steina r. Germany
75 G2 Steinach Germany
80 C3 Steinach am Brenner Austria
81 G2 Steinakirchen am Forst Austria
83 D1 Stein am Rhein Switzerland
74 E2 Steinau an der Straße Germany
137 K5 Steinbach Manitoba Canada
87 H2 Steinbach Germany
81 E3 Steinbach am Attersee Austria
75 G2 Steinbach am Wald Germany
81 F4 Steindorf am Ossiacher See Austria
74 C5 Steinen Germany
80 D3 Steinernes Meer mts Austria
80 E4 Steinfeld Austria
87 H3 Steinfeld Germany
72 D3 Steinfeld (Oldenburg) Germany
69 D5 Steinfort Luxembourg
72 C3 Steinfurt Germany
75 F5 Steingaden Germany
73 H1 Steinhagen Mecklenburg-Vorpommern Germany
72 D3 Steinhagen Nordrhein-Westfalen Germany
128 B3 Steinhausen Namibia
75 G4 Steinheim Germany
80 D2 Steinhöring Germany
72 E3 Steinhuder Meer l. Germany
56 C2 Steinkjer Norway
87 H2 Steinkopf h. Germany
130 A4 Steinkopf South Africa
155 H5 Steins New Mexico U.S.A.
56 C2 Steinsdalen Norway
73 K3 Steinsdorf Germany
58 A1 Steinsland Norway
130 D5 Stekaar South Africa
69 C3 Stekene Belgium
52 F2 Steksovo Rus. Fed.
130 E3 Stella South Africa
127 □5 Stella Matutina Réunion Indian Ocean
72 F2 Stelle Germany
130 B6 Stellenbosch South Africa
68 C3 Stellendam Netherlands
108 B2 Stello, Monte mt. Corse France
107 E2 Stelvio, Parco Nazionale dello nat. park Italy
106 E2 Stelvio, Passo dello pass Italy
59 G3 Stenåsa Sweden
76 E5 Stěnava r. Poland
87 E3 Stenay France
55 A3 Stenbjerg Denmark
59 G3 Stenbo Sweden
73 G3 Stendal Germany
54 C3 Stende Latvia
55 A4 Stenderup Denmark
59 G2 Stenhamra Sweden
12 D3 Stenhouse Bay S. Australia Australia
27 □ Stenhouse, Mt h. Hong Kong China
66 E4 Stenhousemuir Scotland U.K.
107 E2 Stenico Italy
114 E4 Steni Dirfios Greece
55 D4 Stenlille Denmark
55 E4 Stenløse Denmark
66 E2 Stenness, Loch of l. Scotland U.K.
115 D5 Steno Greece
115 E7 Steno Antikythiro chan. Greece
115 D6 Steno Elafonisou chan. Greece
115 B4 Steno Ithakis chan. Greece
115 F5 Steno Kafireos chan. Greece
113 F6 Steno Karpathou chan. Greece
113 F7 Steno Kasou chan. Greece
115 F5 Steno Keas chan. Greece
115 F6 Steno Kimolou-Sifnou chan. Greece
115 F5 Steno Kythnou chan. Greece
115 E5 Steno Petasi chan. Greece
115 F6 Steno Polyiagou-Folegandrou chan. Greece
115 F5 Steno Serifou chan. Greece
115 F5 Steno Sifnou chan. Greece
59 F4 Stenshuvuds Nationalpark Sweden
55 E5 Stensved Denmark
58 D2 Stenungsund Sweden
77 N5 Stenyatyn Ukraine
77 N5 Stenzharychi Ukraine
53 B1 Stepan' Ukraine
Stepanakert see Xankändi
114 C1 Stepanci Macedonia
53 B1 Stepanivka Khmel'nyts'kyy Ukraine
53 F1 Stepanivka Sumy Ukraine
53 F3 Stepanivka Persha Ukraine
52 E1 Stepantsevo Rus. Fed.
73 G2 Stepenitz r. Germany
80 D2 Stephansposching Germany
137 K5 Stephen Minnesota U.S.A.
8 D4 Stephens, Cape c. New Zealand
8 D4 Stephens I. i. New Zealand
148 D3 Stephenson Michigan U.S.A.
136 C3 Stephens Passage chan. Alaska U.S.A.
139 J4 Stephenville Newfoundland Canada
151 D5 Stephenville Texas U.S.A.
52 A3 Stepne Ukraine
76 E2 Stepnica Poland
47 H2 Stepnogorsk Kazakhstan
53 G3 Stepnohirs'k Ukraine
51 H5 Stepnoye Rus. Fed.
112 C3 Stepojevac Yugoslavia
47 G4 Step' Shaidara plain Kazakhstan
7 □13 Steps Pt pt American Samoa Pacific Ocean
52 B1 Sterpurino Rus. Fed.
77 L3 Sterdyń Osada Poland
114 D4 Sterea Ellas div. Greece
131 G2 Sterk r. South Africa
131 G4 Sterkfontein Dam dam South Africa
131 G2 Sterkrivierdam dam South Africa
131 F5 Sterkspruit South Africa
131 F5 Sterkstroom South Africa
131 G2 Sterkwater South Africa
77 K1 Sterławki-Wielkie Poland
152 G3 Sterling Colorado U.S.A.
148 C5 Sterling Illinois U.S.A.
150 C2 Sterling N. Dakota U.S.A.
155 G2 Sterling Utah U.S.A.
130 C5 Sterling South Africa
151 C6 Sterling City Texas U.S.A.
149 F4 Sterling Hgts Michigan U.S.A.
46 E2 Sterlitamak Rus. Fed.
73 G2 Sternberg Germany
78 G2 Šternberk Czech Rep.
115 F7 Sternes Greece
72 E1 Sterup Germany
76 E3 Stęszew Poland
78 D1 Štětí Czech Rep.
136 G4 Stettler Alberta Canada
148 D2 Steuben Michigan U.S.A.
146 C4 Steubenville Ohio U.S.A.
63 F3 Stevenage England U.K.
8 D4 Stevens, Mt mt. New Zealand
12 C1 Stevenson Cr. watercourse S. Australia Australia
137 K4 Stevenson L. l. Manitoba Canada
148 C3 Stevens Point Wisconsin U.S.A.
64 D2 Stevenston Scotland U.K.
134 D3 Stevens Village Alaska U.S.A.
55 E4 Stevns Klint cliff Denmark
136 B2 Stewart r. Yukon Terr. Canada
136 D3 Stewart B.C. Canada
14 C1 Stewart, C. headland Northern Terr. Australia
136 B2 Stewart Crossing Yukon Terr. Canada
171 B7 Stewart, I. i. Chile
9 A7 Stewart Island i. New Zealand
135 K3 Stewart Lake l. N.W.T. Canada
66 D5 Stewarton Scotland U.K.
159 □1 Stewart Town Jamaica
148 A4 Stewartville Minnesota U.S.A.
72 E3 Steyerberg Germany
131 F3 Steynrus South Africa
131 E5 Steynsburg South Africa
81 F3 Steyr r. Austria
81 F2 Steyr Austria
81 F3 Steyr-Land div. Austria
130 E6 Steytlerville South Africa
76 F1 Stężyca Poland
107 F5 Stia Italy
79 H3 Štiavnické Vrchy mts Slovakia
62 B4 Stibb Cross England U.K.
68 D1 Stiens Netherlands
109 J4 Stigliano Italy
136 C3 Stikine r. Canada/U.S.A.
136 C3 Stikine Ranges mountain range B.C. Canada
130 C7 Stilbaai South Africa
131 F3 Stilfontein South Africa
65 G3 Stillington England U.K.
64 B4 Stillorgan Rep. of Ireland
148 A3 Stillwater Minnesota U.S.A.
154 C2 Stillwater Nevada U.S.A.
151 D4 Stillwater Oklahoma U.S.A.
153 C4 Stillwater Ra. mountain range Nevada U.S.A.
111 F4 Stilo Italy
111 F4 Stilo, Punta pt Italy
63 F2 Stilton England U.K.
112 C3 Štimlje Macedonia
108 A4 Stintino Sardegna Italy
112 D4 Štip Macedonia
87 F3 Stiring-Wendel France
66 D4 Stirling div. Scotland U.K.
12 D3 Stirling S. Australia Australia
66 E4 Stirling Scotland U.K.
154 B2 Stirling City California U.S.A.
14 B3 Stirling Cr. r. Northern Terr. Australia
17 B6 Stirling, Mt h. Western Australia Australia
17 B7 Stirling Ra. mountain range Western Australia Australia
17 B7 Stirling Range Nat. Park nat. park Western Australia Australia
106 D4 Stirone r. Italy
56 C3 Stjørdalshalsen Norway
66 D4 Stob Choire Claurigh mt. Scotland U.K.
78 C1 Stochov Czech Rep.
75 G4 Stockach Germany
59 E4 Stockamöllan Sweden
73 F2 Stockelsdorf Germany
81 H2 Stockerau Austria
75 G2 Stockheim Germany
59 G2 Stockholm div. Sweden
147 J1 Stockholm Maine U.S.A.
59 H2 Stockholm Sweden
82 C2 Stockhorn mt. Switzerland
13 F3 Stockinbingal New South Wales Australia
131 F1 Stockpoort South Africa
65 F4 Stockport England U.K.
65 F3 Stocks Res. resr England U.K.
74 D3 Stockstadt am Rhein Germany
63 G3 Stocks, The England U.K.
154 B3 Stockton California U.S.A.
150 D4 Stockton Kansas U.S.A.
155 F1 Stockton Utah U.S.A.
148 B2 Stockton I. i. Wisconsin U.S.A.
151 E4 Stockton L. l. Missouri U.S.A.
65 G3 Stockton-on-Tees div. England U.K.
65 G3 Stockton-on-Tees England U.K.
147 J2 Stockton Springs Maine U.S.A.
77 K4 Stoczek Łukowski Poland
78 C2 Stod Czech Rep.
57 E3 Stöde Sweden
25 C4 Stœng Sângke r. Cambodia
25 D4 Stœng Sên r. Cambodia
25 D4 Stœng Trêng Cambodia
66 C2 Stoer, Point of pt Scotland U.K.
131 G2 Stoffberg South Africa
114 B1 Stogovo Planina mountain range Macedonia
55 B3 Stoholm Denmark
62 D1 Stoke-on-Trent div. England U.K.
62 D1 Stoke-on-Trent England U.K.
62 C4 Stoke St Mary England U.K.
62 D2 Stokesay England U.K.
65 G3 Stokesley England U.K.
9 E4 Stokes, Mt mt. New Zealand
13 E5 Stokes Pt pt Tasmania Australia
14 B2 Stokes Ra. h. Northern Terr. Australia
53 A1 Stokhid r. Ukraine
56 L7 Stokkseyri Iceland
56 D2 Stokkvågen Norway
56 D1 Stokmarknes Norway
81 E4 Stol mt. Slovenia
104 F4 Stolac Bos.-Herz.
73 F4 Stolberg Germany
74 B2 Stolberg (Rheinland) Germany
76 F2 Stołczno Poland
79 K3 Stolica mt. Slovakia
53 B1 Stolin Belarus
75 H2 Stollberg Germany
76 G2 Stolno Poland
128 □3 Stoltenhoff I. i. Tristan da Cunha Atlantic Ocean
68 C3 Stolwijk Netherlands
72 E3 Stolzenau Germany
114 D3 Stomio Greece
109 J1 Stončica, Rt pt Croatia
62 D2 Stone England U.K.
62 D3 Stone England U.K.
141 G3 Stonecliffe Ontario Canada
147 F5 Stone Harbor New Jersey U.S.A.
66 F4 Stonehaven Scotland U.K.
15 E5 Stonehenge Queensland Australia
64 E2 Stonehouse Scotland U.K.
136 E3 Stone Mountain Prov. Park res. B.C. Canada
155 H3 Stoner Colorado U.S.A.
147 F4 Stone Ridge New York U.S.A.
128 □2 Stone Top B. b. St Helena Atlantic Ocean
137 K4 Stonewall Manitoba Canada
146 C5 Stonewall Jackson Lake l. W. Virginia U.S.A.
140 D5 Stoney Point Ontario Canada
60 K1 Stongfjorden Norway
147 J2 Stonington Maine U.S.A.
154 A2 Stonyford California U.S.A.
159 □1 Stony Hill Jamaica
128 □3 Stonyhill Pt pt Tristan da Cunha Atlantic Ocean
147 E3 Stony Pt pt New York U.S.A.
137 H3 Stony Rapids Saskatchewan Canada
77 J5 Stopnica Poland
55 B5 Stör r. Germany
55 A3 Stora r. Denmark
59 F2 Stora Åby Sweden
59 G2 Stora Ålö i. Sweden
59 G3 Stora Alvaret i. Sweden
59 G3 Stora Askö i. Sweden
59 E3 Stora Färgen l. Sweden
59 E2 Stora Gla l. Sweden
55 E2 Stora Horredssjön l. Sweden
56 E2 Stora Inlevatten l. Sweden
59 G3 Stora Karlsö i. Sweden
58 D2 Stora Le l. Sweden
59 H2 Stora Nassa skärgård is Sweden
56 E2 Stora Sjöfallets National Park nat. park Sweden
56 E2 Storavan l. Sweden
58 A2 Stord i. Norway
55 C4 Store Bælt chan. Denmark
58 A1 Storebø Norway
55 E5 Store Damme Denmark
58 B1 Store Granatunane mt. Norway
58 B1 Store Grånosi mt. Norway
55 E4 Store Heddinge Denmark
58 C1 Store Jukleeggi mt. Norway
59 E3 Store Moss Nationalpark nat. park Sweden
56 C3 Støren Norway
58 B2 Store Nup mt. Norway
58 B1 Store Shrekken mt. Norway
58 A1 Store Sotra i. Norway
58 B2 Store Urevatnet l. Norway
58 A1 Storfjellet mt. Norway
56 G1 Storfjordbotn Norway
178 □3 Storfjorden inlet Svalbard Arctic Ocean
58 C1 Storfjorden l. Norway
59 F2 Storfors Sweden
56 D2 Storforshei Norway
81 E5 Štorje Slovenia
56 D2 Storjord Norway
59 G1 Storjungfrun i. Sweden
59 E1 Stor Kallberget h. Sweden
58 B2 Storkarshei h. Norway
73 J3 Storkow Germany
13 F5 Storm Bay b. Tasmania Australia
131 F5 Stormberg mt. South Africa
131 F5 Stormberg mt. South Africa
131 F5 Stormberg r. South Africa
131 F5 Stormberg South Africa
150 E3 Storm Lake Iowa U.S.A.
130 D6 Stormsrivier South Africa
141 K4 Stornoway Québec Canada
66 B2 Stornoway Scotland U.K.
107 E3 Storo Italy
50 K2 Storozhevsk Rus. Fed.
53 A2 Storozhynets' Ukraine
63 F4 Storrington England U.K.
147 G4 Storrs Connecticut U.S.A.
66 B3 Storr, The h. Scotland U.K.
56 E2 Storseleby Sweden
58 D1 Storsjøen l. Norway
59 G1 Storsjön l. Sweden
56 D3 Storsjön l. Sweden
58 B1 Storskavlen mt. Norway
57 C3 Storskrymten mt. Norway
56 F1 Storslett Norway
55 D5 Storstrøm div. Denmark
55 D5 Storstrømmen chan. Denmark
63 G3 Stort r. England U.K.
68 D1 Stortemelk chan. Netherlands
56 E2 Storuman l. Sweden
56 E2 Storuman Sweden
59 G1 Storvik Sweden
55 C2 Storvorde Denmark
59 G2 Storvreta Sweden
63 F2 Stotfold England U.K.
75 F5 Stötten am Auerberg Germany
55 B4 Stouby Denmark
148 C4 Stoughton Wisconsin U.S.A.
69 D4 Stoumont Belgium
63 H3 Stour r. England U.K.
63 G3 Stour r. England U.K.
63 E2 Stour r. England U.K.
62 D2 Stourbridge England U.K.
62 D2 Stourport-on-Severn England U.K.
138 B3 Stout L. l. Ontario Canada
55 B3 Støvring Denmark
66 F5 Stow Scotland U.K.
54 E5 Stowbtsy Belarus
147 F4 Stowe Pennsylvania U.S.A.
63 G2 Stowmarket England U.K.
63 E3 Stow-on-the-Wold England U.K.
77 N5 Stoyaniv Ukraine
107 G3 Stra Italy
73 H4 Straach Germany
131 F2 Straatsdrif South Africa
67 D2 Strabane Northern Ireland U.K.
64 C1 Strachur Scotland U.K.
77 N1 Stračiūnai Lithuania
76 E2 Strączno Poland
67 D3 Stradbally Rep. of Ireland
63 H2 Stradbroke England U.K.
106 D3 Stradella Italy
63 G2 Stradishall England U.K.
64 A4 Stradone Rep. of Ireland
63 G2 Stradsett England U.K.
72 B4 Straelen Germany
13 F5 Strahan Tasmania Australia
155 G3 Straight Cliffs cliff Utah U.S.A.
69 D5 Straimont Belgium
108 A3 Strait of Bonifacio str. France/Italy
63 H4 Strait of Dover str. France/U.K.
136 E5 Strait of Georgia chan. B.C. Canada
111 H2 Strait of Otranto str. Albania/Italy
158 B2 Straits of Florida str. The Bahamas/U.S.A.
78 C2 Strakonice Czech Rep.
112 F3 Straldzha Bulgaria
81 G3 Strallegg Austria
73 J1 Stralsund Germany
82 C3 Strambino Italy
69 D3 Stramproy Netherlands
130 B7 Strand South Africa
56 B3 Stranda Norway
58 B1 Strandavatnet l. Norway
145 E7 Strangers Cay i. The Bahamas
67 F2 Strangford Northern Ireland U.K.
67 F2 Strangford Lough inlet Rep. of Ireland
59 G2 Strängnäs Sweden
14 C2 Strangways r. Northern Terr. Australia
64 B2 Stranocum Northern Ireland U.K.
67 D2 Stranorlar Rep. of Ireland
66 C6 Stranraer Scotland U.K.
110 B5 Strasatti Sicilia Italy
87 G4 Strasbourg Bas-Rhin France
87 G4 Strasbourg-Entzheim airport France
146 D5 Strasburg Virginia U.S.A.
73 J2 Strasburg Germany
112 G1 Strășeni div. Moldova
53 C3 Strășeni Moldova
81 F4 Straßburg Austria
69 E5 Strassen Luxembourg
81 G2 Straßengel Austria
81 H2 Strasshof an der Norbahn Austria
80 E3 Straßwalchen Austria
140 E5 Stratford Ontario Canada
151 C4 Stratford Texas U.S.A.
13 F4 Stratford Victoria Australia
148 B3 Stratford Wisconsin U.S.A.
8 E3 Stratford New Zealand
63 E2 Stratford-upon-Avon England U.K.
12 D3 Strathalbyn S. Australia Australia
66 D5 Strathaven Scotland U.K.
64 D2 Strathblane Scotland U.K.
66 F3 Strathbogie reg. Scotland U.K.
66 D3 Strathcarron v. Scotland U.K.
136 D5 Strathcona Prov. Park nat. park B.C. Canada
66 D3 Strathconon v. Scotland U.K.
66 D3 Strath Dearn v. Scotland U.K.
65 E1 Strath Earn v. Scotland U.K.
66 D2 Strath Fleet v. Scotland U.K.
66 D3 Strathglass v. Scotland U.K.
66 E2 Strath Halladale v. Scotland U.K.
66 D2 Strathmore r. Scotland U.K.
136 G4 Strathmore Alberta Canada
66 D2 Strathnaver v. Scotland U.K.
136 E4 Strathnaver B.C. Canada
66 E2 Strath of Kildonan v. Scotland U.K.
140 E5 Strathroy Ontario Canada
66 E3 Strathspey v. Scotland U.K.
65 E1 Strath Tay v. Scotland U.K.
66 E2 Strathy Scotland U.K.
66 D2 Strathy Point pt Scotland U.K.
66 D4 Strathyre Scotland U.K.
114 E2 Stratoni Greece
114 E2 Stratoniki Greece
114 C4 Stratos Greece
62 B4 Stratton England U.K.
147 H2 Stratton Maine U.S.A.
63 E3 Stratton St Margaret England U.K.
75 H4 Straubing Germany
56 L6 Straumnes pt Iceland
73 K4 Straupitz Germany
73 J3 Strausberg Germany
73 F4 Straußfurt Germany
114 B2 Stravaj Albania
148 B4 Strawberry Point Iowa U.S.A.
155 G1 Strawberry Reservoir resr Utah U.S.A.
112 E3 Strazhitsa Bulgaria
81 F1 Stráž nad Nežárkou Czech Rep.
75 J3 Strážov Czech Rep.
79 L3 Strážske Slovakia
12 C3 Streaky Bay b. S. Australia Australia
12 C3 Streaky Bay S. Australia Australia
63 E3 Streatley England U.K.
148 C5 Streator Illinois U.S.A.
78 D2 Středočeský div. Czech Rep.
79 J3 Středoslovenský div. Slovakia

62 D3 Street *England* U.K.
112 D2 Strehaia Romania
73 J4 Strehla Germany
78 C1 Střela r. Czech Rep.
114 B2 Strelcë Albania
112 E3 Strelcha Bulgaria
52 D3 Strelets Rus. Fed.
53 G1 Streletskoye Rus. Fed.
81 H1 Střelice Czech Rep.
45 R3 Strelka Rus. Fed.
16 B4 Strelley *Western Australia* Australia
50 F1 Strel'na r. Rus. Fed.
81 H3 Strem Austria
53 C1 Stremyhorod Ukraine
54 D3 Strenči Latvia
80 B3 Strengen Austria
106 C3 Stresa Italy
63 G2 Stretham *England* U.K.
111 E4 Stretta di Messina str. Italy
55 □1 Streymoy i. Faeroes
44 J3 Strezhevoy Rus. Fed.
78 B2 Stříbro Czech Rep.
66 F3 Strichen *Scotland* U.K.
6 □1 Strickland r. P.N.G.
140 E2 Strickland *Ontario* Canada
81 H4 Štrigova Croatia
68 C3 Strijen Netherlands
75 L3 Strimilov Czech Rep.
114 E2 Strimonas r. Greece
81 G5 Strmec Croatia
81 E3 Strobl Austria
55 E4 Strøby Egede Denmark
173 F6 Stroeder Argentina
115 C5 Strofades i. Greece
114 E4 Strofylia Greece
80 C2 Strogen r. Germany
53 C3 Stroieşti Moldova
53 G1 Stroitel' Rus. Fed.
67 C3 Strokestown Rep. of Ireland
66 E2 Stroma, Island of i. *Scotland* U.K.
111 E4 Strombolicchio, Isola i. Italy
111 E4 Stromboli, Isola i. Italy
66 C3 Stromeferry *Scotland* U.K.
66 E2 Stromness *Scotland* U.K.
171 □ Stromness *S. Georgia* Atlantic Ocean
150 D3 Stromsburg *Nebraska* U.S.A.
58 D2 Strömstad Sweden
56 D3 Strömsund Sweden
64 D1 Stronachlachar *Scotland* U.K.
83 E3 Strone r. Italy
111 G3 Strongoli Italy
146 C4 Strongsville *Ohio* U.S.A.
115 F6 Strongyli i. Greece
66 F1 Stronsay i. *Scotland* U.K.
66 F1 Stronsay Firth chan. *Scotland* U.K.
81 H2 Stronsdorf Austria
66 C4 Strontian *Scotland* U.K.
79 L2 Stropkov Slovakia
81 F2 Stropnice r. Czech Rep.
83 D3 Stroppiana Italy
91 F4 Stroppo Italy
62 D3 Stroud *England* U.K.
13 G3 Stroud Road *New South Wales* Australia
147 F4 Stroudsburg *Pennsylvania* U.S.A.
114 C1 Strovija Macedonia
55 A3 Struer Denmark
114 B1 Struga Macedonia
54 F2 Strugi-Krasnyye Rus. Fed.
130 C7 Struis Bay South Africa
67 D2 Strule r. *Northern Ireland* U.K.
75 F3 Strullendorf Germany
114 E1 Struma r. Bulgaria
62 A2 Strumble Head headland *Wales* U.K.
114 D1 Strumeshnitsa r. Bulgaria
114 D1 Strumica r. Macedonia
114 D1 Strumica Macedonia
52 D1 Strunino Rus. Fed.
81 F1 Strunkovice nad Blanicí Czech Rep.
130 D4 Strydenburg South Africa
131 E3 Strydpoort South Africa
131 G2 Strydpoortberg mt. South Africa
77 H4 Stryków Poland
114 E1 Strymoniko Greece
57 B3 Stryn Norway
53 D3 Stryukove Ukraine
79 N2 Stryy r. Ukraine
77 M6 Stryy Ukraine
53 C2 Stryzhavka Ukraine
76 E5 Strzegom Poland
76 E5 Strzegomka r. Poland
77 J3 Strzegowo-Osada Poland
77 H3 Strzelce Poland
76 D3 Strzelce Krajeńskie Poland
76 G5 Strzelce Opolskie Poland
77 H4 Strzelce Wielkie Poland
12 E2 Strzelecki Cr. watercourse *S. Australia* Australia
14 C4 Strzelecki, Mt h. *Northern Terr.* Australia
76 F5 Strzelin Poland
76 G3 Strzelno Poland
77 K6 Strzyżów Poland
145 D7 Stuart *Florida* U.S.A.
146 C6 Stuart *Virginia* U.S.A.
14 C4 Stuart Bluff Ra. mountain range *Northern Terr.* Australia
136 E4 Stuart Lake l. *B.C.* Canada
9 A6 Stuart Mts mts New Zealand
12 C2 Stuart Ra. h. *S. Australia* Australia
146 D5 Stuarts Draft *Virginia* U.S.A.
80 C3 Stubaier Alpen mountain range Austria
80 C3 Stubaital v. Austria
81 F3 Stubalpe mt. Austria
55 E5 Stubbekøbing Denmark
55 C3 Stubbe Sø l. Denmark
10 □2 Stubbings Pt pt *Christmas I.* Indian Ocean
63 E4 Stubbington *England* U.K.
83 F2 Stuben Austria
81 G3 Stubenberg Austria
64 D1 Stuchd an Lochain mt. *Scotland* U.K.
73 L2 Stuchowo Poland
81 G1 Studená Czech Rep.
52 H1 Studenka Rus. Fed.
63 F3 Studham *England* U.K.
9 C6 Studholme Junction New Zealand
63 E2 Studley *England* U.K.
56 E3 Studsviken Sweden
151 C6 Study Butte *Texas* U.S.A.
83 D1 Stühlingen Germany
72 D2 Stuhr Germany
137 L4 Stull L. l. *Manitoba/Ontario* Canada
80 C3 Stumm Austria
25 D4 Stung Chinit r. Cambodia
52 D2 Stupino Rus. Fed.
109 J1 Stupišće, Rt pt Croatia
77 J2 Stupsk Poland
106 C3 Stura r. Italy
82 C3 Stura di Ala r. Italy
106 B4 Stura di Demonte r. Italy
82 C3 Stura di Lanzo r. Italy
82 C3 Stura di Viù r. Italy
179 A6 Sturge I. i. Antarctica
148 D2 Sturgeon r. *Michigan* U.S.A.
137 K4 Sturgeon Bay b. *Manitoba* Canada
148 E3 Sturgeon Bay b. *Michigan* U.S.A.
148 D3 Sturgeon Bay *Wisconsin* U.S.A.
148 D3 Sturgeon Bay Canal chan. *Wisconsin* U.S.A.
141 F3 Sturgeon Falls *Ontario* Canada
138 B3 Sturgeon L. l. *Ontario* Canada
140 B2 Sturgeon River *Ontario* Canada
144 C4 Sturgis *Kentucky* U.S.A.
148 E5 Sturgis *Michigan* U.S.A.
150 C2 Sturgis *S. Dakota* U.S.A.
62 D4 Sturminster Newton *England* U.K.
79 H4 Štúrovo Slovakia
63 H3 Sturry *England* U.K.
16 D3 Sturt Cr. watercourse *Western Australia* Australia
14 E6 Sturt Desert desert *Queensland* Australia
13 E2 Sturt, Mt h. *New South Wales* Australia
12 E2 Sturt Nat. Park nat. park *New South Wales* Australia
14 C3 Sturt Plain plain *Northern Terr.* Australia
59 E4 Sturup airport Sweden
87 G3 Sturzelbronn France
131 F6 Stutterheim South Africa
74 E3 Stuttgart div. *Baden-Württemberg* Germany
151 F5 Stuttgart *Arkansas* U.S.A.
74 E4 Stuttgart Germany
56 L6 Stykkishólmur Iceland
114 D4 Stylida Greece
51 C5 Styr r. Ukraine
169 G3 Suaçuí Grande r. Brazil
119 G4 Suakin Sudan
68 E1 Suameer Netherlands
125 D5 Suana Congo(Zaire)
99 F1 Suances Spain
33 H3 Su'ao Taiwan
128 D3 Sua Pan salt pan Botswana
156 C2 Suaqui Mexico
153 E6 Suaqui Gde Mexico
173 G1 Suardi Argentina
163 D2 Suata r. Venezuela
54 D4 Subačius Lithuania
22 A3 Subang Indonesia
37 G4 Subankhata India
37 H3 Subansiri r. India
109 E1 Subasio, Monte mt. Italy
54 D3 Subate Latvia
119 G2 Şubayḩah Saudi Arabia
126 D2 Şubayḩī reg. Yemen
107 F5 Subbiano Italy
112 E1 Subcetate Romania
119 G3 Şubḩ, J. mts Saudi Arabia
109 F3 Subiaco Italy
25 E7 Subi Besar i. Indonesia
76 G1 Subkowy Poland
79 J5 Subotica Yugoslavia
126 D2 Subucle mt. Eritrea
92 D3 Suc-au-May h. France
112 F1 Suceava Romania
166 D1 Sucesso Brazil
112 E1 Suceviţa Romania
77 H6 Sucha Beskidzka Poland
76 D2 Suchań Poland
78 D3 Suchdol nad Lužnicí Czech Rep.
77 J4 Suchedniów Poland
82 B2 Suchet mt. Switzerland
77 M2 Suchowola Poland
77 L3 Suchożebry Poland
103 C7 Sucina Spain
67 C3 Suck r. Rep. of Ireland
73 G2 Suckow Germany
164 C3 Sucre Bolivia
162 C2 Sucre Colombia
162 D3 Sucuaro Colombia
163 F5 Sucunduri r. Brazil
168 B4 Sucuriú r. Brazil
124 B3 Sud div. Cameroon
51 E6 Sudak Ukraine
116 G4 Sudan country Africa
50 G3 Suday Rus. Fed.
52 C3 Sudbishchi Rus. Fed.
63 G2 Sudbury *England* U.K.
140 E3 Sudbury *Ontario* Canada
126 B3 Sudd swamp Sudan
163 F2 Suddie Guyana
73 F2 Sude r. Germany
72 E1 Süderbrarup Germany
72 E1 Süderhastedt Germany
72 D1 Süderlügum Germany
72 D1 Süderoog i. Germany
76 D5 Sudety mountain range Czech Rep./Poland
52 B3 Sudimir Rus. Fed.
50 G3 Sudislavl' Rus. Fed.
147 F5 Sudlersville *Maryland* U.S.A.
68 E3 Südlohn Germany
72 C3 Süd-Nord-Kanal canal Germany
52 E2 Sudogda r. Rus. Fed.
52 E2 Sudogda Rus. Fed.
54 F3 Sudomskiye Vysoty h. Rus. Fed.
52 A3 Sudost' r. Rus. Fed.
124 A3 Sud-Ouest div. Cameroon
127 □4 Sud Ouest, Pt pt Mauritius
77 M6 Sudova Vyshnya Ukraine
43 B5 Sudr Egypt
56 M6 Suðurland div. Iceland
55 □1 Suðuroy i. Faeroes
55 □1 Suðuroyarfjørður chan. Faeroes
53 F1 Sudzha r. Rus. Fed.
53 F1 Sudzha Rus. Fed.
124 E2 Sue watercourse Sudan
103 C5 Sueca Spain
112 E3 Sŭedinenie Bulgaria
108 B5 Suelli *Sardegna* Italy
89 G4 Suèvres France
43 B5 Suez Egypt
119 F1 Suez Canal canal Egypt
119 F2 Suez, Gulf of g. Egypt
63 G2 Suffolk div. *England* U.K.
146 E6 Suffolk *Virginia* U.S.A.
42 F2 Sūfiān Iran
148 C4 Sugar r. *Wisconsin* U.S.A.
147 H2 Sugarloaf Mt. mt. *Maine* U.S.A.
10 □4 Sugarloaf Pass. chan. *Lord Howe I.* Pacific Ocean
13 H3 Sugarloaf Pt pt *New South Wales* Australia
128 □2 Sugar Loaf Pt pt *St Helena* Atlantic Ocean
23 C4 Sugbuhan Point pt Philippines
22 A1 Sugi i. Indonesia
43 A1 Suğla Gölü l. Turkey
47 J5 Sugun China
23 A5 Sugut r. Malaysia
126 C4 Suguta r. Kenya
127 B5 Suguti B. b. Tanzania
23 A5 Sugut, Tg pt Malaysia
112 E3 Suhaia Romania
30 C5 Suhait China
81 F5 Suha Krajina reg. Slovenia
41 J5 Şuḩār Oman
30 E3 Sühbaatar div. Mongolia
30 C2 Sühbaatar Mongolia
75 F2 Suhl Germany
73 F3 Suhlendorf Germany
82 D1 Suhr Switzerland
122 D5 Suhum Ghana
42 B2 Şuhut Turkey
36 B3 Sui Pakistan
166 B3 Suiá Missur r. Brazil
31 J3 Suibin China
33 G2 Suichang China
33 F3 Suichuan China
30 D5 Suide China
31 J3 Suifenhe China
36 B4 Suigam India
31 H3 Suihua China
32 C2 Suijiang China
31 H3 Suileng China
33 E3 Suining China
32 D2 Suining China
33 G1 Suining China
33 F1 Suiping China
86 D3 Suippe r. France
86 D3 Suippes France
67 D4 Suir r. Rep. of Ireland
28 K2 Suishō-tō i. Rus. Fed.
89 E3 Suisse Normande reg. France
33 G1 Suixi China
33 E4 Suixi China
33 F1 Sui Xian China
Sui Xian *see* Suizhou
32 D3 Suiyang China
31 G4 Suizhong China
33 F2 Suizhou China
30 C4 Suj China
36 C4 Sujangarh India
36 C2 Sujanpur India
36 B4 Sujawal Pakistan
22 A3 Sukabumi Indonesia
22 A3 Sukadana Indonesia
22 B2 Sukadana Indonesia
22 B2 Sukadana, Tk b. Indonesia
29 H5 Sukagawa Japan
22 B2 Sukaramai Indonesia
23 A5 Sukau Malaysia
31 H5 Sukchŏn North Korea
112 F3 Sukha Reka r. Bulgaria
30 C1 Sukhaya Rus. Fed.
52 B2 Sukhinichi Rus. Fed.
52 G1 Sukhobezvodnoye Rus. Fed.
77 N6 Sukhodil Ukraine
50 H2 Sukhona r. Rus. Fed.
24 B3 Sukhothai Thailand
31 H2 Sukhotino Rus. Fed.
52 B1 Sukhoverkovo Rus. Fed.
Sukhumi *see* Sokhumi
Sukkertoppen *see* Maniitsoq
50 E2 Sukkozero Rus. Fed.
36 B4 Sukkur Pakistan
38 C2 Sukma India
118 C2 Sūknah Libya
22 B3 Sukoharjo Indonesia
79 J5 Sükösd Hungary
36 C4 Sukri r. India
52 B1 Sukromlya Rus. Fed.
52 C1 Sukromny Rus. Fed.
128 B3 Sukses Namibia
28 D7 Sukumo Japan
58 A1 Sula i. Norway
53 E2 Sula r. Ukraine
36 B3 Sulaiman Ranges mountain range Pakistan
51 H7 Sulak r. Rus. Fed.
39 B3 Sūlār Iran
66 B1 Sula Sgeir i. *Scotland* U.K.
22 E2 Sulawesi i. Indonesia
22 D2 Sulawesi Selatan div. Indonesia
22 E1 Sulawesi Tengah div. Indonesia
58 B2 Suldalsvatnet l. Norway
76 D3 Sulechów Poland
76 D3 Sulęcin Poland
76 F3 Sulęcinek Poland
77 K3 Sulęcin Szlachecki Poland
76 F1 Suleczyno Poland
39 B1 Suledeh Iran
123 F5 Suleja Nigeria
77 H4 Sulejów Poland
77 K3 Sulejówek Poland
66 D1 Sule Skerry i. *Scotland* U.K.
76 D4 Sulików Poland
122 B5 Sulima Sierra Leone
112 G2 Sulina Romania
72 D3 Sulingen Germany
73 L2 Suliszewo Poland
56 D2 Sulitjelma Norway
57 H3 Sulkava Finland
162 A4 Sullana Peru
63 F4 Sullington *England* U.K.
150 F4 Sullivan *Missouri* U.S.A.
Sullivan I. i. *see* Lanbi Kyun
137 G4 Sullivan L. l. *Alberta* Canada
147 J1 Sully *Québec* Canada
62 C3 Sully *Wales* U.K.
89 H4 Sully-sur-Loire France
81 G4 Sulm r. Austria
76 F4 Sulmierzyce Poland
109 F2 Sulmona Italy
88 C4 Sulniac France
112 F4 Süloğlu Turkey
76 F4 Sułów Poland
151 E6 Sulphur *Louisiana* U.S.A.
151 E5 Sulphur Springs *Texas* U.S.A.
169 G4 Sul, Pico do mt. Brazil
140 D3 Sultan *Ontario* Canada
118 D1 Sultan Libya
Sultanabad *see* Arāk
42 C2 Sultanhanı Turkey
113 F4 Sultaniça Turkey
37 E4 Sultanpur India
23 B5 Sulu Archipelago is Philippines
37 H4 Sulung India
118 D1 Suluntah Libya
118 D1 Sulūq Libya
23 A4 Sulu Sea sea Philippines
47 G4 Sulutobe Kazakhstan
53 D1 Sulymivka Ukraine
80 C1 Sulz r. Germany
80 B1 Sulzach r. Germany
74 D4 Sulz am Neckar Germany
80 D2 Sulzbach r. Germany
74 E3 Sulzbach am Main Germany
74 E3 Sulzbach an der Murr Germany
80 A2 Sulzbach-Laufen Germany
75 G3 Sulzbach-Rosenberg Germany
74 C3 Sulzbach/Saar Germany
83 F1 Sulzberg Germany
179 A4 Sulzberger Bay b. Antarctica
112 C2 Šumadija reg. Yugoslavia
20 D6 Sumatera i. Indonesia
22 A2 Sumatera Selatan div. Indonesia
Sumatra i. *see* Sumatera
78 C2 Šumava mountain range Czech Rep.
78 C2 Šumava nat. park Czech Rep.
23 □2 Sumay *Guam* Pacific Ocean
22 D4 Sumba i. Indonesia
55 □1 Sumba Faeroes
39 C1 Sumbar r. Turkmenistan
22 D4 Sumbawa i. Indonesia
22 D4 Sumbawabesar Indonesia
127 B6 Sumbawanga Tanzania
164 B3 Sumbay Peru
125 B6 Sumbe Angola
102 B1 Sumbilla Spain
127 B6 Sumbu Zambia
127 B6 Sumbu Nat. Park nat. park Zambia
66 □2 Sumburgh *Scotland* U.K.
66 □2 Sumburgh Head headland *Scotland* U.K.
32 C2 Sumdo China
36 D2 Sumdo China/Jammu and Kashmir
166 E2 Sumé Brazil
81 H5 Šumećani Croatia
22 A3 Sumedang Indonesia
78 G5 Sümeg Hungary
124 E2 Sumeih Sudan
91 B5 Sumène France
22 C3 Sumenep Indonesia
Sumgait *see* Sumqayıt
27 P5 Sumisu-jima Japan
82 C1 Sumiswald Switzerland
31 E2 Sümiyn Bulag Mongolia
42 E2 Summēl Iraq
138 C3 Summer Beaver *Ontario* Canada
139 K4 Summerford *Newfoundland* Canada
148 D3 Summer I. i. *Michigan* U.S.A.
66 C2 Summer Isles is *Scotland* U.K.
139 H4 Summerside *Prince Edward I.* Canada
146 C5 Summersville *W. Virginia* U.S.A.
146 C5 Summersville Lake l. *W. Virginia* U.S.A.
8 F4 Summit h. New Zealand
148 E5 Summit Lake l. *Indiana* U.S.A.
136 E4 Summit Lake *B.C.* Canada
154 D2 Summit Mt mt. *Nevada* U.S.A.
148 A4 Sumner *Iowa* U.S.A.
9 D5 Sumner New Zealand
9 D5 Sumner, L. l. New Zealand
136 C3 Sumner Strait chan. *Alaska* U.S.A.
29 G5 Sumon-dake mt. Japan
28 E6 Sumoto Japan
22 D3 Sumpangbinangae Indonesia
78 F2 Šumperk Czech Rep.
24 B1 Sumprabum Myanmar
42 G1 Sumqayıt Azerbaijan
36 B4 Sumrahu Pakistan
50 E1 Sumskiy Posad Rus. Fed.
145 D5 Sumter *S. Carolina* U.S.A.
43 A5 Sumusta el Waqf Egypt
53 E1 Sumy div. Ukraine
53 F1 Sumy Ukraine
32 B2 Sumzom China
152 D2 Sun r. *Montana* U.S.A.
50 J3 Suna Rus. Fed.
28 H2 Sunagawa Japan
36 C3 Sunam India
37 G4 Sunamganj Bangladesh
30 A5 Sunan China
31 H5 Sunan North Korea
66 C4 Sunart, Loch inlet *Scotland* U.K.
152 E1 Sunburst *Montana* U.S.A.
146 B4 Sunbury *Ohio* U.S.A.
146 E4 Sunbury *Pennsylvania* U.S.A.
13 F4 Sunbury *Victoria* Australia
173 G1 Sunchales Argentina
80 D2 Sünching Germany
31 H5 Sunch'ŏn North Korea
31 H6 Sunch'ŏn South Korea
131 F2 Sun City South Africa
147 H3 Suncook *New Hampshire* U.S.A.
59 J1 Sund Finland
152 F2 Sundance *Wyoming* U.S.A.
37 G5 Sundarbans reg. Bangladesh/India
37 F5 Sundargarh India
36 D3 Sundarnagar India
175 M4 Sunda Trench sea feature Indian Ocean
130 E6 Sundays r. *Eastern Cape* South Africa
131 H4 Sundays r. *Kwazulu-Natal* South Africa
173 F3 Sundblad Argentina
58 A2 Sunde Norway
65 G3 Sunderland *England* U.K.
72 D4 Sundern (Sauerland) Germany
90 F1 Sundgau reg. France
22 B3 Sundoro, G. volcano Indonesia
59 H3 Sundre Sweden
141 F4 Sundridge *Ontario* Canada
55 B3 Sunds Denmark
57 E3 Sundsvall Sweden
131 H4 Sundumbili South Africa
30 D2 Sunduyka Rus. Fed.
127 C5 Sunga Tanzania
25 C7 Sungaiapit Indonesia
22 A1 Sungaiguntung Indonesia
25 C7 Sungaikabung Indonesia
22 B2 Sungaikakap Indonesia
22 A2 Sungailiat Indonesia
25 C7 Sungai Pahang r. Malaysia
20 D7 Sungaipenuh Indonesia
22 B1 Sungaipinyuh Indonesia
22 A2 Sungaiselan Indonesia
Sungari r. *see* Songhua
25 C6 Sungei Petani Malaysia
25 □ Sungei Seletar Res. resr Singapore
22 D3 Sungguminasa Indonesia
Sungqu *see* Songpan
22 A2 Sungsang Indonesia
124 C4 Sungu Congo(Zaire)
112 F3 Sungurlare Bulgaria
42 C1 Sungurlu Turkey
108 A4 Suni *Sardegna* Italy
104 F3 Sunja Croatia
37 F4 Sun Kosi r. Nepal
59 F1 Sunnansjö Sweden
56 C3 Sunndalsøra Norway
59 E2 Sunne Sweden
60 K1 Sunnfjord reg. Norway
58 A2 Sunnhordland reg. Norway
152 C2 Sunnyside *Washington* U.S.A.
154 A3 Sunnyvale *California* U.S.A.
29 G6 Suno-saki pt Japan
148 C4 Sun Prairie *Wisconsin* U.S.A.
165 E3 Sunsas, Sa de h. Bolivia
153 □1 Sunset Beach *Hawaii* U.S.A.
155 G4 Sunset Crater National Monument nat. park *Arizona* U.S.A.
45 N3 Suntar Rus. Fed.
39 E4 Suntsar Pakistan
152 D3 Sun Valley *Idaho* U.S.A.
31 H2 Sunwu China
122 D5 Sunyani Ghana
51 H7 Sunzha r. Rus. Fed.
56 G2 Suolijärvet l. Finland
148 C1 Suomi *Ontario* Canada
54 C1 Suomusjärvi Finland
56 H2 Suomussalmi Finland
28 C7 Suō-nada b. Japan
56 G3 Suonenjoki Finland
24 C2 Suong r. Laos
25 D5 Suŏng Cambodia
50 E2 Suoyarvi Rus. Fed.
38 A3 Supa India
155 F3 Supai *Arizona* U.S.A.
37 F4 Supaul India
86 C4 Superbe r. France
47 G5 Superfosfatnyy Uzbekistan
155 G5 Superior *Arizona* U.S.A.
150 D3 Superior *Nebraska* U.S.A.
148 A2 Superior *Wisconsin* U.S.A.
83 F3 Superiore, Lago l. Italy
157 G5 Superior, L. l. Mexico
148 B2 Superior, Lake l. Canada/U.S.A.
107 J4 Supertarska Draga Croatia
104 F4 Supetar Croatia
25 C4 Suphan Buri Thailand
42 E2 Süphan Daği mt. Turkey
109 F3 Supino Italy
53 D2 Supiy r. Ukraine
52 B3 Suponevo Rus. Fed.
179 B3 Support Force Glacier gl. Antarctica
77 M2 Supraśl Poland
51 G7 Sup'sa r. Georgia
31 H4 Supung North Korea
119 H4 Sūq al Inān Yemen
42 F4 Sūq ash Shuyūkh Iraq
33 G1 Suqian China
119 G3 Sūq Suwayq Saudi Arabia
126 □ Suqutrā i. Yemen
80 D3 Sur r. Germany
41 J5 Şūr Oman
52 H1 Sura r. Rus. Fed.
52 G3 Sura Rus. Fed.
36 A3 Surab Pakistan
22 C3 Surabaya Indonesia
52 G2 Suradeyevo Rus. Fed.
36 C3 Surajgarh India
39 D4 Sūrak Iran
22 B3 Surakarta Indonesia
22 D2 Suramana Indonesia
112 E2 Şura Mare Romania
90 D2 Suran r. France
43 D2 Şūrān Syria
79 H3 Šurany Slovakia
15 G5 Surat *Queensland* Australia
36 C5 Surat India
36 C3 Suratgarh India
25 B5 Surat Thani Thailand
51 E4 Surazh Rus. Fed.
15 F4 Surbiton *Queensland* Australia
7 □16 Sur, Cabo c. *Easter I.* Chile
42 F3 Sūrdāsh Iraq
112 F2 Surdila-Greci Romania
112 D1 Surduc Romania
112 D3 Surdulica Yugoslavia
69 E5 Sûre r. Germany/Luxembourg
36 B5 Surendranagar India
156 K7 Suretka Costa Rica
69 D5 Sûre, Vallée de la v. Luxembourg
154 B4 Surf *California* U.S.A.
92 B2 Surgères France
158 B2 Surgidero de Bata banó Cuba
44 J3 Surgut Rus. Fed.
68 E1 Surhuisterveen Netherlands
102 E3 Súria Spain
38 B2 Suriapet India
29 □1 Suribachi-yama h. Japan
23 C4 Surigao Philippines
23 C4 Surigao Str. chan. Philippines
25 C4 Surin Thailand
160 G3 Surinam country South America
127 □4 Surinam Mauritius
39 G2 Surkhab r. Afghanistan
37 E3 Surkhet Nepal
47 H5 Surkhob r. Tajikistan
118 B1 Surman Libya
39 C3 Surmāq Iran
42 E1 Sürmene Turkey
112 D4 Sŭrnitsa Bulgaria
52 F2 Surovatikha Rus. Fed.
51 G5 Surovikino Rus. Fed.
6 □2 Surprise, Î. i. *New Caledonia* Pacific Ocean
154 B3 Sur, Pt pt *California* U.S.A.
173 J4 Sur, Pta pt Argentina
100 C1 Surrazala r. Portugal
63 F3 Surrey div. *England* U.K.
146 E6 Surry *Virginia* U.S.A.
82 D1 Sursee Switzerland
83 D2 Surselva reg. Switzerland
52 G3 Sursk Rus. Fed.
52 H2 Surskoye Rus. Fed.
118 C1 Surt Libya
55 E2 Surte Sweden
56 L7 Surtsey i. Iceland
166 C1 Surubiú r. Brazil
42 D2 Sürüç Turkey
29 G6 Suruga-wan b. Japan
23 C5 Surup Philippines
72 C3 Surwold Germany
88 C4 Surzur France
42 F2 Şuşa Azerbaijan
106 B3 Susa Italy
28 C6 Susa Japan
109 J2 Sušac i. Croatia
118 D1 Sūsah Libya
107 J4 Susak i. Croatia
28 D7 Susaki Japan
29 E7 Susami Japan
39 B3 Sūsangerd Iran
50 G3 Susanino Rus. Fed.
154 B1 Susanville *California* U.S.A.
106 A3 Susa, Valle di v. Italy
83 F2 Susch Switzerland
53 B1 Suschany Ukraine
107 G3 Susegana Italy
42 D1 Suşehri Turkey
73 F1 Süsel Germany
78 C2 Šušice Czech Rep.
54 F3 Šuškova Latvia
25 B6 Suso Thailand
33 G2 Susong China
173 K1 Suspiro Brazil
147 E4 Susquehanna r. *Pennsylvania* U.S.A.
170 C1 Susques Argentina
139 G4 Sussex *New Brunswick* Canada
147 F4 Sussex *New Jersey* U.S.A.
69 D3 Susteren Netherlands
22 E2 Susua Indonesia
23 A5 Susul Malaysia
45 Q3 Susuman Rus. Fed.
42 B2 Susurluk Turkey
77 H2 Susz Poland
36 D2 Sutak India
154 C2 Sutcliffe *Nevada* U.S.A.
66 D2 Sutherland reg. *Scotland* U.K.
150 C3 Sutherland *Nebraska* U.S.A.
130 C6 Sutherland South Africa
36 C3 Sutlej r. Pakistan
43 B1 Sütlüce Turkey
108 E2 Sutri Italy
154 B2 Sutter Creek *California* U.S.A.
63 F2 Sutterton *England* U.K.
138 D3 Sutton r. *Ontario* Canada
63 G2 Sutton *England* U.K.
141 J4 Sutton *Québec* Canada
146 C5 Sutton *W. Virginia* U.S.A.
63 G2 Sutton Bridge *England* U.K.
63 E2 Sutton Coldfield *England* U.K.
63 E1 Sutton in Ashfield *England* U.K.
138 D3 Sutton L. l. *Ontario* Canada
146 C5 Sutton Lake l. *W. Virginia* U.S.A.
15 F4 Suttor r. *Queensland* Australia
28 H2 Suttsu Japan
30 C3 Suugant Mongolia
54 D2 Suure-Jaami Estonia
54 C2 Suuremõisa Estonia
54 C2 Suur-Pakri i. Estonia
54 C2 Suur Väin chan. Estonia
47 H4 Suusamyr Kyrgyzstan
6 □8 Suva Fiji
111 F4 Suvero, Capo c. Italy
53 C3 Suvorov Moldova
52 C2 Suvorov Rus. Fed.
112 G2 Suvorove Ukraine
112 F3 Suvorovo Bulgaria
5 L6 Suvurov Island i. *Cook Islands* Pacific Ocean
29 G5 Suwa Japan
22 C2 Suwakong Indonesia
77 L2 Suwałki div. Poland
77 L1 Suwalki Poland
77 L1 Suwalski Park Narodowy nat. park Poland
24 C4 Suwannaphum Thailand
145 D6 Suwannee r. *Florida* U.S.A.
119 H1 Suwayr well Saudi Arabia
43 C3 Suweilih Jordan
31 H5 Suwŏn South Korea
Su Xian *see* Suzhou
162 A4 Suyo Peru
47 G4 Suzak Kazakhstan
29 G5 Suzaka Japan
179 □ Suzanne, Pte pt *Kerguelen* Indian Ocean
52 E1 Suzdal' Rus. Fed.
52 B3 Suzemka Rus. Fed.
33 G1 Suzhou *Anhui* China
33 H2 Suzhou *Jiangsu* China
31 H4 Suzi r. China
29 F5 Suzu Japan
29 F6 Suzuka Japan
29 F5 Suzu-misaki pt Japan
47 K2 Suzun Rus. Fed.
107 E4 Suzzara Italy
59 F1 Svabensverk Sweden
56 G1 Særholthalvøya pen. Norway
178 □3 Svalbard is Arctic Ocean
55 F4 Svalöv Sweden
79 M3 Svalyava Ukraine
59 H2 Svanberga Sweden
58 D2 Svanesund Sweden
59 F3 Svängsta Sweden
52 B4 Svapa r. Rus. Fed.
56 F2 Svappavaara Sweden
59 F1 Svärdsjö Sweden
75 J4 Švareenbersky Canal canal Czech Rep.
59 F2 Svartå Sweden
59 F1 Svartälven r. Sweden
59 E2 Svartån r. *Värmland* Sweden
59 G2 Svartån r. *Västmanland* Sweden
55 □1 Svartbakstindur h. Faeroes
135 N2 Svartenhuk Halvø pen. Greenland
58 B1 Svartenibba mt. Norway
59 H2 Svartlöga-fjärden b. Sweden
51 F5 Svatove Ukraine
25 C4 Svay Chek Cambodia
25 D5 Svay Riĕng Cambodia
173 J3 S. Vazquez Uruguay
178 □3 Sveagruva *Svalbard* Arctic Ocean
55 D4 Svebølle Denmark
50 H3 Svecha Rus. Fed.
54 D4 Svėdasai Lithuania
57 D3 Sveg Sweden
58 A2 Sveio Norway
55 B3 Svejbæk Denmark
54 B4 Švėkšna Lithuania
57 B3 Svelgen Norway
56 C3 Svellingen Norway
58 D2 Svelvik Norway
52 B3 Sven' Rus. Fed.
54 D4 Švenčionėliai Lithuania
54 E4 Švenčionys Lithuania
55 C4 Svendborg Denmark
55 □2 Sveneke Denmark
59 E3 Svenljunga Sweden
56 E1 Svensby Norway
56 D3 Svenstavik Sweden
55 B3 Svenstrup *Nordjylland* Denmark
55 B4 Svenstrup *Sønderjylland* Denmark
77 M1 Šventežeris Lithuania
52 B2 Sverchkovo Rus. Fed.
46 F1 Sverdlovsk Rus. Fed.
Sverdlovsk *see* Yekaterinburg
135 J2 Sverdrup Channel chan. *N.W.T.* Canada
52 A4 Svesa Ukraine
109 H1 Sveta Andrija i. Croatia
81 H4 Sveta Marija Croatia
107 J4 Sveti Grgur i. Croatia
112 C4 Sveti Nikole Macedonia
78 E2 Světlá nad Sázavou Czech Rep.
27 P2 Svetlaya Rus. Fed.
27 Q2 Svetlodarskoye Rus. Fed.
44 K3 Svetlogorsk Rus. Fed.
54 B4 Svetlogorsk Rus. Fed.
51 G6 Svetlograd Rus. Fed.
54 B4 Svetlyy Rus. Fed.
46 F2 Svetlyy Rus. Fed.
51 H5 Svetlyy Yar Rus. Fed.
107 H3 Svetvinčenat Croatia
52 F2 Svezhen'kaya Rus. Fed.
77 N6 Svicha r. Ukraine
79 L2 Svidník Slovakia
78 C2 Švihov Czech Rep.
104 F4 Svilaja mts Croatia
112 C2 Svilajnac Yugoslavia
112 F4 Svilengrad Bulgaria
55 D4 Svinninge Denmark
50 E2 Svir' r. Rus. Fed.
54 E4 Svir Belarus
77 N6 Svirzh r. Ukraine
52 A4 Svisa r. Ukraine
52 F3 Svishchevka Rus. Fed.
112 E3 Svishtov Bulgaria
54 E5 Svislach r. Belarus
77 N2 Svislach *Hrodna* Belarus
54 E5 Svislach *Minsk* Belarus
71 K4 Svit Slovakia
78 F2 Svitava r. Czech Rep.
78 F2 Svitávka Czech Rep.
78 F2 Svitavy Czech Rep.
53 F2 Svitlohirs'ke Ukraine
53 E2 Svitlovods'k Ukraine
77 M4 Svityaz' Ukraine
50 J4 Sviyaga r. Rus. Fed.
52 C4 Svoboda Rus. Fed.
52 H3 Svobodnyy Rus. Fed.
31 J2 Svobodnyy Rus. Fed.
112 D3 Svoge Bulgaria
56 D1 Svolvær Norway
78 F2 Svratka r. Czech Rep.
112 D3 Svrljig Yugoslavia
51 D4 Svyetlahorsk Belarus
131 F3 Swaartplass South Africa
63 E2 Swadlincote *England* U.K.
131 E6 Swaershoek South Africa
131 E6 Swaershoekpas pass South Africa
63 G2 Swaffham *England* U.K.
15 H4 Swain Reefs reef *Queensland* Australia
145 D5 Swainsboro *Georgia* U.S.A.
5 L6 Swains Island i. *American Samoa* Pacific Ocean
128 A3 Swakop watercourse Namibia
128 A3 Swakopmund Namibia
65 G3 Swale r. *England* U.K.
69 E3 Swalmen Netherlands
137 J4 Swan r. *Saskatchewan* Canada
17 B6 Swan r. *Western Australia* Australia
63 E4 Swanage *England* U.K.
130 D6 Swanepoelspoort mt. South Africa
13 E3 Swan Hill *Victoria* Australia
136 F4 Swan Hills *Alberta* Canada
158 B3 Swan Is is Honduras
137 J4 Swan L. l. *Manitoba* Canada
63 G3 Swanley *England* U.K.
64 A3 Swanlinbar Rep. of Ireland
12 D3 Swan Reach *S. Australia* Australia
137 J4 Swan River *Manitoba* Canada
62 B3 Swansea div. *Wales* U.K.
13 G5 Swansea *Tasmania* Australia
62 C3 Swansea *Wales* U.K.
62 C3 Swansea Bay b. *Wales* U.K.
147 J2 Swans I. i. *Maine* U.S.A.
147 G2 Swanton *Vermont* U.S.A.
76 G1 Swarożyn Poland
130 B7 Swartberg mt. South Africa
131 G5 Swartberg South Africa
130 B5 Swartdoorn r. South Africa
131 F6 Swart Kei r. South Africa
130 B5 Swartkolkvloer salt pan South Africa
131 E6 Swartkops r. South Africa
131 E6 Swartkops South Africa
131 F2 Swartruggens mountain range South Africa
131 F2 Swartruggens South Africa
131 G1 Swartwater South Africa
76 F3 Swarzędz Poland
155 F2 Swasey Peak summit *Utah* U.S.A.
140 E2 Swastika *Ontario* Canada
36 C2 Swat r. Pakistan
36 C2 Swat Kohistan reg. Pakistan

64 B3 Swatragh Northern Ireland U.K.
63 E4 Sway England U.K.
117 H8 Swaziland country Africa
48 G2 Sweden country Europe
152 B2 Sweet Home Oregon U.S.A.
152 E3 Sweetwater r. Wyoming U.S.A.
145 C5 Sweetwater Tennessee U.S.A.
151 C5 Sweetwater Texas U.S.A.
130 C7 Swellendam South Africa
77 J2 Światki Poland
76 G1 Świbno Poland
76 E5 Świdnica Wałbrzych Poland
76 D4 Świdnica Poland
77 L4 Świdnik Poland
76 D2 Świdwin Poland
76 E5 Świebodzice Poland
76 D3 Świebodzin Poland
76 G2 Świecie Poland
76 E4 Święciechowa Poland
76 G2 Świekatowo Poland
76 D5 Świeradów-Zdrój Poland
77 J3 Świercze Poland
76 D4 Świerzawa Poland
77 M4 Świerże Poland
76 E1 Świerzenko Poland
76 C2 Świerzno Poland
77 L1 Świętajno Suwałki Poland
77 K2 Świętajno Poland
77 K5 Świetokrzyski Park Narodowy nat. park Poland
147 H2 Swift r. Maine U.S.A.
137 H4 Swift Current Saskatchewan Canada
137 H5 Swiftcurrent Cr. r. Saskatchewan Canada
68 D2 Swifterbant Netherlands
136 C2 Swift River Yukon Terr. Canada
67 D1 Swilly, Lough inlet Rep. of Ireland
63 E3 Swindon div. England U.K.
63 E3 Swindon England U.K.
63 F2 Swineshead England U.K.
67 C3 Swinford Rep. of Ireland
76 C2 Świnoujście Szczecin Poland
66 F5 Swinton Scotland U.K.
83 F2 Swiss National Park nat. park Switzerland
48 F4 Switzerland country Europe
73 K2 Swobnica Poland
67 E3 Swords Rep. of Ireland
15 E4 Swords Ra. h. Queensland Australia
77 N3 Syalyets Belarus
77 N3 Syalyets Vodaskhovishcha resr Belarus
50 D2 Syamozero, Oz. l. Rus. Fed.
50 G2 Syamzha Rus. Fed.
54 F4 Syanno Belarus
77 N2 Syarednenemanskaya Nizina plain Belarus/Lithuania
50 E2 Syas'troy Rus. Fed.
67 A4 Sybil Point pt Rep. of Ireland
148 C5 Sycamore Illinois U.S.A.
76 E1 Sycewice Poland
52 B2 Sychevka Rus. Fed.
52 C2 Sychevo Rus. Fed.
76 F4 Syców Poland
13 G3 Sydney New South Wales Australia
139 H4 Sydney Nova Scotia Canada
11 □1 Sydney B. b. Norfolk I. Pacific Ocean
138 B3 Sydney L. l. Ontario Canada
139 H4 Sydney Mines Nova Scotia Canada
51 F5 Syeverodonets'k Ukraine
72 D3 Syke Germany
115 D6 Sykea Greece
114 E3 Syki Greece
50 J2 Syktyvkar Rus. Fed.
145 C5 Sylacauga Alabama U.S.A.
56 D3 Sylarna mt. Norway/Sweden
37 G4 Sylhet Bangladesh
72 D1 Sylt i. Germany
145 D5 Sylvania Georgia U.S.A.
146 B4 Sylvania Ohio U.S.A.
136 G4 Sylvan Lake Alberta Canada
145 D6 Sylvester Georgia U.S.A.
14 C3 Sylvester, L. salt flat Northern Terr. Australia
136 E3 Sylvia, Mt mt. B.C. Canada
115 □ Symi i. Greece
115 □ Symi Greece
156 E3 Symon Mexico
58 C2 Syndle l. Norway
53 F2 Synel'nykove Ukraine
58 C1 Synhovd mt. Norway
58 C1 Synnfjell mt. Norway
62 B2 Synod Inn Wales U.K.
52 E2 Syntul Rus. Fed.
53 D2 Synyukha r. Ukraine
179 D4 Syowa Japan Base Antarctica
147 E3 Syracuse airport New York U.S.A.
150 C4 Syracuse Kansas U.S.A.
147 E3 Syracuse New York U.S.A.
Syracuse see Siracusa
47 G4 Syrdar'ya r. Kazakhstan
47 G4 Syrdar'ya Uzbekistan
18 E6 Syria country Asia
24 B3 Syriam Myanmar
Syrian Desert desert see Bādiyat ash Shām
113 F6 Syrna i. Greece
115 F5 Syros i. Greece
59 G3 Syrsan l. Sweden
52 D3 Syrskiy Rus. Fed.
57 G3 Sysmä Finland
50 J2 Sysola r. Rus. Fed.
52 E3 Sysoy Rus. Fed.
63 E2 Syston England U.K.
53 C2 Sytkivtsi Ukraine
50 J3 Syumsi Rus. Fed.
46 D1 Syun r. Rus. Fed.
53 F3 Syvas'ke Ukraine
114 B3 Syvota Greece
55 C2 Syvsten Denmark
50 J4 Syzran' Rus. Fed.
79 J5 Szabadszállás Hungary
79 M3 Szabolcsbáka Hungary
79 M3 Szabolcs-Szatmár-Bereg div. Hungary
71 J3 Szadek Poland
79 H5 Szakály Hungary
79 H6 Szalánta Hungary
76 F2 Szamocin Poland
79 M3 Szamos r. Hungary
79 M3 Szamosköz reg. Hungary
76 E3 Szamotuły Poland
78 G4 Szany Hungary
79 K5 Szarvas Hungary
76 D3 Szczaniec Poland
77 J6 Szczawnica Poland
77 L5 Szczebrzeszyn Poland
76 D2 Szczecin div. Poland
76 C2 Szczecin Szczecin Poland
76 E2 Szczecinek Poland
76 D2 Szczecińskie reg. Poland
77 H5 Szczekociny Poland
77 H4 Szczerców Poland
77 K5 Szczucin Poland
77 L2 Szczuczyn Poland
77 J1 Szczurkowo Poland
77 H3 Szczutowo Poland
79 J2 Szczyrk Poland
77 J2 Szczytno Poland
Szechwan div. see Sichuan
79 J3 Szécsény Hungary
79 H5 Szederkény Hungary
79 K5 Szeged Hungary
79 L4 Szeghalom Hungary
79 H4 Székesfehérvár Hungary
79 K5 Székkutas Hungary
79 H5 Szekszárd Hungary
76 G1 Szemud Poland
79 K3 Szendrő Hungary
79 J4 Szentendre Hungary
79 K5 Szentes Hungary
78 F5 Szentgotthárd Hungary
79 G5 Szentlászló Hungary
79 J4 Szentmártonkáta Hungary
81 H3 Szentpéterfa Hungary
78 F5 Szepetnek Hungary
77 L3 Szepietowo Poland
79 L3 Szerencs Hungary
77 K2 Szestno Poland
77 L1 Szeszka Góra h. Poland
79 H4 Szigetcsép Hungary
79 G5 Szigetvár Hungary
79 K3 Szikszó Hungary
78 G4 Szil Hungary
76 F4 Szkaradowo Poland
76 D5 Szklarska Poręba Poland
76 E4 Szlichtyngowa Poland
79 H4 Szob Hungary
79 K4 Szolnok Hungary
78 F4 Szombathely Hungary
79 H4 Szomód Hungary
76 D4 Szprotawa Poland
77 J5 Szreniawa r. Poland
76 D5 Szrenica mt. Czech Rep.
77 J2 Szreńsk Poland
77 M2 Sztabin Poland
77 H2 Sztum Poland
77 H1 Sztutowo Poland
76 F2 Szubin Poland
77 M2 Szudziałowo Poland
77 J4 Szydłowiec Poland
76 E2 Szydłowo Poland
77 K2 Szymonka Poland
76 G4 Szynkielów Poland
77 M1 Szypliszki Poland

T

122 C5 Taabo, Lac de l. Côte d'Ivoire
126 D3 Taagga Duudka reg. Somalia
43 C3 Taalabaya Lebanon
23 B3 Taal, L. l. Philippines
7 □11 Taapuma French Polynesia Pacific Ocean
79 H5 Tab Hungary
23 B3 Tabaco Philippines
119 H2 Tābah Saudi Arabia
22 D1 Tabang Indonesia
131 G5 Tabankulu South Africa
42 D3 Ţabaqah Syria
159 □3 Tabaquite Trinidad and Tobago
98 E3 Tábara Spain
6 □1 Tabar Is is P.N.G.
105 B7 Tabarka Tunisia
39 E2 Ţabas Iran
39 D2 Ţabas Iran
54 D2 Tabasalu Estonia
157 G5 Tabasco div. Mexico
39 D3 Tabāsin Iran
168 D4 Tabatinga Brazil
162 D4 Tabatinga Colombia
23 B2 Tabayoo, Mt mt. Philippines
120 D3 Tabelbala Algeria
137 G5 Taber Alberta Canada
59 F3 Taberg Sweden
101 H3 Tabernas Spain
125 B5 Tabi Angola
124 E3 Tabili Congo(Zaire)
4 J5 Tabiteuea i. Kiribati
54 E2 Tabivere Estonia
23 B3 Tablas i. Philippines
172 B1 Tablas, C. c. Chile
101 G1 Tablas de Daimiel, Parque Nacional de las nat. park Spain
23 B3 Tablas Strait chan. Philippines
8 F3 Table Cape c. New Zealand
130 B7 Table Mountain mt. South Africa
127 □5 Table, Pointe de la pt Réunion Indian Ocean
151 E4 Table Rock Res. resr Missouri U.S.A.
15 F3 Tabletop, Mt h. Queensland Australia
123 E5 Tabligbo Togo
101 F2 Tablillas r. Spain
101 E4 Tablon, Sierra del mountain range Spain
98 C2 Taboada Spain
165 E3 Tabocó r. Brazil
24 B1 Tabong Myanmar
78 D2 Tábor Czech Rep.
127 B6 Tabora div. Tanzania
127 B6 Tabora Tanzania
47 G4 Taboshar Tajikistan
173 H1 Tabossi Argentina
122 C6 Tabou Côte d'Ivoire
123 E3 Tabrichat well Mali
42 F2 Tabrīz Iran
98 B4 Tábua Portugal
98 C3 Tabuaço Portugal
5 M4 Tabuaeran i. Kiribati
102 B3 Tabuenca Spain
119 G2 Tabūk Saudi Arabia
13 H2 Tabulam New South Wales Australia
47 J2 Tabuny Rus. Fed.
6 □2 Tabwémasana mt. Vanuatu
59 H2 Täby Sweden
163 G3 Tacalé Brazil
157 E5 Tacámbaro Mexico
158 C5 Tacarcuna, Co mt. Panama
47 K3 Tacheng China
75 H4 Tacherting Germany
118 A2 Tachiumet well Libya
78 B2 Tachov Czech Rep.
22 E3 Tacipi Indonesia
23 C4 Tacloban Philippines
164 B3 Tacna Peru
152 B2 Tacoma Washington U.S.A.
164 C3 Tacopaya Bolivia
170 D2 Taco Pozo Argentina
164 C3 Tacora, Vol. volcano Chile
173 K2 Tacuarembó div. Uruguay
173 K1 Tacuarembó r. Uruguay
173 K1 Tacuarembó Uruguay
173 L2 Tacuarí r. Uruguay
156 C2 Tacupeto Mexico
168 A5 Tacuru Brazil
76 F4 Taczanów drugi Poland
29 G5 Tadami-gawa r. Japan
65 G4 Tadcaster England U.K.
Tademaït Plateau plat. see Plateau du Tademaït
6 □2 Tadine New Caledonia Pacific Ocean
121 E3 Tadjmout Algeria
126 D2 Tadjoura Djibouti
126 D2 Tadjoura, Golfe de b. Djibouti
121 E2 Tadjrouna Algeria
63 E3 Tadley England U.K.
42 D3 Tadmur Syria
137 K3 Tadoule Lake l. Manitoba Canada
139 G4 Tadoussac Québec Canada
54 C2 Taebla Estonia
31 H5 Taech'ŏn South Korea
31 H5 Taedong man b. North Korea
31 J6 Taegu South Korea
31 H6 Taehŭksan Do i. South Korea
31 H5 Taejŏn South Korea
31 J5 T'aepaek South Korea
62 B3 Taf r. Wales U.K.
5 K6 Tafahi i. Tonga
102 B2 Tafalla Spain
130 C6 Tafelberg mt. South Africa
82 C2 Tafers Switzerland
62 C3 Taffs Well Wales U.K.
39 C3 Tafīhān Iran
42 C4 Tafila Jordan
170 C2 Tafi Viejo Argentina
120 C3 Tafraoute Morocco
39 B2 Tafresh Iran
154 C4 Taft California U.S.A.
39 E3 Taftān, kūh-e mt. Iran
25 A6 Tafwap Andaman and Nicobar Is India
7 □12 Taga Western Samoa
119 F4 Tagab Sudan
29 H4 Tagajō Japan
51 F6 Taganrog Rus. Fed.
51 F6 Taganrog, Gulf of b. Rus. Fed./Ukraine
120 B5 Tagant div. Mauritania
24 B2 Tagaung Myanmar
28 C7 Tagawa Japan
50 H4 Tagay Rus. Fed.
23 B3 Tagaytay City Philippines
123 F3 Tagaza well Niger
23 B4 Tagbilaran Philippines
58 A1 Taget h. Norway
123 F3 Taggart Tegguet well Niger
106 B5 Taggia Italy
121 D2 Taghit Algeria
122 D2 Taghmanant well Mali
67 E4 Taghmon Rep. of Ireland
136 C2 Tagish Yukon Terr. Canada
109 F2 Tagliacozzo Italy
107 G2 Tagliamento r. Italy
107 G3 Taglio di Po Italy
86 D3 Tagnon France
23 C4 Tagoloan r. Philippines
23 B4 Tagolo Point pt Philippines
103 E5 Tagomago i. Spain
168 D1 Taguatinga Distrito Federal Brazil
166 C3 Taguatinga Tocantins Brazil
123 F3 Taguedoufat well Niger
6 □1 Tagula I. i. P.N.G.
23 C5 Tagum Philippines
Tagus r. Spain see Tajo
Tagus r. Portugal see Tejo
7 □10 Tahaa i. French Polynesia Pacific Ocean
136 F4 Tahaetkun Mt. mt. B.C. Canada
101 H3 Tahal Spain
121 E4 Tahalra reg. Algeria
7 □10 Tahanéa i. French Polynesia Pacific Ocean
25 C6 Tahan, Gunung mt. Malaysia
29 F6 Tahara Japan
121 F4 Tahat, Mt mt. Algeria
31 H1 Tahe China
8 D1 Taheke New Zealand
30 A3 Tahilt Mongolia
7 □11 Tahiti i. French Polynesia Pacific Ocean
39 E3 Tahlab r. Iran/Pakistan
151 E5 Tahlequah Oklahoma U.S.A.
154 B2 Tahoe City California U.S.A.
154 B2 Tahoe, Lake l. California/Nevada U.S.A.
134 H3 Tahoe Lake l. N.W.T. Canada
151 C5 Tahoka Texas U.S.A.
123 F3 Tahoua div. Niger
123 F4 Tahoua Niger
39 D3 Tahrūd r. Iran
119 F2 Tahta Egypt
136 D4 Tahtsa Pk summit B.C. Canada
164 C2 Tahuamanu r. Bolivia
23 C6 Tahuna Indonesia
122 C5 Taï Côte d'Ivoire
37 G4 Taiabpur India
27 □ Tai a Chau i. Hong Kong China
31 F5 Tai'an China
32 D1 Taibai Shan mt. China
Taibei see T'ai-pei
101 H2 Taibilla r. Spain
101 H2 Taibilla, Sierra de mountain range Spain
80 D4 Taibòn Agordino Italy
31 E4 Taibus Qi China
33 H3 T'ai-chung Taiwan
9 C6 Taieri r. New Zealand
30 E5 Taigu China
30 E5 Taihang Shan mountain range China
8 E3 Taihape New Zealand
33 F1 Taihe China
33 F3 Taihe China
29 □2 Taiho Japan
33 H2 Tai Hu l. China
33 G2 Taihu China
29 E7 Taiji Japan
32 E3 Taijiang China
33 F1 Taikang China
24 A3 Taikkyi Myanmar
31 G3 Tailai China
27 □ Tai Lam Chung Res. resr Hong Kong China
12 D3 Tailem Bend S. Australia Australia
91 D3 Taillefer mt. France
27 □ Tai Long Bay b. Hong Kong China
33 H3 T'ai-lu-ko Taiwan
39 E2 Taimani reg. Afghanistan
27 □ Tai Mo Shan h. Hong Kong China
66 D3 Tain Scotland U.K.
33 H4 T'ai-nan Taiwan
33 H4 T'ainan Taiwan
33 G3 Taining China
91 C3 Tain-l'Hermitage France
27 □ Tai O Hong Kong China
83 G2 Taio Italy
169 G1 Taiobeiras Brazil
22 E2 Taipa Indonesia
54 E1 Taipalsaari Finland
122 C5 Taï, Parc National de nat. park Côte d'Ivoire
33 H3 T'ai-pei Taiwan
33 E4 Taiping China
33 G2 Taiping China
25 C6 Taiping Malaysia
30 B5 Taipingbao China
31 G3 Taipingchuan China
31 G3 Taiping Ling mt. China
27 □ Tai Po Hong Kong China
37 H4 Taipudia India
29 □2 Taira Japan
28 H3 Tairadate-kaikyō chan. Japan
28 G2 Taisei Japan
28 J2 Taisetsu-zan mountain range Japan
28 J2 Taisetsu-zan National Park nat. park Japan
28 D6 Taisha Japan
33 F4 Taishan China
30 E5 Taishan China
33 G3 Taishun China
120 B3 Taïssa, Jbel mt. Morocco
86 D3 Taissy France
9 D5 Taitanu New Zealand
171 B6 Taitao, Península de pen. Chile
171 A6 Taitao, Pta pt Chile
33 H4 T'ai-tung Taiwan
56 H2 Taivalkoski Finland
56 G1 Taivaskero h. Finland
54 B1 Taivassalo Finland
19 O7 Taiwan country Asia
Taiwan Haixia str. see Taiwan Strait
33 H4 Taiwan Shan mountain range Taiwan
33 G3 Taiwan Strait str. China/Taiwan
33 H1 Tai Xian China
33 H1 Taixing China
30 E5 Taiyuan China
30 E5 Taiyue Shan mountain range China
Taizhong see T'ai-chung
33 G1 Taizhou China
33 H2 Taizhou Wan b. China
126 D2 Ta'izz Yemen
36 B4 Tajal Pakistan
118 B3 Tajarḩī Libya
22 A2 Tajem, G. h. Indonesia
18 H6 Tajikistan country Asia
29 G5 Tajima Japan
29 F6 Tajimi Japan
156 B2 Tajito Mexico
100 D1 Tajo r. Spain
99 H4 Tajuña r. Spain
24 B3 Tak Thailand
39 A1 Takāb Iran
126 D4 Takabba Kenya
22 E3 Taka'Bonerate, Kep. atolls Indonesia
29 H5 Takahagi Japan
28 D6 Takahashi Japan
28 D6 Takahashi-gawa r. Japan
8 D4 Takaka New Zealand
36 D5 Takal India
127 C6 Takaloi well Tanzania
127 □2 Takamaka Seychelles
28 E6 Takamatsu Japan
29 H3 Takanosu Japan
29 F5 Takaoka Japan
8 F4 Takapau New Zealand
7 □10 Takapoto i. French Polynesia Pacific Ocean
8 E2 Takapuna New Zealand
7 □10 Takaroa i. French Polynesia Pacific Ocean
28 E6 Takasago Japan
29 G5 Takasaki Japan
28 B7 Taka-shima i. Japan
128 C3 Takatokwane Botswana
29 E6 Takatsuki Japan
28 D7 Takatsuki-yama mt. Japan
24 B2 Ta-Kaw Myanmar
29 F5 Takayama Japan
25 C6 Tak Bai Thailand
29 F6 Takefu Japan
28 D6 Takehara Japan
28 C7 Takeo Japan
59 F2 Tåkern l. Sweden
Take-shima is see Tok-tō
39 B1 Takestān Iran
28 C7 Taketa Japan
25 D5 Takêv Cambodia
42 F4 Takhādīd well Iraq
46 E4 Takhiatash Uzbekistan
25 D5 Ta Khmau Cambodia
46 F5 Takhta-Bazar Turkmenistan
47 G2 Takhtabrod Kazakhstan
46 F4 Takhtakupyr Uzbekistan
39 F3 Takhta Pul Post Afghanistan
36 B3 Takht-i-Sulaiman mt. Pakistan
137 G1 Takijuq Lake l. N.W.T. Canada
28 H2 Takikawa Japan
28 J1 Takinoue Japan
22 C2 Takisung Indonesia
9 A6 Takitimu Mts mts New Zealand
136 D3 Takla Lake l. B.C. Canada
136 D3 Takla Landing B.C. Canada
Takla Makan desert see Taklimakan Shamo
47 K5 Taklimakan Shamo desert China
122 D6 Takoradi Ghana
37 H3 Takpa Shiri mt. China
79 L3 Takta r. Hungary
136 C3 Taku r. B.C. Canada
28 C7 Taku Japan
123 F5 Takum Nigeria
7 □10 Takumé i. French Polynesia Pacific Ocean
36 C2 Tal Pakistan
43 A4 Tala Egypt
173 K3 Tala Uruguay
172 C1 Talacasto Argentina
50 D4 Talachyn Belarus
36 C2 Talagang Pakistan
38 B4 Talaimannar Sri Lanka
92 A3 Talais France
38 A1 Talaja India
31 G2 Talakan Rus. Fed.
31 K2 Talakan Rus. Fed.
53 E1 Talalayivka Ukraine
108 D2 Talamone Italy
31 J2 Talandzha Rus. Fed.
22 A2 Talangbatu Indonesia
22 A2 Talangbetutu Indonesia
172 F1 Tala Norte Argentina
37 H4 Talap India
162 A4 Talara Peru
39 E4 Talar-i-Band mountain range Pakistan
101 E1 Talarrubias Spain
47 H4 Talas div. Kyrgyzstan
47 H4 Talas r. Kazakhstan
47 H4 Talas Kyrgyzstan
47 H4 Talas Ala-Too mountain range Kyrgyzstan
6 □1 Talasea P.N.G.
52 A2 Talashkino Rus. Fed.
Talas Range mountain range see Talas Ala-Too
43 B4 Talata Egypt
43 D2 Ţal 'at Mūsá mt. Lebanon
100 D1 Talaván Spain
99 F5 Talavera de la Reina Spain
100 D2 Talavera la Real Spain
14 E3 Talawanta Queensland Australia
24 B1 Talawgyi Myanmar
45 R3 Talaya Rus. Fed.
23 C5 Talayan Philippines
98 E5 Talayuela Spain
103 B5 Talayuelas Spain
36 D4 Talbehat India
135 L2 Talbot Inlet b. N.W.T. Canada
13 G3 Talbragar r. New South Wales Australia
172 B3 Talca Chile
172 D6 Talcahuala Argentina
172 A4 Talcahuano Chile
172 B2 Talca, Punta pt Chile
37 F5 Talcher India
52 C1 Taldom Rus. Fed.
47 J3 Taldykorgan div. Kazakhstan
47 J4 Taldykorgan Kazakhstan
47 H5 Taldyk P. Kyrgyzstan
47 G3 Taldysayskiy Kazakhstan
Taldysu see Taldy-Suu
47 J4 Taldy-Suu Kyrgyzstan
39 B2 Taleh Zang Iran
6 □5 Taleki Tonga i. Tonga
6 □5 Taleki Vavu'u i. Tonga
88 D3 Talensac France
103 C5 Tales Spain
39 B1 Tālesh Iran
47 J4 Talgar Kazakhstan
62 C3 Talgarth Wales U.K.
98 B4 Talhadas Portugal
21 H7 Taliabu i. Indonesia
91 E4 Taliard France
23 C4 Talibon Philippines
38 B2 Talikota India
47 G5 Talimardzhan Uzbekistan
38 A3 Taliparamba India
126 B3 Tali Post Sudan
23 B4 Talisay Philippines
22 D1 Talisayan Indonesia
23 C4 Talisayan Philippines
42 G2 Talış Dağları mts Azerbaijan/Iran
172 E2 Talita Argentina
50 H3 Talitsa Rus. Fed.
52 D3 Talitsa Rus. Fed.
52 E3 Talitskiy Chamlyk Rus. Fed.
52 F1 Talitsy Rus. Fed.
22 D4 Taliwang Indonesia
43 A4 Talkha Egypt
107 F5 Talla Italy
145 C5 Talladega Alabama U.S.A.
42 E2 Tall 'Afar Iraq
145 C6 Tallahassee Florida U.S.A.
13 F4 Tallangatta Victoria Australia
145 C5 Tallassee Alabama U.S.A.
119 G4 Talla Talla Seghir I. i. Sudan
17 A6 Tallering Pk h. Western Australia Australia
42 E3 Tall Fadghāmī Syria
54 D2 Tallinn Estonia
42 D3 Tall Kalakh Syria
42 E2 Tall Kayf Iraq
90 E3 Talloires France
67 C4 Tallow Rep. of Ireland
151 F5 Tallulah Louisiana U.S.A.
42 E2 Tall'Uwaynāt Iraq
112 E2 Tălmaciu Romania
90 D1 Talmay France
47 K2 Tal'menka Rus. Fed.
43 D3 Tal Misma h. Jordan
92 B3 Talmont France
92 A2 Talmont-St-Hilaire France
53 D2 Tal'ne Ukraine
36 C5 Talod India
126 B2 Talodi Sudan
23 □2 Talofofo Guam Pacific Ocean
24 B2 Ta-long Myanmar
139 G2 Talon, Lac l. Québec Canada
39 G1 Tāloqān Afghanistan
108 B4 Talora r. Sardegna Italy
36 C2 Tal or Shohi P. pass Pakistan
53 E2 Talova Balka Ukraine
46 D2 Talovaya Kazakhstan
51 G5 Talovaya Rus. Fed.
135 J3 Taloyoak N.W.T. Canada
30 A3 Talshand Mongolia
54 C3 Talsi Latvia
170 B2 Taltal Chile
137 G2 Taltson r. N.W.T. Canada
42 F3 Talvar r. Iran
107 F2 Talvera r. Italy
56 F1 Talvik Norway
15 G6 Talwood Queensland Australia
53 D2 Tal'yanky Ukraine
13 E3 Talyawalka r. New South Wales Australia
Talyshskiye Gory mts see Talış Dağları
50 K1 Talyy Rus. Fed.
148 A4 Tama Iowa U.S.A.
24 A2 Tamadaw Myanmar
52 F3 Tamala Rus. Fed.
162 C2 Tamalameque Colombia
122 D5 Tamale Ghana
22 C2 Tamalung Indonesia
98 D4 Tamames Spain
28 C7 Tamana Japan
173 H5 Tamangueyú Argentina
118 B2 Tamanhint Libya
28 D6 Tamano Japan
121 F4 Tamanrasset Algeria
24 A1 Tamanthi Myanmar
162 C2 Tama, Parque Nacional el nat. park Venezuela
147 F4 Tamaqua Pennsylvania U.S.A.
62 B4 Tamar r. England U.K.
127 □4 Tamarin . Mauritius
112 F1 Tămășeni Romania
77 M4 Tamashowka Belarus
79 H5 Tamási Hungary
112 F1 Tamași Romania
157 F3 Tamaulipas div. Mexico
126 C3 Tama Wildlife Reserve res. Ethiopia
156 D3 Tamazula Mexico
157 F5 Tamazulápam Mexico
157 F4 Tamazunchale Mexico
127 C4 Tambach Kenya
75 F2 Tambach-Dietharz Germany
122 B4 Tambacounda Senegal
37 F4 Tamba Kosi r. Nepal
22 E3 Tambalongang i. Indonesia
22 B2 Tambangmunjul Indonesia
168 E4 Tambau Brazil
123 E4 Tambawel Nigeria
22 A1 Tambelan Besar i. Indonesia
17 B7 Tambellup Western Australia Australia
172 C1 Tamberías Argentina
39 B3 Tambiān Iran
172 C2 Tambillo, Co mt. Argentina
23 A5 Tambisan Malaysia
13 F4 Tambo r. Victoria Australia
164 B3 Tambo r. Peru
15 F5 Tambo Queensland Australia
162 A4 Tambo Grande Peru
129 G2 Tambohorano Madagascar
22 D4 Tambora, G. volcano Indonesia
173 J1 Tambores Uruguay
166 D1 Tamboril Brazil
124 E2 Tamboura Central African Rep.
52 E3 Tambov div. Rus. Fed.
52 E3 Tambov Rus. Fed.
31 J2 Tambovka Rus. Fed.
98 B2 Tambre r. Spain
22 D2 Tambulan Indonesia
124 E2 Tambura Sudan
22 D1 Tambu, Tk b. Indonesia
23 A5 Tambuyukon, G. mt. Malaysia
120 B5 Tâmchekkeţ Mauritania
46 F4 Tamdybulak Uzbekistan
162 C2 Tame Colombia
98 C3 Tâmega r. Portugal
123 E3 Tamesna reg. Niger
157 F4 Tamiahua Mexico
157 F4 Tamiahua, L. de lag. Mexico
38 B4 Tamil Nadu div. India
22 C2 Taminglayang Indonesia
83 E2 Tamins Switzerland
30 B3 Tamirin Gol r. Mongolia
112 C2 Tamiš r. Yugoslavia
166 B3 Tamitatoala r. Brazil
50 F1 Tamitsa Rus. Fed.
43 A5 Tâmîya Egypt
24 E4 Tam Ky Vietnam
109 G3 Tammaro r. Italy
54 C1 Tammela Finland
59 G1 Tämnaren l. Sweden
98 C1 Támoga r. Spain
145 D7 Tampa Florida U.S.A.
145 D7 Tampa Bay b. Florida U.S.A.
22 A3 Tampang Indonesia
39 D4 Tamp-e Gīrān Iran
57 F3 Tampere Finland
157 F4 Tampico Mexico
25 □ Tampines Singapore
31 F3 Tamsagbulag Mongolia
30 B4 Tamsag Muchang China
54 E2 Tamsalu Estonia
162 C4 Tamshiyacu Peru
81 E3 Tamsweg div. Austria
81 E3 Tamsweg Austria
24 A1 Tamu Myanmar
157 F4 Tamuín Mexico
23 □2 Tamuning Guam Pacific Ocean
37 F4 Tamur r. Nepal
63 E2 Tamworth England U.K.
13 G2 Tamworth New South Wales Australia
127 C5 Tana r. Kenya
29 E7 Tanabe Japan
168 D4 Tanabi Brazil
56 H1 Tana bru Norway
132 D3 Tanacross Alaska U.S.A.
56 H1 Tanafjorden chan. Norway
111 E2 Tanagro r. Italy
126 C2 T'ana Hāyk' l. Ethiopia
22 D2 Tanahgrogot Indonesia
22 E3 Tanahjampea i. Indonesia
23 A6 Tanahmerah Indonesia
25 C6 Tanah Merah Malaysia
22 B3 Tanah, Tg pt Indonesia
22 D3 Tanakeke i. Indonesia
36 E3 Tanakpur India
22 D2 Tanambung Indonesia
15 B3 Tanami Northern Terr. Australia
14 B3 Tanami Desert desert Northern Terr. Australia
25 D5 Tân An Vietnam
134 C3 Tanana Alaska U.S.A.
91 C4 Tanargue, le mt. France
106 C4 Tanaro r. Italy
62 C2 Tanat r. Wales U.K.
23 C4 Tanauan Philippines
6 □8 Tanavuso Pt pt Fiji
15 E5 Tanbar Queensland Australia
29 □2 Tancha Japan
33 G1 Tancheng China
31 J4 Tanch'ŏn North Korea
122 D5 Tanda Côte d'Ivoire
37 E4 Tanda India
59 E1 Tandådalen Sweden
23 C4 Tandag Philippines
112 F2 Tăndărei Romania
125 C7 Tandaué Angola
23 A5 Tandek Malaysia
80 C2 Tandern Germany
36 D2 Tandi India
173 H4 Tandil Argentina
173 H4 Tandil, Sa del h. Argentina
124 C2 Tandjilé div. Chad
36 B4 Tando Adam Pakistan
36 B4 Tando Alahyar Pakistan
36 B4 Tando Muhammmad Khan Pakistan
13 E3 Tandou L. l. New South Wales Australia
59 E1 Tandövarn h. Sweden
67 E2 Tandragee Northern Ireland U.K.
38 B2 Tandur India
8 F3 Taneatua New Zealand
29 H3 Taneichi Japan
121 F3 Tan Emellel Algeria
24 B3 Tanen Taunggyi mountain range Thailand
77 L5 Tanew r. Poland
146 E5 Taneytown Maryland U.S.A.
121 D4 Tanezrouft reg. Algeria
121 E4 Tanezrouft Tan-Ahenet reg. Algeria
64 A4 Tang Rep. of Ireland
127 C6 Tanga div. Tanzania
118 C4 Tanga well Chad
30 D2 Tanga Rus. Fed.
127 C6 Tanga Tanzania
8 E2 Tangaehe New Zealand
37 G4 Tangail Bangladesh
129 H3 Tangainony Madagascar
6 □1 Tanga Is is P.N.G.
38 C5 Tangalla Sri Lanka
127 A5 Tanganyika, Lake l. Africa
39 C1 Tangar Iran
124 C2 Tangaray Chad
38 B4 Tangasseri India
32 C3 Tangdan China
Tangdan see Dongchuan
39 C1 Tangeli Iran
58 D1 Tangen Norway
179 D4 Tange Prom. headland Antarctica
120 C1 Tanger Morocco
22 A3 Tangerang Indonesia
73 G3 Tangerhütte Germany
73 G3 Tangermünde Germany
55 B3 Tange Sø l. Denmark
32 C1 Tanggor China
37 G2 Tanggula Shan mountain range China
37 G2 Tanggula Shankou pass China
33 F1 Tanghe China
Tangier see Tanger
147 E6 Tangier I. i. Virginia U.S.A.
22 A3 Tangkittebak, G. mt. Indonesia
37 G4 Tangla India
25 □ Tanglin Singapore
32 A2 Tangmai China
29 E6 Tango Japan
37 F3 Tangra Yumco salt lake China
31 F5 Tangshan China
23 B4 Tangub Philippines
123 E4 Tanguieta Benin
31 J2 Tangwanghe China
31 E5 Tang Xian China
33 F2 Tangxianzhen China
32 E2 Tangyan r. China
24 B2 Tang-yan Myanmar
33 F1 Tangyin China
31 J3 Tangyuan China
56 G2 Tanhua Finland
25 D5 Tani Cambodia
32 A2 Taniantaweng Shan mountain range China
90 E2 Taninges France
Tanintharyi see Tenasserim
23 B4 Tanjay Philippines
Tanjore see Thanjavur
22 C2 Tanjung Indonesia
22 A1 Tanjungbalai Indonesia
25 B7 Tanjungbalai Indonesia
22 A1 Tanjungbatu Indonesia
22 D1 Tanjungbuaya i. Indonesia
22 D2 Tanjunggaru Indonesia
22 A3 Tanjungkarang Telukbetung Indonesia
22 A2 Tanjungpandan Indonesia
22 A1 Tanjungpinang Indonesia
22 A2 Tanjungraja Indonesia
21 G6 Tanjungredeb Indonesia
22 B2 Tanjungsaleh i. Indonesia
22 B2 Tanjungsatai Indonesia
21 G6 Tanjungselor Indonesia
36 B2 Tank Pakistan
30 C2 Tankhoy Rus. Fed.
122 B4 Tankon mt. Guinea
36 D2 Tankse India
130 C6 Tankwa r. South Africa
130 B6 Tankwa-Karoo National Park nat. park South Africa
90 C1 Tanlay France
75 H4 Tann Germany
6 □2 Tanna i. Vanuatu
66 F4 Tannadice Scotland U.K.
57 D3 Tannäs Sweden
90 B1 Tannay Bourgogne France
86 D3 Tannay Champagne-Ardenne France
58 D1 Tannfjell h. Norway
80 B2 Tannhausen Germany
80 B3 Tannheim Austria
55 C2 Tannis Bugt b. Denmark
26 F1 Tannu Ola, Khrebet mountain range Rus. Fed.
122 D5 Tano r. Ghana
23 B4 Tañon Strait chan. Philippines
36 B4 Tanot India
123 F4 Tanout Niger
120 C2 Tanout-ou-Fillali pass Morocco
73 K2 Tanowo Poland
156 E3 Tanque Alvarez Mexico
37 E4 Tansen Nepal
33 H3 Tan-shui Taiwan
119 F1 Tanta Egypt

153 E6 **Tepachi** Mexico
8 D1 **Te Paki** New Zealand
156 E5 **Tepalcatepec** Mexico
7 □11 **Tepati** French Polynesia Pacific Ocean
156 E4 **Tepatitlán** Mexico
156 D3 **Tepehuanes** Mexico
157 F5 **Tepeji** Mexico
114 B2 **Tepelenë** Albania
157 F5 **Tepelmemec** Mexico
78 C2 **Tepelská Vrchovina reg.** Czech Rep.
22 D1 **Tepianlangsat** Indonesia
156 D4 **Tepic** Mexico
9 C5 **Te Pirita** New Zealand
78 B1 **Teplá r.** Czech Rep.
75 H3 **Teplá** Czech Rep.
75 J3 **Teplá Vltava r.** Czech Rep.
78 C1 **Teplice** Czech Rep.
79 K3 **Teplička** Slovakia
50 K2 **Teplogorka** Rus. Fed.
31 J2 **Teploozersk** Rus. Fed.
52 H3 **Teplovka** Rus. Fed.
52 D3 **Teploye** Rus. Fed.
52 C3 **Teploye** Rus. Fed.
53 C2 **Teplyk** Ukraine
156 B2 **Tepoca, C. headland** Mexico
7 □10 **Tepoto i.** French Polynesia Pacific Ocean
109 E3 **Teppia r.** Italy
8 F2 **Te Puke** New Zealand
157 G5 **Tequisistlán** Mexico
157 F4 **Tequisquiapán** Mexico
102 G2 **Ter r.** Spain
100 C2 **Tera r.** Portugal
98 E3 **Tera r.** Spain
123 E4 **Téra** Niger
5 L4 **Teraina i.** Kiribati
36 D2 **Teram Kangri mt.** China/Jammu and Kashmir
109 F2 **Teramo div.** Abruzzo Italy
109 F2 **Teramo** Teramo Italy
152 E4 **Terang** Victoria Australia
68 F2 **Ter Apel** Netherlands
36 B3 **Teratani r.** Pakistan
77 M5 **Teratyn** Poland
9 E4 **Terawhiti, Cape c.** New Zealand
68 E3 **Terborg-Silvolde** Netherlands
52 D3 **Terbuny** Rus. Fed.
42 E2 **Tercan** Turkey
100 □ **Terceira i.** Azores Portugal
173 F2 **Tercero r.** Argentina
83 D3 **Terdoppio r.** Italy
52 B3 **Tereben'** Rus. Fed.
53 A2 **Terebovlya** Ukraine
112 D2 **Teregova** Romania
51 H7 **Terek r.** Rus. Fed.
51 H7 **Terek** Rus. Fed.
47 L2 **Terektinskiy Khr. mountain range** Rus. Fed.
79 K6 **Teremia Mare** Romania
50 J4 **Teren'ga** Rus. Fed.
25 C6 **Terengganu div.** Malaysia
168 A4 **Terenos** Brazil
46 F3 **Terenozek** Kazakhstan
22 B2 **Terentang** Indonesia
162 D2 **Terepaima, Parque Nacional nat. park** Venezuela
168 C6 **Teresa Cristina** Brazil
51 H4 **Tereshka r.** Rus. Fed.
166 D2 **Teresina** Brazil
169 G5 **Teresópolis** Brazil
77 M3 **Terespol** Poland
25 A5 **Teressa I. i.** Andaman and Nicobar Is India
7 □16 **Terevaka h.** Easter I. Chile
164 D3 **Terevinto** Bolivia
75 K2 **Terezín** Czech Rep.
80 C3 **Terfens** Austria
100 B3 **Terges r.** Portugal
86 C3 **Tergnier** France
107 F3 **Tergola r.** Italy
83 G2 **Terlano** Italy
109 J3 **Terlizzi** Italy
53 C1 **Termakhivka** Ukraine
172 B4 **Termas de Chillán** Chile
172 B3 **Termas de Flaco** Chile
173 J1 **Termas del Arapey** Uruguay
172 B1 **Termas de Socos** Chile
172 B5 **Termas de Tolhuaca** Chile
172 C2 **Termas de Villavicencio** Argentina
42 D1 **Terme** Turkey
102 D4 **Terme, Cap de pt** Spain
111 E3 **Terme Luigiane** Italy
102 D3 **Térmens** Spain
47 G5 **Termez** Uzbekistan
91 E3 **Termignon** France
110 C5 **Termini Imerese** Sicilia Italy
110 C4 **Termini Imerese, Golfo di b.** Sicilia Italy
109 E2 **Terminillo, Monte mt.** Italy
157 H5 **Términos, Lag. de lag.** Mexico
123 G3 **Termit well** Niger
123 G3 **Termit-Kaoboul** Niger
109 G3 **Termoli** Italy
64 B4 **Termonfeckin** Rep. of Ireland
62 D2 **Tern r.** England U.K.
21 J6 **Ternate** Indonesia
81 F3 **Ternberg** Austria
69 B3 **Terneuzen** Netherlands
109 E2 **Terni div.** Umbria Italy
109 E2 **Terni** Terni Italy
90 C1 **Ternin r.** France
81 H3 **Ternitz** Austria
53 G2 **Ternivka** Dnipropetrovs'k Ukraine
53 E3 **Ternivka** Mykolayiv Ukraine
53 C2 **Ternivka** Vinnytsya Ukraine
86 B2 **Ternois reg.** France
53 A2 **Ternopil' div.** Ukraine
53 A2 **Ternopil'** Ukraine
52 E4 **Ternovka** Rus. Fed.
53 G3 **Ternuvate** Ukraine
53 E1 **Terny** Ukraine
114 B3 **Terovou** Greece
12 D3 **Terowie** S. Australia Australia
168 B5 **Terra Boa** Brazil
169 G2 **Terra Branca** Brazil
136 D4 **Terrace** B.C. Canada
140 B2 **Terrace Bay** Ontario Canada
17 C6 **Terraces, The h.** Western Australia Australia
109 F3 **Terracina** Italy
102 F2 **Terrades** Spain
130 D2 **Terra Firma** South Africa
56 D2 **Terråk** Norway
108 A5 **Terralba** Sardegna Italy
111 F3 **Terranova da Sibari** Italy
111 F3 **Terranova di Pollino** Italy
139 K4 **Terra Nova Nat. Pk nat. park** Newfoundland Canada
107 F5 **Terranuova Bracciolini** Italy
168 B5 **Terra Rica** Brazil
168 A6 **Terra Roxa d'Oeste** Brazil
98 B3 **Terras do Bouro** Portugal
110 C4 **Terrasini** Sicilia Italy
102 F3 **Terrassa** Spain
92 D3 **Terrasson-la-Villedieu** France
179 B6 **Terre Adélie reg.** Antarctica
151 F6 **Terre Bonne Bay b.** Louisiana U.S.A.
159 □5 **Terre de Bas i.** Guadeloupe Caribbean
159 □5 **Terre de Haut i.** Guadeloupe Caribbean
144 C4 **Terre Haute** Indiana U.S.A.
139 K4 **Terrenceville** Newfoundland Canada
90 B1 **Terre Plaine plain** France
103 B4 **Terriente** Spain
101 E4 **Terril mt.** Spain
63 G2 **Terrington Marsh marsh** England U.K.
100 C2 **Terrugem** Portugal
152 F2 **Terry** Montana U.S.A.
51 G5 **Tersa r.** Rus. Fed.
47 G2 **Tersakkan r.** Kazakhstan
68 D1 **Terschelling i.** Netherlands
47 J4 **Terskey Ala-Too mountain range** Kyrgyzstan
50 F1 **Terskiy Bereg reg.** Rus. Fed.
53 F3 **Tersyanka** Ukraine
108 B5 **Tertenia** Sardegna Italy
Terter r. see Tärtär
69 B5 **Tertry** France
102 C4 **Teruel div.** Spain
103 B4 **Teruel** Teruel Spain
25 B6 **Terutao i.** Thailand
54 D1 **Tervakoski** Finland
112 F3 **Tervel** Bulgaria
92 B2 **Terves** France
56 G2 **Tervola** Finland
69 C4 **Tervuren** Belgium
104 F3 **Tešanj** Bos.-Herz.
81 H1 **Tešany** Czech Rep.
93 D5 **Tescou r.** France
126 C1 **Teseney** Eritrea
52 F2 **Tesha r.** Rus. Fed.
52 F2 **Tesha** Rus. Fed.
28 K2 **Teshikaga** Japan
28 H1 **Teshio** Japan
28 J2 **Teshio-dake mt.** Japan
28 H1 **Teshio-gawa r.** Japan
28 H1 **Teshio-sanchi mountain range** Japan
107 F2 **Tesimo** Italy
30 A2 **Tesiyn Gol r.** Mongolia
104 F3 **Teslić** Bos.-Herz.
136 C2 **Teslin r.** Yukon Terr. Canada
136 C2 **Teslin** Yukon Terr. Canada
136 C2 **Teslin Lake l.** Yukon Terr. Canada
166 B3 **Tesouras r.** Brazil
168 B2 **Tesouro** Brazil
50 D3 **Tesovo-Netyl'skiy** Rus. Fed.
123 E2 **Tessalit** Mali
123 F4 **Tessaoua** Niger
89 E3 **Tessé-la-Madeleine** France
69 D3 **Tessenderlo** Belgium
123 F3 **Tesséroukane well** Niger
73 H1 **Tessin** Germany
92 B3 **Tesson** France
123 E2 **Tessoûnfat well** Mali
89 D3 **Tessy-sur-Vire** France
63 E3 **Test r.** England U.K.
110 D6 **Testa dell'Acqua** Sicilia Italy
59 G1 **Testeboån r.** Sweden
98 B2 **Testeiro, Montes de mountain range** Spain
99 G5 **Testillos r.** Spain
105 B7 **Testour** Tunisia
93 E6 **Têt r.** France
79 G4 **Tét** Hungary
164 B4 **Tetas, Pta pt** Chile
62 D3 **Tetbury** England U.K.
129 E2 **Tete div.** Mozambique
124 D2 **Tété r.** Central African Rep.
129 E2 **Tete** Mozambique
91 E4 **Tête de l'Enchastraye mt.** France/Italy
91 E4 **Tête de l'Estrop mt.** France
8 F3 **Te Teko** New Zealand
6 □1 **Tetepare i.** Solomon Is.
53 C1 **Teteriv r.** Ukraine
73 H2 **Teterow** Germany
112 E3 **Teteven** Bulgaria
7 □10 **Tetiaroa i.** French Polynesia Pacific Ocean
101 H3 **Tetica mt.** Spain
53 C2 **Tetiyiv** Ukraine
53 F1 **Tetkino** Rus. Fed.
65 H4 **Tetney** England U.K.
152 E2 **Teton r.** Montana U.S.A.
152 E3 **Teton Ra. mts** Wyoming U.S.A.
120 C1 **Tétouan** Morocco
112 C3 **Tetovo** Macedonia
36 B5 **Tetpur** India
74 E5 **Tettnang** Germany
Tetuán see **Tétouan**
50 J4 **Tetyushi** Rus. Fed.
75 H3 **Teublitz** Germany
28 B8 **Teuchi** Japan
170 D1 **Teuco r.** Argentina
72 D2 **Teufels Moor reg.** Germany
83 E1 **Teufen** Switzerland
81 F3 **Teufenbach** Austria
108 A5 **Teulada** Sardegna Italy
108 A6 **Teulada, Capo pt** Sardegna Italy
108 A6 **Teulada, Golfo di b.** Sardegna Italy
73 J3 **Teupitz** Germany
28 H1 **Teuri-tō i.** Japan
72 D3 **Teutoburger Wald h.** Germany
73 G4 **Teutschenthal** Germany
57 F3 **Teuva** Finland
109 E3 **Tevere r.** Italy
109 E2 **Teverone r.** Italy
43 C2 **Teverya** Israel
66 F5 **Teviot r.** Scotland U.K.
66 F5 **Teviotdale v.** Scotland U.K.
65 F2 **Teviothead** Scotland U.K.
9 A7 **Te Waewae Bay b.** New Zealand
22 C2 **Tewah** Indonesia
15 H5 **Tewantin** Queensland Australia
22 C2 **Teweh r.** Indonesia
8 F3 **Te Whaiti** New Zealand
9 □1 **Te Whanga Lagoon lag.** Chatham Is New Zealand
9 E4 **Te Wharau** New Zealand
62 D3 **Tewkesbury** England U.K.
77 N3 **Tewli** Belarus
32 C1 **Têwo** China
64 B2 **Texa i.** Scotland U.K.
136 E5 **Texada I. i.** B.C. Canada
151 E5 **Texarkana** Texas U.S.A.
151 D6 **Texas div.** U.S.A.
15 G6 **Texas** Queensland Australia
151 E6 **Texas City** Texas U.S.A.
68 C1 **Texel i.** Netherlands
151 C4 **Texhoma** Oklahoma U.S.A.
151 D5 **Texoma, Lake l.** Oklahoma/Texas U.S.A.
131 F4 **Teyateyaneng** Lesotho
52 E1 **Teykovo** Rus. Fed.
39 F2 **Teyvareh** Afghanistan
52 E1 **Teza r.** Rus. Fed.
157 F5 **Teziutlán** Mexico
37 H4 **Tezpur** India
37 H4 **Tezu** India
120 B3 **Tfaritiy** Western Sahara
137 K2 **Tha-anne r.** N.W.T. Canada
131 G4 **Thabana-Ntlenyana mt.** Lesotho
131 H3 **Thabankulu mt.** South Africa
131 F4 **Thaba Putsoa mt.** Lesotho
131 G4 **Thaba-Tseka** Lesotho
131 F2 **Thabazimbi** South Africa
24 B2 **Thabeikkyin** Myanmar
24 C3 **Tha Bo** Laos
131 F3 **Thabong** South Africa
91 E3 **Thabor, Mt mt.** France
43 C5 **Thabt, G. el mt.** Egypt
25 B4 **Thagyettaw** Myanmar
Tha Hin see **Lop Buri**
24 D2 **Thai Binh** Vietnam
36 B3 **Thai Desert desert** Pakistan
19 L8 **Thailand country** Asia
25 C5 **Thailand, Gulf of g.** Asia
24 D2 **Thai Nguyên** Vietnam
6 □6 **Thakau Matathuthu reef** Fiji
6 □6 **Thakaundrove Pen. pen.** Fiji
6 □6 **Thakau Vuthovutho reef** Fiji
37 G4 **Thakurgaon** Bangladesh
36 E5 **Thakurtola** India
74 F2 **Thal** Germany
36 B2 **Thal** Pakistan
121 F1 **Thala** Tunisia
25 B5 **Thalang** Thailand
Thalassery see **Tellicherry**
80 C1 **Thalbach r.** Germany
73 G4 **Thale** Germany
25 C6 **Thale Luang lag.** Thailand
73 F3 **Thalfang** Germany
80 E3 **Thalgau** Austria
75 H2 **Thalheim** Germany
24 C3 **Tha Li** Thailand
15 G6 **Thallon** Queensland Australia
75 G3 **Thalmässing** Germany
39 F3 **Thalo** Pakistan
83 D1 **Thalwil** Switzerland
118 C2 **Thamad Bū Hashīshah well** Libya
128 D3 **Thamaga** Botswana
41 H6 **Thamarīt** Oman
126 E2 **Thamar, J. mt.** Yemen
63 F3 **Thame r.** England U.K.
63 F3 **Thame** England U.K.
63 G3 **Thames est.** England U.K.
63 E3 **Thames r.** England U.K.
8 E2 **Thames** New Zealand
140 E5 **Thamesville** Ontario Canada
24 B3 **Thanatpin** Myanmar
24 B4 **Thanbyuzayat** Myanmar
36 C5 **Thandla** India
63 H3 **Thanet, Isle of pen.** England U.K.
36 B5 **Thangadh** India
24 E4 **Thăng Binh** Vietnam
16 C3 **Thangoo** Western Australia Australia
15 G5 **Thangool** Queensland Australia
24 D3 **Thanh Hoa** Vietnam
38 B4 **Thanjavur** India
Thanlwin r. see **Salween**
90 F1 **Thann** France
74 F4 **Thannhausen** Germany
36 A4 **Thano Bula Khan** Pakistan
128 C2 **Thaoge r.** Botswana
87 F4 **Thaon-les-Vosges** France
24 C3 **Tha Pla** Thailand
25 B5 **Thap Put** Thailand
25 B5 **Thap Sakae** Thailand
36 B4 **Tharad** India
75 J2 **Tharandt** Germany
68 D2 **'t Harde** Netherlands
15 E5 **Thargomindah** Queensland Australia
36 B4 **Thar or Indian Desert desert** India
24 A3 **Tharrawaddy** Myanmar
24 A3 **Tharrawaw** Myanmar
100 C3 **Tharsis** Spain
114 F2 **Thasopoula i.** Greece
114 F2 **Thasos i.** Greece
114 F2 **Thasos** Greece
63 E3 **Thatcham** England U.K.
155 H5 **Thatcher** Arizona U.S.A.
24 D2 **Thât Khê** Vietnam
24 B3 **Thaton** Myanmar
24 A1 **Thaungdut** Myanmar
24 B3 **Thaungyin r.** Myanmar/Thailand
80 C3 **Thaur** Austria
63 G3 **Thaxted** England U.K.
81 G2 **Thaya r.** Austria/Czech Rep.
81 G2 **Thaya** Austria
25 B4 **Thayetchaung** Myanmar
24 A3 **Thayetmyo** Myanmar
83 D1 **Thayngen** Switzerland
24 A3 **Thazi** Myanmar
24 B2 **Thazi** Myanmar
155 F5 **Theba** Arizona U.S.A.
119 F2 **Thebes** Egypt
150 C3 **Thedford** Nebraska U.S.A.
25 B5 **Theinkun** Myanmar
24 B3 **Theinzeik** Myanmar
88 C4 **Theix** France
137 H2 **Thekulthili Lake l.** N.W.T. Canada
89 G2 **Thelle reg.** France
137 J2 **Thelon r.** N.W.T. Canada
137 J2 **Thelon Game Sanctuary res.** N.W.T. Canada
55 B3 **Them** Denmark
75 F2 **Themar** Germany
130 E6 **Thembalesizwe** South Africa
131 G3 **Thembalihle** South Africa
92 B2 **Thénezay** France
121 E1 **Theniet El Had** Algeria
92 D3 **Thenon** France
15 G5 **Theodore** Queensland Australia
165 D1 **Theodore Roosevelt r.** Brazil
155 G5 **Theodore Roosevelt Lake l.** Arizona U.S.A.
150 C2 **Theodore Roosevelt Nat. Park** N. Dakota U.S.A.
92 E2 **Théols r.** France
91 E5 **Théoule-sur-Mer** France
86 B3 **Thérain r.** France
147 F2 **Theresa** New York U.S.A.
15 F4 **Theresa Cr. r.** Queensland Australia
127 □2 **Thérèse I. i.** Seychelles
114 D2 **Thermaïkos Kolpos g.** Greece
154 B2 **Thermalito** California U.S.A.
115 E5 **Thermisia** Greece
114 C4 **Thermo** Greece
152 E3 **Thermopolis** Wyoming U.S.A.
114 D4 **Thermopyles** Greece
86 B2 **Thérouanne** France
134 F2 **Thesiger Bay b.** N.W.T. Canada
115 E4 **Thespies** Greece
114 B3 **Thesprotia div.** Greece
114 B3 **Thesprotiko** Greece
114 C3 **Thessalia div.** Greece
140 D3 **Thessalon** Ontario Canada
114 D2 **Thessaloniki airport** Greece
114 D2 **Thessaloniki div.** Greece
114 D2 **Thessaloniki** Greece
63 G2 **Thet r.** England U.K.
63 G2 **Thetford** England U.K.
141 K3 **Thetford Mines** Québec Canada
24 D3 **Theun r.** Laos
131 F4 **Theunissen** South Africa
69 D4 **Theux** Belgium
12 C3 **Thevenard** S. Australia Australia
16 A4 **Thevenard I. i.** Western Australia Australia
93 B5 **Thèze** France
87 E4 **Thiaucourt-Regniéville** France
89 F2 **Thiberville** France
86 D4 **Thibie** France
151 F6 **Thibodaux** Louisiana U.S.A.
137 K3 **Thicket Portage** Manitoba Canada
86 D4 **Thiéblemont-Farémont** France
150 D1 **Thief River Falls** Minnesota U.S.A.
90 E2 **Thielle r.** Switzerland
179 B4 **Thiel Mts mts** Antarctica
74 J3 **Thiendorf** Germany
107 F3 **Thiene** Italy
86 C3 **Thiérache reg.** France
80 B2 **Thierhaupten** Germany
82 B2 **Thierrens** Switzerland
90 B3 **Thiers** France
122 A4 **Thiès** Senegal
73 J1 **Thießow** Germany
92 E3 **Thiézac** France
127 C5 **Thika** Kenya
35 D9 **Thiladhunmathee Atoll atoll** Maldives
37 G4 **Thimphu** Bhutan
56 L6 **Þingvallavatn l.** Iceland
69 C5 **Thin-le-Moutier** France
6 □2 **Thio** New Caledonia Pacific Ocean
87 F3 **Thionville** France
115 G6 **Thira i.** Greece
115 G6 **Thira** Greece
115 G6 **Thirasia i.** Greece
119 F4 **3rd Cataract rapids** Sudan
65 E3 **Thirlmere l.** England U.K.
89 F3 **Thiron Gardais** France
89 G3 **Thironne r.** France
65 G3 **Thirsk** England U.K.
17 C7 **Thirsty, Mt h.** Western Australia Australia
Thiruvananthapuram see **Trivandrum**
90 E1 **Thise** France
55 A3 **Thisted** Denmark
55 A3 **Thisted Bredning b.** Denmark
56 N6 **Þistilfjordur b.** Iceland
12 D3 **Thistle I. i.** S. Australia Australia
115 E4 **Thiva** Greece
92 C3 **Thiviers** France
90 C2 **Thizy** France
137 K2 **Thlewiaza r.** N.W.T. Canada
137 H2 **Thoa r.** N.W.T. Canada
24 C3 **Thoeng** Thailand
131 H1 **Thohoyandou** South Africa
90 D2 **Thoirette** France
89 G3 **Thoiry** France
90 C2 **Thoissey** France
90 C1 **Thoisy-la-Berchère** France
68 C3 **Tholen i.** Netherlands
69 C3 **Tholen** Netherlands
74 C3 **Tholey** Germany
90 B1 **Tholon r.** France
17 B5 **Thomas r.** Western Australia Australia
146 D5 **Thomas** W. Virginia U.S.A.
12 D1 **Thomas, L. salt flat** S. Australia Australia
145 C5 **Thomaston** Georgia U.S.A.
147 J2 **Thomaston** Maine U.S.A.
147 K2 **Thomaston Corner** New Brunswick Canada
67 D4 **Thomastown** Rep. of Ireland
145 D6 **Thomasville** Georgia U.S.A.
69 E4 **Thommen** Belgium
136 E4 **Thompson r.** B.C. Canada
150 E3 **Thompson r.** Missouri U.S.A.
137 K3 **Thompson** Manitoba Canada
148 D3 **Thompson** Michigan U.S.A.
147 F4 **Thompson** Pennsylvania U.S.A.
152 D2 **Thompson Falls** Montana U.S.A.
9 A6 **Thompson Sound inlet** New Zealand
15 E5 **Thomson watercourse** Queensland Australia
145 D5 **Thomson** Georgia U.S.A.
24 D3 **Thôn Cư Lai** Vietnam
90 E3 **Thônes** France
24 B3 **Thongwa** Myanmar
90 E2 **Thonon-les-Bains** France
25 E5 **Thôn Sơn Hai** Vietnam
91 E4 **Thorame-Basse** France
93 E5 **Thoré r.** France
153 E5 **Thoreau** New Mexico U.S.A.
86 C4 **Thorigny-sur-Oreuse** France
81 G3 **Thörl** Austria
65 G3 **Thornaby-on-Tees** England U.K.
148 E4 **Thornapple r.** Michigan U.S.A.
62 D3 **Thornbury** England U.K.
131 G1 **Thorndale** South Africa
65 H4 **Thorne** England U.K.
154 C2 **Thorne** Nevada U.S.A.
141 F3 **Thorne** Ontario Canada
136 C3 **Thorne Bay** Alaska U.S.A.
66 E5 **Thornhill** Scotland U.K.
65 F4 **Thornton** England U.K.
148 D5 **Thorntown** Indiana U.S.A.
131 H2 **Thornybush Game Reserve res.** South Africa
148 B3 **Thorp** Wisconsin U.S.A.
179 D3 **Thorshavnheiane mountain range** Antarctica
131 F4 **Thota-ea-Moli** Lesotho
89 E4 **Thouarcé** France
92 B2 **Thouars** France
37 H4 **Thoubal** India
89 E4 **Thouet r.** France
16 B4 **Thouin Pt pt** Western Australia Australia
69 A5 **Thourotte** France
147 E2 **Thousand Islands is** Ontario Canada
155 G2 **Thousand Lake Mt mt.** Utah U.S.A.
154 C4 **Thousand Oaks** California U.S.A.
114 F2 **Thrakiko Pelagos sea** Greece
63 F2 **Thrapston** England U.K.
152 E2 **Three Forks** Montana U.S.A.
136 G4 **Three Hills** Alberta Canada
13 F5 **Three Hummock I. i.** Tasmania Australia
8 D1 **Three Kings Is is** New Zealand
148 C3 **Three Lakes** Wisconsin U.S.A.
148 D5 **Three Oaks** Michigan U.S.A.
24 B4 **Three Pagodas Pass pass** Myanmar/Thailand
122 D6 **Three Points, Cape c.** Ghana
148 E5 **Three Rivers** Michigan U.S.A.
151 D6 **Three Rivers** Texas U.S.A.
152 B2 **Three Sisters mt.** Oregon U.S.A.
130 D5 **Three Sisters** South Africa
115 G7 **Thrifti Oros mts** Greece
Thrissur see **Trichur**
151 D5 **Throckmorton** Texas U.S.A.
17 D5 **Throssell, L. salt flat** Western Australia Australia
16 C4 **Throssel Ra. h.** Western Australia Australia
137 G2 **Thubun Lakes l.** N.W.T. Canada
25 D5 **Thu Dâu Môt** Vietnam
91 C4 **Thueyts** France
69 C4 **Thuin div.** Hainaut Belgium
69 C4 **Thuin** Belgium
93 E6 **Thuir** France
36 B3 **Thul** Pakistan
Thule see **Qaanaaq**
129 D3 **Thuli** Zimbabwe
9 C5 **Thumbs, The mt.** New Zealand
82 C2 **Thun** Bern Switzerland
15 E5 **Thunda** Queensland Australia
17 B6 **Thundelarra** Western Australia Australia
149 F3 **Thunder Bay b.** Michigan U.S.A.
140 A2 **Thunder Bay b.** Ontario Canada
140 A2 **Thunder Bay** Ontario Canada
158 B3 **Thunder Knoll sea feature** Caribbean
82 C2 **Thuner See l.** Switzerland
25 B5 **Thung Song** Thailand
25 B6 **Thung Wa** Thailand
87 G5 **Thur r.** France
83 D1 **Thur r.** Switzerland
92 C2 **Thuré** France
90 B3 **Thuret** France
83 E1 **Thurgau div.** Switzerland
73 F4 **Thüringen div.** Germany
83 E1 **Thüringen** Austria
73 G4 **Thüringer Becken reg.** Germany
75 F2 **Thüringer Wald mts** Germany
73 H2 **Thürkow** Germany
67 D4 **Thurles** Rep. of Ireland
146 E5 **Thurmont** Maryland U.S.A.
75 G2 **Thurnau** Germany
65 E3 **Thursby** England U.K.
66 E2 **Thurso r.** Scotland U.K.
141 H4 **Thurso** Québec Canada
66 E2 **Thurso** Scotland U.K.
179 A3 **Thurston I. i.** Antarctica
89 E3 **Thury-Harcourt** France
82 C2 **Thusis** Switzerland
73 E3 **Thüster Berg h.** Germany
82 A3 **Thusy** France
65 F3 **Thwaite** England U.K.
179 A3 **Thwaites Gl. gl.** Antarctica
55 A3 **Thy reg.** Denmark
114 B3 **Thyamis r.** Greece
55 B3 **Thyborøn** Denmark
55 A3 **Thyholm i.** Denmark
15 E5 **Thylungra** Queensland Australia
113 F6 **Thymaina i.** Greece
89 G3 **Thymerais reg.** France
164 C3 **Tiahuanaco** Bolivia
159 E5 **Tía Juana** Venezuela
30 A4 **Tiancang** China
33 G1 **Tianchang** China
32 D4 **Tiandeng** China
32 D4 **Tiandong** China
32 D3 **Tian'e** China
33 G2 **Tianfanjie** China
166 D1 **Tianguá** Brazil
122 B4 **Tiânguél Bôri** Guinea
31 F5 **Tianjin div.** China
31 F5 **Tianjin** China
30 A5 **Tianjun** China
32 D3 **Tianlin** China
33 F2 **Tianmen** China
33 G2 **Tianmu Shan mountain range** China
31 J4 **Tianqiaoling** China
32 C2 **Tianquan** China
Tian Shan mountain range see **Tien Shan**
31 H4 **Tianshifu** China
32 D1 **Tianshui** China
36 D2 **Tianshuihai** China/Jammu and Kashmir
33 H2 **Tiantai** China
31 F4 **Tiantaiyong** China
32 D4 **Tianyang** China
33 E3 **Tianzhu** China
30 B5 **Tianzhu** China
7 □11 **Tiarei** French Polynesia Pacific Ocean
121 G2 **Tiaret well** Tunisia
121 E1 **Tiaret** Algeria
6 □2 **Tiari** New Caledonia Pacific Ocean
15 H5 **Tiaro** Queensland Australia
122 D5 **Tiassalé** Côte d'Ivoire
7 □12 **Tiavea** Western Samoa
168 C6 **Tibagi r.** Brazil
168 C6 **Tibaji** Brazil
42 E3 **Tibal, Wādī watercourse** Iraq
124 B2 **Tibati** Cameroon
36 B3 **Tibba** Pakistan
122 C5 **Tibé, Pic de summit** Guinea
Tiber r. see **Tevere**
Tiberias see **Teverya**
43 C3 **Tiberias, L. l.** Israel
152 E1 **Tiber Res. resr** Montana U.S.A.
118 C3 **Tibesti plat.** Chad
Tibet Aut. Region div. see **Xizang Zizhiqu**
163 F2 **Tiboku Falls waterfall** Guyana
13 E2 **Tibooburra** New South Wales Australia
37 E3 **Tibrikot** Nepal
59 F2 **Tibro** Sweden
156 B2 **Tiburón i.** Mexico
23 B3 **Ticao i.** Philippines
63 G3 **Ticehurst** England U.K.
141 G4 **Tichborne** Ontario Canada
120 C5 **Tîchît** Mauritania
120 B4 **Tichla** Western Sahara
83 D2 **Ticino div.** Switzerland
106 C3 **Ticino r.** Italy
83 D2 **Ticino r.** Italy/Switzerland
63 E2 **Ticknall** England U.K.
112 D2 **Ţicleni** Romania
147 G3 **Ticonderoga** New York U.S.A.
157 H4 **Ticul** Mexico
59 E2 **Tidaholm** Sweden
59 E2 **Tidan r.** Sweden
123 E3 **Tidarmène** Mali
24 A2 **Tiddim** Myanmar
25 A6 **Tiden** Andaman and Nicobar Is India
123 E3 **Tidjerouene well** Mali
120 B5 **Tidjikja** Mauritania
106 D4 **Tidone r.** Italy
93 A6 **Tiebas** Spain
81 E2 **Tiefenbach** Germany
87 H4 **Tiefenbronn** Germany
83 E2 **Tiefencastel** Switzerland
73 J3 **Tiefensee** Germany
68 D3 **Tiel** Netherlands
122 A4 **Tiel** Senegal
31 H3 **Tieli** China
31 G4 **Tieling** China
36 D2 **Tielongtan** China/Jammu and Kashmir
69 B3 **Tielt div.** West-Vlaanderen Belgium
69 B4 **Tielt** Belgium
69 C4 **Tienen** Belgium
74 D5 **Tiengen** Germany
47 J4 **Tien Shan mountain range** China/Kyrgyzstan
Tientsin see **Tianjin**
89 E4 **Tiercé** France
131 F4 **Tierfontein** South Africa
102 B3 **Tierga** Spain
59 G1 **Tierp** Sweden
162 B2 **Tierra Alta** Colombia
153 F4 **Tierra Amarilla** New Mexico U.S.A.
170 B2 **Tierra Amarilla** Chile
157 F5 **Tierra Blanca** Mexico
157 F5 **Tierra Colorada** Mexico
99 F3 **Tierra de Arévalo reg.** Spain
100 D2 **Tierra de Barros reg.** Spain
99 F2 **Tierra de Campos reg.** Spain
171 C7 **Tierra del Fuego div.** Argentina
171 C7 **Tierra del Fuego, Isla Grande de i.** Argentina/Chile
98 E3 **Tierra del Pan reg.** Spain
98 E3 **Tierra del Vino reg.** Spain
100 D3 **Tierra Llana de Huelva plain** Spain
101 E3 **Tiesa h.** Spain
98 E5 **Tiétar r.** Spain
99 E4 **Tiétar, Valle de v.** Spain
168 C4 **Tietê r.** Brazil
168 E5 **Tietê** Brazil
12 C1 **Tieyon** S. Australia Australia
146 B4 **Tiffin** Ohio U.S.A.
Tiflis see **T'bilisi**
145 D6 **Tifton** Georgia U.S.A.
6 □2 **Tiga i.** New Caledonia Pacific Ocean
46 D4 **Tigen** Kazakhstan
53 C3 **Tighina** Moldova
64 C2 **Tighnabruaich** Scotland U.K.
47 K2 **Tigiretskiy Khr. mountain range** Kazakhstan/Rus. Fed.
37 F5 **Tigiria** India
107 E3 **Tignale** Italy
124 B2 **Tignère** Cameroon
90 E3 **Tignes** France
139 H4 **Tignish** Prince Edward I. Canada
162 C4 **Tigre r.** Ecuador/Peru
163 E2 **Tigre r.** Venezuela
173 H3 **Tigre** Argentina
172 C1 **Tigre, Sa mountain range** Argentina
42 F3 **Tigris r.** Iraq/Turkey
121 E3 **Tiguelguemine well** Algeria
120 A5 **Tiguent** Mauritania
118 C4 **Tigui** Chad
86 B5 **Tigy** France
119 H4 **Tihāmah reg.** Saudi Arabia
79 G5 **Tihany** Hungary
43 B5 **Tīh, Gebel el plat.** Egypt
55 A3 **Tihøje h.** Denmark
118 B1 **Tījī** Libya
101 H3 **Tíjola** Spain
156 A1 **Tijuana** Mexico
168 D3 **Tijuco r.** Brazil
157 H5 **Tikal** Guatemala
36 D4 **Tikamgarh** India
134 C3 **Tikchik L. l.** Alaska U.S.A.
7 □10 **Tikehau i.** French Polynesia Pacific Ocean
124 C2 **Tikem** Chad
52 D1 **Tikhmenevo** Rus. Fed.
51 G6 **Tikhoretsk** Rus. Fed.
50 E3 **Tikhvin** Rus. Fed.
50 E3 **Tikhvinskaya Gryada ridge** Rus. Fed.
8 G2 **Tikitiki** New Zealand
6 □8 **Tikituru h.** Fiji
8 F3 **Tikokino** New Zealand
4 H6 **Tikopia i.** Solomon Islands
42 E3 **Tikrīt** Iraq
56 H3 **Tiksheozero, Oz. l.** Rus. Fed.
45 O2 **Tiksi** Rus. Fed.
114 C1 **Tikveš reg.** Macedonia
114 C1 **Tikveš Ezero l.** Macedonia
131 E3 **Tikwana** South Africa
37 E3 **Tila r.** Nepal
172 B2 **Tilama** Chile
43 D1 **Tilbeşar Ovasi plain** Turkey
15 F5 **Tilbooroo** Queensland Australia
68 D3 **Tilburg** Netherlands
63 G3 **Tilbury** England U.K.
170 C1 **Tilcara** Argentina
90 D1 **Til-Châtel** France
79 M4 **Tileagd** Romania
63 E3 **Tilehurst** England U.K.
123 E3 **Tilemsès** Niger
123 E3 **Tilemsi, Vallée du watercourse** Mali
93 B5 **Tilh** France
36 D4 **Tilhar** India
24 A2 **Tilin** Myanmar
172 E2 **Tilisarao** Argentina
65 F2 **Till r.** England U.K.
123 E4 **Tillabéri div.** Niger
123 E4 **Tillabéri** Niger
93 C5 **Tillac** France
152 B2 **Tillamook** Oregon U.S.A.
25 A5 **Tillanchong I. i.** Andaman and Nicobar Is India
90 D1 **Tille r.** France
123 E3 **Tillia** Niger
66 E4 **Tillicoultry** Scotland U.K.
86 D3 **Tilloy-et-Bellay** France
140 E5 **Tillsonburg** Ontario Canada
66 F3 **Tillyfourie** Scotland U.K.
89 E2 **Tilly-sur-Seulles** France
123 E3 **Tiloa** Niger
164 C4 **Tilomonte** Chile
113 F6 **Tilos i.** Greece
13 F2 **Tilpa** New South Wales Australia
121 E2 **Tilrhemt** Algeria
172 B2 **Tiltil** Chile
54 E3 **Tilža** Latvia
55 A3 **Tim r.** Denmark
52 C3 **Tim r.** Rus. Fed.
52 C4 **Tim** Rus. Fed.
119 F2 **Tima** Egypt
97 □ **Timanfaya h.** Canary Is Spain
44 F3 **Timanskiy Kryazh h.** Rus. Fed.
9 C6 **Timaru** New Zealand
51 F6 **Timashevsk** Rus. Fed.
107 H2 **Timau** Italy
166 E2 **Timbaúba** Brazil
131 H2 **Timbavati r.** South Africa
131 H2 **Timbavati Game Reserve res.** South Africa
120 C5 **Timbedgha** Mauritania
14 B2 **Timber Creek** Northern Terr. Australia
154 D3 **Timber Mt mt.** Nevada U.S.A.
146 D5 **Timberville** Virginia U.S.A.
167 B6 **Timbó r.** Brazil
13 E4 **Timboon** Victoria Australia
129 F2 **Timbué, Pta pt** Mozambique
81 E2 **Timelkam** Austria
123 D3 **Timétrine reg.** Mali
123 D3 **Timétrine** Mali
123 F3 **Timia** Niger
121 E4 **Timiaouine** Algeria
121 E3 **Timimoun** Algeria
47 G2 **Timiryazevo** Kazakhstan
52 F1 **Timiryazevo** Rus. Fed.
79 L6 **Timis div.** Romania
112 D2 **Timiş r.** Romania
79 L6 **Timişoara** Romania
123 F3 **Ti-m-Meghsoi watercourse** Niger
59 E3 **Timmele** Sweden
107 F2 **Timmelsjoch pass** Italy
73 F2 **Timmendorfer Strand** Germany
140 E2 **Timmins** Ontario Canada
50 F3 **Timokhino** Rus. Fed.
67 E4 **Timolin** Rep. of Ireland
166 D2 **Timon** Brazil
21 J8 **Timor i.** Indonesia
4 D6 **Timor Sea sea** Australia/Indonesia
173 F3 **Timote** Argentina
169 G3 **Timóteo** Brazil
121 D3 **Timoudi** Algeria
57 E3 **Timrå** Sweden
43 B4 **Timsâh, L. l.** Egypt
145 C5 **Tims Ford L. l.** Tennessee U.S.A.
47 G4 **Timur** Kazakhstan
36 D5 **Timurni Muafi** India
80 C4 **Tina r.** Italy
131 G5 **Tina r.** South Africa
162 D2 **Tinaco** Venezuela
122 D3 **Ti-n-Aguelhay** Mali
97 □ **Tinajo** Canary Is Spain
118 B3 **Tin Alkoum** Algeria/Libya
123 E3 **Ti-n-Azabo well** Mali
120 C4 **Ti-n-Bessaïs well** Mauritania
89 E3 **Tinchebray** France
123 D2 **Ti-n-Didine well** Mali
38 B3 **Tindivanam** India
120 C3 **Tindouf** Algeria
79 L5 **Tinea** Romania

124 C4 Tumba, Lac l. Congo(Zaire)
22 C2 Tumbangsamba Indonesia
22 B2 Tumbangtiti Indonesia
23 C5 Tumbao Philippines
13 G3 Tumbarumba New South Wales Australia
162 A4 Tumbes Peru
172 A4 Tumbes, Punta pt Chile
136 E3 Tumbler Ridge B.C. Canada
52 F2 Tumbotino Rus. Fed.
12 D3 Tumby Bay S. Australia Australia
30 D4 Tumd Youqi China
30 D4 Tumd Zuoqi China
31 J4 Tumen r. China/North Korea
31 J4 Tumen China
30 B5 Tumenzi China
163 E2 Tumeremo Venezuela
163 E2 Tumereng Guyana
23 A5 Tumindao i. Philippines
169 H3 Tumiritinga Brazil
38 B3 Tumkur India
66 E4 Tummel r. Scotland U.K.
66 E4 Tummel, Loch l. Scotland U.K.
118 B3 Tummo, Mts of mts Libya/Niger
23 □2 Tumon Bay b. Guam Pacific Ocean
39 E4 Tump Pakistan
22 C2 Tumpah Indonesia
100 D1 Tumuja r. Spain
13 G3 Tumut New South Wales Australia
47 J4 Tumxuk China
59 F1 Tuna-Hästberg Sweden
145 □3 Tuna, Pta pt Puerto Rico
159 □3 Tunapuna Trinidad and Tobago
158 C2 Tunas de Zaza Cuba
173 F3 Tunas, L. l. Argentina
39 C4 Tunb al Kubrā i. Iran
39 C4 Ţunb aş Şughrá i. Iran
63 G3 Tunbridge Wells, Royal England U.K.
42 D2 Tunceli Turkey
33 E5 Tunchang China
13 H3 Tuncurry New South Wales Australia
119 E4 Tundubai well Sudan
123 F4 Tundun-Wada Nigeria
127 C7 Tunduru Tanzania
73 F3 Tundzha r. Bulgaria
170 B3 Tunel la Cumbre tunnel Chile
123 F5 Tunga Nigeria
38 B3 Tungabhadra r. India
38 A3 Tungabhadra Reservoir resr India
37 H3 Tunga Pass India
126 B2 Tungaru Sudan
23 B5 Tungawan Philippines
27 □ Tung Chung Wan b. Hong Kong China
56 M6 Tungnaá r. Iceland
136 D2 Tungsten N.W.T. Canada
6 □5 Tungua i. Tonga
22 C1 Tungun, Bukit mt. Indonesia
45 L3 Tunguska, Nizhnyaya r. Rus. Fed.
27 □ Tung Wan b. Hong Kong China
178 □2 Tunheim Bjørnøya Arctic Ocean
38 C2 Tuni India
87 H4 Tuningen Germany
140 E2 Tunis Ontario Canada
121 G1 Tunis Tunisia
121 G1 Tunis, Golfe de g. Tunisia
116 E2 Tunisia country Africa
162 C2 Tunja Colombia
30 B2 Tunka Rus. Fed.
30 B2 Tunkinskiye Gol'tsy mountain range Rus. Fed.
30 E5 Tunliu China
93 C6 Tunnel de Bielsa tunnel France/Spain
59 F2 Tunnerstad Sweden
58 C1 Tunnhovdfjorden l. Norway
56 D2 Tunnsjøen l. Norway
55 C4 Tunø i. Denmark
52 E1 Tunoshna Rus. Fed.
63 H2 Tunstall England U.K.
56 H2 Tuntsa Finland
56 H2 Tuntsayoki r. Rus. Fed.
139 H2 Tunungayualok Island i. Newfoundland Canada
172 D2 Tunuyán r. Argentina
172 C2 Tunuyán Argentina
Tunxi see Huangshan
33 G1 Tuo r. China
32 D2 Tuo r. China
31 G5 Tuoji Dao i. China
25 D5 Tuŏl Khpos Cambodia
154 B3 Tuolumne California U.S.A.
154 C3 Tuolumne Meadows California U.S.A.
32 D3 Tuoniang r. China
32 G2 Tuotuo r. China
37 H2 Tuotuoyan China
168 C4 Tupã Brazil
168 D3 Tupaciguara Brazil
Tupai i. see Motu Iti
147 K2 Tupambaé Uruguay
167 B6 Tupanciretã Brazil
151 F5 Tupelo Mississippi U.S.A.
163 F4 Tupinambarama, Ilha i. Brazil
168 C4 Tupi Paulista Brazil
166 C2 Tupiratins Brazil
54 F2 Tupitsyno Rus. Fed.
164 C4 Tupiza Bolivia
76 C4 Tuplice Poland
147 F2 Tupper Lake l. New York U.S.A.
147 F2 Tupper Lake New York U.S.A.
172 C2 Tupungato Argentina
172 C2 Tupungato, Co volcano Argentina
42 F4 Tuqayyid well Iraq
31 G3 Tuquan China
162 B3 Túquerres Colombia
33 E5 Tuqu Wan China
37 G4 Tura India
45 M3 Tura Rus. Fed.
119 H3 Turabah Saudi Arabia
8 E4 Turakina New Zealand
9 E4 Turakirae Head headland New Zealand
39 D2 Turan Iran
30 B2 Turan Rus. Fed.
31 J2 Turana, Khrebet mountain range Rus. Fed.
8 E3 Turangi New Zealand
46 E5 Turan Lowland plain Asia
76 G5 Turawa Poland
119 G1 Turayf Saudi Arabia
54 D2 Turba Estonia
162 B1 Turbaco Colombia
77 J6 Turbacz mt. Poland
126 D1 Turbah Yemen
39 E4 Turbat Pakistan
83 D1 Turbenthal Switzerland
53 C2 Turbiv Ukraine
162 B2 Turbo Colombia
80 E3 Türchlwand mt. Austria
98 E2 Turcia Spain
79 H3 Turčianske Teplice Slovakia
87 G4 Turckheim France
112 G2 Turcoaia Romania
112 D1 Turda Romania
52 C3 Turdey Rus. Fed.
90 C3 Turdine r. France
17 B4 Turee Cr. r. Western Australia Australia
99 F3 Turégano Spain
76 G3 Turek Poland
54 D1 Turenki Finland
Turfan see Turpan
46 F3 Turgay r. Kazakhstan
46 F3 Turgay Kazakhstan
47 G2 Turgay div. Kazakhstan
47 H2 Turgay Kazakhstan
46 F3 Turgayskaya Dolina v. Kazakhstan
46 F2 Turgayskaya Stolovaya Strana reg. Kazakhstan
52 E2 Turgenevo Rus. Fed.
141 F2 Turgeon, Lac l. Québec Canada
112 F3 Tŭrgovishte Bulgaria
46 F1 Turgoyak Rus. Fed.
42 A2 Turgutlu Turkey
113 F6 Turgutreis Turkey
42 D1 Turhal Turkey
164 C4 Turi Chile
54 D2 Türi Estonia
111 G2 Turi Italy
103 C5 Turia r. Spain
112 C1 Turiaçu r. Brazil
166 C1 Turiaçu Brazil
Turin see Torino
44 H4 Turinsk Rus. Fed.
103 C5 Turis Spain
53 A1 Turiya r. Ukraine
31 J3 Turiy Rog Rus. Fed.
53 A1 Turiys'k Ukraine
26 J1 Turka Rus. Fed.
77 M6 Turka Ukraine
126 C4 Turkana, Lake salt lake Ethiopia/Kenya
113 F4 Türkeli Adası i. Turkey
80 C2 Türkenfeld Germany
47 G4 Turkestan Kazakhstan
47 G5 Turkestan Range mountain range Asia
79 K4 Túrkeve Hungary
18 E6 Turkey country Asia
148 B4 Turkey r. Iowa U.S.A.
16 E3 Turkey Creek Western Australia Australia
75 F4 Türkheim Germany
52 F4 Turki Rus. Fed.
46 D4 Turkmenbashi Turkmenistan
42 B2 Türkmen Daği mt. Turkey
18 G6 Turkmenistan country Asia
39 E1 Turkmen-Kala Turkmenistan
46 D5 Turkmenskiy Zaliv b. Turkmenistan
42 D2 Türkoğlu Turkey
133 L8 Turks and Caicos Islands territory Caribbean
159 E2 Turks I. Pass. chan. Turks and Caicos Is Caribbean
159 E2 Turks Is is Turks and Caicos Is Caribbean
59 J1 Turku r. Finland
57 F3 Turku Finland
54 B1 Turku-Pori div. Finland
126 C4 Turkwel r. Kenya
154 B3 Turlock California U.S.A.
154 B3 Turlock L. l. California U.S.A.
169 G2 Turmalina Brazil
119 H2 Turmus, W. at watercourse Saudi Arabia
8 F4 Turnagain, Cape c. New Zealand
79 K3 Turňa nad Bodvou Slovakia
81 G3 Turnau Austria
66 D5 Turnberry Scotland U.K.
155 G5 Turnbull, Mt mt. Arizona U.S.A.
157 J5 Turneffe Is is Belize
84 F3 Turner r. Western Australia Australia
149 F3 Turner Michigan U.S.A.
69 C3 Turnhout div. Antwerpen Belgium
69 C3 Turnhout Belgium
81 G3 Türnitz Austria
137 H3 Turnor Lake l. Saskatchewan Canada
78 E1 Turnov Czech Rep.
112 E3 Turnu Măgurele Romania
47 L2 Turochak Rus. Fed.
13 G3 Turon r. New South Wales Australia
101 F4 Turón r. Spain
77 L4 Turów Poland
26 E3 Turpan China
26 E3 Turpan Pendi depression China
158 C3 Turquino mt. Cuba
108 A5 Turri Sardegna Italy
66 F3 Turriff Scotland U.K.
42 F3 Tursāq Iraq
109 J4 Tursi Italy
77 N4 Turs'kyy Kanal canal Ukraine
46 F4 Turtkul' Uzbekistan
148 B2 Turtle Flambeau Flowage resr Wisconsin U.S.A.
137 H4 Turtleford Saskatchewan Canada
15 H3 Turtle I. i. Coral Sea Islands Terr. Pacific Ocean
23 A5 Turtle Islands is Philippines
122 B5 Turtle Islands is Sierra Leone
148 A3 Turtle Lake Wisconsin U.S.A.
47 J4 Turugart Pass pass China/Kyrgyzstan
44 K3 Turukhansk Rus. Fed.
163 F3 Turuna r. Brazil
30 C1 Turuntayevo Rus. Fed.
168 C2 Turvo r. Goiás Brazil
167 B6 Turvo r. Rio Grande do Sul Brazil
168 D4 Turvo r. São Paulo Brazil
168 D5 Turvo r. São Paulo Brazil
167 C6 Turvo Brazil
77 N5 Turynka Ukraine
77 J2 Turza Wielka Poland
110 D5 Tusa r. Sicilia Italy
110 D5 Tusa Sicilia Italy
155 F4 Tusayan Arizona U.S.A.
145 C5 Tuscaloosa Alabama U.S.A.
108 D2 Tuscania Italy
146 C4 Tuscarawas r. Ohio U.S.A.
146 E4 Tuscarora Mts h. Pennsylvania U.S.A.
148 C6 Tuscola Illinois U.S.A.
151 D5 Tuscola Texas U.S.A.
39 D2 Tusharīk Iran
52 C4 Tuskar' r. Rus. Fed.
145 C5 Tuskegee Alabama U.S.A.
80 B2 Tussenhausen Germany
146 D4 Tussey Mts h. Pennsylvania U.S.A.
77 H4 Tuszyn Poland
39 D3 Tūtak Iran
42 E2 Tutak Turkey
52 D1 Tutayev Rus. Fed.
63 E2 Tutbury England U.K.
38 B4 Tuticorin India
166 D1 Tutóia Brazil
112 F2 Tutrakan Bulgaria
150 D4 Tuttle Creek Res. resr Kansas U.S.A.
74 D5 Tuttlingen Germany
135 Q2 Tuttut Nunaat reg. Greenland
7 □13 Tutuila i. American Samoa Pacific Ocean
128 D3 Tutume Botswana
157 F5 Tututepec Mexico
75 G5 Tutzing Germany
30 C2 Tuul Gol r. Mongolia
54 D1 Tuulos Finland
31 H4 Tuun, Mt mt. North Korea
56 H3 Tuupovaara Finland
56 H3 Tuusniemi Finland
54 D1 Tuusula Finland
7 □16 Tuutapu h. Easter I. Chile
Tuva div. see Tyva
4 J5 Tuvalu country Pacific Ocean
6 □7 Tuvuca i. Fiji
6 □8 Tuvutau h. Fiji
22 D1 Tuwau r. Indonesia
43 D4 Tuweiyil esh Shiqāq mt. Jordan
80 C3 Tuxer Gebirge mountain range Austria
63 F1 Tuxford England U.K.
156 E5 Tuxpan Jalisco Mexico
157 F4 Tuxpan Veracruz Mexico
157 G5 Tuxtla Gutiérrez Mexico
25 D4 Tuy Đưc Vietnam
24 D2 Tuyên Quang Vietnam
25 E4 Tuy Hoa Vietnam
46 D2 Tuymazy Rus. Fed.
39 B2 Tūysarkān Iran
42 C2 Tuz Gölü salt lake Turkey
50 H3 Tuzha Rus. Fed.
112 B3 Tuzi Yugoslavia
155 F4 Tuzigoot National Monument nat. park Arizona U.S.A.
42 F3 Tuz Khurmātū Iraq
Tuz, L. salt lake see Tuz Gölü
42 E2 Tuzla r. Turkey
43 C1 Tuzla Adana Turkey
104 G3 Tuzla Bos.-Herz.
112 G3 Tuzla Romania
51 F6 Tuzlov r. Rus. Fed.
81 H4 Tužno Croatia
118 C3 Tuzugu well Libya
59 E3 Tvååker Sweden
81 H1 Tvarožná Czech Rep.
58 C2 Tvedestrand Norway
58 C2 Tveit Norway
58 A1 Tveitakvitingen mt. Norway
52 B1 Tver' div. Rus. Fed.
52 B1 Tver' Rus. Fed.
55 C2 Tversted Denmark
52 B1 Tvertsa r. Rus. Fed.
55 □1 Tvøroyri Faeroes
112 E3 Tvŭrditsa Bulgaria
76 F4 Twardogóra Poland
66 E1 Twatt Scotland U.K.
65 F2 Tweed r. England/Scotland U.K.
141 G4 Tweed Ontario Canada
65 E2 Tweeddale v. Scotland U.K.
68 E2 Tweede Exloërmond Netherlands
65 F2 Tweedmouth England U.K.
65 E2 Tweedsmuir Scotland U.K.
136 D4 Tweedsmuir Prov. Park res. B.C. Canada
131 G3 Tweeling South Africa
130 B2 Twee Rivier Namibia
130 C3 Twee Rivieren South Africa
131 F4 Tweespruit South Africa
68 F2 Twello Netherlands
68 E2 Twente reg. Netherlands
68 E2 Twentekanaal canal Netherlands
154 D4 Twentynine Palms California U.S.A.
139 K4 Twillingate Newfoundland Canada
152 D2 Twin Bridges Montana U.S.A.
151 C6 Twin Buttes Res. resr Texas U.S.A.
152 D3 Twin Falls Idaho U.S.A.
139 H3 Twin Falls Newfoundland Canada
16 D4 Twin Heads h. Western Australia Australia
136 F3 Twin Lakes Alberta Canada
147 H2 Twin Mountain New Hampshire U.S.A.
146 C6 Twin Oaks N. Carolina U.S.A.
154 B2 Twin Peak summit California U.S.A.
12 C2 Twins, The S. Australia Australia
72 C3 Twist Germany
72 D3 Twistringen Germany
13 G4 Twofold B. b. New South Wales Australia
155 G4 Two Guns Arizona U.S.A.
148 B2 Two Harbors Minnesota U.S.A.
137 G4 Two Hills Alberta Canada
152 D1 Two Medicine r. Montana U.S.A.
148 D3 Two Rivers Wisconsin U.S.A.
76 G5 Tworóg Poland
63 F3 Twyford England U.K.
112 D1 Tyachiv Ukraine
37 H5 Tyao r. India
53 E2 Tyasmyn r. Ukraine
28 L1 Tyatya mt. Rus. Fed.
76 E2 Tychówko Poland
76 E2 Tychowo Poland
77 L6 Tyczyn Poland
56 C3 Tydal Norway
59 F1 Tyfors Sweden
146 D5 Tygart Lake l. W. Virginia U.S.A.
146 D5 Tygart Valley v. W. Virginia U.S.A.
31 H1 Tygda Rus. Fed.
58 C1 Tyin l. Norway
58 C1 Tyinkrysset Norway
113 F4 Tykhero Greece
53 E1 Tykhonovychi Ukraine
77 K6 Tylawa Poland
151 E5 Tyler Texas U.S.A.
151 F6 Tylertown Mississippi U.S.A.
53 D3 Tylihul r. Ukraine
59 G2 Tyllinge Sweden
55 B2 Tylstrup Denmark
53 F3 Tymchenky Ukraine
114 B2 Tymfi mts Greece
53 F3 Tymoshivka Ukraine
115 F7 Tympaki Greece
45 O4 Tynda Rus. Fed.
136 A2 Tyndall Gl. gl. Alaska U.S.A.
66 D4 Tyndrum Scotland U.K.
66 F5 Tyne r. Scotland U.K.
65 G3 Tyne and Wear div. England U.K.
75 L2 Týnec nad Labem Czech Rep.
78 D2 Týnec nad Sázavou Czech Rep.
65 G2 Tynemouth England U.K.
59 E1 Tyngsjö Sweden
53 D2 Tynivka Ukraine
78 D2 Týn nad Vltavou Czech Rep.
53 B1 Tynne Ukraine
57 C3 Tynset Norway
77 L6 Tyrawa Wołoska Poland
Tyre see Sour
13 E3 Tyrell, L. l. Victoria Australia
137 H2 Tyrell Lake l. N.W.T. Canada
59 H2 Tyresö Sweden
58 D1 Tyrifjorden l. Norway
58 D1 Tyristrand Norway
80 D2 Tyrlaching Germany
31 J2 Tyrma r. Rus. Fed.
31 K2 Tyrma Rus. Fed.
56 G2 Tyrnävä Finland
114 D3 Tyrnavos Greece
52 D2 Tyrnovo Rus. Fed.
Tyrol div. see Tirol
67 D2 Tyrone div. Northern Ireland U.K.
146 D4 Tyrone Pennsylvania U.S.A.
13 E3 Tyrrell r. Victoria Australia
13 E3 Tyrrell, L. l. Victoria Australia
108 C4 Tyrrhenian Sea sea France/Italy
112 D1 Tysa r. Romania/Ukraine
53 D2 Tyshkivka Ukraine
53 D2 Tysmenytsya Ukraine
58 A2 Tysnesøy i. Norway
58 A1 Tysse Norway
58 A1 Tyssebotnen Norway
58 B1 Tyssedal Norway
59 G2 Tystberga Sweden
55 D4 Tystrup Sø l. Denmark
77 M5 Tyszowce Poland
45 Q3 Tyubelyakh Rus. Fed.
47 H1 Tyukalinsk Rus. Fed.
46 D4 Tyuleni, O-va i. Kazakhstan
46 E2 Tyul'gan Rus. Fed.
47 G1 Tyumen' Rus. Fed.
44 H4 Tyumen' Rus. Fed.
47 G4 Tyumen'-Aryk Kazakhstan
47 K2 Tyumentsevo Rus. Fed.
45 N3 Tyung r. Rus. Fed.
Tyuratam see Leninsk
56 J1 Tyuva-Guba Rus. Fed.
30 A2 Tyva div. Rus. Fed.
53 C2 Tyvriv Ukraine
73 K2 Tywa r. Poland
62 B3 Tywi r. Wales U.K.
62 B2 Tywyn Wales U.K.
131 H1 Tzaneen South Africa
131 H1 Tzaneen Dam dam South Africa
68 D1 Tzummarum Netherlands

U

163 E3 Uacauyén Venezuela
7 □12 Uafato Western Samoa
125 D7 Uamanda Angola
163 D4 Uarini Brazil
163 F4 Uatumã r. Brazil
166 E2 Uauá Brazil
162 D4 Uaupés r. Brazil
162 D4 Uaupés Brazil
157 H5 Uaxactún Guatemala
112 C2 Ub Yugoslavia
47 K2 Uba r. Kazakhstan
169 G4 Ubá Brazil
123 G4 Uba Nigeria
69 E4 Übach-Palenberg Germany
47 F2 Ubagan r. Kazakhstan
169 F2 Ubaí Brazil
118 E5 Ubaid well Sudan
166 E3 Ubaitaba Brazil
46 E4 Ubal Karabaur h. Uzbekistan
124 C3 Ubangi r. Central African Rep./Congo(Zaire)
53 C1 Ubarts r. Belarus
162 C2 Ubate Colombia
169 F5 Ubatuba Brazil
126 D1 Ubaydīyah Yemen
91 E4 Ubaye r. France
42 E4 Ubayyia, Wādī al watercourse Iraq/Saudi Arabia
42 E3 Ubayyid, Wādī al watercourse Iraq
55 D4 Ubby Denmark
28 C7 Ube Japan
101 G2 Úbeda Spain
168 D3 Uberaba r. Brazil
168 E3 Uberaba Brazil
165 E3 Uberaba, Lagoa l. Brazil
168 D3 Uberlândia Brazil
74 E5 Überlingen Germany
83 E1 Überlinger See l. Germany
75 H5 Übersee Germany
25 □ Ubin, Pulau i. Singapore
47 J1 Ubinskoye Rus. Fed.
47 K1 Ubinskoye, Ozero l. Rus. Fed.
168 B6 Ubiratã Brazil
24 C3 Ubolratna Res. resr Thailand
131 J3 Ubombo South Africa
25 D4 Ubon Ratchathani Thailand
53 B1 Ubort' r. Ukraine
101 E4 Ubrique Spain
74 D3 Ubstadt-Weiher Germany
124 E4 Ubundu Congo(Zaire)
172 F2 Ucacha Argentina
42 F1 Ucar Azerbaijan
43 B1 Uçarı Turkey
162 C5 Ucayali r. Peru
69 C4 Uccle Belgium
99 C3 Ucero r. Spain
39 E1 Uch-Adzhi Turkmenistan
46 E2 Uchaly Rus. Fed.
39 B1 Üchān Iran
47 K3 Ucharal Kazakhstan
28 D7 Uchiko Japan
28 C8 Uchinoura Japan
52 C1 Uchinskoye Vdkhr. resr Rus. Fed.
28 H2 Uchiura-wan b. Japan
164 A1 Uchiza Peru
46 F4 Uchkuduk Uzbekistan
39 F1 Uchkyay Uzbekistan
46 E4 Uchsay Uzbekistan
73 G3 Uchte r. Germany
72 D3 Uchte Germany
38 A4 Uchto r. Pakistan
99 F2 Ucieza r. Spain
73 K1 Ückeritz Germany
73 J2 Uckermark reg. Germany
63 G4 Uckfield England U.K.
55 E5 Uclés Spain
136 D5 Ucluelet B.C. Canada
153 E3 Ucolo Utah U.S.A.
152 F2 Ucross Wyoming U.S.A.
30 D1 Uda r. Rus. Fed.
53 G2 Uda r. Ukraine
46 C3 Udachnoye Rus. Fed.
45 N3 Udachnyy Rus. Fed.
38 B4 Udagamandalam India
36 C4 Udaipur India
37 G5 Udaipur India
36 D5 Udaipura India
37 F4 Udaipur Garhi Nepal
37 H4 Udalguri India
37 E5 Udanti r. India/Myanmar
173 H4 Udaquilla Argentina
79 M2 Udava r. Slovakia
53 E1 Uday r. Ukraine
38 B3 Udayagiri India
59 E1 Uddeholm Sweden
58 D2 Uddevalla Sweden
66 D5 Uddingston Scotland U.K.
64 E2 Uddington Scotland U.K.
56 E2 Uddjaure l. Sweden
68 D3 Uden Netherlands
38 B2 Udgir India
36 C2 Udhampur India
50 H2 Udimskiy Rus. Fed.
107 H2 Udine div. Friuli - Venezia Giulia Italy
107 H2 Udine Udine Italy
139 J2 Udjuktok Bay b. Newfoundland Canada
50 E3 Udomlya Rus. Fed.
24 C3 Udon Thani Thailand
76 F1 Udorpie Poland
45 P4 Udskaya Guba b. Rus. Fed.
38 B4 Udumalaippetai India
38 A3 Udupi India
6 □6 Udu Pt pt Fiji
53 G1 Udy Ukraine
45 P4 Udyl', Ozero l. Rus. Fed.
Udzhary see Ucar
73 J2 Uecker r. Germany
73 K2 Ueckermünde Germany
29 G5 Ueda Japan
22 E2 Uekuli Indonesia
124 D3 Uele r. Congo(Zaire)
124 B3 Uelen Rus. Fed.
134 A3 Uel'kal Rus. Fed.
68 E2 Uelsen Germany
73 F3 Uelzen Germany
131 J2 Uembje, Lagoa l. Mozambique
29 F6 Ueno Japan
124 E3 Uere r. Congo(Zaire)
82 C2 Uetendorf Switzerland
72 E2 Uetersen Germany
74 E3 Uettingen Germany
72 F3 Uetze Germany
46 E1 Ufa r. Rus. Fed.
46 E2 Ufa Rus. Fed.
126 B2 Uffat r. Sudan
73 F3 Uffenheim Germany
75 G5 Uffing am Staffelsee Germany
128 B3 Ugab watercourse Namibia
54 C3 Ugāle Latvia
127 B6 Ugalla r. Tanzania
127 B6 Ugalla River Game Reserve res. Tanzania
117 H5 Uganda country Africa
172 B2 Ugarteche Argentina
30 E1 Ugdan Rus. Fed.
55 B5 Uge Denmark
111 H3 Ugento Italy
58 A1 Uggdal Norway
55 C2 Uggerby r. Denmark
111 H2 Uggiano la Chiesa Italy
123 F5 Ughelli Nigeria
131 G5 Ugie South Africa
101 G4 Ugíjar Spain
90 E3 Ugine France
27 Q2 Uglegorsk Rus. Fed.
52 D1 Uglich Rus. Fed.
104 E3 Ugljan i. Croatia
31 J2 Uglovoye Rus. Fed.
47 K2 Uglovskoye Rus. Fed.
45 Q3 Ugol'naya Zyryanka Rus. Fed.
45 T3 Ugol'nyye Kopi Rus. Fed.
52 B2 Ugra r. Rus. Fed.
52 B2 Ugra Rus. Fed.
79 M3 Uh r. Slovakia
79 G2 Uherské Brod Czech Rep.
78 G2 Uherské Hradiště Czech Rep.
74 E4 Uhingen Germany
78 C2 Úhlava r. Czech Rep.
74 E5 Uhldingen Germany
130 A1 Uhlenhorst Namibia
75 L3 Uhlířské Janovice Czech Rep.
77 M5 Uhniv Ukraine
146 C4 Uhrichsville Ohio U.S.A.
53 F1 Uhroyidy Ukraine
73 K4 Uhyst Germany
106 B3 Uia di Ciamarella mt. Italy
Uibhist a' Deas i. see South Uist
Uibhist a' Tuath i. see North Uist
66 B3 Uig Scotland U.K.
125 C5 Uíge div. Angola
125 C5 Uíge Angola
6 □5 'Uiha i. Tonga
31 H5 Ŭijŏngbu South Korea
31 H4 Ŭiju North Korea
46 E3 Uil r. Kazakhstan
46 D3 Uil Kazakhstan
51 G7 Uilpata mt. Rus. Fed.
56 H3 Uimaharju Finland
155 F3 Uinkaret Plateau plat. Arizona U.S.A.
142 D3 Uinta Mts mts Utah U.S.A.
28 B6 Ŭiryŏng South Korea
128 A3 Uis Mine Namibia
31 J5 Ŭisŏng South Korea
131 E6 Uitenhage South Africa
68 C2 Uithoorn Netherlands
68 E1 Uithuizen Netherlands
139 H2 Uivak, Cape headland Newfoundland Canada
76 G5 Ujazd Poland
79 L4 Újfehértó Hungary
36 D4 Ujhani India
29 E6 Uji Japan
28 B8 Uji-guntō is Japan
127 A5 Ujiji Tanzania
36 C5 Ujjain India
78 F4 Újkér Hungary
76 E2 Ujście Poland
79 K4 Újszász Hungary
78 F5 Újudvar Hungary
22 D3 Ujung Pandang Indonesia
29 □2 Uka Japan
123 F4 Ukata Nigeria
127 B5 Ukerewe I. i. Tanzania
119 H4 Ukhdūd Saudi Arabia
52 E3 Ukholovo Rus. Fed.
77 N4 Ukhovets'k Ukraine
37 H4 Ukhrul India
50 K2 Ukhta r. Rus. Fed.
50 K2 Ukhta Rus. Fed.
54 E1 Ukhtokhma r. Rus. Fed.
54 F4 Ukhvala Belarus
154 A2 Ukiah California U.S.A.
152 C2 Ukiah Oregon U.S.A.
135 N2 Ukkusissat Greenland
76 D2 Ukleja r. Poland
54 D4 Ukmergė Lithuania
49 H4 Ukraine country Europe
53 D1 Ukrayinka Ukraine
79 M3 Ukraynis'ki Karpaty mountain range Ukraine
104 F3 Ukrina r. Bos.-Herz.
50 J2 Uktym Rus. Fed.
125 B6 Uku Angola
28 B7 Uku-jima i. Japan
128 C3 Ukwi Pan salt pan Botswana
36 D2 Ul r. India
54 F4 Ula r. Belarus
54 F4 Ula Belarus
113 G6 Ula Turkey
30 C3 Ulaanbaatar Mongolia
30 D3 Ulaan-Ereg Mongolia
26 F2 Ulaangom Mongolia
30 C3 Ulaanhudag Mongolia
30 B3 Ulaan Nuur l. Mongolia
30 D3 Ulaan-Uul Mongolia
53 C2 Uladivka Ukraine
13 G3 Ulan New South Wales Australia
34 J3 Ulan China
Ulan Bator see Ulaanbaatar
47 H4 Ulanbel' Kazakhstan
30 C4 Ulan Buh Shamo desert China
30 C1 Ulan-Burgasy, Khr. mountain range Rus. Fed.
51 H6 Ulan Erge Rus. Fed.
Ulanhad see Chifeng
Ulanhot see Horqin Youyi Qianqi
53 C2 Ulaniv Ukraine
77 L4 Ulan-Majorat Poland
52 B4 Ulanove Rus. Fed.
30 D4 Ulansuhai Nur l. China
30 B4 Ulan Tohoi China
30 C2 Ulan-Ude Rus. Fed.
37 G2 Ulan Ul Hu l. China
172 D1 Ulapes Argentina
42 D2 Ulaş Sivas Turkey
113 F4 Ulaş Tekirdağ Turkey
108 A4 Ula Tirso Sardegna Italy
6 □1 Ulawa I. i. Solomon Is.
47 K2 Ul'ba Kazakhstan
55 B3 Ulbjerg Denmark
66 E2 Ulbster Scotland U.K.
31 J5 Ulchin South Korea
112 B4 Ulcinj Yugoslavia
130 E4 Ulco South Africa
30 D2 Uldz r. Mongolia
30 D2 Uldz Mongolia
58 C2 Ulefoss Norway
54 E2 Ulenurme Estonia
30 E2 Ulety Rus. Fed.
55 A3 Ulfborg Denmark
68 E3 Ulft Netherlands
31 F3 Ulgain Gol r. China
47 G2 Ul'gili Kazakhstan
38 A2 Ulhasnagar India
30 A3 Uliastay Mongolia
79 M3 Ulič Slovakia
124 E4 Ulindi r. Congo(Zaire)
21 L4 Ulithi i. Fed. States of Micronesia
46 F3 Ul'kayak r. Kazakhstan
98 B2 Ulla r. Spain
13 G3 Ulladulla New South Wales Australia
66 C3 Ullapool Scotland U.K.
59 E3 Ullared Sweden
56 F3 Ullava Finland
102 D4 Ulldecona Spain
55 C4 Ullerslev Denmark
99 H2 Ullivarri, Emb. de resr Spain
65 F3 Ullswater l. England U.K.
31 J5 Ullŭng South Korea
31 J5 Ullŭng do i. South Korea
74 E4 Ulm Germany
31 J2 Ul'ma r. Rus. Fed.
13 H2 Ulmarra New South Wales Australia
100 B1 Ulme r. Portugal
74 B2 Ulmen Germany
112 F2 Ulmeni Călăraşi Romania
112 D1 Ulmeni Maramures Romania
104 G4 Ulog Bos.-Herz.
129 E1 Ulongue Mozambique
12 D1 Uloowaranie, L. salt flat S. Australia Australia
59 E3 Ulricehamn Sweden
81 E2 Ulrichsberg Austria
59 F2 Ulrika Sweden
68 E1 Ulrum Netherlands
31 J6 Ulsan South Korea
56 C3 Ulsberg Norway
66 □2 Ulsta Scotland U.K.
67 C2 Ulster div. Rep. of Ireland/U.K.
67 D2 Ulster Canal canal Rep. of Ireland/U.K.
55 C4 Ulstrup Vestsjælland Denmark
55 B3 Ulstrup Viborg Denmark
13 E3 Ultima Victoria Australia
113 G4 Ulubat Gölü l. Turkey
42 B2 Uluborlu Turkey
42 B1 Uludağ mt. Turkey
47 H5 Ulugqat China
6 □6 Uluiqalau mt. Fiji
25 C7 Ulu Kali, Gunung mt. Malaysia
42 C2 Ulukışla Turkey
131 H4 Ulundi South Africa
47 L3 Ulungur Hu l. China
25 □ Ulu Pandan Singapore
Uluru h. see Ayers Rock
14 B5 Uluru Nat. Park nat. park Northern Terr. Australia
51 E7 Ulus Turkey
66 B4 Ulva i. Scotland U.K.
Ulvéah i. see Lopévi
65 E3 Ulverston England U.K.
13 F5 Ulverstone Tasmania Australia
59 F2 Ulvettern l. Sweden
58 B1 Ulvik Norway
56 D3 Ulvsjön Sweden
52 C1 Ul'yanikha Rus. Fed.
50 H4 Ul'yankovo Rus. Fed.
53 D2 Ul'yanovka Ukraine
52 B3 Ul'yanovo Rus. Fed.
52 H3 Ul'yanovsk div. Rus. Fed.
50 J4 Ul'yanovsk Rus. Fed.
47 H2 Ul'yanovskiy Kazakhstan
31 F2 Ulyatuy Rus. Fed.
151 C4 Ulysses Kansas U.S.A.
47 G3 Ulytau Kazakhstan
47 G3 Ulyzhilanshik r. Kazakhstan
31 G1 Uma Rus. Fed.
107 H3 Umag Croatia
157 H4 Umán Mexico
53 D2 Uman' Ukraine
170 C2 Umango, Co mt. Argentina
36 A3 Umarao Pakistan
36 E5 Umaria India
38 B2 Umarkhed India
38 C2 Umarkot India
36 B4 Umarkot Pakistan
23 □2 Umatac Guam Pacific Ocean
152 C2 Umatilla Oregon U.S.A.
50 E1 Umba Rus. Fed.
131 H2 Umbabat Game Reserve res. South Africa
147 H2 Umbagog Lake l. New Hampshire U.S.A.
124 D2 Umbelasha watercourse Sudan
62 C4 Umberleigh England U.K.
107 G5 Umbertide Italy
6 □1 Umboi i. P.N.G.
9 B6 Umbrella Mts mts New Zealand
159 □1 Umbrella Pt pt Jamaica
109 E2 Umbria div. Italy
111 F3 Umbriatico Italy
129 D2 Ume r. Zimbabwe
56 F3 Umeå Sweden
56 D2 Umeälven r. Sweden
43 C3 Um ed Daraj, J. mt. Jordan
52 F3 Umet Rus. Fed.
52 F2 Umet Rus. Fed.
131 J4 Umfolozi r. South Africa
131 H4 Umfolozi Game Reserve res. South Africa
131 H4 Umgeni r. South Africa
80 B3 Umhausen Austria
131 H4 Umhlanga South Africa
98 B2 Umia r. Spain
134 H3 Umingmaktok N.W.T. Canada
138 E2 Umiujaq Québec Canada
131 H5 Umkomaas r. South Africa
131 H5 Umkomaas South Africa
131 H4 Umlazi South Africa
119 G3 Umm al Birak Saudi Arabia
39 C4 Umm al Qaywayn U.A.E.
73 J1 Ummanz i. Germany
119 H2 Umm at Qalbān Saudi Arabia
39 B4 Umm Bāb Qatar
119 E5 Umm Bel Sudan
43 B5 Umm Bugma Egypt
80 A2 Ummendorf Germany
118 C2 Umm Farud Libya
119 F3 Umm Gerifat waterhole Sudan
119 E5 Umm Keddada Sudan
119 G2 Umm Lajj Saudi Arabia
43 C5 Umm Mafrūd, G. mt. Egypt
43 C5 Umm Nukhaylah well Saudi Arabia
42 F4 Umm Qasr Iraq
119 E4 Umm Qurein well Sudan
119 F5 Umm Rimtha well Sudan
119 F5 Umm Ruwaba Sudan
118 E1 Umm Sa'ad Libya
Umm Sa'id see Musay'īd
119 F5 Umm Saiyala Sudan
43 D5 Umm Shajtiya waterhole Saudi Arabia
43 B5 Umm Shomar, G. mt. Egypt
119 E4 Umm Sunaita well Sudan
43 B5 Umm Tināşşib, G. mt. Egypt
119 G2 Umm Urūmah i. Saudi Arabia
43 B5 Umm Zanatir mt. Egypt
132 B4 Umnak I. i. Alaska U.S.A.
129 F1 Umpilua Mozambique
152 A3 Umpqua r. Oregon U.S.A.
125 C6 Umpulo Angola
36 D5 Umred India
38 A1 Umreth India
131 G5 Umtamvuna r. South Africa
131 G5 Umtata r. South Africa
131 G5 Umtata South Africa
131 G5 Umtata Dam resr South Africa

131 H5 **Umtentweni** South Africa
123 F5 **Umuahia** Nigeria
168 B5 **Umuarama** *Paraná* Brazil
6 □3 **Umuna i.** Tonga
113 F4 **Umurbey** Turkey
131 H4 **Umvoti r.** South Africa
131 G5 **Umzimhlava r.** South Africa
131 G5 **Umzimkulu r.** South Africa
131 G5 **Umzimkulu** South Africa
131 G5 **Umzimvubu r.** South Africa
131 H5 **Umzinto** South Africa
131 H5 **Umzumbe** South Africa
104 F3 **Una r.** Bos.-Herz./Croatia
169 J1 **Una** Brazil
43 D4 **'Unāb, W. al watercourse** Jordan
169 E2 **Unaí** Brazil
39 G2 **Unai P. pass** Afghanistan
134 B3 **Unalakleet** *Alaska* U.S.A.
134 B4 **Unalaska** *Alaska* U.S.A.
134 B4 **Unalaska I. i.** *Alaska* U.S.A.
127 C7 **Unango** Mozambique
81 H2 **Únanov** Czech Rep.
66 C2 **Unapool** *Scotland* U.K.
42 C4 **'Unayzah** Jordan
119 H2 **'Unayzah** Saudi Arabia
102 B2 **Uncastillo** Spain
36 E4 **Unchahra** India
164 C3 **Uncia** Bolivia
153 E4 **Uncompahgre Plateau plat.** *Colorado* U.S.A.
31 F2 **Unda r.** Rus. Fed.
31 F2 **Unda** Rus. Fed.
59 F2 **Unden l.** Sweden
59 F2 **Undenäs** Sweden
131 G4 **Underberg** South Africa
12 E3 **Underbool** *Victoria* Australia
150 C2 **Underwood** *N. Dakota* U.S.A.
22 E4 **Undu, Tg pt** Indonesia
54 B2 **Undva** Estonia
51 D4 **Unecha** Rus. Fed.
52 H2 **Unga r.** Rus. Fed.
134 B4 **Unga I. i.** *Alaska* U.S.A.
13 F3 **Ungarie** *New South Wales* Australia
139 G2 **Ungava Bay b.** *Québec* Canada
138 F1 **Ungava, Péninsule d' pen.** *Québec* Canada
31 J4 **Unggi** North Korea
53 B3 **Ungheni** Moldova
112 C1 **Ungurași** Romania
127 D5 **Ungwana Bay b.** Kenya
98 C4 **Unhais da Serra** Portugal
50 J3 **Uni** Rus. Fed.
166 D1 **União** Brazil
167 B6 **União da Vitória** Brazil
166 E2 **União dos Palmares** Brazil
36 D4 **Uniara** India
76 G4 **Uniejów** Poland
107 J4 **Unije i.** Croatia
134 B4 **Unimak I. i.** *Alaska* U.S.A.
163 E4 **Unini r.** Brazil
164 B2 **Unini** Peru
159 G4 **Union i.** St Vincent
147 J2 **Union** *Maine* U.S.A.
145 D5 **Union** *S. Carolina* U.S.A.
146 C6 **Union** *W. Virginia* U.S.A.
172 E3 **Unión** Argentina
165 E4 **Unión** Paraguay
146 A4 **Union City** *Ohio* U.S.A.
146 D4 **Union City** *Pennsylvania* U.S.A.
145 B4 **Union City** *Tennessee* U.S.A.
130 D6 **Uniondale** South Africa
155 F4 **Union, Mt mt.** *Arizona* U.S.A.
145 C5 **Union Springs** *Alabama* U.S.A.
146 D5 **Uniontown** *Pennsylvania* U.S.A.
127 □4 **Union Vale** Mauritius
149 F4 **Unionville** *Michigan* U.S.A.
76 G2 **Unisław** Poland
152 E3 **Unita Mts. mts** *Utah* U.S.A.
18 G7 **United Arab Emirates country** Asia
48 E3 **United Kingdom country** Europe
132 H6 **United States of America country** North America
107 G4 **Uniti r.** Italy
147 J2 **Unity** *Maine* U.S.A.
152 C2 **Unity** *Oregon* U.S.A.
137 H4 **Unity** *Saskatchewan* Canada
128 A3 **Unjab watercourse** Namibia
36 C5 **Unjha** India
80 D3 **Unken** Austria
72 C4 **Unna** Germany
59 F1 **Unnan r.** Sweden
36 E4 **Unnāo** India
31 H5 **Ŭnp'a** North Korea
172 E1 **Unquillo** Argentina
31 H5 **Ŭnsan** North Korea
66 □2 **Unst i.** *Scotland* U.K.
72 F4 **Unstrut r.** Germany
29 □2 **Unten** Japan
83 D1 **Unterägeri** Switzerland
83 G1 **Unterammergau** Germany
83 F2 **Unter Engadin reg.** Switzerland
74 E2 **Unterfranken div.** Germany
81 E2 **Untergriesbach** Germany
75 G4 **Unterhaching** Germany
80 C3 **Unter Inn Thal v.** Austria
82 D1 **Unterkulm** Switzerland
74 F2 **Untermaßfeld** Germany
80 A1 **Untermünkheim** Germany
81 G4 **Unterpremstätten** Austria
80 D2 **Unterreit** Germany
80 C2 **Unterschleißheim** Germany
83 E1 **Untersee l.** Germany/Switzerland
75 G2 **Untersteinach** Germany
83 F1 **Unterthingau** Germany
73 J2 **Unterueckersee l.** Germany
81 F2 **Unterweißenbach** Austria
37 G2 **Unuli Horog** China
28 C7 **Unzen-dake volcano** Japan
93 A6 **Unzue** Spain
29 F5 **Uozu** Japan
78 E1 **Úpa r.** Czech Rep.
52 C2 **Upa r.** Rus. Fed.
37 F5 **Upar Ghat** India
163 E2 **Upata** Venezuela
63 E3 **Upavon** *England* U.K.
125 E5 **Upemba, Lac l.** Congo(Zaire)
125 E5 **Upemba, Parc National de l' nat. park** Congo(Zaire)
135 N2 **Upernavik** Greenland
135 N2 **Upernavik Kujalleq** Greenland
68 F1 **Upgant-Schott** Germany
23 C5 **Upi** Philippines
162 C3 **Upía r.** Colombia
78 F1 **Úpice** Czech Rep.
130 C4 **Upington** South Africa
54 D1 **Upinniemi** Finland
36 B5 **Upleta** India
62 D4 **Uplyme** *England* U.K.
56 H2 **Upoloksha** Rus. Fed.
7 □12 **Upolu i.** Western Samoa
146 B4 **Upper Arlington** *Ohio* U.S.A.
136 F4 **Upper Arrow L. l.** *B.C.* Canada
Upper Chindwin *see* **Mawlaik**
122 D4 **Upper East div.** Ghana
9 E4 **Upper Hutt** New Zealand
148 B4 **Upper Iowa r.** *Iowa* U.S.A.
147 K1 **Upper Kent** *New Brunswick* Canada
152 B3 **Upper Klamath L. l.** *Oregon* U.S.A.
152 B3 **Upper L. l.** *California* U.S.A.
154 A2 **Upper Lake** *California* U.S.A.
136 D2 **Upper Liard** *Yukon Terr.* Canada
67 D2 **Upper Lough Erne l.** *Northern Ireland* U.K.
159 □3 **Upper Manzanilla** Trinidad and Tobago
146 E5 **Upper Marlboro** *Maryland* U.S.A.
126 B3 **Upper Nile div.** Sudan
25 □ **Upper Peirce Res. resr** Singapore
139 J4 **Upper Salmon Res. resr** *Newfoundland* Canada
146 B4 **Upper Sandusky** *Ohio* U.S.A.
147 F2 **Upper Saranac Lake l.** *New York* U.S.A.
9 D4 **Upper Takaka** New Zealand
122 D4 **Upper West div.** Ghana
63 F2 **Uppingham** *England* U.K.
59 G1 **Upplanda** Sweden
59 G2 **Upplands-Väsby** Sweden
59 G1 **Uppsala div.** Sweden
59 G2 **Uppsala** Sweden
138 B4 **Upsala** *Ontario* Canada
36 D2 **Upshi** India
15 F3 **Upstart B. b.** *Queensland* Australia
15 F3 **Upstart, C. headland** *Queensland* Australia
147 H2 **Upton** *Maine* U.S.A.
62 D2 **Upton upon Severn** *England* U.K.
8 E1 **Upua** New Zealand
43 D2 **'Uqayribāt** Syria
43 C4 **'Uqeiqa, W. watercourse** Jordan
42 F4 **Uqlat al 'Udhaybah well** Iraq
119 H2 **'Uqlat aş Şuqūr** Saudi Arabia
Uqturpan *see* **Wushi**
162 B2 **Urabá, Golfo de b.** Colombia
Uracas i. *see* **Farallon de Pajaros**
30 D4 **Urad Qianqi** China
30 D4 **Urad Zhonghou Lianheqi** China
39 D3 **Ūrāf** Iran
29 G6 **Uraga-suidō chan.** Japan
29 G5 **Uragawara** Japan
28 J2 **Urahoro** Japan
168 C5 **Uraí** Brazil
78 F4 **Uraiújfalu** Hungary
28 J2 **Urakawa** Japan
13 F3 **Ural h.** *New South Wales* Australia
46 D2 **Ural r.** Kazakhstan/Rus. Fed.
13 G2 **Uralla** *New South Wales* Australia
Ural Mts mountain range *see* **Ural'skiy Khrebet**
46 D2 **Ural'sk** Kazakhstan
44 G4 **Ural'skiy Khrebet mountain range** Rus. Fed.
127 B6 **Urambo** Tanzania
13 F3 **Urana** *New South Wales* Australia
13 F3 **Urana, L. l.** *New South Wales* Australia
14 D4 **Urandangi** *Queensland* Australia
169 G1 **Urandi** Brazil
137 H3 **Uranium City** *Saskatchewan* Canada
163 E3 **Uraricoera** Brazil
163 E3 **Uraricoera r.** Brazil
108 A5 **Uras** *Sardegna* Italy
29 □2 **Urasoe** Japan
114 A2 **Ura Vajgurore** Albania
155 H2 **Uravan** *Colorado* U.S.A.
52 G2 **Urazovka** Rus. Fed.
87 G2 **Urbach** Germany
148 C5 **Urbana** *Illinois* U.S.A.
146 B4 **Urbana** *Ohio* U.S.A.
107 G5 **Urbania** Italy
166 D1 **Urbano Santos** Brazil
99 G2 **Urbel r.** Spain
87 H3 **Urberach** Germany
107 G5 **Urbino** Italy
99 H2 **Urbión mt.** Spain
90 B2 **Urbise** France
164 B2 **Urcos** Peru
51 H5 **Urda** Kazakhstan
101 G1 **Urda** Spain
173 G4 **Urdampolleta** Argentina
173 H2 **Urdinarrain** Argentina
50 J2 **Urdoma** Rus. Fed.
83 D1 **Urdorf** Switzerland
93 B6 **Urdos** France
47 K3 **Urdzhar** Kazakhstan
65 G3 **Ure r.** *England* U.K.
54 E5 **Urechcha** Belarus
50 H3 **Uren'** Rus. Fed.
44 J3 **Urengoy** Rus. Fed.
52 H2 **Ureno-Karlinskoye** Rus. Fed.
58 B2 **Urenosi mt.** Norway
8 E3 **Urenui** New Zealand
6 □2 **Uréparapara i.** Vanuatu
68 E1 **Ureterp** Netherlands
8 F3 **Urewera National Park nat. park** New Zealand
81 F2 **Urfahr-Umgebung div.** Austria
43 B6 **'Urf, G. el mt.** Egypt
74 B2 **Urft r.** Germany
52 G2 **Urga r.** Rus. Fed.
31 K2 **Urgal r.** Rus. Fed.
102 D3 **Urgell reg.** Spain
46 F4 **Urgench** Uzbekistan
42 C2 **Ürgüp** Turkey
47 L3 **Urho** China
56 G1 **Urho Kekkosen kansallispuisto nat. park** Finland
83 D2 **Uri div.** Switzerland
36 C2 **Uri** India
9 C5 **Uriah, Mt mt.** New Zealand
162 C1 **Uribia** Colombia
172 F4 **Uriburu** Argentina
66 F3 **Urie r.** *Scotland* U.K.
83 D2 **Uri-Rotstock mt.** Switzerland
13 E2 **Urisino** *New South Wales* Australia
47 G2 **Uritskiy** Kazakhstan
52 D4 **Uritskoye** Rus. Fed.
126 C2 **Uri Wenz r.** Ethiopia
57 F3 **Urjala** Finland
68 D2 **Urk** Netherlands
42 A2 **Urla** Turkey
112 F2 **Urlați** Romania
67 C3 **Urlaur Lough l.** Rep. of Ireland
67 D4 **Urlingford** Rep. of Ireland
30 C2 **Urluk** Rus. Fed.
31 K2 **Urmi r.** Rus. Fed.
Urmia *see* **Orūmīyeh**
Urmia, L. salt lake *see* **Daryācheh-ye Orūmīyeh**
27 □ **Urmston Road chan.** *Hong Kong* China
83 E1 **Urnäsch** Switzerland
58 B1 **Urnes** Norway
79 J4 **Üröm** Hungary
123 F5 **Uromi** Nigeria
112 C3 **Uroševac** Yugoslavia
47 G5 **Üroteppa** Tajikistan
172 E5 **Urre Lauquén, L. l.** Argentina
102 B2 **Urroz** Spain
37 F3 **Urru Co salt lake** China
93 A5 **Urrugne** France
99 H2 **Urrúnaga, Emb. de resr** Spain
52 E2 **Urshel'skiy** Rus. Fed.
59 F3 **Urshult** Sweden
77 M4 **Urszulin** Poland
93 A5 **Urt** France
30 B4 **Urt** Mongolia
82 C1 **Urtenen** Switzerland
168 D1 **Uru r.** Brazil
156 C3 **Uruáchic** Mexico
166 C3 **Uruaçu** Brazil
163 E4 **Uruana** Brazil
156 E5 **Uruapan** Mexico
164 B2 **Urubamba r.** Peru
163 F4 **Urubu r.** Brazil
163 F4 **Urucara** Brazil
52 A3 **Uruch'ye** Rus. Fed.
163 F5 **Urucu r.** Brazil
169 J1 **Uruçuca** Brazil
166 D2 **Uruçuí** Brazil
169 F2 **Urucuia r.** Brazil
169 F2 **Urucuia** Brazil
166 C2 **Uruçuí Prêto r.** Brazil
163 F4 **Urucurituba** Brazil
167 B6 **Uruguai r.** Brazil
170 E2 **Uruguaiana** Brazil
165 F3 **Uruguatos r.** Brazil
161 G7 **Uruguay country** South America
173 H2 **Uruguay r.** Argentina/Uruguay
31 H2 **Uruhe** China
Uruk *see* **Erech**
23 □1 **Urukthapel i.** Palau
43 D1 **Urūmaş Şughrá** Syria
Urumchi *see* **Ürümqi**
26 E3 **Ürümqi** China
13 H2 **Urunga** *New South Wales* Australia
51 G6 **Urup r.** Rus. Fed.
45 R5 **Urup, O. i.** Rus. Fed.
109 H3 **Ururi** Italy
51 H7 **Urus-Martan** Rus. Fed.
52 F3 **Urusovo** Rus. Fed.
46 D2 **Urussu** Rus. Fed.
168 D2 **Urutaí** Brazil
8 E3 **Uruti** New Zealand
47 L3 **Uryl'** Kazakhstan
28 H2 **Uryū-gawa r.** Japan
31 G1 **Uryupino** Rus. Fed.
51 G5 **Uryupinsk** Rus. Fed.
77 L5 **Urzędów** Poland
50 J3 **Urzhum** Rus. Fed.
112 F2 **Urziceni** Romania
108 B4 **Urzulei** *Sardegna* Italy
50 J4 **Usa r.** Rus. Fed.
28 C7 **Usa** Japan
100 D2 **Usagre** Spain
113 G5 **Uşak div.** Turkey
82 D2 **Uşak** Turkey
128 B3 **Usakos** Namibia
179 B5 **Usarp Mts mts** Antarctica
171 E7 **Usborne, Mt h.** Falkland Is.
112 C3 **Ušće** Yugoslavia
106 D4 **Uscio** Italy
73 K2 **Usedom i.** Germany
73 J2 **Usedom** Germany
17 A5 **Useless Loop** *Western Australia* Australia
108 A5 **Usellus** *Sardegna* Italy
119 G3 **Usfān** Saudi Arabia
54 E5 **Usha r.** Belarus
44 J1 **Ushakova, O. i.** Rus. Fed.
119 H3 **'Ushayrah** Saudi Arabia
30 A2 **Ush-Bel'dyr** Rus. Fed.
54 F3 **Ushcha r.** Rus. Fed.
28 C7 **Ushibuka** Japan
53 G1 **Ushinka** Rus. Fed.
52 F3 **Ushna** Rus. Fed.
52 E2 **Ushna r.** Rus. Fed.
47 J3 **Ushtobe** Kazakhstan
171 C7 **Ushuaia** Argentina
31 H1 **Ushumun** Rus. Fed.
54 C3 **Uši** Latvia
74 D2 **Usingen** Germany
108 A4 **Usini** *Sardegna* Italy
62 D3 **Usk r.** *Wales* U.K.
62 D3 **Usk** *Wales* U.K.
54 E5 **Uskhodni** Belarus
53 D2 **Usk Res. resr** *Wales* U.K.
72 E4 **Uslar** Germany
78 C2 **Úslava r.** Czech Rep.
52 C3 **Usma** Latvia
52 D3 **Usman' r.** Rus. Fed.
52 D3 **Usman'** Rus. Fed.
53 E2 **Usmas Ezers l.** Latvia
101 E1 **Uso r.** Spain
50 J2 **Usogorsk** Rus. Fed.
26 H1 **Usol'ye-Sibirskoye** Rus. Fed.
52 B3 **Usozha r.** Rus. Fed.
172 C2 **Uspallata** Argentina
53 G3 **Uspenivka** Ukraine
47 J2 **Uspenka** Kazakhstan
53 E1 **Uspenka** Ukraine
47 H3 **Uspenskiy** Kazakhstan
51 G6 **Uspenskoye** Rus. Fed.
108 B5 **Ussassai** *Sardegna* Italy
106 B3 **Usseglio** Italy
92 E3 **Ussel** *Auvergne* France
92 E3 **Ussel** *Limousin* France
90 D2 **Usses r.** France
92 C2 **Usson-du-Poitou** France
Ussuri r. *see* **Wusuli**
31 J4 **Ussuriysk** Rus. Fed.
50 H3 **Usta r.** Rus. Fed.
47 M2 **Ust'-Abakan** Rus. Fed.
50 H2 **Ust'- Alekseyevo** Rus. Fed.
36 B3 **Usta Muhammad** Pakistan
93 A5 **Ustaritz** France
46 F1 **Ust'-Bagaryak** Rus. Fed.
27 J1 **Ust'-Barguzin** Rus. Fed.
50 K2 **Ust'- Chernaya** Rus. Fed.
31 F1 **Ust'-Chernaya** Rus. Fed.
51 G6 **Ust'-Donetskiy** Rus. Fed.
78 D1 **Úštěk** Czech Rep.
83 D1 **Uster** Switzerland
58 B1 **Ustevatn l.** Norway
110 C4 **Ustica** Italy
110 C4 **Ustica, Isola di i.** Italy
45 M4 **Ust'Ilimsk** Rus. Fed.
50 E2 **Ust'-Ilya** Rus. Fed.
44 G3 **Ust'-Ilych** Rus. Fed.
78 D1 **Ústí nad Labem** Czech Rep.
78 F2 **Ústí nad Orlicí** Czech Rep.
Ustinov *see* **Izhevsk**
76 E1 **Ustka** Poland
45 S4 **Ust'-Kamchatsk** Rus. Fed.
47 K3 **Ust'-Kamenogorsk** Kazakhstan
47 K2 **Ust'-Kan** Rus. Fed.
31 F2 **Ust'-Karsk** Rus. Fed.
46 E2 **Ust'-Katav** Rus. Fed.
47 L2 **Ust'-Koksa** Rus. Fed.
50 K2 **Ust'-Kulom** Rus. Fed.
45 M4 **Ust'-Kut** Rus. Fed.
45 P2 **Ust'-Kuyga** Rus. Fed.
51 F6 **Ust'-Labinsk** Rus. Fed.
31 G1 **Ust'-Lubiya** Rus. Fed.
54 F2 **Ust'-Luga** Rus. Fed.
45 P3 **Ust'-Maya** Rus. Fed.
45 N3 **Ust'-Mukduyka** Rus. Fed.
31 F1 **Ust'-Nachin** Rus. Fed.
45 Q3 **Ust'-Nera** Rus. Fed.
31 F1 **Ust'-Niman** Rus. Fed.
45 N2 **Ust'-Olenek** Rus. Fed.
45 Q3 **Ust'omchug** Rus. Fed.
30 C1 **Ust'-Ordynskiy Buryatskiy Avt. Okrug div.** Rus. Fed.
93 D6 **Ustou** France
45 S3 **Ust' Penzhino** Rus. Fed.
112 F3 **Ustrem** Bulgaria
76 G6 **Ustroń** Poland
76 D1 **Ustronie Morskie** Poland
77 L6 **Ustrzyki Dolne** Poland
52 F4 **Ust'-Shcherbedino** Rus. Fed.
47 J1 **Ust'-Tarka** Rus. Fed.
31 J2 **Ust'-Tyrma** Rus. Fed.
31 F2 **Ust'-Umalta** Rus. Fed.
50 H2 **Ust'-Ura** Rus. Fed.
31 K2 **Ust'-Urgal** Rus. Fed.
46 F2 **Ust'-Uyskoye** Kazakhstan
50 G2 **Ust' Vayen'ga** Rus. Fed.
50 H2 **Ust'-Vyyskaya** Rus. Fed.
50 H2 **Ust'ya r.** Rus. Fed.
52 D1 **Ust'ye r.** Rus. Fed.
52 E3 **Ust'ye** Rus. Fed.
50 F3 **Ust'ye** Rus. Fed.
53 A1 **Ustyluh** Ukraine
53 E3 **Ustynivka** Ukraine
46 D4 **Ustyurta escarpment** Kazakhstan
50 F3 **Ustyuzhna** Rus. Fed.
47 K4 **Usu** China
29 G5 **Usuda** Japan
28 C7 **Usuki** Japan
156 H6 **Usulután** El Salvador
157 H5 **Usumacinta r.** Mexico
131 J3 **Usutu r.** Africa
50 D4 **Usvyaty** Rus. Fed.
77 J5 **Uszwica r.** Poland
155 G2 **Utah div.** U.S.A.
155 G1 **Utah Lake l.** *Utah* U.S.A.
56 G2 **Utajärvi** Finland
28 J2 **Utashinai** Japan
Utashinai Rus. Fed. *see* **Yuzhno-Kuril'sk**
6 □3 **'Uta Vava'u i.** Tonga
119 H3 **'Utaybah reg.** Saudi Arabia
39 B4 **Utayyiq** Saudi Arabia
58 A2 **Utbjoa** Norway
102 C3 **Utebo** Spain
91 F5 **Utelle** France
125 D7 **Utembo r.** Angola
54 D4 **Utena** Lithuania
127 C6 **Utete** Tanzania
36 A4 **Uthal** Pakistan
43 D2 **'Uthmānīyah** Syria
25 B4 **U Thong** Thailand
165 E2 **Utiariti** Brazil
147 F3 **Utica** *New York* U.S.A.
103 B5 **Utiel** Spain
136 F3 **Utikuma Lake l.** *Yukon Terr.* Canada
166 D3 **Utinga r.** Brazil
58 C1 **Utla r.** Norway
59 F3 **Utlängan i.** Sweden
131 E3 **Utlwanang** South Africa
53 F3 **Utlyuks'kyy Lyman est.** Ukraine
59 H2 **Utö i.** Sweden
28 C7 **Uto** Japan
77 J3 **Utrata r.** Poland
37 E4 **Utraula** India
68 D2 **Utrecht div.** Netherlands
68 D2 **Utrecht** Netherlands
131 H3 **Utrecht** South Africa
100 E3 **Utrera** Spain
58 A2 **Utsira i.** Norway
58 A2 **Utsira** Norway
56 G1 **Utsjoki** Finland
29 G5 **Utsunomiya** Japan
51 H6 **Utta** Rus. Fed.
24 C3 **Uttaradit** Thailand
36 D3 **Uttarkashi** India
36 D4 **Uttar Pradesh** India
80 E2 **Uttendorf** *Oberösterreich* Austria
80 D3 **Uttendorf** *Salzburg* Austria
75 G4 **Utting am Ammersee** Germany
63 E2 **Uttoxeter** *England* U.K.
Utu *see* **Miao'ergou**
145 □3 **Utuado** Puerto Rico
47 L3 **Utubulak** China
7 □11 **Utuofai** *French Polynesia* Pacific Ocean
7 □10 **Uturoa** *French Polynesia* Pacific Ocean
46 D2 **Utva r.** Kazakhstan
73 J2 **Utzedel** Germany
54 D2 **Uulu** Estonia
135 M2 **Uummannaq** Greenland
135 N2 **Uummannaq Fj. inlet** Greenland
135 O4 **Uummannarsuaq c.** Greenland
57 G3 **Uurainen** Finland
30 B2 **Üür Gol r.** Mongolia
57 F3 **Uusikaupunki** Finland
54 D1 **Uusimaa div.** Finland
128 A2 **Uutapi** Namibia
151 D6 **Uvalde** *Texas* U.S.A.
75 K2 **Úvaly** Czech Rep.
52 B2 **Uvarovka** Rus. Fed.
52 G3 **Uvarovo** Rus. Fed.
52 F4 **Uvarovo** Rus. Fed.
58 C1 **Uvdal** Norway
58 C1 **Uvdalselvi r.** Norway
127 B6 **Uvinza** Tanzania
125 E4 **Uvira** Congo(Zaire)
52 E1 **Uvod' r.** Rus. Fed.
131 H5 **Uvongo** South Africa
26 F1 **Uvs Nuur salt lake** China
28 D7 **Uwa** Japan
28 D7 **Uwajima** Japan
119 D2 **'Uwaynāt Wannīn** Libya
118 E3 **Uweinat, Jebel mt.** Sudan
22 A1 **Uwi i.** Indonesia
63 F3 **Uxbridge** *England* U.K.
69 E4 **Üxheim** Germany
30 D5 **Uxin Ju** China
30 D5 **Uxin Qi** China
166 A1 **Uxituba** Brazil
157 H4 **Uxmal** Mexico
46 F2 **Uy r.** Rus. Fed.
46 F4 **Uyaly** Kazakhstan
30 C3 **Üydzin** Mongolia
45 Q3 **Uyega** Rus. Fed.
123 F5 **Uyo** Nigeria
24 A1 **Uyu Chaung r.** Myanmar
47 H4 **Uyuk** Kazakhstan
43 B5 **'Uyûn Mûsa spring** Egypt
51 H4 **Uza r.** Rus. Fed.
18 H5 **Uzbekistan country** Asia
55 E5 **Uzda** Belarus
88 C3 **Uzel** France
46 D4 **Uzen'** Kazakhstan
92 D3 **Uzerche** France
91 C4 **Uzès** France
53 C1 **Uzh r.** Ukraine
79 M3 **Uzhhorod** Ukraine
52 G2 **Uzhovka** Rus. Fed.
112 B3 **Užice** Yugoslavia
52 D3 **Uzlovaya** Rus. Fed.
50 G3 **Uzola r.** Rus. Fed.
42 B2 **Üzümlü** Turkey
47 J4 **Uzunagach** Kazakhstan
42 A1 **Uzunköprü** Turkey
54 D3 **Uzvara** Latvia
54 C4 **Užventis** Lithuania
53 D2 **Uzyn** Ukraine
46 F4 **Uzynkair** Kazakhstan

V

124 D2 **Va r.** Central African Rep.
130 E4 **Vaal r.** South Africa
56 G2 **Vaala** Finland
130 E4 **Vaalbos National Park nat. park** South Africa
131 G3 **Vaal Dam dam** South Africa
131 G3 **Vaal Dam Nature Reserve res.** South Africa
69 E4 **Vaals** Netherlands
69 E4 **Vaalserberg h.** Netherlands
131 G2 **Vaalwater** South Africa
56 F3 **Vaasa div.** Finland
56 F3 **Vaasa** Finland
68 D2 **Vaassen** Netherlands
54 D4 **Vabalninkas** Lithuania
46 F4 **Vabkent** Uzbekistan
52 A3 **Vablya r.** Rus. Fed.
93 E5 **Vabre** France
93 E5 **Vabres-l'Abbaye** France
79 J4 **Vác** Hungary
173 K1 **Vacacaí** Brazil
169 F4 **Vacaré r.** Brazil
169 G2 **Vacaria r.** Brazil
168 A4 **Vacaria r.** Brazil
167 B6 **Vacaria** Brazil
154 B2 **Vacaville** *California* U.S.A.
108 A6 **Vacca, Isola la i.** *Sardegna* Italy
74 F2 **Vacha** Germany
52 F2 **Vacha** Rus. Fed.
82 B2 **Vacheresse** France
127 □4 **Vacoas** Mauritius
81 E1 **Vacov** Czech Rep.
52 F2 **Vad r.** Rus. Fed.
52 G2 **Vad** Rus. Fed.
38 A2 **Vada** India
54 C3 **Vadakste r.** Latvia/Lithuania
112 F2 **Vădeni** Romania
58 D2 **Vaderöarna is** Sweden
58 C2 **Vad Foss** Norway
58 A1 **Vadheim** Norway
52 F3 **Vadinsk** Rus. Fed.
58 B2 **Vadla** Norway
58 B2 **Vådlandsknuten h.** Norway
36 C5 **Vadodara** India
106 C4 **Vado Ligure** Italy
56 H1 **Vadsø** Norway
59 F2 **Vadstena** Sweden
83 E1 **Vaduz** *Vaduz* Liechtenstein
55 D5 **Væggerløse** Denmark
56 D2 **Værøy i.** Norway
50 G2 **Vaga r.** Rus. Fed.
55 □1 **Vágafjørður b.** Faeroes
57 C3 **Vågåmo** Norway
104 E3 **Vaganski Vrh mt.** Croatia
55 □1 **Vágar i.** Faeroes
59 F3 **Vaggeryd** Sweden
109 H4 **Vaglio Basilicata** Italy
59 G2 **Vagnhärad** Sweden
98 B4 **Vagos** Portugal
56 E2 **Vågsele** Sweden
55 □1 **Vágur** Faeroes
79 G3 **Váh r.** Slovakia
56 F3 **Vähäkyrö** Finland
54 C1 **Vahto** Finland
107 F5 **Vaiano** Italy
7 □11 **Vaiau, Pte pt** *French Polynesia* Pacific Ocean
54 D2 **Vaida** Estonia
38 B4 **Vaigai r.** India
74 D4 **Vaihingen an der Enz** Germany
7 □16 **Vaihu** *Easter I.* Chile
54 E3 **Väike Emajõgi r.** Estonia
54 E2 **Väike-Maarja** Estonia
54 C2 **Väike-Pakri i.** Estonia
155 G5 **Vail** *Arizona* U.S.A.
86 C3 **Vailly-sur-Aisne** France
90 A1 **Vailly-sur-Sauldre** France
7 □12 **Vailoa** Western Samoa
6 □4 **Vaina** Tonga
54 C2 **Väinameri b.** Estonia
54 B3 **Vainode** Latvia
87 E4 **Vair r.** France
109 G3 **Vairano Scalo** Italy
7 □11 **Vairao** *French Polynesia* Pacific Ocean
91 D4 **Vaison-la-Romaine** France
7 □13 **Vaitogi** *American Samoa* Pacific Ocean
176 G6 **Vaitupu i.** Tuvalu
7 □12 **Vaiusu** Western Samoa
82 B1 **Vaivre-et-Montoille** France
79 G6 **Vajszló** Hungary
6 □3 **Vaka'eitu i.** Tonga
124 D2 **Vakaga div.** Central African Rep.
44 K3 **Vakh r.** Rus. Fed.
36 C1 **Vakhan** Tajikistan
47 G5 **Vakhsh** Tajikistan
39 D3 **Vakīlābād** Iran
58 A1 **Vaksdal** Norway
38 C5 **Valachchenai** Sri Lanka
82 C2 **Valais div.** Switzerland
50 K3 **Valamaz** Rus. Fed.
110 D1 **Valandovo** Macedonia
89 E4 **Valanjou** France
102 B2 **Valareña** Spain
79 H2 **Valašská Polanka** Czech Rep.
79 H2 **Valašské Klobouky** Czech Rep.
79 G2 **Valašské Meziříčí** Czech Rep.
114 F4 **Valaxa i.** Greece
141 H3 **Val-Barrette** *Québec* Canada
59 G1 **Valbo** Sweden
106 E2 **Valbondione** Italy
91 D4 **Valbonnais** France
93 C5 **Valcabrère** France
172 D6 **Valcheta** Argentina
140 D2 **Val-Côté** *Ontario* Canada
107 F3 **Valdagno** Italy
90 E1 **Valdahon** France
82 C2 **Val d'Anniviers v.** Switzerland
99 F2 **Valdavia r.** Spain
50 E3 **Valday** Rus. Fed.
52 A1 **Valdayskaya Vozvyshennost' reg.** Rus. Fed.
101 F2 **Valdeazogues r.** Spain
91 F4 **Valdeblore** France
101 E1 **Valdecaballeros** Spain
99 E4 **Valdecarros** Spain
99 F2 **Valdecebollas mt.** Spain
99 G1 **Valdecilla** Spain
103 B4 **Valdecuenca** Spain
100 D1 **Valdefuentes** Spain
99 F2 **Valdeginate r.** Spain
100 D3 **Valdelamusa** Spain
102 C3 **Valdelinares** Spain
54 C4 **Valdemārpils** Latvia
59 G2 **Valdemarsvik** Sweden
103 B4 **Valdemeca** Spain
101 J1 **Valdemembra r.** Spain
87 E4 **Val-de-Meuse** France
102 B4 **Valdeminguete, Sierra de mountain range** Spain
99 G4 **Valdemoro** Spain
99 H4 **Valdeolivas** Spain
101 G2 **Valdepeñas** Spain
101 G3 **Valdepeñas de Jaén** Spain
98 E3 **Valderaduey r.** Spain
99 E2 **Valderas** Spain
89 G2 **Val-de-Reuil** France
110 B4 **Valderice** *Sicilia* Italy
93 E4 **Valderiès** France
102 D4 **Valderrobres** Spain
173 G3 **Valdés** Argentina
82 C2 **Val des Bagnes v.** Switzerland
141 H4 **Val-des-Bois** *Québec* Canada
171 D5 **Valdés, Península pen.** Argentina
99 F3 **Valdestillas** Spain
99 E5 **Valdeverdeja** Spain
98 E2 **Valdevimbre** Spain
134 D3 **Valdez** *Alaska* U.S.A.
162 B3 **Valdez** Ecuador
82 C2 **Val d'Hérens v.** Switzerland
83 F2 **Valdidentro** Italy
110 B5 **Val di Mazara v.** *Sicilia* Italy
82 B3 **Val-d'Isère** France
106 E2 **Valdisotto** Italy
172 A5 **Valdivia** Chile
92 C2 **Valdivienne** France
107 F3 **Valdobbiadene** Italy
90 E1 **Valdoie** France
86 B3 **Val-d'Oise div.** France
141 G2 **Val-d'Or** *Québec* Canada
99 G3 **Valdosa mt.** Spain
145 D6 **Valdosta** *Georgia* U.S.A.
58 C1 **Valdres v.** Norway
63 □2 **Vale** *Guernsey* Channel Is.
152 C2 **Vale** *Oregon* U.S.A.
51 G7 **Vale** Georgia
79 M4 **Valea lui Mihai** Romania
100 C3 **Vale de Açor** *Beja* Portugal
100 C1 **Vale de Açor** *Portalegre* Portugal
98 B4 **Vale de Cambra** Portugal
100 B2 **Vale de Gaio, Barragem de resr** Portugal
100 C1 **Vale do Peso** Portugal
107 E3 **Valeggio sul Mincio** Italy
136 F4 **Valemount** *B.C.* Canada
169 G5 **Valença** Brazil
166 E3 **Valença** Brazil
98 B2 **Valença do Minho** Portugal
166 D2 **Valença do Piauí** Brazil
89 G4 **Valençay** France
93 C4 **Valence** *Midi-Pyrénées* France
91 C4 **Valence** *Rhône-Alpes* France
93 E4 **Valence-d'Albigeois** France
93 C5 **Valence-sur-Baïse** France
103 C5 **Valencia div.** Spain
103 C5 **Valencia** *Valencia* Spain
159 □3 **Valencia** Trinidad and Tobago
162 D1 **Valencia** Venezuela
100 C1 **Valencia de Alcántara** Spain
98 E2 **Valencia de Don Juan** Spain
100 D2 **Valencia de las Torres** Spain
100 D2 **Valencia del Ventoso** Spain
103 D5 **Valencia, Golfo de g.** Spain
67 A5 **Valencia Island i.** Rep. of Ireland
159 F5 **Valencia, L. de l.** Venezuela
86 C2 **Valenciennes** France
112 F2 **Vălenii de Munte** Romania
91 D5 **Valensole** France
90 E1 **Valentigney** France
155 F4 **Valentine** *Arizona* U.S.A.
150 C3 **Valentine** *Nebraska* U.S.A.
151 B6 **Valentine** *Texas* U.S.A.
106 C3 **Valenza** Italy
23 B3 **Valenzuela** Philippines
58 D1 **Våler** Norway
162 C2 **Valera** Venezuela
99 H5 **Valera de Arriba** Spain
91 D4 **Valernes** France
58 A2 **Valestrand** Norway
169 J2 **Vale Verde** Brazil
109 E1 **Valfabbrica** Italy
87 F4 **Valfroicourt** France
54 E3 **Valga** Estonia
91 E4 **Valgaudemar reg.** France
54 D2 **Valgejõgi r.** Estonia
82 C3 **Valgrisenche** Italy
110 D5 **Valguarnera Carapepe** *Sicilia* Italy
98 C4 **Valhelhas** Portugal
93 D6 **Valier, Mont mt.** France
114 B1 **Valikardhë** Albania
6 □6 **Valili Pk h.** Fiji
102 E2 **Valira r.** Andorra/Spain
141 J2 **Val-Jalbert** *Québec* Canada
112 B2 **Valjevo** Yugoslavia
86 D2 **Val Joly, Lac du l.** France
102 D4 **Valjunquera** Spain
54 E3 **Valka** Latvia
57 G3 **Valkeakoski** Finland
69 D4 **Valkenburg** Netherlands
69 D3 **Valkenswaard** Netherlands
77 N1 **Valkininkai** Lithuania
54 D2 **Valkla** Estonia
54 E1 **Valko** Finland
53 F2 **Valky** Ukraine
179 C4 **Valkyrjedomen ice feature** Antarctica
91 C5 **Vallabrègues** France
99 F3 **Valladolid div.** *Castilla y León* Spain
157 H4 **Valladolid** Mexico
99 F3 **Valladolid** Spain
87 E4 **Vallage reg.** France
55 E4 **Vallåkra** Sweden
156 D4 **Vallarta, Pto** Mexico
109 H3 **Vallata** Italy
91 F5 **Vallauris** France
103 C4 **Vall d'Alba** Spain
93 C6 **Vall d'Arán reg.** Spain
103 F5 **Valldemossa** Spain
103 C5 **Vall de Uxó** Spain
58 B2 **Valle** Norway
99 F1 **Valle** Spain
172 E4 **Valle Daza** Argentina
163 D2 **Valle de la Pascua** Venezuela
100 E2 **Valle de la Serena** Spain
100 D2 **Valle de Matamoros** Spain
110 C5 **Valledolmo** *Sicilia* Italy
108 A4 **Valledoria** *Sardegna* Italy
162 C1 **Valledupar** Colombia
141 K3 **Vallée-Jonction** *Québec* Canada
172 C1 **Valle Fértil, Sa de mountain range** Argentina
164 D3 **Valle Grande** Bolivia
171 C6 **Valle Hermosa** Argentina
157 F3 **Valle Hermoso** Mexico
97 □ **Vallehermoso** *Canary Is* Spain
90 D2 **Valleiry** France
154 A2 **Vallejo** *California* U.S.A.
83 D2 **Valle Leventina v.** Switzerland
110 C5 **Vallelunga Pratameno** *Sicilia* Italy
82 D3 **Valle Mosso** Italy
157 F5 **Valle Nacional** Mexico
170 B2 **Vallenar** Chile
74 C2 **Vallendar** Germany
59 H2 **Vallentuna** Sweden
91 B4 **Valleraugue** France
108 A5 **Vallermosa** *Sardegna* Italy
93 E6 **Vallespir reg.** France
88 D4 **Vallet** France
111 □ **Valletta** Malta
62 B1 **Valley** *Wales* U.K.
150 D2 **Valley City** *N. Dakota* U.S.A.
152 B3 **Valley Falls** *Oregon* U.S.A.
23 B2 **Valley Head pt** Philippines
146 C5 **Valley Head** *W. Virginia* U.S.A.
119 F2 **Valley of The Kings** Egypt
159 G3 **Valley, The** *Anguilla* Caribbean
136 F3 **Valleyview** *Alberta* Canada
102 E3 **Vallfogona de Riucorb** Spain
107 G4 **Valli di Comacchio lag.** Italy
107 E3 **Valli Giudicarie v.** Italy
102 E3 **Vallmoll** Spain
59 G3 **Vällö i.** Sweden
109 H4 **Vallo della Lucania** Italy
91 E3 **Valloire** France
107 F5 **Vallombrosa** Italy
92 E2 **Vallon-en-Sully** France
91 C4 **Vallon-Pont-d'Arc** France
82 B2 **Vallorbe** Switzerland
90 E2 **Vallorcine** France
91 E4 **Vallouise** France
102 E3 **Valls** Spain
83 E3 **Valmadrera** Italy
137 H5 **Val Marie** *Saskatchewan* Canada
101 F2 **Valmayor r.** Spain
54 D3 **Valmiera** Latvia
99 F4 **Valmojado** Spain
89 F2 **Valmont** France
109 E3 **Valmontone** Italy

86 D3 **Valmy** France
99 G1 **Valnera mt.** Spain
88 D2 **Valognes** France
86 B3 **Valois reg.** France
98 B3 **Valongo** Portugal
101 G4 **Valor** Spain
99 F3 **Valoria la Buena** Spain
54 E4 **Valozhyn** Belarus
98 C3 **Valpaços** Portugal
102 C2 **Valpalmas** Spain
141 F2 **Val-Paradis** *Québec* Canada
172 B2 **Valparaíso div.** Chile
148 D5 **Valparaiso** *Indiana* U.S.A.
168 C4 **Valparaíso** Brazil
172 B2 **Valparaíso** Chile
156 E4 **Valparaíso** Mexico
106 B3 **Valpelline v.** Italy
82 C3 **Valpelline** Italy
104 G3 **Valpovo** Croatia
107 F2 **Val Pusteria v.** Italy
91 C4 **Valréas** France
101 F1 **Valronquillo mt.** Spain
131 F3 **Vals r.** South Africa
83 E2 **Vals** Switzerland
36 C5 **Valsād** India
82 C3 **Valsavarenche v.** Italy
106 B3 **Valsavarenche** Italy
99 F3 **Valseca** Spain
83 F2 **Val Senales v.** Italy
90 D2 **Valserine r.** France
109 J4 **Valsinni** Italy
112 C2 **Valška** Yugoslavia
91 C4 **Vals-les-Bains** France
130 E3 **Valspan** South Africa
131 G4 **Valsrivier** South Africa
107 F3 **Valstagna** Italy
21 L8 **Vals, Tg c.** Indonesia
107 E2 **Valsura r.** Italy
90 C1 **Val-Suzon** France
50 H1 **Val'tevo** Rus. Fed.
81 H2 **Valtice** Czech Rep.
99 G3 **Valtiendas** Spain
102 B2 **Valtierra** Spain
56 H3 **Valtimo** Finland
127 □4 **Valton** Mauritius
114 C3 **Valtou mountain range** Greece
106 B3 **Valtournenche** Italy
6 □8 **Valukoula** Fiji
107 J4 **Valun** Croatia
52 A3 **Valuyets** Rus. Fed.
51 F5 **Valuyki** Rus. Fed.
107 E2 **Val Venosta v.** Italy
97 □ **Valverde** *Canary Is* Spain
99 H5 **Valverde de Júcar** Spain
100 D3 **Valverde del Camino** Spain
100 D2 **Valverde de Leganés** Spain
98 D4 **Valverde del Fresno** Spain
83 F3 **Valvestino, Lago di l.** Italy
59 F1 **Våmån r.** Sweden
78 F1 **Vamberk** Czech Rep.
25 D5 **Vam Co Tay r.** Vietnam
55 B4 **Vamdrup** Denmark
127 D7 **Vamizi, Ilha i.** Mozambique
57 F3 **Vammala** Finland
55 B3 **Vammen** Denmark
115 F7 **Vamos** Greece
79 H4 **Vámosmikola** Hungary
79 L4 **Vámospércs** Hungary
54 C1 **Vampula** Finland
38 C2 **Vamsadhara r.** India
114 E1 **Vamvakofyto** Greece
42 E2 **Van** Turkey
42 F1 **Vanadzor** Armenia
54 D1 **Vanajavesi l.** Finland
59 E1 **Vanån r.** Sweden
86 D4 **Vanault-les-Dames** France
45 M3 **Vanavara** Rus. Fed.
141 J3 **Van Bruyssel** *Québec* Canada
151 E5 **Van Buren** *Arkansas* U.S.A.
147 K1 **Van Buren** *Maine* U.S.A.
25 E4 **Vân Canh** Vietnam
147 K2 **Vanceboro** *Maine* U.S.A.
146 B5 **Vanceburg** *Kentucky* U.S.A.
136 E5 **Vancouver** *B.C.* Canada
152 B2 **Vancouver** *Washington* U.S.A.
17 B7 **Vancouver, C. c.** *Western Australia* Australia
136 D5 **Vancouver Island i.** *B.C.* Canada
136 B2 **Vancouver, Mt mt.** *Alaska/Yukon Territory* Canada/U.S.A.
8 □3 **Vancouver Rock i.** *Snares Is* New Zealand
144 B4 **Vandalia** *Illinois* U.S.A.
145 D5 **Vandalia** *Ohio* U.S.A.
80 A3 **Vandans** Austria
55 B4 **Vandel** Denmark
102 D3 **Vandellós** Spain
90 B2 **Vandenesse** France
131 F3 **Vanderbijlpark** South Africa
148 E3 **Vanderbilt** *Michigan* U.S.A.
146 D4 **Vandergrift** *Pennsylvania* U.S.A.
136 E4 **Vanderhoof** *B.C.* Canada
14 D2 **Vanderlin I. i.** *Northern Terr.* Australia
155 H4 **Vanderwagen** *New Mexico* U.S.A.
55 A2 **Vandet Sø l.** Denmark
14 B1 **Van Diemen, C. c.** *Northern Terr.* Australia
14 D3 **Van Diemen, C. c.** *Queensland* Australia
14 C1 **Van Diemen Gulf b.** *Northern Terr.* Australia
87 F4 **Vandœuvre-lès-Nancy** France
107 F2 **Vandoies** Italy
54 D2 **Vändra** Estonia
141 J3 **Vandry** *Québec* Canada
131 G3 **Vandyksdrif** South Africa
59 E2 **Vänerborgsviken b.** Sweden
59 E2 **Vänern b.** Sweden
59 E2 **Vänersborg** Sweden
131 J2 **Vaneteze r.** Mozambique
146 E3 **Van Etten** *New York* U.S.A.
129 H3 **Vangaindrano** Madagascar
54 D3 **Vangaži** Latvia
42 E2 **Van Gölü salt lake** Turkey
58 C1 **Vangsmjøsi l.** Norway
58 B1 **Vangsvatnet l.** Norway
6 □1 **Vangunu i.** Solomon Is.
151 B6 **Van Horn** *Texas* U.S.A.
141 H4 **Vanier** *Ontario* Canada
82 C2 **Vanil Noir mt.** Switzerland
6 □1 **Vanimo** P.N.G.
27 Q2 **Vanino** Rus. Fed.
38 B3 **Vanivilasa Sagara resr** India
38 B3 **Vaniyambadi** India
112 D2 **Vânju Mare** Romania
134 A3 **Vankarem** Rus. Fed.
141 H4 **Vankleek Hill** *Ontario* Canada
Van, L. salt lake *see* **Van Gölü**
56 E1 **Vanna i.** Norway
56 E3 **Vännäs** Sweden
86 C4 **Vanne r.** France
88 C4 **Vannes** France
47 H4 **Vannovka** Kazakhstan
107 F2 **Vanoi r.** Italy
91 E3 **Vanoise, Parc National de la nat. park** France
131 G4 **Van Reenen** South Africa
130 B5 **Vanrhynsdorp** South Africa
130 B5 **Vanrhyns Pass pass** South Africa
15 E3 **Vanrook** *Queensland* Australia
15 E3 **Vanrook Cr. r.** *Queensland* Australia
59 F1 **Vansbro** Sweden
16 D2 **Vansittart B. b.** *Western Australia* Australia
135 K3 **Vansittart I. i.** *N.W.T.* Canada
131 F4 **Vanstadensrus** South Africa
57 G3 **Vantaa** Finland
6 □7 **Vanua Bailavu i.** Fiji
6 □2 **Vanua Lava i.** Vanuatu
6 □6 **Vanua Levu i.** Fiji
6 □8 **Vanua Levu Barrier Reef reef** Fiji
4 H6 **Vanuatu country** Pacific Ocean
146 A4 **Van Wert** *Ohio* U.S.A.
130 C6 **Van Wyksdorp** South Africa
130 C5 **Vanwyksviei l.** South Africa
130 C5 **Vanwyksvlei** South Africa
24 D2 **Văn Yên** Vietnam
130 D3 **Van Zylsrus** South Africa
6 □2 **Vao** *New Caledonia* Pacific Ocean
93 D4 **Vaour** France
53 C2 **Vapnyarka** Ukraine
91 E5 **Var div.** *Provence - Alpes - Côte-d'Azur* France
91 F5 **Var r.** France
106 D4 **Vara r.** Italy
54 E2 **Vara** Estonia
59 E2 **Vara** Sweden
38 A3 **Varada r.** India
89 D4 **Varades** France
91 D5 **Varages** France
93 D4 **Varaire** France
106 B4 **Varaita r.** Italy
54 E3 **Varakļāni** Latvia
122 D5 **Varalé** Côte d'Ivoire
106 C3 **Varallo** Italy
39 B2 **Varāmīn** Iran
37 E4 **Varanasi** India
56 H1 **Varangerfjorden chan.** Norway
56 H1 **Varangerhalvøya pen.** Norway
106 D4 **Varano de'Melegari** Italy
109 H3 **Varano, Lago di lag.** Italy
54 E4 **Varapayeva** Belarus
101 F2 **Varas r.** Spain
78 F5 **Varaždin** Croatia
81 H4 **Varaždinske Toplice** Croatia
106 C4 **Varazze** Italy
59 E3 **Varberg** Sweden
54 C2 **Varbla** Estonia
91 D3 **Varces** France
39 B2 **Varcheh** Iran
115 C4 **Varda** Greece
38 B2 **Vardannapet** India
112 C4 **Vardar r.** Macedonia
55 A4 **Varde r.** Denmark
55 A4 **Varde** Denmark
42 F1 **Vardenis** Armenia
59 J1 **Vårdö** Finland
56 H1 **Vardø** Norway
114 D4 **Vardousia mts** Greece
52 D1 **Varegovo** Rus. Fed.
72 D2 **Varel** Germany
172 D3 **Varela** Argentina
77 N1 **Varėna** Lithuania
89 F2 **Varengeville-sur-Mer** France
106 D2 **Varenna** Italy
89 G2 **Varenne r.** France
141 J4 **Varennes** *Québec* Canada
87 E3 **Varennes-en-Argonne** France
90 D2 **Varennes-St-Sauveur** France
90 B2 **Varennes-sur-Allier** France
90 B1 **Varennes-Vauzelles** France
104 G3 **Vareš** Bos.-Herz.
106 C3 **Varese div.** *Lombardia* Italy
106 C3 **Varese** *Varese* Italy
83 D3 **Varese, Lago di l.** Italy
106 D4 **Varese Ligure** Italy
79 M5 **Vârful Bihor mt.** Romania
112 E1 **Vârful Bivolu mt.** Romania
112 E2 **Vârful Cozia mt.** Romania
53 A3 **Vârful Harghita-Mădăra mt.** Romania
112 C2 **Vârful Leordişu mt.** Romania
79 M5 **Vârful Malului h.** Romania
112 E2 **Vârful Moldoveanu mt.** Romania
79 M6 **Vârful Padeşu mt.** Romania
53 B3 **Vârful Şandru Mare mt.** Romania
79 M5 **Vârful Vlădeasa mt.** Romania
79 M5 **Vârfurile** Romania
59 E2 **Vårgårda** Sweden
172 C3 **Vargas** Argentina
166 E2 **Vargem r.** Brazil
169 E4 **Vargem Grande do Sul** Brazil
169 F4 **Varginha** Brazil
59 E2 **Vargön** Sweden
58 A2 **Varhaug** Norway
93 D5 **Varilhes** France
164 B4 **Varillas** Chile
59 F2 **Väringen l.** Sweden
44 D3 **Varkaus** Finland
59 E2 **Varmeln l.** Sweden
59 E2 **Värmland div.** Sweden
59 E2 **Värmlandsnäs i.** Sweden
112 F3 **Varna div.** Bulgaria
112 F3 **Varna** Bulgaria
80 C4 **Varna** Italy
52 F1 **Varna** Rus. Fed.
46 F2 **Varna** Rus. Fed.
59 F3 **Värnamo** Sweden
59 E1 **Värnäs** Sweden
52 G1 **Varnavino** Rus. Fed.
54 C4 **Varniai** Lithuania
54 E2 **Varnja** Estonia
78 D1 **Varnsdorf** Czech Rep.
43 B2 **Varosia** Cyprus
104 F3 **Varoška Rijeka** Bos.-Herz.
79 G4 **Városlőd** Hungary
56 G3 **Varpaisjärvi** Finland
79 H4 **Várpalota** Hungary
91 E4 **Vars** France
39 G1 **Varsaj** Afghanistan
54 E3 **Varska** Estonia
68 E3 **Varsseveld** Netherlands
59 G2 **Vårsta** Sweden
Vartashen *see* **Oğuz**
54 G1 **Vartemyagi** Rus. Fed.
115 C5 **Vartholomio** Greece
42 E2 **Varto** Turkey
112 D2 **Vârtop** Romania
37 E4 **Varuna r.** India
53 E1 **Varva** Ukraine
172 B4 **Varvarco Campos, L. l.** Argentina
112 C3 **Varvarin** Yugoslavia
53 G1 **Varvarivka** *Kharkiv* Ukraine
53 B1 **Varvarivka** *Khmel'nyts'kyy* Ukraine
146 D3 **Varysburg** *New York* U.S.A.
39 C2 **Varzaneh** Iran
42 F2 **Varzaqān** Iran
167 C6 **Varzea r.** *Paraná* Brazil
167 B6 **Varzea r.** *Rio Grande do Sul* Brazil
169 F2 **Várzea da Palma** Brazil
169 F1 **Varzelândia** Brazil
106 D4 **Varzi** Italy
106 C2 **Varzo** Italy
50 F1 **Varzuga** Rus. Fed.
90 B1 **Varzy** France
78 F4 **Vas div.** Hungary
166 E3 **Vasa Barris r.** Brazil
79 M3 **Vásárosnamény** Hungary
100 C3 **Vascão r.** Portugal
79 M5 **Vaşcău** Romania
54 D2 **Vaselemma** Estonia
50 H1 **Vashka r.** Rus. Fed.
53 A2 **Vashkivtsi** Ukraine
Vasht *see* **Khāsh**
114 B2 **Vashtëmi** Albania
50 H2 **Vasilevo** Rus. Fed.
114 B4 **Vasiliki** Greece
115 B5 **Vasilikos** Greece
77 N2 **Vasilishki** Belarus
115 C6 **Vasilitsi** Greece
52 H1 **Vasil'sursk** Rus. Fed.
51 G5 **Vasil'yevskiy Mokh** Rus. Fed.
52 G1 **Vasil'yevskoye** Rus. Fed.
52 E1 **Vasil'yevskoye** Rus. Fed.
54 E2 **Vasknarva** Estonia
53 C1 **Vas'kovychi** Ukraine
112 F1 **Vaslui** Romania
149 F4 **Vassar** *Michigan* U.S.A.
92 D3 **Vassivière, Lac de l.** France
59 G3 **Vassmolösa** Sweden
78 F4 **Vas-Soproni-síkság h.** Hungary
169 G5 **Vassouras** Brazil
89 E3 **Vassy** France
54 C1 **Västanfjärd** Finland
54 E2 **Vaste-Kuuste** Estonia
59 G2 **Västerås** Sweden
56 E2 **Västerbotten div.** Sweden
59 E1 **Västerdalälven r.** Sweden
56 E2 **Västerfjäll** Sweden
59 H2 **Västerhaninge** Sweden
56 E3 **Västernorrland div.** Sweden
59 G3 **Västervik** Sweden
59 F2 **Västmanland div.** Sweden
109 G2 **Vasto** Italy
59 E2 **Västra Silen l.** Sweden
54 E3 **Vastseliina** Estonia
78 F4 **Vasvár** Hungary
53 E2 **Vasylivka** *Kirovohrad* Ukraine
53 F1 **Vasylivka** *Sumy* Ukraine
53 F3 **Vasylivka** *Zaporizhzhya* Ukraine
53 D1 **Vasyl'kiv** Ukraine
53 G2 **Vasyl'kivka** Ukraine
53 B2 **Vasyutyntsi** Ukraine
79 M5 **Vaţa de Jos** Romania
89 G4 **Vatan** France
Vaté i. *see* **Éfaté**
59 H3 **Väte** Sweden
114 C2 **Vatero** Greece
66 A4 **Vatersay i.** *Scotland* U.K.
74 E5 **Vaterstetten** Germany
38 A2 **Vathar** India
115 D6 **Vathia** Greece
115 E4 **Vathy** Greece
114 C2 **Vathylakkos** Greece
6 □8 **Vatia Pt pt** Fiji
109 E3 **Vatican City country** Europe
111 E4 **Vaticano, Capo c.** Italy
115 □ **Vatio** Greece
56 M6 **Vatnajökull ice cap** Iceland
6 □7 **Vatoa i.** Fiji
114 C2 **Vatolakkos** Greece
129 H2 **Vato Loha mt.** Madagascar
129 H2 **Vatomandry** Madagascar
112 E1 **Vatra Dornei** Romania
112 E1 **Vatra Moldoviţei** Romania
79 K4 **Vatta** Hungary
59 F2 **Vättern l.** Sweden
59 G1 **Vattholma** Sweden
6 □8 **Vatu-i-Ra Channel chan.** Fiji
6 □8 **Vatu-i-Thake i.** Fiji
6 □8 **Vatulele i.** Fiji
53 D2 **Vatutine** Ukraine
6 □6 **Vatu Vara i.** Fiji
89 E2 **Vaubadon** France
86 C4 **Vauchassis** France
90 B1 **Vauclaix** France
91 D4 **Vaucluse div.** France
90 E1 **Vaucluse, Monts de mts** France
90 D1 **Vauconcourt-Nervezain** France
87 E4 **Vaucouleurs** France
82 B2 **Vaud div.** Switzerland
153 F5 **Vaughn** *New Mexico* U.S.A.
90 C3 **Vaulx-en-Velin** France
162 C3 **Vaupés r.** Colombia
91 D5 **Vauvenargues** France
91 C5 **Vauvert** France
87 F5 **Vauvillers** France
89 F4 **Vaux du Loir, Les v.** France
86 B4 **Vaux-le-Pénil** France
92 A3 **Vaux-sur-Mer** France
69 D5 **Vaux-sur-Sûre** Belgium
129 H2 **Vavatenina** Madagascar
6 □3 **Vava'u Group is** Tonga
122 C5 **Vavoua** Côte d'Ivoire
38 C4 **Vavuniya** Sri Lanka
54 E4 **Vawkalata** Belarus
77 N2 **Vawkavysk** Belarus
77 N2 **Vawkavyskaye Wzvyshsha h.** Belarus
59 H2 **Vaxholm** Sweden
59 F3 **Växjö** Sweden
59 E3 **Våxtorp** Sweden
38 B3 **Vāyalpād** India
44 G2 **Vaygach, O. i.** Rus. Fed.
92 D4 **Vayrac** France
169 E2 **Vazante** Brazil
50 H1 **Vazhgort** Rus. Fed.
52 B2 **Vazuza r.** Rus. Fed.
52 B2 **Vazuzskoye Vdkhr. resr** Rus. Fed.
159 □7 **V.C. Bird airport** *Antigua and Barbuda* Caribbean
81 F2 **Včelná** Czech Rep.
47 K1 **Vdovino** Rus. Fed.
25 C4 **Veal Vêng** Cambodia
59 E4 **Veberöd** Sweden
91 B4 **Vebron** France
72 F3 **Vechelde** Germany
68 E2 **Vecht r.** Netherlands
72 D3 **Vechta** Germany
72 B3 **Vechte r.** Germany
98 E4 **Vecinos** Spain
72 E4 **Veckerhagen** Germany
79 J4 **Vecsés** Hungary
78 E2 **Vectec h.** Czech Rep.
54 D3 **Vecumnieki** Latvia
38 B4 **Vedaranniyam** India
59 E3 **Veddige** Sweden
112 E2 **Vedea r.** Romania
112 E3 **Vedea** *Giurgiu* Romania
91 C5 **Vedène** France
59 E3 **Vedevåg** Sweden
42 F2 **Vedi** Armenia
173 G3 **Vedia** Argentina
50 E2 **Vedlozero** Rus. Fed.
91 B3 **Védrines-St-Loup** France
148 D5 **Veedersburg** *Indiana* U.S.A.
68 E1 **Veendam** Netherlands
68 D2 **Veenendaal** Netherlands
68 D1 **Veenwouden** Netherlands
68 B3 **Veere** Netherlands
68 B3 **Veerse Meer resr** Netherlands
56 C2 **Vega i.** Norway
151 C5 **Vega** *Texas* U.S.A.
145 □3 **Vega Baja** Puerto Rico
98 D2 **Vega de Espinareda** Spain
98 C1 **Vegadeo** Spain
98 D2 **Vega de Valcarce** Spain
58 C2 **Vegar l.** Norway
98 D2 **Vegarienza** Spain
58 C2 **Vegarshei** Norway
58 C1 **Veggli** Norway
68 D3 **Veghel** Netherlands
114 C2 **Vegoritis, L. l.** Greece
89 E4 **Vègre r.** France
137 G4 **Vegreville** *Alberta* Canada
57 G3 **Vehkalahti** Finland
36 B3 **Vehoa r.** Pakistan
75 F2 **Veilsdorf** Germany
166 B1 **Veiros** Brazil
100 C2 **Veiros** Portugal
39 G4 **Veirwaro** Pakistan
77 M1 **Veisiejis** Lithuania
74 E3 **Veitshöchheim** Germany
108 E2 **Vejano** Italy
55 B3 **Vejby** Denmark
55 B4 **Vejen** Denmark
100 E4 **Vejer de la Frontera** Spain
55 B4 **Vejle div.** Denmark
55 B4 **Vejle** *Vejle* Denmark
55 B4 **Vejle Fjord inlet** Denmark
75 J3 **Vejprnice** Czech Rep.
75 J2 **Vejprty** Czech Rep.
55 D4 **Vejrø i.** Denmark
55 C4 **Vejrø i.** Denmark
55 C5 **Vejsnæs Nakke pt** Denmark
39 E1 **Vekil'-Bazar** Turkmenistan
162 C1 **Vela, Cabo de la pt** Colombia
99 F5 **Velada** Spain
104 F4 **Vela Luka** Croatia
38 B4 **Velanai I. i.** Sri Lanka
162 □ **Velasco Ibarra** *Galapagos Is* Ecuador
170 C2 **Velasco, Sa de mountain range** Argentina
91 D5 **Velaux** France
91 B3 **Velay reg.** France
173 K3 **Velázquez** Uruguay
72 C4 **Velbert** Germany
75 G3 **Velburg** Germany
130 B6 **Velddrif** South Africa
75 H4 **Velden** Germany
69 E3 **Velden** Netherlands
81 F4 **Velden am Wörther See** Austria
69 D3 **Veldhoven** Netherlands
104 E3 **Velebit mountain range** Croatia
104 E3 **Velebitski Kanal chan.** Croatia
72 B4 **Velen** Germany
79 H4 **Velence** Hungary
79 H4 **Velencei-tó l.** Hungary
112 B4 **Velenje** Slovenia
112 C4 **Veles** Macedonia
81 F2 **Velešín** Czech Rep.
114 B1 **Velešta** Macedonia
52 F2 **Velet'ma** Rus. Fed.
104 F4 **Velež mts** Bos.-Herz.
101 F4 **Vélez r.** Spain
162 C2 **Vélez** Colombia
101 H3 **Vélez-Blanco** Spain
101 G4 **Vélez de Benaudalla** Spain
101 F4 **Vélez-Málaga** Spain
101 H3 **Vélez-Rubio** Spain
73 H1 **Velgast** Germany
169 E3 **Velhas r.** *Minas Gerais* Brazil
169 F2 **Velhas r.** *Minas Gerais* Brazil
51 H6 **Velichayevskoye** Rus. Fed.
53 A2 **Velika Berezovytsya** Ukraine
81 H5 **Velika Gorica** Croatia
53 A1 **Velika Hlusha** Ukraine
104 E3 **Velika Kapela mountain range** Croatia
112 C3 **Velika Kruša** Yugoslavia
81 H5 **Velika Mlaka** Croatia
53 B1 **Velika Ozera** Ukraine
112 C2 **Velika Plana** Yugoslavia
50 J3 **Velikaya r.** *Kirov* Rus. Fed.
50 D3 **Velikaya r.** *Pskov* Rus. Fed.
50 E2 **Velikaya Guba** Rus. Fed.
81 F5 **Velike Lašče** Slovenia
53 A2 **Veliki Birky** Ukraine
112 C3 **Veliki Jastrebac mts** Yugoslavia
107 J3 **Veliki Risnjak mt.** Croatia
50 D3 **Velikiye Luki** Rus. Fed.
53 A2 **Velikiy Hlybochok** Ukraine
53 D1 **Velikiy Lystven** Ukraine
77 M6 **Velikiy Lyubin'** Ukraine
50 H2 **Velikiy Ustyug** Rus. Fed.
53 B2 **Velikiy Zhvanchyk** Ukraine
52 E2 **Velikodvorskiy** Rus. Fed.
112 C2 **Veliko Gradište** Yugoslavia
38 B3 **Velikonda Ra. h.** India
52 A1 **Velikooktyabr'skiy** Rus. Fed.
112 E3 **Veliko Tŭrnovo** Bulgaria
52 D1 **Velikoye** Rus. Fed.
52 C1 **Velikoye, Oz. l.** Rus. Fed.
52 E1 **Velikoye, Oz. l.** Rus. Fed.
99 F2 **Velilla del Río Carrión** Spain
101 G3 **Velillas r.** Spain
107 J4 **Veli Lošinj** Croatia
93 C4 **Vélines** France
122 B4 **Vélingara** *Kolda* Senegal
122 B3 **Vélingara** *Louga* Senegal
112 D3 **Velingrad** Bulgaria
109 F2 **Velino r.** Italy
109 F2 **Velino, Monte mt.** Italy
50 D4 **Velizh** Rus. Fed.
78 F2 **Velká Bíteš** Czech Rep.
75 K2 **Velká Dobrá** Czech Rep.
79 J2 **Veľká Fatra mts** Slovakia
78 F2 **Velká Haná r.** Czech Rep.
79 G3 **Velká Javořina mt.** Czech Rep./Slovakia
79 L2 **Veľká Javořina mt.** Slovakia
79 J3 **Veľ'ká nad Ipľ'om** Slovakia
81 H2 **Velké Bílovice** Czech Rep.
79 M3 **Veľké Kapušany** Slovakia
81 J2 **Veľké Leváre** Slovakia
78 F2 **Velké Meziříčí** Czech Rep.
81 H2 **Velké Němčice** Czech Rep.
81 H2 **Velké Pavlovice** Czech Rep.
54 B1 **Velkua** Finland
79 J3 **Veľký Krtíš** Slovakia
79 G4 **Veľký Meder** Slovakia
6 □1 **Vella Lavella i.** Solomon Is.
38 B4 **Vellar r.** India
80 A1 **Vellberg** Germany
109 E3 **Velletri** Italy
82 B1 **Vellevans** France
59 E4 **Vellinge** Sweden
38 B3 **Vellore** India
98 C3 **Vellos r.** Spain
115 E6 **Velopoula i.** Greece
69 D5 **Velosnes** France
69 C4 **Velp r.** Belgium
68 D3 **Velp** Netherlands
73 F3 **Velpke** Germany
50 G2 **Vel'sk** Rus. Fed.
73 J3 **Velten** Germany
78 D1 **Veltrusy** Czech Rep.
68 D2 **Veluwe reg.** Netherlands
68 D2 **Veluwemeer l.** Netherlands
68 D2 **Veluwezoom, Nationaal Park nat. park** Netherlands
137 J5 **Velva** *N. Dakota* U.S.A.
75 K2 **Velvary** Czech Rep.
52 C2 **Vel'yaminovo** Rus. Fed.
53 E2 **Velyka Bahachka** Ukraine
53 F3 **Velyka Bilozerka r.** Ukraine
53 E2 **Velyka Burimka** Ukraine
53 D3 **Velyka Korenykha** Ukraine
53 E3 **Velyka Lepetykha** Ukraine
53 C3 **Velyka Mykhaylivka** Ukraine
53 E2 **Velyka Novosilka** Ukraine
53 E3 **Velyka Oleksandrivka** Ukraine
53 F1 **Velyka Pysarivka** Ukraine
53 F2 **Velyka Rublivka** Ukraine
53 B1 **Velyka Tsvilya** Ukraine
77 N6 **Velyka Tur''ya** Ukraine
53 D2 **Velyka Vys' r.** Ukraine
53 D2 **Velyka Vyska** Ukraine
79 M3 **Velykyi Kom''yaty** Ukraine
53 C2 **Velyki Korovyntsi** Ukraine
53 E2 **Velyki Krynky** Ukraine
53 A1 **Velyki Mosty** Ukraine
53 E1 **Velyki Sorochyntsi** Ukraine
53 E2 **Velykyi Khutir** Ukraine
53 D2 **Velykodolyns'ke** Ukraine
53 G3 **Velykomykhaylivka** Ukraine
79 M3 **Velykyy Bereznyy** Ukraine
53 G1 **Velykyy Burluk** Ukraine
112 E1 **Velykyy Bychkiv** Ukraine
174 G5 **Vema Fracture sea feature** Atlantic Ocean
175 J4 **Vema Trough sea feature** Indian Ocean
55 A3 **Vemb** Denmark
38 B4 **Vembanād L. l.** India
59 E1 **Ven i.** Sweden
59 F3 **Vena** Sweden
66 D4 **Venachar, Loch l.** *Scotland* U.K.
108 B2 **Venaco** *Corse* France
173 G2 **Venado Tuerto** Argentina
109 G3 **Venafro** Italy
92 A2 **Venansault** France
90 C1 **Venarey-les-Laumes** France
106 B3 **Venaria** Italy
91 F5 **Vence** France
168 D5 **Venceslau Bráz** Brazil
77 N1 **Venčiūnai** Lithuania
169 H4 **Venda Nova** Brazil
100 B2 **Vendas Novas** Portugal
92 A3 **Vendays-Montalivet** France
92 A2 **Vendée div.** *Pays de la Loire* France
92 B2 **Vendée r.** France
92 C2 **Vendeuvre-du-Poitou** France
86 D4 **Vendeuvre-sur-Barse** France
111 E6 **Vendicari, Isola i.** *Sicilia* Italy
50 H2 **Vendinga** Rus. Fed.
89 G4 **Vendôme** France
55 B2 **Vendsyssel reg.** Denmark
53 B2 **Vendychany** Ukraine
91 D5 **Venelles** France
93 E5 **Vénès** France
107 G3 **Veneta, Laguna lag.** Italy
115 C6 **Venetiko i.** Greece
107 F3 **Veneto div.** Italy
50 F4 **Venev** Rus. Fed.
107 G3 **Venezia div.** *Veneto* Italy
107 G3 **Venezia** *Venezia* Italy
107 G3 **Venezia, Golfo di g.** Italy
160 F3 **Venezuela country** South America
162 C1 **Venezuela, Golfo de g.** Venezuela
38 A3 **Vengurla** India
68 D2 **Venhuizen** Netherlands
98 E3 **Venialbo** Spain
145 D7 **Venice** *Florida* U.S.A.
Venice *see* **Venezia**
83 E2 **Venina r.** Italy
90 C3 **Vénissieux** France
59 E1 **Venjan** Sweden
59 F1 **Venjanssjön l.** Sweden
38 B3 **Venkatagiri** India
38 C2 **Venkatapuram** India
69 E3 **Venlo** Netherlands
114 G1 **Venna** Greece
58 B2 **Vennesla** Norway
58 C1 **Vennisfjellet mt.** Norway
55 A3 **Venø Bugt b.** Denmark
109 H4 **Venosa r.** Italy
109 H4 **Venosa** Italy
90 B1 **Venoy** France
69 D3 **Venray** Netherlands
7 □10 **Vent, Îles du is** *French Polynesia* Pacific Ocean
7 □10 **Vent, Îles sous le is** *French Polynesia* Pacific Ocean
54 B3 **Venta r.** Latvia/Lithuania
99 F3 **Venta de Baños** Spain
98 E1 **Venta de las Ranas** Spain
101 G2 **Venta de los Santos** Spain
173 F5 **Ventana, Sa de la mts** Argentina
98 D1 **Venta Nueva** Spain
101 G3 **Ventas de Huelma** Spain
101 F4 **Ventas de Zafarraya** Spain
91 D4 **Ventavon** France
131 F4 **Ventersburg** South Africa
131 F3 **Ventersdorp** South Africa
131 F3 **Venterskroon** South Africa
131 E5 **Venterstad** South Africa
106 B5 **Ventimiglia** Italy
171 B5 **Ventisquero mt.** Argentina
63 E4 **Ventnor** *England* U.K.
109 F4 **Ventotene, Isola i.** Italy
91 D4 **Ventoux, Mont mt.** France
31 J3 **Ventselevo** Rus. Fed.
54 B3 **Ventspils** Latvia
163 D3 **Ventuari r.** Venezuela
154 C4 **Ventucopa** *California* U.S.A.
154 C4 **Ventura** *California* U.S.A.
13 F4 **Venus B. b.** *Victoria* Australia
7 □11 **Vénus, Pte pt** *French Polynesia* Pacific Ocean
107 H2 **Venzone** Italy
81 H3 **Vép** Hungary
170 D2 **Vera** Argentina
103 B7 **Vera** Spain
157 F4 **Veracruz div.** Mexico
164 C1 **Vera Cruz** Brazil
157 F5 **Veracruz** Mexico
102 B1 **Vera de Bidasoa** Spain
165 E5 **Verá, L. l.** Paraguay
36 B5 **Verāval** India
53 A1 **Verba** *Rivne* Ukraine
77 N5 **Verba** *Volyn* Ukraine
106 C3 **Verbania** Italy
86 B3 **Verberie** France
111 E3 **Verbicaro** Italy
82 C2 **Verbier** Switzerland
52 C1 **Verbilki** Rus. Fed.
53 F3 **Verbove** Ukraine
53 A2 **Verbovets'** Ukraine
52 E2 **Verbovskiy** Rus. Fed.
53 F3 **Verby** Ukraine
83 E2 **Verceia** Italy
106 C3 **Vercelli div.** *Piemonte* Italy
106 C3 **Vercelli** *Vercelli* Italy
90 E1 **Vercel-Villedieu-le-Camp** France
141 J4 **Verchères** *Québec* Canada
91 D4 **Vercors reg.** France
52 E3 **Verda r.** Rus. Fed.
91 E4 **Verdaches** France
56 C3 **Verdalsøra** Norway
155 G4 **Verde r.** *Arizona* U.S.A.
171 C5 **Verde r.** Argentina
166 D3 **Verde r.** *Bahia* Brazil
168 C2 **Verde r.** *Goiás* Brazil
168 C3 **Verde r.** *Goiás* Brazil
168 B2 **Verde r.** *Goiás* Brazil
168 D1 **Verde r.** *Goiás* Brazil
168 E2 **Verde r.** *Goiás/Minas Gerais* Brazil
165 E2 **Verde r.** *Mato Grosso* Brazil
165 E2 **Verde r.** *Mato Grosso* Brazil
168 B4 **Verde r.** *Mato Grosso do Sul* Brazil
168 D3 **Verde r.** *Minas Gerais* Brazil
169 F4 **Verde r.** *Minas Gerais* Brazil
170 E1 **Verde r.** Paraguay
101 G3 **Verde r.** *Andalucia* Spain
101 G4 **Verde r.** *Andalucia* Spain
169 G2 **Verde Grande r.** Brazil
159 F3 **Verde, Isla airport** Puerto Rico
23 B3 **Verde Island Pass. chan.** Philippines
72 E3 **Verden (Aller)** Germany
173 F5 **Verde, Pen. pen.** Argentina
169 G1 **Verde Pequeno r.** Brazil
151 E4 **Verdigris r.** *Kansas* U.S.A.
114 C3 **Verdikoussa** Greece
168 C2 **Verdinho r.** Brazil
91 E5 **Verdon r.** France
114 B2 **Vërdovë** Albania
87 E3 **Verdun** France
93 D5 **Verdun-sur-Garonne** France
90 D2 **Verdun-sur-le-Doubs** France
110 C5 **Verdura r.** *Sicilia* Italy
131 G3 **Vereeniging** South Africa
53 E2 **Veremiyivka** Ukraine
131 G2 **Verena** South Africa
141 G3 **Vérendrye, Réserve faunique La res.** *Québec* Canada
79 J4 **Veresegyház** Hungary
52 C2 **Vereya** Rus. Fed.
93 D5 **Verfeil** France
122 B4 **Verga, Cap pt** Guinea
173 L2 **Vergara** Uruguay
107 F4 **Vergato** Italy
130 E2 **Vergelee** South Africa
15 E4 **Vergemont Cr. watercourse** *Queensland* Australia
147 G2 **Vergennes** *Vermont* U.S.A.
102 G2 **Verges** Spain
86 C5 **Vergigny** France
91 B3 **Vergongheon** France
92 C3 **Vergt** France
52 D1 **Verigino** Rus. Fed.
98 C3 **Verín** Spain
54 E2 **Veriora** Estonia
168 D3 **Veríssimo** Brazil
131 F4 **Verkeerdevlei** South Africa
53 F2 **Verkhivtseve** Ukraine
46 E2 **Verkhne-Avzyan** Rus. Fed.
52 A2 **Verkhnedneprovskiy** Rus. Fed.
44 K3 **Verkhneimbatskoye** Rus. Fed.
50 H3 **Verkhnespasskoye** Rus. Fed.
56 H1 **Verkhnetulomskiy** Rus. Fed.
52 D4 **Verkhneturovo** Rus. Fed.
46 E2 **Verkhneural'sk** Rus. Fed.
45 O3 **Verkhnevilyuysk** Rus. Fed.
52 A1 **Verkhnevolzhskoye Vdkhr. resr** Rus. Fed.
52 G2 **Verkhneye Talyzino** Rus. Fed.
51 H5 **Verkhniy Baskunchak** Rus. Fed.
53 G2 **Verkhniy Byshkyn** Ukraine
51 J5 **Verkhniy Kushum** Rus. Fed.
52 F1 **Verkhniy Landekh** Rus. Fed.
52 F3 **Verkhniy Lomov** Rus. Fed.
53 F3 **Verkhniy Rohachyk** Ukraine
30 D2 **Verkhniy Shergol'dzhin** Rus. Fed.
46 F1 **Verkhniy Ufaley** Rus. Fed.
30 E2 **Verkhniy Ul'khun** Rus. Fed.
50 E1 **Verkhniy Vyalozerskiy** Rus. Fed.
53 F2 **Verkhn'odniprovs'k** Ukraine
53 D2 **Verkhnyachka** Ukraine
52 C4 **Verkhnyaya Grayvoronka** Rus. Fed.
47 K2 **Verkhnyaya Irmen'** Rus. Fed.
52 D4 **Verkhnyaya Khava** Rus. Fed.
31 E2 **Verkhnyaya Khila** Rus. Fed.
56 J2 **Verkhnyaya Pirenga, Oz. l.** Rus. Fed.
50 H2 **Verkhnyaya Toyma** Rus. Fed.
52 C1 **Verkhnyaya Troitsa** Rus. Fed.
50 J3 **Verkhoshizhem'ye** Rus. Fed.
50 G2 **Verkhovazh'ye** Rus. Fed.
52 C3 **Verkhov'ye** Rus. Fed.
53 A2 **Verkhovyna** Ukraine
45 P3 **Verkhoyansk** Rus. Fed.
45 O2 **Verkhoyanskiy Khrebet mountain range** Rus. Fed.
52 H3 **Verkhozim** Rus. Fed.
31 E1 **Verkh-Usugli** Rus. Fed.
56 H2 **Verkhneye Kuyto, Oz. l.** Rus. Fed.
50 H2 **Verkola** Rus. Fed.
131 G3 **Verkykerskop** South Africa
69 D4 **Verlaine** Belgium
130 C7 **Vermaaklikheid** South Africa
86 C3 **Vermand** France
86 C3 **Vermandois reg.** France
168 C1 **Vermelho r.** Brazil
166 C2 **Vermelho r.** Brazil
166 C2 **Vermelho r.** Brazil
90 B1 **Vermenton** France
148 C5 **Vermilion r.** *Illinois* U.S.A.
137 G4 **Vermilion** *Alberta* Canada
155 F3 **Vermilion Cliffs cliff** *Utah* U.S.A.
148 A2 **Vermilion Lake l.** *Minnesota* U.S.A.
148 A2 **Vermilion Range h.** *Minnesota* U.S.A.
150 D3 **Vermillion** *S. Dakota* U.S.A.
138 B4 **Vermillion Bay** *Ontario* Canada
114 C2 **Vermio mt.** Greece
147 G3 **Vermont div.** U.S.A.
52 F3 **Vernadovka** Rus. Fed.
179 B2 **Vernadsky Ukraine Base** Antarctica
107 F2 **Vernago, Lago di l.** Italy
152 E3 **Vernal** *Utah* U.S.A.
91 F4 **Vernante** Italy
89 F4 **Vernantes** France
82 C2 **Vernayaz** Switzerland
140 E3 **Verner** *Ontario* Canada
75 K2 **Verneřice** Czech Rep.
93 D5 **Vernet** France
93 E6 **Vernet-les-Bains** France
89 F3 **Verneuil-sur-Avre** France
130 C4 **Verneuk Pan l.** South Africa
82 B2 **Vernier** Switzerland
58 D2 **Verningen** Norway
107 F4 **Vernio** Italy
93 D5 **Verniolle** France
111 H2 **Vernole** Italy
155 H4 **Vernon** *Arizona* U.S.A.
136 F4 **Vernon** *B.C.* Canada
147 G4 **Vernon** *Connecticut* U.S.A.
151 D5 **Vernon** *Texas* U.S.A.
155 F1 **Vernon** *Utah* U.S.A.
89 G2 **Vernon** France
89 G3 **Vernouillet** France
91 C4 **Vernoux-en-Vivarais** France

45 M3 Vilyuy r. Rus. Fed.
45 O3 Vilyuysk Rus. Fed.
45 M3 Vilyuyskoye Vdkhr. resr Rus. Fed.
102 E3 Vimbodí Spain
70 D3 Vimercate Italy
89 G1 Vimeu reg. France
100 C2 Vimieiro Portugal
98 D3 Vimioso Portugal
59 F3 Vimmerby Sweden
89 F3 Vimoutiers France
78 C2 Vimperk Czech Rep.
86 B2 Vimy France
154 A2 Vina *California* U.S.A.
172 B2 Viña del Mar Chile
106 B4 Vinadio Italy
102 D3 Vinaixa Spain
147 J2 Vinalhaven *Maine* U.S.A.
103 C6 Vinalopó r. Spain
129 H2 Vinanivao Madagascar
102 D4 Vinaròs Spain
59 F1 Vinäs Sweden
91 D3 Vinay France
93 E6 Vinça France
127 □5 Vincendo *Réunion* Indian Ocean
144 C4 Vincennes *Indiana* U.S.A.
179 C6 Vincennes Bay b. Antarctica
11 □1 Vincent, Pt pt *Norfolk I.* Pacific Ocean
87 F4 Vincey France
109 G3 Vinchiaturo Italy
55 C4 Vindeby Denmark
56 E2 Vindelälven r. Sweden
56 E2 Vindeln Sweden
55 A3 Vinderup Denmark
36 C5 Vindhya Range India
52 F2 Vindrey Rus. Fed.
147 F5 Vineland *New Jersey* U.S.A.
89 G4 Vineuil France
147 H4 Vineyard Haven *Massachusetts* U.S.A.
79 L5 Vinga Romania
59 F2 Vingåker Sweden
90 D1 Vingeanne r. France
93 E6 Vingrau France
24 D3 Vinh Vietnam
98 D3 Vinhais Portugal
24 D3 Vinh Linh Vietnam
25 D5 Vinh Long Vietnam
25 D5 Vinh Rach Gia b. Vietnam
24 D2 Vinh Yên Vietnam
81 H4 Vinica Croatia
112 D4 Vinica Macedonia
151 E4 Vinita *Oklahoma* U.S.A.
68 C2 Vinkeveen Netherlands
53 B2 Vin'kivtsi Ukraine
81 G4 Vinkovci Croatia
54 E2 Vinni Estonia
74 C3 Vinningen Germany
53 C2 Vinnytsya div. Ukraine
53 C2 Vinnytsya Ukraine
91 D5 Vinon-sur-Verdon France
179 B3 Vinson Massif mt. Antarctica
53 C3 Vinstra Norway
59 G1 Vintjärn Sweden
148 A4 Vinton *Iowa* U.S.A.
99 H3 Vinuesa Spain
38 B2 Vinukonda India
125 B4 Vinza Congo
73 G3 Vinzelberg Germany
47 G1 Vinzili Rus. Fed.
72 E1 Viöl Germany
16 D3 Violet Valley Abor. Reserve res. *Western Australia* Australia
130 A4 Vioolsdrif South Africa
89 G2 Viosne r. France
81 E5 Vipava Slovenia
127 B7 Viphya Mountains mts Malawi
107 F2 Vipiteno Italy
73 H2 Vipperow Germany
104 E3 Vir i. Croatia
23 C3 Virac Philippines
36 C5 Viramgam India
42 D2 Viranşehir Turkey
36 B4 Virawah Pakistan
54 C3 Vircava r. Latvia/Lithuania
137 J5 Virden *Manitoba* Canada
89 D2 Vire r. France
89 E3 Vire France
125 B7 Virei Angola
69 C4 Vireux-Molhain France
86 D2 Vireux-Wallerand France
79 L5 Virful Highiş h. Romania
169 G2 Virgem da Lapa Brazil
80 D3 Virgen Austria
102 B3 Virgen, Sierra de la mountain range Spain
141 F2 Virginatown *Ontario* Canada
145 □3 Virgin Gorda i. *Virgin Is* Caribbean
146 D6 Virginia div. U.S.A.
148 A2 Virginia *Minnesota* U.S.A.
67 D3 Virginia Rep. of Ireland
131 F4 Virginia South Africa
146 E6 Virginia Beach *Virginia* U.S.A.
154 C2 Virginia City *Nevada* U.S.A.
133 M8 Virgin Islands (U.K.) territory Caribbean
133 M8 Virgin Islands (U.S.A.) territory Caribbean
155 F3 Virgin Mts mts *Arizona* U.S.A.
169 G3 Virginópolis Brazil
145 □3 Virgin Passage chan. Caribbean
90 D2 Viriat France
90 D3 Virieu France
90 D3 Virieu-le-Grand France
82 A3 Virignin France
54 D4 Virinta r. Lithuania
57 G3 Virkkala Finland
25 D4 Vîrôchey Cambodia
69 C4 Viroin r. Belgium
54 E1 Virolahti Finland
148 B4 Viroqua *Wisconsin* U.S.A.
78 G6 Virovitica Croatia
54 C3 Virpe Latvia
57 F3 Virrat Finland
59 F3 Virserum Sweden
69 D5 Virton div. *Luxembourg* Belgium
69 D5 Virton Belgium
54 C2 Virtsu Estonia
164 A1 Virú Peru
38 B4 Virudunagar India
124 E4 Virunga, Parc National des nat. park Congo(Zaire)
90 E2 Viry *Rhône-Alpes* France
82 A2 Viry *Rhône-Alpes* France
109 J1 Vis i. Croatia
109 J1 Vis Croatia
57 G5 Visaginas Lithuania
154 C3 Visalia *California* U.S.A.
36 B5 Visavadar India
23 B4 Visayan Sea sea Philippines
72 D3 Visbek Germany
59 H3 Visby Sweden
169 G4 Visconde do Rio Branco Brazil
134 G2 Viscount Melville Sound str. *N.W.T.* Canada
69 D4 Visé Belgium
104 G4 Višegrad Bos.-Herz.
80 D4 Visentin, Col pass Italy
44 J2 Vise, O. i. Rus. Fed.
107 G4 Viserba Italy
98 C4 Viseu div. Portugal
166 C1 Viseu Brazil
98 C4 Viseu Portugal
112 E1 Vişeu de Sus Romania
107 J3 Viševica mt. Croatia
38 C2 Vishakhapatnam India
47 H2 Vishnevka Kazakhstan
52 F3 Vishnevoye Rus. Fed.
112 E2 Vişina Romania
55 E2 Viskafors Sweden
55 E2 Viskan r. Sweden
54 E3 Viški Latvia
109 J1 Viški Kanal chan. Croatia
59 F3 Vislanda Sweden
58 D1 Vismunda r. Norway
36 C5 Visnagar India
81 F5 Višnja Gora Slovenia
75 L2 Višňová Czech Rep.
81 H2 Višňové Czech Rep.
101 G2 Viso del Marqués Spain
104 G4 Visoko Bos.-Herz.
106 B4 Viso, Monte mt. Italy
82 C2 Visp Switzerland
131 E5 Visrivier South Africa
59 F3 Visselfjärda Sweden
72 E3 Visselhövede Germany
55 C4 Vissenbjerg Denmark
109 F2 Visso Italy
82 C2 Vissoie Switzerland
154 D5 Vista *California* U.S.A.
167 A4 Vista Alegre Brazil
59 E2 Visten l. Sweden
Vistula r. *see* Wisła
54 C4 Vištytis Lithuania
53 E3 Visun' r. Ukraine
112 E3 Vit r. Bulgaria
36 B3 Vitakri Pakistan
Vitebsk *see* Vitsyebsk
108 D2 Viterbo div. *Lazio* Italy
108 E2 Viterbo *Viterbo* Italy
104 F3 Vitez Bos.-Herz.
164 C4 Vitichi Bolivia
98 D3 Vitigudino Spain
6 □8 Viti Levu i. Fiji
45 N4 Vitim r. Rus. Fed.
27 K1 Vitimskoye Ploskogorye Rus. Fed.
81 G2 Vitis Austria
79 G2 Vítkov Czech Rep.
114 C1 Vitolište Macedonia
164 B3 Vitor Peru
99 H2 Vitoria airport Spain
169 H4 Vitória *Espírito Santo* Brazil
166 B1 Vitória *Pará* Brazil
Vitoria *see* Gasteiz-Vitoria
169 H1 Vitória da Conquista Brazil
166 D1 Vitória do Mearim Brazil
88 D3 Vitré France
82 A1 Vitrey-sur-Mance France
91 D5 Vitrolles France
86 B2 Vitry-en-Artois France
86 D4 Vitry-la-Ville France
86 B2 Vitry-le-François France
90 B2 Vitry-sur-Loire France
54 F4 Vitsyebsk div. Belarus
50 D4 Vitsyebsk Belarus
56 F2 Vittangi Sweden
90 C1 Vitteaux France
87 E4 Vittel France
110 D6 Vittoria *Ragusa* Italy
107 G3 Vittorio Veneto Italy
111 □ Vittorisa Malta
109 G3 Vitulano Italy
109 G3 Vitulazio Italy
176 F3 Vityaz Depth depth Pacific Ocean
91 C4 Vivarais, Monts du mountain range France
98 C1 Viveiro Spain
102 C4 Vivel del Río Martín Spain
173 F3 Vivero Argentina
91 B3 Viverols France
106 C3 Viverone, Lago di l. Italy
101 H2 Viveros Spain
69 C5 Vivier-au-Court France
91 C4 Viviers France
91 C5 Viv-le-Fesq France
131 G1 Vivo South Africa
92 C2 Vivonne France
12 D4 Vivonne B. b. *S. Australia* Australia
173 J4 Vivoratá Argentina
6 □8 Viwa i. Fiji
53 F2 Viys'kove Ukraine
Vizagapatam *see* Vishakhapatnam
99 H1 Vizcaya div. Spain
42 A1 Vize Turkey
90 B3 Vizézy r. France
50 H1 Vizhas r. Rus. Fed.
50 H1 Vizhas Rus. Fed.
77 M6 Vizhomlya Ukraine
38 C2 Vizianagaram India
91 D3 Vizille France
52 H1 Vizim"yary Rus. Fed.
52 J2 Vizinga Rus. Fed.
112 F2 Viziru Romania
79 G2 Vizovice Czech Rep.
110 D5 Vizzini *Sicilia* Italy
114 B2 Vjosë r. Albania
69 C4 Vlaams Brabant div. Belgium
68 C3 Vlaardingen Netherlands
115 B4 Vlachata Greece
115 D5 Vlachokerasia Greece
79 M5 Vlădeasa, Munţii mts Romania
112 F1 Vlădeni Romania
112 C3 Vladičin Han Yugoslavia
51 H7 Vladikavkaz Rus. Fed.
52 E2 Vladimir div. Rus. Fed.
52 E1 Vladimir Rus. Fed.
52 A2 Vladimirskiy Tupik Rus. Fed.
52 G1 Vladimirskoye Rus. Fed.
78 E2 Vladislav Czech Rep.
31 J4 Vladivostok Rus. Fed.
50 F3 Vladychnoye Rus. Fed.
68 F1 Vlagtwedde Netherlands
112 E1 Vlăhiţa Romania
104 G3 Vlasenica Bos.-Herz.
104 F3 Vlašić mt. Bos.-Herz.
112 B2 Vlašić Planina mts Yugoslavia
78 D2 Vlašim Czech Rep.
53 E2 Vlasivka Ukraine
112 D3 Vlasotince Yugoslavia
52 D2 Vlasovo Rus. Fed.
68 E2 Vledder Netherlands
68 C1 Vlieland i. Netherlands
68 D3 Vlijmen Netherlands
69 B3 Vlissingen Netherlands
113 B4 Vlorë Albania
72 D3 Vlotho Germany
78 D1 Vltava r. Czech Rep.
114 B4 Vlycho Greece
81 F4 Vnanje Gorice Slovenia
81 E3 Vöcklabruck div. Austria
81 E2 Vöcklabruck Austria
75 J4 Vöcklamarkt Austria
104 E4 Vodice Croatia
107 J3 Vodice Croatia
50 F2 Vodlozero, Ozero l. Rus. Fed.
79 L2 Vodná Nádrž Veľká Domaša l. Slovakia
78 D2 Vodňany Czech Rep.
81 H1 Vodní nádrž Dalešice resr Czech Rep.
78 D3 Vodní nádrž Lipno l. Czech Rep.
81 H2 Vodní nádrž Nové Mlýny l. Czech Rep.
79 L3 Vodní Nádrž Ružin resr Slovakia
78 E3 Vodní nadrž Vranov l. Czech Rep.
107 H4 Vodnjan Croatia
66 □2 Voe *Scotland* U.K.
131 E6 Voël r. South Africa
72 B4 Voerde (Niederrhein) Germany
55 C2 Voerså Denmark
114 C2 Vogatsiko Greece
87 F4 Vôge, la reg. France
73 J2 Vogelsang Germany
74 D2 Vogelsberg h. Germany
74 C3 Vogelweh Germany
130 B2 Vogelweide Namibia
106 D4 Voghera Italy
107 F4 Voghiera Italy
83 E1 Vogt Germany
75 H2 Vogtland reg. Germany
91 C4 Vogüé France
6 □2 Voh *New Caledonia* Pacific Ocean
54 E3 Võhandu r. Estonia
75 G4 Vohburg an der Donau Germany
75 H3 Vohenstrauß Germany
129 H3 Vohilava Madagascar
129 H3 Vohimena, Tanjona c. Madagascar
129 H3 Vohipeno Madagascar
129 H3 Vohitrandriana Madagascar
72 D4 Vöhl Germany
54 D2 Võhma Estonia
74 D4 Vöhringen *Baden-Württemberg* Germany
74 F4 Vöhringen *Bayern* Germany
127 C5 Voi Kenya
87 E4 Void-Vacon France
64 D1 Voil, Loch l. *Scotland* U.K.
112 D2 Voineasa Romania
122 C5 Voinjama Liberia
52 C3 Voin Pervyy Rus. Fed.
115 D4 Voiotia div. Greece
86 D4 Voire r. France
91 D3 Voiron France
89 G3 Voise r. France
90 D2 Voiteur France
81 G3 Voitsberg div. Austria
81 G3 Voitsberg Austria
55 B4 Vojens Denmark
81 G4 Vojnik Slovenia
79 H6 Vokány Hungary
50 H3 Vokhma Rus. Fed.
124 B2 Voko Cameroon
78 C3 Volary Czech Rep.
152 F2 Volborg *Montana* U.S.A.
172 B4 Volcán Antuco volcano Chile
156 K7 Volcán Barú volcano Panama
162 B3 Volcán Cayambe volcano Ecuador
172 A6 Volcán Choshuenco volcano Chile
172 B1 Volcán, Co del mt. Chile
172 B4 Volcán Copahue mt. Chile
162 B3 Volcán de Purace volcano Colombia
172 B3 Volcán Descabezado volcano Chile
172 B4 Volcán Domuyo mt. Argentina
172 B5 Volcán Lanín volcano Argentina/Chile
172 B5 Volcán Llaima volcano Chile
172 B5 Volcán Lonquimay volcano Chile
172 C3 Volcán Maipó volcano Argentina/Chile
Volcano Bay b. *see* Uchiura-wan
127 A5 Volcanoes National Park nat. park Uganda
Volcano Is. is *see* Kazan-retto
172 B3 Volcán Overo volcano Argentina
172 B3 Volcán Peteroa volcano Argentina/Chile
173 H4 Volcán, Sa del h. Argentina
172 C2 Volcán San José volcano Argentina/Chile
172 B3 Volcán Tinguiririca volcano Chile
172 B4 Volcán Tromen volcano Argentina
172 A5 Volcán Villarrica volcano Chile
47 K2 Volchikha Rus. Fed.
57 B3 Volda Norway
50 K2 Vol'dino Rus. Fed.
68 D2 Volendam Netherlands
148 B4 Volga r. *Iowa* U.S.A.
50 H5 Volga r. Rus. Fed.
52 D2 Vol'ginskiy Rus. Fed.
51 G6 Volgodonsk Rus. Fed.
51 G5 Volgograd div. Rus. Fed.
51 H5 Volgograd Rus. Fed.
52 E1 Volgorechensk Rus. Fed.
53 C3 Volintiri Moldova
81 F4 Völkermarkt div. Austria
81 F4 Völkermarkt Austria
83 D1 Volkertshausen Germany
83 D1 Volketswil Switzerland
50 E3 Volkhov r. Rus. Fed.
74 B3 Völklingen Germany
72 E4 Volkmarsen Germany
131 G3 Volksrust South Africa
68 D2 Vollenhove Netherlands
87 G3 Volmunster France
31 J4 Vol'no-Nadezhdinskoye Rus. Fed.
53 G3 Volnovakha Ukraine
45 L2 Volochanka Rus. Fed.
53 B2 Volochys'k Ukraine
53 C2 Volodarka Ukraine
52 F1 Volodarsk Rus. Fed.
53 G3 Volodars'ke Ukraine
51 J6 Volodarskiy Rus. Fed.
47 G2 Volodarskoye Kazakhstan
53 C1 Volodars'k-Volyns'kyy Ukraine
53 B1 Volodymyrets' Ukraine
53 A1 Volodymyr-Volyns'kyy Ukraine
50 F2 Vologda div. Rus. Fed.
50 F3 Vologda Rus. Fed.
112 E1 Voloka Ukraine
52 B1 Volokolamsk Rus. Fed.
53 G1 Volokonovka Rus. Fed.
91 E4 Volonne France
114 D3 Volos Greece
77 M6 Voloshcha Ukraine
50 G2 Voloshka Rus. Fed.
54 F2 Volosovo Rus. Fed.
50 D3 Volot Rus. Fed.
52 D3 Volovo Rus. Fed.
52 C3 Volovo Rus. Fed.
52 B2 Voloye Rus. Fed.
82 C3 Volpiano Italy
80 C3 Völs Austria
73 J2 Völschow Germany
51 H4 Vol'sk Rus. Fed.
130 D6 Volstruisleegte South Africa
130 D5 Volstruispoort pass South Africa
123 E5 Volta div. Ghana
123 E5 Volta r. Ghana
Volta Blanche watercourse *see* Nakambe
16 D2 Voltaire, C. headland *Western Australia* Australia
122 D5 Volta, Lake l. Ghana
107 E3 Volta Mantovana Italy
Volta Noire r. *see* Mouhoun
169 F5 Volta Redonda Brazil
Volta Rouge r. *see* Nazinon
107 E5 Volterra Italy
99 F4 Voltoya r. Spain
109 H3 Volturara Appula Italy
109 H4 Volturino, Monte mt. Italy
109 G3 Volturno r. Italy
112 F2 Voluntari Romania
114 F2 Volvi, L. l. Greece
52 D4 Volya Rus. Fed.
53 A1 Volyn div. Ukraine
78 C2 Volyně Czech Rep.
75 J3 Volyňka r. Czech Rep.
53 E1 Volynka Ukraine
53 B2 Volytsya Ukraine
50 J4 Volzhsk Rus. Fed.
51 H5 Volzhskiy Rus. Fed.
109 F2 Vomano r. Italy
59 E4 Vombsjön l. Sweden
6 □8 Vomo i. Fiji
80 C3 Vomp Austria
129 H3 Vondrozo Madagascar
50 G1 Vonga Rus. Fed.
90 D1 Vonges France
114 B4 Vonitsa Greece
54 E2 Võnnu Estonia
68 C2 Voorburg Netherlands
68 C2 Voorschoten Netherlands
52 A2 Vop' r. Rus. Fed.
56 N6 Vopnafjörður b. Iceland
56 N6 Vopnafjörður Iceland
56 F3 Vörå Finland
81 F3 Voralm mt. Austria
77 O1 Voranava Belarus
80 A3 Vorarlberg div. Austria
114 C2 Voras mt. Greece/Macedonia
81 G2 Vorchdorf Austria
68 E2 Vorden Netherlands
81 F3 Vorderberg Austria
83 D2 Vorderrhein r. Switzerland
55 D4 Vordingborg Denmark
114 B2 Voreia Pindos mountain range Greece
114 F3 Voreio Aigaio div. Greece
114 E3 Voreioi Sporades is Greece
114 D4 Voreios Evvoïkos Kolpos chan. Greece
91 D3 Voreppe France
91 B3 Vorey France
52 A2 Vorga Rus. Fed.
44 H3 Vorkuta Rus. Fed.
54 C2 Vormsi i. Estonia
58 D1 Vormsund Norway
53 D3 Vorob'yevka Rus. Fed.
53 A2 Vorokhta Ukraine
52 F2 Vorona r. Rus. Fed.
51 F5 Voronezh div. Rus. Fed.
52 D4 Voronezh r. Rus. Fed.
52 D4 Voronezh Rus. Fed.
52 A4 Voronizh Ukraine
53 B1 Voronky Ukraine
50 G1 Voronov, Mys pt Rus. Fed.
52 D3 Voronovo Rus. Fed.
53 C2 Voronovytsya Ukraine
Voroshilovgrad *see* Luhans'k
52 A2 Vorot'kovo Rus. Fed.
52 G1 Vorotynets Rus. Fed.
53 F1 Vorozhba Ukraine
53 F1 Vorozhba Ukraine
73 H1 Vorpommersche Boddenlandschaft, Nationalpark nat. park Germany
81 G3 Vorsau Austria
53 F1 Vorskla r. Ukraine
52 F2 Vorsma Rus. Fed.
69 D3 Vorst Belgium
130 D2 Vorstershoop South Africa
54 D2 Võrtsjärv l. Estonia
54 E3 Võru Estonia
47 H5 Vorukh Tajikistan
82 B2 Vorya r. Rus. Fed.
77 N4 Vosa Belarus
130 D5 Vosburg South Africa
47 G5 Vose Tajikistan
87 F4 Vosges div. *Lorraine* France
87 F5 Vosges mountain range France
52 D1 Voshchazhnikovo Rus. Fed.
52 F2 Voskhod Rus. Fed.
114 B2 Voskopojë Albania
52 B2 Voskresensk Rus. Fed.
52 D2 Voskresensk Rus. Fed.
52 G1 Voskresenskoye Rus. Fed.
50 F3 Voskresenskoye Rus. Fed.
52 C1 Voskresenskoye Rus. Fed.
58 B1 Voss Norway
47 K3 Vostochno-Kazakhstan div. Kazakhstan
45 R2 Vostochno-Sibirskoye More sea Rus. Fed.
46 E4 Vostochnyy Chink Ustyurta escarpment Uzbekistan
26 G1 Vostochnyy Sayan mountain range Rus. Fed.
5 M6 Vostok Island i. Kiribati
54 D2 Võsu Estonia
78 D2 Votice Czech Rep.
6 □8 Voti Voti Pt pt Fiji
44 G4 Votkinsk Rus. Fed.
58 C1 Votna r. Norway
52 A2 Votrya r. Rus. Fed.
6 □2 Vot Tandé i. Vanuatu
168 D4 Votuporanga Brazil
115 F6 Voudia Greece
92 E2 Voueize r. France
92 C4 Vouga r. Portugal
90 C1 Vougeot France
90 D2 Vouglans, Lac de l. France
92 C2 Vouillé *Poitou-Charentes* France
92 B2 Vouillé *Poitou-Charentes* France
115 E7 Voukolies Greece
114 C3 Voulpi Greece
86 B4 Voulx France
92 C2 Vouneuil-sur-Vienne France
115 D4 Vouraïkos r. Greece
114 C2 Vourinos mt. Greece
90 B1 Voutenay-sur-Cure France
115 D5 Voutianoi Greece
92 B2 Vouvant France
89 F4 Vouvray France
82 B2 Vouvry Switzerland
98 B4 Vouzela Portugal
86 D3 Vouziers France
89 H4 Vouzon France
53 G2 Vovcha r. Ukraine
53 G1 Vovchans'k Ukraine
89 G3 Voves France
53 B2 Vovkovyntsi Ukraine
124 E2 Vovodo r. Central African Rep.
77 M3 Vowchyn Belarus
144 A1 Voyageurs Nat. Park nat. park *Minnesota* U.S.A.
50 H2 Voynitsa Rus. Fed.
77 N6 Voynyliv Ukraine
50 K2 Voyvozh Rus. Fed.
52 G1 Vozdvizhenskoye Rus. Fed.
52 D2 Vozha r. Rus. Fed.
50 J2 Vozhayel' Rus. Fed.
50 G2 Vozhega Rus. Fed.
50 F2 Vozhe, Ozero l. Rus. Fed.
50 J3 Vozhgaly Rus. Fed.
50 J1 Vozhgora Rus. Fed.
53 D3 Voznesens'k Ukraine
53 D3 Voznesens'ke Ukraine
52 F2 Voznesenskoye Rus. Fed.
50 E2 Voznesen'ye Rus. Fed.
52 E1 Voznesen'ye Rus. Fed.
46 E3 Vozrozhdenye Uzbekistan
46 E4 Vozrozhdeniya, O. i. Uzbekistan
53 E3 Vozsiyats'ke Ukraine
46 F5 Vozvyshennost' Karabil' reg. Turkmenistan
52 G2 Vozvyshennost' Mezhp'yan'ye reg. Rus. Fed.
77 O3 Vozyera Chornaye l. Belarus
31 J2 Vozzhayevka Rus. Fed.
55 B2 Vrå Denmark
79 H3 Vráble Slovakia
115 B5 Vrachionas h. Greece
115 C4 Vrachnaiika Greece
58 C2 Vrådal Norway
53 D3 Vradiyivka Ukraine
53 B Vrancea div. Romania
57 T2 Vrangelya, O. i. Rus. Fed.
104 F4 Vranica mts Bos.-Herz.
112 C3 Vranje Yugoslavia
112 D3 Vranjska Banja Yugoslavia
81 H2 Vranovice Czech Rep.
79 L3 Vranov nad Topľou Slovakia
81 F4 Vransko Slovenia
107 J4 Vransko Jezero l. Croatia
112 C4 Vrapčište Macedonia
112 D3 Vratsa Bulgaria
58 C2 Vråvatnet l. Norway
115 F5 Vravona Greece
104 F3 Vrbanja r. Bos.-Herz.
104 F3 Vrbas r. Bos.-Herz.
112 B2 Vrbas Yugoslavia
78 G1 Vrbno pod Pradědem Czech Rep.
81 H5 Vrbovec Croatia
104 E3 Vrbovsko Croatia
78 E1 Vrchlabí Czech Rep.
87 E4 Vrécourt France
131 G3 Vrede South Africa
131 F3 Vredefort South Africa
72 B3 Vreden Germany
130 A6 Vredenburg South Africa
130 B5 Vredendal South Africa
130 B3 Vredeshoop Namibia
55 C4 Vresen i. Denmark
69 C5 Vresse Belgium
115 D5 Vresthena Greece
59 F2 Vretstorp Sweden
81 F5 Vrhnika Slovenia
38 B4 Vriddhachalam India
68 E1 Vries Netherlands
68 E2 Vriezenveen Netherlands
59 F3 Vrigstad Sweden
90 B1 Vrille r. France
112 C3 Vrnjačka Banja Yugoslavia
86 A2 Vron France
104 D2 Vrontou Greece
68 E2 Vroomshoop Netherlands
114 B3 Vrosina Greece
115 G7 Vrouchas Greece
112 C2 Vršac Yugoslavia
107 H3 Vrsar Croatia
130 E3 Vryburg South Africa
131 H3 Vryheid South Africa
79 G2 Vsetín Czech Rep.
50 D2 Vsevolozhsk Rus. Fed.
52 B2 Vskhody Rus. Fed.
45 S3 Vstrechnyy Rus. Fed.
79 H3 Vtáčnik mt. Slovakia
79 H3 Vtáčnik mts Slovakia
52 E3 Vtoryye Levyye Lamki Rus. Fed.
6 □7 Vuagava i. Fiji
112 C3 Vučitrn Yugoslavia
68 D3 Vught Netherlands
53 G3 Vuhledar Ukraine
104 G3 Vukovar Croatia
44 G3 Vuktyl' Rus. Fed.
131 G3 Vukuzakhe South Africa
112 D2 Vulcan Romania
53 C3 Vulcăneşti Moldova
110 D4 Vulcano, Isola i. Italy
112 D3 Vulchedrŭm Bulgaria
112 F3 Vŭlchidol Bulgaria
109 H4 Vulture, Monte mt. Italy
155 F5 Vulture Mts mts *Arizona* U.S.A.
6 □6 Vuna Pt pt Fiji
6 □8 Vunidawa Fiji
6 □7 Vunisea Fiji
57 G3 Vuohijärvi Finland
54 F1 Vuoksa r. Rus. Fed.
54 F1 Vuoksa, Oz. l. Rus. Fed.
56 G3 Vuolijoki Finland
56 F2 Vuollerim Sweden
56 G2 Vuostimo Finland
52 H2 Vurnary Rus. Fed.
112 F1 Vutcani Romania
53 A1 Vuzlove *L'viv* Ukraine
79 M3 Vuzlove *Zakarpats'ka* Ukraine
52 E1 Vveden'ye Rus. Fed.
127 B6 Vwawa Tanzania
77 N2 Vyalikaya Byerastavitsa Belarus
77 N2 Vyalikaya Mazheykava Belarus
54 F4 Vyalikiya Dol'tsy Belarus
54 G2 Vyal'ye, Oz. l. Rus. Fed.
36 C5 Vyara India
77 M3 Vyarkhovichy Belarus
50 J3 Vyatka r. Rus. Fed.
50 J3 Vyatskiye Polyany Rus. Fed.
52 F3 Vyazemka Rus. Fed.
31 K3 Vyazemskiy Rus. Fed.
52 F3 Vyazhlya r. Rus. Fed.
52 B2 Vyaz'ma r. Rus. Fed.
52 B2 Vyaz'ma Rus. Fed.
52 G3 Vyazmino Rus. Fed.
52 F1 Vyazniki Rus. Fed.
52 G4 Vyazovka Rus. Fed.
54 F3 Vybor Rus. Fed.
54 F1 Vyborg Rus. Fed.
54 F1 Vyborgskiy Zaliv b. Rus. Fed.
50 J2 Vychegda r. Rus. Fed.
50 H2 Vychegodskiy Rus. Fed.
78 E1 Východočeský div. Czech Rep.
79 L3 Východoslovenský div. Slovakia
77 O4 Vyderta Ukraine
77 N4 Vydranytsya Ukraine
30 C2 Vydrino Rus. Fed.
77 N4 Vydrychi Ukraine
54 E4 Vyerkhnyadzvinsk Belarus
54 F4 Vyetryna Belarus
52 B3 Vygonichi Rus. Fed.
50 E2 Vygozero, Ozero l. Rus. Fed.
52 F2 Vyksa Rus. Fed.
52 H2 Vyla r. Rus. Fed.
90 E1 Vy-lès-Lure France
112 G2 Vylkove Ukraine
79 M3 Vylok Ukraine
50 J2 Vym' r. Rus. Fed.
53 A2 Vynnyky Ukraine
79 N3 Vynohradiv Ukraine
53 D3 Vynohradne Ukraine
53 E3 Vynohradove Ukraine
50 E3 Vypolzovo Rus. Fed.
54 F2 Vyra Rus. Fed.
50 D3 Vyritsa Rus. Fed.
62 C2 Vyrnwy, Lake l. *Wales* U.K.
53 F1 Vyry Ukraine
51 F6 Vyselki Rus. Fed.
52 F3 Vysha r. Rus. Fed.
52 F3 Vysha Rus. Fed.
53 D1 Vyshcha Dubechnya Ukraine
52 G2 Vyshche Solone Ukraine
52 G3 Vysheley Rus. Fed.
52 E3 Vyshgorod Rus. Fed.
53 D1 Vyshhorod Ukraine
52 B1 Vyshkovo Rus. Fed.
53 E2 Vyshneve *Dnipropetrovs'k* Ukraine
53 D1 Vyshneve *Kyyiv* Ukraine
50 E3 Vyshnevolotskaya Gryada ridge Rus. Fed.
52 C3 Vyshneye-Ol'shanoye Rus. Fed.
77 N4 Vyshniv Ukraine
53 A2 Vyshnivets' Ukraine
50 E3 Vyshniy Volochek Rus. Fed.
53 E2 Vyshnyaky Ukraine
78 G2 Vyškov Czech Rep.
78 G3 Vysoká h. Slovakia
81 F2 Vysoká mt. Czech Rep.
53 C1 Vysoka Pich Ukraine
81 H2 Vysoká pri Morave Slovakia
77 M3 Vysokaye Belarus
78 F2 Vysoké Mýto Czech Rep.
52 D1 Vysokovo Rus. Fed.
52 F1 Vysokovo Rus. Fed.
53 G1 Vysokovsk Rus. Fed.
52 C1 Vysokoye Rus. Fed.
53 B1 Vysots'k Ukraine
81 F2 Vyšší Brod Czech Rep.
114 C2 Vyssinia Greece
53 C1 Vystupovychi Ukraine
50 F2 Vytegra Rus. Fed.
115 D5 Vytina Greece
45 S3 Vyvenka Rus. Fed.
52 F2 Vyyezdnoye Rus. Fed.
77 N4 Vyzhivka r. Ukraine
53 A2 Vyzhnytsya Ukraine
54 D4 Vyžuona r. Lithuania

W

122 D4 Wa Ghana
72 E1 Waabs Germany
126 D4 Waajid Somalia
80 C3 Waakirchen Germany
68 D3 Waal r. Netherlands
75 F4 Waal Germany
69 D3 Waalre Netherlands
68 D3 Waalwijk Netherlands
68 C2 Waarland Netherlands
69 B3 Waarschoot Belgium
126 B3 Waat Sudan
140 B1 Wababimiga Lake l. *Ontario* Canada
6 □1 Wabag P.N.G.
138 B3 Wabakimi L. l. *Ontario* Canada
136 G3 Wabasca r. *Alberta* Canada
136 G3 Wabasca *Alberta* Canada
148 E5 Wabash r. *Indiana* U.S.A.
148 E5 Wabash *Indiana* U.S.A.
148 A3 Wabasha *Minnesota* U.S.A.
140 C2 Wabatongushi Lake l. *Ontario* Canada
126 D4 Wabē Gestro r. Ethiopia
126 D3 Wabē Shebelē Wenz r. Ethiopia
137 K4 Wabowden *Manitoba* Canada
76 G2 Wąbrzeźno Poland
138 C2 Wabuk Pt pt *Ontario* Canada
139 G3 Wabush *Newfoundland* Canada
139 G3 Wabush L. l. *Newfoundland* Canada
154 C2 Wabuska *Nevada* U.S.A.
145 D6 Waccasassa Bay b. *Florida* U.S.A.
81 G2 Wachau reg. Austria
69 B3 Wachtebeke Belgium
74 E2 Wächtersbach Germany
75 H3 Wackersdorf Germany
151 D6 Waco *Texas* U.S.A.
36 A4 Wad Pakistan
28 E6 Wadayama Japan
119 E5 Wad Banda Sudan
13 G4 Wadbilliga Nat. Park nat. park *New South Wales* Australia
118 C2 Waddān Libya
118 C2 Waddān, Jabal h. Libya
68 C1 Waddeneilanden is Netherlands
68 D1 Waddenzee chan. Netherlands
63 F1 Waddington *England* U.K.
136 D4 Waddington, Mt mt. *B.C.* Canada
68 C2 Waddinxveen Netherlands
62 B4 Wadebridge *England* U.K.
43 D4 Wad ed Dirwāh watercourse Jordan
150 E2 Wadena *Minnesota* U.S.A.
137 J4 Wadena *Saskatchewan* Canada
119 F5 Wad en Nail Sudan
83 D1 Wädenswil Switzerland
74 B3 Wadern Germany
72 D4 Wadersloh Germany
38 A2 Wadgaon India
74 B3 Wadgassen Germany
119 F4 Wad Hamid Sudan
63 G3 Wadhurst *England* U.K.
118 D5 Wadi Abu Hamra watercourse Sudan
42 F4 Wādī al Bāţin watercourse Asia
118 D1 Wādī ál Fārigh watercourse Libya
118 D1 Wādī al Hamīm watercourse Libya
119 F4 Wadi 'Amur watercourse Sudan
43 C5 Wādī 'Araba v. Jordan
118 D5 Wadi Aradeib watercourse Sudan
118 B2 Wādī ash Shāṭi' watercourse Libya
42 D4 Wādī as Sirḥān watercourse Jordan/Saudi Arabia
42 E3 Wādī ath Tharthār r. Iraq
118 D5 Wadi Azum watercourse Sudan
118 D5 Wadi Barei watercourse Sudan
118 B2 Wādī Barjūj watercourse Libya
118 B1 Wādī Bayy al Kabīr watercourse Libya
119 F4 Wadi Bitia watercourse Sudan
124 D1 Wadi Bulbul watercourse Sudan
119 F3 Wâdi el 'Allâqi watercourse Egypt
43 A4 Wâdi el Gafra watercourse Egypt
124 E1 Wadi El Ghalla watercourse Sudan
118 E5 Wadi el Ku watercourse Sudan
119 E4 Wadi el Milk watercourse Sudan
119 E4 Wadi er Ril watercourse Sudan
43 C4 Wadi es Sir Jordan
43 B5 Wâdi Feirân Egypt
124 D1 Wadi Gandi watercourse Sudan
43 D4 Wādī Hadraj watercourse Saudi Arabia
119 F3 Wadi Halfa Sudan
119 G3 Wâdi Hodein watercourse Egypt
124 D1 Wadi Ibra watercourse Sudan
119 E4 Wadi Magrur watercourse Sudan
118 D4 Wadi Mugarib watercourse Sudan
119 F4 Wadi Muheit watercourse Sudan
43 C4 Wādī Mūsā Jordan
119 G3 Wadi Oko watercourse Sudan
118 E5 Wadi Shaqq el Giefer watercourse Sudan
118 D4 Wadi Umm Saggat watercourse Sudan
118 D5 Wadi Uyur watercourse Sudan
118 B1 Wādī Zamzam watercourse Libya
77 H4 Wadlew Poland
119 F5 Wad Medani Sudan
77 H6 Wadowice Poland
76 E4 Wądroże Wielkie Poland
154 C2 Wadsworth *Nevada* U.S.A.
130 C7 Waenhuiskrans South Africa
31 G5 Wafangdian China
42 F4 Wafra Kuwait
29 H4 Waga-gawa r. Japan
14 B2 Wagait Abor. Land res. *Northern Terr.* Australia
72 D3 Wagenfeld Germany
73 F3 Wagenhoff Germany
68 D3 Wageningen Netherlands
135 K3 Wager Bay b. *N.W.T.* Canada
13 F3 Wagga Wagga *New South Wales* Australia
74 D3 Waghäusel Germany

17 B7 Wagin Western Australia Australia
75 H5 Waging am See Germany
80 D3 Waginger See l. Germany
83 D1 Wägitaler See l. Switzerland
72 F1 Wagrien reg. Germany
76 F3 Wągrowiec Poland
36 C2 Wah Pakistan
21 J7 Wahai Indonesia
123 E5 Wahala Togo
153 □1 Wahiawa Hawaii U.S.A.
72 F2 Wahlstedt Germany
150 D3 Wahoo Nebraska U.S.A.
150 D2 Wahpeton N. Dakota U.S.A.
73 F3 Wahrenholz Germany
155 F2 Wah Wah Mts mts Utah U.S.A.
38 A2 Wai India
153 □1 Waialee Hawaii U.S.A.
153 □1 Waialua Hawaii U.S.A.
153 □1 Waialua Bay b. Hawaii U.S.A.
153 □1 Waianae Hawaii U.S.A.
153 □1 Waianae Ra. mountain range Hawaii U.S.A.
9 A6 Waiau r. New Zealand
9 D5 Waiau r. New Zealand
8 F3 Waiau r. New Zealand
9 D5 Waiau New Zealand
74 E4 Waiblingen Germany
74 D3 Waibstadt Germany
75 H3 Waidhaus Germany
81 G2 Waidhofen an der Thaya div. Austria
81 G2 Waidhofen an der Thaya Austria
81 F3 Waidhofen an der Ybbs Austria
21 K7 Waigeo i. Indonesia
9 C6 Waihao Downs New Zealand
8 E2 Waiharoa New Zealand
8 E2 Waiheke Island i. New Zealand
8 E2 Waihi New Zealand
8 E2 Waihou r. New Zealand
22 D4 Waikabubak Indonesia
9 B6 Waikaia r. New Zealand
9 B6 Waikaia New Zealand
9 E4 Waikanae New Zealand
153 □1 Waikane Hawaii U.S.A.
8 E2 Waikare, L. l. New Zealand
8 F3 Waikaremoana, L. l. New Zealand
9 D5 Waikari New Zealand
8 E2 Waikato div. New Zealand
8 E2 Waikato r. New Zealand
8 F2 Waikawa Pt pt New Zealand
12 D3 Waikerie S. Australia Australia
153 □1 Waikiki Beach beach Hawaii U.S.A.
9 C6 Waikouaiti New Zealand
6 □6 Wailagi Lala i. Fiji
6 □6 Wailevu Fiji
6 □8 Wailotua Fiji
153 □2 Wailuku Hawaii U.S.A.
9 D5 Waimakariri r. New Zealand
8 F3 Waimana New Zealand
153 □1 Waimanalo Hawaii U.S.A.
9 C4 Waimangaroa New Zealand
22 D4 Waimanguar Indonesia
8 F3 Waimarama New Zealand
9 C6 Waimate New Zealand
8 D1 Waimatenui New Zealand
153 □1 Waimea Hawaii U.S.A.
153 □2 Waimea Hawaii U.S.A.
22 E2 Waimenda Indonesia
69 E4 Waimes Belgium
80 B2 Wain Germany
63 G1 Wainfleet All Saints England U.K.
38 B1 Wainganga r. India
22 E4 Waingapu Indonesia
62 B4 Wainhouse Corner England U.K.
163 F2 Waini r. Guyana
163 F2 Waini Pt pt Guyana
6 □6 Wainunu B. b. Fiji
134 C2 Wainwright Alaska U.S.A.
137 G4 Wainwright Alberta Canada
8 F3 Waioeka r. New Zealand
8 E1 Waiotira New Zealand
8 E3 Waiouru New Zealand
8 E3 Waipa r. New Zealand
9 B7 Waipahi New Zealand
153 □1 Waipahu Hawaii U.S.A.
8 F3 Waipaoa r. New Zealand
9 B7 Waipapa Pt pt New Zealand
9 D5 Waipara New Zealand
8 F3 Waipawa New Zealand
8 E1 Waipu New Zealand
8 F3 Waipukurau New Zealand
8 F3 Wairakei New Zealand
9 E4 Wairarapa, L. l. New Zealand
9 D4 Wairau r. New Zealand
9 D4 Wairau Valley New Zealand
8 E1 Wairoa r. New Zealand
8 F3 Wairoa r. New Zealand
8 F3 Wairoa New Zealand
8 F3 Waitahanui New Zealand
9 B6 Waitahuna New Zealand
8 E2 Waitakaruru New Zealand
9 C6 Waitaki r. New Zealand
9 □1 Waitangi Chatham Is New Zealand
36 C2 Waitar Pakistan
8 E3 Waitara New Zealand
10 □3 Waite, Mt h. Macquarie I. Pacific Ocean
8 E2 Waitoa New Zealand
8 E3 Waitotara New Zealand
8 E3 Waitotari r. New Zealand
8 E2 Waiuku New Zealand
9 B7 Waiwera South New Zealand
6 □6 Waiyevo Fiji
81 E2 Waizenkirchen Austria
28 E7 Wajiki Japan
29 F5 Wajima Japan
126 D4 Wajir Kenya
124 D3 Waka Équateur Congo(Zaire)
124 D4 Waka Équateur Congo(Zaire)
28 E6 Wakasa Japan
29 E6 Wakasa-wan b. Japan
9 B6 Wakatipu, Lake l. New Zealand
137 H4 Wakaw Saskatchewan Canada
6 □8 Wakaya i. Fiji
29 E7 Wakayama div. Japan
29 E6 Wakayama Japan
150 D4 Wa Keeney Kansas U.S.A.
65 G4 Wakefield England U.K.
148 C2 Wakefield Michigan U.S.A.
141 H4 Wakefield Québec Canada
147 H4 Wakefield Rhode Island U.S.A.
146 E6 Wakefield Virginia U.S.A.
159 □1 Wakefield Jamaica
9 D4 Wakefield New Zealand
Wakeham see Kangiqsujuaq
4 H3 Wake Island i. Pacific Ocean
24 A3 Wakema Myanmar
36 C1 Wakhan reg. Afghanistan
36 C1 Wakhjir P. pass Afghanistan/China
28 E6 Waki Japan
28 H3 Wakinosawa Japan
28 H1 Wakkanai Japan
131 H3 Wakkerstroom South Africa
13 F3 Wakool r. New South Wales Australia
13 F3 Wakool New South Wales Australia
139 G2 Wakuach, Lac l. Québec Canada
125 C6 Waku-Kungo Angola
127 B6 Wala r. Tanzania
63 H2 Walberswick England U.K.
76 E5 Wałbrzych div. Poland
76 E5 Wałbrzych Wałbrzych Poland
13 G2 Walcha New South Wales Australia
75 G5 Walchensee l. Germany
69 C4 Walcourt Belgium
76 E2 Wałcz Poland
83 D1 Wald Switzerland
87 H4 Waldachtal Germany
81 F2 Waldaist r. Austria
74 C3 Waldböckelheim Germany
87 G2 Waldbröl Germany
87 H2 Waldbrunn-Lahr Germany
83 E1 Waldburg Germany
17 B5 Waldburg Ra. mountain range Western Australia Australia
81 H3 Waldegg Austria
82 C1 Waldenburg Switzerland
147 F4 Walden Montgomery New York U.S.A.
80 D1 Walderbach Germany
87 G2 Waldesch Germany
74 C3 Waldfischbach-Burgalben Germany
73 J4 Waldheim Germany
72 E4 Waldkappel Germany
74 C4 Waldkirch Germany
81 E2 Waldkirchen Germany
75 H4 Waldkraiburg Germany
87 G3 Waldmohr Germany
75 H3 Waldmünchen Germany
62 B4 Waldon r. England U.K.
146 E5 Waldorf Maryland U.S.A.
69 E5 Waldrach Germany
179 C6 Waldron, C. c. Antarctica
75 H2 Waldsassen Germany
74 D5 Waldshut Germany
83 E1 Waldstatt Switzerland
80 A2 Waldstetten Germany
81 G2 Waldviertel reg. Austria
83 E1 Walenstadt Switzerland
62 C2 Wales div. U.K.
122 D4 Walewale Ghana
69 E5 Walferdange Luxembourg
13 G2 Walgett New South Wales Australia
179 A3 Walgreen Coast coastal area Antarctica
36 B3 Walhar Pakistan
124 E4 Walikale Congo(Zaire)
76 E5 Walim Poland
154 C2 Walker r. Nevada U.S.A.
148 B4 Walker Iowa U.S.A.
150 E2 Walker Minnesota U.S.A.
130 B7 Walker Bay b. South Africa
145 E7 Walker Cay i. The Bahamas
15 E3 Walker Cr. r. Queensland Australia
154 C2 Walker Lake l. Nevada U.S.A.
179 A3 Walker Mts mountain range Antarctica
154 C4 Walker Pass pass California U.S.A.
140 E4 Walkerton Ontario Canada
150 C2 Wall S. Dakota U.S.A.
15 E2 Wallaby I. i. Queensland Australia
152 C2 Wallace Idaho U.S.A.
140 D5 Wallaceburg Ontario Canada
16 C3 Wallal Downs Western Australia Australia
15 G6 Wallangarra Queensland Australia
12 D3 Wallaroo S. Australia Australia
65 E4 Wallasey England U.K.
15 G5 Wallaville Queensland Australia
13 F3 Walla Walla New South Wales Australia
152 C2 Walla Walla Washington U.S.A.
74 D3 Walldorf Baden-Württemberg Germany
74 F2 Walldorf Thüringen Germany
74 E3 Walldürn Germany
130 A5 Wallekraal South Africa
75 G2 Wallenfels Germany
72 D3 Wallenhorst Germany
147 F4 Wallenpaupack, Lake l. Pennsylvania U.S.A.
83 E1 Wallensee l. Switzerland
81 H3 Wallern im Burgenland Austria
75 H4 Wallersdorf Germany
80 E3 Wallersee l. Austria
74 F4 Wallerstein Germany
75 G5 Wallgau Germany
147 G4 Wallingford Connecticut U.S.A.
63 E3 Wallingford England U.K.
176 H6 Wallis, Îles is Wallis and Futuna Pacific Ocean
5 K6 Wallis and Futuna territory Pacific Ocean
83 D1 Wallisellen Switzerland
13 H3 Wallis L. b. New South Wales Australia
147 F6 Wallops I. i. Virginia U.S.A.
152 C2 Wallowa Mts mts Oregon U.S.A.
66 □2 Walls Scotland U.K.
13 G3 Wallsend New South Wales Australia
15 G5 Wallumbilla Queensland Australia
63 H3 Walmer England U.K.
137 H2 Walmsley Lake l. N.W.T. Canada
65 E3 Walney, Isle of i. England U.K.
148 C5 Walnut Illinois U.S.A.
155 G4 Walnut Canyon National Monument nat. park Arizona U.S.A.
151 F4 Walnut Ridge Arkansas U.S.A.
80 C2 Walpertskirchen Germany
17 B7 Walpole Western Australia Australia
6 □2 Walpole, Î. i. New Caledonia Pacific Ocean
17 B7 Walpole-Nornalup Nat. Park nat. park Western Australia Australia
80 D3 Wals Austria
63 E2 Walsall England U.K.
153 F4 Walsenburg Colorado U.S.A.
15 F3 Walsh r. Queensland Australia
73 H3 Walsleben Germany
72 E3 Walsrode Germany
38 C2 Waltair India
74 F5 Waltenhofen Germany
145 D5 Walterboro S. Carolina U.S.A.
145 C6 Walter F. George Res. resr Alabama/Georgia U.S.A.
75 F2 Waltershausen Germany
15 F6 Walter's Ra. h. Queensland Australia
141 G4 Waltham Québec Canada
63 F2 Waltham on the Wolds England U.K.
146 A5 Walton Kentucky U.S.A.
147 F3 Walton New York U.S.A.
63 H3 Walton-on-Naze England U.K.
63 F3 Walton-on-Thames England U.K.
128 A3 Walvis Bay b. Namibia
128 A3 Walvis Bay Namibia
174 K7 Walvis Ridge sea feature Atlantic Ocean
127 B4 Wamala, Lake l. Uganda
125 C4 Wamba r. Congo(Zaire)
124 D4 Wamba Équateur Congo(Zaire)
124 E3 Wamba Haute-Zaïre Congo(Zaire)
123 F5 Wamba Nigeria
21 L7 Wamena Indonesia
36 B2 Wana Pakistan
13 F2 Wanaaring New South Wales Australia
9 B6 Wanaka New Zealand
9 B6 Wanaka, L. l. New Zealand
33 F3 Wan'an China
158 □3 Wanapa Bonaire Netherlands Ant.
140 E3 Wanapitei Lake l. Ontario Canada
147 F4 Wanaque Reservoir resr New Jersey U.S.A.
12 E3 Wanbi S. Australia Australia
9 C6 Wanbrow, Cape c. New Zealand
31 K3 Wanda Shan mountain range China
135 R1 Wandel Hav sea Greenland
75 F2 Wandersleben Germany
72 E1 Wanderup Germany
73 J3 Wandlitz Germany
31 H6 Wando South Korea
15 G5 Wandoan Queensland Australia
63 F3 Wandsworth England U.K.
8 E3 Wanganui r. New Zealand
8 E3 Wanganui New Zealand
13 F4 Wangaratta Victoria Australia
12 C3 Wangary S. Australia Australia
32 D1 Wangcang China
33 F2 Wangcheng China
37 G4 Wangdu-Phodrang Bhutan
82 C1 Wangen Switzerland
74 E5 Wangen im Allgäu Germany
72 C2 Wangerooge i. Germany
22 E4 Wanggamet, G. mt. Indonesia
33 E3 Wanggao China
31 G4 Wanghai Shan h. China
83 D1 Wängi Switzerland
33 G2 Wangjiang China
31 H3 Wangkui China
Wang Mai Khon see Sawankhalok
33 E4 Wangmao China
32 D3 Wangmo China
31 J4 Wangqing China
32 D1 Wangziguan China
24 B2 Wan Hsa-la Myanmar
124 E3 Wanie-Rukula Congo(Zaire)
36 B5 Wankaner India
72 F1 Wankendorf Germany
126 D4 Wanlaweyn Somalia
72 D2 Wanna Germany
17 A6 Wanneroo Western Australia Australia
33 G2 Wannian China
33 E5 Wanning China
31 E4 Wanquan China
33 F4 Wanshan Qundao is China
69 E3 Wanssum Netherlands
8 F4 Wanstead New Zealand
63 E3 Wantage England U.K.
140 E3 Wanup Ontario Canada
32 E2 Wan Xian China
32 E2 Wanxian China
32 E1 Wanyuan China
33 F2 Wanzai China
69 D4 Wanze Belgium
73 G3 Wanzleben Germany
146 A4 Wapakoneta Ohio U.S.A.
148 B5 Wapello Iowa U.S.A.
68 E2 Wapenveld Netherlands
138 C3 Wapikopa L. l. Ontario Canada
136 F4 Wapiti r. Alberta Canada
77 J2 Waplewo Poland
151 F4 Wappapello, L. resr Missouri U.S.A.
148 A5 Wapsipinicon r. Iowa U.S.A.
32 C1 Waqên China
126 E3 Warabeye Somalia
126 D4 Waradi waterhole Kenya
36 C2 Warai Post Pakistan
126 D3 Warandab Ethiopia
38 B2 Warangal India
13 F4 Waranga Reservoir resr Victoria Australia
36 E5 Waraseoni India
13 F5 Waratah Tasmania Australia
13 F4 Waratah B. b. Victoria Australia
63 F2 Warboys England U.K.
15 E5 Warbreccan Queensland Australia
72 E4 Warburg Germany
12 D1 Warburton watercourse S. Australia Australia
13 F4 Warburton Victoria Australia
17 D5 Warburton Western Australia Australia
131 H3 Warburton South Africa
137 G2 Warburton Bay b. N.W.T. Canada
69 E4 Warche r. Belgium
87 E3 Warcq France
15 F5 Ward watercourse Queensland Australia
12 D3 Wardang I. i. S. Australia Australia
127 D4 Wardeglo waterhole Kenya
131 G3 Warden South Africa
72 D2 Wardenburg Germany
36 D5 Wardha India
38 B1 Wardha r. India
9 A6 Ward, Mt mt. New Zealand
9 B5 Ward, Mt mt. New Zealand
65 F3 Ward's Stone h. England U.K.
136 D3 Ware B.C. Canada
147 G3 Ware Massachusetts U.S.A.
69 B4 Waregem Belgium
62 D4 Wareham England U.K.
147 H4 Wareham Massachusetts U.S.A.
69 D4 Waremme div. Liège Belgium
69 D4 Waremme Belgium
73 H2 Waren Germany
72 C4 Warendorf Germany
68 E1 Warffum Netherlands
13 G2 Warialda New South Wales Australia
73 G2 Warin Germany
25 D4 Warin Chamrap Thailand
77 K4 Warka Poland
65 G2 Warkworth England U.K.
8 E2 Warkworth New Zealand
32 C2 Warli China
63 F3 Warlingham England U.K.
86 B2 Warloy-Baillon France
76 G2 Warlubie Poland
137 H4 Warman Saskatchewan Canada
128 B4 Warmbad Namibia
130 B3 Warmfontein Namibia
77 J1 Warmia reg. Poland
63 E2 Warmington England U.K.
62 D3 Warminster England U.K.
147 F4 Warminster Pennsylvania U.S.A.
154 D2 Warm Springs Nevada U.S.A.
146 D5 Warm Springs Virginia U.S.A.
73 H1 Warnemünde Germany
147 H3 Warner New Hampshire U.S.A.
152 B3 Warner Mts mountain range California U.S.A.
145 D5 Warner Robins Georgia U.S.A.
165 D3 Warnes Bolivia
80 C3 Warngau Germany
76 C2 Warnice Poland
13 H2 Warning, Mt mt. New South Wales Australia
73 H2 Warnow r. Germany
73 G2 Warnow Germany
68 E2 Warnsveld Netherlands
17 A7 Waroona Western Australia Australia
36 D5 Warora India
15 G5 Warra Queensland Australia
14 C4 Warrabri Abor. Reserve res. Northern Terr. Australia
13 E4 Warracknabeal Victoria Australia
13 F4 Warragul Victoria Australia
12 D1 Warrandirinna, L. salt flat S. Australia Australia
16 C4 Warrawagine Western Australia Australia
13 F2 Warrego r. New South Wales Australia
15 F5 Warrego Ra. h. Queensland Australia
151 E5 Warren Arkansas U.S.A.
149 F4 Warren Michigan U.S.A.
150 D1 Warren Minnesota U.S.A.
13 F2 Warren New South Wales Australia
146 C4 Warren Ohio U.S.A.
140 E3 Warren Ontario Canada
146 D4 Warren Pennsylvania U.S.A.
146 C4 Warrendale Pennsylvania U.S.A.
67 E2 Warrenpoint Northern Ireland U.K.
150 E4 Warrensburg Missouri U.S.A.
147 G3 Warrensburg New York U.S.A.
146 E5 Warrenton Virginia U.S.A.
130 E4 Warrenton South Africa
123 F5 Warri Nigeria
17 B6 Warriedar h. Western Australia Australia
12 D2 Warriners Cr. watercourse S. Australia Australia
65 F4 Warrington England U.K.
145 C6 Warrington Florida U.S.A.
9 C6 Warrington New Zealand
13 E4 Warrnambool Victoria Australia
150 E1 Warroad Minnesota U.S.A.
13 G2 Warrumbungle Ra. mountain range New South Wales Australia
15 E6 Warry Warry watercourse Queensland Australia
148 E5 Warsaw Indiana U.S.A.
146 A5 Warsaw Kentucky U.S.A.
150 E4 Warsaw Missouri U.S.A.
146 D3 Warsaw New York U.S.A.
146 E6 Warsaw Virginia U.S.A.
Warsaw see Warszawa
126 E4 Warshiikh Somalia
63 E1 Warslow England U.K.
63 E1 Warsop England U.K.
72 D4 Warstein Germany
77 K3 Warszawa div. Poland
77 K3 Warszawa Poland
76 C3 Warta r. Poland
76 G4 Warta Poland
76 D4 Warta Bolesławiecka Poland
81 F3 Wartberg an der Krems Austria
80 C2 Wartenberg Germany
74 E4 Warthausen Germany
22 D2 Waru Indonesia
63 E2 Warwick England U.K.
147 F4 Warwick New York U.S.A.
141 K4 Warwick Québec Canada
15 H6 Warwick Queensland Australia
147 H4 Warwick Rhode Island U.S.A.
65 F3 Warwick Bridge England U.K.
14 D2 Warwick Chan. chan. Northern Terr. Australia
63 E2 Warwickshire div. England U.K.
32 C2 Warzhong China
153 E4 Wasatch Range mountain range Utah U.S.A.
131 H4 Wasbank South Africa
154 C4 Wasco California U.S.A.
150 E2 Waseca Minnesota U.S.A.
39 E4 Washap Pakistan
148 C5 Washburn Illinois U.S.A.
147 J1 Washburn Maine U.S.A.
150 C2 Washburn N. Dakota U.S.A.
148 B2 Washburn Wisconsin U.S.A.
36 D5 Wāshīm India
152 B2 Washington div. U.S.A.
65 G3 Washington England U.K.
145 D5 Washington Georgia U.S.A.
148 C5 Washington Illinois U.S.A.
144 C4 Washington Indiana U.S.A.
148 B5 Washington Iowa U.S.A.
150 F4 Washington Missouri U.S.A.
145 E5 Washington N. Carolina U.S.A.
147 F4 Washington New Jersey U.S.A.
146 C4 Washington Pennsylvania U.S.A.
155 F3 Washington Utah U.S.A.
172 E2 Washington Argentina
179 B5 Washington, C. c. Antarctica
146 B5 Washington Court House Ohio U.S.A.
146 E5 Washington D.C. U.S.A.
148 D3 Washington Island i. Wisconsin U.S.A.
135 M1 Washington Land reg. Greenland
147 H2 Washington, Mt mt. New Hampshire U.S.A.
151 D5 Washita r. Oklahoma U.S.A.
63 G2 Wash, The b. England U.K.
39 F4 Washuk Pakistan
69 C5 Wasigny France
77 M2 Wasilków Poland
42 F3 Wāsiţ div. Iraq
43 C5 Wasit Egypt
138 E3 Waskaganish Québec Canada
137 K3 Waskaiowaka Lake l. Manitoba Canada
76 E4 Wąsosz Leszno Poland
77 L2 Wąsosz Łomza Poland
156 J6 Waspán Nicaragua
122 B4 Wassadou Senegal
28 J1 Wassamu Japan
87 G4 Wasselonne France
83 D2 Wassen Switzerland
68 C2 Wassenaar Netherlands
72 B4 Wassenberg Germany
130 B3 Wasser Namibia
75 H4 Wasserburg am Inn Germany
74 E2 Wasserkuppe mt. Germany
75 F3 Wassertrüdingen Germany
86 C2 Wassigny France
154 C2 Wassuk Range mts Nevada U.S.A.
86 D4 Wassy France
65 E3 Wast Water l. England U.K.
74 F2 Wasungen Germany
141 G2 Waswanipi r. Québec Canada
141 H2 Waswanipi Québec Canada
141 G2 Waswanipi, Lac l. Québec Canada
22 E3 Watampone Indonesia
22 D3 Watansoppeng Indonesia
62 C3 Watchet England U.K.
147 G4 Waterbury Connecticut U.S.A.
147 G2 Waterbury Vermont U.S.A.
137 H3 Waterbury Lake l. Saskatchewan Canada
67 D4 Waterford div. Rep. of Ireland
146 D4 Waterford Pennsylvania U.S.A.
67 D4 Waterford Rep. of Ireland
131 E6 Waterford South Africa
67 E4 Waterford Harbour inlet Rep. of Ireland
62 A4 Watergate Bay b. England U.K.
67 C4 Watergrasshill Rep. of Ireland
137 H4 Waterhen r. Saskatchewan Canada
14 C5 Waterhouse Ra. mountain range Northern Terr. Australia
68 C2 Wateringen Netherlands
148 A4 Waterloo Iowa U.S.A.
147 H3 Waterloo Maine U.S.A.
146 E3 Waterloo New York U.S.A.
14 B3 Waterloo Northern Terr. Australia
140 E5 Waterloo Ontario Canada
141 J4 Waterloo Québec Canada
148 C4 Waterloo Wisconsin U.S.A.
69 C4 Waterloo Belgium
122 B5 Waterloo Sierra Leone
159 □3 Waterloo Trinidad and Tobago
63 E4 Waterlooville England U.K.
66 F4 Saughs, Water of r. Scotland U.K.
131 G1 Waterpoort South Africa
148 C2 Watersmeet Michigan U.S.A.
136 G5 Waterton Lakes Nat. Park nat. park B.C. Canada
147 E3 Watertown New York U.S.A.
150 D2 Watertown S. Dakota U.S.A.
148 C4 Watertown Wisconsin U.S.A.
131 G3 Waterval r. South Africa
12 D3 Watervale S. Australia Australia
147 J2 Waterville Maine U.S.A.
137 G3 Waterways Alberta Canada
63 F3 Watford England U.K.
140 E5 Watford Ontario Canada
150 C2 Watford City N. Dakota U.S.A.
137 H3 Wathaman r. Saskatchewan Canada
17 B6 Watheroo Western Australia Australia
72 F3 Wathlingen Germany
43 C5 Watîr, W. watercourse Egypt
146 E3 Watkins Glen New York U.S.A.
63 E3 Watlington England U.K.
151 D5 Watonga Oklahoma U.S.A.
137 H4 Watrous Saskatchewan Canada
124 E3 Watsa Congo(Zaire)
148 D5 Watseka Illinois U.S.A.
124 D4 Watsi Kengo Congo(Zaire)
15 E2 Watson r. Queensland Australia
137 J4 Watson Saskatchewan Canada
136 D2 Watson Lake Yukon Terr. Canada
154 B3 Watsonville California U.S.A.
66 E2 Watten Scotland U.K.
66 E2 Watten, Loch l. Scotland U.K.
82 C2 Wattenwil Switzerland
137 J2 Watterson Lake l. N.W.T. Canada
64 A3 Wattlebridge Northern Ireland U.K.
136 F3 Watt, Mt h. Yukon Terr. Canada
63 G2 Watton England U.K.
148 C2 Watton Michigan U.S.A.
69 B4 Wattrelos France
83 E1 Wattwil Switzerland
6 □1 Wau P.N.G.
124 E2 Wau Sudan
148 D3 Waucedah Michigan U.S.A.
13 H2 Wauchope New South Wales Australia
145 D7 Wauchula Florida U.S.A.
22 D2 Waukara, G. mt. Indonesia
16 C4 Waukarlycarly, L. salt flat Western Australia Australia
148 D4 Waukegan Illinois U.S.A.
148 C4 Waukesha Wisconsin U.S.A.
148 B4 Waukon Iowa U.S.A.
148 C3 Waupaca Wisconsin U.S.A.
148 C4 Waupun Wisconsin U.S.A.
151 D5 Waurika Oklahoma U.S.A.
148 C3 Wausau Wisconsin U.S.A.
146 A4 Wauseon Ohio U.S.A.
148 C3 Wautoma Wisconsin U.S.A.
148 C4 Wauwatosa Wisconsin U.S.A.
14 B3 Wave Hill Northern Terr. Australia
63 H2 Waveney r. England U.K.
8 E3 Waverley New Zealand
148 A4 Waverly Iowa U.S.A.
146 B5 Waverly Ohio U.S.A.
145 C4 Waverly Tennessee U.S.A.
146 E6 Waverly Virginia U.S.A.
69 C4 Wavre Belgium
24 B3 Waw Myanmar
140 C3 Wawa Ontario Canada
123 E5 Wawa Nigeria
118 C2 Wāw al Kabīr Libya
118 C3 Wāw an Nāmūs crater Libya
148 E5 Wawasee, Lake l. Indiana U.S.A.
22 E2 Wawo Indonesia
6 □1 Wawoi r. P.N.G.
154 C3 Wawona California U.S.A.
73 L3 Wawrów Poland
151 D5 Waxahachie Texas U.S.A.
69 E4 Waxweiler Germany
6 □8 Waya i. Fiji
6 □8 Waya Lailai i. Fiji
145 D6 Waycross Georgia U.S.A.
17 C5 Way, L. salt flat Western Australia Australia
146 B6 Wayland Kentucky U.S.A.
148 B5 Wayland Missouri U.S.A.
150 D3 Wayne Nebraska U.S.A.
145 D5 Waynesboro Georgia U.S.A.
151 F6 Waynesboro Mississippi U.S.A.
146 E5 Waynesboro Pennsylvania U.S.A.
146 D5 Waynesboro Virginia U.S.A.
146 C5 Waynesburg Pennsylvania U.S.A.
151 E4 Waynesville Missouri U.S.A.
151 D4 Waynoka Oklahoma U.S.A.
120 B3 Wayn Targat watercourse Western Sahara
124 B1 Waza Cameroon
24 B1 Waza Myanmar
124 B1 Waza, Parc National de nat. park Cameroon
69 B4 Waziers France
39 G2 Wazi Khwa Afghanistan
36 C2 Wazirabad Pakistan
76 G2 Wda r. Poland
123 E4 W. du Niger, Parcs Nationaux du nat. park Niger
138 B3 Weagamow L. l. Ontario Canada
63 G3 Weald, The reg. England U.K.
65 G3 Wear r. England U.K.
14 D3 Wearyan r. Northern Terr. Australia
15 F2 Weary B. b. Queensland Australia
151 D5 Weatherford Texas U.S.A.
62 D1 Weaverham England U.K.
152 B3 Weaverville California U.S.A.
140 E3 Webbwood Ontario Canada
138 C3 Webequie Ontario Canada
136 D3 Weber, Mt mt. B.C. Canada
126 D4 Webi Shabeelle r. Somalia
147 H3 Webster Massachusetts U.S.A.
150 D2 Webster S. Dakota U.S.A.
148 A3 Webster Wisconsin U.S.A.
150 E3 Webster City Iowa U.S.A.
146 C5 Webster Springs W. Virginia U.S.A.
68 F1 Wedde Netherlands
171 D7 Weddell I. i. Falkland Is.
179 B2 Weddell Sea sea Antarctica
72 E2 Wedel (Holstein) Germany
62 D3 Wedmore England U.K.
152 B3 Weed California U.S.A.
141 K4 Weedon Québec Canada
63 E2 Weedon Bec England U.K.
146 D4 Weedville Pennsylvania U.S.A.
131 H4 Weenen South Africa
72 C2 Weener Germany
80 C3 Weer Austria
68 E2 Weerribben, Nationaal Park De nat. park Netherlands
68 E2 Weerselo Netherlands
69 D3 Weert Netherlands
83 E1 Weesen Switzerland
68 D2 Weesp Netherlands
13 F3 Weethalle New South Wales Australia
13 G2 Wee Waa New South Wales Australia
68 E3 Weeze Germany
73 G3 Weferlingen Germany
72 B4 Wegberg Germany
163 F2 Wegeningen Surinam
76 D4 Węgliniec Poland
77 K1 Węgorzewo Poland
76 D2 Węgorzyno Poland
77 L3 Węgrów Poland
73 L3 Węgrzynice Poland
81 G3 Wegscheid Austria
75 J4 Wegscheid Germany
68 E1 Wehe-den Hoorn Netherlands
68 E3 Wehl Netherlands
74 C5 Wehr Germany
80 B2 Wehringen Germany
33 F1 Wei r. Henan China
33 E1 Wei r. Shaanxi China
31 F5 Wei r. Shandong China
69 F4 Weibern Germany
31 F4 Weichang China
75 H2 Weida r. Germany
75 H2 Weida Germany
75 G3 Weidenberg Germany
75 H3 Weiden in der Oberpfalz Germany
74 C3 Weidenthal Germany
75 H3 Weiding Germany
31 F5 Weifang China
31 G5 Weihai China
74 E3 Weikersheim Germany
74 D2 Weilburg Germany
87 G3 Weilerbach Germany
74 B2 Weilerswist Germany
75 G5 Weilheim in Oberbayern Germany
74 D2 Weilmünster Germany
75 G2 Weimar Germany
33 E1 Weinan China
73 J4 Weinböhla Germany
83 E1 Weinfelden Switzerland
74 E5 Weingarten Germany
87 H3 Weingarten (Baden) Germany
74 D3 Weinheim Germany
32 D3 Weining China
74 E3 Weinsberg Germany
81 F2 Weinsberger Wald forest Austria
69 E4 Weinsheim Germany
74 E4 Weinstadt Germany
15 E2 Weipa Queensland Australia
15 G6 Weir r. Queensland Australia
141 H4 Weir Québec Canada
137 L3 Weir River Manitoba Canada
146 C4 Weirton W. Virginia U.S.A.
75 H2 Weischlitz Germany
73 G2 Weisen Germany
152 C2 Weiser Idaho U.S.A.
32 C3 Weishan China
33 G1 Weishan China
33 G1 Weishan Hu l. China
69 E5 Weiskirchen Germany
80 C3 Weißach r. Germany
75 H2 Weiße Elster r. Germany
80 B3 Weißenbach am Lech Austria
73 K4 Weißenberg Germany
75 J2 Weißenborn Germany
75 F3 Weißenburg in Bayern Germany
73 G4 Weißenfels Germany
74 F4 Weißenhorn Germany
81 E4 Weißensee l. Austria
75 G2 Weißer-Main r. Germany
75 J3 Weißer Regen r. Germany
73 K4 Weißer Schöps r. Germany
82 C2 Weisshorn mt. Switzerland
81 F3 Weißkirchen in Steiermark Austria
83 F2 Weißkugel mt. Austria/Italy
145 C5 Weiss L. l. Alabama U.S.A.
82 D2 Weissmies mt. Switzerland
128 B4 Weissrand Mts mts Namibia
73 K4 Weißwasser Germany
69 E4 Weiswampach Luxembourg

X

Y

47 L3 Youyi Feng mt. China/Rus. Fed.
30 E5 Youyu China
47 G5 Yovon Tajikistan
42 C2 Yozgat Turkey
165 E4 Ypané r. Paraguay
114 D4 Ypati Greece
165 E4 Ypé-Jhú Paraguay
89 F2 Yport France
Ypres div. see Ieper
114 A3 Ypsos Greece
115 D5 Ypsous Greece
152 B3 Yreka California U.S.A.
Yr Wyddfa mt. see Snowdon
86 B2 Yser r. France
91 C3 Yssingeaux France
59 E4 Ystad Sweden
62 C3 Ystalyfera Wales U.K.
62 C2 Ystwyth r. Wales U.K.
47 J4 Ysyk-Köl div. Kyrgyzstan
47 J4 Ysyk-Köl salt lake Kyrgyzstan
Ysyk-Köl see Balykchy
66 F3 Ythan r. Scotland U.K.
58 B2 Ytre Vinje Norway
59 H3 Ytterholmen i. Sweden
59 E1 Yttermalung Sweden
45 P3 Ytyk-Kyuyel Rus. Fed.
33 E4 Yu r. China
33 H4 Yüalin Taiwan
33 E2 Yuan r. Hunan China
32 C4 Yuan r. Yunnan China
33 E2 Yuan'an China
33 E3 Yuanbao Shan mt. China
32 C4 Yuanjiang China
33 F2 Yuanjiang China
33 H3 Yüanli Taiwan
33 E2 Yuanling China
32 C3 Yuanmou China
30 E5 Yuanping China
33 E1 Yuanqu China
30 A5 Yuanshanzi China
32 C4 Yuanyang China
29 E6 Yuasa Japan
154 B2 Yuba r. California U.S.A.
154 B2 Yuba City California U.S.A.
28 H2 Yūbari Japan
28 J2 Yūbari-sanchi mountain range Japan
28 J1 Yūbetsu Japan
28 J2 Yūbetsu-gawa r. Japan
157 H4 Yucatán div. Mexico
157 H5 Yucatán pen. Mexico
158 A2 Yucatan Channel str. Cuba/Mexico
155 E4 Yucca Arizona U.S.A.
154 D3 Yucca L. l. Nevada U.S.A.
154 D4 Yucca Valley California U.S.A.
31 F5 Yucheng China
30 E5 Yuci China
52 C1 Yudino Rus. Fed.
31 G1 Yudi Shan mt. China
33 F3 Yudu China
32 D2 Yuechi China
31 H3 Yueliang Pao l. China
14 B4 Yuendumu Northern Terr. Australia
14 B4 Yuendumu Abor. Reserve res. Northern Terr. Australia
27 Yuen Long Hong Kong China
33 H2 Yueqing China
33 G2 Yuexi China
32 C2 Yuexi China
33 F2 Yueyang China
33 G2 Yugan China
Yugo-Osetinskaya Avtonomnaya Oblast' see South Ossetia
49 H4 Yugoslavia country Europe
45 R3 Yugo-Tala Rus. Fed.
33 H2 Yuhuan China
31 F5 Yuhuang Ding mt. China
45 R3 Yukagirskoye Ploskogor'ye plat. Rus. Fed.
54 F3 Yukhavichy Belarus
52 B2 Yukhnov Rus. Fed.
125 C4 Yuki Congo(Zaire)
136 B2 Yukon r. Canada/U.S.A.
136 B2 Yukon Territory div. Canada
42 F2 Yüksekova Turkey
28 C7 Yukuhashi Japan
14 B5 Yulara Northern Terr. Australia
46 E2 Yuldybayevo Rus. Fed.
16 B4 Yule r. Western Australia Australia
145 D6 Yulee Florida U.S.A.
33 H4 Yüli Taiwan
33 E5 Yulin China
33 E4 Yulin China
30 D5 Yulin China
32 C3 Yulongxue Shan mt. China
155 E5 Yuma Arizona U.S.A.
155 E5 Yuma Desert desert Arizona U.S.A.
172 A4 Yumbel Chile
124 C4 Yumbi Bandundu Congo(Zaire)
124 E4 Yumbi Kivu Congo(Zaire)
162 B3 Yumbo Colombia
26 G4 Yumen China
47 K3 Yumin China
43 C1 Yumurtalık Turkey
159 E3 Yuna r. Dominican Rep.
17 A6 Yuna Western Australia Australia
42 B2 Yunak Turkey
53 F1 Yunakivka Ukraine
33 E4 Yunan China
33 E1 Yuncheng China
99 G4 Yuncler Spain
99 G4 Yuncos Spain
17 C6 Yundamindera Western Australia Australia
33 F4 Yunfu China
164 C3 Yungas reg. Bolivia
164 C4 Yungay Antofagasta Chile
172 B4 Yungay Biobío Chile
164 C3 Yungayo Peru
32 C3 Yun Gui Gaoyuan plat. China
33 G2 Yunhe China
33 E4 Yunkai Dashan mountain range China
32 B3 Yun Ling mountain range China
32 B3 Yunlong China
33 F2 Yunmeng China
24 B1 Yunnan div. China
28 C7 Yunomae Japan
101 F4 Yunquera Spain
99 G4 Yunquera de Henares Spain
33 F2 Yun Shui r. China
12 D3 Yunta S. Australia Australia
33 E4 Yunwu Shan mountain range China
33 E1 Yunxi China
33 E1 Yun Xian China
33 G4 Yunxiao China
32 E2 Yunyang China
33 F1 Yunyang China
33 E3 Yuping China
31 F4 Yuqiao Sk. resr China
33 D3 Yuqing China
164 C4 Yura Bolivia
29 E6 Yura-gawa r. Japan
54 D4 Yuratsishki Belarus
47 K1 Yurga Rus. Fed.
162 B5 Yurimaguas Peru
52 H1 Yurino Rus. Fed.
50 H1 Yuroma Rus. Fed.
52 H1 Yuronga r. Rus. Fed.
52 F1 Yurovo Rus. Fed.
162 D1 Yurubi, Parque Nacional nat. park Venezuela
47 J5 Yurungkax r. China
50 J3 Yur'ya Rus. Fed.
52 F1 Yur'yevets Rus. Fed.
52 E1 Yur'yevets Rus. Fed.
52 D1 Yur'yevo Opol'ye reg. Rus. Fed.
52 D1 Yur'yev-Pol'skiy Rus. Fed.
53 G2 Yur"yivka Dnipropetrovs'k Ukraine
53 G3 Yur"yivka Zaporizhzhya Ukraine
46 E1 Yuryuzan' r. Rus. Fed.
46 E2 Yuryuzan' Rus. Fed.
156 J6 Yuscarán Honduras
33 H4 Yü Shan mt. Taiwan
33 G2 Yushan China
33 H2 Yushan Liedao is China
30 E5 Yushe China
50 E1 Yushkozero Rus. Fed.
31 H3 Yushu China
32 B1 Yushu China
Yushuwan see Huaihua
51 H6 Yusta Rus. Fed.
42 E1 Yusufeli Turkey
28 D7 Yusuhara Japan
33 G1 Yutai China
165 D3 Yuti Bolivia
37 E1 Yutian China
173 F4 Yutuyaco Argentina
165 E5 Yuty Paraguay
87 F3 Yutz France
30 C5 Yuwang China
32 C3 Yuxi China
33 E2 Yuxiakou China
33 F1 Yu Xian China
30 E5 Yu Xian China
33 H2 Yuyao China
29 H4 Yuzawa Japan
52 F1 Yuzha Rus. Fed.
53 D3 Yuzhne Ukraine
47 G4 Yuzhno-Kazakhstan div. Kazakhstan
28 K1 Yuzhno-Kuril'sk Rus. Fed.
27 Q2 Yuzhno-Sakhalinsk Rus. Fed.
51 H6 Yuzhno-Sukhokumsk Rus. Fed.
53 D3 Yuzhnoukrayinsk Ukraine
46 F2 Yuzhnoural'sk Rus. Fed.
27 Q2 Yuzhnoye Rus. Fed.
47 K2 Yuzhnyy Rus. Fed.
46 E2 Yuzhnyy Ural mountain range Rus. Fed.
30 C6 Yuzhong China
42 F3 Yūzīdar Iran
88 C3 Yvel r. France
89 G3 Yvelines div. France
82 B2 Yverdon Switzerland
89 F2 Yvetot France
88 C3 Yvignac France
69 C4 Yvoir Belgium
82 B2 Yvoire France
82 B2 Yvonand Switzerland
24 A2 Ywamun Myanmar
24 B2 Ywathit Myanmar
59 G3 Yxern l. Sweden
59 G2 Yxnerum Sweden
59 F2 Yxningen l. Sweden
59 G2 Yxnö i. Sweden
90 B2 Yzeure France
92 C2 Yzeures-sur-Creuse France

Z

130 D6 Zaaimansdal South Africa
69 B3 Zaamslag Netherlands
68 C2 Zaandam Netherlands
31 F2 Zabaykal'sk China
111 Zabbar Malta
42 F2 Zab-e Kuchek r. Iran
73 J4 Zabeltitz-Treugeböhla Germany
124 E3 Zabia Congo(Zaire)
126 D2 Zabīd Yemen
126 D2 Zabīd, W. watercourse Yemen
76 E5 Ząbkowice Śląskie Poland
77 M2 Zabłudów Poland
81 H5 Žabno Croatia
77 J5 Żabno Poland
78 E5 Zabok Croatia
39 E3 Zābol Iran
39 E4 Zāboli Iran
53 A2 Zabolotiv Ukraine
53 A1 Zabolottya Ukraine
76 D4 Zabór Poland
76 D2 Żabowo Poland
122 D4 Zabré Burkina
78 F2 Zábřeh Czech Rep.
77 K3 Zabrodzie Poland
76 G5 Zabrze Poland
52 A3 Zabyalyshyna Rus. Fed.
123 E5 Zabzugu Ghana
157 H6 Zacapa Guatemala
157 E5 Zacapu Mexico
166 B3 Zacarias r. Brazil
156 E4 Zacatecas div. Mexico
156 E4 Zacatecas Mexico
157 F5 Zacatlán Mexico
115 C5 Zacharo Greece
80 E2 Zachenberg Germany
53 F2 Zachepylivka Ukraine
77 M3 Zaczopki Poland
104 E3 Zadar Croatia
25 B5 Zadetkale Kyun i. Myanmar
25 B5 Zadetkyi Kyun i. Myanmar
32 A1 Zadoi China
52 D3 Zadonsk Rus. Fed.
76 G4 Zadzim Poland
42 C4 Z'afarâna Egypt
111 E5 Zafferana Etnea Sicilia Italy
110 C4 Zafferano, Capo c. Sicilia Italy
113 F6 Zafora i. Greece
100 D2 Zafra Spain
120 C3 Zag Morocco
81 E4 Žaga Slovenia
76 D4 Żagań Poland
54 C3 Žagarė Lithuania
43 A4 Zagazig Egypt
37 H2 Zagēn China
39 D2 Zaghdeh well Iran
42 F3 Zāgheh-ye-Bālā Iran
121 G1 Zaghouan Tunisia
114 E3 Zagora Greece
120 C2 Zagora Morocco
81 G4 Zagorje reg. Croatia
81 F4 Zagorje ob Savi Slovenia
77 K5 Zagórów Poland
75 F6 Zagórz Poland
77 L6 Zagórz Poland
52 G3 Zagoskino Rus. Fed.
101 F3 Zagra Spain
81 H5 Zagreb airport Croatia
78 E6 Zagreb Croatia
76 D4 Zagrodno Poland
39 B2 Zagros Mountains mountain range Iran
112 C2 Zagubica Yugoslavia
37 G2 Za'gya Zangbo r. China
79 K4 Zagyva r. Hungary
129 H2 Zahamena, Réserve de res. Madagascar
77 N3 Zaharoddzye reg. Belarus
39 E3 Zāhedān Iran
39 G2 Zahidabad Afghanistan
43 C3 Zahlé Lebanon
78 H4 Záhony Hungary
79 M3 Záhony Hungary
78 F3 Záhorská Ves Slovakia
119 H4 Zahrān Saudi Arabia
121 E2 Zahrez Rharbi salt pan Algeria
102 D3 Zaidín Spain
54 C4 Žaiginys Lithuania
30 D2 Zaigrayevo Rus. Fed.
39 B2 Zaindeh r. Iran
Zainlha see Xiaojin
46 D1 Zainsk Rus. Fed.
Zaire country see Congo
125 B5 Zaire div. Angola
Zaïre r. see Congo
114 B1 Zajas Macedonia
112 D3 Zaječar Yugoslavia
73 L2 Zajezierze Poland
129 E3 Zaka Zimbabwe
30 B2 Zakamensk Rus. Fed.
78 F5 Zákány Hungary
79 M3 Zakarpats'ka div. Ukraine
Zakataly see Zaqatala
52 D2 Zakharovo Rus. Fed.
53 A2 Zakhidnyy Buh r. Ukraine
46 F5 Zakhmet Turkmenistan
42 E2 Zākhō Iraq
77 L5 Zaklików Poland
77 H6 Zakopane Poland
124 C1 Zakouma Chad
124 C1 Zakouma, Parc National de nat. park Chad
115 H7 Zakros Greece
76 F2 Zakrzewo Piła Poland
76 G3 Zakrzewo Włocławek Poland
53 B2 Zakupne Ukraine
75 K2 Zákupy Czech Rep.
115 B5 Zakynthos div. Greece
115 B5 Zakynthos i. Greece
115 B5 Zakynthos Greece
78 F5 Zala div. Hungary
78 F5 Zalaegerszeg Hungary
78 F5 Zalai-domsag h. Hungary
54 E2 Zalakhtov'ye Rus. Fed.
78 G5 Zalakomár Hungary
78 F5 Zalalövő Hungary
100 E2 Zalamea de la Serena Spain
100 D3 Zalamea la Real Spain
123 G4 Zalanga Nigeria
31 G3 Zalantun China
81 H4 Zalaszentbalázs Hungary
78 G5 Zalaszentgrót Hungary
78 F5 Zalaszentiván Hungary
78 F5 Zalaszentmihály Hungary
112 D1 Zalău Romania
77 K4 Załazy Poland
81 G4 Žalec Slovenia
52 C3 Zalegoshch' Rus. Fed.
47 K2 Zalesovo Rus. Fed.
77 H2 Zalewo Poland
76 C2 Zalew Szczeciński b. Poland
77 H1 Zalew Wiślany b. Poland
119 H3 Zalim Saudi Arabia
118 D5 Zalingei Sudan
53 A2 Zalishchyky Ukraine
53 A2 Zalissya Ukraine
27 Q2 Zaliv Aniva b. Rus. Fed.
46 D4 Zaliv Kara-Bogaz Gol b. Turkmenistan
46 D3 Zaliv Komsomolets b. Kazakhstan
134 A3 Zaliv Kresta b. Rus. Fed.
46 F3 Zaliv Paskevicha b. Kazakhstan
27 Q3 Zaliv Petra Velikogo b. Rus. Fed.
45 R3 Zaliv Shelikhova g. Rus. Fed.
27 Q2 Zaliv Terpeniya g. Rus. Fed.
53 E3 Zaliznyy Port Ukraine
53 A2 Zaliztsi Ukraine
76 F2 Żalno Poland
68 D3 Zaltbommel Netherlands
77 J3 Załuski Poland
77 N2 Zal'vyanka r. Belarus
29 G6 Zama Japan
131 G3 Zamani South Africa
42 D2 Zamanti r. Turkey
76 F2 Zamarte Poland
23 B3 Zambales Mts mountain range Philippines
78 F1 Żamberk Czech Rep.
125 D6 Zambeze r. Angola
128 E2 Zambeze r. Mozambique
125 D7 Zambezi r. Zambia
125 D6 Zambezi Zambia
129 F2 Zambézia div. Mozambique
117 G7 Zambia country Africa
23 B5 Zamboanga Philippines
23 B5 Zamboanga Peninsula pen. Philippines
99 H2 Zambrana Spain
77 L3 Zambrów Poland
129 E2 Zambue Mozambique
100 B3 Zambujeira do Mar Portugal
73 L2 Zamęcin Poland
123 F4 Zamfara watercourse Nigeria
98 D3 Zamora div. Castilla y León Spain
162 B4 Zamora r. Ecuador
162 B4 Zamora Ecuador
98 E3 Zamora Spain
156 E5 Zamora de Hidalgo Mexico
77 M5 Zamość div. Poland
77 K2 Zamość Ostrołeka Poland
77 M5 Zamość Zamość Poland
29 Zampa-misaki b. Japan
83 F1 Zams Austria
32 C1 Zamtang China
162 D1 Zamuro, Pta pt Venezuela
125 B4 Zanaga Congo
101 H1 Záncara r. Spain
36 D3 Zanda China
163 F2 Zanderij Surinam
69 C3 Zandhoven Belgium
68 C2 Zandvoort Netherlands
146 C5 Zanesville Ohio U.S.A.
122 C4 Zangasso Mali
47 J5 Zangguy China
36 D2 Zangla India
30 E5 Zanhuang China
39 B1 Zanjān div. Iran
39 B1 Zanjān Iran
172 D2 Zanjitas Argentina
109 F4 Zannone, Isola i. Italy
Zante i. see Zakynthos
127 C6 Zanzibar Tanzania
127 C6 Zanzibar Channel chan. Tanzania
127 C6 Zanzibar I. i. Tanzania
52 C2 Zaokskiy Rus. Fed.
99 H4 Zaorejas Spain
33 F2 Zaoshi China
121 F4 Zaouatallaz Algeria
31 F1 Zaoyang China
29 H4 Zaō-zan volcano Japan
52 D1 Zaozer'ye Rus. Fed.
33 G1 Zaozhuang China
42 F2 Zap r. Turkey
112 C3 Zapadna Morava r. Yugoslavia
50 D3 Zapadnaya Dvina r. Rus. Fed.
50 E3 Zapadnaya Dvina Rus. Fed.
112 D4 Zapadni Rodopi mountain range Bulgaria
46 D3 Zapadno-Kazakhstan div. Kazakhstan
27 Q1 Zapadno-Sakhalinskiy Khrebet mountain range Rus. Fed.
44 J4 Zapadno- Sibirskaya Ravnina plain Rus. Fed.
54 F1 Zapadnyy Berezovyy, O. i. Rus. Fed.
46 D4 Zapadnyy Chink Ustyurta escarpment Kazakhstan
56 J1 Zapadnyy Kil'din Rus. Fed.
26 F1 Zapadnyy Sayan mountain range Rus. Fed.
78 C2 Západočeský div. Czech Rep.
79 G3 Západoslovenský div. Slovakia
53 B2 Zapadyntsi Ukraine
172 B5 Zapala Argentina
164 C4 Zapaleri, Co mt. Chile
172 B2 Zapallar Chile
77 L5 Zapałów Poland
99 F3 Zapardiel r. Spain
151 D7 Zapata Texas U.S.A.
172 C2 Zapata Argentina
158 B2 Zapata, Pen. de pen. Cuba
162 C2 Zapatoca Colombia
100 D1 Zapatón r. Spain
173 K2 Zapicán Uruguay
164 C3 Zapiga Chile
54 F2 Zaplyus'ye Rus. Fed.
112 F1 Zăpodeni Romania
31 F2 Zapokrovskiy Rus. Fed.
56 H1 Zapolyarnyy Rus. Fed.
53 F1 Zapol'ye Rus. Fed.
53 F3 Zaporizhzhya div. Ukraine
53 F3 Zaporizhzhya Zaporiz'ka Oblast' Ukraine
54 G1 Zaporozhskoye Rus. Fed.
162 B4 Zapotal Ecuador
114 D3 Zappeio Greece
109 H3 Zapponeta Italy
78 E6 Zaprešić Croatia
52 C1 Zaprudnya Rus. Fed.
77 N3 Zaprudy Belarus
36 E2 Zapug China
77 N6 Zapytiv Ukraine
42 F1 Zaqatala Azerbaijan
32 A1 Zaqên China
32 A1 Za Qu r. China
42 D2 Zara Turkey
46 F4 Zarafshan Uzbekistan
102 B3 Zaragoza div. Spain
153 F6 Zaragoza Chihuahua Mexico
157 E2 Zaragoza Coahuila Mexico
102 C3 Zaragoza Zaragoza Spain
162 C2 Zaragoza Colombia
39 B2 Zarand Iran
39 D3 Zarand Iran
79 M5 Zarandului, Munții mountain range Romania
39 E3 Zaranj Afghanistan
76 D2 Zarańsko Poland
54 E4 Zarasai Lithuania
99 F3 Zaratán Spain
173 H3 Zárate Argentina
99 H1 Zarautz Spain
52 D2 Zaraysk Rus. Fed.
163 D2 Zaraza Venezuela
103 B7 Zarcilla de Ramos Spain
47 H5 Zardaly Kyrgyzstan
56 H2 Zarechensk Rus. Fed.
77 O3 Zarechka Belarus
53 D3 Zarechnyy Rus. Fed.
39 B2 Zāreh Iran
136 C3 Zarembo I. i. Alaska U.S.A.
39 G2 Zarghūn Shahr Afghanistan
36 A3 Zargun mt. Pakistan
123 F4 Zaria Nigeria
53 B1 Zarichne Ukraine
47 K2 Zarinsk Rus. Fed.
77 H5 Żarki Poland
73 K4 Żarki Wielkie Poland
39 E2 Zarmardan Afghanistan
112 E2 Zărnești Romania
79 H3 Žarnovica Slovakia
77 J4 Żarnów Poland
81 H1 Žarošice Czech Rep.
76 E5 Żarów Poland
43 C3 Zarqā' r. Jordan
42 D3 Zarqā' Jordan
39 C3 Zarqān Iran
39 C2 Zarrīn Iran
31 J4 Zarubino Rus. Fed.
162 A4 Zarumilla Peru
76 D4 Żary Poland
46 E3 Zarya Oktyabrya Kazakhstan
101 E2 Zarza Capilla Spain
121 F3 Zarzaïtine Algeria
98 D5 Zarza la Mayor Spain
121 G2 Zarzis Tunisia
54 D3 Zasa Latvia
52 G3 Zasechnoye Rus. Fed.
56 H3 Zasheyek Rus. Fed.
36 D2 Zaskar reg. India
36 D2 Zaskar Mts mountain range India
54 E4 Zaslawye Belarus
75 L3 Žasmuky Czech Rep.
53 A2 Zastavna Ukraine
131 F5 Zastron South Africa
52 H1 Zasur'ye Rus. Fed.
42 D3 Zatara watercourse Jordan
78 C1 Žatec Czech Rep.
46 F2 Zatobol'sk Kazakhstan
53 D3 Zatoka Ukraine
76 C1 Zatoka Pomorska b. Poland
76 G1 Zatoka Pucka b. Poland
53 E3 Zatoka Syvash b. Ukraine
77 H6 Zator Poland
53 A1 Zaturtsi Ukraine
53 C3 Zatyshshya Ukraine
73 H3 Zauche reg. Germany
46 E4 Zaunguzskiye Karakumy desert Turkmenistan
173 G2 Zavalla Argentina
53 D2 Zavallya Ukraine
39 C2 Zavareh Iran
106 D4 Zavattarello Italy
129 E2 Zave Zimbabwe
69 C4 Zaventem Belgium
104 G3 Zavidovići Bos.-Herz.
31 J2 Zavitinsk Rus. Fed.
47 G1 Zavodoukovsk Rus. Fed.
53 A2 Zavods'ke Ukraine
52 F1 Zavolzhsk Rus. Fed.
52 F1 Zavolzh'ye Rus. Fed.
129 F3 Zavora, Pta pt Mozambique
77 M6 Zavydovychi Ukraine
30 B5 Zawa China
76 D4 Zawada Poland
84 B2 Zawgyi r. Myanmar
77 K5 Zawichost Poland
76 D4 Zawidów Poland
77 H3 Zawidz Kościelny Poland
77 H5 Zawiercie Poland
118 C2 Zawīlah Libya
43 D2 Zāwīyah, J. az h. Syria
118 D1 Zāwiyat Masūs Libya
79 J2 Żawoja Poland
46 D1 Zay r. Rus. Fed.
81 H2 Zaya r. Austria
126 D1 Zaylah Yemen
47 K3 Zaysan Kazakhstan
47 K3 Zaysan, Oz. l. Kazakhstan
32 B2 Zayü China
32 B2 Zayü China
32 B2 Zayü Qu r. China/India
129 H3 Zazafotsy Madagascar
53 A2 Zbarazh Ukraine
76 D3 Zbąszyn Poland
76 D3 Zbąszynek Poland
77 H2 Zbiczno Poland
76 G2 Zblewo Poland
53 A2 Zboriv Ukraine
81 H1 Zbraslav Czech Rep.
78 E2 Zbraslavice Czech Rep.
53 B2 Zbruch r. Ukraine
75 J3 Zbůch Czech Rep.
77 L3 Zbuczyn Poduchowny Poland
81 H1 Ždánický Les forest Czech Rep.
78 E2 Žďar nad Sázavou Czech Rep.
78 F2 Žďárské Vrchy h. Czech Rep.
79 K3 Ždiar Slovakia
75 J3 Zdíkov Czech Rep.
78 E2 Zdírec nad Doubravou Czech Rep.
53 B1 Zdolbuniv Ukraine
76 G4 Zduńska Wola Poland
76 F4 Zduny Kalisz Poland
77 H3 Zduny Skierniewice Poland
47 J2 Zdvinsk Rus. Fed.
53 D1 Zdvyzh r. Ukraine
Zealand i. see Sjælland
39 G1 Zēbāk Afghanistan
42 F2 Zēbār Iraq
111 Zebbieh Malta
111 Żebbug Malta
111 Żebbug Malta
131 G2 Zebediela South Africa
119 G3 Zebirget I. i. Egypt
78 C2 Žebrák Czech Rep.
98 C5 Zebreira Portugal
76 G6 Zebrzydowice Dolne Poland
107 J4 Zeča i. Croatia
33 F1 Zecheng China
108 A5 Zeddiani Sardegna Italy
69 B3 Zedelgem Belgium
81 E3 Zederhaus Austria
79 J6 Žednik Yugoslavia
69 B3 Zeebrugge Belgium
13 F5 Zeehan Tasmania Australia
69 B3 Zeeland div. Netherlands
68 D3 Zeeland Netherlands
131 F2 Zeerust South Africa
69 B3 Zeeuwsch-Vlaanderen reg. Netherlands
68 D2 Zeewolde Netherlands
43 C3 Ze'fat Israel
83 D1 Zegama Spain
77 J6 Żegiestów Poland
73 J3 Zehdenick Germany
75 F2 Zeil am Main Germany
54 D3 Žeimelis Lithuania
81 H2 Zeiselmauer Austria
68 D2 Zeist Netherlands
43 B6 Zeit, G. el h. Egypt
73 J4 Zeithain Germany
73 H4 Zeitz Germany
111 Zejtun Malta
32 C1 Zêkog China
69 C3 Zele Belgium
77 K4 Żelechów Poland
53 A2 Zelena Ukraine
51 G6 Zelenchuk, B. r. Rus. Fed.
104 G4 Zelengora mts Bos.-Herz.
53 E3 Zelenivka Ukraine
56 J2 Zelenoborskiy Rus. Fed.
50 J4 Zelenodol'sk Rus. Fed.
53 E3 Zelenodol's'k Ukraine
54 F1 Zelenogorsk Rus. Fed.
52 C1 Zelenograd Rus. Fed.
54 B4 Zelenogradsk Rus. Fed.
53 D3 Zelenohirs'ke Ukraine
51 G6 Zelenokumsk Rus. Fed.
50 H3 Zelentsovo Rus. Fed.
47 H2 Zelenyy Gay Kazakhstan
52 G1 Zelenyy Gorod Rus. Fed.
81 G1 Želetava Czech Rep.
78 C2 Železná Ruda Czech Rep.
78 E2 Železné Hory h. Czech Rep.
81 F4 Železniki Slovenia
78 E1 Železný Brod Czech Rep.
121 E2 Zelfana Algeria
68 E2 Zelhem Netherlands
79 H3 Želiezovce Slovakia
78 F6 Zelina Croatia
75 L3 Želivka r. Czech Rep.
75 F2 Zella-Mehlis Germany
74 D4 Zell am Harmersbach Germany
80 D3 Zell am See div. Austria
80 D3 Zell am See Austria
80 C3 Zell am Ziller Austria
81 E2 Zell an der Pram Austria
81 G2 Zellerndorf Austria
80 D3 Zeller See l. Austria
74 C5 Zell im Wiesental Germany
74 E3 Zellingen Germany
74 C2 Zell (Mosel) Germany
79 J3 Želovce Slovakia
77 H4 Zelów Poland
69 F5 Zeltingen-Rachtig Germany
81 F3 Zeltweg Austria
77 N2 Zel'va Belarus
77 N2 Zel'vyenskaye Vodaskhovishcha resr Belarus
69 B3 Zelzate Belgium
54 B4 Žemaičių Naumiestis Lithuania
79 H3 Žemberovce Slovakia
32 C1 Zêmdasam China
112 D3 Zemen Bulgaria
112 F1 Zemeș Romania
52 F3 Zemetchino Rus. Fed.
124 E2 Zémio Central African Rep.
73 J2 Zemitz Germany
44 F1 Zemlya Aleksandry i. Rus. Fed.
44 G2 Zemlya Frantsa-Iosifa is Rus. Fed.
44 F2 Zemlya Georga i. Rus. Fed.
52 D4 Zemlyansk Rus. Fed.
44 H1 Zemlya Vil'cheka i. Rus. Fed.
69 E5 Zemmer Germany
124 E2 Zémongo, Réserve de Faune de res. Central African Rep.
79 L3 Zempléni-hegység h. Hungary
79 M3 Zemplínska šírava l. Slovakia
157 F5 Zempoala Pyramids Mexico
157 G5 Zempoaltepetl mt. Mexico
69 C4 Zemst Belgium
33 F4 Zengcheng China
31 J4 Zengfeng Shan mt. China
79 H5 Zengő mt. Hungary
154 A1 Zenia California U.S.A.
104 F3 Zenica Bos.-Herz.
62 A4 Zennor England U.K.
28 D6 Zentsūji Japan
121 E1 Zenzach Algeria
73 J3 Zepernick Germany
154 C2 Zephyr Cove Nevada U.S.A.
47 G5 Zerayshan r. Uzbekistan
74 H3 Zerbst Germany
74 B3 Zerf Germany
121 F2 Zeribet el Oued Algeria
76 F3 Żerków Poland
82 C3 Zermatt Switzerland
83 F2 Zernez Switzerland
73 F2 Zernien Germany
73 H3 Zernitz Germany
51 G6 Zernograd Rus. Fed.
Zestafoni see Zestap'oni
51 G7 Zestap'oni Georgia
37 G3 Zêtang China
53 A3 Zetea Romania
72 C2 Zetel Germany
75 G2 Zeulenroda Germany
73 J3 Zeuthen Germany
72 E2 Zeven Germany
68 E3 Zevenaar Netherlands
68 C3 Zevenbergen Netherlands
115 D5 Zevgolateio Greece
83 G3 Zevio Italy
31 J2 Zeya r. Rus. Fed.
27 N1 Zeya Rus. Fed.
39 E4 Zeyarat-e Shamil Iran
39 C3 Zeydābād Iran
39 D1 Zeydar Iran
39 D3 Zeynalābād Iran
31 J2 Zeysko- Bureinskaya Vpadina depression Rus. Fed.
45 O4 Zeyskoye Vdkhr. resr Rus. Fed.
113 F5 Zeytindağ Turkey
98 C4 Zêzere r. Portugal
43 C2 Zgharta Lebanon
77 H4 Zgierz Poland
76 D4 Zgorzelec Poland
53 B2 Zgurița Moldova
77 N3 Zhabinka Belarus
53 C2 Zhabokrychka Ukraine
52 H3 Zhadovka Rus. Fed.
Zhaggo see Luhuo
32 B1 Zhaglag China
32 B2 Zhag'yab China
46 F2 Zhailma Kazakhstan
47 G2 Zhaksy Kazakhstan
47 G3 Zhaksykon r. Kazakhstan
47 H3 Zhaksy Sarysu watercourse Kazakhstan
47 G2 Zhaltyr Kazakhstan
46 D3 Zhaltyr, Oz. l. Kazakhstan
77 N2 Zhaludok Belarus
46 F3 Zhamanakkol', Oz. salt lake Kazakhstan
46 D3 Zhamansor Kazakhstan
47 H4 Zhambyl div. Kazakhstan
47 H4 Zhambyl Kazakhstan
47 G3 Zhanabas Kazakhstan
46 F3 'Zhanakentkala Kazakhstan
46 F4 Zhanala Kazakhstan
37 G3 Zhanang China
47 J3 Zhanaortalyk Kazakhstan
47 J4 Zhanatala Kazakhstan
47 G4 Zhanatas Kazakhstan
46 D3 Zhanbay Kazakhstan
31 E4 Zhangbei China
Zhangde see Anyang
31 H3 Zhangguangcai Ling mountain range China
Zhanghua see Changhua
33 E4 Zhanghuang China
47 K3 Zhangiztobe Kazakhstan
31 E4 Zhangjiakou China
32 C1 Zhangla China
31 G1 Zhangling China
33 G3 Zhangping China
33 G3 Zhangpu China
31 G4 Zhangqiangzhen China
31 F5 Zhangqiu China
31 F5 Zhangwei Xinhe r. China
31 G4 Zhangwu China
32 D1 Zhang Xian China
30 B5 Zhangye China
33 G3 Zhangzhou China
30 E5 Zhangzi China
31 H2 Zhanhe China
31 F5 Zhanhua China
33 E4 Zhanjiang China
46 D3 Zhanterek Kazakhstan
32 C3 Zhanyi China
33 G4 Zhao'an China
31 H3 Zhaodong China
30 A5 Zhaojiaxia China
32 C2 Zhaojue China
33 E3 Zhaoping China
33 F4 Zhaoqing China
47 K4 Zhaosu China
31 G4 Zhaosutai r. China
32 C3 Zhaotong China
31 E5 Zhao Xian China
31 H3 Zhaoyuan China
31 G5 Zhaoyuan China
31 H3 Zhaozhou China
33 E4 Zhapo China
37 F3 Zhari Namco l. China
46 E3 Zharkamys Kazakhstan
47 K4 Zharkent Kazakhstan
52 A2 Zharkovskiy Rus. Fed.
47 K3 Zharma Kazakhstan
47 H3 Zharyk Kazakhstan
53 D2 Zhashkiv Ukraine
33 E1 Zhashui China
46 E4 Zhaslyk Uzbekistan
46 G2 Zhasminnaya Rus. Fed.
37 F2 Zhaxi Co salt lake China
30 D2 Zhaxigang China
47 H3 Zhayrem Kazakhstan
52 H2 Zhdamirovo Rus. Fed.
52 D3 Zhdankovskiy Rus. Fed.
53 E1 Zhdany Ukraine
79 N3 Zhdeneve Ukraine
52 F2 Zhegalovo Rus. Fed.
32 C2 Zhêhor China
33 G2 Zhejiang div. China
44 H2 Zhelaniya, M. c. Rus. Fed.
52 F2 Zhelcha r. Rus. Fed.
47 J2 Zhelezinka Kazakhstan
54 B4 Zheleznodorozhnyy Rus. Fed.
52 B3 Zheleznogorsk Rus. Fed.
47 J2 Zheltorangy Kazakhstan
33 E1 Zhen'an China
32 D1 Zhenba China
32 D3 Zhenfeng China
32 C1 Zheng'an China
30 E5 Zhengding China
33 G3 Zhenghe China
31 F4 Zhenglan Qi China
33 E1 Zhengning China
31 E4 Zhengxiangbai Qi China
33 F1 Zhengyang China
33 F1 Zhengzhou China
33 H2 Zhenhai China
33 G1 Zhenjiang China
32 C1 Zhenjiangguan China
32 B4 Zhenkang China
31 G3 Zhenlai China
33 D3 Zhenning China
33 F1 Zhenping China
32 C3 Zhenxiong China
31 G3 Zhenxi China
32 D3 Zhenxiong China
32 C4 Zhenyuan China
32 D3 Zhenyuan China
30 C6 Zhenyuan China
52 E4 Zherdevka Rus. Fed.
33 G3 Zherong China
50 J2 Zheshart Rus. Fed.
46 D4 Zhetybay Kazakhstan
33 E2 Zhexi Sk. resr China
47 G3 Zhezkazgan Kazakhstan
47 H3 Zhezkazgan div. Kazakhstan
33 E2 Zhicheng China
30 D5 Zhidan China
32 A1 Zhidoi China
45 O3 Zhigansk Rus. Fed.
33 E4 Zhigong China
46 C2 Zhigulevsk h. Rus. Fed.
33 E3 Zhijiang China
33 E3 Zhijiang China
32 D2 Zhilevo Rus. Fed.
52 C3 Zhilino Rus. Fed.
Zhi Qu r. see Tongtian
31 F1 Zhireken Rus. Fed.
51 H5 Zhirnovsk Rus. Fed.
52 A3 Zhiryatino Rus. Fed.
54 F1 Zhitkovo Rus. Fed.
114 B2 Zhitom Albania
52 E3 Zhizdra r. Rus. Fed.
52 B3 Zhizdra Rus. Fed.
Zhiziluo see Bijiang
51 D4 Zhlobin Belarus
53 C2 Zhmerynka Ukraine
36 B3 Zhob r. Pakistan
36 B3 Zhob Pakistan
54 F4 Zhodzina Belarus
45 R2 Zhokhova, O. i. Rus. Fed.
47 H2 Zholymbet Kazakhstan
37 F3 Zhongba China
32 B3 Zhongdian China
32 D2 Zhongjiang China
30 C5 Zhongning China
179 D5 Zhongshan China Base Antarctica
33 E3 Zhongshan China
33 F4 Zhongshan China
33 E1 Zhongtiao Shan mountain range China
30 C5 Zhongwei China
32 D2 Zhong Xian China
33 F3 Zhongxin China
30 D5 Zhongyang China
31 H2 Zhongyaozhan China
32 C3 Zhongyicur China
33 E5 Zhongyuan China
33 H2 Zhongze China
77 M4 Zhorany Ukraine
53 E2 Zhorte Ukraine
53 E1 Zhortneve Ukraine
32 D2 Zhou r. China
30 B5 Zhoujiajing China
33 F1 Zhoukou China
33 G3 Zhouning China
33 H2 Zhoushan Dao i. China
33 H2 Zhoushan Qundao is China
30 E4 Zhouzi China
53 A1 Zhovkva Ukraine
77 N6 Zhovtantsi Ukraine
53 D3 Zhovten' Ukraine
53 E2 Zhovti Vody Ukraine
53 F2 Zhovtneve Poltava Ukraine

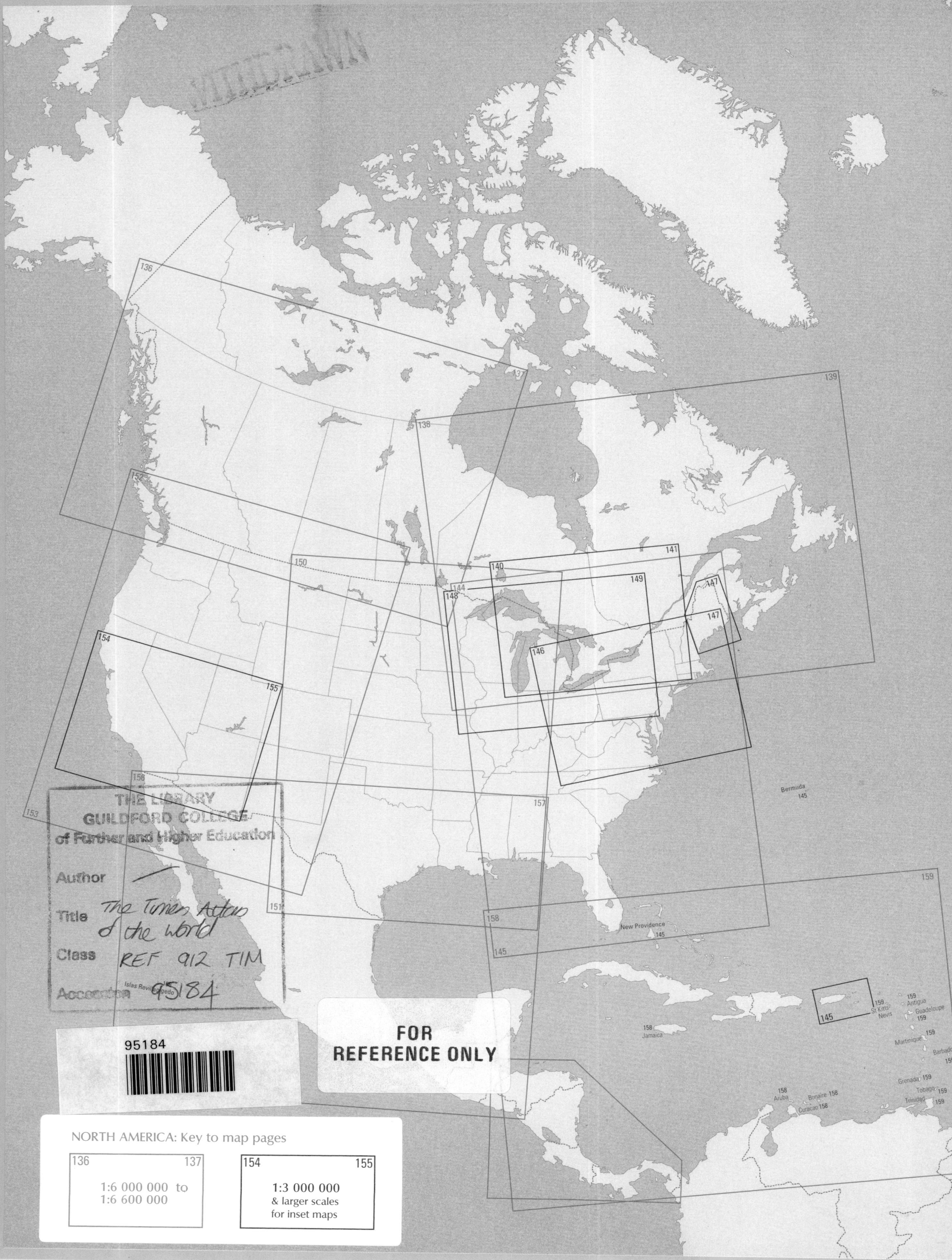

WITHDRAWN
THE LIBRARY
GUILDFORD COLLEGE
of Further and Higher Education
Author
Title The Times Atlas of the World
Class REF 912 TIM
Accession 95184
95184
FOR REFERENCE ONLY